D0209659

HARPER'S
BIBLE DICTIONARY

HARPER'S BIBLE DICTIONARY

by
MADELEINE S. MILLER
and
J. LANE MILLER
revised by eminent authorities

Drawings by Claire Valentine

HARPER & ROW, PUBLISHERS

NEW YORK, EVANSTON, SAN FRANCISCO, LONDON

HARPER'S BIBLE DICTIONARY

EIGHTH EDITION

Library of Congress Cataloging in Publication Data

Miller, Madeleine (Sweeny) 1890-
Harper's Bible dictionary.
1. Bible—Dictionaries. I. Miller, John Lane, 1884-1954, joint author. II. Title.
BS440.M52 1974 220.3 73-6327
ISBN 0-06-065673-5
ISBN 0-06-065674-3 (thumb indexed ed.)

TO THE USER

An asterisk (*) after a word in any article indicates that supplementary material is to be found under the word so marked.

The chronology for the United Monarchy and the Kings of Judah and of Israel used throughout this book is that of W. F. Albright.

A complete list of illustrations and a set of maps is to be found at the back of the book.

ABBREVIATIONS

Contributors

B.W.A.	Bernhard W. Anderson	R.C.D.	Robert C. Danton
W.P.A.	William P. Anderson	R.M.G.	Robert M. Grant
G.W.V.B.	Gus W. Van Beek	E.L.	Edwin Lewis
J.A.B.	Julius A. Bewer	P.L.M.	Paul L. Maier
P.W.B.	Paul W. Brand, M.D.	R.H.P.	Robert H. Pfeiffer
R.W.C.	Richard W. Corney	R.B.Y.S.	R. B. Y. Scott
G.E.W.	G. Ernest Wright		

Publications and Sources

AASOR — *Annual* of American Schools of Oriental Research

AJA — *American Journal of Archaeology*

AJSL — *American Journal of Semitic Languages and Literature*

ANEP[2] — Pritchard, *Ancient Near East in Pictures*, 2d ed.

ANET[3] — Pritchard, *Ancient Near Eastern Texts*, 3d ed.

Antiq. — Josephus, *Antiquities of the Jews*

AOTS — Thomas, *Archaeology and Old Testament Study*

ARI — Albright, *Archaeology and the Religion of Israel*

AS — Anatolian Studies

ASOR — American Schools of Oriental Research

BA — *The Biblical Archaeologist*

BANE — Wright, *The Bible and the Ancient Near East*

BASOR — *Bulletin* of American Schools of Oriental Research

BDB — Brown, Driver and Briggs, *Hebrew and English Lexicon of the Old Testament*

BJPES — *Biblical Journal* of Palestine Exploration Society

BMB — *Bulletin* du Musée de Beyrouth

CAH[3] — *Cambridge Ancient History*, 3d ed.

HTR — *Harvard Theological Review*

IEJ — *Israel Exploration Journal*

JAOS — *Journal* of American Oriental Society

JBL — *Journal of Biblical Literature*

JEA — *Journal of Egyptian Archaeology*

JNES — *Journal of Near Eastern Studies*

JPOS — *Journal* of Palestine Oriental Society

JQR — *Jewish Quarterly Review*

OI — *Oriental Institute*, University of Chicago

PEFQS — Palestine Exploration Fund *Quarterly Statement*

PEQ — *Palestine Exploration Quarterly*

RB — *Revue biblique*

VT — *Vetus Testamentum*

Wars — Josephus, *Wars of the Jews*

ZAW — *Zeitschrift fur die alttestamentliche Wissenschaft*

Chronological Periods

Neo.	Neolithic Age	(c. 8000—4000 B.C.)
Chalco.	Chalcolithic Age	(c. 4000—3200 B.C.)
EB	Early Bronze Age	(c. 3200—2150 B.C.)
MB	Middle Bronze Age	(c. 2150—1550 B.C.)
LB	Late Bronze Age	(c. 1550—1200 B.C.)
Iron	Iron Age	(c. 1200— 587 B.C.)
Hell.	Hellenistic	
Strat.	Stratum or Strata	

Miscellaneous

Accad.	Accadian
A.D.	*anno domini* (in the year of our Lord)
Arab.	Arabic
Aram.	Aramaic
art.	article
Assyr.	Assyrian
A.S.V.	American Standard Version
A.V.	Authorized Version (King James)
b.	date of birth
Bab.	Babylonian
B.C.	before Christ
c.	*circa* (about)
Canaan.	Canaanite
cen.	century
cf.	*confer* (compare)
chap.	chapter
d.	date of death
e.g.	*exempli gratia* (for example)
Egypt.	Egyptian
Eng.	English
et al.	and others
f., ff.	following verse(s) or page(s)
Ger.	German
Gk.	Greek
Heb.	Hebrew
ibid.	*ibidem* (in the same place)
i.e.	*id est* (that is)
illus.	illustration
Lat.	Latin
L.L.	Late Latin
m.	mile
marg.	marginal reading
Moff.	Moffatt
MS., MSS.	manuscript, manuscripts
N.T.	New Testament
O.F.	Old French
O.T.	Old Testament
p., pp.	page, pages
Pers.	Persian
Phoen.	Phoenician
pl.	plural
Rom.	Roman
R.S.V.	Revised Standard Version
Sem.	Semitic
sing.	singular
Syr.	Syrian
Targ.	Targum
v., vv.	verse, verses
vs.	versus
Vulg.	Vulgate

PRONOUNCING-MARKS

ā	as in fate	ȧ	as in sofa	ī	as in ice	ŏ	as in connect
ǻ	as in chaotic	dū	as in verdure	ĭ	as in ill	o͞o	as in moon
â	as in care	ē	as in mete	ĭ	as in charity	ū	as in cube
ă	as in add	ḗ	as in event	ō	as in note	ǘ	as in unite
ă	as in infant	ĕ	as in met	ṓ	as in obey	û	as in urn
ä	as in arm	ĕ	as in silent	ô	as in orb	ŭ	as in up
ȧ	as in ask	ẽ	as in maker	ŏ	as in odd	ŭ	as in circus

The heavy accent mark (ʹ) indicates the primary stress in a word. Many long words require a secondary accent, which is indicated by a light mark (ʹ).

PUBLISHER'S FOREWORD TO THE EIGHTH EDITION

It will perhaps be useful to the reader of this book, the librarian, and the bibliographer to have a statement from the publisher setting forth first, the history of publication of the work, and secondly, the nature and extent of the revisions incorporated in this Eighth Edition.

When Dr. J. Lane Miller and his wife, Madeleine S. Miller, were asked by the publisher to undertake a one-volume Bible dictionary, Dr. Miller was minister of the Hanson Avenue Methodist Church in Brooklyn, N. Y. (He would later become minister of the Methodist Church of Rye, N. Y.) Dr. and Mrs. Miller had already published a useful reference book called *Encyclopedia of Bible Life.* They began their work on *Harper's Bible Dictionary* in 1946, and it was published in 1952. Dr. Miller died in 1954. Mrs. Miller had to lay aside her direction of revisions during the preparation of the Seventh Edition, issued in 1962. This is the first revision since that date.

As Mrs. Miller wrote in her forewords to previous editions, "We were confident that we could call upon generous friends in the world of Biblical scholarship to help us over rough spots. Our confidence in them was not misplaced, as the paragraphs immediately following clearly demonstrate." Those paragraphs of acknowledgments of assistance were fifteen in number, some of them naming a dozen or more experts in various fields. In this Eighth Edition it has been decided to forego the printing of the entire list of acknowledgments for reasons of space. Here we will offer another word of thanks only to those whose help was truly basic to the success of the book as we remember it.

In the case of three Biblical scholars of first rank, we will quote directly from a previous foreword: "Consultants without whom completion of this book would have been most difficult include William Foxwell Albright and G. Ernest Wright. . . . We are also particularly grateful to . . . Robert H. Pfeiffer, who in addition to contributing articles, made countless constructive suggestions." Also making substantial contributions to the First Edition were (alphabetically): Millar Burrows, Morton Enslin, Nelson Glueck, Frederick C. Grant, James L. Kelso, Harold N. Moldenke, and Allen P. Wikgren. Edwin Lewis, a longtime friend of Lane Miller's, wrote all the major theological articles. Extremely helpful also were the American Schools of Oriental Research (Jerusalem and Baghdad) whose directors freely gave permission to quote from their Bulletins, Annuals, and *The Biblical Archaeologist.*

Revisions were made nearly every time this work was reprinted during the 1950s, as the copyright notice attests. The largest of these revisions was the one that resulted in the Seventh Edition in 1962. Again the late W. F. Albright and G. E. Wright were both actively helpful. New contributions, generally in the form of a thorough revision or replacement of articles in the light of new understandings, were made by Bernard W. Anderson, Robert M. Grant, Emil Kraeling, R.B.Y. Scott, Farley W. Snell, Gus W. Van Beek, and Theophilus Taylor. A valuable contribution to accuracy in regard to the Jewish calendar and festivals was made by Rabbi Morris Silverman and Rabbi David Mirsky of Yeshiva University, New York. Alice Parmelee and Eleanor K. Vogel, archaeological assistant to the late Nelson Glueck, were constant contributors in various ways during the ten years following first publication.

We turn now to the nature and extent of the revisions: how this edition differs from its immediate predecessor.

This 1973 revision is by far the most comprehensive to date. This is the first time that the illustrations and line drawings have been reviewed. But more important is the fact that the past dozen years have seen significant rethinking within Biblical archaeology and theology, calling for a thorough reexamination of the articles in these fields.

In revising the articles on archaeological sites and other Biblical localities, the initial step was to bring up to date and expand the Table of Archaeological Sites (p. 33). This involved the insertion of additional information concerning sites already included in the table (i.e., excavations carried out since the last edition) and the addition of other important sites of a more recent excavation date. Care was taken to check the date inserted in this edition with the original excavation reports.

The revised table was then used as a guide in redoing individual articles throughout. All of the articles on archaeological sites and Biblical cities were reviewed and rewritten or edited where necessary, with primary attention given to sites which appear in the table. Articles that were entirely satisfactory (e.g., Samaria, Shechem) were left as they stood. If an article needed only minor additions or revisions, the new material was worked into the framework of the original article. In most cases, however, the articles needed extensive revision and were revised entirely (e.g., Megiddo) or thoroughly overhauled (e.g., Jerusalem).

Guiding principles throughout the revision of the archaeological material were: (1) to bring the articles up to date; (2) to correct whatever had been misrepresented in the previous edition or needed to be altered in the light of more recent study and excavation; (3) to provide as much information about the site as possible (including Biblical data, information from extra-Biblical sources such as Assyrian and Egyptian annals, and archaeological results) in a scholarly and credible manner, without becoming technical or detailed.

The final principle was that this revision should be done with both the genuinely interested layman and the more seriously interested student and minister in mind. For the layman the intent is to provide a concise description of the site, its significance, and its archaeological importance in a readable manner; for the student and minister, to provide substantiation for the claims and arguments presented, as well as references for further study.

The revision work in the area of archaeology and Biblical sites was done by William P. Anderson, in consultation with James B. Pritchard.

FOREWORD TO THE EIGHTH EDITION

Another area that called for major revision was theology. The changes in the theological scene over the past two decades have been greater than the average reader may have realized, and they required the rewriting of many of the theological articles. The original articles reflected to a large extent the theological liberalism that prevailed during the period prior to World War II. Liberalism was displaced in the United States during the mid-century decades by neo-orthodoxy, a movement which in its turn has recently undergone dissolution without as yet giving rise to any clearly definable new tendency. It was thought best, therefore, to eliminate as much as possible the speculative and apologetic elements in the older articles and to make them more factual and purely informative. This work has been done by Robert C. Dentan.

Scores of Old Testament historical and biographical articles have been made more precise and conformant to recent findings of Biblical scholars by Richard W. Corney.

In the case of illustrations and maps (an area pioneered in one-volume dictionaries by *Harper's Bible Dictionary*), Denis Baly has reviewed all 500, and 58 pictures have been replaced for various reasons, ranging from changes in how a famed Biblical site looked in 1940 and 1973 to changes in design of automobiles and ladies' hats. Several spot maps and tables have also been revised and updated. Owners of the previous edition might, for example, compare the new map of Jerusalem on p. 318 with the map of preceeding editions—a revision required by the major investigations within the Holy City by British and Israeli archaeologists in the decade following the last revision of this work in 1962. Claire Valentine is again the artist.

The practice of printing the initials of the contributors of articles at their end has been continued. Where such an article has been revised, the initials of the revising writer have been added. A very few signed articles of earlier editions have been replaced by articles initialed by the current contributor. The names of the various contributors and their initials are printed near the front of the book.

Short bibliographies have been added to the articles on archaeological sites, and the abbreviations of technical works and journals used in the articles can be found in the front matter also.

In their work, Madeleine S. Miller wrote, "We sensed that a Presence over and outside us was encouraging and strengthening us to plod ahead with what otherwise would have seemed an overwhelming task. This sense revived us like a cup of cool water which retains the freshness of God's grace." This revision has been done in the spirit with which J. Lane and Madeleine S. Miller undertook and carried out the challenge offered them: to produce a sound, popular, and interesting Bible Dictionary, based on first-rate scholarship.

September 1973 — THE PUBLISHERS
New York, New York

A

A, the first letter of the alphabet, used to designate the Codex Alexandrinus, famous Gk. MS. of the Bible, prepared in the fifth century A.D., possibly at Alexandria, Egypt. The document was presented in 1624 to James I of England; it is now in the British Museum. Portions of this Codex* have been lost, but 773 parchment leaves remain (10½ in. by 12¾ in.). The Table of Contents indicates that in addition to the O.T. and the N.T. the four Books of the Maccabees, two Epistles of Clement, and other matter were included. See TEXT.

Aaron (âr′ŭn) (Heb. meaning uncertain), the first head of the Hebrew priesthood. He was the son of Amram the Levite and Jochebed (Ex. 6:20), born in Egypt a few years before the persecutions of the Hebrews current at the birth of his brother Moses* (Ex. 7:7). He was the younger brother of Miriam. He had four sons by Elisheba—Nadab, Abihu, Eleazar, and Ithamar; the first two were failures, see NADAB (1); Eleazar* became his successor. Because of his eloquence, Aaron became the spokesman for Moses (Ex. 4:14); and was regarded by Pharaoh as co-leader with Moses (Ex. 8:25). Aaron helped Hur hold up the hands of the rod-bearing Moses, insuring that Israel would prevail in their battle against the Amalekites (Ex. 17:12). (For the golden calf incident see CALF.)

The priestly narratives stress Aaron's function as the founder of the priesthood*, which he served for almost 40 years. Anointed (see ANOINT) by Moses, together with his four sons (Num. 3:1–3), Aaron was consecrated to a higher order than the Levites, who were to perform the menial tasks in connection with the furnishings and service of the Tabernacle*. Aaron and his family were to receive generous heave offerings of meal, first fruits of oil and wine, and first-born animals offered as holy things (Num. 18:8–14). Unlike the secular tribesmen, Aaron would receive no inheritance in Canaan because God was his portion (Num. 18:20). He joined his sister Miriam in taunting Moses about his Ethiopian (A.S.V. Cushite) wife (Num. 12:1). He was punished apparently because, near the end of the arduous Wilderness wanderings, he had doubted God's ability to bring water from the rock at Meribeh. Aaron died at an advanced age and was buried at Mt. Hor, whose site on the border of Edom among the wilderness crags has not been identified. The garments of succession (see DRESS) were placed on his son Eleazar (Num. 20:28) and a month of mourning ensued.

The elaborate accounts of mitre, head tire, breeches, embroidered coat, jeweled ephod, golden plate engraved like an Egyptian signet, "Holy to Jehovah," ascribed to Aaron in the P narratives, indicate the desire of certain writers to account for the equipment of Hebrew high priests through later centuries (Ex. 39:1–31). Yet this equipment need not be entirely an anachronistic "throwback." For in the Sinai desert, at Serabit el-Khadem, in the era of Moses, turquoise was being mined for Egyptian jewelers, as was copper. And in Ex. 11:2 we read of Israelites "borrowing" from the Egyptians "jewels of silver, and jewels of gold." Gold and jeweled ornaments excavated from the ruins of Sumerian Ur and used many centuries before Aaron and Moses are to be found in the University Museum (Philadelphia). The anointing and appareling of Aaron suggest a kingly rank foreshadowing the civil authority vested in the high priest of post-Exilic times when there was no secular Hebrew monarch. The apparent contradictions in delineating Aaron in the Pentateuch narratives are due to the splicing of several source (see SOURCES) accounts devoted to the founder of the Hebrew priesthood. They do not necessarily destroy the historicity of Aaron. In the earlier Pentateuch narratives Aaron is mentioned in connection with the Exodus, the supporting of Moses' hand, the making of the golden calf, and the criticism of Moses for marrying "the Ethiopian woman." But in the P document he becomes the center and founder of the whole priestly system. Records from the S. seem to make no mention of Aaron until after the Exile. Ezekiel centers the priesthood in the family of Zadok. The Priestly Code tells in Lev. 8 of the ordination of Aaron and his son Eleazar to the priesthood, in agreement with Ex. 29.

The oldest known art depiction of Aaron is a mural found by the Yale Dura Expedition to Dura-Europos, Syria, where it ornamented a wall in the 2d century A.D. synagogue (now in the Museum at Damascus).

For Aaron's rod see ROD; see also ALMOND.

Aaronites (âr′ŭn-īts), priestly descendants of the House of Aaron (I Chron. 12:27; Ps. 115:10). The word was not used earlier than the priestly portions of the Pentateuch (as Lev. 3:5). The parents of John the Baptist, Zacharias and Elisabeth, were both Aaronites, thus giving full priestly descent to John.

Ab (ăb) (from Accad. word *abu*), was the 5th month of the Hebrew sacred calendar and the 11th of the civil year—parts of July and August. See TIME.

Abana (ăb′à-nȧ), (**Amana** in Heb. text), a river in Syria, also called Chrysorrhoas, meaning "Golden River" to the Greeks, and identical with the modern Barada, which means "The Cold Stream" to Arabs. It rises near Baalbek in the high valley between the Lebanon and the Anti-Lebanon Mts., flows SE., tumbling through the gorge of Wâdī Barada, watering golden fruit orchards along its banks; divides into seven branches, which further subdivide. From the days of the founding of "the oldest city in the world," it has brought life to Damascus and its oasis. Cf. Rev. 22:1 f. Naaman, the leprous Syrian captain, knew the curative properties of the Abana (II Kings 5:12). See PHARPAR.

Abarim (ăb′ȧ-rĭm) ("regions beyond"), a region E. of the Jordan, S. of Bashan. The mountains of Abarim overlook the Dead Sea and Jordan Valley. Cf. Num. 27:12; 33:47.

Abba (ăb′ȧ) (transliteration of Aram. word for "father", used by Jesus in his Gethsemane prayer, Mark 14:36). See also its use in direct address, in Rom. 8:15; Gal. 4:6. In the Gk. N.T. it retains the flavor of sanctity; servants were forbidden to use it in addressing the master of the home, though children might.

Abdon (ăb′dŏn) ("servile"), a judge of Israel (Judg. 12:13–15). Other men of this name are mentioned in I Chron. 8:23, 8:30, 9:36; II Chron. 34:20. Also a town in the territory assigned to Asher (Josh. 21:30; I Chron. 6:74).

Abednego (ȧ-bĕd′nē-gō) (Azariah), one of the three Heb. companions of Daniel*, miraculously delivered from the fiery furnace into which they were tossed for refusal to bow down to the golden image of King Nebuchadnezzar (Dan. 1:7, 2:49, 3:12 ff.; and I Macc. 2:59). The Bab. name of Azariah means "servant of Nego (or Nebo)," a Bab. god of wisdom, sometimes represented as the planet Mercury in the role of a scribe.

Abel (ā′bĕl) (1) (Heb. "breath," "vanity"), second son of Adam (Gen. 4:2), and brother of Cain, who slew him in jealous rage because Abel's gift to God—the firstlings of his flock—seemed more acceptable than Cain's offering of "the fruit of the ground." This primitive story of "the first murder" is included in the J portion of the Pentateuch. Reference is made to the story by Jesus, who speaks of "the blood of innocent Abel" (R.S.V. Matt. 23:35) in his lament over Jerusalem; and by the author of Hebrews (11:4). Whether the gift of Abel was more acceptable because it was blood, the essence of life, instead of grain, or because it was offered with greater sincerity, is not clear. In the story of Abel's death we read of the struggle between pastoral and agricultural phases of society.

(2) Abel (Heb. "meadow"), used in place names, as *Abel*-cheramim, "meadow of vineyards," Judg. 11:33, probably near Rabbah of Ammon, later Philadelphia; *Abel*-maim, "meadow of waters," II Chron. 16:4, possibly the same as *Abel*-beth-maachah (see MAACHAH), a fortified site in northern Palestine W. of Dan; *Abel*-mizraim, "meadow of Egypt," mentioned in Gen. 50:11 as a halting place of Jacob's funeral procession; *Abel*-shittim, "meadow of acacias," possibly

1. Abel-beth-maachah (*Tell Abil*), a typical unexcavated *tell* in N. Palestine.

Tell el-Hammâm, in the plain NE. of the Dead Sea, from which Joshua dispatched spies to Jericho (Josh. 2:1). (See SHITTIM; ABEL-MEHOLAH.)

Abel-meholah (ā′bĕl-mē-hō′lȧ) ("vale of dancing," cf. Judg. 21:20 f.), a site identified by Nelson Glueck as Tell el-Maqlub (which is no longer considered to be Jabesh-gilead*). Abel-meholah, mentioned in the story of Gideon (Judg. 7:22), is in the present Hashemite Kingdom of Jordan, overlooking the copious waters of Wâdī Yabis (reaches of which may be the Brook Cherith of I Kings 17:3–7, since the Cherith is no longer to be considered as the Wâdī Qelt, W. of the Jordan River). Abel-meholah, possibly the scene of Elijah's visit to Elisha, narrated in I Kings 19:15–21, was the home of Elisha, son of Shaphat. It was only a short distance E. of Elijah's birthplace at Jabesh-gilead (Tell el-Meqbereh and Tell Abu Kharaz). Its several occupation levels were protected by an early wall. The mound, when first studied, was strewn with Israelite and earlier pottery fragments. It is planted with terraced grain patches and overlooks garden areas and vineyards. Its fertility may explain I Kings 4:12. See Nelson Glueck, *The River Jordan*, pp. 166–174, The Westminster Press.

Abel-shittim (ā′bĕl-shĭt′ĭm). See ABEL; SHITTIM.

Abiathar (ȧ-bī′ȧ-thȧr) ("father of abundance"), son of Ahimelech, priest at Nob, slain by Saul's henchmen. Abiathar was protected by David (I Sam. 22:23), whom he joined at Keilah. Having carried the priest's ephod from Nob, he remained as religious consultant to David. He took part with the priest Zadok in bringing the Ark up to Jerusalem. With Joab he supported Adonijah, the fourth son of David, in the intrigue over the succession. Solomon banished him to Anathoth for suspected treachery (I Kings 1:7, 19, 25).

Abib (ā′bĭb) ("an ear of corn"), the first month of the Hebrew Year (March–April); after the Exile called Nisan. The Passover* fell in it. Cf. Ex. 12:1 f., 13:4. See TIME.

Abigail (ăb′ĭ-gāl), wife of "Nabal the fool," rich landsman who grazed sheep and goats on slopes at Carmel, near Hebron on the edge of the Wilderness. As related in I Sam. 25, Abigail saved her husband from hot-tempered young David, who had vainly demanded a share of wool in return for the protection he and his freebooters had extended to Nabal's shearers and flocks. On a convoy of asses she brought David an appeasement gift of raisins, bread, wine, sheep, grain. Observing her beauty and her generous sagacity, David found it convenient to marry Abigail soon after the death of her apoplectic husband. She was taken captive by Amalekites raiding near Ziklag, but was rescued along with David's other wife, Ahinoam of Jezreel (I Sam. 30:18). Abigail bore David a son, Chileab, at Hebron (II Sam. 3:3). She shared David's life at Gath.

Abihu (*a*-bī′hū), one of the sons of Aaron (I Chron. 24:1 f.). He died childless before the death of Aaron, and therefore had no part in the succession of the priesthood.

Abijah (*a*-bī′j*a*) ("Jehovah is my father"). (1) King of Judah (also called Abijam) who ruled c. 915–913 B.C.; the son of Rehoboam and Maacah, daughter of Abishalom. His war against Jeroboam I is recorded in I Kings 15:7 and II Chron. 13. (2) Son of Jeroboam (I Kings 14:1 ff.). (3) Son of Samuel the prophet; a judge in Beer-sheba (I Sam. 8:2). (4) Descendant of Haran who served as head of the 8th course of priests, to which Zacharias, father of John the Baptist, belonged (Luke 1:5). (5) Wife of King Ahaz, and mother of Hezekiah (II Chron. 29:1).

Abijam (*a*-bī′j*a*m). See ABIJAH (1).

Abimelech (*a*-bĭm′ĕ-lĕk) ("My father is Melech [Molek]"). (1) King of what became the Philistine city-state Gerar*. His name is pure Heb. He made a covenant with Abraham at Beer-sheba (Gen. 21:22–34), which he renewed with Isaac (26:26–31). Similarities in the stories of his relations with Sarah (Gen. 20) and Rebekah (26:6–11) appear in both the J and E narratives. (2) Son of Gideon (Jerubbaal), made king by his murder of all but one of his half-brothers. His bloody career is recorded in Judg. 9.

Abinadab (*a*-bĭn′*a*-dăb), a man of Kirjath-jearim, who kept the Ark in his house from the time of its return by the Philistines until David came to remove it (I Sam. 7:1 f.; II Sam. 6:3 ff.). (2) 2d son of Jesse (I Sam. 16:8, 17:13). (3) Other men of the same name: I Sam. 31:2; I Kgs. 4:11.

Abishag (ăb′ĭ-shăg), a fair young Shunammite woman, nurse or companion of the aged King David (I Kings 1:3). She was later sought after by his son Adonijah, but was retained by Solomon as a heritage from his royal father.

Abishai (*a*-bĭsh′ā-ī), son of Zeruiah, David's sister(?); brother of Joab and Asahel. He was one of David's "mighty men" (II Sam. 23:18) and a close companion in his military adventures. He sought to kill the sleeping Saul (I Sam. 26:5–9); served under Joab (II Sam. 2:18; 10:10); pursued Abner after the death of Asahel (II Sam. 2:18–24); remained loyal at the time of the revolts of Absalom and Sheba (II Sam. 16, 20): was ready to slay the cursing Shimei (II Sam. 16:9; 19:21); defeated the Edomites (I Chron. 18:12 f.); and slew the Philistine giant, Ishbibenob, in one of David's last battles (II Sam. 21:15f.).

Abner (ăb′nẽr), son of Ner and cousin of King Saul, whose forces he commanded (I Sam. 14:50). Upon the death of Saul, Abner championed prince Ish-bosheth at Mahanaim (II Sam. 2:8) and helped establish him as ruler of Israel. "But the house of Judah followed David" (II Sam. 2:10). Transferring his allegiance to David at Hebron, Abner was soon after slain by Joab, who was jealous lest Abner supplant him, and was irked by the murder of Asahel (II Sam. 3:27). David mourned Abner as "a prince, and a great man" (II Sam. 3:38).

abomination, whatever is offensive to God and His plan for man's righteous way of life: whether "unclean" items of tabooed food (Lev. 11); idols (I Kings 11:5); or dishonesty (Mic. 6:10). Rev. 17:5 (R.S.V.) calls Babylon "mother of harlots and of earth's abominations." The gods of other nations were "abominable" to the Hebrews, whether Ammonite and Moabite (I Kings 11:5), or Sidonian (A.V. Zidonian) (II Kings 23:13). One who dissembles is described in Prov. 26:25 as having "seven abominations in his heart."

abomination of desolation (R.S.V. "abomination that makes desolate"), referred to several times in Daniel* (9:27, 11:31, 12:11), now generally refers to the proscription of the Jewish religion by Antiochus Epiphanes and to his setting up in the Temple of an altar to the Olympian Zeus, just prior to the Maccabean revolt (see MACCABEES). Just what Jesus had in mind when he spoke of an "abomination of desolation" (Mark 13:14f.) which would be a sign of the beginning of the Messianic Age is uncertain. It may have been a statue of a Roman emperor, an inappropriate figure, or an event.

Abraham (ā′br*a*-hăm), known earlier as Abram (Heb. "exalted father"), was called "father of many nations" (Gen. 17:5), founder of the Hebrew people, and friend of God (II Chron. 20:7). The delineation of Abraham, as well as of other Patriarchs* in the J source* of the Genesis narratives which preserve early oral poems, is too individual to admit of his being regarded as merely a folk hero, a type, or a tribe. He was a son of his age—the Middle Bronze. Archaeologists call "The Age of Abraham" the era of transition from the last kings of Sumer, Isin, and Larsa, to the First Dynasty of Babylon, whose greatest king was Hammurabi, the Amorite codifier of laws resembling many Hebrew laws. W. F. Albright dates Hammurabi some time between c. 1728 and 1686 B.C. The migration of the family of Terah, father of Abraham, from Ur to Haran as told in Gen. 11 is dated in the 20th or 19th century B.C. The tablets unearthed at Mari on the Euphrates, the finds of Sir Leonard Woolley at Ur, probably the early home of Abraham (Gen. 11:28, 31), and the calendaric research of L. Borchard, help set the approximate dates in Mesopotamian history during the 2d millennium B.C. with greater accuracy than before, and place Israelite "tradition" on historic footing in relation to the homogeneous culture of Mesopotamia, Asia Minor, and Syria. The rich collection of clay tablets found at Ur* reveal what life was like in the moon-worshipping city Abraham forsook for nomadism en route around the Fertile Crescent into Canaan. Examples of the Mesopotamian *ziggurats* (see ZIGGURAT) (artificial hills or stage towers) crowned with temples that he saw, have been excavated. The Mari tablets give information about Haran* (Gen. 11:31). The Beni-hasan painting tells us how Abraham and his clan may have looked. The language spoken by Abraham is thought to have been either the Sumerian or the Accadian tongue. In any case, the racial origins of the Hebrews are complicated and confused. They may have included Hurrian elements. But in the light of recent excavations at Mari, which have enabled scholars to locate the mound of "the city of Nahor" (Gen. 24:10), we seem to have clear evidence of Abraham's forebears corresponding to names of towns located near Haran. Social customs indicated in the Patriarchal narratives fit into the Nuzu* civilization now known to have existed

2. Abraham's cenotaph, Cave of Machpelah.

in eastern Mesopotamia. Northeastern Mesopotamia is more closely knit into the pre-priestly narratives of the Patriarchs than Canaan or Egypt. Nelson Glueck has explored in Transjordan (the Hashemite Kingdom of Jordan) sites of towns extant when Abraham (Gen. 14) followed enemies with his trained retainers, all the way from Hebron "as far as Dan," which has been identified as a mound (el-Qâdī) at the foot of Mt. Hermon (Judg. 18:29). The narrative of Gen. 14 concerning Abraham's triumph over Mesopotamian kings contains many enigmas, including that of his meeting with Melchizedek at Salem (? Jerusalem).

The name of Abraham is identified with Hebron and the Mamre oaks (Gen. 18:1 ff.), even as the name of Isaac is associated with Beer-sheba and that of Jacob with Bethel. The tombs of the Patriarchs are within the very conservative Moslem mosque at Hebron, over the Cave of Machpelah which Abraham bought from Ephron the Hittite (Gen. 23).

The story of Abraham's willingness to sacrifice his son is from the main document of the Genesis narrative, commonly dated in the 8th century B.C., and is therefore one of the early strands of the book. It indicates that human sacrifice was not acceptable to God even at this early age, in contrast to II Kings 3:27.

Main Events in the Life of Abraham

Born, son of Terah	(Gen. 11:26)
Marries Sarah	(Gen. 11:29)
Migrates from Ur to Haran and west	(Gen. 11:31)
Called by God	(Gen. 12:1–5)
Descent to Egypt	(Gen. 12:10,13,20)
Separates from Lot	(Gen. 13:7–11)
Renewal of God's promise	(Gen. 13:14–18)
Rescues Lot	(Gen. 14:14)
God's Covenant	(Gen. 15:18; 17; Ps. 105:9)
Name changed; circumcision	(Gen. 17)
Entertains angels	(Gen. 18)
Pleads for Sodom	(Gen. 18:23)
Banishes Hagar, Ishmael	(Gen. 21:14)
Offers Isaac	(Gen. 22)
Buys Machpelah	(Gen. 23)
Seeks wife for Isaac	(Gen. 24)
Succeeded by Isaac	(Gen. 25:8)
Descendants	(Gen. 25)
Faith reflected in N.T.	(Rom. 4:9–16; Heb. 7:2, 11:8–17; James 2:23)

Thus far, no secular record of Abraham has come to light. But Mesopotamian documents now enable scholars to establish the conditions in which the Patriarchs lived. The Ras* Shamra texts have also shed light on the background of Abraham's era.

Abraham's Bosom, a figure of speech for paradise, it being popularly conceived that Abraham, Isaac, and Jacob would welcome the souls of the righteous (Luke 16:22; IV Macc. 13:17).

Abram, see ABRAHAM.

Absalom (ăb′sȧ-lŏm), ? Abishalom (I Kings 15:2, 10) ("the father is peace"), third son of David, grandson of a king of Geshur named Talmai. His mother, Maacah, bore him at Hebron (II Sam. 3:3). He was noted for his physical beauty, especially his abundant hair which he cut only at the end of every year (II Sam. 14:25f.). After killing his half-brother Amnon to avenge the ruined honor of his sister Tamar, he fled to Geshur in Aram; but returned to Jerusalem after three years and was reconciled to his father. Later he organized a plot to seize the throne of his father (II Sam. 13, 14). Gathering about him Judah's malcontents, he moved on his father's capital but met no resistance, because David and his adherents had fled across the Jordan, accompanied by Philistine mercenaries. When battle was joined in the woods of Ephraim in Transjordan, Absalom's badly organized army was defeated by David's seasoned commanders. The fleeing Absalom was caught by the neck in the fork of a branch (or possibly by his hair) as his horse passed under a tree. Joab, his attention called to the entrapped prince, dispatched him with darts (II Sam. 18). David, informed of his son's death, indulged in the grief recorded in the famous words of v. 33: "O Absalom, my son, my son Absalom! Would I had died for thee, O Absalom, my son!"

The prince is said to have been buried in a pit in the forest, beneath a cairn of stones. The so-called "Absalom's Tomb" in the Kidron Valley opposite the southern half of Jerusalem's Temple enclosure is a beautiful piece of probably Herodian architecture, having a scent-bottle cupola and a style mixing Doric, Ionic, and Egyptian elements.

3. "Absalom's Tomb," Jerusalem.

abyss (*ȧ*-bĭss′), the place of the dead, Hades (Rom. 10:7); the dwelling place of evil spirits under Apollyon (Satan) (Rev. 9:11, 17:8, 20:1–3). Sometimes rendered "the bottomless pit" or "the deep."

Accad (ăk″ăd), Agade, Akkad. (1) An ancient town which, according to the author of Gen. 10:10, was part of the kingdom of Nimrod, the mighty hunter. It is possibly the same city as Agade, established as the capital of an early Semitic Dynasty by Sargon I (c. 2371–2316 B.C.). The site of Agade is believed to be on the Euphrates a short distance SW. of modern Baghdad. (2) The narrow plain of Babylonia lying N. of Sumer, base of the Accad Dynasty (c. 2371–2230 B.C.), builders of the world's first great empire. In Accad, named from its capital, lay great cities in antiquity. Some of these are listed in Gen. 10. (3) The period during which the early Semitic Dynasty founded by Sargon I flourished. It is known archaeologically mainly by cylinder seals and monumental sculpture, some from the Sargonid graves at Ur. Artistic unity can be seen in the "Victory Stele" of Naram-Sin (c. 2291–2255 B.C.) found at Susa and now in the Louvre (*ANEP*², No. 309). Building remains of the period include the so-called "Palace" of Naram-Sin at Tell Brak, and the later stages of the Abu temple at Eshnunna (Tell Asmar). An Old Babylonian tablet (c. 18th century B.C.) bears an account of a legend concerning the calamity that befell Accad while Sargon's grandson, Naram-Sin, was king (*ANET*³, pp. 646–651). (4) The Accadian language, written in cuneiform*, was a Semitic tongue related to Hebrew, Arabic, and Aramaic. Ashurbanipal called the Accadian language "beautiful, obscure, and hard to master." The dialect of the Dynasty of Agade is designated "Old Accadian."

W. P. A.

Accho (ăk′ō), Acre, or Acco. (1) Phoenician seaport on the N. end of the broad Bay of Acre, 8 m. N. of Mt. Carmel. The city was "assigned" to the tribe of Asher, but they were unable to capture it (Judg. 1:31). It served as an approach to the rich Plain of Esdraelon and southern Galilee. Accho (Egypt. *'ky*) is mentioned in an Egyptian execration text of the 18th century B.C. (*ANET*³, p. 329, n. 8), in topographical lists of Tuthmosis III and Sethos I (*ANET*³, pp. 484-85, 487), and in the "Satirical Letter" of the late 13th century B.C. (*ANET*³, p. 477). It was captured by Sennacherib of Assyria in his Palestinian campaign of 701 B.C. (*ANET*³, p. 287). At the end of the 3d century B.C. its name was changed to Ptolemais, mentioned by Paul (Acts 21:7). Accho was fought for by Crusaders, some of whose fortifications are seen today. It was captured by Saladin in 1187 and held in 1229 by the Knights of St. John. (2) The Bay of Acre, N. of Mt. Carmel. (3) The northernmost coastal plain of Palestine, which was densely populated in antiquity.

W. P. A.

Aceldama (*ȧ*-sĕl′d*ȧ*-m*ȧ*) (A.S.V. Akeldama). Gk., "field of blood," adopted by transliteration from Aram. The potter's field referred to in Acts 1:19; a parcel of ground possibly on the S. slope of Hinnom Valley near Jerusalem. See POTTER'S FIELD.

Achaia (*ȧ*-kā′y*ȧ*), a Rom. senatorial province organized 140 B.C., consisting of Gk. mainland S. of "Macedonia" which included Thessaly, Epirus, and Acarnania. Its capital was Corinth*. Gallio was governor (A.S.V. proconsul) of Achaia c. A.D. 51 or 52, before whose judgment seat Paul was haled by turbulent Jews of Corinth (Acts 18:12–17). Christians of Achaia sent financial help to "the poor saints which are at Jerusalem" (Rom. 15:26). Paul mentions Stephanas and Fortunatus as first converts in Achaia, delightful personalities who "refreshed" him and gave him generous aid (I Cor. 16:15 f.). Paul was in Achaia more than once.

Achan (ā′kăn), a greedy member of the Tribe of Judah, whose seizure of dedicated spoils from the siege of Jericho was blamed for Israel's defeat at Ai* (Josh. 7). He was stoned to death in the Valley of Achor for the catastrophe he had brought upon Israel.

Achish (ā′kĭsh), son of Maoch and king of Gath, to whom David twice fled from Saul's wrath (I Sam. 21:10–15, 27:1–12, 28:1 f., 29:1–11). He is probably the Achish who was king of Gath at the beginning of Solomon's reign (I Kings 2:39).

Achor (ā′kôr), **Valley of,** S. of Jericho, formed part of the northern boundary between Judah and Benjamin. It was the place of Achan's stoning (Josh. 7:24–26). It was named by Hosea (2:15) as a symbol of fruitful hope.

acropolis, a fortified height overlooking certain Graeco-Roman towns, notably Athens.

Acts of the Apostles, The, fifth book of the N.T. It is a sequel to the story of "all that Jesus began both to do and to teach" (Acts 1:1) as narrated in Luke, and was written by the same author. It begins soon after the Crucifixion, and records outstanding events in the spread of the Gospel from Jerusalem to Rome, from the Jewish to the Gentile world. It is a historical record of the period, written in superb literary form.

The book adheres to the compressed, threefold outline of 1:8, as follows:

Introduction, 1:1–26. The risen Christ and the Apostles

1. "In Jerusalem"—
   2:1–47—Experiencing the Holy Spirit
   3:1–4:31—Activities of Peter and John
   4:32–5:11—The Church at Jerusalem
   5:12–6:7—Activities of "The Twelve"
   6:8–8:3—Activities of Stephen
2. "In all Judaea, and in Samaria"—
   8:4–11:18—Philip, Paul, Peter
   11:19–30—The Gentile Problem
   12:1–24—The Church and Herod's State
3. Paul's labors to carry the Gospel "unto the uttermost part of the earth"—
   12:25–15:39—Barnabas and Saul
   15:40–18:11—Paul and Silas
   18:12–28:13—Paul
   28:14–31—The Church in Rome

Both the Gospel of Luke and the Acts were addressed to the "most excellent Theophilus," who (from his name) was evidently a distinguished Gentile. Whether he sponsored this account, or whether he was a friendly official whom the author wished to win, is not known.

The numerous "we" sections in Acts where the narrative slips into vivid accounts by an eyewitness (Acts 16:10–17, 20:5–21:18, 27:1–28:16) suggest that the author may have been a traveling companion of Paul. The vivid first-hand recollections begin at Troas, where this author may have joined Paul. This has led some to identify the author as the "man of Macedonia," who appealed to Paul to cross the waters separating Asia and modern Europe. If Luke was the "man of Macedonia," this would account for two characteristics shared by the Gospel and Acts: their clear, Greek, literary style, and their appeal to the Graeco-Roman rather than to the Jewish world.

Acts gives a good picture of many phases of 1st-century life in the E. Mediterranean world. Some of the major characteristics of certain cities are disclosed, viz., the poverty of Jerusalem (Rom. 15:26; Acts 3:6) and one of the attempted solutions of this economic problem (Acts 2:44 f.); the philosophical talkativeness of Athens (Acts 17:17 f.); the highly intrenched business monopoly of the silversmiths centering in the Temple of Diana at Ephesus (Acts 19:24–34). A clearer picture of methods of travel is given than in the *Odyssey.* By land it was on foot or horse (Acts 23:24, 31 f.). Philip accepted a ride in a chariot (Acts 8:27–38). Coastal freighters took Paul aboard as a passenger (Acts 21:1–3; 27:1–5). The story of the wreck of the ship carrying grain from Alexandria to Rome, part of the last "we" passage, is the most vivid narrative of sea adventure in ancient literature (Acts 27, 28). The contrast between the hostility of the Jews (Acts 6:8–14, 23:12, 21:27) and the friendliness of Roman officials to Christians (Acts 18:12–16, 26:30–32, 28:30) is evidence of the author's purpose to commend Christianity to the Gentile world. The remarkable similarity in the language and structure of numerous speeches (Acts 2–5, 13) may be due to the author, or to a definite pattern all Apostolic preaching followed. These speeches proclaim: (1) that the new age promised by the Prophets has come; (2) that this age has arrived through the life and death and resurrection of Jesus, of which the Apostles are all witnesses; (3) that the gift of the Holy Spirit is a consequence of Christ's coming; and (4) that the outpouring of the Spirit proves that the new age has actually dawned. The Apostolic preaching included an appeal to repent and turn to God.

Acts portrays the Apostles, guided and empowered by the Holy Spirit, going forth to proclaim their message, first in Jerusalem, and later, as Paul and others realized the universality of their proclamation, to the Gentile world.

Adah (ā′dȧ) (Heb. "ornament"). (1) One of Lamech's wives (Gen. 4:19 ff.). (2) One of Esau's wives (Gen. 36:2, 4).

Adam. (1) ("ruddy," from Heb. word for "red," or coming from Accad. word designating "creature"), the first man (Gen. 1, 2), created in the image of God, i.e., having a measure of God's spirit. Husband of Eve, father of Cain, Abel, Seth. He was privileged to assign names to the animals. After he had disobeyed God's command to refrain from the fruit of a certain tree, Adam was expelled with Eve from his fair Garden of Eden* and condemned to earn his bread in the sweat of his brow. The sin of Adam continues to be mentioned in books later than Genesis, as in Job 31:33 (A.V.); I Cor. 15:22, 45. I Tim. 2:14 excuses Adam and stresses the woman's role in his disobedience.

There are apparently three distinct and quite different accounts of the life of Adam: Gen. 1:1–2:3; 2:4–4:26; 5:1–9:29 ("genealogy" = "history"). In the first of these the "man" is unnamed. In the second, he is referred to in the Hebrew merely by the term *hā'ādām,* "the man," and not by any proper name; not until the Septuagint Version (c. 250 B.C.) was the term regarded as a proper noun in this account. It is clear that Genesis considers the first man as the type of all mankind.

In the N.T., Adam's story is used to illustrate or explain certain points of Christian doctrine: marriage (Matt. 19:4–6); the subordinate position of women in the church (I Cor. 11:7–12; I Tim. 2:13 f.); the universality of grace (Rom. 5:12–21); the resurrection of the body (I Cor. 15:21 f.); the nature of the glorified body (I Cor. 15:45–49). Paul saw, in "the first, the old, the earthly Adam" (Rom. 5:14) a foreshadowing or "type" of Christ, who is "the second, the new, the heavenly Adam." For "original sin," see SIN.

(2) Adamah (ăd′*a*-m*a*), a town 10 m. S. of Succoth (Tell Deir Alla) overlooking the Jordan. It has been identified by Glueck as Tell ed Dâmiyeh, a flat-topped mound seamed with courses of ancient roads, overlooking rich bottomland. As the Israelites arriving from their desert wanderings at last came near Jordan, the miraculously timely damming up of the earthquake-ridden river enabled them to cross with the Ark (Josh. 3:16 f.). Glueck maintains that the 12 m. region between Adamah and Zarethan is the only spot in the Jordan Valley where such a damming up and "going over on dry land" could have occurred. He believes that in the copper-smelting region near Adamah—teeming with industry in Solomon's time (I Kings 7:46)—the two famous Temple pillars, Jachin and Boaz, were fashioned in the valley clay suitable for molds (see JACHIN, illus. 201).

adamant (ăd′*a*-mănt), a mineral or exceptionally hard metal, capable of sharpening or pointing graving tools.

Adar (ā′där) (Accad., probably "darkened"), 12th month in the post-Exilic Jewish calendar (Feb.-Mar.). See Ezra 6:15; also TIME.

adder, A.V. word rendering four different Heb. words, each probably representing a distinct species of snake with a venomous bite.

Adlai (ăd′lā-ī) ("Jehovah is justice"). Father of SHAPHAT (3), one of David's herdsmen (I Chron. 27:29).

Adonijah (ăd′ō-nī′j*a*), son of David (his fourth) and Haggith. His abortive attempt to succeed David, instead of the favored Solomon, was frustrated by the secret anointment of Solomon at Gihon, a spring outside the E. wall of Jerusalem. Requesting Bathsheba, mother of Solomon, to use her influence to secure him Abishag the Shunammite, companion and nurse of David (I Kings 1:4) for wife, he was put to death by Solomon for his designs on the throne (I Kings 2:24, 25).

adoption, a N.T. term used several times by Paul to express the Christian's experience of entering into sonship with the Father, through Jesus Christ. Paul, familiar with the process of Roman law by which a person was adopted with full privileges of sonship, carried over into his theology a legal usage (see Gal. 4; Rom. 8:15, 23, 9:4; Ephes. 1:5). The O.T. mentions two cases of adoption of persons in the usual social meaning of the word: Moses by Pharaoh's daughter (Ex. 2:10); and Esther by her cousin Mordecai (Esther 2:7). Josephus viewed Lot as having been adopted by Abraham while the latter was yet childless. The system of levirate marriage is somewhat akin to the system of adoption, since children of a childless widow taken in marriage by a brother-in-law inherited the name of the deceased (Deut. 25:5 f.).

Adramyttium (ăd′r*a*-mĭt′ĭ-*ŭ*m), a harbor in Mysia, the NW. portion of the Roman province of Asia, located on a gulf at the base of Mt. Ida and E. of Troas. At Caesarea Paul boarded a ship of Adramyttium (Acts 27:2–6).

Adria (ā′drĭ-*a*), the sea in which Paul was "driven up and down" for fourteen days (Acts 27:27) in his tempest-tossed ship. The Sea Adria probably took its name from the town near the mouth of the Po, as does the Adriatic. Some geographers make Adria connote the gulf between Illyria and Italy. Those of N.T. times make it refer to the Ionian Gulf and also the sea between Crete and Sicily. Luke intends Adria to designate that portion of the Mediterranean between Crete and the Peloponnesus, and Malta (Melita) and Sicily.

Adullam (*a*-dŭl′ăm), a town SW. of Jerusalem, approximately midway to Lachish and 9 m. NE. of Beit Jibrîn; now known as Tell esh-Sheikh Madhkur. It is first mentioned as a Canaanite city, but is best known for its cave in which David the fugitive hid (I Sam. 22:1). See also I Chron. 11:15; II Chron. 11:7.

adultery, voluntary sexual intercourse between one person and another not the lawful spouse, condemned by the law* codes and seen as detrimental to family* welfare (see Ex. 20:14; Deut. 5:18). Both guilty parties were punished by being stoned to death (Deut. 22:22 ff.). Jesus went a step beyond the O.T. Law by insisting that even he who so much as cast lustful looks at a woman not his wife had already committed adultery with her in his heart (Matt. 5:28). For his teaching concerning divorce, adultery, and marriage see Matt. 5:31 f. Adultery was one of the vices inveighed against by the writers of the N.T. Letters, as in Rom. 13:9; Gal. 5:19; Jas. 2:11. Symbolically, adultery expressed the sins of backsliding Israel (Hosea; Matt. 12:39). See FORNICATION; MARRIAGE, p. 422.

Adummim (*a*-dŭm′ĭm), a pass that was the shortest route from Jerusalem to Jericho through the Judaean wilderness, the scene of Jesus' parable of the Good Samaritan (Luke 10:30). It was near the boundary between Benjamin and Judah (Josh. 15:7); a hill in this neighborhood is today known as Tal'at ed-Dumm ("ascent of blood").

adversary, a term used to denote the force of evil as it attacks individuals seeking to walk in the ways of Yahweh. It is used simply as "the adversary" in I Tim. 5:14. I Pet. 5:8 refers to "your adversary the devil, as a roaring lion," seeking "whom he may devour." Political enemies described as adversaries of Israel and Judah are frequently referred to in the O.T., as in Ezra 4:1. See SATAN.

Aeneas (ē-nē′ăs), a man who had suffered long with palsy, but was healed by Peter (Acts 9:33–35).

Aenon (ē′nŏn) ("full of springs"), scene of baptisms by John the Baptist (John 3:23).

This reference is the only Biblical mention of Aenon, generally believed to have been "near to Salim," whose site has not yet been identified. Two locations have been suggested: one 8 Rom. m. S. of Beth-shan (Scythopolis) south of border between Galilee and Samaria, and a short distance W. of the Jordan; the other, the Salim of eastern Samaria NE. of Sychar. The abundance of water suggests that the candidates for baptism may have been here immersed, as they were at the Jordan.

Agabus (ăg′ȧ-bŭs), a Christian prophet from Jerusalem who at Antioch c. A.D. 44 predicted a famine (Acts 11:28); and also the "binding" of Paul (Acts 21:10 f.).

Agag (ā′găg), a king of the Amalekites* whom Samuel ordered Saul to exterminate. Saul spared Agag and much booty, however, and precipitated the hewing of Agag to pieces by the prophet himself at Gilgal (I Sam. 15).

Agape (ăg′ȧ-pē) (Gk., "love"), in the early Church denoted definite manifestations of brotherly love among believers, and particularly certain meals taken in common which had a more or less religious character. The Agape rites preceded celebration of the Lord's Supper. Jude 12, possibly II Peter 2:13 and I Cor. 11:34, indicate that "love feasts" (A.V. feasts of charity, Jude 12) required certain disciplinary measures for their purification. See LOVE.

agora, at first the name given the general assembly of common Gk. free men, and later applied to the market place or public square where they met to hear debates and conduct civic business, as Romans did in their forums. Paul was familiar with the great agora of Athens*, the one at Corinth*, etc. In the Athenian agora he disputed daily with those who met with him (Acts 17:17).

The Athenian agora has been fully excavated by the American School of Classical Studies (in the 1930's and from 1946 on to completion). The structures found in this vast area have been studied and published. Small objects recovered, as ostraca, pottery, jewelry, and urns from a Mycenaean chamber c. the 14th century B.C., are now housed in a modern museum containing recovered portions of the ancient Stoa* of Attalos, which closed the square toward the E. (see map).

Structures excavated in the Athenian agora include the round *Tholos* where standard weights and measures were stored and where the Council's executive committee ate; the colonnaded *Metroon*, repository of state archives; the *Bouleuterion* or council chamber; a small temple of Apollo; and possibly an armory. The Stoa of Attalos, among whose colonnades Socrates conducted some of his dialogues, is mentioned above (see AREOPAGUS). The whole group of agora buildings was overlooked by the temple of Hephaistos, god of metal-workers (often called the Theseion). The remarkable preservation of the latter is due to its having been used as a Christian church.

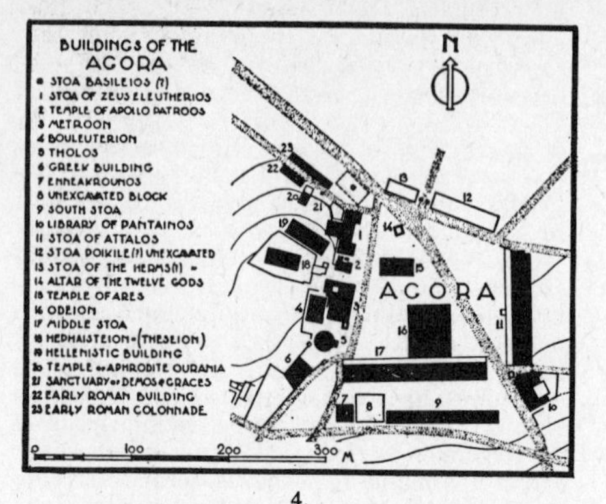

4.

agriculture. See FARMING.

Agrippa, Herod Agrippa I, called "Herod the King," grandson of Herod the Great; son of Aristobulus and Bernice. He was educated in Rome, having as schoolmates such royal youth as Drusus, son of Tiberius, and Claudius. In A.D. 37 he again visited Rome to further his fortunes. Drusus had died, so he attached himself to Caius (later Emperor Caligula). For some incautious remarks he was imprisoned by the Emperor Tiberius; upon the latter's death a few months later he was freed by Caligula, who made him king of the region in Abilene which had been ruled by Lysanias, and also of the realm of Philip the Tetrarch. Two years later (A.D. 39) he wrested Galilee and Peraea from his brother-in-law, Antipas. In A.D. 41 the Emperor Claudius added the province of Judaea to his kingdom, which then equalled that of Herod the Great. Agrippa I was an extravagant

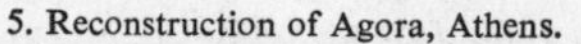

5. Reconstruction of Agora, Athens.

builder, beginning a project by which the N. wall of Jerusalem would include suburbs. Portions of this wall have been excavated. Generally friendly to the Jews in Palestine as against the Roman overlords, this grasping ruler nevertheless appears in Acts 12:1 as ordering the death of James "the brother of John with the sword"; in Acts 12:3 as precipitating the famous arrest of Peter which resulted in his miraculous delivery from prison; and in 12:23 as seized with a loathsome and fatal illness while attending games at Caesarea at the age of 53 (A.D. 44). Agrippa, Bernice, and Drusilla were three of his children mentioned by name in the N.T. See HEROD.

Agrippa, Herod Agrippa II, son of Herod Agrippa I and Cypros, born c. A.D. 27, becoming the seventh and last ruler of the Herod the Great family. Only 17 at the time of his father's death, he was not appointed by Claudius to the throne, but remained at Rome in the Emperor's household; Judaea was again placed under a procurator. Upon attaining his majority and upon the death of his uncle, Herod, King of Chalcis, he had bestowed on him by Claudius that small realm on the Anti-Lebanon slopes (Chalcis). Later he was transferred to the larger territory which had been ruled by Philip the Tetrarch. During the reign of Nero certain Galilean and Perean cities were added to his territory. His relationship (probably indiscreet) with his sister Bernice created a scandal, according to Josephus. He enlarged the Hasmonaean palace at Jerusalem, and beautified Caesarea* Philippi. While Paul was imprisoned at Caesarea (at the N. end of the Plain of Sharon), Agrippa II and his sister Bernice came to salute Festus, who had succeeded Felix as procurator of Judaea (Acts 25:13). Expressing their desire to hear the famous prisoner, Agrippa and Bernice amid "great pomp" (Acts 25:23) went to the place of trial. When Festus admitted that he found "nothing worthy of death" in Paul, Agrippa authorized the famous statement of defense spoken by Paul (Acts 26), after which the king uttered his notable words—whether in derisive sarcasm or wistful yearning: "Almost thou persuadest me to be a Christian" (A.V. Acts 26:28), or, as the R.S.V. says, "In a short time you think to make me a Christian!"

Herod Agrippa II moved to Rome with Bernice after the capture of Jerusalem, enjoyed the rank of praetor, and died there in A.D. 93. See HEROD.

Ahab (ā′hăb). (1) Son of Omri, King of Israel, second in the dynasty reigning at Samaria. His rule lasted from 869 B.C. to 850 B.C. and paralleled that of King Jehoshaphat of Judah. Few personalities of the O.T. have more melodramatic incidents related of them than Ahab. Marrying Jezebel, Phoenician princess, daughter of a king of Zidon (Sidon), he allowed his wife's religion—that of the Phoenician Baal* Melkarth—to be practised. Ahab did not wholly abandon Yahweh, but he encouraged the Baal cult, for which he built a temple on the palace hill. Rebuked by Elijah, who predicted a punitive drought for the kingdom (I Kings 17:1), Ahab saw his fertile terraces and orchards wither—then blamed the "troubler of Israel." In the 3d year of the devastating drought, Elijah called on Ahab to witness a contest at the SE. end of the ridge of Mt. Carmel (El-Muhraqah, "Place of the Burning") (see illus. 128) between the prophets of Baal and the prophet of Yahweh (I Kings 18:19–46). The outcome established Yahweh as "God in Israel." Yahweh instructed Elijah to anoint Jehu* to succeed Ahab. The unpopularity of Ahab was brought to a head by the judicial murder of Naboth and the appropriation of his vineyard (I Kings 21). Ahab allied himself with Benhadad*, King of Damascus, and other local rulers, to resist the advance of Shalmaneser III of Assyria, who was checked at the Battle of Karkar (853 B.C.). Ahab later was fatally wounded between the plates of his armor, as he stood in his chariot during a battle to regain Ramoth-gilead E. of the Jordan.

A historic rock record of Shalmaneser III on the upper Tigris refers to Ahab's having sent 2,000 chariots and 10,000 infantrymen into battle against him. Some of the carved ivories which trimmed Ahab's palace and furniture at Samaria (see IVORY) have been excavated and may be seen in the Fogg Art Museum, Harvard University, and the Palestine Archaeological Museum, Jerusalem. Other archaeological finds related to Ahab are the ruins of the palace complex constructed by Omri and Ahab on the hilltop in Samaria.

(2) A prophet, the son of Kilaiah, of whom Jeremiah predicted that Nebuchadnezzar, King of Babylon, would roast him in a fire because of his misdeeds and lying words Jer. 29:21).

Ahasuerus (ȧ-hăz′ū-ē′rŭs). (1) Son of Darius Hystaspes and Atossa, daughter of Cyrus the Great, identified by many as the Achaemenid Persian King Xerxes I (486–465 B.C.) who was defeated by the Greek fleet at Salamis in 480 B.C. The Book of Esther depicts the impulsive ruler as having for his queen the Jewish Esther*, cousin or niece of Mordecai. But so many attacks have been made upon the historicity of this book that the whole narrative is open to question. In Esther 1:1 Ahasuerus is described as reigning "from India even unto Ethiopia, over an hundred and seven and twenty provinces." Grotefend's deciphering of inscriptions at Persepolis indicates that Ahasuerus was Xerxes. The Hebrew name in Esther 1:1 corresponds to the Aram. and Bab. spelling of the Persian Xerxes.

(2) Another Ahasuerus—son of Darius the Mede—is mentioned in Dan. 9:1.

Ahava (ȧ-hā′vȧ), the small river or canal on whose banks Ezra assembled the Jews to prepare them spiritually for their journey out of Babylonian captivity back to Jerusalem. There they awaited the Levites whom Ezra sent for, and there they kept a fast, asking God's protection on their journey (Ezra 8:15, 21, 31).

Ahaz (ā′hăz) (Jehoahaz I), King of Judah (c. 735–715 B.C.), was the son of King Jotham and was succeeded by Hezekiah*. Throughout his reign, during which he became a vassal of Assyria, he was exposed to the noble prophecies of Micah, and especially Isaiah*, yet he "made his son to pass through the fire. . . . And he sacrificed and burnt incense in the high places . . . and under every green tree" (II Kings 16:3 f.). He failed to invoke Yahweh's aid in the Jerusalem crisis precipitated by the attack of Rezin, King of Syria, and Pekah, King of Israel, a situation which evoked the masterful utterance of Isaiah voicing the Messianic hope (Isa. 7:1–9:7). Instead of placing his faith in the Lord, Ahaz turned to the Assyrian king, Tiglath-pileser, for succor, purchasing his aid with Temple and palace treasures. Ahaz was responsible for the construction of an altar (from a model he had seen in Damascus, possibly of Assyrian origin) which he set up in the Jerusalem Temple Area (II Kings 16:10–13).

Ahaziah (ā′hȧ-zī′ȧ). (1) King of Israel c. 850–849 B.C., son of Ahab and perhaps Jezebel. As corrupt as his father, he consulted Baal-zebub* rather than the God of Israel, and was denounced bitterly by Elijah, who prophesied his death (II Kings 1:2 ff.). The highlight of his short but futile reign was the abortive expedition in cooperation with Jehoshaphat of Judah to Ophir for gold; the naval vessels were broken at Ezion-Geber (I Kings 22:48–49; II Chron. 20:35–37). Leaving no son, Ahaziah was succeeded by his brother Jehoram (II Kings 1:17).

(2) King of Judah c. 842, son of King Jehoram, and grandson or nephew of King Ahab of Israel, through his mother Athaliah*. The chronicler blamed his evil ways on his mother's counsel (II Chron. 22:3). He was allied with King Jehoram of Israel against the Syrians (II Kings 8:28–29). While visiting Jehoram in Jezreel, he was wounded in his chariot by the Israelite rebel Jehu and escaped to Megiddo only to die there (II Kings 9:14-28) after a reign of only a year.

Ahijah (ȧ-hī′jȧ), the name of at least 9 men in the O.T. The most prominent of these was the prophet of Shiloh*, contemporary with Jeroboam I, King of Israel (c. 922–901 B.C.). Even while King Solomon lived, Ahijah had demonstrated his disapproval of this ruler's extravagances and his patronage of Sidonian and Ammonite gods. In the presence of Jeroboam*, Ahijah cut his prophetic cloak into twelve pieces, demonstrating visually his pronouncement that the kingdom would be torn from Solomon and his heirs, and that ten Tribes would come under the leadership of Jeroboam (I Kings 11:29–40), with two remaining for Solomon's heirs, "for Jerusalem's sake." In his blind old age Ahijah of Shiloh spoke against Jeroboam and prophesied the death of his son (I Kings 14).

Ahimaaz (ȧ-hĭm′ā-ăz). (1) Father of Ahinoam, wife of Saul (I Sam. 14:50). (2) Son of Zadok the priest, who participated in the events narrated in II Sam. 17:17–21. Chap. 18 is viewed by some as by the author of early source (see SOURCES) in Samuel—a masterpiece of historical writing. As an agent of the party in Jerusalem loyal to David during the revolt of Absalom (II Sam. 15:27, 36) he, with Jonathan the son of Abiathar, carried vital information to David (17:17 ff.). This Ahimaaz may have been the son-in-law of Solomon stationed in Naphtali (I Kings 4:15).

Ahimelech (ȧ-hĭm′ĕ-lĕk) ("the brother is king"). (1) Son of Ahitub and a chief priest at Nob, where the Ark was guarded after its removal from Shiloh. I Sam. 21 records his giving hallowed "shewbread" (highly illegal by ritual law) and the sword of Goliath to the fugitive David. Doeg the Edomite reported the incident to Saul, who slaughtered Ahimelech and 85 of the priestly group (I Sam. 22:19). His son Abiathar* was a priest at Nob under David (II Sam. 8:17). (2) A Hittite in the service of David (I Sam. 26:6).

Ahinoam (ȧ-hĭn′ō-ăm). (1) Daughter of Ahimaaz and wife of Saul (I Sam. 14:50). (2) A native of the town of Jezreel; wife of David; mother of Amnon, his eldest son (I Sam. 25:43, 27:3; II Sam. 3:2).

Ahiram (ȧ-hī′răm). (1) A son of Benjamin (Num. 26:38). (2) A Phoenician king whose capital was coastal Byblos (see GEBAL). His elegant excavated sarcophagus is inscribed with Phoenician writing (c. 11th century B.C.), which affords an important link in the development of the alphabet (see WRITING). The sarcophagus and jewels of Ahiram are in the National Museum at Beirut. "Ahiram" is probably the same name as "Hiram," but he is not to be identified with Hiram, King of Tyre, who figures in Solomon's trade annals. Byblos was N. of Tyre.

Ahithophel (ȧ-hĭth′ō-fĕl) ("brother of folly"), David's counselor, whose wisdom was highly rated (II Sam. 16:23). Disloyal to David during the revolt of Absalom (II Sam. 15, 17), he committed suicide, when his advice to Absalom was not followed (17:23).

Ahola (ȧ-hō′lȧ). See OHOLAH.

Aholibah (ȧ-hŏl′ĭ-bȧ). See OHOLAH.

Ahura-Mazda (ä′hōō-rȧ-măz′dȧ) (*Ormazd*, "Lord Wisdom"). The chief god in the Zoroastrian (ancient Aryan) religion of Iranian peoples. See illus. 6, p. 11.

'Ai (ā′ī) (Heb. *ha'ay*, "The Ruin"), a city mentioned in Gen. 12:8 as E. of the mountain near Bethel where Abraham pitched his tent on his arrival in Canaan. Its site (et-Tell) 2 m. from Bethel was excavated in 1933–35 by Mme. Judith Marquet-Krause, who uncovered an Early Bronze Age city of the 3d millennium B.C. with an elaborate system of defenses, a shrine built against the city wall, numerous pottery vessels, and alabaster bowls attesting Egyptian contact. This city was destroyed c. 2400 B.C. and the site remained unoccupied until a small Iron I village was erected over the earlier ruins in the 12th century B.C. Recent excavations directed by J. A. Callaway (1964–69) have confirmed the earlier results, revealing more of the fortifications and buildings of the early city, and outlining the extent of the small, unfortified, Iron I settlement on the acropolis.

Since no city existed on the site of 'Ai in the 13th century B.C., the probable date of the Hebrew Conquest, various attempts have been made to explain the apparent discrepancy between the archaeological evidence and the account of the destruction of 'Ai given in Josh. 7:2–5 and 8:1–29. M. Noth, among others, believes the story to be etiological. Some suggest that the site of Biblical 'Ai is to be located elsewhere (see *Biblica* 42, 1961, pp. 201–216). The majority follow Albright (*BASOR* 74, 1939, p. 17) and suppose that Josh. 7 and 8 reflect the capture of Late Bronze Age Bethel, and that later tradition confused the two. Recently, Callaway has

6. Bas-relief of Ahura-Mazda.

proposed that Josh. 8:1–29 describes the conquest of the small Iron I village at 'Ai in the 12th century B.C. (*JBL* 87, 1968, pp. 312–320). No completely satisfactory solution has as yet been proposed. See J. Marquet-Krause, *Les fouilles de 'Ay*, Paris, 1949, and *Syria* 16, 1935, pp. 325–345; L. H. Vincent, *RB* 46, 1937, pp. 231–266; J. A. Callaway, *BASOR* 178, 1965, pp. 13–40; 196, 1969, pp. 2–16; 198, 1970, pp. 7–31. W. P. A.

Aijeleth hash-Shahar (ā′jĕ-lĕth hăsh-shā′här) (A.V. Aijeleth Shahar), probably the melody to which Ps. 22 was set: "Hind of the dawn" or "The hind in its swiftness."

Ajalon (ăj′à-lŏn) (A.S.V. Aijalon), **Valley of,** runs from Jerusalem down toward the Mediterranean, cutting across the hills of Shephelah N. of Emmaus, curving toward Lydda; the site of Joshua's challenge to the sun and moon (Josh. 10:12 f.).

'Ajjûl, Tell el- ("mound of the little calf"), a tremendous mound on the S. side of the Wâdī Ghuzzeh c. 4 m. S. of modern Gaza. Formerly identified as the site of ancient Gaza (Petrie), it is now considered to be Beth-eglaim. See *AJSL* 55, 1938, pp. 337–359.

Akhenaton (ä′kĕ-nä′t′n) ("it is well with Aton"), the 8th Pharaoh (c. 1370–1353 B.C.) of the Eighteenth Egyptian Dynasty, the first dynasty of the brilliant new kingdom. He was earlier known as Amenophis (or Amenhotep) IV, son of the invalid Amenophis III, with whom he was for a time coregent). His mother was Queen Tiy. He was probably educated by the learned priesthood at Heliopolis, the Biblical On* (Gen. 41:45, 46:20). In the 6th year of his reign he renounced the state worship of the Theban Amun* and adopted the pure worship of the Heliopolitan Re-Harakti, or Aton. The striking similarity between Akhenaton's Hymn to the Aton and the Hebrew Psalm 104 has led some to argue that the former was the source of the latter, possibly through a translation into a Semitic tongue of the Egyptian's work, preserved for centuries after the decline of Atonism in Egypt. (See John A. Wilson, *The Burden of Egypt*, pp. 227f., The University of Chicago Press.) Halfway between Thebes and Memphis he established a new capital, which he named Akhetaton (Amarna), "City of the glory of Aton." He displaced the old priesthood of Amun with devotees of a new faith, marked by spiritual beauty and a tendency toward monotheism, which renounced all images—depicting Aton, the world creator and universal ruler, as the sun disk, whose rays terminated in small hands extending blessings. The "monotheism" came to an end when Akhenaton himself rose to a position of deity. After his death Eye, an "elder statesman," guided into the anarchy-ridden kingdom the 9-year-old protégé of Akhenaton's wife Nofretete, Tut-ankh-aton (the later Tut-ankh-amun), who abandoned Amarna and the faith of its founder; returned the royal capital to Thebes; and restored the priesthood of Amun. It expressed its gratitude by giving Tut-ankh-amun a costly burial. Breasted called Akhenaton "the first *individual* in human history." See AMARNA; EGYPT (4).

Akkad, see ACCAD.

7. Alabaster ointment jars; greatest height, approx. 9 in.

alabaster, a cream-colored or white mineral carbonate of lime, resembling marble, used in Bible times for fashioning unguent containers and other *objets d'art*. It is mentioned in connection with the anointing of Jesus (Luke 7:37; Mark 14:3; Matt. 26:7) (see ANOINT). Ancient people made alabaster columns and trimmings for temples. Egyptians used it for canopic jars in which organs of the embalmed were stored. A famous alabaster lamp of hedgehog shape, fashioned more than 1,000 years before Abraham, excavated at Ur, is in the University Museum, Philadelphia. See LAMP, illus. 237.

Alamoth (ăl′ă-mŏth) ("maidens"), a nebulous musical or liturgical term used in I Chron. 15:20 and in the title of Ps. 46. It may refer to use of young women's voices or a musical instrument for accompaniment, or the word may belong with Ps. 45.

Alcimus (ăl′sĭ-mŭs) (Gk. "strong"), a high priest sympathetic to the Greeks and hated by the Jews; he destroyed the inner wall of the Temple, 159 B.C. (I Macc. 7).

aleph, first letter of the Phoen. and Heb. alphabets, represented by an ox head. In Heb. *aleph* is a consonant, indicated in transliteration by an apostrophe, as 'HYH(I am). The Gk. *alpha*, a vowel, is derived from *aleph*.

Alexander. (1) Alexander the Great, one of the most brilliant men of ancient times, King of Macedonia, founder of Hellenism, military genius, propagator of Greek culture. Son of Philip of Macedon, he was born at Pella in Macedonia 356 B.C., died in Babylon 323 B.C. After his defeat of Darius at Issus (333 B.C.), he mastered Asia, advancing through Syria as he took Damascus, Sidon, Tyre, Gaza. He gave privileges to the Jews in Alexandria. He may be mentioned cryptically in Dan. 7:7 and 11:3. See GREECE.

After Alexander's death his empire was broken up into five provinces, each ruled separately by a general: Ptolemy in Egypt, Seleucus in Babylonia, Antipater in Macedonia, Lysimachus in Thrace, and Antigonus in Phrygia. Later further splitting up occurred, but three dynasties became established: in Macedonia, Egypt and Syria.

Though Alexander's empire fell apart, the Greek kingdoms that appeared throughout Asia lasted for centuries. More important than Alexander's conquests—especially in the history of the Hebrews—was the resultant breaking down of barriers between the East and the West and the rapid expansion of Greek civilization throughout the Near East. Hellenistic influences let loose in Palestine offered a severe challenge to Judaism; by the 2d century B.C. Jerusalem was split into pro-Hellenists and less fashionable, conservative anti-Hellenists. When Antiochus* IV Epiphanes adopted the policy of promoting, officially, some of the most abhorred Greek notions and practices, the Jewish reaction became open revolt under the Maccabees*.

(2) Alexander, son of Simon "a Cyrenian" (Mark 15:21), possibly well known in the Roman Church. Whether this is the same Alexander mentioned in I Tim. 1:20 is controversial.

(3) Alexander, a relative of the high priest at Jerusalem (Acts 4:6).

(4) Alexander of Ephesus, a Jew pushed forward by other Jews to avoid their being involved in the fury which broke upon the Christians when Paul protested against their profitable business of making silver shrines to Diana (Acts 19:33).

(5) Alexander the coppersmith (II Tim. 4:14) who did Paul "much evil."

Alexandra, daughter of the Maccabean leader John Hyrcanus. She was the pro-Pharisee wife of the Maccabean ruler Alexander Jannaeus (103–76 B.C.), and the mother of two other Hasmonaean rulers, Hyrcanus II and Aristobulus II. Her reign (76–67 B.C.) was a golden age for the Jews of Palestine, for whom elementary schools* were established (c. 75 B.C.) under the able leadership of her brother, Rabbi Ben-shetach.

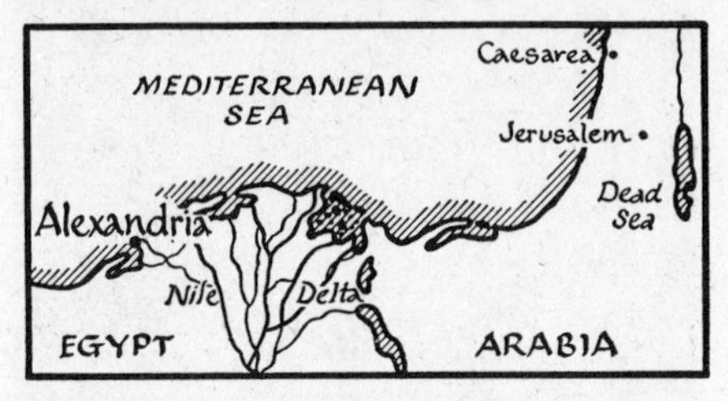

8. Alexandria.

Alexandria. (1) Egyptian city founded by Alexander the Great 332 B.C., on the Mediterranean 14 m. W. of the Canopic mouth of the Nile; one of the three greatest Mediterranean cities in the era of Jesus and Paul. It was a center of Greek culture; the site of the most famous library (see LIBRARIES) of antiquity; and the seat of astronomical investi-

9. "Pompey's Pillar," the most impressive monument (70 ft.) of modern Alexandria. May be a pillar which once stood in the Temple of Serapis. Ivan Dmitri for American Export Lines.

gations from the 3d century B.C. to the 3d century A.D., long after the Ptolemaic Age. It was marked by the "Pharos" lighthouse, one of the "Seven Wonders of the World." It became the home of a large Greek-speaking colony of Jews who demanded the translation of the Scriptures into Greek; this translation, the Septuagint, was begun under Ptolemy Philadelphus (285–246 B.C.), perhaps completed by 132 B.C. (see TEXT, VERSIONS, MANUSCRIPTS; etc.) Early Christian scholars, like Clement of Alexandria and Origen, edited early N.T. texts in the shadow of the vast library, and played a part in recovering original manuscripts. A grain ship from Alexandria bound for Rome (Acts 27:6) had Paul for a passenger when wrecked off Malta (Melita); and another ship from Alexandria, "The Castor and Pollux," took the Apostle three months later on the final lap of his cruise to Rome (Acts 28:11). Jewish merchants there conducted much of the corn trade with Rome. Their benefactions may have built the Alexandrian synagogue at Jerusalem (Acts 6:9). Paul seems never to have visited Alexandria, possibly out of deference to Alexandrian-born Apollos (Acts 18:24), who may have written the Epistle to the Hebrews and directed it to Alexandrian Jews. Alexandria is today a prosperous port, but has almost no traces of her ancient splendor.

(2) Alexandria Troas, simply called Troas, is in the Troad c. 10 m. S. of the W. end of the Dardanelles. It has a good harbor, from which Paul sailed into Macedonia after his night vision of the man calling for help (Acts 16:9). Incomplete excavations have brought to light ruins of an aqueduct, theater, and city walls 6 m. in circumference.

algum, possibly juniper (II Chron. 2:8). See ALMUG.

almond, *Amygdalus prunus* (Linn. *Amygdalus communis*), a delicately flowering white-blossomed tree blooming in January. The almond may have been introduced into Palestine from India or Persia. The bitter type of almond was prized for the flavor of its oil as well as for its beauty. When old Jacob sent native condiments down to Joseph, his package included almonds (Gen. 43:11). Because of its early blooming it is known as *shakedh*, or "wakener," "watcher," and was used by

10. Almond.

Israel as a symbol of hope. Almond blossoms bloomed on Aaron's rod (Num. 17:8) (see ROD). Shekels of the brief period of independence under the Maccabees bore the budding almond and the pot of manna. The golden seven-branched candlestick had cups shaped like almond blossoms (Ex. 25:32–38), whose pattern Moses had seen in the Mount. The almond trees known to the Tribes while fashioning their lamps and vessels were probably ones seen in Egypt and remembered after the Exodus. The flowering almond was sometimes a token of times "out of joint" (Eccles. 12:5).

alms, donations for the poor, are not mentioned under this name in the O.T., although the Mosaic Law (Deut. 24:19, for example) directed that at harvest some sheaves be left uncut "for the stranger, for the fatherless, and for the widow." In N.T. times alms giving marked the spiritually minded Christian, and was efficacious in securing the remission of sin. Jesus specifically enjoined secrecy in alms giving (Matt. 6:1–4). Further references to the giving of alms are found in Acts 24:17, 3:3, 10:2; Luke 21:1–4.

almug, "a great amount of" (I Kings 10:11); possibly the very famous rosewood or red sandalwood which was brought as part of Hiram* of Tyre's cargo to Solomon for building enterprises at Jerusalem. Almug from Ophir was prized for harp frames, and for trim in palace construction. Solomon evidently believed that the timber of Lebanon* included algum (II Chron. 2:8).

aloes (Ps. 45:8; Song of Sol. 4:14), perhaps the "eaglewood" native to India, sold by eastern traders, and popular for its fragrance when burned. It is not the common bitter aloes plant. (See John 19:39.)

alpha, first letter of the Gk. alphabet. It has special significance in the Bible, as expressing the timelessness and eternal existence of God, especially when used in connection with omega, the last letter of the alphabet, as in Rev. 1:8, 21:6, 22:13, denoting "the beginning" and "the end." See ALEPH; OMEGA.

alphabet. See WRITING.

Alphaeus (ăl-fē′ŭs). (1) The father of Levi, a tax collector (Mark 2:13–17 R.S.V.; cf. Matt. 9:9). (2) The father of James the Less (Matt. 10:3; Mark 3:18; Luke 6:15; Acts 1:13). See JAMES (2); MARY (4).

altar (Heb. "place of sacrifice"). The O.T. contains more than 400 references to altars. Primitive ones in Palestine, some of which are still seen on mounds in Jordan, were dolmens or piles of man-arranged stones, the top one of which was flat enough to receive offerings of sacrificed animals, grain, etc. Some early altars were of clay. The author of the J narrative tells of the Patriarchs' erecting altars, but never states that they burned sacrifices on them; prayer, in J, takes the place of burnt offerings. Some of the earliest altars of the O.T.—usually built on sites where God had spoken or an appearance of Deity had taken place (a theophany)—are: Noah's (Gen. 8:20); Abraham's (Gen. 22:9), erected at Bethel* after he had pitched his tent there; and those built by Moses when the Lord spoke after his victory over the Amalekites (Ex. 17:15) and before he went up into the Mount (Ex. 24:4–8). Mosaic Law specified unhewn stones or native earth for altar construction. Levitical law contains many instructions about the proper use of altars.

One of the most important altar narratives of the O.T. concerns the one erected by David

11. Abraham offers sacrifice.

on Jerusalem's Mt. Moriah, at a threshing floor of natural stone which he bought from Araunah the Jebusite (II Sam. 24:15–25). This sacred rock became the central place of sacrifice in the Temple* of Solomon, and is seen today in Jerusalem under the Moslem prayer-place, "The Dome of the Rock." It is 51 ft. broad and 4 to 6½ ft. high, and is surrounded by an elegant metal grille erected by Crusaders. The holes and channels down which blood from legions of sacrificed animals flowed to the Kidron are plainly visible.

Saul built a field altar during his conquest of the Philistines (I Sam. 14:31–35); on it he sacrificed to Yahweh the booty of sheep, oxen, and calves.

Altars to deities other than Yahweh appear in the O.T.—to the Baals (II Chron. 33:3); to various other Canaanite gods (Deut. 12:3 f.); to Chemosh, national deity of Moab, for whom Solomon built an altar near Jerusalem to please his foreign wives; and to the Ash-

12. The Great Altar for burnt offering, Megiddo.

toreth of the Zidonians (I Kings 11:5–7). Almost every elevation in the Promised Land had been a Canaanite "high place"* for a major or a minor god. Some of these sites were taken over for worship by Hebrews, as at Beer-sheba, Bethel, Shechem. But Yahweh gave specific instructions for throwing down pagan altars before new ones were reared; for hewing down cultic pillars (Deut. 12:2 f.); and for burning groves where Asherim (see ASHERAH) were worshipped. Manasseh (c. 687–642 B.C.), vassal king under Esar-haddon, reared altars to "the host of heaven" even in the Jerusalem Temple.

Greatest interest is attached to altars of the Tabernacle and the Temple, chief centers of Hebrew worship for many centuries. Strands of narrative concerning these altars are tangled and often confused. No vestige of the Tabernacle has come down the centuries, and no contemporary art portrayal of it. The description in Ex. 25–31 and 35–40, possibly by post-Exilic authors, indicates three altars: a small portable structure for the burnt offerings, a table of acacia ("shittim wood"), overlaid with metal and used for shewbread (the bread shown to God); and an altar of incense dedicated to the act of worship. So, too, the elaborate Temple built by Solomon at Jerusalem from a Phoenician model had three altars, but on a grander scale than the simple woven equipment of the Tent of Meeting.

(1) The great altar for burnt offering was in the outer court, at the E. end of the Temple structure. The narrative of I Kings 8:64 suggests that the tremendous number of oxen and sheep sacrificed at Solomon's dedication of the Temple were burned on the ground "in the middle of the court". The sacred Rock now encased by the Dome of the Rock may be the Holy of Holies (Albright, De Vaux). The enormous "brazen" altar described in II Chron. 4:1 may have been of later construction, although there is much evidence also in favor of its having been made by Hiram's Phoenician artisans.

(2) The table of shewbread, in the Holy Place or *Hekal*, was in a sense an altar.

(3) The small, gold-plated cedar altar of incense stood in front of the flight of steps leading up into the Holy of Holies, *Debir*, where God abode (I Kings 7:49). Concerning the "horns of the altar" affixed to tne great altar of burnt sacrifices there has been much speculation. They follow a Canaanite pattern. Possibly they were reminiscent of actual horns of sacrificed animals. A horned limestone altar dating c. 1050–1000 B.C. was excavated from Stratum V of Megiddo (Biblical Armageddon).

A new altar was built in the year of the Return (538 B.C.), followed by the restoration of the Temple itself (520–515 B.C.) by Zerubbabel.

An interesting incident in the altar lore of Jerusalem concerning King Ahaz is narrated in II Kings 16:10–15.

Recent archaeological explorations have unearthed numerous historic altars of early date in Bible lands. One is attached to the S. wall of an Egyptian Canaanite temple in the fosse or fortification trench at the foot of the fortress mound at Lachish (Tell ed-Duweir) near the Palestine-Egyptian border. It was constructed between 1475 and 1223 B.C., in times of relative security, by the citizens of the town. Near the small sanctuary altar is a bench on which objects of worship were placed. At the N. Syrian coastal city of Ras Shamrah (Ugarit) an altar dating from before 1906–1887 B.C. has been excavated from a temple of Baal. The altar stands in a court, approached by steps from a portico. From similar sanctuaries in centers of Canaanite religion radiated influences upon Hebrew ways of worship.

Excavated Megiddo* has yielded a great altar for burnt offerings, made of unhewn stones (Ex. 20:25) and rubble and measuring 26 ft. in diameter and 4½ ft. high. This unique specimen lies within levels dated between 2500 and 1800 B.C. Megiddo has also supplied a number of unique horned incense altars carved from limestone on which round pottery bowls or chalices once stood.

Egyptian art has preserved a record of one of the most impressive altars of Bible times—the high altar of young Akhenaton* at Amarna. It was reached through several outer courts all open to the sky.

There are only about 24 references to altars in the N.T. Of these, 6 are made by Jesus as in Matt. 5:23 f. In the record of Paul there are 5 allusions to altars, including the significant observation he made at Athens (Acts 17:23). An altar of this type has been excavated at Ephesus. Eight of the other N.T. allusions to altars occur in Revelation.

Altashheth (ăl-tăsh'hĕth) (A.V. Altaschith), possibly a familiar melody, "Do not destroy," to which the words of Pss. 57–59 and 75 might be sung.

Amalekites (ăm'*ă*-lĕk-īts), an ancient group of nomadic marauders, descendants of Esau's grandson Amalek (Gen. 36:12), called "the first of the nations" (Num. 24:20). They occupied the desert S. of Canaan, E. of the Wilderness of Shur in Sinai Peninsula, and penetrated into N. Arabia and the Arabah N. of Ezion-geber. They were chronic enemies of early Israel, from the time when they attacked the Hebrews migrating from Goshen under Moses (Deut. 25:17–19) and were defeated by Joshua at Rephidim (Ex. 17), through the period of the Judges, when Gideon conquered them (Judg. 6:33, 7:12). These people "of the south" continued to be a scourge, apparently used by Yahweh to punish wayward Israel when the people worshipped Baalim, and from whom He delivered them when they cried for help (Judg. 10:12). King Saul smote them but failed to destroy their rich booty of livestock as God commanded, thus evoking the bitter rebuke of Samuel the prophet, who himself hewed to pieces Agag, the Amalekite ruler (I Sam. 15:33). David was forced to rescue two of his wives from Amalekite bandits (I Sam. 30:18). Descendants of David fought a remnant of Amalekites down in the weird fastnesses of Mt. Seir in Edom, S. of the Dead Sea (I Chron. 4:43). This rough Negeb ("southland") tribe is listed (Ps. 83:7) as an inveterate enemy of the people of God. Archaeology has thus far revealed nothing concerning them.

Amarna, Tell el-, artificial name for the ruins of Akhetaton, the new capital of Egypt founded by the religious revolutionary Akhenaton, located in the district of El-Amarna c. 190 m. S. of Cairo. Its library, discovered accidentally by a peasant woman in 1887 and subsequently excavated, has yielded 379 clay tablets inscribed in Accadian cuneiform. The majority (356 tablets) are letters addressed to the Egyptian court by kings in western Asia (Nos. 1–44) and by vassal princes in Syria and Palestine during the final years of Amenophis III (c. 1417–1379 B.C.) and the reign of his son, Amenophis IV (Akhenaton, c. 1379–1362 B.C.), i.e., from c. 1388–1362 B.C. These letters constitute the earliest known international diplomatic correspondence.

The Amarna Letters reveal much about conditions in Palestine in the era just prior to the arrival of the Hebrews, and contain names of cities, rulers, and peoples useful in the reconstruction of the political geography of Palestine at this time. The constant intrigue and political complexities of the mid-14th century B.C. are well illustrated (see *ANET*[3], pp. 483–490). Letters from 'Abdu-Heba, prince of Jerusalem (Nos. 285–290), relate the menace of certain peoples called *Ḫabiru*, once thought to be identical to the term Hebrew, but now recognized as possibly related but not equivalent.

Besides the documents from El-Amarna, a small number of texts have been found at sites in Palestine, such as Taanach (12) and Shechem (2), and most recently at Kamid el-Loz (ancient Kumidi) in the Lebanese Beqa 'a. See J. A. Knudtzon, *Die El-Amarna-Tafeln;* W. F. Albright, "The Amarna Letters from Palestine," *CAH*, Vol. II, chap. XX, 1966; E. F. Campbell, *The Chronology of the Amarna Letters*, 1963; and *BA* 23, 1960, pp. 2–22. W. P. A.

Amasa (ăm'*ă*-s*ă*). (1) Son of Abigail, David's half-sister, and Jether (I Chron. 2:17); cousin of Joab and his successor as commander-in-chief, despite his defection at the time of Absalom's revolt (II Sam. 19:13). He failed to take prompt action against Sheba, and was therefore murdered by Joab (II Sam. 20:1–13).

(2) A prince of Ephraim, and son of Hadlai (II Chron. 28:12).

Amaziah (ăm'*ă*-zī-*ă*) ("the Lord strengthens"). (1) King of Judah c. 800–783 B.C. Son of King Joash, who was slain ill in his bed by his servants in revenge for his murder of the high priest Zechariah (II Kings 12:20; II Chron. 24:25). After disposing of his father's murderers and consolidating his position, he hired an army of 100,000 Israelitish mercenaries for a venture against the Edomites; these he discharged at the direction of a man of God and proceeded with his own Judahite forces to a victory in the Valley of Salt and the capture of Edom's Capital, Sela. The discharged mercenaries, meanwhile, plundered the N. cities of Judah as they drifted homeward. After the campaign against Edom Amaziah's ill-considered challenge to King Jehoash of Israel precipitated the breakthrough of Jerusalem's defenses, the spoliation of its treasures, and the reduction of

Judah to virtual subjection to Israel. Amaziah was murdered at Lachish where he had fled following an intrigue (II Kings 14:1–14, 17–20). He was succeeded by his 16-year-old son, Azariah. (2) A priest at the Bethel sanctuary of Jeroboam II, who tried to thwart the prophetic ministry of Amos* (Amos 7:10 ff.) and was answered by the famous words of Amos in 7:14.

Amen, from a Heb. word whose root suggests "So be it." Used to indicate confirmation or agreement, as in I Kings 1:36. Also used in a liturgy by people and leader (Neh. 8:6) and in conclusion of a prayer, as in Matt. 6:13; I Cor. 14:16; and many other prayers and benedictions of the N.T. In Rev. 3:14 "the Amen" is used as a name for Jesus, the word of affirmation for God's promises.

Amon (ā′mŏn). (1) A governor of the city of Samaria in the reign of Ahab (I Kings 22:10, 26). (2) A king of Judah, son of and successor to Manasseh, and father of Josiah. After a reign of two yrs. he was murdered in his palace by servants (II Kings 21:19–26; II Chron. 33:21–25).

Ammonites, inveterate enemies of Israel and a force for spiritual corruption, even though considered somewhat akin, as descendants of Lot, nephew of Abraham (Gen. 19:38). Their country, part of what is now the Hashemite Kingdom of the Jordan, lay E. of Jordan and the Dead Sea, in the watershed of the Jabbok River, on whose banks was located their capital, Rabbath-Ammon (Deut. 3:11), with its strong acropolis. It lay N. of Moab and S. of Gilead, and contained few large cities, which is still true of this part of Jordan today. At the time of Israel's conquest c. the 13th century B.C., the Kingdom of Sihon* lay between Ammon and the Jordan. In the period of the Judges Ammon was bounded on the W. by Gad and Manasseh and on the E. by desert. There were times when Ammonites passed over the Jordan to fight against Judah, Benjamin, and Ephraim and "sore distressed" them. Saul defeated the troops of Ammon (I Sam. 11). David, who had suffered insult, besieged and took the capital through the good generalship of Joab, who made possible the crowning incident (II Sam. 12:30).

The Ammonites not only rejoiced in the misfortunes which overtook the pious of Israel, but delighted in spreading their "abominations" of false gods and debasing ideals through intermarriage which corrupted the faith even of King Solomon (I Kings 11:5, 7). Ezra decried Israel's apostasies "according to abominations of the Ammonites." Nehemiah was annoyed by Ammonite taunts as the rebuilding of Jerusalem's walls went on. Ezekiel foretold an era when Rabbath-Ammon would become "a stable for camels, and the Ammonites a couching place for flocks" (25:5). The government disappeared c. the 3d century A.D.

Rabbath-Ammon lives on today in Amman, capital of the Kingdom of Jordan, a busy trading center of Arabs and goal of travelers, who delight in its Roman hillside theater and other marks of ancient occupation of the city. It was rebuilt by Ptolemy Philadelphus in the 3d century B.C., and named Philadelphia.

13. Amman Amphitheater, main surviving monument of the Graeco-Roman city.

Amorites (ăm′ō-rīts), early Semitic inhabitants of Palestine whose early history is obscure, but some of whose blood probably ran through Hebrew veins. Their country lay at the head of the Fertile* Crescent, and extended from the N. border of Babylon to the edge of Syria. In the 3d millennium B.C. Syria and Palestine were called by Babylonians "the land of the Amorites." Hammurabi conquered Mari, the Amorite capital, in the 17th century B.C. The Amorites occupied Canaan, along with Jebusites, Girgasites, and other families of the land (Gen. 10:15 f.). At the time of the Exodus they lived in the mountains (Num. 13:29), while Canaanites (later Phoenicians) lived along the Mediterranean and the Jordan. The Amorites had also extended their territory E. of Jordan (Num. 21:26). Even after the Hebrew Conquest Amorites continued to live in Palestine (Judg. 1). After the Ark was returned to Israel from the Philistines "there was peace between Israel and the Amorites" (I Sam. 7:14). Their racial and military strength is revealed by the fact that down to Solomon's time (c. 961–922 B.C.) certain Amorites remained unconquered and paid a levy of tribute (I Kings 9:21). Ps. 136:19 records the last appearance of the Amorites in the Bible.

The Louvre Museum under M. A. Parrot has turned up thousands of clay tablets from archives of an Amorite king at Mari* on the middle Euphrates NW. of Babylon. Our picture of how the Hebrew Patriarchs looked and lived is pieced out by information recorded at Nuzi* in N. Mesopotamia and by paintings of Amorites possibly contemporaneous with them on the tomb of an Egyptian nobleman at Beni-hasan. These portray the bearded Amorites, with their shaven upper lips, their elaborately woven striped garments, their transport asses, their musical instruments, spears, bows, and skin water bottles.

Amos. (1) The man. He was a native of the mountain-top Judaean village of Tekoa* two hours S. of Bethlehem by donkey in a wild, rock-strewn wilderness. He was by trade a "herdsman" of sheep and goats, and "a dresser of sycomore [fig] trees," the pricking of whose fruit hastened ripening (Amos 7:14 f.). He denied any connection with prophetic fraternities. Nevertheless, the accurate information he received concerning the economic, social, moral, political, and religious conditions in distant cities and in surrounding

14. Amos, *by John Singer Sargent.*

nations was so disturbing to him that he was moved to action (Amos 3:8, 7:15), with the result that a new chapter in Hebrew prophecy* began some time during the reign of Jeroboam II (c. 786-746 B.C.).

(2) The book. The book naturally falls into three divisions: (a) The indictment of foreign nations (1, 2); (b) the indictment of Israel (3–6); (c) a series of visions and narratives (7–9). The verses of 2:6–16 may be called the thesis of the whole book. This fiery preacher from the Southern Kingdom steppes, with his vivid images drawn from rural life (3:4, 5, 8, 12, 4:2, 9:13), exposed the extravagant and callous ways of living among lords and ladies of sophisticated Samaria* (4:1, 5:11, 6:4–6) in the Northern Kingdom. Ivories (see IVORY) such as Amos denounced have been excavated and are in the Fogg Museum, the Palestine Archaeological Museum, etc. The elaborate offerings made in the shrines of Yahweh at Gilgal and Beer-sheba were no substitutes for moral decencies and the good life (5:14 f.); ritual could not take the place of righteousness. Amos moralized religion without substituting morality for religion; righteousness meant both right relation to God in whole-souled loyalty and right relation to men in social behavior. The religion of Israel before Amos was national in its appeal. Amos was the first to extend over all nations (1:3, 6, 9, 11, 13, 2:1, 4, 6) the moral jurisdiction of Yahweh, who imposed upon all peoples His holy will. Thus Amos prepared Israel for the imminent fate which befell it at the hands of the Assyrians (5:1–3, 6:4), and planted the roots of universal monotheism in the Jewish-Christian-Moslem worship of God.

The convictions of Amos were as different from those of his contemporaries as the convictions of Luther from those of the monks of his day. Amaziah of Bethel (Amos 7:10–13) was so hostile to the point of view of Amos that he accused the prophet of sedition.

It is evident that Amos 1:1 was added by a later writer. Some critics claim other interpolations (1:2, 9–12, 2:4 f., 10, 3:7, 10 f., 4:13, 5:3, 8 f., 13–15, 20, 6:2, 7, 9–11, 8:8–13, 9:8b–15). But the distinctive personality of Amos, discernible throughout most of the book, is a strong argument for its substantial unity and integrity.

Amphipolis (ăm-fĭp′ō-lĭs), a city of Macedonia on the River Strymon, 53 m. SW. of Philippi, situated on the famous Egnatian Way between Philippi and Thessalonica, visited by Paul on his Second Missionary Journey (Acts 17:1). In 1920 vestiges of an early Christian basilica were excavated—possibly a center for believers who came under Paul's preaching at Philippi or Thessalonica (Acts 16, 17).

Amram (ăm′răm), a Levite, son of Kohath. and founder of the family of the Amramites. He was an ancestor of Aaron and Moses (Ex. 6:20; Num. 3:19).

amulet, a tiny representation in clay, metal, faïence or semiprecious stone of dogs, chickens, crocodiles, crescents, etc., used by people in all Bible lands in ancient times, and believed to have magical or religious powers. Some from c. 4000 B.C. found at Tepe Gawra in the Tigris Valley, near Nineveh, Assyria, are now in the University Museum, Philadelphia. See illus. 15, p. 18.

Amun (Amen, Amon), chief god of Egyptian Thebes, known also as Amun Re. A great temple was erected in his honor at Karnak. Amun-Re was the sun god against whose powerful priesthood at Thebes the youthful reformer Akhenaton* rebelled when he built Amarna.

Anakims, sons of Anak, a race of giants (Num. 13:22, 28, 32 f.; Deut. 1:28, 9:2; Josh. 11:21 f., 15:13 f., 21:11; Judg. 1:20.

15. Amulets and figurines (Canaanite and Israelite).

Anani (ȧ-nā′nī), a descendant of David (I Chron. 3:24).

Ananiah (ăn′ȧ-nī′ȧ), a city of Benjamin, mentioned along with Anathoth and Nob (Neh. 11:32).

Ananias (ăn′ȧ-nī′ăs). (1) A member, with his wife Sapphira, of the early Christian community at Jerusalem which owned all things in common, distributing to each according to his need. The story of his dishonesty is related in Acts 5:1–10. (2) A Damascus Christian who played a part in restoring the sight of Saul* and who baptized him (Acts 9:10–18). (3) The Jerusalem high priest before whom Paul was brought by Claudius Lycias for a hearing before the full council. Paul, not recognizing him as high priest, called him "a whited wall" (Acts 23:3), violating the law against criticizing a religious leader.

Anat (Anath), a N. Semitic goddess of the Astarte type, patroness of war and sex. Figurines and pottery plaques of the nude Anat have been dug from Palestinian levels of the 2d and 1st millennia B.C. Such were probably known to Hebrew settlers in Canaan. In N. Syria Anat was sister and sweetheart of Aliyan Baal*. See ASHERAH.

anathema (ȧ-năth′ĕ-mȧ) (Gk. *anathĕma*, anything devoted, esp. to death in sacrifice; "accursed") (A.S.V. Rom. 9:3), a denunciation of a person or thing as accursed; a person or thing cursed by ecclesiastical authority.

anathema maranatha (măr′ȧ-năth′ȧ), I Cor. 16:22, once thought to be a double curse. "Maranatha," however, is now viewed as an independent phrase (Aram. *Marana tha*) meaning probably, "O our Lord, come!" which may have been an early Christian watchword of mutual encouragement and hope. Cf. Phil. 4:5; Rev. 22:20.

Anathoth (ăn′ȧ-thŏth), a "city of refuge," in territory allotted to the Levites from the tribe of Benjamin (Josh. 21:18; I Chron. 6:60; see I Chron. 7:8). It was the home of Abiathar, a priest (I Kings 2:26); of two of David's warriors, Jehu (I Chron. 12:3) and Abiezer (II Sam. 23:27; I Chron. 11:26, 27:12); and of the prophet Jeremiah (Jer. 1:1, 11:21, 23), who purchased a field there (Jer. 32:7–9). It was repopulated after the Exile (Neh. 7:27, 11:32; Ezra 2:23). It has been identified as Râs el-Kharrûbeh near the village of 'Anāta, 3 m. NE. of Jerusalem (*BASOR* 62, 1936, pp. 18–26; 63, 1936, pp. 22–23). W. P. A.

Andrew, a follower of John the Baptist (John 1:35–40), and the first-called of Jesus' disciples, according to John, who records him as bringing his brother Peter to the Lord (John 1:41 f.). The summons to the work of a disciple came later to Andrew and Peter, when they formally forsook their fishing business (Mark 1:16–18). Andrew's character was revealed when, in contrast to the perplexed Philip, he thought it worth while to tell the Lord of the lad's five loaves and two fishes (John 6:5 ff.); and again when he helped the hesitant Philip to inform Jesus of the presence of the inquiring Greeks (John 12:22). Andrew thus qualifies as the first home missionary (John 1:41), and also the first foreign missionary (John 12:22). His "day" is November 30, because, according to tradition, he was crucified then at Patrae in Achaia, upon a *crux decussata* (X), thereafter known as St. Andrew's cross. The Order of St. Andrew is an association of church ushers with obligations to be courteous to strangers. See APOSTLE.

angel (Gk. *angelŏs*, "messenger"), one of the types of spiritual attendants of God (see also CHERUB, SERAPHIM), believed to convey the authority of the sender as if he himself were present. In some passages it is difficult to determine whether it is God's angel that appears to man, or Yahweh Himself.

Belief in angels was prevalent in Biblical times and was accepted by Jesus in his teaching (Luke 15:10, 16:22; Mark 8:38). They were generally thought of as blameless (I Sam. 29:9; "sons of God," Job 1:6), yet they could fall from grace (see SATAN). Even among fallen angels there were differences in rank (thrones, dominions, principalities and powers, Rom. 8:38; Eph. 1:21; Col. 1:16).

Angels frequently appear in the story of Jesus: to Mary (Luke 1:26 ff.); to Joseph (Matt. 1:20); to shepherds (Luke 2:9 ff.), etc. They ministered to Jesus after his Temptation (Matt. 4:11) and strengthened him in Gethsemane (Luke 22:43). Heb. 1:14 (R.S.V.) describes them as "ministering spirits sent forth to serve, for the sake of those who are to obtain salvation."

The earliest known art depiction of angels, on the stele of Ur-Nammu, a Sumerian king, shows them flying over his head as he stands at prayer.

See also APOCALYPTIC LITERATURE; DEVIL.

angel of the Lord (or of Yahweh), a messenger of God, almost equivalent to Deity, yet distinct from Him. This theophanic (see THEOPHANY) visitor appeared to Hagar (Gen. 16:7–12); to David at the threshing floor of Araunah (Ornan) (I Chron. 21:16, 18, 20). He also appears in narratives dealing with Moses at Horeb (Ex. 3:2); Balaam (Num. 22:22); the mother of Samson (Judg. 13:3 ff.); Zechariah (Zech. 1:10–13); to shepherds at Bethlehem (Luke 2:9–15). The "angel of the Lord," having always the same personality, seems a specific one, apart from angels in general.

anger. See WRATH.

animals. To animals, wild as well as domestic, there are hundreds of references in the Bible (see ASS, CAMEL, DOG, OX, SHEEP, etc.). Domestic animals especially—ass, camel, ox, sheep, and goat—played an important role in the lives of people in Bible lands. Before coinage was invented, riches were measured in terms of the animals owned. The Patriarch Abraham in nomadic days had so many sheep, cattle, oxen, and asses that he and his nephew Lot fell into strife over the control of wells and pasture (Gen. 13:6). When settled occupation of portions of Canaan was established, families lived in villages adjacent to grazing lands, as is still the case at Bethlehem. A righteous man regarded "the life of his beast" (Prov. 12:10).

The wide range of animal types indicated in Scriptures is due to the great variety of topography and climate in Palestine. The use of animal forms in religious art objects now excavated suggests the reverence in which many ancient worshippers held them. Among the Sumerian people from whom Abraham emigrated to Canaan, animal motifs play a larger role in religious art than any other design. These are seen in the tiny incised cylinder seals* now housed in our great museums, and in such notable animal friezes as those found at Babylonian al-'Ubaid. Egypt honored animals by giving several of her chief gods the heads of animals; Horus was a hawk god; Hathor's head was that of a cow. In Crete, Egypt, and elsewhere bulls were worshipped. In the Serapeum of Memphis sacred bulls were buried in huge sarcophagi, many of which are still seen there. Fertility cults of Canaan and Babylonia used the serpent in their iconography. The horse was a symbol of Persia, as the lion was of Babylon.

Some of the Animals Referred to in Scripture

(Note: the names vary in A.S.V. and R.S.V. in certain instances. Zoölogists, though not always agreeing on A.V. translations, accept the general accuracy of the ancient writers in describing traits of the animals intended.)

ANIMAL	SPECIMEN SCRIPTURE REFERENCES
ape	I Kings 10:22
ass (domestic and wild)	Judg. 5:10; Job 39:5–8
badger	Ex. 26:14; Ezek. 16:10
bat	Lev. 11:19
bear	I Sam. 17:34
beasts (in general)	Lev. 26:22; Mark 1:13
behemoth (? hippopotamus)	Job 40:15
boar	Ps. 80:13
bull (see ox)	
camel (see CAMEL)	
cattle (see CATTLE)	
chamois (? antelope)	Deut. 14:5
coney (rock badger)	Lev. 11:5
deer (? roebuck, hart)	Deut. 12:15
dog (species perhaps akin to collie)	Ex. 11:7
(scavenger)	I Kings 21:19
(pet)	Mark 7:27
(greyhound)	Prov. 30:31
dromedary (or swift horses)	Jer. 2:23
ewe	II Sam. 12:3
fox	Neh. 4:3; Judg. 15:4
fallow deer (? roebuck)	I Kings 4:23
goat*	
hare	Deut. 14:7; Lev. 11:6
hind	Gen. 49:21
horse	
Assyrian	II Kings 18:23
Egyptian	Ex. 15:21; Gen. 41:43 (implied)
Syrian	I Kings 20:20
Persian	Esther 6:8
Roman	Acts 23:32
(Note: finest description)	Job 39:19–25
hyena (possible meaning of Zeboim)	I Sam. 13:18
jackal (possible meaning of dragon)	Job 30:29
lamb (see SHEEP)	
leopard	Jer. 5:6
lion	Ps. 34:10; Dan. 6:7
mole	Lev. 11:30
mouse	Isa. 66:17
ox	Isa. 1:3; I Tim. 5:18
wild ox (A.S.V. antelope)	Deut. 14:5
pygarg (? antelope)	Deut. 14:5
ram (see SHEEP)	
roe (gazelle)	II Sam. 2:18
roebuck	I Kings 4:23
sheep (see SHEEP)	
swine	Lev. 11:7; Luke 15:15, f.
unicorn (fabulous; ? wild ox)	Deut. 33:17
weasel	Lev. 11:29
whale	Gen. 1:21
wolf	Isa. 11:6; Matt. 7:15, etc.

The most famous animal passages in the Bible occur in Job, whose descriptions are welcomed by zoölogists:

wild goat and ass	Job 39:1–8
ostrich	Job 39:13–18
horse	Job 39:19–25

The most important role played in the religious life of Israel by animals is in connection with the rites of sacrifice in atonement for sin. Incredible numbers of unblemished creatures were laid upon Hebrew altars, as illustrated in the narrative of Solomon's dedication of the Temple at Jerusalem (I Kings 8:62–64). Only certain animals (Lev. 11) were "clean," i.e. fit for food or sacrifice

16. The Annunciation, *by Fra Angelico.*

(later Heb. *kosher*). The general rule was that they must have hooves (thus excluding amphibians, reptiles, rodents, and carnivorous animals generally); that the hooves be cloven (thus excluding the rabbit and camel) and that they chew the cud (thus excluding swine). Fish must have both scales and fins (thus excluding shellfish). Only non-carnivorous birds were allowed; certain insects were acceptable.

Fabulous animals met in Jewish literature include the behemoth (? hippopotamus) in Job 40:15–24; the dragon (A.S.V. serpent) (Deut. 32:33; Ps. 91:13); leviathan (? crocodile) (Job 41, cf. 3:8); phoenix.

There is a Biblical Zoo in Jerusalem which includes as complete a collection as possible of the beasts and birds mentioned in the Bible. Each exhibit is labeled with a Biblical verse mentioning the creature. Among those exhibited are: badgers, Syrian bears, conies, foxes, gazelles, hyenas, jackals, kites, leopards, lions, monkeys, and griffin vultures (the "eagle" of the A.V.). See LEOPARD, LION, VULTURE, illus. 243, 248, 468.

anise, a garden plant mentioned by Jesus (Matt. 23:23) as being scrupulously tithed by hypocrites. It may be dill, or possibly *Pimpinella anisum*, which yields seeds similar to caraway.

Anna, a prophetess or holy woman (Luke 2:36) of the tribe of Aser (R.S.V. Asher), who witnessed the dedication of the infant Jesus and "spake of him to all them that looked for redemption" (Luke 2:38).

Annas (ăn′ăs) ("Jehovah hath been gracious"), former high priest to whom Jesus was taken for trial* (John 18:13). Appointed by Quirinius* about A.D. 6, he had been succeeded by his son-in-law, Caiaphas*; but his prestige was still such that out of deference the Galilean was taken to him before he was led to the officiating high priest. Annas was in office when John the Baptist began his wilderness preaching (Luke 3:2), and was in the group of "kindred" before whom Peter and John were haled for examination after they had healed a lame man (Acts 4:6). All five sons of Annas became high priests.

Annunciation, the announcement by Gabriel to Mary* of Nazareth that she was to bear a son Jesus, to whom God would give the throne of David (Luke 1:28–32). March 25 is observed as a festival in commemoration of the Annunciation, Lady Day. The 15th-century artists Fra Angelico and Benozzo Gozzoli, as well as the 19th-century D. G. Rossetti, painted famous canvases of the Annunciation.

anoint, to apply oil or ointment to the head or person. People in Bible lands used unguents as a sign of hospitality, as in Luke 7:46. Many carved or jeweled cosmetic and ointment containers have come down from Bible times. Jesus mentions anointing the head as part of the routine toilet, along with washing the face (Matt. 6:17). But there was also an official religious anointing of prophets, priests, and kings; as of Aaron (Ex. 28:41); Saul (I Sam. 10:1); Elisha (I Kings 19:16); Jehu (I Kings 19:16). "God anointed Jesus of Nazareth with the Holy Ghost and with power; who went about doing good, and healing" (Acts 10:38). The word "Christ" is from the Gk. word meaning "anointed"—the equivalent of Heb. and Aram. "Messiah." Women from Galilee prepared ointments with which to anoint the dead body of Jesus (Luke 23:56). The bruised and sick were anointed with oil or ointment (Isa. 1:6; Luke 10:34; Rev. 3:18). In addition to this medical treatment, anointing had a spiritual significance, as suggested in James 5:14 f., where

17. Anointing of David.

anointing of the sick by elders of the Church, and "the prayer of faith," were confidently expected to effect cures in the name of the Lord. See ALABASTER.

ant, the small insect immortalized in Prov. 6:6 and 30:25.

antelope, A.S.V. word for A.V. "wild ox" (Deut. 14:5) and "wild bull" (Isa. 51:20). Greek versions and the Vulgate render the word "oryx," which is much more like the antelope than the ox or bull. The antelope was a favorite motif in early ceramic art in the Middle East, and has been found on pre-Dynastic Egyptian ware, well executed.

anthropomorphism, the ascription of human form, personality, or attributes to God*. Much of the success of the religion of early

Israel was due to its naive anthropomorphic conception of Yahweh, whose altogether righteous nature was in marked contrast to the fluid personalities of the gods of Egypt, Mesopotamia, and Canaan, who changed their natures and names, and were at times portrayed as zoömorphic—that is, having animal forms. The Hebrews apparently thought of their God as possessing human though unseen form, and as being characterized by capacity for love, hate, sympathy, on a universal scale. Yahweh frequently spoke to individuals, instructing them as to procedure: to Noah (Gen. 8:15), Moses and Aaron (Ex. 6:13), the child Samuel (I Sam. 3:4), Solomon (I Kings 3:5; 11:9). He spoke at the Baptism of Jesus (Mark 1:11) and at his Transfiguration (Matt. 17:5); but was silent at the agony of Christ in Gethsemane and at his Crucifixion.

Vivid as Yahweh was to Israel—He was often believed to be seen—he was *depicted* only as an effulgent, undefined glory, speaking from a burning bush to Moses* in the desert, or hovering above the heads of worshippers, enthroned higher than the cherubim* in the Jerusalem Temple. Completing Israel's abhorrence of any iconographic portrayal of God, was the ancient conviction that no man would live if he saw Yahweh. So far, no archaeological or epigraphic evidence has demonstrated that Yahweh was ever represented in material form. Even in the N. T. God is anthropomorphic, with loves and hatreds. But His emotions have been spiritualized and made universal. See THEOPHANY.

Antichrist (Gk. *antichristos*, "instead of Christ"), an antagonist of Christ, who denies that Jesus is the Christ, but who will be conquered for all time by the Second Coming of Christ. Although mentioned by name only in I John 2:18, 22, 4:3; II John 7, it is thought to be referred to as "man" in II Thess. 2:1–12 and as "beast" in Rev. 13 and 17. The concept of a conflict between the forces of good and evil appeared in a very early Babylonian myth, became a dominant part of Persian thought, and made its way into Jewish beliefs and Christian doctrine concerning the Second Advent. Early Christians associated Antichrist with false teachers and disciples and with apostasies and impious denials of God. Some students have identified Antichrist with the Roman Empire or with such rulers as Nero, Titus and Caligula, while others interpret II Thess. 2 to show the Roman Empire as a force restraining Antichrist.

Anti-Lebanon, the eastern of two parallel mountain ranges extending about 95 m. NNE. to SSW., visible from the Mediterranean. Mt. Hermon* (Jebel esh-Sheikh) rises 9,166 ft. in this range. See LEBANON.

Antioch (ăn'tĭ-ŏk). (1) Pisidian Antioch, a city in Asia Minor, founded by Seleucus I Nicator (312–280 B.C.), a Macedonian cavalry general of Alexander the Great, in honor of his father, Antiochus. This Galatian city, 3,600 ft. above sea level, was a center of Hellenistic influence, and commanded the great trade route between Ephesus and the Cilician Gates. The Romans made it a free city. Paul's notable success here and in this Galatian region (Acts 13:49) was in part due to the colonizing of friendly Jews whom the Seleucid kings had planted throughout Asia Minor for business, cultural, and political purposes. The more liberal-minded enthusiastically heard Paul in their synagogue and spread his message among their Gentile neighbors (Acts 13:14–48), while the more conservative displayed hostility, enlisted the tongues of influential women, and drove Paul and Barnabas out of town (Acts 13:50 f.). This same vicious opposition trailed them to Lystra (Acts 14:19 f.). But Christianity, in spite of these tribulations, had taken firm root among the Jewish and Gentile converts of Paul and Barnabas in Antioch (Acts 14:21–23). Some believe that Paul's Letter to the Galatians was addressed to all four cities of the Roman province of Galatia—Antioch, Iconium, Lystra, and Derbe. The ruins of Pisidian Antioch are near the modern Turkish town of Yalovach.

(2) Syrian Antioch was about 20 m. from the Mediterranean at the point where the Orontes River turns abruptly to the W., as it enters a fertile plain separating the Lebanon

18. Antioch-on-the-Orontes, modern Antioch in background.

from the Taurus Mts. It was c. 300 m. N. of Jerusalem. Here at the foot of Mt. Sylphus, Seleucus I Nicator, after his victory over Antigonus at Ipsus (310 B.C.), built (c. 300 B.C.) the most famous of the sixteen Antiochs which he founded in honor of his father. A navigable river and a fine seaport, Seleucia Pieria, made Antioch a maritime city. Pompey captured Antioch in 64 B.C. Under Roman control it was the capital of the province of Syria. The earlier emperors often visited it and embellished it with new colonnaded, lamp-lighted streets and buildings, fragments of which are built into many present-day houses. In later times the city suffered damage from attacks and earthquakes, and was reduced to ruins by the Persian King Khosrau I in A.D. 540. From 1098 to 1269 Antioch was the seat of a Christian kingdom founded by European Crusaders. Since then, Moslem influence has dominated it. Today it is an unimportant town in Syria (Antakiyeh), with a population of c. 46,000. Ancient Antioch was noted both for its culture and for its bad moral reputation. The groves of Daphne (from which the city was sometimes called "Antioch-by-Daphne"), with waterfalls, cypress trees, and gardens (10 m. in circumference), and a sanctuary to Apollo, were a huge pleasure area where orgiastic rites were performed in the name of religion. Known as "Antioch the Great" and "Queen of the East," it was the third largest city in the Roman Empire, with many Jews enjoying the excellent commercial privileges and citizenship granted them in this free city. With its suburbs, it may have had a population of some 800,000. Its patron was "Fortune" (*Tyche*), a statue of whom (dated c. 300 B.C.) has been excavated.

Antioch was also an important center of early Christianity. Nicolas was one who repudiated his Greek religion and became a member of the Jewish synagogue at Antioch (Acts 6:5). No other city but Jerusalem was so closely associated with the Apostolic Church. The martyrdom of Stephen brought many fugitive Jewish-Christian disciples to Antioch, where they found hearing among not only Jews, but also Greeks (Acts 11:19–21). Barnabas was the first apostle and Paul his assistant to the Antioch church, where the disciples were first called Christians (Acts 11:26), possibly in derision. Here foreign missions were born (Acts 13:1–3). On the completion of the first journey by Barnabas and Paul (Acts 14:26 f.) and the second trip by Paul (Acts 18:22), the missionaries returned to report to the church at Antioch. While Antioch was respectful to the mother church at Jerusalem and sent alms for its poor, it definitely broke with the conservative outlook at Jerusalem in favor of universal evangelism. Paul fought with Peter for this principle, and won at Antioch (Gal. 2:11). Subsequent to the apostolic period, Antioch was the residence of several important bishops and theologians, including Ignatius, Lucian (who compiled a critical edition of the Septuagint), and John Chrysostom.

Excavations at Antioch, carried out by Princeton University and the Musées Nationaux de France between 1931 and 1939, uncovered numerous fragments of mosaics dating from the 4th–6th century A.D. One of the best preserved examples has a phoenix standing on a mountain of rocks in its center, surrounded by a floral design within a border of pairs of rams. Fragments from another building portray mythological scenes, possibly related to the Mysteries of Isis. One mosaic, discovered in a 6th-century floor N. of St. Paul's Gate, contains a phrase which may be the only Biblical allusion yet found in Antioch: "Peace be your coming in, you who gaze [on] this; joy and blessing be to those who stay here" (*LXX* rendering of I Kings 16:4). Besides the mosaics, a score or more of early Christian churches have been identified from excavated ruins. Most famous are Constantine's 4th-century octagonal one (probably very influential in later ecclesiastical architecture); a cruciform one dated A.D. 387, in suburban Kaoussie; and the Martyrion at the seaport of Antioch (Seleucia Pieria) 5 m. N. of the mouth of the Orontes, the earliest portions of which date to the late 5th century.

See *Antioch-on-the-Orontes*, I–IV, 1934–52; C. R. Morey, *The Mosaics of Antioch*, 1938; D. Levi, *Antioch Mosaic Pavements*, 1947; G. Downey, *Ancient Antioch*; B. M. Metzger, *BA* 11, 1948, pp. 69–88. M. S. M./W. P. A.

Antioch, Chalice of, a piece of early liturgical silver said to have been found by Arabs digging a well near Syrian Antioch in 1910. The Chalice, of carved silver openwork, once gilded, rises c. 7½ in. from a narrow stem on whose lotus-flower base the cup rests. The ovoid inner cup appears to have been roughly hammered out from one piece of silver. It holds more than two quarts of liquid. The Chalice is now in the Barnard Cloisters (Metropolitan Museum of Art).

19. Chalice of Antioch.

Claims for a 1st-century origin provoked long and stubborn controversy as to the date, place of origin, and iconography of the unique silver case decorated with figures of 12 men and with symbolic designs. The figures probably represent Christ and ten of the N.T. apostles or writers. It dates from the 4th or 5th century A.D., and is a valuable example of early Near Eastern Christian art.

For details of the debate surrounding this piece, see H. H. Arnason, *BA* 4, 1941, pp. 49–64; 5, 1942, pp. 10–16; F. V. Filson, *BA* 5, 1942, pp. 1–10. W. P. A.

Antiochus (ăn-tī′ŏ-kŭs), the name of several Syrian kings in the line of Seleucus* I, who ruled southern Asia Minor, Syria, and other parts of the empire left by Alexander the Great. The stormy Maccabean (see MACCABEES) era of Palestine fell within the era of the Seleucids. The revolt was precipitated by efforts of Antiochus IV (Epiphanes) to Hellenize Palestine, which had fallen into Syria's hands following the victory of Antiochus III ("the Great") over Egypt (198 B.C.).

Antipas (ăn′tĭ-păs). (1) See ANTIPATER. (2) Herod Antipas, son of Herod the Great, ruled Galilee and Peraea as Tetrarch (4 B.C.-A.D. 39). (3) A Christian martyr (Rev. 2:13). See HEROD.

Antipater (ăn-tĭp′ȧ-tẽr), father of Herod the Great, also known as Antipas the Idumaean. He was Procurator of Judaea (c. 55–43 B.C.), ruling virtually all Palestine by Roman grant. See HEROD.

Antipatris (ăn-tĭp′ȧ-trĭs) (from Antipater, father of Herod the Great), a town on the route of prisoner Paul when sent from Jerusalem to Caesarea for trial before Felix, Governor of Judaea (Acts 23:31). In O.T. times it was Aphek (Josh. 12:18; I Sam. 4:1), the battleground where the Israelites lost the Ark to the Philistines (I Sam. 4:1 f.). Excavations conducted in 1946 by the Palestine Department of Antiquities prove that this site was occupied from 2000 B.C., when it was a 40-acre Canaanite stronghold, until the Middle Ages. Its inexhaustible springs of water (Ras el-'Ain), now piped 30 m. upland to Jerusalem, are one explanation of its long existence.

Antonia (ăn-tō′nĭ-ȧ), **Tower of,** residence and guard tower rebuilt by Herod the Great on a rocky precipice at the NW. corner of the Temple court, Jerusalem. Possibly the *Birah* (Assyr. *birtu*, "fortress") repaired by Nehemiah (Neh. 2:8). Strategic in the defense of the Temple, having underground passageways for the escape of rulers, turrets for guards, barracks, and baths, it was at times the residence of Persian governors and

20. Caravanserai at Antipatris, dating from medieval times.

Maccabean priest-kings. Herod strengthened it and changed its name to the Tower of Antonia in honor of his friend Mark Antony. Herodian masonry is still visible in the lower courses of the present structure. A pavement found below the present surface may be a portion of the ancient courtyard, to be identified with Gabbatha, where Jesus appeared before Pilate (John 19:13). The Antonia (called "barracks" in Acts 21:34–37, 22:24, 23:10, 16, 32, R.S.V.) was the scene of Paul's dispute with Jewish leaders and his subsequent arrest. W. P. A.

ape, not indigenous to Palestine, but mentioned as one of the luxuries imported to the court of Solomon (I Kings 10:22).

Apharsachites (ȧ-fär′săk-īts). The Hebrew word so rendered in A.V. (Ezra 5:6, 6:6) is a Persian loan word, denoting some kind of judicial officer or investigator, appointed by the king. The A.V. word is only a transliteration; A.S.V. and R.S.V. read "governors." Exegetes once erroneously interpreted the word as

21. Ancient masonry incorporated into tower, Jerusalem.

denoting a tribe from beyond the Euphrates, relocated by Asnapper (Osnappar) in Samaria.

Aphek (ā′fĕk) (I Sam. 4:1). See ANTIPATRIS.

Apocalypse. See REVELATION.

Apocalypse of Lamech, the Aramaic, at first tentatively identified, from a fragment, as one of the documents found among the first of the Dead Sea Scrolls* to be discovered in the 'Ain Feshkha cave at Qumran. The Scroll was in such a fragile condition that it could not be unrolled and translated for some time, but it was eventually found to be an Aramaic version of several chapters of Genesis, with little bearing on Lamech.* See *BA*, XIX (1956), 22–24.

apocalyptic literature, a class of literature common in Judaism at the beginning of the Christian era. Efforts have been made to trace the influence of other peoples, especially Persian, upon apocalyptic literature, but the main source seems to have been Jewish. It was an outgrowth of prophetic literature, both having in common the inspiration of the Divine Spirit and belief in the ultimate reign of God. The apocalyptic style is evidenced early among the Prophets in Isa. 24–27; Jer. 24:1–3; Ezek. 1–37; Joel; and Zech. 12–14. It attained its maturity in Daniel, Enoch (200–64 B.C.), Jude (14 f.), and many of the noncanonical books. It supplied many of the thought forms used by Jesus in addressing the people of his day (Matt. 25:31–46); and reached its fullest expression in Christian literature in Revelation* or the Apocalypse of John.

Apocalyptic literature grew out of despair over human conditions. When the Prophets found that their moral prognostications of the reward for the righteous had failed, they were led to extend the operation of a just, righteous, loving God to realms beyond the earthly. When this moral impulse was visualized, faith was retained, but imagination was taxed to the utmost, and issued in angels' (see ANGEL) aerial flights to tops of pinnacles (Matt. 4:5, 8), and many expressions which defied the accepted measurements of time and the universe (Rev. 20:1). Apocalyptic literature endeavored to show that the righteousness of God in respect to a nation, as well as to an individual, would ultimately be fully vindicated. The just would yet inherit their due, either in an eternal or in a temporal Messianic (see MESSIAH) kingdom. The "second coming of Christ" in the early Christian Church was the outgrowth of this literature and teaching in Judaism, which continued to look forward to the appearance of the earthly Messiah, even after Jesus had come (Luke 24:21). The conception of Jesus' *parousia** (Gk. "sudden arrival"), as to its time, duration, character, etc., varies with each N.T. writer (Mark 8:38; Matt. 10:23; Luke 12:40; Acts 3:20 f.; II Thess. 2:2–12; I Cor. 15:25 f.; I Peter 3:1–13; John 14–16).

Among the noncanonical apocalyptic books of both Jewish and Christian origin, in addition to the Ethiopic Enoch mentioned above, are the Slavonic Enoch and the following:

- The Sibylline Oracles
- The Assumption of Moses
- Fourth Ezra
- The Syriac Baruch
- The Greek Baruch
- The Psalter of Solomon
- The Testaments of the Twelve Patriarchs
- The Book of Jubilees
- The Ascension of Isaiah
- Histories of Adam and Eve
- The Apocalypse of Abraham
- The Apocalypse of Elias
- The Apocalypse of Zephaniah
- The Prayer of Joseph

Apocrypha (*ȧ*-pŏk′rĭ-*fȧ*) (Gk. "hidden, spurious [books]"). Noncanonical literature in general, and specifically, for Protestants, the books included in the Greek ("Septuagint") and Latin ("Vulgate") Christian Old Testaments, but excluded from the Hebrew Bible. The Apocrypha were included in Wyclif's Bible (c. 1382) and in the A.V.O.T. (1611), being scattered among the canonical books; but Luther in his German Bible (1534) had relegated them (omitting I and II Esdras) to the end of the O.T. under this superscription, "Apocrypha: these are books which are not held equal to the sacred Scriptures, and yet are useful and good for reading." Coverdale (1535) followed Luther's arrangement, but added I and II Esdras. These three Christian attitudes toward the Apocrypha are also represented in the ancient Church: their full canonicity (Roman Catholicism; cf. Origen and Augustine), their usefulness without being canonical (the Lutheran, Zurich Reformed, and Anglican Churches; cf. Jerome), and their complete omission from the Scriptures (the Calvinistic and other Protestant Churches; cf. Julius Africanus).

All the books of the Apocrypha were written by Jewish authors (only II [IV] Esdras 1–2 and 15–16 have been added by Christians). All (except II [IV] Esdras, extant in the Latin Vulgate [following the New Testament], as well as in Syriac and other Oriental languages) have been preserved in the Greek Bible (as well as in the Lat. translations from the Gk.) and in the Syriac ("Peshitta") Bible (as well as in some other Oriental translations). We may class these books according to their original language and probable date as follows, noting that they all originated in the last two centuries B.C. except I (III) Esdras (shortly before 200 B.C.) and II (IV) Esdras (c. A.D. 90).

(1) *Written in Hebrew.* Ecclesiasticus (180 B.C.), Judith (c. 150 B.C.), I Maccabees (c. 100 B.C.), Baruch (c. 100 B.C.), Prayer of Manasses (100–50 B.C.).

(2) *Written in Aramaic.* The Story of the Three Youths (I [III] Esdras 3:1–4:63; earlier than 200 B.C.), Additions to Daniel (Susanna, etc.; c. 130 B.C.), The Rest of the Book of Esther, except for 13:1–7 and 16:1–24 (c. 100 B.C.), II Maccabees 1:1–2:18 (? 100 B.C.), Epistle of Jeremy (c. 100 B.C.), II (IV) Esdras 3–14 (A.D. 90).

(3) *Written in Greek at Alexandria.* Wisdom of Solomon (c. 80 B.C.), Greek Esther 13:17 and 16:1–24 (c. 80 B.C.), II Maccabees 2:19–15:39 (c. 50 B.C).

It seems probable that these books (except II [IV] Esdras) in a Gk. text were included in the Bible of the Alexandrian Jews when it was adopted by the early Christians as their Bible—the so-called Septuagint (LXX). But when the Palestinian Jews fixed the canon of the Hebrew Bible (at the Council of Jamnia in A.D. 90) they did not regard them as divinely inspired for one of the following reasons: Because they were known to have been written after the time of Ezra and Nehemiah, when divine inspiration was thought to have ceased (Ecclesiasticus and I Maccabees); or because no Hebrew text of a book was known, either because it had been written in Gk. (Wisdom and II Maccabees) or because in A.D. 90 the Hebrew or Aramaic text was lost (Judith, Tobit, Baruch, and the Epistle of Jeremy).

Thus the Apocrypha, though never included in the Scriptures of the Palestinian Jews, were part of the Christian (Greek) Bible from the beginning of St. Paul's mission to the Gentiles. Allusions to them are found in the N.T., in the Didache, the Epistle of Barnabas, I Clement, etc. But objections to the canonicity of the Apocrypha began in 238 (Julius Africanus), so that the Councils of Hippo (393) and later ones down to the Council of Trent (1546) found it necessary to stress the canonicity of all books in the Vulgate Bible. In the Greek Church the Apocrypha were declared canonical at the Council in Trullo (692), although (aside from I Esdras, and the Greek Esther and Daniel) the Council of Jerusalem (1672) specifically mentioned only Tobit, Judith, Ecclesiasticus, and Wisdom as canonical.

In the Protestant Churches, however, the views of Jerome tended to prevail. He distinguished between "canonical" and "ecclesiastical" books, limiting the O.T. canon to the Hebrew Bible and placing all other books "*inter apocrypha*" (among apocryphal writings); nevertheless he was forced to include the Apocrypha in his edition of the Latin Bible (the Vulgate). A. R. Carlstadt (1520) distinguished "hagiographic apocrypha" (Wisdom, Ecclesiasticus, Judith, Tobit, and I–II Maccabees) from "worthless apocrypha" (the others), and his conclusions were accepted by Luther. In the Forty-Two (1553) and Thirty-Nine (1563) Articles, the Church of England quoted Jerome in deciding that the Apocrypha were read "for example of life and instruction of manners" but were not used "to establish any doctrine." As early as 1629 some English Bibles appeared without the Apocrypha; and since 1827 the British and Foreign Bible Society excluded them from all editions of the Bible, except for some pulpit Bibles. The American Bible Society (founded in 1816) has never printed the Apocrypha in its Bibles.

In addition to the Books of the Apocrypha, summarized below, some of the Oriental Christian Churches accepted in their Bibles (or in their ecclesiastical literature) certain other books of Jewish origin, now usually called the Pseudepigrapha; they date from 200 B.C. to A.D. 100, and may be classified as follows:

(1) *Written in Hebrew.* The Testaments of the Twelve Patriarchs, the Psalms of Solomon, The Lives of the Prophets.

(2) *Written in Aramaic.* Jubilees, the Testament of Job, Enoch, the Martyrdom of Isaiah, the Paralipomena of Jeremiah, the Life of Adam and Eve, the Assumption of Moses, Syriac Baruch, the Apocalypse of Abraham.

(3) *Written in Greek.* The Letter of Aristeas, Sibylline Oracles III–V, III and IV Maccabees, Slavic Enoch, Greek Baruch.

The subject matter of the principal Apocrypha may be summarized as follows:

(1) *I (III) Esdras.* Except for changes in order (Ezra 4:7–24 comes before 2:1), omissions (Ezra 4:6; Neh. 1:1–7:5, 8:13b–13:31), and additions (I Esdras 1:23–24, and the Story of the Three Youths in 3:1–5:6), this book is a Gk. version, more idiomatic than the one in the Gk. Bible, of parts of Chronicles-Ezra-Nehemiah (II Chron. 35:1–36:21; Ezra 1:1–10:44; Neh. 7:73–8:13a). The Story of the Three Youths relates that three pages of Darius I of Persia competed for a prize for the best answer to the question, What is the strongest thing in the world? The first said "wine," the second said "the king," the third said "woman," and received the prize when he added that "truth" was the strongest.

(2) *II (IV) Esdras*, omitting the Christian apocalypses in chaps. 1–2 and 15–16. After the destruction of Jerusalem by Nebuchadnezzar, Shealtiel lamented the tragic fate of the Jews and God's failure to reward the piety of the righteous (3:1–9:25). Through the visions of the mourning mother, the eagle, and the Son of Man (9:26–13:58) he was assured that God would manifest His justice in the age to come, through the rule of the Messiah for 400 years, the Resurrection and the Judgment, and the eternal rewards and punishments in Paradise and Gehenna. In chap. 14 Ezra restores the sacred books: 24 in the O.T. and 70 esoteric apocalypses.

(3) *Tobit.* Exiled to Nineveh by Shalmaneser V (727–722), Tobit of the tribe of Naphtali observed the Law but was blinded after burying a dead Jew; he quarreled with his wife and wished to die (1:1–3:17). At the same moment Sara longed for death in Ecbatana (Media) because the demon Asmodeus had killed in succession her seven husbands on the nights of their weddings (3:7–15). Guided by Raphael (disguised as Azarias), Tobias, son of Tobit, drove away Asmodeus (3:16–8:3), married Sara (8:4–21), brought back to Nineveh ten talents of silver lent by Tobit to Gabael, and restored Tobit's sight by means of the gall of a fish caught in the Tigris (9–11). Raphael returned to heaven (12), and Tobit praised the Lord (13). Tobias, on the advice of Tobit, moved to Ecbatana before Nineveh was destroyed in 612 (14).

(4) *Judith.* Nebuchadnezzar defeated Arphaxad, King of Media (1), and sent Holophernes to punish the Jews in Palestine who had not provided troops, and to force on them the worship of himself (2–3). Holophernes besieged the Jews in Bethulia (4–7). A pious young widow named Judith assured the Jews that the Lord would deliver their city (8–9). She enticed Holophernes, cut off his head while he was in a drunken stupor (10:1–13:10), and thus delivered the Jews (13:11–15:13). She praised the Lord (16:1–17), and lived happily ever after (16:18–25).

(5) *The Rest of the Chapters of the Book of Esther.* (a) The dream of Mordecai, predicting the triumph of the Jews (cf. f), and his discovery of a conspiracy (11:2–12:6). (b) The edict of Artaxerxes against the Jews (13:1–7). (c) The prayers of Mordecai (13:8–18) and Esther (14:1–19). (d) Esther's audience with the king (15:1–16). (e) The edict of Artaxerxes in favor of the Jews (16:1–24). (f) The interpretation of Mordecai's dream (10:4–13; cf. a) and the colophon (11:1).

(6) *The Wisdom of Solomon.* (a) The rewards of wisdom (1–5). In this life the ungodly Jews enjoy worldly pleasures and persecute the Jews who are pious and needy. But after death the ungodly will vainly repent, while the righteous will enjoy bliss "in the hand of God" forever. (b) The nature and attainment of wisdom (6–9). Solomon obtained wisdom from God, for she is an emanation of His glory, and praises wisdom for her gifts. (c) The heroes of wisdom, from Adam to Moses, contrasted with the wicked (10–12). (d) Paganism is foolish (13–15). (e) Contrast between the Israelites and the Egyptians (16–19; the conclusion 11:2–14).

(7) *The Wisdom of Jesus the Son of Sirach or Ecclesiasticus.* Wisdom is the fear of the Lord, attained through observing His Law

(1). On resignation, honoring parents, humility, kindness (2:1–4:10). Tests and rewards of wisdom, wrong conduct, friendship (4:11–6:17). Search for wisdom, right behavior (6:18–9:16). The upper classes (9:17–14:19). The blessings of wisdom (14:20–15:10). God's justice and mercy (15:11–18:14). Kindness, foresight, and self-control (18:15–20:26). The wise and the foolish (20:27–23:28). Wisdom is identical with the Pentateuch (24). Good and bad wives (25:1–26:27). The troubles and sins of rich men (26:28–29:28). The education of children (30:1–13); the dangers of wealth (30:14–31:11); table manners (31:12–32:13). On teachers, and on the excellency of Israel (32:14–33:18). The father should rule the family (33:19–31). On dreams (34:1–8). On travel (34:9–17). True piety (34:18–35:20). A prayer for Israel's deliverance (36:1–17). On helpful persons (36:18–38:15). On mourning (38:16–23). The value of a higher education (38:24–39:15). The Creator (39:16–35). Despite the miseries of human life, the lot of the pious is the best (40:1–41:13). Wisdom should not be concealed (41:14–15, same as 20:30–31). On shame (41:16–42:8). Fathers worry about their daughters (42:9–14). The praise of God (42:15–43:33); of "the Fathers of Old" from Adam to Nehemiah (44–49); and of the high priest Simon (50:1–24). Denunciation of Edomites, Philistines, and Samaritans (50:25–26). Colophon (50:27–29). Praise of God for His help (51:1–12); a liturgy with the refrain, "Give thanks unto the Lord," is found here in the Heb. text. Reminiscences of the author (51:13–30, an alphabetic acrostic poem). Final doxology (in the Heb. and Syr. only).

(8) *Baruch.* (a). Repentance of the Jews after the destruction of Jerusalem (1:1–3:8). (b) A poem in praise of wisdom (3:9–4:4). (c) The Jews should find comfort in the imminent return of the Exiles and in the ruin of Babylon (4:5–5:9).

(9) *The Epistle of Jeremy* (Baruch, chap. 6 in the Vulgate and in the A.V.). A sarcastic denunciation of the folly of idolatry.

(10) *The Song of the Three Holy Children* (following Dan. 3:23 in the Gk. and Lat. Bibles). The prayer of Azarias (1–22); the heating of the fiery furnace (23–28); the song of praise of the three children (29–68, 35–65 are the *Benedicite* [Bless ye!] of the Prayer Book).

(11) *The History of Susanna* (at the beginning of Daniel in the Gk. Bible; Dan. 13 in the Vulgate). Susanna, the wife of Joakim (a wealthy Jew in Babylonia), refused to lie with two Jewish elders who approached her as she was preparing to bathe in her garden pool (1–27). They accused her of adultery with an imaginary youth and she was condemned to death (28–44). But Daniel convicted the elders of false testimony, and they were executed (45–64).

(12) *The History of the Destruction of Bel and the Dragon* (at the end of Daniel in the Gk. Bible; Dan. 14 in the Vulgate). (a) Bel (1–22). By scattering ashes secretly on the floor of the temple of Bel (Marduk) in Babylon, Daniel proved—by the footprints of priests and their families—that by entering through a trap door at night the priests, not Bel, consumed the food offered to this idol. (b) The Dragon (23–42). After Daniel killed the dragon of Babylon, by feeding him a vile concoction, he was cast into the den of lions; Habakkuk was flown from Judaea by angels to bring him his dinner. Eventually Daniel was delivered.

(13) *The Prayer of Manasses.* A penitential psalm composed as a supplement to II Chron. 33:11–13.

(14) *The First Book of the Maccabees.* This is our best source for Jewish history 175–135 B.C. The antecedents of the Maccabean rebellion (1) and its beginning (2). A poem praising Judas Maccabaeus (3:1–9). The wars of Judas for religious liberty (3:10–4:61), and against the enemies of the Jews (5). The campaign of Lysias following the death of Antiochus IV Epiphanes 164 B.C. (6). Demetrius I sent Bacchides to support Alkimus in Jerusalem (7:1–20); Judas defeated Nicanor, but fell at Adasa (7:21–9:22). Jonathan was forced to sign a treaty with Bacchides (9:23–73). Jonathan supported Alexander Balas against Demetrius I, and defeated Apollonius (10). At first Jonathan allied himself with Demetrius II against Tryphon and Antiochus VI, but later turned against them (11). Despite his alliance with the Romans and the Spartans, Jonathan was captured by Tryphon (12). Simon supported Demetrius II and made Judaea independent (13). Although Demetrius II was captured by the Parthians, Simon consolidated his power (14). Simon defied an ultimatum of Antiochus VII, but was assassinated by his son-in-law Ptolemy; John Hyrcanus, son of Simon, succeeded him (15–16).

(15) *The Second Book of the Maccabees.* Letters to Egyptian Jews from Palestine reporting the rededication of the Temple in 164 B.C., and Nehemiah's discovery of naphtha (1:1–2:18). II Maccabees is the summary of the five books of Jason of Cyrene (2:19–32). Under Seleucus IV (187–175 B.C.) Heliodorus was miraculously prevented from entering the Temple in Jerusalem (3); Jason displaced Onias III as high priest, and Hellenized Jerusalem, but Menelaus took his place (4). Antiochus IV Epiphanes (175–164 B.C.) plundered the Temple, proscribed the practice of Judaism, and persecuted the Jews (5–7). The initial victories of Judas Maccabaeus (8); and the death of Antiochus (9). The rededication of the Temple (10:1–9). Lysias was forced to come to terms (10:10–11:38). The victories of Judas over various enemies (12); again over Lysias (13), and over Nicanor (14:1–15:36): thus was Jerusalem delivered forever (15:37). The epitomist of Jason's five books presented the facts somewhat fancifully (15:38 f.). R.H.P.

Apollonia (ăp′ŏ-lō′nĭ-*ȧ*), name of several towns in the Mediterranean world, named in honor of the Greek sun god Apollo. The most noted was located on the Egnatian Way, 28 m. W. of Amphipolis in Macedonia; visited by Paul on his Second Missionary Journey (Acts 17:1).

Apollos (*ȧ*-pŏl′ŏs), a Jew steeped in the eloquent culture of Alexandria*, who came in touch with the Messianic (see MESSIAH) hope voiced by John the Baptist. Familiar with Scripture, enthusiastic in spreading the gospel of repentance and baptism, he arrived, probably in the summer of A.D. 54, at Ephesus where Priscilla and Aquila, after hearing him in the synagogue, "expounded unto him the way of God more perfectly" (Acts 18:26). In Greece his missionary zeal effectively used Scripture to win other Jews to the Messiahship of Jesus. While Apollos was at Corinth Paul arrived in Ephesus, where he told men who were probably pupils of Apollos of the Holy Spirit. So popular did Apollos become at Corinth, that against his wishes a clique attached itself to him in rivalry to Paul. The situation only served to give Paul occasion to preach the gospel of Christian unity (I Cor. 1:12 f., 3:4–6, 22 f.) and of the mastery of Christ. Admirers of Apollos give him credit for being the real founder of the Corinthian Church; many, including Martin Luther, have attributed to him the Epistle to the Hebrews. Paul trusted him, "greatly desired him" to return to Corinth (I Cor. 16:12), and urged Titus to make easier Apollos' journey (possibly to Crete) (Titus 3:13).

Apollyon (*ȧ*-pŏl′yŭn) (Gk. "the destroyer"), the angel of the abyss* (Rev. 9:11).

Apostle (Gk. *apóstolos*, "ambassador," "messenger," "envoy," "one who represents the sender"), a term applied to the 12 more intimate disciples of Jesus, who, because of their familiarity with his personality, teaching, and methods, were to be his witnesses before mankind everywhere. The number 12 corresponds to the 12 Tribes of Israel and their historic role in establishing the first Jewish commonwealth. There are 4 listings of the Twelve Apostles in the N.T.: Matt. 10:2–4; Mark 3:16–19; Luke 6:14–16; Acts 1:13. Jesus gave specific instruction to "the Twelve" (Mark 6:7–13; Acts 1:8). (See chart, THE TWELVE APOSTLES, p. 28, for their lives, labors, and symbols.)

22. The Calling of Apostles Peter and Andrew, *by Duccio di Buoninsegna.*

The original Apostles were young men, perhaps the same age as Jesus, each different from the others in taste and temperament. Because their comprehension of Jesus' mission was deeper than that of the other 9, Jesus singled out Peter, James, and John for special privileges and intimacies. They were in the room at the raising of Jairus' daughter (Mark 5:37), were present at the Transfiguration (Matt. 17:1), and were in the Garden of Gethsemane during the agony (Mark 14:33). Speaking Aramaic and Greek, with minds quickened by knowledge of the Hebrew Scriptures learned in synagogue schools and services, these first Apostles, while not as well educated as Paul, were not as "unlearned and ignorant" as their enemies believed (Acts 4:13).

The first qualification for being an Apostle was to have "seen the Lord." Matthias (Acts 1:23–26), Paul (I Cor. 9:1), and James (I Cor. 15:7) met this qualification, when the original group was enlarged after the Resurrection. The witnessing of those who had "seen the Lord" supplied material for the N.T. writings (Luke 1:2), and gave spirit and power to the early Church (Acts 4:33). See also individual entries.

apothecaries, perfumers in a society to which unguents and cosmetics were well-pleasing; they compounded the incense and holy anointing oils used in religious ceremonies; also, flavoring extracts and medicinal herbs (mentioned as early as Ex. 30:25). The medical arts developed in very ancient times in Babylonia, Egypt, and other Bible lands. An old drugstore of Nippur, situated between the Tigris and the Euphrates, has come to light through a long-neglected clay tablet housed in a drawer of the University Museum in Philadelphia. It gives a formula for balsam prescribed for a metal-worker who has been burned. Apothecaries also prepared spices used in burials (II Chron. 16:14), and did their bit to repair the walls of Jerusalem (Neh. 3:8). See also DISEASE.

apparel. See DRESS.

Apphia (ăf′ĭ-*ȧ*), a Christian, wife of Philemon* (Philem. 2).

Appian Way, famous road from Capua to Rome, built by Appius Claudius 312 B.C., used by Paul when walking to the capital (Acts 28:15). Long portions of this narrow but well-paved road are extant, lined with tombs and grazing ground, where Roman villas stood in ancient times, and with catacombs or series of underground galleries where early Christians sought refuge from persecutors, for worship and the burial of their dead. Paul certainly saw the huge, round,

23. The Appian Way, at outskirts of Rome. At left, Tomb of Caecilia Metulla.

The Twelve Apostles

No.	Name	Surname	Parents	Home	Business	Writings	Work	Death	Symbol
1	SIMON	Peter } "Rock" Cephas }	Jonah	Bethsaida; Capernaum	Fisherman	Source of 1 Peter 2 Peter (?Mark)	Missionary to Jews far as Rome. 1 Peter. 5:13 probably refers to Rome	Crucified c. 68 A.D. head downward, at Rome (tradition)	Keys saltire
2	ANDREW		Jonah		Fisherman		Preached in Scythia, Greece, Asia Minor (tradition)	Crucified on St. Andrew's cross (X) (tradition)	X-shaped cross
3	JAMES, the elder	Boanerges, or Sons of Thunder	Zebedee and Salome	Bethsaida; Jerusalem	Fisherman		Preached in Jerusalem and Judaea	Beheaded by Herod A.D. 44, at Jerusalem (Acts 12:2)	Pilgrim's staff and wallet
4	JOHN, the beloved disciple				Fisherman	Source of Gospel	Labored among the churches of Asia Minor, especially Ephesus	Died a natural death (tradition)	Chalice with serpent
5	JAMES, the less or younger		Alphaeus or Cleophas and Mary			Epistle of James	Preached in Palestine and Egypt	Crucified in Egypt (tradition)	Saw
6	JUDE	Same as Thaddaeus and Lebbaeus				Epistle of Jude	Preached in Assyria and Persia (tradition)	Martyred in Persia (tradition)	Sailboat with cross-mast
7	PHILIP			Bethsaida			Preached in Phrygia, Caesarea	Died at Hierapolis in Phrygia (tradition)	Two loaves of bread
8	BARTHOLOMEW	Nathaniel		Cana of Galilee				Flayed to death (tradition)	Flaying knife on Bible
9	MATTHEW	Levi	Alphaeus	Capernaum	Tax collector (publican)	Source of Gospel		Died a martyr in Ethiopia (tradition)	Three money bags
10	THOMAS	Didymus		Galilee			Claimed by Syrian Christians as founder of their Church	Martyred—shot by shower of arrows while at prayer (tradition)	Spear and carpenter's square
11	SIMON	The Cananaean or Zelotes		Galilee				Crucified (tradition)	Fish on hook
12	JUDAS	Iscariot		Kerioth of Judea				Suicide (Matt. 27:5)	Blank shield of yellow

marble-faced tomb of Caecilia Metulla (built in the period of Augustus). Archaeologists uncovered (1850–53), about 2½ m. from Rome's Gate of St. Sebastian, the picturesque stretch of road Paul paced between the 3d and 11th milestones.

Appius, the Market of, the point on the Appian Way where Paul was met by "brethren" who came out from Rome to greet him on his arrival from Puteoli (Acts 28:15). In R.S.V., "Forum of Appius."

apple, indigenous to Armenia, and called in Greece "golden apple," may be the apricot, more at home in the Middle East than the apple. But some scholars claim the early origin of the apple was in Asia Minor, saying it was distributed by Hittite traders all round the Mediterranean. It grew in the Anti-Lebanon valleys and possibly on Mt. Hermon—probably in Solomon's time. (See Prov. 25:11; Song of Sol. 2:5, 7:8; Joel 1:12; cf. Deut. 32:10; Ps. 17:8; Prov. 7:2; Lam. 2:18; Zech. 2:8.)

Apples were anciently recognized to be aids to health (Josephus and the Talmud).

The "apple of Sodom" is a disappointing fruit growing in the weird region of the Dead Sea, expressive of the general, bitter desolation meted out on the cities of the Plain as a judgment of Yahweh against their wickedness. This *colocynth* looks like an orange or yellow apple, and contains dried filaments and seeds.

aprons, originally loin cloths or wide girdles (Gen. 3:7), often the only garment of the toiler. From them developed the Egyptian kilt and the tunic of Near Easterners. The apron of the priest was his ephod*. The aprons mentioned in Acts 19:12 as brought from Paul's person to effect the cure of the sick were the napkins of Luke 19:20 and John 20:7.

Aqabah (ä'kȧ-bä), **Gulf of,** a northern arm of the Red Sea, at whose head Ezion-geber, seaport of Solomon (I Kings 9:26), was located (excavated by Nelson Glueck for the

ASOR). The Sinai Peninsula is W. of the Gulf of Aqabah and Midian, whence came the traders by whom Joseph was sold to the Ishmaelites (Gen. 37:28).

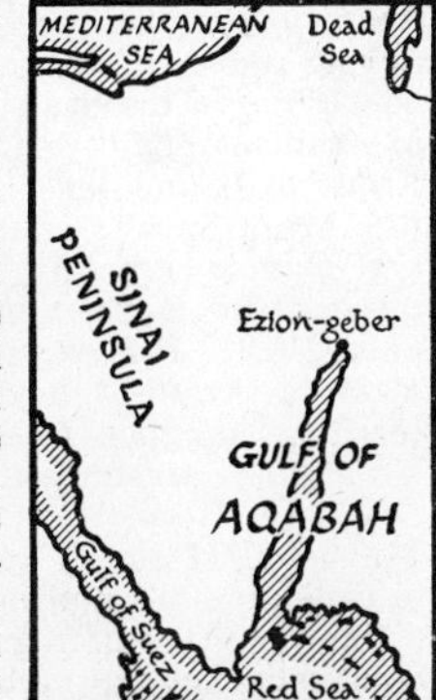

24. Gulf of Aqabah.

aqueduct, a word not appearing in the Bible, but denoting usually an elevated structure of stone arches, with a channel to convey water from storage basins to the desired destination. One of the best extant examples is the Aqueduct of Claudius, certainly seen by Paul as he journeyed to Rome (Acts 28:15) along the Appian Way. A famous aqueduct, or a pair of them, carried water from "Solomon's Pools" (three reservoirs built in Roman or pre-Roman times about 3 miles S. of Bethlehem) to the Temple enclosure at Jerusalem 7 miles north. See RESERVOIR, illus. 344.

Aquila (ăk′wĭ-lȧ), husband of Priscilla; a widely-traveled Jew born in Pontus, a section of northern Asia Minor bordering the Black Sea, and living for a time in Rome, whence he came to Corinth after the anti-Semitic edict of Claudius in A.D. 49. Pursuing their craft of looming tent cloth, Aquila and Priscilla added Paul, an expert Cilician tent-cloth weaver, to their staff; and they joined him in his great mission of Christian teaching (Acts 18:1–3). Whether they had become Christians in Rome is not clear. Traveling with Paul from Corinth to Ephesus (Acts 18:18 f.), they established there a home which was hospitable headquarters for new converts, all of whom sent greetings to old friends on the isthmus in Paul's First Letter to the Corinthians (16:19). One of their famous pupils was Apollos (Acts 18:24–28). Aquila and Prisca were greeted by name in Romans* 16:3–5, evidently addressed by Paul to Ephesus. Possibly these two traveled E. again, for Paul's Second Epistle to Timothy, dispatched from Rome, sends salutation to Aquila and Prisca (diminutive of Priscilla). then living probably at Ephesus (II Tim. 4:19). See p. 623 left, lines 26 ff.

Arabah (ăr′ȧ-bȧ) (Heb. "desert plain"). (1) The entire deep rift extending from the Sea of Galilee and the Jordan Valley, through the Dead Sea and on to the Gulf of Aqabah*. (2) More narrowly, the dry desert between the S. end of the Dead Sea (including the Kingdom of Edom, founded in the 13th century B.C.) and Ezion-geber*. The mines of the Arabah (Deut. 8:9), the largest anywhere yet found in the ancient Near East, furnished iron and copper for Solomon and wealth for his commerce. Research among Early Iron Age sites of the Arabah shows the presence of a large population as early as the 13th or 12th century B.C. The 42 stations indicated as having been visited by Israel during the wanderings toward Canaan included halts in the Arabah, then populated with villagers and seminomadic Arab tribes who terrorized the homeless Israelites. The Arabah is 1,275 ft. below sea level at the Dead Sea, and 300 ft. above at a point just W. of Petra, which controlled caravan trade between the desert and Gaza. Josh. 18:18 mentions the Arabah. Numerous other O.T. references (A.V.) to this region appear under other designations, as "the river of the wilderness" (Amos 6:14). See also Ezek. 47:8.

25. The Arabah.

Arabia, world's largest peninsula, lies in the SW. corner of Asia; bounded on the N. by Jordan and Iraq enclosed on the other three sides by water—Red Sea, Arabian Sea, Persian Gulf. On this oil-rich, desert plateau live 12 million people in an area one-fourth the size of the U.S. In ancient times Arabia was divided into Arabia Deserta (N. interior region), Arabia Petraea (rocky NW. region), and Arabia Felix (fertile S. region, generally limited to Yemen). Today Arabia comprises the large kingdom of Saudi Arabia; small kingdom of Yemen in the SW.; British colony of Aden and Aden Protectorate on the S. coast; independent sultanate of Muscat and Oman in the SE.; two N. Neutral Zones; British-protected Persian Gulf States—Kuwait, Bahrain, Qatar, and Trucial Coast Shiekdoms.

From Arabia in ancient times wave after wave of Semites* erupted into Palestine and its peripheral areas, and carried into Canaan, Babylonia, and Assyria their desert ideals and customs. The Arabic language (belonging to the S. Semitic linguistic group) spread through a large section of the Near East. Recovered inscriptions in S. Arabian script shed light on customs of the last millennium B.C., and include names and cult terms paralleling those found in the Bible. Many patriarchal customs and ideals appear to have counterparts in Arabian nomadic ways. It is thought that in the era of the Judges of Israel, Aramaeans swept in from Arabia under the name "Syrians" and played roles recorded in Scripture. Up through Arabia ran one of the busiest caravan routes of the Biblical period, coming up along the Red Sea to the coastal plain of the Mediterranean, where it branched off to Egypt. Arabian merchants sold flocks, spices, gold, frankincense, and horses to Israel. The earliest people of Arabia named in Scripture are possibly Ishmaelites (Gen. 37:25), Midianites (Gen. 37: 28a, 36) or Kedarites (Gen. 25:13), whose black Arabian tents were proverbial. Arabians were always dreaded as enemies of Israel, whose lands and people they often marauded as fanatical highwaymen (Jer. 49:28 f.). Yet there were eras when they brought tribute of flocks to Hebrew kings, as they did to Jehoshaphat of Judah (c. 873–849 B.C.) (II Chron. 17:11). And the story of the SW. Arabian Queen of Sheba* who brought gifts to the famed court of Solomon (c. 961–922) probably reflects an early commercial-political alliance between the two Semitic peoples. Arabians constantly traded with Tyre* (Ezek. 27:21). They ridiculed the rebuilding of Jerusalem's wall after the Exile (Neh. 2:19).

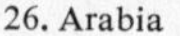
26. Arabia

Arabia is represented in Scripture as a lonely desert conducive to great spiritual revelations, like those to Moses and Israel in Sinai at its NW. tip, and to Paul, who went "away into Arabia" (Gal. 1:17)—probably the region where the Syrian desert runs off to meet the northern section of the Arabian peninsula. Arabians were in the Jerusalem throng at Pentecost (Acts 2:11).

The Arabian Expedition of the American Foundation for the Study of Man undertook campaigns of excavation in South Arabia from 1950 on, led by Wendell Phillips. W. F. Albright was chief archaeologist, and the Carnegie Museum of Pittsburgh and other organizations were patrons. (See TEMPLES, illus. 426.)

Before this expedition there had been only one small systematic dig in all South Arabia, and chronological reconstructions of its history differed by a thousand years in some instances. This work has stabilized the chronology of South Arabia from about 1000 B.C. to the 2d century A.D., and pottery, masonry, forms of writing, etc., can now be dated within a century or two. The history of ancient Qataban (modern Beihan and contiguous areas) is particularly well established, since the excavations were carried out in and around the ancient capital of Timna.

Aram (ā′răm), son of Shem, son of Noah (Gen. 10:22 f.; I Chron. 1:17), thought to be the progenitor of the Aramaeans. These references reflect an effort to explain the ancient origin of a people dwelling between the Taurus Mts. and the region of Damascus, and from Lebanon to E. of the Euphrates—known as Aram. Out of Arabia came the Aramaeans shortly before the time of Abraham. They settled down in the era of the Judges. Several Aramaean states or districts N. and E. of Canaan are distinguishable in the Bible: (1) Aram-naharaim ("of the 2 rivers") (see PADAN-ARAM), home of the Patriarchs before they moved into Canaan. (2) Aram-Damascus, enemies of the N. Kingdom during most of its existence (see REZON, DAMASCUS). This city-state became the center of Aramaean culture and influence W. of the Euphrates, and later the capital of Syria. (3) Aram-Zobah, contemporary with Saul and David, extending from Hamath to Damascus and E. toward the Euphrates. Cf. I Sam. 14:47; II Sam. 8:3, 10, 10:6; I Chron. 18:3. (4) Aram-Maacah, E. of the Jordan, in territory assigned to Naphtali (Josh. 12:5, 13:11). (5) Geshur, also E. of the Jordan, near Mt. Hermon, in territory assigned to Manasseh (Deut. 3:14). Absalom fled here in exile after his murder of Amnon.

The identity of the Aramaeans with the Syrians is clearly indicated in the O.T., though the Gk. word for the region, "Syria," is never used in the Heb., but always "Aram." Septuagint, however, renders "Syria." At times the Aramaeans were enemies of Israel; at other times they were regarded as kin. Abraham sent among the Aramaeans to secure a wife for his son Isaac (Gen. 24). Laban, brother of Rebekah, appears in Gen. 24:29 ff. as a shrewd Aramaean. David's attack on their powerful center, Zobah, helped save Assyria from the Aramaean advance. Aramaeans were a chief enemy of Israel in the 9th and 8th centuries B.C. Tiglath-pileser III overthrew the kingdom of Damascus in 732 B.C., Hamath was taken by Sargon II, c. 722. Henceforward the small states of Aram were at all times subject to one or other of the great world-empires.

Aramaic (ăr′*ȧ*-mā′ĭk), the language of the Aramaeans, sprang from a W. Semitic tongue spoken in NW. Mesopotamia early in the 2d millennium B.C., and probably therefore by the Hebrew Patriarchs before their entry into Palestine. It was spread by Aramaean merchants journeying throughout W. Asia, until it became in all its dialects virtually the *lingua franca* of the Near East. After the decline of Phoenician sea power, the Phoenician alphabet was supplanted in popularity for commercial communications throughout W. Asia by the Aramaic. The history of the use of Aramaic letters may clearly be traced from Nineveh in the 7th century B.C. by study of the letters on coins struck by Persian petty rulers in Asia Minor; on tomb inscriptions; and in Egyptian papyri.

Several Aramaic dialects were used in Bible lands. After 500 B.C. Aramaic was the official language of the Persian Empire. Jesus spoke Galilean Aramaic. Aramaic portions of the O.T. include: Gen. 31:47; Jer. 10:11; Ezra 4:8–6:18, 7:12–26; Dan. 2:4b–7:28. Ezekiel shows Aramaic influences. Job, certain Psalms, the Song of Solomon, Jonah, Esther, and Hebrew parts of Daniel contain Aramaic words. In fact, Job is strongly Aramaic. The N.T. quotes some Aramaic words. The Jews translated their Scriptures into Aramaic when Aramaic became their vernacular, using square characters. The Gk. version, therefore, except the Pentateuch, was prepared from the cursive Aramaic, with the use of almost square Hebrew letters. See WRITING; also TEXT.

Ararat (ăr′*ȧ*-răt). (1) A section of E. Armenia W. of the Araxes River, somewhat N. of Lakes Van and Urmia, today belonging to Turkey. Ararat provides part of Euphrates' source. To this region the sons of Sennacherib

27. Turkish captain and his patrol on eastern slope of Ararat, a few miles from Russian border.

fled after killing their father at worship (II Kings 19:37). A Kingdom of Ararat was summoned by Jeremiah to fight against Babylon (51:27). (2) Mt. Ararat, a twin-peaked, majestic massif (Agri Dagh) rising 17,000 ft., in territory that belonged to Hurrians (Horites) before 1700 B.C. It is named in Gen. 8:4 as the resting place of Noah's Ark. A Babylonian Flood record places the event east of Mesopotamia, on Mt. Nizir.

Aratus, a minor Greek poet from Cilicia (315–245 B.C.) whose writings Paul briefly quoted at Athens (Acts 17:28).

Araunah (*ȧ*-rô′n*ȧ*) (Ornan in I Chron. 21, II Chron. 3), Jebusite landsman from whom David bought the stone threshing floor which became the base of the altar dedicated by David to Yahweh (II Sam. 24:16–25). Araunah's threshing floor may be the rugged, natural scarp preserved under the Dome of the Rock, on or near the site of Solomon's Temple.*

archaeology (Gk. *archaios*, "ancient," and *logos*, "discourse"), the rapidly developing science whose aim is the excavation, examination, and interpretation of the material record of man's past. The recovery of the remains of the ancient cities and civilizations of the Middle East has greatly revolutionized our understanding of the Bible, its peoples, and their history.

Early interest in Palestine and its neighboring lands is reflected in the many accounts and descriptions left by pilgrims in their search for its holy places. Critical inquiry into the ancient topography of Palestine, however, can be said to have begun only with the explorations in 1838 and 1853 by Edward Robinson, who was able to identify many Biblical places correctly. A few years later, the era of regular excavation in the Near East began with the excavation by P. E. Botta, a Frenchman, at Khorsabad in 1842, and that by A. H. Layard, an Englishman, at Nimrud in 1845—both sites in ancient Mesopotamia. The foundations of the modern science of Palestinian archaeology were laid when W. M. Flinders Petrie, an Egyptologist, carried out excavations at Tell el-Hesi in southern Palestine in 1890. His careful attention to the recording of the successive occupational levels of the mound (stratigraphy) and his demonstration that the history of Palestine could be traced through changes in the forms of broken fragments of pottery (typology) were of great significance. Subsequent excavation, such as that at Tell Beit Mirsim*, Samaria*, Beth-shan*, Lachish*, Megiddo*, Jericho*, and Tell Deir 'Allā, has resulted in a reasonably accurate and efficient chronology*. Moreover, increased use of specialists (e.g. geologists, ceramicists, palaeontologists), and the growth of modern technology (e.g. radiocarbon dating, metallurgical and petrographical analysis, geophysical surveying, computer analysis), have broadened the potential of archaeology as a historical and cultural tool (see D. Brothwell and E. Higgs, eds., *Science in Archaeology*, London, 1969; R. G. Bullard, "Geological Studies in Field Archaeology," *BA* 33, 1970, pp. 98–132).

In addition, surface exploration since the time of its initial use by W. F. Albright in the regions of Samaria and Galilee in 1921, has greatly increased the number of archaeological sites known and places identified, leading in many cases to actual excavation. Among the more important endeavors, mention should be made of the systematic survey of Eastern Palestine (Trans-Jordan) by N. Glueck, 1932–47, and the current archaeological survey of the Holy Land by the Israel Exploration Society.

Work in areas outside Palestine has also contributed to our understanding of the Bible. Many ancient civilizations have been rediscovered, such as those of the Assyrians, the Babylonians, the Sumerians, and the Phoenicians. Lost languages have been recovered and deciphered, such as Accadian, Hittite, and Ugaritic. Thousands of clay tablets have been translated broadening the understanding of literary form and style in the ancient world (see the variety of texts translated in

28. The Palestine Archaeological Museum, Jerusalem, gift of John D. Rockefeller, Jr.

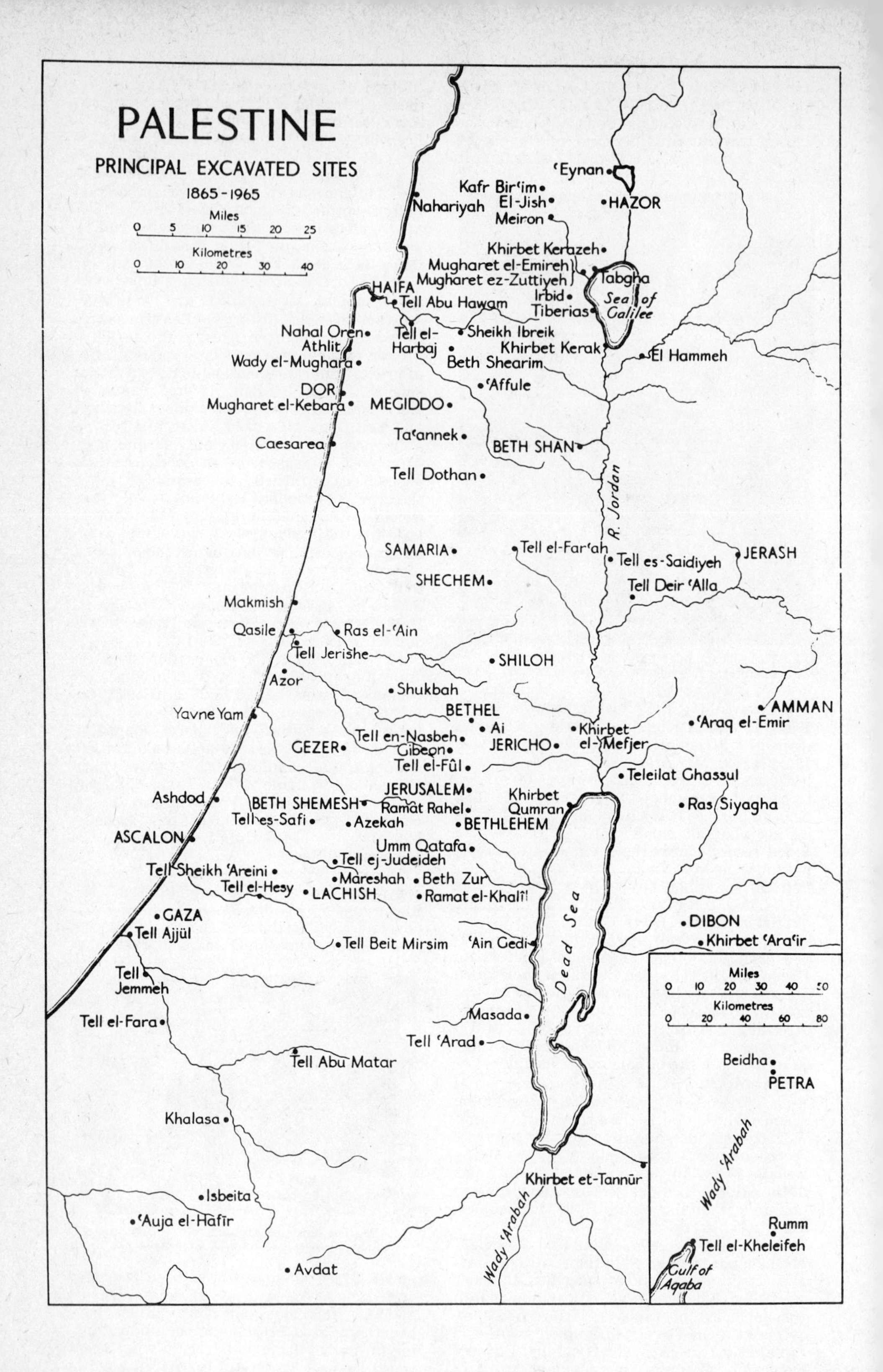
PALESTINE
PRINCIPAL EXCAVATED SITES
1865-1965
Miles
0 5 10 15 20 25
Kilometres
0 10 20 30 40
ʿEynan
Kafr Birʿim
El-Jish
HAZOR
Meiron
Nahariyah
Khirbet Kerazeh
Mugharet el-Emireh
Mugharet ez-Zuttiyeh
Tabgha
Irbid
Sea of Galilee
Tiberias
HAIFA
Tell Abu Hawam
Nahal Oren
Athlit
Tell el-Harbaj
Sheikh Ibreik
Khirbet Kerak
El Hammeh
Wady el-Mughara
Beth Shearim
ʿAffule
DOR
Mugharet el-Kebara
MEGIDDO
Taʿannek
BETH SHAN
Caesarea
Tell Dothan
R. Jordan
SAMARIA
Tell el-Farʿah
Tell es-Saidiyeh
JERASH
SHECHEM
Tell Deir ʿAlla
Makmish
Qasile
Ras el-ʿAin
Tell Jerishe
SHILOH
Azor
Shukbah
Yavne Yam
BETHEL
AMMAN
Ai
Khirbet el-Mefjer
ʿAraq el-Emir
Tell en-Nasbeh
GEZER
Gibeon
JERICHO
Tell el-Fûl
Teleilat Ghassul
JERUSALEM
Ashdod
BETH SHEMESH
Ramat Rahel
Khirbet Qumran
Ras Siyagha
Tell es-Safi
Azekah
BETHLEHEM
ASCALON
Umm Qatafa
Tell ej-Judeideh
Tell Sheikh ʿAreini
Mareshah
Beth Zur
Tell el-Hesy
LACHISH
Ramat el-Khalîl
GAZA
Dead Sea
DIBON
Tell Ajjül
Tell Beit Mirsim
ʿAin Gedi
Khirbet ʿAraʿir
Tell Jemmeh
Miles
0 10 20 30 40 50
Kilometres
0 20 40 60 80
Tell el-Fara
Masada
Tell ʿArad
Tell Abu Matar
Beidha
PETRA
Khalasa
Wady ʿArabah
Khirbet et-Tannūr
Isbeita
ʿAuja el-Hafīr
Rumm
Tell el-Kheleifeh
Avdat
Wady ʿArabah
Gulf of Aqaba

ANET[3]). Fragile papyri have shed light on both the O.T. and N.T., such as those found at Qumran, in the desert of Judaea, and at Elephantine.

As a result of these efforts, hundreds of Biblical places have been reasonably firmly identified and a number of them excavated. Chronologies have been worked out for the entire ancient Near East which put the Biblical narratives in proper historical perspective. Ancient texts and manuscripts have shed light on both lexicographical and syntactical problems, and on the cultural setting of the Bible. Though archaeology has raised certain problems, such as with the reliability of the "conquest" narratives in Joshua and Judges in the case of Jericho and 'Ai, more often the evidence has attested to the historical reliability of the Bible, such as for the social background of the Hebrew Patriarchs, and the economic background of the Hebrew monarchy.

For an excellent assessment of the changes which archaeology has brought about in viewing the Biblical past, see J. B. Pritchard, *Archaeology and the Old Testament*, Princeton, 1958. For basic introductions of the archaeology of Palestine, see W. F. Albright, *The Archaeology of Palestine*, Baltimore, 1960, with a brief discussion of the method of excavating a tell*, and K. M. Kenyon, *Archaeology in the Holy Land*, New York, 1970. A good source book of excavated sites in Palestine and elsewhere, and the contributions they have made to our understanding of the Bible, is *Archaeology and Old Testament Study*, ed. by D. Winton Thomas, Oxford, 1967.

The following chart lists some of the more important sites in Palestine (Israel and Jordan) and its peripheral regions. For an assessment of our present-day knowledge of ancient Palestine, see P.W. Lapp, "Palestine: Known but Mostly Unknown," *BA* 26, 1963, pp. 121–134. W. P. A.

Archelaus (är′kĕ-lā′ŭs). son of Herod the Great, who bequeathed him the title of king (4 B.C.). He ruled Judaea, Samaria, and northern Idumaea 9 years. He was deposed by the Emperor Augustus A.D. 6, and was succeeded by procurators. See HEROD.

archers, one of the chief groups of warriors in O.T. times (Gen. 49:23 f.; I Chron. 8:40). "Call the archers together against Babylon, all them that bend the bow" (Jer. 50:29) was a typical rallying cry in Israel. In Shalmaneser's attacks on Syrian cities, and Sennacherib's assault on Lachish, archers formed conspicuous units. Philistine archers "greatly distressed" Saul (I Sam. 31:3). An Egyptian archer of Pharaoh-necho took the life of Israel's King Josiah (II Chron. 35:23). Persian archers with bows and arrows were

TABLE OF EXCAVATED SITES IN BIBLE LANDS

Palestine

(Israel and Jordan)

Name	*Location*	*Major Excavations*	*Major Periods or Discoveries*	*Bible References*
Acre (Acco; Ptolemais; Tell el-Fukhkhar)	Bay of Acre, 8 m. N. of Haifa	Dept. Antiq., Israel (Z. Goldman, 1855–56) (S. Applebaum, 1959) (E. Linder, G. Edelstein, 1966) (V. Tsaferis, Y. Margovsky, 1967)	Crusader ruins of A.D. 1104–1291	Judg. 1:31; Acts 21:7
'Ai (et-Tell)	2 m. SE. of Bethel	Pal. Dept. Antiq. (J. Garstang, 1928) Rothschild Expedition (J. Marquet-Krause, 1933–35) ASOR Consortium (J.A. Callaway, 1964–69, 1972)	EB Age (3rd mill. B.C.) defenses and architecture; small unwalled Iron I village (12th cent. B.C.)	Josh. 7:2–5, 8, 9:3, 10:1 f., 12:9
'Ammân (Rabbath-ammon, Philadelphia)	Highlands of E. Palestine, SE. of Jerash (Jordan)	Museo Nazionale Romano (G. Guidi, 1927) Dept. Antiq., Jordan, 1947– (G.L. Harding, R.W. Dajani, J.B. Hennessy, F. Zayadine, and others)	Palaeolithic flints; tombs of MB II and Iron Ages; Late Bronze Age temple; Graece-Roman theater	Deut. 3:11; II Sam. 12:26 ff.; Jer. 49:2–3
Anathoth ('Anāta; Râs el-Kharrûbeh)	3. m. NE of Jerusalem	ASOR (E.P. Blair, A. Bergman, 1936)	Soundings revealed Iron II and Persian-Hell. remains	Josh. 21:18; Jer. 1:1, 29:27, 32: 7–9
Aphek (Antipatris; Râs el-'Ain)	10 m. NE. of Jaffa	Pal. Dept. Antiq. (J. Ory, 1934–36) Dept. Antiq., Israel (A. Eitan, 1961)	Evidences of intermittent occupation, 3000 B.C.-Middle Ages; Canaanite stronghold; caravanserai	Josh. 12:18; I Sam. 4:1; Acts 23:31
Arad (Tel Arad)	East. Negev, 20 m. NE. of Beersheba	Hebrew Univ.; IES (R. Amiran, Y. Aharoni, 1962–)	EB I-II walled city; Iron Age citadel and Israelite sanctuary (10th–6th cent. B.C.)	
'Arō'er (Arâ'ir)	E. of Dead Sea, 1½ m. SE. of Dibon (Jordan)	Casa de Santiago (E. Olávarri, 1964–66)	2 phases of EB IV-MB I (c. 2250–1900 B.C.); Iron Age (Moabite) and Nabataean fortress	Josh. 12:2, 13:16; II Sam. 24:5; Jer. 48:19
Ashdod (Azotus; Isdud; Tel Mor)	Coastal plain, 9 m. NE. of Ashkelon	Carnegie Mus.; Pitts. Theo. Sem.; Dept. Antiq., Israel (D.N. Freedman, J.L. Swauger, M. Dothan, 1962–)	EB Age to Byzantine; Philistine private houses and high place (12th–10th cent. B.C.); city wall and pottery kilns of Iron II Pd.	Josh. 13:3; I Sam. 5:1 ff.; Neh. 13: 23 f.; Jer. 25:20; Amos 1:8
Ashkelon (Ascalon; 'Ashqelon)	Plain of Sharon 12 m. N. of Gaza	BSAJ; Pal. Explor. Fund (J. Garstang, W.J. Phythian-Adams, 1920–22) Dept. Antiq., Israel (R. Gophna, 1968)	Traces of Philistine city and much light on Roman Palestine	Judg. 14:19; Jer. 25: 20; Zeph. 2:4, 7; Zech. 9:5

Palestine (*Continued*)

Name	*Location*	*Major Excavations*	*Major Periods or Discoveries*	*Bible References*
Beersheba (Tell es-Seba; Tell Abu Matar; Bir es-Safadi; Khirbet el-Bitar)	Negev, 27 m. SW. of Hebron	Dept. Antiq., Israel (J. Perrot, 1951–60) (M. Dothan, 1953–55) (Y. Israeli, 1967) Tel Aviv Univ. (Y. Aharoni, 1969–)	Subterranean dwellings of mid-4th mill. B.C.; walled city of 10th–8th cent. B.C., with city gate and storehouses; fortress of Persian-Roman times	Gen. 21:14, 31–33, 22:19, 26:23, 33, 28:10, 46:1; Josh. 19:2; I Kings 4:25
Bethel (Beitin)	10 m. N. of Jerusalem	ASOR; Pitts.-Xenia Theo. Sem. (W.F. Albright, 1927, 1934) ASOR; Pitts. Theo. Sem. (J.L. Kelso, 1954, 1957, 1960)	MB I-end LB Age (destroyed 13th cent. B.C.); well-built domestic structures of LB Age; Hell.-Roman coins	Mentioned more often than any other city except Jerusalem
Bethlehem (Beit Lahm; Ephrath)	5 m. S. of Jerusalem	British Museum (E.W. Gardner, 1934–36) Pal. Dept. Antiq. (R.W. Hamilton, E.T. Richmond, 1932–35) Dept. Antiq., Jordan (B. Bagatti, 1962–64)	Palaeolithic flints and geological deposits of early Pleistocene; Constantinian floor mosaics, Church of Nativity	I Sam. 17:2; II Sam. 23:15; Matt. 2:1 ff.; Luke 2:4
Beth-shan Beisān; Tell el-Ḥuṣn; Scythopolis)	E. end of Jezreel Valley	Univ. Mus., Univ. of Penna. (C.S. Fisher, A. Rowe, G.M. FitzGerald, 1921–33) Dept. Antiq., Israel (N. Zori, S. Applebaum, 1951–53, 1957–64, 1972)	18 occupational strata from 4th mill. B.C.-6th cent. A.D.; most important series of Canaanite temples, 14th–11th cents. B.C. (Levels IX-V)	Judg. 1:27 f.; Josh. 17:11, 16; I Sam. 31:10, 12; II Sam. 21:12
Beth-shemesh ('Ain Shems) Tell er-Rumeileh)	16 m. SW. of Jerusalem	Pal. Explor. Fund (D. Mackenzie, 1911–12) Haverford College (E. Grant, 1928–31, 1933)	Superb Philistine pottery; 8 occupation strata from c. 2200 B.C.; cave tombs; fragments of proto-Hebrew script; light on late Canaanite and early Heb. occupation	Josh. 15:10, 19:22, 21:16; Judg. 1:33; I Sam. 6:9 ff.; II Kings 14:11 ff.; II Chron. 28:18
Beth-zur (Khirbet et-Tubeiqah)	4½ m. N. of Hebron	ASOR; McCormick Theo. Sem. (O.R. Sellers, 1931, 1957)	MB II citadel (18th–16th c. B.C.); Maccabean fortress	Josh.15:38; II Chron. 11:7; Neh. 3:16
Bozrah ('Buseirah)	24 m. S. of Dead Sea (Jordan)	BSAJ (C.M. Bennett, 1971–)	Large multi-roomed bldg. (palace?), and other structures of 1st mill. B.C. Edomite city; city wall	Gen. 36:33; Isa. 34: 6; 63:1; Jer. 49: 13, 22; Amos 1:12
Caesarea Maritima	Med. coast, 23 m. S. of Haifa	Pal. Dept. Antiq. (J. Ory, 1948) Hebrew Univ. (M. Avi-Yonah, 1951–56) Miss. Arch. Italiana (A. Frova, 1959–64) Heb. Univ.; S. Bapt. Theo. Sem. (M. Avi-Yonah, A. Negev, J. J. Vardaman, 1959–62) ASOR Joint Exped. (R. Bull, 1971-	Well-planned Roman city with aqueduct, theater, harbor, and sewage system; Crusader fortress	Acts 8:40, 10:1, 24, 18:22, 23:23, 33, 25:4, 6, 13
Capernaum (Tell Hûm; Kfar Naḥum)	NW. shore Sea of Galilee	Deutsch Orient-Gesellschaft (H. Kohl, C. Watzinger, 1905–14) Franciscan Custody Holy Land (G. Orfali, 1921) (V. Corbo, S. Loffreda, 1968–)	Fine synagogue ruins, c. 3rd c. A.D. Early Christian "House-Church"	Matt. 4:13, 8:5–13, 11:23, 17:24; Mark 2:1–22; John 6:59
Dan (Laish; Tell el-Qāḍi)	Source of Jordan, 25 m. N. of Sea of Galilee	Dept. Antiq., Israel (A. Biran, 1966–)	MB II fort. wall and glacis; city gate of 9th cent. B.C.; poss. "high place" (c. 600 B.C.)	Deut. 34:1; Judg. 18:27–29; I Kings 4:25; Amos 8:14
Debir (Kiriath-sepher) (? Tell Beit Mirsim)	13 m. SW. of Hebron	ASOR; Pitts.-Xenia Theo. Sem. (W.F. Albright, M.G. Kyle, 1926–32)	Imp. sequence of occupation from late 3rd mill. (EB III) to 6th cent. B.C.	Josh. 10:38 f., 15: 15, 21:15; Judg. 1:11–12
Dibon (Dhībân)	E. of Dead Sea, 40 m. S. of Amman	ASOR; Dept. Antiq., Jordan (F.V. Winnett, W.L. Reed, A.D. Tushingham, W.H. Morton, 1950–52, 1955–56)	EB I-III; heavy occupation during Iron I-II, inc. massive city defenses; Nabataean temple; Byz. church	Num. 21:30; Isa. 15:2
Dor (Dora; et-Tantūrah)	Med. coast, 17 m. S. of Haifa	BSAJ (J. Garstang, W.J. Phythian-Adams, 1923–24) Dept. Antiq., Israel (J. Leibovitch, 1951–52)	Hellenistic and Roman remains	Josh. 12:23, 17:11; Judg. 1:27; I Chron. 7:29
Dothan (Tell Dotha)	13 m. N. of Samaria	Wheaton College (J.P. Free, 1953–60)	Continuous occupation c. 3000 B.C.–Iron Age; Hell. and Roman remains	Gen. 37:12–36; II Kings 6:13
'En-Gedi (Tell ej-Jurn; Tel Goren)	W. shore Dead Sea, 18 m. E. of Hebron	IES; Hebrew Univ. (B. Mazar, I. Dunayevsky, T. Dothan, 1949, 1961–)	Chalc. high-place; Israelite (c. 9th–6th cent. B.C.) and Hell. citadels; Roman baths	Josh. 15:62; I Sam. 23:29; 24:1; Ezek. 47:10
Ezion-geber (Elath, Tell el-Kheleifeh)	Head of Gulf of Aqabah	ASOR (N. Glueck, 1938–40)	5 phases of occupation from 10th–5th cent. B.C.; major structure probably a fortified storehouse, rather than a refinery	I Kings 9:26; II Chron. 8:17, 20:36

Biblical Palestine (*Continued*)

Name	*Location*	*Major Excavations*	*Major Periods or Discoveries*	*Bible References*
Gerasa (Jerash)	Transjordan plateau, 26 m. N. of Amman	BSAJ; Pal. Dept. Antiq. (J. Garstang, G. Horsfield, 1925–27) BSAJ; ASOR; Yale Univ. (J.W. Crowfoot, C.S. Fisher, C.C. McCown, C.H. Kraeling, 1928–34) Dept. Antiq., Jordan (T. Canaan, D. Kirkbride, 1953–56) (F.S. Ma'ayeh, 1959)	Well-preserved Roman city (1st cent. B.C.–3rd cent. A.D.); Forum, columned street, temples of Artemis and Zeus; 13 churches from 4th–7th cent. A.D.	cf. Mark 5:1; Luke 8:26, 37
Gezer (Tell Jezer; Tell Abu Shusheh)	Shephelah, 18 m. W. of Jerusalem	Pal. Explor. Fund (R.A.S. Macalister, 1902–9) (A. Rowe, 1934) HUCBASJ;HarvardSemiticMuseum (W.G. Dever, 1964–71) (J.D. Seger, 1972–)	Occupation strata from c. 3000 B.C. to post-Exilic; unique water tunnel and cave spring; Gezer calendar; "High Place"; city gate and casemate wall of Solomon-date (10th cent. B.C.)	Josh. 21:21; Judg. 1:29; I Kings 9: 15–17
Gibeah (Tell el-Fûl)	3 m. N. of Jerusalem	ASOR (W.F. Albright, 1922–23, 1933) ASOR; Pitts. Theo. Sem. (P.W. Lapp, L.A. Sinclair, 1964)	Polygonal masonry of fortress "castle" of King Saul (shortly before 1000 B.C.); cook pots; spinning-whorls; game board	I Sam. 13:2, 16, 14:2, 5, 16
Gibeon (el-Jib)	8 m. NW. of Jerusalem	Dept. Antiq., Jordan (A.K. Dajani, 1950) Univ. Mus., U. of Penna.; Church Div. School of the Pacific; ASOR (J.B. Pritchard, 1956–62)	MB I tombs (21st–20th cent.), reused in MB II and LB IIA; two water systems, city wall, and winery of Iron Age; inscribed jar handles of 7th–6th cent. B.C.	II Sam. 2:13; Jer. 41:12
Hazor (Tell el-Qedaḥ; Tell Waqqaṣ)	5 m. SW. of Lake Huleh	Pal Explor. Fund (J. Garstang, 1928) J.A. de Rothschild Expedition; Hebrew Univ. Y. Yadin, 1955–58, 1968–69, 1971–72)	EB-Hell. occupation; large fortified "Lower City," MB II-LB II (destroyed 13th cent. B.C.); Solomonic city gate and casemate wall; Imp. series of Iron Age ("Israelite") levels	Josh. 11:1; Judg. 4:2; I Sam. 12:9; I Kings 9:15
Hebron (el-Khalil)	19 m. SW. of Jerusalem	Dept. Antiq., Jordan; Princeton Theo. Sem. (P.C. Hammond, 1964–66) HUCBSAJ; Dept. Antiq., Israel (W.G. Dever—tombs W. of Hebron, 1967–68, 1971–)	Late Chalc. to Byzantine and late Arab; MB II (c. 18th cent. B.C.) fortification wall and tower; MB I tombs (c. 2150–1900 B.C.)	Gen. 13:18, 23:2, 35:27; Josh. 10: 36, 14:13–15; II Sam. 2:1–3, 11
Heshbon (Tell Ḥesbân)	Transjordan, 14 m. SW. of Amman (Jordan)	Andrews Univ.; ASOR (S.H. Horn, R.S. Boraas, 1968, 1971–)	Excavation just beginning; good sequence of Byzantine and Arab remains	Num. 21:25–30; Josh. 12:2, 13: 17; Judg. 11:26
Jericho (N.T.) (Tulûl Abū el-'Alâyiq)	Two *tells*, near entrance of Wâdī Qelt into Jericho Plain	ASOR; Pitts.-Xenia Theo. Sem. (J.L. Kelso, 1950) (J.B. Pritchard, F.V. Winnett, 1951)	Roman structures of this winter capital of Herod the Great and Herod Archelaus, including a unique military tower	Matt. 20:29–34; Mark 10:46–52; Luke 10:30–37
Jericho (O.T.) (Tell es-Sultau)	West side of Jordan Valley, 15 m. NE. of Jerusalem	Pal. Explor. Fund (C. Warren, 1868) Deutsche Orient-Gesellschaft (E. Sellin, C. Watzinger, 1907–9) BSAJ; Univ. of Liverpool (J. Garstang, 1930–36) BSAJ; Pal. Explor. Fund; British Academy; ASOR (K.M. Kenyon, 1952–58)	Largest early fortified village known (8th mill. B.C.); Early Bronze walls; massive MB II fortification and well-sealed tombs with food and furniture	Num. 22:1; Deut. 34:1, 3; Josh. 2–6; II Kings 2:4, 15; Neh. 3:2; Heb. 11:30
Jerusalem	Highlands of Judaea	Excavated more than any other site in Palestine, it has until recently yielded little of scientific value; below are listed some of the more significant endeavors:		
		Pal. Explor. Fund (C. Warren, 1864–68)	Herodian masonry of Temple Mount explored using tunnels and shafts	Josh. 15:8; II Sam. 5:5–9; II Chron. 1:4, 2–8, 36:19; Ezra 2:1; Matt. 2:1, 16:21, 23:37; Luke 24:52; Acts 4:6
		(F.J. Bliss, A.C. Dickie, 1894–97)	S. wall traced from W. ridge across the Tyropoean Valley	
		BSAJ; Pal. Dept. Antiq.; Hebrew U.; ASOR (R.A.S. Macalister, J.C. Duncan, J.W. Crowfoot, E.L. Sukenik, 1923–29)	Maccabean fort. wall and tower uncovered along top of SE. ridge; fill of Central Valley probed; "Third Wall"	
		Pal. Dept. Antiq. (C.N. Johns, 1934–47)	Hellenistic fort. explored in area of Citadel	
		Franciscan Custody Holy Land (B. Bagatti, J.T. Milik, 1954–57)	Excavated Dominus Flevit	
		BSAJ; Pal. Explor. Fund.; British Academy; Royal Ont. Mus. (K.M. Kenyon, 1961–67)	Earliest remains (Jebusite, Davidic, etc.), along E. slope of SE. ridge	
		BSAJ; Dept. Antiq., Jordan (C.M. Bennett; J.B. Hennessy, 1964–66)	Early phases of Damascus Gate excavated	
		IES; Hebrew Univ. (N. Avigad, 1967–) (B. Mazar, R. Amiran, A. Eitan, 1968–)	Excavations in area of Temple Mount, the Citadel, and the Jewish Quarter of the Old City, revealing occupation as far back as 7th cent. B.C.	
Joppa (Jaffa; Yâfō)	Med. coast, 35 m. NW. of Jerusalem	Dept. Antiq., Israel (P.L.O. Guy, 1950) (J. Bowman, B.S.J. Isserlin, 1952) Mus. Antiq., Tel Aviv-Jaffa (J. Kaplan, 1955–)	Continuous occupation from as early as 5th mill. B.C.; MB II fort. wall and glacis; gateway of Ramesses II of Egypt (13th cent. B.C.); Iron Age ("Israelite") sequence	Josh. 19:46; II Chron. 2:16; Ezra 3:7; Acts 9:36 ff., 10:5 ff.

Palestine (*Continued*)

Name	*Location*	*Major Excavations*	*Major Periods or Discoveries*	*Bible References*
Khirbet Qumran ('Ain Feshkha Cave)	NW. corner of Dead Sea, 8 m. S. of Jericho	Dept. Antiq., Jordan; Ecole Biblique; Pal. Arch. Mus. (G.L. Harding, R. de Vaux, A.K. Dajani, 1949–58)	Dead Sea Scrolls; Essene community center, c. 140 B.C.–A.D. 68; scriptorium, cisterns, potter's workshop	Copies of and commentaries on O.T. books, (Isaiah, Habbakuk, etc.)
Lachish (Tell ed-Duweir)	Judean foothills, 15 m. W. of Hebron	Wellcome-Marston Arch. Exped. (J.L. Starkey, 1932–38) Hebrew Univ. (Y. Aharoni, 1966, 1968)	LB Age sanctuary blt. in MB Age fosse; Iron Age city wall and gateway; 21 ostraca written in Heb. script of Jeremiah's time	Josh. 10:3, 31 f.; II Kings 18:14, 17; II Chron. 11:9; Isa.36:2,37:8;Jer. 34:7; Neh. 11:30
Mareshah (Marisa; Tell Sandahannah; Beit Jibrin; Eleutheropolis)	13 m. NW. of Hebron	Pal. Explor. Fund (R.A.S. Macalister, F.J. Bliss, 1900) École Biblique (W.J. Moulton, W.G. Masterman, 1921–24) Dept. Antiq., Israel (E. Oren-survey, 1961–63)	Hellenistic city uncovered; tombs of Sidonian colony; "painted tomb" marvels; mosaic pavement; Rom. and Byz. remains	Josh.15:44;IIChron. 11:8, 14:9 f.
Masada	W. of Dead Sea 10 m. S. of En-Gedi	Dept. Antiq., Israel (M. Avi-Yonah, 1955) Hebrew Univ.; IES (Y. Yadin, 1963–65)	Herodian fortress-palace; synagogue, ritual baths and schoolroom of Zealot stronghold; 12 scroll frags., inc. piece of Heb. book of Jubilees	
Megiddo (Tell el-Mutesellim)	Plain of Esdraelon SE. of Haifa	Deutsche Orient-Gesellschaft (G. Schumacher, C. Steuernagel, C. Watzinger, 1903–5) Oriental Inst., Univ. of Chicago (C.S. Fisher, P.L.O. Guy, G. Loud, 1925–39) Hebrew Univ. (Y. Yadin, 1960, 1966–67)	20 Levels; earliest Chalc. (c. 3500 B.C.); series of EB Age Canaanite temples; early hoard of invories (13th cent. B.C.); gateway and casemate wall from time of Solomon (10th cent. B.C.); large public bldgs. (not stables!) from time of Ahab (9th cent. B.C.)	Josh. 12:21; I Kings 4:12, 9:15; II Kings 9:27; II Chron. 35:22
Mt. Carmel (Caves) and Vicinity (Wâdī el-Mughârah; el-Wad; Abu Uṣba; Kebarah; et-Tabun; Naḥal Oren; etc.)	SE. slopes of Mt. Carmel, overlooking Sharon Plain	BSAJ (F. Turville-Petre, 1925–26) BSAJ; Am. School Prehist. Res. (D. Garrod, T. McCown, 1929–34) ASOR; Hebrew Univ.; Dept. Antiq., Israel (M. Stekelis, 1940–41, 1951–60, 1964) Dept. Antiq.. Israel (E. Wreschner, 1962, 1964) Univ. Arizona; Univ. Michigan (A.J. Jellink, 1969, 1972)	Numerous caves provide rich sequence of deposits from the Middle Palaeolithic to the Mesolithic; skulls of classic Neanderthal hominide, and other vestiges of "Mt. Carmel Man"; burials and deposits of Natufian culture Mesolithic, c. 10th mill. B.C.)	
Mt. Gerizim (Jebel et-Tur; Tell er-Râs; Tananir)		Survey of Western Palestine (C.W. Wilson, 1866) Gottingen Univ. (A.M. Schneider, 1927–28) ASOR Joint Expedition (R.J. Bull, 1964, 1966, 1968) (R.G. Boling, 1968)	MB II sanctuary on lower slopes; Found. of temple of Zeus Hypsistos (4th-6th cent. A.D.); 5th cent. A.D. church of Theotokos	Deut. 11:29, 27:12; Josh. 8:33; Judg. 9:7
Nazareth (en-Naṣireh)	Galilean hills, 20 m. SE. of Haifa	Franciscan Custody Holy Land (P.M. Vioud, A. Mansur, 1890–1909) (B. Bagatti, 1953–59)	Cultic installations from early Christ. era; Greek, Hebrew and Aramaic graffiti and art-motifs	Matt. 2:23, 4:13, 21:11; Luke 1:26, 2:4, 39, 4:16
Petra (Umm el-Biyerah)	Highlands E. of Arabah, 50 m. S. of Dead Sea	Melchett Expedition (G. Horsfield, A. Conway, W.F. Albright, 1929–36) British School Arch. Egypt (M.A. Murray, 1937) Dept. Antiq., Jordan; BSAJ (P.J. Parr, D. Kirkbride, G.L. Harding, G.R.H. Wright, C.M. Bennett, P.C. Hammond, 1955–68)	Nabataean temples, palaces, tombs; "Conway High Place"; Palaeolithic flints; Edomite fortress (8th–7th cent. B.C.)	
Ramat Raḥel (Beth-haccherem?)	Midway between Jerusalem and Bethlehem	IES; Hebrew Univ.; Univ. of Rome (Y. Aharoni, 1954,1956, 1960–62)	Royal palace and citadel of Judah (late 7th cent. B.C.), similar in plan to that at Samaria	Jer. 6:1; Neh. 3:14
Samaria (Sebaste)	7 m. NW. of Shechem	Harvard Univ. (G.A. Reisner, C.S. Fisher, D.G. Lyon, 1908–10) BSAJ; Pal. Explor. Fund; British Academy; Hebrew Univ. (J.W. Crowfoot, *et al.*, 1931–33, 1935) Dept. Antiq., Jordan (F. Zayadine, P.W. Lapp, 1965–67) BSAJ (J.B. Hennessy, 1968)	Continuing history of occupation from its founding by Omri (c. 880 B.C.) to Crusader times; Israelite royal palace and citadel; ivory inlays from time of Ahab; Heb. ostraca from time of Jeroboam II; Hell. fortress; Roman Temple of Augustus	I Kings 16:24; II Kings 3:1, 17:5–6; II Chron. 28:8–9; Isa. 10:9–11
Sharuhen (Tell el-Far'ah)	15 m. S. of Gaza	Brit. School Arch. Egypt (W.M.F. Petrie, 1928–30)	MB II embankment; tombs with Phil. pottery and anthropoid clay coffins	Josh. 19:6

Palestine (*Continued*)

Name	*Location*	*Major Excavations*	*Major Periods or Discoveries*	*Bible References*
Shechem (Tell Balâtah)	7 m. SE. of Samaria	German Arch. Inst.; Deutsche-Evangelischen Inst.; Vienna Acad. of Science (E. Sellin, G. Welter, 1913–34) Drew-McCormick Expedition (G.E. Wright, *et al.*, 1956–69, 1972)	Temenos area and fort. from early stage of MB II (c. 1800 B.C.); so-called 'Fortress-temple" (*miḡdāl*) of late MB and LB Age (c. 1650–1100 B.C.) fort. of Jeroboam's time	Gen. 33:18, 37:12–14; I Kings 12:1, 25; II Chron. 10:1
Shiloh (Tell Seilûn)	12 m. S. of Shechem	Natl. Museum of Denmark (A. Schmidt, 1922) (H. Kjaer, 1926, 1929, 1932) (S. Holm-Nielsen, 1963)	Middle Bronze, Iron I, Hellenistic to Arab remains (dest. by Philistines c. 1050 B.C.); mosaic floors of two Byzantine churches	Josh. 18:1, 8–10; Judg. 18:31; I Sam. 1:24, 3:21
Taanach (Tell Ta'annak)	Pl. Esdraelon, 5 m. SE. of Megiddo	Vienna Academy of Science (E. Sellin, 1902–4) ASOR; Concordia Theo. Sem. (P.W. Lapp, 1963, 1966, 1968)	EB Age fort. and debris (c. 2700–2500 B.C.); MB IIC glacis; cun. tablets (15th cent. B.C.); series of LB-Iron Age structures	Josh. 12:21; Judg. 5:19
Tell Deir 'Allā (? Succoth)	E. bank of Jordan, N. of Wâdī Zerqa	Dutch Arch. Expedition (H.J. Franken, 1960–64)	LB Age sanctuary; imp. sequence of Iron I pottery; Aramaic inscriptions on plastered wall	Gen. 33:16, 17; Josh. 13:27; Judg. 8; I Kings 7:46
Tell el-Hesi (? Eglon)	On edge of Coastal Plain, W. of Hebron	Pal. Explor. Fund (W.M.F. Petrie, 1890) (F.J. Bliss, 1891–93) ASOR; Oberlin College; Hartford Sem. Found. (J.E. Worrell, L.E. Toombs, 1970–)	Group of copper weapons of EB Age (c. 2600 B.C.); 14th cent. clay tablet (City III); initial pottery chronology for Pal. established; immense mud-brick fort. wall (10th–9th cent.); Persian-Hell. sequence	Josh. 10:3, 34, 15:39
Tell en-Naṣbeh (? Mizpah)	8 m. N. of Jerusalem	Pacific School of Religion; ASOR (W.F. Bade, J.C. Wampler, 1926–35)	Unique city gate, illus. Bib. allusions to activities; 26 ft. walls, remnants to 25 ft. high; rich evidences Heb. life; tombs	Josh. 18:26; I Kings 15:22; Neh. 3:7
Tell eṣ-Sâfi ('Blanche Garde') (? Libnah) (? Gath)	Edge of Coastal Plain, 10 m. N. of Lachish	Pal. Explor. Fund (F.J. Bliss, R.A.S. Macalister, 1899)	Sections of ancient city wall traced; structure with 3 standing monoliths	Josh. 10:29 ff., 15:42, 21:13; II Kings 8:22, 19:8
Tirzah (Tell el-Far'ah)	6 m. NE. of Shechem	École Biblique (R. de Vaux, 1946–55, 1958–60)	EB Age town with well-preserved gateway; typical house-plans of Early Iron Age; "unfinished" bldg. of 9th cent. B.C.	I Kings 14:17, 15:21, 16:6; II Kings 15:14
Zarethan (Tell es-Sa'idiyeh)	1 m. E. of Jordan R., c. midway between Sea of Galilee and the Dead Sea	Univ. Mus., Univ. of Penna. (J.B. Pritchard, 1964–67)	Tombs of 12th cent. B.C.; Iron Age tunnel from inside city wall to spring at base of *tell*; 4th cent. B.C. "palace"	Josh. 3:16; I Kings 4:12, 7:46

For bibliography, see: E. Vogel, "Bibliography of Holy Land Sites," *Hebrew Union College Annual* XLII (1971), pp. 1–96; and the annual *Elenchus Bibliographicus Biblicus* (pub. as an appendix to *Biblica* prior to 1969). For current excavations, see: "Chronique archéologique," in *Revue biblique*; and "Notes and News," in the *Israel Exploration Journal*. See also current issues of the *Biblical Archaeologist, Bulletin of the American Schools of Oriental Research*, the *Palestine Exploration Quarterly, Levant, Annual of the Department of Antiquities of Jordan*, and other relevant periodical literature.

Mesopotamia and Elam

(Assyria, Babylonia, and Persia)

(Iraq and Iran)

Name	*Location*	*Major Excavations*	*Major Periods or Discoveries*	*Bible References*
Assur (Qal'at Sherqat)	W. bank Tigris R., 60 m. S. of Mosul	British Museum (H. Rassam, 1853) Deutsche Orient-Gesellschaft (W. Andrae, 1903–14)	Archaic temples of Ishtar and Ashur (c. 3000 B.C.); Anu-Adad temple and ziggurat (12th cent. B.C.); Assyrian copy of Creation Epic (c. 1000 B.C.)	Ezek. 27:23; cf. refs. to Assyria
Babylon (Babel; Qasr; Homera; Merkes; 'Amran ibn 'Ali)	Ancient course of Euphrates R., 54 m. S. of Baghdad	East India Company (C.J. Rich, 1811, 1817) (R. Mignan, 1829) British Museum (A.H. Layard, 1850) (H. Rassam, 1879–80, 1882) Expéd. scientifique français (F. Fresnel, J. Oppert, 1852–54) Deutsche Orient-Gesellschaft (R. Koldeway, 1899–1917) (H.J. Lenzen, 1956–58, 1963–64) Directorate-General Antiq., Iraq (since 1968)	City of Nebuchadnezzar; Ishtar Gate and "Processional Way"; palace; Ziggurat Entemenanki; Esagila, the temple of Marduk; numerous other temples and shrines, city gates and fortifications; clay tablets with description and maps of city	Gen. 10:10, 11:3–9; II Kings 17:30; 24; 25; Ezra 2:1; Ezek. 12:13

Mesopotamia and Elam (*Continued*)

Name	*Location*	*Major Excavations*	*Major Periods or Discoveries*	*Bible References*
Calah (Kalḫu; Nimrud)	E. bank Tigris R., 20 m. S. of Mosul	British Museum (A.H. Layard, 1845–51) (H.C. Rawlinson, 1852–54) (W.K. Loftus, 1854–55) (G. Smith, 1872–73) (H. Rassam, 1878) British School Arch., Iraq (M.E.L. Mallowan, 1949–63)	Assyrian capital (c. 883–727 B.C.); palace of Ashurnasirpal II; stone colossi, *lamassu* and *šedu* (winged lion and bull figures with head of a man); Nabu temple (Ezida); military fort built by Shalmaneser III; black obelisk of Shalmaneser III; superbly carved Nimrud ivories	Gen. 10:11–12
Erech (Uruk; Warka)	S. Iraq, 40 m. NW. of Ur	Deutsche Orient-Gesellschaft (J. Jordan, 1912–13, 1928–30) (A. Noldeke, E. Heinrich, 1931–39) (H.J. Lenzen, 1954–)	Early Sumerian city (4th–3rd mill. B.C.); monumental architecture; ziggurat of Eanna; earliest imprints of cylinder seals; earliest Sumerian documents	Gen. 10:10; Ezra 4:9
Mari (Tell el-Harīrī)	Middle Euphrates, 6 m. N. of Abu Kemal, near Iraq border (Syria)	Musée du Louvre (A. Parrot, 1933–39, 1951–55, 1960–)	Ziggurat and adjoining shrines of 3rd and 2nd mill. B.C.; series of temples dedicated to Ishtar; Old Babylonian palace of Zimri-Lim; administrative records (20,000 tablets) of 18th cent. B.C.	
Nineveh (Tell Kuyunjik; Tell Nebi Yunis)	Upper Tigris, on E. Bank, opposite Mosul	Musée du Louvre (P.E. Botta, 1842) British Museum (A.H. Layard, 1845–51) (H. Rassam, 1852–54, 1878–82) (E.A.W. Budge, 1889–91) (L.W. King, 1903–5) (R.C. Thompson, 1927–32) Directorate-General Antiq., Iraq (M. d-A. Mustafa, 1954) (T.A. Madhloom, *et al.*, 1965–70)	Occupational strata from 5th mill. to 7th cent. B.C.; palaces of Assyrian kings Ashurbanipal and Sennacherib; temples of Ishtar and Nabu; important library of Ashurbanipal with some 26,000 fragments of cuneiform tablets ("first systematically collected library in the ancient Near East" —Oppenheim)	Gen. 10:11 f.; II Kings 19:36; Isa. 37:37; Jonah 1:2; Nah. 1:1 ff.; Matt. 12:41
Nippur (Tell Nuffar)	Central Iraq, 60 m. SE. of Babylon	British Museum (A.H. Layard, 1850) Univ. Mus., Univ. of Penna. (J.P. Peters, 1888–90) (J.H. Haynes, 1893–96) (H.V. Hilprecht, 1898–1900) Oriental Instit., Chicago (D. McCown, R. Haines, 1948–61) (J. Knudstad, 1964–67)	Sumerian cultural and religious center; E-kur temple and ziggurat of Enlil; temple library and scribal quarter, yielding some 40,000 cuneiform tablets in the Sumerian language, inc. a Sumerian account of the Flood	

30.

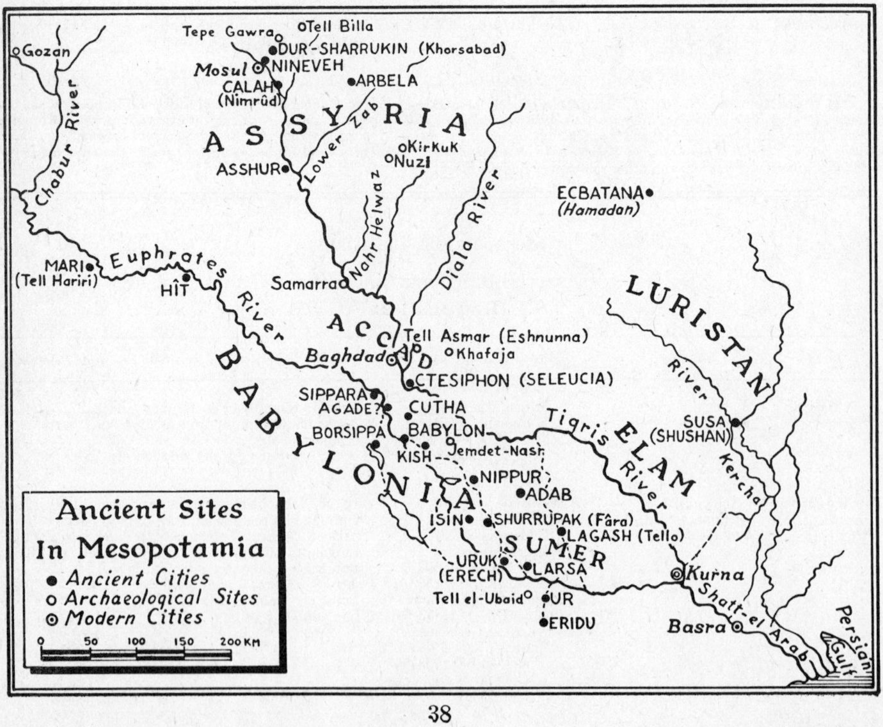

Ancient Sites In Mesopotamia

- Ancient Cities
- Archaeological Sites
- Modern Cities

0 50 100 150 200 KM

Mesopotamia and Elam (*Continued*)

Name	*Location*	*Major Excavations*	*Major Periods or Discoveries*	*Bible References*
Nuzi (Nuzu; Yorghan Tepe)	10 m. SW. of Kirkuk	ASOR; Iraq Mus., Boston and Harvard Univ., (E. Chiera, 1925–28) (R.H. Pfeiffer, 1928–29) (R.F.S. Starr, 1930–31)	Temple, palace and several domestic structures; several thousand clay tablets of mid-second mill. B.C. shed light on Hurrian society and provide parallels to Patriarchal customs	
Shushan (Shush; Susa)	In ancient Elam E. of Tigris (Iran)	British Museum (W.K. Loftus, 1851–52) Musée du Louvre (M. Dieulafoy, 1884–86) Délégation en Perse français (J. de Morgan, 1897–1908) (R. de Mecquenem, 1908–14, 1920–33) (R. Ghirshman, 1946–67)	Ancient capital of Elam; uninterrupted sequence of occupation from c. 4th mill. B.C.–c. 12th cent. A.D.; elaborately decorated prehistoric painted pottery of Susa A necropolis (c. 4000–3600 B.C.); ex. of early semi-pictographic script (Proto-Elamite); palace of Darius I; copy of Code of Hammurabi	Neh. 1:1; Esther 1:2 etc.; Dan. 8:2
Ur (Tell al-Muqaiyar)	S. Iraq, 100 m. NW. of Bosra	British Museum; Univ. Mus., Univ. of Penna. (J.E. Taylor, 1854) (R.C. Thompson, 1918) (H.R. Hall, 1919) (C.L. Woolley, 1922–34)	Ziggurat of Ur-Nammu (Ur III c. 2100 B.C.); temple of moon god, Nanna; residential area of Isin-Larsa Pd.; royal tombs of E. Dyn. III (c. 2500 B.C.); excellent examples of jewelry, weapons, art-work	Gen. 11:28, 31, 15:7; Neh. 9:7

For additional information, see: A.R. al-Haik, *Key Lists of Arch. Excavations in Iraq 1842–1965* (1968); S.A. Pallis, *The Antiquity of Iraq* (1956); and relevant chapters in the revised *Cambridge Ancient History*. Also useful are: S.N. Kramer, *The Sumerians* (1963); A.L. Oppenheim, *Ancient Mesopotamia* (1964); H.W.F. Saggs, *The Greatness that was Babylon* (1962). For current research in the area, consult reports on Iran and Iraq in *COWA Surveys and Bibliographies*, Area 15: *Western Asia*, pub. triennially, and more detailed surveys and articles appearing in current issues of *Orientalia, Sumer, Iraq, Iran*, and other relevant periodical literature.

Egypt

(United Arab Republic)

Name	*Location*	*Major Excavations*	*Major Periods or Discoveries*	*Bible References*
El-Amarna (et-Till; el-Hag Qandil)	E. bank of Nile, 190 m. S. of Cairo	Egypt Explor. Fund/Society (W.M.F. Petrie, 1891–92) (N. de G. Davies, 1902–7) (T.E. Peet, *et al.*, 1920–36) Deutsche Orient-Gesellschaft (L. Borchardt, 1907–14)	Houses and royal palace of Akhenaton's capital; tombs of royal officials; diplomatic correspondence (Amarna Letters) of great importance for the political background of Canaan during the 14th century B.C.	
Memphis (Mit-Rahineh; Giza; Saqqara; Abu Roash; Abu-sir; Dahshur)	W. bank of Nile, 13 m. S. of Cairo	Service des Antiq.; Cairo Mus. (A. Mariette, J.E. Quibell, and others—periodically since 1854) Universität Leipzig (G. Steindorff, 1903–14) Harvard; Mus. Fine Arts, Boston (G.A. Reisner, 1905–27) Österreichische Akademie (H. Junker, 1926–32) Egyptian University (S. Hassan, 1928–39) Egypt Explor. Fund/Society (W.M.F. Petrie, 1880–82, 1906–12) (C.M. Firth, 1924–31) (W.B. Emery, 1935–39, 1945–46, 1952–56, 1964–71)	Old Kingdom capital of Egypt; early dynastic mastaba-tombs; Step Pyramid of Zoser at Saqqara (Dyn. III); Great Pyramid of Cheops (Khufu) and those of Chephren and Mycerinus at Giza (Dyn. IV); Great Sphinx; New Kingdom Temple of Ptah; other remains and pyramids	Isa. 19:13; Jer. 2:16, 46:14, 19; Ezek. 30:13, 16; Hos. 9:6
Thebes (Karnak; Luxor; Biban el-Moluk; Deir el-Bahari; Medinet Habu; etc.)	E. and W. banks of Nile, 450 m. S. of Cairo	Service des Antiq.; Cairo Mus. (A. Mariette, G. Legrain, H. Chevrier, and others, since 1858) Egypt Explor. Fund/Society (W.M.F. Petrie, 1898; T.M. Davis, 1902–14; H. Carter, 1907–28; others Metrpolitan Mus. of Art, N. Y. (H.E. Winlock, 1911–31) (A. Lansing, W. Hayes, 1931–36) Oriental Institute, Chicago (H. Nelson, U. Hölscher, 1924–36) Univ. Mus., Univ. of Penna. (C.S. Fisher, 1921–23) (D. O'Connor, *et al.*, 1966–) Deuts. Arch. Institut, Kairo (D. Arnold, 1963–)	Temples of Amun at Karnak and Luxor; Theban necropolis; Valley of the Tombs of the Kings, including the Tomb of Tutankhamun (c. 1361–1352 B.C.) with its valuable treasure of burial furnishings now in the Cairo Museum; mortuary temple of Ramesses III at Medinet Habu; temple of Queen Hatshepsut at Deir el-Bahari; worker's village at Deir el-Medineh	Jer. 46:25; Ezek. 30:14–16; Nah. 3:8?

For additional archaeological work in Egypt, see: B. Porter and R.L.B. Moss, *Topographical Bibliography of Ancient Egyptian Hieroglyphic Texts, Reliefs, and Paintings*, 7 Vols.; and J. Leclant, "Fouilles et travaux en Egypte et au Soudan," pub. annually in *Orientalia*. For overviews, see: *A General Introductory Guide to the Egyptian Collections in the British Museum* (1969); W.C. Hayes, *The Scepter of Egypt*, 2 Vols. (1953–59); H. Kees, *Ancient Egypt* (1961); and the revised *Cambridge Ancient History*.

Syria and Phoenicia

(N.W. Syria and Lebanon)

Name	Location	Major Excavations	Major Periods or Discoveries	Bible References
Antioch and its harbor, Seleucia Pieria (Antakya)	On the Orontes, 20 m. from the Med. (Hatay, Turkey)	Princeton Univ.; Musée National de France (G.W. Elderkin, R. Stillwell, *et al.*, 1931–36)	Floor mosaics in villas, baths, etc. (from c. 100 A.D.); sculptures; Antioch Chalice; altar to unknown gods; Temple Demeter	Acts 11:19 ff.; 13:1, 14:26, 15:35; Gal. 2:11
Carchemish (Jerablus)	Upper Euphrates, 63 m. NE. of Aleppo (Syria)	British Museum (D.G. Hogarth, R.C. Thompson, 1911) (C.L. Woolley, 1912–14, 1920)	Neolithic to Roman; MB Age earthen embankment; fortification walls and gateway of 1st mill. B.C.	II Chron. 35:20; Isa. 10:9; Jer. 46:2
Gebal (Gubla; Byblos; Jebeil)	25 m. N. of Beirut on Med. coast (Lebanon)	(P. Montet, 1919, 1921–24) (M. Dunand, 1925–)	Occupied as early as Neo. Pd.; temples of EB and MB Age city; royal tombs of Princes of Gebal; sarcophagus of Ahiram with early Phoenician inscription (11th cent. B.C.); Persian palace; Roman city; Crusader fortress	Josh. 13:5; I Kings 5:18; Ezek. 27:9
Hamath (Hama; Epiphania)	W. bank Orontes R., 28 m. N. of Homs (Syria)	Fondation Carlsberg, Mission Arch. danoise (H. Ingholt, 1931–38)	Neolithic to Arab; large Neo-Hittite Aramaean citadel and cemetery with cremated burials (12th–8th cent. B.C.)	II Sam. 8:9; II Kings 14:28, 17:24; Amos 6:2
Ras Shamra (Ugarit)	S. of Antioch, on old Syrian coast 8 m. N. of Latakia (Syria)	Strasbourg Mus.; Acad. des Inscript. et Belles-Lettres; Centre Nat. Rech. Scient. (C.F.A. Schaeffer, 1929–38, 1948–)	Neo. Pd. to end of LB Age (c. 1200 B.C.); temples of Baal and Dagon; palace; literary and administrative texts in alphabetic cuneiform (Ugaritic) with numerous points of contact in the O.T.	
Sidon (Saïda; Eshmun)	Med. coast, 25 m. N. of Tyre (Lebanon)	Mission de Phénicie (E. Renan, 1860) (J.C. Gaillardot, 1861–63) Imperial Ottoman Museum (O. Hamdy Bey, 1887) (T.C. Macridy Bey, 1901–3) Mission archéologique à Sidon (G. Conteneau, 1913–14, 1920) Service des Antiquities (P.E. Guigues, *et al.*, 1937–38) (A. Poidebard, G. Lauffrey, 1946, 1950) (M. Dunand, 1924, 1968–)	Chalcolithic dwellings; Iron Age tombs; Roman-Byzantine necropolis; sarcophagus of Esmunazar (5th cent. B.C.), inscribed with well-preserved Phoenician inscription; temple dedicated to the Phoenician god Eshmun (Gk. Asclepius); Crusader Castle of the Sea	Josh. 11:8, 19:28; Judg. 1:31; I Kings 17:9; Isa. 23:2, 4, 12; Joel 3:4–8; Matt. 11:21; Acts 27:3
Tyre (Sur)	Med. coast, 25 m. S. of Sidon (Lebanon)	Mission de Phénicie (E. Renan, 1860) Imperial Ottoman Museum (T.C. Macridy Bey, 1903) Mission archéologique à Tyr (Mme. D. LeLasseur, 1921) Service des Antiquities (A. Poidebard, 1934–36) (M. Chehab, 1947–)	Columned streets, baths, sports arena, palaestra, hippodrome and other remains of the extensive Roman city. Vast Roman-Byzantine necropolis with many sculptured sarcophagi; traces of earlier (Phoenician remains; cathedral of Crusader period	Josh. 19:29; II Sam. 5:11, 24:7; I Kings 5:1, 7:13 f., 9:11 f.; Ezek. 26–28, f.; Isa. 23:1, 5, 13 ff.; Ezek. 26–28; 29:18; Amos 1:9 f.; Zech. 9:3; Matt. 15:21; Mk. 7:31; Acts 12:20, 21:3
Zarephath (Sarepta; Sarafand)	Med. coast, 8. m. S. of Sidon (Lebanon)	Univ. Mus., Univ. of Penna.; National Geographic Society (J.B. Pritchard, 1969–)	First stratified Phoenician city excavated in Phoenician homeland; Numerous pottery kilns, one with roof preserved; Shrine with altar and cache of religious objects; Seal inscribed with anc. name of city (SRPT); Late Roman-Byz. port	I Kings 17:9 f.; Obad. 20; Luke 4:26

For further information, see: R. Dussaud, *Topographie historique de la Syrie antique at médiévale* (1927); relevant chapters of the revised *Cambridge Ancient History*; and reports on Lebanon and Syria in *COWA Surveys and Bibliographies*, Area 15: *Western Asia*, pub. triennially. For current work in Lebanon, see the relevant articles and bibliog. pub. in *Berytus* and the *Bulletin de Musée de Beyrouth*. For Syria, the pub. *Syria* and *Annales archéologiques Arabes Syriennes.*

Asia Minor

(Anatolia; Turkey)

Name	Location	Major Excavations	Major Periods or Discoveries	Bible References
Boğazköy (Hittite Hattusha; Büyükkale, Kizlarkaya, Yazilikaya, etc.)	N. Cappadocia, 100 m. E. of Ankara	Deutsche Orient-Gesellschaft (H. Winckler, T. Macridy, 1906–7, 1911–12; O. Puchstein, 1907) with Deutsche Arch. Institut (K. Bittel, 1931–39, 1952–)	Small settlements of late EB Age; old Assyrian trade colony; Hittite capital (16th–13th cent. B.C.); huge fortifications, gateways; sculptured reliefs; cuneiform tablets with Hittite myths, historical annals, treaties, etc.	Cf. ref. to Hittites in O.T.

Asia Minor (*Continued*)

Name	*Location*	*Major Excavations*	*Major Periods or Discoveries*	*Bible References*
Ephesus (Seljuk; Panajir Dagh; Bülbül Dagh)	W. Turkey, 35 m. S. of Izmir along Cayster R., 4 m. from Aegean	British Museum (J.T. Wood, 1863–74) (D.G. Hogarth, 1904–5) Austrian Arch. Institute (O. Benndorf, 1898–1913) (J. Keil, 1926–35, 1954–59) (F. Miltner, H. Vetters, 1960–)	Great Temple of Artemis (Diana) (6th cent. B.C.–3rd cent. A.D.); baths, agora, library, gymnasiums, city gates, theater, and main street ("Arkadiane"); Byzantine churches and other remains	Acts 18:19, 21, 24, 19:1–20:1; I Cor. 15:32, 16:8; I Tim. 1:3; Rev. 1:1, 2:1 ff.; Eph. 1:1 (KJV)
Miletus (Balat; Palation; ? Millawanda)	W. Turkey, near mouth of Lycus (Meander) R,. 5 m. from Aegean	Berlin Museum (T. Wiegand, 1899–1914) (C. Weickert, G. Kleiner, *et al.*, 1938, 1955–)	LB Age Mycenean citadel; Classical Greek city (c. 5th cent. B.C.), with agora, palaestra, Nymphaeum, etc.; city of Roman imperial times; Byzant. church	Acts 20:15, 17; II Tim. 4:20
Sardis (? OT Sepharad)	W. Turkey Hermus R. Valley, 50 m. E. of Izmir	Am. Soc. for Excav. of Sardis (H.C. Butler, T.L. Shear, 1910–14, 1922) Harvard, Cornell, ASOR (G.M.A. Hanfmann, 1958–)	Lydian material (7th–6th cent. B.C.), including altar and refinery of time of King Croesus; extensive Roman remains (theater, gymnasium, "Marble Court"); massive synagogue (3rd–6th cent. B.C.)	Rev. 1:11, 3:1–6 (Obad. 20?)

For additional information on archaeological sites in Turkey, see relevant chapters (under Anatolia) of the revised *Cambridge Ancient History*. For current work, consult: M.J. Mellink, "Archaeology in Asia Minor," in the *American Journal of Archaeology* (annually since 1955); and "Recent Archaeological Research in Turkey," appearing in the annual *Anatolian Studies*.

Greece

Name	*Location*	*Major Excavations*	*Major Periods or Discoveries*	*Bible References*
Athens (port, Piraeus)	c. 5 m. from Aegean on peninsula of Attica	Early visitors and descriptions (e.g., 1436–Curiac of Ancona) French in 17th cent. (e.g., J. Giraud) British in 18th cent. (J. Stuart, N. Revett, 1751–54) Greek Arch. Society (since 1837) German Excav. (1907–16, 1926–39) Am. School of Classical Studies (O. Broneer, T.L. Shear, 1931–39) (H.A. Thompson, 1946–)	Strongly fortified Late Helladic citadel (c. 1600–1100 B.C.); cemeteries and other remains of Geometric Pd. (c. 1100–750 B.C.;) Gk. and Rom. marketplaces; stoa of Attalus; Kerameikos; Theater of Dionysus; archaic temples on acropolis; Erechtheion; Parthenon; Propylea; Areopagus ("Mars Hill"); Byz. churches; Temple of Olympian Zeus; sculpture	Acts 17:15–34; I Thess. 3:1
Corinth	On isthmus, C. Greece 5. m. SW. of modern canal	(W. Dörpfeld, 1886–91) Am. School Class. Studies (Richard Stillwell, Oscar Broneer, *et al.* since 1896) Univ. of Texas (J. Wiseman, 1965–)	Roman city of c. 1st cent. A.D.: Lechaeum Rd., Basilica; vast agora springs; arcaded shops; workers' quarters; Sanctuary of Aesculapius; theater; Temple of Apollo (built 6th cent. B.C.); gymnasium; subterranean "Fountain of the Lamps"	Acts 18:1–17; I Cor. 1:2 ff.

For Mycenaean and other Pre-Classical archaeological sites in Greece, consult relevant chapters of the revised *Cambridge Ancient History*. For current excavations in Greece, see the following periodical literature: *Archaeology;* the *American Journal of Archaeology; Annual of the British School of Archaeology at Athens;* and *Hesperia* (the latter three are more technical).

defeated by Greek spearmen in the epochal Battle of Marathon (490 B.C.). Mesopotamian archers rode to the battle or the hunt in chariots. Most Near Easterners relied on bow and arrow for hunting game. Young Ishmael in the Wilderness of Paran became an archer (Gen. 21:20). For the famous O.T. story of Jonathan and David, in which archery played a major role, see I Sam. 20:17–42.

Archippus (är-kĭp′ŭs). See PHILEMON, EPISTLE TO.

architecture. The word does not appear in Scripture; but many evidences of architecture appear in the background of events. Hebrew spiritual leaders were not primarily interested in developing architecture, but godly personalities. The architectural beauty they knew came from Egyptian, Mesopotamian, Syrian, Asiatic, Phoenician, Greek, Roman, and other skills. Often the extravagance of "environments" thrust upon them by overlords was repugnant to devout Jews. Jesus, hearing his disciples exclaim over the massive beauty of the Herodian Temple and its area—"what manner of stones and what buildings!"—minimized their abiding value, saying, "Seest thou these great buildings? there shall not be left one stone upon another, that shall not be thrown down" (Mark 13:1 f.).

Castles. Gen. 25:16 refers to 12 castles of the 12 princes, sons of Ishmael (A.S.V. "encampments"). I Chron. 27:25 mentions David's officers in charge of storehouses "in the castles." When Saul "went home to Gibeah" (I Sam. 10:26) he went to a crude rustic stone stronghold. Jehoshaphat's castles in Judah are mentioned in II Chron. 17:12. Moses commanded Israel to burn the castles of the Midianites (Num. 31:10). King Jotham of Judah erected castles "in the forests" (II Chron. 27:4). The Castle of Antonia*, scene of Paul's defense, stood at the N. edge of Jerusalem's Temple Area. The castle fortress of Machaerus on a grim mountain E. of the Dead Sea was "the prison" (Mark 6:27) in which Herod the Great beheaded John the Baptist.

Forums. Acts 28:15 (A.V.) mentions the "Appii forum"—Market of Appius (A.S.V.) —as the rendezvous where Christian brothers welcomed travel-weary Paul on his way into Rome from Puteoli harbor. Every Graeco-Roman city of Christ's time had its forum. Many were of sumptuous beauty, as the Forums at Rome, the Agora* of Athens and Corinth, the oval one at thousand-columned Jerash (Gerasa). Ezekiel wrote of the markets of Tyre (27:13, 27). Market places are mentioned by Jesus (Matt. 20:3; Luke 7:32).

31. The Roman Forum, seen through Arch of Septimius Severus, looking to Triumphal Arch of Titus. Rostra or speakers' platforms are at lower right; the circular Temple of Vesta, where the sacred fires of the state were kept burning, is the three-columned structure just above and beyond Rostra. The House of the Vestals, where virgins spent their consecrated life of service, adjoins Temple.

Gates. Towered entrances through stone walls into cities often attained architectural beauty, like the Ishtar Gate of Babylon; the 18th-century B.C. gate of Megiddo (Stratum XIII); several of the Jerusalem gates—whose grandeur we guess today when we look at their successors—the Jaffa Gate, the Golden Gate, the Damascus Gate. I Kings 22:10 mentions the gate of Samaria. One of the gates into Jerusalem's Temple was called "the Beautiful Gate" (Acts 3:10). The King's Gate at the Persian palace city, Shushan, is mentioned in Esther 2:19. Casemated gates of Biblical cities were often noble pieces of military architecture.

Palaces. A palace usually consisted of complex fortified structures surrounding a court, leaving noncommittal walls facing the street. Palaces housed kings, governors, and high priests, and were centers of administration and revolt. Many have been excavated, as at Samaria (I Kings 22:39), Persepolis, Megiddo, and Lachish. A Canaanite palace fort of c. 1400–1000 B.C. has been excavated at Gezer, and Amorite palace forts have been found at Taanach in the Plain of Esdraelon. Dr. W. F. Albright has excavated what appears to be Saul's fortress castle at Gibeah (Tell el-Ful) 4 m. N. of Jerusalem, erected between c. 1020 and 1000 B.C. with "casemated walls and separately bonded corner towers." It measured 170 by 155 ft., had two stories and a strong stone stairway (I Sam. 15:34). (See also JERICHO—Tulûl Abū el-'Alâyiq.) See *Praetoriums*, p. 40 rt.

The first "palace" of King David was at Hebron, where he ruled seven years—probably a flat-roofed stone house. After his siege of Jebusite Jerusalem he probably prepared something better at Millo, the SE. corner of what became Jerusalem. To date nothing of this crude palace has been excavated. We glimpse it in II Sam. 7:2: "I dwell in an house of cedar" (meaning trimmed with cedar, supplied by Hiram from Lebanon).

The site of Solomon's sumptuous palaces for himself and his harem (I Kings 7) and the scene of the visit of the Queen of Sheba (II Chron. 9:3) appears to be near the present Mosque El Aksa in Jerusalem's Temple Area. Ivory* which decorated the palaces and furniture of Omri and Ahab at their capital, Samaria (Amos 3:15), has been brought to light by George Reisner, C. S. Fisher, the Crowfoots, and other archaeologists. A palace, possibly constructed by Jeroboam II, has yielded a strong rectangular tower and extensive court. The "pool of Samaria" (I Kings 22:38) may be the one found at the N. end of the palace courtyard.

The O.T. has numerous references to palaces in Mesopotamia, as in Isa. 39:7 and II Kings 20:18, "the palace of the king of Babylon," to which Israelites dreaded being taken as eunuchs, perfumers, and servants. The Persian palace at Shushan (Susa), often mentioned in Esther, and the scene of Nehemiah's cup-bearing, still waits adequate excavation. Examination of a dizzying complex of palaces at Babylon and Persepolis (Oriental Institute) enables us to imagine the court life that was familiar to the captives and prophets of Israel and Judah after 587 B.C. Arches believed to be part of Belshazzar's palace walls (Dan. 5) have been dug up at Nineveh. The palace of Sennacherib (705–681 B.C.) at Nineveh "on a grander scale than any" has been revealed by archaeologists. Palaces of Sargon II (722–705 B.C.), who took captive thousands of Israelites, have been revealed at Khorsabad by the Oriental Institute. Egyptian palaces seen by Joseph and the oppressed Hebrews are revealed by excavated tomb reliefs. We know the ground plan and appearance of the Palace of Merenptah (c. 1224–1216 B.C.).

Praetoria, headquarters of Praetorian guards, Rome; or of judicial governors, such as Pilate (Matt. 27: 19–27), i.e., wherever praetor's chair was set up as judgment seat. In Jerusalem the praetorium where Jesus was tried was either that in the Tower of

Antonia or the one adjacent to Herod's palace. See GABBATHA. Caesarea had a praetorium (Acts 23:35) where Paul was safeguarded by Felix (Acts 23:35). A praetorium might house a ruler or be headquarters of a praetorian guard (Phil. 1:13).

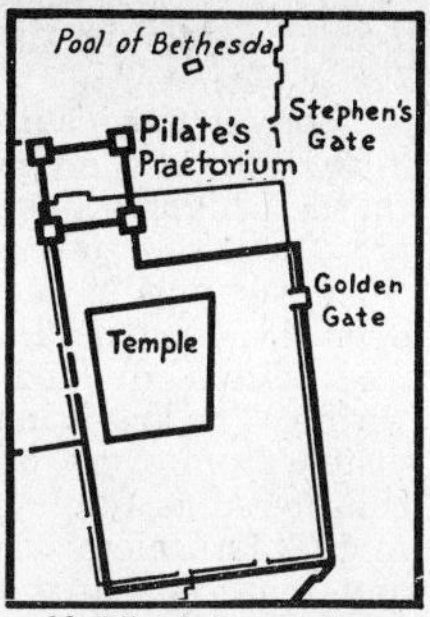

Pool of Bethesda
Pilate's Praetorium
Stephen's Gate
Golden Gate
Temple
— During Time of Christ
— Present Wall

32. Pilate's Praetorium.

Synagogues Their forms varied with their location—whether in Palestine, Asia Minor, Greece, or Egypt. For Jews built them wherever they were scattered. At more than 40 sites in Palestine ruins have come to light, more in Galilee than elsewhere. The elegant white limestone synagogue at Capernaum (Tell Hûm) has been excavated and partly restored. See CAPERNUM.

The synagogue at Kefr Bir'im, 25 m. NW. of Chorazin, reveals a spacious basilica plan. It, too, was rectangular, with a columned porch running along its entire façade. The Beth-shearim synagogue, recently excavated, 10 m. W. of Nazareth, was oriented SE. toward Jerusalem, and not only had the form of a basilica, but appears to have been used also as a place where civil decisions were made. The relation between basilica and synagogue of the first 3 centuries is marked.

Christian churches are more closely related to early synagogues than synagogues were to the Temple. At Gerasa in Trans-Jordan we can trace the evolution of the synagogue into the Christian church. A synagogue floor is a few inches below the mosaic floor of the church which succeeded it; some of the columns of one were used to support the other. Church and synagogue are related as the N.T. is to the O.T.

For functions of the synagogue see SYNAGOGUE.

Famous Tombs of the Bible. Abraham's tomb, and those of other Patriarchs and their wives, were in the Cave of Machpelah* in a field near Hebron, bought from Ephron the Hittite (Gen. 23:10 ff.). The site is covered today by an extremely restricted Moslem mosque. The tomb of Rachel is shown today on the right side of the road from Jerusalem to Bethlehem (Gen. 48:7), now covered by a Moslem mosque and a small Jewish prayer-place. The tombs of the Hebrew kings in the City of David have not yet been located in spite of eager search. They are covered by too much sacred and privately owned debris to make investigation possible at present. The most famous tombs of early Bible times were the Egyptian pyramids, of which no mention is made in Scripture. Darius, Xerxes, and other Persian kings were interred in rock-hewn sepulchers. The simple tomb of Cyrus, who treated Hebrews with clemency, has been found aboveground at Pasargadae. Lazarus' tomb (John 11:38) was in a cave at hilly Bethany. "And a stone lay upon it." It may have resembled the one in which Jesus was interred at Jerusalem. The rock-hewn tomb of Joseph (of Arimathaea) became (Matt. 27:60) the tomb of Jesus; it was in a garden, with a "great stone" for a door rolled against the opening. Its site is believed by many today to be covered by the Church of the Holy Sepulcher. See CALVARY. See THEATER, TEMPLES.

Arcturus (ärk-tu'rŭs), one of the three brightest stars of the Southern Hemisphere, part of the constellation Boötes, in line with the tail of Ursa Major (Great Bear); referred to in Job 9:9 (A.V.), 38:32. In the A.S.V., not Arcturus but the Bear is named, with Orion and the Pleiades.

Areopagus (ăr'ē-ŏp'ȧ-gŭs) (Mars Hill), the city court of Athens. This word also applies to ridge of rock SE. of the Athenian Acropolis* where the council of the Areopagus met at certain seasons to pass on questions pertaining to welfare. Sometimes it met downtown in Royal Stoa. An inscription discovered in 1952, as Homer A. Thompson reported, reveals that it had its own meeting place—the as yet undiscovered Bouleterion on the Acropolis (Hesperia-XXI, 1952). Paul was called before Areopagus to give ideas official hearing (Acts 17:18 f.). One member, Dionysius the Areopagite, "joined him and believed". Also, a woman, Damaris; and others (Acts 17:34). See illus. 38 and 259.

Aretas (ăr'ē-tăs) **IV,** a Nabataean king (9 B.C.–A.D. 40) who defeated Herod Antipas, Tetrarch of Galilee, whose first wife was a daughter of Aretas. See HEROD.

Ariel (ăr'ĭ-ĕl). (1) The Moabite father of two sons (A.S.V. II Sam. 23:20), etymology uncertain. Cf. Moffatt, "two lion cubs in their lair." (2) One of the chief men with Ezra at the River Ahava (Ezra 8:16). (3) A name applied to Jerusalem (Isa. 29:1, 2, 7 and A.S.V. marg. Ezek. 43:15 f.), perhaps meaning "God's altar" or "altar-hearth of sacrifice" (*Ariel*). (4) In post-Exilic times an angel who appears as a water-demon in occult mediaeval literature.

Arimathaea (ăr'ĭ-mȧ-thē'ȧ), home of Joseph, the rich counselor (Matt. 27:57; Luke 23:50 f.) who was a secret disciple of Jesus. The Jewish town may perhaps be identified with Ramathaim-zophim, lying in the hill country of Ephraim NW. of Jerusalem, and sometimes called Ramah, the home of Samuel the prophet. See JOSEPH.

Aristarchus (ăr'ĭs-tär'kŭs), a Macedonian from Thessalonica, arrested in the Ephesus riot following Paul's protest there against Diana worship (Acts 19:29); a faithful traveling-companion of Paul, who shared his journey to Rome (Acts 27:2) and his imprisonment there (Col. 4:10; Philem. 24).

Ark (from Heb. word for "chest" or "box"). (1) Noah's, described in Gen. 6:14–16, a houseboat in which family and animals together sought refuge from the Babylonian Flood. The pitch caulking is typical of Mesopotamian work (Gen. 6:14). (2) The ark of the infant Moses (Ex. 2:3), made of Nile bulrushes (papyrus) smeared with mud and pitch (bitumen) and hidden in flags on the river brink, has a counterpart in the story of another great Eastern leader whose lowly origin led his mother to hide him in a bulrush ark on the Euphrates—Sargon I, founder of the First Dynasty of the Semitic kings of Accad (Akkad) in N. Babylonia (cf. Gen. 10:10).

(3) The Ark of Yahweh, or Ark of God (in the J and E narratives), also known as the Ark of the Covenant (Heb. *'aron haberith*)

33. The Ark of the Covenant being carried around walls of Jericho, depicted on bronze doors by Lorenzo Ghiberti, the Baptistry, Florence.

and (in the P record) the Ark of the Testimony, is described in Ex. 25:10–22 as made of shittim (acacia) wood, overlaid with gold, and having four rings into which carrying-staves were inserted. The gold lid was known as the mercy seat, over which hovered two golden cherubim gazing downward toward the place where the Presence of Yahweh was believed to dwell as He communicated with His people (Ex. 25:22). The contents of the Ark were believed to be the two tablets of stone on which were recorded the Law* considered the basis of the covenant between Yahweh and Israel. The Ark was housed in the Holy of Holies of the Tabernacle* and of the Temple*. Its craftsman is called Bezaleel (Ex. 37:1). The history of the Ark parallels many of the vicissitudes of Israel. It was carried by the sons of Levi on the Wilderness wanderings (Deut. 31:9); borne over the Jordan by the priests (Josh. 3:17); participated in the fall of Jericho (Josh. 6:4–11); deposited at Shiloh (Josh. 18:1); captured by the Philistines (I Sam. 4); brought to Jerusalem by David (I Chron. 13:3–14, 15:1–28). After being kept in a tent-like sanctuary, it was finally installed in the holiest chamber of Solomon's Temple (*Debir*) beneath the cherubim.

Nothing is known of what became of the Ark. Did a conqueror of Jerusalem confiscate it? Did Jeremiah hide it? At any rate, it was not available for the second and third Temples. And in the synagogues which sprang up in great numbers after the Exile and the Return, a chest or ark containing the rolls of the Law (Torah) and other sacred books was placed in a niche shut off by a curtain from the rest of the building. Some authorities believe that the first Ark, like the synagogue Torah arks, looked not like a chest, but like a miniature building. A frieze found at Capernaum shows such a small-columned structure, flanked by lions. Other likenesses of the synagogue arks have been found in mosaics from Beth Alpha near Beth-shan, S. of the Sea of Galilee (later than the 4th century A.D.). The synagogue of c. A.D. 200 removed from Dura-Europos on the middle Euphrates to the Damascus Museum has murals depicting the Ark, and has also a Torah shrine.

Today in most synagogues the ark is placed in the wall of the structure facing Jerusalem (in the United States, the East) toward which prayers are directed. The congregation rises whenever this holy portion of the wall is opened to remove the sacred scrolls of the Law (see SCROLL OF THE LAW) which are kept within. The ark is usually so placed as to be visible from every part of the hall, and it is considered as symbolic of the Holy of Holies in the Jerusalem Temple. The architecture and materials used for arks in synagogues vary. Many are richly ornamented with art metal or carved wood or marble.

Armageddon (är′mȧ-gĕd′ŭn) (Gk. transliteration from Heb. Har Megiddon, "Mountain of Megiddo") in W. portion of the Great Plain of Esdraelon; symbolic battlefield where final contest between forces of good and evil is ultimately to take place (Rev. 16:16). This apocalyptic use of the word is based on the fact that Armageddon or the Plain of Megiddo* (Esdraelon) time and again has been the scene of violent conflicts, even before those recorded in Judg. 5:19, II Kings 9:27, 23:29.

arms, armor. Before the Hebrew Monarchy, weapons in Palestine were primitive. Then, as now, stones were commonly used; balls of limestone or flint, hurled in slings, proved effective (I Sam. 17:40–50). (See SLING, illus. 389 and 390.) These forerunners of hand grenades were c. 30 centimeters in diameter. Battle-bows, which had been used in Mesopotamia 1,000 years before Joshua, were popular in the warfare of early Israel (Gen. 21:20; I Sam. 2:4; I Chron. 12:2). An Egyptian arrow killed good King Josiah at Megiddo (II Chron. 35:23) (see ARCHERS). Swords were few before David's time, but cf. Josh. 11:11 f. Not even Saul and Jonathan always had swords to fight the Philistines (I Sam. 13:19–23); but cf. I Sam. 31:4, 9 f. Spears were available (I Sam. 26:7). Armor was owned by the fortunate few, as indicated by Saul's offer to David (I Sam. 17:38 f.). Philistines were heavily armed (I Sam. 17:4–7), and controlled the weapon-sharpening monopoly (I Sam. 13:19–22). Before the Monarchy, armor was of leather or quilted fabric. David's arms were built up by booty from Philistines, Syrians, and Edomites; so, too, were Solomon's (I Kings 10:25). By the time of Solomon, who had access to metals in the Arabah, weapons were common among the Hebrews (I Kings 10:16–18). Roman armor was elegant and elaborate. (For armor-bearers see I Sam. 14:6–17, 16:21, 31:4 ff.) From personal observation of his armed escort, etc., Paul drew details for his allegory of "the whole armor" (Eph. 6:13–17). See CHARIOTS; WEAPONS.

Egyptians in Solomon's era (c. 961–922 B.C.) used corselets made of scales of iron. Before the New Kingdom (began 1546 B.C.) Egyptian warriors seem to have used little armor, but protected their bodies with bands of linen or leather. Scale armor seems to have come in from Oriental sources. (See SHISHAK, illus. 381.)

army, the military forces of a nation; a great host or multitude. The first army of Israel consisted of every able-bodied male "from twenty years old and upward" from every tribe except the Levites, who were not numbered but might bear arms if necessary (Num. 1; II Sam. 24:9; I Chron. 12:26–28). During the period of the Judges armed warriors began to join forces for defense and for military exploits (see WAR; also DEBORAH, GIDEON). Saul, the first king of Israel, assumed leadership of the first organized army c. 1020–1000 B.C.; David, his successor, greatly enlarged the troops and gained access, through his victories, to metals suitable for making weapons of a more advanced type than the improvised spears, slings, bows and arrows previously used. Solomon inherited his father's army and enlarged it to defend his chariot and store cities; the armies of subsequent kings were organized into "thousands," "hundreds," "fifties," "tens" (I Sam. 10:19; II Chron. 25:5; II Kings 1:9). In addition to the king's guard, like David's Gittites and his "mighty men" (II Sam. 15:18, 23:8–19), the organization included brilliant generals like Joab (II Sam. 10 ff.), food commissaries, and scribes to record the important booty. Other well-equipped armies were those of the Canaanites, Egyptians, Assyrians, and Neo-Babylonians. For Roman armies in Palestine, see CENTURION; LEGION. See also ARCHERS, ARMS, BATTLE, SOLDIER, WEAPONS.

Arnon (är′nŏn), **the River** (Wâdī el-Môjib), pours its perennially clear waters down from mountains of the Kingdom of Jordan through a deep gorge whose grandeur suggests that of the Grand Canyon in miniature. It enters the Dead* Sea at about the central point of its eastern shore. The Arnon was the boundary between the kingdoms of Sihon and of Moab (Num. 21:13). Both banks were heavily fortified at the time of Israel's wanderings en route from Egypt to Canaan. Sihon, king of the Amorites, held the N. bank of the Arnon in that period. Between the Arnon gorge and the Nahaliel runs a spur, on which stand ruins of the giant Machaerus fortress where John the Baptist was beheaded, according to many authorities. "The City of Moab" on the border of the Arnon is mentioned in Num. 22:36, in the Balaam and Balak story.

Aroer (*ȧ*-rō′ĕr), name of three towns. (1) Modern 'Arâ'ir, built by the children of Gad (Num. 32:34), later given to the Tribe of Reuben, and forming the S. boundary between Israel's territory E. of the Jordan and that of Moab. It lies a short distance N. of the Arnon R. It is mentioned in line 26 of Mesha's Moabite Stone (9th century B.C.). (2) A town of Judah (I Sam. 30:28). (3) A settlement adjacent to Rabbath-ammon, Ammonite fortress (Josh. 13:25) (see AMMONITES).

Arphaxad (är-făk′săd) (Arpachshad) (är-păk′shăd), a son of Shem, son of Noah, born "two years after the flood" (Gen. 11:10), and considered important in priestly genealogy; a connecting link between Shem and Abraham, tenth in the family line.

Artaxerxes (är′tăk-sûrk′sēz) **I** ("Longimanus"). King of Persia, a younger son of Xerxes; ruled 465–424 B.C. He granted permission to his Hebrew cupbearer Nehemiah* to return to Jerusalem from Shushan and rebuild Jerusalem's walls (Neh. 2). The return of Ezra, leading back Exiles who had not taken advantage of the edict of Cyrus (Ezra 7–10) is dated by some scholars within the reign of Artaxerxes I, by others in the era of Artaxerxes II.

artificer, a craftsman, especially in metalwork, as Tubal-cain, son of the Cainite Lamech and Zillah (Gen. 4:22). Artificers are usually mentioned in connection with working gold, silver, iron, copper, or bronze for the House of God. See BEZALEEL; HIRAM (2).

Arvad (är′văd), modern Ruād, site of the most northern of the Phoenician cities, located on an island 2 m. off the Syrian coast and 125 m. N. of Tyre. During the time of Ezekiel, its men served in the navy and army of Tyre (Ezek. 27:8, 11).

Arumah (*ȧ*-rōō′m*ȧ*), a village near Shechem, where Abimelech lived (Judg. 9:41).

Asa, third king of Judah (c. 913–873 B.C.). Following the short war-filled reign of his father Abijam (Abijah), his 40-year reign began with a decade of peace (II Chron. 14:1), and in its entirety overlapped the reigns of Jeroboam I, Nadab, Baasha, Elah, Zimri, and Omri in the Northern Kingdom. His "mother" (I Kings 15:10; actually his grandmother) was Abishalom's daughter, Maacah, who as queen mother had erected an image for an Asherah* (v. 13). Asa removed her from influence, banished the male prostitutes (v. 12), and abolished the idols of his predecessors. Though his "heart was perfect all his days," not all the high places were removed. While the land was at peace, he fortified cities in Judah (II Chron. 14:6 f.). An invasion of Ethiopians under Zerah was beaten off at Mareshah (v. 9–15). Later, encouraged by Azariah, Asa returned to the work of religious reformation (15:8–15). It was probably soon afterward (and not in the 36th year of his reign, as 16:1) that Baasha of Israel occupied a part of N. Judah, fortifying Ramah on the main road from Jerusalem N. Instead of meeting this threat with his own (inferior) army, Asa bribed Ben-hadad, King of Syria, to attack Baasha's northern borders. Baasha subsequently withdrew from Judah and Asa used the building materials intended for Ramah to strengthen Geba and Mizpah (16:1–6). Asa was reproved by Hanani for trusting in Ben-hadad instead of Yahweh, became wroth, and put Hanani in prison (16:7–10). His last years were marked by poor health. In the assessment of the religious historians who compiled the books of Kings and Chronicles, Asa was one of the few "good" kings, though "the high places were not removed."

Asahel (ăs′*ȧ*-hĕl). (1) Nephew of David, brother of Joab* and Abishai, slain by Abner in self-defense, and later avenged by Joab (II Sam. 2:18). (2) A Levite under Jehoshaphat, King of Judah (II Chron. 17:8). (3) A Levite under King Hezekiah (II Chron.

31:13). (4) Father of Jonathan in the time of Ezra (10:15).

Asaph (ā′săf), a cymbal-playing Levite, appointed leader of David's choir, who founded a family guild of singers, and was possibly author of certain Psalms (I Chron. 16:4, 5, 7).

Ascension of Christ, his final post-Resurrection manifestation to his followers. The forty-day period after the Resurrection, recorded by Luke in Acts 1:3, was climaxed with an emotional valedictory which greatly impressed the Twelve, and motivated them for their empowered ministry recorded in Acts. The great beauty of this disappearance of Christ, believed by many to have taken place on the summit of the Mount of Olives (see OLIVES, MOUNT OF) overlooking Jerusalem, was a preparation for the Day of Pentecost. Matthew does not mention the Ascension. A.V. Mark 16:9–20, which records it, is generally considered a later addition. John refers to the event (6:62, 20:17) but gives no narrative of it. Luke 24:51 need not mean that the Ascension took place on the day of the Resurrection. There is nothing in the O.T. to parallel the Ascension of Jesus. Nearest to this manifestation was the "translation" of Enoch* and the assumption of Elijah.*

Ashdod (ăsh′dŏd), one of the five chief cities of the Philistines (Josh. 13:3), near the ruins of the village of Isdud, 18 m. NE. of Gaza, 3 m. from the coast. Apportioned to Judah (Josh. 15:46–47), it was never possessed (Josh. 11:22). The Ark was captured by the Philistines and placed in the temple of Dagon in Ashdod (I Sam. 5:1–8). Uzziah "broke down the wall" of Ashdod (II Chron. 26:6), and in 711 B.C. Sargon II sent a military expedition against the city (Isa. 20:1; see *ANET*³, pp. 286–287). The subsequent fate of Ashdod is reported by several of the prophets (Amos 1:8; Jer. 25:20; Zeph. 2:4; Zech. 9:6). The Ashdodites opposed the rebuilding of the walls of Jerusalem after the Return (Neh. 4:7–8), and Nehemiah protested against marrying their women (13:23–25). As Azotas, it was attacked twice by the Maccabees (I Macc. 5:68, 10:83–84) and visited by Philip (Acts 8:40).

Excavations directed by M. Dothan at Tel Ashdod since 1962 have uncovered 20 levels of occupation, the earliest dating from c. 1700 B.C. Of particular interest are three strata of Philistine occupation (c. 1170–1000 B.C.), with its buildings, including a possible fortress and a "high place," pottery, and many small finds to enhance our knowledge of Philistine life and culture. The latter include a cult stand decorated with the figures of five musicians (*Archaeology* 23, 1970, pp. 310–311), and the first inscriptions excavated in a context that is undoubtedly Philistine.

See *BA* 26, 1963, pp. 134–139; *Archaeology* 20, 1967, pp. 178–186; M. Dothan, "Ashdod of the Philistines," in *New Directions in Biblical Archaeology*, 1969, pp. 15–24; *Ashdod*, I, 1967. W. P. A.

Asher (ăsh′ẽr) ("happy"), son of Jacob* and Leah's handmaid Zilpah. He became the head of a Hebrew tribe "assigned" to a strip of coast along the Mediterranean, reaching from Mt. Carmel to Phoenicia, a fertile territory supplying food to royal tables, but never wholly subdued by Asher, for it included such powerful cities as Accho, Tyre, Sidon (Judg. 1:31). In Solomon's time, the Asher territory was a dependency of Phoenicia. Anna, who saw the infant Jesus dedicated, was of the tribe of Asher (Luke 2:36).

Asherah (*ȧ*-shē′*ra*) (pl. Asherim, Asheroth), akin to Asherat, "Lady of the Sea," consort of El in Ras Shamrah* literature, was a pagan goddess whose name in various forms is found some 40 times in the O.T., especially in Kings and Chronicles. "Asherah" is used in a fluid manner, at times denoting the goddess herself, or her image (of wood), or the tree or pole used as her symbol, even as the *masseba* (stone pillar) may have stood for the male pagan god Baal (cf. Judg. 6:28). In the A.V. the word is translated "grove"; better would be "sacred tree" or "wooden pole," or still better, "Asherah image." The "prophets of the groves" in A.V. I Kings 18:19 reads in R.S.V. "prophets of the Asherah." Jezebel* had 400 such "prophets of the Asherah" eating at the table of her husband, King Ahab of Israel. Asherah had long been the chief goddess of Tyre, one of whose kings was her father. (See *The Asherah in the Old Testament*. by W. L. Reed, T.C.U. Press.)

34. Astarte represented and named in cylinder-seal impression from Bethel (c. 1300 B.C.).

" 'Astart" is the Canaanite pronunciation of " 'Ashtart," "Ashtarot" in Heb. and Phoen., equivalent to Astarte of the Greeks. Ashtaroth is the plural of Ashtoreth. In Canaan there was a tendency to use the plurals Ashtaroth, Astartes, Anatot, Anaths to summarize all the various manifestations of this deity. Similarly Israel took over the Canaanite plural *elohim* ("gods") to express their idea of their one God.

Ashtoreth, Anath, Astarte, and Asherah are manifestations of a chief deity of W. Asia, sometimes regarded as wife, sometimes as sister, of the principal Canaanite god El. This female deity was often represented as a virgin yet pregnant goddess. A center dedicated to her has been excavated at Byblos (see GEBAL) on the Mediterranean coast between Tripoli and Beirut. She and her colleagues specialized in sex and war. Her temples were centers of legalized vice, which appealed even to daughters of Israel to engage in sacred prostitution. These goddesses correspond to Aphrodite and Venus of the Greeks and Romans. The Hebrews backslid to Ashtoreth throughout their national experience—Solomon (I Kings 11:5), and Ahab (I Kings 16:33). In Palestine Ashtoreth was the wife of Baal, as war-loving Anath was in N. Syria. Canaanite poems on clay tablets describe the martial adventures of Anath—

called in the O.T. Asherah, but known to Phoenicians as "Ashirat of the Sea." The latter was also worshipped by S. Arabians and Amorites as "the bride of heaven." Philistines maintained a temple of Ashtoreth at Ashkelon.

A typical clay cultic shrine-house of Ashtoreth has been excavated outside a Canaanite temple of the goddess at Beth-shan (Scythopolis), Palestine, from c. the 13th century B.C., the period when Israel was beginning to settle down during and after the Conquest. It shows the earth goddess seated in a lewd posture outside a window, holding two symbolic doves; two warring male deities who are courting her favor; a serpent, symbol of fertility; and the lion of power. This crude glorification of prostitution in the name of religion is one of the evils which Jewish and Christian faiths struggled to uproot (see I Sam. 31:9 f.). The hundreds of Astarte plaques which have been recovered are far more base than those of the Egyptian fertility goddesses depicted during the same period. The one found at Tell ed-Duweir (Lachish) from c. 1000 B.C. is typical in its emphasis on prominent breasts, sensuous smiles, accented eyes, and nudity.

Akin to the Canaanite Ashtoreth was the Babylonian Ishtar* (Venus of the Romans). The names, personalities, and relationship of the fertility goddesses of the Middle East are extremely fluid and confusing. The Biblical Asherah of I Kings 18:19 was the wife of El, chief Canaanite god, "creator of creatures," and mother of many offspring, including Hadad (as son or grandson) called by the people "Baal," meaning "Lord." A similar goddess was known to N. Arabians and Aramaeans as Atar. Many scholars believe that the beginning of the fertility cult was Babylonia, whose Queen of Heaven was not the moon god (which was Sin, male) but Ishtar. The most famous Gate of Babylon, through which historic processions passed to the Tower of Babel, was the Ishtar Gate. (See BABYLON, illus. 44.) Albright finds an enormous impact of "cultural internationalism" spreading into the religious concepts of W. Asia as early as the Late Bronze Age.

The Egyptian pantheon "adopted" Canaanite Astarte and Anath in the Empire period.

A center of Ashtoreth or Astarte worship existed in the kingdom of Og*, ruler of Bashan, E. of the Jordan. It has been identified as Tell 'Ashtarah, c. 20 m. E. of the Sea of Galilee, a hillock on a fertile plain, in territory "allotted" to Manasseh during the Conquest.

ashes, in the usual sense of residue from a fire or a furnace (Ex. 9:8, 10), or from a body burned together with ceremonial objects, were spread upon the heads of mourners (II Sam. 1:2). Cf. the story of Tamar (II Sam. 13:19). Ashes were also used to disguise the face (I Kings 20:38). To wear sackcloth and sit in ashes expressed grief (Gen. 37:34), humility and penitence (Neh. 9:1; Jon. 3:6).

Jeremiah mentioned "the valley of the ashes," near the Kidron (31:40). A solid mound, c. 500 ft. long, 200 ft. wide, and 60 ft. deep, represented this ancient dumping place of accumulated ashes, carried out from the Temple sacrifices every evening by Temple staff members.

Ashkelon (ăsh'kĕ-lŏn) (Askalon, Askelon, Eshkalon; Ascalon in N.T. times), one of five chief Philistine (see PHILISTIA) cities (Josh. 13:3), located c. 12 m. N. of Gaza, on a ridgy amphitheater commanding a seascape, flanked by sand dunes on the S. and gardens on the N. Limited excavation shows the site to have been occupied from the Neolithic to the late Arabic period. Mentioned in the execration texts (*ANET*³, p. 329) and the Amarna Letters (*ANET*³, pp. 488, 490), Ashkelon was stormed by Ramesses II (*ANET*³, p. 256) and had a sanctuary of Ptah (*ANET*³, p. 249). It was captured by Judah (Judg. 1:18), but by the time of Samson belonged to the Philistines (14:19). The city became a vassal to Assyria, and was sacked by Nebuchadnezzar, an event spoken of by Jeremiah (47:5–7) and Zephaniah (2:4–7). Herod the Great was born at Ashkelon and his sister Salome resided there. The town is mentioned in David's lament for Saul and Jonathan (II Sam. 1:20).

Ashkenaz (ăsh'kĕ-năz) (or Ashchenaz), eldest son of Gomer and great-grandson of Noah (Gen. 10:3; I Chron. 1:6). In the time of Jeremiah it was the name of a people near Ararat (Jer. 51:27).

Ashtaroth (ăsh'tȧ-rŏth) (plural of Ashtoreth). See ASHERAH.

Ashtoreth (ăsh'tō-rĕth). See ASHERAH.

Ashurbanipal (ă'shŏor-băn'ĭ-păl). See ASNAPPER.

35. Detail of amber statuette of Assyrian Ashurnasirpal.

Ashurnasirpal (ä'shōōr-nä'zĭr-päl') **II.** A cruel ruler in the first phase of the Assyrian

Empire of the 9th century B.C. He raised the quality of provincial administration, improved such military equipment as battering-rams* and siege engines, and built a magnificent new capital on the ruins of ancient Calah* (cf. Gen. 10:11 f.), represented today by the mound of Nimrud.

Ash Wednesday, first day in Lent.

Asia, a Roman province in W. Asia Minor, bounded on the W. by the Mediterranean. In it Paul did his most important work, as at Ephesus (Acts 18:19 ff., 19), the capital city from which the Gospel spread to other cities of Asia, like Colossae, Laodicea, and Hierapolis. Pergamum and Sardis, mentioned in Revelation as cities of this fair Roman province, which included Mysia, Caria, Lydia, part of Phrygia, as well as coast cities and islands. Asia was governed by a proconsul, was allowed much local autonomy, and was famous for the weaving and dyeing of seamless garments and rugs. The "seven churches of Asia" listed in Rev. 1:11 were Ephesus, Smyrna, Pergamum, Thyatira, Sardis, Philadelphia, and Laodicea.

Asiarchs (ā′shī-ärk), officials appointed by towns of the Roman province of Asia to superintend the yearly festival and public games in honor of the Roman Emperor. The Asiarchs of Ephesus were friends of Paul (Acts 19:31, R.S.V.).

Asnapper (ăs-năp′ẽr) (Osnappar, R.S.V.), the name sometimes used (see Ezra 4:10) for Ashurbanipal, grandson of Sennacherib and son and successor of Esar-haddon. He ruled the Assyrian Empire 669–c. 633 B.C. Excavation of his vast clay-tablet library at Nineveh, his capital on the Tigris (see LIBRARIES) revealed a wealth of information concerning the life and literature of Assyria. Ashurbanipal was reigning during the 36 years which approximately paralleled the regimes of Manasseh*, Amon, and Josiah* of Judah. Israel had already fallen (II Kings 17 f.) to the Assyrian Sargon* II (721 B.C.).

asp, a venomous snake, probably *Naja haje*, found in Egypt but rare in Palestine (Deut. 32:33; Job 20:14, 16; Isa. 11:8; Rom. 3:13).

ass, in Bible times, as well as today in many Mediterranean countries, was the family's tractable burden bearer, needing only a bridle to guide it, and frequently finding its own way. Eating only one-fourth as much barley as a horse, an ass was available to the poorest families, like Joseph's at Nazareth. It is not a stupid animal, but with sure-footed efficiency picks its way across stony deserts where man's eye can scarcely detect paths. The family ass was not only a transport animal for nomads, but helped with plowing and hauled the threshing sled. The Bible forbade hitching ass and ox together (Deut. 22:10). The ass was tamed long before the camel, which may be considered an anachronism in Patriarchal narratives. The ass was considered unclean for food.

Asses appear in the famous Bible stories of Balaam's talking ass, Num. 22:21–30; Saul seeking his father's lost asses, I Sam. 9 f.; gift-bearing asses, I Sam. 16:20, 25:20, II Sam. 16:1; Jesus' use of an ass on Palm Sunday, John 12:14.

White asses were mounts of royalty, as suggested in the Song of Deborah (Judg. 5:10). Jesus' use of the ass was a symbol both of Messianic kingliness (see MESSIAH) and of humility.

Wild asses, *Asinus onager*, once numerous in the Sahara and in Arabia, are described in Job 39:5–8. Syrian wild asses, *Asinus hemippus*, wander in Mesopotamia, Syria, and sometimes N. Palestine.

The ass, an ever-willing burden bearer, was the symbol of Issachar* (Gen. 49:14).

Assassins (Gk. *sikarioi*, "daggermen"), a secret society opposed to Roman rule. They concealed a small sword beneath their cloak and at festivals stabbed their opponents. Bands of assassins pillaged villages and terrorized Judaea A.D. 50–70 (Acts 21:38, R.S.V.).

Assos (ăs′ŏs), a seaport of Mysia not far from Troas (Acts 20:13, 14).

Assur (ăs′ẽr) (Asshur). (1) The national deity of the Assyrians, king of their gods, and incarnation of war, to whom even militarist Assyrians lifted prayers for help. A "deified patriarch," he supplanted the triad of Babylonian gods, and foreshadowed the trend toward monotheism. As chief protector of the Assyrian people, he was represented in art by the sun disk, topped by an archer shooting a shaft. His home is thought to have been on the site which was occupied by the Assyrian capital. (2) The first capital of the Assyrians, on the W. bank of the Tigris, occupied by Amorites* c. 1748 B.C. An archaic temple of Ishtar*, in the Sumerian style, has been excavated and dated c. 3000 B.C. Assur was regarded with affection even after the founding of Nineveh, its successor. (3) The country Assur (Asshur, Assyria) took its name from its capital. Gen. 10:11 tells of Nimrod going to Assur from the Plain of Shinar to establish Nineveh. Ezra 4:2 mentions Esar-haddon, King of Assur. Merchants of Assur appear in Ezek. 27:23. At Assur in 1914 an Assyrian bilingual poem was found which deals with the creation of the world and the beginnings of mankind. It carries alongside the text what may be "musical notations." See ASSYRIA.

assurance, the Biblical doctrine that a believer may be conscious of personal fellowship with God through Jesus Christ. An intimation of such an ideal was expressed by The First Isaiah (32:17). The Fourth Gospel stressed assurance in its teachings concerning "the Comforter" (John 15:26, 16:7). The purpose of the Gospels is salvation of men through reconciliation to God (I Thess. 1:5); and those who know themselves to possess this salvation possess assurance (1) directly through the witness of the Spirit (Rom. 8:16); (2) indirectly, through deeds they are able to accomplish (I John 3:14).

Assyria, Empire of, a great domain centered along the upper Tigris River in Mesopotamia. Several cities, including Assur, Calah, Nineveh, and Khorsabad, served as capital of this Empire, and the excavation of their remains has yielded quantities of data for the reconstruction of the political, economic, and cultural history of Assyria. The

Empire achieved its greatest expansion during the reign of Ashurbanipal*, extending southward into northern Arabia and as far as Thebes in Egypt, westward into Cappadocia, northward to Lake Van and Lake Urmiah, and eastward into Elam. Beyond its territorial boundaries, its influence reached Lydia in the west and Urartu in the north. Racially, Assyrians contained Semitic and Hurrian elements. Their history is intertwined with that of Babylonia*. To Israel and Judah Assyria was synonymous with mighty dread. Assyrian aggressions were interpreted by the Prophets as scourges of God to punish apostasy. Assyria and its vigorous people are mentioned some 150 times in Scripture. The names of Assyrian kings who raided Israel and Judah are known to us through Biblical records; and Assyrian sieges of Samaria and of Jerusalem have been found depicted on alabaster slabs, clay prisms, and tablets from the Assyrian libraries of Calneh, Nineveh, Khorsabad, etc. Recent achaeological finds contain the names of nine or ten Hebrew kings:

Israel	*Judah*
Omri	Uzziah ?
Ahab	Ahaz
Jehu	Hezekiah
Menahem	Manasseh
Pekah	
Hoshea	

Some Asian Aggressors

Ashur-nasir-pal II (883–859 B.C.)

Shalmaneser III (858–824 B.C.) went against Israel's King Ahab and his Syrian ally, Ben-hadad II, and was defeated at Karkar 853 B.C.

Tiglath-pileser III (745–727 B.C.), first Assyrian ruler mentioned in Scripture (II Kings 15:29). To him Menahem had paid tribute. When Pekah refused tribute, he took N. Israel and carried many N. Israelites into captivity. This first Assyrian victory in "Holy Lands" left Israel pushed into a small area around Samaria. Tiglath-pileser III is called Pul in II Kings 15:19.

Shalmaneser V (727–722 B.C.) besieged the capital city of Samaria for 3 years.

Sargon II (722–705 B.C.) completed the task of taking Israel captive, including thousands of leading citizens, as an excavated inscription reveals. They were deported to Assyria (II Kings 17:6), where they were concentrated in Halah, in the Habor River Valley, and the "cities of the Medes." In their abandoned homes among the olive orchards were settled a mixed population from Babylonia, Elam, and Syria, who mingled with the Israel remainder and became Samaritans. Sargon's palace has been unearthed at Dur-Sharrukin by the Oriental Institute; treasures found there offer vivid commentary on II Kings 17.

Sennacherib* (705–681 B.C.), son of Sargon II, marched against Judah 701 B.C., and took mighty Lachish* on the border between Palestine and Egypt and numerous other "fenced cities," but failed to seize Jerusalem because of plague in his army. A clay prism bought by the Oriental Institute confirms Bible narrative (II Kings 18) about spoils—including gold from the Temple doors—demanded of King Hezekiah*, whom Sennacherib "shut up in Jerusalem."

Asshurbanapal (c. 669–633 B.C.). See entry under this name, p. 48 right.

Assur* was captured in 614 B.C. and Nineveh in 612 B.C. by Chaldaeans (Semitic nomads) who had gained control of Babylonia and allied themselves with the Medes (see Nah. 3). The Chaldaean-Babylonian Empire (612–539 B.C.) succeeded the Assyrian, and was followed by the Persian line, including Cyrus and his successors.

36. Assyrian human-headed winged bull from palace of Sargon II at Khorsabad (ancient Dur-Sharrukin), 722–705 B.C. Carved from single block of limestone weighing c. 40 tons. Associated with similar winged bulls and human figures which flanked portal leading from the courtyard to throneroom.

Assur was Assyria's chief god, but Babylonian deities were also honored: the triad Anu, Bel, and Ea; Shemash the sun god; Sin the moon god; Hadad, god of thunder; and Ishtar*, influential female deity.

See ASHURBANIPAL; NINEVEH.

Astarte (ăs-tär′tē). See ASHERAH.

astrologers, those who profess to foretell events by the position and movements of the stars, were a part of the court of Nebuchadnezzar (Dan. 1:20); and were called in by Herod when Jesus was born (Matt. 2:7). They were classed by Isaiah along with the stargazers, "monthly prognosticators," sorcerers, and enchanters that were characteristic of the courts of Babylon and Chaldaea (Isa. 47:12 f.). Astrology was practiced in most of the nations mentioned in Scripture, but found no encouragement among the Israelites.

Atad (ā′tăd) ("thorn" or "bramble"), the name of the threshing floor E. of the Jordan where the descendants of Jacob mourned for seven days on their journey from Egypt with Jacob's body to his burial place at Hebron (Gen. 50:9–13).

Ataroth (ăt′*a*-rŏth). (1) A town E. of Jordan (Num. 32:3, 34; Josh. 16:2).

(2) A town on the edge of the Jordan Valley on the border of Ephraim (Josh. 16:7).

(3) A village near Bethlehem (I Chron. 2:54).

Athaliah (ăth′*ā*-lī′*ā*), wife of Jehoram*, King of Judah (c. 849–842 B.C.), daughter or sister of Ahab, king of Israel. She seized the government after her son Ahaziah had been killed by Jehu (II Kings 11); put to death "all the royal seed," missing only the young prince Joash* (II Kings 11:2). Athaliah was slain by supporters of Joash (Jehoash) c. 837 B.C., whom they proclaimed king. She is the heroine of Racine's great tragedy *Athalie*. The reign of this early feminist at Jerusalem is dated c. 842–837 B.C.

Athens, capital of modern Greece. In ancient times Greece was a cluster of small states dominated by cities. Beginning c. 600 B.C., Athens quickly developed political vigor, civic interest, extensive sea power, and colonial possessions, which, combined with brilliant intellectual and artistic attainments, made it a great world center in ancient times. In the 1st century A.D. it was a virtually free city-state under the protection of Rome, many of whose leading sons studied in the famous Athenian schools. It remained a center of learning until Justinian banned the study of philosophy in A.D. 529.

The Acropolis*, a hill 500 ft. high, had been in earliest times a fortified settlement. In the "Golden Age" (5th century B.C.) it became a religious center, with glorious temples dedicated to Athena, the city's patron goddess, and Nikē ("victory"), etc. In Paul's time, as now, the town circled the base of the Acropolis. Among pagan temples still standing in the city are the Temple of Hephaistos dominating the market place; the Temple of Olympian Zeus, with ornate Corinthian columns, begun by Peisistratus (530 B.C.), and completed under the Roman Emperor Hadrian (A.D. 130); and topping all, the world-famous architectural wonders on the Acropolis—the Temple of the Wingless Victory, the Erechtheum with its graceful Ionic columns, and the Parthenon, with its severely plain Doric pillars. See TEMPLES, illus. 424.

During Paul's Second Missionary Journey he sojourned for days at Athens (I Thess. 3:1), and beheld its wonders, experienced its dominant spirit (Acts 17:15–34), and preached to its citizens with only partial success.

37. Temple of Hephaistos, god of metalworkers ("the Thesion"), overlooking one end of the excavated Agora, Athens.

Paul may have docked at the Ionian port of Piraeus. As he journeyed to Athens, he passed by an altar dedicated "To an Unknown God" (Acts 17:22 f.). The 2d century Greek writer Pausanias also told of seeing altars to "gods called unknown," probably on the same road to Athens.

N. of the Acropolis was the market place or agora* of Athens, with shops and shrines where Athenian citizens met to transact business, visit, and dispute (Acts 17:18). The American School of Classical Studies has excavated the agora, and completely charted the buildings and streets with which Pericles, Phidias, Plato, and Paul were familiar (see AGORA, illus. 4, 5). Mars Hill (R.S.V. Areopagus*), usually the meeting place of the

Areopagus court and councils, was at the W. approach to the Acropolis. Here Paul came to present what was a new philosophy to those who were then devotees of three current schools of Greek thought: Platonic, Epicurean, and Stoic. Paul argued against polytheism, already losing favor with some advanced Greek thinkers, and for a monotheistic religion, closely akin to the best theology of Judaism, with only a minimum emphasis on Jesus Christ. Dionysius, an Areopagite, was impressed. A few converts were secured elsewhere in the city, and from Paul's synagogue contacts (Acts 17:17). But no church at

38. Athens, the Acropolis from the Hill of the Muses. Mt. Lycabettus (920 ft. high) at right. The Acropolis (520 ft. high) is a hill-plateau 990 ft. long and 429 ft. wide. The 8-columned frontal colonnade of Parthenon, right of center. The Erectheum with its "Porch of the Maidens," left; Propylaea gateway-temple, on sloping W. main approach to elevation. Mars Hill (The Areopagus), hidden in picture, behind Propylaea. In foreground, the Odeion (Music Hall) of Herodes Atticus. The Stoa of Eumenus II (195–159 B.C.), King of Pergamum, joined the Theater of Dionysus (off at right) and the Odeion, and served as covered promenade and shelter for theater and concert patrons when it rained. The Boulevard of Dionysius the Areopagite (Acts 17:34) is in foreground.

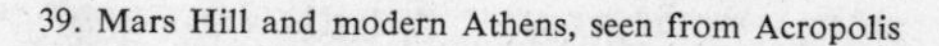

39. Mars Hill and modern Athens, seen from Acropolis

once sprang up in Athens to which Paul afterward could write, as he wrote to the societies in Thessalonica, Corinth, Ephesus, etc.

Among other architectural wonders of Athens were the music hall or Odeion of Pericles (see MUSIC); the Stadium, with its foot races and wrestling contests; and the impressive Tower and Waterclock of Andronicus. It was in Athens that Paul revealed his Hellenistic culture by quoting (Acts 17:28) from an invocation to Zeus written by Aratus, a minor Greek poet (315–245 B.C.). In the pottery-making section for which Athens was famous, Paul, himself a craftsman (weaver), made contacts with fellow workmen.

Excavations continue under the direction of the American School of Classical Studies. The first part of Pausanias' *Description of Greece*, written a century after Paul's visit, provides a good guide to the antiquities of Athens. See *BA* 21, 1958, pp. 1–28.

Athlit, an impressive site on the shore of the Mediterranean S. of Haifa, whose excavated pottery indicates occupation from the Late Bronze Age through the Hellenistic period. It was known in the Biblical period as a place along the ancient coast road to Egypt. Its most impressive feature today is the ruined Crusader castle (*Castellum Peregrinorum*) built on a *tell* not yet fully excavated.

atonement, a cardinal doctrine of the Christian Church, concerning the means and condition of the reconciliation by which man returns into complete communion with God. The basic assumptions of atonement are that, through man's fault, the natural relation between God and man has been broken; and that this communion can be restored by the removal of sin*. The means of restoration in O.T. references are considered to be by payment of compensation for wrong, in sacrifices (see under WORSHIP) or offerings, by the performance of ritual pleasing to God, by the acceptance of suffering, by intercessory prayer (Gen. 18:23–32), and occasionally, in the prophetic writings, by repentance. The various N.T. writings relate atonement to the suffering and sacrificial death of the sinless Jesus Christ on the Cross. By this act man is emancipated from judgment and the consequences of sin, and new life "at-one-ment" (regeneration) is made possible. In this light, the atonement is Christ's unique glory and service to mankind.

The Gospels do not make clear just how Jesus viewed his death as a means of "ransoming" others, but the doctrine is clearly foreshadowed by his sayings (Mark 10:45, 14:24). Traditional theology has presented three theories, based on various interpretations of Scripture: (1) "the satisfaction theory"; (2) "the governmental"; (3) "the moral influence theory." "Constraining love" is the most satisfying explanation offered by scholars—a perfect, complete, and sinless love which reveals the enormity of man's sin and demonstrates how far God is willing to go to win estranged sons back into communion with Himself. To this Jesus adds his oft-repeated injunctions to repentance* and amendment of life.

The word "atonement" occurs only once in the N.T., in Romans 5:11 (R.S.V. "reconciliation"). Other major references to the concept are found in I Cor. 5:7; Rom. 5:6–11, 15–19; Heb. 2:9, 17, 9:14; and I John 2:2.

Atonement, Day of (*yŏm kippurim*), prior to A.D. 70 was the climax of the purification rites cleansing the individual from the defilement of sin (Lev. 16). The priest, clad in holy linen garments, was to make atonement for himself, his family, and "for all the assembly of Israel," killing the "bullock of the sin-offering," sprinkling the blood on the mercy seat, killing the goat of the sin-offering, and selecting the scapegoat*, over whose head were confessed the transgressions of Israel before that creature was sent away into the Wilderness of Judaea, carrying the people's sins "unto a solitary land." The Day of Atonement, marking the culmination of ten days of penitence at the beginning of the New Year (see NEW YEAR FESTIVAL) celebration, was the most solemn of all Hebrew fasts (see FEASTS). It fell on the 10th day of the 7th month (Tishri, Sept.-Oct.), five days prior to the Feast of Tabernacles. Christ, as eternal high priest, entered not "into the holy places made with hands" (Heb. 9:24) but into heaven itself, offering his own blood—not merely sacrificing animals—for men's redemption. Some authorities claim that no observance can be traced prior to 444 B.C. In Acts 27:9 this solemn fast is called "the fast." The Day of Atonement saw the only entry of the high priest into the Holy of Holies. It involved abstinence from all labor, food, and drink, and the calling of a holy convocation to recite penitent prayers beseeching forgiveness. Modern Judaism still so observes it.

Attalia (ăt-*ȧ*-lī′*ȧ*), a seaport of Pamphylia from which Paul sailed on his way to Antioch at the end of his First Missionary Journey (Acts 14:25).

Augustus, Gaius Julius Caesar Octavianus, or Octavian, 1st Roman Emperor, known as Augustus Caesar. He ruled 27 B.C.–A.D. 14; the ruler by whom the decree was issued "that all the world should be taxed" (Luke 2:1)—a decree which took Joseph and Mary to be enrolled at Bethlehem, shortly before the birth of Jesus. Peace, culture, and good government characterized his reign. The "Augustan band," to which belonged Julian the centurion who guarded Paul (Acts 27:1), was probably named in his honor.

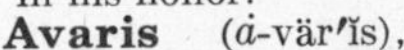

40. Head of Caesar Augustus.

Avaris (*ȧ*-vär′ĭs), capital of Egypt during Hyksos regime (c. 1720–1550 B.C.) and used by pharaohs of Nineteenth Dynasty after 1300 B.C. Near the Mediterranean, eastern mouth of Nile. (G. E. Wright) See RAAMSES; ZOAN.

Aven (ā′vĕn) ("emptiness," "an idol"). (1) The Egyptian city On or Heliopolis (Ezek. 30:17).

(2) The name Hosea gave to Bethel to show it had become a place of idolatry (Hos. 10:8).

(3) A plain N. of Damascus (Amos 1:5).

avenger, the individual or group who wreaked punishment on him who had wronged a kinsman; usually the nearest blood relative of the wronged. Blood revenge was looked upon with favor in the O.T. (Gen. 9:5; Num. 35:19; Josh. 10:13). But there was a gradual toning down of this spirit as Israel advanced in its ethical code. Provision was made for mercy toward unintentional murders. "Cities* of refuge" were set up by Moses or by David and Solomon, three on each side of the Jordan: Hebron, Shechem, and Kadesh on the W.; Bezer, Ramoth-gilead, and Golan E. of the river. In these cities criminals could live safely until fair trial was arranged. At last the long stride was taken to the merciful attitude expressed in Rom. 12:19 (R.S.V.): "Beloved, never avenge yourselves, but leave it to the wrath of God. . . . Vengeance is mine; I will repay, says the Lord. . . . If your enemy is hungry, feed him."

ax, battle-ax. See WEAPONS.

Ayin ('ä′yēn) ("eye," "spring") (ain in A.V.). (1) The 16th letter of the Hebrew alphabet (see WRITING). It heads the 16th section of the acrostic Psalm 119.

(2) A place near Riblah on N. boundary of Palestine (Num. 34:11).

(3) A town near Rimmon (Josh. 15:32; I Chron. 4:32).

Azarel (ăz′ȧ-rĕl) ("God has helped") (A.V. Azareel). The name of six men: I Chron. 12:6; I Chron. 25:18; I Chron. 27:22; Ezra 10:41; Neh. 11:13; Neh. 12:36.

Azariah (ăz′ȧ-rī′ȧ), a king of Judah. See UZZIAH.

The name of many other men: a man of Judah (I Chron. 2:8); an ancestor of Samuel (I Chron. 6:36); a son of Zadok (I Kings 4:2); a grandson of Zadok (I Chron. 6:9); an official over the district rules of Solomon (I Kings 4:5); a prophet (II Chron. 15:1–8); two (?) sons of Jehoshaphat (II Chron. 21:2); a grandson of Obed (I Chron. 2:38, 39); two captains (II Chron. 23:1); a prince of Ephraim (II Chron. 28:12), two high priests (I Chron. 6:10, 13); two Levites (II Chron. 29:12); an opponent of Jeremiah (Jer. 43:2); four people in Nehemiah's time (Neh. 3:23 f., 8:7, 10:2, 12:33). It is also the Hebrew name of Abednego (I Chron. 6:10, 13–14; Ezra 7:1, 3; Dan. 1:7).

Azazel (ȧ-zā′zĕl), used in R.S.V. for the "scapegoat" of A.V. (Lev. 16:8, 10, 26), to designate an evil spirit living in the Wilderness of Judaea, which played some part in the ritual of ridding Israel of sin. A goat, chosen by lot and symbolically laden with the sins of the people, was led to a cliff and tossed over. His expiatory death, in some way originally connected with Azazel, was believed to rid people, priests, and sanctuary from impurity. The ceremony, deeply rooted in ancient folk practice, was embodied in post-Exilic legislation for Yom Kippur (see ATONEMENT, DAY OF).

Azekah (ȧ-zē′kȧ) (Tell ez-Zâharîyeh), a fortified city a short distance NE. of the strong border fortress city of Lachish*. It was occupied before Israel entered Canaan (Josh. 10:10–11; 15:35). Goliath and the Philistines encamped "between Succoth and Azekah" (I Sam. 17:1). Rehoboam strengthened Lachish and Azekah for the defense of Judah (II Chron. 11:9). When Nebuchadnezzar, King of Babylon, attacked Zedekiah, King of Judah, at Jerusalem, only Azekah and Lachish remained among Judah's fortified cities (Jer. 34:7).The famous Lachish Letters in ink on broken bits of pottery found at Tell ed-Duweir were written by an officer in charge of an outpost between Azekah and Lachish, to the commandant of the latter fortress (*ANET*[3], p. 322).

B

Baal (bā′ăl) (Canaan.-Phoen., "master," "lord"), a chief member of the Canaanite pantheon; offspring of Dagon, consort of Baalat (Asherah, Astarte, Anath of the O.T.); identified with the storm god, Hadad; and known in various communities as their own local Baal. The sum total of such community Baals made up the Baalim, whose worship was Baalism.

The name Baal occurs in many place names such as: Baalah, Baalath, Baalhamon, Baalhazor, etc.

Baal was the farm god, responsible for the germination and growth of crops, the increase of flocks, and the fecundity of farm families. Canaanites (see CANAAN), as revealed in the recovered literature of this influential people, believed that in summer heat Baal died, but with the winter rains was resurrected after Anath had killed Mot (death).

The worship of Baal, as it existed when Israel began to filter into Canaan, was conducted by priests in fields and on mountain "high places" (see HIGH PLACE), where communities brought "taxes" to their favorite deity, in the form of wine, oil, first fruits, and firstlings of flocks. The cult included joyous, licentious dances and ritualistic meals. Austere Hebrews, accustomed to nomadic desert ways, were attracted by the gay but demoralizing Baal worship around rustic altars flanked with sacred poles or trees of Astarte and symbolic stone pillars (*maṣṣeboth*). They felt the rigorous exactions of their own God, whose demands for righteousness had been revealed at Sinai*. Not only did they fall into an alluring trap in their habits of worship, but often compounded town names and those of their sons with Baal—as in Ish-baal, which remained until reforms some many centuries after his death revised it to Ish-bosheth.

For three centuries Hebrew prophets protested against the wide acceptance of Baalism among their people. They saw Baalism eating into the morality and the theology of their adherents. The backsliding recorded in Judg. 2:11–14 was typical of oft-repeated crises in the experience of Israel. Even the Hebrew kings divided their loyalty between Yahweh and Baal. Two of the most fanatical protagonists of Baal were wives of Hebrew kings. Jezebel, daughter of the priest-king of Tyre, Eth-baal, imported with her to Israel's capital at Samaria an elaborate entourage of Baal cultists such as were typical of her great commercial harbor home with its worship of the Tyrian Baal (Melkarth). The contest between her prophets and those of Elijah* on Mt. Carmel, and the vindication of the supremacy of Yahweh, was epochal in the religious history of Israel (I Kings 18). Athaliah, daughter of Jezebel and wife of Jehoram, King of Judah, was another notorious champion of the fertility cult of Baal. Among the worst idolatries of royalty were those of Manasseh* (II Chron. 33). Hosea (2:8) denounced deflections to Baal in the 8th century B.C. Not until the reforms of Josiah (c. 640–609 B.C.), who tossed Baal images into the Kidron, burned them, and sent the ashes to Bethel (II Kings 23), did Baal worship loosen its grip on Judah. Even just before the Exile Jeremiah was still voicing stern denunciations of his people's apostasy. Yet Israel's conflict with Baalism strengthened her own sense of religious destiny.

41. Gold-covered statuette (c. 1500–1200 B.C.), probably of Baal, found at Megiddo. Cap and robe characteristic of Canaanite gods.

A certain amount of syncretism was inevitable, as Israel faced the religious and cultural forces of its Canaanite neighbors. Grosser elements were sloughed off, others refined and assimilated. The definite influence of Baal festivals on the three great Hebrew agricultural festivals is easily discernible. The Feasts* of Unleavened Bread, of Harvest, and of Ingathering were adopted and given significance based on the Hebrew experience of God; particularly the Passover attached significance to the first of these three.

Baal is mentioned only once in the N.T. (Rom. 11:4, quoting I Kings 19:18); monotheism was by that time taken for granted. Hebrew culture was becoming more urban, and less subject to old customs associated with the field.

The discovery of the Ugaritic myths recorded on clay (c. 14th century B.C.) at Ras Shamrah* on the N. Syrian coast, has enabled scholars to trace the roots of many religious ceremonies adopted by the Hebrews after their entry into Canaan. Excavations of many Canaanite levels in Palestine have yielded "likenesses" of the Baals and Anaths.

Baalbek ("lord of the Beqa 'a"), an ancient center of Baal worship situated in the Beqa 'a (Coele Syria) between the Lebanon and the Anti-Lebanon mountains, N. of Damascus. Its position on the watershed separating the Litani and the Orontes Rivers made it very early a popular place of worship; later it became highly syncretistic. Greeks, associating Baal with Helios, called it "Heliopolis." Recent soundings in the Central Court of the Roman Temple of Jupiter Heliopolitanus have uncovered remains of the Achaemenid period, the 18th century B.C., and the late 4th and early 3d millennia B.C., attesting to the antiquity of the site. Albright suggests an identification with Ṭubikhi of Papyrus Anastasi I (*ANET*³, p. 477) and the Amarna Letters (*ARI*, 1942, p. 131, n. 8). Ṭubikhi, in turn, may be the Betah (Tibhath) from which David took bronze after he defeated Hadadezer, king of Zobah (II Sam. 8:8; I Chron. 18:8). The genius of Greek architects and of Rome's imperial builders from Augustus to Caracalla was lavished on Baalbek, making it one of the wonders of the Mediterranean world. The acropolis, propylaea, and great court (later a Christian basilica) are a maze of beauty. Most imposing are the Temple of Bacchus (or Atargatis), with its 52-ft. Corinthian columns and majestic doorway, and the lofty Temple of Jupiter Heliopolitanus, six of whose 54 Corinthian columns, 60 ft. high, remain as reminders of the Roman builder, Antoninus Pius.

Baal-gad ("Lord of good fortune"), a town near Mount Hermon (Josh. 11:17).

Baal-hamon ("Lord of abundance"), a town location unknown (Song of Sol. 8:11).

Baal-hazor ("Baal of Hazor"), a town near the town of Ephraim (II Sam. 13:23).

Baal-hermon ("Lord of Hermon"), a town near Mount Hermon (I Chron. 5:23). It may be the same as Baal-gad.

Baal-meon ("Lord of the habitation"), a town in N. Moab (Num. 32:38).

Baal-peor (bā′ăl-pē′ôr), probably Chemosh, a Moabite god (Num. 25:3; Ps. 106:28; Hos. 9:10). See CHEMOSH.

Baal-perazim ("Lord of breaking through"), a town near the Valley of Rephaim (II Sam. 5:20).

Baal-shalisha ("Lord of the palm"), a town near Shechem (II Kings 4:42–44).

Baal-tamar ("Lord of the palm"), a town near Gibeah of Benjamin (Judg. 20:23).

Baal-zephon ("Lord of the North"), a station of the Exodus in NE. Egypt (Num. 33:7).

Baal-zebub (bā′ăl-zē′bŭb) ("lord of flies"), also Beelzebub, a Philistine god worshipped at Ekron*, believed to be creator and controller of flies. He was consulted by King Ahaziah* of Israel (c. 850–849 B.C.), who had fallen from a lattice in his room at the Samaria* palace (II Kings 1:2 f., 6, 16). In the N.T. the name is spelled Beelzebub by the A.V., where the Pharisees call him "the prince of the devils" (Matt. 12:24), and Beelzebul by the R.S.V. Jesus denied that he cast out devils by the power of Beelzebub (Luke 11:19 f.). Many Jews of the period of the second Temple believed that heathen deities were demons; it was easy for them to regard as leaders of demons such deities as were mentioned in Scripture. See SATAN.

42. Ruins of Baalbek.

Baasha (bā'ȧ-shȧ), a son of Ahijah of the Tribe of Issachar. He conspired against and slew Jeroboam's son Nadab, and succeeded him as the 3d king of Israel (I Kings 15:27 f.). His long reign of 24 years (c. 900–877 B.C.) paralleled part of the 41-year reign of his far greater contemporary and enemy, Asa*, King of Judah. He was succeeded by his son Elah (c. 877–876 B.C.). Baasha's attempt to build a strategic military stronghold within the border of Judah, his defeat at the hands of Asa and Ben-hadad* of Damascus, and his provocation of Yahweh to anger, are narrated in I Kings 15 f. and II Chron. 16.

Babel (bā'bĕl) ("the gate of God"), Heb. name for Babylon*, polyglot city in the Plain of Shinar. The name "Babel" became synonymous with such confusion of tongues as characterized cosmopolitan Babylon (Gen. 11:4–9). Moffatt's reading of Gen. 11:9 is: "Hence it was called Babylon, because it was there that the Eternal made a babble of the language of the whole earth, and there that the Eternal scattered men all over the wide earth."

The Tower of Babel (*Etemenanki*—"House of the Terrace-platform of Heaven and Earth") was a seven-story *ziggurat** or zoned tower-temple of sun-dried brick faced with kiln-dried brick. Each of the lower six stories formed a platform on which the next was built. The priests used stairways from the court to the top of the second story, and proceeded by a continuous ramp on the outer surface of the *ziggurat* to the temple on the top. This shrine played a part in the worship of the chief god of Babylon, Marduk, whose large temple was one of the prominent sites of the city. It is believed that the temple on top of the Tower of Babel contained nothing but a large, elegant bed and a golden table. No one was permitted to enter that sanctuary except the Babylonian woman whom the god had chosen.

The Tower of Babel, long ago in ruin, had a ground plan 300 ft. square. Begun by Hammurabi* and developed by several other rulers, it was completed by Nebuchadnezzar in the 6th century B.C. Alexander the Great ordered the rubble of its ruins cleared away to prepare for reconstruction; but he died in 323 B.C. and his dream went unfulfilled.

Architects see in the tower-temple a stage in the development of minaret and spire.

See BABYLON.

Babylon. In the O.T., Babylon (from Accad. *Bab-ilu*, "Gate of God") referred to the city as well as to the country of which it was capital. Babylon influenced Hebrew life and religion more than any other city except Jerusalem; and ancient Babylonia molded Jewish thought more than any other land outside of Palestine. They are mentioned in Scripture about 300 times. The impact of Babylon on Palestine and Syria was caused by three facts. (1) From the now excavated

Sumerian city Ur in the lower alluvial plain of Babylonia, tradition claimed that Abraham began his journey to Canaan, carrying with him language, culture, and faith which deposited influences in the stream of future Hebrew life (Gen. 11:26–12:5). (2) Babylonia influenced "The Holy Land" by being the source of wave after wave of attacks by which aggressive Babylonian and Assyrian rulers extended thier borders (see lists below). (3) Babylon, as the scene of the Captivity* of Judah, exerted formative influences upon the later thought, business, and worship of the Jewish people.

Geography is the key to Babylonian history and religion. All the area bounded by the Tigris and the Euphrates is aptly called Mesopotamia ("the land between the rivers"). Its mountainous N. portion became Assyria* —which in some eras dominated Babylonia, whose territory lay S. in the unbelievably fertile alluvial plain extending down to the Persian Gulf and including in ancient times

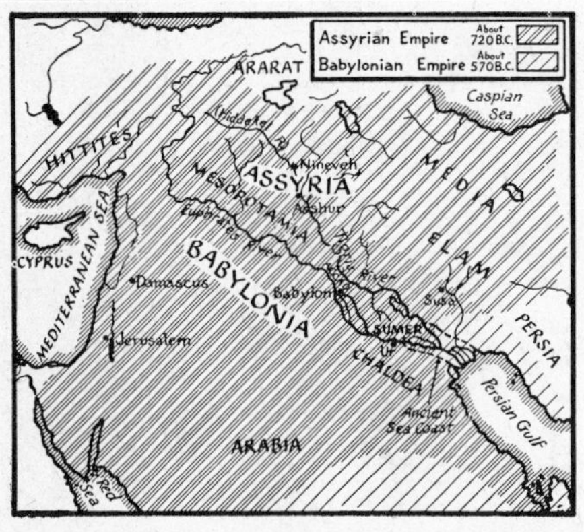

43. Babylonian and Assyrian Empires.

Accad and its southern neighbor, Sumer. The history of Babylonia is intertwined with that of Assyria. Babylonia proper was no larger than New Jersey—a strip 40 m. wide and comprising c. 8,000 sq. m. Contrary to past opinion, the coastline of the Persian Gulf does not appear to have changed since ancient times (Lees and Falcon, *Geographical Journal* 118, 1952, pp. 24–39). But in the years of its greatest power Babylonia dominated much of the Middle East. The well-tended network of irrigating canals (see IRRIGATION) made possible amazing crops which enriched priest-kings, toilers, bankers, and traders alike. Study of the geography of Babylonia calls into consideration the possible location of the Garden of Eden within its borders. Gen. 2:14 mentions the river Hiddekel (Tigris) and the Euphrates*. And a Babylonian deluge is described in various cuneiform clay tablets. There is every evidence of the dawn of history in Babylonia, great rival to Egypt in this claim.

The city of Babylon conformed to the city-state pattern of very early Mesopotamia, whose borders included such cities as Ur, Babel (Babylon), and Erech (Uruk, Warka) (cf. Gen. 10:10). All these cities have become tangibly real through excavations, some of which reveal occupation in the 4th millennium B.C. Not mentioned in Scripture, but influential in early Babylonia, were the cities of Lagash, Nippur*, Borsippa, Fara, Jedmet Nasr, Kish, etc. Some of these

44. Babylon in the time of Nebuchadnezzar. Ishtar Gate in center foreground, leading to temple area. Hanging gardens and *ziggurat* (Tower of Babel) upper right. Painting by M. Barden, after Unger.

reveal Neolithic occupation; others have Chalcolithic ("copper-stone") vestiges. Ur revealed an astonishingly high culture level in its First Dynasty (c. 2600-2360 B.C.). Babylon attained its most dazzling appearance during the prosperous reign of Nebuchadnezzar (c. 605–562 B.C.). The mounds which cover its former glories (cf. Jer. 51:37) extend for miles along the E. bank of the Euphrates, which in ancient times bisected the city. Reconstructions of Babylon, based on meticulous excavations, help modern Bible students to envision the heavily walled, massively moated city with its twin Citadel and famous Ishtar Gate

45. Babylonian lion of glazed brick, 6th century B.C.

adorned with glazed-tile lions and dragons, through which ran a festival avenue or "Procession Street" to the quarter of the city where stood the vast palace of Nebuchadnezzar, with its "hanging gardens" on the roof (one of the Greeks' Seven Wonders of the World); the stepped Tower of Babel (Gen. 11:1–9), supporting a temple associated with the worship of Marduk, chief god of Babylonia. Procession Street led also to the Temple of Ishtar (comparable to Ashtoreth, the Canaanite Astarte). The Genesis name for Babylonia was Shinar (11:2).

The political history of Babylonia is confusing because it was ruled by several different peoples, notably by the Sumerians Mes-Anni-pada; Accadians (see ACCAD), whose Sargon I founded the capital, Agade; Amorites, of whom Hammurabi*, an able executive and codifier of laws, was the greatest; Assyrians, of whom Asshurbanapal was typical; Chaldaeans, most famous of whom was Nebuchadnezzar II; and Persians, led by Cyrus*, whose empire eventually reached to India.

The following list names some of the Assyrian, Neo-Babylonian, and Persian (Chaldaean) Kings whose acts of aggression are specifically mentioned in the Hebrew O.T.:

Assyrian Kings

Shalmaneser III (859–824 B.C.) waged repeated campaigns in Syria and Palestine during the reign of Ahab at Samaria; was checked at the battle of Karkar (853 B.C.)

Tiglath-pileser III (745–727 B.C.) (called "Pul" in II Kings 15:19 and I Chron. 5:26). Asked by King Ahaz of Judah, from whom he collected tribute, to help against Damascus, he attacked Israel; carried captives from Gilead, Galilee, Naphtali (II Kings 15:29); and reduced this territory to "provinces."

Shalmaneser V (727–722 B.C.) besieged Samaria* for three years (II Kings 18:9-10).

Sargon II (722–705 B.C.) continued the siege of Samaria, took it, carried Israelites captive to the Habor River region and cities of the Medes (II Kings 18:10–11).

Sennacherib (705–681 B.C.) attempted the siege of Jerusalem (701) against King Hezekiah; failed (II Kings 18:13 ff.); but removed enormous tribute, including Temple* treasures (v. 16).

Esar-haddon (681–669 B.C.) (Ezra 4:2, II Kings 19:37).

Ashurbanipal (669–? 633 B.C.), referred to in Ezra 4:10 as Asnapper (A.V.) or Osnappar (R.S.V.), replaced citizens of Samaria with immigrants.

Chaldaean Kings (Neo-Babylonians)

Merodach - baladan (Berodach - baladan) had two reigns (722–710 B.C., and 703–702 for 9 months) at Babylon. He sent envoys to Jerusalem (II Kings 20:12). He was defeated by Sargon II and Sennacherib.

Nebuchadnezzar* II (605–562 B.C.), to whom there are over 90 references in Scripture, reduced Syria and Palestine to vassal states; came against Jerusalem; made King Jehoiakim* dependent; exacted fines; returned in 598 B.C.; carried young King Jehoiachin* to Babylon with thousands of captives, leaving only the "poorest sort of the people," with Zedekiah in control of Jerusalem (II Kings 24:12–16); came again in 587 B.C., destroying Jerusalem and its Temple (II Kings 25). A third deportation, of some 745 men, occurred in 582 B.C.

Persian Kings

Cyrus (c. 550–530 B.C.) founded the Persian Empire. He conquered Babylon in 539. He was called "anointed of the Lord" by Isaiah (45:1). He gave the Jews permission to return to Jerusalem (c. 538 B.C.). (See CHRONOLOGY.)

Darius I (c. 522–486 B.C.), mentioned in Ezra 6:1, was reigning during the rebuilding of the Jerusalem Temple (c. 520–515 B.C.), which had begun in 537 and been interrupted.

The greatest impact of Babylonian influence on Palestine came from what the Hebrew Exiles (see EXILE) saw and experienced between c. 597 B.C. and c. 538 B.C., when Cyrus authorized the first Return. The lot of the displaced Jews was not without hardship (cf. Psalm 137), yet following the advice of the prophet Jeremiah, many settled down to hard-working careers of farming, weaving, dyeing, metal-working—skills which they improved and brought back home with them. Many married women of the rich alluvial plain and reared families there. Their villages were near Nippur, from which a goodly number of Jews acquired financial skill under expert Babylonian bankers. They amassed money which enabled them to contribute ultimately to the rebuilding of the Temple when they returned to their own towns (Ezra 2). Even the Hebrew King Jehoiachin, who had been taken captive by Nebuchadnezzar, was at last given greater freedom in the 37th year of the Captivity by King Amel-Marduk, and not only received a definite ration from the king's warehouse, but a seat of honor (Jer. 52:31–34). The Hebrews in Babylon became acquainted with coined money, and astronomy also came to their attention. Most important of all, the captives developed a synagogue system during their Exile which they carried back to Palestine. This system developed further in the N.T. times of Jesus and Paul. Laws, narratives, and prophecies which now form part of our O.T. were first written down during the Babylonian captivity, when absence from well-loved sacred scenes gave time to ponder in clear perspective the events of Hebrew history and God's will for the race: for example, the Pentateuch in its enlarged form; Second Isaiah; possibly Ezekiel. The last portions of II Kings must have been composed during the Exile or after the Return. The books of Haggai and Zechariah are valuable sources of historic material concerning the little-known years between 561 B.C. (events narrated at the close of II Kings) and the years when Nehemiah was active.

The religion of Babylonia centered in a pantheon of gods, whose traits and names varied through the millennia. Anu was the Accadian "Heaven," lord of Uruk. "Lord Wind," or Enlil, was prominent in Nippur. Enki (Accad. Ea) was god of the sweet waters and the earth. Ninhursag was a goddess of mountains and motherhood. The moon god, Sin, was ruler of Ur. Inanna was the Accadian Ishtar. Marduk, an old "hoe" deity, became the most powerful god of later Babylonia. Worship rites included divine marriage, in which the king, assuming the role of Dumuzi, god of vegetation, espoused a priestess in the role of the goddess Inanna. The elaborate New Year celebration featured a battle between the king, symbolizing Marduk, and Kingu, god of Chaos. M.S.M./R.W.C.

Baca (bā′kȧ) ("balsam tree" or "weeping"), an unknown valley in Palestine (Ps. 84:6), possibly named for its balsam.

badger, the word used in the A.V. for the animal whose skin was used for the outer covering of the Tabernacle (e.g. Ex. 25:5; Num. 4:6) and for women's shoes (Ezek. 16:10). The meaning is uncertain; the R.S.V. speaks of "goatskin" in all cases except Num. 4:25 and Ezek. 16:10, where it is referred to as "sheepskin" and "leather."

bags, made of skin or woven material, or formed by folds in a girdle, had various uses in Bible times. In them merchants sometimes carried their weights (Deut. 25:13). A shepherd's bag contained everything from food to stones from the brook, used to attract the attention of sheep or to frighten off wild animals. Water bags were made of tanned whole skins of animals. Prov. 7:20 refers to a money bag (not necessarily coined money, but lumps of metal). Isaiah refers to a bag containing gold (46:6). The most famous bag of the N.T. is that in which Judas carried the disciples' money (John 12:6). The bag to which Jesus referred (Luke 12:33) was probably the scrip or wallet-for-the-journey type. Money bags are the art symbol for Matthew, the tax collector.

46. Bags.

Bahurim (bȧ-hū′rĭm) ("young men"), a village just E. of Jerusalem on the road to the Jordan. It figures in the history of David (II Sam. 3:16, 16:5, 17:18, 19:16; I Kings 2:8).

baker, one who baked cakes or bread. The first baker mentioned in Scripture is Sarah, wife of Abraham, who made cakes "upon the hearth" for the three angelic visitors announced by Abraham (Gen. 18:6). The hearth was probably red-hot stones or ashes kept glowing at Sarah's kitchen tent. The unleavened cakes prepared during Israel's Wilderness journeys could have been baked similarly, or by pressing the dough against the side walls of a conical clay pit oven which had been filled with coals. Sometimes the oven looked like an inverted bowl, heated by heaping burning dung on its outside. Isaiah 44:19 refers to baking "bread upon the coals." Num. 11:8 refers to baking manna in pans—plates of metal serving as griddles. Even though women were bakers for their families, villages had public ovens into which bakers inserted the home-made, flat, round loaves brought on trays by children. Bakers were supposed to watch their ovens at night, lest by morning they become "flaming fire" (Hos. 7:6–8). As in Mediterranean towns today, there were bakers' streets in Bible times (Jer. 37:21). Bakers were important when directing the bread* and cake supply for a pharaoh as Joseph's fellow prisoner did (Gen. 41:1 ff.). Yet for a family's daughters to be summoned to be bakers or confectionaries (see FOOD) (I Sam. 8:13) for a king, was considered menial. (See BREAD, illus. 68, and OVEN, illus. 305.)

Balaam (bā′lăm), son of Beor, a heathen occultist or soothsayer living between the Jordan Valley and the Euphrates at Pethor. He was summoned by Balak, King of Moab, to invoke a curse upon Israel, whose tribes were advancing into the Jordan Valley by way of the country of the Amorites. His story (Num. 22–24) presents the strange spectacle of a pagan man sensitive to commands of the Lord God. The characteristics of Balaam are presented with confusing contradiction. In Num. 24:5–9 he displays exemplary obedience to Jehovah and pronounces blessings instead of curses upon the Lord's people. He utters oracles about the rising "star of Jacob" as he sees the Israelites approaching below his observation posts at Pisgah and the high places of Baal worship. But he later falls from grace by inducing Israel to commit sensuous sin and to eat food sacrificed to idols (Num. 31:8, 15 f.). The Midianitish seer is remembered for this disgrace in all subsequent references, even in the N.T. (Jude 11; Rev. 2:14). Psychological discrepancies in the character of Balaam are attributable to the fact that strands of three sources from the J, E, and P narratives are woven into the story. The miracle of the friendly, talking ass of Balaam (Num. 22:21–33) is one of the most interesting animal stories in Scripture.

The story of Balaam illustrates how Israelites regarded their God as universal, not national. He spoke through a Mesopotamian, as well as through such Hebrews as Moses*.

Balak (bā′lăk), a king of Moab who sought to avoid conflict with Israel by having Balaam invoke a curse upon them (Num. 22–24).

balances or scales were used in Egypt and Palestine to weigh money and produce. On one side was placed a metal ring of known value; or a lump of metal stamped with a recognized weight, or fashioned in the shape of a stone or metal pig, gazelle, duck, or some other animal. Before coinage, values were in terms of weighed gold, etc. The 600 shekels which David paid Araunah for his threshing floor (I Chron. 21:25) were "of gold by weight." See also Jer. 32:9. Scripture stresses the necessity of having honest balances (Prov. 16:11). The phrase of Dan. 5:27, "Thou art weighed in the balances, and art found wanting" suggests that illustration in the Egyptian "Book of the Dead" where the human heart is shown on one side of the scale, weighed against the symbol of righteousness (the feather of Maat). Cf. Ps. 62:9.

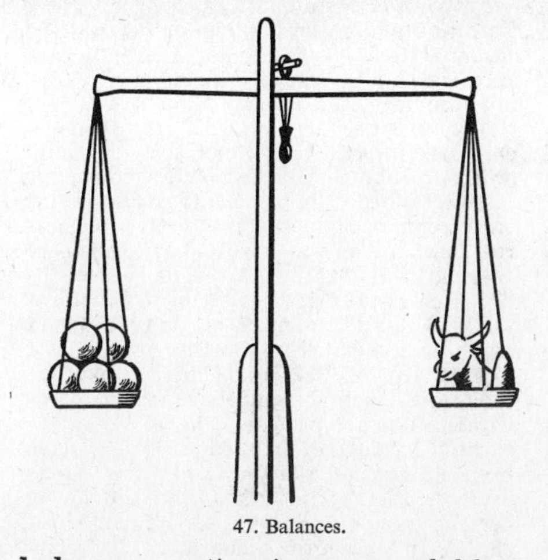

47. Balances.

balm, an aromatic resin or gum exuded from a bush growing so plentifully in O.T. times in Gilead* that it was exported from Judah to Tyre (Ezek. 27:17) and Egypt (Gen. 37:25). It cannot definitely be identified, as formerly believed, with *Balsamodendron opobalsamum* or *gileadense,* for this tree does not grow in Gilead now and perhaps never did. It is native to Arabia* and might have been brought from there by traders. Balm was part of the cargo of the Ishmaelite (see ISHMAEL) caravan drivers who bought Joseph for twenty pieces of silver (Gen. 37:25). Sometimes "balm of Gilead" is identified as mastic, *Pistacia lentiscus.* It was prized for its healing properties (Jer. 51:8), and for use in cosmetics and embalming*. When aged Jacob wanted to send a choice gift to Joseph in Egypt he included "balm, and a little honey, spices, and myrrh, nuts, and almonds" (Gen. 43:11). When Jeremiah the prophet wailed, "Is there no balm in Gilead; is there no physician there?" (8:22) he expressed the sum total of Judah's calamities.

Bani (bā′nī). (1) One of David's mighty men (II Sam. 23:36). (2) A descendant of Judah (I Chron. 9:4). (3) Head of a family of returned exiles (Ezra 2:10, 10:29; Neh. 10:14). (4–7) Four Levites (I Chron. 6:46; Neh. 11:22, 3:17, 9:4). (8) Founder of a family (Ezra 10:38).

bank, mentioned in Christ's Parable of the Pounds (Luke 19:12–27), does not indicate an establishment for the custody of money. The Gk. word used for "bank" in v. 23 suggests a counter or table upon which money matters were transacted. The agricultural society of O.T. times frowned upon a Hebrew's loaning money to a Hebrew (Ex. 22:25; Lev. 25:37). In N.T. times, however, bankers who loaned money at interest to enable people to engage in legitimate business were not condemned even by Jesus (Luke 19:23; Matt. 25:27). Most people hid their capital in the ground—hence the numerous ancient coins still being unearthed by farmers.

banner, a symbol set up on a pole to rally tribes or armies. God instructed Moses and Aaron to have every man of Israel pitch camp by his own tribal standard (Num. 2:2). Moses' serpent upon a pole was an ensign to which life-giving powers were ascribed (Num. 21:8 f.). Banners are also mentioned in Ps. 20:5, 60:4; Isa. 13:2; Song of Sol. 2:4, 6:4 f. A famous standard surviving from antiquity is a mosaic, inlaid with shell and lapis lazuli, from the royal Sumerian tombs of Ur*, dating from c. 2900 B.C. The first Christian Roman emperor, Constantine the Great, was said to have seen a flaming cross in the sky and to have adopted it on his banner (*labarum*) as the sign by which he determined to conquer.

banquets and feasts run through Bible narratives from Genesis to Revelation. Hospitality* has always been part of life in the Middle East, e.g. the Patriarchal narrative of Gen. 18:1–8. In the A.V. banqueting is synonymous with wine-drinking following the feast. The Book of Esther describes four such banquets at the sumptuous Persian court of Ahasuerus (Esther 1:5–12, 1:9,

48. Restoration drawing of carved ivory panel found at Megiddo (c. 1350–1150 B.C.), showing a feast with ruler and two courtiers attended by three servants.

5:4, 9:17–32). Job (41:6) shows himself conversant with the popularity of banquets. Song of Sol. 2:4 indicates a spring supper party in a banqueting house. The typical banquet denounced by Amos (6) at Israel's hilltop court in Samaria is historically accurate.

Jesus knew his people's taste for merrymaking and did not categorically denounce all feasting. He recognized its function in a drab and hard-working routine, and accepted invitations to large dinners (as in Matt. 9:10–17). Even some of these occasions ap-

49. A Palestinian banquet.

pear to have carried the O.T. connotation of the A.V., for Jesus said that he was upbraided by critics as "a man gluttonous, and a winebibber" (Matt. 11:19). Christ's presence at the Sabbath dinner table of "one of the chief Pharisees" (Luke 14) gave rise to his utterance of two great parables (Luke 14:8–14, 16–35). Narratives of Jesus' dinners reveal customs current in his day, as the use of couches, in contrast to the floor mats used by earlier Hebrew society—sloping couches (*triclinia*) placed around three sides of a table, leaving one side open for servants; the custom of having one side of a dining room separated from the street only by curtains, so that passersby peered in and criticized what was going on within (Matt. 9:11). Dining with Simon the Pharisee, Jesus was seen from without by a woman who ventured in and washed his feet with tears and anointed them (Luke 7:36–50). Jesus approved such wholesome merrymaking as the family banquet celebrating the prodigal's return (Luke 15:11–32).

The author of the Petrine Epistles, who had seen much of the widespread Graeco-Roman festal boards and their extravagant carousings, decries banqueting as a Gentile vice (I Pet. 4:3). In contrast is John's lofty conception of the marriage supper of the Lamb (Rev. 19:9), to which all the faithful are eligible. The Messianic banquet conceived of by Jesus (Matt. 8:11; Luke 13:29 f.) had a cosmic guest list, including Hebrew Patriarchs and "the righteous" from all quarters of the Kingdom of God.

See also FEASTS.

baptism was a rite characteristic of John the Baptist's ministry (Mark 1:4, 11:30; Luke 7:29), and was also imposed upon converts

50. Baptism in River Jordan, Epiphany ceremony.

from the beginning of the Christian Church (Acts 2:38–41, 19:3–5). Analogies to this use of water in religious ceremonies are found in the Eleusinian Mysteries in Greece, certain Babylonian religious rituals, and Jewish priestly ordinances (Num. 19:7). Just prior to the Christian era proselytes from the Gentiles qualified for membership in Israel by baptism. John the Baptist took this ceremony and adapted it as purification for the reign of the Messiah (Luke 3:3–6). By means of this rite, the people were consecrated to receive salvation*; while Jesus, in submitting himself to John's ritual, was consecrated to bestow it (Matt. 3:13–15). Tradition places the baptism of Jesus in the Jordan* River near Jericho. Although baptism was not specifically included in Jesus' instructions to the Twelve (Luke 9:1–5), nor to the Seventy (Luke 10:1–16), the Disciples employed it as the initiation into a new moral order, as John the Baptist had, even though Jesus refrained from personally administering the ceremony (John 4:2). After Jesus' resurrection, baptism was regarded as a means of sharing in his death and the renewal of his life (Rom. 6:13). It brought men the gift of the Holy Spirit* (John 1:33; Acts 19:2–6) and made them members of Christ's own body (I Cor. 12:13; Gal. 3:27). So Christian baptism took on a spiritual significance which John's baptism did not profess to have. While the earliest formula of baptism seems to have been "in the name of the Lord Jesus" (Acts 8:16, 10:48) the trinitarian formula obviously became standard at a very early time (Matt. 28:19). In view of the solidarity of the family in Jewish-Christian thought, it later became customary to baptize infants as well as adults, but whether or not this practice began in the New Testament period is something that can be neither proved nor disproved.

E. L./R. C. D.

bar, (1) any piece of wood or metal, longer than it is wide or thick, used as a support, fastening, barrier, lever, etc. This is the usual sense of the word in the Bible. The "bars" of the Tabernacle (Exod. 26:26–29, 36:31–34, etc.) were used in the framing of the superstructure and were of acacia (A.V. shittim) wood. Bars were used to secure the two-piece gates of cities (Deut. 3:5; Judg. 16:3, etc.), which needed more stiffening against assault, because of their width, than a smaller bolt-and-lock fastener could provide. Figuratively, bars were employed by poets and prophets to connote security (e.g., Ps. 147:13), and the reverse for broken bars (e.g., Amos 1:5). Peace obviates the need of gates and bars (Jer. 49:31).

(2) Aram. for "son." In the N.T. it is the first component of several names like Barnabas, Bartholomew, and Bartimeus, and of contrived surnames like Bar-Jesus (Acts 13:6) and Bar-Jona (Matt. 16:17).

Barabbas (bär-ăb'*ă*s) ("son of Abba" or "son of father"; see BAR), named by all four Evangelists as "a robber" (John 18:40), a murderer (Luke 23:19), an insurrectionist (Mark 15:7), held as a "notable prisoner" (Matt. 27:16), and released by Pilate at the Trial of Jesus, in response to the clamor of the mob incited by Christ's priestly accusers. One such act of clemency was a Roman sop to Jewish unrest at each Passover. Moffatt's translation, following ancient authorities, including the Sinaitic Syriac version and other MSS. known to Origen, gives his full name as Jesus Bar-Abbas (Matt. 27:16 f.). The R.S.V. records this in a footnote as a possible reading. The drama of the trial increased when the choice Pilate submitted to the multitude was not only between the robber and the righteous one, but as to *which Jesus* they preferred.

Barak (bâr′ăk) ("lightning flash"), of Kedesh-naphtali, once a prisoner of the Canaanites (Judg. 5:12). On the initiative of Deborah* of Ephraim he formed an alliance to drive out the Canaanites who had made the N. land unsafe for Israelites. Barak marshalled 10,000 men from Zebulun and Naphtali on the slopes of Mt. Tabor, while Deborah with her forces lured the Canaanites commanded by Sisera* to the Plain of Esdraelon. The armies of this coalition, aided by weather and the swollen Kishon R., completely routed the Canaanites. The prose account of this 12th century B.C. episode (Judg. 4), dating from the 8th century B.C., lacks some of the picturesque details and historical facts included in the earlier (12th century) poetic war Song of Deborah and Barak (Judg. 5)—one of the oldest folk epics of Israel. The Song was recited by word of mouth for centuries before it was reduced to writing in its present form. See also HEBER; JAEL.

barbarian (Gk. *barbaros*, "foreign," "ignorant"), an uncivilized foreigner. Because Israelites had been taught to regard themselves as being more precious to God than other people (A.V. Ex. 19:5; Isa. 43:20) they looked on non-Hebrews as "strangers," "aliens," "sojourners," "Gentiles." The word "barbarian" is not used in the O.T. In the N.T. it connotes: (1) The "unwise" peoples of the E. Mediterranean world who were not a part of the Graeco-Roman cultural sphere (Rom. 1:14; Col. 3:11). The Greek-speaking Luke praised "the barbarous people" of Melita (Malta) who showed no little kindness to Paul and his party (Acts 28:2–4). (2) Those using a language not familiar to the hearer (I Cor. 14:11).

barefoot, without sandals or shoes, which were removed when the individual felt he was standing in the presence of Deity, like Moses at the burning bush (Ex. 3:5); or to express humiliation and regret, like David at Absalom's revolt (II Sam. 15:30), and Isaiah, who went barefoot for three years (Isa. 20:2–4); or as an evidence of mourning (Ezek. 24:17, 23); or as a feature of the marriage ceremony whereby a dead kinsman's wife was redeemed (Ruth 4:7). It is believed that priests removed their sandals when ministering. Pious Moslems praying today place their sandals beside them.

Baris (băr′ĭs), a strong fortress erected by the Maccabeans on high ground at the NW. corner of the Temple Area, connected to the courts of the Temple* by bridges. Herod renovated it and called it "Antonia".* It was here on a stairway that Paul made his defense (Acts 21:34–39).

Bar-Jona (bär′jō′nȧ) ("son of Jona" or "son of John"), a surname of Simon Peter (Matt. 16:17).

barley, a food* grain of major importance in Bible lands, used largely for cattle, horses, and donkeys, for whom oats were seldom available. Combined with better grain, or used alone, it was baked into round, flat loaves by poor village people. It was not the food of city-dwellers, who preferred wheat. The small Galilean loaves turned to miraculous use by Jesus were of barley (John 6:9, 13). Israel in Egypt saw barley "smitten" in the ear by a plague (Ex. 9:31). It was to be one of the features of the Promised Land (Deut. 8:8). Barley was sown as soon as the October rains had set in; furrows were upturned by the plowman, followed by the sower, who dropped the valuable seeds by hand and saw them plowed in for protection (Matt. 13:3–8). The barley harvest on the fertile Jericho Plain might be under way in March; later in the highlands near Jerusalem. The time of the barley harvest (Ruth 1:22) is not specified, but was familiar to people living near Bethlehem. The reaping and binding of barley sheaves usually lasted about seven weeks—from Passover to Pentecost.

Barnabas (bär′nȧ-bȧs) ("son of exhortation" or "of prophecy"), member of the primitive church at Jerusalem; classified as prophet, teacher (Acts 13:1), and apostle (14:14); a close associate of Paul. Comparison of him to Jupiter (Acts 14:12) suggests his robust, magnetic appearance. Barnabas, otherwise known as Joses or Joseph, a Levite of Cyprus, sold his land and donated the proceeds to the early Church (Acts 4:36 f.). The friendship between Barnabas and Paul may be explained by the proximity of the island of Cyprus to Tarsus, and the association which Barnabas could have with one of his own age and interest in the mainland's cultural and commercial center at Tarsus. Barnabas guaranteed the genuineness of Paul's conversion when the Christians in Jerusalem were distrustful (Acts 9:26 f.), and sought him out in Tarsus when the church in Antioch needed more helpers (Acts 11:25). Together they carried a contribution from the church at Antioch to Jerusalem for the poor of Judaea (Acts 11:22–30). Then they teamed up as partners in the First Missionary and evangelistic tour through Cyprus and S. Asia Minor. During this tour Paul's name began to appear first in the narratives (Acts 13:46–50) and Barnabas's second. After a rest in Antioch from their arduous missionary labors, Paul and Barnabas for a second time were commissioned to go to Jerusalem to present to the Mother Church the views of this Gentile-minded group concerning circumcision. As a result, an important step was taken in democratizing the Gospel (Acts 15:1–31). When Paul and Barnabas were planning their Second Missionary Journey, Barnabas insisted that his nephew Mark go with them (Col. 4:10). Paul objected because Mark had quit them during the First Journey (Acts 12:25, 15:36–38). This contention led to the separation of Paul and Barnabas, Paul choosing Silas as his companion and Barnabas teaming up with Mark. The faith of Barnabas in Mark was a strong factor in the development of the second Evangelist and the monumental literary work which bears his name. See also Acts 11:24; I Cor. 9:6; Gal. 2:1 f.

Barsabas (bär′sȧ-bȧs). (1) The Joseph surnamed Justus on whom the lot did not fall when Matthias* was chosen to succeed Judas (Acts 1:23–26). Tradition says that he had been one of the Seventy (Luke 10:1) sent out by Jesus to be his helpers. (2) The surname of Judas who was sent to Antioch as a delegate from the Jerusalem church. He accompanied Paul, Barnabas, and Silas (Acts 15:22).

Bartholomew (bär-thŏl′ō-mū), a son of Talmai (see BAR), one of the Twelve Apostles*, mentioned in all four of the lists (Matt. 10:3; Mark 3:18; Luke 6:14; Acts 1:13), always in the second of the three groups of four disciples. He may be the Nathanael of the Fourth Gospel. To have a surname in addition to one identifying the family origin was common. The Synoptists always list Bartholomew immediately after Philip, as if desirous of preserving the link between him and the evangelistic agent by whom he was led to Christ (John 1:45).

John's Gospel affords us the only insight we have into this disciple's personality. Nathanael was a mystic, inclined to meditate (John 1:48). His hesitation about accepting Jesus as Messiah because of Jesus' Nazareth background was not based on the common Judaean scorn for Galileans, but rather on a humble doubt that anyone so extraordinary should come out of a village adjacent to his own rural home, Cana (John 21:2). His willingness to meet Jesus, together with his prompt declaration of faith (John 1:49), is in keeping with a frank, honest, spiritual nature. Nathanael was present in the choice company that went fishing after the Crucifixion (John 21:1–14). Open-mindedness, trained by comradeship with Jesus, qualified him to receive additional revelations about the resurrected Lord whom at first he had hailed as "Rabbi . . . Son of God . . . King of Israel" (John 1:49).

Bartimaeus (bär′tĭ-mē′ŭs) ("son of Timaeus"), the blind beggar who was cured by Jesus near Jericho (named only in Mark 10:46–52). Parallel narratives (Matt. 20:29–34; Luke 18:35–43) reveal divergences in details but aid in the portrayal of the central fact of the records.

Baruch (bâr′ŭk) ("blessed"). (1) Son of Neriah; secretary and close friend of Jeremiah* at Jerusalem in the reigns of the vassal Jehoiakim (609–598 B.C.) and Zedekiah (598–587 B.C.). Legend ascribed admirable traits to Baruch, apparently of notable lineage. While Jeremiah was receiving messages from God concerning Israel on the eve of the Captivity, he summoned Baruch to bring ink and rolls to his prison and take dictation recording his oracles. At the prophet's request, Baruch went into the Temple Area "upon the fasting day" (Jer. 36:6) and read what he had written, so that all Judah might hear. Learning of this incident, King Jehoiakim demanded that the document be brought to him. Resenting its warnings, the ruler burned Baruch's record of the prophet's words. Undiscouraged, Jeremiah dictated again his message from the Lord, with more prophecies added. The material dictated to Baruch apparently forms the nucleus of the Book of Jeremiah: chaps. 1–9, 10:17–25, 46–49:33, and possibly portions of chaps. 11–20. Baruch acted as the prophet's business manager in the interesting transaction recorded in Jer. 32:9–14. He was carried into Egypt with Jeremiah (43:6). One tradition says that he died there; another, that he went to Babylon and died c. 574 B.C. He may have been an author, as well as a secretary. See BARUCH, BOOK OF.

(2) Baruch, son of Zabbai, earnestly repaired a section of the Jerusalem wall near the door of Eliashib the high priest (Neh. 3:20). He may be the same Baruch who was a signer of the covenant drawn up in Nehemiah's time (Neh. 10:6), agreeing to walk "in God's law." This may also be the same Baruch whose son Maaseiah lived at Jerusalem after the Return (Neh. 11:5).

Baruch, Book of, a prophetic document which is one of the Apocryphal* or extra-Canonical books. It was written originally in Heb., at an unknown date—possibly in the 3d century B.C. It contains anonymous material attributed to Baruch, as well as matter composed by others who used his name as a tribute to his literary ability. It consists of two dissimilar parts: chaps. 1–3:8 purport to have been written in Babylon; the second half (3:9–5:9) is a poem or psalm giving glimpses of captive Israel. The Apocalypse of Baruch, written in Aram., is also attributed to him. It includes visions, one of the most interesting being that of the forest, the vine, the cedar, and the fountain. The scene is the vicinity of Jerusalem, just before and just after its capture by the Chaldaeans.

Barzillai (bär-zĭl′ā-ī) ("man of iron"), a wealthy Gileadite who sent provisions to David's army at Mahanaim during Absalom's rebellion (II Sam. 17:27–29). Barzillai was invited to David's court at Jerusalem, but refused the honor because of his eighty years (II Sam. 19:31–40).

Basemath (băs′ē-măth) (A.V. Bashemath). Two of Esau's wives (Gen. 26:34, 36:3, 4, 13, 17). A daughter of Solomon (I Kings 4:15).

Bashan (bā′shăn), a region E. of the Sea of Galilee, S. of the Pharpar R.; high, rich, grain-producing land at c. 2,000 ft., from which camel caravans came at harvest time W. into Galilee; now occupied by fanatical Druse people. The powerfully built people of Bashan, known in the age of Abraham as Rephaim*, terrified the Israelites. Their best known king was Og*, who in the time of Moses was slain together with "all his people" (Num. 21:35). During the Conquest Bashan was "assigned" to the half-tribe of Manasseh, who found 60 walled cities within its boundaries (I Kings 4:13). The wealth acquired from grain was taxed by Solomon. Bashan connoted to Israel a country of mountains, oaks, lions, huge cattle, sheep, and rugged men. The "strong bulls of Bashan" (Ps. 22:12) are proverbial.

basin (A. V. bason), a utensil for holding water for washing (John 13:5), for receiving the blood of sacrifices (Ex. 24:6), or for domestic purposes (II Sam. 17:28). Basins of gold, silver, or bronze were used in the Tabernacle and Temple (Num. 4:14; Jer. 52:19).

bath, basic unit of liquid measure in O.T., probably 5.8 U.S. gals., equivalent of dry measure ephah*; see Ezek. 45:11.

bathing was primarily a ceremonial act in O.T. times, part of the purification in preparation for approaching the altar. Neither priest nor worshipper was permitted to approach until he had bathed himself in running water and washed his clothes (Lev. 15:13). This was a matter of protective hygiene as well as reverence for Yahweh. Bathing and washing also played a curative role in Bible narratives, as when Elisha ordered Naaman of Damascus to dip himself "seven times in Jordan" (II Kings 5:14); and when Jesus told a blind man to wash in the Pool of Siloam* (John 9:11). In both of these cases faith, obedience, and the will power of the patient were as much involved as the water itself—or more so. Egyptians, meticulous about their grooming, bathed frequently—priests 4 times each 24 hours. A few Egyptian palaces had bathrooms. The Nile bathing of a pharaoh's daughter (Ex. 2:5) is true to custom. Palestinians did not as a rule bathe in public. Bath-sheba's bathing on a Jerusalem housetop had far-reaching consequences. The elaborate and vast public baths and gymnasia of Graeco-Roman times were known to Jesus and to Paul. Mineral springs near the Sea of Galilee (see TIBERIAS) and the Dead Sea possessed curative values, and dissolute rulers frequented them, as they did those on the edge of Puteoli and Corinth. Jesus criticized the Jews and Pharisees for washing their hands too many times before eating, while inwardly their hearts were unclean (Mark 7:2–6).

For the symbolic hand-washing of Pilate (Matt. 27:24) see PILATE, PONTIUS.

Bath-sheba (băth-shē′bȧ) ("daughter of the oath, or seventh day, or Sabbath"), daughter of Eliam, wife of Uriah the Hittite. Coveted and seduced by David*, who beheld her bathing on the roof top while her husband was with Joab warring against the Ammonites E. of the Jordan at Rabbah (II Sam. 11:1–4). This adultery, repented of by the king, may be reflected in the great penitential Psalm 51. After David had ordered Uriah sent into the forefront of battle, where he was killed, he elevated Bath-sheba to the position of queen. The Bath-sheba adultery was rebuked by Nathan the prophet (II Sam. 12:1–23). Bath-sheba became the mother of Solomon (II Sam. 12:24), for whom, when David was very old, she begged assurance of succession (I Kings 1:15–17). She interceded for Adonijah, Solomon's half-brother, who had requested to be given Abishag the Shunammite (I Kings 2:19 f.).

battering ram, a siege device used in heavy assaults on Near Eastern town walls, gates, and mounds from O.T. times (cf. II Sam. 20:15) to the 1st-century siege of Jerusalem by the Romans. Few defenses could withstand repeated poundings by rams.

The simplest form was a heavy pole or beam of timber, shod with an iron tip resembling the pointed head of a ram. This was thrust repeatedly against the defenses by a squad of attackers, who were usually protected by movable wooden shelters—sometimes by towers several stories high, from which archers fired at the besieged. A more efficient battering ram, as much as 100 ft. long, was suspended from a beam supported by two posts, thereby reducing the manual labor. The type Ezekiel knew (4:2, 21:22) may have been the tank-like device shown on extant reliefs of Assyrian attacks on Syria. These were small carts, carrying men armed

51. Shalmaneser Campaign in Northern Syria, 854 B.C.

with bows and arrows, and equipped in front with metal beaks. Soldiers behind the cart pushed the ram against the wall. Protection was given this type of ram and its men by independent towers full of archers. Medieval Christian Crusaders besieged the N. walls of Jerusalem with battering rams mounted on elevations near the present Palestine Archaeological Museum.

battle, a state of conflict constantly referred to throughout the Bible, both physical and spiritual. Palestine lies at the crossroads of the ancient Middle East. Never of great value in itself, it has always been an essential bridgehead coveted by conquerors tramping across from E., S., or N. The Plain of Esdraelon*—Armageddon—has witnessed epochal battles, participants in which include Deborah and Barak (Judg. 4); Midianite chiefs (Judg. 6:1–5); Syrian armies (I Kings 20:25); those of successive pharaohs in the turbulent years between Abraham and David; Canaanites; Romans like Vespasian, Titus;

52.

Arabs; Turks; British. The Valley of Jezreel, dominated by the fortress Beth-shan, Mt. Gilboa, the highlands of Samaria, the wadies of Judaea, Canaanite farmlands, and the coastal plains have all borne the heat of furious battle. The almost legendary "four kings vs. five kings" battle in the Dead Sea Plain, following which Abraham is said to have swept N. as far as Damascus to rescue Lot (Gen. 14) heads the list of struggles, which continued through the Conquest of Canaan and the turbulent period of the Judges (c. 1200–1020 B.C.), when waves of Canaanites, Midianites, Philistines, Hivites, Gileadites, etc., were in constant joust with Israel. Battles among tribes and even within palace families (II Sam. 15) increased the national unrest. The people lived in constant dread of invasion from Egypt (as Shishak, c. 922 B.C.); from Assyria (as Tiglath-pileser III, 745–727 B.C.); from Babylonia (as Nebuchadnezzar, 605–562 B.C.). The only time of independence in Palestine was the Maccabean Period (167–63 B.C.), following a revolt against Syrian domination and ending when Pompey lifted Roman standards in 63 B.C.

The inner battles of Israel were precipitated by contacts with enemy ideals and standards. Prophets interpreted national woes as judgments sent by God in punishment for apostasies and lewdnesses (II Kings 17:1–23). The Armageddon battleground of Rev. 16:16 took its name from the actual Armageddon.

See DEFENSE; WAR; WEAPONS.

battlement. (1) A low parapet ordered built (Deut. 22:8) around the flat roof of the typical Palestinian stone house, to prevent people from falling into the street or field and involving the owner in accidental homicide. Since much domestic work was done on roof tops—grinding meal, cooking, weaving—this provision was a practical safety law. (2) Towered stretches of city walls, wide enough to allow rows of troops to stand at arms in defense (Jer. 5:10).

bay tree (Ps. 37:35) may be a cedar. The A.S.V. reads "a green tree in its native soil."

beam. (1) A weaver's beam—the cylindrical, heavy wooden roller on which cloth or woven carpets are wound as they come from the loom. Goliath's spear staff was likened to a weaver's beam (I Sam. 17:7). (2) Squared timbers, like the cedar beams used by Solomon in the inner court of the Temple* (I Kings 6:36); and the cedar beams on pillars of the same wood in his House of the Forest of Lebanon (I Kings 7:2, 3, 12). (3) The beam, or absurdly large piece of timber referred to by Jesus in his little Parable of the Critic (Luke 6:41).

53. Beards: 1. Egyptian; 2. Hittite; 3. Amorite; 4. Assyrian; 5. Syrian; 6. Median; 7. Philistine.

beards, facial hair customarily worn by Hebrew men. One of the most humiliating penalties an enemy could inflict was to cut off their beards, as Hanun did to David's servants (II Sam. 10:4). Cf. Isa. 15:2. Rending beards was a sign of mourning, although decried by Levitical law as heathenish. Hebrew priests were forbidden to shave the corner of the beard (Lev. 21:5). Romans and Greeks preferred closely shaved faces and short hair. Egyptian rulers wore artificial ceremonial beards, as a mark of royalty. Even queens, such as Hatshepsut, used this accessory. Babylonians and Assyrians gave meticulous attention to the grooming of their long hair and well-set, curly beards, as clearly shown in excavated bas-reliefs.

beasts, used symbolically in Daniel and Revelation for empires and powers hostile to God and His people. The "four beasts" of Rev. 4:6–9, A.V., are more correctly rendered "living creatures" in A.S.V. and R.S.V. See ANIMALS.

Beatitudes (Lat. *beatitudo*, from *beatus*, "made happy"), grouped sayings or *Logia* of Jesus (Matt. 5:3–12; Luke 6:20–23). In them he gives clear-cut statements with regard to the blessedness of those possessing certain virtues or experiences. It is generally held that these are the qualities of character which he expected in his followers. Whether the longer wording of Matthew is earlier than the briefer Luke summary is not known. Nor do scholars agree as to which account represents more exactly what Jesus actually said. Both appear to spring from a common written source. The Beatitudes in their present form are a preface to the Sermon* on the Mount, but may have been spoken at various times when Jesus in his teaching ministry found it convenient to describe characteristics of the ideal believer. Matthew gives 8, if we do not include 10–12 as separate Beatitudes. Luke gives only 4 attributes of the perfect personality. Matthew states his Beatitudes in the 3d person; Luke, in the 2d. Luke adds "woes" (6:24–26), which dramatically stress the blessedness of those possessing the traits named in vv. 21–23. Taken together, the two lists of moral ideals include: the poor in spirit, those tested by sorrow, the lowly, those who hunger for righteousness, the merciful, the pure in heart, the peace-seekers.

In addition to these gathered Beatitudes, there are isolated Beatitudes scattered through Matthew, Luke, and John, quoting sayings of Jesus concerning those whose action is exemplary. Some of these are: "Blessed is he, whosoever shall not be offended in me" (A.V.) (A.S.V., " . . . shall find no occasion of stumbling in me") (Matt. 11:6; Luke 7:23); "Blessed are your eyes, for they see" (R.S.V., Matt. 13:16); "blessed are they that have not seen, and yet have believed" (John 20:29). Paul (Acts 20:35) quoted a Beatitude of Jesus when he said, "It is more blessed to give than to receive."

bed, couch, in early O.T. times, as in rural Palestinian villages and Bedouin tent colonies today, mats or sacks filled with straw piled by day on roofs or on the ground. In many modern Arab homes in Jerusalem families sleep on mats on the floor. Such was the bed which the cured man picked up when he walked (Luke 5:25). By the time depicted in II Kings 4:10 (the widow offering her guestchamber to the prophet, with its bed, table, stool, and candlestick), living conditions were occasionally more comfortable. Numerous examples of palace beds and bedchambers are found in the O.T.: that of Prince Ish-bosheth (II Sam. 4:7), and of the King of Syria where Elisha eavesdropped (II Kings 6:12). (See also II Chron. 22:11; Amos 6:4; Esther 1:6; Ps. 6:6.)

Sick were carried on couches, or pallets, to Jesus and Peter for healing (Luke 5:19, 24; Acts 5:15). In O.T. times a man's bedding was usually his hand-woven, seamless cloak—the *abayeh* of the shepherd, which he threw on the ground at night and used as a sleeping bag. Such was the use to which Jesus put his mantle (John 8:1; 19:23).

The giant king, Og of Bashan, had a bedstead of iron (Deut. 3:11). Egyptians used low, couch-like beds the size of modern day beds, some of which are in museums today; so, too, are Roman metal beds such as Paul knew. See FURNITURE, illus. 157.

Banquet* couches were part of the equipment of every palace and well-furnished home of the 1st century (John 13:23).

The words "couching," "couching-place" (Job 38:40; Ezek. 25:5) are used with reference to lions and flocks.

Beelzebub (bē-ĕl′zē-bŭb). See BAAL-ZEBUB.

Beelzebul (bē-ĕl′zē-bŭl) ("Baal Prince"). See BAAL-ZEBUB.

Beer (bē′ĕr) ("a well"), a place on the borders of Moab where the leaders of the Israelites dug a well (Num. 21:16).

Beeri (bē-ē′rī). (1) The Hittite father of one of Esau's wives (Gen. 26:34). (2) The father of Hosea (Hos. 1:1).

Beeroth (bē-ē′rŏth) ("wells"), a town about 9 m. N. of Jerusalem. Evidently an ancient caravan site, with springs and traces of old caravansaries, Beeroth is suggested as the possible site where the parents of Jesus discovered at the close of the first day out from Jerusalem that their son had remained in the city (Luke 2:44–49). It had been "assigned" to the tribe of Benjamin (Josh. 18:25). It was the home of Ish-bosheth's murderer (II Sam. 4:2), and of Joab's armor-bearer (II Sam. 23:37). The modern Moslem town El-Bireh is on its site. It is sometimes identified as the Palestinian Berea. A Beeroth (site uncertain) is mentioned in Josh. 9:17.

Beer-sheba (bē′ĕr-shē′bȧ), "the well of the seven" (Gen. 21:22–34; incorrectly "the well of the oath" through misunderstanding of Hebrew; see Gen. 26:17–33), a favorite dwelling place of the nomadic Hebrew Patriarchs Abraham, Isaac, and Jacob (Gen. 22:19, 26:23–25, 28:10) and possessing sacred significance (Gen. 21:33, 46:1). Identified with Tell es-Seba (Tel Beer-sheba), NE. of the modern town, c. 27 m. SW. of Hebron, in the Negeb. Both Abraham (Gen. 21:30–31) and Isaac (Gen. 26:32–33) dug wells in its vicinity. Part of the inheritance of Simeon (Josh. 19:2), it was judged by Samuel's sons (I Sam. 8:2). During the time of the monarchy, Beer-sheba became the probable center of royal administration in the south. "From Dan to Beer-sheba" reflects the classical definition of the borders of the Israelite kingdom (Judg. 20:1; II Sam. 24:2, I Kings 4:25; etc.). Elijah fled to Beer-sheba (I Kings 19:3). In the time of Amos it was a sanctuary frequented by Israel

54. A well of Beer-sheba.

(Amos 5:5). On the return from the Exile it was peopled by Jews (Neh. 11:27–30). In Roman times it was a strong frontier garrison (recent excavations have located a fortress and Roman bath); and in early Christian centuries, the seat of a bishopric. The persistence of water in and near the present town of Beer-sheba makes it a key to irrigation projects in this section of Palestine. Excavations in the vicinity of Beer-sheba (Tell Abu Mater, Bir es-Safadi, etc.) by J. Perrot (1951–1960) have uncovered subterranean dwellings and other remnants of a Chalcolithic culture ("Ghassulian") dating to the 2d half of the 4th millennium B.C. Tell es-Seba' itself has been excavated since 1969 by Y. Aharoni, bringing to light archaeological remains extending from the time of the monarchy (10th century B.C.) down to the Roman period. Especially interesting are the remains of a walled city of the 8th century B.C., with a city gate, water system and storehouses similar in plan to that of Megiddo (Stratum IV, c. 850–750 B.C. M. S. M./W. P. A.

beggar, a forlorn and ubiquitous figure in the society depicted in the Bible. He sat along dusty roads, on dunghills (I Sam. 2:8), or awaited the charitably inclined at gates of temples. Jesus immortalized in a parable "a certain beggar named Lazarus" (Luke 16:19–31). He restored sight to a blind beggar at the Pool of Siloam (John 9:8) and to blind Bartimaeus, begging along the Jericho road (Mark 10:46). Jesus, like all great Hebrews who preceded him, considered the cause behind the beggars' condition; taught kindly treatment of them, as the Levitical Law prescribed (Lev. 19:10, 25:25); expressed God's consideration of them (Ps. 69:33); indicated God's mercy (Luke 16:19–25).

behemoth (bē-hē′mŏth) ("colossal beast"), possibly the hippopotamus. The description given in Job 40:15 ff. suggests that this was a creature of the Nile and other great river valleys. Job uses him to indicate the amazing creative powers of God.

beka(h), unit of weight for precious metals, a half *shekel*, ⅕ oz. avdp.; later a half shekel coin, a didrachma. A half shekel was the amount of the annual head tax paid to the Temple, Ex. 30:13; Matt. 17:24. See MONEY.

Bel (bāl), Babylonian-Assyrian form of Baal ("lord"), used as a title for Marduk, called

Merodach* by the Hebrews (Jer. 50:2).

Belial (bē′lĭ-ăl) ("not profitable," "wicked"), rendered in the O.T. literally, as if a proper name; and used in derogatory phrases with "son of," "daughter of," etc., to designate a very wicked character (Deut. 13:13; Judg. 19:22; I Sam. 1:16, 10:27, 25:25). In Apocalyptic literature Belial, under the form of Beliar, is personified. In the N.T. (II Cor. 6:15) it is identified with the genius of all evil, synonymous with Satan*.

bells, made of gold and fastened to the hem of the ephod or robe of the high priest made a sound when he went into the Holy Place (Ex. 28:33–35, 39:25). Bells were attached to horses' bridles (Zech. 14:20).

Belshazzar (bĕl-shăz′ẽr) ("Bel protect the king") in the Bible is called the son of Nebuchadnezzar (Dan. 5:2) and the last Chaldaean king of Babylon (5:30 f.). The feast given by Belshazzar to a thousand of his nobles, featured by colorful Oriental splendor, bacchanalian orgies, and climaxed by the interpretation by Daniel* (4:9) of the words which appeared on the walls of the banquet hall, is unsurpassed in vividness in ancient literature (Dan. 5).

Cuneiform inscriptions make clear that Belshazzar was not the son of Nebuchadnezzar but the eldest son of Nabonidus (Nabuna'hid, c. 556–539 B.C.), the last king of neo-Babylonia. Nabonidus was so preoccupied by Arabian wars and antiquarian pursuits in Ur* that his year-after-year absence from Babylon led him to name Belshazzar as prince regent. On a cuneiform cylinder describing the completion of a *ziggurat* started by a predecessor, Nabonidus concludes with a prayer for life for himself and his son, Belshazzar. Nabonidus did not actually relinquish his rule until Babylon was conquered by Cyrus*. The prince, or co-regent, was active in business and temple affairs, and made generous offerings to Babylonian sanctuaries.

Many view Belshazzar as a lineal descendant of Nebuchadnezzar, perhaps a grandson. In that case, to refer to him as "son" is in keeping with Semitic custom, if not with actual fact.

Belteshazzar (bĕl′tē-shăz′ẽr) ("protect the life of the king"), the name given to Daniel by his Babylonian captors (Dan. 1:7, 2:26, 4:8, 9, 19, etc.).

Benaiah (bē-nā′yȧ) ("Jehovah has built"), the son of Jehoiada*. He performed valiant acts (II Sam. 23:20–22; I Chron. 11:22–24); was a member of David's bodyguard (II Sam. 8:18) who remained loyal to David during the rebellions of Absalom (II Sam. 20:23), and of Adonijah (I Kings 1:10). He escorted Solomon to Gihon to be anointed king (I Kings 1:38). He carried out the executions of Adonijah, Joab, and Shimei (I Kings 2:25–46). He succeeded Joab as commander of the army (I Kings 2:35).

The name of eleven other men: II Sam. 23:30; I Chron. 4:36, 15:18, 24; II Chron. 20:14, 31:13; Ezek. 11:1; Ezra 10:25, 30, 35, 43.

Ben-ammi (bĕn-ăm′ĭ) ("son of my kinsman"), the son of Lot's younger daughter and founder of the tribe of the Ammonites (Gen. 19:38).

benediction, a blessing, specifically that pronounced at the close of public worship. For two well-known benedictions, see Num. 6:24–26; II Cor. 13:14.

benevolences, carried over by Christians from the almsgiving characteristic of Israel from its very beginnings, are glimpsed in such passages as Acts 6:1–6; Rom. 15:25–29.

Ben-hadad (bĕn′hā′dăd) ("son of Hadad"), the name of three kings of Damascus* in the O.T. (1) Ben-hadad, son of Tab-rimmon, was bribed by Asa*, King of Judah, with the gold and silver treasures of the Jerusalem palace and Temple, to attack Baasha, King of Israel (c. 900–877 B.C.). He did so with success (I Kings 15:18–20; II Chron. 16:2–4).

(2) Ben-hadad II, son and successor of Ben-hadad I, continued hostility to Israel by making war on King Ahab (c. 869–850 B.C.) (I Kings 20:1–21). At Aphek (see ANTIPATRIS) Ben-hadad was defeated and compelled to restore the cities taken by his father, as well as to grant Israel, by a commercial clause in the peace treaty, a bazaar or trading street in Damascus (I Kings 20:26–34). In 853 B.C. Ahab was numbered among Ben-hadad's allies against Shalmaneser III of Assyria at Karkar on the Orontes. Ben-hadad, when the allies evidently fell out, seized Ramoth-gilead. It was Ahab's attempt to recover the city that cost his life. (I Kings 22:1–38). Later Ben-hadad, when ill, sent Hazael to the prophet Elisha, who was in Damascus, asking him if he could expect to recover. But Hazael, informed by Elisha that he would be the next king of Damascus, the next day took the life of his master and seized the crown (II Kings 8:7–15).

(3) Ben-hadad III, son of Hazael, lost all the Israelite conquests his father had made (II Kings 13:25). The "palaces (R.S.V. "strongholds") of Ben-hadad" were the palaces of Damascus (Jer. 49:27; Amos 1:4).

Benjamin ("son of the right hand"), the 12th and last son of Jacob, though only the 2d son of Rachel. The boy was renamed thus after his dying mother had called him "Ben-oni" ("son of my sorrow"). Full brother of Joseph, Benjamin was the only son of Jacob whose birth took place in Canaan (on the outskirts of Bethlehem). He was precious to Jacob because Rachel had been his favorite wife. He figures in the story of Joseph (Gen. 42–44). Benjamin's descendants formed the Tribe of Benjamin, concerning whose allotted territory at the Conquest of Canaan the records are confused. Its boundaries in general seem to have been the Jordan on the E., to a point SW. of Beth-horon on the W.; and from near Ai on the N. to Gibeah on the S. But these boundaries are only approximate. The boundary between Benjamin and Judah seems to have run through the city of Jerusalem (cf. Judg. 1:8, 1:21), with the Temple in Benjamin and its arcaded courts in Judah. Several prominent towns are listed in the narrative of Josh. 18 (P source) as belonging to Benjamin: Jericho, Jerusalem, Bethel,

Beeroth, Gibeon, Gibeath, Mizpah, Ramah, and Kiriath (Kirjath). The men of Benjamin were rugged mountain warriors, and were ever champions of freedom. They supplied Israel's first king, Saul, and were intensely loyal to his house (II Sam. 2:9, 15). At times their loyalty to David wavered, but when Jeroboam led away the Ten Tribes, Benjamin remained true to Judah. Its warriors had fought with Deborah and Barak against the Canaanite Sisera (Judg. 5:14) and had broken the back of the Philistine incursions. The Apostle Paul was from the Tribe of Benjamin.

Berea (R.S.V. Beroea), a Macedonian town c. 24 m. from the Aegean Sea, 50 m. W. of Thessalonica, the most populous center of the province. Berea had a Jewish synagogue whose members gave ready ear to Paul when he stopped there on his Second Missionary Journey, after rough treatment at Thessalonica. The Bereans gave him safe escort as far as Athens, when carping enemies from Thessalonica came stirring up enmity (Acts 17). Berea is Verria today. The N.T. Beeroth in Palestine is sometimes called Berea.

Berechiah (bĕr′ē-kī′*ȧ*). (1) The father of Asaph (I Chron. 6:39, 15:17). (2) A doorkeeper for the Ark (I Chron. 15:23 f.). (3) An Ephraimite in the reign of Pekah (II Chron. 28:12). (4) A son of Zerubbabel (I Chron. 3:20). (5) A descendant of Elkanah (I Chron. 9:16). (6) The father of the prophet Zechariah (Zech. 1:1, 7).

Bernice (bẽr-nī′sē) ("bearer of victory"), daughter of Herod* Agrippa I, and sister of Herod Agrippa II. She was twice married; was suspected of sexual intimacy with her own brother; and while in Rome was mistress of Titus, sharing his Roman palace before he became emperor. She was a recognized evil woman of the N.T., who entered with pomp (Acts 25:23) the judgment hall at Caesarea where Paul was on trial before Governor Festus and King Agrippa II; but was numbered with those who declared Paul unworthy of death and bonds (Acts 26:30).

Berodach-baladan (bē-rō′dăk-băl′*ȧ*-dăn), also called Merodach-baladan, a Chaldaean king of Babylon* who ruled c. 12 years; sent a spying expedition to King Hezekiah at Jerusalem (II Kings 20:12; Isa. 39); was defeated by Sargon II of Assyria; fled to Elam, but resumed his reign at Babylon for 9 months. In Assyr., his name is spelled Marduk-bal-iddina ("Marduk has given a son"). See list of Chaldaean kings under BABYLON.

beryl, a precious stone of great hardness, belonging to the mineral species that includes the emerald; pale green, fusing into light blue, yellow, and white. It was the 1st stone in the 4th row of the high priest's breastplate (Ex. 28:20); and the 8th foundation wall of the heavenly Jerusalem (Rev. 21:20).

beth, the 2d letter of the Heb. and Proto-Sinaitic alphabets; the numeral 2. Its original form was a crude drawing of a Middle Eastern house (see WRITING). In the sense of "house," "dwelling," "place of" it enters into many compound proper names, as in Bethany ("house of the poor"), Bethel ("house of God"), Bethlehem ("house of bread"), Beth-shemesh ("house of the temple of the sun"), Beth-zur ("house of Zur" [a god] or "rock house"). See also BETHESDA; BETHPHAGE; BETHSAIDA; BETH-SHAN; BETHUEL.

Bethabara (bĕth′ăb′*ȧ*-r*ȧ*), scene of John's baptizing (A.V., John 1:28 f.). The best MSS. and the R.S.V. have "Bethany." The church father Origen favored Bethabara, which, like Bethbarah of Judg. 7:24, means "ford-town." The Madeba Mosaic shows Bethabara W. of the Jordan, Ainon E. of the river; both near the main Jordan ford SE. of Jericho, traditional site of Christ's baptism.

Bethany (Aramaic, "house of poverty") (1) A little suburb of flat-roofed stone houses, around the shoulder of the Mount of Olives, "fifteen furlongs" (about 1¾ m.) from Jerusalem (John 11:18). John calls it "the town of Mary and her sister Martha" (11:1). Jesus resorted to Bethany for refreshing rest among his friends, Lazarus, Mary, and Martha. After the events of Palm Sunday he was accompanied there by the Twelve (Mark 11:11). His raising of Lazarus from the dead may have precipitated his arrest (John 11:47). His entertainment at Bethany by Simon the leper, and his anointing there, stirred jealousy among Pharisees and scribes. In Jesus' time, the route from Bethany to Jerusalem was a footpath over the Mount of Olives; on this path the triumphant Palm Sunday procession began. Today Bethany lies on a motor road from Jericho to Jerusalem. Modern Bethany (el-'Azariyeh, or Lazarus' village) is a squalid little town, jarred by earthquakes and poverty-stricken. A cave-tomb with a rolling stone, similar to the one from which Jesus raised Lazarus (John 11:38), is found there.

(2) Bethany beyond Jordan. See BETHABARA.

Beth-arabah (bĕth′ăr′*ȧ*-b*ȧ*), boundary between Judah and Benjamin (Josh. 15:6) in the Jericho Plain between that city and Jordan.

Beth-eglaim, a large city-state situated near the Palestinian terminus of the desert road from Avaris, Egyptian capital of the Hyksos rulers, and the lands NE. Its mound is thought to be Tell el-'Ajjûl, identified by Sir W. M. F. Petrie as ancient Gaza*. The original site extended over an area of 28 to 30 acres, and the city left a mound several times as large as Troy, twice as large as Megiddo. The terrain was so low—possibly only 15 ft. above the plain—that Hyksos defenders engineered one of their typical fosse defense works, *terre pisée*. They dug a ditch 3¾ m. long around three unprotected sides of the *tell* and threw the earth up onto the mound, so that encroaching enemies found a deep moat, beyond which there was a 150-ft. slope at an angle of 35 degrees to the summit. This characteristic Hyksos glacis is similar to the construction at Lachish a short dictance NE.

Although valuable material has been found in the excavation of Tell el-'Ajjûl, it would require years of examination to make a proper study of Beth-eglaim. Five successive phases of a "Palace" (the last three actually Egyptian fortresses) were uncovered, together with two city-levels corresponding in date to Palace I (Late Hyksos, 17th–16th cen. B.C.) and Palace II (16th–15th cen. B.C.). Numerous burials, including two large cemeteries (MB I and MB IIA, respectively) were also cleared. Beneath one palace were evidences of what seems to have been a Hyksos horse burial in a 5-ft. pit. Two other horses were killed, eaten, and their bones placed beside the pit. This "hippophagy" has not been found elsewhere in Palestine. It was part of the ritual of the aggressive Hyksos chiefs, who introduced horses into Palestine and later became pharaohs of Egypt. One of the outstanding art works of the Late Bronze Age (c. 1500–c. 1200 B.C.) excavated at Tell el-'Ajjûl was a vase painted with sensitive and charming depictions of animals. Finely wrought gold jewelry, imported to Tell el-'Ajjûl from the W., is in the Palestine Archaeological Museum at Jerusalem. Huge granaries were found, evidently prepared in the 5th century B.C. against the Persian advance on Egypt. See W. F. Albright, *AJSL* 55, 1938, pp. 337–359.

Bethel ("House of God"), a town mentioned in Scripture more often than any other except Jerusalem. According to the evidence of excavated potsherds, the site began to be occupied as a town in the 21st century B.C. Tell Beitin, the site of ancient Bethel, lies 10 m. N. of Jerusalem on the road to Shechem, 10 m. S. of Shiloh, and 2 m. W. of 'Ai, with whose history Albright believes that of Bethel to have been sometimes confused, assigning the narrative of the capture of 'Ai* (Josh. 8) to Bethel. The town stood on the watershed of Palestine at the head of passes E. and W. through the hills of Judaea. Being more exposed than Jerusalem, well-built Canaanite Bethel fell to Israel before Lachish. Present evidence dates the fall of Bethel in the early 13th century B.C. (Albright). Sometimes it was "assigned" to Benjamin (Judg. 18:22–25), sometimes to Ephraim (I Chron. 7:28). It was destroyed four times in intertribal disputes, c. 1200–1000 B.C. After the division of Solomon's kingdom Bethel lay in Samaria.

Bethel's history revolves about several O.T. personalities. Abraham pitched his tent and built his first Palestinian altar there (Gen. 12:8); there Jacob had his dream of angels and revelation of God, after which he erected a pillar and pledged loyalty to Yahweh, calling the place "God's house" (Gen. 28:11–13, 22). The aged prophet Samuel included Bethel in his circuit of towns visited annually to settle the spiritual problems of the people (I Sam. 7:16). King Saul singled out for his service a detachment of Bethel men (I Sam. 13:2). David sent Bethel a portion of war booty (I Sam. 30:27). Jeroboam I, ruler of the Northern Kingdom (c. 922–901 B.C.), erected a shrine at Bethel near the border of Judah, to rival the religious prestige of Jerusalem with its central Temple (I Kings 12:29, 32, 33). The golden calves mentioned in I Kings 12:32 were probably not representations of Yahweh in the form of a bull god, but rather a golden bull pedestal above which hovered the invisible God, even as His presence was believed to preside above the cherubim in the Jerusalem Temple. This bull pedestal was offensive to the orthodox prophets of Yahweh, who found further objection to Jeroboam's appointment of "the lowest of the people, who were not of the sons of Levi" to be priests at Bethel. Not even the reforms of Jehu removed the golden calves from Bethel (II Kings 10:29), although Josiah cleansed the high places of Baal worship there (II Kings 23:15). Elijah passed through Bethel (II Kings 2:1–3); Elisha was taunted there after the death of Elijah (II Kings 2:23–25). Abijah of Judah ended Jeroboam's rule soon after his capture of Bethel. Ezra (2:28) and Nehemiah (7:32) mention a small group of men as returning from Exile to resettle at Bethel. Hosea (10:15) uses Bethel almost in the sense of conscience. In the last O.T. mention of Bethel, according to the arrangement of the books, the prophet Amos protested against Israel's sins, was challenged by Amaziah, the priest of Bethel, and retorted with the famous words in Amos 7:4–17.

Excavations at Bethel have revealed two Hyksos phases of history with excellent defenses. Then two phases of Late Bronze represent the finest house masonry in ancient

55. Masonry of Late Bronze Age, Bethel.

Palestine. Next comes a terrific burning (greatest in the city's history), the work of Joshua's conquest. Bethel did not fall with Samaria or Jerusalem but remained influential until about the time world power was shifting from Babylonia to Persia. Bethel prospered in the inter-Testament period and in Christ's day was larger than in O.T. times.

(Last paragraph by James L. Kelso)

See *BA* 19 (1956), pp. 36–43; *BASOR* 151 (1958), pp. 3–8; 164 (1961), pp. 5–19.

Bethesda (bē̇-thĕz′dȧ) ("house of grace," "house of kindness"), a rectangular, spring-fed pool with five porches where invalids waited their turn to step into the mysteriously "troubled" waters. Bethesda, where Jesus empowered a man who had been an invalid for 38 years to take up his bed and walk, is now thought to be the pool found during repairs in 1888 near St. Anne's Church in the Bezetha Quarter of Jerusalem not far from the Sheep's Gate and Tower of Antonia. It is below the slippery-stepped crypt of a ruined 4th-century Church of St. Mary Probatica, and has a five-arched portico with faded frescoes of the miracle of Christ's healing (John 5:2 f.).

Beth-horon (bĕth'hō'rŏn) ("house of Hauron," a Canaanite god of the underworld), twin towns built by Sheerah, daughter of Ephraim (I Chron. 7:24; see Josh. 16:3, 5), along the northernmost of three passes over the Shephelah from the Plain of Ajalon leading to Gibeon and Jerusalem. The lower Beth-horon, 1,240 ft. above sea level, is 1¾ m. from the upper Beth-horon, 1,730 ft. above sea level. These strategic towns controlled the pass. Joshua, after relieving the besieged Gibeonites, chased the Amorites from upper Beth-horon to lower Beth-horon, where a providential hailstorm contributed to their disastrous defeat (Josh. 10:8–11). Solomon fortified these towns (II Chron. 8:5). Judas Maccabaeus fought two battles there (I Macc. 3:16–26; 7:39–50). The army of Cestius Gallus, Governor of Syria, was almost annihilated there by Jews about two centuries later. The modern names of the towns are Beit 'Ur et- Tahtā (Beth-horon Lower) and Beit 'Ur et-Foqā.

Bethlehem (from Heb. and Aram. words, "house of bread"). (1) a city 5 m. S. of Jerusalem, overlooking a main highway to Hebron and Egypt. A steep valley drops from the S. side of Bethlehem's rock spine down to the Dead Sea. A stony donkey path to the wilderness Tekoa, home of Amos, descends S. from the E. edge of the town. A pass to the Valley of Sorek runs W. to Adullam with its mountain caves (I Sam. 22:1) SW. of Bethlehem, and the artificial, truncated mound of Frank's Mountain is SE.; there Herod's pleasure palace stood.

Bethlehem's site on a limestone ridge of Judaean highland, running ENE. above the Shepherds' Field and the Dead Sea rift, has never been disputed. It was a walled town as early as David's time. Many of its narrow streets, lined with substantially built, cubical, flat-roofed stone houses, reveal how the prosperous settlement may have looked when Mary and Joseph applied for lodging at the overcrowded inn. Today, Bethlehem has a population of over 20,000, the majority of which are Arab Christians.

Ephrath, the ancient name of Bethlehem (modern Beit Lahm), is to be associated with Rachel's burial place (Gen. 35:19, 48:7). The traditional tomb is a short distance N. of the town—a small, domed stone structure sacred to Christians, Jews, and Moslems. Bethlehem was the home of Ruth and her first husband Mahlon (Ruth 1:1, 2, 4, 22), and the setting for the love idyll of Ruth and Boaz (2–4). The hills of Bethlehem witnessed the development of David, son of Jesse, and his anointing for kingship by Samuel (I Sam. 16:1–13, 17:12, 20:6). A Bethlehem well—possibly reached by a small footpath, or one of the cisterns at the Church of the Nativity near the ancient gate site—gave occasion for the courageous errand narrated in I Chron. 11:17–19. Bethlehem was one of the places considered suitable for the Tabernacle (Ps. 132:7). Rehoboam, son and successor of King Solomon, fortified Bethlehem to guard the approach to Jerusalem (II Chron. 11:6). Families returned to Bethlehem after the Exile (Ezra 2:21).

Bethlehem, the city of David's birth (I Sam. 17:12), was to be the birthplace of the Messiah (Mic. 5:2; see Matt. 2:5–6; John 7:42). Matt. 2 records Christ's birth at Bethlehem, the arrival of the Wise Men from the East, and the departure from Bethlehem of the Holy Family when intimidated by Herod's threat to the infant's life. Luke tells the story of the manger child at Bethlehem, the angels and shepherds, and the meditative Mary.

56. Bethlehem, from belfry of the Church of the Nativity.

Bethlehem was devastated in the 2d century A.D. by the Roman Emperor Hadrian. Some two centuries later, the Church of the Nativity was begun by the Byzantine Emperor Constantine the Great over a hillside grotto believed then, as now by most authorities, to be over the site of Christ's birth. Inns often had hillside caves for their stables, and could have supplied a low stone manger lined with warm straw. The church, looking more like a complex of fortified structures than a church — except for the three cupolas for relatively modern Bethlehem bells, rung by Latin, Greek, and Armenian Christians—was enlarged and beautified by Justinian in the 6th century A.D. and by many subsequent rulers. In no other church has worship proceeded for so many consecutive centuries. Its elegant, cheerful, five-aisled basilica has an attractive interior, reached through the 4-ft. Door of Humility, the only front entrance.

Excavations carried out during the 1930's by the Department of Antiquities of Palestine in the Church of the Nativity revealed several phases of its construction, including a basilical form with octagonal sanctuary erected by Constantine.

(2) A city in Galilee belonging to the inheritance of Zebulun (Josh. 19:15), identified with Beit Lahm, 7 m. NW. of Nazareth. M. S. M./W. P. A.

Beth-pelet (bĕth′pē′lĕt) (A.V. Beth-palet), a town in the Negeb of Judah (Josh. 15:27; Neh. 11:26). Its exact location is unknown (? Tell es-Saqati).

Beth-peor (bĕth′pē′ôr) ("house of Peor"), a site E. of the Jordan in the land of Moab, near Mt. Pisgah, in the vicinity of which the Israelites encamped before crossing the Jordan (Deut. 3:29, 4:46). Moses was buried nearby (34:6); later the site was assigned to the tribe of Reuben (Josh. 13:20). The Moabites worshipped a god Baal-Peor (Num. 25:1–5), and it is possible that Beth-peor is to be connected to the Peor where Balaam built 7 altars (23:28–30). The exact location is uncertain, but may be Khirbet esh-Sheikh Jayil.

Bethphage (bĕth′fȧ-jē) ("house of unripe figs"), the village to which Christ dispatched Disciples to commandeer an ass for use as his mount for the triumphal entry into Jerusalem (Matt. 21:1; Mark 11:1; Luke 19:29). Its site on the Mount of Olives near Bethany and the road from Jericho has never been exactly located.

Bethsaida (bĕth′sā′ĭ-dȧ) ("house of fishers"), a town on the N. shore of the Sea of Galilee, the home of Peter, Andrew, and Philip (John 1:44, 12:21), near the place where Jesus fed the five thousand (Mark 6:45; Luke 9:10) and healed a blind man (Mark 8:22). For his capital, Philip the Tetrarch (see HEROD) rebuilt Bethsaida and named it Bethsaida-Julias after Julia, daughter of Caesar Augustus. When Jesus denounced Bethsaida for its unbelief (Luke 10:13, Matt. 11:21), he referred not to the older Jewish section, a settlement composed largely of fishermen situated on the lake shore, but to the pagan section which was Philip's capital.

Beth-shan (bĕth′shăn′) (Tell el-Husn, "Mound of the Fortress"), known also as Beth-shean ("house of rest," or possibly "temple of the Serpent God"); in N.T. times known as Scythopolis; and to modern Arabs as Beisan. One of the largest of the chain of ten Greek cities, the Decapolis; now merely a huge mound on the Wâdī Jalud at the throat of the Valley of Jezreel where it impinges on the deep Jordan Valley. No site in Palestine is more strategic. Occupied intermittently for more than 5,000 years, its 18 explored levels have given up a mass of archaeological evidence. It has been analyzed down to virgin soil by the University Museum of Philadelphia (1921–1933).

Beth-shan's long history is due to its position at the junction of two valleys, overlooking a rich food-producing area. Solomon's organization of commissary depots placed one of his 12 officers of provisions in charge of this region (I Kings 4:12).

Beth-shan was "assigned" to Issachar and then to Manasseh, who found it impossible to drive out the chariot-riding Canaanites (Judg. 1:27). King Saul and three sons, including Prince Jonathan, were killed in the battle against the Philistines at Mt. Gilboa and their bodies fastened to the city wall of Beth-shan. Their armor was placed in the temple of Ashtaroth (I Sam. 31:10). I Chron. 10:10 (A.V.) reads: "they put his armour in the house of their gods, and fastened his head in the temple of Dagon." Later David gave Saul and Jonathan suitable burial (II Sam. 21:12–14).

No mound in Palestine is more impressive than Beth-shan. A deep sounding yielded the remains of settlements dating to the 4th millennium B.C., and to the Early Bronze Age. The main excavations, however, were focused on the upper 9 levels, which dated from the late 14th century B.C. down to Islamic times. Most impressive were a series of temples roughly contemporary to the Ramesside period in Egypt. Level IX, of the late 14th century B.C. (the original dates of the excavators have been discarded in favor of a more exact chronology based on the pottery sequence), yielded a temple complex dedicated to "Mekal, the great god, the lord of Beth-shan" (see *ANEP*[2], Nos. 487 and 732). The remains of Level VIII were very fragmentary, but Levels VII

57. Beth-shan mound, with entrance to Roman theater in foreground.

(13th cen. B.C., Ramesses II) and VI (12th cen. B.C., Ramesses III) revealed temples of Egyptian type. To the E. of the temple in Level VII (c. the time of the Hebrew settlement) was a fort tower ("migdol"), a large house and a 1000-bushel-capacity brick-lined underground silo. A number of pottery sarcophagi with images of the deceased on the lids were found in the city cemetery, and are contemporary with Level VI (Ramesses III). It has been suggested that perhaps these belong to Philistine mercenary troops stationed by the Egyptians at Beth-shan (see *BA* 22, 1959, pp. 53–66). Level V (11th cen. B.C.) yielded two temples, the S. one dedicated to Resheph, and the other to the goddess Antit. Rowe suggested that these are the temples of Dagon and Ashtaroth (I Chron. 10:10; I Sam. 31:10). Little is left of the remains of the settlement (Level IV) from the end of V (c. 800 B.C.) to the Hellenistic period (Level III), when it was rebuilt as Scythopolis.

See *BA* 30, 1967, pp. 110–135; *AOTS*, 1967, pp. 185–196; A. Rowe, *The Topography and History of Beth-shan, 1930; The Four Canaanite Temples of Beth-shan*, 1940; F. James, *The Iron Age at Beth-shan*, 1966.
M. S. M./W. P. A.

Beth-shemesh (bĕth′shē′mĕsh) ("house [or temple] of the sun"), the name of four Biblical towns, all of which may have practiced the sun cult. (1) In the Valley of Sorek, 16 m.

SW. of Jerusalem on the highway to Ashdod and the Mediterranean; a site known today as Tell er-Rumeileh ('Ain Shems). Part of the inheritance of Judah, on its N. border with Dan (Josh. 15:10), it was set aside as a Levitical city (Josh. 21:16; I Chron. 6:59). Excavations in 1911–12, and more extensively by Haverford College between 1928 and 1932, indicate that the city was first settled at the end of the Early Bronze Age, c. 2200 B.C. It flourished as an important Canaanite city during the Middle Bronze (Stratum V, c. 1700–1500 B.C.) and Late Bronze Ages (Stratum IV, c. 1500–1200 B.C.). A tablet written in the alphabetic cuneiform of Ugarit comes from the latter (*BASOR* 173, 1964, pp. 51 ff.). Philistine pottery from Stratum III (Iron I, c. 1200–1000 B.C., the period of the Judges) suggests that Beth-shemesh was occupied by Philistines at this time, but I Sam. 6 indicates that it belonged to the Israelites. The city was destroyed (Stratum IIb), possibly by Shishak (I Kings 14:25–28), but the stratification is unclear. Joash, King of Israel (c. 801–786 B.C.), captured Amaziah, King of Judah, at Beth-shemesh (II Kings 14:11–13). Philistines took Beth-shemesh during the war between Ephraim and Syria (II Chron. 28:18). It was destroyed (Stratum IIc) in the 6th century B.C., probably by Nebuchadnezzar. See *AOTS*, 1967, pp. 197–206; E. Grant and G. E. Wright, *'Ain Shems Excavations*, I–V, 1931–39. (2) The Canaanite city of Beth-shemesh named in Josh. 19:22, possibly Khirbet Shemsin or el-'Abeidiyeh, S. of the Sea of Galilee, along the Jordan. (3) A town in the N. Naphtali (Josh. 19:38). (4) A center of sun worship, possibly the Egyptian On (Heliopolis) (Jer. 43:13). M. S. M./W. P. A.

Bethuel (bê-thū'ĕl) ("house of God"). (1) The father of Rebekah and nephew of Abraham (Gen. 24:15), called "Bethuel the Syrian of Padan-aram" (Gen. 25:20). (2) A town of Simeon (Josh. 19:4; I Chron. 4:30), possibly Khirbet er-Ras, N. of Beer-sheba.

Beth-zur (bĕth' zûr') ("house of rock"), a city in Judah (Josh. 15:58) settled by the descendants of Caleb (I Chron. 2:45), identified as Khirbet eṭ-Tubeiqah, 4 m. N. of Hebron. Excavations by O. R. Sellers in 1931 and 1957 unearthed a Maccabean fortress and earlier ruins, including a Middle Bronze Age wall (c. 19th–16th cen. B.C.). Rehoboam fortified Beth-zur (II Chron. 11:7), and its later ruler helped to repair the walls of Jerusalem (Neh. 3:16). Beth-zur was a strategic stronghold during the Maccabean wars (I Macc. 4:26–34, 61; 9:52).

Beulah (bū'lȧ) ("married"), name given to Palestine after the exile when it was repeopled and restored to God's favor (Isa. 62:4).

bewray (bē-rā'), to expose or betray (Isa. 16:3). Cf. Prov. 27:16, 29:24; Matt. 26:73.

Bezaleel (bĕ-zăl'ē-ĕl) ("in the shadow of El"). (1) The divinely inspired craftsman (Ex. 31:1–5, 35:30–35; II Chron. 1:5), teacher of the arts (Ex. 35:34), and architect of the Tabernacle* (Ex. 36, 37, 38). The interpretation of God as the Spirit in the world which inspires the beautiful—characteristic of the P document—made Bezaleel's group the patrons of sacred art in Israel's development and culture. (2) One of the eight sons of Pahath-moab who married foreign wives in the days of Ezra (10:30).

Bezer (bē'zẽr) ("fortress"). (1) Head of a family of the tribe of Asher (I Chron. 7:37). (2) A city described in Deut. 4:43 as "in the wilderness, in the plain country, of the Reubenites"—a city of refuge set apart by Moses, where men who had killed neighbors accidentally might find shelter. The site is unknown. Ramoth in Gilead and Golan in Bashan performed similar functions.

Bezetha (bĕz'ē-thȧ) a quarter of Jerusalem N. of the Temple area. In it are situated the Pool of Bethesda and portions of the Via Dolorosa; cf. Luke 23:27–33.

Bible, the sacred book of Christians. The name ("little books") is derived from an O.F. word, based on Lat. *biblia,* from Gk. *biblia* ("books"), plural of *biblion* (diminutive of singular *biblos*). The Gk. word *byblos* ("papyrus") was given to a coastal city between Sidon and Tripoli (Gebal of the O.T.). For in that seaport was carried on an extensive manufacture and trade in papyrus writing material, made from the inner layers of papyrus* reed grown in Egypt in ancient times. As early as the 11th century B.C., or earlier, papyrus rolls were shipped from the Delta to Gebal. Many books of Scripture were first written on papyrus leaves. The word "Bible" is not used in the Bible; the O.T. is referred to in the N.T. as "the scriptures," as in Luke 24:32. Sometimes the N.T. use of the singular, "scripture," refers to the entire O.T. (Gal. 3:22); again, to a portion of it (Mark 12:10; Acts 1:16).

The composition of the Bible took more than 1,000 years. The O.T. developed from c. 1200 B.C. to 100 B.C., the only surviving portion of the national literature of early Israelites. The N.T. was written during the 1st century A.D. and possibly the early 2d century. All the O.T. authors were Jews, as were those of the N.T. except possibly Luke. Lawgivers, soldiers, wise men, prophets, kings, priests, peasants, poets, story-tellers, farmers, officials, one physician, several missionaries, and Christ himself contributed to the Bible. The writing of the O.T. took place in Palestine, Babylonia, and peripheral areas. Of the N.T., the Gospel of John and the Epistles of John appear to have sprung from Ephesus or its vicinity; the locale for the other N.T. books cannot be stated with certainty.

The Bible incorporates much oral material which was repeated from father to son in very ancient days, reworked time and again, then put into written form by various editors and redactors. There is scarcely an O.T. book surviving today in the form in which it was originally written—or left in the hearts of the people to whom it was addressed—by the person to whom its authorship is attributed. (See SOURCES.) Moreover, there are numerous instances now definitely established of additions having been made to the original, like John 7:53–8:11 (omitted entirely from most of the ancient authorities) and Mark 16:9–20.

The books of the Bible are not arranged now in the order in which they were written. It would be almost impossible to work out a perfect chronology of their composition. Poems incorporated in historical matter are the oldest parts of the Bible, like the Song of Miriam, the Song of Deborah, and the Song of the Well. Genesis is not as old as many other portions of the Bible; the Creation story was written later than the Eden and Temptation portions. Amos, written probably c. 750 B.C., antedates numerous books which precede it in the printed Bible. The Book of Daniel was not composed in the era of Nebuchadnezzar. Many of the Psalms attributed to David have undergone much rewriting. The oldest specimens of the various types of literature in the O.T. are the best in their spontaneous perfection of style: the Song of Miriam, the Ode of Deborah, the elegy of David for Jonathan and his biography (II Sam. 9–20), and the earliest Psalms and pieces of Wisdom* literature.

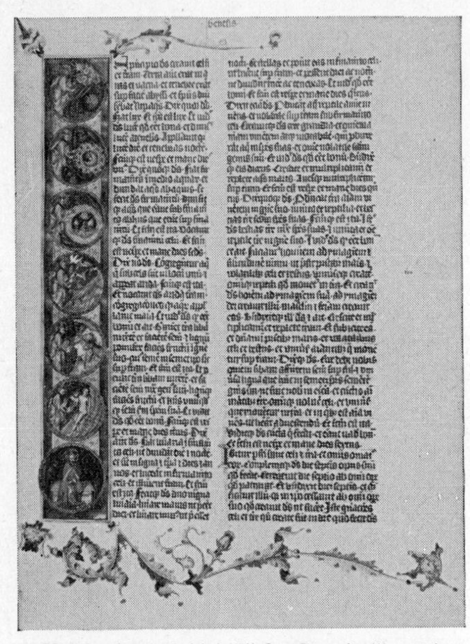

58. Illuminated initial "I" for Genesis, illustrating the Creation, from Latin Bible written and illuminated in Bohemia and dated 1391 by the scribe Andreas of Austria. The miniatures throughout were painted by artists of the celebrated Bible of King Wenceslaus at Vienna.

The various narratives, laws, songs, oracles, prayers, and prophecies making up the tapestry of the O.T. show several distinct strands, sometimes very tangled strands, known as the J, S, E, JE, D, and P sources. The S source, probably originating in the South or Seir about the 10th century, is divided into 2 parts: myths of the beginnings of mankind, including the story of the Garden of Eden (Gen. 3), and legends of the peoples of Southern Palestine and lands E. of the Dead Sea. It ends with a summary of Edom's early history. Although possibly the earliest of the strands, it was the last to be incorporated into the Pentateuch not long before 400 B.C. The J or Jehovistic (Yahwistic) strand, dating from Judaea c. 850 B.C., tells the story of Israel from the origin of its people to the Conquest. J, called "the most comprehensive history of a people that had yet been written in any land," was a remarkable narrative. It had for its theme, "Canaan is to be subject to Shem and Japheth." This Judaean strand stresses with inimitable art the story of Abraham, and concludes with the peril from the Philistines. The writer of J has never been identified, but he had amazing skill in making epics out of oral traditions (Julius A. Bewer). So, too, did the writer of the E or Elohist strand, using "Elohim" (not "Yahweh" or "Jehovah") for God until the time of Moses. Written c. 750 B.C. in the Northern Kingdom, as J had been in the Southern, E lifts old theological ideas to higher levels; it may have been influenced by Elijah. Its masterpiece is the Joseph saga. Its teaching method is the gifted use of stories. A later editor combined the J and E strands into a more complete JE narrative. Another strand is known as D, the Deuteronomic Code, or Book of the Covenant found by Josiah* during Temple repairs at Jerusalem c. 622 B.C. This Deuteronomy was the first book to be canonized, at about the time of its rediscovery (see II Kings 22–23:3). JED together are called "an embryonic Pentateuch." Another document, known as P, gives from written, priestly narratives "a charter of Judaism" (R. H. Pfeiffer).

The strands are not distinguished in a King James Bible, but in the Moffatt Bible the use of italics for J, brackets to enclose material from E, wherever it is necessary to disentangle two separate forms or fragments of a story, and double brackets to denote editorial additions—all this helps the readers to understand the manner in which the text was put together, and the reason for repetitions and variations in material contributed by the two sources.

Through the long, conscientious work of an inspired group of men and a few women attempting to record the revelation of God in its profound, basic workings as best they understood it, the Bible came to be and has been preserved, outliving and outselling all other published books. Throughout the process there has been the consistent guidance of one Mind—"God, who at sundry times and in divers manners spake . . . unto the fathers by the prophets" (Heb. 1:1).

Viewed as a whole, the Bible is a library of 66 books arranged in two alcoves—the Old Testament (or Covenant, centering in Moses) and the New Testament (or Covenant, centering in Christ).

The 39 books of the O.T. may be grouped thus:

(1) *Law:* Genesis, Exodus, Leviticus, Numbers, Deuteronomy—5.

(2) *History:* Joshua, Judges, Ruth, I Samuel, II Samuel, I Kings, II Kings, I Chronicles, II Chronicles, Ezra, Nehemiah, Esther—12.

(3) *Poetry:* Job, Psalms, Proverbs, Ecclesiastes, Song of Solomon—5.

(4) *Prophecy:* (a) Major Prophets—Isaiah, Jeremiah, Lamentations, Ezekiel, Daniel—5; (b) Minor Prophets—Hosea, Joel, Amos, Obadiah, Jonah, Micah, Nahum, Habakkuk, Zephaniah, Haggai, Zechariah, Malachi—12.

(For dates of the O.T. books see CHRONOLOGY.)

The 27 books of the N.T. may be grouped thus:

(1) *Historical:* The Gospels—Matthew, Mark, Luke, John, Acts—5.

(2) *Doctrinal:* The Epistles—Romans, I Corinthians, II Corinthians, Galatians, Ephesians, Philippians, Colossians, I Thessalonians, II Thessalonians, I Timothy, II Timothy, Titus, Philemon, Hebrews, James, I Peter, II Peter, I John, II John, III John, Jude—21.

(3) *Apocalyptic:* Revelation—1.

There is of course poetry in some of the historical books and history in many of the books of prophecy.

(For dates of the books of the N.T., see CHRONOLOGY.)

These books are all canonical (see CANON). The Bible of Jews at Alexandria (see SEPTUAGINT) had interspersed through it non-canonical books such as I and II Esdras, the Wisdom of Solomon, Ecclesiasticus of Ben Sirach, etc. Luther's Bible relegated these Apocryphal (see APOCRYPHA) books to the end, as inferior to the Canon, though useful and good. Some early English translations included the O.T. Apocrypha. Most Protestant Bibles today (except the Lutheran) contain only the canonical Hebrew books and the N.T. The Roman Catholic Rheims-Douai O.T. contains 46 instead of 39 books; it includes Apocryphal books.

The Hebrew O.T. divided its 24 books as below. Note the combination of I and II Samuel; I and II Kings; I and II Chronicles; Ezra and Nehemiah. "The Twelve" Minor Prophets were counted as one book. Note also the order, differing from the O.T. of Christian usage.

The Law

Genesis, Exodus, Leviticus, Numbers, Deuteronomy.

The Prophets

"The Former Prophets": Joshua, Judges, Samuel, Kings.

"The Latter Prophets": Isaiah, Jeremiah, Ezekiel.

"The Twelve" ("Minor Prophets"): Hosea, Joel, Amos, Obadiah, Jonah, Micah, Nahum, Habakkuk, Zephaniah, Haggai, Zechariah, Malachi.

The Writings

Psalms, Proverbs, Job, Ruth, Song of Solomon, Lamentations, Ecclesiastes, Esther, Daniel, Ezra-Nehemiah, Chronicles.

Three languages were used in the original Bible: Heb. (for most of the O.T.), with a few Aram. passages; Gk. for the N.T., with Aram.-based material incorporated. The trilingual superscription above the head of the crucified Saviour included one line in Latin (Luke 23:38). Today the Bible, in part or entirety, has been published in more than 1,151 languages, as reported by the American Bible Society, 1960. A 20-volume Braille Bible, a 12-volume Braille Commentary, and 169 Talking-Book Bible records of the complete Scriptures are available to the blind.

The *materials* on which the Bible was written were rolls of perishable papyrus, and more lasting scrolls made from very thin, treated skins of sheep and goats. (See BOOKS; SCROLLS, THE DEAD SEA.) Of papyri only a few fragments remain, as the Nash Papyrus (Heb. fragment, 2d century B.C.) and the Chester Beatty Papyri from the 2d to the 4th century A.D. The Ten Commandments and other laws may possibly have had their first recording on tablets of stone (see SERABIT for inscriptions in Sinai); for Moses, educated in the wisdom of the Egyptians, may have been able to write (Ex. 31:18, 32:15). (See WRITING; CODEX.)

The following are some of the O.T. passages which appear to be based on non-Jewish sources or are closely akin to them:

- Isaiah 16, 17—from a Moabite elegy.
- Psalm 104—suggests the Sun Hymn of the Egyptian Akhenaton.*
- Proverbs 22:17–23:14—akin to Egyptian maxims of Amen-em-ope.
- Legislation in Exodus 22, 23—of Canaanite origin.
- Laws in Exodus 20:23–23:33—related to the Code of the Babylonian Hammurabi.
- Job and Psalms 88:89—Edomite.

The earliest prayer of a spiritual quality and high literary value is "Solomon's," at the dedication of the Temple (I Kings 8:14–61). It dates from c. 600 B.C. (Solomon reigned c. 961–922 B.C.).

Originally no chapter and verse numbers were indicated in the Bible. About 1250 Cardinal Hugo de Sancto-Caro divided the Latin Bible into 1,189 chapters (929 in the O.T., 260 in the N.T.). In 1551 a French printer, Robert Stephens, divided the Greek Bible into 23,214 verses for the O.T. and 7,959 for the N.T. The Geneva Bible of 1560 was the first English Bible to carry chapter and verse numbers—the same as those used today. The King James Bible contains 773,692 words.

See ENGLISH BIBLE; TEXT.

Bible lands, the countries where events narrated in Scripture occurred. Their modern names include Israel, Syria, Lebanon, the Hashemite Kingdom of the Jordan, Egypt, Iraq, Iran, Saudi Arabia, Turkey, Greece, Italy, and the islands of the Mediterranean. See GEOGRAPHY.

Bildad ("son of contention," or "Bel has loved"), a Shuhite, one of Job's three friends (Job 2:11, 8, 18).

Bilhah (bĭl′hȧ) ("modesty" or "simplicity"), maidservant of Rachel*, who persuaded her to become a secondary wife of Jacob; mother of Dan and Naphtali (Gen. 30:1–8).

birds (fowls in many Biblical allusions) are listed in Mosaic law as "clean" and "unclean" (Deut. 14:12–18). Clean birds were considered suitable for food. Various characteristics of birds are mentioned in Scripture: *peacock*, *eagle* (more properly vulture), *ostrich*, *hawk* (Job 39:13–30). The hunting of wild birds is indicated in Job, who mentions four ways of trapping (18:8–10). Ps. 91:3, 124:7; Hos. 9:8; Amos 3:5 all tell of fowls caught in the snare (a trap made with a loop of cord to

59. Swan and cormorants depicted in mosaic floor of Church of the Loaves and Fishes, by the Sea of Galilee.

entangle the feet). The *swallow* (swift; A.V. crane) nests on altars of the Lord (Ps. 84:3).

Song birds, seldom mentioned in Scripture (Song of Sol. 2:12), use the Jordan Valley as a migration corridor, even though they do not sing as they pass through. They include the *bulbul* (E. song thrush) in Jericho's subtropical fruit orchards and the Rehoveth section on the coastal plain; the migrating *redstart* in Galilee; *warblers* near Lake Huleh and in the Jordan Valley; and *larks* in the Syrian desert.

At the headwaters of the Jordan live more than 100 species, many of them similar to the water birds portrayed in the 4th century A.D. floor mosaics of "The Church of the Multiplying" at Tabgha near Capernaum. Among the 300 species of birds which have been found in Palestine, 26 are estimated to be unique there. Jesus, a man of the open who knew the birds of Palestine, used them in his parabolic teaching; see Matt. 13:4, 6:26, 23:27; Luke 13:19, 9:58, 12:6, 12:24.

See also DOVE; QUAIL. For use of birds as offerings see WORSHIP. See Section 16, "Ornithology," in *An Encyclopedia of Bible Life*, Madeleine S. and J. Lane Miller (Harper & Brothers).

birthright, the rights or inheritance of the first-born. According to Hebrew Law (Deut. 21:17) it involved inheritance* by the eldest son of a double portion of the father's wealth —even when that son was the child of a "hated" wife. From earliest times the first-born of flocks and of human families was expected to be dedicated to Yahweh, either literally or by paying "redemption" money (Ex. 13:11–16). Hence the abhorrence of Esau's conduct in despising his birthright to the point of selling it to his brother Jacob for "bread and pottage of lentils" (Gen. 25:34; see Heb. 12:16). I Kings tells of a younger son of David (Solomon) preferred to one born earlier (Adonijah, son of Haggith).

bishop (from Gk. *epīskopos*, "overseer"), an official of the early Christian Church whose qualifications are stated in I Tim. 3:1–7; Tit. 1:7–9; mentioned five times in the N.T. Paul expected every city where there were groups of believers to have elders or overseers. Acts 20:28 states their function: "to feed the church of God." In I Pet. 2:25 Christ is called "the Shepherd and Bishop of souls." Acts 1:20 (A.V.) refers to the "bishoprick" of Judas, implying that the Twelve were all bishops.

Bithynia (bĭ-thĭn′ĭ-*ȧ*), in Paul's time a Roman province in N. Asia Minor along the Black Sea, W. of Pontus. It was the center of early Christian groups whose founders are not accurately known. Paul was led to avoid Bithynia, possibly to prevent encroaching on the ter-

60. Bithynia.

ritory of another missionary (Acts 16:7). I Peter (1:1) is addressed to "the strangers scattered throughout Pontus . . . and Bithynia." Within this province was held in A.D. 325 the historic Council of Nicaea, and in A.D. 451 the great ecumenical Council of Chalcedon.

bitter herbs (Heb. *maror*), eaten by Jews, along with unleavened bread, at the Seder or home Passover* meal, to remind them of Israel's bitter lot in Egypt prior to the Exodus (Ex. 12:8; Num. 9:11). The symbolic bitter herbs, sometimes including horseradish, lettuce, endive, parsley, water cress, etc., in salad form, were eaten before the Passover lamb was tasted.

bittern, perhaps a porcupine or some sort of lizard (Cheyne and Guthe), though not definitely identified. It was to have a part in the devastation prophesied for "the Lord's day of vengeance" upon Israel (Isa. 34:11). It appears again in Zephaniah's details of the desolation of Nineveh (2:14). A marsh bird known as "bittern" is found in the Lake Huleh section N. of the Sea of Galilee.

bitumen, mineral pitch or asphalt, used to calk seams of boats, as Noah's ark (Gen. 6:14), and the bulrush ark fashioned by the mother of Moses (Ex. 2:3). Babylonian builders of the al-'Ubaid period (c. 2900 B.C.) used bitumen in which to set tiny tesserae of limestone or lapis lazuli, thus forming the mosaic decoration applied to columns and panels for temples. One such column is in the University Museum at Philadelphia. The reference in Gen. 14:10 to slime pits in the "vale of Siddim" (the Dead Sea region) was probably meant to designate bitumen pits or wells of liquid pitch oozing from the earth. Isaiah envisioned the Day of the Lord as turning the land to burning pitch (34:9).

blasphemy (Gk. *blasphemia*, "abusive or scurrilous language"), language directed against God. Mosaic Law decreed death by stoning as punishment for blasphemy. False accusations of blasphemy were brought against Naboth (I Kings 21:9–13), Jesus (Matt. 9:3, 26:65 f.; John 10:36), and Stephen (Acts 6:11).

Blasphemy against the Holy Spirit is attributing the work of God's spirit to Satan (Matt. 12:22–32; Mark 3:22–30).

blindness in Bible times, as today in Palestine, was tragically prevalent. Two types of blindness are mentioned in Scripture—highly infectious ophthalmia, accentuated by dirt, dust, and glare; and blindness incident to old age, like that of Isaac (Gen. 27:1), Eli (I Sam. 3:2) and Ahijah (I Kings 14:4). Lev. 26:16 mentions blindness that results from malaria. Paul's temporary blindness along the Damascus Way may have been amaurosis affecting the optic nerve (Acts 9:8). O.T. writers noted the pity felt for the blind, and recorded the prohibition against placing stumbling blocks in their way (Lev. 19:14). A curse was invoked against those who willfully made the blind wander "out of the way" (Deut. 27:18).

Jesus in his peripatetic ministry was daily in intimate touch with afflicted blind sitting along the highways of Palestine, devoted much of his healing ministry to them, and from their stories dramatized many of his most urgent messages. To bring "recovering of sight to the blind" (Luke 4:18–22) was one of the declared purposes of his anointment by the Lord. Some of the blind whom Jesus cured included the man born blind (John 9:1–41), whose healing gave rise to Christ's historic declaration, "I am the light of the world" (v. 5); the man whose recovery was gradual (Mark 8:24); the two men who together were relieved of blindness and given opportunity to abandon enforced poverty (Matt. 9:27–31); the man who was not only blind, but dumb and possessed of a devil (Matt. 12:22 ff.); two blind men sitting by the wayside (Matt. 20:30–34); Bartimaeus of Jericho (Mark 10:46–52); and the occasion when many blind were cured at one time (Luke 7:21). In these case reports three characteristics are notable: (1) the extraordinary cure was effected by the miraculous, positive therapeutics of Christ's first-hand touch with the afflicted; (2) Christ shunned spectacular acclaim by insisting that the cured should not "tell it to any in the town" (Mark 8:26)—with one notable exception (Luke 7:22); (3) the cured were stirred by desire to follow their great benefactor immediately. Sometimes their cure provoked heated attack by jealous Pharisees (John 9:15 ff.).

Blindness was often attributed to sin. A curse involving blindness as punishment for evil-doing was superlative, as with the men of Sodom (Gen. 19:11); the Syrian army (II Kings 6:18); Elymas at Paphos (Acts 13:11).

See BIBLE for Braille Scriptures and Talking-Book records.

blood is referred to hundreds of times in Scripture. Its use for food was forbidden from the earliest days of Israel (Gen. 9:4; Lev. 3:17). In the O.T. ritual, the blood of sacrificed animals was poured on altars* to atone for men's sins. Ex. 24 tells that Moses took blood from slain oxen, placed half of it on the altar, and used the balance for sprinkling worshippers, saying, "Behold the blood of the covenant which the Lord hath made with you" (Ex. 24:8). The sanctity of the human life stream of blood was early recognized in Hebrew laws against murder (Deut. 5:17), and in the system of blood-avenging. (See AVENGER.)

In the N.T. the function of the atoning blood (see ATONEMENT) of slain animals was assumed by Christ (I John 1:7). This is made clear in many N.T. passages such as: Luke 22:20; John 6:56; Rom. 5:9; Heb. 9:11–14.

Jesus used the fact that blood is essential to human life not only as a symbol, but also as a summary of his whole personality and life purpose. He said, in effect, as he poured out the wine at the Last Supper (see LORD'S SUPPER, THE): "My blood is about to be poured out as this wine is poured out" (Mark 14:23–25). The death of Christ was a "price," or "ransom" paid for others. The result of the sin and unresponsiveness of indifferent man, it revealed not only the terrific cost of sin, but showed how far God would go to reconcile sinners to Himself (John 3:16). When Jesus "poured out his soul unto death" (cf. Isa. 53:12) it cost him his own blood.

See REDEMPTION; SACRAMENTS; SIN; SALVATION.

Boanerges (bō'ă-nûr'jēz) ("sons of thunder"), Christ's appellation of James and John (only in Mark 3:17). Jerome says that it refers to their fiery eloquence; others assert that it connotes their disposition to use violence (Luke 9:52–56).

boats, water craft. The Hebrew people were not sea-minded; their natural penchant was for agriculture. The allusions of Judg. 5:17 admit of various interpretations. The coastal strips of the great marine nations, Phoenicia* and Philistia*, were out of their control. Solomon turned to sailors of Tyre* and the famous Phoenician commercial fleet of Hiram* when sending to Ezion-geber* for ore (II Chron. 8:17 f.), to Ophir for "ivory, apes, and peacocks" (II Chron. 9:21), or to the mountains of Lebanon for cedar. The ships of Tarshish, once thought to have sailed to Spanish Tartessus and to English Cornwall (for tin) at a very early date, now seem to indicate "a smeltery fleet," since excavations at Ezion-geber. Jehoshaphat, trying to imitate Solomon, made "ships of Tarshish to go to Ophir for gold: but they went not; for the ships were broken at Ezion-geber" (I Kings 22:48 f.).

Even if few Hebrews were mariners, Bible writers were aware of other men's ships. See Ps. 107:23 f., 104:26; Prov. 31:14.

Boats actually operated inside Palestine include Jordan ferryboats (II Sam. 19:18), and the "little ships" of fishermen on the Sea of Galilee, propelled by oars and sails (Mark 4:36). Christ used such small boats as these many times, not only for transportation (John 6:1, 21, 23) but also for pulpits (Luke 5:1–3). Luke, whose voyages took him across the Mediterranean to Italy, wrote the best ship's log of N.T. times (Acts 27). It supplies detailed descriptions of the appearance and equipment of the Alexandrian (see ALEXANDRIA) grain ships which plied between Egypt and Italian Puteoli* (Acts 28:13), a great wheat port. Excavated floor mosaics at the Italian port of Ostia*, near Rome, reveal such heavy sailing ships, lighthouses, and granaries as Paul saw on his Mediterranean voyages. The winter storms dreaded by sea-wise sailors were feared not only for rough waters, but because they obscured the stars by which alone navigation was possible before discovery of the compass. Paul in his Second Corinthian Letter (11:25 f.) refers to three shipwrecks and frequent "perils of waters" and "perils in the sea."

61. Boats: 1. Egyptian, 1250 B.C.; 2. Galilaean; 3. Phoenician.

Paul used wretched little coastal freighters for many stages of his missionary journeys. Acts refers to his taking a ship from Phoenicia, or for Cyprus, or returning to Antioch by boat, or landing at Tyre, or departing for Italy in the lee of Crete, or going "over the sea to Cilicia." He landed at Tyre, went on to Ptolemais, sailed from Corinth to Syria, said farewell to friends on beaches while the ship was being loaded. His observation of sailors helped him give sound advice to the crew when his Alexandrian grain ship was wrecked (Acts 27:30, 33). So sensible a passenger was Paul that the centurion, desiring to save him, ordered that none of the prisoners be slain, but allowed to swim or float on boards safe to the land.

Israel's neighbors Egypt and Mesopotamia were using river traffic at the dawn of history. Egypt's earliest boats were wooden dugouts. Prehistoric Egyptians of 4000 B.C. had lashed bundles of papyrus reeds together to make boats with upturned prows. Isaiah (18:2) refers to bulrush boats. It is known that such craft made the 100-m. trip from the Delta to Gaza in the 7th century B.C.; they were 30 ft. long or more. In Amratian times 100-ft. Egyptian ships with 8-ft. cabins and 60 oars were trading with Aegean islands for gold and obsidian. Boats resembling "two long cigars lashed together" did business in the Red Sea. In very ancient times, a regular trade by sea went on between Egypt and Phoenician Byblos (see GEBAL) in sailing boats called "Byblos travelers," because they unloaded Nile reeds for papyrus-papermaking on the Phoenician coast, and took to Egypt wines and fancy wood for furniture, for mummy cases, masts, and flagpoles. While Israel was in Egypt, flat-bottomed Nile boats such as are still doing business conveyed heavy stone for obelisks and temples for hundreds of miles (the Nile being navigable for 2,900 m.). Egyptian postage stamps today show ships of Queen Hatshepsut (1504–1482 B.C.) operating before Israel's Egyptian Exodus. They imported luxury wares from "Punt," possibly along the Red Sea.

Egyptian boats in the Biblical period were propelled by sails, oars, or poles. In some dynasties, they had deck cabins for the ladies, sheltered by awnings. The *dahabiyeh* of every rich man was luxurious after the manner of the day. Boats were used for heavy cargoes, for funeral craft, and—in very narrow, long shape—for fishing with seines. Eighteenth Dynasty ships were influenced by the designs of Syrian traders, and had central masts stayed by straddle masts. Both stern and prow turned straight up. Screens of matting were stretched along the sides to break the force of wind and spray. People alighted by a plank ladder with steps.

Bas-reliefs in Egyptian tombs give accurate views of Egypt's royal navy at war with

Philistine ships. Thutmose III, conqueror of Palestine, Syria, and Phoenicia in the 15th century B.C., commandeered cedar boats built behind the Lebanons and had them hauled on carts overland as far as the Euphrates.

Mesopotamian river traffic on the Tigris-Euphrates began in prehistoric times. Round boats of bitumen-calked basketwork, and rafts of timber floated on inflated skins, proved as satisfactory as the "guffahs" used there today. Sea-borne cargoes for Babylon were brought to the mouth of the rivers, from India via the Persian Gulf. See TIGRIS.

The last book of the Bible refers to ship captains, sailors, passengers, and traders, who saw smoke from the burning of a great city ("Babylon," Rome?) and lamented her loss (Rev. 18:2, 10, 16 ff.).

Modern Lebanon stamps show Phoenician boats of Solomon's era, with upturned prows. Carefully stamped ancient coins give excellent pictures of ships used in Bible times. Some of these show the many-oared Roman war galleys which plied E. in N.T. times.

Boaz (bō′ăz) (prob. "swiftness" or "strength"), a wealthy, land-owning, influential Bethlehemite (Ruth 2:1), with a deep concern for the welfare of his workers (Ruth 2:8 f.), and an appreciation of family obligations. Ruth, the alien, Moabitish widow of his kinsman, Mahlon, subjected Boaz to a severe moral test in which he was triumphant (3:8–12). He acquired Ruth according to the usages of the levirate marriage* (Ruth 4:1–11; Deut. 25:5–10). The narrative brings out the strong character of Boaz, shows how Hebrew marriage was a concern of the family* involving property interests, undermines the tradition against mixed marriages, and stresses the mixture of foreign blood which is in the Hebrew and Christian lineage. Boaz and Ruth were ancestors of David (Ruth 4:22), and of Jesus (Matt. 1:5; Luke 3:32).

Tell Boaz is the name of the Jerusalem Y.M.C.A. property in the Shepherds' Field below Bethlehem. It includes a large cave. Services are held there on Christmas Eve. Herodian potsherds have been found in the vicinity.

Boaz and Jachin. See JACHIN AND BOAZ.

book, a written or printed narrative or document. Many more books than the 66 in the Bible* existed in the religious and historical literature of the Hebrew people (see APOCRYPHA.) The first O.T. record of a book's being written occurs in Ex. 17:14, after the Hebrews' return from Egypt, where they saw papyrus* rolls such as had been common in the Delta region from earliest dynastic times. Materials used for records in the centuries during which the Bible developed were: clay* tablets; stone (Ex. 24:12), of which specimens dating from the 13th to the 9th centuries B.C. have been excavated; potsherds (like the Lachish* letters); papyrus paper, in long rolls; fine skins, allowing script to be written on both sides; wooden tablets covered with wax, on which a stylus wrote messages (Luke 1:63); and parchment, developed at Pergamum in Asia Minor, from the finest skins of sheep or goats. Vellum came later, made of the skins of young calves and lambs, durable and smooth. Much of the O.T. was written on skins. Torah scrolls are still so written today. Such a one was handed to Jesus to read in the Nazareth synagogue (Luke 4:17). The Dead Sea Scrolls* found at 'Ain Fashka were sheets of leather sewn together with linen thread. Metal scrolls exist.

Records of events in the reigns of Hebrew kings were listed, together with genealogies, "in the book of the kings of Israel and Judah, who were carried away to Babylon for their

62. Silver-gilt, jeweled cover of a lectionary executed at Westphalia, Germany, 13th century. Shows Christ enthroned, blessing.

transgression" (I Chron. 9:1). These chronicles narrated events beginning with the era of Rehoboam and Jeroboam and continuing through the time of Jehoiachin (II Kings 24:5).

Several books are specifically mentioned in the O.T. The book of the Covenant Code* (Ex. 20:22–23:33) is a series of civil, religious, sanitary, and humanitarian laws which developed after Israel abandoned nomadic for more settled ways. These were long attributed to Moses' transmission of the revelations he received from God. The "book of the covenant" (Ex. 24:7), read by Moses to the children of Israel, is now thought to be only one of seven distinct codes of law within the Pentateuch*, material which is based upon documents known as J, E, JE, D, RD, P—written between c. 850 and c. 400 B.C. (See SOURCES.) The lost "book of the law," found by the high priest Hilkiah in the collection box during Temple repairs at Jerusalem in 622 B.C. and read to the people (II Kings 22–23) by King Josiah, was probably not the Pentateuch, but Deuteronomy (possibly Deut. 5–26 and 28). "The Book of the Law of Moses" which Ezra read to the great assembly of Hebrews at Jerusalem after the Return (Neh. 8) was actually the Pentateuch—the Mosaic Law as expanded by scribes, lawyers, and priests during the Exile at Babylon.

Some books now lost are mentioned in Scripture: "the book of the wars of the Lord" (Num. 21:14); "the book of Jasher"* (Josh. 10:13; II Sam. 1:18); the "book of Shemaiah the prophet, and the book of Iddo the Seer" (II Chron. 12:15). Vivid, lively quotations from writings now lost forever freshen many a tedious narrative. Evidently memoirs of Jesus are intended by Luke 1:1—"sayings" which found their way into the earliest written narratives.

Writing was not always done by authors. Scribes* were employed in Palestine, Egypt, and Babylonia. Such a scribe was Baruch.

The Book of Life, believed to be kept by God (Dan. 12:1 ff.; Ps. 69:28) grew out of a concept indicating a list of those who would partake of the joys of the Messianic Age (see MESSIAH). Several N.T. allusions refer to the books of those who will inherit eternal life (Luke 10:20; Phil. 4:3; Heb. 12:23; Rev. 3:5). The "Lamb's book of life" lists the inhabitants of the heavenly Jerusalem (Rev. 21:27).

Of ancient Egyptian books, religious works are the most numerous. These were written in hieroglyphic pictograms; or the more cursive hieratic script, on papyrus rolls; or were chiseled on stone. The three most famous collections known today are the "Pyramid* Texts," the "Coffin Texts," and the "Book of the Dead," all of which contain magical (see MAGIC) formulae and instructions for reaching the hereafter. The first of these three was written in the Old Kingdom (c. 2700–2200 B.C.); the second, during the Middle Kingdom (c. 1991–1786 B.C.); the third in the New Kingdom (c. 1570–1065 B.C.). Egyptians produced rich Wisdom Literature strikingly similar to portions of the Hebrew Proverbs and the Apocryphal Book of Sirach. One of these was compiled by Amen-em-ope, the "Scribe of the Granary of Egypt." Another was "The Maxims of Ptah-hotep."

See WRITING.

booth, a leafy structure made of branches by a farmer, so that he could rest in its shade while drinking water from his earthen or skin bottle as he ate his noon meal, and at the

63. Vine-dresser's booth overlooking Plain of Esdraelon.

same time keep a watchful eye on his crops. In harvest time, booths in fields and vineyards were occupied even at night by some member of the family. Jonah built a booth at Nineveh (Jon. 4:5).

Booths, Feast of, celebrated by the Hebrews for eight days during the great autumn agricultural festival of thanksgiving, following Lev. 23:39–44, starting on the 15th day of the 7th month. They re-enacted the time when they came up from Egypt and lived in leafy tents or booths, and gathered "boughs of thick trees, and willows of the brook," and erected booths—usually on their roof tops. This custom, influenced by an old Canaanite (see CANAAN) agricultural harvest festival, took on new meaning when revived after the Return from the Babylonian Exile (Neh. 8:13–18, describing its first observance since their restoration to their homeland). The Feast of Booths was also called the Feast of Tabernacles and Sukkoth*, and was the most popular and joyful of Jewish festivals. At a Feast of Tabernacles Solomon dedicated his Temple. See FEASTS.

bottles. (1) Skin bottles, prepared by removing whole hides from kids, goats, cows, or buffaloes, and drying them slowly. A small skin bottle is implied in Gen. 21:14 and in

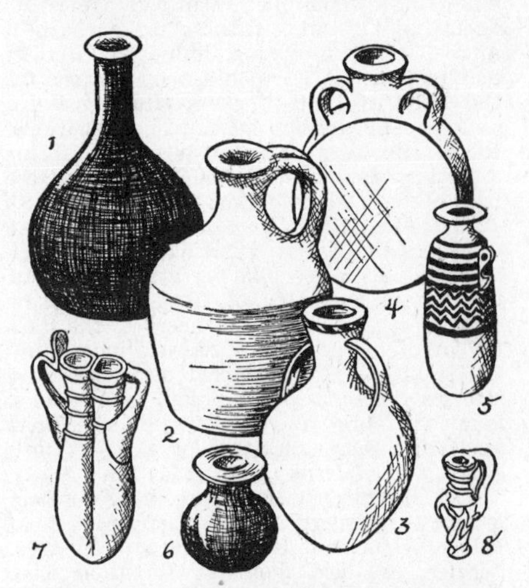

64. Bottles: 1. Egyptian, 1800 B.C.; 2. Palestinian, c. 1600 B.C.; 3. Egyptian, 1580 B.C.; 4. Persian, 500 B.C.; 5. Greek, 500 B.C.; 6. Roman, 300 B.C.; 7. Ink bottle; 8. Egyptian tear bottle.

Josh. 9:4. The image of the wine bottle which bursts when new wine gases work was used in the O.T. (Job 32:19), and was employed by three Gospel authors to record Christ's parable of new wine in old skins (Matt. 9:17; Mark 2:22; Luke 5:37). Skin bottles are still used in the streets of Jerusalem by men dispensing cups of water during droughts, or selling rose water and licorice beverages in summer. Fountains in the Jerusalem Temple Area are surrounded by men and children filling their skin bags. The skin bottle was also used to "bring" butter, by tossing milk back and forth until it thickened, when it was removed and boiled or melted into the honey-like winter butter or the oily summer variety. Egyptians, Greeks, and Romans all used skin bottles. (2) Earthen bottles, so easily broken that their shards remain our best evidence for dating periods of time, are referred to in

Isa. 30:14 and Jer. 48:12. Tear bottles, sometimes of decorated glass, were cherished in Egypt and Palestine (Ps. 56:8); these, containing tears of the bereaved, were placed in tombs.

boundary stones, like ancient landmarks*, were deemed important in the Near East of the Biblical period; especially in agricultural Babylonia, where demarcation of fields flooded by irrigation canals was important to the wealthy farmers, attention was given to substantial boundary stones. One of these, surviving from the era of Nebuchadnezzar I, was excavated at Nippur and is in the University Museum at Philadelphia.

65. Boundary stone of Nebuchadnezzar I.

bow. See ARCHERS; WEAPONS.

bowl, a round dish, often shallow, used to contain liquids, as wine, broth, or water. (1) Bowls were part of the altar equipment in the Tabernacle and the Temple, used to convey libations or oblations (Ex. 25:29; Num. 7:79). Zechariah wrote of "bowls before the altar" (14:20). Such bowls, sometimes fashioned of gold or of silver, were among the first treasures seized by invaders of temple areas, like Jerusalem's (Jer. 52:19). (2) Bowls formed the upper part of the seven-

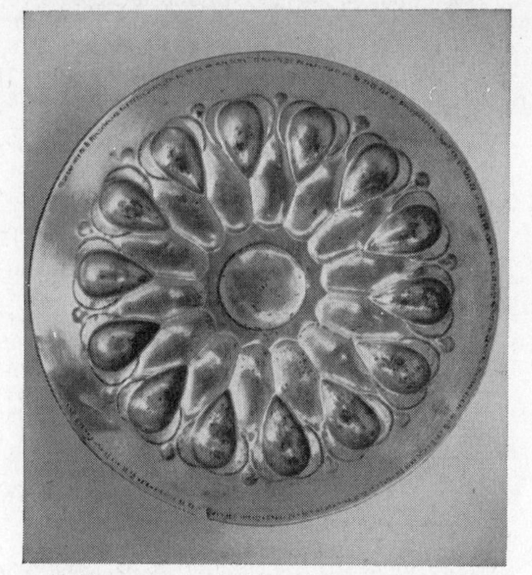

66. Silver wine bowl of Iran Achaemenian period. Engraved inscription reads, "Made for Artaxerxes I" (462–424 B.C.).

branched candlesticks (Zech. 4:2 f.) and of the capitals of the Temple pillars (I Kings 7:41) (See TEMPLE, illus. 421). (3) Bowls of ordinary pottery were used for water (Judg. 6:38) or for serving the family's juicy foods. (4) Costly silver bowls, sometimes ornamented around their edge with cuneiform writing, like the recovered one of Artaxerxes I, were used for wine vessels at banquets (see Amos 6:6). Fine bowls were often presented with oblations by tribute-bearing prisoners. See CUP.

Bozrah (bŏz′ rȧ) ("fortress, sheepfold"). (1) The home of King Jobab of Edom* (Gen. 36:33; I Chron. 1:44). Israel's prophets announced its destruction (Isa. 34:6; Jer. 49:13, 22; Amos 1:12). It appears to have been noted for its sheep (Mic. 2:12, A.V.), and possibly its weaving and dyeing industry (Isa. 63:1–3). Bozrah was the northern metropolis of Edom (c. 1200–700 B.C.) and later of the Nabataean Kingdom (see NABATAEA) (c. 100 B.C.–A.D. 100). It is identified with Buseirah, in Jordan, c. 35 m. N. of Petra, along the "King's Highway" which runs the length of the Transjordanian highlands. Many sections of this road as it existed during the Roman period are still intact. Bozrah during the era of the Constantines was the seat of a Christian bishopric.

(2) A city in Moab (Jer. 48:24), possibly to be identified with the Levitical city Bezer of the tribe of Reuben (Deut. 4:43; Josh. 20:8; 21:36), the latter identified with Umm el-'Amad 12 m. S. of 'Amman. (3) A town in Gilead (I Macc. 5:26, 28), also known as Bosora, or Bostra, in the Hauran. An oasis city and trading post on the edge of the Syrian desert, possibly modern Busra eski-Sham, c. 60 m. E. of Beth-shan.

bracelets, of iron, gold, or silver, often with inset gems, were popular among both sexes. They were worn on the wrists or upper arms. Many splendid examples from Bible times have been excavated and are in museums. Bracelets worn by Ashurnasirpal of Assyria, Esarhaddon, Tiglath-pileser, and the Assyrian god Shamash are well-known from carved reliefs. (See Gen. 24:22 for Rebekah's bracelets.) Bracelets were sacrificed to make Taber-

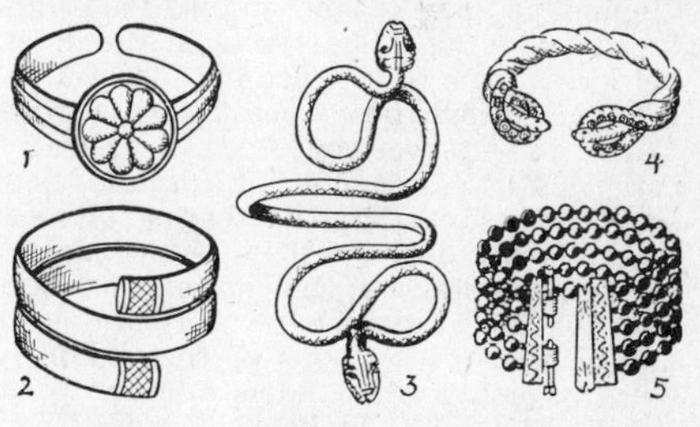

67. Bracelets: 1. Assyrian, 885–856 B.C.; 2. Assyrian, 772–705 B.C.; 3. Egyptian, 332–30 B.C.; 4. Phoenician; 5. Silver link.

nacle vessels (Num. 31:50). These may have been acquired in Egypt—ever the source of coveted bracelets (Ex. 12:35 f.). The usual type of ancient clasp was a pin which slipped between hinges.

brambles appear in Scripture under different names (see THORNS). The bramble in Jotham's fable (Judg. 9:7–15) may have been a boxthorn, or some other prickly plant ubiquitous in Palestine, and used for hedges, fuel, and food for camels and goats.

See the allusion of Jesus to brambles (Luke 6:44).

brass, a malleable, long-lasting metal alloy consisting basically of copper and zinc, used erroneously in some versions, like the A.V. and the A.S.V., in passages which should read "bronze," as in Ex. 38:3 ff., describing Tabernacle equipment, and I Sam. 17:5, the mail of Goliath. Solomon had access to vast quantities of copper from his Arabah mines. His Temple was equipped with articles made of bronze. (See Moffatt in such passages as II Chron. 4.) There is only one Heb. word for "copper" and "bronze."

bray, to pound or crush, as with a mortar and pestle (Job 30:7; Prov. 27:22).

bread in Bible lands was the minimum for human subsistence (Isa. 3:1). It was made of wheat or barley ground with mortar and pestle or on a saddle-shaped quern or between two revolving stones at the tent or house door or between the miller's larger stones, and was baked daily or several times a day. (See Luke 11:3. For methods of preparation see BAKER; MILL.) Bread was sometimes leavened (Matt. 13:33; 16:6). The round, pancake-like loaves were so pliable that they could be bent spoon-shape for

68. Bread baking, Palestine.

dipping up gravies and juices. Palestinian bread loaves look like stones in the desert, hence the logic of the Temptation of Jesus: "Command that these stones be made bread" (Matt. 4:3). It was convenient for a man to carry his loaves in his fabric girdle. Some scholars suggest that the sharing of men's travel supply of bread may be one explanation of the miracle of the loaves and fishes—men beholding a small boy's sacrifice of bread and being moved to open up their supply at Christ's prayer of confidence (Mark 6:41). When grain failed in Palestine and Jacob's sons went searching it in prolific Egypt, they were given by Joseph a gift including bread, to carry back to his father (Gen. 45:23). Bread was always a popular gift in Palestine (Gen. 14:18; Judg. 19:19; I Sam. 16:20; II Sam. 16:1). It found its way into many famous Hebrew proverbs (see Prov. 20:17, 28:19, 31:27; Eccles. 11:1). Christ climaxed all proverbial wisdom concerning bread when he said, "Man shall not live by bread alone" (Matt. 4:4); and made one of his greatest identifications of himself as "the bread of life" (John 6:48–51). O.T. miraculous supplies of bread include the Wilderness manna (Ex. 16:4 ff.); Elisha and the man of Baal-shalisha (II Kings 4:42–44); the supply brought to Elijah in the wilderness near the brook Cherith (I Kings 17:6). Paul in his First Corinthian Letter (5:6, 8) spoke figuratively of "a little leaven" leavening the whole lump, and of "the unleavened bread of sincerity." The symbolism of bread reached its highest point during Christ's Last Supper with his Disciples (I Cor. 11:24). See LEAVEN; PASSOVER.

breastplate. (1) The front panel of a soldier's cuirass. In early Bible times it was made of leather. In Roman times, a soldier's breastplate was a tough leather jacket padded at the shoulders, or made of metal, or formed of two broad plates for back and breast respectively. Royal armor, as revealed by the marble torso of Emperor Hadrian excavated in the agora of Athens, was metal, embossed with mythological figures. (2) The breastplate of righteousness (*hoshen*) was part of the Hebrew high priest's vestment, worn over his ephod* (Ex. 28:13–30, 39:8–21), especially when he entered the most high sanctuary at New Year's—after the manner of Babylonian priests. This pectoral was of the same material as the ephod, fine gold, blue, purple, and scarlet hand-loomed textile, trimmed with four rows of three jewels, each having carved upon it the name of one of the Twelve Tribes of the Children of Israel, as well as the names of Abraham, Isaac, and Jacob. The back of the breastplate was fastened to the front with gold rings, chains, and blue lacers of the woven bands (Ex. 28:22 ff.). The jewels included sardius for Reuben, topaz for Simeon, carbuncle for Judah, emerald for Dan, sapphire (? lapis lazuli) for Naphtali, diamond (crystal) for Gad, ligure for Asher, agate for Issachar, amethyst for Zebulun, beryl for Benjamin, onyx for Manasseh, jasper for Ephraim. Identification of these stones, and their order, is speculative. But their symbolism (see SYMBOL) denotes the priest's carrying upon his heart the names of the Children of Israel. Other references to breastplates are found in Isa. 59:17; Eph. 6:14; I Thess. 5:8; Rev. 9:9.

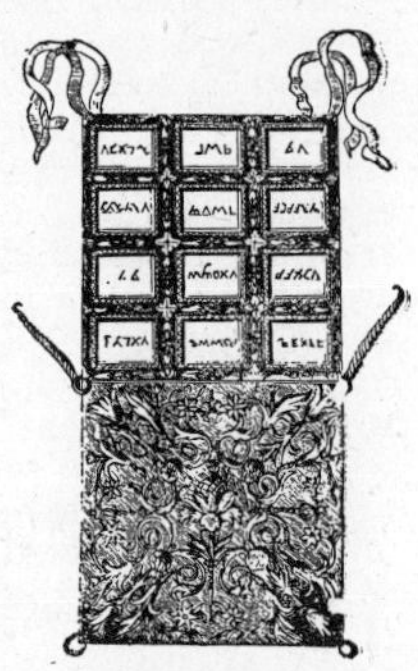

69. High priest's breastplate.

In a pouch behind the breastplate of righteousness, and resting on the breast of the high priest while he was officiating, were the enigmatic Urim* and Thummim, believed by many to have oracular powers—more formal than real. The Urim and Thummim described in the P Code as worn (in the second Temple) after the Exile are to be distinguished from those worn in the pre-Exilic period, when they had no connection with the high priest's breastplate.

brick, made of native clay mixed with water and kneaded by thorough foot-treading, was shaped in molds into oblong or square units, sometimes measuring as much as 21x10x4 in. or 16x16x5 in. It was originally baked in the sun, but early Babylonian brick (Gen.

70. Sun-dried brick stamped with name of Ramesses II (c. 1301–1234 B.C.). Made of Nile mud mixed with straw and sand, shaped in wooden mold, stamped while soft, and dried in sun. Found in wall of the Ramesseum, great Mortuary Temple at Thebes.

11:3) was apparently kiln-fired. When brick was bound by mixing straw with the clay to prevent cracking, sun-drying was essential. Mud or "slime" (probably bitumen in Mesopotamia) was used for mortar. Sometimes houses and shrines of mud brick literally dissolved in prolonged rains. Again, vestiges of cities of sun-dried bricks have outlived 30 centuries, as at Ezion-geber*, called the "City of Bricks with Straw." Great skill was developed by bricklayers in Bible times. Rows of headers and stretchers were often laid in intricate patterns. Houses (see HOUSE) of the period of Abraham at Ur have been found, having lower walls of burnt brick and upper portions of sun-dried units, with the change in material hidden by application of plaster or whitewash to the two-story dwelling. Rulers often had their brickmakers stamp the royal marks on the still wet mud. Nebuchadnezzar's bricks are often found in peasant huts near the ruins of his magnificent capital. Isaiah voiced the orthodox Hebrew protest against those who used brick instead of native stone for altars (65:3). When David wished to impose punishment upon captive towns, he compelled citizens to "pass through the brickkiln" (II Sam. 12:31), as his Hebrew ancestors had long been forced to do in Egypt (Ex. 5) where their output of brick was used in the vast public works of the pharaohs, like the store-cities. See RAAMSES (Tanis).

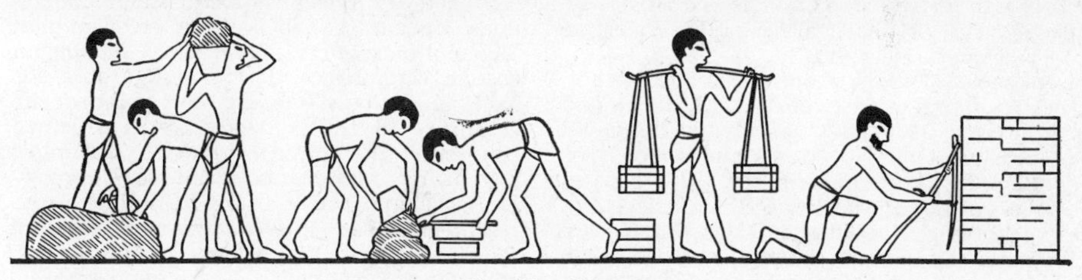

71. Brickmaking.

bride, bridegroom. See MARRIAGE; WEDDING.

bridge, a structure erected over a stream, depression, or chasm, to carry a roadway for pedestrians, vehicles, and other traffic. Only masonry bridges were used, and those in late Bible times. The approved way of crossing streams was by fords (Judg. 3:28) and by ferries (II Sam. 19:18). Ruins of stone bridges constructed by Roman engineers survive, like the one N. of Dog River near Beirut, Lebanon, along the highway over which warriors marched for centuries.

An ancient vestige of the type of bridge which spans a chasm can be seen today in Robinson's Arch, adjoining the W. wall of the Temple Area at Jerusalem. This fragment was once the E. head of a bridge of masonry spanning the 350 ft. of the Tyropoeon Valley between the hill Zion and the Temple Area on Mt. Moriah. John Hyrcanus (134–104 B.C.), one of the Hasmonaean Dynasty, built a palace in Zion, and because the Hasmonaeans were both kings and priests, he constructed a bridge to connect palace and

72. Tyropoeon Bridge, showing "Robinson's Arch" (after restoration by J. E. Hanauer).

Temple. Eight spans of 42 ft. each arched the valley. During the siege by Pompey (63 B.C.) the adherents of Aristobulus retreated from Zion into the Temple, breaking down the bridge behind them. Under Herod the bridge was reconstructed. Without a doubt Jesus used this short cut into the Temple Area. Edward Robinson (1794–1863) discovered the arch fragment which now bears his name (see JERUSALEM, illus. 212). Another venerable bridge, fragments of which have been excavated, was N. of the one just described, known as "Wilson's Arch."

brigandine, armor consisting of overlapping metal plates fastened to leather, linen, or some other fabric (Jer. 51:3).

broad places, protected areas c. 30 ft. square, formed by the extension of one segment of city wall (see WALLS) beyond another, usually near a guardroom or tower. Rulers, religious leaders, and people met in broad places to conduct local business (Jer. 5:1; Lam. 5:14; I Sam. 9:18).

Bronze Age, an era characterized by the extensive use of bronze, extending roughly from the Chalcolithic Age (copper [or bronze]-[and]-stone), c. 4000–3300 B.C., to the Iron Age (began c. 1200 B.C.). Simple subdivisions of the Bronze Age, during which was made a great variety of pottery* whose excavation in abandoned mounds E. and W. of the Jordan helps identify Biblical sites and establish their dates, are as follows:

Early Bronze (first historical era) c. 3300–2000 B.C.

Middle Bronze (called by G. E. Wright "The World between the Ages of Abraham and David") c. 2000–1500 B.C.

Late Bronze (during which Palestine was controlled by Egypt, and the first wave of the Hebrew Conquest of Canaan took place) c. 1500–1200 B.C.

(See also W. F. Albright's Bronze Age date chart, p. 84, *The Archaeology of Palestine*, Pelican Books.)

"Bronze" may be the correct translation of the word "brass," used in II Chron. 4 in connection with the furnishing of the Jerusalem Temple. Some scholars prefer "brass."

Excavations, as at Tell Beit Mirsim, Shechem*, and Tell el-'Ajjûl*, have made Bronze Age Palestine, Syria, and peripheral areas as well known as the Iron Age was a few years ago.

brook, a small stream of water which in Palestine characteristically dries up in summer and floods in winter. Some are narrow and gentle (Ps. 42:1); others rush between stony banks and halt at pools where shepherds graze sheep. Some of the famous brooks of the Bible are: the Kidron*, flowing at the foot of the Mount of Olives below the Jerusalem wall (I Kings 15:13; John 18:1); the Cherith* (I Kings 17:3); and the Wâdī Nimrim* (Isa. 15:6). The Brook of Egypt (Gen. 15:18; Ezek. 47:19) is the tiny river (today the Arish) separating SW. Palestine from Egypt. See WADI.

brothers. (1) Sons of one father and mother, like Cain and Abel (Gen. 4:1 f.), Jacob and Esau (Gen. 25:24–26), Joseph and Benjamin (Gen. 30:25, 35:18), Moses and Aaron (Ex. 2:10, 4:14), Peter and Andrew (Matt. 4:18), James and John (Matt. 4:21; Mark 1:19). The "brethren" of Jesus (Matt. 13:55) are believed by some students to have been younger sons of Mary and Joseph, by others to have been sons of Joseph by a former marriage, or cousins of Jesus (sons of Mary of Clopas and Alphaeus). At any rate, they were critical of the early ministry of Jesus (John 7:3–5), though James later became prominent in the leadership of the Jerusalem Church and a martyr in Christ's cause. Jesus once minimized the blood relationship of his brothers (Mark 3:35). After the Resurrection the brothers of Jesus, together with Mary his mother, continued "in prayer and supplication" with the Disciples at Jerusalem (Acts 1:14). (2) The term "brother" was used of coreligionists, like Ananias, who addressed Saul as his brother (Acts 9:17). (3) Men who were cousins referred to each other as brothers, like Abraham and Lot (Gen. 14:16).

Bul (bōōl), the ancient Heb. name of the 8th month (I Kings 6:38), the same as Marchesvan (Oct.–Nov.). It was known as "the rainy month."

bull, an animal prominent throughout Near East mythology. Egypt had many local divinities in this animal form, including the apis bull at Memphis known to the Hebrews. Begotten, it was believed, by a ray of sunlight which descended from heaven and impregnated a cow, this black and white spotted bull calf, with a white triangle on its forehead and a crescent moon on its right side, had priests assigned to it as far back as the Old Kingdom (c. 2700–2200 B.C.). The theological importance of Memphis made this bull cult very strong. The opposition of Moses to the golden calf was an effort to rid Israel of contaminating Egyptian mythology (Ex. 32:1–24). Winged bulls were conspicuous in Babylonian art.

The bull was a popular symbol of fecundity and worship in Canaanite mythology. One of the names for El, the generic Canaanite word for God, was "father bull." The fluid state of Canaanite mythology led to many confusing references, viz.: bulls fighting among themselves and mating with other symbolic but lesser deities, the birth of the bull calf, etc.

In the Canaanite, early Hebrew, and Arab calendars, the grouping of twelve oxen (sterilized bulls) in four groups of three each, represents the four seasons of the year. The bull supports as bases for figures, sacred objects, thrones, beds, etc. were popular in the Early Iron Age (c. 1200–1000 B.C.). In spite of the Second Commandment (Ex. 20:4 f.), the bull and other "likenesses" found their way into Israelitish architecture. Under Solomon, during the building of the Temple, a paganizing movement took place when, encouraged by Phoenician craftsmen, indigenous Canaanite beliefs were incorporated. The molten sea* (I Kings 7:23–26) had pagan cosmic significance, for it rested upon 12 oxen, in groups of 3 facing the 4 points of the compass. In the N. Jeroboam I tried to counteract the political influence of the new Temple by founding two shrines to Yahweh—at Bethel and Dan—where Yahweh was represented as an unseen presence standing upon a young bull (I Kings 12:26–33). This syncretism furnished the text for many sermons by Hebrew prophets.

The bullock, like the ox, was a young castrated bovine used in Hebrew burnt offerings from early times (Ex. 29:1). There may be traces of bull worship in the horns attached to some altars (see ALTAR) (Ex. 27:2). See TEMPLE, illus. 423.

Bulls of Bashan (Ps. 22:12) were famous. They were raised in the rich land E. of the Sea of Galilee.

See CALF.

burden. (1) A literal load of heavy weight (Jer. 17:21 f.). The burden bearer or porter in Bible lands today (called *hammâl*) is one of the most underprivileged members of the community. (See Christ's invitation, Matt.

11:28–30.) The objective burden came to mean a load of heavy spiritual responsibility, as in Ps. 55:22; Gal. 6:2, 5. (2) An oral prophecy, oracle, or utterance, often foretelling doom; as the "burden of Moab" (Isa. 15:1), the "burden of Damascus" (Isa. 17:1), "the burden of Nineveh" (Nah. 1:1). Such oracles are often accompanied by the name of a specific seer, like Isaiah, or Nahum the Elkoshite.

burial, according to Hebrew law, followed as soon as possible after death, at least within 24 hours. This was a sanitary precaution in hot Eastern climates, and was also a safeguard against violating the law of cleanness by touching the corpse (Num. 19:11–14). Provision for prompt burial is indicated in the narratives of Sarah (Gen. 23) and of Rachel (Gen. 35:19 f.). The burial of Deborah, nurse of Rebekah, under an oak at Bethel (Gen. 35:8), suggests the custom of placing graves under trees, which became sacred shrines, as are the *welys* of Moslems. Prompt burial is usual in Palestine today.

In ancient Palestine coffins were not generally used, but bodies were placed in open graves and covered with stones to prevent marauding by jackals and wolves, or in caves or shafts, as at Megiddo. Joseph's being placed in a coffin in Egypt (Gen. 50:26) is as exceptional as his and Jacob's being embalmed (Gen. 50:2 f.); embalming was done by physicians.

Some of the oldest burials traced thus far in Palestine were in the caves of Mt. Carmel. There, at Mughâret el-Wâd, skeletons of Natufian men and women who lived 10,000 years ago were found lying on their backs in extended positions, or lying in groups in tightly flexed positions, with knees under chins. Many wore bone or shell pendants and dentellium caps. At Teleilât el-Ghassûl infants who died several thousand years ago were found buried in jars. The jar burial of adults is indicated by a skeleton found at Tell Judeideh, Turkey (500–300 B.C.).

In N.T. times the body, washed, anointed with aromatic unguents, and treated with spices (John 19:39, 11:11–18), was wrapped in linen (Mark 16:1), and a bandage or napkin placed over the face (Luke 23:53). Professional wailers were hired to amplify the mourning of relatives (Mark 5:38). Such mourners—often blind singers—sit today at city gates waiting for employment. Egyptians brought gifts of food to the deceased, but Jews did not.

Throughout Bible times, rocky hillsides were favorite burial places. (See MACHPELAH Cave, a family sepulcher.) The numerous large burial chambers found in levels at Beth-shan have revealed facts and dates of Hebrew history. Both Canaanites and Hebrews were buried with implements or vessels deemed useful for their future life. Early Bronze graves in the Kidron Valley hillside below Jerusalem walls have suggested that this city, and not Damascus, is the world's oldest city with continuous occupation. Pious Jews for many centuries have wished to be buried there, because they believed the Messiah* would appear on earth at that place.

The rock-hewn garden tomb which Joseph* of Arimathaea used for Jesus is typical of a 1st-century burial place. It had a rolling stone placed against its entrance (Mark 16:3, 4), as did the cave tomb of Lazarus at Bethany (John 11:38 f.). The Tombs of the Hebrew Kings have not yet been found at Jerusalem, but are probably in a Kidron Valley hillside of the sacred city. Monumental tombs, like the "Tomb of St. James" in

73. The Pyramids of Gizeh. Left to right: The Pyramid of Mycerinus (or Menkaure), the Pyramid of Chephren (or Khafre), the Great Pyramid of Cheops (or Khufu).

the Kidron at the foot of the Mount of Olives, erected in the time of Herod the Great, were seen by Jesus, and may have suggested his words about "whited sepulchres" (Matt. 23:27). The "Tomb of Absalom" is considered a funerary monument associated with the "Tomb of Jehoshaphat." The façades of these structures have much in common with the mausolea hewn in cliffs at Nabataean Petra.

Anthropoid sarcophagi, resembling Egyptian mummy cases but having beautiful Hellenistic faces (5th to 4th century B.C.), have been found at Beth-shan and in the hills near Sidon. Tremendous and elegant stone sarcophagi have come down from antiquity—like that of Ahiram of Byblos (11th century B.C.), and the famous carved sarcophagus of a general of Alexander the Great in Istanbul.

"The painted tombs" of Marisa (Mareshah) date from the 3d century B.C. They were cut in limestone for executives of a colony from Sidon. Sometimes Hebrews were buried in their own homes, like the prophet Samuel (I Sam. 25:1); Joab (I Kings 2:34); and Manasseh (II Kings 21:18). Devout Jews, like Nehemiah in Babylon, yearned to return to the city of their fathers' sepulchers (2:5). Joseph begged his Pharaoh to let him take Jacob to Palestine for burial (Gen. 50).

Cremation, practiced in the early 4th millennium B.C. in some quarters of the Near East, was virtually unknown among Hebrews until N.T. times, except in unusual circumstances (cf. Amos 2:1 f.). Greeks burned the bodies of their dead, and deposited the ashes in graceful urns or under stelae (tall tablets). Cremation was used also by the Romans, who deposited the ashes in box-like repositories placed in columbaria at the edge of cities; or in elaborate tombs, such as the mausolea along Rome's old Appian Way or Pompeii's Via dei Sepolcri. The earliest Christian burials at Rome were in underground passages known as catacombs.

Ossuaries*, or small boxes of stone or baked clay, sometimes inscribed, have been found in N.T. Palestine. Into these the burned bones of families buried in hill chambers were gathered.

Other types of burial found in Palestine and Jordan include deep shaft-tunnels of Jericho's Bronze Age dug into Wilderness Wall; ancient cairns in Sinai, used by nomads; dolmen construction of stone slabs set up to form open-air chambers (c. 6000–4500 B.C.); and the clay bone-boxes in the form of houses on stilts, found in a cave near the Plain of Sharon.

Babylonians and Egyptians alike made elaborate preparations for burial. Future life depended on preservation of the body; ease was attained through material objects placed in the graves—little figures of servants or even living servants being buried with their royal masters, as in tombs of the First Dynasty at Ur. Egyptian tomb walls were painted or carved with scenes depicting conditions desired in future life. In old Egypt, tombs were simple trenches with flat stones

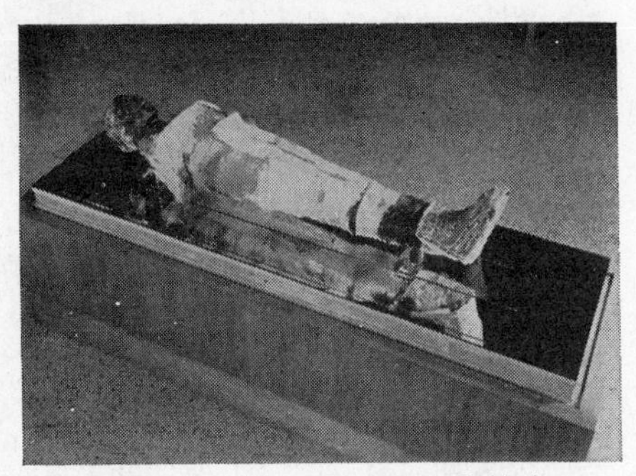

74. Partially unwrapped mummy of elderly woman of 7th century B.C. or later.

(*mastaba*) placed over them, with space left for offerings of food and drink. When several *mastabas* were placed one on top of another, a stepped pyramid resulted. At Sakkara a Second Dynasty pyramid has been found that is 6,500 years old and considered the world's oldest stone structure. From stepped pyramids the square-based, perfect pyramidal forms developed, like those at Gizeh, whose three Great Pyramids of the Fourth Dynasty were among the wonders of the ancient world. The Great Pyramid covers 13.1 acres, and is built of 2,300,000 blocks of stone, each weighing on an average of about 2½ tons. It is 481.4 ft. high, and the sides of its bases measure: N., 755.43 ft.; S., 756.08 ft.; E., 755.88 ft.; W., 755.77 ft. The Pyramid itself was part of an elaborate tomb-complex, which typically included a mortuary temple, a valley building, a causeway, enclosure walls, and accessory structures. It was built of huge blocks of native stone which must have required 100,000 men per year to quarry, transport, and elevate into place. For authoritative information see *The Pyramids of Egypt*, by I. E. S. Edwards, Pelican Books, and detailed reports of George A. Reisner's study of the Gizeh Pyramid area.

Among the maze of corridors and chambers far within the pyramid mummified bodies of royalty were placed. Mummification, including embalming, was an elaborate process, requiring 70 days for removal of the viscera (except the heart) to canopic or animal-headed jars, removal of the brains, and insertion of resinous paste and linen to enable the body to retain its shape. The body was wrapped in linen sheets that were wound lengthwise and crosswise and attached with linen bandages and cords. After the last wrappings were attached, often a gorgeous flat necklace and a heart scarab were put over the chest of the deceased. These scarabs have helped date royal mummies. The mummified body was placed in a cartonnage, usually decorated with sacred eyes, the keys of life (*ankhs*), and other indigenous symbols. The face of the deceased was painted on the cartonnage, for identification. After the era of the Ptolemies the anthropoid or human-headed coffin developed.

Sometimes, as in the case of Tut-ankh-amun, a series of coffins of fine metal, including one of solid gold inlaid with lapis lazuli and carnelian, were used. In the New Kingdom to which this monarch belonged, rock-cut tombs in the remote Valley of the Kings provided the cemetery.

In the "land between the rivers" early graves were in underground passages, as at Ur*. Later Babylonians cremated their dead and placed the ashes in elaborate funerary urns. The tombs of seven of the nine great kings of Persia have been identified in rock hills behind Persepolis—all bearing historic inscriptions. The tomb of Cyrus of Persia (II Chron. 36:22, 23) is an extant, free standing, small stone structure near his palace at Pasargadae NE. of Persepolis. Persian-level tombs excavated in Palestine have often proved very rich.

Poor strangers of Bible lands were usually buried in areas outside the city, on ground useless for other purposes. The potters' field at Athens—the *kerameikós*—was where pottery makers found their materials, as in Jerusalem and other Biblical cities (Matt. 27:3–10).

E. L. Sukenik of Jerusalem became the leading authority on Jewish tombs. His research doubled the number of known tomb inscriptions from c. 30 B.C. to A.D. 70.

For light on early Christian burials at Rome, see *BA*, Vol. XII, No. 1, "Recent Excavations Underneath the Vatican Crypts," by Roger T. O'Callaghan, S. J.

See EMBALMING; IMMORTALITY; MUMMIFICATION; RESURRECTION.

burnt offerings. See WORSHIP.

business customs current in Bible times are revealed in numerous Scripture passages. Many transactions took place in connection with the administration of wealthy temples and industries conducted for their maintenance by priests and priestesses.

One of the big businesses among Hebrews

at Jerusalem was the building and maintenance of the Temple* (see II Kings 12).

Egypt, with whom Solomon traded his horses, had proverbially rich bazaars, granaries, and store-cities (see CITIES) stocked with the fabulous yields of inundated Nile Delta fields—granaries whose scribes kept meticulous business records. Joseph the Hebrew overseer was a unit in this business (Gen. 41). Caravansaries (see CARAVAN) of the entire Middle East were constantly receiving and distributing wares from both Mesopotamia and Egypt. Ezekiel (27) gave a graphic inventory of exports and imports of Tyre. John of Patmos referred to Rome (under the guise of "Babylon") as having merchants who were princes of the earth. In the era of Abraham Babylonian traders were traveling merchants who peddled not only their wares but their language and their gods. Countless recovered clay* business records reveal great Babylonian mercantile families, such as the Egibi. The Hebrew prophet Nahum (3:16) said that in Sennacherib's Assyrian capital merchants were more numerous than "the stars of heaven." Phoenicians plied cargo boats between Byblos (see GEBAL) and Egypt from at least 2500 B.C. Their system of numbers (later adapted by the Greeks) may have developed from sales records scribbled on Mediterranean sands.

Women played prominent roles in the business of Bible lands (see Prov. 31:14, 24). The noted Egyptian Queen Hatshepsut, who ruled Egypt in the 15th century B.C., dispatched trading expeditions to Punt—possibly to tropical East Africa. Lydia (Acts 16) was a seller of the purple-dyed cloth for which Thyatira was noted. Prisca, wife of Paul's colleague Aquila, not only produced but also sold cloth.

Jesus was aware of the business transacted under his eyes in busy Capernaum and other shore towns of Galilee, and drew many keen deductions about 1st-century trade practices. Some of these he incorporated into his parables (see PARABLE), as in Matt. 13:46, 22:5. In his Parable of the Talents Jesus probably had in mind a wholesale merchant departing on an extensive business trip (Matt. 25:14–30). Luke 16:1–8 gives a parable of a steward who worked on commission and mismanaged his employer's affairs.

Interesting business procedures of O.T. times are indicated by Deut. 25:7–10; Ruth 4:7; Neh. 5:6–13; and Jer. 32:6–15.

One of the most famous mercantile contracts of the Bible was that arranged between Solomon and King Hiram* of Tyre. Hiram agreed to send Solomon cedar and fir for the construction of the Temple at Jerusalem in return for 20,000 cor of wheat every year for his vast royal household, and 20 cor of pure high-grade oil beaten from choice olives grown in Palestine (one cor equalled c. 11⅔ bu.). That 20-year business contract between the two kings provided also for close collaboration among their workmen (I Kings 5:18). Solomon also became a copper magnate, with a smelting and refining center at Ezion-geber and a long string of smelting centers down the great desert rift of the Wâdī Arabah. Solomon built ships at Ezion-geber, "and Hiram sent in the navy his servants, shipmen that had knowledge of the sea, with the servants of Solomon" (I Kings 9:27). Glueck cites amazing evidence of the shipping activities at Solomon's seaport. Large copper and iron nails were excavated by his expedition from the 3d and 4th layers of towns on this site, pointing to the fact that each succeeding settlement here went in for boatbuilding. Pitch for calking and fragments of thick ropes used only in boats have also come to light.

See CUNEIFORM; DEBT; INTEREST; USURY.

butter. See FOOD; BOTTLES.

Byblos. See GEBAL.

C

cab, a Heb. unit of dry measure, approximately equal to two quarts (A.V. II Kings 6:25); see "kab" (R.S.V.).

Caesar (sē′zĕr), the family name of Gaius Julius Caesar, his grandnephew Octavian, later Emperor Augustus Caesar, and of the four succeeding emperors. The Caesars referred to in the N.T. are: (1) Augustus* (Luke 2:1); (2) Tiberius* (Luke 3:1; Mark 12:14); (3) Claudius* (Acts 11:28); and (4) Nero* (Acts 25:11 f.).

Caesarea (sĕs′ȧ-rē′ȧ), a magnificent Roman city, 23 m. S. of Mt. Carmel and 64 m. NW. of Jerusalem, constructed on the site of Strato's Tower by Herod the Great and named in honor of Caesar Augustus. Skillful engineering developed this harbor into the virtual capital of Palestine. Twelve years of building thrust a pillared mole and stout

75. Caesarea: Roman theater.

stone breakwater N. and S. of the crescent-shaped harbor; threw a wall around the city's landward side; and developed an enormous amphitheater (recently cleared), high-level aqueduct (*IEJ* 14 (1964), pp.237–252), palaces and other structures.

Pontius Pilate occupied the governor's residence there. Philip brought the Gospel to Caesarea, his home (Acts 8:40, 21:8). Peter preached to a Gentile congregation there (10:1, 24). Paul landed in Caesarea twice (Acts 18:22, 21:8); there he was sent for trial and imprisoned (23:23–33, 24:27); appeared before Festus and Agrippa (Acts 25, 26); and from there he sailed in chains for Rome (27:1). Eusebius, historian of the early Church, was born there c. A.D. 260. The city was a Crusader fortress in the 12th century but was destroyed by the Moslems in A.D. 1291.

Caesarea has been excavated by both Israeli and Italian archaeologists, who have uncovered remains of the Byzantine period, a synagogue, a Herodian fortress, and a theater of the 1st–5th centuries A.D. In 1961, an inscription bearing the name of Pontius Pilate was found on a stone in the theater. A new series of excavations, directed by R. J. Bull, were begun in 1971 under the auspices of the ASOR. Aerial photography, geophysical prospecting, and the cleaning out of the sewage system of the city are being used to reconstruct its plan. See *Archaeology* 8, 1955, pp.122 ff.; *BA* 24, 1961, pp. 50 ff.; 34, 1971, pp. 88 ff.; Finegan, *The Archaeology of the N.T.*, 1969, pp.70 ff.

Caesarea Philippi, a Gentile city at the S. tip of Mt. Hermon in the Anti-Lebanons, constructed by Philip, son of Herod the Great, while tetrarch of the region NE. of the Sea of Galilee (4 B.C.–A.D. 34), named in honor of Philip's Caesar, Emperor Tiberius. Its site (Banias had long been a favorite seat of the Greek and Roman nature-cult god Pan, and of Canaanite fertility deities, worshipped in a cave from which issued a main source of the Jordan River. Matthew (16:13) and Mark (8:27) both mention Caesarea Philippi as the scene of Peter's great confession.

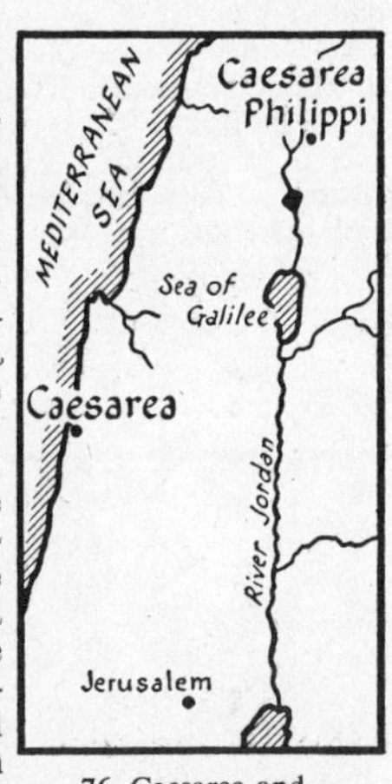

76. Caesarea and Caesarea Philippi.

Caiaphas (kā'yȧ-făs), Joseph, son-in-law of Annas, high priest (see PRIESTS) of Jerusalem, and his successor in that influential office (A.D. 18–37), served during the ministry of John the Baptist (Luke 3:2). Following the marked popularity of Jesus, caused by the raising of Lazarus, Caiaphas in a jealous council of priests and Pharisees posed the famous remark which led to the Crucifixion of Jesus: "It is expedient for us, that one man should die for the people" (John 11:50). During his Trial* Jesus was brought from the residence of Annas to the palace of Caiaphas (John 18:24), before being led to the judgment hall of Pilate (see ARCHITECTURE; JUDGMENT SEAT; PRAETORIUM).

Cain ("smith," "artificer,"), son of Adam, brother of Abel, whom he slew. Differing pictures of Cain are combined by the J source in Gen. 4. That of vv. 1–15 presents Cain as a fugitive murderer, becoming a wanderer and a "vagabond." But the Cain of v. 14 is not the man of v. 17; vagabonds do not establish cities. The second picture suggests (vv. 17–22) the beginning of the ancient craft of traveling metalsmiths (see TUBAL-CAIN).

Calah (kā' lȧ), one of the capital cities of Assyria (Gen. 10:11–12), Assyrian *kalḫu*, modern Birs Nimrud, situated on the E. bank of the Tigris, 20 m. S. of Mosul in N. Iraq. It was first excavated by A. H. Layard (beginning in 1845), who wrongly identified the site as Nineveh (see his *Nineveh and Its Remains*), and more recently by M. E. L. Mallowan from 1949–63 (*Nimrud and Its Remains*, 1966). Calah was rebuilt by Shalmaneser I (1274–1245 B.C.), and again by Ashurnasirpal II (883–859 B.C.), who established it as the new Assyrian capital in 879 B.C. (A stele discovered in 1951 describes this event; *ANET*^{3}, pp. 558–560.) His palace (*ANEP*^{2}, Nos. 758 and 882) covered more than 6 acres of ground. Among other items found in it was a collection of letters from Assyrian governors, some stationed in Phoenicia, to Tiglath-Pileser III (Pul of the O.T.) concerning the administration of the Assyrian provinces (see II Kings 15:19–20, 29; 16:7–10). In the SE. corner of the outer town stood "Fort Shalmaneser" (*ANEP*^{2}, No. 881), where numerous fragments of carved ivory were found (*ANEP*^{2}, Nos. 131–132). Of further interest is the "Black Obelisk" of Shalmaneser III (858–824 B.C.), found in 1846, on which subject rulers are depicted bearing tribute, including "Jehu, son of Omri" (*ANEP*^{2}, No. 355; see II Kings 9, 10). See *AOTS*, 1967, pp. 57–72. W. P. A.

Caleb (kā' lĕb) ("dog"), one of 12 spies sent with Joshua to survey the strength of Canaan (Num. 13, 14). The son of Jephunneh the Kenizzite (see KENAZ), he was named as certain to see the Promised Land because he had "wholly followed the Lord" (Deut. 1:36). The JE document indicates Caleb as the only one of the spies who believed that Israel was strong enough to occupy the land (Num. 13:30, early J source—see SOURCES). The late P document mentions both Joshua and Caleb as spared for the privilege of inheritance (Num. 14:38). The confusion about the Calebs is due to divergent sources. Joshua (15:13–14) assigned Hebron and its adjacent villages to Caleb. Caleb gave his daughter Achsah to Othniel (Josh. 15:15–19) as a reward for help in capturing Kiriath-sepher (see DEBIR). Calebites became one of the most important elements in the Tribe of Judah.

calendar. See TIME; GEZER.

calf. (1) An image of worship made of gold earrings and other jewelry for rebellious Hebrew wanderers under the direction of Aaron during the absence of Moses on the Mount (Ex. 32:1–6; Deut. 9:16), and worshipped as the god of their deliverance from Egypt. The image probably was small, with a wooden core. The design does not necessarily reflect the bull worship witnessed in Egypt, for there the bull was a living animal (Apis). (2) Two calves were made of metal by order of Jeroboam when he established worship centers at Bethel and Dan in rivalry to Jerusalem (I Kings 12:29). These symbols were probably bases supporting the throne of an invisible god. They reflect Canaanite bull cults common among all Semitic peoples. (3) Calves—unblemished and under one year of age—were burned as sin offerings (Lev. 9:2 f., 8). (4) The most famous N.T. calf is the one featured in the Parable of the Prodigal Son (Luke 15:23, 27, 30). A "calf tender and good" had been characteristic of Hebrew hospitality ever since the days of Abraham the Patriarch (Gen. 18:7).

calkers, laborers of Tyre skilled in stopping the seams in ships with tow, bitumen, or pitch (Ezek. 27:9, 27).

call, an invitation from God to an individual to become a part of His eternal plan for man's salvation*. Examples in the O.T. include the calls of Abraham (Gen. 12), Moses (Ex. 3), Isaiah (6:9), Jeremiah (1:2), Ezekiel (1:1), Hosea (1:2) and Amos (7:15). Calls in the N.T. include those of Peter, Andrew, James, and John (Matt. 4:18–22), and of Paul (Acts 9:1–22). To be "worthy of this calling" (II Thess. 1:11) was the goal of earnest followers of Jesus. See also Heb. 3:1; Phil. 3:14; Mark 2:17.

In another sense the word "call" is used in the O.T. with reference to seeking God in time of emergency (Ps. 18:6, 99:6). Psalm 116:1 indicates the answering of Yahweh, in contrast to the silence of Baal.

Calneh (kăl′nĕ) (Calno). (1) Possibly a Syrian city N. of the Euphrates town of Tiphsah (Amos 6:2; Isa. 10:9). (2) A city founded "in the land of Shinar" (S. Babylonia) by Nimrod along with Babel*, Erech*, and Accad* (Gen. 10:10). G. E. Wright suggests that the word "Calneh" here may not mean a town at all, but "all of them." Others have identified Calneh with Nippur. For excavation at Nippur see NIPPUR.

Calvary, the place of Christ's Crucifixion; its exact site is unknown; it is mentioned in the Bible only once (Luke 23:33). It is the *kranion* (meaning "skull") of the original Gk. N.T., whence "Golgotha" (from Aram. for "skull") (Matt. 27:33; John 19:17). "Calvary" is derived from Lat. *calvaria.* The R.S.V. of Luke 23:33 reads "The Skull." Calvary was evidently an elevation (Mark 15:40; Luke 23:49), although the word "hill" is not used, much less "Mount" Calvary. It was near a highway (Matt. 27:39) and "without the gate" (Heb. 13:12). If and when the line of Jerusalem's N. wall in the era of Jesus is located, and an inscription found, the mystery may be solved. There is little to substantiate the view of those who accept the skull-like hillock called "Gordon's Calvary," with its eye-socketed caves recognized in 1849 by Otto Thenius, and its adjacent garden suggesting John 19:41. Many scholars accept the 4th-century tradition of a site inside the present N. wall, covered by the Church of the Holy Sepulcher, begun c. A.D. 326 following the visit to Jerusalem of Helena, mother of Constantine the Great. Inside the tottering structure of this historic church shared by 6 Christian groups, a darkly impressive 14-ft. hillock called "Calvary" rises to the balcony level. The term "Place of the Skull" may have sprung from the shape of this hillock, from skulls seen in ancient times on the site, or from a legend that the "skull of Adam" was buried in this place. A grotto under the Chapel of the Syrians (Jacobites) which is a part of the Church of the Holy Sepulcher, contains tombs which may have been in the garden of Joseph of Arimathaea outside the city wall.

camels (the one-humped variety, *Camelus dromedarius*) have been used for transport and farm work in Bible lands for at least 30 centuries; wild camels have been known since more ancient times. W. F. Albright is authority for the statement that our earliest certain evidence of the widespread domestication of the camel does not antedate the end of the 12th century B.C. Evidence is scanty before the 11th century B.C., but the beast was previously known. Although this fact does not prove the allusions to camels in the Patriarchal narratives to be anachronistic, it certainly does suggest such an explanation. Israelites of the early 2d millennium were ass nomads. Ass caravans preceded the later caravans* of camels used in trade between

77. Camel train on Plain of Dothan.

Arabia and Palestine. The Exodus was probably a phase of ass nomadism, with the route dependent upon the location of wells. Judges 7:12 speaks of NW. Arabian peoples—Amalekites and Midianites—as having countless camels. See SABA, pp. 630 ff.

Camels are frequently mentioned in Genesis and Exodus; Lev. 11:4 lists them as "unclean." The reference to Job's having 3,000 camels (Job 1:3) is probably correct, for the breeding of camels in great numbers E. of the Jordan continues today on a large scale. Camels appear in impressive pageants of gift-bringing, like that of the Queen of Sheba, conveying, in a "very great train" of camels, offerings of spices, gold, and precious stones—all products of her native Arabia—to Solomon (I Kings 10:1 f.); and the forty-camel train of gifts sent by Ben-hadad to the prophet

Elisha (II Kings 8:9). Scripture narratives of the nativity of Jesus do not mention the picturesque camel in connection with the arriving Wise Men frequently depicted by artists, but camels, as well as horses, were probably their mount. Jesus twice made parabolic use of the camel: in his "eye of the needle" proverb (Matt. 19:24); and in his facetious "swallowing of the camel" allusion (23:24).

Camels are prized in the East because, unlike horses, they need little grain or fodder, subsisting on the commonest food, even thistles; and because, since they have two collections of cells in the paunch for storing a water supply, and can carry a reserve of food in the hump, they can conveniently endure long desert journeys. Their well-cushioned soles, encased in hard skin, are suitable for treks over fiery sand, though helpless in slippery mud. Young camels (sometimes "dromedaries" in Scripture) are capable of great speed (I Sam. 30:17; Esther 8:10). Camels were coveted for booty (Jer. 49:32) because of their valuable products: milk and cheese; hides for shoes and bags; manure for fuel cakes; meat in emergencies; hair, clipped in summer, for weaving into rugs and garments (see CAMEL'S HAIR). Camels are still occasionally used by farmers in plowing and threshing. They also transport heavy wood, bales of goods, rugs, tents, and household utensils. They bear young one at a time, taking 12 mo. to bear. Camels are full-grown at 16 yrs., and live to an old age. The cameleer sometimes rides atop the cargo, but more often rides a small donkey leading the caravan. Palanquins resembling wooden boxes were used by passengers, who placed in them such treasures as teraphim (Gen. 31:34). When saddles were used they were strapped to the animal by crosswise girths. It is common to see several people riding one camel.

An Arabian camel driver, Mohammed, founded the Moslem religion.

The earliest known art depiction of a Near Eastern camel (one-humped) is a late Hurrian work (c. 1000 B.C.) from Tell Halâf, in the Walters Art Gallery, Baltimore.

camel's hair, a coarse, durable textile used since early Bible times for garments. The hair is clipped from the animal's neck, back and hump, and woven on hand looms. The camel's-hair mantle or *abayeh* of a Patriarch or wealthy shepherd lasted a lifetime, serving as protection against heat, cold, and rain; as a desert carpet; or an extra tent. It is still prized by Palestinians and Arabians. The garment used by John the Baptist (Mark 1:6) was probably a wide girdle or loincloth worn next the skin, as part of his program of austerity.

Cana (kā'nȧ), a Galilean village, site of two miracles of Jesus reported in John: the water-into-wine incident of the wedding feast (John 2:1–11), and the healing-at-a-distance of the Capernaum nobleman's son (John 4:46–54). There are two suggested sites: Khirbet Qânā, c. 8 m. N. of Nazareth, from which the Plain of Achotis drops down to the Sea of Galilee; and Kefr Kenna, considerably nearer Nazareth among the fertile hills, on the main highway dropping down to Tiberias on the lake. The latter, partly excavated, is now regarded as the less likely site.

78. Spring at Kefr Kenna, traditional site of Cana at Galilee which, however, was more probably at Khirbet Qana.

A Latin chapel on the site of a Crusaders' Church at Cana (Kefr Kennā) claims to be the place where a church was erected in the 4th century A.D. at the order of Constantine.

Canaan, Canaanites (possibly from "the Land of Purple," suggested by the murex molluscs of coastal Palestine, used for dyeing). In the O.T. Canaan connoted all the land between the Jordan and the Mediterranean, from Egypt into Syria. It was bordered on the E. by the 13th-century kingdoms of Moab and Sihon, and on the S. by the 13th-century Kingdom of Edom. The first Canaanites may have been migrants from NE. Arabia before 3,000 B.C., for by that date several of their cities had already been established, like Jebus (Jerusalem), Megiddo*, Byblos (see GEBAL), Gezer*, Hamath, and Beth-shan*. The boundaries of Canaan suggested in Gen. 10:19 were "from Sidon . . . unto Gaza . . . unto Sodom, and Gomorrah, and Admah, and Zeboim, even unto Lasha." The subjugation of this land and its inhabitants was the goal of Israel's Conquest of the 14th–13th centuries B.C. The spies sent out by Moses (Num. 13) returned with a report which, in the light of recent archaeology, was scientifically accurate. In spite of the "milk and honey" aspect of the land, the spies stated: "The people be strong that dwell in the land, and the cities are walled, and very great" (Num. 13:28). (For the various steps of Israel's campaigns in Canaan see CONQUEST, and Num. 21:10 ff. and Josh. 1–24.) The Conquest was much more gradual and incomplete than a cursory reading of O.T. narratives suggests. Jerusalem did not fall to Israel until the era of David; Gezer, not until the time of Solomon.

Many walled cities surmounting high mounds have now been excavated, and their walls of polygonal blocks found to be vastly superior to the Israelites' later construction, as at Bethel. The Canaanites were Semites, called by the E document "Amorites."* But Canaanites took to low shore lands, suitable for their iron-shod chariot warfare (Judg. 1:19), while Amorites were mountain dwellers (Judg. 1:35 ff.). Some scholars believe that the Amorites preceded the Canaanites, and merged with the Hittites* to form the Canaanite people. The Canaanites were only one of several groups occupying Canaan at the time of Israel's invasions; but they were far stronger than the Palestinian Hittites (from Asia Minor); the Hivites (Horites, from N. Mesopotamia and the Mitanni country); the obscure Perizzites; and the Girgashites (Josh. 3:10).

After the gradual Conquest of Canaan by Israel, the Canaanites were pushed seaward by "sea peoples" (early 12th century B.C.), retaining only the coastal strip of N. Palestine and S. Syria which the Greeks called "Phoenicia" (again, "Land of Purple"). The Phoenicians were one of the greatest Mediterranean peoples of the 8th century B.C., when Greek civilization was dawning. They exerted on the Greeks incalculable cultural influences, not the least of which was an alphabet (see WRITING). Phoenician Canaanites were famous merchants, not aggressive warriors. In Prov. 31:24 (A.S.V. margin), the word "merchant" is synonymous with Canaanite.

Canaanite city-state culture contributed much to Israel. According to W. F. Albright, the proto-Sinaitic inscriptions indicate an alphabet used by Canaanites between 1800 and 1600 B.C. (see SERABIT). Excavated inscriptions show further that at the time of Israel's entry the Canaanites were able to write also in Ugaritic (N. Syrian) cuneiform alphabetic script (c. 1500 B.C.), as well as in Egyptian hieroglyphics.

Since the epochal excavations at Ras* Shamrah (Ugarit) in N. Syria, spectacular revelations of Canaanite culture have come to light. Thousands of clay tablets were found stored in a structure (? library) between two huge Canaanite temples dating from c. the 15th and 14th century B.C., written in a cuneiform alphabet, in the Ugaritic language. Most of the Ras Shamrah messages are poetic statements of Canaanite mythology; a few deal with such subjects as veterinary treatments. O.T. writers appear to have been unaware of such Canaanite creation epics as came out of Mesopotamia.

The Canaanites contributed to their Hebrew successors not only the basis of the language in which the Hebrews wrote their Scripture, but also ceramic arts, music and musical instruments, and architecture. Solomon's Temple at Jerusalem was built from a Canaanite (Phoenician) model; Phoenician craftsmen, loaned by King Hiram of Tyre, executed much of the work (I Kings 7:13 ff.). The tremendous, well-built fortifications, palaces, and temples now fully excavated in various cities are in marked contrast to the layers of inferior Hebrew masonry. Art treasures in ivory, gold, and alabaster from a layer of Megiddo destroyed before the arrival of Israel in Palestine bear testimony to Canaanite elegance in royal residences. Albright describes a priceless battle-ax found at Ras Shamrah from the early 14th century B.C., showing that Canaanites used steel and damascened copper, decorated with gold inlay of floral designs.

79. Canaanite carinated bowl (18th century B.C.).

Canaanite fertility cults, which were more lewd and influential than any other nature cults of the Middle East, made incursions into the austere, Wilderness-born faith of Israel. Whether in crude clay altars decorated with gross goddesses, serpents, cultic doves, and bulls, or in well-constructed temples, the ritual of fertility gods was rampant in the land which Israel entered. The pantheon consisted mainly of El, the highest god; his consort, Ashirat (often "Ashirat of the Sea"), known to Israel as Asherah; Baal, or Haddu, the active storm god, son of Dagon, who was possibly a brother of El. The word "Elohim," in Hebrew, for Canaanites or Israelites, meant either "deity" or "gods." Moreover, it is possible to trace many Canaanite words and concepts in Proverbs and certain Psalms.

Some of the Canaanite "high places"* were taken over by Israel and adapted to their own worship ways. There are similarities between the Canaanite system of sacrifice and that of the Hebrews, as suggested by evidence found in Canaanite temples at Lachish*.

Among the Canaanite cities excavated are Jericho*, which fell for its last destruction soon after the Exodus (Josh. 6); Bethel-Ai (Josh. 8); Libnah (Josh. 10:29); Lachish, seized by Israel c. 1220 B.C. (Josh. 10:31); Eglon, SW. of Lachish (Josh. 10:34 f.); Debir (Kiriath-sepher) (Josh. 10:38 f.), which fell in the same wave of attack as Lachish; Beth-shan*, one of the most elaborate excavations in Palestine, among whose ruins is a temple of Astarte that may be the one in which Saul and Jonathan's armor was placed (I Sam. 31:10); Megiddo and Taanach, dominating the Plain of Megiddo (Judg. 5:19); Beth-shemesh (Judg. 1:33); Byblos; and Ras Shamrah in N. Syria. Beth-shan, Megiddo, and Gezer were too strong for Israel's 13th-century invasion.

Cananaean (kā′nȧ-nē′an) (Aram. *qana'i*, "zealous"), A.V. Canaanite. The epithet of the Disciple Simon (Matt. 10:4; Mark 3:18), who is elsewhere (Luke 6:15; Acts 1:13) called the Zealot (Zelotes in A.V.). Simon may have belonged to the extreme Jewish patriotic party of the Zealots.

Candace (kăn′dȧ-sē), a title given to Ethiopian queens. See Acts 8:27. The eunuch treasurer of one of these Candaces was baptized by Philip at a water-hole in the Gaza Desert on his way from Jerusalem (Acts 8:26–38). Pyramid tombs of reigning Candaces of Kush (Ethiopia) were identified by George Reisner at Meroe in the Anglo-

80. Candaces' tombs.

Egyptian Sudan, c. 133 m. N. of Khartoum on the Nile. They were constructed between c. 300 B.C. and A.D. 350.

candle, in Scripture a clay or metal lamp* with a nozzle through which a flax wick carried oil. It was not a taper. The candle was placed on a clay or stone stand, called the candlestick* (see II Kings 4:10). Poorer homes kept the candle in a wall niche. It usually burned day and night. The night-burning candle of the thrifty woman (Prov. 31:18) may indicate night weaving or embroidering of girdles, garments, and tapestry. All three synoptists record the parable of the lamp kept on its stand and not under a bushel (Matt. 5:15; Mark 4:21; Luke 8:16, 11:33). Figurative use of the candle is suggested in Ps. 18:28; Prov. 20:27, 24:20.

From Israel's early celebrations of Yom Kippur to the present observances by orthodox Jews, a special candle is lighted on the eve of the Sabbath and other sacred days.

candlestick (*menorah*), a stand of clay, stone, or metal, made to hold small lamps of similar material. In the Tabernacle was one of pure gold beaten work, with a central shaft and three branches on each side (Ex. 25:31–40) illuminating the altar with perpetual fire. In Solomon's Temple there were five golden tree-like candlesticks in the Holy Place on the right and five on the left, in front of the oracle (I Kings 7:49; II Chron. 4:7). These may have been added after Solomon's time. Jer. 52:19 records their being carried away to Babylon. One seven-branched candlestick appears to have been brought back by Zerubbabel—probably the one depicted on the marble Arch of Titus in Rome. This representation is the earliest extant and the most authentic example of the seven-branched candlestick. (See LAMP.)

Private use of the candlestick is mentioned in II Kings 4:10. The joyous winter festival of the Hanukkah, established in connection with the rededication of the Temple by Judas Maccabaeus and still celebrated by Jews, uses four lamps on each side of the stand and a central kindling light.

Excavations have shown how the candlestick was used in synagogues in the early

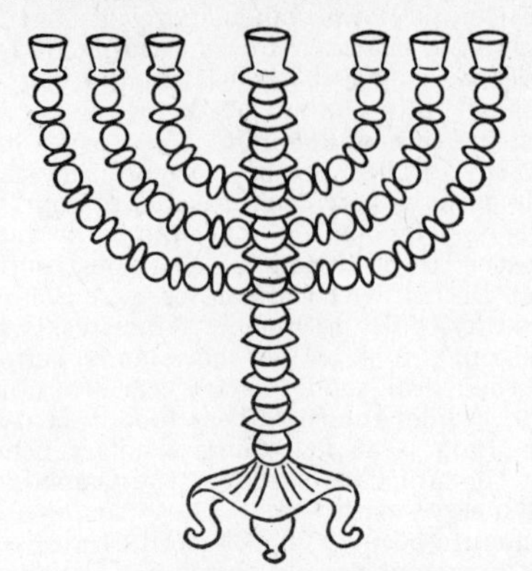

81. Representation of the seven-branched candlestick used in the Temple.

centuries of the Christian era, as at Hammath near Tiberias. From Megiddo came a clay lamp with seven nozzles. A menorah from Gadara is in the Musée du Louvre, Paris.

candy. See FOOD.

Canon (from Gk. *kanōn*, perhaps from the Semitic *qaneh*, "reed," suggesting a measuring reed, whence a list of things in a straight column), a collection of authoritative sacred books composing the O.T. and N.T. of Christians; also applied to the sacred books of the Hebrews. For centuries many more than the 39 books finally selected for the Christian O.T. and the 27 for the N.T. were considered canonical. Some were eliminated because they were deemed spiritually unworthy of inclusion with the inspired masterpieces upon which all authorities agreed, or because they did not appear to be true statements of what Yahweh was trying to communicate to His people. The O.T. Canon was the first collection of sacred literature ever assembled. Egyptians and Babylonians had many writings of a religious character, but they had never gathered them into one standard body of belief. The N.T. does not contain the word "canon," but refers to the canonical books under the term "Scriptures." A description of what is meant by canonical literature is found in II Tim. 3:15–17.

The *O.T. Canon* was agreed upon only after long pondering and debate. A thousand years went into its formation. The sacred literature was first oral, then reduced to writing, then it became literature. The three sections of the Hebrew Bible—the Book of the Law (Torah), the Prophets, and the Writings—each progressed to a definite form in an era of great historic events. The first canonical material was Deuteronomy*, compiled after the rediscovery by King Josiah's high priest, Hilkiah, c. 622 B.C., of the lost Book of the Law (II Chron. 34:9 ff.). When Josiah* called an assembly of Israel, read the recovered book, and pledged himself to accept it as the will of God, the people also "stood to the covenant," and witnessed the adoption of the first canonical literature of the Hebrews—ultimately Deuteronomy (II Kings 23:1–3). The next addition to the O.T. Canon came about two centuries later, c. 400 B.C., when the Law (or Pentateuch*) was canonized in the era of Nehemiah and Ezra. This occurred in the period following the Captivity in Babylon, during which absence from the Jerusalem Temple had fostered the development of synagogues (see SYNAGOGUE) and had given leisure for pondering and formulating the great utterances of God's revealed truth. Next came the canonizing of the Prophets—the "Former" (Joshua, Judges, Samuel, Kings) and the "Latter" (Isaiah, Jeremiah, Ezekiel, and the twelve Minor Prophets). This development probably was spurred by the recording of Hellenistic culture following Alexander the Great's career of the 4th century B.C. The Hebrew Writings or Hagiographa, forming the third part of the O.T., and including the Psalms, Proverbs, Job, Song of Solomon, Ruth, Lamentations, Ecclesiastes, and Esther; Daniel, Ezra, Nehemiah, and Chronicles, began to be collected c. 300 B.C., but were not wholly included in the Canon until after 150 B.C., when some of the latest Psalms were written. Not until early in the Christian era did the Writings attain complete canonicity. (See *An Introduction to the Old Testament*, Robert H. Pfeiffer, Harper & Brothers.)

At Jamnia, near Joppa, c. A.D. 90 a synod of rabbis declared the O.T. Canon completed; the possibility of adding more was ended. The writing of new Christian literature probably spurred the advocates of the O.T. to a defensive attitude. But the world will always be debtor to the Jews, who gathered the greatest treasury of religious literature which had ever been assembled.

The *N.T. Canon* was compiled by Christians who already knew the importance and the possibility of having an authoritative body of literature embodying their tenets. They had received the O.T. Canon, and proceeded from that point. Jesus had referred to the written testimony of God (Matt. 5:17 f.); and read from Isaiah's prophecy, for example, in his home synagogue at Nazareth (Luke 4:17). Numerous allusions by the Apostles to what we call the O.T. Canon appear, as in II Tim. 3:15–17.

But the N.T. Canon was slow in developing. Near the end of the 1st century some books were recognized as canonical. The four Gospels were everywhere accepted as authoritative as early as the 2d century A.D. Justin Martyr (b. Shechem, c. A.D. 100), Clement of Alexandria (A.D. 150–215), Eusebius (d. c. A.D. 340), and Jerome (d. A.D. 420) were influential in the selection of the N.T. Canon. After Eusebius had had 50 elaborate vellum copies of the N.T. prepared for the churches of Constantinople, few major changes were made. Athanasius in 367 issued a list of 27 books which tally with the present N.T., which was accepted as canonical by the synods of Hippo Regius (393) and Carthage (397, 419). There was much opposition to including the Apocalypse, because of aversion for this form of literature. The Apocrypha were never included in the Protestant Canon. See BIBLE.

Canticles. See SOLOMON, SONG OF.

Capernaum (kȧ-pûr′nā-ŭm) (*Kephar-Nahum*, "village of Nahum"), a small lake port on the NW. shore of the Sea of Galilee, about 2½ m. W. of the entrance of the Jordan to that lake. Because of "many mighty works" accomplished there while Jesus was using this center for his busy Galilean ministry, Capernaum, rather than Nazareth, was called "his own city" (Matt. 9:1). Its site, now generally accepted as Tell Hûm, is a tumbled mass of stones (cf. Jesus' prediction, Matt. 11:23). A fishing harbor, it was also the seat of tax

82. Ruined shore line of Capernaum.

collectors (Matt. 9:9–11, 17:24), and apparently the site of a Roman military garrison, as indicated by the presence there of a centurion, whose servant Jesus healed (Matt. 8:5–13; Luke 7:1–10). For other healings by Jesus at Capernaum see Matt. 8:14 f.; Mark 2:3–11; John 4:46–54. His popularity after these miracles, and his teachings to "great multitudes," necessitated his escape time and again to "the other side" of the lake (Matt. 8:18). The Capernaum headquarters of Jesus were probably Peter's house (Matt. 8:14; Mark 1:29, 9:33; Luke 4:38). He also taught in the synagogue at Capernaum (Mark 1:21—possibly that erected by the centurion (Luke 7:5).

The excavation of Capernaum has yielded the ruins of one of the most elegant white limestone synagogues in Palestine—now partly restored, and dating from the 3d century A.D. Like other synagogues, it faced Jerusalem; its main portion was a rectangular, columned basilica with a porticoed trapezoidal porch on its E. It had a main and two side entrances, was paved with limestones, many of which are still visible, and had two rows of stone benches, one above the other, running around three sides. On these—or on floor mats—the men sat. A gallery used by women ran around the NW. and E. sides. It was elaborately decorated with sculptured representations of animals, plants, and mythological and geometric figures. Minor excavations in 1953–54 uncovered the foundations of an earlier structure underlying the 3rd-century synagogue, possibly its 1st-century A.D. predecessor.

Excavations since 1968 by V. Corbo have concentrated on the remains of the central octagon of a 5th-century A.D. Byzantine church, first cleared in 1921. Underneath were the ruins of a domestic complex, with some rooms adapted for Christian worship.

The beginning of this "House-Church" are dated by the excavator to the 1st century A.D., but this is debatable (see *IEJ* 21, 1971, pp. 207–211).

Caph (käf) or kaph, the 11th letter of the Hebrew alphabet. See WRITING.

Cappadocia (kăp′*ȧ*-dō′shĭ-*ȧ*), a region of central Asia Minor made a Roman province by Emperor Tiberius, S. of Pontus, W. of Armenia, E. of Galatia, and adjoining Cilicia, in which was located Paul's birthplace,

83. Cappadocia.

Tarsus*. I Peter was addressed to believers scattered through Cappadocia, Galatia, and the Pontus (I Pet. 1:1). Cappadocian silver mines sent ores to Assyria as early as 1900 B.C. Cappadocians long kept secret their technique for smelting iron from the Taurus Mountains, which in the early Hebrew Monarchy was valued almost as much as silver. Cappadocia was at the heart of an old Hittite (see HITTITES) state (c. 1700–1400 B.C.), whose trade records on recovered clay tablets reveal commerce in minerals, fine horses, and wheat. Possibly some of King Solomon's thoroughbred steeds were imported from Hittite centers in Cappadocia. There were Hittites in Palestine in 1600 B.C. and during the Hebrew Conquest (Josh. 3:10). Cappadocia was the center of Anatolian Hittite culture, whose pottery is related to types at Troy. See CARCHEMISH.

captain, a word appearing frequently in the O.T. and the N.T., as a translation of 13 different Heb. and four Gk. words. In Num. 31:14 a captain is "over thousands" and "over hundreds." In Deut. 1:15 he is also "over fifties" and "over tens." Leaders of tribes were captains (Deut. 29:10). II Kings 8:21 mentions "captains of chariots." "Officer" or "chief leader" might better translate the original word. Acts 4:1 mentions "the captain of the temple"—probably not a military officer, but a Levite in charge of priestly guards. See also Mark 6:21; Luke 22:4, 22:52. The "Carites" of A.S.V. II Kings 11:19 may have been captains who served as executioners.

The "chief captain of the band" (Acts 21:31–23:30) was a Roman officer, Claudius Lysias*.

Captivity. See EXILE.

caravan, a company of merchants, pilgrims, or immigrants traveling together for safety in the Middle East and N. Africa. In Bible narratives the animals used were asses, camels (see CAMELS for date), or horses. Joseph was sold to a caravan of Ishmaelites (A.S.V., Gen. 37:25; A.V., "a company of Ishmaelites") going to Egypt. The "very great train" of the Queen of Sheba was a camel spice caravan from Arabia. Job spoke of caravans (A.S.V. 6:18 f.) from his observations of the ancient Edomite routes. The A.S.V. of this passage is much preferable to the A.V. translation "paths of their way," or "troops." See also A.S.V. Ezek. 27:25.

Caravan routes of more than 4,000 years ago through Bible lands followed the Way of the Sea from Damascus across Esdraelon* to the Mediterranean and on to Egypt; or N. and S. from Carmel to Antioch; or over the spice routes of Arabia to the E. coast of the Gulf of Aqabah; or from the Persian Gulf to Petra and Gaza. There was an Early Bronze trade route across Trans-Jordan to Sinai. A chain of *caravan cities*, offering *caravansaries* or

84. Caravansary between Baghdad and Babylon.

lodgings for drivers and beasts, became fabulously rich: Palmyra (Tadmor), existing c. 1100 B.C.; Jerash, Damascus, Amman (the present capital of Jordan); Tyre and Sidon; and Homs, an ancient Syrian wheat caravan center. See TRADE, TRANSPORTATION.

Carchemish (kär′kē-mĭsh), an important 18th-century B.C. trade center, Hittite fortress, and later "Neo-Hittite" state and Assyrian province, situated on the W. bank of the Euphrates, near Jerablus in N. Syria, c. 63 m. NE. of Aleppo. It guarded the main ford across the Euphrates on the route from Assyria to the Mediterranean. In 1912 and 1914, its importance in history was revealed by archaeological investigations into the gigantic mound conducted by Sir Leonard Woolley and T. E. Lawrence for the British Museum. The finds include a remarkable assortment of Hittite pottery and sculpture, cremation burials, sections of the city's fortifications, and hundreds of cylinder seals used in signing clay business documents. An independent center of late Hittite culture at the beginning of the 1st millennium B.C., Carchemish later became an Assyrian province. Sargon II defeated Pisiris, its king, in 717 B.C. and replaced him by a governor (*ANET*^{3}, p. 285; see Isa. 10:9). In 609 B.C. Pharaoh Necho II of Egypt marched to capture Carchemish (see II Chron. 35:20), but it was controlled by Nebuchadnezzar II with his decisive victory there in 605 B.C. (Jer. 46:2).

Carmel ("garden," "orchard"). (1) A hilly range, 15 m. long rising to as much as 1,742 ft., along the W. border of Asher (Josh. 19:26), extending from the hill country of Samaria to the Mediterranean, where the Mt. Carmel headland rises 556 feet above the improved harbor of modern Haifa. N. of the headland curves the crescent Bay of Acre. Because the 200-ft.-wide shore below the promontory is extremely vulnerable, defenders throughout history have held the passes running over Mt. Carmel to the coastal plain and the Valley of Jezreel (Esdraelon). The ridge at its E. end is watered by the Kishon River (cf. Judg. 4:7). The scene of the contest between Elijah and the 450 prophets of Baal and the 400 prophets of Asherah (I Kings 18:19) took place on the slopes of Mt. Carmel. Carmel with its famous olive and fruit trees was holy ground to ancient oracles and to Baal*. Its luxuriant foliage is reflected in Amos 1:2; Isa. 33:9; Nah. 1:4. Excavations in caves along the Wadi el-Mugharah overlooking the Plain of Sharon, and in other sections of the limestone ridge of Carmel, have provided evidence of prehistoric habitation. See CAVES, illus. 85.

(2) A town in Judah (Josh. 15:55), modern Khirbet el-Kirmil (or Kermel), 8 m. SE. of Hebron, where Saul set up a monument to commemorate his victory over the Amalekites (I Sam. 15:12). Near this Carmel, Nabal, husband of Abigail, who became the wife of David, engaged in extensive sheep-raising (I Sam. 25:2).

carpenter, an artisan whose ordinary work in Bible times was the building of houses, boats, synagogues, yokes, threshing boards, benches, etc. For Temple* construction and repairs, master carpenters were brought from the Lebanons, along with the fine cedarwood they were expert in working (II Sam. 5:11; Ezra 3:7). Isaiah gives details of a carpenter's fashioning of idols (44:13–17). Jesus was known as "the carpenter's son" (Matt. 13:55), but also as "the carpenter" (Mark 6:3).

Carpenters' tools* were compass, plane, pencil, saw, hammer, and nails. The earliest saw was made by mounting, in a curved frame, flint teeth with serrated edges. Small handsaws were pulled against the wood, in the opposite direction from that used by modern carpenters. Many carpenters' tools from ancient times in Bible lands have been excavated; the University Museum at Philadelphia has predynastic Egyptian axheads, chisels, and adzes. The shaft-hole ax had already been invented in Sumerian Ur* by 2900 B.C. Egyptians were using the flange-bladed copper chisel in the time of Queen Hetep-heres, mother of Khufu (Cheops), the Fourth Dynasty (c. 2550–2450 B.C.) pyramid builder. Petrie believed that the largest wood constructions undertaken by Egyptian carpenters were giant boats 150 ft. long for transporting obelisks. Large-scale carpentry was utilized in temples, palaces, and tombs, where columns and painted panels were prominent features. Carpenters in Egypt also made wooden coffins, joining surfaces with wooden pegs, and conserving precious lumber by the use of mummy cartonnages. For the countless irrigation pumps (*shadûfs*) carpenters were always needed along the Nile, and for repairing sluice gates in the network of Delta canals.

Carpus (kär′pŭs), the man with whom Paul left his cloak in Troas (II Tim. 4:13).

carriage, as used in the A.V., meant not a vehicle but baggage, or heavy goods. These were often enclosed in a storing place guarded by a circle of carts around a camp (Judg. 18:21; I Sam. 17:22; Isa. 10:28). The "we took up our carriages" of Acts 21:15 is more accurately rendered "we took up our baggage" (A.S.V.) and "we made ready" (R.S.V.).

cart, an early vehicle used in Mesopotamia and Egypt 5,000 years ago, having four or two wheels (usually solid wooden disks), drawn by oxen, mules, or men, and occasionally horses. Those mentioned in Gen. 45:19 ("wagons") were probably not unlike the crude two-wheeled ones occasionally seen in modern Cairo. A new cart for transporting the Ark from Gibeah to Jerusalem is mentioned in I Sam. 6:7; II Sam. 6:3; I Chron. 13:7. The agricultural use of the cart as a threshing sledge is indicated in Isa. 28:27, and as a means of transporting sheaves in Amos 2:13. Grape-laden carts at Zikhron Ya'aqov still play a part in the production of Hebrew sacramental wine.

cassia, the aromatic bark of a tree similar to cinnamon, though less delicate in flavor. The oil of cassia was one of the ingredients of the holy anointing oil (Ex. 30:24) and of a valued perfume for garments (Ps. 45:8). Cassia, which was also ground as a spice, was an important product of trade with Tyre (Ezek. 27:19).

castle. See ARCHITECTURE; GIBEAH.

Castor and Pollux, in Greek and Roman mythology, sons of Leda, brothers of Helen and Clytemnestra; in later tradition sons of Zeus and Leda, whence Dioscuri, "lads of Zeus." They were friends of sailors, taking form in "St. Elmo's fire," a brush-like discharge of atmospheric electricity which sometimes appears as a light on masts of ships during storms. They formed the figurehead of the Alexandrian ship on which Paul sailed from Malta to Italy (Acts 28:11).

caterpillar, cankerworm, palmerworm—larvae of such migratory insects, as locusts. Like hail, frost, mildew, blasting, and pestilence, caterpillars were regarded as plagues sent to punish Israel. See I Kings 8:37; II Chron. 6:28.

Catholic Epistles. The name given by the early Church to seven epistles: James, I and II Peter, I, II, and III John, and Jude. The A.V. adds the word "general" to the titles of all these epistles except II and III John. See EPISTLES.

cattle, in the O.T., include varieties of oxen, bullocks, heifers, goats, sheep; and even asses, camels, and horses. In the nomadic and early agricultural society wealth was measured in terms of cattle (Gen. 13:2), or a lump of metal similar to a shekel (LXX, Vulg. translate *lamb*), as in Job 42:11 (*kesitah*). Firstlings of all cattle were sacred to Yahweh (Ex. 34:19; Lev. 1:2). The tribes of Reuben and Gad saw in the land E. of the Jordan "a land for cattle," of which they had a "multitude" (Num. 32:1, 4). Cattle supplied the chief offerings on O.T. altars to Yahweh (I Kings 1:19). (Cf. also Ps. 50:10.) The N.T. refers to cattle (Luke 17:7 A.V.); and John 4:12 (A.V. and R.S.V.).

Cauda (A.V. Clauda), a small Mediterranean island SW. of Crete, in whose lee Paul sailed W. to Malta (Melita) (Acts 27:16).

caves in the limestone hills of Palestine have been used for human shelter since prehistoric times. Typical are the almost inaccessible 'Ain Feshkha caves NW. of the Dead Sea, where two goatherds accidentally discovered the Dead Sea Scrolls* in 1947. Edomites at Petra, even down to the Roman period, lived in caves, some of which still show imposing architectural façades. The home of the Holy Family at Nazareth may have been built over a hillside cave, of which there are many in Galilee. Jesus' knowledge of these may explain Luke 4:30. Scripture contains numerous mention of cave refuges: Gen. 19:30; Josh. 10:16; Judg. 6:2; I Sam. 13:6, 22:1, 24:3; II Sam. 23:13; Heb. 11:38. Caves were commonly used for burial places (as in Gen. 23:19; John 11:38, 19:41).
The necropolis at Sidon* was extensive. Caves in Bible lands were also used for dungeons (Jer. 37:16 f.), cisterns, and in very early times for places of worship, as at Gezer and Jerusalem. Caves under Ophel Hill in the latter city have yielded pottery from c. 2500–2000 B.C.

85. Ancient caves of Wâdī el-Mughârah.

Investigation of the cave homes of prehistoric man in Palestine is in its infancy, but has already yielded priceless information concerning his development. Deposits on successive occupation levels of artifacts, worked flints, human and animal bones are the ABC of paleontologists. The now famous series of caves excavated in Mt. Carmel* overlooking the Mediterranean at Wâdī el-Mughârah indicates occupation by man through twelve cultures, from the Recent Bronze Age to what C. C. McCown calls a "primitive Tayacian culture" resting on bedrock. Theodore McCown found in the Carmel "Cave of the Kids" eight giant skeletons of *Paleanthropus palestinensis*—Carmel man. A cave at Shukba in W. Judaea has also proved to be a home of paleolithic man. M. Stekelis has investigated a series of rock shelters at Mugharet al-Watuat in the Ramleh subdistrict, and others at Wâdī Fallah. A short distance N., at Wâdī Abu Hadid, is one of the most beautiful prehistoric caves yet found in Palestine, containing two large, domed chambers with walls covered with stalactites (cf. *Bulletin* ASOR No. 86, pp. 22 ff.). In 1949 at the entrance of the Dog River into the Mediterranean a cave was examined and found to contain prehistoric materials.

In a cave terrace at the N. side of the Plain of Gennesaret Mr. Turville-Petrie discovered the four small pieces of skull now famous as "the Galilee Man," dating from at least 40,000 and possibly 100,000 years ago, and representing a new species related to the genus homo—one of the Neanderthal race, the first ever discovered outside of Europe. In 1947 the Dead Sea Scrolls* were found in a cave by the Dead Sea. Since then many more fragments of the O.T. have been found.

An almost complete sequence of cultural deposits from the Old Stone Age to recent times has been found in the Hotu cave in northern Iran (ancient Persia), below 40 feet of sand and gravel of the glacial period. This cave supplied Carleton Coon of the University of Pennsylvania and his colleagues with evidence of 75,000 years of its use as shelter. Three partial skeletons may prove to be the earliest known forebears of the human race.

Several important traditional Biblical sites which may well be historic, and which are now covered with churches, are identified with caves: the rock-walled cave on Mt. Tabor, associated by some with the events of Christ's Transfiguration (Matt. 17:1–8); the Grotto of the Nativity, beneath the church at Bethlehem, thought to have been the hillside cave stable of the inn (Luke 2:7); the grotto garden tomb of Joseph of Arimathaea, now believed by many to be under the Church of the Holy Sepulcher at Jerusalem; and the grotto under the Church of the Pater Noster on the Mount of Olives.

cedars, especially cedars of Lebanon (*Cedrus libani*, Heb. *'erez*), were sought for construction of palaces, temples, courts of administration, masts (Ezek. 27:5), images, chests (Ezek. 27:24), musical instruments, and coffins. Cedar was considered "incorruptible," capable of taking a fine polish, fragrant, and long-lasting. Its very name means "strength" or "worth" (see Isa. 2:13, 14:8, 35:2, 60:13). It appears today on the flag and certain stamps of the Lebanese Republic.

David and Solomon both made trade alliances with Tyrian kings (II Sam. 5:11; I Kings 5:8), whereby choice cedar was hewn and floated down the Mediterranean to Joppa and hauled upland 25 m. to Jerusalem. There it was incorporated into a royal house for David (II Sam. 5:11, 7:2); and into the palace and "House of the Forest of Lebanon" (I Kings 7:2 f.) of Solomon. Solomon and

Hiram* honored cedar by using it for Temple* vault beams, ceiling, support for chambers, flooring, wall lining, court beams, and altar (I Kings 6:9 f., 15 f, 18, 20, 36). Of the interior of this famous sanctuary it was written: "all was cedar; there was no stone seen" (I Kings 6:18). Temple repairs under Ezra also called for cedars of Lebanon (3:7). To build temples at Ephesus and Utica and palaces in Assyria, Lebanon cedars were carried away for centuries.

86. Cedars of Lebanon. Ivan Dmitri for American Export Lines.

Today the chief colony of ancient cedars, some 400, remains near Bsherreh in the Republic of Lebanon, about 100 m. N. of Beirut and 75 m. NE. of Byblos (see GEBAL). The Bsherreh cedars, 6,000 ft. above the Mediterranean at the head of the deep Qadisha Valley, show characteristics of their ancient forebears: course, rough, reddish-brown bark frosted with white; trunks sometimes 40 ft. in girth, with a branch circumference of 200 or 300 ft.; flat boughs, sometimes as wide as the tree is high, and bearing egg-shaped cones 4 to 5 in. long. Their bright green needles are c. ½ in. long. Other small groups of *Cedrus libani* still grow in the region of Beirut and in the Taurus Mts.

Millions of cedar, pine, and spruce seeds have been sown in the Lebanons from United States Army airplanes, co-operating with the Near East Foundation and the Lebanese Government; but the *Cedrus libani* grows very slowly.

Cenchreae (sĕn′krē̇-ȧ), a port of Corinth at the E. end of the isthmus on the Saronic Gulf, connected with the great commercial center of central Greece by a system of forts. It was visited by Paul on his way to Ephesus (Acts 18:18). It was the seat of an early Christian church (Rom. 16:1).

censer, a metal container holding incense ignited by live charcoal taken from an altar (Lev. 10:1, 16:13). The censers of the Tabernacle* were probably of bronze, those of Solomon's Temple of gold (II Chron. 4:22). In atonement worship rites sometimes as many as 70 elders, each with his own censer, lifted clouds of incense (Ezek. 8:11).

census, an enrolling or numbering of the population preparatory to taxation. The most famous census in the Bible is that which took Joseph and Mary to Bethlehem from Nazareth to be enrolled in the ancestral town of Joseph (Luke 2:1–5). In the O.T. a numbering of the secular tribes of Israel took place, according to the record of Num. 1:1–49, shortly after the arrival at Mt. Sinai. (Cf. the numbering recorded in Num.

87. Cenchreae and entrance to Corinthian Canal.

26; also Ex. 30:11–16.) The census "from Dan even to Beer-sheba" ordered by David (II Sam. 24:1–10) was considered a sin, and was drastically punished (11–15; cf. I Chron. 21:1). Yet the incident took a constructive turn when the king bought the threshing floor of Araunah the Jebusite (I Chron. 21:15–25), which became the historic center of Israel's religious capital (v. 26). See TEMPLE; TRIBUTE, TAX, TOLL.

centurion, the commander of a "century" (100 men) in the Roman Army. Five are mentioned in the N.T., and three became followers of Christ. (1) The unnamed centurion whose servant was healed by Jesus at Capernaum (Matt. 8:5, 8, 13; Luke 7:2, 6). He was characterized by humility, in spite of his position of leadership; by faith in Christ such as the Master had not found even in Israel; and by devotion to his sick servant; by generosity possibly expressing itself in the gift of a synagogue to the Jews of Capernaum—perhaps near the shore of the Sea of Galilee, where vestiges of a later one are extant. (2) The Roman centurion assigned to duty close to the cross of Christ during his Crucifixion. Witnessing his prisoner's demeanor, he declared, "Truly this man was the Son of God" (Mark 15:39; cf. also Luke 23:47). (3) The centurion named Cornelius, stationed with the Italian band at Caesarea (Acts 10:2). Receiving the gift of the Holy Spirit following a sermon by Peter, Cornelius and his family were baptized, and became the first Gentile converts to Christ through the Apostle's influence. (4) A Jerusalem centurion who reminded his chief, the captain, that Paul was a Roman citizen and might not be scourged uncondemned (Acts 22:25). (5) A centurion of Augustus' band, named Julius, assigned to guard Paul on his journey across the Mediterranean from Caesarea to Rome, who thwarted the counsel of soldiers who wanted to kill the prisoners during the shipwreck (Acts 27:43).

88. Roman centurion.

Cephas (sē′făs) (from Aram. *kephâ*, "stone"), the name given to Simon Peter* by Jesus (John 1:42).

chaff, the worthless husk of grain threshed on old stone threshing* floors in Bible lands. Wind blows it away from the grain as it is tossed by harvesters using forks. The Psalmist used this familiar scene as a symbol of the wicked man—blown away like chaff in the wind (1:4, 35:5). Similar figures of speech are found in Isa. 5:24; Jer. 23:28; Hos. 13:3; Zeph. 2:2; Matt. 3:12; Luke 3:17.

chain. (1) Of gold or jewels, worn to designate rank. Joseph was given such a chain by Pharaoh (Gen. 41:42); also Daniel at Belshazzar's court in Babylon (Dan. 5:29). Chains were among the atonement oblations of the Children of Israel (Num. 31:50). (2) Chain work made into wreaths was used in the Temple pillar decoration (I Kings 7:17). (3) Chains as fetters are mentioned frequently, as in Lam. 3:7; Ezek. 7:23; Acts 28:20; II Tim. 1:16.

chalcedony (kăl-sĕd′ō-nĭ) (Rev. 21:19), a translucent quartz, with wax-like lustre, sometimes blue or white. The original stone to which the name was applied appears to have been green, possibly dioptase from the copper mines near Chalcedon in Asia Minor. The *chrysoprasus* of Rev. 21:20, A.V. (R.S.V. "chrysoprase") was an apple-green chalcedony.

Chalcolithic (kăl′kō-lĭth′ĭk) **Age.** See COPPER.

Chaldaea (kăl-dē′ȧ) (from Accad. *Kaldū*), the land of aggressive Semitic Aramaean nomads who gradually wandered into S. Babylonia and, aided by the Medes, conquered Assur in 614 B.C. The line of Chaldaean rulers included Nabopolassar, founder of the New Babylonian or Chaldaean Kingdom, and his son Nebuchadnezzar* (II Kings 24:2, 25:4–13; Jer. 37:5–12). (See ASSYRIA; BABYLON.) Chaldaeans founded the exact science of astronomy. They kept careful records of their observations over a long period, and are said to have estimated a year of 365 days, 6 hrs., 15 mins., 41 secs.—within less than 30 min. of what modern instruments have worked out. "Of the Chaldees" was the region later known as Chaldaea. It was the birthplace of Abraham (Gen. 11:28) and his point of departure for Mesopotamia and Canaan (Gen. 11:31, 15:7).

chalice. See ANTIOCH, THE CHALICE OF; CUP.

chapman, one who buys and sells; merchant; trader (A.V. II Chron. 9:14).

chapiter (chăp′ĭ-tẽr), an archaic word for "capital," the uppermost part of a pillar; in the Tabernacle, A.V. Ex. 36:38, 38:17–19, 28; in Solomon's Temple, A.V. I Kings 7:16 ff.: II Chron. 4:12 f.; Jer. 52:22.

charger, a large, shallow dish or platter, sometimes brought as a sacred offering to Tabernacle or Temple (Num. 7:13, 19, 25, 85; Ezra 1:9). A charger was used to carry the head of John the Baptist (Matt. 14:8, 11).

chariots, two-wheeled vehicles (sometimes four-wheeled in ancient Sumer) used principally for war, though very early Syrians and Egyptians used them also for hunting and for driving to supervise estates. They originated in Asia, where Cappadocian and Cilician horses were bred and exported to Egypt, whence Palestine adopted them. They were used also as ceremonial or royal vehicles (Gen. 50:9; II Kings 5:9; Acts 8:28). War chariots used by Canaanites in the plains of Palestine terrified approaching Israel (Judg. 1:19). These "chariots of iron," 900 of which engaged Deborah and Barak (Judg. 4:3, 13) and became embogged in the muddy Kishon, had their wooden frames reinforced with metal plates. David first introduced them as booty from a campaign waged against an Assyrian province N. of Damascus (II Sam. 8:4). Solomon had many chariots housed in several chariot cities (I Kings 4:26; II Chron. 9:25). Chariots became symbols of power to writers of Scripture (II Kings 2:11, 6:14; Ps. 20:7, 68:17).

The usual occupants of a war chariot were the driver and the bowman; sometimes a third carried a shield to protect the fighter.

89. Assyrian chariot, 858 B.C.

In a royal chariot an attendant would carry an umbrella over the monarch. Archaeology has excavated decorated royal chariots of Eighteenth Dynasty Tut-ankh-amun, one having its light wooden body covered with gold stucco, another having leather tires; and has also found heavy, eight-spoked Assyrian chariots of war, and embossed, metal-faced Estruscan chariots. One of the earliest known depictions of a chariot (c. 2500 B.C.) is on a plaque (University Museum, Philadelphia); it shows a two-wheeled chariot from Sumerian Ur with solid wooden wheels made of three pieces of wood joined together by wooden pegs. A high upright panel protected the front, from which the pole rises in a high curve to support a rein ring before descending to the yoke of the four asses.

charity, a word appearing 28 times in the A.V., as an inadequate rendition of a quality expressed in the Gk. word *agape*. The A.V. use of the word is a poor translation of the Vulgate "*caritas*" ("high esteem"), which itself failed to capture the meaning of *agape*, for which our best English word is "love." In the Bible "charity" is never used in the sense of "alms-giving." See I Cor. 8:1, 13:1–8, 14:1; Col. 3:14; I Thess. 3:6; I Tim. 1:5, 2:15, 4:12; II Tim. 2:22; I Pet. 4:8; Jude 12; Rev. 2:19.

Chebar (kē′bär), a small stream or canal of Babylon; the scene of Ezekiel's visions among the Hebrew captives: Ezek. 1:1, 3, 3:15, 23, 10:15, 20, 22, 43:3.

Chedorlaomer (kĕd′ŏr-lā-ō′mẽr), King of Elam, a land E. of Babylonia, S. of Media, at the head of the Persian Gulf. He controlled a large part of W. Asia, including Babylonia and S. Palestine (Gen. 14:1, 4, 5, 9, 17). In the latter area he had made several vassal allies, who helped him in the four-kings vs. five-kings war in the Dead Sea region (Gen. 14), when the Canaanite sovereigns of Sodom, Gomorrah, Admah, Zeboiim, and Zoar rebelled against Chedorlaomer. All efforts thus far to identify the four Mesopotamian kings of the narrative of Genesis 14 have been futile. But the story is not altogether unhistorical. Its material appears to be very ancient, and some of its allusions are believed by Albright to refer to customs of the Middle Bronze Age (c. 2000–1500 B.C.).

Chemosh (kē′mŏsh), the national deity of Moab*, who was worshipped with rites similar to those of Molech, to whom living children were sacrificed by burning. Moabites were known as "people of Chemosh" (Num. 21:29). The anger of Chemosh is said (in the Moabite Stone inscription) to be the reason for Israel's conquest of Moab (cf. Judg. 11:24). Solomon built at Jerusalem—possibly for political reasons—an altar to Chemosh (I Kings 11:7), which was not destroyed until Josiah's reformation almost three centuries later (II Kings 23:13).

Cherethites (kĕr′ē-thīts) or Cherethims, probably Cretans living in Philistia (I Sam. 30:14; Ezek. 25:16; Zeph. 2:5). David's bodyguard included Cherethites (II Sam. 8:18, cf. 23:23).

Cherith (kē′rĭth), a brook, not definitely identified, but believed to have flowed into the Jordan past Gilgal, SE. of Jericho. Possibly a wadi* running into the River Jabesh*. Its tangled underbrush made an excellent hiding place for the fugitive Hebrew prophet Elijah (I Kings 17:3, 5). Nelson Glueck's studies in E. Palestine (the Kingdom of Jordan) dispose of the old identification of the Brook Cherith with the Wâdī Qelt* (which runs down to Jericho). It is certain that when Elijah fled from the rage of the Phoenician princess Jezebel he went eastward (I Kings 17:3).

90. Ivory cherub found at Samaria.

cherub (plural, cherubim), symbolic, mythological "living creatures": guarding the tree of life in Eden (Gen. 3:24); placed in pairs at each end of the mercy seat of the Tabernacle*, protecting the sacred articles in the Ark* (Ex. 25:18–22); embroidered on the veil of the Temple (II Chron. 3:14); and sacred symbols in Solomon's Temple (I Kings 6:23 ff.; cf. I Chron. 28:18). Cherubim made a frieze around the wall of the Temple, and decorated the bases of the molten sea (I Kings 7:29). Ps. 18:10 speaks figuratively of Yahweh's riding upon a cherub. As to their appearance, W. F. Albright points to an excavated representation of a pair of cherubs supporting the throne of King Hiram of Byblos (see GEBAL) (era of the Judges, c. 1200 on). This design indicates a creature with a lion's body, human face, and conspicuous wings. The Byblos depiction jibes well with Ps. 80:1. Neighbors of Israel had symbolic winged creatures, such as winged lions and bulls, guarding the temples and palaces of Mesopotamia, and the Egyptian winged creatures in the temple of the Zodia of Dendar. Hittites had griffins—winged sphinxes having lions' bodies and eagles' heads and wings. Ezekiel's description of 4 composite "living creatures" (chap. 10) seen by the River Chebar may reflect Babylonian observations. Heb. 9:5 speaks of cherubim overshadowing the mercy seat. They guarded, veiled, and denoted Deity.

chest. (1) The chest of Joash (Jehoash) (c. 837–800 B.C.) was ordered made to receive moneys from the people to repair breaches in the Jerusalem Temple (II Chron. 24:11; II Kings 12:9 f.). (2) The chests of Tyre were famous for their storage of rich apparel (Ezek. 27:24). They were of carved cedar, bound with cords.

Cheth (kāth), Heth in R.V., the 8th letter of the Hebrew alphabet. See WRITING.

child, children, regarded as gifts from God (Gen. 4:1). To be childless was considered a reproach (Gen. 16:4; Luke 1:25). Children were legally adopted as heirs even in the Patriarchal period (cf. Gen. 15:2). Jesus referred to the joy of a woman at the birth of her son (John 16:21). Child training was given attention by early Israel, filial respect being enjoined as a prerequisite to long dwelling in the inheritance (Ex. 20:12). Prov. 22:6 supplied a program which has never been surpassed: "Train up a child in the way he should go, and when he is old he will not depart from it." II Tim. 3:15 elevates that policy of character training by a program of religious education*.

Jesus clearly expressed his evaluation of children (Mark 9:36 f.). He used childhood to define entrance requirements for the Kingdom of God (Mark 10:14 f.). He thanked God for revealing to babes what He had hidden from "the wise and prudent" (Matt. 11:25). Cf. also Luke 6:20–38.

The Hebrews practiced several deeply ingrained ceremonial and hygienic customs in connection with child-bearing: the use of midwives (Ex. 1:19); washing new-born infants with water, rubbing them with salt, and wrapping them in swaddling clothes (Ezek. 16:4; Luke 2:12); the observance of laws for ceremonial cleanness and atonement gifts after childbirth (Lev. 12:1–8); festivities at weaning (Gen. 21:8) (see CIRCUMCISION). Early home training was managed by mothers, professional guidance by fathers. Wealthy families employed nurses (II Sam. 4:4) and tutors (II Kings 10:1, 5), called "bringers up of the children."

children of God, a distinctive N.T. conception of redeemed individuals in relation to the Father-God revealed by Jesus Christ. ("We are children of God, and if children, then heirs . . . with Christ." Rom. 8:16 f.)

Chileab (kĭl'ē-ăb), the second son of David born at Hebron, of Abigail (II Sam. 3:3). Identified as Daniel in I Chron. 3:1.

Chilion (kĭl'ĭ-ŏn), a son of Elimelech and Naomi, apparently native of Bethlehem in Judah. With his parents he migrated to Moab, married Orpah, and died of a disease suggested by the literal meaning of his name, "wasting away," possibly tuberculosis (Ruth 1:2, 5).

Chimham (kĭm'hăm), the son of Barzillai*. He went to Jerusalem as David's guest in place of his father. He may have built a caravanserai near Bethlehem (A.S.V. note at Jer. 41:17 reads "the lodging-place of Chimham.").

Chinnereth (kĭn'ē-rĕth) (Chinneroth) ("lute," "harp"), a fortified city on the NW. shore of the Sea of Galilee (Josh. 19:35). It gave its name to the surrounding plain and to the harp-shaped lake (Num. 34:11) known later as Gennesaret or Galilee.

Chios (kī'ŏs), an Aegean island off the W. coast of Asia Minor opposite Smyrna, on Paul's route to Rome (Acts 20:15). It claims to have been the home of Homer. It is famous for figs, mastic, and marble.

Chislev (kĭs'lĕv) (A.V. Chisleu), the 9th month of the Hebrew year, November-December (Zech. 7:1; Neh. 1:1).

Chittim (kĭt'ĭm), a term used several times in the A.V., as in Num. 24:24, Isa. 23:1, Jer. 2:10, etc., for Kittim, a name associated with Cyprus*.

Chloe (klō'ē), a woman of Corinth or Ephesus, whose servants told Paul of contentions in the church at Corinth (I Cor. 1:11). Whether she herself was Christian or pagan is not known.

Chorazin (kō-rā'zĭn), a town N. of Sea of Galilee c. 2½ m. N. of Capernaum (Tell Hûm) denounced by Jesus because it had remained unrepentant (Matt. 11:21; Luke 10:13). For two centuries the black basalt ruins of the Chorazin synagogue have been known. Its "Moses seat" (Matt. 23:2), reserved for distinguished guests or its elder, has been found.

Christ (Gk. *Christos*, "the anointed"). See JESUS CHRIST; MESSIAH.

Christian, the name carried by followers of Christ since N.T. times; possibly first applied in derision by non-Christians. Early Christians called themselves "brethren" (Acts 14:2), "disciples" (Acts 20:30), "they . . . which believed" (Acts 10:45), men and women "of this way" (A.V.) or of "the Way" (R.S.V.) (Acts 9:2). "Christians" is first mentioned in Acts 11:26, in connection with the ministry of Barnabas and Paul at Antioch. Evidently the name soon spread beyond the Antioch of A.D. 40–44, for it is used in the first General Epistle of Peter (4:16) as though widely understood. Its use by Agrippa (Acts 26:28) may or may not have been in derision. Historically, "Christian" came to designate not a sect of Judaism, but a separate religion based on the person of Jesus Christ, rather than on a book of law, a dogma, or an institution.

Christianity, a word not appearing in the N.T., but designating the Christian faith as founded on the life and teachings of Christ and his Apostles. The first extant use of the word is in the 2d-century letters of Ignatius, Bishop of Antioch. Christianity, though rooted in Judaism (Matt. 5:17), was an entirely new religion, the "new song" of Ps. 33:3, the "new heart" and "spirit" of Ezek. 36:26, the new covenant* or "testament" of Matt. 26:28, the "all things new" of Rev. 21:5. It is a revelation of God through His Son Jesus* Christ; a way of life based on a personal experience of Christ (Acts 16:30 f.); obedience to his commandments (John 15:10); and a determination to increase the brotherhood of his followers into a redeemed world society made up of perfected individuals (Matt. 5:48).

Christmas (Christ-mass), the anniversary of the birth of Jesus, celebrated by Protestants generally and Roman Catholics on December 25, a fixed date, in contrast to the variable Easter. Christmas is observed by Orthodox Churches of the East on December 25 and by the Armenian Church on January 6. The first celebration of Christmas on December 25 was in Rome c. A.D. 336. It is by no means certain that Christ was born in December. The Christian era (indicated by "A.D.," Anno Domini, "in the year of the Lord") should logically begin with the birth of Jesus. But when the Roman monk Dionysius Exiguus attempted to work out a Christian chronology without disturbing the Roman year and months, he began it with January 1, 754 A.U.C. (*ab urbe condita*—referring to the foundation of Rome). Emperor Charles III of Germany was the first to adopt (A.D. 879) *Anno Domini*. Because of an error of Dionysius, the anomaly exists of Christ's having been born several years before the era which bears his name. Herod "the king," in whose reign Christ was born (Matt. 2:1), ruled 37–4 B.C. Orthodox Jews refer to the Christian era as "the common era" (C.E.).

Christology, the study of Christ's understanding of his mission and his relation to God, as impressed on his early followers; and of men's estimate of that understanding.

Chronicles I and **II** are historical books of the O.T. which originally, like Samuel and Kings, were a single volume, called in Hebrew *The Things of the Days* (or *Events of Past Time*). The 12 preceding books terminated with the Hebrew nation in captivity (II Kings 25). I Chronicles parallels in part II Samuel; and II Chronicles parallels in part I and II Kings. Jerome (c. A.D. 342–420) called them "a chronicle of the whole of sacred history," from Adam to Cyrus (538 B.C.), thus naming the books for our English Bible.

The author is known only as "the Chronicler." The books of Ezra* and Nehemiah* were written by him. W. F. Albright believes that Ezra was the Chronicler, but it is generally thought that "Chronicles-Ezra-Nehemiah" was penned some time between 350 and 250 B.C. About half of Chronicles is based on material from the canonized books Genesis-Kings (omitting Judges); and the other half may have been derived from the 21 books mentioned in I Chron. 29:29; II Chron. 9:29, 13:22, 27:7, 33:18, 24:27, 26:22. Some of these are in the O.T. Canon*. Others have been lost.

The contents of I and II Chronicles are as follows:

(1) I Chron. 1–10, an outline of history from Adam to Saul, chiefly through genealogical lists.
(2) I Chron. 11–29, reign of David.
(3) II Chron. 1–9, reign of Solomon.
(4) II Chron. 10–36, history of the Southern Kingdom to the Babylonian Captivity.

The character of the books, as well as of the Chronicler, can be ascertained by the study of what he selects, omits, and alters from his sources. He uses the facts not so much to write history as to defend a point of view and establish an apology. He was "a son of the law," wrote as a devotee of the priestly cause, and continued on a level of high enthusiasm the priestly strand of literature so easily discernible in the O.T. (See SOURCES.) The Levitical order in charge of the Temple music is extolled. Compare II Sam. 6 with I Chron. 15:2, 13–28, or I Kings 8 with II Chron. 5:11 ff., and observe the new emphasis the Chronicler places on the Temple services of the Levites. The service of praise led by the Levites is exalted (I Chron. 16:4, 23:30). Only a keen musical knowledge and interest would record such details as I Chron. 15:16 ff., 25:1 ff. Priests were their brothers and superiors in the hierarchy; but the Levites were always placed out front. Music in the Temple service was regarded by the Chronicler as outstanding. Prophets are treated by him with deference, but they too become ecclesiastical, and their messages deal with worship more than with the great social duties.

David is pictured as the founder of the Jewish Church (I Chron. 21:18 ff.). He is a second Moses, exalted as the promoter of the Temple (I Chron. 21:18 f., 28:1 f.). He ordered the music (I Chron. 6:31, 25:1) and organized the Levites (I Chron. 23:27). All personal aspects of David's life are subordinated to his ecclesiastical leadership. But David's military glory was retained, for the Chronicler without difficulty combined the military and the ecclesiastical. Of the 29 chapters of I Chronicles, 19 are devoted to David. When Solomon died and the Kingdom was divided, the Chronicler saw this break as a wicked rebellion of the Northern Kingdom against the legitimate Davidic dynasty in the Southern (II Chron. 10:16–19, 11:13–17, 13:4 ff.). It was this attitude of narrow devotion to Jerusalem and of pugnacious hatred of everything in the N., including hostility to the Samaritans, that created the religious schism (II Chron. 13:4–12). A more tolerant interpretation of history in the days of the Chronicler would likely have made unnecessary the erection of a temple on Mt. Gerizim as a rival to that on Mt. Zion (John 4:20). The Books of Chronicles mirror less the days of David and his successors than the attitude of the later Jewish community, the exclusiveness of their Temple worship, and the sacred ecclesiastical institutions centered in Jerusalem after the Exile.

The Chronicler had an indiscriminate love for fantastically big numbers. David was made king by 6,800 men of Judah, 7,100 Simeonites, 4,600 Levites (I Chron. 12:23 ff.). Temple donations were huge, indicated by I Chron. 22:14. He had opinions as to what made war justifiable, successful, or disastrous (II Chron. 13:4–20, 14:9–15, 20:1–30). Retribution was one of his controlling ideas (I Chron. 10:13). He stressed monotheism (I Chron. 29:10–19) and condemned idolatry (I Chron. 14:12; II Chron. 14:3 f.). To the Chronicler, Yahweh was a liturgically minded God whose ritual worship did not center in sacrifices (see WORSHIP), but in ritual, music, and prayer. The ethical demands of God upon man he does not stress as the prophets do. The sins for which kings were punished were: corrupting worship; seeking other gods; depending on foreign alliances; and in one case summoning a physician instead of seeking Yahweh (II Chron. 16:12).

Chronology

Archaeological Periods of Palestine in Terms of Pottery Chronology (based on data by J. L. Kelso and J. P. Thorley, *BA* Vol. VIII No. 4.)

Carbon-dating results in accuracy.

Neolithic Age c. 5500–4000 B.C. Toward the close of this period pottery first appears.

Chalcolithic Age c. 4000–3300 B.C. The great period of irrigation culture in Palestine and the time when copper was introduced into use there.

Early Bronze Age c. 3300–2000 B.C. These years saw Egyptian Dynastic history begin and Egypt exert a strong cultural influence on Palestine. "The first historical period."

Middle Bronze Age c. 2000–1500 B.C. Palestine was under Egyptian political domination when this period opened, and remained so through the time of Abraham. The Hyksos captured Palestine and Egypt in the days of Joseph and controlled both lands until Egypt again became a world power about the end of this period.

Late Bronze Age c. 1500–1200 B.C. The close of Israel's Sojourn in Egypt, the Exodus, and Joshua's Conquest of Palestine.

Iron Age I c. 1200–1000 B.C. The Period of Judges to the time of David, during which iron came into common use.

Iron Age II c. 1000–587 B.C. From the time of David to the destruction of Jerusalem.

Iron Age III 587–333 B.C. The Exilic and Post-Exilic period; predominantly Persian.

Hellenistic Period 333–63 B.C. From the time of Alexander the Great to the Roman conquest of Palestine.

Roman Period 63 B.C.–A.D. 325. The time of the N.T. and the Early Church.

Using pottery alone for calendar purposes, the date of any city of Bible times can be worked out to within about fifty years.

Some Convenient O.T. Date Pegs (based on W. F. Albright)

Migration of the descendants of Terah (the Terachids) from Ur N. to Haran and on to Canaan—20th–19th century B.C., "The Patriarchal Age."

Song of Miriam (parts)— c. 13th century B.C.

Descent of the Jacob tribes to Egypt—18th (or more likely 17th) century B.C., in connection with the Hyksos occupation.

Jacob may be dated c. 1750 B.C. (Middle Bronze II).

Fall of Jericho (incident to the Conquest)—c. 1250 B.C.

Song of Deborah—c. 1125 B.C.

Philistine destruction of Shiloh—c. 1050 B.C.

Hiram of Tyre, ally of Solomon—c. 969–936 B.C.

Tiglath-pileser III destroys Megiddo—733 B.C.

Siloam Tunnel construction and inscription—701 B.C.

Lachish Letters—c. 589 or 588 B.C.

Period of the Maccabees (Hasmonaeans)

Revolt of Palestine against Syria—167 B.C.
Judas Maccabaeus—166(165)–160 B.C.
Jonathan—160–142
Simon—142–134
John Hyrcanus—134–104
Aristobulus I—104–103
Alexander Jannaeus—103–76
Alexandra—76–67
Aristobulus II—66—63

Note: Mariamne, wife of Herod the Great (37–4 B.C.) was a Maccabee.

Pompey established Roman control of Palestine—63 B.C.

Some Rulers of Palestine in the Time of Christ and Paul

Caesar Augustus, Roman Emperor—27 B.C.–A.D. 14

Tiberius, Emperor—A.D. 14–37

Herod the Great, Idumaean King of Judaea under the Romans—37–4 B.C.

Herod Antipas, Tetrarch Galilee and Peraea—4 B.C.–A.D. 39

Herod Agrippa I, King of Judaea—A.D. 41–44

Herod Agrippa II—A.D. 50–93

Roman procurators ruling Palestine for the Romans:

Pontius Pilate—A.D. 26–36
Felix—52–60
Festus—60–62

A Bird's-Eye View of Historical Periods in Palestine

Hellenistic—c. 333–63 B.C.
Roman—63 B.C.–A.D. 324
Byzantine—A.D. 324–636
Arabic—A.D. 636–1516
Turkish—A.D. 1516–1917

Approximate Dates in the Life of Christ

Birth—c. 7–4 B.C. (some scholars prefer 5 B.C.)

Baptism—c. A.D. 26 (some scholars prefer 25 or 27)

Ministry—3 or 2 years (some scholars prefer 2 years or 1)

Crucifixion—A.D. 29 Friday, Nisan 14th day (some prefer 30)

Chronology of Hebrew Rulers

(Based on dates of W. F. Albright, *Bulletin 100*, ASOR, used by permission of W. F. A. and ASOR): United Israel—Saul, c. 1020–1000 B.C.; David, c. 1000–961 B.C.; Solomon, c. 961–922 B.C.

The Divided Monarchy

Judah			*Israel*		
Ruler	*No. of years reigned*	*Dates*	*Ruler*	*No. of years reigned*	*Dates*
Rehoboam	8 (17)†	c. 922–915	Jeroboam I	22	c. 922–901
Abijah (Abijam)	3	c. 915–913			
Asa	41	c. 913–873	Nadab	2	c. 901–900
			Baasha	24	c. 900–877
			Elah	2	c. 877–876
			Zimri	7 days	c. 876
Jehoshaphat	25	c. 873–849	Omri	8 (12)	c. 876–869
			Ahab	20 (22)	c. 869–850
Jehoram	8	c. 849–842	Ahaziah	2	c. 850–849
Ahaziah	1	c. 842	Joram	8 (12)	c. 849–842
Athaliah	6 (7)	c. 842–837	Jehu	28	c. 842–815
Jehoash	38 (40)	c. 837–800	Joahaz	15 (17)	c. 815–801
Amaziah	18 (29)	c. 800–783	Joash	16	c. 801–786
Uzziah (Azariah)	42 (52)	c. 783–742	Jeroboam II	41	c. 786–746
Jotham (regent)	8 (?)	c. 750–742	Zechariah	6 mos.	c. 746–745
			Shallum	1 mo.	c. 745
Jotham (king)	8 (16)	c. 742–735	Menahem	8+ (10)	c. 745–738
			Pekahiah	2	c. 738–737
Jehoahaz I (Ahaz)	21± (16)	c. 735–715	Pekah	6— (20)	c. 737–732
Hezekiah	29	c. 715–687	Hoshea	9	c. 732–724
			Fall of Samaria		722–1
Manasseh	45 (55)	c. 687–642			
Amon	2	c. 642–640			
Josiah	31	c. 640–609			
Jehoahaz II (Shallum)	3 mos.	c. 609			
Jehoiakim (Eliakim)	11	c. 609–597			
Jehoiachin (Jeconiah)	3 mos.	c. 598			
Zedekiah (Mattaniah)	11	c. 598–587			

† Numbers in ( ) are those of the Hebrew Bible.

(Jerusalem was stormed and destroyed by Chaldaeans in August 587 B.C. after 1½ years' siege. See EXILE.)

Some Subsequent Dates in Jewish History

Jews under Babylonian rule: in Judaea, poor; in Babylon, prosperous—587/6–538 B.C.

Jews under Persian rule—538–333.

Jerusalem Temple reconstructed—520–515.

Jerusalem's walls rebuilt and the Law* enforced; Nehemiah*—c. 447, 433.

Jews controlled by Alexander*—333–323.

Jews controlled by Egyptian Ptolemies*—323–198.

Jews controlled by Seleucids (see SELEUCUS) (Judaea annexed to Syria)—198–167.

Maccabean Period (see MACCABEES)—166–63.

Roman rule in Palestine—63 B.C.–A.D. 324.

Approximate Dates Suggested for the Apostolic Age

Pentecost—c. A.D. 29 or A.D. 30

Stoning of Stephen—c. A.D. 31

Jerusalem Council—c. A.D. 48 (or 50)

The Life of Paul

Conversion—between A.D. 32 and A.D. 35 (some say 37–38)

First Missionary Journey—A.D. 47–48

Second Missionary Journey—(Acts 15:36–18:22) 49–52

In Corinth—(arrived) c. 50 (Gallio, proconsul at Corinth)—51 or 52

Third Missionary Journey—(Acts 18:23–21:19) 52–56

After 2 yrs. in prison, appeal to Caesar, following accession—Festus 61

Starts to Rome— fall of 61

Arrives Rome—spring of 62

2 yrs. in Rome 62–64

Death—64/65

James, death—61 or 63

Peter, death—64–65 (some prefer 80)

Fall of Jerusalem—70

Persecutions under Emperor Domitian, evidenced in Revelation, 93–96

For additional dates, see suggestions in ASSYRIA; BABYLON; EGYPT; HEROD; HITTITES; PHILISTINES; WRITING, etc. Carbon-dating process helps to fix dates of early mss., but cannot establish them exactly.

Old Testament Books in Approximately Chronological Order

(According to Robert H. Pfeiffer, in *Encyclopedia of Religion*, pp. 84 f., quoted by permission of Vergilius Ferm and *Philosophical Library*)

Genesis (1200–450 B.C.)
Exodus (1200–450)
Judges (1150–550)
I, II Samuel (1000–500)
Numbers (850–400)
Joshua (850–350)
Kings (850–350)
Amos (750)
Hosea (745–735)
Isaiah 1–39 (740–700; 550–250)
Micah (702; 500–250)
Deuteronomy (630)
Jeremiah (626–586)
Zephaniah (625: 600–300)
Nahum (614; 300)
Habbakuk (600)
Job (600)
Proverbs (600–200)
Ezekiel (593–571)
Lamentations (570–450)
Leviticus (560–450)
Isaiah 40–66 (546–400)
Haggai (520)
Zechariah 1–8 (520–518)
Psalms (500–100)
Obadiah (470)
Malachi (460)
Nehemiah (432)
Ruth (400)
Joel (350)
Jonah (350–300)
Zechariah 9–14 (300–200)
Song of Solomon (250)
I, II Chronicles (250)
Ezra (250)
Daniel (164)
Ecclesiastes (160)
Esther (125)

The O.T. Apocrypha date from 180. Some of the books contain writings of different dates. The period covered by the most important of them is indicated.

The oldest written portions of the O.T. are poems—once oral utterances; such as Gen. 4:23 f.; Ex. 15:21 ("The Song of Miriam"); Josh. 10:12b–13a; Judg. 5 ("Song of Deborah"); and laws, like the "J Decalogue."

For more detailed statement of dates of O.T. books, see *An Introduction to the Old Testament*, Robert H. Pfeiffer, pp. 20 ff. (Harper & Brothers).

New Testament Books in Approximately Chronological Order

Scholars find it impossible to agree on the exact dates when the N.T. books were written. Not even the authorship and place of writing are certain in all cases. But for the convenience of students the following table has value. It is based on the opinions of Dr. Albert E. Barnett, in *The New Testament: Its Making and Meaning*, pp. 17 f. (Abingdon-Cokesbury Press). Dates at the right indicate various views of other scholars (see also NEW TESTAMENT). Albright feels there is little basis for dating any N.T. book after A.D. 80.

Galatians	A.D. 49	A.D. 53–58
Thessalonian Letters	50	52
Corinthian Letters	53–55	57
Romans	56	57–58
Philippians	(? 55) 60	63
Colossians, Philemon	(55) 61–62	58–60
Mark	65–67	68–70
Matthew	75–80	70–85
Luke, Acts	90–95	before 63–96
Ephesians	95	58–60
Hebrews	95	80
Revelation	95	96
I Peter	95–100	61–63
Fourth Gospel	95–115	95–115
Johannine Epistles	110–115	98
James	125–150	58–60
Jude	125–150	81
II Peter	150	98
Timothy, Titus	160–175	64–67

Church. The English word is a translation of the Gk. *ekklēsia*, which means literally "assembly of citizens called out" and is used in the Gk. version of the O.T. (the Septuagint) to translate the Hebrew word *qahal*, which the O.T. applies to the people of Israel when assembled for a religious purpose. The concept underlying these words is, therefore, an important link between the O.T. and N.T. In both Testaments, the life of the religious person, whether Jew or Christian, is not understood in terms of a merely individual salvation, but as involving membership in a divine community. The N.T. places the word on the lips of Jesus only in Matt. 16:18 and 18:17, but his choice of 12 apostles, corresponding to the 12 tribes of Israel, and his sense of a mission directed chiefly to Israel (Matt. 15:24) show that the thought of establishing, or rather re-establishing, a community was central to his thinking. The relationship of the idea of "the Church" to that of "the Kingdom of God"* is not entirely clear, but probably the Church is to be thought of as the chosen group which is to wait, patiently and obediently, for the coming of the Kingdom and is, perhaps, to be conceived as in some sense the nucleus of it.

Outside the Gospels, the word Church occurs many times and in two different senses. It can refer to the congregation of Christians situated in a particular locality, such as at Cenchreae or Corinth or at someone's house (Rom. 16:1; I Cor. 1:2; Col. 4:15), or to the universal Church of Christ which includes all local congregations (Eph. 5:27; I Tim. 3:15). The word is never used in the N.T. for a church building. It is the concept of the church as a universal community that is theologically significant for N.T. writers. For them (at least for Paul and his "school"), the church is in some very real sense the earthly "body" of Jesus Christ. He is the "head" of the body, and individual Christians, each with his own function, are the "members" (I Cor. 12:12–27; Eph. 5:23; Col. 1:18). The conception resembles the one found in the Fourth Gospel which pictures Christ as the vine and individual Christians as the branches (John 15:5).

The Church began to take shape only after the Resurrection of Jesus. Its birth and spread, under the guidance and by the power of the Holy Spirit, is the main theme of the Book of Acts. Following Jesus' Ascension* (Acts 1:9), the little company of his faithful returned from the Mt. of Olives (v. 12) to an upper room, probably in the home of John Mark's mother, where the eleven and the believing women, a company numbering about 120, met, with Peter as the spokesman (Acts 1:12–15). This cell of first Christians was multiplied after Pentecost* to numerous groups meeting in other homes, as possibly that of James (Acts 21:18). Thus grew the Church, with only occasional large group meetings in the Temple arcades, where all citizens were permitted to gather for expression of ideas. The first Church was still "in the house" when Pentecost came with its supernatural accompaniments (Acts 2); the preaching of Peter (2:14–36); and the addition of "three thousand souls" who were initiated into active membership in the first Church body by baptism* (v. 38), "the breaking of bread" (v. 42), and the voluntary sharing of possessions for mutual service based on actual need (v. 45). Even after Pentecost, the Apostles were free to go into Solomon's Porch of the Temple to heal and preach the Resurrection of Jesus, until their very success drew official rebuke (Acts 4:5–7). The rapid growth of the Church is clearly stated in Acts 5:12–42. Even a "great company of the priests were obedient to the faith" (Acts 6:7). The Church in Jerusalem, and in every other city to which the new faith was carried, was composed of house congregations, over which officials (see below) presided.

The growth of the Church is vividly indicated in Acts and in the N.T. Epistles. The baptism of Cornelius and other Gentiles by Peter at Caesarea, the seat of Roman government in Palestine, astonished those "of the circumcision" (Acts 10:45), and a step forward was taken when Gentiles who had received the Holy Ghost were admitted into the Christian body. This step was not taken until after Peter was rebuked for his unorthodox eating with Gentiles (Acts 11:1 f.). But after the voice of the Jerusalem Council had spoken through James (Acts 15:13) there was joy and a glorifying of God because Gentiles, as well as Jews, had been granted "repentance unto life" (Acts 11:18). The only entrance requirements for Gentiles, in addition to faith in the living Lord, was that "they abstain from pollutions of idols, and from fornication, and from things strangled, and from blood" (Acts 15:20). Paul, Silas, Barnabas, and John Mark went through Syria, Asia, Cyprus, and Achaia, organizing and confirming churches (Acts 15:25–36), and preaching even in Jewish synagogues, as at Damascus (Acts 9:20) and Salamis (Cyprus) (Acts 13:5). Remaining at Antioch for a whole year, and in Corinth for as much as 18 months at one time, Paul and his colleagues laid substantial foundations for permanent groups of people in the Way. The churches to which the N.T. Epistles were addressed took form, and others which were never honored with letters, as at Athens (Acts 17:16–34. See Rev. 1:4).

The early Church at worship met daily in the Temple as well as in homes (Acts 5:42). Later, in recognition of Christ's Resurrection on the first day of the week, that day became the principal occasion of public worship (I Cor. 16:2). At these public worship services missionary teaching was offered to all who were within reach, whether in the Temple arcades, along a river bank, in jails, or in private homes. Prayer was offered (Acts 4:31) not only on the Lord's Day, but whenever special occasion demanded it (Acts 12:5). Scripture was read (James 1:22; I Thess. 5:27). The all-important ritual of "the breaking of bread" and the sharing of "the cup" on the Lord's Day was interpreted as a continuing proclamation of Jesus' death, an anticipation of his coming, and a participation in his "body and blood" (I Cor. 11:20–29, 10:16). It was celebrated as a part of a common meal or agape* ("feast of love") to which only believers were admitted. Offerings for the needy were received (I Cor. 16:2). Individuals frequently took the floor, under the influence of the Holy Spirit, as they believed, to "speak in tongues" or "interpret" (I Cor. 14:26–32).

Church organization was fluid at first, developing to meet the need for dependable instruction in the faith, the regulation of worship, and the administering of financial relief to the poor. There is insufficient evidence to show how the uniform, stabilized ministries of the post-Apostolic Age developed out of the more "charismatic" ministries described in the N.T.(1) The Church officers of the Apostolic Age, some of whose duties no doubt overlapped with others, were these:

Apostles—those who had seen the Lord (Luke 1:2; Matt. 10:2; Acts 1:21 f.; I Cor. 9:1 f.) and felt specially appointed by him to continue his work. This group included the original eleven, plus Matthias, Paul, James, and probably Barnabas. Upon these natural leaders fell the greatest responsibilities and decisions.

"*The Seven*" (Acts 6:1–6)—men "of honest report, full of the Holy Ghost and wisdom," appointed by the Apostles as helpers or almoners to look after "the widows" and other needy, and to "serve tables." These are sometimes identified with the deacons mentioned below.

Prophets or inspired speakers (forerunners of "preachers")— animated by divine impulses and "god-called" (Acts 11:27 f.).

Ministers—teachers endowed not so much with inspiration as with knowledge and "the word of wisdom" (I Cor. 12:8).

Evangelists (Eph. 4:11) or missionaries—like Philip (Acts 21:8) and Timothy (II Tim. 4, 5).

And in addition to these there were workers gifted in healing-miracles, "helps," "tongues" (I Cor. 12:28–31).

(2) *Local officials*, as the Church grew rapidly in numbers and needed definite organization, included:

Elders (Acts 14:23), not only in Jerusalem, but wherever the Church was spreading, entrusted with pastoral and moral supervision, shepherding the flock ("pastors," Eph. 4:11).

Bishops were also known as "elders" (Titus 1:5–9). Some see in the N.T. a tendency toward the monarchical episcopate.

Deacons and deaconesses (Rom. 16:1, I Tim. 3:8–11) who attended to Church charities—people of character and common sense.

And in addition to these there were workers gifted in healing-miracles, "helps," "tongues" (I Cor. 12:28–31).

E. L./R. C. D.

Chuza (kū'ză) (Chuzas in A.S.V.) the steward of Herod the tetrarch. His wife,

Joanna, was one of the ministering women who followed Jesus (Luke 8:3).

Cilicia, in N.T. times a Roman province at the NE. corner of the Mediterranean, bounded on the N. and W. by the Taurus Mts. (see TARSUS); a plain well watered by rivers, with a marshy coast. The chief city of the Cilicia Plain was Tarsus, described by Paul (Acts 21:39). Cilicia was famous for the goat's-hair textile *cilicium*, loomed from strong wool cut from flocks grazing in the Taurus during winter. Cilicia in Paul's day was busy with traders and travelers using

91. Cilicia.

the famous Cilician Gates. This series of narrow passes through the Taurus Mts. was the historic highway which for 4,000 years carried armies of invaders—Hittites, Assyrians, Greeks, Romans, etc., into Syria, Mesopotamia, and Asia Minor. Paul passed through the Cilician Gates, as he went to found and to revisit the Christian Churches (Acts 15:40 f., 18:23). (See map under CYPRUS.)

circumcision, a very ancient Semitic rite, involving the removal of the foreskin (*praeputium*) of male members of the community. Among Hebrews the custom is based upon Abraham's example, the procedure being a token of the covenant between the Patriarch and Yahweh (Gen. 17:10–14). The narrative of Ex. 4:24–26 (J) associates its origin with Moses. The use of a flint knife indicated in this passage points to the early date at which the ceremony was practiced. The Hebrews may have adopted the custom from Egyptian sources, for Egyptians and Canaanites, as well as Moslems, Polynesians, and many primitive tribes of America, Africa, and Australia have practiced circumcision or still do. Originally, Hebrews did not circumcise boys until they reached puberty. Later, they performed the operation on the 8th day after birth (Lev. 12:3), at which time the name was given the son (Luke 1:59, 2:21). In early times, circumcising was done by a parent; later, as now, by a professional *mōhēl*. There are several theories offered to explain the ancient custom: hygienic considerations (like the prevention of venereal diseases), preparation for sexual life, ritual for initiation into a tribal group, dedication of the generative organs, acknowledgment of the male's life-giving god. One of the issues on which Jewish and Gentile Christians split was the matter of circumcision. Paul and Barnabas won the debate before the Jerusalem Council in the whole matter of Mosaic Law with reference to the new Christian faith, and liberalized the requirements for admission (Acts 15:20).

In the O.T. as well as in the N.T. circumcision is mentioned symbolically; "uncircumcised lips" (Ex. 6:12), "the circumcision made . . . in putting off the body of the sins of the flesh by the circumcision of Christ" (Col. 2:11).

cisterns, reservoirs for the storage of rain water; necessary to the inhabitants of Palestine because seasons of heavy rainfall are followed by months of virtual drought, and the geological formation makes water run off rather than seep and accumulate below the surface. Water was also conducted by pipe from distant sources. Sometimes cisterns honeycombed rocks near ancient settlements, as at Gezer. These were constructed with circular shafts, widening as they sank to a chamber 10 to 25 ft. wide and 20 ft. deep. The walls were usually plastered. The reference of Eccles. 12:6 to the wheel broken at the cistern implies a hand-manipulated wheel for elevating the water. The public works system of Solomon brought millions of gallons of water from the vicinity of Bethlehem, where it was stored in giant reservoirs (see RESERVOIR, illus. 344), to the area of his Temple and palaces. Today below the Dome of the Rock in that same area, under a fountain called "The Cup," there are giant cisterns or storage tanks. Another cistern or reservoir of old Jerusalem is near the Church of the Holy Sepulcher—the so-called Pool of Hezekiah (II Kings 20:20), 250 ft. x 150 ft., drawing water by conduit from the Birket Mamilla Pool at the Hinnom Valley entrance. Prof. Solomiac of the Hebrew University has recently excavated some of the cisterns which supplied soldiers guarding watchtowers of "The Third Wall of Jerusalem."

Sennacherib promised the people of Judah a cistern for every man (II Kings 18:31).

cities are referred to more than a thousand times in Scripture, though the interests of the Hebrews were largely pastoral. Their important cities were acquired by conquest from skillful Canaanite city builders, Philistines, Syrians, or by inheritance. Even Jerusalem had been a Jebusite (see JEBUS) center before its conquest by David. Masonry erected by Hebrews at Lachish*, or walls in any other complex construction, is inferior to that of Canaanites. Dwellers in the Mesopotamian Valley, and in areas E. and W. of the Jordan where Graeco-Roman civilization flourished, were city builders par excellence.

The existence in the Age of Abraham of such cities as Shechem, Bethel, Ai, Jerusalem (? Salem), Gerar, Dothan, and Beer-sheba has been archaeologically proved. The earliest settlements in Palestine were along the Mediterranean and in the Jordan Valley (see

JERICHO). In the latter region Nelson Glueck has found more than 70 villages which flourished from 3500 B.C. to A.D. 1200, and which contained three times as many people as inhabit the area today. The Dead Sea cities of Sodom and Gomorrah (Gen. 14:2, 10) had a Chalcolithic history (c. 4000–3300 B.C.) antedating most other city sites in Palestine. Jericho, said to be the oldest city in Palestine, has been explored down to the 19th level of human occupation.

Before the Hebrew Monarchy in Iron Age Palestine, from the 11th century on, many separate cities were small states ruled by local kings and citizen assemblies. The five kings of the Jordan Valley cities (Gen. 14) were independent chieftains. Petty local rulers had the right to grant land and make treaties; this was the sequel to the Patriarchal system of tribes settling down after nomadic wanderings. Saul was a rustic chief who became a gloomy king.

Several historic lists of cities of Palestine are extant, in addition to those in the Bible. The Tell el-Amarna Letters mention numerous Biblical towns. Another famous city list was found on the temple wall at Egyptian Karnak, in a huge relief depicting Shishak*, at war—the Pharaoh who raided Palestine c. 918 B.C. (II Chron. 12:2–9). Behind him are listed 156 districts and towns he claimed as tribute payers—most of them in Palestine: Gaza, Taanach, Shunem, Gibeon, Beth-horon, Aijalon, Megiddo, etc. Jerusalem was not listed, but only because the inscription was mutilated. The cities which the Book of Joshua cites as captured from many powerful kings and "allotted" to Hebrew tribes form an over-colored roster compiled from various sources*—J, E, P, etc.—and written down between the 10th and 2d centuries B.C. Yet the city lists in Joshua are the best we have of the towns in which Israel settled.

The "great and goodly" *cities of the Canaanites* (Deut. 6:10) practically all later became Hebrew cities, including Gezer, Hazor, Megiddo, Beth-shan, Lachish, Kadesh-naphtali, and Kiriath-sepher. Canaanite cities were small, independent states, whose failure to link together was one cause of the fall of Canaan* to the invading Hebrews.

Five *cities of the Philistine Plain* (see PHILISTINES) which were at their height during the Hebrew monarchy were: Gaza, Ashkelon, Ashdod, Ekron, Gath.

*Cities of coastal Phoenicia**, reaching N. from the present Haifa and Mt. Carmel, included Tyre, city of Hiram (II Sam. 5:11); Sidon (Matt. 15:21), mother of "the virgin daughter Tyre"; Sarepta (Zarephath), where Elijah healed the daughter of a Phoenician (Luke 4:26); Berytus (now Beirut); Gebal or Byblos (Ezek. 27:9); and Arvad, an island city famous for rowers (Ezek. 27:8). Phoenician cities were in their prime from c. 950–750 B.C.—great sea-powers reaching out for trade as far W. as Cadiz, Spain.

Cities of refuge were organized among the Hebrews, to afford sanctuary for unintentional murderers seeking escape from the O.T. law of life for life (Num. 35:11). These six cities included Hebron in S. Palestine, Shechem in the mountains of Samaria, Kadesh on Mt. Naphtali, Bezer, Ramoth Gilead, and Golan.

Royal cities (I Sam. 27:5) were centers of kingly government, such as Hebron, Shechem, Rabbah (now Amman, capital of the Kingdom of Jordan), Gibeon, Gibeah, Samaria (capital of Israel), Jerusalem (capital of Judah), and Damascus (capital of Syria).

The *Decapolis chain of 10 cities*—nine E. of the Jordan and one W. (Beth-shan)—represented the onrush of Greek influence in the wake of Alexander the Great in the 4th century B.C. Some may have been founded by the great Macedonian conqueror himself, or by his generals. Christ knew and probably visited some of these. Multitudes from the Decapolis region followed him (Matt. 4:25; see also Mark 5:20, 7:31). The original Decapolis cities (listed by Pliny) were: Beth-shan (Scythopolis), Pella, Dion, Kanatha, Raphana, Hippos, Gadara, Philadelphia (Rabbath-ammon), Damascus, and Gerasa (Jerash)—the latter now extensively excavated, revealing the typical city-plan of this sumptuous League. At times the Hellenistic city-league included as many as 18 cities.

Store-cities, to receive surplus stocks of grain, were typical of Egypt in Bible times. Hebrew forced labor went into the construction of some of them, like Pithom (Tell Retabah); and Ramesses (Tanis), which may have been the Hyksos capital (built c. 1720 B.C.). David the Hebrew king also erected depots of treasures in fields, villages, and "in the castles" (I Chron. 27:25, 31). Solomon's commissariat were assigned to towns from which they levied supplies, like Taanach, Megiddo, and "the region of Argob, which is in Bashan, three score great cities with walls and brazen bars."

Chariot cities were established by Solomon to accommodate his horses and chariots (I Kings 9:19; 10:26; II Chron. 1:14; 8:6; 9:25). Unfortunately, none of Solomon's "chariot cities" can be readily identified, despite some attempts to do so on the basis of I Kings 15–19. See GEZER, MEGIDDO).

Levitical cities, mentioned in the P source as having been assigned to Levites in various sections of Palestine (see Num. 35:1–8; cf. Josh. 13:33), are at variance with the tenet that Levites were to have no inheritance of land in Canaan, because the Lord was their heritage (Josh. 13:14; cf. Num. 18:20). In the period of the second Temple some sort of provision of land seems to have been made for priests and others engaged in Temple worship rites. This fact may have given rise to a theory that "Levitical cities" had existed earlier.

Jerusalem today gives us many clues as to the appearance of any city of Bible times: the immensely stout stone walls, 70 ft. high in some places, crenelated at the top to allow standing room for archers; gates that are massive pieces of impressive architecture; moats which gave extra strength near the citadel; broad places inside the gates for public assembly (Amos 5:16 A.S.V.); places of worship; government buildings; synagogues, shrines, and temples; high elevation above valleys, with steep glacis on the E. and S.; very narrow streets, paved with stone, and stepped to facilitate traffic in rainy weather; houses having high stone walls and flat roofs; quarters for goldsmiths, for leather and metal workers; cloth bazaars; animal markets; and food stalls. Biblical cities had small areas—6 to 10 acres being the average—to make defense easier. The oft-repeated O.T. phrase "cities and their suburbs" (Lev. 25:34; Num. 35:2–5, Josh. 21:33) connotes adjacent grazing land, running out in strips from the town site; or dependent but not necessarily contiguous villages, as in Josh. 19:38 f.

The oldest cities of Bible lands and the first known urban centers, according to such an authority as Samuel Noah Kramer, were in the Plain of Shinar, now S. Iraq. Several of these cities are mentioned in Gen. 10:10, 11:28. Erech (Uruk), Calah and Kish, Nippur and Ur, Larsa and Eridu have revealed early chapters in the history of man.

Cities, Towns, and Villages Visited by Jesus

Name	*Dist. from Jerusalem*	*Gospel Ref.*
Bethlehem	5 m.	Matt. 2:6
Sidon	120	Matt. 15:21
Tyre	105	Matt. 15:21
Caesarea Philippi	104	Mark 8:27
Bethsaida Julias	80	Luke 9:10
Capernaum	77	Matt. 4:13; John 4:46
Bethsaida	75	Mark 6:45; John 1:44, 12:21
Dalmanutha	75	Mark 8:10
Cana	65	John 2:1
Nazareth	63	Matt. 2:23, 13:54; Luke 4:16
Nain	57	Luke 7:11
Ephraim	10	John 11:54
Bethany (on Mt. of Olives)	2	Matt. 21:17; John 11:1
Jerusalem	0	Luke 2:22; Matt. 21:1, 23:37
Sychar	27	John 4:5
Bethany (E. of Jordan)	24	John 1:28
Jericho	21	Luke 19:1
Emmaus	7–8	Luke 24:13

Clauda (more correctly R.S.V. Cauda), a small, treeless island S. of Crete (Acts 27:16).

Claudia, a Christian woman who sent from Rome a message of greeting to Timothy (II Tim. 4:21).

Claudius. The 4th Roman emperor (reigned A.D. 41–54), son of Nero Claudius Drusus and Antonia Minor, daughter of Mark Antony and Octavia, sister of Augustus. Ill and despised, he nevertheless gave the provinces good government (see Acts 11:28; 18:2).

Claudius Lysias (klô′dĭ-*u*s lĭs′ĭ-ăs), the "chief captain," the chiliarch or commander of 1,000 men guarding Jerusalem. His second name indicates that he was a Greek, but he had bought Roman citizenship (Acts 22:28). When Paul was endangered by a mob in the Temple Area, Claudius ordered him to be carried into the fortress ("castle") Antonia and there scourged, to draw testimony from him (Acts 22:24). Discovering that Paul was a Roman citizen, Lysias timidly washed his hands of the case and turned it over to the chief priests and their council (22:30). See also Acts 23:17–30, 24:27.

clay, an earthy material, the cheapest and most essential available to people of Bible times, used for the following purposes: (1) *Houses.* Clay mud was used for both bricks (see BRICK) and mortar. When straw, shells, fish bones, or wood fragments were added to clay, it became a good binder. Houses fashioned of plastic, unfired clay were perishable, actually melting in rain, and easily crushed (Job 4:19). (2) *Pottery**. Water jars, cooking vessels, bowls, pitchers, and storage vats for oil, wine, and grain were made of clay characteristic of geographical areas and in styles typical of various periods. Thus pottery has become a scientific yardstick for dates and peoples of excavated sites (see POTTERY, illus. 328). (3) *Idols* (see IDOL). These were fashioned of clay, as well as of wood, metal, stone, and ivory, to express primitive concepts of deity (Jer. 22:28). (4) *Medicinal* use of clay is hinted in John 9:11. (5) See CLAY TABLETS.

O.T. writers made parabolic use of clay (Isa. 29:16, 41:25; Job 10:9; Ps. 40:2).

clay tablets, imprinted with cuneiform* writing done with a wedge-shaped stylus and baked as hard as pottery, constituted one of the chief writing materials of people in the Near East for thousands of years. They were probably first used by Sumerians (see SUMERIA) and their successors, the Accadians (see ACCAD) in what is now Iraq. They were almost indestructible. Many thousands of them have been excavated from Ur, Nippur, Sippar, Mari, Susa, Ras Shamrah*, etc. The Babylonian collection at Yale University is the largest in America, but the University Museum of Philadelphia also has hundreds of valuable tablets. Many of the clay tablets, carrying business and literary and religious records, have been cleaned by being rebaked in an electric oven for 3 days at a temperature of 1,400° F. until they are hard enough to permit foreign matter (mud, dirt, salt, crystals, etc.) to be picked off under a microscope with a needle, so that the scholar can finally compare the wedge-shaped, meticulously written characters with his Sumerian dictionary and learn whether the tablet gives an account of a temple transaction of perhaps 2500 B.C., or carries the record of a boy's adoption. The subject matter of clay tablets deals with sales of land, leases, mortgages, bankruptcy, wills, notes, determination of boundaries, records of commodities brought to a temple as tithes and offerings, mathematical tables, religious poems, etc. Codes of law, like the Code of Hammurabi, were meticulously recorded in beautiful cuneiform on large clay tablets.

The tablets were cushion-shaped, and usually rectangular, measuring c. 3x4x½ in. Some were cone-shaped. For protection of the message, the tablet was placed in a clay envelope carrying a duplicate imprint. While the tablets were still soft, tiny cylinder seals (see SEAL) were rolled over them, incised with signatures of the senders or addresses of consignees in cuneiform or pictograms. Intaglio seals were similarly used.

92. Clay tablet.

Tablets found near Babylon's Ishtar Gate list Hebrew captives mentioned in the Bible.

One of the famous Tell el-Amarna tablets owned by the Metropolitan Museum of Art is a letter written by King Asshur-Uballit of Assyria to Akhenaton of Egypt to accompany a gift of a chariot and horses.

See WRITING.

clean. See ANIMALS; PURITY.

Cleopas (klē'ŏ-păs), one of the two disciples who met the resurrected Jesus on the Emmaus road (Luke 24:18).

Cleophas (klē'ŏ-făs) (R.S.V. Clopas), husband of one of the Marys at the cross of Christ (John 19:25).

cloak. See DRESS.

clothing. See DRESS.

clouds, conspicuous in the skies of Palestine between the Mediterranean and the Jordan rift at certain seasons, were used widely by writers of the Bible as symbols. For example, God's covenant with a post-Flood world was his "bow in the cloud" (Gen. 9:13); "a pillar of a cloud" led the wandering Israelites by day (Ex. 13:21); when Moses was in Sinai, a cloud covered the mount for 6 days, "and the seventh day he (Yahweh) called unto Moses out of the midst of the cloud" (Ex. 24:16). See also Job 38:9; Ps. 97:2, 104:3; Matt. 17:5; Rev. 14:14.

Cnidus (nī'dŭs), a city on Cape Krio, the SW. tip of Asia Minor, adjacent to Rhodes and Cos, connected with the mainland by a causeway. It boasted a temple to Aphrodite (Praxiteles). Jewish inhabitants dwelt in this free city in the 2d century B.C. See Acts 27:7.

code, a systematic body or compilation of laws. There are several codes of ancient Hebrew law embodied in the O.T., developed over a long period of time and arranged by many minds in a complicated series of editorial revisions. Various redactors picked up material which had originally appeared in one place in Scripture and set it down in a connotation consistent with their own development of thought. In the Pentateuch as now arranged, there are 7 codes of law. Robert H. Pfeiffer identifies them thus:

The Covenant Code (Ex. 20:22–23:19, plus appendix 23:20–33).

The Ritual Decalogue (Ex. 34:10–26 and 22:29b–30, 23:12, 15, 19).

The Twelve Curses (Deut. 27:14–26).

The Ten Commandments (Ex. 20:1–17 and Deut. 5:6–21).

The Deuteronomic Code (Deut. 12–26).

The Holiness Code or H (Lev. 17–26).

Priestly Code or P (in its legal portions) scattered throughout Genesis, Exodus, and Numbers.

The following dates have been suggested in connection with the formulation of the O.T. codes:

Deuteronomic Code c. 622 B.C.—RD (Redactor) c. 550.

Priestly Code c. 450 B.C.—RP (Redactor) c. 430 B.C.

S (South or Seir) material—non-Israelite source of Pentateuch, incorporated in Pentateuch c. 400 B.C.

Holiness Code (H) compiled possibly 6th century B.C.

See also COVENANT; DEUTERONOMY; SOURCES.

codex (pl., codices), a manuscript volume of ancient Bible text. First used by Christians to supplant old parchment scrolls (see SCROLL) and tablets used by Hebrews for writing their Scriptures. Hebrews did not use codices until the 2d or 3d century A.D. A codex or book was formed by taking quires of four or five sheets of vellum or papyrus* and folding them once to make pages, which were then stitched together.

Some of the most famous ancient codices are:

Codex Vaticanus or B, written in Gk. c. 4th century A.D., now in the Vatican Library, Rome. The text, though mutilated, is the most important extant, and is the basis of the printed editions of the Bible.

Codex Sinaiticus, or Aleph, written in Gk. in the 4th or 5th century A.D., in brown ink, on 326½ leaves found in 1844 in the Monastery of St. Catherine on Mt. Sinai; now in the British Museum.

Codex Ambrosianus, in the Peshitta,* 6th century, now in Milan, includes not only the O.T. with most of the Apocrypha, but also the Apocalypses of Baruch and Ezra, and Book 7 of Josephus' *Wars of the Jews.*

Codex Alexandrinus, or A, dating from 5th-century (A.D.) Egypt, contains most of the O.T. and N.T.; also some non-canonical works. It follows Origen's edition of the Septuagint for the most part. It is now in the British Museum.

Recently in a ruined church on the way to Mt. Sinai, at 'Aujā el-Hafîr, extensive fragments of N.T. manuscript from the 7th century have been discovered, including 30 consecutive pages of John's Gospel and portions of Paul's Epistles. They are on papyrus, in Gk.

See TEXT.

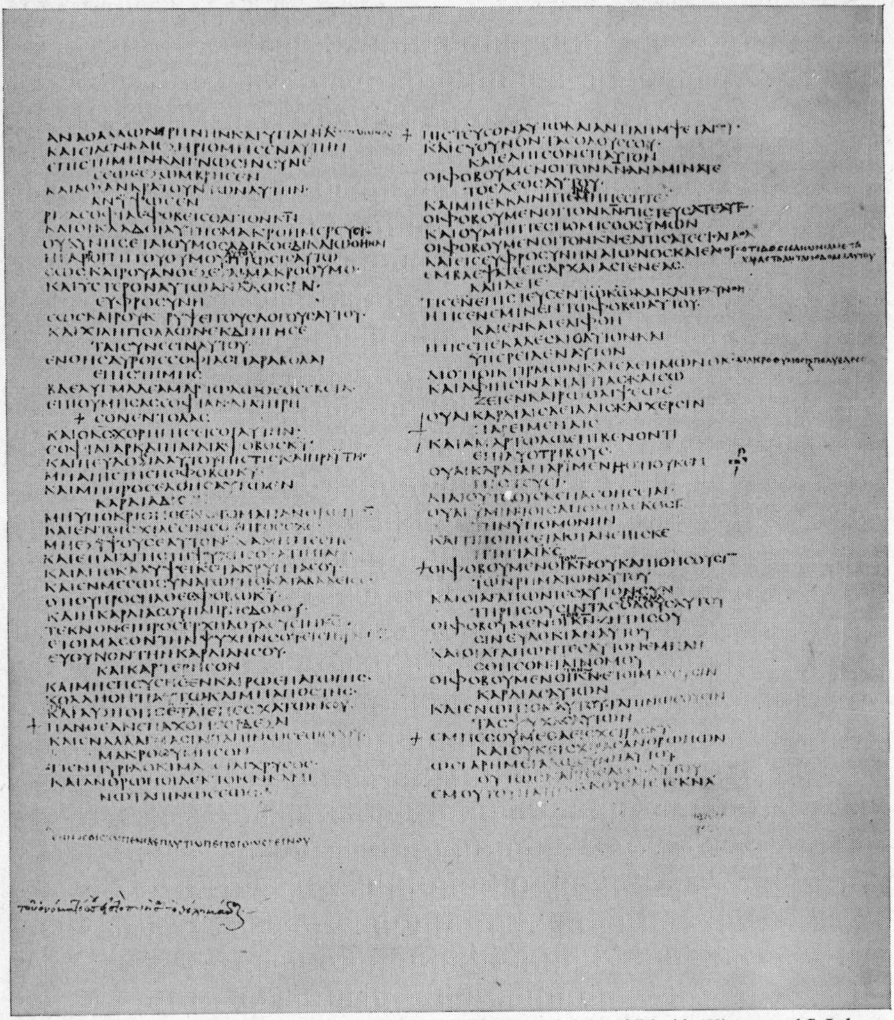

93. Codex Sinaiticus, British Museum. Portion containing Eccles. 1:18–3:1, published by Kirsopp and S. Lake.

Coele Syria (Gk. "hollow Syria"), the area between the Lebanons (see LEBANON) and Anti-Lebanons (see ANTI-LEBANON), referred to in Apocryphal books.

coins. See MONEY.

college, used in A.V. II Kings 22:14 and II Chron. 34:22 to indicate the "second quarter" (A.S.V.) of Jerusalem, where Huldah the prophetess lived. The Heb. text has *mishnah,* from which the connotation of a center of instruction crept into the A.V.

collop (kŏl′ŭp), a protuberant roll of flesh (Job 15:27).

Colossae (kō̆-lŏs′ē), an ancient Phrygian city located on the S. bank of the Lycus River, tributary of the Meander; mentioned only in the introduction to Paul's Letter to the Colossians. Colossae, together with sister cities, Laodicea* and Hierapolis* (Col. 4:13), was on the important trade route between the seaport Ephesus* and the Euphrates Valley. Its polyglot population made race prejudice a live local question (Col. 3:11). Jewish and Greek merchants traveling the highway made the city buzz with philosophical and religious arguments, and later it became a battlefield of early Christian theology. Paul during his Second Missionary Journey was "forbidden of the Holy Ghost" to preach in Asia, where Colossae was located (Acts 16:6); but during his two years at Ephesus (Acts 19:10, 26) his evangelistic zeal reached Colossae through Epaphras, though the Apostle himself had never been there (Col. 2:1). Tychicus (Col. 4:7), Onesimus (4:9), Philemon (Philem. 10, 11), and Archippus (Col. 4:17) were all Greek Christians identified with Colossae. Down through the 4th century A.D. this section of Asia Minor, according to the records of early councils and Church Fathers, was a hotbed of fantastic theological theories.

Colossians, the Epistle of Paul the Apostle to the, was written while the Apostle was in prison (4:3, 18). Three other Epistles were written in prison, Philippians, Philemon, and Ephesians (if genuine). The last two are closely related to Colossians. (See EPHESIANS.) Colossians and Philemon were evidently written at the same time and sent to Colossae by the same messengers. Tychicus delivered the letter addressed to the church at Colossae (Col. 4:7 f.). He was accompanied by Onesimus, a runaway Christian slave from Colossae (Col. 4:9) who was returning to his former master, Philemon, with a letter from Paul.

It cannot be taken for granted that the four prison Epistles were written while Paul awaited trial at Rome, for, since Paul was frequently in prison (II Cor. 11:23), this Epistle might have been written from Caesarea (Acts 23:35, 24:27), from Ephesus (I Cor. 15:30–32; II Cor. 1:8), or from Rome. Among the arguments in favor of Ephesus are these: (1) Paul writes in the name of himself and Timothy, his companion during his Third Missionary Journey. (2) He mentions as men who were with him those associated with that earlier period. (3) He requests Philemon, in v. 22, to prepare a guest room for him. (4) The fugitive slave Onesimus could hardly have made his way the long distance from Colossae to Rome. Though Ephesus is thought by some to be the most likely place of origin of the prison Epistles, the generally accepted view is that they were written from Rome. There Paul might easily have found many of his old friends. Runaway slaves often made for the great city to escape detection. Other imprisonments of Paul were probably of short duration, but at Rome in his own hired house he would have had leisure to compose these letters.

Colossae, together with Laodicea and Hierapolis, was situated in Asia Minor, about a hundred miles east of Ephesus, in the valley of the Lycus. Paul had never visited these cities, but in each of them a church had been founded by the labors of Epaphras, probably one of Paul's Ephesian converts.

The occasion for this Epistle was the report Epaphras brought to Paul of the religious situation in Colossae. The Christians there had been confused by false teaching, the nature of which is known only from Paul's references to it in this letter. The age was one of religious experiment brought about by the breakdown of ancient beliefs, by the introduction of Eastern cults, and by the influence of Greek philosophy. Everywhere men attempted to create new religions out of different combinations of the old. This phenomenon, known as "syncretism," seems to have been responsible for the new Colossian teaching in which Christianity had been "improved" by additions from Judaism and paganism. The errorists appear to have taught that Christ delivered man's spiritual nature from sin, but that this was not enough, for as a creature of earth man is imprisoned in the material world by hostile powers. Men need the help of angelic beings to gain freedom. By ascetic discipline men must rid themselves from the contamination of matter, and by mysterious rites they must counteract the forces working for their destruction. Ascetic notions were apparently accompanied by moral laxity, which in part occasioned the strong moral injunctions of Paul in this letter. This teaching was a forerunner of Gnosticism*, which in the 2d century A.D. threatened the existence of the Church. The basic question raised by the new Colossian teaching was: over against the tremendous visible forces of the world, what is the significance of Christ?

Paul's answer was that Christ is preeminent. He is not one power among many, for he includes in himself all powers. Not only is he supreme over angels, but they owe their existence to him. He is the ultimate reality, so that his work for us is all-sufficient. "For in him dwelleth all the fulness of the Godhead bodily. And ye are complete in him, which is the head of all principality and power" (Col. 2:9, 10). Christianity was primarily an ethical religion, but the Colossians confronted it with speculative problems interesting to the Greek mind. This caused Paul, who had already touched on the idea of Christ's cosmical significance in I Cor. 8:6, to state explicitly in Col. 1:15–17 that "by him were all things created." This teaching is in substantial agreement with the Logos doctrine as found later in John and in Hebrews.

The Epistle opens with a salutation, thanksgiving, and prayer (1:1–14). In the main section Paul explains Christ's significance for the new life (1:15–23); inserts an account of his own labors (1:24–2:3); contrasts true Christian teaching with what was being taught at Colossae (2:4–15); warns against practices associated with the false teaching (2:16–23); describes the real nature of the spiritual life (3:1–4); warns against heathen vices (3:5–11); and explains the requirements of the new life (3:12–17). This is followed by practical advice on the ordering of the household (3:18–4:1) and general counsels (4:2–6). He concludes with an introduction of the messengers and with salutations.

commandment, that which is commanded by one who has the right to be obeyed; like Pharaoh (Gen. 45:21), Moses (Ex. 36:6), David (II Chron. 29:25), Hezekiah (II Chron. 31:13), Festus (Acts 25:23). Commandments of Yahweh, other than the Ten* Commandments, were frequently heard by the conscience of Israel, as in Num. 9:20; Nah. 1:14. The Psalmist summarized the attitude of the righteous man toward the commandments of Yahweh (112:1, 119:127). Jesus enumerated the two greatest commandments (Matt. 22:36–40), and established the relation of the new commandment of love to the old commandments of law (John 13:34).

communion. See LORD'S SUPPER, THE.

concubines, or secondary wives, acquired by purchase or as war booty, and protected by laws of rightful inheritance (Deut. 21:15–17), were commonly accepted in O.T. society. But it is possible to trace in the O.T. a trend toward monogamy. The Deuteronomic Law (remembering Solomon's excesses) forbade kings to take several wives (17:17). Prophets like Hosea preached monogamy as a symbol of the faithful union between God and His people. Malachi (2:14 ff.) took monogamy for granted. For security large families (see FAMILY) were essential in early Hebrew society, and concubinage contributed to this end. Although O.T. law codes discouraged polygamy, perpetuation of the family often necessitated it. In the case of Abraham's polygamy, an explanation was offered (Gen. 16:1–3). The ideal woman of Prov. 31 moved in a monogamous society. By N.T. times Jewish husbands usually had one wife; N.T. teaching advised monogamy.

conduit (from Fr. *conduire*, to lead), a channel or duct to carry water from external sources to a desired destination. "The conduit of the upper pool" in Jerusalem (II Kings 18:17; Isa. 36:2) was apparently a well-known landmark, a site where plenty of water was available for craftsmen who cleaned, bleached, pressed, and dyed cloth. Conduits were in the form of channels cut in rock to convey water to gardens, as at Sidon; or underground tunnels, as at Gezer and Canaanite Megiddo (now excavated), possibly at Lachish, where an enigmatic shaft has been explored; and at Jerusalem, where Hezekiah in 701 B.C. built the Siloam* Tunnel. Solomon's Pools beyond Bethlehem may have been designed to feed conduits to his gardens. Authorities are divided about his conveying a supply to Jerusalem, as was done by Roman engineers 10 centuries later. Aqueducts (see AQUEDUCT) were also conduits—like the stone-paved causeway built by Sennacherib at Jerwan across the Gomer River, to conduct water* 30 m. for his Nineveh gardens. Water pipe lines of stone units such as engineers of Pontius Pilate built, and metal ones such as today convey water 30 m., from Râs el-'Ain (Antipatris) on the Mediterranean coast, up the Judaean mountains to Jerusalem, are also among the conduits of Palestine.

coney See ANIMALS.

confection (Ex. 30:35) (confectionaries I Sam. 8:13). See FOOD.

confectioner. See FOOD.

congregation (Lat. *congregatio*) is used scores of times in the O.T. to denote the sum total of Israel's men, women, and children during the Wilderness experience (Ex. 12:3). *Qāhāl* designated "assembly." In the A.V. the portable worship center is called "the Tabernacle of the congregation" (Ex. 33:7), or "the tent of the congregation" (Ex. 39:40; A.S.V., "the tent of meeting"). See also Ex. 35:1; Josh. 8:35; II Chron. 6:3; Ps. 74:2. There is probably no justifiable distinction between the congregation as a whole and the assembly (Lev. 4:13). There is close connection between "congregation" and "synagogue,"* signifying assembly, as well as place of meeting, in post-Exilic (see EXILE) times. "Congregation" is used only twice in the N.T., in Acts 13:43 and Heb. 2:12 R.S.V. (A.V., "church"). The Christian Church stemmed from both synagogue and *ekklēsia* (Gk. for "an assembly of citizens called out"). (See CHURCH.)

Conquest of Canaan* by Israel was one of the most important phases of Hebrew history and the archaeological evidence is open to different interpretations. The Scriptural records are contained mainly in the Book of Joshua and opening chapters of Judges. Strands of the almost lost but valuable J source (see SOURCES), based on early historical material, and from E (c. 750 B.C.), are combined with interpretations of Deuteronomistic writers (c. 550 B.C.), and of priestly redactors eager to make individual interpretations stressing the completeness of Israel's occupation of Canaan. The occupation was not as swift, complete, or permanent as some chapters of Joshua suggest (see Judg. 1). Yet the main theme remains unchallenged: a part of the Hebrew people went down to Egypt; suffered bondage; was marvelously released by Yahweh; finally entered the land which had traditionally been promised as early as the time of Abraham (Gen. 12:6 f., 13:14–17, 17:6–8, 24:7). To establish his people there, the Patriarch had renounced his home in well-established Ur* and become a voluntary nomad (Heb. 11:8–10). The records of the Conquest were written down on the basis of historical oral narratives, over a long period of time. The topographical data furnished by this 6th book of the O.T. has been valuable as a guide to many later conquerors and travelers. It is regrettable that no complete contemporary record of the Conquest survives, like the Song of Deborah, which is contemporary with the events it narrates—events of a slightly later period (c. 1125 B.C.) than the first waves of the Conquest.

The steps of Israel's Conquest were as follows:

Campaign I (*E. Palestine*). (1) God's early promises of a homeland for the Hebrews (see above). (2) Moses sends 12 spies, one for each tribe (Num. 13). (3) The occupation of portions of *Jordan* (Num. 21 ff.). (4) Joshua succeeds Moses as leader (Num. 27:22 f.).

Campaign II (*S. and Central Palestine*). (5) Joshua sends spies to Jericho (Josh. 2). (6) Israel crosses the Jordan, conveying the Ark (Josh. 3). (7) The siege of Jericho (c. 1250 B.C.) (Josh. 6). (8) Israel captures Ai (? Bethel) (Josh. 8). (9) The league with the royal city of Gibeon (Josh. 9). (10) The five kings defeated (Josh. 10). (11) The capture of Mak-kedah (10:28); Libnah (10:30); Lachish, c. 1220 B.C. (10:33); Hebron (10:36); Debir (10:39).

Campaign III (*Galilee and N. Palestine*). (12) Galilee invaded; Hazor taken (Josh. 11); advance to Mt. Hermon. (13) The allotment of territory to the Tribes, by lot (Josh. 13–17). (14) The establishment of six cities of refuge (20); and Levitical cities (21).

In the summary of Josh. 11:23 the "whole land" seems in the hands of Israel (Josh. 10:40–42, 11:23). But Judg. 1, 3 deflates this claim, stating that the Conquest was not completed by Joshua, and telling of certain nations being left in the land "to prove Israel"; and again, "the children of Israel dwelt among the Canaanites, Hittites, and Amorites, and Perizzites, and Hivites, and Jebusites" (Judg. 3:5 f.). The Judges narrative confesses that Israel did not drive out the inhabitants from Beth-shan, Taanach, Dor, Megiddo, Gezer, Accho, Sidon, or Beth-shemesh. The usual pattern was for Israel to settle down among the Canaanites and exact tribute from them. But by 1200 B.C. the Canaanites had been pushed out of most of Palestine except a coastal strip in N. Palestine and S. Syria. Aramaeans took what is now known as Syria, E. of the Lebanons.

Thus portions of the Conquest narrative claim the completion of the occupation within the lifetime of Joshua, as the P emphasis stressed the religious aspect of the experience as God's plan for Israel, His chosen people. Others indicate a slow process covering the three centuries between Joshua and the Hebrew Monarchy. There are overlappings and inconsistencies in allotments and boundaries; yet Joshua remains the best available record.

Three weaknesses of Israel's campaign methods were: compromise with the Gibeonites (Josh. 9), failure to take strategically located Jerusalem (II Sam. 5), and inability to control Philistia and the approach to the Mediterranean (II Sam. 5:25).

Conditions among the Canaanites which contributed to the gradual reduction of their territory included debased moral standards of the population; development of too many city-states not federated; existence of a benighted feudal system of wealthy princes and the absence of a thrifty lower class; and long-continued and unscrupulous exactions by bureaucratic Egyptian commissioners or "inspectors," collecting tribute of grain, timber, and man power, as indicated in the Tell el-Amarna* Letters.

In estimating the Conquest one must ever remember that not all the Hebrews in Palestine subsequent to the arrival of the descendants of Terah* (see ABRAHAM) descended to Egypt with the Jacob tribes. Those who remained behind probably amalgamated with those who entered at the Conquest.

conscience (Gk. *syneidēsis*, "joint knowledge") was defined by the Greeks as a sense of "oughtness," an evaluation of divergent ways of conduct, and a censuring of the self that chose the lower way. But beyond these ethical considerations of the pagan moralist was a higher step recognized by intelligent Christians like Paul and Peter. God's* voice, not man's mind, issues the moral commands. Conscience registers what God reveals as right. The word is used 30 times in the N.T., chiefly in the writings and speeches of Paul, in Hebrews, and in I Peter. Paul's most detailed discussion of conscience is I Cor. 8–10. He summed up his evaluation of his own Christian effort when he said before the Jerusalem council, "I have lived in all good conscience before God until this day" (Acts 23:1); and before Felix, "I exercise myself, to have always a conscience void of offense toward God, and toward men" (Acts 24:16). The author of I Peter (3:21) writes that baptism is not a mere outward washing, but a prayer for a good conscience before God. Sins which burden the conscience are cleansed in baptism. Conscience is the voice of God within us, urging us to do right and reproving us for doing wrong. The author of I Tim. 4:2 speaks about seducing spirits, doctrines of devils, and hypocritical lies that sear the conscience "with a hot iron."

conversation, meaning behavior or manner of life, is used in the A.V. in these passages: Ps. 37:14, 50:23; Phil. 3:20; I Tim. 4:12; Heb. 13:5; James 3:13; I Peter 2:12, 3:16; II Peter 3:11.

conversion (Gk. *epistrophē*, "a turning to") is a specific, remembered consciousness of hearing God's voice and of responding to that hearing; or, as Millar Burrows defines it, "God's calling and man's response." The experience, stemming from personal initiative, is generally considered essential to full

94. Roman road between Damascus and Antioch. Paul almost certainly traveled this road after his conversion.

entry into the Christian life. The word appears once in the N.T. (Acts 15:3), referring to the conversion of Gentiles. In the R.S.V. the A.V. word "conversion" is almost always translated "turn," "turning" away from false gods, toward the true God. O.T. references to conversion appear in Isa. 6:10; Ps. 51:13. Numerous instances of true conversion or turning to the Lord appear in the N.T.: Paul (Acts 9:1–22), the jailor at Philippi* (Acts 16:27–34), many at Antioch* (Acts 11:21). The reward of a Christian who aids a sinner to turn "from the error of his way" is stated in James 5:19 f. Some believers distinguish between "resurrection" (I Pet. 1:3), stressing the supernatural source of a religious rebirth, and "conversion," as a psychological activity of the soul involving repentance and faith, and consequent blotting out of sin and "refreshing . . . from the presence of the Lord" (Acts 3:19).

convocation (Heb. *miqra'*), a solemn festival gathering of the congregation* of Israel; a holy assembly during which no servile work was to be done, but burnt offerings were to be presented. Holy convocations were scheduled as follows:

Every Sabbath (Lev. 23:1–3).

1st month, Nisan (March–April): The first and last days of Passover (Ex. 12:16; Lev. 23:5–8; Num. 28:18, 25).

3d month, Sivan (May–June): Pentecost (Lev. 23:21).

7th month, Tishri (September–October): New Year's Day (Lev. 23:24). Day of Atonement (Lev. 23:27; Num. 29:1). The first and last days of the Feast of Tabernacles (Lev. 23:34–36; Neh. 8:18).

See TIME.

copper (from "Cyprus") has given its name to the Chalcolithic ("copper—or bronze—and stone") Age (c. 4000–3300 B.C.). It was the most important metal in O.T. times, even after the introduction of iron* during the early Hebrew Monarchy. Its most common use in Bible lands was in the form of its alloy, bronze, for cups, utensils, knives, and weapons (Ex. 38:3; Num. 16:39; II Chron. 12:10; Jer. 52:18). W. F. Albright believes that "brass" in both A.V. and A.S.V. translations of the above passages, and wherever it appears in narratives dealing with Temple* construction and equipment, should be translated "copper." Millar Burrows prefers "bronze." If we change the brass mentioned in Deut. 8:9 to "copper," we get a really scientific statement. An amazing number of large copper-mining and smelting centers have been found in the Arabah* by Nelson Glueck, with slag heaps, ruins of workmen's quarters and towns, flues for draughts up the deep wâdīs (see WÂDI), and furnaces producing metal in the 10th century B.C., helping build up the fabulous wealth of Solomon*. The king's own industrial and shipping center at Ezion-geber* at the head of the Gulf of Aqabah was excavated by Glueck, exploring from 1932 for several seasons for the Jordan Department of Antiquities and the American Schools of Oriental Research. The Hebrew copper king had at Ezion-geber (I Kings 9:26) a "Pittsburgh" or a "Duluth" exporting metal, the proceeds from which bought luxury wares for his court and ornaments for the Temple which Hiram* of Tyre and his craftsmen helped build on Mt. Moriah. The copper-mining sites are all rich in broken pottery fragments which date accurately the eras of activity. Some of the slag heaps are spotted with green, from copper never refined out of it. One of Solomon's greatest copper centers was Khirbet Nahas, c. 25 m. S. of the Dead Sea—the "City of Copper" in the "Valley of the Smiths." There lived the Kenezites (see KENAZ), related to the Kenites* (Gen. 15:19), who may first have told the Hebrews about rich ore deposits in their highlands. Albright believes that the traveling groups of bellows-working Kenites were related to the ancestral Hebrews.

95. Archaeologist Nelson Glueck at opening of an ancient copper mine shaft at Mene'iyeh (Timna).

Throughout Bible times the traveling metal smiths, like Tubal-Cain, spread religious beliefs as well as wares.

Egyptian copper mines also played a role in O.T. life. Sir Flinders Petrie believed that copper was the oldest metal used in Egypt and that bronze was not an intentional alloy before the Eighteenth Dynasty. First-Dynasty Egyptians went to the copper mines of the Sinai* Peninsula and fought the Sinai people to possess the mines. Hebrews may have supplied corvée (forced labor). (See SERABIT and WRITING.) Ancient Egypt used soft copper for hand-beating many useful and ornamental articles—from mirrors to drain pipes.

The oldest Chalcolithic occupation evidences thus far found are at Jericho* VIII, a stratum dating possibly toward the end of the 5th millennium B.C.

cor. A unit of liquid measure. See WEIGHTS AND MEASURES.

coral, the hornlike skeleton, usually red, of a sea animal, found in the Mediterranean and the Red Seas and made into beads or ornaments. It was considered of great value (Job 28:18), and was brought by Aramaean traders to the merchants of Tyre in exchange for "abundant goods" (Ezek. 27:16, R.S.V.). The word translated as "rubies" in the A.V. at Lam. 4:7 is rendered "coral" in the R.S.V.

Corban (kôr' băn), an offering or oblation dedicated to God and therefore not available for other purposes. The word appears in the Hebrew text in Lev. 1:2; Num. 7:13; etc., where it is translated as "offering." The practice came to be misused in order to avoid an obligation, such as to one's parents, and it was this misuse that Jesus spoke of in Mark 7:11–13, where he used the word "Corban." See also JESUS CHRIST (b).

coriander, *Coriandrum savitum* (Ex. 16:31; Num. 11:7), an annual growing wild in Egypt and Palestine and bearing small spicy white seeds used as seasoning and for medicinal purposes. See MANNA.

Corinth, one of the great commercial centers of ancient Greece, situated in command of trade routes at the W. end of the isthmus between central Greece and the Peloponnese. Its two harbors, Lechaeum, 1½ m. W. on the Gulf of Corinth, and Cenchreae, 8½ m. E. on the Saronic Gulf, made it a noted and cosmopolitan seaport. Only 10 m. to the E. were the temples of Poseidon and Palaimon, and their associated stadia and theaters—the site of the Isthmian Games (see *BA* 25, 1962, pp. 1–31). Corinth was a crossroads, a center of trade and of industry, and had a reputation for moral corruption as well. Dominating the town is the Acrocorinth, a steep, rocky outcrop, rising 1,750 ft. above the city, on the summit of which stood a temple of Aphrodite.

Excavation of ancient Corinth was begun in 1896 by the American School of Classical Studies in Athens, and is continuing. Flint tools, stone implements, and pottery indicate settlement here as early as the Neolithic period, and metal tools the transition into the Early Bronze Age. The site was devastated c. 2000 B.C., and reoccupied again only at the beginning of the 1st millennium B.C. It was a prosperous city, famous for its pottery, metallurgy, and shipping, from the 8th–5th centuries B.C., and flourished again in the Hellenistic period, until as part of the Achaean League it came into conflict with Rome and was demolished by the consul, L. Mummius, in 146 B.C. Julius

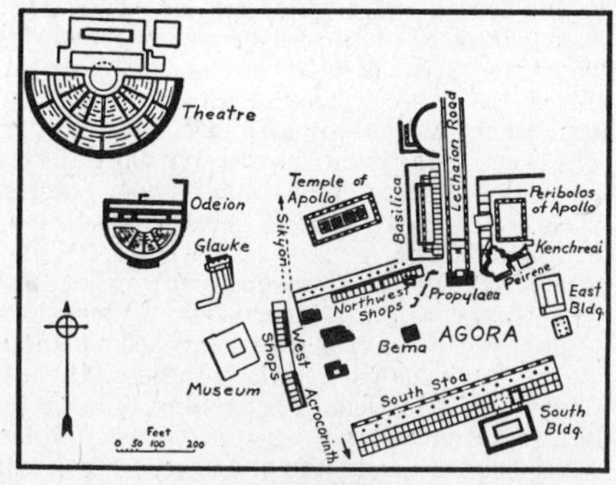

96. Corinth.

Caesar refounded the city as a Roman colony in 44 B.C., and it was named the capital of the new province of Achaea in 27 B.C. The 18-month sojourn of Paul during his Second Missionary Journey (Acts 18:1–18) can be dated by an inscription from Delphi which indicates that Gallio (Acts 18:12–17) became proconsul of Achaea in A.D. 51 or 52.

Because of the destruction wrought by Mummius, it is mainly the ruins of Roman Corinth that have been preserved, for which the second book of Pausanias' *Description of Greece*, c. A.D. 174, has been a useful guide. The center of Roman Corinth was reached by the Lechaeum Road, which led from its W. harbor. Lined with colonnades and shops, it was paved with blocks of hard limestone, and was c. 20 ft. wide as it approached the propylaea, which gave access to the agora. Near the propylaea, on the Lechaeum Road, was found an inscription, partly destroyed, which reads "Synagogue of the Hebrews," and is probably the lintel of such a building. Though the style of its letters indicates a date later than the time of Paul, it is possible that the inscription belongs to the successor of the synagogue in which Paul preached (Acts 18:4). To the E. of the propylaea stood a structure enclosing a natural spring, the "Fountain of Peirene." To the W., beyond a basilica which stood above the shops on the W. side of the Lechaeum Road, stood the archaic Temple of Apollo, founded in the 6th century B.C. The agora, which lay below the temple and at the head of the Lechaeum Road, was divided into a lower (N.) and an upper (S.) part, and surrounded by colonnades, shops, and other monumental remains. The S. stoa measured 500 ft. in length, and the many drinking vessels recovered here, inscribed with such words as Health, Zeus, Dionysus, and Love, suggest that some of these shops served as taverns. Inscriptions discovered in the vicinity of the agora identify shops as *macellum* (Lat., "meat market") and *piscario* (Lat., "fish market"). Paul used the Gk. form of the former, *makellon* (I Cor. 10:25). The division of the agora was marked by a row of shops, in the midst of which stood the bema, a high, broad platform with a superstructure and benches. Built of white and blue marble, it functioned as a platform for public speaking. Its construction is to be dated to the 1st half of the 1st century A.D. This bema, translated "tribunal" in the N.T., is no doubt the place where Paul was brought before Gallio (Acts 18:12–17). To the NW. of the agora was a theater, originally constructed in the 5th century B.C., and rebuilt several times by both Greeks and Romans. Near the theater, on one of the blocks of a limestone-paved square probably of mid-1st century A.D. date, was an inscription which records that for his aedileship (signifying a Roman official in charge of various public works), Erastus laid the pavement at his own expense. Paul mentions an Erastus who was the "city treasurer" (Rom. 16:23), and it is held by

97. Lechaeum Road (Corinth) with Acrocorinth in background.

some that, since the term rendered "treasurer" can have the broader meaning "steward, manager," the two may be the same. This is far from certain, however. One m. W. of the agora was the potters' quarters, where craftsmen produced the Corinthian ceramics. It is possible that Paul resided in similar quarters in practicing his trade as a tentmaker (Acts 18:2–4).

The strong Corinthian Church established by Paul and his colleagues and fostered by Apollos* (Acts 18:24, 19:1; I Cor. 1:12, 3:4) flourished among the Gentile Christians, in spite of their dissensions and abuses in public worship. By the 2d century the bishop of Corinth exerted wide influence. W. P. A.

Corinthians, First and Second Epistles of Paul the Apostle to the, the 7th and 8th books of the N.T. There is evidence that Paul wrote four letters to the church which he had founded at Corinth* (Acts 18:1–17; I Cor. 3:6, 4:15). Two letters and fragments of two others are believed to be embodied in I and II Corinthians. The "first" letter (I Cor. 5:9), written from Ephesus*, has been lost, but a portion is thought to be preserved in II Cor. 6:14–7:1. In it Paul warned the Corinthians against associating with immoral persons. News had evidently reached him that the Christians in the notoriously dissolute city of Corinth were tolerating vices among their own members and disregarding the moral demands of the Gospel. "Be ye separate" (II Cor. 6:17), he urged, realizing that the Church is of necessity in the world, but that the world must not be in the Church.

The second letter, our canonical I Corinthians, was also written from Ephesus c. A.D. 54, partly because of disturbing reports brought to him by members of Chloe's household (I Cor. 1:11); and partly in answer to questions asked him in a letter from Corinth (I Cor. 7:1), probably brought by Stephanas, Fortunatus, and Achaicus (I Cor. 16:17). Paul first dealt with the disturbing situation in Corinth, which was largely due to a pagan background of unrestrained individualism and lack of moral standards. He rebuked the Corinthians for their party quarrels, showing that it was disloyal to Christ to become partisans of either himself, or Apollos, or any other human leader (I Cor. 1–4). He demanded discipline for a member guilty of incest; denounced taking quarrels between Christians to pagan law courts; and warned against toleration of immorality (I Cor. 5, 6). Next he dealt with problems on which they had asked his advice: marriage, meat offered to idols, and the ordering of public worship. His discussion of marriage (I Cor. 7) is historically interesting as showing (1) the difficulties encountered in a community of both Christians and pagans; and (2) the influence Paul's belief in the imminent end of the age had upon his ideas of marriage. He gave practical advice on a typical 1st century problem of whether Christians should eat meat sacrificed to idols (I Cor. 8–10). As to their conduct in church, he said that women must be veiled (I Cor. 11:1–16), and he rebuked the Corinthians for irreverence at the Lord's table, reminding them of the authentic tradition (I Cor. 11:17–34). In discussing spiritual gifts, among which were such ecstatic phenomena as trances, visions, and "speaking with tongues," all at that time highly regarded in Corinth, Paul declared that these are of less value than love and consideration for others (I Cor. 12–14). He explained the Christian doctrine of the resurrection of the dead (I Cor. 15); and closed with personal instructions and greetings (I Cor. 16).

This Epistle is outstanding (1) for its picture of life in a 1st-century Christian church; (2) for its application of the principles of the Gospel to complex situations; and (3) for some of Paul's deepest insights into the meaning of the Gospel, such as his message on the Cross (I Cor. 1:18–2:2). It contains the oldest account of the Last Supper (I Cor. 11:23–26) and of the Resurrection (I Cor. 15:3–9), both written only 25 years after these events and long before the parallel passages in the Gospels. Its hymn to love (I Cor. 13) and the magnificent passage on immortality (I Cor. 15:42–58) are among Paul's most inspired utterances.

A fragment of the 3d or severe letter (II Cor. 2:4, 7:8) is believed to be II Corinthians 10–13. A crisis had arisen in Corinth, apparently caused by Jews (II Cor. 11:22) who defied Paul's authority (II Cor. 10:10) and claimed that they were "the very chiefest apostles" (II Cor. 11:5). After a short visit to Corinth (II Cor. 2:1, 12:14, 13:1–3), during which he was unsuccessful in dealing with this crisis, Paul returned to Ephesus and wrote the third letter. In it he reproached the Corinthians for their unfaithfulness, and defended his apostleship by telling of what he had endured for the cause of Christ. Titus*, who probably delivered the letter to Corinth, met Paul in Macedonia with news that the Corinthians had accepted the severe letter in good part (II Cor. 7:5–8).

Paul's 4th letter, II Corinthians 1–9 (exclusive of 6:14–7:1, as noted above), was written in Macedonia c. A.D. 55. Now that the crisis was happily ended he wrote this very personal and discursive Epistle in a mood of gratitude and rejoicing. He began by defending his conduct against the charges of his opponents. In chaps. 3–5 personal feeling gave place to a meditation on the nature of his apostleship, "We are ambassadors for Christ" (II Cor. 5:20), and on life in Christ, "If any man be in Christ, he is a new creature" (II Cor. 5:17). He ended the latter with an appeal for contributions to the collection for the Jerusalem church (II Cor. 8, 9).

cormorant, a large, voracious sea bird of the pelican family, listed as "unclean" in Lev. 11:17 and Deut. 14:17. The bird referred to in Isa. 34:11 was probably a hawk, while the meaning of the Hebrew word used at Zeph. 2:14 is not clear (R.S.V. "vulture").

corn in the A.V. (A.S.V. and R.S.V. "grain") refers generically to the seeds of any of the cereal grasses used for food, including wheat, millet, barley, spelt, fitches, lentils, beans, and pulse. See references in Gen. 41:49; Josh. 5:11; Isa. 21:10; Mark 2:23. The word "corn" often refers to the chief cereal crop of a given region, so that in England it refers to wheat, in Scotland and Ireland to oats, and in the U.S.A. and Canada to Indian corn or maize. "Corn and wine" (Gen. 27:28) (R.S.V. "grain and wine") is a symbolic phrase representing the entire produce of the fields.

Cornelius, a centurion (captain) of an "Italian band" stationed in Caesarea*, c. 40 m. N. of Joppa. Though reverent, generous, just, and acceptable to the Jews even in synagogue worship, he was looked upon by them as an outsider. Simultaneous visions coming to Peter* at Joppa*, and to Cornelius at Caesarea (Acts 10), led to Peter's acceptance of God's breaking down the barriers between Jew and Gentile believers in Christ (Acts 10:34); to his broader outlook on "clean" foods (10:15); to the rebuke by "apostles and brethren that were in Judaea"; and to his own defense of his liberal policy (11:1–18).

The baptism of Cornelius and others at Caesarea marked the first Gentile converts through Peter.

cornerstone, an important foundation stone laid at a front angle or corner. In foundations of city walls or public structures, the cornerstone was usually selected for its strength (Job 38:6). Psalm 118:22 refers to a stone which had been rejected by builders, yet had become the head stone of the corner. Jesus quoted this ancient saying, implying that he was that cornerstone (Matt. 21:44; Mark 12:10; Luke 20:17). Peter, when haled before "rulers, elders, and scribes" to justify the cure of the lame man, boldly proclaimed Christ as "the stone which was set at naught of you builders, which is become the head of the corner" (Acts 4:11). The Ephesian Letter (2:20) speaks of Christians as a building, erected upon the foundation (see FOUNDATIONS) "of the apostles and prophets, Jesus Christ himself being the chief cornerstone." I Peter (2:5–7), still more explicit, calls Christians a spiritual house, erected in Zion upon Christ the chief cornerstone, once "disallowed" by the builders. The gigantic stones still seen at the SE. corner of Jerusalem's walls are an impressive illustration of Mark 12:10. These or others immediately under them may have been seen by Jesus.

cornet, used in A.V. to translate the Heb. word *keren* (lit., *horn*), a trumpet made of an animal's horn, such as the shophar*. In II Sam. 6:5 the Heb. word is different (*mena'an-'im*) and is better translated "castanets."

Cos (A.V. Coos), a small Aegean island off the SW. tip of Asia Minor where Paul* spent one night on his way from Miletus* to Rhodes on his Third Missionary Journey (Acts 21:1). Its alliance was valued by Egyptian Kings, who used it as an outpost for their navy to watch the Aegean, and it became a favorite resort for the education of Ptolemaic princes. The religious history of Cos dates back to the 4th century B.C. when Greek worship and the practice of healing went hand in hand. Because of its sacred spring, hospital, and temples to Asklepios, god of healing, Hippocrates, "father of medicine," was attracted to Cos. The symbolic snake of Asklepios has been found in various ruins of Cos. Genoese Christian Crusaders are represented by vestiges of their mediaeval castle.

cosmetics, beautifying applications valued by Egyptians and other peoples of the ancient Near East (Prov. 27:9; Rev. 18:13). Ivory combs, alabaster ointment boxes, and mirrors of polished metal have turned up in great numbers. In the University Museum at Philadelphia are an ivory rouge pot found at Beth-shan in the 1479 B.C. level of Thutmose III; an archaic (c. 3000-2800 B.C.) Egyptian wooden toilet box retaining its original metal lid-rivets on a lid carved in a Maltese cross design; bronze razor blades 4 to 6 in. long; ivory and bone hairpins; bodkins; and a little stone mill for grinding eye paint. What appear to be a curling-rod and an ivory comb have been found in the Lachish mound at the level of an Amenhotep ruling c. 1400 B.C. Jezebel of Samaria painted her eyes and attired her head (II Kings 9:30). Toenails and fingernails were tinted with henna juice. Rouge and paint were applied to faces of men and women, and heavy black lines were traced under their eyes to make them look larger. Anointing (see ANOINT) guests with

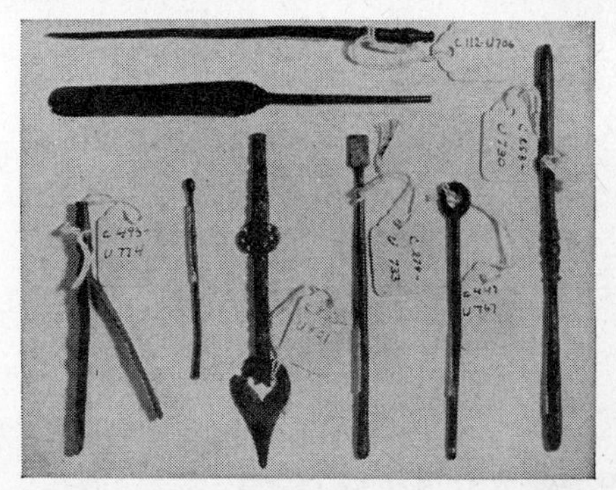

98. Bronze toilet articles excavated at Antioch. Top, reading down: Hairpin, knife; Left to right: Tweezers, Hairpin, Arrow-pointed ornament, Ear spoon, Ornament, Knife.

unguents was a part of Palestinian hospitality in the time of Jesus (Luke 7:37 f.).

coulter (kōl′ter), used in A.V. and A.S.V. for colter, the sharp metal point attached to a plow beam. Israelites had to take them to the Philistines for sharpening before metal became plentiful in Palestine (I Sam. 13:20 f.).

council. (1) The Sanhedrin* (from Gk. *synedrion*, reduced to Aram.) was the highest court of justice and supreme council at Jerusalem after the return from the Babylonian exile. When the Gk. word came in use is not known. At first the supreme body was called the Great Synagogue*, later the "senate" (Acts 5:21). During the period of the Roman procurators, and therefore in the lifetime of Jesus, the council or Sanhedrin was the supreme authority of the Jewish people. Its aristocratic membership was drawn from old established families, particularly from noble Sadducees*. In the latter half of the 1st century B.C. the council included also Pharisees* (scribes and elders). The council was presided over by the high priest in the Temple Area (Mark 14:55). As a religious tribunal its jurisdiction extended to the entire Jewish world (Acts 9:2, 22:5, 26:12). As a court of justice its jurisdiction was limited after Herod's death; it retained the authority of judging in matters of life and death, but was obliged to turn over execution of sentence to Romans. The trial of Jesus as recorded in the Gospels is historically correct. The 71 Sanhedrin members—a number suggesting the personnel of the old court of Israel's elders—could order arrests (Matt. 26:47; Mark 14:43); and could sit in such cases as those of Peter, John, and other Apostles (Acts 4:5 f., 15, 5:21, 27, 34, 41). It tried Stephen for blasphemy (Acts 6:12–15); and Paul for transgressing Mosaic Law (Acts 22:30). It had its own police and made arrests (Matt. 26:47). In Judaea it could levy taxes, whose collection it farmed out to publicans* (Luke 18:10). After the fall of Jerusalem (A.D. 70) the Sanhedrin, though claiming descent from the earlier body, lost its authority, becoming merely a learned school (*yeshiva*).

(2) The term "council" was also used for informal but official consultations, as of Pharisees (A.V. Matt. 12:14; Matt. 22:15; Mark 3:6; John 11:53), and prominent persons at Caesarea (Acts 25:12). Their findings were sometimes called "counsel," in the sense of Luke 23:51; Matt. 27:1.

(3) Local communities of Jews had councils of their own (Matt. 5:22; Mark 13:9). In large towns councils had as many as 23 members or "elders." These apparently had authority to scourge offenders in their synagogues. Jesus referred to such councils (Matt. 10:17).

counsel, in the sense of advice, appears frequently in Scripture: Saul sought God's counsel (I Sam. 14:37); Rehoboam that of "the old men that had stood before Solomon his father" (II Chron. 10:6). Scoffers demanded "the counsel of the Holy One of Israel" (Isa. 5:19). See also Ps. 1:1.

counsellor (A.V. Mark 15:43; Luke 23:50, A.S.V., councillor R.S.V. "member of the council"), a member of the Sanhedrin or council*, like Joseph* of Arimathaea. The counsellors of Artaxerxes (Ezra 7:14) were his princely advisers (cf. Esther 1:14). "Counsellor" is one of the names given the Messiah*—an indication of the high esteem in which counsellors were held (Isa. 9:6).

covenant, an agreement or compact between individuals or, in Scripture, between God and individuals or people. (1) Covenants between individuals: Abraham and Amorites (Gen. 14:13); Abraham and Abimelech (21:27); Laban and Jacob (31:44); Jonathan and David (I Sam. 18:3); Solomon and Hiram (I Kings 5:12). In primitive times covenants were sealed by exchanging drops of each other's blood—a custom later refined into the procedure in Jer. 34:18 f.; or by exchanging handclasps; or by setting up pillars of stone (Gen. 31:44–48); or by accepting a covenant token of salt* (Num. 18:19)—symbolic of sacred hospitality*, still used by Palestinian nomads. (2) Covenants between Yahweh and individuals: God and Noah, with the rainbow for token (Gen. 9:13); God and Abraham, with circumcision for token (Gen. 15:18–21, 17:4–14). (3) Covenants between God and Israel: The *Sinaitic Covenant*, Israel's "constitution," regarded as having been given at Sinai* or Horeb*, renewed in the plains of Moab (Deut. 29:1 ff.), and sealed by the ritual described in Ex. 24:1–8. According to Josh. 24 (see v. 25), this covenant was renewed again at Shechem after the Conquest of Canaan. Some scholars believe that this was, in fact, the original covenant. Many modern scholars believe the covenant between Yahweh and Israel was modeled on ancient "suzerainty treaties" which were imposed by Assyrian and Hittite kings on their vassals. In both cases there is the promise of protection in return for exclusive loyalty and obedience to specific commands. In the O.T., the commands are found in two different, parallel collections, Ex. 20:22–23:19 (called "the book of the covenant" in 24:7) and 34:10–26 (sometimes called "the ritual Decalogue"). The essence of the covenant is the pledge that Yahweh will be the God of Israel and they His people (Ex. 19:5; Deut. 26:17 f.).

The *Covenant Code*, or "book of the covenant" (Ex. 24:7, see above), is considered by many scholars to be the oldest extant body of Hebrew law. It developed over a period of several centuries, in the hands of many codifiers and redactors, and became the first strand in the great Deuteronomic Code*, developed in the era when Israel, in from the desert Wanderings, was settling down in agricultural society in Canaan, and feeling the influence of already existing bodies of civil and criminal laws, such as the Code of Hammurabi* (c. 1690 B.C.) and the Assyrian and Hittite codes of c. 1350 B.C. The Covenant Code consists of (a) *mishpātim* or judicial decisions, such as: with reference to murder (Ex. 21:12–15); injuries to cattle (vv. 33–36); breach of trust (22: 7–13); (b) *debārim* or commands, related to those of the Decalogue, and dealing with treatment of strangers (22:21), offerings of first fruits and firstlings (vv. 29 f.); and the Sabbath (23:10–12). Redactors who placed the Covenant Code in a Sinaitic setting did so to give it Mosaic authority.

The *New Covenant* of the prophets grew up in the centuries after Israel had entered Canaan, and through experiences of personal and national suffering attained a spiritual awareness of the need for salvation. Israel had broken her covenant with God, but He was willing to write in their hearts a new compact (Jer. 31:31–34) which would be universally available (Isa. 49:6). Ezekiel (37:21–28) connects the re-establishment of the covenant with expectations of a Messiah*

The *N.T. Covenant*, as indicated in I Cor. 11:25, in connection with the institution of the Lord's* Supper, showed Christ, the Passover, as the latest covenant between God and His people. Every time Christians today observe Communion and accept the cup they partake of "the new covenant" (R.S.V.) (A.V. "testament") in his blood, "shed for remission of sins." See also Heb. 7:22, 8–10, 9:15 for Christ, R.S.V. "the mediator of a new covenant," A.V. "new testament."

The *Ark of the Covenant* (Num. 10:33, 14:44) was the repository of the *Tables of the Covenant* on which the Sinai laws were believed to have been inscribed (Deut. 9:11). See TEN COMMANDMENTS; ARK. E. L./R. C. D.

cow. See CATTLE.

cracknel, a hard, brittle kind of biscuit (A.V. I Kings 14:3, cf. "cakes," A.S.V. and Moff.).

crafts. See individual entries.

crane, a large water bird, mentioned in connection with its chattering (Isa. 38:14), and with its knowledge of the seasons (Jer. 8:7). The elegant European crane and the demoiselle crane both migrate through Palestine, but may winter in Egypt.

Creation, the act whereby God brought into existence the heavens, the earth, their luminaries, life forms, and elements. In addition to the two stories of Creation found in Gen. 1 and 2, there are accounts in Ps. 104, probably influenced by the "Hymn to the Sun" of Akhenaton* (1370–1353 B.C.), and in the Book of Job (see especially ch. 38).

As elsewhere in the Pentateuch*, there are two or three strands or sources* in the Creation story of Genesis. The material of Gen. 1:1–2:4a is part of the P document; Gen. 2:4b ff. of the earlier J (Jehovistic) document. Some scholars believe the J account belongs to a source older than the completed J document which is variously called L, S, or J[1]. The first of the two documents deals with the creation of heaven, earth, the firmament, and all that inhabit them, culminating (Gen. 1:26 ff.) in the creation of man; in the second account, the main concern of the writer is the creation of man and woman and the placing of them in Eden. The P account is believed to be the work of priestly writers with highly developed theological interests who lived during, or immediately after, the Babylonian Exile*.

Genesis 1–2:4a tells of eight creative acts, one for each of six days of God's work, except that two works fell on the 3d and 6th days.

Gen. 1:14 alludes to the nature of the Hebrew festival calendar, based on the position of the heavenly bodies and the succession of days, seasons, and years.

The Creative Acts of God
(Gen. 1–2:4a, P Code)

(1) Light (1:3–5)
(2) The waters divided by the firmament (1:6–8)
(3) (a) Dry land separated from the seas (1:9 f.)
    (b) Vegetation (1:11–13)
(4) Lights: sun, moon, stars (1:14–19)
(5) Fishes, birds (1:20–23)
(6) (a) Land animals (1:24 f.)
    (b) Man (1:26 ff.)
(7) The Sabbath of rest (2:2 f.)

It is futile and unnecessary to try to reconcile the Genesis Creation accounts with modern science. The authors of Genesis used the cosmogony of their day, and could not be expected to use that of the 20th century. Their aim was spiritual. They strove reverently to summarize the steps by which a personal, intelligent, ethical God, by several clear-cut fiats, fashioned heaven, earth, and "all that in them is" (Ex. 20:11). Their aim was not to write charts of geology, biology, paleontology, or astronomy, but to predicate the omnipotence of the one God, who in the beginning created all that was created and that had never existed before.

There are Babylonian Creation epics older than the Hebrew narratives of beginnings. These tell how Marduk* killed the repulsive dragon Tiâmat, and shaped heaven and earth from the two halves of her body. This myth is referred to in Ps. 89:10, where Tiâmat is called "Rahab"; in Ps. 74:14; and in Job 41:1 ("leviathan"). A text of the Babylonian Creation epic was found in the library of Asshurbanapal at Nineveh in 1872, on 7 clay tablets inscribed in cuneiform*. Whether there is any direct relationship between the Babylonian and O.T. stories of Creation is uncertain. There are similarities, but the differences are even greater, and the theological superiority of the Hebrew account is beyond any question. E. L./R. C. D.

creatures, all created, animate beings—human and animal—which were part of God's total act of Creation. The "new creature" in Christ was Paul's description of the redeemed man (Gal. 6:15).

creeping things, the term used for any creeping animal (Gen. 1:24–25); it may be a land or water reptile (Gen. 6:7; Ps. 104:25); or it may creep on four or more feet or crawl on its belly. It is unclean (Lev. 22:5); it is considered an "abomination" and is not to be eaten (11:41–42). In the latter reference the R.S.V. calls it a "swarming thing." In Deut. 14:19 "every creeping thing that flieth" (A.V.) is rendered by the R.S.V. as "all winged insects."

Crescens (krĕs′ĕnz), a Christian mentioned in II Tim. 4:10 as going to Galatia or Gaul.

Crete, a mid-Mediterranean island lying almost equidistant from Europe, Asia, and Africa, about 60 m. S. of the Greek peninsula. Its location made inevitable its use as a seed bed and distributing center for the religions and cultures of Near Eastern peoples between 3400 and 1200 B.C. Its E.-W. mountain chain, from which Mt. Ida, legendary birthplace of Zeus, rises 8,000 ft., was as famous as its Minoan civilization (and the Mycenaean which sprang from it). In O.T. times Crete was known as Caphtor (Deut. 2:23). Jeremiah (47:4) and Amos (9:7) are among those who believe that the Philistine (see PHILISTINES) sea lords were emigrants from Crete—part of a stream that flowed out from the island soon after a great catastrophe of c. 1200 B.C. (to the labyrinthine palace of Minos?) and overran Palestine, Syria, and part of Egypt. Extra-Biblical knowledge of Cretan culture in this period is based on the discovery of pottery* displaying characteristics of Minoan civilization, of which much is now known through the extensive excavations at Knossos and elsewhere, by Sir Arthur Evans and others. The Minoans (c. 3400–1200 B.C.) spread their pottery, their elegant script (only partially deciphered from thou-

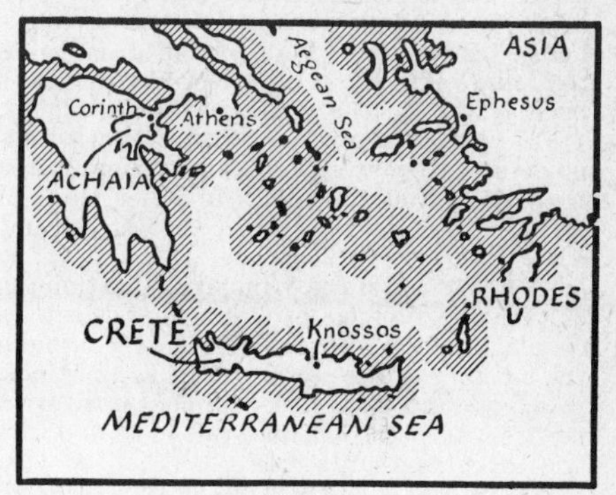

99. Crete.

sands of tablets found at Knossos and other sites), their famous bull sports, and their nature cults through the Middle East during the period of Israel's occupation of Palestine. The Philistines did not control their coastal plain much longer than three centuries. Yet, because of their monopoly of the import of iron—owing to their control of coastal shipping—and of their hereditary skill in forging weapons (I Sam. 13:19–22), they troubled Israel exceedingly through the period of the Judges (Judg. 13–16), but were finally defeated by Saul and David. As wave after wave of invaders passed over their land, the Philistines lost their identity and were absorbed. Peoples who had first appeared in Biblical history in the period of the Judges bowed from the stage after Assyrian aggressions. But the Philistines from Crete left behind the name by which the Holy Land has ever since been known. "Palestine" comes from the Gk. *Palaistine*, "Philistina," used originally only for the coastal region S. of Phoenicia, later for the larger area. Palestine in the A.V. of the O.T. is "Palestina" (Ex. 15:14; Isa. 14:29, 31).

Jews from Crete were in Jerusalem on the 1st Pentecost (Acts 2:11). The date and circumstances of the introduction of Christianity to the island are uncertain. Paul may have visited Crete, and left Titus to supervise and extend the Christian centers there (Tit. 1:5). Paul sailed all along the S. coast of Crete before his wreck on Malta (Melita) en route to Rome (Acts 27:7, 12 f., 21). Cretans have been belied by the characterization of Tit. 1:12 (quoted from the Cretan poet Epimenides); they were probably no more evil than their contemporaries in other parts of the Mediterranean world of the 1st century A.D.

After the fall of the Minoan civilization the culture and prestige of Crete diminished. In classical times Crete survived mainly through the memory of the sea power of King Minos. It exerted no influence commensurate with its size, and played a small role in the Persian and Peloponnesian wars.

Crispus, the chief ruler of the synagogue at Corinth*, who with his whole household accepted Jesus as the Messiah, and was baptized by Paul (Acts 18:8; I Cor. 1:14).

cross. (1) An instrument of execution, used by Assyrians, Persians, Phoenicians of Carthage, Egyptians, Greeks, and Romans. A stake, *staticulum*, was early employed for impaling criminals. By the time of Christ's Crucifixion a crossbar, *patibulum*, had been added—sometimes carried by the condemned man and fastened to the upright. The crosses used for 1st-century executions were of two types: the *crux commissa* (also called the "anticipatory," or "O.T." cross, and later "St. Anthony's cross"), shaped like a letter T; and the *crux immissa* (later known as the "Latin" or the "Roman" cross), having unequal arms. Since a superscription (Mark 15:26) was nailed above the head of the crucified Saviour, the instrument of his torture was probably of the latter variety. Sometimes a small saddle (*sedile* or *cornu*) supported the body. Greek and Russian crosses, many centuries after Christ's Crucifixion, had a third crossbar, the *suppedaneum lignum*, to which the pierced feet were attached. The upright stood usually not more than 10 ft. above ground, near a roadway (Mark 15:29) for the convenience of executioners, and outside the city wall (cf. John 19:20). For other varieties of cross, see (4), p. 120.

100. The Crucifixion, *by William Hole.*

(2) *The Cross of Christ.* The Crucifixion of Jesus, precipitated by political influences exerted on the Roman authorities by the priesthood and the Sanhedrin*, followed immediately after sentence had been pronounced by the procurator of Judaea, Pontius Pilate*.

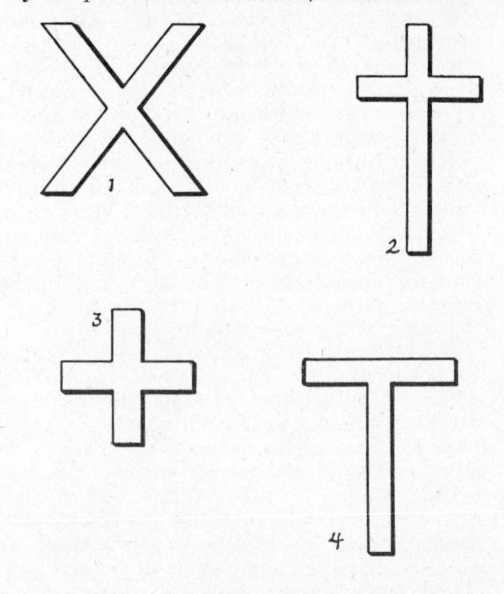

101. Basic Crosses: 1. St. Andrew's; 2. Latin; 3. Greek; 4. Tau.

Mark (15) gives the briefest and most awesome account of the Crucifixion. After Jesus had been clothed in purple and crowned with thorns came the mock worship, the walk to Calvary, with Simon* of Cyrene commandeered to bear the cross; then the refusal of Christ to drink a sedative of wine and myrrh; the affixing of his body, and of the superscription; the taunting by passers on the nearby roadway; the reviling by his fellow victims; the darkness over the whole land until the 9th hour; and the one utterance of the Saviour recorded by Mark (15:34): *Eloi, Eloi, lama sabachthani* (see ELI); the crying of Jesus with a loud voice and his giving up the ghost; the rending of the Temple veil; and the declaration by the Roman centurion, "Truly this man was the Son of God." See also the more detailed accounts of Matthew, Luke, and John.

(3) The *religious message of the Cross of Christ.* During his ministry, Christ had made clear the power that comes to any life which nobly takes up daily its cross of service, hardship, and consecration (Mark 8:34; Luke 9:23 f.). But his own voluntary going to the atoning cross was something far more profound, universal, and mystical. Christ thought of himself as fulfilling on his cross the prophecy of Isa. 53 concerning the "suffering servant." Christ on his cross became the "great instrument of reconciliation" between God and sinful men. The preaching of his Cross became the central emphasis of N.T. evangelism. The Cross was the necessary preface to the Resurrection of Jesus and the resultant immortality of man. Christ's vicarious, undeserved suffering made it possible for the first martyrs to endure hardship in obedience to God's plan. The atonement* was not understood, but it was accepted as part of God's will, the principle of "constraining love." To Paul belongs credit for formulating N.T. thought concerning the Cross. To him even the Incarnation was a step in the direction of the Crucifixion. The Cross demonstrated both the enormity of sin, and how far God would go to bring sinners back to Himself. When Paul failed to mention the Cross in his preaching (as in Acts 17:16–34) he won few converts, and was overwhelmed with disappointment and self-reproach; so that, as he

102. 1. French cross of thorns; 2. Celtic cross with circle of immortality; 3. Cyprus Greek cross; 4. Excavated from a Crusader's tomb in Jerusalem, but clearly a Byzantine piece, possibly purchased at Constantinople; 5. St. Martin's cross (English) with vine and grape motif; 6. Jerusalem or Crusader's Cross. The five crosses symbolize the five wounds of Jesus; or Christ and the four quarters of the earth; or the five nations which joined the Crusades to free the Tomb of Jesus from the Moslems. Adopted by Godfrey de Bouillon, perhaps based on old Armenian form; 7. English Canterbury cross, a consecration cross used on altars; 8. Bethlehem cross—Greek, with four groups of three palms (victory) representing the Twelve Disciples. Note spears (used at the Crucifixion), the flower at center, the suggestion of a star or sunburst, and the concealed circle of immortality; 9. Scotch cross; 10. French cross of thin gold, a general's heirloom; 11. Old Damascus cross, stylized palm pendants; 12. 17th-century Russian enamel and silver, once owned by Grand Duchess Tatiana, daughter of the last Russian Czar; 13. Simple Palestinian Arab (Latin type); 14. Romsey Abbey (England) cross, showing Byzantine influences: the living Saviour, head erect and feet outstretched, hand of God above head; 15. Greek cross patonce on ancient silver amulet (box for relics). (From author's collection)

later wrote to the Corinthians, he resolved that when he came to their city he would not use "the wisdom of words" (I Cor. 1:17), "lest the cross of Christ should be made of none effect," but would not "know anything . . . save Jesus Christ, and him crucified" (I Cor. 2:2). Other statements of Paul concerning the Cross appear in Gal. 6:12, 14; Phil. 2:8; Col. 1:20, 2:14; and Eph. 2:16 (whether Ephesians was written by Paul in Rome, or by Onesimus* in Ephesus, the doctrine is Paul's). The First General Epistle of John amplifies the message of Christ's propitiatory love. In a mystical sense Paul felt that his old self had been "crucified with Christ" (Rom. 6:6; Gal. 2:20).

The ignominy of the Redeemer nailed to a cross stirred the early Church to zealous expansion of Christ's teaching, including the Resurrection, and the telling of his life story. New believers endured hardship in his name. The Cross became a symbol proudly worn even when it brought persecution (Gal. 6:14). The centrality of the Cross in the total account of Christ's life as it appears in the Gospels is indicated (a) by the prominent space given it—about half the Gospel of Mark, for example; and (b) by the fact that the passion narratives were the first portions to attain a "definite, consecutive form," probably because they were used in celebration of the communion sacrament.

(4) *The Cross in Christian symbolism.* Iconography ("the expression in art of an idea, a person, or an event") early adopted the Cross as its key symbol. Nations have worked out their own forms of cross—hundreds of varieties down the centuries. But all conform to five fundamental shapes: the X or St. Andrew's, *crux decussata;* the Latin or Roman, unequal-limbed *(immissa);* the square, equal-limbed Greek cross (or "St. George's"); the Tau, T-shaped, or anticipatory cross; the hooked or swastika, of Sanskrit origin, denoting "object of well-being." The 1st-century ossuaries* found between Jerusalem and Bethlehem were marked in charcoal with what are no longer believed to be Christian crosses designating the tomb of a witness to the Crucifixion. Instead the crosses are now thought to be space-fillers, or signs that the box is full, or marks made in an effort to ward off demons. Coins of Constantine the Great show him lifting aloft a Christian cross. After the era of Constantine there came a wide and diverse development of the Christian cross; worn by worshippers as pectorals; carved on Byzantine sarcophagi, such as survive at Ravenna; looming on church domes, gables, towers, and spires; erected as market, wayside, or preaching crosses; and set in countless numbers of graveyards. Churches were erected having beautiful cruciform ground plans, like the Church of the Apostles in Constantinople, and surviving in the architecture of St. Mark's, Venice; the Armenian Greek-cross types of church, as at Salonika; the triapsidal cruciform Church of the Nativity at Bethlehem*, begun by Constantine in the 4th century A.D. No more beautiful cross has been developed than the perfectly balanced Byzantine crosses of the 6th century Constantinople of Emperor Justinian, seen in the recently uncovered mosaics of Sancta Sophia, and on handles of Byzantine lamps, as well as in extant bronze pectorals in the bazaars of Istanbul.

See SYMBOL.

crown, the translation of several Heb. words in the O.T. (1) *Zer* indicates twisted bands or fillets such as formed a gold cincture around the Ark, the table of shewbread, and the altar of Moses' Tabernacle (Ex. 25:11, 24, 30:3). (2) *Nezer,* the crown or plate of gold worn by the high priest, carrying the words "Holy to Jehovah" (Ex. 28:36 f.), or by a Hebrew king, like Jehoash (see JOASH) (II Kings 11:12), whose crowning was accompanied by anointing (see ANOINT). (3) The *Atarah,* the crown of any king, like that of the Ammonite monarch brought to David and used for his crowning (I Chron. 20:2). (4) The *kether* or diadem of any ruler, such as Vashti (Esther 1:11).

In the N.T. the Gk. word *stephanos* (Lat. *corona*) indicates the garland or wreath awarded the victor in a contest (I Cor. 9:25). In derision, a "stephanos" of thorns platted by soldiers was placed on Christ's brow (John 19:5) (see also II Tim. 4:8; Rev. 12:1). *Diadema* in the N.T. denotes royalty, as in Rev. 19:12.

Since neither Hebrew crowns nor carved likenesses of them have been found, we have no way of knowing the appearance of the royal crowns of Israel. We do know, however, the elaborate, double-emblem-trimmed crowns of such Egyptian kings as Tut-ankh-amun, and the truncated, conical crown of such Assyrians as Esarhaddon, revealed on stele bas-reliefs.

Crucifixion. See CROSS; JESUS CHRIST.

cruse, a small pot or jar for holding liquids (I Sam. 26:11; I Kings 14:3, 17:12, 19:6; II Kings 2:20).

crystal (Gk. *krystallos,* "ice"), transparent quartz, colorless or slightly tinged, prized by the ancients for ornamentation. See Job 28:17; Ezek. 1:22; Rev. 4:6, 21:11, 22:1.

cubit, basic unit of linear measurement, 17.5 in. See WEIGHTS AND MEASURES.

cucumber, a creeping plant and its fruit, grown in Palestine in Bible times and now. Two varieties are known: *Cucumis sativus,* whitish, smooth-skinned; and one called by Arabs *faqqus,* long and slender, an Egyptian vegetable (Num. 11:5). The allusion to Zion being as desolate as an abandoned cucumber booth* (Isa. 1:8) refers to an old custom of owners erecting leafy watch places for guarding their crops against thieves, and letting them fall down after the season was over.

cults, systems of worship centering in devotion or homage to a person or an object. The developing religion of the Hebrew people triumphed over the base cults of their neighbors: Syrian and Canaanite fertility cults, common throughout W. Asia, and leading to sexual immorality between priests and women cultists; sun-god cults of Egypt, centering in Heliopolis; pillar cults prevalent along Edomite caravan routes; cults of the dead; bull and calf cults from Crete; and many others. See WORSHIP.

cummin, a plant cultivated for its seeds which were used as spice in bread and meat and as a medicine (Isa. 28:25, 27), Jesus criticised the Pharisees for tithing trifles such as cummin, while neglecting weightier matters (Matt. 23:23).
See FLOWERS.

cuneiform (kū-nē′ĭ-fôrm) **writing** (Lat. *cuneus*, "wedge") was recorded on small, cushion-shaped, wet clay tablets, later baked, with a stylus of reed, wood, ivory, bone, or metal having a three-sided prism point. Sometimes more durable materials than clay were used for cuneiform records (see below). Cuneiform was the successor of the impractical pictographic, which had devised thousands of symbols made to resemble the house, man, or animal, etc., indicated. In the transition from pictographs to phonetics, the number of symbols was gradually reduced, for the sake of speed, from several thousands to about 150 arbitrary groups of lines; which were still further reduced, after contact with the old Hebrew alphabet, to about 39. The writing was done in neat columns, originally read downward from right to left, but after the era of Hammurabi read horizontally from left to right. Many scribes became meticulous masters of cuneiform writing, so that extant tablets recording syllabaries, mathematical tables, and literary compositions amaze modern epigraphists. The word "cuneiform" was first applied by Kämpfer early in the 18th century.

	A	B	C	D	E
	Original pictograph	*Pictograph in position of later cuneiform*	*Early Babylonian*	*Assyrian*	*Original or derived meaning*
1					bird
2					fish
3					donkey
4					ox
5					sun day
6					grain
7					orchard
8					to plow to till
9					boomerang to throw to throw down
10					to stand to go

103. Diagram showing pictorial origin of ten cuneiform signs. From J. H. Breasted, *Ancient Times*, fig. 86, 2nd edition.

Cuneiform writing is the gift of the great Sumer-Accadian peoples who were living in the alluvial plain at the head of the Persian Gulf in the 4th millennium B.C., and who developed what many believe to have been the world's first culture. Cuneiform tablets have been excavated from Uruk (the Biblical Erech* of Gen. 10:10), 50 m. NW. of Ur*, home of Abraham. Unearthed tablets from the 3d millennium B.C. supply impressive evidence of the historicity of such disputed O.T. passages as Gen. 10:10. Cuneiform spread from the most ancient city centers all over the Middle East, and provided means of communicating business, religious, and literary messages. Just as Roman letters today are used to write modern Turkish as well as English and other languages, so cuneiform was employed by Egyptians, Assyrians, Anatolians, Canaanites, Hebrews, Hittites, and many other Near Easterners. It is likely that some of David's official documents were written in cuneiform by skillful Babylonian scribes* such as the Shavsha of I Chron. 18:16 (Seraiah, II Sam. 8:17; Sheva, II Sam. 20:25). The Hebrews, however, had been in possession of an alphabet ever since the time of Moses (see SERABIT; WRITING). The Ugaritic people of Ras Shamrah* in N. Phoenicia had been writing in their cuneiform alphabet since c. 1500 B.C. The "Standard Assyrian Cuneiform Writing" was in vogue c. 650 B.C.; the "Ancient Persian," c. 520 B.C. The diplomatic correspondence contained in the Tell el-Amarna* tablets was in cuneiform of c. 1400–1350 B.C. The reduction of cuneiform signs to an alphabet of 39 "letters" was accomplished by the 6th century B.C. Just as cuneiform replaced pictographic writing, so it was replaced by more cursive forms when pen, ink, and papyrus became popular shortly before the Christian era. But cuneiform was still employed side by side with the modern Aramaic alphabet until the very end of the pre-Christian period.

Although cuneiform was characteristically written on clay tablets, thousands of which survive (see CLAY), and have been published and are displayed in many museums, it was sometimes committed to rock surfaces, incised across the garments of Babylonian kings carved on stone, or even chiseled on metal.

The deciphering of cuneiform has proceeded for two centuries. One great step, corresponding to the decoding of the trilingual Rosetta Stone which unlocked ancient Egyptian literature and historical records, was Rawlinson's deciphering of the 12-ft.-high columns carved at Behistun Rock 300 ft. above the caravan road between Ecbatana and Babylon. These recorded the feats of Darius I in three languages, so that all might read of Achaemenid greatness. The characters were carved in Old Persian, Elamite, and Accadian. Rawlinson's work (1835–47) and that of recent scholars have unlocked priceless records of Asia.

Students of the Bible find great interest in 300 clay tablets from 590–570 B.C. found near Babylon's* Ishtar Gate. Some of these mention captives bearing Hebrew names that appear in Scripture, as "Yaukin, king of Judah"—the Jehoiachin of II Kings 25:27–30. Another cuneiform message, written on a six-sided clay cylinder now in the Oriental Institute of the University of Chicago, tells of Sennacherib's campaign, when he boasted of shutting up King Hezekiah in Jerusalem "like a caged bird" (cf. II Kings 19).

The deciphering of cuneiform has brought to the world not only historical records and business accounts important in the evolution of commerce, but ancient versions of Babylonian and Canaanite epics of Creation, and prayers, hymns, and penitential psalms which challenge comparison with the sacred literature of the Hebrews.

cup, the common drinking utensil which plays an uncommon part throughout the Bible. The one in the dream of Pharaoh's butler (Gen. 40:11) was of the ordinary size, the sort into which the responsible court attendant pressed fresh grapes. It may have been of carved gold or silver. The cup hidden in Benjamin's sack (Gen. 44:2 ff.) was probably Joseph's silver divining bowl or goblet. The brim of a cup gave the design for the rim of the molten sea (II Chron. 4:5) (see MOLTEN SEA, illus. 273). The overflowing cup of happiness in Ps. 23:5 was suggested by the smaller stone drinking trough into which the shepherd dipped water for his sheep from the too large cistern or pool. In a figurative sense the cup in O.T. writings signifies man's earthly lot, as the cup of bitterness (Ps. 11:6), and the cup of salvation (Ps. 116:13). In a similar sense Jesus used the word "cup" in his prayer for escape from earthly suffering (Matt. 26:39). When Jesus asked his disciples if they were able to drink the cup that he drank of, he referred to the experience of sacrificial death (Matt. 20:22). Jesus gave

104. Gold libation cups of Queen Shubad.

lasting religious significance to the ordinary cup when he made of it a chalice* symbolically filled with his blood of "the new testament" (Luke 22:20; I Cor. 11:25).

See ANTIOCH, THE CHALICE OF.

Libation cups of choicest materials were used by various ancient peoples of the Near East, for drink offerings, like the famous gold libation cups of Queen Shubad of Ur*, found in the royal tombs built almost 5,000 years ago.

cupbearer, the drink-giver at Eastern courts; the butler charged with testing wines served to his royal master, as in Gen. 40:11; I Kings 10:5. Nehemiah, a Jew, was cupbearer to Artaxerxes (Neh. 1:11), an evidence of unusual trust of a foreigner. The importance of the cupbearer is indicated by depictions of him on palace reliefs. Median provincials carried some of their tribute to Achaemenid Persian kings in cup-like bowls.

curse, an imprecation or utterance invoking deity to destroy; frequently used in the O.T. The Levites uttered a number of legitimate curses from Mt. Ebal*, the Mount of Cursing, opposite Mt. Gerizim*, the Mount of Blessing, in Samaria (Deut. 27). Certain curses were forbidden, as the cursing of a deaf person; worst of all was an imprecation against parents (Ex. 21:17; Matt. 15:4). The lofty idealism of Psalm 109:28 led the way to the words of Jesus (Luke 6:28): "Bless them that curse you"—a great advance over the O.T. attitude (Num. 22:6, 17).

Cush. See ETHIOPIA.

cylinder seals. See SEAL.

cymbal. See MUSIC.

cypress (*Cypressus semper virens*), mentioned only in Isa. 44:14, and possibly identical with the fir named as flooring in Solomon's Temple (cf. A.V. I Kings 6:15 with A.S.V. margin). Cypress wood is very hard, and suitable for such carving as craftsmen of Damascus have been doing for centuries. Cypress trees grow near shrines, as in the Jerusalem Temple Area, or in cemeteries and terraced gardens.

105. Cypress.

Cyprus ("copper"), a Mediterranean island 60 m. W. of Latakia on the Syrian coast, and 45 m. S. of Turkey. It is shaped like a fist, with forefinger pointing toward Antioch* and the Orontes, to which it distributed cultural and religious influences. Known in O.T. times as "Chittim" (Jer. 2:10), it was coveted by one civilization after another for the copper* and timber of its two mountain ranges, separated by a low plain. Its first N.T. mention (Acts 4:36) is in connection with Joseph Barnabas*, evidently a Jew driven abroad by persecution. To Cyprus, where Christianity gained a start soon after Stephen's persecution, Barnabas and Saul* sailed on their First Missionary Journey, landing at Salamis*, the largest port of the island, facing Syria, and proceeding W. to Paphos*, capital of the island (Acts 13:2–6). In that place occurred the conversion of Sergius Paulus, a Roman proconsul ("deputy") (Acts 13:7–12). An inscription bearing the date "A.D. 52–53" has been found at Paphos, inscribed with "in the time of the proconsul Paulus." The Acts narrative calls "Saul" "Paul" after the event narrated in 13:12. Another N.T. man of Cyprus was Mnason, an early disciple, with whom Paul lodged at Jerusalem (Acts 21:16). The presence of numerous synagogues in Cyprus to whose congregations Barnabas and Paul preached (Acts 13:5) is attributable to the immigration of Jews to the island when Herod* the Great farmed out the famous copper mines (reopened by modern American engineers). Not much is known of apostolic Christianity in Cyprus after the tour of Barnabas and John Mark (Acts 15:39).

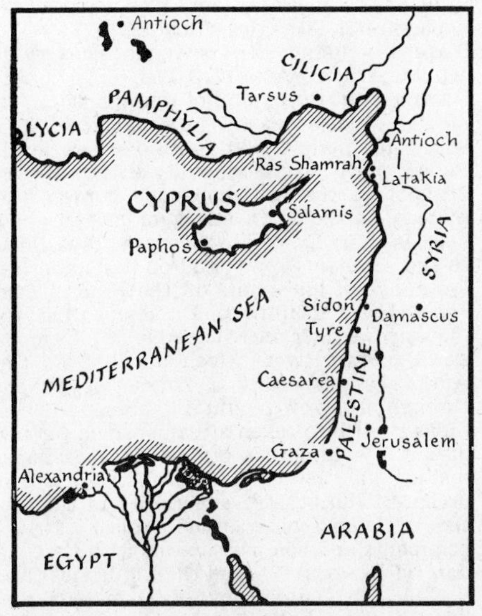

106. Cyprus.

At both Salamis and Paphos archaeological investigations are under way; in the latter place, by the University of Pennsylvania Museum (whose *Bulletin* see). Ruins of structures and "objects of worship" have already been uncovered which may well have been seen by Paul as he walked through Cyprus in the direction of Paphos. Cyprus offers promise of rewarding evidence of the N.T. period.

Cyrene (sī-rē′nē̇), the principal city of Libya, later Cyrenaica, in N. Africa. Simon of Cyrene carried the cross of Jesus (Mark 15:21). Cyrenian Jews had a synagogue in Jerusalem (Acts 6:9). Cyrenian Christians preached to Greeks in Antioch (Acts 11:20). Lucius of Cyrene was prominent in the church of Antioch (Acts 13:1).

Cyrus II ("the Great"), founder of the Persian Empire, son of Cambyses I, King of Anshan, and of Mandane, daughter of King Astyages of the Medes. He succeeded to the throne of Anshan c. 559 B.C., and made rapid conquests of the surrounding territories, so that he became ruler of the largest empire the world had yet seen—the Persian (see PERSIA). By 550 Cyrus had united his own people and conquered the Medes; by 547 he had subdued Lydia; and in 539 B.C. he had defeated the Chaldean army at Babylon*. When he was succeeded (530 B.C.) by his son Cambyses II, who took Egypt, his Achaemenid house held the entire East as far as India.

Cyrus was known for his clemency to all subdued peoples. His leniency in authorizing the return of the captive Jews* to rebuild the Jerusalem Temple (II Chron. 36:22 f.; Ezra 1:1–8) led them to write of Cyrus as Yahweh's "shepherd" (Isa. 44:28) and His "anointed" (Isa. 45:1); but there is no evidence that Cyrus himself accepted the Yahweh of the Hebrew captives. An excavated cylinder carrying priceless cuneiform* historic records refers to Marduk, the chief god of Babylon, associated with the planet Jupiter, as the one who had accepted Cyrus as "righteous prince," appointing him king "over the whole world." This cylinder also confirms Cyrus' edict authorizing the return of captives to "the other side of the Tigris." The efficiency of his administration is suggested by Ezra 6,

107. Tomb of Cyrus the Great at Pasargadae, Iran.

which tells of a search by Darius* in the archives house of Cyrus, for the roll recording the decree permitting reconstruction of the House of God at Jerusalem. The capital of Cyrus was Pasargadae, N. of Persepolis (built by Darius and now excavated by the O.I.). There meager ruins of a terraced city have been found, and a few buildings on which inscriptions still claim the structures as the work of "Cyrus the king of the Achaemenids." The small, simple tomb of Cyrus, with its pathetic inscription, survives on the plain at Murghab.

A part of the story of Daniel's career is set within the reign of Cyrus (Dan. 1:21, 6:28, 10:1).

D

D, symbol for the D document of material in the O.T. See SOURCES.

dagger. See WEAPONS.

Dagon (dā′gŏn) (Heb., dâgân, "grain"), an ancient Canaanite deity (prob. vegetation deity) associated with agriculture; identified by N. Syria Ras Shamrah* texts as father of the great god Baal*; and honored in early Phoenician times. He was worshipped as a national god of the Philistines, who erected temples to him at Gaza and Ashdod. His name was incorporated in town names, as in Beth-dagon (Josh. 15:41). He was praised during martial victories. A temple of Dagon has been found in N. Syrian Ugarit— a shrine similar to the adjacent one to Baal. It has a naos, an altar court approached by three steps, and other features found later in Hebrew architecture. Some authorities, like W. F. Albright, believe that Dagon was an early Accadian deity, to whom homage was paid throughout the Euphrates Valley as early as the 25th century B.C.

Three O.T. incidents center in a shrine of Dagon. (1) A Philistine temple of Dagon at Gaza was the scene of Samson's death (Judg. 16:23–30). (2) Philistines at Ashdod were killed when the Hebrew Ark was carried into their temple of Dagon (I Sam. 5:1–7), and the statue of the god tumbled to the ground. (3) Following the battle of Israel against the Philistines at Mt. Gilboa, the head of slain King Saul was fastened "in the temple of Dagon" (I Chron. 10:10) at Beth-shan. This shrine may be the "south temple" of stratum V, in the now fully excavated "Mound of the Fortress," Beth-shan, at the E. end of the Valley of Jezreel (U. of Pa.).

dainties, toothsome foods and sweetmeats associated with royal tables (Gen. 49:20), and with workers of wickedness—as part of the extravagant living abhorrent to ascetic Hebrews (Ps. 141:4; Prov. 23:3, 6). Babylonian dainties may have been delicate meats, rich cakes, or confectionery, made by Hebrew women captives (I Sam. 8:13). See also Rev. 18:14.

Daleth (dä′lĕth), the 4th letter of the Hebrew alphabet. See WRITING.

Dalmanutha (dăl′mȧ-nū′thȧ), an unidentified village, perhaps Magdala, on the W. shore of the Sea of Galilee; or Khan el-Minieh near Tabgha*. To it Christ and his Disciples sailed after the feeding of the 4,000 (Mark 8:10). In a cave in this vicinity the famous skull of a Neanderthal man was found in 1925.

Dalmatia (dăl-mā′shĭ-ȧ), a region along the E. shore of the Adriatic, comprised today in Yugoslavia; once part of Illyricum, under which name Paul referred to it (Rom. 15:19). Dalmatia became tributary to Rome in 180 B.C., but under Augustus it attained the rank of province. II Tim. 4:10 records the departure of Titus to Dalmatia.

Damaris (dăm′ȧ-rĭs), a woman convert of Paul at Athens (Acts 17:34).

Damascus, the capital of Syria, c. 65 m. E. of the Mediterranean, in the center of a 30x10 m. plain 2,300 ft. above sea level. Snowcapped Mt. Hermon is on its W.; an offshoot of the Anti-Lebanons borders the plateau on the N.; a string of marshes and lakes is on its E., before the plain drops down to the Arabian Desert; and on its S. another low range of hills shuts off the Hauran (the Jebel Druse country). Damascus and its plateau owe their life to the Abana* (the modern Barada) River, which bursts from the Anti-Lebanons, runs a course of 10 m. through a narrow mountain gorge, and then flings itself into seven streams which further divide into hundreds of smaller waterways, making all this area a fruitful garden and orchard. The boasted superiority of the waters of Damascus was the subject of rival comments and comparisons, as with the Jordan (II Kings 5:12), and the Euphrates (Isa. 8:5–8). The supremacy of Damascus was due to the fact that it was the highway terminus of 3 caravan routes: (1) SW. through Galilee via the Mediterranean coast to Egypt; (2) S. to the Arabian peninsula—for centuries the Moslem pilgrim route to Mecca; (3) E. to Baghdad and the Euphrates. Thus Egypt, Arabia, and Mesopotamia were the trade neighbors which made Damascus "the head of Syria" (Isa. 7:8).

Damascus goes back to the prehistory era of myth. Uz, grandson of Shem (Gen. 5:32, 6:10, 10:23), was its legendary founder. It is the world's oldest city having continuous habitation. Though it has experienced devastating misfortunes of war, its long history shows that its successive masters have risen from pivotal battles fought elsewhere, a fact which frequently spared the city from destruction. Abraham traveled via the Fertile Crescent from Ur to Canaan (Gen. 11:31 f., 12:4 f.), passing through Damascus (see also Gen. 14:14 f.). Eliezer, an important personage in Abraham's household, was a Damascene (Gen. 15:2). In the period of Hebrew empire expansion, David captured and garrisoned Damascus (II Sam. 8:5 f.; I Chron. 18:5 f.). Rezon (I Kings 11:23 f.) led a revolution, seized Damascus, and founded a Syrian dynasty which for 200 years, i.e., 940–732 B.C., was frequently in conflict with Israel and Judah; and then in alliance with Judah against Israel.

Damascus made reciprocal trade treaties with cities in the orbit of its conquests (I Kings 20:34). King Ahaz of Judah visited Damascus to pay homage to victorious Tiglath-pileser III, where he saw the great altar, a duplicate of which he ordered erected in the Jerusalem Temple (II Kings 16:10, 16). When Tiglath-pileser III (Pul) conquered Syria (732 B.C.), overthrew the dynasty, and killed Rezin (II Kings 16:9), he brought on Damascus the destruction so vividly depicted by the prophets (Isa. 8:4, 17:1; Amos 1:4; Jer. 49:23–27).

108. Damascus: traditional site of Paul's escape.

Syria flourished under the Persians. But in the Hellenistic era Damascus was superseded by Antioch. Damascus prospered under Greek and Roman control, becoming in Christ's time a favored city of the Decapolis. The presence of a considerable colony of Jews in Damascus, presumably merchants, led Saul of Tarsus to journey there, determined to purge the city of Christian heretics (Acts 9:1 f.). His conversion occurred outside Damascus (Acts 9:3, 22:6).

The Christian quarter in present-day Damascus, with its "street called Straight" (*Sûk et-Tawîleh*, "The Long Street"), has not changed its general location since Paul's time (Acts 9:10 f.). See WALL, illus. 473, which illustrates Acts 9:23, 25, II Cor. 11:32. The most important building in Damascus is the Great Mosque, since the 8th century A.D. a Moslem shrine, modified from the cathedral church of Syria dedicated to John the Baptist by Constantine the Great. It still shows above its S. door the Greek inscription: "Thy kingdom is an everlasting kingdom, and Thy dominion endureth throughout all generations." In this unchanged city the Great Mosque is believed to be on the site of the Temple of Rimmon (II Kings 5:18). In the picturesque but odorous bazaars the same sorts of wares are sold today as were marketed in Bible times. Arranged in long avenues, roofed over to protect buyers from sun and rain, the cell-like shops are zoned, with the saddlers' bazaar, the silk bazaar, the silversmiths' bazaar, the coppersmiths', woodcraft, slipper, tobacco, and sweetmeat bazaars, and the warehouses. "Damask"—a reversible figured fabric—came originally from Damascus; and Damascus steel was famous throughout Europe for swords and other small arms.

Aramaean Kingdom of Damascus

c. 940–920 Rezon (I) B.C.	I Kings 11:23 f.
c. 920–910 Hezion B.C.	1 Kings 15:18 f.
c. 910–900 Tabrimon	
c. 880–842 Ben-hadad I	II Chron. 16:2 f.
c. 869–850 Ben-hadad II (Hadadezer)	II Kings 6:24, 8:7.
c. 842–806 Hazael	I Kings 19:15–17; II Kings 8:8–15, 9:14, 15.
c. 770–750 Ben-hadad III	II Kings 13:3–5, 24 f.
c. 740–732 Rezon (II) (A.V. Rezin)	II Kings 15:37, 16:5 f; Isa. 7:1, 4.

Dan ("he judged"). (1) Son of Jacob* and Bilhah, Rachel's handmaid (Gen. 30:1–6), and the eponymous ancestor of the tribe of Dan. (2) One of the 12 tribes of Israel, assigned a small territory during the Conquest*, bounded on the N. by Ephraim, on the S. by Judah, on the E. by Benjamin (Josh. 19:40–48). The tribe may have reached the Mediterranean, but this is uncertain (see Judg. 5:17). Unable to retain their inheritance, the Danites migrated N. to an area near the source of the Jordan River (Josh. 19:47; Judg. 1:34; 18). A part of the tribe remained in the original territory, as evident by the sagas about Samson, a Danite hero (Judg. 13–16). (3) A Danite city, near

109. Jordan River, S. of site of Dan.

one of the sources of the Jordan, identified with Tell el-Qadi (Tel Dan), the "mound of the judge." Prior to its seizure by the Danites (Josh. 19:47; Judg. 18:27–29), it was known as Laish (Leshem). The latter name appears on a clay tablet from Mari, in the Egyptian execration texts of the 19th century B.C., and in the topographical lists of Tuthmosis III (c. 1504–1450 B.C.; see *ANET*[3], pp. 242 and 329, n. 8). A cult center was established in Dan by Moses' grandson, Jonathan (Judg. 18:30), later made a national sanctuary of Israel by Jeroboam I (I Kings 12:26–30). Dan was recognized as the N. boundary of Palestine in the classic phrase, "from Dan to Beer-sheba" (Judg. 20:1; II Sam. 24:2; I Kings 4:25; etc.).

Since 1956, A. Biran has directed excavations on Tell el-Qadi, the site of ancient Dan. Included among the remains are a fortification wall and glacis of the MB II ("Hyksos") period, beneath which lie strata belonging to the Early Bronze Age and 7 strata spanning the length of the Late Bronze and Iron Ages. The remains of a city gate dating to the 1st half of the 9th century B.C. were excavated, and a large structure of the late 7th–early 6th century B.C., possibly a *bamah*, or "high place" (see Notes and News in issues of *IEJ* since 1966). W. P. A.

dancing in Scripture usually had a religious function. It was also employed in celebrations of victory, as in the timbrel-accompanied dance of Miriam and her maidens, celebrating the crossing of the Sea of Reeds (Ex. 15:20 f.; see also Judg. 11:34; I Sam. 18:6, 30:16). The Bible also depicts the happy folk-dancing of the grape gatherers of Shiloh at the old vintage festival, when women were courted (Judg. 21:21). These merrymakings were more wholesome than the Canaanite fertility dances, akin to Greek bacchanalia. But many of the dances in Scripture were ritualistic, as when David brought the Ark to Jerusalem and "danced before the Lord with all his might" (II Sam. 6:14, 16). Dancing before calf idols and at shrines was common in O.T. times (Ex. 32:19). The Psalms reveal dances and music used to praise the Lord (149:3, 150:4). Jeremiah pictured rejoicing over a restored Israel in terms of merry dancing (31:4). Jesus referred to children dancing (Luke 7:32), and to music and dancing at the homecoming feast of the Prodigal Son (Luke 15:25).

In the Graeco-Roman world of his day professional women dancers were employed, like Salome at Herod's birthday banquet (Mark 6:22). Greek dancing gods are suggested by Isaiah's allusion to satyrs (13:21). Among Egyptians, banquets were featured by dainty women and child dancers, swaying to the music of harp, flute, lyre, or lute, or to the rhythm of clapped hands; tomb art depicts such scenes.

Daniel. (1) A son of David and Abigail (I Chron. 3:1), called Chileab in II Sam. 3:3. (2) A priest who signed the covenant in the time of Nehemiah (Ezra 8:2; Neh. 10:6). (3) A king of ancient times who appears as the hero in an epic poem recorded on clay tablets found at Ras Shamrah*. He dispensed judgment at the gate of the city, and belonged to the same age of hero-tradition as did Noah and Job. He is referred to in the 6th-century B.C. Book of Ezekiel (14:14, 20, 28:3), where the name is spelled as on the Ras Shamrah tablets, not as in the Book of Daniel. (4) The prophet of the Book of Daniel, taken captive, educated, and later made ruler of Babylon by Nebuchadnezzar, whose court gave him the name of Belteshazzar. Daniel is unknown except for what appears in the book bearing his name, although he is mentioned in Matt. 24:15; Mark 13:14 (A.V.); II Esdras 12:11; I Macc. 2:60. See DANIEL, THE BOOK OF.

Daniel, the Book of, in the Hebrew Canon is placed among the Hagiographa or Writings, the 3d section of their Canon (finally closed c. A.D. 90); but in the Greek, Latin, and English Bibles it is one of the four Major Prophets, following Ezekiel. It is divided into the story of Daniel (1–6) and the visions of Daniel (7–12). It is written in Hebrew, except Dan. 2:4–7:28, which is in Aramaic. With its symbols, imaginative forms, religious enthusiasm, and predictions of apocalyptic events at the end of the world it is unique in the O.T., but the forerunner of the Revelation of St. John. Portions of MSS. of Daniel, which may date less than a century from the original, are among the Dead Sea Scrolls* acquired by the Hebrew University in Jerusalem.

To some the book is a cryptogram of history written early in the 6th century B.C. Daniel was a historical character, they say, a youthful Jew in Babylon loyal to the Levitical law (chap. 1). He ably interpreted the royal dreams (2, 4) and visions (5). His three companions survived the fiery furnace (3), and he the lions' den (6). Then through four visions he revealed the course of history from c. 600 B.C. to 164 B.C. The four beasts (7:3–7) are Babylon, Media, Persia, and Greece. The "other horn" (7:8, 20, 24) is Antiochus IV Epiphanes, also identified by some with the anti-Christ, the Roman papacy, Hitler, Stalin, etc. Daniel himself was mystified by his lack of understanding of what he saw (8:15). There are allusions to Cyrus, Cambyses, Darius I, Xerxes I (or Cyrus, Xerxes I, Artaxerxes I, and Darius III) (11:2), Alexander the Great (11:3), Ptolemy I of Egypt ("the king of the south"), and Seleucus I (11:5); Berenice, the daughter of Ptolemy II (11:6); Seleucus II (11:7–9); Seleucus III and Antiochus III the Great (11:10–19); Seleucus IV (11:20); and Antiochus IV Epiphanes (11:21–45). Daniel closes his sketch of world history with the Resurrection (12:1–3) and the end of this age 12:4–13). Certain types of interpretation have made this book, together with Revelation, the arsenal of millennialism— a forge where through the centuries the weapons for religious controversy about the last things have been shaped.

For those who view Daniel as an apocalypse written in the 2d century B.C. the book contains a message of comfort to the faithful and courageous in terrible times of persecution (168–165 B.C.). This viewpoint permits an explanation of some of the inconsistencies. Some of the historical references in Daniel are correct, others erroneous. From Jehoiakim, King of Judah (1:1) (c. 609–598 B.C.), to King Cyrus (6:28), or from 609 to 539 B.C., the successive kings in Babylon were:

According to Daniel	*According to Secular Records*
Nebuchadnezzar (2:1)	Nabopolassar
	Nebuchadnezzar
Belshazzar (5:1)	Evil-Merodach
Darius the Mede (5:31)	Neriglissar
	Nabonidus and Belshazzar
Cyrus (6:28)	Cyrus

Darius did not precede Cyrus, but followed him 20 years later. Belshazzar was not the son of Nebuchadnezzar, but of Nabonidus (Nabuna'id) (556–539 B.C.). Darius, instead of being the son of Ahasuerus or of Xerxes (9:1), was the father of Xerxes. The historical accuracy of the book improves as it moves through the Babylonian, Persian, and Greek kingdoms and comes into the days of Antiochus Epiphanes (175–163 B.C.), whose persecutions of the Jews are vividly portrayed (Dan. 8:9–12, 23–25, 11:21–39). After a successful campaign in Egypt, Libya, and Ethiopia, Antiochus was expected to meet his death somewhere between Jerusalem and the Mediterranean (Dan. 11:40–45); in fact, Antiochus died in a campaign against the Parthians in the east (163 B.C.). In view of all the evidence, the Book of Daniel was probably written c. 164 B.C. Its place in the Hagiographa rather than among the Prophets favors this date. Some Jewish writers presented messages for the current day as given in the past, as in the case, e.g., of the Law of Deuteronomy, the Book of Ecclesiastes. etc. Just so, this unknown gifted author assumed the role of a young Jew, Daniel, at Babylon, extolling in accordance with traditional legends (Ezek. 14:14, 20, 28:3) his courage, piety, and wisdom; and he made Daniel predict accurately the history up to the time the book was written, in order to bring comfort and encouragement to Jews in the persecutions of Antiochus Epiphanes, at the time of the Maccabean Revolt.

Among the influential theological ideas characteristic of Daniel are angelology (8:16, 9:21, 10:13, 20); the Resurrection (12:2); and the reign of "the Son of Man"* (7:13 f.; Mark 14:62).

Darda (där′dȧ), one of the sons of Mahol, widely known for his wisdom (I Kings 4:31). In I Chron. 2:6 the name is given as Dara.

daric, a Persian gold coin common in the time of the Chronicler (R.S.V. Ezra 2:69, 8:27; Neh. 7:70–72), and thus referred to by him in expressing the value of the gold contributed for the Temple in David's reign (R.S.V. I Chron. 29:7). The A.V. uses the word "dram."
See MONEY.

Darius (dȧ-rī′ŭs), the name of two or of three rulers mentioned 26 times in the O.T. (1) Darius the Great (Darius I, son of Hystaspes), King of Persia*, instigator of the campaign against Greece which resulted in his defeat at Marathon 490 B.C.; reigned 522–486 B.C. He recorded his deeds in the famous trilingual inscription at Behistun Rock. Restoring the realm of Cyrus*, he continued that ruler's tolerant policy toward the Jewish captives in Babylon, and encouraged them to continue their restoration of the Jerusalem temple. When complaints were lodged against the building by Tatnai, a governor appointed by Persia, and others (Ezra 5:3 ff.), Darius searched the well-kept archives of Cyrus, found the original decree roll authorizing the work (Ezra 6:1–5), and issued a new edict forbidding hindrance of the Jewish project and ordering a generous contribution to it (6:6–12). The Temple was

110. Darius the Great, detail of portrait cut in limestone cliff near Behistun, Iran.

finished in the 6th year of his reign (Ezra 6:15). Darius I was contemporary with the Hebrew prophets Haggai (1:1, 2:1, 10) and Zechariah (Zech. 1:1, 7, 7:1). The Darius referred to in Neh. 12:22 may be Darius the Great, or Darius Codomannus, last king of Persia (336–331 B.C.).

Recently Dr. George Cameron of the University of Michigan used steeplejack methods to reach the almost inaccessible limestone rock above the Iranian village of Behistun to copy the trilingual inscription left 2400 yrs. ago by Darius the Great boasting of his triumphs and the organization of his far-flung Empire. These inscriptions, which became a key to the little-known languages of W. Asia, are accompanied by carved depictions of the Persian's power, and of his worship of Ahura-Mazda in the presence of royal prisoners.

(2) Darius the Mede, concerning whose identity there is much confusion, appears in the Book of Daniel*. He is mentioned in Dan. 5:31 as succeeding Belshazzar to the throne of Babylon; in Dan. 9:1 he is called the "son of Ahasuerus, of the seed of the Medes"—not a historical person. Whatever his identity, this Darius made the pious Hebrew prisoner Daniel the first of three presidents having authority "over the whole kingdom" (Dan. 6:1–3). Daniel's popularity precipitated the decree of Darius which sent him into the lions' den (6:7–23), an episode which resulted in the authorization of the worship of the God of Daniel (6:26).

darkness, most often in Scripture a metaphor. Physical "darkness upon the face of the deep" was an ancient way of describing the pre-Creation state (Gen. 1:2). Darkness symbolically denoted wickedness (Isa. 5:20; Matt. 4:16; John 3:19); ignorance (Isa. 42:7; Psalm 82:5); the unknown (Psalm 18:11; I Cor. 4:5); woe (II Sam. 22:29; Job 18:18; Psalm 88:6); and eternal sin* (Jude

13). Having always identified darkness with evil, the Hebrews thought of God and Christ in terms of light shining in darkness: Psalm 27:1, 119:105; Isa. 60:1; John 1:4–9. Christ called himself "the light of the world" (John 8:12). "Dark speeches" (Num. 12:8) meant enigmatic utterances from God to man. The parables of Jesus were called "dark sayings."

dark saying. See PARABLE.

dart. See WEAPONS.

date, the fleshy, ovoid, one-seeded fruit of the date palm (*Phoenix dactylifera*). It was highly prized as a food in the Biblical period, as now, and was an important trade commodity. The departure on Mesopotamian rivers of the

111. Date grove at Aqabah.

first boats of a season laden with dates occasioned shouts of joy, as it still does in Iran. Dates still grow in oases of North Africa, the Nile Delta, and across Mesopotamia to India. They have always characterized well-watered Jericho ("the city of palm trees"), and such regions as Sidon. In Arabia, dates are a main source of national income. They grow in huge clusters of golden tan, dark brown, or mahogany-colored fruits which develop from flowers branching from the high crown of feathery palm leaves. The flowers are female only, and must be artificially fertilized. To pick a date crop requires deft climbing of tall, rough trunks. Dates are best when eaten fresh. Since ancient times people of the Near East have also pressed them into cakes prized for their sugar content. Recovered clay tablets record business transactions in which dates were used in payments. "Old dates for grinding" were sometimes used in paying temple dues in Sennacherib's Assyria.

Dathan (dā′thăn), a Reubenite who joined the rebellion of Korah the Levite against Moses and Aaron in the Wilderness (Num. 16:1–35, 26:7–11; Ps. 106:17).

David ("beloved"), the 2d Hebrew king (1000–961 B.C.), successor to Saul*. The Biblical material on David is found in I Sam. 16 to I Kings 2; I Chron. 2, 3, 10–29; Ruth 4:18–22; and in titles of many Psalms—seventy-three Psalms bear the title "To David." Many such dedications, however, were eulogistic of David's great influence, were written years after he lived, and offer little or no historic data on his life. The same remoteness from actual events characterizes the glorification of David and his regime by the Chronicler (see CHRONICLES), who used generously the material of I Sam. 16 to I Kings 2. This latter is of great historical value. It consists of several strands of narrative often giving divergent versions of the same event, but these strands may be harmonized in an accurate, historic picture of David.

A Summary of David's Life

David the Man—	
A Judaean of Bethlehem	Ruth 4:18–22
shepherd	I Sam. 16:11 ff.
musician	I Sam. 16:14–23
poet	II Sam. 1:17–27
warrior	I Sam. 17
friend (of Jonathan)	I Sam. 18:1–4, 19:1–7, 20:1–42
enemy (of Saul)	I Sam. 18:5–22
saved by Michal, Saul's daughter	I Sam. 18:20,-29, 19:8–17
David the Fugitive and Outlaw—	
At Naioth in Ramah	I Sam. 19:18–24:42
Nob	I Sam. 21:1–9,
Gath	I Sam. 21:10–15,
Cave of Adullam	I Sam. 22:1 f.
Mizpeh	I Sam. 22:3 f.
Forest of Hareth	I Sam. 22:5
Keilah	I Sam. 23:1–13
Wilderness of Ziph	I Sam. 23:14–24, 26:1 ff.
Maon in the Arabah	I Sam. 23:24–28
En-gedi	I Sam. 23:29–24:22, 26:4 ff.
Wilderness of Paran	I Sam. 25
Gath (Achish)	I Sam. 27:1–5
Ziklag	I Sam. 27:6 ff. Cf. I Chron. 12:1–22
Death of Saul and Jonathan—	I Sam. 31; II Sam. 1. Cf. I Chron. 10
David as King of Judah and United Israel	
Anointed King of Judah at Hebron	II Sam. 2:1–11
Abner's counter-revolution and death of Ish-bosheth	II Sam. 2:12–4:12
David elected King of all Israel	II Sam. 5:1–5; cf. I Chron. 11:1–3, 12:23–40
Captures and establishes Jerusalem as political capital	II Sam. 5:6–10; cf. I Chron. 11:4–9
Alliance with Hiram, King of Tyre	II Sam. 5:11; cf. I Chron. 14:11

Makes Jerusalem the religious capital of all Israel	(a) By transferring Ark: II Sam. 6:1–19; cf. I Chron. 13:1–14, 15:1–16:42
	(b) By prayers and preparation for Temple: II Sam. 7.; cf. I Chron. 21:18–22:19
Personalities and Events of David's Reign—	
His family	II Sam. 3:2–5, 5:13–16; cf. I Chron. 3:1–9, 14:3–7
The Bath-sheba episode	II Sam. 11:2—12:25
Court officials	II Sam. 8:16–18, 20:23–26; cf. I Chron. 18:15–17, 27:25–34
Treatment of the sons of Saul	II Sam. 21:1–14
Treatment of the sons of Jonathan	II Sam. 4:4, 9:1–13
Illustrious warriors	II Sam. 23:8–12, 18–39; cf. I Chron. 11:10–14, 20–47, 27:1–24
Wars of Conquest—	
Philistines	II Sam. 5:17–25, 8:1, 21:15–22, 23:13–17; cf. I Chron. 11:15–19, 14:8–17, 18:1, 20:4–8
Moabites	II Sam. 8:2; cf. I Chron. 18:2
Zobah	II Sam. 8:3f., 7f.; cf. I Chron. 18:3, 7
Syrians	II Sam. 8:5–13; cf. I Chron. 18:5–10
Edomites	II Sam. 8:13–14; cf. I Chron. 18:12–13
Ammonites	II Sam. 10:6–11:1, 12:26–31; cf. I Chron. 19:6–20:3
David Takes the Census—	II Sam. 24; cf. I Chron. 21
Rebellions—	
Of his son Absalom	II Sam. 13–19.
Sheba	II Sam. 20:1–22.
Adonijah	I Kings 1.
David's Charge to Solomon—	I Kings 2:1–9.

David's influence over all kinds of people was due to his personal charm. His character was a mixture of good and bad, with the former predominating. The prevailing polygamy of the times was the cause of most of his family difficulties. David was passionately loyal to Yahweh, the God of battles, a Providence which had led and cared for him, and which in return received his thanks. He felt an ethical responsibility to God. For when Nathan confronted him with the charge, "Thou art the man," David's only answer was, "I have sinned against the Lord" (II Sam. 12:13). In spite of David's imperfections, Samuel's summary of David as a man after God's "own heart" (I Sam. 13:14) has become the verdict of history as to the genuineness of his religion. I and II Chronicles idealize David as the one who established the Jewish "Church," inaugurated the ritual of worship, and especially the musical features of the ceremony. As a leader of men, military organizer and tactician, diplomat, deliverer of his people, founder of a dynasty, and unifier of the nation, David demonstrated his enormous talents. He was a resourceful executive. and a wise administrator (II Sam. 8:15). He established Jerusalem as capital of all Israel. When oppression and injustice in subsequent years became common among the Hebrew people, the great prophets looked forward to a time when again a righteous king would sit on the throne (Jer. 23:5), and took the name of David as a symbol of this ideal ruler (Jer. 30:9; Ezek. 34:23 f.; Luke 1:32, 2:11).

112. David, in stained-glass window, the Hanson Place Central Methodist Church, Brooklyn, N. Y.

The so-called David's Tower at the Jerusalem Citadel near the present Jaffa Gate is Phasael Tower, built by Herod the Great in honor of his brother. Courses of its extant masonry were doubtless seen by Jesus.

David, City of. (1) The most ancient portion of the Jerusalem site, lying S. of what became the city of Solomon and the Temple* Area. The City of David was excavated by the Palestine Exploration Fund (whose *Quarterlies* for 1924, see). Because of proximity to two springs—En-rogel* and Gihon* (see map)—the small S. hillock above the Kidron attracted human beings at least as early as the 3d millennium B.C. Amorite pottery and Egyptian Twelfth Dynasty scarabs (c.1991 1786 B.C.) have been excavated in this area. Long before these articles were placed there, crude shepherds fought to possess the highland spring of Gihon. Abraham may have journeyed this way (Gen. 14:17–20) and visited Melchizedek the priest when the place was called "Salem." The reason why Jebusites who occupied what we now call "the City of David" did not build on the higher and better N. portion of the plateau was probably because they respected a shrine already there, near the stone threshing floor, which became altar and heart of the Hebrew Temple, and is still a place of prayer on Mt. Moriah, controlled by Moslems. For the account of David's capture of "the strong hold of Zion . . . in the city of David," on its 1000-ft.-high scarp, see II Sam. 5:6–8; cf. I Chron. 11:4–8. Joab's strategic scaling of the 50-ft.-high watercourse, whose location is now definitely known ("Warren's Shaft"), to enter the haughty Jebusite fortress with its 20-ft.-thick wall and bastions, has been verified by British archaeologists. It is possible to descend the very steps to the spring cave and follow along the tunnel by which Joab and his men made their way to enter the fortress. When Hezekiah three centuries later dug his (Siloam*) tunnel, he started it from the bend in the old Jebusite tunnel (II Chron. 32:30). A bastion of the Jebusite wall has been exca-

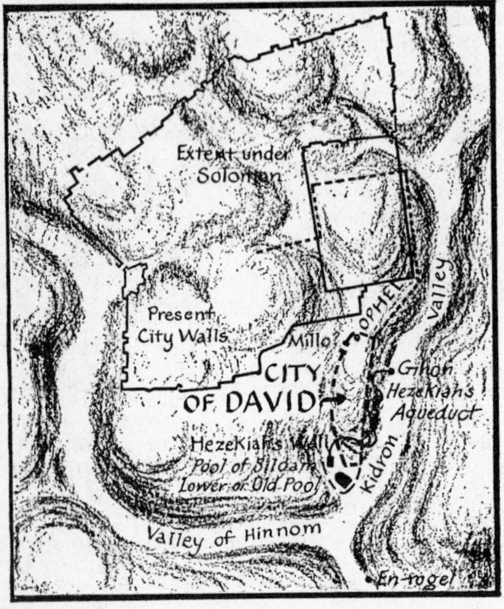

113.

vated. "The City of David" situated S. of the Dung Gate in the E. city wall overlooks an area of tombs and narrow clefts of the Kidron and Hinnom valleys. It is rich in unexcavated historical material.

The City of David came to be known as "Millo" ("filling") after Solomon had filled in the broken defense walls which David had breached but did not have time to repair. British archaeologists have found the roughly constructed masonry thrown up by David (II Sam. 5:9). R. A. S. Macalister described it as being just the sort which would be hurriedly run up by the use of rubble alternating with courses of large stones. The captor of the Jebusite town did nothing to enlarge or beautify it. To Solomon fell the task of building a worthy Hebrew capital.

Other Events at the City of David

The arrival of the Ark at Zion	II Sam. 6:12, 16; cf. I Chron. 15
The departure of the Ark for Mt. Moriah	I Kings 8:1; II Chron. 5:2
The burial of David	I Kings 2:10
The building of a palace for Pharaoh's daughter	I Kings 7:8
The burial of Solomon	I Kings 11:43
The burial of other kings of Judah	
Rehoboam	I Kings 14:31
Abijam	I Kings 15:8
Asa	I Kings 15:24
Jehoshaphat	I Kings 22:50
Joram	II Kings 8:24
Ahaziah	II Kings 9:28
The slaying of Joash in "the house of Millo"	II Kings 12:19–21
The building of Manasseh's wall	II Chron. 33:14

Efforts have been made to find the tombs of the kings of Judah, but the fanaticism of the present owners of the land has prevented scientific exploration.

(2) Bethlehem of Judah was sometimes called "the City of David" (Luke 2:4, 11) because it had been the boyhood home of David.

day. See TIME.

Day of Atonement. See ATONEMENT.

Day of Judgment, Day of the Lord. See ESCHATOLOGY.

daysman, a mediator or arbiter (Job 9:33).

dayspring, the beginning of day; dawn; the beginning of a new era (Job 38:12; Luke 1:78).

deacon, deaconess. See CHURCH.

Dead Sea, also called "the salt sea" (Gen. 14:3; Num. 34:3, 12; Josh. 3:16, 12:3, 15:2, 5, 18:19); "the sea of the plain," A.V., or "of the Arabah," A.S.V. (Josh. 3:16, 12:3); "the east sea" (Ezek. 47:18; Joel 2:20); "the former sea" (Zech. 14:8). It is not mentioned in the N.T. Josephus called it "the Sea of Asphalt" and "the Sea of Sodom"; Arabs know it as *Bahr Lut* or "the Sea of Lot." Greeks in the 2d century A.D. gave it its present name.

The Dead Sea is 46 m. long, with a maximum width of 9½ m.; its measurements vary with rainfall and season. It lies 1,292 ft. below sea level, and has a mean depth of 1,200 ft., which makes it the lowest sheet of water in the world. It is in the middle of a great geological fault extending from Mt. Hermon to the Gulf of Aqabah*; and is all that remains of an arm of the sea which once

114. The Dead Sea, showing Jordan Delta salt pans and mountains of Moab.

extended from the Red Sea to the Lebanons. It is fed by the Jordan* and lesser streams, viz., the Zerka and the Mojib (the Arnon of Scripture, Deut. 2:24). There is no exit for its waters except through evaporation. The intense heat of the Ghor speeds this. Fantastic geological formations characterize the region (Gen. 19:26). The saline content of the water is 5 times greater than that of the ocean, resulting in a correspondingly increased buoyancy. No fish can exist in the Dead Sea. Rich chemical accumulations in the form of potassium chloride, magnesium chloride, magnesium bromide, etc., in solution are now being extracted and exported.

Salt* has always been marketed from Dead Sea water. Modern resorts along its shores are profiting from its curative properties. Since World War I the Dead Sea has been commercially alive. The diverting of its Jordan source waters for irrigation purposes would alter its contours, contents, and usefulness.

Some authorities assert that vestiges of the devastated cities of Sodom* and Gomorrah lie beneath the waters of the SE. portion of the Dead Sea. Throughout Scripture this section has been associated with divine judgment (Matt. 10:15). Ezekiel (47:1–12) makes it the scene of one of the most lively and stupendous hopes of prophecy.

Dead Sea Scrolls, the. See SCROLLS, THE DEAD SEA; also under HABAKKUK; ISAIAH: TEXT.

death, the cessation of life—a mystery early recognized by the Hebrews. Yet their sacred writings reveal oddly little about what they believed concerning life after death. They seemed most concerned about Sheol (Hades*, A.V. hell*), a distinct place of silent forgetfulness (Ps. 88:12) in the depths of the earth (Ps. 86:13; Prov. 15:24). Immortality seemed to them to be a vague, shadowy existence not necessarily characterized by consciousness. They looked upon death not as annihilation, but as transition to something of which they knew nothing. They believed that death was caused by the escape of the soul* from the body. They sometimes thought of death as being "gathered unto their fathers" (Judg. 2:10; II Kings 22:20; cf. Jesus, "Abraham's bosom," Luke 16:22). They associated death with sin*, basing their belief on Gen. 3:19, 22, where the infliction of toil on the guilty pair was accompanied by "dust thou art, and unto dust shalt thou return." This philosophy was clearly stated by Ezekiel (18:20 f.), with an attendant promise of life to the repentant (see PAUL). The concept of the dead rising to a reward or a punishment* did not find expression in their literature until very late in the O.T. period (Daniel 12:2 f.).

Many scholars believe that the Hebrew hope for immortality* was a national one, something to be enjoyed by posterity, even if the individual himself fell short of its attainment. Even Hos. 6:1–3 may refer to a national, not a personal resurrection.

The Wisdom writers of the O.T. make such comments as the following: Job, with his Edomite background, finds hope only in the dark silence of the underworld or pit (17:13–16); knows that his redeemer lives, expects God to vindicate the righteous after death (19:25–27); and admits that death strikes rich and poor alike, and does not necessarily mete just judgment upon the wicked (21:23–26, 24:20, 22–24). Jeremiah was the first to call death a harvestman or "grim reaper" (9:22); his mourning is for the nation (9:1); he refuses to participate in funerals, and urges as part of his prophecy of doom for Jerusalem that corpses be left for wild beasts (16:4). The author of Ecclesiastes (c. 250–150 B.C.) alludes to the bitterness of death (7:26); feels the futility of life (1:2, 12:8); and calls God's acts incomprehensible, since they allow the fate of death to overtake both good and evil men, as well as beasts (3:18–21). Therefore he adopted almost an Epicurean attitude (8:15, 9:9). Death and oblivion, he finds, come to the individual regardless of how evil or how righteous he is (2:14b, 16). His pessimism rises to a climax in 4:2. His term for the grave—man's "long home" (12:5)—is akin to the Egyptian concept.

Hebrews, like Babylonians and Egyptians, placed in tombs objects which they hoped would be useful to the deceased (see BURIAL).

Even the Egyptians, a brilliant people, failed to work out a logical group of ideas concerning man's life after death (Steindorff and Seele, *When Egypt Ruled the East*). After death man would continue to live exactly as on earth, provided that a large supply of food, drink, and representations of servants be placed in the tomb to serve the soul as they had the man, and provided that the body was well preserved through embalming and mummification. The body, as well as the soul, persisted in the hereafter, but the soul would not recognize the body unless it had escaped decomposition. The soul was believed to take the form of a bird, which after the death of the body, flew at will through the world, yet could also return to the tomb. These views, some of which exerted influence upon their Hebrew neighbors, explain the elaborate mortuary temples, pyramids, and rock sepulchers of the Valley of the Tombs of the Kings. Not only sacred bulls were mummified and preserved in sarcophagi, seen today in the Serapeum at Sakkara, but family pets and minor sacred animals (see DOGS). Egyptians believed in death as an entrance to the judgment chamber, where the heart of the individual was weighed by Anubis and Thoth, on a scale balanced by the symbol of Maat, or righteousness (the Egyptian Book of the Dead). The chief extant literary works of the Egyptians are the Pyramid* Texts, the Coffin Texts, and the Book of the Dead, which contains spells to facilitate passage to the hereafter.

In the N.T., as stated above, death is frequently associated with sin, although at times it is difficult to determine whether the writer is indicating physical or spiritual death, or both. Yet there are many deaths recorded in the N.T. where there is no special implication of sin, like those of Jairus' daughter, the son of the widow of Nain, Lazarus, and Dorcas. On the other hand, the frightful death of Herod is laid to sin (Acts 12:23). The most constructive N.T. thought concerning death in relation to evil is "The sting of death is sin" (I Cor. 15:56)—hence the urge to a life of virtue. Man's forgiveness by God depends upon his own willingness to forgive those who had wronged him (Matt. 6:12, 14 f.; Mark 11:25 f.).

What Jesus actually said about death includes his reference to the beggar Lazarus as "carried by angels to Abraham's bosom" (Luke 16:22)—an apparent identification of eternal life with the Hebrew destiny. He regarded death as the entrance to eternal friendship with God—something as natural as the growing of new wheat from grain sown in the ground (John 12:24). This fellowship was different, more powerful, more complete than it had been even for him in his life on earth. Of the nature of life after death, he revealed little. He shared the Pharisees' belief (Luke 14:14 f.); but see his controversy with the Sadducees (Mark 12:24–27). To the dying thief on the cross he promised immediate companionship with himself in Paradise (Luke 23:43). To his intimate disciples, on the eve of his Crucifixion, he very naturally made his most profound utterances about death and the endless life, as going to the Father (John 16:28); preparing mansions for his followers (14:2 f.); sending them an empowering Comforter (14:26); admitting the tribulations of this world, and the joyous "overcoming" he felt even on the threshold of death (16:33); and stressing that "this is life eternal, that they might know thee the only true God, and Jesus Christ, whom thou hast sent" (17:3). The greatest utterance of Jesus about death and its sequel, is "I am the resurrection and the life" (John 11:25). Since resurrection and judgment are concomitant, the avoidance of sin is the best preparation for eternal life*.

Paul considered sin as closely related to death (Rom. 5:21, 6:16). Going back to the Genesis promise, he declared that "by man came death" (I Cor. 15:21), but that "in Christ shall all be made alive" (22), since death is the last enemy he will subdue (26). "Death is swallowed up in victory" (54); therefore the steadfast, unmovable course of right conduct, "abounding in the work of the Lord," is the best guarantee against the vanity of life and labor (v. 58).

Debir (dē′bẽr) (1) A city in the highlands of Judah, also known as Kiriath-sepher (Josh. 15:15), or Kiriath-sannah (Josh. 15:49). It was conquered by Othniel, the Kenizzite, as part of the inheritance of Caleb (Josh. 15:15–17). Its conquest was also related within the more inclusive traditions about Judah (Judg. 1:11–13), and of Joshua and all Israel (Josh. 10:38–39). It was later established as a Levitical city (Josh. 21:15; I Chron. 6:58). Debir was identified with Tell Beit Mirsim, c. 13 m. SW. of Hebron, by W. F. Albright in 1924. This identification has not been universally accepted, but nevertheless, his excavations at the site from 1926 to 1932 have provided the basis for the standard pottery chronology of Palestine for many years. The geographical situation of Tell Beit Mirsim and its occupational history coincide well with O.T. references to Debir. The earliest remains date from the later part of the EB III period (c. 2200 B.C.). After a slight gap MB I strata (I and H) are present (c. 2000–1800 B.C.), followed by a continuous sequence of MB II material (Stratum G–D, c. 18th–16th century B.C.), including battered fortification walls characteristic of the Hyksos period. Following a gap during the LB I period, the site was again reoccupied some time after 1400 B.C., with two phases of Canaanite occupation, ending with a general destruction at the end of the LB II period, which can be attributed to the coming of the Israelites. Five phases of Iron Age occupation, from c. 1225 B.C. to c. 587 B.C., provide a wealth of information about Hebrew pottery, house plans, dye vats (see DYEING), and day-to-day activities. A jar handle inscribed, "Belonging to Eliakim, boy [steward] of Yokin [Jehoiachin]" suggests that this site was occupied by Hebrews until the carrying off to Babylon by Nebuchadnezzar of the young King Jehoiachin in 597 B.C. (See Albright, *AOTS*, 1967, pp. 207–220). (2) An unidentified location on the N. border of Judah (Josh. 15:7). (3) A place E. of the Jordan, in the territory of Gad, near Mahanaim (Josh. 13:26), Heb. Lidebir. Possibly Lo-debar (II Sam. 9:4–5, 17:27; Amos 6:13), identified with Umm ed-Dabar, c. 10 m. S. of the Sea of Galilee. (4) A king of Eglon, one of five Amorite kings defeated by Joshua (10:3). W. P. A.

Deborah (dĕb′ô-rȧ) ("a bee"). (1) Rebekah's nurse (Gen. 35:8). (2) The wife of Lapidoth; judge, prophetess, and co-ordinator with Barak of Israel's victorious allied forces against the Canaanites under Sisera. Deborah became famous and influential for the manner in which she held court and settled disputes among the Israelites (Judg. 4:5). She repeatedly heard complaints about atrocities inflicted upon Israelite travelers and homesteaders by Canaanites in the N. country; these stirred her to drastic action. From Kedesh-naphtali she summoned Barak, with whom she covenanted to lead a military attack against the Canaanites (Judg. 4:9). To her appeal to the Tribes for help in this united effort, Ephraim, Benjamin, West Manasseh, Zebulun, Naphtali, and Issachar responded (Judg. 5:14 f.); Reuben, men of Gilead (Gad and the half tribe of Manasseh), Dan, and Asher refused to co-operate (5:16 f.). Simeon and Judah in the south are not mentioned in the roundup. The decisive conflict took place near Taanach and Megiddo (5:19). The fighting was along the right bank of the River Kishon* (4:7, 5:21); the Plain of Esdraelon* as far as Mt. Tabor (4:6) was the area of maneuver for the Israelite allies and the Canaanites (4:13). Thunderstorms and heavy rains made the Canaanite chariots useless in the mud of the plain and the overflowing streams. The Canaanites were routed and massacred by the pursuing Israelite horsemen, and the Canaanite general, Sisera, fled on foot and was assassinated by Jael, whose husband Heber was believed to be a friendly ally (4:11 f.).

There are two accounts of these events—a prose version (Judg. 4) from the E document, and a poetic version (chap. 5) considered the choicest masterpiece of Hebrew poetry*, and one of the earliest monuments of Hebrew literature (c. 1125 B.C.). This poem was probably part of the J source. The earlier poetic account is one of the first songs in Hebrew literature, and one of the oldest passages in the Bible. Its author was probably not Deborah, but a contemporary who supplied many picturesque details about social and economic as well as religious and political conditions in N. Israel early in the 12th century B.C. The position of leadership accorded Deborah gives an important clue to the position of noble women in Hebrew society during the period of the Judges. Deborah was a dynamic personality, gifted for leadership in peace and war; she broke down tribal isolationism; and for the sake of bringing peace to harassed Israelites waged, in the name of Yahweh, a successful conflict in which Providence was an important factor.

debt, an obligation; something owed. Because O.T. Hebrews were not usually merchants, commercial debts were few. Small loans were usually promptly repaid. Deuteronomic laws protected borrowers (Deut. 24:6, 17). Every 7th year was a time of "the Lord's release," when debts were forgiven and their proceeds used for support of the poor, widows, and aliens. Yet debtors among the poor were always present as elements of discontent, like the families who joined David in his flight (I Sam. 22:2). Property and members of the clan could be sold by creditors (II Kings 4:1–7; Matt. 18:25). In N.T. times debtors were cast into prison (Matt. 5:25; Luke 12:58). Christ told a parable of "the Two Debtors" (Luke 7:41, 42); and one of "The Two Creditors" (Matt. 18:23–25). In the prayer he taught his Disciples mercy to an individual is contingent on leniency granted by him (Matt. 6:12).

Decalogue. See TEN COMMANDMENTS.

Decapolis (dē-kăp′ō-lĭs). See CITIES.

Decision, Valley of, the scene in Joel 3:14 of the judgment* day of Yahweh definitely expected at the time this book was written. It was envisioned as the Kidron* Valley, or Valley of Jehoshaphat, lying between the impressive elevation of walled Jerusalem and the opposite summit of the Mount of Olives (Ezek. 37). Moslems today believe that Mohammed will return to this scene, and compel all souls to walk across the valley on a wire, from which the condemned will fall into the valley and on which the saved will walk safely across. See ESCHATOLOGY.

decrees of the political masters of the Middle East were familiar to the people of the Bible, like the edicts of Hezekiah (II Chron. 30:5), of Cyrus (Ezra 5:13), of Cyrus and Darius (Ezra 6:1, 3), of Ahasuerus (Esther 1:20), of Nebuchadnezzar (Dan. 3:10), of Caesar Augustus (Luke 2:1), and of Claudius (Acts 17:7). (See the individual entries.) The decree of the Lord is mentioned in Ps. 2:7 as an exhortation to the kings of the earth to accept the Kingdom of the Son.

Dedan (dē′dăn), a people of NW. Arabia* along the Red Sea, claiming descent from Noah (Gen. 10:7) and Abraham (Gen. 25:3); merchants in luxury wares (Ezek. 27:20, 38:13). They shipped goods to the Phoenician Tyre (Ezek. 27:15); and were included in the categories of doom pronounced by Jeremiah (25:23, 49:8).

dedication of shrines and public structures gave occasion for popular public gatherings. Some of these were a combination of political and religious factors, like the dedication of the golden image set up by Nebuchadnezzar in the Plain of Dura (Dan. 3:1 f.). The dedication of Israel's altar in the Tabernacle* (Num. 7:84, 88) was characterized by such lavish gifts as vessels of heavy silver, golden spoons full of incense, and hundreds of bullocks, rams, goats, lambs, and kids for the burnt offering (vv. 85–88). The dedication of the altar of Solomon's Temple is described as marked by a solemn assembly and a 7-day ceremony of feasting (II Chron. 7:9 f.). Secular occasions, such as the rededication of the Jerusalem city wall, were observed with pomp and circumstance (Neh. 12:27–47). The dedication of private houses is commanded in Deut. 20:5.

Dedication, Feast of the, a celebration each 25th day of Chislev (November-December) in commemoration of the reconsecration of the Jerusalem Temple*, which had been desecrated by pagan ceremonies; it was instituted by Judas Maccabaeus 165 B.C. The feast lasted eight days, and was marked by joyous meals, by extra illumination of houses (whence the "Feast of Lights"), by uplifting synagogue services, and by the carrying of branches, as at the Feast of Tabernacles. Jesus, present in Jerusalem during the Feast of the Dedication (John 10:22 f.), was walking in Solomon's Porch of the Temple when Jews demanded if he were the Christ; his reply, "I told you, and ye believed not . . . that the Father is in me, and I in him," is given in John 10:25–38.

Jews today still celebrate the Feast of the Dedication, called in Hebrew Hanukkah, with special prayers and by lighting oil lamps or candles (one on the first day, two on the second, etc.).

See FEASTS, FESTIVALS, AND FASTS.

defense was a serious necessity for early Israel, which had forcibly taken over the lands of armed and aggressive neighbors provided with metal weapons and chariots of war. The Hebrews took comfort in the thought that it was "better to take refuge in Jehovah than to put confidence in man" (A.S.V. Ps. 118:9). Confidence in a Power stronger than themselves developed a morale which accounted for the amazing exploits of Joshua, Barak, Samson, Jonathan, David, Abner, and Joab. After David acceded to the kingship (c. 1000 B.C.) there was not sufficient wood to make bows for his militia until he worked out an economic trade treaty with Phoenicia. Nor did Israel have enough metal to make spear points until Solomon sealed a reciprocal treaty with Hiram* of Tyre and took advantage of the Arabah* mines and the smeltery at Ezion-geber* (I Kings 9:26). The army of David was modeled after that of the Philistines. Joab was commander-in-chief, having under him twelve divisional commanders. Benaiah was captain of the bodyguard of the king. There was also an "elite guard," consisting of "the Order of the Three" and "the Order of the Thirty" (see II Sam. 8:18, 20:23–26; I Chron. 27). (For the important role of city walls, towers, and gates, see WALLS; also ARMOR; FORTS; TOWERS; WEAPONS.)

Evidence of the elaborate preparations for defense made by nations which encroached on Israel is found in two inscribed clay tablets which have been brought to the Iraq Museum, telling that Nebuchadnezzar II had built moat walls to protect Babylonia from invaders.

degrees, a word appearing in the titles of Ps. 120–134 which form a collection called Songs of Degrees (R.S.V. Ascents). These psalms are believed to have been sung by processions of pilgrims during their ascent of Mt. Zion at the time of the great Temple festivals. See PSALMS.

Deity. See WORSHIP.

Delaiah (dē-lā'yȧ) (A.S.V. Dalaiah, as also A.V. I Chron. 3:24). (1) A descendant of David (I Chron. 3:24). (2) The head of the 23d order of priests (I Chron. 24:18). (3) A prince who begged King Jehoiakim not to burn the roll of Jeremiah's prophecy of doom (Jer. 36:12). (4) The founder of a post-Exilic family (Ezra 2:60). (5) A son of Mehetabeel and father of Shemaiah (Neh. 6:10).

Delilah (dē-lī'lȧ) ("coquette"), a Philistine woman from Sorek, a valley town whose site is near the rail route from Jaffa and Tel Aviv to Jerusalem. Playing paramour with Samson*, she inveigled from him the secret of his strength and betrayed him to the Philistine lords, who blinded and imprisoned him at Gaza (Judg. 16).

deluge. See FLOOD.

Demas (dē'măs), an inconstant fellow worker with Paul. After sharing the first Roman imprisonment of the Apostle and sending greetings through him to Philemon and Colossian friends (Col. 4:14; Philem. 24), he forsook Paul (II Tim. 4:10) and went to Thessalonica, possibly his home.

Demetrius (dē-mē'trĭ-ŭs) ("belonging to Demeter," Greek goddess of agriculture). (1) A silversmith of Ephesus*, who, finding his trade in miniature models of the great shrine of Diana thwarted by Paul's preaching of Christianity, incited a riot against the Apostle (Acts 19:24–41). (2) A Christian reported in III John 12 as being approved by "all men."

democracy, national self-government. Democratic procedure characterized the society of early Israel. Democracy in the modern West stems from the Judaeo-Christian tradition that stresses the intrinsic value of every human personality. National problems in early Israel were decided by "all the people," "the congregation," in an assembly near the town gate or before the Tent of Meeting. When communities grew too large to have every male in the population exert his right in a *vox populi*, elders represented communities (Josh. 24:1 f., 19, 21). "All the people," "the congregation," "the assembly," "all the inhabitants," were identical in meaning. The theocracy of the period of the Judges was essentially democratic, for "every man did that which was right in his own eyes" (Judg. 21:25). Even the anarchies which came between eras of good judges were forms of democracy. "The whole congregation" was the ultimate source of political authority; true sovereignty rested on the people, not on the king. It was "the voice of the people" which Yahweh told Samuel to heed when they clamored for their first king (I Sam. 8:7). (See study by C. Umhau Wolf, *JNES*, Vol. 6, No. 2.)

Some Decisions Made by "All the People"

Punishment of criminals	Num. 15:35 f.; Judg. 20–21:18
Rights of inheritance	Num. 27:1–5
Judgments between slayer and avenger	Num. 35:24 f.
Deciding for war or peace	Judg. 20:3–8
Confirmation and election of monarchs:	
Saul	I Sam. 10:24
David	II Sam. 3:36
Participation in conquest:	
David	II Sam. 12:29
Rehoboam	I Kings 12:1
Joash	II Kings 11:12
Acting jointly with the king for the new covenant	II Kings 23:1–3
The accounting of the work of the prophets (Samuel)	I Sam. 12:1–5

Even kings were responsible to the people, as in I Kings 12:3. Even so eminent a prophet as Samuel was called to report on his holy office.

N.T. emphasis on democracy was inaugurated by the angelic heralding at Bethlehem of "good tidings of great joy, which shall be to all people" (Luke 2:10). The fulfillment of the democratic prophecy was enunciated by Jesus when he declared, "I, if I be lifted up from the earth, will draw all men unto me" (John 12:32). (Cf. also Matt. 6:6, 10:30–32, 11:11, esp. 25:40.) In Revelation representative elders stood before the throne of God in heaven (4:4); the palm-bearing, praising throng was "a great multitude, which no man could number, of all nations, and kindreds, and people, and tongues" (Rev. 7:9).

demon. See DEVIL.

demonology. See DEVIL.

deputy, in the O.T. an officer of lower rank than a king or governor of a province, as in I Kings 22:47. In the N.T. "deputy" appears to be synonymous with proconsul, like Sergius Paulus (Acts 13:7, 12), and Gallio (Acts 18:12). In the R.S.V. "deputy" is uniformly translated "proconsul," as in Acts 19:38.

Derbe (dûr'bē), an inland city in the Roman province of Galatia*, visited by Paul (Acts 14:20) on his First Missionary Journey. On his Second Journey Paul once more visited Derbe, and met Timothy there—or at Lystra (Acts 16:1). Gaius, who later joined him (Acts 20:4), was from Derbe. It is to be identified with the mound of Kerti Hüyük, c. 60 m. SE. of Lystra in S. Turkey, based on an inscription found there (see *AS* 7, 1957, pp.147–151).

desert, sparsely settled, arid, unproductive country, with scanty rainfall. Much of the Bible land is desert. Some is level, like the Gaza desert (Acts 8:26), and the beautiful palm-dotted belt along the Mediterranean at the approach to the Egyptian border near Gaza, and the band 15 m. deep that edges the Sinai peninsula along the Red Sea. Some is mountainous, like the Sinai Desert, the Desert of Zin, and the deserts of the Judaean highlands. Four Heb. words are used in Scripture—one 280 times in the O.T.—to denote a desert or wilderness (terms frequently interchangeable), as in Ps. 106:14; Num. 33:16. The great Arabian Desert bounded Palestine on the E. and the S. From it came the Hebrew Patriarchs, nomads having the austere, simple ideals of desert peoples. The Canaanites, Israelites, Assyrians, and Babylonians were all Semitic wanderers who pushed, in wave after wave, out of desert Arabia into the Fertile Crescent and its adjoining territory. The Bible is a record of conflicts between desert and highland peoples, and of the ways of life which these established. Caravans of traders were constantly crossing the vast Arabian desert, passing through such threshold cities as Petra, which controlled the trade between Arabia and Gaza and the West. A caravan route ran all the way across Sinai from Ezion-geber (I Kings 9:26), at the head of the Gulf of Aqabah, across the present Gulf of Suez, and on to Egyptian Memphis. A branch ran S. to the important turquoise and copper mines of W. Sinai's desert mountains. (See SERABIT.)

When Paul went "into Arabia" (Gal. 1:17) he probably went no farther than the arid region E. of Damascus, known as the Desert of Damascus. The Sinai Desert or Wilderness (Ex. 19:2; Num. 33:16) and the Wildernesses of Shur, Paran, and Zin were portions of the barren mountain deserts in the Sinai Peninsula—an offshoot of the main Arabian desert peninsula. When Moses went to Midian (Ex. 3) he was in W. Arabia.

The deserts of Bible lands were sparsely peopled by nomads constantly on the move, trekking along from well to well in search of water and food for their animals. Resentful of law and domination, as well as of strangers, these shy but persistent enemies of "the sown" contributed rigorous virtues to the developing ideals of the Hebrews. Probably the Negeb* ("parched land"), S. of Judaea, destined in modern times for irrigation, gives the best idea of Biblical desert country. The Desert of Beer-sheba* and the Desert of Tekoa* are similarly lonely wastelands. The desert where John the Baptist lived until he began his ministry (Luke 1:80) was probably the sparsely settled but not treeless area near Jericho, at the head of the Dead Sea. The authors of Matt. 14:13, 24:26, and Mark 6:31 had the same topography in mind when they spoke of Jesus taking ship "to a desert place."

Writers of Isaiah (35:1 and 51:3) yearned for a time when God would make deserts blossom, would send streams through baked wâdīs (35:6, 43:19 f.), and would transform winding labyrinths into straight highways (40:3).

Jeremiah wrote of "the mingled people that dwell in the desert" (25:24). Animals inhabiting the arid places include the owl (Ps. 102:6), wild beasts (Isa. 34:14), foxes (Ezek. 13:4), and the ostrich (Lam. 4:3).

Deuteronomy ("The Second Law" or "Repetition of the Law") is the final book of the Pentateuch. It can be briefly summarized thus:

(1) The first address of Moses in Moab (chaps 1–4).
(2) The second address of Moses:
  (a) introduction (5–11).
  (b) exposition (12–26).
  (c) peroration, with curses and blessings (27, 28).
(3) The third address of Moses (29, 30).
(4) The farewell of Moses (31–33).
(5) The death of Moses (34).

Scholarship holds that the original edition of Deuteronomy (most of 5–26, 28) was the 1st book ever canonized as the Word of God. Its authors were priests of Jerusalem deeply influenced by the great Prophets, eager to lead Israel to a higher ethical and religious level. To Moses the lawgiver (Ex. 24:12) and the prophet (Deut. 18:15 f.) the work was attributed in all sincerity, for he united these two distinct basic streams of divine revelations to Israel. Jerome in the 4th century of our era realized that "the book of the law" (II Kings 22:8) dramatically discovered in the Temple in 622 B.C. was to be found in Deuteronomy. Written earlier, in the reign of Manasseh (II Kings 21:1–18), it was hidden away until found in the Temple collection box (II Kings 22:3–13); and eventually it was enlarged to its present form by later writers. Sweeping reforms in accordance with this book were ordered by King Josiah* (II Kings 23:3–24; cf. Deut. 12:2–5, 16:21, 17:2–7; etc.).

Three influences are blended in Deuteronomy: (1) The Covenant Code (Ex. 20:22–23:19). (2) The teachings of the Prophets Amos, Hosea, Isaiah, and Micah, whose books (not yet in the form in which we now know them) contributed to the rise of a higher religion. (3) The original contributions of the Deuteronomists: the centralization of the worship at Jerusalem; and the homiletic (Deut. 12) style, spirit, and emphasis which is unmistakable and later permeates parts of Joshua, Judges, and Kings. The Deuteronomist, by blending priestly and prophetic ideals, profoundly influenced the religious life of the Hebrews.

Deuteronomy, with its many authors, editors, and varied time elements, uniformly places right motives above correct forms in sacrifice. The love and service of Yahweh and of one's fellow men is the supreme demand, together with the undivided loyalty of all to the one and only God of Israel (Deut. 6:4–9).

Jesus and the N.T. writers used Deuteronomy frequently:

Jesus	*N.T. Writers*
Matt. 4:4—cf. Deut. 8:3	Acts 3:22—cf. Deut. 18:15, 18
Matt. 4:7—cf. Deut. 6:16	I Cor. 9:9—cf. Deut. 25:4
Matt. 4:10—cf. Deut. 6:13	II Cor. 13:1—cf. Deut. 19:15
Matt. 5:31—cf. Deut. 24:1	Gal. 3:13—cf. Deut. 21:23
Mark 12:30—cf. Deut. 6:5	Rom. 10:6–8—cf. Deut. 30:12, 14

The laws of the Deuteronomic Code* pertain to religious practices, civil authorities, judicial procedure, military edicts, the family, chastity, exclusion, various ritualistic and humane laws, ritual formulae, etc. All these belong to an agricultural and settled community life in Canaan.

See SOURCES.

devil. The English word is used to translate two different Gk. words, with different meanings: *diabolos*, "the accuser," "Satan" (e.g. John 8:44); and *daimonion*, "demon," one of the numerous evil spirits believed to infest the world and to be the cause of many disasters, especially physical and mental illness. The present article deals principally with the second of these (for the other, see SATAN). Belief in demons is rarely attested in the O.T., but by N.T. times had become an important part of Jewish thinking.

Demonology is based on the animistic belief in malignant spirits which primitive man accepted as originators of disaster, disease, evil, etc. Its counterpart in Biblical literature is angelology, which deals with spirits that bring good to men. Judaism, surrounded by the animistic ideas of primitive people, absorbed some of these from Assyria, Babylonia, Greece (Isa. 34:13 f.), and developed a distinct crop of its own. According to one Jewish tradition, demons were created by God before the world was made. Satan*, identified by post-Biblical Jewish writers (Wisd. of Sol. 2:24), with the serpent, was the chief demon (Gen. 3:1–3; Rev. 12:9, 20:2). In another theory, based on Gen. 6:1–8, certain angels (see ANGEL) forsook their allegiance to God, descended to earth, and married attractive daughters of men, and their offspring were demons. Azazel* was the demon who dwelt in the desert and made traveling dangerous for unaccompanied pilgrims; the scapegoat dispatched into the Wilderness, laden with the sins of the people, was an offering to Azazel (Lev.16:8, 10, 26, R.S.V.). Thus early man's fear of desert solitude was absorbed in the ritual of Judaism. Apocryphal literature, especially the Book of Enoch, did much to fasten animism in the popular thinking of late Judaean and early Christian times.

In the N.T., Satan "the adversary" (Job 1–2; Zech. 3:1) is identical with Beelzebub (see BAAL-ZEBUB), the "chief of the devils" (Matt. 10:25; Mark 3:22; Luke 11:15), and with "the devil," who was so dramatically personalized in the narrative from Christ's own lips concerning his temptation. Jesus in the Parable of the Tares defined the devil as "the enemy," "the wicked one" (Matt. 13:38 f.). He taught the disciples to pray for deliverance from "the evil one" (N.E.B. Matt. 6:13); and acclaimed Satan as "the prince of this world" (John 12:31, 14:30, 16:11), who, with his demoniacal angels, constituted the kingdom which in the Last Judgment would be destroyed (Matt. 25:41). Demons were associated with abnormal forms of human life, especially disease*. Dumbness (Luke 11:14–16), deafness (Mark 9:25), blindness (Matt. 12:22), and epilepsy (Mark 1:26; Luke 9:39) were manifestations of demonic influence. Mary Magdalene had "seven devils" (Luke 8:2). The Gadarene demoniac possessed "a legion" (Luke 8:30). Jesus accommodated himself to current demonology, and by the power of his word, presence, and prayer, readjusted the distorted to life (Mark 9:25; Luke 11:20). How much the authors of the Gospels colored their accounts by their own belief in demons is hard to determine. Though the personification of evil is present in the Fourth Gospel, demonology is almost entirely absent.

Jesus commissioned his disciples to minister especially to those who are maladjusted to life because dominated by demons (Matt. 10:1, 8; Mark 16:17; Acts 8:7). Though demonology presents difficult problems, the record of Christianity testifies to the power of the Gospel to correct distorted mental states. Paul shared the conceptions of his day in regard to the personal source of evil, and made the offerings to heathen gods synonymous with sacrifices to devils (I Cor. 10:20, 21). See BELIAL; ESCHATOLOGY.

devoted thing meant the booty of people or possessions captured in war and dedicated to Yahweh (Num. 18:14). Women and children were redeemable (Num. 31:7 ff.), but men and animals were expected to be slaughtered in a sacrifice of gratitude for victory. Israelites who violated this law were severely punished, like Achan (Josh. 7).

dew, atmospheric vapor condensed in small drops on cool areas between evening and morning, thus saving the vegetation of Palestine in the hot, dry months (cf. Hag. 1:10). Dew symbolized the word of God (Deut. 32:2); the freshness of youth (Ps. 110:3); the beauty of fraternity (Ps. 133:3); and the life-giving power of God (Isa. 26:19). See also Isa. 18:4; II Sam. 1:21.

dial, the sundial of King Ahaz (II Kings 20:11; Isa. 38:8). It may have been an instrument with graduated lines, called steps or degrees, and a projecting gnomon to cast a shadow, like the sundials of Babylonia.

Diana of the Ephesians, the goddess worshipped in the great temple or Artemision in Ephesus*, the capital city of the Roman province of Asia in Paul's time—and long before. Diana to Greeks and Romans was a chaste goddess of the hunt, maiden sister of the sun god Apollo; more correctly called Artemis. But in Asia Minor Artemis was a very ancient Anatolian fertility or nature goddess worshipped long before the rise of Greek culture. Her great statue—as also a sacred stone "from the sky" (Acts 19:35)—was enthroned magnificently in the temple at Ephesus, and duplicated in miniature by the silversmiths (Acts 19:23 ff.). The image depicted her as a lewd goddess having four rows of breasts, with a garment whose front was trimmed with rows of sphinxes, nymphs, shells, bees, and roses. Her aegis crown was decorated with signs of the zodiac, suggesting the influence of the seasons upon agriculture. The richest and most elaborate extant statue of Diana of the Ephesians is in the National Museum at Naples; it dates from Hadrian's reign.

The Temple of Diana which Paul saw at Ephesus was the 5th on the site, completed probably soon after the visit of Alexander the Great to Ephesus (c. 334 B.C.). The Ephesus temple (see EPHESUS, illus. 133), which was listed as one of the seven wonders of the ancient world, and to which Croesus contributed, was the 4th (dedicated between 430 and 420 B.C. after 120 years of building). British scholars excavating the Artemision at Ephesus have discovered dazzling riches of foundation deposit gifts brought to the shrine of Diana (Artemis), some of which are now in the British Museum, others in Istanbul. The early part of Paul's three-year residence in Ephesus (Acts 19:8, 10, 20:31) brought converts to Christianity without conflict with the votaries of the Artemis cult. Only when he incurred the antagonism of Demetrius and other silversmiths who made their living by fashioning statuettes of the goddess for pilgrims, was he haled into the theater by an uproarious mob. The tactful town clerk exonerated him as a blasphemer of Artemis or "a robber of churches" (Acts 19:35–40).

Dibon (dī'bŏn) ("wasting away"). (1) A city of Moab, identified with the modern ruins of Dhībân, in Jordan, 13 m. E. of the Dead Sea, and 4 m. N. of the River Arnon (Wadī Mojib). Dibon had been captured from the Moabites by Sihon, King of the

115. Excavated wall of ancient Dibon.

Amorites (Num. 21:26), and was taken in turn by the Israelites at the time of the Exodus (Num. 21:30). Given to the tribes of Reuben and Gad (Num. 32:2–3), it was rebuilt by Gad (Num. 32:34; thus it was also known as Dibon-gad, Num. 33:45–46), though it is assigned to Reuben (Josh. 13:17). According to information supplied by the Moabite Stone, found on the site in 1868 and dated c. 830 B.C. (*ANEP*², No. 274; *ANET*³, pp. 320–321), Omri reconquered Moab and for 40 years Israel occupied the area of Dibon. With the death of Ahab (c. 850 B.C.), Mesha re-established Moabite independence (cf. II Kings 3), and built Qarhoh, probably to be identified with the citadel of Dibon. Isaiah (15:2) and Jeremiah (48:18, 22) knew it as a Moabite city. Excavations between 1951 and 1956 show that the occupational history of Dibon began in the Early Bronze Age, with no succeeding Middle or Late Bronze Age remains. The Iron Age ("Moabite") is represented by a complex system of defenses, an entranceway, and the foundations of an official building on the acropolis. The heaviest period of occupation during this time is from the 10th–8th century B.C. (See *BASOR* 125, 1952, pp. 7–20; 133, 1954, pp. 6–25; Winnett and Reed, *AASOR* 36–37, 1964; Tushingham, *AASOR* 40, 1972.) (2) A town of Judah (site unknown), occupied after the Return (Neh. 11:25). W. P. A.

Didymus (dĭd'ĭ-mŭs) (from Gk. for "twin"). See THOMAS.

dill. See ANISE.

Dinah, a daughter of Jacob by Leah (Gen. 30:21); raped by Shechem, son of Hamor the Hivite (34:2); avenged by the sons of Jacob (34:25).

Dionysius (dī'ŏ-nĭsh'ĭ-ŭs) (from Gk. god Dionysus), a member of the Areopagus* Court at Athens, converted by Paul (Acts 17:34).

Diotrephes (dī-ŏt'rĕ-fez), a member of the church to which Gaius* belonged. John's Third Epistle mentions the difficulties Diotrephes caused (III John 9, 10).

disciple (from Gk. "learner"), a follower of such leaders of thought as Moses (John 9:28), John the Baptist (Luke 11:1; John 1:35); or the Pharisees (Mark 2:18). It was used in the N.T. of the followers of Jesus, especially the Twelve (Matt. 20:17), but also of the more numerous and less intimate group of all who clung to his person and his teachings (Matt. 14:26) (see APOSTLES). Paul made disciples for Jesus; and on his journeys met many at Ephesus (Acts 20:1), at Troas (Acts 20:7), and at Caesarea (Acts 21:16).

discus. See GAMES.

disease and healing.

(1) *Disease.* The following diseases are identifiable in the Bible from the symptoms described. Those treated by Jesus are preceded by an asterisk.

*Blindness	(see BLINDNESS)
Cancer (?)	II Kings 20:1; II Chron. 21:18
Consumption	Lev. 26:16; Deut. 28:22
Cutaneous diseases (boils, tumors, itch, sores)	Ex. 9:9; Lev. 13:18; Deut. 28:27, 35; II Kings 20:7; Isa. 1:6
*Dropsy	Luke 14:2
*Dumbness	Matt. 9:32, 12:22
Dysentery	II Chron. 21:15; Acts 28:8
Endocrine disturbances	Lev. 21:20; I Sam. 17:4
*Epilepsy	Matt. 17:15 R.S.V.
Eye diseases	Gen. 27:1, 29:17; Prov. 23:29
*Fevers	Luke 4:38 f.; John 4:46–54
Gonorrhea (?)	Gen. 20:17 f.
Gout or foot disease	II Chron. 16:12

*Lameness	Acts 3:2
*Leprosy	Ex. 4:6; Lev. 13:1–17; Num. 12:10; II Kings 7:3, 15:5; Matt. 8:3; Mark 1:41; Luke 5:12. 17:12–17
*Mental disorders	I Sam. 21:13; Matt 4:24, 17:15; Mark 3:11; Acts 26:24
Malaria (Paul's thorn in the flesh?)	II Cor. 12:7
Paralysis*:	
Infantile (?)	II Sam. 4:4
Palsy	Matt. 4:24; Mark 2:1–12
Atrophy	Matt. 12:10
Pestilence (plague, cholera?)	Jer. 21:6; Ezek. 6:11
*Plagues (scourges, marginal A.S.V.)	Mark 3:10
Sunstroke (?)	II Kings 4:18–32
Worms	Acts 12:23

Hebrews recognized the following causes of disease: (1) sin of the individual (Prov. 23:29–32) punished by God (Gen. 12:17; Num. 12:10; II Kings 8:8–10); (2) sin of parents (II Sam. 12:15; implied also in John 9:3); (3) seduction by Satan (Matt. 9:34; Luke 13:16; II Cor. 12:7). Yet Job (34:19 f.) and John (9:1–3) suggest that there is no explanation for some diseases.

(2) *Healing*. Among people of Biblical times, healing was associated with divinity. For example, Malachi (4:2) spoke of the Sun of Righteousness arising "with healing in his wings," and the Psalmist praised a God who "healeth . . . diseases" (103:3).

Egyptian physicians were consulted even by Babylonian and Persian rulers. The Egyptian god of healing was Imhotep—royal architect and Wisdom writer. Medicine in Egypt was attributed to Apis of Memphis. Isis, sometimes depicted as a nursing mother, was a healing deity of the highest rank. Much Practical Egyptian medical information doubtless found its way into Hebrew laws of health and sanitation (see below).

Medicine was developed in the Early Babylonian dynasties to such an extent that Hammurabi included in his Code a tariff of fees varying with the financial status of patients and a law against malpractice. The clay-tablet library (see LIBRARIES) of Asshurbanapal contains some 800 texts. (See *The Healing Gods of Ancient Civilizations*, by Walter A. Jayne, for priestly rites, exorcism, and education of physicians in temples.) The chief Babylonian god of healing was Ea, god of curative springs. Next to him, Marduk was the most successful god of healing. The medical role of Ishtar was related to childbearing. The Babylonian sun god, Shamash, helped prolong life.

Greek physicians drew early inspiration from the god Asklepios (Aesculapius) (see CORINTH), from Hygeia, goddess of health, and from spring nymphs who cured skin diseases. Orpheus with his flute allayed mental disorders.

Many medicines, compounded from herbs, minerals, animal substances, wines, fruit, and leaves, were known to people in Biblical times. Balm* of Gilead was especially prized (Jer. 8:22). Fig poultices were used for boils (II Kings 20:7); mineral baths in the Dead Sea and Galilee regions, Jordan water, and thermal treatments popular among the Romans (as at Baiae and Pompeii) were resorted to. Charms, such as Egyptian *ankhs*, scarabs, depictions of the "hand of God," amulets (see AMULET) of the varieties still used in Egypt and Palestine "to keep the evil eye away" were relied upon. Elements of magic* were confused with *materia medica*. Priests were doctors and prophets were diagnosticians (II Kings 8:8). Sometimes the pious condemned those who sought advice from doctors instead of from prophets (II Chron. 16:12). Ahaziah (who had sent a messenger to consult a god of Ekron) received an unfavorable prognosis from Elijah (II Kings 1:4); Ben-hadad inquired of Elisha (II Kings 8:7 f.); Isaiah prescribed for Hezekiah (II Kings 20:7). (See also APOTHECARIES.)

In the O.T. physicians are mentioned in Gen. 50:2; Jer. 8:22; II Chron. 16:12. In the N.T. only the able Luke, "the beloved physician" (Col. 4:14) with his Greek (? Antiochan) background of knowledge, is mentioned by name. (See also Mark 2:17, 5:26; Luke 4:23; Ecclus. 38:1–15.)

The positive therapeutics of Christ included: the power of prayer* alone, at a distance from the patient (Matt. 8:13); the use of clay-and-spittle ointment applied to eyes (John 9:6); the encouraging influence of his presence (woman with issue of blood, Luke 8:43); personal touch—as with the little daughter of the synagogue ruler (Mark 5:41), and Peter's wife's mother (Matt. 8:15).

Although surgery is represented in the Bible only by circumcision*, this science achieved a high point of skill at an early date in Egypt, as indicated by the Edwin Smith Surgical Papyrus from Egypt of probably the Hyksos era. This remarkable papyrus, a 17th century B.C. copy of an original from c. 3000–2500 B.C. and now in the Library of the N. Y. Academy of Medicine, may have been a surgeon's notebook or a professor's lectures.

In N.T. times physicians received stated fees, as indicated in Luke's narrative of the woman who had "spent all her living upon physicians" and remained an invalid, until her faith elicited Jesus' healing power (Luke 8:43–48).

Mosaic law forbidding the touching of the dead prevented post-mortem study of anatomy and causes of disease. But many sensible laws of hygiene and sanitation contributed to the prevention of disease, as concerning sex life (Lev. 12, 15:19–24), circumcision (Gen. 17:11–14), the disposal of excreta (Deut. 23:10–14), and the prevention and care of leprosy (Lev. 13, 14) (see TEETH).

dispersion (Gk. *diaspora*) of Jews outside Palestine began at least as early as the reign of Ahab, when an Israelite colony existed at Damascus (I Kings 20:34). The Assyrian deportations and the Babylonian Exile* effected a large-scale dispersion of the 10 tribes of the Northern Kingdom and the 2 of the Southern. Many of the choicest families of Judah never returned from Babylonia, but developed industries there, and under such leaders as Ezekiel and Ezra organized their old tenets of faith into forms which spread far and wide. From Babylonia Jews of the dispersion found their way over ancient trade routes into Media, Persia, Egypt, Cappadocia, Armenia, and the Pontus. They penetrated into every important city of the Roman Empire, retaining their burning faith and establishing their synagogues (see SYNAGOGUE). They had sometimes been strongly influenced by Hellenistic culture, yet they long continued to pay the half-shekel tax for maintenance of Temple worship; and participated in the great festival pilgrimages to Jerusalem (Acts 2:9–11), coming from Parthia, Media, Mesopotamia, Egypt, Libya, Rome, Crete, and Arabia. The scattering of Jewish Christians assisted the rapid spread of Christianity; for in the 1st century more Jews lived outside of Palestine than in it. There was a time when mystified Jerusalem Jews asked whether Jesus was about to go "to the dispersed among the Gentiles" to teach (John 7:35). The General Epistle of James and the First General Epistle of Peter both open with greetings to the "tribes which are scattered throughout Pontus," etc. Because Jews of the dispersion used other languages than Hebrew, especially Greek, the famous Greek Version of the O.T. (the Septuagint, LXX) was prepared for their use by a group of scholars at Alexandria, Egypt, between c. 250 and c. 132 B.C.

distaff. See WEAVING.

Dives (dī′vēz), a name commonly applied to the unnamed man of wealth in Jesus' parable of the beggar Lazarus (Luke 16:19–31), because of the use of the Lat. adjective *dives*, "rich," in this passage in the Vulgate. See PARABLE.

divination. See MAGIC AND DIVINATION.

divinity, of Jesus. See JESUS CHRIST.

divorce. See MARRIAGE.

doctor. See DISEASE AND HEALING.

document. See ACTS; Q; NEW TESTAMENT; SOURCES (for J, E, D, P, S, etc.).

Dodanim (dō′dȧ-nĭm), probably Rodanim*, early sea-isle people of the Mediterranean—of Cyprus*, Rhodes*, and other regions inhabited by Ionian Hellenes; called descendants of an eponymous ancestor, Javan, fourth son of Japheth, son of Noah (Gen. 10:2, 4 f.; cf. I Chron. 1:7). At the time when Gen. 10 was written, Ionian peoples were in competition with the Phoenicians (see PHOENICIA).

Doeg (dō′ĕg), a man from Edom, S. of the Dead Sea, whom Saul placed in charge of his herds or runners (I Sam. 21:7). Doeg reported to his king matters he overheard concerning David's activities and aid received from the priest Ahimelech; whereupon, at Saul's command, Doeg killed Ahimelech and 85 priestly companions, as well as women and children of Nob* (I Sam. 22:9, 18).

dogs in Job 30:1 were evidently useful to the shepherds of Edom; elsewhere the dog is uniformly pictured in the Bible as a pariah, without admirable characteristics. This attitude persists in remote areas of the Middle East today. Bible dogs were scavengers (Ex. 22:31), received only the unclean (Matt. 7:6; 15:26), were indolent and stupid (Isa. 56:10 f.), and at night noisily took over the streets of the town (Ps. 59:6, 14). Their disgusting eating habits (Prov. 26:11; II Peter 2:22) were noted; "dog" was a term of contempt (Deut. 23:18). Man treated them cruelly (Prov. 26:17; Isa. 66:3); their ferocity caused him to fear for the safety of his loved ones (Jer. 15:3; Ps. 22:20; Phil. 3:2). When Naboth was stoned to death outside Samaria, dogs lapped up his blood (I Kings 21:14, 19). At the same gate, when the chariot of slaughtered King Ahab was about to be washed, dogs licked his blood from its floor (I Kings 22:35–38). On the ramparts of Jezreel, where Jezebel met her end, only her skull, feet, and hands were found; dogs had devoured her body (II Kings 9:35 f.). The licking of a helpless beggar's sores by dogs was not an act of canine sympathy, but to Lazarus an additional aggravation and an example of dogs' bloodthirstiness (Luke 16:21). Rev. 22:15 indicates the prevailing habitat of dogs in a community. The Greek word *kunarion*, meaning "little dog," in contrast to *kuon*, translated "dog" elsewhere in the N.T., indicates that puppies of the ferocious Bible dogs were friendly enough to associate with children of a household and pick up crumbs from the master's table (Matt. 15:26 f.; Mark 7:27 f.). Nowhere in Scripture is the dog portrayed with admirable characteristics.

That dogs hunted with their masters is seen in extant Mesopotamian art. Egyptian reliefs show dogs accompanying their owners on inspections of estates. Greyhounds, similar to the modern *saluki* hound, appear in reliefs of Egyptian hunting scenes, from the predynastic period on. There was also a low-slung dog erroneously identified as a dachshund. Several dogs' names are known from ancient Egyptian records, containing the syllable "bw", which of course recalls the familiar childish word "bow-wow." George Reisner found at Giza a slab which indicates that a dog was buried with honor in the cemetery there. The inscription reads: "The dog which was the guard of His Majesty. Abuwtiyuw is his name. His Majesty ordered that he be buried [ceremonially], that he be given a coffin from the royal treasury, fine linen in great quantity, [and] incense. His Majesty gave perfumed ointment, [and] ordered that a tomb be built for him by the gangs of masons. His Majesty did this for him in order that he [the dog] might be honored [before the great god Anubis]."

dominion, or lordship, was shared with the first man made in God's image (Gen. 1:26). But elsewhere in Scripture this relationship is generally ascribed to the Lord Himself, except where political dominion is indicated, as in the Philistine mastery of Israel (Judg. 14:4). The authors of Ps. 72:8; Dan. 4:3; Zech. 9:10; I Pet. 4:11 reach sublime heights in efforts to express the majestic lordship of the eternal God, climaxed in Rev. 1:6.

doorkeepers of the House of Yahweh were "keepers of the threshold" (A.V. marg., II

Kings 22:4). Doorkeepers for the Ark* were appointed (I Chron. 15:23), and Levites were doorkeepers for the Temple* (Ps. 84:10). It was the duty of "keepers of the threshold" to gather money from Temple worshippers (II Kings 22:4). Private houses sometimes had women porters (Acts 12:13; cf. Mark 14:66).

doors. (1) Domestic. Doors to the tent homes in the nomadic period were mere openings in the heavy fabric, closed by an extra flap; see Gen. 18:1 f., for Abraham in his tent door; Num. 11:10 for Israel weeping in tent doors. After Israel settled down in Canaan, doors of Hebrew homes were of metal or of wood, boltable against intruders (Judg. 19:26). They had two square doorposts and lintels, such as the ones on which blood was smeared by the Hebrews in Egypt on the eve of their Exodus, to indicate to the death angel which households were to be spared (Ex. 12:1, 7, 23, 26 f.). Small wooden or metal boxes containing parchment inscribed with Deut. 6:4–9, 11:13–21 were placed on the doorposts, as is still customary today. (See also FRINGES; PHYLACTERIES.) The threshold or sill was peculiarly sacred. Connected to the sill and to the lintel were metal pivot sockets into which were fitted hinge pivots which allowed the low door to swing. The lock was strong and ingenious, of a type still used in Syria—a short wooden upright fastened on the inside of the door, through which passes a square bolt at right angles, into the door-jamb socket. When the bolt is shot, several small iron pins drop from the upright into holes in the bolt, hollow at this point. Only the proper flat wooden key, containing pins to correspond to holes in the bolt, can open the door. The common Hebrew desire for privacy led to keeping bolted the doors from the street to the courtyard of the home. A metal knocker was customary (Luke 13:25; Rev. 3:20). The houses of Bethlehem and old Jerusalem today have doors and walls rising flush from the stone-paved streets. Palace doors were often double-leaved, carved, and metal-trimmed. At their threshold stood the porter or doorkeeper, usually a royal official.

(2) Sanctuary doors of Ezekiel's ideal Temple are fully described (8:3, 7, 8, 14, 16, 10:19, 41:16, 24), and of Solomon's Temple (I Kings 6:31–35, 7:50). Doors were also prominent in city gates, as in the Joppa Gate of Jerusalem today; in prisons (Acts 5:19, 23, 12:6, 16:25 f.); at rock-hewn tombs, where a stone was rolled against the opening to form a sealed door (Matt. 27:60).

(3) Symbolic use of the door is frequent in the Bible: the door of hope (Hos. 2:15); the door of one's lips (Ps. 141:3); the door of faith (Acts 14:27); the door of utterance (Col. 4:3); the open door of opportunity (Rev. 3:8); and the door of beseeching fellowship (Rev. 3:20).

Dor, an old Canaanite seaport on the Mediterranean between Carmel headland and Caesarea, modern Khirbet el-Burj, N. of Tanturah. Its king was one of those defeated by the Israelites in the battle by the waters of Merom (Josh. 11:1–2, 12:23). Allotted to Manasseh (Josh. 17:11; cf. I Chron. 7:29), it was never possessed (Judg. 1:27). Dor is referred to as a "town of the Tjeker" (one of the Sea Peoples associated with the Philistines) in the Egyptian Tale of Wen-Amon, dating to c. 1100 B.C. (*ANET*³, p. 26). It appears as the 4th district in the list of Solomon's district officials, supervised by the ruler's son-in-law (I Kings 4:11). Dor formed the center of an Assyrian province established during the reign of Tiglath-Pileser III (c. 733 B.C., see Aharoni, *The Land of the Bible*, 1967, pp. 329–331), and was granted to Baal of Tyre in a treaty with Esar-haddon (c. 680–669 B.C.; *ANET*³, 1969, p. 534). In the 5th century B.C., Eshmunazar, King of Sidon, received Dor and Joppa as grants from the Persian king (*ANET*³, p. 662). Dor continued as a seaport during the Graeco-Roman period, besieged by Antiochus Sidetes in 138 B.C. (I Macc. 15:11–14, 25).

Dorcas (Gk. "gazelle"; also "Tabitha"), a disciple at Joppa, characterized by "good works and almsdeeds" (Acts 9:36). The Church, distressed over her death, sent to nearby Lydda for Peter, who restored her to life through prayer, while the widows who had received garments from her displayed these gifts. Dorcas was the forerunner of bands of Christian women ("Dorcas Societies," etc.) engaged in social service through the churches.

Dothan, a town and a plain traversed by the main caravan route from Damascus to Egypt. The low mound Tell Dothan, hiding under deep debris the once pleasant settlement, lies 6 m. S. of Jenin—SW. of the Plain of Esdraelon—and c. 13 m. NE. of Samaria. Dothan was the scene of the Joseph narrative of Gen. 37:12–36. Cistern pits like the one into which the jealous brothers tossed Joseph (v. 22) are still to be seen nearby. Elisha was at Dothan when Syrians encompassed the town (II Kings 6:13) and were smitten with blindness in response to the prophet's prayer (v. 18).

Excavation of Dothan, begun in 1953 by J. P. Free, showed that the mound was occupied as early as the beginning of the Early Bronze Age (c. 3000 B.C.) and that occupation continued through the Iron Age, with Hellenistic and Roman remains also present. See *BA* 19, 1956, pp. 43–48; *BASOR* 131, 1953, pp. 16–29; 135, 1954, pp. 14–20; 139, 1955, pp. 3–9; 143, 1956, pp. 11–17; 152, 1958, pp. 10–18; 160, 1960, pp. 6–15.

116. Dove symbol on mosaic cross.

dove, a bird of the *Columbidae* family, easily distinguishable from the pigeons of the same family. Sometimes "dove" is applied to the smaller and "pigeon" to the larger birds. Biblical translators probably had no distinction in mind, and it is not unlikely that a single Hebrew and a single Greek word appear in the original text. This bird was included among the animals of even poor families in Palestine, such as that of Jesus. Mary had brought a pair of turtledoves or young pigeons for her offering as she and Joseph came to Jerusalem in Jesus' infancy (Luke 2:24). From the beginning of history, doves have been used as messengers (Gen. 8:8–12). In fertility cults practiced for centuries throughout the Middle East, the dove adorned temples and statues of Venus, Astarte, and other sensual goddesses. At Beth-shan an excavated cult-stand shows doves flying from a Canaanite Ashtaroth center of the 13th century B.C.

dowry. See MARRIAGE.

drachma (drăk′mȧ). See MONEY.

dragon, a mythical monster depicted in the literature of the ancient Middle East. It is akin to the subtle serpent of Gen. 3, and is openly called in Rev. 12:9 "the great dragon . . . that old serpent called the Devil, and Satan, which deceiveth the whole world." The dragon wars with the seed of the woman (Rev. 12:3–6, 13–17), but is overcome "by the blood of the Lamb" (12:11), and is cast into a bottomless pit unto perdition (17:8). The N.T. antichrist is the same subtle beast that destroyed man's first Eden. The dragon was pictured sometimes as a river-dwelling monster like the alligator or crocodile, inhabiting the Nile and denoting Pharaoh himself (Ezek. 29:3) or the sea (Isa. 27:1); again, he had "seven heads and ten horns" (Rev. 12:3), and drew stars from heaven and cast them to earth; again he was drawn to resemble a jackal; once a whale. See also Dan. 7:3–7. The dragon appears in other Apocalyptic* passages, as in Isa. 27, 51:9, and in prophetic literature, as in Jer. 51:34, where Nebuchadnezzar is likened to a dragon. On certain pages of O.T. literature the dragon connotes specific rulers: the four beasts of Daniel's Apocalyptic vision (7:1–8) symbolize world powers in a seething sea of unrest, as the Babylonia of Nebuchadnezzar; the Median Kingdom, its successor; Persia; and the kingdoms of Alexander the Great and Antiochus Epiphanes, persecutor of Syria. The dragon contest depicted in Rev. 12 resembles the Assyrian Creation epic, featuring the struggle between Marduk and Tiâmat. The art of the Mediterranean world today retains vestiges of the mythical dragon of sin, slain by the medieval hero St. George. The iconography of the Far East, however, depicts the dragon as a symbol of strength and virtue, denoting the coming of spring and rain—a once-worshipped river beast.

The Dragon's Well of Jerusalem (Neh. 2:13) was probably En-rogel*. (See DAVID, CITY OF, illus. 113.)

dreams were not relied on by the great Hebrew prophets to foretell God's will; but visions they did rely on and attempt to interpret. Yet Scripture reveals that a few persons believed dreams had meaning—particularly Joseph* (Gen. 37:5–11, 40:5–23, 41:1–36), and Daniel* (2:25–30). The angel of God is mentioned as speaking to Jacob in a dream (Gen. 31:11–13); and an "angel of the Lord" advised Joseph (Matt. 2:13, 19). See also Matt. 27:19 for the dream of Pilate's wife and Acts 27:23 for Paul's dream of deliverance. Babylonians had such trust in dreams that on the eve of important decisions they slept in temples, hoping for counsel. Greeks desiring health instruction slept in shrines of Aesculapius, and Romans in temples of Serapis. Egyptians prepared elaborate books for dream interpretation. See MAGIC.

dress of Biblical people we know about less from the Bible itself than from excavated material and outside sources; for the Biblical descriptions are usually generalized or rendered poetically, and use Hebrew and Greek words difficult to translate into modern terms. It is easy to discern, however, the attitude of people toward their garments.

Because of their scarcity, garments were stolen as spoil by poor Hebrews (Achan, Josh. 7:21). Thirty linen* garments and "thirty changes of raiment" were held out by Samson as a prize (A.S.V. Judg. 14:12). Captain Naaman of the Syrian army offered "two changes of garments" to the greedy servant of the prophet Elisha (II Kings 5:23). Women expected booty of clothing, as in Judg. 5:30. Even in early Patriarchal times Israelites were garment-conscious, as when Rebekah dressed up her younger son Jacob in the "goodly raiment" of Esau (Gen. 27:15). Hebrews were enjoined by ancient law to wash their clothes (Ex. 19:10), especially if they had touched an unclean animal (Lev. 11:25) (see ANIMALS).

Jesus made several references to clothing in his teaching, usually to stress a new attitude toward material things and their use: Matt. 5:40, 6:25, 9:16, 10:10, 23:5; Luke 15:22.

Palestine.—(1) *Materials* in Palestine were similar to those used by all Near East people. Animal skins were successors to the mere belts or aprons which constituted men's first garments and held their first tools. When the grazing era began, sheepskins were common. Rarer and more valuable leopard skins were used in Egypt by priests for ceremonial attire. But wool was the staple source of Palestinian and Syrian clothing. Home-grown, hand-beaten to free it from foreign matter, home-combed, homespun and woven on family-made looms, wool provided every-day attire for the entire family (Prov. 31:13, 19, 21–22). Wool garments were handed down from one generation to another. Goats' hair cloth and camel's hair, such as John the Baptist wore with a leather girdle (Matt. 3:4), were also popular, durable, and warm. Silk, coveted by rich rulers, may have been imported from China via such ports as Berytus or Tyre, both of which were equipped to weave and dye it (see DYEING; WEAVING). Persians and Medes so prized silk coats and skirts that Greeks called silk "Median garments." Ezek. 16:10 refers to silk as a luxury given to Jerusalem by Yahweh. In later centuries Syria grew mulberries for her own larvae. Linen—an Egyptian influence—was popular in Canaan even before Israel's entry. The flax which produced linen is mentioned in Josh. 2:6. The worthy wife of

Prov. 31:24 sold home-made linen girdles to Canaanite merchants. Ancient Hebrew law forbade mixtures of wool and flax yarn (Lev. 19:19). Materials not processed at home were sent to establishments of the affiliated craftsmen—weavers (I Sam. 17:7), dyers (Ezek. 23:15), and fullers (see FULLER) (Mark 9:3), who bleached, washed, shrank, and pressed cloth.

(2) *Articles of apparel* in Palestine and Syria included a loincloth, worn by everyone from laborers to priests; an inner shirt of wool or linen reaching to the ankles and close-fitting at the neck, worn by both men and women, as seen in the bas-relief of Sennacherib's Jewish captives from Lachish. This shirt corresponded to the Roman tunic and the Greek chiton. A tunic of "many colors" constituted Joseph's famous garment (Gen. 37:3); and a seamless coat "woven from the top throughout" was worn by Jesus (John 19:23). A long mantle of striped wool and goat's hair, with seams only at the shoulders, was useful as a storm garment, or a covering at night during journeys. This *abayeh* or *simlah* is worn today by Syrian shepherds and Arab Bedouin sheikhs. The mantle used in Graeco-Roman Palestine was often a long rectangle with tassels at the four corners known to Romans as a pallium, and to Greeks as a himation. Jesus probably wore the *abayeh* (John 19:23), since it was both comfortable to wear in travel and useful for shelter. The scarlet robe in which soldiers derisively attired Jesus (Matt. 27:28) was a military cloak worn over armor by officers. Paul's cloak (II Tim. 4:13) was probably the circular cape worn by 1st-century travelers. The mantle of the prophet Elijah was worn over a leather girdle (II Kings 1:8, 2:13). The royal robe of a ruler or of a high priest (see below) was made of superior fabric, worn as a long chest protector or chasuble over the ephod (I Sam. 2:18), and having a skirt (I Sam. 15:27).

Sandals, made of cowhide or other sorts of leather, even badgers' skins (Ezek. 16:10), were universally worn. They consisted of a sole having a thong or latchet passing across the top of the foot and around the ankle (Mark 1:7). Indoors, sandals were removed. Priests officiated barefoot. Travelers often carried their shoes until they entered cities, as Bedouins do today. See SHOES, illus. 382.

Girdles, usually made of leather (Matt. 3:4) or a square of stuff folded diagonally to make a strip about 5 in. wide, were worn by both men and women. Linen was too perishable (Jer. 13:1). Slits in the girdle provided pockets for carrying coins, knives, inkhorns, and even food. Longer garments were pulled up and bloused over girdles during hours of field labor or on journeys along dusty roads.

Headdress developed in the form of a folded square of cloth worn as a veil for protection against the sun, or wrapped as a turban. Women's veils, like Rebekah's (Gen. 24:65), were probably long mantles; see I Cor. 11:4–7, 15. Headcloths of Egyptians were distinctive, as seen in extant statues and reliefs. See under (3) below.

Many village and Bedouin women today wear garments as simple as those worn by the average woman in Palestine during the Biblical period. The dress (*khurkah*) was made of blue or black homespun, long and full, sometimes with touches of colored handwork at the neck. The sleeves were often long and pointed at the outer edge, so that they could be fastened back while the wearers were engaged in harvesting or domestic tasks. Sometimes the dress was tucked up to serve as a receptacle for the cut grain. A girdle of folded material, often gayer or more valuable than the gown itself, was worn at the waist. The woman's veil was similar to the man's headcloth, and may have been held in place by inherited coins like those lost by the woman of Christ's parable (Luke 15:8–10). The women wore home-made sandals similar to their husbands'.

(3) *Priestly habits* were "finely wrought" holy garments prescribed in the Levitical Law. From Ex. 28 and Lev. 8:6–8 are derived details of priestly attire: linen breeches (Ex. 28:42) and an undershirt. Over the shirt and breeches went the robe, entirely of blue fabric, with a hole for the neck and with a border of blue, purple, and scarlet pomegranates—either appliquéd or woven—alternating with golden bells, which tinkled as the high priest walked. Over the robe was worn the ephod*, a sort of vest, from the armpit to the waist. This vest might be either of white linen, worn by temple assistants like Samuel (I Sam. 2:18), or of skillfully woven gold, blue, purple, and scarlet thread combined with "fine twined linen," and held to the shoulders by two bands. A girdle of similar material attached this vest-ephod to the body. A breastplate* elaborately jeweled was worn over the ephod. The headtire of the high priest was a mitre or turban with the sacred inscribed gold plate at the front (Lev. 8:9)—"the holy crown."

In accordance with Num. 15:37–39, Deut. 22:12, the *simlah* or robe featured *zizith*, fringed tassels fastened to each corner (see FRINGES). The striped prayer shawl, or *tallith*, still worn by orthodox Jews at worship, evolved from the *simlah*, which was drawn over the head when the man was at prayer. From the time that the *simlah* went out of style, orthodox Jewish men have worn a small *tallith* in the form of a vest under their outer clothing, to be able to carry out the commandment of fringes even when not at prayer.

(4) *Royal attire*, such as David's, consisted of a linen ephod and a fine linen robe (I Chron. 15:27). Kings of Israel and of Judah, notably Solomon, Ahab and Jehoshaphat, were always decked in voluminous, richly colored robes of scarlet or purple when they were enthroned. A tasseled overgarment and a conical turban were essentials. Ezekiel described the merchant princes at Tyre, who removed their gorgeous robes and broidered garments as they came down from their thrones in the ruined city. Royal princesses, like Tamar, daughter of David, wore gowns "of divers colors" (II Sam. 13:18)—A.S.V. margin, "a long garment with sleeves."

(5) *Soldiers' mail* in Palestine and Syria during Bible times consisted of an upper

breastplate and a lower armor. The area between was vulnerable, as King Ahab found when fatally wounded by an arrow at Ramoth-gilead (I Kings 22:34). Some authorities believe that solid-metal armor was not used until the 2d century A.D.

Armor (see ARMS) or military apparel worn in Jesus' day is known from Graeco-Roman art. A heavy cuirass of leather studded with pieces of metal and fringed with leather at the bottom was worn over a short, pleated tunic. Wealthy Romans wore all-metal cuirasses in

117. Dress: 1a. One type of loincloth (Semite, c. 1800 B.C.); 1b. Animal skin; 2. Men's tunic or coat; 3. Men's mantle; 4. *Himation*; 5. 1st-century cloak or cape; 6. Women's dress; 7. High Priest; 8. Type of Prayer Shawl; 9. Hebrew royal attire; 10. Roman toga; 11. Roman *stola* and *pallium;* 12. Egyptian loincloth (c. 1300 B.C.); 13. Egyptian sheath-like dress (c. 2000 B.C.); 14. Babylonian (c. 2025 B.C.); 15. Assyrian (c. 900 B.C.); 16. Persian.

some periods. They were equipped with the voluminous rectangular cloak which was useful for disguise. Leather sandals or buskins were worn over socks.

In early Egypt militia wore a short linen skirt, to the center of which was attached a narrow, heart-shaped guard of leather. Egyptian militia used "scale armor" from the Eighteenth Dynasty on, i.e., after c. 1546 B.C. This was a corselet having metal or leather scales in bands, attached to a shirt of leather or heavy fabric. See SHISHAK, illus. 381.

Rome.—Roman men in Christ's time—and long before and after—wore a basic tunic to the knees, with a top layer formed by the voluminous, rectangular pallium or the even more famous toga, a semicircular cape whose straight side was worn uppermost, the balance falling in rich folds. Senators and emperors wore embroidered or striped tunics of wool, linen, or silk. The toga was an encumbrance and was laid aside at home. A long rectangular cloak was also worn by Roman men. Paul, a Roman citizen, wore such a cloak.

Roman matrons wore a stola over an inner tunic to the ankles, and over the stola a pallium, or rectangular woolen garment they could draw up over their heads. Their hair was piled high with stiff little "*croquignole*" curls, bound with a series of fillets.

Egypt.—Egyptian apparel constitutes material too rich for full discussion here. All through the Old Empire and feudal times (c. 2700–2000 B.C.) the loincloth or *sheuti* was worn by toilers and kings alike. It was like a wide scarf, tied about the hips, usually white, but sometimes in royal hues. In later times the kilt was made with a sunburst of pleats, indicating rays of the sacred sun. Sometimes a dalmatic tunic was worn under the kilt. The second traditional garment of Egypt was the squared-off headcloth or *nemes*. The tall, symbolic headdress of the pharaohs was conspicuous. Women of feudal times wore long tunics held up by shoulder straps. Sometimes they used a rectangular cloth draped as a mantle. When the New Kingdom came in with the Eighteenth Dynasty (c. 1570 B.C.), more elaborate modes, using patterned materials, appeared, indicating Asiatic influences, after conquests of Thutmose III in Syria. Men wore long, goffered skirts and flat, jeweled necklaces. The elaborate wigs of earlier times gave way to shaven heads to accommodate high headdresses. Ceremonial aprons of gazelle skin were used. Women's apparel was similar to men's, but of the sheerest material, that showed the form beneath. Fragments of textiles worn by Egyptians while Israel was in Egypt have been excavated from tombs. Egyptians have always abhorred woolen garments as unclean and hairy; men were impious if they entered temples dressed in wool. They preferred white linen, woven 160 threads to the inch in the warp and 120 in the weft. Joseph in Egypt wore linen (Gen. 41:42).

Mesopotamia.—Mesopotamian styles for men in the era of Hammurabi and Abraham included a robe flowing to the ankles, draped to leave the right arm bare. The round turban was popular. Assyrians who invaded Palestine wore short kilts, and long-fringed capes harking back to early Sumerian nubbly fringes (cf. Hebrew fringed garments) (Num. 15:38 f.). Sculptured friezes show how Persians looked in the era of the Hebrew Captivity: men wore ankle-length gowns with wide, pleated sleeves and graceful folds at the left side of the skirt. Textiles were elegantly woven, and patterned with rich harmonies of color. Long, curled beards and well-set wigs (Isa. 3:24) were typically Persian.

See COSMETICS; JEWELRY.

drink, moisture for human consumption. Water*, for the family and its animals, was man's most necessary beverage in Biblical times. The search for and discovery of wells* determined the route of patriarchal migrations into Canaan, as well as the Exodus of the Tribes from Egypt a few centuries later. When towns developed, each family strove to have its own cistern, but in times of scarcity bought water (Deut. 2:28; Isa. 55:1), as is still done in periods of drought even in Jerusalem. The preciousness of water adds poignancy to Jesus' references to it, in John 19:28, 4:14; Matt. 10:42; Luke 16:24. Milk was always a valued drink. (See FOOD.) Wine (see VINE), frequently squeezed directly into a cup from the vines, was a common beverage throughout the ancient East, where royal households had special attendants to serve their drinks (see CUPBEARER), and where the lowliest citizens aimed at having their own vines. (See DRUNKENNESS.)

Drink offerings accompanied gifts of meal in connection with sacrificed animals. Ex. 29:40 and Num. 28:7 suggest that wine was the customary libation, though Judg. 6:19 f. mentions broth and I Sam. 7:6 suggests the use of water.

dromedary. See CAMEL.

dropsy. See DISEASE AND HEALING.

drunkenness, alcoholic intoxication; inebriety. "Strong drink" is denoted in Scripture by *shekar* ("intoxicating liquor"); alcoholic beverages made from grapes are called *yayin*. Intoxicants were made not only from abundant grapes, but also from pomegranates, apples, dates, grain, and honey. There is evidence throughout Scripture that excessive drinking existed among rich and poor. The instances of Noah (Gen. 9:21), Lot (Gen. 19:30–35), and Nabal (I Sam. 25:36) indicate typical conduct of men in primitive Israel. The books having a Persian background paint drunkenness as part of the court routine: Esther 1:7, 3:15; Daniel 1:5, 8, 5:1, 3 f. The Syrian king Ben-hadad and his 32 allied kings drank in their huts during their wars against Ahab of Israel (I Kings 20:16). Egypt made and exported a famous quality of beer. Yet the O.T. contains many injunctions against strong drink: Lev. 10:9; Deut. 21:20; Ezek. 23:33; Job 12:25; and also Gal. 5:21; I Cor. 5:11. In spite of the common acceptance of drink at patriarchal feastings (Gen. 27:25; Gen. 43:34) there were early protests, as voiced in Prov. 23:21. The society of Nazirites*, to which Samson belonged, was based on an ancient law whereby members separated themselves "unto the Lord" and foreswore not only all manner of intoxicants, but even fresh and dried grapes. The drunkenness of the Roman age as Jesus

118. Drunkenness of Noah, a 17th-century carving on the Palace of the Doges, Venice.

observed it in Palestine found reflection in such comments as Luke 12:45 and 21:34.

See VINE.

Drusilla (drōō-sĭl'ȧ), the youngest daughter of Herod* Agrippa I, granddaughter of Herod the Great, and third wife of the Roman procurator Felix*, for whom she deserted her husband, King Aziz of Emessa, contrary to Jewish law. While still probably in her teens, this famous Hebrew beauty heard Paul speak at Caesarea (Acts 24:24). She and Felix had a son, Agrippa, who in manhood perished during an eruption of Vesuvius.

dulcimer. See MUSIC.

Dumah (dū'mȧ) ("silence"). (1) A tribe of Ishmaelites living in the desert of N. Arabia (Gen. 25:14). (2) The name given to Edom (Isa. 21:11) in reference to the silence of death in store for her. (3) A town in Judah 10 m. SW. of Hebron (Josh. 15:52).

dumbness. See DISEASE AND HEALING.

dung, made into cakes, was a common fuel even for baking food (Ezek. 4:12). It was used also as a fertilizer, as in Christ's parable of the vinedresser (Luke 13:8). The Dung Gate of Jerusalem (Neh. 2:13, 3:13 f., 12:31) was near the SE. corner of the city wall, on the hill Ophel. Through an area of refuse still existing outside the city, the portal led to Siloam. Dung is used figuratively as a term of contempt (Ps. 83:10; Mal. 2:3).

Dura (dū'rȧ), a plain in Babylon where the golden image was set up (Dan. 3:1).

dyeing, a craft in which Hebrews early excelled, though the Bible makes few references to this skill. They secured rich and permanent colors from murex shellfish obtained near Tyre*, which gave them coveted purple reds, and from vegetable matter. Almond leaves supplied yellow dye. Pomegranate bark furnished black. Red was secured from roots of the madder plant. Green was not popular, but was secured by blending an umbelliferous plant with indigo. Indigo dye contained not only blue powder from plants of the genus *Indigofera*, but also potash, lime, and grape treacle.

To process wool in the popular purple tones, they placed it in grape juice, sprinkled powdered madder on it, left it all night without washing, and continued the dyeing with ashes of wood or goat's dung.

Dr. W. F. Albright (in *The Archaeology of Palestine and the Bible*, Revell) describes dye vats found in Stratum A, Tell Beit Mirsim (Debir*, or Kiriath-sepher), a center of cloth industry developed by the Hebrews some 600 years after their arrival in S. Palestine: "The dye-vats are made of single stones about 3 ft. high and the same in diameter, hewn round, but with flat tops and bottoms. The interior is hollowed out to form a roughly spherical basin, about 1½ ft. across. Around the rim there runs a deep circular channel with a hole in its bottom communicating with the interior of the vat; we generally found a stone fitting into the hole. The purpose of the channel was naturally to catch the precious dye when it was spilled on the rim, and to return it to the vat. Near the vats . . . we generally found a number of large stones, about 15 or 16 in. across, all pierced with a hole through the center. . . . The standard vat was made to last forever. . . . The perforated stones . . . [probably] were employed as pressure weights,

119. Dye vats at Tell Beit Mirsim.

perhaps to press the dye out of the cloth, in order to conserve it" (pp. 119–121).

The Children of Israel were commanded by the Lord to bring for the Tabernacle "rams' skins dyed red" (Ex. 25:5, 26:14, 39:34). The dyed garments for which desert people near Bosrah in the Hauran, E. of Jordan, were famous, are mentioned in Isa. 63:1. Ezekiel refers to the dyed turbans of Babylonians and Chaldaeans (23:15).

dysentery. See DISEASE AND HEALING.

E

E, the symbol for the Ephraimitic document of Biblical material, stemming from Bethel and Shechem (in the territory of Ephraim) and characterized by the use of *Elohim* for Jehovah (*Yahweh*) in the patriarchal stories. For fuller discussion of E, and comparison with J and other contributory documents, see SOURCES.

Ea ("house of water"; in Sumerian called *enki*, "lord of the earth"), a Babylonian god worshipped from at least 2200 B.C. With Anu and Enlil (Bel), he formed the first triad in the Mesopotamian pantheon. His principal temple was at Eridu, not far from Ur, traditional home of Abraham. In Babylonian creation stories the formation of the universe is ascribed to Ea, god of sweet waters; later to his son Marduk. (See NEW YEAR FESTIVAL.) Ea was not related to the primordial ocean, but was the fertilizing element in water. He presided over wisdom, music, and the magical arts; played an important role in the council of the gods; and was a friend of man. Seated in his watery shrine, he appears on one of the choicest Accadian cylinder seals ever recovered. He was the father of Adapa, also identified with Atrakhasis, who was honored as the savior of mankind from catastrophes.

eagle, an unclean bird of prey whose flesh was forbidden to Israel (Deut. 14:11), probably because of his carnivorous habits. Ornithologists identify some of the Biblical references to "eagle" as more properly the "vulture," related to the lammergeier. (Cf. Matt. 24:28, R.S.V. margin "vultures.") True eagles of the Middle East do not eat carrion. Traits of this bird are his wide cruising range (Deut. 28:49; Prov. 23:5), nurture of his young (Deut. 32:11), speed (II Sam. 1:23; Lam. 4:19), recuperative powers (Ps. 103:5), and ability to reach great heights (Isa. 40:31). The four living creatures of Ezekiel's vision had "faces" of eagles (Ezek. 1:10; cf. Rev. 4:7). Storm-loving eagles, regarded by ancient Greeks as messengers from Zeus, appeared on silver staters from Elis in W. Greece as early as the 5th century B.C. Storm eagles were also stamped on Egyptian coins of the Ptolemies c. 316 B.C. An eagle sat by the throne of Phidias's Olympian Zeus. In Christian symbolism the eagle denotes the Ascension of Christ, immortality, and John.

earrings, ornaments made of gold and silver, worn by women and men of Bible lands. They were given as offerings to Yahweh (Ex. 35:22, Num. 31:50), and melted for the golden calf (Ex. 32:3). Men of Ishmael characteristically wore "golden earrings" (Judg. 8:24–26). The first earring mentioned in the O.T. was the one given to Rebekah by Abraham's servant—probably a nose ring (A.S.V.), or possibly an ornament for her forehead (Gen. 24:22), weighing half a shekel (112 or 224 grains) (see MONEY). The prophets Ezekiel (16:12) and Hosea (2:13) used earrings to symbolize meticulously clad persons or vain women. One of the choicest golden earrings from antiquity is in the Boston Museum of Fine Arts—an amazingly wrought little two-horse chariot driven by an exultant Nike figure whose wings are full spread in

120. Earrings: 1. From Tell el-'Ajjûl, 1600 B.C.; 2. Of Gideon times. Gold, 1100 B.C.; 3 and 4. Assyrian, 900–800 B.C.; 5. Egyptian, 800 B.C.; 6. Egyptian, 100 B.C. (Meroitic); 7. Greek, 100 B.C.

victory (c. 450 B.C.). This object illustrates how an ornament could possess religious significance, like the amulets (see AMULET) which Jacob stripped from his household, together with "strange gods" (A.V. Gen. 35:4; R.S.V. "foreign gods").

earthquake, a phenomenon which in the varied geological formation of Palestine and Syria has been frequent from prehistoric times. Craters are found in the Hauran, in Midian, E. of the Gulf of Aqabah, on the E. rim of the Jordan, and in Trachonitis—locations which all reveal deposits of black basalt and lava, products of volcanic actions.

Two types of earthquake are found in Scripture—historical events, and imaginative conditions accompanying impressive spiritual events:

Historical—

In the Vale of Siddim (Gen. 19:24–29).
At Sinai (Ex. 19:18).
When Korah was destroyed (Num. 16:31).
In the reign of Saul (I Sam. 14:15).
On the flight of Elijah (I Kings 19:11).
In the reign of Uzziah (Amos 1:1; Zech. 14:5).
In the reign of Herod (31 B.C.) (Jos. *Antiq.*).
At the Crucifixion (Matt. 27:51).
At the Resurrection (Matt. 28:2).
At the Philippi prison (Acts 16:26).

Imaginative or Prophetic—

At Zion (A.S.V. Isa. 29:6).
Foretold by Christ (Matt. 24:7).
In the Apocalypse (Rev. 6:12, 8:5, 11:13).

east, the, with Hebrews the determining point of the compass—the direction of sunrise, the way that was "before," as the W. was "behind." The E. gate of the Jerusalem Temple was so built that at the spring and fall equinoxes sunrise rays entered the Holy of Holies. The "gate that looketh toward the east" was prominent in the visions of Ezekiel

(Ezek. 43:1–5; see also his allusion to sun worshippers, 8:16). Children of the E. (Gen. 29:1; Ezek. 25:4; Jer. 49:28) were nomadic tribes of the Syrian Desert (Judg. 6:3, 33, 7:12) including Aramaeans (see ARAM) and Kedar (Jer. 49:28) associated with Midian and Amalek (see AMALEKITES), and were noted for their wisdom (I Kings 4:30). Job was one of them (Job 1:3). People of the farther E. were Babylonians, Assyrians, Persians. The E. Sea was the Dead* Sea. The east wind (see WINDS), fatal to vegetation (Gen. 41:6) and perilous for shipping, was the hot sirocco (Ps. 48:7; Ex. 10:13), bringing periodic locust invasions. Out of the E. came the Wise Men to the manger of Christ (Matt. 2:1), whose star they had seen in the E. (2:2).

Easter (A.-S. *Ēastre,* Norse goddess whose festival was observed at the vernal equinox, akin to Lat. *aurora,* "dawn," Gk. *ēōs,* "east"), the Christian festival observed on the first Sunday after the full moon on or following the vernal equinox (c. March 21). Not mentioned in Scripture (except in the erroneous translation of A.V. Acts 12:4, of which the original Greek reads *pascha,* "passover"). Christians very early carried over the Hebrew Passover into their celebration of the Resurrection of Jesus, whom they regarded as the true Paschal Lamb and first fruits of the dead. The W. kept it on the first day of the week. But the E., clinging to the Jewish custom, celebrated it on the 14th day of the moon at evening. The Council of Nicaea (A.D. 325) decided that Easter should be observed on a Sunday, and fixed the method of determining its date in any year. Easter

121. Easter; a typical tomb with stone rolled away (Luke 24:2).

closes the 40-day Lenten period opened by Ash Wednesday. Unsuccessful efforts have been made to establish a "fixed" Easter for the whole Christian world.

East Sea. See DEAD SEA.

Ebal (ē′băl). (1) Traditional founder of a Horite clan (Gen. 36:23). (2) A descendant of Eber (1 Chron. 1:22, 40).

Ebal, Mt., a peak conspicuous in the Samaritan (see SAMARIA, DISTRICT OF) highlands, c. 1,207 ft. above the valley and 2,077 ft. above sea level. Together with Gerizim*, Ebal forms the narrow mouth of a strategic pass through which migrants and military and commercial bands have passed N., S., E., and W. since the dawn of history. Ancient Shechem, S. of Ebal, guarded the pass. In obedience to the instruction of Moses (Deut. 27:13), Joshua,

122. Mt. Ebal, from Nablus.

who built an altar on Ebal and erected stones inscribed with the Law (Josh. 8:31 f.), pronounced to assembled Israel (Deut. 11:29, 27:13; Josh. 8:33) the curses that would follow breaches of the Law. Thereafter Ebal was known as the Mount of Cursing. On the summit of Mt. Ebal are ruins of a fort and a small church.

Ebedmelech (ē′bĕd-mē′lĕk), the Ethiopian eunuch who drew the prophet Jeremiah out of a dungeon by cords. He was rewarded for this deed by being told that he would be saved when Jerusalem was captured (Jer. 38:7–13, 39:15–18).

Ebenezer (ĕb′ĕn-ē′zĕr). (1) The scene, location unknown, of a great defeat of Israel by the Philistines, who captured the Ark (I Sam. 4:1, 5:1). (2) The name given by Samuel to a stone set up to commemorate a victory of Israel over the Philistines (I Sam. 7:12); it may be Mejdel Yāba, adjacent to Antipatris, or a place N. of Bethel.

Eber (ē′bĕr) ("other side"). (1) The imaginary, eponymous ancestor of Hebrews and certain Arab and Aramaean tribes, which are believed to have developed E. of the Euphrates and possibly E. of the Tigris. The region "on the other side" of the river became personified in this son of Shem, son of Noah (Gen. 10:21). Eber was the father of Peleg and Joktan (Gen. 10:25; I Chron. 1:18). In Gen. 11:15 his genealogy is traced to Salah, son of Arphaxad, son of Shem. He was the 6th ancestor of Abraham. He was listed in the ancestry of Jesus (Heber A. V. Luke 3:35). (2) A Gadite (A.S.V. I Chron. 5:13). (3) A

Benjamite (I Chron. 8:12). (4) A member of a priestly family who returned from the Exile (Neh. 12:20).

Ecclesiastes (ĕ-klē′zĭ-ăs′tēz) (Gk. *ekklēsiastēs*, "preacher," translation of the original Heb. *koheleth*, "one who convenes an assembly"), the 21st book of the O.T.; part of the Wisdom* Literature. "The Preacher" was an alternative title; a marginal reading for "the Preacher" in the English A.S.V. is "the Great Orator." Moffatt's translation is "the Speaker."

Because of the tradition of Solomon's wisdom and the assemblies of learned minds he addressed (I Kings 4:29–34), the book was attributed to him; this literary device was used to give additional prestige to what was written. Evidence against this attribution to Solomon is abundant. Solomon, who reigned until his death, could not have written 1:12. The references to kings are inconceivable as the words of Solomon (4:13–16; 10:16 f.). The book abounds in Aram. words and phrases that place it in the post-Exilic (see EXILE) period—probably c. 200 B.C. In 2:12 the real author permits the reader to see him with the same realism with which he strives to view life. He lived in or near Jerusalem (8:10), in a time of oppression (4:1, 13–16); beyond that, the period is unrecognizable (10:16 f.). Though the name of the author remains unknown, his thought identifies him as a vigorous mind at the headwaters of realistic humanism.

Ecclesiastes 1:4–7, 3:1–8, 15 is the Hebraic version of the theory that history and nature move in a circle, an ever-revolving and recurring cycle—a philosophical idea widespread in the non-Jewish world of the Babylonians, Egyptians, and Greeks. Such a philosophy led to a sense of futility, cynicism, and pessimism; and these abound in this book. Probably Koheleth, in contact with Greek influence, was deflected from the traditional faith of his fathers, went "all out" for something new, and lost the hope which had earlier characterized the leaders of his nation.

It is impossible to outline the Book of Ecclesiastes. The circle of repetitions which the author sees in life's ever-revolving nature has its counterpart in the repetition of ideas throughout the book. He conducted on himself experiments in living and noted their results. The pursuit of wisdom (1:12–18, 7:23 f., 9:17–10:3), pleasure (2:1–5, 10:12–15), wealth (2:6–11, 5:10–20), labor (2:18–23, 11:1–8), evil-doing (7:23–29) all led to vain ends. At the very outset he states his conclusion (1:2): "All is vanity" is his verdict for the whole of life. The sorry plight of the oppressed (3:16–22, 5:8 f.), the discontented (4:1–3), and the lonely (4:7–11) are pictured. The shocking incongruities in society (10:4–7), hazards in daily work (10:8–11), despotism in government (10:16–20) are evils which depress him. The Epicurean philosophy, "Eat, drink, and be merry, for tomorrow we die," is the logical conclusion of his pessimistic outlook (8:15–9:9). The infirmities of old age, minutely described in a famous allegory (12:1–8) are cynically introduced by an appeal to youth to have a good time (11:9 f.). Caught in the whirl of blind pagan faith, with God imprisoned in the machinery of His own making, man should be pious, but not too good (5:1–7). The name "Jehovah," the God of Israel, who is love, mercy, and justice, is not mentioned. "Elohim" dwells afar, has no contact with man (5:2), and never interferes in the moral machinery of the universe. Prayer is nowhere mentioned as an aid to man in his sorry plight.

The pessimism of Koheleth is due to the fact that he rejected both current conceptions of the hereafter, the immortality of the soul and the resurrection of the body (3:19–21, 9:4–6, 10, 12:7) (see DEATH). The epilogue (12:9–14) was penned later by some devout, admiring intellectual. Ecclesiastes won a place in the Hebrew Canon* because of its popularity and its attribution to Solomon. It is not referred to in the N.T.

Ecclesiasticus. See APOCRYPHA.

Eden (possibly from Sum. and Bab. *edinu*, "plain").

(1) The extremely fertile first home of man (Gen. 2:8), from which Adam* and Eve were expelled because of their disobedience to God (Gen. 3). It was an earthly paradise, E. from the viewpoint of the Hebrew writer, well-watered by a tremendous river which divided into four branches, of which one was the Euphrates* and another the Tigris* (Hiddekel Gen. 2:14). Vain efforts have been made to identify the other two, possibly as the Nile (? Gihon) and the Persian Gulf (? Pishon). Several sites have been suggested for Eden, the most widely accepted being Mesopotamia and Armenia. But Eden belongs less in the realm of geography than in the soul of man. Eden continued to represent, in O.T. writings subsequent to Genesis, a land of trees that were "a glory and a greatness" (Ezek. 31:18), in contrast to the burning wilderness of Judaea; the paradisaic scene which distraught prophets promised to a redeemed society, as in Isa. 51:3; Ezek. 36:35; Joel 2:3. There is no mention of Eden in the N.T., despite efforts to identify such allusions as Luke 23:43. Paradise is a Persian word, indicating lush gardens surrounding royal palaces.

New light on Eden has been shed by Samuel Noah Kramer's brilliant translation of a hexagonal cylinder recovered from Mesopotamia, revealing a Sumerian (see SUMER) story parallel to the Genesis narrative, handed down from Sumerian culture to the Babylonian with which Hebrews were ultimately in contact. Though the Sumerian Eden story is as inferior to the Biblical narrative as the Canaanite epics are to their Hebrew parallels, in spiritual quality and literary excellence, the old clay record well illustrates "the Hebrew marvel" which transformed static motifs, as Dr. Kramer states, and old, conventionalized patterns, "into the most vibrant and dynamic literature known to man." The 278 lines of text on the cylinder have Enki, the water god, for their hero and Ninhursag for his goddess. They contain also a woman-from-rib story, which in the Sumerian is a play on words; for the word "*Nin-ti*" means both "the lady of the rib" and "the lady who makes live"—the oldest known pun. Eight fruits instead of one were forbidden to the Sumerian pair; the animal who misled Enki was a fox, not a serpent. The Sumerian Eden was located, apparently, near the Hebrew Eden, in SW. Persia.

(2) A section of Mesopotamia, occupied by "the children of Eden . . . in Thelasar" (II Kings 19:12; Isa. 37:12, A.S.V. Telassar). Ezekiel refers to merchants of Eden doing business with Tyre (27:23).

(3) A son of Joah, who lived in the era of Hezekiah, a Levite who helped assign offerings to the "brethren" (II Chron. 29:12, 31:15).

Edom ("red") sometimes refers to a people (Num. 20:18–21; I Sam. 14:47) (see EDOMITES); again, to the land (Num. 20:23; II Kings 3:20). "Seir" (Gen. 32:3; Num. 24:18; Judg. 5:4) is another name for the same country used interchangeably. The territory of the Edomites contracted and expanded with their national fortunes. Edom is first mentioned in the records of the Egyptian Merenptah (c. 1224–1216 B.C.). But throughout most of the O.T. it was the land S. of the Dead* Sea, extending to the Gulf of Aqabah*, including mountains and fertile plateaus on both sides of the Arabah*, especially the towering 5,000-ft. ridge of Mt. Seir*, where the national life of Edom was cradled, an area of c. 100 sq. miles. At the time of the Hebrew Exodus its N. boundary was the Nahal Zered* (Wâdī Hesa), flowing into the S. end of the Dead Sea. Its N. neighbor was Moab*. The rose-red wonder city of Petra, a monument of the skill of its later Nabataean (see NABATAEA) inhabitants, was formerly Selah (II Kings 14:7), the early capital of the Edomites. Secure in fortified mountain settlements which communicated with each other by fire, the nation grew by agriculture, industry, and the levying of tolls on caravans which crossed their country, especially on "the King's Highway," used by every historical people of the Jordan, between the Arabian Desert, Egypt, and the Mediterranean, and from Damascus to the Red Sea. The wealth of Edom is shown by the heavy tribute they paid Esar-haddon of Assyria. Edom's opposition to the Israelites en route from Egypt (Num. 20:14–21) helps establish the date of the Exodus as not before the 13th century B.C. (probably c. 1290 B.C.), for Edomites were not living before then in the area traversed.

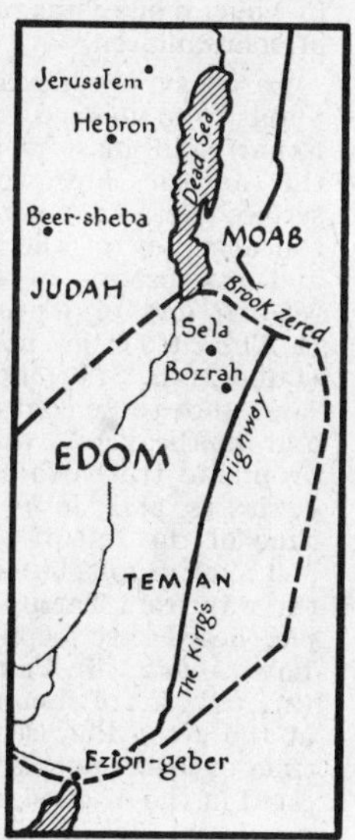

123. Edom.

Archaeologists have discovered there mines, mining camps, and slag-heaps from which copper* and iron* in large amounts had been extracted. This Edomite ore explains why Edom was economically important to the ancient world, and why David and Solomon risked armies in this difficult terrain to gain control of the country's output of copper and iron, which W. Palestine lacked (II Sam. 8:13–15; I Kings 9:26, 11:15 f.). Solomon's navy and merchant marine were based on Ezion-geber* (I Kings 9:26–28). Edomite pottery excavated by Nelson Glueck's expeditions tells of a highly developed civilization from the 13th to the 6th century B.C.

Edomites, inhabitants of Edom, descendants of Esau* (Edom). Esau overcame the former inhabitants of the mountains of the Arabah, the Horites (Horim, Hivites) (Gen. 14:6; Deut. 2:12), married their daughters (Gen. 36:2, 20), and settled there. Gen. 36 charts the development of these Semites* into families (9–14), into clans (15–19), and under kings or dukes (31–39). The old feud between Jacob and Esau emerged when the Edomites refused passage to the Israelites (Judg. 11:17 f.) (see above). The bitterness between these two branches of Semites was intense and never-ending (Gen. 25:23; Num. 20:14; II Kings 8:20–22, cf. II Chron. 25:11 f.; II Kings 14:22, cf. II Chron. 26:1 f.; Mal. 1:2 f.). Historians (II Kings 8:20–22) played up the faults of the Edomites (I Sam. 21:7, 22:9 f., 18; I Kings 11:14–22). The Psalmist remembers their derision when Jerusalem fell (Ps. 137:7). The prophets pronounced doom on Edom for holding Israelites as slaves (Amos 1:6, 9, 2:6, 9:11 f.); for mistreating innocent merchants and travelers (Joel 3:19); for pride in their rocky fastnesses (Obad. 3); for vindictiveness (Ezek. 25:12–14, 35:1–15). Divine justice appears as the avenger of Edom's wrongs (Isa. 63:1–6). Yet Edom was famous for its Wise Men (see WISDOM) (Obad. 8; Jer. 49:7); and the background and thought of the philosophical poem that is the Book of Job* are probably a contribution from Edom. Edom, and the experiences of the early Israelites in it, contributed much to Hebrew understanding of Yahweh (see GOD), whose home Edom was (Deut. 33:2; Judg. 5:4 f.; Hab. 3:3).

In the post-Exilic period the Edomites, due to the pressure of Nabataean Arabs, were gradually pushed N., and finally occupied the S. half of Judaea, including the region around Hebron, an area which the Greeks later called S. Judaea, Idumaea (Mark 3:8). Judas Maccabaeus fought them; fifty years later, John Hyrcanus completely conquered them, imposed circumcision, and invoked the old Jewish law of assembly (Deut. 23:7 f.). In c. 55 B.C. Julius Caesar appointed an Idumaean, Antipater, procurator of Judaea, Samaria, and Galilee. In 37 B.C. Herod, son of Antipater, was crowned King of the Jews. When the Romans under Titus besieged Jerusalem in A.D. 70 the Idumaeans joined the Jews in rebellion against the foe. According to Josephus 20,000 Idumaeans were admitted as defenders of the Holy City. Once within, they proceeded to rape, rob, and kill, sparing neither priests nor populace in their orgy of blood. These traitors-at-arms received the same fate as their few surviving brothers when Rome took over Jerusalem; Idumaea or Edom ceased to be; Gen. 27:40 was fulfilled in the words of Jesus (Matt. 26:52).

Edrei (ĕd′rē-ī), an important city of Bashan* where the Israelites fought the giant King Og* and killed him. (Num. 21:33–35; Deut. 1:4, 3:1, 10; Josh. 12:4, 13:12, 31).

education, in the Bible, dealt not only with moral and religious instruction, a field in which the Hebrews excelled their contemporaries, but with manners, practical living, and science. Jesus, whom Nicodemus* of the Sanhedrin called a "teacher come from God" (John 3:2), continued the educational functions of Ezra and Nehemiah*, but taught with an authority exceeding that of the scribes* (Luke 4:32). He was addressed more frequently as "Teacher" than anything else; and he himself referred to the fact that he sat "daily in the temple teaching" (Mark 14:49). (See FAMILY; SYNAGOGUE; SCHOOL.)

There are many evidences that people of ancient Bible lands got off to an earlier educational start than scholars formerly believed. At Mari on the Middle Euphrates two well-built schoolrooms dating from the 3d millennium B.C. have been unearthed. Great numbers of clay tablets in the Stephens Library at Yale and in the University Museum at Philadelphia evidence the literacy of the peoples from whom the Patriarchs came, and their interest in mathematics and cuneiform word lists pricked on wet clay. Many of the Psalms were put in writing long before David; maxims in Egypt were set down a thousand years before Solomon.

In O.T. times the education of children devolved upon parents, and was pre-eminently religious training. Solomon is credited with the proverb, "Hear, ye children, the instruction of a father" (Prov. 4:1). This entire chapter is a discussion of gaining wisdom* through parental indoctrination. Time and again in Proverbs the text runs, "My son, keep my words" (7:1), etc. Mothers, too, performed functions of education (Prov. 1:8, 6:20, and notably, Prov. 31:1; cf. II Tim. 1:5, 3:15). To early Hebrews the beginning of knowledge was the "fear" of the Lord; this theme recurs constantly throughout the O.T.

Formal education among Jews developed during and after the Exile, during which Ezra and others codified the Law* and placed in the hands of the people written drafts of what had before been transmitted orally from father to son (Deut. 6:7–25). The events recorded in Neh. 8 are epochal in the history of religious education. After the Return professional teachers and synagogue schools functioned all over Palestine, stressing the memorizing of portions of the sacred writings, such as the opening chapters of Leviticus, portions of the Deuteronomic Code, certain psalms and proverbs, and Scripture that gave the origin of the Hebrew festivals (see FEASTS). Boys went to synagogue schools at the age of six for elementary instruction.

In the 1st century B.C. Pharisees saw to it that even country towns had schools for youths of 16 or over. There must have been elementary schools in the time of Jesus, though none at Nazareth is mentioned specifically in Scripture. Yet consider what must have lain behind the situation described in Luke 2:46–50. In every synagogue there was an attendant (Luke 4:20), who, sitting on a low platform in the midst of a group of boys on the floor, taught them the Law and the Prophets, and the elements of reading. The teacher gave out a verse, and the pupils repeated it after him in unison. Sometimes an advanced pupil read the verse and the others followed, word for word. Pupils were given small wooden tablets covered with wax, on which they copied passages from scrolls* of sacred writings. Teachers were held in respect. They were paid by local congregations. Expenses were met by voluntary contributions. The Temple provided a receptacle in which money was placed for the education of poor children.

Larger synagogues had classes for advanced pupils who desired to become rabbis (see RABBI) and masters. Figures prominent in the Jewish educational system included scribes (Ezra 7:6), concerned with preserving the accuracy of the written Law; copyists and interpreters of the same; teachers of reading and of writing this same material (I Tim. 1:7); learned doctors of the Law (Luke 2:46, 5:17; Acts 5:34); wise men or sages (not to be confused with necromancers and soothsayers), whose work of applying prophetic truths to everyday life (as in Ecclesiastes and Job) culminated about the time of the fall of the Persian Empire (c. 330 B.C.). Pupils like Paul, who had come all the way from Tarsus to the Jerusalem Temple, heard discussions of theology and the Law (Acts 22:3). Paul's professor, Gamaliel* (2), was a son of Simon and probably grandson of the great Pharisee scholar Hillel. In the time of Jesus people were profoundly interested in the discussion of religious and moral problems. The restless yearning for an authoritative teacher paved the way for the educational impact made by Jesus on the multitude (Luke 4:22, 32).

The wider learning characteristic of the Graeco-Roman world in which Paul lived worked its way into the education even of rabbis. In Jerusalem there had been schools based on the Greek type for two centuries before Christ's birth.

See "Synagogues," under ARCHITECTURE.

Eglon (ĕg′ lŏn). (1) A city SW. of Lachish* in S. Palestine, whose king, Debir, was one of the five Amorite kings defeated by Joshua (10:3, 34–35, 12:11). It was allotted to Judah (15:39). Albright (*BASOR* 17, 1925, p. 7) and most observers identify Eglon with Tell el-Hesi, W. of Hebron. Excavations were carried out by Petrie (1890) and Bliss (1891–93) and a new series begun in 1970. The site contains the ruins of a fortress, standing on the remains of a large Early Bronze Age city, which was totally destroyed at the close of the Late Bronze Age; it yielded a clay tablet of the Amarna period (14th century B.C.). See *BA* 34, 1971, pp. 76–86. (2) A king of Moab, who occupied territory W. of the Jordan and who was assassinated by Ehud (Judg. 3:12 ff.). W. P. A.

Egypt, a country lying along the Nile* beyond the SW. border of Palestine and Syria, which exerted from earliest times a profound influence upon her northeastern neighbors. In this brief account Egypt will be considered only in relation to the people and the lands of the Bible, and not with regard to her own greatness.

(1) *Geographical relations.* The boundary between Palestine and Egypt consists of no mountain range or conspicuous river, but the merest trickle of a wâdī, the El Arish ("River of Egypt"), whose wide valley drains seasonally into the Mediterranean 50 m. SW. of Gaza; this brook is the "river of Egypt" (Num. 34:5; Josh. 15:4, 47). On the map the Suez Canal appears a more natural boundary, for the barren highland of the Sinai* Peninsula belongs rather with Palestine and the Arabian (see ARABIA) Peninsula, of which it is a part, than with the Nile Delta. From a geographical viewpoint there has never been anything formidable to deter Egyptian military forces from driving NE., in spite of difficulties sometimes encountered by Pharaoh's chariot cavalry (Ex. 14:22–28).

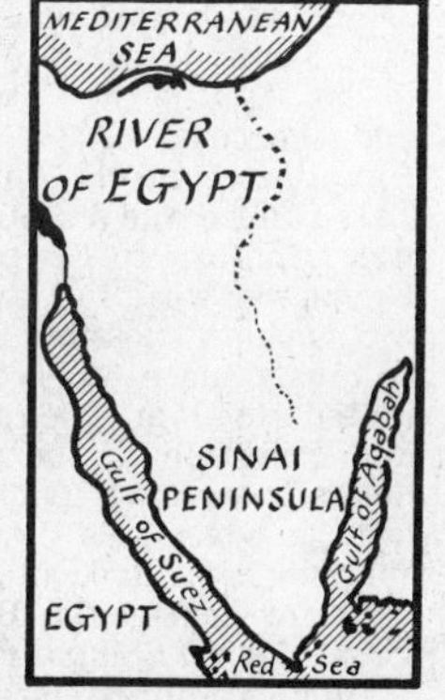

124. River of Egypt.

(2) *Economic relations.* In O.T. times Palestine had little to offer Egypt except a coveted bridgehead leading to Syria and the Tigris-Euphrates Valley, and a not-too-rich source of taxes in the form of livestock, oil, wine, honey, labor, etc. Palestine farms, except in the Plain of Sharon, were not worth fighting for. Timber was scarce, except for the mighty cedars of the Lebanon Range, transshipped for construction works, boats, and mummy cases. Egypt herself was regarded as a fat granary, to which hungry nomads, like Abraham, trekked (Gen. 12:10–20) whenever their less fruitful lands suffered from a brief local famine. The motivation of the four-centuries-long Sojourn* of the Jacob tribes while Joseph was "over all the land of Egypt" (Gen. 41:41–45) was likewise food shortage. All "countries came into Egypt to Joseph to buy corn; because that the famine was so sore in all lands" (Gen. 41:57). It is not surprising that extant Egyptian records contain no reference to the long settlement of Hebrew tribes in Egypt, since tolerant pharaohs several times ordered displaced persons to be admitted to the Delta for food. Well-known were the famous storehouses (see "store-cities," under CITIES), kept filled with local and imported goods, ever ready for foreign campaigns. From Syria came levies of horses, chariots, slaves, incense, gold, copper, and even elephants—many wares being transshipped from more distant emporiums. Egyptian bas-reliefs show Syrian tribute bearers arriving—easily recognizable by their beards, high cheekbones, and prominent noses. Economic relations between Egypt and her two northern neighbors included an enriching coastal trade from very early times, especially with such ports as Byblos (see GEBAL) and Ugarit (see RAS SHAMRAH). Caravan cargoes were steadily pouring riches into Egypt from every direction, so that the gay, luxurious courts at Memphis, Thebes, and Akhetaton (Tell el-Amarna*) enjoyed a standard of living not often exceeded in ancient times. (See TRIBUTE, illus. 458.)

(3) *Political relations.* Egypt made political impact on Palestine in two ways: (a) through the long Sojourn of the Jacob tribes; (b) through repeated invasions.

(a) The *Sojourn,* according to Ex. 12:40, lasted "four hundred and thirty years"—an estimate oddly in line with archaeological findings concerning construction projects in progress during their residence, and with the date of the Exodus*. The Sojourn began soon after the Patriarch Jacob dispatched his sons from Canaan to seek food in the land where Joseph their brother was enjoying unprecedented prestige as prime minister of Pharaoh (Gen. 41:37–42:6). The date c. 1700 B.C. has been suggested by some scholars as the time of Joseph's arrival in Egypt; others place it later. The Sojourn is believed to have taken place during the 15th–17th Dynasties

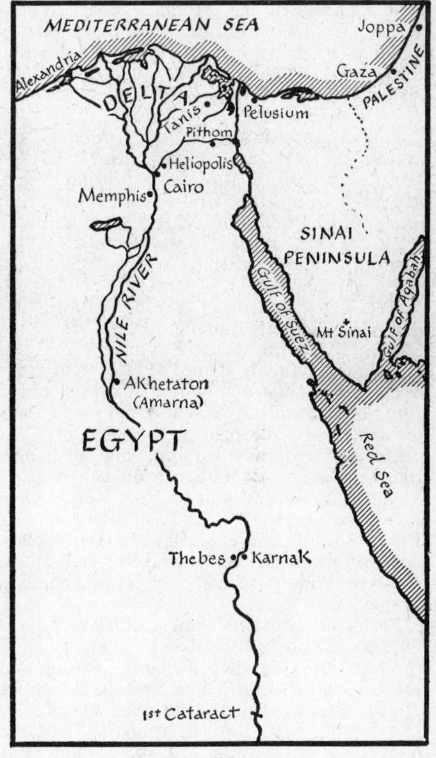

125.

in Egypt—namely, the Dynasties of Hyksos* horsemen who swept across Palestine to the Nile Valley (c. 1720–1550 B.C.), and who, though ranked as barbarians, possessed cultural abilities, brought to Egypt chariot and cavalry warfare, and probably popularized bronze (see BRONZE AGE). Their era was a "dark age" for Egypt; but they were sympathetic to the Hebrew tribes, and allowed them to settle near their capital "in the plain of Tanis" (Zoan of Ps. 78:12, 43) in the NE. Delta. The Hyksos (c. 1720–1550 B.C.) (meaning "rulers of foreign lands") were probably of mixed W. Semitic or Canaanite stock. When they were expelled by Eighteenth Dynasty Egyptian rulers other kings arose, who "knew not Joseph" and his kin (Acts 7:18) (i.e., who were not familiar with his record of service to his adopted country), followed at length by the reign of "the Pharaoh of the Oppression." Then began the long siege of forced labor in building projects, continued by the cruel aggressor Ramesses II (c. 1290–1224 B.C.)—accepted by many as "the Pharaoh of the Exodus." For two centuries the Jacob tribes were enslaved by taskmasters in charge of rebuilding Pithom (excavated in modern times, at Tell Retabeh) and Ramesses (Tanis—Per Re'emasese or "House of Ramesses") (Ex. 1:11). The Exodus of Hebrews from Egypt probably occurred c. 1290 B.C. Moses, leader of the Exodus, not only bore an Egyptian name, *Mōsheh*, from the abbreviated Egyptian name *Mâse*, but was reared by Pharaoh's daughter (Ex. 2:10). He was trained in "the wisdom of the Egyptians" (Acts 7:22), possibly at the religious center of Heliopolis (On*). The grandson of Aaron, Phineas, also had an Egyptian name, *Pi-nehase*, "the Nubian." Joseph, whose Egyptian name was Zaphnath-paaneah (Gen. 41:45), had married, at the peak of his official career at the court of Pharaoh, Asenath, daughter of Potipherah, priest (or prince) at Heliopolis, the center of sun-god worship, one of whose temple obelisks still stands on the edge of modern Cairo, and one in New York's Central Park. Asenath bore Joseph two sons in Egypt—Ephraim and Manasseh (Gen. 46:20), both of whom became heads of tribes and received "assignments" in the Promised Land.

Scripture contains many allusions to the Sojourn of the Jacob tribes in Egypt in addition to the Exodus account—throughout Deuteronomy and Kings and Samuel; Ps. 78:43, 51, 81:10, 105:23, 38, 106:7, 21, 114:1, 135:8, 9, 136:10; Amos 9:7; Micah 6:4; Hag. 2:5; Acts 7:9–40, 13:17; Heb. 3:16, 8:9, 11:26 f. The following prophets advised against turning to Egypt for help, when their people were hard pressed by other foes: Isaiah (30:1–7, 31:1, 36:6, 9); Jeremiah, who himself was ultimately carried off to Egypt (42, 43:6); and Hosea (7:11).

After the fall of Jerusalem in August of 587 B.C., groups of Jews descended to Egypt (Jer. 43). Papyri recovered from Elephantine, where a colony settled at the First Cataract, reveal that Jews there were observing the Passover* in 419 B.C. with standard procedure. In the Egypt of the era of the Jewish philosopher Philo (c. 20 B.C.–A.D. 50) there may have been 1,000,000 Jews. Alexandria* under the Ptolemies (323–30 B.C.) offered great privileges to Jews—even state offices. Nowhere else could Jews live as happily as at Alexandria, which made frank efforts to blend Hebrew and Hellenic cultures. To the presence of Jewish minds in Alexandria we owe the Septuagint translation of the O.T. and some of the Apocrypha from Hebrew to Greek.

(b) *Military aggression.* Before and after the forced residence of the Hebrew tribes in Egypt, Delta people made wave after wave of aggression into Palestine, robbing it and establishing bases in it for more distant conquests. During the Patriarchal Age Palestine and the coast of Syria were largely under Egyptian control. Almost throughout the Late Bronze Age (c. 1500–1200 B.C.) Palestine was tributary to Egypt. Only the fact that Egypt was weak in David's day (c. 1000–961 B.C.) made it possible for this able executive to amalgamate the N. and S. tribes into a united kingdom. The relation between Egypt and Palestine in the reign of David's son Solomon is shown by the fact that one of the latter's wives was daughter of the current Pharaoh, and lived in Jerusalem in a palace built for her by the Hebrew king (I Kings 7:8). (See WAR, illus. 474.)

(For the approximate dates of the Egyptian conquerors and their Palestinian invasions see chart under PHARAOH.)

(4) *Religious relations.* The influence of Egypt on the religion of Palestine was not as profound as might have been expected. Egypt was so unsympathetic toward her subjects that she felt no missionary impulse to spread her gods. In fact, she rather drew to herself her neighbors' deities. For example, she equated the Canaanite Baal with Seth; "the Lady of Byblos" with Hathor; and during the New Empire drew into her pantheon Astarte and Anath. Although the triad of Isis, Osiris, and Horus remained popular with Egyptian families, the roster of official Egyptian gods was fluid, and varied with successive rulers and their priesthoods. One of the greatest religious revolutions occurred when the spiritual young Pharaoh Akhenaton* or Amenophis IV (1370–1353 B.C.) displaced the powerful and menacing priesthood of Atum, centering at Karnak, with one which promoted the worship of the Heliopolitan Aton, an uncontaminated name for the Re-Harakhti of Heliopolis, symbolized by the burning sun disk surrounded by a uraeus serpent. Since the Hebrews of the Sojourn were in Egypt during this radical religious revolution, they could scarcely have been entirely ignorant of the innovation. Akhenaton, "the world's first monotheist," dreamed of banishing superstition and of establishing his new deity, Aton, as the one universal god, endowed with attributes in keeping with the size and magnificence of his vast empire, which extended throughout Egypt, Palestine, Syria, and the Euphrates basin. Marked parallels have been found between Akhenaton's great Hymn to the Aton and the Hebrew Psalm 104, both possibly

based on a common Syrian source. Parallels may be found between Akhenaton's beliefs concerning Aton and those of Judaism concerning Yahweh. Aton was the tender creative father of all, intangible yet ever-present; he was addressed by the young king as the "Father which art in Heaven"; he had no form of which graven images could be made, but he had as supreme symbol the sun disk, even as Christianity later adopted its emblem of the cross; he was known as "the God of Love," was compassionate, tender, merciful; was associated with joy; was one whose kingdom was "within" the hearts of men; was "the Lord of peace" and of truth. His advocate, Akhenaton, was such a pacifist that he

126. Egyptian canal.

lost wide realms rather than go to war. As Arthur Weigall says, "The Aton of Akhenaton has scarcely a quality which we do not attribute to God.'

But Hebrew slave laborers were probably not aware of religious revolutions in the upper social levels. The Jacob tribes in Egypt undoubtedly knew the local gods worshipped in individual cities. Ptah was honored at Memphis; Osiris at Abydos; the Apis bull at Memphis, where elaborate galleries of sarcophagi for mummified holders of the title of sacred bull have survived to modern times. And Horus was known to every Egyptian. At the first union of Upper and Lower Egypt in the prehistoric period, this hawk-headed god attained honor on a national scale which he never surrendered down through the Dynasties. (See HAWK, illus. 176.)

The countless gods of polytheistic Egypt cannot be enumerated here. Every aspect of nature, every object beheld, was thought to be inhabited by a spirit which could choose its own form—crocodile, tree, man, fish. The pantheon of Heliopolis included Temu, Shu, Tefnut, Seb, Nut, Osiris, Isis, Set, and Nephthys, besides the mighty Re-Harakhti and a vast company of minor gods. Other cities had their local pantheons; with the earth goddess Hathor, the fertility goddess Isis, Osiris, patron of agriculture, and his son Horus being universally adored.

The increased belief in magic, especially in the power of amulets (see AMULET) worn on the person, and the spiritual retrogression which led—despite the work of Moses—to the construction of the golden calf during the Exodus of the Jacob tribes, are reflections of the Sojourn experiences of the Hebrews—though Aaron's golden calf is not to be confused with the Mnevis or the Apis bulls of Egypt. Cf. Jeroboam's calves (I Kings 12:28 ff.).

The most important N.T. references to Egypt are in connection with the flight of Joseph, Mary, and the infant Jesus to its safety and their return to Palestine (Matt. 2:13–19; cf. Hos. 11:1, reflecting Ex. 4:22). Acts 2:10 indicates the presence of Egyptians in Jerusalem at Pentecost. Stephen summarized the Sojourn experience in his reply to the high priest (Acts 7); and in Acts 21:38 Paul is confused with an Egyptian insurrectionist. See also Rev. 11:8.

During the first Christian centuries Egypt was one of the most productive seed-beds for the new faith—according to the Eusebius tradition—under the evangelizing influence of John Mark and Apollos. Few historical data have come to light as yet concerning the birth of Coptic Christianity, influential in Egypt today.

(5) *Cultural relations.* The ancient Egyptian language was of the Hamitic family, closely related to the Semitic, of which Hebrew is a member. However, other than a few words of Egyptian origin found in the Bible there seems to have been little influence of Egyptian language or literature on the Hebrews.

Similarly, Egyptian art and architecture had little influence on ancient Israel. While Egyptian handicrafts were famous (Dan. 11:43), especially ivory, jewelry, pottery, metal work and textiles (Prov. 7:16; Ezek. 27:7), and many small art objects imported by the Hebrews and Canaanites have been found in Palestine, native artists rarely imitated them. The public buildings of Israel were generally constructed according to styles prevalent in Asia Minor, not Egypt. The Temple at Jerusalem, for example, bore no similarity to Egyptian structures but was built in accordance with ancient native Palestinian convention. Furthermore, when Solomon built his palaces and Temple he did not turn to Egypt for advice and assistance but to Phoenicia (see I Kings 5:18; 7:13, 14).

Belief in life after death and the practice of circumcision have been suggested as possible examples of Egyptian cultural influence on Palestine. However, these customs and beliefs were probably common over the entire ancient Near East. The calendars of the Hebrews and other inhabitants of Asia Minor were lunar or luni-solar and were little influenced by the Egyptian calendar, which was regularized about 2780 B.C. as a strictly solar calendar (see TIME). It must therefore be concluded that the Hebrews brought little or no cultural baggage from Egypt.

Egypt, River of, a broad, shallow wâdī or valley, rather than a stream, forming the S. boundary of Judah, draining the seasonal surplus water from the Wilderness of Paran* into the Mediterranean. Known today as Wâdī el-Arish, this line of demarcation between Sinai and Palestine (Num. 34:5) is 96½ m. NE. of Kantara, the point of ferrying over the Suez Canal into Egypt proper.

Ehud (ē'hŭd), a left-handed Benjamite who killed Eglon* king of Moab and 10,000 Moabites, and "judged" Israel (Judges 3:15–4:1).

Ekron (ĕk′rŏn), the northernmost of the five important cities of the Philistine plain (Josh. 13:3). On the boundary of Judah, it frequently changed hands between the Tribe of Dan and the Philistine lords (Josh. 15:11, 45 f.; Judg. 1:18; I Sam. 17:50–52). To it the Ark of the Covenant was carried after it had been transported by Philistines to Ashdod and Gath, with dire results for the inhabitants (I Sam. 5:10–12, 6:17). At Ekron the god Baal-zebub was "consulted" by agents of Israel's King Ahaziah (c. 850–849 B.C.) (II Kings 1:2–6). Ekron is mentioned in judgments of doom pronounced by Amos (1:8); Zephaniah (2:4); and Zechariah (9:5, 7). It is probably now Khirbet al-Muqanna', between the Mediterranean coast and the Judaean highlands, S. of the Valley of Sorek. Surface exploration indicates a 40-acre, fortified Iron I settlement with some Philistine pottery. See *IEJ* 8, 1958, pp. 87 ff., 165 ff.; *PEQ*, 1958, pp. 27–31.

El (Canaanite, "*the* god"; Heb., "the divine being"), *El Elyon* (to Hebrews, "the Highest God," "Possessor or Creator of heaven and earth," as in Gen. 14:19), *El Elôhê Yisrael* ("the God of Israel" as in Gen. 33:20; cf. Josh. 8:30), *Elohim* (to Hebrews, "Deity," pl. of Canaanite *El*). When waves of Hebrews migrated into Palestine from Mesopotamia in the Patriarchal Age (c. 20th–19th centuries B.C.), they found Canaanites worshipping El, *the* god, "generally a rather remote and shadowy figure, like Sumero-Accadian Anu, god of heaven; or Egyptian Re, the sun-god" (Albright, *Archaeology and the Religion of Israel*), and a storm-god son named Shaddai. While in Babylonia the Hebrews had also known El Shaddai, god of mountain(s), a word whose etymology is uncertain but which may root in "to act violently," indicating primordial strength. The Genesis passages mentioning El Shaddai are often inaccurately translated "God Almighty," whereas El Elyon does literally connote "highest God," and may have been understood as "God Most High" even before Moses'* revelation at Horeb identified him with Yahweh.

The Canaanite El, whom arriving Hebrews saw honored at many shrines, was probably the counterpart of the Syrian Hadad and the Hittite Teshub. As revealed in recovered Ras Shamrah clay tablets from c. 1400 B.C., the Canaanite El lived in a remote region called "the Source of the Two Deeps"; he was a passive father who received dependents and sent forth messengers. The god whom Abraham saw being worshipped by the priest-king Melchizedek in Salem (? the later Jerusalem) (Gen. 14:18) was "the most high God." When Jacob built an altar at Shechem* he called it "El, the God of Israel" (*El Elôhê Yisrael*, Gen. 33:20).

The people who became Israel used in various eras different names for Him who ultimately became their revealed God. In the P document the following development is indicated:

(1) From Adam through Noah to Abraham, God was "Elohim" (pl., "Deity"), as in Gen. 33:20.

(2) From Abraham to Moses. He was called "El Shaddai," (Gen. 35:11, A.S.V. marg.).

(3) Beginning with Moses' experience at Horeb, God was Yahweh (Eng., "Jehovah"), the El Shaddai of shepherds, and the "I am the Lord" of Ex. 6:29.

The Jacob tribes which descended to Egypt found the Delta-dwelling people worshipping a powerful old sun god, Re*, most popular of Egyptian cosmic deities. (Syncretism* may explain the festivities of Israel depicted in Ex. 32, and the bull-cult shrines erected at Bethel and Dan after the division of Solomon's kingdom).

But Israel's real and vital discovery of God* came from their community experience following the revelation of Yahweh to Moses when Deity spoke from a burning desert bush (Ex. 3:6, 14, 16), declaring himself to be the God of the fathers Abraham, Isaac, and Jacob; the "I AM THAT I AM" (3:14); the one known to Jethro, Midianite father-in-law of Moses, as Yahweh, "the Lord . . . greater than all gods" (18:11); the God whom Hebrews had known when shepherds became, as chanted in the Song of Moses at the Sea of Reeds (Ex. 15:3–11), the all-powerful Lord of strength, "a man of war," overwhelming His enemies. At this point the patriarchal experiences and the divine wisdom acquired by Moses in Egypt and at Sinai fused into a glorious revelation of Yahweh. For the time being the new people—who a few centuries later divided into two kingdoms, one of whom worshipped El in N. Palestine or Israel, and the other of whom preferred the Yahweh aspect of God in Judah—were united in a largely monotheistic conception of the Almighty. The two trends became vocal in the J or Jehovistic (Yahwistic) document of Judah and the E or Elohistic source (see SOURCES) which developed largely in Ephraim or the N. Kingdom.

It took several generations for heathen beliefs to be weeded out from Israel's religious life and a true Yahwistic monotheism established. Even as late as the Monarchy, apostasies were rampant (I Kings 11:5–8). These were protested by Hebrew prophets until the carrying away to Babylon in the 6th century B.C. Backsliding was the easier because the Hebrews lived among the Canaanites; indeed patriarchal Hebrews took over many shrines once used for the worship of Canaanite gods, and rededicated them to El Shaddai. Proper names such as El-bethel ("the El of the House of El") (Gen. 35:7); El-paran (A.S.V. Gen. 14:6); El-berith (A.S.V. Judg. 9:46)—already assigned to worship when the Patriarchs reached Canaan—indicate the very early use of these centers for worship. It is evident that Hebrews settling in Palestine during the Conquest were often influenced by what the Canaanites thought of their supreme deity. Clay tablets excavated from the 1400 B.C. level at Ras Shamrah on the N. Syrian coast speak of El as "the father of men and gods," the influential "father of years" (*abu shanîma*). But when the political disintegration of the always loose-knit Canaan occurred under 15th-century Egyptian pharaohs, the national El declined in influence and was seriously challenged by local Baals (see BAAL), to whom Canaanites looked for agricultural production. Baalism influenced Israel, which found it easy to adopt its neighbors' religious customs, along with many of their social and economic standards.

Scores of Hebrew personal names embody El as a syllable, like Elead ("God has testified"); Eleazar ("God has helped"); Eliakim ("God will establish"); Eliezer ("God is a helper"). In the Book of Job, El, Eloah, and Shaddai are all names for God, used interchangeably to avoid repetition. Elohim (God) is used so many times in Ps. 42–83 that this section of the Hebrew hymnal is known as the Elohistic Psalter. Here Elohim is used four times as often for God as Yahweh; in the rest of the Psalter Yahweh is used twenty times as frequently as Elohim.

Elah (ē'lȧ). (1) A valley of Central Palestine (Wâdī es-Sant) about half way between Bethlehem and the Mediterranean, protected by the fortified towns Libnah and Azekah. It was used by Philistines and others to gain access to Central Palestine. There David slew Goliath (I Sam. 17:2, 19 ff.). (2) A son of Baasha*, the 4th king of Israel, who acceded to throne and ruled less than two years (c. 877–876), and was killed while drunk by Zimri, his successor, in his capital, Tirzah (I Kings 16:6–14). (3) The father of Hoshea, the last king of Israel (c. 732–724 B.C.) (II Kings 15:30).

Elam (ē'lăm) (Accad. "highland"). (1) A land across the Persian Gulf from old Babylonia, SE. of what became Assyria, SW. of Media, on the main caravan routes to India, Babylon, Palestine, and Egypt; a province of modern Iran, in the Zagros Mts.; occupied by a very ancient people, which may have been part of the pre-Sumerian population of Babylonia. The Biblical listing of a man named Elam as son of Shem and grandson of Noah (Gen. 10:22) is an effort to express the writer's knowledge of the early origin of the Elamites, though he was inaccurate in implying that they were Semites (*Shem*itic). They had their own Anzanite language and a system of writing used for centuries. The Elamite capital was Susa (Shushan*) (Neh. 1:1; Esther 1:2, etc.; Dan. 8:2). The Biblical allusion to Elamites as a wild, plundering people, skillful with bow and arrow (Jer. 49:35–39), tallies with modern archaeological discoveries. For example, in their mountain fastness capital at Susa—a safe storage place for booty—the priceless stone inscribed with the Code of Hammurabi* was found in A.D. 1901–1902, where it had lain ever since Elamite warriors had carried it there many centuries before. Yet Elamite culture has been revealed in pottery excavated by the French in a cemetery at the foot of the Susa citadel, on a level immediately above virgin soil. This pottery is claimed to be older than the al-'Ubaid (pre-Sumerian) painted types. Elam was the scene of pioneer excavations in the Middle East (1849–1853).

From Elam the first invaders entered old Sumeria; yet sometimes Elam was under Sumerian rule, allied by marriage. But an Elamite, Ibi-Sin, ended the famous Third Dynasty of Ur, and an Elamite dynasty ruled a united Sumer and Accad*, paving the way for the great Amorite ruler of Babylonia, Hammurabi. In an Elamite raid on Ur*, the famous stele of Ur-Nammu telling of construction of the *ziggurat* (temple foundation tower) at Ur was broken and the pieces scattered. In modern times archaeologists from the University Museum at Philadelphia found it, pieced it together, and placed it in their Babylonian collection as a chief treasure.

127. Bronze head of Iranian ruler, 2d century B.C., from Tiklon Teppeh, Azerbaijan, Iran.

Genesis (14:1–11) tells how Chedorlaomer*, king of Elam, the acknowledged head of several Babylonian states, kept the Dead Sea-Jordan region under tribute and precipitated the trek of Abraham to rescue his nephew, Lot. During the 8th and 7th centuries B.C. Elamites allied with Chaldaeans against Assyria, but saw their capital, Susa, fall (c. 640 B.C.). This winter capital of Darius I and his successors, and the capital of the Persian Empire, has left to posterity masonry outlining its foundations, some of its pavements, and glazed tiles from the reign of Artaxerxes II. Fierce Elamites helped Assyria invade Judah (Isa. 22:6; see also Isa. 11:11, 21:2). Ezekiel pictured Elam as aiding Egypt (32:24). Elam is a fine example of the shifting political alignments of borderland nations throughout history. Jeremiah (25:25) listed "outcasts of Elam" among those to feel God's "judgments" (49:35).

Cyrus* the Great (born c. 598 B.C.), founder of the Persian Empire and conqueror of Babylonia, was 4th hereditary prince of Anshan, the section of Elam S. of Susa, but spoke Persian rather than Elamitic, and considered himself a Persian.

Elamites were in Jerusalem on the Day of Pentecost (Acts 2:9).

(2) A Jew whose descendants are listed (Ezra 2:7, 31 8:7) in the registry of those who returned from Exile with Zerubbabel (520–516 B.C.) and Ezra (458 B.C. or later). Some Elamites acknowledged their sin in marrying "foreign wives" and made atonement for it. Elam agreed to the reform covenant (Neh. 10:14).

(3) A priest who took part in the dedication of the repaired walls of Jerusalem (Neh. 12:42).

Elath (ē′lăth). See EZION-GEBER.

El-Bethel (ĕl′ bĕth′ ĕl) ("God of Bethel"), an altar built by Jacob at Bethel after he returned from Mesopotamia, commemorating God's appearance to him when he was fleeing from his brother (Gen. 35:7; cf. 28:10 ff.).

Eldad (ĕl′dăd) ("God has loved"), one of the seventy elders summoned to assist Moses. Though Eldad did not go to the Tabernacle with the others, he also received the gift of the Lord's Spirit and prophesied. Moses, rebuking Joshua who would have forbidden Eldad to prophesy, said: "Would God that all the Lord's people were prophets, and that the Lord would put his spirit upon them!" (Num. 11:24–29).

elder, the head of a family or of a tribe (I Kings 8:1–3; Judg. 8:14, 16). Since usually it was men of mature age who came into these positions of responsibility, they were known as "elders." See also CHURCH.

Eleazar (ĕl′ ē-ā′ zẽr) ("God has helped"), the name of at least 11 men in the O.T. (1) The most prominent was the 3d son of Aaron* (Ex. 6:23; Num. 3:2) and father of Phinehas (Ex. 6:25). He became chief of the Levites and overseer of the sanctuary custodians (Num. 3:32), and succeeded Aaron as high priest (20:25 ff., Deut. 10:6), an office he held during the remainder of Moses' life and under Joshua's leadership. He cooperated with Joshua and the tribal heads in allotting territory to the Children of Israel in Canaan (Josh 14:1). (2) An Eleazar who was an ancestor of Joseph appears in Matthew's list of the ancestors of Jesus (1:15).

election, the doctrine that God chooses certain individuals or groups to be the agents of His purpose. In the O.T. it is primarily Israel which He chooses to be His own people (Ex. 19:5) and the mediators of His salvation to the rest of the world (Isa. 49:3, 6). Israel's election first became manifest in the election of its ancestor Abraham (Gen. 12:1–3). In the N.T. God's election is a call to individuals to have faith in Christ and thereby become Abraham's true descendants (Gal. 3:7) and members of the elect community, committed to a certain kind of life (Col. 3:12 ff.). Neither the O.T. nor the N.T. conceives of election as foreordination to a privileged status. It involves, rather, choice to accept moral responsibility and serve God in special ways (Amos 3:2). The Christian must therefore work to make his election sure (II Peter 1:10). Nevertheless, God's elect live with a consciousness of God's special love and favor (Mark 13:20; Rom. 8:33). R. C. D.

Elephantine. See EGYPT; PASSOVER; SYENE; TEMPLE.

Eleusis. See MYSTERY.

Eleven, the, a term applied to the original Twelve Disciples, minus the traitor Judas (Mark 16:14; Matt. 28:16; Luke 24:9, 33; Acts 1:26, 2:14).

Elhanan (ĕl-hā′năn). (1) Son of Dodo of Bethlehem; one of David's thirty men, II Sam. 23:24, I Chron. 11:26. (2) Son of Jair, who slew Goliath (A.S.V., R.S.V., Moff., II Sam. 21:19) or the brother of Goliath (I Chron. 20:5, A.V. II Sam. 21:19). This contradiction may be explained by a corruption in the Heb. text of the Books of Samuel or by an effort to ascribe to the hero David an achievement of Elhanan.

Eli (possibly a contraction from "God is high"), a weak judge and priest at Shiloh*, where the Ark reposed for a time. To him Hannah and Elkanah brought young Samuel to serve "unto the Lord" (I Sam. 3:1). His line came to an end when his two evil sons, Hophni and Phinehas, were slain while vainly trying to guard the Ark during the Philistine siege. When the old man heard the news, he fell backward from his seat by the gate, his neck was broken, and he died. He had judged Israel 40 years (I Sam. 2:22–4:18). With his death the office of judge lost its importance for a long time, and Samuel became the religious leader of the people. As prophesied, the priesthood of the house of Eli then ended (I Kings 2:27).

Eli (Eloi), **Eli** (Eloi), **lama sabachthani** ("My God, my God, why hast thou forsaken me?"), 4th cry in the series of seven uttered by Christ from the cross. It was addressed to God, and spoken "with a loud voice" (Matt. 27:46; Mark 15:34). Confusion has attended its interpretation, not because it was not heard, but because it was not understood. If Psalm 22:1 is here quoted, it is a free Aram. translation of the Heb., suggesting the familiarity of Jesus with the vernacular Aram. version of the O.T. The oldest MSS. reflect this confusion of language, even as do Matthew and Mark, who alone record it. Mark preserves the Aram. *Eloi;* Matthew, its Hebrew equivalent, *Eli.* Similarity in sound led those of the multitude who did not understand Galilean Aramaic, but only Hebrew, to believe that Jesus was calling to Elijah for help (Matt. 27:47). This belief in the second coming of the prophet was current in the apocalyptic thought of the day. The absence of this cry from the Fourth Gospel has been attributed to the fact that when it was spoken John was busily absorbed fulfilling the mission entrusted to him by Jesus (John 19:26, 37). Luke, who used Greek sources for his Gospel, may have been so distressed by what to him was a cry of desertion that he omitted it as offensive to his readers. No Galilean, no apostle, or well-educated man like Paul, who understood Aramaic, felt called upon to explain or defend this phrase. The Jews would willingly have used the claim that Jesus had been deserted by God if such had been the meaning of this utterance. If the word *sabachthani* comes from the Aram.

verb *sabach*, and the suffix *ni* is the first person singular, the passage could be translated according to some Aramaic authorities, "My God, my God, for this was I kept [spared, reserved]." Such a translation from the Aram. would be in complete harmony with Christ's earlier utterance (John 16:32). Without some such understanding of the confused text at this point, the theological interpretation must suffice. God did not desert Jesus in the sense that He shut Himself off from the reach of the Saviour; but the sin of the world which Christ here voluntarily assumed, momentarily clouded the Son's vision of the Father. Christ's despair and misery, however, were not enough to keep him from addressing God as "My God." Such faith resulted in the 7th cry from the cross (Luke 23:46).

Eliab (ē-lī'ăb), the name of six O.T. men. (1) The son of Helon and captain of the children of Zebulun (Num. 1:9, 2:7, 7:24, 29, 10:16). (2) A Reubenite, father of Dathan and Abiram (Num. 16:1), and son of Pallu (Num. 26:8). (3) A descendant of Levi (I Chron. 6:27). (4) David's eldest brother (I Sam. 16:6, 17:13, 28; I Chron. 2:13). His granddaughter was taken to wife by Rehoboam (II Chron. 11:18). (5) A Gadite captain who joined David's forces at Ziklag (I Chron. 12:8, 9). (6) A Levite musician at the sanctuary (I Chron. 15:20, 16:5).

Eliakim (ē-lī'a-kĭm) (Heb. "my God establishes"). (1) A son of Hilkiah, steward of King Hezekiah's palace, and one of three of the king's delegation to confer with the Assyrian Rabshakeh bearing Sennacherib's demands for surrender (II Kings 18:18–37; Isa. 36:3–22). Thereafter Eliakim was sent by Hezekiah to Isaiah (Isa. 37:2), and reported to the king the prophet's advice. Prior to these events Isaiah had prophesied (Isa. 22:20–25) that Eliakim would displace Shebna "over the house" of the king. (2) A brother of Jehoahaz*, whom he succeeded as King of Judah (c. 609 B.C.) under the name "Jehoiakim" when the Egyptian Pharaoh-nechoh carried off Jehoahaz to Egypt (II Chron. 36:4). He raised the tribute of silver and gold for Pharaoh (II Kings 23:35) from the people. He reigned 11 years, until c. 598 B.C.; and was succeeded by his son, Jehoiachin*. (3) A priest participating in the rededication of the Jerusalem walls (Neh. 12:41). (4) A son of Abiud and ancestor of Joseph (Matt. 1:13). (5) A son of Melea, ancestor of Jesus (Luke 3:30).

Eliam (ē-lī'ăm) (Heb. "my God is kinsman"). (1) The father of Bath-sheba (II Sam. 11:3). (2) A son of the Gilonite Ahithophel, one of David's mighty men (II Sam. 23:34). The two may be the same.

Elias. See ELIJAH.

Eliashib (ē-lī'ȧ-shĭb) ("my God brings back"), name of several O.T. men, most of whom were associated with the Temple services. (1) A son of Elinoenai, descendant of Zerubbabel (I Chron. 3:24). (2) The head of a priestly house to whom fell the 11th lot in line of Temple service (I Chron. 24:12). (3) A high priest second in succession from Jeshua (Neh. 12:10), contemporary with Nehemiah; father of Joiada. He assisted in rebuilding Jerusalem's walls (Neh. 3:1, 20, f.). He was allied to the Ammonite Tobiah (Neh. 13:5) and did not oppose foreign marriages (13:28). (4) A singing Levite who put away his foreign wife (Ezra 10:10, 19, 24).

Eliel (ē'lī-ĕl) ("my God is God"). (1) Ancestor of Samuel (I Chron. 6:34). See ELIHU. (2, 3) Two of David's mighty men (I Chron. 11:46, 47). (4) A Gadite who joined David (I Chron. 12:1, 8, 11). (5) A Levite of David's time (I Chron. 15:9, 11). (6, 7) Two Benjamites (I Chron. 8:20, 22). (8) A chief man of Manasseh (I Chron. 5:24). (9) An overseer of tithes in Hezekiah's reign (II Chron. 31:13).

Eliezer (ĕl'ĭ-ē'zẽr) ("my God is helper"), the name of numerous O.T. men, including a steward of Abraham (Gen. 15:2); the younger son of Moses (Ex. 18:4); a priest who was in the escort of the Ark to Jerusalem (I Chron. 15:24); a prophet who predicted the shipwreck of Jehoshaphat's vessels (II Chron. 20:37); and an ancestor of Jesus in the Luke genealogy (3:29). Cf. also I Chron. 7:8, 27:16; Ezra 10:10, 18, 23, 31.

Elihu (ē-lī'hū) ("my God is he"). (1) Ephraimite, son of Tohu and great-grandfather of Samuel (I Sam. 1:1). (2) The eldest brother of David, called also Eliab*. (3) A Manassite captain who joined David's forces (I Chron. 12:20). (4) A doorkeeper in David's reign (I Chron. 26:7). (5) A disputant with Job (Job 32–37).

Elijah (Heb. *Elīyāh*, Gk. *Elias*, "Jehovah is my God"), a great prophet of the Northern Kingdom in the 9th century B.C.; one of the most dynamic of Israel's religious leaders, who shaped the history of his day, and dominated Hebrew thinking for centuries later.

The story of Elijah (I Kings 17–19, 21; II Kings 1, 2) was recorded probably by a member of the prophetic school founded by Elijah and Elisha* (I Kings 19:19; II Kings 2:15), and represents the popular oral tradition passed on for half a century. Unlike Amos, Isaiah, Jeremiah, and the later prophets, Elijah and Elisha left no personal written words or records. The unnamed editor of Kings has entwined this Elijah cycle (written c. 800 B.C. in the Northern kingdom, with information derived from the "Chronicles of the Kings of Israel" (I Kings 22:39; II Kings 1:18), the official records from the court in Samaria. These are blended with other contemporary materials from the time of Ahab.

Elijah was a Tishbite (I Kings 17:1), but the location of Tishbeh is uncertain. It may have been Lisdīb in the Kingdom of Jordan, SE. of the Sea of Galilee. Glueck, correcting a small scribal error, believes that Elijah came from Jabesh-gilead*, and calls him "Elijah the Jabeshite" (see Glueck, *The River Jordan*, p. 170). The prophet's unconventional appearance and dress (II Kings 1:8), his fleetness of foot (I Kings 18:46), his rugged constitution, which resisted famine (I Kings 19:8), his cave-dwelling habits (I Kings 17:3, 19:9) all point to his being a robust outdoor man. These outdoor tastes were emphasized when Elijah made his long trek across the desert to Mt. Horeb, where he relived some of the cosmic experiences which had attended the original giving of the law to Moses about four centuries earlier on that same mount, and in addition, received his theophany* (I Kings 19:8–13). The authority of the still, small voice was added to that of the Ten Commandments. Thus the historic process of the revelation* of God for matters of conduct was carried from fixed laws applicable to a simple agrarian state into the more complex forms of society through the direct revelation which the individual could receive from God Himself (I Kings 19:15 f.).

Israel was the laboratory where Elijah demonstrated the power of this direct contact with God. King Ahab* (869–850 B.C.) had married Jezebel of Tyre, and while giving nominal allegiance to Yahweh, had permitted Jezebel to promote the worship of her Phoenician Baal* (Melkarth), with its colorful ritual and lax and vulgar immoralities.

One of the periodic famines had been cursing the land of Ahab. Elijah pronounced this as one of the direct cosmic consequences of Israel's sin (I Kings 17:1, 18:18). The food shortage of this period is indicated by Elijah's being fed by "ravens" (I Kings 17:2–7); by the scanty oil and meal supply of the Zarephath widow (I Kings 17:8–16); and by Ahab and his court official Obadiah looking for pasture land to keep horses and mules alive. Near the wooded SE. headland of Mt. Carmel* a dramatic contest between Elijah and the prophets of Baal was held, to determine the true God (I Kings 18:17–38). God answered Elijah's prayer (I Kings 18:36 f.; James 5:17 f.). The result was the end of much theological uncertainty among the people (I Kings 18:21; cf. 18:39) and the conclusion of the drought (I Kings 18:41–45). This checking of Baal worship in Israel was a blow to immorality, occasioned a restatement of the priority of Yahweh over all other gods. and was an important step in strengthening monotheism* (I Kings 17:8–16; Luke 4:26; I Kings 18:26; cf. I Kings 19:15). Elijah's

128. Elijah's "Place of the Burning," showing Plain of Jezreel (Esdraelon) and mountains of Samaria.

prophecy that the wicked Omri dynasty would end (I Kings 21:21–24; II Kings 1:16) was fulfilled when King Ahab died in the battle of Ramoth-gilead (I Kings 22:1–40), Ahaziah, his son, perished from a fall in the palace at Samaria (II Kings 1:1–17), and Jezebel, Joram, Ahaziah's brothers, and the decendants of Ahab living in Samaria were slaughtered during Jehu's revolt (see JEHU) (II Kings 9:24–26, 30–37; 10:1–11).

Elijah selected Elisha as his disciple (I Kings 19:19–21). The transfer of spiritual leadership from the elderly Elijah to young Elisha is dramatically described in II Kings 2:1–15. In this same Jordan country, Moses had died, though his grave was never found. Here, now, Elijah neither died nor was buried. Enoch* alone shared the translation experience of Elijah (Gen. 5:24). The word of the Lord, which "he spoke by his servant Elijah," lived on (II Kings 9:36, 10:10, 17). Even the

Chronicler, not always accurate as to history, but always a good propagandist for his Judaean point of view and laudable spiritual objectives, made use of Elijah's prestige (II Chron. 21:12–15) (see CHRONICLES I and II). It became a fixed belief that this Elijah, who had never died, would appear again to restore Israel, before "the great and dreadful day of the Lord" (Mal. 4:5 f.).John the Baptist* was identified with Elijah (Luke 1:17).Many people thought Jesus was Elijah (Matt. 16:14). When Jesus cried on the cross, "Eli, Eli," etc. (Matt. 27:47; Mark 15:35), the multitude mistook his Aramaic for a call to the Tishbite. At the Transfiguration* Moses and Elijah, both of whose passings from this life were more spiritual than earthly, were seen sharing the event with Jesus (Matt. 17:3; Mark 9:4; Luke 9:30). These two prophetic attendants were fitting companions for Jesus who was also to ascend into heaven.

In Palestine at the SE. end of the Mt. Carmel Ridge, 12 m. from Haifa, the supposed "Place of the Burning" (El-Muhraqah) is pointed out. Also a majestic Mediterranean headland has been consecrated as the onetime habitation of the prophet. Both sites at least bring vividness to the re-enacting of the drama presented in I Kings 18:21–39. In the Wâdī el-Qelt, a monastery named for Elijah see QELT, illus. 336) is a monument to his name near the Jordan Valley. Greek Christians keep his memory green with a happy summer festival. At the Jewish Passover the door is opened in expectation of his return and a cup of wine is poured for him.

Elim (ē′lĭm), the refreshing oasis of 70 palm trees and 12 wells of potable water which was the 2d camp site of wandering Israel (Ex. 15:27, 16:1; Num. 33:9 f.) after crossing the Sea (Lake) of Reeds, S. of the Great Bitter Lake, misnamed by some O.T. translators of Heb. *Yam Suph*, "Red Sea." Elim may be the Wâdī Gharandel, 63 m. SE. from the present Suez, and 7 m. S. of 'Ain Hawarah (Marah) on the main caravan route from Egypt to the turquoise and copper mines of Sinai. Short palms, acacias, and tamarisks shaded the wanderers as they drank safely from the abundant water holes. The presence of Egyptian guards along the copper route may account for Israel's short sojourn in Elim (Ex. 16:1); this too prompt departure for the Wilderness contributed to the protests of "the whole congregation . . . against Moses and Aaron" (Ex. 16:2).

Elimelech (ē-lĭm′ĕ-lĕk) ("my God is king"), a Bethlehemite, husband of Naomi* and father of Mahlon (husband of Ruth) and Chilion (Ruth 1:2). In time of famine he fled to Moab with his family, and died there (v. 3). His Bethlehem property was purchased by his kinsman Boaz, who married Ruth (Ruth 2:1, 3, 4:3, 9).

Eliphaz (ĕl′ĭ-făz), the eldest and most moderate of Job's disputants, bears a name stemming from Eliphaz, son of Esau and father of Teman. For his part in the dialogue with Job, see chaps. 3–8, 15, 22–24. Eliphaz and his two friends were rebuked (42:7–9) for their indignation against Job.

Eliphelet (ē-lĭf′ĕ-lĕt), alternate forms: Eliphal, Eliphalet, Elpalet, Elpelet ("my God delivers"). (1) One or possibly two sons of David (II Sam. 5:16; cf. I Chron. 3:5 f.). (2) One of David's mighty men (II Sam. 23:34). (3) A descendant of Saul and Jonathan (I Chron. 8:39). (4) A son "of Adonikam," who returned from Babylon with Ezra (Ezra 8:13). (5) A Hebrew who took a foreign wife during the Captivity (Ezra 10:33).

Elisabeth, of the house of Aaron, married a prophet, Zacharias (R.S.V. Zechariah), living in the hill country of Judaea, possibly near 'Ain Karem, 4 m. N. of Jerusalem. To him she bore in her old age a son, later known as John the Baptist*. She occasioned two of the

129. 'Ain Karem, a traditional scene of Luke 1:39.

greatest poems in the N.T.—the "Magnificat"* of Mary, who was to become the mother of Jesus, and who visited Elisabeth before the birth of John, and responded to her kinswoman's exultant greeting with the remarkable words of what has been called "The Song of Mary" (Luke 1:46–55); and the "Benedictus" of Zacharias, pronounced prophetically after the birth of John (Luke 1:68–79). Both of these poems are parts of the ritual of the Christian Church today. Elisabeth and Mary have always been associated in sacred art.

Elisha ("my God is salvation"), (Eliseus, A.V. Luke 4:27), son of Shaphat, successor to Elijah*, and prophet of the Northern Kingdom, Israel. Fulfilling a divine commission, Elijah found Elisha at Abel-meholah ("meadow of the dance"), a hill town (Tell el-Maqlub) E. of the Jordan on the Wâdī Yabis, a little NE. of Elijah's birthplace at Jabesh-gilead (Glueck). There, on his father's extensive estate, Elisha was driving one of the 12 yokes of oxen plowing the fertile plain (I Kings 19:15 f., 19). When the elder prophet cast his mantle upon Elisha, this well-to-do farmer's son understood the invitation implied in the ritual; sacrificed the team of oxen at a farewell feast for his friends and neighbors; kissed his father and mother goodbye; and became the lowly but devoted helper and disciple of Elijah (I Kings 19:20 f.; II Kings 2:2, 12, 3:11). That mantle was the symbol of prophetic succession and power when it fell on Elisha from Elijah, who mysteriously made his exit from this life on the banks of the Jordan (II Kings 2:8–14).

Elisha was in striking contrast to his master. He was bald (II Kings 2:23; cf. II Kings 1:8); wore conventional garments (II Kings 2:12, cf. II Kings 1:8); and carried a walking stick (II Kings 4:29), a staff which at times was his proxy. Unlike Elijah, he frequented towns (II Kings 6:13, 19), and had his own house in Samaria (II Kings 6:32). A Shunammite woman reserved a furnished room in her home for the itinerant man of God, who enjoyed such comfortable accommodations (II Kings 4:8–13). He resembled the group prophets in his use of music to induce an ecstatic condition in which he would receive the word of the Lord (II Kings 3:15; cf. I Sam. 9:5 f.). The historian records only a few scenes in Elijah's life; but he fills the record of Elisha with undated daily ministries of human helpfulness. Springs, so necessary for man and beast, were sweetened by Elisha,

130. Elisha's Spring.

and the whole Jericho community (as at 'Ain es-Sultan NW. of modern Jericho) benefited and was grateful (II Kings 2:19–22). A home devastated by death, hunger, debt, and slavery was economically rehabilitated (II Kings 4:1–7). He miraculously restored the Shunammite's son after a fatal sunstroke (II Kings 4:8–37. See also II Kings 4:38–41, 42–44, 5:1–19, 6:1–7).

The ministry of Elisha lasted for a half century during the reigns of Joram (c. 849–842 B.C.), Jehu (c. 842–815 B.C.), Jehoahaz (c. 815–801 B.C.), and Joash (c. 801–786 B.C.). Elisha had such wisdom and popularity that kings sought his counsel. He took an active part in political affairs. At the earnest solicitation of the coalition leaders of Israel, Judah, and Edom in their war against Moab, Elisha outlined a practical plan of irrigation by building trenches which channeled the rainfall of the uplands into the wâdīs of Edom, bringing relief for the soldiers and animals of the allied troops (II Kings 3:9–20). Elisha repeatedly warned the imperiled King of Israel in time for him to escape capture by marauding Syrians (II Kings 6:10). Once the prophet's advice, to return good for evil, was heeded by the king, who fed the trapped Syrians and sent them home unharmed (II Kings 6:21–23). Later, the king of Syria, with a great force, returned to besiege Samaria. This time Elisha counseled resistance to the bitter end. The city was reduced to famine. Revolt among the defenders threatened. Unseen spiritual forces, in which Elisha had encouraged Israel to believe, rescued the defenders over night, and the Syrians fled in panic (II Kings 6:24–7:20).

Elisha's services to Israel were on such a high spiritual plane, and his ministries so favorably known everywhere, that when he visited Damascus Ben-hadad, the sick Syrian king, sought his counsel. Elisha courageously diagnosed the illness of the king as fatal, and finished Elijah's work by anointing Hazael, Ben-hadad's messenger, as King of Syria, one who was destined to be the bitter enemy of Israel (II Kings 8:7–15; I Kings 19:15). Elisha, in arranging the anointing of Jehu*, King of Israel, toppled Joram from his unsteady throne, and brought to an end the Omri-Ahab-Jezebel dynasty in the Northern Kingdom (II Kings 9:1). King Joash, grandson of Jehu, grateful for the service rendered to his country and his royal line, visited the aged, dying prophet, who dramatically revealed to the young king the fate which awaited the fatherland (II Kings 13:14–19). So wonderful was Elisha's reputation for wisdom and miracles of service and helpfulness to all classes, that incredible tales were circulated concerning what happened around the burial place of the prophet.

Three periods in Bible history are especially characterized by stories of miracles. Each was an era of religious crisis and progress. The first was under Moses; the second, in the time of Elijah and Elisha; the third, in "the days of His flesh."

Elishah, son of Javan (Gen. 10:4), whose name was given to an ancient people and their land, identity unknown. The reference in Ezek. 27:7 suggests Carthage, S. Italy, or Greece.

Elkanah (ĕl-kā′n*ȧ*) ("God has acquired"). (1) An Ephraimite who married Hannah and Peninnah; father of Samuel (I Sam. 1:2, 20). (2) A warrior who joined David at Ziklag (A.S.V. I Chron. 12:6). (3) An official at the court of Ahaz of Samaria (II Chron. 28:7).

Ellasar (ĕl-lā′sär), a city-state (Gen. 14:1) whose king, Arioch, was allied with Chedorlaomer in the "four kings vs. five kings" warfare near the Dead Sea (Gen. 14). It may possibly be identified with ancient Larsa in lower Babylonia. Abraham's participation in the events precipitated by this contest (Gen. 14:12–17) synchronizes with recent knowledge gained through material excavated from the level of the transition from the kings of Isin and Larsa and the First Dynasty of Babylon—a period known as "the Age of Abraham." A remarkable seated statuette of Ningal, wife of the moon god Nannar, whose temple stood on the famous *ziggurat** (staged tower), is now in the University Museum, Philadelphia. This work of art was carried from Ur* to Susa c. 2000 B.C. by Elamites and their allies; then was brought back 40 years later to take part in the revival of the moon cult in Ur, rebuilt by the rulers of Larsa and Isin.

Elnathan (ĕl-nā′thăn), a man of Jerusalem whose daughter Nehushta became mother of King Jehoiachin* (II Kings 24:8).

Elohim (ĕl-ō′hĭm). See EL.

Elohist (ĕ-lō′hĭst). See SOURCES; E.

Elon (ē′lŏn). (1) The father of Bashemath*, one of Esau's Hittite wives (Gen. 26:34). (2) A son of Zebulun and founder of a tribal family (Gen. 46:14; Num. 26:26). (3) A "judge" of Israel (Judges 12:11 f.). (4) A village of Dan (Josh. 19:43).

El Shaddai (ĕl shăd′ī), the name assigned by the Hebrew Patriarchs to their family god, as indicated time and again in the Priestly Code, where El Shaddai—improperly translated in A.V. Gen. 17:1 and Ex. 6:3 "the Almighty God" and "God Almighty"—should be rendered to bring out the meaning of the old Mesopotamian words, "The Mountain One." "Shaddai" was incorporated in personal names, as seen in Numbers. After Moses' experience at Horeb Israel identified El Shaddai with Yahweh (Jehovah). See EL; EXODUS; GOD.

Elul (ĕ-lōōl′), 6th month of the Hebrew year, corresponding approximately to September. See TIME.

Elymas (ĕl′ĭ-măs) or Bar-Jesus ("son of Jesus" or "Joshua"), a false prophet and sorcerer whom Paul encountered in Cyprus on his First Missionary Journey (Acts 13:6–12).

embalming, the preparation of bodies for the tomb, usually by Egyptians (see BURIAL; MUMMIFICATION). Gen. 50:2 is the only direct reference in the Bible to Hebrew use of this rite. Spices were inserted in certain body cavities, and corpses were put through 70 days of processing to prevent decay. Cf. II Chron. 16:14 (Asa) and John 19:39 (Jesus). From embalmed and mummified Egyptian bodies of animals and people much historic information has come.

embroidery. See NEEDLEWORK.

emerods (ĕm′ĕr-ŏdz), hemorrhoids (archaic). Deut. 28:27 and I Sam. 5:7 *passim*. "Tumours" (Moff.).

Emmanuel. See IMMANUEL.

Emmaus (ĕ-mā′ŭs), a village "from Jerusalem about threescore furlongs," of uncertain site, the goal of Jesus' walk on the first Easter afternoon (Luke 24:13–32). Unrecognized by "two" (Cleopas* and another) whom he joined on the 6- or 7-mile journey (60 furlongs), he was known when he broke bread with them in a village home. Several sites claim to be the original Emmaus, each a long round-trip walk from Jerusalem (Luke 24:33): (1) El-Qubeibeh, 7 m. NW. of Jerusalem on the Roman road, where the ruins of a Crusaders' church are now covered by a Franciscan one. (2) Abū Ghôsh ("village of grapes"), 4 m. SW. of El-Qubeibeh on the Roman road, whose milestone is still standing, also has a church built over the ruins of a Crusader church. (3) Kuloniah, 3 m. S. of El-Qubeibeh, a point where Titus stationed soldiers 60 furlongs from Jerusalem. (4) the 'Amwâs (Nicopolis) in the Shephelah, 20 m. from Jerusalem on the highway to Joppa, is too remote to be considered for the Luke 24 narrative, though its ruined church is of great antiquity. If, however, textual evidence that the figure in Luke 24:13 was originally 160 stadia instead of 60 should prove to be correct, 'Amwâs may be the village intended.

131. The Supper at Emmaus, *by D. R. Velazquez.*

encampment. (1) The areas where the wandering children of Israel halted en route from Egypt to Canaan, as along the Sea of Reeds (Num. 33:10); in the Wilderness of Sin (Num. 33:11); at Ezion-geber (Ezion-gaber, A.V. Num. 33:35). (For sanitary regulations, see Deut. 23:9–14.) (2) Headquarters of armies, like the encampment of Philistines (I Sam. 13:16; II Chron. 32:1). (3) The symbolic encampment of the angel of the Lord (Ps. 34:7).

enchantment, the use of magic arts, spells, or charms. Mosaic Law forbade the practice of enchantment (Deut. 18:10; Lev. 19:26; Isa. 47:9).

Endor ("fountain of habitation"), a small town c. 6 m. SE. of Nazareth, on the shoulder of Little Hermon, c. 4 m. S. of Mt. Tabor. Famous because its witch was visited by King Saul* on the eve of the fatal battle of Gilboa (I Sam. 28:7–25). It was associated by the author of Ps. 83:10 with the battle of Sisera vs. Deborah and Barak. Near Endor are important ancient caves of Galilee. In early Palestine Endor was a town of those of Manasseh's* tribe who were living in the territory of Issachar (Josh. 17:11).

En-gannim (ĕn-găn′ĭm) ("fountain of gardens"). (1) A town of Judah SW. of Jerusalem, possibly near Beth-shemesh (Josh. 15:34). (2) A town on the border of Issachar and Manasseh (Josh. 19:21, 21:29), probably "the garden house" of II Kings 9:27, possibly the modern Jenin, c. 7 m. SW. of Mt. Gilboa, on the main road from Esdraelon through Samaria to Jerusalem.

En-gedi (ĕn-gē′dĭ) ("spring of the young goat"), an oasis fed by warm, fresh-water springs, on the W. shore of the Dead Sea near its center, c. 18 m. SE. of Hebron. It was allotted to Judah (Josh. 15:62), and its beauty and fertility were often praised (Song of Sol. 1:14; cf. Sirach 24:14). The surrounding wilderness afforded refuge for fugitives (David, I Sam. 23:29–24:6), ascetics, and rebels (e.g., recently discovered letters of Bar-Kokhba found in a cave of Nahal Hever addressed to his commanders at En-gedi). The Hebron–En-gedi road was used in an attempt to invade Judah during the reign of Jehoshaphat (c. 867–852 B.C.; II Chron. 20:2). Excavations in the area (1961–64) have revealed, in addition to a Chalcolithic "high place" and a Roman bath, the remains of a fortress at Tell el-Jurn, the oldest settlement of which (Stratum V) dates to the period of Josiah and his successors (c. 640–587 B.C.). The succeeding level (IV) dates to the post-Exilic period. See *AOTS*, 1967, pp. 223 ff. W. P. A.

engines of war, as distinguished from the light arms of infantry, included armored shelter set up on battlements to encase battering rams—a device used as late as the 12th-century Crusades—and instruments for hurling missiles. They were used in defensive warfare by King Uzziah of Judah (II Chron. 26:15), and by such invaders as Nebuchadnezzar (Ezek. 26:9). Sometimes the siege engines were set up on mounds adjacent to city walls. They were a favorite device of Assyrian and Babylonian warfare. Romans developed battering-ram* engines 150 ft. long; Josephus describes one used by the Romans against Jerusalem, as requiring 300 oxen to move it and 1,500 men to drive it against the walls in assault.

English Bible, the Bible used in Great Britain after the 14th century; until then the Latin version was generally used. Illiteracy and the many dialects of the British Isles retarded the production of vernacular versions.

Anglo-Saxon versions took the form of metrical paraphrases, interlinear glosses, and short translations. In the 7th century Caedmon and other poets composed verses on Biblical subjects; Aldhelm, Abbot of Malmesbury and later Bishop of Sherborne, translated the Psalms into Anglo-Saxon; and Egbert, Bishop of Holy Island, the Gospels. No trace remains of the Gospels translated by Bede, who died in 735. King Alfred is said to have translated the Ten Commandments and other laws from the Pentateuch and the Psalms. The earliest surviving manuscripts of Anglo-Saxon versions are interlinear, word-for-word renderings of the Old Latin text. The oldest is a Latin Psalter now in the British Museum, written about A.D. 700, and at the close of the 9th century supplied with an interlinear gloss in the Kentish dialect. The Lindisfarne Gospels, also in the British Museum, were supplied with a gloss in the dialect of Northumbria about 950, by the priest Aldred. A little later "the Rushworth Gospels," of the Bodleian Library, Oxford, were supplied with an interlinear gloss in Yorkshire. The earliest copies of translations of the Gospels, with no accompanying Latin text, come from the 10th century. Six such copies are known—2 at each of the libraries of Oxford, Cambridge, and the British Museum. The variants of these MSS. are so slight as to indicate a common original Anglo-Saxon version of the Gospels. Two manuscripts survive of the free translations of the O.T. made by Abbot Aelfric at the end of the 10th century.

The *Middle English period*, during which the Anglo-Saxon language fused with the Norman of the conquerors, saw the production of "The Ormulum," a metrical paraphrase of the Gospels and Acts. It uses Teutonic words, but its cadence and syntax have Norman characteristics. It was made by the monk Orm, and is in the Bodleian Library, Oxford. In the 14th century three translations of the Psalter appeared: a metrical version in a northern dialect; William Shoreham's West Midlands prose translation; and another prose version with commentary by Richard Rolle, the "hermit of Hampole" in Yorkshire.

Wyclif's version of 1382 or soon afterward is the 1st translation of the entire Bible into English. Though made under Wyclif's leadership, the actual translating was largely done by Nicholas of Hereford and other scholars of the Lollard movement. It is a word-for-word rendering of the Vulgate into a Midland dialect. About 30 manuscripts of it are known. The revision which soon followed, attributed in part to John Purvey, Wyclif's former curate, supplanted the first translation, and became so popular that many copies were made, about 140 of which survive. Though the Wyclif Bible profoundly influenced English life in the 15th century, and crystallized the long evolution of Norman and Anglo-Saxon into early English, it remained a manuscript volume until 1731, when Purvey's N.T. was first printed. The entire Bible was not printed until 1850, when Forshall and Madden brought out their edition of both the Wyclif and Purvey versions.

Tyndale's version, the 1st printed English N.T., determined the character and style of subsequent versions. A student of Latin and Greek at Oxford and Cambridge, William Tyndale determined to translate the Scriptures so that everyone could understand them. He left London practically as an exile, planning to complete his N.T. translation and find a printer on the Continent. In Cologne Peter Quentel began printing the 1st quarto edition, but this was interrupted by Cochlaeus, an enemy of the Reformation. Tyndale, taking the sheets already printed, escaped up the Rhine to Worms. There Peter Schoeffer printed 3,000 copies of an octavo edition of Tyndale's N.T. This, and the quarto edition begun at Cologne but completed in Worms, were shipped to England, arriving early in 1526. The books, eagerly bought by the common people, were burned by the authorities. Today only three copies exist: 31 leaves of the quarto begun at Cologne and completed in Worms are in the British Museum; a copy of the octavo edition, perfect except for a missing title page, is in the Baptist College at Bristol, England; an imperfect octavo copy is in the library of St. Paul's, London. In 1530 Tyndale translated the Pentateuch from the Hebrew, and published it with controversial marginal notes. In 1531 his translation of Jonah appeared. His revisions of the Pentateuch and of the 1525 N.T. were published in 1534. His subsequent N.T. revision and his translations of Joshua to II Chronicles are thought to have been left with his friend, John Rogers. In 1535 Tyndale was arrested in Antwerp, and the following year he was put to death as a heretic. His N.T. marked an epoch in the history of the English Bible. Unlike Wyclif's, it was not a translation of the Vulgate but of Erasmus' Greek text of 1516 and 1522. The Vulgate, Erasmus' Latin translation of his own Greek text, and Luther's German translation aided Tyndale. He combined exactness with breadth of scholarship. The grace, simplicity, and directness of style which make his version outstanding molded the English language during the Elizabethan era. About 90% of his translation is retained in the Authorized Version.

Coverdale's Bible of 1535, the 1st complete English Bible to be printed, was produced with the encouragement of Thomas Cromwell, the Secretary of State, and dedicated to Henry VIII. The sheets of this black-letter Bible are believed to have been printed on the Continent but bound in London by Nycolson. As Miles Coverdale was a scholar in neither Heb. nor Gk., his Bible is not a new translation from the original texts, but a compilation of other versions, modified to meet the demands both of the public and of the church authorities. It is based on Zwingli's Zurich Bible, Luther's German version, the Vulgate, the Lat. text of Pagninus, and Tyndale's Pentateuch and 1534 N.T. It achieved immediate popularity, and some of its felicitous renderings were retained in the Authorized Version. Coverdale's translation of the Psalms later appeared almost without change in the *Great Bible*, from which it was taken for *The Book of Common Prayer* of the Church of England and the Protestant Episcopal Church. Two revised editions of Coverdale's Bible appeared in 1537 under royal license.

Matthew's Bible, printed in 1537, probably at Antwerp, was dedicated to the king and licensed by him. It bears the name "Thomas Matthew," which is probably the name assumed by Tyndale's associate, John Rogers, in order to hide his identity. Rogers edited this Bible, which includes Tyndale's Pentateuch, his version of Joshua to II Chronicles, left in manuscript at the time of his death, Coverdale's Ezra to Malachi and his Apocrypha, and Tyndale's 1535 revision of the N.T.

Taverner's Bible of 1539 is a revision of Matthew's Bible by the able Greek scholar Richard Taverner. It had little influence on subsequent translators, and was entirely superseded by the Great Bible.

The *Great Bible* of 1539, so called because of its size, 10 by 15 in., was Coverdale's revision of Matthew's Bible, undertaken at the behest of Thomas Cromwell. The printing, begun by Regnault in Paris, was halted by the Inquisition, but the sheets were transferred to London and completed by Richard Grafton and Edward Whitchurch. The second edition, often called "Cranmer's Bible" from its preface by Archbishop Cranmer, was issued in 1540, and bore on its title page: "This is the Byble apoynted to the use of the churches." For the 1540 edition Coverdale revised his own 1539 revision of Matthew. The seven editions which appeared within two years indicate its great popularity.

The *Geneva Bible*, a scholarly revision of Tyndale and the Great Bible, was made by a group of English refugees, including Coverdale, who fled to Geneva from Queen Mary's persecutions. The N.T., which appeared in 1557 and is ascribed to William Whittingham, a brother-in-law of Calvin, is basically Tyndale's revised N.T. with changes from the Great Bible and many new renderings from Theodore Beza's Latin translation and commentary. The entire Bible, published in 1560, included the O.T. of the Great Bible revised on the evidence of the best texts and a revision of the 1557 N.T. It was often called the "Breeches Bible" from its use of the word "breeches" in Gen. 3:7. Because of its quarto size, its clear roman type, its verse divisions (the first in an English Bible), and its superiority over previous versions, it became so popular that by 1611 120 editions had appeared. This was Shakespeare's Bible.

The *Bishop's Bible* of 1568, issued under the leadership of Archbishop Parker, was an attempt to supplant the popular Geneva Bible, which was unacceptable to the religious authorities because of its controversial notes. A group of scholars, including 9 bishops, revised the Great Bible. Because they lacked editorial supervision, they produced a version of unequal merit. It was a large volume, in appearance like the Great Bible except for the verse divisions borrowed from the Geneva Bible. As it was authorized by the bishops, it soon displaced the Great Bible, and copies were set up in many churches. The 1572 edition became the official basis for the Authorized Version.

The *Rheims and Douai Bible* was the English Bible translated from the Vulgate for Roman Catholics. William Allen, founder of the English college at Douai, Flanders, saw the need for providing such a volume, in view of the popularity of the Protestant versions. Gregory Martin, an Oxford scholar, translated the N.T., which was issued in 1582 at Rheims, where the English college had moved. The O.T. was published in 1609–10 at Douai. Its extremely literal translation carried over into English many Latin words and expressions. Many of the Latinisms of the Rheims N.T. were used in the Authorized Version.

The *Authorized Version* of 1611, also called the King James Version, has been the Bible of English-speaking people for three centuries. The suggestion that it be made came from Dr. John Reynolds, president of Corpus Christi College, Oxford. At the Hampton Court conference, held in January, 1604, to consider the complaints of the Puritans against the Anglicans, Dr. Reynolds moved that a new translation of the Bible be made, for he found the 16th-century versions "corrupt and not answerable to the truth of the original." James I, a Biblical scholar himself, responded favorably to the suggestion, and appointed 54 outstanding Biblical scholars to undertake the task; only 47 worked on the revision. The revisers were organized in 6 groups, 2 at Westminster, 2 at Oxford, and

ENGLISH BIBLE

2 at Cambridge. Each group sent its work to all the other groups for review and suggestions. The Bishop's Bible was to be followed, but where another version agreed better

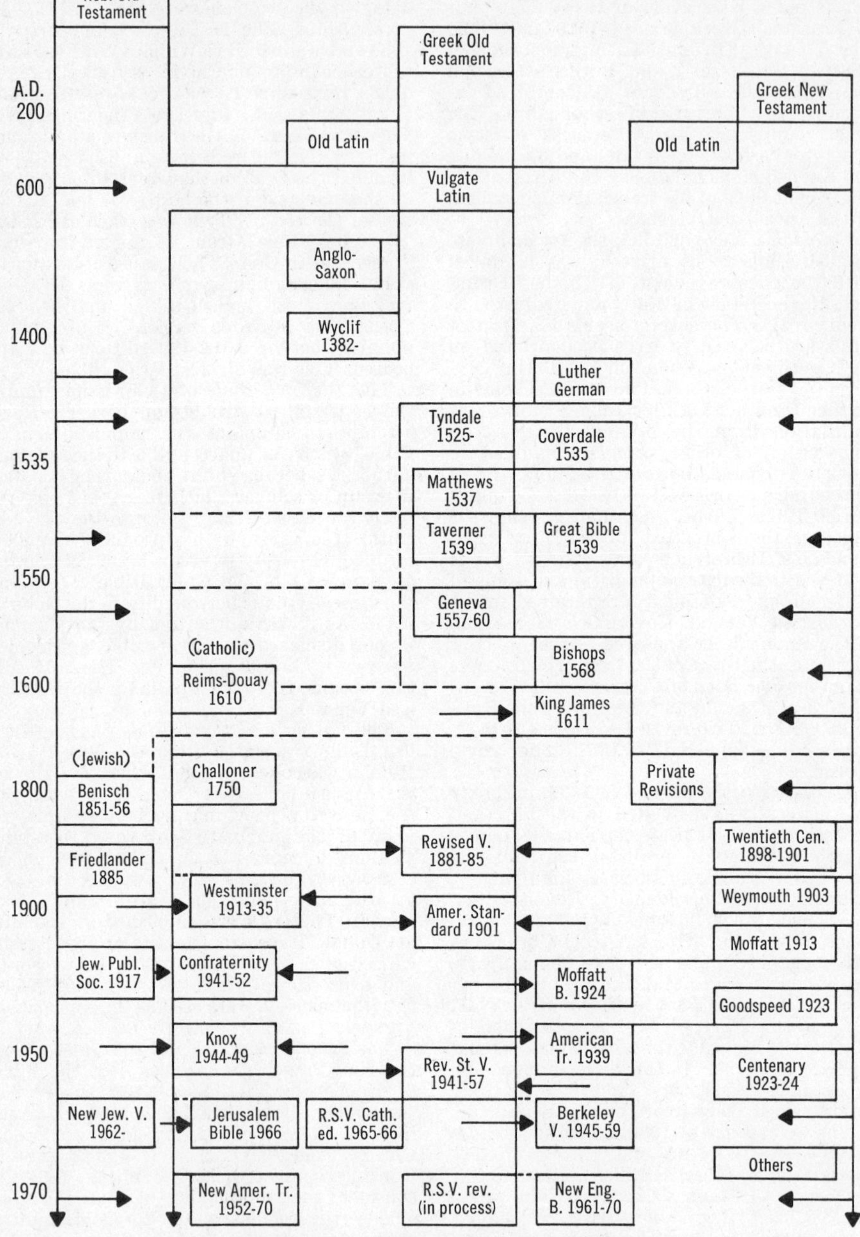

132. Chart of the English Bible, *by Allen P. Wikgren.*

with the original text it was to be used. The first three years (1604–1607) were occupied in preliminary arrangements and private study by some of the translators. The next two or three years were spent in the individual and co-operative labor of the six groups of translators. During the following nine months the final revision was made in London. In 1611 the version appeared from the press of Robert Barker in a large folio volume similar to the Bishop's Bible. Miles Smith, a translator, explained the purpose of the version in the preface. Though ordered by King James and effusively dedicated to him, there is no record that he authorized its use, as the words on the title page, "Appointed to be read in Churches" imply. The title page describes this as "newly translated out of the original tongues," but it is actually a scholarly revision on the basis of the Hebrew and Greek. It is the final achievement of nearly a century of translating, but 90% of its N.T. is Tyndale's. It soon became so popular that the Bishop's Bible was not reprinted, and in 50 years it replaced the Geneva Bible, the last edition of which appeared in 1644. Its O.T. far surpassed any English translation in its faithfulness to the Hebrew text and the simplicity of its style. Its N.T. is so expressive in language and form that it is said to rival the original Greek as literature. Its majestic, direct, forceful prose has never been surpassed in English literature. For more than two centuries the Authorized Version held undisputed sway in the English-speaking world.

The *Revised Version*, produced through the co-operation of about 75 leading Biblical scholars of Great Britain and America, is a revision of the Authorized Version. Biblical scholarship, stimulated by the discovery of ancient manuscripts, had recovered a N.T. text superior to that used for the Authorized Version. (See TEXT.) Progress had been made in the study of the Hebrew and Greek languages. The defects of the Authorized Version had become evident. In February 1870 Bishop Wilberforce in the Convocation of Canterbury moved that a revision of the Authorized Version be made, and in June 54 revisers, organized in 2 companies, one for each Testament, met in Westminster. Thirty American scholars co-operated, meeting in Bible House, New York. On May 17, 1881, the Revised N.T. was published, and within a year an estimated 3,000,000 copies in all editions were sold in England and America. The O.T. was completed in 1884, and was published with the N.T. on May 19, 1885. In 1901 the American Committee issued the American Standard Version. In it they incorporated their preferred readings, which had not been adopted by the British Committee but had been printed in an appendix. They revised antiquated or typically English words, and substituted Jehovah for Lord or God where YHWH appears in the Heb. text. Inferior to the Authorized Version in beauty of expression, the Revised Version is superior in scholarship. A Gk. N.T. text had been used which was better than that underlying the Authorized Version, and differing from it in 5,788 readings, though only one in four of these substantially affects the meaning. It is estimated that the Revised N.T. differs from the Authorized Version in about 36,000 places. A better understanding of N.T. Gk. made possible a clearer translation of difficult passages, especially in the Epistles. The Heb. text for the O.T. was similar to that on which the Authorized Version was based, but the revisers' mastery of Heb. enabled them to make sense out of many passages which had been obscure in 1611. Other commendable features include the abandonment of verse paragraphing in favor of paragraph divisions according to sense, poetry (except in the prophets) printed as such, and the omission of descriptive chapter headings and chronological material.

Recent versions are for the most part independent, modern-speech translations. They are numerous, and include: *The Bible in Modern English*, by Ferrar Fenton, 1900; *The New Testament in Modern Speech*, by Richard F. Weymouth, 1903; *The Twentieth Century New Testament*, published anonymously in 1904; *The Bible: A New Translation*, by James Moffatt, whose N.T. appeared in 1913, and his O.T. in 1924; *The Holy Scriptures According to the Masoretic Text—a New Translation*, by Jewish scholars headed by Max L. Margolis, 1917; *The Complete Bible—An American Translation*, 1939, incorporating Edgar J. Goodspeed's New Testament of 1923, the 1927 Old Testament of A. R. Gordon, J. J. Meek, Leroy Waterman, and J. M. Powis Smith, editor, and Professor Goodspeed's Apocrypha of 1938; *The Westminster Version of the Sacred Scriptures*, by Roman Catholic scholars, from Greek and Hebrew texts, 1913–1935; *The New Testament of Our Lord and Savior Jesus Christ Translated from the Latin Vulgate*, the "Confraternity" version by Roman Catholic scholars, 1941; and *The New Testament*, 1944, *Psalms*, 1947, and *The Old Testament* in two volumes issued respectively in 1948 and 1950, all from the Vulgate, by the late Ronald Knox.

The *Revised Standard Version*, stemming from the great English Bibles beginning with Tyndale, is a revision of the American Standard Version in the light of the Authorized Version by a group of American scholars. The project was initiated in 1929 by the International Council of Religious Education. Only changes receiving a two-thirds vote of the entire committee were made. The consonantal Heb. text of the O.T. was used. For the Gk. text the revisers studied the variant readings and adopted or rejected them according to their merits. "The Greek text of this Revision is not that of Westcott-Hort, or Nestle, or Souter; though the readings we have adopted will, as a rule, be found either in the text or the margin of the new (17th) edition of Nestle (Stuttgart, 1941)," says F. C. Grant in the introduction. Matters of English style were carefully considered. "Jehovah" was changed to "Lord." On February 11, 1946, the *Revised Standard Version of the New Testament* was published. The Revised Standard Old Testament was published in 1952.

In the summer of 1947 an interdenominational committee was set up by the Church of England, the Church of Scotland, and the Free Churches of Great Britain, with representatives from Ireland and Wales, to prepare a new translation of the whole Bible, including the Apocrypha, into modern English. It is to be not a revision, but an entirely fresh translation from the originals into good modern English. Jewish scholars are making a new translation of the Heb. Bible and the Gk. Apocrypha. All this is momentous for students and teachers of the Bible.

(For the facts in the above article the authors are chiefly indebted to Ira M. Price's *The Ancestry of Our English Bible*, 3d revised edition. They also consulted the writings of F. G. Kenyon.)

En-lil, a Sumerian god next in rank to An, the sky god; a wind deity, regarded at Nippur* as "Lord of the Storm." Probably known to Abraham.

Enoch, a prophesying Patriarch, listed in J as son of Cain and 3d from Adam (Gen. 4:17 f.), and in P as 7th from Adam (Jude 14). Father of Methuselah (Gen. 5:21). Cain named a city (site unknown) in honor of Enoch (Gen. 4:17). His manner of departure from this life—translation (conveyance to heaven without death), because his walk with God was pleasing to the Deity (Heb. 11:5)—exercised considerable influence on O.T. views of immortality*. See APOCRYPHA for Three Books of Enoch.

Enoch, Books of. See APOCRYPHA.

En-rogel (ĕn-rō′gĕl) (poss. "Spy's Spring," but not "Fuller's Well" as formerly thought), a well or spring outside the Jerusalem walls, at the juncture of the Kidron and Hinnom Valleys; possibly the same as Dragon's Well (Neh. 2:13), near the Dung Gate; on the border between Judah and Benjamin (Josh. 15:7, 18:16). A rendezvous of Jonathan (II Sam. 17:17); and the scene of Adonijah's celebration when he attempted to seize the kingdom (I Kings 1:9). En-rogel is sometimes confused with Gihon Spring farther N.

En-shemesh (ĕn-shē′mĕsh) ("spring or fountain of the sun"), a spring on the boundary between Judah and Benjamin, but the exact location is uncertain; possibly just beyond Bethany, on the Mount of Olives, en route to Jericho, the last watering place before the Jordan. Sometimes called "the Apostles' Fountain." Cf. Josh. 15:7, 18:17.

Epaphras (ĕp′*ȧ*-frăs) (short form of "Epaphroditus"), a citizen of Colossae*, where he labored "fervently" to establish the Church in a center apparently never visited by Paul (Col. 4:12). Epaphras carried to imprisoned Paul a report of heresy at Colossae (see COLOSSIANS) which occasioned a prison Epistle directed to the believers of that city and possibly also of nearby Laodicea and Hierapolis. Epaphras was esteemed as Paul's "dear fellowservant" (Col. 1:7), "faithful minister" (Col. 1:7); and "fellow prisoner in Christ Jesus" (Philem. 23). His personal greetings were forwarded in Paul's Epistle (Col. 4:12).

Epaphroditus (ē-păf′rŏ-dī′tŭs) (Gk. "charming"), a Christian of Macedonian Philippi*, greatly valued by Paul (Phil. 2:25) and by friends at Philippi. Their anxiety for him during his serious illness, incurred while he was assisting Paul, occasioned the Apostle to send his homesick assistant back to them after his providential recovery (Phil. 2:27).

ephah, a dry measure—⅗ U.S. bushel, also the liquid measure *bath**. See Ezek. 45.11; WEIGHTS AND MEASURES.

Ephesians, the Epistle of Paul the Apostle to the, is popularly believed to have been written c. A.D. 59–61, during Paul's imprisonment in Rome (Eph. 3:1, 4:1, 6:20) (see COLOSSIANS) and carried by Tychicus* (Col. 4:7–9; Eph. 6:21), together with Colossians and Philemon*, to their respective destinations within the same district of Asia Minor. Paul's authorship of Ephesians has been questioned on the grounds of (1) its style, which is diffuse and involved, rather than concise; (2) the suspicious similarity of its language and ideas to those of Colossians, 78 of whose verses contain phrases which appear in Ephesians; and (3) the more developed form of its ideas as compared with Paul's authentic epistles. A theory has been advanced that a late 1st-century Christian, using Paul's name as a pseudonym, and borrowing freely from Colossians, wrote Ephesians as an introduction to the first published collection of Paul's letters. Parallels from all nine Pauline writings and from Revelation, I Peter, Pastoral Epistles and Acts suggest that Ephesians was written too late to be by Paul. E. J. Goodspeed nominates Onesimus (Col. 4:9), C. L. Mitten, Tychicus (Col. 4:7; Eph. 6:21) as the likely author. Whoever he was, he faithfully presented the Gospel according to Paul, and his ideas concerning the Church universal are a logical development from Paul's local churchmanship.

Ephesus was clearly not the destination of this Epistle. Paul had labored more than two years in Ephesus (Acts 19:8–10), but this Epistle contains no personal greetings to his many friends there. Furthermore, the words "at Ephesus" (1:1) are omitted in the two chief New Testament MSS., the Codex Sinaiticus and the Codex Vaticanus, as well as in the Chester Beatty papyrus, the oldest known copy of Paul's letters. These facts are reflected in the R.S.V. translation of 1:1: "to the saints who are also faithful in Christ Jesus." This was possibly a circular letter written for all the churches of the province of Asia. As Ephesus was the chief city of the province, the words "in Ephesus" became attached to the letter; or they may have been inserted in place of an obliterated name. Some scholars believe this to be the letter to Laodicea (Col. 4:16).

Colossians and Ephesians, in their underlying conception of Christ as central in the universe, and of the Church as the body of Christ (Col. 1:16–19, 2:9,10; Eph. 1:21–23), are companion epistles; but their aims are different. In Colossians Paul was combating false teachings, and his purpose was controversial. Controversy is absent from Ephesians, and the ideas that appeared in Colossians are developed for their own sake. Ephesians meditates on the ultimate purpose of God in reuniting all things in Christ, and in the light of this it discusses the nature and meaning of the Church.

The two sections of Ephesians, the doctrinal and the hortatory, are concerned with two aspects of the same theme. The doctrinal section explores the divine purpose at the heart of the Christian message. The key verses, 1:9, 10, state that God's ultimate purpose is to reunite all conflicting forces of the world into a final unity in Christ. The second half of the Epistle deals with the significance of the Church in the light of the divine purpose. The Church is seen as an extension of the incarnation and as the body of Christ (1:23, 5:30–32). It is through his body, the Church, that Christ accomplishes his work of reconciliation; as members of the Church Christians must by their love, understanding, and mutual service bring unity to the Church, and through it harmony into a disordered world.

The Epistle may be outlined as follows:

(1) The salutation, 1:1–2.

(2) God's purpose to unite all things in Christ, 1:3–3:21—

- (a) thanksgiving for membership in Christ, 1:3–14.
- (b) prayer that they may understand their salvation, 1:14–19.
- (c) the supremacy of Christ, 1:20–23.
- (d) God's gift of salvation to Jew and Gentile, 2:1–18.
- (e) the unity of the "household of God," 2:19–22.
- (f) Paul's mission as Apostle of the Gentiles, 3:1–13.
- (g) a prayer that Christ may dwell in their hearts, 3:14–19.
- (h) a doxology ending the doctrinal section, 3:20 f.

(3) The Church as God's instrument in reconciling all things in Christ, 4:1–6:18—

- (a) the unity of the Church amid its variety of gifts and functions, 4:1–16.
- (b) the difference between Christian and pagan behavior, 4:17–24.
- (c) practical exhortations, showing how unity may be attained in the Church and how Christians may act worthy of their calling, 4:24–5:20.
- (d) mutual service as the guide to relationships in the Christian family, 5:21–6:9.
  - husband and wife, 5:22–33.
  - children and parents, 6:1–4.
  - servant and master, 6:5–9.
- (e) an exhortation to Christians, equipped with God's armor, to do their part for the Church, 6:10–17.

(4) The conclusion: personal matters and benediction, 6:18–24.

Ephesus, the metropolis of the Roman Province of Asia, sharing with the Syrian Antioch and the Egyptian Alexandria the honor of being one of the three great cities of the eastern Mediterranean. It was situated 3 m. from the sea, on the left bank of the Cayster River, at the head of one of the four river valleys traversed by highways that run from the seacoast up into the high plateau that forms Asia Minor. Ephesus was a transportation junction between E. and W., between sea lanes and highways (Acts 19:21, 20:1, 17; I Tim. 1:3; II Tim. 4:12). Paul took advantage of the constant sea traffic between Ephesus and Corinth (cf. II Cor. 12:14, 13:1). The Cayster River carried down much silt, which was deposited in and around the city, with the result that at certain seasons it was advantageous for deep-draught vessels and passengers to use the nearby port of Miletus* (Acts 20:16–17).

Croesus of Lydia and Cyrus of Persia in the 6th century B.C., and also Alexander the Great in the 4th century, had left their mark on the Asiatic peoples and the Ionian Greeks who originally made up its population. Under liberal Roman rule, which began about 190 B.C., Ephesus became a racial melting pot, a cosmopolitan commercial center of the Empire, and a battlefield of religion. From the days of Croesus (c. 560 B.C.), a Lydian fertility goddess similar to the Phoenician Astarte (see ASHTORETH), and identified by Greeks

133. Temple of Diana at Ephesus, one of the Seven Wonders of the World. A reconstruction based on a recovered coin.

with their Artemis (R.S.V.) and by the Romans with their Diana*, had dominated the life of the city, with legalized prostitution, commercialized subsidiaries, and a wonder temple. "The city of Ephesus" was not only "a worshipper" (A.V.) but "temple keeper" (A.S.V.) or "warden" (Moffatt) of the goddess (Acts 19:35). Magic had its followers and its commercial promoters in Ephesus. Fees were charged by charlatans for consultation (Acts 19:13–16, 19). Inscriptions on walls and buildings indicate the prevalence of superstition; one of these reads: "If the bird is flying from right to left, and settles out of sight, good luck will come. But if it lifts up its left wing, then, whether it rises or settles out of sight, misfortune will result." Paul recalled these local conditions (Eph. 4:19, 5:3–12). On the W. slope of Mt. Pion overlooking the old city stands the Great Theater where was held the mass meeting of protest against Paul organized by Demetrius to represent the local silversmiths, whose trade in images of Diana was hurt by Paul's preaching. It was 495 feet in diameter and seated 25,000. The Asiarchs—Roman officials appointed to further emperor worship throughout the Empire and to engineer public festivals—were friendly to Paul because he had made such progress against the monopolistic local cult as they, with all their official prestige, had not been able to do (Acts 19:31). The main street (Arkadiane) connecting the theater with the harbor has been excavated. It is marble paved, 36 ft. wide and 1,735 ft. long, and was lined with colonnaded shops. It ends in a sumptuous arched gate at the harbor.

In this cosmopolitan atmosphere of fabulously wealthy Ephesus, with its cross currents of interest and loyalties, the people recognized that Paul's ethical message was a positive way of life (Acts 19:9); listened to him in the synagogue (Acts 19:8), in the school of Tyrannus (Acts 19:9), and in their homes and market places. His message, free from invective and frontal attack (Acts 19:37), won converts. In spite of opposition Paul realized that Ephesus offered him an open door to all Asia Minor (Acts 19:26; I Cor. 16:9). He knew that at festival times devotees of Artemis came from all over Asia, especially in the Artemision month (March-April). His farewell to church officials at Miletus presents as high an ideal of the pastorate as has ever been recorded. The substantial worth of those who responded to his ministry is reflected not only in his words but in their actions (Acts 20:17, 36–38).

134. Theater at Ephesus, with orchestra (left center) and spectators' seats. At center, the street (*Arkadiane*) leading to the Aegean Sea and Smyrna.

Associated with the early Church at Ephesus were Priscilla and Aquila (Acts 18:18 f.), Timothy (I Tim. 1:3), Erastus (Acts 19:22), and especially John the Apostle and John the Presbyter. Among the churches of Asia Minor in the Apostolic Age, Ephesus came first. The summary of its condition in Rev. 2:1–7 is fairly complimentary. Ephesus had a long line of bishops, and was the seat of the council which condemned Nestorius in A.D. 431. The ruins of Christian churches, especially the tremendous Church of Saint Mary, and the many crosses (see CROSS) which decorate tombs in the cemeteries of Ephesus, indicate how complete was the victory of Christianity over the worship of Diana. Many inscriptions found at Ephesus, studied along with Egyptian papyri, throw light on Acts 19. They attest the accuracy of Luke in portraying the Ephesus in which Paul worked.

ephod ("a covering"), an apron-like garment worn under the breastplate of the high priest* Aaron and his successors. It had shoulder straps and an embroidered girdle, and was worn over a robe; see Ex. 28 for details. Sometimes it was merely a linen waist cloth (I Sam. 2:18; II Sam. 6:14). The references in Judg. 8:27, 17:5, 18:14–20 to an ephod used for cultic purposes are enigmatic; in these instances it may not have been a garment. See I Sam. 23:6–12, 30:7; see also BREASTPLATE; URIM AND THUMMIM.

135. Ephod.

ephphatha (ĕf′ȧ-thȧ) (Aram. "be opened"), an Aram. word spoken by Jesus to a man whose hearing and speech were impaired, effecting a cure (Mark 7:31–37).

Ephraim (ē′frā̇-ĭm) ("fruitfulness"). (1) An Egyptian-born son of Joseph and Asenath, daughter of the priest Potipherah; younger brother of Manasseh. He was adopted by his sick grandfather Jacob (Gen. 48:5), and received the blessing customarily bestowed on the eldest. History fulfilled the judgment of Jacob—the younger became the greater (v. 19); his tribe grew to a "multitude" (v. 16), and the land allotted to him was some of the best in Palestine.

(2) The territory "assigned" to Ephraim at the Conquest* was bounded on the N. by Manasseh's land extending to the S. edge of the Plain of Esdraelon, on the E. by the Jordan rift as far S. as Jericho, on the S. by Dan

and Benjamin, and on the W. by the Mediterranean. Its most important city was Shechem* (Josh. 21:20), for a time the capital of the Northern Kingdom (I Kings 12:1). Such Canaanite strongholds as Gezer, however, did not fail to Ephraim for centuries (I Kings 9:16). The rugged, olive-clad terrain of Ephraim, in the central range of Palestine, led to its being called Mount Ephraim, which became the scene of the fierce battle between David and Absalom (II Sam. 18:6).

(3) The half-tribe of Ephraim, together with that of Ephraim's brother Manasseh, formed one of the Twelve Tribes*. After the Ten Tribes had revolted against Rehoboam, Ephraim became pre-eminent within the Northern Kingdom; indeed Israel was often called "Ephraim." To offset the popular influence of Jerusalem, which was the religious as well as the political capital of the rival Southern Kingdom (Judah), Jeroboam I had made rival shrines at ancient Dan and Bethel (I Kings 12:28–33). The Ephraimites joined Syria in the war against Judah (II Kings 16:5) causing King Ahaz of that country to call upon Tiglath-pileser for aid against Israel and Syria (v. 7). Amos and Hosea uttered vehement protests against the intemperate, immoral, skeptical, and idolatrous traits of Ephraim, and announced that a patient God would visit calamity upon this country of excesses, corrupt politics, intrigue and idolatry (Hos. 8:4b–6). Ephraim was carried into captivity in 722 B.C. by Sargon II.

The important Ephraimitic document E, written c. 750 B.C., uses Elohim* (instead of Yahweh) to designate God. Like the J document, the E source (see SOURCES) forms one of the main strands of the O.T. It stresses morality and religion, rather than the patriotic aspects of faith often emphasized in J.

(4) Cities called Ephraim are recorded as N. of Jerusalem and also "near the wilderness"—possibly E. of the Jordan (John 11:54).

Ephraimite, a member of the tribe of Ephraim.

Ephrath (ĕf′răth) (Ephrata, Ephratah, Ephrathah, A.S.V.). (1) The town of Bethlehem* in Judaea (Gen. 35:16, 19, 48:7; Ruth 4:11; Mic. 5:2). (2) The wife of Caleb and mother of Hur, "the father of Bethlehem" (I Chron. 4:4, 2:19, 24, 50). (3) The territory of Ephraim (Kirjath-jearim) in the Ark story (Ps. 132:6).

An Ephrathite was a citizen of Bethlehem, Jesse, e.g. (I Sam. 17:12); or a member of Ephraim's tribe, like the father of Jeroboam (A.V. I Kings 11:26).

Ephron (ē′frôn) ("fawn"). (1) Son of Zohar, a Hittite living at Hebron. From him, by a meticulous business transaction witnessed by all who came through the city gate, Abraham purchased for 400 shekels of weighed silver money (coinage did not yet exist) the Cave of Machpelah in Ephron's field, surrounded by oaks of Mamre (Gen. 23:8, 10, 13–17). This cave became the burial place not only of Sarah but of Abraham (25:9), Isaac, and Rebekah (49:31), and of Jacob (50:13). (2) A mountain spine on the border of Judah between Kirjath-jearim and Nephtoah (Josh. 15:9). (3) A city E. of the Jordan in the territory of Manasseh, on the road between Beth-shan and Karnaim, captured by Judas Maccabaeus (I Macc. 5:46-52).

Epicureans (ĕp′ĭ-kū-rē′ănz), members of a leading school of Greek philosophers founded by Epicurus, who died 270 B.C., but whose school near the Dipylon Gate survived until the 4th century A.D. His ethics made sensation the criterion of good and evil. Happiness lay in mental quiet, free from the fear of death or of the gods. He did not believe in the life to come, since the soul on leaving the body was dissolved into the primordial "indivisible" atoms from which it had been compounded in space. Hence the reaction of his followers, as accurately stated in Acts 17:32. Representatives of the Stoics* and the Epicureans heard Paul dispute in the synagogue and market place (see AGORA) of Athens daily, and belittled him as a babbler and setter forth of strange gods (Acts 17:17 f.). They led Paul to the Areopagus and there precipitated his famous speech (17:22–31). The barren soil of Greek Epicurean ethics, exalting chance and belittling deity, is evidenced by Paul's sudden departure (v. 33).

Epiphany, Feast of, the commemoration on Jan. 6 (Twelfth Night) of the appearance of the Wise Men.* (See also STARS.)

Epistles, apostolic letters constituting 21 of the 27 books of the N.T. (For subject, see discussions of the individual books.) Most of them consist of an opening greeting, a message of discussion, and a closing salutation, wishing the readers a divine blessing, extending a benediction, or dispatching personal remembrances from the writer and his Christian associates. The Epistles—some of which antedate the Gospels—were written between c. A.D. 49 and A.D. 160–175, the first-written appearing to be Thessalonians, Galatians, the Corinthian correspondence, and Romans. The last penned were possibly the Epistles to Timothy and Titus, though authorities differ on the dates of these. II Peter was also one of the last-written N.T. books. The subject matter of the Epistles includes doctrinal instruction, exhortations to Christian conduct, sometimes pastoral advice, and news of personal matters. When an Epistle like Ephesians was intended for "round-robin" circulation among several communities it was an encyclical. Paul did not intend his Epistles for publication. They probably remained in possession of the group to whom they were addressed, unknown in Christian history until published as a collection.

Sometimes the names of prominent apostles were appended as pseudonyms, to compliment one admired, or to impress the readers with authenticity, like II Peter, which bears the Apostle's name but probably was not written until long after his death. The long scholarly disputes concerning the authorship, date, place of writing, and point of destination of letters makes futile any attempt to chart them authoritatively, but the following table may prove helpful.

Epistles

Name	*By whom*	*Where written*	*To whom*
I Thess.	Paul	Corinth	Thessalonian Christians
II Thess.	"	"	Church at Thessalonica
I Cor.	"	Ephesus	Corinthian Christians
Galatians	"	Antioch, Ephesus or Corinth	Christian groups named in Acts 13, 14
II Cor.	"	Ephesus, Macedonia	Corinthian Christians
Romans	"	Corinth or Cenchraea	Roman Church
Philippians	"	Rome, Caesarea or Ephesus	Christians at Philippi
Philemon	"	Rome	Philemon
Colossians	"	"	Colossian Christians
Ephesians	(? Philemon or Tychicus as Introd. to Paul's letters)	Unknown	Groups of non-Jewish Christians
		Pastoral Epistles	
I Timothy	Prob. follower of Paul	Unknown	Church officers
II Timothy	" " " "	"	" "
Titus	" " " "	"	" "
	Catholic or General Epistles Destined for Wide Reading		
James	Unknown Christian teacher	Unknown	Christians of Dispersion
I Peter	? Apostle Peter	"In Babylon" (Rome)	Christians in Asia Minor
II Peter	Unknown using pseudonym Peter	Unknown	Christians everywhere
Jude	Brother of Jesus or James using pseudonym Jude	Unknown	Christian groups divided by dissension
I John	Author of Fourth Gospel or one of his disciples	? Ephesus	Early Christians, Asia Minor
Hebrews	Unknown Christian teacher	Unknown	Jewish Christians
		Asiatic Epistles	
I John	(see above)		
II John	"The Elder"	? Ephesus	"Elect lady" (? Church Universal)
III John	"The Elder"	? Ephesus	Gaius (? Church Universal)

See CHRONOLOGY; LETTERS; NEW TESTAMENT.

Erastus ("amiable"), a man who "ministered unto" Paul and was sent by him into Macedonia from Ephesus, just before the riot (Acts 19:22). He may be the same Erastus who was chamberlain (R.S.V. "treasurer") probably of Corinth (II Tim. 4:20) and sent greetings to Roman Christians (Rom. 16:23).

Erech (ē′ rĕk) (Accad., Uruk), an ancient Sumerian city, represented today by a group of mounds known collectively as Warka, 40 m. NW. of Ur in S. Babylonia on the Plain of Shinar. The author of Genesis (10:10) attributed its foundation to Nimrod, great-grandson of Noah. Some of the citizens of Erech were deported to Samaria in the 7th century B.C. by Ashurbanipal (see Ezra 4:9–10). More or less continuous excavations by the Germans from 1912 have shown that the site was founded c. 4000 B.C. and have uncovered the remains of two ziggurats and several temples dating to the late 4th and early 3d millennia B.C. The "Anu Ziggurat" (really a raised platform rather than a stage-tower), on which rests the "White Temple," represents in its earliest phases the beginnings of the Mesopotamian ziggurat (c. 3500 B.C.). Erech was regarded as the home of Gilgamesh, hero of the great Babylonian epic (*ANET*[3], pp. 45 ff., 266). Writing was in use here at an early date, as was the seal*, whose earliest known use is exhibited on two small tablets of gypsum plaster found in the "White Temple" at Erech. A small limestone pavement found at Erech is the oldest known stone construction in Babylonia.

Esaias (ĕ-zā′yăs). See ISAIAH.

Esar-haddon (e′sär-hăd′ŏn) ("Asshur has given a brother"), favorite son of the Assyrian King Sennacherib. He ruled 681–669 B.C. (II Kings 19:37; Isa. 37:38). He was father of Ashurbanipal, who succeeded him (669–633 B.C.). He was mentioned by Ezra (4:2) in connection with the story of the opponents of Zerubbabel at Jerusalem. He pillaged the coastal city of Sidon and deported its inhabitants. He marched through Tyre en route to a powerful campaign against Egypt (675 B.C.). He subdued Syria; colonized Samaria (Ezra 4:2); laid tribute on Manasseh, King of Judah, whom, it is said, he took captive to Babylonia (II Chron. 33:11), which he controlled as well as Assyria.

Esau ("hairy"), a son of Isaac and Rebekah,

and older brother of Jacob* (Gen. 25:25 f.). Ruddy and hairy, Esau was a "cunning hunter" and "man of the field" (v. 27), his father's favorite. The Genesis narrative of fraternal relations is skillfully and dramatically drawn: the hungry Esau's loss of birthright privileges when crafty Jacob offered to buy them with a mess of lentil pottage (25:34); the loss of his father's "preferred stock" of blessings by Jacob's crafty deception of his blind parent (27:1–29); the estrangement of Esau, and his murderous intent (v. 41) after he had received a minor inheritance (vv. 39 f.); his marriage with Hittite women "a grief of mind" to his parents (Gen. 26:34 f.). The climax of the story comes with the reconciliation of Esau and Jacob, near the rugged, picturesque Wâdī Jabbok in E. Palestine. Both brothers conducted themselves graciously (Gen. 33:1–15). Esau, "who is Edom"* (Gen. 36:1), took his family and possessions to Mt. Seir (Gen. 33:16) in ancient Edom—a heritage of wilderness waste—and Jacob pushed on to Shechem (v. 18) and Hebron* (35:27). The two brothers symbolize the supremacy of younger Canaan over the older Edomite country. Hence the allusion, "the elder shall serve the younger" (Gen. 25:23; Rom. 9:12). See also Rom. 9:13; Mal. 1:1–4, for the indignation of Yahweh against Edom. Esau's descendants are listed in Gen. 36:9 ff. and I Chron. 1:35 ff.

eschatology (from Gk. "last things"), teaching or belief about the ultimate destiny of mankind. It has been called "the otherworldly aspect of salvation."* It deals with the Day of the Lord; the Day of Righteous Judgment*; with death and immortality*; the millennium;* the *Parousia** or sudden coming again of Jesus, and the eternal reign of the Lord throughout the universe. Eschatology is of greater concern to the Christian than is cosmogony, theories about how the universe and the human race began. Since ancient, pre-scientific man had so few means with which to change his world and combat its injustices, it is natural that he gave more of his attention than modern man would do to theories about the final destiny of the righteous and the wicked and the possibility of a future golden age. In view of this general fact it is surprising that the early Hebrews actually had so little concern with eschatology, either as respects the individual or the universe. Most of the O.T. is centered upon this world and its problems, and ideas of a universal judgment and restoration, and of a resurrection after death, appear only at a late period and, partly at least, as the result of foreign influence.

(1) *In the O.T. Period.* The first clear indication of the existence of some kind of eschatological ideas among the Hebrews is found in a casual reference of Amos (5:18) (c. 750 B.C.) to a belief in "the day of the Lord," but no one knows exactly what this involved. The 8th-century prophets all spoke of God's intention to judge Israel itself in the near future. The prophet Zephaniah (1:14–18) (c. 625) gives the classic picture of this "day of wrath." From time to time most of the other prophets brought certain other nations within the scope of God's judgment as well (Amos 1:3–2:3; Isa. 17–19; Jer. 46–51), but the idea of a universal judgment upon all nations seems to have been a much later development and is related more to apocalyptic* literature than to prophecy (Isa. 24; Zech. 12, 14). The developed eschatological drama took various forms. Sometimes it included the coming of a Messiah* (Isa. 11:1–10; Zech. 9:9); sometimes judgment and salvation are simply attributed to the direct intervention of Yahweh (Ezek. 38–39; Isa. 2:12–21). Daniel (7:13) introduces the mysterious figure of "one like a son of man" into the picture. Post-Exilic Israel's increasing concern with individual, as distinguished from national, life culminated in belief in a final resurrection of the dead (Isa. 26:19; Dan. 12:2 f.). The Daniel passage speaks of the resurrection of both the righteous and sinners, for eternal reward and eternal punishment.

Many O.T. passages, especially in Second and Third Isaiah, describe idyllically the peace, prosperity, and happiness of the recreated world of the future (Isa. 60, 65:17–25). Israel, of course, will be specially favored. Jeremiah (31:31 f.) says Yahweh will enter into a new covenant with her. In some passages, however, other nations are represented as sharing in her blessings (Isa. 2:2–4; Zech. 14:16), and, in at least one passage, are placed on an equality with her (Isa. 19:24 f.). The comprehensive term for the glorious future that lies beyond the judgment is "the Kingdom of God" (although precisely that term does not appear in the O.T.), for in that day God will reign over all as King (Isa. 24:23; Zech. 14:16).

(2) *In the Inter-Testamental Period.* In the period between the Testaments keen interest in eschatology is apparent in such apocryphal books as II Maccabees, filled with the belief in Judaism that accompanied the succession of independent Jewish political rulers (167–63 B.C.). In this period "the Messiah" was thought of as a Davidic leader who would restore Israel's fortunes. Under Maccabean rule, from Judas Maccabaeus to Aristobulus II, a deliverer who combined the functions of priest and king was heralded. Then, with the end of Hasmonaean rule and Pompey's approach in 63 B.C., Jews returned to the Davidic type of expected royal leader. Again the fires of hope for a sudden coming of a Messiah were kindled by the Jewish revolt against Rome (A.D. 66–70), which resulted in the destruction of Jerusalem. Current history time and again colored the eschatology of Israel. Sometimes her hopes were set upon the coming of a military and political "Messiah"; sometimes, as in Enoch, on a heavenly "Son of Man." There is no evidence that the "Suffering Servant" of Isa. 52:13–53:12 ever played a role in Jewish eschatology, although it certainly does in the N.T.

(3) *In the N.T. Age.*

(a) Some of the *views expressed by Jesus*

himself at first appear contradictory. If his actual words had been preserved, we should have a clearer conception of what he actually thought about things to come; but we are dependent upon what his recorders transmitted. It is not possible to make all passages tally. The Gospels offer various views, none of which is all-inclusive concerning the final state of the righteous. As stated in each of the first three Gospels (Matt. 16:28; Mark 13:30; Luke 17:20–24), Jesus considered that the future coming of the Son of Man was identical with the sudden coming of the Kingdom* of God. Yet he also believed that the Kingdom was already at work "within" the hearts of earnest seekers after it (Luke 17:21, A.V.), and that they would share in the eternal, universal Kingdom of God which would finally expel Satan and establish cosmic redemption of all who had ever lived. It has sometimes been said that Jesus was "mistaken" in his timing of the sudden coming of the "end of the age" (Matt. 24:36–44) and the initiation of the Kingdom of God by the Parousia. But if he foreshortened the time, it was possibly because he had counted on the prompter response of mankind to his revelation of the Father's plan than he received. The individual's freedom of choice and the Father's infinite patience are factors in the timing of the coming Kingdom of God which are too important to be hurried. The Kingdom, as Jesus described it, would have come at once if Israel—as well as the Gentile world—had proved ready and worthy to have it come. It is not for man to know the hour (Acts 1:7). Meantime there remains the challenging advice of Jesus to all his disciples, "be ye also ready," like the faithful servant of his lord's household (Matt. 24:44).

(b) The *authors of all the Gospels* expressed themselves concerning "things to come." *Matthew* was persistently interested in the judgment, and climaxed his views in the statements of 19:1–25:46. He taught that agreements made on earth would be carried through in heaven (18:15–20); and spoke enigmatically about children having angels continually beholding the face of the "Father which is in heaven" (18:10). His Gospel made it possible to interpret the destruction of Jerusalem (A.D. 70) as a tragic signal of the coming of the Lord. This catastrophe was a rebuke to Jews for rejecting Jesus. He optimistically urged believers to profit by the example of disfranchised Jews, and to take advantage of the situation by making "disciples of all the heathen."

Mark 13 ("the Little Apocalypse") may represent the efforts of a Jewish Christian to apply to the world picture what Daniel had prophesied. This chapter makes Jesus speak of wars and rumors of war, brothers betraying each other, false prophets arising, and the failure even of heavenly bodies to play their appointed role. Yet in the midst of all this Mark quotes Jesus; the Son of Man would be coming "with great power and glory," at an hour which no man and not even angels knew, but only the Father. Meantime, wrote Mark, Jesus urged constant watching, lest any be caught sleeping at the coming.

For the record of *Luke* concerning what Jesus taught about "the end," see Luke 13:29, 19:41–44, 21:5–38, 22:28–30, 69.

The author of the *Fourth Gospel* has very different views from the other three concerning "things to come." He finds the Comforter ever present in a mystical and eternal fellowship with the followers of Christ. He does not look to the Parousia. He states his eschatology in the "supper discourses" of 13–17 rather than in the presupper talks of Mark 13 and Matt. 24–25. See also Luke 21.

(c) *Paul's* eschatological views were rooted in his sure belief in Christ's Resurrection. He was not able to tell his hearers the nature of immortality, but he assured them that God would surely equip those who desired immortality with the qualifications of attaining it (I Cor. 15:35–38). He stressed the O.T. faith fulfilled in a Christian revelation of one who, as God's representative, would return to judge the world and give eternal life to those who keep His commandments (I Thess. 3:13). Many of Paul's writings concerning eschatological matters were directed to those who were frankly puzzled about "things to come." The despondent ("faint-hearted," R.S.V. I Thess. 5:14), whom he exhorted Thessalonian Christians to encourage, were troubled about friends who had met sudden death and might not have been ready to meet Christ; and about themselves, because Christ might come so suddenly that they would be unqualified for entry into his Kingdom To such Paul gave the practical advice of I Thess. 5:1–11. The eschatology of II Thessalonians does not contradict that of I Thessalonians, but shows that the Parousia is yet to be, "after the lawless one . . . be revealed" (R.S.V. II Thess. 2:8). The eschatology of Thessalonians and of Revelation both show the influence of Daniel.

(d) The unknown author of the *Epistle to the Hebrews* felt that Christianity's greatest message was not concerned with "things to come," but with teaching man how he can have access to God at all times (10:19–25). He wishes to make Christians, who for generations have vainly expected the coming, feel proud of their unshakable faith and make it a thing of growth.

(e) *Revelation* contains the most elaborate and spectacular N.T. symbolism concerning the ushering in of the millennium—the binding of Satan for 1,000 years (20:2) while the righteous dwell with Christ (v. 6); and after those 1,000 years the loosing of Satan, who will be cast into a sea of fire along with the beasts and false prophet (v. 10), while the new heaven and new earth come down from God, Who makes all things new (21:5), and places a river and tree of life at the disposal of all who have obeyed His commandments (22:14). The Apocalypse of John was written in the enthusiastic expectation that Jesus was coming again quickly. His followers were eager to have him do so; "Even so, come, Lord Jesus," is the penultimate verse of the Bible.

In modern times two groups hold divergent beliefs about the millennium with reference to the second coming of Christ. *Premillennarians*, including Mormons, Adventists, and others, maintain that Christ must return before the world is converted; and that the "millennium" of world-wide holiness which is to precede the end of the world, and during which world conversion will occur, will follow the coming of Christ. *Postmillennarians*, on the other hand, maintain that the Kingdom of God has already begun, and that world conversion through evangelism will take place during the present age (commonly called a millennium) before Christ returns for his final advent, ushering in the eternal state.

See JUDGMENT, DAY OF.

Consult *An Outline of Biblical Theology*, Millar Burrows, ch. XI (Westminster Press).

E.L./R.C.D.

Esdraelon (ĕs′drȧ-ē′lŏn) (Gk. modification of Jezreel, "God sows"), a vast plain not mentioned in scripture, but forming one of the most conspicuous geographical features of Palestine. The plain measures c. 20 m. NW. to SE. and 14 m. NE. to SW. Its right angle touches Mt. Tabor* below Nazareth; its long side runs from Jenin (En-gannim) to the N. slope of Mt. Carmel*; and its E. side runs from Tabor along two lower mountains to Jenin. Its famed fertility is due to down-washed soil from the Galilee hills forming its N. border, and the highlands of Samaria hemming it in on the S.; and to ancient deposits of volcanic material and decayed basaltic subsoil.

Despite its mountain walls caravans have always crossed the Plain N. and S. between Nazareth and Jerusalem, and E. and W. from the deep Jordan Valley to the Carmel headland and the coastal cities. And over the head of the Megiddo hillock, at the E. end of the long Carmel ridge, runs one of the most famous passes of history, leading from Damascus and the Tigris-Euphrates across Palestine and to Egypt. Mary, Joseph, and Jesus crossed the Plain of Esdraelon, going from Nazareth to Jerusalem, unless they followed Jordan thicket paths. The E. portion of Esdraelon is often called the Valley of Jezreel, whose bastion city, Beth-shan, commanded the approach to the Jordan and the Decapolis.

Esdraelon drains into the Mediterranean by the Wâdī Kishon of Deborah's ancient battle (Judg. 4:7, 5:21) and of Elijah's contest (I Kings 18:40). *

Esdras (ĕz′drăs), **Books of.** See APOCRYPHA.

Esh-baal (ĕsh′bā′ăl). See ISH-BOSHETH.

Eshcol (ĕsh′kŏl) ("cluster"). (1) one of three Amorite brothers, confederate with Abraham in the battle of the kings near the Dead Sea (Gen. 14:13, 24). (2) One of the wâdīs (brooks or dry valleys, depending on the amount of rainfall) near Hebron. From it spies sent by Moses brought back the cluster of grapes so heavy that two men were required to carry it (Num. 13:23 f., 32:9; Deut. 1:24).

Essenes (Greek for Aramaic *ḥasên*, *ḥasayyâ* = Hebrew *ḥasîdîm*, "pious"). According to Josephus, one of three orders of Jews in antiquity, the others being the better known Sadducees* and Pharisees*. The chief ancient sources of information about them are Philo Judaeus (as quoted by Eusebius in *Praep. evang.* VIII. 11–12), Josephus (*Antiquities* XIII, 171–3; XV, 371–9; XVIII, 18–22; *Jewish War* II, 119–61), and Pliny the Elder (*Natural History* V, 17). Other accounts in the Church Fathers are dependent on these sources. The Dead Sea Scrolls* and the excavation of Qumrân have brought to light such a wealth of fresh information that the most considered scholarship has identified the Qumrân sect with the Essenes, and now suggests that the Scrolls have become the standard source against which the information in the ancient writers is to be interpreted.

The excavations of Qumrân between 1951 and 1958 and the exploration of its vicinity have brought to light a large center for a community, many members of which lived in caves among the cliffs nearby and at 'Ain Feshkhah, c. 1½ miles south. It was established during the latter part of the 2nd century B.C. (Level Ia), with an elaborate building and all the accompanying installations for a fairly self-contained community being erected during the early 1st century B.C. (Level Ib). An earthquake interrupted the site's occupation and destroyed the center in 31 B.C. Level II represents its rebuilding and occupation until destroyed by the Roman army of Vespasian, evidently in the early summer of A.D. 68. The "last days" of the site were its occupation by a Roman garrison for a time after this event (Level III).

Qumrân is surely the Essene "city in the wilderness" described by Pliny. Philo and Josephus agree that there were about 4000 Essenes but that they did not all live at Qumrân. The scrolls clarify the situation by referring to the main community at Qumrân as the *Yáḥad*, to other communities elsewhere as the "camps" or *maḥanôt*, and to all together as the "congregation" or 'ēdâ. Qumrân was the sect's original place of exile "in the wilderness," established by a founder known as "the teacher of righteousness," and governed by a celibate rule. Not all of the "camps" appear to have been celibate, because some at least followed "the order of the earth."

The Essenes were the true eschatological or apocalyptic branch of Judaism. They were *ḥasîdîm* who between c. 145 and 130 B.C. retired to the "wilderness," disgusted and outraged at the secularization of Judaism in the Maccabean wars. There they lived a communal life with intense absorption in the Law, preoccupation with the quality of life needed for the New Age about to dawn, an organization modelled on the old rules for Holy War in early Israel, and an expectant interpretation of the fulfillment of prophecy in their own day. Their "ascetism" was a tactical return to the desert simplicity of the Mosaic era while preparing for the coming of the Messiah and the end of the age. The Essenes had little to do with the Jerusalem temple or its cultus because they felt them defiled. They were the new Israel of the new covenant. G.E.W.

Esther (? "star"), Jewish heroine of the Biblical book which bears her name. Cousin and adopted daughter of Mordecai (Esther 2:15), she became Xerxes'* queen (1–2:18); delivered her people from their destruction planned by Haman (2:19–4:17); and saw him hanged on the gallows he had had made for Mordecai (5–7), who thereafter became the grand vizier (8–9:16). To commemorate these episodes the Feast of Purim* was instituted (9:17–10:3). (see FEASTS.)

The Book of Esther in the Jewish O.T. Canon belongs among the Writings or Hagiographa*. In the Greek Bible it usually stands after the historical books (or after the poetical books), before the prophetic books; in the English Bible it stands between the historical and poetical books.

The Heb. names of the chief characters in the book are of Mesopotamian origin. Esther (whose Jewish name was *Hadassah*, "myrtle") is Ishtar, the Babylonian goddess of love. Mordecai is Marduk, the chief Babylonian god. Vashti is the name of an Elamite goddess. Ahasuerus was the Persian Xerxes I (486–465 B.C.). The story is set in Susa (Shushan*) (Esther 1:2). The author shows an authoritative familiarity with Persian life: the architectural plan of the palace and court (1:5, 2:11, 21, 7:8); banquet customs (1:6–8, 5:5 f.); court protocol (4:11, 8:4, 5:1, 2, 3:10, 8:2); the royal harem (2:8, 12–18); and palace intrigues (2:21–23; 7:9 f.). Exaggeration, a characteristic of imaginative fiction, is much in evidence throughout the narrative, viz., the 83-ft. high gallows (5:14); the 6-months' feast (1:4); a year's beauty treatment for the court maidens (2:12); the 10,000-talent (c. $18,000,000) bribe for permission to conduct the pogrom (3:9), etc. No historical records disclose that Xerxes ever had a queen by the name of Esther or one who was a Jewess. As historical fiction the book had a purpose and fulfilled its mission.

Esther had exceptional physical beauty, personal charm, and courageous character, all of which she used on the king with great effectiveness. By her militant defense of her race she demonstrated that she had "come to the kingdom for such a time" (4:14). Haman's edict against the Jews displays anti-Semitic feeling in the ancient world. But in this narrative the Jews took matters into their own hands, and forced non-Jews to become proselytes under fear of death (Esther 8:17–9:5). This may reflect the Maccabean reign of John Hyrcanus (135–105 B.C.), who forced the conquered Idumaeans to adopt Judaism by compulsory circumcision. The probable date of the writing of Esther is believed to be c. 125 B.C.

The unnamed author of the Book of Esther was more patriotic than religious. There was "fasting" but no prayer (4:15 f.). God's help and leadership, so prominent in the best earlier Jewish thought, are referred to only in veiled language, as if the author were unwilling to speak of God's providence (4:14). This charmingly written, romantic, and sometimes noble story reflects racial jingoism characterized by secularization. Even Esther herself is guilty of the racial intolerance which the book aims to condemn. The slaying of 75,510 Gentiles by the Jews in a single day (9:6–9, 16) is an exaggeration which makes this story acceptable as fiction rather than believable as history. Martin Luther said, "I am so hostile to . . . Esther that I wish [it] did not exist; for [it] Judaizes too much and has too much heathen naughtiness."

The purpose of the Book of Esther may have been to propagandize the Feast of Purim, for which there are no other Scriptural sanctions. The origin of Purim is uncertain. Perhaps a national Persian festival was celebrated by the Jews during their Captivity and Dispersion. A Jew with a Persian background in the time of Hyrcanus wrote the story of Esther to promote in Jerusalem and the homeland what had been a day of joyous celebration among Judaea's scattered children, and synchronized it with the Jewish political revival of his time. The book was so unsatisfactory that *The Rest of the Chapters of the Book of Esther*—an apocryphal addendum of 107 vv.—was written for the purpose of adding to the Greek version the religious motive lacking in the original.

The book is out of sympathy with the teachings of the prophets; it bristles with hatred and revenge. It is no preparation for the Gospel, but rather an indication of the great need for the Gospel's coming. Jesus (so far as we know) did not quote from it. Nowhere is it mentioned in the N.T.

Etam (ē′tăm). (1) A village of Simeon (I Chron. 4:32). (2) A rock in whose cleft Samson lived (Judg. 15:8, 11, A.S.V.). (3) A town c. 2 m. SW. of Bethlehem (II Chron. 11:6).

eternal life has various meanings and connotations in the Bible. The usual idea conveyed by "eternal" is that of continuous duration, but there are various modifications. When, for example, God is spoken of as "the Eternal," it means that He is a Being who has no "before" or "after." He never began to be, and He will never cease to be: He is without beginning or end. He is therefore a necessary existence, Himself uncreated, but the Creator of all else. The name Yahweh (Jehovah), by which God told Moses He was to be known (Ex. 3: 13–15), carries this idea among others. Moffatt follows the French custom of rendering the name "the Eternal." Thus Moses, in his final blessing upon his people, said, "The eternal God is thy dwelling-place, and underneath are the everlasting arms" (A.S.V. Deut. 33:27); Ps. 90:2 reads, "Even from everlasting to everlasting, thou art God." Isaiah, whose descriptions of God—as, for example, in chap. 40—are without parallel in the O.T., speaks of God as "the high and lofty One that inhabiteth eternity" (57:15).

But in both the O.T. and the N.T. the word frequently rendered as "eternal" actually means "an age." It was as though the idea of changeless eternity was too elusive to grasp, as indeed it is. The idea of a succession of ages (aeons) helped the imagination. "Eternal" therefore sometimes means simply "age-long," and this is the usual meaning in the N.T. An "age" has other "ages" before it and other "ages" after it. In the N.T. the Greek rendered "for ever" or "for ever and ever" means literally "unto the ages" or "throughout all (remaining) ages"; and the same is true of the Hebrew equivalent in the O.T. "Age-long" or "age-lasting" therefore may not mean "eternal" in the sense of unbeginning and unending. Even when all future ages are meant, which is frequently the case (Ps. 89:36; I John 2:17), past ages are not necessarily included. Looking forward, there is no discernible end; but there may have been a beginning, and this precludes eternity in the classical sense. Such expressions as "life everlasting," "everlasting punishment" (Matt. 25:31–46; Mark 9:42–48; Luke 16:19–31), look only to the future. The condition described may be "age-long," it may even be "unto the ages of the ages," without necessarily being endless, though in some usages endlessness is definitely intended.

There are references in the N.T. to an "eternal purpose" of God (Eph. 3:11), a purpose which He had "before the foundation of the world" (Eph. 1:4; cf. Matt. 25:34; John 17:24; I Pet. 1:20). This is the purpose for whose fulfillment God created the world and mankind. Christ was involved in this purpose, because what God desired was a family of sons made possible through the eternal Son who existed in the very being of God. "In the fulness of the time" (Gal. 4:4) this eternal Son was to be "made man," that through him the purpose of God might be fulfilled (see Eph. 2:10, 3:9; Col. 1:13–20, 3:9–11). This eternal Son came among men, who knew him as Jesus of Nazareth, but some at least recognized him for what he was, the Lord and Saviour of men, the bringer of redemption.

According to the Fourth Gospel, Jesus declared to men that he was come to make possible for them eternal life. This Gospel is less a biography of Jesus than the writer's own interpretation, expressed in his own language, of what Jesus said, and did, and meant. The validity of the interpretation is bound up with the whole question of Christian experience. Jesus certainly called upon men to surrender themselves wholly to him, and he said that if they did this they would possess the Kingdom of God. Speaking generally, the "Kingdom of God" of the Synoptics becomes in the Fourth Gospel "eternal life." The distinctive metaphors of the Fourth Gospel, such as that Christ is the Water of Life, the Bread of Life, the Door of the Fold, are intended to express the significance of Christ for a new relation of men to God. Submission to "the Son" is submission to "the Father." Frequently this new relation is described as "eternal life," or a life securely grounded in the eternal God. This thought is frequent throughout the N.T. By contrast there is "everlasting" or "eternal" death, sometimes called "punishment" (Matt. 18:8, 25:46), sometimes "destruction" (Matt. 7:13; II Thess. 1:9). Here what is chiefly stressed is "loss": the soul has lost that life for which God created it in Christ.

When this "qualitative" sense of the term is grasped, whether of "eternal life" or "eternal death," then it is proper to add the note of "age-long" or "duration." Life in Christ is life according to the eternal divine intent, and its duration is a natural consequence. Failure to find this is loss indeed: it is "age-long" loss.

See IMMORTALITY; HEAVEN; HELL; PUNISHMENT; REDEMPTION; RESURRECTION.

E.L.

Ethan ("permanent"). (1) An Ezrahite possessed of great wisdom (I Kings 4:31), born of the family of Zereh (? Ezrahite), in the line of Judah; associated with Ps. 89. (2) A Levite, of the household of Merari (I Chron. 6:44), appointed as a Temple singer.

Ethiopia, an ancient region in NE. Africa, bordering on Egypt and the Red Sea; at one time Abyssinia. Hebrews knew it as Kush or Cush, established by a son of Ham (Gen. 10:6–8). Gen. 2:13 describes it as encompassed by the river "Gihon" (? Nile). Esther (1:1) mentions it as a border of Ahasuerus (Xerxes I) the Persian. The four rivers of Ethiopia (Zeph. 3:10) may have been the White and Blue Niles, the Atbara, and the Takkaze. The inhabitants of E. Ethiopia were often straight-haired; those of the W. woolly-haired. A mighty army of Ethiopians set out against King Asa of Judah (c. 913–873 B.C.), but after amassing great spoil was defeated (II Chron. 14:9–15) by "Asa and the people." In the 8th century B.C. Ethiopia conquered Egypt and her rulers, and formed the Twenty-fifth Egyptian Dynasty. To this Dynasty belonged Tirhakah, who fought against Sennacherib (II Kings 19:9). Job knew the fame of Ethiopian topaz mines (28:19). Isaiah wrote of the merchandise of Ethiopia (45:14). Greek and Latin writers mention a line of Ethiopian queens known by the title or family name of Candace*. (See CANDACE, illus. 80). One such Candace is mentioned in Acts 8:27, whose eunuch treasurer accepted Jesus after hearing Philip teach (Acts 8:28–40).

136. Ethiopian and Abyssinian Christian crosses, the center one made by natives from silver coins.

Christianity seems to have come to Ethiopia c. A.D. 341. Coptic Christians of Egypt have exerted a profound influence on Abyssinian Christians, and today foster the little colony of black-faced, lean, bearded Ethiopian priests whose simple chapel is on the roof of the Church of the Holy Sepulcher in Jerusalem.

Eucharist. See LORD'S SUPPER, THE.

Eunice, the mother of Timothy (II Tim. 1:5). As the devout Jewish wife of a Greek (Acts 16:1), she trained her son in the faith inherited from her mother Lois.

eunuchs, emasculated males employed in Oriental harems as bedroom attendants, but also given positions as trusted officials and commanders. Hebrew kings and princes aped their royal neighbors by having eunuchs guard their women's quarters (Jer. 41:16; Esther 1:10, A.V. margin; Dan. 1:3). Isaiah warned that Hebrew captives might be made eunuchs in the palaces of Babylon (II Kings 20:18; Isa. 39:7). An old law forbade eunuchs to worship in the Temple, either because the maimed were regarded as unfit for worship, or because some men had deliberately mutilated themselves in pagan rites. Isaiah advocated restoring to worship privileges those eunuchs who strove to keep covenant with God (56:4 f.), even though their lack of heirs cut them off from future inheritance in Israel. Two Ethiopian eunuchs appear in Scripture. (1) Ebed-melech, who plead before King Zedekiah on behalf of the imprisoned Jeremiah (38:7–13). (2) The pious Ethiopian eunuch who had great power under the ruling Candace*, and was baptized by Philip into the Christian faith (Acts 8:27–38). Jesus' reference to eunuchs in Matt. 19:12 may refer to voluntary and involuntary celibacy. Eunuchs were permitted to marry.

Euodias (û-ō'dĭ-ăs) (A.S.V., R.S.V. Euodia) ("fragrance"), a quarrelsome Christian colleague of Syntyche in Philippi, where both may have served as deaconesses after Paul's second visit to Macedonia (Phil. 4:2 f.).

137. Euphrates-Tigris Basin.

Euphrates, the longest river of SW. Asia, one of the four streams of Eden* (Gen. 2:14). It was called in the O.T. "the river" (Deut. 11:24) and "the great river" (Josh. 1:4). A natural boundary between the empires of Egypt and Babylonia (II Kings 24:7), it was the border aspired to by the Hebrew Monarchy at its height (II Sam. 8:3, 10:16; I Kings 4:24). Its source is two headstreams, the longest of which is the Turkish Murat rising in Kurdistan highlands between Lake Van and the Black Sea. As the Murat it flows westward until at Keban it joins the Turkish Firat (otherwise known as the Kara Su and Euphrates proper) and makes a wide, sweeping turn southeasterly. Below Hit, in its lower course, the Euphrates wastes itself in vast marshes and ruined canals, joining the Tigris at Al Qurna, about 40 miles NW. of Basra and 60 miles NW. of the Persian Gulf, to form the Shatt-al-Arab. The delta region formed by the combined silt burden of the Euphrates and Tigris has been advancing into the Gulf at the rate of approximately 72 feet per year. Great cities of the Euphrates Valley included Carchemish* (II Chron. 35:20); Babylon*, Accad* (Agade), Kish*, Erech*, Ur*, Mari*, and Dura-Europos.

Euroclydon (û-rŏk'lĭ-dŏn) (more accurately A.S.V. "Euraquilo"; R.S.V. "the northeaster"), a NNE. wind of great violence, typical of the Mediterranean spring off the Cretan coast (Acts 27:14 ff.).

Eutychus (ū'tĭ-kŭs) ("fortunate"), a youth of Troas who fell from a third-story window where he was listening to Paul, and was restored by the Apostle (Acts 20:7–12).

evangelist ("one who proclaims good tidings") is the name given in the N.T. to one who travelled from place to place proclaiming the Gospel. Philip*, one of the Seven chosen by the Twelve to look after benevolent work among widows and the needy (Acts 6:1–5), is perhaps the best example of the Christian evangelist. After the martyrdom of Stephen he went into Samaria, preaching Christ, and into the desert, as well as to the coastal cities between Azotus and Caesarea (Acts 8:5, 12, 25, 35, 40); with the result that joyous believers in Christ were baptized. The most famous convert of Philip the Evangelist was the treasurer of the Ethiopian Candace* (Acts 8:36–39). Paul referred to helpers whose gifts were those of evangelists (Eph. 4:11), who, without holding any office in the Church, or possessing the responsibilities of apostles or prophets, performed a vital role, as Timothy did, when traveling from place to place, before settling down to one congregation under his moral supervision (II Tim. 4:5).

Evangelist	*Symbol*	*Meanings*	
		Mystery	*Virtue*
Matthew	man	incarnation	reason
Mark	lion	resurrection	courage
Luke	ox or bull	sacrificial passion	renunciation
John	eagle	ascension	expectancy of immortality

In the first Christian centuries, though not in the N.T. era, the authors of the four canonical Gospels were called "Evangelists." Their individual symbols (see SYMBOL), based upon imagery in Ezekiel and Revelation, found their way early into Christian art.

Eve (from Heb. *hawwāh*, "life," connected by some with Arab. word for "serpent"), the name given by Adam* to his wife, who became the "mother of all living" (Gen. 3:20). Beguiled by a subtle serpent, Eve induced Adam to eat the fruit of a tree forbidden by God (Gen. 3:3), and thus precipitated their expulsion from the Garden of Eden* (v. 24). After this tragedy Eve bore Cain (4:1), Abel (4:2), and Seth (5:3). Paul quoted the material of Gen. 3 in II Cor. 11:3. Ideas expressed in I Tim. 2:11 f. about the subordinate position of women may be based on the primacy of Adam.

evil, the antithesis of good, and the possibility of its eradication from the soul of man, were prominent in the thought of the minds which produced the Bible. The Eden tree "of the knowledge of good and evil" (Gen. 2:17) was an early effort to express man's freedom to make moral choices. This freedom was still being stressed in I Thess. 5:22. Time and again in the O.T. this pattern repeats itself: "the children of Israel did evil in the sight of the Lord . . . and provoked the Lord to anger" (Judg. 2:11, 13, 3:7, 4:1). Some kings were evil: Solomon (I Kings 11:6), Jehoahaz (II Kings 13:1, 2, 11), Jeroboam (II Kings 14:24), Zechariah (II Kings 15:9), and Ahaz (II Kings 16:2). The Lord was recognized as being outside the possibility of being subject to evil (James 1:13); yet He was frequently regarded as the source from which evil descended upon the heads of evil-doers, as in Josh. 23:15; II Sam. 17:14. Yet men knew that He would forestall the evil they merited on the slightest evidence of their regret for evil-doing (Jer. 26:3). (Cf. the Abraham saga of Sodom, Gen. 18:23–32). God was also regarded as the sender of evil spirits, as to Saul (I Sam. 19:9). For the work of Jesus and Paul in purging evil spirits see Matt. 8:28–34; Acts 19:12. (See also DEVIL.) Ancient thinking about the source of evil was vague, as in a proverb quoted by David, "wickedness proceedeth from the wicked" (I Sam. 24:13). The author of I Tim. 6:10 indicated "love of money" as the source of all evil. Mark believed that evil is "from within" (7:23).

The recognition of God's ability to inflict evil upon sinners led people to implore Him to "deliver us from evil" (Matt. 6:13); hence the injunction of Amos (5:14) and the summary of III John 11.

The origin of evil remains one of the greatest moral problems, which challenges man to heroic quests for the truth concerning it. The following tenets bearing upon evil have been accepted by many Christian thinkers: (1) Physical evil is radically different from moral evil, though much of it is due to moral evil and might be avoided. Many physical evils have value, however, in training character. (2) Evil began when spirits, created free, chose to do evil rather than right, and thus condemned themselves (John 3:19). (3) This does not discourage God, Who has ready a plan of redemption through a self-sacrificing Saviour* (Gal. 1:4). (4) The revelation of this saviourhood could not have taken place without a conflict between good and evil. (5) Evil is thus made a partner of good, which will ultimately triumph through the infinite patience of God, Who allows His creatures to mature into holiness. (6) Man learns to trust God so completely in Christ that he is confident that even a universe with evil in it will finally crown God's total creative acts with a complete vindication of His purpose (Rom. 5:20).

Evil-Merodach (Accad. "man of Marduk"), son and successor (562 B.C.) of Nebuchadnezzar. This lawless and indecent ruler of Babylon is given credit for granting generous privileges to his prisoner King Jehoiachin of Judah (II Kings 25:27–30; Jer. 52:31–34). His brother-in-law Nergal-sharezer* (sometimes known as Neriglissar) conspired against him, put him to death, and seized the throne in 560 B.C.

evil spirits. See DEVIL.

ewe, a female sheep. The most famous Bible mention of the "ewe lamb" is found in Nathan's rebuke of David in II Sam. 12:1–14. See also Gen. 21:30. For the use of ewes in sacrifice, see Lev. 14:10, 22:28; Num. 6:14.

excavation. See ARCHAEOLOGY.

Exile, the period of the Captivity, when the Hebrews were subjected to deportation and supervised living under alien powers in Mesopotamia and Persia. Israel first encountered this treatment when the cities of Naphtali were captured by Tiglath-pileser III (745–727 B.C.), and its citizens "carried captive to Assyria" (II Kings 15:29). The Tribes of Reuben, Gad, and Manasseh shared the same fate (I Chron. 5:26). Samaria was besieged by Shalmaneser V (727–722 B.C.) and Sargon II (722–705 B.C.). It fell in 722, and many of its inhabitants were deported (II Kings 17:6, 18:11). These Biblical passages briefly summarize the Captivity of the Ten Tribes. There was "none left but the tribe of Judah" (II Kings 17:18).

Forecasts of a similar fate for Judah (Isa. 6:11 f., 39:6; Mic. 4:10; Jer. 25:11) were later fulfilled. During the conflict between her great neighbor powers, Egypt and the Babylonian Empire (successor of the Assyrian Empire), Judah was forced to ally herself with Egypt, who immediately dictated the internal policies by naming Jehoiakim (Eliakim) King of Jerusalem (II Kings 23:34). Nebuchadnezzar (605–562 B.C.) decisively defeated Pharaoh-nechoh at Carchemish in 605 B.C. (Jer. 46:1–12). When Jehoiakim refused to pay tribute to Nebuchadnezzar (II Kings 23:34, 24:1), the Chaldeans marched on Judaea; the unpopular king died; and Jehoiachin*, the 18-year-old son and successor of Jehoiakim, surrendered in 597 B.C. (II Kings 24:8–13). The king, court, men of valor, craftsmen, and ironworkers were exiled to Babylonia. The record suggests that only the poor and incompetent remained in Jerusalem (II Kings 24:14–16; Jer. 27:20, 29:2). Jeremiah was permitted to stay; Ezekiel was taken (Ezek. 1:1–3). King

Zedekiah, the new appointee of Nebuchadnezzar (II Kings 24:17), rallied the remaining inhabitants, who developed a false sense of security and importance. In spite of Jeremiah's warning, strong nationalistic feelings led Zedekiah to rebel against Nebuchadnezzar (II Kings 24:20). After a siege attended by famine (II Kings 25:3; Lam. 2:11–20, 4:3–12), Nebuchadnezzar captured Jerusalem in July 587 B.C. King Zedekiah was killed, the Temple and palaces were plundered and burned, and the entire population, save "the poor of the land"—farmers and vinedressers—taken to Babylonia (II Kings 25:4–21).

The Exiles were usually planted in colonies, like Tel Abib by the River Chebar, near Nippur (Ezek. 1:1, 3:15). The treatment they received and their reactions to their new home varied. Some possessed houses (Ezek. 8:1, 12:1–7; Jer. 29:5); married (Jer. 29:6); made money (Isa. 55:1 f.; Zech. 6:9–11); and obtained high positions in the state (Neh. 1:11). Others, probably the poor, suffered harsh treatment (Isa. 14:3, 47:6). Nostalgia (Ps. 137) bred despair (Ezek. 37:11). Among the exiles were Temple priests (Jer. 29:1), who, because of their hereditary position, possessed wealth, influence, and ability. During this period, they collected, codified, and reduced to writing the Temple laws, some of which appear in the Holiness Code (Lev. 17–26). They dreamed of Temple restoration, but they organized the synagogue* as a substitute during the Exile. At the same time, many active minds among these displaced persons were in contact with Babylonian ideas, especially mythology and astrology, which cropped out in later Jewish literature. Worshippers, cut off from their Temple and its sacrifices, continued to pray, to circumcise their sons, to develop their writings, and to prepare for a future. In 539 B.C., Babylon fell into the hands of Cyrus the Great, the tolerant Persian, who issued a decree permitting the Jews to return to the land of their fathers and to rebuild their Temple (Ezra 1:1–4). Many, however, preferred to remain in Babylonia, and, together with the Israelites scattered elsewhere, formed what became known as the Diaspora (see DISPERSION) (Acts 2:5–11; I Pet. 1:1).

See ISRAEL; RETURN, THE.

Exodus ("a way out," from Gk. *exodos*; in Heb. *Yetzi'ath Mitzraim*, "exodus from Egypt"; the title in the Hebrew Bible is *Ve'eleh Shemoth*, or *Shemoth*, "and these [are] the names").

(1) *The experience* was the deliverance of Israel from bondage in Egypt by God's power working through the human agency of Moses*. Not until this deliverance did Israel emerge as the people of Yahweh, for the slaves in Egypt did not even know the name of the God Who sent Moses to deliver them (Ex. 3:13). The God of the Patriarchs, "God Almighty" (El Shaddai) (Ex. 6:3) was revealed as "Yahweh" to Moses from a burning bush (Ex. 3:14 f., 6:1–3). When Israel experienced the workings of the Lord in their delivery from Pharaoh, they were ready to worship Him as their God, in gratitude for what He had led them out from and was leading them into. If they did their part, He would conduct them into a "land flowing with milk and honey" (Ex. 3:17) and would use them down the centuries in the spiritual services of revealing their God to other peoples. Under the convincing leadership of Moses, and the morale born of a revelation of Yahweh (Ex. 19:1–8), the Tribes were held together through the exigencies of a 40-year period, including a trek across wilderness sands and mountains and a prolonged residence at the oasis of Kadesh. The exact date of the Exodus and of the entry of Israel into Palestine is not of supreme importance, although heated debate has centered on it. Present opinion, guided by archaeological findings in Edom* and at Jericho*, suggests the latter half of the 13th century B.C., or c. 1250, for the entry into Palestine. An inscription on a bowl found in the ruins of Lachish suggests that the city was destroyed c. 1220 B.C., and the Israel Stele of Merenptah (c. 1220 B.C.) indicates that Israel was already in W. Palestine at that time.

(2) *The Route of the Exodus*. For the route of the Exodus there are two or three theories, each with plausible features. The traditional itinerary took the migration across the N. end of the Red Sea. But, as pointed out by the 1948 African Expedition of the University of California, the "Red Sea" of Ex. 13:18 and "the sea" of Ex. 14 are probably the Lake of Reeds, which was N. of the present town of Suez in the marshy area between Suez and the Great Bitter Lake. The Lake of Reeds may appear as the "Papyrus Marsh" in Egyptian documents. Probably, then, the crossing of Israel took place somewhere along the present Suez Canal. The journey proceeded into the apex of the rugged projection of the Arabian Peninsula known as the Plateau of Sinai, between the Gulf of Suez and the Gulf of Aqabah at the head of the Red Sea; and continued by way of Aqabah. Two peaks of Sinai are among those suggested as the site of Israel's encampment—Serbal and Mûsā. Several years may have been spent at Kadesh-barnea (see KADESH), with its famous springs, near the S. frontier of Palestine. The route from Kadesh into Edom, Moab, and the grazing lands of E. Palestine (now the Kingdom of Jordan) was probably along trails still used by nomadic sheikhs with their flocks.

The baffling part of the journey is its first stage out of Egypt. Major Jarvis, who served nine years as an official in the Sinai Peninsula, and had rare opportunities for knowing its roads and topographical peculiarities, advanced a belief in a northern route—despite the Philistine peril which led many to discard this route as the likely one (Ex. 13:17). But the Philistine peril, pointed out in Ex. 13:17, did not appear before the Philistines settled in coastal Palestine soon after 1200 B.C.—later than the time now accepted for the Exodus. Jarvis felt that Israel may never have visited the S. tip of Sinai or its Jebel Mûsā (Mount Moses), which became sacred as late as the 4th century A.D. He believed that Israel came out of Egypt via Bardawil Lake, which he thought was the 45-m.-long "Sea of Reeds" (the *Yam Suph* of the Hebrew text) that played havoc with Pharaoh's chariots. This beautiful marshy stretch is along the modern train route from Palestine to Egypt. Near here in Israel's day were grazing lands capable of supporting a large population of migrants. And from the alluvial plain, S., rises 2,000-ft.-high Mt. Hellal, more impressive for "the Mount of the Law" than the Jebel Mûsā in S. Sinai.

EXODUS

Outline of the Book of Exodus

(*a*) *To Sinai*—1–18:

The death of Joseph, rise of a hostile ruler (1:8, 2:23), increase of Hebrew population, oppressive measures (1:1–22).

The birth and rearing of Moses; his flight to Midian (chap. 2).

The burning bush revelation to Moses at Horeb; the identity of Yahweh; the call of Moses to establish the nation and conduct it to the Promised Land (chap. 3).

Moses receives his rod of authority (4:17);

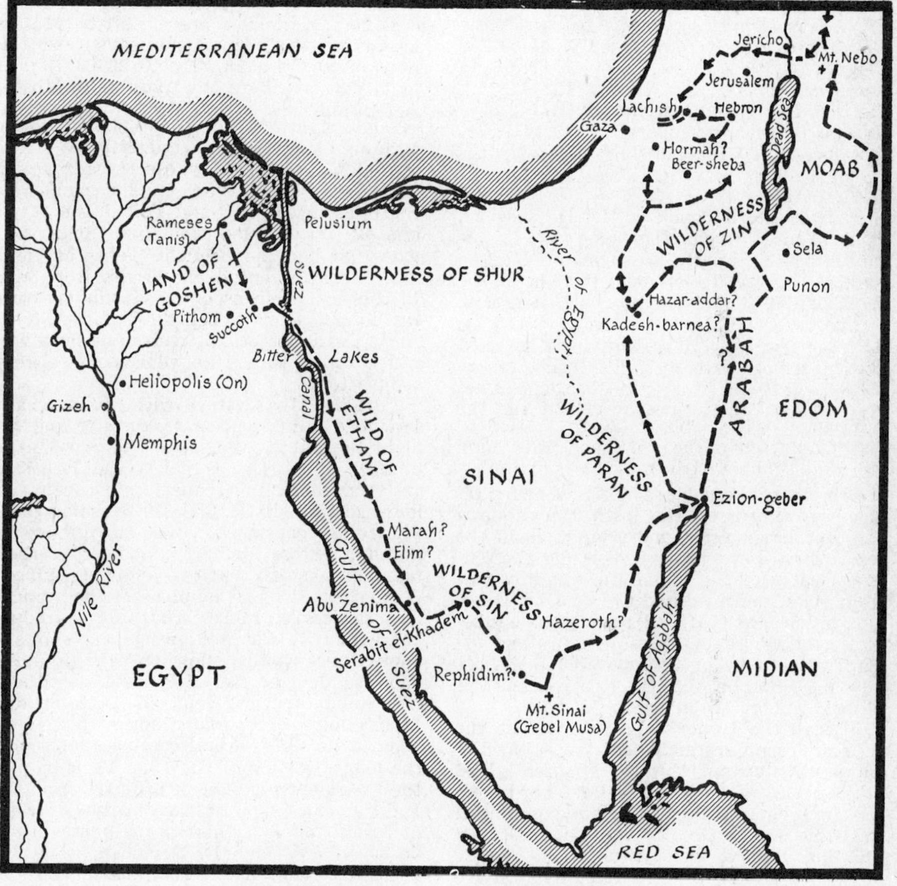

138. Tentative route of the Exodus.

Jarvis envisioned Israel as living in the triangle between the present El Arish, Rafa, and Kosseima, near the Mediterranean coast, until they turned sharply SE. to Kadesh-barnea, thence by the traditional route. He objected to the S. Sinai route because Israel would have feared Egyptian troops guarding the turquoise and copper mines at Serabit. (See ISRAEL; WILDERNESS.)

(3) *The Book*. Exodus is subheaded "The Second Book of Moses, commonly called Exodus" in both the A.V. and the A.S.V. There is no such title in the original text; in Hebrew the Pentateuch was originally a single work in five volumes.

returns from Midian to Egypt (4:20); circumcision (4:25–26).

Interviews with Pharaoh; the ten plagues (5–11); the departure of Israel from Egypt; the Passover (chap. 12).

The crossing of the Sea of Reeds and the journey through the Wilderness to Sinai (14:1–18); Moses' song (15:1–18); the Song of Miriam (15:21); quails and manna; the visit of Jethro, declaring "the Lord is greater than all gods" (18:11), and aiding Moses to organize courts of law (vv. 13–27).

(*b*) *At Sinai*—19:

The encampment of Israel at Sinai; Moses with Yahweh on the Mount (19:20); Yahweh reveals His plans for His "holy nation" (19:6).

God gives the Law (chaps. 20–24, 32–34).

The Lord's instructions about the priesthood and the sanctuary (25–31; 35–40)—the Sabbath and offerings (chap. 35); furniture (chaps. 36, 37); vestments (chap. 39); the erection of the Tabernacle and its presence during journeys (chap. 40).

(Note. Exodus closes with Israel still journeying, led by Moses and the cloud-covered Tabernacle filled with the glory of the Lord. The entry to Palestine is not mentioned until Josh. 3, after the death of Moses.)

Notable Passages in Exodus

Call of Moses at Horeb	3:1–4:17.
Plagues	7–11.
Passover	12:1–13:16.
Songs of Moses and Miriam	15:1–21.
Visit of Jethro and Zipporah	18.
Decalogue and "Book of the Covenant"	20–23; cf. 24:7.
Golden Calf	32.

Exodus, the 2d book of the Hexateuch*, contains in its 40 chapters some very important material, from the death of Joseph to the building of the Tabernacle. It tells of the formation of Israel as a people (Ex. 6:6, 7:14, 16); their discovery of Yahweh (15:11, 17); the genesis of Hebrew divinely revealed law, developed later in fuller form (20:22–23:33, 34:10–26); the origin of the greatest Hebrew festival, the Passover (12), and the ordinances of the Sabbath (20:8–11, 34:21); the organization of the priesthood (28f.); and the establishment of the movable community shrine, the Tabernacle (25–27). When similarities to already existing institutions appear, those of Israel prove more lofty, as in the resemblance between Yahwism and the religion of Jethro* the Midianite, which he saw so happily confirmed and elevated by Moses and his people (18:1–12); the parallels between the Hebrew Codes (see CODE) and the Babylonian Law of Hammurabi* (c. 1728–1686 B.C.), and between the Passover and the old Babylonian Moon or Sin festival.

Not all the Hebrews in Palestine at the time of Joseph descended for the Sojourn in Egypt. For example, Judah apparently did not, nor part of the Tribe of Levi, nor others who were found already occupying central Palestine at the time of the Conquest and did not need to be subdued, but merely amalgamated. There were living in Palestine after the Exodus, therefore, pre-Israelite Hebrews, Israelites, and Canaanites. Nor did all who made the Exodus do so at the same time. For example, Manasseh and Ephraim (sons of Joseph) may have trekked N. at the time of Jacob's funeral (Gen. 50:7) and remained in Palestine. Or they may have left Egypt after the expulsion of the Hyksos*. Some may have crossed the Jordan and seized land in Palestine in Amarna times. The journeying out of Egypt and into Palestine was a slow process, as wave after wave emerged, conquered, and settled down. While their kinsfolk were in Egypt, the groups which "stayed behind" in Palestine felt the impact of very ancient religious concepts pressing in from the E., impacts from possibly Yahweh-worshipping Kenites*. These experiences were later blended with the profound spiritual revelations which came to Israel during the bondage and escape. In the long run, the Hebrews in Palestine who had been oppressed by the Pharaohs were knit together by a consciousness of the protective power of Yahweh—the God of the Mount and of the Desert. Some scholars believe that the "Ritual Decalogue" of Ex. 34:10–26 and 23:15–19 originated in a more primitive source (possibly Kenite) than that from which sprang the "Ethical Decalogue" of Ex. 20:1–17 (cf. Deut. 5:6–21). Be this as it may, the oldest portion of the Mosaic Law is the Covenant Code, called also the Book of the Covenant (Ex. 20:22–23:19 plus 23:20–33), attributed by tradition to Moses. See SOURCES.

Scholars, attempting to get the maximum meaning from Exodus, have analyzed it into several main strands whose threads are at times chaotically tangled. The men who centuries ago wrote and edited the J, E, and P documents from oral epics and codes, all had independent points of view, sources of information, and locales. But above all the controversies of critics, and beyond any possible effort to belittle the facts, Moses looms as the historic deliverer and lawgiver; and Yahweh towers above His nonexistent competitors.

J begins Moses' story with his indignant slaying of an Egyptian taskmaster and his flight to Arabia, whereas E begins with the infancy of Moses. J makes the Israelites cattle-breeders living apart in Goshen and increasing rapidly (1:6, 8–12). E makes them Pharaoh's "pensioners" in an Egyptian community, deletes the cattle, and makes their numbers so small that two midwives sufficed (1:15–20a; 21 f.). E emphasizes the miraculous powers of Moses' rod and a gradual concession by Pharaoh; whereas J shows a more direct participation by Yahweh and a more sudden reversal of Pharaoh's attitude. The very ancient Song of Miriam—one stanza only—in its original form (15:21), expanded possibly several centuries later into the longer version of Ex. 15:1–18, is part of the E strand. As might be expected from the P document, much of this "learned" strand of Exodus offers a "historical commentary' on the J, E, and D Documents (R. H. Pfeiffer). It contains the laws of a holy nation, and gives instructions for the building of the Tabernacle; the establishment of the priesthood of Aaron and his successors; and various rites. Written during the 5th century B.C. while many Jews were living in Babylonia, P "made of the Jews a sort of monastic order living in the world but apart from outsiders and under their own rules." Israel, as shown by P, dreamed of a "purely ritualistic, ideal Kingdom of God, belonging to the dim past." P, called by R. H. Pfeiffer the "charter of the new Jewish church," was written either toward the end of Darius' reign (522–486 B.C.)—after the rebuilding of the Temple—or in the reign of Xerxes (486–465 B.C.). P stresses the cultus, the Passover, the Sabbath, and the importance of the high priest Aaron.

(R. H. Pfeiffer, *An Introduction to the Old Testament*, p.257, Harper & Brothers.)

Criticism has not depreciated but enhanced the readers' understanding of the facts behind Israel's record of her national history. The findings of archaeology have at times proved a corrective to some of the unfounded tenets of criticism. W. F. Albright considers that four centuries of oral transmission of the stories of Moses' life preceded their being put into final form. He stresses the fact, however, that from the Patriarchal Age on alphabetic Hebrew writing was employed in Canaan and the surrounding regions. Before the Exodus, in the 14th and 13th centuries B.C., the Hebrew alphabet was being written in ink, for everyday communications; later written records have been found at Lachish*, Samaria, Beth-shemesh*, Megiddo*, etc. Moses could conceivably but not certainly have prepared written documents. (See SERABIT; SINAI.) Even if Exodus in its present form did not come from the hand of Moses, the Mosaic origin of its nucleus need not be doubted. See MONOTHEISM.

exorcism. See MAGIC.

eye, the organ of sight or vision, frequently used in the Bible in colorful figures of speech. Jesus called it "the light of the body," whose health governed that of the whole person (Matt. 6:22). Again, he used an evil eye to express a man's jealousy (Matt. 20:15)—a phrase not synonymous with the "evil eye" of Eastern superstition, warded off by wearing an amulet*. Jesus showed himself a true Easterner when he used such phrases as "if thy right eye offend thee, pluck it out" (Matt. 5:29), for his hearers knew that the eye was the symbol of envy and desire. Cf. his words, "whosoever looketh on a woman" (Matt. 5:28). Lustful use of the eye is referred to in Ezek. 6:9; II Pet. 2:14; I John 2:16.

In Bible lands people have always been subjected to many ophthalmic diseases due to dust, glare, and germs. See AMULETS, illus. 15; BLINDNESS.

Ezekiel (ē-zēk′yĕl) ("God strengthens"). (1) A 6th century major prophet of the Exilic period; the son of Buzi (1:3), of a priestly family. He grew up in Jerusalem, was familiar with the Temple, and probably heard Jeremiah preach. In 598 B.C. he was among those of the elite who were deported with King Jehoiachin to Babylon (II Kings 24:11–16). Fourteen dates scattered through the book bearing his name, peg 23 years of Ezekiel's history (c. 593–571 B.C.). He lived in a colony of exiles at Tel Abib on the Chebar, an important canal in the Euphrates irrigation system (3:15); he was married (24:15–18), and had a house of his own (3:24, 8:1). His prophetic mission began five years after his captivity (1:2), when he was perhaps 30 (cf. 1:1; Num. 4:3). The dual role of prophet-priest makes Ezekiel's position unique among O.T. personalities. His position as "watchman" over the exiles is defined in terms of a pastor's concern for the spiritual welfare of his flock.

Ezekiel was a preacher whose sermons, reduced to writing, read well. He performed many symbolic acts (4:1–15, 12:1–20). His deep introspective and religious nature found expression in visions (8–11, 37:1–14, chaps. 40–48). Babylonian art—winged creatures (1:8), etc., seen on gates and palaces—stimulated his imagination. Ezekiel, like Hosea, used personal experiences to dramatize his teachings, bearing, for example, a tragic domestic loss with fortitude (24:15–18). Some also think he suffered a nervous affliction (perhaps epilepsy or paranoid schizophrenia) (3:25 f., 4:4, 24:27), of which he was cured with the announcement in 587 B.C. that Jerusalem had fallen (33:21 f.); such was the release from the tension under which the prophet had been working. His congregation of exiles in Chebar did not always like to hear Ezekiel expound so pointedly the moral causes of their national downfall (3:11). But the elders appreciated his character and insight (8:1, 14:1, 20:1), and crowded his little mud-brick house. His picturesque eloquence in time won him many hearers (33:30–33), who admired his art, if not the substance of his message. Even though his congregation was small, remote, and relatively unimportant, Ezekiel continued to address the whole of Israel over and beyond them. His data concerning the history, politics, and commerce of the neighboring nations demonstrate his breadth of interest (25–32). His informa- is an important literary source of our knowledge of the trade of the ancient maritime center of Tyre.

Jeremiah and the youthful Ezekiel were together in Jerusalem before its fall, and Ezekiel may well have received inspiration from the utterances of the older prophet. Their affinity, sometimes in language as well as in thought, may be traced to such common concerns as the overthrow of Jerusalem and the Temple (Jer. 7, 27; cf. Ezek. 4, 7, 19, 24); to despair for the people of Judah and hope for the exiles (Jer. 24, 29:10 ff.; cf. Ezek. 11:16–21, 36:24 ff.); to confidence in the return of the dispersed (Jer. 23:3, 29:14; cf. Ezek. 11:17, 20:34, 41 f.); to belief that a descendant of David, even a second David, would come to rule a united people (Jer. 23:5 f., 33:14–16; cf. Ezek. 34:23 f., 37:24 f.). Though both Jeremiah and Ezekiel stressed individual responsibility (Jer. 31:29 f.; cf. Ezek. 18) and recognized the heart as the starting place for a new way of life (Jer. 4:4, 31:31–34), Ezekiel held that conversion* would bring salvation* to the individual (36:26 f.). The destruction of the Temple led Jeremiah to maintain his religion (Jer. 29:5–7, 11–14). But Ezekiel believed that the religious future of the Jews could be maintained only in a theocracy, expressed in a sanctuary (40–43), with a priesthood and laws (44–48). Ezekiel was the bridge between the ritualistic institutions of Deuteronomy and those of the P Code; the national religion of the Prophets and the personal religion of the Psalms; faith in the Temple which was once seen and the sanctity of the sanctuary unseen but spiritually real (47:1 f.).

(2) The Book of Ezekiel stands in the English Bible between Lamentations and Daniel, but in the Hebrew Bible it immediately follows Jeremiah. It consists of the prophet's utterances written either before or after they were delivered, and arranged in a topical and usually also chronological scheme. There is some evidence that some verses represent the work of a redactor; but the book is generally considered the work and arrangement of Ezekiel in Babylonia. A fourfold division of the book is possible:

(1) Chaps. 1–24: prophecies of judgment prior to the destruction of Jerusalem.

(2) Chaps. 25–32: prophecies against seven foreign nations—Ammon, Moab, Edom, and Philistia (25); Tyre (26–28:19); Sidon (28:20–26); Egypt 29–32.

(3) Chaps. 33–39: discourses after Jerusalem's fall.

(4) Chaps. 40–48: the ideal theocracy: sanctuary (40–43); ritual (44–46); the river of holiness (47); the holy land (48).

The book teaches that God is holy, calling to high moral standards not only individuals but nations. When peoples fail to live up to God's standards they will experience His judgment and they shall know that I am the Lord" (26:6; 29:21; 30:19). Hebrew angelology was furthered by the teachings of this book (cf. 1:4–26). But Ezekiel, though he presented a universal, monotheistic God, did not present a universal religion; Yahweh and Israel belonged together.

Many of the teachings of this book are discernible in the N.T. God as a shepherd, seeking the lost sheep (Ezek. 34:11–16), was used by Jesus (Matt. 18:12–14). Paul clarified conversion and the change of heart (II Cor. 3:3; cf. Ezek. 11:19). The visions of the prophet profoundly influenced the writer of Revelation: the city foursquare (Ezek. 48:16, 30; cf. Rev. 21:16), the river of life (Ezek. 47:1; cf. Rev. 22:1), etc.

Ezion-geber (ē′zĭ-ŏn-gē′bẽr) (Elath, Eloth) (? "grove of tall trees"), a settlement at the head of the Gulf of Aqabah, which served as a port throughout most of the Iron Age. Two contiguous sites appear to be indicated in some passages (Deut. 2:8; I Kings 9:26), but in others merely a change of name from Ezion-geber to Elath (Eloth), apparently some time between the reigns of Jehoshaphat and Uzziah (cf. I Kings 22:48 with I Kings 14:22). Ezion-geber/Elath is to be identified with Tell el-Kheleifeh, c. 2 m. W. of the modern village of Aqabah. Excavations directed by Nelson Glueck between 1938 and 1940 uncovered five phases of occupation dating from the 10th–5th century B.C. Ezion-geber is first mentioned in the O.T. as one of the campsites of the Israelites during their wilderness journeys (Num. 33:35–36; Deut. 2:8). Later, Solomon founded an important port, and possible industrial center, at Ezion-geber (I Kings 9:26; II Chron. 8:17; Phase I at Tell el-Kheleifeh, according to Glueck; Rothenberg, however, considers this too late a date; see below). The site was burned down, and rebuilt (Phase II), probably by Jehoshaphat (c. 860 B.C.), whose fleet was wrecked there (I Kings 22:48; II Chron. 20:36–37). It was again rebuilt (Phase III) by Uzziah (c. 780 B.C.), this time as Elath (II Kings 14:22; II Chron. 26:2). A seal signet ring was found in this level bearing the inscription "belonging to Jotham," the successor of Uzziah (*BASOR* 163, 1961, pp.18–22). The Edomites recovered Elath during the reign of Ahaz of Judah (c. 730 B.C.; II Kings 16:6), and it remained in Edomite control from the 7th–4th cen. B.C. (Phases IV–V). Tell el-Kheleifeh was subsequently abandoned, the Nabataean settlement being located further E., at Aila, near Aqabah.

Considerable controversy has evolved over the function, and even the date, of the large mud-brick structure, with two rows of horizontal apertures penetrating its walls, discovered in the NW. corner of Tell el-Kheleifeh. Glueck at first suggested that the structure was a type of smelter-refinery, the apertures being flue holes which furnished a natural draft by taking advantage of the prevailing winds at the head of the Gulf of Aqabah. As a result, Ezion-geber/Elath had been somewhat hastily, and incorrectly, dubbed the "Pittsburgh of Palestine" (Glueck, *Rivers in the Desert*, 1940, ch. 4). Further study has shown that the apertures are nothing more than the resulting void left by decayed wooden crossbeams (see Glueck, *The Other Side of the Jordan*, 1970, pp. 111–113; *AOTS*, 1967, pp. 438–439). Glueck nevertheless still insisted that (a) it was a metallurgical-industrial city, and (b) the remains dated from the 10th–5th centuries B.C. and that it was founded by Solomon, to complement the copper-smelting sites in the Wâdī Arabah which Glueck believed were Solomonic (*The Other Side of the Jordan*, chaps. III–IV; *BA* 28, 1965, pp. 70–87). B. Rothenberg, on the other hand, prefers to call the structure at Ezion-geber a "storehouse/granary," and has shown with considerable proof that the copper mining sites are pre-Solomonic, dating from the 14th to mid-12th century B.C., and has rejected any suggestion that copper refining was practiced at Tell el-Kheleifeh, interpreting the central structure there as a large storehouse and fortress built by Solomon along the route from Arabia to Egypt and Syria (*PEQ*, 1962, pp. 44–56; *Archaeologia Austriaca* 47, 1970, pp. 91–130). While the latter interpretation seems preferable, more work needs to be done to settle the question. W. P. A.

Ezra ("help"; Esdras in Gk. and Lat.). (1) *The man.* Ezra was a Jewish priest who returned to Jerusalem during the reign of Artaxerxes (Ezra 7:1). He played a prominent part in instituting reforms which rehabilitated the Jewish church and state. The source for his life story is primarily the "Ezra Memoir" (Ezra 7–10; Neh. 8–10).

Ezra belonged to a high-priestly family; was "a ready scribe" (Ezra 7:6, 10) and in the Apocrypha was called "a prophet" (II

EZRA

Esdras 1:1). Though many exiled Jews were satisfied with making money in Babylon, Ezra embodied the interests of those who in the Babylonian atmosphere cherished thoughts of their distant Temple and meditated on their nation's sacred writings and traditions. Under the tolerant policy of the Persian regime, Ezra with the aid of influential Jewish courtiers enlisted the help of Artaxerxes, who by imperial edict permitted this priestly leader to conduct home to Jerusalem such of his countrymen as desired to rehabilitate the Temple and the religious life of their people. The hazardous pilgrimage of over 1500 men and their families across the desert was completed in four months. These returned exiles presented gifts and sacred vessels for the embellishment of the Temple ritual. Ezra was shocked at the mixed marriages in Jerusalem, and commanded faithless men to separate from "strange wives" (Ezra 10:11). During the governorship of Nehemiah* Ezra led a revival in reading and obeying the Book of the Law (Neh. 8:1–12), and in reviving the thanksgiving festival, "The Feast of the Booths" (Neh. 8:13–18).

Ezra the priest and Nehemiah the layman dominate this period of Jewish history. Ezra as an ecclesiastical leader influenced the Jewish people for centuries after his time. His efforts to have Jews divorce foreign wives (Ezra 10:1–17), with its resultant misery and unhappiness, was an integral part of his program for the revival of Judaism. It may have completed the schism with Samaria. When he restored the sacred vessels to the Temple he proved himself a priestly patron of ecclesiastical art in ritual. He led the people into a new understanding of and devotion to the Law of Moses. The acceptance of this emphasis furthered the organization of the synagogue; the rise of the rabbinate in Judaism following the professional scribes; and ultimately the Sanhedrin*, with its powerful judicial prerogatives. In Ezra are found the elements of reform, ritual, and religious education. A contagious joyousness was the dynamic which made Ezra's stiff program possible and acceptable to the people (Neh. 10).

(2) *The book.* Together with Nehemiah, this constitutes one volume in the early Jewish canon. In the Vulgate I Esdras is Ezra; II Esdras is Nehemiah. Both deal apparently with the same period, present the same problems, and were put in their present forms by the same editor. The history in I and II Chronicles is continued in Ezra and Nehemiah, which relate the story of the Jews during the century and a half following the edict of Cyrus permitting the Exiles to return (538 B.C.). The following is a summary of these books as they now are:

(a) Ezra 1–6, return of the Exiles (538 B.C.); rebuilding the Temple.

(b) Ezra 7–10, activities of Ezra (continued in Neh. 8–10).

(c) Neh. 1–12, Nehemiah's administration in Judaea (445–433 B.C.).

(d) Neh. 13, his second visit to Jerusalem (433 B.C.).

Haggai and Zechariah prophesied during this period (Ezra 5:1). Most scholars, basing their belief on diction and viewpoint, hold that the author of Ezra and Nehemiah was "the Chronicler"; W. F. Albright believed that Ezra alone should be considered "the Chronicler," as does the Talmud. II Chron. 36:22 f. is repeated in Ezra 1:1–3. For many, however, the Chronicler remains anonymous.

It is impossible to harmonize chronologically or logically the events of these books, since the Chronicler did not write with the modern motive of historical accuracy uppermost. He was a propagandist for the priesthood, an historic fact important in the revival of the Jewish church and state in the 3d century B.C., when this was written. His record is an accurate reflection of the ecclesiastical revival of his day. The Chronicler for his purpose used as material (a) Nehemiah's personal memoirs (Neh. 1–7:5a, 13:6–31); (b) data on Ezra (Ezra 7–10; Neh. 8–10); (c) Aramaic official documents (Ezra 5:3–6:13; 7:12–26); (d) genealogical lists (Neh. 7:5b–65, etc.); (e) his own information with its marked ecclesiastical bias (Neh. 9–13:5).

Some scholars place the return of Ezra in the reign of Artaxerxes I (Longimanus) (465–424); others, in the reign of Artaxerxes II (Mnemon) (404–358). The former date Ezra before Nehemiah, as in the present Scripture sequence; the latter make Ezra follow him. Perhaps Ezra and his activity would more logically come after that of Nehemiah, who, as the Persian-appointed governor of Jerusalem, would probably have been sympathetic to his reforms and have offered strong support. This later date is supported by the conflict between Ezra 10:6 and Neh. 12:23–26. The Chronicler, in his use of the Ezra material, exercised considerable liberty. Some of it is recorded in the first person (Ezra 7:27–9:15); other passages are in the third (Ezra 7:1–10; Neh. 8–10). Evidently the Chronicler, throughout Ezra and Nehemiah, used all his literary talents to portray Ezra not only in terms of his historical background but as the benefactor and dispenser of the great Nehemiah influence. This is in keeping with the clerical characteristic of the Chronicler.

In this confused narrative, which contains much that is historic fact, the memoirs of Nehemiah emerge from literary rubble as the earliest autobiography extant, with the exception of the grave inscriptions of the Egyptian nomarchs of the Middle Kingdom. Written by Nehemiah emerge from literary rubble. Written by Nehemiah himself after 432 B.C. (Neh. 5:14), and recounting acts during his governorship, these memoirs report fully and vividly, as one would do in a diary not intended for publication, the actual facts and emotions they aroused in the writer. They throw much light on the political history of the Jews during the foggy Persian period. The Chronicler incorporated in full the Nehemiah saga, because this great layman was so sympathetic to the religious ideals of the reconstructed Jewish church and state.

F

fable, a fictitious story, usually having animals or plants for characters, designed to emphasize moral maxims. There are only two fables in the Bible: that of the trees who sought a king (Judg. 9:8–15); and that of the thistle and the cedar (II Kings 14:9).

Fair Havens, a small bay on the S. coast of Crete, exposed on the E., protected on the SW. by two small islands. There Paul's ship, after sailing W. under the lee of the island, found shelter in rough fall weather (Acts 27:8). In this roadstead the grain ship remained a considerable time, covering the Fast (Acts 27:9), i.e., the Day of Atonement (Lev. 16:29 f.), which in A.D. 59 fell on Oct. 5. Mediterranean navigation was increasingly dangerous at this season, and was often suspended entirely by winter storms from Nov. 11 to Feb. 8. At a ship's conference Paul (Acts (27;9–12) advised remaining at

139. Fair Havens on Muros Promontory, Crete.

Fair Havens for the winter to ensure the safety of cargo, passengers, and crew. But the ship's owner argued that the port of Phenice, 50 m. W., whose landlocked harbor faced E., would be a more commodious and safer winter haven; and his nautical argument won out. A gentle S. wind enabled the vessel to leave Fair Havens and round Cape Matapan (Acts 27:13). The vessel failed to reach Phenice because the Euraquilo—a violent northeaster—drove it off its course, with disastrous results (27:14–44). The harbor is still called Fair Havens.

faith, in a religious sense, is variously defined: (1) an act or state of acknowledging the existence and power of a supreme being and the reality of a divine order; (2) the acceptance as real or true of that which is not supported by evidence of the senses or by rational proofs; (3) an affirmative response of the will to God as revealed, especially by Jesus Christ. It is thus compounded of belief, trust, and an attitude of mind, will, or spirit.

Faith so varies in its connotation throughout the Bible that any accurate interpretation of a passage where the idea or the word for faith occurs requires consideration of when it was recorded; who wrote it; and the use made of the same word elsewhere.

In the Authorized Version of the O.T., the word "faith" occurs only twice (Deut. 32:20; Hab. 2:4), and in both cases it should be translated "faithfulness" (see R.S.V., N.E.B.). Nevertheless, examples of the *attitude* of faith involving belief and trust abound, viz.: Gen. 15:6; Ex. 4:1–9, 19:9; Isa. 53:1; Jer. 17:7; II Chron. 20:20. Belief in the prophets' words is equivalent to faith in God (Ex. 14:31; II Kings 17:14). In the devotional literature particularly, trust and belief are identical with faith (Ps. 22:4, 25:2, 37:3, 52:8, 84:12, 2:12, 34:8, 40:4, 71:1, 141:8). When Judah faced the military might of the Babylonian Empire, trust was demanded (Isa. 12:2, 26:1–4; Jer. 39:18), and the efficacy of such naïve nonmilitaristic faith was questioned (Isa. 36:12–15; II Kings 18:30).

In the N.T. Jesus made faith, expressed in terms of belief, the first condition for entering the Kingdom* of God (Mark 1:15); specified it as a prerequisite for his miracles of healing (Matt. 9:28; Mark 9:23; Luke 8:50, 17:19); taught it as an essential in efficacious prayer (Mark 11:22–24); and rebuked his disciples for their lack of it (Matt. 6:30, 8:26, 14:31, 16:8, 17:20, 21:21; Mark 4:40, 5:36; Luke 8:25, 12:28, 18:8, 22:32, 24:25). John put definite content into his understanding of faith. Sometimes this belief is reposed in God (John 5:24, 12:44, 14:1); again, in the name of Christ (John 1:12, 2:23), or his spoken word (John 2:22, 4:50), or in the works of Christ (John 10:38); but more frequently, in Christ himself (John 2:11, 3:16, 4:39, 7:31, 9:35–38). Although there is no exaltation of faith in an objective, theological sense in the earliest N.T. books, faith is the human attitude which brings man all kinds of blessings (John 3:16, 18, 6:35, 12:36, 14:12).

Paul in his Epistles uses the noun "faith" and the verb "believe" almost 200 times. Thus faith becomes as clearly identified in the literature of the Bible as hope or love (I Cor. 13:13). Faith brings to man a union with God through Christ (Gal. 5:6); expresses itself in confession (Rom. 10:9); furnishes the very lifeblood for the Christian experience (Gal. 2:20); and creates righteous living (Rom. 1:17; Eph. 2:8; Phil. 3:9). Paul, the foe of the Jewish legal system designed to inculcate spirituality, contrasted faith and its fruits with obedience and its results, and declared that the latter was inferior to the faith in and through Christ, whom God had sent to supersede Judaism. So it was that in the Apostolic Church faith was hailed as an attitude (Heb. 12:2) possessing a certain definite intellectual content (I Pet. 5:9), and attended by a subjective, inner assurance (Heb. 11:1; Col. 2:2). This inner "substance" or "assurance" is a deposit of God's grace in the heart of the believer, and represents the divine gift through faith from God to man (Eph. 2:8). The classic statement of man's climb to this Christian position, acknowledging Jesus as the author and finisher of our faith, is Hebrews 11:1–12:2.

The bitter condemnation of heresy in Jude 3 and II Pet. 2:1–3, 3:3, together with the exhortations to the faithful to hold fast to what they had been taught (I Tim. 1:19, 4:1, 6, 6:3, 20; II Tim. 2:14–18, 3:14; Tit. 1:3, 10–13, 2:1) are indications that faith was very early under assault.

While Jesus put devotion to his way of life above correct beliefs, and at no time denied fellowship to any because of erroneous belief or because of conformity to traditional orthodoxy, he expected us to remember always that he is truth (John 14:6). Adherence to him and his way of life means a constant search for the true. A willingness to learn, as well as a fidelity to the highest ideals and to the fullest truth one knows, are the surest way to gain greater truth and attain a satisfying faith (John 7:17).

"Believing where we cannot prove" characterizes experience in both science and religion. Just as faith in a scientific principle is justified when tests have shown that its application leads to correct or useful conclusions, so faith in God, Christ, and the Christian way of life establishes their validity, and brings satisfying results. The Bible demands faith in the sense of recognizing and accepting new truth when apparent (Mark 4:9–12); condemns the refusal to believe anything without a conclusive demonstration (John 20:29); honors faith which may be accompanied by honest doubt (Mark 9:23 f.); and condemns dogmatism at the price of dishonesty (Job 13:7, 42:7).

In traditional Christian doctrine faith is reliance on God's testimony regarding the mission and atoning death of His son, Jesus Christ, the Redeemer of sinful men, and on the testimony of Jesus regarding himself. The system of doctrine built around such revelation is termed "the faith" (Acts 6:7, 24:24; Rom. 1:5, etc.).

Fall, the, the lapse from innocence and goodness, the first apostasy: the loss of Adam's position of integrity, virtue, and innocence, after his sin, as related in the Genesis accounts of the Eden* tragedy. Adam's Fall is represented as a legacy of proclivity toward sin, upon being given freedom of will; the result of the Fall is "original sin," handed on to the population of the earth by natural generation, so that all human beings are conceived and born in sin. There is no O.T. doctrine of the Fall. But the Fall and the atoning grace* of Christ are the core of the N.T. theology of Paul (Rom. 5:12–21; I Cor. 15:45–49). Paul believed that, just as man's sinfulness is the result of Adam's fall, so the righteousness of the atoning (see ATONEMENT) Christ brings grace to all. At one end of the human spectrum are Adam and sinful mankind; at the other, Christ and redeemed mankind.

Two slightly divergent narratives concerning the tree of life and the tree of the knowledge of good and evil, both taken from the J document, appear in Gen. 2:9, 17; cf. Gen. 3:1–22, 24. Genesis accounts of the Fall parallel vastly inferior Babylonian myths. The chief similarity between the Hebrew and the Mesopotamian accounts consists in the proffering of food determining death or immortality. Failure of the Babylonian Adapa to eat food offered him by the gods caused his death, even as Adam's eating of the forbidden fruit brought about his spiritual death. Psychologically viewed, the Genesis story of man's experience in the Fall is true. It also suggests early efforts to explain symbolically such sources of human suffering as man's hard toil, woman's travail, and her subordination to man. Freedom to obey or to disobey God is inherent in Gen. 2, 3. The idea of Satan* is much later than the serpent story.

See SIN; REDEMPTION.

familiar spirit, the spirit of a dead person, allegedly consulted by mediums who issued prophetic advice of a secular sort. Consultation of mediums was forbidden in the O.T. (Lev. 19:31, 20:6, 27; Deut. 18:11) as apostasy from Yahweh. Mediums were punishable by death. King Saul had put "those that had familiar spirits, and the wizards, out of the land" (I Sam. 28:3); but he himself, in an overwrought state because of threatening Philistines, consulted the witch of Endor, who summoned the prophet Samuel from the dead and staged a consultation with him (I Sam. 28:7–25). Similar consultations were held by King Manasseh (II Kings 21:6). Josiah put away familiar spirits, together with many other "abominations" (II Kings 23:24). Isaiah (8:19, see also Isa. 19:3, 29:4) protested against consultation with those who had familiar spirits, and "wizards that peep, and that mutter"—a phrase suggesting the windy ventriloquism of the talking Memnon at the Egyptian Thebes and the oracles at the Cave of the Cumaean Sibyl near Naples, and at the Greek shrine in Delphi. Belief in the occult powers of mediums, charmers, sorcerers, and magicians still characterizes the Middle East (see also Isa. 29:4).

family, the (in Scripture, usually Heb. *mishpachah*, "clan," or *bayith*, "house"), a group descended from a common ancestor, or consisting of the near kinsfolk, comprising the fundamental social unit. Efforts to trace the origins of prehistoric family life have proved futile and speculative.

The first human beings mentioned in Genesis were a family; and the history of Israel began with the history of a Hebrew family, even as O.T. religion was inaugurated by a single family—Abraham's—which developed into a tribe and then into a nation with a distinctive faith. As early as the Wilderness wanderings of Israel family life was safeguarded by such injunctions as Ex. 20:14–17, 21:15–17. Long genealogical lists, from

Gen. 5 and 36 to Matt. 1:1–17 and Luke 3:23–38, reflect concern for primogeniture. The Hebrew Wisdom Literature is full of injunctions calculated to ensure happy home life: Prov. 13:1, 15:5, 19:13, 26, 15:20, 13:22.

The narratives of Abraham's family life (Gen. 15–19) are unsurpassed annals of early home life, out of whose desert chastities, rugged moralities, and occasional lapses (Gen. 20) developed a clan which became the seed of a nation founded on an everlasting covenant with Yahweh (Gen. 17:1–9). From such tent-dwelling beginnings emerged later family life, protected by laws enjoining children's esteem of parents (Ex. 20:12), protection of inheritance* rights (Deut. 18:8, 21:15–17; Ruth 4:1–12; Jer. 32:6 ff.), justice to neighbors (see NEIGHBOR) (Ex. 22:26), kindness to strangers (Lev. 19:33 f.), and child welfare and prenatal protection (Ex. 21:22 f.).

140. Mother and baby from Palestinian village.

Over and above all was the dominating position of the house-father, who was guardian of the group, business manager, and judge, enjoying the rank almost of deity (Ex. 21:15, 17), as sheikhs still do among Bedouin tribes. Thus the long experience of Hebrew families in their tent life not only developed parental authority, but also gave every member of the large household of wives, children, and servants a group sense of warm security. Jesus and Paul, however, both took occasion to rebuke the overemphasis of the father's* position (Luke 2:48–50; Col. 3:21).

The position of the mother in the patriarchal family, though naturally below that of the father, was worthy and often revered, as seen in the stories of Sarah, Rebekah, and Rachel. The O.T. depicts some mothers who enjoyed the prestige of matriarchs, like Deborah (Judg. 4, 5), Abigail (I Sam. 25:14–42), and Huldah (II Kings 22:14–20). Queen mothers, important in Near Eastern society, are met on O.T. pages: Maacah, mother of Jeroboam (I Kings 15:10, 13); and wicked Athaliah, mother of Ahaziah (II Kings 11:1). Isaiah paid the comforting reassurance of mothers a glowing tribute (66:13).

Marriages (see MARRIAGE) were the concern of the entire family, for they involved not only the perpetuation of the group and its religious faith, but matters of property. Hence the emphasis given to the courtships of Rebekah and Rachel (Gen. 24:29). Polygamy was not forbidden by O.T. law. Large families were essential for protection against outside enemies; and secondary wives, like Sarah's handmaid, Hagar (Gen. 16:1–6), and Leah (Gen. 29:23), and concubines were common, especially when the principal wife was barren. For Hebrew families knew no more bitter experience than the inability of the wife to produce seed for future generations. Yet even in the O.T. there were trends toward monogamy (Deut. 17:17). Ruth and Naomi were remembered as paragons of marital faithfulness. Even in the period of the Judges adultery was often ruthlessly punished (Judg. 20). Hosea stressed monogamy as a symbol of the abiding union of God and His people. By N.T. times monogamy was largely taken for granted (see CONCUBINES); Jesus spoke a stinging condemnation of a woman whose husbands were five (John 4:16–18).

Early legislation against the marriage of Hebrews with aliens is stated in Deut. 7:3. Yet such kings as David and Solomon, as well as commoners, engaged in it, and by the era of Ezra it was common even among the sons of the priests (Ezra 10:18–24) at the time of his ritualistic reforms. In the long run, Ezra was fighting a lost battle.

But in spite of its shortcomings, the Hebrew family for many centuries remained the purest known in antiquity. When N.T. teachings were added to the foundation of the home as already worked out, the family achieved a less rigid and nobler position as a social group.

Jesus set his approval upon the family as a fundamental social group by remaining in his own at Nazareth until his maturity, cooperating in the family carpentering trade. His teachings are full of figures that reveal the lasting impressions made upon him by home life: Luke 6:36, 13:21; Matt. 5:45, 10:21; John 4:44, 7:3–5, etc. In spite of his consciousness that he at times had foes within his own household (Matt. 10:36), and in spite of his grief over the unbelief of some of his own brothers (John 7:1–8), Jesus continued to recognize his family obligations, until, from his cross, he entrusted his mother to John (John 19:27). After that his work was continued by at least one brother, James. Yet Jesus declared, and proved by his own example, that an individual is justified in surrendering family ties when called to engage in efforts to usher in the Kingdom of God (Matt. 10:35–39, 12:49; Luke 2:49, 8:21, 18:29 f.).

In his teachings, and in his revelation of the nature of God, the main emphasis of Jesus was upon God as Father, and men as a brotherhood of God's sons. He constantly used the family as a symbol of the relation of God to humanity. The Gospel of John alone has more than 130 references to God as Father. Jesus, like Paul (Eph. 3:15), declared that from the Father "the whole family in heaven and earth is named."

Long before the formulation of the Mosaic Law and the recording of the Hebrew Wisdom Literature, Egyptians had set on the Saqqarah tomb reliefs near Memphis history's first record of happy, wholesome family life, and disclosed the close association of family affection with the nascence of all other moral feelings. And in the world's oldest written record of rules of conduct—the *Maxims of Ptah Hotep*, Grand Vizier to Pharaoh Isesi of the Fifth Dynasty—the value of a son's hearkening to the wisdom of his father, that he may bespeak the same to his children, is made clear. Moses, living in Egypt 1,000 years later, may have had an awareness of the deeply rooted principles of noble family relationships.

famine, scarcity of food, endemic in unproductive Palestine, was caused by deficient rainfall or by pestilence and "the sword," and frequently determined the course of history. The pantry of Palestine has never had reserve supplies; and the literature of the Near East is studded with accounts of this situation. The very ancient Hebrew or Amorite Deluge story, the Atra-hasis Epic (of which the Pierpont Morgan Library has a clay tablet cuneiform copy written in 1966 B.C.), tells of a famine of several years' duration which preceded the Flood. In fact, the Deluge was deemed to have been sent to relieve the unproductive nature of the land in which people had been multiplying too rapidly (cf. A. T. Clay's *The Hebrew Deluge Story in Cuneiform*). The Genesis narratives omit this pre-Flood famine, but include several other periods of serious drought: the vast famine which sent Abraham to Egypt (Gen. 12:10); the one which gave his son Isaac a similar experience (Gen. 26:1); and the sore famine of the Joseph saga (Gen. 41:27–43), felt both in productive Egypt and scanty Canaan. Ruth 1:1 gives a Judaean famine as the cause of Elimelech's migration to Moab. Palestine during David's reign felt a three-year famine, whose cause was attributed to Saul's slaying of the Gibeonites (II Sam. 21:1). In usually fruitful Samaria a famine came in the era of Elijah and Ahab (I Kings 18:2). Jesus referred (Luke 4:25) to a famine in Israel in the days of Elijah, which lasted 3½ years—possibly the same as the above.

Local famines were caused in besieged cities by foes who prevented provisions from entering, especially during the siege of Samaria by the Syrian Ben-hadad (II Kings 6:24 ff.) and of Jerusalem by the Babylonian Nebuchadnezzar (II Kings 25:1 ff.; Jer. 52:4–6).

fan, a six-pronged wooden fork used by fanners on Palestinian and Egyptian threshing floors to toss grain into the air to let the chaff blow away. The winnowing afternoon wind from the sea (Ps. 35:5; Dan. 2:35; Hos. 13:3) blew the chaff away (Isa. 41:16, cf. Ps. 1:4). John the Baptist foretold the coming of the great fanner, Jesus, who would thoroughly cleanse his floor, garnering the grain and burning the chaff (Matt. 3:12; Luke 3:17). Small wooden shovels, with holes cut to reduce wind resistance, were used along with the fans. The same methods are in use today in remote sections of the Middle East. See THRESHING.

141. Fans: 1. Egyptian; 2. Egyptian official fan, 1350 B.C.; 3. Winnowing fan; 4. Winnowing shovel.

Fâr'ah, Tell el-. See SHARUHEN; TIRZAH.

farming, the cultivating of land, so highly regarded among Hebrews that Yahweh Himself was regarded as the founder of husbandry (Isa. 28:26). Farming by Israel was widely engaged in after the nomadic Patriarchal (see PATRIARCH) groups—primarily herdsmen—began to settle down in Canaan (Gen. 26:12), and received per family as much land as a yoke of oxen could plow in a day (I Sam. 14:14), or as much as was needed to plant a specified amount of seed (Lev. 27:16). The Hebrews emulated the long-successful farming methods on which the substantial Canaanite (see CANAAN) wealth was built. Farmers lived in villages adjacent to their fields. Some of these villages became walled towns in which farm families lived during the winter, overlooking their fields. Boundary* stones were respected.

Plains and terraced mountains had been cultivated so long when Israel arrived that the soil—not dependent on irrigation (see WATER), as in Mesopotamia and Egypt—was well tamed. Palestine man has probably been farming for almost 10,000 years. The most fertile acreages lay in the Maritime Plain, the Plain of Esdraelon, and the Jordan Plain, together with lower Galilee and such areas of rugged Samaria—famous for its olive orchards (Isa. 28:1)—as the Plain of Dothan. The highlands of Jordan and the Hauran were noted for wheat crops. Agricultural folkways exerted a profound influence on Canaanite religion, which impressed its stamp on the susceptible souls of Israel. (See FEASTS.) Many laws (see LAW) of early Israel reflect an agricultural milieu.

The rains of autumn and early winter—called "former" or "early" because the old

142. Farming: 1. Plowing; 2. Sowing; 3. Irrigating; 4. Reaping; 5. Transporting to threshing floor; 6. Threshing; 7. Sifting; 8. Winnowing; 9. Fruit and vegetable markets in Bethlehem; 10. Animal market in Bethlehem.

civil year began in autumn—and the "latter" rains of March and April justified Israel's belief that Yahweh would provide adequate water supply for their crops (Deut. 8:7). The porous limestone of Palestine topsoil allows heavy rains to filter through, so that earth is prepared for the final stages of growth. From underground water sources the supply trickles into wâdīs, many of which do not dry up completely even in burning summer. The Jordan overflow irrigates some of its plains. (See VINE; WEATHER.)

The program of the Palestine farmer in the era of Saul and David is revealed by the famous Gezer Calendar, a limestone plaque from c. 950–918 B.C., discovered in 1908 by R. A. S. Macalister, and translated as follows by W. F. Albright:

"His [or a man's] two months are [olive] harvest;
his two months are grain-planting;
his two months are planting;
his month is hoeing up of flax;
his month is barley harvest;
his month is harvest and festivity;
his two months are vine-tending;
his month is summer-fruit."

See Isaiah 28:23–29 for a classic description of the processes of farming.

Jesus, reared among the fertile farmlands and orchards of Galilee, recorded in parables and sayings numerous farming procedures known to him.

Crops: Barley, Deut. 8:8; corn, Gen. 27:37, Ps. 4:7; flax, Ex. 9:31, Josh. 2:6, Prov. 31:13, 22; fruit (see FOODS, VINE); honey (see FOOD); millet, Ezek. 4:9; olives (see OLIVE), Deut. 8:8; spelt (rye), Ex. 9:32; vegetables (see FOOD, VINE); wheat, Ps. 81:16, Joel 2:24, Matt. 3:12, 13:25.

Rotation of crops was effected by fallowing the seventh year (Ex. 23:10 f.).

Cultivation: Plowing (opens the farm season in November, after the early rains), Luke 9:62, 17:7, 8, I Cor. 9:10, cf. I Kings 19:19; sowing, by hand, or from a box attached to the plow, Matt. 13:1–8, Luke 8:5–15; fertilizing, usually by excrement left on the field, Luke 13:8; growth, Mark 4:26–32; tasks of the farmer, Luke 14:16–19; labor relations, Matt. 20:1–16, 21:33 ff., Luke 19:12–27, John 4:36–38; reaping, usually by cutting with sickles, often flint, Mark 4:29; binding into bundles to cart to the threshing floor, Matt. 13:30; threshing*, Matt. 13:30, cf. II Sam. 24:16–18; winnowing in the wind, Matt. 3:12, Luke 3:17; sifting, with round screened trays, Luke 22:31; gleaning, by the poor, for harvest remnants, cf. Lev. 19:9 f., Ruth 2:2 ff.; storing, Matt. 3:12, 9:37, 38; hidden field treasures, Matt. 13:44; transportation to markets by caravans, cf. Isa. 30:6.

Pests: Cankerworms, palmer worms, caterpillars, Joel 2:25; field mice, ants, tares, II Kings 19:35 (cf. Herodotus II 141), Prov. 6:6, Matt. 13:25–40; locusts, Ex. 10:14, 15; wind, mildew, hail, Hag. 2:17.

Agriculture continues to be a principal occupation in Palestine, whose fertile areas have caused long and bitter contests between Jewish and Arab segments of the population. Additional irrigation would greatly increase production, and support heavier population. Archaeologists have found ample evidence that the perennial streams of Trans-Jordan in Biblical times were used for irrigation, and made possible intensive cultivation of its highland plains, which supported far larger populations than inhabit them today. Irrigated Moab was the fairest portion of the N.T. Peraea.

farthing. See MONEY.

fasting, abstinence from food, a rigor undertaken to evoke the favor of God, to ward off evil, to chasten the soul, or to discipline oneself in time of stress. It was practiced both corporately and individually throughout Bible times. (For national prescribed fasts, see FEASTS.) During fasting, prescribed or voluntary, no work was done, sackcloth and ashes were often used, and garments were rent, although prophets like Joel (2:13) and Isaiah (ch. 58) stressed spiritual rather than external disciplines. The following list includes the more important fastings recorded in Scripture:

Moses, before approaching Yahweh, Ex. 34:28, Deut. 9:9, 18; men of Jabesh-gilead, grieving for Saul and Jonathan, I Sam. 31:13; David, while his child was ill, II Sam. 12:16; Elijah, before reaching the mount of God, I Kings 19:8; Ahab, when Elijah reproached him, I Kings 21:27; Nehemiah, in sorrow for the state of Jerusalem, Neh. 1:4; the Jews in Shushan, on the eve of Esther's interview, Esther 4:16; Nineveh, Jon. 3:5; Anna, serving God, Luke 2:37; Jesus, during his temptation, Matt. 4:2, Luke 4:2; Paul, following conversion, Acts 9:9; the Antioch Church, before selecting Paul and Barnabas, Acts 13:3.

The N.T. did not condemn fasting, though the act was considered inconsistent with the imminent approach of the Messiah (Matt. 9:14 f.). Jesus, ever simple in his own habits, probably fasted frequently; but he asked his followers to avoid the self-advertised piety of the fasting Pharisees (Matt. 6:16–18). Not fasting, but joy, was the keynote of Christ's message (John 15:11; Heb. 12:2).

The R.S.V. of the N.T. rightly omits the A.V. "fasting" from the following passages: Matt. 17:21; Mark 9:29; Acts 10:30; I Cor. 7:5.

fat, as an offering to Yahweh, is first mentioned in the story of Abel (Gen. 4:4). According to Mosaic Law, "All the fat is the Lord's" (Lev. 3:16), and neither fat nor blood of sacrificed animals was to be eaten (v. 17). The fat of firstlings is frequently recorded as burned on the altar of Yahweh as a sacrifice (Ex. 29:13, 22–25; Lev. 3:3–5, 4:8–10; Num. 18:17). Even after 622 (Deut. 12), the fat of animals slaughtered for food without sacrifice continued to be burned at the altar as Yahweh's portion of the sin and peace offerings.

The adjective "fat" is used to refer to pasture (I Chron. 4:40); to land (Neh. 9:25); and to people (Judg. 3:17). Isaiah's phrase, "the head of the fat valley" (28:4), as one of the beauties of Israel, is classic.

father. (1) In the sense of an earthly parent,

see FAMILY. Important fathers of Scripture include Abraham, Gen. 16:15, 21:3; David, father of Absalom and Solomon, II Sam. 3:3, 12:24; Isaac, Gen. 25:26; Jacob, Gen. 29:32–35, 35:22–27, 35:18; Jephthah, father of the sacrificed daughter, Judg. 11:30–40; Jesse, father of David, I Sam. 16, Ruth 4:17; Jethro, father-in-law of Moses, Ex. 3:1, 4:18, 18:1–27; see also Num. 10:29; Joseph, father of Manasseh and Ephraim, Gen. 41:51 f., Num. 26:28; Joseph, foster-father of Jesus, Luke 2:41; Nun, father of Joshua, Ex. 33:11; Publius' father, occasion of a Pauline healing, Acts 28:8; Saul, father of Jonathan, I Sam. 13:16; Simon, a Cyrenian, father of Alexander and Rufus, Mark 15:21; Zacharias, father of John the Baptist, Luke 1:59; Zebedee, father of James and John, Matt. 4:21. See individual entries.

(2) For Father-God, see GOD.

(3) Used in the Bible in the sense of an ancestor of a tribe or nation (Gen. 10); or the male parent of a "house" or family* (Ex. 2:1; Josh. 17:17). When a man was buried with his "fathers" (II Kings 15:38) he was sepulchered with his ancestors. In Ecclesiasticus 44–49 "fathers" means "distinguished forebears," like Enoch, Noah, and Elijah. The Talmud uses "fathers" to mean "distinguished teachers of the Law." The Apostolic Fathers were those who helped formulate its doctrines through their writings, which became a chief source for the beliefs, history, and observances of the first Christian centuries. They include Barnabas, Hermas, Clement of Rome, Ignatius, Polycarp, Papias, etc.

fear of the Lord, used in the Bible for reverential awe of the majesty and holiness of God (Ps. 34:11; Prov. 1:7; Eccles. 12:13), rather than to express an emotion of painful apprehension concerning Him. Moffatt translates this phrase as: "true religion" (Ps. 34:11); "reverence for the Eternal" (Prov. 1:7); "awe of God" (Eccles. 12:13). In N.T. times Gentile adherents of the synagogue were called "God-fearers" or those who "feared God" (Acts 10:2, 22, 13:26).

feasts, festivals, and fasts were an important part of the usually joyous religious life of the Hebrew people. They were landmarks in their faith, anniversaries of their salvation, and celebrations rooted in ancient lunar and solar feasts which they had adapted and spiritualized to celebrate events in their own national history. (See MOON; SUN.) Religious festivals were occasions of refreshment for hard-working agricultural people, even as in rural countries of Europe today. They knit together the developing soul of Israel, and promoted her sense of union with God. Although fasting and penitence had their place, especially on the Day of Atonement*—observed after the Exile (Lev. 23:2, 24, 27)—the singing of Psalms that made "a joyful noise unto the Lord" (Ps. 100:1), dancing (Judg. 21:21), and folk processions to the Temple and other shrines (Ps. 42:4) characterized Hebrew festivals. Occasionally these festivals ended in excesses (I Sam. 1:13–15; Amos 2:7; II Kings 23:7; Isa. 1:29).

From the most ancient times people in Palestine believed that through their sacrificial feasts they entered into communion with their gods. In the chief agricultural festivals rituals sought to invoke the co-operation of fertility processes by sympathetic magic*. One of the earliest Hebrew festivals of which a record exists is the "wave offering" (Lev. 23:10 f.), wherein the first harvested sheaves were presented to the Lord of harvests. Offerings of animals, wine, bread, and oil (Gen. 4:4; I Sam. 1:24, 21:6, 10:3) were carried to sanctuaries by tithing farmers. (See WORSHIP.)

When Israel brought to Canaan their lunar festivals, characteristic of nomadic shepherds who depended on the light of the moon for convenient movement of their flocks, they merged these with the ancient Canaanite agricultural feasts whose chronometer was the life-giving sun. This new cycle of sacred festivals was later affected by the Babylonian New Year and other Mesopotamian influences during the Exile. Both Jewish and Babylonian calendars consisted of twelve lunar months, but the Hebrew sacred year differed from the civil year in beginning six months earlier. For example, Abib or Nisan (March-April) was the 1st month of the sacred year, but the 7th of the Jewish civil year; Adar (Feb.-March) was the 12th of the sacred year, and the 6th of the civil. (See TIME.)

There were *three great historic feasts* enjoined by Mosaic Law, at which every adult male in good health was enjoined to present himself to his God at the sanctuary: (1) The *Passover** (Num. 28:16), a lunar pastoral festival of the lambing season, which fell on the 14th day of the 1st month of the sacred year—Nisan. The *Feast of Unleavened Bread* began on the 15th day and lasted 7 days (Lev. 23:5–8; Num. 28:17–25). (2) The *Feast of Weeks*, or *Pentecost**, or *of Harvest*, or *First Fruits*, 50 days after the beginning of the Passover season (Ex. 23:16, 34:22; Num. 28:26–31), on the 6th day of the 3d month. This was the 1st of two great agricultural feasts, timed to coincide with the first fruits of the wheat harvest, a few weeks after the April barley harvest—seven weeks after the first sickle went into the barley (Deut. 16:9 ff.). New meaning was given Pentecost by the events of Acts 2:1 ff. (3) The *Feast of Tabernacles*, or *of Booths*, or *of Ingathering* (*Sukkoth*), starting the 15th of the 7th month (Tishri)—Sept.-Oct., five days after the Day of Atonement, and lasting a full eight days (Lev. 23:34–36). This autumn festival (Deut. 16:13–17), at the grape vintage and final harvest of olives and fruits, was most important, as the beginning of the new civil year. It corresponds to the New England Harvest Home and Thanksgiving festivals. It was celebrated by families tenting in booths, remembering the 40 years' wanderings of their nomadic forebears who lived in tents. See also John 7:2, 8.

In addition to these three great feasts, *minor feasts* were later instituted, of which the following are the most important: (1) The *Feast of Dedication** or *of Lights* (Hanukkah, also Chanukah), began on the 25th day of Chislev, the 9th sacred month (Nov.-Dec.), ran eight days, and was celebrated by carrying torches and lighting houses and places of worship. It celebrated the rededication of the Temple by Judas Maccabaeus 165 B.C. (I Macc. 4:52–59; see also John 10:22). (2) *Purim** was observed on the 14th and 15th days of Adar, the last month of the sacred year (Feb.-March), to mark the deliverance of the Jews from Haman's plots (Esther 9:21–28). It may be of Persian origin. (3) The *Feast of Wood Offering* came on the 15th day of Abib or Nisan (March-April), the 1st month of the sacred year, at which time people brought wood to the Temple for altar use (Neh. 10:34). (4) *Sheep-Shearing* (I Sam. 25:4–11; II Sam. 13:23, 27).

Certain feasts were also instituted in connection with the Sabbath: (1) The *Sabbath*, whose origin is not definitely known, though it is mentioned in Gen. 2:2 f. as following God's six days of creative acts, and is stressed in the Decalogue and in Ex. 23:12. The word is first mentioned in the list of festivals found in Lev. 23. This day of rest and gladness was observed especially after the Exile, to separate Jews from Gentile ways. Rules for its observance are stated in Ex. 23:12; Deut. 5:12, 14, 15; Neh. 13:15–22. Jesus placed human welfare above the hair-splitting regulations of the Pharisees for the Sabbath (Mark 1:21–25, 2:27). Man was Lord of the Sabbath (Luke 6:5). Whether the Christian Sunday succeeded the Jewish Sabbath in N.T. times or later is not clear. See also Matt. 12:9–13; Mark 3:1–5; Luke 6:6–10, 13:10–17; John 5:1–16, 9:14–16. (2) The *Sabbatical year* was a year of rest every 7th year, intended to benefit laborers, owners, farm animals, land, and strangers (Lev. 25:4–6 f.). (3) The *Jubilee year*, the 50th year (or the year after seven Sabbatic cycles), brought the liberation of slaves and the return of mortgaged property (Lev. 25:8–13). See also Luke 4:18–21. (4) The *New moon*, at which time burnt offerings and sin offerings were increased. See also Col. 2:16. (5) The New Year Festival, also called *The Feast of Trumpets*, the 1st (later also the 2d) of Tishri (Sept.-Oct.), the 1st civil month or the 7th sacred month (Lev. 23:24, 25; Num. 29:1–6), was celebrated by the blowing of trumpets in convocation.

Closely related to the feast days are the *fasts:* (1) *Atonement Day* is the only fast commanded by the Law (Lev. 16:29, 23:27–32). It was instituted at the time of the priestly reform; there is no mention of it in pre-Exilic literature. In the N.T. it is called "the fast" (Acts 27:9). See also Heb. 4:14–16, 5:1–10. (See ATONEMENT, DAY OF.) (2) Minor fast days, instituted after the Babylonian Exile, included one in memory of the destruction of the Jerusalem Temple by Nebuchadnezzar (II Kings 25:1, 8), observed on the 9th of Ab; and one in commemoration of the destruction of the Jewish state (Jer. 41). (3) The *Fast of Esther*, on the 13th of Adar, the day before Purim.

It is probable that Jesus, in obedience to ancient Hebrew law (Ex. 34:23), went three times a year to observe the historic festivals of his people (Matt. 26:17; Mark 14:12; Luke 22:8; John 2:23, 7:2–37, 13:1). The Fourth Gospel represents much of his teaching and public activity as taking place during the great Jewish festivals.

As to Christian festivals, Easter* and Christmas both developed after N.T. times, possibly as spiritualized successors of pagan and Jewish spring and winter festivals.

For social banquets and feasts, see MEALS. For a detailed account of the Jewish festivals see *The Jews*, ed. by Louis Finkelstein, Vol. II, pp. 1361 ff. (Harper & Brothers).

Felix, Antonius, appointed procurator or governor of Judaea by the Emperor Claudius, probably in A.D. 52. Paul was tried before him at Caesarea c. A.D. 60, whither he had been sent for protection after a Jerusalem riot in which he had been accused of being an insurgent Egyptian who had led a motley band against Jerusalem (Acts 21:38). Although Felix was known to be a cruel and despotic governor, he was moved by Paul's cheerful and irrefutable defense (Acts 24:10–21); and ordered him to be safeguarded and given considerable freedom (v. 23), until his second hearing—witnessed this time by Drusilla, Jewish wife of Felix. The powerful impression made upon Felix by Paul (v. 25) resulted in no action on Felix's part beyond two years of procrastination, of invitations to bribery, and of "communing" interviews (v. 26). Felix, succeeded by Porcius Festus, left Paul bound (24:27).

felloe (fĕl′ō), the circular rim into which spokes of a wheel are set (A.V. and Moff. I Kings 7:33).

fellow was used in the O.T. for "brother" or "companion" (Ex. 2:13); and often in derision, as "the vain fellows" (II Sam. 6:20); also in the N.T., "the fellow was with Jesus" (Luke 22:59). The multitude that brought Jesus before Pilate called him "this fellow" (Luke 23:2). But "fellow" has a worthier connotation in its use to mean "partner," "helper," "companion in faith," "fellow heirs, members of the same body" (R.S.V. Eph. 3:6). Mention is made of "fellowservants" (Matt. 24:49); fellow disciples (John 11:16); fellow prisoners (Rom. 16:7). See FELLOWSHIP.

fellowship, A.V. and A.S.V. translation of Gk. *koinonia*, meaning a communion of persons on equal terms, or a "sharing" of experience and of possessions, as in II Cor. 8:4. The word appears seldom in the O.T. But the idea of fellowship with God is inherent in the close relationship with Him of such personalities as Abraham, the friend of God (Isa. 41:8; II Chron. 20:7; James 2:23); Moses, who talked face to face with Him (Ex. 33:11); David (I Sam. 30:6); Nehemiah (2:8, 12, 7:5); and in the spiritual associations between the worshipper and God expressed in many of the Psalms, as in Ps. 40, 62, 63, 69:3, 71:1.

Fellowship between God and believers reaches the climax of its expression in the N.T. writings, stressing fellowship with Christ and the Holy Spirit (II Cor. 13:14). It is a supernatural relationship, involving an association of persons who have attained fellowship with God through forgiveness of sin. The "moral partnership with the Redeemer" (Millar Burrows) is clearly stated in Matt. 20:22 f., Rom. 8:17; and especially in John 1:3, 6 f. The cornerstone of Paul's theology, and the high peak of N.T. thought, is "union with Christ," who, in contrast with the heroes of current mystery cults, was remembered by many who were still living in Paul's time, as the historic, spiritual Christ who had actually dwelt in Galilee and was able to develop astonishing moral powers in those who accepted his fellowship. Life to Paul was living with the eternal Christ (Phil. 1:21 ff.). Such fellowship was the guarantee of the hereafter (II Cor. 1:22, 5:5).

Fellowship with God and Christ inevitably led to the establishment of little cells of believers, brothers, comrades in faith, fellows —the *koinonia* closely knit by common experience of the living, resurrected Christ. These fellowships became the *ekklēsiae*, or earliest Christian churches, enjoying what Paul described as "the fellowship in the Gospel" (Phil. 1:5).

Fellowships of Christians were expected to show themselves worthy of that experience by shining with good works in the eyes of the non-Christian community (Matt. 5:16; Rom. 12:17; I Pet. 2:12). Their belief that Jesus would soon come again led many 1st-century fellowships to behave with exemplary conduct. See PAROUSIA.

fenced city (Josh. 14:12; II Chron. 8:5; Jer. 5:17). See FORTS; WALLS.

Fertile Crescent, a now widely used term, coined by James H. Breasted, to indicate the great arch or semicircle of fertility constituting a cultivable fringe between the mountains on one side and the desert on the other, extending from the head of the Persian Gulf, NW. around the Tigris-Euphrates valley to Haran and Carchemish (situated at its head), and SW. through Syria, Phoenicia, and Palestine. Along the Fertile Crescent Patriarchal nomads such as Abraham grazed their way into the Promised Land. This arable arch includes the modern entities of Palestine (Israel and Jordan), Lebanon, Syria, and Iraq, even as in ancient times it included Phoenicia, the Kingdoms of Judah and Israel, part of the Hittite Empire (see HITTITES), and the empires of the Mitanni*, the Babylonians (see BABYLON), and the Assyrians (see ASSYRIA).

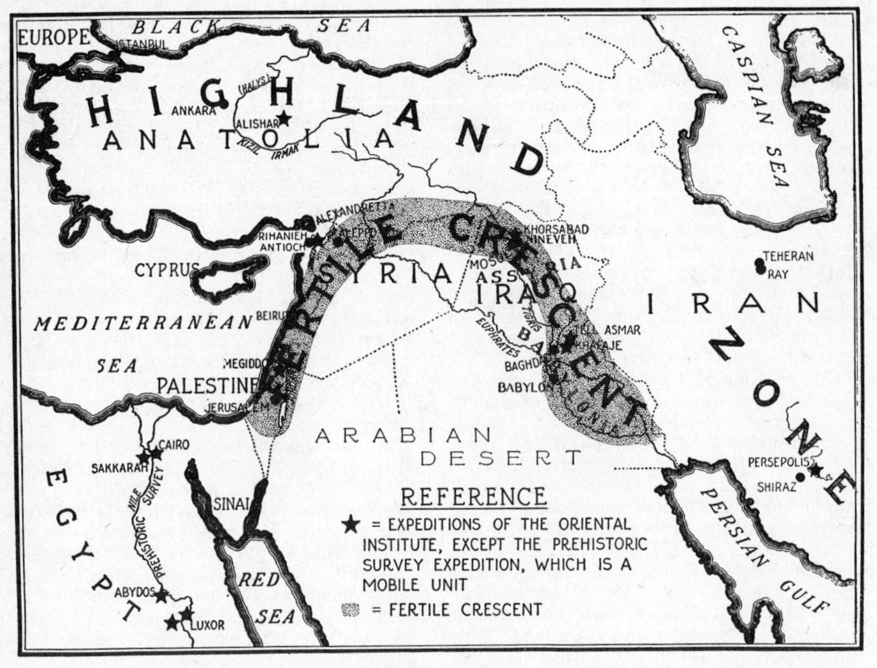

143. Fertile Crescent.

fertility cults. See WORSHIP.

Festus, Porcius, appointed by Nero to succeed Felix as governor of Judaea (Acts 24:27), administered affairs in the judgment hall built by Herod (Acts 23:35). A better administrator than Felix*, Festus heard Paul's defense, and though convinced of his innocence suggested that Paul go to Jerusalem for trial before the Sanhedrin, whereupon the prisoner asked to be sent to Rome for trial before Caesar. Festus arranged a hearing before his friend, King Agrippa II, who with his sister Bernice had come down from Jerusalem to Caesarea to salute the new governor (Acts 25:13). Festus was a witness of Paul's memorable defense before Agrippa* (Acts 26). Agrippa declared to Festus that the prisoner might have been set at liberty if he had not appealed to Caesar (Acts 26:32).

Festus died in office and was succeeded by Albinus.

fig. (1) The *Ficus carica* is common in the high-lying sections of Palestine, and occurs in several kinds and colors identified by native *fellahin*. Fig trees are usually not culti-

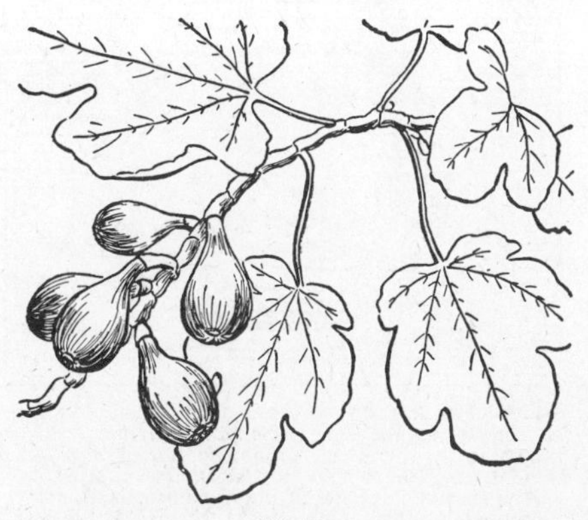

144. Fig.

vated in groves, but singly or in small groups, often adjacent to pomegranates (see POMEGRANATE), as at well-watered Cana of Galilee, or in the corners of vineyards. Figs grow well

145. Fig tree at Cana.

near dwellings (I Kings 4:25). They shed copious, cool shade, sprawling like vines or growing to trees 20 to 30 ft. tall. Their longevity is remarkable. Unless man-sown, fig trees are not certain to produce fruit. Standing leafless through the winter, figs put out their first fruit buds in February or in March (Matt. 24:32), most of whose immature fruits are blown to the ground; the leaves appear in April or May. Fruits that mature are called "early figs" (Micah 7:1), prized for their flavor. Some figs produce several times a year. The great crop of "late figs" usually comes in August or September; they are purplish, green, whitish, or nearly black. Their thick, wide, palmately lobed leaves are sizable enough to suggest use as aprons (Gen. 3:7)—as often in art depictions of Adam and Eve. The miracle of Jesus, disappointed in the fig tree's productivity (Mark 11:12, 13, 20 f.) expressed his disillusionment about the apparent fruitlessness of Israel. Figs, both fresh and dried (I Sam. 25:18), or pressed into cakes, are popular for food. They also make admirable poultices for boils (II Kings 20:7). The very large leaves of the fig tree (cf. Gen. 3:7) make delightful shade in which to sit, as Nathanael was doing when noticed by Jesus (John 1:47–50).

(2) The sycomore or mulberry fig (*Ficus sycomorus*) cultivated by Amos was an evergreen dressed by making incisions in its inch-long fruit, which was of poor quality; this puncturing was done three or four days before picking, to speed ripening. The wood, rather than the fruit, was the chief value of this wild, mountain-loving fig tree common in the Shephelah (Amos 7:14; Isa. 9:10). This was the tree Zacchaeus climbed (Luke 19:4).

figurines, small statuettes of man-made gods, animals or persons, made of clay, bone, ebony, semiprecious stones, precious metals, or wood, and used throughout Bible lands for cultic purposes. Akin to teraphim (Gen. 31:19, 34; Lev. 26:1), they were worn on the person or placed in shrines for protection (Jer. 10:4; Acts 19:24). Crude ones of a sensual nature have been found in excavations of the pre-Flood level at Ur*. Egyptians placed lifelike figurines (*shawabti*) in their tombs, to surround themselves with proxy servants. Archaeological explorations have revealed Kassite (rulers of Babylonia) figurines dating from c. 1300 B.C.—human figures praying perhaps for relief from bodily ills, or carrying petitions to a goddess of healing, precursor of the Greek Hygeia. See TERAPHIM, illus. 431.

fine, verb, meaning to refine, to remove dross from silver and gold (Job 28:1; Prov. 25:4, 27:21).

finer, a workman who refines.

fining-pot, a utensil used in refining silver and gold (Prov. 17:3). The jeweler bending over his fining-pot, testing precious metals for jewelry, can still be seen in the silver markets of Jerusalem and Damascus.

fir tree (possibly also denoting the cypress and varieties of pine, but not the ash, as in A.S.V. Isa. 44:14 margin), a tree which was imported along with cedar from the forest of Hiram by Solomon for the building of the Temple (I Kings 5:10). It was used in the flooring (I Kings 6:15), in doors (6:34), and in ceilings (II Chron. 3:5). Fir was a favorite wood of coastal shipbuilders known to Ezekiel, who states that this wood was brought from Senir, probably the northern portion of the Anti-Lebanons (Ezek. 27:5). The old names of fir and pine have not yet been ascertained. Hosea (14:8) makes Ephraim liken his vitality to that of the green fir tree.

Many commentators identify the "pine" of many O.T. passages as *Pinus halepensis* ("the Aleppo pine"), abundant on the dry hills of ancient Palestine. It grows to 60 ft. and is "scarcely inferior to cedar."

fire, the active principle of burning, recognized early by Israel as a purifying agent. The Israelites associated it with deity, as did their Prometheus-worshipping Greek neighbors; the Persian Zoroastrian advocates of Atar, the sacred fire, son of Ahura Mazda; and the cultists of Mithraism's mysteries, a chief rival to Christianity in the first two centuries after Christ. God manifested His presence with wandering Israel in a pillar of fire by night (Ex. 13:21). On His altars (see ALTAR) of burnt offerings they kept fire burning continuously (Lev. 6:13), seeing in its consumption of offerings their acceptance by Him (Judg. 6:21; I Kings 18:38). They challenged Him to manifest His presence by descending in fire, as in the contest at Carmel (I Kings 18:24). Israel's theophanies saw God in fire (Gen. 15:17; Ex. 3:2, 13:21 f., 24:17; Ps. 78:14). His indignation against the sins of men was like fire (Deut. 4:24; Ezek. 38:19; Amos 5:6). In the N.T. as well as in the O.T. fire was associated with punishment (Lev. 20:14; Isa. 47:14; Jer. 51:58; Matt. 5:22, 18:8; Rev. 19:20). Unproductive Christians deserved the fate of barren fruit trees, "cast into the fire" (Matt. 3:10).

Secular uses of fire included cooking (Ex. 12:8 f.; John 21:9); heating (Isa. 44:16; Jer. 36:22; Mark 14:54); refining of metals and manufacturing from them (Ex. 32:24; Isa. 44:12, cf. I Pet. 1:7; Mal. 3:2); burning refuse (Lev. 8:17, 13:52); and destroying captured enemy cities (Josh. 6:24, 7:15; Judg. 9:15).

For "fire offerings," a general term used more than 60 times in the Bible, see WORSHIP, "Sacrifice and Offerings."

For "cloven tongues as of fire" at Pentecost, see Acts 2:3.

firebrands, usually pieces of bent stick set on fire, as in Samson's feat (Judg. 15:4); tossed over city walls in time of siege, as the olive boughs were at Lachish; or hurled as missiles by madmen (Prov. 26:18). Plucked by God "from the burning," they symbolized individuals rescued by the Lord (Amos 4:11).

firepan, a pan of copper, or other durable metal, used to carry fire to altars (Ex. 27:3); sometimes the equivalent of brazier or censer (Lev. 16:12; Num. 16:46; Jer. 52:19, margin).

firkin (Eng. rendering of Gk. *mētrētes*), a Greek liquid measure, roughly equivalent to the Hebrew liquid measure *bath*; approximately 10 U.S. gals. Cf. John 2:6. See WEIGHTS AND MEASURES.

firmament, the vault of the sky, the heavens; a word appearing only in the O.T. The Semitic cosmogony of Gen. 1 deemed it to be a rigid vault, arch, or dome, called by God "Heaven"* (Gen. 1:8), rising above the earth and its watery ocean. Above the firmament was a heavenly ocean of controlled clouds (Gen. 7:11; II Kings 7:2; Ps. 78:23). The firmament was the lofty area in which God placed sun, moon, and stars (Gen. 1:16 f.), and across which He enabled fowls to fly (v. 20). The poet-author of Ps. 104:2 thought of it as a gigantic tent or curtain.

THE HEBREW UNIVERSE

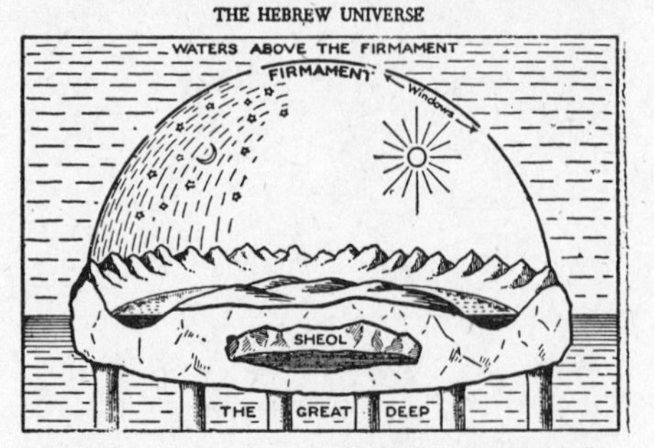

146. The diagram represents a cross-section of the Universe as the ancient Hebrews imagined it. The world was round and flat and supported on pillars (Job 9:6; I Sam. 2:8; Ps. 104:5). Over it stretched the great solid dome of the firmament held up by mountain-pillars (Job 26:11, 37:18). Above the firmament and under the earth was water, divided by God at Creation (Gen. 1:6, 7; cf. Ps. 24:2, 148:4). The floods came up from "the great deep" below the earth, and the rain came through windows in the firmament (Gen. 7:11, 8:2). The sun, moon and stars moved across, or were fixed in, the firmament (Ps. 19:4, 6). Within the earth lay *Sheol*, the realm of the dead (Num. 16:30–33; Isa. 14:9, 15). (H. Martin, *The Teachers' Commentary*, Harper & Brothers)

The firmament was believed to rest upon "foundations" or "pillars" (II Sam. 22:8; Job 26:11, 37:18), and as having several chambers, in the highest of which God dwelt (Deut. 26:15). "Firmament" was a favorite word of Hebrew writers when they wished to surround an incident with the atmosphere of the majestic presence of the Creator. They spoke of the firmament as showing His handiwork; of praise being lifted to Him "in the firmament of his power" (Ps. 150:1). The firmament is a feature of Ezekiel's vision (1:22). Daniel (12:3) used the "brightness of the firmament" to describe the man of wisdom.

first-born, the eldest child; **first fruits,** the earliest fruits; **firstling,** the earliest offspring. Israel attached especial value to the eldest son. He received the right to inherit (see INHERITANCE) family leadership and a double portion of his father's estate (Gen. 43:33; Deut. 21:17). This is what gives special significance to the Jacob-Esau story (Gen. 27), and to the tragedy of the last Egyptian plague (Ex. 11:4–6, 12:12–29). Mosaic law in the nomadic era stated the claim of Yahweh upon the first-born of nomads (Ex. 13:2; cf. Gen. 4:4; Ex. 22:29), to Whom they were consecrated. One purpose of the story of Abraham's near-sacrifice of Isaac (Gen. 22) may have been to protest against the killing of children. When Israel settled down in Canaan they found Canaanites sacrificing first-born sons to gain the favor of the fertility and agricultural deities of the land, on the assumption that gods had a right to the best, and would continue their favor only if worshippers sacrificed their choicest. (See MOLECH; II Kings 23:10; Amos

FISH

5:26.) The fundamental law concerning the sacrifice of the first-born of men is found in Ex. 22:29 (see also Ex. 34:19 f.).

Hebrew laws of sacrifice early provided that the firstlings of beasts were the Lord's (Ex. 13:2, 34:19; Lev. 27:26), to be turned over to the sanctuary; the clean animals to be sacrificed, the unclean ones to be destroyed or replaced (but see Deut. 15:19 f., 21–23.) These laws were extended in time to include the offering of the first fruits of the harvest and the newly sheared wool (Ex. 23:16, 34:22; Deut. 18:4). As Israel's worship system developed, offerings came to be a chief source of support of the priesthood (Num. 18:12).

The N.T. brought to a climax the protest against sacrificed firstlings which had been voiced by such prophets as Hosea (6:6). The sacrificial death of Jesus completely wiped out the need for burnt offerings. Spiritual holiness, not the spilled blood of firstlings, was desired by the Lord. There is no record that Jesus ever engaged in burnt offerings.

fish abound in Bible lands; more than 40 species have been found in the inland waters of the Near East; 22 are peculiar to Palestine and Syria, and 14 of these are known only in the Jordan* River system. Many of the latter swarm in immense schools in the warm fountains of the Sea of Galilee*, particularly along the shores adjacent to Tabgha. Jesus evidently was familiar with this phenomenon (John 21:6). "St. Peter's fish," 6 to 10 in.

147. Fishing boat in Sea of Galilee.

long, from the Sea of Galilee, are still an appetizing breakfast or lunch (John 6:9, 21:9–12) for the native or traveler. Barbel, bream, bleak, dace, and loach prevail. The landlocked Jordan River system has perpetuated its characteristic species unchanged from earliest times. Josephus was first to note the similarity between the fish of this basin and African species, a fact which corroborates the contention of modern geologists that the Jordan-Dead Sea rift once continued into Africa. The fresh, sweet waters of the Jordan River frequently in times of flood carry great quantities of fish down into the Dead Sea, whose salty waters kill them.

The Hebrew Bible, though it names many specific land animals and birds, is not at all scientific with regard to fish. The fish of the Jonah story is called simply a "great fish" (Jonah 1:17). The only attempt to classify fish was as clean or unclean (see ANIMALS (Lev. 11:9–12). All scaleless water animals like eels, were unclean. Jesus used this selective process as an illustration of divine judgment (Matt. 13:47–50). The distinction is exemplified also in Matt. 7:10. Fish was a cherished article of diet throughout Egypt and the Near East (Num. 11:5; John 21:11–13). Jesus described the devotion of a provident father to his son in terms of the gift of a fish (Matt. 7:10). The Jerusalem seafood market, whose lucrative business after the Exile was in the hands of lawless Phoenician (see PHOENICIA) fishmongers (Neh. 13:16), was located near the fish gate (Neh. 3:3, 12:39). The prophet describes the smelly atmosphere of the costermongers' stand (Ezek. 29:4 f.).

When Palestinian people fished, it was not as a sport, nor comparable to the large social parties of Egyptians, boating in the reedy marshes of the Nile, trying to capture birds with boomerangs and spearing fish with long spears, together with bronze fishhooks and harpoons used in hunting hippopotamuses in papyrus thickets. Palestinian fishermen sought fish for food or commerce. The loss of the pure Nile drinking water and its fish, together with the stench of putrid fish, constituted the first Egyptian plague (Ex. 7:20–24; cf. also Isa. 19:8).

All four methods of fishing used today in Near Eastern waters are recorded in the Bible: (1) *Spearing* a fish with a harpoon or trident (Job 41:7). In the Egyptian Museum at Cairo there are statues of a fishing party of young Tut-ankh-amun, standing in a boat with spears poised ready to hurl. Spears of such antiquity are extant in museums. Today torches or electric lights are held over the stern of boats on the Sea of Galilee to attract fish. (2) *Angling* with a hook on a line (Isa. 19:8; Amos 4:2). Jesus authorized Peter to use this method to secure money to pay his taxes (Matt. 17:27). (3) *Casting a seine or drag-net.* This was done in two ways: either by letting the net down into the water and

148. Casting a drag-net.

drawing it together in a narrowing circle, as it is pulled into the boat (Luke 5:4–9); or in a semicircle, drawn to the shore (Matt. 13:47–50). Both are still seen daily in Galilee. (4) *By small hand net.* In this type of casting the net is draped on the arm of the fisherman, who stands on the shore or in shallow water. The net is then skillfully whirled around and allowed to fall in a tent shape or cone. Its lead weights pull it to the bottom so that it encloses fish. The haul is removed from the net and placed in a smaller receiving net, draped about the body of the fisherman. Habakkuk (1:15) mentions methods (2), (3), and (4). Drying the expensive nets in the warm sun is an important part of the fisherman's craft. He suspends them from underbrush or lays them over his boats.

149. Drying nets near Capernaum.

The challenge of Jesus to Peter and Andrew, and James and John, the sons of Zebedee, to "follow" him and become "fishers of men" (Matt. 4:19, 21; Mark 1:17; Luke 5:10) involved the breakup of a family industry and the sacrifice of a capital inheritance.

In symbolism (see SYMBOL) the fish was prominent. Canaanite fertility cults, because of the multitude of fish eggs in a single spawn, selected the fish as one of their art symbols. The Hebrew prohibition against the worship of images included "any thing . . . that is in the water under the earth" (Ex. 20:4; cf. Deut. 4:18). In the days of the early Christian Church, however, the fish was a symbol whose secret meaning during the persecution era was shared only by the initiated. The Greek word for fish is ἰχθύς ("ichthus") whose five component letters are a sacred acrostic for the initials of the five Gk. words that mean "Jesus Christ, Son of God, Saviour." The anchor, symbol of hope, is sometimes shown resting on the fish symbol.

The Mediterranean supplies more than 80% of the fish of Palestine. The Sea of Galilee is capable of being stocked with large quantities. The Gulf of Aqabah is believed to be rich in unexploited supplies of excellent fish.

fitch, an herb cultivated for forage and regarded as tares (Isa. 28:25); in some versions wrongly identified as black commin, *Nigella sativa*, whose aromatic seeds are beaten out with a staff and used for seasoning, especially on top of bread. The "fitches" of Ezek. 4:9 (A.V.) are more properly "spelt" (A.S.V.), an inferior wheat.

150. Eelgrass (*Zostera marina*).

flags, a general A.V. term for several blade-leaf plants growing in moist ground, especially several varieties of iris, rushes, and coarse sedgy grass (*suph*), such as line the Nile today. The Red Sea (Ex. 15:4) is properly the Sea of Reeds (*suph*). The flags mentioned in the story of Moses' infancy (Ex. 2:3, 5) were reed-grass (*'āchū*). Job used the figure of flags which wither soon after being removed from water to express the fate of men who forget God (Job 8:11–16). Isaiah (19:6) foretells doom for Egypt in terms of her river flags and reeds, withering along foul, dry canals.

flax (*Linum usitatissimum*), a plant cultivated in Egypt and Palestine yielding fibre desired by industrious women for weaving into linen* (Prov. 31:13; Hos. 2:5, 9; Isa. 19:9). Flax is the oldest textile fiber and one of the earliest plants cultivated in Egypt and Palestine. Like wool, it was a chief textile material, antedating the cotton for which modern Egypt is famous. Flax was also made into girdles and garments (Isa. 3:23); nets (Isa. 19:9); measuring lines (Ezek. 40:3); napkins (John 11:44), etc. It was not commonly used for rope—this was made from animal hides and twisted rushes and other plants. When its seeds were ripe and the small plants ready to harvest, the pods were "bolled" (for linseed oil) (Ex. 9:31), and the stalks were dried carefully on flat roofs, as on Rahab's at hot Jericho (Josh. 2:6), for the fine fibre. Isaiah's allusion to slow-burning flax (42:3) was quoted by Jesus (Matt. 12:20).

151. Flax.

flesh, a word normally applied to (1) the soft

parts of the body of a man or animal (Gen. 2:23; Lev. 13:2; II Kings 4:34), but in Scripture also containing various specialized meanings. (2) The edible portions of animal food (Ex. 16:8; Num. 11:4, 18). (3) The portions of animals used in sacrifice at altars (Lev. 7:15 ff.) (see WORSHIP). (4) The physical nature of man in contrast to his spirit (Mark 4:38; Gal. 1:16; Rom. 8:8). (5) The evil or carnal aspect of lustful man (Gal. 5:16; Eph. 2:3). See FLESH AND SPIRIT.

flesh and spirit may indicate the recognition of a contrast between "body" and that part of man which is not body. Sometimes in place of "spirit" we find the word "heart" (Ps. 51:10; Matt. 15:19), or "soul" (Ps. 42:1, 2; Matt. 16:26); or "mind" (Eph. 2:3, cf. A.S.V. margin). Sometimes two of these are used together, as "heart and soul" in Deut. 13:3; "heart and mind" in I Sam. 2:35; Deut. 6:5 (but cf. Matt. 22:37, "heart and soul and mind"). Sometimes "flesh" is used for the entire man, or for all mankind, as in Gen. 6:12; Num. 16:22; Ps. 145:21; cf. John 17:2. In the important statement "The Word was made flesh" (John 1:14) the meaning is that the Son of God became a complete man: "flesh" here means "human being." The general thought of the O.T. is clearly that a man consists of two elements, physical and psychical, but the two are regarded as inseparable; but in the use of such terms as "heart," "soul," "mind," "spirit," and "flesh" there is considerable looseness.

This looseness carries over into the N.T. Paul seems to have a definite psychology which distinguishes "spirit, and soul, and body" (I Thess. 5:23). It is usually supposed that Paul thought of the psychic life as related both to the body and to God. Under the body relation he called it "soul"; under the God relation he called it "spirit." A "spiritual" man would be concerned with the things of God (Gal. 6:1); a "soulish" man would be concerned with the things of the body. Sometimes, however, Paul seems to fall back on the older Heb. idea that man is an animated body—a living whole, with the consequence that whatever the man does, *the whole man* does it.

This fits into the sharp contrast of "flesh" and "spirit" which is frequent in the N.T., especially in Paul. The "soulish" man would be the "carnal" man of Rom. 7:14, perhaps the same as the "natural" man of I Cor. 2:14 (cf. A.S.V. margin). Paul implies that human nature is torn between good and evil. He speaks of an inward "warring" (Rom. 7:22, 23), and of a "lusting" of flesh and spirit against each other (Gal. 5:17). The seat of evil is "the flesh," and the seat of good is "the spirit"; yet both belong to the same man. "The mind of the flesh is enmity against God" (A.S.V. Rom. 8:7). What Paul calls "the works of the flesh" and "the fruit of the Spirit" (see the lists in Gal. 5:19–23) are not from different parts of the man: they involve the use of all the human powers, the difference being in how the powers are used and for what purpose. The "spirit" recognizes "the law of God," but "the law [is] weak through the flesh" (Rom. 8:3). Paul can mean only that man is not "naturally good," but suffers from a natural defect. Salvation* is bringing a man from the domination of the flesh (the principle of evil) and putting him under the domination of the spirit (the principle of good). This experience is made possible through Jesus Christ, who, having "condemned sin in the flesh," enables the man of faith to "walk not after the flesh, but after the Spirit" (Rom. 8:3, 4). Elsewhere Paul uses the terms "the old man" and "the new man" to express the same contrast (Eph. 4:20–24). In the Gospel of John the contrast is of "the once-born" and "the twice-born" (3:3–8), and of "the children of darkness" and "the children of light" (8:12, 12:35 f.; cf. I John 2:9–11). See IMMORTALITY; RESURRECTION; SALVATION. E. L.

fleshhooks, forks of copper, bronze ("bright brass"), or gold (Ex. 27:3, 38:3), part of the priest's equipment at the altar of sacrifice. From David the design of the golden fleshhook for the Temple was handed down to Solomon (I Chron. 28:17), who had the work fabricated by the craftsman-architect Hiram of Tyre (II Chron. 4:16).

flint, a hard stone of almost pure silica, steel gray inside a whitish crust, common in the limestone of Palestine, and found in great abundance in skillfully worked artifacts, at the mouth of prehistoric caves of Natufian man at Mount Carmel. It was used for arrowheads, knives (Ex. 4:25), hand-axes, and sickle blades. Flint balls, thrown as hand grenades in O.T. times, have also been found, helping us to visualize what David may have planted in Goliath's forehead (I Sam. 17:49). Flint implements were used to bore underground water tunnels like the one at Gezer (c. 2000 B.C.).

152. Egyptian flint knife. Predynastic period.

"Flint" is also used in figures of speech to represent any intractable rock, especially one from which water was caused to flow (Deut. 8:15, 32:13; Ps. 114:8); also firmness of character (Isa. 50:7; Ezek. 3:9).

flock. See SHEEP.

flood, flowing water, the term being used in several senses: (1) A particular river, like the Euphrates* (Josh. 24:2); the Nile* (Amos 8:8); the Jordan (Ps. 66:6); (2) a beneficial inundation for irrigation (see FARMING; WATER) (Isa. 44:3); or (3) a destructive force in nature (Ps. 90:5; Dan. 9:26; Nah. 1:8; Matt. 7:25; Luke 6:48). Disastrous flash floods are common throughout Bible lands, where long dry spells are followed by torrential rains. Prayer (Ps. 32:6) and the consciousness of the divine presence (Isa. 43:2) are man's protection in such troubled times. In Hebrew poetry "flood" is synonymous with "sea" (Ex. 15:8; Ps. 24:2, 93:3; Jonah 2:3).

Popularly the word is identified with the Deluge story (Gen. 6:5–8:22). Because of man's wickedness God decided to cleanse the earth and destroy the race, except for Noah*, whom He commissioned to build an Ark* into which his family and animals of every species would embark and be preserved from the destruction which the Deluge would cause. When the water finally abated, the ark rested on Mt. Ararat (Gen. 8:4), and life on the earth began all over again (Gen. 9:7). Noah sacrificed to God, Who by the rainbow in the clearing skies covenanted never again to destroy the race by flood.

Two distinct accounts are found closely woven together in this story. The J narrative, characterized by the use of "Jehovah" throughout, is from Judah in the 10th century B.C. The other, P, is a late priestly strand written at about the time of the Exile*. Though agreement is general, each presents variations as to the number of animals saved (Gen. 7:2 f.; cf. Gen. 6:19 f.), the cause of the Flood (7:12; cf. 7:11), and its duration (7:12, 8:6–12; cf. 7:24, 8:4, 13 f.). J credits Noah with inaugurating sacrifices to Yahweh upon leaving the ark (8:20); P omits the sacrifices but records the covenant with God (Gen. 9:13–17). The two strands are characterized by the editorial slants of their compilers, and are evidently different versions of the same events spliced or edited by a final redactor into the present Genesis form. (See SOURCES.)

Flood stories are frequent in the ancient literature of many of the world's peoples. Efforts to link them all together as evidence of one universal event in which all life suffered are, however, futile. Egypt, where the annual flooding of the Nile is considered a blessing, has no such catastrophic legends. The literary links between Genesis and the Babylonian Flood narratives are unmistakable. A Babylonian clay tablet from the library of Ashurbanipal (669–? 633 B.C.) written at Nineveh, a part of the Gilgamesh epic, tells how Ut-naphishtum (the Babylonian Noah) built a houseboat calked with pitch (cf. Gen. 6:14) according to specific dimensions (6:15), on which he loaded his possessions, his family, and the "seed of life of all kinds," and escaped the Deluge by which "mankind was turned to clay." A dove, swallow, and raven were sent out (8:6–12) and helped to determine the safe hour for the company's disembarking. This Babylonian account pictures the gods as disagreeing, quarrelling, crouching in fear like dogs, and swarming about the sacrifice like hungry flies, all of which is in striking contrast to the Genesis deity. Who is sovereign, and, while picturesquely anthropomorphic, is not repulsive; is interested in humanity, and merciful. An earlier version of this story appears on a fragment of a Sumerian tablet (before 2000 B.C.) found at Nippur, SE. of Babylon, and now in the University Museum at Philadelphia. This older account in one respect agrees more nearly with the Biblical story than the one from the library at Nineveh, for it represents Ziusudra as a very pious man.

Archaeology has made clear that great floods devastated Babylonia, due to the nature of its valley. At Ur traces of a great flood have been found. An 8-ft. deposit of water-laid clay, covering remains of the al-'Ubaid period, was discovered at the bottom of the great pit in the Royal Cemetery. Near the Ishtar Temple at Kish (Uhaimir) a red stratum of sterile earth 3 to 5 ft. deep and at a later date than the "flood" stratum at Ur, extended over the whole city area, perhaps a deposit left by a great flood. The debris below was 25 ft. thick, showing the extent of the destruction. Thus both literary and archaeological evidence join with the only geographical testimony in the Genesis narrative (8:4) in localizing the catastrophe in the Tigris-Euphrates Valley, whose streams originate in the snows of Mt. Ararat.

153. The only known dated fragment of Hebrew (Amorite) cuneiform Deluge story, copied c. 1966 B.C. from one written perhaps 2000 years earlier. This indicates that West Semitic peoples, as well as Babylonians, had a Deluge legend.

Early Patriarchal contacts with Haran (Gen. 11:31 f., 27:43, 29:4) may have furnished the earliest channel through which the Flood story passed into the consciousness of the Hebrews by word-of-mouth, from parent to child. The variations in the northern and southern Mesopotamian versions indicate how adaptable the legend is to a local or purposeful objective. Noah, in Mari and other texts, is the name of a god. In the skillful hands of the inspired writers of Genesis the Flood story, whatever its origin, has been the medium through which large sections of the human family, from its earliest childhood, have gained fresh and higher conceptions of God and religion. Throughout the Bible no question is ever raised as to whether it happened. Wherever the Flood story is referred to it is used in a context aimed to promote some practical religious objective, e.g., evangelism and the judgment to come (Matt. 24:36–41; Luke 17:26 f.); salvation and baptism (I Pet. 3:20 f.); God's righteousness (II Pet. 2:5).

floor. (1) The floor of a building. Two unusual floors of the Bible were the floor of Solomon's temple, described (I Kings 6:15, A.S.V.) as "overlaid with boards of cypress"; and the *gabbatha*, the paved open court of square stones outside the palace of Herod in Jerusalem, where the governor held court seated upon the judgment seat or high bema (John 19:13).

(2) A threshing floor; a round, outdoor space with a smooth surface, built on a rocky base and covered with packed-down mud, used for threshing and winnowing grain (Ruth 3:2).

flour. See BREAD, MILL.

flowers, the glory of Palestinian springtime, bloom in greater variety in Palestine than almost anywhere else in the world. Palestinian and Syrian deserts are said to contain 400 varieties of wild flowers not found elsewhere. Many in the Kingdom of Jordan have never yet been classified. Yet the Bible makes few references to specific flowers, but groups them comprehensively as symbols of life's brevity (Isa. 28:1, 4; James 1:10 f.; I Pet. 1:24); or mentions their use as decorative motifs in the Tabernacle and the Temple (Ex. 25:31 ff., 37:17 ff.; I Kings 7:26, 49). In his reference to lilies of the field (Matt. 6:28–30), (which in the brief and sudden springtime "clothe the grass of the field" in the Plain of Gennesaret, the slopes below Nazareth, etc.), Jesus probably referred to all spring flowers, just as Arabs do today when they speak of *sushan* or *hannum*, designating the anemone, the cyclamen, the daisy, the tulip, the star of Bethlehem, and many others.

The greatest plant list in Scripture is in the Song of Solomon, which contains 74 references to various plants—not identified satisfactorily, however, by modern botanists. This "herbarium" corresponds to the jewel list of Ezekiel and the animal catalogue of Job.

Among the commonest flowers of Palestine is the anemone (*Anemone coronaria*), which is related to the buttercup, and which grows in all parts of Palestine in brilliant reds, delicate pinks, purple, blue, white, and cream. Acres of these grow along the Sea of Galilee after the February and March rains bring them out in a delicate tapestry thrown across the bare brown shoulders of the ancient countryside. The anemone, sharing the deep hues of royal robes, is often identified as the "lily of the field," although Dr. Ha-Reubeni, of the Hebrew University in Jerusalem, thought the latter was the *ahib leban*, or "white flower," possibly the common field daisy. The "rose of Sharon" has been identified by some as the crocus of the plain; by others, as the yellow or white narcissus or red tulip, the *Tulipa montana*, one of the oldest members of the ancient tulip family, whose name comes from the Persian word for "turban." Gladioli in Palestine belong to the iris family, and are called "sword lilies" because their spiky stem curves like a scimitar. Their five or seven dark purple or pink flowers grow all on one side of the stem. Lilies of many varieties grow in swampy regions like the Huleh marshes. Roses (see ROSE) have always bloomed in Palestine, among rocks, in cultivated gardens, in clay pots on flat-roofed houses. Acres of damask roses are cultivated for attar perfume. Some flowers called "roses" are bulbous; some may be narcissi (see NARCISSUS). Salvia was suggested by the late Eleanor A. King and others as the inspiration of the seven-branched golden candlestick. Almond*-blossom calyxes were models for the cup of this famous lamp (Ex. 37:17 ff.), just as the calyx of pomegranate flowers suggested ancient crowns. Larkspur, loosestrife, mallows, jasmine, squills, pink flax, and stars of Bethlehem add their color to the short spring glory. The dominant wild flower of late autumn is the pink, crocus-like *Colchicum* (meadow saffron), which appears abundantly amid thorn bushes.

Egyptian fields grow some of the above flowers, but the water lilies, *Nymphaea alba*, *Nymphaea caerulea*, and *Nymphaea lotus*, were the chief glory of Nile gardens in Bible times. Entwined with the papyrus of Lower Egypt, the lotus of warm Upper Egypt made the emblem of the United Egypt. It also provided the design of the famous lotus-column capitals as early as the Fifth Dynasty—capitals which became ancestors of the Greek Ionic 800 years later.

The flat, muddy Babylonian river reaches did not produce flowers; but in the high steppes between the Tigris and the upper loop of the Euphrates a blaze of gay spring flowers carpeted the meager, stony soil, which was too arid for crops.

The Greece Paul knew produced flowers which found their way into the rites of the Eleusinian Mysteries of the flower-picking Persephone, and into Greek myths associated with Narcissus, Hyacinthus, Ceres, Pluto, and others.

See entries under individual names—FLAX; MUSTARD; and various trees—ALMOND; FIG; OLIVE; etc.

For detailed data consult *Plants of the Bible*, Harold & Alma Moldenke (The Chronica Botanica Co., Waltham, Mass.); also the works of early Biblical botanists, Carolus Linnaeus (1757); F. Hasselquist; and G. E. Post, author of the monumental *Flora of Syria, Palestine, and Sinai* (1883–1893).

Check-List of Flowers† Mentioned in the Bible

almonds. *Amygdalus communis*. Gen. 43:11: "Carry down the man a present, . . . spices, and myrrh, nuts, and almonds."

†These names, which are based on the work of Dr. H. N. Moldenke, former Curator and Administrator of the Herbarium, N. Y. Botanical Garden, are alphabetized according to the form in which each occurs in the Bible. The words in brackets indicate the plant that is believed today to have been represented. Its botanical name follows, and after that, in parentheses, its present-day common name, if one exists in English. Reproduced by permission of the Journal of the New York Botanical Garden (March 1941) and of Dr. and Mrs. H. N. Moldenke, who prepared the list.

algum trees. *Sabina excelsa* (juniper). II Chron. 2:8: "Send me also cedar trees, fir trees, and algum trees."

almug trees. *Pterocarpus santalinus* (rosewood or red sandalwood). I Kings 10:11 f.: "And the navy also of Hiram . . . brought in from Ophir great plenty of almug trees."

aloes (N.T.). *Aloë succotrina*. John 19:39. "And brought a mixture of myrrh and aloes."

aloes (O.T.). *Aquilaria agallocha* (eaglewood) and *Santalum album* (sandalwood). Ps. 45:8: "All thy garments smell of myrrh, and aloes, and cassia."

anise [dill]. *Anethum graveolens*. Matt. 23:23: "For ye pay tithe of mint and anise and cummin."

apple [apricot]. *Prunus armeniaca*. Song of Sol. 2:3: "As the apple tree among the trees of the wood, so is my beloved among the sons."

aspalathus. *Alhag: camelorum* var. *turcorum*. Ecclus. 24:15: "I gave a sweet smell like cinnamon and aspalathus."

balm [balsam]. *Balanites aegyptiaca*. Jer. 8:22: "Is there no balm in Gilead. . . ?"

balm [balsam]. *Commiphora (Balsamodendron) opobalsamum*. Ezek. 27:17: "They traded in thy market wheat of Minnith, and Pannag, and honey, and oil, and balm."

barley. *Hordeum distichon*, *H. hexastichon*, and *H. vulgare*. Deut. 8:8: "A land of wheat, and barley, and vines, and fig trees, and pomegranates."

bdellium. *Commiphora africana (Balsamodendron africanum)*. Gen. 2:12: "And the gold of that land is good: there is bdellium and the onyx stone."

beans. *Vicia faba (Faba vulgaris)*. Ezek. 4:9: "Take thou also unto thee wheat, and barley, and beans, and lentiles, and millet, and fitches, and put them in one vessel, and make thee bread thereof."

bitter herbs. *Cichorium endivia* (endive), *C. intybus* (chicory), *Lactuca sativa* (lettuce), *Nasturtium officinale* (watercress), *Taraxacum officinale* (dandelion), *Rumex acetosella* var. *multifidus* (sorrel). Num. 9:11: "And eat it with unleavened bread and bitter herbs."

box tree. *Buxus longifolia*. Isa. 41:19: "I will plant in the wilderness the cedar . . . and the oil tree; I will set in the desert the fir tree, and the pine, and the box tree together."

briers. *Rubus sanctus* and *R. ulmifolius* (blackberries), *Solanum sanctum* and *S. sodomoeum* (nightshade). Isa. 55:13: "Instead of the thorn shall come up the fir tree, and instead of the brier shall come up the myrtle tree."

bulrushes. *Cyperus papyrus* (papyrus). Ex. 2:3: "And when she could not longer hide him, she took for him an ark of bulrushes."

burning bush [crimson-flowered mistletoe]. *Loranthus acaciae*. Ex. 3:2: "And the angel of the Lord appeared unto him in a flame of fire out of the midst of a bush."

calamus; sweet calamus; sweet cane. *Andropoton aromaticus*. Song of Sol. 4:14: "Spikenard and saffron; calamus and cinnamon, with all trees of frankincense." Jer. 6:20: "To what purpose cometh there to me incense from Sheba, and the sweet cane from a far country?"

camphire. *Lawsonia inermis* (henna). Song of Sol. 4:13: "Thy plants are an orchard of pomegranates, with pleasant fruits; camphire, with spikenard."

cassia (of Exodus and Ezekiel). *Cinnamomum cassia*. Ezek. 27:19: "Bright iron, cassia, and calamus, were in thy market."

cassia (of Psalms) [Indian orris]. *Saussurea lappa*. Ps. 45:8: "All thy garments smell of myrrh, and aloes, and cassia."

cedar. *Sabina phoenicia* (juniper). Num. 19:6: "And the priest shall take cedar wood, and hyssop, and scarlet, and cast it into the midst of the burning of the heifer."

cedar; cedar of Lebanon. *Cedrus libanotica*. Ps. 92:12: "The righteous . . . shall grow like a cedar of Lebanon."

chestnut [oriental plane]. *Platanus orientalis*. Gen. 30:37: "And Jacob took him rods of green poplar, and of the hazel and chestnut tree."

cinnamon. *Cinnamomum zeylanicum*. Song of Sol. 4:14 (see *calamus*).

cockle. *Agrostemma githago* (corn-cockle). Job 31:40: "Let thistles grow instead of wheat, and cockle instead of barley."

coriander. *Coriandrum sativum*. Ex. 16:31: "And it was like coriander seed, white."

corn [wheat]. *Triticum aestivum*. Gen. 41:57: "And all countries came into Egypt to Joseph for to buy corn."

cotton. *Gossypium herbaceum*. Esther 1:5 f. (Moffatt): "There were hangings of white and violet cotton, corded with white and purple linen." (This word appears only in the Revised Version of the Bible, and is believed to have been correctly rendered by Moffatt.)

cucumbers. *Cucumis sativus* and *C. chate*. Num. 11:5: "We remember the fish, which we did eat in Egypt freely; the cucumbers, and the melons, and the leeks, and the onions and the garlick."

cummin. *Cuminum cyminum*. Matt. 23:23 (see *anise*).

cypress. *Cupressus sempervirens* var. *horizontalis*. Ecclus. 50:10: "And as a cypress tree which groweth up to the clouds."

desire [caper]. *Capparis sicula*, or possibly *C. spinosa*. Eccles. 12:5: "And the grasshopper shall be a burden, and desire shall fail."

dove's dung [star-of-Bethlehem]. *Ornithogalum umbellatum*. II Kings 6:25: "And there was a great famine in Samaria: and, behold, they besieged it, until an ass's head was sold for fourscore pieces of silver, and the fourth part of a cab of dove's dung for five pieces of silver."

ebony. *Diospyros ebanaster*, *D. ebenum*, and *D. melanoxylon*. Ezek. 27:15: "They brought thee for a present horns of ivory and ebony."

fig. *Ficus carica*. Prov. 27:18: "Whoso keepeth the fig tree shall eat the fruit thereof."

fir. *Pinus halepensis* (Aleppo pine). Isa. 37:24: "And I will cut down the tall cedars thereof, and the choice fir trees thereof."

fitches. *Nigella sativa* (fennel- or nutmeg-flower). Isa. 28:27: ". . . the fitches are beaten out with a staff, and the cummin with a rod."

flax. *Linum usitatissimum.* Prov. 31:13: "She seeketh wool, and flax."

frankincense. *Boswellia thurifera, B. papyrifera, and B. carterii.* Song of Sol. 3:6: ". . . perfumed with myrrh and frankincense."

galbanum. *Ferula galbaniflua* (a kind of fennel). Ex. 30:34: "Take unto thee sweet spices, stacte, and onycha, and galbanum."

garlick. *Allium sativum* and *A. ascalonicum* (shallot). Num. 11:5 (see *cucumbers*).

gourd. *Ricinus communis* (castor-bean). Jonah 4:6: "And the Lord God prepared a gourd, and made it to come up over Jonah, that it might be a shadow over his head, to deliver him from his grief."

green bay tree. *Laurus nobilis* (sweet bay). Ps. 37:35: "I have seen the wicked in great power, and spreading himself like a green bay tree."

heath [Savin juniper]. *Juniperus oxycedrus.* Jer. 17:6: "For he shall be like the heath in the desert."

holm tree; mastic tree. [Lentisk]. *Pistacia lentiscus.* Sus. 54 (Goodspeed): " 'So now, if you saw this woman, tell us, under which tree did you see them meet?' He answered, 'Under a mastic tree.' "

husks [Carob-tree or St. John's bread]. *Ceratonia siliqua.* Luke 15:16: "And he would fain have filled his belly with the husks that the swine did eat."

hyssop [reed]. *Holcus sorghum* var. *durra.* John 19:29: ". . . and they filled a sponge with vinegar, and put it upon hyssop, and put it to his mouth."

hyssop [marjoram]. *Origanum aegyptiacum.* I Kings 4:33: "And he spake of trees, from the cedar tree that is in Lebanon even unto the hyssop that springeth out of the wall."

ivy. *Hedera helix.* II Macc. 6:7: "And when the feast of Bacchus was kept, the Jews were compelled to go in procession to Bacchus, carrying ivy."

Judas tree. *Cercis siliquastrum.* Matt. 27:5: "And he cast down the pieces of silver in the temple, and departed, and went and hanged himself." Some legends say that Judas hanged himself on this kind of tree, which is a native of Palestine; others say it was a fig tree.

juniper [broom]. *Retama raetam.* I Kings 19:4: "But he himself went a day's journey into the wilderness, and came and sat down under a juniper tree."

juniper roots. *Cynomorium coccineum.* Job 30:4: ". . . and juniper roots for their meat." The actual reference is probably to the fungus, which grows upon the roots of the "juniper" of the Holy Land.

leeks. *Allium porrum* and *Trigonella foenum-graecum* (fenugreek). Num. 11:5 (see *cucumbers*).

lentiles. *Lens esculenta.* Ezek. 4:9 (see *beans*).

lilies [iris]. *Iris pseudacorus.* Ecclus. 50:8: "And as the flower of roses in the spring of the year, as lilies by the rivers of waters, and as the branches of the frankincense tree in the time of summer."

lilies. *Lilium chalcedonicum* (scarlet lily). Song of Sol. 5:13: ". . . his lips like lilies, dropping sweet smelling myrrh."

lilies of the field. *Anemone coronaria* [poppy, or St. Brigid, anemone] or *Anthemis palaestina.* Matt. 6:28: "Consider the lilies of the field, how they grow; they toil not, neither do they spin."

mallows [saltwort]. *Atriplex halimus,* also probably *A. dimorphostegia, A. tatarica* and *A. rosea.* Job 30:4: "Who cut up mallows by the bushes."

manna. *Lecanora esculenta, L. fruticulosa,* and *L. affinis* (lichens). Ex. 16:14 f.: "And when the dew that lay was gone up, behold, upon the face of the wilderness there lay a small round thing . . . And when the children of Israel saw it, they said . . . It is manna."

manna. *Nostoc* (an alga which appears on the surface of the ground under moist conditions). Ex. 16:21: "And they gathered it every morning, every man according to his eating . . . when the sun waxed hot, it melted."

manna. *Tamarix mannifera* (tamarisk), *Fraxinus ornus,* and *Alhagi maurorum* (camel-thorn) (incense-producing plants). Bar. 1:10: ". . . and prepare ye manna, and offer upon the altar of the Lord our God."

melons. *Cucumis melo* (muskmelon) and *Citrullus vulgaris* (watermelon). Num. 11:5 (see *cucumbers*).

mint. *Mentha longifolia.* Matt. 23:23 (see *anise*).

mulberry [poplar]. *Populus euphratica.* II Sam. 5:23: ". . . and come upon them over against the mulberry trees."

mustard. *Brassica nigra.* Mark 4:31: "It is like a grain of mustard seed."

myrrh. *Commiphora (Balsamodendron) myrrha* and *C. kataf.* Prov. 7:17: "I have perfumed my bed with myrrh, aloes, and cinnamon." Mark 15:23: "And they gave him to drink wine mingled with myrrh: but he received it not."

myrrh [fragrant gum]. *Cistus villosus* (rock-rose), *C. creticus* and *C. salvifolius.* Gen. 37:25: ". . . a company of Ishmeelites . . . bearing spicery and balm and myrrh."

myrtle. *Myrtus communis.* Zech. 1:8: ". . . he stood among the myrtle trees."

nettles. *Sinapis arvensis* (charlock). Prov. 24:31: ". . . all grown over with thorns, and nettles had covered the face thereof."

nuts. *Juglans regia* (walnut). Song of Sol. 6:11: "I went down into the garden of nuts."

nuts. *Pistacia vera* (pistachio). Gen. 43:11 (see *almonds*).

oak. *Quercus aegilops.* Isa. 44:14: "He heweth him down cedars, and taketh the cypress and the oak."

oak. *Quercus ilex.* Gen. 35:8: ". . . she was buried beneath Beth-el under an oak."

oak. *Quercus coccifera* and *Q. lusitanica.* Zech. 11:2: "Howl, fir tree; for the cedar is fallen; because the mighty are spoiled: howl, O ye oaks of Bashan."

oak. *Quercus pseudococcifera.* I Kings 13:14: "... and found him sitting under an oak."

oil tree [oleaster]. *Elaegnus angustifolia.* Isa. 41:19 (see *box tree*).

olive. *Olea europaea.* Deut. 28:40: "Thou shalt have olive trees throughout all thy coasts."

onions. *Allium cepa.* Num. 11:5 (see *cucumbers*).

onycha. *Styrax benzoin* (benzoin). Ecclus. 24:15: "A pleasant odor like the best myrrh, as galbanum, and onycha."

palm. *Phoenix dactylifera* (date palm). II Chron. 28:15: "... and brought them to Jericho, the city of palm trees."

pannag [millet]. *Panicum miliaceum.* Ezek. 27:17 (see *balm*).

pine. *Pinus brutia.* Isa. 60:13: "The glory of Lebanon shall come unto thee, the fir tree, the pine tree, and the box together."

pomegranate. *Punica granatum.* Song of Sol. 4:13: "Thy plants are an orchard of pomegranates, with pleasant fruits."

poplar. *Populus alba.* Gen. 30:37 (see *chestnut*).

reed. *Arundo donax.* Job 40:21: "He lieth under the shady trees, in the covert of the reed, and fens."

reed. *Holcus sorghum* var. *durra.* Mark 15:36: "And one ran and filled a sponge full of vinegar, and put it on a reed, and gave him to drink."

rolling thing ("Rose of Jericho"). *Anastatica hierochuntica* (resurrection plant) and *Gundelia tournefortii.* Isa. 17:13: "... like a rolling thing before the whirlwind."

rose [narcissus]. *Narcissus tazetta.* Isa. 35:1: "... and the desert shall rejoice, and blossom as the rose."

rose [oleander]. *Nerium oleander.* Ecclus. 39:13: "... and bud forth as a rose growing by the brook of the field."

rose. *Rosa phoenicia.* II Esd. 2:19: "And seven mighty mountains, whereupon there grow roses and lilies."

rose of Sharon [tulip]. *Tulipa montana* or *T. sharonensis.* Song of Sol. 2:1: "I am the rose of Sharon, and the lily of the valleys."

rue. *Ruta graveolens* and *R. chalapensis* var. *latifolia.* Luke 11:42: "But woe unto you, Pharisees! for ye tithe mint and rue and all manner of herbs."

rie [rye]. *Triticum aestivum* var. *spelta* (spelt). Ex. 9:32: "But the wheat and the rie were not smitten."

saffron. *Crocus sativus.* Song of Sol. 4:14 (see *calamus*).

scarlet [oak]. *Quercus coccifera.* Num. 19:6 (see *cedar*). The scarlet dye used in Biblical days was made from an insect, *Coccus ilicis*, which infests this oak species.

seven-branched candlestick [sage plant]. *Salvia judaica.* Ex. 37:18: "And six branches going out of the sides thereof." It is believed that the Hebrews derived the design of their golden candlestick directly from the form of this plant.

shittim (or shittah). *Acacia seyal* and *A. tortilis.* Ex. 25:10: "And they shall make an ark of shittim wood."

sope [soap]. *Salsola kali* and *S. ineumis* (saltwort) and *Salicornia fruticosa* and *S. herbacea* (glasswort), the ashes of which, after burning, were used for making soap. Jer. 2:22: "... wash thee with nitre, and take thee much sope."

spices. *Astragalus gummifer* and *A. tragacantha* are probably referred to, though many other plants with pungent flavor may have been meant. Gen. 43:11 (see *almonds*).

spikenard. *Nardostachys jatamansi.* Mark 14:3: "There came a woman having an alabaster box of ointment of spikenard very precious."

stacte [sweet storax]. *Styrax officinalis.* Ex. 30:34 (see *galbanum*).

strange vine. *Ampelopsis* (*vitis*) *orientalis.* Jer. 2:21: "How then art thou turned into the degenerate plant of a strange vine unto me?"

sweet cane [sugar cane]. *Saccharum officinarum.* Isa. 43:24: "Thou hast bought me no sweet cane with money." (See also *calamus.*)

sycamine [black mulberry]. *Morus nigra.* Luke 17:6: "If ye had faith . . . ye might say unto this sycamine tree, Be thou plucked up by the root . . . and it should obey you."

sycomore (not *sycamore*, which is another name for the native American plane tree). *Ficus sycomorus.* Ps. 78:47: "He destroyed . . . their sycomore trees with frost."

tares [darnel grass]. *Lolium temulentum.* Matt. 13:24 f.: "But while men slept, his enemy came and sowed tares among the wheat."

teil tree, turpentine tree. *Pistacia terebinthus.* Isa. 6:13: "... as a teil tree, and as an oak." Ecclus. 24:16: "As the turpentine tree, I stretched out my branches."

thistles. *Silybum marianum* (holy thistle); also *Centaurea calcitrapa*, *C. iberica*, and *C. verutum.* Hos. 10:8: "The thorn and the thistle shall come up on their altars."

thorns. *Paliurus spina-christi* (Christ or Jerusalem thorn). Matt. 27:29: "And when they had plaited a crown of thorns, they put it upon his head."

thorns. *Rhamnus palaestina* (buckthorn). Prov. 15:19: "The way of the slothful man is as an hedge of thorns."

thorns [jujubes]. *Zizyphus spina-christi* and *Z. vulgaris.* Matt. 7:16: "Do men gather grapes of thorns, or figs of thistles?"

thyine wood. *Tetraclinis articulata* (*Callitris quadrivalvis*) (arar tree, an arborvitae relative). Rev. 18:12: "The merchandise of gold, and silver, and precious stones, . . . and all thyine wood . . ."

tree [tamarisk]. *Tamarix pentandra*, *T. tetragyna*, or *T. articulata.* I Sam. 22:6: "... now Saul abode in Gibeah under a tree in Ramah."

vine. *Vitis vinifera.* Judg. 9:12: "Then said the trees unto the vine, Come thou, and reign over us."

water lily. *Nymphaea alba*, *N. lotus* and *N. caerulea.* I Kings 7:19 f.: "And the chapiters that were upon the top of the pillars were of lily work in the porch."

weeds [seaweeds]. *Zostera marina.* Jonah 2:5: "The depth closed me round about, the weeds were wrapped about my head."

wheat. *Triticum aestivum* and *T. compositum.*

Judg. 6:11: "And his son Gideon threshed wheat by the winepress."

willow. *Salix alba*, *S. acmophylla*, *S. fragilis*, and *S. safṣaf*. Isa. 44:4: "And they shall spring up ... as willows by the water courses."

willow [poplar]. *Populus euphratica*. Ps. 137:2: "We hanged our harps upon the willows in the midst thereof."

wormwood. *Artemisia judaica* or *A. herba-alba*. Jer. 23:15: "Behold, I will feed them with wormwood, and make them drink the water of gall."

flute. See MUSICAL INSTRUMENTS.

fly, a winged insect. Many varieties of flies plagued people of Bible lands, as they do today, carrying the microörganisms of cholera, malaria, sleeping sickness, ophthalmia, and enteric fever. The flies of Eccles. 10:1 were *zebūb*, whence the name of the god Baalzebub, lord of the flies, whose worship was thought by Ekronites to avert the evil done by flies (II Kings 1:2). The plaguing insects of Ex. 8:21 ff. were *'ārōb*—sand flies, lice, cockroaches, mosquitoes, or some of the "divers sorts of flies" which still torment Egypt and whose eradication is inhibited by religious taboo. The Egyptian fly plague of the Exodus is reflected in Ps. 78:45, 105:31.

food in Palestine was in many areas as scarce in Bible times as now, due to the nature of the soil and shallow cultivation; and as plentiful in Egypt as today, because of the dependable, fertilizing overflow of the Nile*. Ample food in well-irrigated, alluvial Babylonia was the basis of the early civilization and the dawn of political power. Palestine people, never far above the subsistence level, prized their food and dreaded recurrent famines (see FAMINE). Whenever possible, festivities included feasting (see FEASTS.)

Hebrews of the Patriarchal period used foods similar to those of desert nomads today: parched grain; vegetables, such as beans and lentils, cucumbers, squash, mixed with seasonings; occasional meat; milk products from their flocks; fruit from trees passed on treks, such as figs*, olives*, pomegranates*, and grapes (see VINE). Flat, round loaves of coarse bread* made in the open was their "whole stay" (Isa. 3:1). The introduction of animal foods is attributed to Noah in the narrative of Genesis 9:3 ff. The "red pottage" (Gen. 25:30) prepared by Jacob, and savory dishes of kids' meat and venison such as were offered to Isaac (Gen. 27:1–33), are still enjoyed by Bedouins.

Hebrews who settled in villages and towns aimed to have a vine and a fig tree for each family (I Kings 4:25). To this food source they added a few pet sheep, which yielded milk, cheese, meat for special occasions, and many pounds of sweet fat from their heavy tails to put down for winter use. Kids—cheaper than sheep—were relished by the poor (Luke 15:29). The "fatted calf" offered to the returned prodigal was a luxury (Luke 15:23), whose use angered the elder brother.

Food from unclean animals was forbidden by Hebrew law. Swine, camel-meat, and rabbits were taboo. But partridge, quail, geese—the national dish of Egypt—and pigeons were permitted (Num. 11:32; I Sam. 26:20). Table fowls were introduced after the Persian period (II Esd. 1:30; Matt. 23:37, 26:34). Fish* was eaten, and was plentiful along the Mediterranean and the Sea of Galilee. The Jordan furnished more than thirty varieties. Phoenician merchants shipped seafood to Jerusalem markets, sold near the Fish Gate (Neh. 3:3). Fish products from Galilee were salted and dried and sent great distances.

Butter was a delicacy which even poor nomads afforded. The Aramaic word "oil" may in some cases be translated "butter," often used in payment of bills and taxes in regions where butter could be shipped in skin sacks. All sorts of cheeses were prized, especially those made from camel's milk, with its life-giving lactic acid. *Leben*, a sort of yogurt made from soured milk, is one of the oldest and best loved foods of Bible lands. When a bit of *leben* is added to fresh milk to make it ferment, the resultant *ghaib*, when violently shaken in a goatskin bag, turns to butter and to *sheninah* (buttermilk). The latter is put into little cloth sacks and the water squeezed out of it; and the cheese-like *leben* when rolled into balls keeps indefinitely, and saves lives in arid regions where potable water is unavailable. The gift of Judg. 5:25 was probably *leben*.

154. Produce market in Jerusalem.

In addition to the fruit of trees, mulberries and melons were relished. Vegetables included beans, lentils, peas, lettuce, cucumbers, squash, onions, and garlic. Salt* was secured by evaporation of water from the Mediterranean and the Dead Sea. Seasonings included horehound, bitter aromatics, and spices* brought from Arabia by caravans.

Honey was extensively produced in the highland apiaries and shipped abroad. Candies made of dates, honey, nuts, and gum arabic were plentiful and were exported to Tyre (Ezek. 27:17). Women were confectioners as well as bakers of fancy cakes (I Sam. 8:13). In Bible times, as now, sticky sweetmeats were displayed in the bazaars.

Food is still sold in the markets (see AGORA) of towns and cities, in bountiful Bethlehem and in Jerusalem's David Street. In early morning hours peasants from Judaean villages bring vegetables and fruits to the city gate, and by midmorning are gone. Jerusalem still knows a Cheesemongers' Valley (the Tyropoeon); damp, dark wine cellars; and animal markets near the Damascus Gate. The provision stalls of Corinth were called "the shambles" (A.V.), or the "market" (R.S.V.) (I Cor. 10:25).

Food was so scarce in Palestine that it was deemed worthy to be sacrificed in worship*. It was a highly acceptable gift for notables, as well as for people in emergency situations. And it played a major part in the happy times accompanying national celebrations.

Jacob sent fruits, balm, honey, spices, myrrh, and nuts to Pharaoh (Gen. 43:11), and received from him "good things of Egypt" (Gen. 45:23). Jesse sent bread, a bottle of wine, and a kid to Saul (I Sam. 16:20), and ten cheeses to his son's captain (I Sam. 17:18). David received bread, wine, sheep, parched corn, raisins, and figs from Abigail (I Sam. 25:18), and similar gifts from Mephibosheth (II Sam. 16:1); his henchmen brought him grains, flour, vegetables, butter, cheese, and meat (II Sam. 17:27–29). Ahijah sent gifts of bread, cake, and honey to Jeroboam's wife (I Kings 14:3). A man from Baal-shalisha brought first fruits, loaves of barley, and ears of corn to Elisha (II Kings 4:42). On a day of feasting the Jews sent "portions" to one another (Esther 9:19), as did the Jerusalemites (Neh. 8:12).

The Messianic age was pictured by Isaiah (49:10) as a time when there should be no lack of food (cf. Luke 1:53). The greatest gift of actual food mentioned in the Bible is recorded in John 6:1–14, where Jesus symbolized himself as "the living bread" (John 6:31–58). In another instance, Jesus spoke of having "meat to eat" that others knew nothing about (John 4:32–34). Paul defined superlative good will in terms of feeding one's enemy (Rom. 12:20).

For customs in connection with eating, see BANQUETS; FURNITURE; HOSPITALITY; MEALS.

fool, foolishness, folly. A *fool* is one in whom there is no wisdom or judgment. *Foolishness* is the absence of wisdom, the antithesis of qualities found in the Wisdom* Literature of the O.T. and the ideals stated by Jesus (Matt. 5–7). *Folly* is usually synonymous with unwise action or conduct, frequently with wickedness, which represents total want of understanding. A fool is "right in his own eyes" (Prov. 12:15); rages, is overconfident (14:16); fastens his eyes upon the ends of the earth, instead of minding his own business (17:24); hates understanding (18:2); is contentious and given to wrath (18:6, 27:3); is "perverse in his lips" (19:1); meddles (20:3); trusts in his own heart (28:26); has a raucous laugh (Eccles. 7:6). The fool of the N.T. is characterized by lack of intelligence, like the avaricious accumulator of Luke 12:20, classed by Jesus as a fool. The foolishness of the five wedding guests (see WEDDING), on the other hand, was revealed by their improvidence in not carrying sufficient oil. The only other use of "fool" in the Gospels is in the Sermon on the Mount, where Jesus states that he who calls his brother a fool shall "be in danger of hell fire" (Matt. 5:22). See also Matt. 23:17, 19; Luke 11:40, 24:25.

foot, a human member which was more important in Scripture metaphorically than physically. In various figures the foot is used to connote subjugation—when it is placed on the neck of the vanquished (Josh. 10:24; I Cor. 15:27); humility—when it is kissed (Luke 7:38); reverence for a teacher (Luke 10:39; Acts 22:3); rejection of an inhospitable locality (Matt. 10:14). Removal of sandals from the feet in holy places denoted proper reverence, from the days of Moses in Sinai (Ex. 3:5) to the usage of present-day Moslems in their mosques. Frequently Scripture uses "foot" to indicate the stumbling of the whole man (Prov. 3:23; Luke 4:11). Barefootedness denoted mourning (II Sam. 15:30), or slavery (Isa. 20:2); it also meant economy, as Bedouins today walk barefooted through wilderness wastes, carrying their shoes until their arrival in town. The allusion to "foot watering" an Egyptian herb garden (Deut. 11:10) may refer to a kind of treadmill.

footman. (1) An infantryman (II Sam. 8:4), in contrast to a horseman or charioteer (I Chron. 18:4; cf. Jer. 12:5). (2) A messenger who ran ahead of chariots (I Sam. 8:11).

footstool, a simple wooden seat in Palestinian houses; made of gold for the royal throne (II Chron. 9:18). The word appears in metaphors, as in I Chron. 28:2; Ps. 110:1; Isa. 66:1; Matt. 5:35.

forehead, the brow, which in Scripture had special significance. On it the priest was to wear the golden plate inscribed "Holiness to the Lord" (Ex. 28:38). Ezekiel (9:4) writes of a mark ordered by God to be placed on the foreheads of all who protest against public abominations and sins—the mark of the Hebrew letter *taw* (*tau*), in its old form, X or +, known in ancient times as the symbol of perfection and of the end of all creatures (see SYMBOL, CROSS). The mark on the harlot's forehead is mentioned in Jer. 3:3 and Rev. 17:5 (cf. the practice of branding women in modern warfare.) Revelation makes several symbolic allusions to marks of righteousness on the foreheads of the saints (14:1, 22:4), and the mark of the beast (20:4) on those of transgressors.

Red marks on the forehead were often recognized as symptoms of leprosy (Lev. 13:42; II Chron. 26:19 f.). The forehead, as a particularly vulnerable spot, was the aim of sling-shot warriors (I Sam. 17:49). Jewels were worn on the foreheads of women (Ezek. 16:12).

foreigner, a stranger, a Gentile (see GENTILES), a person of another race, acknowledging another God (Ex. 20:10). In exclusive Israel, God's "holy people" (Deut. 14:2), foreigners, such as Canaanites, Egyptians, Philistines, etc., were regarded as a possible political menace (Obad. 11) and a threat to racial purity and religious integrity. The presence of foreigners from many lands in the tiny bridgehead of the Middle East—Palestine—who were left there as deposits of endless waves of conquest and of trading enterprises, accounts for Israel's strict legislation against foreign marriages (see MARRIAGE) (Ex. 34:15 f.) and foreign gods (Deut. 12:2 f.). "Foreigner" appears only four times in Scripture: Ex. 12:45, regarding the "ordinance of the passover"; Deut. 15:3, dealing with the exaction of the "release" at the

Sabbatical year; Obad. 11 (see above); and Eph. 2:19, a passage that expresses yearning for a time when there would be "no more strangers and foreigners, but fellow-citizens."

In the O.T. a stranger or sojourner was one who, though not an Israelite, lived permanently among the Hebrews (Ex. 20:10). The stranger thus had a more intimate position in Hebrew society than the foreigner who was only a temporary visitor. Under Mosaic Law strangers had rights (Ex. 22:21) and duties (Ex. 12:19). Israelites were to treat the stranger kindly (Lev. 19:33 f.; Deut. 10:18 f.).

The throngs of foreigners—many of them devout Jews—who were dwelling at Jerusalem on the day of Pentecost are mentioned in Acts 2:5–11.

forerunner (Gk. *prodromos*, "one who goes before") appears in Heb. 6:20, where it pictures Jesus entering the inner shrine or Holy of Holies (see TEMPLE), as a forerunner on our behalf, not pre-empting the entry privilege for himself, as did the O.T. high priest. Cf. R.S.V. Heb. 6:20. This verse makes clear the distinction between O.T. and N.T. emphasis. The best example of a forerunner in the N.T. is John* the Baptist (Matt. 3:11, 11:10; cf. Mal. 3:1), who "went before" Jesus, as a messenger was customarily sent before the chariot of an arriving royal person to clear the path of obstructions (I Sam. 8:11).

forest in O.T. times covered the hill country of Canaan—forests of cypress, oak, pine, cedar, ash, box, gopher, plane, and other trees, with excellent grazing areas interspersed. Scripture mentions the forest of Hareth, possibly near Keilah in S. Judaea, SW. of Bethlehem (I Sam. 22:5); the Forest of Lebanon* (I Kings 7:2); the forest of Carmel* (II Kings 19:23; Isa. 37:24), whose olive groves are still healthy; the wood of Ephraim, probably E. of Jordan, near Mahanaim (II Sam. 18:6). The "forest in Arabia" (Isa. 21:13) was possibly a mere thicket where merchant caravaneers lurked. The mention in Neh. 2:8 of a "king's forest," apparently near Jerusalem, points to abundant trees in Judaea in the post-Exilic period. The marshy Plain of Sharon had large forests, whose beauty lives on in modern citrus groves. Jericho has always been noted for its palms and balsam, and the Jordan Valley jungle for low, tangled underbrush of tamarisk and willows. S. Babylonia and ancient Egypt both lacked forests, and imported their timber from Assyrian highlands or the mountains of Lebanon. In spite of the centuries of spoliation for war and the constant use of wood for fuel, numerous forests remained until Crusader times. Until recently, large oak forests grew W. of Hebron. Today, in spite of the planting of millions of young trees, whose seedlings are sometimes dropped from airplanes, 200 years would be required for the proper reforestation of Palestine. The oak and pine forests of Carmel have been destroyed almost entirely within the last three decades. Scrub forests of Galilee are constantly under attack. Large forests of oak have vanished within the past century from the region between Jaffa and Carmel. Grazing is a chronic enemy of forest growth. Charcoal burners cut down young trees and strip even dunes of their vegetation.

forgiveness, the restoration of fellowship where sin has caused an estrangement, has both a human and a divine aspect. In the social relationships of the O.T. the idea of forgiveness appears early, as in the forgiveness accorded by Joseph to his once jealous brothers, at the request of the aged Jacob (Gen. 50:17); and the forgiveness sought by Pharaoh from Moses and Aaron (Ex. 10:17). God's forgiveness of disloyal Israel was sought by Moses (Ex. 32:32). Joshua expressed in clear-cut terms that the righteous, jealous God who had brought His people up from Egypt would not tolerate apostasy nor forgive transgressions willfully committed against His holy nature (24:19).

Hebrew Law* specifically prescribes the procedure to rid one's self of guilt (Lev. 4–6), and makes clear the forgiveness available to him whose trespass was unintentional (5:17–19; see also Num. 35). Forgiveness is the only way to Biblical salvation*, the only channel through which the sinner who has offended the righteous nature of God can return to fellowship. God must take the initiative, although man, through his penitence, prepares himself for the divine approach. Occasionally, however, instances occur in Scripture where individuals other than the sinner intercede with God for forgiveness, as in "Solomon's prayer" at the dedication of the Temple (I Kings 8:30, 34, 36); and the matchless intercession of Jesus on his cross for those who had put him there (Luke 23:34). The latter incident implies that the repentance (see REPENT) of the sinner is not essential to the extension of forgiveness. The idea is generally expounded thus: if Christ, the advocate, who paid on his cross the price of mankind's sin, interceded on behalf of a sinner, God would hear that plea out of consideration for him who had been injured. This is certainly one of the most sublime ideas found anywhere in sacred literature.

Just as numerous words in the Bible convey the idea of sin*, so numerous phrases contain the idea of forgiveness: the covering of iniquity (Ps. 78:38); the paying of a debt (Luke 7:43); the act of healing (Ps. 103:3); forgetting iniquity (Jer. 31:34); the overlooking of wrong-doing—stated only in Rom. 4:25.

Forgiveness is the high peak in the ethics of Jesus. It is best expressed in his Parable of the Unmerciful Debtor (Matt. 18:21–35; see also Luke 11:4, 17:3 f.; Mark 11:25 f.). Jesus made it clear that the sinner's forgiveness by God was dependent upon his own willingness to forgive those who had wronged him (Matt. 6:12, 14 f.; Mark 11:25 f.). Restitution* had its place in N.T. theology (Luke 19:8), as it had in the O.T. (Ex. 22:1–9; Luke 19:8). The question as to whether Jesus, or only God, had power to forgive sins aroused heated controversy in Christ's day. The answer is stated in Christ's own words (Mark 2:5–12). John 20:23 suggests that Jesus delegated to his disciples also the authority to remit (A.V.) or forgive (R.S.V.) sin.

God's forgiveness of the sinner is called "justification"* in Rom. 5:16. "Reconciliation"* is the acceptance by man of God's forgiveness.

Paul's doctrine of forgiveness is that redemption came by Christ's atoning death on the cross, as the victim of the sins of men (Eph. 1:7). The author of Hebrews 9:22 has a similar viewpoint. See ATONEMENT.

fornication, illicit sexual intercourse on the part of an individual, clearly violated the Seventh Commandment, set up to protect the permanency and sacredness of the family. There are more allusions to illicit sexual relations in the N.T. than in the O.T., e.g., I Cor. 5:9, 6:9; II Cor. 12:21; Eph. 5:5; Col. 3:5; I Thess. 4:3; I Tim. 1:9 f.; Heb. 13:4; Jude 7. Freedom from unchastity was one of the four minimum entrance requirements for aspiring candidates to Christian groups, as stated in a letter sent from the elders and apostles at Jerusalem to Antioch Christians, via Judas Barsabas and Silas (Acts 15:20, 29).

fortification. See DEFENSE; FENCED CITY; FORTS; WALLS.

forts in prehistoric Palestine were banks of earth and stone, such as Natufian men tossed up against their Carmel cave homes. In pre-Hebrew Jerusalem Jebusites made a rock-scarp fort or stronghold. This fort, Millo*, David captured and dwelt in, calling it "the city of David" (II Sam. 5:7–9). Strong Amorite (see AMORITES) forts existed N. of Beer-sheba, so tall that they seemed to reach up to heaven (Deut. 1:28). Isaiah (25:12) referred to "the fortress of the high fort of . . . walls" (at Jerusalem). Typical siege forts are mentioned in II Kings 25:1 and Ezek. 4:2. Babylonian emergency forts used in foreign campaigns are spoken of in Jer. 52:4 and Ezek. 26:8; Syrian ones, in Dan. 11:19.

Outstanding Biblical examples of forts are Lachish*, guarding the approach to Jerusalem from the S.; and Megiddo*, guarding the Plain of Jezreel, both of which have been excavated. So, too, Beth-shan* ("Mound of the Fortress"), dominating an approach to the Jordan at the E. end of the Valley of Jezreel. Gezer* and Jericho* were also notable fortress towns (see also 'AJJÛL, TELL EL-). In southern Jordan Nelson Glueck found a chain of powerful Iron Age (began 1200–1000 B.C.) Edomite forts guarding caravan routes, approaches to mines, and town sites. The powerful fort of Umm el-Bayyârah near Petra* was the Biblical Sela (Isa. 16:1). Khirbet Tawil Ifreij, built of cut basalt rocks, is a typical border fort. Khirbet Remeil is a notable Moabite fort of the Iron Age. The typical Trans-Jordan fort had a central blockhouse, around which stationary houses and tents clustered, and an all-inclusive fortification wall. Such an enclosed fort town might measure about 115 yds. by 70 yds., and would have a dry moat and a masked gateway. Just in front of the blockhouse was the community's open space, where judges sat to hear complaints of villagers and travelers. (See *The Other Side of the Jordan*, Nelson Glueck). The border forts of Edom and Moab explain why Israel, arriving from Egypt en route to Canaan, had to detour (Judg. 11:17; cf. Josh. 12:3).

See ANTONIA; WALLS.

Fortunatus (fôr-tū-nā′tŭs), a messenger sent with Stephanas and Achaicus from the Corinthian Christians to Paul, probably at Ephesus. The three probably brought a letter from an apparently neglectful group in Corinth (I Cor. 16:17), which Paul answered in I Corinthians.* The messengers "refreshed" Paul's spirit (v. 18).

forum. See ARCHITECTURE.

foundations, the masonry substructure of a building, which Hebrews always laid with serious feelings of their importance. This was true whether the builders were constructing a simple clay-brick house like the one recently excavated at Ezion-geber*, where a woman's treasured jewelry had been placed in a pottery jar beneath her house along with olive pits and fishbones; or the magnificent Temple of Solomon at Jerusalem, whose foundations were of "costly stones," eight and ten cubits long (I Kings 7:10; cf. Jesus as cornerstone, Luke 20:17). This was true also of the figurative foundation stones of Paul, expressed enduringly in I Cor. 3:10–17. The Apostle knew of the customary foundation deposits in temples, like that of Diana at Ephesus, which contained hoards of precious jewels. This information may have been the background of Paul's thinking when he uttered his famous words about life's only sure foundation—faith in Christ—on which men build with different qualities ("gold, silver . . . hay, stubble") (I Cor. 3:11–13). The foundation deposits of the vast audience hall of Darius the Great at Persepolis, excavated by the Oriental Institute of the University of Chicago, are duplicate sets of solid gold and silver records of his achievements engraved in cuneiform, placed by architects in shallow, square stone boxes at the NE. and SE. corners of the hall, and covered with stone lids concealed by large, rough stones. (For unique horse burials by the Hyksos, see BETH-EGLAIM.) Christ spoke of his followers in terms of a builder using a rock foundation (Matt. 7:25). The custom of immuring bodies of small children in foundations may be indicated in Josh. 6:26 and I Kings 16:34.

founder, one who casts metal (Judg. 17:4; Jer. 6:29, 10:9, 14, 51:17).

fountain, a spring of living water, in contrast to a cistern which stores rain. Fountains were prized as precious boons in dry Palestine. Fountains in Palestine rise from under banks or rocks. The porous, chalky soil filters the water supply brought by winter rains. Only occasionally are wells or fountains walled in for the convenience of users and for the protection of the water, as at Nazareth, where Mary's fountain (see WATER, illus. 477) is still in daily use; and at Jacob's stone-curbed one in Sychar*, preserved in the crypt of a church. En-rogel* and Gihon* are two famous fountains outside the S. and E. walls of Jerusalem. Fountains are numerous in Upper Galilee; in the SE. Plain of Esdraelon; near Shechem; and S. of Hebron. Ownership of fountains determined the course of history. Herdsmen fought for them (Gen. 26:18–33). Migrations followed routes along them (Ex. 15:27). Life was lengthened when fugitives found a desert fountain (Gen. 8:2). Many towns have names compounded with "En," meaning "fountain."

Fountains were sometimes channeled into tunnels and conducted to locations safe from enemy attack, as the Virgin's Fount at Jerusalem in Hezekiah's time (II Chron. 32:3, 4). (See SILOAM.)

Because water was essential to life, fountains were given symbolic meaning, as in Prov. 13:14, 14:27; Rev. 7:17. Yahweh was the supreme fountain of life (Psalm 36:9; Jer. 17:13). Genesis picturesquely refers to the "fountains of the deep" (7:11). Cf. "a well of water springing up into everlasting life" (A.V. John 4:14), R.S.V. "a spring of water welling up to eternal life."

Fountain Gate, in the Jerusalem wall, near the Siloam fountain, at the point where the wall crossed the Tyropoeon Valley. It was mentioned in connection with repairs in Neh. 2:14, 3:15, 12:37. It was the same as "the gate between the two walls" (II Kings 25:4).

fowler, one who hunts game birds, snaring them in light traps made with noose cords which entangle the feet of the bird. Hence allusions to the "snare of the fowler" (Ps. 91:3, 124:7; Hos. 9:8), ensnaring or luring the unwary.

fowls, used in Scripture to mean birds of any kind (Gen. 1:20; Deut. 4:17; Psalm 8:8). Scavenger fowls which devoured carcasses appear in Gen. 15:11. Fowls of the heavens were described as wise by Job (35:11). They appeared in Peter's housetop vision (Acts 10:12). Fowls of the mountains (Isa. 18:6); fowls of the branches (Dan. 4:14); fowls which were "clean" for food (Deut. 14:20); fowls fed by the heavenly Father (Matt. 6:26); and fowls that picked up newly sown seeds (Matt. 13:4) all have their place in Scripture.

foxes of two varieties are known in Palestine; and the fox's propensity for holes (Matt. 8:20) and deserted ruins (Lam. 5:18), his cunning marauding (Song of Sol. 2:15), and his slyness (Ezek. 13:4; Luke 13:32) must have been commonly observed. The Heb. word *shūʿāl* covers the jackal* as well as the fox. In certain Scriptural instances (Judg. 15:4; Ps. 63:10; Neh. 4:3) the marginal rendering "jackal" is distinctly preferable.

frankincense was a white, aromatic gum resin exuded in tears often an inch long, from trees (*Boswellia carterii, B. papyrifera, B. thurifera*) related to the terebinth, which grew in abundance in SW. Arabia*, Abyssinia, and India. Hebrews bought it in wholesale quantities for use in worship* and fumigation. Frankincense trees built up the great wealth of ancient traders along the spice routes out of S. Arabia which ran along the Red Sea, along the Arabah to Petra, Gaza, and Damascus (Isa. 60:6). Frankincense from India and the Somali section of Africa may also have found its way into Palestine, by dromedary or camel caravan. The frankincense capitalists of the Bible may have included the Queen of Sheba (II Chron. 9:9), through whose S. Arabian country frankincense importers' caravans moved. Frankincense was one of the four ingredients of the holy oil used for anointing (see ANOINT) priests (Ex. 30:34). It was also burned as incense; the perfumed smoke which rises

155. Frankincense (*Boswellia thurifera*).

from frankincense and other ingredients (Lev. 16:12 f.) was used in connection with the meal offering (Lev. 2:1 f., 15 f., 6:15); and frankincense was placed pure on the shewbread (Lev. 24:7 f.). Isaiah (60:3) and Jeremiah (6:20) protested against use of such "foreign" substances in the worship of Yahweh. The wise man who brought frankincense to the infant Jesus may have financed his long journey by trading (Matt. 2:11). The "frankincense" of A.S.V. Jer. 17:26 reads "incense" in Moffatt and A.V. The A.V. "hill of frankincense" (Song of Sol. 4:6), referring to the Lebanon, reads more accurately in Moffatt, "scented slopes."

freeman, freewoman, men and women of the towns during the Hebrew monarchies who, along with slaves, sojourners (see FOREIGNER), and strangers made up the population (cf. Rev. 6:15). Freemen enjoyed the full privileges of citizenship, including a voice in community decisions (see DEMOCRACY) and public events, including certain acts of worship. Slavery (see LABOR) was an accepted but deplorable relationship in both O.T. and N.T. times, in spite of the enlightenment of Graeco-Roman culture. Sarah, wife of Abraham, was a freewoman, while Hagar was a bondwoman (Gen. 21:10; Gal. 4:22). Paul of Tarsus was a freeman because born of a father who, though a Jew, was a Roman citizen. But the chief captain Lysias, before whom he was haled, stated that "with a great sum" he (Lysias) had bought his freedom (Acts 22:27, 28). Throughout the N.T. the words "bond" and "free" are in juxtaposition, as in I Cor. 12:13; Eph. 6:8; Rev. 13:16. But Christ unified both classes in the social order of his Kingdom (Gal.

3:28); he was "in all" (Col. 3:11). See also LIBERTY.

fret, an archaic verb used in Lev. 13:55 A.V., A.S.V. to describe the state of being "eaten into," in this instance garments or leather articles exposed to the unwholesome biological organisms of leprosy.

friendship, the amicable association of individuals, was early and long regarded by Near Eastern peoples as one of the noblest and most enduring values in life. In the Bible it is expressed by various terms, some of which are used interchangeably, to convey the idea of brotherly love, companionship, neighborliness, or mutual assistance. Friendship in the O.T. reaches its height in Abraham, called the Friend of God (II Chron. 20:7; Isa. 41:8; cf. Jas. 2:23), A.S.V. Job 29:4 ("the friendship of God was upon my tent"); and in the N.T. in the words of Jesus (John 15:12–15), who defined friendship with him in terms of doing his commands.

Of friendship between men there are many examples in the Bible, as seen in the classic examples of David and Jonathan (I Sam. 18:1, 19:1; II Sam. 1:25–27); the three friends of Job (Job 2:11, etc.) and the friendship of Jesus for Lazarus of Bethany (John 11:11). Friendship between women is seen in the Book of Ruth.

Wisdom Literature is rich in comments on the ways of friendship—especially in Proverbs and the Apocryphal Book of Ecclesiasticus (6:1–17, 9:10, 19:8 f., 37:1–6). Friends love "at all times" (Prov. 17:17, 18:24); and wound for correction (27:6). Yet the prophet warned of their fickleness (Mic. 7:5; cf. Ps. 41:9). Behind the frequent allusions of Jesus to friends we feel the ancient wisdom of his people (Luke 11:5 ff., 14:10, 15:9, 29). He himself was known as the friend of sinners and of publicans (Luke 7:34); and called even Judas "friend" (Matt. 26:50). Political friends are suggested in the strange amity of Pilate and Herod (Luke 23:12); cf. "Caesar's friend" (John 19:12); and the Asiarchs who were friends of Paul at Ephesus (Acts 19:31).

See FELLOW; FELLOWSHIP; LOVE; LOVING-KINDNESS; NEIGHBOR.

fringes (A.S.V. "tassels", A.V. "borders") or twined cords were ordered to be fastened with blue ribbons to the four lower corners of the outer garments of the Children of Israel (Num. 15:37–39; Deut. 22:12), garments which resembled the *simlah* or *abayeh* worn by many Arabs today. These fringes were intended to remind the Hebrews to do "all the commandments of the Lord."

In telling of the woman who touched the hem of Christ's garment (Matt. 9:20) and the Gennesaret throng who did likewise (Matt. 14:36), the R.S.V. uses "fringes" instead of "hem"; similarly in Matt. 23:5, where the Pharisees are criticized for making long, conspicuous fringes (A.V. "borders") on their garments. Fringes, whether on the fleece skirts of ancient Sumerian neighbors of Abraham, or worn around the edges of Assyrian ceremonial robes of warrior-kings, had a deeply rooted religious significance, as well as an effective decorative purpose. Fringes or tassels were also worn, as they still are, on the prayer shawl (*tallith*) of men in traditional synagogues, and on the small undervest, reminding them of their obligations under the Law—the purpose also of the phylactery and the mezuzoth boxes on their door-posts.

frog, an amphibian common today in Palestine and Egypt. A plague of them was the second in the series visited by Yahweh on Pharaoh and his subjects before the Exodus of Israel (Ex. 8:1–15). Allusions to this pestiferous experience appear in Ps. 78:45, 105:30. Like the rats in "The Pied Piper," frogs invaded even the kneading troughs of cooks and the bedroom of the king (Ex. 8:3 f.). Pharaoh appealed to Moses and Aaron for relief, even as the mayor of Hamelin appealed to the piper; but when the respite was granted he resumed his oppressions (Ex. 8:15).

frontlet (Ex. 13:16; Deut. 6:8 f., 11:18), a jewel or amulet worn between the eyes. See PHYLACTERIES.

fruit. See FOOD; also individual entries, FIG TREE; POMEGRANATE; etc. For grape, see VINE.

fuels most commonly used in ancient Palestine were wood; useless vine branches (Ezek. 15:4, 6); cakes of dung (Ezek. 4:15); quick-burning thorns and brambles gathered from wilderness wastes and carried on the heads of nomadic women to their earthen stoves; chaff from threshing floors (Matt. 3:12); withered field grass (Matt. 6:30); broom or juniper (Ps. 120:4). Figuratively, Ezekiel referred to Israel as "the fuel of the fire" (21:32). "Coals of fire" were braziers filled with charcoal (John 18:18); or piles of charcoal burned on a beach (John 21:9).

fuller, one who fulls or thickens, cleanses, bleaches, and sometimes dyes cloth in process of its manufacture and its upkeep. Hand-woven garments of people in Bible times were costly and not numerous in anyone's wardrobe, hence the importance of the fuller, who often was also a trader in textiles (II Kings 18:17; Isa. 7:3, 36:2). In Jerusalem ample space was allotted to fullers, outside the E. wall, in a "fuller's field" at the conduit of the upper pool of the Spring Gihon*, where they spread out garments to dry after washing them in copper tubs where feet trod out the grime which had been loosened by lye or soap (Mal. 3:2). The fullers' guild was an important organization in 1st-century Roman towns like Pompeii, where today the ruins of their headquarters are still seen facing the principal forum. The radiance of the transfiguration garments of Jesus was whiter than any fuller could have bleached them (Mark 9:3).

funeral. See BURIAL.

furlong. See WEIGHTS AND MEASURES.

furnace, A.V. translation for several kinds of enclosed places for fire, designed and used for such different purposes as baking bread and pottery, for warming a house, or for melting ores. Behind this one English word lie several Hebrew words. The "smoking furnace" of Gen. 15:17 in Abraham's vision and the "fiery oven" of Psalm 21:9, as well as the towered furnaces of Neh. 3:11 and the "burning fiery furnace" of Dan. 3:6 ff., are *tannūr*, or oven. The kiln or furnace to which burning Sodom and Gomorrah were likened (Gen. 19:28), the furnace of Ex. 9:8, and the appearance of smoking Sinai (Ex. 19:18), were *kibhshān*, or kiln. The fining furnaces of Prov. 17:3, 27:21, and Ezek. 22:20 were *kūr*, crucibles for working gold, silver, etc. The Gk. word used in Matt. 13:42 signifies various sorts of furnaces.

The elemental impressiveness of crackling furnaces found its way into such Apocalyptic expressions as Ezek. 22:18, 20, 22; Matt. 13:42; Rev. 9:2.

Furnaces for refining ores were constructed by Asia Minor Hittites c. 1400 B.C. and also by early Edomites, who knew the resources of the Wâdī Arabah* and taught Israel metallurgy. Nelson Glueck, exploring in the Kingdom of Jordan, discovered vestiges of foundries near Adamah (see ADAM), Succoth*, and Zarethan*, in the area where Hiram of Tyre probably cast the famous pillars, Jachin* and Boaz, for Solomon's Temple (I Kings 7:13, 21 f., 45 f.). Numerous small iron furnaces and their slag heaps dot the Arabah between the Dead Sea and the Red Sea. In the Jordan Valley also Glueck found numerous smelting furnaces and foundries which had been used by Hiram's workmen in the Early Iron Age for making castings. This location had abundant water, charcoal, proximity to mines, and access to Jerusalem. The greatest copper and iron furnaces yet found from antiquity were discovered by Glueck at Solomon's industrial center at Ezion-geber*. Consult *The River Jordan*, Nelson Glueck, pp. 145–147 (The Westminster Press).

156. Egyptian furniture, 2000–1400 B.C. Cane-seated chair at left; at center, table (about 18 in. high) set for game of *senet;* at right, low stool and folding leather stool.

furniture. (1) Of Rachel's camel (Gen. 31:34), more properly translated "saddle," of the cushioned, curtained, palanquin type. (2) Of the Tabernacle* (Ex. 31:7–9, 35:14, 39:33), and of the Temple* (I Kings 7:48–50), referring to vessels. (3) Of palaces, such as the throne of Solomon in its cedar-lined porch (I Kings 7:7); the ivory-trimmed furniture, portions of which have been excavated, at palaces of Samaria; the gold-covered, jeweled throne and stool of Tut-ankh-amun, now in the Egyptian Museum, Cairo.

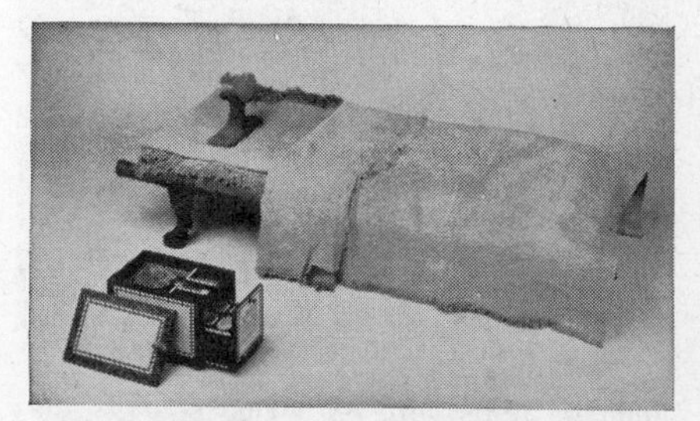

157. Egyptian furniture, 2000–1800 B.C. Bed (about 63 in. long) with head-rest, "springs" of interlaced cord, and mattress of folded linen sheets. Beds were marks of unusual refinement. At left, toilet chest of ebony and ivory with silver mountings, containing mirror and ointment jars.

(4) Of the average dwelling. Household furniture in Biblical Palestine was extremely simple, consisting of hand-woven curtains, separating men's from women's quarters, as in a tent; bed rolls or sleeping mats, piled against the wall in the daytime (Mark 2:9); baking equipment, including stone or basalt grinding mills (Matt. 24:41) for grain and spices, kneading bowls, convex baking sheets, stoves of clay, or a mere pan to contain charcoal, or a brazier; short-handled brooms (Luke 15:8); wooden cradles slung from the ceiling; lamps (see LAMP) of clay, set into wall niches, or on a table, in candlesticks (see CANDLESTICK) (Matt. 5:15); low stools; low, tray-like tables for the common dish (John 13:26) and smaller bowls; water pots (John 2:6); and cooking vessels, often of copper. The Jerusalem "large upper room furnished and prepared" (Mark 14:15) probably contained no more than tables, dining couches or stools, and lamps and vessels for the Passover. The guest room on the wall of the Shunammite, used by Elijah (II Kings 4:10) included a bed, a table, a stool, and a candlestick. For banquet (see BANQUETS) *triclinia* see MEALS. See HOUSE, illus. 187.

G

Gabbatha (găb′ȧ-thȧ) (originally "ridge" or "elevated terrain"), a Heb. (Aram.) word equivalent to the Gk. *lithostroton* ("the stone pavement"). This carefully laid "pavement par excellence," 2,500 meters square, was designed as a parade ground for Roman horses and for the approach to Pilate's judgment seat, to which Jesus was led (John 19:13). The best scholarship locates Pilate's judgment seat near the ancient Tower of Antonia*, of which it may have been a part, NW. of the Temple Area. The Gabbatha is near the Via Dolorosa. Part of its paving has been identified by Père H. Vincent, beneath the present Church of the Dames de Sion. Scratched on the paving is a Roman gaming board, one of the most valuable archaelogical

158. Gabbatha gaming board, second century A.D.

finds in Jerusalem, on which soldiers may have whiled away their time while awaiting Pilate's verdict (cf. John 19:23 f.). Long after the fine paving of the Gabbatha had been buried under the ruins of the Antonia area, Roman emperor Hadrian (A.D. 117–38) erected a triple arch, of which the so-called "Ecce Homo" was a part, leading into the new city. The accurate local coloring in the Fourth Gospel is seen in use of such words as the Gk. *lithostroton* and the Aram. *Gabbatha*—a fact which points to the early authorship of at least part of the Gospel.

Gabriel ("man of God," or "God has shown himself mighty"), one of the seven archangels in the Hebrew celestial hierarchy, akin to the Babylonian and Persian counterparts. Gabriel's function was that of a revealing messenger from God. To Daniel he explained a vision and a decree (Dan. 8:15 ff., 9:21 ff.). To Zacharias and Elisabeth* Gabriel announced the coming of a son and declared his name (Luke 1:5–17). To Mary he heralded the birth of a son and announced his name (Luke 1:26–38). See also Luke 1:19.

Gad ("good fortune"). (1) Eldest son of Zilpah and Jacob (Gen. 30:10 f., 35:26). He was the eponymous ancestor of one of the Twelve Tribes of Israel (Num. 2:14). Gad's territory, granted by Moses (Num. 32; Deut. 3:16–20), lay NE. of the Dead Sea, bounded on the W. by the Jordan, on the E. by the territory of Ammon, on the S. by Wâdī Râmeh, and on the N. by land just N. of the Wâdī Jabbok. Its boundaries shifted with the destinies of the warlike Gadites, who were pressed by the Ammonites* as early as the 11th century B.C., and were delivered by Jephthah* (Judg. 11, where they are called Gilead). Gadites, together with other eastern tribes, supported David against Saul, and after Solomon's death supported the revolt of Jeroboam. The tribe was deported by Tiglath-pileser III in 733 B.C. (See DIBON; MOABITE STONE.) (2) A seer or prophet who served David (I Chron. 21:9 ff.; I Sam. 22:5), who, evidently condemning the king's census, recommended erecting an altar on the Jebusite (see JEBUS) threshing floor (II Sam. 24:11 ff.). According to the Chronicler, he participated in David's organization of the Levitical Temple services (II Chron. 29:25), and prepared a record of David's reign (I Chron. 29:29). (3) A fortune god worshipped in the post-Exilic period (Isa. 65:11, A.V. "troop," A.S.V., R.S.V. "Fortune").

Gadara (găd′ȧ-rȧ), **Gadarenes** (găd′ȧ-rēnz′), a Decapolis city and its people "over against" or "opposite" Galilee (R.S.V., Moff. Matt. 8:28; A.V. Luke 8:26). Scholars have not yet identified positively the site of this town, where Jesus healed a man with an "unclean spirit" (A.V. Mark 5:1–20; Luke 8:26–39) or "two demoniacs" (R.S.V. Matt. 8:28–34). The "Gadara" of the A.V. Mark and Luke accounts may be Muqueis (? Umm Keis) on a headland 5 m. SE. of the S. tip of the Sea of Galilee. Some ancient authorities translate the name of the town as "Gergesa" (? Kursī) and that of the people "Gergesenes" (A.V. Matt. 8:28), while the R.S.V. has "Gerasenes" in Luke 8:26. Most authorities now believe that this does not refer to the great excavated city called "Gerasa"* by the Greeks (Sem. "Jerash"), which lies 37 m. SE. of the Sea of Galilee, in a locale which does not fit the Synoptics' account. The location of the town is unimportant, however, in comparison with the fact that the cured man's testimony of his restoration by Jesus (Mark 5:20) is the only N.T. account of the foundation of a great company of Christians in the Decapolis.

Gaius (gā′yŭs), a common Roman name appearing frequently in the N.T. (1) A Macedonian travel companion of Paul haled into the theater during the Ephesus* riot (Acts 19:29). (2) A man of Derbe who accompanied Paul into Asia (Acts 20:4). Some authorities believe (1) and (2) to be the same. (3) A convert baptized by Paul at Corinth (I Cor. 1:14). (4) The man called "mine host" by the author of Rom. 16:23. If Rom. 16 was written at Corinth, this Gaius may be the same as (3). (5) The man to whom III John was addressed (see v. 1), "well beloved" member of the church to which this Epistle was addressed. Some scholars believe that (2), (3), and (4) are identical; others, that (3), (4), and (5) are the same; (5) and (1) seem to be two different men.

(6) Gaius of Rome (not mentioned in the N.T.) was a presbyter of the last quarter of the 2d century, who rejected the apostolic authorship of the Revelation, believing that it had been written by Cerinthus and then attributed to John.

Galatia (gȧ-lā′shĭ-ȧ), a section of the interior of Asia Minor, named for the warlike Gauls, kindred to the tribes of N. Italy and France, who lived there. In the early years of the 3d century B.C. a violent racial eruption from Europe disturbed Greece, Macedonia, and Asia Minor. Celtic tribes moved E., fighting and bargaining their way, crossed the Hellespont, and finally became masters of the valley of the Halys River and the Asiatic hinterland of NE. Phrygia, reaching almost to the Black Sea. Surrounded by alien tribes, the immigrant Gauls by war, treachery, diplomacy, and peaceful penetration became masters of a vast area, which included the cities of Ancyra (the modern Ankara, capital of Turkey), Pessinus, and Tavium. This area was the original Galatia (from Gk. *Galateia*). Later, when Rome under Pompey (64 B.C.) finally subjected the last of these Celtic chieftains as well as the other barbarian tribes of Asia Minor, a new Roman province was formed with the same name,

159. Galatia.

but now also including Phrygia*, Pisidia*, and Lycaonia*, in which were located the cities of Iconium, Lystra, Derbe, and Antioch in Phrygia (see individual entries). This enlarged S-shaped province stretched across the whole of Asia Minor, from Bithynia and Pontus on the Black Sea to Pamphylia on the Mediterranean.

The word "Galatia" occurs six times in the N.T. In I Cor. 16:1; Gal. 1:2; and I Pet. 1:1 the reference is probably to the Roman province, and I Pet. may perhaps chart the itinerary of the bearer of the Epistle, who landed at some Black Sea port in Pontus, and traveled in Galatia, Cappadocia, Asia, and Bithynia—divisions which correspond to 1st-century geography. There are differences of opinion among scholars regarding the exact territory meant by "Galatia" in Acts 16:6, 18:23. II Tim. 4:10, where the text is defective, may be "Gaul" or "France," the motherland (at least in name) of the Asia Minor Galatia.

Galatians, the Epistle of Paul the Apostle to the, is a vindication of Paul's apostleship and a vigorous statement of the essentials of Christian faith; it has been called the Christian declaration of independence. Its first two chapters are historically important for their first-hand testimony of the beginnings of Christianity; this is our oldest account, written much earlier than Acts and the Gospels. Paul's authorship of Galatians has never been seriously questioned, but its destination, occasion, and date are surrounded by critical difficulties. It was sent to "the churches of Galatia" (Gal. 1:2). The Roman province of Galatia included not only the formerly independent Kingdom of Galatia, situated in the N. interior of Asia Minor and inhabited largely by a Celtic people from Gaul, but also parts of Lycaonia, Pisidia, and Phrygia, all lying to the S. The theory that Paul addressed the churches in the southern part of Galatia is supported by the following evidence: (1) Paul and Barnabas had visited the cities of Iconium, Lystra, Derbe, and Pisidian Antioch, all in S. Galatia, and had founded churches there on the First Missionary Journey (Acts 13:4–14:28). (2) In these cities at this time there were Jews (Acts 13:14–51, 14:1, 16:1–3) who might have caused the situation reflected in the Epistle. (3) Familiar references to Barnabas (Gal. 2:1, 9, 13) would have been pointless in a letter addressed to N. Galatia, where Barnabas was probably unknown.

If the S. Galatian destination of this Epistle is accepted, it may have been written either at Antioch in Syria at the end of the First Missionary Journey (Acts 14:26–28), or at Ephesus during the Third Missionary Journey (Acts 19:10). Paul's visit to Jerusalem, described in Gal. 2:1–10, is believed by many to be that mentioned in Acts 11:30. If this is so, Galatians may have been written from Antioch c. A.D. 48 and before Paul's third visit to Jerusalem to attend the Apostolic Council (Acts 15). According to this theory Galatians would be the earliest of Paul's letters. There is much support, however, for the theory that Galatians was written in Ephesus c. A.D. 52 in the same period as the other great Epistles.

The difficulty that brought forth this Epistle was caused by Jewish Christians, possibly from Judaea, who preached to the Galatians a narrower kind of Christianity than Paul's and questioned his apostolic authority. Paul had preached the gospel of redemption for all men through the death of Christ. The Judaizers preached that Christianity could operate only within the framework of Jewish Law. According to them, it was not enough for Gentiles to be baptized in Christ's name and receive the gift of the Spirit; salvation required obedience to the Mosaic Law (Gal. 2:16, 21, 3:2, 8, 11, 5:4), which included circumcision, observance of feasts (Gal. 5:3, 6:12 f.), and rigid Sabbath observance (Gal. 4:10). This teaching would have made Christianity merely a sect within Judaism.

This situation not only challenged Paul's apostleship and the truth of his gospel, but endangered his entire mission to the Gentiles. With passionate earnestness Paul appealed to historical facts to support his claim to be an apostle. He made it clear that if the Law was still valid, as the Judaizers claimed, then Christ had died in vain and Christianity offered nothing more than Judaism. At the heart of Paul's appeal was his belief that Christ's death redeemed all men. On the sole basis of men's acceptance of and faith in Christ, God receives ("justifies") men and gives them the Holy Spirit. Men must learn to live "in the Spirit" in order that their justification may be real.

The Epistle may be outlined as follows:

(1) Introduction, 1:1–10:

(a) Assertion of his apostleship and of redemption through Christ, 1:1–5;

(b) Reasons for the letter, 1:6–10.

(2) Historical vindication of Paul's apostolic authority, 1:11–2:21:

(a) given directly by Christ, not by man, 1:11–24;

(b) recognized by the Jerusalem authorities, 2:1–10;

(c) his rebuke of Peter on the Gentile issue, 2:11–14;

(d) the point of his argument with Peter, and transition to the doctrinal section: "if righteousness come by the law, then Christ is dead in vain," 2:15–21.

(3) Defense of the doctrine of justification by faith alone, 3, 4:

(a) appeal to the Galatians' own experience of receiving the Spirit through faith, not by obedience to the Law, 3:1–5;

(b) the case of Abraham, who was justified by faith, 3:6–9;

(c) the curse of the Law, with its requirement of perfect obedience, impossible for men, 3:10–12;

(d) Christ's redemption of men from the Law's curse, 3:13 f.;

(e) God's promise not conditioned by later demands of the Law, 3:15–18;

(f) the temporary character of the Law: a "schoolmaster to bring us unto Christ, that we might be justified by faith," 3:19–29;

(g) attainment of freedom as sons of God, 4:1–11;

(h) a rabbinical argument, from the allegorized story of Ishmael and Isaac, that liberty is superior to law, 4:12–31.

(4) Practical implications of freedom from the Law, 5:1–6:10:

(a) the freedom of the Christian life, 5:1–12;

(b) the manifestation of freedom in loving service, rather than in selfish indulgence, 5:13–15;

(c) subjection of the flesh to the Spirit, 5:16–18;

(d) the difference between domination by the flesh and by the Spirit, 5:19–6:10:

(*a*) works of the flesh, 5:19–21;

(*b*) fruits of the Spirit, 5:22–24;

(*c*) social relationships governed by the Spirit, 5:25–6:10.

(5) Conclusion, summarizing his doctrine and defense, 6:11–18.

galbanum (găl′bȧ-nŭm), a yellowish-brown gum resin with an aromatic odor, one of the four specified ingredients of incense used in Hebrew worship (Ex. 30:34); derived from Syrian fennel, a carrot-like plant. Plants producing galbanum were also grown in India, Arabia, and Persia.

Galilean, a native or resident of the district of Galilee*; also of or pertaining to Galilee.

Galilee. (from Heb. *Glil ha-goyim*, "circle of the Gentiles"), a name applied to the N. section of Palestine, W. of the Jordan (Josh. 20:7; I Kings 9:11; II Kings 15:29; I Chron. 6:76). In the original partitioning of Canaan it was "allotted" to Zebulun (Josh. 19:10–16), Asher (Josh. 19:24–31), and Naphtali (19:32–39), but none of these was successful in driving out the original Canaanite residents (Judg. 1:30–33), in spite of bloody battles (Judg. 4, 5). During the Hebrew Monarchy Galilee suffered in the Syrian wars. It was ravaged by Ben-hadad (I Kings 15:20), and overrun again by the Aramaeans under Hazael (II Kings 12:18, 13:22). It was the highway for the conquering Assyrian armies of Tiglath-pileser III in 733 B.C. (II Kings 15:29), who carried many of its inhabitants into captivity. In Isa. 9:1 (A.S.V. margin) it is designated as the "district of the nations." I Macc. 5:15 indicates its Gentile complexion by calling it "Galilee of the Gentiles." Some Jews settled in Galilee on their return from Exile. The varied political fortunes of Galilee caused mixed populations, and led to linguistic and dialectic mannerisms which enabled the Jerusalem Jews to identify them easily (Matt. 26:69–73; Mark 14:70); Galilean pronunciation of Aramaic had peculiarities—e.g., identification of the 4 guttural sounds.

The exact territory included in Galilee varied in different periods. In Christ's time it was a well-defined Roman province with two main topographical divisions, Lower and Upper Galilee, the former including portions of the Plain of Esdraelon, the Jordan River, and the Sea of Galilee, 680 ft. below sea level; and the latter, the hill and mountainous plateau with peaks 2,000 to 4,000 ft. high (Matt. 28:16). Nazareth* was centrally located, giving Jesus access to a wide range of geographical environments. Well watered by streams, Galilee is extremely fertile, with rich grain and grass fields in the valleys, and pomegranate, olive, and other fruit orchards on the elevations. The district was netted with roads. The great O.T. "way of the sea" (Isa. 9:1) crossed through Lower Galilee. The commerce of Egypt, Arabia, and Syria flowed along camel caravan routes which can be followed today, and later over paved Roman roads. The material abundance and wide outlook characteristic of Galilean life in Christ's time are reflected in his parables (Matt. 20:1–8, 21:33, 25:14; Mark 4:3, 13:34; Luke 13:6–9).

During Christ's life Galilee was ruled for the Roman emperors by Herod Antipas*, the Tetrarch of Galilee (4 B.C.–A.D. 39) (Luke 23:5–7). (See HEROD.) After his appointment Herod Antipas built a capital city near the site of Rakkath, which he christened Tiberias*, in honor of his royal benefactor.

More than 60 cities are mentioned as existing when the original "partition" of the land took place. Among the cities of Galilee were Hazor (Judg. 4:2); Sepphoris, the capital of the province prior to the building of Tiberias; Safed, resembling "the city set on a hill whose light cannot be hid" (Matt. 5:14); Cana (John 2:1–11), still a lively agricultural village; Kadesh (Josh. 21:32), a "city of refuge"; Megiddo, the fortress mound controlling the Jezreel plain; Nazareth (Luke 2:39, 51) where Jesus grew up; Capernaum

(Matt. 4:13, 9:1; Luke 10:15), whose ruins are extant today; Chorazin (Kerazeh) (Matt. 11:21); Hammath (? present Mamman) in Naphtali (Josh. 19:35). (See towns; also ARCHAEOLOGY for Galilee excavations.)

The people of Galilee were devoted to their religion and their country; they made pilgrimages to Jerusalem (John 4:45), but were looked down on with patronizing contempt by their pure-blooded and more strictly orthodox brother Jews of Jerusalem. From this Galilean strain of Judaism, with its daily contacts with Greek and Roman life, Jesus recruited his earliest disciples. Peter, Andrew, James, John, Philip, Bartholomew, Thomas, Matthew, James the Less, Thaddaeus, and Simon the Zealot were Galileans. One of the Marys was from Magdala (the present Mejdel). At Pentecost, from which Judas, the lone Judaean among the original Twelve, had eliminated himself, the 100% Galilean composition of the Apostles' group is corroborated by the testimony of the onlookers (Acts 2:7). Jesus appealed to this people of Galilee, with their larger experience and broader ways of thinking, and from them he gathered the multitude who "heard him gladly" (Mark 12:37). Memories of his words and works lingered in the minds of Galileans, and made possible the many recordings of his Galilean ministry in the Gospels. The mystical experience of the resurrected Christ by the Galilean Peter launched Christianity on its triumphant way (Mark 14:28; John 21:1–23).

When Pilate at the Trial of Jesus asked whether his prisoner was a "Galilean" (Luke 23:6), he had in mind his own unpopular verdict on the Galilean troublemakers (Luke 13:1–3), and therefore transferred jurisdiction over the Nazarene to Herod Antipas. In A.D. 6 Judas the Galilean revolutionary (Acts 5:37) taught, "We have no Lord or Master but God." The gibe, "Out of Galilee ariseth no prophet," (John 7:52) overlooked Deborah, Jonah, and Elisha, and was less a reflection on the religious or patriotic character of Galileans, than it was an exposure of the prejudiced mind of the metropolitan and bureaucratic Jew. In the war against Rome, when the upper highlanders, unaided by Judaea, stood out for a year against the Roman legions, 150,000 Galileans perished. When Jerusalem was finally destroyed (A.D. 70) the homeless rabbinical schools sought refuge in despised Galilee, where Sepphoris* and Tiberias* became their chief centers. The Mishnah and the "Jerusalem Talmud" were written in Galilee in the early centuries of the Christian era.

Galilee, Sea of, a heart-shaped fresh-water lake in N. Palestine, and an integral part of the Jordan River waterway. It appears in the Bible under various names. The N.T. calls it the Sea of Galilee (Matt. 4:18, 15:29; Mark 1:16, 7:31; John 6:1); "the Sea of Tiberias" (John 6:1, 21:1); the Lake of Gennesaret (Luke 5:1); in four instances "the lake" (Luke 5:2, 8:22 f., 33); and in several others, "the sea" (John 6:16–25). In the O.T. the lake is known as "the sea of Chinnereth" (? harp) (Num. 34:11; Josh. 13:27) or "Chinneroth" (Josh. 12:3). The lake is approximately 13 m. long and 8 m. wide, and is 680 ft. below sea level. Its greatest depth is about 200 ft. On its E. side 2,000-ft.-high mountains rise from its shores, while on the W. the mountain wall is less abrupt, and toward the N. blends gradually into the fertile garden plains of Gennesaret in the NW. and those of El Batila in the NE., where the Jordan with its waters from the snow-capped Hermon and the Lebanons empties into the lake.

160. Sea of Galilee near biblical Magdala, north of Tiberias.

Pliny corroborates the impression the N.T. gives, that the sea "was surrounded by pleasant towns." Among those associated with Jesus are: Capernaum (Matt. 4:13; John 6:17); Bethsaida (Mark 6:45); Chorazin (Luke 10:13); Magdala (Matt. 15:39); Gadara (Mark 5:1). (See these town names; also GALILEE; JORDAN.) Among the other cities flourishing in his day but not mentioned in Scripture are Sennabris; and Tarichaea (literally "pickle town"), where fish were salted, dried, preserved and shipped even to such remote markets as Spain—perhaps one of the first purely industrial towns in Palestine economic history.

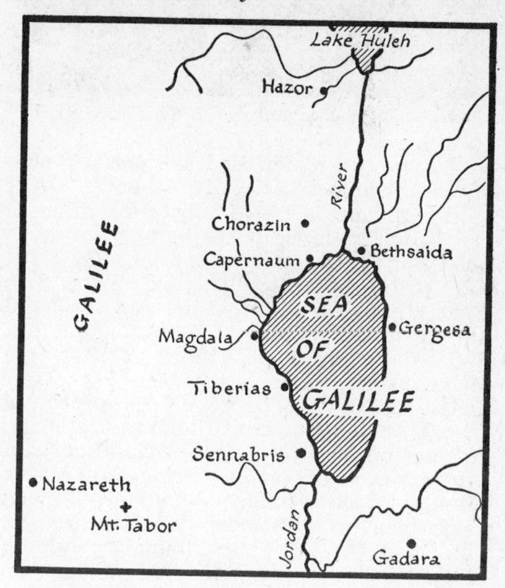

161. Sea of Galilee.

Warm sulphur springs on the outskirts of Tiberias, along the sea, have through the centuries possessed medicinal value. Herod built his palace near its beneficial waters. (See HEROD.) These curative baths, together with the tropical climate of this sub-sea-level lake, made it popular as a health resort, which may help to explain the large number of sick around the lake shore who appealed to Jesus for his healing touch (Mark 1:32 f., 6:53–56).

Boats engaged in fishing and transportation plied between the lake towns. The demand for carpenters in shipbuilding may have led to Christ's change of residence from Nazareth to the seaport town of Capernaum. His close association with the sea made Jesus familiar with boats* (Mark 4:38), navigation (Mark 4:35), and fishing (see FISH) (John 21:6). The lake is subject to violent storms (Matt. 8:24), caused by the difference in temperature of the land immediately around it and that of the mountains and tablelands far above it. The winds are shut off from the edge of the lake by the mountains close to the shore, but descend on the center, and are often violent on the opposite shore. The N. end, being less protected, is more subject to storms; Jesus encountered them in traveling from Capernaum to Gadara (Matt. 8:23; Mark 4:37; Luke 8:23, 26), and from Bethsaida to Capernaum (Matt. 14:24; Mark 6:48; John 6:17 f.).

162. Sea of Galilee near exit of the Jordan River.

gall, variously understood as "poison" (Job 20:16), "hemlock" (Hos. 10:4), or "poppy"; used to denote a bitter substance, often in connection with the bitter herb wormwood* hence anything bitter to endure (Jer. 8:14; Acts 8:23) (see also "travail," Lam. 3:5; Amos 6:12). On his cross Jesus was offered vinegar mixed with gall as an anodyne, but declined to drink it (Matt. 27:34). Cf. Psalm 69:21.

Gallio (găl'ĭ-ō), deputy (A.V.) or proconsul (R.S.V.) under Emperor Claudius, of Achaia, Roman province of Greece (Acts 18:12), in probably A.D. 51 or 52, during Paul's first sojourn in the teeming isthmus city. When Corinthian Jews attacked Paul and brought him before Gallio, at the tribunal or rostrum of the basilica or judgment hall on the edge of the shops of the harbor city, the amiable Roman official found him not guilty of "wrong or wicked lewdness" (A.V. Acts 18:14). Uninterested in the charge that Paul was persuading "men to worship God contrary to law," Gallio dismissed the case and drove the Jewish prosecutors from the tribunal. He was equally unconcerned about the beating of Sosthenes, ruler of the synagogue in which Paul preached, immediately thereafter. (See JUSTUS.)

Gallio, whose original name was Marcus Annaeus Novatus, before his adoption into the family of Lucius Junius Gallio, was brother of Seneca, the Roman philosopher. Pliny tells of his going to Egypt after finishing his term at Corinth—a victim of lung hemorrhage. One tradition holds that Gallio committed suicide in A.D. 65; others that both Gallio and Seneca were put to death by Nero. George Barton called attention to an inscription discovered at Delphi, giving A.D. 51–52 as the dates of Gallio's term at Corinth, helping to fix a point in N.T. chronology from which other dates can be established. Portions of Gallio's tribunal, which faced the agora or marketplace, have been excavated at Corinth by the American School of Classical Studies. These include fragments of a rostrum (bema), quite possibly the one to which Paul was brought by the Jews for a hearing before the Roman governor (Acts 18:12–17). On the nearby Lechaeum Road a stone lintel, inscribed in Hebrew, has been found which may come from the synagogue succeeding the one where Paul preached (Acts 18:4).

Gamaliel (gȧ-mā'lĭ-ĕl) ("reward of God"). A son of Pedahzur and prince of the Children of Manasseh, who took part in making a census of Israel in the wilderness (Num. 1:10, 2:20, 7:54, 59, 10:23). (2) A son of Simon and grandson of Hillel, a "Pharisee," doctor of the Law, member of the Sanhedrin* (Acts 5:34), and early teacher of Saul of Tarsus (Acts 22:3). He intervened successfully at the trial of Peter and the Apostles, with a plea for a more tolerant "wait and see" policy (Acts 5:38–40). This noble attitude of forbearance was not exemplified by his pupil in dealing with Christians (Acts 8:1, 22:20) before his conversion. While there is much in 1st-century writings about this first of seven teachers who received the honored title "Rabban," which in the form of "Rabboni" is applied to Christ in John 20:16, there is no evidence that he ever became a Christian. He represented the most liberal wing of the Pharisees*, the school of Hillel, as opposed to that of Shammai. Gamaliel died c. A.D. 57–58.

games, though not mentioned in Scripture, are known by archaeological evidence to have been popular in Bible lands since 5000 B.C., to which date belongs an Egyptian gaming board recovered with its clay "men," and a child's game of skittles, along with its balls and cone-shaped "men." In ancient Bible times, as today, people of the Middle East spent much time playing draughts, backgammon, and chess. In almost every excavated tell gaming boards have been found, often of limestone, ruled into squares. The "men" were pebbles, small conical stones, or of clay. Dice, often of choice materials, were used. In Crete was found a gaming board 1 yd. long ablaze with gold, silver, ivory, and crystal trim. Hyksos horsemen (c. 1600 B.C.) played on square draught boards, using two spool-like truncated dice with only four numerals—like those of Palestine.

Hebrews were less interested in games than their neighbors. The lot (*pur*) cast at Shushan* gave its name to a Hebrew festival (Esther 9:24, 26). Casting lots was to them a means of determining God's will (Acts 1:24–26). The most eloquent gaming board unearthed to date, from the Christian viewpoint, is that scratched on the stone paving of Herod's Jerusalem *praetorium* (see ARCHITECTURE), seen today under the Church of the Dames de Sion on the Via Dolorosa. (See GABBATHA.) Many believe that the Roman guard played here during the Trial of Jesus. We do not know what sort of "dice" were used by those who cast lots for the robe of Christ (Matt. 27:35).

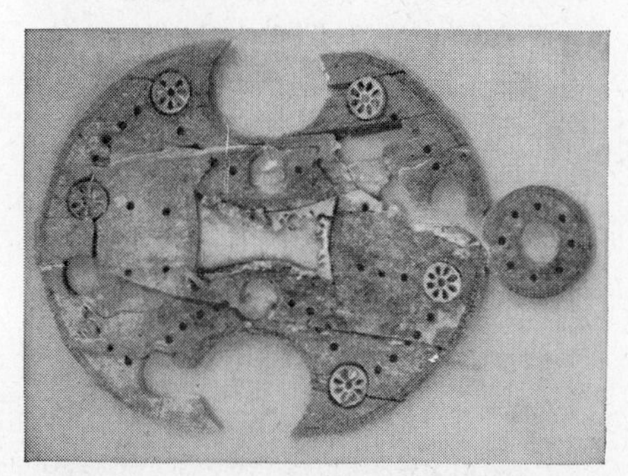

163. Ivory gaming board inlaid with gold (c. 1350–1150 B.C.), found at Megiddo.

Both Jesus and Paul were familiar with the Graeco-Roman flair for athletic contests, including wrestling, running, and discus throwing, conducted in stadia, amphitheaters, and gymnasia like those Antiochus Epiphanes and Herod introduced into Judaea to win popular favor—not always accorded by serious-minded Jews. In the great amphitheater of Corinth, or at the scene of the Isthmian Games, or in Puteoli, Ephesus, and other cities, Paul witnessed the games and quoted from them such metaphors as in I Cor. 9:24–27. See also Acts 20:24; Gal. 2:2, 5:7; Phil. 2:16; II Tim. 2:5, 4:7 f.; Heb. 12:1, 2.

Children in Jerusalem streets were known by Jesus to play at "wedding" and "funeral" (Matt. 11:17). The picture of the restored Jerusalem includes boys and girls playing in the streets (Zech. 8:5). Riddle asking was a favorite pastime (Judg. 14:12 ff.; Ezek. 17:2). Storytelling was a recreation and art in which Hebrews excelled. Babies' rattles and clay horses have been excavated from Gezer.

garden, an enclosed plot of ground (Jer. 52:7) intensively cultivated (Isa. 61:11; Luke 13:19), usually irrigated (Gen. 2:10; Isa. 1:30, 58:11; Jer. 31:12), and highly prized by its Middle Eastern owner for its flowers, vegetables (Isa. 1:8), herbs (I Kings 21:2; Deut. 11:10), fruits (Gen. 3:2 f.), trees (Eccles. 2:1–6; Ezek. 31:8), shade (Gen. 3:8), and quiet (John 18:1). See illus. 229.

The garden planted eastward in Eden* (Gen. 2:8) was a paradise whose loss was deplored (Gen. 3:23 f.). Any hoped-for boon for the individual or the race was frequently expressed in garden terminology (Gen. 13:10; Jer. 31:12; Ezek. 36:35; Mic. 4:4; Rev. 22:1, 2).

When not enclosed within walls of stone, brick, or mud, the enclosure might be given privacy by a hedge (Eccles. 10:8) of cactus or thorns, as often seen today in such towns as Bethany and Nazareth. Mary's expectation of meeting Joseph's gardener on the first Easter morning is evidence of the care expended on a garden's upkeep (John 20:15). People were free to tarry or pass through orchards (see GETHSEMANE), except during the fruit-bearing and -gathering periods (Luke 22:39; John 18:1).

Kings and men of wealth had extensive gardens adjoining or near their residences (II Kings 25:4; Neh. 3:15), where they entertained in splendor (Esth. 1:1–8). This was specially true of the brilliant gardens of Egypt, Assyria, Persia, and Syria, whose patterned walks, trees, and flowers became designs in Near Eastern ceramics and textiles. Sennacherib built his famous aqueduct at Jerwan to give gardens to the citizens of Nineveh*. Gardens were often family burial plots. Manasseh and his son Amon were buried in the garden of their royal ancestor (II Kings 21:18, 26). In the private garden of Joseph of Arimathaea, in an unused sepulcher, the body of the crucified Jesus was placed (John 19:38–42).

garment. See DRESS.

gate. See WALLS.

Gath, one of the five chief Philistine (see PHILISTINES) cities (Josh. 13:3), the nearest of the large Philistine cities to Hebrew territory. The Israelites frequently raided it in spite of its reputation for having huge men, Anakim, like Goliath (I Sam. 17:4–50). Achish, King of Gath, befriended David (I Sam. 27) during Saul's hostility, and gave the Hebrew hero the town of Ziklag (v. 6). Later David captured Gath (I Chron. 18:1). During the reign of Jehoash (c. 837–800 B.C.), Hazael, King of Syria, seized Gath (II Kings 12:17). Uzziah (c. 783–742) destroyed the city (II Chron. 26:6), apparently bringing about the downfall of Gath as a major Philistine city (Amos 6:2; note absence of Gath in list of Amos 1:6–8). After Sargon II conquered Gath in 712 B.C. (*ANET*[3], p. 286), its name is absent from references to the Philistine cities (Jer. 25:20; Zeph. 2:4; Zech. 9:5). Because of this, and the fact that the name "Gath" is a common one, the location of Gath of the Philistines is uncertain. Albright (*AASOR*, 1923, pp. 11 ff.) identified it with Tell esh-Sheikh Ahmed el-'Areini, but excavations at the site argue against this, as well as the suggestion that Gath be located at Tell en-Nagileh (*IEJ* 11, 1961, pp. 101 ff.). Other locations have been proposed, but several authorities have fallen back to an earlier suggestion, Tell es-Safi (generally held to be the site of Libnah), c. 10 m. SE. of Ekron (Aharoni, *The Land of the Bible*, p. 250). The question is far from settled. (2) The name of several cities, generally combined with an ethnic designation, but not always, making identification difficult. Such are Gath-rimmon (Josh. 19:45; ? Tell el-Jarisheh on the Yarkon), Gath-gittaim (II Sam. 4:3; Ras Abu Humeid, N. of Gezer). See *IEJ* 4, 1954, pp. 227 ff. W. P. A.

Gaza (gā'zȧ) (Heb. *'azzāh*), southernmost of the five chief cities of the Philistines (Josh. 13:3), marking the S. boundary of Canaan (Gen. 10:19), c. 3 m. from the Mediterranean. It turned its attention E. to the great caravan routes, rather than to the maritime lanes favored by such ports as Ashdod, Caesarea, and Joppa. Its commercial importance was recognized by Egypt before the Hebrew Conquest. From c. 1550–1200 B.C. it was an administrative center of the pharaohs, and continued to be a commercial prize through Roman times, when it was detached from the Palestine of the procurator Pontius Pilate and included as an enclave within the Roman Province of Syria. Gaza, the greatest trade center of Biblical Palestine, was surrounded by a productive food belt. It had a stranglehold on the busy caravan highways SW. to Egypt, S. to Arabia by way of Beer-sheba, N. along the Great Sea and overland to Damascus, as well as SE. to Edom, rich in coveted copper and iron ores. Its light-fabric textiles have given us the word "gauze." Modern Gaza (Ghazzeh), on the site of the ancient city, is still a congested trading center, whose streets are always picturesquely thronged.

During the time of Ramesses III of Egypt, the Philistines occupied Gaza (Deut. 2:23). It was allotted to (Josh. 15:47) and supposedly captured by (Judg. 1:18) Judah, but the Samson narratives indicate that this is idealistic (Judg. 16:21). Gaza marked what was usually considered the S. boundary of Judah (as in I Kings 4:24). Successive masters of the coveted commercial and military prize included Tiglath-pileser III (745–727 B.C.); Sargon II (721–705 B.C.); Pharaoh Necho II (609–593 B.C.) (see Jer. 47:1); the Persian Cambyses (530–522 B.C.); and Alexander the Great, who took it in 332 B.C.

A chief Biblical interest in Gaza is in connection with the Danite folk hero Samson*, whose involvement with Delilah resulted in his capture by the Philistines. The Gaza city gate whose doors he is credited with carrying off (Judg. 16) is thought to have been Bab el-Mountar, now covered with Moslem tombs, about 15 min. walk SE., and commanding from its 270-ft. elevation a view to the hills of S. Judaea and the beginning of the Sinai Desert. For Samson's destruction of the Gaza temple and of himself, see Judg. 16:23–31, and DAGON. See also Acts 8:26.

Petrie's identification of Tell el-'Ajjûl* as "ancient Gaza" is no longer accepted. Tell el-'Ajjûl, lying on the coast SW. of Gaza, is now believed to be Beth-eglaim.

gazelle, A.S.V. word for the small, soft-eyed antelope* called in the A.V. "roe,"* "roebuck." It was "clean" in the sense of being eatable under food regulations (Deut. 12:15, 22, 14:5, 15:22). Solomon's commissary kept a goodly stock in the royal larder (I Kings 4:23). Its graceful swift-footedness was used metaphorically (II Sam. 2:18; I Chron. 12:8; Song of Sol. 2:7, 17). The graceful, horned, fawn-colored *Gazella dorcas* (cf. the N.T. woman's name, Dorcas or Tabitha, Acts 9:36) was very early a favorite motif used in decorating Egyptian and Palestinian pottery and in wall paintings and low reliefs.

Geba (gē'bȧ) ("hill"), modern Jeba', a town situated in the Biblical period on the N. border of Benjamin (Josh. 21:17), across the valley from Michmash. It is to be distinguished from Gibeah*, with which it is sometimes confused in the Heb. text. "Geba" in II Sam. 5:25 should be "Gibeon."*

Gebal (gē'băl) ("mountain"). (1) Ancient Canaanite and Phoenician seaport (Egypt. *kpn;* Accad. *Gubla;* modern Jebeil), 25 m. N. of Beirut. Because Gebal was the intermediary of an extensive papyrus* trade between Egypt and Greece during the 1st millennium B.C., the Greeks called it Byblos, from *biblos,* "book." Its territory is mentioned among the "land that remains" in Joshua (13:5). The men of Gebal were employed as stonecutters by Solomon for the building of the Jerusalem Temple (I Kings 5:18), and their skill as shipbuilders was noted by Ezekiel (27:9). As early as the Sixth Dynasty (c. 2340 B.C.), reference is made in Egyptian texts to special "Byblos ships." These and later texts, as well as numerous objects of Egyptian origin discovered at Byblos, attest to the close relationship between the two throughout most of the 3d and 2d millennia B.C. This was due mainly to Egypt's need to obtain cedar logs for shipbuilding, tomb construction, and use in funerary ritual (see *ANET*³, pp. 227, 240, 241, 243, 441). Gebal is mentioned in the earlier series (19th century B.C.) of Egyptian execration texts (*ANET*³, p. 329), and the close relationship between Byblos and Egypt is reflected in the letters addressed to the Egyptian court by Rib-addi, King of Byblos, during the Amarna period (14th century B.C.; *ANET*³, pp. 483–484). The Tale of Wen-Amon (c. 1100 B.C.) relates the adventures of an Egyptian envoy to Byblos in his attempt to procure cedar wood (*ANET*³, pp. 25 ff.). During the 1st millennium B.C., Assyrian and Babylonian interest in the port is reflected in the many campaigns against the city and tribute brought from Tiglath-pileser I to Nebuchadnezzar II (*ANET*³, pp. 275 ff.).

Excavations on the site of ancient Byblos from 1921 to the present (P. Montet, 1921–1924; M. Dunand, since 1925) have provided detailed information on the earliest settlements at Byblos, those of the Neolithic period (5th millennium B.C.) and the Chalcolithic period (c. 3500–3100 B.C.), the latter producing over 1200 jar burials. The remains of the Early Bronze Age (c. 2900–2300 B.C.) and the Middle Bronze Age (c. 1900–1600 B.C.) indicate the existence of a prosperous and important city, and attest to the close ties with Egypt at this time. To the Early Bronze Age belongs the initial construction of the temple of Baalat-Gebal, the Lady of Byblos, which as the shrine of the chief goddess of Byblos continued to be rebuilt as late as the Roman period. To the Middle Bronze Age belong the cut tombs of the Byblite rulers, whose funerary offerings included many gifts from Egyptian pharaohs of the Middle Kingdom. Later remains, though important, are scattered, due to the characteristic use in later times of

164. Crusader tower at Gebal.

the stone building blocks of earlier periods. This is no more evident than in the construction of the 12th century A.D. Crusader castle. Mention should be made of the remarkable sarcophagus of Ahiram, King of Byblos (*ANEP*², Nos. 456–459), found in one of the tombs of the Royal Cemetery, the lid of which bears the oldest Phoenician inscription known (c. 10th century B.C.; see *ANET*³, p. 661). See N. Jidejian, *Byblos Through the Ages*, 1968 (rev. 1971).

(2) NE. Edom, mentioned in Ps. 83:7; known also as Teman. It was allied with Moabites and Arabian nomads against Israel.
W. P. A.

Geber (gē′bēr), son of Uri, and one of Solomon's twelve commissary officers (I Kings 4:19).

Gedaliah (gĕd′ȧ-lī′a) ("Jehovah is great"), the name of five men mentioned in Scripture, the most important of whom were: (1) The son of Ahikam, the adviser of Josiah (II Kings 22:12); the Jewish governor appointed by the Babylonian Nebuchadnezzar (II Kings 25:22) over "the poor of the land" after the destruction of Jerusalem, 587 B.C. Gedaliah befriended the prophet Jeremiah (Jer. 39:14), and shared his views with regard to serving the Babylonian king (II Kings 25:24; Jer. 38, 39). While administering his duties at Mizpah he was killed by Ishmael, of the royal Hebrew line (II Kings 25:25; Jer. 40, 41); and the remnant he had tried to govern was carried off to Egypt, along with Jeremiah* (Jer. 43). The murder of Gedaliah has ever since been commemorated on its anniversary (the 3d day of the 7th month, Tishri) as one of the four Jewish fasts (see FEASTS). (2) The eldest "son" of Jeduthun, appointed in the musicians' guild for Temple service (I Chron. 25:3).

Gehazi (gḗ-hā′zī) ("valley of vision"), the servant (II Kings 4:12, 8:4) or associate of Elisha* the prophet, though without the prestige which Elisha bore with reference to Elijah. As intermediary between Elisha and his Shunammite hostess (II Kings 4:8 ff.), he displayed irritation when she sought the prophet's help (v. 27), and proved ineffective in restoring her child (v. 31). He falsely represented his master as requesting a reward of "a talent of silver, and two changes of garments" from Naaman, the Syrian commander cured of leprosy by Elisha, and was smitten with the leprosy of which Elisha had cured Naaman (II Kings 5:20–27).

Gehenna. (1) The N.T. Gk. name for the Valley of the Son of Hinnom* (Arab. Wâdī er-Rabābi), surrounding Jerusalem on the W. and S. One of its steep scarps of rocky soil supported a portion of the city walls. The highest point of the Gehenna Valley slope lies 2,379 ft. above the Mediterranean, but 200 ft. lower than Jerusalem's highest point. The valley itself is open, and is approached from the Zion Gate. It joins the narrower Kidron* Valley at a point S. of the spring Gihon*. Gehenna separated Judah from Benjamin (Josh. 15:8, 18:16) as it ran down between the Hill of Evil Counsel, associated with Caiaphas, and the Rephaim Plain on the S. The road from Jerusalem to Bethlehem intersects the Hinnom Valley. Excavations indicate that in the Biblical period approach was made to Gehenna by way of the Valley Gate (Neh. 2:13), near the SW. corner of the present city wall. (See also the "east [sun] gate," Jer. 19:2.) Because children, in Solomon's "golden age" and the eras of Ahaz and Manasseh, were burned in sacrifice to Molech* in this "valley of slaughter" (Jer. 7:32; see also Lev. 18:21; I Kings 11:7; II Chron. 28:3, 33:6), the area took on a sinister significance. Later it was desecrated and made into a garbage and rubbish heap that was kept burning; these flames were an image of the fires of hell, and Gehenna thus came to mean "hell" (cf. Matt. 5:22, 25:30, 46, 10:28). (2) Thus the foul Valley of Gehenna supplied the imagery for Sheol, the Hebrew counterpart of the gloomy Greek and Roman underworld, *Tartaros, Tartarus*. In Hebrew eschatology Gehenna was the region under, but more extensive than, the earth, where sinners were punished by "hell fire" (Matt. 18:8 f.) and by worms immediately after death (see HELL). According to late Talmudic teaching, Jews who had once gone through such purification were released from further torture. Gehenna was the antithesis of heaven, the blissful state of all who had experienced resurrection (see ESCHATOLOGY). Just as the Valley of Gehenna was to ancient Jews the Valley of Woe, so to Hebrews, as well as to later Moslems, the Valley of the Kidron (Jehoshaphat) was the Valley of Judgment (Joel 3:2, 12). See TOPHETH and JUDGMENT, DAY OF.

Gemariah (gĕm'ă-rī'ă) ("Jehovah has completed"). (1) Hilkiah's son who was one of two messengers sent by Zedekiah to Nebuchadnezzar. They carried a letter from Jeremiah to the exiles in Babylon (Jer. 29:3). (2) Shaphan's son who requested the king not to burn Jeremiah's scroll (Jer. 36:10, 12, 25).

genealogy, the history of the descent of an individual or a group from a common ancestor, was of great interest to Hebrews, as indicated by the numerous genealogical lists in Scripture. Even the words "genealogies" (I Chron. 5:17; II Chron. 12:15), "pedigrees" and "generations" (Num. 1:18, 20) appear in the O.T. There are signs of great interest in "the generations of Adam" (Gen. 5, etc.). Inheritance* from father to eldest son was the basis on which claims to kingship, the high priesthood, the leadership of clans and "houses" and property rights were established by descendants of the Patriarchs in Canaan. To be "chief of the fathers of the priests and Levites" (I Chron. 24:31) was a coveted honor. The importance placed on the continuance of an unbroken male line is the chief reason that polygamy was general and uncondemned. In post-Exilic times genealogy was recorded with special care to line up claimants to the high priesthood, to re-establish property rights which had lapsed during the owners' absence in Babylon (Neh. 7), and to check the denationalizing processes due to mixed marriages (Neh. 13:23–30; Ezra 9 f.).

Family lists in the O.T. are not always literally accurate. "Son of" meant "heir of," as well as one physically descended; this led to confusion in records. Not many of the lists in the O.T. were written down currently. Several genealogies appear to be drawn from information in Kings and Chronicles (as from I Chron. 1–9). The "book of the kings of Israel and Judah" was considered an "official" roster (I Chron. 9). The lines of Saul (I Chron. 8) and of David (I Chron. 2:1–15, 3; Ruth 4) appear in the main to be correct.

Gen. 10 ("Generations of the sons of Noah") is an example of how towns, localities, and countries were spoken of as if they were individuals descending from eponymous ancestors. Sidon was the eldest son of Canaan (Gen. 10:15). Ethiopia, Egypt, Put, and Canaan were "the sons of Ham" (v. 6). Thus, while these statements are not literally true, they supply valuable ethnological information about the foundation and relationships of communities (cf. I Chron. 1). Twelve Aramaean tribes are represented in Gen. 22:20–24 as descendants of Nahor, brother of Abraham, even as 12 N. Arabian tribes are claimed in Gen. 25:12–16 to be sons of Ishmael, son of Hagar. Apparently specific ancestors were invented at times to account for the establishment of a nation, as when Esau was hailed as the ancestor of the Edomites (Gen. 36:1). The Hebrew Patriarchs, however, were probably historic personalities, and not mere folk types.

In the N.T. the most important genealogical record is that of Jesus, as recorded by Matthew (1:1–17) and Luke (3:23–38). Divergencies in the two lists raise questions as to whether the writer of either Gospel had access to the material of the other, whether both had access to the same archives, and whether the points of difference may be attributed to the purpose each had in mind when writing. Both lists agree in the main between Abraham and David. But Matthew's list begins with Abraham and ends with Joseph, whereas Luke's extends from Jesus and Joseph back to Adam. No women are mentioned in Luke; but in Matthew several women are mentioned: Tamar (R.S.V., Thamar A.V., Matt. 1:3); Rahab (R.S.V., Rachab A.V. Matt. 1:5); Bath-sheba, "that had been the wife of Urias" (Matt. 1:6); and Ruth (Matt. 1:5). Some interpreters assert that these were included to show how the universal mission of Jesus, even from its human beginnings, included repentant sinners and non-Israelites. The fact that four women are mentioned as ancestors of Jesus in the Matthew list leads one to question why the ancestry of Mary is not included. One explanation offered is that Mary, like Joseph, was of the tribe of Judah; both had common ancestors in the line of physical descent from David. Jesus himself laid less stress upon his Davidic descent than early Christians did.

Matthew's list, with some ingenuity, arranges the ancestors of Jesus in three groups of 14 generations each: from Abraham to David, from David to the Exile, from the Exile to Jesus.

The age-long interest of Palestinians in the genealogy is shown by the 12th-cen. mosaics of "the tree of Jesse" on the S. wall of the Church of the Nativity at Bethlehem, begun in the 4th century over the site of Christ's birth.

generation, a word whose frequent use in the Bible indicates the interest taken in matters of genealogy*. The phrase "these are the generations of" (e.g., Num. 3:1), is virtually synonymous with "this is the genealogy of" or "these are the descendants of." Used in the singular, generation usually signified the sum total of individuals forming a contemporary group (Ex. 1:6). I Chron. 5:7 refers to reckoning "a genealogy of their generations." John the Baptist called his contemporaries "a generation of vipers" (Luke 3:7). Jesus referred to his age as "an evil and adulterous generation" (Matt. 12:39), more worldly wise than "the children of light" (Luke 16:8). He waxed justly impatient with his "faithless and perverse generation" (Luke 9:41), and admitted that he would be rejected by his own generation (Luke 17:25). Peter shared his view, calling his contemporaries an "untoward generation" (Acts

2:40). When writers wished to express the thought of God's power functioning over a long sweep of time, they used such phrases as "throughout all generations" (Ps. 145:13; cf. Dan. 4:3). Mary in her "Magnificat" sang, "all generations shall call me blessed" (Luke 1:48).

Genesis. (1) A Gk. word meaning "origin" or "beginning."

(2) The 1st book of the Bible, also of the Pentateuch ("five books"), and the Hexateuch* ("six books"). It is known in Heb. as *bereshith* ("in the beginning"), which is the book's first word. It can be outlined thus:

(1) The origin of the world and of man (1–11):
- (a) The Creation (1:1–2:17);
- (b) Adam and his descendants (2:18–5:32);
- (c) Noah and his sons (6–11).

(2) The Patriarchs (12–50):
- (a) Abraham and Isaac (12–25:18);
- (b) Jacob (25:19–36:43);
- (c) Joseph (37–50).

The first 11 chapters present the antecedents of Hebrew history, from Adam to Abraham. What they lack in scientific accuracy they more than make up in sublime religious truth. Apparent similarities between Gen. 1 and 2 and modern scientific theories are interesting but entirely coincidental; the supreme religious revelation in these passages does not imply their scientific and historical accuracy. Whether dependable history begins with chap. 12 is debated; one of the questions is whether the Hebrew people, through their relationship with God in covenants (see COVENANT), began their distinctive religious mission to mankind before Moses.

By the Persian period Jewish scribes attributed the authorship of Genesis and the Pentateuch to Moses—a theory which was later taken over from Judaism by Christianity. It was incorporated in the book captions of the A.V., in spite of abundant internal evidence indicating a much later pen (Gen. 36:31). While evidences increase that Hebrew writing prevailed during, and even before, the time of Moses (see WRITING and chart; and SERABIT) these have probably not shaken the composite documentary theory as the best explanation of the formation of the book. In this theory Genesis is the result of the blending of accounts that express varied points of view, emphases, and characteristics which make it the product not of one, but of many inspired minds. Just as the Spirit of God at Pentecost came upon many peoples who formed the Christian Church, so in Genesis that same Spirit operated through many personalities, using such varied materials as written records (Gen. 10:5); tribal traditions (Gen. 12:2, 15:5, 24:3–8); sacred shrine lore (Gen. 14:18, 35:1–15); and poetry (Gen. 4:24, 25:23, 27:27–29), etc. This analysis of Genesis began in 1753, when two names for God—"Elohim" (Gen. 1:1) and "Yahweh" (2:4)—were first noted as indications of different sources. Repetitions of the same story with variations also furnished clues for the analysis (Gen. 1:26 f., cf. Gen. 2:7, 21–23; Gen. 7:1–5, cf. 6:18–21). Since 1880 the Graf-Wellhausen theory of the composite make-up of Genesis has been held by most students of the Bible investigating the literary elements present in inspired Scriptures. This study has enhanced the value of the book, and has added to the interest of events which are not necessarily historic.

At least three sources*, J, E, and P, are woven together to make Genesis. Robert H. Pfeiffer points out a fourth, which he calls S, for South or Seir. J material can be recognized because it uses Jehovah ("Yahweh") for God (Gen. 2:4–3:24, etc.); represents the Judaean point of view; is majestic, yet simple in style; and has a flowing, easily traceable narrative. Its date is c. 950 B.C. E uses "God" ("Elohim") instead of "Jehovah"; represents the point of view of the N. Kingdom; and its characters are more inclined to outbursts of joy and sorrow (Gen. 37:29 f., 42:21–24, 45:26). Its date is c. 850–750 B.C. J and E often use the same material but with variations (Gen. 12:9–17, J, cf. Gen. 20:1–16, E; Gen. 28:10–11, 13–16, J. cf. Gen. 28:12, 17, E). J and E were combined into JE c. 650 B.C.

The Priestly Code of P (c. 500–450 B.C.) stresses the revelations to Adam, Noah, Abraham, and Moses, and the covenants with Noah, Abraham, and Moses, showing how Israel was separated from the Gentiles and became the chosen nation. P in Genesis records the following stories: Creation (1:1–2:4); the Flood (parts of 6–9); the covenant with Abraham (17); and the 10 genealogies (see GENEALOGY). The latter include: (1) Heaven and Earth (Gen. 2:4); (2) Adam (5); (3) Noah (6:9); (4) Noah and his sons (10:1–7, 20, 22–23); (5) Shem (11:10–26); (6) Terah (11:27, 31); (7) Ishmael (25:12–17); (8) Isaac (25:19, 26b); (9) Esau (36:1–8, 40–43); (10) Jacob (37:2; cf. 35:22b–26). These genealogies constitute the framework of Genesis, an unbroken chronological and statistical chain. Frequently the P material cites the religious practices basic for the Jews in the Babylonian Exile, without a temple; the establishment of the Sabbath (Gen. 2:3); the prohibition to partake of blood (Gen. 9:3–6); and the rite of circumcision (17:22–27).

The 5th-century B.C. date ascribed to the Genesis we know may explain the parallels with Babylonian literature, with which the Jews became familiar during the Exile, detected in the Genesis stories of Creation, the Garden, and the Flood. The Moffatt translation of the Bible uses different type to show different literary strands of Genesis. Priceless religious values are available to all readers of Genesis, whatever may be their theories of its origin. But the documentary theory will disclose new insights into the growth of the Jewish-Christian religion, by consideration of the historical process ten centuries long that is hidden below the surface of this book.

Gennesaret (gĕ-nĕs′ȧ-rĕt). See GALILEE, SEA OF.

Gentiles ("people," "nations") in Jewish thought included all non-Hebrews. As early as Gen. 10:5 and Judg. 4:2, 13, 16 allusions to Gentiles appear in Scripture. Deuteronomic theology taught that Israel, as God's favorite people (Deut. 7:6), had no responsibility for outsiders. Yet this people later conceived themselves as playing the martyr role to save all nations, as revealed in the "Servant Songs" of Isa. 42:1–4, 49:1–6, 50:4–9, 52:13–53:12 (c. 540–500 B.C., J. A. Bewer). The books of Ruth and Jonah also broke down the narrow doctrine of "the chosen people." The prophets continually expanded the Hebrew concept of God, Mal. 1:11 saying that the Lord's name "shall be great among the Gentiles." The Third Isaiah (56:7) saw the Temple as "an house of prayer for all people." Some scholars, like C. C. Torrey, believe that Isa. 34, 35, 40–66 taught that the principal mission of dispersed Israel was to establish world salvation, with Jew and Gentile both worshipping Yahweh on Mount Zion.

Although Jesus is represented by Matthew as criticizing Gentiles for being materialistic (Matt. 6:32) and domineering (20:25), he had spent so much of his time in cosmopolitan Galilee with its Gentile cities like Sepphoris, Tiberias, and Magdala, that he manifested no prejudice against Gentiles, though he did recognize his mission as directed first to the "lost sheep of the house of Israel" (Matt. 10:5 f.). He realized that he was fulfilling Isaiah's prophecy that Gentiles ultimately would trust in his name (cf. Matt. 12:21). The aged Simeon had declared at his presentation in the Temple that Jesus would "lighten the Gentiles" (Luke 2:32). Part of Christ's personal ministry was spent among the Greek cities E. of the Jordan—in the Decapolis (Mark 5) and Peraea. He did not hesitate to minister to individual Gentiles (cf. Matt. 8:5–13, 15:21–28). Although Jesus, like Paul, lived in a society composed of three classes—Jews, Graeco-Roman people of culture, and barbarians (Col. 3:11)—to him all men were brothers, sons of one Father (John 8:41). Christ's Disciples at first continued to meet in the Temple with other Jews. But the rejection of Christ by the nation as a whole led to the development of separate groups, companies of disciples, soon to be called "the church"* (Acts 2:47).

Paul, a Jew of the seed of Abraham and the tribe of Benjamin, gave as his credentials for working among the Gentiles the commission received at his conversion (Acts 26:17 f.). When he went into a new community, he went first into the synagogue to teach, as at Thessalonica (Acts 17:1), Berea (Acts 17:10), Corinth (Acts 18), and Iconium (Acts 14:1), where he made converts both Jewish and Gentile. Yet some of his most hateful persecutors were Jews (Acts 13:44–52, 17:5, 13). The envious hostility of Antiochian Jews and the joyful acceptance of "the word of the Lord" by the Gentiles of this same city led to an appeal by Paul and Barnabas to the Jerusalem Council (Acts 15:1–4) for a statement of entrance requirements for the admission of Gentiles. The simple exactions of Acts 15:20 proved satisfactory. They enabled the apostolic group to push ahead with unmitigated zeal, establishing Christian *ekklēsia* in Syria, Asia, Macedonia, and Greece. Lydia of Thyatira, a Gentile merchant in Philippi, became Paul's first European convert. Paul at times gave private instruction to Gentiles "of [good] reputation" (Gal. 2:2), lest his free leadership be challenged by narrow-minded Jewish converts. By the time that Paul, the Jewish Apostle to the Gentiles, addressed the Areopagites of Athens he was far along the road of leading men to a universal religion and a way of world peace. He spoke of God's having "made of one blood all nations" (Acts 17:26), and said He is "not far" from every one of us (v. 27), "For in him we live, and move, and have our being" (v. 28). Paul included "all men everywhere" (v. 30) in God's call to repentance, and proclaimed a Lord who would judge the entire world "in righteousness by that man [Jesus] whom he hath ordained" (v. 31) and whose authority God had certified by resurrecting him from the dead.

Gentiles were predominant in the 1st-century Christian churches. Yet Paul frankly warned them that even if the divine rejection of Jews, because of their sin, was the good fortune of the Gentiles, they should not become "wise in [their] own conceits" (Rom. 11:25); Israel's separation from God would not be permanent. The broken-off branches (Jews) would again be grafted into the original stem of God's tree, along with the wild olive branch (Gentiles); God at the last would have "mercy upon all" (Rom. 11:32). See also HEATHEN.

Gentiles, Court of. See TEMPLE, THE.

gerah, smallest O.T. unit of weight, 1/50 oz. avdp. See Ezek. 45:12; WEIGHTS AND MEASURES.

Gerar (gē′rär), an ancient inland town on the S. side of Wâdī Ghazzeh, SE. of Gaza on the border between Palestine and Egypt, situated on an inland route more protected than the coastal path used through the centuries by contending armies. It figures in the Patriarchal sagas of Abraham (Gen. 20:1 f.) and of Isaac (Gen. 26:1, 6, 17, 20, 26), both of whom had similar experiences concerning their wives and King Abimelech of Gerar (perhaps based on only one actual incident). Asa (c. 913–873 B.C.) defeated Zerah, the invading Ethiopian, near Gerar (II Chron. 14:9–14).

Gerar was identified by W. M. F. Petrie with Tell Jemmeh (Tell Gamma), 8 m. S. of Gaza, and partially excavated by him in 1927 (earlier work had been done on the site in 1922 by W. J. Phythian-Adams). Petrie found in levels from the Late Bronze Age through Byzantine times myriads of objects which indicated a comfortable cultural standard. A new series of excavations was begun in 1970 under the direction of G. W. van Beek, so far working mainly on the Persian levels. Recently, the identification of Gerar with Tell Jemmeh has been discarded in favor of Aharoni's suggestion that it should be located at Tell Abu Hureira, 11 m. SE. of

Gaza (*IEJ* 6, 1956, pp. 26–32). This is based on a survey of the site by D. Alon, which indicated that a prosperous settlement existed on Tell Abu Hureira during the Middle Bronze Age (the age of the Patriarchs).

M. S. M./W. P. A.

Gerasa (Gerasenes [gĕr′ȧ-sēnz]) (R.S.V. Mark 5:1 and Luke 8:26; A.V. "Gadarenes," cf. Gergesenes, Matt. 8:28). There is disagreement as to the site of the place where Christ healed the Peraean demoniac. The likelier one seems to be the present Kersa (? formerly Gergesa), opposite Magdala on the E. shore of the Sea of Galilee, and having an embankment satisfying the details of the narrative (Luke 8:33). There was a Gadara (Muqeis) c. 6 m. SE. of the S. end of the Sea of Galilee, but this does not fit Mark 5:13. Few people continue to identify the incident with Gerasa, the ancient name of Jerash (a Semitic name called by Greeks "Gerasa"), c. 40 m. SE. of the Sea of Galilee in Trans-Jordan, because the distance seems too great for Christ to have traversed afoot in his Peraean ministry.

But there is nothing to disprove his having been in this elegant city, which was still under construction in his day, nor to deny that there were people from its homes among the multitudes who thronged about him after the healed demoniac and others published in the Decapolis "how great things" the Lord had done (Mark 5:20). Mosaic floor pictures found here, depicting other cities which had early Christian structures, point to some very dynamic force behind what now appears at Gerasa. The meticulously excavated Graeco-Roman city of Jerash, the "Pompeii of the East"—the best preserved Palestinian city of Roman times—and the largest excavation of Roman and Byzantine ruins in Palestine, rivalled in size only by Palmyra, and in importance by Syrian Baalbek, was conducted by the British School of Archaeology in Jerusalem, Yale University, and the American Schools of Oriental Research, for whose detailed report see *Gerasa, City of the Decapolis*, edited by Carl H. Kraeling, published by the American Schools of Oriental Research, New Haven, Conn.

Jerash, called by Romans "Antioch on the Chrysorroas," reveals today the typical, symmetrically laid out Roman city during and just after the N.T. period and the Byzantine era. At Jerash it is possible to trace from extant masonry the downfall of pagan temples and the reincorporation of some of their fabric into Christian churches; e.g., St. Theodore's and the Cathedral. The latter was erected over a temple of Dionysus, the wine god, whose worship flourished on the fruits of local vineyards. Behind the Temple of Artemis (or the Sun) is a small church superimposed upon a synagogue. Fragments carved with a 7-branched candlestick, a vase, and a fowl, have been found in the interior filling of the great Triumphal Arch erected in A.D. 130—an indication of the liquidation of Jews when Vespasian's Lucius Annius in A.D. 68 attacked the city.

Iron Age and Early Bronze Age pottery found near Jerash indicates the early occupation of this isolated region, which later developed into a teeming Roman caravan city and its suburbs. Ruts are seen today in the well-paved street along which was brought fabulous merchandise from distant points. Jerash has an ideal location, in a fertile valley on the W. bank of a small "golden river" or wâdī emptying into the Jabbok and finally into the Jordan. Jerash was in the Peraea where Jesus ministered.

To this section Greek culture had been introduced by survivors of Alexander the Great's campaigns. The prosperous citizens of Nabataea were attracted to the city, and found there all the public structures loved by Graeco-Romans. Its wall, c. 3 m. around, was approached through a sumptuous triumphal arch c. 400 yds. outside the wall as one comes from Amman—a structure comparable to Trajan's Arch at Rome. Inside the S. gate now stand vestiges of the Temple of

165. Temple of Artemis at Gerasa.

Zeus; and near it is the large theater, some of whose seats still bear their numbers. Below is the oval forum, many of whose Ionic columns still carry their architrave. From the forum stretches the long "Street of Columns," 75 of whose 520 columns remain, with Corinthian capitals and plain columns. Ruins of the shops that once lined this famous street, as shops lined Corinth's Lechaeum Road, remain. The amazing propylaeum leads up to the Temple of Artemis, which has two fine rows of Corinthian columns still standing, and the base of its altar. Baths, stadium, hippodrome for 15,000 spectators, fountains, and intersecting crossroads marked by a charming tetrapylon, all help moderns to appreciate the master architects who created captivating Roman cities during the first Christian centuries.

Gergesenes (gûr′gĕ-sēnz). See GADARA, GADARENES.

Gerizim (gĕ-rī′zĭm) (Jebel el-Tōr), a peak 2,849 ft. above the Mediterranean in the highlands of Samaria. With Mt. Ebal* it encloses the valley where the ancient Canaanite Shechem lay. Gerizim forms the S. wall of this pass, which controls the main N.–S. road approaching Jerusalem. The blessings for obedience to the law were pronounced from its slopes (Deut. 11:29, 27:12; Josh.

166. Mt. Gerizim, from Mt. Ebal.

8:33–35; see Mt. Ebal). Jotham uttered his famous fable of the trees (Judg. 9:7 ff.) to the elders of Shechem from its summit. Mt. Gerizim is the sacred mountain of the Samaritans (ref. to in John 4:20–21), on whose central peak a temple was built, destroyed by John Hyrcanus (c. 128 B.C.). The dwindling colony of Samaritans who today live in Nablus and guard a very ancient copy of the Pentateuch still observe the Passover on Mt. Gerizim with impressive rites. Mt. Gerizim is a limestone massif with three peaks. On the SE. peak, the highest, are the tomb of Sheikh Ghanim, the Samaritan sacred place, and the ruins of the 5th century church of Theotokos (excavated by A. M. Schneider in 1930). Recent archaeological work on the E. peak (at Tell er-Ras), has uncovered the foundations of a peripteral temple of the 4th–6th centuries A.D., the temple of Zeus Hypsistos, built by Hadrian, and depicted on coins struck at Neapolis (Nablus), A.D. 138–253 (see *BA* 31, 1968, pp. 58–72). On the lower slopes of Mt. Gerizim, at a place called Tananir, c. 300 m. from ancient Shechem, a MB II temple (dated c. 1650–1543 B.C.) has been re-excavated (see *BA* 32, 1969, pp. 81–103). W. P. A.

Gershom (gûr′shŏm) (by folk etymology "stranger"). (1) The first-born son of Moses and Zipporah, born during the sojourn of the fugitive Moses in Midian (Ex. 2:21 f.). The youth may have been fostered by his grandfather, Jethro, while Moses was preparing the Exodus of Israelites from Goshen. The circumcision referred to in Ex. 4:25 may refer to Gershom or to his younger brother, Eliezer*. One of Gershom's descendants served at the idolatrous Dan shrine, although Judg. 18:30 refers to this "Jonathan" as the grandson of Manasseh rather than of Moses (cf. A.S.V., R.S.V.). (2) A son of Levi (I Chron. 6:16 ff., 15:7 ff.), in some passages called "Gershon"*. (Cf. I Chron. 6:1,16.) (3) The head of a house descended from Phinehas the priest (Ezra 8:2).

Gershon (gûr′shŏn), the name of the eldest son of Levi according to some sources (see GERSHOM). His descendants were apparently influential Levites: families of Libnites and Shimeites descended from him were assigned a camp site W. of the Tabernacle during the Wilderness wanderings (Num. 3:23), and were given specific tasks in the care of the sacred tent (Num. 3:25, 26, 4:24–28; cf. Josh. 21:6). The Asaphite group of Gershonites led the music at the rededication of the Temple after the Return (Ezra 3:10). They were prominent in David's musical organization (I Chron. 6:39, cf. v. 43). Gershonites participated in Hezekiah's reforms (II Chron. 29:12 ff.) between c. 715 and 687 B.C.

Geshem (gē′shĕm) (Gashmu, A.V. Neh. 6:6), an Arabian opponent of the Jews, who ridiculed Nehemiah's plan to rebuild the walls of Jerusalem. When the work was continued, Geshem plotted against Nehemiah; failing in this, he then spread the rumor that Nehemiah was fortifying the city in preparation for making himself king. (Neh. 2:19, 6:1 ff.).

Geshur (gē′shẽr). (1) A small but ancient tribe of Aramaeans, whose territory formed part of the W. border of Bashan*, E. of the Sea of Galilee (Josh. 12:5). It proved difficult for Israel to win (Josh. 13:11, 13), and was still independent in the time of David, who took to wife Maacah, daughter of Talmai, a king of Geshur (II Sam. 3:3). She bore Absalom, who fled to his grandfather's territory after the death of Amnon (II Sam. 13:37 f.). (2) A region at the S. border of Palestine, mentioned in Josh. 13:2 as yet to be won; and in I Sam. 27:8 f. as conquered by David while he was with the Philistines. Some critics doubt the existence of this second Geshur.

gesture, a word not mentioned in Scripture, but indicated by scores of allusions. Middle Easterners are given to visual expressions of emotion. The following chart suggests a few.

Gestures and Other Bodily Expressions of Emotion

The Act	*Meaning*	*Scripture References*
dancing	joy	Ex. 15:20; I Sam. 30:16
	worship	II Sam. 6:16; I Chron. 15:29; Ps. 149:3
	amusement	Matt. 14:6
expressions of eyes	flashing anger	Mark 3:5
	glancing reproach	Luke 22:61
	Uplifted in prayer	Job 22:26; Mark 6:41
	wantonness	Isa. 3:16

The Act	Meaning	Scripture References
facial expressions	mockery	Ps. 22:7; Matt. 27:29
hand—		
beating breast	horror	Luke 23:48
blow of	violence	Gen. 37:22
open	generosity	Ps. 104:28; Prov. 31:20
pointed	scorn	Isa. 58:9; Hos. 7:5
head—		
bowed	reverence	Gen. 18:2; Ex. 20:5; I Chron. 21:21; Ps. 95:6; Isa. 60:14
	submission	Josh. 10:24
shaken	scorn, derision	II Kings 19:21; Ps. 109:25; Mark 15:29
hand laid on	blessing	Gen. 48:14
	preparation of sacrifice	Lev. 16:21
	mourning	II Sam. 13:19
	consecration	Acts 6:6
kissing	affection	Gen. 33:4; Ruth 1:14; Luke 15:20; Acts 20:37
	betrayal	Matt. 26:48, 49
kneeling	homage	Matt. 2:11, 4:9
	worship	I Kings 8:54; Ezra 9:5; Dan. 6:10; Luke 22:41; Eph. 3:14
laughing	scorn	Gen. 17:17, 18:12; II Kings 19:21; Ps. 22:7; Mark 5:40; Luke 8:53
rending garments	consternation	Gen. 37:29; Josh. 7:6; II Chron. 23:13; Matt. 26:65; Acts 14:14
	grief	Judg. 11:35; II Sam. 1:11
shaking dust from feet or garments	alienation	Matt. 10:14
shouting with loud voice	despair	Matt. 27:46
spitting in face	infliction of shame	Num. 12:14; Isa. 50:6; Matt. 26:67, 27:30
weeping	woe or sin	Job 16:16; Ezra 10:1; Jer. 9:10; Mal. 2:13
	joy	Gen. 46:29

(See also MOURNING.)

Gestures and Attitudes Used in Prayer

The Act	Meaning	Scripture References
kneeling	Solomon	I Kings 8:54
	Ezra	Ezra 9:5
	Daniel	Daniel 6:10
	Jesus	Luke 22:41
	Stephen	Acts 7:60
standing	Hannah	I Sam. 1:26
	Solomon	I Kings 8:22
	hypocrites	Matt. 6:5
	Pharisee	Luke 18:11
sitting	David	II Sam. 7:18
bowing to ground	Eliezer	Gen. 24:26
	Elijah	I Kings 18:42
	the people	Neh. 8:6

Hands during prayer were usually "spread up to heaven" (I Kings 8:54; cf. Ps. 141:2) or stretched forth (Ps. 143:6).

Gethsemane (gĕth-sĕm′ȧ-nē) ("oil press"), "a place" (Matt. 26:36; Mark 14:32) frequented by Jesus on the "Mount of Olives" (Luke 22:39), and further identified in John 18:1 as a "garden" over the Brook Cedron (A.V.;) ("across the Kidron valley" R.S.V.; "an orchard," "across the Kidron ravine," Moffatt), where Jesus went with his disciples to agonize in prayer*, and where his midnight arrest took place (Matt. 26:36–56; Mark 14:32–52; Luke 22:39–53; John 18:1–14). The location of this site is believed by many to have been identified by Queen Helena on her visit to Jerusalem (A.D. 326). Today olive groves owned by the Armenian, Greek, and Russian churches, and the Franciscans of the Latin Church, presumably mark this sacred site. Trees of great age are in the beautifully cared-for Franciscan Garden. To the modern visitor the proximity of the Jerusalem city walls and the Kidron Valley ravine, and the quiet of the olive trees with their deep shadows, especially after dark under the full Paschal moon, add to the record of the events which took place here an increased vividness. (See illus. 167, p. 224.)

Gezer (gē′zẽr) (Gazer twice in A.V.; I Macc., Gazera or Gazara), an ancient Canaanite city, known by archaeological investigation to have been first settled during the Late Chalcolithic period (33d century B.C.; see *IEJ* 5, 1955, pp. 240–245). It is to be identified with Tell ej-Jazar (Tell Gezer), situated in the Shephelah along the main N.–S. coastal road (Via Maris), guarding the juncture with the trunk road leading from Jaffa into the hills to Jerusalem, 18 m. NW. of the latter. Excavations were conducted by R. A. S.

Macalister from 1902–09, but though the material was carefully published, the poor excavation and recording methods employed make the historical value of the work nearly useless (*BA* 30, 1967, pp. 47–62). Current excavations undertaken by the Hebrew Union College Biblical and Archaeological School, beginning in 1964, have moved to correct this. At the beginning of the Early Bronze Age at Gezer (c. 3100 B.C.), caves were used as residences — Macalister's "Troglodyte Dwellings" (*PEQ*, 1937, pp. 67–78). The Early Bronze Age city was destroyed c. 24th century B.C., and after a short hiatus rebuilt at the beginning of the MB II period (c. 1850 B.C.). Dating to the Middle Bronze Age are a massive fortification wall, entranceway, and glacis (c. 16th century B.C.) and the enigmatic Gezer "high place" (16th–15th century B.C.), excavated by Macalister and consisting of a line of 10 monoliths running roughly in a N.–S. direction (see *BA* 35, 1972, pp. 34–63). During the Late Bronze Age, Gezer came under Egyptian control, the earliest reference to the city coming from a list of conquered cities of Tuthmosis III (*ANET*³, p. 242). Three rulers of Gezer are known from the Amarna Letters of the 14th century B.C. (*BA* 30, 1967, pp. 62–70; *PEQ*, 1965, pp. 140–143). The capture of Gezer (c. 1220 B.C.) is mentioned in Merenptah's "Hymn of Victory," the only Nile Valley inscription yet found to mention the name Israel (*ANET*³, p. 378). A large rock-hewn water tunnel at Gezer is dated to the Late Bronze Age (*BA* 32, 1969, pp. 71–78), and a Late Bronze Age tomb cleared in 1970 (dated c. 1400 B.C.) produced scarabs of Tuthmosis III and Amenophis II and III, zoomorphic figurines, a ceramic sarcophagus, and one of the earliest whole examples of sand-core molded glass to be found in Palestine (*BA* 34, 1971, pp. 104–108).

167. Gethsemane: Russian church in the garden.

168. Gezer Calendar.

The king of Gezer is reported to have been slain by Joshua (10:33, 12:12), but though the city lay in territory assigned to Ephraim, it was never occupied (Josh. 16:10; Judg. 1:29). The occurrence of Gezer in the list of Levitical cities (Josh. 21:21; I Chron. 6:67) may indicate that Gezer belonged to the Israelites under David (see Aharoni, *The Land of the Bible*, p. 272). It was certainly part of the realm of Solomon, as attested by the remark that the Pharaoh of Egypt (? Siamun) destroyed Gezer and gave it as a dowry when Solomon married his daughter (I Kings 9:16). Solomon rebuilt the city (I Kings 9:15, 17; note that it only states that he rebuilt Gezer—there is no direct link between this statement and the "chariot-cities" of v. 19!), a fact illustrated by the 10th-century B.C. casemate wall and 4-buttress gateway discovered during excavation (*IEJ* 8, 1958, pp. 80–86; *BA* 34, 1971, pp. 112 ff.). Another interesting piece of evidence from this period is the late 10th-century B.C. "Gezer Calendar" (*ANET*³, p. 320; see illus. 168). Remains of the 8th–7th centuries B.C. are present at Gezer, including a number of royal stamped jar handles (7th century), providing a context for a relief of Tiglath-pileser III of Assyria depicting an assault on *Gazru* (Gezer; *ANEP*², No. 369). The Persian period is represented by a tomb with silver vessels

of fine Phoenician workmanship, and a group of seal impressions of late Persian and early Ptolemaic date (*BASOR* 172, 1963, pp. 22–35). Simon Maccabeus captured Gezer in 142 B.C., constructed a fortified castle, and settled Jews there. Numerous Roman and Byzantine tombs are found in the area, but occupation of the tell had ceased by this time. See R. A. S. Macalister, *The Excavation of Gezer*, 3 vols., 1912; *BA* 30, 1967, pp. 34–70; 33, 1970, pp. 98–132; 34, 1971, pp. 94–132; W. G. Dever *et al.*, *Gezer*, vol. I (1964–66 seasons), 1970.
W. P. A.

Ghor, the. See JORDAN.

ghost, (cf. Ger. *geist*), the spirit of a man as distinguished from the physical body. The Bible speaks of giving up or yielding up the ghost when it refers to death, as of Abraham (Gen. 25:8), Isaac (Gen. 35:29), Job (3:11), Jesus (Matt. 27:50, A.V.; R.S.V. "his spirit"), Ananias and Sapphira (Acts 5:5, 10). Holy Ghost is used in the A.V. for the third person of the Trinity. See HOLY SPIRIT.

giant, an abnormally tall or powerful human being affected by endocrine abnormalities or certain environmental factors. (1) In ancient times giant Nephilim were considered demigods (Gen. 6:4; cf. A.S.V.), produced by the marriage of "sons of God" with "daughters of men," even as in Greek myths giant Titans were the offspring of Uranus (Heaven) and Gaea (Earth). Nephilim were "sons of Anak" (Num. 13:33), those formidable Anakim (Deut. 9:2) in comparison with whom the timid spies of Israel felt like grasshoppers. (2) Rephaim*, mentioned in Deut. 2:10 as giant Anakim (v. 11) were the aborigines of Philistia, S. Judaea, and Moab, where they were called Emims (v. 11); early Ammonite Zamzummims (v. 20); and early inhabitants of Bashan E. of the Jordan-Sea of Galilee section. The latter included the famous giant Og*, of iron bed (or sarcophagus) fame, one of the last of his race (Deut. 3:11, 13). Rephaim are mentioned (Gen. 14:5) as struck down by the "four kings." Arba, progenitor of Anakim and legendary founder of Hebron (Josh. 15:13), David's first capital, was one of the widespread race of Rephaim. Jerusalem's Rephaim Valley ("valley of the giants," A.V. Josh. 15:8, 18:16) immortalized an early struggle in the ravine, which begins SW. of the elevation separating it from the Valley of Hinnom and reaching S. toward Bethlehem. In the Valley of the Giants Philistines hid during the outlaw incidents of David's early ascendancy and cut him off from his favorite well (II Sam. 23:13–17; cf. I Chron. 11:15). Its slopes today are being rapidly covered by modern building developments outside the old walls of the capital. (3) In II Sam. 21:16–22 (A.S.V. marg.; cf. I Chron. 20:4–8) Raphah of Gath is the father of several Philistine giants, including Goliath* the Gittite (or "Lahmi the brother of Goliath") and three other tremendous men of this region who featured in stories of the early career of David. The popular story of Goliath is the classic O.T. tale of the giant foes of early Israel. The twelve-fingered, twelve-toed giant of I Chron. 20:6 is picturesque. Apocryphal allusions to giants are found in Wisd. of Sol. 14:6; Ecclus. 16:7, 47:4; Bar. 3:26–28.

Gibeah (gĭb′ē-*ȧ*) (*gibeah*, "hill"). (1) The early home (I Sam. 10:26) and capital of Saul*, and first political center of Israel, located in the territory of Benjamin 4 m. N. of Jerusalem on the side of the main road leading N. to Samaria, on an elevation 2,754 ft. above sea level, at the summit of the central range. It was for centuries a military watchpost looking across to Jerusalem (I Sam. 14:16). It was the headquarters of Saul vs. the Philistines, and the base of Jonathan (I Sam. 13, 14). It was 3 m. NW. of the religious center of Nob* (I Sam. 22:6 ff.). While Saul was ruling at Gibeah in the early 11th century B.C. Jebusites still held Jerusalem. After David captured their stronghold, Gibeah continued to be an outpost. A bloody chapter in its history, the hanging of seven sons of Saul, is recorded in II Sam. 21:6.

The Gibeah of Saul has been identified by W. F. Albright as Tell el-Fûl ("hill of beans"), where the ASOR unearthed evidence of the Biblical history of Saul's capital. The two-acre site, excavated in 1922 and 1933, showed 5 periods of occupation. Period I ("Pre-Fortress," 12th cen.) was found to have been destroyed by fire (Judg. 19, 20). The first of 4 fortresses (Period II, late 11th cen. B.C.), appears to have been the stronghold of Saul. Its sturdy polygonal masonry had evidently been erected not long before 1000 B.C., and allowed to deteriorate when the capital was moved to Jerusalem. The outer walls of the 170x155-ft. citadel were 8 to 10 ft. thick. These vestiges of Saul's fortress illustrate the typical Hebrew construction of that period—"casemated walls and separately bonded corner towers." An iron plow tip was discovered, possibly indicating the introduction of iron, the monopoly of the Philistines up to this time (see I Sam. 13:19–22; *AJA* 43, 1939, pp. 458–463). In the cellars of Saul's royal dwelling of 3,000 years ago, storage jars for wine, oil, and grain still held their contents when excavated. The fortress was later rebuilt on a smaller scale (Period IIIA, 8th cen.), burned, rebuilt again (Period IIIB), and destroyed c. 597 B.C. A final use of the tell is evident for the 4th–2d centuries B.C. (Period IV). See *AASOR* 4, 1924; 34, 1960; *BA* 27, 1964, pp. 52–64.

(2) A city in the hill country of Judah (Josh. 15:5–7), possibly to be identified with el-Jeba, near Bethlehem. (3) Geba of Benjamin, built by Asa (I Kings 15:22). Also called Gibeath-elohim (I Sam. 10:5), site of a Philistine garrison. Sometimes identified with Gibeah of Saul, it is probably Jeba, 2 m. N. of Tell el-Ful. M. S. M./W. P. A.

Gibeath (gĭb′ē-ăth) (Josh. 18:28), a town perhaps the same as the Gibeah of Saul.

Gibeon (gĭb'ē-ŭn) ("a hill"), one of the cities of the Hivites ("Horites") (Josh. 9:17, 11:19), identified with the mound of el-Jib, 8 m. N. of Jerusalem. Its people deceived Joshua (9:3 ff.) into making a covenant with them, thus precipitating an attack on Gibeon led by the king of Jerusalem (10:1–5), and Joshua's victory over the 5 Amorite kings (10:6 ff.). Gibeon was allotted to Benjamin (18:25) and named a Levitical city (21:17). There, during David's reign, Abner was defeated, assuring David's accession to the throne (II Sam. 2:12–17); Amasa died at the hands of Joab (20:7–10); and 7 of Saul's descendants were sacrificed to end a famine (21:1–9). In the early days of Solomon's reign, Gibeon was a cult center for Israel (I Kings 3:4–5; II Chron. 1:3, 13; cf. I Chron. 16:39–40, 21:29). The prophet Hananiah came from Gibeon (Jer. 28:1). After Jerusalem fell in 587 B.C., Ishmael, the assassin of Gedaliah, was caught at Gibeon and his captives released (Jer. 41:12, 16). Gibeonites were among those who returned after the Exile (Neh. 7:25; see Ezra 2:20) and helped to rebuild Jerusalem's walls (Neh. 3:7).

Archaeological work at el-Jib was conducted from 1956–62 by J. B. Pritchard for the University of Pennsylvania. The site was first occupied in the Early Bronze Age, coming to an end when destroyed by fire. Tombs, cut into bedrock during MB I (21st–20th cen. B.C.), showed re-use during MB II B (17th cen.) and LB II A (14th cen.). No remains were found which can be dated to the time of the Hebrew Conquest. Gibeon was resettled c. 1200 B.C., encircled by a wall, and reached its peak of prosperity during the 8th and 7th centuries B.C. Two water systems have been excavated, the first a rock-cut tunnel (c. 10th cen. B.C.), the second a large circular recess cut out of the rock (last used early 6th cen. B.C.). From the latter came 56 inscribed jar handles, 27 of them bearing the name of the city of Gibeon (Pritchard, *Hebrew Inscriptions and Stamps from Gibeon*, 1959). A 7th-century B.C. winery was also cleared, yielding presses, jars, etc., and 63 bell-shaped underground storage cellars. See Pritchard, *Gibeon: Where the Sun Stood Still*, 1962; *Archaeological Discoveries in the Holy Land*, pp. 139–146; *The Water System of Gibeon*, 1961; *The Bronze Age Cemetery at Gibeon*, 1963; *Winery, Defenses and Soundings at Gibeon*, 1964; *BA* 23, 1960, pp. 23–29; *VT, Supp.* 7, 1959, pp. 1–12; W. L. Reed in *AOTS*, 1967, pp. 231–243.

W. P. A.

Gideon (gĭd'ē-ŭn) ("hewer"), also called Jerubbaal ("contender against Baal"), son of Joash of the Manassite clan of Abiezer. Gideon delivered Israel from the Midianites (Judg. 6–8). His life story, preserved in the blending of at least two literary sources (J and E), describes the struggle in early Israel between the settled farmers and invading nomads, between Yahweh and the prevailing Baalism, and the reaction of Gideon to the social and religious influences of his day.

"Midianites, Amalekites, and the children of the East" from the Arabian peninsula (Judg. 6:3) overran central Palestine as far west as Gaza in search of water, food, and plunder (Judg. 6:4–6). Many of the Israelite homesteaders hid for safety in mountain caves and dens (6:2). To preserve his father's scant crops from the invaders, Gideon threshed the grain secretly in a wine press with a hand flail (Judg. 6:11). Such intolerable conditions aroused in Gideon a social concern for his fellows (Judg. 6:15).

Gideon was also stirred by deepening religious zeal. When Israel settled in Canaan, the idolatrous Baal practices associated with fertility were adopted by the Israelites from their neighbors; and this departure from Yahweh was blamed for their misfortunes (Judg. 6:1, 7–10). In spite of opposition, Gideon purified his own immediate family environment of Baalish practices and paraphernalia (Judg. 6:25–32) and revived faith in Yahweh. His strong social and religious motives made Gideon an effective leader. By eliminating the fearful and the less alert, he reduced the 32,000 who responded to his call to 300 men, who attacked the Midianite camp in the Jordan Valley (Judg. 7:1–8). The panic that followed was a victory for faith and an example of applied psychology (Judg. 7:16–22). The neighboring tribes responded to Gideon's call for help (7:23). Ephraim on the south blocked many of the Jordan fords, took several sheikhs captive, and much plunder (Judg. 7:24–8:3). The 300 men "faint yet pursuing" followed the Midianites beyond the Jordan, where Gideon captured and punished two of their "kings" (Ps. 83:11) for their murder of his brothers; they penallized the towns of Penuel and Succoth for refusing to give them food (Judg. 8:4–17).

Gideon refused to become king of all Israel, preferring to return to his village (Ophrah), his family, and his farm (Judg. 8:22–32). The ephod of Judg. 8:27 appears to have been a cone-shaped object made from the golden earrings taken by the Abiezrites from the Midianites and set up by Gideon in Ophrah, and apparently had associations with Baalism of which the later editor did not approve. Gideon died at a "good old age" and was buried in the sepulcher of his father in Ophrah (8:32).

Gideon demonstrated the former power of the Lord (Judg. 6:7–9) to rally Israel and unite them against the oppressor (Isa. 9:4), something the local Baal cults never did. His public spirit, daring, modesty, and good temper made him a brilliant personality.

gier eagle (jēr'ē'g'l), a bird referred to in Lev. 11:18, Deut. 14:17 A.V.; more accurately "vulture."*

Gihon (gī'hŏn) ("a bursting forth"). (1) One of the four branches of the river of Eden, said to have encompassed "the whole land of Ethiopia" (Gen. 2:13). (2) The intermittent Spring Gihon, which constituted the main water supply of the most ancient Jerusalem, situated in the Kidron Valley, below the

Eastern Hill (Ophel), immediately E. of what became "the City of David" (Millo). Gihon, also known as "The Virgin's Fount" ("or 'Ain Sitti Miriam"), together with En-rogel* Spring a bit farther S., determined the site of Jerusalem. The first human occupants of the land near Gihon must have been shepherds watering their flocks. At an early date (possibly c. 2000 B.C.) Jebusites living in what later became Jerusalem protected their women water carriers by having them stand on a platform behind the bastioned height above the Kidron and let their skin or pottery containers down a 40-ft. shaft cut through the rock (now called "Warren's Shaft," from its modern discoverer). The shaft ended in a cave reservoir into which the spring waters ran through a horizontal tunnel driven back c. 36 ft. W. and 25 ft. N. of the fountain in the valley. With jars filled, the women could walk up a sloping ramp into

169. Spring Gihon (Virgin's Fount).

the sheltered area of the city. It may have been up this shaft that General Joab, when his master David and the main troops were lurking in the valley near the spring, made his doughty entrance into the Jebusite city (II Sam. 5:8; I Chron. 11:6). Those who do not accept Warren's Shaft as the entry propose the funnel-like entrance to the cave reservoir which has an E. exit in the hill above the Spring Gihon.

There appear to have been an upper and a lower spring at Gihon; Hezekiah* walled off the upper (II Kings 20:20) when he dug his famous tunnel, 1,777 feet through rock, to conduct the city water supply to the safe Pool of Siloam* during Sennacherib's* approach to Jerusalem (701 B.C.). (See WATER; GEZER.) Remains of a small water tunnel—previously constructed, possibly by Solomon or David, but sometimes claimed for Hezekiah (Isa. 22:11)—ran outside the city wall from S. of the Spring Gihon and entered the "Old Pool of Siloam" near "The King's Garden."

Many historic events took place at or near the Spring Gihon. From the bastions above it Jebusites hurled down vain taunts at David's men (II Sam. 5:6). Beside its almost sacred waters Solomon was anointed king, while the aged David remained in his palace. Nathan the prophet, Zadok the priest, and "all the people," witnessed the picturesque ceremony (I Kings 1:33–45).

Gilboa (gĭl-bō'*ă*), a mountain ("mountains" II Sam. 1:21) forming the NE. spur of Mt. Ephraim and guarding a key pass from the Plain of Esdraelon* or Valley of Jezreel to the Jordan at an elevation of 1,698 ft. Although its W. slopes are gentle enough for pasture, Gilboa's eight miles afford rough terrain for such battles as Saul's against the Philistines (I Sam. 28:4). The chief Biblical allusions to Gilboa are in connection with the death of Saul and his three sons (II Sam. 1:6; I Chron. 10:1, 8). The mountain was cursed by David in a lament for the loss of Jonathan and his kin (II Sam. 1:21). Towns adjacent to Mt. Gilboa include Jezreel, Shunem, and Beth-shan (guarding its SE. limits), to whose walls the body of the vanquished Saul was affixed.

Gilead (gĭl'ē-*ăd*) ("hard, firm"). (1) A son of Machir and grandson of Manasseh (Num. 26:29 f.; Josh. 17:1). (2) The father of the mighty Jephthah* (Judg. 11:1). (3) A son of Michael, a Gadite (I Chron. 5:14). (4) An iniquitous city near Mizpah (Hos. 6:8). (5) The rugged, scenic, highland grazing-ground—in certain areas—grain-producing region of the Jordan situated S. of the River Yarmuk and N. of the Arnon River, with gorges of the Jabbok* (Zerqa) running through its center, down canyons of weird beauty to the Jordan, its W. boundary. Within Gilead lay Heshbon and Mt. Nebo 2,644 ft.). The well-watered tablelands appealed to the Gadites and Reubenites as suitable for their flocks, and they were allowed by Moses to stake claims here in E. Palestine rather than W. of the Jordan (Josh. 13:8–11). At the time of Israel's advance to Canaan, Sihon, King of the Amorites, gave them trouble (Num. 21: 21–24).

In the division of territory among Israel's tribes, Gad was given Gilead S. of the Jabbok, and the half tribe of Manasseh land N. of it (Josh. 13:24–31). Gilead produced sturdy trees, and was famous for its medicinal balm* (Jer. 8:22, 46:11), which was in the camel cargo of the Midianite traders when they took Joseph from the Dothan Plain on their way to Egypt (Gen. 37:25). Picturesque incidents that took place in Gilead include the dramatic reconciliation of Jacob and Esau at the Jabbok (Gen. 32:22 ff.); the touching farewell of Laban and his nephew Jacob (Gen. 31:45–48); the revolt of Absalom based in Gilead (II Sam. 17:26); the rule of Ish-bosheth (II Sam. 2:9); the harboring of David (I Kings 2:7); and oppressions by Aramaeans ("of Damascus") and Ammonites, denounced by Amos (1:3, 13). Jephthah, a judge of Israel, was a man of Gilead (Judg. 11); as was the prophet Elijah (I Kings 17:1).

Gilgal (gĭl'găl) ("circle of stones," or "rolled away"), the name of several towns mentioned in the O.T., all probably having circles of sacred stones, cromlechs. (1) Gilgal SE. of Jericho,* between that city and the Jordan, where Israel's twelve symbolic stones were set up (Josh. 4:1–9, 20), and where Joshua's first camp was pitched in W. Palestine (Josh. 4:19, 5:10). From this Gilgal spies were dispatched to Jericho. Numerous incidents in

Joshua's conquest of Canaan occurred at Gilgal (whose location has not yet been proved by archaeological examination) (Josh. 5:2–9, 9:6, 10:6). Some authorities believe that this Gilgal, along with Mizpah and Bethel, was on the annual circuit of Samuel the prophet (I Sam. 7:16); others believe it was the Gilgal between Shechem, Samaria, and Bethel; see (2). At Gilgal Saul saw "all the people" confirm his kingship (I Sam. 11:15); and there, because he had presumed on Samuel's prophetic prerogatives (I Sam. 13:4–15), he forfeited the kingdom. A sanctuary of Yahweh at Gilgal in the period of the Judges later became a place of debased religion and was denounced by Hosea (4:15, 9:15, 12:11), by Amos (4:4, 5:5), and by Micah (6:5). Here also David was welcomed after Absalom's death (II Sam. 19:15, 40). (2) An important town in SW. Samaria, with a sacred place, the basis of whose influence is not known. The school of the prophets that centered in Elijah and Elisha (II Kings 2:1–4, 4:38) is thought by some to have been at this Gilgal.

The several other O.T. Gilgals have too little identification to warrant discussion here.

girdle. See DRESS.

Girgashites (gûr′gȧ-shīts), one of the seven peoples whose eradication from Canaan was promised to Abraham (Gen. 15:21; cf. Deut. 7:1), and whose delivery into the hands of Israel is attributed to Joshua (Josh. 3:10, 24:11). Nehemiah (9:8) confirms God's honoring of this covenant. Little is known of the Girgashites. "The Girgasite," listed as a son of Canaan (Gen. 10:16), is the same as the Girgashite in the genealogical list of I Chron. 1:14.

Gittith (gĭt′ĭth), a musical term used in the titles of Ps. 8, 81, 84; the feminine form of the Heb. word for "Gittite" (inhabitant of Gath), which may refer to a musical instrument characteristic of Gath, or may derive from a Heb. word for "winepress." The Psalms named above are "vintage songs," possibly sung at the Feast of the Tabernacles. "Gittith" may be a reference to "The March of the Gittite Guard."

glass. See MIRRORS.

gleaning. See FARMING.

glede (glēd) (*Milvus milvus*), the common European kite bird (A.V. and A.S.V. Deut. 14:13).

glory, splendor of a very high degree; also used of those qualities or facts which cause the splendor. Various applications of the word include the following. (1) Visible appearance, both of persons and of things. Examples: the face of Moses (Ex. 34:29–35) after the "glory" of God had been indirectly disclosed to him on Sinai (Ex. 33:19–23); the representation of the divine as "seen" by Ezekiel (1:1–28, especially 26–28); the angel who brought to the shepherds the news of the birth of Christ (Luke 2:9); the "transfiguration" of Christ (Matt. 17:2) and the manner of his revelation to Saul of Tarsus (Acts 22:6–11); the body of the future life (Phil. 3:21); the New Jerusalem of John's vision (Rev. 21:10, 11, 23). (2) Intrinsic excellence of qualities and character, especially true of God, though not exclusively so (cf. Prov. 4:9). Frequently when the glory of God is spoken of in this sense, there is included its manifestation or expression. Thus the glory of God is both in what He is, in Himself, and in His activities, creative, providential, and redemptive, in nature and history. Christ supremely reveals God's glory by the grace and truth which were his (John 1:14, 2:11, 17:4, 5, 22) and by what he does for men (II Cor. 3:7–11). (3) Possessions—material, intellectual, and spiritual—of a man or of a nation. A man's soul (Ps. 16:9), his wealth (Ps. 49:16), his reputation (Prov. 3:35; cf. John 8:50), his Christian experience (Phil. 2:16, 3:3), his Christian service (I Thess. 2:20), are all spoken of as his glory. See the meaning of "Ichabod" in I Sam. 4:21, 22, and cf. Dan. 4:19–37, 5:17–31. (4) The act of recognizing God's majesty, power, and worth through worship and praise, and the act of seeking to carry out His will in personal character and in the service of others, are spoken of as giving God glory (I Pet. 4:11; Rev. 14:7, 19:7; cf. Ps. 29:9; Phil. 2:11). By contrast, "vainglory" is the act of self-boasting or of seeking for oneself the praise of others (Jer. 9:23, 24; Matt. 6:2; Eph. 2:8, 9; Jas. 4:16).

E. L.

gnat, identified by some as the mosquito, by others as a species of *Culex*, a hairy, bloodsucking insect. The picture of a man "straining at a gnat" but swallowing a camel (A.V. Matt. 23:24) is more accurately rendered by R.S.V., "straining out a gnat." The phrase holds up to ridicule the man who scruples at the inconsequential but violates major moral issues.

Gnosticism, a religious movement in early Christian times which claimed that salvation came through knowledge ("gnosis") of one's true self as explained in a myth revealed by a savior (usually Jesus). The importance of the movement lies in its claim to be the true Christianity, understood only by those "by nature saved" and in the stimulus it provided in the development of theology. Only a few adherents called themselves Gnostics or were so called; generally they were given labels from the names of the leading teachers, such as Simon Magus (*q.v.*), Basilides, Marcion, Valentius, etc. To know the myth of the particular sect (usually traced back through one of the apostles to Jesus after his resurrection) meant to be free from the evil world and especially from the evil "flesh;" the notion of matter as evil is present only in the more philosophical systems. In short, one's true existence was that of a divine spark imprisoned here below but destined to escape above. Meanwhile one could follow either of two paths. One could seek to triumph over the flesh either by extreme asceticism, the road of denial, or by total experience, thus rejecting moral demands (such as those of the O.T.) as derived from a creator-god inferior to the true Father. In most instances Gnostic teachers denied the reality of the Incarnation, either by the claim that Jesus, merely seemed to suffer and die or by the separation of the Christ-power from the man Jesus.

In most Gnostic systems there is a significant concern with the O.T. as a problem and with Jesus as a revealer misunderstood by most disciples. This concern suggests that there is a close relation between Gnosticism and heterodox Judaism and Christianity, though undoubtedly Gnostic teachers made use of philosophical language and of Hellenistic-oriental mythology.

The most difficult question about Gnosticism concerns its origin and development. It is difficult to see that Gnostic ideas are reflected in Paul's letters to the Corinthians and the Colossians (also Ephesians), as some critics have held; but many ingredients of later systems were present in the communities. Their presence made the task of the Church's theologians more difficult, and the Gnostic emphasis on "knowing" is still present, in attenuated form, in the works of Clement and Origen.

Conflicts with Gnostic teachers gave impetus to the crystallization of Christian doctrine concerning the unity of God, the unity of Jesus Christ, the unity of scripture, and the importance of the apostolic succession and of apostolic formulas of faith. By the middle of the third century the victory was largely won. See GOSPEL OF THOMAS.

R.M.G.

goad, a pole, sometimes 9 ft. long, fitted at one end with a sharp spike or metal prong, carried in one hand by a plowman to prick the oxen, while he guided the plow with the other. See Acts 9:5. In the period of the Judges, before arms were available, Shamgar, son of Anath, slew "six hundred men" (3:31) with his ox goad. Before the period of the Monarchy Israel had to rely on the metal monopolists, the Philistines, to sharpen goads (I Sam. 13:21). Words of the wise were considered goads to right conduct (Eccles. 12:11).

goat, a member of the large sheep family, the *Caprinae* section of the *Bovidae*, or hollow-horned ruminants (chewers of the cud), and appearing in Scripture in various Hebrew words, translated "he-goat," "she-goat," "young goat," "satyr," and "hairy goat." The Palestine goat is the *Capra hircus*. Goats can be tended along with sheep, but not bred with them; and often are separated for milking, feeding, and herding, hence Christ's parable (Matt. 25:32 f.). The male goat's horns differ from those of the ram; his odor is stronger. A goat's energy is greater than that of the sheep, which prefers lower pasturage and soft grasses rather than the heights to which the nimbler goat leaps, content with rough herbage. Goats usually are in forefront of the flock (Jer. 50:8). The poorest Palestinian family usually had at least one goat. Children carried kids in their arms, together with wisps of grass for food. Rich men in O.T. times measured their wealth in terms of goats (and other animals), like Nabal with his thousand goats (I Sam. 25:2). The uses of the goat, whether by tent-dwelling patriarchal families, or villagers living in houses of mud or stone, were diversified. This cheap but valuable animal provided sometimes as much as 3 qts. of milk per day, and the popular sour-milk delicacy leben; meat (Lev. 7:23); hair for weaving into tent fabric (Ex. 26:7) and coarse garments (Num. 31:20); skins for clothing (Heb. 11:37); filling for pillows (I Sam. 19:13); horn vials for oil; offerings for the Tabernacle (Ex. 25:4); material for Israel's sacrifice in worship*

170. Goat in Judaean Wilderness.

(Lev. 4:22–26; cf. Heb. 9:13 f.). The killing of a kid was—and still is among rural Palestinians—a gesture of hospitality (Luke 15:29). The wild goat is common on lonely cliffs above the Dead Sea, as at En-gêdi (I Sam. 24:1 f.), whose name means "well of the wild goat." The satyrs referred to in Isa. 13:21 (cf. 34:14) may have been wild goats or other wild beasts.

For scapegoat, see AZAZEL; ATONEMENT, DAY OF.

God. The usual name for the supreme power in the universe, the source of all other existences, the controller of the creative process, the moving influence in the pattern followed by history, and the object of man's highest reverence and aspiration. Many believe that the reality of such a God is a demand of the pure reason. Most of the great religions, especially the Jewish and the Christian, teach that God is known only as He reveals Himself, and that the organ of this revelation is faith. If the Scriptures be regarded as a record of this revelation, then we must regard it as progressive; there is a profound difference between the God of the Book of Judges and the God of the Gospel of John.

In the earlier books of the O.T. several words are used to designate God, among them *El** or *Elohim*, indicating vital power. This word is used in the first creation narrative (Gen. 1), and is common throughout the Pentateuch. It is sometimes used in compounds, as in *El-elyon* ("the most high God," Gen. 14:18–22) and *El* Shaddai* ("the Almighty God," Gen. 17:1). The prophets commonly use *Yahweh* for God, Englished sometimes as Lord, sometimes as Jehovah, the latter being a hybrid form which should be written *Yahweh* (YHWH). According to Ex. 3:13 f. the name *Yahweh* originated in the revelation of God to Moses; it there appears as the so-called imperfect tense of the verb "to be," and is rendered accordingly, "I am that I am." That is to say, God is One Who exists and Who can never cease to exist. The claim of Ex. 3:13 f., however, represents only one tradition, the so-called Priestly (P). A different tradition, the so-called Jahwist (J), makes the name a great deal earlier than Moses (see Gen. 4:26, 12:8, 26:25). What Moses learned at the burning bush was the complete dependability of this *Yahweh*, the certainty that He will carry out His agreements. *Yahweh* is One Who can be relied upon; He is utterly trustworthy. He is not fickle, like the gods of other nations; He is the same yesterday, today, and forever.

This was the God who had called Abraham (Gen. 12:1 f.). He was the God Whom the early Hebrews thought of as their own national God and special guardian, without disputing the right of other peoples to have gods of their own. (See Josh. 24:14 f.) It was the great prophets who put into the name *Yahweh* its universal significance, and who saw in the God of Israel the God of the whole universe. This extension of God's dominion was due to the prophetic insight into His character. The more the prophets were brought to realize what God was in Himself, the more they realized that ultimately everything went back to Him. Nothing could be independent of the power and purpose of the everlasting God—"the Eternal."

This very exaltation of God, however, gave rise to a tendency to put Him farther and farther away from men. His greatness limited His accessibility. Hence the necessity of devising means both whereby men could approach "the awful and august God," and whereby this God could disclose Himself to men. Hence angelic messengers and elaborate priestly ceremonies. There had always been these devices in Israel, as among most other peoples, but they greatly increased according as God's "holiness"* was held to imply His complete "separation" from all that was earthly and human. Israel had long had a doctrine of the Spirit of God (see HOLY SPIRIT), which provided for the approach of God to man and of man to God, but the priestly and legalistic mind could not be content with this. Later Judaism, with its complicated system of worship and excessive glorification of the Law (as in Ps. 119), assumed God's remoteness, although there were "the quiet in the land" who realized God's "nearness."

According to the Christian view, the gulf between man and God is bridged by Jesus* Christ, who partakes of the nature of both. He is both Son of God and Son of Man. This implies that God is self-revealed in Jesus Christ, consequently that the qualities of God's character and the nature of His purpose are fully seen in him. The great terms of the O.T., such as righteousness, kindness, grace, longsuffering, compassion, and holiness, take on a deeper significance when they are read in the light of Christ as God's living Word. God is therefore not only the source of creation, and the guiding power in history; He is also "the God and Father of our Lord Jesus Christ" (I Pet. 1:3), hence the God of redeeming love and the power Who seeks to make all men His sons (John 1:12, 13), a household of faith and a habitation of God in the Spirit (Eph. 2:19). These terms, Father, Son, and Spirit, all applied to God and expressing some form of His nature and activity, were eventually brought together in the doctrine of the Trinity. See INCARNATION; MONOTHEISM; POLYTHEISM; REVELATION; WORSHIP.

E. L.

godlessness, the state of being without a god, and therefore impious and wicked. The idea is frequent in the Scriptures. In Job 8:13 the word is in effect defined. This verse is an example of Hebrew parallelism: the thought in one line is repeated in the next, with slight verbal changes. The phrase "all that forget God," in the first line of the verse, is equated with "the godless man" (A.S.V.) in the second. To forget God is to live and act without any reference to God, as regards either His existence or His will and purpose. This is "the godless man," though the Heb. word thus rendered in Job could also be rendered "hypocrite." Luther used this rendering in his German Bible. The word therefore means more than "atheism." The godless man does not necessarily deny the existence of God: it is his complete indifference to God that constitutes his godlessness (see Job 13:16, 27:8, 36:11–14). Actually he *believes* that God exists, but his belief does not affect him.

In Deut. 6–8 "forgetfulness" of God is described at length, and we see there exactly what is meant by "godlessness" and why it involves the idea of "hypocrisy." Jesus' scathing indictment in Matt. 23 is uttered against men who ostensibly believe in God, but who deny Him in all their acts: hence he calls them "hypocrites," literally "play-actors," or "pretenders." Similarly with Paul in Rom. 1:18–2:29; Paul here speaks of those who "knowing God, glorified him not as God" (1:21), and "refused to have God in their knowledge" (1:28), and knowing what God commands do it not, but do rather the contrary (2:17–23). Those who say "Lord, Lord," but do not the Lord's will, are not merely ungodly; they are the really "godless" (Matt. 7:22; cf. 25:31–46). E. L.

godliness is the quality of life and experience that arises from faith in God and obedience to His will. The word itself occurs chiefly in the later epistles of the N.T., namely, I and II Timothy, Titus, and II Peter. But, as in the case of "godless," the same idea is expressed by other words, such as righteousness, sanctity, and God-fearer (cf. I Tim. 6:11). Godliness is more than mere formally correct behavior. Many who scrupulously observed the requirements of the ceremonial law were still without true godliness. The prophets frequently affirmed this (Isa. 1:10–20; Amos 5:21–24), and Jesus did later

(Matt. 5:20). Paul speaks, in I Tim. 3:16, of "the mystery of godliness." He is not saying that godliness itself is a mystery; the "mystery" he refers to is the means by which true godliness is made possible. For Paul, this means is Christ; godliness comes to pass according as the purpose for which Christ lived and died is fulfilled. It is "profitable" not only for this life but for the next (I Tim. 4:8; cf. 6:3–7). According to Peter, godliness includes more even than "holy living": it includes as well that faith and devotion which is expressed in holy living, and that goal at which the holy living is aimed (II Pet. 3:11–13). E. L.

godly is usually the adjectival form of "godliness,"* but there are exceptions. The godly man is the man who sets himself to understand and to do the will of God. A description of what in the O.T. is regarded as a godly man may be read in Ps. 32 (cf. Ps. 1). The term has a deeper meaning in the N.T., because it may include in its reference the new disclosure of God and His will that came with Jesus Christ (see II Tim. 3:12). This new disclosure is what makes possible that kind of "godly man" implied in "the Beatitudes"* (Matt. 5:3–12), and in Rom. 12 and I Cor. 13. The description of the conduct and character of the Roman centurion Cornelius, who was neither a Jew (by race) nor a Christian, is essentially O.T.: "a devout man ... that feared God ..., who gave much alms ..., and prayed to God always" (A.S.V. Acts 10:2). E. L.

Gog. (1) Eponymous founder of a Reubenite family (I Chron. 5:4). (2) Name used by Ezekiel (38:1 f., 14, 16, 18, 39:1, 11) to denote a leader of peoples who were enemies of Israel—a host of northern nations, whom scholars have tried to identify historically with Gyges, a King of Lydia* in Asia Minor, whose hordes reached Palestine; with Gagaia of the Amarna* Tablets; or with Scythian barbarians from the N. Possibly Ezekiel, calling Gog "chief prince of Meshech and Tubal," (38:2), used him only as a symbol, even as Rev. 20:8 connotes assailants of the Kingdom of God as "Gog and Magog." Gog in this case is associated with Magog (a son of Japheth) of Gen. 10:2.

Golan (gō′lăn), a city and its district (Gaulanitis) in Bashan, a section E. of the Sea of Galilee, in modern Syria. Golan (? Sahem el-Jōlân) was one of the three cities* of refuge (for accidental homicides) E. of the Jordan established by Moses (Deut. 4:43). It was assigned to Levites, "sons of Gershom," out of the territory of Manasseh (Josh. 20:8, 21:27; I Chron. 6:71).

gold, a metal known to people of Bible lands in very ancient times, and early recognized as precious (Num. 31:22; Ps. 19:10; Rev. 21:18). Gold was mined nowhere in Palestine, but imported from the Arabian Havilah (Gen. 2:11) and Sheba* (I Kings 10:22; Ps. 72:15); Ophir (I Kings 9:28), which has been variously placed in E. Africa, W. Arabia, or India; and Tarshish*—I Kings 10:22 may indicate the type of ship which brought the metal. Hebrews acquired gold as booty from Egypt (Ex. 12:35), Midian (Judg. 8:26) and Jericho (Josh. 7:21), as well as by the elaborate merchandising enterprises of Solomon* (I Kings 10:14–24). (See EZION-GEBER.) Gifts of gold from rich neighbors also came to the great Hebrew builder and developer (I Kings 10:25). His "golden cups" are quite as plausible as those still extant of the far earlier Sumerians (see SUMERIA).

Expert craftsmanship went into the fashioning of fluted vases and bowls of pure gold (such as were found in the "Royal" tombs of Sumerian Ur by Woolley) and into ornaments as charming as the golden leaves and 9 yds. of intricate gold metal ribbon in the headdress of Shubad from the same deposit, rarely surpassed in any age. See CUPS, illus. 104; and JEWELRY, illus. 219.

Gold is mentioned in the Bible as used for jewels (Ex. 3:22; Song of Sol. 1:10); idols (Deut. 29:17; I Kings 12:28; Isa. 2:20; Rev. 9:20); royal shields, although some other metal, or gold trim, seems more likely (I Chron. 18:7); money*, in post-Exilic times, after coinage had been devised by King Croesus of Lydia and well-developed in Persia—wedges, rings, or lumps of gold by shekels' weight (see WEIGHTS AND MEASURES) having been used before coinage was developed; the mercy seat of the Tabernacle (Ex. 25:19); and various portions of both this ancient Hebrew shrine and the Jerusalem Temple*, as well as their fixtures and candlesticks (Ex. 25:31–39; I Kings 7:48–50). Gold was one of three gifts brought to the infant Jesus at Bethlehem by Wise Men from the E. (? Arabia) (Matt. 2:11). Jesus alluded to gold coins (Matt. 10:9), of which he had very few and to which he attached slight value. The worth of Temple gold, he taught, lay only in the spiritual influence of the sanctuary of which it was a part (Matt. 23:16 f.). Cf. Peter's declaration of Acts 3:6.

Golgotha (gŏl′gō-thȧ). See CALVARY.

Goliath (gō-lī′ȧth), the 9-ft. Philistine giant* of Gath*, possibly a descendant of the giant Anakim. Recovered skeletons prove that men as tall as Goliath lived in Palestine. His slaying by David was one of the early exploits of the future king (I Sam. 17), and encouraged timid Israel to give chase to the dreaded foe. That David's victory had a religious aspect (I Sam. 17:43, 45) is borne out by the fact that the victor placed Goliath's sword in the sanctuary at Nob. (See also II Sam. 23:9–12; I Chron. 11:12 ff.) A second account of the slaying of Goliath (II Sam. 21:19, A.S.V.), states that it was Elhanan, another Bethlehemite, who killed Goliath. An editorial addition in the A.V. makes this read: "Elhanan . . . slew *the brother of* Goliath." See also I Chron. 20:5.

Gomer (gō′mẽr). (1) A son of Japheth, son of Noah (Gen. 10:2; I Chron. 1:5), father of an ancient people, possibly inhabitants of the N. country (Ezek. 38:6)—Cimmerians (Moffatt). (2) The wife of the prophet Hosea*.

Gomorrah (gō-mŏr′ȧ) See SODOM.

Good Friday, anniversary of Christ's crucifixion.

gopher wood, the material of which the Ark* was constructed (Gen. 6:14).

Goshen (gō′shĕn). (1) The section of NE.

Egypt where the hungry Jacob* family of 70 persons settled at the behest of the pharaoh's prime minister Joseph (Gen. 46:28 f.). To Goshen "in the land of Rameses" (47:11) Joseph drove in his chariot and gave welcome to the shepherds (46:28 f.). The description of Gen. 47:11 tallies with the known quality of this region (not called Goshen except in Scripture): excellent for grazing and certain types of agriculture, but unwanted by the pharaohs because of its distance from the Nile irrigation canals. Goshen was a valley 30 to 40 m. long, centering in Wâdī Tumilat, and extending from Lake Timsah to the Nile. It was the part of Egypt nearest Palestine, and the one from which the Exodus* naturally took place across the Sea of Reeds (not Red Sea, Ex. 15:4). On its S. edge were the cities Pithom and Succoth. SW. of it was On (Heliopolis), home of Joseph's wife, daughter of a priest (Gen. 41:45 f., 46:20). As G. Ernest Wright points out, it is not remarkable that thus far no Egyptian record of the Jacob tribe's sojourn in Goshen has been found; pharaohs often allowed hungry groups to settle in Egypt, therefore such an instance would hardly have been noteworthy.

(2) A section of S. Judah conquered by Joshua (Josh. 10:41, 11:16). (3) A town in Negeb or the Shephelah (Josh. 15:51).

Gospel; the Gospels. The two terms are best considered together, since the purpose of the Gospels is to describe the origin, the character, the processes, and the requirements of the Gospel. The Gospel is the provision which God made in Jesus Christ for the salvation and transformation of the life of mankind. It is the means whereby the true relation between God and man, disrupted by sin, might be restored. Divine-human reconciliation is through the Gospel, and the initiative in the Gospel is with God. It is God who sent the Son of Man "to seek and to save that which was lost" (Luke 19:10; John 3:16, 17; Rom. 5:8–11; I Cor. 15:55–57; II Cor. 5:14–19; Gal. 1:3–5; Eph. 2:4–10). The Gospel is the gift of the grace* of God for sinful men.

The Gk. word for "Gospel" is put into English as "evangel." What is called "evangelism" is therefore preaching or teaching or otherwise presenting the Gospel. The word means literally "good news." It is a message intended to rejoice the hearts of those who hear it. Jesus' quotation from Isa. 61:1 is often supposed to be the Gospel in essence, because the phrase "good news" occurs in it (Luke 4:16 ff.). But the Gospel is not in any one message or action of Jesus. The Gospel is Jesus Christ himself, in all that he represented and was, and in all that he accomplished through his death and resurrection. So far as any one brief statement of Scripture may be said to give us the Gospel, it is John 3:16, which declares that men under condemnation ("perishing") because of sin may find "eternal life" through faith in Christ as the "only begotten Son," whose presence in the world was a revelation of the holy love of God. He is "the one Mediator between God and men . . . who gave himself a ransom for all" (I Tim. 2:5, 6; cf. Matt. 20:28).

The four Gospels are to be understood accordingly. We have these Gospels because, before they were written, the Gospel itself, as described above, was already a living power in the world. The Gospels bear witness to the Gospel. Christ is the Gospel (see Rom. 1:16), and the Gospels served to make him known, as they do still. The story of how these Gospels were slowly constructed, especially those of Matthew, Mark, and Luke—known as the Synoptic Gospels because they follow so similar a pattern that they can be compared in an overall view ("synoptically")—is a long and complicated one, and involves many critical questions on which opinion is divided.The Gospels were written to meet the needs of the expanding Church. The Church of the earliest days had no written Gospels. It depended entirely on word-of-mouth testimony and the guidance of the Holy Spirit (see Matt. 28:18–20; cf. John 16:13–15). The first Christians became Christians not because they had documents to read, but because they heard the testimony of the Apostles (Acts 2:37–42). These first converts became, in their turn, witnesses to the same Gospel they had accepted (Acts 8:1–4, 18:24–28). The historical relation between the Gospel and the Synoptic Gospels is therefore approximately as follows: (1) the living fact of Christ himself, with his message, his ministry, his crucifixion, and his resurrection; (2) his acceptance by a little group of men (and women—see Acts 1:14), considerably larger, however, than the original Twelve (Acts 1:15; cf. Matt. 10:1–4; Luke 10:1, 17); (3) the Church as constituted in these first disciples; (4) the preaching of the disciples "in the power of the Spirit" (Acts 2:1–14), by which others came to repentance and faith (2:37–41); (5) the necessity of instructing these new believers in the facts of the Gospel and their significance (2:42); (6) the consequent preservation among men of these facts and meanings, but at the same time their modification, at least in "form," as they were spread by word of mouth; and finally (7) the putting of it all into writing at different times by different persons, a writing, however, which reflected not only the original Gospel facts, but also the "forms" which these facts assumed during the period of oral transmission and instruction.

This process accounts, at least in part, for the differences we find in the Gospels. All the Gospels bear a common testimony. They undeniably deal with the life, work, message, and sufferings of the same person, Jesus of Nazareth. Even a casual reading of the Gospels reveals that some omit what others contain: for example, only Matthew (2:1–23) tells of the visit of the Wise Men and of Herod's massacre of the Innocents; only Luke (2:40–52) tells of the visit of the boy Jesus to the Temple; Mark does not give the details of Jesus' Temptation recorded in Matt. 4:1–11 and Luke 4:1–13; the testimony of Jesus to John the Baptist as given in Matt. 11:7–19 is wanting entirely in Mark and is considerably modified in Luke, who gives it in 7:24–28, 31–35, and 16:16; only Luke (8:1–3) tells of the ministering women and of the Mary and Martha incident (10:38–42); only Matthew (25:31–46) gives the detailed account of the Last Judgment. There are often verbal differences in the account of the same incident or of the same teaching: for example, Matt. 7:1–5 compared with Luke 6:37–42; Matt. 7:16–20 compared with Luke 6:43, 44; Mark 3:23–27 compared with Matt. 12:25–29 and Luke 11:17–22; Mark 6:17–29 compared with Matt. 14:3–12 and Luke 3:19, 20; Mark 10:13–16 compared with Matt. 19:13–15 and Luke 18:15–17. The parables of the "talents" in Matt. 25:14–30 and of the "pounds" in Luke 19:11–27 are doubtless meant to be the same. Luke tells of a cure of leprosy in 5:12–16, and he tells in a different way in 17:11–19 of what was apparently the same cure. Some of the parables which for some reason only Luke records are especially suggestive: they include the parable of the Unjust Steward (16:1–12), of Dives and Lazarus (16:19–31), of the Prodigal Son (15:11–32), and of the Good Samaritan (10:29–37). We can hardly be too grateful to Luke for preserving these. Similarly with some of the miracles which only Luke records: they include the cure of the afflicted woman (13:10–17); of the dropsiac (14:1–6); the restoration of the widow's son (7:11–17); the healing of the high priest's servant (22:49–51); and the postresurrection appearance to the disciples at Emmaus (24:13–35; cf. Mark 16:12 f., which, however, is part of the later composite addition to Mark which begins at 16:9).

The most systematic of the evangelists is Matthew. He brings together as "The Sermon on the Mount" (chaps. 5, 6, 7) a collection of the teachings of Jesus, probably derived from a document called "The Sayings." Little of this teaching is found in Mark. Much of it is found in Luke, except that in Luke the "sayings" are scattered throughout the account rather than gathered at one point. The material common to Matthew and Luke, but not Mark, is often called "Q" (from the German *Quelle* or "source"). Matthew also makes some classification of the parables, especially of "the parables of the Kingdom," as in chap. 13, and of "the parables of judgment," as in chap. 25. Matthew also brings together in chap. 23 much of Jesus' criticism of the scribes and Pharisees, which Mark hardly mentions, and which Luke records here and there.

A comparison of Mark and Matthew re-

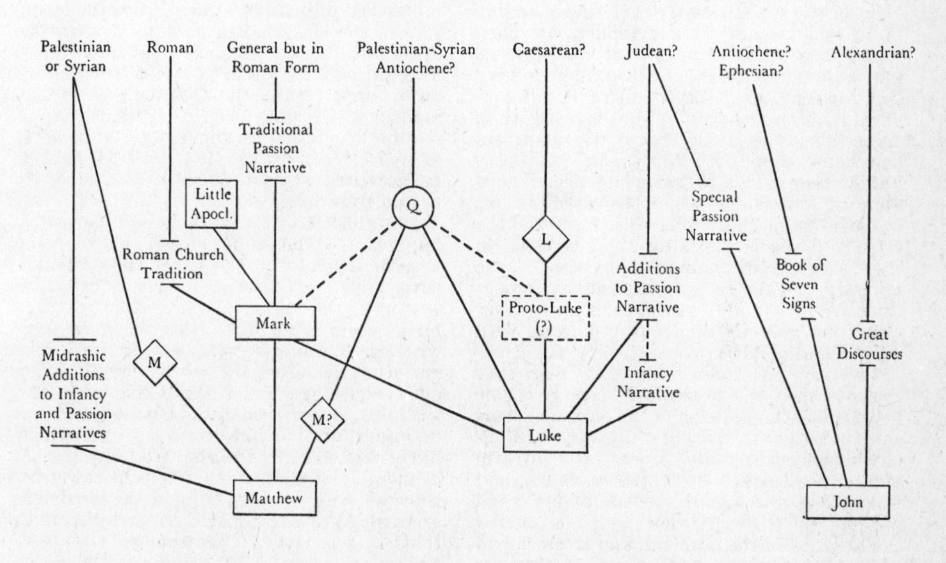

171. The Four Gospels. From *The Gospels, their Origin and Growth*, by F. C. Grant, Harper & Brothers, publishers.

veals that almost the whole of Mark is included in Matthew, but that there is also in Matthew, besides the "Sayings" and the criticisms of the Pharisees, a considerable amount of material not found in Mark. It seems probable that Mark drew from Peter most of his account of the ministry of Jesus. It is also probable that the Gospel of Matthew was compiled chiefly by the Church in Jerusalem, where Peter, James, and John were central (Acts 3:1 f., 4:1 f., 12:1 f.; cf. Gal. 2:9). The Jewish and ecclesiastical character of Matthew's Gospel is apparent (see 5:17 f.). This Gospel uses the word "church" twice (16:18, 18:17), and it occurs in no other Gospel. The compilers attached to it the name "Matthew," but the evidence that he was the disciple of that name is very slim indeed. Luke, the friend of Paul, compiled his account by a firsthand investigation, as he himself tells us (1:1–4). He doubtless had before him both Mark and Matthew, but he seems also to have had access to a separate document which he used as his basis; he is especially full in his account of the infancy of Jesus; he is deeply interested in the human and "humane" aspects of the ministry (see the parables and miracles mentioned above); and more than any other writer he tells us of Jesus' relations with women and children.

These are only a few hints of the facts that create what is known as "the Synoptic Problem"—the problem of the origin, authorship, constituent elements, differences, similarities, inconsistencies, processes of growth, etc., of the Gospels of Matthew, Mark, and Luke. The problem has been further complicated by a recent view which is offered as a solution of the problem, known as "form-criticism." As suggested above, it supposes that during the period preceding the final writing of the Gospels the message of Jesus and the incidents of his life were the basis of oral Christian testimony and instruction, given according to the necessities of time, place, and circumstances. These factors tended to determine the "form" of the testimony and instruction, and the "forms" tended by use to become permanent. When at last the Gospels were written, the material put on record was that which had already undergone this modification, rather than direct transcripts of the original.

This view seems to throw over the written Gospels an embarrassing uncertainty; and it does, if the only consideration is verbal exactitude. But we have to inquire into the motive and purpose of those who first "preached Jesus." That preaching had its immediate inspiration in the Resurrection. The Cross had seemed to put an end to all that Jesus had said and done (Luke 24:17–21). The Resurrection not only revived confidence, but it transformed the very meaning of the Cross; it invested the risen Christ with a significance which reached back over his entire life and work; it was the evidence of his "exaltation" to the right hand of God (Acts 2:33; cf. Phil. 2:5–11); in a word, it created in the hearts of the little band of Disciples a faith that in Christ God had indeed visited His people in a "mighty act" that was the promise of a universal salvation.

This is the faith that created the Church. It is the faith that the disciples at once began to proclaim. All their witnessing, whatever form it took, was motivated by the single purpose to present Christ as Lord and Saviour. When the Gospels were at last written, even if they showed such modifications as are referred to above, the Church of Jesus Christ, nurtured in this faith and committed to it, was already a reality in the world. Hence the important truth comes to light: no critical difficulties arising from the structure of the Gospels can possibly destroy the faith to which the Gospels were intended to bear witness. Christianity is not the result of an attempt to add the Gospels and to harmonize their differences; Christianity is, instead, the presupposition of the Gospels. It existed before they did; it is what led to their being written; it is what they exist to testify to and to propagate.

It is this that makes the Fourth Gospel so important. The differences between the Fourth Gospel and the other three are apparent. "John," as the author is called, is writing at the end of the 1st century, perhaps forty years after the other Gospels were written. His motive was not to write one more life of Jesus; the world already knew all it would ever know about that life. John wrote to declare who Jesus Christ *was*, what he *meant*, and how he came out of the very life of God in order to bring God into the life of men. John simply repeats in his own distinctive way the faith that inspired the original Apostolic preaching, and the faith that is everywhere present in the N.T. Epistles.

The Gospels, therefore, like the Church and like the Epistles, bespeak the prior fact of the Gospel. Criticism of the Gospels as literary documents must necessarily leave untouched the faith respecting Christ from which they sprang and to which they testify. See INSPIRATION; JESUS CHRIST; NEW TESTAMENT; REVELATION. E. L./R. C. D.

Gospel of Thomas, a collection of approximately 114 sayings ascribed to "Jesus the Living" and supposedly recorded by his disciple Didymus Judas Thomas. This work, entitled at the end "The Gospel according to Thomas," belongs to a library of Gnostic writings discovered about 1945 in a jar unearthed near Chenoboskion in upper Egypt. The library consists of thirteen leather-bound volumes which contain forty-nine works written in various dialects of Coptic during the 4th and 5th centuries. Among these works are treatises used by various Gnostic sects and a few "gospels" somewhat more closely related to orthodox Christianity; the gospels include those ascribed to Thomas and to Philip (see last portion of this article); the work which begins with the words "the Gospel of Truth" is not really a gospel.

The Coptic text of Thomas was published photographically by P. Labib in 1956; an improved text and a translation were published in 1959 by A. Guillaumont, H.-C.

Puech, G. Quispel, W. Till, and Yassah 'abd Al Masīh; a translation and a commentary were provided in 1960 by R. M. Grant, D. N. Freedman, and W. R. Schoedel.

(1) *Literary history.* After inspecting the Coptic text of Thomas, H.-C. Puech discovered that three papyri, found about sixty years ago at Oxyrhynchus in Egypt, really contained fragments of this work. Since they come from the third century, it is now possible to see that Thomas underwent editing as it was handed down; it seems to have become slightly more Gnostic. On the other hand, it must be remembered that early patristic quotations are very different from the Coptic version, and it may be that the process of editing is so complicated that we cannot trace it. Later, the Manichees liked the book, since it gave them a Gnostic Jesus.

(2) *Form.* The words of Jesus are presented as "secret," i.e., not known to the common tradition of the church. "Whoever finds the interpretation of them will not taste death" (Preface). The true interpreter will not cease seeking until he finds the hidden meaning; for all the sayings, including those uttered in Jesus' lifetime, according to the church's gospels, were spoken after his resurrection.

The literary (or pre-literary) forms in which the various words are cast are identical with those found in the four gospels, especially the three synoptics. They include parables, aphorisms, brief dialogues, and pronouncements beginning with "I." (The dog in the manger of Saying 102 is proverbial, as in Aesop's fables.) As in some parts of the synoptic gospels, a good many of the sayings seem to be linked by verbal association rather than by similarity of subject matter. And in Thomas we find reflections of the Semitic parallelism often encountered in the Bible. This feature is due either to an authentic Semitic source or to imitation.

It should also be observed how different this collection of secret sayings is from the church's gospels. Naturally there is no historical framework, for all the sayings come after the resurrection, and hence there are no miracles, no passion narrative; there is also no correlation with the Old Testament. Is it really a gospel at all? It speaks only of "secret words" or of the "mysteries of Jesus" (62) or of "the word of the Father" (79); only in the title added at the end does the word "gospel" appear.

(3) *Date and provenance.* The earliest references to Thomas occur about 230, when it is mentioned unfavorably by Origen and Hippolytus; the latter says that it was used by the Gnostic Naassenes, and therefore it must have existed somewhat earlier. We do not know how much earlier, however. It may have been written as early as 140, as some scholars hold; it may have been written a generation later.

The name Didymus Judas Thomas probably points toward Syria as the place of origin—or of editing, since the Greek fragment of the preface, while broken, does not contain enough space for all three names. The affinities with traditions and apocryphal books known to Clement of Alexandria (such as the gospels of the Hebrews and the Egyptians), and the existence of the Greek and Coptic versions in Egypt, may suggest an Egyptian origin instead.

(4) *Sources.* Many of the sayings in Thomas are very much like those in the four gospels, especially the synoptics. It is a question whether he derived synoptic-type sayings from our written gospels or from oral traditions which they too reflect. Similarly, when he uses sayings also found in apocryphal gospels (1, 22, 37, 104; perhaps 12 and 61) he may be using either these books or their sources. But in some cases at least he probably uses the synoptic gospels.

We conclude that, like Gnostic interpreters, Thomas made use of the canonical gospels and of Gnostic materials. In spite of interesting textual variants, there is no reason to suppose that he gives us an earlier or a more reliable version of any saying of Jesus.

(5) *Environment and theology.* Some sayings can be traced back to a Jewish-Christian (though probably Gnostic) origin; for example, Jesus tells his disciples that after he departs they are to "go to James the Just, for whose sake heaven and earth came into existence" (12), and James was prominent in Jewish Christian thought. On the whole, however, Thomas is radically anti-Jewish. If circumcision were "profitable," men would be born circumcised (53); fasting, prayer, almsgiving, and dietary observances—the cardinal duties of Jews—are explicitly condemned (6, 14); Jesus will destroy the temple (71), since external rites are irrelevant (27).

The book is marked by an extreme Gnostic inwardness. The goal, and in part the present possession, of the true believer is the Kingdom, also called the Kingdom of Heaven or of the Father. This kingdom is not in heaven or (for that matter) in the sea (cf. Rom. 10:6–8); instead, it is within the Gnostic (cf. Luke 17:21) and the Gnostic is within it; he comes to it by knowledge of himself, i.e., of his true nature as a son of the Living Father (3). He enters it again because he has come from it (49), from the Light (50). In other words, Thomas has removed most of the eschatological element from Christian teaching; he substitutes the notion that the kingdom can be entered only when sexual distinctions have been overcome or obliterated (22). In this way one becomes like a child (37, 46). But women must become male in order to enter (114).

The doctrine of Christ is sometimes set forth in Christian terms, but he was not "born of woman" (15); he is the Son of the Living One (37) and is himself the Living One (52, 59). "I am the Light that is above all, I am the All; the All came forth from me and the All attained to me. Cleave wood, I am there; lift up the stone and you will find me there" (77). Even "God" is subordinated to Jesus. "Give what is Caesar's to Caesar, give what is God's to God, and give what is mine to me" (100; cf. Mk. 12:17 and paras.).

Another work which should be mentioned is the *Gospel of Philip*, an apocryphal treatise only partly in gospel form, ascribed to the evangelist or, more probably, the apostle

Philip and containing fragmentary discussions of the origin of mankind, the wickedness of the separation of woman from man, and the necessity for the reintegration of humanity (at least of Gnostics) by means of baptism, unction, eucharist, and sacred marriage (perhaps developed from the church's kiss of peace). Like the Gospel of Thomas (*q.v.*), with which it shares some apocryphal sayings, this work was found at Chenoboskion in upper Egypt. The Coptic text was published photographically by P. Labib (*Coptic Gnostic Papyri in the Coptic Museum at Old Cairo*, I, Cairo, 1956, plates 99–134) and translated into German by H.-M. Schenke (*Theologische Literaturzeitung*, LXXXIV, 1959, 1–26).

Previously known only from a quotation by Epiphanius (c. 374) which is not found in our text, the book reflects a kind of Gnosticism principally Valentinian; the spiritual-eschatological idea of marriage and the allegorical exegesis of Philip are close to what Irenaeus and Clement relate about the Valentinians. On the other hand, the notion that Gnostics were formerly Hebrews resembles what Irenaeus ascribes to Basilides: "we are no longer Jews." Philip often explains biblical and Gnostic terminology by Hebrew and Syriac etymologies, though ultimately he believes that most of the theological language of Christianity is inadequately spiritual. Where he quotes sayings of Jesus he uses the gospels and apocryphal sources without distinction. The book was probably composed (in Greek) at the end of the second century or early in the third. The somewhat later Gnostic work called *Pistis Sophia* (42–44) regards Philip, Thomas, and Matthew (or Matthias) as the only true witnesses to the teaching of the risen Lord.

More explicitly Gnostic than Thomas, Philip seems to come from the same environment; it has no direct value for N.T. studies, though it provides new information about later Gnostic syncretism. R. M. G.

gourd, the fruit of any species of *Cucurbita*, or of the bottle gourd (*Lagenaria vulgaris* and varieties); any plant producing such fruit. This may have been the rapidly growing plant that shaded Jonah (4:6–10), although A.S.V. reads *Palma Christi*.

government, a word used in Scripture to express the royal authority and dignity resting upon the Messiah, who is fully competent to develop his Kingdom (Isa. 9:6, 22:21). "Government" A.V. II Pet. 2:10 is R.S.V. "authority," I Cor. 12:28 "administrators."

governor, a term used to designate any one of a variety of officials in Scripture whose differentiated functions, caught in the original by specialized Heb. and Gk. words, are lost in the A.V. word "governor."

Gozan (gō′zăn), a city on the River Habor, a branch of the Euphrates*; at the head of the Fertile Crescent arch, E. of Haran, NW. of Nineveh, Sennacherib's capital. One of the cities to which Assyrian forces deported the Israelites after the fall of Samaria (II Kings 17:6, 18:11, 19:12; I Chron. 5:26; Isa. 37:12).

grace, a favorable disposition on the part of God, usually without reference to any merit or desert in the object of the favor, and, especially in the N.T., even when the object is entirely lacking in merit or desert. The grace of God is therefore that quality of God's nature which is the source of men's undeserved blessings, in particular those blessings which have to do with their salvation from sin. There are variations from this central meaning, as in the word "comeliness" (cf. Jas. 1:11). The Gk. word is *charis*, which we see reflected in the English "charm," a pleasing manner of bearing, and in the English "charity," spontaneous helpfulness to the needy. Paul's frequent greeting "Grace to you!" (Rom. 1:7; I Cor. 1:3; II Cor. 1:2; Gal. 1:3) may be taken to mean "May you have joy and gladness!" but always with the thought that the source of the joy is God.

The idea of finding grace or favor in the eyes of God (or of men) is common in the O.T. It expressed the hope that one may be treated with kindness, or even with mercy* (Gen. 19:19; Ex. 33:13). In the N.T. the grace of God is not only fully disclosed by Christ, but Christ is himself its complete expression (Eph. 2:4–9). He is the chosen means whereby God shows His favor to sinful men: "where sin abounded, grace did abound more exceedingly" (A.S.V. Rom. 5:20). Christ is God's assurance to the rebellious that he seeks only their good, and will give of himself to the utmost to persuade them to receive it (II Cor. 8:9; cf. Eph. 1:3–10). The expression "The grace of our Lord Jesus Christ" is very common in the N.T. (Rom. 16:20), especially in benedictions (II Cor. 13:14; Gal. 6:18). It is to be taken in two different ways: the grace of Christ means not only his own personal attitude toward needy and sinful men; it means also that Christ is himself the sacrificial expression of grace.

To be in "a state of grace" is to know that one's relation to God is determined not by merit—"by the works of the law"—but by faith in Christ as the revealer of God's merciful love. This is the burden of Paul's testimony in Rom. 5 and 6. The Gospel is "good news," because it is the assurance of the grace of God (see Acts 20:24; cf. Luke 4:16–19). Men, says Paul, are "justified freely," or brought to forgiveness and reconciliation, "through God's grace" (Rom. 3:24). It is fundamental Christian teaching that salvation is a free gift, whose source is the undeserved favor, or grace, of God.

One of the important differences, however, between Roman Catholic and Protestant teaching concerns the method of the conveyance and appropriation of divine grace. The very idea of grace is a factor in these differences. In the Catholic view, the Church is regarded as the "depository" of grace and the sacraments as the "channels" through which it may reach the soul. Normally, the efficacy of the sacraments for this purpose depends on a properly constituted priesthood. The Protestant view fully recognizes the importance of the Church, and, in most cases, of the ordained ministry and of the sacraments, but it insists on the possibility of the "direct access" of the soul to God and His grace, expressed in the phrase "the priesthood of all believers." The implication is that the Holy Spirit, whose office it is to bring the grace of God to bear upon the souls of men, is not limited to any one organization or to any one group of men, much less to the use of any one man-made "form" or ceremony. See FORGIVENESS; SACRAMENTS. E. L.

gracious, having the qualities and characteristics of grace*. The word seldom occurs in the N.T.; examples of it are Luke 4:22 (A.V.) and I Pet. 2:3. It is, however, common in the O.T.; and except in Prov. 11:16 and Eccles. 10:12 is applied only to God, as describing His attitude toward men. No man can be "gracious" in the sense that God is. Even the disciplines and punishments God lays upon men express His graciousness, since their purpose is to win men from their evil ways (see Isa. 30:18–21). Frequently the graciousness of God means His mercifulness, although in the Psalms God is often described as both "merciful and gracious" (103:8), "gracious and full of compassion" (145:8), and "gracious and righteous" (112:8). That grace is righteousness tempered with mercy, was eventually elaborated by Paul in Romans. According to Paul, it was of God's gracious mercy in the gift of Christ that the possibility of a true righteousness came to men. The familiar blessing in Num. 6:24–26, beginning, "The Lord bless thee and keep thee" is an affirmation of God's graciousness. See LOVINGKINDNESS. E. L.

graft. See OLIVE.

grain, whose sifting is mentioned by Amos (9:9), is used here in a generic sense. Jesus referred to the very small "grain of mustard seed" (Matt. 13:31). Sown seeds of various sorts of grain gave Paul a figure to describe the resurrection* (I Cor. 15:35 ff.). See BARLEY; CORN; MILLET; RYE; WHEAT.

granary, a structure for storing threshed or husked grain, especially typical of the Egyptian Delta store-cities* in whose construction Hebrew slave labor played a part, like Rameses (Avaris, Zoan*). Egyptian carved reliefs and tomb models have left us accurate representations of granaries and their meticulous accountants. Portions of rich agricultural cities in Palestine were also given over to granaries, where wheat, barley, and other foods were stored in huge earthen jars, as at the Early Bronze Age Jericho*. Some of these jars, still containing grain, have been recovered by excavators. In early Palestine there were no barns for storing grain or housing animals, except allocated portions of the hillside home. Pits and abandoned cisterns made good storage places.

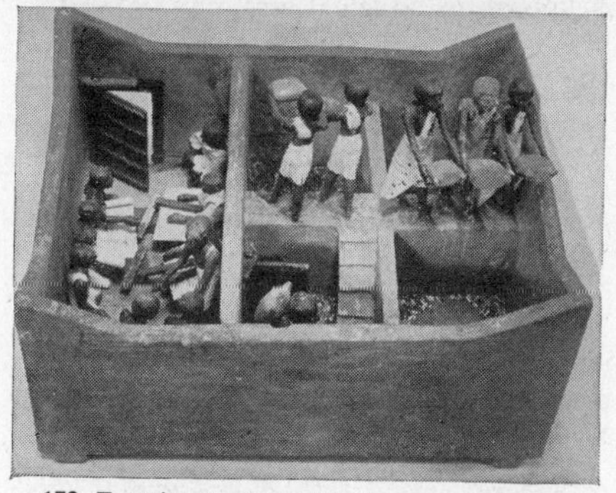

172. Egyptian tomb model of granary, showing scribes keeping account of filled sacks.

grape. See VINE.

grasshopper. See LOCUST.

grave. See ARCHITECTURE; BURIAL.

graven images. See IMAGE.

graving, engraving or carving "gold, or silver, or stone . . . by art and man's device" (Acts 17:29), with a sharp tool, in contrast to casting in a mold. Examples of using the graving tool are Aaron's making the golden calf (Ex. 32:4) and the works of the Hiram family of Tyre (II Chron. 2:14). Materials on which graving was done include onyx stones (Ex. 28:9), and gold for the high priest's head plate (Ex. 28:36). As motifs in the Temple decoration, cherubim, lions, and palms were "graven" (I Kings 7:36; II Chron. 3:7). Hebrews were adept in the gravers' art; yet see Ex. 20:4. Many artisans of the Middle East were proficient in carving cylinder seals (see SEAL) as small as a half inch high and a quarter inch in diameter, used for rolling over wet clay* tablets to make "signatures" on business contracts. Mesopotamia was especially adept in seal making. From pictorial representations on thousands of glyptic specimens recovered from a period of more than 3,000 years, we know more of the religious symbolism and iconography of the Tigris-Euphrates Valley than from any other source. Seals were of semiprecious stones.

greave (grēv), armor for the leg, usually extending from knee to ankle. Goliath wore metal greaves (I Sam. 17:6).

Grecia, a Biblical name for Greece, most prominently in Daniel's vision at Susa of the ram and the goat (Dan. 8:21, 10:20, 11:2).

Greece, in N.T. times usually called "Achaia"*; but cf. Acts 20:2: Paul "came into Greece." In Zech. 9:13 "Greece," listed as an adversary of the Jews, may be a later insertion in the text. The name Hellas, as used by the Greeks, meant all Greek settlements everywhere, not only Greece proper.

Greek culture and interpretation of life exerted a profound influence on Palestine in the great Hellenistic Period (333–63 B.C.) inaugurated by Alexander* the Great (356–323 B.C.), son of Philip of Macedon. The brilliant military genius of this pupil of Aristotle aimed to make a single community out of deadly rivals, East and West. A bridgehead of Hellenistic culture was built in the various empires which developed from his conquests. Jews who had adopted Hellenistic standards carried the young Christianity into the West ruled by the Roman Empire. Meanwhile Hellenistic culture left imposing architectural deposits in Bible lands, as at Jerash (see GERASA) and Samaria*, and supplied the language (Hellenistic Greek, Koine, "common" tongue) of the N.T. writings.

Greek, the language (of the Indo-European family) spoken by ancient Greeks and, in the common idiom, Koine, by Jews of N.T. times (Acts 21:37), as well as by the whole Mediterranean world for c. 6 centuries. The O.T.

had already been translated from Hebrew into Greek (the Septuagint; see BIBLE; TEXT) before the birth of Christ. The N.T. was written in Greek, parts of it based on some Aramaic sources now lost. The Greek language gave Paul and other early Christian propagandists a common language such as no other faith had ever had for its expansion. The Jewish Apostle to the Gentiles acknowledged his debt to the Greeks (Rom. 1:14). The Greek religious spirit influenced the Christian faith. The naïve anthropomorphism which Homer had made a common bond among all Greeks, the Eleusinian Mysteries of Demeter, the orgiastic rites honoring Dionysus, and the highly spiritual philosophies of Socrates, Plato, and Aristotle—all touched the life of the Middle East in the realms of worship, faith, and art. Temples once dedicated to Athena, Zeus, and Artemis became Christian worship centers at Athens, Jerash, Carthage, and Alexandria. The Greeks who came questioning Jesus received from him a delicate allusion to their own mystery cult, which was courtesy on his part and a compliment to Hellenistic intellectual curiosity (John 12:20–26). The most eager converts to the new faith were from the Hellenized world (Rom. 1:16; Acts 14:11 f., 17:4, 19:10, 20:21; I Cor. 1:24). The Greek spirit breathed through the Gospel of John*. Greek remained the language of the Church until about the middle of the 2d century.

Greek versions. See TEXT.

Greeks, persons of Greek descent. The Greeks called persons of true Greek descent "Hellenes" (Acts 16:1, 18:4; Rom. 1:14). They were looked upon as the highest type of Gentiles, guardians of an unsurpassed culture, the opposites of "barbarians" (see BARBARIAN). "Grecians" in such passages as Acts 6:1, 9:29 A.V. (*Hellenistai*) means Greek-speaking Jews, the presence of whom in Jerusalem was verified in 1914 by the finding of the Theodotus synagogue inscription in Gk. on the hill Ophel. The presence of both Jews and Gentiles in the church at Syrian Antioch* marked a new stage in Christian development. Mention of "Grecians" in Joel 3:6 indicates a late date for this passage, since Greeks were not mentioned in Jewish literature until after the Exile.

grisled ("grizzled"), streaked with gray (Gen. 31:10, 12; Zech. 6:3, 6).

grove, a mistranslation in A.V. (following the LXX and Vulgate) for (1) *ēshel*, tamarisk tree (Gen. 21:33; cf. I Sam. 22:6 A.S.V., R.S.V.); (2) Hebrew Asherah*, Asherim and Asheroth, the Canaanite fertility goddess associated with Baal. "Groves" mean the cultic poles of the female deity set beside "high place"* altars along with the stone pillars of Baal—possibly survivals of ancient tree worship. Such "groves" tempted Hebrew worshippers in every age, and were denounced by every spiritual leader from Moses to Malachi: Deut. 16:21; Judg. 6:25–30; I Kings 15:13, 16:33; II Kings 21:3, 7; II Chron. 15:16; Isa. 17:8; Jer. 17:2; Mic. 5:14.

grudge, a feeling of ill will in contrast to the love of one's neighbor enjoined by Levitical Law (Lev. 19:18). Ps. 59:15 and James 5:9 should read "growl" or "grumble" (R.S.V.), not "grudge" (A.V.). A cheerful generosity is enjoined by II Cor. 9:7 and I Pet. 4:9.

guard, bodyguard, soldiers selected for their reliability for the guarding of persons or property; occasionally civilians. Their functions included guarding royal personages and households, like Pharaoh's guard and its captain (Gen. 37:36, 39:1, 40:3 f.); David's foreign guard (II Sam. 23:23, cf. II Sam. 20:23); Arioch, guard to the Babylonian king (Dan. 2:14); Nebuzaradan*, captain of Nebuchadnezzar's guard, an officer prominent in the deportation of Judah (II Kings 25:8–20; Jer. 39:9–13, 40:1, 2, 5, 41:10, 43:6). Rehoboam's guard was in charge of the royal shields in the palace-Temple area of Jerusalem (I Kings 14:27 f.), where a later royal guard protected young King Jehoash (c. 837–800 B.C.) when he was threatened by Athaliah (II Kings 11:19). Sometimes a people's bodyguard protected such valuable citizens as Nehemiah, during the wall repairs (Neh. 4:22 f.). N.T. guards include the one sent to execute John the Baptist (R.S.V. Mark 6:27); the Roman guard watching the tomb of Jesus (Matt. 27:65 f.); the Roman Praetorian guard, defenders of the emperor (R.S.V. Phil. 1:13); Paul's lenient guard in Rome (Acts 28:16).

guest, a word used only once in the N.T. (Luke 19:7), in connection with the visit of Jesus to sinful Zacchaeus. See HOSPITALITY; HOUSE (for guest chamber). Cf. Prov. 9:18.

guest chamber. See HOUSE.

guilt, the condition of an individual or of a community because of the violation of the moral law. God, not man, determines whether there is guilt. One of God's problems is to bring man to realize and confess his guilt.

According to certain parts of the Bible, there is collective or racial guilt. Many hold that the sin of Adam* (Rom. 5), regarded as the race representative, brought guilt upon all his posterity (Rom. 5:12, 15, 17, 19). This is known as "original sin" or "natural depravity": men are sinful "by nature," and guilt accompanies this natural state.

Properly speaking, there can be no individual guilt of this sort. Guilt and punishment presuppose responsibility—voluntary assent to, or commission of, sin. The painful consequences one man may suffer for another's sin should not be regarded as punishment, although a man may consent to be treated as though he were guilty for another's sin.

But every man incurs guilt before God. The very imperfections of his nature lead to deliberate wrongdoing. Rites of sacrifice and penance show how widespread is man's sense of guilt. A sense of guilt reflects a conviction of sin, but even if these are absent, guilt before God may be a fact.

The O.T. emphasizes both individual guilt and collective guilt. It also shows us one man seeking to take upon himself the guilt of others. The fall of Adam was primarily individual, whatever its later consequences (Gen. 3:17–19). The Flood evidenced collective guilt (Gen. 6:5–7). Sodom and Gomorrah could have been spared had there been as few as ten righteous men living in them (Gen.

18:20–33). Judah offered to take upon himself the consequences of the sin of Jacob's ten sons in selling Joseph (Gen. 44:33 f.). Moses later did the same in respect of the people's sin of the golden calf (Ex. 32:31 f.). The cities of refuge were designed to prevent the unintentional manslayer from falling into the hands of the avenger (Num. 35:9–25). Yet the entire family of Achan was put to death; though only Achan had sinned, all were deemed guilty (Josh. 7:22–25).

The Bible shows these various principles becoming increasingly clarified, but not one of them ever entirely disappears. In Leviticus the various forms of guilt offering are described in great detail: they bespeak a keen sense of sin (4:1–7:10). The teaching of the prophets, that the Exile was a national punishment for national sin, makes the guilt collective, since it does not except even children (Jer. 9:1–22). Ps. 51, on the other hand, is a moving confession of individual sin. It is from a prophet of the Exile itself that we get both the declaration that the sinful soul must bear its own burden (Ezek. 18) and the declaration that the presence of even the most righteous of men will not suffice to turn aside punishment for the unrighteous (14:12–20). But it is also from a prophet of the Exile, the so-called Second Isaiah, that we get the description of one who is called the Suffering Servant of God, whose office it is to take upon himself the sin and guilt of others, and so accomplish their salvation.

This conception of the Sin-bearer is central in the N.T. The Son of God, by becoming a man, identifies himself with the sin and guilt of the human race, while yet himself sinless (see SAVIOUR). He was "made to be sin" on our behalf (II Cor. 5:21). In Hebrews the Jewish system of guilt offerings is treated as both symbolic and anticipatory of Christ, who was equally the priest and the sacrifice, "once for all" (Heb. 7:27). The metaphor of "the Lamb of God" (John 1:29) has the same significance, as do Jesus' words at the Last Supper about his broken body and shed blood (Luke 22:14–20). See JUSTIFICATION; PROPITIATION; RECONCILIATION; SIN. E. L.

guilt offerings. See WORSHIP.

H

H or **Holiness Code** (Lev. 17–26). See CODE; SOURCES.

Habakkuk (hȧ-băk'ŭk) ("embrace"), mentioned only in Hab. 1:1, 3:1; perhaps a Levitical Temple musician (3:19), author of the 8th book of the Minor Prophets.

The dates of his life can be approximated. The Temple still stood (Hab. 2:20). Its musical services were intact (3:19). The Chaldaeans (1:6) in 626 B.C. secured their independence from Assyria and ruled in Babylon; in 612, with the Medes, they destroyed Nineveh; in 605, under Nebuchadnezzar, they defeated the Egyptians at Carchemish; in 587 they destroyed Jerusalem and the Temple. Therefore the situation referred to by the prophet corresponds to the triumphant conquests of the Chaldaeans (c. 600 B.C.) prior to the fall of Jerusalem.

Habakkuk was a philosophical prophet, who, looking out on the history-making events of his day, asked why the ruthless overcame the righteous and whether goodness paid.

The three-chapter book is a unit which can be outlined and interpreted as follows: Chap. 1: For sinful Judah (1:2–4) to be punished by the far more wicked, barbaric, Chaldaeans (5–11)—which some prophets declared was their role in history (II Kings 24:2; Jer. 36:31)—was not in keeping with a holy, righteous, loving God (1:12–17). Chap. 2: The cogitating Habakkuk looks down from his watch-tower on events in the making and hears God's answer to his question (2:1 f.). In time, evil will be overthrown (2:3). Righteousness lives on its own inner integrity (2:4). Meanwhile, with confidence let man declare the doom of evildoers (five "woes," 2:5–20), as the true knowledge of God multiplies over the earth (2:14, 20) (cf. WOES). Chap. 3: Habakkuk, "embracing" God in prayer, expresses in a psalm the only possible answer to his "why." He beholds God triumphant over the heathen in the troubled history of Judaea's past (3:2–15), and is frightened by this vision (3:16); in spite of hard times and disaster (3:17), he rejoices in the God he knows (vv. 18 f.).

173. Portion of the commentary on Habakkuk found in Cave I at Qumran.

Quotations from this book in universal use are 2:2, 4, 14, 20, 3:17–19.

The Heb. MS. of a commentary or midrash on the Book of Habakkuk, written earlier than commentaries were known to have existed, is among the DSS. found in the 'Ain Fashka Cave. (See SCROLLS, THE DEAD SEA; and various issues of *BA* and *Bull. ASOR;* also *The Dead Sea Scrolls of St. Mark's Monastery*, Vol. 1, *The Isaiah Manuscript and the Habakkuk Commentary*, published by

ASOR, New Haven, Conn., 1950.) The Habakkuk commentary was, as that volume indicates, written by a Jewish sectarian of Palestine in an effort to reveal that the religious situation foretold by Habakkuk was realized in his day. The author's comments end with what is chap. 2 of our Book of Habakkuk. The badly multilated scroll is two strips of leather joined with linen thread, c. 141.9 cm. long. The writing is on the smoothly dressed hair side, which is ruled with lines.

habergeon (hăb'ĕr-jŭn), obsolete word for a hauberk or short coat of mail or military breastplate (A.V. Ex. 28:32, 39:23; Job 41:26; II Chron. 26:14; Neh. 4:16).

Habiru (Khapiru, Khabiru). See HEBREWS.

Habor (hā'bôr), a river flowing S. through the Gozan region of Mesopotamia, to meet the E. branch of the Euphrates*; identified with modern Khabur. On its banks were settled Israelites deported from Samaria by Tiglath-pileser III, King of Assyria (745–727 B.C.) (I Chron. 5:26); and by Sargon II (722–705 B.C.) (II Kings 17:6, 18:11) in the "ninth year of Hoshea king of Israel" (722 B.C.).

Hachilah (hȧ-kī'lȧ) ("dark"), a wooded stronghold on a hill in the Wilderness of Ziph, possibly near Tell Ziph, SE. of Hebron in the Judaean mountains. There David and later Saul hid (I Sam. 23:19, 24–26, 26:1–3).

Hadad (hā'dăd). (1) An ancient Aramaean deity, the Semitic storm god generally called "Baal" or "lord" by Canaanites, of whose pantheon we know more than formerly, through texts excavated at Ras Shamrah* in N. Syria and elsewhere. Hadad was believed to dwell in a high mountain of the N. and to bring desired rains. He was sometimes called Baal-shamem; known to Phoenicians of the 15th century B.C. as Addu and to N. Mesopotamians of the era depicted in II Kings 17:31 as Adad-milki, to whom children might be sacrificed. He had been known as Adad to Accadians, who sometimes built a joint temple for him and Anu, worshipped also by the peoples of N. and S. Arabia. In Middle Eastern art Hadad is shown standing on a young bull; cf. the golden calves of Jeroboam (I Kings 12:28). Although Hadad as a deity is not mentioned in the O.T., his name is compounded with that of several other men or deities. (See HADADEZER; HADAD-RIMMON.)

(2) A son of Ishmael (I Chron. 1:30). (3) Son of Bedad, a ruler of Edom*, with his capital at Avith (Gen. 36:35; I Chron. 1:46 f.).

(4) A king (A.V. Hadar) of Edom, with capital at Pau (Gen. 36:39), possibly to be identified with (5), a prince of Edom who, when threatened by David's general Joab, fled to friendly Egypt. He attempted to free Edom from the control of Solomon (I Kings 11:14–22).

Hadadezer (hăd'ăd-ē'zĕr) ("Hadad is helper"), a king of Zobah* in David's time (II Sam. 8:3 ff.; I Kings 11:23) who headed unsuccessful Aramaean resistance to David and was made subject to him. His chariot horses were the ones hocked by David in the well-known strategy (I Chron. 18:4). Hadadezer was erroneously called "Hadarezer" in this A.V. passage.

Hadad-rimmon (hā'dăd-rĭm'ŏn) the combination of Syrian gods Hadad and Rimmon (II Kgs. 5:18) mourned at Megiddo (Zech. 12:11) with rites similar to those observed, chiefly by women, at the annual departure of the Accad. god Tammuz* (Ezek. 8:14).

Hadar (hā'där). See HADAD.

Hadassah (hȧ-dăs'ȧ) ("myrtle"), the Jewish name of Queen Esther*, mentioned only in Esther 2:7.

Hades, the underworld inhabited by the departed. Biblical thought conceives a three-story universe: the upper world, the lower world, and the earth in between. Hades was the lower world. The common name for it in the Hebrew O.T. is "Sheol." The new English translations usually retain the word Sheol, as they also retain, in the N.T., the Greek equivalent, Hades (see A.S.V.). The A.V. renders the two terms in various ways, as "grave" (Gen. 44:29, 31; Job 7:9; Ps. 30:3), "hell" (Ps. 16:10, 18:5; Prov. 27:20; Ezek. 32:21), "pit" (Num. 16:30, 33; Job 17:16). The word rendered "pit" in the A.V. of Rev. 9:1, 2, 20:1–3 is the Greek word "abyss," and it is so rendered in A.S.V.

In early times the Hebrews seem to have been uncertain about continued life after death. They believed rather that a man survived in his descendants; hence the passionate desire for children (see the story of Abraham in Gen. 15, 16, 17). The story of Saul and the witch of Endor at the grave of Samuel, however, suggests a belief even that early in continued individual life (I Sam. 28:3–19). However that may be, there is no doubt as to later O.T. thought (see II Sam. 12:15–23; Job 19:25–27, but cf. 14:7–10; Ps. 49:14, 15, 73:24–26; Eccles. 12:7, but cf. 9:10). In Apocryphal and Apocalyptic literature, written for the most part "between the Testaments," the events connected with a future life are a common theme: resurrection, judgment, rewards, and penalties. (See IMMORTALITY; JUDGMENT, DAY OF.)

It is this later conception of the nature and life of the underworld that is carried over into the N.T., where Hades is the usual word for the underworld, though "Gehenna" (A.S.V.; usually "hell" in the A.V.) occurs repeatedly in the Gospels (Matt. 5:22, 29, 30; Mark 9:43, 45, 47; Luke 12:5; see also Jas. 3:6). There is one example of the use of the classical Greek word "Tartarus" (II Pet. 2:4, A.V. "hell"). Jesus' use of "Gehenna" is understandable. Outside of Jerusalem was a gorge known as Ge-Hinnom, or Valley of Hinnom*, which for centuries had borne an evil reputation, and eventually it became the place where the refuse of the city was thrown. The perpetual burning and the numerous crawling things were used by Jesus as suggesting the sufferings of "cast out" souls: Hades, or hell, was like Gehenna, "where their worm dieth not and the fire is not quenched" (Mark 9:48; cf. Luke 16:19–31). The glorified Christ declared that he held "the keys of death and of Hades" (Rev. 1:18), which throws light on the statement in I Pet. 3:19 that after his crucifixion Christ "went and preached unto the spirits in prison," i.e., to the dead. See APOCALYPTIC; ESCHATOLOGY; GEHENNA; IMMORTALITY; JUDGMENT; PUNISHMENT. E. L.

Hagar (hā′gär) (Agar in the A.V. of the N.T.) (possibly from "to flee"; cf. Hegira, or flight, of the Arabian Mohammed), the Egyptian or N. Arabian handmaid of Sarah, wife of Abraham, who may have acquired this bondwoman during an Egyptian sojourn (Gen. 12:10–20). The moving story of Hagar is effectively narrated in the J and E sources, based on still earlier written and oral tales of Israel. P makes brief references (Gen. 16:1a, 3, 15 f.) for purposes of chronology. J (Gen. 16:1b, 2, 4–14) tells how Sarah*, finding God's promise of a son still unfulfilled after years in Canaan, gives her maid Hagar to Abraham for a concubine so that through Hagar Sarah may claim an heir. But when Sarah learns that her handmaid is pregnant, she sends her harshly away into the Wilderness of Shur, between Philistia and Egypt, where the despondent Hagar sees in a theophany near a desert well (Gen. 16:7) "the angel of the Lord" (the first time in the O.T. such an appearance is recorded), who advises her to return to her mistress, and promises her a long generation of descendants through her heir, the "wild" Ishmael* (16:11, 12). Hagar names the place of her theophany Beer-la-hai-roi ("the well of Him that liveth and seeth me"). In the masterful narrative of the E document (Gen. 21:8–21) Hagar's son Ishmael years later is shown mocking Isaac, the puny son of Sarah and Abraham, on the day of his weaning (21:8 f.), whereupon he and Hagar are cast out by Sarah, who was determined not to have the slave's son "heir with" her son (v. 10). This time the father himself is placed in the trying position of sending away the one who had borne his first son. The E author penetrates with skill the emotions of Abraham (vv. 11–14). Again a well plays a conspicuous place in the story—this time near Beersheba, where "the angel of God" (v. 17) shows Hagar water just in time to save the life of Ishmael. Hagar later selected an Egyptian wife for Ishmael (v. 21).

Haggai (hăg′ā-ī) ("festal," perhaps "born on a feast day"), a post-Exilic prophet, contemporary and co-worker of Zechariah* (Hag. 1:1; Zech. 1:1), who aided in the rebuilding of the Temple at Jerusalem (Ezra 4:24, 5:1 f., 6:14 f.). His family background is not recorded, but later tradition declares that he came from the tribe of Levi, was a founder of the Great Synagogue, and was born in Babylon during the Exile*. Others think that he was an old man who remembered the splendor of the Temple and the city before its destruction (Hag. 2:3).

His book presents authoritatively the social and economic conditions of Jerusalem 18 years after the first Return (Ezra 1:5–2:2). Luxurious private houses had been erected (Hag. 1:4). The Temple remained in ruins (1:2, 4, 2:3). Weather conditions (1:10 f.), shortage of food, inferior merchandise, and lack of workers had brought about inflation, characterized as "wages" in a "bag with holes" (Hab. 1:6–9). The Samaritans at the N. were hostile (Ezra 4:1–5; Neh.6:9).

Two short chapters of this tenth Minor Prophet present only outlines of his thought-provoking messages to the people. "Consider" is his favorite word (Hag. 1:5, 7, 2:18). Exact dates (three or four months of the year 520 B.C.—1:1, 15, 2:1, 10, 18, 20) connect his oracles:

(1) The call to build (chap. 1);
(2) encouragement to the builders (2:1–9);
(3) contagion of evil (2:10–19);
(4) the Messianic (see MESSIAH) hope (2:20–23).

Private housing projects, important as they are to individual families, provide no adequate excuse for failure to complete God's house (1:4), whose continuous care alone promotes community decency, security, and welfare for all (1:6–11). Haggai, in his enthusiasm over Zerubbabel's leadership in the restoration of the Temple, saw the Governor of Judaea as the future Messianic king of Judaea, free from Persian control (2:23).

Hagiographa (Gk., "sacred writings"), the 3d division of the Hebrew O.T., known as *Kethubhim* or *Ketubim,* and comprising a miscellany of eleven books which are grouped in the Hebrew Bible in this way: (1) Poetical Books (Psalms, Proverbs, Job); (2) the Five Scrolls (*Megilloth*): Song of Solomon, Ruth, Lamentations, Ecclesiastes, Esther; (3) History (Daniel, Ezra-Nehemiah, Chronicles). Each of these books was canonized (see CANON) separately, instead of being considered in a group like the Prophets. The inclusion of each book was determined by its popularity, and upon anonymous authorship, so that it could be considered as having been divinely inspired to a prophetic transmitter. Ezra-Nehemiah was canonized before I and II Chronicles. Ruth and Lamentations, the earliest of the Five Scrolls, were canonized before the other three.

Hai (hā′ī) (A.V.). See AI (R.S.V.).

hail may fall even in tropical climates, causing great damage to crops and trees (Hag. 2:17). The storms may be local, one district suffering severely while another escapes (Ex. 9:22–26; Josh. 10:11).

hair and beards* were worn long by Hebrew men of Bible times; they abhorred baldness (Lev. 21:5). Women wore their hair bound or veiled. Laws provided for the removal of hair, even of eyebrows, from lepers (Lev. 14:8 f.); for plucking hair at times of mourning (Amos 8:10); for the tonsure of priests (Ezek. 44:20); for Nazirites' hair being worn long during their vows (Num. 6:5; Judg. 16:17); for leaving the "corners" of the hair and beard uncut—not as the heathen did (Lev. 19:27, 21:5). The hair was anointed with oil as part of the regular toilet (Ps. 23:5; Matt. 6:17). Side locks (see next page, illus. 174) are still worn by pious Jews of the Hassidic sect. Today Palestinian Bedouin shepherds often wear long braids of hair. N.T. Christian men were opposed to long hair (I Cor. 11:6 ff.). They did not cover the head when praying or prophesying (I

Cor. 11:4). (For women's coiffures of this period see I Cor. 11:5 f.; I Tim. 2:9; cf. I Pet. 3:3.)

Ancient Egyptians, to whom cleanliness and coolness were important, wore hair very short or shaved, using elaborate wigs for

174. Hair: 1. Egyptian wig, 2630 B.C.; 2. Egyptian wig, 2590 B.C.; 3. Sumerian, 2000 B.C.; 4. Assyrian, 800 B.C.; 5. Roman; 6. Bedouin; 7. Hebrew side-lock.

women and men in public appearances. Kings—and some queens, like Hatshepsut—wore ceremonial beards held on by straps. Men and women kept their bodies free from superfluous hair. Many ancient Egyptian razors, tweezers, and combs have been unearthed, as well as hairpins and hair curlers not unlike those used today. Egyptians feared baldness, and filed on their medical papyri prescriptions for lotions and salves to prevent falling hair.

Elamite kings wore pointed, well-curled beards and burnsides.

Mesopotamian men enjoyed elaborate arrangement of hair and beards, set in intricate croquignole curls, as seen in sculptured portraits of Ashurnasirpal. Ancient Accadians wore their hair stiffly set in parallel waves. The great Sumerian, Gudea of Lagash Province (c. 2200 B.C.), was smooth shaven, bald, and partial to a tight round turban with upturned brim. The "hair-do" of the famous winged bulls from King Sargon's palace reflects the mode of Assyrian rulers.

Greek men wore fairly long hair and beards; women wore it in becoming simplicity, in knots at the nape of the neck. Roman men preferred smooth-shaven faces and short hair; women wore hair bound with fillets.

Halah (hā′lȧ), a region of N. Mesopotamia, location unknown, but possibly near Gozan*, to which captives from the Ten Tribes were carried by kings of Assyria (II Kings 17:6; I Chron. 5:26).

hallel ("praise"). See HALLELUJAH.

hallelujah ("praise Jah," "praise ye Jehovah"), a liturgical ejaculation urging all to join in praising Yahweh. It occurs at the beginning of eleven Psalms (106, 111–113, 117, 135, 146–150) and at the close of thirteen, (104–106, 113, 115–117, 135, 146–150) as an additional exhortation to worship (appearing in the A.V. as "Praise ye the Lord"). These had a specified part in the morning synagogue service, forming a "benediction of song." In some segments of the early Christian Church the "Hallelujah Psalms" were recited daily. Pss. 113–118 formed the "Egyptian" Hallel, and were sung within family circles at the Passover and in Temple and synagogue on the Feast of Tabernacles, Pentecost, and the Feast of Dedication of the Temple. The hallel was the "hymn" used by Jesus and his disciples at the Lord's Supper (Matt. 26:30; Mark 14:26). Pss. 146–150 are considered as a doxology for the Psalter as a whole (Pfeiffer). In the A.V. the form "alleluia" (R.S.V. hallelujah) occur in Rev. 19:1–6, from which it made its way into Christian hymns (as "Christ the Lord is risen today, Alleluia") and liturgies.

hallow, to make holy; used in the O.T. in connection with things as varied as the holy gifts of Israel (Ex. 28:38); the altar hallowed by special rites on the Day of Atonement (Lev. 16:19); the 50th or Jubilee Year (25:10); articles "hallowed" (R.S.V. "dedicated") to the Lord (22:2 f.); the firstborn (Num. 3:13); the head (6:11); the middle of the court that was before the House of God (I Kings 8:64); "the house of God" (I Kings 9:3, 7). Therefore when Jesus prayed "Hallowed be thy name" he used an ancient word which had long been used by his people to indicate special reverence. Matt. 6:9 and Luke 11:2 are the only N.T. uses of "hallowed."

Ham (possibly from word meaning "hot"), a son of Noah (Gen. 5:32, 6:10, 7:13, 9:18, 22), and "father of Canaan" (Gen. 9:22). He was regarded as the eponymous ancestor of the peoples from Phoenicia through W. Palestine into Africa and W. Arabia. Ham's sons listed in I Chron. 8 were "Cush, Mizraim [Egypt], Put, and Canaan." The land of Ham connotes Egypt in Ps. 78:51, 105:23, 27, 106:22; the Ham territory of Gen. 14:5 (cf. Deut. 2:20), where the tribe of Zuzim lived, may be Ammon.

Haman (hā′măn), a son of Hammedatha (Esther 3:1), prime minister and favorite of Ahasuerus* (Xerxes) and villain of the Esther* narrative, in which book alone he appears in Scripture. He was a persecutor of the Jews (chap. 3), and received the punishment he plotted for them (chap. 7). On Feasts of Purim in later times it was apparently customary to hang or burn Haman in effigy.

Hamath (hā′măth) (Hemath, A.V. Amos 6:14). (1) A city on the Orontes R. in Syria, 28 m. N. of Homs, known in Graeco-Roman times as Epiphania, modern Hama. Listed as one of the descendants of Ham (Gen. 10:18; I Chron. 1:16), and the center of an independent kingdom touching the N. border of Israel (Num. 13:21, 34:8; Josh. 13:5; Judg. 3:3). Toi, King of Hamath, sent gifts to David (II Sam. 8:9–10; I Chron. 18:9–10). Jeroboam II (c. 780 B.C.) extended the borders of Israel to Hamath (II Kings 14:28; cf. Amos 6:14). After the Syrian campaign of Tiglath-pileser III (*ANET*[3], pp. 282–283), Hamath became the center of an Assyrian province (cf. Ezek. 47:15 ff.). Under Sargon II, people from Hamath were planted in Samaria when Israel was taken into captivity (II Kings 17:24, 30), and some Israelites were settled in Hamath (Isa. 11:11).

The excavation of Hamath by a Danish team, 1932–38, revealed 12 periods of occupation, the earliest of Neolithic date. A large citadel, with monumental entranceway, palace, and shrine, and a vast cemetery with cremated burials attest to the Neo-Hittite and Aramaean state which existed from c. 1200 B.C. to its destruction by Sargon II in 721 B.C., and which was in constant interaction with ancient Israel. W. P. A.

Hammath (hăm′ăth) (Hemath, A.V. I Chron. 2:55) ("hot spring"). (1) The father of the founder of the house of Rechab* (I Chron. 2:55). (2) A fortified city in Naphtali (Josh. 19:35), probably the same as Hammoth-dor (21:32). It was later known as Ammathus, and is probably the present Hammam Tabariyeh, widely known for its hot, medicinal springs, on the W. shore of the Sea of Galilee, about a mile S. of Tiberias.

hammer, a tool used for driving tent pins (Judg. 4:21, 5:26), in woodworking (Jer. 10:4), in metalworking (Isa. 41:7, 44:12), and for breaking rocks (Jer. 23:29; I Kings 6:7). It was the symbol of destructive power (Jer. 50:23). See TOOLS.

Hammon (hăm′ŏn) ("hot spring"). A village of Asher (Josh. 19:28).

Hammoth-dor (hăm′ŏth-dôr′). See HAMMATH.

Hammurabi (häm′ōō-rä′bē), the 6th king of the First Dynasty of Babylon*. He had Amorite (see AMORITES) background; and is no longer considered to be Amraphel of Gen. 14:1. New information, based on the Khorsabad List and confirmed by sensational finds in some of the thousands of clay tablets recovered from the Mesopotamian city of Mari* in 1936, fix Hammurabi's dates as c. 1728–1686 B.C., rather than two or more centuries earlier. Some authorities make "the Age of Abraham" the period of transition between the kings of Isin and Larsa, and Hammurabi. Hammurabi is listed in one record as having reigned 43 years as King of Babylon. The ascendancy of his kingdom began when he achieved victories over Larsa, Eshnunna, and Mari, which placed him in control of all the territory which had formerly been Sumer* and Accad*. His kingdom endured for about 1½ centuries, when it was thrown into a dark age by incursions of Hittites* from the Taurus and by Kassite horsemen from the eastern mountains.

The great Babylonian was not only a man of marked military ability, but a developer of civic centers. He raised Babylon from an unimportant village to capital of a nation; laid out its streets in straight lines intersecting at right angles; a city some of whose houses have been recently excavated. The staged tower or *ziggurat** of his day at Babylon was known to the Hebrews who wrote the Tower of Babel* narrative of Gen. 11:4–9. Hammurabi was also the beautifier of Asshur and Nineveh. He improved systems of canals; developed river navigation; stabilized wage scales; regulated economy; raised new temples; and fostered his people's gods. He gave his land such security and prosperity that its scholars were able to prepare treatises on astronomy, philology, lexicography, mathematics, and magic which were standard for centuries. They were also able to edit the early Babylonian Flood* story and the creation* epic in a form used for more than 1,000 years, and in the form familiar to modern scholars. Clay tablets containing portions of these epics have been found in the library of Asshurbanapal at Nineveh (650 B.C.), at Kish, and at Uruk. The culture of Hammurabi's era spread over Asia Minor and Syria. Its versatility is evidenced by the fact that the black stele of Hammurabi from Ur (not the Code) was inscribed both in a Semitic language (used by temples and schools) and in Sumerian.

175. Hammurabi Code.

Hammurabi is best known today as the sponsor of the Code of Hammurabi (c. 1690 B.C.), the oldest and most complete recording of which is now in the Louvre at Paris, having been found by Scheil at Susa, where raiding Elamites had deposited it. It is a round-topped, 8-ft.-high stele of black diorite. At its top an incised relief shows Hammurabi standing before the enthroned sun god Shamash, patron of justice. Beneath the relief were about 51 columns of beautiful and meticulous Babylonian cuneiform* characters which recorded almost 300 paragraphs of civil, criminal, and commercial laws, framed by a prologue and an epilogue.

The Code of Hammurabi and the Hebrew Covenant* Code both belong to the class of codes prevalent in the Mesopotamian Valley in the 3d and 2d millennia B.C. See TEN COMMANDMENTS.

As pointed out by R. H. Pfeiffer, the author of D (the Deuteronomic Code) used the same style of framing the laws by an introduction and a conclusion as Hammurabi's Code, which had been written about a thousand years earlier. Moreover, Hebrew codes followed the characteristic form used not only by Hammurabi, but also by Assyrian and Hittite codifiers, as illustrated by such passages as: "If a bird's nest chance to be before thee in the way . . . thou shalt not . . . But thou shalt," etc., (Deut. 22:6–7); again, in the matter of heirs (Deut. 21:15–17) the same form appears, "If . . . then . . . but . . ."

Pfeiffer argued that an ancient and now lost original of the Hebrew Code of the Covenant had a form corresponding to the main divisions of the Code of Hammurabi:

The Law of Procedure (Ham. 1–5; missing from the Covenant Code, but at least partially present in Deut. 19:16–20).

The Law of Property (Ham. 6–126) (see below).

The Law of Persons (Ham. 127–282) (see below).

But the Covenant Code reversed the order and developed first the Law of Persons, including liabilities (as, in part, Ex. 21:2–11; Deut. 15:12–18; cf. Ham. 228–282); edicts pertaining to the family, as inheritance (Deut. 21:15–17; cf. Ham. 162–193); marriage (as in portions of Deut. 22, 24, 25; cf. Ham. 127–161); then the Law of Property (Ex. 21:33 f., 35 f.; cf. Ham. 53–65 ff.); and third, the Law of Procedure (as, for example, Deut. 19:16–20, 25:1–3; cf. Ham. 3–4). For fuller chart of parallels see Pfeiffer, *Introduction to the Old Testament* (Harper), pp. 214 f.

The most popularly known parallels are the *lex talionis* pronouncements (Lev. 24:19 f.; cf. Ham. 196 f.) ("an eye for an eye") and laws concerning incest (Lev. 20:11 f.; cf. Ham. 154–158).

Hamor (hā′môr) (Emmor, A.V. Acts 7:16), a prince of Shechem (Gen. 33:19; Josh. 24:32; Judg. 9:28) whose son, Shechem, seduced Dinah, the daughter of Jacob. In revenge, both Hamor and his son were slain by Dinah's brothers, Simeon and Levi (Gen. 34).

Hanon (hā′nȧn) ("gracious"), the name of numerous O.T. men, among them: (1) Ezra's assistant in explaining the Law (Neh. 8:7, cf. Neh. 10:10); (2) a faithful assistant to the temple treasurers (Neh. 13:13); (3) a prophet whose "sons" had space in the Temple near the "chamber of the princes" (Jer. 35:4); (4) a chieftain of the Tribe of Benjamin (I Chron. 8:23); (5) a descendant of Saul through Azel (I Chron. 8:38, 9:44); (6) one of David's strong men, son of Maacah (I Chron. 11:43).

Hananeel (hȧ-năn′ē-ĕl) (A.S.V. Hananel, hăn′ȧ-nĕl) ("God hath been gracious"), a tower in the N. wall of Jerusalem, location unknown. It stood on a cliff near the "gate of the corner" (Jer. 31:38), "the king's winepresses" (Zech. 14:10), the "fish gate," and the tower of Meah, and was restored by Nehemiah (3:1, 3, 12:39).

Hanani (hȧ-nā′nī) ("gracious"), the name of five men in the O.T.: (1) a seer imprisoned by King Asa (II Chron. 16:7–10) and father of the prophet Jehu* (I Kings 16:1, 7); (2) a musician appointed by David for the sanctuary (I Chron. 25:4, 25); (3) a relative of Nehemiah who carried word of Jerusalem's fate to Susa (Neh. 1:2), and later was in charge of the gatekeepers at Jerusalem (Neh. 1:2, 7:2); (4) a priest who had married a foreign woman but who pledged to put her away (Ezra 10:20); (5) a prominent musician who played an instrument at the dedication of the Jerusalem walls (Neh. 12:36).

Hananiah (hăn′ȧ-nī′ȧ) ("Yahweh hath been gracious"), the name of several men of the O.T., the best known of whom are: (1) the false prophet who publicly contradicted Jeremiah and was doomed to death (Jer. 28); (2) the governor of "the castle" appointed by Nehemiah to help Hanani rule Jerusalem (Neh. 7:2).

hand, a word which appears scores of times in Scripture (see GESTURE). In many passages it expresses the power and participation of God in the affairs of men (I Chron. 21:17); His upholding providence (Matt. 4:6); or His severe chastisement (I Sam. 5:6). Isaiah mentions hiding in "the shadow of his hand" (49:2). The physical might of a political oppressor, like Shishak of Egypt, is also spoken of in terms of his "hand" (Jer. 22:3). God empowered the hand of Moses to effect a miracle at the Sea of Reeds (Ex. 14:27). The laying on of hands by men endued with spiritual gifts (Matt. 9:25) effected healings (Mark 16:18; Acts 3:7); and ordained Christian workers (Acts 8:17, 18). The washing of hands was intended to convey innocence, whether real or assumed (Deut. 21:6–8; Matt. 27:24). Clean hands were a corollary of the pure heart of the ideal Hebrew (Ps. 24:4). Pharisees* were overpunctilious about washing the hands before eating (Mark 7:2, 5; Matt. 15:2, 11). The Bible mentions hands holding various articles: weapons (Neh. 4:17); censers (II Chron. 26:19); scepters (Esther 5:2); potter's clay (Jer. 18:6); winnower's fans (Luke 3:17); stars (Rev. 2:1); palms (Rev. 7:9); "a little book" (Rev. 10:2). The seat of honor, whether for a guest, or of the Son with relation to the Father, was on the right hand (Mark 12:36; Acts 2:25, 7:55; Eph. 1:20; Col. 3:1; Heb. 1:3, 13).

In Christian iconography the commonest and possibly oldest symbol* for God the Father is the hand, denoting power, protection, and possession. It is usually shown emerging from a cloud of mystery. Sometimes it is wide open, or with three fingers extended, in blessing. It may have the nimbus of deity surrounding it. Sometimes the hand of God is upright, again reaching down to proffer help.

handkerchief, a small napkin used by Jews, following a custom of the Romans, for wiping the face and hands, and for wrapping about the head of the dead. The only A.V. use of the word occurs at Acts 19:12, where handkerchiefs or aprons which were carried from Paul to the sick effected miraculous cures. The A.V. uses the word "napkin" in John 11:44 (R.S.V. "cloth") and 20:7, as well as in the parable of the pounds (Luke 19:20).

hanging, as a means of suicide, is mentioned twice in Scripture. Ahithophel the Gilonite, counsellor of David, entered into conspiracy with Absalom and plotted the king's death, but when this plot failed he hanged himself (II Sam. 17:23). Judas Iscariot, betrayer of Jesus, hanged himself in remorse (Matt. 27:3–6).

Hanging on a high gallows (A.S.V. margin "tree"), as capital punishment for wrongdoing, was the fate of Haman, enemy of the Jews at the Persian court of Ahasuerus (Esther 7:9 f.). The hanging on trees of bodies of slain criminals was resorted to in O.T. times to increase their ignominy, as in the case of the 5 Amorite kings slain by Joshua (Josh. 10:26). Such bodies were removed at sundown for burial in caves or elsewhere, for it was believed that a hanged man was accursed, and would defile the land unless interred promptly (Deut. 21:23; cf. Gal. 3:13). Hanging of the living was introduced by Romans.

hangings. (1) Curtains thrown over wooden

framework constituted the Tabernacle* (Ex. 26:1–37). The first layer of 10 curtains was of fine-twined linen, "and blue, and purple, and scarlet" and embroidered with cherubim (v. 1). Each measured 4x30 cubits. The hangings were attached to acacia pillars in 2 sets of 5 each. The second layer of hangings was woven of goats' hair. Hangings also constituted the doors of the holy tent (v. 36). All the hangings were free-will offerings of "wisehearted" women (Ex. 35:25 f.) who spun the goats' hair; and of skillful men, who turned out such generous quantities of blue, purple, and scarlet textiles that Moses had to restrain them (Ex. 36:6). The total weight of the Tabernacle hangings may have exceeded a ton. (2) Hangings for Baal's grove adjacent to the Jerusalem Temple in the apostate age reformed by King Josiah (640–609 B.C.) were woven by pagan women in unwholesome surroundings (II Kings 23:7).

Hannah (from Heb. word for "grace"), the favorite wife of Elkanah of Mt. Ephraim, and devout mother of the prophet Samuel*, who was born after years of bitter barrenness (I Sam. 1:6–8) and intercession for a son (vv. 15, 19 f.). Hannah expressed her gratitude to God by "returning" the little boy at three years of age to Yahweh for service at the Shiloh sanctuary, c. 25 m. N. of Jerusalem (I Sam. 1:24–28). This narrative is from the finest portion of the late source (see SOURCES) material of the Book of Samuel. The lyric prayer or psalm uttered by Hannah at the hour of her son's dedication, probably written in the 4th or 3d century B.C., was inserted in I Sam. 2:1–10 (omitting 2:2a and 8b) from an anthology. It foreshadowed the Magnificat of Mary of Nazareth (Luke 1:42–45), and may have been familiar to the mother of Jesus. The story of Hannah, told with idyllic charm, reveals the pure and happy home life of pious Israelites. Three sons and two daughters were born to Hannah and Elkanah after she had given Samuel to the Lord (I Sam. 2:20 f.).

Hanukkah. See FEASTS.

Hanun (hā'nŭn), an Ammonite who insulted David's servants (II Sam. 10:1–11:1).

Haran (hā'răn) (cf. Accad. word for "caravan"). (1) An important N. Mesopotamian commercial city at the head of the W. horn of the Fertile Crescent on the Belikh River 60 m. above its confluence with the Euphrates. It was situated in the region called Padan-aram in the O.T. Haran in ancient times flourished as a junction of the rich caravan trade between Nineveh and Carchemish, Mesopotamia, the central Hittite Empire, and the Mediterranean shores. Ezekiel mentioned it as a merchant community (27:23). Like Ur, Haran was a center of the moon god Sin worship popular among Semitic nomads. To Haran Terah and his son Abraham and other kinsmen fared from Ur en route to Canaan (Gen. 11:31, P). In Haran Terah died (v. 32). Acquiring "substance" and offspring in the rich city (Gen. 12:5, P), Abraham and Lot with their families continued SW. into Canaan by way of Shechem and Bethel. Even after establishing themselves in the Promised Land, Abraham and his clan kept in touch with Haran. From its neighbor city Nahor Abraham's servant selected Rebekah (Gen. 24) to become the wife of Isaac. From the old Padan-aram region came also Jacob's wife Rachel (Gen. 28, 29).

Haran is a pivotal point in the history of the Hebrew people, where Biblical and archaeological material converge. Cuneiform* tablets found at Nuzu*, a small Hurrian city, shed light on Patriarchal customs recorded in Genesis: deathbed blessings (Gen. 27); the custom of using concubines to insure heirs (Gen. 16, 30); such relations as existed between Jacob and Laban (29:13); the use of family teraphim (A.V. "images") (Gen. 31:19, 34 f.). Such records establish confidence in the social customs depicted in early Genesis narratives, which are authoritative pictures of life in the 2d millennium B.C., between the centuries when Amorite princes of the eras of Abraham and Hammurabi were in control. The "city of Nahor" (Gen. 24:10) is mentioned in the Mari* tablets as Nakhur, a settlement which evidently lay S. of Haran. As W. F. Albright points out in *From the Stone Age to Christianity*, p. 181 (Johns Hopkins Press), Hebrews brought from NW. Mesopotamia to the West the Creation epic of Gen. 2, the story of Eden, the saga of the Patriarchs before the Deluge, the Flood* narrative, and the Tower of Babel story. There appear to be no parallels between Canaanite or Egyptian literature and this Mesopotamian Genesis material.

Haran continued important in history down the centuries. The Assyrians* (see II Kings 19:12) made their last stand there, when the city was held by Ashur-uballit (609 B.C.), but three years later it fell to the Medes, who destroyed it (cf. Zeph. 2:13–15; Nah. 3:1–3), and drove the Assyrians back across the Euphrates. This was the struggle in which the Egyptian Pharaoh-nechoh, marching to help the Assyrians, met the Judaean King Josiah at Megiddo and slew him (609 B.C.). Haran held out against Pharaoh-nechoh. It survives today as the little village of Harran. Moslems living there revere Abraham as an Islamic saint.

The J source connects the Patriarchs with the Aramaeans of Haran (Gen. 24) rather than with the Eastern Bedouins of the E document (29:1). The latter is faithful to oral traditions.

Several ancestors of Abraham have the same names as towns located near Haran: Peleg (Gen. 11:16); Serug (11:20 ff.); Terah (11:24 ff.); Nahor (11:22 ff.).

(2) Haran was a brother of Abraham and son of Terah. He died at Ur, but left a son, Lot (Gen. 11:27), who entered Canaan, and two daughters, Milcah and Iscah (Gen. 11:29). (3) A Gershonite Levite (I Chron. 23:9).

hare (*Lepus judaeae, Lepus sinaiticus, Lepus aegypticus, Lepus syriacus*), classed by Hebrews as an "unclean" (inedible) animal because it does not have divided hoofs (Lev. 11:6; Deut. 14:7).

harlot (Heb. *zonah*), a loose woman; a prostitute. The practice of harlotry was an ancient evil against which the developing conscience of Hebrews and Christians protested. Deuteronomic Law condemned harlotry (Deut. 22:28 ff.); high priests were forbidden to marry prostitutes (Lev. 21:14); Wisdom writers knew and denounced their traits (Prov. 7:5 ff., 29:3). Major prophets likened the apostasies of Israel and Judah to the harlotries of whores who frequented green trees and cultic mountain centers (Jer. 3:6, 8; Ezek. 16:15, 17, 20, 22, 30–52; Hos. 4:15). The Canaanite temples and Syrian shrines that Israel knew were often brothels where priests, priestesses, and cultists engaged in impure rites glorifying reproductive processes. The early Christian Church soon made a pronouncement against harlotry (Acts 15:20, 29), and combated it in cosmopolitan centers by teaching that the body is the temple of the Holy Spirit (I Cor. 6:12–20). Jesus, recognizing that adultery* was only one of the many social sins of his day, said that harlots would enter the kingdom before some priests and elders (Matt. 21:31 f.); and taught leniency to the woman condemned by sinners (John 7:53–8:11) and the harlot who manifested her repentance (Luke 7:37–50). The harlot Rahab and her family were spared when Joshua invaded Jericho, because she had concealed his messengers and helped them escape (Josh. 2:1–22, 6:17, 22, 25; Heb. 11:31; Jas. 2:25); her name appears in Matthew's genealogy of Jesus (1:5; A.V. "Rachab").

Harod (hā′rŏd) ("trembling"), a spring (not a well, as in the A.V.) where Gideon* mustered his men in a pitched camp before his pursuit of the Midianites (Judg. 7). This spring, on the NW. side of Mt. Gilboa about 1 m. SE. of Jezreel, rises in a cave and rushes down to the valley; one of the most copious in Palestine, and frequently a coveted military prize. It may be the site, now identified as 'Ain Jalūd, where Saul camped before his final battle against the Philistines (I Sam. 29:1). The Harod spring is one of the sacred sites not covered by a shrine.

Harosheth (hȧ-rō′shĕth) ("carving") **of the Gentiles** may be the impressive mound Tell 'Amr, 16 m. NW. of Megiddo, or its neighbor, Tell Harbaj, on the N. bank of the Kishon, which together command the entrance to the Plain of Esdraelon at the E. end of the Mt. Carmel ridge. This defile, where Jabin's commander-in-chief Sisera gathered his chariots, offers topographical confirmation of Judg. 4:13, 16. Harosheth was part of the Plain of Acre.

harp. See MUSIC.

hart (hind), a "clean" (edible) animal, a deer (Deut. 12:15, 14:5, 15:22), probably *Cervus dama*, once plentiful in Palestine. "Hart" is masculine; "hind," feminine. The O.T. refers to its traits: love of freedom (Gen. 49:21); thirst for water brooks (Ps. 42:1); beauty (Song of Sol. 2:9, 17, 8:14); ability to leap (Isa. 35:6); habits in rearing young (Jer. 14:5; Job 39:1; Ps. 29:9).

harvest. See FARMING.

Hashabiah (hăsh′ȧ-bī′ȧ), the name of nine men: I Chron. 6:44, 45, 25:3, 19, 26:30, 27:17; II Chron. 35:9; Ezra 8:19, 24; Neh. 3:17, 11:22, 12:21.

Hasmonaeans (hăz′mō-nē′ănz) (sometimes Asmonaeans), descendants of Hashmon, ancestor of the Maccabees*.

Hattîn (hăt′ēn), **Horns of,** a saddle-shaped, twin-peak elevation overlooking the Sea of Galilee and the Plain of Gennesaret, between Cana and Tiberias; identified by ancient tradition as a likely place for the open-air teaching of the multitudes by Jesus on various occasions (Matt. 5:1 ff.; cf. Luke 6:17–20). From Hattîn, believed by Crusaders to be the Mount of Beatitudes, a magnificent panorama spreads N. to Mt. Hermon, E. to Tiberias and the lake.

Hattush (hăt′ŭsh). (1) A descendant of David (I Chron. 3:22). (2) The head of a house who returned (Ezra 8:2) from Babylon —possibly the same as (1). (3) A prominent priest who returned with Zerubbabel (Neh. 12:2). (4) A son of Hashabnia, who participated in repairing the Jerusalem wall (Neh. 3:10). (5) One of the priests who sealed the covenant after the Return (Neh. 10:4).

Hauran (hä′o͞o-rän′) ("hollow land" or "black land" of basaltic rock), a flat plateau of E. Syria dotted with mounds of extinct volcanoes, 2,000 ft. above sea level, S. of the River Pharpar, E. of the Sea of Galilee, S. of Damascus and Mt. Hermon. This rich, treeless granary, from which loaded camel caravans even now move out to the W. and N., lies amid abandoned cities of black basalt in a region roughly identical with the Biblical Bashan*. In Graeco-Roman times the outpost Hauran, comprising a smaller area than formerly, was Auranitis, one of four districts. Augustus gave it to Herod the Great c. 23 B.C.; later it was included in the tetrarchy of Philip. Hauran is mentioned in the O.T. only by Ezekiel (47:16, 18), as a boundary envisioned for restored Israel. E. Hauran is today occupied by fanatical Druses.

Havilah (hăv′ĭ-lä), a vaguely defined region described as territory encompassed by the Pison branch of Eden's* river, and as being rich in gold, onyx, and aromatic gums (Gen. 2:11 f.). It is thought by some to have lain between Ophir and Hazarmaveth, N. of Sheba, in Arabia. Because of the nomadic habits of its people (Ishmaelites, Gen. 25:18), its boundaries were fluid, and may have extended into N. Arabia, as suggested by the narrative of Saul's warfare with the Amalekites (I Sam. 15:7). The P source makes the inhabitants of Havilah descendants of Cush (Gen. 10:7, I Chron. 1:9); J makes them the offspring of Joktan of Shem's lines (Gen. 10:29; I Chron. 1:23).

Havoth-jair (hăv′ŏth-jā′ĭr), small towns of Gilead captured by Jair the son of Manasseh (Num. 32:41).

hawk, an "unclean" or inedible bird mentioned in Lev. 11:16 and Deut. 14:15, along with the owl and the cuckoo. There are at least 18 species in Palestine, the commonest of which are the kestrel (*Falco tinnunculus*) and the sparrow hawk (*Accipiter nisus*). Job referred to the migratory habits of some Palestine hawks (39:26). In Egypt the hawk or falcon was sacred; Horus, the chief deity of united Egypt, had the body of a man and the head of a falcon, and was viewed as the sun god illuminating the world. Pharaoh in some dynasties was considered as the incarnation of Horus. Together with Isis and Osiris, the hawk god formed the great triad or "holy family" of the Egyptian pantheon.

176. Horus the Hawk God (18th-24th Egyptian Dynasty).

Hazael (hăz′ā-ĕl) ("God sees"), an Aramaean courtier of the house of Damascus, who became King of Syria (c. 842–806 B.C.), succeeding Ben-hadad II, whom he murdered at the instigation of Elisha (II Kings 8:7–15), in harmony with a command of the Lord to Elijah (I Kings 19:15–18), as a means of uprooting the baneful influence of the Tyrian Baal-Melkarth apostasy which long had cursed the Omri line of Israel's rulers at Samaria. The stories of the two prophets' relationship to Hazael is confused, probably owing to blended accounts. So vigorous and so competent was Hazael that during a lull in Assyrian aggressions against him he dominated both Israel and Judah. He seized Israel's land E. of the Jordan (cf. Amos 1:3) and spared Jerusalem only at the high price of carrying off everything portable from both city and Temple (II Kings 12:17 ff.; cf. II Chron. 22:5 f.)—the first of many rapes of the capital. Amos in his prophecy of doom predicted the destruction of Hazael's line (1:4).

Hazor (hā′zôr) ("an enclosure"). (1) A city of N. Galilee, SW. of Lake Huleh, identified by John Garstang in 1926 as Tell el-Qedah (Tell Waqqas). Dominating the S. edge of the Huleh Valley, the site controlled the main N.–S. route from N. Palestine to Damascus, which crossed the Jordan River just S. of Lake Huleh at the only possible ford. Other roads led N. to the Lebanese Beqa'a and to Tyre on the Phoenician coast. The site consists of two elements: a 30-acre acropolis (the "Upper City") and a large, 175-acre rectangular plateau to the N. (the "Lower City"), bounded on the W. by a massive rampart of beaten earth. Several soundings were made on the site by Garstang in 1928. Major excavations were carried out with much success under the direction of Y. Yadin in 1955–58, 1968–69, and 1971–72.

The main tell was first occupied in the Early Bronze Age (Strata XXI–XIX, 27th–24th cen. B.C.), and later used by a seminomadic people during MB I (Stratum XVIII, 21st–19th cen. B.C.). A major change occurred at Hazor with the founding of the lower city at the beginning of MB IIB (c. 1750 B.C.), the use of which continued until its final destruction at the end of the Late Bronze Age (c. 1230 B.C.). The outlines of several important structures were recovered from the ruins of the five phases of the lower city (for chronology and correlation with the main tell, see *BA* 32, 1969, p. 54), including a series of city gates, important sections of the city defenses, a shrine with a row of small basalt stelae preserved *in situ*, and four superimposed Canaanite temples , the latest (Lower City Strata I–LB II) of which is regarded as a forerunner of the Solomonic temple. The Hazor example is composed of three elements aligned on a central axis—a porch, with two pillars set near the inner entrance; a hall, or sanctuary; and an altar room, or holy of holies. Throughout the existence of this lower city, Hazor remained an important international and economic center, as attested by the appearance of its name in a number of texts from the 18th-century B.C. Mari archives (see *JBL* 79, 1960, pp. 12–19). The city's dominant role in N. Palestine is again revealed in several Amarna Letters of the 14th century B.C., and is recalled in the Biblical description of Hazor as "the head of all those kingdoms" (Josh. 11:10). Hazor is also mentioned in an execration text of the 19th century B.C. (*ANET*[3], p. 329), in Egyptian topographical lists (*ANET*[3], p. 242), and in 13th century B.C. Papyrus Anastasi I (*ANET*[3], p. 477).

he (hā), the 5th letter of the Hebrew alphabet. See WRITING.

head is mentioned scores of times in Scripture, usually with obvious but sometimes with metaphorical meaning, as "lifting up the head" in arrogant pride (Judg. 8:28; Ps. 83:2); "the head of Syria," Damascus (Isa. 7:8); the head of a "fat valley" (Isa. 28:1, 4); or of a city gate (Ezek. 21:19; Ps. 24:7); or of a river (Gen. 2:10). Saying that someone's blood was "upon the head" of an individual was tantamount to charging him with responsibility for life or death (Josh. 2:19; I Kings 2:37). Returning good for evil was "coals of fire" on an enemy's head (Prov. 25:22; Rom. 12:20). The "head stone" of the corner of a wall was its noblest and most massive masonry (Ps. 118:22; Luke 20:17; Acts 4:11). Shaving the head might witness a vow (Acts 18:18), though shaving the head (except by priests, and in tabooed foreign fashion) was common. Egyptians shaved the head for coolness at home and wore ceremonial wigs in public. An uncovered or disheveled head indicated mourning (Lev. 10:6; Ezek. 24:17). See ANOINT; BEARDS; GESTURE; HAIR.

heart, in its physiological activity, was recognized by writers of Scripture: fainting (Gen. 45:26; Isa. 1:5); heart failure (I Sam. 4:13–18); healthy heart action (Prov. 14:30); longevity (Ps. 22:26). Yet in the O.T., and those portions of the N.T. which were influenced by the O.T., the heart was metaphorically regarded as the source of man's intellectual activities (I Kings 8:48; Isa. 10:7; Ezek. 36:26). The laws of God were considered as written in man's heart (Ps. 37:31). Out of the heart were the issues of life (Prov. 4:23). When Solomon prayed for the greatest gift he could think of, he asked for "an understanding heart" (I Kings 3:9). Wisdom writers referred to the heart as acquainted with wisdom (Eccles. 2:3). Paul in Romans spoke of believing in the heart (Rom. 10:9 f.). Jesus challenged the scribes, "Why reason ye these things in your hearts?" (Mark 2:8). The heart was also regarded as the seat of emotion (Lev. 19:17; I Kings 8:38; Prov. 14:10; Isa. 30:29). It was the switchboard communicating messages from the conscience (Josh. 11:20; I Sam. 24:5; Job 27:6; I Tim. 4:2 A.S.V.). Jeremiah recognized the heart as the source of sin (7:24, 11:8, 16:12); so did Jesus (Mark 7:6 f.). The heart is conspicuous in the teachings of Jesus: the "pure in heart" are to see God (Matt. 5:8); those of "honest and good heart" are the good soil from which production comes (Luke 8:15); a man brings good or evil from "the abundance of the heart" (Luke 6:45; cf. Matt. 12:34 ff.). In the Bible, in brief, the heart is the repository and directive center of thought, will, feeling, and conscience*. The right spirit was the clean heart (Ps. 51:10), practically synonymous with soul.

O.T. theology makes a new heart necessary to the new man (I Sam. 10:9)—a very old statement, dated from near the beginning of the Hebrew Monarchy. Jeremiah writes of the new covenant between God and His people as written in the hearts of the people (31:31–34). Ezekiel amplified this concept (11:19 f., 36:25–27). Joel enlarged it further to include the whole nation in the "outpouring" of new heart (2:28–32). Paul used the Gk. word *nous* ("mind") for "inner man" renewed in the Christian (Rom. 7:23, 25, 12:2; I Cor. 2:16).

So vital did the Egyptians consider a man's heart integrity to his chances for immortality, that one of their favorite depictions in the papyrus rolls of "The Book of the Dead" showed a man standing before a set of balances, watching his heart being weighed on one side, over against the feather, symbol of righteousness (Maat).

Plato (c. 427–347 B.C.) located the soul of man in his heart, and made it ruler of the intelligence and of emotion.

heathen (A.S.V. "nation"; R.S.V. "Gentiles" or "people," "peoples"), a word applied frequently in the O.T., A.V., to pagan or idolatrous nations surrounding Israel (Jer. 49:15) during her formative years, when she was desperately in earnest about establishing the supremacy of Yahweh and of Israel as His chosen people (Isa. 43:20). Protests against "heathen" are prominent in post-Exilic writings. Heathen were non-Jews, Gentiles*, whose "filthiness" in the matter of foods (Ezra 6:21); "abominations" in worship (II Kings 16:3); idolatry and wealth (Ps. 135:15) were reflected in utterances of prophets and reformers. Yet even in the O.T. were notes of yearning to reach "the heathen," or "the nation," as in Isa. 49:6 (and entire chap.) and the Book of Jonah*. In spite of the exclusiveness of the Temple precincts, with its "Court of the Gentiles," the door was always open to heathen proselytes who accepted circumcision and other Jewish rules of life, like the Ethiopian eunuch (Acts 8:26–39); and Timothy (Acts 16:1–3). In the N.T. Paul, who knew "perils by heathen" (II Cor. 11:26), was eager to preach to them (Gal. 1:16; 2:9, A.V.; R.S.V. "Gentiles") and believed that "God would justify the heathen through faith" (Gal. 3:8). He became a "light to the Gentiles" (Isa. 49:6), their Apostle.

heave offering (from Heb. word meaning "to be high"), a portion "lifted," or "separated" in early Israel for Yahweh's portion, and later for the priests and Levites (Ex. 29:27 f.; Deut. 12:6, 11; Ezek. 45:6–16). Heave offerings may have originated in the heaved or tossed up forkfuls of grain dedicated to God on ancient threshing floors (see FARMING). In later Israel heave offerings included first fruits of oil, fruit, and grain; flesh of redeemed fatlings (Num. 18:15–18); "devoted things" (Num. 18:14); cakes from new meal dough (Num. 15:20 f.). Heave offerings also included the tithe mentioned in Num. 18:21–24. See WORSHIP.

heaven, the upper region of the universe according to the common Hebrew three-story conception. The Hebrew word is always plural, but is frequently translated as singular (see Ps. 19:1; cf. Job. 22:12). The belief in a plurality of heavens was common in the ancient world (cf. II Cor. 12:2). It found support in the speculations of Aristotle and of the Pythagoreans, and it provides the framework for Dante's description of Paradise in *The Divine Comedy*. The "highest" heaven was the habitation of God (Ps. 57:5); but the belief grew that even "the heaven and heaven of heavens" could not contain Him (II Chron. 2:6; cf. Job 22:14). Many of the Biblical figures describing heaven are physical. It is a great concave—"the firmament" (Gen. 1:6–8)—overarching the earth, "stretched out like a curtain" (Isa. 40:22; Jer. 51:15), and supported by pillars (Job 26:11). It could on occasion "open" for various reasons, such as to allow the descent of angelic messengers (Gen. 28:12); of bread or manna (Ex. 16:4; cf. John 6:31–33); of fire (II Chron. 7:1); of rain and snow (Isa. 55:10); of numerous other blessings (Mal. 3:10); even of God Himself (Isa. 64:1).

This general view carries over into the N.T., but features are added there which tend to spiritualize it. Heaven is still thought of as "up," as it is today, but the emphasis is less geographical and more qualitative, as in "the kingdom of heaven." The Holy Spirit came from heaven at the baptism of Jesus (Matt. 3:16, 17), as he did at other times (I Pet. 1:12). As in O.T. times, "heaven" is still used as a substitute for God: "a sign from heaven" (Mark 8:11) is a sign from God (cf. II Chron. 32:20). Though in the N.T. heaven is still largely a place, it is a place to be anticipated by the righteous: the desired "better country" of Heb. 11:16 is "a heavenly" one (cf. II Tim. 4:18). It is the abode of "the Father" (Matt. 6:9, 7:21). There the Christian will find his "reward" (Matt. 5:12); there he keeps his lasting "treasure" (Matt. 6:19–21). It is the realm of "joy" (Luke 15:7) and of "peace" (19:38).

The names of the redeemed are recorded there (Luke 10:20; Heb. 12:23)—a metaphor suggesting the right of entrance when the time comes to possess the imperishable heritage (I Pet. 1:4; cf. Matt. 25:14–23). The description of heaven in the Revelation of John (4:1–6, 7:9–17, 14:1–5, 21:1–22:5) is highly pictorial, and it has provided much of the language of Christian hope, but it is intended to represent the ultimate triumph of the purpose of God in a redeemed mankind (7:9) forever secure in "a holy city" (21:10; cf. Ezek. 40:1–4, 48:35). E. L.

Heber (hē′bĕr) ("associate"). (1) A grandson of Asher (Gen. 46:17; Num. 26:45; I Chron. 7:31 f.). (2) A Kenite, husband of Jael (Judg. 4:17, 5:24). The Kenites were a tribe of nomadic smiths in S. Judaea. Heber migrated N. to Kedesh, W. of the Sea of Galilee (Judg. 4:11), possibly because he found the armaments business profitable among the Canaanites with their "nine hundred chariots of iron" (Judg. 4:13). But when Sisera was routed by the Israelites and sought asylum in the tent of his ally Heber, Jael, wife of Heber, killed the Canaanite chieftain with a tent peg and a workman's hammer (Judg. 4:21, 5:26). (3) A man of Judah (I Chron. 4:18). (4) A Benjamite (I Chron. 8:17).

Hebrew, one of the Semitic tongues. It belongs to the NW. group of Semitic languages, including the Aramaic and the Amoritic or Canaanitic (Hebrew, Phoenician, Punic, Moabitic). It is related to Arabic. The Hebrew alphabet contains 22 letters representing consonants (vowels not having been written before the 7th century B.C.). "The vocabulary of Hebrew, although very limited and only partially known, is concrete and vivid. Words still paint a picture and seldom reach the stage of pale abstractions." Sentence after sentence of co-ordinated. impressive, cumulative phrases mark such typical passages as Isa. 5:1 f. Frequent metaphors, vividly realistic phrases, and poetic characterizations are typical of Biblical Hebrew, whose imagery, as Robert H. Pfeiffer points out, is "delightfully bewildering" to Western readers.

The finest form of Hebrew was used in the golden age which produced the historical books (with the exception of Chronicles, Ezra, Nehemiah, and Esther). The less pure post-Exilic was used for most of the books of the Hagiographa* and the latest prophets. Yet in spite of changes in style, which make the Books of Kings, for example, so much more brilliant than Chronicles, the Hebrew language shows consistency over a period of 1,000 years.

Near the beginning of the Christian era Aramaic supplanted Hebrew as the spoken language of the people. Hebrew continued in use during the development of the Rabbinic literature.

See WRITING.

Hebrews, apparently an Aramaean branch of the large Semitic family which originally came out of Arabia, the purest surviving representatives of which are the true Arabs. They are grouped with the NW. Semites (in contrast to the E. Semites, who include the Accadian (see ACCAD) and Assyro-Babylonians (see BABYLON)), and are classified with Amoritic or Canaanitic peoples (including Phoenicians, Carthaginians, and Moabites). (For their language, see HEBREW.) The Aramaean Hebrews seem to have been shepherds at the desert edge of the Fertile Crescent. Though Aramaeans contributed only a small part of the ultimately very mixed blood of Israel, yet the early traditions of the nation's ancestry go back to Aramaeans (A.V. "Syrian," Gen. 25:20, 28:5; A.S.V. margin "Aramaean"). When Abraham desired to secure a suitable wife for his son Isaac he sent to Padan-aram (the region near Haran) for Rebekah, daughter of the Syrian Bethuel (Gen. 24:10, 25:20). So too Jacob sought his wife Rachel from the people of Padan-aram (Gen. 28, 29). Hebrews long maintained relations with their E. Aramaean kinsfolk. They also felt, during their N. Mesopotamian sojourn, a mixed Accadian, Hurrian, and Amorite influence.

Abraham, regarded by Hebrews as their progenitor, according to Gen. 11:27–32 had lived in Ur of the Chaldees, a very ancient city of high culture in S. Babylonia. From Ur, according to this narrative, Abraham with his father Terah migrated to Haran, in NW. Mesopotamia. From Haran Abraham and his family ultimately moved S. and W. into Canaan, the land promised him by Yahweh (Gen. 12:1–3, 15:18–21). Some critics place so much stress on the formative influence of Haran in the Padan-aram region on the subsequent personality, faith, and thought of the Hebrews—as indicated by rich archaeological evidence from the Nuzi, Mari, Hittite, and Amarna tablets—that they consider the experiences of the Hebrews of Ur at the most that of nomads who merely passed through the great southern culture, and did not tarry as residents. There is too much archaeological evidence linking the customs of Hebrew Patriarchs (see PATRIARCH) and those of N. Mesopotamia in the 19th and 18th centuries B.C. to allow us to ignore the Haran theory. There is a wealth of material pointing to the original home of the Hebrew patriarchs as Padan-aram, "field of Aram" (Gen. 25:20, 28:2), in NW. Mesopotamia, where they were under Accadian, Hurrian, and Amorite influences. The names of several of Abraham's forefathers tally with names of towns near Haran: Serug (Gen. 11:20), Nahor (Gen. 11:26, 24:10), and Terah (Gen. 11:24). W. F. Albright and others feel that the Hebrew folk tales and beliefs sprang neither from Canaanite nor from Egyptian sources. On the other hand there are many Mesopotamian parallels to such Biblical stories as the Creation, Eden, the Patriarchs who lived before the Flood, and the Flood story. These parallels all came from NW. Mesopotamia into the W. before the middle of the 2d century millennium B.C. Throughout their history the Hebrews retained contacts with the Baby-

HEBREWS

lonians, to whom they were more closely related than to the Assyrians.

There are evidences in the O.T. that the Hebrews knew themselves to be a composite race (see Deut. 26:5, indicating their claim to descent from a fugitive Aramaean (A.V. Syrian), related, for example, to N. and S. Arabian tribes with Abraham's line through his offspring by Hagar (Gen. 16:15) and Keturah (Gen. 25:1–4; I Chron. 1:32). Not only in the old tribal days, through marriage with Kenites, Kenizzites, etc., but all through their residence in Canaan, Hebrews experienced admixtures of Arabian blood. Egyptian strains appear in the Joseph family with Asenath's two sons, Ephraim and Manasseh (Gen. 41:50–52). Moses had a Midianite wife, Zipporah (Ex. 18:1–7), and an unnamed Ethiopian (Cushite) one (Num. 12:1). A clan of Kenites and other "outsiders" joined in the Conquest* of Canaan (Judg. 1:16), and were counted an important family among Hebrews (I Chron. 2:55). See ISRAEL.

177. Shield of David.

Many critics favor the close association of Hebrews or their identification with the roaming aggressive Habiru (Khapiru*, Khabiru) who are mentioned in tablets from the entire 2d millennium B.C.; the Tell el-Amarna Letters of the 14th century tell of their capture of "the king's cities" in Palestine. R. H. Pfeiffer accepts the Habiru of the Amarna Letters as identified with the Hebrews (*Introduction to the Old Testament*, p. 162). W. F. Albright points out that a Habiru origin would check amazingly well with Hebrew traditional history, and would provide answers to many unsolved enigmas. But other critics see serious difficulties in identifying the Biblical Hebrews with the Habiru of the Amarna letters, as in the taking of Jerusalem —represented as imperiled in the correspondence of Abdi-Hiba with Egypt; whereas we now know from archaeological and textual evidence that Jerusalem was not taken by Israelites until the time of David (II Sam. 5:6–9). Besides, the date of Israel's entry into Canaan cannot apparently be made to tally with the coming of the Habiru.

Distinctions are to be made between the words "Hebrew," "Israelite," and "Jew." Though "Hebrews" and "Israelites" are often used synonymously, Israel was only a part of a larger group called Hebrews, descendants of Eber*, according to the later J narrative of Gen. 10:24; in contrast to the tribes which descended from Israel, the alternate name of Jacob in the early J narratives of Gen. 32:28 and the late P narrative of Gen. 35:10. According to the Bible, the Hebraic ethnic groups included, in addition to Hebrews, the Edomites, Moabites, and Ammonites—their nearest neighbors on the S. and E. In Gen. 25 genealogical traditions were personified in eponymous ancestors. Edom (Esau) was brother to Israel (Gen. 36:1); Moab and Ammon were his second cousins (Gen. 19:37 f.). Moabites spoke a dialect very closely related to Hebrew, learned by the Moabites, as well as by the Hebrews, from the Canaanites. Some critics say, following Deut. 15:12 and Jer. 34:9, 14, that "Hebrew" and "Israel" are synonymous in the code of civil law (Pfeiffer). To state merely that the Israelites were the Twelve Tribes descended from the 12 sons of Jacob is oversimplification, because the Tribes varied in various periods. For the history of Israel in the sense of the Northern Kingdom of 10 Tribes, see ISRAEL (3); for the history of Judah, in the sense of the Southern Kingdom, see JUDAH, KINGDOM OF.

Moreover, it is to be noted that not all the Hebrews who were living in Palestine descended into Egypt. Probably some remained in Palestine, and therefore never took part in the Exodus and Conquest experiences of the Israelites; but after the settlement of those who had come up from Egypt with Moses and Joshua these merged with the "new" settlers and contributed their blood, their ideas, and their very ancient concepts of God (see EL SHADDAI) which they had safeguarded from times even more remote than the Sinai revelations to the wandering Hebrews.

The word "Israel" is often used when the religious aspect of the people is emphasized.

"Jew" was used during and especially after the Exile; it is derived from "Judah," where Jews lived.

A dispersion* (*diaspora*) of Jews from crowded Palestine took place in the expanding world following the conquests of Alexander the Great. Some of these went to Egypt, especially Alexandria, others to Rome, Byzantium, and Mesopotamia. From Egypt the Jews spread to North Africa and Spain, and later France. The French Jews later went to England and Germany, and the German Jews eventually spread to Central and Eastern Europe. There they found a small settlement of Jews who had come from the Byzantine Empire and from Crimea, once held by the Khazars, an oriental people whose ruling family adopted Judaism c. A.D. 740. Most American Jews are of East European descent.

The Hebrew tribal nomads came late into history, in comparison to the peoples whose civilization has been archaeologically proven in lower Mesopotamia (as at antediluvian Eridu, Tell al-'Ubaid, and Ur), and the N. Nile region. Yet their gifts to the world—ethical monotheism and Jesus—have never been exceeded by any single contribution from any source since man emerged from the Stone Age. Their wide-reaching influence has flowed through history, not only from the creative religious thinkers of Israel, but also from Christianity and Islam. When the first great event of Israel's national history occurred—the main phase of the entry into Palestine probably soon after 1300 B.C.—Egyptian prestige was dwindling;

and the rich culture of Sumer was almost forgotten.

For events in the career of the Hebrew people in Palestine and for their religious contribution, see ISRAEL (2).

Hebrews, the Epistle to the, the 19th book of the N.T. Its thesis is that Christianity is the final and absolute religion because Jesus is the true high priest and final mediator between God and man. Christ once and for all wrought forgiveness and Christianity alone can offer salvation. Jesus Christ is superior to the angels; he far surpasses Moses and Joshua in the history of redemption; he is greater than one of the Aaronic priesthood, where one priest follows another, for Jesus is the high priest forever after the order of Melchizedek*. Finally, Christ is "an high priest, who is set on the right hand of the throne of the Majesty in the heavens, a minister of the sanctuary, and of the true tabernacle, which the Lord pitched, and not man" (8:1 f.).

The authorship of this writing was not attributed to Paul until the end of the 2d century. In A.D. 225 Origen thought that Paul was the author of the material, but that someone else—who he was "God only knows"—put the material into written form. Today most scholars agree with Calvin's statement: "Who then composed it is not to be discovered, however hard one labors, but that the nature of the thought and that the style are quite unlike Paul's is abundantly evidenced." The title in the A.V. contains the words "of Paul the Apostle," but these do not appear in the A.S.V. and the R.S.V. As the book is Pauline neither in style nor in theology, many other possible authors have been suggested, among whom are: Barnabas, Timothy, Aquila, Priscilla, Luke, and Clement. Luther believed Apollos possessed the qualifications necessary to this author (Acts 18:24–28). From internal evidence the unknown author was a man of literary training whose Greek is the purest in the N.T. His diction is faultless; his sentences rounded and polished. He displays familiarity with the Greek philosophical ideas of Plato and of Philo of Alexandria as well as with the teachings of Paul.

Hebrews begins with a magnificent paragraph that contains no salutation such as is customary in N.T. epistles. Only in the final chapter is there anything which resembles either a personal letter or a more formal epistle. This has given rise to the theory that Hebrews was originally a homily or treatise written for Christians everywhere, not a letter addressed to one particular group. According to this theory, the final epistolary chapter was added later to endow the writing with the stamp of Pauline authority. The title "To the Hebrews," was given to the work probably at the same time. If the last chapter was part of the original writing, 13:19 suggests that a definite community is addressed. Whether this community was in Antioch, Caesarea, Alexandria, Ephesus, or Rome cannot be determined. The closing greeting (13:24) suggests that the author was a Roman teacher who was somewhere outside Italy, whence he and certain Italians who shared his company sent greetings to their associates.

Hebrews appears to have been written for readers who had become Christians, not by contact with Christ in the days of his flesh, but through the witness of others (2:3). The early days of Christianity were now far behind. Evidences of this lapse of time can be seen: (1) in the reference to "former days, in which, after ye were illuminated, ye endured a great fight of afflictions" (10:32); (2) in the absence of reference to the Parousia*; and (3) in the separation of the leaders from the rest of the saints (13:24). A date between A.D. 85 and 110 would fit these conditions.

The purpose of this writing was to rekindle the faith of those who were drifting away from their Christian convictions (2:1). The author undertook to prove by closely reasoned argument that Christianity is the perfect form of religion, while Judaism, fine though it is, is only an imperfect form. The angels, Moses, and the high priests were all mediators between God and man, but Jesus is greater than them all and is the true high priest (8:1, 9:11). By virtue of his earthly life and his sympathy with human suffering Jesus became the final mediator between God and man (2:5–8, 4:14–16). "Wherefore in all things it behoved him to be made like unto his brethren, that he might be a merciful and faithful high priest in things pertaining to God, to make reconciliation for the sins of the people" (2:17). Except in the Gospels, the N.T. nowhere else emphasizes the human life of Jesus. Instead of a daily sacrifice of the blood of animals, Christ, the great high priest, poured out his own blood once for all. This was effective for man's forgiveness, for this sacrifice is never to be repeated. The author exhorts his readers to be loyal to their faith, for he saw faith as an essential quality of a Christian. Paul understands faith as man's receptivity to God, while the author of Hebrews sees it as man's apprehension of the unseen: "Now faith is the substance of things hoped for, the evidence of things not seen" (11:1). Faith is the quality by which great things were achieved by the heroes and heroines of the O.T. Chapter 11, in which this is recorded, has been called "The Hymn of Faith." The author, returning to his original theme from this digression which illuminates his main argument, declares that Jesus is the perfect example and the goal of faith (12:2). Hebrews may be outlined as follows:

(1) The supremacy of Jesus Christ—1:1–5:10:
 (a) Above the angels;
 (b) Superior to Moses;
 (c) Excels Joshua;
 (d) Superior to the Levitical high priest;
 (e) Christ as the author of eternal salvation.
(2) The dangers of apostasy—5:11–6:12.
(3) The finality and effectiveness of Christ's sacrifice—6:13–10:39:
 (a) Christ, a high priest after the order of Melchizedek;

(b) Supersedes the Levitical priesthood and the daily sacrifices;
(c) Christ's sacrifice was once for all;
(d) The effectiveness of the sacrifice.
(4) Faith as seen in heroes of old—11:1–40.
(5) Practical exhortations—12:1–29.
(6) Appendix and salutations—13:1–25.

Hebron (hē'brŏn) ("union," "league," "association"), a city 19 m. SW. of Jerusalem, one of the oldest continuously inhabited communities in Palestine, claiming to antedate Zoan (Avaris, see RAAMSES) in Egypt, famed for its greatness and antiquity (Num. 13:22). Hebron was adjacent to the oaks or terebinths of Mamre* (Gen. 13:18, 35:27). It was also called Kiriath-arba, a name revived after the Exile (Gen. 23:2; Josh. 14:15; Neh. 11:25). Crusaders called it "the Castle of St. Abraham." To Arabs it is El Khalil, "the Friend," a designation for Abraham (Jas. 2:23).

In the earliest Patriarchal stories Abraham is closely associated with Hebron (Gen. 13:18, 18:1 ff.), as Isaac is with Beer-sheba (Gen. 26:23–25) and Jacob with Bethel* (Gen. 28:10 ff.). Sarah died at Hebron, and Abraham bought the Cave of Machpelah from Ephron the Hittite (Gen. 23:7–16) for her sepulcher, which became the family vault of the Patriarchs and matriarchs of Israel—Abraham, Isaac, and Jacob; Sarah, Rebekah, and Leah (Gen. 49:31, 50:13).

The spies found the giant Anakim among Hebron's inhabitants (Num. 13:22). Hoham, King of Hebron, was part of the Amorite confederacy defeated by Joshua (Josh. 10:3, 23, 36, 39, 11:21). Caleb took it as part of his inheritance (Josh. 14:13–15, 15:13 f.; Judg. 1:20). It became one of the six cities* of refuge (Josh. 20:7, 21:11; I Chron. 6:55, 57). David was anointed king in Hebron (II Sam. 2:11); and there six of his seven sons were born (II Sam. 3:2–5). Absalom raised his standard of rebellion against his father in this his birthplace (II Sam. 15:10). Hebron was fortified by Rehoboam (II Chron. 11:5, 10). During the Captivity Edomites occupied S. Judah, including Hebron, which may explain why the later P writers included among the various narratives that make up Genesis their detailed accounts of the sanctity of Hebron to Israel's Patriarchs Abraham (Gen. 25:7–11), Isaac (Gen. 35:27), and Jacob (Gen. 50:12 f.), and matriarchs Sarah (Gen. 23:1–19), Rebekah (Gen. 49:31), and Leah (Gen. 49:31). Judas Maccabaeus took Hebron from the Edomites.

Brief notices on excavations carried out on Djebel er-Rumeide in Hebron, 1964–66, indicate several main periods of occupation, from the Late Chalcolithic to Byzantine and late Arabic times. Portions of a MB II fortification wall and defense tower, from Patriarchal times, were traced. Today Hebron is a Moslem town. Ancient oaks on its outskirts give it the atmosphere of Mamre. An enclosure 198x111 ft. built on the traditional site of the Cave of Machpelah is most sacred. The ancient wall rises to a height of 40 ft., above which modern walls rise still higher. The construction resembles that of the Haram (Temple Area) in Jerusalem. Within the enclosure is a mosque, formerly a 12th-century Crusader church, which was on the site of the 6th-century basilica of Justinian's era. Inside the mosque are the cenotaphs of Abraham, Isaac, and Jacob, covered with elaborate gold-embroidered green textiles, and of Sarah, Rebekah, and Leah, covered with crimson. The cenotaphs are presumed to be over their tombs in the rocky cavern below. The cave has not been entered since Crusader times.

178. Moslem mosque at Hebron.

hedge, often of thorn (*mesūkah*) (Prov. 15:19; Hos. 2:6; Mic. 7:4), used to separate a man's property from his neighbor's; or privately owned orchards and vineyards from the highway (Mark 12:1; Luke 14:23). Hedges were to be respected (Eccles. 10:8; Ps. 80:12). Today hedges in Palestine are often of cactus, whose "prickly pears" are enjoyed.

heifer, a cow less than three years old that has not produced a calf (Judg. 14:18; Jer. 50:11; Hos. 10:11; see CATTLE). Heifers were also used in Hebrew religious ceremonials of sacrifice and purification (Gen. 15:9; Num. 19:2, 5, 6, 9, 10, 17; I Sam. 16:2; Heb. 9:13). In Egypt the influential goddess Hathor had the horned head of a heifer. The sky goddess Nut was depicted as a heifer held up by gods, with stars attached to her body. Possibly this exalting of the heifer reflected the agricultural Egyptians' appreciation of this valuable farm animal. Jeremiah described Egypt as "a very fair heifer" (46:20).

heir. See INHERITANCE.

Heldai (hĕl'dā̆-ī). (1) David's captain for the 12th month (I Chron. 27:15). (2) A Jew returned from Babylon (Zech. 6:10).

Heli (hē'lī) (Gk. form "Eli"), the father of Joseph the husband of Mary (Luke 3:23); another interpretation, arrived at by punctuating the Greek differently, is that he was the father of Mary, mother of Jesus. See GENEALOGY.

Heliopolis. See ON.

hell, the usual Biblical translation (in the A.V.) of the Heb. "Sheol" and the Gk. "Hades"*. From being merely the shadowy abode of departed spirits the conception of hell was elaborated until it stood for a place of unspeakable terrors, especially in the so-called Apocalyptic* Literature, of which the Revelation of John is the chief example in the N.T. (see 14:9–11, 21:8, 22:15). The concept occurs in some of the sayings of Jesus (Matt. 5:29 f., 23:33), and in several of his parables (Matt. 25); and it is implied in such teaching as John 3:16–18, 36, 15:6. Though the language used is often figurative—like the "fire" and "worm" of Mark 9:48—this does not mean that it is to be taken lightly, as expressing nothing real. The possibility that the results of sin may follow the soul into the next life is plainly taught in the N.T. (Luke 12:10, 16:19–31; Heb. 6:4–8, 10:26–31; II Pet. 3:17). Biblical scholars differ on such questions as to whether the N.T. definitely teaches that the unrepentant wicked will eventually be annihilated; or that the sufferings of the hereafter will suffice to purify the soul and fit it for the hereafter; or that, at last, by the irresistible force of Divine grace and love, all are to be saved. See ESCHATOLOGY; PUNISHMENT.

E. L.

Hellenists (hĕl′ĕn-ĭsts), Greek-speaking Jews of the Dispersion who had adopted Greek habits and customs. They are called "Grecians" in the A.V., "Grecian Jews" in the A.S.V., and "Hellenists" in the R.S.V. (Acts 6:1, 9:29). See GREEKS.

helmet, the metal head-protecting portion of a fighter's armor, used as early as the time of Saul (I Sam. 17:5, 38), of King Uzziah (II Chron. 26:14), and throughout the Biblical period. Helmets of Persians, Ethiopians, and Libyans are mentioned by Ezekiel (27:10, 38:5). The figurative "helmet of salvation" was mentioned in Isaiah (59:17) and by Paul (Eph. 6:17; I Thess. 5:8). Among the historic helmets excavated from ancient sites, the splendid gold one of Mes-kalam-dug of

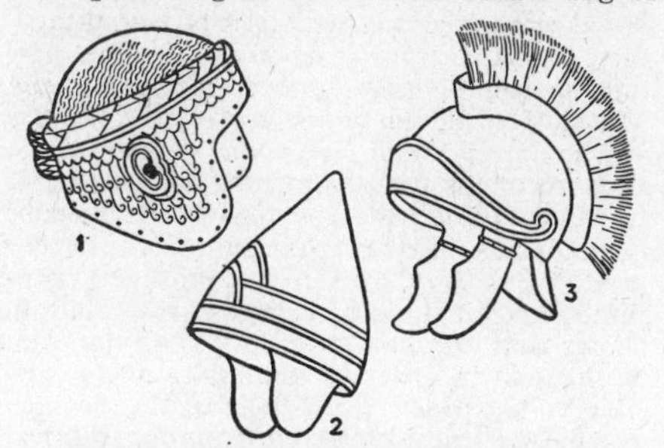

179. Helmets: 1. Sumerian, 3000 B.C.; 2. Assyrian, 700 B.C.; 3. Roman, 200 B.C.

Sumer, excavated at Ur, is considered one of the choicest pieces of goldsmith's art from all antiquity (British Museum, replica in University Museum, Philadelphia).

Heman (hē′măn), a wise man of Solomon's time (I Kings 4:31). According to its title, he composed Psalm 88.

Hemath. See HAMATH; HAMMATH.

hemlock. See GALL.

hems, the edge, fringe, border, or margin of a garment. In the O.T. the word usually appears in connection with high priest's robes (Ex. 28:33, 34, A.V. 39:24–26 A.S.V. "skirts of the robe"); and in the N.T. in connection with those seeking to touch Christ's garments to secure healing, like the invalid woman (Matt. 9:20), and the crowd at Gennesaret (Matt. 14:36). See FRINGES.

hen, a fowl commonly raised in Palestine, mentioned only in Matt. 23:37; Luke 13:34.

henotheism. See POLYTHEISM.

Hepher (hē′fẽr) ("pit"). (1) A town W. of Jordan (Josh. 12:17). (2) A son of Gilead (Num. 26:32, 27:1). (3) A man of Judah (I Chron. 4:6). (4) One of David's worthies (I Chron. 11:36).

Hephzibah (hĕf′zĭ-bȧ) ("my delight is in her"). (1) The mother of Manasseh (II Kings 21:1). (2) A name for Jerusalem (Isa. 62:4).

Heptateuch, the first seven books of the O.T. See HEXATEUCH.

herbs, mixed or used separately at the first Passover supper (Ex. 12:8), may have been lettuce, chicory, endive, watercress. "Bitter herbs" are still used at the Passover meal, symbolizing the sufferings of enslaved Israel.

herd. See CATTLE; SHEEP.

hereafter, the. See ESCHATOLOGY; GLORY; HADES; HEAVEN; HELL; PARADISE.

heresy (Gk. *hairesis*, "a taking," "choosing"), not used in the N.T. in the later Church sense of a departure from orthodoxy like the 2d century Gnosticism*, but to mean a sect, party, or school, like the Sadducees (Acts 5:17) or Pharisees (Acts 15:5). "Heresy" was applied to Christianity by its opponents (Acts 24:14). Paul used "heresy" in the sense of the "division" of the body of Christ, caused by breaches of the law of love rather than by matters of doctrine (Rom. 16:17; I Cor. 11:19; Gal. 5:20). In II Pet. 2:1—written later—"heresy" meant "damnable" false teachings brought in by pernicious leaders in disregard of "the way of truth." Many N.T. passages express violent opposition to teachings out of line with the Gospel without mentioning "heresy."

Hermas (hûr′măs), a Christian at Rome—possibly a slave—greeted by Paul (Rom. 16:14). Origen identified him as author of "The Shepherd of Hermas," an early Christian work.

Hermes (hûr′mēz), (1) The Greek name for the god known to Romans as Mercury (Acts 14:12, A.S.V. margin). (2) A Christian at Rome greeted by Paul (R.S.V. Rom. 16:14).

Hermogenes (hûr-mŏj′ĕ-nēz), an unfaithful follower of Paul in Asia (II Tim. 1:15).

Hermon (hûr′mŏn) ("forbidden [place]"), a mountain called "Sirion" by Sidonians (Deut. 3:9) and "Senir" by the Amorites (Deut. 3:9; Ezek. 27:5; I Chron. 5:23). Another name for it is "Sion" (Deut. 4:48). Its sacred character is evidenced in another name—"Baal-hermon" (Judg. 3:3).

Majestic Hermon constituted the N. limit of Israel's conquests (Deut. 3:8; Josh. 11:3, 17, 12:1, 13:5, 11). It is the culmination of the Anti-Lebanon* Range, and extends NE. to SW. for nearly 20 m. Its principal peak resembles an immense truncated cone, divided into three summits, the highest of which is 9,101 ft. above sea level. Ps. 42:6, where "Hermonites" (preferably A.S.V. "Hermons") are mentioned, perhaps alludes to this conspicuous characteristic. A panorama of Lebanon, Damascus, Tyre, and Carmel, the mountains of Upper Galilee and the Jordan rift to the Dead Sea, appears from its summit. Hermon is covered with snow the year round. From the Dead Sea, 120 miles away, its cool heights can be seen on a torrid summer day. Its snowy whiteness is reflected in the waters of the Sea of Galilee. Its melting snows are the main source of the Jordan.

It figures in Hebrew poetry as an inspirational high point (Ps. 89:12, 133:3; Song of Sol. 4:8). By many it is regarded as the "high

180. Mt. Hermon and the Sea of Galilee.

mountain" of Matt. 17:1; Mark 9:2; Luke 9:28. Its proximity to Caesarea Philippi is an argument for its being the site of Christ's Transfiguration (Matt. 16:13). The phrases in the Transfiguration narratives—"white as the light" (Matt. 17:2); "white and glistering" (Luke 9:29); "intensely white, as no fuller on earth could bleach them" (Mark 9:3 R.S.V.) are possible reflections of the Hermon setting.

In the 10th century A.D. Hermon became the center of the Druse religion, and is now called by Arabs "Jebel esh-Sheikh."

Herod (hĕr′ŭd), the name of a dynasty of princes who in various capacities ruled all or parts of Palestine and neighboring regions from c. 55 B.C. to c. A.D. 93. The house was founded by Antipater (or Antipas), an Idumaean governor, whose family may have come from Ashkelon*. Antipater, with others of his community, was forced by John Hyrcanus the Maccabean (see MACCABEES) to be circumcised and to adopt Judaism. None of the Herods were Jews by blood. Antipater's son Antipater became, by Roman grant in time of Julius Caesar, virtual ruler of all Palestine (c. 55–43 B.C.). His five children included the tetrarch Phasael (41 B.C.) and Herod the Great (also known as Herod I). The following members of the family appear in the N.T.:

(1) *Herod the Great* (probably the Herod of Matt. 2:1), ruling at the time of Jesus' birth. The power and achievements of the Herod family were due not alone to the innate talents of some of their number, but also to opportunities for prestige which the world situation afforded. Civil war gave Antipater a chance to champion the Maccabean Hyrcanus II and to display the qualities which led to his being made Procurator* of Judaea. The Hasmonaean (see HASMONAEANS) house was decaying, Egyptian and Syrian power was gone, the Roman Empire had not yet been established, and when the stage was set for a strong-handed ruler of Palestine Herod the Great was ready for the office (37 B.C.–4 B.C.). His brilliant mind and enterprising boldness were marked by astuteness, as illustrated by the adroitness with which he and his relatives won the favor of the Roman Cassius by collecting the tribute soon after the assassination of Julius Caesar in March, 44 B.C. Through bribery Herod gained the backing of Antony soon after the victory of Antony and Octavian (Caesar Augustus 27 B.C.) following the battle of Philippi (42 B.C.). He was made king of the Jews by Augustus (40 B.C.), to whom he was consistently loyal. Even after Herod was virtually King of Judaea he had to use for three years every possible wile to make his tenure secure. Having conquered first Idumaea, then Samaria and Galilee, he finally after a three months' siege took Jerusalem (37 B.C.) and requested Antony to behead Antigonus, who had been appointed king and high priest by the Parthians. Herod ruled the Jews—who detested his Edomitic blood—with an iron hand, yet he catered to them by reconstructing with magnificent splendor the dilapidated Temple of Zerubbabel's time, so that it could at least hold its own in comparison with the resplendent Hellenistic temples then being erected all over Palestine. Herod's Temple*, begun evidently c. 20–19 B.C., was not finished until A.D. 62 or 64. It was therefore not complete at the time of Christ's death. Jesus saw it develop. Its vast vistas and courts were the scenes of some of his acts of worship, teaching, and healing. There too the first Christians worshipped for a time. There walked the Apostles and Paul. To pay for this shrine the Jews were taxed unbearably. Yet Herod tactfully omitted statues from the Temple and images from his coins, out of deference to the Mosaic Law against such portrayals.

The family life of Herod was melodramatic because of his temperamental flare-ups, and intrigues among his ten wives. His murder even of his beloved Mariamne (I), of her grandfather Hyrcanus, of her brother Aristobulus, and of some of Herod's own children, shows that the plot to kill all the infants of Bethlehem in order to annihilate every possible rival (Matt. 2:16 ff.) fits the pattern of what we know of Herod from non-Biblical records, even though this crime has not been found elsewhere than in the Gospel account. It was one of the last acts of Herod's life.

Herod I contributed his full share to the total construction program achieved by his dynasty. He rebuilt the Mediterranean port "Strato's Tower," renaming it "Caesarea"* in honor of his patron, Caesar Augustus. Until recently, Mediterranean sands had left few traces of the elegant colonnaded city, "Roman in law, Greek in culture." Its once perfect harbor had for centuries been useless to Palestine. Approach by land had been impossible save by foot or mount. Equally extensive reconstructions were sponsored by Herod on the beautifully situated "fat" hilltop city of Samaria, which he renamed "Sebaste" in honor of (Sebastos) Augustus. Tangible evidences of its colonnaded street, the huge temple of Augustus on the site of an early Baal shrine, the Basilica, etc., were excavated by Harvard University

SIMPLIFIED FAMILY TREE OF THE HERODS

(As Related to N. T. Events)

Antipater (Antipas), Governor of Idumaea

Antipater, Idumaean, Procurator of Judaea, virtual ruler of all Palestine (55–43 B.C.)

Phasael, Tetrarch of Judaea (41 B.C.)

Herod the Great ("the king") (Matt. 2:1; Luke 1:5). Tetrarch (41 B.C.); King of Judaea by consent of Rome (37–4 B.C.)
m. Mariamne (I), granddau. Hyrcanus II
m. Mariamne (II), dau. Simon, High Priest
m. Malthace, Samaritan
m. Cleopatra of Jerusalem

Aristobulus, m. Bernice d. 7 B.C.

Herod, m. Herodias

Salome, m. Philip the Tetrarch, son of Herod the Great and Cleopatra of Jerusalem. Husband was Tetrarch of Ituraea and Trachonitis (Luke 3:1)

Herod Antipas ("the tetrarch") of Galilee and Peraea (4 B.C.–A.D. 39) (Matt. 14:1; Luke 3:1, 19; Mark 6:14); deposed A.D. 39

Archelaus (Matt. 2:22), Ethnarch of Judaea, Samaria, Idumaea (4 B.C.–A.D. 6)

Philip, Tetrarch of Ituraea and Trachonitis, (4 B.C.–A.D. 34) (Luke 3:1)

Herod, King of Chalcis (A.D. 41–48)

Herodias, wife of
(1) Herod (son of Mariamne II)
(2) Herod Antipas (Matt. 14:3–11; Mark 6:17–28; Luke 3:19)

Herod Agrippa I (Acts 12:1), made king by Caligula (A.D. 37) over territory formerly held by Philip and Lysanias; A.D. 41 King of Palestine; d. A.D. 44

Herod Agrippa II (Acts 25:13), King of Chalcis (c. A.D. 50); extended territory; d. c. A.D. 93

Bernice, m. uncle, Herod, King of Chalcis; later returned to brother, Herod Agrippa II, with whom she heard Paul's defense before Festus (Acts 25:13, 23, 26:30)

Drusilla (Acts 24:24) m.
(1) Aziz of Emessa
(2) Felix

(George Reisner), the Hebrew University in Jerusalem, the Palestine Exploration Fund, and the British School of Archaeology. Herodian walls 10 ft. thick have been exposed. Priceless ivory trimming from palace furniture (Amos 3:15) has been recovered. Masonry from the era of kings Omri and Ahab (9th century B.C.) is again seen. At Jerusalem and in other cities Herod erected stadia, theaters, and amphitheaters. All in all, Herod the Great was one of the most influential princes in the Middle East of his day.

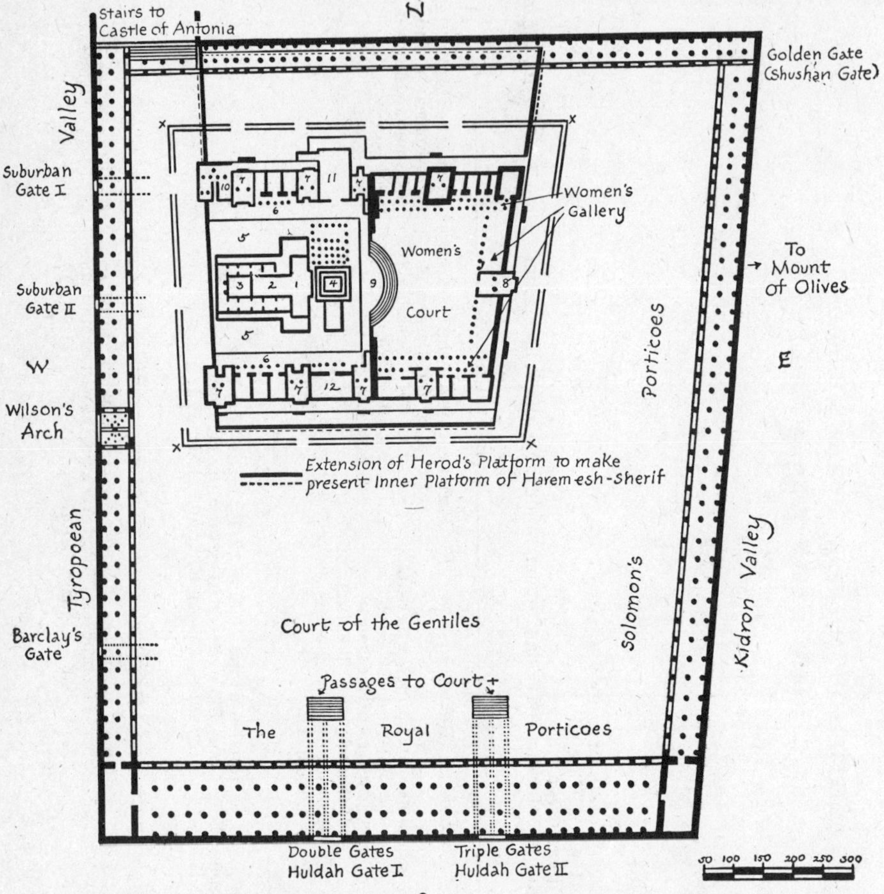

181. Conjectural Plan of Herod's Temple and the Courts. 1. Porch; 2. Holy Place; 3. Holy of Holies; 4. Altar of Burnt Offering; 5. Court of the Priests; 6. Court of Israel, or Men's Court; 7. Sanctuary Gates; 8. Nicanor Gate or Gate Beautiful (?); 9. Nicanor Gate (?); 10. Guardhouse; 11. The northern edifice that was between the gates; 12. Chamber Gazith. (Crosses indicate surrounding Balustrade.)

In 1950, Herod's palace area was excavated on the large mound Tulûl Abū el-'Alâyiq, near the exit of the Wâdī Qelt adjacent to Jericho. See JERICHO, illus. 210.

(2) *Herod Antipas*, son of Herod the Great and Malthace, a Samaritan—and therefore not a Jew by blood—Tetrarch of Galilee (Luke 3:1) and Peraea (4 B.C.–A.D. 39). This Herod is mentioned in the N.T. more frequently than any other. Jesus, knowing Herod's skulking treachery, aptly characterized him as "that fox" (Luke 13:31 f.), and when he heard certain Pharisees report Antipas' threat to kill him, referred to this ruler's evil, permeating influence as "the leaven of Herod" (Mark 8:15). Herod Antipas, holding almost as much power as if he had been king, forfeited his prestige among the Jews when he illegally married his niece Herodias*, former wife of his half-brother, Herod—an outrage which precipitated the beheading of John* the Baptist (Matt. 14:1–12). Herod Antipas was "perplexed" about Jesus and "desired to see him" (Luke 9:7, 9); and questioned Jesus when the prisoner was sent to him from Pilate (Luke 23:7–15). Herod Antipas, when the chief priests and scribes accused the Galilean of many things, "set him at nought, and mocked him, and arrayed him in a gorgeous robe, and sent him again to Pilate" (v. 11). From that day the two estranged authorities "were made friends together" (v. 12). Antipas was the Herod of Acts 4:27.

His chief building works included the reconstruction of Sepphoris, 4 m. N. of Nazareth, and therefore possibly a work site of Jesus and Joseph his carpenter father. Galilean toilers on the aqueduct and amphitheater benefited from its destruction by Varus after the death of Herod the Great. Herod Antipas also constructed a new seaport along the SW. shore of the Sea of Galilee, in a region still famous for its mineral baths, and named it Tiberias* in honor of Emperor Tiberius. The city had no sentimental value for Jews, and is not mentioned in connection with the ministry of Jesus, although it was only a short distance from Magdala, Capernaum, and Bethsaida. Tiberias, a fine specimen of colonnaded Hellenistic city, succeeded Sepphoris as the chief city of Herod Antipas. This ruler was banished to Gaul c. A.D. 39—a fate voluntarily shared by Herodias.

(3) *Herod Archelaus*, Ethnarch of Judaea, Samaria, and Idumaea (4 B.C.–A.D. 6), son of Herod I and Malthace of Samaria; brother of Herod Antipas. His removal by Rome was requested by dissatisfied subjects, a fact to which Jesus evidently referred (Luke 19:12–27). He was banished to Gaul, and his realm placed under the first of a series of Roman procurators (A.D. 6–41). Joseph and Mary, wishing to avoid living in the disturbed territory of Archelaus (Matt. 2:22 f.), bypassed Judaea and went on to Nazareth, which, according to Luke 2:4, 39, was their home.

(4) *Herod*, son of Herod the Great and Mariamne (II). He was half-brother to Herod Antipas, who was later to marry his wife Herodias. (The references in Matt. 14:3 and Mark 6:17 are to him and *not* to Philip the Tetrarch.) Salome was their daughter, and therefore niece to Herod Antipas.

(5) *Herod Philip II*, a half-brother of Herod Antipas; he was the son of Herod the Great and Cleopatra of Jerusalem and was rated the best of Herod's sons. Philip was tetrarch of regions in NE. Palestine, including Ituraea and Trachonitis. He rebuilt in Graeco-Roman style the city of Caesarea Philippi* at the foot of Mt. Hermon. He also rebuilt Bethsaida* and renamed it Bethsaida-Julias, honoring the daughter of Caesar Augustus. Philip died A.D. 34 without heirs. His territory was assigned to Syria. He is mentioned in Scripture only in Luke 3:1.

(6) *Herod Agrippa I*, son of Aristobulus, was grandson of Herod the Great and Mariamne (I). He is called "the king" in Acts 12:1; and "Agrippa the Great" by Josephus. As a youth he went to Rome, became bankrupt, and was satisfied to accept the position of marketmaster at Tiberias. Caligula made him king over what had been his uncle Philip's domain, and he subsequently (A.D. 41–44) ruled practically all that had been governed by Herod the Great.

An enthusiastic Hellenist, Herod Agrippa I built public baths, theaters, amphitheaters (as at Berytus, the later Beirut); and commenced a wall to enclose the N. suburb of Jerusalem. He persecuted Christians, pursuant to his zeal for the Hebrew Law. His orders put James to the sword and persecuted Peter (Acts 12:3–19). His spectacular death after accepting divine honor is narrated in Acts 12:20–23.

(7) *Herod Agrippa II*, son of Herod Agrippa I, and great-grandson of Herod the Great and Mariamne (I), was King of Chalcis (A.D. 50), a small realm in the Lebanons. C. A.D. 53 he exchanged this for what had been the territory of Philip the Tetrarch and the nearby territory E. of Galilee and the Upper Jordan. This Herod did not succeed his father as King of the Jews. Failing in his attempt to dissuade the Judaeans from revolt (A.D. 66), Herod Agrippa II sided with the Romans and fought alongside Vespasian. To this Herod, "expert in all customs and questions which are among the Jews," Paul was brought at Caesarea by Festus (Acts 25:13–26:32). After the fall of Jerusalem he went to Rome, along with his sister Bernice, and died there c. A.D. 93, holding the rank of praetor. He was the 7th and last king of the family of Herod the Great.

(8) The women of the Herodian dynasty were notoriously wicked. Three of them are mentioned in the N.T.: Bernice, eldest daughter of Herod Agrippa I; Drusilla, Bernice's youngest sister; and Herodias, granddaughter of Herod the Great, daughter of Aristobulus and sister of Herod Agrippa I. Though the name of Herodias' daughter who danced before Herod and demanded the head of John the Baptist (Matt. 14:3–11; Mark 6:17–28) is not given in the N.T., it was probably Salome.

Herodians (hē-rō′dĭ-ănz), influential Jews who supported the dynasty of Herod and centered their hopes in Antipas. Opposing all Messianic agitations of the people (Mark 3:6). they joined the Pharisees in an effort to ensnare Jesus in a captious question involving his loyalty to Caesar (Matt. 22:16; Mark 12:13). It is thought that Herodians were pro-Hellenistic and endorsed Herod's promotion of Hellenism in Palestine. They were not a religious sect like the Sadducees* nor an organized social group like the Pharisees*.

Herodias, daughter of Aristobulus, granddaughter of Herod the Great, and half-sister of Herod Agrippa I, King of Judaea. She was first married to her uncle, Herod, son of Herod the Great and Mariamne (II) and then deserted him for another uncle, Herod Antipas, who divorced his wife to marry her. Herodias drew reproof from John the Baptist. After Salome* danced before Herod and gained from him the promise to grant her whatever she asked, Herodias instructed her to demand the head of John the Baptist (Matt. 14:1–12; Mark 6:17–29; Luke 3:19 f.). Josephus states that Herodias went into exile with Herod Antipas.

heron, an "unclean" bird probably related to the stork (Lev. 11:19, Deut. 14:18).

Heshbon (hĕsh′bŏn) (N.T. Esbus, Essebon) ("reckoning"), an ancient city of Moab, modern Tell Ḥesbân, located between the Arnon* and the Jabbok* rivers, 14 m. SW. of Amman. Sihon, King of the Amorites, took it from Moab and made it his royal city (Num. 21:26; Deut. 2:26; Josh. 12:2). Following Sihon's defeat by Israel (Num. 21:25 ff.), Heshbon was rebuilt by Reuben (Num.

32:37), but became part of the inheritance of Gad (Josh. 13:26), who assigned it to the Levites (21:39). By the time of Isaiah and Jeremiah, the Moabites had retaken Heshbon (Isa. 15:4, 16:8–9; Jer. 48:2, 34, 45), probably under Mesha (see Moabite Stone, *ANET*[3], p. 320). In the Herodian period, it was a fortress city, Esbus. By the 4th century A.D. it was the seat of a Christian bishop.

Archaeological excavations begun in 1968, directed by S. H. Horn for Andrews University, have revealed the remains of several Mameluke structures (13th–14th cen. A.D.), a Byzantine church, the latest phase of which is dated to the late 6th century A.D., and rock-cut tombs and occupational debris of the Roman period. As yet, no architectural elements earlier than the Roman period have come to light. See *BA* 32, 1969, pp. 26–41; Borass and Horn, *Heshbon 1968*, 1969.

W. P. A.

Heth (hĕth). (1) Son of Canaan and great-grandson of Noah (Gen. 10:15; I Chron. 1:13). (2) The pre-Hebrew inhabitants of Hebron (Gen. 23), a colony settled in this southland by the great Anatolian group of Hittites*. The sons of Heth witnessed the purchase of the Cave of Machpelah by Abraham from Ephron (Gen. 23:6, 16, 18). They treated the Patriarch courteously, calling him "a mighty prince" (Gen. 23:6). Rebekah was annoyed by Esau's marriage to a "daughter of Heth" (Gen. 27:46).

Hexateuch ("six scrolls" or "[the book] in six scrolls"), a term used to indicate the first six books of the Old Testament. The Hexateuch is, in place of the canonical Pentateuch (see SOURCES), a modern critical invention; it was never considered a unit by the Jews, ancient or modern, and it was created primarily because the P code comes to its end in the Book of Joshua. Joshua seems to cohere equally well with the books both preceding and following it, for the Deuteronomistic edition of 550 B.C. included the books Genesis-Kings (omitting P). In other words, the earliest grouping, in 550, was Genesis-Kings (without Leviticus and the rest of P); after 400, when the Pentateuch was canonized, the grouping was Genesis-Deuteronomy (canonical law of Moses) and Joshua-Kings (canonized as the Former Prophets c. 200 B.C.).

The contents of the Hexateuch include the Creation of man and of the universe (Gen. 1–11); the origins of Israel and the narration of the Patriarchal saga (Gen. 12–50); the organization of the Hebrew people and of their laws governing individuals and society (Ex. 1:1–Num. 10:10); the journey of God's people from Mt. Sinai to the land conquered in E. Palestine (Num. 34:12); and the Conquest of Canaan (Josh.).

The Pentateuch ("the five scroll [book]") contains the first five books of the Old Testament; the Heptateuch contains the first seven books of the O.T.

The discovery by archaeologists of ancient written records dating from before Moses brings added credibility to the early date at which portions of the Hexateuch could have been reduced to writing. Literary fabrications were few in the ancient Middle East. But when scholars put the Hexateuch under analytical scrutiny they found it to be composed of four major strands—five, according to R. H. Pfeiffer—which sometimes overlap, duplicate, and at times apparently contradict one another, but which woven together result in a great document recording God's dealings with His people and His plan for their salvation. If the Hexateuch, as composed over a period of many centuries by many hands, had been compiled with scrupulous truthfulness and unbiased point of view, the O.T. would in many sections read differently from the way it does now. Editors and redactors rewrote from their own viewpoints. For example, the author of the P or priestly strand or source in the Hexateuch used history to teach the origin and inviolability of Israel's religious rites and institutions, viewed from his priestly angle. P in its original form was completed not earlier than 500 B.C. Additions continued to be made to P until the translation of the LXX c. 250 B.C. The theological ideas of P are in advance of those expressed in JE; its aim was to develop a nation which God would find acceptable. It combined history with law, but subordinated history to its aim of directing the Jewish people to salvation through religious institutions associated with the Temple and its priest-administered rites.

An analysis of the Hexateuch strengthens the reader's faith in God's way of speaking "in many fragments and in many manners" to the fathers (Heb. 1:1), climaxing His majestic revelation in the life and teachings of His Son Jesus.

Many scholars today accept the following summary of documents as sources or strands woven into the Hexateuch:

J document (c. 850 B.C.)
E " (c. 750 B.C.); combined by a redactor as JE (c. 650 B.C.)
D Deuteronomic Code (622 B.C.)
P Priestly Code (c. 500–450 B.C.)

To these Pfeiffer and others add a non-Israelitic source in Genesis—S, for S. or Seir, its place of origin, the same region which produced the great poem of Job. Into these main strands several distinctive minor threads have also been knit, like H, the Holiness Code in P; K, the Kenite Code in J; and C, the Book of the Covenant in E.

The Hexateuch contains (1) at least three independent bodies of law: C, the Book of the Covenant (Ex. 20–23); D, the Deuteronomic Code (described in II Kings 22, 23, as having been found in the Temple in the reform reign of Josiah (622 B.C.) and containing those portions of the Law now found in Deuteronomy); and P, the Priestly Code, stressing the Priesthood and the Sanctuary. P was canonized in the time of Ezra*. S material from the South inserted abruptly into JEP is distinguishable. It reveals "indifference or hostility to Israel and its religion" (Pfeiffer, *Introduction to the Old Testament*). (2) Narratives: J and E contain most of the remaining portions of the Hexateuch—E, the Elohist or Ephraimitic source of the histories having been prepared in N. Israel; and J, the Jahvistic document, apparently in Judah.

J and E, the work of unknown authors, are the two oldest of the several Hexateuch sources; together they are known as JE. Which of the two was first committed to writing is not certain. Both were crystallized from very ancient oral narratives some time after the beginning of the Hebrew monarchy.

Hezekiah (hĕz′ē-kī′*ȧ*) ("Jehovah strengtheneth"), the 14th king of Judah (c. 715–687 B.C.), son and successor of Ahaz*, and father of King Manasseh*. Information concerning him is found in (1) II Kings 18–20, to most of which Isa. 36–39 is parallel; (2) II Chron. 29–32—a post-Exilic version of his reign; (3) certain oracles of Isaiah (1, 22:15–25, etc.); (4) messages of the prophet Micah (cf. Jer. 26:17–19); (5) inscriptions of Sargon II, King of Assyria (722–705 B.C.), and of Sennacherib (705–681 B.C.), which illumine Palestine and world political conditions of the time; (6) the Siloam* inscription.

Upon his accession, Hezekiah, under the moral leadership of Micah, initiated a series of reforms that eliminated from current religious practices certain Canaanitish cult places and idolatrous Jewish objects (II Kings 18:4; Num. 21:8 f.), reforms which the later Chronicler considered so monumental that he attributed to Hezekiah the authority for some of the ritual of the second Temple (II Chron. 29:3–31, 31). Hezekiah is credited with a psalm (Isa. 38:9–20), whose thought resembles Job and the later Psalms. The "men of Hezekiah" are said to have copied certain proverbs of Solomon (Prov. 25:1).

His reign was also one of marked material prosperity for the nation. Under his leadership control of the Philistine Plain cities (see PHILISTIA) was re-established for a time (II Kings 18:8); agriculture and trade were encouraged by the establishing of warehouses and stalls for livestock (II Chron. 32:28 f.); and an adequate water supply for the capital in event of siege was made effective by an elaborate engineering scheme involving a tunnel which brought the waters of Gihon Spring inside the Jerusalem walls (II Kings 20:20; II Chron. 32:4, 30). See SILOAM.

Hezekiah was involved in the struggle for supremacy between the empires of the Nile and Mesopotamian valleys. King Ahaz had made an alliance with Assyria which Hezekiah inherited (II Kings 16:7–9). While Assyria was involved in the suppression of revolts elsewhere in the ancient Near East, Hezekiah had found freedom to build up his country. He was inclined to sever the relations inaugurated by his father, and seek a diplomatic compact with the Ethiopian pharaohs of Egypt in the Twenty-fifth Dynasty. Isaiah always opposed such a compact (18:1–6, 30:1–5, 31:1–3). In 721 B.C. Merodach-baladan established himself as King of Babylon and also sought to woo Hezekiah away from the Assyrian fold. The events of II Kings 20 come earlier than those of II Kings 18:13 ff. The sickness of Hezekiah reveals a medical treatment for the king similar to that used for horses, as recorded in the Ras Shamrah tablets (II Kings 20:7). Sargon II (722–705 B.C.) overran the coastal cities of Judah, while Isaiah, naked and barefooted, walked the streets of Jerusalem as a prophetic sign of the sure defeat of Egypt and all her allies (Isa. 20). In 701 B.C. Sennacherib, son of Sargon II, also invaded the coastal plain and laid siege to Lachish, the great fortified city close to the Egyptian border (II Kings 18:13 f.). Jerusalem was next on his list. This realization made Hezekiah regret his pursuit of an Egyptian alliance, as he tried to regain the favor of Sennacherib with gifts (II Kings 18:14–16). Sennacherib's version of this phase of his Judaean campaign is recorded with exaggerated listings of the gifts and their value in the Taylor Cylinder, col. 3, lines 1–41. But the Assyrian general nevertheless sent

182. Hezekiah's pool in old Jerusalem.

his army to reduce Jerusalem. Meanwhile the defenders, now with an adequate water supply, stood ready behind the stout walls of the capital. The besiegers used psychological warfare to disrupt the morale of the besieged (II Kings 18:17–37), while the good king resorted to prayer (II Kings 19:1). The fervor of the king's faith in prayer in such an hour, as well as his conception of God, is noteworthy. Assur (Asshur) was the god of Assyria. Yahweh (see GOD), however, was not only the God of the Hebrews, but of "all the kingdoms of the earth" (II Kings 19:15). In this threatened national crisis a new revelation of the nature of God had become clear.

The Assyrian army was destroyed by the "angel of the Lord" (II Kings 19:35; Isa. 37:36). In Herodotus (Book II, 141) this debacle was due to field mice (cf. II Sam. 24:15; I Chron. 21:12) which devoured quivers, bowstrings and thongs, and spread fatal bubonic plague. Herodotus locates this catastrophe to Sennacherib's army at Pelusium, which commands the entrance to Egypt. This devastating pestilence, coupled perhaps with political unrest at home, compelled the withdrawal of Sennacherib's armies from Jerusalem. This event was viewed by the Jews as a national deliverance ranking in importance with the Exodus from Egypt and the Return from Babylon. While Isaiah was the Yahweh-inspired man who provided the faith to meet the crisis, Hezekiah, the praying sovereign, who shared the prophet's spirit and brought to pass during his life many of the material achievements of a national Messiah, has become the dominating figure in this historic episode as reflected in the tradition of subsequent Jewish people, particularly in the work of the Chronicler, as well as in the sober summary of his life by the Jewish historian (II Kings 18:5).

Hezron (hĕz′rŏn) (Esrom, A.V. Matt. 1:3). (1) A place S. of Judah (Josh. 15:3). For Kerioth-hezron (Josh. 15:25) see HAZOR (3). (2) A son of Reuben (Gen. 46:9; Ex. 6:14; Num. 26:6; I Chron. 5:3). (3) A son of Perez (Gen. 46:12; Num. 26:21; Ruth 4:18; I Chron. 2:5).

Hiddekel (hĭd′ē-kĕl), the name used in Gen. 2:14 for the Tigris* River.

Hiel (hī′ĕl), a man of Bethel who fortified Jericho (I Kings 16:34) and so caused Joshua's curse to be fulfilled (Josh. 6:26).

Hierapolis (hī′ĕr-ăp′ō-lĭs) (from the mythical Amazon queen Hiera), a center of Christian influence located in the Lycus River Valley of Phrygia, near Colossae and Laodicea, mentioned in the N.T. only in Col. 4:13; cf. Acts 19:10. Although apparently never visited by Paul, it felt the impact of his teaching. It is believed that Philip the Evangelist and John preached in this prosperous center of rich dyers' (see DYEING) guilds and hot medicinal springs which at-

183. Theater at Hierapolis.

tracted worshippers of Cybele and patrons of the Plutonium ("Entrance to Hades"). The wealth of the city is demonstrated by its vast ruins, including two theaters, baths, and a gymnasium. It is claimed to have been "wholly Christian" early in the 4th century. Its cosmopolitan population included descendants of Greek colonists from Macedonia, Pergamum, Rome, and Phrygia. It had a large Jewish community. Its famous citizens included Epictetus, contemporary of Onesimus, and Papias, author of *Exploration of the Oracles of the Lord.* Four early Christian churches have been identified at Hierapolis.

higgaion (hĭ-gā′yŏn), (? "musical note"), a word transliterated in Ps. 9:16; translated "solemn sound" in Ps. 92:3, "meditation" in Ps. 19:14.

high place (from Canaanite *bamah*, pl. *bamōth*, "back" or "ridge," possibly from a Phoen. term having as its basic meaning "elevated platform on which cultic objects were placed"; Heb. "elevation of land"), an elevation used by Near Eastern religionists for a temple or altar. When nomadic Israel began to settle down in Palestine several centuries before Solomon built the central Temple at Jerusalem, religious leaders established wholesome rustic shrines, often centering at an unhewn or earthen altar. After the Conquest the Twelve Tribes associated themselves in a league whose center was a shrine where the annual festival was celebrated (Judg. 21), where the Tabernacle was safeguarded, and where spiritual advice was given. Early shrines were usually on elevations, for impressiveness and for the cool afternoon breeze. This was true also with the Greeks, with their lofty Mt. Olympus and low Acropolis hillock; with the Babylonians, who devised artificial hills called *ziggurats* for temple platforms; and with the builders of the Temple of Wâdī Serabit el-Khadem, on the cliffs in the Sinai Peninsula. To look unto the hills for divine help (Ps. 121:1) was natural, even to ancient Israel at Sinai-Horeb. The elevated site of Jerusalem was an ideal choice for the Temple—a high place "beautiful for situation" (Ps. 48:2), "whither the tribes go up" (Ps. 122:4). In the period of the Judges and later people "went up" and came down (I Sam. 9:11–25; Isa. 15:2) from well-known shrines, where they prayed, tithed, sacrificed to Yahweh, consulted priestly oracles, and met their friends, as at Ramah (I Sam. 7:17, 9:12–14, 19, 25); at Shiloh, to which Hannah and Elkanah went annually (I Sam. 1:3); at Bethel in Samuel's time (I Sam. 7:16, 10:3), before the apostasies of Jeroboam were promoted there; at Dan (Judg. 18:27–29); at Mizpah in Jephthah's day (Judg. 11:11); at Nob, where the Ark once rested (I Sam. 21:1); at Bethlehem (I Sam. 20:28, 29); and at Gibeon in Judaea, at whose "great high place" Solomon sacrificed and dreamed before he built the Temple (I Kings 3:4–9). Hebrew open-air shrines were not always on elevations—witness Hebron (II Sam. 5:1 ff., 15:7); Beer-sheba (Gen. 21:33; Amos 5:5); and the Valley of Topheth near Jerusalem (Jer. 7:31; 19:6).

As Israel settled down among the Canaanites and Amorites an inevitable cross-fertilization of cultures took place. Not only did the Hebrews capture sites of ancient worship on high places which had long been used by the Canaanites, but, contrary to God-inspired pronouncements of Israel's religious seers, they adopted immoral cultic rites popular among agricultural groups who pinned their faith to the Baals (see BAAL) which gave rain and crops, and to Asherah* associated with fertility. Israel, weary of ascetic wilderness ways, enjoyed the sociability, dances, and religious picnics at the high places, even as today Mediterranean peoples cherish summer farm-folk festivals at shrines of local saints, like the Rhodian San Silvano. At some of the adopted high places Yahweh was duly worshipped by legitimate rural festivals (J Ex. 34:22, 23, E 23:14–17); at others the whoredoms of Canaanites predominated (for procedure there, see below). Such syncretism as is indicated in I Kings 12:31, 32, 13:2, 32, 33 fully justified the protests of 8th-century prophets. The purifying emphasis of the Deuteronomists, who edited the Book of Kings, continued to influence thought after the adoption of Deuteronomy in 622 B.C. under King Josiah*. The Chronicler was more lenient than the Deuteronomists. Blasting reproofs of apostasy came from Hosea (4:15, 9:15, 10:5, 8), Amos (2:8, 5:5), and Ezekiel (6:1–14, 14:6, 11, 15, 16:16, 20:27–29, 22:9, 23:39, 44:10–12). Some of the most severe came from Jeremiah (7:31, 19:13, 32:35). Many of the protests lashed at worshippers were unjustified, because they were retroactive criticisms directed at people who had lived before the Temple was built (I Kings 3:2).

After the division of Solomon's realm, and the establishment of the Northern Kingdom centering in Samaria under Jeroboam and his successors, rulers conducted apostate rites, especially at Bethel* and Dan*. These centers of worship and political activity were designed to rival the southern capital at Jerusalem (I Kings 12:26–33). Many who found it difficult to journey to Jerusalem were glad of an excuse to join in the lewd pagan rites at northern high places. So widespread were immoralities at high places, especially in the Northern Kingdom, that there were "images and groves in every high hill, and under every green tree. And there they burnt incense in all the high places, as did the heathen" (II Kings 17:10 f.). Such a condition is given as the reason for Yahweh's sending Israel into captivity (vv. 22 f.), so that only Judah was left, and that for less than two more centuries. For Judah had plenty of cultic centers even within the shadow of the Temple. Jehoram is said to have restored high places in the Judaean mountains (II Chron. 21:11) which Amaziah (II Kings 14:4, 15:4), Uzziah (II Kings 15:34, 35), and Jotham (II Kings 15:35) did not remove. Kings were rated not so much by their political power as by their attitude toward the high places, whose history is really the history of Israel's old religion. Pious Hezekiah (II Kings 18:3–5) was praised unconditionally for having removed high places. His reforms won him Isaiah's backing in his defiance of Assyria. In the large-scale reforms instituted by King Josiah after the finding of the lost Book of the Covenant (621 B.C.), false priests and adulterous rites at high places in and near Jerusalem, like Beth-aven, were extirpated (II Kings 22:2–23:10). Then was celebrated, in the purified atmosphere, such a Passover as had not been observed for generations (II Kings 23:21–23).

Little mention is made of high places after the fall of Judah. What Israel experienced during the Captivity was more effective purification than all the prophets had been able to bring about. When the Exiles returned, they were not interested in restoring high places, but in rebuilding the Temple.

What was once believed to be a great "high place" at Gezer* is identified by W. F. Albright as a "mortuary shrine." One of the most famous high places of the Near East is the "Conway High Place" at Petra (see NABATAEA), excavated by Agnes Conway Horsfield and her associates. (For an excellent brief account see *The Archaeology of Palestine*, pp. 161–165, W. F. Albright, Penguin Books.) Dr. Albright believes that the equipment and arrangement of Iron Age "high places" in Palestine were similar to that of the Nabataean "high places," some of which had rock-cut *triclinia* providing sloping couches for three participants, and a system of storage bins and stalls for foods and animals brought for offerings and sacrifices.

Tablets excavated at Ras Shamrah indicate what animals were sacrificed at Baal high places in N. Syria. Always near the rock altar was a sacred pillar, *mazzebah*, close to a sacred pole, capped with the symbol of the *asherah*, probably denoting female fertility. The mother goddess at some high places was indicated by a short, cone-shaped stone symbolizing the female breast. High places maintained chambers for sacred prostitution by *kedeshim* ("male prostitutes") and *kedeshoth* ("sacred harlots") (I Kings 14:23, 24; II Kings 23:7). Sometimes first-born infants were slain and their bodies placed, with food, in jars near the high place, as at Gezer, where many such jars have been found (cf. Isa. 57:5). Cup holes in the rock, measuring from a few inches to 5 ft. in diameter, have been found at Ophel in Jerusalem and at Gezer, suggesting that the broth or blood of slain animals flowed below the ground to "spirits" (cf. I Sam. 7:6). At the Rock Moriah under the Dome of the Rock at the old Temple site in Jerusalem the blood of slain victims flowed similarly through channels down to the Kidron Valley.

A somewhat novel interpretation of Hebrew high places is offered by C. C. McCown in *JBL*, Sept. 1950, pp. 205–219. He is impressed with the fact that in spite of numerous prophetic protests against high places, built "on every green hill," none has been found. Not even at such large sites as Megiddo, he remarks, has a public temple or shrine emerged from excavated ruins. There appears to be more evidence for household rites than for community worship.

high priests. See PRIESTS.

Hilkiah (hĭl-kī′ȧ) ("my portion is Yahweh"). (1) The son of Hosah, a porter in David's bureaucracy (I Chron. 26:11). (2) The father of Eliakim, steward of King Hezekiah (II Kings 18:18 ff.). (3) The son of Shallum and high priest in Josiah's reign (I Chron. 6:13). His discovery of the lost Book of the Law led to a reformation and the temporary abolition of idolatry (II Kings 22). (4) The Anathoth priest who was father of Jeremiah (Jer. 1:1). (5) A priest associated with Ezra and Nehemiah (Neh. 8:4, 12:7).

hill country, the typical, round-knobbed elevations in Judah, (Heb. *gibh'āh*), in contrast to a range or region of mountainous land (Heb. *har*), illustrated by the central range, extending from the Lebanons (see LEBANON) to the Negeb*. Armageddon* (A.S.V. Har-

Magedon Rev. 16:16) means "mountain of Megiddo". "Hill country" (Luke 1:39, 65—probably N. of Jerusalem; Josh. 21:11—Hebron area) meant local elevations of the rocky spine of the central range of Palestine. Mt. Naphtali was spoken of as "the hill country of Naphtali" (R.S.V. Josh. 20:7), but the hill country occupied by Ephraim was usually called Mt. Ephraim (Josh. 17:15).

hin. See WEIGHTS AND MEASURES.

hind, the female deer, especially red deer, in or after the third year (Gen. 49:21; Prov. 5:19; Jer. 14:5).

Hinnom (hĭn′ŏm), **Valley of** (also known as "valley of the son of Hinnom," Jer. 7:32; II Chron. 28:3, or "valley of the children of Hinnom," II Kings 23:10, and as "the valley," II Chron. 26:9, Neh. 2:13, 15, 3:13, and possibly Jer. 2:23), lies S. and W. of Jerusalem, joining the Kidron* brook at a point just N. of En-rogel* Spring, near the traditional Aceldama*. The Valley of Hinnom separates Mt. Zion on its N. from "the Hill of Evil Counsel" and the Plain of Rephaim W. of Jerusalem. The Valley of Hinnom was the boundary between Judah and Benjamin (Josh. 15:8, 18:16). Between the broad Hinnom Valley and the narrow Kidron rose the plateau, joined with the central mountain ridge, on which Jerusalem stood. A third valley, the Tyropoeon, joined the encircling Hinnom and Kidron just below the Pool of Siloam. The original N.T. word "Gehenna,"* hell, is a corruption of Ge-Hinnom.

184. Hinnom Valley.

Hiram (also sometimes "Huram," "Hirom"; possibly from Phoen. and Heb. "Ahiram," "the brother is exalted").

(1) A series of kings of the great merchant port of Tyre*, located about midway between the present Haifa and Beirut. Most noted of the Hirams was the son and successor of Abibaal. The kingdom he established is vividly pictured by Ezekiel (26, 27). This Hiram was the devoted friend and ally of King David* (I Kings 5:1), to whom he sent masons and carpenters, and cedars and firs from the forests of Lebanon (II Sam. 5:11; I Chron. 14:1) for the Jerusalem palace. The trade alliance of the Tyrian king was continued with David's son Solomon*, whose 20-year building program for Temple and palaces was realized only through Hiram's co-operation. The terms of their memorable contract are given in I Kings 9:11; II Chron. 2. In addition to this contract there were other bargains which furnished skilled Tyrian craftsmen (Ezek. 27:8 f.; also Hiram below). Groups of Tyrian sailors manned Solomon's navy and Tarshish ships (? refinery fleets) for the great copper smeltery port of the Hebrew king at Ezion-geber.*

The mariners of Tyre were famous in Bible times. They docked their long-range merchant ships in twin harbors developed by King Hiram of Tyre in the golden age of Phoenician Mediterranean power—a Sidonian one on the N. and an Egyptian basin on the S.

Scholars wonder whether there is any relationship between this Hiram of Tyre and the famous King Ahiram of the Phoenician Byblos (see GEBAL) (c. 1000 B.C.), whose sarcophagus (not later than 975 B.C.) in Beirut Museum bears the notable inscription that forms a link in the evolution of alphabetic writing. But present information is too scanty to identify this Ahiram with the Hiram contemporary of David (c. 1000–961 B.C.) and Solomon (961–922 B.C.). II Chron. 2:11 says: "Huram the king of Tyre answered in writing, which he sent to Solomon." There was also an 8th-century King Hiram of Tyre, mentioned in a Tiglath-pileser inscription.

(2) Hiram the architect-artisan-artist, son of a woman of the tribe of Naphtali (I Kings 7:13) or of Dan (II Chron. 2:14) and a man of Tyre, was summoned from Tyre by King Hiram himself to cast the bronze (? copper) pillars, the molten sea, and other furnishings of the Jerusalem Temple* (I Kings 7:13 ff., 40–46; II Chron. 2:13, 4:16) in specially suited clay found between Succoth and Zarethan.

hireling, a lowly servant employed for wages (Job 7:2), of which he was sometimes defrauded (Mal. 3:5). His rights were protected by the Law (Deut. 24:14 f.). In his Parable of the Prodigal Jesus indicated that the father's many hired servants had "bread enough and to spare" (Luke 15:17). The hireling's term of service was specified, e.g., "three years" (Isa. 16:14; cf. Job 7:1). The comment of Jesus concerning a faithless hireling, in contrast to the devoted owner-shepherd (John 10:12 f.), is not derogatory to hirelings in general.

Hittites (Heb. *Hitti*, pl., *Hittim*; also Heb. *Heth*), so called in accordance with the O.T., were regarded by Hronzý and others as one of the three most influential peoples of the Middle East, rivaling the Egyptians and Mesopotamians. But many other scholars give the third pivotal place to the Hebrew people (see Irwin, *The Intellectual Adventure of Ancient Man*, Univ. of Chicago Press). Israel dreaded the Hittites as they looked forward during their Wilderness wanderings to conquests in Canaan. Yet upon arrival they found the Hittites less formidable than other early inhabitants; for the Hittites by then had moved N., with their stronghold in central Asia Minor and their capital at Boghazköy-Khattushash, not far E. of what became Ankara, capital of modern Turkey. Hittites were non-Semites, the first Indo-Europeans to cross the Caucasus into Armenia and Cappadocia, bringing a pre-Indo-European language (which they called *Nashili*) that was related to Sanskrit, Greek, Latin, Slavonic, and Teutonic tongues. Thus they formed a cultural link between Europe and Mesopotamia. Two kingdoms of Hittites existed: the Old or Proto-Hittite Kingdom, from c. 1700–1400 B.C., of which little is known, but which was alive in the era of the Hebrew Patriarchs; and a New Kingdom, awakened after two centuries of shadowy existence, and lasting from c. 1400 B.C. to c. 1200 B.C. The Hittite Kingdom developed several small states in Asia Minor, each with its own king; pushed its borders into Syria and Mesopotamia; and reduced the strong feudal Mitanni* kingdom to a buffer state by c. 1370 B.C. C. 1530 the Hittites destroyed the Babylonian capital of Hammurabi*, with its Tower of Babel. It planted colonies in Palestine, representatives of which were met by the Hebrews (Gen. 23). Time and again the Hittite Empire clashed with Egypt, sometimes coming out on an equal footing. It was victorious against Ramesses II, but too weak internally to follow up its advantage. The Hittites were succeeded late in the 13th century B.C. by Aegean peoples, possibly from Thrace or Phrygia. When Sargon II seized their eastern capital at Carchemish in the 8th century B.C. the Hittites bowed out of history.

They are mentioned 47 times in the O.T. under their own name, and 14 times as descendants of Heth*. Heth was a son of "Canaan," the son of Ham, the son of Noah (Gen. 6:10, 9:18, 10:15). "Sons of Heth" lived in Hebron in the era of Abraham (Gen. 23), who bought from the co-operative Ephron the Hittite the field of Machpelah with its cave for Sarah's burial place. Num. 13:29 implies that Hittites lived in the mountains of Canaan. Josh. 1:4 tells of Hittites living in the land bounded by the Mediterranean, the Euphrates, the Lebanons, and the eastern wildernesses. Individual Hittites mentioned in Scripture include two wives of Esau, Judith and Basemath (Gen. 26:34), and Uriah the Hittite, wronged by David (II Sam. 11). Yet some O.T. men called "Hittites" have names which seem Hebraic (see Ezek. 16:3, 45).

Hittite states carried on extensive commerce with Solomon, for the Hebrew king transshipped fine horses* from Asia Minor's breeding grounds to Egypt, and brought up from Egypt choice hand-made chariots, at the rate of one chariot for four horses, if we follow the more correct translation now accepted for I Kings 10:28, 29, which should read "And Solomon's horses were exported from Cilicia," not "brought out of Egypt." The Hittites, like other peoples of E. Asia Minor, such as the Mitanni and the Hyksos*, were noted for fine horses, many of which were exported for the Persian cavalry. Data about horses appear on Hittite clay tablets.

Hittite aggressiveness is shown in their careful guarding of the secret of smelting iron when it was still regarded almost as precious as silver and gold. This was two centuries before the Philistines controlled its monopoly in the period of the Hebrew judges and the early Monarchy.

Present knowledge of the hitherto obscure Hittites—who are related to the Khurri, as well as to the Khatti and the Hyksos—has been vastly increased since the excavation of thousands of clay* tablets from Boghazköy by Winkler in 1906–07 and 1911–12; and since 1915, when the Czech scholar Hrozny interpreted the Hittite cuneiform*, used between 1900 and 1100 B.C. Hittites wrote their annals, religious texts, and myths in Sumero-Accadian characters received from the Hurrians (see HORITES). Vestiges of Hittite from the 2d millennium B.C. belong to one of the oldest known Indo-European languages.

Portions of Hittite legal codes have been found, which belong to the same class of secular laws as those contained in the Hammurabi Code and the Hebrew Code of the Covenant.

The religion of the Hittites was highly syncretistic. It borrowed gods from Sumer-Accad*, and transported Ishtar of Nineveh as far as W. Asia Minor. One tablet tells of the Babylonian Marduk's having gone to the land of the Hittites, where he set up his throne for 24 years. Hittites took over the chief gods of Egypt also, and the gods of Syria and Asia Minor. Texts in clay reveal an Anatolian ritual used by the Hittites. The Diana of Ephesus may have been a Hittite Artemis, for Hittites were early located in what later became prominent Asiatic cities—Tarsus, Iconium, etc. Often Hittites depicted gods standing on the backs of animals or enthroned between them, but not actually portrayed as animals (cf. the golden calves of Jeroboam, possibly supports of an invisible God, not portraits of Him.) No great Hittite temples have been excavated yet in Anatolia; our information thus far is gleaned only from rock carvings and cuneiform texts. Carchemish* has given some light; and the Cappadocian tablets from the modern Kul-tepe in E. Asia Minor tell about Hittite business and other matters. Modern Turkey is proud of Hittite strains, and preserves in its museums Hittite treasures in stone and clay.

185. Hittite carved ivory plaque (1350–1150 B.C.) and restoration drawing. Probably carved by a Hittite and imported to Megiddo from Asia Minor, it represents Hittite gods and semi-gods.

Hivites (hī′vīts). See HORITES.

Hobab (hō′băb) ("beloved"), a Midianite (Num. 10:20–32, J source), or a Kenite (E Judg. 4:11) whom Moses impressed to guide Israel through the Wilderness. In E Hobab is Moses' father-in-law; in J his brother-in-law.

holiness, the state or condition of being holy, sanctified, saintly, consecrated. The root idea is that of "separateness" or "apartness." For this reason holiness is originally a quality of divinity, because of its "apartness" from what is not divine. When the term is used of places, things, ceremonies, times and seasons, and the like, it is because of the association these have with something that is in itself holy. In such cases usage or purpose bestows the quality of holiness. The Sabbath is holy not merely as a period of time: one twenty-four hour period is no holier than another, considered simply as time; the Sabbath is to be "kept holy" by the way in which the day is used. In the Christian view, therefore, every day may be a holy day, as Paul himself says (Rom. 14:5).

Holiness in this derived sense is common in the O.T. Often there goes with it the idea of "dread," to indicate the effect on the person who feels himself to be in the presence of the divine. An example is in the experience of Job described in Job 4:12–17. Jacob, after his vision at Bethel, exclaimed, "How dreadful is this place!" and he erected there an altar to indicate that henceforth the place was holy (Gen. 28:10–22). The numerous offerings and sacrifices so carefully prescribed in Leviticus were regarded as holy: it was a consequence of their being "set apart." The members of the priesthood were holy for the same reason; and the holiness extended even to their garments (Ex. 28:2–4). Observe that the words translated "in the beauty of holiness" in the A.V. of I Chron. 16:29 are translated in the A.S.V. "in holy array." It is not so much the character of the worshipper that is holy (in the ethical sense), as the services he performs and the way in which he performs them. The body of regulations that covered these numerous ceremonies became known as "the Code of Holiness," and the term will mislead us unless we keep in mind the reference to forms and ceremonies. Even the terms "to sanctify" and "to consecrate" carry the meaning of "setting aside" for some special use (cf. Ex. 19:10, 29:1–9; see also "cleanse" in Isa. 52:11);

it is the use that is significant. The Temple itself was holy, not by virtue of the materials of which it was built, but by virtue of its purpose as a place where men could worship God. The innermost shrine of the Tabernacle or Temple was "the Holy of Holies" or "the most holy place" (Ex. 26:33; Lev. 16:2 f.; I Kings 7:50; Heb. 9:1–9), because only the high priest could enter it, and only the most solemn rites could be performed there.

But holiness also came to mean that kind of separateness or apartness which could mark personal character. This was holiness in its ethical sense, and it applied both to God and to men. We meet it as early as in the Songs of Moses (Ex. 15:11) and of Hannah (I Sam. 2:11). When Isaiah declares that "God the Holy One is sanctified in righteousness" (5:16) he is stressing the attribute of righteousness, and it is holiness of this sort which Isaiah was led to see he so greatly needed, and which the touch of the live coal so vividly symbolized (6:1–7). It was this ethical holiness that all the prophets pleaded for in protest against the priestly tendency to be content with ceremonial holiness. Indeed, the more the prophets came to realize the ethical quality of the divine holiness the more they saw that God required nothing less in His worshippers. The behavior described by Amos (5:21–23) and by Isaiah (1:10–14) resulted in part from the failure of the priests to apprehend God's real character. The prophets called for something different, because of their truer apprehension of God (Micah 6:6–8). In the priest-prophet Ezekiel we see an attempt to unite the ceremonial with the ethical (36:25–31).

This more ethical conception of the divine holiness meets us everywhere in the N.T. It was from this standpoint that Jesus so sharply criticized the scribes and Pharisees (Matt. 23:16–28). His demand for a new kind of righteousness was in effect a demand for a new kind of holiness (Matt. 5:20, 6:33). Often he was condemned for his association with "publicans and sinners" (Luke 15:1, 2), and for his indifference to ceremonial law (Matt. 12:2–8). But what he was doing sprang from his conviction that God was not simply a "holy" God, separate and apart, but a God of holy love. It was this holy love that he himself knew and exemplified; because of it he could mingle with all sorts and conditions of men, and remain uncontaminated thereby. Holy love involves complete separation from sin, but at the same time profound concern for the sinner and devotion to the task of rescuing him.

Christian holiness is the quality of life and character which comes from being "in Christ" (II Cor. 5:17), from being "indwelt" by Christ (Gal. 2:20), from being made thereby "a habitation of God in the Spirit" (Eph. 2:22). The very mission of Christ was indeed to make men holy, to bring them to sanctity (John 17:17–19; cf. Heb. 9:11 f., 13:11, 12). The Christian, says Paul, is "called to be a saint" (Rom. 1:7; I Cor. 1:2), and his sanctification* or holiness comes through Christ. Indeed, "the saints" is a common designation in Paul for the Christians (II Cor. 1:1; Eph. 1:1; Phil. 1:1). Yet he never thinks of the holiness or sanctification as complete: it is always something yet to be perfected (II Cor. 13:9; Eph. 4:12). Since holy love is God's own deepest and most characteristic quality, and since this was revealed and exemplified in Christ, and since the Christian man seeks Christlikeness, it is as the Christian attains to holy love that he attains to saintship. There is a holiness that tends to austerity, and a love that tends to sentimentalism. It is when holiness is love, and when love is holy, that the Christian man is most like his Lord. Since "justification" is conditioned as a "faith-association" with Jesus Christ, it is not to be sharply distinguished from "holiness" or "sanctification." See CODE; JUSTIFICATION; SANCTIFICATION; WORSHIP.

E. L.

Holy of Holies. See TABERNACLE; TEMPLE.

Holy One of Israel, the, a term for God*, used frequently by Hebrew prophets, especially the Isaiahs, to whom the holiness of Yahweh rather than His power was His central attribute (30:12, 15, 31:1, 41:14). The phrase also appears frequently in the Psalms (71:22, 89:18) and in Jer. 50:29, 51:5. The term "Holy One of God" is applied to Jesus in Mark 1:24; Luke 4:34.

Holy Sepulcher (of Jesus). See BURIAL; CALVARY; JERUSALEM.

Holy Spirit, the, God as present and active in the spiritual experience of men. The term in its later sense does not occur in the O.T. The underlying Heb. words mean also "breath" or "wind," as in the Gk. It is as though men were aware of a form of existence which had no material shape or form; the closest analogy they could think of was that of breath or wind. Jesus himself used the analogy in his conversation with Nicodemus about being "born of the Spirit" (John 3: 5–8). The less God was thought of as having a physical form, the more emphasis was laid on His being "a Spirit," as invisible but as real as wind or breath.

In Ps. 51:11 and Isa. 63:10 f. we find the expressions "thy holy Spirit" and "his holy Spirit," but the meaning is not that of later Christian thought. All that is meant is that God deals with men by his Spirit, and that this Spirit is holy because it is the Spirit of the God who is Himself holy. This, indeed, is the characteristic thought of the O.T.; the distinction is made between God as a Spirit and the spirit of this divine Spirit. The spirit of the divine Spirit is his very life principle, whereby He can carry on all His diverse activities, in creation (Gen. 1:2; Job 26:13; Ps. 104:27–32), in the affairs of men (Zech. 4:1–6), in endowing men with special gifts (Ex. 31:3; Judg. 3:10, 14:6; I Sam. 16:13, 14; Isa. 11:2, 61:1–3), and in rebuking, convicting, and encouraging them (II Chron. 15:1–3; Isa. 63:10; Micah 3:8).

In the N.T. the Spirit of God is still spoken of in this same way. Jesus was baptized with power by the Spirit of God (Matt. 3:1–17); he was led by the Spirit (4:1); he cast out demons by the Spirit (12:28); he carried on his work by the Spirit (Luke 4:16–21). All this is in the tradition of the O.T. But more and more we meet the term "the Holy Spirit," and it is clear that it has a much deeper connotation than that of simply "the Spirit of God." The turning point in the usage is largely provided by the events of the Day of Pentecost, described in Acts 2. The prophet Joel had long since predicted a special outpouring of the Spirit of God to the accompaniment of many signs and wonders (Joel 2:28–32). Peter saw in the sudden empowering of the Disciples the fulfillment of this prediction (Acts 2:16); but he also saw it as the fulfillment of a promise made by Christ himself (2:33–36). The experience of this day was often repeated in the early Church, but always under certain conditions, namely, faith in Jesus Christ as Saviour and in his immediate accessibility as living Lord.

In a word, with the coming of Christ and faith in him as Saviour there came to men a fuller knowledge of God and of His innermost nature. God had disclosed His love in Jesus Christ. Though Christ was no longer among them as he had once been, what he had brought and what he had made possible remained; it remained in the form of a new experience. As the experience continued and deepened and extended in the Church, men saw with increasing clearness its connection with Christ himself, and with what he had said about his abiding presence in the world. The Crucifixion had seemed to invalidate all he said, but the Resurrection gave it a new meaning.

It is chiefly in the Fourth Gospel that this meaning is set forth. John talks about Jesus as the eternal Son of God become a man (1:14–18). He writes of the intimate relation between the Incarnate Son and the eternal Father (17:1–5, 20–26). He writes of what the Son would continue to do for men, as Companion (14:3), as Helper (14:16), as Teacher (14:26); but in some deep mysterious sense this continued work will be a work in which the Father, the Son, and the Holy Spirit will all be involved (14:25–29). They will not all be involved in the same way, yet it is a work that would be impossible except as each did his own part.

This recognition of the Holy Spirit as distinguishable from the Father and the Son, and yet as inseparable from them in the total life of God, becomes more and more evident in the N.T. Epistles and in early Christian thought. The Holy Spirit is regarded as a personal reality—"he" rather than "it"—whose special office it is to bring to fulfillment in human experience the whole meaning of Jesus Christ as Son of God and Redeemer of the world. The Holy Spirit is therefore "God-with-man"; but this is not God in His totality, any more than the Incarnate Son is God in His totality. In due time the problem that was set by these distinctions was met by the formulation of the doctrine of the Trinity. See PAROUSIA; PENTECOST; TRINITY.

E. L.

home. See HOUSE.

homer. See WEIGHTS AND MEASURES.

honey—from bees as well as from dates and grapes (Arab. *dibs*)—was relished by Israelites and used for gifts (Gen. 43:11; II Sam. 17:29; I Kings 14:3). Wild honey was found in rocks (Deut. 32:13), in trees (I Sam. 14:25), and occasionally in animal carcasses (Judg. 14:8). It was prized for making cakes and condiments. Canaan was described as "flowing with milk and honey" (Ex. 3:8 and often). Bee culture may have been known to early Palestinians. See FOOD.

hope, a desire accompanied by the expectation of obtaining what is desired. (1) In the O.T. hope is expressed by several different words. It is at times marked by a reaching out for health and prosperity. In the later O.T. books hope becomes connected with man's spiritual yearning; man's true hope is not in riches but in God (Ps. 39:7). Such a man is happy (Ps. 146:5), secure (Job 11:18), and blessed (Jer. 17:7). By an unconquerable hope and an experience of divine fellowship Job won his victory over the problem of evil, though the problem itself remained unsolved (Job 42).

Hope in the sparing of a righteous "remnant" in the society of Israel was voiced by many of the prophets (Amos 5:15; Isa. 1:9, 11:11; Jer. 44:28; Ezek. 6:8; Micah 2:12, 4:7; Joel 2:32). Isaiah organized and taught a group of disciples so that they might be the seed of the righteous "remnant" (8:16). In thus separating a small nucleus of believers Isaiah laid the foundations of a spiritual community which was later realized in Judaism and Christianity. When Hebrew hope for national independence faded, it oriented itself afresh around the expectation of a Messianic Kingdom (see KINGDOM OF GOD). Isaiah expressed this hope in an ideal age (2:1–4, 9:2–7, 11:1–9, 32:1–8, 15–18, 20). In Job 19:25–27 is the first groping demand for a life after death to correct the injustices of this world.

(2) In the N.T. hope is shown springing from the Resurrection of Jesus (I Pet. 1:3). This hope became a characteristic quality of the early Christians, in sharp contrast to the pervading despair of the pagan world. Paul listed hope as one of the three basic qualities of the Christian (I Cor. 13:13), and declared that the hope of salvation was a helmet (I Thess. 5:8). He said that men are saved by hope (Rom. 8:24 f., 35–39), and described God as the "God of hope" (Rom. 15:13). In Colossians Paul writes of the "hope which is laid up for you in heaven" (1:5), mentions the "hope of the gospel" (1:23), and declares that "Christ in you" is the "hope of glory" (1:27). The author of I Pet. 3:15 exhorted Christians to "be ready always to give an answer to every man that asketh you a reason of the hope that is in you." Hope as portrayed in late N.T. books is marked by an eschatological quality, i.e., a concern for "the last things" (e.g., Titus 2:13).

Hophni (hŏf′nī), a degenerate son of the good priest Eli* of the Shiloh* sanctuary, where the Ark rested for a time. With his brother Phinehas he officiated when his father was too decrepit. Guilty of misappropriating portions of food offerings (I Sam. 2:13–17), and of immoral conduct with women worshippers (v. 22), he met his prophesied doom

(I Sam. 2:34) in the battle of Aphek, when the Ark was lost and the death of the aged Eli followed (I Sam. 4).

Hor (hôr), **Mt.** ("mountain"). (1) The burial place of Aaron*, location uncertain (Num. 20:22–28); probably N. of Kadesh-barnea, on the route followed by Moses to storm Canaan from the E. Claims that Hor is Jebel Harun, the highest peak in Edom, near Petra, have been discounted. (2) A mountain at the N. border of Palestine, near the approach to Hamath, possibly a peak in the Lebanons (Num. 34:7 f.)—but identified by R.A.S. Macalister as Mt. Hermon.

Horeb (hō′rĕb), **Mt.** ("desert," "mount of God"), used in E and D sources for the mountain called "Sinai" in J and P. The exact site is unknown; it may be Jebel Mûsā at the southern tip of the Sinai* Peninsula. It is described in Deut. 1:2 as being "eleven days' journey" from Kadesh-barnea, and in Ex. 17:6 it is the scene of Moses' smiting the rock. It is mentioned in Ex. 33:6; Deut. 1:6,

186. Moses smiting the rock, bronze doors by Lorenzo Ghiberti, Baptistry, Florence.

19, 4:10, 15; and named in Ps. 106:19 ff. as the scene of the making of the golden calf. Elijah fled to Horeb from Beer-sheba in his despondency (I Kings 19:1–21).

Horites (hō′rīts) (Heb. Horim), Hivites, Hurrians, possibly inhabitants of Mt. Seir. The Hori people of Gen. 36:22 may have been a tribe of Horites, living in the land of Seir in Edom* (Gen. 36:30). Horims are mentioned in Deut. 2:12, 22 as having been pushed out from Seir by "the children of Esau." Horites (Gen. 14:6, 36:21, 29) were probably the same as the Hivites of Joshua's day (Josh. 9); they were living in Palestine when Israel arrived. Many scholars believe that Horites were Hurrians, non-Semites who had come into northern Mesopotamia and the eastern highlands from an Indo-Iranian source, about the time that the proud Mitanni* horsemen came in from the same region and established a feudal state, occupying the land extending from the Mediterranean at a point now S. of Syria, E. to Media. By the second millennium B.C. Hurrians were scattered over most of the Middle East, but they have been known to moderns for only about thirty years. Their language is still in process of translation from thousands of recovered clay tablets, texts written in the 15th century B.C. in the Canaanite alphabet, and conveying information about deities, ritual, magic, and other religious matter ferreted out from archives recovered at Ras Shamrah* in N. Syria, in the Hittite center at Boghazköy, and at Nuzu and Mari. W. F. Albright believes that Hurrians, who exerted a profound influence in W. Asia until the end of the second millennium, were Armenoids, related to Urartians of Iron-Age Armenia, and possibly to Georgians in later history. He believes that they originated therefore S. of the Caucasus, made their appearance in history c. 2400 B.C. in the Zagros region, and carried the gods, myths, and general culture of the Sumero-Accadians into the zone later dominated by Hittites and other Anatolians. Hurrian society in the Nuzu region was not feudal, nor was it absorbed in the Mitanni state until very late, and then only partly. The Hurrians were conquered by the Hittites (c. 1370 B.C.), and their land was finally subjugated by the Assyrians (c. 1250 B.C.).

Eminent scholars in the field of ancient languages are still translating and publishing Hurrian tablets, of which the Semitic Museum of Harvard University alone has more than 4,000. Texts on clay found at Nuzu in the land of the Horites present parallels to Patriarchal customs revealed, for example, in Gen. 27, 30, 31:19, 34 f.

Hormah (hôr′mȧ) ("destruction," or "accursed"), a town in the rugged hill country of S. Judaea not far from the border of Edom. Its site is unknown, but is believed to have been not far from Ziklag and Beer-sheba, possibly Tell esh-Sheriah; sometimes called Zepheth. The Israelites were defeated there by Canaanites and Amalekites (Num. 14:45; "Amorites," Deut. 1:44) in an early phase of the Conquest after the discouraged wanderers had murmured against God. Later Hormah was captured and razed by Israel (Num. 21:3; Josh. 12:14). After being originally "assigned" to Judah (Josh. 15:30) it was given to Simeon (Josh. 19:4; I Chron. 4:30). The town was friendly to David, and accepted some of his spoil (I Sam. 30:30).

horn (Heb. *qeren*). (1) Horn of cattle or other animals were hollowed into flasks for oil used in anointing bruised animals (Ps. 23:5), or in royal consecration ceremonies (I Kings 1:39) (see ANOINT). Horn flasks also contained cosmetics* (see KEREN-HAPPUCH). (2) Highland peaks, like the Horns of Hattîn, possibly the Mount of Beatitudes (cf. Isa. 5:1, A.S.V.). (3) "Horn" (sing.) was used to describe the arrogant might of a king or a warrior (Ps. 75:4 f., 92:10, 112:9), because horned animals like the one-horned rhinoceros and the bull were symbolic of strength. Such a passage as Ps. 89:24 refers to God's granting prosperity or power to an individual. Kings and deities of the Middle East often wore horns to denote prosperity as well as power (I Sam. 2:1, 10). When Jeremiah wished to express the breaking of a nation's prestige he said, for example, "The horn of Moab is cut off" (Jer. 48:25). (4) There were horn-like projections at the four corners of the altar* of burnt offering in the Tabernacle and the Temple (Ex. 30:10; I Kings

1:50 f.). Several of these horned limestone altars have been excavated from Megiddo of the era of the early Hebrew Monarchy. The first use of horns on altars is surrounded with mystery, but may have developed from the hooks which held sacrificed animals (Ps. 118:27), or from skulls of animals hung there. Throughout Hebrew history altar horns were smeared with the blood of slain victims (Ex. 29:12; Lev. 4:7). These horns were sacred and afforded sanctuary to criminals who clung to them (I Kings 2:28; cf. Ex. 21:14). (5) Horned beasts signified in prophetic writings a king or kingdom, as in Dan. 7:7 f., 8:3 ff.; Rev. 5:6, 13:1, 17:3. (6) The first instrument that called Hebrews to worship was made by heating, flattening, and straightening a ram's horn. This *shophar*, still used in synagogues (see SYNAGOGUE), may originally have been intended as a memory of the ram's horns caught in the thicket when Isaac was spared (Gen. 22:13). Rams' horns were also used as military bugles in Israel's battles (Josh. 6:4, 6, 13). See INCENSE, illus. 193, MUSIC, illus. 278. TEMPLE, illus. 423.

hornet, an insect of the same genus as the wasp, but larger and more pugnacious. It is common in Palestine. The use of the word in Ex. 23:28; Deut. 7:20; Josh. 24:12 may be literal, or it may symbolize the power of Egypt.

horseleach (hôrs′lēch) (R.S.V. "leech"), a parasite common in Palestine, believed to lodge in the throats of animals as they drink from pools (Prov. 30:15).

horses, according to some authorities, were roaming wild in Palestine in Natufian times, 8,000–10,000 years ago. Their place of origin may have been inner Asia. James H. Breasted believed that the horse was first domesticated near the bend of the Euphrates, where it crosses the arch of the Fertile Crescent, between Assyria and the Syrian coast. There the fierce and aristocratic Mitanni*, who may earlier have known domestic horses in the Indus Valley, bred steeds which enabled them to dominate their neighbors. They wrote treatises on horses in Hittite cuneiform. The horse importers spread into what is now Russian Armenia and into Turkish Anatolia, overcoming the Hittites*, who also were great horse-lovers. Egyptians did not know the horse as a dray animal even in the great Pyramid Age, for their wall reliefs depict legions of small asses and donkeys bearing loads of stone and earth. Horses were apparently introduced to Egypt by the Hyksos*. From these invaders (c. 1720–1550 B.C.) from the N. the Egyptians acquired their enthusiasm for horse-drawn chariots, such as Joseph the Hebrew probably used when prime minister of Pharaoh (Gen. 41–43)—the first mention of chariots in the O.T. Horse-drawn chariots were still such a novelty in Egypt that their participation in the pursuit of fleeing Israel was emphasized by the author of Ex. 14:8 f., 23–28, 15:1, 19. Henri Frankfort believed that maned horses were used in the Mesopotamia of the al-'Ubaid or flood-level era of the Tigris-Euphrates, and that they began to appear in glyptic and other art forms c. 3000 B.C. Some authorities believe that Kassites from the eastern mountains, who forced themselves on Hammurabi's successors, may have introduced the horse into Babylonia, which they ruled for 400 years (c. 1530–1150 B.C.). Assyrians loved horses, and not only used them in their wars of aggression but depicted them with consummate art on their massive stone reliefs and on their delicate seals. Assyrians ranked with the Greeks as the greatest animal sculptors of the ancient world. Persians boasted of their three gifts to man: riding horses, shooting the bow, and telling the truth.

In Palestine horses for freight cargoes and farm work appeared later than the ass*, ox*, and camel*. Early Israel found conquest impeded by foes of the plains who used horses and chariots (Judg. 1:19). Not until the Hebrew Monarchy did hill-dwelling Israel obtain horse-drawn chariots such as their neighbors used in their iron-shod attacks. David boasted of slaying 40,000 Syrian horsemen, whose matériel he doubtless confiscated (II Sam. 10:18). He resorted to the strategy of crippling the horses of Syrian enemies (I Chron. 18:4). His son Solomon equipped his army with thousands of horses and chariots (II Chron. 9:25), for which he built well-equipped stables and quarters for their horsemen in such centers as Megiddo* and Gezer*, from which stone mangers and well-worn hitching posts have been excavated. He also engaged in an elaborate commerce in horses. Controlling the N.-S. trade routes, he imported and transshipped horses from Cilicia to Egypt, and brought up from Egypt hand-made chariots desired in the N.

In peace times horses were sometimes used in Palestine for hunting. Mules* were royal mounts (II Sam. 18:9; cf. Matt. 21:5). Horseback riding never appealed to the Egyptians, as it did to the Assyrians (Hos. 14:3). Syrian kings sometimes rode to escape enemies, like Ben-hadad fleeing from Ahab (I Kings 20:20). Naaman of Damascus came in a horse-drawn chariot to consult the prophet Elisha (II Kings 5:9), for chariots were used not only for war but as vehicles of civilian conveyance (see also Acts 8:28).

When the Persian court, depicted in the Book of Esther, wished to honor a man like Mordecai, they placed him in royal apparel, crowned, upon the king's horse and escorted him through the streets (Esther 6:9, 11). Young Assyrians riding on horses were the acme of harlots' desires (Ezek. 23:6). Romans used cavalry escorts for such prisoners as Paul, en route to Antipatris (Acts 23:23, 32); and bred powerful horses for the racing chariots of their amphitheaters.

Horses in Bible times were not shod. They were driven with bit and bridle. Often they wore bells (Zech. 14:20). Rich men's steeds wore elegant hand-woven riding cloths (cf. Mark 11:7).

O.T. writers made homiletic use of horses, contrasting men's trust in these to the confidence they ought to place in Yahweh (Ps. 20:7, 33:17; Isa. 30:16, 36:9). James recommended bridling men's tongues (Jas.

1:26). Horse-drawn chariots of God were seen by the discouraged prophet Elijah (II Kings 6:17). Revelation 6:2, 4 f., 8 dramatizes the "Four Horsemen of the Apocalypse."

Hosah (hō′sȧ) ("refuge"). (1) A porter (gatekeeper) in the time of David (I Chron. 16:38, 26:10). (2) A village of Asher (Josh. 19:29), possibly the same as Uzu, near Tyre*.

hosanna (Gk. transliteration of Heb. word meaning "save, we beseech thee," used to invoke a blessing) occurs 6 times in the Gospels in its later usage as an acclamation, in each case hailing Jesus on Palm Sunday as he entered Jerusalem. The simplest form appears in Mark 11:9 and John 12:13. The enlarged phrases of Matt. 21:9, 15 and Mark 11:10 may have been added as the Gospels developed. "Hosanna" in its original supplicatory sense had been used (cf. Ps. 118:25 f.) during joyous processions at the Feast (see FEASTS) of the Tabernacles, during the waving of branches, especially on the seventh day of the festival.

Hosea (hō-zē′ȧ) ("salvation"), the son of Beeri (Hos. 1:1); an 8th-century prophet of the Northern Kingdom (Hos. 1:2), identical in name only with Hoshea, the last king of Israel (II Kings 15:30, 17:1–6). The name also appears as a shortened form of Joshua in Num. 13:8. The few known facts of Hosea's life are discernible in his book, the first in the printed order of the Minor Prophets.

Hosea prophesied after Amos* in Northern Israel; his work began before the death of Jeroboam II c. 746 B.C. Inasmuch as the prophet may make mention of the events of Isa. 7:1 and II Kings 16:5, and of the accession of Hoshea in 732 B.C. (cf. 17:3–7), Hosea's mission may be assumed to have been concluded after that date. The contents of his book show him ardently in love with the land and familiar with its geography (2:22, 4:15, 5:1, 8, 6:8 f.), particularly Bethel (4:15, 5:8, 10:5, 12:4). Like Amos, his observations were those of a country man, concerned with wild and domestic animals (2:18, 4:3, 5:14, 7:11 f., 8:9, 9:11, 10:11, 13:7 f.); their capture (5:1, 9:8); the details of agricultural life (4:16, 8:7, 10:11 ff., 11:4, 13:3); fruits, flowers, and thistles of the fields (9:10, 10:1, 4, 8, 13:15); weather (6:4); winds (13:15); and rains (see FARMING) (6:3). Hosea was keenly aware of the hazards of life in the unprotected open spaces (6:9), and championed respect for landmarks (5:10). His observations of the priesthood have led some to believe that he knew this profession from the inside (4:6–14, 5:1, 6:9 f., 8:11). With all this he disclosed a keen knowledge of political conditions (5:13, 7:11, 8:9, 12:1) and the dangers of alliances with foreign neighbors. But it is around his marriage with Gomer and the birth of their three children that the first part of the Book of Hosea (chaps. 1–3) turns.

The Book falls into two parts: (1) Chaps. 1–3: the marriage of Hosea and the birth of his children, to whom ominous names were given. (2) Chaps. 4–14: discourses of Israel's sins and their punishment, reluctantly inflicted by a merciful God.

The interpretations of the domestic life of Hosea (chaps. 1–3) are: (1) that the narrative is an allegorical parable; (2) that Gomer was a prostitute; (3) that Gomer became a prostitute. Whether parabolic or historic, the prophet makes his personal love for the allegedly adulterous wife akin to that of God, Who continued to love a wicked and unfaithful Israel. Her alleged desertion and recovery by Hosea in the slave market, and her segregation in his home (chap. 3), according to a current but questionable interpretation of a symbolical action dramatize the divine love for an unfaithful nation.

The attitude of Hosea toward his supposedly wayward wife, and the use made by the prophet of his alleged tragic experience to reveal God's love for His wayward people, are said to be unique as a pattern of rare human behavior by a high-minded man, and to constitute a revelation of God's forgiveness which was new in the Hebrew conception of the Almighty.

The second half of the book (chaps. 4–14) is an indictment of Israel. Poor textual transmission and interpolated material in these chapters cause confusion but do not entirely obscure the strong personality of Hosea. They may be roughly summarized as follows: Chap. 4 describes the gross immortality of the people, sanctioned by the priests. Chap. 5 describes the guilt, and the punishment from which there is no escape except in repentance. Chap. 6 shows how evanescent is Israel's repentance, compared with her persistent sinfulness. Chap. 7 pictures Israel's inner depravity and outward signs of decay. Chap. 8 announces the imminence of the judgment*. Chap. 9 pictures the calamity which Israel has been drawing down on her head. Chap. 10 gives examples of Israel's guilt and punishment. Chap. 11 shows how God has pursued Israel with His love. Chaps. 12–14 record the issue of the divine judgment, with the door of mercy still open, but not entered.

Hosea glorified the Exodus and the Wilderness experiences of Israel as the nation's happiest period, because it then acted most like a trusting child under a father's loving protection (Hos. 2:15, 11:1 ff., 12:9, 13:4). The image (see IDOL) worship of his day—said to be a feature of Canaanite fertility cults—drew from him expressions of derision and contempt (4:17, 8:4–6, 11:2, 13:2, 14:8). More than 15 direct and indirect quotations from Hosea are contained in the N.T. The Christian anticipations in the book consist mainly of the far-reaching intuition of God's forgiving love proclaimed by Hosea, but revealed in its fullness in Jesus Christ, Savior of mankind. The name Hosea is found in the Latin form "Osee," A.V. Rom. 9:25.

J. L. M./R. W. C.

hosen (pl. of hose), stockings. (A.V. Dan. 3:21.) The meaning of the Aram. word used here is uncertain; it may mean very tight-fitting trousers.

Hoshea (hō-shē′ȧ) ("salvation"). (1) A shortened form of the name of Joshua (Deut. 32:44). (2) The last king of Israel (c. 732–724

B.C.), son of Elah (II Kings 15:30), a contemporary of Ahaz* and Hezekiah* (17:1, 18:1). After murdering king Pekah*, Hoshea was kept as a vassal ruler of the Northern Kingdom by Tiglath-pileser of Assyria, to whom he paid heavy tribute. Conspiring with Egypt against the Assyrian power, he was incarcerated by Shalmaneser* V, who for three years laid siege to Samaria (II Kings 17:4–5). The ultimate fate of Hoshea is not known. (3) An Ephraimite chief in David's bureaucracy (I Chron. 27:20). (4) A Levite who with others sealed the Covenant after the Return (Neh. 10:23).

hospitality, the kind reception of guests, a quality characteristic of the various peoples of Bible lands, including Mesopotamians, Syrians, Egyptians, Greeks, and Romans, as well as Palestinians. It was a feature of the semi-nomadic life of the Patriarchal era depicted in Genesis narratives, which reveal customs still observed by Bedouins. The entertainment of strangers was a sacred obligation, based on something more than supplying food, lodging, and fellowship for the wayfarer in a land where there were no inns until late Biblical times, and then very wretched ones. Hospitality was offered with the feeling that one might be entertaining "angels unawares" (Heb. 13:2; cf. Gen. 18:2, 19:1); and that one might himself become as dependent as the person who was now seeking it. Patriarchs had comfortable standards of living. They pitched groups of hand-woven tents under trees, near an inherited well, surrounded by grazing land and grain acreage. Wealth was often measured by the number of guests a man was able to entertain (Job 31:32). Even an enemy or a blood avenger could claim protection if he so much as touched friendly tent cords; he might remain for three days and four hours, as his just due —the amount of time the host believed his guest to be sustained by his food—and he might then claim immunity for another 36 hours after his departure.

A gracious attitude toward kinsmen and strangers appears in many O.T. narratives. Details of Patriarchal hospitality appear in the story of Abraham entertaining angels (Gen. 18:1–8). The host himself extends the invitation (v. 3); provides water for their feet (4), and rest under a tree (5), and prepares the heavy part of the feast (7 f.), summoning Sarah to bake fresh "cakes upon the hearth" (coals on the ground, probably, outside the tent). Company was always welcome in such a household. The host's responsibility for the safety of his guests was carried to such extremes that Lot offered to turn over his unmarried daughters to the rabble if they would spare his guests (Gen. 19:6, 9). Again, in the exquisite idyll of the courtship of Rebekah (Gen. 24:11–61) details of hospitality are happily sketched; a pitcher of water from the family well is offered to the new arrival and all his beasts by the daughter of the house; golden jewelry is presented to Rebekah (v. 22), whose brother Laban runs out to greet the guest, offers the hospitality of his father Bethuel's home, ungirds the traveler's beasts, feeds and beds them down for the night, and brings cooling water for the dusty feet of Abraham's emissary and his servants (vv. 22–32). An elaborate meal is prepared meanwhile by the women of the household.

Even when Israel had settled down in towns the proverbial hospitality persisted. The king's tables were shared by many guests (II Sam. 9:7). Solomon's palace dinners were sumptuous (I Kings 4:22 f.). Nehemiah, governor of Jerusalem, entertained 150 men at a time, from many nations. The hilltop court of Ahab and Jezebel extended hospitality to as many as 400 Baal prophets and 400 Asherah prophets. Hospitality among the people was widespread, like the entertainment of the fugitive King Saul by a witch of Endor (I Sam. 28:24 f.); and of the prophet Elisha by the woman of Shunem (II Kings 4:10) on the wall.

Jesus extended hospitality to hungry multitudes (Mark 8:1–9), and accepted it from a ruler of the Pharisees (Luke 14:1–11); from the family at Bethany (Matt. 21:17; John 12:2); from the penitent Zacchaeus at Jericho (Luke 19:5–10); and from his bewildered hosts at Emmaus (Luke 24:29–31). The beginning of the Lord's Supper was a shared meal in a Jerusalem guest chamber, prepared under Christ's direction (Mark 14:15; Luke 22:7–13). The historic events of Pentecost also occurred in a large guest room in Jerusalem (Acts 2:2).

In N.T. times Paul, realizing the evil atmosphere of most 1st-century inns, urged his followers to accept private hospitality, and expected Christians to extend it to traveling believers (Rom. 12:13; I Pet. 4:9), as Jesus expected it for his Disciples (Matt. 10:9–15; Luke 10:4 ff.). (Cf. II & III John.)

Despicable breaches of hospitality are illustrated by the Jael incident of Judg. 4:17, 5:24 and by the spying Babylonian guests to whom Hezekiah foolishly showed all that was in his house (II Kings 20:12 ff.). The refusal of Samaritans to be hospitable to Jesus (Luke 9:53) has gone down in history. The Judas betrayal was all the more infamous because it took place immediately after the man had been guest at a Passover meal where Jesus was host (John 13:1 f., 21, 26–30).

Egyptian hospitality toward both men and women was sumptuous, from the transparent gowns and jewels of the guests and their lotus-flower favors, to the viands and condiments of the menu, the games, and the slender dancing girls and women musicians known through extant bas-reliefs. Some of this traditional hospitality overflowed to reach the unkempt nomad relatives of Joseph at Pharaoh's court, even though the snobbish servants arranged one table for Joseph, another for his guests, and separate places for the meticulous Egyptians of the host's retinue because they had scruples against eating with disheveled Hebrews, whose very presence was distasteful (Gen. 43:31–34). The same sort of scaling down of hospitality prevails in Bible lands today, where the sheikh resting under an olive tree eats first, passes on what is left to his servants, who share the remnants with hungry passersby and give their animals what is left.

Canaanites were so hospitable that they subsidized local gods to protect strangers among them, as revealed in a Ras Shamrah text. Cruel Assyrian conquerors delighted in feasts; Asshurbanapal appears in a carving of c. 650 B.C., banqueting with his wife in a Nineveh garden, surrounded by servants and entertainers. The Book of Esther portrays Persian royal hospitality. For Greek and Roman hospitality, see *An Encyclopedia of Bible Life*, Madeleine S. and J. Lane Miller, Chapter 15 (Harper & Brothers).

See BANQUETS; inns, under ARCHITECTURE.

host, a multitude, as: an army (Gen. 21:22); the angels or the heavenly host (I Kings 22:19; Luke 2:13); the stars (Deut. 4:19). The Lord of hosts is the title given to God as the leader of the armies of Israel (I Sam. 17:45). The word "hosts" in this title later included angels, heavenly bodies, and all the forces of nature (Ps. 46:7; Amos 4:13).

hour. See TIME.

hough (hŏk), the tarsal joint or its region in a quadruped's hind leg; to disable by cutting the tendons of the hock; to hamstring. (See Josh. 11:6).

187. Reconstruction (model) of a house found at Tell en-Nasbeh, believed to have been biblical Mizpah.

house. (1) A family line, like "the house of Levi" (Ex. 2:1); a tribal group, like Israel* (Num. 1:2, 12:7; Josh. 24:15; Neh. 1:6) and Judah* (II Sam. 2:7). (2) "The house of God" in O.T. times, conceived as the dwelling of God, sometimes a cloth Tabernacle (Gen. 28:22; Ex. 40:19–35) or a stone temple (I Kings 6:1 ff.). Jesus spoke figuratively of the Temple as "the house of prayer" (Matt. 21:13). The Canaanite god Dagon is mentioned as having a house or temple (I Sam. 5:2).

(3) A family dwelling. Houses in Bible lands developed first as "houses of hair," tents of stout rain-and-wind-resistant textiles hand-woven on family looms (see WEAVING) from wool and animal hair. These were popular in Patriarchal Israel, and are still used by desert nomads (see TENTS). As nomads settled down in villages they built huts of sun-baked mud brick or mud and stone; some very early sun-baked mud bricks examined by archaeologists are uniform in size, have parallel sides, and are superior to many made in the Near East today. Clay was used for mortar and sometimes for an extra coating. Kiln-baked bricks were also widely used. Some bricks were "bound" with straw, shells, fishbones, like those found at Solomon's port of Ezion-geber*. (See Ex. 5:1–21 for Israel's brickmaking task in Egypt.) Sometimes foundations were of kiln-baked brick, and walls of sun-dried. Hebrews developed skill in laying systematic headers and stretchers of brick, as seen in excavations at Bethel.

The earliest houses excavated in Palestine are at Jericho*, where apartment houses were built close to the rampart, or between the city walls or on them, like Rahab's near the oasis spring. The normal shape of such Jericho houses was square, with an entrance hall, store chamber, large bedroom or living room, and guest chamber opening into an open, walled court, where domestic animals were kept except in bad weather, when smaller animals were led down narrow steps to the lower level of the house, under the arches. Two flights of steps led from the court to the roof. Opposite the entrance hall clay divans have been found. Food bins and storage pits in Jericho houses have yielded grains and vegetables evidently abandoned during a sudden summer siege before the Israelites took the city (Josh. 6).

Stone houses in Palestine and Syria tended to be built in the highlands, even as mud houses characterized the plains. Ancient hills provided plenty of stone for the construction of solidly built towns like Bethlehem, Safed, or Jerusalem (Ps. 122:3). Some old stone houses still standing have walls three ft. thick,

188. Typical Palestinian village stone house c. 1900 A.D.

protecting their occupants equally against heat, cold, and military attack. Ai* has yielded portions of stone dwellings from c. 2900 B.C. No finer type of Hebrew stone house from the Late Bronze Age (c. 1500–1200 B.C.) has been excavated in Palestine than the domestic structures found at Bethel*, which were built in one or two rows around a central court. Some of their floors were of smooth flags. Stone drains carried off surplus water. Stone houses often had their own enclosures, outer staircases, and flat roofs, where the guest chamber was located (II Kings 4:10; Acts 10:9), and booths erected for festivals. Shouting from housetops (Matt. 10:27; Luke 12:3) was one means of giving publicity. Doors, at first of wattle or reed or textile, were later made of wood or metal, sometimes with hinges of leather; they were securely bolted with wooden or iron bars pulled through an inside socket. Metal hinges were fitted to temple, gate, and palace doors. The threshold had sacred significance; doorposts supported the lintel, on which Israelite families sprinkled symbolic blood at Passover (Ex. 12:22 f.). To the door of the pious was fastened a tube-like amulet*, *mezuzah*, containing on parchment the words of Deut. 6:4–9, 11:13–21. A parapet around the roof of the stone house, where many family activities—conversation, prayer, weaving, sleeping—went on, was required by law (Deut. 22:8). Stone houses built on Palestinian hillsides (Matt. 5:14) were ramped terrace-wise, so that families could walk from the roofs of one tier to the street level of the next; this scheme provided easy means of escape. Windows, when present, were high above the street, and latticed. In houses too simple for even a small inner court, the one room had two levels, the upper platform (*mastabeh*), where the family cooked, slept, and wove; and a lower level (*rowyeh*), where the animals ate from stone mangers and rested on straw. A depression in the middle of the room, in which a clay vessel of charcoal was set, constituted the "fireplace" (cf. Jer. 36:23). Arches supported the mezzanine *mastabeh*. (For furnishings see FURNITURE; and Section 11, *Encyclopedia of Bible Life*, Madeleine S. and J. Lane Miller, Harper. For ground plans of Palestinian homes in ancient times see *What Mean These Stones?* Burrows, ASOR.)

Greek and Roman dwellings of the 1st century A.D., such as Paul and his companions knew, probably conformed to the Mediterranean court style. Villas were luxurious, gardened, decorated with intricate mosaic* floors, such as are seen today at Beit Jibrîn and Antioch. Ancient houses dating from c. 6,000 years ago have been excavated at Persepolis, where walls stand five and six ft. high. The earliest known extant windows are in Persian houses. Egyptian houses ranged from the luxurious, gracious palaces of the Pharaohs to wretched mud hovels used by Hebrews during the Sojourn—types that are still being built in Nile villages. During the Biblical period Egyptian houses were usually built of unfired brick, of which little evidence remains. City houses were generally near the markets. The more pretentious houses, often more than one story high, were likely to be close to the palace and the temple.

189. Typical Israelite house, Stratum A (c. 600 B.C.) at Tell Beit Mirsim (Kiriath-sepher). City wall at left, with narrow street at right angles.

Country houses were built close to water and to food-producing areas. The servants' quarters were at the rear, entered from the street, and separated from the rest of the house by silos stocked with food reserves. Akhenaton's palace at Amarna seems to have had a central room surrounded by a block of higher ones and lighted by clerestory windows. The master's suite, at the right, included bedroom, bathroom, and anointing chamber. The house also contained a chapel, servants' quarters, stables, and a granary court.

Specific houses mentioned in the O.T. include those of Jephthah (Judg. 11:34); Micah (Judg. 18:2); Absalom (II Sam. 13:20); Solomon (I Kings 7:1 ff.); and Haman (Esther 8:1). "Householders" of the N.T. include Zacharias (Luke 1:23); Martha (Luke 10:38), cf. Simon the leper (Matt. 26:6); Zacchaeus (Luke 19:5 f.); Peter

(Matt. 8:14); the man in whose upper room was celebrated the last Passover of Christ (Matt. 26:18); Mary, mother of Mark (Acts 12:12); Lydia at Philippi (Acts 16:15); Titus Justus at Corinth (Acts 18:7); Philip the evangelist at Caesarea (Acts 21:8); and Paul for three years at Rome (Acts 28:30). Jesus frequently referred in his parables to houses and homes (Matt. 7:26 f., 10:6; Luke 12:52, 13:25, 15:8, 25, 18:14), which makes the more poignant John's words, "every man went unto his own house. Jesus went out unto the Mount of Olives" (John 7:53, 8:1). He spoke of preparing a place in "my Father's house" (John 14:2). Houses of prosperous Christians were the first meeting places of the Church (Acts 2:46, 5:42; Rom. 16:5; Col. 4:15; Philem. 1:2).

190. Middle-class house at Ur (c. 2100 and 1885 B.C.), reconstruction based on material excavated by Sir Leonard Woolley. First story of burnt brick, second of mud brick, built around a central court, from which stairs went up to the balcony. Behind the stairs, a lavatory with a terra-cotta drain and a kitchen. Lower right, domestic chapel with brick altar and niche for picture or clay figurine (cf. TERAPHIM, illus. 431). Such a house sometimes had a vaulted brick tomb beneath the floor for family burial.

Huldah (hŭl′dȧ), the wife of Shallum the wardrobe keeper (II Kings 22:14), a reputable prophetess ranking with Deborah and Hannah. When consulted by King Josiah's deputation after the Book of the Law had been accidentally found (v. 8), Huldah confirmed its authoritativeness, thus encouraging the reforms of Josiah* (vv. 17, 20; cf. II Chron. 34:22–33).

hunting as a pastime was not widespread in O.T. times in Palestine. Life was austere. When wild animals were sought it was usually at the impulse of hunger, or of danger from wild beasts (Ex. 23:29; I Kings 13:24). Venison, such as Esau hunted for Isaac (Gen. 25:28), roebuck and hart (Deut. 12:15, 22), fallow deer, wild goat and ox, and chamois (Deut. 14:5), as well as game birds like the partridge (I Sam. 26:20), were "clean" for food, and found their way onto tables of the poor as well as of royal families (see also FISH).

In Egypt pleasurable ways of living popularized the bagging of falcons, vultures, buzzards, kites, and crows. Greyhounds participated in Egyptian hunting (see DOGS). Large-scale hunting of lions was a favorite pastime of Babylonian and Assyrian kings, who, standing in chariots with poised bows, felled their prey, and then recorded their exploits on glazed tiles and carved reliefs of palaces, temples, and city gates.

Scripture alludes to the hunter's bows and arrows (Gen. 27:3), slingstones and darts (Job 41:28 f.), nets (Job 19:6), fowlers' snares (Ps. 64:5, 91:3, 124:7), and pits for trapping bears (Ps. 9:15; Ezek. 19:8).

A 7,000-year-old hunter's camp, with weapons, tools, and storage jars, has been found at Hassuna, the earliest of the sites excavated by the Iraqui Directorate in "the cradle of civilization."

Hur (hûr) (probably an Egyptian name). (1) An Israelite who with Aaron held up the hands of Moses during battle against Amalek (Ex. 17:10, 12) so that the sacred staff might prevail. He helped control the people while Moses was in the Mount (Ex. 24:14); he may have been the husband of Miriam*, sister of Moses. (2) One of the commissary officers of Solomon (I Kings 4:8 A.S.V. "Ben-hur"). (3) An officer in charge of half of Jerusalem, who helped rebuild the city walls (Neh. 3:9).

Huram (hū'răm). See HIRAM.

Hurrians. See HORITES.

husband. See FAMILY.

husbandman, A.V. word for farmer, like Noah (Gen. 9:20); King Uzziah's cultivators (II Chron. 26:10); the "poor of the land" left behind when Judah went into Exile (II Kings 25:12); and the tenant vinedressers of Christ's parables (Mark 12:1, 2, 7, 9; Luke 20:9, 10, 14, 16). In John 15:1 God is the husbandman and Christ the "true vine." See FARMING.

husks (Luke 15:16), eaten by the Prodigal Son, were probably the sweet pods of the carob, often called the locust tree. When green, the long legumes, ripe from May to August, are used for cattle and swine. They are sweet, and are eaten by poor people. Their pulp is made into syrup. Many call carob pods "St. John's bread," because they believe the ascetic prophet ate these—and not animal locusts—in the Jordan jungles (Matt. 3:4).

Hyksos (hĭk'sōs) (Egypt., for "rulers of foreign lands"), a mixed and predominantly NW. Semitic (Canaanite or Amorite) people, not mentioned by name in Scripture, but influential contemporaries of the Hebrews between c. 1720 and 1550 B.C. Their powerful kingdom included Palestine and Syria, and for a time Egypt, which they overran and ruled as the Fifteenth and the Sixteenth Egyptian Dynasties, with their capital at Avaris-Tanis in the Delta, rather than at Thebes, which was the capital of Egypt before and after the Hyksos regime. Their domination of Egypt included the period when Joseph* the Hebrew became prime minister of Pharaoh (Gen. 47:11), lenient to other foreigners. Details of the remarkable Genesis narratives of the Sojourn tally well with what external history has revealed about the Hyksos Egyptian period. (See *Westminster Historical Atlas to the Bible*, pp. 27–29, for excellent brief statement.) W. F. Albright believes that the migration of Hebrews from Mesopotamia may have occurred just before the Hyksos age.

Recent excavations have revealed tangible evidence of great material prosperity during the Hyksos era, whose innovations included the introduction to Egypt of horses and war chariots, as well as the composite bow; the erection in Palestine and Syria of huge earthen enclosures for their horses; the construction of the unique defense glacis seen at Jericho*, Shechem, Lachish*, and Tell el-'Ajjûl*. The Hyksos were evidently among the first to separate the dead from the living by providing cemeteries outside the town. Shaft burials were customary. Their attitude toward the dead may have influenced the Hebrew "clean and unclean" legislation (Num. 19:11 ff.). The jar burials of infants, under floors or in foundations, was also a Hyksos custom. Possibly they sacrificed their first-born (cf. Ex. 22:29). They not only erected many temples to Baal* and 'Anat*, traces of which are extant, but also left deposits of fertility-cult influences and evidences of worship of the mother goddess. Cultic objects such as nude figurines with prominent sex features, serpents associated with winding streams and fertilizing elements (cf. II Kings 18:4), and doves of the mother goddess are common in excavated Hyksos levels. (Cf. Lev. 12:6 for possible infiltration of Hyksos rites into those of Hebrews.) This warlike people shared with the Israelites the concept of a "mountain god."

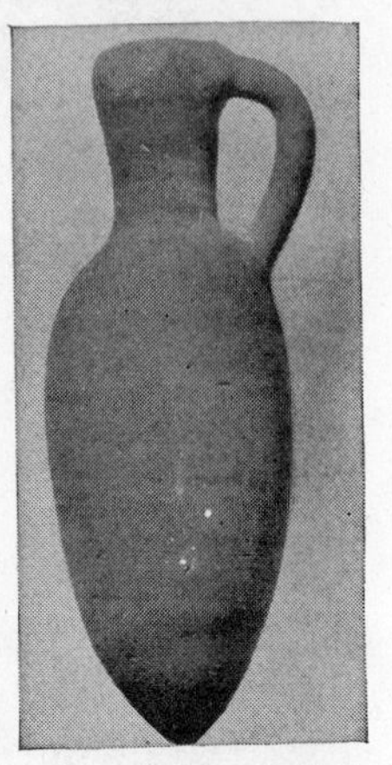

191. Hyksos Period pitcher (c. 1600 B.C.), Tell ed-Duweir.

The Hyksos Dynasties of Egypt ended when Khamose and Ahmose drove them back into Asia during a war of liberation (c. 1600–1550 B.C.), and when Amenophis (Amenhotep I) inaugurated the brilliant Eighteenth Egyptian Dynasty (1570–1310 B.C.). The statement of Ex. 1:8 about a new king arising in Egypt who "knew not Joseph" may describe the transition from Hyksos to native rulers, less friendly to foreigners. It was during the Nineteenth Dynasty that the Exodus* of the Hebrews took place.

Excavations at Mari* and in Ugarit (see RAS SHAMRAH) have recently shed new light on the Hyksos people. (See also EGYPT.)

Hymenaeus (hī'mĕ-nē'ŭs) ("pertaining to the god of marriage"), a heretic denounced by Paul for having made shipwreck of his faith (I Tim. 1:20; II Tim. 2:17). Possibly he was dabbling in Gnosticism*, which was eating into the life of the Christian Church.

hymn (Gk. *hymnos*), a song or ode in praise of the Deity. (1) In O.T. times the Psalms* constituted the hymn treasury of the Temple. The Psalter was recognized as the Temple hymnbook of the post-Exilic Jewish community, which nourished its faith on these religious lyrics developed in artistic form. At least a portion of the Psalter was later used also in synagogues, as for example the Pilgrim

Songs (Ps. 120–137). When the Psalms were canonized their contents were distinguished from other hymns. The following O.T. hymns outside the Psalter have been preserved: the Songs of Moses (Ex. 15:1–19; Deut. 32:1–43); the Song of Deborah and Barak (Judg. 5); and the Song of Hannah (I Sam. 2:1–10).

(2) In the N.T. the word "hymn" first appears in Matt. 26:30 and Mark 14:26—the record of Jesus and his companions singing a hymn (probably the Hallel, Ps. 113–118) before going from the upper room to Gethsemane. This act inspired hymn singing by the earliest Christian groups as a means of expressing their adoration of God and aspiration to holy living. The use of "psalms and hymns and spiritual songs" in joyous worship is recorded in Eph. 5:19 and Col. 3:16. In group worship and in personal devotional life hymns were sung for encouragement (Acts 16:25; I Cor. 14:26; see also Jas. 5:13). Study of their original forms suggests that the following passages contain hymn fragments: Eph. 5:14; I Tim. 1:17, 3:16, 6:16; II Tim. 4:18. It is possible to feel the atmosphere of early Christian worship in the *Magnificat** of Mary (Luke 1:46–55); the *Benedictus* of Zacharias (Luke 1:68–79); the *Gloria in Excelsis* of the Angels' Song (Luke 2:10–14); the *Nunc Dimittis* of Simeon (Luke 2:29–32), as well as in the songs of the Apocalypse (Rev. 4:11, 5:9 f., 12 f., 11:17 f., 15:3 f.). The latter fragments reveal the devout piety of the early Jewish Christians, whose first hymns were sung or chanted in Hebrew. The "Hosanna Hymn" of Palm Sunday appears in its simplest form in Mark 11:9 and John 12:13—the actual cry of the throng (cf. Ps. 118:25 f.). As O.T. times merged into the N.T. era, many old Hebrew hymns were preserved by Christians, who also developed a liturgy of their own. A bit of early Christian hymnody appearing in I Tim. 3:16 is classed as a semiliturgical confession of faith, for the first Christians believed that such a confession should be sung, not merely assented to or signed.

In time "hymns" included all types of composition intended to be sung or recited rhythmically in Christian worship for the expression of emotion and conveying of instruction. After A.D. 600 the clergy tended to reserve for themselves the function of hymn singing. But after the Reformation and the liberating work of Martin Luther the privilege of song was again opened to the people, who during the English Revival were prompt to take up the great hymns created by Isaac Watts and Charles Wesley. It is estimated that there are today more than a half a million Christian hymns.

hypocrisy (from Gk. *hypokrisis*, "playing a part on the stage"), pretending to be what one is not, or to feel what one does not feel. Under Jewish and Christian influences this word came to mean "dissimulation," or the simulating of qualities of personality and character, religious convictions or other beliefs, not actually present in the person assuming the appearance. In the A.V. throughout the O.T. wherever this word is used it might be more accurately translated "godless," "profane," or "impious," as it is in later versions. Though dissimulation and moral and religious insincerity were widely prevalent and recognized throughout the O.T. (as in Isa. 1), in the N.T., under the moral discernment of Jesus, this sin received its real name. Matthew especially, writing for Jewish Christian converts, reports the blasts of Jesus against hypocrites and hypocrisies in those Jewish ceremonial practices which were insincerely enacted (Matt. 6:2, 5, 16, 15:7, 23:13–15, 23, 25, 27, 29).

Hyrcanus (hûr-kā'nŭs). John I, son of Simon Maccabaeus (see MACCABEES), king and high priest (134–104 B.C.). Under him the post-Exilic Jewish State attained its greatest material prosperity, and minted Maccabean bronze coins, as seen from material excavated at Beth-zur*. Hyrcanus tried to reconquer territory which had been David's. He compelled the conquered Idumaeans to become circumcised and adopted into Judaism (see HEROD). Hyrcanus and his ideals are somewhat revealed in the Book of Esther, of whose author he is the ideal, exemplified in Mordecai*.

John II, a Hasmonaean high priest (76–66 and 63–40 B.C.); a weak figure dominated by Antipater*.

hyssop, a plant mentioned several times in the O.T., but not always suggesting the same species. Botanists are baffled in efforts to identify it in Scripture. Maimonides thought it was thyme; Tristram, thorny caper; others, marjoram (as in I Kings 4:33; cf. Heb. 9:19). Ps. 51:7 refers to its purifying quality. Hyssop is described in I Kings 4:33 as springing out of a wall. This may not be the same hyssop shrub (? *Sorghum vulgare*) as the one used for sprinkling the blood of sacrificed animals on lintel and doorposts at Passover* time (Ex. 12:22). Hyssop, together with cedar and scarlet wool, was part of the equipment for purification rites: for lepers (Lev. 14:4, 6); for plague (Lev. 14:49, 51 f.); for the red heifer ceremonial (Num. 19:6, 18; cf. Ex. 24:8; Heb. 9:19). The reed (*Kalamos*) used to lift a vinegar-soaked sponge to the lips of Jesus on his cross was called "hyssop" (John 19:29). This may be the reed-like, 5-ft.-tall sorghum.

I

Ibleam (ĭb′lē-ăm) (Tell Bel'ameh), one of the heavily fortified Canaanite cities which extended from Beth-shan near the Jordan to Acre on the coast, and separated the Joseph tribes from the Plain of Esdraelon. It is situated ¼ m. S. of En-gannim (probably the later Jenîn) and 13 m. NE. of Samaria, on the road to Megiddo. Its pivotal position was demonstrated by tragedies that took place there: the fatal wounding of King Ahaziah of Judah (c. 842 B.C.) by Jehu of Israel; and the murder of the last of the Jehu dynasty, King Zechariah (c. 745 B.C.) by his successor Shallum (LXX IV Kings 15:10). Josh. 17:11 tells of the city's being "assigned" to Manasseh, although the next verse and Judg. 1:27 state that the tribe was not able to clear it of Canaanites.

Ichabod (ĭk′ȧ-bŏd) (meaning uncertain; possibly "no glory" or "inglorious"), a son of Phinehas and grandson of Eli; born at the hour of the capture of the Ark by the Philistines (I Sam. 4:17–22) and shortly after the death of his father in battle and the accidental death of his grandfather.

Iconium (ī-cō′nĭ-ŭm) (Turkish Konya), a populous town since early times, situated in an oasis at the SW. edge of the great central plain of Asia Minor, among famous plum and apricot orchards. Its prosperity in Paul's day was due to its location on the main trade route connecting Ephesus with Syria. Today the railroad from Konia connects Istanbul (via Scutari) with Baghdad. Its people have long been skilled in weaving* rugs and textiles from materials supplied by Taurus mountain flocks, and in cultivating farm produce and highland fields of flax*. In the Roman and Greek empires it was regarded as the capital of Phrygia*, of which it was the easternmost city. It became a Roman colony under Hadrian.

Paul and Barnabas visited Iconium on the First Missionary Journey, after they had been cast out from Pisidian Antioch by citizens stirred up by jealous Jews (Acts 13:51). Iconium yielded "a great multitude," both Jews and Greeks, to the Christian Way (14:1–7), and the Apostles during their prolonged stay were so successful as to divide the city. Ultimately, however, a group of Jews and Gentiles united to stone Paul, who fled into the district of Lycaonia, to Lystra, and Derbe. Persisting in their enmity, Iconium Jews hunted him down in Lystra, 18 m. S., in the midst of his successful preaching there. The Apostle was dragged from the city almost dead (14:19), but returned to Iconium soon after to encourage his converts to hold fast in their Christian faith (14:21). If the Epistle to the Galatians* is interpreted as having been addressed to "Phrygia and the region of Galatia" (Acts 16:6) and "the country of Galatia and Phrygia" (Acts 18:23), we must recognize two later visits of Paul to Iconium. "Brethren of Iconium" were mentioned by him as having given a favorable recommendation to Timothy (Acts 16:2). Paul referred to Iconium's persecution of him (II Tim. 3:11). I Peter was addressed to the people of Iconium and other towns of the Province of Galatia.

Inscriptions at Iconium reveal the presence there of a vigorous colony of Christians from the 3d century on. One of Iconium's notable citizens was Thecla, who (according to the 2d-century monuments of Christian literature *Acts of Thecla* and *Acts of Paul and Thecla*, which were time and again condemned for their fabulous character) was converted through the Apostle's teaching, and is today one of the most honored saints of the Greek and Latin Churches, the first woman martyr. Some have suggested that the Martyrion church at Seleucia Pieria (the port of Syrian Antioch), begun in the 5th century and studied by Princeton University in the 20th, was dedicated to Thecla.

iconography. See SYMBOL.

Iddo. (1) The father of Ahinadab, an official in Solomon's regime (I Kings 4:14). (2) A Levite (I Chron. 6:21). (3) David's chief over the Manassites in Gilead (I Chron. 27:21). (4) A man with a foreign wife (A.S.V. Ezra 10:43; A.V. Jadau, R.S.V. Jaddai). (5) A seer who recorded events in the reigns of Kings Rehoboam, Jeroboam, and Abijah (II Chron. 9:29, 12:15, "concerning genealogies"). (6) A name assigned in the Hebrew Bible to the grandfather of Zechariah (Zech. 1:1, 7). (7) The head of a family which returned from Exile (Neh. 12:4, 16). (8) The head of a Nethinim group (Ezra 8:17).

idol, an image ("likeness") fashioned in human or symbolic form and used as an object of worship. All idols are images, but not all images are idols. For example, images include amulets (see AMULET), worn for both magical and ornamental purposes, and fetishes believed to possess desired powers through an indwelling spirit. The miniatures of servants, pets, foods, vehicles, etc., buried with Egyptians were not idols but images, quite distinct in significance from the god symbols (see SYMBOL) found in the innermost sanctuary of Egyptian temples. The Graeco-Roman world was full of images and idols that were a tangible part of the post-Homeric anthropomorphic polytheism of Greece, which influenced the eastern Mediterranean world until the beginning of the Christian era. To many Babylonians idols were the actual embodiment of gods. Of Israel's pagan neighbors, the Persians alone did not worship idols. Canaanites were especially given to their worship. Many crude specimens of the idols of Hittites* and other peoples of Asia Minor have been found in their excavated occupa-

IDOL

tion levels, as at Ras Shamrah. Although many female images have been found in excavated levels inhabited by Hebrews, no male ones even attempting to portray an anthropomorphic Yahweh have been found.

The struggle of Hebrews against idolatry is believed by many to have begun early in their career as a people. The departure of Abraham from Ur was motivated by the desire to rid himself of his ancestors' gods (Josh. 24:2), as well as by nomadic hunger for more territory. Jacob and his household are also credited by the author of Gen. 35:1–4 with a purpose to "put away strange gods." That Laban and Rachel continued to cherish the simple family idols (teraphim*) is narrated in Gen. 31:30, 32–35, with a suggestion of ancestor worship. The Second Commandment as it now stands in the document of Ex. 34:16–28 J (c. 850 B.C.) probably embodies an earlier Decalogue whose traditional Mosaic legislation may have tolerated the use of certain simple images in contrast to the abhorred cultic idols of molten metals (Ex. 34:17). Many believe that in its austere desert years Israel was not aware of the need for fighting idols or protecting a Sabbath (possibly a Canaanite institution) until it began to settle down. This viewpoint leads to an interpretation of the episode of Aaron's golden calf (Ex. 32) as an exceptional rather than a usual event. At any rate, the O.T. records an unwavering protest against idols and gods other than Yahweh, as the Hebrew people patiently and courageously groped their way toward ethical monotheism—their greatest gift to the world. From the time they settled in Canaan during the Conquest until the Exile, when experience had taught them for all time the folly of idolatry, Israel fought the contaminating influences of idols honored by their polyglot neighbors. These influences were abetted by (1) mixed marriages, even of monarchs (Solomon, I Kings 11:1–13, and Ahab, I Kings 16:30–33)—marriages which continued to be denounced down through the era of Ezra's reforms (Ezra 10); (2) the popular belief that the local gods of Canaan exercised proprietorship; and (3) association with idol-worshipping Egypt (Ezek. 20:7) and Assyria (23:7, cf. 36:18, 19).

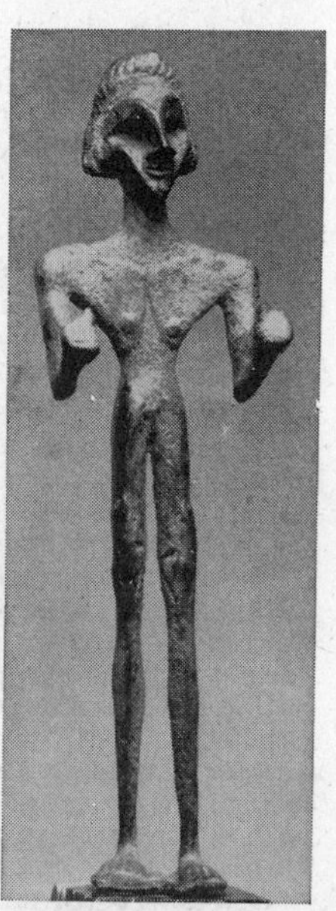

192. Syrian idol, c. 1000 B.C.

The constantly repeated denunciations of idolatry in the O.T. give an indication of the persistence and extent of the apostasies. These protests are found in the various Codes of Law, like the Deuteronomic (Deut. 12:3, 16:22, cf. 5:8); the Covenant Code* (Ex. 20:23); the Holiness Code (Lev. 26:1 f., 26:30). They are also a constant theme of the Hebrew prophets for five centuries: I Kings 21:25 f.; Amos 2:4, 5:26; Hosea 8:4b–6; Isa. 2:8a; Zeph. 2:11; Jer. 7:16–20, 7:29–34, 8:1–3; Hab. 2:18–20; Ezek. 6:4–6, 8, 20:39; Zech. 10:2, 13:2; Isa. 40:19 f., 41:29, 44:9–20, 57:1–13, 65:1–15, 66:15–17. Cf. also Ps. 115, 135:15–21.

The basest idolatries (II Kings 21:2–7) existed during the reign of Judah's King Manasseh (c. 687–642 B.C.), vassal to Assyria. King Josiah (c. 640–609 B.C.) effected reforms (II Chron. 34:1–7) by encouraging the formulation of the Deuteronomic legislation which summarized scattered, uncodified earlier efforts to extirpate idolatry and immorality. It promulgated punishment by death to those who worshipped idols (Deut. 17:2–7); and a curse was pronounced upon the maker of idols (27:15).

Typical Idols

Asherah*—sacred wooden post, tree fetish, possibly with phallic significance.

Baals (see BAAL)—"lords" of hills, streams, fields (Num. 22:41; I Kings 16:31; Jer. 7:9, and *passim* in the O.T.).

Bulls (see BULL)—symbol of divine strength (especially deified at Memphis).

Calves—symbols of deity (Aaron's, Ex. 32; those of Jeroboam I, I Kings 12:28 f.).

Human forms (Ezek. 16:17 f.; Isa. 44:13; Ps. 115:4–8; I Sam. 19:16).

Serpents (see SERPENT)—associated with fertility (as excavated at Beth-shan).

Statues—often on a colossal scale (Dan. 3).

Various animals (especially in Egypt, where gods were given human forms with heads of hawk, falcon, ape, cow, etc.).

Teraphim—figurines or small charms, possibly a reflection of ancestor worship (Gen. 31:34, 35:1–4), or perhaps lots in the sacred box used for divination. See MAGIC.

Typical Materials. Biblical passages show that idols were made of stone (Lev. 26:1; Hab. 2:18–20); gold (Isa. 40:18–20; Dan. 3; Ps. 115:4); silver (Jer. 10:9; Judg. 17:2–4, 18:18); and wood (Hab. 2:18–20; Isa. 37:19, 44:13–17). Archaeological excavations have also unearthed idols made of bone, clay, ivory, and iron.

Idols were made by pouring melted metal over an inner core, whence "molten images" (Isa. 41:29, 44:10); and by engraving with a graving tool, whence "graven images" (Deut. 12:3; Jer. 10:14; Isa. 44:15, 45:20). Various steps of fashioning are described in Isa. 44:9–20 and Jer. 10:1–14).

The idols were put to various uses in worship. Biblical passages indicate at least the following. They were given food (Isa. 65:11); incense (Isa. 65:7; Jer. 7:9; Hos. 11:2); and kisses (Hos. 13:2). They were carried in processions (Isa. 46:7), protected in shrines (Judg. 17:5), and safeguarded against toppling over (Isa. 41:7; Jer. 10:4).

The teachings of Jesus do not inveigh

against idolatry, for idols had ceased to be a problem in the Palestine of his day. As Christianity spread into the Gentile world, however, the problem reappeared. The early Christian Church decreed by its Jerusalem edict that members should abstain from food sacrificed to idols (Acts 15:29). The embarrassments which guests in pagan homes encountered and a guide for their dilemma are suggested in I Cor. 10:18–33.

Paul ran headlong into idolatrous communities in every Graeco-Roman city where he preached. Their temples were adorned with lavish idols, like that of Diana at Ephesus* (Acts 19:35), or with godlike statues of the "saviour-god" of healing, Aesculapius, whose Asklepium (hospital temple) was one of the sights of Corinth. The main square in these cities ordinarily contained the statue of an emperor god like one of Caesar Augustus. The Apostle's interpretation of an idol was not limited to a beautiful material image, but to anything which aimed to place itself between man and God (Eph. 5:5; Phil. 3:19; I John 5:20 f.). He anticipated Cowper's hymn stanza:

"The dearest idol I have known,
Whate'er that idol be,
Help me to tear it from Thy throne,
And worship only Thee."

See GOD; WORSHIP.

Idumaea (ĭd'ū-mē'*ā*) (Idumea, A.V. O.T. and Apocrypha, and R.S.V.) ("pertaining to Edom"), the name used by the Greeks and Romans for the country of Edom (Mark 3:8; A.V. Isa. 34:5–6, Ezek. 35:15, 36:5). It was also known as Seir, e.g. Gen. 32:3. See EDOMITES; HEROD.

Igal (ī'găl) (Igeal, A.V. I Chron. 3:22). (1) The representative of the tribe of Issachar sent to spy out the land of Canaan (Num. 13:7). (2) One of David's mighty men (II Sam. 23:36). (3) A descendant of David (I Chron. 3:22).

Illyricum (ĭ-lĭr'ĭ-kŭm), the official Roman name of the province also, and later officially, known as Dalmatia. It lay on the E. coast of the Adriatic Sea. Its boundaries often changed, but much of Illyricum is now in Yugoslavia. Illyricum was mentioned by Paul as a region "unto which" he had "fully preached the gospel of Christ" (Rom. 15:19). Whether or not Paul or his associates did extensive work within Illyricum is not known, but Christianity spread early and rapidly there. It is evident that in Paul's time there were already Christians on the coast W. of Macedonia and Achaia. Illyrian Salona (Spolato) was a Christian center as early as the 2d century. In such places Roman temples were adapted for Christian churches. Illyricum was the birthplace of Jerome (c. A.D. 342–420), translator of the Old Testament into Latin (Vulgate).

image. See IDOL; SYMBOL.

image of God, in connection with the creation of man (Gen. 1:26, 27, 9:6), suggests that man differs from all other creatures in possessing a self-conscious personality by which he is related to the nature of God*, who throughout Scripture is revealed as a living, feeling, acting Being. The "image" emphasizes man's responsibility under God for the entire Creation. Man is able to know, serve, and love God because he is in His image (I Cor. 11:7; Col. 3:10).

The theology of the N.T. also shows Jesus as "the image" (*eikon*) of the invisible God (Col. 1:15), the perfect revelation or incarnation* of the Father (John 1:14). When man conforms to the image of Christ he is renewed in God's image (Rom. 8:29). The N.T. word for "image" is the same that appears in "iconoclasm," or image-shattering, such as took place for example when Emperor Leo in the 8th century issued edicts against using images in Christian churches for ornament or instruction, a custom which had begun c. A.D. 300. (*Eikon* also appears in "iconography"—see SYMBOL—and in the modern iconoscope element of television.)

Immanuel ("God is with us"), the name of a child whose birth Isaiah* (7:14) predicted to Ahaz during the Syro-Ephraimitic war as a sign. It was given to confirm God's message to him that the enemy plan would not succeed—indeed, if Ahaz believed and trusted in the Lord he and his people's welfare would be firmly established. But he did not dare to believe, in the face of the advancing army of the confederates, and had already declined to ask for a confirmatory sign from the Lord. Indignant at his refusal, Isaiah gave him a sign anyway: a young woman would soon bear a boy and call his name Immanuel, "God is with us." It was to be a sign to him that God was with His people and that His message was true; at the birth of the child salvation would be near, greeted with the joyful cry, "God is with us!" which would be given the child as his name; and within a short time after, "before the child knows how to refuse what is bad and to choose what is good for him" (7:16), the land of the enemy kings would be abandoned. Ahaz would see this fulfilled and pass safely through this crisis. But since he did not believe, he and his kingdom lacked the firm foundation which is faith in God; therefore they would not be established (7:9). They would see the deliverance from Syria and Ephraim, but "when the child knows how to refuse what is bad and to choose what is good for him," not much later, their own land would be devastated as the result of the Assyrian invasion. They would then have only the food of nomads to eat (7:15, cf. 7:21–25).

In this historical situation the mother is unnamed and remains unknown. She is not called a virgin in the Hebrew but a young woman, and a miraculous conception or birth is not indicated. The boy does nothing; he is not the saviour. The boy's significance is in his name. He is mentioned once more in 8:8 in a message from the same time; here also he does nothing. Most likely "Immanuel" is not meant here as a proper name, but a word to be translated by "God is with us." For it is the beginning refrain of 8:9 f., where Isaiah in high exaltation proclaims his own indomitable faith in God. He had given the people a sign, even as he had given one to the king, the name of another boy, Maher-shalal-hashbaz (8:1–3), and had tried to rouse them to a great faith. But here also he met unbelief and fear, and so proceeded to warn the people also of the coming Assyrian danger (8:4–8).

The Immanuel prediction was not intended by Isaiah as a Messianic prophecy; but already Micah (5:3) interpreted it as referring to the Messiah, i.e., the ideal king. Matthew (1:22 f.) used it as a confirmation of the virgin birth of our Lord: Jesus the son of the virgin Mary is the predicted Immanuel; the true *God with us*, the Saviour, the Christ. And Jesus is this to the Christian Church, whether predicted by Isaiah or not. J. A. B.

Immortality, deathlessness; unending existence. As applied to man, the word implies that he will still continue to exist even though he passes through the experience of death. The ancient Greeks believed in "the immortality of the soul," that is, that there is an immortal element in man that will survive even though the body dies. Although this view has been held by Christians throughout much of the Church's history, the fact that the Greek words meaning "immortality" occur only five times in the N.T. (Rom. 2:7; I Cor. 15:53 f.; I Tim. 6:16; II Tim. 1:10) shows that the concept is not particularly congenial to Biblical thinking. Both O.T. and N.T. think of survival after death in terms of resurrection* of the *complete* man, soul and body (in some sense), rather than of the continued existence of the soul alone (Isa. 26:19; II Macc. 7:10 f.; Matt. 27:52 f.; I Cor. 15:35–44; Phil. 3:21). The doctrine of man's natural immortality appears only in the apocryphal Wisdom of Solomon (2:23–3:4).

The idea of a continuing and happy existence after death was a very late development in O.T. thought and is certainly attested only in Isa. 26:19 and Dan. 12:2 f. In the intertestamental period it was widespread and became one of the distinctive tenets of the Pharisees (Acts 23:6–8; John 11:24). But the doctrine takes on a new depth in the N.T. because the possibility of a life after death for the believer is connected with his relationship to the risen Christ. In the apocalyptic sections of the N.T., such as Matt. 24; I Thess. 4:14–18; Rev. 20, as also in other sections where the language is less picturesque, the dead are raised in order to continue their existence, but the character and conditions of the continued existence are determined by the relation to Christ (Matt. 7:22, 23, 10:32, 33, 25:31–46; John 12:48; Rom. 8:35–39). Sometimes the main emphasis is not so much on the soul surviving the experience of death as on its possessing in Christ a new life which nothing can destroy. (See especially Rom. 6:1–14, 8:6–11; cf. II Cor. 4:7–15.) What is important is "the renewal day by day of the inward man"; there naturally follows "an eternal weight of glory." The true life is "life in the Spirit," and over this even death has no power (Gal. 5:22, 6:8). To be made "alive together with Christ" is to be assured of "the heavenly places" (Eph. 2:1–10). For Paul, to live or to die was all one, because he knew himself to be "in Christ" (Phil. 1:21). His one desire was to attain unto that which had been made possible by the resurrection of Christ; to attain it was indeed a "resurrection from the dead" on his own account (Phil. 3:7–14). Dying with Christ, raised with Christ, living with Christ, is the sequence which Paul describes in Col. 2:11–13. This is described as a present experience; it is the realization of that purpose for which the soul was created in Christ "in the beginning" (Col. 1:12–23). A similar thought is expressed in I Peter 1:3–12. The true immortality is an eternal life possible here and now. It is something that death cannot destroy, because it is the life for which men were intended in God's eternal purpose and which led Him to create them "in his own image." This is the usual meaning of "eternal life" in the Gospel of John (17:3). See ETERNAL LIFE; INHERITANCE; RESURRECTION. E. L./R. C. D.

Incarnation (Lat. *carnis*, "flesh"; lit., "enfleshment"), **the,** that process whereby the Eternal Son of God appeared in history as the man Jesus Christ, to reveal God to men in the fulness of His holy love, and to become the means of their salvation. The term itself does not occur in the Scriptures, but it translates the Greek of John 1:14 by an almost exact equivalent. John there writes, "The Word became flesh." The concept "Word" (Gk. *logos*) has a long history behind it, in both Greek and Hebrew thought, and refers to a rational and dynamic element in deity which is responsible for the creating and ordering of the visible universe. It is often conceived of as personal, and is reflected in the nature of man, especially in his reason and conscience (1:4, 9). This "Word," who is later described by John as the Eternal Son of the Eternal Father (1:18), "became flesh," that is, became a man—the "incarnate" one, the "enfleshed" one. In Christ the divine participated in the human.

While it cannot be said that the doctrine of the Incarnation is literally anticipated in the O.T., it is certainly congruous with certain O.T. ideas. This is particularly true of the priestly literature, which puts so much emphasis upon the fact of Yahweh's tabernacling presence in the midst of His people (Ex. 25:8, 22; Num. 5:3). For the author of John 1:14 the incarnation of the Word was the ultimate realization of God's purpose to "dwell" among men. The idea that the Redeemer of men is God incarnate is also suggested by the attributing of divine or semidivine qualities to Israel's king in passages traditionally regarded as "Messianic" (Pss. 2:7, 45:6, A.V.; 72:5 f.; 110:1; Isa. 9:6, 11:2–8). Another part of the background lies in the fact that "Wisdom," which is both a divine (Ps. 104:24) and a human (Prov. 10:31) quality and is an important part of the O.T. background to the idea of the "Word," is pictured as personally present among men (Prov. 8:1 ff., 31).

Although the materials from which the doctrine is drawn can be found in the O.T. and elsewhere, the doctrine itself grew out of the early Church's unique experience of Jesus Christ. In the N.T., it is expressed in a variety of ways. Among the most impressive passages are these: John 1:1–18; Phil. 2:5–11; Col. 1:15

f.; Heb. 1:1–4. All agree in declaring that Jesus Christ was no mere accident of history—the root meaning of the Virgin Birth (Luke 1:26–38)—but that he was one who came out of the very being of God in order to be made "like unto his brethren" and become their Saviour (Heb. 2:14–18). There would have been no such person as Jesus of Nazareth but for the purpose of God to save men from sin, and to save them by the gift of His own Son. While he existed of native right in the form of God, he consented to lay aside his glory and be found in the style and fashion of a man. He did this "to make purification for our sins." Paul expresses this most simply when he says, "God was in Christ reconciling the world unto himself" (II Cor. 5:19; see 5:21).

The N.T. therefore makes the fact of salvation depend on the fact of the Incarnation; the human can be saved only through a sacrificial action of the divine. Later Christian thought may have indulged in overfine speculation concerning this; but the truth—"the Son of God made flesh"—with which the speculation deals is inseparable from the N.T. See JESUS CHRIST; LOGOS; REDEMPTION; SAVIOUR; SON OF GOD. E. L./R. C. D.

incense, a compound of sweet gums and spices burned in the ritual of the Tabernacle and the Temple. Its fragrant smoke, an important part of religious ceremonial, was believed to veil the presence of the Deity. Its principal ingredients are specified in Ex. 30:34–36 as equal parts of pulverized sweet spices: stacte*, onycha*, galbanum*, and frankincense*. A small amount of salt was added. The Talmud (Kerithoth 6a) and Josephus state that smaller quantities of seven other spices were included as well, plus amber of Jordan and a smoke-producing herb. About two pounds of incense per day were consumed in the Temple. Apothecaries compounded incense as well as holy anointing oils (Ex. 37:29). References to incense are characteristic of source P, not J (see SOURCES), a fact that suggests the late introduction of incense, which was condemned by certain prophets because of its association with idolatrous rites (II Chron. 34:25; Jer. 6:20, 48:35). Ezekiel wrote of its use by apostate elders of Israel (8:11). Cults celebrated on high places featured incense (I Kings 13:2; II Kings 17:11; II Chron. 28:25; Jer. 44:18; Hos. 11:2). Incense also belonged in luxurious standards of living (Rev. 18:13).

Every morning the Hebrew high priest burned incense when he dressed the lamps (Ex. 30:1–9). A special altar of incense was located in front of the Most Holy Place in the Tabernacle and the Temple (Ex. 38:1 f.). On the Day of Atonement the priest carried a censer of burning incense when he entered the Holy of Holies (Lev. 16:12 f.). In later times Sadducees held that the priest should light the incense *before* entering the Most Holy Place, lest he see the glory of God; Pharisees maintained this to be superstition, and contended that the priest might light the incense *after* he had entered. Incense was also burned with meat offerings (Lev. 2:1, 2, 15, 16)—possibly with pleasing effect when quantities of odorous animals were slain; and with shewbread (Lev. 24:7–9). Incense was thought to have purifying effect in times of plague (Num. 16:17, f.).

193. Horned limestone incense altar, attributed to Megiddo, Stratum V, c. 1050–1000 B.C. Now in Oriental Institute.

A typical Canaanite clay altar of incense from the era just prior to Solomon has been excavated at Megiddo. Another was found at nearby Taanach, where it had probably been used in domestic worship, possibly by Hebrews, in the 8th or 7th century B.C. This altar was a tapering hollow box of terra cotta 3 ft. high, with hornlike handles; the incense was burned on top, in a basinlike depression 11 in. across. Ventilation holes allowed the smoke to escape from under the incense tray. Reliefs showed crude cherubs, lions, a youth holding a snake, and hoofed animals grazing.

In N.T. times incense was still burned by the priest at the Temple, while the people prayed in a court (Luke 1:8–10). Frankincense offered the infant Jesus was an acknowledgment of his deity (Matt. 2:11).

India, a country mentioned as the eastern boundary of the empire of Ahasuerus (Esther 1:1, 8:9). "India" in O.T. times was used to designate the territory through which the river Indus flows (not Hindustan). This region had been conquered by Darius and annexed to the Persian Empire. Caravans from India brought luxury wares to Palestine in O.T. times: ivory, ebony, cassia, broidered work, and "rich apparel" (Ezek. 27:15, 19, 24). Currents of language and of ethnic strains flowed from India into Anatolia, Syria, and Palestine.

infidel, an unbeliever or disbeliever, especially in the N.T. (A.V.), one who disbelieved in Christianity (II Cor. 6:15; I Tim. 5:8, A.S.V. "unbeliever").

inheritance, the acquisition of property by one person as heir to another, played a prominent part in the family* and national life of Israel. Every Jew considered himself an heir in the land of Canaan, which had been given to the Hebrew people by God, as part of His covenant plan for using them to extend universally the Messianic blessings. Disinheritance from the Promised Land was a corollary of the Exile, occasioned by Israel's spiritual sins. Thereafter Yahweh was regarded by the pious as their greatest inheritance.

As an aid in the settling down of nomadic Hebrew tribes, each family was at least theoretically assigned by lot a parcel of ground based on the population of the group (Num. 26:52–54, 33:50–56; Josh. 13 ff.; cf. Ezek. 45:1–6, 48). (See ISRAEL.) Land, the chief form of property in early Israel, belonged to the tribe (see TRIBES) and was inherited by members of that natural group. Israel's laws of inheritance have much in common with the old Babylonian codes (see HAMMURABI, and cf. Ham. 127–161 with Deut. 21:15–17). The law of levirate marriage, whereby, in case a man left no male heir, his brother was expected to marry the widow (Deut. 25:5–10), is similar to provisions of Assyrian and Hittite codes. The story of Ruth illustrates the safeguards taken to preserve a family's ownership of valuable land (4:1–12). For an interesting account of the "redemption of land" and a detailed record of procedure in making and preserving deeds, see Jer. 32:6–17. Long genealogical lists were kept in order to establish inheritance rights, as seen especially in the later sources like P. P also enjoined approved inheritance by daughters, based on a decision attributed to Moses concerning the heirs of Zelophehad (Num. 27:1–11, P; Josh. 17:3–6). But in such cases daughters were expected to marry within the tribe.

Inheritance of a double share of property was the right of the eldest son, whether he was the child of a favorite wife or of a hated concubine (Deut. 21:15–17). Possibly the origin of the double portion goes back to the extra expense borne by the eldest son in entertaining the clan and its guests at his own tent and in offering expensive sacrificial gifts as representative of the family. This double-portion aspect of a father's heir is opposed to the more ancient institution (*peter rehem*), whereby the first-born of the mother was put to death as a "taboo sacrifice."

Instances where, for one reason or another, the eldest son did not receive the largest inheritance, or, in later times, the throne, include Ishmael and Isaac (Gen. 21:10); Esau and Jacob (27:37); Manasseh and Ephraim (Gen. 48:8–20); Reuben and Joseph (I Chron. 5:1 f.); Adonijah and Solomon (I Kings 1:11 ff.); and Eliab and David (I Sam. 16:6, 7; II Sam. 2:4). If a man had neither son nor daughter the legacy went to his brothers or his father's brothers (Num. 27:9–11). There is ground for believing that a son-in-law was logical successor to a royal throne; hence, possibly, Saul's jealousy of David, husband of his daughter Michal*.

In addition to land, inheritances included slaves, household goods, cattle (Deut. 21:16), and wells. Before the Exile a man could inherit his father's wives, with the exception of his own mother, and his concubines; but later the inheritance of a father's wives began to be considered incestuous and was forbidden (Lev. 18:8, 20:11; Deut. 27:20). To the pious of Israel, and to Christians later, God was regarded as the chief inheritance of the faithful (Gal. 3:7–4).

iniquity. See SIN.

ink, writing fluid used by scribes who prepared the parchments, papyri, and ostraca (pottery fragments) on which the Bible and other important documents of the Biblical period were written (see BOOK; CLAY). Black ink was made of soot mixed with gum arabic, and red ink was made from ochre. Egyptian ink proved exceptionally lasting; and ink found in buildings of 1st-century Herculaneum is of much finer quality than that used in the Middle East, though ostraca from Lachish show ink that has survived many centuries. Sometimes ink was shaped into small cakes tied to the writer's palette and moistened with water at the time of writing; or it was carried in an inkhorn of metal or wood (Ezek. 9:2 f.) slipped into the girdle. Miniature models of scribes' desks, excavated from Egyptian tombs, show palettes and hollow pens of reed, *juncus maritimus*, cut slanting or frayed out, brush-wise. This may have been the equipment of Jeremiah's scribe Baruch* (Jer. 36:18). The N.T. refers to the use of ink (II Cor. 3:3; II John 12; III John 13).

inn. See ARCHITECTURE; CARAVAN.

inspiration, the action of the Spirit of God, or, more exactly, of the Holy Spirit, on the minds and hearts of chosen men in such wise as to make them the instruments of divine revelation. It is customary, and proper, to distinguish inspiration in this sense, whose purpose is a more complete disclosure of the nature of God and of His ways with men, from that inspiration which results in the quickening of the natural powers of the mind. We should not confuse the inspiration of an Isaiah or a Paul, whose significance falls in the area of religious faith, with that of a Shakespeare in literature or a Mendelssohn in music.

Nor should we fail to recognize degrees of inspiration, even when what is being revealed is the truth of God. Inspiration is necessarily conditioned by two factors. One is the experience, capacities, and responsiveness of the human instrument; the other is the divine purpose itself: God will make known to the men of a given time only as much of the truth of Himself as is suitable for that time. If revelation is "progressive," moving toward a goal, then inspiration will correspond in degree. This is what is meant by the "divers portions" and "divers manners" of the divine speaking referred to in Heb. 1:1 f., and the climax of the speaking or revelation in "a Son," and it is what is meant in Gal. 4:4 by Christ having come in "the fulness of the time."

This difference in the degree of inspiration is also held to account for the differences between religions. We no longer speak of "false" religions, but of "imperfect" religions. We make the same distinction among Sacred Books. The Holy Spirit has always been seeking to teach men the truth of God, as Paul says in Acts 14:17 (cf. Rom 1:18–20), but in His own way, and according to His own purpose. The distinction holds even within the Bible itself. There is a difference between the religion of the O.T. and that of the N.T.; there are even differences within the O.T. The religion we meet in the Books of Kings is very different from that which we meet in some of the Prophets and in the greatest of the Psalms (cf. I Kings 18:16–40; Isa. 6:1–7; Jer. 31:31–34; Ps. 34, 51, 103). The difference is chiefly in what is believed about God. This difference in turn bespeaks a fuller revelation of God on the one hand, and a higher degree of inspiration on the other. These differences are reflected in the O.T., because the O.T. is a record of the dealings of God with Israel, His chosen people, and of the reactions of the people to these dealings.

The N.T. presupposes, supplements, and consummates the O.T. It came into existence for just one reason: the fact of Jesus Christ and what men came to believe about him. In him the Holy Spirit found at last a perfect instrument. But there was a reason for this, stated briefly in John 1:14: Jesus Christ was the Eternal Word come alive. This was no longer an imperfect messenger: this was the Perfect Message. In him inspiration and revelation are no longer to be distinguished; here is an inseparable partnership between the Holy Spirit and the Living Word.

But more than this was necessary. It was not enough for God to reveal Himself perfectly and finally: men must be brought to apprehend Him. It was the work of the Holy Spirit to bring about this apprehension. Indeed, Jesus himself assured his Disciples that this is what would take place; the Holy Spirit, he said, would "teach them all things," and would "guide them into all truth" (John 14:26, 16:13 f.).

The N.T. is the record of what took place in the minds and hearts of men as they came under the influence of the Holy Spirit in their consideration of Jesus Christ. They were inspired to a fuller understanding of the revelation which God had made of Himself in His Son. The N.T. gives us the result of that inspiration. This does not mean that the Holy Spirit gave the writers all the *words* they used; He gave them the *truth*, which they then expressed in their own way. Our task is through those words to apprehend that truth. See HOLY SPIRIT; REVELATION.

E. L.

instruction. See EDUCATION; FAMILY; RABBI; SCHOOL; SYNAGOGUE.

instrument, a word used in the O.T. (A.V.) for various tools*, weapons*, or implements, frequently more accurately translated in the A.S.V. by specific terms, as in Gen. 49:5, where A.V. "instrument of cruelty" is translated in the A.S.V. "weapons of violence." Threshing instruments are so translated in both the A.V. and the A.S.V. (I Chron. 21:23; Isa. 28:27, 41:15; Amos 1:3; see FARMING). The Gk. word translated "instruments" in Rom. 6:13, A.V. and A.S.V., means "weapons." (For musical instruments see MUSIC.)

intercession. See PRAYER.

interest, a sum paid by a borrower for the use of money, was not exacted of "brothers" or fellow Jews; but Deuteronomic law permitted interest to be charged to strangers or foreigners (A.S.V. Deut. 23:19 f.). The Christian Church frowned on the exacting of interest, except from non-Christians.

Babylonian clay tablets record in cuneiform sums of heavy interest. One from Nippur indicates a rate of 20% demanded by merchant priests. Bankers were usurers who loaned their wealth for the extension of canals, or for mortgages, or expansion of business, or financial emergencies. Deputies of Persian rulers were persuaded by Nehemiah to desist from burdening the Jews with high interest rates after their return from Exile, so that they might regain possession of their houses and vineyards (Neh. 5:6–12); he even asked for refunds. Mesopotamian rates were usually from 12% to 20%; at Athens in the 5th century B.C. they rose as high as 20%. At the beginning of the Christian era Rome had so much capital that her rates were low; but in her provinces interest was oppressively high.

See BUSINESS; DEBT; USURY.

Ira (possibly "the watchful," or "young ass"). (1) A Jairite, chief minister or priest to David (II Sam. 20:26). (2) A son of Ikkesh of Tekoa and a hero of David's entourage (II Sam. 23:26). (3) Another of David's heroes, known as "an Ithrite" (II Sam. 23:38).

Iran (ē-rän′), the modern name of the territory known in Biblical era as Persia* and Media, or the Persian Empire (greatest extent, 500 B.C.).

iron. (1) The first-known iron of the Middle East was meteoric, distinguishable by the presence of a small amount of nickel. As W. F. Albright pointed out, both the Egyptian name and the cuneiform ideogram for iron implied that it was a "metal of heaven." From c. 4000 B.C. copper was the basic material used for tools and weapons. The Late Bronze Age (c. 1500–1200 B.C.) was followed by the Iron Age, whose earliest phase in Bible lands is reckoned between c. 1200 and 1000 B.C. It lasted until c. 330 B.C. (including the Israelite-Edomite period).

Dr. Albright's simplified chronology of the Iron Age in Palestine (*The Archaeology of Palestine*, p. 112, Pelican Books) is:

Iron I—12th-10th centuries B.C., inclusive, era of the Judges and the united Monarchy.

Iron II—9th century to the opening of the 6th, the divided Monarchy.

IRON

Iron III—c. 550–330 B.C., the Exile and the Return.

Within the Iron Age came the reigns of all the kings of Israel and Judah. Iron Age industrial developments contributed largely to the material prosperity of the reigns of David and Solomon.

Before 1200 B.C. iron had been almost as valuable in western Asia as the silver and gold jewelry of that era; the anklet found by Elihu Grant at Beth-shemesh (from about the time of David) was made of iron. The Hittite monopoly of this metal was not broken until c. 1200 B.C. David's conquest of the Philistines marked the beginning of the general use of iron by the common man of Israel; theretofore iron manufacture had been a monopoly of the Philistines—the Israelites had been unable to secure iron weapons, and even had to journey to the Philistine city of Gerar* to have their iron plowshares sharpened. Sir Flinders and Lady Hilda Petrie found at Gerar four iron furnaces and a sword factory, and near this city spearheads, daggers, chisels, and other iron implements—excellent confirmation of I Sam. 13:19–22. The Philistines probably learned iron smelting from the Hittites*, who secured ore from the Taurus Mountains. David's victory over the Philistines, coupled with triumphs in Edom (see below), at last enabled his people to have plenty of iron for everyday use. No longer did they need to dread their enemy's iron-tired chariots as in the days of the Judges (Josh. 17:16; Judg. 1:19, 4:2, 3).

After David conquered the Edomites (II Sam. 8:14) he exploited the mines of the Arabah*. He "prepared iron in abundance" (I Chron. 22:3) for the Temple his son built, and inspired Israel's leaders to bring 100,000 "talents of iron" (29:7) for coupling and nails. He made available from his day forward raw materials for weapons and implements used in everyday life. Iron Age industry helps explain why he and Solomon were able to finance the building of 10th-century Jerusalem as recorded in the Books of Kings and Chronicles, a royal city whose "wisdom and prosperity exceedeth the fame" (I Kings 10:7; cf. II Chron. 9:6).

Thanks to the brilliant explorations of Nelson Glueck and the joint expeditions of the American Schools of Oriental Research and of the Smithsonian Institution, more is now known of what was going on in Iron Age Palestine, the Jordan Valley, and the Arabah than ever before (*The Other Side of the Jordan*, and *Explorations in Eastern Palestine*, 4 vols., Nelson Glueck, ASOR). The archaeologist-ceramists cleared up the long-baffling problem of the source of Israel's iron. This people did not need to rely on distant Spain (via Tyre), Crete, the Black Sea, the highlands of Assyria, the Taurus Mountains, or even the Lebanons, for ore, as had been believed. The Wâdī Arabah all the way S. to the Red Sea was a drafty corridor teeming with industrial communities which were mining and smelting iron and copper during the Iron Age. Glueck found many tangible evidences of these elaborate yet primitive towns and their powerfully fortified hilltop citadels and blockhouses. From the wealth of Edomite and Hebrew pottery strewn over their sites their occupation dates have been reckoned. Seen from the air, these fortified production centers are tremendously impressive. They shed gratifying light on Deut. 8:9. It is possible today to look into slag heaps still rich in ores; small furnaces, abandoned labor villages, and quarters occupied by *corvée;* and to verify the fact that the fuel of the smelteries was charcoal, brought by donkey caravans from the wooded slopes of Edom. At the tremendous plant in Feinan, Glueck identified levels of continuous occupation from the 13th to the 6th century B.C. He found that copper* continued to be mined at extensive centers like Khirbet Nahas on into the reign of Solomon. He discovered an important Iron Age site near Petra-Tawilan (the Biblical Teman, Amos 1:12) at the intersection of trade routes near abundant water. The area was strewn with thousands of potsherds from shortly before Solomon's day to seven centuries later. Quantities of the Trans-Jordan Iron Age pottery he found are in the Smithsonian Institution, Washington.

The same sort of frenzied industrial activity was going on in the Jordan Valley in Solomon's time—in Biblical Succoth*, for example.

The Hebrews, as well as their predecessors at the Jordan-Arabah mines, partly smelted iron near the veins and then further refined it in the centers where ingots and commodities were fashioned, as at Ezion-geber*—an industrial site unsurpassed anywhere in the ancient world.

The uses of iron in Scripture include: the bed of the giant Og (Deut. 3:11); axheads and hatchets (Deut. 19:5); instruments of violence (Num. 35:16); vessels for the tabernacle (Josh. 6:19, 24); chariots and chariot rims (Josh. 17:16); weapons (I Sam. 17:7); chains and fetters (Ps. 105:18, 107:10, 149:8); graving tools ("pens") (Job 19:24; Jer. 17:1); barbs on hunting weapons (Job 41:7); idols (Dan. 5:4); bars of prison gates (Acts 12:10).

What Glueck discovered about life in Trans-Jordan during the Iron Age confirms Scripture at several points, notably Deut. 8:7–9 and Gen. 4:22. The tremendous strength of the fortified sites on lonely hilltops, as at Qasr el-Al, explains why the wandering tribes of Israel dreaded approaching the territory of Sihon, King of the Amorites, who controlled the whole eastern corridor of the Jordan Valley (Num. 21:21–31; Josh. 12:2), and compelled the immigrants to avoid his land and enter Palestine farther N. above the River Arnon. The Iron Age forts all along the boundaries, at such places as Rabbath-ammon (the present Amman) were too much for them. Had they come before the 13th century B.C. these strongholds would not have been there to block their progress. Therefore Glueck argues for a date not earlier than the 13th century B.C. for the Exodus through eastern Palestine (Trans-Jordan).

Pottery of the Iron Age Trans-Jordan tells

of highly developed civilization in all its Iron Age kingdoms—like that of Mesha*, King of Moab. The chronicle of the regaining of his land from Ahab, King of Israel, is told on the Moabite Stone, whose Iron Age inscription is the longest, outside the O.T., dealing with the early history of Palestine and Trans-Jordan in the Iron Age.

(2) Iron, a town in Naphtali (Josh. 19:38), called Yiron in the R.S.V.

irrigation. See FARMING; WATER.

Isaac ("one laughs"), the 2d of the Patriarchs, the 2d son of Abraham*, and the only son of Sarah* (Gen. 21:1–7). Genesis provides the following data about Isaac.

Abraham was 100 years old and Sarah 91 when Isaac was born, a situation which occasioned smiles and laughter (Gen. 17:17, 18:12, 21:6). Isaac's earliest days were spent in or near Beer-sheba (Gen. 22:19). His weaning feast was the occasion of the expulsion of Hagar and Ishmael* (Gen. 21:8–21). In the "land of Moriah" (traditionally located at the site of the Temple in Jerusalem) Abraham, at a command from God designed to test Abraham's faith, was about to kill Isaac as a human sacrifice (Gen. 22:1–19) when Providence intervened and provided a ram in the thicket. This intervention registered deeply in the Hebrew conscience, later to issue as a protest against human sacrifices (cf. Mic. 6:7–8). (The command to blow a ram's horn, a shophar, in synagogue worship at the New Year is a memorial of this incident.) The submission and obedience of Isaac to paternal authority are emphasized in the narrative as well as the faith of Abraham.

As a result of Abraham's matchmaking Isaac at the age of 40 married Rebekah, of the N. Mesopotamian country and kindred of his father (Gen. 24, 25:10). They were childless for 20 years and then had sons, Esau and Jacob (Gen. 25:19–26). Because of famine in the Negeb, Isaac moved to Gerar (Gen. 24:62, 26:1 f.). Here he was persecuted by the Philistines, but blessed by God with abundant grain, flocks, and herds (26:12–14, 20–22). The peace covenant between Isaac and Abimelech the Philistine was marked by the digging of a new well at Beer-sheba, where Isaac had built an altar (Gen. 26:23–33).

When Isaac became blind and feeble from old age he desired to give his blessing and chief inheritance* to his oldest and favorite son, Esau, but the cunning of Rebekah caused Jacob to receive it (Gen. 27:1–40). This resulted in long and bitter family enmity. Isaac survived Jacob's long sojourn into N. Mesopotamia and his return to Trans-Jordan; he died at the age of 180; and was buried by his two sons, reconciled for the occasion, in the Cave of Machpelah* at Hebron (Gen. 35:28–29, 49:31 f.).

Contradictions in the Genesis narrative are due to the blending of the J, E, and P sources*, without any editorial effort to harmonize them. Among the duplicate entries are: Gen. 17:15–22, 18:9–15; 20 and 26:7–11; and 21:22–24 and 26:26–31. Very little of the material is assigned by critics to the P source. It is possible that the Isaac story was stripped in favor of the Abraham saga as early as the E document. Isaac seems to have had a greater importance in Patriarchal history than the present Bible narrative indicates. The name "Isaac" appears in the oft-recurring Patriarchal formula throughout Hebrew history, as in I Kings 18:36; Jer. 33:26; Matt. 22:32; Acts 3:13. The oldest prophetic references to Isaac (R.S.V. Amos 7:9, 16) make "Isaac" the poetic equivalent of "Israel."

Isaiah ("Jehovah is salvation"), the 8th-century B.C. Hebrew prophet, whose name is given to the longest O.T. prophetic book. The book of Isaiah, covering three different historical periods, originated with the man who so strongly influenced subsequent prophecy that the anonymous work of others was added to his book. The Book of Isaiah can therefore be divided into three main sections: (1) chaps. 1–39, First Isaiah, in the 8th century B.C.; (2) chaps. 40–55, the Second or Deutero-Isaiah—after 580 B.C., during the Exile; and (3) chaps. 56–66, the Third or Trito-Isaiah, prior to the arrival of Nehemiah in Jerusalem in 444 B.C. The oracles in Third Isaiah may come from more than one prophet.

A brief outline of the subject matter:

First Isaiah

(1) Messages of Isaiah (chaps. 1–11); a psalm of thanksgiving (chap. 12).

(2) Prophecies concerning the nations (chaps. 13–23).

(3) Later apocalyptic oracles (chaps. 24–27).

(4) Oracles on Judah and Assyria (chaps. 28–31); the Messianic age (chap. 32); a psalm of triumph (chap. 33).

(5) Judgments on the nations and promises for Zion (chaps. 34, 35).

(6) Historical account (chaps. 36–39) of Sennacherib's siege of Jerusalem (from II Kings 18:13–20:19).

Second Isaiah

(1) Israel's salvation and her Saviour God (chaps. 40, 41).

(2) "The Servant of the Lord" (chaps. 42–44).

(3) God manifests His power through Cyrus and in the fall of Babylon (chaps. 45–48).

(4) The new Israel in its mission as servant (49:1–13); as comforter and the one comforted (49:14–50:11).

(5) Warnings and encouraging words to Zion (51–52:12).

(6) The suffering, death, and exaltation of the Servant (52:13–53:12).

(7) The new Zion (chap. 54).

(8) Exhortations and promises (chap. 55).

Third Isaiah

(1) Problems of the restored community:
  (a) foreigners and eunuchs (56:1–8).
  (b) worthless leaders (56:9–57:2).
  (c) idolatry (57:3–21).

(d) hypocritical fastings (58:1–12).
(e) sabbath observance (58:13 f.).
(f) sin (chap. 59).

(2) Praises for the New Jerusalem and its mission (60:1–64:12).

(3) Blessings for the faithful and punishment for the faithless (chaps. 65, 66).

The Life of Isaiah.—Our information concerning Isaiah is derived from the book that bears his name and from II Kings 19, 20. The facts of his life and labors are not recorded in chronological sequence. His father's name was Amoz—not to be confused with Amos. Isaiah was born c. 770–760 B.C.; lived in Jerusalem, with whose Temple (6:1–7), ritual (1:11–15), and environs (7:3, 8:6) he was intimately familiar. He married a woman whom he called "the prophetess" (8:3), and their two sons were given names associated with prophetic pronouncements (7:3, 8:3). His call to a prophetic career was a definite and vividly recorded experience (6), and his known activities for about 40 years (742–700 B.C.) were during the reigns of 3 Judaean kings:

Jotham	c. 742–735 B.C.
Ahaz (Jehoahaz I)	c. 735–715 B.C.
Hezekiah	c. 715–687 B.C.

Jerusalem was his watchtower, and an effective listening post for news concerning neighboring nations. He was an outstanding figure of his day—a friend and counselor of kings (37:1 ff.) and a prophetic critic of national policies (7:3–9, 18:1–6); a teacher with disciples; but preeminently a prophet, embodying high ethical, social, and spiritual qualities which made his utterances the voice of God to the people. Amos and Hosea were prophesying in Israel (the Northern Kingdom), and Isaiah as a young man may have been influenced by their reactions to social conditions common to both kingdoms. Nothing certain is known of his death, some time after c. 700 B.C.

The Times of Isaiah.—When Isaiah began to prophesy Judah was of much less account than the Northern Kingdom, Israel, but was more secure than her neighbor because of her geographical position. Both kingdoms were of small importance compared with Assyria to the NE. and Egypt to the S. About the middle of the 8th century Assyria under Tiglath-pileser* III began to threaten the security of her small western neighbors, her ultimate objective being her rival Egypt. Both Judah and Israel lay across the trade routes and age-old war paths of these two mighty rival powers. Judah, high up on her plateau, was less exposed than Israel, which sprawled over the plains; this fact accounts in part for Judah's survival for about 135 years after the fall of Samaria. This Assyrian threat to the security of the Palestine states could be met in one of three ways: (1) submission to Assyria and purchase of exemption from molestation, by homage and tribute; (2) help from Egypt, which was eager to secure the allegiance of these buffer states; (3) a confederation of the small Palestinian and other Middle Eastern states, with or without the aid of Egypt, to oppose Assyria.

The Northern Kingdom at first paid tribute to Assyria. But c. 736 B.C. the kings of Israel and Damascus attempted to form a confederacy. Ahaz, King of Judah, refused to join this alliance, and therefore was threatened by attack from Israel and Syria. The appeal of Ahaz to Assyria for intervention led to the subjection of Damascus and Samaria by Assyria in 732 B.C. Ten years later the kingdom of Israel came to an end; and Tiglath-pileser III was determined to bring all the smaller neighboring states into subjection to Assyria. During the career of Isaiah there was constant peril from the Mesopotamian aggressor. The peace policy toward Assyria advocated by Isaiah was followed by King Ahaz, but with less earnestness by King Hezekiah*. In 711 B.C. Ashdod on the Philistine coast was destroyed by the Assyrian Sargon II as a result of a revolt of Palestine states fomented by Egypt. Isaiah was anxious lest Hezekiah be drawn into alliance with the kingdom of the Nile, and he dramatized his warnings by walking through Jerusalem without garments and shoes, like a captive (Isa. 20). Merodach-baladan, driven by Sargon from his Babylonian throne, made an effort when Sargon died to regain his crown, and sought to induce Hezekiah to join a rebellion against Assyria. Isa. 39, the events of which preceded those narrated in chaps. 36 and 37, tells of an embassy sent to Hezekiah c. 705–704 B.C. At the same time Egypt renewed her efforts to stir up revolt against Assyria among the Palestine states, and Hezekiah was persuaded to join. Isaiah opposed this reliance on Egypt (30:1–5, chap. 31). But the towns of Philistia and the Palestine states, including Judah, were determined to oppose Sennacherib, Sargon's successor, in spite of Isaiah's protests (14:29–32). Sennacherib reduced a large number of cities, advanced to Lachish (36:2), and besieged Jerusalem. Hezekiah was in a panic (Isa. 37:1–4). The prophet offered the king strong counsel (37:5–7, 21–35; cf. 10:24–27, 14:24–27, 31:8 f.). Jerusalem did not fall. Sennacherib, after extracting tribute from Hezekiah, was compelled to withdraw to Mesopotamia because of disturbances at home and (presumably) the outbreak of plague among his soldiers (37:36–38).

The Message of Isaiah.—The message of First Isaiah is characterized by three outstanding features: (1) God is in universal history. Isaiah goes further than any previous teacher in stating that God's power extends beyond Israel to all other nations. Israel is His people and He is their God; but the other nations are also instruments of His purpose. Assyria is a tool in God's hands and her conquests are part of His purpose (10:5–12). To rely upon Egypt is political folly and disloyalty to God (19:11–15, 30:2 f., 31:1–3). Judah must trust in her God and not in material defenses (22:9–11). (2) The holiness* of God. As Amos had insisted upon the righteousness of God, and Hosea upon His loving kindness, Isaiah emphasized that "the Holy God shows himself holy in righteousness" (R.S.V., 5:16). In the Southern Kingdom during the time of Isaiah the same evils existed as were denounced by Amos and Hosea in the Northern Kingdom: the amassing of real estate by the rich at the expense of the poor (5:8 f.); the corruption of legal process (10:1–4); luxury, complacency, and pride (3:16, 32:9–12); heathen worship (2:6–9, 31:6 f.). (3) The remnant and the Messiah. Isaiah saw, in spite of Judah's persistent wickedness and imminent punishment, the ultimate preservation of a righteous remnant (10:20–22). In connection with this hope, Isaiah gave Ahaz a sign of faith in the form of the birth of a child called Immanuel* ("God is with us") (Isa. 7:14).

The Second (Deutero) Isaiah

No specific biographical material concerning the identity of the author or authors of the Second or Third Isaiah is apparent in chaps. 40–66. The literary style, historical background, and theology of these chapters differ so greatly from chaps. 1–39 as to compel belief in different authorship. There is no interpretation of Isaiah's oracles nor allusion to his times after chap. 39. Some passages in chaps. 40–55 rise to heights not surpassed anywhere in the O.T. Jeremiah and Ezekiel, in their historic settings, should be studied before these chapters of Second Isaiah are read. The fall of Jerusalem in 587 and the deportation of the best part of its population to Babylon made some Jews question the strength of their own national God and increased the appeal of the Babylonian religion. Second Isaiah, who wrote his spiritual epic after Ezekiel and Jeremiah, during the Exile*, faced this danger. Yahweh was proclaimed to be the only god (43:10, 44:6, 24), and was omnipotent (40:12–18, 43:15–17). He could—and would—deliver His people (41:11–13). Cyrus, King of Persia, would be Yahweh's instrument to bring this to pass (45:1–7). The chief note of Second Isaiah is joy amid sorrow, defeat, and disaster. God's care of His people is tender (40:11). Their sins hurt His love (43:22–24).

Four great passages, the "Servant songs" (42:1–4, 49:1–6, 50:4–9, 52:13–53:12), highlight this second section of the book. The "Servant" in the Jewish interpretation is Israel (41:8), the purified remnant whose sufferings will have a vicarious efficacy for the sins of others and will be finally vindicated by God (53:4–6, 10–12). Jesus Christ, according to Christians, realized in his own life and death this ideal of the Servant of God suffering and dying for the sins of mankind. A harmony of these two views has been expressed in the figure of a pyramid: the base of the pyramid is the people, Israel; the middle areas, the Israel of the spirit; and the apex, Christ the Redeemer.

This Second Isaiah through his monotheism furnished the basis for the theology of Judaism, Christianity, and Islam. His interpretation of suffering, its purifying and redeeming effects on Israel, and through them on the world, made the atoning suffering and death of Christ on the cross an acceptable truth. Christianity cannot be fully understood without Second Isaiah. He is the most evangelical of the prophets. He also passed on to all humanity the element of hope, the outlook on a coming Golden Age, and the doctrine of the Kingdom of God on earth, to which all men without distinction of race are called.

The Third (Trito) Isaiah

Chaps. 56–66 reflect the period just before or during Nehemiah's return to Jerusalem. This 3d section of Isaiah is a composite of many moods and teachings. Inconsistencies and irreconcilable positions are frequently found in these pages. Hope at times possesses the people. The Exile had broken their isolationism. Instead of living in dread of surrounding peoples, they now included them in their missionary zeal (56:6–8). Ritual requirements are stressed (56:2, 7). The sins renounced are partly religious apostasy (57:3–13, 65:1–7), partly moral and social (56:9–12, 57:1, 59:1–8). Chap. 61 reaches the same lofty pitch as the Servant poems of Second Isaiah, but here the prophet speaks of himself. Christ quotes from this passage (Luke 4:18–21). The hereditary enmity of Edom (63:1–6) crops out. The Third Isaiah is less spiritual, cosmopolitan, and idealistic than the Second; there is more concern with the externals of religion, more nationalism, more legalistic zeal.

However purely coincidental some of the events of Christ's life seem to be with passages in the Book of Isaiah, such parallels were hailed by N.T. writers as the fulfillment of the prophetic pattern. An outline of the life of Christ may be charted from the references to Isaiah in the N.T. Following are a few:

Christ's birth	Matt. 1:23—Isa. 7:14.
His Nazareth citizenship	Matt. 2:23—Isa. 11:1.
His Nazareth labors	Matt. 4:12–16—Isa. 9:1 f.
John, his forerunner	Matt. 3:3; Luke 3:3–6—Isa. 40:3 ff.
His program	Luke 4:17-21—Isa. 61:1 f.
His entry into Jerusalem	Matt. 21:4 f.—Isa. 62:11.
His death	Acts 8:32–35—Isa. 53:7 f.

Two almost complete, oldest known manuscripts of the Book of Isaiah were found in the spring of 1947 by Bedouins of the Ta'amira tribe, in a cache of documents and fragments which had been secreted in a remote cave above the W. shore of the Dead Sea. These priceless MSS., dated by eminent scholars as having been written in the 2d or 1st centuries B.C., were acquired (four of them plus fragments) by Mar Athanasius Yeshue Samuel, Syrian Orthodox Metropolitan of St. Mark's Monastery in Jerusalem, and (six of them plus fragments) by Prof. E. L. Sukenik of the Hebrew University. The

St. Mark's Isaiah scroll (now designated "DSIa") has 54 columns of well-written and beautifully preserved Hebrew on neatly ruled skins refined into coarse parchment. The skins show many evidences of long, active use. Yet, in spite of tears and stains, and various corrections and interlineations made by successive scribes, there are only a few small portions missing. These scrolls* form part of what W. F. Albright called "one of the greatest manuscript finds of modern times." Since then many more O.T. fragments have been found.

The St. Mark's Isaiah scroll is 7.34 meters long, and is made up of 17 sheets of parchment sewed together. The portion exposed in the photograph accompanying this article measures 15⅝" x 10⅜"; the left-hand column contains Isa. 40:2b–28a, with Isa. 40 beginning at the bottom of the right-hand column. The only indication of the division between chapters 39 and 40 is a small symbol (covered by the right-hand roll) in the margin just above the line of writing, beginning at the end of chapter 40. The original scribe mistakenly omitted vv. 7b–8a, which were later inserted, by another hand, between the 7th and 8th lines of the left-hand column and extending into the left margin. Another insertion, by a third scribe, can be seen between the columns. The darkened portions show that many hands have held the scrolls. (See SCROLLS, illus. 365.)

For complete plates and Hebrew transcription of the St. Mark's Isaiah Scroll and data relating to it, see *The Dead Sea Scrolls of St. Mark's Monastery*, Vol. I, edited by Millar Burrows, assisted by John C. Trever and William H. Brownlee (ASOR, New Haven, Conn., 1950).

194. Isaiah Dead Sea Scroll, opened to Isa. 40.

Iscariot. See JUDAS.

Ish-bosheth (ĭsh'bō'shĕth) ("man of shame," II Sam. 3:14 f.), the fourth son of Saul*; in public reading of Samuel, name used for Esh-baal ("man of Baal"; I Chron. 8:33, 9:39), to avoid use of "Baal" (Hos. 2:16 f.). On Saul's death Ish-bosheth attempted to rule all the tribes. Judah refused allegiance. With Abner* as general Ish-bosheth set up his capital E. of Jordan at Mahanaim (II Sam. 2:8 ff.). After a stormy career, during which Abner deserted him, Ish-bosheth was murdered by two of his own henchmen, Rechab and Baanah, who took his head to David at Hebron, expecting a reward. But David's sense of justice led to the execution of the criminals and the burial of the head of Ish-bosheth at Hebron (II Sam. 4). This marked the end of Saul's brief dynasty.

Ishi (ĭsh'ī) ("my husband"), a name used by the Israelites for God, in place of the synonymous Baali, which had pagan connotations (Hos. 2:16 f.).

Ishmael (ĭsh'mā-ĕl) ("may God hear"). (1) The son of Abraham and his Egyptian concubine Hagar*, who was the slave of his wife Sarah* (Gen. 16:3, 16). Such a birth was legitimate according to prevalent Babylonian law when the head of a family* had no male heir and the perpetuity of the line was at stake. Ishmael was circumcised (Gen. 17:25 f.) at 13, the age at which many ancient Arab tribes performed the rite. Jealousy between Abraham's wives, Hagar and Sarah, led to the departure of Hagar (Gen. 21:9–14), with her son Ishmael, into the deserts near the

Egyptian border, where the timely discovery of a miraculous well saved their lives (Gen. 21:15–19). In Gal. 4:21–5:1 the narratives of Ishmael and Isaac are expounded allegorically.

The story of Ishmael is considered not only as a personal narrative, but as a tribal story. His character is that of the tribe whose eponymous ancestor he is (Gen. 16:12, 21:20). Ishmael was the eponymous progenitor of 12 princes (Gen. 25:12–16), many of whom gave their names to tribes or localities mentioned elsewhere in the Bible, like Nebaioth (Isa. 60:7); Kedar, a wealthy pastoral and trading tribe (Ezek. 27:21), famous for its archers (Isa. 21:17, 60:7; Jer. 49:28–32); Tema (Isa. 21:14; Jer. 25:23; Job 6:19); Jetur and Nephish (I Chron. 5:19). The region held by Ishmael and his sons "in the presence of all his brethren" (Gen. 16:12) includes E. Palestine (kingdom of Jordan) and territory around the Gulf of Aqabah. The Assyrians called the land "Arabia." Throughout the Bible the descendants of Ishmael, because of their origin, are considered of lower rank than the sons of Isaac. But by the Moslems Ishmael is hailed as an ancestor of Mohammed, buried with his mother in the Kaaba at Mecca.

(2) A son of Azel, descendant of Jonathan (I Chron. 8:38, 9:44). (3) A father of the Zebadiah who was an official of Jehoshaphat (II Chron. 19:11). (4) A military officer in the time of Joash (II Chron. 23:1). (5) A member of the Judaean royal family, and chief participant in the murder of Gedaliah (Jer. 41:1 f.). (6) A priest persuaded by Ezra to put away his foreign wives (Ezra 10:22).

Ishmaelites, mentioned by source J (Gen. 37:25–28, 39:1) as caravan traders carrying gums from Gilead to Egypt, are called by E in a parallel narrative "Midianites" (Gen. 37:28, 36). The term "Ishmaelite" was applied, irrespective of geography, to a desert mode of life followed by itinerant caravan traders, tent-dwellers and cameleers (I Chron. 27:30; Ps. 83:6). The Hebrews classified all their neighbors genealogically, according to their relationship to themselves. Though the Twelve Tribes of Ishmael were traced to Abraham, yet, because they were descendants of the Egyptian-born handmaid Hagar, Ishmaelites were inferior to Hebrews, from the standpoint of racial purity, as well as in standards of living. Ishmaelites were a numerous and a great people (Gen. 17:20), yet Hebrew historians considered them beneath them. This is one of the racial attitudes that has persisted in the Middle East.

Ishtar, the chief female deity of the Assyrian and Babylonian pantheons, with more power in her own right than the usual co-ruler of male gods in the Middle East. In her role of the goddess who goes to the underworld to restore her youthful consort, Tammuz, god of vegetation, she plays a role parallel to that of the Greek Aphrodite seeking Adonis. There is evidence that Ishtar was an ancient Semitic mother goddess, who became associated with Sumerian deities known as "Ishtars" of various communities. Zarpanit was Babylon's Ishtar; Nin-Lil, that of Nippur; Nana, that of Erech. Down the centuries the characteristics of Ishtar became so fluid and complex that she was regarded in such contradictory roles as goddess of sexual love, giver of crops, and patron of waterways, war, and storms. Arab peoples called Ishtar "Attar," "Ashtar," "Athtar"; Abyssinians knew her as Ashtar; Egypt, as Hathor; Greeks, as Aphrodite; Romans, as Venus; Greeks, as Astarte; Canaanites and apostate Hebrews, as Asherah* (later Ashtoreth), goddess of fertility, companion of the Baalim (see BAAL).

195. Ishtar Gate, Babylon.

Assyrians regarded Ishtar next in importance to their national god Asshur, and honored the Ishtar of Nineveh, the Ishtar of Arbela, etc. Ashurnasirpal and Esar-haddon ascribed tremendous powers to Ishtar, "lady of heaven and earth," "lady of battle and of justice." The "queen of heaven" mentioned in such O.T. passages as Jer. 44:17–19 is Ishtar. "Esther" has the same root as "Ishtar." The famous Ishtar Gate of Babylon led to Festival Avenue or Procession Street, the temple quarter, the palace area, and the Tower of Babel. The "Hanging Gardens" were on a royal roof at the right of the Ishtar Gate. (See BABYLON, illus. 44.)

island (isle), mentioned several times in Scripture in spite of the Hebrews' lack of wide first-hand acquaintance with the Mediterranean islands—because of their disinterest and inexperience in maritime affairs.

Though most O.T. allusions are to islands in general, represented as being in the remote west, two exerted a long and profound cultural, religious, and commercial influence on Palestine and its neighbors—Cyprus* nearer, and Crete* more powerful. Some twelve islands figure in N.T. narratives, identified either by their own name or by those of towns situated on them—Cauda, Chios, Cos, Crete, Cyprus, Lesbos, Malta, Patmos, Rhodes, Samos, Samothrace, and Sicily. (See also PAUL; and Section 12, "Islands," *An Encyclopedia of Bible Life*, Madeleine S. and J. Lane Miller, Harper.)

Many O.T. allusions are to islands in general, introduced to bring impressiveness into Messianic and apocalyptic passages by referring to what was unknown territory at "the ends of the earth" (Isa. 41:5, 49:1, 66:19; Jer. 31:10). Remote islands were represented as being the dwelling-places of beasts (Isa. 13:22, 34:14; Jer. 50:39); as sources of luxury commodities sent as gifts to such rulers as Solomon (Ps. 72:10) and the kings of the merchant city Tyre (Ezek. 27:15); as the residence of "heathen" who will some day worship God (Zeph. 2:11) but were temporarily living in the careless confidence characteristic of insular peoples (Ezek. 39:6). When an O.T. writer wished to ascribe impressive power to God, he declared that even the multitude of the isles shall rejoice in the reign of the Lord (Ps. 97:1) and shall wait upon Him (Isa. 51:5), Who will send them a sign (66:19). God bids the islands keep silence before Him (Isa. 41:1); and picks them up as if they were small things (40:15). The island has again a prophetic function in the vision of Daniel (11:18). The climax of apocalyptic use of islands for divine revelation comes in connection with Patmos, scene of the Apocalypse of John (Rev. 1:9, 6:14).

Ezekiel shows a direct knowledge of the island character of the famed merchant city of Tyre, which he declares dwells "at the entry of the sea" and is a "merchant of the people for many isles."

In a few passages of the A.V. "island" should read "coastland," as in A.S.V. Isa. 20:6. But in A.V. Isa. 23:2, 6 "isle" is literally correct, for both Tyre* and Sidon* were island cities connected by causeways with the main coast of Phoenicia.

Israel (ĭz′rā̆-ēl) (probably from the imperfect or jussive of an old Amorite verbal root of c. 2000 B.C. or earlier—"s-r-y" or possibly "s-r-w," to which *el*, for God, has been added). The meaning of the word in Jacob's time, to which it goes back, is not definitely known, and will not be, until the verb is found in some early inscription. The best guess thus far is: "May God strive, contend, or rule," not "he strives or contends with God," as suggested by Gen. 32:28 and Hos. 12:4.

(1) *The name given Jacob* by an angel at the Jabbok ford (Wâdī Zerka in Trans-Jordan) on the eve of his reunion with his brother (Gen. 32:28, J); and also by Yahweh at Bethel (Gen. 35:10, P). The Genesis accounts of the activities of Jacob and his sons make the Patriarch the direct ancestor of the Hebrew nation; and his 12 sons the progenitors and heads of the Twelve Tribes* of Israel. The vicissitudes of the Twelve Tribes are described in the poem contained in Gen. 49:2–27. See JABBOK.

The Twelve Sons of Israel (Jacob) Who Became Heads of Tribes

Son	*Mother*	*Scripture*
Reuben	Leah	Gen. 29:32
Simeon	Leah	29:33
Levi	Leah	29:34
Judah	Leah	29:35
Dan	Bilhah (Rachel's maid, "foreign blood")	30:5, 6
Naphtali	Bilhah	30:8
Gad	Zilpah (Leah's maid, "foreign blood")	30:11
Asher	Zilpah	30:13
Issachar	Leah	30:18
Zebulun	Leah	30:20
Joseph (father of Ephraim and Manasseh)	Rachel	30:24
Benjamin	Rachel	35:18

The Leah Tribes are considered by some to have been established in Palestine before the Rachel Tribes entered Canaan. Deborah mentions only 10 tribes (Judg. 5); elsewhere as many as 13 are listed.

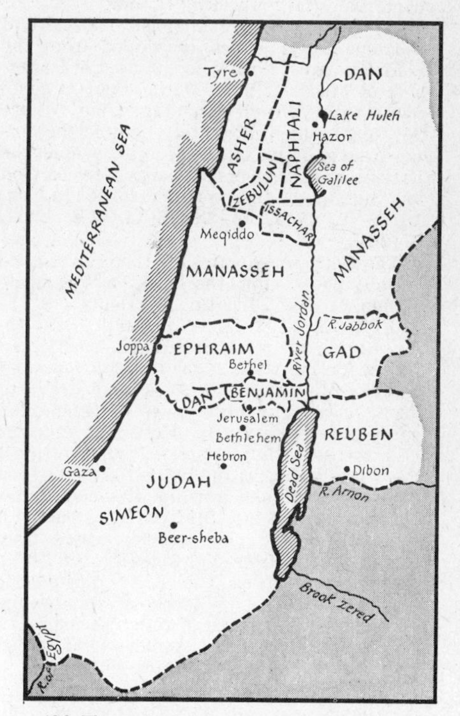

196. The territories of the twelve tribes of Israel as listed in the Book of Judges. Incomplete boundary lines indicate undetermined boundaries.

Each of the Twelve Tribes of Israel, with the exception of Levi, received inheritances in "the Promised Land" during and following the Conquest*. Reuben and Gad, together with the half Tribe of Manasseh, received from Moses territory E. of the Jordan (Josh. 12:6, 17:5). The other 9½ tribes received their shares when lots were drawn by Eleazar the priest and Joshua at Shiloh (Josh. 1–2). The influential Joseph Tribe was represented in the "allotment" by the two half Tribes of his sons, Ephraim and Manasseh, both of whom probably had Egyptian blood. The priestly house of Levi acquired cities and land in the territories of the other Tribes (Josh. 21). The boundaries of the "assignments" were fluid (Josh. 13–19). Dan, possibly pushed out by the Philistines, moved from his original territory on poor land in the N. Shephelah to fertile acreage near the headwaters of the Jordan. The Joseph Tribes and Benjamin held the region of the central highlands, which became the nucleus of the Kingdom of Israel established when the Hebrew Monarchy was divided (c. 922 B.C.). For the 10 Tribes included in this state. see below, *The Kingdom of Israel* (4).

"The Children of Israel" was used from the era recorded in Genesis until the death of Solomon to mean the whole company of Hebrews, regardless of Tribes. Sometimes the term is shortened to "Israel," connoting the total body of those who stemmed from Israel (Jacob).

"The land of Israel" designates what became Palestine, "the Holy Land."

(2) *The People of Israel*, the political and religious entity which developed from the confederated Tribes who, under the leadership of Moses at Sinai-Horeb, made a covenant* with Yahweh (Ex. 19 ff.; Deut. 5:2 ff., 26:16 ff.) which ultimately became the cornerstone of Judaism, the Hebrew people, the nation Israel. Earlier covenants between God and individual Hebrews are recorded in Gen. 15:18 ff., 17:1, 14, 28:13–15. (Cf. Ezek. 37:26 f.)

The Sinai confederates felt themselves to be "a holy people unto the Lord," a "peculiar" people "above all nations" (Deut. 4:37 f., 7:6, 10:15, 14:2, 26:17–19, 28:1–6, 9, 13; Ex. 6:4–8; cf. Ezek. 34:11–16, 25–31). In return for Yahweh's favor Israel covenanted to obey His commandments, and strove to keep "clean" by observance of ceremonial rites and chastity. By sacrificial offerings (Ex. 24:3–8) they expressed their pledged loyalty to Yahweh; and by shared meals they demonstrated their kinship with each other before God (Ex. 18:12). They constructed a tent of meeting (Tabernacle) where they sought oracles from Yahweh (Ex. 33:7–11), where they stored the Ark* during the long years of their Wilderness* wanderings, and where they offered, through their priests, prayers for forgiveness. Israel's goal was to establish not only a pure race, but a body of true believers.

What the Genesis narratives tell of Israel in Egypt tallies well with the framework of known history. The sons of Israel (Jacob) the Patriarch, with their families and flocks, descended into Goshen in a time of famine (Gen. 42:5, 46:1–7). Their Egyptian Sojourn*, with its privations, ended in the Exodus* led by Moses, chosen by God from the tribe of Levi, who had been born in Egypt. This pivotal event occurred, according to much scholarly opinion, in the reign of Ramesses II (1290–1224 B.C.). The Joseph Tribes (Ephraim and Manasseh), in whose veins flowed the Egyptian blood of their mother (Gen. 41:45, 50–52, E), had been adopted into the family of Israel while in Egypt (Gen. 48:14–22, J, E), and probably formed the nucleus of the Exodus. Some scholars believe that at least a portion of Ephraim and Manasseh left Egypt soon after the expulsion of the Hyksos (c. 1550 B.C.). (Cf. the dates suggested for the Exodus and for the final destruction of Jericho*; recent discoveries have brought many scholars to the conclusion that Jericho fell in the latter part of the 13th century B.C. or c. 1250.)

Probably not all the Hebrew tribes went down to Egypt or took part in the Exodus (possibly between 1290 and 1224 B.C.); many scholars believe that the Jacob Tribes went down but that some Semitic clans remained in Canaan. The ultimate union of the two groups is expressed through the identification of Jacob with Israel. (See W. F. Albright, *Archaeology and the Religion of Israel*, p. 112; and *From the Stone Age in Christianity*, 2d ed., pp. 277 f., Johns Hopkins Press.)

It is believed that the "mixed multitude" (Ex. 12:38; Num. 11:4) who joined with the Israelite tribes under the leadership of Moses in the wilderness included Kenites, Calebites (Num. 13:30; Josh. 14:6–15; I Sam. 30:14), Kenizzites, Jerameelites, and possibly Amalekites. These scattered tribes were held together by disasters, threats, and arduous nomadic experiences which cemented them into a federated group with the hope and indomitable courage which throughout history characterized the Hebrew people. After the revelation and covenant at Sinai-Horeb*, an enthusiastic faith in Yahweh was the creative force that cemented a wandering, conquering people who almost 1,000 years later in the post-Exilic era became a "church-state" (c. 537–400 B.C.).

J's record of the Conquest is the main source for a period of history which is obscure and confusing, but very important in view of what Israel became. Many thinkers believe there were 3 waves of immigrants who entered Canaan and settled there in the period known as "the Conquest": one from the N., near Lake Huleh; one into Central Palestine from E. of the Jordan, under Joshua; one from the S., a composite group which comprised the later Judah. Israel never did wholly conquer or expel the native Canaanite O.T. population from the coast, the Esdraelon*, and the Jordan Valley, or the Amorites from their highlands; though by the end of Solomon's reign the Canaanites had been incorporated into the Hebrew Kingdom. The ardently patriotic narratives of the Book of Judges tell how the exploits of the judges* helped Israel entrench itself more securely in Canaan, the promised land.

Events in the History of United Israel before the Monarchy

(a) Abraham's call in Haran to go to the

ISRAEL

land of Canaan (Gen. 12:1–5).

(b) Patriarchal activities of the seminomads (Gen. 13–36).

(c) Descent of the Tribes to Egypt and their Sojourn (Gen. 45–48).

(d) Exodus from Egypt (Ex. 12–15).

(e) Wilderness wandering (the desert years) (Ex. 15:22–ch. 40; Num. 33; Deut.).

(f) Conquests—in Trans-Jordan (Num. 32); the Jordan Crossing (Josh. 3, 4); in Palestine (Josh. 6–21).

(g) Settlement in "the Promised Land," and partial conquest of the Canaanite inhabitants.

(h) Troubled period of the Judges (c. 1225–1020 B.C.) (Judg. 1–21)—thirteen leaders, including Deborah, Gideon, Jephthah, Samson.

(3) *The United Kingdom of Israel* came into being when the people, faced with the threat of Philistine domination, clamored for such a king as their neighbors had. This demand led to the anointing by Samuel of Israel's first king, Saul, and to his analysis of the clamor as a rejection of God, Israel's true king. The United Monarchy lasted about 100 years. Then at the death of Solomon it split into what became the Northern Kingdom, or Kingdom of Israel, and the Southern Kingdom, or Kingdom of Judah.

Kings of United Israel, the Hebrew Monarchy

Saul (c. 1020–1000 B.C.)
David (c. 1000–960 B.C.)
Solomon (c. 960–922 B.C.)

This independent, relatively unified state, presided over by a native king, occupied a little more than 6,000 sq. m., extending from Dan at the fertile headwaters of the Jordan in the N. to Beer-sheba at the desert's edge. Its population may have totaled a million. The Sinai confederacy was able to hold its own without much interference from disintegrating neighbor empires to their E. and N. By the time of David and Solomon a well-organized bureaucracy was established, providing a central Temple*; a ceremonial ritual of worship; a professional priesthood; flourishing agriculture, advantageous foreign trade pacts, opportunities for social diversions, and a relatively comfortable standard of living. The three kings of United Israel were regarded as Yahweh's representatives, "the anointed of the Lord" (I Sam. 24:6, 26:9, 11; II Sam. 1:16). King and people were united in their years of prosperity, famine, war, and peace, in a mystical and political solidarity. In the great story of Solomon's dedication of the Jerusalem Temple—the palace chapel which became the nation's prayer place—the monarch is shown as high priest offering intercessory prayer and a sacrifice to Yahweh for all His people (I Kings 8:15 ff.).

(4) *The Kingdom of Israel* (the Northern Kingdom) consisted of the 10 tribes which revolted from the United Kingdom after the death of Solomon (c. 922 B.C.) because they were disgusted with the monarch's lavish extravagances, inordinate political ambitions, alliances with foreign wives who followed alien gods, and conscription of labor. When Rehoboam, son of Solomon, refused to promise the Northern tribes relief from the heavy demands which had been made on them by his father, and tactlessly sent Adoram "who was over the tribute" (I Kings 12:18) to quell the resulting revolt, the long-standing jealousy between N. and S. came to a head. Jeroboam came back from exile in Egypt and was crowned (c. 922 B.C.) Jeroboam I, King of Israel (I Kings 12:20); he ruled until c. 901. The 10 Tribes which seceded—leaving only Judah and a small part of Benjamin to merge into the Southern Kingdom of Judah—were Reuben, Gad, the half Tribe of Manasseh E. of the Jordan and the half Tribe of Manasseh W. of the Jordan, Ephraim, Issachar, Zebulun, Naphtali, Asher, Dan, and Benjamin—part of whose territory lay within the Kingdom of Judah, but whose important towns (Bethel, Gilgal, and Jericho) were inside the Kingdom of Israel. The Kingdom of Israel (or of Ephraim) lasted for two centuries, until its leading citizens were deported to various places inside Assyria (see below). (For list of the kings of Israel see CHRONOLOGY.)

The division of the United Monarchy which occurred c. 922 B.C. was not the first instance of a divided Hebrew kingdom. After the death of Saul (c. 1000 B.C.) the southern portion had made David king at Hebron, where he ruled over Judah for 6 years (II Sam. 5:5); and the northern Tribes had made Saul's son Esh-baal (Ish-bosheth) king (II Sam. 2:10). When he was murdered (II Sam. 4:7) David was made king of all Israel, and reigned about 33 years (c. 1000–960 B.C.). Sometimes the rulers of the two kingdoms were affiliated in a defensive alliance, as with Ahab and Jehoshaphat; at other times they were at swords' points, as with Amaziah and Joash, and Pekah and Ahaz.

Israel had twice the population and three times the area of Judah. It was a little smaller than Connecticut and Rhode Island (see map for boundaries). It was more productive than its southern neighbor. In fact, as Pfeiffer states, "The kingdom of Israel ranked high above Judah not only in size but in culture, power, splendor, foreign relationships, commerce, and even religion, for (except for Amos, who, however, delivered his message in the Northern Kingdom) the prophetic movement before Isaiah is confined to North Israel. Even the pious Judaean author of Kings, who had no love for North Israel, unwittingly admits this."

Israel was strategically located on the main caravan routes that carried a heavy traffic of ideas and wares. The principal routes from Egypt to Damascus and the ever-coveted states N. of Syria, crisscrossed through Israel. Its accessibility laid it open to enemy raids and the interplay of economic and political forces; its co-operation was sought by first one, then another, of its greedy, warring neighbors. Syria was Israel's only buffer. And when this fell to Assyria, nothing remained to protect Israel against this powerful aggressor.

The two small nations which had been United Israel under a line of three kings had as much in common as in disagreement. Yahweh was the God of both, however vacillating they both might be in loyalty to Him. For His honor both kingdoms fought time and again against pagan nations and cultures which sought to influence them. He had long remained the Yahweh of the desert, of its sheep and tribes; but He also became the God of the farmer, the power who gave oil, grain, wine, social festivals, and wholesome family life. To Israel-in-towns as well as to Israel-in-tents God was the abiding reality. Israel's desire to be loyal to Him was at the core of the codes of sound social, ethical, and religious laws which the state gradually developed. Even the introduction of foreign cults did not deter Israel from expecting Yahweh's help. So while Judah gloried in her Temple and its beautiful ritual, Israel maintained a fierce loyalty to the Yahweh Who had brought its forebears up from Egypt. (For the major prophets of the Kingdom of Israel see AMOS; ELIJAH; ELISHA; HOSEA. See also cities within the kingdom of Israel, e.g., SAMARIA; SHECHEM; MEGIDDO; DAN.)

Some Events in the History of the (Northern) Kingdom of Israel

(a) The northern tribes make Jeroboam I, the Ephrathite, their king (I Kings 11:26–12:1–24).

(b) Jeroboam's capitals: Shechem (I Kings 12:25); Penuel, on the Jabbok, E. of the Jordan (I Kings 12:25); Tirzah, NE. of Shechem (I Kings 14:17).

(c) Jeroboam I builds shrines at Dan and Bethel to rival Jerusalem (I Kings 12:28 f.).

(d) Omri builds a new capital, Samaria (I Kings 16:24).

(e) The cultivation by Omri of friendly relations with Tyre, Sidon, Jerusalem—the marriage of King Ahab of Israel to Princess Jezebel, daughter of Eth-baal, King of Tyre (I Kings 16:31); and of Ahab's daughter or sister Athaliah to King Jehoram of Judah (II Kings 8:18, 26), with the resultant introduction of Baal worship. This apostasy was protested by Elijah (I Kings 18, 19).

(f) The usurpation of Jehu; end of Omri Dynasty (II Kings 9:1–10:27).

(g) The protests of the Prophets—Elijah's victory over Baal prophets (I Kings 17–19, 21; II Kings 1 f.); Elisha's miracles and role in the downfall of the Omri Dynasty (II Kings 2–9); Hosea chastises national corruption and apostasy at the time of Assyria's greatest power (Hos. 1–14); Amos of Judaea protests at Israel's court against injustice, corruption, extravagance, immorality (Amos 1–9).

ISRAEL

(h) The relations between Israel and Judah—frequent frictions, yet peaceful alliance by Kings Ahab and Jehoshaphat vs. Ben-hadad II of Syria, to recover Ramoth-gilead (I Kings 22:1–38), in the course of which Ahab dies; strife between Joash and Amaziah (II Kings 14:8–14).

(i) Relations between Israel and Syria—Ben-hadad I of Syria attacks Israel (I Kings 15:20); after two defeats in battle, Ben-hadad II of Syria makes a covenant with Ahab (I Kings 20:1–34); Israel scourged by Hazael of Syria (II Kings 9:14, 10:32 f., 13:22), is completely dominated by Syria in the reign of Jehoahaz (815–801 B.C.) (II Kings 13:1–3, 22).

(j) Relations between Assyria and Israel—

(*a*) Israel participates in the Syrian coalition of Ben-hadad II vs. Shalmaneser III (859–824 B.C.), checking him at the Battle of Karkar (853 B.C.).

(*b*) Jehu pays tribute to Assyria to secure protection vs. Hazael of Damascus.

(*c*) The rapid decline of Israel.

(*d*) Tiglath-pileser III (Pul) (745–727 B.C.) invades Syria-Palestine. Menahem pays tribute (II Kings 15:19 f.).

(*e*) Pekah, King of Israel, sees Tiglath-pileser III invade a large portion of Israel, incorporate it into his kingdom, and deport groups of citizens to Assyria (II Kings 15:29).

(*f*) Hoshea conspires against Pekah, slays, and succeeds him (II Kings 15:30) (732 B.C.), becoming a vassal of Assyria until the fall of Samaria (722/1 B.C.).

(*g*) Shalmaneser V besieges Samaria 3 yrs. (724–722 B.C.) (II Kings 17:5), dies during the course of the siege; is succeeded by Sargon II (722–705 B.C.) when Samaria is reduced some time between the accession of Sargon II, Dec. 722, and the end of his accession year, spring of 721 B.C. Thousands of leading citizens are deported to "Haleh and on the Habor the river of Gozan, and in the cities of the Medes" (R.S.V. II Kings 17:6).

(*h*) Men brought to Samaria by king of Assyria to take the place of the deported Israelites (II Kings 17:24), the basis of the mixed group later known as "Samaritans,"* of whom a small colony remains today at Nablus.

(k) The scattering of "the ten lost Tribes of Israel," never to return to their kingdom (cf. Post-Exilic Judah's Return as a national group.)

Sources of information concerning the Kingdom of Israel include the O.T. (especially I and II Kings, Hosea, and Amos); the writings of Josephus; Assyrian and Egyptian inscriptions; and excavated clay letters.

R. H. Pfeiffer points out that Kings is a work which "spans the history of less than four centuries and a half," and that it is "a repository of documents ranging from the days of Solomon to those of Judas Maccabeus—a period of eight centuries during which time almost all of the Old Testament was written." (*Introduction to the Old Testament*, p. 412, Harper & Brothers.)

(5) *The name of the holy nation, God's chosen people* (Deut. 7:6–8), used in a religious rather than a political sense.

No scholar has been able to give a rational explanation of why God chose Israel to be the repository of ethical monotheism, His chosen people, whose indestructible loyalty to Him served mankind by spreading their faith to the uttermost corners of the Gentile as well as the Jewish world. As R. H. Pfeiffer states, when the P authors reached such insoluble mysteries as this they accepted what others might call inconsistencies and thus established a successful church. "Cold reason is poison to religion." The Hebrews worshipped with limitless courage an absolute Deity. The Second Isaiah gave to Israel the contradictory concept of Yahweh, King of the Jews (48:12), and the unique, universal God of all mankind 45:6, 22; cf. 42:10–12). As implied in Deutero-Isaiah, God is Israel's father (43:6); He is Israel's creator (43:1, 44:2, 24, 45:11), and husband (50:1, 54:5 f.). His love for Israel is that of a mother (49:15). He holds her hand (42:6). He was loyal to His covenant with David (55:3); resided with Israel (45:14); and empowered the Jews to be His witness (43:10, 12, 44:8). His anger was temporary, but His love is eternal (54:7–10). He poured out His wrath upon the heathen, but proved His love for Israel (42:14–16). He led Israel like a shepherd (40:11, 49:9–13), and granted merciful pardon to sinners (55:7, cf. 43:25). In brief, the very character of Yahweh demanded that Israel be restored and serve to redeem mankind (45:5, 6). Judaism interprets the "suffering servant" in the poems of Isa. 42:1–4, 49:1–6, 50:4–9, 52:13–53:12 as the nation Israel; Christianity interprets him as the individual Jesus Christ.

When Israel, "God's holy people" (Ex. 19:5 f., 24:7 f.), failed to keep her covenant with Yahweh, disasters, viewed as divine judgment, followed (Judg. 2:1–23; II Kings 17:7–23; Neh. 9:6–31). For the chosen people were not exempt from punishment when they were guilty of wandering from their covenant relationship with God. Prophet after prophet protested, warned, and interpreted Babylonia and Assyria as instruments of judgment. The Deuteronomic and the Holiness Codes (see CODE) both stressed unmistakable warnings. Yet Hosea viewed Israel's punishments as redemptive rather than retributive.

To Paul God's chosen people were not Israel—who had rejected the Gospel in spite of having received the Law and the Messiah —but Christians. To him the "elect" and the "saints" were Abraham's spiritual but not physical descendants (Rom. 2:28 f., 4:9 ff.). "The New Testament supplanted Israel with the church." Israel had failed, but not God (Rom. 9–11). God's redemption* of wayward Israel is expressed in such passages as Jer. 31:23–30 and in what Pfeiffer calls an "eschatological drama" of the destruction of neighbor nations and the restoration of a redeemed Israel, returned to a rebuilt Jerusalem (Jer. 33), in an era when God shall have written His laws in the hearts of both Judaeans and Israelites (Jer. 31:33). (Cf. Ezekiel's writings *re* the national rebirth.)

(6) *The name given a Jewish state* proclaimed in Palestine May 5, 1948. The first two paragraphs of the proclamation read:

"The land of Israel was the birthplace of the Jewish People.

"Here their spiritual, religious, and national identity was formed. Here they wrote and gave the Bible to the world."

See also such entries as COVENANT; DRESS; FAMILY; FOODS; GOVERNOR; HOUSE; ISAIAH.

Israelite, a descendant of Israel (Jacob), a Hebrew, a Jew. Also sometimes used in the O.T. with a strictly religious connotation, meaning a spiritual heir of the covenanted promises of God. Hebrews* were in Palestine in Patriarchal times before Israelites proper arrived from the S. (See ISRAEL.) In the N.T. "Israelite" has a definitely spiritual meaning, as when Jesus referred to Nathanael as "an Israelite indeed, in whom is no guile" (John 1:47). The word was associated with fulfillment of the Messianic hope. Paul, who calls himself both a "Hebrew" and an "Israelite" (II Cor. 11:22), declares in his Epistle to the Romans (9:4–13) that not all who are of the seed of Israel are children of God; children of God are followers of Christ, the Church.

Issachar (ĭs'ȧ-kär) ("hired laborer"), Jacob's 9th son, his 5th by Leah (Gen. 30:14–18), the eponymous ancestor of one of the northern inland Tribes of Israel (Gen. 49:14 f.; Josh. 19:17–23).

Issachar, accompanied by his four sons (Gen. 46:13; Num. 26:23 f.; I Chron. 7:1), went down into Egypt with Jacob (Ex. 1:3). The significance of his name and the circumstances of his birth are brought out by Jacob in his death-bed charge, when he likened Issachar and his family to an ass whose love of ease resulted in its becoming the hired burden-bearer of others (Gen. 49:14 f.).

The extent of Issachar's territory in Palestine is uncertain. Its description in Josh. 19:17–23 is from P, a late source. It lay S. of Zebulun and Naphtali, N. of Manasseh, and W. of the Jordan. The Plain of Esdraelon was within its lot, but the Canaanites disputed this claim. This circumstance explains why Judges (1) is silent concerning Issachar's prompt settlement in Palestine. The *Via Maris* ("Way of the Sea") passed through Issachar, and was a source of easy revenue to those who lived there. Deborah and Barak were probably of Issachar (Judg. 5:15), as was the judge Tola (Judg. 10:1 f.). The blessing on Issachar voiced by Moses was for the sacrifices which the Tribe maintained on mountain high places patronized by the neighboring Phoenicians, who possessed "the abundance of the seas" and "treasures hid in the sand" (Deut. 33:18 f.).

Unfortunately no dependence can be put on the recorded figures concerning the Tribe (Num. 1:29, 26:25; I Chron. 7:2).

Isshia (ĭ-shī'*ȧ*). (1) A Levite, chief of the family of Rehabiah (I Chron. 24:21). (2) A Levite, second son of Uzziel (I Chron. 23:20; A.V., "Jesiah"). (3) A man of the tribe of Issachar (I Chron. 7:3; A.V., "Ishiah"). (4) One of the "mighty men" of King David (I Chron. 12:6; A.V., "Jesiah").

issue. (1) As a man's disease, the Heb. word so translated in A.V. (e.g., Lev. 15:2) is in A.S.V. and R.S.V. rendered "discharge," as from a suppurating sore or wound, or a secretion of the body, venereal or otherwise. (2) In the case of women ("issue of blood," Lev. 15:25–30; Matt. 9:20), a hemorrhage is meant. (3) The A.V. also uses "issue" in the legal sense of a child or children, offspring.

Italian Band. See ITALY.

Italy, the central Mediterranean peninsula extending SE. between the Adriatic and Tyrrhenian Seas. Its capital, Rome*, governed the world in which Jesus and the Apostles lived. Its roads ran in every direction, carrying officials, soldiers, teachers, and travelers S. to the Campania and Brundisium, for example, whence they sailed across the Adriatic to pick up the Egnatian Road to Thessalonica and points beyond; or across the Gulf of Corinth to Lechaeum, along the Isthmus to Cenchreae and by boat to Alexandria, Ephesus, or Seleucia Pieria, port of Antioch on the Orontes. Italy is mentioned several times in the N.T.: (1) the place from which Claudius had banished Jews, including Aquila and Priscilla, Paul's helpers at Corinth (Acts 18:2); (2) the destination of Paul and his companions in the most famous N.T. journey to Rome (27:1, 6); (3) the homeland of the group of people mentioned in Heb. 13:24, as sending greetings to those to whom the Epistle to the Hebrews was addressed. The A.V. "They of Italy" is more accurately translated "Those who come from Italy" (R.S.V.).

Italy gave its name to a band on military assignment at Caesarea under Cornelius, a centurion who became a Christian convert through Peter's influence (Acts 10:1 ff.).

Towns of Italy mentioned in the N.T. include: Rome; Rhegium, near the SW. tip of the peninsula, opposite Messina (Acts 28:13); Puteoli, 8 m. W. of the present Naples (28:13); Appii Forum (the Market of Appius) a small market town (the modern Foro Appio), 10 m. from the Three Taverns (28:15). See also ROMAN EMPIRE.

Ithai (ĭth'ī), son of Ribai of Gibeah of the Benjaminites; one of the heroes, the "mighty men," of King David, known as the Thirty (I Chron. 11:31). In II Sam. 23:29 he is called Ittai.

Ithamar (ĭth'*ȧ*-mär), the 4th and youngest son of Aaron and Elisheba (Ex. 6:23), was consecrated to the priestly office with his father and brothers (Ex. 28:1). His duties included tabulating gifts for the Tabernacle* (Ex. 38:21) and supervising the tasks of Gershonite carriers (Num. 4:22–28) and Merarite construction attachés of the Tabernacle (4:31–33). Late priestly circles viewed him as founder of one of the two principal priestly lines (I Chron. 24:1–6). His descendants returned from Exile (Ezra 8:2). Eli belonged to his line (cf. I Kings 2:27 with I Chron. 24:3).

Ithmah (ĭth'mă). A Moabite member of King David's palace guard (I Chron. 4:7).

Ithnan (ĭth'nan). A town in S. Judah, near Ziph. Its site is unknown. (Josh. 15:23).

Ithra (ĭth'ra). Father of Amasa, who married David's sister Abigail (II Sam. 17:25; I Kings 2:5, 32; I Chron. 2:17). In the first of these references he is called "the Israelite"; but in I Chron. 2:17 his name is given as "Jether the Ishmaelite," and the latter is probably correct.

Ithran (ĭth'răn). (1) A Horite, son of the clan chief, Dishon (Gen. 36:26; I Chron. 1:41). (2) Son of Zophah, an Asherite (I Chron. 7:37).

Ithream (ĭth'rē-ăm) ("the kinsman is abundance"), the 6th son of David, born at Hebron (mother, Eglah) (II Sam. 3:5; I Chron. 3:3).

Ithrite (ĭth'rīt), a member of a family from Kirjath-jearim, an important town in Judah (I Chron. 2:53). Ira and Gareb, members of David's guard (II Sam. 23:38; I Chron. 11:40) were Ithrites. The name may more accurately be "Jattirite," from the hill town of Jattir (I Sam. 30:27).

Ittai (ĭt'ā-ī) (perhaps "with," or "companion," or "with me"). (1) A brave Philistine of Gath who with 600 henchmen joined David at the time of Absalom's rebellion and accompanied him in his flight E. of the Jordan, in the course of which he made the noble expression of loyalty stated in II Sam. 15:21. He was elevated to the captaincy of one-third of David's army (II Sam. 18:2 ff.). (2) A Benjamite in David's palace guard (II Sam. 23:29), Ithai A.S.V. I Chron. 11:31.

Ituraea (ĭt'ū-rē'*ȧ*) (from Jetur, Gen. 25:15; possibly "the country of mountaineers"), a region S. of Mt. Hermon, NE. of the Sea of Galilee, E. of the Jordan sources, adjoining (or overlapping) Trachonitis and Gaulanitis in N.T. times. Its wild border warriors of the Anti-Lebanon* range, considered by the author of Gen. 25:15 to be descendants of Ishmael, fought the Israelites E. of the Jordan (I Chron. 5:19). The Maccabees knew an independent kingdom of Ituraea, which was conquered by Aristobulus I (c. 105 B.C.), who virtually annexed it to Judaea and converted many Ituraeans to Judaism. Ituraea was part of the Tetrarchy of Philip (see HEROD); Caligula gave it to Herod Agrippa I, along with Trachonitis and the title of king. C. A.D. 40 there was added to this territory the region which had been held by Herod Antipas. Claudius (A.D. 41) also gave Herod Agrippa I all that had belonged to his grandfather, Herod the Great. When Herod Agrippa died Ituraea was incorporated into the Province of Syria, under procurators. The allusion to Ituraea in Luke 3:1 is accurate. Ituraea today is part of Syria.

197. *Top:* Woman holding staff: Megiddo ivory, c.1350-1150 B.C. *Bottom:* Man holding lotus tree in left hand, with right hand raised in salute; Ivory from Nimrud, 8th century B.C.

ivory, a hard, white substance derived from the tusks of the elephant, hippopotamus, and other animals. It is mentioned in Scripture as a greatly prized luxury ware. Solomon's navy went on three-year cruises with the navy of his trade ally, Hiram of Tyre, to bring ivory, gold, apes, and peacocks (II Chron. 9:21) from Punt, Somaliland or Ethiopia, and possibly also India—the sources which had supplied such luxury-loving Egyptian sovereigns as Queen Hatshepsut 1490–1469 B.C.). Solomon's "great throne" at Jerusalem was ivory-trimmed, overlaid with gold. or of ivory panels inlaid with gold (II Chron. 9:17) and flanked by 12 lions on 6 steps. This ivory throne was probably one of the sights which dazzled the Queen of Sheba (II Chron. 9:1–4).

When O.T. writers wished to create an

198. Woman at a window, possibly a representation of Astarte; Ivory from Nimrud, 8th century B.C.

atmosphere of majesty, exotic beauty, or graciousness, they worked ivory into their descriptions, as in Ps. 45:8, Song of Sol. 5:14. The fabulous wealth of Tyre is evidenced by the tale that even the rowers' benches on her ships were decorated (Ezek. 27:6) with ivory from the Mediterranean isles and N. Africa. Beds and couches decorated with ivory were condemned by prophets. Merchants of Babylon (? Rome) retailed dishes or "vessels" made of ivory (Rev. 18:12). Hezekiah, according to a cuneiform inscription, included "beds of ivory" as well as tusks and hides of elephants in his tribute to Sennacherib.

Rich evidence of the skill of ivory craftsmen in Bible lands has come from excavated sites. The famous Samaria ivories include thousands of fragments which have been cleaned, studied, and recorded by John and Grace Crowfoot. They are described in the Samaria-Sebaste Reports of the Joint Expedition of Harvard University, the Hebrew University of Jerusalem, the Palestine Exploration Fund, the British Academy, and the British School of Archaeology in Jerusalem. These small objects, fashioned in the 9th or 8th centuries B.C., put moderns in touch with what the 9th century prophet Elijah and the protesting prophet Amos knew of the "ivory houses" and the ivory-trimmed furnishings and paneled palaces of King Ahab (Amos 3:15, 6:4). These ivory fragments, among the most valuable finds in the costly excavations in Samaria, once formed borders and inlay for couches, thrones, and stools. One group shows Egyptian influences; the other, including the famous "woman at the window" motif, may

199. Syrian ivory ornament, probably from piece of furniture, c. 1500 B.C.

have been derived from Damascus and its vicinity. Many of the carved pieces are inlaid with gold and lapis lazuli. One of the most famous medallions shows the Egyptian god Horus as a child sitting on a lotus leaf, naked save for a wide jeweled collar and a pair of bracelets. Other Egyptian motifs may have been carved by itinerant Syrian or Phoenician artists from Hama, Damascus, and Phoenician cities. Elephant tusks were procurable from E. Syria, whose Upper Euphrates was the hunting ground of such pharaohs as Thutmose III. The Samaria ivories are the most revealing extant record of art created during the Hebrew Monarchy. In some instances they are signed with names of craftsmen, written in Hebrew-Canaanitish or Aramaic.

At Megiddo, 400 pieces of ivory were found in a half-underground treasury of three rooms of a palace suddenly abandoned c. 1150 B.C. These sensational "collectors' pieces" are chiefly 12th-century Phoenician art, but among them are Hittite and Egyptian articles. They include ivory panels carved with consummate skill, gaming boards, plaques incised with processions of captives and lotus blossoms, boxes, figurines, and a human-headed sphinx clasping a cup.

Egypt, situated near the elephant hunting grounds, had access to an inexhaustible supply of ivory, and used it for fan handles, such as are seen today in the Egyptian Museum, Cairo; ointment boxes, statuettes of gods, jewel caskets, combs, chair legs, statuettes of royalty, dishes, pen cases, headrests, bracelets, castanets, and game boards whose ivory squares alternate with ebony ones.

The Assyrian palace of Tiglath-pileser III has yielded quantities of ivory art pieces, one of which, from the late 9th century B.C., carries an Aramaic inscription mentioning Hazael, King of Damascus, contemporary of Ahab and Elijah, mentioned in I Kings 19:15.

J

J, the symbol for the Jehovistic (Yahwistic) strand of Biblical material originating in Judaea c. 950 B.C. See BIBLE and SOURCES.

Jaazaniah (jā-ăz'ȧ-nī'ȧ) (Jezaniah, A.V. Jer. 40:8, "Jehovah heareth"). (1) A Macaathite guerilla captain in Judaea who offered allegiance to Gedaliah (II Kings 25:23). (2) A Rechabite whose loyalty to his tribe's vow Jeremiah tempted as an object lesson to Judah (Jer. 35:3 ff.). (3) Shaphan's son, who with other Jerusalem elders appeared in Ezekiel's vision offering incense to idols (Ezek. 8:11). (4) Azzur's son, against whose advice Ezekiel prophesied (Ezek. 11:1).

Jabal ((jā'băl), a son of Lamech and Adah (Gen. 4:20), credited by the author of J with founding nomadic ways of life characterized by tent-dwelling and cattle-raising. With his brothers, Jubal* and Tubal-cain*, he was regarded as a designer of man's early social pattern.

Jabbok (jăb'ŏk), the most important river of ancient Gilead (now the Hashemite Kingdom of Jordan). It rises in a spring near Amman (old Rabbath-ammon) on the edge of Biblical Moab c. 18 m. from the Jordan but E. of the watershed; and flows E. and N. before cutting through its impressive canyon to the Jordan at a point opposite the highlands of Samaria, c. 23 m. N. of the Dead Sea. It has always been a natural boundary, as between the 13th-century kingdoms of the Amorite Sihon (Num. 21:24; Josh. 12:2, Judg. 11:22) and Og, King of Bashan (Num. 21:33; Deut. 3:1) which later were "assigned" to Gad and the half Tribe of Manasseh. The deep Jabbok Valley supplied an impressive locale for Jacob's wrestling with an angel and for his reunion with the estranged Esau (Gen. 32:22 ff.). The Jabbok is always shallow enough to ford (Gen. 32:23). Portions of its slopes are wooded, and dotted with patches of orchard, vineyard, and vegetable cultivation. Wheat is cultivated in its upper reaches. Flocks are usually within sight of travelers. Its modern name, Nahr

200. Jabbok Wâdī.

ez-Zerqâ, is suggested by its blue-green color. On one of its tributaries the important city of Jerash (Gerasa) was built.

Jabeash. (1) The father of Shallum, King of Israel for one month c. 745 B.C. (II Kings 15:10). (2) A town. See JABESH.

Jabesh (jā′bĕsh), **Jabesh-gilead** (jā′bĕsh-gĭl′ē-ăd), a famous O.T. city in the highlands E. of the Jordan, c. 10 m. SE. of Beth-shan and S. of Pella. Nelson Glueck has identified it as lying on twin mounds, Tell el-Meqbereh ("burial place"), anciently used as a residential quarter, and Tell Abū Kharaz, its overshadowing fortress. The site (in Perea of the N.T. era) is on the Wâdī Yabis (Jabesh) flowing into the Jordan S. of the Sea of Galilee. The formerly accepted site, Tell el-Maqlub, is now thought to be Abel-meholah*, the home of Elisha. The archaeological method applied by Glueck in the identification of Jabesh-gilead consisted in comparing the O.T. narrative with topography, and in searching for potsherds which indicated occupation here in the Israelite period (13th to 6th century B.C.) (see *The River Jordan*, pp. 159–167, Nelson Glueck, Westminster Press).

Several O.T. passages deal with Jabesh-gilead. (1) Because none from Jabesh-gilead came to the assembly of Israel at Mizpah (Judg. 21:8), the city was destroyed by the indignant faithful and only 400 citizens were spared—maidens, given to Benjamites for wives (v. 14). (2) When Nahash, King of Ammon, threatened to put out the eyes of all the men of Jabesh, they appealed to Saul for help (I Sam. 11:5); Saul's victory did much to bring about his confirmation as king of united Israel at Gilgal (I Sam. 11), and the favor he did the men of Jabesh-gilead was not forgotten. (3) When news of the killing of Saul and his sons in the Battle of Mt. Gilboa reached the men of Jabesh-gilead they hurried across the Jordan, took down the decapitated body of Saul from the walls of Beth-shan (I Sam. 31:12), and carried it, with the bodies of his slain sons, back across the Jordan to Jabesh-gilead. There they ceremonially mourned and buried the bones under an oak tree (I Chron. 10:11 f.), where they remained until they were removed to the tomb of Saul's father Kish in Benjamin's territory farther south (II Sam. 21:12–14). (4) David, successor of Saul, when informed of the courage of the men of Jabesh-gilead, commended them and promised them compensation (II Sam. 2:5–7). (5) Tell el-Meqbereh, according to Glueck, was possibly the home of "Elijah the Tishbite," as recorded in I Kings 17:1, a passage which should read, "Elijah the Jabeshite, from Jabesh-gilead." He believes that the Brook Cherith may be one of the small E. branches of the Wâdī Yabis (Jabesh), and certainly not the Wâdī Qelt W. of the Jordan; for when Elijah fled to Cherith he naturally turned to the desert E. of his old home, where as a youth he had doubtless tended flocks.

Jabin (jā′bĭn) (possibly "God perceives"). (1) A Canaanite king whose capital was the powerful Hazor*. He leagued with other local kings against Joshua, was killed, and his territory was taken by the victorious Hebrew leader (Josh. 11). (2) A Canaanite king, possibly a descendant of (1), who sent his iron-shod chariots and a "multitude" of warriors against Israel, led by Deborah* and Barak*. Jabin's army, led by Sisera, was defeated at the River Kishon in a battle recorded in prose and poetry (written c. 1125 B.C.) (Judg. 4 and 5; cf. Ps. 83:9). This victory ended 20 years of oppression by Jabin in the period of the Judges (c. 1200–1020 B.C.).

Jabneel (jăb′nē-ĕl) ("a god causes to build"). (1) The most westerly village on the N. border of Judah (Josh. 15:11), S. of Joppa, 4 m. inland on the road from Gaza; probably Yebuā today. Jabneel is the Jabneh of II Chron. 26:6 and the Jamnia of the Apocrypha (I Macc. 4:15, 5:58; II Macc. 12:8, 9). Here the Jewish Sanhedrin sat just after the destruction of Jerusalem (A.D. 70). It is believed that the O.T. Canon was established at Jabneel. (2) A town on the N. boundary of Naphtali (Josh. 19:33), today probably Yemmā, W. of the S. end of the Sea of Galilee.

Jachin (jā′kĭn) ("he establishes"). (1) The head of a Simeonite clan (Gen. 46:10; "Jarib"—possibly a scribe's error—in I Chron. 4:24). Cf. "Jachinites" (Num. 26:12). (2) The eponymous ancestor of a priestly family (I Chron. 9:10; Neh. 11:10). (3) For the Temple pillar, see JACHIN AND BOAZ.

Jachin (jā′kĭn) **and Boaz** (bō′ăz) (origin of names uncertain; possibly Jachin means "firmness" or "He [God] establishes"; and Boaz "in him is strength"; or perhaps Jachin is "Jachun," a Phoenician verbal form akin to Heb. *Yahweh*, and Boaz is based on Baal—conventional efforts of Phoenician craftsmen and Hebrew planners to represent the presence of God), twin pillars of burnished copper (not the "brass" of A.V. and A.S.V.) flanking the steps of Solomon's Temple* porch (I Kings 7:21; II Chron. 3:17; cf. Ezek. 40:49). Confused texts of I Kings 7 and II Chron. 3, 4 make it difficult for scholars to know the appearance of the two free-standing "personality" pillars which were cast (I Kings 7:15) in the clay of the Jordan Valley, probably between Adamah and Zarethan, by the noted Phoenician artisan-artist-architect

201. Jachin and Boaz, from Howland-Garber scale model.

Hiram (Heb. *Huram-abi*) (II Chron. 2:13 f.). Each pillar was wrought in one piece. Jachin and Boaz stood c. 31 ft. high, or c. 40 ft. including base and capital; their diameter was c. 6½ ft. They were hollow (Jer.

52:21), and seem to have stood on ovoid bases, looking like inverted mushroom caps. Their 8-ft.-high spheroidal capitals were ornamented with the popular lotus or lily motif (? "checkerwork"), with delicately wrought networks of copper over which hung two festoons of pomegranates, 100 to a row (Jer. 52:20–23). See SOLOMON'S TEMPLE, illus. 421.

"There are strong reasons to believe," says I. G. Matthews in *The Religious Pilgrimage of Israel* (Harper), "that they [Jachin and Boaz] were related to the Asherah poles dedicated to Astarte, that stood beside the high places in Canaan. Fertility rites were so prevalent in all the country that, had there been no recognition of them in the temple, many worshipers would have felt the loss as seriously as if all evidence of the cross were removed from Christian churches. . . . Their unquestioned importance is indicated by the fact that on official occasions, such as coronation, and covenant making, the king stood by the pillar, *as the manner was* (II Kings 11:14, 23:3, II Chron. 34:31)" (p. 103). (See ASHERAH.)

The pillars were apparently not intended to support lights, but were lofty cressets whose bowls contained smoking incense. (See II Chron. 29:7, 11.) Their significance to Hebrew worshippers remains conjectural; possibly they played a multiple role. They may have appeared to some as the tree of life, for in Near Eastern religion and art pillar and tree tended to mingle; sacred trees often stood beside sanctuaries, and there are no other "trees" known to have been at Solomon's sanctuary. But W. F. Albright saw in Jachin and Boaz a cosmic significance. They caught the gleam of Jerusalem sunrise, and their incense wicks smoked and burned; and this may have reminded worshippers of the pillar of fire and the pillar of cloud that led their ancestors through the Wilderness (Ex. 13:21).

jackal, a common animal of the dog kind (*Canis aureus*), the size of a fox. It appears several times in A.S.V. for "fox" in the A.V.

202. Jackal amulet.

In the Biblical period jackals were as great a bane to farmers and wayfarers as they are today. Even on the outskirts of large towns like Nazareth their mournful laughter is heard at night. By day they emerge in packs, searching for carrion and devastating vineyards (cf. Judg. 15:4; Song of Sol. 2:15).

203. The god Anubis as a jackal, lying on funerary chest; from the tomb of Tut-ankh-Amon at Thebes.

The "wild beasts" of A.V. Isa. 13:22 are "jackals" in the A.S.V.; and the "dragons" of A.V. Isa. 34:13 are "jackals" in the A. S.V. The "howling creatures" implied in A.S.V. Jer. 50:39 may be "jackals." So too the "doleful creatures" of Isa. 13:21 A.V. and A.S.V. The Hebrew word *shūʿāl* is used for both fox and jackal.

Jacob (Heb. *Yaʿaqob*, a shorter form of *Yaʿaqub-'el*, "May El protect"), a place name, y-'-q-b'-r (Yaqob-el), in Palestine seen on a list of Thutmose III of Egypt (c. 1470 B.C.) and on tablets of the early 18th century B.C. from Chagar Bazar in N. Mesopotamia, where it appears as *Ya-ah-qu-ub-il (um)*. By a later interpretation the name means "he grasps the heel" (Gen. 25:26; cf. Hos. 12:3).

(1) The 3d of the Hebrew Patriarchs, ranking high in the rabbinic traditions of the Midrash*. He was the younger of two sons born to Isaac and his wife Rebekah (Gen. 25:21–26), and was Rebekah's favorite son (see ESAU). In the interwoven passages from sources* J and E "Jacob" is an individual; but in later passages he designates the nation Israel*, of whom the man Jacob was considered the eponymous ancestor (25:23). The oral traditions which lie behind Gen. 25:19–50:13, where the Jacob material is found, date from antiquity and center in several national shrines, like Bethel, Shechem, and Penuel.

Though tribal memories are embodied in the Jacob narratives, the man himself is so vividly portrayed that the reader is convinced of the Patriarch's reality as a person. His characteristics would not fit the other Patriarchs. He is much more definitely depicted than Isaac. Nothing in Near Eastern literature surpasses the grief of Jacob over Joseph and Rachel. No effort is made to gloss over his weaknesses; he is not a character of uniform excellency, like Joseph or Enoch. Though the ancient saga portrays the shrewd craftiness of this picturesque, "plain" (R.S.V. "quiet") man, dwelling in tents (25:27), it also stresses his deep love for Rachel and his scrupulous attention to the complicated business of owning large flocks and protecting many children (32:5). It shows him in communion with God, Who in specific theophanies (see THEOPHANY) covenanted with this man of destiny, as at Bethel (28:10–16) and the Jabbok (Wâdī Zerqā) (32:24–32). The sufferings of Jacob, such as those caused by the kidnapping of his favorite son Joseph, were brought about by faults in his own nature. In his struggles, like those against Esau and Laban*, he received from God the help available to one who is essentially good and can be used by Him for a great destiny. Bereshith Rabbah 68:18 (Midrash*) says "his image was engraved in heaven"—i.e. was essentially good. Jacob in his old age deplored his early sins, and stressed the grace of God and his own utter faith (Gen. 48:15 f., Heb. 11:21).

Historians see in Jacob, who was renamed "Israel" after his experience wrestling with an angel (Gen. 32:28, 35:10), the personification of the national Israel.

Important Events in the Life of Jacob

Fraudulent grasping of Esau's birthright and Isaac's blessing	Gen. 25:29–34, 27:1–29
Hegira to Padan-aram, Haran*, traditional N. Mesopotamian homeland of his people, to visit his uncle Laban (in JE, to avoid Esau; in P, to be safeguarded against marrying a Hittite wife)	27:41–29:12
Dream experience, angels on ladder, Bethel; vow to God; erection of a stone pillar. (Bethel was to become an important Yahweh sanctuary.)	28
20 yrs. service to Laban (31:41); marriage to Leah and Rachel; birth of children; acquiring of nomadic wealth	29, 30
Escape from Laban's exactions; pilfering of family gods (cf. 31:30–35)	31:1–21
Quarrel and reconciliation covenant with Laban; Mizpah benediction (31:49)	31:22–55
Return to the edge of Canaan, welcomed by angels	32:1
Wrestling with an angel on the Jabbok, Trans-Jordan; receiving new name "Israel"; reconciliation with Esau	32:24–32, 33:4
Residence at Succoth, E. of the Jordan	33:17
Purchase of ground at Shechem, erection of altar *El elohe-Israel* ("God, the God of Israel")	33:18–20
Journey to Bethel; erection of another pillar; receiving God's promise of prosperity; renewal of name	35:1–15
Arrival at Hebron, old family home, where with Esau he attends Isaac's funeral	35:27–29
Incidents centering in his son Joseph, including the descent to Egypt, the Sojourn of 17 years in pastoral Goshen (47:28)	ch. 37–48
Blessing (49:1–27); death; embalming in Egypt; impressive burial in ancestral Cave of Machpelah near Hebron	49:1–50:13

Apparent contradictions in the Genesis epic of Jacob are due to its three strands or sources; the accounts are not "retrojections" from the age of the Dual Monarchy (10th–8th centuries B.C.). As R. H. Pfeiffer indicates, in the E accounts, which stem from Ephraim (Northern Israel) in the 8th century B.C., Jacob's ruse (Gen. 25–27) is either lost or closely interwoven with the J narrative. It is only in chap. 27 (the account of how he obtained Isaac's blessing), that E seems to form a substantial part of JE. E probably gave a fuller narration of the dream of Jacob at Bethel (28) than now appears in the JE account. In some instances E seems to preserve the oral tradition in purer form than J. Its Ephraimite author considered Isaac's blessing of his younger son natural (48:20), and stressed the Bethel shrine as the only one to which tithes were brought (28:22). E makes Jacob receive his wealth not by cunning but through the blessing of God. E describes Jacob's characteristic outbursts of emotion, such as his joy at finding Joseph alive. In E the blessing of Ephraim and Manasseh by their grandfather Jacob is in meter (Gen. 48:15, 20). Sometimes J and E are knit together. J is not blind to the crafty sins of Jacob, but vividly relates Jacob's schemes for acquiring wealth. The scholarly P source (sometimes called a 5th-century B.C. Midrash or historical commentary) is interested in the genealogy of Jacob and his line (Gen. 35:22b–26; Ex. 1:1–5); and stresses the marriages of Esau and Jacob as a protest against mixed marriages, as in Ezra's time (Ezra 10).

(2) The father of Joseph, husband of Mary (Matt. 1:15–16).

Jacob, the Blessing of (Gen. 49:2–27), one of the most important poems in the Pentateuch. Using the form of predictions, it describes the fortunes and woes of the Twelve Tribes of Israel and their traits in the period of the Judges when each Tribe was fighting its own battles. This poem may date from the era of David and Solomon. Its unity indicates a single author (c. 960 B.C.), using in part early oral traditions. The old poem was inserted at the close of the Patriarchal stories probably by some redactor of the 6th or 5th century B.C.—a hint of whose date is given by his use of the eschatological phrase "in the last days" (49:1). The Blessing of Jacob is characterized by its puns on the names of the Tribes, and its comparison of five of the Tribes to animals—Judah "a lion's whelp" (v. 9); Issachar "a strong ass" (v. 14); Dan a "serpent" (v. 17); Naphtali a "hind let loose" (v. 21); and Benjamin a "wolf" (49:27)—and its comparison of Joseph to a "fruitful bough" (v. 22).

Jacob's Well, one of the most exactly identified sites in O.T. Palestine, c. ½ m. S. of 'Askar, once widely accepted as N.T. Sychar*, ESE. of Nablus. Many experts now prefer Shechem* for Sychar, between Mt. Gerizim and Mt. Ebal, on the highway from Beth-shan over the highlands of Samaria via Shechem to Jerusalem. Gen. 33:18 f.; 37:12; Josh. 24:32; John 4:5 f. imply this location for Jacob's Well, at the center of a parcel of grazing land purchased by Jacob for a "hundred pieces of silver" and inherited by Joseph. It was here that Jesus, "being wearied with his journey," asked the Samaritan woman for a drink of water (John 4:5–12). The ancient stone well curb (7½ ft. in diameter) is covered today by an uncompleted chapel, successor of several ancient ones that protected the site. The shaft is still "deep" (John 4:11)—c. 85 ft. today, and formerly deeper. The quality of the cool water is excellent. The Gk. word translated "well" in vv. 11 f. really means "cistern," whose waters are accumulated rainfall, which adds point to Jesus' words in v. 14 (R.S.V.): "the water that I shall give him will become in him a spring of water welling up to eternal life."

204. Jacob's well near Sychar.

Jael (jā'ĕl) ("wild goat"), the wife of Heber the Kenite. The Kenites* were a nomadic tribe friendly to the Israelites at the time of Moses (Judg. 1:16, 4:11); but allies of Jabin, King of Hazor in the days of Barak and Deborah (Judg. 4:17). The Kenites were itinerant metal-smiths, which explains in part the relationship between Heber and Jabin, with his "nine hundred chariots of iron" (Judg. 4:2 f.). When Sisera, the Canaanite general, was defeated by the coalition of Israelite forces under Barak and Deborah he hid from his pursuers in the tent of Heber the Kenite, whose wife Jael extended hospitality. She gave the exhausted warrior not water, as he requested, but curdled milk—loved by Middle Easterners today—covered him with a rug to hide him from his pursuers, and then while he slept took a workman's hammer and drove a tent pin through his temple. Such a deed violated the ancient code of hospitality*, but the Israelites commended and celebrated her act (Judg. 5:24–27).

Jah (jä). A form of Yahweh used in poetry (A.V. Ps. 68:4).

Jahweh (jä'wĕ), a variation of Yahweh. See GOD.

Jair (jā'ẽr) ("he enlightens," cf. Jairus, Mark 5:22; Luke 8:41). (1) A man descended probably from Manasseh. Tradition makes him the conqueror, possibly in a post-Mosaic age, of some Amorite land E. of the Jordan, on the border of Gilead and Bashan, N. of the Jabbok—"the small towns" or tent villages he called Havoth-jair (Num. 32:41, cf. Deut. 3:14). Josh. 13:30 ascribes to Jair 60 cities in Bashan (cf. I Kings 4:13). (2) A man who judged Israel 22 years (Judg. 10:3–5), possibly a descendant of (1). (3) A forebear of Mordecai* (Esther 2:5). (4) The father of Elhanan* (I Chron. 20:5).

"The Jairite," i.e., descendant of Jair, is the term used to designate the ancestry of Ira*, II Sam. 20:26.

Jairus (jā'ĭ-rŭs) (Gk. *Iaeiros*), ruler of a Galilee synagogue who asked Jesus to cure his only daughter who lay at the point of death (Luke 8:42). In spite of Christ's request that no publicity be given to the miracle, performed in the presence of Peter, James, John, and the parents, of restoring the little girl to life (Mark 5:37, 40), the story was spread throughout the countryside (Matt. 9:26; Mark 5:43). Matthew omits the name of the synagogue ruler.

James (Eng. equivalent of the Gk. word for "Jacob"). (1) James the son of Zebedee, one of the Twelve, and elder brother of John. Their father was a fisherman of Galilee (Mark 1:19 f.). Comparison of Mark 15:40 with Matt. 27:56 (see also Mark 16:1) indicates that the Salome who witnessed the Crucifixion may have been the mother of James and John. James forsook his fishing business to follow Christ (Luke 5:10; Matt. 4:21 f.; Mark 1:19 f.). In the list of Apostles his name is always

JAMES, THE GENERAL EPISTLE OF

paired with John, his partner in service (Matt. 10:2; Mark 3:17; Luke 6:14); the men were kindred in spirit (Mark 10:35–45), and were so designated by Jesus (Mark 3:17). Together with Peter they were on terms of special intimacy with the Lord (Matt. 17:1; Mark 9:2; Luke 9:28; Matt. 26:37; Mark 14:33). James suffered martyrdom (Acts 12:2) in the early days of the Apostolic Church.

(2) James the son of Alphaeus (Acts 1:13) and son of the Mary named in Mark 16:1, is styled "the less" in A.V. Mark 15:40; "the younger," R.S.V. He was perhaps a brother of Matthew (Mark 3:18) and Joses (Mark 15:40). He was certainly a member of a remarkable Christian family. He stands at the head of the third group in each listing of the Apostles*.

(3) James the brother of Jesus (Matt. 13:55; Mark 6:3), the eldest of the three brothers, all of whom opposed Jesus' work (Matt. 12:46–50; Mark 3:31–35; Luke 8:19–21; John 7:3–5). He was won to faith by a special manifestation of the risen Lord (I Cor. 15:7). He appears as head of the Church at Jerusalem, rivaling Peter in importance (Gal. 1:18 f.), presiding over and making decisions at the council of the Church (Acts 15:13–34), and receiving the report of Paul's Third Missionary Journey (21:18 f.). According to tradition he was a strict Nazirite (see NAZIRITES); was called "the just"; had calloused knees like the camel's because of his long intercessions for the people; and was cruelly martyred by the scribes and Pharisees. The N.T. Epistle which bears his name and in which the author modestly refers to himself as "the servant of the Lord Jesus Christ" is ascribed by some scholars to him (James 1:1).

(4) James the "brother" (A.V. Luke 6:16; A.S.V. and R.S.V. "father") of Judas.

James, the General Epistle of, the first of five Epistles called "General" or "Catholic" Epistles in their titles in the A.V. (James, I and II Peter, I John, Jude); they were addressed not to individual churches, as were most of Paul's Epistles, but to Christians in general.

This book is a tract or homily written "to the twelve tribes which are scattered abroad." Though this apparently refers to Jews of the Dispersion or to Jewish Christians living in the pagan world, the words are more probably a symbolic reference to the Christian Church in general, which believed itself to be the true Israel. The author's purpose was to recall Christians from their worldliness and from their misconceptions of Christianity to the moral demands of their faith. He wrote not about its mystical or philosophical aspects but about the practical, every-day aspects of Christianity. The style is terse and forceful, abounding in imperatives; here, according to Zahn, "is a preacher who speaks like a prophet." The author was influenced by two Apocryphal books—Ecclesiasticus and the Wisdom of Solomon. From these books of Wisdom Literature he drew material for his treatise on Christian wisdom and the philosophy of everyday life. The Epistle is close to the Synoptic Gospels in its Christian spirit; and it often shows marked similarity to the Sermon on the Mount. The following comparisons are not actual quotations, but the reproduction of truths accepted and restated in the author's own words: the blessings of adversity, 1:2, 3, 2:5, 5:7 f., 11—Matt. 5:3–12; the dangers and uncertainty of wealth, 1:10 f., 2:6 f., 4:4, 6, 13–16, 5:1–6—Matt. 6:19–21, 24–34; the futility of mere profession, 1:26 f.—Matt. 6:1–7; the contrast between saying and doing, 1:22–25, 2:14–26—Matt. 7:15–27; the nature of true prayer, 1:5–8, 5:13, 18—Matt. 6:6–13; love of the world and love of God, 2:5, 4:4–8—Matt. 6:24; the forgiveness of others and of ourselves, 2:12 f.—Matt. 6:14 f.

Five main themes recur throughout the Epistle—endurance under trial; the superiority of deeds to theory; just dealings with the poor; the perils of evil speech; the qualities of humility and sincerity. Moral maxims are used to develop these themes and provide a guide to Christian living.

The author's distinctive teaching is that Christian action is more important than faith: "Ye see then how that by works a man is justified, and not by faith only" (2:24). This, which at first sight appears to be an attack on Paul's great doctrine of justification by faith (Rom. 3:28), led Luther to criticize this letter as "that Epistle of straw." The conflict, however, between Paul and the author of James is more apparent than real, for Paul also demanded an active faith that showed itself in deeds (Rom. 2:13). In James 2:14–26 the author is correcting, not Paul's doctrine of justification, but a misconception of Paul's antithesis between faith and works that led some people to substitute an empty profession of faith for a faith that expresses itself in Christian living. The fact that Paul's teaching had been distorted and now needed correcting throws light on the date of this Epistle.

The Epistle may be outlined as follows:

(1) Endurance under trial and temptation—1:1–16.

(2) The true word and true worship—1:17–27.

(3) Abuses in contemporary worship—2:1–13.

(4) Refutations of merely formal faith—2:14–26.

(5) The vices of the tongue—3:1–12.

(6) The true wisdom of life—3:13–18.

(7) Conflicts and worldliness in the church—4:1–12.

(8) Censure of scheming traders and profiteers—4:13–5:6.

(9) Exhortation to patience—5:7–11.

(10) Scattered counsels—5:12–20.

According to the traditional view the author of this Epistle is "James the Lord's brother" (Gal. 1:19), who was a leader of the Jerusalem church (Acts 15:13) until his martyrdom in A.D. 62. Some of the arguments supporting this view are these: (1) Many of the 230 words used by James in Acts 15:13–30 are in the vocabulary of the Epistle; (2) the silence of James concerning his blood relationship with Jesus is in keeping with Christ's statement (Matt. 12:47–50) and the early practice of the Church; (3) the similarity in spirit, style, and thought of the Epistle to the Sermon on the Mount. Moreover, there is internal evidence that the book was written at an early date, c. A.D. 45: (1) There are no references to the decision of the Jerusalem Council (A.D. 51) (Acts 15:13–21). (2) There are no allusions to the destruction of Jerusalem in A.D. 70. (3) Believers are still meeting in the "synagogue" (Luke 12:11; Acts 9:2; A.S.V. Jas. 2:2), where "elders" were the officials. (4) Belief in the early Parousia of the Lord prevailed (Jas. 5:8).

There are difficulties, however, in ascribing this Epistle to Jesus' brother: (1) Its Hellenistic Greek language is not what one would expect from the leader of an Aramaic-speaking church in Jerusalem. (2) There are no references to the Law, of which James was a champion (Acts 15:13 ff., 21:18 ff.; Gal. 2:12). (3) Its denunciation of wealth does not belong to the early days of Christianity, when few rich men were Christians. (4) There is no clear evidence of its authorship until the 3d century, when Origen hesitatingly spoke of it as "the so-called Epistle of James." These arguments support the theory that it was written by an unknown Christian teacher c. A.D. 90. This comparatively late date is necessary to provide for a lapse of time during which Paul's teachings about faith and works had become greatly garbled. In the 4th century the Epistle won a place for itself in the Canon by its high ethical teaching and by the fact that the Church read Jas. 1:1 as an allusion to James the Apostle.

Japheth (jā′fĕth) (etymology uncertain, possibly from Heb. *yafah*, "to be beautiful," *Yepheth*), the 3d son of Noah in both P and J sources (Gen. 5:32, 6:10, 9:18, 10:1); but possibly the 2d, if the enumeration of Gen. 9:24 ff., 10:2, 6, 21 is accepted. Japheth was regarded as a forebear of Gomer, Magog, Madai, Javan, Tubal, Meshech, and Tiras (Gen. 10:2). These inhabitants of the W. highlands of Asia Minor, from the rugged plateaus S. of the Caspian Sea and around the Black Sea to the NE. shores and islands of the Mediterranean—a large part of the known world—were largely of Indo-European stock. Some of them have been "identified," like Madai (Medes); Javan (Ionians or Greeks), etc.

Japheth's 4th son was Javan, ancestor of "the coastland peoples" (R.S.V. Gen. 10:5); A.S.V. "the isles (footnote "coastlands") of the nations"; A.V. "isles of the Gentiles."

Noah's prophecy (Gen. 9:27) suggests that the descendants of Japheth would get along well with Shem (Semites) and would have Canaanites for their servants.

Japhia (jȧ-fī′ȧ). (1) A king of Lachish* in S. Judaea, allied against Gibeon (Josh. 10:3), and executed by Joshua at a Makkedah cave (vv. 22–26). (2) A son of David (II Sam. 5:15; I Chron. 3:7, 14:6). (3) A town on the S. edge of Zebulun (Josh. 19:12), a short distance SW. of the Nazareth of Jesus' day.

Jareb (jā′rĕb) (possibly connected with the root of the Heb. word for "to strive"), the name used in Hos. 5:13, 10:6 to ridicule the love of conflict characteristic of the Assyrian king mentioned by this Hebrew prophet, "King Combat." But a different division of the consonants of the word gives the meaning "the great king" (cf. Accad. "*sharru rabū*"). Identification with Sargon is not acceptable to scholars today. Some authorities believe him to be Tiglath-pileser* III.

Jarmuth (jär′mŭth) ("a height"). (1) Khirbet Yarmûk, a royal Canaanite city (Josh. 10:3) at the time of Israel's Conquest, in the Shephelah c. 8 m. from Beit Jibrîn (Eleutheropolis), on the road to Jerusalem, S. of Beth-shemesh. It became a part of Judah (Josh. 15:35). (2) A town of Issachar (Josh. 21:29) given to Gershonite Levites, the Remeth of Josh. 19:21; cf. Ramoth, I Chron. 6:73.

Jashar (jā′shẽr) (A.V. Jasher), **the Book of** (*Sefer Hayashar*, etymology uncertain; possibly from a word meaning "victorious," but probably not the attributed "upright"), apparently a collection of poems. Fragmentary extracts from this work appear in the song of Joshua (10:13); the elegy of David over Saul and Jonathan (II Sam. 1:18–27); and in I Kings 8:53b (LXX), probably Solomon's Temple dedication speech (A.V. I Kings 8:12 f.). The Song of Deborah* (Judg. 5) may also be from this source. In form, the ballads and their prose introductions—and perhaps also prose conclusions—resembled Ps. 18 and 51 and the Book of Job. The excellence of the fragments incorporated in the O.T. raises the hope that the entire Book of Jashar will eventually be recovered. It cannot have been written before the time of David or of Solomon.

Jason (jā′sŭn) (a popular Gk. name meaning "healing," adopted by Hellenized Jews to designate "Joshua," "Jeshua," or "Jesus"). (1) The name of several individuals mentioned in the Apocrypha. (2) A "kinsman" (probably fellow Jew) of Paul, who entertained him at Thessalonica. Consequently Jason's house was assaulted by a mob which dragged him and "certain brethren" to the rulers of the city because they had proclaimed Jesus to be king, "contrary to the decrees of Caesar" (Acts 17:5–7). Jason was released on bail (v. 9). His ardor for the new faith apparently was not lessened, for in Paul's Letter to the Romans Jason sent salutations from Corinth (Rom. 16:21).

jasper. See BREASTPLATE; JEWELRY.

Jaulan. See GOLAN.

Javan (jā′văn) (from Heb. *Yāwān*, "Greece," "Greeks"), the 4th son of Japheth and father of Elishah (possibly regarded as the people of Hellas, Italy, or a region near Cilicia), Tarshish (perhaps a distant people carrying on a refinery fleet business), Kittim (possibly Cyprus and nearby Mediterranean isles), and Dodanim (cf. Rodanim) (Gen. 10:2, 4; I Chron. 1:5, 7). This name is intended to account for the origin of early island and coastland peoples known to have traded slaves, copper, iron, spices, etc., with merchant cities like Tyre (Isa. 66:19; Ezek. 27:13, 19; cf. Joel 3, A.V. "the Grecians," A.S.V. "sons of the Grecians"). The Heb. of Javan is identical with *Iōn* (*Iawōn*), the eponymous ancestor of the Ionian Hellenes. From Mesopotamian sources Ionians are known to have traded in the bazaars of such cities as Tyre in the 8th century B.C., before Greeks appeared on the scene. Ionians were important trade partners of Persia in the 5th century B.C., to which era the writing of Gen. 10 is ascribed.

javelin. See WEAPONS.

Jazer (jā′zẽr) (Jaazer) (jā′ȧ-zẽr), a town in Ammon, E. of Jordan, possibly a short distance W. or NW. of Rabbath-ammon (the Hellenistic Philadelphia, the modern Amman). The region around what became the town of Jazer was in the midst of highlands so well suited for cattle grazing that the Tribes of Reuben and Gad requested it (Num. 32:1–5). After Israel had captured it (Num. 21:32) it was granted by Moses to Gad on the terms stated in Num. 32: 20–25. Men of Gad's tribe fortified it. Later it became a Levitical city (Josh. 21:39; I Chron. 6:81). Its luxuriant grapevines were treasured (Isa. 16:8 f.; Jer. 48:32). Jazer became a part of Moab (Isa. 16:8 f.), and in the Maccabean period was an Ammonite town (I Macc. 5:8).

jealousy, suspicion or resentment arising from fear or mistrust of another. (1) This appears in the O.T. as an attribute of God, in the sense of His desiring to maintain a unique and pure relation between Himself and Israel (Ex. 20:5; Deut. 5:9; Josh. 24:19; I Kings 14:22, etc.). The almost fanatical zeal for the Lord displayed by some of His adherents is sometimes described as "divine" or "godly" jealousy on their part (II Cor. 11:2). (2) Jealousy in the sense of an undesirable human trait appears in the A.S.V. and the R.S.V. (Rom. 13:13; I Cor. 3:3; II Cor. 12:20, etc.).

Jebus (jē′bŭs) (Jebusi), the city which became Jerusalem*. The E source mentions Jebusites only once (Num. 13:29); P, only in Josh. 15:8. In the Amarna Letters Nos. 179–185 and 285–290, which voice complaints to Egyptian pharaohs from petty Palestinian rulers concerning the arrival of Khabiru (Hebrews probably) c. 1400 B.C., the town is called "Uru-salim" (? "City of Peace"). "Jebusite" may be the late name of a tribe which had earlier been known as the people of Uru-salim. Just when the Jebusite mountain dwellers (Josh. 11:3) arrived is not known. They were of Canaanite extraction and are included in various O.T. "nations" lists, as in Gen. 10:16, 15:21; Ex. 3:8, 17, 13:5, 23:23, 33:2; Deut. 7:1, 20:17; Josh. 3:10, 12:8. The Jebusite is mentioned as a "son" of Canaan (Gen. 10:16; cf. I Chron. 1:14). Ezekiel (16:3) represents the forebears of Jerusalemites as a mixed stock: "Thy birth and thy nativity is of the land of Canaan; thy father was an Amorite, and thy mother an Hittite" (cf. Josh. 10:5). These suggestions tally with the Abrahamic picture. It is not certain whether the Salem visited by Abraham, who there presented tithes to the Amorite priest-king Melchizedek (Gen.14:18–20), was the Jebusite town or some other place.

Several O.T. passages take pains to identify Jebus with what became Jerusalem. Most specific is Josh. 18:16, which tells of Benjamin's territory being bounded by "the end of the mountain that lieth before the valley of the son of Hinnom, and which is in the valley of the giants on the north, and descended to the valley of Hinnom, to the side of Jebusi on the south, and descended to En-rogel." A cartographer could map the city site from these details. To climax the location of what became the site of Israel's capital, the author of Josh. 18 concludes, "Jebusi, which is Jerusalem" (v. 28); and Judg. 19:10 refers to "Jebus, which is Jerusalem." In the era of the Judges this city was already settled. It was a place where wayfarers might lodge overnight on the desert's edge. Hebrews hesitated to stay in this "city of a stranger" (Judg. 19:12). I Chron. 11:4 identifies the later Jerusalem with "Jebus, where the Jebusites were, the inhabitants of the land."

The small town of the Jebusites lay S. of the superb higher area on the eastern hill which in the 10th century B.C. became Solomon's Temple Area and is still a place of prayer. Possibly the Jebusites did not select the better location because this high place overlooking the Kidron Valley was already occupied by a Canaanite shrine they did not wish to displace. The site they developed was a tiny triangle bounded by the Kidron, Tyropoeon, and Zedek Valleys. It was relatively impregnable because of natural rock scarps, and practical because it was near the copious spring Gihon which had been used as far back as man could remember.

During the Hebrew Conquest* the Jebusite King Adonizedek conspired against Gibeon (Josh. 10:1–5) and was slain by Joshua, along with the other four kings of the conspiracy (10:16–26), but Jerusalem was not captured at this time. Somewhat later the men of Judah, whose territory bordered that of the Jebusites (Josh. 15:8), took the city and set it on fire (Judg. 1:8). But the Jebusites were a persistent people, whom neither Judah (Josh. 15:63) nor Benjamin (Judg. 1:21) could expel; the Children of Israel "dwelt among" them (Judg. 3:5). Several centuries after Joshua's day the Jebusite city fell to the Hebrews, when David sent his doughty general Joab and his henchmen up the long-used rock-cut watercourse at Gihon Spring and gained entrance to the high city (II Sam. 5:7–9; I Chron. 11:4–9). David's capture of Jerusalem was the beginning of his conquests in all directions from this center; with the Lord's help "David went on and grew great" (II Sam. 5:10). Meanwhile he had brought up the Ark to Jerusalem (II Sam. 6:4 ff.), and had set in motion forces which led to the establishment here by his son Solomon of the great Temple precincts and the royal palace area (I Kings 6 ff.).

The Jebusites as a people gradually disappeared by merging with the Hebrews. Solomon kept them as bond servants (I Kings 9:20 f.).

David's respect for the property rights of the conquered people is illustrated by his purchase from Araunah* (II Sam. 24:16–24, A.V. "Ornan" I Chron. 21:15–28) of his ancient stone threshing floor that paved the summit of the breeze-swept eastern hill. That large flat rock became the altar of burnt offering in the Temples of Solomon and Herod, and is today encased by the tile-lined, 7th-century Byzantine Dome of the Rock, a most sacred Moslem place of prayer.

"Jerusalem underground" has few more interesting segments than the small area excavated by the Palestine Exploration Fund S. of the hill Ophel, a short distance SE. of the present Dung Gate, a few yards NW. of the Virgin's Fount which it overlooks, commanding the Kidron Valley. In this area British archaeologists laid bare what R. A. S. Macalister termed "an ensemble of remains of building," including an E.-W. rock scarp, apparently a portion of an ancient line of defense; remains of a wall which had been constructed over the scarp, and which clearly had been broken through in an attack; a long stretch of wall within the area originally included in the breached wall, and constructed to fill in or mask the breach; a round fortress bastion built above the breach with stone debris from the breach; and a later building made of the rubble from the above mentioned structure. Here, according to Macalister, are evidences of the breach made by David when his men attacked the Jebusite Jerusalem, and the temporary barricade hurriedly constructed by David across the breach when he was building his city on Ophel. Here was the original Hebrew Jerusalem, c. 200 yds. S. of the present S. wall of the city, and running roughly parallel to the Kidron: "So David dwelt in the fort, and called it the city of David. And David built round about from Millo and inward" (II Sam. 5:9)—"Millo" means "filling"—an accurate description of the material employed in the new stronghold. The text would more accurately read, "round about from what later was called Millo, and inward." When Solomon came to the throne his buildings were more leisurely and carefully constructed than David's emergency work at Millo.

"Zadok the priest" (I Kings 1:8) is believed by some scholars to have been a Jebusite priest of Nehushtan* just before the Davidic development of Jerusalem. Jebusite "abominations" long remained among the people of Israel, and were protested by Ezra (9:1). Nehemiah at the rebuilding of the wall (see WALLS) gave praise to God for having given the land of the Jebusites to the seed of Israel (Neh. 9:8).

Jeconiah (jĕk′ō-nī′*ă*). See JEHOIACHIN.

205. Jebusite bastion, Jerusalem.

Jeduthun (jē-dū′thŭn), the head of one of the groups of sanctuary musicians who had been appointed in charge of sacred music (I Chron. 25:1, 3, 6; cf. 15:17, 19); the father of Galal (I Chron. 9:16). R. H. Pfeiffer views him as the eponymous ancestor of a guild of sanctuary porters or gatekeepers (I Chron. 16:38, 42b), and the "mythical 'father' " of Obed-edom*, the Philistine from Gath living in the territory of the Gibeonites, who sheltered Israel's Ark for three days in his house. The Obed-edom guild of gatekeepers were later promoted to be musicians (I Chron. 16:40–42; II Chron. 5:12, 29:14, 35:15), presumably in the time of Jeduthun. Jeduthun was also called a royal "seer" (II Chron. 35:15). He was "Ethan" of I Chron. 6:44. The P Code of the 5th century B.C. added to the three chief Levitical families the branches of Asaph, Heman, and Jeduthun. But Jeduthun does not impress readers of the O.T. as being a man of flesh and blood, so much as an ancestor of a line of musicians connected with Hebrew sacred music. His name appears in the titles of three Psalms

(39, 62, 77), but the heading would more accurately read "after the manner of Jeduthun"—what Pfeiffer calls a "musical tonality or mode," to show how the music was to be rendered.

The repeated appearance of the name "Jeduthun" in connection with Temple music at historic occasions in the regimes of Solomon (II Chron. 5:12 f.), Hezekiah (II Chron. 29:14), Josiah (II Chron. 35:15), and in the list of those who returned to Jerusalem from Exile and were officials in Jerusalem (Neh. 11:17) accents the importance of musicians in Hebrew worship.

It was formerly believed that the musical guilds attributed to David were of later origin. But W. F. Albright says, in *Archaeology and the Religion of Israel*, that we are justified in believing in the institution at a very early date of groups—possibly hereditary—of sanctuary musicians. Ancient records of the Near East from Egypt and Mesopotamia reveal that Palestine and Syria were noted for their musicians. Recent archaeological evidence from N. Syria indicates the early date at which Canaanite music and musical instruments (copied by Greeks and others) came into wide use. There was pre-Israelite sacred music among Semites in Canaan. Critics need no longer question the historical accuracy of the Chronicler, who gave David credit for organizing guilds of temple musicians (I Chron. 25:1, 3, 6). See MUSIC.

Jehiel (jē-hī′ĕl) ("God lives"). (1) A Levite who played the psaltery when the Ark was moved to Jerusalem (I Chron. 15:18, 20, 16:5). (2, 3) Two other men of David's time (I Chron. 23:8, 27:32). (4) A son of Jehoshaphat (II Chron. 21:2–4). (5) A Levite who aided Hezekiah (II Chron. 29:14, 31:13). (6) A ruler of the Temple in Josiah's reign (II Chron. 35:8). (7, 8, 9) Three men in the time of Ezra (Ezra 8:9, 10:2, 21, 26).

Jehoahaz (jē-hō′*ȧ*-hăz). (1) See AHAZ. (2) See SHALLUM.

Jehoash (jē- hō′sh). See JOASH.

Jehohanan (jē′hō-hā′năn) ("Jehovah is gracious"). (1) One of David's Tabernacle gatekeepers (I Chron. 26:3). (2) A captain under the Judaean King Jehoshaphat) (c. 873–849 B.C.) (II Chron. 17:15, cf. 23:1). (3) A son of Bebai who had married a foreign wife (Ezra 10:28). (4) A priest in King Jehoiakim's time (c. 609–598 B.C.) (Neh. 12:13). (5) A priest contemporary with Nehemiah (Neh. 12:42). (6) A son of Eliashib (A.V. "Johanan") (Ezra 10:6). (7) A son of Tobiah (A.V. "Johanan"* Neh. 6:18).

Jehoiachin (jē-hoi′*ȧ*-kĭn) (abbreviated to "Joiachin," "Yqukin," also appearing as "Jeconiah," Jer. 24:1, 27:20; I Chron. 3:16 f. and "Jechoniah," R.S.V. Matt. 1:11 f., A.V. "Jechonias"; and "Coniah," Jer. 22:24, "Jehovah establishes"), son and successor of King Jehoiakim of Judah. He mounted the throne in 598 B.C. at 18. He was father of seven sons (I Chron. 3:17 f.). After reigning three months and ten days he was taken captive by Nebuchadnezzar and deported to Babylon, along with his mother, wives, and thousands of "men of might," smiths, and craftsmen, and the precious vessels of the Temple (II Kings 24:12–16; II Chron. 36:10 f.). The Chronicler recorded him as one who followed the evil pattern of his predecessors (II Chron. 36:9). While his uncle Zedekiah* was left in charge at Jerusalem the captive monarch resided at Babylon, and apparently never returned to his kingdom. Archaeological finds reported by W. F. Albright, Elihu Grant, L. H. Vincent, and E. F. Weidner (see *BA* Vol. V, No. 4, Dec. 1942) have led to a revision of our knowledge of Jehoiachin. Three clay jar handles unearthed at Beth-shemesh* and at Kiriath-sepher (see DEBIR) all bear the imprint of a seal carrying in the old Hebrew or Phoenician script the phrase, "Belonging to Eliakim, steward of Yqukin." Albright believes that these seals show that crown property was in charge of Eliakim* during Jehoiachin's exile, and that Zedekiah, believing in the possible return any day of his royal nephew, did not seize the property of the rightful ruler. The Ernest F. Weidner find was a "vaulted building" near the Ishtar Gate of Babylon, whose 14 rooms contained almost 300 clay tablets (595–570 B.C.) carrying receipts of oil, barley, and other supplies which had been rationed to captive workmen and exiles from many lands. King Jehoiachin ("Yqukin") is mentioned on the tablets as receiving rations. Therefore it is believed he was free to move about the city and was not in prison—at least not in the early years of his exile, as had previously been thought. The imprisonment from which he was released in the 37th year of his captivity (II Kings 25:27), when Evil-Merodach (Amel-Marduk) succeeded Nebuchadnezzar (562 B.C.), was due to some incident after his first years of exile. Moreover, the "vaulted room" tablets carry the names of five sons of Jehoiachin and their Jewish attendant, Kenaiah. These sons are thereby shown to have been born before 592 B.C., with the eldest, Shealtiel*, father of Zerubbabel, probably born c. 598 at the latest. This conclusion makes Prince Zerubbabel of the Second Temple reconstruction (c. 520–515 B.C.) older than had been supposed when the prophecies of Haggai were delivered, as Albright points out. The Weidner tablets also reveal (contrary to C. C. Torrey's former opinion that the Jewish Exiles were not free to be farmers and craftsmen) that rations were issued to one Jewish gardener and probably to many more whose receipts have not yet been found, and to hundreds of skilled craftsmen assembled from the whole Middle East (cf. II Kings 24:14 ff.).

It is interesting to speculate about the reasons for Jehoiachin's being given "preferential treatment" above other kings captive at the same time in Babylon. He was addressed kindly by Evil-Merodach; his throne or chair was "above the throne of the kings that were with him in Babylon"; he had changes of garments; and plenty of food to eat all the days of his life, "a daily rate for every day" (II Kings 25:27–30). This passage tallies with the evidence of the Weidner clay ration receipts.

The clay tablet mentioning Jehoiachin dates from 592 B.C., the same year when

Ezekiel had his vision of "abominations" (Ezek. 8). The Jews of the Exile dated events in such-and-such a year of the exile of King Jehoiachin, perhaps an indication of his royal status. It is also possible that the Babylonians looked upon Jehoiachin as Judah's legitimate ruler, who might some day be restored to his Jerusalem throne.

Jehoiada (jē-hoi'ā-dā) (R.S.V. Joiada, Neh. 3:6) ("Jehovah knows"). (1) The father of the Benaiah* who served as commander of David's bodyguard (II Sam. 8:16, 18, 20:23) and under Solomon as army head (I Kings 4:4). Jehoiada's name is usually linked with that of his son, who was powerful enough to slay a lion on a snowy day (I Chron. 11:22 ff.). It was probably this Jehoiada, a leader "of the house of Aaron," who led many to join David at Ziklag (I Chron. 12:27). Some think the text of I Chron. 27:34 seems to confuse Jehoiada with Benaiah, which perhaps should read "Benaiah (son of Jehoiada)." But it is possible that a grandson of Jehoiada with the same name may here be intended as one high among David's officials.

(2) The chief priest of the Temple under Ahaziah, Athaliah*, and Joash, and the husband of Jehoshabeath, daughter of King Jehoram and sister of King Ahaziah of Judah, who saved the seven-year-old heir Joash* (Jehoash) from the murderous rage of Athaliah (II Kings 11:2; II Chron. 22:11). After six years Jehoiada executed a *coup d'état* which not only helped save Judah from Israel, but put Jehoiada in a position to champion the religion of the Lord. He set Joash, descendant of David, on the throne (II Kings 11:4–16), made a covenant between the king, Judah, and God (vv. 17 ff.), and instituted reforms that included the destruction of Baal shrines (v. 18). He trained the young King Joash in the ways of righteousness (II Kings 12:2); and at his request repaired the Temple and financed it from offerings placed in a large chest which he put beside the altar (12:9–16). Jehoiada died at an advanced age, and as a tribute to his effective service to the state he was buried in David's original "city" of Jerusalem in the tombs of the kings (II Chron. 24:15 f.). But after his death Joash turned away from God, and when reproved by the priest's son Zechariah (v. 20) Joash had Zechariah stoned to death (v. 21), thus inviting God's judgment in the form of a Syrian invasion (v. 23), his own murder in the royal bed (v. 25), and his burial elsewhere than in the tombs of the kings.

(3) A priest in Jeremiah's era who was replaced by Zephaniah (Jer. 29:26). (4) Paseah's son, who took part in repairing the walls of Jerusalem, A.V. Neh. 3:6 (R.S.V. "Joiada"). (5) Eliashib's priestly son, who held office in the regime of Nehemiah (Neh. 12:10 f. "Joiada"), but whose son married a daughter of Sanballat the Horite (13:28).

Jehoiakim (jē-hoi'ā-kĭm) (abbreviated "Joiakim" and "Yauqim," "Jehovah raises up"; originally "Eliakim"), king of Judah in Jerusalem; given this name by the Egyptian Pharaoh-nechoh, who placed him on the throne of Judah (II Kings 23:34) after deposing his brother Jehoahaz II (Shallum) after his three months' reign c. 609 B.C. (II Chron. 36:4). Jehoiakim was the 2d son of King Josiah of Judah. His mother was Zebudah, daughter of Pedaiah of Rumah (II Kings 23:36). His brother was the Zedekiah* who later was set up as vassal king at Jerusalem by Nebuchadnezzar (II Kings 24:17; I Chron. 3:15). Determining to keep in the good graces of his Egyptian overlord, Jehoiakim levied heavy taxes on his people and turned them over to the pharaoh (II Kings 23:34 f.). However, within seven years Egyptian control was superseded by that of the Chaldaeans. Jehoiakim's 11-years' reign (609–598 B.C.) was marked by apostasy from Yahweh which was repeatedly censured by the prophet Jeremiah (Jer. 25, 26) at the risk of his life. Jehoiakim's bold irreverence displayed itself in the manuscript-burning incident described in Jer. 36:1–26—a dramatic event whose sequel was the preparation of a fresh roll and appendix, pronouncing again the doom prepared by the Lord for the king and his evil subjects at the hand of the King of Babylon. Jeremiah's prophecy was fulfilled with the arrival of Nebuchadnezzar (II Kings 24:1), whom Jehoiakim served three years, but against whom he at length rebelled. The might of Chaldea, pressed heavily against the capital and the king died or possibly was assassinated (II Kings 24:6). He was succeeded (598 B.C.) by his young son Jehoiachin*, who in his father's stead was carried captive to Babylon (597 B.C., II Kings 24:15), while Zedekiah, brother of Jehoiakim, became Nebuchadnezzar's puppet ruler.

Jehonadab (jē-hŏn'ā-dăb) (Jonadab) ("Jehovah is bounteous"), the son of the Kenite Rechab, whom Jehu of Israel took into his chariot and made his assistant in a religious reform aimed at exterminating Baal worshippers (II Kings 10:15, 23). Jehonadab, by emphasizing the values of the ascetic life of tent dwellers and of total abstinence from wine, decried the building of houses, cultivation of vines, and sowing of fields. Jeremiah saw in the obedience of Jehonadab's later disciples to their founder's precepts (Jer. 35:3–19), during the corrupt regime of King Jehoiakim of Judah, the model for Israel's obedience to the commands of the Lord.

Jehonathan (jē-hŏn'ā-thăn) ("Jehovah hath given"). (1) Son of Uzziah, appointed by David as overseer of the king's treasures (I Chron. 27:25; R.S.V. "Jonathan"). (2) A Levite sent by Jehoshaphat to teach in Judah (II Chron. 17:8). (3) A priest in Jehoiakim's time (Neh. 12:18). See also JONATHAN.

Jehoram (jē-hō'răm) (abbreviated Joram, "Jehovah is exalted"), the name of two partly contemporaneous kings of Israel and Judah. (1) King of Israel (c. 849–842 B.C.), the son of Ahab (II Kings 3:1), succeeding the brief reign of his brother Ahaziah. He was a contemporary of three kings of Judah including Jehoshaphat (II Kings 3:1), who aided him in dealing with a revolt of Moab (II Kings 3:7–27). Events in connection with this revolt are commemorated in the Moabite Stone inscription of Mesha. Possibly the siege of Samaria by the Syrians (II Kings 6, 7) should be dated in his reign. Elisha* was active in his reign and accompanied the expedition against Moab (II Kings 3:11–20). Jehoram may have been the king to whom the Syrian king sent his leprous general, Naaman, to seek a cure from Israel's God (II Kings 5:1–27). Wounded in the siege of Ramoth-gilead by Hazael of Syria, Jehoram went to recuperate at the well-watered Jezreel (II Kings 8:29), where he was murdered by the usurper Jehu*, who succeeded him.

(2) King of Judah (c. 849–842 B.C.), the eldest son of King Jehoshaphat (I Kings 22:50; II Kings 1:17; II Chron. 21:1, 3), with whom he was associated on the throne for about five years before succeeding him at the age of 32 during the reign of King Jehoram of Israel. He reigned eight years (II Chron. 21:5). He married Athaliah*, daughter of Ahab, and under her influence encouraged Baal worship in Judah (II Kings 8:18, 26). He warred against the Philistines and Arabians (II Chron. 21:16–17, 22:1), who captured his wives and all his sons except Ahaziah. He died unmourned of an incurable bowel disease foretold by Elijah (II Chron. 21:18 f.). Many doubt the historicity of the Chronicler at this point.

(3) A priest appointed by Jehoshaphat to teach the Law (II Chron. 17:8). See JORAM.

Jehoshabeath (jē′hō-shăb′ē-ăth) (Jehosheba [jē-hŏsh′ē-bȧ] II Kings 11:2) ("Jehovah is an oath"), the daughter of King Jehoram and wife of the priest Jehoiada (II Chron. 22:11 f.). She saved her young nephew Joash* (Jehoash) from the murderous wrath of Athaliah by hiding him during the six-years' reign of the wicked queen, mother of the slain Ahaziah.

Jehoshaphat (jē-hŏsh′ȧ-făt) ("Jehovah judges"). (1) A son of Ahilud who served as recorder under David and Solomon (II Sam. 8:16, 20:24; I Kings 4:3). (2) A son of Paruah, stationed in Issachar as one of Solomon's commissary officers (I Kings 4:17). (3) A son of Nimshi and the father of King Jehu of Israel (II Kings 9:2, 14). (4) A priest who blew a trumpet before the Ark in David's organization (I Chron. 15:24, R.S.V. Joshaphat).

(5) The 4th king of Judah after the division of Solomon's kingdom; a son of King Asa and Azubah, daughter of Shilhi (I Kings 15:24; II Chron. 20:31). He was apparently associated with his diseased father on the throne for five years, then succeeded him and reigned at Jerusalem a total of 25 years (c. 873–849 B.C.). He was contemporary with the kings Omri, Ahab, and Jehoram of Israel; and early in his reign cemented cordial relations between the two rival kingdoms by marrying the crown prince Jehoram to Ahab's daughter Athaliah (II Kings 8:18, 26; A.S.V. margin, "granddaughter" of Omri). This act, openly inviting Baal worship, was inconsistent with the reforms attributed to Jehoshaphat by the Chronicler (II Chron. 19:3); but Jehoshaphat is depicted as on the whole a good king. He continued the reforms of his father; and his reign enjoyed the type of security often linked with prosperity. He invoked the protection vouchsafed such rulers as Solomon (II Chron. 20:9, cf. II Chron. 6:24–30). He increased the strength of his walled cities, forts, army, and business enterprises; and then was prepared for such military enterprises as his alliance with Ahab of Israel against Ramoth-gilead (II Chron. 18:28); assistance to Jehoram (II Kings 3:4–27) against Mesha of Moab; and an advance against a strong confederacy of Edomites, Ammonites, and Moabites (II Chron. 20:1–30). He organized a maritime commercial expedition to Ophir which was wrecked near Ezion-geber (I Kings 22:48).

His religious reforms swept away much of the Asherah* worship, though he failed to remove all the high places (I Kings 22:43; II Chron. 20:33), and was rebuked by the prophet Jehu* for assuming regrettable attitudes (II Chron. 19:2 f.). Yet he is given credit for reorganizing his nation's judicial system. R. H. Pfeiffer points out that the Chronicler represents him as organizing the Sanhedrin*. He sent Levites and priests to teach in the cities of Judah, expounding the Book of the Law of the Lord (II Chron. 17:7–9). Neighbor nations were so impressed with him that in some instances they refrained from war and sent him gifts—the Philistines, silver; the Arabians, rams and goats. Jehoshaphat was buried in the tombs of the kings in David's city at Jerusalem, and was succeeded by his son Jehoram (II Chron. 21:1).

Jehoshaphat, Valley of, of uncertain location, though from the 4th century A.D. it has been identified by many Christians and Jews as part of the wide Kidron* Valley, extending between the plateau where Jerusalem lies and the Mount of Olives, the scene where all nations must stand before the Lord on the Day of Righteous Judgment (Joel 3:2) (see ESCHATOLOGY). Moslems today regard this Jerusalem Valley as the scene where God will compel the soul of every man to walk on a wire, with angels to aid the good, while the evil drop into the cleft below. The belief of countless thousands in Kidron as the scene of the Last Judgment is attested by the presence of thousands of Jewish and Moslem tombs lining both sides of the Valley. Since pre-Exilic times Jews chose to be buried here, that they might be near the place of "the last day."

Jehovah. See GOD.

Jehovah-jireh ("Jehovah sees"), a name given by Abraham to the place where the providential ram appeared in the thicket (Gen. 22:14).

Jehovah-nissi ("Jehovah is my banner"), the name given by Moses (Ex. 17:15) to the altar he erected after defeating the Amalekites.

Jehovah-shalom ("Jehovah is peace"), the name attached to an altar at Ophrah by Gideon (Judg. 6:24).

Jehovah-shammah ("Jehovah is there"), the name joyously attached to the restored Jerusalem (A.S.V. Ezek. 48:35; cf. Isa. 60:14–22, 62:2; Rev. 21:2 f.).

Jehovah-tsidkenu ("Jehovah is our righteousness"), the name given by Jeremiah (23:6, 33:16) to the wholly Righteous King who would reign over Israel after their Return from Captivity.

Jehu (jē′hū) ("Jehovah is He"). (1) One of David's heroes from Anathoth, near Jerusalem (I Chron. 12:3). (2) A prophet, a son of Hanani, who protested against King Baasha (c. 900–877 B.C.) of Israel and his house for their violations of the Lord's will (I Kings 16:1–4, 7, 12). A "book of Jehu" (II Chron. 20:34) is cited by the Chronicler as his source for events in the reign of Jehoshaphat, King of Judah (c. 873–849 B.C.).

(3) A son of Jehoshaphat (not the King of Judah), son of Nimshi (II Kings 9:2), anointed by a member of a prophetic guild at

206. Jehu, King of Israel, or his ambassador, kneeling with tribute at the feet of Shalmaneser III, Assyrian king and conqueror (c. 859–824 B.C.), from obelisk in British Museum.

the command of Elisha at Ramoth-gilead and commissioned to overthrow the Ahab dynasty and take over the throne of the Kingdom of Israel (v. 6). He and his loyal henchmen killed King Jehoram* of Israel (c. 849–842 B.C.), who was recovering in Jezreel from wounds received in a war against Hazael of Syria (II Kings 8:29); King Ahaziah of Judah (c. 842 B.C.), who was visiting his uncle Jehoram; the evil queen mother Jezebel (II Kings 9:33), with all the heirs and officials of Ahab (10:11); and prophets of Baal (10:25). In this wholesale slaughter the swift chariot driver Jehu's motives were mixed. His moral purge was colored by political intrigue designed to insure the throne of Israel for himself. Though Elisha* is represented as sanctioning his procedure at a later time, Hosea deplored it (Hos. 1:4). Jehu lived to see Hazael of Syria seize part of his land E. of the Jordan, areas within the territories of Manasseh and Gad. Jehu also paid tribute to Shalmaneser* III, as depicted on the Black Obelisk of the Assyrian ruler. His dynasty, the 4th of Israel, was continued by kings Jehoahaz (c. 815–801 B.C.); Joash (801–786); Jeroboam II (c. 786–746); and Zechariah (c. 746–745). (4) A man of Judah (I Chron. 2:38). (5) A Simeonite (I Chron. 4:35).

Jehudi (jĕ-hū′dī) (possibly a naturalized Jew), an officer in the service of King Jehoiakim of Judah (609–598 B.C.), who was sent by the court to ask Baruch, the secretary of Jeremiah*, to read Jeremiah's writings, later burned by the king (Jer. 36:14–23).

Jemimah (A.V. Jemima) ("dove"), the first of Job's three daughters born after the return of his prosperity (Job 42:14).

Jephthah (jĕf′thȧ) (A.V. Jephthae Heb. 11:32, "he opens"), one of Israel's most important judges (an official so-called from Canaanite *shôphet*, meaning a trustworthy, popular magistrate who was a court of appeal for civil disputes among tribesmen). According to the J source (see SOURCES) Jephthah was the son of a Gileadite and a harlot (Judg. 11:1), who, when cast out by the legitimate sons of his father, fled to the land of Tob and gathered about him sturdy if unscrupulous henchmen. The E source makes Jephthah a respectable house owner at Mizpah (Judg. 11:34). When in the 11th century B.C. Gilead was hard pressed by the Ammonite foe, fellow tribesmen came to Jephthah begging him to return and be their champion, and offering him the leadership of the clan (Judg. 11:4–8). Something about the man W. F. Albright has called a "bastard adventurer" must have made his hateful kinsmen detect in him some special power believed to be an outpouring of God's grace (Judg. 11:29)—a quality associated with other judges of early Israel, like Ehud, Barak, and Gideon. In the long conversation between the King of Ammon and Jephthah (Judg. 11:12–28)—probably originally addressed to the Moabites (cf. Num. 20–22) and dated from the 7th century B.C.—events in Israel's Conquest are rehearsed and a statement made (Judg. 11:24) which raises the question whether Jephthah recognized the existence of other gods than Yahweh. But the late date of these verses, together with the ad hominem character of the argument, means that henotheism in the era of the Judges is not here demonstrated.

Tragedy lurked in the decisive victory won by Jephthah. He had made a vow to devote, as a burnt offering to God, whatever he first saw coming out of the door of his house. It proved to be his only child, a young girl (Judg. 11:34). Loyal to his vow, the brokenhearted Jephthah became a donor of a living sacrifice, common in his age, but protested against by the code of Israel. The departure of the girl to the mountains for two months to bewail her virginity (Judg. 11:37) was perhaps an indirect way of stating that the young woman had no husband to spring to her defense and no offspring to perpetuate her memory. The story may have been incorporated in Judges out of the background of the pagan custom of human sacrifice practiced by the neighbors of early Israel; perhaps it was suggested by the Tammuz rites long popular in the Middle East, as at Byblos, where a youthful fertility god (cf. Adonis), responsible for renewed vegetation, was worshipped with ceremonies that involved bewailing the "dead" deity. The E account of 11:34–40 explains the custom of Gilead women who mourned four days every year for Jephthah's daughter.

Jephthah's last campaign was a victorious one against the Ephraimites, who were disgruntled because he had not invited them to go on the campaign against Ammon (Judg. 12:1–6). For an interesting use of "accent detection" see Judg. 12:6. Jephthah judged Israel six years; he was buried in a town of his native Gilead (v. 7). Because Jephthah had no heirs and left no dynasty, the tribes he had controlled fell apart after his death.

Jerah (jē′rȧ), a descendant of Joktan (Gen. 10:26; I Chron. 1:20), a forebear of people in an unidentified district, probably in SE. Arabia.

Jerahmeel (jĕ-rä′mē-ĕl) ("may God have compassion"). (1) The eponymous ancestor of a group of non-Israelites, Jerahmeelites, living in the extreme S. of Palestine, where David came into contact with them after his flight from Saul (I Sam. 27:10, 30:29). The Chronicler (I Chron. 2:9, 18) makes Jerahmeel a descendant of Judah and a brother of Caleb*. (2) A Levite, son of Kish (I Chron. 24:29). (3) One of three ordered to arrest Baruch and Jeremiah; called "the king's son" (Jer. 36:26), but this may be an official title and does not necessarily mean he was Jehoiakim's son.

Jerash See GERASA.

Jeremiah ("Jehovah lifts up" or "Jehovah loosens [the womb]"). (1) The head of a family of Manasseh E. of the Jordan (I Chron. 5:24). (2) A Benjamite efficient in the use of the bow and sling, who joined David at Ziklag (I Chron. 12:4). (3), (4) Two Gadites, swift of foot and users of shield and buckler, who enlisted with David (I Chron. 12:8, 10, 13). (5) A priest who went up to Jerusalem with Zerubbabel (Neh. 12:1); sealed the Covenant with Nehemiah (10:2); and joined in the procession dedicating the wall (Neh. 12:34). It may be that the Jeremiah of 10:2 is a different individual. (6) The father of a Rechabite (Jer. 35:3). (7) A man of Libnah, the father of Hamutal, wife of Josiah and mother of two Judaean kings—Jehoahaz (II Kings 23:31) and Zedekiah (II Kings 24:18; Jer. 52:1).

(8) ("Jehovah establishes or lifts up"), one of the three Major Prophets. His prophecy is the 24th book of the O.T., and the chief source of information concerning the 7th-century seer who gives the book its name.

Jeremiah, a century after Isaiah, lived during the subjection of Jerusalem in 609 B.C., its capture in 597B.C., and its destruction in 587. His life (c. 640–587 B.C.) brought him in touch with the events in the reigns of the last of the Judaean kings:

Manasseh (c. 687–642 B.C.)	II Chron. 33:1–20; Jer. 15:4
Amon (c. 642–640 B.C.)	II Kings 21:18–26; II Chron. 33:21–24
Josiah (c. 640–609 B.C.)	II Kings 21:24 23:30; Jer. 25:3
B.C., 3 mo.)	22:10–12
Jehoiakim (c. 609–	II Kings 23:34–24:6;
Jehoiachin (598–597 B.C., 3 mo.)	II Kings 24:6–15; Jer. 52:31–34
Zedekiah (597–587 B.C.)	II Kings 24:17–21; Jer. 21:1–7, chap. 34,

The domestic troubles in Judah were chiefly the result of international crisis; a three-cornered contest for world supremacy was on between Assyria, Babylonia, and Egypt. Assyria had dominated for 200 years but was growing weak. Babylon (under Chaldaean leaders) was becoming more powerful. Egypt was staging a comeback. Judah's foreign policy, based on expediency, was mercurial. Hordes of Scythians from S. Russia—once allies of Assyria—were also threatening the former empire of Ashurbanipal, but despite Jeremiah's fears did not overrun Judah. Pharaoh-nechoh imposed the Egyptian yoke on Judah (II Kings 23:29–35), but at Carchemish* (605 B.C.) he was defeated by Nebuchadnezzar*, the Chaldaean crown prince, and Palestine became a Babylonian province (II Kings 24:7; Jer. 46:1–12). These fluctuating forces made little Judah, eager for its independence, an arena where political, moral, and religious convictions clashed.

As with many Bible personalities, the events of Jeremiah's life are not chronologically arranged in Scripture—many attempts have been made to rearrange in correct sequence the biographical data concerning any of the prophets. Jeremiah was born at Anathoth* of an old priestly family (Jer. 1:1) which held landed estates (Jer. 32:6–15). Anathoth was in the territory of Benjamin in the Northern Kingdom, and Jeremiah was a N. Israelite at heart (cf. Jer. 3:11 f.), though he eventually lived in Jerusalem. Hosea, the only northerner among the

207. Jeremiah and the potter, *by William Hole.*

reforming prophets, profoundly influenced Jeremiah. He was called to his prophetic mission as a "child" (1:2, 6 f., 25:3); the Lord had selected him for this task even before his birth (1:5). Confidence in his divine mission asserted itself over his natural timidity (1:6, 8–10, 18); he was more like an oak than a weeping willow. Throughout his career he attacked the apostasy of the people, the immoralities of life, the self-deception of superficial reformers, and dangerous international alliances. Among those whom Jeremiah attacked were: (1) the townsmen of Anathoth (Jer. 11:21); (2) the temple priests (20:1–6); (3) false prophets (5:31, 23:9–40, chap. 28); (4) vindictive rulers (36:29–31); (5) the military authorities (38:4). The people's behavior so nauseated Jeremiah that he longed for a place of quiet escape (9:2). His life of strife so wearied him that he mourned his combative nature (15:10); even cursed the day of his birth (20:14); but could not put out the burning fire within, which drove him on (20:9). He won for himself adherents and friends, such as the better men of the community (26:16–24), an Ethiopian in the king's service (38:7–13), etc. In vain he pleaded with King Zedekiah to put his trust in the Lord and submit to the Chaldeans (ch. 27–29). When Jerusalem was taken by the Chaldeans in 587 the aging prophet was treated with great consideration by the orders of Nebuchadnezzar (39:11–14). Whether he was freed in Jerusalem at the time of its fall, or later at Ramah from a caravan of exiles (two interwoven accounts of his release conflict), he was allowed to go without hindrance to Gedaliah*, the new Israelite governor whose headquarters were at Mizpah (40:1–6). After the evil plot which led to the assassination of the governor, Jeremiah and his secretary, Baruch*, in a company of Jews fearful of Nebuchadnezzar's vengeance, were forced to flee to Egypt (40:7–43:7). At Tahpanhes, believed to be 2 m. W. of the modern El Kantara on the Suez Canal, Jeremiah laid stones in one of Pharaoh's palaces in a dramatic act of prophetic significance (43:8–13), and in his last oracle denounced the pagan cults in Egypt to which the Jews had succumbed (chap. 44). He probably died in Egypt.

The Book of Jeremiah has three main parts and a historic appendix:

(1) Chaps. 1–25—The words of Jeremiah, many perhaps written or dictated by himself. These include data on his call (1:4–19), his reaction to current events (2:1–15:9), his confessions and speeches (15:10–20:18), his denunciation of kings and prophets (21–23), and a vision (24).

(2) Chaps. 26–45—Biographical material concerning the prophet, probably written by his secretary, Baruch. This section records a Temple address by Jeremiah and its consequences (chap. 26), his dramatic effort to influence Judaean foreign policy (27–29), his hopes for the future of the land and its peoples (30–33), his experiences under Jehoiakim and Zedekiah (34–36) and the destruction of Jerusalem (37–39), and finally his last years (40–45).

(3) Chaps. 46–51—Oracles against foreign nations attributed to Jeremiah (46:1) but put in their present form by a later editor or editors: Egypt (chap. 46); Philistia (47); Moab (48); Ammon (49:1–6); Edom (49:7–22); Damascus (49:23–27; Kedar and Hazor (desert Bedouins) (49:28–33); Elam (49:34–39); and Babylon (50:1–51:64).

The order of the oracles differs radically in the Hebrew and the LXX versions.

(4) The historical appendix (chap. 52) on the fall of Jerusalem quotes from II Kings 24:18–25:21, 27–30.

208. Hebrew clay stamp used for sealing wine jars, with reversed inscription of Jer. 48:11. Found in Babylonia, it dates from the early Christian era.

Jeremiah's dictations to his secretary Baruch were written down upon a scroll of leather or more probably of papyrus (36:2) which King Jehoiakim cut up with a knife and burned column by column (36:23, 28). Some think much of the book was edited by Baruch, to whom they attribute the sections in prosaic, legalistic, Deuteronomic diction, yet the spirit, style, and unique character of Jeremiah are obvious. Jeremiah made abundant use of symbols taken from the life of the day, among which were the loincloth (13:1–11); the wine jars (13:12–14); the potter (18:1–11); the broken jar (19); and the figs (24:1–10). He often dramatized his message (27–28). The "confessions" (11:18–23, 12:1–3, 5 f., 15:10–20, 17:14–18, 18:18–23, 20:7–12, 14–18; cf. 1:4–19, 6:11, 8:21–9:1) inaugurated a style of introspective expression that was followed in many of the Psalms and that also marked a shift of religious emphasis from the nation to the individual. With Jeremiah it was only a matter of time before the Temple and its worship would cease to be. But he could do without them because he had discovered God was not confined to human institutions; religion had continued without Shiloh* and would continue without Jerusalem (26:9). Jeremiah was the prophet of spiritual religion. This individualism, after repentance, would be the basis of a new covenant* with God (31:31 ff.). Fresh expression of conceptions of God is found in such choice passages as 3:4 f., 19, 4:2, 9:24, 14:8 f., 17:10, 20:12, 31:3, 34.

The mistaken attachment of Jeremiah's name to the authorship of Lamentations* has given him an undeserved reputation for weeping.

Jesus was thought by some to be the returned Jeremiah (Matt. 16:14).

Jericho (jĕr′ĭ-kō) (meaning uncertain; *BDB*, "place of fragrance"; Albright, NW. Semitic moon god, *Yariḥ;* but see Accad. *jarḫu*, "water hole, pool"), an ancient city located near an oasis on the W. side of the S. Jordan Valley, 10 m. NW. of the Dead Sea, and 825 ft. below sea level. It controlled the important E.–W. route across the Jordan Valley from Jerusalem, 15 m. to the SW., to Transjordan (see Josh. 2:7). Two mounds in the area are important for the history of ancient Jericho; (1) Tell es-Sultan, the site of O.T. Jericho, 1½ m. NW. of er-Riha (modern Jericho). E. of the tell lies 'Ain es-Sultan, a copious water supply still known as "Elisha's Fountain," whose brackish waters the prophet once purified (II Kings 2:19–22; cf. Josh. 16:1). To the W. rise the hills of Judaea (see Josh. 18:12). (2) Tulul el-'Alayiq, the site of Herodian and N.T. Jericho, c. 2 m. S. of the earlier city.

209. Excavation of O.T. Jericho.

(1) *O.T. Jericho* has been excavated three times: by Ernst Sellin and Carl Watzinger (1908–11), by John Garstang (1930–36), and by Kathleen Kenyon (1952–58). The history of the site sketched below is based on these most recent discoveries.

The earliest definite evidence for occupation of ancient Jericho consists of a curious structure, interpreted as a sanctuary, consisting of a rectangle of natural clay resting immediately above bedrock, surrounded by a wall of stones in which wooden posts were set at intervals. Associated flints show that these remains are Mesolithic (9th millennium B.C., latest radiocarbon dates). Elsewhere on the site are traces of a hitherto unknown culture, provisionally labeled "proto-Neolithic," with no evidence of any permanent structures. This phase was followed by the remains of two pre-pottery Neolithic cultures which can be described as true towns. The earliest, which dates to the 8th millennium B.C., is one of the most ancient urban settlements in the world. At this early date, houses were round with earth floors. A high level of community organization is attested by massive stone fortifications, which included a great tower built against the inside of the wall (see Kenyon, *Archaeological Discoveries in the Holy Land*, 1967, pp. 19–28; also *BASOR* 167, 1962, pp. 25 ff.).

This phase was followed by a second pre-pottery Neolithic culture which is distinguished by houses of rectangular plan, built of elongated, rounded, thumb-impressed bricks, and highly burnished, colored plaster floors. As many as 19 building phases of this period have come to light, and this settlement was also surrounded by a large town wall which was rebuilt several times. From this period come nine human skulls discovered beneath the floor of a house; they were covered with plaster, which was modeled in the form of human facial features, and the eyes were inset with shells. These skulls, together with one building which may have served as a temple, illustrate early religious practices. This phase dates to about the 7th millennium B.C.

The next Neolithic culture is distinguished by the presence of pottery. The people of the first phase of this period (Garstang's Level IX; Kenyon's Pottery Neolithic A; c. 6th millennium B.C.), lived in pits cut into the ruins of the last pre-pottery town. During the second phase (Garstang's Level VIII; Kenyon's Pottery Neolithic B; 5th millennium B.C.), houses were again built on the site, and at least three building phases have been distinguished. Plano-convex mud brick, i.e., round bricks with a flat base, was used in these constructions. The pottery of this phase is much more advanced than that of the first phase.

The Early Bronze Age (c. 3300–2300 B.C.) is well represented at Jericho. The evidence for the early part of this period (EB I, or "Proto-Urban") comes from tombs, for the first time cut into the rock. In them were multiple secondary burials of up to 400 individuals. From these beginnings developed a new urban culture (c. 2900–2300 B.C.). Houses were well built of mud brick, and timber; the latter was used for roofing beams and as posts to support the roof. The town wall, constructed of rectangular mud brick set on stone foundations, was rebuilt no fewer than 17 times during this period, having been repeatedly destroyed by enemy attacks and earthquakes. The last Early Bronze town wall was erected in haste and was burned before completion. It was this final phase of the Early Bronze Age defenses that Garstang erroneously dated to the 14th century B.C., ascribing its destruction to Joshua (see *PEQ*, 1951, pp. 101–138). The most recent excavations have clearly shown that it was destroyed c. 2300 B.C.

The Middle Bronze I, or Intermediate Early–Middle Bronze period (c. 2300–1900 B.C.), was quite different from that of Early Bronze. New pottery forms, weapons, building techniques, and burial customs were introduced at this time. The only surviving structures of this period are found on the slopes of the mound and consist of thin walls of greenish mud brick. Virtually all MB I tombs contain only one burial and the meagerest tomb equipment.

Middle Bronze II (c. 1900–1500 B.C.) represents another sharp cultural break. New fortifications were introduced, of which three successive phases have been found at Jericho. Each consists of a massive sloping retaining wall of stone, and a high, plastered slope which was crowned with a mud brick wall. Ten building phases of this period were found on the east side of the mound. Well-built houses contained quantities of jars filled with carbonized grain, loom weights, and saddle querns. But the most exciting discoveries were made in the multiple burial tombs of this period. In several of them, wooden furniture—such as tables, stools, bed, boxes inlaid with carved bone—woven mats and baskets, meat, and even human flesh and hair were preserved. The last MB town was destroyed by fire c. 1560 B.C.

Little evidence of Late Bronze Age occupation (c. 1500–1200 B.C.) has survived, because of erosion of the mound by wind and rain. Only one building (Garstang's "Middle Building") and the foundations and floor of another have been discovered on the mound; no trace of fortifications has been found. Furthermore, even these meager remains date only to the 14th century B.C. There is nothing characteristic of the 13th century, the age of Joshua. No trace exists of the Jericho which plays such a prominent role in the Biblical account of the entry of the Israelites into Canaan (Josh. 6). Any explanation for this apparent discrepancy is purely hypothetical.

The O.T. record states that after being abandoned since its destruction by Joshua, Jericho was rebuilt during the reign of Ahab, King of Israel (c. 869–850 B.C.), by Hiel of Bethel (I Kings 16:34), who lost his sons in accordance with the curse Joshua laid on Jericho (Josh. 6:26). Again, there is no evidence of any occupation on the mound which can be dated to the 9th century B.C., with the exception of a single tomb (*Jericho* II, pp. 482–489). It is only in the 7th century that there is again evidence of occupation, ending about the time of the Exile. Three building phases have come to light at the foot of the W. side of the mound. Judging from their location, it is clear that the site was unwalled in this period. It is the remains of this settlement, the last on Tell es-Sultan, near which Zedekiah was captured by the army of Nebuchadnezzar (II Kings 25:5; II Chron.

210. Part of N.T. Jericho. This section of the *tell* was originally a Hellenistic tower on which Herod the Great erected a cut stone building; a large concrete edifice was built on this soon afterward.

28:15; Jer. 39:5, 52:8). See Kenyon, *Digging up Jericho*, 1957; *AOTS*, 1967, pp. 264–275; prelim. reports in *PEQ*, 1952–57; tombs, *Jericho* I, 1960, and II, 1965; for earlier excavations, see J. Garstang, *The Story of Jericho*, 1948, and *Joshua–Judges*, 1931.

(2) The excavation of *N.T. Jericho* at Tulûl Abū el-'Alâyiq was conducted by J. L. Kelso and D. C. Baramki in 1950, and by J. B. Pritchard and F. V. Winnett in 1951. The site was first occupied in the Chalcolithic and Early Bronze periods, as shown by some of the pottery, but no walls of this period were found. There was no further occupation of the site until Herodian times. The great mounds or *tells* on which the winter capital of Herod and Archelaus was built stand on each side of the Wâdī Qelt* waterway, which, along with the amenities of winter climate and the early coming of spring, attracted the Roman rulers. The city, some of whose buildings were of concrete faced with diamond-shaped stones and brilliantly colored plaster, was patterned after architecture characteristic of Rome from c. 80 B.C. to the death of Augustus Caesar (A.D. 14). One of the early finds was a Hellenistic fortress whose walls were square on the outer reaches and circular on the inner ones. Along the banks of the wâdī were a promenade and sunken garden, as well as a circular theater and terraced area. An imposing grand staircase led to the upper levels

of hillside Jericho near a large government building. The study of the palace of Herod the Great sheds light on a type of architecture of which little was previously known. The city continued to flourish until the end of the 1st three Christian centuries; then it gradually disappeared until Arabs in the 8th century converted it into a military outpost

The largest ancient palace area discovered in Palestine has been excavated at N.T. Jericho, dating from the time of Jesus, and attributed to Herod the Great and his son Archelaus. One building (a gymnasium ?) (284 x 152 ft.) contained 36 rooms around an open court. It was built of cut sandstone plastered over and painted red, black, and gold; portions of this paint remain. The luxurious winter capital, with its Roman baths, mosaic floors, cellars for Mediterranean wines, and repositories for perfumed unguents, was identified by coins and pottery found in the area. The story of the erection and the burning of a palace at Jericho by Herod, and its re-erection by Archelaus, is told by Josephus (see PALACE, illus. 307). See Kelso, Baramki, "Excavations at N.T. Jericho and Khirbet en-Nitla" (*AASOR* 29–30); Pritchard, "The Excavation at Herodian Jericho," 1951 (*AASOR* 32–33).

Several incidents in the life of Jesus are associated with Jericho. The Jordan ford where his Baptism took place is not far from the town (cf. Matt. 3:5 ff.). The stark mountains of his Temptation loom behind Jericho (Matt. 4:1 ff.); the snow-clad slopes of Mt. Hermon, possibly the scene of his Transfiguration (Mark 9:2 ff.), may be seen at certain seasons from a nearby point. At Jericho, shortly before Palm Sunday, Jesus restored sight to Bartimaeus (Mark 10:46–52); here he was entertained by Zacchaeus (Luke 19:1–11); and uttered his Parable of the Pounds (19:12–28).

M. S. M./W. P. A.

Jeroboam I (jĕr′ō-bō′ăm) (possibly "the people increases"), a son of Nebat, an Ephraimite living at Zereda, and of Zeruah (I Kings 11:26), who became the first king of the Northern Kingdom (Israel) after the division of Solomon's territory in the reign of Rehoboam*, and remained on the throne for c. 22 years (c. 922–901 B.C.). He first appears in Scripture as an Ephraimite chief, a competent foreman of Solomon's conscripted labor during the reconstruction and building enterprises at Jerusalem. Jeroboam worked on the Millo* and "closed up the breach of the city of David" (R.S.V. I Kings 11:27). Smarting under Solomon's tyranny, Jeroboam planned revolt but was found out (I Kings 11:26 f.). Encouraged by the prophet Ahijah* of Shiloh, he fled to the Pharaoh Shishak of Egypt. When Solomon died and was succeeded by his son Rehoboam, further tactless oppressions galled the northern tribes (I Kings 12:13 f., 18); and Israel rebelled (v. 19), summoned Jeroboam, whose return from Egypt had become known, and "made him king over all Israel" (v. 20), leaving only Judah and Benjamin for Rehoboam to rule (v. 21). Jeroboam made his capital at Shechem*, and later at Tirzah*. He fortified Shechem as well as Penuel, E. of the Jordan (I Kings 12:25). Even some of Rehoboam's older councilors at Jerusalem sympathized with the complaints of the 10 northern tribes which seceded (I Kings 12:6–15).

War between Jeroboam I and Rehoboam continued "all their days" (I Kings 14:30). Their rivalry was not put aside, even in the face of the invasion by Shishak of Egypt, whose plundering of Judah and Israel the Egyptian recorded on a temple wall at Karnak. The incidents of Jeroboam's reign, including the activities of three prophets and supernatural evidences of the Lord's interest in Israel, are told in I Kings 12:25–14:20.

Jeroboam I allowed the worship of Yahweh outside Jerusalem and set up images (I Kings 12:28–29). At ancient Bethel and at Dan he built calf shrines, whose nature has caused considerable discussion among scholars. Many authorities, including W. F. Albright, believe that the golden calves were not intended to depict Yahweh in the form of bulls, but that the bulls were the pedestals where the invisible Lord was worshipped, just as at Solomon's Jerusalem Temple the invisible deity was enthroned above two cherubim. Nevertheless Jeroboam's use of bulls, long sacred to followers of the Canaanite Baal with "taurine associations," as well as to pre-Hebrews of central Palestine, was retrograde and debasing. Behind Jeroboam's installations at Bethel and Dan was the astute political aim stated in I Kings 12:27—a safety measure hidden behind his reiteration of the calf god's protection at the Exodus.

In addition to his golden-calf innovations Jeroboam allowed other alien cults (I Kings 14:9)—the Sidonian Ashtoreth*, the Moabite Chemosh*, and the Ammonite Milcom* (I Kings 11:33). He maintained high* places (I Kings 12:31).

Orthodox prophets also condemned Jeroboam I for appointing to priestly positions men who were not Levites, but from the whole of the people (I Kings 12:31); and for changing the traditional feast month from the 7th to the 8th (v. 32); but in this change W. F. Albright suggests that Jeroboam was not so much a reformer as the restorer of an almost obsolete alternative date for the festival, intended "to restore older practices (cf. Ex. 32) which had been abandoned by normative Yahwism, or which had been supplanted by the latter."

O.T. writers stressed the baneful effects of Jeroboam's reign; time and time again they declared that "Jeroboam made Israel to sin" and drove them from following the Lord. The long influence of Jeroboam's sinfulness is reiterated in a formula appearing in the O.T. in connection with the evil reigns of all but three of the northern kings. It appears, for example, in the comments on Jehoram, who put away the Baal worship inaugurated by his father Ahab and his mother Jezebel, but persisted in the "sins of Jeroboam" (II Kings 3:3); so too Jehu (II Kings 10:29, 31); Jehu's son Jehoahaz (II Kings 13:1 f.); his son Jehoash, who reigned 16 years at Samaria (13:10 f.); Jeroboam II, great grandson of Jehu, son of Jehoash (II Kings 14:23 f.); Zachariah, son of Jeroboam II (15:8 f.); Menahem, son of Gadi (II Kings 15:17 f.); and Pekahiah, son of Menahem (II Kings 15:23 f.).

Jeroboam I ruled for almost a quarter of a century. He was succeeded by his son Nadab, who reigned only two years (c. 901–900 B.C.).

Jeroboam II, the son of King Jehoash (Joash of Israel), 4th king of the Jehu dynasty, 13th in line of the 19 monarchs of the Northern Kingdom. His long, prosperous and relatively peaceful reign lasted from c. 786 to 746 B.C., when he was succeeded by his son Zechariah*, who was murdered after six months on the throne. The material prosperity of Jeroboam's reign was partly due to his victories over Ben-hadad* III of Syria, which won ancient Damascus and considerable territory formerly held by Israel; whose boundaries now extended from the N. pass between the Lebanons and Hermon, into eastern Palestine and S. to the Dead Sea, and included almost all that Solomon and David had held except Judah. Jeroboam also benefited by having weak Assyrian contemporaries. The brief account of his important reign is contained in II Kings 14:23–29. The oracles proclaimed against the kingdom at this time by the prophets Hosea and Amos show the religious, moral, and economic conditions under Jeroboam II (Hos. 1:2–9, 2:2–15, 4:1–3a, 6–10, 5:1 f.; Amos 2:6–5:27, 7:1–16, 8:4–6). Jeroboam's country was "like a stubborn heifer," "a band of drunkards." His people "sold the righteous for silver, and the poor for a pair of shoes" (Amos 2:6). They were so abominable morally, in spite of extravagant sacrifices, that the Lord hated the feast days (5:21), preferred "mercy" to sacrifice (Hos. 6:6), and prepared punitive captivity for Israel. Jeroboam seems to have profited from the advice of the Yahweh prophet Jonah, son of Amittai, only in matters concerning the expansion of the kingdom. His reign shows the effects of economic prosperity on a people's spiritual life.

The remarkable ostraca (inscribed pottery fragments) unearthed in a palace storehouse at Samaria are believed to date from the reign of Jeroboam II in the 1st half of the 8th century B.C. They reveal, among other things, that Solomon's administrative districts were maintained in principle for a century and a half after his death; and they list many personal names compounded with Baal, as well as with Yahweh, in the ratio of seven for Baal to 11 for Yahweh; but it is possible that "Baal" was sometimes used to indicate "Lord" in the sense of Yahweh. The Samaria ostraca give the names of over 20 places in the Northern Kingdom, of which six appear as O.T. clan names (Josh. 17:2; Num. 26:30–33). The writing on the shards also records royal income from peasants who remitted taxes in the form of jars of wine and oil.

Jerubbaal (jĕr'ŭb-bā'ăl). See GIDEON.

Jerusalem, the chief city of Palestine; a holy city for Christians, Jews, and Moslems. Several reasons for the prestige of the small city are: (1) It could control the ancient N.–S. route along the edge of the Judaean hills, and the southernmost E.–W. thoroughfare to Trans-Jordan. In addition, the earliest city, confined to the eastern spur and surrounded on three sides by steep inclines, could easily be defended, concern being limited only by the narrow neck of the spur to the N., and the protection of its water supply. (2) It possessed a reliable though not copious water supply from its ancient Spring Gihon* (the Virgin's Fount) in the Kidron; and En-rogel* (Job's Well) S. of the junction of the Kidron and the Valley of Hinnom, both in use since ancient times. (3) It was pivotal in a series of sacred places which developed around altars to Yahweh—Beersheba, Hebron, Bethlehem, Bethel, Shiloh, and Shechem. (4) Its Temple Area became the platform for such great prophets and religious leaders as Isaiah, Jeremiah, and Jesus, and the principal scene of Hebrew worship from David and Solomon in the 10th century B.C. to the fall of the city to Titus in A.D. 70. (5) Its central location made it a convenient capital for the United Kingdom of Israel under David and Solomon (c. 1000–922 B.C.), and of Judah from c. 922 B.C. to 587 B.C. (6) It is to Jews "the city which the Lord had chosen out of all the tribes of Israel, to put his name there" (I Kings 14:21); to Christians the place where Jesus was crucified, buried, and rose from the dead; to Moslems the setting for Mohammed's visionary ascent to heaven (Quran 17:1).

Name. The etymology of the name, Jerusalem, is uncertain. Many authorities derive the final part of the word from Heb. *shalem* ("peace"), supporting the traditional interpretation, "city of peace." It has been pointed out, however, that a more accurate derivation might be from an older Semitic *Urusalim*, "foundation of (the god or primeval figure) Salem" (see *PEQ*, 1945, pp. 23 ff.). The city is first identified with Salem (Gen. 14:18; cf. Ps. 76:2), a form which omits the initial particle *Yeru-* ("city of," perhaps more accurately "foundation of"), or possibly *Beth-* ("house of"). The full name first occurs in an Egyptian execration text (19th cen. B.C.) in the form *Urusalimum* (see *JPOS* 8, 1928, pp. 247 f.). The form *Urusalim* appears in the 14th century Amarna Letters, and *Ursalimmu* in Assyrian texts (see *ANET*³, p. 288). In Hebrew (MT) it is *yerûšālaim* (II Sam. 5:5) or *yerûšālayim* (Jer. 26:18), in Aramaic *yerûšālēm* (Ezra 5:14), in Syrian *'ûrišlem*, and in Greek either *Hierosolyma* (Matt. 2:1) or *Hierousalēm* (Matt. 23:37). Other names for Jerusalem are: "the city of David" (e.g. II Sam. 5:7), "Jebus" (Judg. 19:10), "Moriah" (II Chron. 3:1), "Zion" (Ps. 50:2), "Ariel" (Isa. 29:1), and "the city of holiness" (Isa. 52:1). The latter is preserved in the modern Arabic name, *El Kuds*. The Romans renamed it *Aelia Capitolina* in A.D. 135, its original name being restored in the 4th century by Constantine.

Location and Description. Jerusalem is situated in the central highlands of Judah, c. 33 m. E. of the Mediterranean, c. 14 m. W. of the Dead Sea and c. 138 m. SW. of Damascus. The present Old City rests on an irregular quadrangle of rock and ancient debris which to the N. loses its identity in the chief mountain range of Palestine, and slopes perceptibly to the SE. This plateau is enclosed on all sides by higher elevations, poetically described by the Psalmist: "As the mountains are round about Jerusalem. . . ." (Ps. 125:2). Except from the N. where it is possible to view Jerusalem—though only partially—from as far away as el-Bireh, the city remains invisible until closely approached. To the W. rises the main watershed of the Judaean hills, and to the S. the traditional "Hill of Evil Counsel." To the E. runs the ridge of the Mount of Olives (see OLIVES, MOUNT OF), and the Mount of Offense—the traditional place of Solomon's idolatrous sacrifices (I Kings 11:7; II Kings 23:13). Along the W. slopes of this ridge are the remains of numerous rock-cut and monolithic tombs, many hidden from view by the village of Silwan (see Simons, *Jerusalem*, pp. 194 ff.; Ussishkin, *BA* 33, 1970, pp. 34 ff.).

211. Jerusalem from Mount of Olives. Dome of the Rock (old Temple Area) in center; walled-up Golden Gate at extreme right; center background, King David Hotel and Jesus Tower of Jerusalem YMCA; left foreground, Russian Orthodox Church of Mary Magdalene.

The ancient city of Jerusalem, however, can be defined more accurately in terms of its valleys, which isolate the Old City from its surroundings on three sides. To the E. it is bounded by the Kidron* Valley (II Sam. 15:23; John 18:1), and to the W. and S. by the Wâdī er-Rababeh—the Biblical "Valley of Hinnom," the boundary between Judah and Benjamin (Josh. 15:8; 18:16; see HINNOM)—which curves E. to meet the Kidron. Here, at a point SE. of the city, the two valleys join to form the Wâdī en-Nar ("Valley of Fire"), which descends through the Judaean wilderness to the Dead Sea. A third ravine once divided the plateau between the Kidron and Hinnom valleys into an eastern and western ridge. This central valley is not named in the Bible, but it was called by Josephus the Tyropoeon, or "Valley of the Cheesemakers" (see Simons, *Jerusalem*, p. 52, n. 2). The Tyropoeon Valley is at present almost completely filled in by the accumulated debris and rubble of an often destroyed and rebuilt city, and by the deliberate leveling of areas for new construction (see Kenyon, *Jerusalem*, pp. 12 f. and Fig. 1). Today it appears simply as a pronounced hollow in the midst of the Old City, in places covering some 80–90 ft. of debris.

Several smaller valleys subdivided the two main ridges into a number of separately defined areas (see illus. 213). The E. ridge was highest and broadest at its N. end, forming the Temple Hill on which were erected the Solomonic and Herodian temples. The present Haram esh-Sharif ("The Noble Sanctuary") incorporates in part the great platform built by Herod the Great, and houses the al-Aksa Mosque and the Dome of the Rock. The long, relatively low S. end of the E. ridge—separated from the Temple Hill by a narrow saddle—was the site of the earliest city, that of the Jebusites, and later the city of David (see Simons, *Jerusalem*, chaps. 2–3; Kenyon, *Jerusalem*, chap. II). This SE. ridge is often referred to as the Hill of Ophel, though this designation should perhaps be restricted to a small spur projecting SE. of the temple area.

The higher and more massive W. ridge, separated from the original city by the Tyropoeon Valley, was long thought, though erroneously, to be the "Stronghold of Zion" (see Simons, *Jerusalem*, pp. 38 ff.). Without access to a natural water supply, it was not occupied until the period of the Late Monarchy. In Biblical times, it was cut off from the N. by a small valley which descended from the area of the Citadel at the present Jaffa Gate to the Tyropoeon Valley. Beyond this, the NW. portion of the ridge lay completely outside the area of the Biblical city, and is only partially enclosed within the walls erected by Suleiman II. Here, on a small spur which projected into the central valley, is the hill on which is located the Church of the Holy Sepulchre, the traditional site of the crucifixion and burial of Jesus (see Simons, *Jerusalem*, chap. 5; Smith, *BA* 30, 1967, pp. 74 ff.; Wilkinson, *Levant* 4, 1972, pp. 83 ff.).

Two natural sources of water were available to Jerusalem (see Simons, *Jerusalem*, pp. 157 ff.). The first, Bīr 'Ayūb ("Job's Well"), the floor of the Wâdī en-Nâr S. of the original city, is the Biblical En-rogel (Josh. 15:7, 18:16; II Sam. 17:17; I Kings 1:9). Of greater importance, however, is the Biblical Gihon (I Kings 1:33; cf. II Kings 20:20), the "Virgin's Fountain," known also as Umm ed-Daraj' ("Mother of Steps"), or 'Ain Sitti Miryam ("Spring of Our Lady Mary"). It lies at the foot of the E. ridge in the Kidron Valley, and made early settlement possible here. To assure access to the spring in time of siege, the Jebusites cut a water channel, shaft, and tunnel through the rock to the spring from inside their city wall (see Simons, *Jerusalem*, pp. 165 ff.). Channels and tunnels of a later date are also connected with the Gihon (see Vincent, *Underground Jerusalem*, 1911). Hezekiah, for example, constructed the Siloam tunnel through solid rock in order to provide safe access to the water at the time of the Assyrian siege (see Simons, *Jerusalem*, pp. 179 ff.). The waters still flow through this into the Pool of Siloam at the SW. end of the E. ridge. As other means of protecting, transporting, and storing the water supply became available, settlement spread to the W. ridge. Many water channels, pools, and reservoirs exist within the present Old City. A reservoir with a double basin and surrounding portico on the grounds of the 12th-century Church of St. Anne is believed by many to be the Pool of Bethesda (John

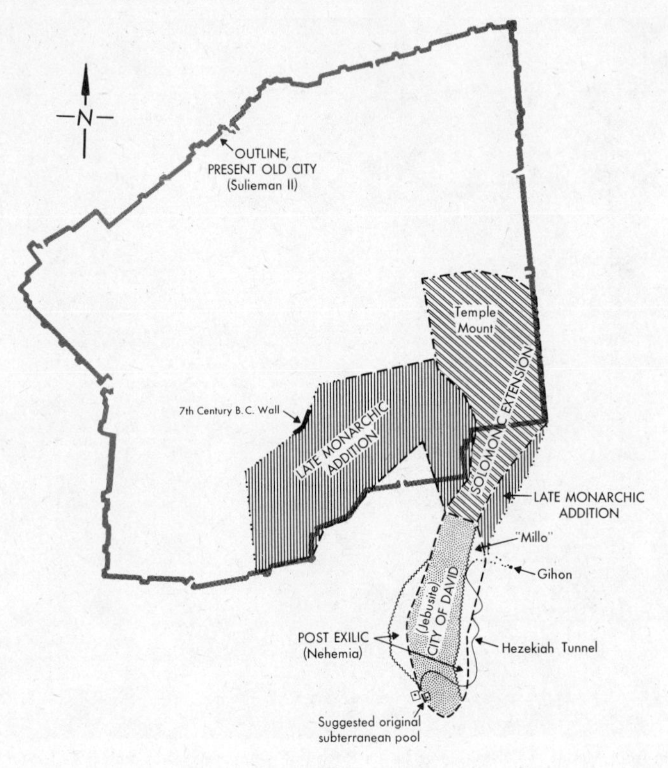

212. City of Jerusalem, Jebusite to Post-Exilic.

5:2 ff.). Other examples include an extensive system of reservoirs under the Haram esh-Sharif, the Mamilla Pool, and the so-called "Bath of the Patriarch," or "Hezekiah's Pool."

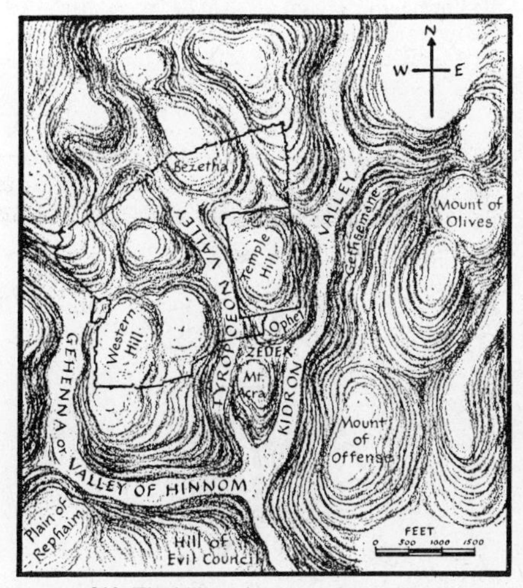

213. The hills and valleys of Jerusalem.

Excavations. The Ordnance Survey of the Palestine Exploration Fund (P.E.F.), begun in 1864 by C. Wilson and completed by C. Warren and C. R. Conder, initiated archaeological work at Jerusalem. Of significance are: C. Warren's probes of the Temple Mound, 1867–70; investigation of the SW. angle of the W. hill by F. J. Bliss and A. C. Dickie, 1894–97; L. H. Vincent's study of the ancient water system based on the work of the Parker Mission, 1909–11; R. Weill's two seasons on the S. end of the SE. ridge, 1913–14 and 1923–24; work on the N. end of the SE. ridge by R. A. S. Macalister and J. G. Duncan, 1923–25; the discovery of the so-called "Third Wall" to the N. of the Old City by E. L. Sukenik and L. A. Mayer, 1925–27 and 1940; excavations along the W. side of the SE. hill by J. W. Crowfoot and G. M. Fitzgerald, 1927–28; C. N. John's extensive exploration of the Citadel at the Jaffa Gate, 1934–40 and 1947; excavations of the SE. ridge and soundings in the Tyropoeon Valley and elsewhere by K. M. Kenyon and R. deVaux, 1961–67, producing the first stratified sequence of materials; and exploration of the Old City in the area of the Temple Mound and the Citadel, by B. Mazar and others since 1968. See bibliography at end of article for references.

History of the City. Uncertainty exists in attempting to describe the physical history of Jerusalem. Because of its unique status as a sacred city, a large body of tradition has accumulated which is difficult to evaluate. Names of existing ruins or localities, such as "Tower of David," "Zion," "Way of the Cross," serve to establish the discontinuity between longstanding tradition and historical reliability. In addition, 4000 years of continuous occupation have made archaeological excavation a hardship. Jerusalem has been excavated more than any other site in Palestine, but dogmatic presuppositions, lack of modern stratigraphical excavation, and the frequent destructions and rebuildings which the city has experienced have combined to produce the poorest results. It is only within the last decade that positive results have been achieved. It is on this evidence that the following sketch of the history of Jerusalem is based, keeping in mind the difficulties and uncertainties mentioned above.

The earliest evidence of occupation consists of a few caves along the slopes of the SE. ridge above the Gihon Spring, in which were discovered cultural remains of Early Bronze Age I (c. 3200 B.C.). In addition, EB II and III ceramics have been found on bedrock along the E. slope of the ridge.

Elements of a Middle Bronze Age city wall discovered some 160 ft. below the crest of the hill on the E. slope of the SE. ridge, provide the earliest architectural remains. Constructed around 1800 B.C., it continued in use until it was superseded by another wall in the 8th century B.C. Related to this is a reference to Jerusalem in one of the Egyptian execration texts of the 19th century B.C. (*ANET*³, p. 329). Perhaps it is with this city that the tradition about Abraham's relationship with Melchizedek, the king of Salem, is to be connected (Gen. 14:18).

Jerusalem continued to exist as an important city during the Late Bronze Age. Among the Amarna Letters of the 14th century B.C. are five written by Abdi-Hiba, king of Jerusalem, to Pharaoh Akhenaton of Egypt requesting assistance in his struggle against the 'Apiru (see *ANET*³, pp. 487–488). The city wall along the E. slope, constructed during the Middle Bronze Age, continued in use during the history of Jebusite Jerusalem. Changes were made during this period when a series of artificial terraces or stone-filled platforms were constructed along the E. slope, between the city wall and the crest of the ridge, which extended the habitation area some 55 ft. These platforms, constantly under stress and in frequent collapse due to warfare, earthquakes, and erosion, were often repaired throughout the history of Jerusalem until the 7th century B.C., when houses (destroyed by Nebuchadnezzar in 587 B.C.) were constructed upon the repair of the last collapse. At the time of the Hebrew conquest, Jerusalem was ruled by Adonizedek (Josh. 10:1), the leader of the Amorite confederacy defeated by Joshua during the battle for Gibeon (Josh. 10:1–27). Although the city is at one place stated to have been captured by the men of Judah (Judg. 1:8), it apparently remained in control of the Jebusites until the time of David (Josh. 15:63; Judg. 1:21).

David seized the Jebusite town and made it his capital, c. 996 B.C. Confident in the defenses of their city, the inhabitants laughed at David's intentions (II Sam. 5:6; II Chron. 4:5). David, however, apparently captured the city when Joab gained access through the shaft—cut into the limestone hill from the Gihon Spring to about 80 ft. from the crest of the ridge—by means of which the Jebusites reached their water supply (II Sam. 5:8). Such a theory was meaningless while it was believed that the Jebusite and Davidic wall was that discovered by Macalister along the crest of the ridge. Since Macalister's wall and tower have now been shown to be Maccabean in date, and since the discovery of the actual Jebusite wall well down the slope, beyond the entrance to the shaft, the suggestion has gained plausibility. David occupied the city, renamed it "the city of David," and "built the city round about from the Millo inward" (II Sam. 5:9; I Chron. 11:8). This Millo, or "Filling," is probably to be identified with the massive stone platforms initially constructed by the Jebusites (see above). It was again repaired by Solomon (I Kings 9:15, 24; 11:27), and also by Hezekiah (II Chron. 32:5). David also built a palace (II Sam. 5:11; I Chron. 14:1), of which no trace remains, and was buried "in the city of David" (I Kings 2:10), as were his twelve immediate successors, but again the actual place has never been located. A "house of David" was known in the S. part of the city in the post-Exilic period (Neh. 12:37). Although the existing archaeological evidence for David's city is meager, the general outline of its walls

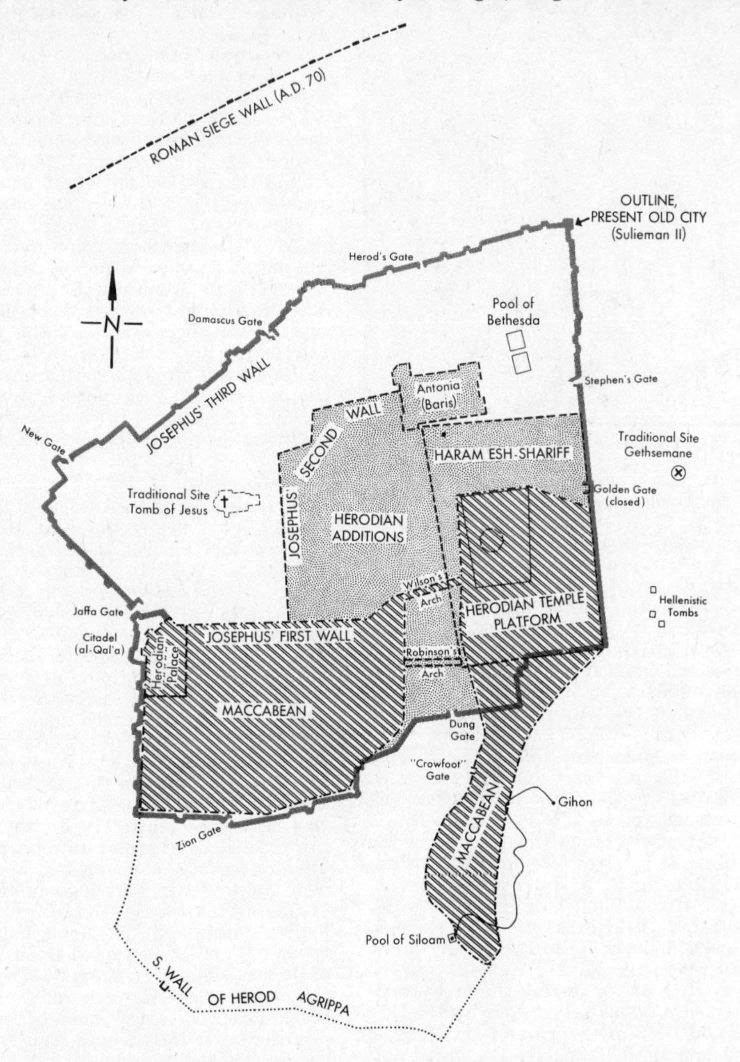

214. The walls of Jerusalem.

can be inferred with reasonable accuracy. Recent excavation (1961–67) has established that the original city—that of the Jebusites and David—was limited to the SE. hill, S. of the Temple area, and that its E. wall ran along the slope of the SE. ridge. Its N. boundary is probably to be located across the narrow neck of the ridge, as excavations N. of that point revealed nothing earlier than the 10th century B.C. (Solomonic), while the area S. of the supposed line of the wall produced pottery of the Late Bronze Age. The same procedure was used to establish the likelihood that the W. and S. walls followed the line of the summit scarp, beginning at the NW. corner in the area of a Maccabean gateway discovered by J. W. Crowfoot in 1927 (see illus. 212 and 214).

Solomon repaired the city walls and rebuilt the Millo (I Kings 9:15). A massive buttressing terrace of large stones, discovered in 1962 at the base of the Late Bronze Age terrace system, may possibly represent Solomon's repair of the latter. Solomon's most important achievement in Jerusalem, however, was the construction of the temple. David had captured Jerusalem, taking it for his own personal possession, and by so doing made possible the political unification of the northern Israelite tribes with southern Judah. His next aim was to make Jerusalem the religious center of the nation, and with this in mind he transferred the Ark of the Covenant from Keriath-jearim to Jerusalem (II Sam. 6), and purchased the threshingfloor of Araunah the Jebusite (II Sam. 24:18–25), which lay outside the Davidic city, with the intention of erecting there a sanctuary for the Ark. The actual building of the temple, however, fell to Solomon (II Chron. 3:1), who also erected an adjacent palace and audience hall N. of the City of David. The position of the Temple enclosure cannot be doubted—beneath the present Haram esh-Sharif, the E., S., and W. walls of which are formed by the platform of Herod's temple. As to the actual structure of the Temple, however, there is no archaeological evidence, and attempts to compensate for this on the basis of (a) the description of its construction recorded in I Kings 5–7 (II Chron. 2–4), and (b) isolated archaeological fragments which appear to fit this mold, are numerous. Certain deductions can, of course, be made: for example, its tripartite form has interesting parallels in the Canaanite temple at Hazor, dated to the 2d half of the 2d millennium B.C., and the 9th century B.C. temple at Tell Ta'yinat in Syria, among others. Furthermore, the many individual objects found in recent years throughout Syria and Palestine serve to indicate the cultural context of Solomon's great achievement, as for example in his use of Phoenician masonry and craftsmanship (I Kings 5:6 ff., 7:13 ff.), and the description of the bronze vessels and ivories. Despite these parallels, however, it must be pointed out that minute reconstructions are highly conjectural and lack positive documentation. Solomon also appeared to have increased the size of the city. What evidence there is suggests that the City of David was joined to the Temple platform constructed by Solomon by an extension of its walls along the N. summit of the SE. ridge (for suggested plan, see illus. 212).

There is little evidence for the Jerusalem of the later monarchy, at least until the 7th century B.C. After the death of Solomon and the division of the kingdom, Jerusalem can be expected to have experienced a decline. In the fifth year of King Rehoboam, Solomon's son, the city was attacked by Pharaoh Shishak of Egypt (I Kings 14:25 f.; II Chron. 12:2–9). During the reign of Jehoash (c. 837–800 B.C.), repairs were made to the Temple (II Chron. 24:4–14; II Kings 12:4 ff.). Warfare between Amaziah of Judah and Jehoash of Israel resulted in the destruction of part of the city wall of Jerusalem and the looting of its Temple and palace (II Kings 14:13 f.; II Chron. 25:23 f.). An interesting feature of this period was the discovery of two caves, an enclosure wall, and a small room with two standing stones (*maṣṣebôth*). This ritual complex, or sanctuary, located on the hill SE. of the Temple, brings to mind the many unorthodox cults which existed in Jerusalem during the time of the Divided Monarchy (e.g., II Kings 12:3, 14:4, 23:4 ff.).

Archaeological evidence indicates that the Jebusite–Davidic city wall continued in use until the 8th century B.C. Its immediate successor has not yet been traced, but a cobbled street built over the top of the original wall must have been retained by a wall farther to the E. (Kenyon, *Jerusalem*, pp.66–67). These levels were cut by a later wall, which cannot date earlier than the 7th century B.C., and show evidence of several stages of repair. Contemporary with this 7th–6th century B.C. city wall are the remains of several domestic structures constructed upon the final rebuilding of the Jebusite terraces along the crest of the SE. ridge. The destruction of these buildings at the time of the Babylonian capture in 587 B.C. terminated the occupation of the city in this area. The construction of this new wall, and subsequent repairs, are probably to be ascribed to the reigns of Hezekiah (II Chron. 32:5) and Manasseh (II Chron. 33:14). The Assyrian military threat of 701 B.C. (II Kings 18:13) compelled Hezekiah to further protect his water supply (II Kings 20:20; II Chron. 32:30), which he accomplished by the cutting of the Siloam tunnel, bringing the waters of the Gihon Spring into the Pool of Siloam in the central valley. The achievement of this marvelous engineering feat is celebrated in the inscription discovered in 1880 (*ANET*[3], p. 321). There is considerable debate concerning the size of Hezekiah's Jerusalem. Evidence indicates a slight expansion along the N. part of the eastern slope of the SE. hill (see Illus. 212) sometime during the 8th–7th centuries B.C., but the debate centers on whether or not the city expanded onto the W. hill at this time. Kenyon has emphatically rejected such an expansion, indicating that probes in the area of the W. hill have provided no evidence of occupation earlier than the time of the Maccabees (Kenyon, *Jerusalem*, pp. 70 f., 110; *PEQ*, 1962, pp. 84–86). More recently, however, the discovery of a massive city wall and other structures of 7th century date W. of the Temple enclosure indicate that at least part of the W. hill was included within Hezekiah's Jerusalem (*IEJ* 20, 1970, pp. 5 f., 129–134). According to the excavators, it may be possible to identify the new evidence, described as a residential quarter, with the "mishneh" or "2d quarter" mentioned in II Kings 22:14 and elsewhere. The line of the city wall as suggested by these recent discoveries is indicated in illus. 212. It should be noted that there is no evidence for its S. extension to include the Pool of Siloam, this being purely conjectural (see Kenyon,

Jerusalem, pp. 70–77).

The Jerusalem of the later monarchy was destroyed by the Babylonian army in 587 B.C., and lay virtually abandoned for about 60 years. With the return to Jerusalem under Cyrus the Great, the reconstruction of the Temple was undertaken by Zerubbabel (Ezra 3–6) and completed c. 516 B.C. (see Haggai 2:18). Recent clearance of the SE. corner of the Temple platform has revealed a straight joint (c. 32 meters to the N.) with typical Herodian masonry to the S. of that joint and an older type of masonry, Persian in style, to the N. The latter may represent the work of Zerubbabel, and in addition mark the position of the SE. corner of the Temple platform of Solomon (*MUSJ* XLVI, 1970–71, pp. 139–149).

The process of reconstructing the city walls was undertaken by Nehemiah in the 20th year of Artaxerxes I (c. 444 B.C.; Neh. 2:1–8). Nehemiah provides a graphic description of the ruined walls during his night-time inspection of the city (Neh. 2:12–16), and during the reconstruction (Neh. 3:1–32, 12:31–43). Despite the detailed description in Nehemiah's list, however, it has been difficult to determine the actual circuit of the walls. Nehemiah's work was doubtless little more than a restoration of the walls destroyed by Nebuchadnezzar in 587 B.C. The E. limit consists of the initial structure of a complex of walls discovered in 1923–25 following the crest of the SE. ridge, which continued to form the E. boundary of the city until abandoned in Roman times. According to Kenyon, the other limits followed the line of the pre-Exilic city walls. This, however, does not take into consideration the recently discovered wall W. of the Temple enclosure (see above) which indicates that at least part of the W. hill was occupied during this time. Since only a small portion of this wall has been cleared, its exact line along the W. hill can be nothing more than conjecture (see illus. 212).

In 168 B.C., Antiochus IV Epiphanes destroyed Jerusalem and defiled and pillaged its Temple (I Macc. 1:20 ff.). He established a fortress, the Akra of the Syrians, on a site dominating the Temple courtyard (I Macc. 1:33). The exact location of this structure is unknown, and debated, though it may have been situated in the NE. sector of the W. spur, near the later Hasmonean palace. Others would locate it on the E. spur, which seems unlikely, or beneath the Maccabean Baris, the later Herodian fortress Antonia (see *BASOR* 176, 1964, pp. 10 ff.).

When the Maccabees gained control of the city in 164 B.C., Jerusalem was in ruins (see I Macc. 3:45), except for the Syrian citadel which held out until 141 B.C., when it finally capitulated to Simon. Jonathan began to rebuild the city in 153 B.C. and refortified the Temple mount, encircling it with "squared stones" (I Macc. 10:10–11). Other works were constructed (I Macc. 12:35–38), later strengthened by Simon (I Macc. 13:10, 52, 14:37). To these measures must be attributed Macalister's so-called "Tower of David" and its associated wall, discovered in 1923–25 along the crest of the SE. ridge, above the Kidron Valley (*PEQ*, 1962, pp. 76 ff.). To the W., the Maccabean wall encroached on the central (Tyropoeon) valley, the line of which includes a gateway discovered by J. W. Crowfoot in 1927 (see illus. 214). Antiochus VII invaded Judah in 134 B.C., and again the fortifications of Jerusalem were destroyed (Josephus, *Antiq.* XIII.viii.2–3). John Hyrcanus rebuilt the walls (I Macc. 16:23), and constructed the fortress (Baris) at the NW. corner of the Temple courtyard, later rebuilt by Herod the Great as the Antonia (Josephus, *Antiq.*, XV.xi.4; XVIII.iv.3). During the period of the Maccabees, the N. sector of the SW. spur was also occupied. Excavations in the area of the Citadel in 1934–47, and more recently since 1968, have revealed the foundations of walls constructed in the 2d century B.C. The "First Wall" of Josephus (see below) is generally assumed to have run from the Citadel on a direct E.–W. line to the point at which "Wilson's Arch" connects to the Temple platform (see illus. 214). In Maccabean times, this viaduct extended from the Temple precinct to a gymnasium on the W. hill, immediately below the Syrian citadel (II Macc. 4:12).

Herod the Great ruled Jerusalem from 37–4 B.C. His building enterprises were on a grand scale, and much Herodian masonry is still visible in present-day Jerusalem. It is the Herodian city that is the Jerusalem of the N.T. period. Of the Temple erected by Herod (Josephus, *Antiq.* XV.xi), nothing remains except the massive platform which dominates the SE. corner of the present Old City. Its beautifully finished walls are composed of large well-cut stones, with a flatly tooled center and shallow marginal draft. The total surviving height of the platform at its SE. corner is c. 128 ft. (75 ft. above present surface), traced in 1867 by C. Warren by means of his "Great Shaft" (see frontispiece of PEQ). Dominating the W. spur was Herod's Palace, or Citadel, later the residence of the high priest, Caiaphas, and the possible site of Jesus' trial (Matt. 26:3, 57 ff., etc.). Included in the present "Tower of David," which forms part of the Citadel structure E. of the Jaffa Gate, is a section of Herodian masonry of considerable height. With the exception of the S. end, the entire W. spur was enclosed within the walls of Herodian Jerusalem, and joined with the Temple area by two viaducts, represented today by "Wilson's Arch" and "Robinson's Arch." At the NW. corner of the Temple courtyard, Herod built the fortress Antonia (Josephus, *Antiq.* XV.xi.4; XVIII.iv.3), which replaced the Maccabean Baris, and was the probable site of Jesus' trial before Pilate (John 18:28, etc.). The Jewish historian Josephus provides an interesting portrait of Jerusalem in the 1st century A.D. in describing in detail the final attack of Titus in A.D. 70 (Josephus, *Wars* V-VI). Here are described three walls which Titus had to storm to capture the city from the N. The "First Wall" is the N. wall of the Maccabean quarter on the SW. spur noted above, running on an E.–W. line from the Temple platform to the Citadel, along the approximate course of present-day David Street. The

"Third Wall," the outermost of the three, was the work of Herod Agrippa (c. A. D. 40–44), and represents a post-Herodian extension of the N. wall (see below). The position of the "Second Wall" (probably Herodian) has been the subject of debate, and is crucial in establishing the site of the crucifixion and tomb of Jesus, both of which lay outside the city walls (John 19:17 ff., and parallels; see Heb. 13:12). Josephus' description (see Simons, *Jerusalem*, pp. 324 ff.) simply states that the wall extended from the fortress Antonia (a known point of reference) to the Gate Gennath in the old ("First") N. wall (the location of which is unknown). Many have thought the Gate to have been situated N. of the present Citadel, placing the line of the "Second Wall" N. of the Church of the Holy Sepulchre, and suggesting that the traditional location of the final events in the life of Jesus are not authentic. Others accept the above location of the gate, but trace a number of disjointed fragments of walls in a series of re-entrant angles which leave the Church, and thus the traditional site, outside the city walls (Vincent and Steve, *Jérusalem*, pp. 90–113). A third suggestion is that the gate lay midway between the Citadel and the Temple platform, the wall extending N. and curving to the E. to join the fortress Antonia (Simons, *Jerusalem*, pp. 295–309). This theory also preserves the traditional sites of Jesus' crucifixion and burial, and appears to be supported by recent excavations, which indicate that the city wall must lie E. of the Church of the Holy Sepulchre (see Kenyon, *Jerusalem*, pp. 151–154; *BA* 30, 1967, pp. 74–90). Other localities in Jerusalem mentioned in the N.T. include the Mount of Olives (Matt. 21:1, 24:3, etc.), Gethsemane (Mark 14:32, etc.), the Pool of Bethesda (John 5:2, near the "Sheep Gate") and the Pool of Siloam (John 9:7).

From A.D. 6, Jerusalem was controlled by Roman governors, the most famous of whom was Pontius Pilate*. During a brief interlude from Roman rule under Herod Agrippa (A.D. 40–44), renewed building activity occurred. A new N. wall (the "Third Wall" of Josephus) was built. In 1925–27, a wall constructed of large stones, c. 1360 ft. N. of the present Old City, was found, and it was concluded that this represented the "Third Wall" (Sukenik and Mayer, *The Third Wall of Jerusalem*). Re-excavation of a section of this wall produced evidence that the wall was constructed after the time of Herod Agrippa. Furthermore, excavations below the present level of the Damascus Gate in the present N. wall of the Old City proved that this wall was first constructed in the mid-1st century A.D., and that therefore the line of the "Third Wall" is the same as the line of the present N. wall of the Old City. Sukenik's "Third Wall" apparently is the remains of a siege wall erected in A.D. 70 by Titus and the Roman Tenth Legion (Kenyon, *Jerusalem*, pp. 162–163, 166–168). It also has been shown that Herod Agrippa was responsible for the inclusion of the S. end of the SW. hill within the city walls (Kenyon, *Jerusalem*, pp. 155–161). This wall, extending from the SW. corner of the present Old City, along the crest of the ridge above the Hinnom Valley, and E. across the Tyropoeon Valley to the S. limit of the original settlement on the SE. spur, has been known since 1894–97, when it was traced by Bliss and Dickie (*Excavations at Jerusalem*, chaps. I–III). It is now clear that the wall in this sector can be dated no earlier than the mid-1st century A.D.

The Jewish rebellion of A.D. 66 brought almost complete destruction to Jerusalem in A.D. 70, when Titus destroyed all but three towers of Herod's Palace, and a portion of the city wall to the S., where a garrison was established. After the second revolt was quieted in A.D. 135, Hadrian (A.D. 117–138) established a Roman city on the site, Aelia Capitolina. A completely new plan in classic Roman style was laid out. It became Jerusalem once again under Constantine (c. 313), and under Byzantine rule numerous churches were erected. The greatest monument of this period was the Church of the Holy Sepulchre, the original structure of which was built by Queen Helena, the mother of Constantine, in c. A.D. 325. In A.D. 636, Jerusalem fell to the Arabs, and by A.D. 691, the city began to take on its present structure, with the building of the Dome of the Rock. A brief Crusader occupation later added certain elements, such as additions to the Church of the Holy Sepulchre. Much of the present appearance of the Old City, however, is due to Suleiman the Magnificent, who in 1538–41 rebuilt the walls which stand today for the most part.

Bibliography. F. J. Bliss and A. C. Dickie, *Excavations at Jerusalem*, 1894–1897, 1898; J. W. Crowfoot and G. M. Fitzgerald, "Excavations in the Tyropoeon Valley, Jerusalem, 1927," *APEF* 5, 1929; C. N. Johns, "Recent Excavations at the Citadel," *PEQ*, 1940, pp. 36–58, and *QDAP* 14, 1950, pp. 121–190; K. M. Kenyon, *Jerusalem: Excavating 3000 Years of History*, 1967; K.M. Kenyon, "Israelite Jerusalem," in J. A. Sanders (ed.), *Near Eastern Archaeology in the Twentieth Century*, 1970, pp. 232–253; R. A. S. Macalister and J. G. Duncan, "Excavations on the Hill of Ophel, Jerusalem, 1923–1925," *APEF* 4, 1926; A. Parrot, *The Temple of Jerusalem*, 1957; J. Simons, *Jerusalem in the Old Testament*, 1952; E. L. Sukenik and L. A. Mayer, *The Third Wall of Jerusalem*, 1930; cf. *PEQ*, 1944, pp. 145–151; L. H. Vincent, *Underground Jerusalem: Discoveries on the Hill of Ophel, 1909–1911*, 1911; H. L. Vincent and A. M. Steve, *Jérusalem de l'Ancien Testament*, 2 vols., 1954–1956; C. Warren, *Notes on the Survey and on Some of the Most Remarkable Localities and Buildings in and about Jerusalem*, 1865; C. Warren, *Underground Jerusalem*, 1876; R. Weill, *La Cité de David, Campagne de 1913–1914*, 1920, and *Campagne de 1923–1924*, 1947. W. P. A.

Jeshanah (jĕsh′ȧ-nȧ) ("old"), one of the cities in the hill country of Ephraim taken in battle by Abijah from Jeroboam (II Chron. 13:19; cf. 15:8). The probable location is Burj el-Isaneh, about 6 m. N. of Bethel and 1. m. W. of Baal-hazor. The Greek and Syriac texts indicate that Shen (A.V. I Sam. 7:12), where Samuel set up the stone he called

Ebenezer*, is an incorrect rendering of the same name.
(3) The family name of a group from Pahath-moab who returned from Exile with Zerubbabel (Ezra 2:6; Neh. 7:11). (4) A Levite entrusted with the distribution of tithes (II Chron. 31:15). (5) A high priest, a son of Jozadak, who came back from Babylon with Zerubbabel (Ezra 3:2, 8), and strengthened the morale of the men restoring the Temple (Ezra 4:3, 5:2, cf. 10:18; Neh. 12:1, 7, 10, 26). (6) The head of a Levitical family who took part in rebuilding the Temple (Ezra 3:9); interpreted the Law (Neh. 8:7); and sealed the Covenant (Neh. 10:9; cf. Ezra 2:2, 8:33; Neh. 3:19, 7:43, 9:4, 5, 12:8, 24).
(7) A S. Judaean settlement (Neh. 11:26), possibly the same as Shema (Josh. 15:26) and Sheba (Josh. 19:2); may be Tell es-Sa'ur, NE. of Beer-sheba.

Jeshurun (jĕsh′ŭ-rŭn) (A.V. Jesurun, Isa. 44:2, "upright one"), a symbolical name for Israel (Deut. 32:15, 33:5, 26).

Jesse (jĕs′ē) (Heb. *Yishay*), the son of Obed and grandson of Ruth and Boaz (Ruth 4:17, 22; Matt. 1:5); and father of eight sons including David (I Sam. 16:10 f., 17:12), or of seven sons (I Chron. 2:15). Two of his daughters (I Chron. 2:16, 17), Zeruiah and Abigail, became mothers of famous warriors. His name appears in the genealogical list of I Chron. 2:12. Jesse was well acquainted with the customs of family worship (I Sam. 16:5 f., 20:29). His sons tended their large flocks grazing over the ancient fields of his ancestors. He was a prosperous farmer who could afford to send gifts to Saul (I Sam. 16:20). His son David's tender concern for Jesse and his wife is shown by his sending them to a prince of Moab for protection when he was being hunted down by angry Saul (I Sam. 22:3 f.). Jesse's son Eliah had a daughter Abihail who married Rehoboam (II Chron. 11:18). Jesse is mentioned in a Messianic prophecy of Isaiah (11:1 and 11:10) and in Matthew's and Luke's genealogies of Jesus (Matt. 1:5 f.; Luke 3:32). In the Bethlehem Church of the Nativity, built over the cave site of Christ's birth, 12th century wall mosaics depict Jesse's family tree and its branches. Paul, in Romans 15:12, indicates that he saw in Jesus the fulfillment of Isaiah's the "root of Jesse" prophecy.

Jesus Christ. The account, which seeks to be at once descriptive, critical, and constructive, elaborates the following outline:
1. The Gospel story itself.
   (1) Jesus' characteristic activities.
   (2) His growth in self-understanding.
   (3) The closing days.
2. The meaning of the story.
   (1) Jesus' genuine humanness.
   (2) The records: their central testimony.
   (3) Jesus' integration with his time.
      (a) The political situation.
      (b) The social situation.
      (c) The religious situation.
   (4) Jesus transcending his time.
      (a) The means of God's saving will.
   (5) Identity of person and teaching.
      (a) Fatherhood; Sonship; Brotherhood.
   (6) The threefold attestation.
      (a) The Resurrection.
      (b) The gift of the Spirit.
      (c) The Church as the redeemed community.

1. The records that tell of the life of Jesus Christ are exceedingly brief. Of the four Gospels, only two of them, those of Matthew and Luke, reveal anything about him prior to the baptism and temptation which marked his entry upon his public career. John, indeed, the latest of the Gospel writers, and by far the most reflective and interpretive, begins by affirming his "pre-existence" with God in the form of "the Word" (or *Logos*), but having done that, he at once passes to the beginning of his public career and the Baptist's hailing him as "Lamb of God" and "Son of God" (1:1–34). The narratives of Jesus' birth and early childhood found in Matthew and Luke contain numerous differences. Both stress the "supernatural" features of the Birth, Matthew with a prosaic literalness designed to connect the event with various O.T. passages (1:23, 2:6, 15, 17 f., 23), Luke with poetic imagery and emotion as befits the mysterious commingling of earth and heaven (2:8–16). The Virgin Birth story represents the later faith of the Church that since Jesus "explained" history he could not be "explained by" history, but stands in an inexplicable relation to God's creative and redeeming will. Both Matthew and Luke give a genealogy of Joseph, whom they trace through David to Abraham. The two genealogies differ in numerous details, which do not, however, affect Jesus' Davidic descent, the undoubted point for the introduction of the tables. The N.T. makes much of the belief in Jesus' Davidic descent: it was regarded as an indispensable qualification of Messiahship (cf. Acts 2:22–36). Both accounts give Bethlehem as Jesus' birthplace, but they differ in the reason for the occurrence there, Luke treating it as accidental (2:1–7), Matthew as predestined (2:1–6). They also differ in their way of relating the family to Nazareth (cf. Matt. 2:19–23; Luke 2:4, 39). From the infancy until the association with John the Baptist, nothing is told of the career of Jesus save the solitary incident of his being "lost," as a boy of eleven or twelve, in the Temple (Luke 2:41 ff.). There are numerous fanciful accounts dealing with this period (the so-called *Legendary and Apocryphal Lives*), but they are wholly without historical value. Our knowledge of Jewish family, social, educational, economic, and religious customs permits us to make certain surmises about these "years of silence," but that is all. That through the normal discipline of childhood, boyhood, youth, and early manhood, he was being "prepared" for his mission, should be obvious, but as to the precise means whereby he came to his unparalleled moral and spiritual insight, we have no information. He breaks upon us at his Baptism and Temptation as a man already gripped by a sense of destiny (Mark 1:9–15; cf. Matt. 4:1–11). From then until he was put to death some two years later, or even less, he spoke those words, performed those

deeds, evoked those antagonisms and loyalties, and set in operation those indestructible redeeming agencies, which are described for us in the few brief chapters of the Gospels. He gradually appears as the key to the O.T., and the very purpose of the diverse and tragic history of Israel. It becomes evident why he was named "Jesus" (Luke 1:30–33), the Grecianized form of the Hebrew name meaning "God Saves," and why he became recognized as "the Christ," the Greek equivalent of the Hebrew "Messiah"*, meaning "the Anointed One." The growth of what is known as "the Messianic hope" eventuated in the expectation of a specific person as that particular "Anointed One" who would indeed prove to be "the Chosen Deliverer."

215. Emperor Justinian kneeling before Jesus. Byzantine mosaic lunette above door to main sanctuary, Sancta Sophia, Istanbul.

(1) Jesus quickly attached to himself a few personal followers—Peter and Andrew, James and John, pairs of brothers (Matt. 4:18–22). According to the account in John 1:35–42, he had already had an understanding with at least two of these, which would explain their ready response to his "call." His early ministry after the departure from the Baptist in Judaea consisted of a series of journeys throughout various parts of Galilee, perhaps centering in the fishing village of Capernaum, the home of his first disciples. What may be regarded as a typical day's activity is described in Mark 1:21–38; there were public preaching, friendly intercourse, works of mercy, private instruction of his followers, personal communion with God his Father. Equally typical is the visit to Nazareth, his teaching there, and its diverse reception (Luke 4:16–30). In fact, the "text" of the Nazareth discourse quite fairly expresses the spirit and purpose of his early period. He was proclaiming "good news." He was accomplishing "mighty works"—both works of healing (Luke 5:12, 13) and works upon nature (Luke 8:22–25; cf. 7:18–23, the reply to the Baptist's deputation). He aroused great popular enthusiasm, although he was not deceived by it (John 6:15). The acclaim was understandable enough. His words and actions, especially his strange power over "evil spirits," inevitably conveyed Messianic suggestions to a people whose eyes had grown weary from long looking for a Deliverer (although cf. the report in Matt. 16:13, 14). Just as certainly they created suspicion and hostility on the part of men in authority (Luke 6:7). A constant theme of his preaching was the Kingdom of God, which he said was "at hand" (Mark 1:15); and in whose coming he was implicated (cf. Mark 4:11). What is known as "The Sermon on the Mount" (Matt. 5–7), actually a collection of the "Sayings" of Jesus used for Christian instruction by the early Church, as also many of the parables (Matt. 13:24–33), dealt largely with the nature, the laws, and the possession of this kingdom. Combined with this teaching, radical as it was, were sharp criticisms of the religious leaders of the day. It was inevitable that Jesus should become a marked man. His words and actions were given a sinister significance. Even his power over evil spirits was declared to arise from his allegiance to Beelzebub, the leader of these spirits—surely the bankruptcy of criticism (Luke 11:14–22).

(2) It is obvious that there must have been considerable development in Jesus' self-understanding as respects both his nature and his mission, but, because of the character of the Gospels, the evidence is confused and sometimes contradictory. What follows here is merely one attempt at a consistent interpretation. Others are equally possible. It

would seem natural that Jesus should come to rely more and more upon his inner circle of friends. He saw that it was only a question of time before they must take over his cause. We are told of the special attention he gave to them (Luke 6:20 f.), and of his instructions as he sent them out to teach and to preach. He sent both the more select group of twelve (Matt. 10:1–5; Luke 9:1–6), and a larger group of seventy (Luke 10:1–23). It may be that the disciples' report on their journeys caused him to stop thinking of himself primarily as Davidic "Messiah" or heavenly "Son of Man" and begin to interpret his destiny rather as that of the "Servant of the Lord" (Isa. 53) who would deliver his people by suffering. The main burden of his teaching had always been the Kingdom of God, sometimes pictured in apocalyptic fashion, connected with the revelation of the Son of Man (see Dan. 7:13 f.), sometimes less spectacularly, as in the parables of the Kingdom (Matt. 13:24–33). In either case, the coming of the Kingdom was to be God's work alone. Jesus' work, and that of his disciples, was merely to proclaim its imminence.

But there was no dramatic result from the disciples' mission. The disciples reported an enthusiastic receptivity to their message, but the Kingdom itself did not arrive. This would be a natural moment for Jesus to begin thinking once more of the purpose of his life and the God-intended way by which he should attain it. This may be the reason why Jesus for a while left Galilee with his disciples for Phoenicia (Matt. 15:21 ff.). He sought more light. That it came to him during this retreat seems apparent from what happened on his return to Galilee. He came to Caesarea-Philippi, and here, in a conversation with his disciples, he elicited what is known as Peter's Confession of the Messiahship. The confession was met with Jesus' startling declaration that as Messiah, that is, as Redeemer, he must go to Jerusalem, there to meet death at the hands of men. In this way alone could he "give his life a ransom for many." It is evident that he had come to apply to himself the profound truth set forth in Isa. 53. The Father would still create the Kingdom, but the means would be not the words of a Teacher or the declaration of a Herald, but rather the sufferings, death, and resurrection of the Son who withheld nothing from the Father's will (Matt. 16:13–21).

In this resolution of Jesus to accept the Cross, everything fuses. It makes intelligible all we know of him up to this point. The actual carrying out of the resolution makes intelligible all that was to happen afterwards. The truth we are faced with is that Jesus Christ came into the world to die for its sins, and that God "raised him from the dead," to be forevermore "at his right hand." This latter is a form of speech meaning that God's dealings with men are in accordance with his self-disclosure in Christ. *The Lamb shares the throne of the universe* (Rev. 22:3).

(3) From the hour that Jesus saw that he must be crucified, until the event itself occurred, there are many episodes, many conversations with the disciples, many mighty works, many clashes with the authorities. He did not at once proceed directly to Jerusalem. Instead, he prolonged the journey all that he could. We know a good many of the details of the journey, but the records are not too clear, and the chronology is uncertain. Even a brief description of it must be received with caution. He lingered in Galilee (Matt. 17:22); he visited Capernaum (17:24); he travelled to the region "beyond the Jordan" (19:1); he entered "the borders of Samaria" (Luke 17:11 f.); and he seems to have exercised a very considerable ministry in Judaea, almost passed over by the Synoptics, but described at length in the Gospel of John (cf. 7:1 ff.). But always in the mind of Jesus there is one settled purpose: to go to Jerusalem to die at the hands of men, because only thus could that "new community," at once a mystery in its nature, a gift from God, and a task for men, the Kingdom of God on earth, come to pass. In all the incidents of the closing week—the so-called Triumphal Entry, the preaching, the relation to authorities, the activities, the Last Supper, the Agony, the Arrest, the Trial, the Crucifixion—we are confronted by a man who is conscious of approaching an inevitable climax of destruction. Yet there is no warrant for this inevitability in the external situation itself. Humanly speaking, the end was avoidable, as Jesus himself seemed to imply (see Matt. 26:51–54). Where then is the warrant? It is in the inscrutable mystery of the will of the Father respecting the Son. The ancient Christian faith that in Jesus Christ, the Living Word of God, Father and Son co-act in the drama of human redemption, is a faith amply justified by the Gospel records themselves. This statement calls for some elaboration.

2. From any point of view, Jesus Christ is the central figure of the Bible. Hosea, Jeremiah, and the Second Isaiah may fairly be said to stand by themselves in the O.T., but he is the blossom of which they were the bud. The prophets proclaimed the word of God as they were given to see it, but at last it was said of Jesus Christ that he was "the Word made flesh" (John 1:14)—the Word of God transmuted into a living person. The O.T. describes the stately ritual by which the priest sought to make atonement for the sins of the people (Lev. 16), but what was said of no other priest was said of Jesus Christ—that being himself without sin, and hence in no need of atonement, he could make atonement for all mankind by the offering of himself (Heb. 9). There may be gathered from the O.T. a body of ethical teaching which is its own authentication, yet the secret of creating a universal community which would incarnate this teaching in all of its life waited for disclosure on Jesus Christ. To a people haunted through long centuries by the dream of a King and a Kingdom never to be superseded, he offered himself as such a King bringing such a Kingdom, and although the response he received was a Cross, it is from that Cross that he reigns, and his Kingdom is

imperishable just because a Cross is both its symbol and the law of its being. The mission of the Bible is to bring this its central figure before the eyes of men. It is to set him in the perspective of time and history, but in suchwise that he is seen to transcend time and to interpret history. He who is God's Living Word to men is also he through whom God purposes to come to redeeming Lordship in all the life of the world, personal, social and political, economic, ethical and religious.

(1) These are high claims, and they are claims which are made of One who, whatever else he was or was not, was a historical actuality. Undeniably the Bible assigns to Jesus Christ a universal significance. The postulate of any justifiable effort to comprehend him under this form is his membership in our race. If he is not a figure of our human history, then Biblical Christianity becomes at once a mythology. In the end, we shall do as the Bible itself does, and read the historical figure in the light of the over-historical, but we do not begin with the over-historical. Instead, we begin with a definite point in time, with a definite human situation—in a word, *with a man*. This very fact has, indeed, been used against the records themselves. For example, early in the present century a famous scholar (Schmiedel) selected from the Gospels a small group of passages which appeared to reflect on Jesus' knowledge, or insight, or perfection, or unique relation to God. Since these passages were contrary to what the early church was declaring respecting Jesus, they could not possibly have been "invented." One of these passages was Jesus' reply to a salutation: "Why callest thou me good? none is good, save one, even God" (Luke 18:19; but cf. Matt. 19:16, 17). The passages in question were therefore to be treated as criteria. Anything not in agreement with them was open to suspicion. Since so much in the Gospel records lacked this agreement, Schmiedel could only conclude that the narratives were of such a character that it was impossible to construct "a critically tenable view of the life of Jesus."

That any life of Jesus is always open to critical objections is simple fact. An element of mystery attaches to him, and to deny this in the name of historical science is to leave us with something less than the historical reality itself. Some of the critical considerations will be referred to below, but variations in the accounts of a man's activities are not to be taken as evidence that there was no such man. The paralytic is not proven not healed, nor Jesus himself proven not possessed of healing power, because the accounts of the event differ. The admitted variations in the Gospels may mean either that we have more than one witness or that "editors" took liberties. The least that the Gospels can be said to call for is a man of flesh and blood. No pretence waits on the humanity of Jesus Christ. Early views that his human nature was in some sense "illusory" agreed with neither Scripture nor reason. He was born as any person was born. He knew helpless infancy. He had to learn to walk and to talk, to read and to write. Such an account as Edersheim, *Jewish Social Life in the Time of Christ*, would by implication tell us much about Jesus himself. He possessed no magic equipment from his birth that guaranteed him against the ordinary perils of life. He knew hunger and weariness, temptation and perplexity, uncertainty and disappointment. He seems to have undergone the whole gamut of human emotions, save those arising from the deepest of personal intimacies—and from these, like many another man, he was precluded by the very nature of his vocation (cf. Jer. 16:2). Unknown to him also was the emotion of repentance, since the consciousness of sin arises from the consciousness of self-will, and he sought nothing but to know and to do the Father's will (see Luke 2:49; John 4:34, 5:30, 6:38). He identified himself with God's people by joining devoutly in the normal religious practices of Judaism. He pondered the Sacred Books of his people; he participated with his people in their worship; he observed their great festivals; he knew the secret of the closed door (see Mark 1:35); fellowship with God was his native breath; trust, confidence, and assurance were not occasional to him, but habitual. As none other ever did, he put holy and sacrificial love, alike to God and to men, at the very center of his being. He revealed the marks of perfect Sonship to God, not in some set of especially favorable circumstances, some "Garden of Eden," but in "the common world, which is the world of all of us."

(2) A true understanding of Jesus Christ, therefore, as the revelation of God to man, does not require any modification of his genuine humanness. Neither does it require a false worship of the letter of the Gospels. The present prevailing view of the structure of the Gospels allows for every critical consideration, while fully protecting the vital relation in which Jesus Christ stood to the original Christian faith. The view puts less stress on the details of the record, which it realizes are often at variance, than it does on that which created the record. It frankly recognizes that some time elapsed before the Gospel story itself was reduced to writing. Christianity began in a witnessing to Jesus Christ on the part of those who had known him, and who, through the impact of his life, death, resurrection, and living presence, had come to recognize him as Saviour and Lord. It did not begin with a written book: it began with a word-of-mouth story. The story had many parts, but one theme. This theme may be discerned by anyone who will read the discourses in the Acts of the Apostles. These discourses represent the earliest Christian preaching. There are two or three verses in Peter's sermon on the day of Pentecost which state the theme exactly (see Acts 2:22, 23, 24, 33, 36). The last of these verses reads: "Let all the house of Israel therefore know assuredly, that God has made him both Lord and Christ, this Jesus whom you crucified" (R.S.V.).

Necessarily, this witnessing to Jesus Christ as the Saviour of the world by reason of his

JESUS CHRIST

death and resurrection as "the Chosen One" of God, included the declaration of the things he had said and done. It was to be expected that variation would occur in the telling. Every new convert became a witness (see Acts 8:4). He had to depend on others for his knowledge of Jesus' words and deeds. There was as yet no verbally authoritative account on which he could depend. The natural

216. Jesus Tower, the Jerusalem YMCA.

consequence was that he gave his testimony and told his story in his own way. In the course of time, certain ways of telling the story came more and more to prevail, and these are what we possess in the Gospels, but it is evident that *there was never one way only*. A comparative study of the Gospels, as already stated above, quickly reveals that the process yielded both similarities and differences. The briefer sayings of Jesus, just because of their brevity, and because they were made very early into a separate collection, were less subject to this modification than were parables, events, and other longer passages, yet even the briefer sayings show differences. Compare, e.g., the Beatitudes in Matt. 5:3–12 with those in Luke 6:20–26; the teaching on divorce in Matt. 5:31, 32 with that in Luke 16:18; and the Lord's Prayer as given in Matt. 6:9–13 and Luke 11:2–4 respectively. Among longer passages, the following with their differences are typical: Death of John the Baptist (Matt. 14:3–12; Mark 6:17–29); Healing of Jairus' Daughter and the Afflicted Woman (Matt. 9:18–26; Mark 5:21–43; Luke 8:40–56); Parable of Talents or Pounds (Matt. 25:14–30; Luke 19:11–27); Speech Against Pharisees (Matt. 23:1–39; Luke 11:37–52, 20:45–47; cf. Mark 12:38–40); Jesus in Gethsemane (Matt. 26:36–46; Luke 22:40–46); Jesus' Tomb found Empty (Matt. 28:1–10; Mark 16:1–8; Luke 24:1–12).

These differences, we must surmise, arose in the very process of the telling, and according to the circumstances of the witnessing, until one "form" or another gradually prevailed, and became "fixed." It is these various finally "fixed forms" that we possess in the Gospels. In a similar way we account for the fact that so much is found in one Gospel that is not found in another. We should be poor indeed without the parables of the Prodigal Son and the Good Samaritan, yet only Luke records them, just as he alone tells us of some of the most lovely of the Infancy and Resurrection traditions (2:8–20, 24:13–35). The fact of these omissions, additions, peculiarities, modifications, is undeniable. Nothing is gained by ignoring them. They clearly mean that the Gospel story passed through a fluid stage before it reached the forms in which we now possess it. But they no less mean that those who received and transmitted the tradition were concerned chiefly to maintain a consistent witness to the central figure. No insistence on divergences in the form of the telling can do away with what was the manifest intent of the telling. All the words of the witnesses were designed to testify to the Living Word, Jesus Christ, in order to evoke toward him faith, obedience and love on the part of others. This was the dominant concern: to this all else was subservient.

(3) The historical actuality of Jesus Christ meant his integration with his own immediate political, social, and religious situation. No man can be unaffected by his time, nor was he.

(a) Jesus was born a Jew, and he lived at one of the dark periods of his people's history. It was the period of Roman supremacy. From the Exile, 587 B.C., until the 2d century B.C., the Jews had been mainly a subject people. They then attained a degree of independence under the heroic leadership of the Maccabee family, only to lose it to Rome at the end of the century. Rome eventually divided the country into various provinces, continuing to exercise its authority, however, in much of the country through the Herodian dynasty, members of which governed different divisions. Jesus' activity fell chiefly in the territories of Galilee, Samaria, and Judaea, although Luke seems to suggest some ministerial activity in territory east of the Jordan. There was also a territory known as Idumaea, south of Judaea, to which Jesus seems not to have gone, although people from Idumaea heard of him, and sought him out (Mark 3:8).

The Herodian dynasty was in power throughout the life of Jesus: the influence of the Herods affected him in many ways. He was born during the reign of Herod the Great, who would have killed the Child had he been able (Matt. 2:16–23). Since Herod is known to have died in what to us is 4 B.C., the birth of Jesus should be dated 5 or 6 B.C., and his death A.D. 28 or 29. The error arose out of an attempt to fix the Christian calendar by a Roman monk in the 6th century.

Jesus was put to death during the rule of Herod Antipas, "that fox," as Jesus once called him (Luke 13:32), who had ordered the murder of John the Baptist (Matt. 14:1-12), and who at least connived at the death of Jesus (Luke 23:6-16). Any man who lived in Palestine was conscious of the restrictions—especially apparent in the system of collecting the imperial taxes, and in the limitation on judicial rights and privileges—laid by Rome on Jewish liberty through the servile Herodians. Jesus was fully aware of the revolutionary spirit that was created in many a Jewish patriot by these restrictions. The disciple known as Simon the Zealot may have shared this spirit. Some have identified the Zealots with the home-rule party that opposed the census ordered by Quirinius which caused Jesus to be born at Bethlehem (Luke 2:1-7), and that harassed Rome in every possible way. During Jesus' ministry, enemies attempted to involve him with the political authorities on the question of taxation (Matt. 22:15-22). His association with tax-collectors, agents of the oppressors, was a common charge against him (Luke 5:27-32; cf. 15:1, 2, 19:1-10). It was by the Roman procurator, Pontius Pilate, that Jesus was turned over to his enemies to be crucified; the brutal conduct of Roman soldiers added to his final sufferings; Roman soldiers gambled for his garments as he was dying (John 19:23, 24); and Rome sealed his tomb and placed there a guard.

(b) Jesus was equally affected by his social situation. Many of the things he said and did are unintelligible apart from some knowledge of the prevailing customs. He wore the "tunic" of the time immediately above the undergarment or linen shirt; and the "cloak," the seamless "robe" or mantle, easily laid aside (cf. Mark 14:51, 52), mentioned in the crucifixion story. This "tunic" and "robe" are the "coat" and "cloak" of the saying in Matt. 5:40 (cf. John 13:4); and it was the "hem" or tassel of the mantle that was "touched" by the woman (Matt. 9:20). He also wore the conventional leather sandals fastened with a thong (Matt. 3:11). As a traveling teacher, he counted on the hospitality of others (Luke 8:3, 10:38-42; the "baskets" mentioned in Matt. 14:20 were possibly those in which the disciples carried what alms they received). He slept where the occasion found him (but cf. Matt. 8:20). Pictures of the Last Supper are frequently misleading, in that they show the group seated at table in Western fashion, and not, as was the custom, reclining; only this custom can explain the reference to the disciple as "reclining in Jesus' bosom" and as "leaning back on Jesus' breast" (John 13:23, 25). The parables especially reflect contemporary life and activity—the Prodigal Son, the Good Samaritan, the Sower, the Hired Laborers in the Vineyard, the Hidden Treasure, the Wedding Garment, the Wise and Foolish Virgins. Many of Jesus' briefer sayings are equally allusive. A striking example is the "one and two mile" of Matt. 5:41. The reference is to the legal right of a Roman soldier to compel a passing Jew to carry his burden a mile. The "Corban" of Mark 7:11-13 refers to the device whereby a man, by claiming that his substance, or part of it, was "given to God," and hence was no longer his own, could claim that he was not able to support his needy parents.

(c) The contemporary religion is also echoed in many of Jesus' words and deeds. The frequent reference in the Gospels to "the Scribes, Pharisees, and Sadducees" is of the nature of the case, considering the significance of these groups. Silence concerning them would constitute a grave objection to Gospel historicity. The *scribes*, who had their origin in the legalistic development during the Exile (6th-5th century, B.C.), were the official expositors of the vast body of the Law—the Torah—which controlled Jewish life and activity. They "sat in Moses' seat." They were sometimes men of admirable character; three of the greatest of them, Hillel, Shammai, and Gamaliel (see Acts 22:3; cf. 5:34 ff.), were contemporaries of Jesus. But the scribe's chief reverence was for the written word and its traditional meaning. His approach to religion was quite different from that of the prophet: there could be for him no new truth. Only tradition had authority. Between such a man and Jesus Christ there was bound to be antagonism, and the record everywhere reveals it. Closely associated with the scribes, and often the same persons, were the *Pharisees*. The word meant "Separatist," much in the sense of "Puritan." The group came into existence in the 3d century B.C., as the champions of a complete Jewish exclusiveness. They eventually stood in sharp opposition to the *Sadducees*, who became the dominant priestly party, and in many matters of legalistic and ceremonial interpretation were more "conservative" than the Pharisees. They were not, however, averse to other cultures; and there is evidence that by the time of Jesus, if not before, they had developed markedly worldly interests, and could even be described as latitudinarian. It was they who encouraged the traffic within the Temple precincts, and who benefited from the prices charged and the profits made. It was they who, as Jesus declared, had made the Temple into "a den of thieves," and those "chief priests" who were so deeply angered when they heard what he had said and done were in general Sadducees. The Gospels usually speak of the scribes and Pharisees together (see Matt. 23) as an indication of their intimacy, but, presumably, there were Sadducean scribes as well. Although the Pharisees were the best element in the Judaism of their time their preoccupation with the Law frequently led to narrowness, rigidity, and intolerance. Noble Pharisees of the type of Nicodemus (John 3:1; 7:50 ff.) were undoubtedly far more typical of the movement than the Gospels seem to suggest, but, even at their best, their conservatism was inflexible and their conception of goodness was not open to new patterns of conduct. Jesus did not question their basic "righteousness," but insisted that his disciples must somehow have the imagination to go beyond that (Matt. 5:20). The spirit that animated Jesus was that of the ancient prophets, free, spontaneous, and liberating. It is not surprising that, like the prophets, he was frequently in conflict with the religious leaders of his day.

(4) This varied integration of Jesus with his time and place in the way described is simple fact, but the more it is stressed the more it is seen to be not everything. He was, in the striking phrase of a great Biblical and theological scholar (H. R. Mackintosh), "rooted in the fruitful depths of history," but he just as certainly bears the marks of One who transcended history. He was both in the world and above it. He saw himself and his mission and the meaning of Israel as parts of one whole, and this whole he read in the perspective of the eternal purpose of God. One who wishes to do so may call this sheer audacity: it has, indeed, been so described; but the fact itself is as stated. Jesus' use of the term "I" is without parallel in human history. "I came to fulfill the law and the prophets" (Matt. 5:17). "Ye have heard that it was said by them of old time [i.e., by Moses] but I say" (cf. Matt. 5:21 f., 27 f., 33 f., 43 f.). See also the instructions in Matt. 10:16–42, and the portrayal of Jesus in John 14–18. What was declared above to be the faith of the Church respecting Jesus Christ is, by all the testimony of the records, grounded in his conviction respecting himself. He had an awareness of his relation to God and God's will for human salvation which sets him apart from the rest of mankind. His self-consciousness agrees with the known actualities. The mistakenness of Jesus Christ would constitute the postulate of a complete skepticism, and so of a complete despair. In relating himself to the religious reformation of John the Baptist, he did what many other earnest-minded men were doing (Matt. 3:1–17); yet the issue of the relation in his case was unique, namely, a baptism by the Spirit, accompanied by a profound conviction of Messiahship.

(a) As shown above, this did not at once settle everything for him. Instead, the conviction set the problem which the rest of his life would be devoted to solving. He never wavered in the profound belief that he had come into the world to "save" it, but he was to learn only through great tribulation of mind and heart (Heb. 5:7–10) what this "salvation" was, and how it was to be accomplished. There is no least evidence that he saw the end from the beginning, and all the steps he must take between. His master-conviction was expressed in the words, "The Son of Man came to seek and to save that which was lost" (Luke 19:10); but what that involved for him of dire and tragic experience is suggested in another saying of his as he approached his last days: "The Son of Man came not to be ministered unto, but to minister, and to give his life a ransom for many" (Matt. 20:28). It is true that he made this "giving of the life" a condition to discipleship, but the phrase may be taken in two senses. It may mean devoted service to others, selfless love; and this is the usual meaning. But it may also mean the surrender of the life in death itself, and it was by this "giving of life" that Jesus came to believe that he was to "save" the world. This is why he saw in the determination of men to put him to death a determination that could not have prevailed save for its coincidence with the will and purpose of God.

(5) Jesus' conviction concerning his divine-human centrality greatly serves to illuminate his teaching. Many show an appreciation of Jesus' teaching who do not share his view of himself or that view which, because it united men to him after his death, humanly speaking created the Church. This separation, however, between the man and the message, not only does violence to the records: it weakens the teaching by failing to recognize how completely it "came alive" in Jesus himself. In the end, the Gospel is not in anything that Jesus said, but in who he was and what he did. The "Good News" is not merely in Jesus' declaration of the finality and absoluteness of love. Power is not in love spoken but in love acted. "God is love"; but according to the Bible the ultimate evidence of that love to faith is the fact that Jesus Christ is "God's only begotten Son" who came into the world to save it, and who saved it by what this coming made it possible for him to endure. There is no Gospel apart from Jesus Christ himself, and even this "togetherness" of Jesus and the Gospel is credible only as Jesus himself is the holy love of God sacrificially and savingly expressed in the very being of Jesus, and exemplified by him in all his conscious life (cf. Phil. 2:5–11).

Speaking broadly, Jesus' teaching may be expressed in terms of Fatherhood, Sonship, and Brotherhood, and of what they imply. He declared these in many ways, but always underlying the declaration was the reality itself. His own existence mirrored the divine Fatherhood, which can be known only through sonship, in action: that is, in Christ's perfect sonship the divine Fatherhood was perfectly disclosed. Hence the words: "He that hath seen me hath seen the Father" (John 14:9). The completion of sonship is in brotherhood, and in the case of Jesus the marks of the perfect Son and the marks of the perfect Brother were inseparable. It could not be otherwise. Brotherhood is the logic of sonship according to the teaching of Jesus, and love is the driving power in both, and all his relations to men exemplified this. He could be severe enough on occasion, but the severity was love channeled through holiness, and therefore intolerant of evil. Love that is indifferent to the moral condition of its object is defective. The love of God is holy love; the love of Jesus Christ is holy love; the love he set forth as the promise and power of human salvation is holy love. A holy Fatherhood, a holy Sonship, a holy Brotherhood—this is the "trinity" which Jesus Christ perfectly represented, and in which the whole Biblical revelation of God and man was brought to final focus. Christianity is concerned with the proclamation of this "trinity" of truth and reality, and there is no complete Christianity otherwise.

(6) The threefold attestation of the revelation in Christ was the Resurrection, the gift of the Spirit, and the Church.

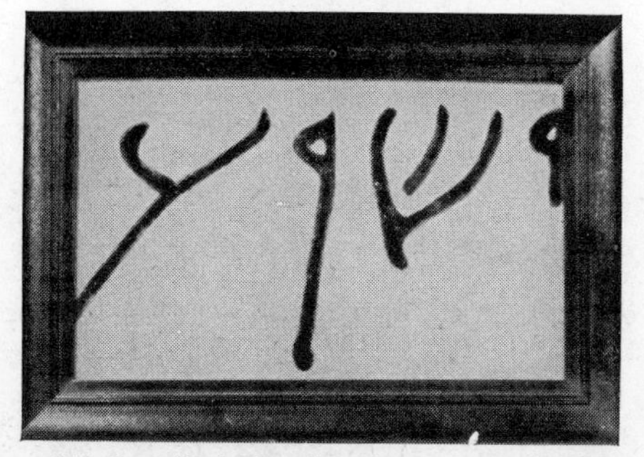

217. Jesus (Yeshua), a 1st-century ossuary inscription showing the form in which Jesus would have written his name.

(a) It is with the *Resurrection* as it is with the miracles. The accounts of the miracles can only mean that Jesus accomplished "mighty works" which men were unable to deny. The separate "miracles" may all be "explained away," and often are: what cannot be "explained away" is the presence in the ministry of Jesus of deeds which filled the observers with awe. Similarly with the accounts of the Resurrection. What chiefly matters is what the accounts are *about*. The least they can fairly be held to mean is that a group of men and women, overwhelmed by the tragedy that had befallen their Lord, became the subjects of an experience that convinced them that he was still alive, still active, still available. It is this experience which led to the perpetuation among men of the knowledge of Jesus Christ, and of the things he said and did.

(b) *The gift of the Spirit* was an attendant of the Resurrection experience and faith. Speaking broadly, the Spirit was the form under which the living Christ made himself known to believing men and was himself known by them. "The Lord is the Spirit" (II Cor. 3:17). It is not possible to reduce to complete consistency the Biblical teaching on the Spirit, especially the teaching on the Holy Spirit in the N.T. What is perfectly clear, however, is the teaching that faith in Christ as Redeemer and Lord gives rise to a form of experience known as "having the Spirit," or being "led by the Spirit." The teaching pervades both Rom. 8 and II Cor. 4. "Christ in me," "I in Christ," "filled with the Spirit," "led by the Spirit"—for the early Christians these were ways of describing the same experience.

(c) The final attest of God's revelation in Jesus Christ was *the Church*. The Resurrection, the Spirit, and the Church are inseparable. Without a doubt, the term "church" is used in various senses in the N.T., but the basic sense is that of a Fellowship initiated by God's revealing and redeeming activity in the gift of His Son Jesus Christ. The Church quickly needed some organization, but the Church is not primarily in the organization but in the reality that is organized. This reality is Jesus Christ and believing men in spiritual unity. *Life* hidden with Christ in God, appropriated by faith, nurtured by the offices of love, disclosing itself in transforming activity among men—this is the Church which Christ "purchased with his own blood" (Acts 20:28). The Acts of the Apostles shows us this Church in its beginnings and early expansion. The various Epistles indicate that it was already putting its faith into definite confessional forms. These forms served both as a means of proclaiming the faith and of deepening the sense of the Church as constituting that Kingdom which God had purposed from the beginning and had at last established in Jesus Christ.

From this point, the Christ of the Scriptures passes over into the Christ of theology. The resultant story is long and complicated enough, not to be entered into here. One observation only is called for. Christian theology, with all its errors, has at least sought to keep Jesus Christ in organic relation to mankind on the one hand and to God Himself on the other hand. Hence the persistent phrases, "truly man" and "truly God." In so far as it has done this, it has but continued to witness to what gives the Bible its true unity, to what is seen to underlie all else, especially in the N.T., and to what by every evidence we possess as the vital source whence the Church itself came into being. See GOSPELS; MESSIAH; SON OF GOD; SON OF MAN; TRINITY.

E. L./R. C. D.

An Outline of the Life of Christ

The period of Christ's ministry, estimated at three years, is difficult to arrange in chronological order because of the different points of view expressed in parallel passages of the four Gospels. By checking the points at which the narratives agree, however, a logical sequence of events can be arrived at. One-third of the Gospel record is devoted to Christ's death and resurrection.

Birth, Infancy, and Childhood	MATT.	MARK	LUKE	JOHN
The genealogies of Jesus	1:2–17		3:32–38	
The birth announcement to Mary			1:26–38	
Joseph and the Incarnation	1:18–25		2:1–7	
The Word made flesh				1:1–18
The birth of Jesus—shepherds			2:8–20	
Circumcision and presentation in the Temple			2:21–40	
Visit of the Wise Men	2:1–12			
Flight to Egypt and return to Nazareth	2:13–23			
The boy Jesus visits Jerusalem			2:41–52	

JESUS CHRIST	JESUS CHRIST			
Preparation for His Ministry	MATT.	MARK	LUKE	JOHN
Jesus is baptized by John the Baptist—	3:13–17;	1:9–11;	3:21, 22;	
The Temptation—	4:1–11;	1:12, 13;	4:1–13.	
His Early Ministry				
He calls his first followers—				1:19–51.
His first miracle—				2:1–12.
His cleansing of the Temple—				2:13–25.
Nicodemus visits Jesus—				3:1–21.
He baptizes in Judaea—				3:22–36.
He teaches at Sychar in Samaria—				4:1–42.
He returns to Galilee—				4:43–54.
His first rejection at Nazareth—			4:16–30.	
His Galilean Ministry				
His headquarters at Capernaum—	4:13–16;		4:31.	
Peter, Andrew, James, and John are called to discipleship—	4:18–22;	1:16–20;	5:1–11.	
He teaches in the synagogue—		1:21, 22.	4:31 f.	
He heals the sick—	8:14–17;	1:23–34;	4:33–41.	
He tours Galilee and preaches—	4:23–25;	1:35–39;	4:42–44.	
His fame grows—	8:1;	1:40–45;	5:12–16.	
The Developing Opposition				
He heals a paralytic, and is criticized for forgiving sins—	9:1–8;	2:1–12;	5:17–26.	
He calls Matthew to discipleship, and is criticized for associating with sinners—	9:9–13;	2:13–17;	5:27–32.	
He is criticized for his attitude toward fasting—	9:14–17;	2:18–22;	5:33–39.	
He is criticized for desecrating the Sabbath—	12:1–14;	2:23–28, 3:1–6	6:1–11;	5:1–18.
The Christian Movement Takes Form				
His widespread fame—	4:24, 25, 12:15–21	3:7–12;	6:17–19.	
He commissions the Twelve*—	10:1–4;	3:13–19;	6:12–16.	
Christian standards for living (the Sermon on the Mount)—	5:1–8:1;		6:20–49.	
Opinions about Jesus				
A Roman centurion—	8:5–13;		7:1–10.	
The common people—			7:11–17.	
John the Baptist—	11:2–30;		7:18–35.	
A sinful woman and a Pharisee—			7:36–50.	
The women of Galilee—			8:1–3.	
His friends—		3:20, 21		
The religious leaders—	12:22–45;	3:22–30;	11:14–32.	
The Basis of Real Relationship to Jesus and His Cause				
Jesus designates his true relatives—	12:46–50;	3:31–35;	8:19–21.	
Parables of the Kingdom—	13:1–53;	4:1–34;	8:4–18.	
The place of faith in his program—				
(1) The stilling of the tempest—	8:24–27;	4:35–41;	8:22–25.	
(2) The Gadarene demoniac—	8:28–34;	5:1–20;	8:26–39.	
(3) Jairus' daughter and the woman with a hemorrhage—	9:18–26;	5:21–43;	8:40–56.	
(4) Two blind men and a dumb man—	9:27–34.			
His second rejection at Nazareth—	13:54–58;	6:1–6.		
He instructs and commissions the Twelve—	9:36–11:1;	6:7–13,	9:1–6.	
The Disciples report to him—		6:30;	9:10.	
He teaches and feeds the multitude—	14:13–21;	6:32–46;	9:11–17;	6:1–14.
He refuses to be king, walks on the sea, and returns to Gennesaret—	14:22–36;	6:45–56;		6:15–24.
His discourse on the bread of life—				6:25–71.
He condemns the traditionalism of the elders—	15:1–20;	7:1–23.		

JESUS CHRIST	JESUS CHRIST			
The Acts and Teachings Associated with the Various Journeys of Jesus	MATT.	MARK	LUKE	JOHN
Into Tyre and Sidon; the daughter of a Syro-Phoenician healed—	15:21–28;	7:24–30.		
The Decapolis; a deaf-mute healed—		7:31–37.		
Four thousand fed; he departs to Dalmanutha—	15:32–39;	8:1–10.		
He warns against the spirit of the Pharisees and Sadducees—	16:1–12;	8:11–21.		
He journeys into the Caesarea Philippi district—	16:13;	8:27.		
Peter's confession—	16:14–20;	8:28–30;	9:18–20.	
He first foretells his death and Resurrection—	16:21–28;	8:31–9:1;	9:21–27.	
His Transfiguration—	17:1–13;	9:2–13;	9:28–36.	
An epileptic boy healed—	17:14–21;	9:14–29;	9:37–43.	
He again predicts his death and Resurrection—	17:22, 23;	9:30–32	9:44, 45.	
He returns to Capernaum; the half-shekel tax—	17:24–27.			
Discourses on humility, self-denial, the young, and forgiveness—	18;	9:33–50;	9:46–50.	
He attends the Feast of Tabernacles at Jerusalem and meets his enemies—				7:1–52.
He debates with the Jews in the Temple—				8:12–59.
He heals the man born blind—				9:1–41.
Discourses on the sheep and the shepherd—				10:1–21.
He attends the Feast of Dedication at Jerusalem—				10:22–42.
His final departure from Galilee for his ministry beyond the Jordan—	19:1, 2;	10:1;	9:51–62.	
The Mission of the Seventy—			10:1–24.	
Concerning marriage and divorce—	19:3–12;	10:2–12.		
He blesses little children—	19:13–15;	10:13–16;	18:15–17.	
The relationship of riches to eternal life—	19:16–30;	10:17–31;	18:18–30.	
The laborers in the vineyard—	20:1–16.			
He forecasts for the third time his death and Resurrection—	20:17–19;	10:32–34;	18:31–34.	
The standards of greatness—	20:20–28;	10:35–45;	22:24–27.	
The blind beggar of Jericho—	20:29–34;	10:46–52;	18:35–43.	
Zacchaeus the tax collector of Jericho—			19:1–10.	
He raises Lazarus at Bethany—				11:1–44.
Plots for his death—				11:45–53.
Supper in his honor at Bethany—				12:1–11.
The Last Week—Palm Sunday, the Day of Triumph				
His entry into Jerusalem—	21:1–11;	11:1–11;	19:29–44;	12:12–19.
Monday, the Day of Authority				
He curses the unfruitful fig tree—	21:18–22;	11:12–14, 20–25.		
He cleanses the Temple*—	21:12–17;	11:15–19;	19:45–48.	
Tuesday, the Day of Controversy				
Priests, scribes, and elders question his authority—	21:23–27;	11:27–33;	20:1–8.	
He parabolizes Israel's unfaithfulness—				
(1) A parable of two sons—	21:28–32.			
(2) A parable of wicked tenants—	21:33–46;	12:1–12;	20:9–19.	
(3) A parable of a marriage feast—	22:1–14.			

(Luke 9:51–18:14 has often been treated as a whole and identified with Christ's Peraean ministry on his last journey to Jerusalem. The material, however, seems too varied to belong entirely to this period of his career. Some incidents reveal the easier relationship with the Pharisees which was characteristic of Christ's early ministry (Luke 11:37, 14:1 f.). The events of Luke 10:38–42 could have taken place during one of Christ's earlier visits to Bethany. The three parables in Luke 15, narrated without indication of time or place, belong in spirit to the middle period of his ministry. His severe denunciation of the Pharisees, and the eschatological sections (Luke 13:22–30, 17:20–18:8) are related by their subject matter to the later period. This material is for the most part only in Luke.)

JESUS CHRIST

	MATT.	MARK	LUKE	JOHN
The Pharisees question him concerning tribute to Caesar—	22:15–22;	12:13–17;	20:20–26.	
The Sadducees and Resurrection—	22:23–33;	12:18–27;	20:27–38.	
A scribe and the greatest commandment—	22:34–40;	12:28–34;	20:39, 40.	
He asks about the Messiah—	22:41–46;	12:35–37;	20:41–44.	
He pronounces woes on the scribes and Pharisees—	23:1–39;	12:38–40;	20:45–47.	
A widow's mites—		12:41–44;	21:1–4.	
Greeks seek him—				12:20–36.
The Jews reject him—				12:37–50.
He talks about what shall be—	24:1–51;	13:1–37;	21:5–38.	
A parable of ten maidens—	25:1–13.			
A parable of talents—	25:14–30.			
He describes the judgment to come—	25:31–46.			
Judas conspires against Jesus—	26:1–5, 14–16;	14:1, 2, 10, 11;	22:1–6.	
Wednesday (no record)				
Thursday, the Day of Fellowship				
The preparation for the Passover—	26:17–19;	14:12–16;	22:7–13.	
Jesus washes the Disciples' feet—				13:1–20.
The Passover and the betrayer—	26:20–25;	14:17–21;		13:21–35.
The Lord's Supper inaugurated—	26:26–29;	14:22–25;	22:14–23.	
Peter and the Disciples forewarned—	26:30–35;	14:26–31;	22:31–38;	13:36–38.
His farewell talk to the Disciples—				14–16.
His intercessory prayer for his Disciples—				17.
Friday, the Day of Suffering				
He prays in Gethsemane—	26:36–46;	14:32–42;	22:40–46;	18:1.
He is betrayed and arrested—	26:46–56;	14:43–52;	22:47–53;	18:2–12.
His Trial (ecclesiastical)—				
(1) Before Annas—				18:13, 19–23.
(2) Before Caiaphas—	26:57–67;	14:53–65;	22:54;	18:24.
(3) Before the Sanhedrin—	27:1;	15:1;	22:66–71.	
He is denied by Peter—	26:69–75;	14:66–72;	22:55–62;	18:15–18, 25–27.
His Trial (legal)—				
(1) Before Pilate	27:2, 11–14;	15:2–5;	23:1–5;	18:28–38.
(2) Before Herod—			23:6–12.	
(3) Before Pilate (resumed)—	27:15–26;	15:6–15;	23:13–25;	19:1.
He is mocked by the soldiers—	27:27–31;	15:16–20;		19:2.
He is sentenced to be crucified—				19:16.
The road to Golgotha—	27:32;	15:21;	23:26–32;	19:17.
He is crucified—	27:33–44;	15:22–32;	23:33;	19:18–24.
His seven last words—				
(1) "Father, forgive them . . ."—			23:34.	
(2) "Today . . . with me in Paradise"—			23:39–43.	
(3) "Woman, . . . thy son! . . ."—				19:25–27.
(4) "My God, my God, why . . ."—	27:46;	15:33–39.		
(5) "I thirst"—				19:28, 29.
(6) "It is finished"—				19:30.
(7) "Father, into thy hands . . ."—			23:44–49.	
His burial—	27:57–61;	15:42–47;	23:50–56;	19:38–42.
Saturday, the Day of Silence				
His guarded tomb—	27:63–66.			
Sunday, the Day of Resurrection				
The empty tomb and the risen Christ—	28:1–10;	16:1–8;	24:1–12;	20:1–10.
His appearance at Emmaus—			24:13–35.	
His appearance at Jerusalem—			24:36–43;	20:19–25.
The Later Appearances of Jesus				
To the Disciples and Thomas—				20:26–29.
To seven Disciples by the sea—				21:1–23.
To eleven Disciples on a Galilean mountain—	28:16–20.			
At his Ascension—			24:50–53.	

Jethro (jĕth′rō) ("excellence") (alternate name Reuel, A.V. Raguel, Num. 10:29 ("friend of God"), a noble shepherd-priest of a Midianite tribe called Kenites*. Moses, fleeing from Egypt after slaying an Egyptian (Ex. 2:15–22), tended Jethro's sheep near Mt. Horeb, and there had his great theophany at the desert's burning bush (Ex. 3, E source [see SOURCES]). Moses married Jethro's shepherdess daughter, Zipporah, who bore him two sons (Ex. 3:1, 18:1 f.). From his 40 years' service with Jethro Moses was summoned by God to lead the Hebrews from their Egyptian bondage (Ex. 3:10). W. F. Albright maintains that there is substantial traditional evidence for the Moses-Jethro story. The Kenite ("belonging to coppersmiths") clan was a partly sedentary people trading with Egypt and Canaan. Jethro, who believed in God, El Shaddai, ("the One of the mountains"), rejoiced to find, during a visit to Moses at the Rephidim camp (Ex. 18:1–12), what "the Lord" had done for Moses and his company. Jethro was the father of Hobab.

jewelry, jewels used for personal adornment. Most Hebrews of ancient Palestine had few jewels—either imported or indigenous semiprecious stones and colorful minerals (I Kings 10:2, 10; Ezek. 27:22). Acquisition by gift was not unusual (II Chron. 32:27).

The first book of the Bible records a betrothal gift of jewelry to Rebekah and her family (Gen. 24:22, 30, 47, 53); and the last book of the N.T. uses jewel terminology to express the radiance of the New Jerusalem (Rev. 21). Between these are numerous allusions to jewels. Exodus 11:2, e.g., tells how the Israelites, on the eve of their departure from Egypt, asked of their Delta neighbors "jewels of silver, and jewels of gold"—which may have found their way into the golden calf (Ex. 32).

Prehistoric Palestinians adorned themselves. Natufian* men who lived c. 10,000 years ago on terraces outside Mt. Carmel's excavated caves wore necklaces and headdresses of shell, bone, and fish vertebrae. In the early Hebrew Monarchy the then scarce iron was used for men's bracelets and anklets, one of which was found by Elihu Grant at Beth-shemesh, dating from about the time of David's accession. During his conquests David acquired such treasures as the jeweled crown of the King of Ammon in E. Palestine (II Sam. 12:30). The crowns of Israel were long treasured; two centuries after David young Joash had "the crown" placed on his head (II Chron. 23:11). By the time of Solomon, foreign trade had increased Israel's resources, so that the king had not only a gold-and-ivory-trimmed throne, but stocks of metals and gems, many of which had been presented by the kings and governors of Arabia. The Queen of Sheba brought Solomon gold and precious stones (I Kings 10:2, 10)—possibly from Ophir and Bahrein. His Temple altar was lighted with golden candlesticks standing near a hundred golden basins (II Chron. 4:7 f.).

Among the prophets, Ezekiel prophesied the seizure of Israel's gems by their enemies whom God would use to punish His apostate people for turning to Asherah and the local Baals (23:26). Hosea told the people that in going to worship Baal decked out in jewels as if after lovers, they had forgotten that it was Yahweh who had given them their silver and gold. The Second Isaiah excoriated those who hired goldsmiths to fashion idols (46:6).

Jewelry among O.T. Hebrews included gem seals (see SEAL), coronets, bracelets, ear and nose rings, armlets and anklets, gold nets for hair, pendants, and fancy cosmetic cases. In early times every important Mesopotamian man wore his personal seal round his neck on a cord; later it was set in a ring. Much has been published concerning the seals of Near Eastern glyptic artists.

218. Rings, earrings, pin, and pendant from Tell el-'Ajjûl (17th-16th century B.C.).

For thousands of years Jews and other Semites have been skilled jewelers, fashioning wires of gold and silver into lacy ornaments, often studded with jewels. These craftsmen can be seen today sitting with their fining pots (Prov. 17:3) in the shadowy *sûks* of old Jerusalem and the jewelry stalls of Damascus. Many Jews who had improved their skills during the Captivity returned to Jerusalem (Neh. 3:31 f.); and it must have been a joy to them to see the gold and silver platters, knives, and bowls which Nebuchadnezzar had confiscated returned to Jerusalem (Ezra 1:9–11, cf. 2:69, 5:14).

There are four famous lists of stones in the Bible. (1) The breastplate* of the Jewish high priest was studded with twelve stones, on each of which was engraved (? incised) the name of one of Twelve Tribes. The stones were set in four rows, three to a row: sardius, topaz, carbuncle; emerald, sapphire, diamond;

ligure, agate, amethyst; beryl, onyx, jasper (Ex. 28:17–21, 39:10–14). (2) Job described the resplendence of wisdom in terms of gold ("it cannot be valued with the gold of Ophir," 28:16) and jewels, known to him from his native highland mines: onyx, sapphire, crystal, coral, pearls, rubies, topaz (28:16–19). (3) Ezekiel, attempting to describe the rich garments of the merchant-king of Phoenician Tyre, mentioned "every precious stone . . . the sardius, topaz, and the diamond, the beryl, the onyx, and the jasper, the sapphire, the emerald, and the carbuncle . . ." (4) The author of Revelation wrote of precious stones incised or engraved with the names of the twelve Apostles, and set into the foundations of the city wall (Rev. 21:12, 18–21). This may reflect the acquaintance of the author with the Near Eastern custom of building foundation deposits of jewels and precious metals in temples, as at Edfu and Ephesus; and in palaces, as at Persepolis.

It seems futile to attempt to identify these stones in modern terms. Among the A.V., the A.S.V., and the R.S.V. there are such variations as topaz for chrysoprase, agate for chalcedony, and onyx for sardonyx. The ancients may have called lapis lazuli "sapphire," red carnelian "ruby," and malachite "beryl."

In the N.T. books appear various attitudes toward jewels. Jesus appreciated their beauty in his Parable of the Merchant seeking the pearl of great price (Matt. 13:45 f.), and in his mention of the signet ring placed on the finger of the Prodigal Son by his father (Luke 15:22). Paul decried the gold and pearls of vain women (I Tim. 2:9). James (2:2) alluded to a man entering a synagogue wearing a ring, but mentioned the ornament merely to indicate the man's station in life; he saw "every good gift" as coming from the Father of lights (1:17).

In O.T. and N.T. times people felt concern for the safety of their jewels and their lumps of metal money or coins. They either wore their jewels or concealed them on their persons; though sometimes they buried their jewels in the ground, as did the man of Christ's Parable of the Hidden Treasure (Matt. 13:44). At Megiddo, under the floor of a palace room, modern investigators turned up as choice a collection of jewelry as has been found in Palestine (now in the Museum of the Oriental Institute, Chicago): the treasure of a prince who ruled Megiddo in the 15th–14th century B.C. Fearing an invasion, such as marked the period just before the Judges and the first kings of Israel, the prince or his servant hid an electrum ring with scarab setting, a gold-mesh chain, a whetstone capped with gold, some lapis lazuli cylinder seals, a heavy gold bowl, beads of granulated gold, twin heads wearing disk crowns, etc.

219. Gold jewelry cached beneath a palace floor in Megiddo, dated to 14th century B.C.; discovered in 20th century A.D. Top row, shell-shaped gold bowl flanked by lapis-lazuli cylinder seals and gold-trimmed cosmetic jars; center, twin heads of gold and rosettes of gold leaf; bottom row, left to right, gold objects joined by gold-mesh chain, ceremonial whetstone with two gold caps, electrum ring with scarab setting, and two gold headbands.

Because of the constant looting and levying of tribute by aggressors in the Middle East, most of the jewels of the Biblical period have been lost; but several collections have been excavated, like the Hyksos golden jewelry from Tell el-'Ajjûl (see 'AJJÛL, TELL EL-) S. of Gaza, and may be seen in museums. For example, the small National Museum of

Lebanon at Beirut displays the hinge-clasped, solid gold and enamel bracelets of King Ahiram of Byblos; silver-soled sandals; scarabs, pins, sceptre, and statuettes, displaying the Egyptian backgrounds of their donors to the Phoenician monarch; and also some Phoenician jewelers' work. The Palestine Archaeological Museum in Jerusalem has jewelry excavated at various sites in Palestine, Trans-Jordan, and other parts of the Middle East. Most resplendent of all are the Egyptian National Museum's unsurpassed treasures of Tut-ankh-amun in Cairo, including his countless rings, flat *useks* or necklaces, bracelets, amulets, diadems, and jeweled breastplates. One of the flat, rounded, jeweled collars of this Eighteenth-Dynasty pharaoh was so heavy that it required a bronze pendant to be worn down his back as a counterbalance. The National Archaeological Museum in Athens houses the Mycenaean gems and rosettes, and the famous Vapphio golden cups with the embossed and gleaming Minoan bull. Such cups recall Joseph's silver cup tucked into Benjamin's grain sack (Gen. 44:2, 5, 8, 17); and Nehemiah, cupbearer at the Persian court (Neh. 1:11). A broad and shallow "Queen Esther" golden cup has been recovered from the palace city of Shushan. The 5th-century B.C. silver bowl of Artaxerxes I is in the Metropolitan Museum of Art. Possibly the most famous cup of the Middle East is the Antioch* Chalice, whose carved metal work encases what some have hypothesized to be the cup used by Jesus at the Last Supper. This chalice (now in The Cloisters, New York) may date from the early Christian centuries. The University Museum in Philadelphia has some of the jewels and precious *objets d'art* from before 3000 B.C., recovered by Sir Leonard Woolley from Ur of the Chaldees, birthplace of Abraham; a group of gold and electrum rosettes and beads from the Mesopotamian Tepe Gawra; and many seals carved in semiprecious stones. The British Museum has early Sumerian jewelry. The Metropolitan Museum of Art (New York) is exceptionally rich in Egyptian jewelry from before and after Joseph. A valuable collection of seals is in the Stevens Library at Yale. (See BOWLS, illus. 66; BRACELETS, illus. 67.)

Jews, members of the Hebrew race. The word was used especially during and after the Exile to mean people who had gone from and returned to Jerusalem and Judaea. See HEBREWS; ISRAEL.

Jezebel (jĕz′ĕ-bĕl), a daughter of King Ethbaal of Tyre ("of the Zidonians," A.V. I Kings 16:31), advocate of the Tyrian Baal* and Astarte (see ASHERAH), and the wife of King Ahab of Israel, of the Omri dynasty (c. 869–850 B.C.). As a champion of Baal worship Jezebel led the king and Israel into the gross immoralities of this popular religion, and brought to the royal table hundreds of priests and prophets of this cult from her Phoenician homeland (I Kings 18:19). From Ahab's luxurious court at Samaria she persecuted the prophets of God, and ordered many slain when they protested against her immoral regime (I Kings 18:4). She clashed with the great Hebrew prophet Elijah*, who demanded a contest on Mt. Carmel between the power of Yahweh and that of Baal—one of the most dramatic passages of the O.T. (I Kings 18:21–46).

Baal's defeat inflamed the rage of Jezebel, who threatened Elijah and caused him to flee into the wilderness (I Kings 19:4 ff.). Another example of Jezebel's evil-doing is found in the tragic story of Naboth's vineyard (chap. 21). The queen's horrible end, prophesied in II Kings 9:10, is narrated in 9:30–37.

In Rev. 2:20 Jezebel's name is applied to a seductive "prophetess" who encouraged immorality at Thyatira. The name is now synonymous with wickedness.

Jezreel (jĕz′rē-ĕl) ("whom God soweth"). (1) The valley better known as the Plain of Esdraelon*—a vast, well-watered, exceedingly fertile plain extending SE. across Palestine from N. of Mt. Carmel to the deep pass leading down to the Jordan. Jezreel's most strategic pass leads S. over the Carmel ridge to the coastal plain, and is guarded by the fortified hillock Tell el-Mutesellim (Megiddo*), excavated by the Oriental Institute of the University of Chicago. Through this pass ran the main highway between Syria and Egypt. N. and S. across the plain of Jezreel ran the main highway from Damascus, through Galilee, and across Samaria to Jerusalem, whence a network of inland roads ran S. to Gaza and Joppa and W. to the Mediterranean. The plain of Jezreel has always been coveted by aggressors, and in countless crises has been the stage for the battles of Armageddon*. In certain O.T. passages the Valley of Jezreel is more narrowly used to indicate the vale dropping SE. from the town of Jezreel to the Jordan, rather than the wider stretch reaching NW. to Carmel. Strong centers of Canaanite culture were located in the plain of Jezreel at Accho (the present Acre), Taanach, Megiddo, and Beth-shan. It was coveted by the sons of Joseph, who complained to Joshua that their wooded highland territory was too small, and that the great plain was held by threatening Canaanites using iron-rimmed war chariots (Josh. 17:16). See ELIJAH, illus. 128.

(2) A town (the present Zer'in) on a NW. spur of the Gilboa Mountains overlooking the plain near a copious fountain (I Sam. 29:1). Its strong watchtower commanded a view to the Jordan pass, used by hungry mobs of desert peoples advancing to seize the fruitful harvest fields of the plain, as in Gideon's time (Judg. 6:33–7:23). It was a royal city of Israel's kings (I Kings 18:45 f., 21:1 ff.), though Samaria was the capital. The main N.-S. highway from Nazareth to Jerusalem ran through the town of Jezreel.

The O.T. contains numerous references to events which occurred in Jezreel:

By its fountain, Israel's forces gathered before the Battle of Gilboa—	I Sam. 29:1
Controlled by Ish-bosheth—	II Sam. 2:10
Administrative district of Solomon—	I Kings 4:12
Naboth's vineyard tragedy—	I Kings 21:1–24

Joram's healing—	II Kings 8:29, 9:15
Joram and Jezebel killed by Jehu—	II Kings 9:24, 30–37
Murder of all Ahab's heirs by Jehu—	II Kings 10:1–11

(3) The town in Judah where David found his wife Ahinoam the Jezreelitess (I Sam. 25:43, 27:3, 30:5). (4) The symbolic name of Hosea's eldest son (Hos. 1:4); and of Israel (Hos. 2:22).

Joab (jō′ăb) ("Jehovah is father"). (1) A son of Seraiah and founder of a group of craftsmen (I Chron. 4:14; cf. Neh. 11:35) in the Valley of Charashim—possibly the Wâdī esh-Shellal, running NW. from Lydda toward Joppa.

(2) A son of Zeruiah, half-sister of David (II Sam. 2:18), and brother of the fleet-footed Asahel and the sturdy Abishai; he became commander-in-chief of David's army. It was his crafty entry into the Jebusite (see JEBUS) stronghold that obtained control of Jerusalem (II Sam. 5:8; I Chron. 11:6–8); Joab helped repair the breaches. But for his loyal devotion to David the Monarchy would have been difficult to establish. Though at times Joab's deeds were marked by savage cruelty, and his motives appeared as mixed as those of most men of the 10th century B.C. in Israel, his magnanimity was equally evident. His murder of Abner, general of the Northern Kingdom under Ish-bosheth, who had slain Joab's brother Asahel (II Sam. 2:18–23), provoked the wrathful rebuke of David, who saw to it that Abner had honorable burial, including an elegy attributed to David himself (II Sam. 3:33 f.). Successful campaigns were led by Joab against the Syrians and the Ammonites. His capture of the citadel at Rabbath-ammon (the present 'Ammân, capital of Arab Jordan) was marked by his insistence that David should have the privilege of taking the acropolis in person, receive credit for the victory, and accept the booty (II Sam. 12:26–31). In his successful contest with Edom Joab was needlessly cruel (I Kings 11:15 f.). Yet he was the mediator who attempted to reconcile David and his rebellious son Absalom (II Sam. 14)—though later, when Absalom revolted against David, Joab drove in the three darts that ended the prince's life as he dangled by his hair from a tree (II Sam. 18:14). Joab carried out David's order to place Uriah, husband of Bath-sheba, in the front line of battle—the equivalent of causing his murder (II Sam. 11:6–25)—and put down the revolt of Sheba; he slew the tardy Amasa, David's general, with his own hand (II Sam. 20:4-22). In David's old age Joab supported the wrong claimant to the successorship, Adonijah (I Kings 1:5–53); later this cost Joab his life (I Kings 2:34). Solomon, applying the law of blood revenge (Ex. 21:14 f.), regarded Joab as a murderer, and declared that David on his deathbed had charged him to dispose of Joab (I Kings 2:5 f.).

(3) The founder of a family, some of whom are listed among those who returned from Exile* (Ezra 2:6, 8:9; Neh. 7:11).

Joanna ("Jehovah hath been gracious"). (1) The wife of Chuza (A.S.V. Luke 8:3 Chuzas), a supervisor of the household of the tetrarch Herod Antipas* at Jerusalem. Like other converts to the Way, she contributed of her means to Jesus (A.V. Luke 8:3) and his company (R.S.V.). Along with Mary called Magdalene and Mary the mother of James and others, Joanna went to anoint the body of Jesus. They found the tomb empty and heard the message of two men "in shining garments" who said: "He is not here, but is risen" (Luke 23:55–24:11). (2) (Joanan A.S.V., R.S.V.) A son of Rhesa, ancestor of Jesus (Luke 3:27).

Joannan (jŏ-ăn′ăn) (A.V. I Macc. 2:2), the eldest son of Mattathias.

Joash (jō′ăsh) (Jo'ash, short form of Jehoash, "Jehovah has given"). (1) Gideon's father (Judg. 6:11). This Joash (with a Yahwistic name) erected an altar to Baal at his home, Ophrah of Abiezer (Judg. 6:11, 24). This place, never identified exactly, was probably on the N. edge of Manasseh's territory in Cis-jordan, a region that was exposed to considerable Canaanite Baal influence. This explains why, when local idolaters threatened Gideon with death because he had broken down the Baal shrine and an Asherah (Judg. 6:28), Joash gave as his shrewd retort the words of Judg. 6:31 f. from which the story derives Gideon's other name, "Jerubbaal." (2) A son of King Ahab of Samaria (unless "king's son" is a mere title). To him Ahab sent the prophet Micaiah (not Micah) for imprisonment after an unfavorable pronouncement (I Kings 22:26 f.; II Chron. 18:25 f.). (3) A descendant of Judah of the family of Shelah (I Chron. 4:22). (4) An adherent of David at Ziklag (I Chron. 12:3).

(5) The 8th king of Judah (c. 837–800 B.C.), a son of Ahaziah*. His story is told in II Kings 11, 12 and II Chron. 22:11–24:27. Joash as a young child was rescued from the murderous plot of Athaliah* by his aunt Jehoshabeath*, the wife of Jerusalem's high priest Jehoiada and sister of the late king. Joash was concealed by his aunt in a bedchamber, then for about six years in the Temple precincts (II Chron. 22:11 ff.). In his 7th year the prince was brought out by Jehoiada and displayed in the Temple court to the civil and military leaders (II Kings 11:4 ff.), who were drawn into a covenant to protect the rightful king (vv. 4–8), and were equipped with royal arms that had been stored in the sacred area (v. 10). Hearing the acclaim that attended the anointing and crowning of Joash, Athaliah came to the Temple crying, "Treason!" But she was slain by the loyal guard (v. 16). As long as Jehoiada was at the young king's side, and had a voice even in the selection of his wives to insure the royal succession (II Chron. 24:3), Joash "did that which was right in the sight of the Lord." He reduced Baal worship, even though he did not remove the high places frequented by his subjects (II Kings 12:3). He promoted extensive Temple repairs (II Kings 12:4–16) out of freewill offerings placed by the people in a chest prepared by Jehoiada (vv. 9–16). But after Jehoiada's death

Joash lapsed from moral reform, and even precipitated the stoning of his sponsor's son Zechariah, who had reproved his evil acts (II Chron. 24:15–22, cf. Matt. 23:35). When he was threatened by Hazael of Syria Joash bought him off with some of the Temple treasures dedicated to the Lord (II Kings 12:18). After a reign of about 40 years (II Chron. 24:1) Joash was murdered in Millo, the section of Jerusalem developed by David. He was not buried, however, in the sepulchers of the kings (II Chron. 24:25). He was in the 23d year of his reign when Jehoahaz ascended the northern throne (II Kings 13:1).

(6) The 12th king of Israel (c. 801–786 B.C.), 3d in the Jehu dynasty, and successor of Jehoahaz (II Kings 13:9–25). He shared the apostasies of Jeroboam* I (II Kings 13:11), but was honored for his recovery of Israelite territory which his father had lost to Syria (II Kings 13:25)—possibly because of Assyrian pressure on his foe. But the words of the dying prophet Elisha*, whom Joash visited in an act of deference (v. 14), reveal that the sage was disappointed in the king for not following up his advantage over the Syrians (v. 19). Challenged by King Amaziah of Judah, Joash went forth to meet his southern neighbor; worsted his army at Beth-shemesh* in Judah (II Kings 14:8–12); and carried back to his capital at Samaria vessels from the Temple, treasures from the palaces, and hostages (v. 14). He is said to have uttered his famous fable of the cedar and the thistle on the occasion of his war with Amaziah (II Kings 14:9–10; II Chron. 25:18–19). Joash was buried with the kings of Samaria and was succeeded by his able and active son Jeroboam II (II Kings 14:16).

(Jo'ash, "Jehovah has come to help"). (7) A son of Becher (I Chron. 7:8). (8) A keeper of David's store of oil (I Chron. 27:28).

Job, the Book of, a superb poem, in dialogue form, with narrative prologue and epilogue in prose, and belonging to the Wisdom Literature of Israel. It is the longest-sustained and finest poetic composition in the Hebrew Canon.

The Book of Job challenged the validity of a doctrine commonly prevalent in the orthodox thought and literature of the ancient world, and found especially in the Book of Proverbs: namely, that the righteous and the wicked receive their just deserts on earth. It was written because an unknown philosopher-poet could not reconcile this doctrine and the observable facts of life. At the time of its writing, the Book of Job was an expression of revolt against the dogma that there is only one cause of suffering—sin. The unknown author took the familiar folk story of Job (perhaps similar to the prologue and epilogue as we have it today; the evidence is inconclusive) and created an immortal poem recording the history of a just soul that suffered, despaired, and yet hoped and battled on until it found peace. To its readers from the first, the book has stood as a most profound questioning of God's justice in His dealings with human beings and study of the universal problem of suffering.

Who the author may have been is a complete mystery. Whether Jew or Edomite is a question much argued on dubious evidence. The case for a Hebrew author rests largely on references to civil and moral prescriptions (22:6; 24:9, cf. Ex. 22:26; Job 24:2, cf. Deut. 19:14), familiarity with a few O.T. writings, and mention of the name of the God of Israel, Yahweh, in the prologue and epilogue, and in the superscriptions of God's speeches and Job's answers. In rebuttal, those who hold that the author was an Edomite state that the references to civil and moral prescriptions represent practices in force among

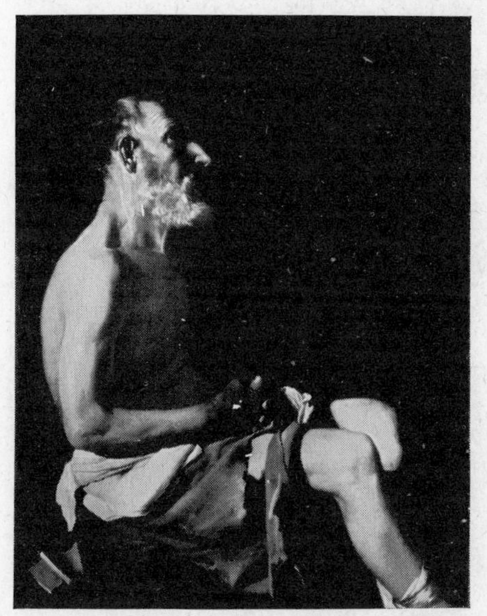

220. Job, *by D. R. Velazquez.*

all ancient civilized nations; that the author was obviously a learned man and consequently familiar with the "wisdom" of other nations, and able to read Israelitic writings easily, since his own language was only dialectically different from Hebrew; and finally that "Yahweh" is never used in the poem proper, where various terms for "God" are used, one of which designates the deity that comes from Teman in Edom. Further, the Hebrew of Job is unusual, being strongly influenced by Arabic and Aramaic; the geographical background of the folk tale is also thought by some to be Edomitic. If the author was a Jew, there was obviously a strong Edomitic influence in his background.

Similarly there is little agreement on the date of the poem in its earliest form. It cannot be later than 200 B.C., while the folk story, in its oral form at least, goes back to remote antiquity. There are in Job no positive allusions to historical events or persons. Dates ranging from 700 to 200 B.C. can be and are supported, precariously. The largest number of scholars narrow the period to 600–400 B.C., when the question of divine earthly retribution, national and individual, was of general concern.

There is complete agreement on the uniqueness of the Book of Job as a literary masterpiece. Although parallels to portions of the form and substance of the Book of Job can be found (e.g. the Babylonian "I will praise the Lord of Wisdom"), there is no close parallel to it as a whole, nor does it fit into any of the standard categories of literature. It is not truly a dramatic poem; it is often lyric and almost epic; reflective or didactic are less adequate classifications for the whole of its structure and content. The general form is that of a debate, yet there are compositions within it which can be read quite independently of the argument: doxologies (5:8–16; 9:4–10; 12:13–25); lyric laments (3:11–19; 7:1–10, 11–21; 9:25–31, etc.); and petitions to God (10:1–22, 13:20–28; 14:13–17). The indictment of Job (22:5–11) and his defense (31) are fine examples of forensic literature. All these gems (and many others) have their place, however, in the general scheme; they are also overwhelming evidence of the greatness of the art of the author. His vocabulary is wider that that of any other O.T. writer; his powers of expression are unmatched; he was a scholar of vast knowledge, an original theological thinker, a careful observer of nature; he was also a man of sensitivity, capable of intense emotion and varying moods, reflected in a style rich in contrast. In understanding, imagination, and art he may be compared with Shakespeare.

Job as a historical Biblical figure is but the shadow of a shadow. Job as a legendary character, the hero of a folk tale, had substance in the Hebrew tradition. The Book of Job starts (1:1–2:13) with this prose tale of the man who withstood every test, and concludes (42:10b–17) with his reward. Whether prologue and epilogue of the book we now have once formed a separate, earlier folk book, or whether it was written by the poet himself, or by later editors, is undecided; the problems are complicated and the evidence slim. The question is far less important than recognition that the legend of Job had existed for centuries, and that the poet borrowed from the folk saga. The story was familiar to Ezekiel and his hearers (Ezek. 14:14, 20) before the middle of the 6th century B.C., and probably circulated much earlier. The prologue and epilogue are generally regarded as a slightly touched-up form of the tale, with insertions (2:11–13, 42:7–10a) to make framework and poem more suitable to each other, and others, by warning the reader what to expect (1:22, 2:10), to harmonize the poet's desperate, insistent Job with the pious, patient Job of legend. Regardless of such problems of literary criticism, the viewpoint of the folk tale with regard to the suffering of an innocent man should not be considered that of the poet. The tale becomes the vehicle for an investigation of theological and philosophical problems that far outstrip the folk tale and its simple folk philosophy.

The basic problem under discussion in the debate between Job and the three dogmatists, Eliphaz, Bildad, and Zophar, was the justice of God in His dealings with human beings. Eliphaz in his first speech (4, 5) presents the case of the friends: No innocent man ever perished through affliction; only the wicked are consumed by God's anger. Job's difficulties are explainable either as punishment for his natural sinfulness (all men being sinful) or as chastisement with intent to improve his character. Anyway, God is just and merciful and will spare Job if the latter will commit himself fully to God. All of the later speeches of the trio only fortify this argument (8:3–7, 20; 18:5–21; 20:4–29; 22:3–11). Job admits the sinfulness of man and the omnipotence of God. But he hotly denies his friends' thesis that human conduct is justly rewarded or punished on earth by a just God, and repeatedly asserts his own innocence in support of his convictions. He infers that in making Job suffer God is unjust and heartless. Job's arguments open many philosophical vistas: Is God responsible for everything in the world, and therefore for evil? Does suffering have a rational purpose and explanation? If not, can God be regarded as just? Thus the author tackles the problem of evil from a philosophical point of view almost unknown in O.T. literature. God, to the author, is an inscrutable, exalted, transcendent force. The author seems at times (9:4–24) to argue that God is almighty, but not just—at least according to man's standards. He does, however, realize that man's understanding is limited, and so no final answer can be reached.

The dramatic climax tends however to turn away from the pessimistic theological position toward which the author had been advancing. The speech of "the Eternal" (Job 38–41, Moffatt) is a series of unanswerable questions on the mysteries of the universe, such as the creation, the marvelous wonders of the world of nature and of animal life, God's government of the world, and the significance of man in the total picture. In the last scene of the drama Job receives the humbling—and yet comforting—revelation of God's interest in him. With a new realization that he, Job, is insignificant within the universe, but still without an answer to the problem of suffering, he accepts the vision itself as the solution for him. His acceptance was based, not on the false theological ideas known to and expounded by others, but on a conviction arrived at through personal experience (cf. Matt. 5:8). Job was rewarded by his inner assurance, "I know that my redeemer [A.S.V. margin "vindicator"] liveth" (19:25). However mysterious His rule may be, God does rule, and for the best; God did appear to him, implying vindication of Job's argument; God is on Job's side. True piety needs no outward attestation, no social approval. Therefore whatever suffering befalls the pure in heart they can endure, because their spiritual integrity, the witness of their own conscience, is its own reward and the surest way to find the peace of God.

The long-winded speeches of Elihu (32–37) are a later addition, perhaps by a poet who found it incredible that Job should be winning the debate. They interrupt the connection between Job's final challenge and God's answer. Many think that the beautiful poem on wisdom (28), and especially the descriptions of the ostrich (39:13–18), hippopotamus and crocodile (40:15–41:34) are additions by other hands.

A brief outline of the book follows:

(1) The Prologue—1, 2.
(2) The Poem—3:1–42:6;
 (a) Job bewails his birth and longs for death—3.
 (b) Three series of debates—
  (*a*) Eliphaz, 4, 5; Job, 6, 7. Bildad, 8; Job, 9, 10. Zophar, 11; Job, 12–14.
  (*b*) Eliphaz, 15; Job, 16, 17. Bildad, 18; Job, 19. Zophar, 20; Job, 21.
  (*c*) Eliphaz, 22; Job, 23, 24. Bildad, 25; Job, 26, 27.
 (c) The poem on wisdom—28.
 (d) Job reviews his life—29–31.
 (e) The speeches of Elihu—32–37.
 (f) Jehovah speaks—38–41.
 (g) Job's submission—42:1–6.
(3) The Epilogue—42:7–17.

Jobab (jō′băb). (1) Mentioned in the ethnological lists of Gen. 10:29; I Chron. 1:23 as a "son" of Joktan, descendant of Shem, and representing an Arabian tribe. (2) An Edomite king (Gen. 36:33 f.; I Chron. 1:44 f.). (3) A king allied with Jabin of Canaanite Hazor who fought against Joshua (Josh. 11:1). (4) and (5) Two men of Benjamin's Tribe (I Chron. 8:9, 18).

Jochebed (jŏk′ĕ-bĕd) ("Jehovah is glory"), the wife of Amram and mother of Aaron and Moses (Ex. 6:20; Num. 26:59, P). The E document calls her simply "a daughter of Levi" (Ex. 2:1).

Joel (jō′ĕl) ("Jehovah is God"). (1) The eldest son of Samuel and the father of Heman (I Sam. 8:2; I Chron. 6:33, 15:17). (2) An ancestor of Samuel (I Chron. 6:36). (3) A Simeonite prince (I Chron. 4:35). (4) A Reubenite (I Chron. 5:4, 8). (5) A Gadite chief (I Chron. 5:12). (6) A man of Issachar (I Chron. 7:3). (7) One of David's heroes (I Chron. 11:38). (8), (9), (10) Levites (I Chron. 15:7, 11, 23:8, 26:22; II Chron. 29:12). Possibly these references concern only two persons. (11) A Manassite chief (I Chron. 27:20). (12) A husband of a foreign wife (Ezra 10:43). (13) An overseer of the laity (Neh. 11:9). (14) A son of Pethuel (Joel 1:1), and author of the 2d book of the Minor Prophets. Nothing is known about him, other than what his book reveals of his remarkable gifts and insights. Judah (probably Jerusalem) was the theater of Joel's prophetic activity.

Joel, the Book of, is the 2d book among the Minor Prophets. It may be divided into three sections:

(1) Chap. 1:1–2:17: The plague of locusts.

(2) Chap. 2:18–27: The Lord shows pity and bestows material blessings.

(3) Chap. 2:28–3:21: The Lord will administer justice and bestow spiritual blessings.

In the Hebrew 2:28–32 is chap. 3, and chap. 3 is chap. 4.

The terrific destruction wrought by a plague of locusts on the agricultural, economic, and religious life of a people is described with almost scientific accuracy, according to many who have witnessed such a scourge (1:5–20, cf. Amos 7:1 f.). Joel 1:4 records under different names four different kinds of locusts—or rather locusts in progressive stages of development. Military invasions from the N. (cf. 2:20) furnished the prophet with poetic and rhetorical phrases to intensify his picture of the devastation wrought by this locust invasion (2:4–11; Rev. 9:3–10). Some view Joel's description as figurative, others as Apocalyptic; but most O.T. students consider the locust plague as a historical event in the prophet's lifetime, a terrible experience from which religious truth and Apocalyptic insight were revealed. Such catastrophes in nature cause religious upheavals in man. Joel, like most O.T. writers, attributed disaster to man's departure from God (2:12–14). Between 2:17 and 2:18 a period of time elapsed during which the people presumably repented. The Lord promised to remove the locusts (2:20); the recuperative forces of nature would operate (vv. 22 f.), prosperity would return (vv. 24 f.), and a repentant people would have their faith in God confirmed (vv. 26 f.). The remaining portion of the book is eschatological in character. The prophet looks forward to a time when the Lord's spirit will be poured out on all flesh (2:28); all Israel will share the intimate knowledge of God and the fruits of the Spirit (cf. Jer. 31:33 f.). The world will suffer judgment (3:1–16a), but Jerusalem can be confident of the Lord's protection (3:16b–21).

At times Joel's Apocalyptic ideas are intermingled with the historical; at other times they stand out alone. Peter saw in the phenomena of Pentecost* the fulfillment of Joel's prophecies (Acts 2:16–21, cf. Joel 2:28–32). The disastrous experience with the locusts was but a preview of "the Day of the Lord" (Joel 1:15, 2:1, 10 f.), an idea used in Amos 5:18–20, Isa. 2:5–22; Zeph. 1:14–18 (see ESCHATOLOGY). The locale of the final judgment* was definitely envisioned (Joel 3:2, 12). The people of Tyre, Sidon, and Philistia would fare ill in this judgment, because they sold Jews as slaves to the Greeks (Joel 3:1–8); Egypt and Edom would also be punished, because they shed Jewish blood (3:19). Throughout the book God's spirit is limited exclusively to Israel. Joel by his cries to arms (3:10 f.) and his paean of joy over the destruction of Judah's enemies (3:19 ff.) is linked with the vengeful and the racially exclusive group in Judaism.

The date of the book must be determined from internal evidence. The Monarchy is not mentioned. Elders and priests are the authorities (1:2, 13, 2:16 f.). Israel consists only of Judah (2:27, 3:2, 16). Jerusalem is the holy place (3:17). The Temple, rebuilt 520–516 B.C., is standing (1:13 f., 2:15–17). The completion of the Jerusalem wall (2:9) dates the book at least after Nehemiah (c. 445 B.C.). In place of the denunciations of specific iniquities characteristic of pre-Exilic oracles, Joel's call to repentance (2:12 f.) mentions no particular sin; he urges the performance of ritual ceremonies, viz., congregational fasting, weeping, and mourning (2:12). Daily offerings and libations in the Temple had become the fixed symbol of the current relations between the Lord and His people (1:9, 13, 2:14). Like other clues in the book, Jewish pride in racial superiority and divine favoritism, tends to date Joel c. 350 B.C.

J. L. M./R. W. C.

Johanan (jō-hā'năn) (short form of Jehohanan*, Heb. "John," meaning "Jehovah is gracious"). (1) A son of Careah (Kareah), who joined Gedaliah* after the fall of Jerusalem (II Kings 25:23; Jer. 40:8), and took part in leading a remnant, with Jeremiah, to Egypt (Jer. 41:11–43:7). (2) The eldest son of King Josiah (I Chron. 3:15, 24). (3) A post-Exilic prince of the house of David (I Chron. 6:9, 10). (4) A high priest (I Chron. 6:9 f.). (5) and (6) Two men who joined David at Ziklag; (a) a Benjamite (I Chron. 12:4); (b) a Gadite (I Chron. 12:12). (7) A man of Ephraim (II Chron. 28:12). (8) A son of Hakkatan who returned to Jerusalem from Babylon with Ezra (Ezra 8:12). (9) A high priest, son of Eliashib (Ezra 10:6, A.S.V., R.S.V. "Jehohanan"; Neh. 12:23). The Johanan of Neh. 12:22 f. was contemporary with Alexander the Great. The one mentioned in the Elephantine papyri was the high priest (c. 408 B.C.) whom the Jews of Egypt begged to bring to Darius* II (Darius the Mede) their complaints against their Egyptian neighbors. (10) See JOANNAN.

John ("Jehovah hath been gracious"), the father of the Apostle Peter (John 1:42), called "Jona" in the A.V., "John" in the A.S.V. and R.S.V. of this passage; "Jonas" in A.V. John 21:15–17, but "John" in the A.S.V. and R.S.V. of this passage. Nothing is known of him except his relationship to Peter and Andrew.

John the Apostle, a son of Zebedee, who was a Galilean fisherman. Both John and his brother James were fishermen also. The family was apparently prosperous, for Zebedee employed hired servants (Mark 1:20). It has been inferred that the mother of John and James was Salome (Matt. 27:56, cf. Mark 15:40, 16:1), and that she may possibly have been a sister of Mary, the mother of Jesus (John 19:25). John was among the earliest disciples "called" to follow Jesus (Mark 1:19 f.; Matt. 4:21 f.). The acts of John and James (Mark 9:38; Luke 9:52–56) reveal their fiery, impetuous nature. Jesus called them Boanerges, "sons of thunder" or "sons of anger" (Mark 3:17). They asked special honors for themselves, but said they were ready to face death (Mark 10:35–41; Matt. 20:20–24). In the lists of the Twelve, John is always among the first four (Matt. 10:2; Mark 3:14–17; Luke 6:13 f.). He was one of the inner circle of three at the raising of Jairus' daughter (Mark 5:37; Luke 8:51); at the Transfiguration (Matt. 17:1; Mark 9:2; Luke 9:28); and at Gethsemane (Matt. 26:37; Mark 14:33).

It has been conjectured that John the son of Zebedee is the unnamed "beloved disciple" who occupies a prominent place in the Fourth Gospel. (1) At the Last Supper he leaned on Jesus' breast (John 13:23); (2) at the Cross he alone was faithful, and was entrusted with the care of Jesus' mother (John 19:26 f.); (3) at the Tomb he was the first to believe in Jesus' Resurrection (John 20:1–10); (4) at the Sea of Galilee he first recognized the Lord (John 21:1–7). Of the three prominent members of the Twelve, Peter, James, and John, only John seems to fit the picture of "the beloved disciple," yet many scholars believe that it is impossible to identify him as "the beloved disciple" of the Fourth Gospel.

Outside the Gospels there are few references to John. He was one of the little company of Jesus' followers who waited in Jerusalem after the Ascension (Acts 1:13). Twice he appeared in company with Peter: when the two went up to the Temple to pray and there healed the lame man (Acts 3:1–4:22); and when they were sent to Samaria to investigate the progress of the Gospel there (Acts 8:14–17). The earliest reference to John is in Galatians 2:9, where Paul states that when he visited Jerusalem (c. A.D. 50) John, together with James and Cephas, "seemed to be pillars" of the mother Church.

Some traditions connect John the Apostle with Ephesus. According to Eusebius, Polycrates (Bishop of Ephesus at the end of the 2d century) claimed Ephesus as the home of John, "who reclined in the bosom of the Lord." Irenaeus, a contemporary of Polycrates, said that in his youth he heard the aged Polycarp speak of having known John personally. Irenaeus says this John, the disciple of the Lord, lived in Ephesus until the reign of Trajan and published his Gospel there.

The tradition of John's residence in Ephesus is seriously undermined by the lack of evidence for it in all the subapostolic writers until A.D. 180. About A.D. 116 Ignatius wrote to Ephesus complimenting the church there for its association with Paul, but not mentioning John. This silence concerning John is inexplicable if he had died there only a few years previously, the outstanding figure of the Christian world. Papias and Polycarp are also silent on John's residence in Ephesus. In a celebrated passage Papias mentions two Johns, one the Apostle, the other an elder or presbyter. It is possible that the late 2d century tradition of John the Apostle living in Ephesus was due to a confusion of the elder with the Apostle.

It seems likely that there is authentic tradition behind a 7th- or 8th-century epitome, probably based on the *Chronicle* of Philip of Side (c. A.D. 430), which states (on the authority of the second book of Papias) that James and John the sons of Zebedee were "killed by the Jews." This presumably occurred in Palestine before A.D. 70. This third-hand evidence seems to be corroborated by Jesus' prophecy in Mark 10:35 ff., which may have been written after the martyrdom.

For the possible relation of the Apostle John to the Fourth Gospel and to the Epistles of John, see JOHN, EPISTLES OF; JOHN, THE GOSPEL OF.

John the Baptist, the immediate forerunner of Jesus; the son of the aged priest Zacharias and his wife Elisabeth (Luke 1:5–24, 56–80). Both parents were of priestly families. Luke 1:36 leads us to infer that his birth occurred about six months before that of our Lord, to whom he was related—Mary and Elisabeth were kin. Tradition has fixed the birthplace of John at 'Ain Karem, a village 4 m. W. of Jerusalem (Luke 1:39). His early religious training and life (1:66) accorded with Gabriel's predictions (1:15). There is no Scriptural evidence that John forsook the high prerogatives of his priestly birthright to become a community-minded Essene*, as some have contended; but his austere life indicates that he followed the pattern of the prophet Elias (Elijah*) (Luke 1:17; Matt. 11:12–14, 17:11 f.); devoted himself to reform (Luke 1:16); and prepared himself to be the forerunner of the Messiah (Luke 1:17). In the desert solitudes of Judaea (Luke 1:80) the ascetic John fed on locusts* and wild honey, and wore coarse garments of camel's hair and a leather girdle (Matt. 3:4; Mark 1:6; II Kings 1:8). After such rugged self-discipline, constant brooding over the Scriptures, especially on Elijah's career, and receiving an experience of God, John began his public ministry (Luke 1:80), which centered in the wilderness (Mark 1:4; "of Judaea" Matt. 3:1) and "all the country about Jordan" (Luke 3:3). The Jordan River was the main scene of his activity, for his baptisms were almost certainly by immersion (Matt. 3:6, 13, 16; Mark 1:5, 9) (see AENON; BETH-ABARAH). John baptized on both sides of the river (John 1:28, 3:23, 10:40). So distinctive was the ceremony that it gave John his unique appellation. Baptism was connected with (1) Jewish ceremonial washings (Lev. 11:40, 13:55–58, 14:8, 15:27; Num. 19, cf. Mark 1:44; Luke 2:22; John 1:25), which under John took on ethical significance (Matt. 3:2, 6); (2) the national cleansings foretold by the prophets (Jer. 33:8; Ezek. 36:25 f.; Zech. 13:1), which under John developed deeper spiritual significance (Matt. 3:11); and (3) the ceremony used by the Jews to initiate proselytes into Israel. John insisted that all must submit to baptism, irrespective of racial origin (Matt. 3:9), and show fruits of repentance, with a desire to flee from the wrath to come (Matt. 3:7 f.; Luke 3:7 f.), because the baptism of the Coming One would be for judgment (Matt. 3:12; Luke 3:17) (see JUDGMENT, DAY OF).

John attracted many hearers. The lower classes accepted baptism (Luke 7:29), but the upper classes rejected his preaching (7:30). John drew around him disciples (Matt. 9:14; Luke 7:18), whom he taught to pray (Luke 11:1); who fasted (Mark 2:18; Luke 5:33); some of whom became Christ's followers (John 1:37); visited him in prison (Matt. 11:2); carried his messages to Jesus (Luke 7:19); and entombed John's decapitated body (Mark 6:29). Twenty-five years later in Ephesus there preached an Alexandrian Jew named Apollos who knew only the baptism of John (Acts 18:25).

The baptism of Jesus by John is recorded by all the Synoptists (Matt. 3:13 ff.; Mark 1:9 f.; Luke 3:21); and the Fourth Gospel corroborates the Messianic sign attending the ceremony (John 1:32; Matt. 3:16; Mark 1:10; Luke 3:22). Jesus insisted on the rite for himself as a part of his Messianic mission (Matt. 3:15). John 1:24–36 is the testimony of John concerning Jesus. "Behold the Lamb of God . . ." (John 1:29) shows the depth of the Baptist's understanding of Christ. (See MESSIAH.)

The career of John the Baptist was cut short by Herod* Antipas, who caused his arrest; any such popular following as John had was certain to arouse the suspicion of the nervous Roman authorities, and Herod had also a personal reason for antipathy to John (Mark 6:17–20; Matt. 14:3 ff.; Luke 3:19). Fear of the people (Matt. 14:5) and of John himself—whom he nevertheless had heard gladly (Mark 6:20)—led Herod to grant the request of Herodias made through her dancing daughter Salome (Matt. 14:6–12; Mark 6:21–28). Josephus declared that the Castle of Machaerus on the E. shore of the Dead Sea was the scene of John's imprisonment and death.

Jesus accorded John the highest praise (Matt. 11:9, 11, 14; Luke 7:25 f.; John 5:35), and attached divine value to John's baptism (Matt. 3:15, 21:25). John adopted baptism as a symbol of his reforming activity and the gateway into the Messianic regime. The early Church transformed it into a sacrament—the token of forgiveness, and the seal of Christian discipleship (Matt. 28:19).

John, the Epistles of, the three short "General" Letters just preceding Jude and Revelation. These so-called Epistles attributed to John are more accurately described as (1) a sermon or homily, (2) a letter or note to a church, and (3) a personal note to an individual. All three reflect a Hellenistic environment, and a period when Christianity encountered an early form of Gnosticism*. Many scholars believe that one person wrote all three.

The First Epistle of John lacks the usual features of a Greek letter: the sender's name, the destination, and the usual closing greetings. Though it is like an informal tract, it seems to have been addressed to some definite group with which the writer was on intimate and affectionate terms. It may perhaps best be understood as a circular letter written to the churches of an entire region where the author was a revered leader; perhaps the churches of Asia Minor in the vicinity of Ephesus. Similarities in phraseology, style, and general outlook between I John and the Fourth Gospel make it possible, as tradition believes, that both were by the same author (for a discussion of his identity see JOHN THE APOSTLE; JOHN, THE GOSPEL OF); but for all their similarities they show some basic differences which could be explained if the author of the Epistle had been a disciple of the Evangelist. The Epistle may have been written before A.D. 80, though opinions vary.

The aim of I John was to recall its readers to their fundamental Christian loyalties, and to counter a distorted form of Christianity preached by certain "false prophets" within the Church itself (4:1–6). The errors seem to have been an early form of Gnosticism. The false prophets denied that Christ had "come in the flesh," for to them physical

JOHN, THE GOSPEL OF

matter was evil. This denial of the Incarnation—characteristic of the Docetic heresy—may have been in the author's mind as he developed the idea of the inseparability of Christ and the historic Jesus (2:22, 4:2, 5:1, 20). The author attacked the false claims to spirituality and mystical experience of those who said, "We have no sin," "We know God." He attacked also the errorists' neglect of Christian morality, Christian fellowship, and Christian charity or love.

But instead of refuting the false ideas the author reinterpreted and applied the original Gospel of primitive Christianity to the needs and outlook of his time. He emphasized three aspects of the Church tradition: (1) Believers possess and experience now and in this world eternal life (5:12–13); they know God and have fellowship with the Father and the Son. (2) To know God is to obey His commandments. Real religion has ethical implications. It is here that the Incarnation is important, for the incarnate life of Christ gives human, personal, and ethical meaning to the concept of eternal life: to dwell in God is to live after the example of Christ (2:6) and to obey God's commands (2:7–11). (3) The essential mark of eternal life is agape, love or charity, as seen in the life and teaching of Jesus Christ. The life of eternity can be lived only in community—therefore "fellowship" is the essential mark of the Church (1:3).

The author's great contribution to Christian theology is his simple as well as profound summary of the Christian revelation of God: "God is love" (4:8).

The argument does not progress in an orderly way, for the author "thinks around" his related topics in what has been called a "spiral" fashion; and his most striking aphorisms come in flashes, seldom as the climax of a line of thought. For these reasons the divisions of any outline are largely arbitrary. The Epistle might be analyzed as follows:

- (1) Theme and purpose—1:1–4.
- (2) What Christianity is—1:5–2:28:
  - (a) criticism of "religious experience"; a digression on sin and forgiveness —1:5–2:6;
  - (b) the new order—2:7–17;
  - (c) the Truth vs. false teaching—2:18–28.
- (3) Living in the family of God—2:29–4:12:
  - (a) the rights and duties of God's children—2:29–3:10;
  - (b) love, the token of the new order—3:11–18;
  - (c) union with God and a digression on counterfeit inspiration—4:1–6;
  - (d) God is love—4:7–12.
- (4) The certainty of the Faith—4:13–5:13:
  - (a) grounds of assurance—4:13–18;
  - (b) love toward our brothers, obedience to God's commands, faith in Christ —4:19–5:5;
  - (c) the witness to the Faith—5:6–13.
- (5) Conclusion—
  - (a) prayer and intercession—5:14–17;
  - (b) the three Christian certainties—5:18–21.

The Second and Third Epistles of John each consist of less than 300 Gk. words; each could have been written on a single sheet of papyrus. Both, in letter form, were sent by the "Elder" or *Presbyteros* (II John 1; III John 1). They originated in the Province of Asia between A.D. 96 and 110. In all probability the "Elder" is the author of I John also.

II John is addressed to the "elect lady and her children." It is not known whether this means a Christian matron and her family or a church; the early churches often gathered in houses, and strong family associations became part of the consciousness of the Christian community. The Epistle, briefly echoing the teaching of I John, emphasizes the "commandment" of love. It issues a sharp warning against roving heretical teachers (v. 7) who were endangering Christian truth, not by opposing it, but by preaching only certain aspects of it. These false teachers are not to be given hospitality (vv. 10 f.).

III John may be a general letter with personal touches, or a genuine personal letter on church affairs from the Elder to his loyal friend Gaius. The situation which called forth the letter was dramatic. Diotrephes, an ambitious and arrogant local church official, had evidently resisted the Elder's authority and rebuffed missionaries sent by him; the conflict seems to have involved the Elder's authority rather than a question of doctrine. The letter was apparently entrusted to Demetrius, who is highly praised (v. 12). This document affords a glimpse of an early church with its worthy members and its ambitious officers; its generous hosts and kindly helpers; and the absent Elder who bears the care of all the churches and is about to pay this one a visit.

John, the Gospel of, the fourth book of the N.T.; the Fourth Gospel. This famous book has a unique quality: historical fact is blended in it with religious interpretation, vivid dramatic narrative, and profound theology, all fused into a literary unity. This difference from the other three or Synoptic Gospels was early recognized. C. A.D. 200 Clement of Alexandria said: "Last of all John, perceiving that the bodily literal facts had been set forth in the other gospels, with the inspiration of the Spirit composed a spiritual Gospel." A study of its contents, its relations to the Synoptic Gospels, and its purpose and method leads to an identification of its author and an understanding of his work.

The contents of the Gospel of John may be briefly outlined as follows:

- (1) The Prelude—1:
  - (a) The prologue: "The Word was made flesh"—1:1–18;
  - (b) Early witnesses to Jesus as the Son of God:
    - (*a*) John the Baptist—1:19–34;
    - (*b*) Andrew and Peter—1:35–42;
    - (*c*) Philip and Nathanael—1:43–51.

JOHN, THE GOSPEL OF

(2) The Manifestation of Christ's glory and power—2–6:
  (a) water turned into wine—2:1–11;
  (b) the cleansing of the Temple—2:12–22;
  (c) Nicodemus and the discourse on the new birth—3:1–21;
  (d) John the Baptist's second witness to Jesus—3:22–36;
  (e) the Samaritan woman and the new Gospel—4:1–42;
  (f) the healing of the nobleman's son in Galilee—4:43–54;
  (g) the healing of the lame man on the Sabbath—5:1–16;
  (h) the proclamation of Jesus' divine authority—5:17–47;
  (i) the feeding of the 5,000—6:1–21;
  (j) Jesus as the bread of life—6:22–71.

(3) Deepening conflicts of the Light with the darkness—7–12:
  (a) the unbelief of Jesus' brothers—7:1–9;
  (b) the perplexity concerning him of the people at the feast—7:10–44;
  (c) the hostility of the chief priests and Pharisees—7:45–52;
  (d) Christ's mercy to the woman taken in adultery—7:53–8:11; (a later addition to the Gospel)
  (e) Jesus as the Light of the world—8:12–30;
  (f) the divine commission—8:31–59;
  (g) the blind man's sight restored—9:1–41;
  (h) the allegory of the Good Shepherd—10:1–42;
  (i) the raising of Lazarus—11:1–57;
  (j) the homage of Mary, the Jews, and the Greeks—12:1–22;
  (k) the way of the Cross—12:23–36;
  (l) the unbelief of the Jews—12:37–50.

(4) Christ's fuller revelation of himself to his Disciples—13–17:
  (a) the washing of the Disciples' feet—13:1–38;
  (b) the promised communion—14:1–31;
  (c) the allegory of the vine—15:1–17;
  (d) the coming separation—15:18–16:33;
  (e) the high-priestly prayer—17:1–26;

(5) The final revelation of Christ's glory—18–20:
  (a) his arrest and Trial—18:1–19:16;
  (b) his Crucifixion—19:17–37;
  (c) his burial—19:38–42;
  (d) his Resurrection—20:1–31.

(6) The appendix—21:
  (a) Jesus with his Disciples in Galilee—21:1–14;
  (b) the reinstatement of Peter—21:15–19;
  (c) the attestation of the Gospel to the beloved disciple—21:20–25.

A comparison with the Synoptic Gospels shows that John knew and used both Mark and Luke, but probably not Matthew. John's dependence on Mark is proved by his use of a number of Mark's unusual phrases (e.g., John 6:7—Mark 6:37; John 12:3, 5—Mark 14:3, 5). When the Synoptics differ among themselves John usually follows Mark. Luke's influence on John is apparent in the similarity of their stories of Martha and Mary; in certain resemblances in their Passion narratives; and in the fact that both Luke and John place Christ's first Resurrection appearance to his Disciples in Jerusalem rather than in Galilee. The evidence for John's use of Matthew is inconclusive, and indicates either that John did not know Matthew or that he rejected it because of its Judaistic and Apocalyptic character.

In spite of its use of Mark and Luke, the Fourth Gospel shows many important differences from them. (1) John's *chronology* differs from Mark's at three points. Mark places the beginning of Jesus' ministry after the imprisonment of John the Baptist, whereas John (3:23 ff.) shows the two ministries overlapping. John mentions three Passovers during Jesus' ministry (2:13, 6:4, 11:55), but Mark's narrative appears to compress the ministry into a year. In the Synoptics the Last Supper is the Passover meal. According to John the Last Supper took place on the evening before the Passover, and the Crucifixion on the 14th of Nisan, the day of preparation while the paschal lambs were being killed for the Passover meal after sunset (13:1, 29, 18:28, 19:14). John's chronology here seems nearer the facts, inasmuch as the arrest, Trial, and Crucifixion would have been impossible during the most sacred hours of the festival, on the 15th of Nisan.

(2) The *scene of the ministry* in the Synoptics is mainly in Galilee, whereas in the Fourth Gospel it is chiefly in Judaea, centering in Jerusalem. This may be due to John's choice of material, or to his dependence on the testimony of one who lived in Jerusalem and recorded only events with which he had a personal connection.

(3) *Miracles* in the Synoptics are performed by Jesus usually out of compassion; but in John they are performed as "signs" of Jesus' divine power (2:11) and as an inducement to faith (14:11).

(4) In the *form and content of Jesus' teaching* John and the Synoptics differ. John contains no parables, his nearest approach to this form of teaching being such figurative discourses as "the vine" (15:1–8) and "the Good Shepherd" (10). The terse, pithy, axiomatic sayings characteristic of Jesus' teaching in the Synoptics do reappear in John, but they are all but lost in their discursive, elaborate settings. In the Synoptics the teaching is practical and connected with actual situations; in John it is abstract and concerns such mysteries as Christ's own person and his relation to God. In the Synoptics Jesus demands of his Disciples "faith" and trust in him; in the Fourth Gospel Jesus demands "belief" in his divinity. This contrast, however, must not be exaggerated, for evidence of Jesus' mystical teaching, so prominent in John, can be found in the Synoptics also (e.g., Matt. 10:32 ff., 11:25 ff.). Both the practical and the mystical elements may have been present in the teaching of Jesus.

JOHN, THE GOSPEL OF

(5) The *human traits of Jesus*, so vividly recorded in the Synoptics, are largely absent from the Fourth Gospel. Though all the Gospels portray Jesus as a majestic figure, in John the divine nature of Christ overshadows his humanity. The Synoptics show Jesus going like any other man to be baptized by John; but the Fourth Gospel omits all human facts from this incident, and records only the descent of the Spirit upon Jesus (1:32–34).

(6) The *perspective* from which the Synoptics view the mission and person of Jesus differs from that of the Fourth Gospel. The Synoptics record a development in Jesus' understanding of his mission and a slowly growing realization by the Disciples of his Messiahship; whereas in John the effect of development is absent, and the perspective is foreshortened to such an extent that at the beginning of the ministry John the Baptist publicly proclaims Jesus to be the Messiah.

(7) *New names and incidents* appear in this Gospel which are not found in the Synoptics: e.g., Nathanael, Nicodemus, the Samaritan woman, Lazarus, etc. Additional insight is given on Jesus' mother, Mary Magdalene, John the Baptist, Peter, Caiaphas, Pilate, and Judas.

The *purpose* of this Gospel is stated at the end of the original document: "But these [signs] are written, that ye might believe that Jesus is the Christ, the Son of God; and that believing ye might have life through his name" (20:31). It was faith rather than fact that was paramount with John; he was concerned with historical events not for their own sake, but for their use in awakening faith. Though this purpose is present to some extent in all the Gospels, it is more consciously and creatively present in the Gospel of John. It explains John's choice of representative materials, many of his differences from the Synoptists, and his unique method.

The *method* of this Gospel is not that of a historical record, but of a drama whose successive scenes reveal Christ's glory. Though it is built on a foundation of history, its superstructure is concerned with spiritual truth. To develop this the author chooses typical miracles, and unfolds their meaning by elaborate discourses. At the heart of these dramatic discourses are brief, vivid sayings which may be authentic sayings of Jesus: e.g., "I am the light of the world" (8:12); "If any man thirst, let him come unto me and drink" (7:37). The discourses are not verbatim records, but a development of the central teaching in a manner like that used by Plato in writing the speeches of Socrates. Ignatius said: "He that truly possesseth the word of Jesus is able to hearken unto his silence." By the inspiration of the Spirit (14:26) John fills the silence of Jesus and interprets him to a later age.

The *authorship* of the Fourth Gospel has long been a matter of discussion. The unmistakable unity of the work presupposes a single author. Tradition names him John, and points to Ephesus as the city from which the Gospel originated. Many believe that this John is the Apostle, the son of Zebedee. Others find difficulties in this view, only a few of which can be stated here. (1) The appendix (chap. 21) in endorsing the Gospel does not claim that John the Apostle was its author. (2) The Gospels and Acts show John as of a fiery temperament, ambitious to be first in the Kingdom, and an adherent of the Jewish party in the Church. The spirit of love pervading this Gospel, and its bias against the Jewish point of view, argue against such an author. (3) External evidence points to John's early martyrdom, before A.D. 70, and fails to connect him with Ephesus.

221. John the Evangelist, in stained-glass window, the Hanson Place Central Methodist Church, Brooklyn, N. Y.

There was a prominent leader in Ephesus around A.D. 100 known as John the Elder. Papias, writing c. A.D. 150, mentions this John and distinguishes him from the Apostle. "When a person came who had been a follower of the Elders, I would inquire about the discourse of the Elders—what was said by Andrew, or by Peter, or by Philip, or by Thomas or James, or by John or Matthew or any other of the Lord's disciples, and what Aristion and the Elder John, the disciples of the Lord, say" (Eusebius, *Hist. Eccl.* III, 39). Many scholars find both external and internal evidence to support the view that the Elder John was the author of this Gospel as well as of the three Epistles of John.

Though the author's individuality pervades the Fourth Gospel, he may well have used an earlier source, either oral or written, that came to him from an actual eyewitness. Such a source would account for (1) the many points at which this Gospel differs from or adds new material to the Synoptic record; (2) the traces of a point of view earlier than the author's own time; and (3) the vividness of detail. The appendix bases its endorsement of the Gospel on the reliability of "the disciple which testifieth of these things" (21:24). This witness, also mentioned in 19:35, is apparently identified with the "disciple whom Jesus loved" (21:20; cf. 13:23).

The *date* of this Gospel may come within the decade A.D. 95–105, though some prefer A.D. 70–80 or earlier. Some time later it was apparently revised, some new material introduced, sections rearranged, and the appendix (chap. 21) added.

The oldest piece of N.T. writing found thus far is a papyrus fragment, 3.5 x 2.3 in., containing two verses of the Fourth Gospel. This precious relic is the Papyrus Rylands (Greek 457), acquired in Egypt, and assigned to c. A.D. 140. This seems to prove that part or all of this Gospel not only existed within the 1st half of the 2d century, but had already become one of the widely circulated standard Christian writings.

The *value* of the Fourth Gospel for its own day was that it reinterpreted the faith in terms a new age could understand. At a time when the bonds with Judaism were broken and many Gentiles had come into the Church, it transplanted the Gospel of Jesus into Greek soil. It went far toward meeting the challenge of Gnosticism, the popular philosophical system which became a dangerous heresy. The dualism of Gnosticism tinges this Gospel and is evident in the contrast between light and darkness (1:5); the children of God and of the devil (1:13, 8:44); spirit and flesh (3:6); and the Church and the world (17:16). But John transcends this dualism by his great universalism: "For God so loved the world, that he gave his only begotten Son, that whosoever believeth in him should not perish, but have everlasting life" (3:16). John rejected the Gnostic system of spiritual beings, intermediaries between God and man. He did not share the Gnostic contempt for the O.T. Above all he opposed the Docetic teaching that Christ was only a divine being, and firmly insisted on the historical reality of the Incarnation: "The Word was made flesh and dwelt among us" (1:14).

John's great doctrine of the Logos or Word of God provides the keynote; and in its aspects of truth, light, and life pervades his work. In this doctrine he takes the Hebrew concept of a personal God, illuminated by the Gospel of Christ and by nearly 100 years of Christian experience, and interprets it in terms of Greek philosophy. Jewish, Christian, and Alexandrian Greek influences meet in the idea of the Logos. Dr. G. H. C. Macgregor says of John: "If he was able adequately to present the Gospel to a heterogeneous Church, it was just because in the forefront of his Gospel so many converging streams of thought are gathered into one clear pool in which is reflected the face of Jesus Christ."

The greatness of the Gospel is, then, not so much in its record of fact, important and authentic though this may be, but in its interpretation of the record in the light of Christian experience. "This indeed is the abiding value of the Gospel, that it brings Jesus before us at once as a historical Person, and as the invisible Lord who is ever present with his people" (E. F. Scott).

Joiada (joi′ȧ-dȧ) ("Jehovah knows"). (1) Paseah's son, who took part in repairing the "old gate" of the Jerusalem walls in the time of Nehemiah; the Jehoiada* of Neh. 3:6 A.V. (2) Eliashib's priestly son, who held office in the regime of Nehemiah (Neh. 12:10 f., 22). His son married a daughter of Sanballat the Horite (13:28).

Jokneam (jŏk′nē-ăm), a royal Canaanite city, ruled by a "king of Carmel," represented in Josh. 12:22 as smitten by the Israelites. The town was on the brook Kishon, at the border of Zebulun (19:11), and was given to Merarite Levites (21:34).

Joktan (jŏk′tăn), a man listed in genealogical tables as a descendant of Noah and Shem; one of the two sons of Eber; the ancestor of 13 old Arabian tribes; and a link between Hebrew and Arab stocks (Gen. 10:25–30; I Chron. 1:19–23).

Jonah (Heb. "dove"; Jonas in the A.V. of the N.T.; twice Jona, Gk. genitive.) (1) A prophet of Israel, son of Amittai, a Zebulunite, a citizen of Gath-hepher, c. 3 m. from Nazareth (Josh. 19:10–13). Tradition points out several of his "tombs" in the Galilee region. Jonah, an older contemporary of the prophets Hosea and Amos, in the days of Jeroboam* II (786–746 B.C.) foretold the recovery of Israel's territory from Hamath on the N. to the Dead Sea in the S. ((II Kings 14:23–25). Such political prognostications of court prophets were pleasing to Israel.

The Book of Jonah, the 5th of the books of the twelve Minor Prophets, is unlike the other 11, which deal almost entirely with prophetic oracles, for it records a prophet's experiences rather than his utterances. A brief outline follows:

(a) Jonah's commission, disobedience, and punishment—1:1–16.
(b) Jonah's wonderful deliverance from drowning—1:17–2:10.
(c) Jonah preaches and Nineveh* repents —3:1–10.
(d) Jonah complains and is rebuked—4.

Much controversy has characterized this book. By various camps it has been hailed (1) as history; (2) as allegory; (3) as a story told with a serious purpose. The ancient Jewish port of Joppa supplies an accurate marine atmosphere to the opening of the book. The history theory involves credulity concerning many debatable questions, viz., the punitive storm (1:4); Jonah's selection by lot (v. 7); the sea calm (vv. 12, 15); the waiting great fish (v. 17); Jonah's ejection safe and sound (2:10); the rapidly growing gourd (4:6). Other incidents of the story are also questioned. Historians have no record on tablets or stelae of the conversion of the Ninevites en masse (3:5); nor has archaeological research revealed any Assyrian king called "the King of Nineveh" (3:6). In the days of Sennacherib the circuit of Nineveh's walls measured c. 8 m. (cf. 3:3). The narrative fails to tell what language Jonah used to make his message intelligible to the Ninevites. Many Jews and Christians, in spite of these difficulties, have accepted the story as history. In the pre-scientific era this literal interpretation was acceptable.

Throughout the centuries, both in Jewish and Christian circles, the book has had many symbolic and mystical interpreters. Jonah stands for the true Israel; Nineveh, for paganism; the sea, for world politics; the vessel, for diplomacy; the crew, for the neighboring nations with whom Israel and Judah were intriguing; the storm, for the disturbance that shook the Middle East when Babylon succeeded the Assyrian power; etc. Thus each item of the story finds a parallel in Jewish history. The Gospel of Matthew used the Jonah story as a symbolic vehicle of the 3-day burial of Jesus (Matt. 12:40). The factual difficulties in the story are of course lost sight of in such an allegorical interpretation.

It is natural that Jewish literature should capitalize on the name of Jonah, son of Amittai (chap. 1), because of his association with the renaissance of Israel—as had been done with other patriots and prophets. But the story belongs to a much later period than the reign of Jeroboam II. Nineveh was a "great city" (3:2), but it had been destroyed (612 B.C.) when the Book of Jonah was written. This fact places the incidents in the narrative beyond the possible prophetic activities of Jonah, son of Amittai. Aram. words in the original text indicate its composition in the 5th or 4th century B.C. The "prayer" (Jon. 2:2–9) is probably a 3d century B.C. psalm of thanksgiving of a man saved, not from the belly of a whale, but from drowning, and may have been inserted here by the editor of the Minor Prophets because it gave a true spiritual climax to a harrowing adventure. The date-scope of this book seems to lie between 600 and 200 B.C.

Those who consider the facts of history, as well as literary and religious data, in their interpretation of the Book of Jonah draw these general conclusions: though the story is associated with a genuine historic personality in order to give it prestige, the supernatural imaginative aspects of the tale have a didactic purpose rather than historical validity. Just as a parable is an account of possible events with a spiritual meaning, and was employed by Jesus without claiming the historicity of any detail, so the Book of Jonah conveys a religious message for all time. It was a protest against Jewish exclusiveness and the dislike of other nationalities during the post-Exilic period. Its position is opposed to the forcible divorce of foreign wives (Mal. 2:11; Ezra 9:1 f.; Neh. 13:23); God, according to this unknown author, cared for all men, and penitent Gentiles could obtain pardon as readily as penitent Jews. The Book of Jonah is read in its entirety as the *Haftarah* for the afternoon service (*Minhah*) on Yom Kippur (Atonement Day). Many Gentiles were ready to repent if only they could be taught. Jonah prepared the way for the clear dawn of the Gospel's day (John 3:16; Gal. 3:28). It is a story of the redemptive God in action—the noblest evangelistic and missionary tract in the Bible.

(2) The father of Simon Peter (John 1:42).

Jonas (jō′nȧs). See JONAH.

Jonathan (Jehonathan) ("Jehovah hath given"). (1) A Levite, a descendant of Gershom* and therefore of Moses, but the Massoretic text of Judg. 18:30 inserted an "n" (the Heb. letter *nun*) to make the passage read "Manasseh," in order to avoid making a man in the line of Moses custodian of "the graven image" honored at Dan until the Captivity. This Jonathan was rated as a wandering Levite, carried by Danites from Ephraim, where he had served as priest at Micah's shrine (Judg. 17, 18).

(2) A son of Saul, who, however, never succeeded to the throne of Israel (I Sam. 13:16, 14:49; I Chron. 8:33). This Jonathan is one of the noblest, most winsome, and self-effacing characters of the O.T., worthy of the friendship accorded him by David. Even after Jonathan was aware that David would occupy the throne he bore no resentment. The friendship between the two men is one of the great ones of history (I Sam. 18:1–4, 19:1–7, 20:41). The elegy of David for Jonathan, killed in the battle of Mt. Gilboa* (I Sam. 31:2), was included in the Book of Jashar* (II Sam. 1:17–27). It is one of the noblest examples of ancient Hebrew poetry.

Young Jonathan's career began with a successful attack against the Philistines at Geba (I Sam. 13:3). He later initiated the attack on the Philistine garrison at Michmash (I Sam. 14:1–15). His unwitting violation of Saul's rash vow brought down the paternal wrath, but evoked the admiring protection of his fellow fighters (v. 45). Great booty accrued to Saul from Jonathan's hard-won victory over the Philistines "from Michmash to Aijalon" (I Sam. 14:31 f.). His devotion to David included not only his gift to David of his own robe, girdle, sword, and bow (I Sam. 18:4), but pledging that he would be loyal to the house of his friend (I Sam. 20:42). David subsequently honored his part of the pledge by showing kindness to Jonathan's lame son, Mephibosheth* (Merib-baal) (II Sam. 9, 21:7). Jonathan risked his father's anger to restore David to favor (I Sam. 19:1–7) and to excuse David's repeated absence from the royal table (I Sam. 20:27–34). When Saul suggested that Jonathan kill David, Jonathan warned David to hide, using arrows as signals (I Sam. 20:20 ff.). With his father and two brothers Jonathan was killed by Philistines at the battle of Mt. Gilboa, and his body was affixed to the walls of Beth-shan* (I Sam. 31:2–12). I Chron. 10:3 ff. states that the royal warriors' armor was placed in the house of the gods, the king's head in the temple of Dagon, and that Saul had asked his armor-bearer to kill him. Jonathan's body, with those of his slain father and brothers, was carried by the kindly and courageous men of Jabesh-gilead, E. of the Jordan, where they were given burial under an oak and mourned for seven days (I Sam. 31:11–13). Jonathan's body was later brought back by David and buried in the sepulcher of Kish in the territory of Benjamin (II Sam. 21:12–14). When David was informed by an escaped Amalekite that he personally had given the death thrust to the royal warriors, and produced Saul's crown and arm bracelet as evidence, David had him killed for ending the life of the Lord's anointed (II Sam. 1:2–16).

(3) A son of the high priest Abiathar who brought David news during Absalom's revolt (II Sam. 15:36, 17:15–22). (4) David's nephew, who killed a tremendous man of Gath (II Sam. 21:20 f.). (5) A son of Jada (II Chron. 2:32 f.). (6) One of David's heroes (II Sam. 23:32; I Chron. 11:34). (7) A son of Uzziah, a treasurer (A.V. Jehonathan) of David (I Chron. 27:25). (8) A kinsman of David, a scribe and counselor (I Chron. 27:32). (9) The father of Ebed (Ezra 8:6). (10) A Levite (Jehonathan) (II Chron. 17:8). (11) A son of Joiada (Neh. 12:11 f.); possibly an error for Johanan (9). (12) A priest (Neh. 12:14). (13) A son of Shemaiah, a Levite (Neh. 12:35). (14) A scribe, in whose home Jeremiah* was imprisoned (Jer. 37:15). (15) A son of Kareah (A.V. Jer. 40:8; R.S.V. Johanan).

(16) Jonathan Maccabaeus, son of the priest Mattathias, and youngest of the five Maccabean brothers, a leader (160–143 B.C.) in Hasmonaean affairs during their revolt against Syria (see MACCABEES). Gaining control of Jerusalem, he was made the first Hasmonaean high priest by Alexander Balas of Syria (153 B.C.). He also served as governor of Judaea (I Macc. 10:46; 59–66). He was murdered with his sons by Diodotus (Trypho) in Gilead (13:12–23). His body was removed to the family sepulcher at Modin (12:25).

Joppa (from Gk. *Ioppē*; Heb. *Yâfō*, "beauty"; Arabic *Yâfā*, whence "Jaffa"), though poorly protected, one of the most important harbors of ancient Palestine, located on the Mediterranean coast in the S. part of the Sharon Plain, 35 m. NW. of Jerusalem. Now a suburb of modern Tel Aviv, archaeological soundings were carried out by P. L. O. Guy in 1950, and continued by J. Bowman and B. S. J. Isserlin. Systematic excavations were begun by J. Kaplan in 1955 for the Museum of Antiquities of Tel Aviv-Jaffa, and have continued to the present.

Excavations have uncovered portions of a large fortified enclosure surrounded by a rampart of beaten earth of the MB II period (18th cen. B.C.). The earliest literary reference to Joppa is in a list of Canaanite cities captured by Pharaoh Tuthmosis III (1504–1450; see *ANET*³, p. 242).

An Egyptian folk tale, preserved on a manuscript dated to c. 1300 B.C., describes the event in terms of a ruse reminiscent of the story of Ali Baba and the 40 thieves (*ANET*³, pp. 22–23). References to Joppa in the Amarna Letters indicate that it served as an Egyptian military base during the 14th century B.C., and it is the setting for the interesting misadventure of Amen-em-Opet described in the late 13th-century B.C. Papyrus Anastasi I (*ANET*³, p. 478). During excavation of the 13th-century B.C. gate (Level V) on the citadel of Jaffa, a number of dressed stones were recovered inscribed with the titles and name of Ramesses II of Egypt (c. 1304–1237 B.C.). This level was destroyed in a violent conflagration, above which another citadel (Level IV) was erected which in turn suffered destruction, possibly at the hands of Philistines whose remains were found in a pit and courtyard built into the debris of Level IV.

At the time of the Israelite settlement, Joppa was outside of the territory assigned to Dan (Josh. 19:46), but probably became a part of Judah when David gained control of the coast. It served as the harbor by

222. Coast line of Joppa.

which Hiram of Tyre transported cedars from Lebanon to Solomon for use in the construction of the Jerusalem Temple (II Chron. 2:16). The 8th-century B.C. prophet Jonah embarked from Joppa in his attempt to flee to Tarshish (Jonah 1:3). The port was captured in 701 B.C. by Sennacherib prior to the siege of Jerusalem (*ANET*³, p. 287). During Persian rule, control of Joppa was granted to Eshmun'azar, king of Sidon (*ANET*³, p. 662), and it was through this port that cedars were brought for the construction of the Second Temple (Ezra 3:7). A section of a 4th-century B.C. wall of dressed masonry was uncovered at Jaffa, as well as part of a Hellenistic fortress in the debris of which was found an inscription of Ptolemy Philopater (221–204 B.C.). The city served as a port and garrison during the Maccabean Wars (see II Macc. 12:3–4; I Macc. 10:76; 12:33–34; 13:11; 14:5, 34; Josephus, *Antiq.* XIII.9.1; XIV.10.6). It was at Joppa that Peter raised Tabitha from the dead (Acts 9:36–42). A mosque now marks the traditional site of the house of Simon the tanner, where Peter stayed while in Joppa (Acts 9:43) and received the vision concerning unclean things (10:1 ff.). Minor remains of this and later periods have been uncovered during the excavation of the city. See *Archaeology* 17, 1969, pp. 270–276; and most recently, *BA* 35, 1972, pp. 66–95. W. P. A.

Joram (short form of Jehoram). (1) A son of King Toi of Hamath (II Sam. 8:10; cf. I Chron. 18:10). (2) A Levite (I Chron. 26:25). (3), (4), (5). See JEHORAM (1), (2), (3).

Jordan ("the river that rushes down," "the descender," "the downrusher"; Arab. *Esh-sheri'a el-qebir*), the chief river of Palestine, and the boundary between E. and W. Palestine, regarded by people of Biblical times as a dread barrier to be crossed rather than as a beauty of nature to be praised.

The river is part of the great rift, a fissure, fault, or depression in the earth's crust extending from the elevated Beka'a Plain between the Lebanons and the Anti-Lebanons down through the Huleh marshes, the Sea of Galilee, the lower Jordan to its mouth S. of Jericho, on through the Dead Sea and the 110 m. of desert bordering the Arabah* (in the narrower sense in which "Arabah" is used) to the Gulf of Aqabah*, thence into the Red Sea and NE. Africa. This subsea-level fissure is the deepest ditch in the world. Sometimes the word "Arabah" is applied to the whole of it. The sources of the Jordan near Banias (the Phoenician Paneas), near Caesarea Philippi of N.T. times, are 1,200 ft. above the Mediterranean; the river drops to 1,286 ft. below sea level at the delta where it enters the Dead Sea, whose bottom is another 1,200 ft. lower. The giant fault was created by what Glueck calls a "geological spasm" that brought into being both the Nile and the Jordan—a disturbance which manifested itself in earthquakes, landslides, contractions of limestone earth crust, and volcanic shakings and deposits. Cretaceous and Eocene patches give clues to the geological era when the convulsion took place.

223. Air view of Jordan River, looking north from Allenby Bridge.

From the air the Jordan looks like a gigantic, mud-colored, twisting serpent between green thickets or white marl hills. It has been called the "liquid backbone of Palestine." It is at the center of a plain enclosed by two long mountain ridges—those of Galilee and Samaria on its W. and of Gilead on its E. The river flows c. 200 m. to cover a distance of 65 m. between the S. end of the Sea of Galilee and the N. end of the Dead Sea, falling 9 ft. per m., and maintaining a depth of 3 to 10 ft. and a breadth of 90 to 100 ft. Its currents are swift, swirling in whirlpools and falling in small cascades over rocks to make its navigation impossible; even canoe travel is perilous. The "ferry boat" translation of II Sam. 19:18 needs correction. Crossings have usually been by fords, of which there are 50 or more, as at the approach to Jericho; at the mouth of the Wâdī Nimrin; at Adamah (Josh. 3:16), Bethabara (John 1:28), etc. Bridges were not built until Roman times, and even now are few; the Allenby Bridge near Jericho, the Jisr Banat Ya'qub ("Bridge of the Daughters of Jacob"), and the Jisr Skeikh Hussein are important. The vista down 2,600 ft. of abrupt canyon walls from such lonely summits as Mt. Nebo in the Kingdom of Jordan to the river and on up to the towers of Jerusalem and Bethlehem is breath-taking, and helps one imagine the feelings of Moses as he looked over the Promised Land which he never entered (Deut. 34:1–4).

The *sources* of the Jordan are four. Three of these enter from the E. (1) The Nahr Banias is the easternmost, flowing only 5½ m. from its cave springs at Caesarea Philippi 1,200 ft. above sea level. (2) The Nahr et-Leddan, shortest and fullest of the four sources, gushes from the famous fountain at Biblical Dan (Tel el-Qâdī) and joins the Banias c. 5 m. from their points of origin. (3) The Nahr Hesbân runs a course of c. 24 m. relatively in line with the future Jordan. (4) The Nahr Bareighit ("Flea River") is the westernmost source. The confluents which form the upper Jordan move 7 m. through papyrus-bearing marshes, now drained and cultivated, to enter Lake Huleh (possibly the waters of Merom of Josh. 11:5, 7), a body 4 m. long at an elevation of only 7 ft. above sea level. The middle Jordan flows 10 m. S. from Huleh to enter the blue-green Sea of Galilee, dropping in those 10 m. to 696 ft. below sea level. The lower Jordan—the main body of the stream—takes on an en-

JORDAN

tirely different character S. of Galilee, almost losing its way as it swirls through the jungles of the Jordan in the Zor N. of Jericho—the region referred to as flooded every harvest time, with consequent enrichment (Josh. 3:15). Two conspicuous plains open out from the Lower Jordan—Beth-shan* in the N. at the debouchement of the Valley of Jezreel down into the Jordan Valley; and one at Jericho.

The *tributaries* of the Jordan are more numerous and more vigorous as they flow in from the E. than the wâdīs which enter from the W. The following, eleven of which are perennial, flow from the E.: the Yarmuk* River, the Mojib (the Biblical Arnon*), the Arab, Ziqlab, Jurm, Yabis, Kufringi, Rajeb, Jabbok, Nimrim*, Kefrein, and Rameh. Of these the Yarmuk, Jabbok*, and Arnon are really rivers. The Arnon, along with the Wâdī or Brook Azeimeh and the Wâdī Zered, flows into the Dead Sea; the others enter the Jordan proper. From the W. no river contributes to the Jordan, but there are numerous stony wâdīs which disappear altogether in summer—the Feggas, el-Bireh, Nahr Jalud, Fara, and Qelt*; the Qelt drops down through the Judaean wilderness, falls over a graceful cascade near the Orthodox Convent of Elijah, and finds its way down toward Jericho's tropical oasis.

The *Jordan Valley*, a long corridor of well-watered lands which appealed to Lot (Gen. 13:10 f.), is sparsely settled today; but, as we now know from the brilliant explorations of Nelson Glueck and the staff of the Smithsonian Institution and the American Schools of Oriental Research in Jerusalem which Glueck directed, the Valley once teemed with town-dwelling populations. If more power plants like the Rutenberg at the Yarmuk were installed the Jordan Valley could be irrigated and again become fertile farmland, a "garden of God." Glueck examined archaeologically for the first time 70 town sites in the Hashemite Kingdom of Jordan between the Sea of Galilee and the Dead Sea; he also investigated the entire E. valley of the Jordan. He dated the sites by means of vast quantities of broken pottery; many of these potsherds are now in the Smithsonian Institution, Washington. Some of the sites were occupied in the 4th millennium B.C.; more than half were occupied within the Israelite period. More than 30 sites between Jisr Mejami and Damieh were occupied between the 13th and the 6th centuries B.C. These are not all mentioned in the Bible; probably in Biblical times many of these town sites had become grazing grounds, as Israel developed occupation areas W. of the Jordan. Glueck has identified the following Biblical sites in the eastern Jordan Valley:

Bible Name	*Modern Name*	*Scripture References*
Abel-shittim*	Tell el-Hammâm	Num. 33:49
Adamah (Adam*)	Tell ed-Dâmiyeh	Josh. 19:36
Beth-haram (Beth-haran)	Tell Iktanû	Num. 32:36
Beth-jeshimoth	Tell el-'Azeimeh	Josh. 12:3, 13:20; Ezek. 25:9
Beth-nimrah	Tell el-Bleibil	Num. 32:36; Josh. 13:27
Jabesh-gilead*	Tell Abū Kharaz and Tell el-Meqbereh	Judg. 21:8; I Sam. 11:1, 9, 31:11; II Sam. 2:4 f., 21:12; I Chron. 10:11 f.
Succoth*	Tell Deir'allā	
Zaphon*	Tell el-Qôs	Josh. 13:27
Zaretan*	Tell es-Sa'īdîyeh	Josh. 3:16

See *Explorations in Eastern Palestine*, I, II, III, IV, Nelson Glueck, ASOR.

The town locations were determined by ample water supply, and in many instances by the presence of iron and copper brought for refinement and manufacture to such centers as 'Ajlûn, NW. of Jerash (Gerasa) and SE. of Beth-shan; these places were not far from charcoal supplies in the mountains of Gilead. Succoth and Adamah manufactured metal furnishings for the Jerusalem Temple built by Solomon. Caravans of donkeys brought crude or partly refined ores up the Arabah from the Dead Sea and the Gulf of Aqabah.

Neither on the E. nor the W. bank of the Jordan did cities rise in the sense in which New York lines the Hudson. But a short distance back from the river glowered the mound of Beth-shan, settled at least as early as 3500 B.C. A few miles W. of the Jordan's edge, on a low hillock near spring-fed oases of palms and tropical fruits, rose historic Jericho. Back several miles from the stream, too, were the Trans-Jordan cities of the Amorite Heshbon, Moabite Qir-hareseth (Kerak), Rabbath-ammon (Amman), Jabesh-gilead, Succoth, Zaphon (Tell el-Qôs), Madeba, and the over-Jordan members of the Decapolis (see CITIES) league, like Jerash, Pella, and Kanatha.

The *fauna and flora* of the Jordan Valley present too much material for inclusion here. In prehistoric times gigantic animals fit to be companions of the sturdy men who lived there roamed the waters and banks of the muddy river—hippopotamuses, rhinoceroses, lions, and elephants. An elephant tusk 6 ft. long, dug from the Jordan bottom, is in the possession of the Palestine Department of Antiquities. Today the Jordan jungle animals are small but plentiful—hyenas, jackals, and foxes.

The river contains more than 30 species of fish*, some like those of the Nile and African lakes, and 14 peculiar to the Jordan. The Valley is a migration corridor for 45 species of birds*, which enjoy the abundant seeds and fresh water; the Huleh section counts more than 100 resident species, including storks, cormorants, pelicans, buzzards, her-

JOSEPH

ons, and kingfishers, such as are pictured in the mosaics of Early Christian basilicas and Graeco-Roman villas. Twenty-three species are peculiar to the Jordan valley, including two owls, a dove, a starling, a thrush, two larks, a martin, a striolated bunting, and six warblers. Jungles of broom, willow, bamboo, oleander, tamarisk, castor-oil plants, acacia, and thorn thrive in the subsea-level Valley, whose temperature rises in August to 118°.

224. The Jordan River at Adam, in the central section of the Jordan valley.

Scripture references to the Jordan, with the exception of reiterated allusions to Israel's crossing of the barrier stream, are not as numerous as might be expected. The following table includes some of the most interesting, centering in spiritual revelations and influential personalities.

Name	*Incident*	*Scripture Reference*
Lot	Selects favored land	Gen. 13:10 f.
Abraham	Probable route to rescue Lot	Gen. 14:12–16
Jacob	Allusion to his crossing	Gen. 32:10
Moses	Allusion to Israel's crossing	Deut. 3:20, 25, 27, 1:1
Joshua and Israel	Crossing the Jordan	Josh. 1:1 ff., 3, 4, and *passim;* Ezek. 47:18
Ehud	Seizing Moabite fords	Judg. 3:28
Gideon	Victory over Midianites	Judg. 7:24 f.
Jephthah	Dispute with Ammon	Judg. 11
David	Flight and return over the Jordan	II Sam. 10:17, 17:22, 24, 19:15–39
Absalom	Flight over the Jordan	II Sam. 17:24
Naaman	Healing of leprosy	II Kings 5:10, 14
Elijah	Crosses and ascends the Jordan	I Kings 17:3–5; II Kings 2:6 ff.
Elisha	Receives mantle	II Kings 2:13–15
Jonathan Maccabaeus	Attack against Bacchides	I Macc. 9:45 ff.
John the Baptist	Preaches and baptizes	Matt. 3:5; Mark 1:5; Luke 3:3
Jesus	Receives baptism, "Beloved Son"	Matt. 3:13 ff.; Mark 1:9–11; Luke 3:21, 22

Joseph ("may he [Jehovah] add," Gen. 30:24). (1) A Patriarch, son of Jacob and Rachel. The account of his birth is given in Gen. 30:22–24, and the events of his life in Gen. 37–50.

Joseph's dreams incurred his brothers' jealousy (37:5–24); he was sold into slavery (37:25–36); became Potiphar's steward (39:1–6); resisted temptation (39:7–23); interpreted the dreams of Pharaoh's servants and of Pharaoh himself (40–41:36); was made a ruler in Egypt and married (41:37–45); prepared for famine (41:46–57); received his hungry brothers and father (42–46), who settled in Goshen*, Egypt (47); and charged his brothers and prepared to die (50:15–26).

The Hyksos* Dynasty, noted for its friendliness to foreigners, ruled Egypt from c. 1720–1550 B.C.; the Joseph saga is set in the early years of the Hyksos regime.

Joseph's "coat of many colors" was a long-sleeved tunic, instead of the short, sleeveless garment of the worker (Gen. 37:3). The Plain of Dothan, where today a modern hard-surfaced highway and an old caravan trail touch, has a dry cistern or pit used for grain storage, into which, tradition says, Joseph was cast (37:17–28). Joseph's tomb, ½ m. N. of Jacob's narrative are woven together artistically, combining J and E material. The Joseph story represents a N. Israel point of view; where J is discernible the Judaean or southern bias prevails. Both present important details of the narrative, viz., J, the caravan of "Ishmaelites" from Gilead (Gen. 37:25); E calls them "Midianite merchantmen" (37:28). There are Egyptian details in the Joseph story. Gen. 39:7–20 is similar to the ancient "Tale of Two Brothers," transcribed in the Nineteenth Dynasty (c. 1225 B.C.), preserved in a papyrus in the British Museum. Gen. 40:19 is a terrible fate for a human body, according to Egyptian standards. Egyptians were clean-shaven (Gen. 41:14). The signet ring with its cartouche, the gold neck-chain with its scarab, and the white cotton clothing are thoroughly Egyptian (Gen. 41:42), as were the fiscal and agrarian measures of Joseph (Gen. 47:13–26). The Egyptian caste system (43:32) and embalming (50:2–6) are accurately described. On*, the site of ancient Heliopolis, now the airport of Cairo, contributed to Central Park, New York, one of the obelisks which once stood before the Temple of Re, the sun god, from whose

JOSEPHUS, FLAVIUS

priestly family Joseph secured his wife (41:45, 50, 46:20). To Joseph God's activity was providential in character (Gen. 50:20).

The name "Joseph" is used to denote the combined tribes of Ephraim* and Manasseh* (Josh. 16:1–4) and the Northern Kingdom (Ps. 80). It is possible that part of his tribe made early settlements in Canaan before the Exodus. It has been argued that I Chron. 7:21 ff. refers to an old invasion by way of the Philistine territory, and to the establishment of the Joseph clans in the Mountains of Ephraim. (See EXODUS; CONQUEST.)

(2) A man of Issachar (Num. 13:7). (3) A son of Asaph (I Chron. 25:2, 9). (4) One of the sons of Bani (R.S.V. Binnui), who married a foreign wife (Ezra 10:42). (5) A priest (Neh. 12:14). (6) and (7) Ancestors of Jesus (Luke 3:24, 30).

225. Joseph in prison, with butler and baker (Gen. 40:2 f.), a decoration found in a 5th-century church at Seleucia Pieria, port of Antioch.

(8) The husband of Mary, mother of Jesus. Joseph of the house of David in Bethlehem (Matt. 1:20) had migrated to Nazareth (Luke 2:4), where he followed the trade of a carpenter (Matt. 13:55). He, Mary's senior, became betrothed to her (Matt. 1:18). The tradition that he was a widower with children by his former wife probably arose in the interest of the dogma of Mary's perpetual virginity (Matt. 1:25). Joseph was a pious Israelite who faithfully observed Jewish ordinances (Luke 2:21–24) and feasts (2:41 f.). He was kindly and chivalrous, for when Mary's condition was discovered, he contemplated breaking the betrothal without publicity and any attendant disgrace for the woman; when he learned the truth he took Mary with him to Bethlehem for the census-taking to save her from the slanders of gossiping neighbors (Luke 2:1–5). He exhibited the characteristics of a noble father at the shepherds' visit (Luke 2:16); in instigating the flight of his family into Egypt for safety (Matt. 2:13); in his full share of the parental supervision of Jesus (Luke 2:48, 51); and in the popular understanding of this relationship (John 1:45, 6:42). Since only Mary appears in the narratives of Christ's public ministry (Matt. 13:55 f.) it is presumed that Joseph died before Jesus began his public ministry; and the death of Joseph would explain the postponement of Christ's public ministry until his 30th year—Jesus, apprentice and eldest son of the carpenter (Mark 6:3) Joseph, probably supported the widowed Mary and her younger children (Matt. 13:55). Matt. 1:18–2:23 is written from the standpoint of Joseph; Luke 1:26–2:20 is from Mary's point of view.

(9) One of the brothers of Jesus (A.S.V. and R.S.V. Matt. 13:55, but A.V. "Joses," the Greek form of the name).

(10) Joseph of Arimathaea*, a wealthy (Matt. 27:57), pious (Luke 23:50) Israelite and member of the Sanhedrin* (Mark 15:43) who was a secret disciple of Jesus (John 19:38). He took no part in the condemnation of Jesus in the Sanhedrin, nor did anything to prevent it. Mark 14:64 and Luke 23:51 indicate that he was absent from the meeting or abstained from voting. The proximity of his own new tomb to the execution place, together with his relationship to Jesus, argue for his presence at the Crucifixion. Fear and personal shame over his neglect of duty gave way to courage (Mark 15:43). According to Jewish law the body of the person executed might not remain on the instrument of torture over night (Deut. 21:22 f.); and according to Roman law relatives could claim the body of the executed person. These considerations moved Joseph to petition Pilate* for the body of Jesus, so that it could be buried before the Sabbath. In the absence of any relatives able to provide a respectable burial he volunteered as a disciple of Jesus to assume that responsibility. Pilate granted his request. Near Calvary was a garden in which was a newly hewn sepulcher intended by Joseph to be his own burial place; there, after the Arimathaean had furnished the linen shroud (Matt. 27:59), Jesus was entombed. Joseph rolled a great stone across the entrance to the tomb (Matt. 27:60; Mark 15:46; cf. Luke 23:53). (See TOMB OF JESUS.) In these last acts Nicodemus* shared some of the honors with Joseph (John 19:40). The garden tomb may well have been on the site now covered by the Church of the Holy Sepulcher.

(11) Joseph Barsabas, one of the two disciples who had been followers of Jesus during his public ministry and were therefore deemed acceptable candidates for the apostolic office left vacant by the treachery and death of Judas Iscariot (Acts 1:23). Tradition says that he was one of the Seventy (Luke 10:1).

Josephus, Flavius (Joseph ben Mattathias), a Jewish historian born in Jerusalem c. A.D. 37 or 38; died at Rome c. 100. Though not mentioned in the Bible he has contributed to the understanding of Scripture a better description of the Jewish background of Christian history than other writers. Though he was a contemporary of authors of the N.T. none of his authentic passages refer to the life of Christ; but many have found what they believe to be allusions to him in *The Antiquities*. His reference to John the Baptist may be authentic; and he supplies data that corroborate statements in the Gospels and Acts about several rulers of Judaea. His few allusions to Messianic expectations of his day have value. But his interpretations of the O.T. are often worthless. Josephus is especially illuminating about Jewish customs and legends; has made us his debtor for information concerning the essential distinctions between Sadducees* and Pharisees*; and has given valuable data about the Essenes (see ESSENE). His treatment of Jewish history is tinged with admiration for the Romans, whom he excuses for burning the Temple, and whose emperors Titus and Vespasian bestowed property and other gifts upon him. He was a friend of Herod Agrippa II.

He was more at home writing in Greek than in Hebrew, and used Aramaic for *Concerning the Jewish War*—written to point out to Jews in Babylonia the greatness of Rome—then translated it into Greek. This volume sheds valuable light on the society in which Jesus lived; *The Antiquities of the Jews* is rated as one of the great literary monuments surviving from ancient times. He also wrote his autobiography, *The Life of Flavius Josephus;* and *Against Apion*, replying to attacks on the Jewish religion by Greek critics, and including descriptions of manners and thought of 1st century Jews throughout the Dispersion as well as in Judaea.

Though not a great historian, this scion of a priestly Maccabean house was regarded almost as canonical by scholars in the Middle Ages. Yet he had little reputation among Jews, and was ignored by rabbis of the Talmud. He wrote of the Jews for the Gentile world, in a language they understood. As a general in Galilee, he was a failure.

Joses (Gk. form of "Joseph"). (1) A brother of Jesus (A.V. Matt. 13:55, "Joseph" A.S.V., R.S.V.; Matt. 27:56 A.V., A.S.V. but "Joseph" in the R.S.V.; Mark 6:3, 15:40–47). Mark 15:47 refers to "Mary, the mother of Joses." Jerome believed that Joses, together with the other "brethren of the Lord," as well as those called "sisters," were cousins, children of Mary* of Clopas, wife of Alphaeus—a theory not accepted by most Protestant scholars, but held by Roman Catholics. (2) The given name of Barnabas (A.V. Acts 4:36, "Joseph" A.S.V., R.S.V.).

Joshaphat. See JEHOSHAPHAT.

Joshua ("Jehovah is salvation"; Gk. "Jesus," Hellenized from Jeshua; cf. Matt. 1:21, and A.S.V. margin Acts 7:45). (1) Joshua, son of Nun, Tribe of Ephraim; first mentioned in Ex. 17, as selected by Moses to rout the Amalekites, whom he defeated in a brilliant victory in Sinai (v. 13). He was placed in charge of the Tent of Meeting, was a member of the tribal representatives sent to survey Canaan (Num. 13:8 A.V. "Oshea"; R.S.V. "Hoshea"; cf. v. 16); and was chosen to succeed Moses as the leader of Israel from Egypt to Canaan (Num. 27:18–23). Unlike Moses, Joshua was fortunate enough to enter the Promised Land. He made immediate plans for advance on Jericho*, which commanded entrance to Palestine from the E. (Josh. 2); participated in the historic crossing of people and Ark (chap. 3); and established the first camp at Gilgal (4:20). (For subsequent events in the life of Joshua, see CONQUEST.) Narratives in the Book of Joshua are a bewildering weaving together of several strands, which some would see as a continuation of the J and E sources* of the Pentateuch (see JOSHUA, THE BOOK OF). Some authorities make Joshua the hero of the whole enterprise of occupying Canaan; others reduce his active military participation to the southern campaigns against Jericho and Bethel* or Ai*, and ascribe the settlement of N. central Palestine to other factors, some of which go back as far as the late Patriarchal Age. There is too much historical evidence of Joshua the hero to allow for the view that he was not an individual, but "a clan in Ephraim." Some scholars believe that certain portions of the Book of Joshua were written during the lifetime of Joshua. The final events in his life include the distribution of land to the Tribes by lot, and the fixing of boundaries (Josh. 13–22); the appointing of six cities of refuge (chap. 20), and Levitical cities (chap. 21); Joshua himself received a town (Timmath-serah in Mt. Ephraim). Late in life he was at Shechem, the site of Abraham's first altar in Canaan, where in a powerful address he challenged Israel to serve Jehovah faithfully (24:1–27). He was buried at Timnath-serah (Josh. 24:30).

(2) A man of Beth-shemesh in whose field once rested the cart bearing the Ark (I Sam. 6:14). (3) A governor of Jerusalem sometime between 640–609 B.C. (II Kings 23:8). (4) A high priest (called also Jeshua*) of Jerusalem during the governorship of Zerubbabel at the Return (c. 520 B.C.) (Ezra 2:2; Hag. 1:1, 12, 14). In his days the Temple was restored and dedicated (Ezra 3).

Joshua, the Book of, the 6th book of the O.T. Since its story of the occupation of Canaan is a fulfillment of the promises expressed in the Pentateuch, Joshua is sometimes called the last book of a hexateuch*, an entity unknown to the ancient Jews, whose canon distinguished the Torah (Gen.-Deut.) and the Former Prophets (Josh., Judg., Sam., Kings). Actually its narratives—sometimes confused because they rest on several documents from various eras—chronicle one of the most important epochs in Hebrew history. Its record of the topographical details of Palestine is invaluable. But its primary purpose is homiletic, to teach God's will for Israel and to tell of the ultimate winning of His goal for the nation—the occupation of a country promised to His people while they were still "strangers and pilgrims on the earth" (Heb. 11:13). The most reliable portions of the book as it now stands are the meager passages from J (c. 950 B.C.); less valuable are the E stories (c. 850 B.C.). W. F. Albright believes that Joshua in its present form dates from the 7th century B.C., and that some parts were written as early as the 10th century B.C.; the Deuteronomistic revision dates from c. 550–400 B.C.

Various editors and redactors blended the documentary strands, giving us the present 24 chapters. Joshua was not one of the various authors; he is the hero of the history. Portions of the book may, however, have been written during his lifetime. The narrative of the Book of Joshua is continued in the next book of the O.T., Judges. The Book of Joshua was canonized with the other "Former Prophets" c. 200 B.C.

Josiah ("Jehovah heals"; "Josias" in the A.V., Matt. 1:10 f.). (1) The son of Amon, King of Judah (c. 642–640 B.C.), and Jedidah, daughter of Adaiah of Boscath (R.S.V. Bozkath) (II Kings 22:1). In I Kings 13:2 a prophecy of his birth is given. Succeeding his young father, who had been murdered in his own palace by his henchmen, Josiah was made king by "the people of the land," who slew the assassins of Amon. He began his reign at the age of eight. His long reign lasted from c. 640 to 609 B.C. (II Kings 22:1), when he lost his life trying to protect the region of Haran (II Kings 23:29) from the Egyptian Pharaoh advancing to help the Assyrians. Falling at the mighty fortress of Megiddo* (II Kings 23:29), Josiah was carried back to Jerusalem in his chariot (v. 30) for burial "in his own sepulchre." He was succeeded by his young anti-Egyptian son Jehoahaz II (Shallum), who, after reigning for only three months, was displaced at the instigation of the Egyptian pharaoh by his pro-Egyptian brother Eliakim, whose name was changed to Jehoiakim (II Kings 23:31 ff.; Jer. 1:3, 25:1).

The outstanding event of Josiah's reign was the discovery during Temple repairs of the lost Book of the Law* (II Kings 22:3 ff.; II Chron. 34:8 ff.), and the consequent religious reforms it inspired. When Shaphan the scribe was paying off the workmen with money donated for the cause (II Kings 22:8; II Chron. 34:15), he was given "the Book of the Law" by Hilkiah the priest, who had found it in the Temple. Shaphan read the document to the king. Because the book contained denunciations of the apostasies of the Jewish people and their rulers, Josiah sent it to Huldah* the prophetess, who announced that its terrible dooms would not be fulfilled in the reign of Josiah (II Chron. 34:28). The discovered book was the core of what we know as Deuteronomy*—not the three addresses of Moses plus groups of laws which proceeded from them, but the brilliant work of a group of prophets, priests, *literati*, and redactors (the Deuteronomists), who over a long period of years (c. 700–500 B.C.) recorded the Yahwistic spiritual ideals. These were adopted by Josiah as the constitution of his state some 600 years after the death of Moses. Josiah used the Book of the Law as an instrument of reform; burned idols and other paraphernalia used by cultists of "the host of heaven" (II Kings 23:4 ff.); and ousted the idolatrous priests. The reforms of Josiah extended also to the Northern Kingdom (II Kings 23:19).

Centralizing religion at Jerusalem, he exalted Levites, a process which unintentionally threw many priests of small shrines out of employment. He led his people to spiritual heights where the ethical character of God, His love to man, and man's duty to love God were emphasized. Then in his cleansed state he led the celebration of such a Passover* (II Kings 23:21–23; II Chron. 35:1–18) as had not been observed "since the days of Samuel the prophet." The Deuteronomic Code, discovered during his reign, restated the theology and religion of some of the great earlier prophets and influenced prophets of later times. Many leaders of post-Exilic Israel followed Josiah's ideals.

Josiah is listed in Matthew's genealogy of Jesus (1:10 f.).

(2) Zephaniah's son, contemporary with the prophet Zechariah (Zech. 6:10).

jot, the smallest letter in the Heb.-Aram. alphabet (*yodh*—"y") and also in the Gk. alphabet (*iota*—"i"). It was used by Jesus, along with "tittle" (Gk. *keraia*), meaning any small mark by which one letter is distinguished from another, like the stroke of a "t" (Matt. 5:18), to emphasize the minute observance of every part of the old Hebrew law.

Jotham (jō′thăm) ("Jehovah is perfect"). (1) The youngest son of Jerubbaal, or Gideon (Judg. 9:5), who, standing on the summit of Mt. Gerizim, uttered his famous fable of the trees which selected a bramble for their king (vv. 7–20). He spoke in tones so loud that men of Shechem in the valley below could hear. He denounced the selection of Abimelech, son of Jerubbaal, by the citizens of Shechem to be ruler of Israel after this man had killed all 70 sons of Jerubbaal; only Jotham, who fled to Beer, escaped (v. 21). Jotham's curse (v. 20) was fulfilled after three years of Abimelech's stormy reign (Judg. 9:57). Jotham's fable (possibly derived from an old Canaanite one) is one of two in Scripture (cf. II Kings 14:8 f.); both fables have settings in Lebanon.

(2) King of Judah for a total of c. 16 years, part of which (c. 750–742 B.C.) were served as regent for his leprous father, Uzziah* (Azariah, II Kings 15:1, 5), and part in his own right (c. 742–735 B.C.). His mother was Jerusha, daughter of Zadok (II Kings 15:33; II Chron. 27:1). The Chronicler represents him as doing "that which was right" in the sight of God for a number of years, even though he did not deter his people from corrupt ways (II Chron. 27:2). He built "the high gate of the house of the Lord," and fortified Judah (II Chron. 27:3 f.). The most complete summary of Jotham's reign is found in II Chron. 27. In his reign Rezin, King of Syria, and Pekah, King of Israel (c. 737–732 B.C.) (II Kings 15:37), formed a coalition to attack Judah. Jotham was contemporary with three Hebrew prophets (Isa. 1:1; Hos. 1:1; Mic. 1:1). He was buried in the tombs of the kings, in the ancient part of Jerusalem known as "the City of David."

journey, a day's, the unit (four to eight hours' walk) by which people measured the distance of their travels in O.T. and N.T. times, like Laban (Gen. 30:36, 31:23); Israel in the Wilderness (Ex. 3:18; Num. 10:33; Deut. 1:2); Elijah (I Kings 19:4); three kings (II Kings 3:9); Jonah (3:3 f.); and Mary and Joseph (Luke 2:44). Journeys were frequent in the history of Israel and her neighbors, like the journey of early dwellers in the Plain of Shinar (Gen. 11:2); of Abraham from Ur* to Canaan (Gen. 12:9); of

Jacob to Succoth (Gen. 33:17); of Israel to Palestine from Egypt (Ex. 12:37 and *passim;* Num. 9:17 and *passim;* Josh. 9:17). An interesting note on food for a journey is found in Josh. 9:4, 14. One of the most interesting N.T. journeys is mentioned in Matt. 2:1–12. It was natural for Jesus, whose ministry was peripatetic, and who regarded himself as "the way" (John 14:6), to make parabolic use of the journey, as in his story of the man travelling into a far country (Matt. 25:14–30); of the hungry traveler arriving at midnight (Luke 11:5–13); of the prodigal wandering to a far country (Luke 15:11–32); and of the Good Samaritan (Luke 10:30–37). Jesus gave his Disciples practical advice on preparation for their journeys in Matt. 10:5 ff.; Mark 6:8–11; Luke 9:3–5. Paul was "in journeyings often" by land and sea (II Cor. 11:26). His conversion had taken place while going from Jerusalem to Damascus (Acts 9:3, 7). He associated the Providence of God with the success and safety of his evangelistic travels (Rom. 1:10; cf. Ps. 37:5). He enjoyed being brought forward on his journeys by friends of the Way (Rom. 15:24).

A Sabbath day's journey (Acts 1:12) was usually reckoned as 2,000 cubits (c. 3,000 ft.). This was the distance which the orthodox were permitted to travel outside their home town on the Sabbath*, as from Jerusalem's E. gate to the Mount of Olives, or from Jerusalem to a spot on this elevation from which Bethany was seen (Luke 24:50). The specification was based on Josh. 3:4 ("yet there shall be a space between you and it, about two thousand cubits in measure"), a passage suggesting that Israel's camps were 2,000 cubits from the Tabernacle, to which everyone was permitted to walk on the Sabbath. However, if travel should be necessary for some religious purpose, it was permissible to establish temporary residence by placing foodstuffs inside the allowed limit, then proceeding 2,000 cubits more beyond that "home." In modern parlance, a Sabbath day's journey would be the distance from one's house to his church. The Sabbath day's journey of the Talmud is 2,000 cubits.

joy, a quality of spirit mentioned frequently in Scripture and expressed by several Heb. and Gk. words. O.T. writers saw joy in the natural world of fields, earth, and trees (Ps. 96:11 f.), and in the reclaimed desert (Isa. 35:1 f.). To them the heavens and the earth were joyful (49:13).

An early O.T. allusion to secular joy is to the pleasure of exultant, singing, dancing women who came out to acclaim the return of David from his slaughter of the Philistines (I Sam. 18:6). The O.T. contains many other allusions to purely social joy, like the three-day feast at Hebron when David was crowned (I Chron. 12:40). Yet in ancient Israel secular joy was often blended with the spiritual happiness that righteous men found in Yahweh (Ps. 97:12, etc.) and that the Lord found in them (Deut. 30:9; Zeph. 3:17, cf. Luke 15:7, 10). The joy of good men was recognized as being a normal state. And many a man mingled his patriotic and bloody joy over military gains with the sacred joy he experienced while celebrating those victories at Tabernacle and Temple (II Chron. 20:27).

Most noteworthy is the joy found by worshippers at the sanctuaries of the Lord. Merely to be within the sacred precincts (Deut. 12:12) of the God of joy (Ps. 104:31) made the heart rejoice. The righteous were recognized as people of light and glad heart (Ps. 97:11). Hebrew worship was essentially a joyous ritual, in contrast with other faiths of the Near East; the good Jew regarded the act of thanking God as the supreme joy of life. The first reference to joy in Israel's worship occurs in I Chron. 15:16, which tells of David's organization of Levites who were to play and sing with joy at the Tabernacle, whose Ark had been brought back with rejoicing (v. 25). The Psalmist exhorted musicians to "play skillfully with a loud noise" (33:3) and to "make a joyful noise unto the Lord" (100:1 f.). Joy also marked the bringing of gifts to God's treasury (I Chron. 29:9, 17). Shouts of rejoicing marked the laying of Zerubbabel's Temple foundations (Ezra 3:12 f.) and its dedication (6:16, 22). The Feast of Tabernacles (see FEASTS) was known as "the time of our joy," when the righteous man had gladness before the Lord for seven days (Lev. 23:40). The Feast of Purim, in which many non-Hebrew elements mingled, was a time of gladness and celebration.

As the spiritual content of Hebrew worship deepened, God himself became "the exceeding joy" (Ps. 43:4); and Jerusalem was prized above a man's "chief joy" (137:6). Though the wise author of Ecclesiastes appreciated the healthy man's joy in his labor as a gift from God (2:10, 26, 5:18 f.), yet to him—and to Isaiah and Jeremiah as well—"the everlasting joy" was of the redeemed, coming to Zion with singing (Isa. 51:11).

The Bible is the most joyous book in sacred literature. The N.T. reveals Christianity as the most joyful of world religions.

Almost at the beginning of the N.T. the note of gladness was sounded. The worshipful Wise Men rejoiced to find again the star that had led them to Bethlehem (Matt. 2:10); Mary rejoiced that God her Saviour had looked upon her lowly estate (Luke 1:47); angels announced their "good tidings of great joy" which was to "all people" (2:10). Jesus came into the world that his joy might be established in men and made complete (John 15:11). He cured paralytics, who leaped for gladness. For the "joy that was set before him, he endured the cross" (Heb. 12:2). When his Disciples found themselves successful in furthering his Kingdom they "were filled with joy" (Acts 13:52, 15:3). To Paul the Kingdom *was* joy, as well as righteousness and peace (Rom. 14:17). The fellowship of 1st century Christians was marked by joy, as stressed in the three letters of John (I John 1:4; II John 12), who felt no greater happiness than in hearing that his "children" were walking in the truth (III John 4). Joy was included in apostolic benedictions, as in Jude 24; Rom. 15:13.

Jubal (jo͞o′bǎl), a son of Lamech and Adah, and brother of Jabal* and Tubal-cain*, legendary inventor of nomadic music (Gen. 4:21), "father of all such as handle the harp and pipe" (A.S.V.; A.V. "harp and organ").

jubile, jubilee (jōō'bĭ-lē) (from Heb. *yōbēl*, "ram's horn," "trumpet"; now spelled "jubilee" except in some editions of the A.V.), meaning originally "a loud trumpet blast" (Moffatt). Its derived O.T. meaning is the institution of the Sabbatical year prescribed in Lev. 25:8–24, ordained to be kept every 50th year, to be announced by a trumpet blast on the Day of Atonement, and to be observed by the return of every Israelite to his own property. It is unlikely that the jubile was ever observed in the elaborate form laid down in Leviticus.

Jubilee, Year of. See FEASTS.

Jubilees, Book of. See APOCRYPHA.

Juda (Joda A.S.V., R.S.V.), an ancestor of Jesus (Luke 3:26). See also JUDAH; JUDAS.

Judaea, the Graeco-Roman equivalent of the old Kingdom of Judah*, first mentioned in the O.T. in Ezra 5:8, which refers to "the province of Judea" (A.S.V. "Judah"; "Juda," A.V. Luke 1:39), a portion of the Roman Empire. Neh. 2:7 uses it to designate the region to which families of the Judah and Benjamin Tribes returned after the Exile. Judaea in the time of Jesus was the southernmost of the three divisions of the Roman Province of Western Palestine, the other two being Samaria and Galilee. The boundaries of this small territory, occupied by descendants of the Tribes of Judah and Benjamin, were fluid. In general, they were on the N., a line extending approximately from Apollonia on the Plain of Sharon to a point on the Jordan c. 10 m. N. of the Dead Sea; on the S., from a point c. 7 m. SW. of Gaza, through Beer-sheba, to the S. end of the Dead Sea; on the E., the cleft of the Jordan-Dead Sea rift; it never fully controlled the Maritime Plain on its W. Its length was only c. 55 m.; its width, about the same. Yet it contained the scenes of Christ's birth, Baptism, Temptation, much of his public ministry, his betrayal, Trial, Crucifixion, and Resurrection. G. A. Smith called Judaea "the throne of Israel's one enduring dynasty." It was the site of the Jews' Temple, and the place where their most important prophets spoke.

Nearly half of Judaea was desert. Its area was never more than 2,000 sq. m. The region had three physical divisions: the rugged plateau of Judah (Josh. 15:48, Luke 1:39); the Maritime Plain; and the lowland or Shephelah (Josh. 15:33 ff.). The Negeb* or south land lay S. of Beer-sheba. Its important towns included Jerusalem, Bethlehem, Jericho, Tekoa, Bethel, Mizpah, Ramah, the Beth-horons, Gibeon, and Emmaus (see individual entries).

The naked, stony hills of the Judaean wilderness are dotted with grazing flocks. In summer the rivulets dry up, yet their courses are lined with pink oleanders. Even now Judaea, more than many other areas of the Middle East, is a land of shepherds. Its slopes are terraced with stone-walled vineyards and olive groves, and a few palms are found in Jerusalem gardens.

Judaea (under the name of "Judah") is referred to in Judg. 1:16; Ps. 63 (title). In I Macc. "Judaea" means the region originally owned by the Judaeans and Benjamites; in later Maccabean times it was a larger area, including Ekron and Ashdod. Josephus sometimes uses "Judaea" to mean Old Canaan.

Judaea was the home of the J (Jehovistic) document or source (see SOURCES).

Judah (Jehudah) (Heb. *Yĕhūdhāh*) (possibly "may God be praised"); the Hellenized form is "Judas," "Juda"; Anglicized, "Jude" (Jude 1). (1) The 4th son of Leah and Jacob (Gen. 29:35), eponymous ancestor of the Tribe of Judah. Not much is revealed in the O.T. concerning this man, whose Tribe, along with that of Ephraim*, was the most important in the history of the Hebrew people. Judah's Tribe was in almost constant conflict with that of Ephraim. From the Tribe of Judah came the line of Boaz, Jesse, and David, which produced Jesus (Luke 3:23–33). In the J document (written c. 950 B.C.), which is especially interested in Judah, Judah, though younger than Reuben, Simeon, and Levi, received from Jacob a more powerful blessing than they (Gen. 49:8). His magnanimous spirit revealed itself twice in the Joseph saga (Gen. 37:26 f., 44:16–34). Judah and Reuben assumed leadership in the family of brothers. During the Exodus the Tribe of Judah encamped with Issachar and Zebulun on the E. side of the sanctuary (Num. 2:3). Its people were many (Num. 2:4, 26:22), and its company was enlarged by additions from the Kenites* (Judg. 1:16), Kennizites (see KENAZ), or Calebites (Num. 32:12; Judg. 1:12–15, 20), and by absorbing the dwindling Simeon (Josh. 19:1–9). Judah was a "lion's whelp" (Gen. 49:9). How Judah's followers entered Canaan, settled near Bethlehem, and acquired most of S. Palestine, is not known. The men of Judah supported Saul; anointed as his successor David, at Hebron (II Sam. 2:4); and supported him and his heirs at Jerusalem (I Kings 12:20), forming the major population group in the Kingdom of Judah, which lasted until the fall of Jerusalem 587 B.C. (See JUDAH, KINGDOM OF.)

(2) A Levite (Ezra 3:9), called Hodaviah in Ezra 2:40. (3) A Levite who returned with Zerubbabel (Neh. 12:8). (4) A Levite who put away his foreign wife (Ezra 10:23). (5) A Benjamite, second in command of Jerusalem (Neh. 11:9). (6) A participant in the dedication of the Jerusalem wall (Neh. 12:34). (7) A musician (Neh. 12:36). (8) A place, now unidentified, on the boundary of Naphtali (Josh. 19:34).

Judah, Kingdom of, the Southern Kingdom of the Divided Monarchy—the Tribes of Judah and most of Benjamin, which remained loyal to the house of David when the other 10 Tribes broke away c. 922 B.C.

Some Events in the Career of the Kingdom of Judah (c. 922–587 B.C.)

(For Judah's participation in the United Monarchy see ISRAEL. Dates of kings used below are based on those of W. F. Albright, *BASOR* No. 100.)

JUDAH, KINGDOM OF

From King Rehoboam through Ahaziah
(c. 922–842 B.C.)

(1) The secession of Israel from the kingdom ruled by Solomon in Rehoboam's reign (c. 922–915), leaving Judah and Benjamin to form the Kingdom of Judah (the Southern Kingdom). Disastrous invasion by Shishak of Egypt in Rehoboam's reign.

(2) *King Abijah* (Abijam) (c. 915–913) regained some of the territory lost to Israel.

(3) *Asa* (c. 913–873), with the help of Ben-hadad of Damascus, repulses an invasion by Baasha of Israel and regains Ramah (I Kings 15:16–22).

(4) Israel's Omrian Dynasty (beginning c. 876) the dominant power in Palestine.

(5) *Jehoshaphat* (c. 873–849) allies himself with Ahab of Israel by marrying his son Jehoram (c. 849–842) to Athaliah, daughter or sister of Ahab, thus accenting Baal worship in Judah and giving rise to two religious parties—the followers of Yahweh and of Baal.

(6) *Jehoram* (c. 849–842) suffers from the rebellion of Edom.

(7) *Ahaziah* (c. 842) is killed by Jehu of Israel, which interrupts the Davidic dynasty on the throne of Judah, now usurped by the evil queen mother.

From Athaliah through Jehoash
(c. 842–800 B.C.)

(8) *Athaliah* (c. 842–837) kills all the royal family except 7-year-old Jehoash (Joash), concealed by his aunt Jehoshebeath, wife of the high priest (II Kings 11:2).

(9) *Jehoash* (c. 837–800) restores the Temple fabric by offerings brought to a chest (II Kings 12); pays tribute to Hazael of Damascus.

From Amaziah through Hezekiah
(c. 800–687 B.C.)

(10) *Amaziah* (c. 800–783) is successful against Edom, but precipitates a disastrous war with Joash of Israel, ending in the dismantling of Jerusalem's defense walls and the plundering of the Temple treasures (II Kings 14:13 f.)

(11) *Uzziah* (Azariah) (c. 783–742) restores Jerusalem's defenses; gains Elath (see Ezion-geber), controlling the head of the Red Sea; feels the prosperity of Jeroboam II. Seized with leprosy (II Kings 15:5), he yields to his son Jotham, associated with him as co-regent (c. 750–742).

(12) *Jotham* (c. 742–735) "did right" yet conserved the cultic high places.

(13) *Ahaz* (Jehoahaz I) (c. 735–715), an evil ruler, becomes the vassal of Assyria, which wins a victory over his enemies, Rezin of Damascus and Pekah of Israel; but he pays tribute to the Assyrian Tiglath-pileser III (745–727). This strategy helps save Judah from the fate of Samaria, which fell to Assyria (722/1).

(14) *Hezekiah* (c. 715–687), a prayerful king, defies Sargon II of Assyria by giving ear to his chief foe, Merodach-baladan; rebels openly against Assyria in reign of Sennacherib and sees the latter plunder 46 of his towns and deport many citizens (701) (II Kings 18:13). Hezekiah is shut up "like a bird in a cage," but Jerusalem is spared for a time, as Isaiah had prophesied, and counts on a "righteous remnant" being saved (II Kings 19:31). The Assyrian army is mysteriously destroyed (II Kings 19:35).

From Manasseh through Zedekiah
(c. 687–587 B.C.)

(15) *Manasseh* (c. 687–642), an evil king, ceases to oppose the Mesopotamian might; advocates the worship of gods of other lands (II Kings 21:1–16). The Assyrianizing of Judah reaches its climax in his reign, the longest in Judah's history.

(16) *Amon* (c. 642–640), after a similar policy, is assassinated and is succeeded by his 8-year-old son Josiah.

(17) *Josiah* (c. 640–609), a good king, who, when he reaches his majority, begins to reform the apostate worship favored by his predecessors. The program of the reform is shaped by the discovery in the Temple in 622 of an ancient law code, which, expanded and edited, became the present Book of Deuteronomy (II Kings 22 f.).

(18) The rapid decline of Judah; *Shallum* (Jehoahaz II) (3 mo. 609) is deposed by Pharaoh-nechoh, who appoints in his place Eliakim, giving him the throne name *Jehoiakim* (609–598). After the defeat of Egypt by Babylon (605), Jehoiakim becomes a vassal of Nebuchadnezzar, but after 3 or 4 years rebels. Jehoiakim perishes, and is succeeded by his young son *Jehoiachin* (Jeconiah), who surrenders to the Chaldean army and goes into Exile with the best of his subjects and craftsmen (597) (II Kings 24:14–16; Jer. 22:24 ff.). (Note: there were at least three deportations of Judaeans: 597, 587, 582 B.C.).

(19) *Zedekiah* (Mattaniah) (597–587), son of Josiah, influenced by those who favor leaning on Egypt, defies Nebuchadnezzar, whose army advances on Jerusalem (589) and destroys it after a siege of 1½ years (II Kings 25; Jer. 39). More Judaeans are deported to Babylon (587). (For the growth of the Torah and sacred Jewish literature during the Captivity, see EXILE.)

(20) *Gedaliah*, former palace official, is appointed governor of Judah by the Chaldeans (II Kings 25:22 f.). After his murder some Jews flee to Egypt, compelling Jeremiah to accompany them.

(21) The third deportation (582).

The Restoration

(22) By edict of Cyrus the Persian (538 B.C.) the Jews are permitted to return to Jerusalem (Ezra 1:1 ff.). Groups return under Sheshbazzar, prince of Judah (Ezra 1:8, 11), identified by some with Zerubbabel, and under Zerubbabel, a grandson of King Jehoiachin, and the high priest, Joshua (Jeshua). Early *emigrés* carry the sacred vessels stolen by Nebuchadnezzar but restored by Cyrus (Ezra 1:7 ff.), make efforts to restore the Temple under the governorship of Zerubbabel (Ezra 3:8 ff.), and complete the task when stirred up by Haggai's first oracle (520 B.C.)

and Zechariah. Ezra 5 and 6 tell of obstacles removed. The Temple is rededicated "in the sixth year of Darius" (Ezra 6:15). During the reign of Artaxerxes I (465–424 B.C.) two more groups of exiles return. A century and a half after the destruction of Jerusalem, the capital is again functioning as the center of Jewish hope and life, and its impact is felt in the Diaspora. But the hoped-for Davidic state does not materialize. After three generations of this small Jewish commonwealth, however, a new impetus is felt, for

(23) *Nehemiah*, cupbearer to Artaxerxes, returns c. 445 B.C. and is followed soon after by Ezra*. Nehemiah leads the citizens to rebuild Jerusalem's walls (beginning in August 439); Ezra institutes needed religious and moral reforms. (See RETURN, THE.) The task requires probably two years and four months (Josephus).

(24) The small semi-autonomous Jewish state is recognized by Persian officials, who allow the minting of coins (some of which are extant) and the levying of taxes.

(25) Palestine and Syria are part of the Hellenistic regimes of the successors of Alexander the Great (after 323 B.C.).

(26) The Maccabean Period (166–63 B.C.) (see MACCABEES).

(27) Judah's territory under the Roman Empire (from 63 B.C.) is known as "Judaea."

The Kingdom of Judaea is ruled by Herod the Great by grant of the Roman Senate (37–4 B.C.). After his death it becomes part of the tetrarchy of Archelaus (4 B.C.–A.D. 6). After Archelaus' banishment Judaea is under Roman governors. Jerusalem, after its destruction in A.D. 70, is rebuilt in the 2d century A.D. as a Roman colony for Gentiles, *Aelia Capitolina*, and is subordinate to Caesarea.

Hebrew prophets active in the Kingdom of Judah included Isaiah and Micah, in the reign of Jotham and on through that of Hezekiah; Jeremiah, in the time of Josiah and until the fall of Jerusalem, when he joined a group fleeing to Egypt; and Ezekiel, in Exile in Babylonia, which he shared with his people.

Five Assyrian kings received tribute from rulers of Judah, according to their own records: Tiglath-pileser II (745–727 B.C.) "Pul," II Kings 15:19); Sargon II (722–705) (Isa. 20:1); Sennacherib (705–681) (Isa. 36:1, 37); Esarhaddon (681–669) (Isa. 37:38; II Chron. 32:1 ff.); and Ashurbanipal (c. 669–626) (possibly the A.V. "Asnapper" or R.S.V. "Osnappar" of Ezra 4:10).

See individual entries for many of the individuals and places mentioned above.

Judaism, the name given to the religion of Israel* after the fall of the Northern Kingdom and the period culminating in the Exile, when only the Tribe of Judah ("the Jews") remained. It was at this time that the religion began to assume the shape, centered in the written Torah* interpreted in the light of an oral tradition, which it has retained ever since.

Judas (Gk. form of Heb. "Judah"), a Late Lat. name widely used in late Judaism, reflecting the prestige of Judas Maccabaeus (I Macc. 2:1–5), founder of the Maccabees (166/5–160 B.C.). (1) Judas Maccabaeus (see MACCABEES). (2) A captain associated with Jonathan at Hazor (I Macc. 11:70). (3) A son of Simon Maccabaeus (142–134 B.C.). With his brother John he led an army (I Macc. 16:2). (4) An official Jewish correspondent at Jerusalem (II Macc. 1:10). (5) A man mentioned in I Esd. 9:23; possibly the same as the Judah of Ezra 10:23.

In the N.T. there are several men named Judas. (6) The brother (or son) of James; one of the Twelve (Luke 6:16), perhaps the Lebbaeus or Thaddaeus of Matt. 10:3; cf. Mark 3:18; the Judas of John 14:22. (7) The brother of Jesus (Matt. 13:55; "Juda," Mark 6:3; Jude v. 1). He was less prominent than James at Jerusalem. He may have been in Paul's company. (See JUDE, EPISTLE OF.)

(8) Judas Iscariot ("Judas, the man of Kerioth"*), son of Simon Iscariot (John 6:71, 13:26 A.S.V., R.S.V.). Kerioth may be Khirbet el-Qaryatein, in rugged SE. Judaea. Judas, always mentioned last in the lists of the Twelve, was probably the only one who was not a Galilean. No more is told of his early life than of the other Apostles; nothing is narrated of the circumstances of his call. Writers of the Gospels were careful to distinguish him from Judas (or Judah), brother of James, by appending "which also betrayed him" (Mark 3:19; cf. Luke 6:16), or "Simon's son" (John 13:2), or, when they were referring to the other Judas, "not Iscariot" (John 14:22).

Judas showed ability to handle the money bag and the financial problems of the busy company of Disciples (John 13:29); but Jesus knew, as time went on, that Judas would betray him (13:11). Yet the Eleven did not identify Judas as the traitor of their group (13:2), for as late as the Upper Room incidents, when Jesus announced that one of them would betray him, each of the faithful sincerely asked, "Is it I?" and did not point the finger at Judas.

Judas's mercenary tendencies fed on the thought that Jesus was about to usher in an earthly political kingdom in which he would be king and Judas would be secretary of the treasury. To a man with such a concept the words of Jesus after the Transfiguration were a bitter disappointment; Judas did not wish his leader to let himself be delivered into the hands of men and killed (Mark 9:31; cf. Mark 8:31), and his loyalty cooled as his disappointment increased. His resentment reached a crisis when Jesus rebuked him at Bethany for his criticism of Mary's extravagance in the alabaster box incident, and unmasked Judas's false pretense of loving the poor (John 12:1–8). Already Caiaphas and the chief priests were seeking a way to rid themselves of Jesus (Matt. 26:3–5). Judas went to them and offered to betray Jesus (Matt. 26:14–16); accepted "thirty pieces of silver,"—the equivalent of twenty dollars, the price of a slave (Ex. 21:32); and set in motion the forces that precipitated the Crucifixion. The next tragic events are narrated by the four Gospel writers, Matthew and John giving the most detailed accounts: the participation of Judas in the last Passover in the Jerusalem Upper Room; the whispered query of John to Jesus, as to which of the group would betray him (John 13:25); the revealing sop-dipping incident (v. 26); the quick dispatch of the betrayer by Jesus (v. 27); the departure of Judas into "the night" (John 13:30) to make final arrangements for turning Jesus over to the high priests; the institution of the Lord's Supper* (Eucharist) (Matt. 26:26–29; Mark 14:22–25; Luke 22:14–20); the arrival of Jesus and the eleven at the Garden of Gethsemane (Matt. 26:36); Judas's traitorous kiss in the shadowy garden (Mark 14:43–45) and the immediate arrest (v. 46) of Jesus, who had addressed Judas as "friend" (Matt. 26:50). It is to be noted that Luke's account places the institution of the Communion before the departure of Judas.

Judas may have believed that Jesus would still perform a miracle and escape from his captors, and the Messianic Kingdom might still come. But as the Trial proceeded and Judas realized the situation he had brought about, he tried to call off the plot of the priests and elders by returning the blood money (Matt. 27:3), but was rebuffed by them, who mocked him, "What is that to us?" (v. 4). Rushing into the Temple Area, he threw the silver on the floor, and later hanged himself (Matt. 27:5). Acts 1:18–20 gives another account of the end of Judas, in the field Aceldama, bought with the blood money.

Numerous attempts have been made to understand Judas. His disappointment in the failure of the Master to usher in at once a successful earthly kingdom has been mentioned. Some interpreters believe that Judas was trying to force the hand of Jesus into claiming the long-anticipated throne of David. Others believe that he felt that if Jesus really were the Messiah* nothing could harm him; and that if he were not it was right that he should perish. One interpretation makes Judas a part of God's foreordained plan to precipitate the death of Jesus, from which issued his Resurrection and the redemption of man. The N.T. explanation is that Satan had entered into him (Luke 22:3. cf. John 6:71, 13:27); one of the faithful Twelve had become "a devil" (John 6:70).

Judas's status is depicted in the Hanson Place Central Methodist Church of Brooklyn, N.Y., whose communion rail has 12 niches, eleven of which contain statuettes of the faithful Disciples, each having his name and his symbol above the figure; but the 12th niche is empty—above it is carved simply, "Judas." In iconography the symbolic color of Judas is yellow, the tint of dung.

Acts 1:22–26 tells how two men worthy to succeed Judas were immediately available. Matthias was chosen by lot, and restored the number of the Apostles to twelve.

(9) The "Galilean" (Acts 5:37), though he came from Gaulanitis, E. of the Sea of Galilee. Some historians believe that he led a revolt against Quirinius' census in the 1st century A.D., inspiring the group that became the Zealots (see ZEALOT). (10) A Damascus Jew in whose house on the "street called Straight" the newly converted Paul was guest (Acts 9:11). (11) Judas Barsabas, a prominent Jerusalem Christian, who was chosen with Silas to accompany Paul and Barnabas to deliver to the churches of Syria

226. Judas, repentant, in hands of Satan, a fresco in a 17th-century Metropolitan Church, Bucharest.

and Cilicia the conditions on which the Jerusalem council would accept Gentiles into the Church (Acts 15:22–33). This Judas was called a "prophet" (Acts 15:32). He may have been a brother of Joseph Barsabas, defeated candidate for the successor to Judas (Acts 1:23).

Jude, possibly one of the Lord's "brethren" (cf. Mark 6:3; Matt. 13:55), a son of Mary and Joseph. Jude has been identified by many with the Apostle Judas (not Iscariot) (Luke 6:16; John 14:22; Acts 1:13); but others deny that the "brethren" included any Apostles (Jude 17). According to the latter view the "brethren" (John 7:5) did not accept Christ until after his Resurrection (Acts 1:13). This Jude, traditionally identified as author of the Epistle (see JUDE, EPISTLE OF), stressed his spiritual relationship with Jesus rather than the fleshly one (v. 1). This verse also indicates that Jude was less important in the early Church than his brother James. Perhaps he was married (I Cor. 9:5).

Jude, the Epistle of, a "General" or "Catholic" Epistle declared to have been written by Jude, "servant of Jesus Christ, and brother of James." Traditionally this Jude is identified with "Judah" or "Judas," A.V. and R.S.V. (Mark 6:3), who was the brother of James and Jesus. Some scholars believe the author was an unknown Jude whose brother was named James. The author does not claim to be an Apostle (v. 17), and looks back on the Apostolic Age. This indicates a date c. A.D. 90 for the Epistle.

Though in letter form it is really a polemical tract against heretical teaching. The author denounces the errorists rather than describes them, but they seem to have believed that spiritual men were exempt from the moral law. Their heresy was an early form of Gnosticism*. They perverted the doctrine of God's free grace into an excuse for immoral living. The author quotes from two popular Jewish Apocalyptic writings evidently well-known in 1st century Christian circles: (1) The Book of Enoch (vv. 6–14 f.) and (2) the Assumption of Moses (vv. 9 f.). The 2d-century Epistle of II Peter contains parallels to Jude 14–17 f., and appears to be an expanded revision of the earlier Epistle. Perhaps the most famous part of this Epistle is its great doxology.

The Epistle may be outlined as follows:

(1) The Salutation—vv. 1, 2.

(2) Reasons for writing—3, 4:
- (a) to exhort Christians to uphold the faith;
- (b) to warn them against those who used God's forgiveness of sins as excuse for immoral living.

(3) Condemnation of false teachers—5–16:
- (a) examples of God's punishment of disobedience:
  - (*a*) Israel in the wilderness;
  - (*b*) the rebellious angels;
  - (*c*) cities of the plain.
- (b) Denunciation of errorists.

(4) The duty of Christians—17–23:
- (a) remember apostolic preaching;
- (b) build their lives on faith, prayer, and the love of God;
- (c) try to save errorists.

(5) The Doxology—24, 25.

Judea. See JUDAEA.

Judges, the 7th book of the O.T., received its name from those who judged Israel (Judg. 2:16), the tribal heroes who governed locally between the eras of Joshua and Samuel and strengthened Israel's hold of Canaan against a variety of enemies.

The book consists of three main divisions:

(1) The Conquest of parts of Canaan by individual Tribes—1:1–2:5.

(2) Exploits under the Judges—2:6–16:31.

(3) Later stories concerning the migration of the Danites and the crusade against the Benjamites—17–21.

The stories and traditions by various authors, gathered and annotated by various editors, are important historical records. It is possible to separate the later comments from the earlier stories, thus contrasting the times of a late editor with the much earlier times when the story originated; viz.: Jerusalem was said to have been captured (Judg. 1:8), but this occurred in David's day (Judg. 1:21; II Sam. 5:6 f.); Gaza, Ashkelon, and Ekron, three Philistine cities (Judg. 1:18), were not subdued during the early years of the Conquest but much later, for the reason given in Judg. 1:19. Archaeological research has confirmed the impregnable nature of the Canaanite sites like Beth-shan* and Megiddo* (Judg. 1:27), whose inhabitants the first Israelite assaults did not dispossess. The Israelites occupied the hill country, where they pursued agricultural tasks. The editors, in presenting the older stories in a framework which reflects their own religious viewpoint, asserted that the reverses and slow progress of Israel in occupying the land were due to religious defections (2:2–3, 3:12, 4:1 f., 6:1, 10:6–8, etc.).

The Biblical total of the period of the Judges is 410 years; but many of these local chieftains were independent of one another, and contemporaneous. This is one explanation given for the incorrect records concerning the length of their sway. The period of the Judges ending with the coronation of Saul (I Sam. 8–12) actually lasted c. 230 years (c. 1200–1020 B.C.). The heroes reported in the Book of Judges are:

Othniel	Judg. 3:7–11
Ehud	3:12–30
Shamgar	3:31
Barak and Deborah	4, 5
Gideon	6:1–8:32
Abimelech	8:33–9:57
Tola	10:1 f.
Jair	10:3–5
Jephthah	10:6–12:7
Ibzan	12:8–10
Elon	12:11 f.
Abdon	12:13–15
Samson	13–16

These stories—without the comments by the religious-minded editor—present a factual picture of Israel's life at the beginning of the Iron Age (c. 1200–1000 B.C.). Though some iron weapons are mentioned, they are possessed by Israel's enemies (1:19, 4:13, cf. I Sam. 13:19–22). Israel was establishing an agricultural economy (6:3, 11, 9:27, 15:1, 18:9, 21:20 f.) in the midst of a nomadic environment (6:5). The worship of Baal, an agricultural deity, affected Israel, and at times a demoralizing syncretism prevailed (5:8, 6:25–27, 8:27, 17:4, 5, 18:18–20). Although it was a time of anarchy (17:6, 21:25), moral indignation was registered (19:30). A dynamic consciousness of God characterized the times (5:4 f., 6:34, 11:29, 13:24 f., 14:6, 19).

The last five chapters of Judges are not a continuation of what precedes, but they add two episodes to the period already recorded. Pfeiffer maintains chaps. 17 and 18 are designed by the author of the J narrative, with his southern bias, to cast contempt on the N. sanctuary of Dan by recording its idolatrous origin. Chaps. 19–21, according to some scholars, add to the account of barbaric historic events reported by early Judaean sources a post-Exilic picture of the theocratic "congregation" acting as directed by God (21:16). Others find here an accurate picture of the manner in which the Twelve Tribes acted in concert in the pre-monarchic periods.

The book, containing various sources, unimpeachable historical data, the great Song of Deborah (Judg. 5)—one of the oldest poems in the O.T., dating from c. 1125 B.C.—and editorial additions, reached approximately its present form c. 500 B.C. As a record of early Israelitic history (disregarding later editorial revisions), this book is a basic historical source and a valuable contribution to our understanding of divine revelation in the O.T. J. L. M./R. W. C.

Judgment, Day of, the time when sin will be followed by loss and penalty and goodness by a promised reward, is taught in the Bible from the beginning. The early stories like those of Adam and Eve (Gen. 3); Cain and Abel (4:1–15); the generation of Noah (6, 7, 8); Sodom and Gomorrah (18:16–19:29); and the sale of Joseph by his brothers (37:12–35) all illustrate the law that "what a man sows, that shall he also reap" (Gal. 6:7). The principle announced to Moses at Sinai, that both the righteousness and the unrighteousness of men will have results that will follow them and their children after them, is everywhere emphasized in the O.T. (Ex. 20:5 f.; Num. 14:18). It was regarded as of the very nature of things, because Yahweh was a righteous God.

The idea of a final day of judgment, involving a "recording angel" and carefully kept "books," grew up through the comparatively late Jewish belief that the present age would be followed by a Messianic age (see MESSIAH). In its earliest form the Messianic age meant little more than the conviction that Yahweh would fulfill His covenant with Israel in the destruction of their enemies. The prophets, however, moralized the concept by announcing a "Day of the Lord," and declaring that it might be a calamity for Israel as well as for Israel's enemies; the Messianic age would be introduced by a great act of judgment.

This is the teaching in Amos (5:18–20). It is carried forward with dramatic intensity in Zephaniah (1:1–2, 3), and hardly less so in Malachi (3:1–6, 4:1–6). The phrase itself is common in most of the prophets, frequently occurring in Isaiah as "that day" (11:10 f., cf. 13:9, 13), and in Ezekiel as "the day" (7:5–10, cf. 7:19). Isaiah felt that any divine visitation, whether to save or to destroy, was in effect a "Day of the Lord" or time of judgment (chap. 10). Similarly in Jer. 30:1–11 and 46:1–10; though these prophets insist that the divine visitation is not necessarily a finality, but the beginning of a process of reformation; the time of judgment may therefore serve to hasten the coming of the Kingdom of God.

The later Apocryphal and Apocalyptic writings usually emphasize the suddenness of the coming of the "Day of the Lord," and the universality of the accompanying work of judgment. They describe the judgment in language characteristically imaginative. By that time (the 2d and 1st centuries B.C.), the Jews had a highly developed angelology and demonology, and this colored the description of the Day of Judgment. The demons were fallen angels, who were to be judged in common with the sinful men whom they had led astray (see the writing known as *The Testament of the Twelve Patriarchs;* cf. Matt. 25:41). There is a graphic description of judgment in Dan. 7:9–14, which contains the first reference to "books" (v. 10, cf. 12:1; Rev. 3:5, 20:12; but see the striking use of "book" in Ex. 32:32 f.). In Daniel the judgment is conducted by "the Ancient of Days"; the same description introduces the figure of "a Son of Man," to whom is assigned an "everlasting dominion." In Apocalyptic writings later than Daniel (c. 190 B.C.) sometimes God Himself is the judge, sometimes the Messiah. In Matt. 25:31 f. it is "the Son of Man," and here "Messiah" is plainly meant. In some accounts, there are two judgments: one introduces a Messianic kingdom of limited duration; the other, introduced by Messianic "woes" or "signs," and usually involving a general resurrection and the transfer of the scene of judgment to "the heavens," issues in the assignment of final destinies for all angels and men alike. This is the pattern followed in Rev. 20.

It is apparent that the teaching about judgment in the N.T. reflects much of the late Jewish apocalypticism. We see it in certain parables, and in other passages. Matt. 24 describes the preliminary Messianic "woes." Matt. 25 contains two parables of judgment, besides the description of "the day" itself. This description carries the important implication that final destiny is to be determined by the relation to Jesus Christ. This is the thought that prevails in the Epistles: the final judgment on a soul, whether made directly by God (Rom. 14:10–12), or through Christ as God's representative (Rom. 2:16), proceeds on a Christian basis; the decisive question is the lack or the possession of what is found in Christ (II Cor. 5:10; Heb. 10:26–31; I Pet. 3:18–22; I John 4:17).

The book of Revelation is deeply colored by Jewish apocalypticism. God on the throne (4:2–11); "the book" and "the seals" and the "sounding" of the seven angels (5:1–11:19); the coming of the Messiah, who is "the Word of God" (19:11–16); the temporary "binding" of Satan (20:1–3); the final judgment (20:11–15); and the renewed heaven and earth (21:1–22:5)—all these are anticipated in earlier Jewish imagery. Even the metaphor of "the books" is repeated in 20:12. But in 3:5 the scrutinizer of "the books" is Jesus Christ, and he also was found worthy "to open the book and the seven seals thereof" (5:1–5, 6:1, 2, 5, 7, 9, 12, 8:1). Whether one's name were found "written in the book of life" (20:15) was, however, no accident. The "redeemed" must be vouched for by "the Lamb" (5:8–10; cf. Luke 10:20). In Revelation, as elsewhere in the N.T., judgment takes place "before the judgment seat of Christ." The metaphor of a great assize, with "all nations" gathered before the Judge on the throne, is only intended to dramatize a solemn truth; and the truth—moral decisions determine future destiny—still stands, even if the metaphor be rejected.

See ETERNAL LIFE; HADES; MILLENNIUM; RESURRECTION. E. L.

judgment hall. See ARCHITECTURE; GABBATHA.

Judgment, the Last, the end of one age and the beginning of another. See ESCHATOLOGY.

judgment seat, the formal chair or bench constituting the tribunal or bema where a governor, judge, procurator, or other authority heard cases and rendered judgments. Solomon built a cedar-lined porch "for the throne where he might judge, even the porch of Judgment" (I Kings 7:7). But the judgment seat was typical of the Roman world. The one that figured in Pilate's trial of Jesus (Matt. 27:19) occupied a "place that is called the Pavement," Gabbatha (John 19:13). Gallio's Achaian judgment seat in Corinth before which Paul was haled (Acts 18:12–17) is thought to have been an open-air bema in the S. half of an open portion of the agora or market place, and subsequently covered by a Christian church. Beneath this church excavators have found a well-built stone platform whose size and imposing position make it likely that this was the speaker's platform where Gallio sat when the rioting Jews demonstrated, rather than a seat in an enclosed audience room of the large basilica or government building N. of this open area. The judgment seat of Felix, procurator of Judaea, before whom Paul was tried in the presence of King Agrippa and Bernice, was at the government house in Caesarea (Acts 25:6–10, 15–17). James 2:6 contains an allusion to the dragging of the poor to judgment seats at the instigation of rich oppressors.

Judith (Heb. fem. of word for Judaean or Jew). (1) A Hittite wife of Esau (Gen. 26:34). (2) A daughter of Merari, of the Tribe of Simeon, widow of Manasses (Jth. 8:1 f.), heroine of the Apocryphal Book of Judith. See APOCRYPHA.

Julia, greeted in Rom. 16:15 as a Christian woman, possibly the wife of Philologus, and mother of Nereus and his sister, part of a devout family group. Julia was a common name, often borne by slaves.

Julius, the courteous Roman centurion of the Augustan cohort who escorted Paul and other prisoners from Caesarea to Rome (Acts 27:1), possibly on a government ship (27:11, 28:16). He and his detachment were possibly in charge of the commissary and prisoners. To Julius Paul owed much (27:3, 43). But Julius did not follow Paul's advice on navigation (27:11). Possibly through Julius came Paul's privilege of living in his own house at Rome (Acts 28:30).

Junia (A.V. Rom. 16:7, R.S.V., A.S.V. Junias and margin Junia), a Hebrew woman or man who was a follower of Christ before Paul was and a fellow prisoner of Paul's at Rome. If the name is feminine and not a contraction of the masculine "Junianus" the lady was probably the wife of Andronicus.

juniper. See FLOWERS.

Jupiter, the Lat. name of the chief Roman god, the Gk. Zeus, by which name he is called in the Gk. text of Acts 14:12 f. He was worshipped in magnificent temples at Rome, Athens, Baalbek, and throughout the Graeco-Roman world, where he was acclaimed with votive offerings, sacrifices, garlands, and rites of an organized priesthood supported by people desiring his favor. Antiochus dedicated a temple to Jupiter Olympius at Jerusalem. When Paul and Barnabas at Lystra were acclaimed as "Mercury" and "Jupiter" they found it intolerable to be considered "gods come down in the likeness of men"; and they disliked to see people, led by their local priest of Jupiter (v. 13), make ready garlands and oxen at the city gates for the sacrifice.

justice. (1) *As an attribute of God* it is referred to in Job 37:23; Ps. 89:14; Jer. 50:7. Righteousness, or moral rightness, is included in any definition of this quality. The divine justice is that part of the divine righteousness which exhibits itself as absolute fairness. This is implied in Abraham's question (Gen. 18:25). For Acts 28:4 the A.S.V. and the R.S.V. use "justice" instead of the "vengeance" of the A.V. Here justice is personified, and represents the exaltation of a divine quality to deity itself, a concept current in Greek, Babylonian, and Phoenician mythology, and readily acquired by the people of Malta.

In the early and nonreflective stage of Israel's progress it was thought that God showed special favor to the righteous; but this concept did not stand up under the strain of national calamities, and Jesus exposed its fallacies (Matt. 5:45, 13:28 f.; Luke 16:25, 18:1–5; John 9:2 f.). An explanation of the sufferings that befall the righteous is given in Rom. 8:18–39 and Heb. 12:11, which goes far in removing what is considered a violation of God's justice. Divine justice requires the next world as well as this one for its operation (II Cor. 4:16 f.; Heb. 5:8); but even here the suffering righteous receive spiritual compensations (I Pet. 2:19 f., 3:12–22).

Because justice and holiness meet in the divine nature, God must take account of human sin (Gal. 6:7). Punishment is the reaction of His holy nature against wrongdoing; without it, the moral order of the world could not be maintained. The reforming influence of punishment is part of the divine purpose, but this influence never takes effect in the sinner until he recognizes the justice of the punishment and confesses the moral authority of God. "The meek will he guide in justice" (A.S.V. Ps. 25:9).

God's justice is shown in the forgiveness of sins when man repents (I John 1:9); both forgiveness and punishment are expressions of His justice; and in justice both His holiness and His mercy, His law and His grace find expression.

(2) *As an attribute of man* justice depends on the fact that man was created in God's image. Justice was early expressed in the social life of Israel by the head of the family, who typified authority in the group and settled questions dealing with right and wrong (Gen. 18:19, 38:24). This pattern for the administration of justice still exists in nomadic groups in the Middle East. In time, the elders of the tribe or clan came to exercise the judicial function (Ex. 18:13–27; Num.

11:16). The leadership of the Judges* rested in part on their ability to dispense justice (Judg. 2:16–18, 4:4 f.; II Sam. 15:4). Justice was a qualification for kingship (II Sam. 18:13, 23:3; I Kings 10:9; I Chron. 18:14; II Chron. 9:8). The prophets democratized this virtue by showing it to be required by God of every man (Mic. 6:8). Among those in the N.T. who were noted for their high ethical sense and ability to discriminate between right and wrong were Joseph (Matt. 1:19); Simeon (Luke 2:25); John the Baptist (Mark 6:20); Joseph of Arimathaea (Luke 23:50); Cornelius (Acts 10:22); and Jesus (Matt. 27:19).

Justice under the Pharisees in Christ's time became a cold, external code of conduct. Christ in the Sermon* on the Mount deepened the meaning of justice by making it an affair of the heart (Matt. 5:22, 28, etc.). His law of justice which was to serve as a basis for men's judgment and conduct was the Golden Rule (Matt. 7:12; Mark 12:30 f.). Love alone can bring into the human heart the perfection of such qualities as characterize the divine nature (Matt. 5:48).

justification, a term found chiefly in Paul, who uses it to mean "to reckon to be righteous." If God regards a man as he actually is in himself, then the man necessarily appears as unrighteous: "There is none righteous, no, not one" (Rom. 3:10). But a man may enter into a certain relation with God through Jesus Christ, and by virtue of this new relation he is "reckoned to be righteous." He is not now in all possible ways a perfect man, judged by the absolute moral law, but he is a man in whom love is coming more and more to prevail; and since what God seeks for men is not rigid conformity to a set of rules but complete domination by love, it follows that "love is the fulfillment of the law" (Rom. 13:10; cf. Mic. 6:8). Love provides for forgiveness, but law does not. To break law is to be unrighteous, and no amount of later obedience can ever change the fact of the earlier disobedience (Jas. 2:10–13). It is love that is merciful, not law. Then, since the law of God necessarily makes men rebels because it creates demands beyond their power to meet, another way for God to deal with men is indicated if His purpose with men—fellowship with Himself—is to be realized.

This way is the way of grace. To deal with a man graciously is to deal with him in a way not provided by law. Grace may "reckon to be righteous" a man whom law declares unrighteous; grace may do this because of the introduction of two factors not recognized by law, namely, faith and love.

This is the burden of much that Paul writes in Romans and Galatians. He contrasts two kinds of righteousness—that of law and that of faith. He even goes as far back as Abraham to prove his point that there is a righteousness of faith (Rom. 4). Paul himself had been brought up in the legalistic religion of later Judaism (Acts 22:1, 3, 26:4 f.; Gal. 1:14), which presupposed a set of regulations whose complete observance made a man right with God. He had learned for himself how impossible this was. He then found himself confronted with "Jesus Christ and him crucified," and he saw in what this crucified Christ brought into the world a different way of becoming reconciled with God. This Christ was the gift of God's love to men, to destroy the terror of the law, to reveal beyond question the divine grace, and to establish between men and God a new relationship.

But there was a condition to the appropriation of this gift: the condition was faith. Christ must be taken to be nothing less than the sin-bearer, for whose sake God would forgive and restore sinful men (Rom. 6:5–11; II Cor. 5:18–21). To do this is to have faith; this, indeed, is what faith is—trust in God's grace revealed in Christ, rather than reliance on one's own observation of God's law. Such faith changes a man's relationship to God, and God's to a man. If the faith be genuine—and it must be that or nothing—love is its inevitable issue, and what happens when love is in command may be seen in Paul's matchless hymn of love (I Cor. 13).

This is that new kind of righteousness which comes of faith. As the Church came to increasing power and influence in the world this simple way of salvation tended to be lost sight of—the Gospel itself became bound in that very legalism from which it had sought to set men free. This largely accounts for the central emphasis of the Protestant Reformation on "justification by faith." What was sought was a recovery of the Pauline doctrine—emancipation from regulations that assumed that a man's salvation lay in "works" which the man himself did, rather than in "faith" in something that God in Christ did for him. This "faith" involved being "in Christ," a participation in his "perfect righteousness." Consequently there is no sharp break between "justification" and "sanctification," as is too often assumed. See GRACE; REGENERATION; RIGHTEOUSNESS; SANCTIFICATION; SON OF GOD. E. L.

Justus (Lat., "just," "righteous"). (1) Joseph Barsabas, the defeated candidate for the successor to Judas (Acts 1:23). (2) The devout and kindly Corinthian Tit(i)us Justus, who shared with Paul his house near the synagogue and was led to the Christian way of life (Acts 18:7 f.). (3) A Jew ("Jesus" or "Joshua") who, as fellow prisoner of Paul in his first Roman imprisonment, was a great "comfort" (Col. 4:11) to the Apostle, and joined him in greetings to Colossian Christians. "Justus" in (1) and (2) is a Gentile surname adopted by Jews; in (3) it is the surname of a Roman who had joined synagogue worshippers at Corinth.

K

kab (kăb), (R S.V.), *cab* (A.V.), an O.T. unit of dry volume measure, 1⅑ dry quarts (U.S.), 1⁄18 of an *ephah**, the standard unit. See WEIGHTS AND MEASURES.

Kabzeel (kăb′zē-ĕl) ("whom God gathers"), a town in S. Judaea, site uncertain, possibly NE. of Beer-sheba, listed (Josh. 15:21) in the inheritance of Judah, home of David's iron-muscled henchman, Benaiah (II Sam. 23:20), and a place to which Exiles returned from Babylon (Neh. 11:25, "Jekabzeel").

Kadesh (kā′dĕsh). (1) Kadesh-barnea (kā′-dĕsh-bär′nē-*ȧ*) or Qadesh, 'Ain Kadeis, 'Ain el-Qudeirat or Gedeirat, the central camp site of Israel during their Wilderness* wanderings, reached by an 11-day trek from Sinai*. It was probably situated in the NE. part of the Sinai Peninsula, in the Wilderness of Paran and the Wilderness of Zin*, some 70 m. S. of Hebron. From here observers sent by Moses spied out the land (Num. 13:21–26; Deut. 1:19–25). The topography of Kadesh-barnea tallies with events narrated of it in the O.T. The camp site was determined by a cave-born spring (Num. 20:2 ff.). But the water and food supply here proved inadequate, and the Hebrew nomads pushed out to the more adequate area, c. 5 m. north, watered by the lively 'Ain Qudeirat (Gedeirat), and to 'Ain Qoseimah. Thus they acquired the best-watered region on the Sinai Peninsula. This fact explains the generation-long settlement here of the wanderers before they moved nearer their Canaan goal (Num. 20:1; 27:14; 33:36; Deut. 1:46). Sometimes the spring of Kadesh was called "En-mishpat," because here tribal decisions were made (Gen. 14:7). Miriam was buried at Kadesh (Num. 20:1). From here messengers were sent to the King of Edom, who refused the migrants permission to pass through his country (20:14 ff.; Judg. 11:16). Kadesh (or 'Ain Gedeirat) today shows evidences of early occupation, including a well-constructed pre-Roman reservoir, 75 ft. square and nine ft. deep. A fort from the 10th century B.C. has also been found here.

(2) Kadesh-on-the-Orontes in Syria was the scene of a great battle fought between the forces of Rameses II* (c. 1286 B.C.) and the Hittites*, who gained the upper hand but failed to follow up their victory. See also KEDESH-NAPHTALI.

Kadmiel (Kăd′mĭ-ĕl) ("El is the ancient one"). (1) The head of a Levitical family who returned from Exile with Zerubbabel (Ezra 2:40; Neh. 7:43, 12:8, 24). (2) One or more Levites who participated in rebuilding the Temple (Ezra 3:9); in the ceremony of repentance (Neh. 9:4,5); and in sealing the covenant (Neh. 10:9).

Kadmonites (kăd′mŏn-īts) ("dwellers to the east," or "ancients"), a primitive Arab people named in the genealogical list of Gen. 15:19–21 along with Kenites* and Kenizzites (see KENAZ). All three groups enriched the blood strains of the people of S. Canaan.

Kain. (1) A clan name for a group known as Kenites*. (2) An ancient village in the Judaean highlands (A.S.V. Josh. 15:57), possibly on a hill SW. of Hebron, site of the supposed tomb of Cain. Yukin has cisterns, tombs, and other signs of early occupation.

Kallai (kăl′ā-ī) ("swift"), a priest and head of a house in the era of the high priest Joiakim (Neh. 12:20).

Kanah (kā′n*ȧ*) (Heb. *qāneh*, "a reed"). (1) A little river flowing between Manasseh and Ephraim (Josh. 16:8, 17:9). Its location is uncertain, but it is probably a brook which flows into the Mediterranean N. of Joppa. (2) A town SE. of Tyre, settled before the Hebrew Conquest*, at which time it fell by lot to the Tribe of Asher (Josh. 19:28).

Kattath (kăt′ăth), a town of Zebulun (Josh. 19:15), site unknown, possibly Khirbet Qoteina, SW. of Jokneam. Possibly the same as Kartah (Josh. 21:34) and the Canaanite Kitron (Judg. 1:30). Kartah may be Athlit, on the Mediterranean coast nine m. S. of Carmel, the picturesque "Pilgrims' Castle" of Crusaders—their last stronghold in Palestine, as it was of the Maccabees in 130 B.C.

Kedar (kē′dẽr) (Heb. *qēdhar*, Assyr. *Kidru*), a name applied both to a region and to the large group of people who lived in it, E. of Palestine, in the NW. portion of the Arabian peninsula where it reaches toward Damascus. The eponymous ancestor of this important group of Bedouins was Kedar, son of Ishmael*, son of Hagar and Abraham (Gen. 25:13; I Chron. 1:29). Families of Kedar, "men of the East" (Jer. 49:28), were noted for their choice flocks (Isa. 60:7; Ezek. 27:21), and for their black tents which gave picturesque similes to the Psalmist (120:5) and the author of the Song of Solomon (1:5). Their prototypes are seen today in villages of black and gray striped tents along the Sea of Galilee, where seminomadic groups raise vegetables and secure fish from the lake, and in S. Judaea and Jordan. In the Assyrian age Kedar represented a considerable group of people, who may have worshipped Syrian deities. They cut their hair, contrary to the usual Bedouin custom, and were noted for skill in archery (Isa. 21:16 f.). Ezekiel (27:21), classing them as true Arabs, mentions their trading lambs, rams, and goats with Tyre*, their nearest port city. The Targums and rabbinical literature sometimes call Arabia "Kedar."

Kedemah (kĕd′ē-m*ȧ*) (Heb. *qēdhmāh*), a son of Ishmael and the head of villagers encamped in tents (Gen. 25:15; I Chron. 1:31); also a clan descended from him.

Kedemoth (kĕd′ē-mŏth) (Heb. *qedhēmōth*, "east," ? ez-Za'ferân). (1) A wilderness E.

of the Dead Sea, N. of Moab, near the upper waters of the Arnon River, from which Moses sent messengers with peaceful greetings to King Sion of Heshbon, asking for the right of way (Deut. 2:26 f.). (2) A town of this region, possibly NE. of Dibon, "assigned" to Reuben by Moses (Josh. 13:15–18), later to Levites (Josh. 21:37; I Chron. 6:79).

Kedes. See KADESH.

Kedesh-naphtali (kē′dĕsh-năf′tȧ-lī), also called Kedesh (kē′dĕsh) (Josh. 12:22) and Kedesh-in-Galilee (Josh. 20:7); may be Kedes, NW. of Lake Huleh in Galilee. (1) This old, fortified hill center of the Canaanites was the home of Barak (Judg. 4:6, 9 f.), and the place where he and Deborah assembled troops to fight the Canaanite Sisera. It was captured by Tiglath-pileser III (II Kings 15:29). For a time it was a city of refuge and a Levitical city of Gershonites (see GERSHON) (I Chron. 6:76). Ancient ruins strew the picturesque site. (2) A Levitical city (I Chron. 6:72) in Issachar, territory lying along the Jordan SW. of the Sea of Galilee. This town may be the "Kishion" of Josh. 19:20.

Keilah (kē-ī′lȧ) (Khirbet Qila), a city of Judah (Josh. 15:44) in the Shephelah, c. 1,500 ft. above the Mediterranean, and c. 7 m. E. of Beit Jibrîn; SW. of Bethlehem and SE. of Adullam, between the Valley of Berachah and the Valley of Zephathah. Used for a short time by David as his headquarters, it was abandoned by him because the Lord told him that its people would deliver him into the hands of Saul (I Sam. 23:7–13). Exiles returned to it in the 5th century B.C.

Kelt, Wâdī. See QELT.

Kemuel (kĕm′ū-ĕl). (1) Ancestor of the Nahorites, from whom Aram sprang (Gen. 22:21; cf. 10:22). (2) A prince of Ephraim (Num. 34:24). (3) A Levite, father of Hashabiah (I Chron. 27:17).

Kenath (kē′năth) ("possession"), the easternmost of the 10 Decapolis cities*; also known as Canatha, Kenatha (I Chron. 2:23), and for a time Nobah, so named for one of its conquerors (Num. 32:42). It was on the W. slope of the rugged Jebel Hauran, at the extreme NE. border of Israel, 16 m. NE. of Bosrah. Today it is inhabited by fanatical Druses, a religious sect founded in the 11th century by el-Hakim, Caliph of Egypt, and embodying tenets of Mosaic Law, teachings from the Gospels, the Koran, and Sufi mysticism. Its site presents a composite of impressive ruins, some of them Graeco-Roman.

Kenaz (kē′năz) (Kenez), a descendant of Esau (Gen. 36:11), and the reputed ancestor of part of the pre-Israelite population of Palestine, the Kenezites (A.V., A.S.V. Kenizzites). They were related to the Kenites*, expert metal workers of the Jordan Valley. Possibly they invaded Canaan from the S. Caleb was the son of a Kenezite (Num. 32:12; Josh. 14:6); Othniel, too, is said to have belonged to this clan (15:17). Gen. 15:19 suggests that part of the Kenizzites merged with Judah. Their center was near Hebron (Josh. 15:13). Another portion of the clan became Edomite.

Kenezites (kē′nĕz-īts), (**Kenizzites**) (kē′nĭz-īts). See KENAZ.

Kenites (kē′nīts) ("belonging to the coppersmith[s]"; cf. Arab. *cain* and Aram. *cainaya*, "smith"), a tribe of prosperous "traveling tinkers" or gypsy smiths who early plied their skills up and down the mineral-rich Wâdī Arabah*, supporting themselves by their metalcrafts, knowledge of which they probably shared with Edom and Israel (Num. 10:29; Judg. 4:11). (See TUBAL-CAIN, and his ability to work the copper and iron [Gen. 4:22] known to have been mined at a very early date in the Jordan Valley.) Kenites belonged to the Midianites*, and were related to the Kenezites.

That Kenites as well as Amalekites were at times affiliated with Judah is evident (I Sam. 27:10). Saul, attacking the Amalekites, advised the Kenites to separate from them, for he recalled the Kenites' kindness to his forebears during the Exodus (I Sam. 15:6). They took up residence along the SW. shore of the Dead Sea, SE. of Hebron (Judg. 1:16). Possibly their joining with Israel in the first place for entry into W. Palestine by conquest (Num. 10:29–32) was due to their having had ancestors in that land. The Kenite Hobab, son of Raguel, became "eyes" for the wandering settlers moving up from their Egyptian bondage (Judg. 1:16, 4:11). The fact that individual Kenites are mentioned in the O.T. as living in various places confirms the impression of their nomadic ways; they were in Wâdī Arabah (Num. 24:20–22); SE. of Hebron (Judg. 1:16); in Naphtali (Judg. 4:11); and in S. Judah in the era of David and Solomon (I Sam. 15:6, 27:10, 30:29). Kenites were confirmed Bedouins.

The father-in-law of Moses was a Kenite (Judg. 1:16), who is credited with having imparted to him deep spiritual truths (Ex. 18:1–12). Nelson Glueck suggests that from him Moses learned to fashion the copper ("brazen") serpent. Another individual Kenite mentioned in the O.T. was Heber* (Judg. 4:11, 17, 5:24), who in the period of the Judges severed himself from the friendly relations with the Hebrews which had prevailed in the time of his ancestor Hobab. The ascetic Rechabites were of Kenite origin (I Chron. 2:55).

Keren-happuch (kĕr′ĕn-hăp′ŭk) ("horn of antimony"), the youngest of Job's three daughters born after the return of prosperity (Job 42:14). Her name suggests "beautiful eyes," since eyelash dye was made from antimony, a bluish-white metallic substance.

Kerioth (kē′rĭ-ŏth) (Kirioth [kĭr′ĭ-ŏth] Amos 2:2). (1) A town in the mountains of Idumaea, W. of the S. shore of the Dead Sea, the Kirioth-hezron of Josh. 15:25; possibly Khirbet el-Qaryatein. (2) A city in Moab (Jer. 48:24, 41), site uncertain, though effort has been made to identify it with Ar, the ancient capital of Moab, because Amos 2:2 refers to its royal palaces. Line 13 of the Moabite Stone refers to its having a principal sanctuary of the god Chemosh.

kesitah, the transliteration of a Heb. word translated "piece of money" in Gen. 33:19 and Job 42:11. Its value is not known, but it was probably an ingot of precious metal of recognized value. The LXX of Gen. 33:19 renders it "lamb." In the ancient Middle East precious metals carved in animal shapes were used in various sizes for standard weights* (see illus. 483) and as currency.

Keturah (kĕ-tū'rȧ) ("frankincense"), the 2d wife (or concubine, I Chron. 1:32) of Abraham, mentioned only by J and the Chronicler. She was the ancestress of six Arab tribes which lived in southern and eastern Palestine: Zimran, Jokshan, Medan, Midian, Ishbak, and Shuah (Gen. 25:1–4), which are represented as having received, through their fathers, gifts of lesser importance than those Abraham gave Isaac, the son of Sarah. During his lifetime Isaac sent Keturah's son away to "the east country" (Gen. 25:6).

key, used in the N.T. as a symbol of authority (Matt. 16:19; Rev. 1:18, 3:7, 9:1, 20:1).

Keziah (kĕ-zī'ȧ) (A.V. Kezia) ("cassia"), the 2d daughter born to Job after the return of his prosperity (Job 42:14).

Khapiru (formerly spelled "Khabiru" in cuneiform, sometimes "Habiri"; more properly "'Apiru"; "'Aperu" in Egyptian texts), an early people of Palestine believed by many authorities to have been related to the Hebrews and to have formed ultimately a part of the nation of Israel. A vague reference to them has been found on a stele excavated at Beth-shan in the Valley of Jezreel, on the level of the era of the Egyptian King Seti I, regarded by many as the pharaoh of the oppression of Israel. The 'Apiru are also mentioned on tablets excavated at Ras Shamrah (Ugarit) in N. Syria, and are there represented as a distinct class of the population living in a certain quarter of the city, the *Khalbi*, on the slopes of a mountain where Ugaritians believed their gods dwelt. The name 'Apiru may have been applied to a group of wandering people who lived on the periphery of society in various lands, including Mesopotamia in the time of Hammurabi. Possibly even the Hebrews were one of a large number of such groups, looked upon as "outsiders." *Habiru* is an old Babylonian word suggesting "bandit" or "Bedouin," one who crosses boundaries, *'Iprî*. The Tell el-Amarna* letters also mention the 'Apiru as a seminomadic people whose occupation of Palestine hill country in the 14th century B.C. was contributing to the insecurity of the country. They were plundering Palestine to such an extent that the governor of Urusalim (Jerusalem) was begging the Egyptian pharaoh for help, especially in view of the fact that the Khapiru were being given food by Gezer, the region of Ashkelon, and Lachish. W. F. Albright states that the Khapiru of the Amarna tablets may represent a pre-Israelite phase of the Hebrew settlement in Canaan, where they were joined by the Israelites proper after their Exodus from Egypt. Some critics believe that some of the events in Joshua occurred when the Habiru overran Palestine. New material found at Nuzu* and Mari* sheds further light on this people.

Kheleifeh, Tell. See EZION-GEBEZ.

Khirbet Kerak, a 60-acre mound excavated near the SW. tip of the Sea of Galilee, just N. of the point where the Jordan emerges from the lake, now identified as Beth-yerah (Temple of the Moon), where as early as the 4th millennium B.C. the cult of moon-god worship was carried on. The city was prosperous between c. 3500 and 2500 B.C.

Khirbet et-Tannûr, a site on the lofty Jebel Tannûr, SE. of the Dead Sea, on the River Zered in the Kingdom of Jordan, excavated by the American Schools of Oriental Research (under Nelson Glueck) and the Jordan Department of Antiquities. Examination especially of the Nabataean (see NABATAEA) temple has brought rich evidence of the eclectic nature of Nabataean religion and civilization, influenced by Hellenistic, Syrian, Egyptian, and Parthian peoples.

Kibroth-hattaavah (kĭb'rŏth-hă-tā'ȧ-vȧ) ("graves of lust"), a site whose exact location is unknown, but which was one day's journey from the Sinai wilderness (Num. 33:16), and accessible to the plain below the traditional Mt. Sinai. It was named in Num. 11:34 as the place where "the people that lusted" were buried (see also Deut. 9:22).

kid. See GOAT.

kidney, the two glands in vertebrates for secreting fluid waste. (1) Two animal kidneys were burned upon the altar as a sacrifice, along with other choice animal portions, in the celebration of the peace offering that expressed friendship between God and man (Ex. 29:13, 22; Isa. 34:6). (2) Biblical people considered the kidneys to be the seat of man's emotions. (A.V. uses the archaic word "reins" —Ps. 7:9, 16:7, 26:2; Isa. 11:5; Jer. 11:20; Rev. 2:23).

Kidron (Kedron, or Cedron of A.V. John 18:1, "torrent valley" or "dark, turbid," though the Gk. form suggests "cedars"), a valley 3 m. long which bounds the E. slope of Jerusalem (I Kings 2:37; Jer. 31:40) and separates it from the Mount of Olives. Through the valley runs a seasonal brook, and the name is applied to both. Nehemiah (2:15) calls it simply "the brook" (cf. II Chron. 32:4). Running (at Jerusalem) NE. to SW., it joins the Valley of Hinnom* N. of En-rogel, S. of the old Pool of Siloam and the City of David. Originally the Spring Gihon* emptied into the Kidron. The Tyropoeon Valley joins it. (See JEHOSHAPHAT.)

The road running down from the NE. corner of Jerusalem, past the Palestine Archaeological Museum, crosses the brook Kidron to join the path up the Mount of Olives and the road to Bethany and Jericho at a point near the Garden of Gethsemane.

The wâdī is dry during many months of each year. Rising c. 1½ m. N. of the NW. corner of the Jerusalem wall, it extends first SE., then, where it is crossed by the path up the Mount of Olives, it runs S., narrowing at En-rogel Spring, and continues as Wâdī en-Nar ("Valley of Fire") to enter the Dead Sea far below Jerusalem. The Tyropoeon Valley enters the Kidron near the Hinnom. Below the E. wall of the city, where the valley is narrow and walled by scarp, the Kidron is called Wâdī Sitti Mariam ("Valley of Lady Mary"). Much of its E. slope is taken up with ecclesiastical holdings and with tombs of poor and rich, Moslem and Jew. Many "hybrid tombs" of the Herodian period are in the Valley, including the so-called Tomb of St. James and the Pyramid of Zacharias. Into the Kidron righteous Hebrew kings dumped idols and refuse from heathen shrines they had cleansed (I Kings 15:13; II Kings 23:4–6; II Chron. 29:16, 30:14). Josephus relates that the wicked queen mother Athaliah was led to the Kidron to be killed, lest she defile the Temple. As stated by C. C. McCown, debris from the hilltops of both sides of the Kidron has been "dumped into it during periods when it was unoccupied by buildings; in places the deposits have grown to a depth of 80 ft. In J. W. Crowfoot's 1927 trench dug across the Valley the depth ran from 35 feet at the east end, just inside the old gate, to 50 feet in the middle of the Valley."

227. Kidron Valley at junction with Hinnom Valley. At left, Mount of Offense; at right, Hill of Evil Counsel. Silwan (Siloam) village across Kidron.

The two most notable crossings of the narrow Kidron Valley were by David on his flight from Absalom (II Sam. 15:23), and by Jesus on his way to Gethsemane (John 18:1).

king, a male monarch invested with chief authority over a country or a people, usually for life and with hereditary succession. Egypt considered its pharaoh as a god incarnate. Mesopotamia looked upon its ruler as the chosen servant of the gods. Kingship in Judah meant a hereditary ruler; in Israel the charismatic and democratic principles also played an important role at various times. The hereditary principle prevailed among Canaanites, Hittites, Mitanni, Medes, and the Persians. Kingship in Egypt was considered as a function of the gods, and in Mesopotamia as a divinely ordained political order. The Hebrews introduced it on their own initiative in imitation of their neighbors, and at a time when Ammonites and Philistines were pressing them hard.

The concept of kingship played an insignificant part in the early stages of Hebrew history, for the people (as a family, clan, or nation), constituted the ultimate authority. After the Exodus the conviction of the Hebrews that they were the chosen people, with whom Yahweh was in covenant* relationship, gave a pre-eminence to their law* and religious institutions—a pre-eminence which outlived the earthly monarchy taken on in imitation of their neighbors. Even when expediency had dictated the wisdom of establishing a kingship, the divine sanction given to such a practice (I Sam. 8:21 f., 24:6) was at times not sufficient to restrain the death (II Sam. 5:5–7) or the repudiation of the royal incumbent and his line by the democratic sanctions inherent in the people (I Kings 12:16). God's covenant with the people antedated and surpassed in importance any earthly kingship. His special covenant with David was a personal affair with him and his descendants, yet a covenant which implied the security of the nation (II Sam. 7:8–16).

Among the possessions characteristic of the kings were: a sceptre (Ps. 45:6); a spear (I Sam. 22:6); a crown (II Kings 11:12); a throne (I Kings 2:19, 10:18–20); a palace (I Kings 7:1–12, 22:39); and royal chariots (I Sam. 8:11; II Sam. 15:1). Among his entourage were those who "saw the king's face" (A.S.V. II Kings 25:19)—that is, who were "the king's council" (R.S.V.); his bodyguard (II Sam. 15:18; II Kings 11:4); and the leading military officials (I Sam. 14:50; I Kings 16:9, 16). His civil attendants were the "recorder" or royal herald (II Sam. 8:16, 20:24) (A.S.V. margin "chronicler");

KINGDOM OF GOD

the scribe or secretary (II Sam. 8:17, 20:25; I Kings 4:3); the officer "over the household" (I Kings 4:6, 18:3; II Kings 18:18, 37); the overseer of conscript labor (II Sam. 20:24; I Kings 4:6, 5:14, 12:18); his "friend" (I Kings 4:5; II Sam. 15:37, 16:16); his "counsellor" (II Sam. 15:12); and many other minor attachés (I Chron 27:25–31).

The Hebrew king normally functioned in the secular sphere. He judged in disputes (II Sam. 14:4–11 f., 15:2; I Kings 3:16–27) and led the preparations for war and in battle (II Sam. 21:15–17; I Kings 12:21; II Chron. 17:1 f., 32:2–8). With his power and wealth he made worship possible (II Sam. 6:12; I Kings 6:2). These subsidies were extended to the cults of Baal and of the deities (I Kings 16:32 f.; II Kings 21:3). The Hebrew king was only occasionally identified with priestly costumes (II Sam. 6:14–18) and customs (I Kings 8:62–64), though in later times the priests*, not the kings, were the functionaries of religion in the Hebrew state (Matt. 12:3 f.). Prophets were free to criticize the king because of their sacrosanct character. The dominant accusation of prophets against kings was that they were faithless to Yahweh (II Kings 21:9–11; I Kings 16:3). Such accusations against rulers were taken up by the compiler of the Book of Kings and reverberate with monotony throughout the book. To the prophets the king was just one of the people, equally subject to moral law (Nathan and David, Elijah and Ahab).

Yahweh was the Hebrews' spiritual king. Deut. 33:1–5 records how the Tribes accepted Him as their sovereign. Gideon rejected the invitation of a grateful people to become their king, because God's kingship leaves no room for human kings (Judg. 8:22 f.). This too was the reason for Samuel's opposition to the establishment of a monarchy (I Sam. 8:7, 10:19, 12:12, 17, 19). When the kingdom was established, both people and king were still required to regard God as their sovereign (I Sam. 12:14). Hosea without reservation denounced the corrupt kings of the Northern Kingdom, and reasserted the primacy of God (Hos. 8:4, 13:10 f.). God was Judge, Lawgiver, and Deliverer (Isa. 33:22). The reign of Yahweh, which was conceived at first as the national possession of Israel, expanded under the teachings of the prophets, and indirectly through contact with the great empires of the Nile and the Euphrates Valley, until it took on universal proportions in the theology of the Hebrews (Jer. 10:7, 10; Ps. 47:8; cf. Amos 1:3–2:16). The Psalmist shouted it jubilantly (Ps. 96:10; cf. I Chron. 16:31; Isa. 42:10–22). Isa. 11:1–16 looks forward to the time when this kingship will be manifested to the nations. To have all people know and worship this sovereign God became a future goal, inspired the Apocalyptic literature, and infused Jewish (and later, Christian) thought and life with ideas which, for Christians, were brought to completion in and by Jesus.

Jesus faced this dual conception of kingship. He possessed the requirements of an earthly king, as evidenced by his lineage (Matt. 1:1–16), in his Temptation (Luke 4:5–7), by the acclaim of the people (John 6:15, 12:13), and in the accusations of his enemies (Luke 23:2) and Caesar's representatives (John 18:33). He clearly defined his personal attitude toward temporal and spiritual authority (Matt. 22:21). He repudiated all overtures of an earthly kingship for himself (Matt. 4:8–10), and declared his allegiance to the unseen Kingdom* of God (John 9:36 f.). The title "king" he applied to God alone (Matt. 5:35, 18:23, 22:2). Only once does Jesus invest himself with the kingdom, and that not immediately, but in the future and in participation with the Divine Sovereign, a participation open to all who accepted the Sovereign (Luke 22:29).

In the early Church, where Jesus was considered as one with the Father (John 17:21), his kingship was acclaimed. The misunderstanding created by this spiritual declaration caused Paul and Silas in Thessalonica to be accused of subversive activity (Acts 17:7). In the N.T. the title of king is applied to rulers of various degrees of sovereignty (Acts 12:1, 25:13; II Cor. 11:32), as well as to the Roman Emperor (I Tim. 2:2; I Pet. 2:13, 17). The apostles recognized obedience to these rulers as earthly authorities under God (Rom. 13:1 ff.). In Revelation, however, as

228. King and queen dining; a late Hittite relief.

hatred for Rome increased, the sovereignty of Christ was strongly emphasized. The throne (Rev. 3:21), the crown (14:14), and the sword (19:15) are among his royal regalia. His ultimate control and triumph over all earthly potentates is declared (1:5, 17:14, 19:16).

For chronological list of kings of Israel and Judah, see CHRONOLOGY; also ISRAEL; JUDAH.

Kingdom of God, that final event of history in which God's will is completely done. In Biblical use, the word "kingdom" means the reign of a king, not a geographical area ruled by one. The Bible teaches that, as Creator, God is already in ultimate control, but man, by the misuse of his God-given free will, has introduced sin and disorder into creation. The Kingdom of God is that anticipated historical event when sin and its consequences have been abolished and God takes up His perfect rule forever, over the world and in the hearts of men (Isa. 24:23; Zech. 14:9; Rev. 11:15). The conception became most important in later Hebrew thought when the historical Hebrew kingdoms had come to an end. Since men had demonstrated their inability to establish the ideal order by their own cleverness, the belief arose that God would some time intervene in the historical process and, by His own power, establish His Kingdom. In the apocalyptic* literature this belief was given a particularly dramatic form (e.g. Dan. 7:9–14, 27). When Jesus began his ministry, his basic theme was "The Kingdom of God is at hand" (Mark 1:15); some of his references to the "Son of man" show how closely his thinking was connected, on one side at least, with the apocalyptic views found in Daniel and other apocalyptic books (Matt. 16:27; Luke 17:24, 21:27).

A less dramatic conception of the coming of the Kingdom is also found in the teaching of Jesus. He sometimes speaks of the Kingdom as though it were a process going on in his own time and connected with his ministry. Wherever men begin to accept his teaching and live by the laws of the Kingdom, he seems to say, the Kingdom is already beginning. This conception has its antecedents in rabbinical rather than apocalyptic thought. Presumably it is this conception that underlies the saying "the kingdom of God is within you," or more correctly, "in the midst of you" (Luke 17:21 R.S.V.). The "parables of the Kingdom" (Matt. 13:24–33) seem to reflect this view rather than the apocalyptic one.

The two ideas of the Kingdom—that it is a future event to be anticipated, and a present reality in the process of arriving—are not necessarily antithetical. Jesus speaks of first one aspect and then another, but underlying both is the firm assurance that God's will must finally prevail. It may be that Jesus expected the perfect realization of the Kingdom only in the future, and used apocalyptic language to describe it, but also taught that even in the present age men could apprehend its coming and enter it in anticipation.

Unfortunately, in modern scholarship there has been a tendency to emphasize exclusively one or the other of these aspects and thus distort the teaching of the Gospels. On the one hand, scholars like Schweitzer have stressed the apocalyptic element so strongly as to make Jesus seem a visionary totally out of touch with the real world. On the other, "liberals" have often emphasized the idea of gradual growth so much as to deprive the Kingdom of its rooting in God's act and identify it with a merely human struggle for social and material betterment. In fact, both elements are present in the teaching of Jesus and are vital to it. While, from one point of view, the task of establishing the Kingdom is so enormous that only God can accomplish it, and men need the assurance that it is His will and intention to do so, from another point of view they also need the assurance that their own efforts at creating a better world are not futile, but are in some real way a foreshadowing of the coming Kingdom and an evidence that it is "at hand." As the N.T. describes it, it is also necessary for each individual to "enter" the Kingdom by being "born again" (John 3:3–8), and by accepting for himself the law of the Kingdom set forth in the "Beatitudes" (Matt. 5:3–12) and elsewhere in the Gospels.

The Church, in the sense of the visible organization and its associated orders, is not itself the Kingdom. There are numerous agencies of the Kingdom, and the Church is one of these. Indeed, all human institutions may serve the Kingdom, as the Kingdom may serve them. The Kingdom does not consist merely in social progress. Such progress is desirable as removing obstacles to it, but the progress is not itself the Kingdom (Rom. 14:17). The Kingdom of God is not a kingdom of this world (John 18:36), but this world provides the sphere in which it is to function (Matt. 6:10). See MESSIAH; PARABLE; SON OF GOD. R. C. D.

Kingdom of Heaven, for all practical purposes a synonym for "the Kingdom of God." The phrase is found only in Matthew's Gospel, where it is used some 30 times. Only four times (6:33, 12:28, 21:31, 43; but cf. 26:29) does Matthew use "the kingdom of God," which is the customary term in Mark and Luke (in John only twice, 3:3, 5), and which is frequent in Acts (1:3, 6, 8:12, 14:22, 19:8, 20:25, 28:23, etc.). Revelation uses it once (12:10; cf. 11:15).

Matthew's preference for the "kingdom of heaven" may reflect Jewish influence. His Gospel represents the Christian faith as it was accepted and declared by the church centered in Jerusalem, many of whose members were also priests of the Temple (Acts 6:7). Jewish priests had long regarded the name of God as much more than a mere name; it was a part of God Himself, and was to be revered as God was. The Levitical law elaborated on the Third Commandment, which forbade profaning the name of God (Ex. 20:7; see Lev. 18:21, 19:12, 21:6, 22:2, 32). One sure way to avoid profaning it was not to use the name at all where it could possibly be avoided; indeed, it was enough to say merely "the Name" (Lev. 24:11). In Ex. 3:14 "I am that I am" (later Yahweh or Jehovah) is not really a name at all, but a description of God's nature and character. Substitute words came into use, such as "the Blessed One," "the Holy One," "the high and lofty One," "the Almighty" (used in Job more than 30 times). One of these substitutes (common among other peoples besides the Jews) was the word "heaven"* (cf. Matt. 5:34). It is therefore reasonable that a Gospel narrative which had its origin in and around Jerusalem should for that reason prefer "kingdom of heaven" to "kingdom of God." The meaning would not be affected in the least (cf. Matt. 13:31 and Mark 4:30 f.).

Another possible explanation is that the term is used to indicate the specifically heavenly character of the Kingdom (cf. Matt. 7:21). In the teaching of Jesus the Kingdom never comes from below, as a creation of man, but from above, as a gift of God. "The Kingdom" means the will of the Father in heaven being done on earth (Matt. 6:9, 10); in that meaning "kingdom of heaven" is less open to misunderstanding than "kingdom of God." E. L.

Kings, I and II, the Book of the, like the two Books of Samuel*, in the Heb. were originally a single volume. In the Gk. Bible, where the divisions first appear, the four books of Samuel and Kings are called "First, Second, Third, and Fourth Kingdoms." In the Lat. Bible the word "Kings" is used, a word preferred by Jerome. Thus arose the superscription to I and II Kings in the A.V., "Commonly called, The Third Book of the Kings," "The Fourth Book of the Kings." These explanatory phrases were dropped in later translations.

I and II Kings relate the history of Israel from the last days of David (c. 961 B.C.) to the release of Jehoiachin* from his Babylonian prison c. 562 B.C. This is the period of Israel's glory, division, decline, disintegration, and fall. The approximately four centuries of recorded history in this book can be outlined as follows:

(1) Accession and reign of Solomon (I Kings 1–11).

(2) Synchronistic account of the divided Kingdoms of Judah* and Israel* until the capture of the Northern Kingdom (I Kings 12–II Kings 17), concluding with a statement concerning the reasons for its capture and an account of the origin of the Samaritans* (II Kings 17:7–41).

(3) The Kingdom of Judah until the Babylonian Exile* (II Kings 18–25).

The data which make up these books are from court, Temple, and literary records; an official "scribe" is mentioned among the ministers of David (II Sam. 8:17, 20:25); of Solomon (I Kings 4:3); of Hezekiah (II Kings 18:18, 37); and of Josiah (II Chron. 34:18). Such records, similar to the Hittite and Assyrian annals on cuneiform tablets, furnish some of the historic material for this book. Specifically mentioned, but lost in the dust of time, are histories based on such official annals: "The Book of the Acts of Solomon" (I Kings 11:41); "The Book of the Chronicles of the Kings of Israel" (I Kings 14:19); "The Book of the Chronicles of the Kings of Judah" (I Kings 14:29). "Temple Annals," written by priests of Jerusalem, may have supplied such data as I Kings 6:2–37, 7:13–51, 14:25–28; II Kings 12:4–16; etc. The stories of Elijah (I Kings 17–19, 21; II Kings 1) and of Elisha (II Kings 2, 3:4–8:15, 13:14–21), though closely interwoven with national events recorded in these excellent histories, were independent of them, and are remnants of the literary productivity of the Northern Kingdom. After the transition to the Divided Kingdom (I Kings 12), the story of each reign is, with few exceptions, fitted into a regular framework consisting of (1) an opening formula giving the date of the reign, its length, the contemporary ruler in the neighboring kingdom, etc. (I Kings 15:1 f., 22:41 f.; II Kings 15:1 f., 18:1 f.); (2) the compiler's judgment of the reign (I Kings 15:26, 22:43; II Kings 15:3, 18:4–6); and (3) a closing formula, including the king's death, the place of his burial, the name of his successor, and a reference to one of the lost histories (I Kings 15:8, 22:50; II Kings 15:7, 20:20 f.). This "paper and paste method" was used to bring together the histories of Israel and Judah from various sources. There are some errors in the dating of the several reigns; but the historical sequence of rulers in I and II Kings is correct, and makes the Book an invaluable historical source. (See CHRONOLOGY; PROPHET.)

Archaeology in its various forms supplements or corroborates I and II Kings. A few examples of this follow: (1) the cedar forests of Lebanon* (I Kings 5:6; II Chron. 2:8 f.) furnished supplies not only to Solomon but also, according to cuneiform inscriptions, to Gudea, ruler of Lagash* in Babylonia (c. 2450 B.C.) for the Temple of Ningursu, and to Ashurnasirpal II, King of Assyria (883–859 B.C.), for his building enterprises; (2) Ezion-geber*, Solomon's harbor city (I Kings 9:26 ff., 10:11 f.), has been excavated; (3) the city of Solomon at Megiddo* (I Kings 9:15) has been examined; (4) Shishak*, founder of the Twenty-second Egyptian Dynasty (I Kings 14:25–28), recorded his Palestinian campagin (c. 918 B.C.) on the walls of the Temple of Karnak; (5) Shalmaneser* III, King of Assyria (859–824 B.C.), in records of his repeated attacks on the revolting kings of Syria and Palestine, states that he erected a stele with his "royal portrait" on the "mountain of Baalrasi" (probably Mt. Carmel), and received "the tribute of the Tyrians, the Sidonians, and of Jehu [I Kings 19:16], son of Omri"*; (6) numerous ivory* fragments from the Ahab period were found in the excavation of Samaria* (I Kings 22:39; cf. Amos 6:4, 3:15); (7) the Moabite* Stone, written by Mesha* (II Kings 3:4 ff.), supplements the Bible account; (8) the records of Tiglath-pileser* III (745–727 B.C.), concerning his extensive conquests in the West, confirm II Kings 15:29 f. and furnish background for the obeisance of Ahaz (II Kings 16:7–16); (9) the siege and fall of Samaria (722/1 B.C.) (II Kings 17:6, 24 f.) is confirmed in the cuneiform records of Shalmaneser V (727–722 B.C.) and Sargon* (722–705 B.C.); (10) the annals of Sennacherib (705–681 B.C.) parallel closely II Kings 18:13–19:36 and Isaiah 36 and 37; (11) the Siloam* Tunnel, with its inscription, definitely corroborates II Kings 20:20 and II Chron. 32:30.

The promotion of religion, however, was the main aim of the editors of the Book of Kings; historical data in their hands served as the vehicle for a larger purpose than history. Solomon was the cornerstone of the book because his Temple (I Kings 5, 6) became after 621 B.C. the only place where sacrifices could be offered to Yahweh (see

Deut. 12). Divine retribution for human deeds (cf. Deut. 28), both individual and national, was an article of faith. Rewards and penalties were still confined to life on this earth. The idea of the punishment* of evil and the reward of obedience to God rings like chimes throughout the Book.

The varied editorial attitudes revealed in Kings disclose, according to modern scholars, redactions of various dates, with corresponding changes in religious convictions. According to some, the original edition consisted of I Kings 2:1–12 and much of I Kings 3:1–II Kings 23:25. Later extracts were added, particularly from N. Israelite sources. On this view, c. 550 B.C. the Deuteronomist (see DEUTERONOMY) not only re-published the Book of Kings, but edited the books of the Pentateuch (except Leviticus) and the historical books of Joshua, Judges, and Samuel. Students believe they can recognize additions made at this period because of a more sympathetic attitude toward N. Israel. In 600 B.C., when Judah was glorying in its own survival, 122 yrs. after the downfall of its northern neighbor Israel, an earlier editor considered the Kingdom of Israel reprobate and accursed. He recorded or composed oracles after the style of Amos*, which proclaimed the inevitable doom of certain Israelite kings: Jeroboam I (I Kings 14:1–18, 15:29); Baasha (I Kings 16:1–4); and Ahab (I Kings 21:20–24). He shed no tears over the end of the Kingdom (722/1 B.C.), since he saw in this calamity a just punishment for the sins of Jeroboam (II Kings 17:21–23). But after the destruction of Jerusalem (August 587 B.C.) the later Deuteronomistic editor could no longer contrast the virtues and security of Judah with the sinfulness and woe of Israel. A more friendly and sympathetic attitude toward N. Israel, discernible elsewhere after 587 (Ezek. 37:15–28), is apparent in Kings (II Kings 13:5, 22 f., 14:25–27). Thus what formerly seemed to be opposing attitudes in one book became, as the result of deeper study, clear evidence of the historical backgrounds of divine revelation, always adapted to the receptive mind of man.

J. L. M./R. W. C.

King's Garden, an open, cultivated space in ancient Jerusalem near "the gate between two walls" (II Kings 25:4; Jer. 39:4, 52:7), adjacent to the Pool of Siloam* (Neh. 3:15) whose overflow waters irrigated it. The space is still used for vegetable gardens outside the SE. wall of Jerusalem.

229. The King's Garden, near the Lower Pool of Siloam, outside present S. wall of Jerusalem. Village of Silwan (Siloam) at upper left.

King's Highway, the, an ancient road through Trans-Jordan used by the four kings who battled against five kings in the region of Sodom and Gomorrah (Gen. 14). Moses desired to use it in leading Israel through Edom (Num. 20:17, 21:22). It was so well paved in Roman times that it is still used, especially since it has been resurfaced by the Hashemite Kingdom of Jordan. It is plainly visible from the air.

Kings of Judea and Israel. See CHRONOLOGY.

King's Pool, the, of Neh. 2:14 was probably the Pool of Siloam*, not far from the palace areas.

King's Vale, the, or King's Dale (A.V.), mentioned in Gen. 14:17 as "the valley of Shaveh," was probably a low-lying area at the head of the Kidron Valley, mentioned in connection with Absalom's setting up of a pillar (II Sam. 18:18).

Kir (kĭr). (1) A people and an unidentified place to which Tiglath-pileser deported Aramaeans from Damascus (II Kings 16:9). Militia was recruited from Kir to fight Israel (Isa. 22:6). Some authorities render the Kir of II Kings 16:9 "Media." Other suggested locations include Armenia; a river basin near the Caspian; Cyrene; Aleppo; and the plain between the Tigris and Elam. Kir is credited by Amos (9:7) as the original home of the Aramaeans, some of whom emigrated to Syria. (2) A Moabite city (Isa. 15:1), also called Kir-hareseth, identified as the modern Kerak, on an impregnable 3,370 ft. elevation of the Jordan, 15 m. S. of the Arnon River, 11 m. E. of the Dead Sea; possibly the ancient Moabite capital. It was a strategic city during the Crusades and also in Roman times, from which era an impressive ruined castle survives, with massive walls, glacis, underground passages, and rock-cut cisterns. Kir of Moab may be the same as Kir-haraseth (II Kings 3:25); Kir-hareseth (Isa. 16:7); or Kir-heres (Jer. 48:31, 36).

Kiriath (kĭr′ĭ-ăth) (A.V. Kirjath, kĭr′jăth) ("city"), the prefix of several site names: Kiriath-arba, Hebron (Gen. 23:2); Kiriath-arim (see Kirjath-jearim); Kiriath-baal; Kiriath-huzoth, location unknown (Num. 22:39); Kiriath-sepher, now identified as Tell Beit Mirsim (see DEBIR; and *The Annual of the ASOR*, Vols. XXI–XXII, "The Excavation of Tell Beit Mirsim," Vol. III, "The Iron Age," for structural, industrial, and pottery remains).

Kiriathaim (kĭr′ĭ-*a*-thā′ĭm) (A.V. Kirjathaim, kĭr′j*a*-thā′ĭm) ("double city"). (1) a town "assigned" to Reuben (Num. 32:37; Josh. 13:19), N. of the Arnon River, E. of the Dead Sea, in ancient Moabite territory; later occupied again by Moabites (Jer. 48:1, 23; Ezek. 25:9). The site is now known as Khirbet el-Qereiyât. The plain of Kiriathaim ("Shaveh Kiriathaim") was probably the elevated land around the city (Gen. 14:5). (2) Kartan (Khirbet el-Qureiyeh), a town of Naphtali (Josh. 21:32), possibly a site in NW. Galilee known as Kirjatham (I Chron. 6:76).

Kiriath-jearim (kĭr′-ĭăth-jē′*a*-rĭm) ("city of forests"), a Gibeonite town (Josh. 9:17) belonging to the tribe of Judah (Josh. 15:9–10, 60; 18:14; cf. Judg. 18:12), on its border with Benjamin (Josh. 18:14–15). It was also called Baalah (Josh. 15:9), Kiriath-baal (15:60; 18:14) and Baale-judah (II Sam. 6:2; cf. I Chron. 13:6). For 20 years the Ark rested in the house of Abinadab here before David conveyed it to Jerusalem (I Sam. 6:21, 7:1 f.; II Sam. 6:2 f.). It was the home of the prophet Urijah (Jer. 26:20 ff.). Some of its people returned from the Babylonian Exile (Neh. 7:29; cf. Ezra 2:25). It is generally identified with Deir el-'Azar in the modern village of Abu Ghosh, 8½ m. N. of Jerusalem.

Kiriath-sepher (kĭr′ĭ ăth-sē′fẽr). See DEBIR.

Kish. (1) An early Sumerian city, modern Tell al-Uhaimer, 8 m. E. of Babylon. Excavations by H. de Genouillac in 1912–14 and S. Langdon in 1923–33 have unearthed chariot burials, two early ziggurats, an early Mesopotamian palace, and numerous clay tablets which shed important light on early Sumerian culture (Early Dynastic period, c. 2900–2370 B.C.). In the Sumerian King List, Kish is designated the first city to receive kingship after the Flood (*ANET*³, p. 265).

During the excavation of Kish, a deposit of sterile fluvial clay was discovered, datable by current estimates to the early 3d millennium B.C. Discussion has arisen about the relationship of this and similar deposits at such sites as Ur and Fara (Shuruppak) with the Babylonian (*ANET*³, pp. 93–95) and Biblical (Gen. 6–9) accounts of the Deluge. While general chronological and literary considerations suggest that the "Flood Deposit" at Kish may perhaps correspond with that described by tradition, it remains hazardous to affirm its absolute identity. See FLOOD.

230. Western wall of Temple of Nabonidus, at Kish.

(2) A wealthy Benjamite, son of Abiel or Ner and father of Saul (I Sam. 9:1; 14:51; I Chron. 8:33; 9:39; cf. Acts 13:21). (3) An uncle of Kish the father of Saul (I Chron. 8:30, 9:36). (4) An ancestor of a Merarite Levite family (I Chron. 23:21 f., 24:29). (5) A Levite, son of Abdi (II Chron. 29:12). (6) A Benjamite, ancestor of Mordecai (Esther 2:5). W. P. A.

Kishon (kī′shŏn) (A.V. Kison, Ps. 83:9, ? "stream of the god Kish" or "curving"), a small river whose N. arm rises in springs W. of Mt. Tabor* in Galilee and whose S. arm flows from near Mt. Gilboa*. The two meet in the Plain of Esdraelon at the foot of Megiddo, whence "the waters of Megiddo" (Judg. 5:19). The Kishon flows W. between Mt. Carmel (I Kings 18:40) and the hills of S. Galilee, and empties into the Acre bay N. of modern Haifa. During many months the stream bed is a waterless ditch, unnoticed until the beholder is almost upon it, except in the westernmost 7 m. of its course, where it gains plentiful waters from Carmel and two small streams which empty into it from the NE. on the Plain of Acre. During the rainy season, however, it becomes that raging torrent of which Deborah sang in the 12th century B.C. poem of the great battle of Taanach between the bogged-down chariots of Sisera's Canaanite warriors, who fled on foot, and Israel during the period of the Judges (Judg. 4:7, 13, 5:21; Ps. 83:9); the whole plain had been engulfed by the Kishon. Armies and villages were safe only on the upper reaches of the hills above Armageddon, for the pools and marshes on the edge of the Acre Bay were always treacherous. The Canaanite camp during the Battle of Taanach, fought c. 1125 B.C. (Judg. 4, 5), and sometimes called "the Battle of the Kishon," was at Harosheth on the Kishon Pass, where the foe not only had paralyzed the commerce of Dan and Asher, but threatened the existence of all Israel. In the great battle hymn of a uniting nation Deborah, the mother-prophetess-warrior, sang with the fervor of Julia Ward Howe (who thirty-two centuries later wrote the battle hymn of an American republic):

"The kings came and fought; . . .
From heaven fought the stars, . . .
The river Kishon swept them away,
That ancient river, the river Kishon.
O my soul, march on with strength."
(A.S.V. Judg. 5:19–21)

By the waters of the River Kishon 2½ centuries after Deborah's battle Elijah slew the priests of Baal (I Kings 18:40) after the epochal victory for Yahweh on Mt. Carmel.

kiss. See GESTURE.

Kittim (kĭt′ĭm) (A.V. Chittim), the O.T. name for the island of Cyprus*, and also for its inhabitants, as in Gen. 10:4. They were regarded as descendants of Javan (4th son of Japheth, son of Noah), "Ionians." "Kittim" was derived from "Kition," a word used by the Greeks to designate the settlement later known as Larnaka. Ionians and Greeks were not the first settlers of Kittim; Phoenicians made it their first western trading post. Ezekiel recognized it as the mother of western maritime colonies (27:6) and a source of coveted boxwood.

I Macc. 1:1 states that Alexander the Great came from "Chittim"; actually his home was Macedonia. In such fashion the name "Kittim" gradually came to be applied in the O.T. to a wider area; ultimately it included inhabitants of the coasts of Greece and Asia Minor, and islands of the Mediterranean other than Cyprus, like Sicily. "Kittim" was used figuratively for Rome in the Apocalyptic book of Daniel (11:30). "Kittim" as used in Num. 24:24 may be a misinterpretation of an ordinary word (Albright).

231. Kyrenia harbor in Cyprus (O.T. "Kittim").

kneading trough, a shallow wooden or pottery vessel in which dough was worked by hand or (in Egypt) by foot (Ex. 8:3; Deut. 28:5, 17 A.S.V.). Migrants carried this essential "bound up in their clothes upon their shoulders" (Ex. 12:34). See illus. 232, p. 373.

kneel. See GESTURE.

knife, an instrument with a sharp edge for cutting. Abraham's "knife" for his sacrifice of Isaac (Gen. 22:6, 10) was probably a piece of sharp flint*. "Knives of flints" were used as circumcision instruments (A.S.V. Josh. 5:2 f.). Ceremonial knives were used by adherents of Baal for cutting their flesh during their contest with Elijah on Carmel (I Kings 18:28). The penknife used by a scribe to sharpen his reed pens and to make erasures is mentioned by Jeremiah (36:23). Ezekiel (5:1) referred to the barber's knife or razor. As late as the Hebrew Monarchy metal knives and daggers were scarce, and when excavated in Israel's occupation levels are likely to be of Philistine making, taken as war booty, for Philistines were making knives with handles of inlaid ivory before the Conquest. Hittite daggers have come to light at Beth-shan, in the level of Thutmose III. An inscribed Hyksos knife has been found at Lachish. Prized Cretan daggers were found in the armory of the Knossos sea kings by Arthur Evans. By the time of the Exile Judah had plenty of knives, some of them fine enough to be included in booty seized by Nebuchadnezzar and returned to the Jews when they were released by Cyrus (Ezra 1:9). The figurative use of knives is found in Prov. 23:2, 30:14. (See FLINT, illus. 152; WEAPONS.)

knop, an archaic word for the "knob" or "bud" of a flower, used to designate the spheroidal ornaments of the seven-branched candlestick* or lampstand of the Temple at Jerusalem (Ex. 25:31, etc.); also ornaments, shaped like eggs or gourds, on the cedar linings of the Temple walls (I Kings 6:18) and the "molten sea" (7:24).

Kohath (kō′hăth), a son of Levi, according to P and Chronicles (Gen. 46:11; Ex. 6:16–18; Num. 3:17); the reputed founder of an important Levite family, the Kohathites, to one of whose four branches the Amramites Moses and Aaron belonged (Ex. 6:20), as did Korah. During the Wilderness wanderings Kohathites had specified duties in connection with carrying Tabernacle equipment (Num. 3:27, 30 f., 4:4–15, 10:21). Hemen, a Kohathite, was listed among David's appointees (I Chron. 6:31–38, 16:41 f.) in connection with music and other activities. Kohathites led the loud singing at the battle of En-gedi (II Chron. 20:19), and participated in Hezekiah's Temple cleansing (II Chron. 29:12).

Koheleth (kō̆-hĕl′ĕth). See ECCLESIASTES.

koph (kōf) (A.S.V. Qoph), the 19th letter of the Hebrew alphabet. See WRITING.

Korah (kō′rȧ). (1) A son of Esau (Gen. 36:5, 14; I Chron. 1:35), possibly the same man mentioned in Gen. 36:16. (2) A tribe apparently descended from Caleb, and therefore Edomitic (I Chron. 2:43). (3) The Levite from whom descended a guild of Temple musicians, the Korahites, who had formerly been doorkeepers (Ex. 6:24). Their name is attached to the headings of several Psalms (42–49, except 43; 84, 85, 87, 88). Korah, son of Izhar, son of Kohath*, led a rebellion against Moses (Num. 16, 17). Its story is told in two layers of document, written in different eras: (a) the earlier shows Korah leading 250 prominent leaders of the congregation against Moses and Aaron—the people vs. the Tribe of Levi; (b) the later tells of Korah heading 250 Levites expressing the opposition of the Tribe of Levi to the priesthood of Aaron. The story of the blossoming of Aaron's rod, the sequel to (a), is told in Num. 17.

232. Egyptian model of bakery from Asyut Middle Kingdom (c. 2000–1788 B.C.). Mixing and kneading dough, placing loaves in pottery oven, from whose heat model at right shields face. Figures are of painted wood.

Kore (kō′rē) (Heb. *qōrē*). (1) The father of Shallum, a member of the Tabernacle gatekeepers' guild (I Chron. 9:19) (see KORAH). (2) A Levite contemporary with Hezekiah (II Chron. 31:14).

L

Laban (lā′bă̆n) ("white," in contrast to dark-complexioned Bedouins), a descendant of Nahor, and brother of Rebekah (Gen. 24:29, 25:20). His home country was Padan-aram, land of the Aramaeans, NE. of the Euphrates. There he welcomed the servant sent by Abraham to secure a wife (Rebekah) for his son Isaac (Gen. 24:29 ff.). A generation later young Jacob was sent to his uncle Laban by his mother Rebekah to escape the murderous envy of his brother Esau, and to find a wife in the ancestral home at Haran* (Gen. 27:43 f.). The subsequent story of the marriage of Jacob to Laban's daughters, Leah and Rachel, and the birth to them and their handmaids of 12 sons who became the nucleus of the Hebrew people, is told in Gen. 29–31. Laban's grasping nature is fully revealed in his tricky dealings with Jacob, culminating in his efforts to detain Jacob and his wives and 11 sons (Benjamin not having yet been born) after his son-in-law had served him 20 years (Gen. 31:41).

Laban is often regarded as a kinsman "sloughed off" by the developing nation of Jacob-Israel, and his story a satire on the typical Aramaean who fleeces even his own family. Yet his final separation from Jacob at mount Ephraim was signalized by the erection of a cairn and a pillar, and the pronouncement of the moving Mizpah covenant (Gen. 31:49). Laban revered the Lord (Gen. 24:50), yet hankered after the man-made family gods ("images," Gen. 31:34) or teraphim*, which Rachel had stolen and concealed under the palanquin or large saddle of her camel when she left Padan-aram. Information gleaned from recently excavated Nuzu tablets justifies Laban's resentment over the abduction of his family gods—possession of which evidently gave title to the inheritance* of family estates. If, as seems likely, Laban adopted Jacob (having at the time no sons of his own) to insure keeping the inheritance within the family, and after that adoption became the father of a son, then such a natural son would have the precedence as his heir. According to the law of the times in Aramaean lands, therefore, Rachel's act of seizing Laban's gods (the symbols of inheritance) and secreting them in Jacob's baggage was legally a fraud. These Nuzu tablets delineate many of the customs of the Patriarchal period (c. 2000–1500 B.C.), and confirm much of the social background of the stories in Genesis. (See *Bulletin* 66, ASOR.)

labor of many sorts is depicted throughout Scripture. Gen. 1 is an effort to describe the creative work of Yahweh in a universe in which He continued to labor (Ps. 104:22–24; Isa. 28:29, 40:28). Human labor took on dignity from God's labor on man's behalf. Toil was honored in Hebrew society, and was recognized as tending to life (Prov. 10:16); idleness was disparaged (Prov. 6:6–11, 24:30–34; Eccles. 10:18). The six days of labor (Ex. 34:21) were as definitely commanded as the day of rest. Labor was not only essential but founded on honorable precedents; the roster of great men included many who had worked with their hands. Labor was protected by ancient laws (Deut. 24:14 f.; Lev. 19:13, 25:6 f.; Jer. 22:13; Mal. 3:5). Jesus worked (John 5:17), and encouraged others to accomplish as much as possible before night came, "when no man can work" (John 9:4). He invited discouraged laborers to the refreshing rest to be found in spiritual activities (Matt. 11:28–30). Paul was an indefatigable worker (Acts 18:3), and urged his fellow laborers not only to toil in Christian tasks, but to labor with their hands (I Thess. 4:11). All the Twelve, and probably most of the early Christian leaders, had a trade or profession at which they worked by day. Many of their worship services were at night, when even Christian slaves might attend.

Four main types of laborers are found in Scripture: (1) the self-employed shepherd and farmer, supervising as well as working with underlings, like Abraham (Gen. 13:2), Jacob (33:17), Boaz (Ruth 2:3), Elisha (I Kings 19:19a); also sons assisting such an independent farmer, like Saul (I Sam. 9:3) and David (I Sam. 16:11); (2) the worker in crafts and trades; (3) the hired laborer of (1) or (2), who received wages and protection; (4) slave laborers. Slave labor, which went into the building of every great empire of the ancient Middle East, is fully documented in clay tablet literature and annals surviving in stone monuments. Hebrews used Israelite slaves (1) bought for terms of 6 yrs. (Ex. 21:2–6) and protected by legislation (Ex. 20:10, 17; Lev. 24:17; Deut. 20:10–18); (2) foreigners, captured (Deut. 20:10–18; Josh. 9:3–27) or purchased (Gen. 17:12; Ex. 12:44).

The Bible is a record of people at work. He that did not work was never sure that he would eat. Ancient Hebrew custom required every boy to learn a trade, to insure himself from want and temptation of stealing. Hence Jesus, like the other youths of Nazareth, joined his father at the carpenter's bench and helped support the family. In Palestine itself, the carpenter* was less important than the stonemason. There was more native material for the latter to work upon. Hebrews became adept masons. They built low walls for farms and sheepfolds, houses, palaces, military and religious buildings, town walls and city gates and cisterns. Local building stones were quarried in nearly every region. At such labor free workers and slaves worked side by side. In periods when Jerusalem was being rebuilt or expanded, or when repairs were being made to the Temple, wages of masons were entirely satisfactory. Other trades that required laborers in significant numbers were farming, fishing, cattle-breeding and shepherding; fruit growing and wine-making, mining, metalworking, pottery making, shoemaking, weaving and dyeing, and carpet-looming.

In early O.T. times Hebrews themselves were victims of forced labor (Ex. 1:10 ff. and *passim*). During the Monarchy the long and excessive *corvée* maintained by Solomon for public works at Jerusalem (I Kings 5:13–18, 11:26–28 f.) played a large part in precipitating the revolt and division of his kingdom when Rehoboam succeeded him. Impressed labor was allowed in Palestine under Roman law in N.T. times, when every Roman soldier could compel a native to carry his pack for one mile (Matt. 5:41). (See FREEMAN.)

Women in lowly homes in the Biblical period drudged not only at their grain mills (Ex. 11:5; Matt. 24:41), hearths (Gen. 18:6), with their brooms (Luke 15:8), at their looms (I Sam. 2:19), and with their water jars (Gen. 24:15), but were shepherdesses (Gen. 29:6), gleaners (Ruth 2:3), and laborers in many fields, even including business, like Lydia (Acts 16:14). Their heads and shoulders transported much of the household effects on nomadic treks, as the Bedouin custom is today. N.T. writers did not denounce slavery *per se*. Believing that either the end of the world or a cataclysmic change was imminent (see PAROUSIA), they advised slaves and household servants to accept their lot with patience (Col. 3:22 f.; I Pet. 2:18–25; cf. Eph. 6:5–8), and masters to be merciful (Eph. 6:9). (See Paul's Epistle to Philemon concerning his runaway slave Onesimus.)

Modern Israel derives inspiration from the injunction of the Midrash* to combine work, study, and prayer in the program of the day.

Lachish (lā'kĭsh), an important fortified city in Judah, correctly identified by W. F. Albright (*ZAW* 6, 1929, p. 3) with Tell ed-Duweir, 30 m. SW. of Jerusalem, 20 m. E. of the Mediterranean, 23 m. NE. of Gaza, and 15 m. W. of Hebron, overlooking the fertile Shephelah lowland and dominating the main road from central Palestine to Egypt. The *tell* itself is part of a limestone ridge surrounded by valleys on four sides, its 18-acre summit being exceeded in size only by Hazor. It was excavated by the Wellcome-Marston Archaeological Research Expedition to the Near East in 1932–38 under the direction of J. L. Starkey, whose murder by bandits brought the excavations to a tragic end. A small trial excavation was carried out in the area of the "Solar Shrine" in 1966 by Y. Aharoni.

The earliest levels of Lachish were barely reached in a step-trench cut along the S.–E. corner of the tell, as little work was done on the city mound before the excavations were suspended in 1938. However, traces of human occupation as far back as 8000 B.C. were discovered in the surrounding ridges, and caves were found in the area which had been occupied at the beginning of the Early Bronze Age (c. 3200 B.C.). These caves were later used as tombs, when it appears that occupation began to be concentrated on the mound itself in the mid-3d millennium B.C. Single burial-shaft graves cut into a spur N. of the tell (the 2000 Cemetery) and traces of occupational remains in caves located to the N.–W. of the mound indicate a change in culture toward the end of the 3d millennium B.C. The tell was again occupied during the Middle Bronze II period when a massive plaster-faced embankment of beaten earth (glacis) and fosse (artificial ditch) were constructed (c. 1750 B.C.) as fortifications, a feature characteristic of Palestinian cities at this time (see *BASOR* 137, 1955, pp. 23–32).

During the Late Bronze Age, Lachish was one of three important political centers in the Judaean Shephelah. Its close relationship with Egypt may be inferred by the occurrence on the site of scarabs of nearly all of the rulers of the 18th Dynasty. A cuneiform tablet of the Amarna Age (14th cen. B.C.) from Tell el-Hesi accuses the prince of Lachish, Zimreda, of being a traitor (*ANET*[3], p. 490; see *BASOR* 87, 1942, pp. 32–38), while another of the Amarna Letters refers to his death (*ANET*[3], p. 489). The Late Bronze Age levels on the city mound have been examined only superficially. This has been somewhat compensated for by the discovery of a Late Bronze Age Canaanite temple constructed in the debris-filled fosse at the base of the massive Middle Bronze II rampart noted above. Three successive phases of construction were evident in the "Fosse Temple," whose main features consisted of an altar in the S. end and a large collection of pottery bowls and other vessels deposited as offerings around the shrine, often containing animal bones, especially the right shoulder of a young sheep or goat (cf. Lev. 7:32). The initial phase (Fosse Temple I, c. 1475–1400 B.C.) consisted of a simple oblong sanctuary of rough undressed stones with a low bench along the S. wall with three rectangular projections which served as an altar. The structure was enlarged in the next phase (Fosse Temple II, c. 1400–1325 B.C.), and a cult room with raised shrine added on the S. In the third phase (Fosse Temple III, c. 1325–1223 B.C.), the shrine consisted of a large plastered platform against the front of which was built an altar of mud brick, and an additional room was added to the S. (see *Lachish*, II. *The Fosse Temple*, 1940). This last phase was brought to an end by a tremendous destruction, an event also attested in soundings on the city mound itself (Level VI). Albright (*BASOR* 58, 1935, pp. 10 ff.; 68, 1937, pp. 22 ff.; 74, 1939, pp. 20 ff.), among others, has interpreted the destruction of Late Bronze Age Lachish as confirmation of Joshua's defeat of the Amorite coalition which included Japhia, King of Lachish, and the subsequent fall of the city to the invading Israelites (Josh. 10:3, 5, 23, 31–32). A reasonably close date for the latter event was proposed (c. 1220 B.C.) based on fragments of a bowl found in the debris of Level VI on which were written in Egyptian hieratic of the late 13th century B.C. tax receipts dating to "Year 4" of an unnamed Egyptian ruler, thought to be Merenptah (c. 1236–1223 B.C.). On the basis of the occurrence in the same debris of a scarab of Ramesses III (1198–1166 B.C.), however, Tufnell, Kenyon, and others are more cautious in the matter, stating that the destruction may have been due to the invading Israelites, to an Asiatic campaign by an Egyptian Pharaoh, or even to the "Peoples of the Sea" (*AOTS*, 1967, p. 302).

233. Site of Lachish guardroom, where Lachish letters were found.

Archaeological evidence, though limited, suggests that Lachish lay deserted during the period of the Judges (12th–11th cen. B.C.). There is nothing on the site to indicate Philistine occupation, though two tombs cut into the counterscarp of the disused Middle Bronze Age fosse contained broken anthropoid clay coffins. Evidence for the period of the early monarchy is also limited. During the 10th century B.C. a large platform (Palace A, Level V) was erected over the remains of an earlier Late Bronze Age building, but nothing of its superstructure was preserved. This platform was later enlarged (Palace B, Level IV), to which an additional element was subsequently added (Palace C, Level III). Little about the chronology and character of the early Iron Age city of Lachish can be established with certainty, however, since clearance of the mound was suspended before the Iron Age levels were more than probed.

Lachish was one of 15 cities fortified by Rehoboam (c. 922–915 B.C.) for Judah's defense (II Chron. 11:5–12), a task which may have been continued by Asa (see II Chron. 14:6). Amaziah (c. 800–783 B.C.) fled in vain to Lachish during the successful conspiracy to place Uzziah on the throne (II Kings 14:19; II Chron. 25:27), and during the latter half of the 8th millennium the prophet Micah condemned Judah's reliance on the fortified city (Micah 1:3). To this age must be assigned the Iron Age city defenses at Lachish (Level III), in use during the 9th and 8th centuries B.C. The summit was surrounded by a solid brick wall about 19½ ft. thick, erected on a stone foundation, while a lower wall or revetment was constructed about halfway down the slope of the mound. Both walls were built with recessed panels, and a large free-standing bastion was constructed near the city gate at the SW. corner. A road ascended along the W. side of the mound to the city gate.

Sennacherib captured the city in 701 B.C. (II Chron. 32:9; see *ANET*³, p. 288), making it his headquarters while he negotiated the surrender of Hezekiah in Jerusalem (II Kings 18:13 ff.; Isa. 36:1 ff.). The siege of Lachish is depicted on a series of reliefs from Sennacherib's royal palace at Nineveh (*ANEP*², Nos. 371–374; see *IEJ* 8, 1958, pp. 165–170), and represented by the massive destruction of the city level and fortifications of Level III (Tufnell, *AOTS*, 1967, pp. 304–305). The plan of the city defenses recovered at Lachish match in remarkable detail the portrait of the city depicted on the Assyrian reliefs. Some authorities prefer to date the destruction of Level III to the initial campaign against Judah by Nebuchadnezzar II, c. 598 B.C. (Albright, *BASOR* 132, 1953, p. 146; Wright, *VT* 5, 1955, pp. 97 ff.; Kenyon, *Archaeology in the Holy Land*, 1970, pp. 287, 290). Because of the limited nature of the archaeological evidence, however, more data are necessary before firm conclusions can be reached, though the earlier date seems preferable.

The city defenses of Lachish were soon rebuilt in stone (Level II) on the remains of the earlier destroyed brick wall. These were totally destroyed by Nebuchadnezzar II, possibly in two attacks, one during his first campaign against Judah c. 598 B.C., the other during his second campaign in 588–587 B.C. (see II Kings 24–25). Lachish was one of the last strongholds of Judah to be captured (Jer. 34:7). One of the most important discoveries made at the site consists of a collection of 21 ostraca (potsherds used for writing) found in the ash and debris of a ruined guard room adjoining the outer gate of the city. Written in black ink and in general dated to the last days of the existence of Judaean Lachish immediately prior to the final siege of 588–587 B.C., they represent the only known corpus of written documents in classical ("Biblical") Hebrew prose (H. Torczyner, *Lachish*, I. *The Lachish Letters*, 1938; *ANET*[3], pp. 321–322). Most of the "Lachish Letters" form part of a file of correspondence from a person named Hoshaiah, apparently in charge of a fortified outpost N. of Lachish, to his superior Yaosh, probably the military commander of Lachish. These provide added insight into the words of the prophet Jeremiah and the history and political intrigue of the last days of Judah. Letter III, the longest of the preserved correspondence, provides the first occurrence of the O.T. word for prophet (*nabi'*) in a non-Biblical text. It has evoked considerable speculation as to the identity of the "prophet," but it must be stated that none of the principals in the Lachish correspondences can be identified with any certainty with Biblical characters. Letter III appears to be Hoshaiah's defense of charges brought against him that he has indiscreetly read the contents of important documents which have passed through his hands. In addition, a report concerning military matters and a note concerning political correspondence is appended. Letter IV supplies information concerning the use of fire signals in ancient Israel, and the breakdown of communication between Lachish and Azekah, possibly due to the advance of the Babylonian army.

Following the destruction of Level II, the mound of Lachish remained virtually abandoned, though a clay sealing was found bearing the name of Gedaliah, possibly the governor of Judah appointed by Nebuchadnezzar (II Kings 25:22 ff.). Lachish was reoccupied in the post-Exilic period (Neh. 11:30). A Persian fortress or residency (c. 450–350 B.C.) was built on the site of the earlier citadel, as well as a "Solar Shrine" of the Persian-Hellenistic Age (*IEJ* 8, 1968, pp. 157–169). See Tufnell, *et al.*, *Lachish*, II. *The Fosse Temple*, 1940; *Lachish*, III. *The Iron Age*, 1953; *Lachish*, IV. *The Bronze Age*, 1958; *AOTS*, 1967, pp. 296–308. W. P. A.

ladder, a translation of the Heb. word in the story of Jacob's vision (Gen. 28:12), more properly rendered "a flight of steps." Rock-cut steps, widely found in mountainous Bethel, must have seemed to worshippers a reasonable means of communicating between heaven and earth. Wooden scaling ladders were commonly used in warfare to mount city walls.

Lagash (Telloh), one of the most ancient and influential Sumerian city-states of S. Babylonia, c. 50 m. N. of Ur. Its vestiges are seen today in a series of mounds along a dry canal c. 10 m. E. of the living city of Shatra. The oldest mound was the prehistoric site of Girsu. That Lagash was an art center as early as the 4th millennium B.C. is evident from such recovered works as an elegant vase bearing the city arms. The discovery by a French consul, De Sarzec, of pure Sumero-Babylonian art at Lagash, together with documents in the Sumerian language older than anything in Assyria, stimulated European nations late in the 19th century to send out expeditions to explore S. Babylonia. Among the notable finds are heads and statues of Gudea of Lagash, a *patesi* or governor and priest who restored the city following the age of the Accadian Semitic Sargon I (24th century B.C.) and sponsored a renaissance of Sumerian culture. A gray-black turbaned head of this large-eyed, small-mouthed, gentle-looking man is in the University Museum in Philadelphia, the remainder of the statue being in the Baghdad Museum. The fervent atmosphere of this Lagash art treasure—classical rather than archaic—helps one understand the deep currents which filtered ultimately into Hebrew spiritual and cultural patterns. If culture began with the Sumerians, certainly Lagash, together with its sister cities—Ur*, Uruk*, and Fara—with which it was in close contact, was one of the nurseries. By the era of Hammurabi Lagash was no longer inhabited. Its once teeming mounds were lifeless until the 2d century B.C.

Lahmi (lä′mī), the brother of Goliath (I Chron. 20:5). Note the similarity between this word and the last part of "Bethlehem" (Heb. Beth-*hallahmi*) (cf. II Sam. 21:19).

Laish (lā′ĭsh), an ancient Phoenician-controlled city, now identified with the bush-covered mound of el-Qâdī, the Biblical Dan*, so named after the tribe of Dan had conquered the town, which abounded in springs (Judg. 18:27; Leshem, Josh. 19:47). It became the northernmost settlement of Israel, and later a border between Palestine and Syria. The story of Dan's seizure of the city of the "quiet and secure" inhabitants (Judg. 18:7), living in a large and "very good land" (v. 9), is told in Judg. 18.

lamb. See SHEEP.

Lamb of God, an epithet applied twice to Jesus by John the Baptist following his baptism: "Behold, the Lamb of God, who takes away the sin of the world!" (John 1:29, 36 R.S.V.). The phrase may have been first recorded by the author of the Fourth Gospel, or it may have been widely used earlier in connection with the redemptive quality of the expected Messiah (Isa. 53:7). In various O.T. passages the lamb had conveyed the idea of persecuted innocence (Jer. 11:19); of vicarious suffering expressed in the burnt offering (Lev. 9:3, 23:12); and of deliverance, as at every Passover (Ex. 12:3–14). In Revelation the lamb is used more than a score of times as a symbol of Christ, "slain from the foundation of the world," but who at the last day would receive "power and riches, and wisdom, and strength, and honor, and glory, and blessing" (Rev. 5:12). The Lamb is represented in the Apocalypse as enthroned (5:13, 7:9, 22:1, 3); as guardian of the "book of life" (13:8); he was honored with his bride (the Church) at the "marriage supper of the Lamb" (19:7–9). In early Christian art the lamb, carrying a cross or a pennon of victory, was a widely used symbol carved on sarcophagi, tinted in fresco, or emblazoned in mosaics. The *Gloria in*

Excelsis in the communion liturgy of various churches includes the words, "O Lord God, Lamb of God, Son of the Father, that takest away the sins of the world, have mercy upon us."

Lamech (lā′mĕk), the name of one or two antediluvian Patriarchs, according to the view taken of two genealogical lists. In that of Gen. 4:1–24, J source, Lamech is the son of Methusael and husband of Adah and Zillah. By Adah he became father of Tubal and Jubal, founders of nomadic ways and of music; by Zillah he became parent of Tubal-cain, inventor of metalcrafts, including the making of swords. In the list of Gen. 5, P source, Lamech is the son of Methuselah (v. 25) and father of Noah. Critics have suggested that the similarity in the two Lamechs may indicate that the list of Sethites may contain borrowings from the Cainite list.

The ancient poem of Gen. 4:23 f., one of the oldest bits of folk song in the O.T., is called "the Song of Lamech," with its unquenchable thirst for revenge, its cruel lack of pity, and its brutal boastfulness. Just how old it is no one can say with assurance. It comes from a primitive civilization in which even the law of blood revenge exerted no restraint, yet (as J. A. Bewer says, speaking of the Hebrew form of it) the rhythm is perfect, and the rhyme (rare in Hebrew poetry) enhances its wild beauty. Such boasts of endless blood feuds have parallels in Arab songs, which are also addressed to women.

One of the Dead Sea Scrolls* was at first tentatively identified, from an extracted fragment, as an Aramaic Apocryphal Book of Lamech, previously known only by casual references in mediaeval literature. Its frail condition delayed translation, but it proved to be an Aramaic version of several chapters of Genesis.

lamed (lä′mĕd) (A.S.V. Lamedh), the 12th letter of the Hebrew alphabet. See WRITING.

lameness disqualified a man from becoming a priest of Yahweh, lest, having a blemish, he defile the altar and the holiest parts of the sanctuary (Lev. 21:18, 23). No lame animal might be offered in sacrifice (Deut. 15:21; Mal. 1:8, 13). Malnutrition caused many spinal afflictions in Palestine and Egypt. Evidently there were many lame in ancient Jerusalem (II Sam. 5:6, 8). Jonathan, son of Saul, had a son Mephibosheth, who became lame in both feet after a childhood accident (II Sam. 4:4, 9:3–13). Jesus cured the lame (Matt. 11:5, 15:30 f., 21:14). His Disciples also effected miraculous cures of the lame: Peter and John in the Temple (Acts 3:2–13); Philip in Samaria (Acts 8:7).

Lamentations of Jeremiah, The, an O.T. book between Jeremiah and Ezekiel in the LXX, Vulgate, and the English Bible; but in the Heb. text found between Ruth and Ecclesiastes among the Hagiographa, as one of "the five scrolls." The Heb. title of the book is *Ekah* ("Ah, how"), derived from its opening word (1:1). But in the Talmud the book is named after its contents, *Qinoth* ("dirges"); the *Threnoi* ("Elegies") in the Gk. LXX; and *Threni* ("Lamentations") in the Lat. versions. In the latter "of Jeremiah" is added.

Five poems, a poem to a chapter, constitute the book. All lament the destruction of Jerusalem in 587 B.C. The first four are alphabetic acrostics. In chaps. 1 and 2 each verse begins with one of the 22 successive letters of the Heb. alphabet, each letter having three stanzas. In the 66 vv. of chap. 3 each group of three verses, as seen in the A.S.V., begins with the same letter, a pattern found elsewhere only in Ps. 119. In chap. 4 each acrostic or letter has two verses. The 5th poem (chap. 5) is a prayer, rather than an elegy, in 22 metrical verses but without acrostic alphabetical arrangement. The elegiac meter of the poems (in which a silence takes the place of the last foot of the distich) was used by the 8th century prophets and later by Jeremiah (Jer. 9:9 f.), Ezekiel (19), and some Psalmists (Ps. 84).

II Chronicles 35:25 is quoted as authority for ascribing the authorship of Lamentations to Jeremiah*, and thus the Chronicler (250 B.C.) is the instigator of the Jeremiah tradition. It was natural to attribute these lamentations over the destruction of Jerusalem to a prophet who witnessed the calamity; but the Chronicler was referring specifically to the death of Josiah (609 B.C.) and not to the 587 B.C. period. Lam. 2:9 does not sound like Jeremiah; he never spoke favorably of Egypt as a deliverer (Lam. 4:17; Jer. 42:13–17, 43:12 f., 44:11–14, 26–30). Lam. 4:20 could not have been a reference to King Zedekiah by the imprisoned Jeremiah (Jer. 37:16–21).

Many believe that a number of authors were responsible for these poems. Lam. 2 and 4 imply that the author was an eyewitness of the dreadful events of 587 B.C.—the plight of the rulers (2:6, 9, 4:19 f.) and of the children (2:11 f., 4:10). The authors (or author) were presumably among the Exiles and wrote these elegies in Babylon, except chap. 5, written in Jerusalem a generation after the catastrophe (Lam. 5:7), but before the Temple was rebuilt (520–516 B.C.) (chap. 5:18)—perhaps c. 530 B.C. Chaps. 1 and 3 are later; there is no longer any mention of a king, but only priests and elders (1:19) and princes (1:6). Here the Temple has been rebuilt (520–515 B.C.), but the Jerusalem community has not yet experienced Nehemiah's reforms (445 B.C.). Chap. 3 was composed as a lamentation of Jeremiah (3:1), but is artificial in style and content. The imagery of woe in 3:2–17 is unnatural. The reflections on the abounding mercies of the Lord (vv. 18–39) are echoes from the Psalter. Lam. 3:55–60 indicates that the situation in Jerusalem has improved over that portrayed in 3:3. The author perhaps lived after the time of Nehemiah*, as late as the 4th century, but still felt the weight of his country's woe and the tragedy of the 6th century prophet.

The Book of Lamentations is read in synagogues during the evening and morning services of the Fast of the Ninth of Ab, which laments the destruction of Jerusalem by the Chaldaeans (587 B.C.)—and also by the Romans (A.D. 70).

The unity of the book may be found in its

attitude toward suffering. It proclaims that suffering is the inevitable result of persistent sin (1:22, 4:13, 22, 5:16). It acknowledges that God is righteous in allowing judgment to be executed (1:18, 2:17, 3:33, 4:11, 12). It appeals to a trust in God, Who will yet turn and be gracious to His people (3:31–36, 5:21). But there is no indication that suffering could be borne on behalf of others; such a solution to the mystery of suffering came to the world first in Isa. 53, but fully in Christ (I Cor. 1:3 f.; I Pet. 2:19–25).

lamp, a vessel with a wick for burning oil to give light. In early Palestine, as in Homeric Greece, the torch antedated other forms of artificial lighting; it was adequate for an "early-to-bed, early-to-rise" way of living. Fire brands were probably the "lamps"

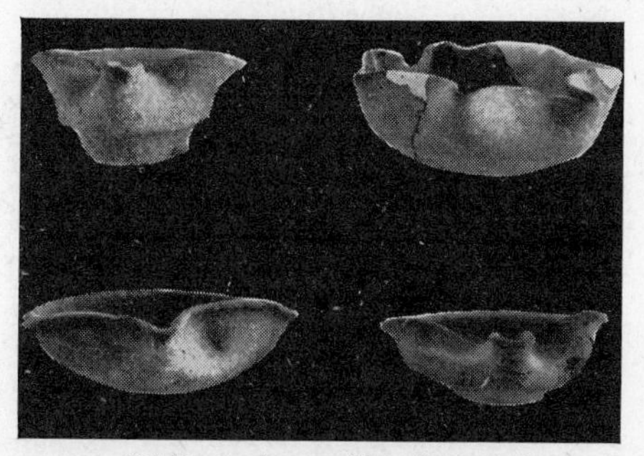

234. Pottery lamps of Israelite Period.

placed by Gideon and his men in their pitchers (Judg. 7:16, 20). Torches and lanterns continued to be used down through Roman times (John 18:3).

Palestine people felt the need of a light in tent and house which would keep a flame easily accessible, night and day. (In many dwellings lamps are still kept burning all night, for fear of thieves and evil spirits.) The earliest Palestinian lamps were of clay, in the Canaanite saucer shape, with brims pinched at one point to make a spout for the wick of flax (Isa. 42:3) or hemp which conducted the olive or animal oil to the flame. One of the oldest lamps yet excavated in Palestine (Elihu Grant) is from a tomb at Beth-shemesh in Samson's Valley of Sorek, in the level of c. 550–500 B.C. It may have been brought back from Babylon by a returned Jew. Its spout is long and it has no handle.

Early Palestinian hand lamps were very small—only 3 or 4 in. long by 2 or 3 in. wide—suitable for carrying in the palm. This is the type of lamp referred to in Christ's parable of the virgins (Matt. 25:1–13). Often a tiny refill vase of oil was suspended from the finger on a string. Lamps intended to be stationary were flat-bottomed. The commonest material was native clay or terra cotta. When metals became plentiful lamps were also made of copper, bronze, or gold. Handles developed, some very short, others sizable, and often in symbolic shape, ultimately taking the form of the sacred monogram (*Chi Rho*) used on certain Christian crosses. There were also foot lamps of clay, with perforations to emit light and heat. These were carried on a stick, for use along dark pathways. Hence the Psalmist's image, "Thy word is . . . a light unto my path" (Ps. 119:105). In later times small chains and rings were attached to lamps to permit their being hung.

In peasant houses the large central wooden or stone pillar which supported the roof usually provided a small shelf for the oil lamp—the only light for the house (Matt. 5:15). In early times, when hillside caves were used for rooms, a niche was cut in the rock wall to hold the tiny lamp. A stand ("candlestick," Luke 8:16) for the lamp was found in well-equipped houses, like that of the Shunammite woman and her husband who entertained Elisha (II Kings 4:10). Sometimes lamps had several spouts—three, four, six, or seven. An interesting multiple lamp has been excavated at Nob near Jerusalem, dating possibly from the era of David; it is of clay, with four spouts.

The graceful alabaster lamp of Tut-ankh-amun in the Egyptian Museum at Cairo has three cups, in the form of an open lotus flower and two buds.

Fanciful shapes were popular among lamp-makers—a lady's foot, or a duck, like the notable one excavated at Gezer; the famous hedgehog lamp found at Ur (c. 3000 B.C.), the ancestral home of Abraham, now in the University Museum, Philadelphia.

In the early development of Hebrew worship, provision was made for a lamp, filled with pure, beaten olive oil, to be kept burning outside the veil of testimony of the Tabernacle (Ex. 27:20). Throughout their national history, the Jews faithfully assigned to the successors of Aaron the task of keeping the Temple lamps trimmed and glowing in

235. Lamp of Roman Palestine.

mystical worship (Num. 4:9). Meticulous care was taken to maintain the supply of olive oil (Ex. 35:14), that the lamps of God might burn continuously (Lev. 24:2). They were cleaned each morning (Ex. 30:7). In the decades of Solomon's glory seven-branched golden candlesticks* were fashioned. Herod's Temple lamps were finally carried off to Rome by Titus, who carved on his arch in the Forum of Rome the only authentic depiction extant. Descriptions of the seven-branched

Temple lamps are found in I Chron. 28:15; II Chron. 4:20–22. Five stood on the right, and five on the left, before the oracle (I Kings 7:49). (See JACHIN AND BOAZ; KNOP.)

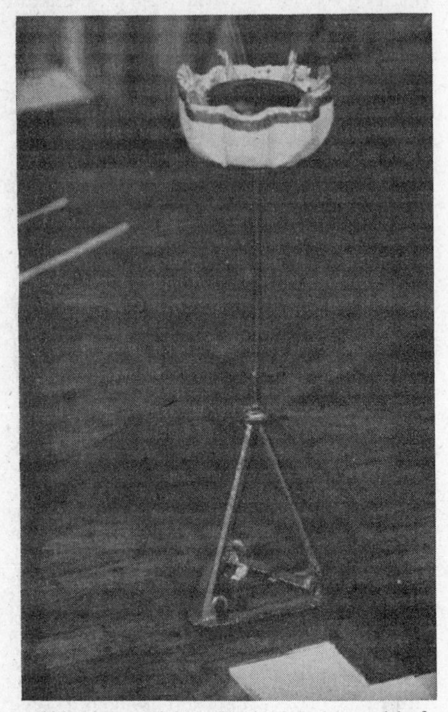

236. Lampstand from Howland-Garber model of Solomon's Temple, patterned after copper lamp found by Nelson Glueck at Ezion-geber. Seven wick-channels supplied the oil.

The burning lamp was regarded as a symbol of the living personality (e.g., the lamp set by God for David at Jerusalem, I Kings 15:4; Ps. 132:17). The snuffing of the flame was equivalent to the snuffing out of life (Prov. 13:9, 20:20; cf. Jer. 25:10). Figuratively and apocalyptically the lamp appears frequently in Scripture: God as the lamp of man (II Sam. 22:29) and the diligent lamp or "candle" of the ideal woman (Prov. 31:18); Ezekiel drew lamps into his vision of living creatures (1:13); Daniel, into the eyes of "a certain man" (Dan. 10:6); Zechariah into the candlestick of his vision (4:2); and the author of the Apocalypse into his conception of the throne of God (Rev. 4:5).

237. Alabaster lamp from Ur, in shape of hedgehog.

Archaeological investigations have brought the world notable collections of early lamps, found in tombs, wells, market places, and domestic ruins. The museum in old Corinth, donated by Americans, exhibits a remarkable sequence of clay lamps from the 6th century B.C. down through the Byzantine period (c. A.D. 300–600). Greek, Hellenistic, late Roman, and Christian types are there—many of the sort which lighted the Corinthian looms of Paul and his dark little preaching places. In the evolution of symbols stamped on the lamps while the clay was still wet, one can trace in the Corinth collection the gradual lessening of pagan influences and the coming of Christian designs, even the use of the cross. A wealth of clay lamps has been excavated in the Athenian agora—more than 3,578 by one group of scholars—ranging from the 7th century B.C. to Byzantine times. Antioch-on-the-Orontes, too, has yielded many lamps, of which F. O. Waage has formed a family tree for the published reports of the Antioch excavations—lamps from those of light-buff Syrian clay down to Roman and Hellenistic lamps covered with a poor quality of red glaze. The "tree" includes the flat Ephesus types, others trimmed with herringbone designs, some with tiny busts of Serapis and Isis.

Egypt was making cup-and-saucer lamps in the Middle Bronze Age. Oil was placed in the cup, and water in the saucer to prevent oil from seeping through the pores; the saucer was spouted. From the early period also comes the tubular or solid ring to which small lamps were fastened. Sometimes oil was placed in the individual lamps, some-

238. Lamp with menorah design, 4th or 5th century A.D.

times in a tube connecting with the lamp. By 1600–1200 B.C. many lamps of this type were in use.

landmarks, boundary* markers, consisted in ancient times of no more than double furrows between allotted fields. Such furrows were to be respected not per se, as were Babylonian boundary stones, but as expressions of respect for hereditary property rights. They were not to be removed (Deut. 19:14) for the purpose of infringing on a neighbor's privileges. (Cf. Hos. 5:10; Prov. 22:28.)

languages spoken in Palestine in the years covered by the O.T. were as numerous as the polyglot peoples who lived at this crossroads of three continents. The mingled tongues did literally produce a "Babel" ("confusion"), so picturesquely accounted for in Gen. 11:1–9—oversimplified though this statement is from the viewpoint of philology. Languages and dialects were carried back and forth through the Middle East by soldiers, merchants, travelers, scribes, and displaced persons—Sumerians, Egyptians, Phrygians, Indo-Europeans, Greeks, Romans, Syrians, etc. The large and important family of Semitic languages (see SEMITES) includes: in the N., Assyrian and Babylonian; in the middle region, Hebrew and Phoenician; in the S., Arabic, Ethiopic, and Amharic. The languages spoken by Moabite, Edomite, Ammonite, Phoenician (Canaanite), and Amorite neighbors have all undoubtedly contributed words or phrases to the languages in which the Bible was written. As I. G. Matthews states in his *Religious Pilgrimage of Israel*, Arabic, the inclusive term for the language of the ancestors of the Hebrews, grew up in the desert; it was a rugged, masculine language, marked by gutturals and sibilants, rich in verbs and nouns rather than adjectives, for lack of which speakers resorted to gestures and eloquent facial expressions. The primitive Semitic language, as well as Hebrew, was comprehended only in the "speech community." Hence one of the difficulties of scribes who reduced oral traditions, laws, and history to writing.

The O.T. was originally written in Hebrew, with a few Aramaic portions and occasional words from Sumerian, Babylonian, Egyptian, Amorite, Sidonian, Greek, and Persian. The Aramaic portions include Gen. 31:47; Jer. 10:11; Dan. 2:4b–7:28; Ezra 4:8–6:18, 7:12–26, plus individual words throughout. The "Syrian tongue" mentioned in Ezra 4:7 is Aramaic. For though Hebrew remained the sacred tongue of Jews, they—like others in the Middle East—began using vernacular Aramaic for everyday conversation and writing some time between the 6th and the 3d century B.C. In the 1st century A.D. Aramaic in one dialect or another was the daily tongue of Palestinian Jews. Good examples of early O.T. Hebrew writing are found in the Gezer* Calendar, the Moabite* Stone, the Siloam* Tunnel inscription, the Samarian ostraca*, and the Lachish* Letters. In the 4th and 3d centuries B.C. a gradual change was made to "square" letters, such as were used in MSS. and early printed versions of the O.T.

The N.T. as a collection of books is "a Greek library," even if some portions may conceivably have been written in a Semitic tongue and translated into Hellenized Greek, or "N.T. Greek," which was quite representative of the Koine or commonly used form of the Greek current in the E. Mediterranean world in N.T. times among semiliterate persons. Although Koine was not on a literary par with the pure Attic Greek of the Golden Age, its idioms were elastic and useful—far more expressive than the Hebrew used by O.T. authors. The N.T. was thus written in a natural and universal language. Even when the O.T. is quoted in the N.T. the words are usually from the Greek LXX—except the quoting of Ps. 22:1 by Jesus on the cross, where use is made of a transliteration of the Hebrew or Aramaic original into the Greek alphabet (Matt. 27:46; Mark 15:34).

Not all N.T. writers conformed to the one "style manual" of Koine Greek; they used latitude, selecting words congenial to their personalities and purposes. Luke, "the most literary of the Evangelists," used "a book language" (Moffatt) that was homogeneous yet with rich and pleasing variety. Some believe that Luke may not have known Hebrew. The Greek of Mark is "tense, frank, naïve, unpolished." He retained a few Aram. words, like *Abba* (14:36). Matthew's Gk. is rated as more "balanced." Matthew or one of his sources appears to have known the Hebrew O.T., from his preoccupation with proof from O.T. prophecy. Paul's Koine is less literary than Luke's. He wrote not in reflection but in the midst of burning issues and practical affairs of local church communities. Paul was fluent in Hebrew and Aramaic, yet quoted the LXX rather than the original Hebrew. He spoke Greek and was able to address Athenians (Acts 17) and his audiences in other Greek centers in their own language. The Gk. of the author of the Fourth Gospel is simple, carefully wrought, and marked by the use of words treasured by mystics— "light," "life," "words," etc. A few scholars have held that this book was written first in Aram. and then translated into Gk. The other N.T. books are wholly Gk.

The language of Jesus in daily contacts was a Galilean dialect of Aram. (Matt. 26:73). He knew Hebrew (Luke 4:16–20). He may have spoken Gk., for in his trial before Pilate, who spoke only Lat. and Gk., he appears to have spoken without an interpreter (Mark 15:2–5). His Disciples all spoke Galilean Aram.—except possibly Judas, who was not a Galilean. But they probably spoke also a second tongue, as did most people of their day in Palestine.

The presence in cosmopolitan Jerusalem at Pentecost of people from "every nation under heaven," with every man speaking in his "own tongue, wherein [he was] born" (Acts 2:5–11), suggests a long language list, whose analysis would challenge any philologist. But all could exchange thoughts in Koine. The fact that there were so many Greek-speaking Jews in the Middle East and throughout the Diaspora in the 1st century A.D. explains why so many Greek-speaking Christians were members of the early Church. With reference to the prophecy of Joel (2:28 ff.), Peter at Pentecost (Acts 2:17–21) explained to the doubting multitude the appeal of Christ to men of all nations and languages, already drawn into the growing Christian fellowship.

The Bible in whole or in part has been translated into more than 1,118 languages or dialects; and there are still many more waiting to receive the "good news" in their own tongue.

See TEXT; WRITING.

Laodicea (lā-ŏd′ĭ-sē′*ȧ*), a city of Asia Minor, situated in the Lycus River Valley at the crossroads of the great trade route from the East to Pergamum and Ephesus; one of the seven churches of Asia (Rev. 3:14). Its prosperity is reflected in the fact that its citizens, after an earthquake in A.D. 60, rebuilt the city without aid from Rome (Rev.

3:17). Its products were a famous black wool cloth made of local sheep's wool (cf. v. 18), embroidered garments, and a well-known eye medicine, called Phrygian powder (cf. v. 18). Its bankers negotiated with the whole empire. Laodicea had a Christian church (in the house of Nymphas, Col. 4:15) at an early date, possibly through the influence of Epaphras (Col. 1:7, 4:12 f.). It was probably one of the cities that received the Epistle to the Ephesians*, or a copy of the original, which some authorities believe may be the lost letter to Laodicea (Col. 4:16). The subscription of I Tim. in the Textus Receptus (see TEXT, VERSIONS), "Written from Laodicea," is an early guess, apparently due to the notion that this was the "letter from Laodicea" of Col. 4:16. Its early Christian zeal cooled through its sense of self-sufficiency, thus provoking the scorching condemnation expressed by the author of Rev. 3:14–22. The city has not been excavated, though the ruins of several Seleucid and Roman structures are still visible, including two theaters, Roman baths, portions of the E. gate, and a stadium, probably dating to c. A.D. 79. See *BA* 13, 1950, pp. 1–18.

Lapidoth (lăp′ĭ-dŏth) ("torches" or "lightning flashes"), the husband of Deborah* (Judg. 4:4).

Lasea (lȧ-sē′ȧ), a town on a tiny island E. of Cape Lithinos on the S.-central coast of Crete, c. 5 m. E. of Fair Havens. It is mentioned in the literature of antiquity only in Luke's account of Paul's voyage to Italy (Acts 27:8).

Last Supper, The. See LORD'S SUPPER, THE.

latchet, a leather thong which fastens the sole of a sandal to the foot (Isa. 5:27; Mark 1:7).

Latin, the language of the Romans, hence the official language of Palestine during the hundred years or so of Roman rule; however, except for a few words such as *praetorium*, it did not take root there. Roman officials caused the superscription on Christ's cross to be written in Latin, Greek, and Hebrew (Luke 23:38; John 19:20). For Lat. versions see TEXT.

laughter, as used in Scripture, usually connotes scornful skepticism, as in the case of Abraham and Sarah (Gen. 17:17, 18:12 f., 15, 21:6), or of derision (II Kings 19:21; Neh. 2:19; Job 12:4; Ps. 2:4, 37:13, 52:6). Sometimes this scornful laughter is of God and the righteous (Ps. 2:4, 37:13, 80:6); or of an obstructionist, like Sanballat (Neh. 2:19), or of incredulous witnesses of Christ's work (Matt. 9:24). Laughter in the joyous sense is mentioned in Eccles. 3:4; Luke 6:21, 25. There is no intentional humor in the Bible, though there is an occasional light touch in the teachings of Jesus (Matt. 19:24; Luke 6:42). The prophets frequently employed wordplay, which abounds in Hebrew, but which is lost in translation (cf., however, Micah 1, Moffatt's translation). Such wordplay, however, was employed for the sake of gravity, not levity. "The laughter of children" was to the prophets of the Exile one of the symbols of the happiness with which God would endow His people upon their repentance and return to Jerusalem.

laver, a large copper or bronze (not brass) vessel for Jewish priests' ablutions in the Tabernacle (Ex. 30:17–21) and the Temple. It stood near the altar (40:7), and according

239. Laver.

to 38:8 was fashioned from the mirrors of women ministering at the door of the tent of meeting. Solomon's Temple had ten lavers (I Kings 7:30, 38, 40) made by the great craftsman Hiram of Tyre.

law (Heb. *torah*, "instruction," from root "to teach," " to cast," sometimes used to include all the O.T., including the Law, the Prophets, and the Writings, John 10:34, 12:34, 15:25), but in Jewish usage specifically the first five books, containing the Mosaic Law.

(1) *In the O.T.*, which is the basic source of Jewish law, the Ten* Commandments (Ex. 20:3–17; Deut. 5:6–21) given to Moses at Sinai remained the core of the elaborate system of legislation, both oral and written, which developed into codes (see CODE) down the centuries of the Hebrews' experience as a people. This core lives today in orthodox Judaism. The Law provided for almost every situation which could arise between man and God, man and man, and man and animals. It began to grow in the hard years of Israel's encampment at Kadesh-barnea after receipt of their covenant* and their short stay near Mt. Sinai. It was recognized as the revealed will of God for His chosen people. Its demands were severe, yet so kindly (Lev. 19:14; Deut. 22:1–3, 8, 24:19, 25:4) that Psalmist poets were able to declare enthusiastically, "O, how love I thy law! it is my meditation all the day," and "I love thy commandments above gold" (Ps. 119:97, 127).

The oldest code in the Hebrew system of law is the Covenant Code (Ex. 20:22–23:19, plus the appendix of 23:20–33). The date accepted for the first committing of the Law to writing, believed by many to have been formed in Canaan at least a century or two after Moses, depends on the date accepted for the introduction of writing* among the Hebrews, on which recent scholarship has shed new light. Moses, using tablets of stone (Ex. 31:18, 34:1) similar to the many inscribed stones now excavated, could have written the Ten Commandments on them. "Skilled in the wisdom of the Egyptians," he was probably as capable of writing as those who have left inscriptions in the mines of Serabit near the border of Egypt.

The written and the oral Law (*Torah Shebichethav* and *Torah Shebe'alpeh*) were both regarded as being God-inspired and not to be changed. But the Hebrews admitted the development of the applications of the Law by creative minds. It centered in three principles: (1) the sacredness of life itself,

240. Moses receiving the law at Sinai, bronze doors by Lorenzo Ghiberti, Baptistry, Florence.

more valuable even than the Law, as Jesus taught (see below, "Law in the N.T."); (2) parental authority, as an eternal social attitude giving stability to the home (Ex. 20:12; Deut. 5:16); (3) the having no other deity before God, an attitude outranking all other issues (Ex. 34:14, 20:3, 5). Thus through the generations the gist of the Law persisted, though changing its specific relevancy, as for example when the agricultural life of the early years in Canaan was succeeded by expanding commercial relationships during the Hebrew Monarchy. Sometimes outside political administrators made it impossible for Israel to obey the Law as they desired to do, as on their return from the Exile, when they were not free to comply with the statute governing the Year of Jubilee and the reversion of property to original owners.

Many personalities of reverent spirit and brilliant mind had a share in preserving and applying the core of the Mosaic Law in its various codes. Moses was believed to have distributed it first to his people, thence to the custody of Joshua, from whose hands it was passed on to the elders of Israel, the prophets, and the men of the Great Assembly.

Down the centuries the following types of people influenced the formulation and application of Israel's Law until it took form in the various Codes: (1) elders or sheikhs of leading families (Ruth 4:2 ff.; cf. Deut. 19:12, 21:3 ff., 22:15 ff.; I Kings 21:8); (2) priests, whose cumulative authority finally was voiced in the P Code, wherein they alone are accredited judges (Ex. 21–23); (3) able kings, like David, Solomon, and Amaziah (I Sam. 30:21–25; II Sam. 14:11; II Kings 14:5); (4) prophets, whose teachings found their way especially into the Deuteronomic (see DEUTERONOMY) Code; (5) scribes, *sopherim*, especially after the return from Babylon, the greatest and most "ready" of whom was Ezra. The *sopherim* laid the foundations for the Massoretic (Heb.) text of the O.T.

A high moment in the history of the Law came when an early draft of Deuteronomy (the Magna Charta of Israel, so to speak), a copy written probably c. 650 B.C., was discovered c. 622 B.C. during the Temple repairs in the time of King Josiah. The religious reforms which followed caused an over-enthusiasm for both Book and Temple, which, directed by a hierarchy, led to the substitution of ceremonial for character, so that when Jeremiah voiced what he believed to be a rebuke from the Lord (Jer. 7:3) he was arrested and his life threatened (26:7 f.). But upon intercession by Ahikam (26:24) he was spared, having vindicated his belief that God's law "in the inward parts" (31:33 f.) is more vital than a man's proximity to the Temple or even to the sacred law book. This view of the "new covenant" between God and Israel is the apex of all Israel's attitude toward the Law; it testifies to the operation of the spirit of truth and light in the total personality of man. During the Captivity which followed on the heels of the destruction of Jerusalem the Law, which had been carried into Exile, not only gave cohesion to the displaced persons, but kept them a courageous group of God's covenanted people until, when they returned, their scribes, especially Ezra, set down in better form than ever before Israel's ideology of covenant, race, and worship of one God, in spite of pressure from outside foes. If Israel had their Law with them, they could survive any exigency.

Following the Persian period, when the governor was the highest political authority, the high priest and his council were supreme administrators of Israel's Law. From this group probably the Sanhedrin* court of justice developed, a powerful organization whose decisions were binding throughout Palestine, but whose functions did not include authority to impose the death sentence without the consent of the Roman governor—as in the trial of Jesus.

It is notable that throughout Jewish history severe penalties were imposed on those who bore false witness. See the Ninth Commandment (Ex. 20:16; Deut. 19:15–21).

Administration of the law in O.T. times generally took place in the open, as it did in most cities of the ancient East. Walled towns provided broad spaces near the main city gate, where the elders, prophets, or even the king sat and rendered decisions (Deut. 22:15, 24, 25:7; I Sam. 9:18; II Sam. 19:8). By the time of the Monarchy, and the creation of the magnificent 10th-century capital of Solomon, more formal provision had been made for royal pronouncements, in the cedar-panelled Porch of Judgment (I Kings 7:7) near the palace and the Temple. This royal audience chamber contained the throne of ivory and gold (I Kings 10:18–20). In the Graeco-Roman period basilicas for law administration were erected. Yet even then trials were often conducted in the open, at or near the market place, where a judgment* seat was provided, as in the case of Paul's hearing before Gallio at Corinth (Acts 18:12).

An interesting instance of the *operation of law outside Palestine* is given in Dan. 6:7–9, indicating that once an edict of the council of princes in the united kingdom of Media and Persia had been formulated and sealed by the king, it could not be changed by a whim of the ruler—a check on absolute monarchy. (See Esther 1:19 and 8 for evidence of more power on the king's part or greater pliancy on that of the council in the time of Ahasuerus—Xerxes I, 486–465 B.C.—than had prevailed at the court of Nebuchadnezzar, 605–562 B.C.)

A late chapter in the evolution of Jewish Law took place at Lydda, Palestine, when in A.D. 135 the council of 70 noted rabbis met in a garret and decided that, since the Law had been given to foster life, not to precipitate death, all laws except those against idolatry, adultery, and murder might be broken under stringent emergencies. In this era, when a Roman settlement, *Aelia Capitolina*, was about to occupy the sacred precincts of Jerusalem, and the worship of Jupiter to supplant that of Yahweh, it is notable that Jewish courage held to the law against idolatry, the only one that might bring it into violent contact with emperor-worshipping Rome. The Jews no longer had a nation, yet their monotheism remained intact as "the religion of the people," guided by the Torah as interpreted by its readers.

The O.T. laws contain much that is universally true and for the good of humanity, regardless of time or place. The Ten Commandments will never be obsolete for Christian or Jew as a summary of man's noblest moral code. Happy is the man whose "delight is in the law of the Lord," and in Whose law he "doth meditate day and night" (Ps. 1:2).

The relation of Hebrew law codes to other great codes of the Middle East offers challenging study. Though the influence of some of these may be overestimated, the conscious or unconscious effect of Babylonian, Hittite, Egyptian, Assyrian, Persian, Greek, Roman, Parthian, and Neo-Persian law bodies must be considered, for these peoples touched the Hebrews in one way or another. Notably the Babylonians had law codes which present numerous parallels to Hebrew codes. Every new fragment excavated from Mesopotamian mud and published by the co-operating scholars of the world arouses fresh interest. A good example is the Lipit-Ishtar Code of King Isin, fragments of which were discovered 50 years ago by the University of Pennsylvania expedition to Nippur (c. 100 m. S. of Baghdad), but, along with thousands of other fragments, were never published (deciphered) until 1919, when three of them were observed to be in script antedating that of Hammurabi—but by how many years it was not known. Nor did the University Museum staff attempt to state the date when the original from which these fragments were copied had been set down. But during a cataloguing process in 1947, some additional pieces of the same code were found, telling that the code had been promulgated by Lipit-Ishtar, who ruled a portion of Mesopotamia c. 164–175 years before Hammurabi. A few of the laws were identical with his. Both codes are cast in the same literary form—a prologue and an epilogue, with the laws sandwiched between. The language is Sumerian. The fragments, comprising possibly a third of the whole, contain 35 laws (the total of Hammurabi's is c. 300). The Lipit-Ishtar Code included regulations about slaves, boats, gardens and houses, feudal and family obligations, and the treatment of oxen. The Sumerian laws appear to have influenced Babylonian statements of almost two centuries later.

Even more important is the "Law of Eshnunna," discovered among numerous tablets from Tell Abū Harmal, near Baghdad, studied by the Iraq Department of Antiquities and Dr. Albrecht Goetze of Yale University, who was serving a term as Director of the Baghdad School of the ASOR. Dr. Goetze says that this law code, in Semitic Old Babylonian (not Sumerian), is considerably older than the other codes of the ancient Near East. The prologue states that this code includes laws of the King of Eshnunna (a section E. of the Tigris, opposite Baghdad), a monarch who reigned c. 150–200 years before Hammurabi. One of its interesting features is the fixing of prices of such basic commodities as oil and grain. The code was published (translated) in 1948. (See the periodical *Sumer*, July 1948, for text).

Nuzu* clay documents also show parallels between certain Nuzu laws of the 15th century B.C. and those of the Hebrews.

But the Hebrew Law has a spirit which makes it uniquely superior to the codes of neighbor nations. It is more than a document to be obeyed; it is a power which lifts the quality of life of those who obey it. It is unflinching monotheism, but has a kindly consideration of all living creatures, and an optimistic realism which enabled the Jews to reinterpret their ancient laws in terms of the needs of successive ages. To know and to do God's will was the primary consideration. Orthodox Judaism today maintains the same viewpoint.

(2) *Law in the N.T.*—The attitude of Jesus toward the O.T. Law was one of respect. He had been cradled in it at the Nazareth synagogue and in his home. He came "not to destroy but to fulfill" it, with a richness of life never before demonstrated (Matt. 5:17). He recognized that the Law had prepared him to receive the profound revelations committed to him by his heavenly Father, for which he would scarcely have been ready but for the

preparatory discipline of the obeyed Law. Yet he had no brief for the excessive legalism of the scribes and Pharisees, who "tithed mint and anise and cummin" but omitted the weightier matters of the Law: "Judgment [justice], mercy, and faith"—blind guides, straining out a gnat and swallowing a camel, washing the outside of the cup but leaving the inside soiled; men who outwardly appeared righteous, but within were full of hypocrisy and iniquity (cf. Matt. 23:25 ff.). To Jesus, who astounded the orthodox by curing a man on the Sabbath, life was of more value than the Law concerning a day: "the Son of man is Lord also of the Sabbath" (Luke 6:5 ff.). He asked his followers to let their righteousness "exceed that of the scribes and the Pharisees"; and when put on the spot by one of the scribes as to which is "the first commandment of all," summed up his attitude toward the Law in terms preserved in Mark 12:29–31, a reply which brought such ready response in the inquirer that Jesus told him he was "not far from the kingdom of God" (v. 34). Also, at the inauguration of the Lord's Supper, Jesus declared, "A new commandment I give unto you, that ye love one another, as I have loved you" (John 13:34 f.).

Jesus left no legal code; unless we take his teachings as summarized and interpreted in the Beatitudes* and the Sermon on the Mount (Matt. 5:1–7:29; Luke 6:20–7:1) as his basic code of spiritual idealism. His own respect for the Roman civil law he demonstrated when, replying to the trick question of chief priests and scribes, "Is it lawful for us to give tribute to Caesar, or no?" he gave his brilliant reply, "Render to Caesar the things that are Caesar's, and to God the things that are God's" (Mark 12:17). For similar loyalty to Roman law, see the incident of the tribute money at Capernaum (Matt. 17:25–27).

Paul, who prior to his conversion to the Christian way had been an advanced student of Jewish Law, came to the point in his Christian experience where he realized that the function of the Law had been temporary, acting as a "custodian" (R.S.V. Gal. 3:24) to lead men to Christ. It has revealed the sinfulness of humanity and its need of redemption (Phil. 3:9 ff.), and stirred up a burning sense of sin, but had provided no delivery from it. His own searching question, as to what good the Law had served, was prevalent among his thoughtful contemporaries, who found help in the long statement in Romans (chaps. 3–7) and the Galatian letter (chaps. 3 f.). They learned that the Law had strict limitations; but that they might attain a state of justification by faith, and freedom from the cramping old restrictions, through Jesus Christ. Paul repeated what Jesus had said concerning the Law (Rom. 13:10), and stressed the freedom of the Christian who is guided by love (Gal. 5:14).

Matthew and James regarded Christianity as a new law destined to produce a richer life. To James it was a "perfect law" of liberty (2:8–13).

The Epistles of Peter and of John contain no reference to the Law, but their authors show the influence of Paul's teaching concerning the Law, sin, and sacrifice (I Pet. 1:18 f., 2:24, 3:18; I John 2:2, 4:10).

(3) *Definition of a few terms* familiar to orthodox Judaism today may be helpful to Christians: The *Torah* includes the Written Law (*Torah Shebichethav*), and the Oral Law (*Torah Shebe'alpeh*), which explains the Written Law in intricate detail. The Torah was more than mere law—it was a way of life. Legal portions of the Torah are known as the *Halacha*. The *Talmud* is the body of the Jewish law and legend comprising the *Mishnah*, prepared by Rabbi Judah the Prince and his disciples (precepts of the elders, codified c. A.D. 200) and the *Gemara* (commentary on the *Mishnah*). It includes seven centuries of growth. Maimonides, mediaeval philosopher, physician, and Talmudist (1135–1204), in his *Mishnah-Torah* compiled a complete digest of the Written and the Oral Law. See also HEXATEUCH; LEVITICUS.

lawgiver. See MOSES.

lawyer. See SCRIBE.

laying on of hands, an act having several implications, but always associated with the idea of blessing, or of identifying oneself with a person or an animal in the presence of God. (1) The donor of an animal destined for a burnt offering to God in absolution from sin pressed his hand on the victim's head (Ex. 29:10 ff.; Lev. 1:4, 4:4 ff.). (2) Hands laid on the heads of children imparted the blessing of parents, as by Isaac upon Jacob (Gen. 48:14); or of dedication, as by Jesus (Matt. 19:13, 15; Mark 10:13, 16). In some N.T. instances the laying on of hands was associated with baptism. (3) In the act of healing, Jesus customarily laid his hands on the sick, as if to communicate God's blessing, or to express his own intimate sympathy (Mark 1:41, 6:5, 8:23; Luke 4:40, 13:13, etc.). Contrast this positive therapy with its opposite in II Kings 4:29, 31. (4) Consecration to God's service: Levites (Num. 8:10); Joshua (Num. 27:18, 23; Deut. 34:9); deacons in N.T. times, like Stephen, Philip, and Nicanor (Acts 6:6); missionaries, like Barnabas and Paul (Acts 13:3 f.); ministers of Christ at ordination, like the ordination of Timothy by Paul (I Tim. 4:14; II Tim. 1:6). Jewish rabbis laid their hands on pupils when these were ready to become teachers. The Book of Hebrews classes the laying on of hands as one of the Christian doctrines (6:2). Augustine regarded it as a symbol of intercessory prayer.

Lazarus (from Heb. *Eleazar*, "God has helped"). (1) The brother of Mary and Martha, who entertained Jesus and his company in their suburban home at Bethany, on the shoulder of the Mount of Olives, just out of sight of Jerusalem c. 2 m. away. Lazarus was taken ill (John 11:1) while Jesus was in a period of retirement E. of the Jordan. When the Master did not return immediately after being summoned, Lazarus died—a tragedy which Martha said would not have occurred if Jesus had been present. But Jesus used the situation to perform a great miracle—restoring to life, in the presence of a great company of witnesses, a man whose body had been in his cave tomb three days. This sensational miracle had three effects: (1) it increased the mounting popularity of Jesus among the people at Jerusalem; (2) it aroused the antagonism of the Sanhedrin so that they at once plotted to do away with the Galilean; (3) it endangered the life of Lazarus, who seems to have fled, possibly to spare Jesus greater danger. The Lazarus narrative appears only in the Fourth Gospel (chap. 11). A rock-cut tomb suggesting how Lazarus' tomb looked is shown in Bethany today.

(2) The beggar in Christ's parable (Luke 16:19–31). His poverty is not praised per se any more than the wealth of Dives is condemned. The one experienced misery while alive, the other "fared sumptuously." In death each received his due reward.

lead, a blue-gray malleable metal, sometimes found pure, but often in the form of sulfide. It was heavy (Ex. 15:10); refined or consumed in the fire (Jer. 6:29, Ezek. 22:18); was listed among metals known to early Israel (Num. 31:22); and was supplied to markets of Tyre* by Tarshish*. Job's allusion to words written in rock "with an iron pen and lead" (19:24) may refer to a filling-in of the inscription with this metal to make it more legible.

Leah ("gazelle" or "wild cow"), the elder daughter of Laban, married by his trickery to Jacob after he had served 7 years for Rachel, her younger sister (Gen. 29:23). Leah bore Jacob six sons and a daughter (Reuben, Simeon, Levi, Judah, Issachar, Zebulun, and Dinah), and became recognized as one of the builders of the house of Israel (Ruth 4:11). She was buried in the family cave of Machpelah in Hebron, before Jacob's descent to Egypt. The Tribes descended from Leah are viewed as a separate group, distinct from the Rachel Tribes. Tradition ascribes large Aramaean additions to the Hebrew stock through Leah. The Midrash regards her as a good and honorable woman, even though she was disliked by Jacob (Gen. 29:33); and explains her "tender" eyes as due to her weeping lest she be compelled to marry Esau.

leather, the skin of such animals as sheep or goat, mentioned as the stuff of girdles (Elijah's, II Kings 1:8, and John the Baptist's, Matt. 3:4). Parchments or treated skins were a favorite writing material in O.T. times. The ancient Dead Sea Scrolls*, found by Bedouins at 'Ain Fashka in 1947, were on leather.

leaven (from two Heb. words meaning "to ferment" and "to sour"; Lat. *levamen*, "that which raises," from *levare*, "raise"), a substance added to dough to cause fermentation. In O.T. times leaven was a piece of highly fermented dough left from a previous baking and inserted in meal in the kneading trough. Unleavened bread was always a sacred reminder to Hebrews of the haste of their Exodus from Egypt, when they did not delay to bake leavened bread, but carried dough and kneading troughs with them, baking as they wandered, as Bedouins do today. This incident became an orthodox custom when Mosaic Law governing the Passover* and the Feast of Unleavened Bread called for use of unleavened dough in the celebration of the Passover anniversary (Ex. 12:15, 19, 13:6–8, 23:18, 34:25). Israel, eating the "bread of bitterness," remembered a high moment in their experience. The 14th day of the month Nisan (or Abib)—approximately April—began a period when the family and its guests used only unleavened bread (Ex. 12:17–20, 23:15). The Feast of Unleavened Bread became one of the three great occasions of the Jewish year. (See FEASTS; KNEADING, illus. 232.)

Levitical law forbade the use of leaven, as well as fermentive honey, as suggestive of decay or taint, in meal offerings made to Yahweh (Lev. 2:4). Leaven was allowed for the peace offering (Lev. 7:13) and the wave loaves (23:17), because these "first fruits unto the Lord" were not burned on the altar as material dedicated to Yahweh. (See Amos 4:5.)

Today for the Passover celebration Jews make flat cakes (*mazzoth*) of unleavened dough about 6 in. square and ⅛ in. thick (Deut. 16:3).

In the N.T. "leaven" is used symbolically in two senses. Jesus, in his Parable of the Leaven (Matt. 13:33), twin to that of the sure-growing mustard seed, meant it to express the pervasive, all-permeating power of the Kingdom of God, transforming the whole world as a housewife's leaven transforms her lump of dough, as he had seen in Mary's home at Nazareth. Again, he used leaven to denote an evil influence at work in society: "Beware of the leaven of the Pharisees, and of Herod" (Mark 8:15), he warned. Luke adds the more explicit explanatory phrase, the leaven "which is hypocrisy" (12:1)—a poison to be avoided by disciples. Some scholars interpret Mark 8:15 as suggesting the determined opposition of Herodians and Pharisees to Christ's work. Paul contrasted the "leaven of malice and wickedness"—a corrupting influence to be purged out—with "the unleavened bread of sincerity and truth," to be eaten at Passover, which is Christ himself (I Cor. 5:6–8). He reiterated the power of a small piece of leaven to influence a mass (Gal. 5:9; I Cor. 5:6).

Leaven in rabbinical literature symbolizes evil desires, regarded in Jewish theology as man's hereditary corruption.

Lebanon (lĕb′ȧ-nŏn), (equivalent, if Sem., to *lābhēn*, "to be white," suggested by snow on the mountains, Jer. 18:14, or gleaming cliffs; the Roman *Libanus*). (1) The 100-m.-long mountain mass of two roughly parallel ranges, the Lebanons and the Anti-Lebanons, extending NNE. to SSW. from the Taurus system in Asia Minor, down through Syria, the Republic of Lebanon, and Palestine, and ending in limestone cliffs at the Gulf of Suez. Between the two Lebanon ranges is the extraordinarily fertile plain, El-Beka (the Beka'a), at an elevation of 2,300 ft. The plain, measuring 30 m. by 10, was known in ancient times as Coele Syria (Hollow Syria), though the latter covered more territory than the Beka'a. A spur of the Anti-Lebanons forms magnificent Mt. Hermon, whose S. peaks climb to 9,383 ft. The two loftiest summits of the Lebanon are Jebel Makmal, towering behind Bsherreh (40 m. E. of Tripolis) and its lonely colony of surviving cedars of Lebanon; and Kurnat es-Sauda, both of which rise to c. 10,200 ft. For miles the Lebanons maintain an average of 6,500–7,000 ft., at times 7,500–8,000 ft. They are the majestic, snow-jeweled backdrop of the approach to Syria from the Mediterranean; they are mirrored in the Sea of Galilee, and are sometimes seen from as far south as Jericho. (See HERMON, illus. 180.)

The Lebanons are not only the focal point of vast Syria, but a determinant feature in the geography of the Middle East. They drop down to become the plateau of Upper Galilee and the lesser hills of Lower Galilee; branch off S. of the Plain of Esdraelon* to form the Carmel ridge; then continue S. through Samaria to become the central mountain range of Judaea, parallel to the Jordan Valley, at an average height of 2,400 ft.; then run past Hebron into the desert plateau where Israel wandered. Down the E. side of the Jordan the mountain mass forms the highlands of the present Kingdom of Jordan, through which the Hebrews trekked to enter Canaan. The elevation crosses the plateau of Hauran grain lands to the deep Yarmuk River Valley, moves through ancient Gilead, forms the Moab tableland, then rolls off into the lofty Arabian desert. The deep Jordan valley is an extension of the Great Rift or Beka'a—"the valley of Lebanon" (Josh. 11:17)—between the Lebanons and the Anti-Lebanons, which, continuing through Palestine, becomes the Arabah.

The Lebanon ranges are the home of countless streams (Song of Sol. 4:15) and of four notable rivers: the Jordan, with its headwaters on the W. slope of Hermon; the Orontes, flowing N. to water almost all of N. Syria, where it created ancient Antioch; the Abana or Barada (II Kings 5:12), running 10 m. from the Beka'a Plain to form 7 streams that feed the Damascus oasis on the edge of the Syrian Desert; the Leontes or Litani, rising near temple-strewn Baalbek (Heliopolis)—the present Nahr el-Qasimieh.

241. The Lebanons. A colony of ancient cedars surviving at the head of the Qadisha Valley shows as a dark mass in center background.

The Lebanons formed the NW. boundary of the "Promised Land" (Deut. 1:7, 11:24; Josh. 1:4, 11:17) but were never the goal of Israel's expansionists after Joshua's theophany (Josh. 13:1–6); or, if held, remained only a short time under Hebrew control. Natural barriers shut the region off from Palestine. But its great scenic beauties inspired many poetic allusions in Scripture (Ps. 92:12; Song of Sol. 4:15, 5:15); and the threat to its magnificent cedars was voiced in Apocalyptic passages, whose writers knew the maraudings of Mesopotamians, Egyptians, Israelites, and Tyrians in search of wood for coffins, palaces, temples, chests, musical instruments, and ship masts (Jer. 22:7; Ezek. 27:5; Zech. 11:2). By the time of Justinian (6th century A.D.) the groves were well nigh exhausted. In recent years a program of reforestation has been in effect. Wild life has always abounded in the Lebanons, but is seldom mentioned in the Bible (Song of Sol. 4:8, Isa. 14:8).

Geologically, the Lebanon region is built of three strata. The lowest is thick limestone (*Cidaris glandaria*); the next layer is Nubian sandstone; then comes a very thick layer of limestone that forms the bulk of the loftiest peaks, and is filled with myriads of fossils. The water-supplying sandstone strata are the most important.

The fragrant, long-lived, sacred cedars* of Lebanon (*Cedrus libani*) were her glory. The admiration felt for Lebanon's forests by peoples of the Middle East is patent in Scripture. Amos praised their height (2:9). Ezekiel, in an oracle pronounced just prior to the fall of Jerusalem, compared the fallen Assyrian to a cedar, high above the other trees, rooted in watery places, broad in branches under which animals brought forth their young and in whose shadow nations dwelt (31:3–8). Psalmists sang of "goodly cedars" (80:10), and compared the righteous to the well-known incorruptibility of their wood (92:12). The poet author of the Song of Solomon lauded their excellence for his house (1:17). Their denudation by successive aggressors was deplored by prophets, and was used by them as a symbol of Israel's destruction (Jer. 22:7; Ezek. 27:5; Zech. 11:2).

The kings of Israel also leaned heavily on the resources of Lebanon. David had a treaty of friendship with the generous King Hiram of Tyre which served him well in his palace construction (II Sam. 5:11), and for the assembling of materials for the Temple built by his son (I Chron. 22:4–10). This trade alliance was continued by Hiram or his successor when Solomon succeeded to his father's throne. (For a full account of this reciprocal treaty, see HIRAM.) When Zerubbabel repaired the sanctuary after the Exile he made further demands on Lebanon's natural resources (Ezra 3:7). (See CEDARS, illus. 86.)

After the region had been occupied by warring Amorites and other highland strong men, who have been succeeded today in some sections by such fanatical types as the Druses, Lebanon-built cities now survive only along the narrow strip of magnificent coast that was the ancient Phoenicia; whose Tyre, Sidon, Byblos, and Sarafand (Zarepta) form a pathetically weak representation of the influence of Lebanon in Mediterranean life between the 10th and 4th centuries B.C.

(2) *The Republic of Lebanon*, occupying much of old Phoenicia, became in 1926 an independent state. It extends along the Mediterranean from a point roughly midway between Tyre and Acre, E. to Mt. Hermon and the Anti-Lebanons, and N. to the small state of Latakia. It is bounded on the E. by Syria. Industrious Maronite and Greek Orthodox Christians cultivate small, terraced mountain farms which produce grain, olives, mulberries, and other fruit coveted by vacationists, who turn to the Lebanon for winter sports in this Switzerland of the Middle East or come up from hot Egypt to their summer mountain villas. Lebanon contains a minority of Moslems, Druses, and Jews.

The Lebanon *Service des Antiquités*, in conjunction with such eminent archaeologists as Maurice Dunand and Pierre Montet, excavated Byblos (see GEBAL).

Lebbaeus (lĕ-bē′ŭs). See THADDAEUS; JUDAS.

leeks, onion-like culinary herbs having cylindrical bulbs, eaten with fish and meat by Hebrews in Egypt and Palestine (Num. 11:5).

lees, dregs or sediment of wine (Isa. 25:6; Jer. 48:11; Zeph. 1:12).

legion (Lat. *legio*), a division of the Roman army made up of 10 cohorts ("bands," in Matt. 27:27; Mark 15:16) of six centuries (or hundreds) each. Each legion had a cavalry complement. In N.T. times the Roman Empire maintained 25 legions, four of which were stationed in Syria. These groups were supplemented by locally-raised provincials, who, however, were not stationed in their own regions. The word "legion" became proverbial among Middle Eastern subjects for any large number of persons. George Adam Smith, after seeing near Gadara the tombstone of a Roman soldier of the 14th Legion, long ago gave an interesting interpretation of the Gadarene demoniac who said that his own name was "Legion" (Mark 5:9, 15); the man, wandering long among tombstones inscribed with the names of members of a lost legion, had developed a fixed idea, so that he declared that his own name was "Legion." But the words of Luke 8:30 are more accurately rendered: "because many devils were entered into him."

242. Tablet of the Tenth Roman legion, built by Crusaders into church wall at Abu Ghosh (perhaps Emmaus).

Jesus in Gethsemane declared to the disciple who had cut off the high priest's ear that he could, by praying to the Father, have the immediate help (Matt. 26:53) of "twelve legions of angels"—three times as many legions as Rome had in Syria.

Lemuel ("belonging to God"), the unidentified king whose mother's wise counsel is preserved in Prov. 31:1–9.

lending. See DEBT; INTEREST.

Lent, forty-days' feast period (Matt. 4:2) from Ash Wednesday to Easter, excluding Sundays. Lent's last seven days are Holy Week.

lentil, the seed of a small leguminous plant which grew wild in Moab and was cultivated in all parts of ancient Palestine for food. It was an ingredient in the pottage served to Esau by Jacob. Because of the reddish color it gives to stew, "lentil" has been suggested as the basis of Esau's alternate name, "Edom" ("red") (Gen. 25:30; but cf. 25:25).

leopard, a spotted, carnivorous animal of the cat family, not common to ancient Palestine, but familiar enough to the Near East to

243. Leopard.

be effectively used in descriptive passages of Scripture depicting a wild, mountainous setting, as in Jer. 5:6, 13:23; Hos. 13:7. Leopards appear in the imagery of Daniel (7:6) and of the Apocalypse (Rev. 13:2). Habakkuk stresses the speed of the leopard (1:8). A leopard, lying down with a kid, is a figure used by Isaiah as a sign of the restored Israel (11:6).

In Egypt leopard skins were worn by priests as part of their ceremonial attire.

leprosy, a disease which is marked by patches of discoloration and thickening of the skin and by loss of sensation. It is caused by a specific micro-organism, discovered in the last century, which can now be controlled by treatment. The Hebrew word, *zara 'ath,* in the Bible was translated "leprosy" long before the modern usage of the term had restricted it to the disease caused by a certain germ. In Lev. 13, the disease *zara 'ath* is described in some detail and is certainly quite different from leprosy as it is known today. For this reason in *The New English Bible* the translators have discarded "leprosy." Unfortunately the term chosen, "malignant skin disease," is also misleading, since physicians use "malignant" to imply cancerous change, and *zara 'ath* was certainly not that.

The Levitical description suggests that more than one disease was covered by the word *zara 'ath:* probably fungus conditions, ringworms. and perhaps psoriasis. Clothing and the walls of houses infected with fungus were also called leprous. (Lev. 13:47–59, 14:33–37). The fact that *zara 'ath* was used by God as a punishment of Miriam. (Num. 12:10–14) and on Gehazi (II Kings 5) has led to the suggestion that the disease was a punishment for sin. It was certainly regarded as ceremonially unclean, and this was a reflection of the laws of hygiene designed to prevent the spread of infections for which there was no effective treatment. The priest had the authority to diagnose and to isolate the patient, and only the priest could pronounce him cured or "clean" again. King Uzziah (II Chron. 26:19–21) had the disease for the latter part of his life. Naaman (II Kings 5) was another distinguished victim, but he was cured by the prophet Elisha. The separate and lonely life that was imposed by leprosy is indicated in the story of the four "lepers" (II Kings 7:3–11).

Jesus healed people with "leprosy" (Matt. 8:2–4; Mark 1:40–45; Luke 5:12–15), and on one occasion cured ten patients, of whom only one returned to thank him (Luke 17:11–15). He also insisted that the Mosaic law of priestly cleansing be observed. P. W. B.

244. Lepers along a Palestine road, c. 1930. Such sights have disappeared in Palestine today, thanks to modern medicine.

Lesbos, an island in the NE. Aegean Sea. Paul stopped there, in Mitylene (Acts 20:14).

letters, in the sense of correspondence, were common in the era when Scripture was being reduced to writing. Many letters—personal and official—are included in the Bible. The name of sender, addressee, messenger (II Sam. 11:14; II Kings 19:14) and means of delivery (II Chron. 30:6; Esther 3) are mentioned. The discovery of thousands of clay letters—some of them still in their unbroken clay envelopes—from Ras-Shamrah, Tell el-Amarna, Lachish, Nineveh, Babylon, Mari, etc., shed light on the Biblical period. Excellent examples of letter style (Persian and Roman) are found in Ezra 4 and Acts 23:26–30. Cf. also the Maccabean appeal by letter to Rome (I Macc. 8) and Rome's reply.

The scribe (see SCRIBES) who wrote letters and other documents was an important member of every court and town, whose citizens hired him to write, witness, and seal communications, as they still do in isolated Near Eastern communities. (See WRITING.) Examples of the letter writer's equipment have been excavated in Egypt. Seals (see SEAL) were used for signatures.

Twenty-one letters, or Epistles*—always an interesting literary form—make up the bulk of the N.T. Lost letters from the Corinthians to Paul are mentioned (I Cor. 7:1). The Book of Revelation contains letters to "the seven churches that are in Asia."

Letters of introduction are referred to (II Cor. 3:1; Acts 18:27; I Cor. 16:3; cf. Rom. 16:1 f.).

As late as Roman times postal service was maintained for official business only; private citizens depended on merchants or friends to deliver their mail (I Pet. 5:12; Eph. 6:21 f.).

Specific letters in the Bible include: that of David to Joab via Uriah (II Sam. 11:14 f.); Hiram to Solomon (II Chron. 2:11); Jezebel to the elders (I Kings 21:8 f.); Jehu to the rulers (II Kings 10:1–7); Ben-hadad to the King of Israel (II Kings 5:5–7); Rabshakah to Hezekiah (II Kings 19); Berodach-baladan to Hezekiah (II Kings 20:12; cf. Isa. 39:1); Jeremiah to the exiles (Jer. 29); Elijah to Jehoram (II Chron. 21:12–15); Hezekiah to the remnants of the Northern Kingdom (II Chron. 30:1, 6); several persons to Artaxerxes (Ezra 4:7); Tatnai to Darius (Ezra 5); Artaxerxes to Nehemiah (Neh. 2:7 f.); Ahasuerus to the provincial rulers (Esther 3:12–15, 9:27 ff.); Mordecai and Esther to the Jews (Esther 9:29); the high priest to the Damascus synagogues (Acts 9:2, 28:21); the Jerusalem Council to Gentile converts (Acts 15:22–29); Claudius Lysias to Felix (Acts 23:25–30).

Levi ("joined"). (1) The 3d son of Jacob and Leah (Gen. 29:34, 35:23), younger full brother of Reuben and Simeon, older full brother of Judah, Issachar, Zebulun, and Dinah; born in Haran, on the Fertile Crescent. When Dinah was raped by Shechem, son of Hamor, Levi and Simeon cut Hamor and Shechem to pieces with their swords, according to the J document. (This version of the episode is badly entangled with another version, in Gen. 34, in which all the sons of Jacob took part.) This family affair is probably a depiction of tribal relations between early Israel and her neighbors. Jacob's disapproval of Levi and Simeon's violence (Gen. 34:30) is echoed in Jacob's blessing (Gen. 49:5 ff.).

Sons of Levi who became heads of tribes were Gershon (or Gershom), Kohath, and Merari (Gen. 46:11; Ex. 6:16). Levi died in Egypt at an advanced age (Ex. 6:16). Miriam, Aaron, and Moses were his great-grandchildren, through Kohath's line. R. H. Pfeiffer views the racial history of Israel, as recorded by the priestly writers, as "a funnel comprising ten rings of decreasing size, down to the extremely small but all-important tube at the bottom—the theocratic community." In the final circle "Levi was singled out among the sons of Jacob . . . ; among the sons of Levi (Num. 3:14–39) the high priest Aaron and his line (3:1–4) marked the exact center of the concentric circles . . ., the climax of Israel's racial history." Rabbinic and Hellenistic literature enhanced the stature of Levi, regarding him as visited by God's special favor because he represented, in a sense, the priesthood. (See LEVITES; PRIESTS.)

(2), (3) Ancestors of Jesus (Luke 3:24, 29 f.). (4) Perhaps another name of Matthew.

leviathan, a mythical, many-headed (Ps. 74:14; cf. Dan. 7:2 ff.), piercing, and crooked (Isa. 27:1) sea monster capable of devouring on a large scale, or conversely, of furnishing food for a large company (Ps. 74:14). Biblical allusions to leviathan are part of an almost universal mythology in which a monster, symbolic of evil, is contending against but ultimately defeated by the power of good. Isaiah, possibly influenced by the Babylonian Creation epic, uses the ancient mythological idea of the destroyed leviathan (27:1) to symbolize the triumphant Day of Judgment, when the righteous Yahweh will triumph over the terrible evil present in the world. But since the discovery of the Ras Shamrah Canaanite texts in N. Syria on the site of Ugarit, it has become clear that there is a closer parallel between the seven-headed Canaanite Lotan of myths current between 1700 and 1400 B.C. and the Biblical leviathan. The names in the two languages are identical.

When the author of Revelation was looking for a vivid symbol to express the violent evils inflicted on Christians in the era of Domitian's last years (c. A.D. 96), he found in leviathan the figure he desired (Rev. 11:7, 12:3, 13:1 ff.).

levirate law. See MARRIAGE.

Levites, the Tribe descended from an eponymous ancestor, Levi*; Aaron and his line were descendants of Levi (Num. 3:1–4). Moses numbered them by families, every male from a month upward (Num. 3:15 ff.), in the Sinai Wilderness; they were a large company before Israel's entry into Canaan. According to the narrative of Num. 3:23 ff. they were assigned to duties in connection with the Hebrew Tabernacle; but their privileges and responsibilities grew rapidly, and changed with the changing conditions of Israel through the centuries. (See PRIESTS.)

Levites (Num. 18:6) were accepted by God as substitutes for the first-born which He might have demanded as His own (Num. 3:11–13, 8:16). In the Priestly Code only descendants of Aaron were to be priests (Ex. 28:1; Num. 18:7). Levites might not come near the altar or its sacred vessels, since only priests could enter the Sanctuary (Num. 4:20). They were regarded as servants of the priests, leaving the latter free for the holy ministry "before the tabernacle of witness" (Num. 18:2 ff.). Levites were organized into three main divisions, descended from Levi's three sons—Gershon, Kohath, and Merari—and cared for and transported the Tabernacle (Num. 3:5 ff.). In certain O.T. passages Levites had charge of the sacred musical service (I Chron. 24–26), and were also doorkeepers. These Chronicle passages cannot, however, be taken as representing the customs of David's time, for they may be retrojections of the Chronicler.

Levitical cities were allotted to the landless Levites in the "assignment" of territory to Israel at the Conquest*. Josh. 21:1 (cf. Num.

35:1–8) tells how the lots were drawn (v. 4), and the towns and their adjoining farm villages or grazing lands allotted to "the children of Aaron the priest," those of the household of Kohath, Gershon, and Merari, the various Tribes contributing a total of 48 valuable towns. Among these were six cities of refuge (Num. 35:6), where unintentional murderers might find shelter. Some scholars view this "assignment" as theoretical—a contradiction of Num. 18:20 f., which narrates how Yahweh revealed to Aaron the priest that he should have no inheritance in the land, because He Himself was the inheritance of Israel's priests; their income was to come from the tithe of Israel (Num. 18:20 f., 26 f.). Levites were expected to pay tithes to the priests (Num. 18:25–32). See also the priests' portions of the meat sacrificed (I Sam. 2:13–17).

A striking O.T. incident in which a Levite figures is narrated in Judg. 17, 18—the story of a young Levite from Bethlehem who was hired by Micah of Ephraim to be his priest, and his role in the capture of the city of Laish which became Dan. R. H. Pfeiffer says that this narrative presents our oldest information concerning the priesthood in early Israel. Another story of a Levite is preserved in Judg. 19–21—the outrage at Gibeah, which led to a war between the Benjamites and Israel. These stories reflect the low state of public order and private morality in the era between the Conquest and the Monarchy.

In the N.T., Christ's Parable of the Good Samaritan tells of an unsympathetic Levite (Luke 10:32).

Levitical cities. See PRIESTS; LEVITES.

Leviticus, the 3d book of the Pentateuch. Its name is the Latin rendering (*Liber Leviticus*) of the Greek title (*Leuitikè Bíblos*, Levitical Book) in the Greek Bible, which occurs at the beginning of our era in the writings of Philo of Alexandria. In Hebrew the title is merely the first word (*wayyiqra'*, "and he called"). Although the book deals with priests more than with Levites, the title is not inappropriate, for the Jewish priesthood was "Levitical" (Heb. 7:11). The contents, mostly legal, are as follows:

The ritual of the five sacrifices	chaps. 1–7
The installation of the priests	8–10
A code on cleanness and uncleanness	11–15
The Day of Atonement*	16
The Holiness Code*	17–26
Laws on vows and tithes	27

The Book of Leviticus is assigned by modern critics to the so-called Priestly Code (designated by "P"), compiled by the priests of Jerusalem in the period 500–450 B.C., but incorporating considerably earlier legislation, like the Holiness Code (11:43–45, 17–26), which seems to date from 650 B.C. in its original form (which was known to Ezekiel). In fact the book contains material dating from very early times, like the scapegoat (Azazel) rite in 16:8, 10, 26, but side by side has post-Exilic laws like 16:29–34. Besides ritual, moral, and civil laws, the Book of Leviticus contains narratives having juristic implications: the ordination of Aaron and his sons (8); the inauguration of their priestly functions (9); the punishment of Aaron's sons, Nadab and Abihu, for offering a sacrifice with strange fire (10:1–7); the error of the surviving sons of Aaron, Eleazar and Ithamar (10:16–20); the stoning of the blasphemer of the divine name (24:10–14, 23).

Leviticus, together with the other portions of the Pentateuch belonging to the Priestly Code (notably in Exodus and Numbers), is the theocratic law of the Jewish Community in the Persian Period (538–333 B.C.) after the rebuilding of the Jerusalem Temple in 515, the ritual of which (in the 5th century B.C.) it records, while attributing its institution to Moses. This is the law of a holy nation whose ruler is the sole God of heaven and earth, who has chosen Israel as His own people. The Persian officials were responsible for law and order under civil law; the Jewish Law under Persian rule could merely regulate Jewish religion and morals. The priesthood, in contrast with Amos and the other reforming prophets, stressed the ritual in the Temple more than other duties towards God; but it thus established, by means of definite ceremonies and obligations, a holy state within an empire, a church whose sole sovereign was God, who had revealed to Moses what He required from His people, fixing exactly public and private devotions. Thus religion became a set of rules, a discipline, a solemn series of sacraments celebrated by a clergy tracing its origin to Aaron. And yet, this religion of observance (characteristic of all sacerdotal religions) preserved the contrasting religion of the prophets, and even stressed, in chap. 19, a high moral standard and the second half of the summary of the Law as given by Jesus: "Thou shalt love thy neighbor as thyself" (Lev. 19:18, cf. 19:34; Luke 10:27; Matt. 19:19, 22:39; Mk. 12:31, 33; Rom. 13:9).

With the destruction of the Temple in A.D. 70, many of the rites enjoined in Leviticus have of course become obsolete and may never be revived in Judaism; the Epistle to the Hebrews had previously interpreted them in a purely allegorical manner for the Christians. Nevertheless, the Book of Leviticus, aside from giving us a notion of Judaism in the Persian period, is still valuable: love for one's neighbor, meaning for Christians and modern Jews love for any human being, will forever remain the hope of "peace on earth"; the holiness of God is a lasting doctrine; the holiness of God requires human holiness, which includes such details as cleanliness, proper foods, and self-discipline: godliness includes hygiene and purity; the relation between medicine and religion is stressed in the regulations about leprosy (13–14).

Five fragments of Leviticus were found in 'Ain Fashka Cave, where the Dead Sea Scrolls* were discovered in 1947. These leather manuscripts are dated by W. F. Albright and S. Yeivin about 100 B.C., and two or three centuries later by other scholars. Some experts regard them as part of a Samaritan MS. of Leviticus. The script resembles that on Hasmonaean coins. The fragments include the following passages: 19:31–34, 20:20–23, 21:24–22:5. R. H. P.

Libertines (literally "freedmen"), members of the Jerusalem synagogue of the Libertines —probably descendants of Jewish freedmen expelled from Rome in the reign of Tiberius— who opposed Stephen (Acts 6:9). In an old cistern on Jerusalem's Hill Ophel has been found a limestone block recording, in what appears to be a 1st-century Gk. inscription, the erection by Theodotus of a synagogue for the reading of the Law and the entertainment of needy Jewish pilgrims to Jerusalem— probably Hellenistic Jews. This structure, given by a Roman freedman of a Jewish family, may be the synagogue of the Freedmen (R.S.V.).

liberty. (1) *Personal liberty* was coveted by the Hebrews in O.T. times, but the heavy hand of foreign oppression often deprived them of freedom (Ex. 5:6 f.; II Kings 24:1, 25) and caused them to work for a pharaoh or go into exile in Babylonia. Hebrews also lost their individual liberty by being sold into slavery for debt (Lev. 25:39). Levitical law provided for a "year of liberty" in connection with the Jubilee every 50 years (Lev. 25:8–17, v. 10 of which is on the Liberty Bell of the United States; Lev. 25:40; Jer. 34:8 f.). Even if this provision freeing Israelites in bondage was never literally and fully carried out, it was more than a gesture toward liberty. (See FREEMAN.) Prophets continually yearned for political captives to be freed (Isa. 61:1). The N.T. records instances of captives being liberated (Acts 12:7–11, 16:25–40; Heb. 13:23) and of a degree of liberty granted such prisoners as Paul (Acts 24:23, 27:3, 28:30).

(2) *Political liberty* in the sense of national independence was lost by the Hebrews in 587 B.C. when Nebuchadnezzar removed the Davidic dynasty from its throne and destroyed Jerusalem. With the exception of the brief period of Maccabean rule, 166–63 B.C., the Jews never again (until 1948) exercised sovereignty over their own land, but were subject to one great empire after another: Persia (538–333 B.C.), the Greek Kingdom (333–166 B.C.), Rome (63 B.C.–A.D. 324), etc. National pride (see APOCRYPHA) found expression in Daniel*, in Judith, and in Esther*. The dreams of a Messianic kingdom were an aspect of the desire for political liberty.

(3) The bestowing of *spiritual liberty* was included in Jesus' conception of his own mission: "The Lord hath anointed me . . . to proclaim liberty to the captives" (Isa. 61:1; cf. Luke 4:18). Here Christ is the liberator: "Stand fast therefore in the liberty wherewith Christ hath made us free" (Gal. 5:1). He liberated men from slavish obedience to the old Hebrew Law by his pointed declaration recorded in Mark 12:29–31. He taught men the truth, and gave them the moral vision which frees men from the power of evil (John 8:32). The spirit of life in Christ liberated men from sin and from the fear of death (Rom. 6:18, 8:2; Heb. 2:15), and endowed them with "the glorious liberty of the children of God" (Rom. 8:21). Paul taught that "where the Spirit of the Lord is, there is liberty" (II Cor. 3:17). Man's spiritual liberty comes from his being in Christ: "our liberty which we have in Christ" (Gal. 2:4). As a Christian a man is guided by love rather than by law, and is interested not in doing such things as the law rightfully forbids but in furthering the Kingdom of God. Paul's Galatian Letter contains his thoughts about bondage to the Law vs. Christian liberty (5:1–6, 13–6:10). He taught that the Christian is freed from such minor rules as those governing food (I Cor. 8 f.), and even circumcision (Gal. 2:4, 6:15). There had been a hint of this provision in Ps. 119:45. Though "called to liberty" (Gal. 5:13), the Christian must not make his freedom a "pretext for misconduct" (I Pet. 2:16, Moffatt) or a stumbling-block to others who have not yet found a deep experience of Christ (Rom. 14:20, 21). (See LAW.)

N.T. theology is neither clear nor entirely consistent in its teachings about man's individual freedom of choice and God's determination for the salvation of men. Perhaps the most that can be said is that God alone is able to give the possibility of salvation and the means by which man can attain it; and that every man is free to accept or reject this salvation.

Libnah (lĭb′nȧ) ("whiteness"). (1) A camp site of Israel during her Wilderness wanderings (Num. 33:20 f.). (2) A strongly fortified Canaanite royal city N. of Lachish (Josh. 10:29), captured by Joshua after he had taken Makkedah and before he stormed Lachish. Libnah was given to the Tribe of Judah and later to the descendants of Aaron, as a city of refuge (Josh. 21:13; I Chron. 6:57). It revolted against Jehoram (II Kings 8:22; II Chron. 21:10); was attacked by Sennacherib on his way toward Jerusalem (II Kings 19:8; Isa. 37:8); was the home of Hamutal, daughter of Jeremiah of Libnah, wife of Josiah and mother of Jehoahaz, King of Judah (609 B.C.) (II Kings 23:31), and of Zedekiah, the last King of Judah (598–587 B.C.) (II Kings 24:18; Jer. 52:1). Libnah was early identified with Tell es-Safi, the site of the Crusader fortress "Blanche Garde," on the basis of its geographical position commanding the entrance from the Philistine Plain into the Vale of Elah, and the surrounding ("white") limestone cliffs (see *BA* 34, 1971, pp. 76 ff.). The site was superficially excavated in 1899 by F. J. Bliss and R. A. S. Macalister, who traced sections of an ancient city wall and uncovered the foundations of a structure enclosing three standing stones (*Excavations in Palestine 1898–1900*, 1902). The exact location of Libnah is uncertain, however, and identification with Tell Bornâṭ, 6 m. to the S., is now preferred (Aharoni, *The Land of the Bible*, 1967, pp. 292 f.; see Albright, *BASOR* 15, 1924, p. 9).

libraries in the ancient Middle East were repositories for clay tablets, parchment scrolls, papyri, and codices on which temple literature and sacred records were written. Much that found its way into the Bible was safeguarded in someone's library. The library of a vast temple school has been excavated at Ras* Shamrah (Ugarit) in N. Syria—a library in the sense not of a building, but of thousands of sand-preserved clay tablets which have opened up to scholars not only the lost Canaanite literature, but documents showing how priests trained acolytes to read and

245. A room suggestive of a library in the Nabu Temple during the reign of Sargon II (722–705 B.C.). Fragments of many tablets, including a complete one inscribed with a syllabary, were found in the debris.

write in the proto-Phoenician or Ugaritic alphabet. Translators will be years tracing the implications of what the Ras Shamrah library has yielded.

About 650 B.C. Ashurbanipal* collected at Nineveh a great library of writings not only in Assyrian but copied and translated from Sumerian and Accadian. Thousands of these clay* tablets have been found, giving much valuable information about the Assyrian Empire and many events recorded in Scripture.

Egypt's most famous library was founded at Alexandria by Ptolemy I in the 4th century B.C. and enlarged by Ptolemy Philadelphus (285–246 B.C.). The staff aimed to have a copy of every work published in the Graeco-Roman world. Catalogues and bibliographies were kept. The Graeco-Roman Museum of Alexandria has reported finding silver, gold, and bronze plaques demonstrating that this city possessed the greatest library of the ancient world. In such an environment the LXX version of the O.T. was prepared and early Christian writings copied.

In Palestine the Temple precincts provided archives for sacred documents, which sometimes, however, were lost (II Kings 22).

Libya (lĭb′ĭ-*ȧ*), a country of N. Africa on the Mediterranean lying W. of Egypt. It is the rendering of *Put* or *Lubim* in Jer. 46:9; Ezek. 30:5, 38:5; Dan. 11:43. In Roman times western Libya was called Cyrenaica (see CYRENE).

life. (1) In the O.T. life was thought of as the gift of God, who "breathed into his nostrils the breath of life; and man became a living soul" (Gen. 2:7; cf. Ps. 36:9). Life was maintained by God (Ps. 66:9, 27:1), and a long life was a satisfying gift (Ps. 91:16). But life was often like a shadow (I Chron. 29:15); it passed swifter than a weaver's shuttle (Job 7:6), or hurrying messengers (Job 9:25). The early Hebrews believed that the life of the flesh was in the blood (Deut. 12:23; Lev. 17:11). This identification of life with blood was the basis of the religious rites in which blood, considered sacred because it belonged to God, was sacrificed on the altar for atonement (Lev. 17:14).

(2) In the N.T. the word "life" usually had spiritual meaning. Jesus said that life was more than meat (Matt. 6:25), and that it was of more value than the whole world (A.S.V. Matt. 16:26). He regarded each human life as precious, and devoted much of his ministry to healing maimed lives, yet he decried too much concern for the physical aspects of life (Matt. 6:25). In the Fourth Gospel "life" is a major word used for the real or spiritual life lived in fellowship with God, now and hereafter. This life was given by God (5:26), and was in Christ: "in him was life" (1:4); "I am the way, the truth, and the life" (14:6). Christ came to give this life to those who believe in him (20:31). To pass "out of death into life" (5:24), out of the sin and evil of man's unregenerate nature into eternal life, one must be "born again" (3:3). Eternal life can begin now through faith in Christ (3:36, 17:3) and continue throughout the future. The N.T. Epistles teach that "he that hath the Son hath life" (I John 5:12). To obey Christ's commandment of love is to pass "from death to life" (I John 3:14). "To be spiritually minded is life and peace" (Rom. 8:6).

Life, the Book of, a figurative term intended to suggest a record of the redeemed fellow workers of Christ (Phil. 4:3). Revelation (21:27) makes it "the Lamb's book of life."

light, in Scripture from Gen. 1:3 through Rev. 22:5, symbolized the presence of God. In Heb. Creation epics, as in those of some other nations, like the Egyptians, the formation of the universe was described as the separation of darkness from light, which the Lord called "day" (Gen. 1:5). In their years of wandering Israel relied on God's "pillar of fire" (Ex. 13:21). When they established their cloth Tabernacle, they attended scrupulously to the burning of the perpetual light (I Sam. 3:3); and throughout their national history, they kept burning the seven-branched lampstands at the Temple (II Chron. 4:7) in obedience to Lev. 6:9. Symbolically, God was the light of their countenance (Ps. 4:6), His word a light to the path of the faithful (Ps. 119:105). To a people who for generations had been taught to think of God as light, it was understandable that a Hebrew ascetic, John the Baptist, announced one who actually came into the world as light, ready to light every man (John 1:4 ff.), a role affirmed by Jesus of himself (3:19–21, 8:12) and extended to include his faithful witnesses (Matt. 5:14–16). This concept was spread through the Roman world by Paul (Eph. 5:8), and reiterated by the author of I John 1:5–7, who here unites N.T. symbolism with that of the O.T. The godless grope in the dark (I John 2:11).

In a world so dreary even humble homes tried to keep a small lamp* burning through the night. When Judas Maccabaeus cleansed the Temple, where for three years to a day sacrifices had been offered to the Olympian Zeus, the worship of Yahweh was inaugurated anew (165 B.C., I Macc. 4:52), and the Feast of Hanukkah (see DEDICATION) has been celebrated annually ever since. Josephus says that it was called "Lights" from the custom of illuminating the houses throughout the 8-day celebration. The use of lights in festivals was common in the various cults of the Hellenized world, especially those honoring Dionysus and Apollo.

lightning, an ever-impressive spectacle in nature which was viewed by the Scripture writers as a manifestation of God's power. The appearance of Yahweh at Sinai was accompanied by lightning (Ex. 19:16, 20:18). Especially in Wisdom literature and other devotional utterances lightning was in the word pictures of the creating, self-manifesting God: Job 28:26, 37:3, 38:25; Ps. 18:14, 77:18, 97:4, 135:7, 144:6. It appears in David's Song of Deliverance from his enemies (II Sam. 22:15). Prophets were awed by the sight of it in their visions (Ezek. 1:13 f.; Dan. 10:6; Jer. 10:13; Nah. 2:4). Flashes of lightning, loud blasts, and earthquakes accompanied the wonders portrayed in Revelation (8:5, 11:19, 16:18). Jesus, speaking of the coming of the Son of man, said that he would come out of the east and shine unto the west, even as lightning (Matt. 24:27; cf. Luke 17:24). To the Seventy returning from a successful mission he said, "I beheld Satan as lightning fall from heaven" (Luke 10:18). Matthew described the face of the resurrected Jesus as "like lightning."

The name of Deborah's general, **Barak***, means "lightning."

Lights, Feast of, see DEDICATION, FEAST OF.

lign aloes (līn ăl′ōz), the resinous wood of an E. Indian tree (*Aquilaria agallocha*), burned as a perfume by Orientals; the name given in the A.V. and A.S.V. (Num. 24:6) to trees called "oaks" by Moffatt.

lily, a bulbous plant and its flower, whose several varieties are abundant in Palestine and Egypt. The "lilies of the field" to which Jesus referred (Matt. 6:28 f.; Luke 12:27) may have included all the spring flowers*

246. Anemone, possibly one of the "lilies of the field."

(Arab. *schôschanna*), including the lily, iris, gladiolus, anemone, daisy, tulip, cyclamen, star of Bethlehem, etc. There has been much speculation about the lilies mentioned in the Song of Solomon. Harold Moldenke suggests in his *Plants of the Bible* (Chronica Botanica, Publishers) that these flowers may have been hyacinths (*Hyacinthus orientalis*). The allusion in Song of Sol. 6:2 may refer to the madonna lily (*Lilium candidum*). The lily-like lips (5:13) may be red anemones (*Anemone coronaria*). The writer may on the other hand have intended mixed spring flowers. The "lily" of Hos. 14:5 may have been the iris.

But the lily par excellence was the Egyptian *Nymphaea—alba, caerulea,* and *lotus*—abundant in flooded Nile fields. The lotus has been more influential in art than any other flower, from prehistoric times on. The stylized lotus motif, seen in the charming little temple at Saqqareh near Memphis, appears to be ancestor to the Greek Ionic, whose lily-like volutes did not appear on capitals for 800 years after the Saqqareh work. The lotus calyx motif, dating from the earliest Dynastic Period at least (c. 3000 B.C.), ornamented one of the two fundamental Egyptian column capitals—the papyrus being the other. The intertwined lily of Upper Egypt and the papyrus of Lower Egypt symbolized the United Kingdom. The brilliant Phoenician artist-architect-craftsman of Solomon's Temple, Hiram of Tyre, incorporated lily work or lotus-headed capitals and the lily brim into pillars (I Kings 7:19, 22, 26) and the "molten sea" (II Chron. 4:5). Many *objets d'art* excavated in Egypt and Egyptian-influenced Palestine are decorated with curving forms suggested by the lily.

The lily was stamped on coins of the Maccabeans, John Hyrcanus (134–104 B.C.) and Alexander Jannaeus (103–76 B.C.).

limestone, a calcium carbonate rock burned for its lime. People of O.T. times knew how to secure lime for plastering walls and other building purposes by burning limestone until it gave off white, caustic, alkaline earth. Prophets of doom pictured times when the bones of men would be "as the burnings of lime" (Isa. 33:12; cf. Amos 2:1).

The mountainous backbone of Palestine is largely limestone, whose rocks protrude through the scanty soil of the hill country E. and W. of the Jordan. In the Kingdom of Jordan common limestone is sometimes seen covered with a layer of black basalt deposited by volcanic action long ago, as in the Hauran. This is also true of sections of Galilee, which have used the basalt for buildings. In the desert S. of Beer-sheba soft chalky limestone is flaked with red flint, which washes out and strews the surface. The limestone of the E. wall of the Arabah is stocked with copper and iron, which was responsible for Edom's early prosperity. Surface limestone in Palestine, breaking down through moisture, becomes productive when fertilized. Natural filters of limestone are valuable in conserving rains for Palestine's water supply. See JERUSALEM.

linen, a finely woven cloth for which several Heb. words are used in the O.T., depending on whether reference is made to the fabric, its thread, or flax (*Linum usitatissimum*). Egypt is credited with producing the finest linen, but Mesopotamia or India is believed to have been the original home of flax*, the oldest known textile fiber. Herodotus mentions four qualities, one so fine that each thread contained 360 fibers. But Hebrews also developed great skill at the linen looms, and even exported their product to the Nile Valley for loincloths. Hot, low areas of Palestine, such as the Jordan Plain near Jericho, where Rahab dried flax "in order" on her roof top (Josh. 2:6), grew flax under conditions similar to those in Egypt.

In the Nile Valley flax is sown in November, pulled 110 days later, separated from its seed capsules, bundled, retted, exposed to the sun, and then covered with water for 10 days to bleach and soften for crushing. A wooden mallet is used to separate the flax fibers from the woody parts; and a comb, such as carders still use, is employed to draw it into thread for weaving in household hand looms (see WEAVING). Loom weights have been excavated from ruins of ancient occupation levels, as at Teleilât el-Ghassûl in the plains of Moab, at the NE. end of the Dead Sea. These had been used before the destruction of the town in the early 4th millennium B.C.

The fullers' guild was important in linen production in O.T. and N.T. times. Men pressed, dyed, cleaned, washed, and bleached new material and old. Fullers' (see FULLER) fields were established outside Jerusalem, conveniently near the water "conduit of the upper pool" (II Kings 18:17) (see also Isa. 7:3, 36:2; Mark 9:3).

Linen was the fabric worn by Egyptian priests and some Palestinian ones, possibly under the influence of nearby Egypt. The presence of foreign matter in wool made it undesirable. Cool, lustrous, smooth linen lent itself to such vestments as the Hebrew ephod (Ex. 28:6, 15; I Sam. 2:18, 22:18; II Sam. 6:14), girdle, coat, miter, and breeches (Ex. 28:39, 39:27 ff.). Mixtures of wool and linen were forbidden (Lev. 19:19). From Egypt, too, may have come the idea of using linen for the Tabernacle hangings (Ex. 25:4, 26:1, 28:5). Egyptian linen was prized for bedding (Prov. 7:16). The industrious Palestinian woman praised in the last chapter of Proverbs wove linen and sold it to the merchants (31:24). Linen was durable enough to be used, embroidered, for the sails of Tyrian ships (Ezek. 27:7).

The comfortable texture of linen, due to the microscopic structure and length of flax fiber, made it popular for the garments of royalty and aristocrats. Pharaoh clothed the Hebrew Joseph in fine linen (Gen. 41:42); Mordecai at the Persian court dressed in "fine linen and purple" (Esther 8:15); the "certain rich man" in Christ's parable of the beggar Lazarus wore fine linen and royal purple (Luke 16:19).

The garments of Jesus at the Transfiguration may have been of hand-woven white linen: "his raiment became shining, exceeding white as snow; so as no fuller on earth can white them" (Mark 9:3).

When Joseph of Arimathaea arranged for the burial of Jesus, he wrapped the body in "clean linen cloth"—perhaps an Egyptian influence (Matt. 27:59; cf. Mark 16:5, "a long white garment"). In Egypt mummy bandages, sometimes hundreds of yards long, were of linen exclusively. Sometimes piles of linen sheets 60 ft. long, beautifully fringed, were piled in the tomb chambers of the deceased. Nicodemus brought "myrrh and aloes"; "they wound it in linen clothes with the spices, as the manner of Jews is to bury" (John 19:39 f.). When Peter looked into the empty tomb on Easter morning, he "saw the linen clothes lying" (John 20:5).

Harold N. Moldenke of the N.Y. Botanical Garden mentions in his *Plants of the Bible* (Chronica Botanica, Publishers), three kinds of linen: (1) the coarsest, intended in Lev. 6:10; Ezek. 9:2; Dan. 10:5; (2) a good quality, as in Ex. 26:1, 39:27; (3) the choicest quality (Esther 8:15; I Chron. 15:27; Rev. 19:8). The best available to Hebrews was much coarser than fine linen known today.

The Dead Sea Scrolls found in 1947 in 'Ain Fashka Cave were wrapped in linen cloth, bundles of which were found on the cave floor. A fragment of this textile was examined by the staff of the Textile Museum and of Dumbarton Oaks in Washington, D.C.; the piece examined was Palestinian linen, whose warp is spun tighter than its weft, which was the normal style except in Egypt. The edges were rolled and sewed. The yarn used appears more woolly than the Egyptian types, and gives somewhat the appearance of flannel. Linen thread was used to sew together the pieces of coarse parchment on which the Scrolls were written.

Another fragment of the cloth was submitted to the Institute of Nuclear Studies at the University of Chicago, to be studied by the new radio-carbon method of dating materials used in the past 20,000 years by measuring the amount of carbon 14 they contain. According to Professor W. F. Libby of the Institute, the measurement of the Dead Sea Scrolls' wrappings indicates that their date is between 167 B.C. and A.D. 233. Thus nuclear physics, epigraphy, and archaeology combine their findings to support the genuineness and the age of the 'Ain Fashka Cave material. Dating by use of the carbon 14 process will enhance the speed and the accuracy with which various archaeological materials can be placed. (See *BA*, Vol. XIV, No. 1, Feb. 1951, pp. 25–32.)

See DRESS; FLAX; TABERNACLE.

lintel, a horizontal piece of wood or stone spanning the doors of Hebrew houses, sometimes projecting out over the entrance, on which blood from the sacrificed Passover lamb was sprinkled at the Exodus (Ex. 12:22 f.). The lintel of the olive-wood doors of the Temple is mentioned (I Kings 6:31). (See illus. 247, p. 396.)

Linus, one of four Christians at Rome who joined Paul in greetings to Timothy (II Tim. 4:21). Early authorities identify him as successor to Paul and Peter as "bishop" at Rome.

lion, a large, mammalian carnivore, numerous in Palestine in O.T. times, but extinct there since mediaeval times. The Heb. language has several words for this beast, depending on whether a full-grown creature is meant (Gen. 49:9; Judg. 14:8), or a vigorous young lion (Num. 23:24; Judg. 14:5; Ps. 104:21; Ezek. 19:2), or a female (Ezek. 19:2);

or a roaring beast (Job 4:10; Isa. 5:29). The warm, moist Jordan Valley was a favorite haunt of lurking lions (Jer. 49:19), but they were plentiful also in the mountains of Judaea

247. Lintel of a church at Subeita in the Negeb. The symbols are Christian.

and Samaria (II Kings 17:25; Song of Sol. 4:8). They menaced men (I Kings 13:24 f.); broke their bones (Isa. 38:13); and killed their flocks (I Sam. 17:34; Amos 3:12). Their terrifying roaring was frequently mentioned (Job 4:10; Prov. 20:2; Isa. 5:29; I Pet. 5:8). Yet they were also hunted for sport (II Sam. 23:20), and their killing was evidence of a man's strength (Samson, Judg. 14:5 f.; David, I Sam. 17:34–37). The most famous lion story in the O.T. is Dan. 6:16–23, climaxed by the declaration accredited to the Persian Darius, that the God of Daniel is the living God whose dominion "shall be even unto the end" (v. 26). In the N.T. the lion sometimes symbolizes Satan (I Pet. 5:8; but cf. Rev. 5:5).

Metaphorically, the lion appears frequently

248. Lion in Jerusalem Zoological Garden.

in Scripture: paired with a lamb and forming a symbol of peace (Isa. 11:6); expressing the vigor with which God pursues Job (Job 10:16); the voice of God (Jer. 25:30); typifying the king's rage (Prov. 19:12); and the boldness of the righteous (Prov. 28:1). Each of the living creatures seen by Ezekiel had a lion's face (1:10; cf. 10:14). The first of the four living creatures seen by John was like a lion (Rev. 4:7). Jesus was the "Lion of the tribe of Judah" (A.V. Rev. 5:5; cf. Gen. 49:9).

As early as the 12th century Western artists were using the lion to symbolize Mark, whose Gospel opens with the "voice of one crying in the wilderness." Mediaeval artists used a lion whose breath gave life on the third day to cubs born dead, to symbolize the Resurrection of Jesus. Mesopotamian art specialized in depicting lions. The walls bordering Babylon's Procession Street (606–539 B.C.) and leading from the Ishtar Gate to the Temple of Marduk were adorned with the famous sixty lions (sacred to the goddess Ishtar), done in relief on bricks, glazed in soft yellow and white, or red and yellow, against a background of deep blue or turquoise. Some of these are extant, and have been restored for museum use. They were probably seen *in situ* by Hebrew exiles, who were given freedom of movement throughout Babylon.

lizard, a reptile having a long body and tail, four legs, and a hide that is granulated or scaly. Lev. 11:29 f. lists as "unclean" several lizards under various names. Palestine has at least 40 recognized species, including the common, beautiful, green lizard, the sand lizard, the crocodile, and the chameleon. Lizards lurk in uninhabited areas, in warm crannies of rocks, on trees, and on walls and ceilings of houses.

loan. See BUSINESS; DEBT; PLEDGES; USURY.

loaves. See BAKER; BREAD; MIRACLES.

locks. (1) Of hair: Nazirites' (Num. 6:5); Samson's (Judg. 16:13, 19); Ezekiel's (Ezek. 8:3); Hebrew priests' (Ezek. 44:20). (2) Of doors (see DOORS).

locust. (1) The English rendering of several Heb. words for certain species of grasshoppers, of migratory habits, travelling in swarms and destructive of vegetation. In the Near East they have always been deemed edible. In the N.T. (esp. Matt. 3:4; Mark 1:6) the Gk. word translated "locust" refers to an insect, not the pod of a tree. Throughout the Biblical period, as today, plagues of locusts swept over Egypt and Palestine from Arabia, Sinai, and the Sudan, causing vast devastation. One such invasion reached the Egyptian Delta at the moment when the oppressed Israelites were pleading for freedom to flee the country. Pharaoh admitted that the locusts were a curse, yet he would not let the toilers go (Ex. 10; Ps. 78:46, 105:34). The account of locusts in Ex. 10 is accurate. They were carried to the coast by the E. wind (v. 14); they were so thick that they "covered the face of the whole earth" and devastated crops, trees, and herbs (v. 15). Locusts invaded in "bands" (Prov. 30:27); they looked like smoke (Rev. 9:3); and they appeared like horses prepared for battle (Rev. 9:7). The same plagues recur in Egypt and Palestine today, but are fought by scientific methods: the use of flame, the destruction of eggs, the digging of chemically treated trenches into which the locusts fall by the bushel, and the spreading of arsenic mixed with damp bran. Locust invasions tend to recur about every ten or fifteen years. Levitical Law permitted the use of locusts for food (Lev. 11:22). John the Baptist ate them. They are still consumed, along with unleavened bread and oil, by Bedouins and the poor while on journeys. Near-Easterners sometimes roast, broil, stew, or preserve locusts in brine, after removing the wings. Yet possession of the land by locusts which "camp in the hedges in the cold" was one of the curses threatened for Israel's disobedience (Deut. 28:42; Joel 1:1–4, 2:3–5; Nah. 3:15–17). Solomon in his traditional prayer at the dedication of the Temple besought for Israel immunity from locust plagues (I Kings 8:37).

249. Locusts devouring a thistle.

(2) The pods of the carob tree, containing a sweet pulp. Some Biblical exegetes have mistakenly suggested that this pulp was the food of John the Baptist in the wilderness (Matt. 3:4; Mark 1:6).

Lod (lŏd), see LYDDA.

Lo-debar (lō′dē′bär) (possibly Debir*), a place E. of the Jordan in Gilead, where Mephibosheth, the lame son of Jonathan, lived until summoned by David to his court (II Sam. 9:4 f.). People from this settlement, apparently near Mahanaim, sent provisions to David when he was a fugitive (II Sam. 17:27).

log. See WEIGHTS AND MEASURES.

logos, a Gk. term, meaning both "reason" and "word." It forms a part of many English words, like geology, biology, etc., in which it indicates that type of reasoning known as science; thus biology is the science of life (*bios*), and psychology is the science of the soul (*psyche*). When the term occurs in the Greek translation (the Septuagint) of the Heb. O.T. or in the Gk. N.T. it is usually with the meaning of "word." In the O.T. a common reference is to the word of God that comes to the prophet or that is spoken by the prophet (Isa. 38:4 f. shows both senses). "The word" is therefore a form of divine revelation, a means used by God to communicate to men the truth of Himself or the knowledge of His will. In Isa. 55:11 "the word" approaches personification, as though it acted of itself, a common note in the prophets (Hos. 1:1; Zeph. 2:5). In what is known as the Wisdom literature of the O.T., which includes Proverbs, this personification of God's self-utterance is carried still further, except that the divine "Word" is substituted by Wisdom (logos may mean "reason"). The classic example is in Prov. 8, where the divine Wisdom, represented as inseparable from God, speaks in the first person.

In John's Gospel, and by implication elsewhere in the N.T., the logos is identified with Jesus Christ, or, more exactly, Jesus Christ is declared (1:14) to be "the Word [logos] made flesh" or "incarnated." Only in John is the term itself actually used in this sense, and even by him only in the introductory section. He declares that the logos is a constituent of the divine nature, to be called otherwise the eternal Son, that "only-begotten" from the bosom of the Father, through whom came to men the divine truth and grace.

John sets forth the Gospel as the story of this "logos in the flesh," the Son of God appearing as the Son of Man. It was, he says, through the logos that men were created; it was with his nature that they were endowed (cf. Gen. 1:26 f.); it was through this same logos that they could apprehend the reality and the truth of God. But because sin had darkened men's minds it was necessary for the logos to "become flesh" to destroy this darkness and bring men to their true sonship to God. Jesus Christ was this logos incarnate. He became thereby "the Way, the Truth, and the Life" (14:6; cf. Heb. 10:20). He disclosed the truth that sets men free (8:32). He was the water of life (4:13, 14, 7:37–39); the bread of life (6:35); the door of the fold (10:7); the Good Shepherd (10:11); the resurrection and the life (11:25); the bearer of eternal life (17:2, 3), that is, of a quality of life that "the darkness" (1:5) could not destroy.

It is clear from all this that John does not use the logos idea merely to solve a philosophical problem about creation (1:3), but to emphasize the significance of Jesus Christ for human redemption. What comes to men through Christ comes from the very being of God Himself. To know the Son is to know the Father (14:9). To be one with the Son is to be one with the Father (17:22). Jesus Christ, "the logos made flesh," came to give men "abundant life" (10:10). It is precisely such life as Paul describes as "life hid with Christ in God" (Col. 3:3), which he says is what God purposed for men from the beginning (Eph. 1:3–10). The logos for John is therefore that Son who is forever inseparable from the Father, who determined the Father's creative method and purpose, and who eventually consented to be "made man" in order to bring the purpose—a family of sons (1:12, 13)—to completion. See INCARNATION; SON OF GOD; TRINITY. E. L.

loincloth. See DRESS.

Lois (lō′ĭs), the grandmother of Timothy.

She is described as a woman of "unfeigned faith" (II Tim. 1:5).

loom. See WEAVING.

lord, used in other senses than reference to God* and Jesus* Christ, includes: "Lords of the high places of Arnon" (Num. 21:28)—cultic figures honored at pagan worship centers, or possibly masters of ceremony at such pagan shrines; "lords of the Philistines"—petty kings, chieftains, or tyrants of the five Philistine city-states of Gaza, Ashkelon, Ashdod, Ekron, and Gath (Judg. 3:3; I Sam. 5:8). The "lord of the vineyard" (Matt. 20:8, 21:40) was the owner, who might let it out to a tenant husbandman, whose task it was to hire laborers and manage production. The "lord of the harvest" (Matt. 9:38) may be regarded as the foreman of the harvesters. The lords whom Herod invited to his birthday banquet (Mark 6:21) were his courtiers (and are so named in the R.S.V.).

Lord's Day, the, was first mentioned in Rev. 1:10. It is to be distinguished from "the day of the Lord" of the O.T. prophets (Amos 5:18–20; Zeph. 1:14–18; etc.), and from the N.T. idea of Christ's second advent. (See ESCHATOLOGY.) The Lord's Day, which became the Christian Sunday, was the 1st day of the week, when the earliest Christians assembled to worship. It was selected because on the 1st day of the week Jesus rose from the dead (John 20:1–19), and one week later visited his Disciples in Jerusalem (v. 26). For a time the Jewish members of the happy Christian company continued to observe the old Sabbath* also, "continuing daily in one accord in the temple" (Acts 2:46); but this observance had no meaning to the Gentile members of the early Church, who gradually outnumbered the Jewish converts. Therefore it was easy to make the transition from the 7th or Sabbath day to the 1st day for worship, cessation from labor, and fellowship. Possibly as early as the late N.T. period the "Lord's Day" came to be known as "Sunday," meaning to pagans "day of the sun" but to Christians the day when the Sun of Righteousness, Jesus, rose from the dead.

Descriptions of the activities of early Christians on the Lord's Day are found in Acts 2:41 ff., 20:7—the breaking of bread together in the observance of the Lord's Supper; preaching; leisurely fellowship; and the "laying in store" of money or other resources collected for needy converts. The earliest Christians at Jerusalem held daily meetings for worship and fellowship. But as the Church grew, the weekly gathering—often at night, when work was over—became more popular.

Today such sects as the Seventh Day Adventists and Seventh Day Baptists still observe the Sabbath on Saturday, the 7th day of the week.

250. The Lord's Prayer, reproduced in 35 languages in the court of the Church of the Pater Noster on the Mount of Olives. In the 4th century A.D. Constantine the Great erected on this site a basilica to mark the traditional spot where Jesus taught his disciples to pray.

Lord's Prayer, the, taught by Jesus to his Disciples, appears in two forms in the N.T. The briefer and probably older form is Luke 11:2–4. The longer form in Matthew 6:9–13 shows greater liturgical fullness, and ends with a doxology which was probably added in the first century to round out the prayer for public worship. Though the doxology appears in some versions of Matthew's Gospel and in the A.V., it is not found in the oldest and best Greek MSS., and is not included in the A.S.V. or the R.S.V., except in a footnote.

The context of the prayer differs in the two Gospels. In Matthew it is given as a model of prayer: "after this manner therefore pray ye" (6:9); and it illustrates the teaching about prayer in the Sermon on the Mount (6:1–8). In Luke it is a form to be used: "When ye pray, say . . ." (11:2). Here it is represented as Jesus' response to a disciple's request, "Lord, teach us to pray, as John also taught his disciples" (cf. 5:33).

Its Jewish background is seen in its echo of the language of synagogue litanies; in its opening ascription of praise; and in its naming of God as Father.

The two parts concern first the glory of God, then man's physical and spiritual necessities. Here God's holiness, His rule, and His will have priority over human needs. The longer form of the prayer may be outlined thus:

(1) Concerning God's glory—
- (a) Hallowed be thy name
- (b) Thy kingdom come
- (c) Thy will be done

} in earth, as it is in heaven

(2) Concerning man's needs—
- (a) Give us this day our daily bread
- (b) Forgive us our debts, as we forgive our debtors
- (c) Lead us not into temptation
- (d) Deliver us from evil

Abba, Father, Jesus' name for God (Mark 14:36; Luke 23:34) is rooted in a belief of late Judaism (cf. Tob. 13:4; Ecclus. 23:4; Wisd. of Sol. 2:16). Jesus filled this belief in God as Father with intense meaning, and bequeathed it to Christianity as its fundamental spirit (Rom. 8:15; Gal. 4:6). *Pater noster*, Lat. for the first two words, became a name for the prayer itself.

Divine forgiveness is contingent in this prayer on human forgiveness. This does not mean that God's forgiveness is limited to the measure of man's, nor that man's forgiveness is the ground on which God bestows His forgiveness; but that only as men are open to bestow forgiveness are they also open to receive it. The Aram. word for "debt" is used in the rabbinic writings to mean "sin," and Jesus' hearers would have understood it so.

"Lead us not into temptation" suggests more deliberate purpose than the Aram. word which Jesus probably used. A better translation would be: "Let us not enter into temptation" (cf. Mark 14:38). This cannot be taken as indicating God as the source and cause of temptation. Christian teaching was clear on this point: "Let no man say when he is tempted, I am tempted of God: for God cannot be tempted with evil, neither tempteth he any man" (Jas. 1:13). This petition does not reflect cowardice, but self-distrust in the face of the trials and temptations of human life; it is an acknowledgement that man's strength is insufficient and that he needs to be upheld by God's power—"but God is faithful, who will not suffer you to be tempted above that ye are able; but will with the temptation also make a way to escape, that ye may be able to bear it" (I Cor. 10:13). "And the Lord shall deliver me from every evil work, and will preserve me unto his heavenly kingdom" (II Tim. 4:18).

Lord's Supper, the (a phrase first used in I Cor. 11:20, where it refers to the love feast, common meal, agape*, commemorating the Last Supper; also called "the eucharist" (from *eucharistia*, "the giving of thanks"), is the Christian development of an old paschal custom of thanksgiving.

The Synoptists all record the institution of the Lord's Supper: Mark 14:22–25; Matt. 26:26–29 (based on Mark's earlier account); and Luke 22:14–20, related to Paul's narrative account of it (I Cor. 11:23–25). The Gospel of John contains no account of the first Lord's Supper.

Whether it was on the usual day, Friday Nisan 14, or on Thursday Nisan 13 that Jesus ate the Passover "with great desire" with his Disciples before his death (Mark 14:14; Matt. 26:17–19; Luke 22:7–13) is not clear. John 18:28 suggests that Jesus died on Friday afternoon, before the Passover of Friday Nisan 14, which began at sunset. Jesus may have been compelled by the swift development of the circumstances that precipitated his death to eat an anticipatory Passover with his disciples. This belief lies back of the Holy Thursday observance of the Lord's Supper in many churches today.

The incidents in connection with Christ's establishment of the Lord's Supper, as told by the three Synoptists, are: the preparation of the Passover in a "large upper room" (Mark 14:15; Luke 22:7–16); the celebration of the ancient Passover by Jesus and his Disciples (Matt. 26:20 f.); the announcement that one of the number would betray him (Matt. 26:21; Mark 14:18); the self-examination of the Disciples (Mark 14:19); the blessing by Jesus of a piece of bread (evidently remaining from the Passover) which he asked his Disciples to eat—his body given for them (Matt. 26:26). Next he took a cup of the remaining wine, gave thanks for it, and asked all his table companions to drink of it (Matt. 26:27), calling it his "blood of the new testament" (A.S.V. and R.S.V. "covenant") which is "shed for many for the remission of sins" (v. 28), and added that he would no more drink of the fruit of the vine until he drank it new in his Father's Kingdom. The words "This do in remembrance of me" (incorporated later in the Christian Communion ritual) are recorded by Paul (I Cor. 11:24 f.) but in the best Gk. manuscripts (cf. Luke 22:19 R.S.V. footnote) do not appear in the Synoptists' account of the first Lord's Supper.

Luke (22:17–20) makes the inauguration of the Last Supper occur before the announcement of Judas's imminent betrayal (v. 21–23), but some scholars believe that these verses are misplaced here. At any rate, neither Luke, Matthew, nor Mark records the departure of Judas; John does (13:30; cf. Luke 22:21–23). In the A.V. the Luke account of the Lord's Supper mentions two cups (22:17 and v. 20), one given perhaps as part of the old Passover, and the other inaugurating the new covenant. In the R.S.V. only one cup is mentioned (v. 20 being omitted except in the marginal reading)—the second being regarded by some authorities as an interpolation.

John omits the giving of the bread and wine, but does tell of the observance of the last Passover by Jesus with his Disciples (13:1 f.); the washing of the Disciples' feet (v. 2–12); the announcement of the betrayal (v. 21); the self-examination of the faithful (vv. 22–25), the entering of Satan into Judas (v. 27); the "do quickly" of Jesus (v. 27); his handing of the telltale sop to the betrayer (v. 30); and the departure of Judas into the night (30). Then the Gospel writer, with a clear sense of relief that the evil one has been purged out, launches into a statement of the new commandment of love (13:34), and his unique record of the profound last utterances of Jesus (chaps. 14–17). Both Jesus and his Disciples must have had in their minds the Suffering Servant poems of Isaiah 53 in the table talk of the one who was about to be sacrificed.

Paul's account of the institution and early observance of the Lord's Supper (I Cor. 11:23–25) is regarded as the earliest written record of it, penned probably not more than 30 years after its institution. But before Paul was even converted the Lord's Supper was actually being observed in the first Christian churches of Jerusalem. Paul's statement is less a detailed account of the first Lord's Supper in the Jerusalem upper room than a protest against the current lighthearted observance of the Lord's Supper, which savored of cultic meals in centers of Greek mystery religions (as at Eleusis, only a few m. E. of Corinth); it is a description of the ideal celebration of the Lord's Supper by Christian brothers (I Cor. 11:27–34).

Despite the variations within the individual records, and the different emphases the writers felt impelled to stress, the meaning of the sacrament is widely agreed on. Celebration of the Lord's Supper leads the faithful (1) to remember his personal redemption* by the blood of Jesus; (2) to remain grateful ("eucharistic") for his salvation; (3) and to keep alert for the ultimate coming of universal redemption.

World-wide observance of the service of Christian Communion, which developed from the Lord's Supper, brings all men into the range of inclusion in the living Christ, the body of the living Lord being the mystical body of the Church, where "we, being many, are one bread, and one body: for we are all partakers of that one bread" (I Cor. 10:17). The Communion service is the cornerstone of the ecumenical Church.

251. The Last Supper, *by Leonardo da Vinci;* detail shows Jesus, with James and Thomas at his left.

In addition to "the Lord's Supper," "the Eucharist," "the breaking of bread," "Thanksgiving," and "the Holy Communion," the following names are given to this sacrament by various bodies of Christian believers: "the divine liturgy" (by the Greek and Russian Orthodox churches), "the Mass" (by the Roman Catholic Church); "the present" or "the oblation" (by the Armenian and Coptic churches); "the consecration" (by the Abyssinian or Ethiopian Church). Each of these terms stresses an aspect of this solemn sacrament of Christendom. (See SACRAMENTS).

Lot, a son of Haran (Gen. 11:27), nephew of the Patriarch Abraham, with whom he migrated from Ur of the Chaldees to Haran and ultimately to Canaan (11:31, 12:5). Lot accompanied Abraham to Egypt (13:1), and after they returned both he and Abraham became so prosperous in flocks and herds that their herdsmen quarreled (13:2, 5–7). Abraham offered him a choice of territory, and Lot, eyeing the fertile plain of the Jordan*—apparently before the cataclysm of nature which caused the great waste around the N. end of the Dead Sea (13:10)—selected what he thought was the better area, well watered, a "garden of the Lord" (v. 10). This choice left Canaan for Abraham, and paved the way for the destiny God had in mind for him as founder of a people in the little strip between the Mediterranean and the Jordan. Lot later benefited again from Abraham's patriarchal goodwill: when he was carried off by Chedorlaomer* and his confederates in the struggle of the four-kings-versus-five-kings in the region of Sodom where Lot had settled, Abraham went as far N. as Dan (Gen. 14) to rescue him. Lot was freed after a struggle at Hobah, W. of Damascus.

The next chapter in Lot's career is told in Gen. 19—his entertainment of two men angels at Sodom; their warning to him to flee with his family from the imminent destruction God had prepared for the evil city; his flight with his daughters; his loss of his wife because when she looked back toward their lost estate she was turned into one of the weird pillars (Gen. 19:26) such as are today seen in the Dead Sea wasteland of mirages. By his own two daughters Lot helped to repeople the devastated world; one bore a son, Moab, "father of the Moabites" (v. 37), and the other Ben-ammi, "father of the children of Ammon" (v. 37 f.)—an uncomplimentary effort of the writer to account for the origin of the Moabites and Ammonites, problem-neighbors of later Israel. Moses could not acquire Moab, because God had given it to the descendants of Lot (Deut. 2:9). Wandering Israel passed across Ammon's border (Deut. 2:19), under instructions from Yahweh not to engage the people in any way.

The fire-and-brimstone tragedy of Lot's land near the Dead Sea was long remembered by Hebrews. Jesus referred to it (Luke 17:28 f.); also the author of II Pet. 2:6–8. The Arab name for the Dead Sea today is Bahr Lût ("The Sea of Lot").

lot, lots, In modern understanding a lot in its primary meaning is an object used in deciding a matter by chance, a number of these being placed in a container and then drawn or cast out at random. In the Biblical world this method of deciding portentous questions had a wide use and great prestige. It was a sort of divination, a method of appeal to one's god, free from all influence of passion or bias, a method of ascertaining the divine will. Among the Hebrews the use of lots, with a religious intention, direct or indirect, persisted into N.T. times, and was never considered a practice bordering on magic, and therefore condemned, as were certain practices of Israel's neighbors (Deut. 18:10–12). The true O.T. estimate of the use of lots is set forth in Prov. 16:33: "The lot is cast into the lap, but the decision is wholly from the Lord." Casting lots was a serious matter: Joshua, for example, states that he will cast lots for the tribes of Israel "before the Lord."

The character and shape of the lot used in the Bible are not known, nor is the method by which they were cast. Possibly smooth stones distinguishable by color or by symbols marked upon them were deposited in a container, which was then shaken until one lot jumped out. The ceremony was commonly preceded by prayer, making the act an appeal to God to decide the matter. The disciples refer to their Risen Lord the question of the successor to Judas (Acts 1:23–26). See MAGIC AND DIVINATION.

love, the chief quality or attribute of ideal character. Its highest O.T. expression is the command to love God with all one's being, part of the so-called Shema (Deut. 6:4 f.), and one's neighbor as oneself (Lev. 19:18), both of which are quoted by Jesus (Matt. 22:37 ff.), Love was emphasized by Jesus in his pronouncement of the greatest law, and his teaching of the "new commandment" at the inauguration of the Lord's Supper (John 13:34). Love in the sense of mutual love between God and people is unique in the religion of Jew and Christian as compared to other faiths.

(1) *In the O.T.* one Heb. word is used for various types of love: (a) parental affection, as "Rebekah loved Jacob" (Gen. 25:28); (b) strong physical desire ("I love Tamar," II Sam. 13:4); (c) the Lord's love of Israel (Deut. 4:37; Mal. 1:2) and Jerusalem (Ps. 87:2); (d) Israel's love of Yahweh, of which there are many expressions throughout Scripture (Ex. 20:6; Ps. 31:23). The first O.T. writer to present God as pre-eminently a God of love, devoted to the well-being of His chosen people, is Hosea*. Out of this prophet's personal suffering came such tender passages as that of the loving Father (Hos. 11:1–4). To Hosea God's love was both tender and firm, a combination of qualities unfamiliar to his people. To Jeremiah also God was a God of love, devoted to His people with an eternal love (31:3), just, truthful, and righteous. The Third Isaiah thought of God's love in terms of lovingkindness and pity (63:7–10).

The O.T. frankly depicts Israel's love to God as frequently wayward, in spite of the covenant made with the Lord in their early group experiences (Ps. 78:17, 32, 56; Isa. 1:2 f.). God's love could be full of the wrath of offended love (Deut. 7:7–11), and could flame up in jealousy at the spectacle of idolatry (Jer. 44:3 f.). His capacity for universal love extending to all peoples and throughout eternity is expressed in Ps. 145:9–13 (cf. Luke 2:29–32; Tit. 3:4).

(2) *In the N.T.* The rich Gk. language in which the N.T. is written has several words for love: *erōs*, for sexual love; *storgē*, for family affection; *philia*, for friendship between man and man or woman and woman; *philanthropia*, for humanitarianism; *agape**, a late word, found in the Septuagint* and adopted by the N.T. writers to express the distinctive character of Christian love. Love in the N.T. includes (a) God's love to man (John 3:16), for whom He has prepared unbelievable blessings (I Cor. 2:9), because

His very nature is love (I John 4:8); (b) man's love to God (Rom. 8:28; I Cor. 8:3; I John 5:2); and (c) man's love of his fellows (John 15:13; Gal. 5:14; Rom. 13:8). This trinity of love is expressed in John 15:9.

In the N.T., love, which finds its loftiest descriptions in I Cor. 13 and I John 4, is best exemplified in the life and attitudes of Jesus, who, having from youth followed the principles of the love of God and the love of man, bound them together in his summary spoken to the lawyer who inquired concerning the greatest commandment (Matt. 22:37–39). A distinctive contribution of the N.T. to the total content of love is the inclusion of affectionate regard for one's enemies. Whereas the O.T. had sanctioned the *lex talionis*, the seizing of eye for eye, as an acceptable principle in civil law (but cf. Prov. 24:17, 25:21), Jesus challenged men unequivocally, "Love your enemies, bless them that curse you, do good to them that hate you, and pray for them which despitefully use you, and persecute you; that ye may be the children of your Father which is in heaven" (Matt. 5:44 f.). His own ability to pray God to forgive even those who brought him to the cross, excusing them because they knew not what they were doing (Luke 23:34), is one of the most convincing witnesses of his divine sonship (cf. Acts 7:60).

For Jesus love asked no reward other than the spiritual satisfaction of knowing that its action was Godlike (Luke 6:35 f.). "Who loveth God love his brother also" (I John 4:21). The Christian life is a working out of the principle of love in all social attitudes and relationships, with a view to doing what will be best for all, for the greatest length of time, in the spirit which Christ brought to the solution of people's wants in his time.

The personality of Jesus himself must have been the original from which Paul painted his great Corinthian portrait of perfect love (I Cor. 13). The love incarnated in Jesus, never failing in any situation of temptation, disappointment, betrayal, or even death, taught Paul, and continues to teach Christians today, how to think concerning the love of God. Love in N.T. theology is the first "fruit" of the regenerated, grateful spirit (Gal. 5:22), responding to God's love, expressed superlatively and for all time in the Crucifixion and the Resurrection of Jesus.

love feast. See AGAPE.

lovingkindness, an expression used in the A.V. of the O.T. to translate a Heb. word (*chesed*) which covers a range of meaning encompassed by no single English word. The A.V. also translates it frequently by "mercy," "pity," "favor," "goodness," etc. Modern studies show that the Heb. word, in its original sense, included the idea of loyalty and steadfastness along with love, and that it often appears in passages having to do with fidelity to covenant obligations (Deut. 7:9; I Kings 8:23—A.V. "mercy"). Some suggest it might be translated consistently "loyal love": R.S.V., more often than not, translates it "steadfast love"; N.E.B. translates variously "constant love," "faith," etc. The moral quality it denotes is proper to God (A.V. uses "lovingkindness" only for this sense: Ps. 40:10; Isa. 63:7; Jer. 9:24), but is often manifested by men also (Josh. 2:12; I Sam. 20:15; I Chron. 19:2—A.V. "kindness"). Unfortunately the English translation often obscures the presence of this richly evocative word in the original and makes comparison of passages difficult.

R. C. D.

Lubim (lū′bĭm), an ancient people, Libyans (cf. Dan. 11:43), living in N. Africa, W. of Egypt, in what today is Cyrenaica in Libya. They are mentioned in II Chron. 12:3 as coming in great numbers with Shishak (Sheshonk), King of Egypt, against Jerusalem (vv. 2–9), with the Sukkiim and the Ethiopians. Some authorities regard the Biblical Shishak as the founder of their dynasty, which invaded Egypt in the 10th century B.C. and headed the Twenty-second Egyptian Dynasty, the first of the Libyan period.

Lucifer (lū′sĭ-fẽr) ("light-bringer"), a name given the planet Venus when it is the morning star. It is used in Isa. 14:12, A.V. to render the Heb. "shining one" applied to the King of Babylon, fallen from his high estate. In the 3d century A.D. the saying of Jesus: "I beheld Satan as lightning fall from heaven" (Luke 10:18) was erroneously supposed to refer to Isa. 14:12. Hence Lucifer came to be regarded as the name of Satan before his fall.

Lucius (not Luke). (1) A man of Cyrene who served in the Antioch Church as teacher and prophet (Acts 13:1). (2) A kinsman of Paul—possibly the same as (1)—who joined the Apostle in sending greetings from Corinth to Christians at Rome (Rom. 16:21).

Lud (lŭd), **Ludim** (lū′dĭm). (1) A place, and a people, of W. Asia Minor, including the Lydians (see LYDIA) but occupying a more extensive territory than Lydia proper. The Ludim are mentioned in the list of peoples in Gen. 10:22 and I Chron. 1:17, along with Elam, Asshur, Arphaxad, and Aram, as children of Shem. Lydians were not Semites. They may have been a lost N. Syrian tribe. (2) In Egypt Ludim are listed as descendants of Mizraim or Egypt (Gen. 10:13), renowned archers employed in the Egyptian and Tyrian armies (Isa. 66:19; Jer. 46:9; Ezek. 27:10).

Luke (from Gk. *Loukas*, a shortened form of the Latin *Lucanus* or *Lucius*, once in A.V. *Lucas*, Philem. 24), a physician and companion of Paul mentioned by name three times (Col. 4:14; Philem. 24; II Tim. 4:11). His identification with Lucius of Cyrene (Acts 13:1) is improbable. The Third Gospel and the Acts* of the Apostles, believed to have been written by Luke, indirectly furnish valuable data concerning his life.

Luke apparently joined Paul as companion on his Second Missionary Journey at Troas, where the account changes for the first time to the first person plural (Acts 16:11). Some believe that the man of Macedonia who appealed to Paul for help was Luke the physician, who urged this first evangelistic venture into the European continent (Acts 16:9 f.). Luke's familiarity with Greek cities was that of one who knew Achaea (Acts 16:12 f., 17:16, 19, 21, 18:8). Luke rejoined the Apostle again at Philippi on the Third Missionary Journey (Acts 20:5), and went with him to Jerusalem. During the two years in which Paul was imprisoned at Caesarea Luke had opportunity to gather data for his Gospel; some scholars believe he may have written a first brief draft of his Gospel at this time. He sailed with the Apostle to Rome. His Gentile background is implied in Paul's listing of his companions (Col. 4:10–14). Because he is believed to be the writer of one of the four Gospels he is called "the Evangelist."

Luke was a much-traveled Greek (a few believe he was Jewish), acquainted with the technicalities of navigation (Acts 27). He had a well-trained mind, excellent literary ability, and marked reportorial skill (Luke 1:1–3). He served as a literary bridge spanning the gulf between the Jewish and the Gentile world. He addressed his literary labors to Romans and Greeks—Theophilus, a Greek, was his patron (Luke 1:3; Acts 1:1).

The relationship between Paul and Luke was based not only on Christian fellowship, but on the ministry of this "beloved physician" (Col. 4:14) to the physically afflicted Paul (II Cor. 12:7; Gal. 4:13–15). The access which the physician has to the realities of life and people gives authenticity to the career of Paul as Luke narrates it in detail. Luke's exclusive narratives concerning the birth of John and of Jesus are such as would interest a physician, to whom such personal disclosures would be confided (Luke 2:19). Among the evidences of the physician's touch in his Gospel, not referred to elsewhere, are the "great fever" (Luke 4:38, cf. Matt. 8:14; Mark 1:30); the ability of the restored daughter of Jairus to eat "meat" after she recovered (Luke 8:55, cf. Matt. 9:25; Mark 5:42); and the Parable of the Good Samaritan, with its first-aid episode (Luke 10:25–37). "Healed" (Acts 28:8) and "cured" (Acts 28:9, A.S.V. and R.S.V.) may refer to recovery through prayer and the medical science of the day as practiced by Luke. The physician includes himself among those who were honored for services rendered to the Maltese (Acts 28:10).

Luke was a kindly, evangelistic literary genius and 1st-century physician who dedicated all that he had to the universal Christ in varied service to his fellow men.

Luke, the Gospel of, the 3d book of the N.T. This Gospel, together with the Acts of the Apostles, originally formed a two-volume treatise on the origin of Christianity and its spread from Jerusalem to Rome. In the 2d century, when the present four canonical Gospels began to be circulated together as "the Gospel," Luke's Gospel and The Acts became separated. Their original close connection, however, is proved by their similarity of vocabulary, style, and outlook, and by their common dedication to Theophilus (Luke 1:3; Acts 1:1).

The author is nowhere mentioned by name in Luke or Acts, but he speaks of himself in the prologue of Luke, and indicates in the "we" sections of Acts that he was present (16:10–17, 20:5–15, 21:1–17, 27:1–28:16). In the prologue he does not claim to have been a personal witness of Jesus, but to have been in touch with those who had been witnesses and to have studied the work of previous Gospel writers. The "we" sections of Acts were in all probability written by the author himself as a travel diary of his journeys with Paul. Since the 2d century tradition has unanimously identified the author as Luke, the travelling companion of Paul (Col. 4:14; Philem. 24; II Tim. 4:11). The fact that Luke was not otherwise a prominent person adds weight to the tradition ascribing authorship to him. Moreover, in Ephesus, Jerusalem, Caesarea, possibly in Antioch and Rome, and from close association with Paul, Luke had opportunities to learn the early facts of Christianity from those who "from the beginning were eyewitnesses, and ministers of the word" (Luke 1:2). While not absolutely proved, the authorship of the Gospel and Acts by Luke, "the beloved physician" and Gentile companion of Paul, is the most probable of the theories of authorship.

The Gospel falls naturally into five sections:

The introduction—1:1–4.
(1) Early years of Jesus—1:5–2:52.
(2) Preparation for the ministry—3:1–4:13.
(3) The ministry in Galilee—4:14–9:50.
(4) Journey to Jerusalem—9:51–19:44.
(5) Crucifixion and Resurrection—19:45–24:53.

A comparison with Mark and Matthew shows Luke's dependence on Mark and many agreements with Matthew. A third of Luke's Gospel is drawn from Mark. Luke treats his sections borrowed from Mark objectively, and follows Mark's chronology. Though Luke condenses the narrative and improves the style, he does not add statements of time or place where these are absent in Mark. The following sections of Luke are based on Mark:

Luke	*Mark*
4:31–44	1:29–39
5:12–6:19	1:40–3:19
8:4–9:50	4:1–9:40
18:15–43	10:13–52
19:29–22:13	9:1–14:17

Many sections of Luke have no parallels in Mark but resemble Matthew. The similarity of the language in the sections common to Luke and Matthew indicates their use of the same source, now lost, but designated by scholars as "Q" (*quelle*, "source"). The following are a few examples of the many parallel sections in Luke and Matthew believed to be derived from Q:

Four Beatitudes—Luke 6:20–23	Matt. 5:3, 4, 6, 11, 12
The law of love—6:27–36	5:38–48
Instructions for mission work—10:2–12	9:37 f. 10:7–16

LUKE, THE GOSPEL OF

The Lord's Prayer—
11:2–4 6:9–13
The promise of the Spirit
to the Disciples—
12:11 f. 10:19 f.

As these and other sections where Luke and Matthew agree deal mainly with the teachings and sayings of Jesus, a subject not fully treated in Mark, it is believed that Q was a collection of the sayings of Jesus drawn up to meet the questions and problems of early Christians.

Nearly half of Luke's material is peculiar to his Gospel. This special material, usually designated as "L," includes such stories as:

The birth narratives—1:5–2:52.
Jesus' sermon at Nazareth—4:16–30.
The Parable of the Good Samaritan—10:29–37.
Mary and Martha—10:38–42.
The Parable of the Friend at Midnight—11:5–8.
The Parables of the Lost Coin and the Lost Son—15:8–10, 11–32.
The Parables of Dives and Lazarus—16:19–31.
The Conversion of Zacchaeus—19:1–10.
The penitent thief on the cross—23:40–43.
The Disciples going to Emmaus—24:13–35.
The Ascension—24:50–53.

From this partial list it can be seen that Luke's special material gives the whole Gospel its characteristic quality. In L are some of Jesus' most memorable parables. Here are evidences of his interest in Samaritans; his teachings about the right use of wealth; his emphasis on prayer; his understanding and sympathy for women; and his graciousness to the penitent.

Luke's method of using his sources is accounted for by several theories. Many scholars believe Mark is the basis for Luke and that to it were added selections from Q and L. Possibly Q and L were already combined in a written document when Luke found them; if so, Luke would have been less an author than an editor combining existing materials. According to another theory, Luke collected his L material in both oral and written form from Christians he met during his sojourn in Judaea and at Caesarea. He combined this material with Q to form the first draft of the Gospel, sometimes called proto-Luke. Later he expanded this by adding sections from Mark.

The Gospel was issued in its final form certainly after Mark and before the publication of Acts, probably c. A.D. 75 or soon thereafter.

Luke's purpose was evidently to compile from the existing miscellaneous records an account of Christian beginnings that would be accurate, well arranged, and authoritative (1:1–4). He aimed to present the historical facts to a Roman official, "most excellent Theophilus," and to the world at large, not merely to allay suspicion of Christianity, but more especially to recommend it to intelligent Gentiles outside the Church. That Gentile readers were addressed is evident from the fact that Hebrew words are explained (6:15, 23:33), and places in Palestine are located (4:31, 8:26, 23:51).

The distinctive features of this Gospel spring from the author's purpose, and may be summarized as (1) its literary quality; (2) its universal appeal; (3) its humanitarian sympathies; (4) its emphasis on prayer; (5) its teaching about the Holy Spirit; (6) and its undercurrent of Christian defense against suspicion by Roman officials. This is the most literary of the Gospels, for it is readable, written in good Greek, carefully arranged, and full of interesting narrative. It displays an absence of theology which indicates that Luke and his readers were not primarily interested in doctrinal questions.

The universal appeal of this Gospel is seen in its inclusion of the Gentiles in salvation—its preaching of the "good tidings of great joy, which shall be to all people" (2:10, cf. 13:29). Paul did much to fashion the universality of Luke's outlook. Luke passes over that part of Jesus' teaching which deals with Jewish interests, but features those aspects of his teaching and life that have universal human appeal, such as the Parables of the Good Samaritan and the Lost Son, and the stories of the woman in Simon's house and of Zacchaeus. Quotations from the O.T. are few, except in the sayings of Jesus (4:4, 8, 7:27). There are only 5 references to prophecy, and of these only one occurs in the narrative of the author. This Gospel opposes exclusiveness and intolerance (e.g., 10:25 ff.) and from beginning to end expresses the universality of Christianity (3:5 ff., 24:47).

The Third Gospel makes a strong humanitarian appeal. Its sympathies are with the poor. This is seen at the outset from Mary's song (1:51–53), from John the Baptist's preaching (3:11–13), and from Jesus' opening announcement that he was sent "to preach the gospel to the poor" (4:18). Special blessings are promised to the poor (6:20) and the hungry (v. 21), while woes are pronounced upon the well-fed, complacent, and socially popular (vv. 24–26). Generosity is recommended toward those in need (vv. 27–38). Such parables as that of Dives and Lazarus reflect sympathy with the poor.

The constant emphasis on prayer is seen in references to Jesus praying (3:21, 6:12, 9:18, 29, 11:1) and in the parables of the Friend at Midnight (11:5–8) and the Unjust Judge (18:1–8).

References to the Holy Spirit, though more numerous in Acts, are a marked feature of this Gospel (1:15, 35, 41, 67, 2:25–27, 3:16, 4:1, 11:13, 12:12).

The Third Gospel displays an undercurrent of Christian defense against Roman objections that Christianity is an unlawful religion with revolutionary tendencies. It showed that Christianity was true Judaism (2:34 f., 3:8), and that it was faithful to the synagogue (4:16), the Temple (19:45–47), and the Scriptures (4:21). Christianity was therefore due the recognition and privileges accorded Judaism under Roman law. From the beginning Christianity was identified with the Empire (2:1–3), was responsive to Roman citizens, law, and custom (3:14, 5:27–32,

7:2–9), and never condoned dangerous methods of action (4:5–8, 20:20–26, 22:50–53). Jesus was never guilty of revolution (23:1–4, 15, 20–24, 47). The revolutionary record of Barabbas (23:19, 25) was given to impress the law-respecting Romans with the injustice done Jesus.

lute. See MUSIC.

Luz (lŭz). (1) A Canaanite town N. of Jerusalem adjacent to Ai*. In Gen. 28:19 and Judg. 1:23–26 it seems an earlier name of Bethel, though Josh. 16:2 suggests that Luz and Bethel were not identical. Possibly Jacob built his Bethel altar (Gen. 35:6) on the outskirts of Luz. (2) A town in Hittite territory, possibly c. 4 m. NW. of Banias, founded by a fugitive from Luz (1) (Judg. 1:22–26).

LXX, the abbreviation commonly used for the Septuagint or Greek Version of the O.T. See SEPTUAGINT; TEXT.

Lycaonia (lĭk′ā-ō′nĭ-ȧ), a district in Asia Minor varying in extent at different times, but usually bounded by Cappadocia, Phrygia,

252. Lycaonia.

Pisidia, Cilicia, and Isauria. This high tableland N. of the Taurus Mts. was annexed to Galatia c. 35 B.C., but was added, along with the Kingdom of Galatia, to the Roman Empire c. 25 B.C. In Lycaonia (Acts 14:6, 11) Paul visited Derbe and Lystra. Lycaonians were wild borderland people, which explains in part their treatment of Paul (Acts 13:50, 14:19).

Lycia (lĭsh′ĭ-ȧ), a province of SW. Asia Minor, today a region of Anatolian Turkey bordering the Mediterranean in a peninsula E. of Rhodes, almost opposite Alexandria, with which Egyptian port its harbor city, Patara, traded in ancient times. Its wooded mountains and fertile Xanthus Valley produced wealth which fostered many cities, like Patara, from which Paul sailed to Phoenicia (Acts 21:1), and Myra, in whose busy harbor he boarded an Alexandrian ship for Italy (27:5 f.). Lycia was the original home of the Philistines, who early migrated to Crete, and then to the plain along the Mediterranean in SW. Palestine. At about the same time that the Hebrews were settling the hill country of Judaea these migrant Lycian Philistines were getting control of Canaanite cities and dominating the coast and the Shephelah. Lycia, after feeling the masterful hand of the Persians, or Alexander the Great, and of the Seleucids, was incorporated into the Roman Empire and later made a self-governing province, possibly by Claudius. Its prosperous citizens developed centers of Hellenistic culture, as attested by the surviving ruins of theaters and other civic structures. (See LYCAONIA, illus. 252.)

Lydda (Lod, Ludd), a town in the fertile Plain of Sharon c. 70 m. S. of Haifa, c. 11 m. SE. of Joppa (Acts 9:38), mentioned in I Chron. 8:12, Ezra 2:33, Neh. 7:37. Its chief interest to Biblical students is because of Peter's cure here of a palsied man, Aeneas (Acts 9:32–35). The man's recovery led to the conversion of "all that dwelt at Lydda."

Lydda was the traditional site of the martyrdom of St. George, reputed to have been buried here c. A.D. 303, revered by Crusaders, adopted through Richard Coeur de Lion as the patron saint of England, and recognized as patron of Syrian Christendom. St. George was the symbol of righteousness, triumphant over the slimy dragon of sin. In this role he was possibly the successor of an ancient spirit of vegetation. The Lydda Church of St. George built by 12th-century Crusaders is represented by surviving fragments. Lydda is a chief airport of Israel.

Lydia. (1) A powerful kingdom of W. Asia Minor, facing the Aegean and W. of Phrygia. Its capital was Sepharad (Sardis*). Ezekiel mentioned it in a "day of the Lord" prophecy (30:5), foretelling the destruction of this ally of Egypt; Jeremiah also (46:9). C. 546 B.C. Sardis fell to Cyrus the Persian, and its King Croesus, associated with the invention of coinage, was prisoner. (See LYCAONIA, illus. 252.)

(2) A "certain woman . . . seller of purple, of the city of Thyatira" (Akhisar), SE. of Pergamum in the Roman Province of Asia (now Anatolian Turkey). Acts 16:14 tells of her being a worshipper of God, who, when Paul came into the Macedonian city of Philippi where she was engaged in selling purple-dyed textiles or the murex secretion from mollusks used for coloring materials, was stirred by the Lord through the preaching of the Apostle. Prosperous Lydia was converted and baptized with her whole household—the first recorded Christian convert in Europe. Immediately her innate hospitality manifested itself with gracious modesty. Because of her "constraining" persuasion, her invitation was accepted (v. 15). To her home Paul and Silas returned (v. 40) after they had been miraculously released from imprisonment for curing a young woman whose soothsaying had brought her masters much gain (v. 16). She possibly became one of the women helpers mentioned in Phil. 4:3 as laboring with him in the spread of the Gospel.

lying was prohibited by Israel's early Law codes as unbecoming in a group which had covenanted to be the chosen people of Yahweh, Whose nature was truth (I Sam. 15:29;

Ps. 89:34 f.; cf. John 17:17). Lying was forbidden in the Ninth Commandment (Ex. 20:16; cf. Lev. 19:11 ff.). The bringing of false reports was forbidden (Ex. 23:1). Falsifying was punishable by the law of revenge ("eye for an eye," Deut. 19:16–21). Breaking a vow accompanied by an oath was a sin, restitution for which was prescribed (Lev. 5). Prophets were constantly warring against lying in its various current forms: in words (Hos. 7:13); in false weights (Mic. 6:11). Jesus taught men not to make any oaths (Matt. 5:33–38); to him the devil was the father of lies (John 8:44). In the N.T. truth was axiomatic for Christians (Eph. 4:24 f. cf. Zech. 8:16 Col. 3:9), though they lived in a corrupt Graeco-Roman world whose paganism, said Paul, was "based on a lie" (Rom. 1:25). The theology of Rev. 21:8 pointed to "the second death" for liars.

lyre. See MUSIC.

Lysanias (lī-sā′nĭ-ăs), tetrarch or governor of a region known as Abilene, watered by the Abana River and situated between Damascus and Heliopolis (Baalbek) on the N. side of Mt. Hermon. The reference to him in Luke 3:1 as a contemporary of John the Baptist is believed by many to be erroneous.

Lysias Claudius. See CLAUDIUS LYSIAS.

Lystra (lĭs′tră), a city in the Lycaonian section of the Roman province of Galatia, c. 25 m. SSW. of Iconium and on the "Imperial Road" to Pisidian Antioch. There Paul and Barnabas were so successful in their ministry of healing (Acts 14:6–19) that they were hailed at the entrance to the city as "Jupiter and Mercury." Ill treatment did not deter the Apostle from visiting the city four times (Acts 14:6, 21, 16:1, 18:23). In Lystra (or in Derbe) he met Timothy, and he sent his Letter to the Galatians* to it, as to other cities where he had founded churches. The site of Lystra was identified in modern times by an altar found standing erect in its original position and carrying a Lat. inscription including the Lat. name of the city, Lustra.

M

Maacah (mā′ă-kă), sometimes in the A.V. Maachah, Beth-maachah; A.S.V. Josh. 13:13 Maacath (mā′ă-kăth) (? "oppression"). (1) A conspicuous, flat-topped city mound, Tell Abil, the Biblical Abel-beth-maachah, overlooking the marshlands of Lake Huleh near the Jordan headwaters, a short distance S. of Dan and Mt. Hermon, and N. of the Geshur region in the time of David and Solomon. II Sam. 20:14–23 tells of the city being so important that it was regarded as "a mother in Israel," "an inheritance of the Lord" (v. 19). It was defended, as was Lachish, by a bank cast up against the city, so that only by the battering of many people could it be cast down (II Sam. 20:15). In the reign of David a man named Sheba led a revolt and fled to Maacah. To seize him, David's general Joab made ready to lay siege to the town, but was dissuaded when a "wise woman" promised that she would toss the rebel's head over the wall if Joab would spare the city; Sheba was destroyed and Maacah spared. Abel-beth-maachah, today one of the most impressive mounds in Palestine, is framed in fig boughs. It substantiates the words of Josh. 13:13: "the children of Israel expelled not . . . the Maachathites: . . . the Maachathites dwell among the Israelites until this day." The region around the Abel-beth-maachah hillock was called Maachah, and the people of its clan Maachathites (Deut. 3:14; Josh. 12:5, 13:11; I Chron. 4:19; Jer. 40:8). See ABEL.

(2) Several men and women of the O.T. were named Maacah. The women were: a concubine of Caleb (I Chron. 2:48); the wife of Machir, son of Manasseh (I Chron. 7:15 f.); the wife of Jehiel and forebear of Saul (I Chron. 8:29, 9:35); a daughter of Talmai, King of Geshur, who became a wife of David and the mother of Absalom (II Sam. 3:3; I Chron. 3:2); the wife of King Rehoboam of Israel, daughter or granddaughter of Absalom (I Kings 15:2; II Chron. 11:20–22), and the mother of King Abijah, serving as queen mother until Asa rejected her for making an image of Asherah (II Chron. 15:16 A.S.V.). Men named Maacah were: the father of Achish of Gath, a contemporary of Solomon (I Kings 2:39); the father of Hanan, a henchman of David (I Chron. 11:43).

Maaseiah (mā′ă-sē′yă), ("the work of Jehovah"), the name of numerous men in the O.T. (1) A Levite singer (I Chron. 15:18, 20). (2) A captain of Jehoiada's forces who went against Athaliah (II Chron. 23:1). (3) One of Uzziah's officers (II Chron. 26:11). (4) A son of Ahaz (II Chron. 28:7). (5) A governor of Jerusalem (II Chron. 34:8). (6) A Temple officer (Jer. 35:4), possibly the same as (7). (7) A priest (Jer. 21:1, 29:25, 37:3). (8) The father of the fraudulent priest Zedekiah (Jer. 29:21). (9), (10), (11) Priests who had foreign wives (Ezra 10:18, 21 f.). (12) A son of Pahath-moab, husband of a foreign wife (Ezra 10:30). (13) The father of Ahaziah, who co-operated in building the Jerusalem wall (Neh. 3:23). (14) A man who stood beside Ezra during the reading of the Law (Neh. 8:4). (15) One who helped the people understand the Law (Neh. 8:7). (16) One who sealed the covenant in Jerusalem after the Exile* (Neh. 10:25). (17) A son of Baruch (Neh. 11:5). (18) A family name among Benjamites (Neh. 11:7). (19), (20) Two priests (Neh. 12:41 f.).

Maccabees, the family which won religious and political independence for the Jews and ruled them from 166 to 63 B.C.—or to 37 B.C. if one considers the priesthood period. The dynasty derives its name from Judas, who was called Maccabee (perhaps from the Aram.

maqqaba, "hammer"). He was 3d of five sons of the aged priest Mattathias, who struck the first blow for religious freedom against Antiochus IV (Epiphanes) of Syria (175–163 B.C.), the Seleucid king who controlled Palestine. The great-grandfather of Mattathias, according to Josephus and Talmudic sources, was Hashmon, and the family is more correctly called Hasmonaeans or Asmonaeans.

The cause of the Maccabean rebellion was the attempt of Antiochus IV to force Hellenistic culture on the Jews and to destroy

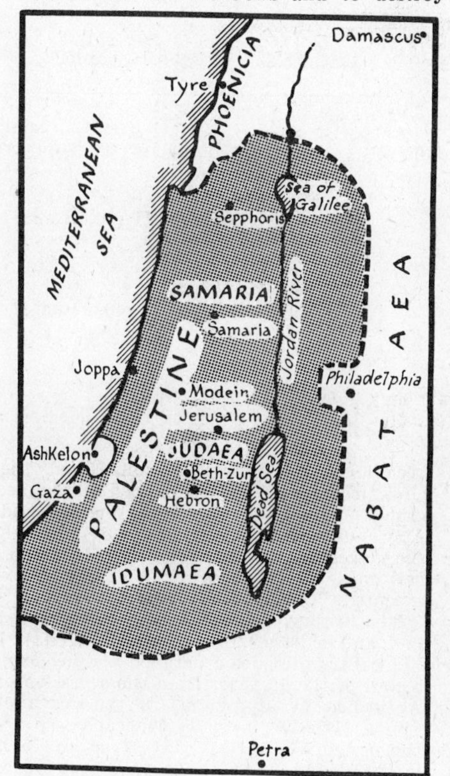

253. Palestine in the Maccabean Period.

Judaism. In December of 168 B.C. Antiochus defiled the Temple at Jerusalem by sacrificing swine to Zeus on a small Greek altar ("the abomination that maketh desolate" Dan. 11:31), erected over the great altar of burnt offerings. Under penalty of death Antiochus prohibited all religious observances ordained in the Law of Moses, such as keeping the Sabbath and circumcision. He had all copies of the Law burned. Heathen altars were erected throughout Palestine, and the worship of heathen gods became compulsory. Some Jews, who had already adopted Hellenistic culture, complied with the royal edict. Others, the Hasidim, or Pious, offered passive resistance. Their attitude is described in the Book of Daniel (3:17 f.), which was written by a Hasid to encourage the faithful during this persecution. A third group, led by the Maccabees, openly defied the royal edict and fought for their faith.

The Maccabean rebellion began when Mattathias, the aged priest at Modin, not only refused to offer heathen sacrifices, but killed an apostate Jew who was about to perform such a ceremony. He and his five sons thereupon fled to their ancestral hill country NW. of Jerusalem, and were joined by many Hasidim. After the death of Mattathias, his son *Judas Maccabaeus* (166/5–160 B.C.) continued the struggle for Judaism against Hellenism. By employing guerrilla warfare Judas and his band defeated the Syrian detachments sent against them, and succeeded in entering Jerusalem. He purified the Temple, where for three years sacrifices had been made to Zeus, and restored the worship of Yahweh and the daily sacrifices. Hanukkah, or Feast of the Dedication* (John 10:22), or "Feast of the Maccabees," was instituted to commemorate the rededication of the Temple on Kislev (-Nov.-Dec.).

Though religious freedom was won and the Hasidim were satisfied, Judas determined to fight on for political independence. When he died in battle his younger brother *Jonathan* (160–142 B.C.), who later became high priest, assumed command of the army. Jonathan was treacherously killed by a Syrian general.

Simon (142–134 B.C.), the last remaining son of Mattathias, was elected leader and succeeded in negotiating a treaty in 142 B.C. with the Seleucid king, Demetrius II, whereby political independence for the Jews was secured. In gratitude for this the independent Jewish state conferred on Simon and his descendants permanent authority as ruling high priests. Thus the Hasmonaean or Maccabean dynasty was established. In 134 B.C. Simon and two of his sons were murdered by

254. Maccabean money. Top shows symbols of palm and fruit baskets; shekel below shows cup for manna or Passover barley and pomegranates (fertility or piety).

his son-in-law Ptolemy, who aspired to succeed him. Ptolemy's plot miscarried, for a 3d son of Simon, *John Hyrcanus* (134–104 B.C.), was warned of it and escaped. He succeeded his father as hereditary head of the state;

Family Tree of the Maccabees

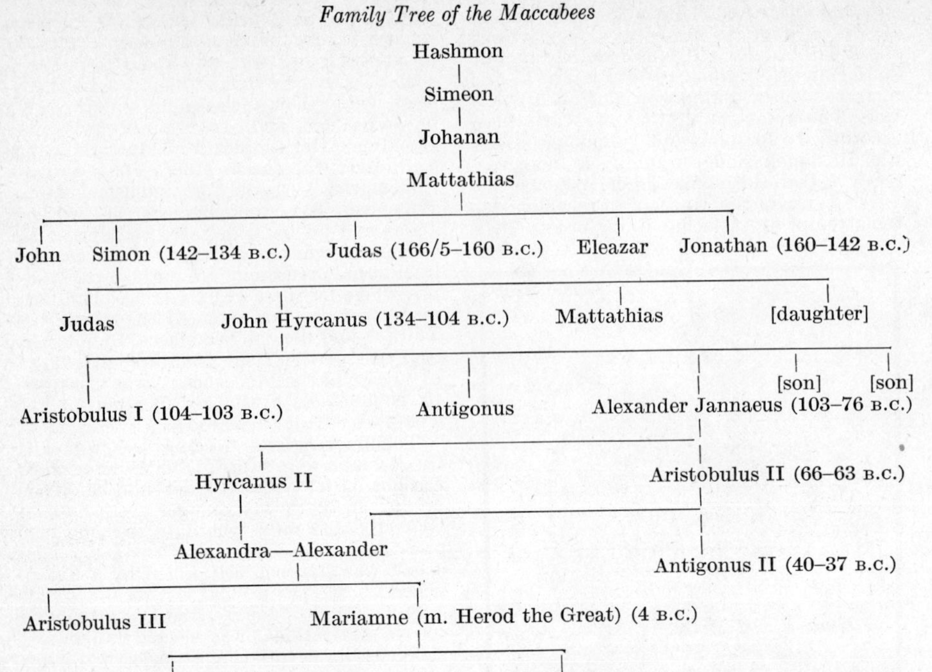

and by military conquest brought Judaea to the height of its power.

Hyrcanus was succeeded by his son *Aristobulus* (104–103 B.C.), who—according to Josephus—secured power by having his mother and brother killed and keeping three other brothers in prison. He was the first of the Maccabees to call himself king, but he retained the high priesthood. Following his death his widow, Salome Alexandra, freed the three brothers and married the eldest, *Alexander Jannaeus* (103–76 B.C.). His reign was marked by wars of conquest and bitter internal strife between Sadducees and Pharisees. At his death *Alexandra* (76–67 B.C.), the widow of two kings, succeeded to the throne, while her son, Hyrcanus II, became high priest. Her reign was peaceful and prosperous; and she was succeeded by her son *Aristobulus II* (66–63 B.C.). For selfish reasons Antipater, military governor of Idumaea, made trouble between Aristobulus II and his brother Hyrcanus. In the war that broke out between the brothers Pompey intervened, 63 B.C. The Roman legions besieged Jerusalem, Pompey captured the city, and entered the Holy of Holies. Thus the Jewish state passed under Roman rule and the kingship was abolished. *Hyrcanus II* (63–40 B.C.) became high priest and his brother Aristobulus II was taken to Rome and forced to march in Pompey's triumph. There were revolts against Rome by Maccabean aspirants. Finally *Antigonus II* (40–37 B.C.), the last son of Aristobulus II, was set on his father's throne by the Parthians, but he was executed at the request of Herod and by order of Mark Antony. The Maccabean dynasty thus became extinct. Antipater's son, Herod* the Great (reigned 37–4 B.C.), married Mariamne, granddaughter of both Hyrcanus II and Aristobulus II, thus uniting the Herods with the Maccabean family. Herod had Mariamne, her sons, and others of the Maccabees executed.

The history of the Maccabees is narrated in I and II Maccabees (see APOCRYPHA). I Maccabees provides a detailed and accurate record of the 40 years from the accession of Antiochus IV Epiphanes to the death of Simon (175–134 B.C.). II Maccabees covers the period 176–161 B.C. III Maccabees is a legendary account of events in the years 221–203 B.C. and has nothing to do with the Maccabees. IV Maccabees is a sermon illustrated with stories of Jewish martyrs in II Maccabees.

Coins of the Maccabean period survive which prove the autonomy of the Jewish state under its high-priest rulers. The earliest Maccabean coins (half, quarter, and third shekels) were probably struck by John Hyrcanus, although his father Simon may also have minted coins. See also MONEY, and *Jewish Symbols on Ancient Jewish Coins*, Paul Romanoff, Dropsie College, Philadelphia, 1944.

Valuable Maccabean structures have been excavated at Beth-zur* by O. R. Sellers and W. F. Albright, on an elevation commanding the N.-S. road from Jerusalem to Hebron. They include a fortress with three construction layers; houses, shops, and reservoirs. More than 300 coins were found, some carrying the name of Antiochus Epiphanes. Beth-zur is mentioned in I Maccabees in connection with the Syrian-Maccabean war.

Maccabees (măk′ȧ-bēz), **Books of the.** See APOCRYPHA.

Macedonia (măs′ĕ-dō′nĭ-ȧ). (1) The state of hardy people ruled by Philip of Macedon (359–336 B.C.), N. of Greece in the present Balkan Peninsula. Its capital was Pella. (2) The Macedonian Empire was expanded by Philip's son, Alexander* the Great (336–323 B.C.), who extended its borders as far E. as India. Alexander and his successors helped frame the Hellenistic world into which Christianity was born.

Macedonia was conquered by Rome (168 B.C.) and made a province (146 B.C.). In Paul's day it extended across what is now the Balkan Peninsula from the Adriatic to the Aegean. It lay S. of Dalmatia (the present Yugoslavia), Moesia, and Thrace; and N. of Achaia (Greece). To its thriving city of Philippi Paul sailed from Troas (Troy) on the Asiatic mainland, after he had seen in a vision a man of Macedonia beckoning him to come to minister to his people (Acts 16:9). Paul's

255. Macedonia.

"straight course" (v. 11) brought him to the little island of Samothrace, then to Neapolis, and soon to the Macedonian Philippi. There he made his first Christian convert in Europe —Lydia of Thyatira, a devout business woman who was baptized with her household. Here Paul and Silas met with such success that a hostile multitude precipitated their arrest (vv. 21–40). Paul and his associates also visited the Macedonian cities of Thessalonica, to which I and II Thessalonians were written, Amphipolis, and Berea (17:10). While Paul was preaching at Athens and Corinth the work in Macedonia was carried on by Silas and Timothy (Acts 18:5). Paul used the great Egnatian Way across the province from Neapolis, through Philippi to Thessalonica. A later visit of Paul and his fellow workers to Macedonia is recorded in Acts 20:1–3; and a 3d sojourn in Macedonia in I Tim. 1:3—possibly after Paul's first imprisonment. Macedonians who risked their lives to further the Christian cause were Gaius and Aristarchus (Acts 19:29) and Secundus (20:4), who remained a faithful friend of Paul. Macedonians, especially in Philippi, were generous to the Christian poor (Rom. 15:26), and to the Apostle himself (II Cor. 8:1–5; Phil. 4:15).

Paul wrote three Epistles to churches in Macedonia: Philippians and I and II Thessalonians. In the latter he gratefully recalls the Thessalonians' reception of the Gospel (I Thess. 1:5 f.), and their proclamation of it in Macedonia and Asia (v. 8). He is ever thankful for their growth (II Thess. 1:3, 2:13), and urges them never to grow "weary in well-doing" (3:13).

Machaerus, a powerful fortress-prison in the N.T. Peraea (in present Jordan) overlooking the NE. shores of the Dead Sea. It was constructed by the Maccabean Alexander Jannaeus, and strengthened by Herod the Great to protect his interests against enemies in Jerusalem and Rome. It overlooks the main N.-S. road to Damascus via the Decapolis cities of Philadelphia (Rabbath-ammon, Amman) and Gerasa (Jerash). Josephus mentions it as the scene of the imprisonment and beheading of John the Baptist (Matt. 14:10 ff., Mk. 6:17–28), but the distance from Machaerus to Jerusalem makes this unlikely if the rapid sequence of events narrated in Matthew and Mark is accepted without question.

Machir (mā′kĭr) ("sold"). (1) The eldest son of Manasseh, son of Joseph (Gen. 50:23; Josh. 17:1; Num. 26:29). (2) The eponymous founder of a warlike group, the Machirites, who conquered and were "assigned" to the Gilead highlands E. of the Jordan (Num. 32:33, 39 f.; Deut. 3:15; Josh. 13:31; cf. Num. 27:1, 36:1). Judges (5:14) tells of Machirites settling originally W. of the Jordan and migrating after the time of Deborah to Gilead (I Chron. 2:21 f., 7:14 f.). (2) A son of Ammiel of Lodebar, who sheltered Jonathan's son Mephibosheth (II Sam. 9:4 f.) E. of the Jordan near Mahanaim, and brought supplies to David when he was a fugitive from Absalom (II Sam. 17:27–29).

Machpelah (măk-pē′lȧ) (possibly "double"), the field and its twin-chambered cave mentioned in P as a tree-dotted plot of ground near ("before") Mamre* (the W. portion of the late Hebron). The cave was purchased by Abraham from Ephron the Hittite for 400 shekels of silver, to be the burial place of his wife Sarah (Gen. 23); cf. Acts 7:16, indicating a sepulcher for Abraham and Jacob at Shechem. According to the P document this cave later became the burial place of Abraham, Rebekah, Isaac, Leah, and Jacob (Gen. 25:9 f., 49:30 f., 50:13). A 4th century traveler, the reliable Bordeaux Pilgrim (A.D. 333), tells about the unusual beauty of the stone enclosure of the cave sepulchers. Some authorities believe that the present mosque is successor of a magnificent structure erected by Herod the Idumaean (Edomite), to whose people Machpelah was as sacred as it was to the Jews. The rectangular wall enclosing the cave mosque is judged by many to be the finest Herodian masonry extant. Others believe it to be older than Herodian. Queen Helena, Byzantines, and Crusaders have left their marks. It is recognized by most scholars as belonging to the same period as the lower courses of the Jews' Wailing Wall at Jerusalem. It is 8½ ft. thick, with some of its stones measuring 24 ft. 8 in. long. It encloses an area 197x111 ft. Machpelah is mentioned in the Talmud. Entrance is forbidden to Jews and Christians, unless they secure permission from the Moslem Supreme Council. Visitors who have been admitted to the mosque describe the cenotaphs of Abraham, Isaac, and their wives, as being covered with elaborately ornamented palls. The cenotaphs of Jacob and Leah are in a small adjacent structure. The tombs are said to be in the cave below the cenotaphs. Moslems claim that the tomb of Joseph is just outside the Cave of Machpelah, represented by a cenotaph W. of the Mosque of the Women. (But see Josh. 24:32.) See ABRAHAM, illus 2.

madness, in the sense of insanity or violent rage, was prevalent in Bible lands, but little understood. Even today in Palestine there are few asylums for the care of the insane. Early writers considered it as the Lord's punishment for disobedience to His laws (Deut. 28:28). Zechariah included madness in his Apocalyptic picture of the coming Day of the Lord (12:4) (see JUDGMENT, DAY OF). Types of temporary madness named were: that of the would-be homicide King Saul (I Sam. 16:14, 23, 18:10 f., 19:9); the mad blundering of intoxication (Jer. 25:16, 51:7); passionate anger, as displayed by Saul of Tarsus against the saints (Acts 26:11) and by the Pharisees against Jesus after he had healed a man's withered hand (Luke 6:11). Festus accused Paul of being mad with learning (Acts 26:24). The damsel Rhoda at the home of Mark's mother in Jerusalem was accused of being out of her mind when she excitedly reported Peter standing at the door (Acts 12:15). Demoniacs were madmen—one of the most pathetic groups healed by Jesus. Their state of mind was believed to have been caused by evil spirits.

Magadan (măg'*ȧ*-dăn). See MAGDALA.

Magdala (măg'd*ȧ*-l*ȧ*) (Matt. 15:39 A.V.; Magadan A.S.V., R.S.V., Moffatt), a town of Galilee at the edge of the Plain of Gennesaret on the W.-central shore of the Sea of Galilee (see illus. 161). It lies on the caravan route from Nazareth via the Horns of Hattîn to Damascus. Its exact location is uncertain, but the narrative of Matt. 15:39 calls for a harbor, such as Khan el-Minieh on the S. edge of Tâbghah provides (but cf. Mark 8:10, "Dalmanutha"). Some authorities locate Magdala at Tarichaea, headquarters for fishing, fish pickling, and boat-building. Others identify it with the squalid little village of Mejdel (see MARY). Any one of the suggested sites makes Magdala adjacent to the scene of Christ's feeding of the 4,000, and a place to which his boat could carry him for rest as the Matthew record suggests. A woman of Magdala is mentioned in Luke 8:2. See MARY (2).

Magdalene, Mary. See MARY (2).

Magi. See WISE MEN.

magic and divination, the beliefs and procedures by which primitive peoples try to induce desired results, or to secure information about the future. These methods, using spells and rites, were popular in the ancient Near East during the Biblical period. Magic entered into all Semitic religions. Canaan, to which Hebrews migrated from the East in the Patriarchal Age, and where the Jacob Tribes settled after their Exodus from Egypt, taught Israel the practice of magic. Isaiah chided the house of Jacob for becoming "soothsayers like the Philistines" (2:6). Belief in magic constantly filtered into Palestine from the Nile and the Mesopotamian valleys (Ex. 7:11, 8:7, etc.). The pseudoscientific efforts of early Egypt to draw specific results from the supernatural world are reflected in the Joseph story (Gen. 41, 44:5), and in the narrative of the court magicians in Moses' day (Ex. 7:10, cf. 8:18). In some of the records of the Exodus the depiction of Moses appears influenced by the role of the Egyptian magicians. I. G. Matthews states in *The Religious Pilgrimage of Israel* (Harper & Brothers) that the brazen serpent (Ex. 4:2–4 E, cf. Ex. 7:9 P)—associated with magic and long worshipped by many eastern peoples—was not inappropriate when used for healing purposes (Num. 21:8 f. J, E; cf. the caduceus of the Greek Aesculapius). This serpent symbol was kept in the Temple until the time of Hezekiah, according to II Kings 18:4. "Such objects have often been associated with vital experiences, and in some cases may have been the stepping stones to more intelligent religious views."

Daniel, God-inspired interpreter of dreams (1:20, 2:2), displaced Babylonian wise men, Chaldaeans, soothsayers, and magicians at the courts of Nebuchadnezzar and Belshazzar. He became the head of the guild of magicians (5:11 f.) because of his "excellent spirit, and knowledge, and understanding, interpreting of dreams, and showing of dark sentences, and dissolving of doubts." He was "ten times better than all the magicians and enchanters that were in all his [Nebuchadnezzar's] realm" (A.S.V. 1:20). Daniel's ability to deal with the occult was partly responsible for his being retained by successive rulers at Babylon.

Among Hebrews magic—a word originally designating the ritual and the learning practiced by Persian Magi (see WISE MEN)—included taboos, spells (cf. blessings and curses, Num. 22:6; Judg. 5:23; Job 3:8), and rites, many of which emerged from the tenuous haze of early tradition, to become religious ceremony and ritual. An example of this is the use of holy water ("water of separation"*) to restore holiness to a tent, object, or person who had become "unclean" by contact with a dead body or a grave (Lev. 5:2–6, 21:1–11; Num. 6:9–12, 9:6–11); the weird formula for such water is given in Num. 19:17 f., 31:21–24. A second sort of holy water, used for treatment of skin eruptions, leprosy, and mildew in houses, has its formula in Lev. 14:1–7, 49–57. Incense was a "holy fumigation" believed to possess magical properties to stave off evil spirits (Wisdom of Sol. 18:21; Baruch 6:43). Examples of magic practices which became religious rituals are the following: blood sprinkling to re-establish cleanness and to give protection, as at the Passover (Ex. 12:7, 13, 22); the scapegoat dedicated to Azazel*, the Wilderness demon (Lev. 16:2–22), on the Day of Atonement*; and the offerings burnt to Yahweh to invite His presence (Lev. 1:8 f., 3:3–16, 4:1–12). Early Hebrews probably made no sharp demarcation between magic and ritual. Opinions differ as to whether religion developed from primitive magic, aiming to draw deities into the affairs of men, and to enable men to control natural forces; or whether religion at certain periods degenerated into magic. Millar Burrows has said that cultic observances were established by God's covenants with His people, who believed that these procedures were what He required. This concept lifted wonder-working and rites from the realm of magic to that of religion. (See the budding of Aaron's rod, Num. 17). The margin between the false appeal of the Baal prophets on Mt. Carmel and that of Elijah, challenging God to send down fire, appears narrow to the superficial observer. The wonder-working mantle of Elijah (II Kings 2:8–14); the manipulation of the widow's cruse of oil by Elijah (I Kings 17:8–16), and the healing of her son by the prophet's personal ritual (17:17–24); the effectiveness of Elisha's presence for curing the sick, in contrast to his staff which proved ineffective in the hands of his agent, Gehazi (II Kings 4:29–36), all call for examination as one tries to distinguish between magic and ritual.

Beneath some ancient features of Hebrew ritual may be seen aspects of magic, like the phylacteries* worn on forehead (*ṭotafoth*) and arm (Ex. 13:2–16; Deut. 6:4–9, 11:13–21, cf. Matt. 23:5), surviving from objects once dedicated to pagan deities; and the boxes (*mezuzoth*) containing the words of Deut. 6:4–9, fastened to the doorposts of Hebrew houses. The moonlike crescents worn by Gideon's camels (Judg. 8:26) still dangle on the beasts of desert nomads to keep away the evil eye. The tinkling ornaments of the daughters of Jerusalem denounced by Isaiah (3:16–21) survive in the amulets (see AMULET) still worn in parts of Palestine and Syria to ward off unfriendly spirits ("jinn"), and in the blue beads worn on the necks of donkeys and the steering wheels of automobiles. Rural populations still live in terror of evil spirits. Moslems will not drive flies from the eyes of infants lest they give offense to a lurking spirit. Even the bells worn on the bottom of the high priest's robe (Ex. 28:33), "that he die not" (v. 35), may originally have been a fetish to ward off evil forces. Ancient Hebrew MSS. in the Museum of the Oriental Institute (Chicago) tell of charms against sickness, sleeplessness, childbirth ills, dreams, and hatred.

A gypsum tablet found at Arslan-Tash in upper Syria, on the route from Haran (dwelling place of the Patriarch Abraham) to Carchemish, proved to be a "Canaanitic" incantation of the 7th century B.C. against night demons in general. Written in pure Biblical Hebrew, translated (Harry Tur-Sinai believes) from an Aramaic original, the incantation is directed not against darkness per se, but against feminine demons of darkness which were believed to threaten men with strangulation in unlighted rooms, especially on their wedding nights. (A small lamp is even today kept burning at night in many Palestinian houses.) This unique tablet (probably a copy of a widely circulated original) supplies the earliest known example of poetic Biblical Hebrew with end rhyme. Its last four lines may be translated thus (courtesy Harry Tur-Sinai):

"Sz, open an olive for me,
that we shall have light,
until the sun rises,
the morning shines."

Limitation of space allows definition of only a few of the many sorts of magic appearing in Scripture. *Sympathetic magic*, found in all early cultures, was the effort to induce the desired results by mimetic dances or gestures—pouring water on the ground to cause rain; burning an image to punish an enemy; using attractive scents or "love apples" (see MANDRAKE) to stimulate passion. Such sympathetic magic, abortive science, made false use of associated ideas. *Black magic* was the resorting to *sorcery*, the calling in of evil spirits for aid. *Witchcraft*, the consorting with evil spirits, enchanters, wizards, and necromancers, was denounced very early in the laws of Israel (Ex. 22:18; Deut. 18:10). Jezebel's witchcraft was castigated by King Jehoram (II Kings 9:22), and denounced along with idolatries and heresies.

Divination, the peering into future events, was brought about by consulting such unseen powers as the talking Memnon of Thebes, the Delphic oracle of Apollo, and the Cumaean Sibyl in her cave near Naples or the oak (terebinth) of Moreh (Gen. 12:6 f.). At Pharaoh's court Joseph divined by means of a cup containing liquids which gave play to light (Gen. 44:5, 15). Diviners sometimes looked for signs in the entrails of sacrificed animals, or the flight of birds, or the way in which talismans fell. Divination by inspection of the livers of sacrificed animals (*hepatoscopy*) was popular at Mari, where 32 clay models of divination livers, dating from the 2d millennium B.C., have been excavated. The witch or woman with "a familiar spirit" consulted by King Saul at Endor (I Sam. 28:3–25), after he himself had illegalized such wizardry (v. 3), resulted in "calling up" Samuel the prophet from the dead (v. 20). *Necromancy* was another name for divination through consultation with the dead. Advice was also sought by shaking arrows in a quiver (*belomancy*), and looking for the direction in which the first one fell (Ezek. 21:21, cf. II Kings 13:14–19). *Soothsaying* (Josh. 13:22; Mic. 5:12; Acts 16:16) may spring from a Heb. word for "crooning" or for "cloud," in the sense of "weather-maker." Soothsaying was associated with divining of future events. The Balaam of Num. 22–24 was a famous soothsayer. *Dreams* were believed to convey a message, like the dreams of Joseph (Gen. 37:5 ff.); of Pharaoh's butler and baker (40:8 ff.); of Pharaoh (41:1–32); and of Daniel. Joseph of Nazareth had confidence in the dream revelations of the "angel of the Lord" prior to the birth of Jesus (Matt. 1:20) and during the massacre of the Bethlehem babies (2:13). Prophets frowned on dream revelations and stressed heavenly visions (see VISION), of which an example is the experience of Saul (Acts 9:3 ff.).

The *casting of lots* was a popular means of divination. The casting of the sacred lot by the priestly soothsayer may provide the root for "Torah" ("instruction," "law," lit. "casting"). The priest's Urim* and Thummim—possibly oracular pebbles carriedin a pouch under the priest's breastplate (Ex. 28:30; Lev. 8:8)—were widely trusted. Lots were used to "assign" territory to the Hebrew Tribes in Canaan (Num. 26:55, 33:54, 34:13; Josh. 21:4, 6, 8). By the drawing of lots (Pur) at the Persian court a policy was determined (Esther 9:24 f.). The Phoenician use of the lot is indicated in Jonah 1:7 to localize a cause of ill luck. People were selected by lot for certain tasks (Judg. 20:9; cf. Saul and Jonathan, I Sam. 14:41 f.). Lots were cast by Roman soldiers for the robe of Jesus (Matt. 27:35); and by the Apostles for a successor for Judas (Acts 1:26).

Ordeals were resorted to, to establish guilt or innocence in marital relations (Num. 5:11–31). Early in Israel's religious experience, as stated above, magic was denounced, because it led people to rely on peeping wizards and muttering soothsayers rather than on God's guidance (Isa. 8:19). False prophets, preying on people's fears, staged frenzied demonstrations which showed how far they were from the true spiritual prophets of Hebrew monotheism, who shunned omens and listened for the "still small voice" of the Lord (I Kings 19:12). Ezekiel was outspoken in denunciation of magic and vain divinations (13:17–23). Second Isaiah emphasized opposition to Babylonian astrologers, stargazers, and monthly prognosticators (44:25, 47:12–15).

In N.T. times magical practices included the bringing to Paul of aprons or handkerchiefs, to be blessed and carried to the sick (Acts 19:12), an instance similar to that when a sick woman touched the hem of Jesus' garment (Matt. 9:20 f.). Jesus clearly dispelled her superstition by commending her faith. Even in the ritual of the laying on of hands (Heb. 6:2) in ordination, there may be a survival of ancient magic.

Exorcism, by the use of a sacred name, formula, or incantation (Acts 19:13, cf. Matt. 12:27), was one of the most popular forms of magic in N.T. times, for the driving out of evil spirits. When Jesus freed people from their feeling of being possessed by evil forces, he was accused of being in league with Beelzebub (Matt. 12:24). Quacks, who attempted to employ the methods of the Apostles, are described in Acts 19:13–20. Simon Magus (Acts 8:9 ff.) and Bar-jesus (Acts 13:6 ff.) were both sorcerers.

magicians. See MAGIC AND DIVINATION.

magistrate, a public civil officer (A.V. Judg. 18:7; cf. A.S.V. "possessing authority"), of lower rank in N.T. times than the judge (Luke 12:58).

"Magnificat" (măg-nĭf'ĭ-kăt), the exquisite hymn of praise (Luke 1:46–55) in the introduction to the birth of Jesus in Luke's narrative. Luke may have learned it from Mary during his two-year sojourn in Palestine, for he was there about 30 years after the Resurrection of Jesus, and Mary may have been living in Luke's time. The song has four strophes, whose verse form is apparent in the revised versions:

(1) Praise of God—vv. 46 f.

(2) Her anticipation of being remembered throughout history, because of her God-given destiny—vv. 48 f.

(3) Her observation of God throughout time, exalting the lowly, disciplining the haughty—vv. 50–53.

(4) Her intimation of the Incarnation*, as the fulfillment of Messianic promises—vv. 54 f.

It is based on Hannah's song (I Sam. 2:1–10), and contains many other O.T. allusions.

There are two views concerning the one who expresses the song. (1) The usual interpretation of the *Magnificat* is that it proceeded from Mary, mother of our Lord. The song may have sprung from Mary's awareness that she was nearer the fulfillment of Messianic prophecy than any other had ever been. It seems to express the simple faith and hope, the humble gratitude and submission, of the one chosen to be the Lord's mother. (2) Some old Latin MSS. ascribe the *Magnificat* to Elisabeth*, in whose home Mary was visiting (Luke 1:56) for three months before the birth of John the Baptist. The original text of 1:46 may have read "she said," so that both "Elisabeth" and "Mary" may be viewed as glosses. Those who accept the Elisabeth theory stress the "with her" of v. 56. But the thoughts in vv. 47–55 suggest the inadequacy of viewing Elisabeth as their source.

The *Magnificat* has been used by the Church as a canticle from at least the 4th century, if not earlier. It is incorporated in the Daily Office of the Roman Catholic Church and the Evening Prayer of the Anglican Communion.

Magog (mā'gŏg). See GOG.

Magus, Simon. See SIMON MAGUS.

Mahalath (mā'hă-lăth) ("sickness"). (1) The daughter of Ishmael and wife of Esau (Gen. 28:9). (2) The daughter of David's son Jerimoth, and a wife of King Rehoboam (II Chron. 11:18). (3) A musical term appearing in the titles of Ps. 53 and 88 ("Mahalath Leannoth"). As in many of the Psalm titles, which were added after the Psalms were written, the meaning of this term is obscure, but it may indicate a tune or an instrument.

Mahanaim (mā'hȧ-nā'ĭm) (possibly "two camps"). An important site E. of the Jordan, not exactly identified, but N. of the Jabbok (or on the N. bank of the Jabbok, as Nelson Glueck stated). Khirbet Mahneh, 2 m. N. of 'Ajlûn, has been suggested; also Jerash (Gerasa*). At Mahanaim Jacob, returning by the main N.-S. highway along the Jordan from Mesopotamia, was met by angels (Gen. 32:2). Mahanaim was a Levitical (see LEVITES) city in the territory of Gad (Josh. 21:38). There Abner made Ish-bosheth, the son of Saul, king (II Sam. 2:8); there David fled E. of the Jordan during the rebellion of his son Absalom (II Sam. 17:24–27, 19:32); and at the gates of Mahanaim David grieved over the death of his disloyal but beloved son (18:33). Mahanaim was the center of one of Solomon's prefectures (I Kings 4:14) and commissary depots.

Mahaneh-dan (mā′hȧ-nĕ-dăn′) ("camp of Dan"), a place where men of Dan seeking new territory pitched camp (Judg. 13:25, 18:12). The site is unknown, but may be between Eshtaol and Zorah, or "behind" (W. of) Kiriath-jearim.

Maher-shalal-hash-baz (mā′hĕr-shăl′ăl-hăsh′băz′) ("spoil speeds, prey hastens"), the symbolic name Isaiah wrote in a public place and later gave to his 2d son as a sign that Syria and Israel would soon be conquered by Assyria (Isa. 8:1–4).

Mahli (mä′lī) (Mahali) (Ex. 6:19) ("weak," "sickly"). (1) A son of Merari*, and founder of a prominent Levitical family (Num. 3:20, 33; I Chron. 6:19, 29, 47, 24:26). One of his descendants, contemporary with Ezra, is spoken of as "a man of understanding," sent "by the good hand of God" (Ezra 8:18). (2) A Levite, son of Mushi, of the family of Mahli.

Mahlon (mä′lŏn) ("sickness"), the son of Elimelech and Naomi of Bethlehem (Ruth 1:2), 1st husband of Ruth the Moabitess (Ruth 4:10), and brother of Chilion.

Mahol (mā′hŏl) (possibly "dance"), the father of famous wise men, probably skilled in music, whose ability was exceeded by that of Solomon (I Kings 4:31).

maid. (1) In the sense of maidservant and bondwoman, see SERVANT. (2) A virgin (Deut. 22:17; Esther 2:12; Ezek. 9:6), or a young woman, often portrayed as being attractive (II Chron. 36:17; Jer. 2:32, 51:22; Esther 2:7). (3) A harlot or sacred prostitute (Amos 2:7). (4) A child (Matt. 9:24 f.).

mail. See DRESS.

Makkedah (mă-kē′dȧ), a Canaanite royal city in the Shephelah N. of Lachish, captured by Joshua (Josh. 10:28, 12:16), following the defeat of the five Amorite kings who hid themselves in a nearby cave (10:16 ff.). It was one of the cities assigned to Judah (15:41). Early identification with El-Mughar ("the cave"), E. of Aijalon, is doubtful. Perhaps it is to be located at Khirbet el-Kheisun, N. of Azekah, or nearby Khirbet Maqdum.

Malachi (măl′ȧ-kī) ("my messenger," used as a proper name only in Mal. 1:1), the last book of the O.T. and the Minor Prophets. Nothing elsewhere is recorded in the Bible concerning "Malachi." This has led many to believe that "my messenger" (3:1) induced the editor of the Book of the Minor Prophets to affix "by Malachi" (1:1), (meaning "my messenger" or an abbreviation of "messenger of the Lord") to the four chapters (three in Heb.) of this book in order to have 12 named authors in the Book of the Minor Prophets. Speculation has identified "my messenger" with Ezra. If Malachi was really the author's name, nothing is known of him except the utterances in the book.

The book may be outlined thus:

Title—1:1.

Preamble—1:2–5.

Denunciation of priests who despise God's name—1:6–2:9.

Four oracles. Jewish men denounced (1) for divorcing wives and marrying Gentiles—2:10–16; for doubting the reality of divine retribution for human deeds—2:17–3:5; for failure to pay Temple tithes in full—3:6–12; for thinking there is no profit in fulfilling the will of God—3:13–4:3.

Later appendix—4:4–6.

The date of the book can be reasonably determined. The Jewish people were under a governor (Mal. 1:8; cf. Hag. 1:1), doubtless appointed by the Persian emperor (Neh. 5:14 f.). The title "great king" (Mal. 1:14) would reflect the magnificence of the Persian court. The second Temple, completed in 515 B.C., had priests who for a number of years (1:10, 3:1, 10) had been performing ritualistic ceremonies and were wearied by them (1:13). The invasion of Edom*, resulting eventually in the organization of the Nabataean kingdom, cannot be exactly dated, but according to 1:2–5 the Edomites were in despair though not yet driven into S. Judaea (called "Idumea" c. 312 B.C.). Therefore the 1st half of the 5th century, c. 460, is a likely date.

Malachi is an invaluable historical source concerning the Judaean Jews in the Persian period (before Nehemiah). A plague of locusts (3:11) caused crop failure and economic distress. The pessimistic outlook of the people in the homeland tallies with the report received by Nehemiah at Susa (Neh. 1:3). No amount of piety seemed to bring relief from disasters (Mal. 2:13, 3:4). Laymen continued to be denounced for their divorces and pagan marriages (2:10–16), and for failure to pay in full their Temple tithes (3:6–12). Evil times would become good times if God's laws were obeyed (3:10, 12, 16). But the people generally doubted the efficacy of ritual (3:14), and thought that God winked at wickedness (3:15). The prophet tried to comfort all by pointing out the far worse plight of their brothers, the Edomites (1:2–5), and the ultimate triumph of the righteous (3:18–4:3).

Because of the book's didactic form some literary critics believe that its author circulated his ideas to the people in writing. In style it marks the beginning of a method of exposition that afterward became universal in the schools and synagogues of Judaism. Its loftiest revelation concerns the universal nature of God (1:11, 2:10). The book is directly or indirectly quoted in the N.T.: Mark 1:2, cf. Mal. 3:1; Mark 9:11 and Luke 1:17, cf. Mal. 4:5; Rom. 9:13, cf. Mal. 1:2 f.

Malchiah (măl-kī′ȧ) (Malchijah) (măl-kī′-jȧ) ("my king is Jehovah"), the name of several O.T. men. (1) A descendant of Gershom (I Chron. 6:40). (2) A priest (I Chron. 9:12). (3) The head of the 5th course of priests at Jerusalem (I Chron. 24:9)—may be the same as (2). (4), (5), (6) Men listed as having married foreign wives (Ezra 10:25, 10:31). (7) One who repaired the Jerusalem Dung Gate (Neh. 3:14). (8) A jeweler who helped rebuild the Jerusalem wall (Neh. 3:31). (9) One who accompanied Ezra during the reading of the Law (Neh. 8:4). (10) A man who sealed the Covenant (Neh. 10:3)—may be the same as (2). (11) A priest who participated in the ceremony of wall dedication (Neh. 12:42).

Malchus (măl′kŭs), the high priest's bond servant in the company which arrested Jesus. His ear, partly struck off by Peter, was healed by Jesus (John 18:10).

malefactor, an evildoer, like the criminals executed with Jesus (Luke 23:32 f., 39). Enemies of Jesus accused him of being a malefactor (John 18:30).

mallow (măl′ō), any plant of the genus *Malva*. In Job 30:4 its leaves were used for food. The A.S.V. reads "salt-wort."

Malluch (măl′ŭk). (1) A Merarite (see MERARI), ancestor of Ethan (I Chron. 6:44). (2), (3) Jews who had married foreign wives (Ezra 10:29, 32). (4), (5) Men who sealed the Covenant in the era of Nehemiah (Neh. 10:4, 27).

Malta. See MELITA.

Mamertine, the Roman prison for criminals and captives awaiting execution. It was adjacent to the imperial forums. An ancient Christian tradition identifies this rock cell as

256. Mamertine Prison, Rome.

the place where Peter (cf. John 21:19) was held pending his crucifixion c. 64/5. (See PETER, illus. 320.) The Mamertine is also associated with the martyrdom of Paul, which took place at about the same time.

mammon (Lat. *mammōna*, from Gk. *mamōnas*, from Aram. *māmōnā*, "riches"). A word used in the N.T. (Matt. 6:24; Luke 16:9, 11, 13) to convey the idea of too great trust in or value attached to material wealth, as against too little concern for God's affairs.

Mamre (măm′rē) (meaning unknown). (1) A plain (Râmet el-Khalîl) very near or in what later became the city of Hebron in S. Palestine. There Abraham pitched his tents (Gen. 13:18) under ancient oaks or terebinths. Pleasant tree-shaded camp sites are still used near there by Bedouins (23:17). There the Lord appeared to Abraham and promised him and Sarah a son (18:1 ff.). In the field of Machpelah* which is "before" (? east of) Mamre Abraham purchased from Ephron, a Hittite dwelling among descendants of Heth, the cave which became the sepulcher of Sarah (23:17, 19) and later his own (50:13) and that of other Patriarchs and their wives. (2) A chieftain of ancient Amorite inhabitants of S. Palestine, brother of Eshcol and Aner (Gen. 14:13, 24), and possibly a former owner of the oaks under which Abraham pitched his camp (but see 23:10–20.) Mamre was Abraham's confederate in rescuing Lot, kidnapped during the four-kings-vs.-five-kings struggle in Chedorlaomer's day in the Dead Sea region.

man in the Bible is significant for his relation to God. The Biblical view of man is concerned primarily with the nature of man and with the relation of this nature to the purpose of the God who created it. To look at man politically, or economically, or scientifically is perfectly proper, and all may be brought under the Biblical view; but the Biblical view is not any one of these.

The Bible sees man as the highest of all God's creatures on the earth, because he is made in the image of God, and possesses qualities that resemble in some degree the qualities of God Himself, and that fit him for a life of fellowship with his Maker (see Gen. 1:26–28, 9:1–7; Ps. 8:1–3; John 1:1–13). This fellowship, however, does not come to pass in the ordinary course of events. The very freedom which is one of God's greatest gifts to man is also the cause of his perversion. He departs from the path he was designed to walk, and introduces confusion not only into his own life but into the life of the world; the potential sonship becomes an actual rebellion (Gen. 3:1–24). Only this can explain such a prayer of repentance and confession as is found in Ps. 51. Reason, conscience, will, and love are all affected by the blight of sin and disobedience. The blight reaches into social relations, and man is at enmity with man as well as with God. (See SON OF GOD.)

This is the Biblical view of "the natural man." He has a nature in which is the promise of both sonship to God and brotherhood with his kind, yet both are rendered impossible by a deep-seated evil that corrupts and perverts his nature (John 3:3–6; I Cor. 2:14, cf. 15:41–49; Rom. 1:18–32; Jas. 3:1–10). The Bible does not hesitate to give concrete examples of the sinful excesses to which men may go. Some of these indeed are as shocking as anything in secular history (e.g., Gen. 19:1–11, 30–38; Judges 9:1–6, 19:1–30; I Sam. 15:1–3; II Sam. 11:1–26; II Kings 25:7; Matt. 2:16–18). There is no cheap optimism in the Bible. Its warnings in respect of the evils that men may do and the results that follow are searching and unmistakable (II Sam. 12:1–14; Prov. 7; Isa. 1:4–15; Jer. 22:1–12; Amos 6:1–11; Gal. 5:16–21).

This helps to create the background for the other side of the Biblical teaching about man. It is nothing less than that man is capable of being saved. God by His creative power maintains in existence rebellious and sinful men, and He brings on them the harvest of their evil-doing (see Gal. 6:7). But He never desists from His ultimate purpose, which even the tragedy of Eden served only to dramatize (Gen. 3:15). The Bible tells not only the story of man's rebellion against God and the consequences that follow—it tells also of the persistent purpose of God to win men from evil. He chooses Israel not merely for the sake of Israel, but that Israel might be the instrument of His grace and love to all men (Jer. 31:31–34; Heb. 11:39 f.).

This emphasis on community is fundamental in the Biblical view. Paul interprets the Genesis narrative of the Fall to mean that the sin of one involved tragedy for all (Rom. 5:12); but he also interprets the Cross to mean that the utter self-giving of one promised blessing for all (Rom. 5:17–19). To come to a new life in Christ is to be obligated to make the new life possible to others (Rom. 1:14–16). There are "two humanities," and Paul describes them in Eph. 4:17–32 (see also Gal. 5:16–24). But the "new man in Christ," for whom all other things have become new, is also, says Paul, "an ambassador on behalf of Christ" (II Cor. 5:17–20). He has come into "the household of God" (Eph. 2:19), but the privilege brings its responsibilities: it is to help spread the spirit of the household into all the world. The logic of such a "new man" as the Bible describes is a "new race," the replacing of hate by love, of hostility by friendship, of divisiveness by unity. This is already anticipated in some of Jesus' most striking metaphors, such as "salt" (Matt. 5:13), "light" (5:14), and "leaven" (13:33; cf. Gal. 5:8).

There is nothing in the Biblical view of man that need be opposed to scientific progress. On the other hand, unless the Biblical view of man, his divine origin, his nature as a reflection of God's, his moral predicament, his need for "regeneration," his ultimate purpose and destiny in the will of God—unless this Biblical view underlies man's individual, social, political, and economic activities, the Biblical pronouncement of the resulting doom can hardly be denied (Matt. 7:24–27; Jas. 3:13–4:10). See GUILT; REDEMPTION; SIN.

E. L.

Manaen (măn′*ă*-ĕn), "a member of the court of Herod the tetrarch" (R.S.V. Acts 13:1), or one who had been brought up with that official (A.V.), who taught or prophesied at Antioch along with other early Christian leaders.

Manasseh (m*ă*-năs′ĕ) (from Heb. *nasheh*, cause to forget"). (1) The Egyptian-born elder son of Joseph—and of the Egyptian Asenath, daughter of the high priest of the Egyptian national temple at On. Joseph, in assigning this name, suggested that God had enabled him to forget his family's troubles (Gen. 41:51). Manasseh's paternal grandfather was the Hebrew Patriarch Jacob. His full brother was Ephraim* (Gen. 46:20). Though Manasseh's prior birth entitled him to expect a major inheritance*, the dying Jacob, sensing the coming greatness of Ephraim's descendants (Gen. 48:1–22, cf. Num. 1:35), gave the younger son his greater blessing. As was often the case in O.T. times, both grandsons had been adopted by their grandfather; adoption insured inheritance. The writer of I Chron. 7:14 makes Manasseh marry a Syrian concubine who became the mother of Machir, father of Gilead. This narrative may reflect Israel's custom of intermarrying with Canaanites after the Conquest. In the "assignment" of territory during the occupation of Canaan and E. Palestine, Manasseh's descendants settled half to the east of the Jordan and half to the west. "The half tribe of Manasseh" refers always to those to the east.

(2) A chief tribe of Israel, divided into two halves and possessing land E. and W. of the Jordan, each portion approximately opposite the other. It was of such an extent in comparison with that allotted to several of the other Twelve Tribes that it enjoyed great prestige, in spite of the superior expectations of Jacob for mighty Ephraim. The seven families of the Manasseh group were descended from his son Machir and his grandson Gilead's six sons. The E. territory of Manasseh extended from the Jabbok on its S., where it bordered the land claimed by Gad, N. to the lower slopes of Mt. Hermon, and NE. to include a large part of the fertile tableland of the wheat-producing Hauran. Its people must often have clashed with Damascus Syrians. Following the defeat of Og*, King of Bashan, Manasseh E. of the Jordan included part of Gilead and all of Bashan. Its area was 65–70 m. wide and 40 m. long. It included numerous large towns and cities, ruins of which have been excavated. Its important centers included Ramoth-gilead*, Ashtaroth, Karnaim, Argob, Nobah, and Jabesh-gilead*. West of the Jordan, Manasseh (which lay within the Kingdom of Israel after the division of Solomon's United Kingdom) included the excellent land immediately N. of Ephraim in its mountain mass, and S. of Zebulun and Issachar. It was bounded on the W. by the Mediterranean, on the E. by the Jordan. It reached to the rich, flat farmlands of the Valley of Jezreel* (Plain of Esdraelon), in which lay the prized cities it could not wrest from their Canaanite holders—Megiddo, Taanach, En-gannim, Ibleam, and Beth-shan (Josh. 17:11 ff.). Yet the record implies that Manasseh sometimes reduced the Canaanites in these powerful sites to taskworkers (v. 13). When Manasseh and his brother Ephraim complained to Joshua that they needed more land, that great strategist rightly told them that they would have enough if they made greater efforts to drive out the Canaanites (v. 18).

The great men of Manasseh included Gideon*, the worthy judge (Judg. 6:15). Many men of Manasseh helped David during his alliance with the Philistines vs. Saul (I Chron. 12:19 f.), and joined him at Hebron (v. 23). Some of the Israelites of Manasseh's territory defected to Asa, King of Judah (c. 913–873 B.C.) (II Chron. 15:9). Some of the people of populous, idolatrous Manasseh were carried into captivity by Tiglath-pileser III (I Chron. 5:18–26) of Assyria, and the remainder were deported after the fall of

Samaria (722/1 B.C.). Manassites are mentioned at Passovers in the era of Hezekiah, King of Judah (c. 715–687 B.C.).

(3) A son of Hezekiah and Hephzibah, who, in spite of being "the most wicked king of Judah," had a long reign of peace and prosperity (c. 687–642 B.C.). His story is narrated in II Kings 21:1–18 and II Chron. 33:1–20. His religious syncretism included Baalism, the exaltation of Astarte on high places, wizardry, sun worship, and adoration of "all the host of heaven" (II Kings 21:3, 5; II Chron. 33:3, 5). He introduced the abominable worship of Molech (Moloch) in the Hinnom Valley, including the rite of causing living children to pass through fire (Deut. 18:10—written during the Exile). This syncretism was believed to have been a main cause in bringing destruction on Jerusalem and the Temple. The II Chron. 33 narrative contains a story not told in Kings, to the effect that Manasseh was deported to Babylon by the Assyrians, repented, prayed to God, was restored to his kingdom, abolished idols, and turned his people to the worship of the true God (vv. 11–16). Some interpreters accept this story because Assyrian kings of this era did spend part of their time in Babylon; others see in it an attempt to explain why Manasseh, though wicked, enjoyed the longest reign in the history of Judah. Rabbinic literature says that Manasseh had Isaiah sawed asunder. Manasseh was succeeded by his son, King Amon of Judah (II Chron. 33:20). The names of various sons—including "Shechem"—and daughters were probably place names.

(4) The name given in Judg. 18:30 to the grandfather of Jonathan, priest of the idolatrous shrine of Micah in Dan.

(5), (6) A son of Pahath-moab, and a son of Hashum, who, influenced by Ezra, put away foreign wives (Ezra 10:30, 33.).

Manasses (mȧ-năs′ēz), a name used in the N.T. for "Manasseh" (Matt. 1:10; Rev. 7:6).

Manasses (mȧ-năs′ēz), **Prayer of.** See APOCRYPHA.

257. Mandrake. Drawing shows flowers and leaves still attached to heavy root.

mandrake (*Mandragora officinarum*), a narcotic, laxative, solanaceous perennial of the nightshade family, related to the potato and tomato and commonly identified with the "love-apple." Throughout the Biblical area it grew plentifully in deserted fields. Mandrakes were associated with magic. The fleshy forked root made it resemble a human form. Superstitions of the E. were attached to its sweetish fruit, which ripens all over Palestine in May. It is slightly poisonous. Mandrakes were believed to arouse sexual desire. Rachel was jealous of the mandrakes presented to Leah by Reuben (Gen. 30:14–16). The Song of Solomon alludes to the fragrance of mandrakes (7:13).

maneh. See WEIGHTS AND MEASURES.

manger, a trough or open box for cattle fodder (from Gk. word for "feeding place." A number of stone basins were found in Stratum IV at Megiddo (see Fig. 258). Thought to be "mangers" for "Solomon's stables (see

258. Stone manger between hitching posts in stable of King Ahab at Megiddo.

STABLE), they have recently been shown to be incongruous with such a function (see J. B. Pritchard, "The Megiddo Stables: A Reassessment," in J. A. Sanders, ed., *Near Eastern Archaeology in the Twentieth Century*, 1970, pp. 271, 273). When caves are used as stables, as in old Bethlehem, the manger is sometimes cut in the rock wall. Many artists have erroneously shown the Christmas manager as a wooden trough or box on a trestle. A stone manger filled with sweet straw made a bassinet for the infant Jesus (Luke 2:7, 12, 16). The "stall" of Luke 13:15 A.V., A.S.V., should be "manger," as in the A.S.V. margin and R.S.V. When a manger is for several animals it is carved from a longer piece of stone, and has partitions

manna, the food miraculously supplied to the Israelites in the Sinai Peninsula. This "bread which the Lord" gave (Ex. 16:15) after serious unrest because of hunger (Ex. 16:1–4, 12) appeared on the surface of the Wilderness as "a small round thing, as small as the hoar frost on the ground" (v. 14), like coriander seed (Ex. 16:31). Its color was that of bdellium resin (Num. 11:7). Though sticky, it quickly solidified so that it could be ground and baked into wafers or cakes, which tasted like "fresh oil" (Num. 11:8) or honey (Ex. 16:31); it was also boiled in pots. When left over night it was eaten by "worms"—

probably ants. Moses allowed each Israelite a ration of one omer of manna per day (c. 3.3 qts.), and two on every 6th day in preparation for the Sabbath (Ex. 16:16, 22). Dr. F. S. Bodenheimer of the Hebrew University, Jerusalem, describes manna as a sweet secretion of various plant lice, cicadas, and scale insects feeding on wilderness tamarisk trees. Insects secrete their excess carbohydrates in the form of the honeydew manna, which evaporates into particles resembling hoar frost. Pre-Exilic J and E narratives tally with his and other observations in Sinai. Later P writers added such apparently mistaken legendary interpolations as the melting "when the sun grew hot"—rather than by 8:30 A.M., as is the case—and the night activity of the worms (ants), actually confined to early evening (Ex. 16:20).

The chemical analysis of manna shows the presence of three basic sugars with pectin (*BA* Vol. X, No. 1, p. 3). The nomadic Israelites craved such sweetness, since they had no dates or beets or sugar cane.

God continued to supply manna until the Israelites entered Canaan and the "fruit of the land" was available (Josh. 5:12). Some observers believe there are not enough tamarisk trees in the southern location suggested for Kadesh-barnea to make possible such manna deposits as Exodus indicates, and they prefer to locate Kadesh farther north at 'Ain Gedeirat, where trees are more plentiful.

Throughout the Bible, references to manna indicate the writers' view of it as a blessing from Yahweh (Deut. 8:3, 16; Neh. 9:15, 20; Ps. 78:24 f.; John 6:31; Rev. 2:17). Jesus referred to the "bread from heaven" given to Israel by Moses, but revealed himself as the "true bread from heaven," which if a man eat he would never hunger or thirst (John 6:32, 35).

The regard early Israel had for the Wilderness manna was expressed by the author of Hebrews, who wrote that a golden pot of it, together with Aaron's budding rod and the tables of the Law, was placed behind the second veil of the Tabernacle in the Holy of Holies (Heb. 9:4; cf. Ex. 16:32–34).

Manoah (mȧ-nō′ȧ), a devout and hospitable man of Zorah, of the Tribe of Dan, father of Samson, the Israelite judge and hero against the Philistines. The story of Samson's unusual birth is narrated in Judg. 13:2–23. Manoah and his wife opposed Samson's marriage to a Philistine woman of Timnath (Judg. 14:2 f.), yet Manoah attended the wedding feast (v. 10). He was buried between Zorah and Eshtaol (16:31).

manservant. See SERVANT.

mansions, stately, pretentious, or impressive houses; used in A.V. John 14:2 in Jesus' allusion to his Father's heavenly home. The R.S.V. has "rooms"; A.S.V. margin has "abiding-places"; Moffatt, "abodes." The figure may have been suggested to Jesus by the common sight in Palestine of an enormous dwelling in which many units of a family had quarters or apartments.

mantle, a loose, sleeveless cloak, often seamless—the *abayeh* of the Palestinian and Syrian man (John 19:23). See DRESS.

manuscript. See TEXT.

Maon (mā′ŏn) ("dwelling"), a town in the inheritance of Judah (Josh. 15:55). In I Chron. 2:45 where the name Maon is that of the "son" of Shammai and "father" of the inhabitants of Beth-zur, it may be used collectively for the inhabitants of Maon (cf. I Chron. 2:54). The town was in the highlands W. of the Dead Sea, S. of Hebron, Ziph, and Carmel; known today as Tell Ma'in. To the Wilderness of Maon, E. of the town, probably, David fled from Saul (I Sam. 23:24 f.). His henchmen were kind to the sheep-shearers of the churlish Nabal of Maon, whose wife Abigail later became David's wife (I Sam. 25:42). The Maonites oppressed Israel (Judg. 10:12).

Mara (mä′rȧ) ("bitter"), the name Naomi applied to herself after the death of her husband and sons (Ruth 1:20).

Marah (mā′rȧ) ("bitter"), the first oasis reached by the Children of Israel after they crossed the Sea of Reeds. It may be 'Ain Hawârah, a few miles inland from the Gulf and c. 47 m. from the town of Suez, on the ancient road S. to the Sinai mines. When the waters proved too bitter to drink—symbolic of future hardships—Moses sweetened them by casting into the well a tree which Yahweh showed him (Ex. 15:22–25; Num. 33:8).

maranatha (măr′ȧ-năth′ȧ), an Aramaic prayer used by early Christians as a watchword signifying, "Our Lord, come!" (R.S.V. I Cor. 16:22). In the A.V. passage "maranatha" follows "anathema"; cf. R.S.V., "If anyone has no love for the Lord, let him be accursed," and Moffatt, "If anyone has no love for the Lord, let God's curse be on him." Cf. Rev. 22:20.

marble, limestone capable of high polish, found in many colors in the Middle East, and popular for temples (I Chron. 29:2), palaces (Esther 1:6), and other public structures. It was used for pillars, flooring, or wall inlay. Marble was included in the list of "precious" or luxury commodities (Rev. 18:12).

Marcus, sometimes used in the A.V. for Mark*.

Marduk. See MERODACH.

Mareshah (mȧ-rē′shȧ) (Marisa) (Josh. and II Macc.). (1) A city of Judah (Josh. 15:44), identified with Tell Sandahannah, 1 m. S. of Beit Jibrîn, on the ancient road from the coastal plain to Hebron (see E. Robinson, *Biblical Researches in Palestine*, II, pp. 51 ff.). It was fortified by King Rehoboam of Judah (c. 922–915 B.C.) to protect Jerusalem (II Chron. 11:8); and was the scene of the battle between Zerah, an Ethiopian invader, and King Asa of Judah (c. 913–873 B.C.) (II Chron. 14:9–12). It was the birthplace of the prophet Eliezer (II Chron. 20:37); and Micah (1:15) prophesied its destruction. In the 3d century B.C., Apollophanes founded a Sidonian colony at Marisa, the decorated tombs of which reveal the extent of Hellenistic cultural and religious influence (see Peters and Thiersch, *Painted Tombs in the Necropolis of Marisa*, 1905). At the time of the Maccabean revolt, Marisa was an Idumean fortress (II Macc. 12:35; cf. I Macc. 5:66). The city was destroyed by the Parthians in 40 B.C. Excavation by F. J. Bliss and R. A. S. Macalister in 1900 (*Excavations in Palestine During the Years 1898–1900*, 1902, pp. 52 ff.) revealed the remains of a complete Hellenistic city, with streets and houses laid out on a regular plan. (2) First-born son of Caleb, and the father of Ziph (I Chron. 2:42). (3) The son of Laadah, a descendant of Judah (I Chron. 4:21). W. P. A.

Mari (mä'rē) (Tell el-Harīrī), an ancient city near Abū-Kemal on the Middle Euphrates*, S. of its junction with the Habor. According to the Sumerian King List, Mari was the seat of the 10th Dynasty after the Flood. Identification with Tell el-Harīrī, first proposed by Albright in 1932, has been definitely established as a result of the excavation of the site since 1933 for the Musée du Louvre by A. Parrot, who completed his 19th season in 1971. Archaeological evidence indicates that Mari was founded at the end of the 4th millennium B.C., and experienced two great periods of prosperity. The first cultural peak occurred in the first half of the 3d millennium B.C. (the "Pre-Sargonic," or Early Dynastic period), and is represented by the remains of a number of monumental buildings: the archaic ziggurat; temples of Ishtar (see *CAH*³, Vol. I, Pt. 2, 1971, pp. 291 ff.), Dagan, Shamash, Ninhursag, and other deities; and the pre-Sargonic palace, under excavation since 1964, with a royal chapel and massive earthen altar (cf. Ex. 20:24). Numerous statues and pieces of shell inlay shed light on the culture, dress, and appearance of the period (e.g., *ANEP*², Nos. 24, 305, 429, 506, 788).

More important for Biblical studies is Mari's second great period of achievement, when it was ruled by Amorite kings during the late 19th and early 18th centuries B.C., until conquered by Hammurabi c. 1760 B.C. ("Middle" chronology; according to the "Low" chronology, c. 1696 B.C.; see CHRONOLOGY). This period is represented by the enormous palace of Zimrilim, the last king of Mari, with an area of over 6 acres and more than 300 rooms and courtyards, including private living quarters, administrative offices, a royal chapel, throne room, reception hall, and scribal school. Details of a large mural painting discovered in one of the courtyards have been interpreted as analogous to the O.T. description of Eden (Parrot, *AOTS*, 1967, p. 139; cf. *ANEP*², No. 610). Over 20,000 clay tablets taken from the palace archives contain information of great importance for the history of the early 2d millennium B.C. and the background of the O.T. Patriarchs. Numerous proper names occur in the Mari texts which are paralleled in the patriarchal narratives. Of particular interest, and controversy, is the Mari tribal designation, *Banū-yamīna* ("sons of the South"), which is similar to the O.T. name Benjamin; the Mari clay documents often mention the city of Nahor (Nakhur), home of Rebekah (Gen. 24:10), and Haran, where Abraham migrated from Ur (Gen. 11:31, 12:4 f.); several tribal and religious practices common to the O.T. are found in the society of Mari, such as the killing of a young animal to establish a covenant, or the expression "the god of my father" (Gen. 28:13, 31:5, etc.; see *ANET*³, pp. 628 f.); the presence at Mari of diviner-prophets who experienced ecstatic trances and acted as the spontaneous mouthpieces of deities, provides new insight into the origins and types of prophecy in the O.T. (see *ANET*³, pp. 623–625, 629–632; *BA* 31, 1968, pp. 102–124; *HTR* 63, 1970, pp. 1–28; *VT Supp.* 15, 1966, pp. 207–227). These examples serve to indicate the significance of the excavations and archives at Mari for the background of the Patriarchal Age. See *AOTS*, 1967, pp. 136–144; *BA* 11, 1948, pp. 1–19; *BA* 34, 1971, pp. 2–22. W. P. A.

mark, a symbolic mutilation of the body; as the "mark of Cain" the murderer (Gen. 4:15), which has been interpreted as a tribal branding, or incision in the forehead, or some sign indicating that he was a repentant sinner and not to be treated as a common murderer; circumcision, the mark of the Israelite (Gen. 17:13); the "mark of the prophet," possibly a distinctive scar on the forehead (I Kings 20:35–43) or wounds in the hands (Zech. 13:4–6) received, ironically, in the house of friends. The latter thought reappears in the words of Paul about bearing in his body the marks (stigmata) of scourgings and ill-treatment received during his witnessing for Christ (II Cor. 11:23 ff.; Gal. 6:17). Revelation mentions in cryptic terms the marks on the right hand and forehead of all Christians, small and great, rich and poor, to distinguish them from pagans (13:16 f., cf. 14:9, 15:2, 16:2, 19:20, 20:4). It also mentions the "mark of the beast" (Rev. 19:20). The Levitical law against making cuttings or marks on the body was probably in protest against the pagan tattooing of pictures of deities. Yet cf. the "memorial" on hand and forehead in Ex. 13:9, probably succeeded by phylacteries* (Deut. 6:8, "frontlets").

Mark (Marcus three times in the A.V.: Col. 4:10; Philem. 24; I Pet. 5:13), John Mark (Acts 12:12, 25, 15:37), designated sometimes only as John (Acts 13: 5, 13); a Jerusalem Jew whose mother, Mary, was a property-owner and hospitable to early Christians (Acts 12:12–17). Mark was a kinsman of Barnabas (Col. 4:10). He accompanied Barnabas and Paul to Antioch (Acts 12:25, 13:1), and later served as their attendant on the First Missionary Journey (13:5); but for some reason Mark deserted the missionary party at Perga and hurried home (13:13). Because of this Paul thought it unwise to take Mark on the Second Journey (15:38). This caused a disagreement between Paul and Barnabas and the end of their missionary partnership (15:36–41 f.). Barnabas gave Mark another chance, and took him to Cyprus as a companion.

After 10 years Mark is next heard of with Paul, who had evidently forgiven him (Col. 4:10; Philem. 24). "If he comes" could refer to the unfavorable impression caused by Mark's earlier defection; or possibly to a lingering fear of Paul's concerning his forgiven but still uncertain protégé. II Tim. 4:11 perhaps indicates that Mark had made good on his visit to the Colossian church, and that Paul wanted him to come to Rome, where he could be useful; that Mark now excelled in "ministering," the same work in which he had once failed the Apostle (Acts 13:5).

Peter is represented as referring to Mark as "my son" (I Pet. 5:13), probably in the sense of his being responsible for Mark's conversion during Peter's intimacy with Mark's Jerusalem home and family (Acts 12:12). The incident of the anonymous young man (Mark 14:51 f.) could easily fit the youthful Mark, who knew Peter, and would love late hours and exciting happenings. Papias of Hierapolis, who wrote c. A.D. 130, says that Mark was the "interpreter" and "attendant" of Peter. The Galilean fisherman needed someone like Mark to translate his sermons to Gentile audiences. There is no doubt that Mark in Rome assisted both Peter and Paul. The Gospel of Mark, attributed to this John Mark, is believed by some scholars to be based on the firsthand authority of Peter; other scholars find evidence of the use of so many other sources within this Gospel as to minimize Peter's influence upon it.

Tradition declares that Mark was the founder of the church in the great Jewish-Greek city of Alexandria, where he is believed to have died and been buried. The supposed transfer of Mark's body from Egypt to Venice in A.D. 832 by devout merchants is depicted in a series of mosaics on the façade of St. Mark's, Venice, beneath whose altar his bones are said to repose.

The lion is the symbol of this Evangelist, who, once weak and unstable, was by God's grace made strong.

Early Christian tradition locates the Jerusalem home of John Mark's mother, the gathering place of the first *ekklēsia* or church, on the S. end of the western hill of Mt. Zion, a residential section in the time of Jesus, which may have been the scene of Pentecost (Acts 2:1 ff.).

Mark, the Gospel according to, the 2d book of the N.T. and the shortest and simplest of the four Gospels. Historically it is the most important of the Gospels, for it is the basis of Matthew and Luke and it underlies John. It is therefore the earliest surviving written record of Jesus' life and virtually the only record.

Mark's Gospel may be outlined as follows:

(1) Beginning of the Gospel—1:1–13
  (a) ministry of John the Baptist—1:2–8
  (b) baptism and temptation of Jesus—1:9–13
(2) The Galilee ministry of preaching and healing, and the conflicts with religious authorities—1:14–8:26
  (a) about the Sea of Galilee—1:14–5:43
  (b) more distant journeys—6:1–8:26
(3) The Messiah and the coming Passion—8:27–10:45
  (a) Peter's confession—8:27–33
  (b) predictions of Passion—8:32, 9:30–32, 10:32–35
  (c) doctrine of discipleship—8:34–9:1, 9:33–37, 10:13, 31, 35–45
  (d) Transfiguration—9:2–13
(4) The Passion Narrative—10:46–15:47
  (a) on way to Jerusalem—10:46–52
  (b) entry into Jerusalem—11:1–11
  (c) ministry in Jerusalem—11:12–13:2
  (d) apocalyptic discourse—13:3–37
  (e) Jesus' death—14:1–15:47
(5) The empty tomb—16:1–8
(6) Appended conclusion—16:9–20

Its date must fall between A.D. 64 and 85. The former date is established from Irenaeus' statement that "after the deaths [of Peter and Paul] Mark, the disciple and interpreter of Peter, also handed down to us in writing the things which Peter had proclaimed." Peter and Paul are believed to have suffered martyrdom in Rome c. A.D. 64/65. Its latest date is determined by the fact that it was used by Matthew and Luke, both of which were written before the close of the 1st century. A more precise dating depends upon the interpretation of the "Little Apocalypse" in chapter 13. The vagueness of Mark (13:13 ff., 24–27, 30, 33) compared with the clarity of Luke (21:20) leads some scholars to believe that Jerusalem had not yet been destroyed when this Gospel was written and that it should be dated just prior to A.D. 70. Other scholars believe the author makes a distinction between the great catastrophe (vv. 14 ff.) and the return of Christ. Mark warns his readers that those who foretold Christ's coming during the great trouble were false prophets (vv. 21 f.). Christ will come "after that tribulation" (v. 24). This seems to indicate that Jerusalem had already fallen, but men were still expecting the coming of the New Age. A date about A.D. 75 agrees with these conditions.

The readers for whom it was written were evidently Christians, for the author does not explain such terms as: "the Spirit," "the Gospel," "the Kingdom of God," which would have been meaningless to non-Christians. Though the Gospel shows the influence of some Aramaic documentary sources (3:17, 5:41, 7:11, 34, 14:36, 15:34), the theory that it is a Greek translation of an Aramaic original is unconvincing. It was written in Greek for Greek-speaking Christians; and its language is not literary, but the popular, spoken Greek of the day. Most of its O.T. quotations are from the Septuagint or Greek translation. It explains details of life in Palestine which would be unfamiliar to Greek readers (7:3 f., 12:42, 14:12, 15:22, 42). Its point of view is that of Hellenistic Christians who felt an obligation to preach Christ's gospel to the whole world.

The tradition that this Gospel was written in Rome for Roman Christians arose at the end of the 1st century. On the authority of the Presbyter John, Papias wrote the following passage quoted in Eusebius' *Church History:* "This also the Presbyter said: Mark having become the interpreter of Peter, wrote down accurately . . . whatsoever things he remembered of the things said or done by

Christ. For he neither heard the Lord nor followed Him, but afterwards, as I said, he followed Peter . . ." This evidence from the end of the 1st or the beginning of the 2d century connects the author of this Gospel with Peter. The First Epistle of Peter, written in Peter's name near the end of the 1st century, says: "The church that is at Babylon [a symbolic name for Rome] . . . saluteth you; and so doth Marcus my son" (I Peter 5:13). This not only connects Mark with Peter, but reflects the early tradition that they both labored in Rome.

The evidence connecting this Gospel with Rome is further supported by the fact of its survival even after the appearance of the fuller and more skillfully written Gospels of Matthew and Luke. In popular favor Matthew and Luke supplanted Mark. But Mark was not discarded, as were other early records which were used as sources and then allowed to disappear. Some influential church must have valued this Gospel for its origin. The only church influential enough to have preserved Mark in the face of its lack of popular favor was Rome.

The author, according to internal evidence, was a Christian Jew, for he shows: acquaintance with Jewish life and thought; knowledge of the Scriptures; understanding of Aramaic, phrases of which he incorporates in his text; and familiarity with the general geography of Palestine and particularly with Jerusalem. The author's point of view belongs, however, not to the Jewish, but to the Hellenistic part of the early Church. This is seen in, e.g.: the endorsement of the Gentile mission; the disapproval of Jewish food laws and strict Sabbath observance; the use of Hellenistic terms; and quotations from the Septuagint.

This internal evidence concerning the author agrees with known facts about Mark, whom tradition identifies as the author (see above; for the facts of Mark's life see MARK). Mark would have gained his acquaintance with Jewish life and thought, his knowledge of Aramaic, and his familiarity with Jerusalem from his residence in that city, where his mother occupied a large house. As far as we know, his adult life was spent in the Hellenistic cities of the Roman Empire, with such Christian missionaries as his relative Barnabas, Paul, and Peter.

The sources used by Mark are thought, by many scholars, to have been early, written documents now lost. Formerly it was believed, on the authority of Papias, quoted above, that this Gospel was virtually the Memoirs of Peter. Doubtless many of the narratives go back ultimately to the testimony of the eyewitness Peter, but before these materials were incorporated in the Gospel they are believed to have had a literary history. Luke stated that "many have taken in hand to set forth . . . those things which are most surely believed among us" (1:1). Such written records as Luke here implies would have been available to Mark. Evidence of written sources underlying this Gospel can be seen: (1) in the blocks of material on one theme interrupting a narrative; (2) and in stylistic differences of certain parts. The following sections are among those thought to rest upon documentary sources: (1) the series of conflicts (2:1–3:6, 12:13 ff.) between Jesus and Jewish authorities; (2) the Apocalyptic chapter (13), which is the only instance in Mark of a long discourse on a single theme; (3) the group of parables (chap. 4); (4) the Passion story (14:1–16:8), which contains exact notes of time and place not found elsewhere in Mark; (5) the names of the Twelve (3:16 ff.); (6) and citations from the Scriptures. In addition to these documentary sources Mark must have used the oral traditions which Papias, in the 2d century, declared he preferred to the written records. The oral tradition would have supplied material for expanding or modifying the documentary sources. It would also have provided a framework (cf. Acts 10:37 ff., 13:23–31) for the general course of Jesus' life to guide Mark in the arrangement of his material.

To these sources Mark brought his crisp, vigorous style and a sense of the dramatic. He made constant use of the words "straightway," "immediately," and "forthwith," giving a sense of urgency to his narrative.

The end of the Gospel (16:9–20), which is lacking in the two oldest Greek MSS. and other authorities, is a later addition. Possibly the Gospel ended abruptly with v. 8 because the author was unable, for some reason, to finish it. Or the original MS. may have suffered mutilation at the end of the scroll. Competent scholars who disagree with these two theories believe that 16:8 is an entirely adequate and artistic conclusion to the Gospel of Mark and the one intended by the author.

The purpose of Mark becomes clear from a study of its contents. It was written for those who already believed in Christ and it was designed to give them information about his deeds and sayings. In order to give unity and meaning to his account Mark had to select his information, explain it, and emphasize certain aspects. Any narrative of Jesus' life necessarily contains interpretation. There is interpretation in this Gospel, though it cannot, because of this, be classified as a theological tract. Mark's narrative blends history and theology. His beliefs, which were those of the early Church, are revealed in the slant and emphasis he gave his narrative. The information he selected had practical religious value for his readers, e.g.: Jesus' teaching about eating with sinners (2:13–17); fasting (2:18–22); keeping the Sabbath (2:23–3:5); requirements of the Law (7:1–23); divorce (10:2–12); civil obedience (12:13–17); the chief commandments (12:28–34); the duties and characteristics of discipleship (8:34–9:1; 9:33–37; 10:35–45). The Gospel also included accounts of the origins and significance of the chief Christian rites, baptism (1:8–11) and communion (14:22–25). Its detailed explanation of how and why Jesus met death was information the early Christians found necessary in meeting controversy. Finally, Mark may have attempted to show Christians of his day, who were fearful of trouble and renewed persecution, how Jesus met opposition and death victoriously. In this Gospel the shadow of the cross appears almost at the beginning (2:6, 7, 3:6), but it is on a note of confident triumph (14:62) that Jesus answers his final enemies.

This Gospel satisfactorily answered the question of Roman Christians: "What was Jesus like?" It revealed him by deeds more than by discourses. It portrayed him in human terms: eating (14:3), drinking (2:16), becoming weary and sleeping (4:38). His personal touch is frequently mentioned (5:41, 6:5, 7:33, 9:27, 10:13). He expressed compassion (5:19), love (10:21), and other emotions (3:5, 6:6, 10:14, 14:33, 15:34).

Beside these vivid human aspects of Jesus, Mark sets his portrait of Jesus as Son of God. From the beginning he is the mighty one (1:7) and God's beloved Son (1:11). Mark makes it clear that Jesus was the Messiah, not in a political sense, but in the sense of the Son of God (8:38, 9:7, 12:1–11, 13:32, 14:36, 61 f., 15:39). This was the belief of the early Church, the announced theme of the Gospel (1:1), one of the turning-points of the narrative (8:27–33).

market place. See AGORA; ARCHITECTURE; ATHENS; CORINTH; STOA.

marriage, the legal union of man and woman for life; safeguarded in Hebrew society by specific laws formulated in ancient times to promote family* welfare and prestige. In the nomadic period and the days of the Judges mothers were often honored matriarchs, presiding over home affairs in the central tent. Often the wife remained among her own people, and her husband visited her occasionally (Judg. 14:19, 15:1 f.; but see Gen. 2:24, 24:5). "Marriage by capture," a frequent basis of marriage in primitive society, did not prevail among the Hebrews. Betrothals and marriages were often arranged at the vintage festivals (Judg. 21:21) and other community celebrations, like those in honor of returning warriors.

In early O.T. times wives were selected for sons by the heads of tribes or families (Abraham for Isaac, Gen. 25:20; Isaac for Jacob, 28:19). Betrothal was effected by the payment of the *mohar* (usually 50 shekels) to the father of the prospective bride, not as a purchase price, but as a compensation for the loss of the daughter (Gen. 34:12; I Sam. 18:25); by the presentation of substantial gifts to the girl (Gen. 34:12; Ex. 21:7, 22:15–17; Deut. 22:28 f.; Ruth 4:5, 10); or by the groom's agreeing to serve the bride's father for a period of time, as Jacob served Laban for Leah and Rachel (Gen. 29:18, 20, 25, 30). The bride often brought considerable means to the new home, e.g., Abigail (I Sam. 25:42). The recently discovered Eshnunna Law Code current in Babylon probably 3,800 years ago (the oldest law code yet known) required the payment of "bride money" by the prospective groom, and a refund of the same plus 20% interest in case the bride died (Albrecht Goetze). In Semitic society cousins might marry: Isaac and Rebekah (Gen. 24:15); Jacob and Leah and Rachel (28:2); Esau and Basemath (36:3). Families liked to keep their land and flocks within their own group, and they went to great inconvenience to arrange marriages that continued this policy (Gen. 24). There was a "Mosaic" law specifying that the daughters of Zelophehad* (who had no sons), must marry within their tribe if they wished to safeguard their rights of inheritance* (Num. 27:1–11).

Among primitive nomads in Palestine, as well as in Mesopotamia, the chastity of the unmarried woman was expected, as it still is among Bedouins. The laws of the Hebrew Deuteronomic code and those of Hammurabi are strikingly similar in this matter (seduction of a betrothed virgin, Deut. 22:23 f.; rape of a betrothed virgin, 22:25–27; rape of an unbetrothed virgin, Deut. 22:28 f.). O.T. laws concerning marriage and chastity are found in the Holiness Code (Lev. 18:1–5, etc.). Incestuous relations with certain relatives were forbidden (mother, Lev. 18:7; sister or half-sister, 18:9; paternal aunt, 18:12; maternal aunt, 18:13; two sisters at the same time, 18:18). Contrast Jacob's marriage to Leah and Rachel. The customs of polygamous Canaanites and Egyptians were denounced.

Ezekiel's marriage restrictions were more drastic than those of Lev. 21:7, 14. Among religious leaders marriage was customary, though with certain restrictions (Lev. 21:14). Priests and Levites married, and bequeathed their offices to their sons. Essenes in the time of Jesus refrained from marriage, but were not necessarily esteemed for so doing. John the Baptist is assumed to have been a celibate. Peter was married (Matt. 8:14); and there is a suggestion that some of the other Apostles were also (I Cor. 9:5). Paul may have remained unmarried (see I Cor. 7).

The laws of the levirate marriage (Deut. 25:5–10) provided that a brother of a deceased man should under certain circumstances marry the widow; and their son would be considered the deceased man's son. (For levirate marriage law in operation see Gen. 38). Leviticus and Numbers express opposition to levirate marriage. If the man refused to marry his deceased brother's widow the woman might, in the presence of elders, remove his shoe from his foot and spit in his face. Ruth 4:7 illustrates how a kinsman of Boaz, by drawing off his shoe and giving it to his neighbor, relinquished his right to marry Ruth. A case of levirate marriage is indicated in Matt. 22:23–30.

Plural marriages were sanctioned in O.T. times, and Deuteronomic law did not forbid them (Deut. 21:15–17). Large families were desirable; polygamy, with concubines, handmaids, and secondary wives, was normal. Though Isaac apparently had no wife but Rebekah, other Patriarchs (Abraham, Jacob, Joseph) had more than one. But O.T. ethics point to one wife for one husband as the ideal (Mal. 2:14–16)—a symbol of God's relation to His people (Hos. 2:19 f.). During the Conquest and the development of town life marriage was a matter of caste, governed by material means and prestige. Kings had several wives—like David (I Sam. 18:27, 25:42 f.; II Sam. 11:3, etc.); and Solomon (I Kings 11:1–3)—for political alliances.

After the Exile polygamy tended to wane; and by N.T. times monogamy was taken for granted.

Hebrew laws discouraged intermarriage with foreigners—not on ethnic grounds, but to avoid religious syncretism and to foster the worship of Yahweh (Ex. 34:15 f.). Marriage with Canaanite neighbors was especially frowned on (Deut. 7:1–3 f., 16, 23:3, cf. Ex. 34:15 f.). Yet Ruth, a Moabite, became the ancestress of David and Jesus (4:22). In the Deuteronomic Code marriage with a captured enemy was tolerated, after suitable rites (Deut. 21:10–14). Nehemiah, returning to Jerusalem after the Babylonian Exile, compelled his followers to cease marrying foreign wives from Ashdod, Moab, Ammon, etc. Ezra the scribe revived an old law (Ex. 34:15 f.; Deut. 7:1–4), and established a divorce court that annulled mixed alliances (Ezra 10:5–44). The sanctity of the home was emphasized in Hebrew religion.

Marriage in O.T. times required no state or religious sanction; it was a private affair, with the good of the total family group paramount. It was not a contract, but a "sanctification" (*kiddushin*) often based on lofty ideals and regulations. Jews, in contrast to Greeks and Romans, saw in marriage more than a means of increasing national power; it was a "building of joy," the founding of a home.

In Jewish marriage the engagement ceremony was very important, marking the beginning of the marriage ceremony (cf. Hos. 2:19 f.). (See in this connection Matt. 1:18–25, the betrothal of Mary and Joseph of Nazareth.) Joseph, knowing the old law that an engagement could be terminated only by divorce, considerately planned a private putting away of Mary (v. 19) before his angelic revelation changed his attitude (vv. 20–25). From early times an engagement had been a period during which the bride was still dependent on her father, though consecrated to the man who was to become her husband, and forbidden to all others; the espoused woman was regarded as already married. She took a period of 12 months to assemble her trousseau and property—a longer interval was frowned upon. During the engagement the groom was exempt from military service (Deut. 20:7, cf. 24:5). In earliest times the engagement began when the groom paid the dowry or *mohar* to the bride's father, in the presence of witnesses, or began to "serve" for her; in post-Exilic times the marriage settlement supplanted the old "purchase price."

After the marriage ceremony the gorgeously attired groom brought the bride home to his family at evening, amid joyous and elaborate celebration (see the Parable of the Wise and Foolish Virgins, Matt. 25:1–13, and the wedding feast at Cana of Galilee, John 2:1–11). Matt. 9:15 refers to the "bridechamber."

Marriage normally guaranteed food, clothing, and shelter for the wife, as well as performance of the marital act. Rabbinical law allowed the wife the privilege of seeking a divorce in the event that any of them were denied.

But despite regulations there was sentiment and romance in marriage. The joys of the family and the sanctity of marriage are stressed in Prov. 5:15–20, 11:16, 12:4, 14:1, 31:10–31; cf. the Song of Solomon, an ancient love song.

Laws governing divorce are stated in Deut. 24:1–4. Mosaic law forbade priests to marry divorced women (Lev. 21:14). But a priest's divorced daughter might return to her father's house (Lev. 22:13). Immorality is the only specified cause for divorce, but other grounds were apparently recognized. Adultery in O.T. law (Ex. 20:14; Deut. 5:18) was the offense of illicit intimacy between a married or a betrothed woman and a man not her husband; and both parties were subject to the death penalty (Lev. 20:10). But intimacy between a married man and an unmarried girl did not constitute adultery; there was a double standard (but see Deut. 22:28 f.). A woman found guilty of premarital unchastity might be stoned to death (Deut. 22:13–21). Written bills of divorcement were given (Deut. 24:1; Isa. 50:1) to divorced women; and this divorce regulation remained valid in the time of Jesus (Matt. 5:31 f., 19:7). The Gospel of Mark, whose words are incorporated into the Christian marriage ceremony, "What therefore God hath joined together, let not man put asunder" (10:9), quotes Jesus as saying, "Whosoever shall put away his wife, and marry another, committeth adultery against her. And if a woman shall put away her husband, and be married to another, she committeth adultery" (10:11 f.). (For laws against adultery, see Lev. 20:10–13; cf. Matt. 5:27 f. See FORNICATION.)

Widows in Palestine were viewed with pity. Consideration for their economic helplessness gave rise to laws of mercy (Ex. 22:22; Deut. 10:18; Isa. 1:17; see II Kings 4:1 ff.).

For a discussion of laws of marriage and divorce in ancient Babylonia and Assyria as compared with those of the Hebrews, see "The Family in the Ancient Near East," I. Mendelssohn, in *BA*, Vol. XI, No. 2, May 1948, pp. 24–40.

Mars Hill, used in A.V. Acts 17:22 for Areopagus*.

Martha ("lady"), the sister of Mary and Lazarus of Bethany (Luke 10:38; cf. John 11:1–12:2), in whose home Jesus and his company sought rest from their work in nearby Jerusalem or hospitality on their way up from Jericho. A woman named Martha appears three times in the N.T.; whether she is one and the same is not entirely clear. (1) Luke 10:38, 40–42 shows her entertaining Jesus in her home and complaining to him because her sister Mary is not helping her with preparations for the meal. Martha's complaint drew rebuke from her guest (vv. 41 f.). (2) John 11:1–39 presents Martha as an admirable woman of faith and action. She went out into the road to meet Jesus when he was returning from a distant preaching mission (v. 7), during which Lazarus had died. With complete faith Martha declared that if Jesus had been present her brother would not have died (v. 21). It was to Martha that Jesus made his great statement about eternal life:

"I am the resurrection and the life; he that believeth in me, though he were dead, yet shall he live" (v. 25). (3) Some authorities have suggested that Martha might have been the wife or widow of Simon the leper, at whose home in Bethany Jesus and his Disciples were present only two days before the last Passover (Matt. 26:6–13; Mark 14:1–3). In view of the scanty evidence, however, it seems more likely that she was simply a capable neighbor who went with her clay cookstove on her head, as women of Bethany still do, to lend a hand when company comes.

259. Mars Hill, Athens.

martyr (Gk. *martys*, "witness"), a witness for Jesus Christ who, rather than renounce his faith, chooses death; like Stephen* (Acts 22:20), Antipas (Rev. 2:13), "the martyrs of Jesus Christ" (Rev. 17:6). The Revised Versions use "witness" instead of "martyr" for Acts 22:20 and Rev. 2:13, but "martyrs" for Rev. 17:6 except in margin, A.S.V., R.S.V.

Mary (Gk. form of Heb. *Miriam*). The name of six women in the N.T.

(1) *Mary, the Virgin*, the mother of Jesus. (See separate article, MARY THE VIRGIN.)

(2) *Mary Magdalene*, identified by the name of her home town, now Mejdel, 3 m. from Capernaum on the NW. shore of the Sea of Galilee, and according to Jewish authorities renowned for its wealth and immorality. This Mary may have been a harlot who had been rescued from her evil life (Mark 16:9), and had followed Jesus out of gratitude (Luke 8:1 f.). Opinion varies as to whether Luke 7:37–50 refers to Mary Magdalene. She, with other devoted women, stood by the cross (Matt. 27:56; Mark 15:40; John 19:25), watched Jesus' burial (Matt. 27:61; Mark 15:47), and came early to the sepulcher on the Resurrection morning (Matt. 28:1; Mark 16:1; Luke 24:10; John 20:1). She was among the last to leave the cross and the first to see the open tomb (Luke 23:55–24:2). She was rewarded by a vision of her risen Lord (Matt. 28:1, 9; John 20:11–18).

(3) *Mary of Bethany*, sister of Lazarus (John 11:1) and Martha (Luke 10:38 f.). She served with her sister, but was not "distracted" (R.S.V.) as Martha was. Mary "also sat at Jesus' feet and heard his word" (Luke 10:39 f.). Jesus commended Mary's wisdom in choosing to seize an opportunity for spiritual instruction rather than to help Martha with an elaborate meal (Luke 10:41 f.). When Lazarus became ill both sisters sent for their friend Jesus (John 11:3). When Lazarus died, many Jews came to comfort the sisters (John 11:19). Martha, true to Luke's portrayal, rushed out to meet Jesus (John 11:20–27), while Mary remained in the house. Many Jews who came with Mary, after seeing the events at the tomb of Lazarus, believed in Jesus (John 11:45). The third and last appearance of this Mary in the Gospel record occurs after the raising of Lazarus, when Jesus was entertained at Bethany; she anointed his "feet" (John 12:1–11). This anointing was used to identify this Mary (John 11:2), and is distinct from another anointing in the Bethany house of Simon the leper by an unnamed woman, and a much earlier anointing by a woman "who was a sinner" [Luke 7:36–50; Mary (2)].

(4) *Mary, the mother of James* the Less and Joses**, followed Jesus from Galilee, witnessed the Crucifixion (Matt. 27:55 f.; Mark 15:40 f.; Luke 23:49), watched the burial (Matt. 27:61; Mark 15:47), and visited the sepulcher on the Resurrection morning (Matt. 28:1; Mark 16:1; Luke 24:10). This Mary was also designated as the wife of Cleophas (A.V.), or Clopas (R.S.V.) (John 19:25), who is identical with Alphaeus (Matt. 10:3; Mark 3:18; Luke 6:15), both names coming from the same Aram. word.

(5) *Mary, the mother of Mark*, the Christian woman whose house in Jerusalem was the meeting place of the early Disciples (Acts 12:12). Her son is believed to be the author of the Second Gospel. According to A.V. Col. 4:10 she was the sister of Barnabas, but in the A.S.V. Mark and Barnabas are cousins (Acts 15:37, 39). Her widowhood is implied in the fact that her real estate holdings were in her own name.

(6) *Mary, a Christian woman* (mentioned in Rom. 16, which many authorities feel was part of the letter to Ephesus). Paul sent his greetings to Mary (Rom. 16:6) "who bestowed much labor on us" (A.S.V. "on you," R.S.V. "among you"); he had not yet visited Rome when this Epistle was written. Perhaps this Mary, whose services were well known, may be compared with Lydia (Acts 16:14 f.). Some believe that she was the mother of Mark.

Mary, the Virgin, the wife of Joseph and the mother of Jesus. It is most difficult to draw a line of demarcation between the many legends and the meager Biblical record of the mother of Jesus Christ. Even the latter has undergone repeated challenges.

First, the Biblical record. Mary, as well as Joseph, may have sprung from Judah and the family of David (cf. Luke 1:32, 69; Rom. 1:3; II Tim. 2:8; Heb. 7:14). Both Matthew and Luke give the genealogy of Jesus from the standpoint of Joseph, the male head of the household (Matt. 1:16; Luke 3:23).

Mary had one sister (John 19:25), probably Salome, wife of Zebedee, mother of James and John (Matt. 27:56; Mark 15:40). Mary was also related to Elisabeth, mother of John the Baptist (Luke 1:36).

During the betrothal of Joseph and Mary—which usually preceded marriage* by a year—the angel Gabriel announced to Mary that she was to be the mother of the Messiah, "the Son of God" (Luke 1:26–35, 2:21). The decision of Mary to leave her Nazareth home and visit her kinswoman Elisabeth in Judaea (Luke 1:38–40) was due to (1) a natural craving for understanding by a trusted woman friend, and (2) the wish to escape the gossip that a birth under such circumstances would precipitate—Joseph later was tempted to yield to the latter (Matt. 1:19). Mary was greeted by Elisabeth as "the mother of my Lord" in a beautiful psalm (Luke 1:42–45). Mary replied in a still more wonderful song, the *Magnificat** (vv. 46–55). For about three months, until the birth of John the Baptist, Mary remained with Elisabeth; then returned to Nazareth.

According to Luke 2:4 f., Joseph and Mary traveled together "from Galilee, out of the city of Nazareth" to Bethlehem as engaged persons, though their marriage had been legalized. Had Mary not been officially "espoused" (A.V. Luke 2:5) or "betrothed" (R.S.V.) to Joseph, Jewish custom would have forbidden her making the journey alone with him. At Bethlehem—possibly in the cave which served as stable to the inn, on or near the site of the present Church of the Nativity—Mary brought forth her "firstborn son." All the circumstances connected with this event were faithfully remembered and pondered by Mary (Luke 2:19). Matthew appears to tell the birth story from the viewpoint of Joseph, and reveals Mary through her husband's eyes.

Some of those who believe that the miraculous element in the birth narratives of Matthew and Luke is not fact but poetry, nevertheless maintain that these stories bear witness to the divine nature of Jesus. They see in the stories of his mysterious origin an attempt to account for the inexplicable in Christ's character and life. The virgin birth is—to them—not a historic proof of Christ's divinity, but a recognition that Christ's divinity found explanation in the 1st century in terms of a miraculous birth. See IMMANUEL.

After the birth there followed a series of events in which Mary participated: (1) the presentation and purification (Luke 2:22–39); (2) the visit of the Wise Men (Matt. 2:11); and (3) the flight into Egypt and the return (Matt. 2:14, 20 f.).

The daily routine of a woman's life in a Nazareth home was interrupted once each year by the family journey to Jerusalem for the Passover (Luke 2:41). Mary's words when she found the lost Jesus revealed not only her motherly solicitude but her discipline (Luke 2:48, 51). Four more sons, all of whom are named (Matt. 13:55), and one or more unnamed daughters (Mark 6:3), were born to Mary; though the Roman Catholic Church and others which teach the perpetual virginity of Mary declare that these children were Joseph's by a former marriage. Others believe that the long-delayed entrance of Jesus into his public ministry was due to the death of Joseph, which placed on Jesus the duties of a breadwinner until the younger brothers and sisters reached the age of self-support. Jesus never abandoned this solicitude for the welfare of Mary (John 19:26 f.).

In the Gospel records no special veneration or authority is accorded Mary. At the feast in Cana of Galilee her authority was shown to be less than her son's (John 2:1–5). When the family moved to Capernaum (John 2:12; Matt. 4:13) Mary joined in a popular demonstration of neighbors, friends, and family to restrain Jesus in his activities (Mark 3:21, 31–35). In answering the unknown woman in the Jerusalem multitude who paid tribute to his mother, Jesus did not deny her blessedness, but refused to put her above all who hear and heed the word of God (Luke 11:27 f.).

After the Gospels the only glimpse of Mary in the N.T. is among those who "with one accord" continued steadfast in prayer (Acts 1:13 f.). Her intercession was not considered distinctive.

These brief references to Mary in Scripture set forth the mother of Jesus as blessed among all women (Luke 1:48), who shared with Joseph the parental responsibility of his upbringing (Luke 2:27, 33, 41, 48, 3:23), solicitously followed him in his life work (Luke 23:49), and at the cross experienced what Simeon had foretold (Luke 2:35).

Roman Catholic tradition and theology have built up through the centuries a series of incidents and doctrines concerning the Virgin which have no foundation in the Bible. Some give to Mary the homage others give only to her Son (Matt. 2:11). The presentation, annunciation, visitation, purification, assumption, and other ceremonial glorifications of the Virgin are official Roman Catholic festivals of Mariolatry. The immaculate conception applies to Mary rather than to Jesus—a dogma, proclaimed by Pius IX in December 1854, which states that the Virgin from the moment of her conception "was preserved free from all stain of original sin."

Maschil (mäs′kĭl) ("attentive"), a Heb. word appearing in the titles of Ps. 32, 42, 44, 45, 52–55, 74, 78, 88, 89, 142. It may stem from a forgotten liturgy, or it may characterize these Psalms as "contemplative" or "didactic."

masons, artisans who build with stones and brick. In Scripture they are usually mentioned with affiliated craftsmen, hewers of stone and carpenters, such as were sent by Hiram of Tyre to David to build his house (II Sam. 5:11; I Chron. 14:1); or to repair breaches in the Temple during the priest Jehoiada's renovations for King Jehoash (II Kings 12:12; II Chron. 24:12); or under the high priest Hilkiah for King Josiah (II Kings 22:6); or during the rebuilding of the Temple after the Exile (II Chron. 3:7). The quality of the work is evidenced by the substantial remains of their work still standing or excavated, like the Omri-Ahab palaces of Israel at Samaria*; the successive city levels and town walls at Lachish*, Byblos (see GEBAL), Megiddo*, Beth-shan*, and Tell en-Nasbeh (? Mizpah).

Masons achieved wonders underground, as at the Siloam* Tunnel in Jerusalem and the water systems at Megiddo, Lachish, and Gezer*.

The ancient city walls of Jerusalem, which survived scores of attacks and experienced countless reconstructions, are eloquent witnesses of the ability and persistence of Jewish masons. Jesus and his Disciples were impressed by the substantial quality of these walls (Mark 13:1 f.).

260. Mason in modern Lebanon, continuing craftsmanship of his Phoenician predecessors. Ivan Dmitri for American Export Lines.

Stone has always been plentiful in rugged Palestine; no man needed to go without building material for his house. Almost every village had stonemasons, quarries, and mortar kilns. Sojourners were impressed to work with native masons, as when David was preparing to build the Temple (I Chron. 22:2). Masons' tasks included the erection of shrines, walls between properties, enclosures for sheepfolds, the hewing out of cisterns and of caves for sepulchers (Mark 15:46); making winevats, millstones, and olive presses; and fashioning idols (Deut. 29:17). Masons were often skilled craftsmen and well paid. Others were impressed for *corvée*. Stoneworkers gave particular consideration to foundations* (Matt. 7:24–27; I Cor. 3:10–13), and rejected stones they judged unfit (Ps. 118:22). Often they reused masonry from earlier buildings, and even dismantled temples to build village houses.

Their tools consisted of a mallet or maul of hard stone; a plumb line (Amos 7:7; II Kings 21:13); a square; boring-rods to check joints; and chisels—the best ones of bronze hardened by long hammering. Some hammers had two faces, one a hammer, the other a pick.

Solomon's era (c. 961–922 B.C.) was the golden age of the mason, as demonstrated in the royal chariot cities like Megiddo; in the repairs to Millo*; and in the Temple and palaces. His masons co-operated with the expert ones of his trade ally, Hiram of Tyre (I Kings 7:9–12). Jewish masons who went to Phoenicia or worked with Phoenicians in Jerusalem learned much from their tutors. Men of Gebal were noted for their stonework (I Kings 5:18, A.S.V. margin). Much of the stone for the Temple was prepared at the quarries, so that the masons erected it without sound of hammer and chisel (I Kings 6:7). Probably local limestone was used for trim. This could have been removed silently by a special process from the tremendous cave beneath the Bezetha section of Jerusalem, not far from the Temple Area.

The better masonry of Solomon's time was partly due to the supplanting of crude hammers by improved ones able to square the ashlar building blocks. Blocks were dressed with more accurate alignment of courses. Even when these were not worked on their whole face, their margins were carefully squared. An example of fine Solomonic masonry survives in the tower of an outer wall at Gezer.

In the huge space beneath the present platform of the Jerusalem Temple Area, misnamed "Solomon's stables," can be seen the work of masons in a system of arches and other supports of the enlarged space needed for the central Temple building, its colonnades, staff houses, archives, and palaces of the kings and their courts.

Examples of excellent Herodian masonry are seen today in city walls at Jerusalem and probably at Hebron.

Archaeologists can easily date the occupation levels of cities by the type and quality of their masonry. (See also illus. 261, p. 426.)

Massa (măs′*ȧ*) ("load"), a descendant ("son") of Ishmael (Gen. 25:14; I Chron. 1:30), eponymous founder of a tribe of N. Arabia, possibly near the Persian Gulf. The A.S.V. margin of Prov. 31:1 reads, "The words of Lemuel, king of Massa," suggesting that this passage is part of the Wisdom Literature of the Hebrew borderland.

Massah (măs′*ȧ*) ("testing"; Meribah, "contention"), a place near Mt. Sinai, location unknown, where Moses produced water by striking a rock with his rod when Israel was restless with thirst and critical of Yahweh (Ex. 17:1–7). This was possibly a year after the Exodus. A similar event is mentioned in Num. 20:1–13, but is ascribed to a much later date, and possibly at Kadesh-barnea; the two events may be the same, confused in the record. Allusions to the smiting occur in Deut. 6:16, 9:22, 33:8; Ps. 95:8; etc.

Massora (m*ȧ*-sō′r*ȧ*) ("tradition"), traditional Hebrew text* of Bible, with notes added to preserve it intact.

master, the translation of several words used in Scripture for one having authority: (1) a Patriarchal sheikh (Gen. 24:9 ff.) or head of a house (Ex. 22:8); (2) an owner of slaves and servants (Ex. 21:4–8; Deut. 23:15; Judg. 19:11–23; I Sam. 30:13; Luke 16:13; Eph. 6:5; Col. 3:22; I Tim. 6:1 f.); (3) a political leader or king (II Sam. 12:8; II Kings 5:1;

261. Masonry of Hebrew Period at Lachish.

Isa. 36:8); (4) a leader of sacred song (I Chron. 15:27); (5) one in charge of eunuchs (Dan. 1:3) or magicians (Dan. 4:9); (6) the owner of a ship (A.V., A.S.V. Acts 27:11, R.S.V. "captain"); (7) the usual name by which Jesus was addressed or referred to (*Rabboni*, "teacher," in some versions): by his Disciples (Mark 4:38, 5:35, 9:5, 17, 38, 11:21; John 9:2, A.V. 20:16, etc.); by seekers (Matt. 8:19, 12:38); and by scribes and Pharisees (Matt. 12:38).

Mattaniah (măt′ȧ-nī′ȧ) ("gift of Jehovah"). (1) The original name of King Zedekiah*, son of Josiah, appointed by King Nebuchadnezzar of Babylon (II Kings 24:17) to rule the remnant of Jews left in Judah during the Exile. He reigned 11 years (598–587 B.C.). (2) A Hemanite in the singers' guild at the Temple (I Chron. 25:4, 16). (3) A Levite, son of Micah an Asaphite (I Chron. 9:15), leader of Temple singers (Neh. 11:17, 12:8). (4) One who helped reform worship under Hezekiah (c. 715–687 B.C.) (II Chron. 29:13). (5) The name of several men who put away foreign wives during the reforms of Ezra (10:26–37). (6) A Temple doorkeeper in the era of Nehemiah (12:25). (7) A priest whose son played his trumpet at the rededication of the walls (12:35). (8) A trusted distributor of offerings of oil and wine to "the brethren" under Nehemiah (13:13).

Mattathias (măt′ȧ-thī′ăs) ("gift of Jehovah"), a name popular in late O.T. and Maccabean times. (1) The Modin priest, father of five Maccabean brothers and founder of the Maccabees family (I Macc. 2:1) (see MACCABEES). (2) A captain in the army of Jonathan Maccabaeus (160–142 B.C.) (I Macc. 11:70). (3) A son of Simon the high priest (I Macc. 16:14–16). (4) An emissary dispatched by Nicanor to Judas Maccabaeus (166/5–160 B.C.). (5), (6) Two ancestors of Jesus (Luke 3:25 f.).

Matthew, one of the Twelve Apostles. His name is given in all four of the official lists. In Mark 3:18 and Acts 1:13 he is paired with Bartholomew; in Matt. 10:3 and Luke 6:15 with Thomas. Outside these records of his Apostolic status he is mentioned only when Christ called him to discipleship (Matt. 9:9; Mark 2:13 f.; Luke 5:27). Mark and Luke give his name as "Levi"—dual names are frequent in the N.T. Mark states that Levi's father's name was Alphaeus, and he implies that Capernaum was his home (Mark 2:1, 13 f.). Matthew may have been brother of the Apostle James*, whose father was Alphaeus (Matt. 10:3; Mark 3:18; Luke 6:15; Acts 1:13).

Matthew evidently was a Jew who entered the service of Rome as a despised tax collector. While seated at his place of toll in Capernaum, on the overland customs route between Damascus and the Mediterranean, he was invited by Jesus to leave his lucrative position and become his disciple. Matthew's "great feast" which followed the call (Luke 5:29–32) revealed the unpopularity of Matthew and his guests, and the willingness of Jesus to disregard prevailing public opinion in order to win such people for God.

For the relationship of Matthew to the First Gospel see next article.

Matthew, the Gospel according to, the 1st book of the N.T. Though written later than Mark, this Gospel was placed first among the collected four Gospels because it was early recognized as the authoritative and most comprehensive record of Jesus' life. Early Christians saw it as an improved edition of Mark, nine-tenths of whose contents it reproduces. To Mark's record it adds stories of Jesus' birth and infancy and accounts of his Resurrection appearances. It contains a full and clear account of Jesus' teaching, which is largely lacking in Mark. Its material, instead of being mingled as in other Gospels, is well arranged and useful for instruction purposes. Finally, it gives many different aspects of Christian thought.

The First Gospel may be outlined as follows:

(1) The Messiah is introduced—1:1–4:16

- (a) genealogy—1:1–17
- (b) birth—1:18–25
- (c) infancy—2:1–23
- (d) call and preparation—3:1–4:16

(2) The ministry in Galilee—4:17–16:28

- (a) beginning of the ministry—4:17–25
- (b) the new Law: Sermon on the Mount—5:1–7:29
- (c) miracles—8:1–9:34
- (d) the evangelistic charge to the Disciples—9:35–11:1
- (e) Jesus and his opponents—11:2–12:50
- (f) parables of the Kingdom—13:1–58
- (g) Jesus in exile—14:1–16:28

(3) The new Messiah—17:1–20:34

- (a) the Transfiguration and after—17:1–27
- (b) discourse on true discipleship—18:1–35
- (c) teachings on the way to Jerusalem—19:1–20:34

(4) Jesus in Jerusalem—21:1–25:46

- (a) the challenge of Christ—21:1–22:46
- (b) denunciation of scribes and Pharisees—23:1–39
- (c) eschatological discourse on the end of the age—24:1–25:46

(5) Jesus' death and Resurrection—26:1–28:20

- (a) final preparations—26:1–16
- (b) the last evening—26:17–46
- (c) arrest and trial—26:47–27:31
- (d) Crucifixion and burial—27:32–66
- (e) Resurrection—28:1–15
- (f) the great commission—28:16–20

The author is not named in this Gospel. According to tradition he was one of the Twelve, the tax collector Matthew (Matt. 9:9), known as Levi in Mark (2:14) and Luke (5:27). This tradition is reflected in the statement of Papias, Bishop of Hierapolis in Asia Minor, writing c. A.D. 130: "Matthew collected the *Logia* in the Hebrew language and each one interpreted them as he was able." Opinions of Bible scholars differ widely as to what these *Logia* actually were, but this Gospel probably embodies some of Matthew's work. It was, accordingly, named for him. It does not, however, impress the reader as being the account of an eyewitness. Moreover, the fact that it was written in Greek and was based on a variety of Greek sources makes it difficult to believe that its author was one of the primitive Disciples. Though scholars do not believe the author can be identified by name, they think he must have been a Christian Jew, for he shows a Jewish viewpoint. (1) He explains how O.T. prophecies are fulfilled in Christ. (2) He traces Jesus' ancestry to David and Abraham. (3) He notes the high regard Jesus had for the Law of Moses (5:17), and (4) the preferential treatment Jesus accorded the Jews (15:24). In compiling the Sermon on the Mount this evangelist refers to Jewish ideas. The Beatitudes* are the new Decalogue (5:3–12); Christ's commandments fulfill the Law of Moses (5:17–48). Christian worship is spiritual, in contrast to synagogue practices (6:1–18). Righteousness is the Christian's chief concern (6:19–34). The Christian community is a brotherhood (7:1–6). The fatherhood of God is the basis of Christian prayer (7:7–12). The teachings of Jesus are the revelations of God's will (7:13–27).

The Gospel's place of origin is unknown. Its Jewish viewpoint suggests a Palestinian origin. But this Gospel also displays a Gentile atmosphere. It tells the story of the Roman centurion of Capernaum whose faith was without parallel in Israel (8:5–13). It also records the witness of another Gentile centurion (27:54). The missionary commission with which it closes is on a universal basis at variance with Jewish orthodoxy, "Go ye therefore, and teach all nations" (28:19 f.). This mingling of Jewish and Gentile aspects suggests that the First Gospel was written in some early Christian center, like Antioch in Syria, where Jewish and Gentile influences met and mingled.

The earliest date at which Matthew could have been written is determined by the date of Mark, on which it is based. This date is usually placed c. A.D. 75. There are internal evidences for a later date than this: (1) references to something which has continued "unto this day" (27:8, 28:15); (2) indication that Christ's second coming was long delayed (24:48, 25:5); (3) reference to Christian persecutions such as became serious at the end of the 1st century (5:11, 10:18, 25:36, 39); (4) developed liturgical and doctrinal statements, e.g., the baptismal formula (28:19). These suggest a period from A.D. 85 to 95, but Dr. Albright and others feel no N.T. book should be dated later than A.D. 80.

The chief sources of this Gospel can be discovered by comparing it with Mark and Luke. (1) Not only does Matthew reproduce ninety percent of Mark's material, but it follows Mark's order of events in the ministry of Jesus, and even copies Mark's language. As the author of Matthew was limited by the length of the ancient book into which he had to fit all his extra material, he was obliged to condense Mark's record. When he does this, he reduces details, but is careful to give the actual spoken words of his source. The evidence of Matthew's dependence on Mark is overwhelming.

(2) Where Matthew and Luke agree, but have no parallels in Mark, scholars believe they are using a common source, now lost, but designated as "Q" (see LUKE). Q* apparently contained sayings of Jesus, and the story of the healing of the centurion's servant.

(3) Besides Mark and Q, this Gospel drew upon a collection of O.T. passages used in controversy with Jews. These O.T. texts are believed to have been compiled in Hebrew, but translated into Greek before the author of Matthew used them. Some scholars think that the *Logia* Papias referred to, in the passage quoted above, was this collection of O.T. prophecies concerning the Messiah. Other scholars think that *Logia* refers to the sayings or teachings of Jesus which Matthew wrote down in Aramaic and which were the source, Q, used by Luke and Matthew. Still another theory is that Papias' reference to the *Logia* is a reference to the Gospel of Matthew itself. (See chart, "Strands of Tradition and Sources," Frederick C. Grant, *The Growth of the Gospels*, Abingdon-Cokesbury Press; and GOSPELS, illus. 171.)

(4) Other material in Matthew, not traceable to Mark, Q, or the O.T. proof-texts, includes stories of: Jesus' birth, Peter walking on the water, the Temple tax, the fate of Judas, the dream of Pilate's wife, Pilate's washing of his hands, the earthquake and ghostly apparitions at Jesus' death, the sealing of the tomb, and the appearances to the women and the Eleven. There is a legendary quality to some of this material, suggesting that it may have been derived from oral tradition. Some indications connect this material with Aramaic-speaking Christians of Jerusalem.

The arrangement of the First Gospel follows two principles. (1) For the order of events in the life of Jesus, Matthew follows Mark's chronology. (2) For the presentation of sayings and miracles, Matthew groups his material in such a way as to give an impressive and apparently organic whole. A series of miracles are grouped together in chapters 8, 9. It is chiefly in the discourses that Matthew shows his skillful fitting together of scattered sayings, some of which are recorded separately in Mark and Luke. There are five great discourses: (1) the Sermon on the Mount, dealing with the contrast between the old and the new righteousness, chapters 5 to 7; (2) duties of Christian missionaries, chap. 10; (3) parables of the Kingdom of heaven, chap. 13; (4) requirements of discipleship, chap. 18; and (5) Apocalyptic teaching about the end of the age, chapters 24, 25. These five discourses are all clearly marked off by the concluding formula: "and it came to pass, when Jesus had finished these sayings" (7:28, 11:1, 13:53, 19:1, 26:1). This repeated formula divides Matthew into five parts, suggesting the five books of the Law of Moses.

The purpose of this Gospel and the special viewpoints it displays are linked to the fact that the evangelist was a Christian Jew. His Gospel, unlike the others, which are addressed to Gentiles, is written for Christians of Jewish origin. His purpose is to demonstrate that Jesus of Nazareth was the Messiah, in whom God's promises to His people were finally fulfilled. The writer links Messianic prophecies with corresponding events in the life of Jesus, and one of his characteristic phrases is: "that the scripture might be fulfilled." Though other evangelists note the correspondence between the expected O.T. Messiah and the actual Jesus, this author carries the principle to such lengths that sometimes he seems to modify his source to accord more closely with the relevant prophecy.

Jewish thought for two centuries had been marked by eschatological interests. These are prominent in the First Gospel. This is seen in the Apocalyptic flavor the evangelist gives to sayings of Jesus which lack this emphasis in other documents: e.g., "there shall be weeping and wailing and gnashing of teeth" (8:12, 13:42, 22:13, 24:51, 25:30).

It is also seen in the extended Apocalyptic discourse in chapters 24, 25.

To the Jew the Jewish nation existed for the sake of God and His worship. This evangelist substitutes for the nation a world-wide Church which would include all who sought entrance to the Kingdom. Matthew is the only Gospel to make two direct references to the Church (16:18, 18:17). He shows his particular interest in the Church by relating the teachings of Jesus to its needs: e.g., almsgiving, prayer, fasting (6:1–18); marriage and divorce (5:27–32); faithfulness under persecution (10:17–36, 16:24–28).

This Gospel, which began with Jesus' descent from Abraham and David, ends in catholicity of spirit on the double note of the world-wide Kingdom and the eternally present Christ (28:19, 20).

Matthew's Bible. See ENGLISH BIBLE.

Matthias ("gift of Jehovah"), the successor to Judas. He and Joseph Barsabas (Justus) were nominated for the vacant place by the Eleven. After prayer had been offered he was chosen by lot. Nothing is known of him except what Acts 1:23, 26 states. He has been identified by various scholars as "one of the Seventy," Barnabas, Zacchaeus, or Nathanael.

mattock, a Palestinian farm tool for loosening soil, especially around trees and bushes (Isa. 7:25). Sometimes its metal end was triangular; again the mattock head had a long, sharp, axlike arm at one end and a short broad one at the other. Hoelike mattocks followed plows, to break up clods; and were also used to fill baskets with earth. Until the Monarchy Israelites had to take their mattocks and other tools to their Philistine enemies for sharpening (I Sam. 13:20), unless they could manage to sharpen them with files (v. 21).

maul (môl), a heavy club or mace, often studded with metal (A.V. and A.S.V., Prov. 25:18; A.S.V. marg. Jer. 51:20, where A.V. and Moffatt give "battle-axe").

Maundy Thursday (from Lat. *mandatum*, "a command"), the day before Good Friday, possibly so named through a corruption of "mandate," for the "new commandment" given the Disciples by Jesus at the Lord's Supper on Thursday evening (John 13:34).

meadow, a tract of low-lying, usually well-watered grassland, like the reed-grass area along the Nile where Pharaoh's cattle were grazing in his dream (Gen. 41:2). The meadows of Gibeah were used for ambush by men of Israel (Judg. 20:33).

meal offering. See WORSHIP.

meals. (1) *In Biblical Palestine.* (For articles consumed, see FOOD.) The fast of the night was broken, as it still is in many sections of Bible lands, by snacks too casual to be called *breakfast.* Workers in Biblical times began their day very early, and carried in their girdles or in donkey or camel sacks handfuls of olives, raisins, flat round loaves, or goat's-milk cheese which they munched on their way to fishing boats, sheepfolds, fields, or construction jobs. The one breakfast mentioned in Scripture (John 21:4–19)—a fishermen's repast on the shores of Galilee—is duplicated there today by men who return with their hauls about daybreak (v. 4). *Noon meals* were primarily for rest rather than for food (but see the Egyptian luncheon of Gen. 43:25–34). Workers in remote fields might mutiny if the "lord of the harvest" (Luke 10:2) compelled them to work beyond 11 o'clock without halting to eat. Like O.T. Patriarchal groups, they sit in their fields among threshed grain, munching food brought from home.

The *evening meal* was the main one of the day, called supper, feast, or "sitting at meat" (Matt. 9:10; R.S.V. "at table"), depending on social status. Work was over, food had been brought from the local market or family garden and flocks, and prepared by wives and servants. The entire family ate together. Guests were frequent, and ate until they rolled over on the floor, asleep. Meals celebrating birthdays, marriages, or the arrival of honored guests were featured by riddles (Judg. 14:10 ff.); music (Isa. 5:12); or dancing (Matt. 14:6; Luke 15:25). Wedding feasts were in charge of stewards or "rulers" (John 2:9), who served as masters of ceremony and regulated the distribution of food and drink. The feast for the returned Prodigal Son (Luke 15:22–32) is a picture of a happy family meal in Bible times. In villages and towns families ate on the roof, or mezzanine—the lower level was devoted to animals. They sat on mats or stools, which were gradually supplanted by low seats surrounding a table. On this rested the large central clay bowl containing meat and vegetables, which were scooped up with the fingers. Spoons of bent brown loaves the size of griddle cakes sopped up (John 13:26) the gravy. By N.T. times the Roman manner of serving meals prevailed among well-to-do Palestinians (see BANQUET, illus. 49.). Guests reclined on couches grouped about a table on a low pedestal. Usually there were three couches (*triclinia*), with room on the 4th side of the table for servants to pass the foods. If there were two couches they were called *biclinia.* Three or four persons could recline (on the left elbow) on each couch, the most important person being given the "highest" place, and the unimportant the lowest (Luke 14:9–11). Several evening repasts at which Jesus was guest are recorded. (1) For the wedding feast at Cana of Galilee (John 2:1–11) invitations had probably been issued—as in Matt. 22:2–10. (2) Matthew's great feast (Matt. 9:10–17) followed the pattern of a more formal dinner of the 1st-century Graeco-Roman world. Jesus "reclined at meat," and publicans and sinners "sat down" with him (v. 10). The dining room had one side open to the street, with adjustable curtains hanging from the lintel or columns; passersby could look in and gossip about the guests, and "when the Pharisees saw it, they said unto his disciples, Why eateth your Master with publicans and sinners?" (3) When he was dining in a similar room with Simon the Pharisee (Luke 7:36–50) a woman passing by saw him, slipped in, "stood at his feet behind him" (v. 38), and anointed his feet with ointment from her alabaster cruse;

she thus supplied the customary unguent of hospitality* omitted by this host, who had also possibly neglected to have a servant bring the basin and towel for hands and feet (Gen. 18:4; John 13:5–10). (4) The dinner served to Jesus by Zacchaeus at Jericho may have been followed by overnight lodging (Luke 19:6). (5) Of the many dinners enjoyed by Jesus and his Disciples at Bethany, the one at the home of Simon the leper was eaten two days before his last Passover (Mark 14:1–3, cf. John 12:1 f.). (6) The frugal repast of broken bread at Emmaus on the first Easter afternoon was marked by the giving of thanks.

People going *on journeys*, in lands where inns were few and wretched, tucked into their girdles as much food as they expected to consume en route and carried an earthen bottle of water, as did Hagar trudging into the desert (Gen. 21:14). This was the manner of the Disciples, who sometimes forgot "to take bread" (Mark 8:14). Such was the case with the multitude fed by Jesus on the Galilean hillside (Mark 8:1–9).

Palace meals in Judah and Israel attracted large numbers of retainers and guests, and were often occasions for intrigues (Prov. 23:1, 6 f.). Saul, in his rustic castle at Gibeah, expected David to be present at dinner, and was enraged when he absented himself to eat at Bethlehem (I Sam. 20:6). When David came to power, he invited Jonathan's lame son Mephibosheth to take all his meals at the royal board for his father's sake (II Sam. 9:7). Solomon's meals were so elaborate that he organized commissary officers to bring food from regional depots, and also imported luxuries served in golden tableware. Doubtless Solomon had his summer meals served in such a garden as appears in the Song of Solomon. Jezebel, at the hilltop court at Samaria in Israel, entertained at her royal table a collegium of 450 prophets of Baal and 400 prophets of the Asherah (I Kings 18:19).

Nehemiah, governor of Jerusalem after the Exile, entertained at his well-stocked table 150 men, "beside those that came unto us from among the heathen" (5:17–19). One day's marketing included an ox, six sheep, many fowls, and much fruit. For this Nehemiah expected no return hospitality, because his guests were poor.

One of the earliest banquet scenes of Bible lands is depicted on a tiny lapis lazuli cylinder seal from Ur. This treasure, in the University Museum at Philadelphia, shows a banquet of Queen Shubad (probably c. 2500 B.C.). Guests are seated on stools, probably of reed, receiving goblets of wine from fleece-skirted servants. Palace attendants attempt to waft away the hot Babylonian air, while one stands playing a bow-shaped harp.

Sacred meals were part of the sacrificial rites of Hebrews, by which God was drawn into fellowship. His favor and forgiveness were asked, and gifts of unblemished "clean" animals*, meal, wine, oil, etc., were presented (see WORSHIP). Blood and fat were reserved for the Lord; priests received their legal portions (Lev. 2:10, 7:6); worshippers ate what was left. At solemn assemblies of the whole congregation of Israel, such as took place when David turned over his kingdom to Solomon (I Chron. 29:20 ff.), thousands of animals were presented as sacrifices, and the people ate and drank "before the Lord with great gladness" (cf. II Chron. 7:8–10). Hebrew worshippers in Samuel's day went to approved high places to eat and sacrifice (I Sam. 9:11–14, 25); they were all too familiar with cultic meals served at pagan high places. These semisocial, semireligious, and often funerary meals were popular, and often accompanied by lewd rites. Rock-cut *triclinia* of Nabataean high places are seen at Petra today. From the Ras Shamrah* tablets (Ugarit) in N. Syria, it is known that Baal temples were dedicated with religious-social gatherings lasting many days, during which enormous amounts of food were consumed. Hyksos temples, like the one found at Shechem, provided festival meals served by shrine attendants whose quarters have been located near the unroofed court. The Lord's* Supper and the agape* were the sacred meals of Christianity.

(2) *In Egypt.* Genesis 40 describes an Egyptian palace birthday banquet in Joseph's day, an occasion when the king elevated to new honors his chief butler and baker, in appreciation for "all manner of baked food" which they served him, and for the fresh grape juice pressed into his golden cup from clusters grown on royal vines. The plentiful foods served at such a feast, as known from wall paintings, included roast beef, chicken, fowls, pigeon, vegetables, barley beer, and elaborate condiments. Servants dragged in huge jars of wine and handed the guests bent glass tubes or siphons, which they dipped directly into the vats, and from which they drank till they fell to their couches near the low tables. Tomb art shows them wearing at festivals cones of perfumed unguents on their heads.

Nowhere in Bible lands were royal meals served with greater finesse than in Egypt. Excavations of the capital of young Akhenaton, the monotheistic reformer, reveal the amenities of his hospitality at Amarna in the 14th century B.C. The state dining hall of Akhenaton, his wife, and their three little daughters was impressively spacious. Garlands hung from the pillars. Slaves cooled the hot evening air by waving ostrich fans with ivory handles. Outlining the pavilion roof were carved cobras, to devour lurking enemies. Under a kiosk at the center of the dining room was the banquet table, with cushioned couches and chairs. Egyptians lived in a happy atmosphere and enjoyed gracious living, a standard which they tried to carry with them beyond the grave by making their tombs miniature models of their homes.

(3) *In Assyria.* An Assyrian relief shows a dining scene where King Ashurbanipal is feasting with his wife in the Nineveh palace garden. The king is stretched on the customary dining coach, with his head and left arm on a round pillow; he is lifting to his lips a handsome bowl. His wife is seated on a sort of glorified infant's high chair, her feet on its

shelf; she too is lifting a brimming bowl to her royal lips. Servants with fly-whisks stand near by. Under the date palms and grape vines musical instruments await the musicians. Belshazzar's infamous feast entertained 1,000 of his lords, who used for their drunken debauchery the precious vessels stolen from the Jerusalem Temple (Dan. 5:1–4).

(4) *In Persia.* Five Persian palace banquets in the Book of Esther reveal customs of the 5th century B.C. at Shushan* (Susa). (a) The king's banquet for princes of Media and Persia (1:3–12) lasted 180 days, after which the entire palace staff was invited to a huge garden party in the king's park. The banquet was served on couches trimmed with gold and silver. The awnings and curtains shielding the company from intense sunlight were of the royal Persian colors, white, green, and blue, attached to marble pillars with purple cords. (b) While this drinking-bout was proceeding, Queen Vashti gave a feast to the palace women. (c) The wedding feast of Queen Esther was tendered to princes and vassals (2:16–18). (d) Esther gave a "banquet of wine" to the king and Haman (5:4, 7:1–8). (e) The feast celebrated by Jews throughout Persia's provinces (9:1–32) was the background of Purim*.

(5) In Paul's era *Greek banquets* were intellectual gatherings at which the keenest minds joined the symposium that followed the meal. The fare consisted of an elaborate stew, with meat cut in small pieces—knives and forks were not yet in common use. For the symposium after the meal the large tables near the couches were removed and smaller ones brought in for nuts and dried fruit. Talk of philosophy and politics continued into the night.

measure. See WEIGHTS AND MEASURES.

meat. See FOOD; MEALS; WORSHIP.

Medan (mē′dăn), named in Gen. 25:2 and I Chron. 1:32 as a son of Abraham and Keturah; but the word here is probably a doublet for "Midian"; cf. A.S.V. Gen. 37:36 margin, where Heb. "Medanites" reads "Midianites" in the correct text.

Medeba (mĕd′ē-bȧ) (Medaba in I Macc., the modern Madeba), an ancient town E. of Jordan, c. 50 m. S. of Jerash (Gerasa, Philadelphia), 6 m. S. of Heshbon, and c. 16 m. SE. of the entrance of the Jordan to the Dead Sea. This old Moabite town, mentioned with Dibon in Num. 21:30 as conquered by Israel, was on a high plain (Josh. 13:16) or tableland from which there is a rise of barren, rocky fields in the direction of Mt. Pisgah and Nebo (Isa. 15:2). It figured in O.T. history as assigned to Reuben (Josh. 13:9–16); used by the Syrian allies of Ammon for a camp site (I Chron. 19:6–15); regained from Ammon by Moab for Israel's King Omri (Moabite Stone, l. 8); held by Israel for 40 years; recovered by Mesha; seized from Moab by Jeroboam II; and apparently held again by Moab (Isa. 15:2). It figured in the history of the Maccabean revolt (I Macc. 9:36–42).

In early Christian times Madeba was an ecclesiastical see. After its destruction—apparently by Persians in the 7th century—it lay in ruins for centuries. In 1882 Christians from Kerak migrated to Madeba. During the construction of their houses they came across several pieces of mosaic floor, among which was the famous Madeba mosaic map of Palestine, now preserved in the Orthodox Church. Biblical archaeologists consider it a contemporary picture of Christian Palestine and Egypt, with sea, plains, and mountains in appropriate colors, and the names of towns in Gk. (many of the mosaic workers in this Byzantine era were Greeks). It shows Jerusalem in such detail that even her principal streets and churches are recognizable. The Madeba portrayal of the Constantinian Church of the Holy Sepulcher is the more valuable because this was greatly damaged by Persians in A.D. 614.

Medes, an ancient Aryan (Iranian) Indo-European people who invaded the rugged mountain territory S. of the Caspian and by 700 B.C. (the age of Isaiah the Hebrew prophet) had built up a prosperous realm, Media. Medes were first mentioned, so far as we know, in records of an Assyrian campaign of Shalmaneser II (c. 836 B.C.) in a war against tribes in the Zagros Mountains, where "Amadai" (Medes) were among those who paid tribute. In their well-watered, parallel mountain ranges, where food and pasture for their famous horses were abundant, Medes grew in strength until they marched down the Tigris in c. 614 B.C. and captured the city of Assur*. In August 612 B.C. the Medes, led by Cyaxares, allied with Chaldaeans (neo-Babylonians, originally Semitic nomads) under Nabopolassar and Scythians, suddenly seized Nineveh*, the proud capital of the Assyrian Empire. The widespread relief occasioned by Nineveh's fall brought such expressions from neighboring nations as are found in the record of the 7th-century Hebrew prophet-patriot Nahum (2:3–3:19), who wrote his ode almost as if he were an eyewitness.

The Kingdom of the Medes enjoyed its greatest extent in the era of the Babylonian King Nebuchadnezzar (the time of Jeremiah), when it extended from near the Persian Gulf (excepting Elam) to the Black Sea. It was bordered on the W. by the Lydian Empire; on the E. by desert; and on the S. by the Babylonian Empire. The Medes and the Lydians constituted the two nations lying E. and N. and NW. of Neo-Babylonia. Media's valuable territory (today part of Iraq, Iran, Anatolian Turkey, and Armenia U.S.S.R.) included Lakes Van and Urmiah, Mt. Ararat, and cities that included two capitals, Ecbatana (the present Hamadan) and Rhagae (S. of Teheran). Its greatest prophet was Zoroaster (probably the 6th century B.C.), to whom the Good was Ahura-Mazda, one of whose helpers was Mithra, a god of light (see MYSTERY). Medes were less open to his teachings than were the Persians after his death.

The Medes dominated the relatively small nation of Persians (see PERSIA) (c. 600–549 B.C.) until Cyrus II ("the Great"), son of Cambyses I, mastered Media (c. 549 B.C.) and made Pasargadae his capital. Media, however, remained the most important province of Persia, a partner in a dual nation. The names "Medes and Persians" were long linked (Esther 1:19; Dan. 5:28). Medes were noted for the immutable character of

262. Median provincial bearing tribute bowls for the king; a Persian relief of the Achaemenid period (6th-4th century B.C.).

their laws, which even a king could not alter without the consent of his government. They used a cuneiform* alphabet of 39 letters to write Persian on clay documents; this alphabet has been discovered at Ecbatana.

The Medes never came into personal contact with the people of Palestine, as did the Assyrians and Babylonians (Chaldaeans). When the Assyrian Empire broke up, the Medes received the greater part of Iran, Assyria, N. Mesopotamia, Armenia, and Cappadocia, while the Chaldaeans (Neo-Babylonians) acquired Syria, Palestine, and S. Mesopotamia. Media is first mentioned in the O.T. as the destination to which Hoshea, King of Assyria, deported the Israelites from Samaria c. 721 B.C.—"cities of the Medes" (II Kings 17:6, 18:11). Medes are mentioned by Ezra in connection with Darius' search for the roll containing the famous decree of Cyrus that allowed the Jews to return to Jerusalem —a roll he found "in the palace that is in the province of the Medes" (Ezra 6:2). Laws of the Medes are mentioned in the Book of Esther (1:19) and in Daniel (6:8, 15).

The history recorded in Daniel is too confused to allow easy interpretation of his allusion to "Darius the Median" (5:31, 11:1), and to "Darius the son of Ahasuerus, of the seed of the Medes . . . made king over the realm of the Chaldeans" (9:1; cf. Daniel's prophecy to Belshazzar, that his kingdom would fall to "the Medes and Persians," 5:28).

Medes were among the polyglot crowd in Jerusalem on the day of Pentecost (Acts 2:9).

mediation, intervention or action of a go-between. In distinction from the work of the more or less priestly mediator, there is a type of mediation which calls for no official status, but which may be exercised by anyone. Several forms of this meet us in the Scriptures.

(1) Mediation by encouraging good will. Misunderstandings, jealousies, and antagonisms may be greatly lessened or done away by men of good will seeking to create good will in others. An example in the O.T. is provided by the Ethiopian eunuch Ebed-melech, whose compassion led him to plead with the king for the release of Jeremiah from the dungeon (Jer. 38:7–13). An example in the N.T. is Paul's letter to Philemon on behalf of Philemon's runaway slave Onesimus.

(2) Mediation by the right use of privilege. This has particular reference to Israel as a chosen people. God chose Israel, not simply for its own sake, but for the sake of the whole world (Gen. 22:18). The function of "the seed of Abraham" was to mediate the knowledge of the true God to all mankind. Often enough it lost sight of this larger mission. The Book of Jonah was written to rebuke this failure: Jonah represents selfish Israel, and Nineveh the needy outside world. Privilege bespeaks responsibility.

(3) Mediation by Christian testimony. This is illustrated in the Acts of the Apostles, the earliest Church history. The book shows how simple Christian testimony may exert a healing and reconciling influence. Peter's act in baptizing the Gentile centurion Cornelius and his household, and his bold defense of his act, was an important factor in "breaking down the middle wall of partition" (Eph. 2:14) between Christian Jews and the Gentile world (Acts 10). The similar attitude displayed by Paul and Barnabas led to official action by the leaders of the church at Jerusalem in declaring that the Gospel was accessible to all men, of whatever race, on the same conditions (Acts 15; cf. Gal. 3:28 f.; Col. 3:11).

(4) Mediation by intercessory prayer. This approaches more nearly to the priestly, but it is always open to those who claim no priestly prerogatives. The Scriptural examples are numerous: Abraham's prayer for Sodom and Gomorrah (Gen. 18:22–33); Moses' prayer for his rebellious people (Ex. 32:30–33); Solomon's prayer of dedication of the Temple (I Kings 8:22–53); the prayer of Jeremiah that God would have pity on Judah (Jer. 14:1–9); the similar prayer of the psalmist (Ps. 80); the long intercessory prayer of Jesus (John 17). The principle involved is stated in Jas. 5:16. E.L.

mediator, in general, one whose function is to bring together persons who are in disagreement with each other, with the purpose of effecting a reconciliation by removing the grounds of hostility. The term, however, has a specifically religious significance, and usually—though not always—involves the priestly office. In religious usage it means one who represents God to men and men to God. He acts in behalf of both, bringing to God the evidences of man's penitence, and bringing to man the assurance of God's forgiving grace.

The Bible is chiefly concerned to describe the long process whereby the holy God was seeking reconciliation with sinful men. Such a process is essentially religious, which explains why the mediator in some form plays so important a part in the account. Mediation is a characteristic Biblical idea; it looks toward an increasing fellowship of God and men. In the O.T. the mediator is conspicuous in the establishing of the various covenants between God and the people of Israel. A covenant* meant a mutual bond, an agreement between two. Chief among these is the covenant mediated through Moses at Sinai (Ex. 19), and renewed after the incident of the golden calf (Ex. 34). How truly a priest Moses was in the renewal of the covenant may be seen in Ex. 32:25–35. Sometimes the prophet played the part of the mediator to bring God and man together. This was the motive of the dramatic act of Hosea in seeking to rescue his unfaithful wife Gomer: he was illustrating the possibility of the restoration of a broken relationship (3:1–5). The principle of the mediator underlies the description in Isa. 53 of the Suffering Servant, who "bore the sin of many, and made intercession for the transgressors."

The most common mediator of the O.T. was, however, the priest. It was chiefly for this that he was appointed. According to Jewish tradition Aaron was the founder of a hereditary priesthood (Lev. 8:1–9; cf. Num. 17:1–18:7); but the hereditary principle could not be maintained, and as occasion arose the priesthood was increased from the Levites, the tribe to which Aaron belonged (see Num. 4; cf. Deut. 10:6–9, 33:8–11). The function of the priest was to minister at the altar (the Levite did the more humble tasks connected with ceremonial worship), to present the various kinds of sacrifice, especially sacrifice for sin (see Lev. 1–7 for the regulations), and to lead the prayers of intercession (see the priestly blessing, Num. 6:22–27). The high priest in particular played the part of the mediator on the great Day of Atonement, the climax of the Jewish sacrificial system (Lev. 16), when atonement was made for all the sins of all the people for the year gone by (cf. Heb. 9:6–10).

All this was a preparation for the work of "the one mediator between God and man, himself man, Christ Jesus, who gave himself a ransom for all" (I Tim. 2:5). He is called "the mediator of a better covenant" (Heb. 8:6) and of "a new covenant" (9:15, 12:24). Christ is so described because he is both the priest and the sacrifice. What he offers in order to effect a reconciliation, and consequently a true fellowship between God and man, is himself. He could be the Mediator for all mankind, because he himself, being without sin (Heb. 7:26–28), needed no mediation, as even the high priest needed it (9:7). He met the requirement of the Levitical system that the sacrifice be "without blemish" (Lev. 22:20; Heb. 4:15, 9:14); he could do this because he was the sinless Son of God (Heb. 2:9–18, 4:14 f., 7:26–28); and for the same reason his self-offering could be "once for all" (7:27), not needing to be offered continually, but "one sacrifice for sins for ever" (10:11–14). This is why the Christian salvation is conditioned on simple faith, not on formal "works" done by oneself. This is why the Christian prays "in the name" of Christ (John 14:13). And this is why he seeks forgiveness not on his own merits, but "for Christ's sake" (John 1:12). See COVENANT; JESUS CHRIST; PARDON; PROPITIATION; RECONCILIATION. E. L.

Mediterranean Sea, the ("the sea of the Philistines," Ex. 23:31; "the sea" to the Hebrews, Num. 13:29; Acts 10:6; "the great

263. Mediterranean Sea from Crusader Castle at Athlit, S. of Haifa.

sea," Num. 34:6; Josh. 1:4, 15:12, 47; also called "the uttermost" or "utmost sea" in A.V. Deut. 11:24; Joel 2:20; the "hinder" or "western" sea in the same A.S.V. passages), the 2,300-m. waterway on which many of the nations prominent in Biblical history faced—with the exception of the Mesopotamian states and Persia. The Hebrews feared it; commerce by water was distasteful to them. They preferred to hire Phoenician (see PHOENICIA) sailors and ships for their maritime trade, as when, during the Monarchy, Solomon and Hiram* of Tyre* became allies. Palestine had few good harbors. Even in the shelter of the Mt. Carmel cape the beautiful crescent bay of Accho (the modern Acre, the Roman Ptolemais) left much to be desired in the way of a safe harbor. In N.T.

times Caesarea* (formerly Strato's Tower) was a port for ships sailing to the harbors of Rome—Puteoli and Ostia. The Phoenician coast had the best harbors; from them ships sailed for ports as distant as the Pillars of Hercules and possibly Britain. Sidon* in the 2d millennium B.C. and Tyre its daughter flourished during the Hebrew Monarchy. From Gebal cargo boats* ("Byblos travelers"), with upturned prows, sailed back and forth between Egypt and Phoenicia. The excellent harbor of modern Beirut was the Phoenician Berytus. Tripolis (the modern Tripoli in Lebanon) dates its port from c. 700 B.C. Though Philistia lay along the Mediterranean between the border of Egypt and the vicinity of Joppa*, the Philistines had been a Greek seafaring people before they migrated from Crete and gave their name (Gk. *Palaistine*) to Palestine.

264. Megiddo. The 13-acre Palestinian mound beneath which, under 40-50 ft. of debris, the fortress city was buried. Farmers in foreground are cultivating grain such as covered the mound before excavation.

In the time of Jesus the Mediterranean was the Roman-controlled *Mare Nostrum.* Its waters carried soldier-laden galleys to the E. to keep order in the provinces, especially Syria. The main area of Paul's missionary activities was an inlet of the Mediterranean at its NE. corner—the Aegean Sea. His headquarters were at Ephesus and Corinth. He used such ports as Caesarea (Acts 9:30); Seleucia (for Antioch) (Acts 13:4); Troas (Acts 16:8); Cenchreae (for Corinth) (18:18); Ptolemais (21:7); Tyre (Acts 21:3); Sidon (27:3); Syracuse (Acts 28:12); and Puteoli (for Rome) (Acts 28:13). He usually avoided stormy winter sailings when possible (Acts 27:9–44, 28:11), but his wreck en route to Rome was due to sailing too late in the autumn.

Megiddo (mė-gĭd'ō), an important ancient city in N. Central Palestine overlooking the Plain of Esdraelon (Valley of Jezreel), identified as Tell el-Mutesellim ("mound of the commander"), 20 m. SE. of Haifa. Excavation of the site, a large oval mound over 54 ft. high with a surface area of about 13 acres, has revealed a history of almost continuous occupation from the mid-4th millennium to the 4th century B.C.

(1) *Location.* Megiddo dominated the Plain of Esdraelon and guarded the N. end of the strategic 'Aruna pass (Wâdī 'Ara), the most direct route through the Carmel Ridge from the Plain of Sharon and a vital part of the important coastal road between Egypt and Syria (see Y. Aharoni, *The Land of the Bible,* 1967, pp. 46 ff.). An indication of the importance of the 'Aruna pass is provided in accounts of the first Asiatic campaign of Pharaoh Tuthmosis III (c. 1482 B.C.), directed against a coalition of Asiatic rulers (*ANET*³, pp. 234 ff.). Though advised by his military commanders to advance on Megiddo by either of two alternate routes, Tuthmosis III elected to use the somewhat more difficult but more direct 'Aruna pass and succeeded in surprising and defeating his enemies. A further description of this route is found in the late 13th century B.C. Papyrus Anastasi I (*ANET*³, pp. 477 f.).

(2) *Bible References.* The first Bible reference to Megiddo occurs in Josh. 12:21, where "the king of Megiddo" is listed among those rulers defeated by Joshua. "The inhabitants of Megiddo and its villages" were subsequently assigned to the tribe of Manasseh (Josh. 17:11; I Chron. 7:29), though Manasseh was unable to occupy Megiddo (Josh. 17:12 f.; Judg. 1:27 f.) and it remained a Canaanite city, probably down to the time of Solomon.

Megiddo next occurs in the Biblical narrative at the time of Solomon (c. 961–922 B.C.), when it was included in his fifth administrative district (I Kings 4:12) and refortified (I Kings 9:15). The frequently held belief that Megiddo was one of Solomon's "chariot cities," however, is problematical. This latter idea came into prominence as a result of the synthetic joining of various Bibilical traditions (I Kings 9:15, 19, 10:29; II Chron.

MEGIDDO

1:14 ff.), combined with the attempt to use these traditions to describe certain features of the archaeological evidence (see section 4, "Israelite Megiddo").

Megiddo is mentioned as the place where Ahaziah of Judah (c. 842 B.C.) died (II Kings 9:27), and was later the scene of the death of Josiah (c. 640–609 B.C.) at the hands of Pharaoh-nechoh II of Egypt (II Kings 23:29 f.; II Chron. 35:20 ff.). The name occurs also in Zech. 12:11 (Megiddon), and in the N.T. Book of Revelation, where Armageddon stands for the Heb., *Har-megiddôn*, "the hill of Megiddo" (Rev. 16:16).

(3) *Extra-Biblical Sources.* The earliest historical reference to Megiddo occurs in the annals of Tuthmosis III, which describe his successful campaign against that city c. 1482 B.C. (see section 1), as well as in the topographical lists of this 18th Dynasty Egyptian pharaoh (see *ANET*³, pp. 242 f.). Megiddo is also mentioned in six 14th-century B.C. Amarna Letters addressed to the Egyptian court by Biridiya, the prince of Megiddo (see *ANET*³, p. 485). One of these tells of the organization of forced labor ("men of the corvée") by Biridiya in the Plain of Esdraelon. From this time may also date a fragment of a cuneiform tablet on which are preserved 40 lines of the Gilgamesh Epic, found in 1955 by a local shepherd in the excavation debris left by the Oriental Institute.

Megiddo next appears in the late 13th century B.C. Papyrus Anastasi I (see section 1). Megiddo is also mentioned in the topographical lists of Sheshonk I (O.T. Shishak, c. 945–924 B.C.; see *ANET*³, pp. 263 f.), and it is possible that he captured the city during his campaign in the fifth year of Rehoboam of Judah (see I Kings 14:25; II Chron. 12:9). A fragment of a stele bearing his name was found during the course of excavation.

(4) *Excavations.* Tell el-Mutesellim was first excavated by the Deutsche Orient-Gesellschaft, under the direction of G. Schumacher, 1902–05. More significant excavations were carried out by the Oriental Institute of the University of Chicago under the successive direction of C. S. Fisher (1925–27), P. L. O. Guy (1927–35), and G. Loud (1935–39). Equipped with the most modern equipment then available, the Institute completely removed the four uppermost Strata (I–IV). Financial considerations, however, restricted the exploration of lower levels to certain select areas. Though for the most part there has been general agreement on the date and sequence of the pottery, controversy has ensued concerning the correlation of the successive building levels at Megiddo (see references cited below). Additional excavations recently carried out by Y. Yadin (1960, 1966–67) have helped to clarify the Iron Age sequence. The following brief survey reflects the major discoveries and discussions which have shed light on the history of ancient Megiddo.

Early History. The earliest levels at Megiddo (Strata XX–XIX) are poorly stratified and contain a mixture of deposits ranging from the Neolithic to the beginning of the Early Bronze Age (see *CAH*³, Vol. I, Part I, 1970, pp. 531 ff.).

265. Reconstruction of Stratum IV Gate at Megiddo.

The full Early Bronze Age is represented by Strata XVIII–XVI, though here too the stratification is far from clear (see *CAH*³, Vol. I, Part 2, 1971, pp. 211 ff.). The evidence suggests that Megiddo was a city of considerable size, with massive retaining walls and terraces, and a sacred area whose main feature consisted of a large circular stone platform enclosed within a rectangular precinct. Animal bones and broken fragments of pottery from the area indicate that this was a sacrificial altar, an early example of a *bāmāh* or "high place."

The succeeding period of Megiddo's history has been a point of confusion and debate, Wright and others believing that the site was abandoned during EB III (c. 2650 B.C.) and not reoccupied for several centuries (*BA* 13, 1950, pp. 31 ff.). Kenyon, however, suggests a more continuous history of occupation based on a reinterpretation of the successive stages of the Megiddo sacred area (*Eretz-Israel* 5, 1958, pp. 55 ff.), while admitting to the difficulty in interpreting the stratification (*CAH*³, Vol. I, Part 2, 1971, pp. 578 ff.). A number of shaft tombs are to be assigned to the end of this relatively unstable period of the late 3d and early 2d millennia B.C. (MB I; Kenyon, "Intermediate Early Bronze–Middle Bronze").

Canaanite Megiddo. The Middle and Late Bronze Age Strata at Megiddo indicate an overall cultural continuity throughout most of the 2d millennium B.C., despite frequent destructions, rebuildings and the occasional introduction of new material. The beginning of the period (Strata XV–XIII; MB IIA, c. 1850–1750 B.C.; Kenyon, MB I) is represented by a number of intramural burials and several building phases which remain difficult to assess (Kenyon, *CAH*³, Vol. II, chap. III, and *Levant* 1, 1969, pp. 25 ff.; Wright, *BA* 13, 1958, pp. 32 f.). Some contact with Egypt is indicated by the recovery of the statuette base of Thuthotpe, a high-ranking Egyptian official c. 1900–1850 B.C. (J. A. Wilson, *AJSL* 48, 1941, pp. 225 ff.).

Strata XII–X (MB IIB–C, c. 1750–1550 B.C.), were enclosed by a substantial city wall, the first phase of which may have been erected toward the end of MB IIA (Stratum XIII). It was subsequently thickened (XII) and later replaced by a wall with internal buttresses (XI). A well-designed gate was approached at a right angle from a sloping ramp adjacent to the wall. It appears that the sacred area continued in use throughout this period, though the evidence is difficult to interpret (see C. Epstein, *IEJ* 15, 1965, pp. 204 ff.).

Late Bronze Age Megiddo (Strata IX–VII) continues the development of the Middle Bronze Age city without cultural break. The transition is represented by Stratum IX (LB I, roughly 1550–1468 B.C.), which is characterized by bichrome painted pottery (C. Epstein, *Palestinian Bichrome Ware,* 1966). Stratum IX is thought to be the city conquered by Tuthmosis III c. 1482 B.C. (*CAH*³) or 1468 B.C. (Wright).

A new fortification system, originating perhaps with Stratum X, remained in use throughout the Late Bronze Age. The city gate consisted of a long passage divided into two chambers by three pairs of internal piers. A large building located just inside the city gate was perhaps the palace of the local ruler. Beneath the floor of a room in its first phase (Stratum VIII, c. 1482–1350 B.C.) was discovered a treasure hoard of objects in gold, ivory, lapis lazuli, and other precious materials. It was during this period that the letters from Biridiya were sent to the Egyptian court at Amarna (see section 3). This palace continued in use through two more phases in Stratum VII (c. 1350–1150 B.C.). An important collection of carved ivories was discovered among the ruins of the palace in its final phase (Stratum VIIA), in a small room suggested to be a basement treasury (G. Loud, *Megiddo Ivories*, 1939). Among these pieces was a pen-case of an Egyptian envoy bearing the name of Ramesses III (c. 1198–1166 B.C.). The latest object found in Strarum VII was a statue base of Ramesses VI (1156–1148 B.C.).

A second building of importance was a temple of simple plan but massive structure, in use throughout the Late Bronze Age. The destruction of this temple at the end of Stratum VII (c. 1150 B.C.) marks the end of the use of the sacred area begun in the 3d millennium B.C.

Israelite Megiddo. Lack of a clear stratigraphical sequence resulted in a confused ordering of certain elements of the Iron Age strata (VI–I) at Megiddo. This was particularly so with the designation of the large pillared structures of Stratum IV as "Solomon's stables" (see section 2), which have since been shown to date a century later than Solomon and probably are not even stables (see J. B. Pritchard, "The Megiddo Stables: A Reassessment," in J. A. Sanders, ed., *Near Eastern Archaeology in the Twentieth Century*, 1970, pp. 268 ff.). Reassessment of the original data, combined with the results of recent excavation carried out by Y. Yadin, suggests the following conclusions (but see Y. Aharoni, *JNES* 31, 1972, pp. 302 ff.).

After the destruction of Stratum VIIA (c. 1150 B.C.), Megiddo was rebuilt (c. 1150/1120 B.C.) on a much restricted scale, with a small but well-constructed city gate (Stratum VI, divided into two phases). Stratum VI was violently destroyed, perhaps as Yadin suggests, by David (but see Wright, *BA* 13, 1958, pp. 36 ff.). The next city (Stratum VA) is poorly built and unfortified.

Megiddo was completely rebuilt (Strata VA–IVB), probably by Solomon (I Kings 9:15), and included a S. and N. residency or fortress, a gallery which gave access to the city's water supply, and other large public buildings—all which were surrounded by a casemate wall with a large six-chambered gate constructed out of ashlar blocks, similar to structures at Hazor and Gezer (Y. Yadin, *IEJ* 8, 1958, pp. 80 ff.). This city was destroyed, probably at the hands of Pharaoh Sheshonk during the reign of Rehoboam (see section 2).

Megiddo was rebuilt on a different plan (Stratum IVA), probably by Ahab (c. 869–850 B.C.), but perhaps partly by Jeroboam I (c. 922–901 B.C.). To this phase are to be attributed the offsets/insets wall (originally ascribed to Solomon), a four-chambered city gate, and the so-called "stables," perhaps better interpreted as storehouses for which parallels have been found at Hazor, Ramat Rahel, and elsewhere. The city was again destroyed, either at the time of the Syrian wars (Albright/Wright, c. 810 B.C.; see II Kings 13:3–7), or by Tiglath-pileser III in 733 B.C. (Kenyon, Yadin; see II Kings 15:19).

The city was rebuilt (Stratum III) with a smaller two-chambered gate and several large buildings with cental court in Assyrian style. Dates for this phase differ, from the time of Jeroboam II (Albright/Wright, c. 810–733 B.C.), to the period of Assyrian domination (Kenyon, c. 733–587 B.C.). This was followed by a phase of general rebuilding (Stratum II) at which time the city became an unwalled settlement with a large fort built on the corner of the mound. It generally has been assigned to the time of Josiah (c. 640–609 B.C.), but may be later. The final Stratum (I) yielded only scattered remains of the Babylonian and Persian periods (c. 587–350 B.C.).

Excavation Reports: R. S. Lamon, *The Megiddo Water System*, 1935; H. G. May, *Material Remains of the Megiddo Cult*, 1935; P. L. O. Guy and R. M. Engberg, *Megiddo Tombs*, 1938; R. S. Lamon and G. M. Shipton, *Megiddo*, I. 1925–34, 1939; G. Loud, *Megiddo*, II. 1935–39, 1948; see also Y. Yadin, *BA* 23, 1960, pp. 62 ff. and *BA* 33, 1970, pp. 66 ff. W. P. A.

Melchizedek (měl-kĭz′ĕ-děk) (Melchisedec) ("king of righteousness"), A.V. Heb. 5:6, etc., the priest-king of Salem (which may be identified with Jerusalem, Uru-salim, "city of peace," as it is called in the Tell el-Amarna tablets of c. 1400 B.C., an older name than Jebus*.) When Abraham returned from his battle with Chedorlaomer he met Melchizedek, who blessed him and refreshed him with ceremonial bread and wine (Gen. 14:17–20), and to whom he gave a tithe (Heb. 7:2). Melchizedek became a symbol of the ideal king-priest of whose order Christ was called a member (Heb. 5:10, quoting Ps. 110:4).

Melita (mĕl'ĭ-tȧ) (Malta) (so named by Greeks of Paul's time because of its honey production), an arid, rocky islet in a group 60 m. S. of Sicily, 140 m. S. of the European mainland, and 180 m. N. of Cape Bon in Tunisia. Paul was wrecked on the island after drifting two weeks in a winter gale (Acts 27:43), and stayed there three months (28:11). His place of landing was at what became "St. Paul's Bay," 8 m. N. of Valetta, where his ship apparently went to pieces between the islet of Salmonetta and the W. shore of the bay. The Christian Knights (of Malta), protected by Charles V, settled there in the 16th century after their expulsion from Palestine. Their 8-pointed, fish-tail-indented cross with equal arms tapering toward the intersection has become a favorite form of the Christian symbol. A bishop of Malta attended the Council of Chalcedon in 451.

266. Melita (Malta). 1899 postage stamp showing Paul's escape from shipwreck.

mem, the 13th letter of the Hebrew alphabet, from which "m" developed. See WRITING.

memorials, designed to commemorate events and personalities, appear in various forms in Scripture: a stone or cairn (Gen. 31:45); 12 stones erected in the Jordan (Josh. 4:3–9, 20 f.). In the singular, a name by which the Lord was to be known throughout the generations (Ex. 3:15); the Passover* feast (Ex. 12:14); a sign worn between the eyes (13:9); a record in a book (17:14); a breastplate* of 12 stones worn by the high priest (28:12, 29); a meat offering (Lev. 2:9); a blowing of trumpets (23:24); the Lord, as memorial of Jacob's experience at Bethel (Hos. 12:5). These expressions are attempts to state Israel's awareness of the Lord's participation in national and personal destinies. In the N.T. Jesus says that the telling about his anointing by an unnamed woman shall be a memorial of her (Matt. 26:13). See LORD'S SUPPER.

Memphis (Noph, A.V. Jer., Ezek.), an ancient capital of Egypt on the Nile, 10 m. N. of modern Cairo. Its greatness began soon after Menes united Upper and Lower Egypt. King Djoser, whose Third Dynasty promoted Memphis, had his architect-physician Imhotep erect the terraced step pyramid for his funerary monument in the Memphis necropolis at Saqqârah—the oldest stone structure in Egypt. Memphis is mentioned by the Hebrew prophets: Hosea linked the apostasy of Israel with the burial places of Memphis (9:6); Isaiah mentioned it in connection with the deceit of its princes (19:13); Jeremiah narrated its outrages (2:16), and prophesied Nebuchadnezzar's conquest of Egypt and the captivity of the Israelites living in Memphis (46:14, 19); Ezekiel prophesied against the city and its falling images (30:13, 16).

Menahem (mĕn'ȧ-hĕm) ("comforter"), a son of Gadi (II Kings 15:14), and King of Israel (c. 745–738 B.C.). In the period of anarchy following the death of Jeroboam II, Shallum seized Samaria. Menahem, Governor of Tirzah*, the older capital of Israel, opposed Shallum, put him to death, and took over the government of Israel (vv. 14 f.). He put down opposition with cruel highhandedness (v. 16), and enjoyed a fairly peaceful rule—in part due to his buying the favor of the Assyrian King Tiglath-pileser* III (the Pul of II Kings 15:19) with a tremendous sum, which he levied on thousands of his subjects. Menahem's Assyrian policy led to the final annexation of Israel by Assyria (II Kings 15:29). The prophet Hosea, contemporary of Menahem, wrote a vivid commentary on the times (chaps. 4–14). Menahem appears in an Assyrian carved relief as bringing tribute (c. 738 B.C.) to Tiglath-pileser III. He ruled during the reign of the Judaean King Jotham at Jerusalem. His son Pekahiah succeeded him.

mene, mene, tekel, upharsin, three Aram. words which mysteriously appeared (Dan. 5:25) on the plaster of Belshazzar's palace walls while he and his lords were desecrating vessels that Nebuchadnezzar had brought from Jerusalem (II Kings 25:14 f.). Daniel deciphered the words after Chaldaean wise men had failed (Dan. 5:8 ff.). Discussion continues as to the meaning of the words and Daniel's interpretation of them. (1) They may be terms used in Mesopotamian counting-houses—"numbered, numbered, weighed, and divisions." (2) They may be related to the names of weighed money*—the mina, shekel, and half-mina. Possibly Daniel made a play on words when he interpreted the message, "God hath numbered thy kingdom, and finished it . . . . Thou art weighed in the balances, and art found wanting. . . . Thy kingdom is divided, and given to the Medes and Persians." Cf. 5:30 f.

Mephibosheth (mē̆-fĭb'ō̆-shĕth). (1) a son of Jonathan and grandson of Saul, originally named Merib-baal (I Chron. 8:34) ("my lord is Baal" or "Baal contends"). When carried as a child of five for refuge to Lo-debar, E. of the Jordan, after the disaster to Saul and Jonathan at Gilboa, Mephibosheth fell from the arms of his nurse and was lamed (II Sam. 4:4). He was graciously called to Jerusalem after David's accession, given his father's inheritance, a permanent place at the royal table, and a staff of servants under Saul's steward Ziba (II Sam. 9:1–13). During Absalom's revolt Ziba tried to ingratiate himself with David at the expense of Mephibosheth (II Sam. 16:1–4). The cripple's gracious spirit, however, did not resent the king's suspicions, which had been fostered by Ziba (19:24–30). Mephibosheth was the father of Mica (II Sam. 9:12, cf. I Chron. 8:35 ff., 9:41). (2) A son of Saul and Rizpah, executed by the Gibeonites with David's consent (II Sam. 21:8).

Merab (mē′răb), the eldest daughter of Saul (I Sam. 14:49), promised to David in appreciation of his prowess against the Philistines (I Sam. 18:17), but given to Adriel (18:19). Their five sons were given by David to the Gibeonites, to be hanged during the barley harvest at Gibeah in atonement for Saul's injustices to this non-Israelite remnant of the early Amorite settlers (II Sam. 21:8, 9). Probably "Michal" in this passage is a scribal error and should read "Merab."

Merari (mē̇-rā′rī), the 3d and youngest son of Levi. His descendants (Merarites) were divided into two groups, Mahlites and Mushites (Num. 3:33, 26:58). During the wanderings the Merarites were assigned duties connected with transporting the less sacred parts of the Tabernacle* (Num. 3:36 f., 4:31 f., 10:17). After the settlement in Palestine they were given privileges of residence in 12 cities in the territories of Reuben, Gad, and Zebulun (Josh. 21:7, 34–40). Members of the Merarite family, according to the Chronicler, had a part in the Temple music (I Chron. 6:44–47, 23:21–23). They were prominent at Hezekiah's Temple cleansing (II Chron. 29:12); and probably at the restoration in Ezra's time (Ezra 8:19).

merchant. See AGORA; TRADE.

Mercurius (mûr-kū′rĭ-ŭs) (A.V., Mercury A.S.V., Hermes R.S.V. Acts 14:12). the name of a Greek deity, messenger of the gods; applied to Paul by the people of Lystra.

mercy, in the sense of compassion, forbearance, grace, long-suffering, providential deliverance, and loving-kindness, is an attribute of God throughout the Scriptures (Judg. 5:11; Ps. 23:6, 106:1, 145:17; etc.). God's justice is inevitably linked to His mercy. The disloyalties of God's chosen people brought into conflict the forces of justice and mercy. Hosea was the first Hebrew prophet to emphasize God's mercy, going so far as to pardon and re-establish wayward Israel (Hos. 2:19, 11:8 f.). Because of man's dependence on the mercy of God he is expected to extend it to his fellows (Mic. 6:8). God esteemed mercy more than the ritual of sacrifice (Hos. 6:6; Matt. 9:13). Jesus showed mercy to lepers (Luke 17:13); and to the blind (18:38); and he made mercy a cornerstone of his teaching (Matt. 5:7, 7:1 f.). N.T. writers believed it was by God's mercy that men were granted hope through the Resurrection of Jesus (I Pet. 1:3). "Mercy" was incorporated into the benedictions of the early Church (I Tim. 1:2; III John 3).

mercy-seat. See ARK.

Merenptah, a son of Rameses II, Pharaoh of Egypt (c. 1224–1216 B.C.), regarded by some as the "Pharaoh of the Exodus," though a predecessor is more likely. A stele of Merenptah indicates that Israel was already in western Palestine c. 1220 B.C. and had been defeated by his forces. An imaginative reconstruction of the throne room of Merenptah's palace is in the University of Pennsylvania Museum.

Meribah (mĕr′ĭ-bä). See MASSAH.

Merodach (mē̇-rō′dăk), Heb. form of Accad. name Marduk (Bel*, Baal*), chief god in the Babylonian pantheon and the Bel of the Apocryphal Bel and the Dragon. He was the patron of the city of Babylon. Merodach was honored by Nebuchadnezzar, and even by the Assyrians and the Persian Cyrus. Cyrus, according to a recovered cylinder seal, had been accepted by Marduk as "righteous prince," and appointed by him to rule as king "over the whole world." Isaiah referred to this deity (46:1); so did Jeremiah (51:44), The names of several prominent persons were compounded with Merodach, for the sake of prestige or protection: Merodach-baladan. Evil-Merodach, and possibly Mordecai.

Merodach-baladan (mē̇-rō′dăk-băl′ȧ-dăn) (Berodach-baladan, II Kings 20:12 ff.) (Assyr., "Marduk has given a son"), a Chaldaean, son of Baladan, ruling originally at the head of the Persian Gulf, and twice ruler of Babylon (722–710 and 703–702 B.C.). Pretending to congratulate the Hebrew King Hezekiah (c. 715–687 B.C.) on his recovery from illness (Isa. 39:1–8), Merodach-baladan tried, with messengers and lavish gifts, to draw the Jews into a confederacy of Near Eastern states against his arch enemies, the Assyrians. Hezekiah's egotistic folly in displaying everything in his palace to the emissaries drew from Isaiah one of his most stinging rebukes. Merodach-baladan initiated the policy of strengthening Chaldaea. This policy eventually made it the most influential state in the Neo-Babylonian Empire under Nabopolassar and his son Nebuchadnezzar II (605–562 B.C.).

Merom (mē′rŏm), **the Waters of,** the vicinity of Joshua's victory over a coalition of kings of the N. (Josh. 11:5). The Lake Huleh section through which the Jordan headwaters flow S. is accepted by many as Merom, but the terrain here is too swampy for battle. Merom may be Wâdī Meirôn, SW. of Hazor in Galilee, 4 m. NW. of Safed; or it may be the village of Marun, 7 m. farther N. Both sites are well-watered. An ancient synagogue has been excavated at Meirôn.

Meroz (mē′rŏz), a town in or near the Valley of Jezreel, condemned in the Song of Deborah* (Judg. 5:23) because it did not ally itself with Israel to fight the Canaanites.

Mesha (mē′shȧ). (1) An Iron Age king of Moab*, whose successful rebellion against King Ahab of Israel (c. 869–850 B.C.) secured the liberation celebrated on the Moabite* Stone. The author of II Kings (3:4) disparages Mesha by calling him a "sheepmaster" who paid to Israel tribute of 100,000 lambs, 100,000 rams, and their wool. These figures, however inaccurate, serve to reveal the prosperity of Moab. Mesha built many well-fortified cities, of which Khirbet Aqrabah is a good example; laid out a commercial road—early forerunner of the one modernized by King Abdullah; and provided for a community water supply—as shown in the Moabite Stone inscription. Nelson Glueck, exploring this land, identified numerous town sites by their pottery. (2) A son of Caleb (I Chron. 2:42). (3) A son of Shaharaim (I Chron. 8:9). (4) A place (Gen. 10:30).

Meshach (mē′shăk), originally Mishael, one of the three men cast into the fiery furnace at Nebuchadnezzar's command (Dan. 1:7, 2:49, 3:13–30).

Meshech (mē′shĕk) (once Mesech, A.V. Ps. 120:5), a son of Japheth; grandson of Noah (Gen. 10:2; I Chron. 1:5). He was founder of a people (Ezek. 32:26) who dwelt perhaps in SE. Asia Minor, W. of the land of Tubal's descendants, their allies. They were mentioned as a merchant nation trading "persons of men and vessels of brass" with Tyre (Ezek. 27:13). Gog* was "a chief prince of Meshech and Tubal" (Ezek. 38:2 f., 39:1). Descendants of Tubal and Meshech were allied against Syria in the 12th century B.C. The Meshech people were gradually driven to the Black Sea region.

Meshullam (mē̇-shŭl′ăm) (? reconciled), the name of more than 20 men in the O.T.—an excellent example of the popularity of certain names in given periods. (1) The grandfather of a scribe during King Josiah's reign (II Kings 22:3). (2) The son of Zerubabbel (I Chron. 3:19). (3) A prominent Gadite in the reign of Jotham (I Chron. 5:13). (4), (5), (6) Three members of the tribe of Benjamin (I Chron. 8:17, 9:7; Neh. 11:7; I Chron. 9:8). (7) A priest, son of Zadok, and father of the high priest Hilkiah, in the reign of Josiah (I Chron. 9:11; Neh. 11:11). (8) A priest (I Chron. 9:12). (9) A Kohathite who helped repair the Temple in Josiah's time (II Chron. 34:12). (10) An important citizen of Babylon who helped Ezra recruit Levites for the Return (Ezra 8:16). (11) One who differed with Ezra on foreign marriages (Ezra 10:15). (12) A man who married a foreign wife (Ezra 10:29). (13) Berechiah's son, who helped rebuild two sections of the Jerusalem wall, one of which adjoined his own living quarters (Neh. 3:4, 30, 6:18). (14) A son of Besodeiah, who helped repair the old gate (Neh. 3:6). (15) One who was near Ezra during the reading of the Law (Neh. 8:4). (16), (17) Two who sealed the covenant (Neh. 10:7, 20); (18), (19) priestly leaders of two families in the time of the high priest Joiakim (Neh. 12:13, 16). (20) A porter (Neh. 12:25). (21) A prince who participated in the procession at the dedication of the repaired wall (Neh. 12:33). The activities of these various Meshullams give clues about life in the two centuries before the Exile and the period just after the Return.

Mesopotamia (mĕs′ō̇-pō̇-tā′mĭ-*ȧ*) (translation in Gen. 24:10 of Aram-naharaim), the name used in the O.T. in a narrow sense for the land E. of the Middle Euphrates*, at least as far as the River Habor*. To Greeks and Romans it meant the vast territory "between the rivers," S. of the Masius mountain range and N. of the Syro-Arabian desert. Today much of the ancient Mesopotamia lies within Iraq. Its N. section was known as Aram-naharaim, or "Syria of the Two Rivers" —now Upper Mesopotamia. There mighty Assyria* developed in ancient times. Lower (Southern) Mesopotamia contained the Biblical Plain of Shinar*, later Chaldaea. There flourished Accad* and Sumer*, and there the Kingdom of Babylonia (see BABYLON) developed. Lower Mesopotamia, whose two rivers provided water for irrigation, yielded fabulous crops ("two hundred fold," Herodotus). To these was due the prosperity of such city-states as Babel, Calneh, Erech, Accad, and Ur*. Upper Mesopotamia was higher ground, and drained by the Tigris and Euphrates from the border of Armenia; it was cooler than S. Mesopotamia and not as well watered, and specialized in huge flocks rather than in farm products. Its rocks encouraged sculpture. Between Palestine and the Upper Euphrates region lay Aram (Syria), whose destiny was intertwined with that of the Hebrew people.

Mesopotamia in its narrower sense is mentioned in the following O.T. passages: Gen. 24:10, which names this region around Haran as the goal of Abraham's servant when he was seeking a wife for Isaac from the N. Mesopotamian homeland of the Hebrew Patriarchs; Judg. 3:8, 10, which tells of Israel serving a king from that land; I Chron. 19:6, which names it as a source of chariots and horsemen drawn upon by the Ammonites to fight David. Acts 2:9 mentions Mesopotamians in Jerusalem on the day of Pentecost; Acts 7:2 refers to Abraham's living in Mesopotamia (evidently with Ur in mind) before his trek to Haran.

The influence of Mesopotamia on Palestine has been inestimable. It was the E. arch of the Fertile* Crescent, where civilization flourished from the New Stone Age to the Golden Age of Greece in the 5th century B.C. Out of Mesopotamia came the arts of irrigation, of cuneiform* writing, of architecture and sculpture, of city-state organization, of efficient business transactions. It produced magnificent textiles, finely carved gems, and seals*. It codified law, and evolved modes of worship which left a deep imprint on the Hebrews. They lived in Mesopotamia during the Exile; and there much of the O.T. as we now know it took form. Out of Mesopotamia swept the conquerors most dreaded for centuries by Palestine—the Assyrians, the Babylonians, and the Chaldaeans.

See ARAM; MARI; etc.

Messiah, the Christ; the looked-for king and deliverer of the Hebrews. The root meaning of the word is "anointed one." It recalls the ancient Hebrew custom of anointing a person who was being set apart for high office, especially a priest or a ruler. In the N.T. it becomes "the Christ," the exact Gk. equivalent of the Heb. "Messiah."

The promise of God to Abraham, that in him and his descendants all the world was to be blest (Gen. 12:1–3, 15:1 f.), created the expectancy of a Kingdom* of God on earth. The O.T. is the story of the growth of this expectancy, and of changes in the way it was understood. One form limited the promise to the physical line of Abraham: "the chosen people" were "the sons of Abraham." With the emergence of Saul as the first Hebrew king, the national and political conception was quickened (I Sam. 8:1–12:25). The brilliance of the reign of David, Saul's successor, and his own personal character, set the pattern of Messianic thought for later centuries (II Sam. 7:1–29). The conviction grew that the Kingdom of God, in which the Abrahamic covenant would be consummated, would be a kingdom like that of David, and its ruler would be "a son of David," a king like David, only greater (Isa. 9:2–7; Jer. 23:5–8; Ezek. 34:20–31; cf. Ps. 89:3, 19–37, 132:1–18).

The checkered history of the kingdom, especially after the division that followed the death of David's son and successor Solomon (I Kings 11:9–12:20), and still later the destruction of the separatist Northern Kingdom by the Assyrians under Shalmaneser* (II Kings 17:1–6), which left the loyalist Southern Kingdom, or Judah, to carry on alone the Davidic tradition and hope (17:18), threw into prominence the idea of a Deliverer. If the promise of Abraham were to be fulfilled, someone must deliver the people of God from their enemies. Hence the important meaning of the word "save" in the O.T., notably in the Psalms (28:9, 69:35, 72:13 f., 106:47), and in Isaiah (25:9, 33:22, 35:4, 37:20, 63:1–5; cf. Jer. 42:11). Often the "salvation" or "deliverance" desired and promised was from "enemies," especially from threatening world powers. A person who could thus "save" or "deliver" would be a king indeed. Sometimes only God Himself would suffice; otherwise it must be "the anointed one" of God, a veritable Messiah. Ps. 72 is believed by many to express the sentiments of the group that supported the reformations of the young King Josiah (II Kings 22:1–23:25); but in due time the psalm was used and cherished, as it still is, for its Messianic significance.

With the great prophets, however, there came a different reading of the promise to Abraham. An occasional prophet retained the national outlook (see OBADIAH; NAHUM; HABAKKUK), but the idea grew that if God is not merely the God of Israel but the God of the whole earth, then His concern was not limited to one people, but extended to all mankind. The collapse of Jerusalem under Nebuchadnezzar in 587 B.C., and the virtual destruction of the Jewish state, gave force to the message already being delivered by Jeremiah, that the promise to Abraham would be fulfilled not in any political organization but in a truly religious "community," a brotherhood broader than race, between whom and God existed "a new covenant written on the heart," and open to every man (Jer. 31:31–33).

The Exile that followed gave force to Jeremiah's words. The priestly influence, however, grew strong among the Exiles, and two Messianic concepts existed side by side. One centered in the thought of a restored nation, essentially Jewish, which found its chief mark in the meticulous observance of "the Code of Holiness," which was largely a product of the Exile. (See the elaborate description in Ezek. 40–48, an Exilic writing.) In this conception there was practically no provision for a personal Messiah; the nearest approach to it is in the figure of "the prince" (Ezek. 44:3, 45:7, 16 f., 22, 46:2–18, 48:21 f.). The prevailing thought is that of a Messianic ritualistic community, a people of God made one by devotion to "the Law." The movement led later by Ezra and Nehemiah in the restoration of Jerusalem, and described in their O.T. books, was a bold attempt to realize this concept.

But the Exile also served to emphasize the more spiritual concept of the great prophets. The Exile saw the production of many of the Psalms; some—like the long 119th, which is really a group of psalms with a common theme—emphasize the centrality of the Law; others emphasize the necessity of spiritual deliverance, and of One able to effect it (102, and possibly 103). The man who is known as the Second Isaiah was an Exile contemporary with Ezekiel. It was he who not only wrote such glittering descriptions of the return to Jerusalem as in chaps. 52 and 55, but who also wrote the so-called "Servant Songs" (42:1–4, 49:1–6, 50:4–9, 52:13–53:12). The "Servant" is a "sufferer"; and whether the reference be to a purified Israel, or to a "remnant" of Israel (cf. Isa. 11:1–5), or to a particular person, this "Servant" would not only point the way to a true "seed of Abraham," an Israel not after the flesh but after the spirit, but would make its realization a universal possibility through his own sacrificial and self-forgetting love (53:10–12).

The priestly and particularistic concept may be said to have prevailed following the Ezra-Nehemiah movement. The more spiritual and universal concept, however, still had its advocates. It obviously inspired the writing of the Book of Jonah (300 B.C.). In the 2d half of Zechariah (chaps. 9–14, not written by the man who wrote 1–8), probably not before 300 B.C., the emphasis is markedly on a national restoration, and on Jerusalem as the center of the world (chap. 14); but there is no reference to the Law or to the Temple (except perhaps 14:20). On the other hand, the section contains the words quoted at Jesus' entry into Jerusalem: "Thy king cometh unto thee," etc. (9:9; cf. Matt. 21:5). But in the next verse we are told that this king will create a universal peace, and that "his dominion shall be from sea to sea" (cf. Ps. 72, and the note on it above). In the still later Book of Daniel (about 167 B.C.) is the teaching about "an everlasting kingdom" to be granted to one called "a Son of Man," a kingdom embracing "all peoples and languages" (7:13, 14).

In the Jewish writings that followed Daniel (dated c. 167 B.C.) not included in the O.T.

proper, the teaching about the Messiah and the Messianic kingdom is frequently associated with "the Day of the Lord" of early prophecy, with a dreadful conflict, and with a general resurrection. Sometimes the Messiah himself is the head of the armies of heaven; sometimes he is the Judge; sometimes he is the ruler of the kingdom that follows the resurrection and judgment; and sometimes he does not personally appear at all, it being taught that God would save His people either through their obedience to the Law or by the power of His own Word (cf. Rev. 19:13). Always, however, in these writings the Messiah, no matter how he is described, is conceived as an instrument of God. God provides the Deliverer, and through him achieves the deliverance.

It is natural that such ideas should have been extant at the time of Jesus. Current Messianic belief included all of the above. There was one party, the Zealots, who would achieve the national deliverance by force, in the conviction that this would reveal a Messiah. Judas Iscariot may have been a Zealot*. The Pharisees, on the contrary, did not approve of revolution; they believed that the Messiah would appear in God's own good time, that he would be "a Son of David," and that through him the Law, which the Pharisees so deeply reverenced, would be fulfilled. The Apocalyptic form of the Messianic hope, however, was especially widespread, and it strongly influenced early Christianity.

Many are convinced that Jesus came to regard himself as the promised Messiah; though in what sense he was to be the Messiah he may not at first have understood. His Messiahship was apparently revealed to him at his Baptism (Mark 1:11). In the Temptation* that followed he wrestled with the problem of what his Messiahship involved (Matt. 4:1–11). In his address in the synagogue at Nazareth (Luke 4:16–21); in what he said about his conquest of Satan (Mark 3:22–27); in his reply to John the Baptist's question (Luke 7:18–23); and in his acceptance of Peter's "confession" (Matt. 16:15–17) he clearly revealed his own thought about himself.

A more difficult question is whether he extended his Messianic function to include also the eschatological feature of Apocalypticism. It is undeniable that eschatological language—the language of "the end"—is frequently ascribed to him (see Matt. 19:28–30, 20:20–23 f.), especially in the parables (Matt. 13:36–43, 22:1–14, 25:1 f.). Certain scholars suppose that we owe this language not directly to Jesus himself, but to the disciples, who put his teaching into these forms; but this is to take extreme liberties with the records. It is better to suppose that on certain occasions Jesus actually used the language—not so much because he meant the descriptions to be taken literally, but because the descriptions were effective means of telling the people that he was the expected Judge and Saviour of men.

What is more important, however, is the fact that he saw his mission as essentially that of bringing to men a moral and spiritual deliverance, and that to do this he must suffer and die. "My kingdom," he said to Pilate, "is not of this world" (John 18:36). He was a king, but one who ruled by serving (Matt. 20:25–28). He was a priest, but one who offered not the blood of an animal, but his own blood—his life (John 10:11–18; Heb. 9:11–28). He was a prophet, but one whose message was himself, "the Word made flesh" (John 1:14). He would set up a kingdom, but it would be one of love and good will (Matt. 18:1–4; cf. 9:35–38; Luke 12:31–34; cf. Col. 1:13 f.), from which none need be excluded (Matt. 11:29 f.; John 6:34–40). It was at this point chiefly that Jesus transformed the traditional Jewish Messiahisms; and though their influence, through the numerous Jewish converts, lingered in early Christianity for some time, Jesus' own understanding of his Messiahship came increasingly to prevail. The proof of that is in the fact that the N.T. epistles as a whole teach that Jesus Christ came into the world to deliver all men from the reign of sin and bind them into a family of God (Acts 2:36–42; Gal. 3:26–29; Eph. 2:11–22). See APOCALYPTIC; APOCRYPHA; JESUS CHRIST; KINGDOM OF GOD; SAVIOUR; SON OF MAN. E. L.

metals were prevalent in all later Bible times. Ore deposits in E. Palestine have been reported and analyzed by Nelson Glueck; the veins known in ancient times are still rich in iron and copper (Deut. 8:9). The abundant yield of many ancient mines is indicated in such passages as Ezra 1:9–11. The figure of 5,000 articles of gold and silver which had been accumulated at the Jerusalem Temple before the Exile may, however, be hyperbole. See COPPER; GOLD; IRON; LEAD; SILVER; also MINES; MONEY. See also AQABAH; EZION-GEBER, JORDAN, SERABIT EL-KHADEM.

meteyard (mēt′yärd′), archaic for measuring-stick (Lev. 19:35).

Methuselah (mē-thū′zĕ-lȧ) ("man of the dart"), a man descended from Seth and Enoch who lived to an almost incredible age, 969, after having begotten many sons and daughters, including Lamech (Gen. 5:21–27). His name appears in genealogical lists, as in Gen. 4:18 (A. V. Methusael) and in Luke 3:37 (A.V. Mathusala).

mezuzah (mĕ-zōō′zä), a small wooden or metal case attached to the doorpost of the houses of devout Jews. It contains a parchment inscribed on one side with Deut. 6:4–9 and 11:13–21, and on the other *Shaddai* (one of the names of God*). Its purpose is to stimulate piety. See DOORS.

Micah (mī′kȧ) ("who is like Jehovah?"), a proper name frequently found in the O.T., with such variant spellings in the different English versions as Mica and Micha. (1) Micah of Ephraim, at the instigation of his mother, equipped a shrine in his house. At first his son, and later an itinerant Levite, was made its officiating priest (Judg. 17). When the Danites* migrated northward (Judg. 1:34) they kidnapped Micah's Levite priest and removed the contents of his private chapel to their new home in Laish* (Tell el-Qâdī) (Judg. 18:1–29). Thus Micah's

Levite became the accredited founder of the Danite priesthood, and the religious objects from his chapel furnished Israel's northernmost shrine (Judg. 18:30). (2) A Reubenite ancestor of Beerah, who was carried into captivity by Tiglath-pileser III (I Chron. 5:5). (3) A son of Merib-baal (Mephibosheth) (II Sam. 9:12; I Chron. 8:34 f., 9:40 f.). (4) The father of Abdon (II Chron. 34:20).

(5) The prophet Micah was probably a native of Moresheth (Mic. 1:1; Jer. 26:18), identified with Moresheth-gath in the Shephelah of Judah, against which town the prophet inveighed (1:14). He was a prophet from the countryside, a younger contemporary of Isaiah (Isa. 2:2–4; cf. Mic. 4:1–3). Like Amos, he saw the evils of urban life (1:5). He was familiar with life in Samaria, and especially with that in Jerusalem (3:10). During Hezekiah's reign (c. 715–687 B.C.) he noted that wealthy landowners took advantage of the poor (2:1 f., 4; Isa. 5:8); that mercenary religious leaders were corrupt (2:11); and that justice miscarried (3:10 f.)—all in an atmosphere of pious platitudes and loud acknowledgments of God (3:11). Micah, like Isaiah, Amos, and Hosea, emphasized the righteousness of Yahweh and the ethical implications of this righteousness for individual and community life. He had nothing to say about idolatry and immortality, as Amos and Hosea did, but was concerned about the social injustices that befell the peasant, the farmer, and the small landowners. He prophesied during the reigns of Jotham (742–735 B.C.), Ahaz (735–715 B.C.), and Hezekiah (715–687 B.C.). Micah did not regard the fall of Samaria in 722/1 B.C. in its broad political aspects, as Isaiah did, but in terms of a threat to his immediate neighborhood (1:10–15) and the already unfortunate "little people" (2:3). One hundred years later Micah's prophecy about Jerusalem (3:12) was still remembered and referred to by Jeremiah (26:18, 19). See MICAH, THE BOOK OF.

Micah, the Book of, the 6th of the 12 books of the Minor Prophets. It receives its name from its title (Mic. 1:1; cf. Jer. 26:18). The book may be divided, according to subject matter, into three parts: chaps. 1–3, judgment; 4, 5, comfort; 6, 7, salvation. When outlined in its literary pattern, the words "hear ye" introduce three slightly different subdivisions—1:2–2:13, 3–5, 6 and 7. Though the emphasis in prophetic writings is on the spoken word, yet their preservation is due to the fact that they were reduced to writing by the prophet or by some devoted listener. Thus the name standing at the head of a collection of writings became a convenient label for the identification of the particular scroll, though not every saying on that scroll may have been by that author.

Most modern scholars believe that only a part (certainly Mic. 1:2-2:10, and probably portions of chaps. 4 and 5) proceeded from Micah himself. According to this theory, additions covering later periods were added. The diversity of background conditions discernible in the book supports this theory. Others believe that the forceful, picturesque style seen in every chapter argues for a unity of authorship. Whatever its origin, there runs through the book a consistent revelation of divine judgment, hope, and mercy.

Judgment is portrayed as the march of a devastating army through the country (1:10–16, 7:12), leaving the cities leveled like a plowed field (3:12). Hope is expressed for a universal religion (4:1–5); a personal, Bethlehem-born Messiah* (5:2 f.); and an age of peace (5:3–7). Salvation* is to be obtained not by ritualistic offerings, but by fulfilling the simple requirements of justice, mercy, and humility (6:6–8). The severity of divine judgment is to be softened by God's forgiving mercy (7:16–19).

Many evidences of a late date for the last portions of the book may be found in Israel's Exilic contacts and outlook (7:11 f.). Just as Baal and Marduk, deities of Canaan and Babylonia, overcame their monstrous foes, Mot and Tiâmat, so will God "cast all their sins into the depths of the sea" (Mic. 7:19). These closing verses of the book, with their promise of forgiveness, are read annually by Jews in the afternoon service of Yom Kippur (the Day of Atonement*).

The birth of Jesus at Bethlehem was more than a fulfillment of Micah's hope for a deliverer of the common people, by one of their own kind.

Micaiah (mī-kā'yȧ) (A.V. Michaiah, except in I Kings 22:8–28; II Chron. 18:6–27). (1) A prophet of Israel, son of Imlah. When Micaiah was summoned to appear before Kings Ahab of Israel and Jehoshaphat of Judah, meeting to discuss the advisability of an attack on Ramoth-gilead, the prophet at first did what was desired of him and concurred with the prophets of Baal who had forecast victory. But Ahab detected irony in Micaiah's statement and pressed for his true opinion. Micaiah in solemn imagery then forecast the sorry fate which would befall the enterprise. This true prophet of an unpleasant forecast was sentenced to prison by Ahab (I Kings 22:8–18; II Chron. 18:6–27). Ahab was killed at Ramoth-gilead, and Israel was defeated. The final fate of Micaiah is unknown. (2) One of Jehoshaphat's princes, sent by him to teach in the cities of Judah (II Chron. 17:7). (3) The father of Achbor (II Kings 22:12). (4) A son of Gemariah (Jer. 36:11 f.), one of the nobles of Judah in the days of Jeremiah. When Micaiah heard Baruch reading the roll of Jeremiah's prophecies to the people, he reported it to his father and his colleagues gathered in the "scribes' chamber" in the "king's house." This act led to its subsequent reading before all the princes and the king himself (Jer. 36:13–26). (5) A son of Zaccur (Neh. 12:35, 41), a priest who participated in the dedication of the Jerusalem walls. (6) Probably a corruption of Maacah* (I Chron. 3:2).

Michael ("who is like God?") (1) The name of several men mentioned in I Chronicles, none of whom was outstanding; and of a son of King Jehoshaphat of Israel (II Chron. 21:2). (2) An angel of the Persian period, mentioned in Dan. 10:13, 21, 12:1 as guarding Israelites against the influences of Persia and Greece; in Jude (v. 9), where he is an archangel contending with the devil to secure the body of Moses (cf. Deut. 34:6); and in Rev. 12:7, where he is at war with the dragon of evil, Satan.

Michal (mī'kĕl) (short form of "Michael"), a daughter of Saul (I Sam. 14:49). She was offered to David on condition that he slay 200 Philistines (I Sam. 18:27 f.). When Saul plotted against him, Michal helped David escape. During his flight Michal was given to Phaltiel, but was later restored to David (II Sam. 3:15). She rebuked David for dancing ceremoniously before the Ark (II Sam. 6:16–23). She died childless. (The reference to Michal in II Sam. 21:8 is probably a scribal error for Merab*.)

Michmash (mĭk'măsh) (Michmas) (possibly "a hidden place"), a town in the Tribe of Benjamin E. of Bethel, 7 m. N. of Jerusalem. It was situated 1,900 ft. above sea level, on the hill N. of the deep Wâdī es-Suwenit on the E. slope of the hilly central backbone of Palestine. The military episode at Michmash marked the expulsion of the Philistines* from this E. hill-country (I Sam. 13, 14). The Philistines occupied the hills of Benjamin with superior numbers and military equipment (13:5); they took Michmash (I Sam. 13:11), and the poorly armed Hebrews retreated in disorder (vv. 6 f.). Six hundred under King

267. Michmash Gorge.

Saul were concentrated at Geba (or Gibeah*) (13:15 f., 14:2). The Pass of Michmash (Wâdī es-Suwenit) separated the two encampments (I Sam. 13:23), and two rocky crags, Bozez and Seneh, lay before Michmash and Geba, respectively (14:4 f,). Jonathan and his armor-bearer scaled the rocky crag Bozez, created panic in the Philistine camp (14:6–15), and aided by their captured countrymen and Saul's small force, overran the Philistine garrison (14:16–23). Josephus elaborates in his *Antiquities* on the details of the assault (*Antiq.* VI. vi). By following the accurate topographical description found in I Sam. 14:4 f., General Edmund H. H. Allenby was able to develop a strategy which dislodged the Turks from Michmash in the campaign of 1917. This height is represented by Isaiah as occupied by the Assyrians in their attack upon Jerusalem, with the same geographical details and maneuvers, but in reverse direction (Isa. 10:28). After the Exile members of the Jewish community lived in Michmash (Ezra 2:27; Neh. 7:31, 11:31). It was the residence of Jonathan Maccabaeus (160–142 B.C.) (I Macc. 9:73; Josephus, *Antiq.* XIII.i.6). The name is preserved as modern Arabic Mukhmâs.

Michtam (mĭk'tăm), an obscure word appearing in the titles of Ps. 16, 56–60, which may indicate "for private meditation," in contrast to a song intended for public ministry, or may suggest a meticulously-fashioned psalm or one designed to help the worshipper atone for sin. Moffatt translates it, "A golden ode of David."

Midianites, a people living in the NW. Arabian Desert, E. of the Gulf of Aqabah, opposite the Sinai Peninsula, and S. of Moab. Their nomadic (see NOMADS) habits led this Bedouin company to wander W. into Sinai and N. into the eastern Jordan Valley and Canaan. They were perhaps among the first to use domesticated camels* (cf. Isa. 60:6). The genealogical list of Gen. 25:1 ff. makes Midian a son of Abraham and Keturah. Judg. 8:24 identifies the Midianites of Gideon's day as "Ishmaelites"*, the name given by the author of Gen. 37:25 to the camel-using merchants en route from Gilead to Egypt to whom Joseph's brothers sold him (v. 27); the text of v. 28 uses "Midianites merchantmen" and "Ishmaelites." Their attitude toward Israel varied. Moses, who fled to them from Egypt, found hospitality with the Midianite shepherd Jethro (Reuel), whose daughter Zipporah he married (Ex. 2:15–3:1), and from whom he later received spiritual guidance (18:1–12) and advice about governing the wandering Israelites (vv. 14 ff.). The Lord of the Midianite Jethro was the Yahweh of Moses. The scene of this narrative suggests the Sinai area across the Gulf of Aqabah from the Midianite homeland. Since one group of Midianites were the metal-working Kenites* (Judg. 1:16, 4:11), the Midianites may have been attracted to Sinai by its famous copper mines. (See SERABIT EL-KHADEM.)

In the period of the Judges the Midianites and the Amalekites* entered into territory claimed by Israel, and during seven years of oppression caused the Israelites to flee to strongholds in mountain dens and caves (Judg. 6:1 ff.). This was interpreted as punishment by the Lord for Israel's evil ways. The striking victory of Gideon over this roaming Bedouin people in the valley between Jezreel and the Jordan is narrated in Judg. 6–8. The Midianites did not merge with the peoples of Palestine; instead they are represented as typical, picturesque nomads, whose kings wore golden earrings, ornaments and purple garments, and ornamented their camels (Judg. 8:26), as Bedouin chiefs do today.

Midrash (mĭd′răsh), the traditional Jewish interpretation of and commentary on the Scriptures, often arranged according to the order of the text. There are halachic as well as aggadic midrashim (see LAW). Besides the separate volumes of midrashim, many midrashic passages are incorporated in the Talmud*.

migdal (mĭg′ dăl), a Semitic term designating a "fortified tower" (cf. Judg. 8:9, 17, 9:46 ff.; for an Egypt. rep., see *ANEP*², No. 329). It occurs in a number of place names: (1) Migdal-el ("tower of El"), a town of Naphtali in Upper Galilee (Josh. 19:38), site unknown. (2) Migdal-gad ("tower of Gad"), a town of Judah in the Shephelah, near Lachish (Josh. 15:37). (3) Migdol ("fortress, tower"), the proper name of various military stations on the Egyptian frontier (see *ANET*³, pp. 243, 259, 485): (a) a place on the route of the Exodus (Ex. 14:2; Num. 33:7); (b) the seat of a Jewish colony at the time of Jeremiah (Jer. 44:1, 46:14), perhaps modern Tell el-Ḥeir, between Pelusium and Sile (see *JEA* 6, 1920, pp. 107 ff.); (c) a place in N. Egypt mentioned by Ezekiel (29:10, 30:6), possibly the same as (b).

Migron (mĭg′rŏn) (possibly "steep"). (1) A site, possibly near Geba, where Saul during his feud with Jonathan tarried on a threshing floor or under a pomegranate tree (I Sam. 14:2). (2) A place mentioned by Isaiah (10:28) as on the route of the invading Assyrians, N. of Michmash and possibly on the opposite side of "the valley" (A.S.V. Isa. 10:29, "the pass") from Migron (1).

Milcah (mĭl′kȧ) ("queen"), corresponding to the N. Mesopotamian Malkatu ("princess"). (1) A title of the Babylonian goddess Ishtar*. (2) A daughter of Haran, sister of Lot, wife of Nahor, and mother of eight, including Bethuel, who was the father of Isaac's wife Rebekah (Gen. 11:29, 22:20, 23, 24:15, 24, 47); the eponymous ancestress of a tribe. (3) A daughter of Zelophehad, descendant of Joseph (Num. 26:33, 27:1; Josh. 17:3). (4) A town, site unknown.

Milcom (mĭl′kŏm) (from *malk, milk*, "king," epithet of Baal; Malcam, probably a corruption), a Semitic deity sometimes identified with Molech* (Moloch, but cf. I Kings 11:5, 7, "in the hill," and II Kings 23:10, "in the valley"). Milcom was an "abomination" adopted by Solomon (I Kings 11:5, 33), abandoned by Josiah (II Kings 23:13).

mildew, a destructive growth of minute fungi which attacked the crops of Palestine, and was interpreted as punishment visited by God on the disobedient (Deut. 28:22; Amos 4:9; Hag. 2:17). Deliverance from mildew was one of the blessings prayed for by Solomon (I Kings 8:37; II Chron. 6:28).

mile. See WEIGHTS AND MEASURES.

Miletus (mī-lē′tŭs) (Miletum A.V. II Tim. 4:20), an ancient seaport of SW. Asia Minor colonized by Ionian Greeks at the mouth of the Meander River. From its four harbors ships sailed across the Mediterranean and up into the Black Sea, in which region they established 60 cities before the middle of the 7th century B.C. It declined after its capture by Alexander the Great (334 B.C.), but had recovered by the time of Paul's visit on his way to Jerusalem after his Third Missionary Journey. Paul may have visited it a second time (cf. II Tim. 4:20). At his first visit (Acts 20:16–38), which lasted only two days, Paul was in a hurry to ship for Tyre so that he might reach Jerusalem for Pentecost. He sent 30 m. N. to Ephesus, asking the elders of the flourishing church there to come to Miletus for a farewell message, which, as recorded in Acts, is one of the most touching messages of the N.T.

The extensive ruins of Miletus include an agora* with the typical Hellenistic shops and long street connecting the harbor with the city walls, as at Corinth and Athens; a sacred way lined with tombs; temples to Apollo Delphinus and to Athena; a stadium; and the largest open-air theater in Asia Minor. An inscription in koine Gk. on a block of seats in the theater reads: "Place of the Jews, who are also called the God-fearing."

mill, a combination of two stones, one on the other, for grinding grain. The daily baking of bread in Bible lands, which still prevails in many sections of Israel and Jordan, required frequent grindings of home-grown meal by women slaves, handmaids, or the wives and daughters of the family (Ex. 11:5; cf. Gen. 18:6). The pleasant sound of the mills and the cheerful voices of chattering grinders was common in everyday life (Jer. 25:10). Grain was ground into meal by various methods. (1) A mortar and pestle were used (Num. 11:8). (2) In Egyptian households, as seen in extant models from tombs, a narrow stone 12 to 18 in. long was rubbed over a 2-ft.-long stone slab, usually saddle-shaped. (3) The usual household mill consisted of a stationary lower or nether millstone, very heavy, often of basalt, 17 to 19 in. in diameter, somewhat convex; and an upper millstone, somewhat concave, revolving on a pivot and equipped with a funnel-shaped hole into which the peg from the lower stone fitted, and through which grain could be poured down between the stones. Two women sat on the ground by the mill, opposite each other. With their left hands they turned the upper millstone by means of an upright wooden handle inserted near the outer edge; each gave the stone a half turn. With her right hand each poured in grain from an adjacent basket. The meal flowed onto a cloth which had been placed under the millstones. (4) Two large hollow stone cones were placed one on top of the other, and turned by a pole thrust through holes in the stones. The pole was pushed by a slave, a prisoner—like Samson (Judg. 16:21)—or, especially in N.T. times, by an ass (A.S.V. margin Matt. 18:6).

Scripture makes parabolic use of the familiar millstones. Mosaic Law forbade a credtor's taking a man's upper millstone, because his food depended on it (Deut. 24:6). The firmness of the strong lower stone was proverbial (Job 41:24). The heavy weight of the millstone was mentioned by Jesus as symbolic of a man's responsibility not to put a stumbling block in the way of young Christians (Matt. 18:6; Mark 9:42; Luke 17:2). To symbolize the weight of powerful Babylon's fall the author of Revelation wrote of an angel's tossing a great millstone into the sea (Rev. 18:21).

268. Baker's millstone, Ostia, Italy.

In N.T. times public millers had large wholesale mills and granaries (*horrea*), such as have been excavated at Pompeii and at Ostia*, port of Rome.

millennium, a thousand-year period. In Christian tradition it refers to the period, described in Rev. 20:1–8, during which "the dragon, the old serpent, which is the Devil and Satan," was to be bound, making possible a universal blessedness. During this period Christ would reign, and the martyrs would be raised to reign with him; the remainder of the faithful dead would not be raised until the thousand years were ended. At the end of the thousand years Satan would be temporarily released to devastate the earth, but before long he would be bound again and be "cast into the lake of fire" with "the beast and the false prophet," this time "for ever and ever" (20:10).

This is the sole N.T. basis for belief in the millennium. The passage in I Cor. 15:20–26 can hardly be fitted into the conception. Something approaching the concept occurs in the Jewish Apocalyptic writings produced shortly before the birth of Christ. In the Apocalypse of Enoch, for example, the seven "days" of creation are treated as symbols of later history; each creation "day" represents a thousand years. After six thousand years have elapsed there comes judgment. Judgment is followed by a "Sabbath" period of a thousand years, corresponding to the Creator's "day of rest" (Gen. 2:2 f.); this is the millennium. It is highly probable that John is indebted to these Jewish Apocalyptic writings for his own view.

The early Church was much occupied with the question of future times and seasons. Even during our Lord's lifetime the question was a popular one (Matt. 24:1–31). There was a common expectation among the first Christians of the Lord's return, to judge the wicked and to reward the righteous, and to introduce an era of peace (cf. Acts 1:6 f.)—the millennium, but it was not necessarily conceived according to the pattern of the Revelation of John described above. Indeed, the description written by Paul in I Thess. 4:13–18 is very different from that of John. Paul's words, "so shall we ever be with the Lord" (v. 17), could be held to refer to the millennium, but the reference is much more likely to "heaven."

The millennial hope has always become strong in the Church during periods of tribulation. A very late epistle explains why the Lord delayed his return: 1st, what to the Lord seemed "soon" might be to men a thousand years; 2d, the Lord postponed his return in order to keep open the door of repentance for the indifferent (II Pet. 3:3–13). The millennial hope in one or another of its forms characterizes Second Adventism and various other sects. The two groups who call themselves respectively Premillennarians and Postmillennarians divide on the question whether the return of Christ, the establishing of his universal reign, and the resurrection of the redeemed, will precede or follow the millennium. For most Christians it suffices to believe that Christ will finally reign (Heb. 10:13).

See APOCALYPTIC; ESCHATOLOGY; JUDGMENT, DAY OF. E. L.

millet, a cereal grass extensively used in western Asia, southern Europe, and northern Africa. The stalks are fed to cattle, while the seeds can be fed to poultry or ground for consumption by man. Ezekiel (4:9) was instructed to make bread and to use millet as one of the ingredients.

Millo (Heb. "filling"). (1) The Millo mentioned in connection with the defense works of David, Solomon, and Hezekiah may best be described as a raised platform or terrace of filled-in masonry along the steep E. slope of the Davidic city of Jerusalem*, located on the E. ridge that projects S. of the present Old City (for other suggestions, see J. Simons, *Jerusalem in the Old Testament*, 1952, pp. 131 ff.). Probably originally constructed by the Jebusites, it was repaired by David after he captured the city (II Sam. 5:9; I Chron. 11:8). This terrace system was later repaired by Solomon (c. 961–922 B.C.) as part of his monumental building program (I Kings 9:15, 24, 11:27). Joash (c. 837–800 B.C.) was slain in the "house of Millo" (II Kings 12:20), and Hezekiah (c. 715–687 B.C.) strengthened the Millo against the advance of the Assyrian king Sennacherib (II Chron. 32:5). Recent archaeological excavation has strengthened the above hypothesis. A Late Bronze Age Jebusite terrace system was uncovered, supported by a retaining wall along the E. slope. It consisted of a massive stone fill divided into sections by thin stabilizer walls. A succession of repairs was noted continuing as late as the 7th century

B.C. (see K. M. Kenyon, *Jerusalem*, 1967, pp. 50 f., 79; *Royal Cities of the Old Testament*, 1971, pp. 33 ff., 45). (2) Beth-millo, an unidentified place near Shechem (Judg. 9:6, 20). W. P. A.

mina. See MONEY.

Minaeans, a people of SW. Arabia, living N. of the Sabaeans of Sheba*. Their dialect resembled that of Canaanites, as shown by Ugaritic (see RAS SHAMRAH) inscriptions. S. Arabian-Minaean inscribed documents dating from the 6th or 5th century B.C. provide information on their pantheon and religious usages, which may have influenced Biblical cults. (Cf. Meunim, II Chron. 20:1, A.S.V. margin; Neh. 7:52; Mehunims, II Chron. 26:7; Ezra 2:50.)

mind, the thinking mechanism. In the N.T., especially in Paul's writings, which were influenced by Gk. philosophy, the word *nous* is sometimes employed to denote the total inner man, including his ability to distinguish between right and wrong (Rom. 7:23; Phil. 2:5). Mark uses *dianoia* for "mind" (12:30). Luke uses *boule*, in the sense of "counsel" (Luke 23:51; Acts 5:38) or "purpose" (Acts 20:27). See HEART, often used in the N.T. for "mind."

minerals, substances secured from mines*; ore. See FLINT; JEWELRY; MARBLE; METALS; REFINING.

mines, excavations for the extracting of mineral ores. Deut. 8:9 (cf. Deut. 4:20) characterized Israel's promised land as one "whose stones are iron, and out of whose hills thou mayest dig" copper (not "brass," as *passim* A.V. and often A.S.V.). Although Western Palestine lacks mines, Eastern Palestine (the present Kingdom of Jordan) has been found, as explored by Nelson Glueck and others, to be rich in Iron Age mines of both copper and iron, in the deep cleft of the Jordan Valley and the Arabah*, as far as Aqabah*. (See EZION-GEBER.) In the region of Succoth* (Tell Deir'allā) and Adamah (see ADAM), where equipment for Solomon's Temple was fabricated by Hiram* of Tyre (the craftsman-architect, not the king), there are many slag heaps testifying to the mining activity of this creative age. Glueck pictures (in *The River Jordan*, Westminster Press) interminable lines of donkeys picking their way down the valley from iron mines in the 'Ajlûn region N. of the Jabbok, where the ore was partly refined before being further processed in the S., as at Ezion-geber. The Jordan-Arabah provided plenty of water for miners and mines, and abundant charcoal fuel from the forests of Gilead and Edom. Mining and casting of such equipment as is described in I Kings 7 could have taken place in Trans-Jordan, on sites accessible to Jerusalem. For an account of King Solomon's copper mines, the acropolis heights which defended them, remains of blast furnaces, slave-miners' huts, slag heaps, and abundant Iron Age pottery dumped at Khirbet Nahas ("the Copper Ruin"), Feinan, and the vast Mene'iyeh (c. 24 m. N. of Aqabah), whose slag heaps are still green with copper not fully refined out, see Glueck's *The Other Side of the Jordan*, published by ASOR. Khirbet Hamr Ifdan was a fortress erected in the era of the kings of Israel and Judah to guard the approach to mines and furnaces. David's iron tools are mentioned in I Chron. 20:3; he turned over "iron in abundance" to Solomon for the Temple (I Chron. 22:3). This material was in part due to his conquest of Edom*. Besides the Jordan-Arabah mines there were mines in the Lebanons. N. Syria was an early mining area. The Oriental Institute of the University of Chicago found at Tell al-Judaidah a hoard of copper statuettes which date the beginnings of competent metallurgy earlier than had been supposed. Nehemiah referred to iron from the N. Israel secured some of its metal products from Phoenician markets, notably Tyre, which imported it from afar (Ezek. 27:12).

The greatest mining passage in Scripture is the poem of Job 28:1–11, which depicts the perils of the mines, and suggests personal observation by the author (in Edom or Gilead). Zechariah refers to "mountains of copper" (6:1). The genetic lists of Genesis ascribe to Tubal-cain*, descendant of Cain ("smith" or "miner") the founding of metal-crafts (Gen. 4:22) (see SMITHS), and therefore indicate an early date for mining and metal-crafts.

The Philistines* monopolized iron until the time of David's conquests (I Sam. 13:19–22); during the era of the Judges Israel envied them their supply. Flinders Petrie discovered at Gerar, a Philistine coastal city, four large iron furnaces and a sword factory.

The Hittites* for centuries controlled the chief iron supply of Asia Minor—the Taurus mountains. W. Asia began doing metalwork soon after ores were discovered in the Pontus and Caucasus areas.

Egypt, according to some scholars, did not smelt iron until c. 1300 B.C.; she mined in Sinai. (See SERABIT EL-KHADEM,) Israel may have done mining in the peninsula en route to Canaan. Pharaoh's forces guarded the mines, which had been seized from Sinai people as early as the First Dynasty; they used copper for 6-ft. saws; chisels and drills; drain pipes; and temple ornamentation.

minister (Lat. *minister*, "servant"), a person authorized or licensed to conduct religious worship. (1) In the O.T. one who assisted, not necessarily in a servile manner; like Joseph, overseer at the court of Pharaoh (Gen. 39:4); Abishag at David's court (I Kings 1:4, 15); functionaries at Solomon's table (I Kings 10:5). Particularly in religious offices the minister assisted; thus Joshua was minister to Moses (Ex. 24:13, 33:11; Josh. 1:1); Elisha to Elijah (I Kings 19:21; II Kings 3:11). Priests and Levites in the Tabernacle and Temple were ministers of God, His servants (Ex. 28:35; I Kings 8:11; Ezra 8:17). (2) In the N.T. the minister of the Nazareth synagogue was an "attendant" (as in the R.S.V. Luke 4:20), who aided the officiating teacher by handing him the scroll, etc. In this sense young John Mark was minister to Paul and Barnabas (Acts 13:5). Many instances of "minister" in the N.T. are translations of the Gk. word *diakonos*, suggesting the Christian ministry as a lowly service—in contrast to the pompous priesthood of the O.T.—with *diakonia* as the word for the characteristic Christian ministry. This term is used for the service rendered Jesus by Mary and Martha and other women (Luke 10:40; John 12:2; Matt. 27:55), and Paul by Onesimus (Philem. 13). Anyone who sincerely follows Christ is his *diakonos*, his servant, his minister (John 12:26). Christ's definition of the great in terms of the minister (A.V. Matt. 20:26) is made even more lowly in the R.S.V., which uses "servant" instead of "minister" and "slave" instead of "servant." As the Church grew its ministry was performed by various types of orders having several functions (I Cor. 12:8–10 ff.), but all ministering servants of God—apostles (Luke 6:13) who were with Jesus and went forth to preach, to cast out demons (Mark 3:14 f.), to witness the Resurrection (Acts 1:21 f.); traveling missionaries or evangelists (Acts 21:8; Eph. 4:11; II Tim. 4:5); teachers (Rom. 12:6 f.; R.S.V. Jas. 3:1); pastors (Eph. 4:11); deacons (Acts 6; Phil. 1:1; I Tim 3:8); elders (Acts 14:23, 16:4; I Tim. 5:1, 17–19); and bishops (Phil. 1:1; I Tim. 3:1–7). The "good minister of Jesus Christ" (I Tim. 4:6) is a *diakonos*.

The Christian minister today devotes himself to following the pattern of Christ, who came to minister to the lost, the weary, the bewildered, the wicked, the sick, the indifferent, and the ignorant. Paul's ideals for the minister are stated in II Cor. 6:1–10; I Tim. 4; cf. Mal. 2:5–7 for a beautiful description of the true priest or minister of God.

Minni (mĭn'ī), a people living near the headwaters of the Tigris in Armenia, in a grain-growing region near Lake Urmiah, SE. of Lake Van. They suffered periods of domination by Assyria until they allied themselves with other nations, who seized Nineveh and ended Assyrian power (612 B.C.). The Minni are mentioned by Jeremiah (51:27) as uniting with the kingdoms of Ararat and Ashchenaz against Babylon.

Minnith (mĭn'ĭth), a town of eastern Palestine (now Jordan), the northernmost limit of the territory conquered by Jephthah from the Ammonites (Judg. 11:33); probably situated not far from Rabbath-ammon (now Amman); near the center of the great wheat-growing region referred to by Ezekiel (27:17).

mint, one of the herbs tithed by Pharisees (Matt. 23:23; Luke 11:42). Several varieties grow wild in Palestine.

miracles, events in the physical world outside the operation of known laws. Popularly considered, a miracle contains one of or a combination of several elements. (1) It is an *incomprehensible event.* In Bible times, as in the modern scientific age, man has not fully discerned the ways of God in the universe. An event may be incomprehensible and therefore termed "miraculous," but this is not to say that it never happened. (2) A miracle may be an event involving a real or apparent *upset of law* or ordinary human procedure. A temporary breach in the uniformity of nature or of human behavior, while a superior law or will takes over, is commonplace in the ancient as well as the modern world, as, for example, the law of gravitation is temporarily suspended when a human hand keeps a book from falling to the floor. Modern miracles occur when hitherto unknown laws are discovered and applied, like the use of penicillin to cure disease heretofore incurable. (3) A miracle is the *advent of the supernatural into the realm of the natural.* Some people, under the domination of the scientific method, consider miracles nonessential to Christian faith; others see miracles as the timely participation of the divine in human events.

A man's intellectual assumptions control in large part his attitude toward miracles. Enthusiasts for history, natural law, science, myth, literature, psychology, etc., have all applied their ideas to Bible miracles. Battles over the Bible are usually fought from different basic points of view. The Bible is primarily a religious book, presenting a record of man's faith in God, which raises him above all lesser assumptions. The Bible presents God as master of law as well as of mystery, the known and the unknown, the ordinary and the extraordinary. The miraculous was a popular thought-pattern in the ancient world, in which God was presented as intervening in the ordinary course of affairs in order to express His will and purpose.

In the Bible miracles fall mainly into four great periods, each of which was characterized by extraordinary religious revelations: (1) The establishment of a nation under Moses and Joshua. (2) The ethical reformation of the Jewish people under the leadership of Elijah and Elisha. (3) The humiliating experiences of the Exile. (4) The introduction of Christianity under Jesus and the Apostles. Miracles thus not only spotlight specific events, but reveal a deep and unforgettable experience of God by the people.

Many Bible miracles, especially *in the O.T.*, may be interpreted in the light of magic (Ex. 7:20; II Kings 2:14); poetry (Josh. 10:12 f.); psychology (I Sam. 14); science (Josh. 3:14–17); legend (Dan. 3:19–27); literature (Job 2:1–10); or archaeology (Josh. 6:6–20). Yet when such interpretations seem for the modern mind to eliminate the miraculous, God still remains in the universe—a position not established by miracles, nor disturbed by their repudiation.

The miracles *of the N.T.* are on a higher level. Those by Jesus are intimately woven into his life and personality. Many are manifestations of the power of one personality over another, of spirit over body, of mind over matter. Because of the progress of modern man in this field (John 14:12), such miracles are not considered as marvelous as they once were. But this attitude cannot remove all of Jesus' miracles from the category of his extraordinary power. He performed his miracles in an atmosphere of faith (Mark 2:5, 4:40, 5:34; Matt. 8:10, 13; Luke 7:50) and prayer (Mark 9:19–29; John 11:41 f.). His miracles were characterized by (1) a desire to be helpful to mankind; (2) a high moral purpose which made every miracle not an end in itself but a means toward some divine good; and (3) a restraint lest his power be used for selfish gratification or advantage. Jesus modestly minimized his miracles by calling them "works"—the logical expression of his nature in terms of daily labor. John called them "signs" (see SIGN) of his Messiahship (John 2:11, 3:2, 4:54; etc.).

All other miracles in the Bible are insignificant in comparison with the supreme miracles of the Incarnation and Resurrection of the Lord Jesus Christ. Spiritual experiences in the early Church, like Pentecost, the conversion of Paul, etc., were miracles on the highest level. Faith in miracles is not primarily a mental attitude toward what is recorded, but a spiritual adventure into the release and use of divine power. A personal experience of the living Christ which issues in conversion, guidance, deliverance, and triumph is a miracle which those who experience it never deny, and which those who behold it never doubt.

Miracles in the Old Testament

Under Moses

Aaron's rod becoming a serpent, Ex. 7:10–12
The ten plagues:
- Water made blood, Ex. 7:20–25
- Frogs, Ex. 8:5–14
- Lice, Ex. 8:16–18
- Flies, Ex. 8:20–24
- Murrain, Ex. 9:3–6
- Boils and blains, Ex. 9:8–11
- Thunder and hail, Ex. 9:22–26
- Locusts, Ex. 10:12–19
- Darkness, Ex. 10:21–23
- Death of the firstborn, Ex. 12:29, 30

The Reed Sea divided, Ex. 14:21–31
The waters of Marah sweetened, Ex. 15:23–25
The manna, Ex. 16:14–35
Water from the rock at Rephidim, Ex. 17:5–7
Death of Nadab and Abihu, Lev. 10:1, 2
Fire consuming the people at Taberah, Num. 11:1–3
Death of Korah, Dathan, and Abiram, Num. 16:31–35
Aaron's rod budding, Num. 17:6–8
Water from the rock at Meribah, Num. 20:7–11
The brazen serpent, Num. 21:8, 9

Under Joshua

The Jordan stopped, Josh. 3:14–17
The fall of Jericho, Josh. 6:6–20
Sun and moon stayed, Josh. 10:12–14 (probably an apparent rather than an actual miracle.)

Under the Kings

Death of Uzzah, II Sam. 6:7
Jeroboam's hand withered and altar destroyed, I Kings 13:4–6
By Elijah:
- The widow's cruse supplied, I Kings 17:14–16
- The widow's son raised, I Kings 17:17–24
- The sacrifice at Carmel consumed, I Kings 18:30–38
- Ahaziah's troops consumed by fire, II Kings 1:10–12
- The dividing of Jordan, II Kings 2:7, 8
- Elijah translated to heaven, II Kings 2:11

By Elisha:
- The dividing of Jordan, II Kings 2:14
- The waters of Jericho sweetened, II Kings 2:21, 22
- Mocking children (*Heb.* young men) destroyed by bears, II Kings 2:24
- Water supplied to Jehoshaphat and the allied army, II Kings 3:16–20
- The widow's oil increased, II Kings 4:2–7
- The Shunammite's son raised, II Kings 4:32–37
- Deadly pottage corrected, II Kings 4:38–41
- 100 men fed with 20 loaves, II Kings 4:42–44
- Naaman's leprosy cured and transferred to Gehazi, II Kings 5:10–27
- The axhead floated, II Kings 6:5–7
- The Syrian army smitten and cured, II Kings 6:18–20
- Resurrection of a dead man on Elisha's bones, II Kings 13:21
- Sennacherib's army destroyed, II Kings 19:35
- Return of the shadow on the sundial of Ahaz, II Kings 20:9–11
- Uzziah smitten with leprosy, II Chron. 26:16–21
- Jonah's deliverance, Jonah 2:1–10

During the Captivity

Shadrach, Meshach, and Abednego uninjured in the furnace, Dan. 3:19–27
Daniel uninjured in the lions' den, Dan. 6:16–23

Miracles in the New Testament

Two blind men healed, Matt. 9:27
A dumb demoniac healed, Matt. 9:32
Stater in the mouth of the fish, Matt. 17:27
The deaf and dumb man healed, Mark 7:31
A blind man healed, Mark 8:22
Christ passed unseen through the multitude, Luke 4:30
Draught of fishes, Luke 5:1
Raising the widow's son, Luke 7:11
Healing the crooked woman, Luke 13:11
Healing the man with dropsy, Luke 14:1
Healing the ten lepers, Luke 17:11
Healing the ear of Malchus, servant of the high priest, Luke 22:50
Turning water into wine, John 2:1
Healing the nobleman's son, John 4:46
Healing the impotent man at Bethesda, John 5:1
Healing the man born blind, John 9:1
Raising of Lazarus, John 11:43
Draught of fishes, John 21:6
Demoniac in synagogue cured, Mark 1:23, Luke 4:33
Healing the centurion's servant (of palsy), Matt. 8:5; Luke 7:1
The blind and dumb demoniac, Matt. 12:22; Luke 11:14
Healing the daughter of the Syrophenician, Matt. 15:21; Mark 7:24
Feeding the four thousand, Matt. 15:32; Mark 8:1
Cursing the fig tree, Matt. 21:18; Mark 11:12
Healing the leper, Matt. 8:2; Mark 1:40; Luke 5:12

Healing Peter's mother-in-law, Matt. 8:14; Mark 1:30; Luke 4:38
Stilling the storm, Matt. 8:26; Mark 4:37; Luke 8:22
The legion of devils entering the swine, Matt. 8:28; Mark 5:1; Luke 8:27
Healing the man sick of the palsy, Matt. 9:2; Mark 2:3; Luke 5:18
Healing the woman with the issue of blood, Matt. 9:20; Mark 5:25; Luke 8:43
Raising Jairus' daughter, Matt. 9:23; Mark 5:38; Luke 8:49
Healing the man with a withered hand, Matt. 12:10; Mark 3:1; Luke 6:6
Walking on the sea, Matt. 14:25; Mark 6:48; John 6:19
Curing the demoniac child, Matt. 17:14; Mark 9:17; Luke 9:38
Curing blind Bartimaeus (two blind men, Matt. 20), Matt. 20:30; Mark 10:46; Luke 18:35
Feeding the five thousand, Matt. 14:19; Mark 6:35; Luke 9:12; John 6:5
The Gospels state that Jesus wrought many other miracles of healing.

Recorded in the Acts of the Apostles

The gift of the Holy Spirit at Pentecost, Acts 2:1–4
The cripple at the Beautiful Gate cured, Acts 3:1–10
The death of Ananias and Sapphira, Acts 5:1–11
Various miracles, Acts 5:12
The Apostles freed from prison, Acts 5:21–23
Stephen's miracles, Acts 6:8
Philip's miracles, Acts 8:13
Conversion of Paul, Acts 9:1–9
Paul's sight restored by means of Ananias, Acts 9:17–19
Peter cures Aeneas of palsy, Acts 9:32–35
Peter raises Dorcas to life, Acts 9:36–43
Peter is delivered from prison, Acts 12:5–11
The blinding of Elymas the sorcerer, Acts 13:11
Various miracles by Paul and Barnabas at Iconium, Acts 14:3
Paul heals a cripple at Lystra, Acts 14:8–10
Paul cures the maid with a spirit of divination at Philippi, Acts 16:16–18
Paul and Silas set free by an earthquake, Acts 16:26
Many miracles by Paul at Ephesus, Acts 19:11, 12
The raising of Eutychus, Acts 20:9–11
Paul unhurt by a viper's bite, Acts 28:3–6
Paul cures the father of Publius and others, Acts 28:7–10

Miriam (Heb. equivalent of "Mary"). (1) The daughter of Amram and Jochebed, and older sister of Aaron and Moses* (Num. 26:59; I Chron. 6:3). She suggested to Pharaoh's daughter that a Hebrew nurse be procured to care for the infant Moses, and summoned Jochebed, his mother (Ex. 2:4–8). After the crossing of the Sea of Reeds she led the ceremonial dance and the paean of the grateful Hebrew women (Ex. 15:20 f.). Because she shared Aaron's criticism of Moses for his marriage with an Ethiopian—a rebuke that disclosed their jealousy of his leadership—she was afflicted with a temporary leprous condition which delayed the progress of the Exodus until, after Moses' intercession for her, she was cured and readmitted to the company (Num. 12:2–15). She died in Kadesh-barnea near the close of the Wilderness wanderings and was buried there (Num. 20:1). (2) A son or daughter of Ezra, a man of Judah (I Chron. 4:17).

mirrors, mentioned several times in Scripture, are not to be understood as looking glasses (an anachronism of A.V. Ex. 38:8), or "molten looking glass" (Job 37:18, cf. "molten mirror" Moffatt), or "glasses" (Isa. 3:23, cf. A.S.V. "hand-mirrors"). The mirrors used by people in the Biblical period were usually of highly polished copper, bronze, silver, gold, or electrum, capable of reflecting the face. The mirrors which were melted down to make the laver for the Tabernacle were obviously metal, not glass (Ex. 38:8). Though glass was made at an early date by Phoenicians at the mouth of the Belus River, and by craftsmen in Hebron and in Egypt, it tended to be opaque in most cases (except the clear Roman glass); it was certainly not silver-backed. The "we see through a glass, darkly," of the A.V. (I Cor. 13:12) is now more accurately rendered, "we see in a mirror, dimly" (R.S.V.) or "we only see the baffling reflections in a mirror" (Moffatt; cf. James 1:23).

269. Bronze mirror, with head of Hathor, Egyptian goddess of love and festivity (c. 1500–1200 B.C.).

Mishnah (mĭsh'nȧ) (from Heb. verb, *shanah*, "to repeat"), the collection of Jewish oral laws edited by Rabbi Judah ha-Nasi (c. A.D. 135–220). This was the culmination of various efforts to organize the vast mass of traditions transmitted orally for centuries; the basis of the Talmud*.

mist, mentioned as supplying the first moisture for the growth of vegetation after the Creation* (Gen. 2:6), is still a valuable source of water supply in Palestine. Acts 13:11 tells of mist blinding the sorcerer Elymas so that he sought someone to lead him. The author of II Pet. 2:17 (A.S.V.) likens unsubstantial people to "mists driven by a storm."

Mitanni (mĭ-tăn'ē), a non-Semitic, Indo-Iranian people who invaded N. Mesopotamia from the eastern highlands about the time of Hammurabi* (1728–1686 B.C.), and dominated the region between the Mediterranean and Media. Haran*, to which Abraham and Terah migrated, was Mitanni territory. The Mitanni held a balance of power between the Hittite Empire (including Assyria) (c. 1500 B.C.) and Egypt, with whose royal family they intermarried for political purposes. The horse-breeding Mitanni people were finally reduced by the Hittites (c. 1370) to a position of a buffer state between Assyria and Asia Minor, and were reduced by Assyria c. 100 years later. The Mitanni garrisoned many Syrian cities. They worshipped Indo-Iranian deities, including Varuna, Indra, and Mithra.

mite. See MONEY.

miter, high priest's headdress. See DRESS.

Mithredath (mĭth'rē-dăth) ("given by Mithra"). (1) A treasurer of Persia who at the command of Cyrus turned over to Sheshbazzar, prince of Judah, and the returning Jews precious vessels stolen by Nebuchadnezzar from the Temple (Ezra 1:8). (2) One of a group who protested to Artaxerxes I (Longimanus) against the Jews' rebuilding the Jerusalem walls (Ezra 4:7).

Mitylene (mĭt-ĭ-lē'nē), the most important city on the island of Lesbos, strongly fortified, and a center of early culture. One of its two harbors was used by Paul (Acts 20:14) on his Third Missionary Journey, from Assos on the mainland of Asia Minor to Chios.

mixed multitude, the heterogeneous company of non-Israelites who joined in the Exodus* (Ex. 12:38). Intermarriage led to Nehemiah's reform (13:3), aimed at separating from Israel "all the mixed multitude."

Mizar (mī'zär) ("littleness"), a small hill near Mt. Hermon (Ps. 42:6).

Mizpah (mĭz' pȧ) (Mizpeh), the name of several O.T. localities, often in construct relation, derived from Heb. *sāphāh* ("to keep guard, watch") thus the meaning "watch tower" (cf. II Chron. 20:24; Isa. 21:8). (1) An area below Mt. Hermon, probably near Banias, which was allied with Jabin, King of Hazor, at the time of the Hebrew conquest of N. Canaan (Josh. 11:3, 8). (2) An unidentified city in the Shephelah of Judah (Josh. 15:38). (3) An unidentified city in Moab, where David left his parents with the Moabite king when fleeing from Saul (I Sam. 22:3). (4) A site in Trans-Jordan, where Jacob and Laban solemnized their covenant by erecting a pillar (*maṣṣebah*) and a pile of stones (Gen. 31:45 ff.). Here Jephthah's leadership over the Israelites in their dispute with the Ammonites was confirmed (Judg. 10:17, 11:10 f.), and his own vow fulfilled (11:29 ff.). It may also be the Ramath-mizpeh of Gad (Josh. 13:26). The most probable identification is with Khirbet Jel 'ad, 16 m. NW. of Amman (see M. Ottosson, *Gilead*, 1969, pp. 24 ff.)

(5) The most important of the Mizpahs was a site in the territory of Benjamin (Josh. 18:26), on the boundary between the Northern and Southern Kingdoms, but usually part of the Southern. It was often called "the Mizpah." Its site is a matter of scholarly debate. The Palestine Institute of the Pacific School of Religion, at the instigation of and under the direction of William F. Badè, excavated (1926–35) Tell en-Nasbeh, an 8-acre mound 8 m. directly N. of Jerusalem on the main highway to Samaria and Galilee, N. of Ramah and Gibeah and S. and SW. of Beeroth and the usually accepted site of Bethel. What the Badè expeditions unearthed at Tell en-Nasbeh confirmed their belief and that of many other scholars that this was the Mizpah on the circuit of the prophet Samuel* (I Sam. 7:16); the civil center of the Hebrews who remained after Nebuchadnezzar's deportation to Babylon of the bulk of the citizens from the Southern Kingdom (II Kings 25:23); and the municipality of Gedaliah, the Babylon-appointed Governor of Judah (II Kings 25:23; Jer. 40, 41). It had been the scene of bitter fighting between Israel under Baasha and Judah under Asa (c. 913–873 B.C.), who fortified it heavily (I Kings 15:16–22). Other eminent archaeologists, however including W. F. Albright—and Robinson a generation ago—locate Mizpah at Nebi Samwîl, a 2,900-ft. elevation overlooking Jerusalem, 5 m. SW. of Tell en-

270. Artist's reconstruction of the walled city of Mizpah.

Nasbeh. Buildings erected since the time of Justinian (A.D. 527–565) have so modified Nebi Samwîl that earlier remains do not exist, except for scattered pottery deposits (see W. F. Albright, *AASOR* 4, 1924, pp. 90 ff.; for an excellent survey of the problem of identification, see J. Muilenburg in *Tell en-Nasbeh*, I, 1947, pp. 13 ff.).

Tell en-Nasbeh has revealed little evidence of occupation before the 11th century B.C. Tombs and caves dating to the Early Bronze Age (3d millennium B.C.) were found, but except for a single tomb, no traces of occupation during the Middle or Late Bronze Ages (2d millennium B.C.) were recovered. Scattered remains of a small Iron I settlement established c. 1100 B.C. were cleared, including a thin, poorly constructed fortification wall and examples of Philistine pottery.

The great bulk of the excavated material is from the time of the Hebrew monarchy. Early in the 1st millennium B.C., a massive fortification wall and other structures were erected at the site, perhaps by Asa (I Kings 15:22; II Chron. 16:6). This large wall is one of the strongest yet discovered in pre-Roman Palestine. It was 15 to 20 ft. thick, and in some places is still 25 ft. high; it may have reached 35 to 40 ft. It was of stone, covered with plaster to a height of 15 to 18 ft., and joined to a series of rectangular towers at irregular intervals. A single gate was located on the NE., with overlapping walls. Dated to the 9th century B.C., it is one of the best examples of this type to be found. When unearthed, the gate walls were intact up to 6 to 9 ft. The sill, sockets for pivots on which the gate swung, and the stop against which they closed, were in place. Long stone benches where the town elders may have sat were found just outside the gate, partially enclosed. Buildings were radially arranged along the interior of the city wall, separated by a ring road from the center area, which was little preserved.

Epigraphic finds include a group of seal impressions stamped on the handles of storage jars. A number are inscribed *lmlk*, "(belonging) to the king," and represent the N. limit of the "Royal" seal impressions dated to the 7th century B.C. (see *AOTS*, 1967, pp. 337 f.). Twenty-eight post-Exilic examples are read as either *msp* or *msh*. The former reading provides added support for the identification Tell en-Nasbeh = Mizpah, but the latter is perhaps more satisfactory. Also recovered was a seal inscribed in Hebrew, "(belonging) to Jaazaniah, servant of the king." An official named Jaazaniah is mentioned in II Kings 25:23 (cf. Jer. 40:8).

Additional Bible references indicate that Mizpah was an early cultic site (Judg. 20:1 ff.; I Sam. 7:5 ff., 10:17 ff.). It was also occupied after the Exile (Neh. 3:7, 15, 19), and was the site of an assembly at the time of Judas Maccabaeus (I Macc. 3:46).

See C. C. McCown *et al.*, *Tell en-Nasbeh*, I *Archaeological and Historical Results*, 1947; J. C. Wampler, *Tell en-Nasbeh*, II. *The Pottery*, 1947; D. Diringer, "Mizpah," *AOTS*, 1967, pp. 329 ff. W. P. A.

Mizraim (mĭz′rā-ĭm). (1) A son of Noah's son Ham (Gen. 10:6), and the eponymous ancestor of the Hamitic peoples of Lower Egypt and Africa NW. of the Delta, as well as of the Hamitic people in Canaan; "Casluhim (out of whom came the Philistines)" (Gen. 10:13 f.). Mizraim was also regarded as ancestor of the Raaman peoples of SW. Arabia. (2) The Heb. name for Egypt.

Mnason (nā′sŏn), an early Christian disciple, native of Cyprus, in whose home Paul lodged, either in Jerusalem (Acts 21:16) or in a village between Caesarea and that city.

Moab (etymology uncertain), an ancient kingdom and its people whose territory lay in the fertile, well-watered highlands of the Jordan, E. of the Dead Sea in what became Trans-Jordan, N. of Edom, W. of the desert. It was immediately opposite Bethlehem, birthplace of David and Jesus, both of whom had Moabite blood in their veins through Ruth the Moabitess. Early inhabitants of Moab were the Emim and the Zuzims (Gen. 14:5; Deut. 2:10). The narrative of Gen. 19:30–38 makes Lot the progenitor of the Moabites by incest with his daughter—perhaps a low insinuation of a Hebrew writer to express hate for this rival, rather highly civilized people (cf. Deut. 2:9). Moab's N. neighbor was the Kingdom of Ammon at the time of Israel's arrival from Egypt, but its territory and boundary on the N. fluctuated. The Plains of Moab are down along the Jordan and the Dead Sea, from which Moses climbed to the Moabite Mount Nebo to die (Deut. 34:1–5).

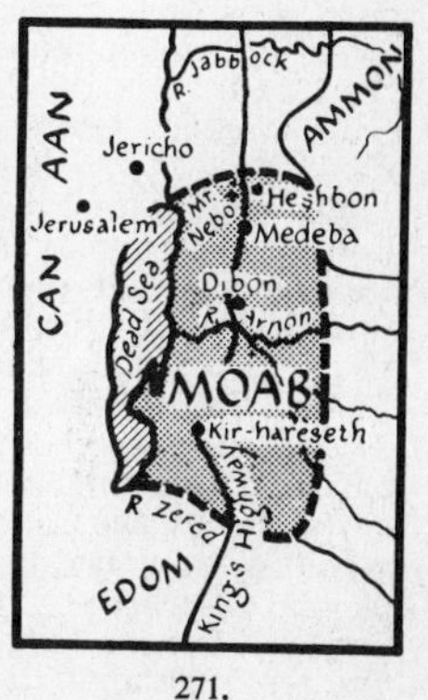

271.

Moab's 3,000-ft. tableland rising abruptly from the Dead Sea sheltered it from invaders in that direction and gave it impressive beauty. Ample rainfall and numerous streams enabled this lovely land to produce grain, fruit, and flocks of sheep on a scale large enough to support a considerable degree of city culture. Irrigation culture was followed in Moab from 5,000 to 7,000 years ago. After a catastrophe c. 1900 B.C. the people of this region temporarily adopted a nomadic life, but from c. 1200 to 700 B.C. the soil was intensively cultivated. Nelson Glueck's explorations in Moab identified hundreds of town sites, including numerous walled fortresses, some of whose Iron Age levels are extant. These made a chain from hill to hill, a barrier to Bedouins from the eastern desert steppes—a defense system retained and improved when the Nabataeans (see NABATAEA) gained control of Moab and Ammon. The towered, strong-gated cities of Moab presented to Israel arriving from Egypt in the 13th century B.C. a barrier so formidable that after the king of Moab had refused passage through his territory (Judg. 11:17 f.; II Chron. 20:10) the wanderers "went around" and sought entry to Canaan through the Amorite territory of Sihon. The Moabite blockhouses and walls of the 13th century B.C. help date the Exodus*; had Israel arrived earlier these would not have been there to block their passage. Excavations in Moab have proved the existence of hundreds of cities, whose broken pottery dates their various levels. One of the best preserved is Qasr Abū el-Kharaq, probably on the site of "the city of Moab." Kir-hareseth (see KIR) was one of its most important cities, situated on the main N.-S. highway running through the heart of the land more than 30 centuries ago—a road which resurfaced is still in use. Other Moabite towns include Madeba (still inhabited) directly E. of Bethlehem in Judaea; Heshbon, etc.; 25 Moabite cities are mentioned in the O.T. (See DIBON.)

In language and general background Moab had much in common with Israel, though her exaltation of the gods Chemosh and Ashtor-chemosh and her wide use of crude fertility gods and goddesses—many of whose figurines* have been excavated from old Moabite farms—indicate how far she fell below the lofty spiritual heights of the pure Hebrew worship.

Hebrew prophets condemned proud, arrogant Moab's low religious level, and cried down "judgments" upon this people (Isa. 15, 16, 25:10; Jer. 9:26, 25:21, 27:3, 48—especially stressing God's judgment for her sins, Ezek. 25:8–11; Amos 2:1, 2; Zeph. 2:8–11).

The history of Moab is intertwined with that of Israel and Judah. When the Hebrews trekked through eastern Palestine toward Canaan from Egypt, Ammonites N. of Moab had already annexed areas of Moab N. of the Arnon. The Reuben tribe was "assigned" land bordering on Moab (Josh. 13:15–21), and Gad for a time held some of its southern cities; but by the 9th century B.C. Reuben as a political unit had been pushed out and his people absorbed by the Moabites. In the period of Israel's Judges Moab oppressed the Tribe of Benjamin (Judg. 3:12–30, 11:15). The Book of Ruth indicates free travel and friendly relations between Judah and Moab. Saul tried to subdue Moab, and David succeeded in doing so (II Sam. 8:2 f.), in spite of Moab's having brought him aid against Saul, and having provided shelter for his parents in time of unrest. Solomon seems to have retained Moab (I Kings 11:1, 7). But Moab evidently regained independence, for on the Moabite* Stone Mesha, King of Moab, records that his land had been subdued by Omri of Israel and held by Omri's son Ahab until almost the close of the latter's reign (c. 869–850 B.C.), when Mesha freed his country and celebrated his victory by erecting the stone at Dibon. A counter-conquest was attempted, possibly by Jehoram of Israel (c. 849–842 B.C.); but it failed, after Mesha's despicable (from Israel's viewpoint) sacrifice of his eldest son (II Kings 3:27) and the rallying of his forces. II Kings (13:20) suggests that Moab subsequently invaded Israel.

Moab paid tribute to Tiglath-pileser III after his invasion of the W. (c. 733–732 B.C.), and to Sennacherib (701 B.C.). It disappeared as a political power when Nebuchadnezzar (605–562 B.C.) subjugated the country, but it continued as a race. Nabataeans held and developed Moab in the first two centuries B.C. and the 1st century A.D.

Moabite Stone, the, an inscribed stele of black basalt found at Dibon* (Dhībân) in Jordan, just N. of the Wâdī Mojib, S. of the Wâdī Zerka and the city of Amman (the Philadelphia of the Decapolis). It is the largest single literary document yet found, outside the Bible, dealing with Palestine and E. Palestine in the Iron Age. It was discovered by a Prussian missionary in 1868, offered for sale at a high price by Arabs to the French Clermont-Ganneau; later it was broken into many pieces by Arabs in the course of a dispute, but it at length found safekeeping in the Louvre at Paris. The pieces were put together again by aid of a squeeze impression which had been taken.

272. A cast of the Moabite Stone (original in the Louvre) showing an inscription in Biblical phraseology from a language which is virtually Hebrew.

Its 34 lines cut in clear, ancient Moabite (Heb.) characters similar to those in the Siloam Tunnel inscription and the Gezer calendar reveal a high degree of culture among the Moabites of the 9th century B.C. Events recorded on the Moabite Stone parallel the account of II Sam. 1 and 3. Many places named in the text occur also in Bible passages —Madeba, Ataroth, Aroer, etc. The inscription tells how Mesha's Moab had been subdued by Omri and Ahab, but was freed because his god Chemosh had commanded him to fight Israel, who had oppressed Moab for 40 years. He fought from dawn until noon, and then dragged the vessels of Yahweh and other booty and captives before Chemosh (cf. II Kings 3:4 ff., which tells that Mesha sacrificed his eldest son "for a burnt offering upon the wall" to secure his god's favor).

This is the 34-line inscription on the Stone:

1. I am Mesha, son of Chemosh . . . king of Moab, the D-
2. aibonite. My father reigned over Moab for thirty years, and I became king

3. after my father. And I made this high place for Chemosh in Krhh with . . . [Sal]vation,
4. because he saved me from all the kings and because he let me see my desire upon all them that hated me. Omr-
5. i king of Israel, he afflicted Moab many days, because Chemosh was angry with his la-
6. nd. And his son succeeded him; and he too said: "I will afflict Moab." In my days he said . . .
7. But I saw my desire upon him and upon his house, and Israel perished with an everlasting destruction. Now Omri had taken possession of all the [la-]
8. nd of Mehēdeba [Medeba], and dwelt in it during his days and half the days of his sons, forty years; but resto-
9. re it did Chemosh in my days. And I built Ba'alme'on and I made in it the reservoir [?] and I built
10. Ḳiriathān (Kiryathaim). And the men of Gad had dwelt in the land of 'Aṭaroth from of old, and had built for himself the king of I-
11. srael 'Aṭaroth. And I fought against the city and took it, and slew all the [people of]
12. the city, a gazingstock unto Chemosh and unto Moab. And I brought back from there the altar hearth of Daudoh [?] and drag-
13. ged it before Chemosh in Ḳeriyyoth [Kerioth]. And I settled the men of Srn therein and the men of
14. Mḥrth. And Chemosh said to me: "Go, take Nebo against Israel," and I
15. went by night and fought against it from break of dawn until noon, and to-
16. ok it and slew all of them, seven thousand men and . . . and women and . . .
17. and maidservants; for I had devoted it to 'Ashtar-Chemosh. And I took thence the a[ltar-hear-]
18. ths of Jehovah and dragged them before Chemosh. Now the king of Israel had built
19. Yahaṣ; and he abode therein while he fought against me. But Chemosh drove him out from before me. And
20. I took of Moab two hundred men, all its chiefs; and led them against Yahaṣ and took it
21. to add to Daibon. I built Ḳrḥh, the wall of the Woods and the wall of
22. the Mound. And I built its gates and I built its towers And
23. I built the king's palace, and made the sluices [?] of the reserv[oir [?] for wat]er in the midst of
24. the city. And there was no cistern in the midst of the city, in Ḳrḥh. And I said to all the people: "Make for
25. yourselves, each one a cistern in his house." And I cut out the cutting for Ḳrḥh with the help of prisoner-
26. s of Israel. I built 'Aro'er and made the highway by the Arnon.
27. I built Beth-bamoth, for it was pulled down. I built Beṣer, for ruins
28. . . . [had it become . . . of] Daibon were fifty, for all Daibon was obedient. And I reigned
29. [over] one hundred in the cities which I added to the land. And I built
30. Mehēdeba [Medeba] and Beth-diblathen and as for Beth-ba'alme'on, I took thither the [herdsmen]
31. . . . the sheep of the land. And as for Ḥauronān, there dwelt in it the so[n] . . . And
32. . . . Chemosh said to me: "Go down, fight against Ḥauronān"; and I went down and . . .
33. . . . and Chemosh [resto] red it in my days. And I . . . thence ten [?]
34. . . .

Modin (mō′dĭn), the ancestral home of the Maccabees*. A suggested site is 13 m. W. of Bethel.

mole, a word used in Scripture to mean any one of several insectivorous animals 6 or 7 in. long, as in A.V. Lev. 11:30, "mole," but A.S.V. "chameleon." The same Heb. word is translated "swan" in A.V. Lev. 11:18, Deut. 14:16, and "horned owl" in the A.S.V. Translators have not always understood the natural history of the Middle East.

Molech (mō′lĕk) (Moloch) (mō′lŏk) (Gk. *Moloch*, Heb. *Mōlekh*, from *melekh*, "King"), a Semitic deity whose worship was characterized by parents' sacrificing their children by compelling them to pass through or into a furnace of fire. In very early times there may have been a sanctuary of Molech in the Jerusalem Hinnom* Valley at Topheth (possibly Aram. for "place of burning"). Molech is sometimes regarded not as a foreign god, but as the king embodying the god in Israel. The Israelites may have absorbed from the Canaanites a feeling that they owed their first-born to Yahweh (cf. Abraham and Isaac, Gen. 22; Jephthah and his only child, Judg. 11:31–39). Though the Hebrews occasionally felt impelled to sacrifice their first-born or other children, the practice was not usual, was contrary to Hebrew Law* (Lev. 18:21, 20:1–5, cf. II Kings 16:3), and was punishable by stoning to death. Excavations in Palestine have revealed piles of ashes and vestiges of infant skeletons in cemeteries around heathen altars. (See also GEHENNA.)

The author of II Kings 21:6 attributes the introduction of Molech worship to King Manasseh (c. 687–642 B.C.) (cf. II Chron. 33). The reformer King Josiah intentionally desecrated the Molech center in the valley of Hinnom in order to prevent its use by the Hebrews (II Kings 23:10, cf. Lev. 18:21, 20:1–5; Deut. 12:31, 18:10). But his son Jehoiakim*, who succeeded him, revived the cult, and it continued until the Exile.

Jeremiah (7:29–34, 19:1–6, 10–13) and Ezekiel (16:20 f., 20:26, 31, 37–39) inveighed against the sacrifices of children. The reference to "Moloch" in A.V. Amos 5:26 (quoted in Acts 7:43 by the Christian martyr Stephen) is translated in the R.S.V. as "your king."

Solomon, influenced strongly by Phoenician and Canaanite practices, strengthened or rebuilt an altar to Milcom* (I Kings 11:5). (The reference to Molech in I Kings 11:7 is believed to be an error for Milcom.)

molten, a condition of metal produced by melting and casting: the molten calf (Ex. 32:4, 8); molten images typical of Canaan (Num. 33:52; Deut. 9:12; Judg. 18:14–18); molten copper (A.V. "brass") capitals of

273. The Molten Sea, from Howland-Garber model of Solomon's Temple.

Temple columns fashioned by Hiram of Tyre (I Kings 7:16); and the molten sea or large metal basin which stood between the porch and the altar of the Temple, containing water for the priests' ablutions (I Kings 7:23, 30, 33; II Chron. 4:2).

money, metals used as a medium of exchange. But minted coins did not circulate in Palestine until long after the time of Solomon (I Kings 5:11). Ionian (see JAVAN, and Gen. 10:4 f.) Greeks minted coins of electrum (a natural alloy of gold and silver), and by 600 B.C. money in the modern sense was current in Aegean cities. The first gold coins were struck probably by King Croesus of Lydia (561–546 B.C.), whose Anatolian mines and stream beds were rich in gold and silver. When Cyrus the Great of Persia conquered Croesus (546 B.C.) he doubtless carried back to Persia the coined-money idea, though some numismatists attribute its introduction there to earlier Greek influences. Darius the Great (522–486 B.C.) minted gold coins and allowed his satraps to mint silver. Money flowed throughout his vast Persian kingdom. During the Exile Jews became acquainted with coined money—Persian *darics* (130 gr.), roughly equivalent to an American $5 gold piece (A.S.V. I Chron. 29:7; Ezra 2:69, 8:27; Neh. 7:70–72); and *siglos* or shekels (86½ gr.), equal to about a U.S. twenty-five-cent piece.

(1) *Egypt* did not influence Palestine in fiscal matters. Some experts believe that the first Egyptian minted state coins appeared during the regime of the Ptolemies (from 323 B.C.). In the O.T. period Egyptian money consisted of weighed rings of gold, silver, iron, or copper of recognized value, or metal wire and small bags of gold dust. When Joseph, the Hebrew prime minister of Pharaoh, "gathered up all the money that was found in Egypt" from hungry Egyptians and exchanged it for grain, he collected moneys of this sort (Gen. 47:14). When he placed "bundles of money" in his brothers' grain sacks (Gen. 42:35) this too was of weighed rings, wedges (thin bars), or crude metal lumps. (Cf. Achan's "wedge" or "tongue" of Babylonian gold, Josh. 7:21, and the "golden wedge of Ophir," Isa. 13:12). Micah's "pieces of silver" (Judg. 17:1–6) were lumps of metal ("shekels of silver"), which could easily be melted into images; so too the "money" brought by the Philistines to Delilah (A.V. Judg. 16:18), and that mentioned to Naboth by Ahab (I Kings 21:6). Royal Egyptian taxes were payable not only in specified weights of precious metals, but in commodities; wall reliefs in tombs at Saqqârah near Memphis (Hos. 9:6) show tenant farmers of c. 2400 B.C. bringing taxes in the form of geese, grain, fruits, wine, and other produce.

(2) *Babylonian* values were standard throughout the ancient Middle East because their customs in fiscal matters influenced the procedure in those neighbor nations with whom they did business. Fully 1,000 years before the world's first coins were struck checks inscribed on clay tablets were being used in ancient Babylonia, where bankers also had an elaborate system of exchange: one ox = one maneh or 15 silver shekels or two tons of barley or 270 pt. of barley or 265 pt. of dates; one sheep = 225 pt. of barley or 265 pt. of dates. One silver shekel = 2½ pt. of oil or 10 pt. of barley. Some of the tables from Ur, signed by the inspector of prices, may be seen in the University Museum at Philadelphia. Tell el-Amarna tablets indicate that Babylonian weight-values based on a sexagesimal system were prevalent in Palestine and Syria in the 15th century B.C.: mina, shekel, and talent, of the "heavy standard" and the "light." The mina is seldom used in Scripture, the shekel being the more usual unit. Down to N.T. times Hebrews continued to use the 252 gr., heavy gold Babylonian shekel (approximately $10) for weighing against Hebrew gold. The Eshnunna Law Code (Baghdad Museum) published by Dr. Albrecht Goetze of Yale in 1949 reveals price controls maintained 3,800 years ago (200 years before Hammurabi). The clay tablet documents list tables of equivalents: one bu. grain = one silver shekel (c. ¼ oz. of white metal); hire for a donkey and remuneration for its driver = 40 qt. of grain.

Monetary transactions in Bible lands centered in (a) the temples, as at Jerusalem and Babylon, to which the people brought dues and sacred offerings for the upkeep of the sanctuary, payment of the priests, charity budgets, etc., and (b) the royal palaces, where taxes for the king or the state were deposited. In Mesopotamian temples the collection cashbox was often a wicker basket, placed near the entrance to the shrine; at the Jerusalem Temple the box stood near the altar. II Kings 12:9 relates that in the reign of Jehoash (c. 837–800 B.C.) "Jehoiada the priest took a chest, and bored a hole in the lid of it." The money that was put in consisted of unminted lumps of metal, usually silver of poor quality, which were melted down once a month—probably in the Temple's own foundry—into bars of standard value that were then stored in the treasury (cf. Mark 12:41 f.). In fertile Mesopotamia and Palestine payment to temple and palace was often made in barley, dates, or other crops.

(3) *Phoenician* money and weights became current among the Hebrews after the Conquest. This coastal trading people, who had access to mines in Cilicia and Spain, circulated their coins as legal tender throughout the Mediterranean area, where they minted in such cities as Aradus, Byblos (see GEBAL), Tyre, and Sidon. The "tribute money" (A.V. Matt. 17:24, A.S.V. "half-shekel"), payable before the Passover Feast, was more plentiful than the specified didrachma (half-shekel) per person, and frequently two individuals joined to pay the didrachma sanctuary tax by using one Phoenician tetradrachma. Judas may have received 30 Tyrian tetradrachmas (c. $25, the price of a slave) for selling Jesus. The Phoenician shekel was a 224 gr. standard silver coin, 15 of which were equivalent to one heavy Babylonian gold shekel of 252 gr. In N.T. times the sanctuary shekel (paid by Jesus) was still the Phoenician Hebrew coin.

(4) *Hebrew money.* Metals were not the only medium of exchange in O.T. Palestine. Barter, the exchange of one commodity for another, was the usual trade method. Abraham and Lot counted their wealth in thousands of cattle, as did Job (1:3). Jerusalem Temple tithes were paid in "first fruits" (Deut. 26).

O.T. allusions to money are confusing because words like "shekel" and "talent" first referred to weights*, but were later used to mean coins. Abraham "weighed to Ephron" 400 silver shekels for the Cave of Machpelah (Gen. 23:16). David paid Ornan (Araunah) "six hundred shekels of gold by weight" (I Chron. 21:25) for the Jebusite threshing floor which became the focal point of Jerusalem (cf. Job 28:15; Dan. 5:27). The half-shekel that "every one that passeth among them" was required to pay after the "shekel of the sanctuary" (Ex. 30:13) was not a coin; pieces of unminted metal served as money for many centuries.

The Jews probably first used coined money during the Exile, and took coins back to Palestine (Ezra 1:4). Except during brief periods of independence, they used their conquerors' coins. The Hebrews tended to be slow in minting money, even when autonomy was briefly granted high priests under the Persian regime; possibly because they would not make the image of a ruler or even an animal (Ex. 20:4). W. F. Albright counts as genuine (*Bulletin* 53 ASOR) at least three known Heb. coins of the 4th century B.C., two carrying the name *Yehud* (Aram. form of the Heb. *Yehudah,* "Judah") in archaic characters, and one (found by Albright and Sellers at Beth-zur) stamped "Hezekiah" (a high priest prior to the era of Alexander the Great). Thus it appears that the Jews in Palestine were permitted autonomous coinage in the high-priestly theocracy of the 4th century B.C., and were probably allowed to raise their own taxes as well. From Beth-zur also came evidence that John Hyrcanus, and not his father Simon, as some had believed, was the first of the Maccabees to mint bronze coins. They were half, quarter, and third shekels. Simon may also have coined money.

Jewish coins were minted (a) in the Maccabean period (166–63 B.C.); (b) during the first revolt against Rome (A.D. 66–70); and (c) during the second revolt (A.D. 132–135). Existing coins from these three periods do not bear portraits, but depict symbols of the fertility of the land: palm, citron, vine, basket of fruit, cornucopia, etc.; utensils and musical instruments used in Temple worship; or aspects of the Temple itself, used for "rebuilding" propaganda, as during Bar Kokba's revolt (see SYMBOL).

It is impossible to chart the coins of the Bible accurately because different versions refer to the same coin in different terms. For example, where the A.V. says "mite" (Mark 12:42), the R.S.V. has "two copper coins"; the "farthing" of A.V. Matt. 5:26 is the "penny" of the R.S.V. The A.V. and R.S.V. both have "pound" (mina) in Luke 19:13–25. The following tables of Biblical coins may prove useful:

O.T. Money (by weight, Babylonian standard)

	Weight in grains	*Approx. Value*
Shekel (silver) a common unit of value, equivalent to 4 Gk. drachmas or 4 Rom. denarii.	224½ heavy or common	$ .64
The minted coin shekel was slightly larger than an American half-dollar	112¼ light standard	32
Shekel (gold) = 15 silver shekels	252⅔ heavy	9.69
	126½ light	4.85
Mina (silver) = 50 shekels	11,225 heavy	32.30
	5612½ light	16.15
Mina (gold)	12,630 heavy	484.75
	6,315 light	242.38
Talent (silver) = 60 minas	673,500 heavy	1940.00
	336,750 light	970.00
Talent (gold)	758,000 heavy	29,085.00
	379,000 light	14,542.50
Dram (A.V. daric, A.S.V. Ezra 8:27; Neh. 7:72), a Persian gold coin	130	5.60

(5) *N.T. money.* The cash drawer of a Jerusalem merchant of the 1st century A.D. might have contained:

(a) A few old Persian silver sigloi or gold darics (equivalent to about one English sovereign) brought back to Jerusalem by returning captives from Babylon and still circulating.

(b) Small bronze and silver coins struck by the Maccabean John Hyrcanus.

(c) Independently minted coins from the great Phoenician mints at Tyre and Sidon, especially shekels and tetradrachmas. (A half-shekel equalled about one Greek didrachma; a whole shekel, one Tyrian tetradrachma).

274. Some coins of Biblical times: 1. Persia; gold *daric*, c. 400 B.C. Shows king kneeling. 12.5 mm. in diameter. 2. Sidon; silver *shekel*, c. 342–333 B.C. Rev., Persian king in chariot; obv., war galley. 25 mm. 3. Corinth; silver *stater*, c. 350 B.C. Rev., Pegasus; obv., Athena in Corinthian helmet. 20 mm. 4. Tarsus; silver *stater*, 361–333 B.C. 22.5 mm. 5. Thrace; silver *tetradrachma*, 302–284 B.C. Alexander or Lysimachus. 25 mm. 6. Rome; copper or bronze *sestertius*, c. A.D. 71. Obv., Vespasian; rev., *Judaea capta*. 32.5 mm. 7. Syria; silver *tetradrachma*, 175–164 B.C. Antiochus Epiphanes. 27 mm. 8. Judaea; silver *shekel*, Second Revolt, A.D. 132–135. Obv., ark and columns; rev., palm branch. 27.5 mm. 9. Judaea; silver *denarius*, c. 54 B.C. Bacchius Judaeus. 17.5 mm. 10. Tiberius; silver *denarius*, A.D. 15. "Tribute penny" (Mark 12:15). 15 mm. 11. Antioch; silver *stater*. Shows Tyche of Seleucia, wearing turreted crown. 17.5 mm. 12. Ephesus; silver *drachma*. Shows bee, symbol of fertility. 17.5 mm. 13. Judaea; silver *denarius*, A.D. 71, time of Vespasian. 15 mm. 14. Rome; gold *aureus*. Obv., Augustus, 31 B.C.–A.D. 14. 17.5 mm. 15. Judaea; copper or bronze *lepton* ("mite," Luke 12:59, 21:2). Shows double cornucopia, poppy in center. 14 mm. 16. Judaea; copper or bronze *lepton* of Procurator Felix, A.D. 52–55. 14 mm. 17. Rome; gold *aureus*. Obv., Claudius, A.D. 41–54. 17.5 mm.

(d) Elegant Greek silver and gold coins from the period of trade expansion under Alexander the Great throughout western Asia in the 4th century B.C., such as silver drachmas, didrachmas and tetradrachmas, gold staters, copper obols (1/6 drachma), and leptons (the smallest Greek coin). Some of these coins were stamped with portraits of Alexander the Great, Antiochus Epiphanes, Tiberius, etc., designed by great artists. As early as c. 650 B.C. Corinth was minting coins, and Paul probably received some of her Pegasus-stamped moneys when working there as a weaver. American scholars in the agora at Athens have excavated more than 80,000 Gk. coins, some minted 572–561 B.C.

(e) Standard coins of the Roman Empire, authorized by currency reforms of Caesar Augustus at the beginning of the Christian era. These alone were acceptable for government taxes. They included the silver denarius (the most-used coin of N.T. times in Palestine, mentioned at least 16 times in the N.T. of the R S.V.; it was usually a day's wage, and was approximately equivalent to the Gk. drachma; brass dupondius; copper as (1/6 of a denarius); half-as (semis); quarter-as (quadrans); and gold aureus. English translators of the Bible have sometimes referred to these coins in the denominational terms of their own country. Thus, at times the drachma has been rendered as "shilling," the copper as "penney," the quadrans as "farthing," and the gold aureus as "pound."

(f) Ptolemaic Egyptian coins, locally minted at Gaza, Joppa, Acre, and Sidon. The silver tetradrachma bore the smiling face of a Ptolemy, the eagle of Zeus, and the name of the mint. Others were the didrachma, or silver shekel or stater (standard coin), and the gold octodrachma.

(6) *Buried hoards.* People who carried money bags (Isa. 46:6; John 12:6, 13:29) in their girdles often lost coins, and money in circulation in Biblical times is frequently turned up today by the plows of farmers in the eastern Mediterranean area. The finding of a single coin may help archaeologists date a whole city level. At Beth-shan a hoard of silver minted by Ptolemy Soter I was found in the ruins of a pagan temple begun possibly at the beginning of the 3d century B.C., when Demetrius I Poliorcetes was king of Macedonia (c. 294–289 B.C.). At Bethel (Beitîn) a number of coins from the period of Alexander the Great (336–323 B.C.) to the fall of Jerusalem were found. At Beth-zur, c. 4 m. N. of Hebron, a cache of coins has been excavated, among them 52 Ptolemaic, 173 Seleucid (including 124 of Antiochus Epiphanes), and 18 Maccabean, of which 16 were from mints of John Hyrcanus. The presence of such money indicates vigorous trade or war booty. A hoard of Maccabean coins was dug from the area of a great gate in Jerusalem, near the Jebusite ramp and the "Solomonic" tower of the E. wall. A coin stamped "L.X.D.," found at Jerusalem, is reminiscent of the Tenth Legion which Titus stationed there as an occupation force when he left the destroyed city (A.D. 70). Near Stephen's Gate, Jerusalem, a valuable hoard of coins of the second revolt period was found in 1935. Phoenician coins excavated from the fortress at Athlit indicate a Phoenician settlement at this pivotal shore point S. of Carmel, from c. 700 to 300 B.C.

Such hoards are graphic illustrations of the custom of burying money mentioned in Jesus' parable of the man who found "treasure hidden in a field" (Matt. 13:44), and in the parable of the buried "talent" (Matt. 25:18, 24 f.).

(7) *Financiers in Bible times.*

(a) *Taxgatherers* like Matthew the publican secured by fair means or foul the right to gather revenue for Rome in Palestine. Taxes paid at Capernaum were based on the Roman denarius. Matthew probably had his toll-booth on the busy caravan road from Syria to Galilee (Matt. 9:9).

(b) *Money-changers* were denounced by Jesus because of their excessively high rates for changing into the Phoenician-Hebrew sacred half-shekel (Mark 11:15, 17) the many kinds of currency brought in for the Temple tax by Jews arriving "from every nation under heaven." The high priest, like Annas, had every opportunity to share profits with the money-changers. The "pieces of silver" given to Judas for the betrayal of Jesus may have come from the coffers of the high priest and his colleagues—30 Phoenician tetradrachmas (about 120 denarii).

(c) *Bankers and usurers* were wealthy men who loaned money for mortgages, purchases, or financial emergency. There were O.T. laws against lending money at usury except to foreigners: "Thou shalt not lend upon interest to thy brother; interest of money, interest of victuals, interest of anything" (A.S.V. Deut. 23:19). Nehemiah (5:6–12) persuaded the Persian deputies to cease usury so that people could again get possession of their homes and vineyards. Babylonian rates of interest ranged from 12 to 20%; at Athens they jumped from 12 to 20% in the 5th century B.C. Interest was somewhat lower in Rome.

The N.T. makes clear that love of money can be the root of all evil (I Tim. 6:10), as with Pharisees (Luke 16:14); Ananias and Sapphira (Acts 5:1–11); Simon the sorcerer, whence "simony" (Acts 8:18–20); Felix the Roman governor (Acts 24:26). The conduct of these people was in contrast to the integrity of Barnabas of Cyprus (Acts 4:35 f.). Jesus wisely advised his Disciples to travel with "nothing . . . neither bread, neither money" (Luke 9:3).

Further details on moneys of the Biblical period can be obtained at the Museum of the American Numismatic Society, New York City.

money-changers. See MONEY.

monogamy. See MARRIAGE.

monotheism, the belief that there is only one God. The remote ancestors of the Hebrew people were probably polytheists (see POLYTHEISM). Hebrew history may be said to begin with the call of Abraham (Gen. 11:31–12:9), a member of the family of Terah, of Ur of the Chaldees. They set out to migrate to distant Canaan. Part of the family remained near the headwaters of the Tigris and Euphrates rivers, where Terah had died; Abraham and his wife, with his nephew Lot, went on to Canaan. Abraham believed he did this at the call of God, whom he afterwards recognized as Yahweh; henceforth this was Abraham's God (cf. Ex. 3:13–15, 6:2–4). This can only mean that he had broken with the polytheism of his ancestors at Ur, and was now a henotheist—henotheism was the worship and service of one God, without necessarily denying that there were other gods, each having his own worshippers.

Even Moses, whom we may regard as the founder of the religion of Israel, was more probably a henotheist than a monotheist. His commission at the burning bush came from "the God of Abraham, the God of Isaac, and the God of Jacob" (Ex. 3:6). He was told that the name of this God was Yahweh (Jehovah); and though the name meant "the Everlasting and Dependable One" Moses still supposed that he was in communion with the God of the people of Israel (Ex. 3:1–17). Later, when the covenant was made at Sinai, it was made between the God Whose abode was Sinai (cf. 3:1) and the nation whom this God had chosen (19:1 f.). Indeed, it remained a belief in Israel for centuries (see I Kings 19:1 f.); and there is a tradition that the Ark, which was carried throughout the Wilderness wanderings (Num. 10:33), carefully guarded when the people reached Canaan (I Sam. 6:1), and later enshrined in the new Temple by Solomon (I Kings 8:1–11), contained stones taken from Sinai as an assurance in the earlier days of Yahweh's abiding presence.

When Israel arrived in Canaan they found there many other tribes, like the Midianites and Philistines, each with its own god or gods (cf. Judg. 11:24; I Sam. 5:1–5; I Kings 11:33). Much of the rivalry between Israel and these other tribes was a rivalry among their various gods. On the other hand, Israel was continually tempted to worship Yahweh according to the licentious customs that attended the worship of these neighboring gods, the Baalim* (see I Kings 16:29–33). The prophet Elijah was among the few loyal souls who passionately opposed this Baalism (I Kings 18:16–40).

In the loyalty of men like Elijah to Yahweh as the one God of Israel were the seeds of a genuine monotheism, which came to maturity with the great writing prophets, the first of whom was Amos. Amos at Bethel uncompromisingly proclaimed Yahweh as the God not only of Israel but of all the earth; He was the God of nature, the God of history, the God of every nation, and there was no other (Amos 4:12 f., 9:5 f.). None of the successors of Amos ever gave up this great truth; instead, they expounded it with increasing fervor. There is a moving description of the universal power and dominion of God in Isa. 40 (cf. also Job 38–41).

Religious monotheism is the contribution of Israel to mankind. Israel came to it slowly, because it was God Himself Who was teaching the great truth, and it could not be comprehended all at once. The Creation narrative in Gen. 1 clearly presupposes a single creative power. The narrative, however, is not itself primitive, but reflects later Hebrew thought about God. There were certain ancient philosophers who saw the universe as the expression of a single principle, but their interest was speculative, not religious. A sporadic monotheism appeared in the religions of Egypt and India, but in the main these religions have many gods. The monotheism of the Mohammedans was borrowed from the O.T. That there is One God only, creative, providential, and redemptive, is proclaimed in the Hebrew and Christian Scriptures as nowhere else.

See GOD; POLYTHEISM; REVELATION.

E. L.

months. See TIME.

moon (in Hebrew called *yareah*, prob. "wanderer," and *lebanah*, "white" or "pale"), the earth's satellite. Semitic nomads of the time of Abraham the Patriarch paid homage to the moon as a safe guardian for the cool night travel of caravans. Abraham must have passed many moon-god shrines en route from Ur to Haran. The moon is still honored by Bedouins, who place crescent amulets on their camels' necks. Early farmers of Bible lands believed that the moon as well as the sun fostered the growth of crops (Deut. 33:14). They relied on the moon also to measure time for planting and for agricultural feasts and religious festivals. The Passover was determined by the full paschal moon of the first spring month, Nisan (March–April).

(1) Early *Hebrews* felt that the moon, like its fiery brother, had power to "smite" (Ps. 121:6), to make men "lunatic" (cf. Matt. 4:24, 17:15). They equated "month" with "moon," but accommodated their months to the solar year and later adopted the Babylonian calendar, based on the early Sumerian one developed at Nippur.

O.T. writers shared with many Near Eastern peoples an appreciation for the moon, though not to the extent of worshipping it. They cherished it as a beautiful creation of God's handiwork (Gen. 1:16; Ps. 8:3, 136:9); and described eternity in terms of "as long as the moon" endures (Ps. 72:5, 89:37). Job, the nature lover, spoke of the moon "walking in brightness" (31:26). Jeremiah regarded it as given by the Lord (31:35). Apocalyptic writings abound in allusions to the moon's behavior (Isa. 13:10; Joel 2:10, 31; Ezek. 32:7). Its abnormal manifestations would herald the Day of the Lord. Jesus spoke of the moon's signs as a token of the Messianic coming (Mark 13:24; Luke 21:25). Peter at Pentecost (Acts 2:16–21) felt the fulfillment of Joel's words (2:28 ff.). But the climax of Biblical allusions to the moon is Rev. 21:23 (cf. Isa. 60:19), which declares the moon will be no longer needed, because the Lamb will light the heavenly Jerusalem. Deuteronomic Law forbade moon worship (Deut. 4:19, 17:3, cf. Jer. 8:2). First Isaiah protested against "new moons and appointed feasts" (1:14). The reformer-king Josiah inveighed against burning incense to the moon (II Kings 23:5). Yet throughout

Hebrew history gatherings partly religious and partly social were held at each new moon—times often mentioned with the Sabbath (II Kings 4:23; I Chron. 23:31; II Chron. 2:4, 8:13, 31:3; Ezra 3:5; Neh. 10:33; Isa. 66:23; Col. 2:16); then labor and commerce halted (Amos 8:5), offerings were increased, rituals were observed. A suggestion of the social meal enjoyed at the new moon is reflected in the story of Saul and David (I Sam. 20:5, 18, 24). After the Diaspora less rigid observance of the Feast of the New Moon prevailed.

Official announcement was made from Jerusalem of the coming of each new moon (until the 1st century A.D. by the lighting of fire signals on the Mount of Olives, and until the 4th by the sending of messengers) after the Sanhedrin had seen the young crescent early on the morning of the 30th or 31st of the month, and had declared, "The new moon is consecrated." The day on which the crescent appeared was the 1st of the new month. While the astronomical calculation of the new moon was known to scholars in Israel following their contact with Babylonian astronomy during the Captivity, the traditional method of declaring its appearance was not abandoned until the 4th century A.D.

Orthodox synagogues still announce the coming of the new moon, offer prayers for God's blessing, and read from the Torah Num. 28:1–5.

(2) In *Babylonia* moon-god worship flourished under the names Nannar (in Sumer) and Sin (in Accad). Nannar's wife was named Ningal in the Sumerian pantheon. Nannar was the parent of the revolving hosts of heaven, guardian of the world at night. The god Marduk (see MERODACH) in certain of his aspects was identified with the god Nannar. His symbol was the crescent—worn in the horned crowns of Assyrian kings.

The most influential center of moon-god worship was the Sumerian Ur*, indicated in the Genesis narrative (11:26–31) as the early home of Abraham. The city was dominated by the Temple of Nannar and its walled complex of nunneries and other auxiliary structures sacred to Nannar and Ningal. The famous staged platform (artificial mountain) and its brick tower, the *ziggurat**, rose immediately behind the Temple of Nannar, to whose service even the daughters and sons of kings were sent. After the fall of Sumer the moon god of Ur remained influential. As late as the 6th century B.C. Nebuchadnezzar renovated this worship center, tearing down old buildings and clearing a space large enough to be used for congregational worship, rather than the mysterious priest-dominated service. (Cf. the Book of Daniel, 3:1–7.)

In the University Museum at Philadelphia is a 10-ft. restored slab, destroyed by Elamites before the time of Abraham, showing in sculptured reliefs scenes connected with the building of the *ziggurat* by Ur-Nammu, a wealthy king of Ur's Third Dynasty. This Museum also contains a charming statuette of the moon goddess Ningal, dedicated by a high priest, Eannatum, who lived before the time of Abraham; and an alabaster disk of En-khe-du-an-na, moon-priestess daughter of King Sargon of Agade.

If Abraham passed his early years at Ur it would have been natural for him to carry with him deeply implanted impressions of moon-god worship. When he reached Haran he met it there. Excavated Mari* tablets prove that there were Sin (Moon-god) temples at Haran in the era of the 18th century B.C. W. F. Albright suggested that Terah, father of Abraham, was a legendary hero who had been honored by the Canaanites and Hebrews as a moon god. (Terah was also the name of a town near Haran.)

The Accad. name for Nannar (Sin) was incorporated into royal names like Ibi-Sin, Narâmsin, Rim-sin. He made an impact on sophisticated central Babylonian literature—inferior to the works of Heb. O.T. writers, as seen in the poetic "Myth of En-lil and Ninlil: the Moon and His Brothers." This saga tells of the rape of the moon goddess Ninlil by the god En-lil, whose son became the moon god Sin (Thorkild Jacobsen, in *The Intellectual Adventure of Ancient Man*).

The grip of moon worship on various parts of the Middle East has been revealed by other archaeological finds. Inhabitants of the Sinai Peninsula—as now known by excavation of a sanctuary at Serabit el-Khadem—were worshipping the moon god Sin in the 15th century B.C., possibly before the time of Moses, in a Semitic cult older than any now known in Arabia or Syria. Some scholars believe that Mt. Sinai contains the root "Sin," though Albright doubts that the word "Sinai" is derived from the moon god worshipped at Ur. It may spring from a place name Sinin, a desert plain; or from *seneh* (Heb. *s'neh*), possibly the sort of bush where Moses experienced his earliest theophany; he recalls that Canaanites worshipped a moon god, but believes that they called the god Yerah. Moon worship is also attested by a small alabaster stele of Rim-sin, telling in the old Sumerian language of this king's rebuilding and endowing the moon god's temple at Ur. Fragments of a black diorite stele from this temple are in the British Museum.

(3) The *Canaanites* began their year with the new moon preceding each fall harvest season. That they observed the new moon and the full moon with festivities is now known from Ras Shamrah texts, which recommend the sacrifice of two sheep to Ashtoreth* as suitable for the new moon's advent. These same N. Syrian documents reveal the 7-day week known to early Canaanites.

Ancient Jericho was dedicated to the moon goddess, who blessed it with what Nelson Glueck calls "unrestrained bounty." The name "Jericho" reflects devotion to a lunar deity.

(4) The *Nabataeans* also at one time worshipped the moon in Petra and decorated their pilasters with crescents. These people, who pushed the Edomites from the mountains of Seir, were devout. The moon god Allat (or al-Lat) was their chief deity, the other being Dusares (or Du-shara), the sun god (Allat may be the feminine form of El).

She is sometimes regarded as a virgin goddess who gave birth to a son, Dusares. Allat, worshipped by Arabs, is mentioned in the Koran.

(5) In the *Egyptian* pantheon the moon was less important than the sun. It was depicted as adorning the body of the sky goddess Nut (Heaven), or the underbelly of the celestial cow. The moon was also one aspect of the series of god-king-pharaohs, who were believed to control the moon and the calendar for the safety of Egypt's crops and terrain.

(6) In the *Greek* world moon worship was directed to Diana, a female deity symbolized by the crescent moon.

Mordecai (from Accad. *Marduk*, *Merodach*, chief male god of Babylon), the cousin and foster father of Esther*. He was not known to history, but was a major character in the Biblical story of the Jewess who became a Persian queen. He saved the life of King Ahasuerus by informing Esther of a plot to kill him (Esther 2:21–23). When he angered Haman, the king's favorite, by refusing to reverence him (3:5), Haman influenced Ahasuerus to order Mordecai's execution and the destruction of all the Jews (3:6–15). During a sleepless night the king commanded that the chronicles of the kingdom be read to him, and was reminded, by the account of the conspiracy, of the fact that no honor had been bestowed upon Mordecai (6:1–3); he directed Haman to array Mordecai in royal apparel and bring him to the palace. At a banquet arranged for Esther, Haman, and the king, Esther named Haman as the enemy of her people, and Ahasuerus ordered him hanged on the gallows prepared for Mordecai (7:6–10). Esther then revealed her connection with Mordecai (8:1), and he became second only to the king (10:3).

Moreh (mō′rĕ) ("soothsayer," "teacher"). (1) The place, known by its sacred tree (oak or terebinth), where Abraham pitched his camp near Shechem* after his arrival in Canaan from Mesopotamia (A.S.V. Gen. 12:6; A.V. incorrectly reads "plain"). The Moreh tree, like many other trees in the Middle East, was thought to possess oracular powers (v. 7), or to have been tended by priests who gave advice. The venerated cedars of Lebanon today are tended by Maronite priests. The Moreh tree may be the one of Gen. 35:4, where Jacob hid "foreign gods" (cf. Josh. 24:26). (2) The hill of Moreh, which figured in the encounter of Gideon and the Midianites (Judg. 7:1), the S. boundary of a pass rimmed on the N. by Mt. Tabor, N. of Jezreel and the spring of Harod (Judg. 7:1), c. 8 m. NW. of Mt. Gilboa, and 1 m. S. of Nain; sometimes called "Little Hermon."

Moriah (mō̇-rī′ȧ). (1) The district where Abraham prepared to sacrifice his son (Gen. 22:2). (2) The hill on which was the threshing floor of Ornan purchased by David. This became the site of Solomon's Temple (II Sam. 24:18 ff.). See JERUSALEM: *Location*.

mortar. (1) A mixture of clay, stone (Gen. 11:3), lime, straw, mud, pebbles, ashes, or bitumen (in Mesopotamia) used in ancient times to cement stones and bricks. When mortar was not treated so that it would harden for safe masonry it was called "untempered" (Ezek. 13:10, 11, 14 f.). It was mixed by treading (Nah. 3:14). In certain types of construction stones were laid "dry" in courses without mortar. (2) A bowl-shaped vessel of hard material like stone or basalt, in which grain, spices, etc., were pulverized by being ground with a pestle (Num. 11:8; Prov. 27:22).

mortgage, a conditional transfer of property to a creditor as security, a last resort of poor Jews in post-Exilic Palestine, and one of the social injustices complained of by Nehemiah the governor (c. 445–433 B.C.). Hearing of the use of mortgages to secure money for "the king's tribute" (Neh. 5:1–5), he angrily demanded that the nobles and local rulers return the mortgaged lands, vineyards, and olive orchards, together with a hundredth part of the money and produce accepted. He called priests to witness their promise to correct the abuse (vv. 6:13). The generous business policy of Nehemiah is indicated in 5:15–19.

mosaic, a picture or design made by laying small pieces (tesserae) of stone, gems, glass, or marble in bases of bitumen (in very ancient times) or plaster, in such a fashion that they tell a story or form a decoration. The earliest mosaics now known were found at al-'Ubaid in a low mound 4 m. W. of Ur, in a Sumerian temple dating from c. 2900 B.C. They adorn small columns, one of which is in the University Museum at Philadelphia. These mosaics consist of small, colorful triangles laid in bitumen and overlaid on the wooden core of the columns. Bands of mosaic-cut figures on bitumen grounds, framed

275. Mosaics in floor, era of Constantine the Great (c. A.D. 330), discovered in 1934 under present floor of the Church of the Nativity, Bethlehem.

sometimes in copper, have been found in temples of the First Dynasty al-'Ubaid (c. 1900 B.C.), antedating Abraham. Some of these, like the milking scene, are also in the University Museum. Such art confirms the belief that Abraham left an atmosphere of culture to trek as a shepherd-sheikh around the Fertile Crescent. Down into early Christian and Byzantine times mosaic art expressed itself in mosaic floors, fragments of which have been excavated in Bethlehem's Church of the Nativity (the Constantinian, 4th century portion); in Beit Jibrîn (Mareshah, a town once fortified by Rehoboam) near Lachish; in Antioch on the Orontes; in Tabgha near Capernaum; in Jerash and Madeba (scene of the famous mosaic map) in Trans-Jordan; in the walls and domes of handsome churches in Ravenna and Istanbul and in the 40,000 sq. ft. of Biblical mosaics in the mediaeval San Marco Basilica, Venice. See index and illustrations in *An Encyclopedia of Bible Life*, Madeleine S. and J. Lane Miller (Harper & Brothers). (See JESUS, illus. 215.)

Moses, the great Hebrew statesman, lawgiver, and leader who led the Israelites from slavery in Egypt to independent, orderly, and religious nationhood in Canaan.

(1) *Name.*—The original Heb. of the name is *Mōsheh*. The Biblical explanation (Ex. 2:10) as coming from the verb *mashah*, "to draw out," is gramatically difficult. It is therefore generally derived from the Egyptian. Many Egyptian names of the 14th and 13th centuries B.C. ended in *-mose*, meaning "to be born," as that of the Pharaoh Thutmose (Thutmosis), "Thoth is born." "Moses" may therefore possibly be the last part of a two-part name whose first has been lost. W. F. Albright believes that it comes from an Egyptian name, *Mâsĕ* (perhaps from Egypt. *mesu*, "child"), pronounced "Môse," after the 12th century B.C. and probably pronounced much the same in the Delta about the time of Moses.

(2) *The Historic Moses.*—There is too much positive evidence in the Pentateuch and other documents bearing on the history of the Middle East in the 2d millennium B.C. to doubt that Moses was a historic personality. He was more than a folk hero or the eponymous ancestor of a tribe; he was as individual as Gudea of Lagash, Hammurabi, or Abraham. Without him it would be difficult to account for the Yahwistic monotheism that culminated in the Solomonic Temple worship, or for the Law, or for the unification of a wandering, discouraged group of nomads. Only by such a new revelation of Yahweh as Moses brought can the history of Israel be understood. Many elements of Hebrew Law remained practically the same from Moses to Ezra. Except Samuel, there was no great spiritual leader between Moses and David. Moses was certainly the first great leader of the Hebrews; he is also regarded by many as the supreme lawgiver (Ex. 34:27–32) and a proponent of Yahwistic monotheism. A likely date for Moses and the Exodus* of the main group of Jacob tribes who left Egypt is some time soon after 1300 B.C. The "pharaoh of the oppression" who figures in the life story of Moses may be Seti I (c. 1309–1290 B.C.), and the "pharaoh of the Exodus" Rameses II (c. 1290–1224 B.C.)—not all authorities agree with this dating.

(3) *Life.*—Moses was born probably near Memphis in NE. Egypt in the 2d half of the 2d millennium B.C., of humble Hebrew parents—Amram a Levite and his wife Jochebed (though the latter may be the name of an ancestress rather than his own mother). He was the brother of Miriam and Aaron. He might have perished in infancy, because of Pharaoh's law against male Hebrew babies (Ex. 1:22); but the clever resourcefulness of his mother, and his sister—who guarded his bulrush cradle among the Nile reeds (2:5–10)—led to his adoption by an Egyptian princess who satisfied her longing for a son by taking him into her royal household and rearing him to young manhood.

At the Egyptian court Moses was trained in "the wisdom of the Egyptians" (Acts 7:22), which reached a high peak in such centers as On* (Heliopolis). This acquiring of "wisdom" probably included: (a) information about such philosophers of ancient Egypt as Ptah Hotep, whose popular maxims had been current long before; (b) knowledge of the solar monotheism of Pharaoh Akhenaton* (cf. Ps. 104); (c) knowledge of the architectural splendors of the NE. Nile country, which may have colored his understanding of the Tabernacle pattern revealed by Yahweh (Ex. 25); (d) a sense of magic* and the semblance of magic in which Egyptians have always excelled (for Moses' rod see Ex. 4:1–17; Aaron's rod, Ex. 7:9–23; Num. 17; the copper—not brass—serpent, whose making Moses may have learned from his Kenite wife's metalworking people, Num. 21:9, 11; II Kings 18:4); and (e) knowledge of writing, not only in current cuneiform and hieroglyphics, but possibly in the alphabetic proto-Sinaitic script now known to have been used by miners of turquoise at Serabit el-Khadem near Mt. Sinai before the time of Moses. The training received by Moses would doubtless have fitted him to become an official of Egypt, as Joseph the Hebrew had been—"a lord of all Egypt" (Gen. 45:9).

On a visit to his family while he was still living at court, Moses' passion for the oppressed was roused by seeing an Egyptian strike a Hebrew laborer (Ex. 2:11). He killed the Egyptian and hid his body in the sand; and when he learned that his deed had been witnessed, he fled precipitately to the grazing lands used by a group of Midianites who lived S. of the Dead Sea, an influential one of whom was Reuel (Ex. 2:18). This priest of Midian, a noble shepherd (also known as Jethro), had a daughter Zipporah, whom Moses married. By her he became the father of two sons, Gershom and Eliezer (18:3 f.). While Moses was tending the flock of his father-in-law Jethro at "the backside of the desert" in Mt. Horeb (3:1) in the Sinai Peninsula, he experienced on the mountain his first theophany—Yahweh speaking from the midst of a flaming but unconsumed desert bush (acacia or "flame of fire") (*Loranthus acaciae*) (Ex. 3:1–17). In this divine communication Yahweh commissioned him to lead Israel out from Egyptian bondage and guide them to a land "flowing with milk and honey" (v. 17); charging him that when he had brought them forth he should again come to the mount and worship Him (3:12). Yahweh revealed Himself as "I am that I am" (v. 14), or, as suggested by Ras Shamrah texts, "the one who speaks"—the same God who had appeared to the Patriarchs (see EL SHADDAI; GOD). After receiving signs confirming the revelation, Moses returned to Egypt to take up his task of uniting his oppressed people and leading them and a "mixed multitude" who had joined the Jacob tribes toward Canaan (Palestine). The accession of a new pharaoh (4:19)—a verse significantly similar to words in the life of Jesus (Matt. 2:20)—made his return safe.

Moses shared the news of his call with his brother Aaron, and was gratified over Yahweh's selection of Aaron to be His eloquent mouthpiece (Ex. 4:10–17). The humility of Moses had expressed itself in four objections he offered to Yahweh before he accepted the call: (a) his own inadequacy to the task—"Who am I, that I should go to Pharaoh?" (Ex. 3:11); (b) his ignorance of God's name (v. 13); (c) his fear that the Israelites would not believe him (4:1); and (d) his lack of confidence in his ability to speak for Yahweh (4:10). All these objections Yahweh met with reassurances, including a series of three wonders (Ex. 7:10–13). When Moses asked Pharaoh to let his people go into the Wilderness for a religious festival, he refused; and added still heavier burdens to the work of the Hebrew slave laborers in brickyard and construction work (5:7 f.).

After a long series of plagues* visited on Egypt because of the stubbornness of Pharaoh, ending with the slaying of the first-born (12:29), Moses led Israel in observing its first Passover* (12:21–28), which it continued to celebrate throughout its history. The Hebrews made a hasty midnight departure (later celebrated each 14th of the month Abib or Nisan). The company followed at first the caravan route out of the Delta, then turned S., making the historic crossing of the watery barrier at the Sea of Reeds (not the Red Sea), believed to have been between the Great Bitter Lake and the present town of Suez (see EXODUS for the route). After their miraculously safe crossing (Ex. 14) the poet-prophet Moses, together with his sister Miriam, broke into eloquent song (indicated in verse in the revised versions of Ex. 15:1–18, 21; see below, *Poetry in the Moses Records*).

Egyptian records make no mention of the departure of the Hebrew slaves, nor of the drowning of the Egyptian army that pursued them (14:28). This is understandable when it is realized that the Exodus was to the Egyptian overlords merely a walk-out of unpaid laborers. To the departing families it was the beginning of their nation, Israel.

The 40 years' trek led by Moses brought the wanderers, fed on manna and quail, to various encampments in the Sinai wildernesses and back again to Mt. Horeb, where Jethro rejoiced to see this people worshipping Yahweh, "who is greater than all gods" (18:11)—confirming a conviction he himself had long held. Jethro helped Moses to organize his motley crowd (18:13).

In the 3d month after the Exodus, while the camp was pitched in the Sinai Wilderness, Moses went up to a high peak of the mountain and there was met by Yahweh. There, in a spectacular setting, Moses received two tablets of stone on which were written—either by "the finger of God" (Ex. 31:18, 32:16, cf. 34:27 f.) or by the hand of Moses—the Ten Commandments (Ex. 20:2–17); these became the core of Israel's subsequently developed elaborate system of Law*. When Moses, after 40 days of communion with Yahweh on the Mount, descended again to his people, he found that they had fashioned a golden calf, made from their golden jewelry, and were worshipping it (Ex. 32). Enraged at such apostasy, he broke the tablets of the Law and "took the calf which they had made, and burnt it in the fire, and ground it to powder, and strawed it upon the water, and made the children of Israel drink of it" (32:19 f., cf. vv. 25–35).

Subsequent events in the life of Moses include: his return to the Mount to make atonement for his people's sin (Ex. 32:30 ff.); Yahweh's gift of a second set of Law tablets (34:1–4); the granting of a covenant between Yahweh and Israel (34:10 ff.); the establishment of the Feast of Unleavened Bread (34:18); the revelation of the Sabbath (35:1 ff.); the organization of the people for making the Tabernacle* and its equipment (chaps. 35–38); and the manifestation of God's presence in that holy center (40:38). Deut. 5 repeats the Commandments and the giving of the Covenant.

Moses' shepherd's rod which became his staff of authority is mentioned in Ex. 4:2, cf. Ex. 14:16, 17:5. (For further events in the career of Moses as he guided his people toward Canaan, see EXODUS; ISRAEL.) Numbers records Aaron's and Miriam's criticism of Moses (12:1) because he had married an Ethiopian (A.S.V. Cushite)—a criticism which really was an outburst of jealousy because of their unappreciated leadership (v. 2). The 4th book of the O.T. also narrates how Moses sent spies into the S. country of Canaan from the Wilderness of Paran (Num. 13:2 f., 17–20). Their glowing report from the Valley of Eshcol at harvest time and the huge clusters of grapes they brought back to the thirsty wanderers (vv. 23–27) made the land seem very desirable. But they also reported the people so formidable and the cities so well fortified that invasion was impossible. Caleb, contradicting his fellow-spies, said: "We are well able to overcome it" (v. 30). His words were unheeded. The abandonment of an invasion from the S. led to a murmuring of the discontented (chap. 14). A decision was made to attempt the entry of Canaan from the E. (Num. 21:21–35) rather than the S. (Deut. 2:18 f.), and to spare thus the Ammonite territory because Yahweh had already given it to Lot's descendants (Num. 2:19). The delay saw the rise of a younger generation. Moses promised land in E. Palestine (now the Kingdom of Jordan) to Reuben, Gad, and the half Tribe of Manasseh, provided they would cross the Jordan and help their brothers win holdings there. Having consecrated Joshua* to be his successor (Num. 27:18–23), Moses, in words seldom surpassed for poignancy, prayed the Lord to let him at least look upon the goodly land "beyond Jordan, that goodly mountain [hill country], and Lebanon" (Deut. 3:25). He was granted from Mt. Nebo (32:49) (now Khirbet el-Mekhaiyet) a glimpse of the panorama which thrills all beholders today, an expanse spreading N., E., S., and W. (Deut. 3:27), down to the Dead Sea, up to Bethlehem and the towers of Jerusalem. Then Moses was gathered to his fathers and buried in Moab (Deut. 34:6). Joshua led Israel across the Jordan, and became the leading figure in the Conquest of a large part of Judaea (some time in the 13th century B.C.).

Analysis of the sources* of the Pentateuch records of Moses leads to bewildering confusion because of interpolations from various sources like J, E, JE, JED, etc., all of whose authors desired to do him full justice.

(4) *Poetry in the Moses Records.*—Several poems are incorporated in the Scriptural story of Moses, some of great antiquity; others were composed several centuries after Moses. All endow the high moments in his spiritual experience with impressiveness. In the revised versions and Moffatt these poems are printed in verse form. The Song of Deliverance or Song of Moses and Miriam (Ex. 15:1–21) is one of the finest passages in Hebrew literature, joyously exulting over escape from their enemies and a newly discovered faith and confidence in Yahweh. Many believe that the first part of the song, ending with v. 11, was composed contemporaneously with the Reed Sea crossing or soon after; the subsequent lines presuppose settlement in Canaan, and must have been set down after Moses' time. The didactic poem (or psalm) known as the Song of Moses (Deut. 32:1–43, in 4:4 meter) makes no claim to be of Mosaic origin, and includes events much later than his time; it may indeed have been written in the 1st half of the 5th century B.C. by a priestly writer who wished to depict Moses declaring to the people on the highlands of Moab the legal and narrative messages of Deuteronomy. From a literary viewpoint this Song is unsurpassed in the O.T. The original part of the Blessing of Moses (Deut. 33) appears in an exordium (33:2–5) and a peroration (33:26–29), composed possibly as late as the 9th century B.C., with portions possibly as late as the 5th. The Song of the Well (Num. 21:17 f.) is a charming folk song from the very early poetry of Israel.

(5) *Moses in the N.T.*—Jesus revealed his deference for the laws of Moses when he taught that he had come not to destroy but to fulfill the law (Matt. 5:17 f.), and that not one jot or tittle was to be subtracted until the whole law was not only fulfilled but had actually been exceeded (vv. 18–20). Jesus amplified his statement in the sayings now collected in the Sermon on the Mount (Matt. 5–7; cf. 22:39 f.). He quoted Moses' law concerning lepers (Matt. 8:4) and divorce (19:8), and paralleled his own being "lifted up" with the lifting up by Moses of the serpent in the Wilderness (John 3:14). Peter and John beheld Moses witnessing Jesus' Transfiguration (Matt. 17:3). The author of the Fourth Gospel credits Moses with giving the Law, whereas "grace and truth came by Jesus Christ" (1:17); he quotes Jesus as saying, "had ye believed Moses, ye would have believed me: for he wrote of me. But if ye believe not his writings, how shall ye believe my words?" (John 5:46 f.). Jesus contrasted the manna given by Moses to Israel with the true "bread from heaven" given by the Father, even himself (6:32 f.). In the Temple, which was symbolized by Moses' Tabernacle in the Wilderness, Jesus said to his carping Jewish critics, "Did not Moses give you the law, and yet none of you keepeth the law?" Jesus, on his walk to Emmaus on the first Easter afternoon, expounded to "two" what the Scriptures had said concerning him, "beginning with Moses" (Luke 24:27).

The charge brought against Stephen was that he was speaking blasphemously against Moses (Acts 6:11). Acts (7:20–44) gives a few details concerning Moses not included in the O.T. narratives. In the dispute concerning circumcision in the early Church, the law of Moses was quoted (Acts 15:1); but Paul taught the insufficiency of relying on the ancient law of Moses for justification* (Acts 13:39, cf. Rom. 10:5), and even urged forsaking circumcision* (Acts 21:21). Yet in his trial before Agrippa he stressed his acceptance of what Moses and the prophets had said would come (Acts 26:22); and at Rome Paul taught such things as he accepted from the Law of Moses (Acts 28:23), ever contrasting, however, the "veiled" revelation of Moses with the free revelation of the Spirit of the Lord through Christ (II Cor. 3:13-18). In his Epistle to the Galatians (chaps. 2–6) Paul said Christ brought freedom from the Law, since justification was by faith.

The Epistle to the Hebrews contains a glorification of the faith of Moses, as illustrated in his choices (11:23–29).

The many Jewish legends about Moses are grouped in three cycles showing him (a) as popular leader, conqueror, and lawgiver; (b) as the intermediary of God's covenant, prototype of the prophet; and (c) as the founder of Israel's two greatest sanctities—the Tabernacle, symbol of the Temple; and the Levitic priestly organization.

(6) *Geographical landmarks* of Moses which may be visited today include two sites claimed for the Mount of the Law: (a) the ancient traditional one, 8,000 ft. high in the Sinai range, towering above the Monastery of St. Catherine where the Codex Sinaiticus was found and many other ancient MSS. were microfilmed in 1949–50; and (b) the northern site suggested for Sinai, at Gebel

Serbal, whose geography seems to harmonize with activities specified in the O.T. narratives of Moses and Israel; Mt. Nebo and Mt. Pisgah near Mâdebā in Trans-Jordan, "the land of Moab" (Deut. 3:27, 34:1–8). A steep trail leads down from Mt. Nebo to "the Springs of Moses" overlooking a fortress old enough to have been there in Moses' day—Khirbet Ayun Mûsā. Archaeologists have located the King's Highway used by the messengers sent by Moses from Kadesh-barnea to the kings of Edom and Moab, to inquire if they would grant safe conduct to the migrating Israelites. It ran all the way from the Gulf of Aqabah to Syria; was later called Trajan's Road; and still later, King Abdullah's. Today it is strategic.

Moses, Assumption of. See APOCALYPTIC.

Most High, a name applied to God* (Ps. 7:17, 9:2, 21:7, 87:5; Mark 5:7; Luke 8:28; Acts 7:48).

mote, a particle of dust (considered sawdust in view of Matt. 7:3–5; Luke 6:41 f.), straw, wool, or any other foreign matter whose trifling importance was contrasted by Jesus with a beam, such as a roofer would use.

moth, a fabric-eating, winged insect, ubiquitous in hot Eastern countries not having adequate exterminating means to protect heavy woolen garments. It appears in Scripture (1) in its literal role of a consumer of clothing (Job 13:28; Isa. 50:9, 51:8; Matt. 6:19 f.; Luke 12:33; Jas. 5:2); and (2) as a symbol of the frailty of the wicked and his clay house (Job 4:19, 27:18; Hos. 5:12).

mother. See FAMILY; MARRIAGE; and such individual entries as ATHALIAH; DEBORAH; ELISABETH; HAGAR; HANNAH; MARY; RACHEL; REBEKAH; RUTH; SARAH; etc. (Note the equality of mother and father in Deuteronomic Law, Deut. 5:16).

mount, mountain, a mass of earth or of earth and rock; usually conical. The A.V. uses "mount," "mountain," and "hill" interchangeably. "Mount" is more frequently applied to some specialized summit, like Hermon (Josh. 11:3; 12:1); Carmel (Josh. 19:26); Sinai (Ex. 19:2); and Seir (Deut. 1:2). "Mountain" is often used to designate an extensive district of high land, like Moab (Gen. 19:30); Gilboa (II Sam. 1:21). Neither Biblical writers nor modern geographers have settled the question as to when a hill, in terms of its elevation above the sea, becomes a mountain.

The mountain systems of Bible lands pursue two general directions: (1) in Asia Minor from the Aegean to the Caspian Sea, they extend from E. to W.; (2) at the NE. corner of the Mediterranean, where the Lebanon* system begins, the mountains pursue a NE.-SW. course through Palestine. Mountains therefore confined the eastern Mediterranean on its N. and E. rims. There are no mountains along the Egyptian shore. Valleys between the ridges and coastal mountain-rimmed thoroughfares provided avenues for trade* and conquest; breaks in the mountain chains at Antioch on the Orontes, the pass of Megiddo, and the Plain of Esdraelon helped to channel that flow. The cliffs along the Dog River Pass 9 m. N. of Beirut, within sight of the Mediterranean, are carved with cartouches of invading conquerors from Rameses II of Egypt (c. 1286 B.C.) to Esar-haddon of Assyria (c. 671 B.C.). They record road improvements and engineers' detachments from the Third Gallic Legion during the reign of Caracalla (A.D. 215), as well as inscriptions relating to the use of this mountain road in recent wars.

All three geological theories of mountain origins are exemplified in Bible lands: (1) Some mountain ranges owe their origin to direct elevation en masse above the surface of the sea or the adjoining lands. The Sinaitic group of mountains between the Gulfs of Suez and Aqaba is of this order, dating from Paleozoic and Tertiary periods. (2) Mountains are caused when uplifted land masses are subjected to erosion which forms valleys. The Lebanon Range with its Beka'a illustrates this. (3) Volcanic activity creates mountains, especially such isolated peaks in the Mediterranean as Vesuvius and Etna, and the Trans-Jordan Plateau with its extinct craterlike peaks and its patches of lava and layers of fertile black basalt over the limestone of earlier foundations.

Throughout the Bible mountains are pictured as dwelling places (Gen. 36:8); places of refuge (Gen. 14:10; Judg. 6:2; Matt. 24:16); lookouts (Isa. 18:3; Matt. 4:8); landmarks (Num. 34:7); assembly sites (Josh. 8:30–33; Judg. 9:7; II Chron. 13:4); military camps (I Sam. 17:3); and cemeteries (II Kings 23:16). For the animal world mountains were sanctuaries (Ps. 11:1); abodes (I Chron. 12:8); pastures (Luke 8:32); and haunts when lost (I Kings 22:17; Jer. 50:6; Matt. 18:12).

Many ancient peoples considered mountains as holy places (see HIGH PLACE). Mt. Sinai was Yahweh's special abode (Deut. 33:2; Judg. 5:4 f.); Mt. Zion was another of the Lord's favorite dwelling places (Ps. 68:16) (see JERUSALEM). The Lord as the God of the hills brought Israel victory (I Kings 20:23, 28). Mountains melted at His presence (Judg. 5:5; Ps. 97:5); leaped in His praise (Ps. 114:4, 6); witnessed His dealings (Mic. 6:2). Israel was lured by the idolatrous hilltop shrines of Canaanite neighbors, but the severe discipline of the Exile destroyed much of this. Jesus made it clear that God could be worshipped elsewhere than on a particular mountain (John 4:2–24); and he often sought mountain solitude and height for his own devotions (Matt. 14:23; Mark 6:46; Luke 6:12, 9:28; John 6:15). His Ascension took place from an unnamed mountain (Luke 24:50; Acts 1:9–12).

For individual mountains see CARMEL; EBAL; EPHRAIM; GERIZIM; GILBOA; HERMON; NEBO; OLIVES; PISGAH; SINAI; TABOR; etc. See also JERUSALEM for the "hills round about Jerusalem"—the Mount of Olives, Bezetha, Moriah, Ophel, Zion, etc.

mourning rites, ceremonials for the dead and for disaster, were practiced in the Middle East in O.T. times. The authors of the Deuteronomic Code* warned against the paganism of excessive rites (Deut. 14:1 f.). The Holiness Code provided that priests should avoid defilement "for the dead" (Lev. 21:1–6, 10 f.). Lev. 19:27 f. condemns such practices even by laymen.

Jeremiah excelled in his preoccupation with mourning and funerals; taught mourning women their dirge (9:17–22); heard nature's laments (9:10, 12:11, 23:10, 12:4); interested himself in the symbolic mourning of Rachel, his "tribal mother" (31:15 f.), yet urged his country to wail for its sins (4:8, 6:26, 7:29); contemplated national mourning (14:2, 22:10); and secretly mourned for the Hebrews (9:1, 13:17). He discouraged funeral rites, as a sign that in the future corpses would be left for beasts to devour (16:4, 6 f.), because God had removed "lovingkindness" from His wayward people.

Eastern mourning customs included the leaving off of ornaments (Ex. 33:4–6), the rending of garments (II Sam. 1:2, 11) or putting on sackcloth (II Sam. 3:31, 21:10); dressing in mourning garments (II Sam. 14:2); neglecting personal grooming (II Sam. 19:24); placing earth or ashes on the head (II Sam. 15:32, cf. Mic. 1:10); cutting the flesh (Deut. 14:1 ff.; Lev. 19:27 f.; Jer. 16:6); shaving the head or beard (Lev. 19:27; Deut. 14:1 f.) and covering the head (II Sam. 15:30); removing sandals in the presence of the deceased (II Sam. 15:30); uttering loud laments, or hiring professional mourners or musicians to do so, as is still the custom in Palestine and Syria (Joel 1:8; cf. Christ's allusion, Matt. 9:23); the offering of sacrificial meals to the dead (Deut. 26:14) and ceremonial feasts eaten by the living, following a fast for the dead; and the burning of spices for the deceased (II Chron. 16:14; 21:19).

Periods of mourning varied, from 30 days (for Moses, for example, Deut. 34:8), to seven for King Saul (I Sam. 31:13). The Egyptians devoted 70 days of mourning to Jacob, who was also mourned seven days more at the threshing floor of Atad (Gen. 50:3, 10). Palestinian mourning customs were largely influenced by those of Egypt, Persia, and Scythia.

Christian belief in the Resurrection of Jesus and the resultant immortality* of all men (I Thess. 4:13) did away with the former customs of barbaric mourning.

It was customary for mourning women to go to a grave very early in the day to anoint* the corpse with sweet spices, as the women did who visited the tomb of Jesus on Easter morning (Mark 16:1 f.). Moslem women still wander among the tombs outside the walls of Jerusalem.

See BURIAL.

Mughârah, Wâdī el- ("The Gorge, or Valley, of the Caves"). A rocky valley 18 m. S. of Haifa and 3½ m. SE. of the Crusader castle at Athlit, on the W. slope of Mt. Carmel overlooking the Plain of Sharon. Here a series of caves—the homes of prehistoric Palestinians—were examined by a joint expedition of the British School of Archaeology in Jerusalem and the American School of Prehistoric Research. From 1929–34, D. A. E. Garrod and T. D. McCown excavated the caves and established a sequence of flint industries for Palaeolithic and Mesolithic (Natufian) times. The earliest deposits come from Mughârat et-Tab'un ("Cave of the Oven"), dated to around 120,000 years ago. From Mughârat es-Sukhul ("Cave of the Kids") came skeletal remains of Mt. Carmel Man, a type intermediate between Neanderthal and modern man, and some 50,000 years old (previously dated to c. 100,000 years ago). Mughârat el-Wād ("Cave of the Valley") produced a good sequence of Upper Palaeolithic materials (c. 32,000–10,000 B.C.), as well as an excellent Natufian assemblage (c. 10,000–8,000 B.C.). The latter included microliths, flint scrapers and sickle-blades, and pieces of art work, such as a carving of a young deer on a bone sickle-shaft and a small human head in calcite. A number of Natufian burials were also uncovered, many

276. Mughâret el-Wâd.

decorated with fan-shaped headdresses of *dentalia* shell and other ornaments. See Garrod and Bates, *The Stone Age of Mt. Carmel*, I, 1937; McCown and Keith, *The Stone Age of Mt. Carmel*, II, 1939; *CAH*³, Vol. I, 1970, chaps. III and V; Anati, *Palestine Before the Hebrews*, 1963, pp. 59–178. W. P. A.

mulberry, the black or white fruit of the mulberry bush. It must be distinguished from the mulberry cultivated in modern Syria and Lebanon for feeding silkworms (before the introduction of artificial silk). Mulberries were grown in ancient Palestine, as they are today, for their fruit, which, when combined with sugar, honey, or spices, makes a favorite drink. The trees mentioned in II Sam. 5:23 f. and I Chron. 14:14 f. A.V. and A.S.V. (margin A.S.V. "balsam trees") are probably inaccurately translated "mulberry"; they may be poplars or aspens. The mulberry was also called "sycamine" (Gk. *sycaminos*), as in certain passages of the LXX. Some recognize the figs cultivated by Amos at Tekoa as "fig mulberries" or "mulberry figs" (*Ficus sycomorus*, not to be confused with the American sycamore or plane tree).

mule, a grain-eating animal, a hybrid of horse and ass, known in Assyria and Egypt in very ancient times, and apparently introduced into Palestine in the time of David. The mule was a royal mount "of all the king's sons" (I Kings 1:33, 38, 44; II Sam. 13:29). It was valued as a pack animal having great endurance (I Chron. 12:40; Ezra 2:66; Neh. 7:68), and was traded in *sûks* ("fairs," Ezek. 27:14). It was popular for gifts (II Chron. 9:24). In Scripture it is often mentioned along with the horse, camel, ass, dromedary, and ox (Ps. 32:9). It was used by Ahasuerus to carry messages throughout Persia (Esther 8:10, 14).

mummification, the preservation of the body of a human being or an animal by an elaborate system of embalming, practiced in Egypt for 30 centuries, and in lands influenced by their culture. Joseph ordered Egyptian court physicians to embalm his father Jacob (Gen. 50:2 f.), and he himself was embalmed and "put in a coffin in Egypt" (50:26). The Egyptians mourned for Jacob 70 days; and 70 days were required for mummification; forty days for Jacob's embalming are specified in Gen. 50:3. Mummification was resorted to as an aid in preserving the identity of the deceased, on which future life was believed to depend.

The elaborate process of readying a body for burial was not regarded as onerous. Details varied in different dynasties, but the technique achieved its finest results during the Egyptian Eighteenth Dynasty. First, the brain was removed and the cranium packed with linen. The viscera (lungs, liver, stomach, intestines), with the exception of the heart, were removed, and in certain eras (from c. 2200 B.C.) placed in four canopic jars. Such jars were of stone, alabaster, marble, or fine wood, and were often carved with the heads of animals believed to be protective custodians of the viscera: the human-headed Imset, the ape-headed Hapi, the jackal Duamutef, and the hawk Kebhsenuf. After the New Kingdom these jars were purely symbolic, and contained no viscera. Nostrils were plugged with linen and pads placed over the eyes. After the cavity was washed out, the body was placed up to the neck in a large jar of salt or natron (hydrated sodium carbonate), to remove fat and epidermis. Then it was straightened out and treated with a paste of resin and spices. Sometimes a packing was inserted under the skin to bring the body back to its original appearance, and in some cases artificial eyes were inserted. Then the elaborate system of winding the mummy with long linen bandages began. Trunk and limbs were wrapped separately, and the arms were laid over the chest or alongside the body. Sometimes the mummy was covered with a net of blue-gray-green faience "mummy beads," many of which survive in sands near Memphis, Saqqârah, etc. Finally a papyrus cartonnage was placed around the mummy and made gay with such painted hieroglyphics and symbolic figures as the *ankh* ("key of life") or the sacred eyes of Osiris. Lifelike cartonnage masks portrayed the deceased. The masks of royal mummies were of gold, as in the case of Tut-ankh-amun. From such masks developed the anthropoid or human-headed coffin, found in recent years in caves near Sidon on the old Phoenician coast.

Religious ceremonies accompanied mummification (cf. Gen. 50:3). The deceased was identified with Osiris, who had been killed by Set. The embalmer became the god Anubis. His helpers impersonated deities who had officiated after the passing of Osiris.

See BURIAL; EMBALMING.

murder, the deliberate slaying of a human being, was a crime against Jewish sacred law, as in secular codes. The Sixth Commandment (Ex. 20:13; Deut. 5:17) states the principle, "Thou shalt not kill," based on the sacredness of human life, made in God's image (cf. Priestly Code* Gen. 9:4–6). The law called for the shedding of the slayer's own blood; the Covenant Code demanded blood revenge (*lex talionis*) (Ex. 21:14 f.). So, too, the Holiness Code (Lev. 24:17, 20) and the Deuteronomic Code, which was specific concerning murder (Deut. 19:11–13, 21:1–9, 22 f.). Distinction is made between intentional murder and accidental manslaughter, as when a woodsman's axhead flew off its helve and fatally injured a fellow worker (Deut. 19:5). Humane considerations provided cities* of refuge, E. and W. of the Jordan, where unintentional killers were secure from vengeance by blood relatives until the death of the high priest (Deut. 19:1–10; Num. 35:11–15). The suspected man was safe in a city of refuge until he was heard by the congregation or assembly of Israel, or until the judges and elders of the community heard his case, and, if he were found guilty, turned him over to the next of kin for slaying (Num. 35:9–34). If the suspect voluntarily left the city of refuge and was attacked and slain by an avenger, the latter could not be punished. No "satisfaction," bail, or buying off of a murderer was tolerated (Num. 35:32). Land, ever sacred to Israel, was impure until blood intentionally spilled on it had been avenged (v. 33). Kindly laws were developed to prevent unintentional killing, such as those about an ox that gored someone (Ex. 21:28–32), and about the building of parapets to prevent anyone from falling from a housetop (Deut. 22:8).

murrain, an infectious disease of cattle (Ex. 9:3; Ps. 78:50, A.S.V. margin).

music, the expression of sound in time, to convey thought and emotion, was enjoyed by people of Bible lands in ancient times, though their first instruments were crude, their rhythms rugged, and their tunes probably not too melodious. The ancient prestige of musicians is hinted at by the author of Gen. 4:21, who credits Jubal*, descendant of Cain, with being "the father of all such as handle the harp and organ." This writer may have been familiar with early Hebrew traveling players (II Kings 3:15, "minstrel") who were also metalworkers and diviners, trekking from one community to another, playing and repairing as they went (cf. KENITES). Music played a role in prophetic ecstasy (I Sam. 10:5; II Kings 3:15; Ps. 49:4). Musicians were honored; and were sometimes spared the death penalty suffered by their brothers. Throughout Bible history the men who furnished the orchestras and choruses for worship stood next to the kings and priests in prestige.

(1) *Sumerian Music.*—The oldest known extant musical instruments from Bible lands are the four Sumerian *lyres* (? harps) found in the great death pit of Ur by Sir Leonard Woolley, preserved and restored in the University Museum at Philadelphia, the Baghdad Museum, and the British Museum. If Abraham spent his early years at Ur he may

have seen religious processions using such instruments at the *ziggurat* shrine of the moon god, and have heard musicians sing the great Sumerian hymn on the creation of man, accompanied by long, vertical reed flutes, short silver ones, and double pipes (oboes) such as were played in Sumerian temples a millennium before his time. The general

277. Reconstruction model of Music Hall (Odeion), built c. 15 B.C., Period 1, in the Athenian Agora. The high central core contained a concert hall with a balcony on three sides.

notation and words of this hymn, and its harp accompaniment, have been set down by Francis W. Galpin (*The Music of the Sumerians and Their Immediate Successors*). From seals and other evidences it is known that Sumerians at an early date also fashioned drums, such as the great *balag*, played with both hands; hourglass drums of gourds; log-drums, and small *balag-di* drums which accompanied singers; sistra—metal rattles—(later popular in Egyptian Isis rites) and animal horns. One of Shub-ad's seals in Philadelphia shows a musician standing at his bow-shaped harp playing for banquet guests. The Mesopotamian orchestra of Nebuchadnezzar in the 6th century B.C. performed on the Plain of Dura in front of the giant image of gold. The instruments listed by the author of the Book of Daniel (3:7) as played on this occasion are Graeco-Syrian, not Babylonian. The late date of Daniel as a piece of symbolic prophetic writing is suggested by this orchestral anachronism.

(2) *Hebrew Music.*—Hebrews did not excel in music as early as they did in some of the other arts. Yet their musicians were esteemed worthy of playing at the Assyrian court of Sennacherib in the 8th century B.C., as suggested by a carved relief, and the account of Sennacherib's 3d campaign in 701 B.C. ("male and female musicians" sent captive to Nineveh). None of their ancient instruments survive (contrast the Sumerian lyres, above). Because of their laws forbidding graphic depictions, the appearance of their musical instruments is not known except through a few Maccabean coins (the six-stringed lyre and the trumpet). (See MONEY; SYMBOL.) Yet a picture scratched on a floor at Megiddo by some non-Hebrew many centuries before David's time shows a woman playing a harp; and bone flutes have been found in a cave near Jericho of the 1st historical period (Early Bronze, 3300–2000 B.C.).

But the names of well-loved early Hebrew songs* are known, like the Song of the Well (Num. 21:17 f.), the Vintage Song (cf. Isa. 65:8), and the March of the Gittite Guard. (Cf. the Song of Solomon; the Psalms; and the Sword Song, Ezek. 21:8–17.) The words of the Song of Moses and Miriam, celebrating the triumph of God in delivering the Hebrews at the Reed Sea (Ex. 15), and the Song of Deborah (Judg. 5), celebrating Israel's victory over the Canaanites, are recorded. The latter poem contains an allusion to music, uttered as a rebuke to Reuben (v. 16). David's lament over Jonathan (II Sam. 1:19–27) is marked by great beauty. (See POETRY.)

Not all the music of the Hebrews was sacred. Folk music is indicated in numerous Biblical passages (Ex. 15; Josh. 6; Judg. 5; I Sam. 16:23). Music contributed merriment to weddings (Jer. 7:34), royal feasts (II Sam. 19:35), house-roofings, sheep-shearing festivals, and war enterprises, even if it was rendered on the crude homemade instruments. Shepherds played their pipes thousands of years ago.

(3) *Hebrew Sacred Music.*—David's part in organizing Hebrew sacred music has been debated by scholars. R. H. Pfeiffer believes that the liturgy of Israel was organized after the Exile, and that the author of I Chron. 16, for example (c. 350–250 B.C.), attributed to David's era the organization of Temple musical guilds because he wished to magnify the role of the singers' and doorkeepers' guilds which were striving for a still higher rank (I Chron. 23–25). Some deprive David of all credit for the Psalms*, and assert that their language and style are later than his time. They believe that his name is attached to these great religious poems to give them the prestige associated with "the sweet psalmist of Israel" (II Sam. 23:1); but cf. Amos 6:5. Others, including W. F. Albright (*The Archaeology and Religion of Israel*, pp. 125 ff.), think that nothing a priori can be said against the view that David was the "patron saint of Jewish music" and organizer of the Temple* music; that there are too many indications of David as a musician and as the founder of liturgical music for Hebrew worship, to toss aside the traditional credit given him. Since Canaanite music contemporary with David is now known through material found at Ras Shamrah, there is no reason to deny that the organization of the Temple musicians might also go back to the 10th century B.C.; or to deny David's authorship, for example, of the short psalm at the beginning of II Sam. 23 (1–7), even if the long "Psalm of Praise" in II Sam. 22 is not his. Such groups as accompanied the Ark to Jerusalem (I Chron. 15:16–28) and played at the dedication of Solomon's Temple (II Chron. 5:12–14, cf. *ibid.* 23:13) originated very early. Phoenicians outshone their contemporaries in music, and Israelites who were influenced by them excelled their neighbors. Musical guilds of Hebrews may be traced back, in some instances, to old Canaanite families whose names became a part of Hebrew family names.

The heads of David's guilds, according to

I Chron. 25, were originally Asaph, Jeduthun, and Heman, who led 24 groups comprising 288 Levite musicians. Hezekiah (c. 715–687 B.C.) and Josiah (c. 640–609) both fostered Temple music (II Chron. 29:25, 35:15). The headings of certain groups of Psalms, "For the Sons of Korah," etc., give the names of ancient musical hereditary guilds. Some Psalms are headed "For the Chief Musician." Many scholars believe that David's actual experiences are expressed in Ps. 23, and also in Ps. 24 and many others. Many certainly belong to his century, and could very well be Davidic.

Curt Sachs found that 3,000-year-old Jewish vocal music persists in ancient Hebrew communities in Yemen, Iraq, and Iran, where colonies settled after the Exile and remained separated from Jerusalem influences. A picture of the musical accompaniment of worship in the Jerusalem Temple in the time of King Hezekiah is given in II Chron. 29:25–30. The Levites stood near the instruments of David, as Nathan the prophet had ordered, and the priests blew the trumpets, as the offering began to burn on the altar and the songs to ascend. The people sang "praises unto Jehovah with the words of David and of Asaph the seer." In spite of the obscurity surrounding himself and his work, Habakkuk has to his credit at least a part of the beautiful religious song in the 3d chapter of the book bearing his name—a song "For the Chief Musician," to be accompanied on stringed instruments, "set to Shigionoth"—a collective term for "stringed instruments." It is a prayer of confidence in God, possibly written in the Chaldaean emergency of c. 600 B.C., or in a Greek crisis of a later period.

To this day certain parts of the Jewish ritual of prayer (especially the *Avoda* used on Atonement Day) retain evidences of ancient remembered music.

(4) *Post-Exilic Temple Music.*—With their return from Captivity the Jews initiated a fully developed Temple liturgy involving music, for which David had laid the cornerstone. When the foundations of the restored Temple were dedicated, priests with trumpets and Levites with cymbals (Ezra 3:10) praised Yahweh "after the order of David king of Israel" (A.S.V.; cf. Neh. 12:45 ff.). The leaders "sang one to another" (Ezra 3:11) and the people shouted with joyous acclaim "heard afar off" (v. 13). Temple music perpetuated the ancient type of antiphonal singing by two choruses, one of men, one of women, or by two mixed groups singing "against" each other, and by a group answering a leader's solo, as in synagogues today. In the first Temple the people did not join in the music, except with "Amen," but they did participate in Herod's Temple music. Of post-Exilic musical organization Ezra and Nehemiah speak specifically—the exemption of musicians from toil and tribute (Ezra 7:24), and their receiving state maintenance through allotment of "holy things" (Neh. 12:47). They were stationed E. of the altar (II Chron. 5:12).

(5) *Hebrew Musical Instruments.*—The Chronicler, as Pfeiffer suggests, was primarily interested in vocal music. He quotes hymns, psalms, and doxologies in his text, and shows that instruments were made primarily to accompany the choirs.

The Temple music involved the use of large orchestral ensembles, as did the shrines of Egypt, Elam, and Babylonia. The unaccompanied singing of modern cantors did not spring from ancient Biblical customs.

The various translators and redactors have led to some confusion in identifying the instruments actually used. (See *The Rise of Music in the Ancient World,* Curt Sachs, W. W. Norton & Co.)

Wind instruments included the single reed pipe, such as David probably used when tending sheep below Bethlehem; and the double pipe (*ugab*) or oboe (*chalil*). "The people" piped with pipes when Zadok anointed Solomon (I Kings 1:40). Trumpets were used as early as the Exodus, at Sinai (Ex. 19:16).

Moses, in obedience to God's command in the Wilderness, had his metalworkers make of beaten or turned silver two long trumpets to call the congregation to the tent of meeting and to give signals on the journeys from one camp to another. One trumpet call was to summon the princes commanding their groups. The first blast meant that the camps pitched on the E. should resume their journey; the second for the camps on the S. Throughout the generations "the sons of Aaron, the priests," continued to sound the worship call on the trumpets of Israel, to remind the people of their deliverance from their enemies and to resound "in the day of gladness, and in . . . set feasts, and in the beginning of . . . months . . . over burnt offerings, and over the sacrifices of peace offerings" (Num. 10:1–10; Lev. 25:8–11; A.S.V. Ps. 81:2 f.; II Chron. 5:12). Israel also used trumpets for war signals. When Gideon wanted to muster followers he blew a trumpet to beat down the "children of the east" encamped in the Valley of Jezreel. The trumpet was also used to signal "cease fighting" (II Sam. 2:28); to announce feasts (Ps. 81:3); and to warn (Jer. 6:1; Ezek. 33:4 f.; cf. Matt. 6:2, the Pharisees sounding trumpets).

No other instruments were as vital to the religious life of the Jews as the two long silver trumpets which Moses fashioned, according to the Numbers record, at God's command. Little wonder that the designer of the Arch of Titus in the Roman Forum, wishing to depict the humiliation of the Jews in A.D. 70, showed their trumpets being carried away along with their golden candlestick. Trumpets appear in Apocalyptic passages (Rev. 8:2, 6).

The shophar or ram's horn (*keren*) (Josh. 6:4, 6, 8, 13) is the oldest Hebrew instrument still in current use in Hebrew synagogues. The shophar, made by flattening and straightening with heat the natural horn of a ram, was adopted as a memorial of that ancient ram caught in the thicket and sacrificed by Abraham in place of his son Isaac. (Gen. 22:13).

Lady Hilda Petrie described a ram's horn

found among vestiges of burnt offerings in a Jewish temple built in the Nile Delta under High Priest Onias c. 154 B.C.

A very old type of Hebrew stringed instrument was known as the *kinnôr*, a lyre "the songs of Zion." A lyre differs from a harp in having two upright arms joined by a crossbar at the top; Hebrew lyres often had **six** strings. The skin, bottle-shaped *nebel* was another stringed instrument (an angular harp like the Egyptian and Assyrian ones); possibly prophets played such "harps" (I Sam. 10:5). Other shapes of harps and lyres in vogue included the widely popular U-shaped lyre seen on Jewish coins, perhaps like the one that David played (I Sam. 16:23). Some believe that the Jewish *nebel* may have been a harp or a dulcimer. The latter, a

278. Palestinian musical instruments: First row, left to right: viol with bow, shophar (horn), cymbal; at rear, zither from Hebron and double pipes.

("harp" in some versions) of almug or other wood, trimmed sometimes with amber or metal, and fitted in earliest times with twisted grass and later with sheep gut strings. *Kinnôrs* were probably small, portable lyres such as the exiled Israelites hung on the trees of Babylon when they sat down to rest after their captors had compelled them to sing zitherlike instrument having a shallow trapezoidal box and as many as 18 quadruple strings tuned by pegs, is popular in Iran and Iraq. John Garstang believed the *nebel* may have been a psaltery which was probably a zither or triangular harp similar to the Greek trigon, or a lute, which in many passages is mentioned along with the lyre as complementing it. George Post believed that the *nebel* was an Assyrian type of triangular harp, carried by a strap around the waist of the player as he held it upright and strummed.

The harp family has led to endless confusion. If we translate the first instrument mentioned in A.S.V. Ps. 33:2 as "harp," then the second one proves to be "a psaltery of ten strings." The A.V. mentions in this one verse three instruments: harp, psaltery, and "an instrument of ten strings."

Percussion instruments included timbrels, or tambourine-like hand drums (Heb. *toph*). These were used in the time of Moses to accompany the song and sacred dance of Miriam and her attendant women (Ex. 15:20). By c. 2500 B.C., as we learn from a cylinder seal of Queen Shubad, eastern neighbors of the Hebrews were accompanying their psalms and enlivening their royal banquets with timbrels or tambourines. Some of these had single heads and were rectangular; others were round, like the large timbrel carried by a woman carved in stone at Nippur about 2000 B.C., now shown at the University Museum in Philadelphia.

The loud-sounding cymbals of David's sacred orchestra accented the rhythm of Temple worship (cf. Ps. 150:5; I Cor. 13:1). Josephus thought these cymbals were flat, and made of heavy bronze, and when clashed together by the musical director led the other instruments. Some Assyrian carvings show cup-shaped cymbals with short handles. A few translators think that the cymbals were castanets, but this seems unlikely.

(6) *Music in the N.T.*—Of four references by Jesus to music, two have secular settings: "We piped unto you, and ye did not dance" (Luke 7:32); and the festal music which greeted the returned prodigal (Luke 15:25).

Matthew (9:23) tells how Jesus, coming into the home of a ruler whose little daughter appeared to be dead, "saw the flute-players, and the crowd making a tumult" (A.S.V.). Professional musicians are still employed at Near Eastern funerals and weddings.

The finest evidence of Jesus' inheritance and use of his people's traditional music is, "And when they had sung an hymn, they went out into the mount of Olives" (Mark 14:26). This was the Hallel* (Ps. 113–118).

Paul, writing to the Corinthians, appealed to their knowledge of music. Denouncing the Greeks' tendency to speak with many words, in mysteries and prophecies not understood by anybody, he said, "Even things without life, giving a voice, whether pipe or harp, if they give not a distinction in the sounds, how shall it be known what is piped or harped? For if the trumpet give an uncertain voice, who shall prepare himself for war?" (A.S.V. I Cor. 14:7 f.).

The author of Revelation, writing of the adoration of the Lamb standing on Mount Zion, mentioned "harpers harping with their harps," surrounded by a multitude of singers pouring forth "a new song before the throne" (14:2, 3); and used music as a metaphor when, picturing the fall of Babylon (Rome), he said that in the great city there were no more harpers, or minstrels, trumpeters, or flute players (18:22).

musical instruments. See MUSIC.

mustard, a plant which, with "the least of seeds" (Matt. 13:32), outstrips other herbs in height, so that birds often perch in it in order to enjoy its seeds (Luke 13:19). The

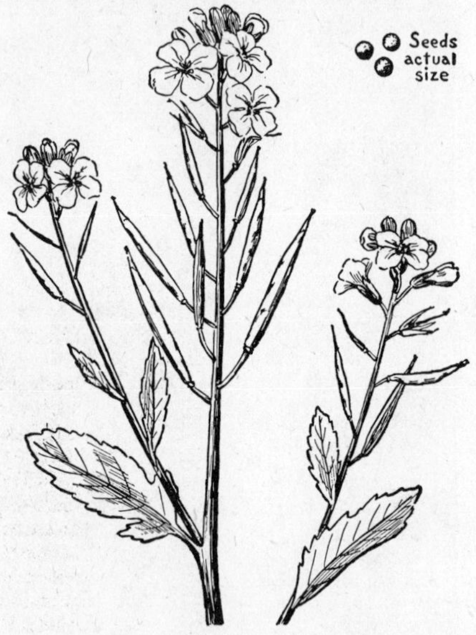

279. Mustard.

marked development of mustard became proverbial for the growth of anything from very small beginnings, like the Kingdom of God in Jesus' parable (Matt. 13:31 f.; Mark 4:31 f.; Luke 13:19); and a man's faith (Matt. 17:20; Luke 17:6). Mustard grows wild along the Plain of Gennesaret, where Jesus taught the multitudes.

Muthlabben (mŭth′lăb′ĕn), probably the opening words of a familiar melody, dealing perhaps with death, to which Ps. 9 was to be sung.

Myra (now Dembre), together with its port, one of the most influential cities of Lycia. It was situated at the SW. tip of Asia Minor. Paul and his centurion escort boarded there an Alexandrian grain ship bound for Italy (Acts 27:6). The brief statement of Acts agrees so well with the best navigation information for this route that it gives the reader added confidence in the accuracy of the author of Acts. Myra remained prosperous several centuries after Paul's time. One of its early bishops, "St. Nicholas," became the patron of sailors in the stormy eastern Mediterranean waters. The ruins of an impressive theater remain in the Myra acropolis cliff.

myrrh (Accad. *murru*, Heb. *môr*), according to most Scriptural allusions, probably the low, scrubby, bushlike tree *Commiphora myrrha*, or the closely related *C. kataf*. These are native to Arabian deserts and African terraces in Abyssinia and Somaliland. Both bark and wood emit a strong odor. Gum exudes from stems and branches—gum which at first is soft, clear, and yellowish, but later turns to oily, yellow-brown resin, which drops on the ground. Myrrh was an ingredient of Israel's holy anointing oil (see ANOINT) (Ex. 30:23–33). It was prized for its perfume (Ps. 45:8; Prov. 7:17; Song of Sol. 3:6, 4:14, 5:1, 5, 13); and was used in purification rites for women (Esther 2:12) and in compounding cosmetics. The Wise Men from the East presented myrrh to the

280. Myrrh.

infant Jesus (Matt. 2:11); and mingled with wine, myrrh was administered to him as an anodyne for pain during his Crucifixion (Mark 15:23, cf. Moffatt Matt. 27:34, "mixed with bitters"). Myrrh and aloes were brought by Nicodemus for embalming his dead body (John 19:39) and by women ("myrrophores") who came to prepare his body for burial (Mark 16:1; cf. Luke 23:56 "spices and ointments"). The "myrrh" carried by Ishmaelite trading caravans to Egypt, as in the Joseph saga (Gen. 37:25, 43:11), may have been commercial ladanum (*lōt*) (see "ladanum" A.S.V. margin), a fragrant perfume oil made from rock roses.

myrtle (Heb. *hadas*, whence "Hadassah," Esther, Esther 2:7), a popular shrub in the highlands and cultivated gardens of Palestine, admired for its white flowers and aromatic, edible berries (Isa. 41:19, 55:13; Zech. 1:8, 10). Its boughs are used at the Feast of the Tabernacles (Neh. 8:15). Emblematic of love, in the Graeco-Roman world it was sacred to Venus (Ishtar-Esther).

Mysia (mĭsh′ĭ-*ȧ*), an ancient land in NW. Asia Minor along the Hellespont and the Aegean, containing Troas and Adramyttium, ports used by Paul (Acts 16:7 f., 27:2). Today it lies within Anatolian Turkey.

mystery (from a Gk. word meaning "to initiate" or "to shut the eyes or mouth"), from its original concept of secrecy, something imparted only to the initiate (*mystes*) and thus a feature of religion. In a scientific age there are still mysteries in the universe as a whole, as well as in religion. Mystery induces awe and wonder, stimulates imagination and investigation, and calls for faith; all of which are requisites for a developing personality.

In the O.T. the possession of a secret is set forth as a special gift of God showing His favor (Dan. 2:17–47).

In N.T. times the secret religious mystery cults of the Middle East supplied some of the terminology in which Christianity was expressed. These cults had certain common characteristics. A family of gods was involved, with chief interest usually in the female. An initiation involving ceremonial washings, the dramatization of their individual myths, and feasts of welcome for the initiated, were part of the ritual of each. Through such rituals the members of the cult entered into a fellowship, partook of the nature of the cult leader, and were assured of life after death. Among the cults current in the 1st century A.D. were the following:

(1) The *Isis cult* originated in Egypt, but maintained temples throughout the Middle East, as evidenced today by ruins in Pompeii and mosaic pictures in floors at Antioch. Isis was a mother goddess of great appeal, with sympathy for human sufferings. Initiation into the mysteries of Isis involved the voluntary "death" of mortals and a symbolic trip to the underworld, followed by a glorious resurrection. A Mediterranean festival called *Navigium Isidis* was celebrated on March 5, when a gay procession carried the statue of Isis from her temple (at Antioch) to the shore, where a new ship *Isis* was launched with rites and vows.

(2) *Mithraism* originated in Persia. Mithra was a foe of evil, a savior of righteousness, and a guarantor of life in the seven heavens to come. He was presented as a mighty hero, and as such made a strong appeal to soldiers, who frequented his shrines—e.g., the one

281. Mysia.

excavated at Ostia, port of Rome. This cult was a formidable rival to Christianity.

(3) *Syrian mystery cults* were numerous. The Aphrodite and Adonis cult centered in Syrian Byblos and at Paphos in Cyprus. The Cybele-Attis cult, which practiced the

wildest, most frenzied orgies, was introduced into Rome (204 B.C.) by action of the Roman senate, in order to invite victory in the Punic Wars.

(4) *The Eleusinian Mysteries*, after flourishing for 1,000 years, were brought to an end by Alaric (A.D. 395). The Hymn to Demeter (c. the 7th century B.C.), furnishes the literary background of this most famous of the state cults of ancient Greece. Persephone (or Cora), while gathering flowers, was seized by Pluto and enthroned in Hades as queen of the underworld. Demeter, earth mother, indignant at the outrage, checked the

282. Hall of the Mysteries (*Telesterion*) at Eleusis, between Athens and Corinth, showing candidates' seats.

sprouting of the sown grain, and deprived the farmer of his harvests until her daughter was restored. Father Zeus compelled Pluto to surrender his bride to her mother, but not before Pluto had made Persephone swallow the seed of the pomegranate*, whose magic properties made her come back to him and remain in the underworld for a part of each year. After Persephone returned the Greeks were taught how to grow corn and wheat. This myth is a milestone in the economic and religious development of the Greeks.

An elaborate ritual originated at Eleusis, and later developed at Athens in the Acropolis celebrations for the whole of Attica. The cult glorified the energies of the natural world—autumn, winter, spring, and summer. Candidates for membership in the Eleusinian cult were initiated into the lesser Mysteries in February. After a year of probation they were admitted into the full Mysteries in the autumn ceremonies, which included a pilgrimage of 12 m. along the Sacred Way from Athens to Eleusis, and bathing in the Bays of Phaleron and Salamis and the two salt lakes en route. A long fast preceded their admission into the *Telesterion*, a hall of initiation seating 3,000, now excavated at Eleusis. There, in silence, the candidate beheld the drama of Persephone against the backdrop of water, island, and Greek landscape. This drama, characterized as "something shown" (cf. I Cor. 15:51), was followed by a feast for the initiated. Cicero, who was initiated, revealed none of the details, but wrote that the rites taught men "not only to live happily, but also to die with a fairer hope." The Roman emperors Hadrian and Marcus Aurelius were adherents of the cult.

Opinions among scholars vary as to the extent to which these "mysteries" influenced Christianity. Jesus implied that religion was not a secret withheld from man deliberately, but, because of man's obtuseness, it was not understood until it was revealed (Matt. 13:11; Mark 4:11; Luke 8:10). His interview with the Greeks, with his reference to the grain of wheat and immortality, if not purely coincidental, implies some knowledge on his part of the Eleusis cult, or is due to strong Hellenistic influence exerted on the author of the Fourth Gospel (John 12:20–24). Paul, because of his contact with the Greek world, and his journeys through Eleusis on his way from Athens to Corinth (Acts 18:1), certainly showed a knowledge of the mystery cults. He used the word "mystery" 21 times in his Epistles; and the word was part of the religious terminology of his audiences. An accredited instructor indoctrinated the Christian candidate (I Cor. 2:7, 15:51, cf. I Cor. 4:1; Col. 1:26, 4:3; Eph. 3:3). The Gospel was something withheld until it was made manifest (II Thess. 2:5 f.), and was known only to the instructed (Rom. 11:25; I Cor. 13:2). I Cor. 15 gives the full meaning of the resurrected life, of which Eleusis gave a faint idea; such an experience resulted in the fellowship of the mystery (Eph. 3:9). Since Paul at no time lays particular stress on baptism (I Cor. 1:13–17), his idea of dying and rising with Christ in connection with baptism (Rom. 6) could have been a figure of speech, borrowed from the initiation rites of cultism, but filled with his own spiritual experience of Christ (Acts 9:1–18). The Apocalypse employs symbols to create the atmosphere of mystery (Rev. 1:20, 10:7, 17:5), as well as to interpret it (17:7).

Each of the pagan mysteries was characterized by a family pantheon of deities; but the Christ of the early Christian era was wholly unaccompanied. Not until 400 years had elapsed did the Virgin Mary assume a relationship to Christ which could suggest the association of female and male deities so characteristic of the mysteries.

mystic, one who attains direct knowledge of God and of spiritual truth through immediate intuition or spiritual insight. His experiences transcend those of the ordinary man. The Hebrew literary prophets were mystics. Jeremiah was the first O.T. mystic to record his inner experiences of despair and his final triumphant faith in God.

N

Naamah (nā′ȧ-mȧ) ("pleasant"). (1) Lamech's daughter, sister of Tubal-cain (Gen. 4:22). (2) A woman of Ammon, mother of Rehoboam (I Kings 14:21, 31; II Chron. 12:13). (3) A town of Judah in the Shephelah (Josh. 15:41), possibly Khirbet Fered. Zophar the Naamathite was one of Job's friends (Job 2:11, 11:1, 20:1, 42:9). The site of his town may be in N. Arabia.

Naaman (nā′ȧ-măn) ("pleasant"). (1) A grandson of Benjamin; eponymous ancestor of the Naamites (Gen. 46:21; Num. 26:40). He may be the same as Naaman, the son of Ehud (I Chron. 8:4, 7).

(2) The successful Syrian commander-in-chief of Ben-hadad*, King of Damascus—who was an arch enemy of Israel (I Kings 20). Naaman was afflicted with leprosy, of a type evidently not considered by Syrians to be communicable. His disease aroused the sympathy of his wife's handmaid, a devout Israelitish girl captured in a border skirmish. The Hebrew servant expressed her longing that Naaman might have access to the healing ministry of God's prophet at Samaria, capital of Israel (II Kings 5:3). Ben-hadad sent a letter to his vassal, the King of Israel, and commended his afflicted officer to him to be cured. The King of Israel suspected that the incident was a ruse for further attack (v. 7), but Elisha*, seeing an opportunity to use his prophetic healing as a witness to God's power, sent to the king to have Naaman, the proud, chariot-driving officer, come to his humble house in Samaria. His prescription of a seven-fold dip in the muddy Jordan* (v. 10), though repugnant to one who knew the clear, rushing waters of Damascus (v. 12), was finally accepted by the sick man.

283. Naaman's Waters, Damascus.

His immediate cure led to his acceptance of the God of Israel as the only "God in all the earth" (v. 15).

The fifth chapter of II Kings, in which Naaman's story is told, is important evidence of the henotheism (belief that nations had their individual gods) prevalent before the time of King Josiah. Naaman's request that he might carry "two mules' burden of earth" from Samaria to Damascus, so that he might worship the God of Israel on Israel's soil, even though he was required to accompany his master to the temple of Rimmon, is characteristic of the thought of his times. The Great Omaiyid Mosque at Damascus, today the city's most magnificent structure, ranking in sanctity with the Dome of the Rock at Jerusalem and the mosques of Mecca and Medina, is built (according to tradition) on the site of the Temple of Rimmon where Naaman deposited his load of earth. Luke mentions the cleansing of Naaman the Syrian (4:27).

Nabal (nā′băl) (epithet, "fool"), a rich, irascible sheikh, possibly from the Clan of Caleb, residing in the town of Maon, SE. of Hebron, and owning farm and grazing lands in adjacent Carmel in the highlands of S. Judaea and the Negeb (not to be confused with Mt. Carmel, farther N.) (I Sam. 25:2 f.). The freebooter David and his men had defended Nabal's sheep shearers from brigands in the wilderness (v. 21). When Nabal refused to give them food supplies, the hot-headed band of 400 outlaws threatened his life (v. 13). Nabal's resourceful wife, Abigail*, hearing of the danger, tactfully averted it (vv. 14, 31) and incidentally deterred David from the crime of bloodguilt (vv. 30 f.). Next morning, when Abigail told Nabal of his narrow escape, the "very drunken" tippler was so shocked that he had a heart attack, from which he died 10 days later (vv. 36–38). Abigail became a wife of David (vv. 39–42).

Nabataea (năb′ȧ-tē′ȧ), **Nabataeans** (năb′ȧ-tē′ănz), an Arabian kingdom and its remarkable people whose period of greatest prominence was between the first two centuries B.C. and the beginning of the 2d century A.D., when Rome made Nabataea the Province of Arabia (A.D. 106). Nabataeans were originally Arabians who between the 6th and 4th centuries B.C. pushed north out of their peninsula, seized and strengthened mountain strongholds and watchtowers that belonged to Edom* and Moab*, commanding intersections of the great caravan trade routes of the Middle East. The movement of this people is reflected in the book of Obadiah, vv. 1–7.

In Jesus' day the kingdom stretched S. of Idumaea (see EDOM), reaching the Mediterranean S. of Gaza, and extended down the Arabah* and N. through Trachonitis almost to Syrian Damascus, which at times it dominated. The mother of Herod the Great was a Nabataean. Though Christ apparently never visited Nabataea, he ministered in the adjoining Peraea and Decapolis when Nabataea was at its peak of prosperity. The Arabians mentioned as present in Jerusalem at

Pentecost (Acts 2:11) may have come from Nabataea. A Nabataean king, Aretas IV (9 B.C.–A.D. 40), appointed an ethnarch (governor) of Damascus who was scheming to arrest Paul, and whom Paul barely escaped by being let down over the city wall in a basket (II Cor. 11:32 f.) (see WALL, illus. 473). A daughter of Aretas IV was the divorced first wife of Herod Antipas of Galilee (the sly "fox," Luke 13:32).

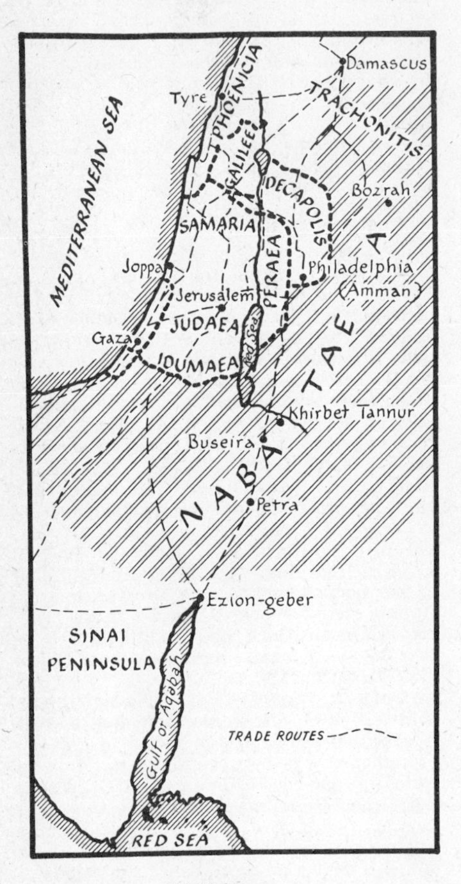

284. Nabataea.

As late as the 3d century B.C. Nabataeans were still nomads*, holding the Sinai Peninsula, resisting agriculture and the construction of houses as vigorously as they resisted wine. They left inscriptions in Sinai (not to be confused with the proto-Sinaitic inscriptions of an earlier date at Serabit* el-Khadem). By c. 100 B.C. they had engineered such ingenious water-supply devices that the parched highlands of what is now the Kingdom of Jordan produced crops and flocks for a large population. There survive today vestiges of amazing aqueducts, reservoirs, cone-shaped water catchments, cisterns, and dams, especially at the rock city of Sela (not the Biblical Sela), a few m. NW. of Buseirah (the Biblical Bozrah, Isa. 63:1; Amos 1:12). At Ummel-jemal the Nabataean-Roman reservoir is still watertight, though unused for centuries for lack of inhabitants. For much of interest concerning Nabataeans, see *The Other Side of the Jordan* and *The River Jordan* by Nelson Glueck, who, with survey expeditions of the American Schools of Oriental Research, examined Trans-Jordan sites once occupied by Edomites and Moabites and found more than 500 Nabataean watchtowers, fortresses, and villages, identified by pottery even where no standing ruins remain. One of the most rewarding sites was Khirbet et-Tannûr, on the River Zered, E. of the S. end of the Dead Sea, on the summit of lofty Jebel Tannûr, reached by a single steep path and rock-cut steps. Its temple area yielded much information about Nabataean religion.

The Nabataeans were much more than astute traders who kept a strangle hold on caravan routes, and profited by trade flowing out of India, China, Arabia, and Syria to markets of many nations. Their unique ceramics have seldom been excelled. Fragments of buff-and-brown bowls, jugs, cups, and fine saucers of eggshell thinness have been excavated as far S. as Aqabah. Many are decorated with modernistic designs of palm, grape, pomegranate. Many pieces have no affinity with other known pottery. Their rock-cut temples, tombs, castles, theaters, and sanctuaries are unique contributions to the history of architecture.

The Nabataean capital was the virtually impregnable Petra (O.T. Sela, Isa. 16:1) a lofty, rock-cut, rose-red city 60 m. S. of the Dead Sea, in the Ash-Shara mountain chain running 120 m. down the Arabah. Petra towers above the Wâdī Musa, is inaccessible except by foot or beast, and was unknown to the Western world until J. L. Burckhardt visited it in 1812. Petra, "city of altars," occupied a rough parallelogram 1 m. long and ½ m. wide, bounded by walls of richly colored sandstone pocketed with ancient caverns—probably used by troglodyte cave dwellers (Deut. 12:2), probably Hivites (see HORITES) (Gen. 36:2). Petra contains several Nabataean "high places" or open-air sanctuaries so violently opposed by prophets and many kings of Israel. The most impressive of these cultic centers (discovered by G. L.

285. Great high-place at Petra.

Robinson in 1900) is Petra's Great High Place that faces the rising sun, and memorializes the early Nabataean faith of nomads who honored both moon and sun. The chief gods were a male deity, Dushara or Dusares (Dionysus), and a female goddess, Allat. Research at Khirbet et-Tannûr reveals numerous other members of a Nabataean pantheon, chief of which are Zeus-hadad; Atargatis (Artemis), depicted at Khirbet et-Tannûr as a fish goddess (reminiscent of trade with coastal Ascalon) and as goddess of grain; and a winged Tyche (Victory). For diagram of the installations of the cultic Great High Place at Petra, see G. L. Robinson's *Sarcophagus of an Ancient Civilization*, which shows the sacred banquet couches (*triclinia*) used for sensuous cultic banquets, a rectangular altar, a circular altar evidently used in preparing material for sacrifices, the water reservoirs, and the *mensa sacra* or "table" such as is found in the many lesser high places of the Near East. The 20-ft.-high twin pillars, cut from solid rock and left free-standing, suggest the Jachin* and Boaz at Solomon's Temple (I Kings 7:21). The Conway High Place (discovered by Agnes Conway Horsfield), examined in 1934 by W. F. Albright and others, is the oldest known datable high place (used from the 1st century B.C.). It is not known whether Nabataean architects and artists created these amazing works, or whether skillful craftsmen from outside were employed. The *Kasneh* mausoleum, cut in the rock at the end of the funnel-like passageway, the *Siq*, is a unique work of possibly the 1st century A.D., attributed by some to the King Aretas IV mentioned above.

Nabataean high places, in the early centuries of Biblical history, were sacred sites of "sons of Esau," Edomites*, of whose worship a little is narrated in I Kings 11:1 f.; II Chron. 25:14 f., 20.

A great Nabataean city in the north was in the Hauran, at the N.T. Bostra (Bosora)—not mentioned in the O.T. Other Nabataean towns include Kerek, Khirbet Dherih, and Qasr Rabbah. See NEGEB.

Nablus. See NEAPOLIS.

Nabonidus (năb'ō-nī'dŭs) (Nabu-na'id), the son of Nabu-balatsuikbi, and the last ruler of New Babylonia (556–539 B.C.); the father of Belshazzar*, who was coregent with him from his 3d year on the throne till the fall of Babylon to Cyrus the Persian (539 B.C.). Nabonidus was the last Semitic ruler to hold a position of world power. He was a "religious antiquary" with a flair for archaeology. The date lists and other information unearthed by his scholars from many early temple sites in Babylonia have helped modern archaeologists to determine Mesopotamian chronology and the nature of early cults and rites. He was the last ruler of Babylon to repair the famous old stage tower or *ziggurat** to the moon god Sin at Ur. Unlike the unscrupulous Ramesses II, who wrote his name across constructions of predecessors, Nabonidus placed in each corner of the tower a cuneiform-inscribed barrel cylinder telling of his modest share in the total. His daughter, sister of Belshazzar, is said to have maintained a small museum of archaelogical finds. Another daughter, Bel-shalti-nannar, was dedicated to the moon-god temple at Ur. Nabonidus withdrew the Babylonian army from Palestine (c. 553 B.C.).

Nabopolassar, the Chaldaean "son of a nobody," founder of the New Babylonian Empire whose rebellion against Assyria (c. 626 B.C.) gave Josiah, King of Judah (c. 640–609 B.C.) courage to carry out religious reforms and an opportunity to regain almost all the former territory of Israel. That Nabopolassar reconstructed the city of Babylon* has been verified by excavation. In the 14th year of his reign (612 B.C.), with Cyaxerxes the Mede and the Scythian king, he captured mighty Nineveh* (Nah. 3:1–3; Zeph. 2:12–14) and laid it waste. Nabopolassar was father of Nebuchadnezzar II, and sent him into the epochal battle of Carchemish against Egypt (Jer. 46) in the "fourth year of Jehoiakim"* (v. 2) (605 B.C.). Nabopolassar died in Babylon at about that time. See NECHOH; NAHUM.

Naboth (nā'bŏth), an influential citizen of the prosperous agricultural town of Jezreel, the town on the Plain of Jezreel* which gave its name to this vast, fertile area. Jezreel (today Zer'in) lies between Nazareth and Jenin on the main N.-S. road from Galilee to Jerusalem. The story of Naboth perfectly fits its setting. Naboth owned a vineyard (I Kings 21:1, A.V., A.S.V., R.S.V.; "field" II Kings 9:25, A.V., A.S.V., where Moffatt has "ancestral field" and R.S.V. "plot of ground") adjoining the property of King Ahab* of Israel. During the years of drought it was feverishly coveted by Ahab (I Kings 21:2–4). Under Hebrew laws which safeguarded a man's inheritance not even Ahab could wrest the land from Naboth for money or exchange. But wicked Queen Jezebel plotted to have Naboth falsely accused of blasphemy against God and disloyalty to Ahab. While presiding at a feast (v. 12) Naboth, with his heirs, was stoned to death by "base fellows" (A.S.V. v. 13). The prophet Elijah, hearing of the outrage, foretold to Ahab that in the very field he had acquired (I Kings 21:18) Jezebel would be eaten by dogs in the place where Naboth had been murdered (I Kings 21:17–25)—a prophecy fulfilled in the incidents narrated in II Kings 9:21–26.

Nadab (nā'dăb) ("generous). (1) The eldest son of Aaron* (Ex. 6:23; Num. 3:2, 26:60) and Elisheba. He was permitted to accompany Moses and Aaron high on Sinai (Ex. 24:1, 9). With his brother Abihu he died (childless) on the day when he was appointed to the priesthood (Ex. 28:1; Num. 3:4; I Chron. 24:2), because he offered "strange fire" (? profane coals) to Yahweh (Lev. 10:1; Num. 3:4). (2) A Jerahmeelite, descendant of Caleb of Hezron (I Chron. 2:28, 30). (3) A Benjamite, son of Gibeon, a chief man at Jerusalem, and Maacah (I Chron. 8:29 f., 9:36). (4) Son and successor of King Jeroboam of Israel (I Kings 14:20). After a short and evil reign (c. 901–900 B.C.) he was slain by Baasha* of Issachar in the Philistine town of Gibbethon, in the 13th year of Asa, King of Judah. He was succeeded by Baasha (c. 900–877 B.C.).

Nahalal (nā'hă-lăl) (Nahalol, nā'hă-lŏl), a town "allotted" to Zebulun (Josh. 19:15), from which that tribe did not drive out the Canaanites (Judg. 1:30). Later it was assigned to the Levites (Josh. 21:35). Its site is possibly Tell en-Nahl, on the plain near the Kishon, SE. of the Bay of Acre.

Nahaliel (nă-hā'lĭ-ĕl) ("torrent-valley of El"), a brook, possibly Wâdī Zerka Ma'in, which enters the Dead Sea N. of the Arnon and S. of Mt. Nebo. Adjacent to a good camp site, it marks an encampment of Israel on the journey from Egypt (Num. 21:19).

Nahash (nā'hăsh) ("serpent"). (1) An Ammonite king whose impossible demands on the men of Jabesh-gilead* stirred Saul* to rescue them in a victory which proved pivotal in establishing him as ruler of the new Kingdom of Israel (I Sam. 11); possibly the same Nahash who was kind to David (II Sam. 10:2), and whose son Hanun insulted him rudely (v. 4). Shobi, another son of this Nahash, brought supplies to David while David was at Mahanaim, E. of the Jordan, during Absalom's rebellion (II Sam. 17:27–29). (2) A kinsman of David, whose relationship is not clear in a corrupt text (II Sam. 17:25; cf. I Chron. 2:16).

Nahor (nā'hôr) (twice Nachor [nā'kôr] A.V. Josh. 24:2; Luke 3:34). (1) A son of Serug (Gen. 11:22), father of Terah, and grandfather of "Abram, Nahor, and Haran" (vv. 24, 27).

(2) A grandson of Nahor (1) and brother of Abraham and Haran. According to Gen. 11:29 he married his niece, Milcah, daughter of Haran. By her and a concubine Nahor became parent of 12 sons—probably heads of tribes in N. Mesopotamia. He was great-grandfather of Rachel and Leah (29:5, 6). To "the city of Nahor" in upper Mesopotamia (Heb. *Aram-naharaim*, Gen. 24:10) Abraham sent his servant to secure a wife for his son Isaac from among his own N. Mesopotamian people (v. 15). He found Rebekah, granddaughter of Nahor (v. 24). The God of Nahor was the God of Abraham (21:33).

The "city of Nahor" was Nakhur (Nahur), S. of Haran, mentioned in clay documents found at Mari* and in Middle Assyrian texts. The site may be Tell Nakhiri ("Mound of Nakhuru"), below Haran in the Balikh Valley. When the wealth of excavated material has been published it will probably shed more light on N. Mesopotamia with reference to the Hebrew Patriarchs. In several instances names of towns near Haran correspond to the names of Abraham's ancestors, e.g., Serug, Nahor, Terah.

Nahor is viewed as the eponymous ancestor of the N. Semites, Aramaean tribes, as Abraham is of the Israelites and Edomites of the southland.

Nahum (nā'hŭm) ("consolation, compassion"), the last of the great Hebrew classical poets of which Deborah was one of the earliest, and an ardent patriot who saw in the destruction of Nineveh* a manifestation of God's punitive justice. He is identified only as "the Elkoshite," a citizen of Elkosh (Nah. 1:1; this place has never been located). Since the 16th century the village of Elkush, 27 m. N. of Mosul, has claimed Nahum's tomb. This late tradition assumes that he was among those led into captivity when Sargon took Samaria (722/1 B.C.). Another unsubstantiated theory is that Nahum was a Judaean who lived near Beit Jibrîn, midway between Jerusalem and Gaza.

The Book of Nahum is 7th in the list of the Minor Prophets. Its three chapters may be outlined as follows:

Chap. 1:1—The prophet and the prophecy:
- 1:2–6—Yahweh's vengeance and wrath.
- v. 7—Stronghold of the faithful.
- v. 8—Pursuer of his enemies.
- vv. 9 f.—Will not fail his people.
- vv. 11–13—Deliverance of Judah.
- v. 14—Destruction of Assyria.
- v. 15—Rejoicing in Mount Zion.

Chap. 2:1–3:19—Ode on the destruction of Nineveh:
- 2:1–5—Attack on Nineveh: its defenses.
- 2:6–10—Capture and destruction of the city.
- 2:11–13—Crimes of Nineveh.
- 3:1–3—The attack.
- 3:4–7—Nineveh's crimes and their punishment.
- 3:8–17—Capture and destruction of the city.

Chap. 3:18 f.—Epilogue.

The 1st section of the book (1:2–15) is a psalm, somewhat mutilated, but with traces of an alphabetic acrostic arrangement (from *aleph* to *samech*). It was appended (according to those who do not attribute it to Nahum) as a sort of theological introduction to the superb ode of Nahum (2:1–3:9). In the midst of the terrifying manifestation of God, outraged because of evil, are the much-quoted verses of beauty and comfort (1:7, 15; cf. Isa. 52:7).

The ode on the fall of Nineveh (chaps. 2, 3) is a graphic depiction of military operations in the 7th century B.C. C. 614 B.C. Assyria was seriously threatened by Cyaxerxes of Media (see MEDES). In June of 612 the Mede, in league with Nabopolassar* of Babylon, began the siege of Nineveh. Nahum pictures the fighting in the suburbs, then the assault on the walls, followed by the capture and destruction of the city. The vivid and sometimes ferocious or unrefined language depicts magnificently scenes of horror and vengeful rejoicing because Assyria is finally suffering the atrocities she had inflicted on others. Two dates implied in the narrative fix the possible time when the main part of this book was written. Thebes (No-Amon) was captured by Ashurbanipal in 663 B.C. (Nah. 3:8); Nineveh fell in August 612 B.C. Since Nineveh had not yet fallen when Nahum wrote his ode, the probable date of chaps. 2–3 (certainly after 663 B.C.) is probably between 614 and 612 B.C., when her end was imminent. This makes Nahum a 7th century contemporary of Zephaniah, Habbakuk, and Jeremiah.

Nahum uses this one isolated event in the life of Assyria—the siege and fall of Nineveh—to describe the fate meted out to the nation which outrages the conscience of humanity. Nahum expresses the moral indignation of a righteous God Who is international in His jurisdiction; and at the same time the relief of the nations of Western Asia when the doom of ruthless, tyrannical Assyria was certain.

nails, small metal spikes, known in Palestine at least as early as the beginning of the Monarchy. Nails of iron as well as of copper were available in large numbers for the construction of the Temple* by Solomon (II Chron. 3:9), because his father David had stock-piled iron for doors and joinings (I Chron. 22:3). These passages show the enthusiasm for metals characteristic of the opening of the Iron Age (c. 1200–1000 B.C.) at the beginning of the Monarchy of Israel. Large iron and copper nails have been excavated at Ezion-geber*, boat-building seaport of Solomon. The nail used by Jael (Judg. 5:26) may have been a tent pin of wood or metal. Stout and cruel Roman nails affixed Jesus to his cross and left their prints in his hands and feet (John 20:25 f.). The allusions of Isaiah (22:23, 25, 41:7) and Jeremiah (10:4) are to pegs driven into house walls to hold utensils or idols.

Nain (nā'ĭn), a small village on "Little Hermon," a hillock 1,690 ft. high in Galilee, overlooking the Valley of Jezreel, 6 m. SE. of Nazareth, 2 m. NNW. of Endor, in the heart of the region of Jesus' Galilean ministry. It is W. of the main NS. highway to Samaria, and looks NE. to Mt. Tabor. The son of a widow of Nain was restored to life by Jesus (Luke 7:11–17).

Naioth (nā'ŏth), a place in or near Ramah* in Benjamin, a short distance N. of Jerusalem, where David, fleeing from Saul, took refuge with Samuel and the prophets associated with him (I Sam. 19:18). Saul's messengers, sent to Naioth to take David, became imbued with the prophetic spirit, as did Saul himself when he followed (I Sam. 19:20–24).

names were considered very important in O.T. society. The long genealogical lists (e.g., Gen. 36; I Chron. 1–2; Luke 3:23–38, etc.) reflect the Hebrew concern to establish inheritance* rights and to prolong the prestige of important individuals. Another characteristic is the devising by early ethnologists of eponymous ancestors to account for tribes and localities, e.g., Shem, Ham, and Japheth (Gen. 10:1–32), Moab (Gen. 19:37), and Ammon (v. 38). Canaan was a "man" (Gen. 5:9) whose eldest son was Sidon, an ancient city; Kittim (Cyprus) was a son of Javan; likewise Rodanim (Rhodes) (Gen. 10:4).

(1) For the various names of God see GOD.

(2) "Jesus" is the Gk. form of the Aram. *Yeshua'* (Ezra 3:2, 4:3), in Heb. *Joshua'* or *Jehoshua'* (Hag. 1:1; Zech. 3:3, etc.). In these passages Jeshua and Joshua are the same person (a high priest). "Christ" is the Gk. rendering of the Aram. *Meshiah* ("anointed"), from which comes the Eng. *Messiah*, a passive participle corresponding to the Heb. *mashuah* or *mashuakh*.

(3) In the days of the Patriarchs names seem to have been given by the strongest character in the situation. Adam's wife named Seth (Gen. 4:25); the daughters of Lot named Moab and Ben-Ammi (Ammon) (Gen. 19:37, 38); Leah named Reuben, Simeon, and Judah (Gen. 29:32–35); Rachel named Bilhah's sons; Leah named Zilpah's; Abraham named Isaac (Gen. 21:3). Names were assigned either at birth, or at the circumcision the 8th day, as in the case of Isaac (Gen. 21:4). Originally the sources of names were limited; parents drew them from animals, like Rachel ("ewe"), Leah ("wild cow"), Deborah ("bee"), and Caleb ("dog"); or from plants, like Hadassah ("myrtle"), and Tamar ("palm"). A later name, Habbakuk, may be based on the Assyrian garden plant *hambaququ*. Traits of the child often suggested his name, like Esau ("hairy"). The names by which many Biblical characters are known reveal what they became, and therefore must have been applied in maturity. Many seem to be prophetic of cherished hopes, like "Saviour" for Jesus (Matt. 1:21). Names often sprang from events in the life of the nation, like Ichabod ("the glory is departed," I Sam. 4:22), or in the life of the family or of the father; frequently names were changed by events, as when King Mattaniah took the name of Zedekiah under Babylon's regime at Jerusalem (II Kings 24:17).

Many names were theophorous, i.e., compounded with the name of a deity. The various names of the God of Israel were popular elements of such compounds—El, as in Bezaleel (Ex. 31:2), Elnathan (II Kings 24:8), and Nathanael (John 1:45); Je, as in Jehoiada (II Kings 11:4) and Jehoshaphat (I Kings 15:24); and Shaddai, as in Ammishaddai ("kinsman of Shaddai," Num. 1:12; see also JEHOVAH-JIREH, etc.). Canaanite deities also appeared in proper names, like Zedek in Melchizedek (Gen. 14:18) and Adonizedek meaning, "my lord is righteousness" (Josh. 10:1). Many Hebrews carried names in which Baal ("lord") was incorporated, such as Esh-Baal, son of Saul (I Chron. 8:33), and Merib-baal (Mephibosheth), son of Jonathan (II Sam. 9:6). In times of reform men in whose names Baal had been incorporated were appropriately renamed (cf. Jerubbaal, Gideon Judg. 6:32). The name Gad was the name of an Aramaean god of good luck.

Many O.T. persons bore names not of Hebrew origin, that reflected foreign groups among whom they lived, e.g., Moses. Joseph had an alternate Egyptian name, Zaphenath-paneah (A.S.V. Gen. 41:45). For Mordecai cf. the Babylonian Marduk. Persian names appear in the Books of Esther and Daniel. Edomitic and Hurrian names may also be traced.

Individuals were frequently more fully identified by appending "son of" to the given name: "Joshua the son of Nun" (Josh. 2:1), "Simon Bar-jona" ("Bar," son) (Matt. 16:17), "Levi the son of Alphaeus" (Mark 2:14). Sometimes a city name was added, as in "Jesus of Nazareth" (Acts 2:22); Mary of Magdala (Luke 8:2); "Simon a Cyrenian" (Mark 15:21); or the name of an occupation, as in "Joseph the carpenter," Levi, "a publican . . . sitting at the receipt of custom"

(Luke 5:27), Simon the sorcerer (Acts 8:9), "Simon a tanner" (Acts 9:43). Often a person's name was changed by a significant event in his life: Abram became Abraham (Gen. 17:5); Sarai, Sarah (v. 15); Jacob, Israel (32:28); Eliakim, Jehoiakim (II Chron. 36:4); Mattaniah, Zedekiah (II Kings 24:17); Simon, Cephas (or Peter) (John 1:42); Saul, Paul (Acts 13:9).

As today, certain names tended to be more popular in one century than in another. There are at least 21 Meshullams and 31 Zechariahs. And just as American presidents, generals, and motion-picture stars have children named for them, so did the Hebrews name their sons for their heroes, especially for David and his court. A score bear the same name as one of David's musicians, Maaseiah.

In N.T. times Romans gave a man three names—his own, that of his house or clan, and his family's: Marcus Antonius Felix. Sometimes the personal name was omitted: Porcius Festus (Acts 24:27). Many N.T. Jews bore Roman names, like Crispus (Acts 18:8). Mark was Marcus; Timothy, Timotheus. The Alexandrian Apollos (19:1) was among those with Greek names.

(4) Names of places and topographical features offer material for the resourceful reader to interpret. Many place names incorporate Beth (house): Bethel ("house of God"); Bethlehem ("house of bread or meat"). Others have a prefix, En ('Ain), to indicate proximity to springs or a fountain, or Beer, to a well. Abel, "meadow," appears in Abel-beth-maachah ("meadow of Beth-maachah") (I Kings 15:20), and in Abel-meholah ("Vale of Dancing") (I Kings 4:12). Gibeah means "a hill"; Ramah, "a height." Mizpah means "a watchtower." The names of many Canaanite and other non-Israelite deities found their way into place names, like Shamash into Beth-shemesh and Anath into Anathoth. Rivers and mountains have very ancient names, like the Semitic Jordan, Yarmuk, Jabbok, and Arnon. The names of many towns show layers of linguistic influence, from the Semitic stratum of the 4th and 3d millennia B.C. to the Canaanite and Amorite forms of the 2d millennium. "Bethlehem," though pronounced almost the same for at least 3,500 years, has meant at various times "Temple of the God Lakhmu" (Canaanite); "House of Bread" (Heb. and Aram.); and "House of Flesh" (Arab.). (See chap. 8, *The Archaeology of Palestine*, W. F. Albright, Pelican Books).

Isaiah gave significant names to two of his sons: (a) Shearjashub ("a remnant shall return," 7:3); (b) Maher-shalal-hash-baz ("the spoil speedeth, the prey hasteth," 8:3 f., 18). Hosea also gave symbolical names to (a) his eldest son by Gomer, Jezreel ("God sows," 1:4); (b) his daughter, Lo-ruhamah ("That hath not obtained mercy," 1:6); (c) another son, Loammi ("not my people," 1:9).

When the State of Israel was established in 1948, many Jewish citizens adopted new names identified with Israel's ancient history or symbolic ones valuable for propaganda. Thus, some took Amikam ("my people rose") or Bar-on ("strong"). Others translated their names: German Schwartz ("black") became Shahor. Sometimes a name similar in sound to the old one was adopted: Prime Minister David Gruen became Ben-Gurion ("son of the young lion"), Foreign Minister Moshe Shertok became Sharett ("servant"), scholar Harry Torczyner became Tur-Sinai ("Mount Sinai").

Nannar, a form of the Accadian male moon god Sin, worshipped at Ur. His shrine originally topped the garden-decked *ziggurat**.

Naomi (nā′ō-mī; nȧ-ō′mī) ("my pleasantness"), the wife of Elimelech the Bethlehemite (Ruth 1:2). Widowed and bereft of her two sons in the land of Moab, whither they had moved during a famine in Judaea, she returned to Bethlehem with Ruth*, her devoted Moabitish daughter-in-law (Ruth 1:14–19). When Naomi returned to her ancestral home (1:20, 21) she successfully arranged the marriage of the young widow Ruth to Boaz, Elimelech's influential kinsman (Ruth 3, 4). Naomi was nurse to their son Obed, who became the grandfather of David (4:16 f.).

Naphtali (năf′tȧ-lī) (from Heb. *naphtulim*, "wrestlings," because Rachel had wrestled with Leah and won, by the birth of a son to her handmaid, or had wrestled with God in petition for a child), the second son of Bilhah, handmaid of Rachel, and Jacob (Gen. 30:7 f.), brother of Dan (35:25), father of four sons—Guni, Jahziel, Jezer, and Shallum (Gen. 46:24; I Chron. 7:13). Naphtali was the eponymous ancestor of one of the Twelve Tribes of Israel; and the story of this clan, as narrated in the O.T., follows the course of the nation of which he was a part, though many scholars regard Naphtali as being already settled when the Israelites arrived. His Tribe, according to the narrative of Ex. 1:4, descended to Egypt with the Jacob tribes; had a princely representative at Sinai (Num. 1:15); was "numbered" on two occasions (Num. 1:42 f., 26:50); offered a beautiful and substantial "oblation" for the Tabernacle (Num. 7:78–83), suggesting ample resources; marched from Sinai, with Ahira leading (10:27); sent a representative with the spies dispatched by Moses from the Wilderness of Paran to survey Canaan (13:14); was in the group assigned to stand on Mt. Ebal "for the curse" (Deut. 27:13); shared Moses' view of the Promised Land from Nebo (34:2); drew the 6th lot for inheritance in Canaan; and was assigned territory whose borders are outlined in Josh. 19:32–39. The men of Naphtali were unable to drive out the Canaanites from such towns as Beth-shemesh* and Beth-anath (Judg. 1:33).

Naphtali as a border territory developed hardy men who took part in such crises as the battle of the 5-tribe confederacy of Deborah and Barak, against Sisera (c. 1125 B.C.), for which they were praised in the Song of Deborah (Judg. 5:18). Barak himself came from Kedesh-naphtali. The tribe also acquitted itself well when summoned by Gideon against the Midianites (Judg. 7:23). The adventurous, free young spirit of the men of

Naphtali led to their being likened in the "blessing of Jacob" to "a hind let loose" (Gen. 49:21).

When David went to Hebron to be crowned, (c. 1000 B.C.), men of Naphtali were adherents (I Chron. 12:34–40); they were represented in the new king's bureaucracy (I Chron. 27:19).

The territory which fell to Naphtali's lot as a member of the northernmost tribal group was all north of the Plain of Esdraelon, and was cut off from the southern tribes by a chain of Canaanite fortresses. It was excellent land along the W. and NW. shores of the Sea of Galilee and the Upper Jordan as far as Abel-beth-maachah and the beginning of the Beka'a Valley between the twin Lebanon ranges. It was bordered on the W. by Asher, on the S. by Issachar and Zebulun, and on the NE. by Dan. Its cities included Kedesh-naphtali, Hazor*, and Beth-shemesh—and a total of 19 "fenced cities." It gave its share of towns to the Levites (Josh. 21:6), and for cities* of refuge (Josh. 20:7, 21:32).

The Tribe of Naphtali became incorporated in the Northern Kingdom (Israel). Its store-cities were attacked by Ben-hadad*, King of Damascus (Aram), c. 877 B.C. (I Kings 15:20); and many of its citizens were carried captive to Assyria by Tiglath-pileser* III (c. 733 B.C., II Kings 15:29).

Naphtali was included in Ezekiel's vision of a restored Jerusalem, and "assigned" a gate on the W. side of the city (48:3 f.).

napkin, a piece of linen or other fabric used to wipe the mouth and fingers, referred to by Jesus in his Parable of the Pounds (Luke 19:20). The face of the entombed Jesus was bound (A.V.) or wrapped (R.S.V.) (John 11:44, 20:7) with a napkin (A.V.) or cloth (R.S.V.).

Narcissus (när-cĭs′ŭs). (1) A Roman whose household included Christians to whom Paul sent greetings (Rom. 16:11); possibly a favorite of Emperor Claudius. Narcissus was killed shortly before the Roman letter was written, and his slaves, still identified by his name, had been seized by Nero (cf. "saints of Caesar's household," Phil. 4:22).

(2) A white and yellow flower growing along the Mediterranean plain, sometimes identified with "the rose of Sharon" (Song of Sol. 2:1).

Nash Papyrus, the. See TEXT (1).

Nathan. (1) A son of David, born in Jerusalem (II Sam. 5:14). His family is listed along with that of David, in Zechariah's prophecy of the Day of the Lord (12:12). (See JUDGMENT, DAY OF.) He appears in Luke's genealogy of Jesus (3:31).

(2) Prophet and chaplain at the court of David, and of Solomon in his early years. He rebuked David for his illicit affair with Bath-sheba*, using the famous parable of the one ewe lamb to express his condemnation (II Sam. 12:1–23). Nathan accepted David's repentance, and when Solomon was born of his union with Bath-sheba the prophet named the boy "Jedidiah" ("beloved of Jah," II Sam. 12:25). He first endorsed David's plan to erect a suitable "house" for Yahweh (II Sam. 7:2 f.); then, after a vision from Yahweh, advised the postponement of construction until Solomon's reign (vv. 12 ff.). Nathan participated with Zadok the priest in anointing Solomon king at the Spring Gihon outside Jerusalem (I Kings 1:8–45). He served David and Solomon by revealing the plot of Adonijah (I Kings 1:5 ff.). The influence of his good life is shown by subsequent O.T. passages. He was father of Zabud, the "principal officer, and the king's friend" (I Kings 4:5), and of Azariah, who was over Solomon's officers. His name is mentioned reminiscently in connection with the restoration of Temple music during Hezekiah's reforms (II Chron. 29:25). The Chronicler refers to a "book of Nathan the prophet," in which he apparently recorded events in the life of David (I Chron. 29:29) and of Solomon (II Chron. 9:29). Rabbinic sources make Nathan a nephew of David, reared by Jesse, Nathan's grandfather. Nathan, God-inspired prophet, illustrates the close connection between the prophetic mission, moral and political reforms, and the true religious revival which took place when the Monarchy was consolidated under David and Solomon. He broke new ground spiritually, and lifted the moral tone of Hebrew life during the early Monarchy.

(3) The father of Igal, an officer of David (II Sam. 23:36; cf. I Chron. 11:38). (4) A "chief" man who returned from Exile with Ezra and was appointed to secure ministers for the house of God (Ezra 8:16). (5) One of those who agreed to "put away" their foreign wives (Ezra 10:39). (6) A Judahite, a son of Attai (I Chron. 2:36).

Nathanael ("God has given"), sometimes identified with Bartholomew*.

nations, a term used by Hebrew writers for non-Israelites, outsiders, Gentiles*, heathen. (See Isa. 43:9 ff.; Jer. 1:10 ff.; Ezek. 5:6 ff., *passim;* II Chron. 13:9, 32:23; Ps. 66:7, 96:5, 108:3; Luke 12:30, 24:47; Acts 17:26; Rev. 22:2). The author of Ps. 106:47 voiced Israel's desire to be great among the nations.

Natufian, a Mesolithic culture of Palestine (c. 10,000–8,000 B.C.), concentrated mainly in the central coastal plain and the Judaean hills. First discovered by D. Garrod in the Wâdī en-Natūf, the sequence is best represented at El-Wād (see MUGHÂRAH, WÂDI EL-). Natufians inhabited caves and open-air sites, were keen hunters and fishermen, perhaps cultivated food, and established early permanent settlements. The best example of the latter is 'Einan, on the W. shore of Lake Huleh, excavated by J. Perrot (IEJ 10, 1960, pp. 14 ff.). The dead were often decorated with ornaments of shell and bone, and a naturalistic plastic art was developed. See E. Anati, *Palestine Before the Hebrews*, 1963, pp. 139–178.

Nazarenes, one of the names applied to early Christians (Acts 24:5).

Nazareth, a town in Lower Galilee, situated on the W. slope of a valley running SSW.-NNE. in the southernmost slopes of the Lebanon Mountains just before the ridge drops to the Plain of Esdraelon. From the top of the W. rim of the 1,600-ft.-high basin, on whose slopes the town sits (Luke 4:29), could be observed the military and commercial routes of antiquity, crossing the Esdraelon to the S. Main highways ran E. to the fords of the Jordan and the Decapolis; S. to Samaria, Jerusalem, and Egypt; W. to Acre and the Mediterranean; and N. to Damascus. The town itself was unimportant, as indicated by the silence of the O.T., Josephus, and the Talmud on the subject, as well as by popular opinion at the time of Christ (John 1:46). In N.T. times, it was overshadowed by Sepphoris, the chief city in the area, 4 m. to the NW., just S. of the main road from Ptolemais (see ACCHO) to Tiberias.

286. Nazareth.

Nazareth was the residence of Joseph and Mary (Luke 1:26 f.), whence they journeyed 85 m. S. to Bethlehem for the Roman enrollment (Luke 2:4 f.). Nazareth, with its busy threshing floors and gnarled olive trees, was the childhood home of Jesus (Luke 2:4; Matt. 2:23; Luke 2:51). Here he received the religious training afforded by his home and synagogue (Luke 2:51, 4:16). On the occasion of his baptism he came from Nazareth (Mark 1:9), and returned to it after the Temptation (Matt. 4:12 f.). The violent reaction of its citizens when he returned to preach (Luke 4:28 f.) led him to make his headquarters in Capernaum thereafter (Matt. 4:13). There is no record that Jesus ever revisited Nazareth (Luke 10:10 f.; Mark 6:11), but its name continued to be attached to him by friend and foe (Matt. 21:11; Acts 10:38).

The hill on which Nazareth stands (Luke 4:29) is honeycombed with tombs and ancient caves. Skeletal remains of Middle Palaeolithic man (c. 70,000 B.C.) have been found at nearby Jebel Qafzah cave.

The chief permanent water supply for Nazareth comes from Mary's Fount or Well ('Ain-sitt Miriam), where Nazareth women and their children carrying water jars daily re-enact the scenes in which Mary and Jesus once participated. The Church of the Annunciation, with its "Chapel of the Annunciation" and "Kitchen of the Virgin"; and the "Workshop of Joseph" in the Moslem quarter of the town objectify the traditions of the Nazareth story. (See WATER, illus. 477.)

Nazirites (from Heb. *nāzar*, "to dedicate," *nāzīr*, "one consecrated"), ascetic individuals who expressed their consecration to God by (1) totally abstaining from products of the vine and all intoxicants—possibly an ancient Hebrew protest against the low ideals of Canaanite agriculturists; (2) refusing to cut their hair lest a man-made tool profane this God-given growth; (3) avoiding contact with the dead; and (4) declining unclean (see PURITY) food. Laws governing their ideals are stated in Num. 6:1–21. But long before this code* existed Hebrews were observing such vows. Nazirites who unintentionally violated their vows could be received back into the Nazirite status—they had no "monastic" community—only by observance of extremely complicated rites (Num. 6:9–20). Many took the vows for life; others to insure success in specific undertakings. A mother who, like Samuel's, dedicated her child to the religious way before his birth (though Samuel did not become a Nazirite), assumed the regulations during her pregnancy. This was true also of the mother of Samson (Judg. 13); Samson best illustrates the lifelong Nazirite, in spite of his romantic disaster (Judg. 14–16).

Nazirite vows continued into N.T. times. John* the Baptist was consecrated from his birth (Luke 1:15), but whether he actually adopted Nazirite vows is uncertain. Anna (Luke 2:36) may have been a Nazirite. Acts 21:23–26 suggests that the Nazirite vow may have been taken by Paul, when his friends warned him of the rising storm of opposition to him at Jerusalem. The "vow" (Acts 18:18) completed at Jerusalem (v. 21) was Paul's way of expressing gratitude to God for some unnamed blessing. When the Apostle agreed to finance the expenses connected with the Temple sacrifices of four poor men who were completing their Nazirite vows, he demonstrated his respect for worthy Jewish ascetic customs but failed to win popular Jewish support (Acts 21:20–30).

Neapolis (nē-ăp'ŏ-lĭs). (1) A Roman town (later Nablus) founded by Vespasian near the site of ancient Shechem*. Shechem was long thought to be on the site of Nablus, but it is now known to be Tell Balâtah, 2 m. SE. of Nablus. Nablus today is the home of a small colony of surviving Samaritans. (2) The Roman name for Naples. (3) The port of Philippi*, in Macedonia, and terminus of the great Egnatian Road. Paul landed at Neapolis (Acts 16:11) after crossing the NE. Aegean from Troas to begin his European mission. Its modern name is Kavalla.

Nebaioth (nē-bā'yŏth) (Nebajoth [nē-bā'-jŏth] A.V. Gen. 25:13, 28:9, 36:3), an eponymous ancestor of a N. Arabian clan or tribe, descended from Ishmael (I Chron. 1:29) and rich in cattle, as were their neighbors, the people of Kedar. Both groups are named in the annals of Ashurbanipal, and were perhaps forerunners of the Nabataeans in this area.

Nebat (nē'băt), an Ephraimite of Zeredah (I Kings 11:26), father of Jeroboam* I, King of Israel (c. 922–901 B.C.) (I Kings 12:2, 15:1; II Kings 3:3; II Chron. 9:29, etc.).

Nebī Samwîl, a strategic elevation 2,935 ft. above the Mediterranean, commanding a view of the main N.-S. road to Jerusalem and Bethlehem, and the approaches to Ramleh, Lydda, and Jaffa on the coastal plain, and E. to the highlands of Trans-Jordan.

The traditional site of the tomb of Samuel (Nebī Samwîl, "the prophet Samuel"), 5 m. NW. of Jerusalem, it is thought by some (Albright, *AASOR* 4, 1924, pp. 90 ff.) to be the site of ancient Mizpah. Topographical and archaeological evidence favors identification with Tell en-Nasbeh. The minaret of the mosque on top of Nebī Samwîl is a Palestinian landmark. See MIZPAH.

Nebo (nē′bō) (Khirbet el-Mekhaiyet). (1) A 2,643 ft. mountain of the Abarim Range in the land of Moab* (in the Kingdom of Jordan), described in the O.T. as "over against Jericho" (Deut. 32:49 f.), i.e., across the

287. View from Mt. Nebo, looking westward over the Dead Sea to the Promised Land.

Jordan from it. It is approached from Madeba by a stony track through almost uninhabited, camel-grazing country. To this conspicuous, lonely, stone elevation of which Pisgah was a part (Deut. 34:1) Moses went in obedience to God's advice to look over the Promised Land of Canaan before he died; his grave is somewhere in this majestic high country. Although Nebo is not as high as Jebel 'Osha near the town of Es-Salt, the panoramic view it commands is more extensive, reaching over the Dead Sea from En-gêdi to Bethlehem and Jerusalem, and up the Jordan Valley N. to the Valley of Jezreel, with Mts. Ebal, Gerizim, Gilboa, and Tabor clearly visible. Churches dedicated to Moses in the Byzantine era have been excavated on Mt. Nebo by Father Saller.

(2) A town E. of Jordan given to the Tribe of Reuben for cattle raising (Num. 32:3, 38), captured by Mesha, King of Moab (lines 14 ff. of the Moabite Stone). (3) "Children of Nebo," i.e., of tribes or towns in the Nebo region, returned from Exile with Zerubbabel (Ezra 2:29, 10:43; Neh. 7:33). (4) Nebo (nā′bō), an influential and popular god in the Babylonian city of Borsippa, patron of culture. An effigy of Nebo was carried about on a beast (Isa. 46:1).

Nebuchadnezzar (nĕb′ŭ-kăd-nĕz′ẽr) (Nebuchadrezzar) ("Nebo, defend the border"). (1) Nebuchadnezzar I, a Fourth Dynasty ruler of the Old Babylonian Empire (c. 1128 B.C.).

(2) Nebuchadnezzar II ("the Great"), son of Nabopolassar*, succeeded his Chaldaean father as ruler of the Neo-Babylonian Empire (605–562 B.C.). Nebuchadnezzar was the ablest Babylonian ruler since Hammurabi, the most prominent figure of his day in the land between the rivers and in W. Asia, and an outstanding personality in Oriental history. After his victory at the battle of Carchemish* in Upper Mesopotamia (605 B.C.) against Pharaoh-nechoh of Egypt and the remnant of the Assyrian army, he moved toward the Nile Valley. News of his father's death hastened his return to safeguard his inheritance at Babylon. Following up advantages he had gained after Carchemish, Nebuchadnezzar's Chaldaean forces occupied the small Kingdom of Judah (c. 603 B.C.) and made it a vassal (Dan. 1:1), but allowed its pro-Egyptian King Jehoiakim* to remain as ruler until he rebelled a few years later (II Kings 24:1 ff.). The annals of Nebuchadnezzar do not record his destiny-fraught Palestinian activities; but the Biblical record is rich in details. (See II Kings 24, 25; Jeremiah 9:11, 10:22, and chs. 24–43 *passim;* Lamentations 4:8–10, for information and atmosphere of the last years of the Kingdom of Judah.)

Nebuchadnezzar was responsible for three deportations of the citizens of Judah. (1) In 598 B.C., after Jehoiakim's uprising, he sent marauding bands of Chaldaeans, Aramaeans, Moabites, and Ammonites into Judah "to destroy it" (II Kings 24:2). Jehoiakim was killed in battle, and was succeeded by his 18-year-old son Jehoiachin* (v. 8), who reigned only three months before his deportation to Babylon, along with 10,000 of the flower of the kingdom (vv. 11–16). The Temple treasures were looted for Nebuchadnezzar (v. 13). Nebuchadnezzar appointed Jehoiachin's 21-year-old uncle, Mattaniah (3d son of King Josiah), whom he renamed Zedekiah*, to be puppet king at Jerusalem (vv. 17–19). (2) The rebellion of Zedekiah (II Kings 24:20) precipitated the 1½-year siege and ruthless destruction of Jerusalem and its Temple and the second deportation of its citizens (August 587 B.C.), graphically recorded in II Kings 25. Nebuchadnezzar's captives from Judah and from neighbor nations augmented the population of Babylon while Nebuchadnezzar was still beautifying this brilliant capital. (3) Nebuchadnezzar's final deportation of the people of Judah took place in c. 582 B.C., after the murder of Gedaliah*, Judaean puppet governor (II Kings 25:22). Throughout these terrible times the prophet Jeremiah* remained in Jerusalem, tolerated by the Chaldaean because he had advised his people to submit to the invader, whom he interpreted as God's scourge for their wickedness. He was finally swept into Egypt with fugitives who feared punishment from Nebuchadnezzar for the murder of Gedaliah.

Nebuchadnezzar had so reduced Jerusalem, as well as Lachish and other outposts, that for more than a century it remained what Isaiah called a wilderness of thorns and briars (7:24). After the close of his reign of more than 40 years, and the eventual succession of Nabonidus and Belshazzar (Dan. 5:1 ff.),

Chaldaean power began to weaken before the advance of the Indo-European Medes and Persians.

The unhistoric Book of Daniel* depicts Nebuchadnezzar as a conceited, domineering king, afraid of his own dreams (4:5), who compelled his subjects to bow down before a tremendous image (? of himself), set up in the Plain of Dura, to the accompaniment of a tremendous orchestra (3:1–7).

No inscriptions of Nebuchadnezzar thus far excavated describe his Palestine campaigns. But in the basement of one of his palaces there has been found a clay tablet that mentions the daily rations allotted (probably by Evil-Merodach*, II Kings 25:27) to King Jehoiachin, his five sons, other Judaean captives, and prominent exiles from Egypt, Phoenicia, and Philistia. This humble evidence tallies with II Kings 25:27–30, which tells of the lenient treatment and prestige of Jehoiachin on a throne higher than those of other captive kings in Babylon: "And Jehoiachin did eat bread continually all the days of his life: and for his allowance, there was a continual allowance given him of the king, every day a portion, all the days of his life." (A.S.V.)

Nebuzaradan (nĕb′ū-zär-ā′dăn), the chief bodyguard of Nebuchadnezzar*, dispatched by the Babylonian (Chaldaean) king to Jerusalem (587 B.C.) to direct the destruction of the Temple and palaces and walls (II Kings 25:8–20). This "captain of the guard" deported "the remnant of the multitude" (v. 11), carried off the metal and utensils of the Temple (vv. 13–17), and led the chief priests and officials to Riblah (v. 20), Babylonian headquarters in Syria. Five years later Nebuzaradan deported another group from Judah (Jer. 52:30). To the prophet Jeremiah*, however, who had advised his people to submit to Nebuchadnezzar (whom he viewed as God's scourge for the sins of the people), the officer showed leniency, releasing him from chains and allowing him to choose between Babylon and the homeland. Jeremiah went to Mizpah, temporary capital of Judaea (Jer. 39:11–14, 40:1–6).

Nechoh (nē′kō) (A.S.V. Neco, Necoh), Pharaoh-nechoh II, the son of Psammetichus I (Psamtik), and 2d king of the Twenty-sixth Egyptian Dynasty (609–594 B.C.). Inspired by the fall of the Assyrian capital, Nineveh, in 612 B.C. (as it is now dated from Nabopolassar's annals, British Museum) and spurred to strengthen Egyptian prestige, Nechoh moved up the coastal plain of Palestine in 609, not to seize that land, against which he said he had no grudge (II Chron. 35:21), but to gain territory from disintegrating Assyria and possibly to strengthen the weakened state as a buffer against the rising "new" Babylonian (Chaldaean) Empire. The statement in II Kings 23:29 that he was going up *against* the Assyrian king at the Euphrates is a mistranslation. The R.S.V. translates, properly, that he "went up *to* the king of Assyria to the river Euphrates." Nechoh took Gaza and Ashkelon and came through the Megiddo* Pass onto the Plain of Esdraelon. When the two narratives, II Kings 23:29 f., 33–35 and II Chron. 35:20–24, 36:4 are placed side by side, it appears either that Nechoh called King Josiah* of Judah to an interview at Megiddo and there assassinated him, possibly because he believed the reformer-king might have territorial ambitions of his own, or because Josiah rashly meddled (II Chron. 35:21) in Nechoh's hurried expedition to the Upper Euphrates (v. 20). When his retainers clashed with Nechoh's men, the Egyptian "slew him" (II Kings 23:29) (cf. "the archers shot at King Josiah" II Chron. 35:23). The fatally injured monarch was conveyed by chariot to Jerusalem, while Nechoh pushed north. Nechoh's expedition resulted in the defeat of his forces and a remnant of the Assyrian army by the Babylonians near Haran in 609. Turning his attention after a few months to Riblah and to a consideration of Judah's affairs, he deposed Jehoahaz II (Shallum), whose loyalty he doubted, exiled him to Egypt (II Kings 23:33 f.), and installed Eliakim (whose name Nechoh changed to Jehoiakim*), who ruled Palestine as an Egyptian vassal (609–598 B.C.). Nechoh was disastrously beaten at Carchemish* on the upper Euphrates in 605 B.C. by the Chaldaean crown prince Nebuchadnezzar* of the New Babylonian Empire (cf. Jer. 46). The Chaldaean took everything "from the river of Egypt unto the Euphrates" (II Kings 24:7), so that "the king of Egypt came not again any more out of his land." Nechoh II was succeeded by his son Psamtik II (593–588 B.C.).

necromancy. See MAGIC AND DIVINATION.

needle's eye, used literally in the parable of Jesus concerning the camel (Mark 10:25 and

288. "Needle's eye" or "straight gate" in Hospice of the Russian Palestine Society, next to the Church of the Holy Sepulcher, Jerusalem.

parallels). There is no basis for interpreting the "needle's eye" as the small pedestrian gate of a broad city portal. But some think so.

needlework, embroidery done with linen, wool, or metal threads of various colors on garments of kings and their families (Ps. 45:13 f.), and often on the single set of attire of very poor Near Easterners. The gorgeously dyed apparel of the Canaanite Sisera was "embroidered on both sides" (Judg. 5:30). Fine needlework trimmed the hangings of the Tabernacle (Ex. 26:36, 27:16, 36:37, 38:18). The coats and girdles of the priests were beautifully adorned with fine needlework and woven work (28:39, 39:29). The ornamental pomegranates on the hem of the priest's ephod robe (Ex. 28:33), must have been appliquéd by fine needlework. Babylonian and Persian garments trimmed with appliquéd needlework, as seen in bas-reliefs, were greatly coveted, as by Achan (Josh. 7:20 f.). Babylonian embroidered needlework, which spread to Phrygia, Greece, and the west, may have influenced Israel's priestly apparel (see DRESS). Egyptians also were skilled needleworkers.

neesings, the snorting of the leviathan (? crocodile), Job 41:18.

Negeb (nĕg′ĕb), **the** ("the dry"), the largely waterless district S. of Judaea. Because of its geographical position in relation to Judaea this area became known as "the South." This fact explains many confusing O.T. passages, e.g., Gen. 13:1.

The Negeb consists of the area, square in shape, each side approx. 60 m. long, in the neighborhood of Beer-sheba* and Kadesh-barnea*. By a series of steps or slightly inclined slopes the land drops from the Judaean highlands down to the Arabian Desert. The ridges run E. and W. in such a way as to make a series of natural barriers against

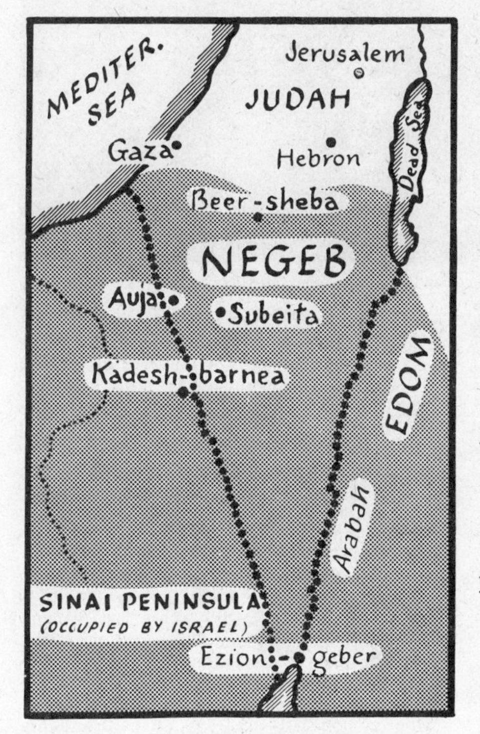

289. Negeb. Shaded portion indicates area in Biblical times; dotted lines show present boundaries.

traffic in a N.–S. direction; a few trade routes crossed it. Armies flowed not through the Negeb but along the highways S. and W. of it. The vegetation is abundant immediately after the winter rainy season (Ps. 126:4), but in summer the land is as barren as the desert itself, except in the wâdīs. By the sinking of wells water is obtainable (Gen. 21:30). Irrigation will increase production, as it did in Nabataean times.

The terrain and the nature of the Negeb were such that Judaea was almost never invaded from the S. through this section. When Israel sought to enter the Promised Land it was repulsed by this formidable barrier and its occupants (Deut. 1:42–46). This rugged section served as the field of operation for David during his life as an outlaw (I Sam. 27:5–10). Among the people associated with the Negeb were the Amalekites* (Num. 13:29; Judg. 6:3; I Sam. 15:1–3), the Kenites*, and the Jerahmeelites (see JERAHMEEL) (I Sam. 27:10). Caleb (Judg. 1:12–15; Josh. 14) and Simeon (Josh. 19:1–9) had claims in the N. Negeb. During the 6th and 5th centuries B.C. the Negeb was occupied by Edomites* (thus began Idumaea, the Gk. name for the new Edom).

Throughout Bible times grazing was the main occupation in the Negeb (Gen. 20:14). Some farming was also done.

Between the 4th and 7th centuries A.D. successful efforts were made to occupy and cultivate the Negeb. Extensive ruins of water systems—reservoirs, cisterns, and dams—and of Christian churches and monasteries, especially at Alusa, Oryba, and Subaita, testify to the extensive civilization current here in this period. During the excavation of the churches at 'Aujā el-Hafîr a mass of papyrus documents written in Gk. and Arab., dating from the 6th and 7th centuries A.D., came to light—the first ever found in Palestine. These documents contain fragments of N.T. Christian legends and business transactions, all in a perfect state of preservation because of the exceeding dryness of the land. Evidently the Negeb was a secluded, out-of-the-world spot which appealed to early Christian ascetics and religious orders until the destruction which attended the Moslem invasion.

The Negeb today is part of the state of Israel. Its geological formation suggests oil, copper, phosphates, manganese, iron, silicon. See *Rivers in the Desert*, Nelson Glueck.

Neginah (nĕ-gē′nä) (pl. *Neginoth*, nĕg′ĭ-nŏth), a word appearing in the titles of Psalms 4, 6, 54, 67, 76, "To the chief Musician on Neginoth." Neginoth are stringed instruments (cf. A.S.V. heading of Ps. 61, "a stringed instrument"). Neginah also means "song," "music."

Nehemiah (nē′hĕ-mī′*ȧ*), a Jew in Susa who amassed a fortune (5:14–18) and attained the influential position of cupbearer (Neh. 1:11b–12:1) to the Persian King Artaxerxes I Longimanus (465–424 B.C.). Our information concerning Nehemiah is confined to his memoirs (Neh. 1:1–7:73), and the last chapters of the book which bears his name (12:27–13:31). Reports reached Nehemiah in 445 B.C. that Jerusalem, his ancestral home, was still in a wretched condition, without the protection of strong city walls and gates. Nehemiah's personal appeal to Artaxerxes resulted in his appointment as Governor of Judaea, with guarantees of safe conduct and letters to the Persian authorities in Syria to provide the materials necessary for the city's reconstruction (2:7–9). Nehemiah made a secret survey of the demolished walls of the city (2:12–16); then, in an assembly of the citizens, secured their co-operation in the task of rebuilding the walls. People in the vicinity (notably Sanballat, 2:19), opposed the undertaking. Jewish papyri discovered at Elephantine in Egypt mention several personalities named in Nehemiah's book—the high priest Johanan (Neh. 12:22), Nehemiah's brother Hanani (7:2), and Sanballat, the governor of Samaria (cf. 2:9). The Samaritan opposition to Nehemiah was based on community jealousies, rival defense programs of two cities, and deep-seated racial conflicts, all of which finally produced the schism of two competing religious groups—the Jews and the Samaritans, both worshipping the same God and obedient to the same divine Law.

290. Nehemiah's ride (2:11–16), re-enacted by a present-day Jerusalem youth.

Nehemiah's evident knowledge of engineering was equaled by his marked organizing ability. Priests, goldsmiths, tradesmen, and apothecaries—as well as those who were familiar with the technical trades (3:15)—were assigned their work on the wall. He tactfully enlisted their self-interest (3:10, 23, 29). Women too joined the laboring squad (3:12). Ridicule (4:1–6), armed opposition (4:7–14), and intrigue (6:1–9) were all unsuccessfully attempted by Sanballat and his allies to halt construction; but Nehemiah had the psychological resources to overcome every attack of his enemies. So great was the patriotic appeal of this project that voluntary workers from such nearby towns as Tekoa, Jericho, Gibeon, and Mizpah left their summer harvests to work on the Jerusalem walls*. The resulting scarcity of farm labor led to food shortages, then to higher living costs, resulting in farm mortgages and the enslaving of children by unscrupulous profiteers. Excessive interest fees were forbidden by the governor (5:1–6). Nehemiah shamed the profiteers into decency by serving himself without compensation (5:6–16). When after 52 days (6:15)—Josephus says 2 years and 4 months—the walls were finished, they were consecrated with as much pomp and ceremony as if they had been the Temple (12:27–47). The Chronicler no doubt embellished his account of this event. Marriage reform (13:23–27); the expulsion of non-Jews from "the congregation of God" (13:1–3); and adherence to the Mosaic Law (8:18), with its festivals (8:17) and Sabbath observance (13:15–18), were all part of Nehemiah's program that involved exclusiveness as the way to strength; isolationism won out over any internationalism the prophets may have advocated.

When Nehemiah returned to Jerusalem after a visit to the Persian king (13:6) he discovered that Eliashib, the priest, because of the housing shortage (7:4), had permitted Tobiah, one of the allies of Sanballat, to occupy the treasury room of the Temple; Nehemiah promptly evicted him (13:4–9). Meanwhile the Temple fees of the priests and Levites were so small that they had been compelled to work in the fields and neglect their Temple tasks. Nehemiah reformed the system of tithes to provide adequate support for the Temple staff (13:10–14). In this narrative the Chronicler may also have exercised his bias for the clergy and taken some liberty with the governor's part in correcting the scandal. But the story is in keeping with the spirit of Nehemiah—a loyal layman; a man of piety, of prayer, and of great faith in God. (See EZRA.)

Several years ago, at the extremity of the Gehenna Valley, archaeologists located the Fountain Gate which Nehemiah noted during his survey and ordered repaired (Neh. 2:14, 3:15, 12:37). (See JERUSALEM, illus. 214.)

nehiloth (nē′hĭ-lōth), wind instruments or pipes; cf. the caption of Ps. 5 (see PSALMS).

Nehushta (nĕ-hŭsh′tȧ), the daughter of Elnathan of Jerusalem and mother of Jehoiachin*. She and her son were carried captive to Babylon in 597 B.C.(II Kings 24:8 f.).

Nehushtan (nĕ-hŭsh′tȧn), the copper or bronze serpent (A.V. "brazen") destroyed during the religious reforms of Hezekiah (II Kings 18:4). See Num. 21:8 f. and John 3:14.

neighbor, one who is near in space or in interests; expressed by several different Heb. words in the O.T.

In nomad society friendliness and neighborliness were essential; tent families lived in such proximity that they had to get along well together or lose all social cohesion. Very early laws, at first unwritten, provided against every contingency that might cause friction. Such laws dealt with false witness (Ex. 20:16; Deut. 5:20); fraud (Lev. 19:13); borrowing and lending (Deut. 15:2); neighbors' landmarks (Deut. 19:14); vineyards and grain fields (23:24 f.); harsh judgments (Lev. 19:15; cf. Matt. 7:1–5); and adultery (Lev. 20:10). It was considered disgraceful to hire a neighbor without paying him current wages (Jer. 22:13). The last of the Ten Commandments, which deals with coveting a neighbor's possessions, is the climax of the four preceding ones (Ex. 20:13–17).

Wisdom literature dealt with the quality of neighborliness (Ps. 28:3; Prov. 3:28). Prophets deepened the idea of helpfulness (Isa. 41:6; Jer. 31:34). The concept of the neighbor rose to a climax in Christ's great commandment, "Thou shalt love thy neighbor as thyself" (Matt. 19:19; Lev. 19:18), and in his Parable of the Good Samaritan (Luke 10:36 f.). Paul preached that the type of love which "worketh no ill to a neighbor" is "the fulfilling of the law" (Rom. 13:9 f.).

Scripture illustrates neighborliness at work. In Bethlehem neighbor women gave the name "Obed" to the child of Boaz and Ruth (Ruth 4:17). The woman who lost and found a coin called in her neighbors to rejoice with her (Luke 15:9), as did the shepherd who had found his sheep (v. 6). Rich neighbors, who would repay hospitality, were not considered ideal guests by Jesus (Luke 14:12), in certain Apocalyptic writings "neighbor" means a fellow Israelite; and in canonical literature such merely geographical neighbors as Egyptians and Assyrians are spoken of disparagingly (Ezek. 16:26, 23:5, 12). But a Christian neighbor may live across the world yet be at one's side spiritually. "Better is a neighbor that is near than a brother far off" (Prov. 27:10).

Neolithic, the Late or New Stone Age, dating in the Near East c. 8000–4000 B.C. Characterized by the initial domestication of plants and animals, and the earliest use of pottery. See *CAH*³, Vol. I, 1970, chap. IXb.

Nephilim (nĕf′ĭ-lĭm), the giant demigods borne by daughters of men to "the sons of God" mentioned in a very ancient fragment (A.S.V. Gen. 6:4) unaltered by later editors, probably preserved from a longer story. Israel's spies to Canaan (A.S.V. Num. 13:33) reported that the stalwart occupants of the land appeared like "the Nephilim."

Nephtoah (nĕf-tō′ȧ), a town c. 2 m. NW. of Jerusalem, a short distance E. of Emmaus, and SW. of Gibeah. Its fountain marked a border between Judah and Benjamin (Josh. 15:9, 18:15). Its modern name is Liftā.

Ner (nûr), a Benjamite, son of Abiel, frequently identified as the father of Abner (I Sam. 14:51; II Sam. 2:8, 12, 3:23, 25, 28, 37; I Kings 2:5, 32; I Chron. 26:28). Varying texts confuse the relationship of Ner to Saul: "uncle" (I Sam. 14:50), or grandfather if Ner was the father of Kish* (I Chron. 8:33, 9:35 f.).

Nereus (nē′rūs), a Christian at Rome who, with his sister, was greeted by Paul (Rom. 16:15).

Nergal-sharezer (nûr′găl-shȧ-rē′zẽr) (Nergal-shar-usur) (meaning "Nergal preserve the king"), King of Babylon 560–556 B.C., the "Rab-mag" present with other high officials at the capture of Jerusalem (587 B.C.) (Jer. 39:3, 13), one of the officers who released Jeremiah* from prison (v. 14). His high rank is stated on a cuneiform tablet excavated at Erech; he was popularly known in Babylon as Neriglissar. He succeeded to the throne of the New Babylonian Empire after slaying his tolerant brother-in-law, Amel-Marduk (the Evil-Merodach of II Kings 25:27). After reigning four years he was followed by his young son, Labashi-Marduk, who was killed by a conspiracy of Babylonian nobles, one of whom, Nabunaid (Nabonidus), came to the throne as the last ruler of New Babylonia (556–539 B.C.).

The first part of his name is that of the Babylonian god, Nergal, variously described as the god of storm, war, pestilence, hunting, or the sun.

Neri (nē′rī), an ancestor of Jesus (Luke 3:27).

Neriglissar. See NERGAL-SHAREZAR.

Nero (Nero Claudius Caesar Augustus Germanicus), Roman emperor, b. A.D. 37, ruled 54–68. He is not mentioned by name in the N.T., but was the "Caesar" to whom Paul appealed at Caesarea (Acts 25:11) after being tried before Nero's Palestinian procurators, Felix (A.D. 52–60) (Acts 21:27–24:27), and Porcius Festus (60–62) (Acts 25:1–12). Paul's Roman imprisonment fell within Nero's reign, and he received his death sentence (c. 64/5) from deputies of this emperor. The great fire at Rome, for which Christians were blamed and tortured by Nero, occurred in July of A.D. 64. Nero was the "Caesar" from whose household its Christian members sent greetings in Paul's Epistle to the Philippians* (Phil. 4:22). The A.V. appends to the last verse of II Timothy, "The second epistle unto Timotheus, ordained the first bishop of the church of the Ephesians, was written from Rome, when Paul was brought before Nero the second time."

Nero, the nephew of Caligula and adopted son of the Emperor Claudius, was greatly influenced by his mother Agrippina, whom he tried to do away with by drowning and later had assassinated. He was tutored by the Roman philosopher Seneca, whom he ultimately had murdered. Nero was a patron of the arts, and a contestant in the historic games of Greece, and his inconsistent traits were ridiculed in secret. He increased the extent of his Palestinian holdings, administered for him by Herod Agrippa II, by annexing towns in Galilee and Peraea. Events of his reign include the beginning of the Corinthian Canal across the Isthmus (A.D. c. 67) and the rebuilding of a large part of Rome, including his "golden house," for which even Achaia* and Asia were taxed. He saw the beginning of the Jewish revolts against the Roman Empire which led to the siege of Jerusalem by Titus (A.D. 70). After Nero's career of intrigue, debauchery, and corrupt administration, which precipitated serious revolts in his provinces, the Senate proclaimed Galba emperor and sentenced Nero to death. He fled to the villa of a freedman 4 m. from Rome and committed suicide June 9, A.D. 68. His sporadic persecution of Christians (widespread tortures came later, under Domitian) were consistent with his other evil deeds. He was regarded by many early Christians as the Antichrist, Satan-slain, but due to return to life (Rev. 13:4, 5, 7). Some see in the cryptic number "666" a symbol of Nero (Rev. 13:18).

291. Nero.

nests, used literally in Scripture, reflect the interest of the Biblical Hebrews in natural history: the eagle stirring up her old nest (Deut. 32:11); building it in high places, "among stars" (Jer. 49:16; Job 39:27; Obad. 4); doves building nests on the "sides of the hole's mouth" (Jer. 48:28); nests of the great owl and vulture on deserted sites (Isa. 34:15); of swallows on altars (Ps. 84:3); nests from which birds are lost like people from their homes (Prov. 27:8; Isa. 16:2). Deuteronomic law forbade taking a setting hen from her nest (Deut. 22:6).

Nests are sometimes used metaphorically: Num. 24:21; Job 29:18. Assyria gathered riches as a hand gathers eggs from a nest (Isa. 10:14); the people of Lebanon make their nests in the cedars (Jer. 22:23); the covetous man strives to set his nest on high (Hab. 2:9). Jesus contrasted his homelessness with the snugness of the bird in its nest (Matt. 8:20; Luke 9:58).

Nethaneel (nē̆-thăn′ĕl) (A.S.V. Nethanel, which is derived from Gk. *Nathanaēl*), borne by ten men in post-Exilic O.T. passages: (1) The son of Zuar, a captain of the Tribe of Issachar (Num. 1:8; 2:5); (2) the fourth son of Jesse, and brother of David (I Chron. 2:14); (3) a priest who blew the trumpet before the Ark (I Chron. 15:24); (4) a Levite, father of Shemaiah (I Chron. 24:6); (5) the fifth son of Obed-edom, a member of the Temple organization (I Chron. 26:4); (6) a prince of Judah in the reign of Jehoshaphat (873–849 B.C.) (II Chron. 17:7); (7) a Levite who gave generous supplies to the Passover celebration (II Chron. 35:9); (8) a "son of Pashur" who had taken a foreign wife (Ezra 10:22); (9) a priest (Neh. 12:21); and (10) a musician who played at the dedication of the repaired Jerusalem wall (Neh. 12:36).

Nethaniah (nĕth′ȧ-nī′ȧ). (1) A prominent Temple musician (I Chron. 25:2, 12). (2) The princely father of the Ishmael who, with his confederates, killed Gedaliah and his associates at Mizpah (II Kings 25:23, 25; Jer. 40:8–16). (3) A Levite sent to teach in the cities of Judah (II Chron. 17:8). (4) The father of Jehudi (Jer. 36:14).

Nethinim (nĕth′ĭ-nĭm) ("the given ones"), a group of persons given or appointed to perform menial tasks in the Temple* service, as early as the time of David (Ezra 8:20). As in neighbor nations, these men were probably slaves or war captives who took over from the priests such distasteful chores as carrying water and wood, removing waste, and cleaning sacred utensils. After the Exile, when separation from the Temple had removed their stigma of lowly service, they were first called "Nethinim" and were usually listed with priests, Levites, singers, and porters (Ezra 2:70). Some may have returned with Zerubbabel (Ezra 2:43–58). Nethinim accompanied Ezra to Jerusalem (7:7). Some of them lived in the city, in their own quarters on the Hill Ophel*, S. of the Temple precinct, adjacent to the Water Gate which gave access to the Spring Gihon (Neh. 3:26, 31, cf. Neh. 11:21). They shared in rebuilding the city wall, were on the committee to get "ministers for the house of our God" (Ezra 8:17), and were exempt from taxes and tribute (7:24). They were among those who joined the new covenant with God (Neh. 10:28 ff.). Their foreign background, suggested by the names of several individual Nethinim, was by this time forgotten. They appear to have been included now with Levites as Temple servants (cf. I Chron. 23:28).

Netophah (nē̂-tō′fȧ), a village in the central hill country of Judah, near Bethlehem (I Chron. 2:54; Ezra 2:22; Neh. 7:26). It was the home of two of David's hardy heroes (II Sam. 23:28 f.). Netophathites were loyal to Gedaliah, vassal governor of Jerusalem under Nebuchadnezzar's occupation (II Kings 25:23; Jer. 40:8 ff.). Some citizens returned to Netophah after the Exile. Several Levites and singers were given homes there (I Chron. 9:16; Neh. 12:28). A possible identification is with Khirbet Bedd Fālûh, a heap of ruins 3½ m. SE. of Bethlehem in the vicinity of the Herodium. A spring in the area, 'Ain en-Naṭūf, may preserve the ancient name.

nets. See FISH.

nettle, any of several thorny plants infesting the desert places of Palestine and vicinity (Job 30:7; Prov. 24:31; Isa. 34:13; Hos. 9:6; Zeph. 2:9).

new birth. See CONVERSION.

new moon. See FEASTS; MOON.

New Testament (or Covenant), the collection of writings which form the second, briefer, and later-written portion of the Christian Bible. It contains accounts of the life and works of Jesus Christ, the beginnings of the Church, and the roots of Christian theology and ethics. The word "Testament" comes from the Lat. *testamentum;* it renders the Gk. *diathēkē*, which means "testament," as in A.S.V. and R.S.V. Matt. 26:28; Luke 1:72; Acts 7:8. The covenant was the divinely initiated entering of God into the destiny of man for his spiritual development.

The N.T. is less than 1/3 as long as the O.T. It was written within about one century, most of it within two generations; the process of writing the O.T. covered a period in excess of 1,000 years. The N.T. consists of 27 short books by an inexactly known number of authors having different temperaments, backgrounds, outlook, and objectives. These writers, who had no opportunity of sitting down together for conference, as do modern revision committees, achieved a remarkable basic unity, which springs from the centrality of the story of Christ, the good news of the Gospel*, which gave the N.T. writers a framework; and from a sense that they had received the Holy Spirit, which carried them forward with their earnest task. None of them wrote with any feeling that they were having a share in preparing what became "The Holy Scriptures." They certainly did not anticipate that their thoughts would be spread throughout the world for centuries in written form. Their ambition was to transmit the facts about Christ's life, teachings, redemptive death, and Resurrection which would assist believers in their worship and their daily life. They crystallized what oral instructors had helped new converts to memorize. No other message has been read by as many people in as many tongues, over as long a period of time, as this "literature of a mission."

The N.T. writings were addressed to people living under different conditions in scattered parts of the Roman Mediterranean world, the people who formed the first little cells of *ekklēsia* from which the Christian Church developed. Many scholars, including Goodspeed, believe that the first group of collected writings these N.T. Christians received was probably Paul's Letters, gathered at Ephesus (after Luke-Acts was in circulation), and possibly with the Letter to the Ephesians as an introduction.

Many members of the first Christian Church were Jews of different nationalities, who brought to their energized faith a reverent regard for the O.T., in which they found prophecies of the long-anticipated Messiah*. Jesus and Peter both evidenced their appreciation of the O.T. by their spoken use of it. For a number of years after the Resurrection of Jesus, Christians and Jews shared the O.T. as their only Bible. Christians were alert to find new light on the book which had led their fathers into paths of righteousness. So much of the O.T. worked its way into the N.T. that many Jews today consider the N.T. part of the literature of Judaism, in spite of its unfavorable reports on the Jews in portions of John, Acts, and the Epistles, which set forth a new religion that had become detached from and opposed to Judaism.

N.T. writers and readers were not primarily men of letters. They eagerly awaited the Parousia* and the end of the world they knew; new literature would not be important, except as it ministered to the new life in Christ. When the return of Jesus did not come as expected (I Thess. 3:13, 5:8), and there were heresies to be fought and controversies to be settled, a demand arose for Christian literature (Luke 1:1–4).

The rapidly growing Christian communities could not all be reached by the few Apostolic missionaries and teachers (Acts 8:30). New converts needed information about Jesus, counsel for conduct, and guidance in formulating beliefs. They felt themselves a part of a new age, and they were not

292. New Testament: Sinai Greek Manuscript #213 photographed by the International New Testament Manuscripts Project, 1951. This folio, which shows a portion of the Lectionary of the Gospels written in uncials, A.D. 967, is the illuminated headpiece and the beginning of the Easter reading (John 1:1-18).

ready for it. Hence the authors of what became the N.T. wrote what they knew of the "signs that Jesus showed," so that people might "believe that Jesus is the Christ, the Son of God, and that believing . . . have life in his name" (R.S.V. John 20:30 f.). N.T. writers were evangelists, apologists, and missionaries before they were authors. The N.T. did not shape the early Church; on the other hand, it was made by the Church. It still is "the church's book" (F. C. Grant).

Even before the earliest N.T. Epistles* had been written (I and II Thessalonians, c. A.D. 50, and Galatians 51 or 49), or the basic Gospel of Mark reduced to writing (c. 65–67), there existed written matter, since lost, dealing with Jesus and his sayings (Luke 1:1) including Q* (*Quelle*) and other material.

Yet in the main Christ's "good news" (Gospel) remained oral for probably 20 years after his death. Had those who were with him in his brief earthly ministry been able to preserve a complete contemporary record of their observations of him, no book as brief as the N.T. would have contained their notes (John 21:25); nor would the problems of scholarship have been so acute.

Scholars have been greatly interested in analyzing the Gk. used in the N.T. They recognized the difference between it and the Gk. of authors like Plato or Sophocles, and attributed the divergence to the fact that the N.T. writers were unlettered men, using the vernacular koine or Greek employed by uneducated men throughout the Greek-speaking or Hellenistic world. This now appears not to have been the true explanation of the divergence between N.T. Gk. and the classical form. Strong Heb. and Aram. influences are seen in the "strange" N.T. Gk. These may explain the apparent Semiticisms in the N.T., as W. F. Albright points out in *The Archaeology of Palestine*, p. 199. Many scholars, however, cannot go as far as C. C. Torrey and C. F. Burney, who believe that much of the Gospels and Acts had first been written in Aram. and translated into Gk.; there is no evidence of an Aramaic-reading public, nor of other contemporary Aram. literature. It becomes increasingly likely that the Aramaicisms of the Gospels crept in through the translation into Gk. of orally transmitted Aram. records of the words and doings of Jesus. This viewpoint harmonizes with the well-known fact that the rabbis, as well as the earliest Christian teachers, handed down their teachings by word of mouth. Thus, as Albright observes, devotees of the N.T. need not fear that serious errors have taken place in translating from Aram. texts to the Gk. of the N.T. The Gospel traditions were crystallized in Aramaic-speaking communities in Palestine, and were not written down in Gk. until the revolt of A.D. 66–70 against Rome had widely dispersed (see DISPERSION) the Jewish Christians of Palestine and thus broken the chain of oral tradition which had tied Jesus to the Apostolic circles by means of first-hand narrations of his deeds and words as witnessed by his disciples.

At this point a word should be said concerning "form history" (*Formgeschichte*). "Form criticism" is the study of how oral tradition developed and was used in the early Church. Martin Dibelius, probably the best known proponent of form criticism, attempted (from 1919) to recover the units of the oral tradition which circulated before the Gospels were written. He believed that narratives about the person of Jesus and the accounts of his parables, miracles, and teachings, took on in many instances a community cast and received an emphasis designed for immediate community use (cf. I Cor. 1:23, 9:14; Matt. 18:18). Sometimes the oral utterances were given a Judaistic or a Hellenistic setting. Such study as that of Dibelius has brought out the rugged, racy Aramaicisms which reveal a Jesus who is forceful, poetic, and Godlike. Form criticism reveals what it believes to be the basic historic core of the N.T., and shows the part played by the community in preserving the original saying or incident handed down in the written N.T. The N.T. is the child of the Church; Jesus of Nazareth is the life of that child.

Form criticism classified five types or forms of oral tradition: paradigms, parables, sayings, miracle tales, and legends. These forms had been preserved by the memorizing by new converts of events in Christ's life and of the elements of his teaching, culminating in his Resurrection.

But even those scholars who agree with the form critics in stressing the practical role played by the Gospels in the life of the early Church—which may account for the survival of some traditions and the deletion of others—cannot ignore the archaeological data which speak against the radical utterances of Dibelius and the extreme views of some of his followers. Form criticism has been especially aimed at the Gospel of John, which has been said to contain virtually no historical matter and only the views of Christians in the early 2d century who were tinged by gnosticism*. Some authorities favor dating John's Gospel between A.D. 70 and 80 (but cf. F. C. Grant's dates below and see also JOHN, p. 345). W. F. Albright finds internal evidence—including local color reflecting events prior to A.D. 70—that the traditions embodied in John were put into practically their present form before A.D. 66–70 (*The Archaeology of Palestine*, pp. 243 f., Penguin Books).

Although the ministry of Jesus has been estimated as covering as much as 550 days, the days identifiable by specific events narrated in Mark account for only 23; and the pages of this Gospel make up only 23 of a printed N.T. whose total contents run to 288 pages.

The N.T. may be outlined as follows:

(1) *Historical*—

(a) The four Gospels ("good news"), containing four records of the life, sayings, works, and redemptive Resurrection of Jesus. The first three Gospels are synoptic (see SYNOPTIC PROBLEM), i.e., when taken together, they present a complementary life of Christ's experience on earth. The Synoptists, drawing part of their material from the "basic" Gospel of Mark (most probably the earliest of the four), deal chiefly with the Galilean ministry of Jesus, using material seldom paralleled in John. They are compiled around a Petrine nucleus. None of them gives a complete list of events in the life of Jesus. The Fourth Gospel, the latest written—possibly as late as A.D. 95–125—uses a very different viewpoint, stressing the metaphysical and mystical concepts growing out of the Hellenistic philosophy of the logos or Word of God (John 1:1–18) which made its impact on the profoundly reverent Hebrew spirit in "a great epic of the salvation of man." It is the viewpoint of a single Apostle rather than the tradition of the Apostolic Church. John is interested chiefly in the Judaean ministry of Jesus, and tells of five visits to Jerusalem in contrast to possibly only one in the Synoptics. John is less concerned with events than with the teachings of Jesus; he is interpretive.

(b) The Acts contains our only vivid history of the beginnings of the Christian Church, with easily identified locales which tie into secular history. It is accredited to Luke, author of the Third Gospel. It supplies a framework in which N.T. Letters can be fitted.

(2) *Doctrinal*—

Twenty-one Epistles or Letters to churches and individuals, written by several authors over a period of almost 100 years. The General Epistles follow Paul's Epistles and Hebrews.

(3) *Apocalyptic:* The Revelation of John—

There is a variety of opinions among scholars concerning the dates when the N.T. books were written; and individual scholars change their dates as new evidence is found. F. C. Grant, believing that the N.T. books developed in groups, suggests the following chronological arrangement (*The Growth of the Gospels*, pp. 34 f., Abingdon-Cokesbury Press; by permission), but he states that the dates are uncertain or approximate. (See also another chronology of N.T. books under CHRONOLOGY; also dates suggested in articles on the individual books of the N.T.)

(1) *The Pauline Epistles*—A.D. 50–51: I and II Thessalonians; Galatians. A.D. 55–56: I and II Corinthians; Romans. A.D. 59–61: Philippians; Philemon; Colossians; (? Ephesians).

(2) *Early Christian Apocalyptic*—A.D. 65–66: Letters to the Seven Churches (Rev. 1–3); Little Apocalypse (Mark 13).

(3) *Synoptic Gospels and Acts*—A.D. 68: Gospel of Mark. A.D. 85: Gospel of Luke. A.D. 95: Book of Acts. A.D. 95–112: Gospel of Matthew.

(4) *Pastoral Epistles*—A.D. 95–112: I and II Timothy; Titus.

(5) *Apocalypse of John*—A.D. 95.

(6) "*Catholic Apostolic*" *Group*—A.D. 95: Hebrews; I Peter; Jude; James.

(7) *Asiatic*—A.D. 100–125: I, II, III John; Gospel of John.

(8) *Apocryphal, based on Jude*—A.D. 150: II Peter.

In most present versions of the N.T. the books are not printed in the order in which they were written. But the present arrangement is preferable, because it gives the reader consecutive narrative from the birth of Jesus to the foundation of the first groups of the People of the Way, and ends with the Apocalyptic hope of a perfect and eternal society in which the "Lord God and the Lamb" are central and spiritual joys are unending (Rev. 21:23).

So-called "criticism" (more accurately "examination") has done service to students of the N.T. by putting personalities and events in their proper historical perspective; by attempting to determine which of the several strands making up the narratives are the most trustworthy; and by making it clear that the writings as we now read them are in part based on earlier, brief documents. Modern criticism has not decreased the prestige or sacredness of the N.T., but has increased our understanding of the historic Christ and of the continuing revelation of religious truth.

Most scholars today accept the following as Pauline: I and II Thessalonians, Galatians, I and II Corinthians, Romans, Philippians, Colossians, and Philemon. Many accept, others reject, a Pauline hand for Ephesians. Some still debate the authorship of II Thessalonians, believing it to have been written under a pseudonym for Paul as much as a generation or more after his death, to explain why the promised return of Christ to earth had not come. But other excellent scholarship views this letter as written by Paul to encourage those who had vainly watched for the Parousia. Textual criticism has stressed the anonymous authorship of many N.T. books. For example, thoughtful students do not usually view the total Gospel of Matthew, as now printed, as having been written by Matthew. Many surrender, though reluctantly, Pauline authorship of I and II Timothy and Titus. Some view II Peter as the last written book of the N.T. (some making it as late as 150 or 175); others place the letters to Timothy and Titus after II Peter by 10 to 15 years.

The N.T. represents a larger body of Christian literature written before the 4th century, when, after long controversy, the present Canon* was adopted; its inclusions are satisfactory to most Christian readers. Some of the rejected writings are found in the N.T. Apocrypha*, which contain information concerning the N.T. era and clues about lost Christian literature.

One of the tasks of N.T. scholars is to reconstruct the text of the N.T. Unfortunately, no complete manuscript of a single N.T. book survives. The fact that they were written on perishable papyrus* has made their preservation less likely than the preservation of the O.T. messages written on skins. Yet papyrus fragments dating from the 3d and 4th centuries have turned up in Egypt (see TEXT). In 1935 fragments of what may be a 2d century writing were found, containing evidences of the author's acquaintance with the Gospel of John, and possibly with the Synoptics. Yet, as Albright points out (*The Archaeology of Palestine*, p. 238) many more very early manuscripts of the N.T. survive than those of any classical writers; in fact the oldest considerable remains now known date from only about two centuries after their original composition. Startling new manuscript finds may be made at any moment; while scholars equipped with modern photographic equipment are working inside the ancient monasteries of the Near East, recording treasures long neglected, and others are investigating the sites of Christian beginnings not yet touched by spade and mattock.

The modern science of Biblical archaeology has placed an incalculable wealth of material at the disposal of N.T. students desirous of visualizing the scenes where the events of the N.T. took place, and the social backgrounds of the men and women who people its pages. Years of brilliant excavation at Corinth, for example, enable the readers of Acts and the Corinthian Letters to know that they can visit the site of the judgment seat before which Paul was haled (Acts 18:12), and walk the Lechaeum Road he knew and on which the synagogue may have faced (vv. 7 f.). Remains of the great Syrian Antioch breathe a new life since they were freed from the layers of the forgotten past. All the cities where Paul and his helpers worked in Asia Minor are known to Turkish and foreign archaeologists; and American, British, French, and Palestinian scholars now know all the N.T. sites of Palestine and the principal roads by which N.T. Christians reached their destinations. They read Herodian masonry as readers do a book. They have discovered that Bethlehem is the birthplace of important prehistory. And their tasks of exploration have only begun.

New Year Festival (Heb. *Rosh Hashanah*, *rōsh*, "head of," *hash-shānāh*, "the year," "the beginning of the New Year"), listed in the Holiness Code (Lev. 23:23–25) as a time when trumpets were to be blown (whence its alternate name, "The Feast of Trumpets"), servile work to be halted, and a holy convocation called (cf. Num. 29:1–6). In pre-Exilic times the Hebrews celebrated the New Year in the autumn, at the close of the old and the beginning of the new harvest, on the 10th (later the 1st) day of the 7th or Sabbatical month Tishri (Sept.-Oct.). During the Babylonian Exile the Jews adopted the date of the great Babylonian New Year celebration in the spring, the first of Nisan (March-April) but also celebrated the old autumn festival. Ezekiel*, in his restoration program (chaps. 40–48), in which the Temple was the supreme agency of the expiation of sins, stressed the bringing of sin offerings on the two New Year days, as well as on the Passover. The Tishri celebration gained solemnity when it was remembered that Jews who returned from Exile brought offerings to the newly erected altar on the 1st of Tishri, and on that date Ezra made an impressive reading of the Torah to the people.

Down the centuries the Jewish New Year retained its emphasis on atonement*, and on the moral quickening which it had stressed in early times. The festival evolved into a solemn introduction to the Day of Atonement* (Yom Kippur), and was the 1st of the "Ten Days of Penitence." It is observed today on the 1st and 2d days of Tishri. The Scripture read in synagogues on New Year's includes Gen. 21 and 22; Num. 29:1–6; I Sam. 1:1–2:10; Jer. 31:2–20.

During the Exile the Jews at Babylon witnessed the elaborate 7-day celebrations of the Babylonian New Year, which had been developing since the 3d millennium B.C. These celebrations included gala festivities when the Babylonian epic of the Creation was retold, and a mock battle staged between Marduk, impersonated by the king, and Kingu, chief of the host of Tiâmat. Then the king buried a lamb in which the latter god was thought to reside. Farmers of the fertile lowlands of Babylonia believed that conscientious observance of the New Year Festival would contribute to the success of crops. Second Isaiah, the great prophet of the Exile, witnessed these celebrations and commented on the Babylonians' futile efforts to bring new life back to the world by carrying idols of the gods Bel and Nebo on the backs of beasts (Isa. 46:1), So important were the Babylonian New Year celebrations that travelers would not think of leaving the capital until the great festival had ended. Not even the Jew Nehemiah, cupbearer to Artaxerxes, would have been likely to start for his authorized trip to Jerusalem until after the New Year. His sad countenance during his functioning at Artaxerxes' court in the gala month of Nisan (Neh. 2:1 ff.) led the monarch to inquire about his depression and authorize his journey (445 B.C.).

Nicanor (nī-kā′nôr). (1) A general of Antiochus Epiphanes, defeated in the war against the Maccabees (I Macc. 3:38, 7:26–32). (2) A deacon in the early Christian Church, one of the seven selected to administer relief to the poor, including Greek widows (Acts 6:1, 5).

(3) The name given in the Mishnaic tractate *Middôth* to an important gate in Herod's Temple area. Apparently it led by an impressive flight of 15 curved steps from the Women's Court to the Inner Court. At the Nicanor Gate offerings were made after cleansings. It is said that side chambers of the gate provided storage space for curtains, thin cakes used in sacrifices, and equipment of the vestment keeper. The Nicanor Gate may have been trimmed with Corinthian brass or copper. Perhaps singers chanted on its steps. (See HEROD, illus. 181.)

Nicodemus (nĭk′ō-dē′mŭs), a Pharisee, a ruler of the Jews (John 3:1), a member of the Sanhedrin* (7:50), and probably a very rich man (19:39). He paid a timid night visit to Jesus (John 3:2, 19:39); he undertook a cautious legalistic defense of Jesus against the Pharisees (7:45–52); and he played a secondary role in the entombment of the body of Jesus (19:38 f.). The conversations of Jesus and Nicodemus reflect Nicodemus's intellectual conservatism (3:4, 9 f.). Yet Nicodemus displays throughout a real interest in and concern for Jesus, in the face of the unanimous hostility of his Pharisee colleagues, which suggests a virtual discipleship within his heart.

Legends without Biblical foundation tell that Nicodemus was baptized by Peter and John, and banished from Jerusalem during the Jewish uprising against Stephen. The Apocryphal Gospel of Nicodemus dates from the 13th century A.D.

Nicolaitans (nĭk′ō-lā′ĭ-tănz), a sect in the churches of Ephesus and Pergamum. They are censured in Rev. 2:6, 14, 15. At Pergamum they are associated with those who taught Christians "to eat things sacrificed to idols, and to commit fornication." Their antinomian teachings are similar to those rebuked by Jude and I John.

Nicolas (nĭk′ō-lăs) (R.S.V. Nicolaus, nĭk′-ō-lā′ŭs) ("victor over the people"), a non-Jewish proselyte at Antioch, selected as one of the seven deacons (Acts 6:5) appointed to administer relief to the Christian poor, including Greek widows (v. 1) (cf. NICANOR).

Nicopolis (nĭ-kŏp′ō-lĭs) ("city of victory"), a Roman town in the Epirus region of NW. Greece on the Ambracian Gulf, 4 m. N. of Preveza; established by Caesar Augustus (31 B.C.) on the site of his camp before the Battle of Actium. The Actian Games celebrated there attracted many visitors. Paul considered Nicopolis so important that he remained there an entire winter (Tit. 3:12). Its extensive ruins include Herodian structures. The subscription of Titus in the Textus Receptus (see TEXT, VERSIONS) arose from a misconception of Tit. 3:12.

Niger (nī′jẽr), the 2d name of Simeon, prominent among the prophets and teachers in the early Church at Antioch (Acts 13:1).

night. See TIME.

nighthawk, an "unclean" bird, unfit to eat; possibly an owl (Lev. 11:16; Deut. 14:15).

Nile (Heb. *Yeor*, whose plural, as in Isa. 7:18, refers to the Nile system; known to ancient Egyptians as *H'p* or *Hapi;* to Romans, translating from Gk., known as *Nilus*, surviving in the Arab. *En-Nil;* known to modern Egyptians as *El-Bahr*, "the sea," cf. Nah. 3:8, "the sea"), the approx. 4050-m.-long river which caused the realm of the pharaohs to be known as "the Empire of the Nile," the world's 2d longest river. In Scripture it is referred to as "the river": the mother of Moses laid the child in a papyrus boat by "the river's brink" (Ex. 2:3); on the eve of Israel's departure from the Nile Valley "the waters that were in the river turned to blood. And the fish that was in the river died" (7:20 f.). Isaiah alluded to the Nile when he mentioned "paper reeds by the brooks" (A.V. 19:7), and Sihor, "the river" (23:3; cf. Zech. 10:11). Jeremiah spoke of Egypt* rising up as a flood (the Nile) whose waters (? irrigating canals) "are moved as the rivers" (46:7 f.). Goshen was the portion of the NE. Delta nearest Palestine. Here Abraham fled to avoid famine (Gen. 12:10–13:1), and here the Jacob tribes settled during their famine Sojourn* (Gen. 46:3–50:26). For the construction of store cities (e.g., Pithom and Raamses) the labor of Hebrew slaves was forced by taskmasters (Ex. 1:11). To the security of Egypt Joseph led Mary and Jesus when threatened at Bethlehem by Herod (Matt. 2:13, 19, 21).

The Nile, unlike the rushing Jordan, is navigable at high water for 2,900 m. inland from the Mediterranean in a N.-S. direction, and for 4,000 m. by small barges and pleasure craft. Its two branches, the White and the Blue Nile, flow from the lakes of equatorial Africa and the mountains of Abyssinia; their confluence is at Khartoum. The Delta is flat. The valley is closely bordered for miles by arid deserts, and in the S. is confined by 1,000-ft. cliffs. Hecataeus, quoted by Herodotus, called Egypt "the gift of the Nile." A modern has described the Nile as " a tremendous garden hose, with its tap at Lake Victoria and its nozzle in the Delta." The fertility of the valley depends on the rich silt washed down from the vast area of NE. Africa and deposited by flood waters on the fields of Egypt. It is easy to see why the Nile Valley and its marginal desert highlands have been occupied continuously since the beginning of the Pleistocene geological period approximately a million years ago. Pleistocene fossils have been found near Cairo, as well as evidences of many later cultures.

In the third millennium many of the city-states that featured Near Eastern society in the era were located on the Nile. On the

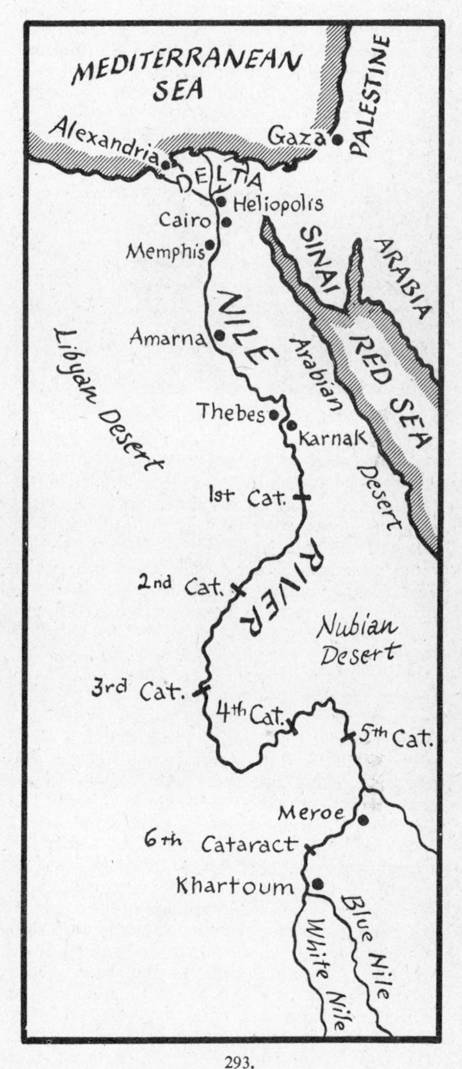

293.

shores, sometimes on both banks of the river, the valley supported a chain of great cities whose monumental remains are architectural wonders of the world—Heliopolis (see ON), Memphis*, Amarna*, Thebes (see NO), etc. The cities were centers of the several districts of Egypt, located "end to end" down the Nile Valley.

Of the seven mouths of the Nile at the Delta in ancient times the most important were the Pelusiac or eastern, nearest Canaan, and therefore most familiar to Palestinians; and the Canopic, or western, used for trade with Greece, the Mediterranean islands, and later with Phoenicia, to and from whose Byblos port sailed some of the first commercial craft of the Great Sea. The guarding of the mouths of the Nile occupied large forces of the armies of the pharaohs.

The Nile itself was a great commercial artery. By the 15th century B.C. it linked trade routes from the Sudan to Asia Minor, the Tigris-Euphrates basin, Syria, and the Aegean world. The small Wâdī Hammamat joined the Nile waterway with the Red Sea, making accessible to the luxury-loving Egyptians the metals, jewels, and foodstuffs of Sinai, Arabia, Nubia, and India. The Execration Texts indicate that Middle Empire kings

294. Boat transporting stone on Nile River.

controlled a vast African and Asiatic Empire from the Second Cataract of the Nile to N. Phoenicia. Without the Nile's facilities for local freight, none of the material for Egypt's stone temples, pyramids, obelisks, tombs, or colossal statues could have been conveyed from quarry to site, as was, for example, the 700,000-lb. obelisk still standing at Thebes—quarried at Assuan. Together with commercial wares, new words poured into the language of Nile peoples, and new gods—Baal, Astarte, 'Anat, etc.—into their pantheon.

The predictable inundations of the Nile formed the basis of Egypt's great wealth in Biblical times, as today. Pharaohs and their stewards (see the narrative of Joseph, the Hebrew prime minister, Gen. 39–50) were kept as well-informed of the flood times of the Nile and the ingathering of its crops as about local taxes and foreign affairs. At Cairo the inundation begins early in June, reaches its height in October, and recedes until April. On the softened and fertilized soil crops are sown as the water recedes. On lower ground a second crop is maintained by the elaborate system of canals supplied with water lifted from the river by *shādūfs* with buckets, or water-wheel pumps. The agricultural year known to Israel in Egypt had three seasons: (1) the inundation (end of June to late October); (2) spring (or winter) crop-growing time (from late October to late February); (3) summer or harvest time, from late February to the end of June.

The Nile Delta in modern times produces more crops than in the Biblical period because a barrage 15 m. from Cairo controls the intricate system of the distribution of water through the network of canals, so that even in midsummer cotton thrives.

The flooding of the Nile aided the development (1) of mathematics (including geometry, a gift of Egypt, not of Greece), because the changing boundaries of flooded fields necessitated accurate measurement to protect ownership; (2) of astronomy, whose observations of heavenly bodies fostered the development of the calendar; (3) of engineering, for working out the intricate canal system; and (4) of writing, for recording acreages, crops, and farm transactions. Nilometers, still used to measure the rise of the flood waters, were made in very early times, and became sacred symbols, hung with god images of blue-green-rose beads of faience.

The Nile became one of Egypt's many gods (Hapi), though not as influential as Re, Osiris, or Isis. It was an androgynous or hermaphroditic deity, though often depicted as a man wearing a hunter's girdle, and a wig entwined with the lotus (symbol of Upper or S. Egypt), and the papyrus* (emblem of Lower or N. Egypt), and carrying a tray of assorted aquatic plants. The isolation of the Nile Valley fostered conservatism in religion. The kindly ferrying of people over the Nile is listed in the sacred papyri of The Book of the Dead as a great virtue. The great Egyptian hymn of praise found in the Tomb of Eye (possibly composed by the monotheistic reformer Akhenaton), mentions the Nile as having been created by Aton in the underworld, whence it mounted to heaven, and descended upon people's fields to bring forth whatever they required.

Archaeological exploration of the Nile Delta, where the Jacob tribes lived, is extremely expensive, because of the flooding of early occupation levels. The first towns and cemeteries are now far down under Nile mud.

See EGYPT.

Nimrim (nĭm′rĭm), Waters of (Isa. 15:6), probably Wâdī Shu'eib, a beautiful valley cutting down into the Jordan from the east, with a plentiful supply of water for Beth-nimrah (in O.T. times Tell Nimrin) at its opening into the Jordan valley. The modern road from Jericho to es-Salt ascends this valley.

(See WÂDĪ, illus. 469.)

Nimrod (nĭm′rŏd), an ancient legendary figure with a fabulous reputation as "hunter," "builder," and founder of "kingdoms" (Gen. 10:8–12). According to some he is the Babylonian god Merodach in human form; others see in him a reflection of Gilgamesh, a national Babylonian hero. The presence in Mesopotamia of many places in which the name "Nimrod" is preserved in varied forms testifies to the popular basis of his widespread fame: Birs Nimrûd, Tell Nimrûd (near Baghdad), the mound of Nimrûd (the ancient Calah), etc.

The Heb. version of Nimrod is from J. Nimrod was the great-grandson of Noah, the grandson of Ham, the son of Cush (Gen. 9:18, 10:8). Babylon was the scene of his first activities; all the cities named in 10:10 are in the geographical or political orbit of Babylon. He colonized Assyria (10:11 f.), to which section of N. Mesopotamia his name was attached (Mic. 5:6). "He began to be a mighty one in the earth" (Gen. 10:8; I Chron. 1:10) may mean that he was considered the originator of the military state based on arbitrary force. The accurate depicting of wild-animal and hunting scenes prevalent in Babylonian and especially Assyrian art indicates a love of sport and understanding of wild life which explains in part the popularity of Nimrod the hunter. The Hebrew author gave Nimrod's hunting a religious slant (Gen. 10:9).

Nimrud. See CALAH.

According to Biblical tradition, Nineveh was founded by Nimrod (Gen. 10:11 f.). A deep sounding cut through the Kuyunjik mound indicates that the earliest material on the site dates from c. 5500 B.C., and shows evidence of contact with Sumer during the Early Dynastic period (Ninevite V, c. 2900–2400 B.C.).

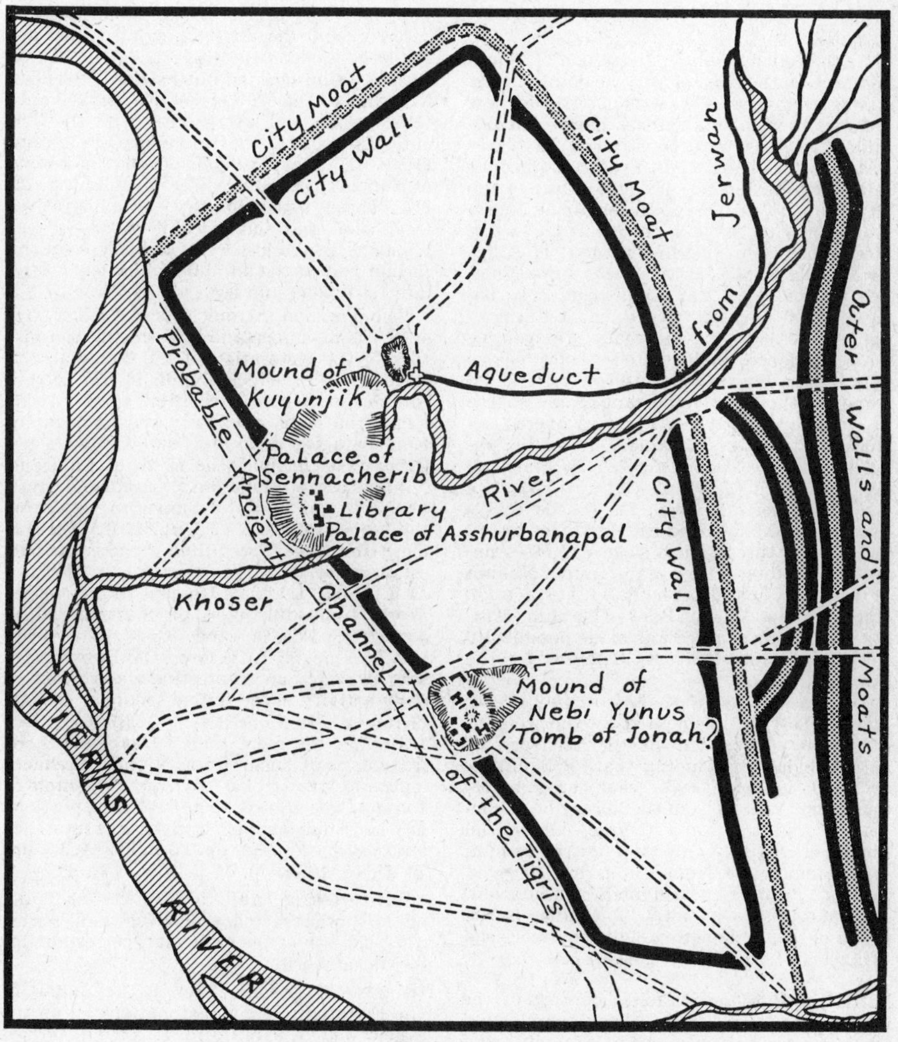

295. Nineveh.

Nineveh (nĭn′ĕ-vĕ) (Assyr. *Ninâ* or *Ninua*) the last capital of the Assyrian Empire, located on the E. bank of the Tigris River opposite Mosul. Its ruins consist of a number of small mounds and two large tells, enclosed within an area of c. 1800 acres by the remains of a 7½-m.-long brick wall. Kuyunjik, the larger of the tells, has been the main focus of excavation. The smaller mound, Nebī Yunus ("the prophet Jonah"), occupied by modern settlement, marks the traditional site of the tomb of the prophet Jonah.

Cuneiform building inscriptions attest to the presence of a temple at Nineveh dedicated to Ishtar as early as the time of Manishtusu (c. 2306–2292 B.C.). Reference is made to repairs carried out by Shamshi-Adad I (c. 1813–1781 B.C.), Tiglath-pileser I (c. 1115–1077 B.C.), and other Assyrian rulers (see ref. in *CAH*[3], under Nineveh). Remnants of the temple and other early buildings have been excavated (*Iraq* 1, 1934, pp. 95 ff.).

During the Neo-Assyrian period, Nineveh was established as an alternate royal residency. Both Ashurnasirpal II (c. 883–859 B.C.) and Sargon II (c. 721–705 B.C.) constructed palaces there. The tribute of Menahem (II Kings 15:20) and Samaria (Isa. 8:4) may have been sent to Nineveh. According to the Book of Jonah, Nineveh was a "great city" (1:2, 3:2 f.) with a population of 120,000 (4:11), best understood as referring to the whole district of Nineveh—"Greater Nineveh" (see A. Parrot, *Nineveh and the Old Testament*, 1955).

Under Sennacherib (c. 704–681 B.C.) Nineveh became the chief city of the empire. New streets and squares were laid out and new defenses, a palace, and vast parks and botanical gardens were constructed. A water system with a canal and the oldest aqueduct in history (at Jerwan) brought water to the city from 30 m. away. Hezekiah of Judah sent tribute to Nineveh (II Kings 18:13 ff.), after which Sennacherib returned (II Kings 19:36; Isa. 37:37). Clay prisms from Nineveh (*ANET*[3], pp. 287 f.) provide Assyrian accounts of the siege of Jerusalem. Ashurbanipal (c. 668–633 B.C.) also made Nineveh his main residence, and erected a new palace with a vast library, the tablets from which comprise the most important single source of Accadian literature. Texts recovered include the Epic of Gilgamesh (*ANET*[3], pp. 72 ff.), the Creation Epic (*ANET*[3], pp. 60 ff.), the Myth of Adapa (*ANET*[3], pp. 101 ff.), and others. Nineveh fell to the Babylonians, the Medes, and the Scythians in 612 B.C. after a three-month siege (*ANET*[3], pp. 303 ff.), as foretold by the prophets Nahum (1:1, 2:8, 3:7) and Zephaniah (2:13). Greek tradition, as well as the Book of Nahum (1:8), asserts that its capture was made possible by the breaches made in its defenses by the flooding Tigris.

Excavations by A. H. Layard in 1845–47 and 1849–51, supplemented by the work of others, have resulted in the recovery of several palaces, including that of Sennacherib, a large quantity of sculptured reliefs and 25,000 tablets from the library of Ashurbanipal and the Nabu temple—all on the mound of Kuyunjik. A palace of Esar-haddon on the mound of Nebī Yunus has received little attention because of modern habitation. An important relief for O.T. studies is the group of scenes depicting Sennacherib's siege of Lachish (*ANEP*[2], Nos. 371–374).

W. P. A.

Ninlil, a Babylonian deity, consort of the great earth god En-lil, whose temple and cult centered at Nippur*. Originally conceived as an aspect of the war god Ninurta*, Ninlil survived as an Assyrian deity, whose temple Ashurnasirpal II (883–859 B.C.) found at Calah* (Gen. 10:11) when he came to that abandoned city to erect his own capital.

Nippur, an ancient Sumerian (see SUMER) city, situated on the E. shore of the old course of the Euphrates, S. of Kish and Babylon, and a short distance NW. of Erech, Larsa, Ur, and Eridu. Because it was the center of the national cult of Enlil, the most important of the Sumerian gods, Nippur occupied a special place in Mesopotamian history up to the mid-2d millennium B.C. No dynasty could maintain prestige without the support of the priesthood of Nippur. This can be seen in the Sumerian historiographic poem entitled "The Curse of Agade," in which the collapse of the Dynasty of Agade (c. 2230 B.C.) is attributed to the sacrilege committed against Ekur, Enlil's sanctuary at Nippur, by Naram-Sin (see S. N. Kramer, *The Sumerians*, 1963, pp. 62 ff.).

Nippur was also a center of intellectual activity from the early Sumerian period on. Tablets found on the site during the course of excavations carried out by the University Museum of the University of Pennsylvania (1888–1900), and later jointly with the Oriental Institute of the University of Chicago (1948–67), provide much of what is known of Sumerian literature (see Kramer, pp. 22 ff.). These texts—literary, administrative, legal, economic, and lexical in nature—cover all stages in the history of the city from the second half of the 3d millennium B.C. to the late 1st millennium B.C.

The Tummal Chronicle (see Kramer, pp. 46 ff.) is an important text tracing the history of the restoration of the Tummal, the shrine of the goddess Ninlil in the temple complex at Nippur. According to this document, the Enlil sanctuary was founded by Enmebaragisi, ruler of Kish (c. 2700 B.C.). Other texts include: the myth of Enki and Ninhursag, a Sumerian "paradise" myth (*ANET*[3], pp. 37 ff.); a Sumerian version of the Flood story (*ANET*[3], pp. 42 ff.); "Gilgamesh and Agga," recording perhaps the oldest political assemblies known (*ANET*[3], pp. 44 ff.); and "Inanna's Descent to the Nether World," shedding light on Sumerian ideas concerning death and the netherworld (*ANET*[3], pp. 52 ff.). A later, Old Babylonian, text provides an interesting description of daily activity in the scribal school at Nippur (Kramer, *The Sumerians*, pp. 237 ff.).

Besides the more than 40,000 tablets, or fragments of such, from Nippur, archaeological excavation has uncovered a temple of Inanna, traced back to c. 3400 B.C., portions of the Enlil temple, and a ziggurat. See *Archaeology* 5, 1952, pp. 70 ff.; 12, 1959, pp. 74 ff.; 15, 1962, pp. 75 ff. W. P. A.

Nisan (nī′săn) (Abib, ā′bĭb), the 1st month of the Jewish sacred year (Neh. 2:1; Esther 3:7), the 7th of the civil year, corresponding to March-April.

No (also No-amon), Thebes, the capital of the Egyptian New Kingdom, located on the Nile c. 330 m. S. of Cairo. It is characterized by two large temple-precincts of the god Amun on the E. side (Karnak and Luxor), and by royal funerary temples (Deir el-Bahari, etc.) and a vast necropolis (Biban el-Moluk) on the W. Both Jeremiah (46:25) and Ezekiel (30:14 ff.) denounced Thebes. Nahum (3:8 ff.) cited the fate of Thebes in predicting the fall of Nineveh. See C. F. Nims, *Thebes of the Pharaohs*, 1965.

Noah (A.V. Noe, Matt. 24:37 f.; Luke 3:36, 17:26 f.) ("rest" or "comfort"), the son of Lamech (Gen. 5:28 f.) and 10th in descent from Adam (5:3–27). Two stories concern Noah in Genesis. In one (Gen. 5.29, 9:18–

27) Noah is the first vinegrower; in the other he is the hero of the Flood* (Gen. 6:5–9:17). In the 1st Noah's sons are unmarried and live with their father in his tent; in the 2d the sons enter the ark* with their wives (Gen. 7:7, 8:18). The shameless drunkenness of Noah does not harmonize, according to our standards, with the character of the "upright" hero of the Flood narrative (6:8 f., 22, 7:5, 8:20, 9:17).

The story of Noah the viticulturist is a continuation of the early J narrative of Gen. 14:19–23, which knows nothing of the later accounts of the Flood; for it states that Lamech's sons were the direct ancestors of nomads, musicians, and metalworkers. Such a statement is incompatible with the tradition that the Flood destroyed all the sons of Lamech except Noah (Gen. 7:23). The Gen. 9:20–26 story (1) explains to whom agriculture, and in particular viticulture, is due; (2) sets forth in the persons of Noah's three sons, Shem, Ham, and Japheth, the eponymous ancestors respectively of the Semites, Hamites, and the Aryan or Indo-European peoples; (3) explains on moral grounds, by its censure of Ham, why the more highly cultured Canaanites were slaves of the Hebrews and Aryans. Noah's poem in Gen. 9:24–26 describes the political situation in 1150–1050 B.C. when the Israelites were beginning to triumph over the Canaanites, and the Philistines were crowding Palestine from the W.

In the Flood story God instructs Noah to build an ark, in which he and his sons, together with every kind of animal, would find security from the destructive waters. Noah obeyed. The rains descended; and the whole earth was engulfed and its wicked inhabitants and all life destroyed. When the waters abated the ark rested on Mt. Ararat*. Noah dispatched a raven and doves to determine the degree of the water's recession. Finally Noah disembarked, erected an altar, and offered sacrifice to God, Who by a rainbow in the sky covenanted never again to inundate the earth and disturb the orderly process of the seasons. This moral and religious classic is a result of the blending of two sources*—the J or Judaean strand and the P or late Priestly narrative; each supplies details the other lacks. The apparent contradictions in the narrative are thus explained, e.g., Gen. 7:2 vs. 6:20, 7:15. The J narrative records the sacrifice of Noah (Gen. 8:20), but the P narrator does not include this feature, because, according to the Priestly theory, sacrifice began with Moses. Mt. Ararat, the only geographical name in the narrative (P), gives the story a N. Mesopotamian locale. The very complete Babylonian account of the Flood found on the 11th tablet of the Gilgamesh epic has many close parallels between its hero and Noah. The construction details of the houseboat, its cargo, the use of scouting birds, and the sacrifices of thanksgiving appear in both. But Noah throughout the Genesis narratives deals with only one God. Evidently the very ancient and widely circulated Flood story, screened of all polytheistic and debasing ideas at the hands of Israel's inspired prophetic and priestly writers, brought Noah a fame which surpassed his lesser claim for remembrance.

Nob (nōb) (I Sam. 22:19 "the city of the priests"), a place mentioned in three passages, all of which may refer to the same site. Père Abel believes Nob to be on Mount Scopus, near the old Augusta Viktoria Hospice, on the edge of Bethphage, and overlooking Jerusalem at a point near the Hebrew University. It was apparently the place to which Yahweh's priests fled with the ephod* after the Ark had been stolen by the Philistines. It was visited by David while Ahimelech, descendant of Eli, was in charge. When Ahimelech gave David food for his men and the sword with which David had killed Goliath, a spy reported to Saul, who ordered the murder of Ahimelech and the inhabitants of Nob (I Sam. 21 f.).

Nob and Anathoth* are listed as places occupied after the return from Exile by "children of Benjamin" (Neh. 11:32). Isaiah prophesied that the Assyrian invaders would advance, town by town, to Nob (10:32), whence Zion would be challenged. Some authorities locate Nob on the ridge from which travelers from the N. get their first impressive view of Jerusalem.

Nod, the unidentified region E. of Eden to which Cain fled (Gen. 4:16).

nomads (nō′mădz) (from a Gk. derivative of a Lat. word meaning "to graze"), wandering herdsmen and shepherds, who led their grass-eating flocks from one green grazing ground to another. Down to about the end of the 12th century B.C., when camels became domesticated, nomads used ass caravans. Nomads were tent dwellers, with no settled homes. They established claims to land by the use of it, as Sinai nomads do today, or by forcible maintenance; or by amicable agreements, like Abraham and Lot when their shepherds quarreled (Gen. 13:5–18). Flocks were owned in common; nomads possessed little private property. Hebrew writers indicated the ancient origin of nomads by making Jabal*, of the 7th generation after Noah, "father of such as dwell in tents, and of such as have cattle" (Gen. 4:20). Thus the O.T. defined nomads as tent-dwelling cattle breeders. "Bedouins" ("desert dwellers") is not an exact synonym for nomads, for many Bedouins now live in houses and do graze flocks.

Semitic nomads, of whom the Hebrew Patriarchs are examples par excellence, were "erupted" from the Arabian Peninsula toward the tempting grazing lands named by J. H. Breasted "the Fertile* Crescent." Such eruptions seem to have come out of Arabia about every 1,000 years, as c. 3500 B.C., when nomads pushed into Assyria and Babylonia, continued perhaps through Palestine-Syria, and deposited non-Egyptian stock in the N. Nile Valley; again c. 2500 B.C., when they followed a similar route, bringing in the men who ultimately established Phoenician trade; c. 1500 B.C., when streams of Semitic nomads (including Hebrews) poured into Palestine; and again c. 500 B.C., when the Nabataeans* were pushing the Edomites from their holdings. By Iron Age III (c. 587–333 B.C.) Arab nomads had taken over control of most of the

Negeb of Palestine and most of southern Trans-Jordan.

Other waves of Indo-European nomads wandered with their flocks into Europe, to gain grasslands stretching from the Danube to the N. shores of the Black Sea and SE.

296. Nomadic herdsmen in Syria.

into Asia and Mesopotamia. Originally Hittites* too were nomads.

The first city-kings of ancient Accad, in the Plain of Shinar, were nomads who "located" and created a cultural pattern which influenced the ancient world. The Hyksos, who provided Egypt with Dynasties XV to XVII (c. 1720–1550 B.C.), were at first nomads. Such nomadic cultures produced little in such fields as the alphabet or the art of writing, for their interests ran instead to the development of the trade that developed from their husbandry. Their occasional visits to markets at the desert's edge for the few essentials in their tent homes led to later trading. Thus gradually evolved the fearless desert caravaneers who developed into Semitic merchants—the greatest businessmen of ancient times. (See TRADE.)

When nomads settled in villages their desert morality weakened, and they were overrun by fresh waves of vigorous nomads. A 14th century student of history, Ibn Khalkun of Tunis, observed that kingdoms founded by nomads lasted only three generations. Notes on similar cycles are found in the O.T., e.g., Deut. 32:15 ("Jeshurun waxed fat"); II Sam. 11–20; I Kings 1, 2; II Kings 17:6–18, which record periods of recurring apostasies, defeats, and religious revivals.

Nomads are usually lean, tall, and powerfully built, having survived desert hardships which carried off the weak. They give total allegiance to their family and tribe. The counsel of their aged sheikhs is respected. They are sullen toward strangers until they test their motives. When they settled down in villages they often proved to be poor citizens, for their extreme independence sometimes led them to ignore the necessities of taxation, census, etc. Nomads love litigation, and cling to their tribal laws of blood revenge, the *lex talionis* of the O.T. codes (cf. Gen. 9:6; Ex. 21:24). They have always been quick to punish violation of their women's chastity. One reason for this is that women do much of the shepherds' work, drawing water, etc., as did Rachel (Gen. 29:6–10); should harm be done them as they move through the desert alone, men would have to do their work, and this would be contrary to nomadic ways of life.

Nomads are the soul of hospitality, whether to strangers arriving at their tents at nightfall, or to travelers halting at a noon harvest floor. If a Sinai nomad robs or murders a guest, he may expect death from his tribesmen.

Often on the Beer-sheba* desert today, or on the high grazing lands of Jordan near Madeba and Amman, one looks into the "ancient" faces of nomads who must resemble Abraham, Isaac, and Jacob. Their dress suggests O.T. apparel—flowing robes, floating veils under goat's-hair rings, girdles carrying food and money; homemade hide sandals; walking sticks carried for protection and guidance of herd or flock. Their houses of hair are hand-woven, with curtains separating the women's quarters from the men's. The tents* of the Patriarchs must have been similar. Even the fiercely barking scavenger dog is there. The heavy feast comes at the end of the day, when guests and family alike sit around the fire and listen to stories told with the quick-moving episodes and shrewd human characterizations that are distinguishing features of many of the sagas of the Patriarchs.

The customs concerning women (Ex. 2:16–21, etc.), hospitality (18:7 ff.), etc., continue among nomads today, and help one understand Israel on trek to Canaan.

Nomads developed profound religious concepts. Pre-Mosaic Hebrew nomads must have shared for a time the W. Semitic deities—El (a father god), a mother god consort (possibly Elat or 'Anat*), and a mountain or storm god, El Shaddai*. Many revered the moon god Sin, protector of their night-moving caravans. The nomads' god was a family god, taken into the intimate family circle, as the nature gods of town-dwelling Canaanites were not. The religion of nomads attained its highest development under Moses, who, while tending flocks of his father-in-law, the nomad priest-shepherd Jethro, "at the back of the wilderness," came to the mountain of God, Horeb (Sinai) and there had his great theophany at the "burning bush" and received from Yahweh his commission to lead Israel (Ex. 3). Moses became the shepherd of his people. Many of the spiritual qualities he had developed as a desert nomad were embodied in the Laws he transmitted to the wandering tribes who became the congregation of Israel.

Noph (nŏf), a word used in several O.T. passages, A.V., for Memphis (Jer. 2:16, 44:1, 46:14, 19; Ezek. 30:13, 16; Isa. 19:13).

numbers, figures representing an arithmetical sum. They were not widely used until after the Exile. So far as is now known early Hebrews spelled out their numbers, as on the Moabite Stone and in the Siloam Tunnel inscription. Letters of their alphabet were used as signs for quantities, as on Maccabean coins (see WRITING). Israel did not use figures as early as the Mesopotamians, who were mathematical experts at a very early date. To the Babylonians a great debt is owed for mathematical data spread by Phoenician traders.

Figures in the Bible must often be considered as "round numbers," not to be interpreted literally, e.g., David's census of "a thousand thousand" (A.S.V. I Chron. 21:5); Zerah's "thousand thousand" Ethiopian warriors (II Chron. 14:9); the "7,000" sheep sacrificed in Jerusalem (II Chron. 15:11); the "ten thousand times ten thousand" angels (A.V., Rev. 5:11, R.S.V. "myriads of myriads"); and Paul's "five" words of understanding, evaluated against "ten thousand words in an unknown tongue" (I Cor. 14:19). Apocalyptic writings, e.g., Daniel and Revelation, are full of "round numbers." Furthermore, in considering the accuracy of numbers in Scripture, we must remember that scribes make more errors in setting down numbers than in almost anything else.

Early Hebrews, like most ancient peoples, used numbers symbolically or with hidden meanings. To push an interpretation of this symbolism too far is to leave the realm of the mystical and enter that of the occult. The following numbers appear to have been especially sacred: *one*, denoting the unity of Yahweh (Deut. 6:4); *three*, which ultimately stood for the Trinity and the formulae of baptismal and apostolic benedictions (Matt. 28:19; II Cor. 13:14), was already sacred in early Babylonian religions, honoring a triad (Anu, Bel, Ea) comprising the component parts of the universe—heaven, earth, the abyss—as Egyptians honored Isis, Osiris, and Horus. David's choices were three (I Chron. 21:12); Christ's inner circle of disciples were three (Mark 9:2; Matt. 26:37); there were three crosses on Calvary (Mark 15:27); and he was three days in the tomb (Mark 16:2). Paul stressed three cardinal Christian virtues (I Cor. 13:13). Three gates were on each side of the foursquare New Jerusalem (Rev. 21:13). *Four*, a square, the symbol of completeness, was the number of letters in YHWH (Yahweh, Jehovah); the number of heads to Eden's river (Gen. 2:10); the winds (Ezek. 37:9); the quarters of the earth (Rev. 7:1); the world kingdoms in Apocalyptic literature (Dan. 7:3, 16 f.); the beasts of destruction (Rev. 4:6, 9:13–15); the horns of the golden altar (9:13). There were four Gospels. *Seven*, the Hebrew sacred number par excellence, may have been influenced by awareness of seven planets. The 7th day completed the creation cycle and became the Sabbath*, on which were based the Hebrew Sabbatical and Jubilee years (see TIME). Seven seven-branched candlesticks are mentioned in Revelation (1:20), as are seven stars (3:1), and seven churches (1:4, 20). *Ten*, the basis of the decimal system and of the Heb. tithe* (Num. 18:24 ff.; Deut. 14:22 f.; Neh. 10:37 f.), acquired sacred meanings. There were Ten Commandments (Ex. 20:3–17); and parables of 10 talents (Luke 19:13) and of 10 virgins (Matt. 25:1–13). *Twelve*, significant to Sumerians, who divided the year into 12 months based on the moon's revolutions, was the number of the sons of Jacob (Gen. 35:22; Acts 7:8) and of the Tribes of Israel (Num. 1) and of Ishmael (Gen.). Jesus chose 12 to be Apostles (Mark 3:14); and had 12 baskets of food left after feeding the multitude (John 6:13). *Forty*, sometimes reckoned as the length of one generation, often appears in Judges (3:11) and the annals of the early Hebrew Monarchy. It was the number of days believed to have been spent by Moses in Mount Sinai (Ex. 24:18, 34:28), and of Jesus in the wilderness of the Temptation (Mark 1:13). Numbers (14:33 f.) records Israel's Wilderness wanderings as covering 40 years. *Seventy* (formed by multiplying two sacred numbers) numbered the elders of ancient Israel (Ex. 24:1; cf. Gen. 46:27). Jeremiah listed the years of Israel's Babylonian Exile as 70 (25:11 f., 29:10). "Seventy times seven" was a round number used by Jesus to express the limitless occasions when a man should forgive (Matt. 18:22). He chose the Seventy to be his helpers (Luke 10:1). A *thousand* years was a round number for God's large-scale view of time and constituted the millennium* of the Apocalypse.

The mystical *six hundred and sixty-six* (Rev. 13:18)—the number of the beast—has been used as a runic number for Nero and many other anti-Christian leaders.

Numbers, the Book of, the 4th book of the Pentateuch*. The name is derived from the census of the people in chaps. 1–4, 26. In all Hebrew editions its title is *Bamidbar*, "In the Wilderness," from the 5th Hebrew word of Num. 1:1. Thirty-nine chapters consist of laws, narratives, and poems which concern Israel's 40 years of desert wanderings, with special emphasis on the beginning and end of this period.

Numbers, divided into three main parts, can be outlined thus:

(1) The camp at Sinai—	1:1–10:10
The census	1–4
Various laws and regulations	5, 6
Levites and their office	7–10:10
(2) The Wanderings—	10:11–22:2
The trek from Sinai	10:11–36
Manna, quails, etc.	11
The sedition of Miriam and Aaron	12
The spies and their report	13, 14
Sundry laws	15
The revolution of Korah	16
The Levites strengthened	17–19
Leadership of Moses	20
Incidents prior to the arrival in Moab	21:1–22:1
(3) On the uplands of Moab—	22:2–36:13
Balak and Balaam	22:2–24
Phinehas and his reward	25
The second census	26
Women's rights	27:1–11
Moses and his successor	27:12–23
Sacrificial laws and vows	28–30
Moses deals with the Midianites, Reubenites, Gadites, etc.	31, 32
Boundaries, cities of refuge, etc.	33–36

There are a few who still hold to the Mosaic authorship of Numbers. Most scholars, however, believe that the book is the final result of a long editorial development. A few obvious indications of its post-Mosaic date are 12:3, 15:32, 22:1, 35:29. (For a detailed analysis of the Book of Numbers see SOURCES.) Some sources employed written data, now lost (21:14 f.); traditions which had gathered about persons and places (11:3, 34, 20:13, 22:3); poems (10:35 f., 21:17 f., 27–30, 23:7–10, 18–24, 24:3–9, 15–24); ritualistic formulae (6:24–26); and fixed habits of life expressed in laws (5, 6, 15, 28–30).

The commanding personality of Moses* is apparent everywhere in this book. We notice his faithfulness to God and devotion to His wayward and intractable congregation; his humility (12:3); his trust in God (10:29–32); his depression and despair (11:10–15); and his indignation and anger (16:15). The religious interpretations of the writers are as important as the historic events they record. Numbers therefore becomes a testimony of the faith of those who wrote concerning events which had occurred 400 to 800 years earlier. The book is not only a record of facts, but the testimony of a continuing faith.

nun, the 14th letter of the Heb. alphabet, used to head the 14th part of Ps. 119. See WRITING.

Nun, an Ephraimite, the father of Joshua* (Ex. 33:11; Num. 11:28; Josh. 1:1; "Non" I Chron. 7:27).

nurse, among Hebrews usually a child's own mother (Gen. 21:7; Ex. 2:7, 9), who suckled it for as much as three years (Hannah, I Sam. 1:23 f.), as is still frequently done in the Near East. Weaning was often the occasion for a happy celebration (Gen. 21:8; I Sam. 1:23 f.). The employed wet nurse is illustrated by Rebekah's Deborah, who long remained an honored attendant even after the betrothal of her charge (Gen. 24:59, 35:8); and by that of the young exiled prince Joash* (II Kings 11:2; II Chron. 22:11). Moses' mother was engaged as his wet nurse by his foster mother, Pharaoh's daughter (Ex. 2:7, 9). After the weaning stage, nurses were employed only by royalty and the wealthy: Saul's nurse for Mephibosheth let the five-year-old boy fall, so that he "became lame" for life (II Sam. 4:4). Naomi attended her grandson Obed as his loving nurse (Ruth 4:16). The good and "gentle" nurse is memorialized by Paul in I Thess. 2:7. Moses referred to himself as a "nursing father" for Israel (Num. 11:12).

Nut (nōōt), the sky goddess of the Egyptian Delta, mother of Seth, identical with the Canaanite Baal*. From the union of Nut with Geb, the earth god, sprang the great sun god Re*. Nut was sometimes depicted in Egyptian art as a cow, held up by various gods, with stars fastened to her belly, and the sun god in his boat traveling across her body.

nuts were enjoyed in Bible lands as food* and flavoring, and were prized as gifts (Gen. 43:11), especially to people living in lands where nut trees did not grow, e.g., Egypt. Families liked to have a few nut trees in their gardens (Song of Sol. 6:11). (See ALMOND.) Pistachio nuts were used in confections; walnuts, from Galilee and elsewhere, in dyeing garments.

Nuzi (Nū′zĭ) (Yorghan Tepe), an ancient city of N. Mesopotamia, E. of Asshur. Its site, near Kirkuk in modern Iraq, was first systematically excavated by Edward Chiera (University of Pennsylvania) in 1925. Subsequent investigations by the Semitic Museum, the Fogg Art Museum of Harvard University, and the American Schools of Oriental Research at Baghdad have gone down almost to virgin soil, disclosing history back to 4000 B.C. In addition to the palace and temple of the Hurrian level, Nuzi has yielded thousands of clay* tablets written when the Mitanni controlled the town (15th century B.C.). These tablets, written in Old Babylonian cuneiform by Hurrian scribes, document customs and laws in N. Mesopotamia which resemble those of the patriarchal period of the O.T. These include the practice of filial adoption (Gen. 29–31), the transference of birthright (Gen. 25:29 ff.), respect for a deathbed blessing (Gen. 27:18 ff., 48:15 ff., chap. 49; I Kings 2:1 ff.), and the giving of a handmaid to the husband to bear children (Gen. 16:2, 30:3). Such similarities attest to the accuracy of the social background of Genesis in the time of the Hebrew Patriarchs. See C. H. Gordon, *BA* 3, 1940, pp. 1–12; C. J. Mullo-Weir, *AOTS*, 1967, pp. 73–86.

Nymphas (nĭm′făs) (A.V. and A.S.V. Col. 4:15; Nympha [fem.] A.S.V. footnote and R.S.V.), a man or a woman whose home at Laodicea was a meeting place for Christians. Paul greets him (her) and directs that the Epistle to the Colossians be read to him (her).

O

oak (O.T. translation of several Heb. words—*'allah, 'elah, 'elon, 'allon*), possibly in the A.V. a generic term for any large tree; in several instances it probably should be translated "teil" (linden) or "terebinth" (turpentine tree). The true oak of Palestine was thick-leaved, as in Absalom's tragedy (II Sam. 18:9 f., 14) and in accounts of idol worship in shady oak groves (Hos. 4:13). The strength of oaks was proverbial (Isa. 44:14; Amos 2:9). Their fall was a sign of the coming day of the Lord (Isa. 1:30). Oaks were prized for oars (Ezek. 27:6; Zech. 11:2). The oaks growing abundantly in the Biblical period in Bashan, and on Mounts Carmel and Tabor and the hills of Ephraim and the highlands of N. Trans-Jordan and the Lebanon, were cut down through the centuries for fuel and war, but today are being replaced.

The O.T. oak was a venerated tree, associated with important events or people, like Abraham's oaks at Hebron (A.S.V. Gen. 13:18); the oak where Jacob hid the people's strange gods and jewelry (Gen. 35:4); the one under which Deborah, nurse of Rebekah, was buried (Gen. 35:8); the oak of the pillar in Shechem (A.S.V. Judg. 9:6); the oak at Ophrah, where an angel appeared to Gideon (Judg. 6:11, 19); the oak of Tabor (A.S.V. I Sam. 10:3); and the oak (margin "terebinth") under which the "man of God" was sitting (I Kings 13:14).

Oaks were used for tanning and dyeing, for fuel, and in the fashioning of images. Tannic acid was obtained from oak galls.

oath (Heb. *shĕbŭ'ah*, from the same root as the sacred number 7; and Heb. *'ālah*, "curse"), a solemn appeal to Yahweh or some sacred object in attestation of the truth of a statement or of one's intention to keep a promise. God Himself was thought of as making an oath when He entered into a covenant* with Abraham (Gen. 24:8; Luke 1:73; Heb. 6:13–20) and with Moses (Deut. 29:12, 14; cf. Deut. 7:8). Joseph took an oath of the children of Israel (Acts 2:30; cf. Ezek. 17:13–16, 18) that they would bring his bones from Egypt to the homeland in Canaan (Gen. 50:25). God was thought of as receiving oaths between two neighbors to guarantee their honesty (Ex. 22:11). Some oaths bordered on a curse, as in Judg. 21:5. The Lord abominated false oaths (Zech. 8:17).

Oaths were so widely used in the time of Jesus that the reform indicated in his rebuke in Matt. 5:34–37 was in order. Peter used an oath to fortify his denial of Jesus (Matt. 26:72). Herod the tetrarch made a rash oath (Matt. 14:3–12); and the 40 men who lay in wait to seize Paul made an evil oath (Acts 23:21).

Oaths were made by calling God to witness (Matt. 5:33); by lifting a hand toward heaven (Gen. 14:22); by placing a hand under the thigh of the individual with whom an agreement was made (Gen. 24:2, 47:29), indicating reverence for posterity; or by appealing to a sacred object (Matt. 5:34–36).

Obadiah (ō′bȧ-dī′ȧ) ("worshipper of Jehovah"). (1) A chief of the tribe of Issachar (I Chron. 7:3). (2) A Gadite who joined David at Ziklag (I Chron. 12:9). (3) The father of the chief of the Zebulunites (I Chron. 27:19). (4) A steward of Ahab, who during the persecution by Jezebel hid 100 prophets of Yahweh in caves, and arranged the interview of Elijah with Ahab (I Kings 18:3–16); the trial on Mt. Carmel resulted from this interview (I Kings 18:17–46). (5) A Levite who supervised workmen employed by Josiah in Temple repairs (II Chron. 34:12). (6) A priest who sealed the covenant made in Nehemiah's time (Neh. 10:5). (7) A Levite credited with founding the family of porters and gatekeepers (Neh. 12:25). (8) The prophet (see next article).

Obadiah, the Book of, the shortest of the prophetic books, consists of only 21 verses. It stands 4th among the 12 Minor Prophets. Nothing is known about its author, and efforts to associate him with any of the other O.T. Obadiahs have proved futile (see the preceding article for a partial list).

The book may be outlined as follows:

(1) The denunciation of Edom	vv. 1–14
(a) the ruin of her rocky fastnesses	1–9
(b) the reasons for her fall	10–14
(2) The restoration of Israel	15–21
(a) God's law of retribution	15 f.
(b) Apocalyptic triumphs	17–20
(c) Yahweh's universal kingdom	21

The book is a fiery denunciation of Judah's traditional enemies, the Edomites, who had taken part in the overthrow of Judah by Nebuchadnezzar (Obad. 11–14) and who later seized the Negeb. The subjugation of Edom by nomadic Arabs (see NABATAEA) is predicted as an act of divine retribution (vv. 15 f.) for Edom's perfidy. Similar feelings of revenge on the part of the Jews for Edom's behavior are vented in Ps. 137:7; Lam. 4:21 f.; Ezek. 25:12–14, 35:1 ff.; Isa. 34:5 ff., 63:1–6. It is to this literature that the book of Obadiah belongs. In vv. 17–21 an historic situation gives way to Apocalyptic prophecies of the deeds and dreams that will be brought to fruition in the reign of the Lord on Zion.

The dwelling "in the clefts of the rock" (v. 3) probably refers to Petra*, the rose-red, rock-cut, supposedly impregnable capital of Edom in the mountains of Seir. Vv. 10–14 almost certainly refer to the destruction of Jerusalem by Nebuchadnezzar (587 B.C.), and in their vivid recollection of events suggest a date for 1–14 in the early part of the Exile. Dates ranging from 587 B.C to 400 B.C. have been assigned to various sections of the book. It is commonly held that at least two authors had a hand in it. The arguments for a composite authorship are: (1) In vv. 1–7 Edom alone, and in vv. 15–20 all nations included in the house of Esau, are under condemnation; (2) in vv. 1–14 the writer prophesies in words of historic realism the defeat and destruction of Edom, whereas vv. 15–21 are in a later, Apocalyptic language.

The similarity between Obadiah 1–4 and Jer. 49:7–22 suggests a common source, but it is equally possible that one borrowed from the other.

Obed ("worshipper"). (1) The son of Ruth and Boaz and the father of Jesse, ancestor of Jesus (Ruth 4:17–22; I Chron. 2:12, 11:47; Matt. 1:5; Luke 3:32). (2) A Jerahmeelite, father of one Jehu (I Chron. 2:38). (3) One of David's heroes (I Chron. 11:47). (4) The son of Shemaiah and grandson of the Korhite Obed-edom (I Chron. 26:7). (5) The father of the Azariah who helped Jehoiada establish Joash on Judah's throne despite the evil design of Athaliah (c. 837 B.C.) (II Chron. 23:1).

Obed-edom ("worshipper of Edom"). (1) A man of Gath (a Gittite), in whose home near Jerusalem David deposited the Ark* for safekeeping for three months before transporting it to Jerusalem. His household was greatly blessed by its presence (II Sam. 6:10–12; I Chron. 13:13 f.). (2) An ancestor of the men who guarded the doors of Israel's place of worship (possibly the same as Obed-edom (1) (I Chron. 15:18 ff., 16:38, 26:4 ff.). (3) The founder of a company of singers at the Temple in post-Exilic times (I Chron. 15:21, 16:5). One of this group was guarding Temple treasures when Joash, King of Israel, invaded Judah in the reign of Amaziah (c. 800–783 B.C.) (II Chron. 25:24).

obedience, compliance with the laws (see LAW) and will of God—prerequisite to membership in the congregation of Israel (Num. 27:20) and in the community of Christ (John 14:21–24; Rom. 6:17). Jesus himself was made perfect through obedience to God (Heb. 5:8 f.). He came into the world to do the will of his Father (Heb. 10:7). His Apostles were obedient to their heavenly visions (Acts 26:19; I Pet. 1:2), and expected people of the Way to be obedient to the Christ (II Cor. 10:5), who through suffering learned obedience to God, and through that experience brought salvation* "unto all them that obey him" (Heb. 5:9).

obeisance (from "obey"), a bow or other movement of the body to show deference or homage. This is portrayed in carved reliefs of prisoners prostrate before their captors, as in the Shalmaneser obelisk where Jehu bows. Subjects bow before their sovereign (I Sam. 24:8; II Sam. 14:4; I Kings 1:16). O.T. writers described the worship of the Lord in terms of "bowing down" (Gen. 24:52; Num. 22:31; cf. Matt. 27:29; Mark 15:19). (See JEHU, illus. 206).

obelisk, a tapering, four-sided, pyramidal-topped shaft, often monolithic, associated with Egyptian temples. (Cf. the cultic pillars* prevalent in Near-Eastern worship.) A group of obelisks stood in front of the great Temple of Re-Harakhti, god of the rising sun, at Heliopolis, the center of Egyptian religion in the Fifth Dynasty—the On* known to Abraham, Joseph (Gen. 41:45, 50, 46:20), and Moses. One obelisk survives *in situ*—the oldest and perhaps the most beautiful in Egypt. It is inscribed, "the king of Upper and Lower Egypt, the lord of the crowns and the son of the Sun, Sesostris (12th Dynasty) whom the spirits of On love . . . erected the obelisk on his first Set festival." Jeremiah (43:16) calls the place Beth-shemesh, Heb. for "the city of the sun." The obelisk, which is still standing, may have been seen by Joseph and Mary, whose Egyptian flight is associated with this section of the Delta. The obelisk from Heliopolis which Caligula set up in his circus at Rome stands now in St. Peter's Square. Of the two obelisks from Heliopolis (erected by Thutmose III, c. 1490–1435 B.C.), which came to be known as "Cleopatra's Needles," one stands on the Thames Embankment, London, and the other in New York's Central Park. Each weighs c. 200 tons and bears hieroglyphic inscriptions. (See PETER, illus. 320.)

oblation, a ritualistic offering presented to God—usually of a nonliving object, in contrast with animal sacrifice: e.g., meal (Lev. 2:4); first fruits (v. 12); or land for the sanctuary (Ezek. 48:9). (See WORSHIP.) Isaiah denounced vain oblations (Heb. "an oblation of vanity") (1:13, 16 f.).

occupations. See individual entries.

Oded (ō′dĕd). (1) Father of the prophet Azariah (II Chron. 15:1). (2) A prophet of Israel in the reign of Pekah. He induced the army of Israel to treat their captives from Judah kindly and return them to their countrymen (II Chron. 28:9–15).

297. Obelisk at On.

offerings. See WORSHIP.

Og (ŏg), the powerfully built King of Bashan* whose defeat by Israel at Edrei, the Bashan capital (Num. 21:33) in N. Trans-Jordan, was considered so decisive in the Conquest* that the event was referred to many times in the O.T. (Deut. 1:4, 3:1–13, 31:4; Josh. 2:10, 9:10, 12:4, 13:12–31; I Kings 4:19; Neh. 9:22). The victory over a ruler said to be a "remnant of the Rephidim"* or giants found its way even into the devotional literature of the Hebrews (Ps. 135:11, 136:20). His bedstead of "iron" (black basalt) 9 cubits long was said in O.T. times to be at Rabbath-ammon (today 'Ammân, capital of Jordan) (Deut. 3:11).

See AMMONITES.

Oholah (ō-hō′lȧ), **Oholibah** (ō-hŏl′ĭ-bȧ), A.S.V.; Aholah, Aholibah, A.V. ("she who has a tent," "tent in her"), the names of two women of evil repute, used allegorically (Ezek. 23:3 ff.) for Samaria and Jerusalem to typify their unfaithfulness to the Lord when they were seduced by the foreign gods of Assyria and Babylon.

oil, in Scripture usually olive* oil, except in such passages as Esther 2:12, where oil of myrrh is meant, and II Sam. 14:2, Ps. 104:15, Ruth 3:3, where a cosmetic ointment (see OINTMENTS) may be intended. Matthew (6:17) implies the daily use of oils to anoint*. Egyptians used unguents and were copied by their neighbors, like the Alexandrian Jews and the Palestinians.

(1) Olive oil was an evidence of prosperity (Deut. 8:8, 14:23; Jer. 31:12, 40:10). It was used as a medium of exchange before coinage was invented. The most ancient Babylonian law codes gave the value of the hours of human labor in units of oil (cf. II Kings 4:7). Solomon paid Hiram of Tyre thousands of gallons of oil for laborers and materials furnished for the Jerusalem Temple (I Kings 5:11; cf. Ezek. 27:17; Hos. 12:1).

Olive oil was used (1) for food, taking the place of butter in cooking (I Kings 17:12–16); (2) mixed with meal (Lev. 2:4 f., 6:15–22) or meat (Lev. 6:15), for offerings to the Deity; (3) for lights (see LAMP) in houses (Matt. 25:1–13) and in the sanctuary (Ex. 25:6, 31 ff., 27:20, 30:25, 31, 37:29); and (4) for anointing (a) a new king (I Sam. 10:1; I Kings 1:39); (b) the sick (Mark 6:13); (c) the bruised (Ps. 23:5); (d) the Tabernacle and its priests (Ex. 30:22–33; Lev. 8:10–12); and (e) guests (Luke 7:46).

Olive oil was produced by knocking the olives from the trees with poles and pounding them in a mortar with a pestle (Ex. 27:20); or by grinding them in a stone olive press. The Garden of Gethsemane (from the Aram. "an oil press") was named for the presses used for the olives from the Mount of Olives. An elaborate underground press has been found at Jerusalem. Often the press was hewn out of solid rock, c. 6 ft. in diameter, like those found at Megiddo and Taanach. A stone roller, often a section of an ancient round pillar, c. 3 ft. long and 18 in. to 3 ft. thick, was laid in the flat-bottomed basin, so that one end nearly touched the side. Through a perforation in the roller a stout stick was passed, terminating at each end with a handle. Olives were dumped from collecting baskets into the circular, flat-bottomed basin of the press, where they were crushed to pulp by the stone roller worked by two people who grasped its handles and walked around the press. The pulp poured through an opening in the side of the press, and was taken up in bags, which were then sewed up. Hot water was added to the matter in the bags, which were placed in a trough and trodden out by bare feet (Deut. 33:24, cf. 32:13) or pressed under a heavy beam, and the oil flowed down into vessels ready to receive it. Newly extracted oil was purified by allowing its impurities to settle in earthen jars or in rock-cut vats. One good tree yields 10 to 15 gal. of oil each year. Some olives are eaten or pickled for family use.

oil tree (Isa. 41:19), possibly the oleaster, or, as G. E. Post suggested, a pine which exudes "oil" or resin (cf. Neh. 8:15 A.V.). The latter would provide more suitable material for two cherubim (I Kings 6:23–26 margin) than the shrubby oleaster. The A.S.V. and R.S.V. of this passage read "olive wood."

ointments and perfumes used in ancient Bible lands (Eccles. 7:1, 9:8; Matt. 6:17) were compounded by perfumers, apothecaries, confectioners (Ex. 30:35), priests, or individual users. Their use originated with the Egyptians, who found them cleansing and cooling, and spread throughout neighbor nations. At banquets small cones of scented ointment were placed on the forehead, and as these melted the ingredients perfumed the face (cf. Ps. 133:2, 92:10). In Jesus' day banquet guests were anointed with oil (Luke 7:46). Such cosmetics were stored in precious jars of alabaster (cf. Matt. 26:7 and Mark 14:3), marble, ivory, or faïence, like those excavated in the tomb of the Sumerian queen Shubad (University Museum, Philadelphia), the jar of Pepi I, Egyptian Old Kingdom (c. 2700–2200 B.C.) (Metropolitan Museum). The Tut-ankh-amun carved chair in Cairo depicts his young queen anointing his flat, jeweled collar with a cosmetic.

298. Ointment jars from Egypt.

To the original olive-oil ointment that shepherds used to soothe the bruised faces of sheep (Ps. 23:5), the Hebrews added the specified ingredients of a formula attributed to Moses (Ex. 30:22–30) to produce the holy anointing oil for the Tabernacle* and its appointments and its priests. A penalty was prescribed for the man who used holy oil to anoint "a stranger" (one not a priest), in the code* of law of Ex. 30:33. Ointments were used by prophets in anointing new kings, e.g., when Elijah anointed Jehu (II Kings 9:3) and Jehoiada anointed Joash (II Kings 11:12). Ointment was also used in anointing the sick (James 5:14) and (often perfumed with myrrh) the dead (Luke 23:56; Mark 14:8). Cedar oil was sometimes used to anoint bodies.

See COSMETICS.

old things generally, and old age particularly, were revered by Hebrews and other Semitic peoples. Concern for parents was considered prerequisite to the individual's own longevity (Ex. 20:12). The aged mother was not to be despised (Prov. 23:22); the old man's hoary beard was a mark of beauty (20:29). Righteousness was deemed a corollary of the "good old age," attributed, for example, to the Patriarchs (Gen. 25:8, 50:22; Deut. 34:7). The aged were viewed as depositories of tested wisdom (Deut. 32:7; but cf. I Kings 12:6–20, Rehoboam). The description of old age in Eccles. 12 is one of the most outstanding in world literature.

The prophets occasionally spoke for a true conservatism that forgot not "the old ways." Jeremiah declared, "Thus saith the Lord, Stand ye in the ways, and see, and ask for the old paths, where is the good way, and walk therein, and ye shall find rest for your souls" (6:16). There was hesitancy too about removing the "old landmark" (see LANDMARKS) (Prov. 23:10).

The overcautious Pharisaical evaluation of the old ways was swept away by Jesus. He found it impossible to put the new wine in old skin bottles, which burst with the force of the new ferment (Mark 2:22). He made "all things new" (Rev. 21:5), and presented a "new commandment" (John 13:34), yet avoided the destruction of the good that was in the old dispensation.

Old Gate, the, an important but not yet exactly identified portal of ancient Jerusalem, restored under Nehemiah (3:6, 12:39). Some authorities believe this should read the "Mishneh" Gate, i.e., the gate which led into the second quarter (see COLLEGE). A location to the E. of the Church of the Holy Sepulcher* is possible.

old prophet, the, an unnamed prophet of Yahweh, who dwelt in Bethel and whose story, set in the period of Jeroboam, is narrated in I Kings 13:11–32.

Old Stone Age, the. See PALAEOLITHIC AGE

Old Testament, the (from Gk. *diathēkē*, "testament"), the earlier and longer portion of the Christian Bible, identical in content with Heb. Bible (but not in arrangement). Not called by Jews "Old Testament," for this title, first used in connection with the Bible by Tertullian and Origen (based on II Cor. 3:14), implies the acceptance of the later covenant (the N.T.) in which Jesus is set forth as the Messiah. The theme of the O.T. is God's covenant with Israel; Israel's history is unfolded, with its discouragements, triumphs, and apostasies, its return to God's love, and its eternal hope through righteousness*.

(1) The *order* of books is not the same in the Hebrew and the Christian Bible. In the Hebrew canon* the Old Testament has three divisions: (a) the "Law"* (Torah), i.e., the five books of the Pentateuch; (b) the "Prophets"—(8 books), arranged in two groups: the "Former Prophets," containing Joshua, Judges, Samuel, and Kings; and the "Latter Prophets," containing the three major prophets, Isaiah, Jeremiah, and Ezekiel, and "the Minor Prophets" or "the Twelve" (see PROPHETS); (c) the "Writings" or "Sacred Writings," i.e., the Hagiographa*, consisting of (a) the poetical books—Psalms, Proverbs, Job; (b) the five Megilloth or "Rolls," from which readings are made during the five Jewish holy days—Song of Solomon, Ruth, Lamentations, Ecclesiastes, and Esther; and (c) the remaining books of the canon, i.e., Daniel, Ezra-Nehemiah, and Chronicles. According to Christian reckoning, the 24 books of the Hebrew Bible have become 39, since each of the Minor Prophets is considered one book; Ezra has been separated from Nehemiah; and Samuel, Kings, and Chronicles have been divided into two books each.

The Law was the first part of the O.T. to be canonized, i.e., recognized as authoritative. Yet is was not "complete" until c. 400 B.C.

(2) The *oldest portions* of the O.T. are poems, quoted from collections now lost, like The Book of Yashar, and The Book of the Wars of Yahweh (see Josh. 10:12–14). The Ode of Deborah, immortalizing Israel's victory over Sisera (Judg. 5), and probably composed at that time (c. 1125 B.C.), is not only the oldest long poem of the O.T., but as an ode is unexcelled in ancient world literature. The first prose literature of the O.T. was probably the narrative of the establishment of the Kingdom of Israel, inspired by the career of David. Much of the historical part of the O.T. was based on such original sources, now lost, as royal Judaean annals, Temple records, the Elijah stories, and a history of the Omri Dynasty (c. 876–869 B.C.) written in Israel during the reign of Jehu (c. 842–815 B.C.).

The writing of the historical books of the O.T. began as early as 600 B.C., when one of the Deuteronomists (see DEUTERONOMY) wrote the history of Israel and Judah from the building of Solomon's Temple to the reformation by which it became the only legitimate sanctuary of Israel (see I Kings 1–II Kings 23:25a).

(a) The story of Solomon (reigned c. 1020–1000 B.C.).

(b) The Divided Kingdom, to the fall of Israel (722/1 B.C.).

(c) The History of Judah until Josiah (640–609 B.C.).

It is certain that this Deuteronomist had access to the lost "Books of the Acts of the Kings of Israel and Judah," as J. A. Bewer has suggested. During the Exile later Deuteronomistic historians carried the work on from Abraham's era; this Deuteronomistic history covered the period from Abraham through to the Babylonian Exile, and included the books known as the "Former Prophets." Though written by many writers, the books show the viewpoint of their final editors, who were sometimes more interested in religion than in historical fact.

(3) The O.T. contains excellent examples of almost every sort of literature. It is difficult to classify the books according to their type, for some are both law and history; others are both poetry and Wisdom literature; or poetry and devotional expressions, like the Psalms. Many prophetic books are poetry. Some books, like I and II Kings, are both history and prophecy. Following is a simplified grouping of the books of the O.T.:

Legal literature, contained chiefly in the Pentateuch, and contributed principally by the priestly class.

Historical literature, contributed by prophets, priests, and historians, and including Joshua, Judges, I and II Samuel, I and II Kings, I and II Chronicles, Ezra, Nehemiah, (?) Esther.

Prophetic literature, prepared both before and after the Exile by the prophets or their followers, and showing co-operation or friction in some cases between prophets and contemporary rulers of Israel.

Wisdom literature, contributed by the Wise Men or teachers, who through appeal to the mind aimed to transform men's actions. It includes Proverbs, Job, and Ecclesiastes; and, according to some, the Song of Solomon.

Devotional literature, contributed by a number of religious poets, in the Psalms.

(4) Old Testament literature took form during the 1st millennium B.C. Almost every book is of composite authorship, and shows marks of having been edited by several hands in successive centuries.

An outline showing the historical development of the O.T. has been prepared by Julius A. Bewer (*The Literature of the Old Testament*, Columbia University Press). Not all critics agree with its details, and as our knowledge increases it may have to be recast.

Order of the Historical Development of the Books of the O.T.

(1) The Pre-Monarchic Period, before c. 1000 B.C. (topically arranged, not chronologically)—

(a) War and march songs—

Song of Lamech (Gen. 4:23 f.); Song of Miriam (Ex. 15:21); Eternal War with Amalek (Ex. 17:16); Incantations to the Ark (Num. 10:35 f.); List of Stations (Num. 21:14 f.); Taunt Song on the Amorites (Num. 21:27–30); Song of the Well (Num. 21:17 f.); Joshua's Appeal to the Sun and the Moon (Josh. 10:12 f.); Song of Deborah (Judg. 5).

(b) Proverbs, riddles, and fables—

David's Proverb (I Sam. 24:13); Samson's Riddles (Judg. 14:14, 18) and Taunt (Judg. 15:16); Jotham's Fable (Judg. 9:7–15).

(c) Prophetic blessings and oracles—

The Blessing of Noah (Gen. 9:25–27) and of Jacob (Gen. 49); the Oracles of Balaam (Num. 23 f.).

(2) The Time of David, Solomon, and Jeroboam I, from c. 1000–910 B.C.—

(a) Poems—

Paean over David's victories (I Sam. 18:7 etc.); Sheba's War Cry (II Sam. 20:1); David's Lamentation over Saul and Jonathan (II Sam. 1:19 ff.), and over Abner (II Sam. 3:33 f.); Nathan's Parable (II Sam. 12:1–4); Solomon's Dedication of the Temple (I Kings 8:12 f.); the Books of Jashar and of the Wars of Yahweh; the Blessing of Moses (Deut. 33).

(b) Narratives—

The Story of the Founding and Establishment of the Kingdom by Saul, David, and Solomon (parts of I and II Sam. and I Kings 1 f.); The Book of the Acts of Solomon (I Kings 3–11 in part); Beginnings of the Royal Annals and of the Temple Records.

(c) Laws—

The Book of the Covenant (Ex. 20:23–23:19); The So-called Cultic Decalogue of Ex. 34.

(3) The 9th and 8th Centuries—

The Elijah Stories (I Kings 17–19:21).

The Elisha Stories (II Kings 2–8 in part, 13:14–21).

The History of the Rise and Fall of the Dynasty of Omri (I Kings 20:22; II Kings 3, 6:24–7:20, 8:7–15, 9:10).

The Yahwist (c. 850 B.C.).

The Elohist (c. 750 B.C.).

Amos (c. 750).

Hosea (from c. 745–735).

Isaiah (from 738–700 and perhaps later).

Micah (from c. 725 till perhaps the 7th century).

(4) The 7th Century—

Combination of the Yahwist and the Elohist.

Deuteronomy (published 621 B.C.).

Zephaniah (c. 627–626).

Jeremiah (from 626 on).

Nahum (c. 615).

The First Edition of the Books of Kings (between 620 and 608).

(5) The 6th Century—

Jeremiah (continued till after 585).

Habakkuk (between 600 and 590).

Ezekiel (593–571).

The Holiness Code (Lev. 17–26).

Lamentations (586–550).

Isaiah (63:7–64:12).

Combination of the Yahwist and Elohist with the Deuteronomist in the Hexateuch. The Second Edition of the Books of Kings (c. 550).

The Deuteronomistic Editions of the Stories of Joshua, Judges, and Samuel.

The Song of Moses (Deut. 32).

Isaiah 13:2 ff., 14:4–21, 21.

Deutero-Isaiah (Isa. 40–55, between 546 and 539).

Haggai (520).

Zechariah 1–8 (? 520–518 and after).

Isaiah 56:9–58:12, 59:1–15a, 65:1–16, 66:1–6, 15–18a, 24 (from 520 on). The Priest Code (c. 500).

(6) The 5th Century—

Isaiah 59:15b–63:6, 65:17–25, 66:7–14, 18b–23.

Jeremiah 3:14–18.

Isaiah 34 f.
Obadiah.
Isaiah 15 f.
Amos 9:8b–15.
Zephaniah 2:7a, c, 8–11.
Isaiah 11:10–16.
Malachi (c. 460).
The Memoirs of Nehemiah (after 432), and of Ezra.
The Book of Ruth.
The Aramaic Story in Ezra 4:8–6:18.
Joel (c. 400).

(7) The 4th Century—
Joel (later elements).
Isaiah 19:1–15, 23:1–14.
Proverbs (older portions).
Job.
Isaiah 24–27.

(8) The 3d Century—
The Chronicler (300–250).
Genesis 14.
I Kings 13.
Esther.
Song of Solomon.
Proverbs 1–9:30 f.
Jonah.
Isaiah 19:18–25.
Ecclesiastes (c. 200).

(9) The 2d Century—
Daniel (165–164).
Zechariah 9–11, 13:7–9.
Isaiah 33.
Zechariah 12; 13:1–6, 14.
Completion of the Psalter.

Jesus thought of his mission as the fulfillment of old Hebrew Scripture (Matt. 5:17); and often quoted passages which were in line with truths he wished to emphasize (e g., Matt. 5:27, 31, 38, 43, 22:40; Mark 14:21). Paul, whose training in the O.T. had made him an enthusiast for it, frequently used it to emphasize his preaching (Rom. 14:3, cf. Ps. 69:9; Rom. 14:11, cf. Isa. 45:23; and elsewhere, marginal notes in the various versions.)

Early Christians preserved the O.T., even in the first enthusiasm over the N.T., for they saw that Christ met the requirements of many O.T. prophecies concerning a Messiah, and they searched the ancient Scriptures for prophecies of him. (For use of the O.T. by early Christians, see NEW TESTAMENT.)

Many aspects of the O.T. are treated under the names of the 39 separate books. See also CANON; CHRONOLOGY; HEXATEUCH; LAW; POETRY; PROPHET; SOURCES; TEXTS.

olive, a tree (*Olea europea*, Heb. *zayit*) and its berry-like fruit, cultivated in the highlands (at seldom more than 2,000 ft.) which rim the Mediterranean from Spain and Greece to Palestine. Many consider the olive native to Syria; it was not originally native to Europe as its botanical name suggests. It thrives in 'Ajlûn in the Kingdom of Jordan, Armenia, Assyria (II Kings 18:32), Samaria, Shechem, and near Bethlehem, Hebron, Lachish, and Gezer. Its groves lined the Phoenician Plain. It impresses travelers in Palestine with its "Biblical" look (cf. II Kings 18:32). Though its bark is gnarled and its contour unsymmetrical, its shimmering veil of misty blue-green lanceolate leaves, whose under surface is scurfy white, contributes an ethereal beauty to many a poor man's garden (Ps. 52:8). The olive tree supplies shelter from the sun, and privacy for those who seek rest and contemplation (Luke 22:39). Almost every garden in Palestine contains one or more olive trees. There are four varieties of olive in the Near East.

299. Olive grove near Jerusalem.

Though it is mentioned in Scripture less often than the fig, and barely a tenth as often as the vine, the olive and the cedars of Lebanon are the Biblical trees par excellence. Moses called Palestine a "land of oil olive" (Deut. 8:8). In the highlands of Samaria during the prosperous 9th-century Omri-Ahab dynasty olives formed a chief source of wealth in this "fat" country; and they still are in the vicinity of ancient Shechem and the present Nablus, which is known for its olive-oil soap.

Cultivation of the olive is not arduous in view of the profit of its yield. It thrives in stony soil, and begins to bear a few berries three or four years after being grafted at the age of three, and yields plentifully at 15 years, continuing to do so often for centuries. It requires grafting if it is to produce good fruit—hence Paul's allusion to the wild olive graft (Rom. 11:17–24). Old trees usually send new shoots up from the ground before they die (cf. Ps. 128:3). The olive groves in Jerusalem's Garden of Gethsemane contain a few trees said to be descendants of the ones beneath which Jesus prayed (Matt. 26:36). People living along the Bethlehem Road near Rachel's Tomb say that the trees there are "the oldest bearing olive trees in the world." Groves are now being carefully tended on the outskirts of Bethlehem and elsewhere in Palestine.

Crops ripen in the fall and are harvested in November and December, when the fruit is often beaten from the trees by poles, a primitive

OLIVES, MOUNT OF, OLIVET

method that injures the trees and makes them yield only every 2d year. In Bible times the poor were allowed to pick a few berries from the top of trees, or glean those left on the ground.

The olive, one of the principal trees of the Bible, is worthy of being called their king (Judg. 9:8 f.). Hosea thought of redeemed Israel as possessing beauty "as the olive tree" (14:6). It became the symbol of the peace essential to its cultivation, and of the comeliness and strength bestowed by God (Ps. 52:8; Jer. 11:16). It has acquired an almost sacred character to Christians from its association with Jesus (Mark 13:3, 14:26, 32; John 8:1; cf. Acts 1:12) (see OLIVES, MOUNT OF).

The olive has many uses. As a food fresh or pickled olives form, along with bread, a chief source of nourishment among Palestinians. Olive oil* fries and seasons food, and feeds the lamp wicks in old-fashioned households. In O.T. times it was a medium of exchange. It supplied the base of ointments and hair tonics, and was used in surgery. The roots of the olive tree make fine fuel. Olive wood, though too brittle and knotty for carving, is workable after it has been seasoned for several years; its deep-amber, fine-grained surface takes a high polish. From

300. Ancient olive press.

olive wood (or perhaps oleaster) were constructed the two decorative cherubim and doors of the oracle of the Tempie, according to the narrative of I Kings 6:23, 31–33. If either of these woods was used, it must have been pieced together in many fragments, for neither is a timber tree. Olive branches were built into booths during the Feast of Tabernacles (Neh. 8:15). Olive wreaths crowned the victors in the Graeco-Roman games witnessed by Paul. Athene's gift of the olive tree to Athens was more highly valued than Poseidon's horse.

Olives, Mount of (Heb. *har hazethim*), **Olivet** (II Sam. 15:30; Acts 1:12), the mile-long ridge of rounded limestone hills roughly paralleling the eastern elevation of Jerusalem. The Mount of Olives is the most conspicuous landmark of Jerusalem. The Mount is separated from the plateau of the city by the deep, narrow cleft of the Kidron* Valley. This "mountain which is on the east side of the city" (Ezek. 11:23) is "a Sabbath day's journey" from it (Acts 1:12). The ridge has several elevations, separated by inconspicuous depressions. The northernmost end joins Mount Scopus, where the British War Cemetery and the Hebrew University are situated. From N. to S. the high points of the ridge are: (1) The northernmost and the highest (c. 2,723 ft. above sea level), sometimes called the *Viri Galiloei* because many people locate the Ascension here (Acts 1:11), was covered with structures in Christ's time, and consequently seems an unlikely site for this event (cf. Mark 16:7). (2) The next and principal hill of the Mount (c. 2,641 ft.) is often called "the Ascension." Here is the enclosure of the Russian Orthodox Church, with its tall Tower of the Ascension, seen from all the approaches to Jerusalem. Near it are the small Moslem Chapel, claimed by Islam to be the place of Christ's Ascension, and the village of et-Tûr, possibly the Biblical Bethphage (Matt. 21:1 ff.), from which one of the conspicuous Y-shaped paths runs abruptly down the face of the Mount to the Kidron. From this point can be seen an unsurpassed panorama of Jerusalem, compactly built (Ps. 122:3) within its ivory-colored, mediaeval walls, showing courses of very ancient masonry. (3) Next is the elevation called "the Prophets," because tombs of Hebrew prophets are believed by the credulous to be there. (4) The "Mount of Offense," sometimes considered separate from the Mount proper, is 2,411 ft. high, about the same elevation as the Temple hill opposite; it is named for Solomon's apostasies carried on there. Clinging to the slope at this point is the squalid village of Silwan (or Siloam, but not to be confused with the Pool of Siloam on the E. slope of Jerusalem).

Four sections of the Garden of Gethsemane*, Franciscan, Armenian, Russian and Greek, are on the lower reaches of the Mount of Olives, marked today by a few ancient olives, palms, and other trees. The lowest part of the Mount is lined with hundreds of Jewish tombs and Herodian sepulchers, assigned without historic justification to Absalom, Jehoshaphat, St. James, and others. Nehemiah's enumeration of olives, pines, myrtles, and "thick trees," stripped to erect booths for the Feast of Tabernacles (8:15), may explain the palm branches associated with the Palm Sunday procession. Only John's narrative describes the "branches" as palms (John 12:13; cf. Matt. 21:8; Mark 11:8).

Around the shoulder of the Mount of Olives, not seen from Jerusalem, is Bethany*, to whose refreshing hospitality Jesus and his company often came to escape the pressures of the hostile city.

The Mount of Olives is mentioned only occasionally in the O.T. King David fled over it barefoot during his son Absalom's revolt (II Sam. 15:30); there was a shrine on its summit (II Sam. 15:32); Ezekiel located a theophany there (11:23); and Zechariah made the Mount of Olives God's vantage point for watching the powers threatening Jerusalem, and prophesied that it would be cleft to form a new valley (14:4).

Until the first century A.D. (when messengers were substituted), Jewish religious leaders announced the coming of each new moon by signals lighted on the Mount of

Olives after the Sanhedrin had observed its first slender crescent.

It was Jesus' custom to go to the Mount of Olives at evening, when other men went to their homes (John 7:53, 8:1). From its top, with its panoramic view of the Holy City and its sumptuous Herodian structures, Jesus pronounced his lament over its impending doom and the judgment of its people (Matt. 24–25). On the slopes of this Mount, perhaps, he had taught his prayer (Luke 11:1–4) to his Disciples—an event memorialized on the E. slope by a chapel on whose walls the Lord's Prayer is written in 35 languages. (But cf. Matt. 6, where the prayer appears following the Sermon on the Mount, in Galilee). From the hilltop village of Bethphage Jesus rode a borrowed colt down the steep slope from the summit of the ridge, across the Kidron, and up the escarpment to walled Jerusalem, entering at an opening that for centuries was said to be the Golden Gate in the E. wall (Matt. 21:1–12). After the Lord's Supper in the Upper Room Jesus and the Eleven went out to the Mount of Olives (Matt. 26:30). Ancient olive groves on the Mount witnessed Christ's agony in the Garden, his betrayal by Judas, and his arrest by the Romans (vv. 47–56). Within view of the Mount, probably, were Calvary and the garden tomb from which he arose, to ascend after 40 days (Acts 1:4, 9, 11 f.).

See LORD'S PRAYER, illus. 250.

On the strategic summit of the Mount of Olives in A.D. 70 the army of the Roman Titus poised for the siege of Jerusalem.

The road from Jerusalem to Jericho via Bethany runs along the base of the Mount of Olives, skirting the Franciscan portion of the Garden of Gethsemane, and branching N. of this area into several paths up the E. face of the Mount, to Bethphage and one Ascension site.

301. Mount of Olives. In foreground, Garden of Gethsemane, with Armenian portion at left of road, Franciscan portion at center foreground; Russian portion, with pencil cypresses, at center right, Orthodox Church of Mary Magdalene at far right. A road to Bethany and Jericho skirts base of picture. Right fork of Y-shaped road leads to Bethphage and Mt. of Ascension.

The Mount of Olives, like Mary's Fount at Nazareth and Jacob's deep well at Sychar, is a Biblical site about which there are no arguments.

Olivet. See OLIVES, MOUNT OF.

Olympas, a member of the Roman Church to whom Paul sent greetings (Rom. 16:15).

omega (ō-mē′gȧ), the last letter of the Gk. alphabet. For symbolic use in the N.T. see ALPHA, SYMBOL.

302. Alpha and Omega.

omer (ō′mẽr), the tenth part of an ephah (Ex. 16:36) (Heb. dry measure; see WEIGHTS AND MEASURES). The small cup seen on the Hebrew silver shekels and half shekels of the First Revolt may represent the omer of barley from the new crop, presented at the Temple as first fruits of the field on the 2d day of the Passover and on *Bikkurim*, 50 days later, at the festival of Pentecost (Lev. 23:9 f.).

Omri (ŏm′rī), the 6th king of Israel (c. 876–869 B.C.), 1st of a dynasty of four, including his son Ahab (c. 869–850), Ahaziah (c. 850–849), and Joram (c. 849–842). When Elah, King of Israel (c. 877–876), was assassinated by Zimri (I Kings 16:9–11), who then proclaimed himself king, the prophetic party under the leadership of Jehu* supported Omri, one of Elah's generals engaged in the siege of the Philistines (16:15–17). Zimri, after a reign of seven days (c. 876 B.C.), sensed his defeat and chose to be burned to death in the palace of his besieged capital, Tirzah (probably Tell el-Fâr'ah). The anti-prophetic party, supporting Tibni, another contender for the throne, was finally exterminated by the Omri forces after four years of civil war.

The reign of Omri was more important than Bible records indicate (I Kings 16:23–28), for Judaean jealousy minimized his achievements. He moved the capital, Tirzah, Israel's first seat of government after the division of Solomon's kingdom, to the 400-ft. hill of Samaria* belonging to Shemer. Archaeology verifies the fact that this site was unoccupied until Omri's time. Its orientation toward the N. and W. indicates Omri's choice of a strategic military location. Here he began extensive defenses, completed by his son Ahab. (Later they proved so formidable that it took the besieging Assyrians three years to break through.) Omri enriched Israel by developing Samaria, fed by its prolific olive orchards, as a commercial center. He negotiated trade concessions, such as caravansaries and bazaars, with neighbor nations (I Kings 20:34). His city prospered as a port on the altered caravan routes. He established lucrative business alliances with western Phoenician neighbors, and married his eldest son Ahab to the Phoenician Jezebel, daughter of the king of Tyre. Ostraca* of this period,

303. Demi-omer, ancient Hebrew stone vessel found on property of Notre Dame de Zion, Jerusalem.

unearthed at the "ostraca house" in Samaria, bear the names of both Yahweh and Baal (I Kings 16:25 f.), indicating syncretism and apostasy. Omri laid the foundation of the long-standing Phoenicia-Israel brotherhood (Amos 1:9). The Moabite Stone tells of Israel's exploits east of the Jordan unmentioned in the O.T. Omri conquered the region near Madeba; and years later Mesha, a wealthy sheep-owning king of Moab, was paying wool tribute to the King of Israel (II Kings 3:4 f.).

During the Omri period Israel was a powerful member of the western states, superior in wealth, military prowess, and international prestige to Judaea. For 100 years after Omri Assyrian records refer to Israel as "the Land of the House of Omri." The regulations inaugurated by Omri were long in force (Mic. 6:16). His liberal attitude toward foreigners and foreign practices became the habit of the Samaritan colony, which later flourished near Omri's capital and was considered unorthodox by the Jews.

On (ŏn), a city of Lower Egypt (Gen. 41:45, 50, 46:20), 6 m. NE. of modern Cairo, the great center of Egyptian sun worship, where Re was enshrined in the 5th Dynasty (c. 2494–2345 B.C.; see *CAH*[3], Vol. I, chap. XIV, Pt. III), and possibly as early as the 2d (c. 2890–2686 B.C.). In Jeremiah (43:13) "Beth-shemesh" ("house of the sun") may refer to On; the Greeks named it "Heliopolis." In the LXX Ex. 1:11 adds "Heliopolis" to Pithom and Raamses as cities where the children of Israel labored.

The sun, dominant in Nile* Valley life, early became the supreme god (see also RE). According to Egyptian tradition the primeval hill on which creation had its beginning was located under the sun temple of On. The sun produced at On the first evidence of new life in the agricultural year; here at the apex of the Delta the inundating Nile waters first began to recede, and the earth, enriched by a new deposit of silt, became fertile under the warmth of the sun. The worship of the sun at Heliopolis was the keystone of the Egyptian ritual. The sun had many cults in On and throughout Egypt expressed in terms of the sun's activities, each having its hieroglyphic symbol.

Potipherah, whose daughter Asenath was given as a wife to Joseph by Pharaoh, was a priest of On (Gen. 41:45, 50, 46:20). The powerful On priesthood was closely identified with the throne, and included some of the leading religious thinkers in Egypt. These priests were subjected to political upsets, due to their close relationship to the rulers. The "ra" (re) compounded in the last syllable of the name of the priest Potiphera (R.S.V. Gen. 41:45), identifies him with the oldest branch of the sun cult in On. Temples were the usual depositories of royal decrees and records, which confirms the remark of Herodotus that the priests of Heliopolis were well-informed on history. If Isaiah (19:18) refers to Heliopolis as "the city of destruction," the statement tallies with the condition of the town in the later centuries of the era before the birth of Christ.

Two obelisks of red Syene granite, erected by Thutmosis III (c. 1504–1450 B.C.) in front of the Middle Kingdom temple of Re in Heliopolis now stand, one on the Thames Embankment in London, and one in Central Park, New York City. The close relationship between Joseph and the priesthood of On has given rise to the belief that Heliopolis always had a Jewish colony, and to the tradition that the Holy Family during its sojourn in Egypt found asylum there. The descendant of the sycamore tree in whose shade Joseph, Mary, and Jesus are said to have slept is pointed out at Matariya, a short distance from the site of ancient Heliopolis. One lone obelisk stands there now (erected by Sesostris I, c. 1946 B.C., in the temple of Re-Atum), marking the grandeur of Biblical On. (See OBELISK, illus. 297.)

Onan (ō′năn), a son of Judah and a Canaanitess, Shuah, slain by God for an act displeasing to Him (Gen. 38:4, 8–10, 46:12; Num. 26:19; I Chron. 2:3). The history of a tribe rather than of an individual is probably the background of this narrative.

Onesimus (ō-nĕs′ĭ-mŭs) ("helpful", "profitable") (Col. 4:9), the slave of Philemon of Colossae (Philem. 10). He proved "unprofitable" by running away from his master (Philem. 11), and perhaps stealing from him (v. 18). This fugitive from the Roman slave law escaped apprehension among the crowds of the capital. A number of causes could have contributed to the meeting of Onesimus and Paul in Rome: (1) an earlier acquaintance between the two; (2) the testimony of love and admiration from his former master, Philemon, for the Apostle; (3) the personal work of a fellow Colossian, Epaphras (Col. 4:12); (4) Paul's well-known attitude toward slaves (I Cor. 7:21 f.; Eph. 6:7–9; Rom. 2:11). As a fugitive in Rome, at any rate, he met Paul, and under the Apostle's influence became a Christian (v. 10), admitted his misdemeanors, and at Paul's insistence returned to his former master. With Tychicus (Col. 4:7–9) as intercessor, Onesimus returned to Colossae bearing the Epistle to Philemon. According to tradition Philemon not only forgave Onesimus but granted him his freedom, as Paul had hoped he would do (Philem. 21).

Onesiphorous (ŏn′ē-sĭf′ō-rŭs), an Ephesian friend of Paul's, who sought out the Apostle and ministered to him when he (Paul) was a prisoner in Rome (II Tim. 1:16–18). Since Paul salutes only his household in this letter (4:19) Onesiphorus had probably died before it was written.

Ono (ō′nō) ("vigorous"), an ancient town of Benjamin, whose building is ascribed to Shamed (I Chron. 8:12). The linking of its name in this reference with that of Lod (Lydda) suggests that Ono was Kefr 'Anā, c. 7 m. SE. of Joppa. It was mentioned in a record of Thutmosis III (c. 1504–1450 B.C.) and in post-Exilic writings (Ezra 2:33; Neh. 6:2, 7:37, 11:35). (See *ANET*[3], p. 243.)

onycha (ŏn′ĭ-kȧ), an ingredient of the holy incense (Ex. 30:34) used in the Tabernacle, believed to have been the operculum, or lid, of a shell mollusk which, when burned, gave off a perfume.

onyx, the translation in some versions of the Heb. *shoham;* in others "sardonyx," "beryl"; according to Flinders Petrie, possibly green feldspar. The *shoham* was regarded as a precious stone (Gen. 2:12), associated with the gold of Ophir (Job 28:16), and was one of the 12 stones set in the high priest's breastplate* (Ex. 28:9, 35:9, 27). Two "onyx" stones, each carrying names of six of the Twelve Tribes, were fastened to the shoulders of the high priest's ephod. Onyx—known to us as a variety of quartz having varicolored bands—was among the materials collected by David for the construction of the Temple (I Chron. 29:2; Ezek. 28:13). See JEWELRY.

Ophel (ō′fĕl) ("hill"), the S. extremity of the eastern or Temple hill at Jerusalem, site of the earliest settlement (II Chron. 27:3, 33:14; Neh. 3:26 f., 11:21). See JERUSALEM.

Ophir (ō′fẽr), a region in SW. Arabia (modern Yemen) and possibly also a portion of the neighboring African coast. Ophir was on the Red Sea, adjacent to Sheba* and Havilah (Gen. 10:29). The fact that "Ophir" occurs after the account of the visit of the Queen of Sheba to Solomon (I Kings 10:1–10) suggests that in the mind of the writer Ophir was associated with the territory of that rich "queen of the south" (Matt. 12:42). The voyages of the Solomon-Hiram navy to Ophir (I Kings 9:26–28; II Chron. 8:18, 9:10) and the visit of the Queen of Sheba to Palestine probably stimulated the overland camel caravan trade, competing with Egyptian sea commerce (cf. II Chron. 9:24 f.). (See SABA; TRADE.)

Ophir is usually associated in the O.T. with fine gold (I Kings 10:11; Job 22:24, 28:16; Ps. 45:9; Isa. 13:12), which Solomon's Phoenician-manned navy of "Tarshish" ships (? smeltery fleet) obtained by sailing from Ezion-geber* on the Gulf of Aqabah down the Red Sea, requiring three years to make the round trip (allowing for halts during excessively hot weather). The fact that the ships brought not only gold, but silver, apes, ivory, and peacocks (I Kings 10:22), does not necessarily mean that they plied as far E. as Indian Ocean ports, for these wares might have come from Punt on the Red Sea, or been picked up at points of transshipment.

Gold of Ophir adorned Solomon's armor, throne, Temple, and "house of the forest of Lebanon" (I Kings 10:14–19; II Chron. 9:20), and from it were fashioned his table vessels (II Chron. 9:20). King Jehoshaphat (c. 873–849 B.C.), attempting to duplicate Solomon's gold-buying project, lost his luxury fleet at Ezion-geber before it set sail for Ophir (I Kings 22:48). See TARSHISH.

Ophrah (ŏf′rȧ). (1) The name of a family of Judah (I Chron. 4:14). (2) A town of Benjamin (Josh. 18:23; I Sam. 13:17), identified with et-Taiyibeh, 4 m. NE. of Bethel; possibly the Ephraim of II Sam. 13:23. (3) A town in the territory of Manasseh (Judg. 6:11, 15), the home of Gideon (Judg. 6–8), and the place of his burial (8:32); the home of Abimelech (Judg. 9:5). Perhaps it is to be identified with et-Taiyibeh, in the Esdraelon Plain NE. of the Hill of Morek, though Aharoni would prefer the site of 'Affûlah, to the SE. (Y. Aharoni, *The Land of the Bible*, 1967, p. 241).

oracle. (1) A divine communication (Rom. 3:2; Heb. 5:12; I Pet. 4:11), or the person or thing through which the message was received (Acts 7:38). Oracles conveyed God's will to man (a) by dreams (I Sam. 28:6); (b) by the Urim* and Thummim (Ex. 28:30) worn on the priest's breastplate; (c) by the prophets' utterances; (d) by divination (see MAGIC). (2) An authoritative or wise utterance, like the oracle taught King Lemuel by his mother) A.S.V. Prov. 31:1; cf. II Sam. 16:23, Ahithophel). (3) The Holy of Holies in the Jewish Temple* (I Kings 6:5 ff., 7:49, 8:6, 8; Ps. 28:2). (4) An utterance by a priest or priestess at the shrine of a god in ancient Greece and in lands influenced by Greece, believed to be the response of deity to the query of a questioner. At Cumae, near Naples, the oracle of the Sibyl issued from her cave in the Acropolis, as described in Virgil's *Aeneid*. This unique cave and its galleries have been excavated by modern archaeologists.

The earliest record of prophetic oracle is in the story of Wen-Amon, an Egyptian emissary at Byblos in Phoenicia (c. 1100 B.C.).

Archaeological examination of Corinth has revealed an oracular shrine c. 30 ft. N. of the sacred spring; its well-matched blocks date from the 5th century B.C. A stele forbade visitors to approach the area. At the upper end of the tunnel a small hole opens like a megaphone below the floor level—evidently the mechanism by which the oracle communicated with the credulous.

oral materials, sources, and traditions, stories in prose or verse, songs, legends, and truths which played a large part in the nomadic culture of the early Hebrews, and which were passed down from generation to generation. Some of these were later captured and preserved in their written literature. Some oral traditions found their way into Genesis 2, 3, 6–8. The most ancient stories, songs*, riddles, and Wisdom utterances incorporated in the O.T. are in poetry*, a form which helped to preserve them. Early Israel honored its singers of folk ballads (Num. 21:27), and encouraged them to reduce their works to writing, as was done in The Book of the Wars of Yahweh, and The Book of Jashar, portions of which survive as quotations in Num. 21:14 f.; Josh. 10:12 f.; and I Kings 8:12 f. Oral literature in the O.T. includes: the Song of Lamech (Gen. 4:23 f.); the Song of Miriam at the Sea of Reeds (Ex. 15:21); the Song of the Well (Num. 21:17 f.); the Amorite taunt ballad (Num. 21:27–30); Joshua's prayer song (Josh. 10:12–14); and the Song of Deborah (c. 1125 B.C.), regarded as the oldest of Israel's poems (Judg. 5), and never surpassed in literature of its type.

As in the literary portions of the O.T.* the oral underlay the written, so in the development of Hebrew Law* the oral Law preceded the written.

The J source (see SOURCES) of O.T. narratives, as Robert H. Pfeiffer points out (p. 150, *Introduction to the Old Testament*, Harper & Brothers), was a national epic composed largely from oral sources. The unique rustic cycle of Samson stories was circulating orally long before J wrote. Similarly, the author of the E document, though he may have known the J document, employed oral traditions popular in N. Israel, as well as Canaanite sanctuary legends, but omitted typically Judaean, Abraham-at-Hebron material. Oral traditions rewritten by the authors of J and E are almost impossible now to identify in the Book of Joshua, for example. The Book of Judges contains two oral forms of the same story: the Song of Deborah (Judg. 5) and a parallel prose version (Judg. 4) based on oral tradition circulating for some centuries after the poem was composed.

(For oral material in the N.T. see LORD'S SUPPER, THE; MARK, THE GOSPEL ACCORDING TO; MATTHEW; NEW TESTAMENT.)

It is evident that in the early Church many sayings not a part of the written Gospel were transmitted by word of mouth. The formula in Acts 20:35, in Paul's farewell at Miletus, "remember the words of the Lord Jesus, how he said," introduces a saying of Jesus' not in the written Gospels; Polycarp and Clement use similar introductions. In I Cor. 11:23 Paul uses words which he may not have had in written form. The compressed records of events (paradigms) found in the Gospels (Mark 2:27, 3:34, 10:16) are an evidence of their oral sources.

orans, the figure of a man praying with extended arms, used in early Christian iconography, as seen in Roman catacomb frescoes. See SYMBOL.

ordain. (1) To appoint authoritatively, as God ordaining stars in their courses (Ps. 8:3), or designating a place for Israel (I Chron. 17:9), or establishing peace (Isa. 26:12). Kings and seers ordained men to certain functions, like David to the kingship, and men to be Tabernacle gatekeepers (I Chron. 9:22). (2) To invest with priestly or ministerial functions, as God did with Jeremiah (Jer. 1:5), or as Jeroboam, without authority, ordained men to be priests for his calves and "devils which he had made" (II Chron. 11:15). Jesus ordained twelve men to be with him, and to preach (Mark 3:14). Titus ordained elders in the cities of Crete (Titus 1:5). (3) The N.T. also uses "ordain" in the sense of foreordination (predestination*), as people ordained to eternal life (Acts 13:48; cf. Eph. 2:10; Jude 4). See also MAGIC.

ordeal. See MAGIC.

ordination, the conferring of holy orders, the setting apart for the Christian ministry, described in the early Church as the "laying on of hands" with prayer, as at Antioch (Acts 13:3) and at Jerusalem (Acts 6:6). Moses gave a "charge" to Joshua (Num. 27:18–23).

Oreb (ō′rĕb) **and Zeeb** (Heb., "raven" and "wolf"), two Midianite princes slain at Gideon's command during the advance of Ephraim to the Jordan (Judges 7:24 f.). A rock "Oreb" and a winepress "Zeeb" where the executions occurred were named for the princes (cf. Ps. 83:11; Isa. 10:26).

Orion (ō-rī′ŏn), the constellation S. of Gemini and Taurus, containing thousands of stars (only a few visible to the naked eye), including the giants Betelgeuse and Rigel. It was early imagined to resemble the form of a hunter, who legend says was slain by Artemis after his pursuit of the Pleiades. God's creation of Orion, Arcturus, and the Pleiades was acknowledged by Job (9:9, 38:31); and Amos

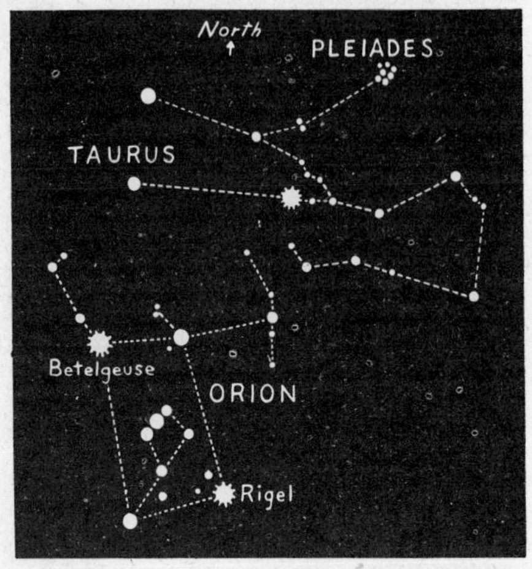

304.

(5:8), made a similar declaration concerning the familiar wonder of the night skies of Palestine. Hebrews and other Semites were early observers of the stars.

ornaments. See AMULET; BREASTPLATE; DRESS; JEWELRY; MAGIC.

Ornan (ôr′năn). See ARAUNAH.

Orontes, the chief river of Syria, also known as the Draco, the Typhon, and the Axius, from which comes its modern name, el-'Asī ("rebel"). Rising in the high Beka'a Valley between parallel ranges of the Lebanons, it pursues a 170-m. course N. through NW. Syria, then W. into the Mediterranean at Seleucia Pieria, ancient port of Antioch-on-the-Orontes. Unlike most Syrian rivers, its channel contains water the year round, and is used for irrigation (see FARMING) by means of huge wooden water wheels. Ancient Antioch, an early Christian center (Acts 11:20 f., 26, 13:1–3), included a district built on an island in the Orontes. This has been excavated by archaeologists for one French and three American organizations. Up the Orontes swept armies contending for the Middle East (see NECHOH). The town of Riblah* on the Orontes appears in the Biblical account of King Zedekiah of Judah and Nebuchadnezzar (II Kings 25:6 f.; Jer. 39:5 f., 52:9 ff.). Hamath, Homs (Emessa), and Kadesh were other influential towns on the Orontes, the latter being the scene of the contest between Ramesses* II and Hittites who almost annihilated the Egyptian forces.

Orpah (ôr′pă). See RUTH.

Osee (ō′-zē). See HOSEA.

Oshea (ō-shē′ȧ). See JOSHUA.

Osiris (ō-sī′rĭs), the son of Geb and Nut, and a member of the triad or "holy family" of Egyptian gods. Osiris was husband and brother of Isis, and father of Horus, a solar falcon god. He was often depicted as an enthroned mummy wearing the crown of Upper Egypt. In protohistoric times the pharaoh was regarded as an incarnation of Osiris, who represented the Nile Valley vegetation, dying in summer when he was submerged under the inundation of the river, but resurrected again when the flood subsided. His home was conceived to be in the fresh-water ocean of the nether regions. Osiris, with his retinue of lesser gods and his mortuary ritual, waned with the rise of the solar monotheism of Akhenaton* and his Aton cult.

In the Egyptian Book of the Dead, known perhaps to the Hebrews in Egypt during their sojourn there, Osiris presided over the underworld, where every deceased person was judged by a court of 42 judges, and had his heart weighed (cf. A.S.V. Prov. 21:2) in a scale (the balances of righteousness), presided over by the god Thoth. If it were found to be true, the soul was permitted to enter the Elysian hereafter, and to become in a sense Osiris himself.

The burial chamber of Tut-ankh-amun was adorned with symbols of the mortuary deity Osiris and his consort Isis. Abydos, called "the city of Osiris," maintained three sanctuaries sacred to his cult of the dead.

The Osiris myths parallel the Tammuz literature of Mesopotamia, that of Adonis of the Hellenistic cultists in Syria, and the saga of Attis in Asia Minor.

Osnappar (ŏs-năp′ẽr) (A.S.V. Ezra 4:10; A.V. Asnapper [ăs-năp′ẽr] but the best Heb. form is Asenappar). See ASSHURBANAPAL.

ossifrage, an unclean (Deut. 14:12) bird, possibly the osprey (large hawk) or lammergeier (vulture, preying on lambs); "gier eagle" A.S.V. margin Lev. 11:13.

ossuaries, small limestone caskets in which the bones of the deceased were placed after the flesh had decomposed. Hundreds of these bone boxes, usually bearing brief inscriptions in Greek or Aramaic, have been excavated in Palestine. The late Prof. E. L. Sukenik of the Hebrew University believed that several ossuaries found in 1945 in a family tomb in the Jerusalem suburb Talpioth, on the road to Bethlehem, date from not later than the 1st century A.D. The tomb contained a coin of King Agrippa from A.D. 42–43. The ossuaries—now in the museum of the Hebrew University and the Palestine Archaeological Museum—are those prepared for the Jerusalem family of Barsaba, whose members bore the names "Miriam, daughter of Simeon"; "Mattathias"; and "Simeon Barsaba" (cf. (Acts 1:23). A symbol resembling a crude cross, accompanied by two Gk. words translated "Jesus, woe!" or "Jesus, alas!" has been found on one of the ossuaries, but at this early date it would not have symbolized Christianity or marked the tomb of a witness to the Crucifixion. It may have been a sign that the box was full or a warning to evil spirits. See *BA* Vol. IX, No. 1, 1946, p. 19.

Ostia, a port of Rome* in Paul's time, situated at the mouth of the Tiber ½ m. below the modern Ostia. It was connected with the capital 14 m. distant by the Ostian Way (still called so—a modern autostrada). As early as c. 338 B.C. Rome maintained a walled fortress at the river mouth to protect lightweight cargo vessels carrying grain from Mediterranean ports up the Tiber to Rome. Virgil's *Aeneid* apparently locates Aeneas's fortress on the Tiber at Ostia. A Roman colony existed at Ostia by 278 B.C. It was the naval base for the Roman navies during the Second Punic War, and after the fall of Carthage was expanded to take care of Rome's Mediterranean expansion during the 2d century B.C. Paul's ship did not land at Ostia, but at Puteoli (Acts 28:13), another port of Rome favored by large Alexandrian grain ships. Paul was probably buried along the Ostian Way, at a point c. 1¼ m. seaward from the extant Pyramid of Cestius in Rome.

Ostia has received expert archaeological examination and restoration (Guido Calza, from 1914 to 1946), and has shed a vast wealth of information concerning life in Rome itself, as well as in this prosperous seaside commercial suburb. Its apartment houses explain how Rome, using similar structures, could house c. 1,200,000 people at the height of the Empire. Paul's "own hired house" at Rome (Acts 28:30) was probably quarters in such an apartment; Ostia's tremendous granaries and warehouses reveal its ancient wealth. Its theater is equalled in Italy only by those of Pompeii. Its several Mithraic sanctuaries of the popular Mithras cult, serious competitor of Christianity; a temple to Hercules Invictus; three temples apparently connected with the Ostian guilds of trading merchants; and five chapels for private worship, have all been excavated, as well as the Campus of the Magna Mater, the Cybele brought from Asia Minor to Rome in 204 B.C. These shrines indicate the religious ideas Paul encountered at Rome. In the autumn of 387 A.D. Augustine, Christian saint and theologian, rented quarters in a balconied apartment at Ostia overlooking an interior garden, where he and his mother Monica had their famous conversations concerning the profundities of the Christian faith. The unique 4th century basilica of Ostia is an example of the architecture of large early Christian churches and baptistries.

In 1940 Prof. Guido Calza of Rome announced the discovery at Ostia of a church assigned to the period of the Antonines in the 2d century A.D., about 150 years before Christianity became the established religion of the Roman Empire. This small basilica is one of the oldest known in Italy. It was humble, and its columns do not match; yet its conspicuous baptistry (designed for immersion, as indicated by water tank and pipes almost intact in the niche) demonstrates that Christians of small means had spent generous sums for marble trim.

ostraca (ŏs′trȧ-kȧ) (plural of Gk. *ostrakon*, "potsherd"), fragments of earthen pots or clay* tablets used by peoples of the ancient Near East for business, personal, and military records and communications. The writing was alphabetic, done in pen and ink. Ostraca were also used for ballots; in Athens the citizens "ostracized" Aristides the Just by casting ostraca against him. Some of these have been found. The 70 Samaria ostraca of the reign of Jeroboam II (c. 786–746 B.C.), excavated in a palace storehouse, are inscribed with personal names, some compounded with "Yah," indicating adherents of Yahweh, and others with "Baal," revealing adherents to Baalism, in the proportion of 11 to 7 for Yahweh. These ostraca also shed light on political organization in the era just prior to the time of the prophet Amos in the early 8th century B.C.; and provide examples of script and orthography in the time of Hosea. The Lachish* Letters found in 1935 and 1938 in S. Palestine were written in ink on ostraca, in the language and spelling of Jeremiah's time.

ostrich, the name used in several O.T. passages to indicate a two-toed, swift-footed bird of the genus *Struthio*, plentiful in ancient times in Africa, Arabia, and wilderness areas of the Near East. Hebrew writers were familiar with the ostrich, and listed it as "unclean," i.e., unfit for food (A.S.V. Lev. 11:16; Deut. 14:15); "cruel" (Lam. 4:3); and "mourning" (R.S.V. Mic. 1:8). In the R.S.V. Isaiah (13:21 and 34:13) and Jeremiah (50:39) list the ostrich as inhabiting the ruins of Babylonian and other palaces; the A.V. reads "owl" at these points. The Wisdom writer whose amazingly vivid observations of natural history are among the most interesting passages of the Book of Job (chaps. 37–41) characterizes the ostrich as rich in plumage (39:13) and capable of spectacular speed in flight (v. 18). He mentions the apparent neglect of the hen ostrich, laying eggs in the hot earth and going away from them with indifferent hardness, forgetting that "the foot may crush them, or . . . the wild beast may break them" (vv. 14 f.). He had perhaps jumped to a hasty conclusion, after seeing an ostrich hen walk off the nest at close of day, just before the cock faithfully took over incubation for the night watch. Or he may have based his remark on his observation of the few eggs left intentionally on the ground near the nest, to supply food for the young after they had been hatched. The mother ostrich is faithful to her task of keeping warm the huge eggs, which would not hatch without her even under the hot rays of the sun. In captivity ostriches are often polygamous, two or three hens sometimes sharing a nest. This may not be true in the wild state.

Ostrich plumes were prized at royal courts of the Near East for fans. Plumes of an ivory-handled fan of King Tut-ankh-amun are still seen largely intact in the National Museum at Cairo, more than 3,000 years after the young king used it.

In Christian symbolism the ostrich egg motif, pendant from lamps for example, suggests that Christ is watchful over his Church, like the ostrich over its eggs.

Othniel (ŏth′nĭ-ĕl), a man of Judah (I Chron. 4:13), son of Kenaz, and younger brother or half-brother of Caleb, who gave him his daughter Achsah and a dowry of land and springs as a reward for his winning Kiriath-sepher (see DEBIR) in the Conquest (Josh. 15:16–19; cf. Judg. 1:13–15). This event in the J narrative is typical of the rise of the leader of oppressed clans or "judge" on whom God poured His grace (*charisma*). The Deuteronomists used this story to illustrate the "charismatic" cycle of Israel's history before the Monarchy: Othniel saved his wayward but penitent people from the Mesopotamian king, Chushan-rishathaim ("Cushan of double villainy"), and established 40 years of peace. After he died Israel did evil again, cried to the Lord for deliverance, and received another deliverer, Ehud, who slew the oppressor Eglon and gave the land rest again for 80 years (Judg. 3:12–30).

A descendant of Othniel was the 12th captain for the 12th month in David's organization (I Chron. 27:15).

ouch (ouch) (pl. "ouches") (Heb. *mishbetsōth*, "woven together," in filigree fashion), an archaic noun signifying (1) the setting for a precious stone, as on the shoulder pieces of the high priest's ephod (A.V. Ex. 28:11; 39:6); or (2) a fastener (clasp or brooch) for the cords of his breastplate (A.V. Ex. 28:13 f., 39:16, 18).

oven, a furnace or hot-air chamber for baking, heated by a fire built within or around it. In a figurative sense enemies were burned in a fiery oven (Ps. 21:9); the skin in famine became "black like an oven" (Lam. 5:10); the

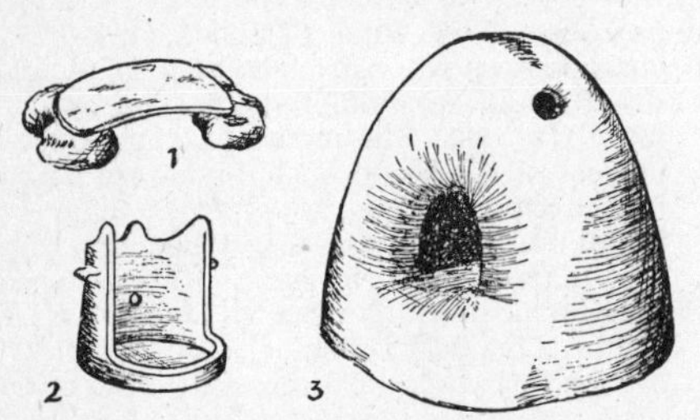

305. Ovens: 1. Type used by nomad tribes; 2. Clay stove still used in many Palestinian villages; 3. Type of community oven.

coming day of the Lord would burn "as an oven," reducing the wicked to stubble (Mal. 4:1). See Matt. 6:30; Luke 12:28. See BAKER.

owl, the name of numerous birds of prey, usually broad-headed and large-eyed. Levitical law listed the owl as unclean, i.e., unfit for food. Scripture mentions the "little owl" (Lev. 11:17; Deut. 14:16); the "great owl" (Lev. 11:17; Deut. 14:16; Isa. 34:15); the "horned owl" (A.S.V. Lev. 11:18); and the "screech owl" (A.V. Isa. 34:14). Owls lurked in desert places (Ps. 102:6) and amid ruins of cities (Isa. 34:11, 14 f.). The small *Athene glaux* was commonly seen in the Palestine countryside at twilight. Athenians esteemed this bird the companion of the wise Athene, and stamped its likeness on their silver coins.

ownership, state or fact of being an owner; safeguarded in early Israel by specific laws, which by the important Talmudic times (after A.D. 200) developed into a complicated body of legislation.

(1) The Jews recognized two types of personal property: (a) possessions (*karka*) which cannot be moved from fixed places, i.e., real estate; and (b) movable personal property (*mitaltelin*), including chattels which are durable, and those which are perishable, like fruits. Animals, which move of their own accord, and slaves (see FREEMAN), had specific laws to govern their ownership. For example, if animals strayed into another man's property they could not be claimed as his unless he could prove that they had been on his land for three years. Money was not regarded as personal property as it is now, because its actual value varied so much that its fixed value could not easily be estimated; it was regarded merely as a convenient means of defraying the cost of a purchase.

(2) Property was acquired (a) by *inheritance** (see also FAMILY) or (b) by *formal purchase*, as Abraham in Patriarchal times acquired the Cave of Machpelah, for which he paid to Ephron the Hittite 400 "weighed shekels of silver, current money with the merchant" (Gen. 23:16), in the presence of witnesses from "the people of the land" (v. 13). Jacob bought the parcel of land where he had pitched his tent from Hamor, father of Shechem, for 100 pieces of money (Gen. 33:18–20 R.S.V. margin, qesitas). The procedure for buying land in the 6th century B.C. is illustrated in detail by the record of the imprisoned prophet Jeremiah's symbolic purchase of a field at Anathoth from Hanameel, his uncle's son (Jer. 32:6–15). First the seller drew up a document and gave it to the buyer. Then Jeremiah weighed out 17 shekels of silver. In return he received two documents, one sealed, the other unsealed. He turned these over to his secretary Baruch in the presence of Hanameel and witnesses. Then he signed "the book of the purchase before all the Jews that sat in the court of the prison" (v. 12). Such documents had to contain the words, "My field is sold to you." Next Jeremiah directed that the two deeds be placed in an earthen vessel—doubtless carefully covered with cloth and sealed with bitumen or clay—"that they may continue many days." After this fashion ancient manuscripts have been preserved for thousands of years (see SCROLLS, THE DEAD SEA). The account also illustrates "the right of redemption" of land by a member of a family.

In connection with this acquisition by purchase Israel used several other symbolic acts, like the handing over of a sandal to denote the transfer of holdings (Ruth 4:4–9); or by "seizure of the cloak" or some other tangible object, the drawing of which to himself by the seller immediately transferred the object to its new owner. This form of acquisition was called *kinyan*. It was used also in drawing up documents for loans or for hiring servants. As Israel's commerce developed, numerous other symbolic customs sprang up to establish ownership, like the shaking of a customer's hand by the merchant in the presence of a witness, to show that bargaining had ceased and the sale was ready to be consummated (Prov. 6:1, 17:18)—a practice still prevalent in the Middle East; or the handing over the keys of a house.

(c) Ownership was also established in early Israel by *covenant* followed by a feast, as when Isaac arranged with Abimelech for the well Sheba (site of the later town Beer-sheba) (Gen. 26:25–33).

(d) Ownership also came about by *confiscation*, as when King Ahab seized his neighbor Naboth's vineyard (I Kings 21). Confiscation on a large scale, and settlement on claimed land, amounted to conquest, as when Israel settled in Canaan—but at God's command (Gen. 13:14–17). This means of establishing ownership is illustrated throughout ancient history, e.g., Nebuchadnezzar's seizure of Judaea, its Temple, and its people (II Kings 24; 25).

3. *Property laws* are found chiefly in Exodus. Deuteronomy omits old property laws, except those against kidnapping (Deut. 24:7; protecting landmarks of property inherited in God's holy land (19:14); and the regulation of honest weights and measures (25:13–16). The Holiness Code contains legislation concerning honesty in buying and selling land (Lev. 25:14–17); the reverting of land to its previous owner every 50 years (the Jubilee), in recognition of freehold being in the hands of God, not of man; and the redemption of the land of the poor by a kinsman or owner, or restoration to the latter in the Jubilee Year (25:23–28). A house in a walled town was transferable, and might be redeemed by the seller any time within a year (v. 29). Houses in unwalled towns were reckoned as part of the fields of the country (v. 31).

See BUSINESS; FEASTS.

ox, the adult castrated male of the *Bos taurus* family, valued throughout the Biblical period (Ex. 20:17) and even today in the Near East as a heavy draft animal. Abraham and Abimelech, for example, used them in Patriarchal times (Gen. 12:16; 20:14). The prophet Elisha plowed with 12 teams of oxen (I Kings 19:19). Oxen were useful for hauling (I Chron. 12:40), plowing (I Kings 19:19), dragging the threshing boards at harvest time (Deut. 25:4; Hos. 10:11); and for food (I Kings 1:25; cf. Matt. 22:4). Oxen in great quantities were offered as sacrifices to Yahweh (I Kings 8:63).

In the Hebrew codes it was unlawful to hitch an ox and an ass together for farm work (Deut. 22:10), or to muzzle an ox when he was treading out the corn to loosen the kernels (Deut. 25:4).

See ANIMALS; CATTLE.

Oxyrhynchus (ŏk′sĭ-rĭng′kŭs), the site of a small Egyptian town in the central part of Lower (northern) Egypt, on the Bahr Jusef stream. Here in 1897 B. P. Grenfell and A. S. Hunt found fragments of a papyrus code containing logia* or sayings of Jesus in Gk. (c. A.D. 200). It includes the sayings concerning the mote, the city set on a hill, the inability of the prophet to influence those of his own community, and the apocryphal "Raise the stone, and thou shalt find me, cleave the wood, and there am I." In one portion of the Oxyrhynchus logia Jesus bids his Disciples live every day as if it were the Sabbath. In 1903 at the same site Grenfell and Hunt found a papyrus roll containing further sayings, written slightly later than those first discovered. Both of these documents lack the simplicity of the words of Jesus recorded in the Gospels. Other Oxyrhynchus papyri, from the 3d to the 5th century A.D., include parts of the 1st paragraph of Romans (now in the Semitic Museum, Harvard University); part of I Corinthians (in Cairo); and fragments of I and II Thessalonians (in the Cathedral Library, Worcester, England). These fragments give an idea of the appearance of early copies of the books of the N.T. These hitherto unknown logia suggest that Jesus uttered many sayings in addition to those preserved in the N.T. (See Q.)

306. Plowing with oxen, Jordan.

P

P, scholar's symbol for that portion of the Pentateuch known as the Priestly Code. See SOURCES.

Padan-aram (pā′dăn-ā′răm) (Paddan-aram [păd′ăn-ā′răm]), ("field of Aram"), a region near the head of the Fertile* Crescent, N. of the junction of the rivers Khabur and Euphrates. In early times it was known as Aram-naharaim ("Aram of the Two Rivers," A.S.V. Gen. 24:10). One of its chief cities was Haran*, to which Isaac and Jacob sent to procure wives (Rebekah and Rachel) from among their kinsmen (Gen. 25:20; 28:2, 6).

paint, painting. The Ten Commandments prohibited the making of images, and there is no trace in the Bible of painting *per se* or in connection with another art form or with Solomon's Temple. King Jehoiakim used vermilion paint on the interior walls of his palace (Jer. 22:14), aping the great palaces of Egypt and Assyria. See COSMETICS.

palace, the large and stately residence of a king or important official. Numerous Middle Bronze Age palaces have been excavated in Palestine, one of the best preserved being that from Stratum D at Tell Beit Mirsim (Debir*), late 17th century B.C. See ARCHITECTURE.

Palaeolithic (Old Stone) **Age,** an early period of human culture (c. 600,000–12,000 years ago), characterized by a subsistence pattern based on hunting and gathering and the use of stone, bone, and flint tools. The earliest anthropoid remains from the Near East come from 'Ubeidiya near the S. shore of Lake Tiberias (dated 300,000–600,000 years ago). Other remains of Palaeolithic man in Palestine come from the Wâdī el-Mughârah, Mughârat ez-Zuṭṭīyah in Galilee, and Jebel Qafzah cave near Nazareth. See E. Anati, *Palestine Before the Hebrews*, 1963, pp. 45–135; also *CAH*², Vol. I, 1970, chaps. III, V.

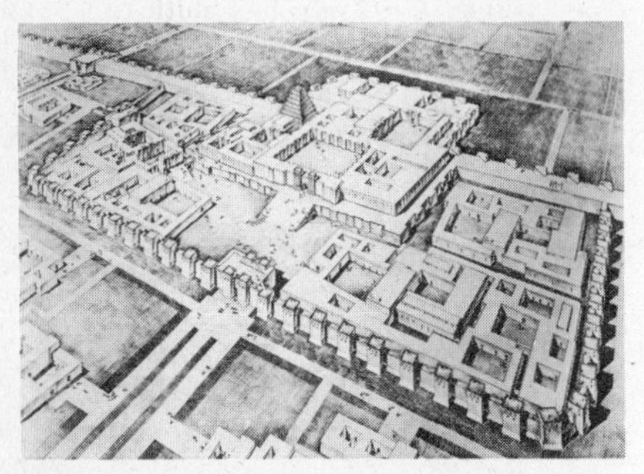

307. Reconstructed drawing of the citadel and palace of the Assyrian king, Sargon II, at Dur-Sharruken (Khorsabad), in modern Iraq.

Palestine, the small land in SW. Asia immediately behind the SE. seaboard of the Mediterranean, where the major events of the Biblical period occurred (from Joshua to Herod, and on through the Apostolic Age). Palestine, regardless of its physical boundaries, has always been thought of as the homeland of Israelites and Jews. Its importance and influence have been out of proportion to its size and resources.

(1) Its *name* stems from that of one of Israel's arch enemies, the Philistines*. Herodotus, the Greek "Father of History," was the first to use "Palestine," when in the 5th century B.C. he referred to "the part of Syria which is called '*Palaistinē*'." The Greeks used *Syria Palaistinē* for all S. Syria including Judaea, to distinguish it from Coele Syria; later they called it simply *Palaistinē*. From the Greeks the Romans derived their Latin name, *Palestina*. *Palestina* appears in A.V. Ex. 15:14; Isa. 14:29, 31; the English derivative, "Palestine," in A.V. Joel 3:4. The name is not mentioned in the N.T.

In the Tell el-Amarna Letters, written in the 14th century B.C. by petty governors and officials in Palestine to their Egyptian overlords, Palestine was called *Kinahni* or *Kinahhi*.

"Canaan" is the name by which Palestine is spoken of in the narratives of the Patriarchal Age, because it was inhabited by Canaanites, a Semitic people who are known today to have possessed a high degree of culture and political power. Abraham's descendants considered the country to be "the promised land," the land of Israel's pilgrimage, guaranteed by the covenant of Yahweh (Gen. 17:7 f.; Ex. 6:4). It is understood as "the promised land" in such passages as Gen. 12:6 f., Ex. 12:25, and Josh. 5:6. After the conquests of Joshua and his successors Palestine was "Israel,"* or "the Land of Israel" ('Eretz Yisra'el) (I Sam. 13:19, etc.). This geographical and political unit never acquired, even under David's expansion, the coastal strip of the Philistine plain inhabited by non-Semites of Aegean background. Not until Israel passed under foreign rule, several centuries after David, did Philistia become a part of Palestine.

The name "holy land" appears in the Bible only in Zech. 2:12 (cf. Ex. 19:5–8), so called because it was Yahweh's country, where occurred events holy to the faithful of Israel.

In the Hellenistic period (333–63 B.C.) and in the Roman era (63 B.C.–A.D. 324), which included N.T. times, the country was called "Judea" (Judaea), a word which originally had connoted only the region about Jerusalem, to which the Jews had returned from Exile.

The official use of "Palestine" did not begin until after A.D. 138, when it referred first to the old SW. coastal strip of the Philistines, and then to all Palestine W. of the Jordan. The land E. of this river was known in the time of Jesus as Perea and the Decapolis; after World War I it was called Trans-Jordan or Eastern Palestine. After the partition of Arab and Jewish Palestine in 1948 the section W. of the Jordan was divided between the Jewish state of Israel and the Hashemite Kingdom of the Jordan (Arab). Boundaries were too irregular and fluid to be listed here.

(2) *Physical Features*—area, boundaries, and population. Biblical Palestine is generally thought of as the region S. and SW. of the Lebanons (including part of what are now the Republics of Lebanon and Syria); NE. of Egypt and the Sinai Peninsula, with the Wâdī el-Arish, the Biblical "river of Egypt" (Gen. 15:18; II Chron. 7:8) as its SW. boundary; E. of the Mediterranean coastal plain; and W. of the Arabian Desert. In terms of "the Fertile* Crescent" ancient Palestine formed the W. portion of the arch lying S. of Mount Hermon. Its latitude, 31°–33° N., corresponds approximately to that of the Atlantic coast between Charleston, S.C., and Jacksonville, Fla. Most of Palestine is in the N. subtropical zone; the Jordan Valley near Jericho is tropical.

Palestine is a rough parallelogram. Its width between Mount Carmel and Tiberias is only 62 m.; it is still narrower between Dan and Tyre. Its average width is 70 m. and its greatest 90 m. The proverbial "from Dan even to Beer-sheba" (Judg. 20:1; II Sam. 3:10, 17:11, 24:2, 15) is a distance of 150 m. The area of Biblical Palestine was c. 10,000 sq. m., made up of c. 6,000 sq. m. in

W. Palestine and c. 3,800 in Eastern Palestine. All of W. Palestine was smaller than Massachusetts, smaller than New Jersey, 1/5 as large as New York State, 9/10 as large as Belgium.

The greatest extent of Israelite control over Palestine was achieved under David and Solomon (c. 1000–922 B.C.), when their kingdom spread N. possibly as far as Kadesh on the Orontes; S. to the Arabian Desert; and W. to the Philistine Mediterranean coast. In that period the Hebrew population of Palestine may have been 1,800,000; tributary groups occupying an area three times as large as Palestine proper may have totalled 3,000,000 persons.

The population of Palestine at the beginning of the Christian era was probably 2 or 2½ million people, half of whom lived in Trans-Jordan or E. Palestine. In the 1st century A.D. more Jews were scattered outside Palestine than lived inside. These figures are interesting to compare with the Jewish population of Palestine at the end of 1937, which was c. 420,000. At the end of 1958, the estimated population of the modern state of Israel was 2,000,000, of which approximately 88% was Jewish. Jordan has c. 1,500,000.

In Jesus' day Palestine was the Roman Judaea, whose principal regions were (a) Galilee—his home province, in the N.; (b) Samaria (Ephraim) in the rugged central highland which had become the Kingdom of Israel after the division of Solomon's United Kingdom; and (c) Judah (Judaea), the southern region ending at the border of Idumaea. S. of Idumaea stretched W. Nabataea.

Seen on a relief map or from the air, Palestine shows four parallel bands between the Mediterranean and the Arabian Desert. These bands are formed by two mountain ranges—(a) the Central Range, which runs down from Mount Lebanon along the west of the Jordan Valley, disappears in the desert, and rises again in the heights of Sinai 250 miles S. of Beer-sheba; and (b) the Eastern Range, which extends S. from the Anti-Lebanon, or Mount Hermon, along the E. of the Jordan; this range forms the heights of Bashan, Gilead, and Moab, and continues as far as Mount Hor in Edom, 250 m. from Dan. These ranges divide the land into four lengthwise sections: (a) a level region along the coast, called the Maritime Plain; (b) the hilly region forming the extension of Mount Lebanon, called the Mountains of Israel or the Central Range; (c) the Jordan Valley; (d) Eastern Palestine.

(a) The Maritime Plain is bounded on the S. by the desert beyond Gaza and on the N. by the Leontes, a river which issues from between the Lebanon and the Anti-Lebanon, and falls into the Mediterranean 5 m. N. of Tyre. The plain is intersected by Mt. Carmel, where that hill juts seaward as a promontory. The N. section forms part of Phoenicia, and is very narrow; the central section has an average width of 5 miles, and includes the Bay of Acre, the only natural harbor of Palestine; and the southern section forms the plain of Philistia, which extends in undulations 32 m. S. from Ekron to Gaza, with a breadth varying from 9 to 16 m. The coastal plain is known as the Plain of Sharon from Carmel to Jaffa, and the Shephelah from Jaffa to the Brook of Gaza, beyond which it becomes the parched plain of the Negeb.

(b) The Central Range and Gilead, the Mountains of Israel, constituted Israel's main holdings in Palestine, and were held longest. The Central Range formed the backbone of the land where Jesus lived. This region extends from Mount Hor in Lebanon to Beer-sheba, interrupted SE. of the Bay of Acre by the Plain of Esdraelon. It is intersected throughout by valleys, called wâdîs, which slope on one side into the Maritime Plain, and on the other into the valley of the Jordan; it is steeper and more barren on the E. than the W.; and includes four prominent points—Mt. Gilboa, the hill of Samaria, Mts. Ebal and Gerizim, and the heights of Jerusalem and Bethlehem. The Central Range area consists of four divisions: (a) Galilee, which reaches from the N. border to the Plain of Jezreel, inclusive. Upper Galilee attains a height of c. 4,000 ft. at Mt. Azmon; Lower Galilee at some points reaches 1,800 ft. above sea level. The ascent from Lower to Upper Galilee is so steep that traffic avoids the hills and takes a roundabout way along the Mediterranean coast or through the Jordan Valley. Low valleys separate the hills of Lower Galilee, where travel from E. to W. is easy. The broad Plain of Jezreel (or Esdraelon) is triangular, with its base on the Carmel Ridge and its apex at Mt. Tabor (1,843 ft.); it is Armageddon, battleground of the ages. (b) Samaria (Ephraim) reaches as far S. as Mt. Ebal (3,077 ft.), and has the same sort of deep valleys as Lower Galilee. The long Carmel Ridge, once heavily wooded, is attached to Samaria in the N. Gilboa (1,698 ft.) has always been bare. Between Mt. Ebal and Mt. Gerizim (2,849 ft.) was Shechem, the principal city of Samaria. (c) Judaea (Judah) continues the Central Mountain Range as far S. as the Plain of Beer-sheba (1,013 ft.). Jerusalem lies 2,593 ft. above sea level. The mountains of Benjamin reach 3,370 ft., and those of Hebron 3,420 ft. (d) The Negeb, S. of Beer-sheba, is a highland region rising to over 4,000 ft.

(c) The Jordan Valley is a gradually depressed extension southward of the plain between Lebanon and Anti-Lebanon, down which flows the Jordan*, a river that rises in several streams at the base of the Anti-Lebanon (the most famous of which is near Caesarea Philippi), and flows into the Dead Sea. The surface of the Dead Sea is 1,290 ft. below that of the Mediterranean, and the bottom 1,300 ft. lower still. The valley varies in width from an average of two or three m. to an average of 12 m., becoming generally wider as it descends. This deep valley, containing the lowest point on the earth's surface, is the N. part of a remarkable geological fault which extends S. through the Gulf of Aqabah, the Red Sea, and E. Africa.

(d) Eastern Palestine is a plateau spreading eastward from Mt. Hermon to Mt. Hor in Edom. It included the densely peopled lands of Bashan, Gilead, and Moab, which, though "allotted" to Israel by her leaders, were always more or less independent.

The Arabian Desert is usually less than 30 m. E. of Palestine, measuring from the Jordan-Dead-Sea-Arabah rift. Along the E. edge of historic Palestine the desert is never more than 100 m. from the Mediterranean.

The Judaean wilderness begins on the very edge of the Mount of Olives in Jerusalem and reaches all along the Dead Sea, except at its N. end, and constitutes the weirdest and most desolate area of Palestine.

The region of the Eastern Range, also known as Eastern Palestine or the plateau of Trans-Jordan, fell naturally into four sections, separated by the River Yarmuk, N. of which lay Bashan; the Jabbok, N. and S. of which was Gilead; the Arnon, S. of which was situated the original land of Moab; and the River Zered, with Edom stretching S. The Yarmuk and the Jabbok flow into the Jordan; the Arnon and the Zered flow into the Dead Sea.

Beyond the S. end of the Dead Sea runs the deep trench of the Arabah, as far as Aqabah at the head of the Red Sea.

Geologically speaking, Palestine soil originated in the Upper Cretacean period. It lacks almost entirely the later Palaeozoic layers which contain the richest deposits of metal and coal. Over primitive rock lies red "Nubian" or "Petra" sandstone, topped by chalky, cretaceous limestone. This limestone, which makes up the mass of Palestine, is overlaid with nummulite limestone and topsoil. NE. Palestine shows huge deposits of volcanic rock, lava and basalt; for though eruptions have not occurred in historic times, traces of violent ones in ancient times are seen in the Hauran and other parts of E. Palestine, which contain the deepest trough in the earth's surface (see DEAD SEA). The weak formation of the earth along the Mediterranean in Palestine is recognized; earth forces are still active there. Earthquakes have been frequent in Palestine, and they occur in modern times, especially in the unstable Jordan Valley and the coastal plain. Such earthquakes were known to writers of Scripture (Ps. 18:7, 114:7; Isa. 13:13, 24:18; Amos 1:1; Zech. 14:5; Matt. 27:51). Quakes are heavier in Syria than in Palestine. Rifts and sinkings in the Tertiary period are responsible for the conspicuous plains of Dothan, Jezreel (Esdraelon), and Zebulun. The deep Jordan rift was formed by a sinking of 5,000 to 6,000 ft. between two lines of fracture, while rocks E. and W. remained in their former positions. The sinking of the Jordan cut some of Palestine's streams in half, so that their upper halves fell into the Jordan and their lower halves became new streams. The Kishon, for example, was part of the Tertiary Jabbok. The weird salt area of Sodom Mountain was formed during a dry interval between the Glacial and the Pluvial periods.

Of the upper and lower layers of limestone around Jerusalem, the upper and harder one is known as *mazi* and the lower, softer one as *malaki*. Heavy structures were built on the former, but the lighter limestone was quarried for building material, much of it from beds near the Damascus Gate.

Water in Palestine finds its way underground to the Mediterranean, rather than into springs which would aid agriculture. The bed of Palestine's largest river, the Jordan, is so deep that the 700,000,000 gal. which it pours annually into the Dead Sea can be utilized only by huge power plants and elaborate irrigation systems. Private wells, dug very deep (as seen at Sychar and Lachish), and underground cisterns of private and public constructions conserve the precious rainfall. Wells and springs determined the location of many ancient cities, like Beer-sheba, Cana of Galilee, Jericho, Jerusalem, En-shemesh, Nazareth, and Sychar.

The *climate* of Palestine is exceptionally varied, owing to the great diversity of level, which embraces a range of over 11,000 ft. from the summit of Mt. Hermon to the surface of the Dead Sea. Consequently among its plants and animals there are representatives of the flora and fauna of almost every other region of the globe from the Arctic circle to the tropics. The plants of northern Europe flourish on Lebanon, those of central Europe at the level of Jerusalem and Carmel, and those of the West Indies on the plain of Jericho near the Jordan. As for the animals, some are denizens of Alpine districts, and others the fauna of the plains of India and the rivers of Africa—there is a symbolic universality about life in little Palestine. (See BIRDS; and entries of individual flowers and trees.)

The prevailing *wind* is from the W., which in winter brings moisture that precipitates into rain in the hill country, creating a rainy season from October to April. Even in summer the W. wind, though dry, makes high temperatures quite tolerable from 11 A.M. until night. Jesus referred to the rain-bringing W. wind (Luke 12:54). Writers of ancient Israel deplored the hot E. wind, "sirocco" (Job 1:19; Ps. 48:7; Jer. 18:17; Ezek. 17:10, 27:26). It manifests itself in blinding sand clouds which make the sky ominous while a high wind roars, or in hot, silent burning. In Ex. 14:21 the E. wind blew back the waters of the Sea of Reeds, so that a path was prepared for Israel's crossing. The S. wind, blowing in from the Arabian Desert, was recognized by Jesus as a bringer of scorching heat (Luke 12:55). People in Palestine were so wind-conscious that believers at Jerusalem described manifestations of Pentecost as a "rushing mighty wind" (Acts 2:2).

Palestine has two *seasons*, determined by the *rains*: summer, from May to October, hot and rainless; and winter, November to April, with mild temperatures and heavy rainfall. The mean temperatures of Tel Aviv, Haifa, Jerusalem, and Beer-sheba are relatively 70°, 69°, 64°, and 67°. The coming of the October rains dated the opening of the plowing season and the civil New Year, with its times of thanksgiving and its Feast of Trumpets, followed by the Day of Atonement. Ps. 65 expresses thanksgiving for the "good earth of Palestine" with its fall rains.

Shortage of water limits agricultural production, except where irrigation is practiced. The "early rains" fall from October to January, the "latter rains" in February through April; the heaviest come in December and January, when most of the total annual rainfall descends. The rainfall follows a pattern similar to that of Los Angeles. Metulla, the northernmost weather station in Palestine, sometimes gets 36 in. of rain, compared to Beer-sheba's 8.8 in. The best-watered lands are too rocky and sloping for successful agriculture. Dew, however, aids crops, especially on the coastal plain, the W. slopes of hills, in the Plain of Esdraelon, and the Negeb (Gen. 27:28; Deut. 33:13; Prov. 3:20).

Lack of water made the grazing of sheep, goats, and cattle a chief industry of Palestine, until farming, fruit-growing, and the industrialization of modern times pushed husbandry farther back into highland and semi-fertile desert sections.

Palestine's *mineral resources* have never been fully exploited. At the opening of the Iron Age (c. 1200–1000 B.C.) Palestine was using little metal. Such utensils as its inhabitants had were usually imported, and in the hands of the upper class. We know now from Nelson Glueck's research in Trans-Jordan and the Arabah that Solomon developed there extensive copper and iron mines, whose slag heaps and refineries Glueck identified and studied. (See EZION-GEBER.) Today Palestine's one abundant mineral source is the Dead Sea, whose potash and bromine supply is unparalleled. Geologists call Palestine a "new country," where coal and the valuable metallic minerals of the Later Paleozoic Age are unknown.

Forests are now lacking, because centuries of uncontrolled grazing and the use of wood for charcoal and war long ago disposed of the trees. In modern times hundreds of thousands of young trees have been planted in an attempt at reforestation. Some seedlings have been sown from the air.

(3) *Historical highlights of Biblical Palestine.*—(a) The antiquity of man in Palestine reaches back into *prehistory*, as demonstrated by research in the caves in Mt. Carmel and Galilee, in areas near Jericho, and on the highlands near Bethlehem. Remarkable progress has been made during a relatively brief period of research into Palestine's prehistory. Anthropologists believe that this small land "presents the most complete and continuous picture of prehistoric human evolution that is at present available in any part of the world" (C. C. McCown). Palestine has furnished a dozen more or less complete Neanderthal or Neanderthaloid skeletons, buried amid tools which these dead and their immediate ancestors used. The skeletons are related to a complete series of successive levels of Stone Age cultures. The "Carmel man" was a Neanderthaler, or man of the Old Stone Age (which began at least 100,000 years ago and ended between 10,000 and 8,000 B.C.). In addition to these, remains of more than 100 Middle Stone Age individuals have been found—people representing the coming to Palestine of *homo sapiens*, "modern man."

The first historical race in Palestine is represented by Natufian man (see CARMEL; MUGHÂRAH, WÂDĪ EL-), who engaged in farming in the Middle Stone or Mesolithic Age (c. 8,000–5500 B.C.). (See CAVES, illus. 85.)

Allusions of O.T. writers to early tribes who inhabited Canaan prior to the conquests by the Hebrews reveal an awareness of the antiquity and the importance of such aborigines as the Canaanites and Perizzites living there in Abraham's time (Gen. 13:7), and of the Kenites, Kenizzites, Kadmonites, Hittites, Rephaim, Amorites, Girgashites, and Jebusites—all listed by the author of Gen. 15:18–21 as groups whose land Yahweh had covenanted with Israel to give to his seed. The narratives of Joshua and Judges suggest that Israel subdued many of these tribes (Judg. 1:4). Some, including powerful groups of Amorites and various Canaanite tribes, were never subdued. (See AMALEKITES; AMMONITES; CANAAN; EDOMITES; GIRGASHITES; HITTITES; HORITES (Hivites); JEBUSITES; KENAZ; KENITES; MOAB; PHILISTINES; REPHAIM (Anakim); ZAMZUMMIMS. Several of these formerly obscure peoples, like the Hittites, Horites, and Hurrians, have become well-known through the research of modern scholars.)

(b) The pivotal position of Palestine at the junction of three continents—Asia, Africa, and Europe—has always made it a bridgehead coveted by advancing conquerors. Palestine has never seemed worth developing for its own sake; its resources are too meager, its rainfall too scanty. Its accessibility to vast oil resources was unguessed in Biblical times. But for 40 centuries—in fact since the dawn of history—it has been the battlefield, sometimes between Israel and her would-be masters, again between powers whose own territory lay far from Palestine.

Egyptians as early as the Old Kingdom (c. 2700–2200 B.C.) became acquainted with their small northern neighbor beyond the "River of Egypt" when they were seeking Lebanon cedars for shipbuilding. Literary reports from Egypt concerning Palestine—the oldest extant mention of the land—include a tomb inscription from the era of Pepi I (c. 2600 B.C.), telling of a war against people in S. Palestine which had been going on so long that a levy of Egyptian manpower was necessary. This war apparently required five campaigns, including a naval attack at "the gazelle's nose" (possibly the spur of Mt. Carmel), resulting in heavy loss to the Semites.

Canaanites, who were living in the land when the several waves of migrating Hebrews arrived and who continued to live alongside of them, deeply influenced the religious and cultural life of the Hebrews. The Bible records the struggles between Israel and Canaan in matters of faith and worship; many images and altars of Canaanites have been excavated at the chief city sites of Palestine. *Phoenician* culture also influenced Hebrew personality; as did later the tastes and beliefs of *Philistines* and *Aegean* peoples—Cretans, Cypriotes, Rhodians, and others.

Syria and N. Palestine were in the *Mesopotamian* sphere of influence following the expansions of Sargon I of Assyria (First Semitic or Accad Dynasty, c. 2360–2180 B.C.). From then on through the various deportations of Israel and Judah to the Tigris-Euphrates Valley (8th–6th centuries B.C.), the story of Palestine is intermingled with that of her aggressive eastern neighbors.

Inscribed records reveal the severity of attacks by Babylonia and Egypt in terms of the fabulous amounts of booty seized. An example of such lists is the statement carved by Thutmose III in a Karnak temple corridor, mentioning 17 invasions of Palestine and Syria. The Tell el-Amarna Letters of the 14th–13th centuries B.C. reveal political conditions in dominated Palestine.

But not all the impacts of Egypt and the "Land Between the Rivers" on Palestine were destructive. Babylon law codes influenced the early codes of Palestine, as did her literature, through epics of the Creation and the Deluge, etc. She fostered the method of writing on clay tablets and broken potsherds; and influenced the architecture of towered fortifications. From Egypt Palestinians probably learned, among many other arts, the use of the potter's wheel, which enabled them to fashion quantities of jars and bowls whose broken remnants furnish archaeologists with their best evidence for dates and phases of Palestinian culture. The cultural and religious influence of both Egypt and Mesopotamia have been inestimable. The impact on Palestine of Hittites, Hurrians, Edomites, and other peoples from the N., E., and NE., concerning whom more is being learned as archaeological and epigraphical research proceeds, is also important.

(See ASSYRIA; BABYLON; EGYPT; also many individual Palestinian cities, like BETHEL; BETHLEHEM; JERICHO; JERUSALEM; MEGIDDO; etc.).

Following the Babylonian Exile, Jews returned to Palestine and formed a majority of the population until c. A.D. 200. The religious revival which took place in Palestine under Nehemiah–Ezra and the codification of the Law were significant in the life of the Jews, who, however, had very little political power. From this era on Hebrews were known as "Jews." The priestly code of their Jerusalem Temple became a standard for Jews throughout the Persian Empire.

(c) *Greek culture*, which had influenced coastal Palestine as early as the 6th century B.C., spread rapidly after the capture of Tyre by Alexander the Great in 333 B.C. Beautiful and powerful Hellenistic cities were founded E. and W. of the Jordan, and old towns were Hellenized. (See GERASA; SAMARIA, etc.) Not until Hellenism interfered with the Jewish religion in Palestine did it meet resistance, which culminated in the Maccabean Revolt. The Maccabees established a short-lived, theocratic Jewish state which after a few years (166–63 B.C.) split into factions. This gave the Romans the opportunity they desired, and Pompey entered Jerusalem. Thus Hellenistic influences in Palestine (333–63 B.C.) paved the way for Roman occupation.

(d) The *Roman period* (63 B.C.–A.D. 325) brought no abrupt changes, but continued the Hellenistic atmosphere. Rome left its imprint chiefly on architecture and engineering. The Romans laid out splendid cities, constructed vast public structures, and built probably the first system of roads worthy of the name. These were marked by milestones, many of which are extant, and guarded by towering castles E. and W. of the Jordan. If Rome robbed Palestine of political independence, it enriched it by architectural glories, seen today in excavated columns, gate arches, walls, and city masonry.

(e) During the *Middle Ages* Palestine felt the blows of European Christendom bludgeoning Islam to secure possession of the Sepulcher of Jesus and his native Palestine. Though nothing was spared in men, money, munitions, and organizations, the Christian Crusaders held Palestine for less than 100 years (A.D. 1099–1187). The collapse of their political and spiritual ambitions precipitated tragic retreats from such key points as Athlit, and led to the failure of a well-organized Christian enterprise. Palestine has always been the land of heartbreak, the eternal land of the cross (Mark 15). The struggle between Arab and Jew—Semitic cousins—in the 20th century is a repetition of what has gone on many times before.

Ancient Hebrew rule in Palestine endured for 6½ centuries, if reckoned from c. 1230 B.C. to 587 B.C.—from Israel's entry from Egypt to the Captivity of Judah. Thereafter

308. Palm tree at O.T. Jericho, "City of Palm Trees."

Palestine was the seat of Jewish political autonomy for only the brief period of Maccabean rule. But since the 6th century B.C.

Palestine has not been the only center of Jewish population (see DISPERSION).

(4) *Spiritual contributions of Palestine.*—The Jews in Palestine before the Christian era developed a faith wherein monotheism* triumphed over the polytheism of their neighbors; produced prophets who revealed, and often left in writing, their understanding of the will of God, not only for His "chosen people," but for His spiritual universe; brought about the triumph of an ethical religion over degrading cultism; built many shrines to Yahweh, including the great Temple at Jerusalem; developed synagogues, especially following the Exile and Return from Captivity; and created a great corpus of sacred literature embodied in the Bible and the Apocrypha.

Palestine was the birthplace of Jesus and the cradle of Christianity.

309. Jesus entering Jerusalem on Palm Sunday (mosaic).

palm (Heb. *tāmār*, Gk. *phoinix*, whence Phoenicia), a tall, stately tree of the *Palmaceae* family, characterized by crown of showy, fan-shaped leaves. It has no true branches. It was regarded by outsiders as characteristic of Palestine, where in the Biblical period, as now, it prospered in oases like Jericho (see p. 518, illus. 308), "the city of palm trees" (Deut. 34:3; Judg. 1:16; II Chron. 28:15). Palms grow with their feet in water and their heads in the sun. Their presence always cheers travelers, as Israel was cheered at Elim with its 70 palms (Ex. 15:27; Num. 33:9). Palestine palms look regal on the Maritime Plain, where they fringe the sand dunes as far S. as the border of Egypt, in whose Nile Delta they are conspicuous. Palms grow in the highlands of Palestine, as at Mount Ephraim, where Deborah presided over Israel's affairs under a palm tree (Judg. 4:5). But they are decorative rather than productive of fruits in such elevations. When watered, they grow in Jerusalem gardens, and in the Garden of Gethsemane, and the lower reaches of the Mount of Olives. In John's account of Palm Sunday the joyous multitude which acclaimed Jesus King of Israel took "palm branches" (12:13) (more properly, "palm leaves"). Matthew (21:8) and Mark (11:8) omit "palm" and use "branches from the trees."

The typical Palestine palm is the date palm, which from June through September yields generous clusters of brown, red, yellow, or mahogany dates. Palms live 100 to 200 years. They are used to thatch roofs and for fences, baskets, and floor mats. They yield wax, sugar, oil, tannin, dyestuffs, resin, and juice for an intoxicant, *arrack*.

Scripture refers to palms and "goodly trees" (Lev. 23:40). They were symbols of prosperity (Ps. 92:12). Their tall "uprightness" was proverbial (Jer. 10:5). In Hebrew art they supplied a conspicuous decorative motif for the Temple (I Kings 6:29, 7:36; II Chron. 3:5; cf. Ezek. 40:16, 41:18).

Palms (*lulab*) were waved at Temple celebrations of the fall festival (Succoth, the Feast of Booths) when the water libation was performed—as if rain makers would invite clouds from the four corners of the earth to bring rain (Lev. 23:40). A weeping Hebrew woman under a palm was stamped on the Roman sestertius minted at Rome by Vespasian in A.D. 71 (see MONEY, illus. 274, No. 6). In Christian and non-Christian symbolism the palm denotes victory. It was frequently carved on early Christian sarcophagi.

palm. See WEIGHTS AND MEASURES.

Palm Sunday, Sunday before Easter. See p. 519.

Pamphylia (păm-fĭl'ĭ-*ȧ*), a district and (after A.D. 74) a Roman province consisting of an isolated coastal plain c. 80 m. long and 30 m. wide, in S. Asia Minor, walled on the N. by the Taurus Mountains. It lay W. of Cilicia and E. of Lycia. After A.D. 74 Pamphylia included a highland region N. of the plain, more accurately called Pisidia. The chief native city of Pamphylia was Perga*. Pamphylians were a mixture of Greek colonists and barbarian aborigines, many of whom were pirates, like those Pompey suppressed (67 B.C.). The climate of this region is notoriously deadly in summer, when fever and malaria are prevalent. Possibly Paul, who visited Pamphylia and made a hasty departure (Acts 13:13), fell victim to such an endemic disease. John Mark separated from Paul and Barnabas there (Acts 13:13, 15:38). They returned there from Pisidia, after ministering at Derbe, Lystra, Iconium, and Antioch of Pisidia (Acts 14:24 f.). Paul again sailed past Pamphylia to Myra in Lycia on his way to Rome (Acts 27:5). Jews from Pamphylia were in Jerusalem at Pentecost (Acts 2:10). Christianity took root slowly in Pamphylia.

310. Pamphylia.

pannag (păn'năg), probably a sweetmeat, shipped with honey from Judaea to Phoenician Tyre (Ezek. 27:17).

paper ("paper reeds by the brooks," Isa. 19:7; "paper and ink," II John 12), a writing material. See PAPYRUS.

Paphos (pā'fŏs), an ancient Phoenician-founded city at the SW. tip of Cyprus*, and its successor, "New Paphos," on a fertile site 10 m. SW. inland; the seat of Roman administration in the 1st century A.D. Here Paul and Barnabas met the proconsul ("deputy" A.V. Acts 13:7) Sergius Paulus, who, in spite of opposition from Elymas the sorcerer (v. 8), sent for the Apostle to tell him "the word of God," and subsequently "believed, being astonished at the doctrine of the Lord" (v. 12); thus Paul first presented Christianity to a Roman official at Paphos. The city was a pagan stronghold of the

311. Legendary birthplace of Aphrodite, on the road between Paphos and Limassol.

Paphian Aphrodite, who, her devotees believed, had sprung from the sea here and was worshipped with sensuous rites centering on a conical meteoric stone. Her famous temple, like that to Artemis at Ephesus, was visited by many pilgrims.

papyrus (Lat. *Cyperus papyrus*, whence "paper"). (1) A tall, graceful aquatic plant ("rush," Job. 8:11) abundant in Egypt in the Biblical period, and in sections of Palestine. It no longer grows in the marshes of Lower Egypt, but it survives in the Sudan. It is still found in the swampy region around Lake Huleh in Galilee, near the Sea of Galilee, and in sections of the Plain of Sharon.

(2) This widely used writing material, the ancestor of paper, was made by removing the outer covering stem and laying the first inner layer of soaked fibers so that they ran vertically. On top of these a layer of soaked fibers was laid horizontally. The layers were glued together with a gummy substance, then they were pressed and allowed to dry to form a sheet of pale yellow papyrus paper. Several sheets fastened together formed a roll usually 9 or 10 in. high and from 10 to 30 ft. long. (The Book of the Dead is 123 ft. long and 17 in. high; the Harris Papyrus measures 133 ft. in length.) Next, the side having its fibers running horizontally (smoother for writing and illuminating) was polished with bone or shell; then it was ready to be written on with pen and ink or brush and ink. This Egyptian discovery that a thin vegetable membrane was the best material to write on is the basis for our use of paper for writing and printing. Papyrus was used in the Egyptian Old Kingdom (c. 2700–2200 B.C.) or earlier, and was available in Palestine at least in the time of Jeremiah (c. 640–587 B.C.) (see Jer. 36). Some Egyptian papyri written in the 3d millennium B.C. are known today, e.g., The Wisdom of Ptah-hotep. The dry, warm air

of Egypt preserved such articles. Papyrus rolls, stored in can-like boxes, were shipped to many parts of the ancient world from Egypt, the world's paper mill for 3,000 years. Bales of papyrus were processed at Byblos (see GEBAL), whence Phoenician middlemen shipped them to Greece. Original manuscripts of Greek dramas and Egyptian treatises, e.g., the Edwin Smith surgical papyrus of c. 5,000 yrs. ago, were written on Egyptian "paper."

Many early O.T. scrolls were of papyrus, though leather and parchment scrolls were used very early (see SCROLLS, THE DEAD SEA). The use of papyrus scrolls of standard size determined, many believe, the division of the

312. Papyrus plant.

Pentateuch* into five scrolls, "Pentateuch" being derived from Gk. *penta* ("five") and *teuchos* ("scroll" or "book"). Later one large parchment scroll sufficed for the whole Pentateuch ("the Book of the Law"). Many N.T. MSS. were on papyrus. (See illus. 314, p. 522.)

The word "papyrus" is used of specific ancient Bible MSS., like the Nash Papyrus, the Turin Papyrus, the Chester Beatty Papyri, and the John Rylands, Oxyrhyncus, the Aramaic Elephantine Papyri, and University of Michigan papyri. (See TEXT.)

(3) Papyrus boats were used in ancient Egypt for hunting and fishing in the marshes, fashioned of papyrus reeds woven and lashed together, with upturned prows like gondolas. Isaiah (18:2) refers to Ethiopia's sending "ambassadors by the sea, even in vessels of bulrushes"; cf. Moses' "ark of bulrushes" ("papyrus" A.S.V. margin Ex. 2:3).

In Egyptian art the papyrus, symbol of Lower Egypt, was carved on column capitals, while the lotus symbolized Upper Egypt.

parable (Heb. *mashal*, "to set side by side," Gk. *parabolē*, "a placing beside, a comparison"), a short fictitious narrative based on a familiar experience and having an application to the spiritual life. It was literally a "throwing alongside." The pithy old definition of a parable as "an earthly saying with a heavenly meaning" has much to recommend it.

The parable is to be distinguished from (a) the *fable*, a short story, not based on fact, in which animals and plants talk as if they were people; characterized often by shrewdness, prudence, and sarcasm, rather than by noble moral quality; (b) the *allegory*, a symbolical narrative in which every detail has a figurative meaning, as in *Pilgrim's Progress;* when effort is made to allegorize the parables of Jesus, i.e., to look for meaning in every detail, rather than to seek the one great truth conveyed by the story, the effectiveness of the intended revelation becomes confused and lost; (c) the *myth*, an invented legend or story concerning imaginary or superhuman beings.

(1) *In the O.T.* there are strictly speaking only two parables: Nathan's story of the poor man's one ewe lamb (II Sam. 12:1–14); and Isaiah's parable of the unproductive vineyard (5:1–7 f.). Many O.T. allegories, similes, and metaphors are often called "parables," however—like the assembly of the trees to elect a king (Judg. 9:8 ff.), and the story of the thistle and cedar (II Kings

313. Papyrus capital, Twelfth Egyptian Dynasty.

14:9), both of which are fables; Ezekiel's "riddle" of eagles and vine (17:2 ff.), and the boiling caldron (24:1–24 ff.), which are allegories; and many poetic proverbs and enigmatic statements (Num. 23 ff.; Job 27:1

ff.). Habakkuk 2:6 contains a "riddle" parable.

(2) *In the post-O.T. period* parables teaching religious truths were used by rabbis and collected in the Talmud and the Midrash. Jesus recognized the parable as an effective means of presenting his good news of God's Kingdom to the story-loving people of his outdoor audiences. Like the rabbis, Jesus often began his parables, "Whereunto shall I liken" (Matt. 11:16).

(3) *The N.T.* parables of Jesus represent the highest development of this narrative form. Parables appear in the three Synoptic Gospels, but not in the Epistles. The "bread of life" and "vine and branches" passages of John 10:7 ff. and 15:1 ff. are sometimes listed as parables, but actually are allegories. The purpose of Jesus in using parables has been variously interpreted as: (a) to reveal truth through them; (b) to conceal the truth except from his close Disciples and those who, by asking for their explanation, manifested a desire to become part of his inner circle; and (c) to spare the unreceptive from the awful responsibility of hearing and rejecting the message of God, which was "the unpardonable sin."

The Synoptic Gospels vary in their concept of the purpose and use of parables. A comparison of Matt. 13:13–17 with the closely related words of Mark 4:10–13 and Luke 8:9 f. shows this, possibly due to the fact that Matthew's words seem to correspond to the spirit of the LXX Version (Gk. from the Heb. of Isaiah) and the words of Mark-Luke to the spirit of the Targum (Aram. from the Heb.). Mark and Luke seem to say just the opposite of what Matthew sets forth when he says, quoting Isaiah, that Jesus taught the multitudes in parables "because seeing they do not see, and hearing, they do not hear," and goes on to quote from Isaiah 6:9 f. (cf. Ps. 78:2), which speaks of people hearing and hearing, yet never understanding, and of actually closing their eyes, "lest they should see with their eyes, and hear with their ears, lest they understand with their heart and turn again for me [God] to cure them" (see Moffatt Matt. 13:13–17). Matthew reinforces this explanation of why Jesus taught in parables by saying that he used them to tell what had been "hidden since the foundation of the world" (Matt. 13:34 f.). Mark and Luke, as these Gospels now read, seem on the other hand to suggest that the purpose of Jesus was not to enlighten through his parables (cf. John 17:8) but actually to conceal and darken men's understanding—which is contrary to our conception of the

314. Fragment of oldest known Greek papyrus of first five verses of Genesis.

total purpose of Christ's coming into the world (John 1:9). (Cf. A.S.V. John 16:29, "no dark saying.")

The purpose of Jesus in telling parables, as he himself stated when questioned by his Disciples (Matt. 13:10–17; Mark 4:10–13; Luke 8:9 f.)—which must be differentiated from the view of the men who wrote the Gospels—was to reveal more and more of the mysteries (R.S.V. "secrets") of the Kingdom to his inner circle of Disciples, and to give his casual hearers arresting stories in the hope that as they pondered the lively imagery of the parables at leisure they might at last see the spiritual point he had intended, and ask for an explanation, as his Disciples had done (Matt. 13:10).

The only true parables are found in the first three Gospels. The parables of Matthew stress the main purpose for which this Gospel was written—to show that Jesus was the expected Messiah*, King of the Jews, Son of David and of Abraham. Matthew's theocratic viewpoint is indicated in his parables of the Kingdom, and in the parable of the Marriage of the King's Son, which in Luke is merely a great supper prepared by an unnamed man. Luke's parables of the Prodigal Son, Dives and Lazarus, and the Good Samaritan embody his emphasis on Jesus not as King but as Saviour of the world (Luke 15). Mark's parables—only two of which are peculiar to him (4:26–29, 13:33–37)—reveal no distinctive viewpoint of the writer.

The number of parables in the N.T. has been debated. Lists vary from 27 to 59; the usual number is about 39.

O.T. Parables

Name	*Location*	*Subject*
Nathan's to David	II Sam. 12:1–6	Deadliness of sin
Unproductive Vineyard	Isa. 5:1–6	Judgment on the fruitful life

N.T. Parables (of Jesus)

Name	*Location*	*Subject*
(1) *In Matthew only—*		
Tares	Matt. 13:24–30	The judgment of good and evil
Hidden Treasure	Matt. 13:44	The Gospel's worth
Pearl of Great Price	Matt. 13:45 f.	The Christian seeks salvation
Drag Net	Matt. 13:47	The mixed character of Church
Unmerciful Servant	Matt. 18:23–34	Forgiveness and ingratitude
Laborers in the Vineyard	Matt. 20:1–17	Reward for all service
Father and Two Sons	Matt. 21:28–32	Insincerity and repentance
Marriage of the King's Son	Matt. 22:1–14	Righteousness a prerequisite
Ten Virgins	Matt. 25:1–13	Spiritual preparedness

N.T. Parables (of Jesus)

Name	*Location*	*Subject*
Talents	Matt. 25:14–30	The use of opportunities
Sheep and Goats	Matt. 25:31–46	The final judgment of good and evil
(2) *In Mark Only—*		
Growth of Seed	Mark 4:26–29	The mystery of spiritual growth
Household Watching	Mark 13:34–36	The expectancy of Christ's return
(3) *In Luke Only—*		
Two Debtors	Luke 7:36–50	Pardon's gratitude
Good Samaritan	Luke 10:25–37	Neighborly compassion
Friend at Midnight	Luke 11:5–8	The effectiveness of persistent prayer
Rich Fool	Luke 12:16–21	Life and property evaluated
Servants Watching	Luke 12:35–40	The expectancy of the Lord's return
Steward on Trial	Luke 12:42–48	Trustworthy service
Barren Fig Tree	Luke 13:6–9	The unworthiness of privilege
Great Supper	Luke 14:16–24	The universality of God's Kingdom
Tower and Warring King	Luke 14:28–33	The cost of serving Christ
Lost Piece of Money	Luke 15:8–10	Joy over the penitent
Prodigal Son and Elder Brother	Luke 15:11–32	God's love for repentant sinners
Unjust Steward, or Dishonest Land Agent	Luke 16:1–13	Aggressive spiritual foresight
Rich Man and Lazarus	Luke 16:19–31	The gulf between selfishness and love
Master and Servant	Luke 17:7–10	Duty a sufficient recompense
Importunate Widow	Luke 18:1–8	The effectiveness of persistent prayer
Pharisee and Publican	Luke 18:9–14	The grace of humility
Pounds	Luke 19:12–27	The reward of diligence
(4) *Common to Matthew and Luke—*		
House Built on Rock and on Sand	Matt. 7:24; Luke 6:48	The importance of spiritual foundations

N.T. Parables (of Jesus)

Name	*Location*	*Subject*
Leaven	Matt. 13:33; Luke 13:20	The Kingdom's permeating influence
Lost Sheep	Matt. 18:12; Luke 15:3–7	The joy of God's redeeming love
(5) *Common to Matthew, Mark, Luke—*		
Candle under a Bushel	Matt. 5:15 f.; Mark 4:21 f.; Luke 8:16 f.	Illuminating spiritual life
New Cloth on old Garment	Matt. 9:16; Mark 2:21; Luke 5:36	The conflict between new and old
New Wine and Old Bottles	Matt. 9:17; Mark 2:22; Luke 5:37 ff.	The power of divine ferment
Soils ("The Sower")	Matt. 13; Mark 4; Luke 8	Christians' responsibility for production
Mustard Seed	Matt. 13:31 f.; Mark 4:31 f.; Luke 13:18 f.	God's Kingdom grows
Vineyard and Husbandmen	Matt. 21:33 ff.; Mark 12:1 ff.; Luke 20:9 ff.	Christ rejected by Jews
Fig Tree and Its Young Leaves	Matt. 24:32 ff.; Mark 13:28 ff.; Luke 21:29 ff.	Christian fruitfulness before Christ's return

The locality in which many of the parables were uttered is hinted at in the persons and the action of the stories, as in the Tares, the Hidden Treasure, the Drag Net, the House on the Sand, the Soils (or the Sower), and the Mustard Seed, which clearly seem to have been part of the Galilean ministry; whereas the Rich Fool, the Friend at Midnight, the Barren Fig Tree, the Prodigal Son, the Great Supper, the Rich Man and Lazarus, the Pharisee and the Publican, as well as the Lost Sheep, belong with the later Jerusalem and Judaean ministry. The parables have a universal meaning independent of the setting or occasion of their first utterance.

Sometimes the parables were told in groups of two or three—like the twin parables of the Friend at Midnight and the Importunate Widow, and the Mustard Seed and the Leaven, and the Hidden Treasure and the Pearl of Great Price; the parables of the Lost Sheep, the Lost Coin, and the Lost Son, repeating the same truth from various points of view. Matt. 13, which introduces the new type of teaching, contains seven parables, uttered near the Sea of Galilee, evidently at Capernaum (vv. 1, 36, 53). The Parable of the Prodigal Son is really two stories—that of the younger son (Luke 15:11–24) and that of the elder brother (15:25–32).

The themes are sometimes akin to those of the Wisdom* literature found in Job, Proverbs, and Ecclesiastes, like those of the House on Rock and on Sand (Matt. 7:24–27), and the Tower (Luke 14:28–33), in contrast to the prophetic parables or parables of the Kingdom, or the apocalyptic Parable of the Last Judgment (Matt. 25:31–46). The parables paint life in the Palestine Jesus knew—a Palestine now almost vanished.

315. The Prodigal Son, *by Puvis de Chavannes.*

They reveal slopes clothed with sheep and shepherds; fields sown with promising seed; roads on which merchants and prodigals traveled; simple houses where women baked and swept; rocks and sands where men built in primitive fashion; weddings to which women guests carried small hand lamps and cruets of extra oil. The parables contain valuable "background material" for understanding N.T. times.

Paraclete (păr′ȧ-klēt) (Gk. *paraklētos*, "an advocate or intercessor summoned to aid"), the Holy Spirit (John 7:39), the Comforter (14:16–18), or Helper whom the Disciples believed Jesus would send to empower them after he had returned to the Father (John 7:39). This Comforter (16:7) or Advocate (I John 2:1) was the Spirit of Truth (John 14:17), who would bear witness of Jesus (15:26). His arrival would enable the faithful to accomplish even greater work than Jesus had done (14:12). In the view of the author of the Fourth Gospel—who regarded Christ's death as his willing casting aside of life's limitations and his return to the inexhaustible glory he had shared with God before his Incarnation—the Paraclete was God's greatest gift to man.

Paradise, literally a "park"—the Garden of Eden was a "paradise" of this sort; it was a garden planted with trees (Gen. 2:8–17). The writer of Ecclesiastes says that he made himself "gardens and parks" and "planted trees in them of all kinds of fruit" (2:5). The word rendered "orchard" in the Song of Solomon (4:13) must be understood literally as "paradise." Ezekiel describes a majestic cedar set in a "plantation," a cedar of such height and beauty that it was envied of "all the trees of Eden, that were in the garden of God" (31:1–9, 16, 18).

The use of a park or a garden to typify the home of the righteous dead is frequent in the later Jewish Apocalyptic writings. This home is indeed called Paradise, in contrast to the abode of the reprobate, which is called Gehenna*.

The term Paradise occurs only three times in the N.T.: (1) Jesus to the penitent thief—"Today shalt thou be with me in paradise" (Luke 23:43). Jewish thought divided Paradise into a lower and a higher—the lower preceded the resurrection of the dead, and was temporary; the higher followed the resurrection, and was permanent. Jesus' words naturally referred to the lower: he was not assuring the thief of "heaven." (2) "Caught up into paradise"—Paul in II Cor. 12:4. The term here may be a simple synonym for "the third heaven," one of the seven into which ancient thought, apparently including Jewish, divided the heavens. (3) "The tree of life . . . in the midst of the paradise of God" (Rev. 2:7). When John writes his final description of the heavenly life he does so under the form of "a holy city, new Jerusalem" (chap. 21); but his mind is under the influence of the traditional conception of the Garden of Eden as a well-watered park. He therefore places in the center of the Holy City "a river of water of life." On its banks is "the tree of life," whose leaves were "for healing" and for removing "the curse" (22:1–3; cf. Gen. 2:15–17, 3:1–6, 17–19). It is almost as if John thought of heaven as a restored Eden or a paradise. This use of Paradise to mean heaven has become common in the language of Christian devotion. See ESCHATOLOGY; GARDEN OF EDEN; HADES; HELL. E. L.

parallelism, a chief characteristic of Hebrew poetry. Basically, it is a reiteration of similar or antithetic thoughts in similar phrases. It is best seen in example:

They hate him that rebuketh in the gate,
and they abhor him that speaketh uprightly.
—Amos 5:10

paralysis (palsy), a disease involving the loss of muscular power, cured by Jesus (Mark 2:1–12 and parallels; Matt. 8:5 ff.; Luke 7:1 ff.; John 5:1 ff.). A man with an atrophied and probably paralyzed hand was healed (Mark 3:1–6 and parallels).

Paran (pā′răn), a wilderness in the E. central region of the Sinai* Peninsula, bordering the Arabah and the Gulf of Aqabah on the E., and possibly including the Wilderness of Zin*, Kadesh*-barnea, and Elath* within its limits. To this lonely tableland Ishmael fled when banished with his mother Hagar from his father Abraham's encampment (Gen. 21:21). In Paran Israel on trek to Canaan from Egypt halted (Num. 10:12; 12:16) and wandered for many years. From Paran Moses dispatched spies to report on conditions in the land of Canaan (Num. 13:1–3, 26). To Paran David went after the death of Samuel the prophet (I Sam. 25:1). The Mount Paran suggested by Deut. 33:2 and Hab. 3:3 is probably a prominent peak of the Sinai wilderness highlands.

parchment. See WRITING.

pardon, the treatment of a guilty person as though he were no longer guilty, and the lifting, within certain limits, of the punishment which the guilt had entailed. For all practical purposes, therefore, pardon may be considered the same as forgiveness or reconciliation. Indeed in the English O.T. the same Heb. words are translated sometimes as "pardon" and sometimes as "forgiveness," as e.g. in Ps. 25:11 ("pardon") and Ps. 103:3 ("forgiveth"). "Pardon" never occurs in the English N.T.; the term preferred is "forgive," which is used to render three different Gk. words (e.g., Luke 6:37, 7:43; Matt. 6:12). The most common of these three Gk. words has the general meaning of "to let go," "to send away," "to release." The Galilean fisherman used the word when he "let go" or "threw off" the painter of his boat as it left the wharf.

Pardon presupposes a fault. When the fault is by man toward God it partakes of the quality of sin (Ps. 51:4); it therefore constitutes a barrier between God and man. The barrier, however, may not be recognized as such, which means that there can be no pardon; a realization of the fault—and with that repentance, confession, repudiation, reformation, and, where possible, restitution—are necessary. But the barrier between God and man may not be the only result of the sin; there may in addition be some effect on the body, or on the social standing, or on the material welfare, even on other people, in ways that can never be fully known. Though pardon may bring restoration to the divine favor, inner peace, and renewed moral sensitivity, it may not be able to change these material and social consequences. David repented sincerely for his sin which led to the death of Uriah (II Sam. 11:1–12:23), but that repentance did not bring Uriah back to life. The prodigal son of whom Jesus told "wasted his substance in riotous living," but his later repentance, and his reconciliation with his father, did not bring back the lost fortune (Luke 15:11–22), any more than the "tears" of Esau sufficed to recover for him the birthright he had so flippantly "sold" to Jacob (Heb. 12:16 f.; cf. Gen. 25:27–34, 27:1–40). God always extends pardon to the true penitent; but nature, society, and the economic order may still continue to exact a penalty.

The Bible also deals with pardon from man to man. In the O.T. this cannot be said to be emphasized (though the Levitical law prescribed the procedure to be followed when one man had wronged another: see Lev. 6:1–5). The teaching of Jesus, however, is quite explicit: a man who will not forgive another can expect no forgiveness from God (Matt. 6:12, 14 f., 18:21–35). The unforgiving remain unforgiven, because they have no true awareness of their own fault, and consequently no true repentance. The essence of forgiveness is the restoration of the broken relationship with God; and there can be no such restoration while bitterness, anger, hatred, jealousy, and the like, remain in the heart (see Eph. 4:31). See GUILT; FORGIVENESS; RECONCILIATION. E. L.

parent. See FAMILY; FATHER.

parental blessings were esteemed by children in the Biblical period as likely to promote the welfare of the household. The hands of the parent were laid on the head of the child (Gen. 48:14). If the child were a son, the words used were: "God make thee as Ephraim and as Manasseh" (v. 20); if a girl, "May God make thee as Sarah, Rebekah, Rachel, and Leah" (cf. Ruth 4:11). These words were followed by the priestly blessing (Num. 6:24–26). Especially prized was the blessing imparted shortly before a parent's death (Gen. 27, Isaac; Gen. 49, Jacob; Deut. 33, Moses). Blessings by very sick persons were sought, because the pious believed that the Shekinah* (reflection of the glory of God) hovered about them.

Parmenas (pär′mē-năs), one of the Seven appointed by the Apostles to administer relief to Greek-speaking widows in the Jerusalem church (Acts 6:1–6).

Parousia (pȧ-rōō′zhĭ-ȧ), a Gk. word meaning literally "being by" or "being near," hence "appearance." Its usual reference is to the second coming of Christ, understood as his return to earth to set up his kingdom, judge his enemies, and reward the faithful (John 14:25–29 refers to a "spiritual" presence). What is known as Adventism is characterized by the belief that the visible return of Christ is to be expected at any moment, and that the expectation should be the normal attitude of the Christian.

Jesus himself appears to have taught that he would return. Many find this teaching in Matt. 24 and 25 (cf. Mark 13; Luke 21:5–26). There is, however, a critical question involved in these passages. We know that descriptions of the coming of the Messiah, or of the Son of Man, to the accompaniment of striking wonders in the heavens and on the earth, were common in the so-called Jewish Apocalyptic writings produced in the two centuries immediately before the birth of Christ. These writings were highly popular; they served to keep faith and hope alive in a time of great difficulty. We cannot doubt that Jesus was familiar with them. This fact has led to two suggestions.

One is that Jesus borrowed from these descriptions, partly to emphasize his own significance as the bearer of the Kingdom of God, partly to give force to his teaching that the Kingdom could come not by any human efforts, but only by the direct and supernatural action of God. In that case the teaching in the N.T., both in the Gospels and in the Epistles, about the return of Christ, would rest back on words actually spoken by Jesus.

It has also been suggested, however, that the first disciples, and the early Jewish Christians in general, were equally familiar with these Apocalyptic writings. The immediate effect of the Crucifixion was to destroy the belief of the disciples that Jesus was the Messiah; but the Resurrection restored their belief (Acts 2:22–24, 32, 36). It also quickened their memory respecting Jesus' assertions that although he was to leave them for a while he would return again, but as a "Presence" (this being the form of the teaching set forth in John 14:18–24, 16:16–22) visible only to the eyes of faith. Influenced, however—so the suggestion goes—by the current descriptions of "the coming of the Son of Man" (cf. Dan. 7:13 f.; Matt. 26:64), the disciples and their early Jewish converts transformed Jesus' teaching about his return into "apocalyptic" language. The conclusion therefore is that this form of the teaching is due rather to an understandable exaggeration of what Jesus said than to his actual words. It would follow from this that Peter's explanation that the gift of the Holy Spirit on the Day of Pentecost was a fulfillment of the "apocalyptic" prediction of the prophet Joel (Acts 2:14–21), is much more in keeping with what Jesus meant than the hopes, common in the early Church (cf. I Thess. 4:13–18), of his return on the clouds of heaven to consummate world history.

Present-day scholars, however, incline to the belief that Jesus definitely anticipated his personal return to inaugurate the Kingdom of God. They feel that this anticipation can be discounted only at the cost of serious violence to the Gospel narrative. The two questions that are really left open are those of the time and the manner. The view that seems best to cover the admittedly wide diversity of the N.T. teaching on the question may be stated as follows: (1) He has already returned in that life of the Spirit which sprang up among believing men, best exemplified in the Church. (2) He is still in process of returning according as men see more clearly and apply more consistently what he can mean for the world. (3) He is yet to return in still greater power as men surrender more completely to his Spirit. (4) There will be a final consummation in the recognition of his universal Lordship, described by Paul as the time when "all things shall have been made subject to Christ" (see I Cor. 15:23–28).

See JUDGMENT, DAY OF; MILLENNIUM; RESURRECTION. E. L.

Parthians, the people of NW. Persia (Iran), living SE. of the Caspian Sea. They were summoned c. 43 B.C. by the Herodian Antigonus, son of Aristobulus II, to help him gain Judaea. They seized Jerusalem 40 B.C. but could not maintain their westward push. Rome, not wishing the formidable Parthian empire to hold Judaea, made Herod King of Judaea (40 B.C.). There were Parthians in Jerusalem on the Day of Pentecost (Acts 2:9); many had abandoned their crude native cults to become proselytes to Judaism. Among such Gentile* converts to Judaism Paul found many prepared to receive the Christian message.

partridge, a common game bird of Palestine. The red-legged or rock partridge is a favorite food. The sand partridge, found in abundance in the Dead Sea region, is probably the inspiration of David's words to Saul concerning himself while a fugitive (I Sam. 26:20). The comparison of an acquisitive person to a partridge sitting on eggs she has not laid (Jer. 17:11) is not based on fact.

paschal, pertaining to the Passover*; later to Easter. In N.T. Christianity the paschal lamb was Jesus Christ.

Pashhur (păsh′hẽr). (1) A son of Malchijah and the father of Jehoram (I Chron. 9:12), dispatched to Jeremiah by King Zedekiah

(598–587 B.C.) to query the prophet concerning the outcome of Nebuchadnezzar's attack on Jerusalem (Jer. 21:1 f.). Subsequently he collaborated in putting Jeremiah into the miry dungeon of a Jerusalem prison (Jer. 38:1–6). (2) A son of Immer the priest, and a chief officer in the Jerusalem Temple under Jehoiakim (609–598 B.C.). He struck Jeremiah and put him in the stocks, but later released him (Jer. 20:1–3). Pashur may have gone into Babylonian captivity with Jehoiachin (597 B.C.). (3) An ancestor of some of those who returned from Babylon (Ezra 2:38; Neh. 7:41) with Zerubbabel. Some of the family had married foreign wives (Ezra 10:22), and one of them sealed the covenant in Nehemiah's time (Neh. 10:3). (4) The father of Gedaliah (Jer. 38:1); possibly the same as (2).

passion, a term used only once in the Bible (A.V. Acts 1:3), to refer to Jesus' "suffering of death, crowned with glory and honor; that he by the grace of God should taste death for every man" (Heb. 2:9). Jesus repeatedly foretold to his Disciples the agony he was to suffer between the Last Supper and his death on the cross (Mark 8:31, 9:31, 10:33 f., and parellels roughly in Matt. 16:21, 20:28; Luke 9:18–62, 18:32 f.; see ATONEMENT; PROPITIATION; REDEMPTION).

The word "passions" appears only in Acts 14:15, where Barnabas and Paul, hailed as gods, professed themselves to be men of "like passions" with those of Lystra; and in a similar sense, James 5:17.

Passion Sunday, second before Easter.

Passover, the, the most important of the three feasts* whose observance was incumbent on every male Hebrew aged 13 and older (Ex. 23:14–17). Jesus went with his parents to observe it in Jerusalem (Luke 2:41 f.). The etymology of "Passover" reaches much farther back into Israel s history than the oldest O.T. records of the feast. The word may possibly be from the Heb. *pāsah* ("to skip" or "to pass over"), to suggest the destroyer "passing over" the Hebrew houses in Egypt to spare them on the eve of the Exodus* (Ex. 12:12–14), or the passing of Yahweh over the sills into the interior of His people's houses to protect them. Some authorities see the derivation of "Passover" in the skipping or leaping done at altars in ancient Semitic rituals (I Kings 18:26); others see it in the Assyr. *pasāhu* ("to propitiate").

The Passover, as recorded in the various sources of the O.T., was instituted to commemorate the events recorded in Ex. 12, which tells of God's deliverance of Israel from Pharaoh's oppressions. In early times the date of the feast was governed by agricultural seasons; ultimately its date was set as the 24-hour period beginning at sundown on the 14th day of Nisan, the 1st month of the Hebrew year (Lev. 23:5)—this corresponds to late March or early April. This spring season was a fitting one in which to observe the beginning of new life for the Hebrew people ("the beginning of months," Ex. 12:2). In Ex. 12:3 "the Lord's Passover" is the 14th day of the 1st month (cf. Num. 9:3).

Back of the Passover also lay an ancient Semitic shepherds' feast of sacrifice (cf. Ex. 5:1–3), which after the entry into Canaan was merged with one or more farm festivals in which tillers paid tribute to the deities of their fields. Thus the Feast of Unleavened Bread was annexed to the Passover, making a double festival (Lev. 23:6–8) at the beginning of the early harvest. "Passover" then came to mean the total eight-day celebration of the Passover 24 hours plus the seven days of the other feast: "the feast of unleavened bread . . . which is called the Passover" (Luke 22:1). The holiday was also called the Feast of Mazzoth, from the unleavened bread eaten during the Passover and the next seven days, in memory of the hasty baking of the "bread of affliction" (Deut. 16:3) by the Hebrews on the eve of their departure from Egypt (Ex. 12:14–28).

The ritual of the Passover developed and its date changed through the centuries. In Israel's early history the Passover was a family festival, presided over by the father. Its ritual is described in Ex. 12:3–20 and elsewhere in the O.T. The reforms of Josiah (c. 622 B.C.), made the feast into a national observance centering at Jerusalem, but retained the two old specifications, that for seven days all leaven was to be removed from the borders, and all the sacrificial flesh consumed before morning (Deut. 16:1–8). Also the sprinkling of blood from sacrificed animals on doorposts and lintels of houses was continued (Ex. 12:7, 13, 22). In the "state church" of Judaism (500–400 B.C.) the Passover was definitely on the 14th day of the 1st month, instead of being controlled by the fluctuating seasons of agricultural life. Animals sacrificed in Temple were not lambs, but bullocks, rams, and a kid (Ezek. 45:21 f.).

Because it was considered important for Jews living in Egypt in the 5th century B.C. to observe the Passover, instructions for the ritual of Ex. 12:1–20 were written for them on papyrus. A set of these from 419 B.C. was found on an Elephantine papyrus—the oldest known allusion to the Priestly Code.

Notable Passovers mentioned in Scripture include the first, or Egyptian Passover (Ex. 12); the one in the Sinai Wilderness, two years later (Num. 9:5); the first in the new homeland, at Jericho, under Joshua (Josh. 5:10); Hezekiah's at Jerusalem (II Chron. 30); Josiah's after "the Book of the Law" was found (622 B.C.) (II Chron. 35:1 ff.); typical ones up to the Exile (Ezek. 45:18–24); upon the return from Exile (Ezra 6:19 ff.); and Christ's last one at Jerusalem (John 12:1).

One of the most significant of the O.T. Passovers was that conducted by King Josiah c. 622 B.C. This occasion was not only "a sacrament, [but] a holy communion," as I. G. Matthews remarks in *The Religious Pilgrimage of Israel* (p. 141, Harper & Brothers), "gladly participated in by those who had harkened so diligently to the voice of Yahweh, their God, to observe and to do all his commandments (Deut. 28:1). By fulfilling the radical conditions they had removed the curse that had overshadowed them (Deut. 28:15–68) and had become a holy people who now could claim prosperity in flock, in field, and in family, and freedom, leadership, and prestige among the nations of the world (Deut. 28:2–14)."

The large crowds which came from the country up to Jerusalem at the Passover (John 11:55) made it necessary for Pilate to go there from Caesarea to prevent disorders. He may have hoped to gain the favor of the populace by freeing some political prisoners (cf. Matt. 27:15 ff.). Passover crowds participated in the tumult of the Trial and Crucifixion of Jesus. Herod, to please the Jews assembled for the "days of unleavened bread," killed James, the brother of John, with the sword and arrested Peter (Acts 12:1–3).

It is evident that Paul took note of the Feast of Unleavened Bread, for he halted at Philippi until it should be over before he sailed on (Acts 20:6).

At the Passover in the time of Christ, observed officially at Jerusalem, the paschal lambs were slain in various sections of the capital and taken to the priests to have their sacrificial portions presented at the altar. The remaining portions of the lambs were taken to the houses, where no fewer than 10 men and usually no more than 20 ate one animal, like Christ and his 12 Disciples. Bitter herbs (? lettuce and endive) reminiscent of the bitterness of Egyptian bondage and unleavened cakes dipped in sweet sauce were also eaten; and four cups of red wine were drunk. The 1st was blessed by the father and passed around. Then the eldest son asked the meaning of the feast, whereupon the father rehearsed the story of the Exodus and the institution of the Passover. The Hallel (Ps. 113, 114) was sung, the 2d cup drunk, and the meal eaten. Then came a prayer of thanksgiving. The 3d cup of wine was blessed; and during the passing of the 4th Ps. 115–118 were sung. Christ's care about observing the Passover is indicated by his being in the vicinity of Jerusalem six days early (John 12:1), and by the preparation he asked his Disciples to make for it in a large upper room (Mark 14:12–16; Luke 22:8–14). He had "desired to eat this passover" with his Disciples (Luke 22:15). In this historic Passover Jesus became the bridge by which this solemn feast of his people progressed into the institution of the Lord's* Supper and the establishment of the Christian Communion (Luke 22:14 ff.). The slain paschal lamb of the age-old Hebrew feast became the symbol of Christ's sacrificed but endless life, which brought redemption* from sin within range of everyone who would reach out for it. In Paul's theology Christ became our Passover, sacrificed for us (I Cor. 5:7). He compares the "old leaven" to malice and wickedness, and urges Christians to keep the feast "with the unleavened bread of sincerity and truth" (v. 8).

Judaism today observes the Passover. Reform Jews keep it only seven instead of eight days, observing the 1st and 7th days as holy. Observance centers in a home service, Seder ("order" or "arrangement"), a family meal observed on the 1st and 2nd evenings of the Passover, continuing customs instituted after the destruction of the Second Temple at Jerusalem. At the Seder the story of Israel's escape from Egypt is retold, and a symbolic meal eaten. On the table are a lamb bone and meat, bitter herbs, unleavened bread (*mazzoth*), parsley (reminiscent of hyssop, cf. Ex. 12:22), and a dish of mixed nuts and apples (symbolic of the mortar used during Hebrew bondage). Wine is used on the Seder table. The narrative of the Exodus (*Haggadah*) is recited—begun by the youngest person present, who asks, "Why is this night different from other nights?" Toward the close of the Seder meal the Hallel Psalms (115–118) are recited.

Through the centuries the ritual of the Passover has been scrupulously followed by the small colony of Samaritans living at Nablus.

Pastoral Epistles. See TIMOTHY I, II, AND EPISTLE TO TITUS.

Pathros (păth′rŏs) (Pathrusim [păth-ro͞o′-sĭm]), a section of Upper Egypt, W. of Mizraim and N. of Cush. It is sometimes understood to be Upper Egypt itself, the home of Menes, traditional founder of the First Egyptian Dynasty. Isaiah prophesied the return of Israelites from Pathros (11:11; cf. 7:18). Jeremiah mentioned refugee Jews living in Pathros after the fall of Jerusalem (44:1 f., 15).

Patmos (păt′mŏs), a 50-m.-square Aegean island in the Sporades group of the Greek Archipelago W. of S. Asia Minor, and opposite the site of ancient Miletus. It is mentioned in the Bible only in Rev. 1:9. The author of the Apocalypse tells of being banished there perhaps in the reign of Domitian, c. A.D. 95, because of his testimony for Jesus Christ. Patmos was the scene of his visions recorded in Revelation. From a passing ship one can see this sparsely settled, penal islet, with its glistening white crags all set in the vast sweep of the Aegean, and one gains new understanding of the mystic's visions: "I saw a new heaven and a new earth . . . (21:1) and there was a rainbow round about the throne, in sight like unto an emerald" (4:3); "a door . . . opened in heaven" (4:1); a "throne . . . set in heaven" (v. 2); "lightnings and thunderings and voices" (v. 5); and a "sea of glass like unto crystal" (v. 6). The sea barred him from his life's work, and he longed for a time when there would be "no more sea" (21:1). Patmos is an excellent example of a geographical setting that helps to interpret Biblical events and experiences associated with it. The Monastery of St. John now owns most of the S. half of Patmos.

patriarch, in general, the male head of a long family line. In the Bible patriarchs are (1) early fathers of the human race, including the antediluvian Patriarchs listed in (a) the Cainite list from the J source (S, R. H. Pfeiffer) (Gen. 4:17 f.) and (b) the Sethite list (5:3–31), assigned to P. One list begins with Cain, the other with Seth; both terminate with Lamech; the former lists six Patriarchs, the latter eight. (2) Early fathers from the Flood to the birth of Abraham (Gen. 11). The Genesis lists offer interesting material to compare with the early Mesopotamian lists of kings, like the one found on a clay tablet at Kish, 8 m. E. of Babylon, compiled c. 2000 B.C. on the site of the First Dynasty after the Deluge; and the 20,000 clay tablets found at Mari*. The incredible number of years during which more than 20 kings reigned at Mari before the kingship passed over to the Sumerian Uruk in the S. may be laid alongside the vast length of years attributed to O.T. Patriarchs, e.g., Methuselah, 969 years (Gen. 5:27). In one Babylonian king list there are only 10 kings covering a period of 456,000 years. Could the P writer have had access to such lists? Long life was so highly valued (Ex. 20:12) that its assignment to Patriarchs was a compliment to their nobility of character.

(3) The progenitors of the Israelites—Abraham, Isaac, Jacob, and sometimes the twelve sons of Jacob from whom the Tribes of Israel descended (Acts 7:8 f.). Acts 2:29 calls David a Patriarch.

Archaeology has helped confirm the historicity of the Patriarchs. These great O.T. figures cannot be regarded as merely folk types, for their personalities and the events of their lives are individual. If their sagas as we read them in Genesis are poetic, it is because countless repetition of these well-loved stories has polished the narratives into the exquisite form we know. The Patriarchal Age is now thought to fall in the Middle Bronze of Palestine (21st to 19th centuries B.C.). Although it is not possible even yet to date the departure of Terah's family from Ur of the Chaldees toward Haran, the migration of the Terachids from Ur may have taken place in the 20th–19th centuries B.C., and Jacob's migration to Egypt may have occurred in the 18th, or more likely, the 17th century B.C. (W. F. Albright). The thousands of clay tablets found by M. A. Parrot, from 1935 on, at Mari on the Middle Euphrates, have told much concerning the life and times of the Hebrew Patriarchs, who were true "children of their age." Data discovered by Mallowan at Chagar Bazar in NW. Mesopotamia and by Chiera and others at Nuzu* in NE. Mesopotamia supplement the evidence from Mari. The rich hoard of tablets found at Sumerian Ur in a well-preserved quarter of the substantially built city reveals "the age of Abraham" as that between the last kings of Isin and Larsa and the First Dynasty of Babylon, of which Hammurabi was the 6th king. Some scholars still consider Abraham a contemporary of Hammurabi; others are not sure whether he preceded or followed Hammurabi. Hammurabi's era, by revised Mesopotamian chronologies, is not 1900 B.C., as formerly thought, but c. 1728-1686 B.C. In appearance and customs the Patriarchs were probably little different from the seminomadic Middle East Arabs today. Abraham, Isaac, and Jacob roamed the hills of central and southern Palestine, occasionally ranging south into the Negeb. They were probably ass-nomads, rather than camel-caravaneers, and allusions to camels in the Genesis narratives (e.g., 24:10 ff., especially v. 63) (see CAMELS) may be anachronistic. The oldest known evidence for the domestication of camels in Palestine does not antedate the 12th century B.C. The Patriarchs' apparel and countenances must have been similar to those seen in the figures with tunics and sandals, lyres and bellows, in the famous Beni-hasan tableau of 1892 B.C., which shows seminomads from Palestine in the Patriarchal Age visiting Middle Egypt (see Fig. 9, *Westminster Historical Atlas to the Bible*). Their weapons were throw-sticks, darts, and bows and arrows. Both the Beni-hasan group and the families of the Patriarchs included members who, like Lamech in an earlier age (Gen. 4:19–22), combined pastoral activities with music and metal-working.

The Hebrew Patriarchs felt that Yahweh was very near and real to them, was even willing to be a guest in their tent, as in Abraham's near Hebron. This Patriarch was known as "the friend of God," Who told him things (Gen. 17; 22:9), provided a way to spare his son Isaac (22:13 f.), and gave his seed an eternal heritage (Gen. 22:14–18). Patriarchs on their nomadic treks carried their ideas about God around the Fertile Crescent into Palestine. The concept of the Parent-God originated among Semitic nomads. The Patriarchs are depicted in the Genesis narrative as living in general the good life as they knew it, the "way of Yahweh." They claimed by settlement the land He gave them as an eternal heritage (Gen. 12:1–3, 13:14–17, 15:7, 18 f., 17:2, 4–8, 49:1–27). They reared altars to Him in places which for centuries were influential in the religious life of Israel, e.g., Shechem, Bethel, Hebron, Beer-sheba, Mahanaim, and Penuel. In the patriarchal period heads of families offered sacrifice in private observances without recourse to a priest at a local sanctuary.

Paul, the Apostle, the most dynamic and influential of early Christians; named in Heb. "Saul," but usually known by his Roman praenomen "Paul." Information concerning this 1st century Jewish convert to Christianity and his contribution to the spread of the new faith is obtained mainly from the Acts of the Apostles and from his Epistles.

Saul was a native and citizen of Tarsus*, capital of Cilicia (Acts 9:11, 22:3). He was proud of his home town (Acts 21:39). His people were Pharisees* (Acts 23:6) of the Tribe of Benjamin (Phil. 3:5), who named this son after their tribe's earliest hero, the 1st king of Israel (I Sam. 11:15; Acts 13:21). Such a religious parentage accounts for his knowledge of the Law, the prophets, and the Aramaic and Hebrew languages (Acts 21:40, 22:2, 23:6; Gal. 1:14); Saul was also familiar with Greek, the language of the streets and shops of Tarsus (Acts 21:37). He may have had a number of brothers and sisters, but we know of only one sister, whose son once performed a real service to his uncle (Acts 23:16–31). In later years Paul applied the Aramaic word "Abba" to God, a term he had used in addressing his own father in their Tarsus home (Rom. 8:15; Gal. 4:6). According to the religious custom of Jewish families of the Diaspora, he made the pilgrimage to Jerusalem (Acts 26:4).

Paul inherited from his father both Tarsian and Roman citizenship (Acts 22:28). In 171 B.C. Jews had been brought to Tarsus to promote business and were given rights of citizenship. Probably at about this time Paul's forebears received their Roman citizenship, an inheritance in which Paul took pride (Acts 22:28). Tarsus was a great commercial and university town, Hellenistic in spirit and Roman in politics. Paul and his family saw the material blessings the Roman Empire brought its people, in roads, bridges, aqueducts, harbors, and trade; and the peace and order that obedience to its law brought its subjects. While some Jews in Palestine were always agitating rebellion against Rome, Paul remained empire-conscious, and appealed for justice to local Roman authorities and even to Caesar in distant Rome (Acts 25:11). Tentmaking may have been the craft Paul inherited from his father, or the trade which the young Pharisee selected as his first step in self-support in preparation for his rabbinical calling. Paul's mastery of the art of weaving the famous goat's-hair cloth called *cilicium*, and his making of it into tents, sails, awnings, and *abayehs* (cloaks) gave him economic independence (Acts 18:3, 20:34, 28:30; II Cor. 11:9; I Thess. 2:9; II Thess. 3:8).

When Saul was about 20 he attended the rabbinical school of the Pharisees under the famous Gamaliel* at Jerusalem. In the capital, despite the liberal influences of Gamaliel (Acts 5:34–39), Saul succumbed to student fanaticism, and aided those who stoned Stephen (Acts 7:58, 8:1) when the latter was charged with fomenting religious change (Acts 6:14). This increased Paul's popularity with the high priest*, made him a leader among the fanatics (8:3), but resulted in inner conflict (Acts 9:4 f., 22:4, 26:10; Rom. 6–7). Armed with letters of endorsement from the high priest, Saul set out for Damascus to search for followers of Jesus of Nazareth, to bring them bound to Jerusalem (Acts 9:2).

The conversion of Saul (A.D. 34) along the sandy, sun-baked road on the outskirts of Damascus was a physical, mental, moral, and spiritual experience which revolutionized his intellectual life, redefined his religious objectives, and turned the vigorous prosecutor of Christianity into its most ardent promoter (Acts 9:19–22). Three detailed accounts of this event (Acts 9:1–19, 22:1–21, 26:1–23) and many references to it in his own writings (I Cor. 9:1, 15:8; Gal. 1:15 f.; Eph. 3:3; Phil. 3:12) indicate its vividness and its lasting importance to Paul. To him, as to many of like temperament, Christ came not as a result of a long educational process, but as in a thunderstorm. The result in Paul's case was an immediate about-face. Ananias and the Christian colony in Damascus forgave their would-be persecutor, interpreted to the bewildered Saul the meaning of what had come to him, and rescued him ingeniously from his own persecutors (Acts 9:10–25). (See CONVERSION, illus. 94.)

Between Paul's conversion and the beginning of his First Missionary Journey came a preparation period of about 13 years, spent partly in some oasis in the Arabian Desert, perhaps not far from Damascus. During

316. Statue of Paul in courtyard of St. Paul's-Without-the-Walls, Rome.

this time began the tremendous intellectual reconstruction of his Jewish theology in the light of his Damascus-road illumination (Gal. 1:17). Later in Jerusalem he interviewed Peter and James, the Lord's brother (Gal. 1:18 f.). Perhaps Paul heard there the oral Gospel in Aramaic, a summary of the words and deeds of Jesus handed down to all new converts. This is believed by some to have been "Q"*. The authoritative knowledge about Jesus which Paul received included (1) the institution of the Lord's* Supper (I Cor. 11:23–25); (2) specific words of the Lord (Acts 20:35; I Cor. 7:10, 25, 9:14), which Paul either quoted directly or used as the basis of instruction; (3) the appearances of the resurrected Lord (I Cor. 15:3–8); and (4) the spirit, character, and life of Jesus, briefly mentioned in two of Paul's letters (II Cor. 10:1; Phil. 2:5–8). Paul spent 10 years of this period of preparation in Cilicia, presumably Tarsus (Gal. 1:21). Here, as was the custom, he probably argued so effectively with Jews in the synagogue and with his Gentile neighbors on the street, in the market place, and in their homes that he began to attract attention at Antioch*, the headquarters of the Christian Church (Acts 11:25 f.), only 80 miles SE. of Tarsus.

The First Missionary Journey (A.D. 47–48) began under the leadership of Barnabas, with Paul as the second member of the party (Acts 13:2), and John Mark as assistant

(13:5). Cyprus, the island home of Barnabas, was its first objective. Until this time missionary and evangelistic efforts had been largely confined to casual contacts made in street, market place, synagogue, highway, etc. (Acts 3:1, 5:12, 42, 8:26–29). This first deliberately organized expedition to Christianize a portion of the Graeco-Roman world was a novel idea. Landing at Salamis at the E. end of the island, the party traversed Cyprus to Paphos in the W., capital and residence of Sergius Paulus, the proconsul. His conversion, which is thought to be indicated in Acts 13:12, had a marked effect on Paul's future career. Whether because of admiration for this distinguished convert or as an indication of a turning away from the Jewish to the Gentile world as his special field of labor, Saul is known from here on by his Roman name *Paulus*, or Paul (Acts 13:9). From this point on Paul replaced Barnabas as leader of the party (v. 13).

The second portion of the First Missionary Journey was in the Asia Minor mainland provinces of Pamphylia, Pisidia, and Lycaonia, the last two being included in the Roman province of Southern Galatia. The communities recorded as being visited were: Perga in Pamphylia (Acts 13:13, 14:25); Antioch in Phrygia on the border of Pisidia (13:14–50, 14:21); Iconium (14:1–5, 21); Lystra (14:6–20), and Derbe (14:20 f.) in Lycaonia. The Asia Minor coast where the party landed is a hot, malarial region. According to one theory Paul's physical infirmity was malaria contracted on this coastal plain; malaria is characterized by headache, fever, and extreme prostration. The journey 100 m. N. inland over the mountains to the 4,000-ft.-high tableland, though full of perils "of waters" and "of robbers" (II Cor. 11:26), was necessary for Paul's health. He never forgot the patience and kindness of these Galatian highlanders (Gal. 4:13 f.), and their willingness to share even their "eyes" with him, if this would bring him relief from the pain (v. 15) of his disease. Eight years later Paul was still afflicted with this "thorn in the flesh" (II Cor. 12:7). Another theory is that Paul's malady was epilepsy. Paul resented John Mark's desertion of their party at Perga (Acts 13:13, 15:38), but later the two men were reconciled (Col. 4:10; II Tim. 4:11). The record of events at Lystra has preserved a candid snapshot of Paul. The Greek-minded populace dubbed Barnabas, the more robust of the two missionaries, "Jupiter," and called Paul, the more agile in body and speech, "Mercury." The missionaries made their contacts with the people through the synagogues in Perga, Pisidian Antioch, and Iconium. But in Lystra and Derbe, where evidently there were no synagogues, they spoke to people whenever there was an opportunity (Acts 14:7–10). In Lystra Jews from the synagogues of Antioch and Iconium stoned Paul, giving him a taste of the same medicine he had once administered to Christians (Acts 14:19). Paul's Epistles to Timothy record Timothy (the Apostle's "son in the faith" I Tim. 1:2) as an eyewitness of Paul's suffering in Lystra (II Tim. 3:10 f.). Timothy, who became Paul's faithful companion and secretary, was the son of a Jewish mother and a Greek father. His conversion to Christianity during Paul's first visit to Lystra (Acts 16:1–3) is symbolic of the two worlds, Jewish and Greek, which Paul and Barnabas labored to synthesize and win for Christ.

The Council at Jerusalem (A.D. 49) was the first ecumenical meeting in the history of Christianity (Acts 15:1–35). When Paul and Barnabas returned to Antioch they found the Church disturbed by propaganda emanating from Jerusalem, calling on all Gentile converts to submit to Mosaic Law and become virtually Jews, as a prerequisite to becoming Christians (Acts 15:1). This was not the view of Paul and Barnabas, nor had they taught it to their Graeco-Roman converts. Antioch forthwith delegated Paul, Barnabas (Acts 15:2), and Titus (Gal. 2:1) to present the more liberal interpretation of the requirements for salvation to the leaders at Jerusalem. The "minutes" of this momentous meeting record a victory for Paul and his position (Acts 15:6–29). Salvation by faith alone won out over the doctrine of salvation by law (Gal. 2:3); and agreement among the leaders was realized (Gal. 2:9). But Paul complained a little later that when Peter visited Antioch he seemed more anxious to please those whose conduct was based on the Jewish Law than those whose fellowship was based on faith (Gal. 2:11–14).

The Second Missionary Journey (A.D. 49–52) brought Christianity into Europe (Acts 15:36–18:22). Paul was accompanied by Silas (Acts 15:40), later by Timothy (Acts 16:1) and Luke* (16:9 f.). From Antioch they traveled by land through Syria and Cilicia (Acts 15:41), where Paul was able to visit Tarsus. Passing through the Cilician Gates to the Anatolian plain, Paul revisited the Galatian churches he had organized on his First Journey (Acts 16:1–6). The Province of Asia, with its leading city, Ephesus*, was the party's objective. But some unnamed circumstance—intuition, or the leading of the Holy Spirit—prevented them from taking this course (Acts 16:6). Circumstances in which God's leading was evident kept them also from going north into the province of Bithynia on the shores of the Propontis (Sea of Marmora) and the Euxine (Black Sea) (Acts 16:7). These two prohibitions emphasized the importance of the decision made at Troas to cross into Macedonian Greece and seize the new and unmeasured opportunity which was open to the Gospel there (Acts 16:8–11; II Cor. 2:12 f.). Paul, like Xerxes and Alexander, used the narrow waterway between Asia and Europe as a thoroughfare, not, like them, for military conquests, but for his crusade for a universal faith.

Philippi was the first city in Europe to be evangelized (Acts 16:12 f.) and to organize a church. Lydia, a business woman, was the Gospel's first European convert. Records of other women touched by the ministry of Paul appear in Acts 17:4, 12, 34, 18:26; Rom. 16:1; I Cor. 16:19. Certain business interests affected adversely by Paul's teaching made charges of an anti-Semitic nature against Paul and Silas and had them imprisoned (Acts 16:16–24). During the night Paul and Silas spent in prison the jailer and his family (16:30–34) were converted and baptized, and became part of the first European Christian fellowship, which met in the house of Lydia (v. 40). The next morning, after Paul had disclosed his Roman citizenship, the authorities released them, and constrained them (v. 39) to leave town. Ten years later Paul wrote an Epistle to the people of this church.

At Thessalonica (modern Salonica) the preaching of Paul and Silas received a responsive hearing from the Greeks (17:1–4). But the Jews agitated violently against them, and entered accusations against some of the new converts for harboring "these that have turned the world upside down" (vv. 5–9). Paul and Silas, in order to avoid further trouble for the Christians, left town under cover of night (Acts 17:1–10). The Apostle, in his Letters to the Thessalonians, mentions some of the events of this early period (I Thess. 1:7, 2:2, 9, 14–18; II Thess. 1:4 f., 3:3, 8).

At Berea both Jews and Greeks gave thoughtful assent to the Gospel until the Jews from nearby Thessalonica interfered (Acts 17:10–13); Paul was their target. By a clever ruse he outwitted them (17:14 f.). Silas and Timothy joined him later (17:14 f., 18:5).

Paul's speech at Athens before the Areopagus (Acts 17:16–31) reveals his broad knowledge of Graeco-Roman philosophy (v. 27 f.), poetry (v. 28), sculpture (vv. 25, 29), architecture (v. 24), and religion (v. 23). He touched on all these in an intellectual appeal which delighted the minds of many but influenced the wills of only a few of his hearers (v. 34). As Paul journeyed on to Corinth he resolved to abandon the learned approach which had failed at Athens and to center his message on Jesus Christ (I Cor. 2:1 f.).

At Corinth (Acts 18:1–7) Paul stayed 18 months and established a church. Aquila and Priscilla (18:2 f.), Justus (v. 7), and Crispus (v. 8) were associated with Paul in this undertaking. Gaius (I Cor. 1:14) and the household of Stephanas (16:15) were among the early converts. While Paul was at Corinth he wrote with the aid of his secretary, Timothy (Acts 18:5; I Thess. 1:1), *I Thessalonians* (A.D. 50), his first Epistle and the oldest book in the Canon of the N.T. When Paul learned that the fanatical portion of the Church had misused his words to stir up increased excitement over the second advent of Christ (II Thess. 2:2) he presently sent another message —*II Thessalonians*. In this he counseled a more temperate faith in the Parousia* (II Thess. 2:15), and a practical program of daily work rather than idle waiting (II Thess. 3:7 f., 10–12). The Gallio episode fixes the date of Paul's sojourn in Corinth (A.D. 50–51) (Acts 18:12–17).

Sailing from Cenchreae (Acts 18:18) by way of Ephesus (vv. 19–21) and Caesarea (v. 22), Paul journeyed "up" (v. 22) to Jerusalem to keep the "feast," then overland to Antioch (v. 22), where he reported the accomplishments of the Second Missionary Journey. From Antioch or Ephesus Paul wrote to the churches of Lystra, Derbe, Iconium, and Pisidian Antioch his *Epistle to the Galatians* (c. A.D. 52) in order to correct their serious deflections from the true Gospel. (See CAESAREA, illus. 75.)

The Third Missionary Journey took Paul through the sections of Asia Minor familiar to him, Macedonia and Greece, and back to Jerusalem (A.D. 52–56) (Acts 18:23–21:19). Paul followed up his written message to the Galatians with a personal visit designed to strengthen the disciples in the "upper coasts" (19:1), the table lands of the interior of Galatia and Phrygia (18:23).

Ephesus was prepared for the Gospel of Christ as preached by Paul (1) through his earlier visit (Acts 18:19–21); (2) by Apollos, the Alexandrian Jewish Hellenist (vv. 24 f.); and (3) the Apostle's converted Jewish friends, Aquila and Prisca (vv. 18, 26). Soon after Paul's arrival at Ephesus "about twelve" were baptized "in the name of the Lord Jesus" in a ceremony marked by the presence of the Holy Spirit (Acts 19:1–7). For three months Paul spoke in the synagogue, and then for two years in the lecture hall of Tyrannus, neutral ground where both Jews and Greeks were free to come (19:8–10). His work was characterized by (1) miracles (19:11 f.); (2) thorough instruction (20:8–31); (3) far-reaching successes (19:10, 17–20, 26); (4) influential official friends (v. 31); and (5) constant and fierce opposition (Acts 19:23–41; I Cor. 15:32, 16:9). To Ephesus came a member of the household of Chloe (I Cor. 1:11) with a story about disturbing conditions in the church at Corinth. This led Paul to write letters which have been preserved in *I* and *II Corinthians* (A.D. 53–55). Paul supplemented his message to the Corinthians by sending a special messenger (II Cor. 8:12, 12:18). But his concern for the Church led him to revisit Corinth (Acts 19:21, 20:1 f.; II Cor. 13:1). During his three months' winter stay in Corinth (A.D. 56) he wrote his *Epistle to the Romans*, setting forth more fully than he had done in Galatians his doctrine of the relation of faith and the Law and the Christian way of salvation.

To symbolize the bond uniting Christians everywhere, and to make the Jewish members of the Church at Jerusalem more conscious of the love of their Gentile Christian brothers for them, Paul promoted a collection to be sent to Jerusalem (Acts 20:35; Rom. 15:26; I Cor. 16:1); and appointed special representatives to solicit the churches (Acts 19:22, 20:4; Rom. 16:1). Paul intended to follow up his Epistle to the Romans, as he had those to the Galatians and Corinthians, with a personal visit. From the city on the Tiber he hoped to continue his missionary activities westward into Spain (Acts 19:21; Rom. 15:22–32). But he believed his immediate task was to take to the Jerusalem Christians the moneys collected for them from the churches of the Graeco-Roman world (Acts 20:16, 24:17). Many unheeded warnings had come to Paul concerning the perils of a Jerusalem trip (Acts 20:22–24, 38, 21:4, 10–15).

The record of the sea journey to Caesarea, written in the first person, indicates that Luke had become a member of Paul's Jerusalem "collection" deputation (Acts 20:5 f., 13–15, 21:1–8). He records the arrival of the missionary party at Jerusalem, where "the brethren received us gladly" (Acts 21:17–19). James and the elders of Jerusalem "glorified the Lord" for Paul's successful work among the Gentiles; but many of the rank and file bitterly opposed the Apostle as a Jewish law-nullifier. To demonstrate his sympathy with the Jews who wished to obey the Law, Paul financed the Temple sacrifices of four poor men who had taken the Nazirite vow, and himself participated in the ceremonies (Acts 18:23–26, 24:18). By thought and action Paul taught that no Gentile or Christianized Jew was compelled to obey the details of the Law, but that the Jews were at liberty to do as they were led to do in regard to regulations and ceremonials. Recognized in the Temple by recalcitrant Asiatic Jews on a pilgrimage to Jerusalem, the Apostle was attacked (Acts 21:27–29); a riot ensued (vv. 30 f.), and he was rescued and arrested as a suspect by Roman soldiers (vv. 31–39). Speaking in Aramaic, Paul quieted the angry multitude—until he mentioned the "Gentiles" (22:1–21). In the bedlam that followed Paul was taken for safety and examination to the Castle of Antonia (vv. 22–24), where his identity as a Roman citizen was established in a speech made in Greek. The situation caused great embarrassment to the military police (v. 25). The next day Paul's speech before the august Sanhedrin was skillfully designed to divide the Jews into their long-standing, bitterly quarreling factions (23:1–9). That night in his prison barracks Paul received another reassuring word from God (23:11, cf. 18:9 f., 27:24). Meanwhile the military, warned of a plot to lynch Paul (23:12–23), hastily transferred the prisoner under heavy guard to Caesarea (v. 23). Hearings before Governor Felix (chap. 24), his successor, Festus (Acts 25:1–12), and King Agrippa* (25:23–26:32) mark Paul's two years of incarceration (A.D. 56–58) in the "Bastille" at Caesarea. The Apostle, knowing the violence of his Jewish enemies at Jerusalem, where Felix suggested he should go for trial, dramatically appealed to Caesar in Rome—as his Roman citizenship entitled him to do—in the firm belief that under Roman law he would receive a fair deal (25:11 f.).

So Paul, with his two attendants (Acts 27:2), began the long journey to Rome in the custody of "Julius, a centurion of Augustus' band" (v. 1). In Acts 27:1–28:13 Luke records one of the most famous shipwreck stories of literature, in which Paul plays a central and heroic role. In Italy he was received cordially, as always, by the brethren (28:13 f.). Because of the non-criminal nature of the charge against the Apostle, and his good behavior and his Roman citizenship, Paul was billeted under military guard (28:16) in a private apartment (v. 30), where all had access to him. The Jewish leaders with whom Paul conferred in the capital had heard nothing of his case, and gave him a divided response (28:17–29). Owing to the crowded court calendar, or the loss of papers in the shipwreck, Paul waited two years for his case to be called. (See MELITA, illus. 266.)

To this period of his Roman imprisonment (A.D. 59–61) some scholars assign the writing of three or four of Paul's epistles. (See PHILIPPIANS, COLOSSIANS, PHILEMON, and EPHESIANS.) Writing, limited evangelistic efforts, and interviews with individual Christians filled up Paul's prison days. The Acts ends without recording his fate.

What was Paul's end? One theory is that Paul was acquitted, and that when he was released he realized his dream of evangelizing Spain (Rom. 15:24); then revisited the Near East, Crete (Tit. 1:5), Asia (II Tim. 4:13), Macedonia (I Tim. 1:3), and Greece (II Tim. 4:20). According to this theory Paul was again arrested, imprisoned in Rome, where he wrote *I* and *II Timothy* and *Titus*, and was finally put to death there. Another hypothesis—and the more probable one—is that Paul's first and only Roman imprisonment ended in his conviction and execution. Luke must have known about Paul's death, but he did not record it, because to have ended his book by narrating how Christianity's chief hero had been put to death as an enemy of the state would have alienated Roman readers, and defeated his purpose of commending Christianity to the Roman world. According to Luke, Acts 20:17–38 was Paul's valedictory. This speech indicates that the Apostle never returned to Asia. I and II Timothy and Titus, according to this theory, included some genuine Pauline fragments of his earlier experiences (I Tim. 1:20; II Tim. 4:10–15) but are pseudonymous. They were written to meet the circumstances of the author's own day; by using the name of the long-dead but still much-loved Apostle the author sought to enhance the authority of his instruction.

As a Roman citizen Paul's death penalty was the sword. Peter was crucified. According to tradition, both were imprisoned for a time in the Mamertine* Prison adjacent to the Roman Forum. When the Roman Church (c. A.D. 95) wrote to the Church at Corinth a letter known as I Clement, Paul and Peter were cherished in memory as great martyrs. Tertullian of Carthage (c. 198–200) declared that Paul was beheaded in Rome. Gaius of Rome (at the beginning of the 3rd century), says that Paul suffered martyrdom on the Ostian Way. Origen, a little later, wrote that Paul suffered martyrdom in Rome under Nero (54–68). Eusebius (326), basing his church history on earlier authentic records, made a similar statement. The magnificent basilica of St. Paul-Without-the-Walls in Rome, near the Ostian Way, replacing small ones built as early as Constantine's time, is a monument to the well-authenticated tradition that the Apostle was buried close to this site. (See ROME, illus. 350.)

Chief Events in Paul's Life

Events	Edgar J. Goodspeed	Conybeare & Howson	David Smith
Birth	A.D. 10–15		1
Conversion	34	36	33
In Cilicia, etc.	36–46	39–43	36–45
In Antioch	46–47	44–47	45–47
1st Miss. Journey	47–48	48	47–49
Jerusalem Council	48	50	50
2d Miss. Journey	49–52	51–54	50–53
In Corinth, etc.	50–51	53–54	51–53
3d Miss. Journey	52–56	54–58	53–57
In Ephesus	52–55	54–57	53–56
Arrest, Jerusalem	56	58	57
In Caesarea	56–58	59–60	57–59
In Rome	59–61	61–63	60–62
Asia, Macedonia, Spain, etc.		63–67	62–67
Second Roman imprisonment		68	67
Martyrdom	61	68	67

Paulus, Sergius, the Roman proconsul of Cyprus, who may have been converted to Christianity by Paul at Paphos on his First Missionary Journey (Acts 13:6–13). Luke's accuracy in naming this proconsul is verified by an inscription at ancient Soli (the present Karavastasi) on the N. coast of Cyprus.

pavement. See GABBATHA.

pe (pā), the 17th letter of the Heb. alphabet.

peace (Heb. *shālōm*) was an early ideal of Israel. (1) In their nomadic stage Hebrews greeted one another on treks, as Bedouins greet friends and strangers on the desert today, "Salaam, Salaam alleikum" ("Peace, peace to every one of you"). To be "peaceable and faithful in Israel" and to "lead a quiet and peaceable life in all godliness" was a deeply rooted ideal (II Sam. 20:19; I Tim. 2:2). "Seek peace and pursue it" (Ps. 34:14) was an eternal challenge. Peaceful conversation among neighbors (Ps. 28:3) and peace within and among the tribes of a patriarchal group were basic to survival. In the O.T. there appear such records of self-control as "Jacob held his peace" (Gen. 34:5). The Patriarchs did not make war on neighbor sheikhs; the military adventure of Abraham to rescue Lot (Gen. 14:1–12) is exceptional. Isaac's policy of nonresistance to the Philistines at his father's wells depicts notable self-control (Gen. 26:18–22). Jacob knew how to appease Laban (Gen. 31:44 ff.) and Esau (32:13 f.). The friendship of the Patriarchs for their neighbors reflects that of Yahweh for such men as Abraham, who was the "friend of God" (Gen. 15).

The O.T. furnishes numerous instances of deliberately peaceful relations between rulers, like those of Israel with the king of Heshbon (Deut. 2:26 ff.); of Jabin, King of the Canaanite city of Hazor, and the house of Heber the Kenite (Judg. 4:17); and of the Phoenician King Hiram of Tyre, and Solomon of Israel (I Kings 5:12 ff.). In times when war between the kings of Judah and of Israel was chronic, occasions were recorded when, for example, "Jehoshaphat made peace with the king of Israel" (I Kings 22:44).

One of the most eloquent prayers for the political peace and prosperity of Jerusalem is Ps. 122:6–9; into the very name of this city of strife is knit the word for peace, *shālōm* (*Yerushalayim*). The Uru-salim mentioned in the Tell el-Amarna tablets of c. 1400 B.C. was "The City of Peace," coveted as a stronghold in S. Palestine.

(2) Though armies of aggression were almost constantly sweeping through Palestine on their way to a prize greater than this unrewarding little country, Hebrews developed a sense of inner, spiritual, God-given peace (Ps. 4:8, 119:165; Isa. 48:18). "Thou wilt keep him in perfect peace, whose mind is stayed on thee" (Isa. 26:3) was an outstanding pronouncement of Isaiah, who even in the face of "hosts encamped" against Judah advised a policy of nonresistance and reliance upon God. "In returning and rest shall ye be saved; in quietness and confidence shall be your strength" (30:15). Peace was the kernel of the Messianic hope for the Kingdom of God (Ps. 72:7; Isa. 2:4, 9:5–7).

(3) Jesus fulfilled his people's longing for peace. The Messiah who had been foretold as a "Prince of Peace" (Isa. 9:6 f.) and whose birth was heralded by angelic acclaims of peace (Luke 2:14) taught the blessedness of the makers of peace (Matt. 5:9); these are the true "sons of God," who know that peace will never come without persistent effort on its behalf. They know that without peace no man can see God (Heb. 12:14), and that without justice peace cannot be permanent:

> "Mercy and truth are met together;
> Righteousness and peace have kissed each other." (Ps. 85:10)

The peace which Jesus coveted for all mankind was that peace of mind and soul that came to one who had sinned or lost his way and been reconciled with God, e.g., the woman of faith whose story is told in Luke 7:50. This was the ultimate peace he left with his faithful Disciples on the eve of his betrayal and Crucifixion; "Peace I leave with you; my peace I give unto you: not as the world giveth, give I unto you" (John 14:27). Paul states that peace with God is the sum total of the blessings experienced in Christ (Rom. 5:1). (See RECONCILIATION.)

(4) Salutations of the Apostolic Church include entreaties for peace from God the Father to fall upon believers (I Cor. 1:3; II Cor. 1:2; Gal. 1:3; Eph. 1:2; Phil. 1:2; Col. 1:2; I Thess. 1:1; II Thess. 1:2; I Tim. 1:2; II Tim. 1:2; II Pet. 1:2; II John 3; Rev. 1:4. Cf. the Hebraistic benedictions of Mark 5:34; Luke 7:50, 24:36; Jas. 2:16. Also see I Sam. 1:17).

(5) The Eighteen Benedictions pronounced in synagogues today incorporate an entreaty for peace in their last prayer and word. (Cf. the benediction of peace committed by Moses to Aaron, Num. 6:24–26.)

For the peace offerings embodied in Israel's early law codes (Ex. 20:24, 24:5, 29:28; Lev. 3:1, 3, 6, 9; Num. 6:14, 17 f., 26) see WORSHIP.

peace offering. See WORSHIP.

pearl, a lustrous concretion formed within the shell of mollusks by deposits of nacreous substances around an irritating foreign body, such as a grain of sand. Pearls were highly prized as gems in N.T. times, as seen in Christ's Parable of the Merchant seeking goodly pearls (Matt. 13:45 f.); in his allusion to casting pearls before swine (Matt. 7:6); and in references to pearls as personal adornments (I Tim. 2:9; Rev. 17:4) (see JEWELRY). Mother-of-pearl, the pearly lining of the mollusk, was probably the substance imagined as forming the "twelve gates" of the Holy City (Rev. 21:21). Bethlehem craftsmen carve mother-of-pearl into stars, crosses, and other objects. Excellent pearls are still obtained from the Arabian coast of the Persian Gulf and off the Bahrein islands.

Pedaiah (pē-dā′yȧ) ("Jehovah hath ransomed"). (1) The grandfather of King Jehoiakim of Judah (II Kings 23:36). Jehoiakim reigned 609–598 B.C. (2) The third son of King Jehoiachin, probably born in Babylon, to which his royal parent was carried captive from Jerusalem 597 B.C. I Chron. 3:18 makes Pedaiah the father of Zerubbabel, listed elsewhere as the son of Shealtiel, brother of Pedaiah. (3) The father of Joel, a ruler under David of the territory of Manasseh, W. of the Jordan (I Chron. 27:20). (4) A son of Parosh who helped rebuild the Jerusalem wall after the Exile (Neh. 3:25). (5) A man who stood at Ezra's left when he read the Law to the people of Jerusalem (Neh. 8:4). (6) A Levite who helped distribute the tithes from the Temple treasury (Neh. 13:13). (7) An ancestor of Sallu, a man who lived in Jerusalem in post-Exilic times (Neh. 11:7).

Peirene (pī-rē′nē), a famous fountain in Corinth*, just E. of the main entrance to the Agora from the Lechaeum Road, between the Propylaea gateway and the Peribolos of Apollo, in the central area of the great commercial city. This spring, with its sources in conglomerate rock, attracted settlers probably as early as the 5th millennium B.C. The Peirene was certainly known to Paul, Prisca, Aquila, and their fellow Christians at Corinth. Women daily filled their water jars of famous Corinthian pottery at this fountain, and temple attendants obtained water here for their sacred ceremonies. There is possibly a reminiscence of the Peirene in Paul's First Letter to the Corinthians (10:4).

The Peirene had six low, square, cave-like chambers from which water flowed N. into an open-air fountain or basin in the middle of a court 20 ft. wide and 30 ft. long. SE. of its arched cave chambers it poured its waters into four long, narrow reservoirs fashioned in native clay rock, two of which measured 65 ft. in length; two others were 80 ft. long. The reservoirs may have contained from 100,000 to 120,000 gallons. They supplied water for the elaborate refrigeration system of the South Stoa (arcaded shops), probably the largest secular structure in Greece.

In Paul's day the Peirene had been rebuilt for the new Corinth of Julius Caesar (44 B.C.)—a center which attracted many Jews who became Christians; this may explain Paul's visit and his two Epistles to the Corinthians. The Peirene Paul knew had Doric columns supporting an architrave, and a second story of engaged Ionic columns. During the lifetime of Herodes Atticus (2d century A.D.) the court was beautified and dedicated by the Corinthians to his wife Regilla, as evidenced by a statue base found in the Peirene, now in the American-given museum at Corinth.

317. Peirene Spring with Acrocorinth in background.

Pekah (pē′kä), a son of Remaliah; he succeeded Pekahiah, whom he murdered at Samaria (II Kings 15:25), and reigned as King of Israel (c. 737–732). The reference to a 20-year reign in II Kings 27 may be due to an error in oral transmission, and needs correction in the light of authoritative Assyrian data that show Menahem of Israel reigning in 738, and Hoshea ascending the throne in 732 as the successor of Pekah.

Pekah's reign was not pro-Assyrian, as that of Pekahiah had been. In fact he went so far as to organize an anti-Assyrian bloc that included Rezin*, King of Damascus, and the rulers of Arvad, Gaza, Ashkelon, Edom, Ammon, Moab, and an Arabian region controlled by Queen Shamsie. This league moved against Jerusalem in the Syro-Ephraimitic War. King Ahaz of Judah (Jehoahaz I, 735–715 B.C.), alarmed at the loss of citizens and damage to property, asked help from Tiglath-pileser, King of Assyria, who moved into Pekah's kingdom, subdued it as far S. as the Sea of Galilee, and deported many citizens (II Kings 15:29). Pekah was murdered by Hoshea*, son of Elah, who succeeded him as the last king of Israel (c. 732–724 B.C.) before the fall of Samaria (722/1 B.C.).

Pekahiah (pĕk′ȧ-hī′ȧ) ("Jehovah opens"), the son and successor of King Menahem of the Northern Kingdom (c. 738–737 B.C.). After a reign of two years, marked by personal iniquities and by inability to retain his father's cordial relationship with the Assyrian Empire, Pekahiah was assassinated in his palace at Samaria by a military and political cabal headed by Pekah*, who followed him as king of Israel (c. 737–732 B.C.) (II Kings 15:22–26). The atmosphere of his reign is reflected in Hosea.

Peleg (pē′lĕg) (from a word meaning "to divide," referring to the early partition of the earth) listed as a son of Eber, descendant of Noah, in the genealogy of Gen. 10:1–25, 11:16; cf. I Chron. 1:19, 25. He had many sons and daughters, and long life (Gen. 11:16–19).

Peleth (pē'lĕth). (1) A man of Reuben's tribe (Num. 16:1). (2) A man of Judah, descendant of Jerahmeel (I Chron. 2:33).

Pelethites (pĕl'ē-thīts), a strong people of S. Philistia, part of David's bodyguard, directed by Benaiah, son of Jehoiada (II Sam. 8:18, 20:23; I Chron. 18:17). These mighty henchmen accompanied David on his flight from the rebellious Absalom (II Sam. 15:18) and on his expedition against Sheba, son of Bichri (20:7). Pelethites took part in Solomon's coronation (I Kings 1:38, 44).

pelican (rendered "cormorant," A.V. Isa. 34:11; Zeph. 2:14), one of the birds considered "unclean" for Israel, i.e., forbidden for food (Lev. 11:18; Deut. 14:17; Ps. 102:6). A wilderness habitat is suggested by Ps. 102:6; unless such waste places were marshy, some other bird may have been intended. Pelicans lived on the shores of the Sea of Galilee, the shallow Egyptian lakes, and the Nile. In Christian symbolism the pelican denotes tender care of the young by the parent, and of the Church by Christ.

Pella (Khirbet Fahil). (1) A Canaanite city-state in what is now Jordan, SE. of and facing the powerful city of Beth-shan across the Jordan Valley. Pella was situated in what became the Kingdom of Og. It is mentioned in the Tell el-Amarna correspondence of c. 1375 B.C. Later, Pella was a member of the confederacy of 10 Hellenistic towns known as the Decapolis (see CITIES). Situated adjacent to the main N.-S. highway E. of the Jordan that linked Gadara with other towns of the Peraea, Pella was the N. gateway to the section of E. Palestine visited by Jesus (Matt. 4:25; Mark 7:31). Travelers journeying from Galilee to Jerusalem via the Jordan crossing near Jericho (Luke 19:1) (rather than through Samaria), would logically go through Pella. This town exported chariot poles (staves) to Egypt. Excavations at Khirbet Faḥil in 1958, 1963, and 1967 have uncovered Late Bronze Age tombs, traces of Iron II occupation, a Byzantine church, and other remains. Pella was a Gentile center to which the Christian group at Jerusalem fled at the beginning of the Jewish revolt against Rome in A.D. 66, and again in 135. It was important as an episcopal see after the Council of Nicaea. As late as the 5th and 6th centuries Christian bishops were functioning at Pella, though the region was outside the main channel of Christian expansion.

(2) A town (the modern Neochori) in Macedonia, a short distance W. of Thessalonica.

pen. See WRITING.

pendant. See AMULET; JEWELRY.

penknife. See WRITING.

penny, the A.V. rendering (Matt. 20:2, 9 f., 13, 22:19; Mark 12:15; Luke 20:24; Rev. 6:6) of a Roman silver coin, the denarius (R.S.V.), translated "shilling" in the A.S.V. The value of the denarius, the commonest coin in the time of Jesus, was c. 19¼ cents, the price of a day's common labor. Jews paid tribute to their conquerors in this coin, which usually bore the head of the emperor (Matt. 22:19–21). It may be the coin intended in Acts 19:19 ("pieces of silver"). See MONEY.

Pentapolis (pĕn-tăp'ō-lĭs). (1) The Gk. term used for the five chief Philistine (see PHILISTIA) cities: Gaza, Ashkelon, Ashdod, Gath, and Ekron. (2) The term used in the Wisdom of Solomon for the five cities of the plain mentioned in Gen. 14:2: Sodom, Gomorrah, Admah, Zeboiim, and Zoar (Bela).

Pentateuch, the first five books of the O.T. See HEXATEUCH.

Pentateuch, the Samaritan. See TEXT.

Pentecost (Gk. *pentēkoste*, "fiftieth" [day]). (1) In O.T. times the 50th day (c. 7 weeks) after the harvest-consecrating, sheaf-waving ceremony of the 16th of the month Nisan (see PASSOVER; FEASTS). Pentecost is also known as "The Feast of Weeks" (Ex. 34:22; Deut. 16:10), "The Feast of Harvest" (Ex. 23:16), and "The Day of the First Fruits" (Num. 28:26). This one-day festival usually fell on the 6th day of the month Sivan (end of May or beginning of June) and was the 2d and least important of the three annual festivals which, by ritual indicated in sources J and E (Ex. 34:18–26, cf. 23:10–17), were to be celebrated at the sanctuary by every male. It opened the fruit harvest, as the Feast of Unleavened Bread opened grain harvest.

Exact dating of Hebrew festivals in the early centuries is difficult if not impossible, for calendars were fixed by methods as unscientific as men's observation of the first moment when the slender crescent moon became visible at Jerusalem. Scholarly arguments about the proper methods of fixing dates are indecisive, and serve only to confuse. Although source D (Deut. 16:11) set a definite day to be celebrated as Pentecost, for centuries before that source was compiled (c. 622 B.C.) Pentecost had been conveniently celebrated at the theoretical close of the barley and wheat harvest, which fell at a different time in the hot Jordan Valley, for example, than in the Judaean uplands.

Some authorities consider Pentecost to have been the development of an ancient Canaanite agricultural festival, naturalized and interpreted by the Hebrews in line with their Yahwistic beliefs. Details of its celebration vary and progress in the various stages of written Law. Source D tends to minimize Pentecost. Specific offerings were not required, but each man brought voluntarily what his harvest justified (Deut. 16:10). Because Pentecost was observed about seven weeks after Passover, it was tied in with the Sabbatical system of feasts; usual labors were halted and people met in a holy convocation (Deut. 28:2–6). Source H (in Lev. 23:15–21) demands that two first-fruit loaves of new, leavened meal prepared from 2/10 of an ephah be waved (whence "wave loaves," v. 17); and seven unblemished yearling lambs, one bullock, and two rams for burnt offerings, and one male goat for peace offerings (v. 18 f.). H further specifies that for Pentecost gleanings of the harvest be left for the poor and the sojourners (v. 22). Ezekiel does not refer to a Pentecost offering, if we regard 45:21 as a later interpolation; he is interested in only two feasts, paralleling the two divisions of the ecclesiastical year. P enlarges the ritual demands of H by including the presentation of two young bullocks, a ram, seven yearling lambs as burnt offering, and a meal offering of three tenth parts mingled with oil for each bullock, two tenth parts for the ram, and one part for each lamb, in addition to a male goat for a sin offering (Num. 28:26–31). When the 15th to the 21st of Nisan was set for the Passover the one-day celebration of Pentecost was established.

Later Judaism added to the meaning of Pentecost by making it commemorative of the anniversary of the giving of the Law at Sinai, thus transforming it into a joint harvest and historical celebration. There is, however, no O.T. record of the Law-giving having occurred 50 days after the first Passover.

(2) In the N.T. the first Christian Pentecost fell on the same day as the old Hebrew festival. The events narrated in Acts 2 mark the beginning of the Christian Church. Multitudes of devout Jews from what seemed "every nation under heaven" (v. 5) had been attracted to Jerusalem. About nine in the morning (cf. v. 15), the Holy* Spirit came upon the Apostles and some 120 disciples gathered together. The cloven "tongues of fire" (Acts 2:3) were analogous to "the burning bush" at Sinai (Ex. 3:2). Not only the disciples but the throng gathered to celebrate the old Pentecost were included in the marvelous happenings (Acts 2:6). As the old Pentecost was a harvest feast, it was appropriate that the new Pentecost brought a harvest of "about three thousand souls" (v. 41). Many Christians saw in the descent of the Holy Spirit upon the disciples, 50 days after the redemption of the world by Christ, an analogy to the gift by God of the Sinai Law, 50 days (traditionally) after the deliverance of Israel from Egypt.

Paul in I Cor. 16:8 spoke of delaying his return to Corinth from Ephesus until after Pentecost; he wished to take evangelistic advantage of the opportunity offered by the crowds assembled for the feast.

(3) In some branches of the Christian Church Pentecost or Whitsuntide is observed as a solemn feast 50 days after Easter (reckoning inclusively), to commemorate the coming of the Holy Spirit. The Church took over from the synagogue the liturgical use of Ps. 29 for Pentecost. In Christian symbolism cloven tongues of fire signify the Day of Pentecost, as well as the Holy Spirit.

Penuel (pē̆-nū′ĕl). (1) The place on the picturesque Jabbok* River in Jordan where Jacob wrestled with a Stranger and obtained an angelic blessing (Gen. 32:30 f.). The fortified tower of this strategic highland position is mentioned in Judg. 8:8–17. Penuel was strengthened by Jeroboam I (c. 922–901 B.C.) (I Kings 12:25).

(2) The father of Gedor (I Chron. 4:4). (3) A descendant of Benjamin (I Chron. 8:25).

people, peoples, racial and national groups. Early interest in the origins of the ancient peoples is evidenced by the genealogical lists of Gen. 5, 10 (a composite of sources J and P, cf. I Chron. 1:1), and the attempts to explain the development of languages (Gen. 11—Babel and the confusion of tongues). The writers confused geography with ethnography, stating that Canaan (a country) begat Sidon (later a city); that Mediterranean islands, Kittim (Gen. 10:4) and Dodanim (Rodanim) (? Rhodes), are the "sons of Javan" (10:4), who was a son of Japheth, son of Noah. The "sons of Ishmael" are named in Gen. 25:12–16 by their villages. The Sumerian king lists discovered in modern times ascribe incredible antiquity to antediluvian rulers, and indicate an interest in the origin of peoples similar to that expressed by authors of certain passages in Genesis.

The peoples of the Bible came from the area stretching from the Mediterranean to the Persian mountains, from Asia Minor and Armenia, from as far S. as the First Cataract of the Nile, and from the estuary of the Tigris-Euphrates on the SE. Palestine's population has always been mixed. (See individual entries, CANAAN; HITTITES; HORITES; HYKSOS; MITANNI, etc.) In spite of many non-Semitic conquerors since the 3d millennium B.C., the ethnic composition of Palestine has been predominantly Semitic (from Shem, eldest son of Noah). Various Semitic peoples settled in Palestine across the centuries. The Hyksos hordes who arrived about the 17th century B.C. brought a non-Semitic people from the N. and NE. Indo-Aryans (descendants of Japheth) also made migrations that left their names and those of their deities. The Egyptians were predominantly Hamitic, descendants of Ham.

The Hebrews, not the oldest or largest group of Semites*, came rather late in the development of the large Semitic family. The Semitic element, prominent in Palestine to the present time, was an offshoot of the Semito-Hamitic stock. (See the more detailed discussion of the closely related Semitic tongues and dialects in W. F. Albright's *The Archaeology of Palestine*, Penguin Books.)

"People" in the O.T. is frequently used in the sense of Yahweh's people. His chosen people, the Israelites (Ex. 8:1; Ezek. 38:14).

The "people of the land" sometimes refers to the popular assembly of freemen of a town (as in Gen. 23:12), at other times to the non-Jewish inhabitants of Palestine (Ezra 4:4, 10:2, etc.). In the N.T. "the people" sometimes means the multitudes (Matt. 4:25, 9:35); the proletariat, or crowd of common people (Mark 11:32; Acts 17:13). Again, it signifies the nation to which Jesus belonged (Matt. 1:21). Cf. Rev. 17:15, "peoples, and multitudes, and nations."

Peor (pē′ôr), a mountain in Moab* to which Balak led Baalam. It evidently overlooked Jeshimon (Num. 23:28), probably a desert waste country in the Jordan Valley N. of the Dead Sea. This may have been the site of the worship of Baal-peor, an apostasy for which Israel was condemned (Num. 25:3, 18; Josh. 22:17).

Peraea (pē̆-rē′ȧ) (Perea) (Gk., "the land beyond"), the name given by the 1st-century A.D. Jewish historian Flavius Josephus to the region referred to in the Bible as "beyond

Jordan," "the land across the Jordan," or "the other side of the Jordan" (Gen. 50:10 f.; Num. 22:1, etc.; Matt. 4:15, 19:1; John 10:40, etc.). It paralleled Judaea and Samaria, and extended N. and S. between Pella and Machaerus. On the E. it was bordered by the Arab Nabataean kingdom (see NABATAEA), on a line passing through es-Salt. It included part of the Decapolis and had within it such cities as Pella, Jabesh-gilead, Succoth, Penuel, Abel-shittim, Gadara (possibly its capital), Gerasa (Jerash), Madeba, and Amathus (see individual entries). The great Decapolis city of Philadelphia ('Ammân) was never included. Maccabean leaders controlled Peraea for a time after 124 B.C., but in Jesus' day it was ruled for Rome by Herod Antipas, Tetrarch of Galilee and Peraea. Its terrain was one of the most picturesque in Palestine, marked by rugged highlands and secluded and fruitful valleys. John the Baptist evidently preached and baptized in Peraea (John 1:28, 10:40). Jesus found that in Peraea many came "unto him . . . And many believed on him there" (John 10:41 f.). From Peraea Jesus was summoned to the sick bed of Lazarus (John 11:3). He apparently liked to use the route from Judaea to Galilee via Peraea and thus avoid Samaria. Early Christianity bore bountiful fruits in Peraea, as illustrated by extensive ruins of churches excavated at Gerasa (Jerash).

perdition (Lat. *perditio*, "the act of destroying"), the state of final destruction of the wicked (Phil. 1:28; I Tim. 6:9; A.V. II Pet. 3:7; Rev. 17:8, 11). Judas was called by Jesus "the son of perdition" (John 17:12, cf. II Thess. 2:3).

Perez (pē′rĕz) ("a breach") (Pharez, A.V. of the O.T. except I Chron. 27:3 and Neh. 11:4, 6; A.V. Phares, A.S.V. and R.S.V. Perez, Matt. 1:3), a twin son of Judah and Tamar (Gen. 38:29). From him the Perezite branch of the Judah tribe descended (Num. 26:20; I Chron. 2:4–5). David was a Perezite and brought prestige to the group (Ruth 4:12, 18 f.), and through this line Perez was an ancestor of Christ (Matt. 1:3).

perfect, perfection, words used in Scripture to express (1) completeness or ideality of quality, as "a perfect and just weight" (Deut. 25:15); (2) the highest attributes of Deity (II Sam. 22:31; Job 37:16); (3) man's sinlessness (I Kings 15:14; A.S.V. Ps. 18:23). Christ believed that man should strive for perfection comparable to that of God (Matt. 5:48). Many Christian teachers have taken an eschatological view of the doctrine of perfection, i.e., that its attainment lies in the future; but because of God's grace* operating through the forgiveness of man in Christ the Christian advances toward perfection. Origen, a great Christian thelogian of the 3d century influenced by neo-Platonic Greek mysticism, believed it was possible for men to attain spiritual perfection; this view is advocated by "holiness" sects and liberal mystical Protestants today.

perfume. See COSMETICS; INCENSE; OINTMENTS AND PERFUMES.

Perga (pûr′gȧ) (the modern Murtana), the chief native city of Pamphylia*, c. 12 m. inland from the Gulf of Pamphylia and the coastal city of Attalia, but having its own harbor on the right bank of the Cestrus River. Never entirely dominated by Gk. influences, it minted its own coins from the 2d century B.C. to A.D. 276. Though Paul stopped briefly in Perga on his First Missionary Journey (Acts 13:13 f., 14:25), Christianity did not take root in this fever-infested center of Artemis, Asiatic nature goddess, "queen of Perga."

Pergamum (pûr′gȧ-mŭm) (the modern Bergama in W. Anatolian Turkey), an ancient city in the district of Mysia. It minted its own coins at least as early as 263 B.C. (reign of Eumenes I). It attained the peak of its culture under Eumenes II (197–159 B.C.), whose kingdom comprised a large part of W. Asia Minor, including Mysia, Lydia, part of Phrygia, Ionia, and Caria. The Romans inherited this realm and formed it into the Province of Asia*, of which Pergamum was capital for a time, and Ephesus and Smyrna the chief cities. Excavations carried out by the Berlin Museum since their instigation

318. Pergamum: ruins of hillside theater.

under G. Humann in 1878 have enabled the plan of much of the Hellenistic city to be reconstructed. On the peak of a 1,000-ft.-high hill were located the royal fortress and residency of the Attalid Dynasty, with its associated barracks, storehouses, and arsenal. Nearby stood the main temple, dedicated to Athena Nicephorus, with its great library. Founded by Eumenes II, it rivaled that of Ptolemy Philadelphus at Alexandria, who, fearing lest his prize be overshadowed, is said to have forbidden the export of papyrus to Pergamum. Whereupon—so legend runs—the people of Pergamum developed what we now know as parchment (from *pergamena*).

To the S. lay the great Altar of Zeus and its richly sculptured frieze with scenes of struggling gods and giants and representations of the defeat of the Gauls by Eumenes —a masterpiece of Hellenistic art. Some Biblical scholars see in this altar the basis for the imagery of "Satan's Throne" in Rev. 2:13. From below the Altar of Zeus a street descended to the central part of the city, where lay the civic buildings—the gymnasium, the agora, and temples of Demeter and Hera. Cut into the W. slope of the hill was the theater, and outside the city to the SW. lay the sanctuary of Asclepius, the god of healing, associated in the 2d century A.D. with the physician Galen. Roman remains include a theater, an amphitheater, a racetrack, and, above the area of the Altar of Zeus, a temple dedicated to the emperors Trajan and Hadrian.

Pergamum was one of the seven churches of Asia to which the Book of Revelation was addressed (Rev. 1:11, 2:12–17). Its pagan cults (2:14) and the teaching of the Nicolaitans were condemned. It was also the site of the martyrdom of Antipas (2:13).

M. S. M./W. P. A.

Perizzites (pĕr′ĭ-zīts), one of the aboriginal groups in Canaan (Gen. 13:7, 15:20; Ex. 3:8; Josh. 9:1, 17:15) whom the Lord expected Israel to displace (Ex. 33:2; Deut. 20:17). In the time of Joshua (11:3) they lived in the hill country; after his death they were defeated by Judah at Bezek (Judg. 1:4–5). Contrary to Mosaic Law, they intermarried with their conquerors (Judg. 3:5–6), leading them into idolatry. Solomon enslaved the Perizzites (I Kings 9:20–21; II Chron. 8:7).

perjury (Heb. *shebu'ath*, *sheker*, "false oath"), swearing to a false statement, viewed in Israel and Judaism as a serious offense against God because it violated the Third Commandment (Ex. 20:7; Deut. 5:11). Punishment in civil cases involved restitution of property plus a fine and a sin offering. A perjurer in a criminal case was punished "as he had meant to do to his brother" (Deut. 19:19). This could mean capital punishment. Perjurers were usually rejected as witnesses.

persecutions, acts of persistent and cruel hostility. The O.T. represents God as One Who will strengthen the upright to meet the persecutions of daily life (Ps. 7:1, 5, 31:15, 119:86). Prophets of Israel were persecuted for their zeal on the Lord's behalf, e.g., Elijah vs. Ahab and Jezebel (I Kings 19), and Jeremiah vs. contemporary monarchs (21:11–23:8)—Jehoiakim (Jer. 37–44). Jesus referred to these persecutions of the prophets in the Beatitudes (Matt. 5:10–12). Jesus was persecuted (John 5:16), and his followers could expect no better treatment (15:20); "a servant is not greater than his lord." In his lament over Jerusalem (Matt. 24:3–25:46) he told his Disciples of cataclysmic persecutions which would signal "the end" and the coming of the Son of man in his glory.

(1) Christ's predictions came to pass. Scarcely had he ascended when the Apostolic group began to feel the blows of Jewish opposition. Peter and other Christian leaders were arrested (Acts 9:23, 5:18 ff.) by Jewish priests and Sadducees (Acts 4:1–3, 5:17 ff.). The stoning of Stephen touched off widespread persecution of Christians by such zealous Jewish Pharisees (Acts 6:8–7:54) as Saul (chap. 8). Saul himself was persecuted at Lystra (14:19; II Tim. 3:11) by Jews from Antioch and Iconium who stoned him and left him for dead, and at many other places such as Berea (Acts 17:10–13).

(2) Roman persecution of Christians drove them underground to the catacombs (tunnelled burial places) for their secret worship. These persecutions are reflected in the stories of Peter and Paul, and throughout the Epistles and Revelation. Vengeance on Christians was wreaked by Nero* (A.D. 54–68)—chiefly at Rome, in the time of Peter and Paul. Under Domitian, who regarded himself as divine (A.D. 81–96), persecutions were extended out into the provinces, and Christians who refused to worship the emperor's statue were banished or put to death and their property was seized. I Peter indicates the treatment of Christians under Domitian, though some scholars assign the writing of I Peter to an even later era—that of Trajan. Persecutions by Trajan (A.D. 98–117) were more extensive, for he equated Christianity with criminality. The Christian persecutions are an aid in dating the N.T. books. For example, many authorities believe that Mark was written at Rome to strengthen the faith of Christians shaken by Nero's persecutions. I Thessalonians mentions the patience and faith of the churches in the midst of persecutions (1:6), and tells of Timothy having been sent to strengthen the afflicted (3:3 ff.). II Thessalonians encourages those who have endured persecutions (1:4–12). The definition of faith in Hebrews is prefaced by a reference to the "conflict of sufferings" (A.S.V. 10:32–39), and an appeal for steadfastness "for yet a very little while" until Christ should return. This Epistle was evidently written to encourage the 3d generation of Christians—those who had experienced the onslaughts of Domitian. Revelation depicts Domitian as "the beast," blended with a sort of Nero and Antichrist; he embodies cosmic evil and antagonism to Christ, and is finally overthrown in his long contest with the people of God, who will live with Christ in a reign of 1,000 years (see MILLENNIUM), while Satan is chained in hell (Rev. 19:19–20:6). The blood of the martyrs became "the seed of the Church."

Persepolis (pûr-sĕp′ō-lĭs) (Takht-i-Jamshîd), a capital of the ancient Persian Empire (Iran), c. 32 m. NE. of Shiraz and c. 25 m. W. of Pasargadae, capital of Cyrus, on a spur of the rugged Zagros Mountains. Its isolation in an "Alpine" region made some Persian rulers prefer Shushan* or Ecbatana, alternate capitals of their realm. The city, which represents the peak of Persian culture, was established by Darius* I ("the Great") (522–486 B.C.), and its development was continued by others of the Achaemenid Dynasty—Xerxes I, Artaxerxes I, and Artaxerxes III. Persepolis is mentioned in II Macc. 9:2. Its architectural grandeur exceeded that of Babylon under Nebuchadnezzar. Its palaces and treasuries were of gray marble from nearby mountain quarries. Excavations conducted by the Oriental Institute of the University of Chicago have revealed the ruins to which Persepolis was reduced when Alexander the Great burned and despoiled the magnificent city in 330 B.C.

Like other cities of Persia (Iran), Persepolis was constructed on a tremendous platform of terraces c. 1,000 ft. x 1,600 ft. Behind the city was a backdrop of majestic mountains—a spur of the "Mountain of Mercy" overlooking a plain, Marv Dasht. One of the most magnificent structures of Persepolis was the great audience hall (Apadana) of Darius and Xerxes (also known as "the hall of a hundred columns"), approached by awe-inspiring formal stairways whose entire face was carved with sculptured reliefs showing emissaries from 23 Oriental nations bringing tribute. This relief is considered the masterpiece of Achaemenid art. It provides evidence of the dress and customs of Biblical peoples. The audience hall included such Egyptian architectural features as colonnades—the earliest in Asia. In its foundation deposits the Oriental Institute found solid gold tablets inscribed with the records of Darius, and a duplicate set in silver. These, with data recently secured by the University of Michigan and the American Schools of Oriental Research from the rock-cut inscriptions at

319. Reconstruction drawing of The Hall of a Hundred Columns, Persepolis, Iran, by Charles Chipiez, from *The History of Art in Persia*, by Perrot and Chipiez.

Behistun along the ancient caravan route from Babylon to Ecbatana, offer scholars historic (if often biased) information concerning the era and the deeds of Darius, self-styled "King of Kings," who credited his successes to his god Ahura-Mazda*. (See DARIUS, illus. 110, and XERXES, illus. 493.)

In addition to the audience halls of Darius and Xerxes, the O.I. found remains of the royal harems, private palaces, treasuries, massive city walls and gates, and colossal bulls which guarded them.

The kings of the Achaemenid Dynasty, with the exception of Cyrus, are buried at Naksh-i-Rustam, a few m. N. of Persepolis. See excavation reports of the Oriental Institute Persian Expedition.

Persia (*Pārsā*, known in antiquity as "Persis"), a country inhabited by Indo-European peoples, Aryans (whence *Eran* and *Iran*). In the Biblical period the Persian Empire was one of the foremost in the world, due to the organizing genius of such rulers as Cyrus the Great and Darius, who had a conviction that they ruled the whole civilized world, and were authorized by Ahura-Mazda ("Lord Wisdom"), chief god of the Zoroastrian religion, to unify and govern it with integrity. Though they never conquered Greece, they dominated Asia for almost two centuries, and as successors of Nebuchadnezzar became masters of Palestine and Syria. Judah was a very small province in the Fifth Persian Satrapy. Its southern frontier fortress, Lachish*, was controlled from the palace of the Persian administrator; it has been excavated by the Marston-Mond-Wellcome Archaeological Expedition.

The Persian kings included Cyrus, who united Media and Persia (549 B.C.), and conquered Lydia (546) and Babylonia (539); Cambyses (530–522); Smerdis (522); Darius I (522–486); Xerxes I (? Ahasuerus) (486–465); Artaxerxes I (465–424); Xerxes II (424–423); Darius II (423–404); Artaxerxes II (404–358); Artaxerxes III (358–338); Arses (338–336); and Darius III (336–331).

The Persian kings who participated in Jewish history in the period following Nebuchadnezzar's destruction of Jerusalem were:

(1) *Cyrus the Great*, recognized by a Hebrew prophet as called to "rule over kings" (Isa. 41:2), anointed of God (45:1), Whose shepherd he was (Isa. 44:28), called by the God of the Hebrews, even though he had not known Him (45:3 f.), to subdue nations. Cyrus reversed the Babylonian policy of deporting conquered peoples, and not only welcomed them at his court and entrusted them with posts of responsibility in his armies, but allowed the Armenians, Lydians, Greeks, and Jews to return home. The Jews began to return to Judah under authorization of an edict of Cyrus (II Chron. 36:20–22) (c. 538 B.C.). Their Return was continued during an extended period (Ezra 1 ff.). Sheshbazzar apparently led the first contingent, and his company began the restoration of the Temple which Nebuchadnezzar had destroyed (Ezra 5:16). Local malcontents belittled and delayed the project (Ezra 5).

(2) *Darius I*, who came to the throne c. 522 B.C., found in the archives the edict of Cyrus concerning the Jerusalem Temple reconstruction (Ezra 6). He appointed Zerubbabel (Ezra 3:8), grandson of King Jehoiachin of Judah, to be governor (c. 520–515) of that portion of his Empire. From that time the enterprise progressed, and the Temple was dedicated (Ezra 6:16–22). Its completion was due in part to the co-operation of an enthusiastic company of priests and Levites (Neh. 12:40), to Joshua the high priest, and to the prophets Haggai and Zechariah (Ezra 5:1). An order from Darius halted the obstructionists (Ezra 6).

(3) *Xerxes I*, son of Darius (486–465), was possibly the Ahasuerus of the Book of Esther (1:1, 2:1, 16, 3:1, 8:1, and frequently "the king"). His palace at Shushan (Susa) was the scene of the incidents in Esther.

(4) *Artaxerxes I* (*Longimanus*), 465–424 B.C., authorized the return of two other groups of exiles. One was led by Ezra (Ezra 7, 8) (c. 458 B.C., or later, according to some scholars), who tried to restore the spiritual ideals of his people, sponsored the publication of the Pentateuch, and brought about reforms in line with its teachings (9, 10). A second group returned in the reign of Artaxerxes I, led by Nehemiah (445), who was appointed Governor of Jerusalem, with authority to rebuild the walls (Neh. 1 ff.).

Persis, "the beloved," a woman whose abundant labor "in the Lord" evoked a greeting from Paul in his Roman letter (16:12).

Person of Christ. See JESUS CHRIST.

Peshitta, See "Syriac Versions," TEXT.

pestle, a short, thick instrument for grinding and pounding grains, spices, etc., in a mortar* (Prov. 27:22).

Peter, the leading Apostle (Acts 1:13, 15, 2:14, I Pet. 1:1; II Pet. 1:1), one of the three favorite Disciples of Jesus (Matt. 16:17 f.; Mark 14:33), and the only person in the Bible bearing this name. He is known by four different names in the N.T.: (1) "Peter," 124 times; (2) "Simon," standing alone in 16 instances; (3) "Simeon" one (Acts 15:14); (4) "Cephas," the favorite designation of Paul, nine times; "Simon" and "Peter" appear together 27 times. "Simeon" (Symeon) and "Cephas" are Sem. in origin, while "Simon" and "Peter" are Gk. John 1:42 indicates that Simon was his surname. "Cephas" is the Aram. equivalent to Greek "*petros*," "rock," symbolic of the man's strong character. When Peter displayed weakness, Jesus addressed him by his old surname rather than the name that meant "rock" (Luke 22:31; Mark 14:37; John 21:15–17).

Peter's father's name was Jona, Jonas, or John (Matt. 16:17; John 1:42, 21:15–17). His mother is unidentified. Peter belonged to Bethsaida, a fishing village or suburb of Capernaum on the Sea of Galilee (John 1:44). He and his brother Andrew were fishermen (Matt. 4:18; Mark 1:16), business partners with Zebedee and his sons, James and John (Luke 5:11; Matt. 4:21). Peter was married (I Cor. 9:5); his mother-in-law and Andrew lived with him. The hospitality of the Capernaum home and family was favorably known (Matt. 8:14 f.; Mark 1:29–31; Luke 4:38 f.).

While Peter was in Bethany beyond the Jordan where John the Baptist was preaching (John 1:28), he first met Jesus through his brother Andrew, one of the Baptist's acknowledged followers, according to the Fourth Gospel. The Lord immediately recognized the latent power of the fisherman and named him "the Rock" (John 1:40–42). Later, when Jesus began his ministry in Capernaum, he enlisted the full-time support of Peter and Andrew, James and John (Matt. 4:18–22; Mark 1:16–20, Luke 5:1–11). In the earliest listings of the Twelve Disciples the two sets of brothers, Peter and Andrew, James and John, were paired, which suggests congeniality and mutual assistance. Andrew's claim to fame was his bringing Peter to Jesus, but the early Church remembered him chiefly as the brother of the more illustrious Apostle (John 1:40, 6:8). Peter's name always heads the Twelve (Acts 1:13).

Peter's remarkable leadership was manifested throughout his life. To his fellow Disciples he declared Christ's Messiahship at a time of doubt and confusion (Matt. 16:13–16; Mark 8:27–29; Luke 9:18–20). He was outspoken in his loyalty when, because of Christ's hard sayings, many turned back and "walked no more with him" (John 6:66–69). On several occasions Peter was chief spokesman for the Disciples, and he is mentioned first among those receiving private instructions and explanations from Jesus (Mark 8:29, 9:5, 10:28, 11:21, 13:3). After the Crucifixion and burial of Jesus, Peter took the lead in investigating the women's story of the open tomb (John 20:2 f.). Although John outran the older Peter to the Garden, Peter was the first to enter the open sepulcher (vv. 4–9). The story of Peter and the resurrected Christ on the shores of Galilee (John 21:1–23) is not only an account of the Apostle's vivid experience (I Cor. 15:5), but an indication of the position of honor and leadership Peter held in the estimation of the Church when the last chapter of the Fourth Gospel was written.

Peter's leadership in the Apostolic Church is apparent in (1) the selection of the successor to Judas (Acts 1:15 f.); (2) his sermon interpreting Pentecost* (2:14–40); (3) his defense of the Christian community before the Sanhedrin (4:8–12); (4) his role as judge when Church discipline was violated (5:3–9); (5) his responsibility when conditions in Samaria needed investigation (8:14); and (6) the hostility which his activities on behalf of the Christians aroused among the Jews and Herod Antipas (12:1–3). Even his shadow was believed to cast a beneficent influence (5:15). Peter was the first to open the doors of the Church to Gentiles (chap. 10). He participated in the first Jerusalem congress, which established membership rules for the growing Church (15:1–35). Paul, who at times opposed him, acknowledged his leadership (Gal. 2:7–9, 11).

Peter was not without weaknesses. His failure to understand the true Messianic (see MESSIAH) program called forth a sharp rebuke from Jesus (Mark 8:33). Rashness rather than courage characterized his conduct in the Garden when Jesus was arrested (John 18:10 f.). His threefold denial of Jesus in the courtyard of the high priest was his greatest failure (Matt. 26:39–75; Mark 14:66–72; Luke 22:54–62; John 18:15–18, 25–27). As this sin was grievous, the sorrow it caused Peter corresponded in intensity (Matt. 26:75; Mark 14:72; Luke 22:62). Christ's loving but pained look (Luke 22:61), his special message to Peter (Mark 16:7), and the experience of the resurrected Christ (Luke 24:34; I Cor. 15:5) cleansed Peter's soul of its guilt but not of his memory of its enormity, as is evidenced by its detailed narration in all the Gospels.

The view that Peter, the man, was the rock on which the Church was built (Matt. 16:16–20) is disputed by some Protestant scholars. The words about Peter found in Matt. 16:18 do not supply a basis for the claims of the Roman Catholic hierarchy to a custody of temporal power proceeding from Peter as its first "pope." The keys which Roman Catholic art frequently shows in Peter's grasp cannot be accepted as either symbols of ecclesiastical government or as the means of unlocking the hidden meaning of Christ's words (Matt. 16:18 f.) concerning "keys of the kingdom of heaven" and the "binding" and "loosing" on earth and in heaven. These Matthaean facets of the incidents are not recorded in the earlier Marcan account of the Caesarea confession (Mark 8:27–30). It is difficult to determine what words Christ actually spoke on this occasion, and what he meant. The Greek words in v. 18 (*petros* and *petra*) are not identical, although both come from the

PETER, THE FIRST EPISTLE OF

same root. Perhaps Christ saw in the man who was declaring him to be "the Christ, the Son of the living God" (Matt. 16:16) the firm, adamant, solidified, petrified personality who would help give the *ekklēsia* ("those that were called out") its permanence and resistance to evil. Peter's *faith* was the rock-like element upon which Christ could build his fellowship of people of "the way."

Matthew's words about Peter may be related to the construction method of ancient temples and palaces, which were often built on a bed of rock, upon which the cornerstone and courses of huge stones were erected. Christ was the chief cornerstone (I Cor. 3:11–15; Eph. 2:20) around which others were "fitly framed together . . . unto an holy temple in the Lord."

According to B. H. Streeter (*The Four Gospels*, Macmillan), Matt. 16:16–20 was inserted into the earlier Marcan account of the incident (Mark 8:27–30) by those who disapproved the conservatism of James and the liberalism of Paul's attitude to the Law, but held Peter in high esteem. This was true of the church at Antioch (Gal. 2:11–14). The Gk. word *ekklēsia*, found in the Gospels only in Matt. 16:18 f. and 18:17, fits better into the church at Antioch than into the situation at the time of Peter's confession at Caesarea Philippi, when the Church in the sense of a congregation had not yet developed. "My church" (Matt. 16:18) here may refer to "the synagogue of the last days" or to the fellowship of all Christians, or to a new element inside Judaism.

The narrative of Peter's travels and labors ends with Acts 12. The indirect testimony of the N.T., the literary evidence in the N.T. Apocrypha, and tradition and archaeology all point to the growing influence of the Apostle in Christian circles everywhere and his final martyrdom in Rome. Clement of Alexandria, Irenaeus, and other Church fathers declare that the Second Gospel was either dictated by Peter or represented the recollections of Peter as compiled by Mark. The writing of this earliest and most Petrine Gospel fits into Peter's sojourn in Rome (Col. 4:10; I Pet. 5:13). The distinctive Petrine material in Matthew (16:17–20, 18:21 f., etc.) reflects perhaps the Apostle's popularity and influence at Antioch. Certainly Peter attains a pre-eminence in that Gospel missing in the others, although the Fourth Gospel does contain passages giving prominence to Peter (see John 1:40, 6:67–69, 13:1–20, 24, 20:3–10, 21:1–23). Peter was the type of person who made and spread news. Further indications that Peter captured the imagination of the early Christians are the Apocrypha bearing his name—The Gospel of Peter, The Apocalypse of Peter, The Epistle of Peter to James, The Preaching of Peter, etc. Miracles credited to him were a natural by-product of such adulation. Enthusiastic devotion to leaders like Peter caused parties to be formed which threatened Church unity (I Cor. 1:12). The Acts of Peter (A.D. 200–220) contains the beautiful *Domine, Quo Vadis?* legend. Peter, leaving Rome, met Jesus coming into the city. "Lord, whither goest Thou?" Jesus replied, "I go to Rome to be crucified." Peter said to him, "Lord, art thou being crucified again?" "Yes," said Jesus to Peter, "I am being crucified again." Peter forthwith returned to Rome.

Confirming the claims of Tertullian (A.D. 200), Eusebius relates in his *Church History* (A.D. 326)—based on information from authorities earlier than Tertullian—that both

320. Supposed site of Peter's execution, Piazza San Pietro, Rome. The obelisk, which is 85 ft. high, was brought from Egyptian Heliopolis by Caligula, who placed it on the *spina* of his Circus. Quadruple colonnade by Bernini is main approach to St. Peter's Basilica.

Peter and Paul suffered martyrdom at about the same time in Rome under Nero (A.D. 64–5). Peter was crucified "downward; not otherwise" at his own request. According to Eusebius the graves of Paul on the Ostian Way and of Peter in the cemetery near Nero's Circus were extant c. A.D. 200. Visitors to Rome today are shown the site of Peter's martyrdom at the base of the Egyptian obelisk* in the Piazza before the Basilica of St. Peter. Nero's Circus, where many Christians met their death, included this site. The grave of the martyred Apostle has long been thought to be nearby, beneath the high altar of the Basilica. Constantine's Basilica of St. Peter was built on this spot in the 4th century A.D., not because of its advantageous terrain, but because of the sacredness of the site. Recent excavations beneath the present Basilica of St. Peter have revealed many tombs, both pagan and Christian, indicating that this was a vast cemetery of ancient Rome —a likely burial place of Peter. Nothing has been unearthed to refute the strong literary and Church tradition that Peter met martyrdom in Rome; no other first-century city has any local tradition concerning the death of this great Christian leader. See *BA*, Dec. 1953.

Peter, the First Epistle of, opens with a salutation from "Peter, an apostle of Jesus Christ" (1:1). It indicates that Peter is "in Babylon" (5:13), the cryptic name used in Apocalyptic literature for Rome (Rev. 14:8, 18:2). It is addressed to Christians living in the five Roman provinces of Asia Minor N. of the Taurus Range. The phrase "strangers scattered" (A.V.) (A.S.V. "sojourners of the Dispersion") does not refer to Jews of the Dispersion but to Christians everywhere who felt themselves to be strangers in the present evil age and exiles from their heavenly home.

These Christians in Asia Minor needed encouragement during a period of tension and persecution. The key idea of this beautiful Epistle is hope. The author describes Christianity as a "living hope" (R.S.V. 1:3) Christ has redeemed Christians (1:18, 19), and will sustain and reward them (1:9, 2:25, 5:4); they may therefore be joyfully confident of salvation (4:13, 14). But the author also points out the responsibility of living worthy of this Christian hope. He lays constant stress on reverently submitting to the will of God and living blameless and peaceable lives.

The authorship of this Epistle is the subject of several theories. Peter's authorship is believed by some scholars to be supported by internal evidence; they find in this Epistle many lines of thought which are parallel to those in other N.T. passages dealing with Peter. Mark's presence in Rome with Peter (5:13) also contributes to the Petrine theory of authorship. But to many N.T. students parallels in thought are not in themselves convincing evidence of Petrine authorship, for there are parallels between I Peter and the writings of Paul, especially Romans. Silvanus (Silas), who was intimate with both Peter and Paul, has been considered a possible author of the Epistle (5:12). Originally he was an outstanding member of the Jerusalem church (Acts 15:22), then a traveling companion of Paul on his Second Missionary Journey (Acts 15:40–18:22), and finally the amanuensis for Peter. He was therefore in a position to understand the two streams of Christian witness stemming from Peter and Paul and to blend them in this General Epistle.

Some scholars believe a Roman Christian, more concerned for the acceptance of his message than the perpetuation of his name, may have written this Epistle under the name of Peter. This theory would explain (1) the excellent Greek in which the book is written; (2) the quotations from the LXX rather than from the Hebrew Scriptures; and (3) the reference to the well-established eldership in the Church (5:1 ff.).

The date of the Epistle of course is connected with its authorship. Those who hold the Petrine theory identify the persecution mentioned in the Epistle as that which took place in Rome under Nero A.D. 64–65; Peter is believed to have died in this persecution. If he is the author of the Epistle, it must be dated A.D. 64-65. But the persecution referred to in the Epistle (4:12–19, 5:9) seems to have been Empire-wide—certainly extended to Asia Minor. The outrages against Christians under Domitian (A.D. 81–96) fit the background of the Epistle also. This may indicate that it was written c. A.D. 96, but most scholars now favor the earlier date.

The impressive feature of the Epistle is its exposition of the intimate connection between faith and conduct in the early Church. The author alternates between doctrine and ethics. "Forasmuch" (4:1), "wherefore" (4:19), "Likewise" (5:5) are connecting links between divine revelation and human action. The Apostolic Gospel is faithfully set forth. Christ, foretold by prophets (1:10–12), lived a sinless life (2:21–23), died a redeeming death (1:18 f., 2:24), gloriously arose (1:3, 21, 3:18), continued his work through the Spirit (4:14), and will appear again (1:7, 13).

Apocalyptic and eschatological factors, characteristic of the literature of this period, appear in the Epistle. The passage concerning "preaching unto the spirits in prison" (3:19–22) is a reference to a story from the Book of Enoch (Ethiopic Enoch) (163–63 B.C.), an Aramaic apocalypse which enjoyed wide circulation among Jews and early Christians. The author of the Epistle used an episode from the Book of Enoch, and then, by processes beyond our patterns of reasoning, made Noah and the Flood the vehicle for teaching that baptism, spiritually and morally experienced in Christ, "doth also now save us" (3:19–21). The preaching "also to them that are dead" (4:6), with which the former passage is associated, is the belief current in the early Church that Christ preached in Hades, the underworld of the deceased, between his Crucifixion and his Resurrection. This belief was embodied in the Apostles' Creed in the clause "He descended into hell." Enoch had a message of doom to fallen angels; Christ had one of hope to souls in the spirit-world. All this fits into the pattern of comfort and hope which the Epistle aimed to bring to a disheartened people.

The Epistle may be briefly outlined as follows:

Address—1:1, 2.

(1) The Christian hope, through the Resurrection of Christ—1:3–2:10:
- (a) security in spite of persecution—1:4–12;
- (b) exhortation to live worthy of hope—1:13–2:3;
- (c) the nature of the Church—2:4–12.

(2) Directions for Christian conduct—2:13–4:6:
- (a) in the state—2:13–17;
- (b) in human relationships—2:18–25;
- (c) in the home—3:1–7;
- (d) under persecution—3:8–4:6.

(3) Instructions concerning present needs—4:7–5:11:
- (a) patience in time of persecution—4:7–19;
- (b) duties of the elders and the people—5:1–11.

Salutations—5:12–14.

Peter, the Second Epistle of, a pastoral letter addressed to Christians everywhere, to warn them against false teachings and to exhort them to hold fast to their faith.

The author of this Epistle declares himself to be "Simon Peter, a servant and an apostle of Jesus Christ" (1:1, 3:1) who had been with Jesus on the Mount of Transfiguration (1:17 f.; Matt. 17:1–13; Mk. 9:2–13; Luke 9:28–36), and whose martyrdom had been predicted (II Pet. 1:14; John 21:18 f.). But internal evidence and historical facts do not support Peter's authorship. Differences in style, language, and point of view between I and II Peter indicate that the books were written by different authors. Perhaps neither was by Peter. (See PETER, THE FIRST EPISTLE OF.) The author of II Peter designates himself and his readers as members of a generation which had been taught by the Apostles then dead (3:2, 4). It was written at a time when Paul's letters were used by heretics to advance their views (3:15, 16). The author knew that Mark's Gospel was based on Peter's recollections (1:15). He was familiar with the Synoptics' account of the Transfiguration, the appendix to John's Gospel concerning Peter's martyrdom, the Pauline collection of letters, and I Peter and Jude. Nearly all of Jude is incorporated in this Epistle. The early Church doubted that it was a genuine letter of Peter's. Origen admitted that "there are doubts about it"; Eusebius stated that of the writings attributed to Peter "only one epistle is genuine"; and Jerome denied its authenticity. Since the discovery and study of the Dead Sea Scrolls*, many scholars have come to the conclusion that most of the N.T. books were written before c. A.D. 80, although opinions still vary.

"Knowledge," the key word of this Epistle, is used so frequently that it suggests the author was combating the false knowledge of the Gnostics. The knowledge of Christ (1:3) which will successfully combat heresy rests on the facts of experience: (1) "exceeding great and precious promises" (1:4); and (2) ethical and Christian conduct (1:5–8). Through the true knowledge of Christ come "grace and peace" and "all things that pertain unto life and godliness" (1:2, 3). Knowledge makes the Christian fruitful in witness (1:8), and free from "the pollutions of the world" (2:20); it enables him to "grow in grace" (3:18).

The author was disturbed by the fading away of hope in the return of Christ, the Parousia*, which had been a vital belief of the primitive Church. The heretical teachings of the Gnostics and the long delay in the fulfillment of this hope were responsible for its disappearance. II Peter, especially in chap. 3, attempts to revive the old belief in the immediate and visible return of Christ.

II Peter 2:1–18, 3:1–3 incorporates most of Jude 4–18, but omits the references in Jude 9 and 14 to Michael and Enoch from the non-Biblical books of the Assumption of Moses and the Book of Enoch respectively. This is in keeping with the purpose of II Peter to denounce unauthorized teaching.

A brief outline of II Peter follows:

(1) Salutation—1:1, 2.

(2) Exhortation to grow in grace and knowledge—1:3–11.

(3) The assurance of Christian salvation—1:12–21:
- (a) through Apostolic teaching—1:12–18;
- (b) by inspired word—1:19–21.

(4) The condemnation and refutation of false teachers—2:1–22.

(5) The certainty of Christ's return—3:1–13.

(6) The duty of Christians—3:14–18:
- (a) to live a pure life—3:14;
- (b) to interpret doctrines correctly—3:15, 16;
- (c) to resist false teachers—3:17;
- (d) to grow in grace and knowledge of Christ—3:18.

Pethahiah (pĕth′ȧ-hī′ȧ). (1) The founder of the 19th course (set, or shift) of priests at Jerusalem (I Chron. 24:16). (2) The son of a Levite who had promised to put away his foreign wife (Ezra 10:23). (3) A Levite who co-operated with Ezra in leading the assembly of praise (Neh. 9:5). (4) A son of Meshezabeel, deputy governor of Jerusalem, responsible for "all matters concerning the people" (Neh. 11:24).

Pethor (pē′thôr), an unknown site in N. Mesopotamia (Aram-naharaim), the home of Balaam, near "the river"—possibly a branch of the Euphrates (Num. 22:5; Deut. 23:4). Pethor was once seized by Thutmose III of Egypt, and again centuries later by Shalmaneser III of Assyria, as the annals of these kings show.

Petra (pē′trȧ), the Gk. name for Sela, capital of Edom and later of Nabataea*.

Phalec (fā′lĕk) (A.S.V., R.S.V. Peleg), the father of Ragau (rā′gô) (A.S.V., R.S.V. Reu [rē′ū]), in the genealogy of Jesus (Luke 3:35).

Phanuel (fȧ-nū′ĕl), the father of the aged Jerusalem prophetess Anna, who recognized the infant Jesus as the Messiah (Luke 2:36–38).

pharaoh (fâr′ō) (Heb. form of an Egypt. word, pronounced approximately *pero*, "the great house"), an honorary title for the chief ruler of Egypt during the early dynasties. With the opening of the brilliant Eighteenth Dynasty of the New Kingdom, (1570–1310 B.C.) "pharaoh" meant "king"—the word is so understood in the O.T., as in I Kings 11:18; Acts 7:10. In the Bible the Egyptian king is often called simply "Pharaoh" (Gen. 12:15, 41:39, 42), or "Pharaoh king of Egypt" (Acts 7:10); or his individual name is added, as Pharaoh-hophra (Jer. 44:30) or Pharaoh-necho (A.V. Jer. 46:2).

At birth a pharaoh was given an individual name such as "Thutmose," or "Amenophis" (Amenhotep), to which were added several other names, like "Splendid of Diadems," "Son of Re," "Mighty Bull," or "King of Upper and Lower Egypt." The name of the pharoah, written in hieroglyphs (pictures of objects denoting a word, syllable, or sound) and surrounded by an oval line, became his cartouche or seal*, and was incised on obelisks, carved in reliefs, or painted as his signature. When engraved on a stone mounted in a ring (often with a swivel setting), the cartouche could imprint his signature on soft clay; the pharaoh who befriended Joseph gave him his ring to use for making official signatures (Gen. 41:42). Symbolic of the pharaoh's authority over Upper and Lower Egypt were two caplike crowns, the white one denoting the former realm, and a red one denoting the latter. Pharaoh's scepters took the form of a flail, a shepherd's crook, a mace, or a scimitar (curved sword). Frequently the pharaoh wore on his forehead, or embroidered at the top of his goffered, kiltlike skirt, the uraeus or cobra, designed to protect him from all enemies.

Most of the land of Egypt belonged to the pharaoh, i.e., to the state. (Cf. Gen. 47:20, "Joseph bought all the land of Egypt for Pharaoh.")

His activities were far more varied than the conventional records on tombs and temples suggest—praying and bringing offerings to the gods. He interviewed his prime minister or vizier (Gen. 41:44–57); received oral or written reports from a multitude of high officials concerning the progress of the Nile* inundation, on which Egypt's prosperity depended; pondered reports of scribes concerning the great granaries and the payment of taxes (in various goods); heard of the progress of foreign wars and state of the army, whose commander-in-chief he was; authorized projects for enlarging networks of canals and their barrages (dams to increase the depth of water and facilitate irrigation); ordered the building of tremendous tombs, temples, or palaces; interviewed prisoners of war to gain information from the outside world; and read such diplomatic correspondence as the Tell el-Amarna* Letters. The pharaoh reserved time for gracious living with such pleasures as all-night banquets, outdoor meals with his family, music, hunting birds in the marshes, and riding out in his chariot to inspect his estate.

As the prestige of a pharaoh depended on the success of his foreign conquests, the kings between Thutmose* III (c. 1490–1435 B.C.) and Amenhotep III (c. 1413–1377) enjoyed the greatest power. During this period Egypt reached her greatest extent abroad and her highest prosperity at home. The Hyksos* had been expelled; the government was reformed; and the bureaucracy of the Old (c. 2700–2200 B.C.) and Middle (c. 1991–1786 B.C.) Kingdoms banished. The pharaoh was "lord of the world," the embodiment of the falcon or hawk* god Horus. Although Egyptians did not often erect temples in which the pharaoh was actually worshipped as a god (except at Nubian Soleb, for example, and Sedeinga, where Amenhotep III and Queen Tiy respectively were worshipped as divine), they believed the pharaoh to be the "son of the sun god Re," or one who had been begotten by Amun of Thebes and was forever under the protection of the gods of Egypt. Viewed in this setting, the pharaohs who oppressed and exploited the Israelites in Egypt are drawn accurately in the narratives of Exodus 1–14.

Biblical scholarship has long interested itself in the problem of identifying the "Pharaoh of the Oppression" and the "Pharaoh of the Exodus" of Israel from Egypt. The evidence in favor of locating the city of Raamses* (Rameses, Ex. 12:37)—Nineteenth Egyptian Dynasty capital—at Tanis (Avaris*) leads many to name Seti (Sethos) I (1309–1290 B.C.) as the pharaoh of the oppression, who forced Hebrew labor for his Tanis construction enterprise. If Seti I is the Pharaoh of the Oppression, his son, Ramesses* II, is the Pharaoh of the Exodus; though Ramesses also was a cruel user of *corvée.* Those who name Merenptah (c. 1224–1216 B.C.) as Pharaoh of the Oppression have insufficient evidence for their claim. An Egyptian monument of Merenptah boasts of his defeat of Israelites living in Palestine in the 5th year of his reign. This indicates Hebrews as already in their new home by c. 1220 B.C.

The following pharaohs were associated with events narrated in the O.T. Some of them are not given an individual name here, and can be identified only by associated events; others, like "Shishak king of Egypt" (II Chron. 12:2), are named specifically. (N.B. Dates are approximate; slight divergencies exist in the various chronologies accepted by outstanding authorities. Cf. alternate dates in *Biblical Archaeology,* by G. Ernest Wright, Westminster Press, Philadelphia, 1957.)

Pharaohs	References
The pharaoh contemporary with Abraham	Gen. 12:14–20
The pharaoh who honored Joseph—possibly one of the Hyksos kings (Fifteenth-Seventeenth Dynasties) resident at Avaris (Tanis) (c. 1720–1550 B.C.). The Hyksos Dynasties included in their empire Palestine, Syria, and Egypt	Gen. 41:37–57
The "new king . . . which knew not Joseph"—expelled the Hyksos and was contemporary with the departure of Ephraim and Manasseh to Palestine	Ex. 1:8
Amenhotep (Amenophis) III (1413–1377) and Amenhotep IV (c. 1370–1353) to whom vassals stationed in Palestine and Syria sent letters (the Tell el-Amarna)	
Seti I (Sethos) (c. 1309–1290), identified by many reliable scholars as "the Pharaoh of the Oppression"	Ex. 1–14
Ramesses II (c. 1290–1224), rated by excellent scholars as "the Pharaoh of the Exodus." His huge construction works in store-cities of the Delta would naturally have led to the oppression of laboring classes	Ex. 1:11–14, 5:4–19, 10:11, 12:29–51
Merenptah (c. 1224–1216 B.C.), defeated Israelites in Palestine and included this victory (c. 1220) in his list of triumphs on a stele in his mortuary temple at Thebes	

Pharaohs	References
Father of an Egyptian wife of King Solomon (c. 961–922 B.C.), and his ally	I Kings 3:1 ,7:8
Shishak* (Sheshonk I), of the Twenty-second (Libyan) Dynasty, who raided and sacked the Jerusalem Temple in the reign of King Rehoboam of Judah (c. 922–915 B.C.). Jeroboam, King of Israel (c. 922–901), fled to the court of Shishak late in the reign of Solomon	I Kings 14:25 *f.*; II Chron. 12:2–9
Zerah, "the Ethiopian," (often identified with Osorkon I), successor of Shishak, suffered defeat at Moreshah in S. Palestine in the reign of King Asa of Judah (c. 913–873)	II Chron. 14:9–15, 16:8
So (possibly not a pharaoh, but a tartan of Egypt), whose help King Hoshea of Israel (c. 732–724 B.C.) endeavored to enlist against Assyria	II Kings 17:4
Tirhakah (Taharka in Egypt. records), Twenty-fifth Dynasty, Ethiopian period (c. 690–664), marched against Sennacherib, King of Assyria, advancing S. through the coastal plain of Philistia toward Egypt	II Kings 19:9
Necho (Pharaoh-nechoh, Pharaoh-necho), of the Twenty-sixth Dynasty, slew King Josiah of Judah (640–609 B.C.) at Megiddo; dethroned his son Jehoahaz, whom the people had chosen, and enthroned in his place Jehoiakim; routed by Nebuchadnezzar, who took "all that pertained to the king of Egypt"	II Kings 23:29–34; II Chron. 35:20–36:4 II Kings 24:7
Pharaoh-hophra (Apries) (c. 588–569 B.C.), reigned during lifetime of Jeremiah and others who fled to Egypt. The prophet declared that God would give this pharaoh into the hands of his enemies, even as He gave Zedekiah into the power of Nebuchadnezzar	Jer. 43:6–13, 44:30

Allusions to unnamed pharaohs are found in: I Kings 11:14–22 (the pharaoh who gave his sister-in-law to Hadad for wife); II Kings 18:21 (contemporary of Sennacherib and Hezekiah); I Chron. 4:18 (father-in-law of Mered).

Phares, Pharez. See PEREZ.

Pharisees (from Heb. *pārūsh*, "separated" or "separatist"), members of one of the three philosophical sects of Judaism in the two centuries before and after the beginning of the Christian era. The name was probably first used in the time of the Maccabean leader John Hyrcanus, because the Pharisees' insistence on scrupulous observance of the Law* led to a separatist attitude toward all of life. They were apparently successors of the *Hasidim* (Pious) who, when Antiochus Epiphanes (168 B.C.) proscribed Judaism, chose to die rather than to defend themselves by fighting on the Sabbath. The two other contemporary sects were the aristocratic Sadducees* and the ascetic Essenes (see ESSENE).

As W. F. Albright points out in *From the Stone Age to Christianity* (pp. 272 f., The Johns Hopkins Press), the Pharisees represent the effect of Hellenism on normative Jewish tradition; many of the divergencies between Sadducees and Pharisees are due to the reactions of these two groups to Hellenism. Pharisees held to a dualism which comprehended God's guiding providence and also the unhampered operation of man's will, which perpetuated O.T. thought and helped to determine orthodox Christianity. Sadducees resisted the Stoic doctrine of predestination, and clung tenaciously to the concept of the freedom of man's will. Although Sadducees, with their princely backgrounds, came into contact with Hellenism earlier than did the scholarly minded Pharisees, the latter became more thoroughly Hellenized.

Pharisees were usually pacifists. Sometimes they sided with the Maccabean leaders, as with Jonathan and Simon, and sometimes broke with them, as with John Hyrcanus. They helped organize resistance against Rome in the struggles under Vespasian and Hadrian.

Though the Pharisees exercised great political power, they were not primarily a political party, but a school or a society of zealous students and teachers of the Law. To them the Law was contained not only in the Pentateuch (which alone the Sadducees recognized), but in the oral* Law, by which they tried to adapt the old codes to new fields and new conditions. The Pharisees "advocated the enlargement of the canon of Scriptures, adding the Prophets (200 B.C.) and the Writings (A.D. 90) to the Torah; they developed exegetical methods by which a scriptural basis could be given to any new law or doctrine; they did not object to new rites in the Temple worship, and new festivals (Hanukkah [Dedication] and Purim); they favored the baptism of the proselytes and the hallowing of the Paschal meal; they were responsible, to a considerable degree, for speculations about wisdom, angels, and demons, as for the flowering of the Messianic hopes and the belief in the resurrection of the body" (R. H. Pfeiffer, *History of New Testament Times*, p. 55, Harper & Brothers). Though criticized by Jesus for their harsh and uncharitable stress on the legalistic aspects of religion, at the expense of emphasis on the loving nature of God as Father, the Pharisees are to be given credit for preserving Judaism. After the Temple and the capital had fallen in A.D. 70 the synagogues and schools of the Pharisees continued to function and to promote Judaism.

The Pharisees were the successors of Ezra* and the early scribes ("Men of the Great Synagogue"). They cherished Ezra—next after Moses (cf. Matt. 23:2)—as the founder of Judaism. The responsibility they felt for preserving, interpreting, and teaching the Law led to a zeal far in excess of that expressed in Ps. 119:97:

"O how love I thy law!
It is my meditation all the day."

The Pharisees opposed the aristocratic Sadducean high priesthood of the Temple. Their strongholds of learning were founded by Shammai and Hillel and later by Ishmael and Akiba. Often there were intense rivalries among these scholarly groups. Saul of Tarsus boasted of being a Pharisee and the son of a Pharisee, brought up "according to the perfect manner of the law of the fathers" (Acts 22:3). He was a pupil at Jerusalem of Gamaliel* (v. 3), a "doctor of the law" (Acts 5:34), probably grandson of the great Pharisee Hillel. Paul was proud of this teacher-pupil relationship of his youth (Acts 23:6, 26:3–7). Usually the Pharisees had two scholarly leaders, one drawn from the aristocratic segment of society, the other from the people.

The Pharisees determined who were worthy of admission to the synagogues. Hence, when many of the chief rulers believed on Christ, these were afraid to confess him "lest they should be put out of the synagogue" (John 12:42).

Although the overscrupulous exactions of the Pharisees had a discouraging effect on those they taught, many Pharisees were sincerely devout. They believed that the Shekinah (Divine Presence) hovered over their deliberations. But they were justly accused by Jesus, according to Matthew's account, of being hypocrites and bombastic persons who, for love of pious display, enlarged the borders of their garments and widened their phylacteries (Matt. 23:5), tithed even wild herbs (23:23), strained their drinking water lest they swallow an impure gnat (23:24), used lengthy intercessions (Mark 12:40), avoided even the appearance of working on the Sabbath (Matt. 12:1 f.), and made large gifts to the Temple funds instead of to their needy parents (Matt. 15:3–6, 23:29). Jesus is said to have regarded them as blind guides, "whited sepulchres," beautiful without but within "full of dead men's bones" (23:27). Luke 18 attributes to him a castigating denunciation of the Pharisees in his Parable of the Publican. Yet Jesus did not hesitate to accept dinner invitations from Pharisees, even though he knew that he was there for scrutiny or condemnation (Luke 11:37, 14:1), even as he was criticized for dining with men whom Pharisees considered "sinners" (Luke 15:1). No more sincere an inquirer is recorded as having sought an interview with Jesus than the Pharisee Nicodemus*, a ruler of the Jews, who came by night (John 3:1–21). His was the only voice in the Sanhedrin advocating legal fairness to Jesus in his Trial (John 7:50–52). Other Pharisees sent officers who tried to arrest him early in his ministry (John 7:32). The Pharisees ultimately had a share in causing his death (Mark 3:6; John 11:47–57). Their own spiritual insight detected in him one who was closer to God than they were. The part played by Nicodemus in the burial of Jesus (John 19:39) suggests that this Pharisee acknowledged all Christ's claims.

Pharpar (fär′pär), the lesser of the two rivers of Damascus (II Kings 5:12) (see ABANA). Close to one of its branches, on the sun-baked desert c. 9 m. S. of the city, is the site associated by ancient tradition with the conversion of Saul (Acts 9:3–8).

Phasael, one of three stone towers built by Herod* the Great in NW. Jerusalem*; the other two were Hippicus and Mariamme. It was named in honor of Herod's brother. It was conspicuous in the city Jesus knew. Archaeology proves that it stood on the site of the later David's Tower adjacent to the Jaffa Gate—an excellent example of ancient Palestinian military architecture. Lower courses of its masonry are ancient, possibly 1st century A.D. or earlier. The second wall of Jerusalem is believed by many to have run N. from Phasael, then E. toward the Tower of Antonia*. From the steps at Phasael Viscount Allenby, who liberated Palestine from the Turks, read his proclamation to the citizens of "Jerusalem the Blessed" on Dec. 11, 1917, declaring that every place of prayer of the three great religions to which the city was sacred (Judaism, Christianity, and Islam) be "maintained and protected according to the existing customs and beliefs of those to whose faiths they are sacred."

321. Citadel tower built on the site of Phasael, near Jaffa Gate, Jerusalem.

Phasaelis (fă-sȧ-ē′lĭs) (Khirbet Fasâ'il), an irrigated, productive Jordan Valley town in Samaria, laid out by Herod the Great, who named it in honor of his brother Phasael, and bequeathed it to his sister Salome; who in turn left this coveted, income-producing site to Livia, wife of the Emperor Tiberius.

Phasaelus. (1) The son of Antipater and elder brother of Herod the Great. He was made prefect or governor of Judaea by Antipater; died 40 B.C. (For structures named in his honor by Herod see PHASAEL; PHASAELIS.) (2) The son of (1); the father of Kypros, wife of Agrippa I.

Phichol (fī′kŏl) (R.S.V. Phicol), commander of Abimelech's army. He witnessed the agreements between Abimelech and Abraham and between Abimelech and Isaac (Gen. 21:22, 26:26).

Philadelphia. (1) See RABBAH.

(2) A city of Lydia (the modern Alashehir) 28 m. from Sardis at a point advantageous for commerce between central Asia Minor and coastal Smyrna, founded by Attalus Philadelphus of Pergamum before 138 B.C. It was prominent in the Roman province of Asia and was one of the seven churches to whom messages in Revelation were addressed (Rev. 3:7–13).

Philemon (fĭ-lē′mŏn), a generous (Philem. 5) citizen of Colossae, in whose house there was a church. He was a convert of Paul's (19). The Apostle (in one of the shortest books of the N.T.) earnestly appealed to Philemon to forgive his valuable runaway, thieving slave, Onesimus. While a fugitive in Rome Onesimus had met the imprisoned Paul, was converted (10), rendered the Apostle valuable service, and willingly returned to Philemon, his master, hoping for freedom and for the higher fellowship possible in Christ (16).

Philemon, the Epistle of Paul to, is concerned with individuals rather than with churches; it is Paul's only private letter in the N.T. (For the reasons this Epistle is connected with Paul's Roman imprisonment [vv. 1, 9] rather than with those at Ephesus or Caesarea, see COLOSSIANS.) The letter is a tactful plea for forgiveness for the runaway slave Onesimus, who, according to the laws of the time, merited severe punishment if not death; Paul attempted to effect his reception as a Christian brother. Onesimus had been a slave in a Colossian household (Col. 4:9), but had stolen property or money (Philem. 18) and had run away from his master. He had met Paul, been converted (v. 10), and had proved of service to the imprisoned Apostle (vv. 9–13). Onesimus means "useful and profitable one," a fact which supplies Paul with material for a pun (v. 11). Though anxious to retain the services of the runaway slave (vv. 11, 13), Paul considered it his duty to send Onesimus back to his master, and accordingly arranged for Onesimus to carry this letter to his master and to travel in company with Tychicus (Col. 4:7–9), who was himself bearing a letter from Paul to the Colossian church (Col. 4:7, 16).

From the 2d century it has been assumed that Philemon was the owner of Onesimus, and that Apphia was Philemon's wife and Archippus their son. A closer study of Colossians and Philemon has led some to believe that Archippus (Philem. 2) was the slave owner who had the special "ministry" to "fulfill" (Col. 4:17); the promixity of the task outlined in Col. 4:17 to "the epistle from Laodicea" (Col. 4:16) suggests this. The phrase "the church in thy house" (Philem. 2) raises no grammatical problem if it was the residence of Archippus that housed the church at Colossae (v. 22). According to this theory Philemon was the minister—"our dearly beloved and fellow laborer" (Philem. 1)—and Apphia was his wife. The Epistle to Philemon would in this case be "the lost" Epistle from Laodicea (Col. 4:16).

The outcome of Onesimus' return is not known; but it may be inferred from the preservation of the letter that Paul's earnest plea on behalf of the runaway slave was successful.

Paul has often been criticized for accepting the Roman institution of slavery (Col. 4:1) rather than making a frontal attack upon it. At a time when the economic system was founded on slavery such an attack could hardly have been successful, and it would have endangered Paul's own mission. Moreover, Paul expected the imminent return of Christ to bring the present order, including slavery, to an end; therefore it seemed unnecessary for a slave to fight for a freedom that would soon be his. Paul believed that Onesimus since his conversion had a new master in Christ, and that this entitled him to be considered on a plane of Christian brotherhood (Philem. 16). This indirect attack on Roman slavery asserted the principle of spiritual equality in Christ—a principle that eventually ended the system of slavery.

Philetus (fĭ-lē′tŭs), one accused by the author of II Tim. 2:17 as teaching an erroneous and upsetting interpretation of the resurrection of believers.

Philip (Gk. *Philippos*, "lover of horses"). (1) King of Macedonia (359–336 B.C.), father of Alexander the Great (I Macc. 1:1, 6:2). (2) The foster brother or friend of Antiochus Epiphanes (II Macc. 9:29); possibly the same as (3) A cruel governor of Jerusalem appointed by Antiochus Epiphanes (II Macc. 5:22, 6:11). (4) A Macedonian king (c. 220–179 B.C.) deposed by Rome.

(5) *Philip the Apostle* (Matt. 10:3; Mark 3:18; Luke 6:14), met by Jesus early in his ministry at Bethany beyond the Jordan where John was baptizing (John 1:28 A.S.V., R.S.V.). The Master personally invited Philip to become a Disciple (v. 43). His home was at Bethsaida on the Sea of Galilee (John 1:44), where he apparently was a friend of Andrew and Peter (12:21 f.). Though Philip was of a retiring disposition he introduced his friend Nathanael to Jesus (1:45 f.), who convinced the man that he was the Messiah* (49 f.), and presently admitted him to his chosen company of the Twelve. Some students have suggested that Philip was the one who, when called by Jesus, asked that he be allowed first to bury his father (Luke 9:57–60). He took charge of the provisions for Jesus and his company (John 6:5 f.). To him certain Greeks who were in Jerusalem on Palm Sunday and reverently desired to meet Jesus appealed for an introduction (12:20–23). Philip was slow to grasp the relationship of Jesus to the Father (14:8–21). He withstood the terrifying experiences of the Crucifixion, and was present with the faithful who prayed in the Jerusalem upper room following Christ's Ascension (Acts 1:12–14).

(6) *Philip the Evangelist.* A man selected as one of the Seven to administer the business affairs of the Twelve and the growing Church, and to distribute relief to the poor, including widows (Acts 6:1–6). He preached and healed effectively at Samaria after the martyrdom of Stephen (Acts 8:4–8); led Simon the sorcerer to become an active believer in Christ (vv. 9–13), and was instrumental in

bringing about the conversion of an Ethiopian convert to Judaism, a eunuch on the staff of Queen Candace (Acts 8:26–39). Through the Ethiopian convert Philip became responsible in part for bringing Christ's message to NE. Africa. He took up residence at Caesarea on the Mediterranean, where he was host to Paul, who stopped there on his last journey to Jerusalem (Acts 21:8–15). Philip had four unmarried daughters who were Christian prophetesses (v. 9).

(7) *Philip the Tetrarch.* Also known as Herod Philip II, he was a son of Herod* the Great and Cleopatra of Jerusalem. He married Salome, the daughter of yet another Herod and Herodias*. Appointed as a tetrarch* by the emperor Augustus, he was still the ruler of Ituraea when John the Baptist began his career (Luke 3:1). The town of Banias, which he enlarged and renamed Caesarea, became known as Caesarea Philippi. He is considered the best of the Herods, and his excellent and just rule lasted from 4 B.C. to A.D. 34. See also HEROD (5).

Philippi (fĭ-lĭp′ī), a city of E. Macedonia on the great E.-W. Egnatian Highway between Rome and Asia, built on a spur of the Pangaean mountain range. It was named in the 4th century B.C. in honor of Philip of Macedon, its conqueror. When Macedonia was taken by the Romans in 168 B.C. Philippi was included in the 1st of the territory's four divisions. In 42 B.C. on the plains below Philippi the forces of Octavian and Antony defeated those of the Roman republic. In commemoration of the victory the city was given unique citizenship privileges and status. Its inhabitants were always proud of their Roman prerogatives (Acts 16:21).

322. Philippi. Ruins of Christian churches, center foreground; Roman forum between churches and road.

The description of Philippi in Acts 16:12 as "the leading city of the district of Macedonia" is certainly incorrect, as Amphipolis* (17:1) was actually the chief city of this district in N.T. times. The Greek text, however, is uncertain and it has been conjectured that in its original form it read "a city of the first district," which would accord with its historical status. The author of Acts, however, appears twice to associate himself with Philippi (the beginning of the so-called "we" sections, Acts 16:10 ff. and 20:5 ff.), and it is possible that Acts 16:12 may be an enthusiastic appraisal of the city.

Philippi was the first city on the continent of Europe to receive the Christian Gospel; and Lydia, "a seller of purple goods," was the Gospel's first European convert (Acts 16:14). A Latin inscription from Philippi provides evidence for such commerce in purple. A syndicate of men who exploited a young woman with a "spirit of divination," variously diagnosed as possibly anything from epilepsy to ventriloquism, had Paul and Silas arrested on a false antireligious charge after the Apostle had liberated her mind from fraudulent servitude and thus interfered with her sponsors' business. The hatred which this "interference" unleashed on the preacher was recalled in later years (I Thess. 2:2; Phil. 1:30). The Apostle's protest on the occasion of his unlawful arrest was perhaps drowned out by the anger of the mob (Acts 16:19–23). The next morning, when the excitement had died down, and word reached the magistrates concerning the Roman citizenship of the two prisoners, Paul and Silas were released and ordered to leave town. Earthquakes, not uncommon in Macedonia, could have furnished the background for the midnight emotional upheaval which characterized the action of the town jailer. The singing of the prisoners supplied the Christian testimony that led the jailer and his family to be baptized (Acts 16:25–34).

The violation of the law concerning the rights of Roman citizens aroused public sentiment. This gave a favorable political atmosphere for the beginning of the first Christian Church in Europe, and made many warm friends for Paul. The Church at Philippi was the Apostle's favorite. Paul revisited Macedonia and kept the Passover with the brethren at Philippi (20:6). The Church sent gifts to Paul on his journeys (Phil. 4:16; II Cor. 11:9) (see EPAPHRODITUS).

According to the narrative of Acts 16 women played an important part in the Church at Philippi. Secular records show that women in this part of Macedonia enjoyed a prominence not accorded them in other sections of the ancient world. The only rebuke administered by Paul in his Letter to these much-loved people was to two women who failed to be of one mind (Phil. 4:2 f.).

The site of Philippi is now deserted. French archaeologists worked there between 1914 and 1938, and uncovered many sections of the city, especially the market place between the acropolis and the basilica (Acts 16:19). The foundations of a great arched gateway at the NW. edge of Philippi were discovered, along with the remains of two large temples. Also uncovered were the foundations of other structures, including a library. Vitrovius, an early Roman writer on architecture, says that the city prison, along with other civic buildings, was adjacent to the agora.

Philippians, the Epistle of Paul the Apostle to the, an informal and friendly letter written from prison by Paul to the

Christians at Philippi. The founding of this first Christian church on the continent of Europe is vividly narrated in the account of Paul's Second Missionary Journey (Acts 16:12–40). Though Paul includes Timothy's name in the salutation (Phil. 1:1) and indicates him as a coauthor, the contents of the Epistle reflect Paul's personal point of view and experiences (1:7, 12, 21, 2:2, 19, 3:8–14, 4:3, 10–17).

The occasion for this Letter was a gift from the Philippians brought by their messenger Epaphroditus to Paul in prison (4:18); Paul wrote the Letter to express his thanks. The Philippians had intended that Epaphroditus should remain with the Apostle as long as he could be of assistance; but Epaphroditus had fallen ill, and on his recovery Paul sent him home bearing this letter (2:25–30). Paul took this occasion to inform the Philippians of his plans for sending Timothy to them and of soon coming himself (2:19–24). He assured them of his welfare, and showed that his imprisonment did not affect his confidence and joy in the Gospel. He encouraged them to be steadfast and even joyful in the face of persecution. He warned them against certain errors. In the midst of practical exhortations he formulated profound statements of doctrine. Though written while Paul was in personal danger (1:20), the Letter expresses the triumph of his Christian faith. Paul uses the word "rejoice" 11 times and "joy" six times—more frequently than in any of his other Epistles.

The place from which this Letter was sent is not stated, though we know that Paul was a prisoner when he wrote it (1:7, 13, 14, 16). Three imprisonments are recorded in the Acts: at Philippi, Caesarea, and Rome. Philippi is ruled out in this case; and the probability of Caesarea is less than that of Rome. Paul refers to the Praetorian Guard (R.S.V. 1:13), whose headquarters were in Rome. He sends greetings from Christians among the imperial slaves in "Caesar's household" (4:22). He includes Timothy with himself in the salutation, as he does in Colossians and Philemon—presumably written from Rome.

Some influential scholars, however, believe that Colossians and Philemon were written during an unrecorded but highly probable imprisonment of Paul in Ephesus (see COLOSSIANS); and they believe that Philippians also was written at Ephesus. The word translated in the R.S.V. as "Praetorian Guard" (1:13) was often used for the official residence of the governor of a province, and Ephesus was the virtual capital of the province of Asia. Associations of imperial slaves (4:22) existed at Ephesus. Among the arguments for Ephesus is Paul's statement that he will go to Philippi if he is released from his present danger (1:26, 2:24); and since he intended to go from Rome to Spain (Rom. 15:28) this could hardly have been his Roman imprisonment.

The date of Philippians is assigned to the closing period of the Roman imprisonment by those who maintain the Roman theory of origin. If the Epistle belongs to an Ephesian imprisonment it must be dated earlier, c. A.D. 55.

Some N.T. students see in the definite break in thought at 3:1b an indication that two letters have been joined together to form Philippians. According to this partition theory 3:1b–19, or 3:1b–4:3, is an earlier letter of warning against errorists, sent possibly to the Philippians and later incorporated in a second letter. Other scholars account for the abrupt change at 3:1b without recourse to the interpolation theory; they explain the break as due to disturbing news from Philippi which reached Paul while he was writing the letter.

The contents of the Epistle reflect Paul's Christ-centered life. His imprisonment is for Christ's sake (1:12 f.), so that he might be able to glorify his Lord (1:20). He is proud to be his slave (1:1). It does not matter to him that he has lost his advantages of birth and station, for in losing them he has won Christ (3:7, 8 f.). His deepest desire is to experience in his own soul the suffering, death, and resurrection of Christ (3:10, 11). He can do and endure all things, because Christ gives him strength (4:13); he can truly say, "For me to live is Christ" (1:21).

The rhythmical cadences of the profound passage about Christ (2:5–11) suggest that it came originally from an early Christian hymn used as a primitive confession of faith. Here the humility and self-abasement of Christ, who took the form of a slave, is contrasted with his exaltation—"at the name of Jesus every knee should bow, of things in heaven, and things in earth, and things under the earth; And that every tongue should confess that Jesus Christ is Lord."

The Epistle may be outlined as follows:

(1) Salutation, thanksgiving, prayer—1:1–11.

(2) Paul's present situation—1:12–26.

(3) Exhortations—1:27–2:18:
- (a) to live worthy of the Gospel—1:27–30;
- (b) to be of one accord—2:1–4;
- (c) to follow the example of Christ's humility—2:5–11;
- (d) to continue in obedience—2:12–18.

(4) Plans for sending Timothy and Epaphroditus—2:19–30.

(5) Counsels—3:1–4:4:
- (a) warning against the legalism of Judaizers—3:1–3;
- (b) Paul's own spiritual experience—3:4–14;
- (c) exhortation to live in harmony—3:15–17;
- (d) warning against worldliness—3:18–21;
- (e) appeal for steadfastness—4:1–3.

(6) Exhortations—4:4–9.

(7) Thanks for their gifts—4:10–20.

(8) Final salutations—4:21–23.

Philistia (fĭ-lĭs′tĭ-*ȧ*), the coastal strip c. 50 m. long and 15 m. wide that stretched along the Mediterranean from Joppa to the S. of Gaza.

Philistines, a sea people who migrated from the Aegean region, especially from Crete* (Caphtor, Amos 9:7) about the first quarter of the 12th century B.C. They became one of

PHILISTINES

the chief rivals of the Israelites, who arrived in Palestine from the opposite direction in about the same era. Philistines were thought by John Garstang to have come possibly from the Dalmatian coast (the present Yugoslavia) and to have made their way gradually to Crete and SE. Asia Minor, where the Hittite kingdom was breaking up, and thence into Palestine, which took its name from the Philistines. W. F. Albright attributed to the Philistines an elemental barbarian energy marked by an exotic culture of the Mycenaean type. Philistines were uncircumcised non-Semites—Aryans, classified by some as Indo-Europeans, a few of whose words lingered in their language. A relief from the temple of Ramesses III at Medinet Habu shows them to have been tall and having the features usually associated with the Hellenes (cf. the story of the Philistine giant Goliath). Their fine, highly decorated pottery has been excavated in various parts of Palestine.

It would seem as if the migrating Philistines had been bound for Egypt, but, repulsed by Ramesses III, chose to land on the attractive plain NE. of Egypt, N. of the site occupied at about the same time by another sea people, the Cherethites (Cretans). Their presence on the ancient coast route N. from the Delta into Canaan led the wandering Israelites to avoid the short cut through their territory (Ex. 13:17, E). Philistine power did not threaten Israel's territory, but it did remain a constant political and economic menace. Although by the time of David and Solomon the Philistines were paying heavy tribute to the Hebrew Monarchy they were never permanently subjugated by Israel.

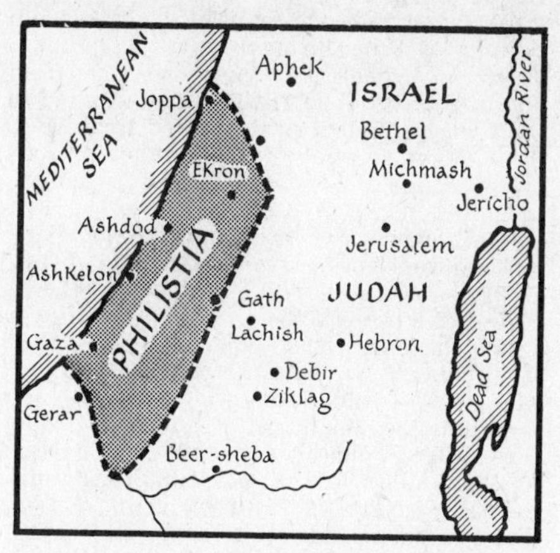

323. Philistia.

The position of Philistia, on the fruitful, well-watered Maritime Plain flanked by sand dunes, gave it an independent supply of agricultural products and fruits, but left it on the highway of conquerors. One powerful economic weapon, however, was theirs—a monopoly of iron, which came into use in Palestine c. 1200 B.C. Philistines not only knew its sources, but had learned its uses from Hittite (see HITTITES) monopolists among whom they had lived in SE. Asia Minor. By importing and forging iron they were able to fashion iron-rimmed chariots and various superior weapons for their own coastal warfare. Moreover they prevented Israel from making iron swords and spear tips, or even sharpening those they had, until the time of David's victories (I Sam. 13:19–22).

Small Philistia's ability to remain a threat to Israel for so long was largely due to her effective political organization based on a league (Pentapolis) of great cities. Much is known of these cities through excavation, and more will be learned when the important mound of Tell Jemmeh, for example (probably Gerar*) has been fully examined. These cities were: (1) Gaza, 3 m. from the Mediterranean, a strategic site from which the Philistines controlled caravan routes to Egypt, Arabia, and the region that later became Nabataea; (2) Gath, NE. of Gaza and farther inland, on the border of the Hebrews' Shephelah holdings; (3) Ashkelon on the coast, also at an intersection of major caravan trade routes whose rocky fortress dominated their approach from three directions; (4) Ashdod, NE. of Ashkelon, on the main road to Joppa and E. to Lydda; and (5) Ekron, a rich market town in the Valley of Sorek, close to the border of the original territory claimed by the Tribe of Dan. Gath, only a short distance NW. of powerfully fortified Lachish, and adjacent to the Hebrew border on its E., was raided more frequently than any other Philistine city; hence the poignant wish expressed by David when he heard of the slaughter of his friend Jonathan and King Saul at Gilboa, that the tragedy should not be talked about in Gath or in the streets of Ashkelon or among "the daughters of the Philistines," lest these rejoice in Israel's disaster (II Sam. 1:20).

These five influential cities of the Philistines were never united into a kingdom; they were ruled by the five "lords of the Philistines" mentioned frequently in Scripture (Josh. 13:3; Judg. 3:3; I Sam. 7:7; etc.). These chiefs composed a council of coequals, of whom a majority could take action against one, as when four opposed the gift of Achish to David (I Sam. 6:18, 27–29). They acted in unison in negotiating with Delilah and planning for the fateful feast of Samson* (Judg. 16:23, J). They often deferred to their citizens (I Sam. 5:7 f., 10 f.). Their chief ruler's office may have been hereditary. Five impressive tombs in the plain have been found—probably of these lords of the Philistines. Some of these contained anthropoid sarcophagi, with lids carved to represent human heads, like those at Sidon.

The Philistine city of Gerar (probably Tell Jemmeh), inland SE. of Gaza on the Wâdī Ghazzeh (possibly the Brook Besor), where Abraham and Isaac lived for a time (Gen. 20:1, 26:1, 20), though not one of the five great Philistine city centers, was important as a royal iron manufacturing place. In this industrial town, to which Israelites took their weapons and tools for sharpening, Sir Flinders and Lady Hilda Petrie found remnants of a sword factory and iron smeltery, with four furnaces. Near one furnace, which evidently had been devoted to the manufacture of swords, they found not only swords, but also spearheads, daggers, and arrowheads, made probably c. 1300–800 B.C.; and pottery models of the iron-shod chariots (c. 970 B.C.) which terrified Israel in the time of David (c. 1000–961 B.C.) (I Sam. 13:19–22).

As John Garstang pointed out (*The Heritage of Solomon*), Philistine lords did not divide their people into tribes or clans as Israel did, but into administrative units. When David, fugitive from Saul, asked the Philistine Achish for a town in which he could live safely, Achish gave him Ziklag (possibly Tell el-Khuweilfeh, SW. of Debir) (I Sam. 27). This fact suggests that the place was within the control of the chief or lord of Gath. Sennacherib's annals imply that Ashkelon similarly controlled Joppa. I Sam. 6:18 refers to the Philistines' "country villages," as distinct from their walled cities.

The Philistines kept peace in the era of Samuel and Saul by maintaining strategic bases that were respected by the peace-minded people of Judah (Judg. 15:11, J). One of these was at Michmash* (I Sam. 13:16), which controlled the approach to the Jordan Valley opposite Geba. This latter place, once held by Saul and Jonathan, was separated from Michmash by a rock-littered valley. Another Philistine base was the garrison on "the hill of God" (I Sam. 10:5), which apparently overlooked Gibeon. In David's day there was a Philistine garrison in hilltop Bethlehem, which kept David from an ancestral spring (II Sam. 23:14–17). All these bases were outer defenses of Jerusalem—then the city of the Jebusites (see JEBUS), allies of the Philistines. Farther from their main holdings on the plain the Philistines maintained a base at Aphek (see ANTIPATRIS). Here they concentrated (I Sam. 4:1) forces against Israelites for the Battle of Ebenezer in the Plain of Sharon, and again for the fateful battle of Gilboa (I Sam. 29:1, 31). Another Philistine base was the historic pass leading to the Plain of Dothan and the W. slopes of Mt. Gilboa, and commanding approaches to the Wâdî Arah, which led into the Plain of Esdraelon (Armageddon) at Megiddo. In spite of these bases overlooking enemy territory, Philistines seemed unaware of the steadily rising power of the Hebrew Monarchy under David, who showed genius for military tactics and organization (I Sam. 18:30, 19:8, 23:5; etc.). Though there were strong Philistine bases nearby, David won the walled Jebusite city which became his capital (Jerusalem).

The strength of the Philistines and other neighbors made Israel urge Samuel to anoint them a king. His choice was Saul, known for his stalwart stature (I Sam. 9:2) and his prowess. His membership in the small central Tribe of Benjamin would not invite antagonism from stronger Hebrew groups. But the new king's jealousy of the freebooter David's popularity following his slaying of the Philistine giant Goliath (I Sam. 17:31–58, 18:6–15), and his protection of Israel's threshing floors from Philistine marauders (I Sam. 23:1–5), evoked murderous threats which precipitated David's flight to the Philistines (I Sam. 27–29). These he served loyally until powerful "lords of the Philistines" (I Sam. 29:7) complained to his friend Achish, lord of Gath, that they did not trust the Hebrew, and objected to his joining them at Aphek for the battle against the Hebrews (I Sam. 29:4). The inability of Achish to withstand the protests of his fellow chiefs is an example of their policy of joint action referred to above. "So David returned into the land of the Philistines. And the Philistines went up to Jezreel" (v. 11).

It was inevitable that the ambitious Philistines and Israelites, both having a sense of destiny, and both arriving in Canaan at about the same time, should clash in their struggle for political and economic control. Meantime the Philistines allied themselves with the Canaanites, and adopted some of their language and gods.

The following events are highlights in the Philistine-Israel struggle:

(1) *The Period of the Judges* (c. 1200–1020 B.C.)—

(a) The folk hero Shamgar (identified as a Canaanite by some scholars) slays "600 Philistines with an oxgoad"—possibly in the original Philistine invasion, or during a local victory over an otherwise unknown N. Philistine group (Judg. 3:31).

(b) Philistine pressure causes the removal of Dan to the NE. (Judg. 18:2).

(c) Israel is defeated and dominated for 40 years by the Philistines (Judg. 13:1).

(d) Israel is delivered by Samson, who later meets death in the Philistine temple of Dagon (Judg. 13–16).

(e) Israel takes the initiative in the hill country of Ephraim against the Philistines, based on Aphek, to bring the Ark from Shiloh (I Sam. 4:4 f.), which is destroyed in the struggle; but loses the sacred treasure to the Philistines, who are sorely afflicted by its presence and return it after seven months (I Sam. 5, 6).

(f) Twenty years later, under Samuel, Israel recovers her territory (I Sam. 7:1–14).

(2) *Under the Hebrew United Monarchy* (c. 1020–922 B.C.)—

(a) The Philistines, defeated by Jonathan at Michmash, are held in check for two decades, with Israel dominating the hills and the Philistines the plain (I Sam. 13, 14).

(b) The Philistines attack at Shochoh (A.S.V. Socoh) (I Sam. 17:1), and their giant, Goliath of Gath, is killed by young David, whose later acclaim arouses the jealousy of Israel's King Saul (I Sam. 17:4–54, 18:6 f., 16–30).

(c) David, threatened by Saul, flees to the Philistines, and receives from Achish, lord of Gath, the town of Ziklag (I Sam. 19, 21:10, 27:1–7); he is absent during the fatal battle of Mount Gilboa when Philistines kill Saul and Jonathan (I Sam. 31).

(d) A powerful Israel rises under David, unobserved by the Philistines, who are taken by surprise by his capture of their ally's capital, Jebus (later Jerusalem). When they hear of his accession they fight him in the Valley of Rephaim and are pursued as far S. as Gezer. They become his mercenaries (II Sam. 5:6–10).

(e) The Philistines make further attacks on David's men (II Sam. 5:17–25, 8:1, 2, 21:15–18).

(f) At the division of his Monarchy they appear independent (I Kings 15:27, 16:15).

(3) *Subsequent to the Hebrew Divided Monarchy*—

(a) Relations vary; Nadab (c. 901–900 B.C.) and other weak kings of Judah invade Philistia (I Kings 15:27, 16:15).

(b) The Philistines appease King Jehoshaphat (c. 873–849 B.C.) (II Chron. 17:11).

(c) They invade during the Judahin reigns of Jehoram (c. 849–842 B.C.) and Ahaz (c. 842) (II Chron. 21:16, 28:18).

(d) They are attacked by Uzziah and Hezekiah (c. 715–687 B.C.) (II Chron. 26:6 f.).

(e) They take part in Antiochus Epiphanes' invasion of Judah (I Macc. 3:41).

The extremely exposed position of the Philistines along the Mediterranean plain laid them open to attacks from Egypt and Assyria, so that in the latter third of the 8th and all through the 7th century B.C. they faced attack after attack, interspersed by rebellions. These attacks are mentioned in the inscriptions of the Mesopotamian aggressors, e.g., Tiglath-pileser III, Sennacherib, Esarhaddon, and Ashurbanipal. The great Philistine city of Gaza fell to Alexander the Great in 332 B.C. after a severe siege. Finally the Philistines were absorbed by other peoples and gradually passed from history.

Though the Philistines were not Semites, their chief god, Dagon* (Judg. 16:23–30; I Sam. 5:3–7), was a Semitic deity—possibly borrowed from the Canaanites; he was worshipped jointly with a fish goddess. Marna, Derketo, Baalzebal or Baal-zebub ("lord of the heavenly mansion"), and Astarte (see ASHERAH) were other Philistine deities. If the Philistines came from the W. they eventually forgot the gods of their European fathers. They were ruthless toward Israel's most sacred possession, the Ark, and its Tabernacle repository at Shiloh. They rejoiced in the death of Israel's judge Samson in the temple of Dagon. It is little wonder that the Philistines were denounced by Hebrew prophets, e.g., Jeremiah (chap. 47), Amos (1:6–8), Zephaniah (2:4–7), and Zechariah (9:5–7).

The Philistines left in Palestine fine, elaborately decorated Aegean types of pottery, the finding of which in excavated city levels helps archaeologists to date their occupation by them, as at the middle phase of Stratum B (c. 1150–1000 B.C.), and at the important Stratum V at Beth-shan*. If the tremendous mound of Tell ej-Jemmeh (probably Gerar) is ever fully excavated, rich revelations concerning Philistine culture will doubtless be discovered.

Philo Judaeus (20 B.C.–A.D. 50), the greatest philosopher of Hellenistic Judaism, who left his mark on Christian theology through the Alexandrian school. Thoroughly trained in Greek philosophy, this fervent Jew stands in contrast to the historian Josephus*, who lost some of his enthusiasm for his religion and his people when disasters befell them. Philo was the bridge between Judaism and Hellenism over which Christian theology advanced. His two outstanding contributions were (1) his conception of the Logos* and (2) his use of allegory, by which he turned Biblical stories into philosophical principles. Orthodox Judaism had seen the value of this type of interpretation, as did later Christians. Philo reduced allegorical interpretation to a system. In his "allegories of the sacred laws" he characterized some of the narratives of the 6-day Creation of the world as purely mythical. Paul employed this literary style in some of his writings (I Cor. 10:4; Gal. 4:24). Philo's influence is seen in the Gospel of John and the Epistle to the Hebrews. He was a contemporary of Jesus.

Phinehas (fĭn'ē-ăs). (1) A son of Eleazar, son of Aaron (Josh. 24:33). His name may be of Egyptian origin. He inherited land in Ephraim. As successor to his father in the high priesthood, Phinehas rose to prominence in the narratives of P and the Chronicler. A post-Exilic clan of priests claimed descent from him (Ezra 8:2). Events narrated of him are: his killing of an Israelite who, by bringing into the encampment a Midianite woman, was responsible for tempting the Hebrews to follow her form of worship (Num. 25); his direction of a band against the Midianites (Num. 10:8 f.); and his witnessing of an arbitrated feud between Benjamin and the larger tribes (Josh. 22:13, 30–32). (2) A younger evil son of the prophet Eli (I Sam. 1:3, 4:17) (see HOPHNI). (3) The father of a priest, Eleazar (Ezra 8:33).

Phlegon (flē'gŏn), a Christian at Rome, greeted by Paul in his Epistle to the Romans (16:14).

Phoebe (fē'bē) (A.V. Phebe), a deaconess or "servant" of the church at Cenchreae, one of the ports of Corinth, mentioned in Paul's Letter to the Romans (16:1) as worthy of receiving assistance from Christians because she had helped many, including Paul. The Apostle requested such a reception for her as would be accorded a saint "in the Lord." Rom. 16:1, 2 may be her introduction to the church at Ephesus. See ROMANS.

Phoenicia (fē-nĭsh'ĭ-ȧ) (A.V. Phenice Acts 11:19, 15:3, Phenicia Acts 21:2, R.S.V. Phoenicia), the very narrow coastal strip along the NE. Mediterranean (now the Republic of Lebanon and S. Latakia), flanked by the magnificent Lebanon Mountains and the hills of Galilee. It was part of O.T. Canaan. Its people were Semites* who called themselves Canaanites as long as Phoenician culture survived in Syria. They themselves believed that they had come in ancient times from Babylonia or NE. Arabia, near the Persian Gulf. After the second millennium B.C. they were called "Sidonians." The boundaries of Phoenicia varied, but they were usually on the N., the region on the mainland opposite the island city of Arvad (now Ruad); and on the S., the Ladder of Tyre, a promontory 14 m. S. of the city of Tyre; Arvad was c. 125 m. from Tyre. Sometimes the boundaries were reckoned from the Orontes River to Mt. Carmel. In the time of Jesus Phoenicia extended as far S. as Dor, 16. m. S. of Mount Carmel. It consisted therefore of a sliver of coast, from c. 150 to 200 m. long; its northern end was opposite the influential island of Cyprus.

(1) *Name.*—"Phoenicians" and "Phoenicia" are certainly derived from the Gk. *Phoinikes* (pl. of *Phoinix*) for the people, and *Phoinikē* for their country; possibly from *phoinios* ("blood-red"), suggested either by the famous reddish-purple dyestuff or purple* (from Tyrian mollusks, *murex*, exported by Phoenicians for coloring garments), or perhaps from the sunburned skin of Phoenician sailors. W. F. Albright traced "Phoenicia" to "palm" (one translation of the Gk. *phoinix*). The word "Phoenicia" appears in Mark 7:26, where Jesus is said to have gone into the "borders of Tyre and Sidon" and ministered to a Greek (or Gentile) woman who was "a Syrophoenician by race" (A.S.V.). The old stock had survived many political vicissitudes.

(2) *Geography and Destiny.*—The narrowness of their coastal strip, which sometimes disappears entirely where a headland drops into the sea, inevitably pushed the Phoenicians seaward. This fact, coupled with their almost inexhaustible supply of cedars, pine, and cypress for ships, and their sturdy, courageous people—like the Lebanese today—made them seafaring merchants. No others knew how to cut timber as the Phoenician Sidonians did (I Kings 5:6); and the men of Byblos (Gebal) were famous shipbuilders (Ezek. 27:9).

Phoenicia faced W., trading at all good ports as far as the Pillars of Hercules, and even venturing out into the Atlantic. She founded centers at Tartessus (? Tarshish) and at what became Cadiz (Gades) in Spain; and in Africa. Some authorities believe that Phoenician ships plied as far as Cornwall, seeking tin; others, that they procured this commodity in the Atlantic Scilly Isles. Phoenicians won prestige not by armed conquest, but through commerce. The skills of her timber cutters, boatbuilders, and crews enabled Phoenicia to equip navies for Sennacherib, Nechoh II of Egypt, and Xerxes the Persian. Isaiah called Sidon "a mart of nations" (23:3). (For Phoenicia's part in the commercial navy of Solomon see EZION-GEBER and HIRAM.) For an idea of her varied imports, see Ezekiel's vivid account (27:28). Cut off from agriculture by abnormal terrain, and having no known mineral resources but iron, Phoenicia became one of the greatest trading nations of history. Few Hebrews joined the Phoenician crews, for Hebrews had little taste for the sea (cf. Jonah, in a Phoenician ship, Jonah 1:3). Phoenicia never made political claims on her eastern neighbor Galilee, nor was she ever possessed by David and Solomon's expanding empire. Her contacts with Hebrews were for purposes of importing grain, which she also bought from Aram (the region around Damascus). She always had plenty of grapes and olives.

(3) *City-Centered Patterns.*—Phoenicians were urban-minded. Their coastal strip was dotted with harbor towns, some of which were powerfully fortified. From S. to N. these cities were: Accho* (the Roman Ptolemais), just N. of the Carmel promontory; Achzib, Misrephathmaim, Zarephath* (Sarepta), Sidon*, Byblos (Gebal*, Jebeil), Arka (mentioned in the Tell el-Amarna Letters), Arvad, and Ras* Shamrah (Ugarit). Of these, Tyre and Arvad were islands (at times made into peninsulas), easily protected and convenient for shipping. The Phoenician cities were not closely federated as were the Decapolis chain of cities. (See TYRE, illus. 461.)

In the 9th century B.C., when Phoenician power was at its height, seafarers from Tyre founded Carthage. They established other ports in N. Africa; in Sicily, as at Heraclea; in Malta, whose priceless harbor they used; in Sardinia; and especially in strategic, mineral-rich Cyprus, source of copper. But between c. 920 and 870 B.C. the Egyptian pharaohs Shishak and Osorkon I brought an end to the independence of Phoenicia. And after 870 Phoenicia felt the oppression of Assyrian masters. The loose federation of Phoenician cities had resisted for centuries the attacks of successive "world empires."

(4) *History.*—Phoenicia came into written history c. 1600 B.C., in records of the Seventeenth Dynasty Egyptian Ahmose I, whose monuments mention Phoenicia as Da-hi. Thutmose III recorded that he had conquered Arvad on his 7th expedition, and claimed Phoenicia as a petty state. The Tell el-Amarna Letters tell much about conditions in Phoenicia in the 15th and 14th centuries B.C.

It is believed that Phoenicia as a state appeared in the period of the Judges of Israel (c. 1200–1020 B.C.). By the time of David and Solomon (c. 1000–922 B.C.) it centered in Sidon and Tyre, which had strong kings. The daughter of Ethbaal, King of Tyre (I Kings 16:31), was Jezebel, royal wife of King Ahab of Israel (c. 869–850 B.C.). Phoenician power was at its height from the David-Solomon era to c. 600 B.C., when its prestige and rich cultural heritage passed to Greece. Carthaginian descendants of the Phoenicians called themselves Canaanites as late as the 5th century A.D.

The obscure beginning of the history of Phoenicia has been somewhat clarified by the excavation of Byblos, her oldest city (cf. "ancients of Gebal," Ezek. 27:9), under the direction of the French archaeologists Montet and Dunand (from 1924), in co-operation with the Lebanese. Byblos appears to have been founded by Egypt, probably not later than the First Egyptian Dynasty (c. 3000–2700 B.C.), whose people were eager to import cedar for mummy cases, oils for use in mummification, timber for masts, flagpoles, and furniture. Some of the first boats to ply the E. Mediterranean were "Byblos Travelers," which carried these wares to Egypt and brought back to Phoenicia and Syria gold, perfumes, and other luxuries, in addition to reeds for papyrus*. Montet discovered that the main temple at Byblos dated from the Old Empire (c. 2700–2200 B.C.) and continued in use as late as the Roman period (63 B.C.–A.D. 324). The town became a "layer-cake" of history, vividly illustrating life during the rise and fall of successive political masters. Sometimes Byblos was subject to Egypt, again independent under Phoenician (Canaanite) princes. The fact that Tyre and Sidon were important centers following the obscure Hyksos Age (c. 1720–1550 B.C.) suggests that they were influential even in that period of foreign-controlled Egypt. The land was never organized as a kingdom, but controlled by successive city kings. Greeks of the Homeric age called all Phoenicians "Sidonians." And after Sidon, declared in Gen. 10:15 to have been "begotten" by Canaan, the grandson of Noah, Tyre ("daughter of Sidon," Isa. 23:12) became the dominant Phoenician center. Jeremiah, prophesying the downfall of Phoenicia, referred to it in terms of the kings of Sidon and Tyre (25:22).

Before her downfall Phoenicia, though absorbed in business rather than war, time and again strongly resisted armed aggressors. In the 9th century B.C. the Assyrian Ashurnasirpal II (883–859 B.C.) exacted tribute from rich Phoenicia, as did Shalmaneser III (c. 859–824 B.C.); for 100 years Assyria drained the resources of Phoenicia. Tiglath-pileser III (734 B.C.) dominated Byblos, and received tribute from Arvad. The 3-year siege of Samaria by Shalmaneser V in the reign of King Hoshea, last king of Israel (732–724 B.C.) (II Kings 17:3 ff.), seems to have included overrunning "all Phoenicia." By the time of Sennacherib's invasion (701 B.C.) Tyre and Sidon had allied themselves. Nebuchadnezzar marched against Phoenicia after the fall of Jerusalem. Tyre (Ezek. 26:1 ff., 29:17 ff.) is said to have held out against his forces for at least 12 years (585–573 B.C.), and then appears to have surrendered on favorable terms, though the family of its King Ithobaal was deported to Babylonia. During the short-lived monarchy of Hiram II the Persians took over control of Phoenicia from the Chaldaeans. Alexander the Great, after attempting for seven months (333 B.C.) to subdue Tyre, succeeded only after making the island city into a peninsula, joined with the mainland by a causeway, traces of which are still visible. Though he sold and killed thousands of Tyrians, the city regained its greatness, and as a prosperous Hellenistic center flourished in Roman times, when various emperors made colonies of Berytus (Beirut), Accho (Ptolemais), Tyre, and Sidon. Even after Tyre's powerful colony at Carthage was severed from her Tyre remained commercially important in the Mediterranean (cf. Ezek. 27:12–25).

After Phoenicia became politically dependent, her merchants continued to trade. They engaged in merchandising and finance in Egyptian Memphis; and in Jerusalem (Zeph. 1:11) they sold their Mediterranean fish and other wares as late as the post-Exilic period (Neh. 13:16). The symbol of a Phoenician fish has been found carved on a shrine in remote Nabataean Petra. Her silver seemed inexhaustible; her coins were heavy and freely accepted as legal tender. The narrative of the Palestine housewife who sold her fine homespun textiles to Phoenician merchants (Prov. 31:24 A.S.V. margin) shows commercial ties between Palestine and the coastal region.

(5) *Religion.*—With their desirable and useful wares Phoenician merchants also brought in undesirable foreign cults, denounced by Hebrew prophets (e.g., Isa. 65:11). Their crude religion was as distinctive as that of the Hebrews or the Egyptians, as is now known from Ras Shamrah (Ugarit) texts (c. 1400 B.C.). Gods of widely traveled Phoenicians exerted a corrupting influence on Israel, as seen in the antagonism between Jezebel and the prophet Elijah (I Kings 18–19:18) and in the apostasies of Solomon (11:5), whose court enjoyed the cultic ritual of orgies administered by male and female Temple prostitutes decried by Hebrew prophets. Tithing was a Phoenician custom. So too was child sacrifice, so difficult to extirpate from Israelite worship. The Phoenician religion was the survival of the system existing in Canaan when the Hebrews arrived. Its gods were male and female nature deities. The head of the pantheon was a male, who blended the personalities of Hadad (Rimmon), the storm god; Shamash, the sun god; and Reshep (Makkal), deity of the earth and the underworld. This chief god, with his fluid characteristics, was usually called Baal ("lord") or Milk ("king"). The goddess honored as the great mother, sponsor of fecundity, was the virgin Astarte (also known as 'Anat*). The popular Phoenician cult of Adonis and Tammuz, which survives in folk festivals in the Lebanon region near Byblos, identified this "lord" Adonis (now known to have been represented as a cedar) with Osiris. Eshmun, especially honored at Sidon, was the god of healing (paralleled by the Greek Asklepios), as was the Nehushtan of II Kings 18:4.

O.T. Biblical personalities associated with Phoenicia include, in addition to Ethbaal, the King of Tyre (I Kings 16:31; cf. Josh. 19:29), and his daughter Jezebel, sponsor of priests and prophets of Baal (I Kings 18:19), the two worthy Hirams (a) King of Tyre, friend and trade ally of David (II Sam. 5:11; I Kings 5:1) and of Solomon (I Kings 5:1–12; II Chron. 2:3–16; and (b) the artisan-craftsman-architect Hiram, the Tyrian whose mother was a widow of Naphtali (I Kings 7:13–47; II Chron. 2:13 f.). Elijah's flight in famine time to Zarephath (cf. I Kings 17:9) was as exceptional as the isolated instance recorded of Jesus going inside Phoenicia to "the parts of Tyre and Sidon." Phoenicia was never regarded as part of Palestine; even its Roman masters included Phoenicia and the area of Carmel with Syria rather than with Palestine.

Phoenicia is mentioned in the N.T. in connection with the visit of Jesus "outside Palestine," "abroad," to a "foreign mission field, the region of Tyre and Sidon" (Matt. 15:21; Mark 7:24, 31), where he healed the young daughter of a Phoenician or Canaanitish woman. Phoenicia is mentioned again in connection with believers who left Jerusalem after the stoning of Stephen (Acts

11:19, 15:3). Paul and his company visited Phoenician ports (Acts 15:3); the farewell given him by Christian friends on the beach of ancient Tyre is a touching incident in his stormy career (Acts 21:2–7).

(6) *Culture.*—The wide travels of the Phoenician "middlemen" resulted in syncretism in art and religion. Many of the discoveries for which they are given credit—the alphabet, making glass, the dyeing of fine textiles, and the use of numbers, weights, and measures—have had a wide and lasting influence upon world culture. What they adopted from other nations is hard to distinguish from what they originated. Eminent scholars believe that Solomon's Temple was built according to a Phoenician model; also the symbolic pillars Jachin and Boaz, and the metal furnishings of the Temple. (See HIRAM.)

Those who believe the Phoenicians discovered the art of glassmaking tell how a ship one day sailed into Byblos harbor at the mouth of the Belus River. After filling their craft with chunks of niter, the sailors saw their fires melt out the salt, which blended with the sand and started a flow of glass. Belus River sand was long used as an ingredient of choice Egyptian glass. Sidon also was famous for its glass. Some French and Lebanese archaeologists believe that the Phoenicians had extraordinary skill in working gold, iron, and copper while Athens and Rome were still in the Bronze Age. Enthusiasts for Phoenician art assert that many a Greek capital, Ionic motif, Assyrian emblem, and Etruscan construction was derived from an old Phoenician concept. Phoenicians made jewelry with unbelievably delicate filigree; the Aleppo Museum and the Museum of the O.I. in Chicago contain some of their remarkable ivories. Though Phoenicians played a large role in evolving the alphabet (see WRITING) used by Hebrews, Greeks, and Europeans, they left no extensive body of literature, except the Canaanite literature recovered at Ras Shamrah in N. Syria. Some of their royal annals have been preserved in Greek by Josephus and others. Their pseudohieroglyphic script may date from the 22d or 21st century B.C. The Iron Age I inscription on the Ahiram sarcophagus found at Byblos was the longest and earliest alphabetic linear inscription known at the time of its discovery during the Montet-Dunand research. It dates from c. 1000 B.C. or a little earlier, and may be seen today in the Lebanon Museum of Beirut, along with the Byblos king's golden bracelets, pendants, silver-soled sandals, gold-trimmed scepter, and fantastic statuettes of animals.

Phoenix (? Lutro), a harbor in S. Crete, looking "northeast and southeast" (Acts 27:12 R.S.V., "south west and north west" A.V.), where Paul and his fellow Mediterranean travelers on the Adramyttium ship hoped to winter safely.

Phrygia (frĭj'ĭ-*ȧ*), a region in W. Asia Minor, now part of Anatolian Turkey. Its boundaries, though varied in early times, included most of the interior of W. Asia Minor and reached to the Black Sea. In 133 B.C. it passed to Rome, and at an unknown date was joined with Cilicia to make a province. Pompey in 67 B.C. drove out the notorious Phrygian pirates. In Paul's day it was a Roman procuratorial province (A.D. 25–50). The portion of Phrygia that included Antioch and Iconium was sometimes called "Phrygia Galatia."

324. Phrygia.

Phrygian inhabitants were mainly Asiatic. In ancient times Aryans speaking an Indo-European language came from Thrace—Phrygians related to the Trojans, who in Homer's account of the Trojan War contended against Greek settlers from Thessaly. Phrygians are said to have aided King Priam in return for his help to them against a powerful people, possibly the Hittites*; it is believed that Hittite culture declined after 1000 B.C. under the pressure of the Phrygians.

Phrygia had a network of major roads, including the "Royal Road" by which Persians connected Susa with Sardis and the Aegean; these roads made it possible for Paul and his companions to travel through this region. A trunk road led up the Lycus Valley to Iconium* and across the Taurus Mountains into Syria—a main commercial route from the Aegean to Syria and Palestine. This way gave access to the iron, copper, mercury, cinnabar, and marble of highland Phrygia, and to the large flocks which supplied wool for the garment looms of Miletus, Pergamum, Laodicea, and Colossae. The textiles and the styles of Phrygians, especially the peaked, loose-fitting Phrygian cap, were influential in the Near East. Phrygia was also known for horses raised for the Roman circus.

Paul went through Phrygia (1) on the First Missionary Journey, when he and Barnabas were going from Perga in Pamphylia to Pisidian Antioch (Acts 13:14–24); (2) on the Second Missionary Journey, when he and Silas and Timothy "went through Phrygia and the region of Galatia" (R.S.V. "the region of Phrygia and Galatia") and proceeded to Troas (Acts 16:6); and (3) on the Third Missionary Journey, when the Apostle went "through all the country of Galatia and Phrygia" (R.S.V. "from place to place through the region of Galatia and Phrygia") (Acts 18:23), and proceeded thence to Ephesus (Acts 19:1).

The five Phrygian cities named in the N.T. are Iconium, Laodicea, Colossae, Hierapolis, and Pisidian Antioch. Jews from Phrygia were in Jerusalem on the Day of Pentecost (Acts 2:10). The labors of Paul and his company in Phrygia bore fruit, for the evangelization of the region was early and extensive; many 2d-century Christian inscriptions have been found; some authorities believe that the people became Christian by A.D. 300. Possibly the gross immoralities of the worship of Cybele, the Asiatic "Earth-Mother," stimulated among new Christians a fighting spirit that won converts.

Phygellus (fĭ-jĕl′ŭs) (A.S.V., R.S.V. Phygelus [fĭ-jē′lŭs]) (II Tim. 1:15), one of the Asiatics who turned away from Paul either for fear of persecution or because they disagreed with his teachings. His name is coupled with that of Hermogenes. The two men are mentioned in the N.T. only here.

phylacteries (from Gk. *phylaktērion*, "safeguard"), the term applied in Matt. 23:5 to the *tephillin* (Aram. pl. of *tephillah*, "prayer") worn by pious Jews; tiny pouches made of skin from ceremonially clean animals, strapped by leather bands to the forehead between and immediately above the eyes, and to the left arm, of males who have reached the age of 13. They are worn during the daily morning prayer, but not on the Sabbath or holy days. Some excessively devout men went beyond the requirement and wore phylacteries all day, or made them more conspicuous by broadening their bands —an ostentatious habit criticized by Jesus.

Phylacteries are made according to instructions thought by many to have been received from Moses. Some scholars, however, believe that phylacteries were not worn until after the division of the kingdom, or even until Maccabean times. They consider the injunctions of Pentateuchal writers concerning "frontlets" (phylacteries) to have been metaphorical (Ex. 13:9, 16; Deut. 6:8, 11:18), and see in these passages suggestions that God's Word is more precious than any jeweled amulet*.

The head phylactery has four small compartments, each of which contains a passage from the O.T. (Ex. 13:1–10, 11–16; Deut. 6:4–9; 11:13–21—see DOORS), written on parchment and tied with hair. The writing is meticulous, without erasures. The knot which ties the headband rests on the back of the neck, is shaped like the Heb. letter *daleth*, and has loops long enough to reach over the shoulders and fall down on the breast. The arm phylactery has one pocket, but contains the same four passages written on one skin; it is fastened to the arm by a long strap, wound seven times around arm and then around middle and ring fingers. When the left arm is bent the pouch lies over the heart. Its knot represents the letter *yōd*, which, together with the *shīn* impressed on the sides of the phylactery and the *daleth* on the head, spelled *Shaddai*, "Almighty." The symbolical sense of the phylacteries is summed up thus: "Put your head, your hand, your heart at the service of God, as a memorial of His having brought you out of Egypt." Traditional Jews still wear phylacteries.

physicians, surgeons, dentists, men skilled in the art of healing practiced in Bible lands at an early date. Their *materia medica* was often not much more than magic*. They knew how to stop nosebleeds; to prescribe curative baths in rivers and pools, as did Israel's prophets (II Kings 5:10; John 5:2 ff.); and to treat boils (cf. II Kings 20:7). (For diagnosis and treatment of various diseases, see DISEASE AND HEALING.)

Babylonian physicians are mentioned in the Code of Hammurabi, which gives a list of their fees and the penalties for malpractice. The clay-tablet library of Asshurbanapal contained some 800 medical texts, most of which are undeciphered. Walter A. Jayne, in *The Healing Gods of Ancient Civilizations*, cites the Mesopotamian belief in the supernatural origin of disease, and traces the relation between priestly sacrificial rites and the exorcism of disease. He tells of the education of doctors in temples, and the carrying of invalids into public squares, as was done in Palestine in the time of Jesus (Mark 2:1–12). The chief Babylonian god of healing was Ea, patron of curative springs and the last resort of sufferers. Ishtar aided women in bearing children; Marduk cured the sick; and Shamash, the sun god, prolonged life.

Egyptians looked to their god-architect-wisdom-writer Imhotep for health, but attributed the art of medicine to the god Apis of Memphis. Isis, depicted in the later dynasties as a nursing mother, concerned herself especially with child health. Her amulets, worn by boys and girls, were similar to "evil eye" charms still worn by many Near Easterners. Physicians were important figures in Egyptian life. As apothecaries* they concerned themselves with everything from cosmetics* and hair pomades to prevent baldness, which Nilotic peoples abhorred, to general tonics compounded of honey and crushed donkey teeth. Egyptian doctors were also embalmers of the dead: "Joseph commanded his servants the physicians to embalm his father" (Gen. 50:2 f.). Evidence that the Egyptians possessed considerable surgical skill is contained in the Edwin Smith Surgical Papyrus, Library of N.Y. Academy of Medicine, possibly from the Hyksos Age (c. 1720–1550 B.C.). This papyrus may be part of a physician-surgeon's handbook, outlines of a medical professor's lectures, or the notebook of some careful student. (See *An Encyclopedia of Bible Life*, Madeleine S. and J. Lane Miller, p. 336, Harper & Brothers.)

Greek physicians drew inspiration from the god Asklepios, whose caduceus is a physician's symbol even today. His Asklepieion and Sanctuary—the nearest equivalent of a general hospital in ancient times—has been excavated and examined by the American School of Classical Studies at Corinth. This structure, where Asklepios and Hygieia, guardian of health, were honored in a cult of the 6th century B.C., includes a temple (? hospital-chapel) restored in early Roman times, probably at the expense of some freedman of Mark Antony; the name of the latter is decipherable on a pointed entablature block. Paul, walking out from Corinth to the outlying gymnasium and theater, may well have seen the colonnade with its ambulatory, dining room, and couches, as well as votive offerings in the form of cured limbs, hands, and other parts of the body, left by grateful patients. Many of these offerings are in the Corinth Museum. A stone collection box was found near the entrance to the Asklepieion precinct, containing 13 ancient bronze coins.

There were other popular Greek shrines of healing, e.g. in the island of Cos, birthplace of the noted Greek Hippocrates, "Father of Medicine" (b. c. 460 B.C.), a man still held in high esteem by medical men. It has been thought that Luke was educated at Cos, or at its rival center, the island of Cnidus. Pergamum was the birthplace of the noble Greek physician Galen (c. A.D. 130–200), founder of experimental physiology, and a believer that God's purposes could be learned by a detailed examination of His works. Many patients in search of health came to Pergamum.

The *Romans* had no special god of healing, but raised altars to minor deities associated with curing specific disorders, e.g., *Febris* for fevers; *Cloacina* for foul-air diseases; *Angina* for heart pains; and *Verminus* for cattle diseases. The father of the family in Roman households doctored his children with herbs, consulted oracles for directions, and relied on hot baths in cheerful and well-equipped thermal establishments, of which many have been excavated.

In *Palestine* of the Biblical period there were physicians. But Scripture is not complimentary concerning their ability to cure patients, e.g., the woman who had "suffered many things of many physicians" (Mark 5:26–29). Job 13:4 expresses a similar distrust. Lack of confidence in doctors, as well as desire to exalt the healing power of the Lord, explains such passages as II Chronicles 16:12 about the sick King Asa of Judah (913–873 B.C.). (For the ministry of Jesus, the Great Physician, see DISEASE AND HEALING.) See also Ecclus. 38:1–4.

Archaeology has disclosed the practice of *dentistry* among Phoenicians at a very early date. C. C. Torrey of Yale University found in 1901 in the sarcophagus of a Phoenician notable in the necropolis of rock-cut tombs SE. of Sidon a specimen of dental art (now in the Archaeological Museum of the American University of Beirut). Fine gold wire was woven around six anterior teeth of the lower jaw to bind them firmly together. This "Torrey Specimen" (known in Lebanon as the "Ford Specimen") dates from the 5th century B.C. The Gaillardot Specimen, in the Louvre at Paris, dating from the 4th century B.C., found in 1862 by Dr. Gaillardot of the Renan Expedition, shows a gold wire retentive prosthesis of a woman's six lower teeth, supporting a replacement of the right central and lateral incisors; the teeth "bridged in" had been removed from the mouth of another person. (See *Bulletin of the History of Medicine*, Vol. XXII, No. 6, November-December 1948, article by Dr. Milton B. Asbell.)

Pi-beseth (pī-bē′sĕth) (Bast or Bubastum), an Egyptian Delta town mentioned in Ezek. 30:17 along with On* (Heliopolis), the residence of the Twenty-second Dynasty of Lybian kings (including Shishak). Its temple ruins are at Tell Basta, near the modern Zakazik (Zagazig).

Pi-hahiroth (pī′hȧ-hī′rŏth), Israel's last camp site in Egypt before they crossed the Sea of Reeds (Ex. 14:2, 9; Num. 33:7).

Pilate, Pontius, the Roman prefect of Judaea from 26 to 36 A.D. Josephus and Tacitus committed anachronisms in calling him "procurator," as proven by an inscription discovered at Caesarea in 1961 which reads, in probable translation: "Pontius Pilatus, Prefect of Judea, has [presented] the Tiberieum [to the Caesareans]." The name "Pontius" denotes Samnite origin in south central Italy, while "Pilatus" means "Armed-with-a-*pilum*" or javelin, the principal offensive weapon in the Roman legion. Governing prefects of the equestrian or middle class at Rome, of which Pilate was a member, would have seen considerable military service.

The Roman emperor Tiberius appointed him as prefect or provincial governor of Judaea in 26 A.D., and the fact that Pilate remained at his post for ten and one-half years—the second longest tenure of any Roman governor of Judaea in this era—shows that he was not the political cripple of popular repute. Tiberius was very concerned that only able men remained in charge of Roman provinces.

Although Pilate is known primarily because of his sentencing Jesus of Nazareth to the cross, five other incidents in his career are reported by Josephus and Philo. The first probably occurred shortly after Pilate's arrival in Judaea, when his auxiliary troops marched into Jerusalem by night, carrying iconic medallions with the imperial image or bust among their regimental standards. Whether or not an intentional provocation, this act occasioned a five-day mass demonstration at the provincial capital, Caesarea, which sought removal of the ensigns as a violation of Jewish law concerning engraved images (Ex. 20:4). Because the people seemed ready to die for their convictions on this issue, Pilate relented and ordered the offensive standards removed.

Later in his administration, Pilate constructed an aqueduct to bring water into Jerusalem from cisterns near Bethlehem, but paid for it with funds from the Temple treasury. This sparked another riot, which was put down only after bloodshed. These vignettes, as well as the reference in Luke to "Galileans whose blood Pilate had mingled with their sacrifices" (13:1–3) have combined to give Pilate a traditionally unflattering portrait. The Mishnah, however, permitted expenditure of surplus Temple funds for such civic needs, and it would seem that Pilate must have had some cooperation from the priestly authorities in Jerusalem, since he could not simply have plundered the treasury in sacred Temple precincts which were forbidden to Gentiles on pain of death. And Jesus' neutral reaction to the Galilean episode suggests that the incident may have been accidental, or the result of a justifiable police action.

On another occasion, Pilate dedicated some golden votive shields in his Jerusalem praetorium, which, Philo states, was located at the palace of Herod in the W. side of the city (i.e., *not* the Tower Antonia). Unlike the standards, these shields had no images on them whatever, only a bare inscription of dedication to Tiberius. And yet the people protested even the imageless shields, although this time Pilate refused to remove them. The Judaeans then informed Tiberius, who ordered Pilate to transfer the shields to Caesarea, and warned him against any further provocations against the Jews.

Pilate seems to have received this threatening letter shortly before the trial of Jesus, which may well explain his finally giving way to the demands of the crowd for Jesus' crucifixion despite his own conviction that Jesus was innocent, in view of which he had tried quashing the case for lack of evidence, change of venue, the Passover amnesty, and even a ceremonial hand-washing. Despite much recent scholarship which seeks to diminish Sanhedral responsibility for Jesus' conviction and enlarge Pilate's, the N.T. version is upheld also by such purely Jewish sources as the Talmud, which requires the death penalty for Jesus (*Sanhedrin* 43a).

In 36 A.D., Pilate used force to prevent a host of credulous Samaritans from an armed ascent of Mt. Gerizim. An unknown pseudoprophet had promised the people he would uncover some sacred temple utensils that Moses had supposedly buried there, and it came to an armed clash. The Samaritan Senate complained to the proconsul of Syria, Vitellius, who ordered Pilate to return to Rome to answer the charges against him. But before Pilate arrived, Tiberius had already died, in March of 37 A.D.

Pilate's subsequent fate has been the subject of numerous grotesque medieval legends, many rooted in Eusebius' claim that Pilate fell into such misfortune that he committed suicide. However, the earlier and more important testimony of Origen contradicts this tradition, and the emperor Caligula probably quashed Pilate's as a carryover case from the previous regime, as he did others. Pilate's true subsequent fate is unknown. His wife, named Procula in an early tradition, attested to Jesus' innocence on Good Friday because of her famous dream (Matt. 27:19) and was later canonized by the Greek Orthodox church, while the Ethiopian church recognizes June 25 as "St. Pilate and St. Procula's Day." P. L. M.

pilgrimage, a journey to a shrine, which was from ancient times a feature of worship in the Middle East. Popular goals were the headwaters of streams, as at Paneas (Banias), sacred to the Greek god Pan, at a source of the Jordan in a cave under the slopes of Mount Hermon, later Caesarea Philippi (Mark 8:27–29); and "high places" dedicated to pagan deities and, at times, to the God of Israel, as at Ramah in Samuel's day (I Sam. 9:12–19, 25). Processions were so important a part of Mesopotamian worship that the chief street of Babylon was named Procession Street. Over it tens of thousands of New* Year celebrants were led by the king and the image of Marduk through the famous

325. Pilgrim amphora from Judaea (9th-8th century B.C.).

Ishtar Gate to the Temple of Marduk. Egyptian temples at Memphis, Thebes, On, and Karnak were scenes of pilgim pageantry. Among the most famous Greek pilgrimages were: the quadrennial pan-Athenaic procession from the agora of Athens to the Temple of Athena on the Acropolis and on to the feast at the Bay of Salamis; and to the Hall of the Mysteries at Eleusis. Romans made pilgrimages along the Sacred Way of the Forum. For Hebrews the chief goal of earthly pilgrimages was Jerusalem with its Temple Hill, Moriah. Many of the Psalms refer to this pilgrimage.

Pilgrimages and the sacrificial feasts at the journey's end were a part of Israel's worship from early times. After the division of Solomon's kingdom Jeroboam's center at Bethel became popular. When Josiah's reform code (622 B.C.) centralized worship at Jerusalem it became the favorite pilgrim goal, though for a time worship at minor altars was permissible for those unable to go to Jerusalem for the three great annual feasts*—the Festival of Unleavened Bread (ultimately made a part of the Passover*); the Festival of Weeks; and the Festival of Booths. Jesus, like all other males of his people, gave heed to such observances (Deut. 16:16).

As more and more participants from towns on the road to Jerusalem joined the festival pilgrimage, joyous songs of worship were sung, e.g., the "Songs of Ascents" (Ps. 120–134). Ps. 24 and 118 are outstanding processional hymns. Among the Psalms expressing the deep religious experiences of the pilgrims when they arrived in Jerusalem are Ps. 84, beginning "How amiable are thy tabernacles, O Lord of Hosts," and Ps. 122, beginning,

"I was glad when they said unto me,
Let us go into the house of the Lord,"

and including the prayer for the peace of Jerusalem.

The pilgrimage theme is pre-eminent in Ps. 48, called "the diary of a Pilgrim to Zion"; in Ps. 87, originating probably in the Diaspora in the early post-Exilic period; in Ps. 46, which gave Martin Luther the theme of "A mighty fortress is our God"; and in Ps. 76, exalting the Lord, Whose capital is in Jerusalem.

Metaphorically, the long journey of Moses and the congregation of Israel from Egypt to Canaan may be viewed as a pilgrimage (Ex. 6:4 A.V.), made under Yahweh's tutelage. So too were such Patriarchal journeys as that of Abraham from Ur and Haran to Shechem and Beer-sheba, when he became by faith a sojourner in the land of promise, by faith going out from his ancestral home, to receive an inheritance in a land not his own, dwelling in tents, and looking for the "city . . . whose builder and maker is God" (Heb. 11:8 ff.).

The aged Jacob spoke to Pharaoh concerning the days of his pilgrimage (life), then totaling 130 years (Gen. 47:9).

In a figurative sense life was viewed by **N.T.** Christians as a journey, in which some attained their goal, and others admitted that they were but "strangers and pilgrims on the earth," bound for "a better country, that is, an heavenly," with its city prepared for them by God (Heb. 11:13-16, cf. I Pet. 2:11).

The first Christians were not interested in religious pilgrimages. They accepted the Johannine view that "God is a Spirit, and they that worship him must worship him in spirit and in truth" (John 4:24). Neither in Jerusalem nor in Samaria was He localized (v. 21); He was everywhere, accessible to all who sincerely sought Him, feeling after Him, to find Him (Acts 17:27).

Before the 4th century, however, Christians were making such journeys to sacred sites as are narrated in "The Diary of the Bordeaux Pilgrim."

Every Friday afternoon nowadays a procession of devout Christians, including archaeologists, members of armed forces, and pilgrims from many parts of the world, retrace the Way of the Cross along the traditional Via Dolorosa, beginning at a Moslem school near the site of the Tower of Antonia and St. Stephen's Gate in the E. wall of the city, on to the Church of the Holy Sepulcher. The level on which Jesus walked was c. 30 ft. below the present stone paving of the narrow way, and the "fourteen Stations of the Cross" are too hypothetical to be labeled confidently. This pious processional is ever impressive as an expression of Christian effort to relive the phases of the tragic hours of Jesus.

pillars appear in the Bible in many forms and with varied significance. (1) Hebrew cosmogony taught that pillars supported the earth (I Sam. 2:8; Ps. 75:3) and the heaven (Job 26:11). The prophet Joel spoke of pillars of smoke in the heavens on the great and terrible day of the Lord (2:30).

(2) The pillar of cloud by day and of fire by night which Israel believed to be God's torch leading them on their Wilderness* trek (Ex. 13:21 f., 14:19, 24, 40:38), was remembered for generations (Ps. 99:7; Neh. 9:12, 19) as a manifestation of His presence among them (Num. 14:14). Yahweh's pillar which hovered at the door of the tent-Tabernacle when Moses entered it (Ex. 33:9; Num. 12:5; Deut. 31:15) was a signal for every man to worship in his tent door (Ex. 33:10).

(3) Pillars or heaps of stone (cairns)—sometimes a single pillar anointed with oil—were erected as memorials of sacred events like the crossing of the Jordan (Josh. 4:19–24) or the making of a vow such as Jacob's at Bethel (Gen. 28:18, 22, 35:14). Jacob erected a pillar in token of the good will restored between him and Laban at what became Mizpah ("This heap is a witness") (Gen. 31:13–52).

(4) A pillar of unworked stone was erected to mark Rachel's grave on the outskirts of Bethlehem (Gen. 35:20), still a sacred spot to Jew, Christian, and Moslem. Dolmens or massive stone slabs have been found in Palestine and Trans-Jordan, set up to make sepulchral chambers, similar to the stone houses in which Neolothic families lived. Menhirs (*masseboth*) similar to the giant stones of the English Stonehenge have been found in the Near East (see GEZER). Burial cairns in Sinai were erected by seminomads before pottery came into general use.

(5) Pillars were occasionally set up as self-monuments, as in the case of Absalom, who had no son to erect a stone in his memory (II Sam. 18:18).

(6) Architectural pillars with carved capitals were used in Egypt and other Bible lands at an early period. Pillars at the Philistine temple of Dagon at Gaza appear prominently in the story of Samson (Judg. 16:25 f., 29). In Solomon's level at Megiddo (Stratum IV) were pilasters having proto-Ionic decoration. Samaria (10th-7th centuries B.C.) also used pilasters (proto-Aeolithic). Solomon's House of the Forest of Lebanon (I Kings 7); the Persian palace where Esther dwelt at Susa (Esth. 1:6, etc.); and various Temple area structures at Jerusalem all contained columns (I Kings 7). Two free-standing, enigmatic metal pillars, Jachin* and Boaz, stood at the main entrance to the Temple (I Kings 7:14 ff.), possibly as incense stands. Some of the Temple pillars seem to have been inlaid with precious metal (II Kings 18:16)—a prey to invaders, as Hezekiah found. The porches and arcades of the Temple area were supported by pillars.

Columns of such stone as marble or alabaster were often taken from one temple and incorporated in another structure. Columns in Bethlehem's ancient Basilica of the Nativity, in Justinian's Sancta Sophia at Constantinople, and in the Church of San Vitale in Ravenna, all may have come from pagan temples, such as Diana's at Ephesus.

(7) Pillars having historic associations figured in the crowning of kings. Abimelech was made king of Israel by the "pillar that was in Shechem" (Judg. 9:6). Young prince Joash was crowned in Jerusalem's palace-sanctuary, standing by a pillar "as the manner was" (A.V. II Kings 11:14). Possibly the pillar signified the old concept of the presence of Yahweh.

(8) Cultic pillars, common in ancient Semitic worship, crept into the worship of early Israel. Moses' command to overthrow heathen altars and break down pillars (Deut. 12:3) indicates that Israel found in Canaan stone pillars, *masseboth*, and cone-shaped objects denoting the female breast. These pillars as worshipped at Asherah shrines were one of the worst apostasies of Israel from the time of Joshua to that of Hosea.

(9) Symbolic mention of the pillar appears in the N.T., which calls the house of God "the pillar and ground of the truth" (I Tim. 3:15), and likens the Apostles James, Cephas, and John to pillars (Gal. 2:9).

pillow. (1) A cushion used under the head of a sleeper (cf. Gen. 28:11; I Sam. 19:13, 26:12). (2) A pad or fillet used in divination (Ezek. 13:18). (3) A piece of padding placed on rowers' seats (Mark 4:38).

pim, ⅔ of a shekel (R.S.V. I Sam. 13:21).

pine, an evergreen tree, possibly the cypress, used to ceil Solomon's Temple (II Chron. 3:5). It is mentioned as growing in the Lebanon (Isa. 60:13). Pine may be elm or plane.

pins used in early O.T. times as pegs for anchoring tent fabric to the ground were of wood (Judg. 4:21 f., 5:26). Jael's tent pins were not "nails" (A.V.); metal did not come into general use in Palestine until David's time (c. 1000–961 B.C.). The "brass" pins used in the construction of the Tabernacle might more accurately be called "wooden pegs" (Ex. 27:19, 35:18; Num. 3:37). The "crisping pin" of Isa. 3:22 (A.V.) was a 16th century English accessory of vain girls rather than an article used by the "daughters of Zion." The "satchels" of A.S.V. and "purses" of Moffatt are other translation efforts.

pipe. See MUSIC.

Piram (pī′răm), King of Jarmuth, was one of five rulers slain and hanged on trees by Joshua after they had hidden in a cave near Makkedah (Josh. 10:3, 16–27).

Pirathon (pĭr′ȧ-thŏn), the home of Abdon (Judg. 12:13, 15) and of Benaiah (II Sam. 23:30), in the hill country of Ephraim (I Chron. 11:31, 27:14). Greek Pharathom (I Macc. 9:50). Identified with Fer'ata, 5 m. SW. of Shechem.

Pisgah, Mt., (Râs es-Siyâghah), sometimes called "the Pisgah" ("the Pisgah plateau," Moff. Num. 21:20), a headland (Deut. 3:27) of the Abarim range in Jordan (ancient land of Moab). It breaks through the ridge and runs out toward the NE. end of the Dead Sea opposite Jericho (Deut. 34:1) (looking toward Jeshimon or "the desert," A. S. V. Num. 21:20). Sometimes Pisgah is referred to as identical with or a part of its neighbor elevation, Mt. Nebo* (Khirbet el-Mekhaiyet); actually it is slightly NW. of Nebo. In ancient times it was prized for its springs (Deut. 4:49). Balak erected seven altars of sacrifice on its slopes (Num. 23:14). From Pisgah the aged Moses had a panoramic view of the Land of Promise, extending from what became Judah, Gilead, Dan, Naphtali and Ephraim "unto the utmost sea," and on the S. the plain of the valley of Jericho ("the city of palm trees") unto Zoar (Deut. 34:1–3). Today the traveler sees the same breathtaking view from the Dead Sea N. to the mountains of Samaria.

Pishon (pī′shŏn), one of the four rivers of Eden* (Gen. 2:11 f.).

Pisidia (pĭ-sĭd′ĭ-ȧ), a region of S. Asia Minor (now Anatolian Turkey) N. of the plains of Pamphylia. Its rugged mountain ranges which here break into the Taurus were peopled with a vigorous, gruff people. In Paul's day Pisidia was part of the Roman province of Galatia*.

326. Pisidia.

Paul and Barnabas passed through Pisidia twice on their First Missionary Journey (Acts 13:14–51, 14:24). Paul's sermon (Acts 13:15–42) at Antioch and their success among the Gentiles merited more substantial results than history indicates. Expelled from Antioch by jealous Jewish opposition, Paul and Barnabas left for Iconium. They "passed through" the Pisidia region, en route to Perga, but little is recorded of this trip. Christianity gained headway in Pisidia, however, in the time of Constantine (A.D. 324–377).

pit, the translation of several words used in the Bible to convey the idea of (1) an excavation dug by man, such as the one into which young Joseph was cast (Gen. 37:20 ff.); (2) a slime pit, or deposit of bitumen, as at the Vale of Siddim (Gen. 14:10); (3) a well or cistern (Jer. 14:3; Luke 14:5); (4) any deep place, such as the pit into which the sheep might fall (Matt. 12:11). "Pit" was also used to mean death, or the grave, or Sheol (Job 33:18; Num. 16:30, 33).

pitch, mineral pitch or asphalt, used to calk the seams of boats; used in Noah's ark (Gen. 6:14), and the bulrush ark built by the mother of Moses (Ex. 2:3). Babylonian builders of the al-'Ubaid period (c. 2900 B.C.) used tiny tesserae of limestone or lapis lazuli set in bitumen to decorate panels and columns of mud or wood for temples; one such column is in the University Museum at Philadelphia. The slime pits in the "vale of Siddim" (Dead Sea) (Gen. 14:10) were probably bitumen pits or wells of liquid pitch. Isaiah (34:9) envisioned "the day of the Lord's vengeance" as turning the land to "burning pitch."

pitcher, a handled pottery* vessel used to carry water (Gen. 24:14; Eccles. 12:6; Mark 14:13); a cruse for oil (I Kings 17:12). Gideon and his men concealed their torches inside pitchers (Judg. 7:16 ff.).

Pithom (pī′thŏm) (from Egypt. Per-Atum or Pi-Atum, "house of Atum," sun god of Heliopolis), an Egyptian store-city traditionally built by Hebrew slave labor (Ex. 1:11), generally taken to refer to the building operations of the 19th Dynasty pharaohs, particularly Sethos I (c. 1318–1304 B.C.) and Ramesses II (c. 1304–1237 B.C.). It was early identified by E. Naville (*The Store City of Pithom and the Route of the Exodus*, rev. 1903) with Tell el-Maskhutah near the E. end of the Wâdī Tumeilat in the E. Delta of Egypt. A.H. Gardiner's identification with Tell er-Retabeh, 8½ m. to the W. (*JEA* 5, 1918, pp. 267 ff.; 10, 1924, pp. 95 f.), has met more general approval. Identification is uncertain, however, and perhaps Heliopolis, the great shrine of Atum (called both Per-Re‘ and Per-Atum, "The House of Re/Atum"), with 19th Dynasty remains, though fragmentary, should be given more careful consideration (see E. P. Uphill, *JNES* 27, 1968, pp. 291 ff.; 28, 1969, pp. 15 ff.). See RAAMSES.

pity, compassion, sympathy, regret for the suffering of an individual or a group; one of the loftiest attributes of God in the O.T. (Ps. 103:13) and the N.T. (Jas. 5:11; I Pet. 3:8). God's pity for His creatures is seen in such narratives as Gen. 12. Time and again He is thought of as extending pity to His chosen Israel (Ex. 15:13; Deut. 13:17; II Kings 13:23); and as urging Israel's enemies to have compassion on them (I Kings 8:50 f.). The corollary of God's pity was the compassion He expected Israel to extend (Ps. 103:13; Isa. 1:17; Mic. 6:8), especially to members of their own race, and to foreigners within their borders (Deut. 7:16; Ex. 22:21; Prov. 19:17, 28:8). Pity and mercy balance the awesome justice of the Almighty.

Jesus exalted pity and compassion for the sinful, the sick, and the individual beaten by life's circumstances (Matt. 18:33, 35). He elevated pity to a dynamic love for the entire world, the love which had led to his Incarnation and the gift of universal redemption (Matt. 5:43–47; Luke 6:27–38).

plagues, the translation of several words (*deber*, *maggefah*, *nega*, etc.) used in Scripture to indicate (a) an affliction or a calamity viewed as a visitation from God (see below, the Ten Plagues of Egypt); (b) a pestilence or epidemic of high mortality (*‘ofalim*), such as afflicted the Philistines after their capture of the Ark (I Sam. 5)—possibly bubonic plague; or the pestilence that followed David's census (II Sam. 24:13–25), or the one threatened in the reign of Judah's King Jehoram (II Chron. 21:14 f.), or the plague of leprosy mentioned frequently in the O.T., e.g., Lev. 13:2–6; (c) any tormenting situation—disease or otherwise—as in Ps. 91:10, "neither shall any plague come nigh thy dwelling."

The first mention of a disease plague visited on an individual and his family is that suffered by Pharaoh because of Sarah, wife of Abraham, who had been represented to the king as Abraham's sister (Gen. 12:17–20). This may be an early record of venereal disease. Plagues were feared as penalties for disobedience to God's laws, as in Ex. 32:35; Lev. 26:21; Num. 11:33 f., 14:37.

The ten plagues of Egypt were the cumulative sequence of events which finally persuaded Pharaoh to let the oppressed Hebrews depart from the Delta, recorded in Ex. 7–12:29. The early J account contained seven plagues: fish and foul water, frogs, flies, cattle murrain, hail, locusts, and death of the first-born. All the plagues are consistent with their Egyptian setting, but their rapid and cumulative succession, mounting to a climax in the death of Egypt's first-born (Ex. 12:29 f.), betokened the operation of miraculous forces. Sometimes God is shown as directly effecting the plague (Ex. 9:6, 12:29); sometimes Aaron at the command of Moses is the agent (Ex. 7:9 f., 20, 8:12 f.); again, Moses himself calls down the plague (Ex. 7:14–18, 9:8, 22 f.).

The role played by Moses' rod to summon and to banish the plagues suggests that prayer—symbolized by the rod—is always suitable when people desire God's help in restoring the kindly processes of His universe.

The ten Plagues of the Exodus narratives are as follows:

(1) The Nile waters are turned to blood (Heb., *dam*): Ex. 7:14–25. Abyssinian red soil comes down the Nile as it rises to flood, and makes the stream appear very red—a situation associated by Egyptians with a period of curse.

(2) Frogs (*tzefarde‘a*): Ex. 8:1–14. Frogs breed as flood water recedes. Birds such as the ibex usually keep them in check, but in this instance the frogs kept on multiplying.

(3) Lice (or gnats or mosquitoes) (*kinnim*): Ex. 8:16–19. Swarms of these pests attack men and beasts in the fields of Egypt.

(4) Flies (or dog flies) (*‘arob*), possibly the tsetse fly (Ex. 8:20–32).

(5) Cattle murrain (*deber*): Ex. 9:1–7, spread by decomposing bodies of frogs, from which bacteria were carried by flies.

(6) Boils (*shehin*): Ex. 9:8–12, on man and beast, "plague-boils," which in Egypt often cause great mortality.

(7) Hail (*barad*): Ex. 9:18–35, a rare occurrence in Egypt.

(8) Locusts* (*‘arbeh*): Ex. 10:1–20, always a bane of the Middle East.

(9) Darkness (*hoshek*): Ex. 10:21–29, such as occurs when the blighting SW. wind (*hamsin*) burns and blinds with dust.

(10) Death of the Egyptian first-born (*makkath bechoroth*): (Ex. 11:1–8, 12:29–42), the climax of all the other plagues.

Sources J, E, and P all believe God's miraculous power caused the plagues, but the oldest source, J, is less emphatic in stressing the miraculous. In P and E the miraculous interest increases, and the text introduces Aaron's rod (P) or Moses' (E). P stresses even more than E the wonder of the supernatural. Whatever degree of the miraculous is expressed, all the writers make it clear that Moses used these events when his people were trying to free themselves from Pharaoh to show that Yahweh was leading them toward a new destiny. Some critics put the plagues in two categories: (1) miracles contrary to nature, like those directed only to Pharaoh (Ex. 7:9); and (2) natural occurrences which took on a supernatural function through their timeliness, severity, and widespread effect on the Egyptians.

Later O.T. mention of the plagues of Egypt is made in Deut. 28:60; I Sam. 4:8; Ps. 78:44–51, 105:28–36, 135:8 f. (Cf. the "last seven plagues," Rev. 15:6, 8, 21:9—"seven" being a symbolic number—see NUMBERS.)

Ever since the plagues led to Israel's escape their story has been repeated in the Haggadah read at every Passover Seder.

N.T. records of the healing ministry of Jesus refer to people who were healed of their "plagues" (Mark 3:10, 5:29, 34; Luke 7:21) in the sense of diseases or infirmities which tormented them, like the woman in Mark 5:29, 34—mental disorder, hemorrhage, dysentery, typhus, or cholera, etc.

plain, cities of the, See CITIES; PHILISTIA. Also individual entries: ASHDOD; ASHKELON; EKRON; GATH; GAZA. Also PLAINS.

plains, level stretches of terrain, suitable for chariot warfare, which were often a decisive factor in Palestine's history.

The plains are flanked by lofty mountains, like the Lebanons, walling in the high Beka'a plain (Coele Syria); or they lie within lower ranges, e.g., the highlands of Judaea, Samaria, Galilee, and Trans-Jordan. Most conspicuous was the long coastal or Maritime Plain along the Mediterranean's eastern seaboard, from the River of Egypt to Cilicia. The most fertile part of the Maritime Plain comprised the old Philistine (see PHILISTIA) plain stretching from S. of Gaza to S. of the Carmel headland. The strip between Joppa and S. of Haifa was known in Biblical times and later as the Plain of Sharon*. N. of Haifa the coastal plain becomes the Plain of Accho (Acre), dotted with important ancient towns. The sea plain extends N. into old Phoenicia (now the Republic of Lebanon), where the shore, always too narrow for agriculture, favored the maritime enterprises of the Phoenicians.

The most conspicuous transverse plain of Palestine is the vast, fertile Plain of Esdraelon* or Valley of Jezreel stretching NE.-SW. from Mt. Carmel, S. of Mt. Gilboa, N. of the highlands of Samaria. It drops down into the deep Jordan Valley. In the Plain of Esdraelon, crossed in early Biblical times by caravan routes from the Plain of Sharon, E. from the Sea, W. from E. Palestine, S. from Galilee and N. from Samaria and Judaea, there were such cities as Megiddo and Taanach in the W. and the powerful fortress Beth-shan in the E. commanding the Jordan Valley. For thousands of years farmers and armies have contended for possession of this plain of Armageddon. The Shephelah ("lowland"), "low plains" (A.V. I Chron. 27:28, A.S.V. "lowland") is not a plain but a district of low hills between the mountains of Judaea and the Maritime Plain.

Conspicuous in the heart of Samaria is the Plain of Shechem, guarded by the twin mounts, Ebal and Gerizim. At a central point in this plain is Jacob's Well at Sychar (John 4:5 ff.). Through the plain roads run N. to Beth-shan and S. to Jerusalem. The Plain of Dothan in the Joseph narrative (Gen. 37:17) lies in Samaria's highlands N. of Shechem, and a short distance S. of the Plain of Esdraelon along the main N.-S. highway to Jerusalem. The pleasant plains of Galilee (Gennesaret), from which Jesus drew many followers, are a short distance N. of Nazareth and along the NW. shores of the Sea of Galilee in a region of intensive cultivation. (See GALILEE, illus. 162.)

The Jordan plains, once evidently "well-watered" (Gen. 13:10), appear at various points in the long, hot, wilderness-lined valley which extends from Mount Lebanon to the Gulf of Aqabah at the head of the Red Sea. The plain "of the valley of Jericho" (Deut. 34:3) has been inhabited and tilled since prehistoric times. The cities of the plain, Sodom, Gomorrah, Zeboiim, and Bela or Zoar (Gen. 13:12), were situated near the now almost uninhabitable Dead Sea plain. The Arabah ("plain" A.V. Deut. 2:8, 3:17) is so translated in the A.S.V.

The Plains of Trans-Jordan are high plateaus watered by streams flowing into the Jordan, e.g., the Zered, the Jabbok, the Arnon, and the Yarmuk. The plains of Moab, of Gilead (where Israel camped before crossing the Jordan, Num. 22:1), and of Ammon were small in comparison to the adjacent areas of rugged highland. In the plain of Madeba (Medeba), which was part of Israel's inheritance E. of Jordan, there flourished in Roman and early Christian times a city, lately investigated by archaeologists.

Most of flat, muddy Babylonia was a plain. Its capital was in "the plain of Shinar" (Gen. 11:2, cf. Dan. 3:1). Many rich cities, of which much is now known, flourished here in early millennia, e.g., Ur, Nippur, Erech, Kish, and Eridu.

Sometimes in the Bible "plain" is used of a vale or a meadow, e.g., Abelcheramin ("meadow of the vineyards") (A.S.V. Judg. 11:33).

plaister (plās'tẽr), archaic variant of "plaster" (A.V. Lev. 14:42).

plane, a tree of uncertain identity, mentioned in A.S.V. and R.S.V. Gen. 30:37, Ezek. 31:8; the A.V. calls it "chestnut."

play. See GAMES.

pledges, personal property offered as security for payment of a debt, because loans on usury to fellow Israelites were forbidden (Ex. 22:25; Lev. 25:35–37). Often the pledge was a commonplace object in the borrower's house, which might not be entered by the creditor. If the pledge was the man's cloak, it was to be returned by sunset, as it might be his only bed covering (Ex. 22:26 f.; cf. Amos 2:8). The debtor's millstone could not be taken as a pledge, for this might be his only means of support (Deut. 24:6). Another humane law forbade taking a widow's clothing for a pledge (v. 17). The Sabbatical (7th) year provided for the return of articles long kept as pledges. The abuse of the pledge, and later of the usury system, was denounced by Israel's prophets (Amos 2:8; Ezek. 18:12, 33:15; cf. Prov. 20:16, 27:13). The word "pledge" in I Sam. 17:18 refers to security offered ("ten cheeses" in this case) for the safety of men in an armed camp. Pledges were demanded by invading kings, like the two thousand horses pledged to Sennacherib of Assyria by Hezekiah of Judah (II Kings 18:23; Isa. 36:8).

Pleiades (plē'yȧ-dēz), a constellation mentioned in Job 9:9, 38:31. Such allusions indicate the interests and knowledge of the Wisdom writer (cf. Job 38:32, "Arcturus"; Amos 5:8, "Orion"). See ORION, illus. 304.

plow, an agricultural implement used to turn and furrow the soil. In primitive Palestine it was merely a forked bough to which a piece of sharp metal was attached. In the days of Saul and Jonathan, when the Philistines monopolized iron, Hebrew farmers had to take the metal shares on their homemade plows to their enemies to be sharpened (I Sam. 13:20.; cf. "swords into plowshares," Isa. 2:4; Joel 3:10; Mic. 4:3). David made it possible for Hebrew farmers to buy metal shares in town market places. The shares had metal points shaped like an arrow or a spear, and a socket in which the wooden part of the plow was fastened by a peg or a nail; the opposite end of the wood was fastened to the yoke*. The primitive Palestinian plow did not turn up the sod, but merely scratched the surface. It is remarkable that by such methods the small land supported so many for so long. In some parts of Palestine and Egypt, whence Palestinians derived it, the primitive plow is still used. It is so light that a farmer can carry it on his shoulders.

The plowing season opens in the middle of October and continues until mid-April, though plowmen may be seen in the hot Jordan Valley even in July. Sometimes in Biblical Palestine the seed was plowed in after it was sowed; again, it was sowed after the land had been plowed. Tilling the sunbaked soil of the Middle East is so arduous that the plowman may be tempted to give up the task; hence the words of Jesus, "No one who puts his hand to the plow and looks back is fit for the kingdom of God" (R.S.V. Luke 9:62). The plowman guided the plow with his left hand, keeping his right one free to apply the sharp ox goad. The sons of foreigners were often allotted the work of plowing (Isa. 61:5); sluggards would not attempt the task (Prov. 20:4). The allusion of I Kings 19:19 to Elisha plowing in the hot Jordan Valley with a group of plowmen "with twelve yoke of oxen before him, and he with the twelfth" is an index of the prophet's vigor. (See FARMING, illus. 142.)

plumb line, a cord to which a plummet, a lump of metal (or stone in ancient times) is attached at one end, used by masons to test the perpendicularity of a wall, etc. Amos had a vision of the Lord, standing with a plumb line in His hand (II Kings 21:13; Amos 7:7–9) to measure Israel. Cf. Zech. 4:10, where the plummet symbolizes the stone used to test integrity.

poetry, the art of expressing in oral or written metrical form lofty and far-visioned thoughts fraught with emotion, exaltation, and imagination. Poetry became part of the written literature of the Hebrew people at a very early date (see chart below). Poems expressing moments of joy, such as the celebrating of a marriage, the naming of a son, the digging of a well, or the winning of martial victory, or those lamenting a fallen hero or a moral defeat, found their way into the O.T. Their verse form preserved them relatively unaltered and made them easier to remember than prose.

The three greatest poetic masterpieces of the O.T. are considered by many to be Judg. 5 (the Song or Ode of Deborah*), the oldest poem of this length in the Bible, written probably contemporaneously or soon after the events it celebrates (c. 1125 B.C.); II Sam. 1:19–27 (David's lament over Saul and Jonathan); and Nah. 1:10–3:19 (the Burden of Nineveh).

(1) *Old Testament Poetry.*—A large part of the O.T. is written in poetry—as much as one third, if we take the view of Edgar J. Goodspeed. In addition to the occasional poetic pieces set among prose passages, entire books, such as Job, Psalms, Proverbs, the Song of Solomon, and Lamentations, are poetry, and also a large part of Isaiah, Jeremiah, and the Minor Prophets*. The oldest books of the O.T., Amos and Hosea, may be regarded as poetry. Several of the Apocryphal books are in poetry. Only in the modern translations of the English Bible and in the original texts does the poetry appear as such.

Jerome (c. A.D. 400), translator of the O.T. from Heb. to Lat. (the Vulgate), was one of the first scholars to interest himself in the meter and style of Hebrew poetry.

Dates of poems. Poetry in the Pentateuch was composed in the centuries between c. 1200 and 400 B.C. Robert H. Pfeiffer in *An Introduction to the Old Testament* (Harper & Brothers), gives a chronological list of much of the poetry in the O.T., though not attempting too exhaustive a list (only a selection of poems later than 600 B.C. are included). Some scholars may differ with his suggested dates, but his list is illuminating. The following chart is based on his longer date list for the various types of O.T. literature (pp. 21–23).

Date	*Subject Matter*	*References*
Before 1200 B.C.	Lamech's sword speech	Gen. 4:23 f.
	Song of Miriam (earliest O.T. hymn to God)	Ex. 15:21
	Blessing of Moses	Num. 10:35 f. (?)

Date	Subject Matter	References
	Concerning the Lord's leadership at the Red Sea	Num. 21:14 f. (?)
	Song of the Well	Num. 21:17 f.
	A Victory of Israel	Num.21:27–30
1200–1000 B.C.	Noah's Curse	Gen. 9:25–27
	Joshua's Victory Shout	Josh. 10:12b–13a
	Song of Deborah	Judg. 5
	Samson's Riddle	Judg.14:14,18
	Samson on Ass's Jawbone	Judg. 15:16
	Women's Boast about David	I Sam. 18:7 = 21:11b =29:5
	David's Lament over Saul and Jonathan	II Sam. 1:18–27
	David's Lament over Abner	II Sam. 3:33 f.
1000–900 B.C.	Blessing of Jacob (possibly other Patriarchal blessings)	Gen. 49; Gen. *passim*
	Balaam's Prophecy	Num. 24:3–9 15–19
	Revolt of Sheba	II Sam. 20:1
	Solomon at the Temple Dedication	I Kings 8:12 f.
	A Psalm of David	Ps. 24:7–10
	The Book of Jashar (The Book of Song)	Ref. II Sam. 1:18
	The Book of the Wars of the Lord	Num. 21:27–30 omitting "to Sihon, king of the Amorites"
900–722 B.C. (in Northern Kingdom)	Baalam to Barak	Num. 23:7–10, 18–24
	Moses blesses tribes	Deut. 33
	Song celebrating king's marriage	Ps. 45
700–600 B.C.	Nahum's Ode	Nah. 1:10 ff.
	Lord's utterance, sedition of Miriam and Aaron	Num. 12:6–8
600–500 B.C.	Poetry in	Lamentations; some Psalms; parts of Proverbs
500–400 B.C.	Song of Moses	Deut. 32
	Moses' Song	Ex. 15:1–18
	Poetry in	Some Psalms; parts of Proverbs
400–300 B.C.	Poetry in	Many Psalms and much of Proverbs
	Speeches	Job 32–37
	Vision of Nahum	Nah. 1:1–9
	Habakkuk's prayer	Hab. 3
	Hannah's song	I Sam. 2:1–10
300–200 B.C.	Poetry in	Song of Solomon; portions of Psalms and Proverbs
200–100 B.C.	Maccabean Psalms	44, 74, 79, 83, etc.
	Hasmonaean Psalms	2, 110, etc.
	Final edition of Psalter	

Types of Poetry.—(a) Lyric. Early forms were secular, and were composed anonymously for some specific occasion, like a marriage (Ps. 45); a birth (Gen. 35:17; I Sam. 4:20); a victory (Gen. 4:23 f.; Ex. 15:21); or digging a new well (Num. 21:17 f.). Taunt songs were also sung (II Kings 2:23). The early lyrics in Genesis were sung to the accompaniment of stringed instruments, before they were incorporated into the S, J, and E documents. The compilers of these sources* themselves frequently used spontaneous rhythm or verse. Later forms included lyrics strictly religious in tone, like the Psalms*. This book, containing the great devotional poetry of the O.T., has sometimes been called "the poetry of the priests," because priests or Levites wrote some of it, and made all of it their own by using it in the Temple ritual. Some Psalms are alphabetical acrostics, i.e., the first line begins with the first letter of the Heb. alphabet, the next with the second, and so on, until all the 22 letters have been used. Examples of this form are Ps. 9, 10, 25, 34, 37, 111, 112, 119, 145. More complicated forms of acrostic poems can also be identified.

Lyric laments and dirges of great beauty are frequent in Scripture, like David's over Saul and Jonathan (II Sam. 1:19–27); and over Absalom (II Sam. 19:1). In prophetic poems laments appear, e.g., Ps. 22, 79, 83; Amos 5:1, 2; Micah 1:10–14; Jer. 9:17–21. The Book of Lamentations consists of four poetic dirges, vividly representing the tragic experiences of the Hebrews during the destruction of their nation and of their capital in 587 B.C.

(b) "Prophetic rhetoric," a form of poetry that alternates with prose in the prophetic books, was especially adapted to the prophets' impassioned protests. The scourges of invading armies were a fruitful theme for poetic utterances, like Nahum's description of the fall of Nineveh (612 B.C.).

(c) Didactic poetry appeals persuasively to the emotions, as in Proverbs, Ecclesiastes, and Job. Many consider Job to be the greatest poem in the O.T., and one of the greatest in literature. It includes lyric, didactic, and dramatic poetry, though in the strict sense of the term neither Job nor any other O.T. book is a drama, since it was not intended to be acted on a stage. Its dialogue, however, has enabled it to be adapted as drama.

The Hebrews did not create epic poems, as did their Canaanite and Babylonian neighbors, or as Sumerians had done in very ancient times.

The outstanding *characteristics of Hebrew poetry* are:

(a) *Emotional content* capable of arousing emotion in the hearer or the reader.

(b) *Imaginative* and often lyric quality, in contrast to the literalism of factual narratives.

(c) *Rhythm*, the measured flow of sounds. Some O.T. passages are rhythmic without being in exact meter. Occasionally the rhythm is accentuated by the use of *rhyme*, i.e., the use of final syllables (in lines) having a correspondence in sound. Although rhyme is not characteristic of Hebrew poetry, and is sometimes used as a play on words, it does occasionally appear in the Heb. text, as in Gen. 12:1–3; Judg. 16:23 f. (a "Philistine poem"); Ps. 105; Isa. 27:3–5.

Hebrew verse has two equal parts divided by accents into two, three, or four feet; the usual Hebrew verse has four accents in each half line (4:4). Pfeiffer suggests that this form sounds like the meter used by Coleridge:

"The lovely lady, Christabel,
Whom her father loves so well,
What makes her in the wood so late,
A furlong from the castle gate?"

Hebrew rhythms are sprightly because they usually combine the iambic foot (consisting of one accented and one unaccented syllable) with the anapest (two unaccented followed by one accented syllable). Much Hebrew poetry is in hexameters; sometimes octameters are used, with 4:4 beats, or 3:2:3 (Ps. 6:7), or 3:3:2 (Ps. 27:11). A 4:4 meter is frequent in the prophets; Job is in 3:3; the prevalent measure of Jeremiah is 3:2; some O.T. poems are in 2:2 meter.

The spontaneity of Hebrew poetry precludes too exact an analysis of its forms.

(d) *Parallelism*, a dominant characteristic of Hebrew poetry, is achieved:

By repeating an idea in successive synonymous lines—

"Examine me, O Jehovah, and prove me;
Try my heart and my mind"
(A.S.V. Ps. 26:2)

By presenting the same notion in antithetical form—

"Many sorrows shall be to the wicked,
But he that trusteth in Jehovah, lovingkindness shall compass him about" (A.S.V. Ps. 32:10)

By using, in a stairlike fashion, "ascending phrases" which repeat with "incremental repetition" the thought of the first line at the beginning of the second—

"Till thy people pass over, O Jehovah,
Till thy people pass over that thou hast purchased" (A.S.V. Ex. 15:16)

By phrasing in parallel form two lines, the second of which contains a thought different from the first, but supplementary to it—

"Answer not a fool according to his folly,
Lest thou also be like unto him"
(A.S.V. Prov. 26:4)

By stating a comparison in parallel form, as:

"As coals are to hot embers, and wood to fire,
So is a contentious man to inflame strife" (A.S.V. Prov. 26:21).

Sometimes the parallel lines occur in pairs, distichs; again, in 3-line groups. Parallelism gives a pleasing sense of balance and greatly facilitates memorization.

(e) The use of refrains seems to indicate that Hebrew poetry was arranged in strophes or stanzas, in the manner of Babylonian and Egyptian poems; these varied from four lines to eight or twelve.

Poetry from sources outside Israel has been identified in the O.T., as in the Moabite elegy added to Isaiah 1:16 f., and Ps. 104, which has much in common with Akhenaton's Hymn to Aton. A Philistine poem seems to be preserved in Judg. 16:23, as Pfeiffer points out (p. 25, *Introduction to the Old Testament*).

(2) *Poetry in the New Testament.*—Most of the poetry in the Bible is in the O.T.; the Gk. N.T. has little poetry, except quoted poetical matter from previous writings, and songs which became incorporated into the hymns and liturgy of the early Church—e.g., the *Magnificat* (Luke 1:46b–55); the *Benedictus* (Luke 1:68–79); the *Gloria in Excelsis* (Luke 2:14); the *Nunc Dimittis* (Luke 2:29–32). Some scholars consider as poetic liturgy such passages as Eph. 5:14; I Tim. 1:17, 3:16, 6:16; II Tim. 4:18.

Polyglot, the Complutensian. See TEXT.

polygamy. See ADULTERY; FAMILY; FORNICATION; MARRIAGE.

polytheism, the belief in many gods, and the worship and service of more than one of them. Most primitive people are polytheistic, because of their natural tendency to assign a separate power or spirit to the various aspects of nature, and to the various forms of their own experience. Thus there will be a god of birth, a god of marriage, a god of fire, a god of the crops, a god of disease, a god of the woods, and so on. The ability to generalize these different powers or spirits into forms of the activity of one and the same universal Power or Spirit bespeaks an advanced stage of culture. It has sometimes been accomplished philosophically before it became characteristic of religion. There were, for example, both Greek and Roman philosophers who explained everything by reference to a single creative Power, while themselves still participating in the current religious practice which assumed many gods.

The Hebrew people, to whom chiefly mankind owes the belief in one God, accounted for their belief not as the result of human speculation, but as due to a revelation in special ways by God Himself. The Semitic ancestors of the Hebrew people were undoubtedly polytheists. The various nations with whom the Hebrew people were in contact during their historical development were all polytheistic. In such books of the O.T. as Judges (2:11 f.), I and II Samuel and I and II Kings we see how the traditional belief of Israel in Yahweh (Jehovah) was continually endangered by contact with the polytheistic beliefs of their idolatrous neighbors. Even

David, when he fled into Philistia to escape the vengeance of Saul, was supposed to serve Philistine gods while he remained in Philistine territory (I Sam. 26:17–19). Solomon, who had built the great Temple for the worship of Yahweh the God of Israel, afterward built within the Temple area altars to other gods, to provide appropriate worship for his numerous wives who had come from other lands; indeed, in his old age he even worshipped at these foreign altars himself (I Kings 11:1–8).

Later, when Jeroboam, an Ephraimite, led a revolt against Rehoboam, Solomon's son and successor, he built rival shrines to Jerusalem in northern territory, at Bethel and at Dan—to destroy the allegiance of the people to the Temple at Jerusalem. The two "golden calves" which he set up were intended to be symbols of Yahweh, but for many people the worship of them seemed pure idolatry, and it at least tended to break down the distinction between Israel's religion and the polytheism of her neighbors (I Kings 12:25–33; cf. Ex. 32:1–14). Open conflict finally broke out when Jezebel (and Ahab) introduced the worship of her own god, Baal-Melkart, into Israel (I Kings 16:30 ff.). This was the beginning of the great struggle between the prophets who were loyal to Yahweh and the forces which tended to polytheism. The temptation to polytheism was by no means limited to the Northern Kingdom, but extended into the Southern Kingdom of Judah which had remained loyal to the house of David. (For a graphic account of the wicked King Manasseh's idolatries, see II Kings 22:1–23:25.) Amos*, the first of "the writing prophets," proclaimed uncompromising monotheism*. The meaning of his first chapter is that Yahweh was the real God of all Israel's neighbors, even though they knew it not: there were no "other" gods (see 4:12, f. 5:4–9, 9:5–7; cf. Ex. 20:1–6, 34:10–17). The definitive repudiation of polytheism is to be found in Deuteronomy (4:35, 6:4 f.) and II Isaiah (Isa. 45:22 f.). See GOD; MONOTHEISM; WORSHIP. E. L./R. C. D.

pomegranate, *Punica granatum*, one of the favorite and most beautiful of Palestinian and Egyptian fruits. It was one of the samples brought from Eschol by Israel's spies (Num. 13:23). Its bright green leaves and its symmetrical fruit, which resembles rose-red, hard-skinned oranges, made it a popular symbol in Jewish life. Its many seeds provide gushing red juice, bitter but satisfying (Num. 20:5), and prized for medicine and beverages. Pomegranates grow abundantly near Cana of Galilee, and must have refreshed Jesus on his hot walks.

Hebrews saw in the many-seeded pomegranate a symbol of rain and fertility. Its abundant seeds denoted many children. In art the pomegranate was to Palestine what the lotus and papyrus were to Egypt. Two hundred of them (I Kings 7:20; cf. Jer. 52:22 f.) are said to have adorned the two free-standing pillars Jachin* and Boaz in the Jerusalem Temple. Blue, purple, and scarlet pomegranates alternated with bells to form the decorative motif on the high priest's robe (Ex. 39:24 ff.). Pomegranates were stamped on several Maccabean coins, the best depiction being on the shekel, which showed a half-budding stage, with blossom.

327. Pomegranate.

Pontius (pŏn′shŭs) **Pilate.** See PILATE, PONTIUS.

Pontus (L., from Gk. *Pontos*, "the sea"), a rugged region of NE. Asia Minor (now Anatolian Turkey) stretching along the Black Sea (*Pontus Euxinus*). Its people were as rough as their land. A dynasty of kings called Mithridates ruled from c. 337 to 63 B.C. In N.T. times the Pontus was a Roman province. In 63 B.C. it was united with Bithynia under proconsular legates, of which the historian Pliny was one. Jews from that region were in Jerusalem at Pentecost (Acts 2:9). Though the Pontus was not Christianized under Paul's influence, it became a strong Christian center, to whose members, along with others, I Peter was addressed. Aquila, husband of Prisca, and fellow worker of Paul, was a Jew of Pontus. A 2d-century shipmaster of Pontus, Marcion, founded an early sect in an effort to reform Christianity by freeing it from its Hebrew background.

pool. See CISTERNS; RESERVOIR; "SOLOMON'S POOLS"; WATER.

poor, the. (1) People lacking minimum economic means did not constitute a social problem in the nomadic and early agricultural periods of Israel's experience. Few lacked simple food, garments, and shelter, when families were organized into clans and tribes under patriarchal sheikhs, who were often just and capable. When Israel, following Canaanite and other neighbors' patterns, settled down in towns and villages, poverty made itself felt, as it always has done in urban communities. Poverty was usually due to calamities, e.g., disturbance of the peace through feud or invasion (Judg. 10:6–17); illness (Num. 16:47–49); failure of crops, due to invasions of locusts or other pests (Ex. 10:4–6; Ps. 105:34 f.; Joel 1:4). Other causes of poverty included: enslavement for *corvée* (Ex. 1:13 f.; Jer. 22:13); oppression by greedy neighbors (II Sam. 12:1–15); slothfulness (Prov. 14:23 f., 20:13), in contrast to the industry of self-supporting toilers (Prov. 28:19), and to the constant creative labors of the Lord (John 5:17); extravagant standards of living (Prov. 21:17, 24:33 f.); and foolhardiness (Prov. 13:18). Israel's early laws contained provisions for ameliorating the condition of the poor by community allotments from vintage and harvests (Lev. 19:9 f., 25:8 ff.); by individual gifts; by exempting the poor man from usury (Ex. 22:25–27); by paying wages promptly (Deut. 24:14 f.); by making Jubilee Year legislation which automatically returned individual property at the end of 50 years (Lev. 25:8 ff.); by including the poor and strangers (foreigners) in joyous community festivals (Deut. 16:11, 14; Esther 9:22). The virtues of the compassionate man were emphasized (Ps. 41:1; Prov. 14:21, 31, 22:22, 29:7). The gross social injustice experienced by the poor of Israel's towns during the later Monarchy and the Divided Kingdom drew stinging rebukes from the prophets (Isa. 1:23, 3:14, 32:7; Amos 2:6, 4:1, 6:1 ff.; Mic. 2:1 ff.).

At the time of the Exile* many Jewish families lost their entire wealth. Some established themselves in prosperous enterprises in Babylon and remained there even after the edict of Cyrus authorized their return to Palestine. Others returned and claimed their ancestral properties, but were poor during the period of economic readjustment. Artisans in Galilee usually lived at the subsistence level, e.g., Joseph and Mary. Levites were poor, but accepted their lot as part of the spiritual guerdon of their calling. Ever since Josiah's reforms (622 B.C.), which centralized worship at Jerusalem, priests at local shrines had been poor. The Jerusalem priests, together with Pharisees and tax-collecting publicans, became rich. In Hellenistic times the expansions which followed the conquests of Alexander the Great built up family fortunes among the Jews of Antioch, Alexandria, and other centers. Affluence continued in Maccabean times.

(2) Jesus revealed a deep and loving concern for the poor (Luke 14:13, 21, 18:22). As a boy in the Nazareth synagogue he learned Israel's traditions of charity. As a man he addressed himself especially to the poor (Matt. 11:5). In his parable of Luke 7:41 ff. he stressed mercy for those who had been oppressed for their debts. (Cf. his parable of Dives and Lazarus, Luke 16:19–31.) He commended the generosity of the poor when he saw a widow cast her tiny contribution into the Temple offering horn; and rebuked the men who paraded their giving in conspicuous places (Matt. 6:1–4; cf. Luke 6:20, 24). He chided the false generosity of Judas, who regretted that the costly ointment and alabaster cruse with which Jesus had been honored had not been sold and "given to the poor," who, as Jesus said, would be with them always (Matt. 26:11).

The Apostolic Church, inspired by Christ's example and its ancient heritage of charity (John 13:29), was conscientious about its poor at Jerusalem and elsewhere; those who had means shared with those who had none (Acts 4:34 ff.; II Cor. 9:6–8; Phil. 4:16). Deacons ("the Seven") were appointed to administer financial relief to widows and other poor; their help was not confined to those of the Way.

The Epistle of James condemns giving an inferior seat to the poor worshipper wearing "vile raiment," and "a good place" to the rich man attired in gay garments and adorned with a gold ring (2:2 f., 5 ff.).

(3) The "poor" in Scripture sometimes means those who for any reason are miserable and unhappy, as in Isa. 61:1. When Jesus blessed the "poor in spirit" (Matt. 5:3) he may have been thinking of those who, for whatever reason, are depressed and low in spirit; or of the humble but invincible meek whose virile inner strength is the true hope of a self-seeking world; or of those who are literally "poor" (see Luke 6:20) and who, unlike the rich, "feel their spiritual need" (Goodspeed), and "come like children to the book of life" (Buttrick). (Cf. II Cor. 8:9.)

poplar, a tree of uncertain identity mentioned in Gen. 30:37; Hos. 4:13. Possibly the storax.

porch. (1) A portion of the house in Biblical times, possibly its forecourt or central court, or an area on its flat roof adjacent to an upper room (Judg. 3:23; Mark 14:68). (2) A colonnaded space sheltering pedestrians from sun and rain, as at the Pool of Bethesda, with its five porches (John 5:2); and the arcaded passages of the Temple court (Ezek. 41:15); or the colonnaded passageways of the stoa* at Corinth and Athens. (3) For Solomon's Porch, see TEMPLE.

Porcius (pôr′shĭ-ŭs) **Festus.** See FESTUS, PORCIUS.

porter. (1) The keeper of a city gate (II Sam. 18:26; II Kings 7:10) or of a house (Mark 13:34, cf. Acts 12:13); or of a sheepfold (John 10:3). (2) A doorkeeper in the Temple (I Chron. 9:22, 23:5; II Chron. 23:4). Ezra and Nehemiah make a distinction between the numerous doorkeepers of the post-Davidic Temple and the Levites (Ezra 2:41 ff.; Neh. 7:44 ff.). The Chronicler calls them Levites (I Chron. 23:1 ff.).

post. (1) A stone or wood upright forming part of a door (see DOORS). The posts were specially significant, for to them were attached the *mezuzah* (Deut. 11:20), a parchment inscribed with the words of Deut. 6:4–9 and 11:13–21. Temple doorposts were of olive wood (I Kings 6:33). (2) A swift messenger or courier carrying urgent business or royal messages (II Chron. 30:6, 10; Esther 3:13). Sometimes the post preceded a great personage (cf. Matt. 11:10).

Potiphar (pŏt′ĭ-fẽr) (possibly Egypt. *Petep-re*, "gift of Re"), the chief of Pharaoh's bodyguard, who bought Joseph from the Midianites and placed him in charge of his household. Later, influenced by his wife's false accusations, he put Joseph in prison (Gen. 37:36; 39:1).

Potipherah (pō-tĭf′ẽr-*ȧ*) (A.S.V. Potiphera, Egypt., "given by the sun god"), the father of Joseph's wife Asenath (Gen. 41:45, 50), probably the powerful head of the sacred college of the sun god Re, in the Delta city of On* (Heliopolis), and therefore prominent in Egyptian life.

potsherd. See POTTERY.

pottage, a thick vegetable soup, made with or without meat, similar to the Italian *minestrone*. It was the dish exchanged by Esau for his birthright (Gen. 25:29 f., 34). Eaten with bread (v. 34), it made a satisfying meal.

potter. See POTTERY.

potter's field, a parcel of ground (Acts 1:19 Aceldama*) on the S. slope of the Hinnom* Valley, near Jerusalem, bought by the chief priests with the 30 pieces of silver cast at their feet by the remorseful Judas after his betrayal of Jesus. This "blood money" secured what became Jerusalem's "potter's field, to bury strangers in" (Matt. 27:6 f.). Peter's account (Acts 1:18 f.) varies in making Judas himself the buyer, and suggesting that Judas died not by hanging, but by falling headlong in the field. In many ancient cities, like Athens and Corinth, the fields from which potters (see POTTERY) derived clay for their vessels are at the edge of occupied areas. It was natural that the poor should be buried in such places.

potter's wheel. See POTTERY.

pottery, dishes and vessels made of clay and other earthy materials. The man who fashioned clay utensils for families, finer wares for palace and ceremonial use, and sundry other clay products, was known as a potter (Heb. *yotsēr*); the articles he made were pottery. His art and technology were ceramics (Gk. *kerameikós*).

The potter's craft was one of the oldest in Bible lands, as proved by pre-Flood specimens from Sumer now in the University Museum, Philadelphia. Some of the oldest pottery of Palestine has been found in the Neolithic or Late Stone Age (c. 5500–4000 B.C.) level at Jericho*. The first mention of pottery in Scripture is in connection with David's flight E. of Jordan, when friends brought him "earthen vessels" of grain (II Sam. 17:28). Pottery was an essential product in all Bible lands, and furnished numerous figures of speech, e.g., Ps. 2:9; Isa. 45:9; Jer. 18:4, 6, 19:1–13.

The field of ceramics must here be limited to a discussion of (1) methods of production in the Biblical period; and (2) its unique contribution to archaeology through broken fragments, "potsherds" ("shards"), which help scholars to read the dates of successive occupation levels. To the archaeologist shards are more valuable than gold. Nelson Glueck surveyed 1,500 sites E. of the Jordan and found cartloads of shards from the Bronze Age and other periods on such sites as Tell el-Meqbereh, for example, surviving from Israel's occupation there from about the 13th century B.C. to the 6th; and at Tell el-Maqlub (probably Abel-meholah*, home of Elisha). This pottery will furnish study material for years to come. (See *The River Jordan*, Glueck, The Westminster Press; reports in *BA*; and the Smithsonian Institution, where many of the Trans-Jordan shards are stored.)

(1) *Pottery Production in Biblical Palestine.*—In their nomad period the Israelite Tribes did not halt long enough to build up skill in and equipment for pottery making, nor could they use breakable articles on trek. As is still done today, nomads used skins for water and milk, and only occasionally acquired metal vessels or pottery at the markets through which they passed. When Israel settled down into seminomadic ways in Trans-Jordan and W. Palestine they began to make pottery. Their best pottery was made during the Divided Monarchy, i.e., in the two centuries following c. 922 B.C.

Though no complete potter's studio from Biblical times has yet been excavated in Palestine, at Lachish* in S. Judaea a late Bronze Age ceramist workshop (c. 1500 B.C.) has been found. It contains a stone seat near a limestone pivot on which a simple potter's wheel once turned. Near it were potsherds worn smooth from having been used to shape revolving masses of wet clay, pebbles probably used to burnish vessels, and a sharp piece of stone for incising designs on the pots. One Lachish red bowl found in a tomb of c. 1295–1262 B.C. carries a few words in white ("His righteousness is my support"), believed to be a link between the Sinai script and the Phoenician alphabet on which European alphabets were based. Jeremiah's reference to the potter's house (18:2–4) reflects a fact historically known, that pottery making was often a family industry, whose skills were passed along from father to son (I Chron. 4:23). I Chronicles (4:23) tells of potters "among plants and hedges: there they dwelt" to do the king's work. (See JEREMIAH, illus. 207.)

How pottery was made. Painstaking study of Tell Beit Mirsim (probably Kiriath-sepher, Debir*) has enabled J. L. Kelso and J. P. Thorley to make an accurate report on the technique of Palestinian pottery making. (See their chapter in *The Annual* of the ASOR, Vols. XXI and XXII (1941–1943), and *BA*, Vol. VIII, No. 4, Dec. 1945, to which we are indebted.)

The clay—an earthy substance of varying chemical composition, containing fine sand, gravel, or foreign animal and vegetable matter—was washed and purified in a series of vats on descending levels. The finest clay was secured by a straining of the contents of the lowest vat through cloth. Red clay, i.e., one which after firing turned red from its original gray, green, black, blue, or yellow, was common in Palestine. Clay was weathered by being spread out in warm weather on a hill.

The steps by which a simple pot was made are as follows. The purified and weathered clay was rendered plastic by long treading with the feet (Isa. 41:25) and by mixing it with water. Next the clay was wedged or tossed into the air to drive out the air. Then it was given a final kneading with the potter's hands for several hours, after which it was "thrown" onto the wheel, which was turned counterclockwise by the potter's hand, or by his apprentice (later by kicks with his feet, after the two-wheeled type had come in). As the wheel rotated, the potter shaped his piece by deft movements of his hand (Isa. 64:8; Jer. 18:6; Lam. 4:2; Rom. 9:21), broadening it out, building it up, sometimes adding one layer to another. By thrusting his forearm into the mass of wet clay, he made the hollow space. The "thrown" piece was

328. Pottery. Based on drawings by Robert M. Engburg in *What Mean These Stones?* by Millar Burrows, and other sources.

sun-dried to a leathery consistency, and returned to the wheel for the turner to remove excess clay and improve the surface, or to reinforce the bottom to prevent leaking. Though no turner's tools have yet been found in Palestine (as they have in Greece), it is known that by the Middle Bronze Age (c. 2000–1500 B.C.) the turner's skill had reached its peak. When quantity production was involved, hollow cones of clay in large numbers were shaped on the board and pinched off at the top, later to be finished off into small jugs or jars; larger cones for larger jars and utensils. Bottoms were smoothed. Handles were added, and sometimes bases. Necks were molded, joints sealed, and decoration applied. The paint was applied either before or after the firing in the clay-mud kiln (as tall as a man). Remains of kilns have been excavated from Tell en-Nasbeh, Megiddo, Gezer, etc. (For discussion of the intricate processes of firing, see Kelso and Thorley, pp. 111–119.)

The *potter's wheel* (Heb. pl. *abnayim*) was, and still is, his chief equipment. Before even its simplest form was devised the Stone Age potter had to sit on the ground, building up and hollowing out with his hands a lump of wet clay; or molding it over a previously made pot or basket, and letting the vessel dry in the sun. Later he found he could improve the shape of his pots by turning them around in a hole dug in the earth. Then he discovered how to make a simple potter's wheel by putting a rectangular (later a round) board on a pivot, and turning it with one hand while he molded the wet clay with the other; sometimes he had an apprentice turn the wheel. It was a great day when the potter's wheel was invented. It came into general use in Palestine c. 1900 B.C., though in Egypt it had arrived considerably earlier, at about the beginning of the dynastic period (from c. 3000 B.C.). The wheel revolutionized the pottery industry by increasing production. In Mesopotamia the slow-moving type of wheel was probably used in the prehistoric period. By 3000 B.C., in the Copper Age, workers at Tell Halaf were producing what some have called "the very finest hand-made ceramics in all antiquity." The double-disked foot-power wheel—possibly a Greek improvement—may not have come into Palestine until about the 2d century B.C. This consists of two wheels joined by a shaft which revolves in a stone or hard earthen socket. The potter turned the lower and heavier wheel with his foot, thus causing the upper wheel or table to revolve; both hands were thus free to shape the clay on the upper wheel into the form desired.

Decoration appears on even cheap cooking vessels of Bible times. Sometimes the design was only parallel grooves scratched around the neck or on the handle with sharp stones or flint while the clay was soft. Twisted cords pressed round a wet vase made a pleasing rope design. Knives and combs made zigzag patterns popular in the Bronze Age. Sticks cut with semicircular ends made half-moons. Many potters painted their wares after the first baking, outlining with black or brown their designs of men and women, animals, scenes, circles, squares, keys, and scrolls. "Slip" or clay veneer was sometimes applied before the 2d firing to make patterns on the original base.

Palestinian potters did not glaze, though they burnished (rubbed) the piece with shells, pebbles, or a tool, sometimes pressed against the vessel as it turned on the wheel.

Ancient Egyptians learned to coat their clay pottery with liquid glass, "glaze." Generally they used a brilliant blue, for which they became famous. Sometimes several glazes were combined by firing one on top of another, with very beautiful results. To mix glazes soda, lead, silver, copper, or tin is required. Green tints require oxide of copper and iron; turquoise comes from copper; deep blue from cobalt; and purple from manganese. One of the finest specimens of Egyptian glazing is the brilliant blue scepter of Amenhotep III (c. 1413–1377 B.C.), 5 in. in diameter and 5 ft. high.

Uses of pottery. From heavy, 5-gal. water jars to delicate ointment jars, Palestinian pottery was functional. Popular shapes were made in quantity; styles changed often. Pottery articles used in the house included all sorts of jars and cooking pots, bowls and sop dishes, handleless cups, ladles and dippers; huge storage jars for grain, wine, and oil; lamps (see LAMP)—both the small hand ones, and the several-branched candlesticks (see CANDLESTICK). Clay stoves were portable. Among the objects made from clay were: spindle whorls, crude jewelry, buttons, theater tickets, voting ballots (ostraca*), figurines of gods, and statuettes of rulers and prominent people like the excavated shell-eyed head made c. 7,000 years ago at Jericho. Clay rattles and toys were fashioned—like the eight little horses and ram now housed in the Pittsburgh-Xenia Museum. Even babies' feeding bottles were made of clay. Pottery fragments were also used as writing* materials, as evidenced by the Lachish Letters and countless clay* fragments excavated in Mesopotamia, Syria, and other parts of the Near East. Ceramic tiles were used to decorate public buildings. It was probably a hot clay shard poultice rather than a scraper that Job used when he was afflicted with boils (Job 2:8). Broken bits of shard were used to dip up ashes from a hearth or water from a pit (Isa. 30:14), or they were ground up on a stone threshing floor to make cement. (See BOTTLES, illus. 64.)

The kerameikós, or Potters' Sections.—Pottery-making centers were at the edge of towns, near open fields, where vessels could be dried in the sun and in kilns. The most famous potters' quarters were the *kerameikós* at Athens, which have given the word "ceramics" to the art of clay-made products.

Athens had two *kerameikós* sections: (1) for selling, near the great Stoa of Attalos or shopping section of the agora (market place), where Paul discussed religion with the Greeks of his day; and (2) the manufacturing *kerameikós* on the edge of Athens, on the way to Corinth, near the Dipylon Gate. The use of the potter's field as burial ground by many cities, originated with the Athenian potter's field, where there remain vestiges of thousands of tombs erected through the centuries. These were not only for the poor and "strangers," whose graves at Jerusalem, for example, might be in the "Potter's field" purchased with Judas's 30 pieces of silver by the chief priests (Matt. 27:7); these Greek potter's field tombs were for wealthy Athenians, who could afford elegant stones or urns. Some of the deceased might have been dealers in Attic pottery, shipped for centuries up the Black Sea and to colonies E. and W. and

329. Potter at his wheel, a limestone statuette from Fifth or Sixth Egyptian Dynasty tomb group of official Nanupkau, probably from Gizeh. Potter turns wheel with left hand, molds clay with right; three finished jars at his left.

to eager neighbor markets, which built up the golden age of Greek art during the 5th century B.C. This period parallels the period when the Jews had returned from Babylonian Captivity to rebuild Jerusalem.

The *kerameikós* of Corinth, as noted as that of Athens, was in the W. quarter of the city, near the weavers' looms where Paul wove tent cloth with Priscilla and Aquila. Hundreds of thousands of pottery fragments have been excavated from the workshops and warehouses of the Corinth *kerameikós*. Its famous white clay came from a ravine adjacent to the quarters. Corinthian water-pots were shipped to distant ports or sold at the long shopping arcade and used at the famous Triglyph and Peirene fountains. Corinthian ware was easily distinguishable from that of Athens, her rival in red-and-black painted pottery.

The museum at Corinth contains a complete series of pottery from earliest prehistoric times to the Byzantine Christian era. Pieces spoiled in the firing, or from being stacked one inside another in the kiln, are included, together with rough clay stands on which the pots were placed while being fired. Lumps of coloring matter found at the studios indicate that pigments were used in painting.

(2) *How broken pottery establishes dates.*— Pieces of broken pottery, tossed out from houses over a period of 7,000 years, tell more about dates of successive occupation levels in the Middle East than any other material thing known to archaeologists. The abundant potsherds or shards are often more eloquent than written records, and they are found on many sites for which no written records are known. Population densities can be estimated from the quantity of a settlement's discarded pottery. Dates can be established within a century or less.

Pieces of well-baked pottery are almost indestructible, unless crushed to powder. The datable fragments need not be large. From fragments found side by side ceramists skillfully piece pottery together, e.g., the elegant gray, burnished, symmetrical pot from the 2500 B.C. level at Beth-shan, which for almost 40 centuries has retained its handle.

Sir Flinders Petrie in 1890 worked out at Tell el-Hesī in S. Judaea "the yardstick of pottery" for dating successive occupation layers (strata) by sequences of broken pottery found in the layer-cake-like mound. By developing "sequence dating" Petrie helped lay the foundation for modern archaeology, by comparing bits of clay with already dated pottery from Egyptian levels and with wares imported from Syro-Palestinian sources, and by considering scarabs (see SEALS) and other man-made articles accompanying the shards, and so setting up a chronology later worked out more accurately by expeditions such as those of the University of Pennsylvania at Beth-shan. In six weeks at Tell el-Hesī Petrie explored 2,000 years of history.

The two principles underlying archaeological research are stratigraphy (study of the sorts of pottery found in a stratum or layer of occupation deposits); and typology (study of the relations of the forms of pottery found in a given level). The value of ceramic evidence to archaeology is well illustrated by Jericho, whose story is being pieced together as more and more shards are found and dated. These include not only native but also foreign deposits—Nabataean, Cypro-Phoenician, Rhodian, Roman, etc. At Jericho there have been found remains of a pottery studio in Stratum X. Glueck in *The River Jordan* reports that by the Middle Bronze Age (1st half of the 2d millennium B.C.) Jericho potters were making finer wares than those made centuries later in Palestine. On a framework of reeds they built up amazingly lifelike pottery likenesses of people. At Jericho the potters made sun-dried pottery of clay mixed with straw for binder, even before they used kilns such as have been found in Stratum IX. By the 17th century B.C. Jericho potters' wheels were turning out vases, one of which, finished by hand, is in the form of a portrait face.

Regional records of pottery show that although Iron Age Hebrew ware was slow in reaching the quality of Bronze Age Canaanite pottery, Jewish craftsmen did learn through the centuries from wares imported from Syria, Egypt, and the Aegean.

Since men were living in the Early Bronze Age in caves on the slope of Megiddo overlooking the Plain of Esdraelon opposite Nazareth, it is not surprising that "Esdraelon culture" pottery has been excavated there. It is gray-black ware, related to that found at the opposite end of the plain at Beth-shan. This "regional pottery," some of which has a grain wash imitating wood, and some has bands of cream, orange, red, and brown, is distinctive. Many of the pots have cylinder-seal impressions giving clues to their dates.

Frequently "date line imprints" were stamped on handles while still wet. Found in a mound in ruins of a definite occupation level, these tell the date of that layer. One pot bearing a two-winged creature, a scroll, and the stamped name of a town, made at Hebron during the Jewish Monarchy (1000–587 B.C.), was found at Lachish in southern Palestine. The winged creature is typical of "royal pottery" stamps. Such ware as this gray earthen fragment with light red slip was stamped to show that its town had sent to the king at Jerusalem its quota of pots filled with oil or wine; or the stamp may mean simply that the piece was wrought in the royal pottery town of Hebron.

Three jar handles marked "belonging to Eliakim, steward of Yokin," one found by Elihu Grant in 1930 at 'Ain Shems, and two by W. F. Albright at Tell Beit Mirsim, have brought us very close to the young King Jehoiachin who was carried off to Babylon by Nebuchadnezzar in 597 B.C.

In the pottery excavated in the five successive cultural levels at the N. Syrian Ras Shamrah, C. F. A. Schaeffer has traced influences of Nineveh, Susa, Turkestan, and other ports of call along the caravan routes. This was the age when Phoenician sailors were bringing to Ras Shamrah perfumes and spices from the Red Sea, and exporting from Syria wood, copper, arms, and utensils, as René Dussaud points out in his *Les Découvertes de Ras Shamra.*

Philistine pottery from the time of David and Solomon has been found in the Shephelah—tan ware, painted with bands of red and brown in spirals, or trimmed with painted birds. This has been classed as "the latest important group of painted pottery in Palestine"; some of it is in the Museum of the University of Pennsylvania.

Egyptian pottery, called "sad stuff" by admirers of the Cretan pots, was always finding its way into Palestine. Much of this was undecorated—suited for heavy everyday use at village wells. (See HYKSOS, illus. 191.)

Greek pottery from its best period, about 500 B.C. or earlier, has been excavated at Tell en-Nasbeh (? Mizpah) in Palestine—both Attic black ware and Attic red-figured specimens. These fragments help date other pottery found with them on this Palestinian site, as discussed in *Bulletin* 83, ASOR.

Pottery excavated in Palestine within recent years furnishes so many evidences of artistic ability that no one is justified in stating that Israel was destitute of creative skills. Had her people been allowed to develop in peaceful environments they would probably have reached as high standards of ceramic art as the Greeks. Experts find in Palestinian pottery more sprightly qualities than in Greek, even though the pots are less precise mathematically than Aegean wares.

See *BA*, Vol. VIII, No. 4, article "Palestinian Pottery in Bible Times," Kelso and Thorley.

pound. See MONEY.

poverty. See POOR, THE.

power, strength, energy, ability to act, suggested in the Bible by various terms and in numerous forms, but with a progressive quality of spiritual content culminating in the ideal of N.T. times associated with the personality of God. (1) The physical power of an individual man to do hurt, e.g., Laban (Gen. 31:29); or to expend accrued resources, e.g., Kish (I Sam. 9:1) or Joab (II Sam. 20:4); or of groups of men, to engage in international power politics, e.g., Egypt (Ex. 32:11; I Kings 14:25) and the Mesopotamian states (II Kings 18:13; Jer. 34). (2) The political prestige of a government, such as Solomon developed by trade and political alliances (I Kings 3, 5, 10). Not only did Israel early in her history feel endowed by Yahweh with peculiar powers (Gen. 15:6 ff.), but her prophets spoke of her being "full of power by the spirit of the Lord" (Mic. 3:8). Zechariah viewed Zerubbabel as equipped for rebuilding the Temple "Not by might, nor by power," but by the spirit of the Lord of hosts (Zech. 4:6).

(3) From Genesis through Revelation the thought of power is attributed to God, Whose creative energy fashioned the universe and holds it together; Who gives of His "strength and power" (II Sam. 22:33) to men who sincerely seek to promote His Kingdom (Gen. 15:6; Ps. 21:13, 147:5); and Who empowers men to become His sons and to usher in His Kingdom, as at Pentecost (Acts 2:1 ff.). This power was the Holy* Spirit, Christ himself, "the power of God" (I Cor. 1:24). The power of the Resurrection of Jesus (Phil. 3:10) became the cornerstone of the Church.

praetor (prē′tŏr), the title given a magistrate next below the consul as a leader of the Roman army. His headquarters was called the praetorium. In Jerusalem the Roman procurators or official rulers, like Pilate (John 18:28, 33, 19:9), had their quarters in the praetorium (Mark 15:16; John 19:9), probably the Castle of Antonia, though Herod's palace was long (but erroneously) so considered. In the court of the Jerusalem praetorium soldiers crowned Jesus with thorns and mocked him with a purple robe and false acclaim (Mark 15:16–20; Matt. 27:27–31), before his Crucifixion. Paul was held in Herod's praetorium or palace (A.V. "judgment hall") at Caesarea (Acts 23:35 A.S.V. margin and R.S.V.).

Praetorian Guard, the, mentioned in A.S.V. and R.S.V. Phil. 1:13, and implied in connection with "Caesar's household" (Phil. 4:22). This unit was housed in the praetorium of Caesar's palace in Rome.

praetorium. See ARCHITECTURE; GABBATHA.

praise, to glorify or extol God, esp. in song; also the act of glorifying and extolling God. See WORSHIP; also HALLELUJAH; PSALMS; SCROLLS, THE DEAD SEA, "The Thanksgiving Psalms."

prayer in the sense of a conscious appeal to the divine, or a conscious effort to hold communion with the divine, is universal. The level and the range of prayer will be determined by the way in which the divine is understood. Prayer that is purely selfish reflects a low conception of God. We sometimes find this in the O.T., especially in such Psalms as 69:19–28, 83, 109:1–20; and it is common in pagan religions.

Prayer takes many forms. It may be simple communion (Mark 1:35); petition (Ps. 25); a "wrestling" (Gen. 32:22–32; Luke 22:39–46); confession (Ps. 51); the uttering of vows (Gen. 28:18–22); praise and thanksgiving (Luke 1:46–55, 67–79); unspoken desire "in the heart" (I Sam. 1:12–15); mere ejaculation (Matt. 8:25); or a prolonged utterance (John 17).

The O.T. contains many examples of great prayers. They include Abraham's intercession for Sodom and Gomorrah (Gen. 18:22–33); Moses' intercession for his people (Ex. 32:11–14, 30–32); David's thanksgiving for God's promise that his "house" should continue forever (II Sam. 7:18–29); Solomon's prayer for wisdom (I Kings 3:4–15) and his long prayer when the Ark was installed in the Temple (I Kings 8:12–53); the prayer accompanying Isaiah's vision and call (Isa. 6:1–11); Jeremiah's prayer after his purchase of the field at Anathoth (Jer. 32:16–25); the Second Isaiah's prayer of confession and petition (Isa. 63:15–64:12); and the prayer of Habakkuk (chap. 3).

The Psalms especially are full of prayers; indeed, the Psalter is a prayer book as much as it is a songbook. Many Psalms are designated as prayers, and assigned to a particular author: e.g., "David" (17, 142); "Moses" (90). Other Psalms have headings which were inserted by translators, including their designation as "prayers": these include such earlier Psalms as 3, 4, 5, 6, 7, 10, 12, 13, and such later ones as 140, 141, 143, 144. Ps. 102 is well called "the prayer of an afflicted one." In some of the Psalms the moral note is supreme (see 51 and the long 119): what is sought is not material good, or victory over enemies, but inward purity and strength. Ps. 88, like Job 10, reveals a soul wrestling with doubt; for Job's victory see 42:1–6. The note of confidence and trust is common in Ps. 27, 39, 40, and especially 73.

The O.T. does not limit prayer to any particular time or place. There were of course certain designated centers, such as the Temple, the village synagogue, and spots which had been made sacred by some special personal experience (see Gen. 35:1–7, cf. 28:10–22). There were stated times for certain forms of prayer; thus Elijah on Carmel waited for "the time of the evening oblation" before he prayed (I Kings 18:29–39, cf. Ps. 141:1 f.); and special prayers were preserved for the great festivals. This is the significance of Ps. 120–134 being described as "Songs of Ascents." Daniel prayed "three times a day" (6:10), and the custom may be indicated in Ps. 55:16 f. In Acts the Jewish times of prayer were the 3d, 6th, and 9th hours—9 a.m., noon, and 3 p.m. (3:1, 10:9, 10:30). Perhaps Paul has a similar regularity in mind when he exhorts the Thessalonians to "pray without ceasing" (I Thess. 5:17, cf. Eph. 6:18). Spontaneous and private prayer, however, and prayer arising from some sudden or immediate need,

330. A man of Jerusalem at prayer.

were not precluded by the fact that there was formalized prayer. This is certainly implied in Joel 2:12–14; in the prayers of Jonah (2, 4:1–3); and everywhere in the Psalms, especially in those that came out of the Exile (79, 89, and 102, all probably Exilic).

N.T. prayer differs from that of the O.T. chiefly because of the influence of Jesus Christ. Prayer changes when religion changes. There are some O.T. prayers the Christian cannot use; others he uses gladly. Jesus strongly rebuked mere formalized praying (Matt. 6:5–8); and it is a grave question whether he ever intended the Lord's Prayer to become a stated form. His own example is unmistakable. He arose early for private prayer (Mark 1:35). After the miracle of the feeding, he went aside to pray alone (Matt. 14:23). He was praying when the Holy Spirit came to him at his Baptism (Luke 3:21). He had spent the whole night in prayer before he "chose" the Twelve (Luke 6:12, 13). Luke says that the Transfiguration occurred "as he was praying" (9:28, 29). The high priestly prayer of Jesus reveals his complete intimacy with the Father (John 17). Prayer carried him through Gethsemane, where he "prayed in an agony" (Luke 22:44); and his last word on the Cross was a prayer (23:46). "He entered heaven with prayer." His example in respect of prayer illustrated his teaching, which stressed importunity (Luke 11:5–13, cf. Mark 7:24–30); a right attitude toward men (Matt. 6:14 f., cf. 18:21–35; Mark 11:25); faith in God (Matt. 8:13; Mark 5:25–34; Luke 8:43–48); submission to God's will (Matt. 7:21–23); and directness and simplicity (Mark 12:40).

The quickening of prayer described in Acts

is due to three causes: the coming of the Holy Spirit; the new understanding of God that came through Jesus Christ; and the use of the "name" of Christ. The Jews tended to identify the "person" and the "name," so that to pray "in the name of Christ" was to pray with implicit confidence in Christ himself (Acts 3:6 f., 16, 4:7–12, cf. 2:1–4, 32–36). The prayer of the early Church was the prayer of men and women who had come to a new knowledge of God and of themselves through Jesus Christ. All the relations of life—individual, social, ecclesiastical—were subjects of this new kind of prayer. In Acts we read of a church at prayer from the beginning (1:14); of prayer for the guidance of Church life (1:24, 6:6, 13:3, 14:23); of prayer as a daily exercise (2:42); of leaders devoted to prayer (6:4); of prayer for the Holy Spirit to be given to converts (8:14–17); of prayer for Peter's deliverance from prison (12:5); of assembling for prayer in the open air (16:13); of Paul and Silas praying in prison (16:25); of prayer for mutual help (20:36, 21:5); and of prayer for recovery from illness (28:8, cf. 9:40; Mark 9:29; Jas. 5:13, 14).

The teaching and exhortation of the Epistles are in agreement with what we find in Acts. Prayer in public is the privilege of all—of women as well as men (I Cor. 11:5; cf. I Tim. 5:5); it is to be "with the understanding," that is, with the head as well as with the heart, not mere emotional raving (I Cor. 14:13–15); it is to be continual (Rom. 12:12; Eph. 6:18; I Thess. 5:17; II Thess. 1:11; I Tim. 5:5); it is to be mutual (Rom. 1:9; Col. 1:9; 4:3; Heb. 13:18); it is to be "in the Spirit" (Eph. 6:18; Jude 20); and it is to be accompanied with thanksgiving (Phil. 4:6; I Tim. 2:1) and with purity of heart and life (I Pet. 4:7).

There is no emphasis on posture in prayer in the N.T., though the Jewish custom of standing was continued for certain occasions (see GESTURE). Kneeling, also a Jewish custom (Ezra 9:5; Dan. 6:10), seems to have been the usual attitude (Acts 7:60, 9:40, 20:36, 21:5, cf. Eph. 3:14; Phil. 2:10). What is chiefly stressed, however, is the attitude of the heart—reverence, sincerity, humility, unselfishness, and faith (see I Pet. 1:17–23). There is catacomb evidence that the early Christians prayed for their dead (cf. I Cor. 15:29). On prayers by the dead for the living the N.T. is silent; see, however, the metaphor in Rev. 5:8, 8:3–5: the "incense" is "the prayers of the saints," but it is uncertain whether the "saints" are living on earth or in heaven. The fact that the censer of prayers was "cast upon the earth" may suggest some interest on the part of the "glorified" in those still living here. See LORD'S PRAYER; WORSHIP.

E. L.

Prayer of Manasses. See APOCRYPHA.

preaching. (1) *In the O.T.* prophets* were preachers, attempting to teach people God's will for their specific situations. Isaiah, Micah, and Amos were all effective preachers, who often blended political guidance with spiritual direction. The preaching of Jonah was mentioned by Jesus (Matt. 12:41).

After the Exile and the establishment of synagogues where the Torah (Pentateuch) was interpreted, preaching with an ethical emphasis was more prominent than eloquent appeals to righteousness. (See ECCLESIASTES for "the Preacher," Heb. *koheleth.*)

(2) *In the N.T.* Apostolic Age preachers set forth the story of Jesus and his teachings as they had first gleaned them from oral accounts based on the testimony of those who had known him. Peter's preaching to the people of Jerusalem (Acts 3:11–26) was testimony. The Acts records 1st-century Christian preaching in various cities (8:40, 9:20–22, 14:7, 21, 25). The objectives of early Christian preaching were (1) winning converts; (2) nourishing faith by witnessing to the Resurrection and the redemptive power of Jesus. Early Church meetings, where the oral material concerning Jesus was repeated for purposes of instruction, not only conserved this for the written Gospels, but helped determine the style of the N.T. writings, in which there is much that sounds "sermonic" or catechetical. The reading of Scripture in present-day public worship often memorializes the sermons of ancient preachers.

The famous sermons of the N.T. include Peter's at Pentecost in Jerusalem (Acts 2:14–40) and at Caesarea (10:34–43), and Paul's at Athens (17).

In the organization of the early Church the preacher, like the teacher, was a member of an order ("prophets," "pastors," cf. Eph. 4:11).

The preaching of John the Baptist in the Jordan Valley (Luke 3:3) was similar to that of the old prophets. When he called the multitude "offspring of vipers" (A.S.V. v. 7) he sounded like a Jeremiah. Like the prophets, he preached of justice (vv. 11–14), repentance (v. 8), and "good tidings" (v. 18); and he heralded the coming of a greater preacher, Jesus (v. 16).

Jesus as preacher attached solemn significance to his preaching function. When John the Baptist had been cast into prison Jesus began to proclaim the gospel of repentance and the coming Kingdom of God (Matt. 4:12, 17). In his first sermon in his home synagogue at Nazareth he read with dramatic significance the words of Isaiah 61:1 f.:

> "The spirit of the Lord is upon me,
> Because he anointed me to preach
> good tidings to the poor" (Luke 4:18).

The discourses of such preachers as Peter, Paul, Philip, and Barnabas as preserved in Acts show that the earliest Apostolic preaching to audiences of the Graeco-Roman world dealt with spiritual problems faced by the devout in a heathen environment (Acts 2:14 ff., 3:12 ff., 13:16 ff.).

An example of preaching in the Apostolic Age is seen in Heb. 3:7–19, 4:1–13: Text (Ps. 95:7–11) and theme (Heb. 3:7–14); exegesis of the text (vv. 15–19); theological idea and promise (4:1–10); application (vv. 11–13).

Origen (c. A.D. 185–c. 254), one of the most influential theologians and writers of the early Church, has been called the father of the Christian sermon. He poured his profound knowledge of the Scripture and his great learning into detailed expositions of specific texts, and used allegorical interpretations to explain them.

precious stones. See JEWELRY; BREASTPLATE.

predestination, "the purpose or decree of God from eternity respecting all events" (Webster). There are many terms and ideas in the Bible which, if they are considered apart from the Bible message as a whole, may easily be misunderstood and misrepresented. Examples are foreknowledge, sovereignty, eternal purpose, election, freedom, providence, and grace. To this list should be added predestination, which has frequently been taken to mean that every person's eternal destiny was fixed, not only before he was born, but even before God had taken the first step in creation. Such an interpretation is a consequence of isolating the term from what the Bible as a whole plainly means. The only defensible approach is one that does justice to the total Biblical teaching.

This teaching is plain enough, and is such as human understanding and experience would seem to call for. It justifies the following general statement: Creation has its origin in a prior purpose on the part of God. This purpose calls for man, and therefore embraces all mankind. The purpose is to bring men, once they exist, into complete conformity to His will, which is a will of holy love. Men, however, being free and responsible, must be won to this conformity, the more so because already their freedom has led to disobedience. All God's dealings with men are designed to produce this conformity. Life follows an order, and God maintains this order. Since, then, all the sequences of life are of God's ordaining, the destiny of the good and evil, or of the "saved" and the "lost"—though the result of human freedom and choice—is still in conformity with God's will. God's purpose is a fixed purpose, and His will is a fixed will in its ultimate intent: this arises from His unchangeable nature. The purpose, however, is necessarily sought through a time process, and this process conditions the realization of God's will. This makes for apparent frustrations of His will, and for apparent failures of His purpose in given cases. But these frustrations and failures are not actually such, when everything involved is considered; their possibility is provided for from the beginning. Like everything else, they are taken up into the order of providence*, and it is through the providential order that the will of God moves forward to the realization of His eternal purpose.

The teaching of the Bible fits naturally into such a view. We can read the Bible in one of two ways: either as a mere record of a succession of events, experiences, changing opinions, and insights, or as a record of how God was moving toward the fulfillment of His creative purpose. The story of Adam and Eve, for example, is significant because it shows that God had to allow for two factors—the pride and rebelliousness of free man, and the subtle power of evil represented by "the serpent" (Satan). These two factors are nowhere long absent from the Biblical record. Always God must reckon with them. From one point of view, they stand in the way of His purpose; from another point of view, they are instruments through which His purpose is still to be carried forward.

The history of Israel is to be understood accordingly. The use of special men in special ways is implicit in God's purpose. He "called" Abraham in order that through Abraham He might secure a people, and through that particular people another people of still wider significance. Abraham's "election" was for the sake of Israel; Israel's "election" was for the sake of mankind. The "choice" of the one is for the good of the many, and "the many" will be seen at last to be "from every tribe, and tongue, and people, and nation" (Rev. 5:9, 7:9, cf. Gal. 3:26–29). To be "called" or "chosen" or "elected" to serve the ongoing of God's purpose is not of itself a "predestination" to salvation. Each in his own way serves God, but service in this sense may still go with rebellion and disobedience.

The nation as a nation clearly failed to meet the divine expectation; it could in no sense be said to be "God's kingdom on the earth." The prophets, however, believed that the Kingdom of God was still to come, even though it was no longer to be identified with Israel. Jeremiah indeed said that God would have to destroy the nation because it had become a hindrance to God's purpose (32:26–44). God would secure "a spiritual people," and He could do that only through "a new covenant written on the heart" (31:31–34). The Second Isaiah saw that such a people would arise according as One whom he called "God's Suffering Servant" became central in men's hearts and lives (see especially Isa. 53). In the followers of the Servant would be fulfilled the promise made to Abraham; but it would be fulfilled not through blood descent or political affiliation, but through a new relation to God available to "many." Such a concept simply has no room for a rigid "predestination" either to "salvation" or to "reprobation." The universal redemption made possible through "the Suffering Servant" sprang from and expressed "the pleasure of Yahweh" (53:10).

It is this conception that lies at the heart of the N.T. In Jesus Christ is realized the character and function of "the Suffering Servant." The fellowship which centers in him, and of which he is the "foreordained" creator (Eph. 1:4, "God chose us in him before the foundation of the world"; cf. 1:11), continues and fulfills the Abrahamic "seed" (Rom. 4:9–13). Paul calls this fellowship "a new Israel," one "not according to the flesh, but according to the Spirit." Christ—with this significance as the mediator of a universal salvation*, one available to all men on the same conditions—was in God's purpose from the beginning (Eph. 3:11). Christ the Redeemer was "predestined" (Acts 2:23) because the Church, as the body of the redeemed, was "predestined." The *time* when the Redeemer should appear was not predetermined: the freedom of man and the contingencies of history precluded this. What was fixed was that he should come; that he should bring salvation; and that the salvation he brought should be available to all. The broad "plan" was of God's eternal counsel; the details of the plan were to be worked out through the clash of human wills and desires, and through the very nature of history as subject to unpredictabilities. Not all the human race at any one time is at the same stage; some have "opportunities" which have not yet come to others. Such differences go with the providential order, but they are not to be taken to mean divine "favoritism." Eternal destiny is not to be determined by the accident of the time and place of birth: "God would have all men to be saved, and come to the knowledge of the truth" (I Tim. 2:4). Predestination does not mean that God is arbitrary, or capricious, or unjust. He rules, but He rules in mercy, righteousness, and love; He also rules according to the situation obtaining at the given time.

The teaching of Paul, especially that in Rom. 8:28–30 (cf. 9:23; I Cor. 2:7; Eph. 1:11) is to be understood accordingly. It is commonly said that Paul teaches that some are predestined to be saved and that all others are therefore "lost," because to be "lost" is the proper and deserved doom of all who are born of Adam. That no man "merits" salvation is true enough; that salvation is the free gift of the grace of God is equally true; but the inference often drawn, that God deliberately withheld His grace from the lost, or the "nonelect," goes in the face of all the N.T. teaching about God's purpose in Jesus Christ. What Paul says about foreknowledge, predestination, election, and reprobation must not be so understood as to take all the meaning out of what he says about human freedom and responsibility, the universality of God's grace, and the reason that Christ came into the world. When Paul says that salvation is for "everyone who believeth" (Rom. 1:16) he assumes that only those who "hear" can "believe," but he has already just declared that he is a "debtor" to others to take to them the Gospel (1:14, see 10:11–21), that they might hear and obey if they will. Paul clearly means that no one is saved apart from the will of God, and that no one is lost apart from the will of God. But the will of God functions through an order which He has Himself established. Salvation and reprobation alike are the results of this order; but that does not mean that a given man is helplessly "predestined" or "foreordained" to follow one set of sequences rather than another.

Much is made of the series of terms used by Paul in Rom. 8:28–30—"foreknowing," "foreordaining," "calling," "justifying," "glorifying." The crucial term is "calling," which many take as the sure proof of "foreordaining" and the sure guarantee of "justification."* If one is "called" nothing else matters. But is the "calling" limited? Are there any whom God has no intention of "calling"? The "calling," says Paul, is "according to God's purpose." But what is this purpose? He tells us that the purpose is to secure men who are "conformed to the image of his Son"; and since elsewhere Paul, in common with the Scripture testimony as a whole, teaches the universality of God's purpose to seek this conformity (Eph. 1:10; Col. 1:14–18), we do not do justice to Paul's complete thought if we suppose he means that there are some whom God has determined beforehand not to "call." He would "call" all, but often the "call" is not heeded, and often it is not even "heard" because God can find no one to extend it. Those who have heard the "call"—that is to say have been confronted with the Gospel—and deliberately turned away from it may well prove to be "reprobate"; but though the reprobation may be the fruit of established sequences, and thus far accord with God's will, the involvement in these sequences rather than in those that issue in salvation will be of the man's own will and choice.

Predestination interpreted according to the total Biblical teaching as to God and the ways of God is therefore a great truth; but it is a truth that provides as much for the freedom and responsibility of men as it does for the sovereign purpose and universal grace of God. See GOD; GRACE; JESUS CHRIST; PROVIDENCE; REDEMPTION. E. L.

presbytery (from Gk. *presbyterion*). (1) Used in I Tim. 4:14 A.V. and A.S.V. (R.S.V. "elders") to designate the group of presbyters or elders in a church. (2) The portion of a church structure in which the chief altar is placed, raised a few steps above the rest of the structure. It is reserved for the clergy.

press. (1) Olive press. See OLIVE. (2) Wine press. See VINE.

priesthood. See PRIESTS.

priests (Heb. sing. *kohēn*, pl. *kohanim*) were highly influential (1) in most of the early cults and religions of the Near East. The father-in-law of Joseph was an Egyptian priest of the great temple at On (Gen. 41:45). Priests often possessed sufficient power to remove and set up kings and to overturn one form of worship in favor of another, as in the Eighteenth Egyptian Dynasty, when priests and officials of the Theban god Amun helped the young Pharaoh Tut-ankh-amun to depose the priesthood of Aton which the monotheistic reformer Akhenaton (c. 1370–1353 B.C.) had established at Amarna. In ancient Sumer priests who had their powerful center in and around the famous *ziggurat* (zoned tower) at Ur functioned as priest-kings (*patesi*). Babylonian kings from Sargon I to Nabonidus, last Chaldaean king of Babylon, sometimes devoted a royal princess to the priesthood of the moon god, whose wife she became and whose secrets she received after spending a night with him in the glazed-tile room which was the empty shrine at the top of the ramped *ziggurat.* A relief incised on an alabaster disk (now in the Museum of the University of Pennsylvania) shows the royal princess pouring libations over sacrifices which have been offered by the shorn priest before an altar shaped like a *ziggurat.* The famous Gudea of Lagash (whose portrait heads are in the Philadelphia Museum of Art, the University Museum, and the Baghdad Museum), was priest-prince of Sumer (c. 2400

B.C.). Through the centuries in Babylonia the palaces and altars of the priests and their well-paid retinue were conspicuous architectural features of cities, as they were later in such centers as the Syrian Baalbek. Many such priestly compounds were places of sacred prostitution, as were many of the Canaanite "high places" of Astarte condemned by Hebrew prophets (Amos 2:8; Ezek. 16:23–39), and similar cultic banquet places in the highlands of Nabataea. The priests of Canaan and Phoenicia were numerous and influential in O.T. times, e.g., the hundreds maintained at the palace table of Ahab's Phoenician Queen Jezebel, patron of Baal-Melkarth of Tyre in the 9th century B.C. (I Kings 18:19, cf. II Kings 10:11 for Jehu's reforms); and by Athaliah, of whom Mattan was chief priest (II Kings 11). The Hebrew priest Jehoiada led the purge of Athaliah's priests from Jerusalem (vv. 4–20). Pre-Israelite Midian had its influential priests, some of them noble and spiritual, like Jethro, father-in-law of Moses (Ex. 3:1, 18:1–24). Ancient Salem (the later Jebus and Jerusalem) had its Gentile priest-king, Melchizedek, who was active when Abraham trekked by that way, rendered "tithes," and was blessed (Gen. 14:17–20).

(2) In the earliest known social pattern of ancient Israel priests as a class did not exist. Any Israelite man could present offerings to God—usually the eldest son or a tribal leader, e.g., Abraham (Gen. 22:13); Isaac (Gen. 26:25); Jacob (33:20); Gideon (Judg. 6:25 f.); and Manoah (Judg. 13:16, 19). Sometimes wealthy landowners maintained their private priests, as Micah of Ephraim employed the traveling Levite Jonathan, and thereby probably established Dan as a sanctuary (Judg. 17, 18, esp. 18:29–31). Samuel, usually thought of as prophet, exercised all the functions of a priest (I Sam. 2:18, 3:1, 9:13–25).

In Israel no other class wielded such great influence through 14 centuries as did the priests (see the eulogy in Deut. 33:8 ff.).

During the early Monarchy (c. 1020–922 B.C.) kings sometimes exercised priestly prerogatives, e.g., David (II Sam. 6:12–19, 24:25) and Solomon (I Kings 3:15), even at such high moments as bringing the Ark up to Jerusalem, and dedicating the Temple (I Kings 8). But an elaborate organization of David's priests at Jerusalem is narrated in I Chron. 24 (cf. also 23:24)—possibly a retrojection by the Chronicler of a later system. Important priests of David were Abiathar (I Sam. 23:6); Ira, a princely state adviser (II Sam. 20:26); and Zadok (I Kings 1:39). Nathan the prophet was his court chaplain and fearless counselor (II Sam. 12). David's son Solomon continued to maintain as leading priests Zadok, who had anointed him (I Kings 4:2, 4 f.), and Abiathar (v. 4).

Certain of the Maccabees were both rulers and priests. Judas Maccabaeus (165 B.C.), son of the high priest Mattathias, brought back the "blameless priest" concept. His brother and successor Jonathan became high priest and general of the army, and was succeeded by his brother Simon. And Aristobulus became king-high priest (104 B.C.), as did Hyrcanus II. From 63 B.C. to A.D. 70 the Jewish high priest was subordinate to Roman rulers and to the various Herods.

(3) *The functions and personnel* of the priesthood varied, and the records concerning them are confused. Their activities were such as laymen could not permanently engage in. Traditionally the priesthood originated at Sinai, with the consecration of Aaron* (descendant of Levi) and his sons, and the recognition of the remainder of the tribe of Levi as assistants to the priests. In source P the Zadokite priests were descendants of Eleazar, eldest son of Aaron; the other priests were descendants of his second son Ithamar. Ezekiel regarded the Zadokites as the legitimate priests (40:46, 44:9 ff.).

The responsibilities of the priesthood changed through the centuries. An interesting account of them in the pre-Monarchy era is the story of Eli and his evil sons (I Sam. 1:3, 9, 2:12 ff.). One difficulty in unraveling the functions of the priesthood concerns itself with the relation between the Tribe of Levi and the priestly or Levitical element of Israel; but it is clear that from Moses' time until after the Exile priests as a class in Israel were known as "Levites." The Jewish tenet that all priests were kinsmen did not apply to pre-Exilic times. Moses set apart the Levites of his day to be priests of his newly organized congregation or people Israel, with the obligation of caring for the Ark, the Tabernacle, and the sacred lot; and teaching the people the ways of God. The great Law Codes which are contained in the various sources of the O.T. offer much information about the functions of Israel's priesthood—J (c. 850 B.C.); E (c. 750 B.C.); and JE (c. 650 B.C.). The D Code, instituted by the reformer-king Josiah, abolished the lesser shrines, centralized worship at Jerusalem (622 B.C.), and recognized the descendants of Zadok as the legitimate priests. The P or Priestly Code (incorporating the older H or Holiness Code) describes in great detail the offices of the priest in the period of the Second Temple. Num. 3 and 4 reveal the elaborate priestly ritual in the 5th century B.C. after the return from Exile.

In general the functions of the Hebrew priests were: to make God's will known through consulting the sacred oracle (the Urim* and Thummim, Ex. 28:30; Ezra 2:63); the oracular ephod* (I Sam. 23:9–12), or the drawing of sacred lots (Lev. 16:8); to teach the Law (Lev. 10:11) and to reduce it to writing (much of the editing and composition of the O.T. was probably done by the priests); to conduct worship, including the receiving and preparation of the materials brought by the people for their sacrifices, and the celebration of the solemn Atonement* Day rites; to care for shrines and the sanctuary; to bless (Lev. 9:22; Num. 6:22–27); and to render judgments—especially for priests of the local shrines prior to Josiah's reforms. For the functions of the priest as stated in the old Holiness Code (incorporated in the Priestly Code) see Lev. 17–26, which goes into detail concerning the slaughtering of animals for the sacrifice at local sanctuaries (Lev. 16:5 f., 21, 22); and the presentation of sheaves for the wave offerings (23:10 f., 20). (See WORSHIP, "Sacrifices and offerings.")

In later Judaism priests pronounced the priestly blessing (prescribed in Num. 6:22–27), which had been used in the Jerusalem Temple, and which is still part of the ritual in the synagogue. In brief, the priesthood was expected to protect the purity and the integrity of Israel. Priests were "ministers of the Lord" (Joel 2:17), and mediators between man and God.

Priests who were derelict and departed from the ideals of their sacred offices met severe rebuke (Lev. 10:1–5, 16–20). They were often no better than those they attempted to lead: "like people, like priest" (Hos. 4:9). The penalty of the sins of Eli and his sons, Hophni and Phinehas (I Sam. 2:12, 22), was the termination of their priestly line. The O.T. contains numerous instances of prophets castigating lax priests, e.g., Amos (2:7 f., 3:4 f.) and Hosea (4:8 f., 5:5) in 8th century Israel; and Isaiah (28:7–22) and Micah (3:5, 11) in Judah. There were times even when drunken priests turned against such outstanding spiritual leaders as Isaiah.

The various sanctuaries were supervised by separate priestly families with no blood relationship. Part of Josiah's reform (621 B.C.) (which removed priests from minor and often corrupt shrines and brought them to Jerusalem to perform menial tasks at the Temple) made the descendants of Zadok priests forever of the Davidic dynasty (cf. the ministry of David's priestly friend Abiathar during his exile, I Sam. 23:6).

The "high priest," called in Lev. 21:10 (H Code) "the priest who is chief among his brethren" (R.S.V. Lev. 21:10) and "the anointed priest" (Lev. 4:3, 5, 16, 6:22, cf. Ex. 29:7–9), was the only priest who was anointed. He was expected to wear "the garments" (see BREASTPLATE; DRESS; EPHOD); and never to "uncover his head, nor rend his clothes" (Lev. 21:10). Though Aaron and his successor, Eleazar, were not called "high priests" their office was a foreshadowing of that influential position (Num. 27:21 ff.). The high priest was viewed as the holiest man in Israel, spiritual head of the congregation, and possessed authority over the highest lay officials. (For the high priest at the Trial of Jesus see Mark 14:53 ff.) He belonged entirely to God. The high priests of Nehemiah's day are listed in 3:1, 12:10, 22—Joiakim, Eliashib, Joiada, Johanan, and Jaddua.

(4) *Levites** (descendants of the Tribe of Levi) in the D Code were synonymous with priests (descendants of Aaron) (Deut. 17:9, 18, 18:1; etc.).

Priestly centers were maintained in early Israel at Shiloh, Nob, Gibeon, Beer-sheba, Hebron, Dan, Anathoth, Bethel, etc. (see individual entries). But with David's capture of Jerusalem from the Jebusites and the establishment of Israel's capital there, Jerusalem became and remained for many centuries the priestly center. But the Temple priests remained subservient to the king. With the division of the Monarchy after Solomon (c. 922 B.C.) the rival religious center set up by Jeroboam I at Bethel was for a time influential; there the king acted as priest-king (I Kings 12:33, 13:1–4). The reforms of King Josiah included the abolition of corrupt rustic shrines at "high places" and the centralization of worship at Jerusalem.

(5) *The Priestly Code.*—Priests contributed to the formulation of the various Law Codes of Israel, notably P, which reveals the priesthood as a well-organized hierarchy (see SOURCES). A separate group of laws has been identified within the Priestly Code, known as "the Holiness Code" (Lev. 17–26). It concerns itself with laws about foods, marriage, religious obligations, sacred festival observance of the Sabbath and the Sabbatical year, and material things offered to God as "devoted things" and tithes. Some scholars believe that its author or authors were priests, deeply attached to sacred traditions and customs, who lived after Ezekiel and followed this priest's accent on the holiness of God, but refused to adopt Ezekiel's innovations in matters of the old Law as promulgated by Moses. Ezekiel played down the power of the "prince" (chaps. 44–46) and before the Exile showed resentment of royal control.

The P Code, called "the charter of the new Jewish Church," is the name applied to strands in the Hexateuch* that are believed by many scholars to have been written by erudite priestly writers as a commentary on the "embryonic Pentateuch" (JED). They used many sources available in the 5th century B.C. It is thought by some scholars to have originated "between Haggai and Nehemiah." It was prepared in Jerusalem, not in Babylonia. Its laws include legislation so old that it is timeless. But P seems to date in its written form from near the close of the reign of the Persian Darius I (521–485 B.C.), several years after the rebuilding of the Temple (516). The earlier strata of P reflect the days of the Second Temple; the later layers were probably written within the next two generations. The Priestly Code is found in Leviticus and the legal portions of Exodus and Numbers. It is considered "the law of a holy nation." The priestly authors of the P Code viewed (1) everything as belonging to God, and (2) the demands of the Law as inexorable. It seems to reflect Nehemiah's reforms at Jerusalem (c. 445 B.C.), as Deuteronomy reflects those of Josiah (622 B.C.). (See *An Introduction to the Old Testament,* Robert H. Pfeiffer, Harper & Brothers.)

Detailed laws concerning the priest's conduct—his marriage, his purification, his tonsure, his freedom from physical blemishes that might desecrate the holy place, and the offerings presented by him to Yahweh for the people—are given in Lev. 21 and 22.

(6) *Priests in Jesus' Time.*—The authority of the priestly caste had become intolerably oppressive by the time of Jesus. Since c. 400 B.C., when Jews had accepted the Torah (the Law) as their canonical guidebook, the high priest at Jerusalem not only received tithes as offerings, but demanded them as legitimate perquisites. In Herod's Temple, where Jesus

taught, there was a Court of the Priests directly in front of the main structure; there stood the stone altar for burnt offerings, with the huge water laver where animals were prepared for the sacrifice. The Court of the Priests was surrounded by the Court of the Men of Israel.

Jerusalem priests, irritated by the barbs of Jesus in such utterances as the Parable of the Good Samaritan, were shocked by his claims to be the Son of God (blasphemy) and the "king of the Jews" (disloyalty to the Roman Government); and they brought about his condemnation and Crucifixion (Mark 14:1, 53 ff.; Matt. 27:57 ff.; Luke 23:5). Jesus healed a leper and suggested that the healed man show himself to the priest (Mark 1:40–45) and make an offering.

The high priesthood which was functioning arrogantly in the Roman Jerusalem of Jesus' time consisted not only of the current high priest, Caiaphas (Matt. 26:3, 65; Mark 14:63), but also the former incumbent, Annas (John 18:13, 24 ff.). Such officials fattened on Temple revenues. They formed an aristocratic priestly party known as the Sadducees*. The old teaching office of the former priests had been assumed by scribes*, most of whom were Pharisees*. The high priesthood at Jerusalem was destroyed with its Temple, but rabbis still teach.

(7) *Christ as Priest Eternal.*—Christ was the world's high priest, as well as the victim sacrificed to bring about God's perfect fellowship with His creatures. Heb. 5–8 makes clear that Christ was a priest forever after the order of Melchizedek (Heb. 7:21), one who did not die as other priests did (v. 23), but continues forever, in "an unchangeable priesthood," living to make intercession for "them to the uttermost that come unto God by him . . ." (v. 25). The old law made priests of men who were subject to infirmity, but the Son of God was consecrated forevermore (v. 28). With the coming of the New Covenant* the infant Church moved away from Judaism, and abolished the laws of the formidable O.T. priesthood. The concept of Israel as a nation of priests (Ex. 19:6) was supplanted by the thought expressed in Revelation (1:6, 5:10), that Christian believers and their Church are "kings and priests" unto God, to reign on the earth.

The long list of priests in the Bible include: Aaron and his sons, Eleazar and Ithamar; Eli and his evil sons; Ahijah; Ahimelech and Abiathar of Nob; Amaziah of Bethel; Abiathar and Zadok; the noble and fearless Jehoiada; Urijah, Hilkiah, Ezekiel, and Ezra; Zacharias, Caiaphas, Annas, and Ananias of Jerusalem (see individual entries).

prince, the translation of several Heb. and Gk. words in the O.T. used to indicate men of authority in a community. A "prince" among the sons of Heth in S. Palestine (Gen. 23:6) was merely a rugged sheikh. The chiefs of Israel's Tribes were "princes" (Num. 1:16, 44, 7:18, 24, 30). The "congregation Israel" had its "princes" (Josh. 9:15, 18 f.). Jonathan, son of Saul, was crown prince of Israel (I Sam. 18, 19). David called his heroic general Abner "a prince and a great man" (II Sam. 3:38). Philistine princes are mentioned in I Sam. 18:30; and Ammonite ones by the Chronicler (I Chron. 19:3). Merchants of Tyre were her princes (Isa. 23:8). In a more accurate sense princes or satraps are mentioned as ruling over Persian provinces (A.V. Dan. 3:2); they were influential officials at the court (Esther 1:14).

The Messiah was "the Prince of Peace" (Isa. 9:6), "the Prince of life" (Acts 3:15).

Hebrew eschatology, quoted in Mark 3:22, provided for a "prince of the devils," Beelzebub.

Prisca (prĭs′kȧ) (Priscilla), was the wife of Aquila, and an influential leader in the early Church in her own right; her name sometimes precedes that of her husband (Acts 18:18; Rom. 16:3; II Tim. 4:19). She has been suggested, though without proof, as coauthor with her husband of the Epistle to the Hebrews. Her homes in the weavers' sections of Corinth and Ephesus were gathering places of Christians, including Paul.

prison, a place of confinement or forcible restraint. In the Biblical period, as now, prisons of the Near East were sordid. Persons believed guilty of violating the usages or laws of a community were detained in (1) *natural pits* or cavelike dungeons where life was eked out by the bread and water "of affliction" (I Kings 22:27). In times of siege even this ration was unavailable to such prisoners as Jeremiah (37:21, 38:9). Examples of natural pits used for holding prisoners are the one on the Plain of Dothan into which Joseph's jealous brothers cast him (Gen. 37:20–28), and the miry dungeon or pit (? abandoned well or cistern) which was one of Jeremiah's Jerusalem prisons (37:16). Sometimes prisoners were pushed into pits where hidden snares caught their feet (Jer. 18:22, 48:43); often they were bound with chains (Isa. 61:1), or held in stocks (Acts 16:24). Prison pits provided places in which to conceal the slain (Jer. 41:7). A rock pit is shown in Cairo today as the traditional state prison of Joseph after the incidents recorded in Gen. 39:20–23, 40:3, 41:45, 42:16–19.

331. Traditional prison of Socrates, looking toward the Parthenon.

(2) Prisons were often *man-made structures*, prison houses, like the one in which the giant Samson was incarcerated at Gaza (Judg. 16:21, 25); and the one provided by King Ahab at Samaria, presided over by the gover-

nor of the capital (I Kings 22:26 f.). Prisons were usually incorporated in government headquarters, like the praetorium (the Tower of Antonia*) at Jerusalem (Mark 15:16), or the Caesarea prison in Herod's judgment hall where Paul was detained for two years (Acts 23:35, 24:27). Jeremiah was evidently held in a cell in the home of Jonathan the scribe (Jer. 37:15); also in the court of the prison (37:21), following the plea of Malchiah for leniency to the great leader (38:6); Jeremiah was in prison "until the day that Jerusalem was taken" (38:28). From his miry dungeon he was drawn by cords of rags by the merciful Ethiopian eunuch Ebed-melech, and freed (38:11–13, 39:15–18).

O.T. kings were held in prison by conquering armies, e.g., the blinded Zedekiah of Judah (598–587 B.C.), who was carried off to Babylon by Nebuchadnezzar (Jer. 52:11); and Jehoiachin (597 B.C.), imprisoned for years at Babylon by Nebuchadnezzar and released, along with other captive kings, by Evil-merodach, in the "thirty-seventh year of the captivity of Jehoiachin" (R.S.V. Jer. 52:31). Hebrew prophets whose utterances were at variance with policies of their kings, e.g., Hanani the seer under King Asa of Judah (II Chron. 16:10) (c. 913–873 B.C.), were thrown into prison. The Messianic prophecy of Isaiah included one concerning "the man of sorrows" committed to "prison and judgment" (53:8), and also of the Messiah who would "proclaim liberty to the captives" (61:1).

Christ showed tender concern for prisoners (Matt. 25:36, 39, 43 f.). His parable of the unmerciful debtor reveals the custom of casting men and their families into prison for their debts (Matt. 18:24–35). Jesus himself became Jerusalem's most notable prisoner—detained first by the Sanhedrin and then at the praetorium.

The Apostolic Age witnessed the arrest and imprisonment by Jewish rulers of such leaders as Peter and John (Acts 4:3), held in a Jerusalem prison from which supernatural events released them (Acts 5:19). Peter was later imprisoned by Herod (Acts 12:1, 4 f.) and guarded by four quaternions. Again he was miraculously released from his chains (6 ff.), and went to the home of Mary, mother of Mark (v. 12). Paul had so many prison experiences—more than all others narrated in the N.T. (II Cor. 11:23)—that he called himself a "prisoner of the Lord" (Eph. 4:1). He and Silas were cast into an inner prison at Philippi, where the jailer "made their feet fast in the stocks" (Acts 16:23 ff.). He was bound with chains at the Jerusalem Tower of Antonia (Acts 21:33, 37), from which his declaration of Roman citizenship released him; and at the Caesarea praetorium (23:35). He was imprisoned in Rome, where he was long under lenient surveillance in his own hired dwelling—possibly quarters in a large Roman apartment house like those found at the surburban port of Ostia (28:30); and again (II Tim. 4:6) in some typical Roman dungeon of Nero's time, such as the Mamertine*, on the slope of the Capitoline Hill, adjacent to the Forum. At such times he must have recalled to his sorrow the occasion when, before his conversion, he had entered the houses of Christians and committed them to prison (Acts 8:3).

Jailers in the Bible offer material for interesting study (Acts 5:23, 12:6 ff., 16:27–34), as do the fellow prisoners of the principal characters (Gen. 40; Acts 16:25).

The Book of Revelation refers to the imprisonment of persecuted Christians (2:10); and to the binding of the fettered Satan in a bottomless prison pit for 1,000 years (20:3, 7).

prize, an award for a contest won; mentioned twice by Paul, who was familiar with races and other athletic contests in stadia and amphitheaters (I Cor. 9:24; Phil. 3:14). He spoke of the Christian way of life as a race in which the contestant sought "an incorruptible crown" (I Cor. 9:25–27).

Prochorus (prŏk′ō-rŭs), one of the Seven appointed by the Apostles to administer relief to the Greek-speaking widows of the Jerusalem church (Acts 6:1–6).

proconsul, in N.T. times, a Roman governor or commander of a province or a region (cf. Sergius Paulus, A.S.V., R.S.V. Acts 13:7 f., 12, A.V. "deputy"), whose powers were similar to those of a consul. Gallio was proconsul of Achaia when Paul was haled before him by the Jews of Corinth (Acts 18:12).

procurator (prŏk′ū-rā′tẽr), a Roman title of the governor of a territory before it was administered as an actual province (see PROCONSUL). In Judaea the Roman governors were "prefects" during the reigns of Augustus and Tiberius. The emperor Claudius first raised their title to "procurator." Hence Pontius Pilate*, who served only under Tiberius, was a prefect, not a procurator. The Greek N.T. very accurately refrains from calling him "procurator," using the word for "governor" instead. English Bibles using "procurator" for Pilate derive their erroneous understanding from anachronisms in Josephus (*Wars*, ii, 9, 2) and Tacitus (*Annals*, xv, 44). That Pilate was "prefect" is further borne out by a dedicatory stone found at Caesarea, engraved for a building erected by Pilate and dedicated to Tiberias in that city, in which Pilate calls himself "prefect of Judaea." See FELIX, FESTUS.

professions and trades. See individual entries; APOTHECARIES; BAKER; BOATS; BREAD; BRICK; CARPENTER; CATTLE; DYEING; FARMING; MASONRY; MAN; METALS; MILL; POTTERY; PREACHING; PRIESTS; PROPHET; PUBLICAN; RABBI; SCRIBE; SHEPHERD; SMITHS; SOLDIER; TAX; WEAVING; etc. (Consult *An Encyclopedia of Bible Life*, Sec. 17, "Professions and Trades," Madeleine S. and J. Lane Miller, Harper & Brothers.)

prognosticators, monthly forecasters mentioned by Isaiah (47:13), along with astrologers and stargazers. See MAGIC.

promise, the, the heart of O.T. prophecy—an awareness of God's design to send to His faithful a Messiah*, an anointed one. Centuries before the Law* had been revealed Patriarchs like Abraham had received a covenant by which the Lord agreed to establish forever the seed of the righteous (Gen. 15). This promise was more than an assurance of a dynasty or eternal inheritance; more than a covenant by which a promised land "from the river of Egypt unto the great river, the river Euphrates" (v. 18) would accrue to the faithful in Israel. It was a spiritual anticipation, fulfilled when Jesus visited his people (Acts 26:6 f.).

In the N.T. Paul explains the concept of "the promise." By faith in the promise, rather than by the Law, men had attained salvation* in O.T. times. The promise was available to men everywhere (Rom. 4:16); not only to those who had known the Law of Israel. The concept of "the promise" rises to a lofty expression in Romans (v. 20 f.), which stresses the strong faith of Abraham in God's ability to perform what He had promised. Just as the Patriarch's faith "was reckoned unto him for righteousness," Paul continues, so for us also who believe in the Resurrection of Jesus who justifies us is the work of "the promise" completed. "Promise" and "gospel" are one and the same to Paul.

Peter in his Pentecost sermon declared that God's promise had been extended to all who repented: "the promise is unto you, and to your children, and to all that are afar off" (Acts 2:39).

property. See BUSINESS; INHERITANCE; OWNERSHIP.

prophet (Heb. *nabi*), divinely inspired preacher. (1) *Prophecy* (Heb. *nebu'ah*) in the Bible does not concern itself primarily with foretelling future events, in the sense in which one speaks of a weather prophet or a financial forecaster. It deals rather with *forth*telling the intuitively felt will of God for a specific situation in the life of an individual or a nation, as Elijah to King Ahab of Israel (I Kings 18:17 ff.), or Amos to the Northern Kingdom at Samaria (Amos 4); or Ezekiel to the Phoenician Tyre (Ezek. 27).

(2) The Heb. word for "prophet" means literally "one who is inspired by God." The Prophets comprise the 2d division of the Hebrew canon: Law, Prophets, Writings. *Prophets* were men to whom God revealed His secrets and who could not resist speaking what they had received from Him (Amos 3:7 f., cf. Ex. 4:16; 7:1). Prophets frequently rose from the ranks of the people, e.g., Elisha, the Jordan Valley farmer (I Kings 19:19–21), and Amos, the herdsman of Tekoa (Amos 1:1, 7:14). All felt themselves to be spiritual leaders commissioned by God to warn their contemporaries of the perils of wickedness, to point the way to true religion, and to give guidance on moral issues. History presents no parallel to the 500 years of the Hebrew prophetic movement initiated by Amos (c. 750 B.C.). Under God, the prophets created Israel's spiritual greatness; they were His messengers, enthusiasts for His program. Luke believed that God had been speaking by "the mouth of his holy prophets" ever since the world began (1:70). "Prophecy came not in old time by the will of man; but holy men of God spake as they were moved by the Holy Ghost" (II Pet. 1:21).

Though prophecy was primarily concerned with current situations, the prophets realized that tomorrow is inherent in today. They foresaw the outcome of Israel's national crises and her evil patterns of living. Time and again their predictions of impending doom were fulfilled. When Jerusalem fell in 587 B.C., as prophets had warned for generations, people saw prophecy fulfilled in history. This gave the post-Exilic prophets great prestige.

(3) *Characteristics of Hebrew prophets.*—They emphasized the holiness of God, fearlessly criticized the morals of their own day, and taught a nobler way of living. They dealt with doomsday, with retribution, and with a return to the simpler, pious life of Israel's pastoral and agricultural period, uncorrupted by Canaanite and Phoenician influences (Amos 5:11, 6:4; Hos. 8:4; Isa. 2:5–11, etc.). They vigorously opposed animal sacrifice (Jer. 7:22; Amos 5:25) and overemphasis of Temple ritual (cf. Matt. 12:6). Yet many prophets admitted that in older times God had been willing to accept the sincere homage of slain animals and first fruits. Joel, in post-Exilic times, was a sacramentarian who urged the renewal of sacrifices to emphasize union between God and His people. The prophet's protests were in general aimed at the extremes of sacrificial activity. Their pleas were for righteousness, mercy, and justice (Amos 4:4–6, 5:22–25; Hos. 6:6; Isa. 1:10–20, 58:3–8; Mic. 2:2, 6:6–9; Jer. 6:20, 7:8–10). "Seek good, and not evil, that ye may live: and so the Lord, the God of hosts, shall be with you," Amos pled (A.V. 5:14); "Hate the evil, and love the good" (v. 15). The patient, nonritualistic, imageless, and essentially moral emphases of the prophets carried Israel a long way toward monotheism*.

The prophets did not separate themselves from the life of the people, though groups known as "the sons of the prophets" maintained headquarters or schools for their coteries in remote places where a nomadic austerity of life was possible, as in the hot Jordan Valley (II Kings 9:1). (For their centers see below, under [5].)

To courts of kings in both Judah and Israel the prophets boldly uttered rebukes, as Nathan did to David (II Sam. 12), and Jeremiah to the princes of Judah (Jer. 26). They castigated the selfish rich (Amos 4:1, 6:4–6). Their intense consecration gave them the sense of partnership with Yahweh in the mysteries of the universe. The Greeks attributed a similar partnership to the Cumaean Sibyl, and to the oracles of Apollo at Delphi and at Didyma near Miletus.

The prophets were intensely patriotic and scornful of all who would invade their land—whether Kenites, Philistines, Aramaeans, or Mesopotamian Valley aggressors. Their written messages declare the ultimate triumph of the good and the downfall of evil. They helped men reach a conviction of Yahweh's concern for His creation (Isa. 18:2 f., 7, 41:25–29); they found God's purpose in their national history, and interpreted the events of their time in terms of God.

They often used stern, caustic tones, yet their judgments were merciful, like those of God; they had pity for the penitent (Isa. 1:18), and charitable concern for the wayward. They yearned for an ideal social order.

They never lost sight of the possibility that a "righteous remnant" (Isa. 10:20–22, 37:32; Ezek. 6:8) would survive catastrophe. Some of their pronouncements were bright with Messianic hopes which were ultimately fulfilled when in the fullness of time the Messiah, Christ, was born in Bethlehem (Matt. 2:1). His coming did what all the prophets of Israel together could not accomplish—he revealed the good life; taught men how to attain it; and died to make it available to all. Jesus felt in himself the fulfillment of what had been written concerning him "in the law of Moses, and in the prophets, and in the psalms" (Luke 24:44).

(4) The *methods* by which the prophets of Israel delivered their God-sent messages were: (a) oral utterances, as with Samuel, Elijah, and Elisha; (b) the written word, developed by the prophet or others from "notes" of his utterances, later edited, amplified by running notes, and now in the books of O.T. prophecy; (c) symbolic acts, like Abijah's rending his garment into 12 pieces (I Kings 11:29 ff.); the casting of Elijah's mantle on his successor, Elisha (II Kings 2:13); placing confidence in "signs" (I Sam. 10:2–10); and using symbolic names. (See also Jer. 27:2, cf. I Kings 22:11.) The contest between Elijah and the priests of Baal may also be classified as a symbolic act (I Kings 18).

(5) Various uses of the word prophet require definition. The *Former Prophets* are the historical books from Joshua through II Kings (except Ruth), which form a sequel to the Pentateuch and contain historical material on the period from the occupation of Canaan (from the 13th century B.C.) to the fall of Jerusalem (587 B.C.). Much of this material was edited in the 6th century B.C. These historical writings were classed as prophetic because they were believed to have been written by men inspired of God. The *Latter Prophets* include orations and incidents in the lives of the three Major Prophets (Isaiah, Jeremiah, and Ezekiel); and the Twelve Minor Prophets.

The *literary* (*or writing*) *Prophets* (see chart below) were those who reduced their messages to writing, or whose utterances were recorded by others. Much of the prophetic literature is in poetic (see POETRY) form. The nonliterary prophets, so far as is known, used only oral messages.

There must have been numerous Hebrew prophets whose names, works, and words have not been preserved, like the unknown prophet whose advice brought victory to King Ahab of Israel; and the one who voiced the people's criticism of Ahab's too soft peace terms to Ben-hadad of Syria (I Kings 20).

The phrase "sons of the prophets" refers to guilds, coteries, or schools of ecstatic prophets such as are mentioned in I Sam. 10:5, 10, 19:20—of which there were many in the Middle East outside of Israel. They were wonder-workers and soothsayers (Deut. 13:1 ff.), who had much in common with the prophets of the Baalim and with the unnamed prophet of Byblos who made a frenzied appeal (c. 1100 B.C.) on behalf of the Egyptian envoy to Byblos, Wen-Amon. They were like the dervishes of the Near East in much later times. The ones mentioned in the O.T. sometimes had marks branded on the forehead, or characteristic tonsures. They gave themselves to rhapsodic music (I Sam. 10:5). Sometimes the "sons of the prophets" traveled as itinerant counselors, or were settled in remote regions, e.g., the hot Jordan Valley, where they were ascetics, like John the Baptist centuries later. They also maintained centers at Bethel, Gibeah, Gilgal, Mount Ephraim, and Ramah. In Ramah Samuel maintained his home and a "company of the prophets," who engaged in worship, fitted themselves for prophecy, and gave helpful advice (I Sam. 19:20–23). Samuel, "the man of God," was the last of the old seers (I Sam. 9:9), and the first prophet in the sense in which Hebrew prophets ultimately became known. Two centuries after his time the ecstatic strain reappeared in the coteries of Elijah and Elisha (II Kings 2:3, 5, 7, 15, 4:1, 38, 5:22, 6:1, 9:1).

The nobler prophets in Israel resented the mercenary motives of many "sons of the prophets," who usually accepted payment for their services, like Samuel (I Sam. 9:7 f.) and Ahijah (II Kings 8:7–9). Elisha's refusal to accept payment for curing Naaman lifts this prophet above the common level. Amos resented being considered a professional prophet (Amos 7:10–17). Many of the true prophets preferred to be called "the man of God."

(6) *The Sequence of the Prophets.*—The so-called *Minor Prophets* are minor only in their brevity, not in their importance. They constitute the last 12 books of the O.T. in the English Bible immediately after Daniel, which is preceded by the three *Major Prophets*, Isaiah, Jeremiah, and Ezekiel; thus all 16 of the O.T. prophetic books are grouped together at the end of the O.T. In the Hebrew Bible the Twelve Minor Prophets together comprise the "Book of the Twelve," which follows Ezekiel. The Twelve were grouped in one volume c. 200 B.C. This was either for the practical reason of preserving 12 slender rolls by bundling them together, or from a consideration of 12 as a "round" or sacred number (see NUMBERS)—12 Tribes, 12 Disciples, etc.

In some of the early Christian manuscripts of the Scriptures (like the *Codices Vaticanus* and *Alexandrinus*) "The Twelve" precede Isaiah, in an effort possibly to establish a better chronological sequence. The order of the twelve as they now appear in English Bibles does not follow the order in which they were written—Amos now being commonly accepted as the earliest (750 B.C.).

The Minor Prophets probably stand in this chronological order (based on *The Modern Message of the Minor Prophets*, p. 2, Raymond Calkins, Harper & Brothers):

Amos	750 B.C.
Hosea	745–734 B.C.
Micah	c. 701 B.C.
Zephaniah	628–620 B.C.
Nahum	614–612 B.C.
Habakkuk	605–600 B.C.

Haggai	520 B.C.
Zechariah (1–8)	520–519 B.C.
Malachi	460 B.C.
Obadiah	400–350 B.C.
Joel	c. 350 B.C.
Jonah	c. 300 B.C.

In the Septuagint the first six of the Minor Prophets appear in a different order: Hosea, Amos, Micah, Joel, Obadiah, Jonah.

Prophets of Israel

(1) *Before the 9th century B.C.*—Moses is regarded by orthodox Hebrews today as father of all the succeeding prophets. In Christian thought he is regarded chiefly as the lawgiver, with Elijah typifying the prophets (see the narratives of Christ's Transfiguration: Matt. 17:3, 10, 12; Mark 9:4 f., 11).

During the United Monarchy and immediately before and after it individual prophets were moral leaders of Israel: Deborah (Judg. 4, 5); an unnamed prophet (Judg. 6:8–10); three Davidic prophets, Samuel, Gad, and Nathan; and Ahijah.

Samuel combined the functions of priest and prophet, and according to one ancient record was influential throughout all Israel "from Dan even to Beer-sheba" (I Sam. 3:20, 7:3, 10:17 ff.), and maintained a circuit that included Bethel, Gilgal, and Mizpah (7:15–17). People found him accessible at home in Ramah (7:17, 8:6) for advice. He was willing to participate in their sacrifices at the high place (9:11–19), and to settle disputes at the city gate (9:18). By his selection and anointing of Israel's first king to lead the Tribes against the Philistines Samuel combined two functions of the prophet—moral counselor and state adviser. He lived in an age when there were still bands of "seer" prophets roving from place to place in a frenzied emotional state—soothsayers, "mad fellows" (I Sam. 10:10–15, 11:1–11, 15, cf. 19:20–24), inspired by music (10:5), relying on dream guidance, omens, and signs (see MAGIC).

Gad exerted great influence over the king (I Sam. 22:5; II Sam. 24:11–14), and is credited with helping establish the musical ritual of the sanctuary (II Chron. 29:25) and with making a record of David's reign (I Chron. 29:29).

Nathan criticized the delay in building the Temple (II Sam. 7); rebuked David in the Bath-sheba affair (II Sam. 12:1–15); and like Gad is given credit for influencing Temple music and writing a history of David's and part of Solomon's reign (I Chron. 29:29; II Chron. 9:29). Gad and Nathan were influential "court chaplains."

Ahijah (I Kings 11:29 ff.) prophesied to Jeroboam of Israel (c. 922–901 B.C.) concerning the division of Solomon's kingdom.

(2) *Ninth-century prophets: Elijah*, contemporary of Ahab, King of Israel (c. 869–850 B.C.) and a member of a school of prophets; *Elisha*, his successor; *Micaiah*, son of Imlah, contemporary of Ahab (I Kings 22); and *Zedekiah*, leader of a band of false prophets in the reign of Ahab (I Kings 22:11).

(3) *Eighth-century literary prophets* stood at the peak of the Hebrew prophetic movement. Their era is characterized by extraordinary economic prosperity, the temptation to adopt pagan cults or Assyrian gods, and wrong conceptions of the nature of their own God.

In Israel	*In Judah*
Amos (c. 750 B.C.)	First Isaiah (chaps. 1–39) (c. 738–700 B.C.)
Hosea (c. 750–735)	Micah (c. 730–722)
Under the Kings	*Under the Kings*
Jeroboam II	Uzziah
Zechariah	Jotham
Shallum	Ahaz
Menahem	Hezekiah
Pekahiah	
Pekah	

(4) *Seventh-century prophets of Judah:*
Jeremiah (b.c. 650 B.C.)
Zephaniah (began c. 626 B.C.)
Nahum (began c. 612 B.C.)
Habakkuk (c. 605–600 B.C.)

(5) *Prophets of the Exile* in Babylon:
Author of Isaiah 13 and 14:4–21
Author of oracles in Isa. 21:1–15
Second Isaiah (Isa. 40–55)
Ezekiel (deported to Babylon 597 B.C.)
Obadiah (prophesied after 586 B.C.)

(6) *Prophets after the Exile:* Earlier—Haggai (c. 520 B.C.); First Zechariah (chaps. 1–8); Third Isaiah (chaps. 56–66), possibly the work of several post-Exilic writers; a nameless prophet (Jer. 3:14–18); conclusion to Amos (9:8b–15); Malachi ("my messenger," c. 460 B.C.). *Later*—Joel; anonymous author of Isa. 24, 25:6–8, 26:20–27:1, 27:2 f.; Jonah (c. 300–200 B.C.). *Last*—Author of Daniel (c. 165 B.C.); Second Zechariah (chaps. 9–11, 13:7–9) (c. 162–1 B.C.).

(To correlate the eras of the kings of Israel and Judah with those of the prophets, see CHRONOLOGY. For lives of the various O.T. prophets see individual entries.)

(7) John the Baptist, last of the prophets under the Old Covenant and forerunner of the Prophet of Nazareth, Jesus the Christ.

Beginning with judgments on Israel, the prophets climaxed their ministry by stressing the individual's value in the sight of God, Whose Kingdom would consist of regenerated individuals. At the outset they viewed Israel as Yahweh's favorite child, but they finally learned that Israel was God's servant, whose sufferings would show the nations the consequences of sin, and cause them to turn with grateful hearts to the God of all nations.

The canonization of the prophets probably began in the era of Nehemiah. It was closed and fully recognized between 180 and 130 B.C., in time to strengthen the Jews against the incursions of Hellenism fostered by Antiochus Epiphanes and the renegade Jews who aided him.

(8) *False Prophets.*—False prophets were to be weeded out by a Temple priest, like Pashhur, who arrested Jeremiah (Jer. 20:1–6), though he had given false prophets liberty to speak. As many as 400 false prophets were defied by Micaiah, son of Imlah (I Kings 22:8 ff.). Micah (chap. 3) protested boldly against mercenary prophets, more interested in their salaries than in true prophetic utter-

ance. False prophets had no inspired message; were motivated by self-interest; and preferred popularity to a truly helpful ministry. Ezekiel denounced false prophets who foretold peaceful security when they knew that this was impossible (Ezek. 13:1–16). False prophets as well as true ones might have visions (Isa. 28:7, 29:11 f.; Jer. 14:14; Ezek. 12:22 f.; Zech. 13:2 f.). There were also false prophetesses as well as true ones (Ezek. 13:17). Jer. 23 contains the longest and sharpest condemnation in Scripture of false prophets. Righteous prophets from the time of Micaiah disassociated themselves from such men. In N.T. times false prophets continued to arise (II Pet. 2:1; Rev. 2:20, 19:20), condemned by the Apostolic leaders. Christ had warned against the "false Christs and false prophets" who would arise, "in sheep's clothing," to confuse and seduce the elect (Matt. 7:15, 24:24; Mark 13:22). In Revelation the false prophet was labeled as one of the evils of the last day (Rev. 16:13 f.); the false prophet, along with the beast, was cast into the lake of fire (19:20, 20:10).

(9) *Jesus and the Prophets.*—The Hebrew prophets from Samuel on had foretold the coming of a Messiah* (Isa. 42:1, 52:13, 53, cf. Deut. 18:15, 22). Jesus belonged to Israel's great line of prophets (Isa. 1:10–17; Mic. 6:6–8; Hos. 6:6). Like them he taught an ethical and spiritual religion. He raised their belief in God's righteousness and love to its climax in his teaching about God, the Father of all men (Matt. 5:38, 43). Jesus fulfilled the qualifications of the ideal prophet as given in Deut. 18:15—words not intended as a specific prophecy of him. He quoted from prophetic writings; e.g., Hos. 6:6, in Matt. 9:13. He evaluated John the Baptist as the greatest prophet of the former age (Matt. 11:11), and referred to himself as a prophet (Luke 13:33). He evidently did not expect the prophet to be popular in his own community (John 4:44).

In N.T. times Christian prophets were recognized (I Cor. 12:28 f.; Eph. 4:11). The prophetic experience was not uncommon in the early Church, e.g., Agabus (Acts 11:27 f., 21:10); and Judas and Silas (15:32). Paul claimed for himself mystical communications (Gal. 1:12, 16, cf. II Cor. chaps. 10–13), as well as guidance direct from God (I Cor. 14:6, 18 f.; II Cor. 12:1–10; Gal. 2:2). The *apostle* was a missionary to the unbelieving (Gal. 2:7 f.); the *prophet* was a "messenger to the Church" (I Cor. 14:4, 22); the *teacher* (Heb. 5:12) explained or interpreted truth already possessed by the believer. Prophesying, in the N.T., included: (1) the ministry of "edification, and exhortation, and comfort" (I Cor. 14:3); (2) special communications from God (Acts 13:1 ff.); and (3) an occasional prediction (Acts 11:18, 21:10).

prophetess, a woman prophet. Women were not excluded from the functions of prophecy in the O.T. period. The following are represented as speaking by divine inspiration: Miriam, sister of Moses (Ex. 15:20, cf. Num. 12:2); Deborah, wife of Lapidoth (Judg. 4, 5); Huldah, wife of Shallum (II Kings 22:14); Noadiah—but not in the LXX, where a man (Noadias) is indicated—(Neh. 6:14); Anna, of the tribe of Asher (Luke 2:23 ff.).

A prophet's wife was also sometimes called "prophetess," as may be meant in Isa. 8:3.

In N.T. times women were recognized prophetesses, like the four daughters of Philip (Acts 21:9). They seem to have been numerous, for rules concerning the veiling of their heads are included in Paul's First Corinthian Letter (11:5). A false prophetess, Jezebel, is mentioned in Rev. 2:20.

propitiation, in its simplest sense, the causing of one who has been justly hostile to another to become favorable to him. The means used to secure this favor is also frequently called "a propitiation." In Rom. 3:25 (A.V.; R.S.V. "expiation," cf. N.E.B.) God's way of restoring the broken fellowship between Himself and men (cf. Heb. 2:17; I John 2:2 A.V.; cf. R.S.V., N.E.B.). Neither "propitiation" nor the allied term "reconciliation"* is common in the Bible, being specially rare in the O.T., but what the terms actually mean is everywhere taught. Sin separates God and man; the separation must be done away; it can be done away only by the use of the appropriate means—this is the Biblical teaching. The means is "a propitiation"; the result is "reconciliation." Sometimes the object of propitiation is a human being, as when Jacob sent a gift to Esau (Gen. 32:13–21, 33:1–8); sometimes it is demons or strange gods (Deut. 32:17; Ps. 106:37, 38; cf. the sacrificing of children to Molech as a propitiation, in II Kings 23:10; Jer. 32:35); but the Biblical interest is chiefly in propitiation as it affects God (but note Matt. 5:23 f.). Noah after the Flood appeased God with offerings (Gen. 8:20–22). Abraham's proposed sacrifice of Isaac was of the nature of an "appeasement," though it is significant that God provided a substitute (Gen. 22:1–19).

The O.T. system of sacrifice was by no means entirely propitiatory. It is generally agreed that the "peace offering" (Lev. 3) was a communion sacrifice, used for thanksgiving and the fulfillment of vows, but the three types of sacrifice that became most important in later times—the burnt offering (Lev. 1:3–17), the sin offering (4:1–5:13), and the guilt offering (5:14–6:7)—all have propitiatory significance; the offering was brought and accepted in place of something else, and the graciousness of God was shown by His acceptance of the substitute. The most impressive example of this was provided by the ritual of the annual Day of Atonement, especially that part of it having to do with the scapegoat. On the head of the scapegoat the high priest symbolically laid all the sins of all the people for the year just passed, and the sin-laden creature was then banished alive into the wilderness to perish (Lev. 16:1–34).

One of the chief points of tension between priest and prophet had to do with the method of propitiation. To the question "How is God made favorable?" the priest was likely to answer: "By the prescribed offerings being brought in the prescribed way." The prophet saw that all too often the ceremony was an excuse for real repentance and real reformation, and he was likely to answer: "The sacrifices of God are a broken spirit: a broken and a contrite heart, O God, thou wilt not despise" (Ps. 51:17, cf. Isa. 1:10–20).

The N.T. may be said to support the priest's conviction of the necessity of propitiation, and the prophet's conviction that an alleged propitiation that was accompanied by no actual repentance, no actual turning away from sin, and no actual transformation of heart and life, was without avail. In the Synoptic Gospels Jesus himself is represented as teaching that God willingly receives all those who turn to Him in true sorrow for their sins. (See the Parable of the Prodigal Son, Luke 15:11–32; though the suffering endured by the father must not be overlooked.) There is to be considered, however, the fact that Jesus also said that he had "come to give his life a ransom for many" (Matt. 20:28), and "ransom" always connotes some sort of exchange (cf. I Tim. 2:5 f.). And at the Last Supper Jesus spoke of his shed blood and broken body as a means of "the remission of sins" (Matt. 26:26–28).

This is the truth that is elaborated by John in the Fourth Gospel. It is John alone who reports the Baptist's declaration about Jesus, that he was "the Lamb of God, that taketh away the sin of the world" (1:29). The words following the interview with Nicodemus can mean only that the Son gave himself to turn the divine judgment against men into a divine acceptance of men (3:16–21). In the discourse on the bread of life in John 6:22–59 Jesus says that he gives himself for the life of the world, to restore men to God as children to their father. The earliest Christian preaching is recorded in Acts, and there is no least doubt that its uniform testimony is that Christ by his death and resurrection has opened the way to the true reconciliation of God and man (2:22–40, 3:11–26).

Paul's teaching is unmistakably in agreement. Sin, he declared, had brought men under the judgment of God (Rom. 3:9, 19, 23; Gal. 3:10 f.). As a righteous God He cannot be indifferent to sin. No man can wipe out his own past, or transform his own nature; to do this is the work of God alone (Rom. 7:8–25). But He cannot do this without at the same time revealing His attitude toward the sin that is to be done away; and this revelation is made "through the redemption that is in Christ Jesus" (Rom. 3:23–26). The nature of sin must be set forth by the very means through which reconciliation is to be brought about: this means is the sacrificial death of Jesus Christ, which is therefore "a propitiation" (v. 25 A.V.). Thus Paul can say elsewhere that Christ, who "knew no sin," was "made to be sin in our behalf" (II Cor. 5:21). Other writers in the N.T., in such passages as Heb. 9:11–28; I Pet. 1:18–21; I John 3:4 f.; and Rev. 5:9 f., repeat this teaching.

What is distinctive in the N.T. teaching, however, is that "the propitiatory" is provided by God Himself. We are not to think of an angry God with Whom Christ is pleading to be merciful; we are to think rather of God pleading with sinful men to make their peace with Him, and of Christ as the form taken by the appeal. "God reconciled us to himself through Christ. . . . We beseech you on behalf of Christ, be ye reconciled to God" (II Cor. 5:18, 20). God's righteousness, which makes sin a barrier to fellowship, and God's love, which would destroy the barrier, are revealed and satisfied in one and the same means, the gift of Christ to be the Mediator* between Himself and men.

See ATONEMENT; GRACE; RECONCILIATION; REDEMPTION; SALVATION; SIN.

E. L./R. C. D.

propylaea (prŏp′ĭ-lē-*ȧ*) (pl. of Gk. *propylaion*, "before the gate"), a vestibule or entrance to a temple area or other enclosure, often of magnificent proportions. The Propylaea of Corinth was an arched gateway by which people mounted from the Lechaeum Road—the main street—into the great agora or forum. In Paul's time the Propylaea of Corinth was in the form of the usual Roman triumphal arch of marble. The extant Athe-

332. Propylaea at Athens.

nian Propylaea, which leads to the temples on the Acropolis, is a magnificent structure rivaling the Parthenon. It was built by Pericles (437–432 B.C.) to replace one erected by Peisistratos in the 5th century. It has five entrances to its central portion; Ionic columned gates; and is adorned with a Doric frieze of triglyphs and metopes. It occupies the whole W. side of the Acropolis, and could have been seen by Paul from Mars Hill. The Great Propylaea at Eleusis, center of the Greek mystery religion, has left extant vestiges near the road from Athens. In Jerash (Gerasa), the best preserved Palestinian city of Roman times and one which may have been visited by Jesus on his Decapolis journeys, the Propylaea Church (A.D. 565) has been found. Its apse incorporates a gateway of the classical period, and its fabric includes columns from the street of that era.

proselyte, one who has been converted to a faith or sect after having been affiliated with a different one. (1) In the O.T., Gentiles living under the protection of Judah or Israel were given certain privileges, and allowed to offer sacrifices to Yahweh (Num. 15:14 ff.). But not until a candidate was circumcised and cleansed (or baptized) and had offered sacrifices did he become a proselyte to Judaism and eligible to partake of the Passover. Many Gentiles were proselytes to Judaism; some of these were in Jerusalem at Pentecost (Acts 2:10), e.g., the Ethiopian eunuch of Queen Candace whom Philip baptized into the Christian fellowship (Acts 8:26–39). (2) In early N.T. times Judaism continued to attract proselytes. Robert H. Pfeiffer attributes the increase of Jews during the last three centuries B.C. to the influx of proselytes; in Nehemiah's time (445 B.C.) the total number of Jews may not have exceeded half a million, but Jews of the Diaspora in the 1st century A.D. probably totaled two millions, half of whom were in Palestine (*A History of New Testament Times*, p. 189, Harper & Brothers). Jesus criticized those scribes and Pharisees who compassed sea and land to make one proselyte (Matt. 23:15). Many non-Israelites who had become "religious proselytes" of Judaism became proselytes of the Christian Way, e.g., many at Pisidian Antioch who followed Paul and Barnabas (Acts 13:43). These readily accepted the Gospel, left the synagogue, and followed the Christ of Paul, who made no ceremonial distinction between Jew and Gentile, bond and free. In this way synagogues of Gentile proselytes to Judaism became living cells which grew into new Christian churches (Acts 13:16, 43, 16:14 f.). Nicolas (Acts 6:5), an Antiochan proselyte to Judaism, was chosen, with Stephen, Philip, Nicanor, and others, to assist the Apostles (Acts 6:5). On the day of Pentecost proselytes from lands as distant as Parthia and the Pontus, Libya, and Rome, were present in Jerusalem (Acts 2:9–12).

prostitute, a woman who earns her living by engaging in illicit sexual intercourse. Such women, condemned in Israel's society (Lev. 19:29; Deut. 23:17), were common in O.T. and N.T. times; prostitution was part of the official worship rites in numerous temples and high places (see HIGH PLACE) of most of Israel's neighbors. Quarters for sacred prostitutes existed at the Sumerian Ur from the 3d millennium B.C. and at the Syrian Baalbek of later centuries. So common was religious prostitution that Jeremiah spoke of Israel's apostasies in terms of harlotry (3:1 f., 6, 8). The story of a forgiven prostitute is told by Luke (7:36–50). See HARLOT.

proto-Sinaitic script. See WRITING.

proverb, a short saying that conveys a familiar truth or useful thought in expressive language. Israelites frequently expressed themselves in such a phrase or saying, called a *mashal.* Sometimes these sayings were positive affirmations (Gen. 10:9); sometimes they took an inquisitive form (I Sam. 10:12b; Isa. 14:4; Hab. 2:6; Mic. 2:4). When an observation became a proverb it expressed a finality of human judgment and history (Deut. 28:37; Jer. 24:9; Ps. 44:14; Job 17:6). Life and environment were epitomized in picturesque phrases (1) from the physical world (Job 14:19; Prov. 25:11, 27:17); (2) from agriculture (Jer. 23:28b, 31:29; Prov. 15:17); (3) from animal life (Deut. 25:4; Jer. 13:23; Prov. 6:6, 14:4, 26:11, cf. II Pet. 2:22); (4) from human nature, as observed (a) in the home (Ezek. 16:44; Prov. 21:9; (b) in business (Prov. 10:2, 14:23); (c) in trades and professions (Job 13:4; Luke 4:23); (d) on the farm (Prov. 20:4, 26:27; John 4:37); (e) in the family of nations (Jer. 13:23).

The Hebrew proverb is often a contracted parable*, and carries a spark of insight which can be labeled "wisdom."

Proverbs, the Book of, the second book of the Hagiographa* (Writings), classified with Job and Ecclesiastes as Hebrew Wisdom Literature. The authors of that Wisdom Literature were early humanists who were primarily interested in human life; therefore this book is concerned not with prophetic or legalistic Judaism, but rather with the wisdom distilled from life itself, taught to young men as a guide to a successful career.

Like the Psalms, the Book of Proverbs is a collection of collections. Its heading is the longest of any book in the Bible (1:1–6). It contains eight divisions:

(1) In Praise of Wisdom, 1:7 to chap. 9.
(2) Proverbs of Solomon, 10:1 to 22:16.
(3) Words of the Wise, 22:17 to 24:22.
(4) "Sayings of the Wise," 24:23–34.
(5) "Proverbs of Solomon, which the men of Hezekiah, king of Judah, copied out," 25:1 to 29:27.
(6) "Words of Agur, the son of Jakeh, even the prophecy," 30:1–33.
(7) "Words of king Lemuel, the prophecy that his mother taught him," 31:1–9.
(8) Praise of a good, efficient wife, 31:10–31.

Tradition attributes Proverbs to Solomon; and such an origin is referred to in 1:1, 10:1, 25:1. Solomon had a reputation for great wisdom (I Kings 4:29 f.), and much Wisdom Literature was assigned to him, as the Psalms were attributed to David. Some of Solomon's wise sayings have doubtless been retained in the Wisdom Literature of Israel; but the Book of Proverbs probably comes from the post-Exilic period. The derogatory manner in which monarchs are spoken of does not represent the Solomonic era (c. 961–922 B.C.), but a later period (Prov. 16:14, 19:12, 20:2, 25:3). Among other evidences that support a post-Exilic date are: (1) monogamy, the prevailing domestic background of that period (5:18 f., 12:4, 18:22, 25:24); (2) emphasis on the individual rather than on the nation, a characteristic of the post-Exilic period of disillusionment when each individual needed a sense of his own personal worth; (3) Aram. words and others of possibly Arab origin; and (4) the alphabetic poem (31:10–31), a relatively late Hebrew literary form. Though many individual sayings of a timeless character may belong to an early date, the book as a whole was not compiled earlier than 400 B.C.; some critics even date it in the Hellenistic period, c. 250 B.C.

One of the oldest parts of Proverbs is 22:17–24:22, which is an echo of the "Wisdom of Amenemope," an Egyptian book exhibiting a common-sense view of life (c. 1000–600 B.C.). Jer. 17:5–8 and Ps. 1 may have been influenced by this same Egyptian source, which had a wide circulation. Israel's relations with Egypt were so varied that it is difficult to say whether this literary influence came through Solomon (II Chron. 8:11), through cultural contacts, or through geographical contacts.

Two schools of thought may be recognized in the Wisdom material of Proverbs—a secular, and a religious. The theology of the secular group is akin to that of Job, Ps. 104, and Ecclesiastes. God is the source of all things (16:9), directing every move of man (21:1), who is powerless against Him (21:30). Wealth is acquired through intelligence (24:3 f.) and hard work (10:4 f.), especially in agriculture (12:11, 28:19). The wise man will retain his property by abstaining from laziness (6:6–11, 24:30–34), profligacy (5:8 f., 6:26), and intemperance (23:20 f.). The pleasures of life, if taken in moderation, are not to be shunned; such pleasures include: perfume (27:9); wine (31:6 f.); honey (25:16); friendship (25:17); and married life (5:15–20). The admonitions of wisdom against adultery, usury, fraud, theft, and ill-gotten gains are not so much moral or religious as expedient; self-interest dictates good conduct.

The religious sections of Proverbs show the influence of Deuteronomic social ideals. There are appeals for the widow and orphan (15:25, 23:10 f.), the poor (14:20 f., 19:17, 21:13), and even one's enemy (25:21 f.). The wisdom of God is accessible to man here and now (1:20–33); the wise are identical with the pious (9:9, 10:31, 23:24); wisdom becomes the supreme goal of life (3:13–18, 8:16–21), by which long life, security, honor, riches, and happiness are won (6:23, 8:18). These pietists firmly believed that wealth and happiness are the reward of righteousness (3:16, 8:18). Many things in life, however, are more precious than riches, namely, wisdom (3:14 f., 8:11); religion (15:16); righteousness (16:8); and a good name (22:1). The proverbs of the religious sections are idealistic, pious, and moral; the proverbs in the secular material are realistic and practical, with an occasional strain of cynicism.

providence is a perplexing idea, made more so by the common supposition that the "providential" implies divine interference in the course of events. This looks like favoritism—or even, on occasion, miracle. It is certainly Bible teaching that God "calls" and "chooses" some as He does not others, and that He does this in keeping with His eternal purpose. But the choice is never exclusively for the sake of the chosen; it is seen at last to be a point on which turns God's purpose for the many. Even a passage like Deut. 7:6–11 is to be read in the light of one like Isa. 42:1–9. The choice of the lad David to be the future king of Israel was connected with some very human motives on the part of Samuel (I Sam. 16:1–13, cf. 15:34 f.), yet in view of all that David is now seen to have meant for the world we have no difficulty in seeing how God used the choice, even if He did not actually dictate it. The sale of Joseph by his jealous brothers, the bitter early experiences of Joseph in Egypt, and the heartache of Jacob over the loss of his favorite son, were directly caused by unworthy emotions, words, and actions; but God took them all into the sweep of His purpose for Israel. Joseph could at last say to his brothers: "It was not you that sent me hither, but God" (Gen. 45:8). Even the destruction of Jerusalem by Nebuchadnezzar served God's ultimate purpose in ways which at the time only one man foresaw, Jeremiah. From any human point of view the Crucifixion marked the end of Jesus Christ; his enemies could now breathe easily, and his few followers were plunged into complete despair. Yet it has long since become apparent that even the Cross furthered that eternal purpose of God to which all the divine ordering of human affairs—the true meaning of "providence"—has reference (Acts 2:22–24; I Pet. 1:18–21).

The first chapter of Job raises the question of the individual and God's providences. What is the relation between God, the calamities that befell Job and his family, and Job the righteous man? Has not a good man the right to expect that "God will take care of him"? The question of course depends on what is meant by "taking care." It certainly does not mean that God stands between a good man and all calamity, for calamity comes to all. But it can at least mean that even in the worst of calamities the good man has in God a resource that will be his support. It should also be remembered that there are many suggestions in the Bible of the activity of a malign evil power that lies in wait to inflict evil on men (Gen. 4:7; Zech. 3:1–5; Matt. 4:1–11, 13:24–30; John 12:31, 16:11; Eph. 2:1 f., 6:12; I Pet. 5:8; I John 3:8–10; Rev. 13:1 f.). To what extent such a power can offer real opposition to God we cannot say; what is evident is that it is a reality to be reckoned with, alike by God and by men. To trace every situation and every event directly to God's will is to go beyond Scripture. Events that were not of God's ordaining, since they sprang so clearly from evil causes, may yet not altogether escape the divine control; and this control by God of situations He did not directly will is another aspect of providence. "His tender mercies are over all his works" (Ps. 145:9). To assert this must always be an act of faith, but it is a faith that rests back on the conviction that the Creator is still Lord of His own creation. The whole of Ps. 145 is a triumphant declaration that a God of goodness and power rules; and Jesus confirmed this in all he said about the fatherly intent of God (Matt. 5:45, 6:25–34, 7:11).

It is customary to distinguish providence as "general" and "particular," but the distinction is really superficial. So-called particular providences—as when a loss that befalls one man passes his neighbor by—are all forms of the working of God's universal oversight and care. The man who can say, "My times are in thy hand" (Ps. 31:15) has arrived at the true understanding of providence as embracing every aspect of his life, even when things are such with him that all he can say is, "Lord, I believe; help thou my unbelief" (Mark 9:24). The Cross was not only in the providential order for mankind—Jesus came to see that it was in the providential order *for himself*, and he accepted it accordingly (Mark 14:36). "We know that to them that love God all things work together for good" (Rom. 8:28) is the classic utterance on this high theme, though it should always be supplemented with verses 35–39 that follow. The modern Babcock hymn with the theme, "This is my Father's world," and the Whittier hymn with the lines, "I only know I cannot drift Beyond His love and care," do but repeat the same profound truth in a different way. See PREDESTINATION. E. L.

provinces, administrative units of a country (Acts 23:34, 25:1), mentioned in the Bible in connection with the empires of the Mesopotamian Valley and the Roman Empire. The Achaemenid Persian Empire of Darius had 20 large provinces or satrapies; the once powerful Media became one of these (Ezra 6:2). The Persian Artaxerxes mentioned in Ezra 7:11 made a province of Babylon. During the early period of the Exile the Jews left in Judaea were ruled by a "governor on this side the river" (A.V. Ezra 5:3–6), but later were organized as a subprovince (Neh. 11:3) under their own governor—Zerubbabel, Nehemiah, and Sheshbazzar (Ezra 2:2, 5:14; cf. "the poor of the land" left in the province, Neh. 1:3, 7:6). The Book of Esther refers to the numerous provinces of the Persian Ahasuerus, each under its local governor (1:22, 3:12–14, 8:9–17, 9:28). The Book of Daniel says that Daniel was made a "chief governor of Babylon" (2:48).

During the Roman Empire and earlier vast provinces were organized from Mauretania in NW. Africa to Mesopotamia. The boundaries and the names of these changed from time to time. Those mentioned in the N.T. are:

(1) *Senatorial* (but imperial in certain years)

	Enrolled	
Macedonia	146 B.C.	Acts 16:12
Achaia	146 B.C.	Acts 18:12
Asia (incorporating several districts, as Cilicia)	133 B.C.	Acts 19:10
Bithynia, with part of Pontus	74 B.C.	Acts 16:7
Crete and Cyrenaica	74 B.C.	
Cyprus	27 B.C.	Acts 13:4, 7

(2) *Imperial*

Syria (which included the subprovince of Judaea, ruled by a procurator or a native king)	64 B.C.	Matt. 4:24
Galatia	25 B.C.	Acts 16:6
Pamphylia and Lycia	25 B.C.	Acts 13:13, 27:5
Egypt	30 B.C.	Matt. 2:13
Cappadocia		Acts 2:9

(See also individual entries for these provinces.)

The *Senatorial provinces* were ruled by men (chosen by lot) from the group who had been either consuls or legates. Asia and Africa were ruled by ex-consuls, and were therefore consular provinces; the other provinces were administered by ex-praetors, but all senatorial governors were ranked as proconsuls (see PROCONSUL). The *Imperial provinces* were under the direct control of the emperor, and governed through his lieutenants. Imperial provinces like Syria were usually frontier areas in which disorders were expected. If senatorial provinces developed civil or financial disturbances they might be converted, at least temporarily, into imperial provinces. Egypt, on whose vast grain supply (Acts 27:6) Rome depended for feeding the home population, was regarded as the emperor's own, and ruled by a prefect of equestrian rank; no senator was allowed within it.

In the Roman provinces land taxes were fixed by the emperor, and collected by imperial officials or men appointed by them. Only the indirect customs taxes were collected by the hated farmer-collectors, the publicans.

In the time of Christ the eastern provinces of Rome, including Judaea, were orderly. Taxation was heavy, but government on the whole was good and peace was maintained. If a province was disorderly, a supergovernor or high official was appointed by Rome. Such possibly was the case when "Cyrenius was governor of Syria" (Luke 2:2).

pruning. See VINE.

Psalms, the Book of, the most important existing collection of Hebrew religious poetry. In the Hebrew O.T. it is the 1st and longest book of the Hagiographa* (Writings), the 3d division of the Canon. Its Heb. title is *Tehillim*, the plural of *Tehillah* ("song of praise"); the English title comes from the Gk. *psalmos* (Luke 20:42; Acts 1:20), meaning "a poem sung to the accompaniment of stringed instruments." "Psalter," another title for the book, comes from Gk. *psaltērion*, used in the Codex Alexandrinus of the LXX.

As early as the Septuagint version the Psalter was divided into five books, a division omitted in the A.V. but indicated in the A.S.V. as follows: (1) Ps. 1–41; (2) 42–72; (3) 73–89; (4) 90–106; (5) 107–150. Each division ends with a doxology, except the last, where Ps. 150 serves as a final doxology. This division was an imitation of the five books of the Pentateuch. Evidence that this division was not made at one time is seen in the way some of the Psalms are repeated, like Ps. 14 and 53; 40:14–18 and 70; 57:7–11, 60:5–12 and 108.

The name of the Deity in "books" (2) and (3) has almost throughout (Ps. 42–83) been changed to *Elohim* (A.V. "God"), whereas elsewhere it is *Yahweh* (A.V. "Lord"). The belief is strong that this Elohistic Psalter was at one time a separate book, by the side of "book" (1) (Ps. 3–41), from which Ps. 53 and 70 were taken. These and many other considerations substantiate the theory of the gradual growth of the Psalter.

The authors of the Psalms are unknown. Suggestions offered in the titles are as follows: (1) Moses (90); (2) David (3–9, 11–32, 34–41, 51–65, 68–70, 86, 103, 108–110, 122, 124, 131, 133, 138–145); (3) Solomon (72,

127); (4) Asaph* (50, 73–83); (5) the Sons of Korah* (42, 44–49, 84, 85, 87, 88); and (6) Ethan* the Ezrahite (89); 101 psalms are thus ascribed; 49 of the 150 are anonymous. The Talmud assigns two of the anonymous group to Adam (92, 139), and one each to Melchizedek (110) and Abraham (89).

David is associated with 73 psalms. Though he was noted for his musical gifts (I Sam. 16:14–23) and his secular poetry (II Sam. 1:17 f., 3:33 f.; see also Amos 6:5), David's great reputation for religious musical verse was given him by the Chronicler (I Chron. 16, where Ps. 105:1–15 is quoted). This reflects a treatment of history used more in the time of the Chronicler than of David. (See MUSIC.) II Sam. 22 (Ps. 18), 23:1–7 can hardly be poetic religious expressions by David, for they reflect conditions at a much later period (22:44 f., 23:5). These and other psalms attributed to David reveal a noble spiritual insight which seems inconsistent with the more primitive views of David's time as recorded in the historical books; the language of some of the Davidic psalms shows Aramaic influence and is evidence of a post-Exilic date (103, 122, 139, 144). See CHRONICLES.

The prevailing critical opinion is that most psalms took their present form between 400 B.C. and 100 B.C.; the date of the final compilation may be later than the date of composition of the whole or part of a psalm. Many lyrics were transmitted orally from generation to generation, as a part of the religious lore of the people; Ps. 24:7–10 was probably sung when the Ark from Shiloh was installed with due ceremony, in the newly built Temple of Solomon. Snatches of ancient verse were revised and applied to current situations in order to recapture the religious faith and emotion of an ancient experience (77–81, 114, 136). The psalms which could possibly have been written by David are 18, 29, 88, and 89. Ps. 68 embodies a number of lyric poems dating from c. 1300–900 B.C. The mention of the Temple (5:7, 27:4; etc.) in any "Psalm of David" shows that it was written after David's time. The lamentations composed during the persecution of the Jews by Antiochus Epiphanes (168–165 B.C.) could have inspired Ps. 108; this period is also mirrored in 44, 74, and 83. The military successes of Judas Maccabaeus (2d century B.C.) against the Syrians may have inspired Ps. 118 and 149. II Chron. 29:30 refers to our Psalter, perhaps "books" (2) and (3).

Besides reflecting the endless variety of historical happenings in Hebrew history, the Psalms also show the influence of Canaanite, Egyptian, and Babylonian cultures on Hebrew customs and thought. The Canaanite festivals (Judg. 9:27) were adopted by Israel (Hos. 2:11–13). The Ras Shamrah texts excavated at Ugarit in N. Syria indicate how the form of Israel's poetry was influenced by that of their early neighbors. There is more than coincidental parallelism between the famous Hymn to Aton (the sun) by Amenophis IV (Akhenaton*, c. 1370–1353 B.C.) written on wall reliefs of chapels in the cliff tombs at his excavated capital, Amarna, and Ps. 104:19–23. This psalm converts the Egyptian solar monotheism into the spiritual monotheism of the Creator-God. From the Sojourn in Egypt and the Exile in Babylon came a great deposit of custom, culture, and experience discernible in the Psalms. Babylonian cosmology is reflected in Ps. 104, and its Epic of Creation in Ps. 136:4–9, 148:1–5. The Akitu festival, during which the priest entered the most holy place and recited the Babylonian epic of Creation, was attended with ceremonies involving all—from king to peasant; and it is believed that this celebration provided the stimulus to the fall festivals copied by Jews from the Canaanites and enlarged after the Captivity into the elaborate New Year celebrations which persist throughout Jewry to this day. These annual festivals required new songs (33, 96, 98, 149), thanksgiving for the past (65, 67, 118, 124), and trustful expectations of God's help in the future (53, 85, 125, 126, 129).

The headings of many of the psalms provided directions for their musical rendition, like "Set to the Gittith," the name of a particular tune, perhaps a vintage song (8, 81, 84), and "On Neginoth" (see NEGINAH) (on stringed instruments) (A.V. 4, 6, 54, 55. 67, 76), and "Nehiloth" (to the accompaniment of wind instruments) (5). (See SELAH.) Ps. 136 records, in the 2d part of each verse, the refrain of the choral response in full; elsewhere it is only implied. Many other words in the headings furnished musical directions (*maschil*, *michtam*, etc.). Memory and usage often supplied the words for the antiphonal hymns. "Hallelujah" and "Amen" were congregational responses.

Some psalms are pre-eminently hymns, sung on pilgrimages, particularly by Passover pilgrims to Jerusalem (84, 121–134). The Hallel (113–118) was sung at the Feast of the Tabernacles, Pentecost, and in the Passover service, half at the beginning and half at the close. Mark 14:26 and Matt. 26:30 refer to the singing of "a hymn" (115–118), the second half of the Hallel, after the Lord's Supper. Liturgies were employed when worshippers entered the sanctuary (15, 24, 100), expressed their praise and thanksgiving (113, 115, 135, 136), and offered supplication (121). This use of the Psalms in Temple worship is well attested from the days of the Chronicler (c. 250 B.C.), who speaks of the musical parts of the ritual with such detailed knowledge (II Chron. 5:11–14) that very likely he belonged to one of the Levitical choirs. The three Levitical guilds of Temple singers, said to be descended eponymously from Asaph, Jeduthun (Ethan), and Heman, are credited to David (I Chron. 25:1–7), but were organized much later. The Psalter as we now have it was the hymnbook of the Second Temple. Though some selections are pre-Exilic in origin, most were collected and edited for use in this post-Exilic period. Many features of sacred music found in the Psalter have survived in the Christian Church; psalms alone are sung in some denominations.

Just as our present-day Church hymnal may serve as a book of devotions, so the Psalter was and is an aid to man in his search for God. Personal thanksgiving finds realistic and picturesque expression here (Ps. 23, 30–32, 34, 66, 92, 107, 116, 138, 139, 146). The desire for security, justice, and vindication, particularly when falsely accused and harassed, led to such prayers as Ps. 7, 11, 26, 42, 43, 52, 54, 56, 64, 70, 120, 140, 142. For mental unrest the "psychiatry" advocated was prayer, sleep, and tarrying in the sanctuary (Ps. 3, 4, 5, 17, 57, 59, 143). Those suffering from physical afflictions, aggravated by a sense of injustice and personal guilt, sought and found help in God (Ps. 13, 22, 28, 31:9–24, 35, 38, 41, 69, 71, 86, 102, 109). Psalms 6, 39, 62, and 83 are mainly prayers for the sick. Throughout the Psalter there is confession of sin and guilt, but the outstanding prayers of penitence are Ps. 51 and 130. "Trust in God," likewise throughout the Psalms, is specially dominant in Ps. 16, 91, and 131. Though the psalmists found God chiefly in the inner realm of the immediate awareness of His spirit, they also felt Him in the world without: (1) in nature (8, 19:1–6, 29, 104, 147, 148; (2) in history (78, 105, 106, 114); and (3) in the Law with its intellectual and moral requirements (19:7–14, 119). Prothero's classic *The Psalms in Human Life* is only a fragmentary record of the power, consolation, and illumination which these inspired creations have brought to man through the centuries.

Everyday life in the Middle East is projected in many of the Psalms: shepherd customs (23, 78:52); hunting practices (22:16, 35:7 f., 69:22, 91:3); bird habits (84:3, 102:6 f., 104:17); nocturnal scavengers (59:6, 14 f.); night patrols (127:1, 130:6); and domestic architecture (128:3, 129:6 f.). Thunderstorms (29:3–9) and forest fires (83:14) are vividly described. Palestine is mapped in terms of its physical geography (104). The so-called "imprecatory psalms" (58, 59, 69, 109, 137, 149) which breathe vengeance on enemies (in violation of Christian teaching) may have their place justified in the book because (1) Christ had not yet spoken; and (2) they realistically present a mood familiar even today, in spite of the full knowledge of the Christian Way.

The words of the Psalms were a part of Christ's intellectual equipment; their spirit guided his life. He used their words at his Temptation (Matt. 4:6—Ps. 91:11 f.); in the Sermon on the Mount (Matt. 5:7—Ps. 18:25, Matt. 5:35—Ps. 48:2, Matt. 7:23—Ps. 6:8). There can be little doubt that Matt. 26:38 and Mark 14:34 are an echo of Ps. 42:5 f. Among Christ's last words on the cross were Matt. 27:46—Ps. 22:1 and Luke 23:46—Ps. 31:6. In his review of the Scriptural Messianic forecast, he at least once included the Psalms with the Law and the Prophets (Luke 24:44). Many phrases throughout the Psalms fit Christ's person and work: Ps. 118:22—Matt. 21:42; Ps. 22:16—John 20:25; Ps. 41:9—John 13:18; Ps. 69:21—Matt. 27:34, 48; cf. Ps. 2:7—Acts 13:33. Some readers "messianize" Ps. 18 and 110, though they may also recognize that these psalms deal with a definite historical situation of an earlier period.

The unifying note in the Book of Psalms is a personal experience of God with wide social and communal implications. No other book in the Bible has ministered so universally to man, and made men of many religions and creeds feel their common spiritual heritage.

Psalms of Solomon. See APOCALYPTIC.

Psalter. (1) The Book of Psalms. (2) A book containing Psalms, used in liturgy. The oldest surviving Anglo-Saxon Psalter is in the British Museum, a 9th-century translation of the Latin Psalter. The Psalter and portions of the Gospels were the chief parts of the Bible translated in Anglo-Saxon times. After the Norman Conquest William Shoreham of Kent translated the Psalter into the dialect of the West Midlands (perhaps c. 1320), and Richard Rolle translated it into the Yorkshire dialect about 1340. These two popular versions of the Psalter spread the new English language and created an interest in the Bible which led to Wyclif's version. The Psalter as printed in the Book of Common Prayer of the Anglican Communion is the translation found in The Great Bible of 1539. See TEXT.

psaltery, a stringed musical instrument plucked with fingers or plectrum. See MUSIC.

pseudepigrapha (sū-dĕ-pĭg′rȧ-fȧ) ("writings under assumed names"), a term applied to books of Jewish literature outside the Apocrypha* of the intertestamental period, to which are attached names of ancient worthies. Some of the books of the Apocrypha were also written under assumed names, like the Epistle of Jeremy, II Esdras, etc.

pseudonym, a fictitious or pen name. The adoption of the name of a prominent person as a pen name was an ancient literary device for acknowledging indebtedness or for securing a hearing for a message. Because pseudonymity was so widely practiced, statements of the authorship of many books of the Bible are unconvincing. Since authorship in antiquity did not involve property rights, pseudonymity involved no ethical problem.

Ptolemais (tŏl′ē-mā′ĭs). See ACCHO.

Ptolemy (tŏl′ē-mĭ). (1) The name of a Macedonian dynasty which ruled Egypt from the breakup of the Empire of Alexander the Great (323 B.C.) to the accession of Augustus after the Roman victory at the Battle of Actium (31 B.C.). The Ptolemies dominated Syria, Palestine, and Phoenicia as part of their Egyptian kingdom for more than a century, until the coming of the Hellenizing Syrian Seleucids*.

333. Ptolemy Philadelphus.

Ptolemy I Soter (323–285 B.C.), a satrap and general of Alexander the Great, added Coele Syria to Egypt after the battle of Ipsus (301 B.C.) and dominated Palestine and Phoenicia. The Jewish historian Flavius Josephus in his *Antiquities* describes Ptolemy's siege of Jerusalem. Ptolemy II (Philadelphus) was king of Egypt (ruled 285–246 B.C.) during the great work of the translation of the Pentateuch into Gk. (the Septuagint or LXX)

(c. 250 B.C.). Ptolemy IV Philopator (221–203 B.C.) figures in the unhistorical tales narrated in III Maccabees* glorifying the Jews. Ptolemy VII Philometor (181–146 B.C.) made Jonathan Maccabaeus governor of Judaea.

Little is known of the Jews under the Ptolemies, but they seem to have paid their taxes and maintained a degree of autonomy in local affairs. Egyptian Jews in Alexandria* under the Ptolemies were given a special quarter of the city, near the royal palace. Later they lived and had synagogues in all five districts of the great cultural center, and dominated two of them. Gk. inscriptions found in Egypt show that Jews settled in various parts of Egypt in the time of Ptolemy III Euergetes (246–221 B.C.).

(2) A son-in-law of Simon Maccabaeus, and governor of Jericho. He assassinated Simon and his sons Mattathias and Judas (134 B.C.).

publicans (R.S.V. "tax collectors"). (1) Originally the *publicani*, who under the Roman Republic contracted to gather taxes in the provinces* and to supervise subordinates entrusted with squeezing as much public revenue as possible from the people. *Publicani* reserved a good margin of profit for themselves, and often formed stock companies whereby they shared it with men of high rank in Rome.

(2) The *telonai* of the Gospels, who functioned after Caesar had abolished the office of the *publicani*, were tax collectors (so translated throughout R.S.V.; A.V. "publicans"); the *telonai* had nothing to do with the major taxes, which were collected through local Jewish sanhedrins co-operating with the procurator*, who, after deducting money for public works, provincial administration, and his own percentage, turned the remainder over to Rome. The Jewish *telonai* or petty tax collectors mentioned in the N.T. were despised by their fellow Jews because they served a heathen government, and because they squeezed all they could from the people. They erected toll gates on roads and at bridges and harbors; they collected duty on goods carried to market, and on wares transported from one city to another; and they taxed many common articles like salt. In current thinking tax collectors were grouped with sinners (Matt. 9:10 f.), harlots (Matt. 21:31), and "heathen" (18:17). They were among those despised by the Pharisees, but baptized by John the Baptist (Luke 3:12 f.), and to whom he said that if they wished to be saved they must "exact no more than is appointed" (Luke 3:13). Jesus was the friend of publicans, as of all who needed his spiritual counsel; and dined with them, as with Matthew (Levi), the tax collector whose office was on the great N.-S. highway along the Sea of Galilee adjacent to Capernaum. He became one of the Twelve Apostles (Matt. 9:9–13; Luke 5:27–31). Jesus went home to dinner with Zacchaeus, tax collector at Jericho, who had been a "chief publican" and

334. Ptolemaic Temple of Serapis, Alexandria, Egypt. Erected by Ptolemy III (246–221 B.C.).

"rich" (Luke 19:2), yet was glad to be saved by Jesus (v. 6). In his Parable of the Pharisee and the Publican (or Tax Collector) Jesus paid his compliment to the sincere humility of this admittedly sinful petty official (Luke 18:9–14).

Publius (pŭb′lĭ-ŭs). The "chief man of the island" of Melita* (Malta) at the time Paul was wrecked there. Paul healed the father of Publius (Acts 28:1–8).

Pul (pŭl). (1) The personal name of Tiglath-pileser* III, used in II Kings 15:19 to designate the Assyrian king who reduced Israel under King Menahem (c. 745–738 B.C.). (2) A region identified by some scholars as that lying along the S. end of the Red Sea and the W. shore of the Indian Ocean and known as Punt (Somaliland), but erroneously copied by a scribe to read "Pul" (Isa. 66:19).

pulse, leguminous plants producing edible seeds, like beans, lentils, and peas—probably vegetable food in general, in Dan. 1:12, 16.

punishment, everlasting, an idea that has come to be associated with horrible physical afflictions, including those caused by fire. There is some warrant for this in the language of the N.T. We are not to overlook, however, the influence of certain great Christian classics, like Milton's *Paradise Lost* and Dante's *Inferno,* the influence of certain great pictures like Michael Angelo's *Last Judgment,* and the influence of a certain type of hymn and sermon dealing with the world to come. Skepticism regarding these descriptions cannot detract from the truth that underlies them, namely, the possibility of irrevocable and permanent loss of the human soul.

Objection to the teaching commonly arises from mistaking symbols for realities. The use of fire, for example, in descriptions of future punishment is clearly metaphorical; we can think of nothing, much less human bodies and souls, that could endure forever the action of fire. As a symbol of the means of suffering or of purification, however, fire is appropriate (cf. I Cor. 3:12–15; I Peter 1:6–9; cf. "a refiner's fire" in Mal. 3:2 f.).

The Christian view of future punishment is to be reached through the Bible teaching that God has designed men for a certain purpose. He is a Creator who would also be a Father: men are made the creatures of His power in order to become, if they will, the sons of His love (John 1:10–13). The various ministries of the Holy Spirit are the means God employs to bring men to this sonship; and central to these means is Jesus Christ, described as "the firstborn among many brethren" (Rom. 8:29; cf. Col. 1:15, 18), the Head of a new humanity (see SONS OF GOD). God will use all His resources to bring to pass this purpose. Either in this life or (if not possible in this life) in another, He will seek to confront every soul with Jesus Christ in such fashion that the soul will be aware of what is taking place (I Pet. 3:18–22, 4:6; II Pet. 3:8–13; cf. Heb. 12:25–29). If faith in Christ is essential to final salvation, we cannot doubt that the opportunity to know this will be given to every man. The acceptance of Christ is, however, like every significant moral act, a free decision on the part of the person concerned. In this right of free decision is both the glory of men and their great danger.

This danger is nowhere more solemnly depicted than in what Jesus said about "unforgivable sin" (Matt. 12:22–34). He had freed a man from an evil spirit. His critics, observing the deed, declared that he could "cast out demons" because he was himself in league with "the prince of the demons." Jesus took this to mean that they were morally blind—so committed to their own evil ideas that they could look on a deed which judged by any standard should be esteemed good, and say that it was evil and wrought by an evil power. He said that men who talked like this were doing far worse than defaming him: they were blaspheming the Holy Spirit by whom eventually every good deed was done. He implied that they had become so "hardened" that they could no longer respond to the appeal of the good. In that case they could not repent, and if they could not repent God could not forgive them. They were, in a word, so impervious to the Holy Spirit that they were beyond redemption.

This incident shows the true meaning of everlasting punishment. In sharp contrast stands the idea of eternal life. The emphasis in the phrase "eternal life" is not on *time* but on *worth.* In the Fourth Gospel it is everywhere evident that what is stressed is the *kind of life* that Jesus promised, not merely its duration. "Eternal life" is, in John's thought, "abundant life" (John 10:10); to refuse the life Jesus came to give is "to abide in death" (I John 3:14). There can be no "eternal life" where men have a hateful spirit (3:15), or where they refuse "the living bread" which is Christ himself (John 6:27, 40). Sometimes the contrast is between having eternal life and "perishing," as in the familiar John 3:16. To "perish" does not mean to cease to exist: it means failure to come to that true life which God intended every man to find. Final failure will come to no man except of his own will: it will be the result of his refusal of eternal life. His continuance in existence will be continuance in "death" (the absence of true life) in a future world as much as in this world. "Everlasting punishment" will consist in the permanent realization of this loss, accompanied by permanent remorse. See APOCALYPTIC; ESCHATOLOGY; JUDGMENT, DAY OF. E. L.

pur (pūr) (Pers. "lot"). See PURIM.

purge, to cleanse of impurities, as to purge a land (II Chron. 34:8); to purge or clean a threshing floor by fanning or sweeping it (Matt. 3:12); to eliminate impure matter like leaven (I Cor. 5:7); or to rid a man of his sins (Ps. 65:3; Heb. 1:3, 10:2; II Tim. 2:21). An altar was purged or purified (Ezek. 43:26). The phrase "purging with hyssop"* indicates a ceremonial cleansing (Ps. 51:7, cf. Ex. 12:22). To purge a fruit tree was to prune it. Purging or eliminating rebels from a group (Ezek. 20:38), was used, as now, to mean ridding a political party of undesirables.

purify, purification. See PURITY.

Purim (pū′rĭm), **the Feast of** (Pers. *pur*, "lot"), a Jewish celebration based on the events of the Book of Esther*, held on the 14th and 15th days of Adar, the 12th month of the Jewish year (Feb.-March). It is characterized by feasting, hilarity, gifts, and alms; the Book of Esther is read in the synagogue on the eve and again on the morning of the 14th, and the congregation participates by making noise when Haman's name is pronounced. Purim has always been popular among Jews when anti-Semitism was prevalent in society.

purity is expressed in the O.T. by several words that range in meaning from "cleanliness," "freedom from foreign bodies," or "salted," to "innocent." Israel was God's chosen people; their land, His holy land; and anything that made a man unclean unfitted him to approach God and His dwelling place. Even certain foods were unclean (Hos. 9:3 f.; Ezek. 4:13). Hebrews regarded sin as defilement, which had to be cleansed or atoned for by such rites as were specified for the Day of Atonement* (Yom Kippur) (Lev. 16).

Purity of nation was an ideal designed to protect Israel from the religious syncretism apt to result from intermarriage with foreigners. (Cf. Obad.; Deut. 23:3 f.; Isa. 34, 62:1–6). Actual racial purity was not sought, and Israel had mixed origins.

Physical cleanliness was practiced by washing the hands and feet before and after eating (John 13:6 ff.), especially on returning from the market place (Mark 7:4). People bathed in the courts of their homes (II Sam. 11:2). Jerusalem pools, like Bethesda*, were popularly used for cleansing as well as healing. Ceremonial bathing for people having discharges is mentioned in Lev. 15:5 ff. Syrians dipped themselves in their cold rivers (II Kings 5:12). Egyptian priests bathed four times daily. Princesses bathed in the rush-lined Nile (Ex. 2:5). Many of Israel's laws concerning purification were wise sanitary precautions, but more than hygienic measures were needed to make a man fit to enter the presence of Yahweh. Purity meant freedom from avoidable and unavoidable sources of contamination.

Ceremonial purification. Israel's Law codes are specific about the purification of land and people. The Deuteronomic Code (Deut. 12–26), for example, provided rites for purifying territory where a murder had been committed by an unidentified criminal (Deut. 21:1–9); about situations arising when unclean food had been eaten (see ANIMALS); and when a leper had come into a camp, and when mold was found on fabric or structure. The Holiness Code (Lev. 17–26) prescribed purification rites, e.g., for those who had eaten the flesh of a dead animal (Lev. 17:15 f., 22:8; cf. Ezek. 44:31). The Priestly Code (all of Leviticus and the legal portions of Exodus and Numbers), like the earlier codes, enjoined purifications: for women after childbirth (Lev. 12; cf. Luke 2:21–24); for skin diseases (Lev. 14); for secretions of the body (15:14 f., 19–30); after touching the dead bodies of unclean animals (5:2 f.), or a corpse (Num. 19). The P Code stressed the rites for the purification of priests (Lev. 8:5–8, 21) and of Levites (Num. 8:6–8).

Christian purity. Jesus denounced the purification rites of the priests and Pharisees, which in his day had become hopelessly burdensome. When accused by them for not washing his hands before eating, he explained that a man is not defiled by what enters into him, but by the evil thoughts and motives which proceed out of his heart (Mark 7:18–23). He denounced those Pharisees who washed the outside of their cups and plates but failed to cleanse the inside of their filthy hearts (Luke 11:39); and told his Disciples that all things were clean to them (v. 41). Jesus abolished ceremonial purifications. He told his disciples at the Last Supper, "Now ye are clean through the word which I have spoken unto you" (John 15:3). He summarized his whole teaching on purity in "Blessed are the pure in heart: for they shall see God" (Matt. 5:8).

Paul wrote to the Church at Philippi concerning purity (I Cor. 5:7; Phil. 4:8).

purple, a rich red-blue color prized by Near Easterners for dyeing garments (Prov. 31:22; Jer. 10:9) and other textiles. Kings arrayed themselves in purple (Judg. 8:26; cf. the robe of purple placed on Jesus by the Roman soldiers, Mark 15:17, 20). Purple textiles were brought for the Tabernacle curtains (Ex. 25:4, 26:1). Hiram*, the craftsman-architect of Tyre, was skillful in dyeing and weaving the purple material Solomon desired for the veil of his Temple (II Chron. 2:14, 3:14). Purple was used for priests' ephods (see EPHOD) (Ex. 28:5 f.), girdles (v. 8), and "breastplate of judgment" (v. 15). Purple pomegranates were appliquéd or embroidered on the hem of the robe of the ephod (v. 33). Purple was a favorite color for accessories and garments in Persian palaces (Esther 1:6, 8:15). Purple was the color of the anemones ("lilies of the field") to which Jesus likened the garments of Solomon (Matt. 6:28 f.). Again, he referred to the "purple and fine linen" of a certain rich man (Luke 16:19). The chief source of the famous Tyrian purple was the tiny mollusks (murex) found along the Phoenician coast and exported far and wide (Ezek. 27:7, 16). Lydia of Thyatira, Paul's first European convert, sold purple dyes or purple-dyed textiles in the market place of Philippi (Acts 16:14).

purse, a small bag or pouch (Prov. 7:20) for carrying money; the Middle Easterner carried it in his girdle. The "bag with holes" used by Haggai (1:6) as the symbol of an inflated economy suggests why many ancient coins are unearthed in Palestine today—they dropped out of poorly made purses. Jesus mentioned the purses of his Disciples (Matt. 10:9; Luke 22:35 f.). Judas "had the bag" containing the common purse of Jesus and his company (John 12:6); from this purse the eleven were accustomed to see him dispense coins to buy their food, or to help the poor (John 13:29). The symbol of Judas in Christian art is three money bags.

Put (pŭt), possibly a corruption of Punt. See PUL (2).

Puteoli (pū-tē′ŏ-lī) (the modern Pozzuoli), an Italian harbor on the W. coast of Italy 8 m. W. of Naples, founded probably by Samian settlers from Cumae (c. 520 B.C.). Though it was much farther from the capital than Ostia*, its excellent roadstead made it a principal port of Rome for ships from the E., especially grain boats. The prisoner Paul

355. Traditional site of John's baptism of Jesus.

landed at Puteoli on an Alexandrian grain ship and was entertained for seven days by Christians living there; from Puteoli he went overland to Rome (Acts 28:11, 16). The huge Puteoli amphitheater, still remarkably well preserved, was completed by Vespasian (A.D. 70–78). Paul probably saw the older structure (426x138 ft.) which preceded it, whose remains have now been found.

pygarg (pī′gärg), a large, light-colored antelope; Moffatt and R.S.V. use the word "ibex" (Deut. 14:5).

Pyramid Texts, the, "the earliest body of religious literature," more than 7,000 lines of hieroglyphics incised on the interior walls of five small royal pyramids erected at Saqqârah, Egypt, near Memphis, c. 2400–2200 B.C. The Texts, some of them pre-Dynastic, came to light in 1880 when the French archaeologists Auguste Mariette and Gaston Maspero discovered the pyramids buried in the sand. They were published in facsimile by Kurt Sethe and associates, and were translated and interpreted by Samuel A. B. Mercer of the University of Toronto. This literature records proverbs, myths, history and all phases of early culture in Egypt. The opening of the deity Nut's utterance on the walls of the Teti Pyramid (Sixth Dynasty), similar to Matt. 3:17, reads, "This is (my) beloved, in whom I am well pleased." See *The Pyramid Texts in Translation and Commentary* (4 vol.), by Samuel A. B. Mercer, Longmans, Green.

pyramids. See BURIAL.

Pyrrhus (pĭr′ŭs), the father of Sopater of Berea, who accompanied Paul on his last journey to Jerusalem (R.S.V. Acts 20:4).

Q

NOTE. Some authors spell with a "q" names that begin with a "k" sound—"Qadesh" for "Kadesh," etc.

Q, an abbreviation for *Quelle* (Ger. "source"), a hypothetical document or documents from which, some scholars believe, the Gospels of Matthew and Luke derived material not found in Mark. Q is sometimes called the "second source," Mark being termed the "first source." It is also known as the "Logia" or "Sayings of Jesus," and may comprise material from oral Aramaic and Greek sources. Q is rich in Christ's discourses, and has been called an "anthology" of his wisdom sayings. Since its existence has never been unquestionably proved, some scholars prefer to attribute material common to Matthew and Luke but not appearing in Mark as due to the borrowing of one of these two writers from the other. See also SOURCES.

Qadisha, a river entering the Mediterranean at Tripolis, the ancient Phoenician port, out of the high Lebanons. Its deep gorge forms the main approach to the 6,000-ft. elevation where a few ancient cedars of Lebanon survive. It is possible that when Hiram of Phoenicia shipped cedars to Solomon for his Temple, his workmen lowered them by way of the Qadisha Valley to the Sea, and there lashed them into floats for their drift S. to coastal Palestine, whence they were hauled c. 25 m. to Jerusalem. (See LEBANON, illus. 241.)

Qain (Arab., from Aram. *quanaya*, "smith"; cf. Cain and Tubal-cain, Gen. 4:22), a word which indicates clans of traveling coppersmiths, such as the Kenites* may have been. The Kenites, one of whose women Moses married, could have imparted to Israel their knowledge of the rich metal deposits of E. Palestine. Their kindred Kenezites lived in the Valley of the Smiths (I Chron. 4:13 f.), whose "city of copper" may have been the vast Iron Age mining center Khirbet Nahas ("Copper Ruin") Nelson Glueck located at the N. end of the Wâdī Arabah.

Qelt, Wâdī, also known as Wâdī Kelt, a deep valley rising in the highlands NE. of Jerusalem. It runs E. through the Wilderness of Judaea by a picturesque canyon seen from the old Jerusalem-Jericho road. The Qelt never fails to water the oasis city generously, before running across the valley to join the Jordan. Wâdī Qelt has been erroneously identified with the Valley of Achor* and with the Brook Cherith* of Elijah. A conspicuous feature of the Wilderness landscape into which its waterfalls bring other-worldly beauty, Wâdī Qelt must have been seen by many Biblical personalities who walked from Jerusalem to O.T. and N.T. Jericho. Today the Orthodox Convent of St. George ("Monastery of Elijah") clings to its precipitous cliffs. See illus. next page.

quail, a small game bird, *Coturnix coturnix*, c. 10 in. long, belonging to the same order as domestic fowl, pheasants, partridges, and grouse. It resembles the American quail or bobwhite. It was supplied providentially to hungry Israel on the trek from Egypt toward Canaan (Ex. 16:3, 8, 13; Ps. 105:40); birds not immediately eaten were spread out to dry (Num. 11:32). Quail was not a constant source of food for Israel through their Wilderness wanderings. This accords with the fact that migrating quails fly with the wind, but often fall exhausted when the wind shifts; Num. 11:31 tells that the Lord brought the quails by a wind from the sea. When Israel moved inland, quails were not available.

336. Wâdī Qelt. Orthodox Convent of St. George ("Monastery of Elijah") near center.

Scientists at Sinai have observed tremendous migrations of quails from the cornfields of Rumania, Hungary, and S. Russia, across the E. Mediterranean to Africa. From the Sinai region alone thousands of quails per day have been exported for the tables of Europe. For 3,500 years Egypt has been catching quails in trammel nets, stretched between 21-ft. poles, or hand nets, thrown down over bushes where the quails rest.

Quarantania, Mt., a traditional name for the "exceeding high mountain" of Christ's Temptation* in the Judaean Wilderness (Matt. 4:1, 8). This elevation, c. 1½ m. W. of ancient Jericho (Tell es-Sultân), presents an almost perpendicular face to the plain. Its location is still isolated.

quarries, open excavations from which is obtained stone for houses, palaces, shrines, idols, cisterns, pits, walls, and roads. Evidence that quarries were worked in ancient times has been found: caves E. and W. of the Jordan have been stripped; masons have left marks of their picks; and crude decorations and writing have been drawn or scratched on quarry walls. Quarries are mentioned in the Bible only in Judg. 3:19, 26, and there perhaps should read "graven images." The so-called "Solomon's quarries" is a tremendous cavern adjacent to the Dome of the Rock (the former Temple Area) between the Damascus Gate and Gordon's "Calvary." Its mouth is 350 ft. across. Its hollow space runs back 250 yds. SE. through the bedrock of a cliff topped by the Bezetha section of Jerusalem. It may have supplied stone for Herod's Temple, but probably not for that of Solomon. Its stone is snow white when freshly quarried, and turns to mellow ivory. Some of its vertical blocks, wedged from the quarry wall and intended to be loosened with water rather than tools, are still in place (cf. I Kings 6:7). In Solomon's quarry some of the early meetings of Freemasons were held. Other extensive ancient quarries and resultant caves exist near Sarafand (Zarephath) (I Kings 17:9 ff.) adjacent to Sidon, and at Caesarea. The latter evidently supplied limestone for Phoenician builders long before the Romans built Caesarea.

Quartus, a Christian "brother" associated with Paul, probably at Ephesus; mentioned as sending greetings in the Epistle to the Romans (16:23).

quaternion, in the N.T., a squad of four soldiers. Peter was put in the custody of four quaternions (Acts 12:4). The quaternion of Roman soldiers assigned to the watches during the detention and Crucifixion of Jesus divided his garments among them in four parts (John 19:23).

337. Monastery of the Temptation, Jericho.

Queen of Heaven, the, an ancient Semitic deity, the Babylonian Ishtar (Venus), popular in Jerusalem and Egypt in Jeremiah's time and earlier, especially among women, who baked cakes used in the ritual of her worship (Jer. 7:18, 44:17–19, 25). The prophet sternly denounced the Queen-of-Heaven cult as offensive to the Lord. When the people attributed their past prosperity to the burning of incense and the pouring out of drink offerings to her (44:19), Jeremiah proclaimed that their present sufferings were due to God's displeasure at their apostasy.

queens, as consorts, normally had little power in Israel and Judah; yet see such allusions as Jer. 13:18, 29:2. When the line of succession was at stake they often interfered (e.g., David's Bath-sheba, Ahab's Jezebel), even murdering to accomplish their ambition (Jehoram's Athaliah). Such heads of ancient states as the Sheba and Candace queens of Arabia and NE. Africa enjoyed great prestige. One of the important pharaohs of Egypt was the Eighteenth Dynasty Queen Hatshepsut (c. 1490–1469 B.C.). Much is known of this Egyptian queen since Howard Carter's excavation of her tomb in the Valley of the Kings. Structures of her reign at Deir el-Bahri present magnificent records of her luxury-seeking expedition to Punt, much like Solomon's some five centuries later for similar wares (I Kings 10:22). See individual entries for Biblical queens, like ATHALIAH; BATH-SHEBA; BERNICE; CANDACE; ESTHER; JEZEBEL; MAACAH; SHEBA; VASHTI. See also ALEXANDRA (mother of the Maccabean rulers Hyrcanus II and Aristobulus II).

quern, a stone hand mill for grinding grain.

quicksands ("the Syrtis," A.S.V. and R.S.V.), the loose, shifting sands and treacherous currents feared by all Mediterranean sailors plying S. of Crete and N. of the African headlands of Tunis and Barca (Tripoli). The captain of Paul's Alexandrian grain ship feared these quicksands when he ran S. of the small island of Clauda (Acts 27:16 f.) in a northeaster.

Quirinius, P. Sulpicius ("Cyrenius"), the Roman propraetor or governor of Syria, who came S. to Judaea in A.D. 6 to enroll the inhabitants as provincials and to assess taxes. A census was necessary. Scholars disagree about the historicity of Luke 2:2, which, after the statement that Caesar Augustus had decreed "that all the world should be enrolled," says: "This was the first enrollment, when Quirinius was governor of Syria" (R.S.V., cf. A.S.V. and A.V.). The coming of Joseph and Mary from Nazareth to their ancestral home at Bethlehem for such an enrollment during the reign of Herod the Great (c. 4 B.C.) throws the established date of Quirinius' census about 10 years too late. Though Quirinius in a capacity other than propraetor of Syria was in the Near East during the Homonadan War (10–7 B.C.), this circumstance would not account for Luke's chronology for the census of Quirinius. There may have been an earlier census of which secular history knows nothing. Scholars await further evidence before accepting Luke's statement that Jesus was born during an enrollment by Quirinius near the close of the reign of Herod the Great. Perhaps Luke was given inaccurate information, or perhaps he was attempting to reconcile the tradition that Jesus was born at Bethlehem with that of his family's coming from Nazareth.

quiver, a case for carrying arrows, seen in many Mesopotamian and Egyptian bas-reliefs. Foot soldiers wore it on the back or left side (Job 39:23; Lam. 3:13); chariot warriors fastened quivers to the sides of their vehicles. Quivers of arrows were also used by hunters. The Psalmist likened the man whose home is full of children to the warrior whose quiver is full of arrows (127:4 f.).

Qumran, Khirbet (kĭr′bĕt koom′răn), ruins of monastic community of Dead Sea Scrolls, located near the NW. corner of the Dead Sea, 8 m. S. of Jericho. See SCROLLS, THE DEAD SEA.

Qurun Hattîn. See HATTIN, HORNS OF.

R

Raamah (rā′ȧ-mȧ), a region and its people in SW. Arabia, listed in source P's ethnological list as a "son" of Cush. Raamah was mentioned as lying across the Red Sea (Gen. 10:7; I Chron. 1:9). The tribe of Raamah has not been identified, but from inscriptions found in Sheba it is believed to have been near Havilah and Sheba* and E. of Ophir. Together with Sheba, Raamah traded with Phoenician Tyre (Ezek. 27:22).

Raamses (Rameses) (răm′ĕ-sēz) (Ex.12:37), **an Egyptian store-city (A.V. "treasure city" Ex. 1:11) built, together with Pithom*, by** Hebrew slave labor, and the starting point of the Exodus (Ex. 12:37; Num. 33:3, 5). It was the residence city in the NE. Delta, "The House of Ramesses—Beloved of Amun —Great of Victories" (see *ANET*³, pp. 470 f. and 255), of Ramesses II (c. 1304–1237 B.C.), generally considered to be the Pharaoh of the Exodus. While a number of identifications have been proposed (Tchel, Tell er-Retabeh, Pelusium, Tanis, Qantir), no conclusive proof has been established. The most widely accepted identification is with Tanis (modern San el-Hagar), supported by P. Montet's archaeological investigations which revealed many examples of the work of Ramesses II (see A. H. Gardiner, *JEA* 19, 1933, pp. 122 ff.; R. Weill, *JEA* 21, 1935, pp. 17 ff.). The 19th Dynasty remains at Tanis, however, do not appear to be *in situ*, suggesting that they had been brought here for re-use in the 21st–22d Dynasty temple (E. P. Uphill, *JNES* 28, 1969, pp. 25 ff.). On the other hand, Qantir, 15 m. S. of Tanis, with ruins of a large urban center and a vast palace establishment, and inscriptional material indicating that Amūn-Re‘ was worshipped here (including an ostracon mentioning "Per-Ramesses-merē-Amūn the royal residence"), appears to offer a better choice (see Uphill, *JNES* 27, 1968, pp. 291 ff.; 28, 1969, pp. 15 ff.).

Rabbah (răb′ȧ) ("great"). (1) A city of Judah (Josh. 15:60), possibly the Rubutu mentioned in the Amarna Letters (EA 289–290, possibly 287; Taanach No. 1; *ANET*³, pp. 488 ff.). It has yet to be identified, though Y. Aharoni suggests Beth-shemesh (*The Land of the Bible*, 1967, pp. 286 f.). (2) (Rabbath-ammon), the chief city of the Ammonites* (Gen. 3:11; Josh. 13:25), modern ‘Ammân, capital of the Hashemite Kingdom of Jordan, located in the highlands of Trans-Jordan c. 24 m. E. of the Jordan River. David's armies besieged and captured the city during the wars with the Ammonites (II Sam. 11:1, 12:26 ff.; I Chron. 20:1). Amos (1:14) later delivered the first of a series of rebukes against the city, followed by Jeremiah (49:2–3) and Ezekiel (21:20, 25:5). In the third century B.C., Rabbah was rebuilt and renamed Philadelphia by Ptolemy II Philadelphus (283–246 B.C.), and later became one of the cities of the Decapolis. The Nabataeans occupied the city for a brief time in the first century B.C., but were driven out by Herod the Great (c. 30 B.C.). After the Roman conquest, it was replanned, erasing nearly all trace of ancient buildings. In Byzantine times it was the seat of a bishopric.

Most of the archaeological remains in 'Ammân are of the Roman, Byzantine, or Umayyad periods, including a Roman temple, Nymphaeum, and theater, a Byzantine church (6th century A.D.) with well-preserved mosaics at Tell es-Swafiyeh on the W. edge of 'Ammân, and an Early Islamic palace. Shards, tombs, and fragments of walls attest to earlier occupation, but the Roman constructions have destroyed most traces on the Citadel Hill (Jebel el-Qala'), the site of the ancient city. In 1955, a Late Bronze Age temple of square plan was discovered at the 'Ammân airport (J. B. Hennessy, *PEQ*, 1966, pp. 155 ff.), and recently a few Middle and Late Bronze and Iron Age levels have been uncovered on the Citadel. See G. L. Harding, *The Antiquities of Jordan*, 1967, pp. 61 ff.
W. P. A.

rabbi (LL., from Gk. *rhabbi*, from Heb. *rabbī*, "my great one," from Aram. *rabb*), and **rabboni** (Heb. *rabbōni*, from Aram. *ribbōni*, from *rabban*, "master"), titles given in N.T. times to learned men. Jesus accepted the salutation "Rabbi" (Matt. 23:8; John 1:38; cf. Matt. 26:25, 49, A.S.V., "Master" R.S.V. and A.V.; Mark 9:5, 11:21, 14:45; John 1:38, 49, 4:31, 6:25, 9:2, 11:8). Nicodemus*, member of the Jewish Sanhedrin, approached Jesus, saying, "Rabbi, we know that thou art a teacher come from God" (John 3:2). "The certain ruler" who inquired of Jesus "the way to inherit eternal life" addressed him "Good Teacher" (R.S.V. Luke 18:18; A.V. "Good Master"). John the Baptist was also addressed as "rabbi" by his pupils (John 3:26). Scribes and Pharisees liked to be greeted as "rabbi" in "the markets," commented Jesus (Matt. 23:7). He did not expect his Disciples to be so called (Matt. 23:8).

"Rabboni" (or "rabban"), implied even more respect than rabbi. This was used from the era of Gamaliel I in addressing the president of the Sanhedrin if he were a descendant of the great Hillel (50 B.C.–A.D. 10). "Rabboni" was used by a blind man to greet Jesus (A.S.V. Mark 10:51, R.S.V. "Master" A.V. "Lord"); and by Mary at the open tomb of Jesus (John 20:16).

In Judaism a rabbi was a graduate of a rabbinical school, an ordained scholar of the Torah, a preacher. The Jews first applied the title "Rabbenu" to their outstanding scholar, Judah ha-Nasi, and have since given the title to leading scholars of every generation. A rabbi was expected to embody the Torah in his own life, conduct himself with dignity, manifest graciousness to all, supply means of charity to the needy, guide his people to the righteous life, preach to men and women in the synagogue on the Sabbath, discuss on other occasions with the more learned the intricacies of the Law*, and study the Torah systematically. Rabbis of the Talmudic period (3d century A.D. in Palestine, 6th in Babylonia) did not accept salaries but engaged in various trades and labors; after the 15th century rabbis received salaries.

Rab-mag (răb′măg) ("great prince"). See NERGAL-SHAREZAR.

Rabsaris (răb′sȧ-rĭs). (1) The title of one of the Assyrian princely emissaries sent by Sennacherib from Lachish to demand of King Hezekiah* the surrender of Jerusalem (II Kings 18:17 ff.). (2) The title of two Babylonian officials, from an Accad. word meaning perhaps "master of eunuchs" (Jer. 39:3, 13).

Rab-shakeh (răb′shă-kē), one of Sennacherib's emissaries (see RABSARIS).

raca (rȧ-kä′) (LL., from Gk. *rhaka*, from Aram. *rēqā*, "empty"), term of scorn (Matt. 5:22), as of the "vain man" of Jas. 2:20.

Rachel ("ewe"), the shepherdess daughter of Laban*, grandson of Nahor, sought by Jacob to be his wife, even as his mother Rebekah had been sought to marry Isaac. Rachel's love story is told by the J author with even more romantic charm than that of Rebekah. She was loved devotedly by Jacob, who was compelled to serve Laban seven years for her elder sister Leah, and then seven years for her. These years of service "seemed unto him but a few days, for the love he had to her" (Gen. 29:20). When Jacob's large family group eluded Laban and started the long trek to Canaan, Rachel took her family's teraphim* or god images and hid them in her tent under her saddle. This surreptitious pilfering is understandable but not excusable in one who was surrendering all her old ties of home and family to live abroad. Rachel's

338. Rachel's Tomb.

life with Jacob in his "house" (tent) at Succoth is described in Gen. 33:17; at Shechem in 33:18 ff.; and at Bethel in 35:1 ff. After a period of childlessness like that of Sarah and Rebekah, she became the mother of Joseph (Gen. 30:24). She died giving birth to Benjamin at Ephrath. Many regard this as a site on the N. edge of Bethlehem of Judaea (Gen. 35:16–19; 48:7). Jacob erected a pillar over her grave, "that is the pillar of Rachel unto this day" (35:20). Though some scholars believe that the Ephrath (Bethlehem) of Gen. 35:19 is the northern Bethlehem near the border of Zebulun and

Asher, SE. of the Mount Carmel ridge (cf. Jer. 31:15), for almost 40 centuries the supposed site of Rachel's grave and of the little pyramid of 12 stones (one for each Tribe of Israel) erected by her husband Jacob (Gen. 35:20) has been pointed out on the right side of the road from Jerusalem to Bethlehem of Judaea. Here is located Rachel's Tomb, a small, Moorish domed structure c. 24 ft. square, erected by Crusaders during their regime at Bethlehem in the 12th century.

The strong family tie felt by Joseph for his mother Rachel and his younger brother Benjamin is recorded in the narrative of Joseph's welcome to Benjamin at the court of Pharaoh (Gen. 43:29–31).

Rachel was mentioned again in the O.T. when the elders of Bethlehem urged Boaz to enable his wife Ruth to emulate Rachel and Leah, "which two did build the house of Israel: and do thou worthily in Ephrath, and be famous in Bethlehem" (Ruth 4:11). The use of Jeremiah's prophecy, 31:15, of "Rachel weeping for her children" at the time of Herod's massacre of the babies of Bethlehem (Matt. 2:18) is tenderly reminiscent of her.

racing, a popular sport and entertainment in O.T. and N.T. times. Ps. 19:5 mentions the joy of the strong man, fit and ready to run his race. Wisdom writers emphasized the fact that the race is not necessarily won by the swift; time and chance determine the outcome (Eccles. 9:11). Paul was familiar with contests in such Graeco-Roman stadia as those at Athens, near Corinth, in Jerusalem, and at Puteoli. He compared the Christian life to a race which many run, but in which only one receives the prize; therefore, he urged, "so run, that ye may obtain" (I Cor. 9:24). He urged Christians to practice self-control, like an athlete in training for a race. He reminded them that they were striving for an eternal crown, not a wreath of laurel leaves (I Cor. 9:24–27; cf. II Tim. 2:5). The Second Letter to Timothy tells of finishing the course in life's race (4:7 f.). The author of Hebrews (12:1) urged Christians to run with patience the race set before them, and to be aware of a great crowd of witnesses, such as at athletic contests.

A race course has been excavated at Corinth, W. of the Julian basilica and parallel with it.

See GAMES.

Raguel (rȧ-gū'ĕl), the father-in-law of Moses (A.V. Num. 10:29; cf. A.S.V. Reuel*); see also JETHRO.

Rahab (rā'hăb) (Heb. Rāhābh, "broad"). (1) A harlot of Jericho* (Josh. 2:1–24) whose house was on the wide city wall, or spanned the space between two concentric walls. (Cf. Paul's escape from a house on the Damascus wall, Acts 9:25.) Josephus and the rabbis considered Rahab to have been not a harlot, but an innkeeper. Willing to cast in her lot with Israel's two spies dispatched by Joshua, Rahab hid the men on the flat roof of her house (Josh. 2:6), under stalks of flax, and let them down from her house on the wall by a rope("cord," v. 15) after identifying her house by a scarlet thread hung from a window. During the siege, as told in Josh. 6, Rahab and her family were brought out of the city, so that they escaped the total destruction of Jericho by fire (evidences of which have been excavated). Rahab is said to have lived among the Israelites long after the siege (v. 25). She is mentioned with honor in Ps. 87:4; Heb. 11:31 because of her faith by which she saved Israel's spies, and is listed in Matthew's genealogy of Boaz and Jesus (R.S.V. 1:5); some authorities question the identity of this Rahab (A.V has Rachab) with the woman of Josh. 2.

(2) A mythological monster mentioned several times in Scripture as an enemy of Yahweh, which was overcome by Him before His creation of the universe (Ps. 89:10 f.). This creature was the dragon, a sea monster, the foe of the good, as was Tiâmat in Assyrian-Babylonian myths. In a figurative sense Egypt was called Rahab (A.S.V. Ps. 87:4; Isa. 30:7; Moffatt "Dragon Do-Nothing").

raiment. See DRESS; GESTURE.

rain. See FARMING; PALESTINE.

rainbow, an arc of prismatic colors appearing opposite the sun, produced by the refraction and reflection of the sun's rays in raindrops. This natural spectacle marked the end of the Flood*, and was a sign* of God's covenant that such a deluge would never again "destroy all flesh" (Gen. 9:12–17). This is the only mention of a rainbow in Heb. literature, except in Ezek. 1:28 and Rev. 4:3, 10:1, where it suggests the effulgent glory of God. The Babylonian account of the Flood does not mention a rainbow.

raise, the translation of numerous words in the Heb. and Gk. texts, e.g., to raise up seed or posterity (Gen. 38:8; I Chron. 17:11; Matt. 3:9, 22:24; Luke 3:8, 20:28); to raise false reports (Ex. 23:1); to prepare leaders for emergencies, as prophets and prophetesses (Deut. 18:15, 18; Jer. 29:15; Acts 3:22, 7:37), judges (Judg. 2:16, 18), deliverers (Judg. 3:9, 15), kings (I Kings 14:14), and a Messiah* and Saviour (Jer. 23:5; Acts 13:23). Afflicted persons spoke of God's raising them up (Ps. 41:10). National income was raised by Solomon's levies (I Kings 5:13, 9:15). Strife and contention were spoken of as rising up (Hab. 1:6).

Numerous statements about the dead being raised or resurrected (see RESURRECTION) are made in the O.T. and the N.T. (Hos. 6:2; Matt. 11:5, 17:23; John 2:19, 6:39, 40, 44; Acts 2:30). The raising of the dead was part of the Apocalyptic* hope (John 6:39 f., 54; I Cor. 6:14; II Cor. 4:14, 5:15; Heb. 11:19).

raisins, dried sweet grapes, widely grown in Palestine for food*. Raisins made popular gifts (I Sam. 25:18; II Sam. 16:1). The raisin cakes used in heathen rites ("love cakes of raisins," A.S.V. Hos. 3:1) were condemned by Hosea; cf. "cakes to the queen of heaven" (Jer. 7:18, 44:19). See VINE.

Ram (1) A son of Hezron, ancestor of David (Ruth 4:19), the "Aram" of Gk. versions. (2) A male sheep, such as the horned ram sacrificed instead of Isaac* as an offering to the Lord by Abraham (Gen. 22:13). A pair of remarkable gold, silver, and shell statuettes of "rams caught in the thicket," dating from c. 2900 B.C., have been recovered from the royal cemetery of ancient Ur*, early home of

Abraham (Gen. 11:31); one is in the University Museum, Philadelphia. They were probably used as supports of an offering table, possibly a Sumerian "cane altar." (For rams as sacrifices, see WORSHIP.) Rams' skins dyed red formed part of the Tabernacle covering (Ex. 36:19, 39:34). Joshua used rams' horns to blow signals when he called Israel to shout at the opening of the siege of Jericho (Josh. 6:5). Heat-flattened rams' horns made the *shophar** which to this day summons orthodox Israel to worship (see MUSIC). (3) A siege ram was a heavy, horizontal beam used for battering down walls in war (see BATTERING RAM.

Ramah (Ramath) (Heb. *rāmāh*, "height"). (1) A town of Benjamin on the border between Judah and Israel (Josh. 18:25; I Kings 15:17 ff.). Deborah, the prophetess, sat under a palm between Ramah and Bethel (Judg. 4:5). The Levite and his concubine planned to stay at either Gibeah or Ramah (Judg. 19:13). Baasha, King of Israel (c. 900–877 B.C.), began to build a fortress here, which Asa, King of Judah (c. 913–873 B.C.), tore down (I Kings 15:17, 21 f.). Isaiah (10:29) traced the route of the Assyrian army (Sennacherib, c. 701 B.C.) past Ramah. After the fall of Jerusalem (587 B.C.), the captives of Judah were gathered at Ramah, and Jeremiah released (Jer. 40:1). Some returned here after the Exile (Ezra 2:26; Neh. 11:33). Rachel was associated with Ramah (Jer. 31:15; Matt. 2:18), and Hosea (5:8) mentions the site. Identification with er-Râm, 5½ m. N. of Jerusalem, is practically certain. (2) The home and burial place of Samuel, in the hill country of Ephraim (I Sam. 1:19, 2:11, 7:17, 8:4, 15:34), also called Ramathaim-zophim (I Sam. 1:1). David fled before Saul to Ramah (I Sam. 19:18 ff.). It may also be N.T. Arimathea (Matt. 27:57; John 19:38). Several identifications have been proposed, including Ramallah, 8 m. N. of Jerusalem; Nebī Samwîl; Rentis (Remphis), 9 m. NE. of Lydda; and Beit Rama, 12 m. NW. of Bethel. (3) A town on the border of Asher (Josh. 19:29), which some propose is the same as that of Naphtali, but which most locate at Ramia, c. 12 m. E. of Ras en-Naqura. (4) A fortified city of Naphtali (Josh. 19:36), usually identified with er-Rameh, 13 m. SW. of Hazor. (5) A town of Simeon, "Ramah of the Negev" (Josh. 19:8; I Sam. 30:27), unidentified. (6) Ramoth-gilead*. W. P. A.

Rameses (răm'ē-sēz). See RAAMSES.

Ramesses (Rameses) (derived from the Egyptian sun god Re* or Ra), the name of 11 Egyptian pharaohs, of whom Ramesses II ("the Great") was the most famous, and the one associated with the oppression and the Exodus* of Israel from Egypt. The Ramessids formed the Nineteenth and Twentieth Dynasties.

(1) *Ramesses I* (c. 1310–1309 B.C.), regarded as the second of the Nineteenth Egyptian Dynasty, was followed by his son, Seti I, and by his grandson,

(2) *Ramesses II* (c. 1290–1224 B.C.). This Ramesses shifted the capital to the Delta, in the region of the old Hyksos capital, Tanis-Avaris, and enlarged the store-cities, Pithom* (Tell er-Retâbeh) and Raamses*. Some authorities identify Ramesses II as the pharaoh of the oppression of Israel, while others view him as the pharaoh of the Exodus, now dated from archaeological evidence c. 1290 B.C. Merenptah (c. 1224–1216 B.C.), son of Ramesses II, and formerly regarded as the pharaoh of the Exodus, would have been too late. Ramesses II wrested a nonaggression treaty from the Hittites* after the Battle of Kadesh in Syria had established the border. He developed the Nile Delta, and built some of

339. Ramesses II.

Egypt's greatest structures: the hypostyle hall at Karnak; the colonnade at Luxor and its giant pylon, in front of which he placed six tremendous statues of himself—"the greatest boaster in Egyptian history." He erased his predecessors' names from the records of royal achievements and inserted his own, as seen on his tumbled statue at Memphis*. This Ramesses also erected the memorial temple "The Ramesseum" W. of Thebes.

(3) *Ramesses III*, son of Sethnakt, came to the throne c. 1175 B.C. During his 31-year reign the aggressions of the seafaring Philistines* were checked (c. 1175 B.C.). Some of the events in his reign may be reflected in Homer's *Iliad*.

(4) *Ramesses IV*, son of Ramesses III, was followed by a series of minor Ramessid pharaohs ending with Ramesses XI. The Twentieth Dynasty and its Ramessids were finally overthrown by Hrihor, high priest of Amun. The decline Dynasties—which, however, included such strong personalities as Shishak* (Sheshonk c. 935–914 B.C.), Psamtik I (c. 663–609 B.C.), and Nechoh* II (609–597 B.C.)—continued to function until the conquest of Egypt by Alexander the Great (332 B.C.), when native rule ended.

When the rulers of the Ramessid Dynasties

(c. 1310 to 1065 B.C.) died they were buried in lavish tombs in the lonely Valley of the Tombs, where young Tut-ankh-amun of the Eighteenth Dynasty had been interred.

The identification of the section of the Delta where Joseph's friendly pharaoh settled the Jacob tribes (c. 1700 B.C.) as "the land of Rameses" is anachronistic (Gen. 47:11), for the first Ramesses did not come to power until c. 1310 B.C.

See also EGYPT; PHARAOH.

Ramoth-gilead (rā′mŏth-gĭl′ē-ăd) ("heights"), an isolated town in Gilead* near the Syrian border, SE. of the Yarmuk, and NE. of Elisha's home at Abel-meholah on the Wâdī Yabis (? Cherith); also called "Ramah" and "Ramoth." Ramoth-gilead appears as a city of refuge (Deut. 4:43; Josh. 20:8) and a city of Levites (Josh. 21:38; I Chron. 6:80) for Gad. It was the center of Solomon's sixth administrative district, overseen by Ben-geber (I Kings 4:13). Control of this frontier town frequently alternated between Aram and Israel (see Josephus, *Antiq.* VIII.xv.3 ff.).

Ahab of Israel (c. 869–850 B.C.), with Jehoshaphat of Judah (c. 873–849 B.C.), attempted without success to recapture it (I Kings 22:3 ff.; II Chron. 18:2 ff.). Another attempt was made by Joram of Israel (c. 849–842 B.C.), with the support of Ahaziah of Judah (c. 842 B.C.), during which Joram was wounded (II Kings 8:28, 9:14 f.; II Chron. 22:5 f.). It was here that Jehu (c. 842–815 B.C.) was anointed King of Israel (II Kings 9:1 ff.). Ramoth-gilead is probably to be identified with Tell er-Rumîth in N. Trans-Jordan, as suggested by N. Glueck (*BASOR* 92, 1943, pp. 10 ff.; *AASOR* 25/28, 1951, pp. 98 ff.). It is not, however, to be equated with Mizpeh of Gilead, the home of Jephthah (see MIZPAH, 4). Excavations by P. Lapp indicate that Tell er-Rumîth was founded at the time of Solomon, supporting Glueck's identification (see *RB* 70, 1963, pp. 406 ff.; 75, 1968, pp. 98 ff.). W. P. A.

ransom. See REDEMPTION.

Rapha (rā′fȧ), the traditional head of a Benjamite clan (I Chron. 8:2).

Ras Shamrah (räs shäm′rȧ) (Ras esh-Shamrah), the ruins of ancient Ugarit (*ugrt*), capital of the N. Canaanite city-state of the 2d millennium B.C., situated on the N. Syrian coast, c. 8 m. N. of Latakia, 59 m. SW. of Antioch, and opposite the eastern tip of Cyprus, with which it carried on a flourishing trade in copper. Accidental discovery by a peasant in 1928 of a vaulted tomb of the 13th century B.C. near Minet el-Beida ("the white harbor"), the port of ancient Ugarit, led to further exploration. Since its inception in 1929, excavation of the site has been directed by C. F. A. Schaeffer, who completed his 30th campaign in 1968. Known also from the Mari texts (8th cen. B.C.) and the Amarna Letters (14th cen. B.C.), excavation has revealed a wealth of information concerning the social structure and commercial activity of Late Bronze Age Ugarit, as well as archaeological evidence for its earlier history (see esp. A. F. Rainey, *BA* 28, 1965, pp. 102 ff.; M. S. Drower, *CAH*[3], Vol. II, chap. XXIb).

Five main levels of occupation have been discerned, subdivided into various stages. The lowest level (V) consists of a pre-pottery and pottery Neolithic settlement. This is followed by a Chalcolithic level (IV) which has similarities with the Halafian culture of N. Mesopotamia. Within the Early Bronze Age level (III), a violent destruction is followed by the appearance of Khirbet Kerak ware. By the Middle Bronze Age (Level II), Ugarit was already a prosperous commercial center, having commercial relationships with the kingdom of Mari on the Middle Euphrates and contacts with Egypt. Several objects with inscriptions of Egyptian pharaohs and officials, such as a statuette of the royal vizier, Senusret-'Ankh (c. 1900 B.C.), come from this level. Important buildings of this period include the temple of Baal on the acropolis, and that of Dagon to the SE., which continued in use through the LB Age —the earliest examples of a tripartite temple with outer court, inner court, and shrine. Also of interest is "the grand stele of Baal," a near life-size representation of the Canaanite rain/storm god (*Ugaritica*, II, chap. III, plates XXIII–XXIV). Foreign contacts at Ugarit reached their peak during the Late Bronze Age (Level I), when the city functioned as a commercial trading center for peoples from Hatti, Egypt, Mesopotamia, Cyprus, Mycenae, and Syria-Palestine (see A. F. Rainey, *IEJ* 13, 1963, pp. 313 ff.). The most impressive remains of this period are those of the stone-built palace of the kings of Ugarit, with an area of c. 10,000 sq. yards. Ugarit's golden age was brought to a close at the end of the Late Bronze Age (c. 1200 B.C.) when it was devastatingly destroyed at the hands of the Sea Peoples.

340. Ras Shamrah. The harbor section of Ugarit and deserted harbor of Minet-el-Beida on Bay of Minet-el-Beida. Ras Shamrah Royal Cemetery in foreground; on horizon, Mt. Casius (Djebel Akra), believed to be the peak revered by Ugaritians as the quarter of Baal and burial place of Aleyin.

Ugarit's primary importance, however, lies in the recovery from its palace archives and temple libraries of numerous cuneiform tablets written in a variety of languages, including Ugaritic, a previously unknown NW. Semitic dialect written in alphabetic cuneiform script. It consists of a simplified combination of wedges which form 29 letters, written like Accadian, from left to right. Deciphered by C. Virolleaud, H. Bauer, E.

Dhorme, and others, these Ugaritic texts are of great importance in reconstructing the cultural life, social institutions, and religious beliefs of coastal Syria and Palestine. Secondarily, they are of value in the appreciation and understanding of the language and imagery of the O.T.

The major texts are mythological epics, copied in the first half of the 14th century B.C., but, because of archaic phrases and religious ideas, believed to date back several centuries. In a number of fragments, the leading characters are Baal, the god of rain and fertility, and the warrior-goddess Anath, which make up the series of poems about Baal and Anath (*ANET*³, pp. 129 ff.). These texts describe Baal's victory over Prince Sea (Yamm), and the tension between Baal (fertility) and Mot ("death," sterility) as mediated by Anath. Similarities in theme and imagery occur in the O.T., especially in the Prophets and the Book of Psalms (cf. Pss. 46, 93, etc.).

A second epic, The Tale of Aqhat (*ANET*³, pp. 149 ff.), relates the death of the young hero at the hands of the goddess Anath, and the mourning and ritual action of his father, King Daniel. The ending of the text is broken off, but probably relates the restoration of Aqhat to his father, perhaps only for the fertile half of the year. Again similarities are found in the O.T. (cf. II Sam. 21:8 ff.), and it is probable that this Daniel, Aqhat's father, is the same as that to whom Ezekiel refers (Ezek. 14:14, 20, 28:3.)

The Legend of King Keret (*ANET*³, pp. 142 ff.) concerns the fulfillment of Keret's desire for an heir and the fluctuations in the provisions for such. In some respects it shows a likeness to the promise of seed to Abraham (Gen. 17).

From these epics and legends, it is possible to reconstruct a great part of the NW. Semitic pantheon: El, the father of mankind and head of the epic pantheon, sometimes represented by a bull; his consort, Asherah — "mistress Asherah - of - the - Sea"; Baal (Hadad), the most active figure of the Ugaritic pantheon, the "Triumphant Lord" and "Rider of the Clouds," god of storm, rain, and fertility; Baal's sister and consort, Anath, "Mistress of Heaven"; Mot ("Death"); Kôshar, patron of crafts; and others (see W. F. Albright, *Yahweh and the Gods of Canaan*, 1968, pp. 115 ff.).

In addition to providing insight into the culture and beliefs of the people of Syria-Palestine at the time of the Hebrews, the Ugaritic texts supply additional information on the terminology and modes of expression used in the O.T. (see H. L. Ginsberg, *BA* 8, 1945, pp. 41 ff.; J. Gray, *AOTS*, 1967, pp. 145 ff.). For example, Yahweh—like Baal—rides on the clouds (cf. Ps. 68:4, 33). Again, R.S.V. "upsurging of the deep" has been accepted as more meaningful than A.V. "fields of offering" in II Sam. 1:21 in the light of similar expressions in Ugaritic. Similarly, lumps of figs are prescribed as a poultice in a Ugaritic text (cf. II Kings 20:7; Isa. 38:21). As a final example, the poetic style of the Ugaritic texts—repetitive, with irregular meter and parallelism—have been used by Albright and others to argue for the early date (13th–10th cen. B.C.) of several O.T. poetic passages, such as the song of Deborah in Judg. 5 (see Albright, *Yahweh and the Gods of Canaan*, 1968, chap. I).

In addition to the references cited above, see: excavation reports, C. F. A. Schaeffer, *Ugaritica* I–VI, 1939–1969; myth. texts published by C. Virolleaud (ref. in *ANET*³, pp. 129 ff.); publications of texts by J. Nougayrol and C. Virolleaud, in *Le palais royal d'Ugarit* (PRU); grammar, C. H. Gordon, *Ugaritic Textbook*, 1967 (UT); trans., C. H. Gordon, *Ugaritic Literature*, 1949; G. R. Driver, *Canaanite Myths and Legends*, 1956; J. Gray, *The Legacy of Canaan*, 1957; M. H. Pope, *El in the Ugaritic Texts*, 1955; M. J. Dahood, *Psalms*, I–III. W. P. A.

raven, any of several large birds in the crow family. A raven, released from the ark by Noah after forty days, flew back and forth until the Flood waters abated (Gen. 8:7). The raven was rated "unclean," unfit for food (Lev. 11:15; Deut. 14:14). Wisdom writers pictured God as providing food even for the unattractive, unwholesome ravens (Job 38:41; Ps. 147:9). Jesus also taught that the Father provides for the ravens, who "neither sow nor reap" (Luke 12:24). Ravens were associated with plundered cities (Isa. 34:11). Their raucous cruelty is mentioned—plucking out the eyes of those who mock or abuse their parents (Prov. 30:17).

Re (Ra), the great sun god, most popular of Egyptian cosmic deities; the son of Geb, male earth god, and Nut, goddess of the sky. He was thought of as traveling across the sky-ocean in a boat each day, and descending by another boat to the underworld every night. The pharaohs (see PHARAOH) regarded themselves as sons of Re, his living image on earth —though kings were not usually worshipped in temples as divine beings. From the life giving Re each pharaoh derived his sovereignty, and by Re's all-illuminating eye was guided on foreign expeditions. Re's name was incorporated into the names of kings, e.g., Menkheperre ("enduring is the form of Re"), a title adopted by the powerful Thutmose III. A cuneiform record of Amenhotep IV (Akhenaton*) names him Nefrkheprure ("beautiful of form is Re"), with the extra title of Wanre ("the unique one of Re"). Queen Hatshepsut was "the daughter of Re." An army division might call itself "the division of Re." The influence of the sun god followed the economic trails of Egypt, as at the Phoenician Byblos (see GEBAL), whose chief trader-prince liked to be called "the son of Re, beloved of the gods of his land." Even the pharaohs of the barbaric Hyksos Dynasty dubbed themselves "sons of Re, the living image on earth of Re, the like of whom does not exist in any other country."

Re worship permeated the Middle East, and may have influenced Hebrew prophetic thought, as, e.g., in the last chapter of the O.T., Malachi's "unto you that fear my name shall the Sun of righteousness arise with healing in his wings" (4:2). This was written long after Akhenaton's famous Hymn to the Sun, found in tomb reliefs near Amarna, which has parallels in Ps. 104:20, 21, 22 ff.

The worship of Re centered chiefly at Heliopolis (the Biblical On*). Here the god was honored as Re-Horakhti (Re-Horus of the Horizon), by some of whose priesthood young Akhenaton may have been tutored. A priest of this powerful temple became the father-in-law of the Hebrew Joseph (Gen. 41:45). Thutmose honored the Re-Horakhti of this city of the sun with a lavish temple, near which, every three or four years, he erected obelisks (see OBELISK).

Re, the cosmic Aton, was immortalized by the young solar-monotheist Amenophis (Amenhotep) IV, who changed his name to Akhenaton and built a new city, Akhetaton (later known as Amarna*), to honor his god. This pharaoh worshipped a less crude sun god than the old Re-Horakhti honored at Heliopolis; he did not tolerate images of Re; worshippers were expected to adore only the visible, burning disk of the sun, which was shown on tomb reliefs, extending radiating beams that terminated in hands offering blessings to the king and his family, or holding out to them the *ankh*, or key of life, *uraeus*. A purer ritual was promoted at Akhetaton than at Heliopolis. The new state religion regarded Aton as the sole god, not only of Egypt, but of the world; it developed a pure—if materialistic—monotheism*, centered in "the lord of all that the sun encircles." The finest expression of praise of the sun god Aton is the great Hymn of Praise found on the Tomb of Eye.

reaping. See FARMING. For the symbolic use of the word see Ps. 126:5; Prov. 22:8; Hos. 8:7; Amos 9:13; Mic. 6:15; Matt. 6:26, 13:30, 25:26; John 4:38; I Cor. 9:11; II Cor. 9:6; Gal. 6:7 ff.; Rev. 14:15.

Reba (rē′bȧ), a Midianite sheikh ("prince") slain by Israel (Num. 31:8; Josh. 13:21).

Rebekah (Rom. 9:10 Rebecca), the daughter of Milcah and Bethuel, son of Nahor, brother of Abraham (Gen. 24:15, 47); sister of Laban the Syrian (Gen. 25:20). Rebekah is prominent in the superb Patriarchal narratives of the J document. She was brought from Abraham's ancestral homeland in Aram* by the Patriarch's trusted servant to be the wife of his son Isaac, lest the Hebrew youth marry a daughter of the Canaanites (Gen. 24). When Rebekah's brother learned of Abraham's desire to have her marry his son, he allowed the girl to make her own decision (v. 57 f.)—a comment on the rights of woman in the upper classes of Patriarchal society. Rebekah journeyed to Isaac in "the south country" (Negeb*) near the well La-hai-roi, under the chaperonage of her nurse or maid Deborah (Gen. 24:59, 35:8).

The courtship of Rebekah is one of the highlights of the sagas of the Patriarchs, even though the camel feature of the romantic cavalcade may be anachronistic (see CAMEL).

Rebekah bore two sons, Esau* and Jacob*. She showed greater affection for the younger, Jacob, and planned his crafty seizing of the traditional birthright* and inheritance* privileges from Esau (Gen. 25:28–34).

Later incidents in the life of Rebekah include her being represented by Isaac as his sister while they were living among King Abimelech's Philistines in Gerar* (Gen. 26:6 ff.). She shared her prosperous husband's life in the Beer-sheba region, where he dug his three famous wells (26:23–33). (See BEER-SHEBA, illus. 54.)

Irked by local Canaanite girls, such as "the daughters of Heth," Rebekah encouraged Jacob to seek a wife from among her own people in Padan-aram (27:46), where he met Rachel, daughter of Laban, son of Nahor (29:5, 10), at her father's well. Rebekah evidently died prior to her son's return with his betrothed. She was buried in the Cave of Machpelah*, near Sarah, her mother-in-law (49:31). Her old nurse Deborah may have survived her, for Deborah's burial at Bethel under the oak Allon-bacuth ("the oak of weeping") is told later in the narrative (35:8). Rebekah's grave is honored today in the sacred Moslem mosque at Hebron.

receipt of custom, the place of toll (A.S.V.), the "tax office" (R.S.V.), where the people of Judaea under Roman rule paid their tribute and customs money to the publicans* or tax collectors, as they did to Matthew at Capernaum (Matt. 9:9; Mark 2:14; Luke 5:27).

Rechab (rē′kăb) (Heb. *rēkhābh*, "rider"). (1) The son of Rimmon, who participated in the murder of Saul's lame son, Ish-bosheth, in his bed—a crime for which David punished him by death (II Sam. 4).

(2) The father of Jonadab (Jehonadab), who, in his zeal to extirpate the Baal-centered idolatry of Ahab, King of Israel (c. 869–850 B.C.) co-operated with Jehu* in annihilating the large household of Ahab at Jezreel, together with his great men, kinsfolk, and priests (II Kings 10:1–28). This successful elimination of Baal worship from Israel resulted from Rechab's Kenite (see KENITES) traditions (I Chron. 2:55). The Rechabites abstained from intoxicating wines, and continued to live in tents long after Israel had settled down in village houses, in protest against the corrupting influences of Canaanite civilization and the worship of Baal, lord of the vines (see VINE). The principles of the Rechabites were commended by Jeremiah, who contrasted their loyalty to their ideals with the faithlessness of Judah to Yahweh (Jer. 35:2–19); some of these ideals survived in the Nazirite (see NAZIRITES) vows. Rechabite trends are said to survive in the Hamathite sections of Syria and in Arabia.

(3) The father of Malchiah*, who repaired the Dung Gate of Jerusalem in Nehemiah's time (Neh. 3:14).

reconciliation implies an estrangement which has been overcome, so that happy relations are again possible for the estranged. Though the O.T. rarely uses the word itself, O.T. religion, both on its priestly or ritualistic side and on its prophetic or ethical side, is largely a religion of reconciliation. Men by disobedience and indifference have made impossible a true fellowship with God; the

RECONCILIATION

hindrance to this fellowship must be removed; with the removal, fellowship is again established—and this is reconciliation. The O.T. also deals with the reconciliation of man and man. The provision for cities* of refuge had to do with this (Deut. 19:4–10; cf. the legislation in Deut. 19:15–21). For examples of human reconciliation, see the story of Jacob and Esau (Gen. 32:1–33:17), and of Saul and David (I Sam. 24:1–22). Jesus taught that men who remained hostile to each other could not hope to be reconciled to God (Matt. 5:21–24; cf. 6:12, and the parable of the unmerciful servant, 18:21–35).

341. Reconciliation (Matt. 5:23 f.), represented by stone reliefs in the Oratory of Jerusalem YMCA: 1. "If thou bring thy gift to the altar," 2. "and there rememberest that thy brother hath aught against thee." 3. "Leave there thy gift before the altar, and go thy way; first be reconciled to thy brother," 4. "and then come and offer thy gift."

The Jewish sacrificial system was intended primarily to bring about reconciliation between man and God (see WORSHIP). The sacrifices were offered as an "expiation" or "propitiation": hence the close connection between reconciliation and atonement. The implication is that the barrier to fellowship really originates on the human side. When man in the prescribed way removes the barrier, reconciliation with God follows. The O.T. priest was inclined to stress the sacrifices as all-important; but the O.T. prophet declared there was no true reconciliation apart from a pure heart and a right spirit—the classical passage is Micah 6:6–8.

In the N.T. it is chiefly Paul who sets forth reconciliation doctrinally. He combines the two emphases of the O.T., namely, a sacrificial offering and a new life. But the sacrifice is not made by the sinner—it is made on his behalf by another; and the new life comes about because by faith the sinner sees the sacrifice as made on his behalf. Moreover, it is God Who provides the sacrifice, and thereby takes the initiative in seeking reconciliation. Through Christ God seeks to "destroy the enmity" (Eph. 2:14–18), and this actually occurs when His appeal through Christ evokes from sinful men repentance, faith, and love. Thus Paul speaks of the work of Christ as "a ministry of reconciliation" (II Cor. 5:18–20), effected through his "satisfying" the righteousness of God (cf. Rom. 3:22–26). The reconciliation is therefore (1) an accomplished fact, as in Rom. 5:10; (2) a fact to be humbly "received," as in Rom. 5:11; (3) a means of coming to peace with God, as in Eph. 2:13–22; and (4) a power to transform the "alienated" into men "holy and without blemish and unreprovable before God," as in Col. 1:21 f.

See FORGIVENESS; PROPITIATION; REDEMPTION; SALVATION. E. L.

red, the color of Esau (Gen. 25:25); of his pottage (25:30); of Judah's eyes (49:12); of the rams' skins in the Tabernacle* covering (Ex. 26:14); of the heifer whose ashes were mixed with the water of purification in Israel's primitive sacrifices (Num. 19:1–22; Deut. 21:3 f.); of apparel (Isa. 63:2); and of the sky (Matt. 16:2 f.). Red symbolizes sin (Isa. 1:18)—the red horses in the visions of Zechariah (1:8, 6:2) and of the writer of Revelation (6:4); and the apocalyptic dragon (12:3). In Christian symbolism, red represents zeal.

Red Sea, the (Heb. *yam suph*, "sea of reeds"—though there are no reeds in the Red Sea—and *yam mitzrayim*, "Egyptian Sea," Isa. 11:15), the 1350-m.-long oceanic gulf extending from the Indian Ocean to the Gulf of Suez. It is over 7,200 ft. deep and c. 127 m. wide. It is bordered on the W. by the Egypt, Cush, and Punt of ancient times, and on the E. by the Arabian peninsula. Its two main arms, both of which figure in O.T. history, are the Gulf of Suez (see EXODUS for comments on "the Sea of Reeds") and the Gulf of Aqabah*. The name "Red Sea" may come from its ancient copper-skinned peoples, or from colorful deposits on its bed and shores. "Red Sea" was applied to the Gulf of Suez (A.V. Ex. 10:19, 15:4) in early times, and later to the Gulf of Aqabah, as well as to the entire body known as the Red Sea (Ex. 23:31). Through the centuries the two arms of the Red Sea may have pushed north. Its long coasts have few good harbors; and sudden storms wrecked frail craft, as evidenced by the wreck of King Jehoshaphat's trade expedition (I Kings 22:48 f.). Egyptian navigators, however, made their way down the Red Sea to Punt on the Somaliland coast, to trade Nile Valley products for the perfumes of Arabia; and the navies of Solomon and Hiram navigated the Sea and brought back luxury wares (II Chron. 9:21). The Red Sea is part of the tremendous geological fault or rift extending from the Beka'a Plain, which divides the Lebanons from the Anti-Lebanon range in Syria, S. through the Jordan and the Gulf of Aqabah and on into Africa. Semitic tribesmen crossed its waters to bring agricultural products to the people of the Nile. The Red Sea region was connected with Syria in Roman times by Trajan's famous road.

Late in 1947 the Red Sea embarkation point for turquoise miners who came across from Egypt to mine at Serabit* el-Khadem was discovered by the University of California African Expedition. It is on the E. shore of the Gulf of Suez, near Merkhah, c. 5 m. S. of Abu Zeneimeh, an Egyptian settlement active in the 15th century B.C. The site, near the present shore of the Dead Sea, suggests that the shore line of the Red Sea has not changed appreciably in 3,500 years. This port adds evidence to the belief that Israel crossed the Sea of Reeds in the N., rather than the Red Sea in the S.

Redeemer. See ATONEMENT; JESUS CHRIST; MEDIATOR; PROPITIATION; RECONCILIATION; REDEMPTION; REGENERATION; SALVATION; SAVIOUR; SON OF GOD.

redemption, the act of redeeming, or the state of being redeemed. The root meaning of the word "redeem" is "to set free," or "to cause to be set free." Sometimes an offering or a gift is required as a condition to the release. Sometimes property is spoken of as being redeemed; this emphasizes the idea of "purchase" or "buying back." In the story of Ruth* her kinsman Boaz fulfilled the part of her "redeemer" (Ruth 4:1–6); and at the request of his cousin Hanameel the prophet Jeremiah* "redeemed by purchase" a field in his native village of Anathoth* (Jer. 32:1–15). Various laws concerning this kind of "redemption," or "buying back," or "setting free," are described in Lev. 25 and 27.

The redemption of poor men who had sold themselves to sojourners or strangers was possible through their purchase by a near kinsman on the payment of a sum by the individual himself, or by the operation of the laws concerning the Year of Jubilee (Lev. 25:47–55).

The Jewish sacrificial system was regarded as having redeeming significance; it provided a means for setting men free from the displeasure of God. His favor, which had been lost by disobedience, was thought of as being "bought back" by these prescribed means. What is emphasized is the idea of a transaction. Closely associated words are those of "ransom," "propitiation," and "atonement." (Cf. Ex. 21:30, 30:12; Job

33:24; Ps. 49:6–8; Matt. 20:28; I Tim. 2:6.) In the O.T. God is frequently spoken of as the Redeemer of His people, and certain of His "mighty acts" are spoken of as the means of redemption; but in such cases there is usually no thought of any transaction: God of His free, unmerited grace, and in fulfillment of His covenant, "redeems" His people from dangers that threaten them (see Deut. 13:5, 21:8; II Sam. 7:23; Ps. 74:2, 77:15). The description of God as Redeemer is especially frequent in Isaiah (41:14, 43:14, 44:6, 24, 47:4, 48:17, 49:26, 59:20, 63:16).

The O.T. recognized corporate redemption: many could be set free because of what was done or suffered by one. Joshua's army was set free—"redeemed"—from the curse by the stoning of Achan* and his family (Josh. 7:1 f.). The ritual of the red heifer (Num. 19:1–10; cf. Lev. 9:1–24) and of the scapegoat was regarded as setting free or redeeming the nation. The belief that God Himself was "Redeemer," that He did not exact an equivalent, and that what was endured by one could avail to set free the many, represents a higher concept than that of redemption as a transaction.

The Bible therefore deals with redemption in two different ways: sometimes it means what men do for themselves or for each other to effect deliverance from danger, and in particular to regain the lost favor of God; and sometimes it means a deliverance that comes to men because of the gracious activity of God on their behalf. The grace of God is not absent from the transactional concept; but it is understood as grace that inclines God to accept one thing in place of another, especially an offering instead of an inflicted loss or punishment. In the concept, however, which sees God as Himself the Redeemer Who effects the redemption or brings about the release, the grace is much more apparent, because God provides on His own account the means necessary to set men free—especially freedom from sin, from sinning, and from the fruits of sin.

It is this second concept that is central in the N.T. God redeems men or sets them free by something He does on their behalf. The redemption, however, is not by mere announcement; it is an accomplishment of God. A costly act on His part is the means whereby He would set men free. The various forms of redemption in the O.T. always cost something. The Christian redemption is a redemption for which God paid the price. The eternal Father gives from within Himself His eternal Son to redeem men from bondage—primarily spiritual bondage. Men need to be "set free" from a power greater than themselves, and it is this that God sets Himself to accomplish in Jesus Christ. It cannot be accomplished without cost; but God lays the cost upon Himself, since what the Son endures the Father also endures, and both endure it from the same motive of holy love. When the means of release is described as a "ransom" (I Tim. 2:6), the "cost" to Christ is implied, but in the unique sense of "giving himself." A similar self-giving is required of the redeemed; he who is himself "ransomed" must be prepared to be a "ransom" (John 10:14–18, 15:13 f.; I John 3:16; cf. Heb. 10:3–18; II Cor. 6:4–10, 11:23–29). This is the practical side of Christian faith, and the side that is so strongly emphasized in the Epistle of James (2:14–26).

See ATONEMENT; GOSPEL; JESUS CHRIST; MEDIATOR; PARDON; PROPITIATION; RECONCILIATION; REGENERATION; SALVATION; SON OF GOD. E. L.

redemption of land in Hebrew society meant the regaining of real estate that had been sold (Lev. 25:24–34) (see OWNERSHIP; FEASTS).

reed, any of various tall, bamboolike grasses. The reed or flag (*qāneh*) and rush (*gōme*) have always grown in numerous varieties in the Jordan jungle and along other low-lying streams, e.g., the Nile, whose papyrus* supplied paper materials in ancient times. The "reed shaken with the wind" of Matthew (11:7), as a symbol of instability or helplessness (cf. "the bruised reed," II Kings 18:21; Isa. 42:3) may have been the *Arundo donax*, whose shining leaves grace the Jordan thickets with pluming flowers rising on stalks six to eight ft. high. This type of reed was used for measuring rods like those in Ezekiel's vision (40:3 ff.). This (or hyssop) may also have been the reed on which the vinegar-soaked sponge was lifted to the lips of Jesus on the cross.

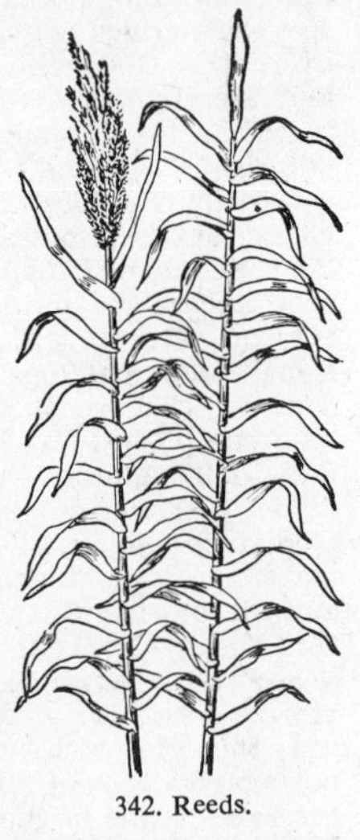

342. Reeds.

Reeds were used in Palestine to fashion rustic musical pipes and for thatching houses. Bundles of reeds, plastered with mud, were the forerunners of columns in the First Egyptian Dynasty, and later copied in stone.

A reed was used for separating the weaver's warp threads and beating up the weft on his looms. A reed was also a Hebrew unit of measure, equal to six cubits.

refining, the process of separating pure metal from alloy and dross, mentioned in the O.T. as a symbol of Yahweh's purification of Israel in the furnaces of affliction (Mal. 3:2; Isa. 48:10; Zech. 13:9). These references are of a relatively late date, for metalworking was not extensively done in Israel until David's day, c. 1000 B.C.; Mesopotamians, Egyptians, Hittites, Canaanites, Phoenicians, Philistines, and Jordan Valley-Arabah peoples were metallurgists long before the Hebrews. The Jordan rift is dotted with ancient refineries, ruins of which have been reported in Nelson Glueck's *The River Jordan* (Westminster Press) (see EZION-GEBER). Today in the native silversmiths' bazaars of Damascus and Jerusalem refiners of silver and gold bend over their small fining pots, or crucibles, as in O.T. times (Prov. 17:3, 27:21).

343. Refinery at Ezion-geber.

refuge. (1) Cities of refuge (see CITIES; PRIESTS). (2) The eternal God is represented as a refuge for men (Deut. 33:27; II Sam. 22:3; Isa. 25:4; Jer. 16:19; Ps. 9:9, 14:6, 46:1, 7; Heb. 6:18).

regeneration, re-creation; revival; re-establishment on a better basis. The literal meaning is "born again." There is a first birth and a second birth; the first birth, as Jesus said to Nicodemus (John 3:1–12), is "of the flesh"; the second birth is "of the Spirit." It is implied that there are two orders of life open to men, one called "natural," the other called "spiritual." Membership in the natural order comes with the gift of life itself; membership in the spiritual order is the result of a decision. The experience may be "sudden," or it may be "gradual," the result of a long period of discipline, meditation, instruction, and moral uncertainty.

Only in the N.T. does the word occur, and it is rare even there (besides John 3:1–12, see John 1:13 and I Peter 1:23; cf. I John 2:29, 3:9, 4:7, 5:1, 4, 18.) But its meaning is common throughout the Bible. Every appeal to men to undergo a radical transformation of life from the self-centered to the God-centered is, in effect, an appeal to be "born again" (see Isa. 1:16 f.; Jer. 31:33; cf. Ps. 51:5–11; Zech. 13:1). A great religious experience like that of Jacob at the ford of the Jabbok (Gen. 32:22–32); or of Moses at the burning bush (Ex. 3:1 f.); or of Josiah on hearing the reading of the Second Law (II Kings 22:8–13); or of Isaiah in the Temple (Isa. 6:1–8), might well be regarded as a "new birth." When Jesus speaks of the necessity of men becoming "as little children" (Matt. 18:1–4) he is declaring that there must be a new kind of life, entered upon in a new way, and lived according to a new principle. When Paul speaks of "adoption" into God's family the thought is that of a new birth (Gal. 4:1–7; cf. Rom. 8:12-17); this "family," according to Paul, is what God set before Himself to secure after the failure of Adam and Eve in Eden (Gen. 3:15). The promise to Abraham marked a step toward that end (Gen. 12:1–3). The process of realizing that promise is characterized by the "flesh and spirit" conflict. Paul saw that there was an "Israel after the flesh," but that this Israel was not the "family" God was ultimately seeking; God sought an "Israel after the spirit," and this was an Israel in which everyone, whatever his race, could participate. But this Israel rested on "the new covenant" (Jer. 31:31 f.; cf. Luke 22:20), not on blood kinship (Rom. 9:6–8; cf. I Cor. 10:14–18). This new Israel, this universal family of God, called for a "new birth," a birth "from above" (the real meaning of the Gk., rendered "anew" or "again" in John 3:3). The means of this rebirth is Jesus Christ, who is "the firstborn among many brethren" (Rom. 8:29); and the conditions to experiencing it are repentance, faith, obedience, and love.

Regeneration is therefore new life made possible to men by Jesus Christ through the power of the Spirit; and it involves a new relation to God, to the things of the world and to men, and by consequence a new quality of experience, describable as "life hid with Christ in God" (Col. 3:1–3).

See SALVATION; SONS OF GOD; REDEMPTION.

E. L.

Rehob (rē'hŏb) ("wide place"). (1) A northern border region searched by Israel's spies before the people entered Canaan (Num. 13:31), possibly near Dan. The people of Rehob fought with the Syrians against David (II Sam. 10:8). Also called Beth-rehob (II Sam. 10:6; Judg. 18:28). (2) A Canaanite town on the Plain of Accho assigned to Asher (Josh. 19:28, 30), which remained unconquered (Judg. 1:31). It was made a city of refuge (Josh. 21:31; I Chron. 6:75). Albright tentatively identified it with Tell el-Gharbi (Berweh), c. 5 m. SE. of Accho (*AASOR* 2/3, 1923, p. 27). (3) A Canaanite city near Beth-shan, known from a basalt stele of Sethos I (c. 1318–1304 B.C.) found at Beth-shan by the University of Pennsylvania (*ANEP*², No. 320; *ANET*³, pp. 253 f.). It is probably to be identified with Tell es-Sarem, c. 3 m. S. of Beth-shan. (4) The father of Hadadezer, King of Zobah, whom David fought when trying to recover his border at the Euphrates (II Sam. 8:3, 12). (5) A man who sealed the covenant in Nehemiah's time (Neh. 10:11).

Rehoboam (rē'hȯ-bō'ăm), a son of Solomon* and Naamah, probably an Ammonite princess whose name suggests a Canaanite goddess. He was the last king of the United Monarchy of David and Solomon, and the first ruler of the Southern Kingdom of Judah after the northern tribes made Jeroboam* I their king. There is disagreement among authorities about the dates of Rehoboam's reign. II Chron. 12:13 states that he reigned in Jerusalem 17 years, which some scholars date c. 937–920 B.C., some 933–917, others 926–907. Egyptian scholars disagree as to the date when Pharaoh Shishak* (Sheshonk I) invaded Palestine—in the "fifth year of king Rehoboam," according to II Chron. 12:2. W. F. Albright, whose chronology for the kings of Judah is followed in the present volume, uses the evidently correct antedating system, by which the 36th year of King Asa of Judah would be the 54th of a Rehoboam era, and arrives at a reign of only eight years for Rehoboam (c. 922–915 B.C.). (See *BASOR* 100, p. 20, note 14.)

The principal record of Rehoboam is found in the narrative of the Deuteronomic historian (I Kings 11:43, 12:1–24, 14:21–31); a longer account is in II Chron. 9:31–12:16.

When all Israel came to Shechem* for his coronation, Rehoboam learned of his subjects' grievances over the forced labor and excessive taxation that had supported Solomon's expensive reign. Rehoboam rejected the advice of his elder counselors to give "good words" to his people (I Kings 12:6 f.), and, following the advice of his contemporaries, told his subjects in "rough" words, "My father made your yoke heavy, and I will add to your yoke: my father also chastised you with whips, but I will chastise you with scorpions" (v. 14). This threat precipitated the revolt of his northern and eastern subjects, and Rehoboam fled in his chariot to Jerusalem for safety. Never again was the Hebrew people a united kingdom (I Kings 12:19).

Rehoboam increased the defenses of towns in Judah. He desisted from war under the persuasion of Shemaiah*, a man of God, who urged him not to fight his brothers, the Israelites (I Kings 12:24). Judah was soon invaded by the Egyptian Pharaoh Shishak (Sheshonk I), because Rehoboam and his subjects had flagrantly offended him (II Chron. 12:5). The apostasies characteristic of Rehoboam's reign are described in I Kings 14:22–24—high* places, the worship of images, groves for illicit rites, and false worship centers "on every high hill, and under every green tree," sodomy, and other immorality. This waywardness continued, though many priests and Levites moved S. into Judah when Jeroboam inaugurated calf worship at Bethel (II Chron. 11:13–17). (See JEROBOAM I for the story of his founding of the Northern Kingdom of Israel.)

Rehoboam witnessed the historic attack of Shishak on Jerusalem and the looting of the Temple treasures, including Solomon's golden shields—which the haughty king replaced with "substitutes" of baser metal (I Kings 14:25–28). His chronic war with Jeroboam and the N. (14:30) explains Rehoboam's policy of internal defense mentioned in II Chron. 11:5–12. The towns he strengthened included Bethlehem, Tekoa, Beth-zur, Gath, Mareshah, Lachish*, and Azekah. Many towns in both Judah and Israel which were despoiled by Shishak are mentioned in his campaign bas-relief at Karnak.

The Chronicler ascribes 18 wives, 60 concubines, 28 sons, and 60 daughters to Rehoboam. He died apparently a few years after the invasion by Shishak, and was buried in the City of David (part of Jerusalem), along with the "good kings" who had been deemed worthy of that honor (II Chron. 12:16).

Rehoboam was succeeded by his son Abijah (c. 915–913 B.C.), whose term fell within the long reign of his father's enemy, Jeroboam I (c. 922–901 B.C.).

Rehoboth (rē-hō'bŏth) ("room" or "open spaces"). (1) A well dug by Isaac (Gen. 26:22), uncontended by herdsmen of Gerar following disputes over two previous wells (Gen. 26:17 ff.). Rehibeh, c. 18 m. SW. of Beer-sheba has been suggested. (2) The home of Shaul, an Edomite king (Gen. 36:37; I Chron. 1:48). The site is unidentified, but "by the river" (A.V.; the context prohibits the translation "Euphrates" as in R.S.V.) suggests a location somewhere near the Wâdī el-Hesa, the N. geographical border of Edom.

Rehoboth-ir (Heb. "broad places of the city"), an Assyrian city whose foundation is ascribed to Nimrod (Gen. 10:11). It may refer to open areas around Nineveh* (i.e., part of "Greater Nineveh"), or describe Nineveh itself as a city of broad streets (see Speiser, *Genesis*, The Anchor Bible, Vol. 1, 1964, p. 68).

Rehum (rē'hŭm) ("compassion"). (1) An exiled Jew who returned from Babylon to Jerusalem with Zerubbabel (Ezra 2:2). (2) The "chancellor" of the Samaritans*, who with Shamsai wrote a letter to Artaxerxes* complaining about the motives of the men rebuilding the Jerusalem wall (Ezra 4:8 ff.). Rehum's charges delayed the completion of the rebuilding until the 2d year of Darius, King of Persia (Ezra 4:24). (3) A son of Bani, a Levite, who helped repair the Jerusalem walls (Neh. 3:17). (4) A man who sealed the covenant presented in Nehemiah's time (Neh. 10:25). (5) A clan of priests and Levites who returned with Zerubbabel (Neh. 12:3).

Rei (rē'ī) (probably "the Lord is a friend"), a loyal member of David's court during the conspiracy of Adonijah (I Kings 1:8).

Rekem (rē'kĕm) (Heb. *reqem*, "friendship"). (1) A Midianite (see MIDIANITES) king slain with four others by the Israelites en route to Canaan (Num. 31:8; Josh. 13:21). (2) An eponymous ancestor of a Calebite (see CALEB) family associated with the man Hebron (I Chron. 2:43 f.). (3) An eponymous ancestor (Rakem) of one of the Machir* clans in Gilead (I Chron. 7:16). (4) A town in the territory of Benjamin (Josh. 18:27).

Release, Year of, a Hebrew institution by which slaves were to be liberated in the 7th year after their purchase (Ex. 21:2–6; Jer. 34:8–15). See SABBATICAL YEAR.

religion for O.T. study may best be thought of as a system embodying the means of attaining and expressing in conduct the values deemed characteristic of the ideal life, including concepts of belief in sacred rites, sacrifices, and offerings. See WORSHIP; also individual entries, ASHERAH; BABYLON; CANAAN; EGYPT; ROMAN EMPIRE; etc.; also such entries as BAAL; RE; etc.

In Hebrew and Christian thought religion is man's recognition of his relation to God and his expression of that relation in faith, worship, and conduct.

remnant (Heb. *shear*). (1) Portions of meat, oil, and other sacrifices, left as the rightful portion for priests (Lev. 2:3, 5:13, 14:18). (2) A term applied to various peoples who survived military or political crises, e.g., the remnants of the race of giants in Bashan* (Josh. 12:4); to the various nations surrounding early Israel (Josh. 13:12); to the Amorites* (II Sam. 21:2); and to the dynasty of Jeroboam (I Kings 14:10).

(3) In prophetic utterances "the remnant," and more specifically "the righteous remnant," denoted the minority of Israel (Ezek. 9:8) who would survive the calamitous purging of the wicked by God at the time of the Exile* and the scattering of Jews in Babylonia (Isa. 10:20–23). The hope of a righteous remnant continued throughout the Exilic and post-Exilic periods. To the nucleus of the remnant within Israel other worthy people would be added from outside nations (Isa. 10:21, 11:11 f., etc.). This residue of fearless people would experience a new prosperity (Zech. 8:12); would become a holy people through obedience to God's laws (Zeph. 3:13) and their acknowledgment of God as Lord (Jer. 32:38 f.; Zech. 13:9). The whole concept of the survival of a righteous remnant presupposed God's care of His "chosen people" (II Kings 19:31; Isa. 10:22 f., 37:12; Ezek. 6:8; Joel 2:32; Mic. 2:12).

Isaiah, one of the chief proponents of the righteous remnant concept, named his son Shear-jashub ("a remnant shall return"). Paul applied Isaiah's teaching concerning the remnant to the Church (Rom. 9:27), but he warned them against overconfidence, lest Israel's fate befall them. He still hoped for the redemption* of Israel, as well as of the Gentiles, in the new universal religion, whose elect were the redeemed of every nation.

repentance in the O.T. means "turning," or—more specifically—"turning to God." In turning to God, however, the penitent also turns away from something—from that which he has come to realize is displeasing to God. The act is accompanied by sorrow for that which makes the repentance necessary. If there is not this sorrow for the evil deed or for the evil condition, then there is no true repentance. How earnestly the great prophets called on the people to turn away from evil to God may be seen in Isa. 1:10–20; Ezek. 33, especially the moving appeal in verse 11, "Turn ye, turn ye from your evil ways: for why will ye die, O house of Israel?"; Hos. 6:1–3; Amos 5:4–6, 21–24. In fact, the Heb. word for "turn" is only occasionally translated "repent" in the English versions: "turn" is the common translation, and it is the context that usually shows that the "turning" involves "repentance." (See Deut. 30:10; I Kings 8:33 f.; Prov. 1:23; Jer. 3:14, 44:4 f.; Jonah 3:7–10).

The last reference (Jonah 3:7–10) illustrates another O.T. use of "turn" or "repent." The term is frequently applied to God Himself. We often meet such expressions as "The Lord repented of the evil which he said he would do unto his people" (Ex. 32:14; cf. Gen. 6:6; II Sam. 24:16; Jer. 26:19), and "The Lord turned from his anger" (Ex. 32:12; Deut. 13:17; Josh. 7:26; II Kings 23:26; II Chron. 12:12; Ezra 10:14; Ps. 85:3). These expressions mean sometimes simply that God is being thought of as subject to human passions and emotions; in others, they mean that God "changes his mind" because the new conditions warrant it. The "evil" from which God is said to "turn" or of which he is said to "repent" is not "moral evil" in the sense of sin*; it is the punishment which He had resolved to inflict on the disobedient. It is not "evil" from God's standpoint—only from the standpoint of men; God is never thought of as doing wrong: "He will not lie," said Samuel, "for he is not a man, that he should repent" (I Sam. 15:29; but cf. 15:35). In the N.T. we have nothing corresponding to these expressions. There it is taught that God will change His attitude toward men when certain conditions are met; this, indeed, is the consistent message of the N.T. But in respect of His character and His purpose, God does not "change." James expresses this truth exactly when he writes that God is One "with whom can be no variableness, neither shadow that is cast by turning" (1:17).

The N.T., however, has much to say about human repentance; where it differs chiefly from the O.T. is in the understanding of sin. This in turn depends on the revelation which God has made of Himself in Jesus Christ. What men take to be sin depends on their belief concerning God and His purpose. There are necessarily degrees of repentance because there are degrees of understanding of God. There are certain gross and palpable sins which are widely recognized as such; it is no matter for surprise that David should repent for adultery and murder; these were not only sins, they were crimes as well (II Sam. 11:1–12:15).

But Christian repentance is by no means limited to crime and vice, or to what is often called "sins of the flesh" (Gal. 5:19–21). This deeper note is of course anticipated in the prophets, who, in opposition to the priests, saw moral fault as something much more serious than ceremonial failure (Mic. 6:6–8; cf. Lev. 5:14–16). But in the N.T. there is special emphasis on the state of the inner life. Men are called on to repent not merely for the evil things they do, but for their evil thoughts and purposes, and for that in themselves which leads them to evil. The standard of goodness in the N.T. is nothing less than Christ himself as the revelation of God's character and will; and this yields a corresponding standard for sin. See, e.g., Jesus' teaching on sin in Matt. 5:21–48. He here contrasts the state of the heart with the outer deed. One may desire to do evil, but for prudential reasons may abstain; Jesus taught that such a man had already done the evil "in his heart."

This also bears on the teaching that the Christian is to pray daily for forgiveness*; the mood of penitence is a normal Christian mood. The more the believer sees himself in the light of Christ, the more he becomes aware of his own imperfection. His penitence is not necessarily an account of gross and open sins; it is rather penitence for wandering thoughts, for uncharitable intentions, for failures of love, for thinking too much of self, for paying too little regard to self-discipline, and for the neglect of what Paul calls "the fruit of the Spirit" (Gal. 5:22 f.). The great saints are always the great penitents, because they are most severe in their self-judgment.

See GUILT; JUSTIFICATION; RECONCILIATION; SIN. E. L.

Rephaim (rĕf′ā-ĭm) (Heb. *rĕphā′īm*, "weak," "ghosts"), aboriginal giants who lived in Canaan, Edom, Moab, and Ammon. Og, King of Bashan, of the fabulous bedstead story (Deut. 3:1–11), was the last of this race. He had ruled, along with Sihon, King of the Amorites, in Jordan, from the Arnon as far N. as Mount Hermon.

Rephaim, Valley of, ("valley of the giants," A.V. Josh. 15:8), a proverbially fertile valley (Isa. 17:5), Baqa', running SW. from Jerusalem to Bethlehem, on the boundary line between Judah and Benjamin. Its productivity and proximity to Jerusalem made it an attractive prize often seized and held by the Philistines, as in the day of David (II Sam. 23:12 f.; I Chron. 11:15, 14:9). Today the railroad station and some of the suburbs of Jerusalem are in the Valley of Rephaim.

Rephidim (rĕf′ĭ-dĭm) (Heb., "plains"), a camp site of Israel en route from the Wilderness of Sin to Mount Sinai (Horeb), site unknown. At this point the wandering Israelites protested against their lack of water for themselves and their cattle. Moses met the emergency by striking a rock in Horeb and making water gush forth (Ex. 17:1–7, 19:2; Num. 33:14 f.). The people's complaints at their lack of water (Ex. 17:1–3) prompted Moses to name the place "Meribah" ("chiding" or "strife"). At Rephidim also occurred the battle between the Israelites and the nomadic Amalekites, during which Aaron and Hur held up Moses' praying hands while Joshua won the fight (Ex. 17:8–16).

Resen (rē′sĕn), an Assyrian town, possibly a suburb of Nineveh*, whose foundation is ascribed to Nimrod (Gen. 10:12). So far no plausible identification has been suggested.

reservoir, a cistern* or other basin where water is collected (see WATER). Remains of

344. The Upper Pool, one of three so-called Solomon's Pools, with ancient caravanserai in distance.

ancient reservoirs are seen at Gadara*, E. of the Jordan, and at the fortress town of S. Peraea*, Machaerus. Solomon's Pools, c. 2 m. beyond the junction of the Bethlehem and Hebron roads, from which Pontius Pilate conveyed water through stone channels to Jerusalem, was an elaborate system of reservoirs. Originally erected during the Hebrew Monarchy, these three reservoirs (the longest being 582 ft. long) were repaired by the Romans. Every Roman town E. of Jordan had several large reservoirs; some of their masonry is still watertight. The Romans knew that the prosperity of arid Palestine depended on conserving the water supply, and constructed aqueducts and underground pipe lines leading to storage cisterns. In modern times tremendous reservoirs have been built to hold the dammed-up waters of the Jordan at its junction with the Yarmuk, S. of the Sea of Galilee.

resh (rĕsh), the 20th letter of the Heb. alphabet.

Resheph (rē′shĕf), a male descendant of Ephraim (I Chron. 7:25).

residue. See REMNANT.

rest. (1) In the sense of cessation from labor, rest is first mentioned in Scripture in connection with God's "resting" from His labors of creating the universe: "he rested on the seventh day, and sanctified it" (Gen. 2:2 f.). From this example sprang the idea of the Sabbath* of rest, the Sabbatical Year, and the rest for the land every seventh year (Lev. 25:4).

345. Rest for camels and camel driver near "Solomon's Quarries," Jerusalem.

Not even the errands of mourners were allowed to interfere with Sabbath rest (Luke 23:56). The necessity for rest in the hot Near Eastern climate is reflected in such passages as Gen. 49:15, telling of Issachar's finding that "rest was good." Kindly O.T. laws provided rest for harvesters (Ruth 3:1) from 11 o'clock in the morning until the mid-afternoon breeze blew in from the Mediterranean. Rest for sheep and shepherds is mentioned in Ps. 23:2; and for people in their tents, in such passages as Num. 9:18. (Cf. Matt. 11:28, 26:45; Mark 6:31.)

(2) In the sense of the termination of long wanderings, rest was promised Israel by settlement in Canaan (Deut. 12:9 f.; Heb. 4:1); but disobedience to God cost many of them their anticipated blessings (Num. 14:23).

(3) Rest is also used to express freedom from war, as "the land had rest for forty years" (Judg. 3:11, 5:31); or "fourscore years" (3:30), from the aggressions of Canaanites or Midianites (cf. II Sam. 7:11).

The Lord promised David a son (Solomon) who would be "a man of rest" (i.e., free from foreign wars—I Chron. 22:9). The "peace and quietness" for Israel during his reign explains in large measure the great prosperity and development of the people under his care. The same deduction may be drawn concerning the city building of King Asa of Judah (c. 913–873 B.C.) who reigned 41 years, because the Lord gave him and his people rest from war (II Chron. 14:6 f.). Jehoshaphat's reign of 25 years in Judah (c. 873–849 B.C.) was marked by what the people recognized as God-given rest.

(4) Rest in the sense of peace of soul, contented mind, and security based on spiritual wholeness is emphasized in the prophetic and devotional literature of the Bible, e.g., Isa. 30:15: "In returning and rest shall ye be saved; in quietness and confidence shall be your strength." The Psalms often describe the rewards of rest offered to the man who trusts in the Lord: "Rest in the Lord, and wait patiently for him: fret not thyself because of him who prospereth in his way" (Ps. 37:7). The Psalmists invite the disheartened to find rest in the bounties of the merciful God, Who delivers, helps, and supports (116:7 ff.). The righteous man of peace finds rest in the house of God (132:14). The man who seeks help in the counsel of the Lord finds rest "in hope," i.e., he shall not be disturbed or moved by circumstances (16:9). Spiritual rest precludes such anxiety as is implied in II Cor. 2:13. To combat anxiety, Christ warned against the restlessness that comes from storing up "treasures upon earth" (Matt. 6:19 ff.), and pointed the way to refreshing peace of mind that is anxious for nothing (6:34). Christ's invitation to the overburdened was to learn of him and find rest for the soul by sharing his yoke of service and his burden of spiritual concern for others (Matt. 11:28–30).

The Book of Hebrews emphasized the rest of "the people of God" (4:9). To gain that spiritual rest involved earnest work, lest the individual fall into unbelief or disobedience to God (v. 11). In the "heavenly rest" pictured in Revelation men's toil is ended, but the fruits of their spiritual work continue with them (Rev. 14:13).

restitution, in general, the return made by an offender to a person against whom he had done an injury. It is to be distinguished from simple restoration and from retribution. Restoration means the return of that which was taken away. Restitution, however, implies a return over and above. The case is exactly stated in Lev. 6:1–7, which deals with a man who has robbed another. The law reads, "He shall restore it in full," but it continues, "and shall add the fifth part more thereto." The addition of a 5th is also specified in Num. 5:7, where it is enacted that if the restitution cannot be made directly to the wronged person it shall be made to a kinsman, or failing that, to the priest. Restoration with a plus becomes restitution. Retribution, on the other hand, has no necessary reference to the injured party. Both restoration and restitution may be refused, but retribution may still follow. There are consequences even of mistakes or wrongs that have actually been forgiven; but these consequences are retribution, not restitution.

Restitution has a large place in the O.T. In the law of holiness, found chiefly in Leviticus, it is the subject of definite legislation. In a passage like Lev. 24:17–24 restitution, restoration, and retribution, are intermingled. In Prov. 6:27 f. what is really being laid down is the principle of retribution, or the law of the harvest (cf. Gal. 6:7 f.); but in 6:30 f. the principle is that of restitution, or "making good" together with an addition —in this case "sevenfold." Zacchaeus told Jesus that he would restore "fourfold" whatever he had taken from a man unjustly (Luke 19:8). This was going beyond any legal requirement; it involved voluntariness, and indicated the depth of his repentance. There is an element of voluntariness in the elaborate "present" which Jacob prepared for Esau, as in effect a restitution for the stolen birthright (Gen. 32:3–33:17; cf. 25:27–34, 27:1–45)—though the probable motive was fear. (See PROPITIATION.) The story of the usurers told in Neh. 5:1–13 illustrates the voluntary principle; pressure, however, was exerted by Nehemiah.

In the Christian view restitution is recognized as implicit in genuine repentance; but it is not limited by mere legalities, because the Christian standard is not law but love. The Christian question is not, "What does law require?" but "What does love require?" Paul states the principle exactly: "Owe no man anything, save to love one another" (Rom. 13:8). In Christianity restitution is not limited to the specific case. This is because a wrong done against one is seen as a wrong done against many; Christian restitution therefore takes the form of sacrificial service rendered to the utmost possible extent. Albert Schweitzer, e.g., said that he went to Africa as a medical missionary in order to make what "restitution" he could to the colored races of the world for the injuries they had received at the hands of the white races. This is lifting restitution out of all the considerations of law, and transforming it into a principle of redemption. Thus Paul called himself "debtor both to the Greeks, and to the Barbarians" (Rom. 1:14). Not only does the Christian recognize the universal obligation of love, but he even regards the sins of others—at least in their social aspects—as committed by himself, and consequently imputes to himself responsibility for the consequences. Paul seems to imply this in the "anathema" reference in Rom. 9:3. This at the deepest possible level is the meaning of the Cross: the sinless Christ, by being "made sin" (II Cor. 5:21), offered to God restitution or satisfaction "on our behalf"; or, in Heb. 9:28, as the perfect sacrifice he was "once offered to bear the sins of many" (cf. Acts 3:21). The Gk. word rendered "restitution" (A.V.) or "restoration" (A.S.V.) in this reference occurs only here in the N.T., and may perhaps be rendered "rectification." See FORGIVENESS; RECONCILIATION; RIGHTEOUSNESS.

E. L.

restoration. See REGENERATION; RESTITUTION.

resurrection, literally, the return to life of the dead. It therefore means more than simple resuscitation; for resuscitation implies that the person was only apparently, not

346. The Resurrection of Christ, *by Giovanni Bellini*, recovered in 1945 by General Patton's Third Army from a salt mine in Germany, where it had been hidden by Germans who had removed it from the Kaiser Friedrich Museum in Berlin.

actually, dead. The teaching is not conspicuous in the O.T. In the early period there was no idea of the persistence of individual identity after death except in the form of a pale, shadowy, hopeless existence in "Sheol*" (Ps. 88:3–12; Ezek. 32:18–32). In general, O.T. belief in life after death took the form of the continuation of one's life in one's descendants (see the promise to Abraham, Gen. 12:1–3, and his concern at having no child, Gen. 15:1 f.). To the Hebrew childlessness was a calamity—a "reproach" (Gen. 30:22–24; I Sam. 1:1–20; Luke 1:25); for it meant that the "name"—meaning the "stock"—would be "cut off" (Ruth 4:10; cf. Ps. 37:28). The concept of corporate life was stronger in Israel than that of individual life. God's choice was believed to be a choice of the nation, which made the permanence of the nation imperative, and, within that, the permanence of the family*. Under such a concept, the survival of individual life would not seem important. The story of Saul bidding the witch of Endor to "bring up" Samuel from the grave indicates at most a belief in Sheol and the power of magic.

With the breakup of the nation at the time of the Babylonian Exile, the individual began to assume a greater importance. The Book of Job raises the question of life after death (14:7–17), only to give a negative answer (14:18–21; if 19:25 f. refers to a resurrection at all, it is only a momentary one). Some scholars see the beginning of a belief in an afterlife in such Psalm passages as 16:11, 49:15, and 73:24. Only in the very latest O.T. literature does the belief appear in unambiguous form, specifically in Isa. 26:19 and Dan. 12:2 f. Because of the Hebrew view of man as an indivisible unity, this belief necessarily took the form of a resurrection of both body and soul rather than the immortality* of the soul alone. In the literature of the intertestamental period, this belief became a fixed article in the creed of the Pharisees, but not the Sadducees (Matt. 22:23 f.; Acts 23:8). Some scholars believe the rise of the doctrine of resurrection was largely due to the influence of Persian religion, where such beliefs were already current. But more important was the suffering and death of many Jewish martyrs in the age of the Maccabees* (II Macc. 7:9–14), which were difficult to harmonize with the justice of God except on the assumption of a retribution after death. The N.T. arose in an atmosphere shaped by this belief (John 11:24), and there are some passages in which it finds expression in almost traditional Jewish form, often connected as in Daniel (7:13) with the coming of the mysterious Son of man (Matt. 25:31–46; I Thess. 4:16; Rev. 20:13).

But there is in the N.T. a teaching about resurrection which is expressed differently from this. The best example is I Cor. 15; and it is significant that Paul definitely associates his teaching here with the Resurrection of Christ. It is true that in vv. 51 f. he reverts to the older type; but the bulk of the chapter deals with resurrection not as the raising of the *same* body as that which was buried, but as the giving of a *new* body. The new body, however, is continuous with the old body as the harvest is continuous with the seed. "It is sown a natural body; it is raised a spiritual body" (v. 44); the first or natural body is in the image of "the first Adam"; the resurrection or "spiritual" body is in the image of "the last Adam," or "the second man"—that is, the risen, glorified, and exalted Christ.

The clue to the Christian resurrection is therefore in the Resurrection of Christ. When we turn to the accounts of his Resurrection it is quite clear that it does not mean a simple resuscitation. In such miracles as those on the dead son of the widow of Nain (Luke 7:11–17), the dead daughter of Jairus (Mark 5:21–24, 35–43), and the dead Lazarus (John 11:1–44) we evidently have a return of the dead to the normal conditions of life. But this is not so with the risen Christ. He is the same Person (Luke 24:29–32), and he bears marks of identification (John 20:24–29); but his body is *differently constituted* (Mark 16:12, "another form"; 16:14, "as they sat at meat"; Luke 24:51, "carried up into heaven"; John 20:19, 26, "the doors were shut"). Such a body as this is not subject to the ordinary laws of the flesh, because it sometimes acts otherwise than flesh can act. The body of the risen Christ lends itself to a new mode of existence and to a new set of relationships; and the resurrection body of the Christian is in the "image" of this (I Cor. 15:49).

Paul works this out more fully in II Cor.

4:7 to 5:10. The "temporal" is to be replaced by the "eternal," the "earthly tabernacle" by "a building from God . . . eternal, in the heavens." Or, as in Phil. 3:21, "the body of our humiliation" is to be "conformed to the body of his glory." Such questions as *when* this "change" will take place—whether at death individually, or at some future time collectively; *how* it will be effected; whether there is a resurrection body for the "lost" as well as for the "saved," are questions which, in the absence of definite Biblical teaching, must be left open. See APOCALYPTIC; ESCHATOLOGY; JUDGMENT, DAY OF; PARADISE.
E. L./R. C. D.

Return, the, a term used for the homecomings of the Exiles (see EXILE) from Babylonia to Palestine and Samaria, as the "Descent" to Egypt was applied to the Delta experience of the Jacob tribes several centuries earlier, and the "Sojourn" to their years of residence there before the Exodus.

Reuben ("see a son," or "the Lord hath looked upon my affliction"), the eldest of the 12 sons of Jacob* (Gen. 29:32; Num. 26:5). His mother was Jacob's less-preferred wife, Leah. Events recorded of his early life include the mandrakes incident (Gen. 30:14 f.), and his immoral conduct with Bilhah, his father's concubine (Gen. 35:22). In the blessing of Jacob (Gen. 49:3 f.) Reuben's instability is ruefully pondered by the dying Patriarch. But his nobler side is vividly brought out in the Joseph* story, for it was Reuben who advised against killing Joseph and suggested instead the casting of the youth into a pit, from which he planned to extricate him later and restore him to their father (Gen. 37:22, 29 f.). A score of years later, when the brothers were imprisoned as spy suspects at Pharaoh's court, Reuben reminded them that their present plight was the result of their crime against Joseph (Gen. 42:16, 21 f.). Reuben offered a guarantee to the aged Jacob for the safety of Benjamin (Gen. 42:36–38). In the era of the Judges Reuben's tribe proved indifferent to the crisis of Israel and the Canaanites, preferring to remain among their sheepfolds while their brothers won the battle against the common foe (Judg. 5:15 f.).

Reubenites, the men who numbered in the Wilderness "46,500" (Num. 1:20), under the leadership of Elizur son of Shedeur (Num. 10:18), and received their tribal heritage as the descendants of Reuben* (according to Num. 32:1–38) shortly before the death of Moses. The Tribe of Reuben, along with Gad, asked that they be allowed to settle east of the Jordan, whose high grazing ground they found excellent for cattle raising. They were allowed to stake out this claim on condition that they accompany the other Tribes over the Jordan and help them win the land God had provided for them in Canaan. When they assented Reuben, Gad, and the half Tribe of Manesseh, son of Joseph, were "assigned" "the kingdom of Sihon, king of the Amorites, and the kingdom of Og king of Bashan, the land with the cities thereof in the coasts, even the cities of the country round about" (Num. 32:33, 38). The Reubenites tried to hold their own against the powerful E. Jordan peoples, in the territory along the Jordan N. of the Arnon River bordered on the S. by Moab* and the NE. by Ammon (Josh. 13:23). The Pisgah*-Nebo* range lay within their holdings. Reubenites are given credit for building the cities of Heshbon, Elealeh, Kirjathaim, Nebo, and Baal-meon (but under new names for these pagan centers), and Shibmah (Num. 32:37 f.). There is evidence that Reuben's Tribe may also have had in its earlier occupation phase a settlement W. of the Jordan, to gain which it had led the Leah tribes in a long-drawn-out invasion from the NE.

In Ezekiel's vision of the rebuilt Temple Reuben's "portion" in the heritage of Israel was recognized (48:6 f.), and a N. gate of Jerusalem named for his Tribe (v. 31).

The Reubenites participated in setting up David as king at Hebron (I Chron. 12:37). Weakened by the wars between Israel and Syria, they were carried into captivity by Tiglath-pileser III of Assyria (II Kings 15:29) c. 733 B.C., and settled in the areas named in I Chron. 5:26; their descendants returned from Exile. The Reubenites seem ultimately to have merged with the Tribe of Dan.

Reuel (ro͞o′ĕl). (1) A son of Esau and eponymous ancestor of an Edomite clan (Gen. 36:4–17; I Chron. 1:35 f.). (2) The Midianite father-in-law of Moses (Ex. 2:18; Num. 10:29, Raguel; but see also Jethro and Hobab). (3) The father of Eliasaph, a "prince" or leader of the tribe of Gad (Num. 2:14). (4) The father of Shephathiah, a descendant of Benjamin (I Chron. 9:8).

revelation, the act of disclosing or communicating the divine to men. Only God can fully know God, and only God can make God known. Revelation is the process whereby God makes Himself known to men. The purpose of God's self-revelation is to confront men with His reality as a God of holy love who seeks their salvation from sin and evil. Revelation presupposes on the part of men a capacity of response. God made men as they are, in order that He and they might come to fellowship. Response calls for faith*—the act of free intelligence both responding to God's self-disclosure and committing itself to all that the revelation and the response are seen to involve.

The Scriptures are the record of God's self-revelation and its results. This does not mean, of course, that all that the Scriptures contain is to be called "revelation." What it means rather is that the experience of revelation, or certain men's apprehension of God in their very souls, created the individual and historical situations that the Scriptures describe. The so-called "inspiration" of the Scriptures is in their vital connection with revelation. Men became aware of the approach of God, and they heard for themselves his "Word," and it led them into certain activities. We must not, however, suppose a perfect equation between the activities and the revelation. Men often wrote and acted out of harmony with the revelation, because men who hear the "Word" of God in themselves, or who accept from others the assurance of this "Word," are still free men, who must carry out, in the circumstances in which they find themselves, their understanding of what this "Word" requires. This explains why they so often attributed to God motives, qualities, and purposes, and so often expressed sentiments and engaged in activities which in due time would need to be corrected. The Scriptures are therefore not merely a verbatim record of revelation; they are as well a record of personal, social, and national experiences arising from the varied responses to revelation, and serving as the means by which revelation was both clarified and perpetuated.

For example, what Moses received directly from God and what he learned from the Egyptians are not to be separated, but neither are they to be identified; his heritage was a factor in his understanding and application of the revelation. He necessarily labored under many handicaps, not least of them being the people whom he must serve, just emerging from slavery. Moreover, we owe not directly to Moses himself, but to a slowly growing tradition, our knowledge of the revelation given him, and of the work it led him to do for Israel. Revelation is one thing; what men did with it and because of it is often another; but the Scriptures record both. Without doubt Samuel had a living fellowship with God; and he expressed an imperishable truth when he declared to the disobedient Saul, "To obey is better than sacrifice, and to hearken than the fat of rams" (I Sam. 15:22); but in commanding Saul to exterminate the Amalekites he was talking entirely as a man of his own time, to whom revenge and vindictiveness seemed perfectly justifiable (see entire chapter). The author of the Book of Jonah* was much ahead of his day in his conviction that God was interested even in hated Nineveh; we can indeed see that conviction as genuine "revelation." But the story he devised as the vehicle of his conviction is another matter; and it would be nothing less than tragic to allow difficulties in his story to lead to a rejection of its central truth —a truth so relevant to our own time.

The process of divine self-revelation came to its climax in Jesus Christ. God can fully disclose Himself to no man; and no man can make fully known to another what has been revealed to him of God. There is always an indirectness about personal testimony to revelation; to be complete, final, and universal, revelation must break out of the limitations of language—it must become a living actuality.

When John wrote, "The Word became flesh" (1:14) he meant that this living actuality had appeared. Historians, prophets, poets, psalmists, evangelists, even missionaries and letter-writers like Paul—these were the messengers of God, each in his own way, and with his own limitations—but they were not the message. They bore witness to the revelation; but they did not and could not directly confront men with the revelation itself.

This direct confronting took place in Jesus Christ. In him God showed men Himself. Thus John puts on the lips of Jesus the words, "He that hath seen me hath seen the Father" (14:9). That can mean only that all other alleged revelations of God, in the processes of nature and of history, in all religions, even in the O.T., are to be brought to the test of this Living Word. The case is exactly stated in Heb. 1:1–4 and in John 1:18.

Our knowledge of Jesus Christ, however, is derived from human testimony and human description. We should not know that Jesus Christ had lived in the world, and that he was the Living Word of God, unless someone had told us so. This witness to him is found primarily in the N.T. (John 20:30 f.). But behind the N.T. is the body of believers, the Church, which embodies a faith that in Jesus Christ the very God had come into the world in behalf of men, to save them from their sins, and to make them "new creatures" (II Cor. 5:17). Revelation is therefore inseparable from faith, and unless a faith response is evoked there is no proper revelation. The function of the Scriptures is to testify to revelation, and at the same time, by so doing, to bring men to the personal apprehension of the Living Word in which alone revelation is complete. See GOD; GOSPELS; HOLY SPIRIT; INSPIRATION. E. L.

Revelation of St. John the Divine, the, the last book of the N.T., which describes the struggle between good and evil and the triumph of Christ and his Church. It is sometimes called "the Apocalypse" from its first word in the Gk. original; it is the chief of all the Apocalyptic* books. The N.T. contains Apocalyptic passages (e.g., Mark 13, II Thess. 2), but Revelation, like Daniel in the O.T., is given over entirely to this type of writing.

The *author* is called John (1:4, 9), but from the available evidence it is impossible to determine who this John was. "Divine" in the A.V. caption means theologian. The book bears the stamp of a single author in its plan, in its splendid descriptions, and in its lofty flights of imagination. From internal evidence come the following facts about the author: (1) He called himself a "servant" of Jesus Christ and a "brother and companion in tribulation" of his readers, who were Asiatic Christians (1:1, 4, 9). (2) He was acquainted with the history and present problems of the seven churches of Asia (2, 3). (3) He called himself a prophet, but there is no hint that he had official status in the seven churches (1:3, 19:10, 22:7, 9). (4) Though the possibility that he was an Apostle cannot be ruled out, he never claimed Apostolic authority or acquaintance with the historic Jesus. His references to the Apostles have a "retrospective tinge" (18:20, 21:14). (5) The author received his visions while he was a prisoner on the island of Patmos, where enemies of Rome were exiled and forced to quarry stone. Subject matter and linguistic considerations make it reasonably clear that the author of the Fourth Gospel was not the author of Revelation. The identity of the latter remains an open question.

Occasion and purpose.—The enforcement of emperor worship in the latter part of the reign of Domitian, A.D. 81–96, threatened the Christians of Asia Minor with a dangerous crisis. The author believed that universal persecution was about to break upon the Church (2:10, 6:10); and he wrote this book, Revelation, to his fellow Christians because he was convinced that Jesus Christ had given him a message for them in this time of terrible urgency (1:1). The message was one of encouragement for the faithful and warning to the complacent. The author's purpose was entirely practical; he had no intention of being obscure. His 1st-century readers understood his message because they were versed in Apocalyptic thought and had the key to its symbolism. Sometimes the author is deliberately cryptic in order to avoid danger from the Church's enemies. But his basic desire to be clearly understood is shown by his frequent explanations of his meaning (1:20, 4:5, 5:6, 7:17, etc.). But the key to the original meaning of Apocalyptic symbolism was soon lost; and unfortunately many of the attempts to find the lost key have been undertaken by those with more enthusiasm than knowledge. To attempt to understand Revelation one must try to discover the author's outlook and his message for his own time.

Message.—The author believed that God was about to intervene in human affairs; this was a basic conception of the Apocalyptic thought of the early Church. A catastrophe or final event would soon take place which would bring the existing world order to an end and usher in the new age. The catastrophe involved supernatural terrors and the arrival of Antichrist. John wrote to prepare his fellow Christians for these terrors, which he believed were already beginning, and to assure them that the outcome would be the triumph of Christ and his Church. His message, like that of all Apocalyptists, was concerned with the future; but it was not a message of doom, but a call to courage and faith.

Revelation is filled with visions and symbols, much of whose meaning can be understood only by studying John's use of Scriptural and non-Scriptural Apocalypses. He was more, however, than an editor of older materials, for he had himself acquired ecstatic experiences. These he attempted to report: "What thou seest, write in a book" (1:11). It was in searching for words to convey his visions that, perhaps unconsciously, he made use of the symbols and conventions of Apocalyptic books familiar to himself and his readers. He brooded over the O.T. prophecies until he believed he saw their message for his own day. Dependent though Revelation may be on Jewish Apocalypses for many of its details, it is basically Christian in its message of God's final victory through Christ.

Contents.—After the preliminary letters to the seven churches of Asia Minor, Revelation reports a series of visions describing the events of the last days and the ultimate triumph of Christ. These visions do not follow a strictly chronological scheme, but are cumulative in their effect. John saw in God's hand a sealed book containing the last woes. Christ begins to break the seals, and as each seal is broken a calamity occurs. After the seventh seal is broken, seven angels appear with trumpets; and the blowing of each trumpet is the beginning of a new woe. Chaps. 12–14 narrate in cryptic language the coming of Antichrist. Next follows another series of woes symbolized by the pouring out of seven bowls of wrath. Finally comes the end; Antichrist and Satan are defeated, and men are brought before God in judgment. The last two chapters picture the opening of the new age when God's people will enter heavenly Jerusalem.

Antichrist is conceived of as Nero coming back from the dead to make war on God's people. He is not named, but the number 666 applied to him represents the sum of the numerical value of the letters in "Nero Caesar" (13:18). Babylon symbolizes Rome. John attached great importance to numbers, especially the number seven, which was the symbol of divine perfection.

Value.—The prophecies of Revelation remained unfulfilled. Domitian was not succeeded by Antichrist, but by the five good emperors. Rome did not fall, but continued to rule for centuries. The end of the world did not come, nor did Christ return to judge men. The supernatural terrors John predicted failed to appear. These prophetic failures have led some commentators to look for the fulfillment of John's prophecies in their own times or in a distant future. Any idea of such a future fulfillment was clearly not in John's mind when he wrote of the "things which must shortly come to pass" (1:1) and declared that "the time is at hand" (22:10). The value of Revelation, then, cannot be found in its prophecies of coming events, but in its great convictions. John is confident that the world is God's creation, and that men cannot break His moral laws without penalty. The power embodied in the Roman Empire John saw as essentially evil, and he knew that the Church which opposed the Empire was small, weak, scattered, and tainted by worldliness. Nevertheless he had superb confidence that in the conflict between these two victory would be won by the Church, because Christ by his death and Resurrection had already won the victory for himself and his Church.

A brief outline of Revelation follows:

(1) The origin of John's revelation—1:1–20.

(2) Letters to the seven churches—2, 3.

(3) The vision of heaven—4, 5.

(4) The opening of the seven seals—6:1–8:5.

(5) The seven angels blowing trumpets and the seven woes—8:6–11:19.

(6) The seven oracles of the last days—12, 13, 14.

(7) The seven last plagues—15, 16.

(8) The fall of Babylon—17, 18, 19:1–10.

(9) The final victory, judgment, and blessedness—19:11–22:5.

(10) Epilogue and authentication of the book—22:6–21.

revenge. See AVENGER.

Revised Versions. See TEXT.

Rezeph (rē′zĕf), an unidentified Assyrian city, Rasappa, an important trade center probably in the Palmyra-Upper Euphrates area. It is listed along with Gozan, Haran, and "the children of Eden that were in Telassar" as destroyed by the King of Assyria (II Kings 19:12; Isa. 37:12).

Rezin (rē′zĭn). (1) A king of Damascus* (740–732 B.C.) who allied himself with King Pekah* of Israel (c. 737–732 B.C.) against King Ahaz* of Judah (c. 735–715 B.C.) because the latter had refused to join their alliance against Tiglath-pileser* III of Assyria (745–727 B.C.) (II Kings 16:5; Isa. 7:1–8). Before joining Pekah, Rezin captured from Judah the important port of Elath on the Gulf of Aqabah (see EZION-GEBER), deported Jews, and settled Syrians there (II Kings 16:6). Rezin and Pekah attacked Jerusalem, and "besieged Ahaz, but could not overcome him" (II Kings 16:5). Meantime Ahaz offered rich treasures from Jerusalem to Tiglath-pileser to buy his help against Rezin of Syria. And "the king of Assyria went up against Damascus, and took it, and carried the people of it captive to Kir, and slew Rezin" (v. 9). The unnatural alliance of the two northern states thus met with disaster, and Syria (see ARAM) was made a vassal of Assyria. The Rezin-Pekah episode is recorded in Tiglath-pileser's inscriptions.

(2) "The children of Rezin" was a name applied to the Nethinim* who returned from Exile (Ezra 2:48; Neh. 7:50).

Rezon (rē′zŏn), a son of Eliadah (I Kings 11:23). He was a general of Hadadezer, Aramaean king of Zobah, and is thought to have founded the Damascus dynasty which produced the Ben-hadads (see BEN-HADAD), Hazael* and Rezin*. See ARAM.

Rhegium (rē′jĭ-ŭm) (the present Reggio), an ancient Greek-founded city on the toe of the Italian boot, 248 m. SSE. of Naples, and opposite Messina in Sicily. Paul reached this port from Syracuse in SE. Sicily. After a day in Rhegium (Acts 28:13) he sailed, with the help of a S. wind, for Puteoli*, where he landed and proceeded overland to Rome. Rhegium was the site of the cave of Scylla, the dreaded sea monster of classical lore.

Rhoda ("rose"), a young girl in the home of Mary, mother of John Mark (Acts 12:13). She may have been a servant, a member of the assembled company of believers, or a relative. When Peter was liberated from prison he knocked at the door of Mary's house; Rhoda knew the Apostle's voice, and was so overjoyed at seeing him that she left him standing outside while she ran to tell the family that "Peter stood before the gate."

347. Ancient harbor of Lindos, Rhodes. Acropolis at upper right.

Rhodes ("island of roses"), an island in the Dodecanese group, situated c. 12 m. S. of Cape Alepo at the SW. tip of Asia Minor at the maritime crossroads of the Aegean and the eastern Mediterranean. Her people may have been the "Rodanim" (Dodanim) of R.S.V. I Chron. 1:7. Cf. Gen. 10:4.

Rhodes had done business with Spain as early as 690 B.C. Her role in the prosperous Graeco-Roman world was comparable to that of Genoa and Venice in Mediterranean traffic during the Crusades. Ships plying from Syria and Greece, or between the Black Sea (Pontus) and Egypt, put in at Rhodes. Her magnificent coins, stamped with the head of the sun god Apollo and the Rhodian rose, reveal the extent of her commerce.

Breezy, picturesque Rhodes, 45 m. long and 22 m. wide, was a brief halting place of Paul on his Third Missionary Journey after his night at Cos (Acts 21:1). His sojourn is immortalized by the Gate of St. Paul overlooking the commercial harbor of the Knights, built by Crusaders after the tragic withdrawal from Palestine of the Knights Hospitaler of St. John of Jerusalem (c. A.D. 1310). On the site of the present capital city of Rhodes these Christian warriors erected a romantic, walled, towered, mediaeval city, much of which remains today. It includes the massive hospital where they ministered to sick pilgrims. Their steep little Street of the Knights is still lined with stone palaces of their Grand Masters. The Christians were expelled from Rhodes on Christmas Eve 1522, by Moslems led by Suleiman the Magnificent; but Christian faith lives on in the churches of Rhodes.

Paul's ship probably anchored, not in the main harbor of the capital at the N. tip of the island, but at Lindos, on the east central side of the island, under the shadow of the high acropolis from which Late Minoan relics have been excavated. Herod the Great had beautified this valuable commercial center, and many Jews were in residence at the time of Paul's visit.

Rhodes was famous for the Colossus—a bronze of Apollo and one of the seven wonders of the ancient world—which fell to the ground in an earthquake in 224 B.C. The Greek Aeschines, rival of Demosthenes, was from Rhodes. Cicero and Julius Caesar studied there. Among the great statues carved there were the Laocoön group, the Farnese Bull, and the Rhodian Venus. From Rhodian sources of Apollonius Virgil drew some of his plot for the *Aeneid*.

The famous resinous wines of Rhodes were exported in jars whose handles were stamped with the name of the maker or administrator and the year when they were made. Thousands of these jar handles have been found scattered over Palestine and Jordan, and are as valuable as coins for determining occupation dates and population density. Many Rhodian jar handles have turned up at Beth-zur, between Jerusalem and Hebron. Two thousand from Rhodes and other Aegean islands have been excavated at Samaria*. Nelson Glueck found them on an ancient Jordan Valley site, revealing Hellenistic occupation in the first part of the 2d century B.C.

Riblah (rĭb′lȧ), an important town on the E. bank of the Orontes R. 50 m. S. of Hamath, in the Assyrian province of Mansuate and in the Hamath satrapy of Persia in Nehemiah's time (c. 445 B.C.); on a main N.-S. highway linking Hamath and points S. with Damascus, and with branches forking W. to the Mediterranean and E. to the Upper Euphrates. Accessible to the broad plain (Beka'a) of Coele Syria, between the parallel Lebanon ranges, Riblah was a strategic military base. It figures in two humiliating phases of Israel's history. (1) In this place the Egyptian Pharaoh-nechoh II (609 B.C.) put King Jehoahaz II (Shallum) of Judah in chains (II Kings 23:33 f.); levied heavy tribute on his kingdom; and set up Eliakim, son of King Josiah, as king, changing his name to Jehoiakim* (c. 609–598 B.C.). (2) Nebuchadnezzar* brought King Zedekiah of Judah (587 B.C.) to Riblah, killed his sons before his eyes, blinded him, and carried him off in fetters to Babylon (II Kings 25:6 f.; Jer. 39:5–7). To this same town Nebuzaradan brought the chief priests of Jerusalem and other high officials, and some of the other people, to be slain (II Kings 25:18–21).

Another Riblah, situated possibly N. of the Sea of Galilee but S. of the above Riblah, is mentioned in Num. 34:11 as a border of Canaan and Israel. Some authorities identify the two places as the same.

riddle, in the Bible, a saying so worded that the meaning is not clear without much thought. In Ezek. 17:2–24 the riddle was to be explained at once; in Judg. 14:12–19 Samson put one forth for men to guess. The "dark speeches" or "dark sayings" of the A.V. are called "riddles" by the R.S.V. in Ps. 49:4; Prov. 1:6.

Righteous One, the, Stephen's term for Jesus Christ* (R.S.V. Acts 7:52).

righteousness, uprightness; rectitude; the quality or state of being righteous. In the Bible God is declared always to do right because He is righteous in Himself. His requirements of men correspond with this: a righteous God will neither demand nor approve anything unrighteous (see GOD). It must be remembered, however, that men came slowly to a full appreciation of God's righteous nature and will. In the early Patriarchal period Abraham could deceive Pharaoh (Gen. 12:10–20), and Jacob could deceive Laban (Gen. 31), with no apparent feeling of guilt. On the other hand, Abraham's prayer for Sodom and Gomorrah is significant for its protest against God's punishing the innocent with the guilty (see Gen. 18:25). This shows a developing sense that, however mysterious God's actions may sometimes seem, He cannot be conceived to be less righteous than fair-minded men would be in a similar situation. Nevertheless, for centuries men continued to expect of God emotions and actions that would not be acceptable among enlightened men (e.g. Ps. 109:6–19). His "righteousness" was too frequently understood to mean simply that He was on the "right" side (i.e., Israel's!), as in Judg. 5:11 A.V. (cf. N.E.B.). The absolute conviction that God is perfectly righteous in an ethical sense is a special contribution of the O.T. prophets, who insisted that He is not only righteous Himself, but demands righteousness of His worshippers (Isa. 5:7; Amos 5:24; Jer. 9:24).

The righteousness of God often means His power and determination to establish that which is right, i.e., to help those who have been wronged. In this sense it can be paired with words like "save" and "salvation." This usage is particularly characteristic of Isa. 40–66 (e.g. 46:12 f., 51:6, 63:1, A.V.; cf. R.S.V., N.E.B.).

Sometimes, especially in the priestly literature, righteousness is understood in terms of ritual or ceremonial. The prophets protested against this tendency; so Isaiah said, in God's name, "Your new moons and your appointed feasts my soul hateth" (1:14). Jesus' attitude was similar (Matt. 23:23 f., 28).

In contrast to ceremonial and legal righteousness is righteousness of the heart. This means the cultivating and expressing such qualities as justice, kindness, sincerity, purity, and unselfish regard for others. Such qualities are held to characterize God Himself, and to be what He supremely wills for men.

The great question in Paul's mind was: How can men be righteous, i.e., "right with God," when it has been so clearly shown that they are incapable of meeting perfectly the ethical demands of God's law? But Paul was sure that in the present age the righteousness of God (i.e., in the active sense described above) is at work in Jesus Christ, destroying the evil and establishing the "right." Men who cannot achieve righteousness by their own power can become righteous by accepting in trust the work that God has done in Christ. This is "the righteousness of God through faith" (Rom. 3:21–26). For Paul this was the kind of faith foreshadowed in the story of Abraham (Gen. 15:6; Rom. 4:3; Gal. 3:6–9) and promised by the prophet Habakkuk (2:4). This is a kind of faith which is closely associated with love (I Cor. 13:13; Gal. 2:19 f.). Where there is true love God's purpose in putting men under law is realized. Law was given to bring men to God (Gal. 3:24); but it failed, because of men's "natural" inability by reason of "the flesh." Love, however, does what law could not do: it does actually bring men to God. Therefore "love is the fulfillment of the law" (Rom. 13:10), and the power of true righteousness.

See FLESH AND SPIRIT; GODLINESS; JUSTIFICATION. E. L./R. C. D.

Rimmon (Accad. "thunderer"). (1) An influential deity in Syria. At his altar Naaman, captain of the royal host, worshipped (II Kings 5:18) before he was cured of leprosy by the Hebrew prophet Elisha (II Kings 5:8–14). The Damascus temple of Rimmon, where the grateful Naaman deposited the "two mules' burden of earth," that he might rear there his own altar to the God of Israel (II Kings 5:17), may have been on the site of the present great Omaiyid mosque. The Rimmon shrine later became a Roman temple of Jupiter; then in the 4th century A.D. a Christian church dedicated to John the Baptist; later a Moslem mosque. In the Assyrian pantheon Rimmon was the storm god, counterpart of the greatest of Syrian gods, Hadad*, with whose name his was sometimes combined (Zech. 12:11). He was symbolized by the thunderbolt, and was analogous to Zeus or Jupiter.

(2) (Heb. "pomegranate"). En-rimmon, a town of Simeon in the Negev of Judah (Josh. 19:7; cf Josh. 15:32 and I Chron. 4:32, where "Ain, and Rimmon" should be read as "Ain-rimmon" or "En-rimmon"). It also appears as a post-Exilic village (Neh. 11:29; cf. Zech. 14:10). Identified with Khirbet Umm er-Ramamin, c. 9 m. N. of Beer-sheba. (3) A rock where 600 Benjaminites from Gibeah sought refuge from the men of Israel (Judg. 20:45 ff., 21:13); identified with Rammûn, c. 8 m. N. of Gibeah. (4) A prominent Zebulunite town, assigned as a Levitical city (I Chron. 6:77, R.S.V. Rimmono; in A.V. Josh. 19:13 Remmon-methoar, "which is drawn"); the present Rummâneh, N. of Nazareth. (5) A man of Beeroth in Benjamin, the father of Baanah and Rechab, who murdered Ish-bosheth, the 4th son of Saul (II Sam. 4:2, 5, 9).

rings, a popular form of jewelry* in Bible times, worn by gentlemen (James 2:2) as well as by nomads. Rings were the crowning touch of apparel, as with the reformed Prodigal Son (Luke 15:22), who received a ring and a new robe from his forgiving father. Rings were incised or engraved with the seal* of the owner so that he might affix his symbol (a cartouche in Egypt) on a damp clay business tablet; or on the mud seal of a corked jar of wine, oil, or grain; or on a decree or state document. Kings and officials used distinctive signet rings. Pharaoh gave Joseph

348. Egyptian scarab seal in swivel mounting on gold ring. Symbol of gods Isis, Osirus, Horus on obverse, sacred beetle on top.

his own seal or scarab ring (Gen. 41:42). In the story of Esther the Persian King Ahasuerus gave his seal ring first to Haman the Agagite, then to the Jew Mordecai (Esther 3:10, 12, 8:2, 8, 10). Gold rings fastened the sacred breastplate* of Israel's high priests to the ephod (Ex. 28:26–28).

rise. See RESURRECTION.

ritual, an accepted order of performing religious rites; or a recorded statement of offices to be used by priests authorized to conduct worship*.

River of Egypt. See EGYPT, RIVER OF.

rivers were important factors in Bible history. Their water made possible the irrigation cultures where religion and civilization developed. Their channels determined the direction of commerce and communication. Their banks were borders coveted by rival nations. Their floods determined the outcome of battles. "Perils of rivers" were experienced by Paul (A.S.V. II Cor. 11:26). See individual entries; e.g., ARNON; AROER; EUPHRATES; GOZAN; JABBOK; JORDAN; NILE; ORONTES; PHARPAR; TIGRIS. See also EDEN; PALESTINE. For the symbolic "river of water of life" see Rev. 22:1 f.

Rizpah, a daughter of Aiah, and concubine of Saul (II Sam. 3:7). When Ish-bosheth (Ish-baal), a son of Saul, accused Abner of illicit relations with Rizpah, a quarrel ensued which led Abner to join David and to offer to "bring about all Israel unto" him (vv. 12 ff.). To appease God, offended by the slaying of Gibeonites (see GIBEON) by the bloody house of Saul, David delivered to the wronged "remnant of the Amorites" (II Sam. 21:2) Rizpah's two sons, along with five sons of Merab*, daughter of Saul, to be hanged. Rizpah spread a sackcloth on a rock, in a symbolic effort to indicate the land's repentance, and watched over the bodies from the harvest until the rainy season, when David ordered their burial (vv. 8–10).

road, an inroad or a raid into enemy country (A.V. I Sam. 27:10). For "road" in the modern sense, see TRADE.

robbery, larceny of property. In spite of the emphasis in ancient Hebrew Law on honesty, crystallized in the Eighth Commandment, "Thou shalt not steal," robbery has always been prevalent in the Middle East.

Israel's Law Codes forbade robbing one's neighbor (Lev. 19:13). Prophets warned against robbing the fatherless (Isa. 10:2; Ezek. 39:10). Wisdom writers deplored robbery of the poor (Prov. 22:22). Malachi's protest against a man robbing God (Mal. 3:8) was amplified by N.T. teaching against robbing the churches of their just due. But men still lay in wait on hilltops, as in Abimelech's time, to rob caravans (Judg. 9:25). People were timid about leaving home after nightfall, lest they be attacked by thieves of their own or outside communities. When families withdrew inside their stone houses and bolted their heavy doors they felt secure until another dawn. This fact may have been in the mind of the author of John 7:53 ("every man went unto his own house"). Highways in Palestine have always been beset by thieves in times of political unrest, as in the period of the Judges when men feared to walk on public roads, and commerce halted (Judg. 5:6; cf. Hos. 6:9). Highway robberies were common in the time of Jesus, who told the story of a Jericho-Wilderness road robbery (Luke 10:30–37). He also denounced robbers of sheepfolds (John 10:7–10), and thieves who broke into houses (Matt. 6:20). The widely traveled Paul mentioned many robberies he had experienced (II Cor. 11:26).

Barabbas*, chosen instead of Jesus for release at the Passover, was a robber (John 18:40).

robe. See DRESS.

Robinson's Arch, fragment of an arch visible on the E. side of the Temple platform in Jerusalem which supported the Herodian viaduct over the Central, or Tyropoeon, Valley connecting the upper city on the W. ridge with the S. part of the Temple courtyard. It was named for Edward Robinson, who first identified it in 1838. Shafts sunk in the area by Captain Charles Warren in the late 19th century disclosed additional Herodian structures, including the corresponding W. pier of the arch some 40 ft. to the W. Recent excavations in the area have uncovered this pier, which is the exact length of the Robinson Arch (see B. Mazar, *BA* 33, 1970. pp. 56 ff.). Four small rooms built into the pier opened to the E. onto a paved Herodian street which passed beneath the arch. Beneath this pavement is an aqueduct of the Herodian period, previously noted by Warren.

Scattered remains of a monumental building were discovered W. of the pier, to which the viaduct presumably passed over. In this same general area were also discovered additional rock cuttings, some of which appear to be tombs of Phoenician type, similar to Iron II (9th–7th cen. B.C.) tombs in the village of Silwân, on the E. slope of the Kidron Valley.

A similar arch was found projecting from the Temple area to the N. of Robinson's Arch by Charles Wilson ("Wilson's Arch"), constituting another access to the Temple court from the royal quarters on the W. hill.

W. P. A.

rock. (1) Used in a physical sense for a rock mass or a cave (see CAVES), like the rock at Horeb*, struck by Moses (Ex. 17:6), or the famous rock Rimmon* (Judg. 20:47). Rocks are said to have contained honey (Deut. 32:13). Conies took refuge in rocks (Ps. 104:18; Prov. 30:26); and wild goats inhabited them (I Sam. 24:2). People (troglodytes) made their homes in caves, as at Mount Carmel (see MUGHÂRAH WÂDĪ EL-), in Galilee, and in the Dead Sea deserts (I Sam. 13:6; Job 30:6; Isa. 2:19, 21, 7:19, 33:16). Rock "necropolises" were burial places in O.T. and N.T. times (Mark 15:46), as at Sidon*. Hence it was natural for men writing of the "Last Day" to picture people fleeing to the rocks for shelter.

(2) In a symbolic sense "rock" was applied to God, the fortress and shelter of Israel (Deut. 32:4, 18, 30 f.; II Sam. 22:2 f., 32, 47; see also Ps. 18:2, 31, 46, 28:1, 31:2, 42:9, 61:2, 62:2, 6, 71:3). God's presence was as welcome as "the shadow of a rock in a weary land" (Isa. 32:2). Jesus also used rocks symbolically, as in his Parable of the Seeds or Soils (Luke 8:6, 13), and of the house built on rock (Matt. 7:24 f.). He spoke of building his Church on "this rock" (Matt. 16:18) (see PETER). N.T. writers carried on the imagery and referred to drinking of the "spiritual rock, Christ" (I Cor. 10:4). (3) For Sacred Rock under Dome of Rock, Jerusalem, see MORIAH (p. 460), p. 731, rt., p. 734, rt.

rod, the translation of three Heb. words (*maqqel*, Gen. 30:37 ff.; *matteh*, Ex. 4:2; 7:15 ff.; *choter*, Isa. 11:1). Sometimes "rod" and "staff" are used interchangeably; the context determines which is intended. (1) The simple shepherd's rod was a stout club c. 3 ft. long, made sometimes of an oak sapling with a bulging joint forming a knob. The rod or club was sometimes tipped with flint or metal to beat wolves away from the flock. With his rod the shepherd guided timid animals over dangerous rocks or difficult wâdīs (stream beds) (Ps. 23:4). At night he "rodded" the sheep, making each pass under his rod (Lev. 27:32) to count it.

The shepherd's rod of Moses in Midian developed into his rod of authority when he became the leader of his people—a rod not without suggestion of the magical properties associated with the rods of Egyptian magicians (Ex. 4:1–5, 7:9–12, 17 f.). Moses' rod was his scepter during the Wilderness wanderings of Israel. Uplifted in his hand during battle, it symbolized God's presence. The *staff*

349. Rod (right) and staff.

(*misheneth*) was usually a pole c. 5 ft. long, on which the shepherd leaned to rest; seeing his repose, the sheep gained confidence as they grazed. (Cf. II Kings 4:29, Elisha's staff, and Isa. 36:6, "unsafe staff" of trust in Egypt).

(2) Each Tribe of Israel had a rod with its name on it (Num. 17:2). Aaron, of the Tribe of Levi, had a special one, used during the Egyptian plagues* and the Red Sea crossing. Left in front of the Ark, in the Tabernacle, Aaron's rod budded miraculously and bore almonds (see ALMOND) (Num. 17:5–11), an incident interpreted as evidence of Yahweh's choice of Aaron to exercise the priestly office and as proof of God's presence. The budding almond was stamped on Jewish coins (see SYMBOL).

(3) The "rod" of God (Job 9:34; Ps. 2:9; Isa. 10:5 f., 24; Ezek. 20:37) chastened wayward Israel; but this painful rod was broken when the covenant was restored between God and His chosen people. Israel's Messianic hopes included the burning of "the rod that has punished it"; the Prince of Peace would inaugurate his new order by burning the judgment rod (Isa. 9:4).

(4) A rod was a club or scourging rod by which a father punished his disobedient son (Prov. 13:24, 22:15), or with which a persecutor or public officer of the law beat his prisoner (Matt. 27:26) into submission (II Cor. 11:25).

(5) A measuring rod (or reed) was used to determine distances (Ezek. 40:3). A rod or reed in Israel's system of measurement was a unit of c. 10 ft. 10 in.

Rodanim (rŏd′ȧ-nĭm), descendants of Javan in the ethnological list of R.S.V. I Chron. 1:7 (Dodanim in the genealogical list of Gen. 10:4 A.V., R.S.V.). Probably "Dedan" in Ezek. 27:15 should read "Rodan" (Rhodians), referring to these island traders with Tyre, for Dedan was a NW. Arabian region and people. "Rodan" seems a logical identification, for Ezek. 27:15 continues, "many isles were the merchandise of thine hand." See RHODES.

roe, roebuck, a gazelle-like animal with branched upright horns. Its fleet-footedness was proverbial (II Sam. 2:18), as was its gentleness (Prov. 6:5). The roe was a clean (see ANIMALS) or edible animal (Deut. 15:22). Solomon's stewards provided the royal tables with several roebucks a day (I Kings 4:23).

roll, a written document on material which was rolled up; a scroll or book (Jer. 36:2–32; Ezek. 2:9, 3:1). Rolls were made of skin, papyrus*, or parchment. See SCROLLS; WRITING.

Roman Empire, the political background of Christ's life and the Apostolic Age. Its capital was Rome*, which gave its name to the Empire. Roman roads, radiating from the Golden Milestone in the *Forum Romanum*, facilitated the ministry of Jesus and his company in Judaea, Galilee, and the Peraea; and the Empire gave them a security which would not have been available in the disturbed 2d quarter of the 20th century in those regions. Christianity could not have developed so rapidly but for the Roman Empire and the "Roman peace." The N.T. world had "a Roman background and a Hebrew foreground," as Harold H. Watts puts it (*Modern Reader's Guide to the Bible*, Harper & Brothers). Christ and his immediate followers moved in a Hellenistic world which was fast becoming Roman. The Romans under Pompey (63 B.C.) assumed power in a world which for more than a century and a half had been dominated by the successors of Alexander the Great. The Romans, failing to exercise their usual farsightedness, placed the Idumaean Herods (see HEROD) on the throne at Jerusalem. Though this family of rulers gave the Jews a new Temple and many material benefits, their regime was uncongenial to their Hebrew subjects. The Herods and their Roman overlords made the Empire the embodiment of what the N.T. meant by the "kingdom . . . of this world" (John 18:36), in contrast to the inner, spiritual Kingdom* of God (Luke 17:20, etc.).

The Roman Republic had developed with amazing rapidity, but its quick growth taxed its powers of administration. The corruption among rich patricians at Rome, the hostility between rich and poor, the corruption of the powerful Roman Senate (comprising, however, some of the most skillful administrators the world has ever known), the landlessness of ambitious farmers, the destruction of farms by war, the decay of wholesome town life, the presence of barbarians admitted legally to towns and armies, the decline of business, the shortage of metal for coinage, excessive taxes, and famine and plague—all these factors led to the overthrow of the Roman

Republic and the rise of able military dictators. Pompey (consul 70 B.C.), Julius Caesar (consul 49 B.C.), and Crassus formed a triumvirate. After the assassination of Caesar on March 15, 44 B.C., his great-nephew and heir Octavian, then a student of 18, formed a second triumvirate with Antony and Lepidus. Elected consul in 43 B.C. at the age of 20, he became "Augustus" in 27, just 17 years after the assassination of Julius Caesar. He became master of the Roman Empire in the E. and the W., and in 30 B.C. added Egypt to his realm. He divided the Empire into imperial and senatorial provinces*, and inaugurated the two centuries of "Roman peace" (*Pax Romana*) within which Christianity was born. The Augustan peace is remembered in Rome today by vestiges of the elegant altar of peace (*Ara Pacis*), erected by the Senate in honor of the *Pax* (113 B.C.), now encased in a protective stone structure.

The extent of the Roman Empire in the reign of Emperor Trajan (A.D. 98–117) embraced the settled Mediterranean world, much of Europe, and the present Middle East. Palestine*, known as "Syria Palestina," lay within the Province of Syria; it had become subject to Rome when Pompey took it over in the process of organizing the Pontus*, Cilicia*, and Syria* as provinces. The emperors in power during the lifetime of Jesus were Caesar Augustus (31 B.C–A.D. 14) (Luke 2:1); and his successor, Tiberius (A.D. 14–37) (Luke 3:1). The emperor to whom Paul appealed was probably Nero (54–68) (Acts 25:11).

In most towns ruled by Rome in the Middle East, Romans occupied the official posts; administered Empire-wide commercial companies (? cartels); formed *colonia* (military settlements); and cultivated eminent natives, whom they honored with citizenship. Evidences of the material benefits and prestige brought to Palestine and Jordan by the Roman Empire in the time of Jesus and the first Christians can be seen in cities from the Mediterranean to the Arabian border: Jerusalem under the Herods, coastal Caesarea, Sebastieh (Samaria), N.T. Jericho (recently excavated at Tulûl Abū el-'Alâyiq), the ring of beautiful towns around the Sea of Galilee from Tiberias to the Jordan, and the chain of Decapolis cities. By means of reservoirs, aqueducts, and dammed streams the Romans made semiarid regions east of Jordan support enormous populations. Temples, theaters, roads, and fortresses all indicate such economic resources and engineering genius as the Middle East has never seen since.

The Christians antagonized the Roman administrators by their intolerance of previously existing cults in the Empire; their fresh enthusiasm for the Way; and most of all by their refusal to participate in emperor worship. Persecution of Christians under Nero (see PAUL; PETER) and Domitian was severe. In Rome they hid in underground galleries cut in the tufa along the Appian Way, and carried on their worship and buried their dead. Persecutions ceased when Constantine the Great, following his cross-illumined vision, cast in his lot with the rapidly growing body of Mediterranean Christians.

The Roman period in Palestine comprises the years between 63 B.C. and A.D. 325, after which the Byzantine Empire was seated at Constantinople.

Roman Emperors	*The Government of Palestine*
Caesar Augustus (27 B.C.–A.D. 14) (Luke 2:1)	Herod the Great, King of Judaea, authority Roman Senate (37–4 B.C.). Temple of Herod begun. Followed by three sons —(1) Archelaus, tetrarch of Judaea, Samaria, Idumaea; (2) Herod Antipas, tetrarch of Galilee, Peraea (4 B.C.–A.D. 39); (3) Philip, tetrarch of Gaulanitis, Trachonitis, Batanaea, Auranitis, Panis (4 B.C.–A.D. 34)
Tiberius (14–37) (Luke 3:1)	Roman procurators (including Pontius Pilate) rule province of Judaea (A.D. 6–41)
Caligula (37–41)	Herod Agrippa I (Acts 12) made king by Caligula A.D. 37 over territories formerly of Philip and Lysanias; 39 or 40, of tetrarchy of Herod Antipas; and 41, all of Palestine; d. 44
Claudius (41–54) (Acts 11:28)	Roman Procurators return (44–66)—Cuspius Fadus (44–?), Tiberius Alexander (?–48), Felix (52–60 or 53–55?), Festus (60–62), Albinus (62–64), Gessius Florus (64–66); Revolt of Theudas (bet. 44–48)
Nero (54–68) (Acts 25:11 f.)	Herod Agrippa II (Acts 25:26), King of Chalcis (50); later, sections of Galilee and Peraea (50–93)
Rivals at Rome—Otho, Vitellius, Galba (68–69)	
Vespasian (69–79)	Jewish Revolt against Rome (66–70); Titus destroys Jerusalem and its Temple September 70
Titus (79–81)	
Domitian (81–96)	Roman Procurators again.
Trajan (98–117)	
Hadrian (117–138)	Revolt of Bar Cochba (132–135); Jerusalem rebuilt as Roman colony, *Aelia Capitolina*, but closed to Jews.
Antoninus Pius (138–161)	

Roman emperors after Antoninus Pius included Marcus Aurelius (161–180); Septimius Severus (193–211); Caracalla (211–217); and Diocletian, archpersecutor of Christians

(284–305—in association with Maximian from 286). Constantine I ("the Great"), sole survivor of the six rival rulers of the Roman Empire, organized the whole under his personal rule (324–337), and established a new capital at Byzantium, christened after himself Constantinople (now Istanbul). Constantine's casting in the lot of his new, eastern-based Empire with the cause of the rapidly growing body of Christians in the Mediterranean world made his establishment of the "New Rome" on the Bosphorus a landmark in Christian history. The Empire's sun had set in the W.; it rose in golden splendor in the E. at Byzantium. When Odoacer became the 1st barbarian king of Italy in 476, a fresh Romano-German civilization developed under which the Christian Church grew and the power of Roman bishops increased.

Following the warfare of Belisarius and Narses against the Goths (535–555), Italy became subject to Constantinople, and was led by an exarch who maintained his seat at Ravenna, where today are magnificent examples of Byzantine art in the mosaic-trimmed churches of S. Vitale (A.D. 525); Sant' Apollinare, the Arian cathedral (500); and the jeweled chapel-mausoleum of the Christian empress Galla Placidia. In 755 the pope accepted from the Frankish King Pippin III (father of Charlemagne), whom he had consecrated as "defender of the Church," the Ravenna exarchate territory and the Pentapolis, and thus laid the foundations of the temporal power of the papacy.

Romans, the Epistle of Paul the Apostle to the, the most important of Paul's epistles, and "the first great work of Christian theology. From the time of Augustine it had immense influence on the thought of the West, not only in theology, but also in philosophy and even in politics, all through the Middle Ages. At the Reformation its teaching provided the chief intellectual expression for the new spirit in religion. For us men of Western Christendom there is probably no other single writing so deeply embedded in our heritage of thought." (C. H. Dodd in the Introduction to *The Epistle of Paul to the Romans*, The Moffatt N.T. Commentary, Harper).

Authorship, date, and *place of writing.*—Paul was undoubtedly the author of Romans; like I and II Corinthians and Galatians, it is marked by his strong and unmistakable individuality. It was written at the close of the Third Missionary Journey, when Paul planned to take relief funds collected from Gentile churches to the poor of the mother church in Jerusalem (15:25–28, Acts 20:2, 3, 24:17). The date assigned to this Epistle by scholars varies from A.D. 56 to 59. In all probability it was written at Corinth in the home of Gaius* (Rom. 16:23; I Cor. 1:14), or at the nearby port of Cenchreae (Rom. 16:1).

The *occasion of writing* is indicated in 1:8 f. and 15:14–33. After six or seven years of traveling through the eastern provinces and establishing churches at key points, Paul had reached a turning point in his missionary program. He looked now toward the W. and planned to carry the Gospel to Spain; for this mission Rome was his natural base of operations. Before he visited Rome he wished to introduce himself to the Roman Christians and to secure their approval and support, so that he might avoid the sort of opposition he had encountered in some Christian circles; and in order to do this he wrote the Epistle to the Romans. In it he stated his Gospel in its full range, explaining the fundamental aspects of Christianity as he saw them and imparting his deepest religious insights. He showed Christianity as a faith for all men, having its roots in earlier divine revelations to the Jews. He met the charge that Christianity was morally inferior to Judaism, and explained the lofty ethics of those "in Christ." It was written at the height of his powers, after years of successful missionary work, and at a time when he looked forward to wider enterprise ahead; but it proved to be his last writing as a free man and active missionary.

The origin of the Roman church which Paul addressed is obscure. "Visitors from Rome, both Jews and proselytes" (R.S.V. Acts 2:10) who were in Jerusalem at Pentecost* could have been among the early bearers of the Gospel to Rome. It is probable that some of the people mentioned in chap. 16 had become Christians in the eastern churches before they went to Rome, taking the Gospel with them. It is clear that by A.D. 49 Christianity was well established in Rome; in that year Claudius "expelled the Jews from Rome because they kept rioting at the instigation of Chrestus" (Suetonius' *Life of Claudius*). This may refer to tumults in the synagogues when Christ was first preached in them. Aquila and Priscilla were victims of Claudius' edict (Acts 18:2). Paul's first converts in Achaia were the household of Stephanas (I Cor. 16:15); this suggests that Aquila and Priscilla were already Christians. It is unlikely that Peter reached Rome before A.D. 49. About this time Paul found Peter in Jerusalem (Acts 15:7; Gal. 2:1–10); a little later Peter was in Antioch (Gal. 2:11). Thus it seems fairly certain that Peter was not in Rome when the church there was founded. Moreover, if Peter had been the founder of the Roman church, Paul would surely have referred to him in this Epistle. The Christian community of Rome came into existence before either Peter or Paul visited the city. In Paul's time it included Jewish Christians (3:9, 9:24), though Gentiles predominated (1:13, 11:13). It must have been a large and important church (1:8). Tacitus described it at the time of Nero's persecutions, c. A.D. 64, as "an immense multitude." By the time of Domitian there were Christians in all classes of society, from the slave population to the imperial family.

The original form of the Epistle to the Romans is believed by many to have undergone editorial changes affecting the last two chapters. Paul unquestionably wrote chaps. 15 and 16 (except possibly the doxology, 16:25–27). There is evidence, however, that in the 2d and 3d centuries Romans circulated in two forms, one of which was shorter than the other because it lacked chaps. 15 and 16. One form of the old Latin version which pre-

ROMANS, EPISTLE OF

ceded the Vulgate ended with chap. 14. The position of the concluding doxology varies in the Greek MSS., but most of them give the concluding doxology at the end of chap. 14. This textual evidence raises the question: did Paul write the short form of the Epistle for general circulation and later adapt it for the Roman Church by adding chaps. 15 and 16? There are difficulties with this theory: (1) the statements in 1:8–13 seem to be addressed to a particular church; (2) the short form ends (14:23) in the middle of a train of thought which logically continues to 15:6. The more probable theory to account for the textual facts is that Paul wrote the long form of Romans which was later cut down, perhaps by Marcion in the second century, or by editors who found little in 15 and 16 suitable for reading in church. The language and thought of the doxology (16:25–27) are not characteristic of Paul; it was probably written by an editor who needed a suitable close for the short form of the Epistle, and later was transferred to the end of the long form.

Chap. 16:1–23, according to many scholars, was not part of the original letter to the Romans, but a separate letter written by Paul to Ephesus. The main arguments for this theory are: (1) it is unlikely Paul knew as many people in Rome as the salutations in this chapter suggest; and (2) Aquila and Priscilla (16:3) when last heard of were living in Ephesus (Acts 18:18 f.; I Cor. 16:19). Though widely accepted, this theory has difficulties. A letter consisting largely of greetings is a strange type of letter. It is possible that many Jews whom Paul had met were temporarily exiled from Rome, but after the death of Claudius, when this letter was written, had returned to Rome. Since the Ephesian hypothesis falls short of proof, chap. 16 (except the doxology) is accepted by some as an integral part of Romans.

This Epistle stands in close relationship to Paul's earlier writings and to his mission. Thessalonians, Corinthians, and Galatians contain passages on similar lines of thought: e.g., the eschatological passages, I Thess. 5:1–10, cf. Rom. 13:11–14; the discussion of the "body" and "members," I Cor. 12, cf. Rom. 12:5–8; the problem of the scrupulous conscience, I Cor. 8–10, cf. Rom. 14:1–15:6; the opposition of "faith" to the "Spirit," "Law" to "works," which is the subject of Galatians, cf. Rom. 3:21–8:39.

In style and matter chaps. 9 to 11 form a unity in themselves; they deal with Israel's rejection. If it was true that Israel had enjoyed a special role in God's plan, how was it consistent with that plan that the new salvation ruled out special privilege for Israel? These chapters discuss this problem, and may originally have been a tract or sermon Paul used when questioned about this matter.

The discourse on the universality of sin and retribution (1:18–3:20) differs from the rest of the Epistle in its style, and in its appeal to a predominantly Jewish group. It may represent a speech Paul used in synagogue debates (Acts 18:4, 19:8).

All the material, whatever its previous history, has been fused into a unity. From the announcement of his theme (1:16–17) to his conclusion (15:13) Paul develops a continuous, coherent argument. All the parentheses and digressions are relevant to his complicated, developing theme, which must have been carefully thought out before being written.

Paul's Gospel, which he was eager to preach in Rome and of which he was proud, was "the power of God unto salvation to every one that believeth; to the Jew first, and also to the Greek. For therein is the righteousness of God revealed from faith to faith" (1:16, 17). The Gospel reveals how God's righteousness justifies sinful men and gives them a new status before Him. It is on the grounds of their faith that men are justified. Justification makes possible men's entrance into salvation, frees them from the power of sin, and gives them a new life in the Spirit. The righteousness first promised to Israel also includes the Gentiles in its scope, and will finally be fulfilled for all men. The Gospel is not morally inferior to the Law, which it supersedes, for it creates a new morality rooted in divine love; the new life in the Spirit empowers men to lead an actually righteous life.

The Epistle, exclusive of the prologue and epilogue, falls naturally into five main sections. It may be outlined as follows:

Prologue—1:1–15:
- (1) Paul's credentials as a missionary;
- (2) brief mention of his Gospel;
- (3) introduction to the letter.

Paul's Gospel—1:6–15:13:

Theme: the righteousness of God is revealed—1:16, 17.

(1) God's righteousness revealed in judgment on man's sin—1:18–3:20:
- (a) the reign of sin and retribution in the pagan world—1:18–32;
- (b) in the Jewish world—2:1–3:20;
  - (*a*) impartiality of retribution—2:1–16;
  - (*b*) moral failure of Judaism—2:17–29;
  - (*c*) God's impartiality vs. Jewish superiority—3:1–8;
  - (*d*) condemnation of the Jews—3:9–20.

(2) God's righteousness revealed in justification—3:21–4:25:
- (a) key passage on the doctrine of justification—3:21–26:
  ("Through the redemption that is in Christ Jesus" all men who believe have been delivered from judgment and enabled to make a fresh start.)
- (b) implications of the doctrine of justification—3:27–31;
- (c) the faith of Abraham—a digression in the rabbinical manner—4:1–25.

(3) God's righteousness revealed in salvation—5:1–8:39:
- (a) the theme: justification and salvation—5:1–11:
  (God's love justifies undeserving

men. At the moment when they become assured of that love it becomes the moral principle of their lives. "The love of God is shed abroad in our hearts by the Holy Ghost which is given unto us. For when we were yet without strength, in due time Christ died for the ungodly.")

(b) the corporate nature of salvation through Christ—5:12–21;

(c) the new life in Christ—6:1–8:13:

(*a*) death of the sinful self and union with Christ—6:1–14;

(*b*) an illustration from slavery—6:15–23;

(*c*) an illustration from marriage—7:1–6;

(*d*) analysis of the experience of salvation—7:7–25;

(*e*) God's saving act—8:1–4;

(*f*) contrast between life in the Spirit and in the flesh—8:5–13;

(*g*) the certainty of salvation—8:14–39;

(aa) sons of God—8:14–17;

(bb) the hope of glory—8:18–25;

(cc) the Spirit as our helper—8:26–27;

(dd) God's aid to those who love Him—8:28–30;

(ee) hymn to God's love—8:31–39.

(4) God's righteousness revealed in history—9–12:

(a) the tragedy of Israel's rejection—9:1–5;

(b) God's freedom to choose the instruments of His purpose—9:6–29;

(c) the human responsibility to respond to God's purpose—9:30–10:21;

(d) a hopeful view of the future—11:1–32;

(e) hymn in praise of God's wisdom—11:33–36.

(5) God's righteousness revealed in Christian living—12:1–15:13:

(a) fundamental attitudes—12:1–8;

(*a*) self-dedication;

(*b*) moral insight;

(*c*) a sense of the social organism.

(b) Love leading to right relations:

(*a*) in the Christian community—12:9–21;

(*b*) in the state—13:1–7;

(*c*) love and duty—13:8–10.

(c) ethics in time of crisis—13:11–14.

(d) an example of Christian charity—14:1–15:6.

(e) concluding statement and prayer—15:7–13.

Epilogue—15:14–16:27:

(1) personal explanations—15:14–33;

(2) an introduction for Phoebe—16:1, 2;

(3) greetings to Roman friends—16:3–16;

(4) final warnings—16:17–20;

(5) greetings from those in Corinth—16:21–23;

(6) doxology—16:25–27.

ROME

Rome, originally a small Latin agricultural and market town on the hills and marshes of a site on the Tiber River 17 m. from its mouth at Ostia*, became the capital of the Roman Republic and Empire. Even in Apostolic times Rome began to be an important center of Christian belief.

Little is known of the origins of Rome. A mythical account attributes its foundation to twin brothers, Romulus and Remus. The Romulus saga sets forth native Latins—Italics of Indo-European origin—as the first kings of Rome. Another claim, however, regards Rome's first kings as Etruscans—non-Indo-European people who pushed W. (c. 750 B.C.) from the territory of the Hittites* in Asia Minor. The Etruscans introduced the round arch, later regarded as typical of Roman architecture; the chariot and enthusiasm for horses; the Phoenician alphabet; and an advanced skill in fashioning delicate gold jewelry. They were seafaring traders who developed strong bases on the W. coast of the Italian peninsula, N. of the Tiber. They walled their towns; and used the square ground plan for buildings, in contrast to the oblong one of the Greeks. C. 500 B.C. the Etruscan kings of Rome were expelled, and the Roman Republic began to take form and expand its power until its destiny touched the borders of the civilized world. Its strong but often harsh Senate made up of experienced statesmen; its efficient military organization; its roads, built so well that miles of them are extant (see TRADE); its engineering projects, including public sanitation and water supply; and its genius for practical affairs—all these factors made Rome unique. The winning of its wars against the Latin tribes (330 B.C.) and over groups of rough Samnite mountaineers (325–290 B.C.) were preludes to its victories over Greek cities in Sicily; only N. African Carthage remained to challenge Rome as mistress of the western Mediterranean—within two and a quarter centuries the small Republic of Rome had mastered the peninsula S. of the Po. The destruction of Carthage in the Third Punic War (146 B.C.) gave her control of the western, as Macedon had of the eastern, shores of the "Inland Sea." Rome was on its way to making the Mediterranean world a Roman Empire*.

Though Rome conquered the Greeks, she herself was conquered by the spirit of the vanquished, and became the chief transmitter of Hellenistic culture. A graphic example of this is the marble torso of Emperor Hadrian, excavated in the agora* of Athens; it shows the proud Roman wearing armor embossed with a figure of the Greek goddess Minerva, patroness of Athens, standing on the traditional wolf of Rome as it suckled Romulus and Remus. As Robert H. Pfeiffer points out (*A History of New Testament Times*, p. 98, Harper & Brothers), both Greek classical culture and the Gospel "passed through Rome before reaching us, losing thereby the sublime purity and beauty of their beginnings but, by being popularized . . . almost beyond recognition and made to serve practical purposes in daily life, they gained universal acceptance and produced our modern civilization."

The Romans were the inhabitants of the Mediterranean-wide Roman Empire (Acts 2:10). To be "Roman born" meant to be born within the Empire. When the Apostle Paul wrote his Letter to the Romans*, Christians living in the city, he addressed a mixed audience from many lands. Roman citizens enjoyed high privileges. Even during the Republic they had been exempt from the death penalty at the hands of a magistrate; they had the right to be heard and sentenced by a general assembly of the people (*comitia centuriata*). They could not be scourged without authorization by the *comitia*. Under the Empire an accused Roman citizen might appeal to the emperor at Rome, as Paul did (Acts 25:11). The Apostle boasted before the authorities in Jerusalem that he was a Roman-born citizen, i.e., son of an honored freedman of Tarsus, who had been given citizenship in return for some service performed for the Empire (Acts 22:28). The Roman chief captain or military tribune in Jerusalem remarked that with "a great sum" he had bought this privilege, and he hurried to release Paul, "because he had bound him" (v. 29). Paul's Roman citizenship often protected him; Empire officials, usually hesitant about participating in local quarrels, often turned Paul over to local administrators, like the town clerk at Ephesus (Acts 19:34–41) or the Sanhedrin* at Jerusalem (22:30), or else dismissed him without sentence (18:12–17).

Roman culture produced the comedies of Plautus (d. c. 184 B.C.) and of Terence (d. c. 159 B.C.), which were clever and popular caricatures of current life. In prose literature and oratory Caesar (d. 44 B.C.) and Cicero (d. 43 B.C.) were masters whose influence on style continues to this day. The poetry of Horace (d. 8 B.C.) is a treasury of Roman life, viewed by a mature mind. Virgil (d. 19 B.C.) produced in his *Aeneid* one of the world's greatest epic poems. Livy's (d. A.D. 17) 242 rolls of Roman history are absorbing reading, even if not scrupulously accurate.

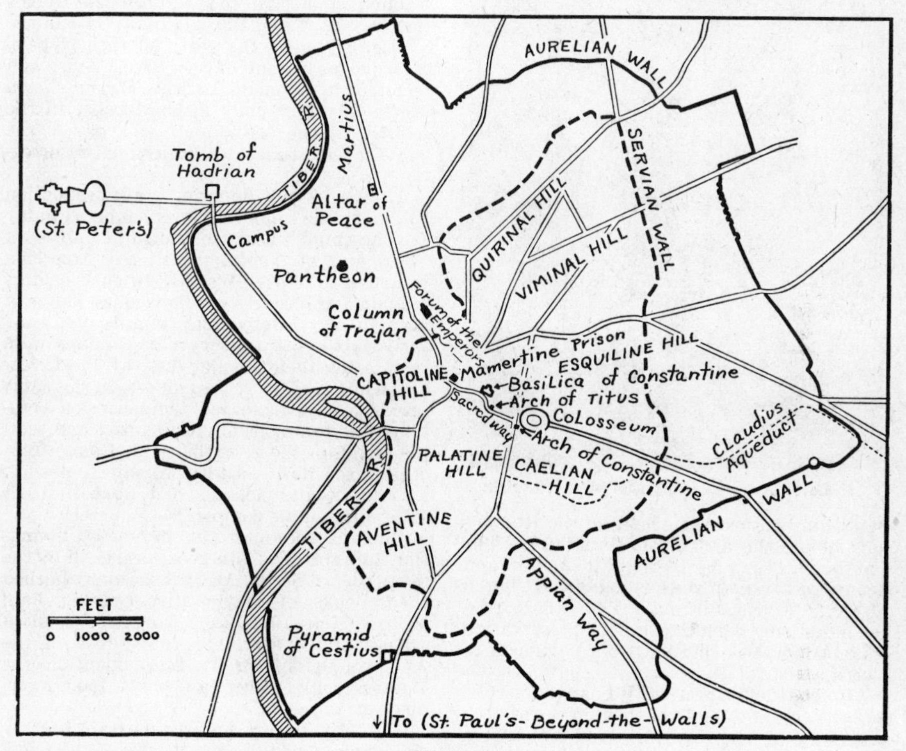

350. Rome.

Roman Religion. (1) In very early times Roman religion centered in the home, with the paterfamilias heading its simple pattern of belief and worship. The lares, embodying the spirits of the family dead, were tutelaries honored in the household, as were the penates, guardians of the food pantry. In 1st-century houses excavated at Pompeii can be seen shelves or niches for the cult of the Penates. (2) Later State gods developed. Janus, originally the god of the family doorsill, became the two-faced deity of the gate to the Roman Forum. Vesta, at first the goddess of home hearths, became the Vesta of the sacred state fires, with her perpetual flame kept burning by patrician vestal virgins. Jupiter, king of the gods, Mars, sponsor of wars, and Ceres, goddess of grain, formed a State triad. The extensive Roman pantheon also exalted Venus, goddess of love; Mercury, messenger of the gods; and Neptune, god of seas and commerce—an example of whose shrines is the extant temple at Paestum, S. of Naples. The Romans knew that these were the counterparts of the Greek gods: the Greek Zeus was the Roman Jupiter; Hermes was Mercury; Hera was Juno, the wife of Jupiter; Aphrodite was Venus, etc. But these deities of the old

351. Caesar Augustus, with god of peace at his right.

pantheon had lost their hold on the Romans long before the arrival of Christianity. The Pantheon, begun by Agrippa in 27 B.C. and dedicated to pagan gods, is today the Church of Santa Maria Rotunda. This structure—the oldest surviving in excellent preservation—embodies the evolution from paganism to Christianity.

(3) The deification of Roman emperors, and the actual worship of them in the eastern provinces of the Empire, is evidenced in the temple remains found, for example, at Samaria, whose broad-stepped *Augusteum* was erected by Herod in honor of his patron, Caesar Augustus, on the probable site of a Baal shrine. Though the actual worship of the emperors was not encouraged by Augustus and his successors, worship of the genius of the reigning house was permitted at the crossroads, along with honors paid to the old lares. The beginning of emperor worship in the W. dates from the erection by Augustus in the old Roman Forum of the Temple of the Divine Caesar (*Templus Divi Julii*), after the murder of his foster father Julius Caesar (March 15, 44 B.C.). Emperor worship was attacked by Jesus (Luke 20:25).

(4) The various mystery cults, such as Paul encountered throughout Asia Minor and in Greece and Italy, were very influential. Fertility cults were practiced at the Temple of Diana at Ephesus* (Acts 19:23–41). The old Eleusinian Mysteries, observed on the Greek mainland between Athens and Corinth, were known to Paul (cf. I Cor. 15:51); they so profoundly impressed the Roman Cicero that he observed, "A man cannot but be nobler for beholding them." Eleusis was only one of many centers where men sought to commune with deity. Egyptian mystery cults were specially popular in Rome. The remnants of a temple of Serapis, a male Egyptian deity, are seen today at Puteoli*, which had a Serapeum as early as 105 B.C.; and temples to the Egyptian Isis were numerous throughout Italy. The influence of the Asiatic "Great Earth Mother" was felt in Rome, as were the mystery rites of Tammuz-Adonis, imported from the Phoenician Byblos (see GEBAL). From Phrygia came (late in the 3d century B.C.) the earth mother Cybele, regarded as parent of the Greek Zeus, and honored by Romans as the *Magna Deum Mater*. Mystery cults fostered belief in the rebirth of the individual, and paved the way for Christian faith in personal resurrection*.

The Greek cult honoring grain production and maritime commerce is remembered today at Paestum, whose columned Temples of Ceres and of Neptune sheltered American wounded in World War II. In such centers religion and business were mixed, as they had been in early Babylonian temple areas. As early as the 5th century B.C. Romans were celebrating their popular festival, the *Cerealia*, in honor of the grain goddess. In this same period a Greek-adorned temple which combined the functions of curb market and temple stood on the Aventine Hill. Roman religion mixed business with worship somewhat as ancient Babylonians had done in their elaborate temple complexes.

Romans were interested in magic*, divination, and sorceries, like those practiced by the seven sons of Sceva. At Ephesus many burned their books of magic after hearing Paul preach (Acts 19:13–20). Romans consulted oracles of the sibylline prophetesses of the Apollo of Delphi. Virgil's *Aeneid* mentions the Cumaean sibyl in her cave above Lake Avernus near Naples.

The Sibylline oracles are an extant literary collection of popular prophecies of the sibyl, regarded as a female counterpart of the Hebrew prophets and widely popular down into Christian times. Some viewed the sibyl as of Babylonian origin; Greeks claimed that she sprang from Ionia. Her prophecies concerned themselves with the history of empire, with coming events like earthquakes, wars, and volcanic disasters; with histories of the Mediterranean peoples, pronouncements of woes on wicked nations, prophecies of a coming Messiah*, and final world judgment.

Mithraism was more influential in the Roman Empire than any other foreign faith before the arrival of the Christian religion. Mithra, an Indo-European deity, was the manifestation in the visible world of Ahura-Mazda, supreme god of Zoroaster, the Persian reformer (c. 650–600 B.C.). Mithra was the universally present guardian of mankind, his cattle, his contracts, and his happiness. Mithraism was popular in the Roman seaport of Ostia at the mouth of the Tiber. The Mithraeum, with its hall and two galleries for the initiated, stood near the theater. Mosaics excavated there show the solar deity, the planets, and signs of the zodiac. Mithraism was carried into Italy by soldiers, sailors, and pirates from Cilicia, Paul's homeland; and Roman emperors honored the cult until it was abolished by Constantine the Great.

(5) Greek and Hellenistic philosophies influenced thoughtful Romans. Teachers taught their pupils as they walked ("peripatetics") or as they sat in the garden or "painted porch." There were Roman enthusiasts for Plato (d. 347 B.C.); Aristotle (d. 322); Epicurus (c. 270); the Cynics' School, led by Crates (d. c. 300); and groups of Skeptics, adherents of Pyrrhus (d. c. 275 B.C.).

Rome, like Rhodes, was for a time the center of Stoic teaching, which emphasized wisdom as the goal of all philosophy, and offered answers to the ever-present problem of securing peace of mind—the objective of most philosophies. But there was incomplete satisfaction and very little comfort in the Hellenistic philosophies; this fact was propitious for the arrival of Christianity with its optimism, joy, hope, purity, its proffer of love, and its promise of eternal life available to everyone. The incompleteness of the Hellenistic philosophies therefore paved the way in some respects for Christian monotheism. They taught men how to cultivate personal relations with Deity through prayer.

Emperor worship did more than anything else to doom the old Roman religion when it came into contact with the fresh, sincere, austere, and exacting Christian faith. Paganism lived on for a time, especially in such centers as Ephesus and Athens, but was conquered before the first three Christian centuries had passed. Constantine's Edict of Toleration freed Christianity and made it an official religion of the Roman Empire.

The first Christians in Rome spoke Greek, which continued to be the language of the Roman Church until the close of the 2d century. The early lists of bishops contained few Latin names. Christianity from the first had an affinity with Greek thought. It established centers in Greek cities, from Seleucia on the Tigris to Lyons on the Rhone. Rome was the first Christian metropolis in the central Mediterranean. Not until almost the middle of the 3d century did the Christian Church at Rome become predominantly Latin, though Roman-born citizens must have had services conducted for them 100 years earlier. In Armenia Christianity had been the state religion c. 300 years before it was tolerated in Rome. As early as the 2d century there were many Christians at Naples, as evidenced by catacombs there.

Constantine the Great established at Constantinople what has been called "the first Christian Roman Empire." Together with Licinius he issued an Edict of Toleration of Christianity (313) after his deliverance of Rome from Maxentian at the Milvian Bridge, Oct. 18, A.D. 312; and his vision on his way to Rome, of a flaming cross in the sky, with the words *in hoc signe vinces* ("in this sign conquer"). Realizing that Rome was a stronghold of paganism, and not wishing to stir up violent opposition from its adherents, Constantine developed a new capital for his new empire at Constantinople, dedicated to Mary the Virgin on May 11, 330. Though the Christian policy of Constantine may have been dictated by political expediency, there is no reason to doubt the sincerity of his conversion—the moral precepts of Christianity influenced his conduct; he gave his sons Christian education; he was baptized on his deathbed. His mother Helena made her famous "site-fixing" and church-building pilgrimage to Palestine in the 4th century.

Of the monuments of ancient Rome few are known by reliable tradition to have been connected with the Apostles. The most eloquent of these landmarks have to do with Paul and Peter. For important recent discoveries concerning Peter in Rome, see PETER.

A review of structures in Rome seen by Paul would include several miles of the narrow, well-paved, straight Appian* Way by which he journeyed from Puteoli; these miles would include those between the 3d and 11th milestones, over which American troops entered Rome in World War II. This Way, paved with polygonal stone, had been begun in 312 B.C. to connect Rome with S. Italy. Some of the dilapidated tombs that line it today must have been noted by Paul. He saw the stately arches of the Aqueduct of Claudius (completed in A.D. 52, some 10 years before Paul's arrival), stretching across the Campagna Plain and carrying water to the palace area of the capital. Along the Appian Way the Apostle passed the tufa quarries in which catacombs were later cut, whose underground labyrinths of vaulted chambers were used for the burial places of early Christians and for secret worship in times of persecution; among these the catacombs of Callixtus and St. Sebastian are notable. Paul's "own hired house," where for two years he received "all that came in unto him" (Acts 28:30 f.), was on an unknown site, but was probably a room or two in some Roman apartment, such as have been excavated recently in Ostia. Paul saw the palaces of the Caesars on the Palatine Hill, and was familiar with the maze of temples and altars of the old *Forum Romanum*, with its Sacred Way, its rostra—birthplace of democracy. Paul's walks through the Forum brought him within the stately shadow of the Temple of Saturn (dedicated 497 B.C), which was converted into the treasury storehouse of the Roman people. As a Roman citizen he may have been interested in the Temple of Castor and Pollux, where weights and measures were tested and metals assayed for coins. He must have stepped into the shops near the Sacred Way, thinking of the vast stoa of Corinth*, where some of his own woven textiles possibly found sale. But the Colosseum, the Arch of Titus, the huge Basilica of Constantine, the elegant forums of Vespasian and Trajan, situated SE. and NW. of the old Forum—none of these had then been built.

Paul must have seen the pyramidal tomb of the nobleman Cestius, standing now beside the Gate of St. Paul.

Early tradition—which is often reliable—places the martyrdom of St. Paul on a site now marked by the Monastery of the Three Fountains, seven minutes' walk from the elegant Basilica of St. Paul's-Without-the-Walls, second only to St. Peter's in size, and supplanting the small basilica erected by Constantine in the 1st half of the 4th century over what he believed to be the tomb of Paul.

roofs of houses provided space for the penthouse guest room, and a place for drying, flailing, and grinding grain; baking and cooking simple foods on clay stoves; and spinning wool and weaving cloth. Rahab of Jericho dried flax* on her roof (Josh. 2:6, 8). During the long hot months families still sleep on mats on Palestine roofs. During the Feast of Booths (see FEASTS) Israelites, remembering days in the tenting experience of their ancestors, sometimes tented under leafy booths on their roofs or in their courts (Lev. 23:40–42; Neh. 8:16).

There is evidence in Jer. 19:13, 32:29 that cultic rites were carried out on people's roofs, like the burning of incense to the host of heaven, or offering incense to Baal and drink offerings to various other gods.

352. Roofs at Safed, Palestine.

Roofs were built of stone, or of mud and cement, rolled smooth with stone rollers, some of which have been excavated; and were renewed after the summer sun had cracked the surface, before the winter rains set in. They were seldom of wood, since trees were scarce except in forested mountain regions and in certain river valleys; though occasional material found on ancient town sites suggests that house roofs had been of wood, laid on stone or mud-brick walls. The heavy weight of stone roofs was supported by the use of such tall arches as are seen in the picturesque houses of Bethlehem today. Sometimes crude roofing was made of bundles of reed thatch; such a roof may have been the type quickly removed in the story in Mark 2:4.

Kindly O.T. laws demanded that roofs have parapets, to prevent people from falling off and involving the family in bloodguiltiness (Deut. 22:8). Watchmen were posted on the roofs of city gates to look for enemies (II Sam. 18:24). In Palestinian hillside villages like Safed roofs of the lowest level formed steps to the next row (cf. Ezek. 40:13). Roofs were popular lookouts for the inquisitive, like the Philistines of Samson's day (Judg. 16:27), and David on the roof of the king's house at Jerusalem (II Sam. 11:2).

An invitation to come under a man's roof was an expression of hospitality, e.g., "I am not worthy that thou shouldest enter under my roof," as the centurion said to Jesus (Luke 7:6). Even a nomad's tent was thought of as having a roof for the protection of guests (Gen. 19:8).

See HOUSE.

room. See HOUSE. For palace rooms, see II Sam. 19:13; I Kings 2:35, 5:1, 5, 8:20; II Kings 15:25, 23:34. For "Upper Room," see Mark 14:15; Luke 22:12; Acts 1:13.

rope, cord made of twisted or braided strands of fiber from hemp or other plant or animal matter, mentioned in the Bible to draw carts (Isa. 5:18); to haul stones (II Sam. 17:13); to bind prisoners (Judg. 16:11); and to rig boats (Acts 27:32). Potters made designs by pressing rope against their wet clay. In Solomon's seaport, excavated by Nelson Glueck at Tell el-Kheleifeh (Ezion-geber) on the Gulf of Aqabah, has been found thick, powerful rope made of bark fiber from palm trees, lying in proximity to 6-in. nails, pitch, and fishhooks. Ramie, a flax-like Asiatic shrub, *Boehmeria nivea*, produced long, strong fibers which in ancient times—as now—made rope three or four times as strong as other materials and was very useful for fish nets. Ramie grows 10 ft. high and produces three or four crops a year.

In the war between Ahab of Israel and Ben-hadad of Syria henchmen of the Syrian put ropes on their heads and sackcloth on their loins when they came as suppliants on behalf of Ben-hadad.

rose, the name given to a plant in several Biblical and Apocryphal passages in the various versions but debated by botanists. The common assertion that there were no true roses in the Near East in the Biblical period seems to be untrue—George Post reported several true roses from the Lebanons and Palestine. There are at least four or five kinds of wild roses in this area, and five extra species of cultivated roses, according to H. L. Moldenke, formerly of the N.Y. Botanical Garden (*Plants of the Bible*, Chronica Botanica Co.). The rose, believed by many to have been introduced from Persia many centuries ago, blooms today along garden pools or in broken jars on peasant roofs. Yet some of the plants translated "rose" in certain versions may not have been roses. Pratt believed that the "rose of Sharon" in Song of Sol. 2:1 may have been a species of rock rose, the *Cistus*, whose flowers resemble the brier rose. Doney regarded the "rose of Sharon" as *Narcissus tazetta*, which is acceptable to Moffatt for the flower in Isa. 35:1. Moffatt translated the passage in Song of Sol. 2:1, "I am only a blossom of the plain" (T. J. Meek, "I am a saffron of the plain"). Moffatt used "rose" for the first "spikenard" in Song of Sol. 4:13 f. The plant now known as "rose of Sharon" is *Hibiscus syricus*—native to China, not Syria, as its name would suggest. The distinguished Jewish botanist Ephraim Ha-Reubeni of Jerusalem regarded the "rose of Sharon" as *Tulipa montana*, though Moldenke viewed it as perhaps the related *Tulipa sharonensis*, rather than the mountain variety.

Some authorities see in the flower of Isa. 35:1 ("the desert shall blossom as the rose") the true rose of the genus *Rosa* (Heb. *chavatzelet* or *chăbatzeleth*). The "rose of Jericho" in II Esdras and the Wisdom of Solomon may be *Rosa phoenicia* ("Phoenician rose").

In Syria today acres of roses are cultivated for perfume and flavoring extract. In symbolism (see SYMBOL) the rose appears on ancient coins, like those of Rhodes ("Island of Roses"), and on crosses and other forms of iconographic art. (See also FLOWERS.)

Rosetta Stone, the famous black basalt slab found in 1799 at the Rosetta or W. mouth of the Nile by a French engineer, Boussard, during Napoleon's expedition to the Delta. Its bilingual inscription in Gk. and in two forms of Egyptian writing (the complicated hieroglyphic and the more popular demotic) provided Champollion with the key to the deciphering of Egyptian. This enabled scholars to read Egyptian monumental inscriptions and reliefs, and thus to gain access to hitherto unknown areas of ancient history and religious thought. The Rosetta Stone has been in the British Museum since it was ceded by the French at their capitulation of Alexandria in 1801. Its message is a decree of priests gathered at Memphis* stating their endorsement of Ptolemy* V Epiphanes.

Rosh (rŏsh) (Heb., "head"). (1) A son of Benjamin listed as descending to the Egyptian Delta with the Jacob tribes (Gen. 46:21). (2) "Prince of Rosh" or "chief prince of Meshech" appears in A.S.V. Ezek. 38:2.

Rosh Hashanah, see NEW YEAR FESTIVAL.

rostrum, a platform or elevation from which a speaker addresses his audience. In Graeco-Roman cities the rostrum was often in the open, as in the various forums of Rome known to Paul, e.g., the extant one in the *Forum Romanum*, whose carved marble balustrade shows a graphic relief of garlanded boar, ram, and bull, ready for the sacrifice. Sometimes

353. Rostrum or Pnyx at Athens.

an orator improvised a rostrum from outdoor steps on the edge of a commanding gathering place, as Paul did when addressing the crowd in Jerusalem from the steps of the Tower of Antonia* (Acts 21:35). In Mediterranean cities where Greek influence predominated the rostrum was known as the bema (Gk. for "step" or "platform"), as in the famous rock-cut Pnyx at Athens, where Pericles addressed his outdoor multitude in view of the Parthenon.

In the N.T. the judgment-seat* or tribunal included an outdoor rostrum or bema from which the presiding government official heard cases. Pilate at the trial of Jesus "sat down on his judgment seat" of the praetorium (castle) (Matt. 27:19; cf. John 18:33), and said of Christ, "Behold the man!" (John 19:5). The judgment seat or tribunal at Corinth, where Gallio* heard Paul's case (Acts 18:12 ff.) was part of a magnificent building in the vast agora* or market place between the long rows of shops in the NW. and S.stoa*.

royal cities. See CITIES.

ruby, a transparent red variety of corundum mineral, prized by ancient peoples for its color (Lam. 4:7) and brilliance. O.T. writers spoke of wisdom as being even more precious than rubies (Job 28:18; Prov. 3:15, 8:11); so too was the virtuous woman (Prov. 31:10). The Second Isaiah used rubies to symbolize the beautiful pinnacles or windows of the ideal Zion (A.S.V. 54:12). Ezekiel referred to Syria's use of rubies (identification doubtful) in her trade with Tyre* (A.S.V. 27:16; cf. "stones of fire," 28:14). Some texts, e.g., the A.S.V. margin, translate *'ōdhem*, the red stone of the high priest's breastplate, as "ruby" (A.V. "Sardius" Ex. 28:17, but A.S.V. margin "ruby").

rue, an herb which might have been any one of several strongly scented plants of the genus *Ruta*, possibly *Ruta graveolens*, a yellowish-flowered herb used for medicine and possibly for flavoring. Jesus mentioned rue as being so inconsequential that its tithing by Pharisees amounted to nothing (Luke 11:42).

Rufus. (1) The son of Simon of Cyrene, the man who was compelled to carry Christ's cross to Golgotha (Mark 15:21). Rufus had a brother Alexander. (2) One to whom, along with his mother, Paul sent greetings in the Epistle to the Romans (16:13). The fact that this Rufus appears to be well known has led many to accept the tradition that he and Alexander accompanied Andrew and Peter on evangelistic trips. Rufus was a popular 1st-century name, however; and the two mentioned in the N.T. may not have been the same.

ruler, one who governs with authority, as head of a group. Head herdsmen were called "rulers over cattle" (Gen. 47:6). Chieftains of Israel appointed by Moses during the Exodus were "rulers over hundreds," etc. (Ex. 18:25). In the period of the Judges such men as Jephthah* were rulers or judges over all Gilead, etc. (Judg. 11:8; cf. Ruth 1:1). King David was "ruler over all Israel" (I Sam. 25:30); his directors of public works were "rulers" over his projects (I Chron. 29:6). Solomon was "ruler over Israel and over Judah" (I Kings 1:35). In Esther's day Persian satraps were "rulers of the provinces" (Esther 8:9). Any governor* (Luke 21:12) or king was a ruler.

The "rulers of the city" in Hezekiah's time were its princely administrators (II Chron. 29:20). In the N.T. "rulers of the city" refers to local Greek magistrates (Philippian *archons*, Acts 16:19, or Thessalonian *politarchs*, 17:6), as distinguished from Roman authorities.

Throughout the O.T. and the N.T. God is regarded as the Ruler (Judg. 8:23) of "the kingdom of men" (Dan. 5:21). (See CHRONOLOGY; PHARAOH; PROCURATOR; ROMAN EMPIRE. For ruler of the synagogue, Luke 8:41; Mark 5:35, see SYNAGOGUE. For ruler of the Jews, A.V. John 3:1, see SANHEDRIN. For ruler of the feast see MEALS.)

run, runners. (1) "Run" is used in the usual sense of going quickly, as when young David at Saul's court said that he wished to run out to Bethlehem to celebrate a family sacrificial feast (I Sam. 20:6), or when fleet-footed Asahel ran after Abner (II Sam. 2:18 f.). Friends of the sick ran to bring them to Jesus (Mark 6:55). Mary Magdalene, after witnessing the Resurrection of Jesus, ran quickly to tell others (John 20:2, 4). Peter ran to the sepulcher to see for himself (Luke 24:12).

(2) Runners were guards who preceded the king's chariot to test the road; to protect the sovereign (I Sam. 8:11; II Sam. 15:1); or to enlist roadworkers to "prepare the way of the Lord" and "make his paths straight." They were guards (A.S.V. I Sam. 22:17; II Kings 10:25) who did errands connected with security. These men were "forerunners" (Heb. 6:20), a term applied to John the Baptist, who paved the way for the coming of Jesus (Mark 1:2).

(3) Runners were also couriers, messengers, heralds, "posts," who conveyed news of peace and war from one ruler to another, or from armies to their leaders and kings (Jer. 51:31; Esther 3:13).

(4) Runners were infantry, in contrast to cavalry and chariot warriors (Acts 23:23).

(5) For runners in the great races of the Graeco-Roman world see RACING.

rush, any of the numerous plants comprising the *Juncus* genus, found abundantly in the miry (Job 8:11) terrain of the Middle East, or along rivers, like the Jordan, Nile (Ex. 2:3, cf. PAPYRUS; Isa. 19:6), Tigris, and Euphrates. It was associated with inhabited areas, in contrast to the devastated wastes described by Isaiah as beast-infested (Isa. 35:7). The rush served many useful purposes in Bible times: for fire under caldrons (A.S.V. Job 41:20); for baskets; for boats (Ex. 2:3; Isa. 18:2); for chair bottoms; and for mats placed on floors for seating during meals. Tied together, bundles of rushes made units for the construction of walls in the mud houses of early Babylonia. *Zostera marina* or eelgrass was probably a rush referred to in Scripture. (See FLAGS, illus. 150.)

Ruth ("companion"), the widowed Moabitess who married Boaz the Bethlehemite and became ancestress of David and of Jesus. Driven by famine from Judaea, the Bethlehem family of Naomi and Elimelech, with their two sons Mahlon and Chilion, emigrated to Moab, where the two boys married two native girls—respectively Ruth and Orpah. Evidently some epidemic destroyed the male members of this family. In the domestic and economic crisis that followed Ruth rose to extraordinary heights of human affection when she chose, in words as beautiful as they are moving, to return to Bethlehem with her mother-in-law, the heart-broken Naomi (1:16 f.). The women arrived during the barley harvest. Ruth sought employment as a gleaner in the fields of Boaz, kinsman of her dead husband. Boaz praised her for her rare devotion to her mother-in-law; gave her wise counsel as to her behavior in the field among the workers; and exercised moral supervision and noble restraint. He purchased Mahlon's share of his ancestral estate; married Ruth to rescue her from widowhood; and thus perpetuated the family line. The first-born son of this union was Obed, grandfather of David (Ruth 4:17). Ruth the Moabitess provided a precedent for receiving Gentile proselytes to the Jewish faith.

Ruth, the Book of, an anonymous historical romance involving chiefly three characters: Ruth, Boaz, and Naomi. Though descriptive of the "former time in Israel" (Ruth 4:7) when the "judges ruled" (Ruth 1:1), it is believed to have been written in the post-Exilic period (c. 400 B.C.). The chief reasons for assigning it to this period are: (1) the language it employs; (2) the obsolete customs it depicts which must be explained to its readers (Ruth 4:7); and (3) its implied protest against Nehemiah's and Ezra's censure of the mixed marriages so popular after the Exile (Ruth 1:4, 4:13; Neh. 13:1–3, 23–27; Ezra 10). The book traced the family origin of Israel's greatest king, David of Bethlehem, and was canonized by the Hebrews among the Hagiographa (see CANON). The fact that it was thus classified, rather than in the Law or the Prophets, is an additional argument for its late origin. The Septuagint and the Vulgate placed it after the Judges. It is a timeless plea for racial tolerance.

rye (A.V. rie), probably spelt (a kind of wheat), as in the A.V. (Ex. 9:32; Isa. 28:25).

S

S, abbreviation for the Seir or South Document in the Pentateuch. See SOURCES.

Saba (sā′bȧ), **Sabaeans** (sȧ-bē′ănz), a kingdom and its Semitic merchant people who lived in W. Arabia in early times, and by the 8th century B.C. had settled in SW. Arabia in a region bordering Ophir* and Havilah, at the crossroads of the Red Sea and the Indian Ocean; modern Yemen*. Romans called it *Arabia Felix* ("Arabia the Happy").

In the O.T. Saba is "Sheba" in several A.V. passages. An employe of Job told of Sabaean raiders having fallen on his flocks and servants, leaving only himself as survivor (1:15). Sabaeans were characterized as men of large stature (Isa. 45:14); and as highway ruffians from the wilderness (Job 6:19) who fancied bracelets and "beautiful crowns" (Ezek. 23:42). They were slave traders (Joel 3:8). They operated camel caravans throughout the Middle East, and as merchantmen they were surpassed only by the Phoenicians. They transshipped goods from India and carried them into the NE. countries.

The Sabaeans appear in O.T. genealogies as sons of Cush, grandson of Noah (Gen. 10:7), or of Joktan, son of Eber (10:25, 28), or of Keturah, wife of Abraham (25:1, 3), who also bore their brothers, the trading Dedanites (see DEDAN). Probably by the 12th century B.C. Sabaeans were pushing their camel caravans out into the N., for by the 8th century their trade had reached the borders of Assyria and the present Hejaz. They had access to luxury wares—gold, perfumes, incense (Jer. 6:20), spices, and precious stones, with which they stocked the bazaars of rich Tyre (Ezek. 27:22 f.).

The Sabaeans were ruled by priest-kings (Ps. 72:10) and eponymous magistrates after whom the years were named. The ruins of their capital, Mariaba (Mareb), (see TEMPLES, illus. 426) reveal the grandeur of their realm. Notable among their monarchs was the Queen of Sheba, whose famous visit to King Solomon* is narrated in I Kings 10:1, 4, 10, 13 and II Chron. 9:1, 3, 9, 12. She made the

354. Part of the huge circular wall of the Temple of Bilquis, near Mareb.

1,200–m. journey to Jerusalem with a very great camel caravan (II Chron. 9:1), laden with gold, precious stones, and spices. First she posed riddles, in true Oriental fashion, to test the proverbial wisdom of Solomon (Matt. 12:42; Luke 11:31). After she got the correct answers, she proceeded to enjoy the entertainment offered at the fabulously brilliant court of the Hebrew; the multitude of his attendants; the richness of their apparel; and the bounty of their table—so dazzling that the heart went out of even this very rich merchant queen—"There was no more spirit in her" (II Chron. 9:4). After she had enjoyed Solomon's royal bounty she returned to her Arabian home. Tradition, however, states that she became a wife of Solomon and bore him a son, Menelek, who later migrated to Abyssinia. The present royal house of Abyssinian (Ethiopian) Christians claims descent from Solomon and the Queen of Sheba. N.T. references to the queen (Matt. 12:42; Luke 11:31) designate her as from "the south."

The real significance of the visit of the Queen of Sheba to Jerusalem is probably the trade zone demarcation and alliance she worked out with Solomon, who with King Hiram of Tyre was then sending a joint merchant marine, "a navy of Tarshish" (I Kings 10:22–25) from Ezion-geber to procure luxury wares from the Arabian Ophir and more distant eastern regions, and depositing their wares in Red Sea ports in competition with the Sabaeans. Certainly the O.T. narratives emphasize the commercial aspect of Solomon's 10th century commercial expansion after the sojourn of the queen at Jerusalem.

N.T. references to Sheba (Matt. 12:42; Luke 11:31) designate the "south" country. Some interpreters of Matthew point out that the gifts of gold, frankincense, and myrrh presented to the infant Jesus (Matt. 2:11) may have been brought by devout merchant princes from the Arabian spice and incense trade-routes of Arabia, out of whose "east" they came to Bethlehem.

The worship of the Sabaeans was of the astral type, their chief god being Attar, the male counterpart of the Babylonian goddess Ishtar (cf. ASHERAH). Judaism won some Sabaean converts after the fall of Jerusalem (A.D. 70). Other gods in the Sabaean pantheon, as now known from excavated tablets, were Almakah, Ta'lab, Kawim, etc. Saba fell to the Moslems in the conquests of the 6th century A.D.

The Sabaean dialects, known from S. Arabian inscriptions, resembled Canaanite, as now known from Ras Shamrah inscriptions which have been compared to deciphered archaic S. Arabian (Himyarite) inscriptions dating from the 8th or 7th centuries B.C.

Many Jews have emigrated from Yemen to Israel. They are expert craftsmen in gold and silver jewelry.

Recent excavations in South Arabia* have clarified its history as follows:

Earliest sedentary occupation—before 1500 B.C.

Southward migration of Sheba and related tribes—before 1200 B.C.

Great expansion of Sheba's power—c. 1000–700 B.C.

Known priest-kings of Sheba—c. 800–450 B.C.

Sheba changed to monarchy—c. 450 B.C.

Kingdoms of Main (Minaeans) and Qatabân flourish—c. 400–25 B.C.

Kingdom of Sheba and Dhu Raydan established—c. A.D. 70 (W. F. Albright).

Sabachthani, an Aram. word (transliterated into Eng. from the Gk.), which formed part of Christ's cry from the cross (Matt. 27:46; Mark 15:34). See ELI, ELI.

Sabaoth (săb′ā-ōth), **the Lord of,** a term used in Rom. 9:29; Jas. 5:4, A.V. and A.S.V., (R.S.V. "the Lord of hosts"). The "Lord of hosts" refers not to the armies of Israel, but to all the forces operating in God's universe (as in Ps. 89:6–8).

Sabbath (Heb. *shabbāth*, from verb *shābath*, "to desist" or "to break off"). The *origin* of the Jewish Sabbath is shrouded in mystery. In spite of the belief of some scholars that it developed relatively late in the experience of the Hebrew people, there is reason to believe that it may have been influenced by an ancient lunar festival of Mesopotamian nomads, which was carried over into Canaanite farm life. Traces of rest days in agricultural festivals appear in the old ritual Decalogue (Ex. 34:10–26; especially v. 21; cf. Ex. 23:12a). If the Hebrews "adapted" a Canaanite rest day, they elevated and spiritualized its meaning. It had little to do with the Bab. *shabbatu*, the day of the full moon; no work or sacrifices were to occur on the unlucky 7th, 14th, 19th, 21st or 28th of the month. Ex. 16:23 is the first reference to a Sabbath. In the P Code (Ex. 31:12–17), as R. H. Pfeiffer points out, God is represented as having instituted the Sabbath at the conclusion of His six days of creative acts, as a perpetual covenant with His people. But men did not observe a Sabbath until Moses had enjoined it on the Children of Israel as an eternal sign of covenant* between them and God. From Moses to the Exile, and on into the Roman era, the Sabbath, like circumcision, served to distinguish Jews from their Gentile neighbors. The P author does not mention Sabbath laws in his Creation narrative of Gen. 2:2 f., but this does not preclude their early existence. The roots of the Hebrew Sabbath may be found in Ex. 20:8–11, where reference is made to God's six days of creation and His rest on the 7th. Cf. Ex. 31:12–17, where Moses is again described as conveying to the Children of Israel the sign of the Sabbath of rest and refreshing (v. 17) as an eternal covenant between God and people. The Book of the Covenant also gives the establishment of the Sabbath (Ex. 23:12), adding the humane provision that servants, farm animals, and strangers are to be included in the rest. This same law prevails in the D statement of the Sabbath law (Deut. 5:12–15). This passage also emphasizes that the Sabbath is to be a reminder of God's having brought Israel out of Egypt.

Characteristics of the Hebrew Sabbath—which began at sundown on Friday and lasted until sundown on Saturday—were complete cessation from labor, even from the buying of food. It was a day of rest and gladness; a pleasant season for searching the soul and meditating on God. It became a tower of strength to the pious. People were expected to attend a holy convocation; Israel's law codes made specific provision for public service on the Sabbath in Tabernacle* and Temple*. The day of rest was designed to be more than a mere resting at home (see Num. 28:9 f.; Lev. 24:1–9; I Chron. 9:32). The worship aspect of the Sabbath was recognized in the period of the kings by visiting the Temple (Isa. 1:13 f.), or a prophet (II Kings 4:23). Exiles in Babylon probably visited Ezekiel's house on the Sabbath for spiritual guidance. Even after the home services were widely prevalent, from the time of the Second Temple public services were continued.

Sabbath in the home. When it was not feasible for people to attend convocations, they were expected to observe the Sabbath in "all their dwellings" (Lev. 23:3). In time the Sabbath became in large measure a home day, when at the blast of the ram's horn (*shophar*) the mother lit a candle of joy, best clothes were put on, and the heartiest meal of the week was served. The father said a special blessing (*kiddush*) over bread and wine. Age-old ritual made each home a sanctuary of the Sabbath. God was talked about, as resting after His work; and Israel, after the rigors of the Egyptian oppression.

The first and the last days of the Feast of the Tabernacles, Atonement Day, Pentecost, and the first and the last days of the Passover were called Sabbaths, i. e., days of rest.

During the Babylonian Exile the Sabbath became a force binding together the displaced families far from the Temple. This sacred rest day kept the Jews aware of God, and protected them from alien beliefs. When Nehemiah* led companies of Jews back to Jerusalem he insisted on a scrupulous observance of the Sabbath (Neh. 13:15–22). Hebrew prophets stressed the importance of respecting the Sabbath (Isa. 56:2, 4, 6; Jer. 17:19–27; Ezek. 46:1–7; etc.).

Jesus and the Sabbath. After the return from Exile, and the development of synagogues in Palestine, services of worship were customary on the Sabbath. Jesus, "as his custom was" (Luke 4:16), went into the synagogue on the Sabbath to worship, to teach, to heal. The company of faithful women who had witnessed his Crucifixion would not even walk to his tomb to anoint his body until the Sabbath had passed (Mark 16:1 ff.; cf. Matt. 28:1). But Jesus liberated many of his people from their hidebound, traditional attitude toward the Sabbath. He taught that man was not to enslave himself to a day, but that the Sabbath was provided for his good (Mark 2:27). He taught that if an ass or an ox fell into a pit on the Sabbath, it should be mercifully rescued (Luke 14:5); and that if men walking through a grainfield on the Sabbath plucked a few grains of ripe wheat to satisfy acute hunger, they should not be upbraided for engaging in harvesting (Luke 6:1–5). Jesus used the Sabbath to minister to human welfare (Mark 1:21–25, 3:4). More of the friction between Jesus and his Jerusalem enemies was based on matters of Sabbath observance than on any other issue, except his claims to be the Messiah (Luke 13:14 ff., 14:1 ff.; John 5:2–13, 7:23, 9:14 ff.; etc.).

In the early Christian Church Paul did not force converts to adopt the Sabbath, but taught that it was a matter for conscience to determine (Rom. 14:5 f.; Gal. 4:9 ff.). The Jerusalem Council did not impose a Sabbath on the Gentile churches (Acts 15:29). Yet Paul, like Jesus, continued to visit synagogues on the Sabbath. On such occasions he presented the Christian message and won many converts, as at Pisidian Antioch (Acts 14:14 ff.), at Philippi (Acts 16:13 ff.), at Thessalonica (Acts 17:1–4), and at Corinth (Acts 18:4). But the hour came when he told his hearers that holy days and new moons and Sabbaths would some day be but "a shadow of things to come" (Col. 2:16 f.).

At first the Christians, many of whom had been Jews, continued to observe the Jewish Sabbath or 7th day of solemn rest, but gradually they also celebrated the 1st day of the week as the anniversary of Christ's Resurrection and the time for breaking bread together (Acts 20:7) and gathering offerings for his poor (I Cor. 16:1 f.). In time the Sabbath disappeared from their observances and the Christian Sunday took its place.

It is notable that the Sabbath is not mentioned in the Psalms (except in the heading of the 92d), nor in Proverbs, nor in Job. The Deuteronomic body of legislation does not discuss it after its incorporation in the Decalogue.

Sabbath day's journey (Acts 1:12, based on Josh. 3:4), the distance of 2,000 cubits which a man was permitted by Jewish Law* to travel on the Sabbath. The Ark traveled 2,000 cubits ahead of the people (Josh. 3:4), and from this came the belief that the Tabernacle was 2,000 cubits from the Israelite camp. Since the people were permitted to go to the Tabernacle on the Sabbath, 2,000 cubits became the distance allowed for a Sabbath day's journey. Jerusalem was a Sabbath day's journey from the Mount of Olives (Acts 1:12).

Sabbatical Year (*shemittah*), the Sabbath among years—i.e., every 7th year. Hebrew legislation stipulated that various activities were to cease temporarily during the Sabbatical Year. In Ex. 23:10 f. the farmer is enjoined to let his fields "rest and lie still," i.e., lie fallow after six years of production. The poor and the beasts of the field were to eat what was available in the resting acres (v. 11). As his entire acreage was required to rest at the same time, his livelihood suffered. Hebrew slaves (see FREEMAN) were also to be freed seven years after their purchase (Ex. 21:2–6). In Deut. 15:1–6 Sabbatical legislation does not specify farm life, but asks that debts be cancelled in the 7th year, to signify that the generous act is "the Lord's release" (v. 2). The loan might be renewed later, if the creditor were a foreigner*, but not if he were a kinsman or neighbor (v. 2). The P Code of Lev. 25:2–7 returned to the demand for the 7th-year rest for farmlands, and established the 50th year as a Jubilee Year when all slaves were to be released.

It is believed that observance of the Sabbatical legislation was current from the 5th century B.C. There were situations when it involved actual hardship and interfered with crop production and commerce. Gradually, the custom of forgiving debts became obsolete, as Jews in various countries developed systems of credit. Many traditional Jews in Israel have reinstated this observance.

Sabbeus (I Esdras 9:32). The Shemaiah of Ezra 10:31.

Sabta (săb′tȧ) (Sabtah), "son" of Cush (Gen. 10:7; I Chron. 1:9); possibly the same name as Sabotah, capital of an extensive region E. of Yemen in S. Arabia, on the Indian Ocean. See ETHIOPIA.

Sabtechah (săb′tē-kȧ), "son" of Cush (Gen. 10:7; Sabtecha, I Chron. 1:9). See ETHIOPIA.

Sacar (sā′kär). (1) A Hararite, the father of Ahiam, one of David's heroes (I Chron. 11:35). (2) The fourth son of Obed-edom, and eponymous founder of a guild of sanctuary doorkeepers (I Chron. 26:4).

sackbut, a mistranslation of *sabbekha*, the Aram. word for an ancient, shrill-toned harp used in Nebuchadnezzar's orchestra (Dan. 3:5, 7, 10, 15). The medieval sackbut was not a stringed instrument, but an early slide trombone.

sackcloth, coarsely woven fabric worn as a girdle around the loins to signify mourning, as when Jacob grieved for Joseph (Gen. 37:34); David for Abner (II Sam. 3:31); the king of Israel for children eaten by his subjects in time of famine (II Kings 6:30); and the elders of Israel for those lost in the pestilence after David's census (I Chron. 21:16). Sackcloth was also worn as a protest against oppressive decrees, as when Mordecai put on "sackcloth with ashes" at the Persian court, in protest against the decree authorizing the murderous purge of Jews (Esther 4:1–4). Girding with sackcloth was a symbol of Judah's lament over calamity sent by the Lord (Jer. 4:8, 48:37). To sit in ashes and to sprinkle ashes on one's head was often an accompaniment of wearing the symbolic sackcloth of repentance (Luke 10:13).

sacraments, religious ceremonies in which visible means are used in the belief that a special divine grace is, or may be, thereby conveyed to the subject. The Bible does not use the term, though the meaning is Biblical. In the most simple sense of sacrament, one thing is regarded as the "sign" of another, and what is signified is then conveyed to the participant. The word is related to "sacred," because it is usually something "sacred" that is "signified," in which the participant shares. The process involved is common to all religions, though it may be used in other than religious connections; for example, in certain fraternal ceremonies that use the insignia of office. In the O.T. olive oil was used in the consecration of the priest or king (Ex. 29:7; Lev. 16:32; I Sam. 9:16, 10:1, 16:13; II Sam. 5:3). The preparation of "the holy anointing oil" for "making holy" both the priests and the furnishings of the Tabernacle*, and to be used for this purpose alone, is described in Ex. 30:22–33. The holy oil made sacred or holy whatever it touched; anointing was therefore a sacrament. The expected Messiah was frequently called "God's Anointed" to indicate his sacred character, and the term was sometimes used of the people of Israel as a whole, as a people set aside for a sacred purpose (Ps. 2:2, 18:50, 20:6, 89:38, 105:15; Hab. 3:13). The principle of "making sacred" reached into the ceremonial system of Judaism. The rite of circumcision* was sacramental, in that it "signified" admission into the people of God; and the Passover, characterized by the slaying and eating of the Paschal Lamb, was a "sign" that, among other things, the relation to God "signified" by circumcision was being attested and renewed by the people as a whole—a "peculiar" people (Deut. 14:2).

A sacrament therefore "makes sacred." In this there is a mystery; and it is suggestive that what appears in the Gk. N.T. as "mystery" (*mystērion*) is sometimes translated in the Latin N.T. as "sacrament" (*sacramentum*). It is commonly supposed that this accounts for the custom of describing the central Christian "mysteries" as "sacraments." For a long time, however, both the term "mystery" and the term "sacrament" were loosely used by the Church. Even the various Christian doctrines were often called "mysteries." During the Middle Ages the number of sacraments was the subject of prolonged controversy. The number was eventually fixed at seven, partly on the ground that the sacramental should accompany life "from the cradle to the grave." The seven were baptism, confirmation, the Eucharist, penance, ordination, matrimony, and extreme unction—the last reserved for the dying, and involving "anointing." Ordination and matrimony were regarded in the Church of the West as excluding each other: the priest must be celibate—though not necessarily in the Church of the East.

355. Traditional site of John's baptism of Jesus.

Protestantism has in general followed the N.T. in recognizing only two sacraments, baptism and the Lord's Supper, it being held that only these two were instituted or commanded by Christ (Matt. 28:19; Mark 16:16; I Cor. 11:23–26; cf. Acts 2:41 f.; I Cor. 10:1–4). The mode of baptism has long been in dispute, but there is rarely any dispute as to its sacramental significance. Water and its purifying power are treated as a "sign" of the Holy Spirit and his cleansing and transforming influence. The "water of baptism" is no different from any other water except in the one regard of that for which it is used; and this is especially so when baptism is by immersion in running water. Nevertheless the water is "the visible sign of the invisible," and it is this "invisible" that gives the rite its significance as a "sign" of a person's entry into the Church as "the community of the redeemed" (John 3:22, cf. 4:1 f.; Acts 2:38, 41, 8:12, 13, 16, 36, 9:18). Infant baptism probably began with the early Apostolic custom of baptizing entire families (Acts 16:32–34), though in the course of time, with the growth of sacramentalism in the Church, the baptism of infants was held to be necessary to assure their salvation*.

In the Lord's Supper the bread and wine are set apart for the special purpose of "signifying" the flesh and blood of Christ. In Roman Catholicism, and among very "high" Protestant churchmen, a mysterious change (transubstantiation) is alleged to take place in the elements by virtue of the priestly "consecration" of them, so that the bread (or wafer) and the wine are now something more than is apparent to the senses. Indeed, the communicant is held to partake actually of the very "substance" of the living Christ. What is known as the evangelical or characteristically Protestant view—which is also the primitive view—does not recognize any such change in the elements. It affirms, nevertheless, that there is by means of the consecrated bread and wine, worthily received, a real participation in the living Christ, but a participation "after a spiritual manner," and not automatic, but only according as there is "a lively faith." Through the bread and wine, the "signs," Christ mediates himself to the believer; and only as this actually occurs is the Supper truly a "sacrament."

There are many related questions, among them whether anyone except an episcopally ordained priest can properly administer the sacraments. In ecclesiastical controversies this question has been given an importance hardly justified by anything in the N.T. What the N.T. makes chiefly important is not the process of consecration, whether of the water for baptism, or of the bread and wine for the Eucharist (an early name for the Lord's Supper, and meaning thanksgiving); but what it makes chiefly important is the desire, intention, and faith of the candidate or communicant (Acts 8:36 f., A.S.V. margin; I Cor. 11:27–29, cf. 10:16 f., 21). See BAPTISM; LORD'S SUPPER. E. L.

sacrifice. See WORSHIP.

Sadoc (sā′dŏk). (1) The same as Zadok (Sadduk), the father of Shallum (Ezra 7:2). (2) An ancestor of Jesus (Matt. 1:14).

Sadducees (săd′ū-sēz) (Heb. *Tzaddūqīm*, possibly named for Zadok, high priest in Solomon's age (I Kings 1:39; I Chron. 12:28), or from *tsaddīqīm*, "righteous ones"). An element in the Jewish society in the 1st century B.C. and the 1st century A.D., composed of educated and wealthy men, but comparatively few in number. Though they were not a political party, nor a sect, nor a school of philosophy, they had characteristics of all three. Their beliefs were limited to those doctrines which they found in the written Law, and these alone were binding. Negatively, these conservatives denied belief in resurrection, angels, and spirits (Mark 12:18; Luke 20:27; Acts 23:8) since they had no basis in Mosaic Law. Their principles were older than those of the Pharisees*, whose chief opponents they became. They attacked the validity of the oral* tradition and the unwritten Torah, which were upheld by the Pharisees. Sadducees backed the Hasmonaeans, and therefore aroused Herod's suspicion. The Sadducees represented the vested interests of the Jews in Jerusalem. Many of them were members of the Sanhedrin*. They were in good standing with the Roman Government, but were unpopular with the people, from whom they kept aloof. Their ranks included nobles and high priests, who dominated the Temple and its ritual, except possibly in their last years. After the destruction of the Temple by the Romans (A.D. 70) the Sadducees were little heard of, except as they continued to combat the beliefs of the Pharisees.

In the N.T. Sadducees and Pharisees were jointly condemned by John the Baptist, who called them "generation of vipers," and challenged them both to "bring forth fruits meet for repentance" (Matt. 3:7 f.). They joined with the Pharisees in posing captious questions to Jesus (Matt. 16:1). Jesus grouped the Sadducees and Pharisees together in his denunciation of their doctrines (Matt. 16:6, 11 f.). They imprisoned Peter and John (Acts 4:1, 5:17; cf. Paul's arraignment by "high priests and Sadducees," Acts 23:6–8). Our estimate of the Sadducees must perhaps be modified when we recall that most of our information concerning them comes from prejudiced Pharisaic sources. At the siege of Jerusalem Sadducees joined with Pharisees and Herodians in pleading with the Romans to save their land and their people from destruction.

saffron (Heb. *karkom*, Ar. *za'farān*), an aromatic herb of the crocus family. The yellow styles and stigmas of its flowers have long been popular in Palestine for dyeing and flavoring.

saints, persons of exceptional holiness, integrity, and consecration, recognized as such by O.T. writers, e.g. in Ps. 106:16, "Aaron, the saint of the Lord"; "O love the Lord, all ye his saints" (Ps. 31:23); "He . . . preserveth the way of his saints" (Prov. 2:8). Saintliness in the O.T. is expressed by two words, *hāsīdh*, ("good," "compassionate," then "godly"); and *qādhash* ("to be holy") (see HOLINESS; SANCTIFICATION). Israel was described as a "congregation of saints" praising the Lord (Ps. 149:1). In the N.T. saints (*hagioi*) were (1) all Christians, "holy ones," like the "saints which dwelt at Lydda" (Acts 9:32, 41), or at Ephesus (Eph. 1:1). Christians were "called to be saints in Jesus Christ" (Rom. 1:7). "Saints" are mentioned 60 times in the N.T. They included many of the worthy poor, people of devout habits, like the "poor saints at Jerusalem" (Rom. 15:26). Those who ministered to the poor saints constituted a fellowship (II Cor. 8:4). (2) Saints in N.T. writings were also supernatural, living souls, who were expected to return with Jesus at his second coming (I Thess. 3:13; Jude 14). Revelation speaks of Jesus as "King of saints" (15:3). The "white linen" of the bride of the Lamb was "the righteousness of saints" (19:8). Satan's armies surrounded "the camp of the saints" (Rev. 20:9), but they were devoured by fire from heaven.

Salamis (săl'ȧ-mĭs), an important city on the SE. coast of Cyprus, where Paul and Barnabas on the First Missionary Journey preached Christ in Jewish synagogues (Acts 13:5). John Mark helped Paul and Barnabas in Salamis (v. 5). Salamis had become Roman almost 100 years before Paul visited it; previously it had been ruled by Assyrians, Egyptians, Persians, and Greeks. Its foundation is popularly ascribed to Phoenician colonizers.

Salchah (săl'kȧ) (A.S.V. Salecah) (the modern Salkhad), a city on the NE. border of the mountainous kingdom of Bashan, E. of the Jordan (Deut. 3:10; Josh. 12:5, 13:11; I Chron. 5:11).

Salem, the city ruled by the priest-king Melchizedek*, who received tithes from Abraham returning from the battle of the kings (Gen. 14:17 ff.), brought him bread and wine, and gave him a blessing in the name of "the most high God" (v. 19; cf. Heb. 7:1–14). Salem seems to be incorporated into the ancient name of Jerusalem*, Uru-salim ("City of Peace"), in the Amarna* letters. If Salem is the same as Jerusalem, the Genesis reference is the first mention of the city in the O.T.

Salim, a place near Aenon*, where John the Baptist was baptizing (John 3:23).

Sallai (săl'ā-ī). (1) One of the men selected to live in Jerusalem after the return from Exile (Neh. 11:8). (2) A priestly family who came back from Babylon (12:20). As the same "father's house" is called "Sallu" in 12:7, one or the other is a misreading of the early Heb. records.

Sallu (săl'ū). (1) A member of Meshullam's line, in the Tribe of Benjamin (I Chron. 9:7; Neh. 11:7). (2) See SALLAI (2).

Salmon (Salma), a son of Nashon (Naasson) (Matt. 1:4 f.; Luke 3:32), and father of Boaz, ancestor of Jesus (Ruth 4:20 f.).

Salmone (săl-mō'nē), a dangerous promontory, now called Cape Sidero, at the NE. tip of Crete, sighted by Paul on his voyage to Rome (Acts 27:7).

Salome (sȧ-lō'mē) (fem. of Solomon). (1) Daughter of Herodias* by Herod*, son of Herod the Great and Mariamne (II), and niece of Herod* Antipas. Her dance before Herod was rewarded by his granting her request for the head of John the Baptist (Matt. 14:3–11; Mark 6:17–28). Her name, not mentioned in Scripture, is found in Josephus, *Antiquities* XVIII:5, 4. (2) A woman who witnessed the Crucifixion of Jesus (Matt. 27:56) with Mary* Magdalene and the mother of James and Joses (Matt. 27:56; cf. Mark 15:40); and who visited his tomb with unguents for his anointing (Mark 16:1). Comparison of Mark 15:40 with Matt. 27:56 has led many to identify Salome with the wife of Zebedee.

salt was valued for seasoning food (Matt. 5:13; Mark 9:50)—whence, "ye are the salt of the earth"—and meat offerings (Lev. 2:13). In the latter instance salt as a preservative was a symbol of the eternal covenant between God and His people (Lev. 2:13; Num. 18:19; II Chron. 13:5; Ezek. 43:24; Mark 9:49). When people ate food (salted) together, they made a pact of friendship. Salt was used by the prophet Elisha to

356. Salt pans along the Mediterranean.

sweeten ("heal") the brackish waters of the Jericho spring (II Kings 2:19–22). Abimelech sowed with salt the ruined area of Shechem, in an effort to keep it fruitless (cf. Ezek. 47:11; Judg. 9:45). Salt was used to rub newborn infants before they were swaddled (see SWADDLING) (Ezek. 16:4).

Salt was secured in the Biblical period, as now, by evaporation in beds or pans, from waters along the rim of the Dead Sea and the Mediterranean. It was also mined from cliffs along the Dead Sea (cf. "salt pits," Zeph. 2:9).

Under the regime of Antiochus* Epiphanes salt was taxed by Syria to pay Rome.

In the Talmud salt symbolizes the Torah, for as a world cannot exist without salt, so it cannot without the Torah (*Soferim* 15:8). For Salt Sea, as in Gen. 14:3, see DEAD SEA. For pillar of salt, see LOT. See also SALT VALLEY.

Salt, city of, a town on the edge of the Wilderness of Judaea, on the Dead Sea, near En-gêdi (Josh. 15:62).

Salt, Hill of, Jebel Usdum ("Mountain of Sodom"), an elevation 5 m. long and 3 m. wide, extending N.–S. at the SW. end of the Dead Sea. It is associated with the pillar of salt into which Lot's wife turned, according to the ancient story preserved in Gen. 19:26.

Salt Sea, the. See DEAD SEA.

Salt Valley, possibly the Wâdī el-Milh, running SE. from Beer-sheba toward the Dead Sea, the scene of David's triumph over the Edomites* (I Chron. 8:12; "Syrians" A.V. II Sam. 8:13); and of King Amaziah of Judah over these same warlike people (II Kings 14:7; II Chron. 25:11, A.V. "children of Seir").

saltwort (A.S.V. Job 30:4) is "mallows" in the A.V. It may refer to any of several bushy plants in salt marshes or alkaline regions, used as food by the very poor.

salutations have always been important to Middle Easterners. The usual greeting in Arabic among Moslems meeting along the way is "es-salam 'aleikum" ("Peace to you"), and the traditional reply is " 'aleikum es-salam" ("to you, peace"). Ostentatious Pharisees in Jesus' day loved to receive "salutations in the market-places" (R.S.V. Matt. 23:7). Merchants and customers still engage in meaningless salutations before getting down to business. Mary saluted her cousin Elisabeth (Luke 1:40 f.). Angels were thought of as bringing salutations, as to Mary of Nazareth (Luke 1:28 ff.). Rulers of cities and kingdoms were saluted (Rom. 16:23) or given homage. Throngs hailed or saluted the healing Jesus (Mark 9:15). Mock salutations were given the condemned Jesus (Mark 15:18). Written salutations or greetings in N.T. literature include Paul's salutations to churches (Acts 18:22); and salutations between churches or groups of believers (Rom. 16:23; I Pet. 5:13).

salvation has both a general and a particular sense. In general, it means release from difficulty, danger, loss, or other crippling circumstance. Persons are spoken of as being saved from illness, starvation, oppression, ignorance, calamity, death. There is much of this in the O.T., chiefly because of the Hebrew tendency to identify God's favor with physical and material well-being (see Ex. 14:30; Deut. 28:29; I Sam. 7:8; II Sam. 22:28; I Chron. 11:14, 16:35; Job 22:29; Isa. 49:25 f., 63:1; Jer. 31:7–9). In the Psalms especially, a prayer to be saved from something dire in common (7:1, 17:7, 44:1–3, 54:1–3, 59:1 f., 106:47, 118:25).

More particularly the word means deliverance from sin and its consequences, and the coming to peace and reconciliation with God. This is the religious meaning; it is what is sometimes called "the salvation of the soul." The O.T. naturally has a place for this, as in Ps. 34:18, and, by implication, 51:1–17. It is frequent in the prophets; see especially Isa. 59 and Jer. 30:4–17. In the N.T. the emphasis is much less on salvation in the general sense, and is correspondingly greater in the religious sense. For Christianity salvation means primarily a right relation to God through Jesus Christ. Jesus is usually called "Saviour" because he has this significance (Acts 5:30 f.; cf. Matt. 1:21). It is quite possible, however, to take too narrow a view here. Jesus showed that he was against evil in all its forms; his miracles of healing and other acts of compassion were a part of his work as Saviour. His words at the opening of his ministry at Nazareth must be understood accordingly (Luke 4:16–21). On this occasion he used the word "good tidings" (gospel) to describe his message, and he made it plain that what he had come to say and to do had meaning for the whole of life.

Nevertheless Jesus recognized that there was a root evil, and that this root evil was sin; a salvation that still left sin in command was not salvation in any proper sense. Even in the O.T. the fact that sin is the cause of

SAMARIA, CITY OF

individual and national ills is common teaching. The banishment from Eden (Gen. 3:22–24); the Flood (6:5–22); the destruction of Sodom (19:1 f.); the Exile* itself (Jer. 29)—all were declared to be the consequences of sin. This truth carries over into the N.T. (cf. Rom. 1:18–2:16), although there it is modified in various ways (cf. John 9:3), and it is recognized that the results of sin may be turned into blessings (Phil. 1:12–20; Heb. 11:32–40; I Pet. 2:11–24, 4:12–19). This, however, still leaves salvation from sin as the fundamental human need. The N.T. nowhere supposes that even the most favored of men is "saved" if he is not right with God (Matt. 19:16–22; Luke 12:16–21; John 3:1–10; Rev. 3:17–19). What every man needs to be saved from is hostility to God and His will. Man was made to live in a relation to God of trust and obedience and love; sin is the denial of this purpose. The intended sons are actual rebels or disobedient sons. Salvation means that the rebels become sons. Jesus himself talked much of fatherhood, sonship, and brotherhood as involved in salvation. (See the Parable of the Prodigal Son, Luke 15:11–32.) Elsewhere the phrasing is sometimes different. In the Fourth Gospel it is being "born from above," "born of the Spirit" (3:3–7), "passing out of death into life" (5:24), finding "eternal life" (6:40). With Paul it is "believing on the Lord Jesus" (Acts 16:31), coming to "peace with God through faith in the Lord Jesus Christ" (Rom. 5:1), being made "a new creature in Christ" (II Cor. 5:17), "putting off the old man and putting on the new man" (Col. 3:9, 10). In Hebrews it is sanctification through the once-for-all offering of Jesus Christ (10:10). These are so many different ways of describing or explaining the same basic fact of salvation.

All this means a direct connection between Jesus Christ, human sinfulness, and salvation. The connection is expressed in the declaration, "He died for our sins" (I Cor. 15:3). But human salvation does not automatically follow on the sacrificial death of Christ. What he did must be appropriated, which is the act of faith (Rom. 5:1); the love that led to the sacrifice must be exemplified (I John 3:9–11); the will of Christ, that all who know him should serve him by service to others, must be carried out (Matt. 25:31–46). Salvation is a gift of the grace of God, but the gift has its own proper conditions, and it lays upon those who receive it its own proper demands (Jas. 2:1–17). See GOSPEL; JESUS CHRIST; REDEMPTION; SONS OF GOD.

Samaria, city of, the capital of the Northern Kingdom (Israel). The city was situated on an easily defensible hill c. 5½ m. NW. of Shechem, overlooking the chief north-south route through the hill country. A village, Sebastiyeh, now occupies the eastern end of the hill. The site was excavated in 1908–10 by G. A. Reisner and C. S. Fisher for Harvard University, and again in 1931–33 and 1935 by J. W. Crowfoot, Kathleen M. Kenyon and E. L. Sukenik for Harvard, Hebrew University (Jerusalem), the Palestine Exploration Fund, and several other organizations.

Pottery found in the lowest levels of the site indicates that the hill was occupied c. 3000 B.C., and again in the late 11th to early 9th centuries B.C. The building remains of these periods were destroyed by subsequent quarrying, leveling, and construction. The first significant occupation (Periods I–II of the excavations) can be attributed to Omri, who purchased the hill from Shemer and built a magnificent city upon it (I Kings 16:24), and to his son, Ahab.

On the summit stood the palace and the courtyard, at the north end of which was found a rectangular pool where possibly Ahab's blood was washed from his chariot (I Kings 22:38). Presumably the temple and altar of Baal (I Kings 16:32) were also located in this area, although their remains have not survived. The summit was surrounded by an enclosure wall, which was augmented by a casemate wall, probably during the reign of Ahab. Two other walls seem to have encircled the lower slopes of the hill. More than 500 fragments of Syro-Phoenician ivory toilet articles and inlays—the latter from wall panels and furniture (I Kings 22:39, Amos 6:4)—were also found in this area.

357. Hellenistic tower in Samaria.

Following Jehu's revolution (II Kings 10:1–7, 12–28), a number of buildings in the city were repaired or replaced (Period III). During the prosperous reign of Jeroboam II, repairs were made to the fortifications, and there were at least three phases of construction in the Royal Quarter (Periods IV–VI), in one of the buildings of which a group of 63 ostraca* were discovered. After a siege of 3 years, Samaria succumbed to the Assyrians (II Kings 17) and at least part of the city was burned, as shown by the excavations. Isaiah and Micah used the fate of Samaria as a warning to Jerusalem (Isaiah 8:4, 10:9–11, Micah 1:1–7).

After many of its inhabitants had been deported, the city was resettled with exiles from other lands. Samaria was built anew and became a district administrative center in the Assyrian Empire (Periods VII and VIIa), a position which it retained in the Babylonian (Period VIII) and Persian (Period IX) Empires.

During Hellenistic times (322–63 B.C.), Samaria was successively a part of the Macedonian, Ptolemaic, and Seleucid Empires, and the Jewish kingdom. The major remains of this period are two massive fortifications: The earlier one, a series of round towers, strengthened the old Omri-Ahab wall on the middle terrace; the second included two walls, one replacing the Israelite wall around the summit and the other protecting the lower slopes of the hill.

Samaria achieved its greatest splendor during Roman times. Herod the Great renamed the city Sebaste, in honor of Augustus, and undertook a great program of construction, including an enormous temple on the summit, a new fortification wall more than 2 miles in circumference, and a stadium in the Doric style. Sebaste was captured and burned during the First Jewish Revolt (A.D. 66–70), and it did not regain prominence again for more than a century. Between c. A.D. 180–230, the city was lavishly rebuilt, chiefly by Severus. The temple on the summit, the temple of Kore, the forum, and the west gate were reconstructed; a number of new structures were erected, including a theater, a large stadium, a basilica at the west end of the forum, a long east-west columned street flanked by shops, and an aqueduct 2¾ miles long. The remains of these buildings still stand above ground level today. In the 4th century A.D., Sebaste became an episcopal see, and the basilica was rebuilt as a cathedral. Two shrines commemorating the death and burial of John the Baptist were revered in the city during this period. In A.D. 634, the Arab occupation of Sebaste began.

See most recently, J. W. Crowfoot, Kathleen Kenyon, E. L. Sukenik, *The Buildings at Samaria* (London, 1942), J. W. Crowfoot, Grace M. Crowfoot, *Early Ivories from Samaria* (London, 1938) and J. W. Crowfoot, Grace M. Crowfoot, Kathleen Kenyon, *The Objects from Samaria* (London, 1957).
G.W.V.B.

Samaria, district of, in the Biblical period was at the geographical center of Palestine. It was one of the three sections of the hill country which runs like a rocky spine from Syria, through Galilee and Judaea, to the desert Negeb in the S. Its name is derived from that of the capital city. In the inheritance of Canaan by the Israelites, much of what became Samaria was allotted to Ephraim and the half Tribe of Manasseh. Samaria was the main portion of what was known after Solomon's time as the Kingdom of Israel, or the Northern Kingdom, in contrast to Judah. It reached from the Mediterranean to the Jordan, and extended S. from the mountain mass of Gilboa and the SE.-NW. ridge of Carmel to Mt. Ephraim. From the narrow pass at Megiddo a network of ancient roads ran in every direction, giving the people of Samaria contact with many other nations, but also exposing them to invasion. Samaria, far better supplied with natural resources than Judaea, led Isaiah to call it "the head of Ephraim" (7:9), and to immortalize its "glorious beauty, which is on the head of the fat valley"—an allusion to its prolific olive orchards (28:4). Mountainous Samaria was well-watered, suitable for the cultivation of vineyards (Jer. 31:5) and farm products (Obad. 19), which enabled it to withstand a three-years' siege by Shalmaneser* V before it fell to Sargon II.

The boundary between Samaria and Judah was an imaginary line passing through the weak buffer territory of Benjamin. Throughout their history Samaria and Judah were rivals rather than neighbors. King Saul (c. 1020–1000 B.C.) held the two regions together for a time, but at his death David acquired Judaea and Ish-bosheth got Israel. The two were reunited by David (c. 1000–961 B.C.), and remained in the United Kingdom of Solomon (c. 961–922 B.C.). But at Solomon's death the units were again separated, with Rehoboam succeeding to the throne of Judah in the S. and Jeroboam taking the ten Tribes which formed the Northern Kingdom. From that time the two political entities were as antagonistic as were their rival religious centers, Bethel and Dan in Israel, and Jerusalem in Judah (I Kings 12:25, 28 f.; Amos 7:10–13).

Important towns in Samaria were Tirzah*, where early kings were crowned (I Kings 15:21, 33, 16:6, 23; cf. Song of Sol. 6:4), Samaria*, founded by Omri as his capital (c. 876–869 B.C.), Shechem, Shiloh, Dan, Megiddo*, Taanach, En-gannim, and Hazor. In the SW. corner of Nablus is the small Samaritan synagogue presided over by a hereditary priest and guarding the *Samaritan Codex* of the Pentateuch. Only a few Samaritans* survive.

The history of Samaria in the Biblical period is mainly that of the ten Tribes of the Northern Kingdom, Israel. (See ISRAEL for events; also CHRONOLOGY.) The succession of the kings of Israel is given in the Books of Kings, in which the author and the editors attempted to synchronize the reigns of the kings of Israel and of Judah, e.g.: "In the three and twentieth year of Joash the son of Ahaziah, king of Judah, Jehoahaz the son of Jehu began to reign over Israel in Samaria, and reigned seventeen years" (II Kings 13:1); the chronologies are not always accurate. The peak of Samaria's material prosperity was reached during the 41-year reign of Jeroboam II (c. 786–746 B.C.), in the course of which he restored "the coast of Israel from the entering of Hamath unto the sea of the plain" (II Kings 14:24–27). When the capital city of Samaria fell in 722/1 B.C. and its people were carried off by Assyria in a series of deportations, and 10 nationalities of colonists were brought in, the independent history of the district ended. From this time also dates the animosity of the Jews toward the racially mixed Samaritan remnant left behind and the foreigners who were brought in. In the Persian period the province of Samaria was larger than Judah (c. 444 B.C.).

Many great names in Hebrew history are associated with Samaria. The prophets associated with Samaria are: Elijah (I Kings

17–19, 21, and possibly II Kings 1:2–4, 17a); Elisha (II Kings 5:3–9, 6:32); Amos (3:1, 10 f., 4:1, 5:1, cf. 8:14, and portions of chaps. 3, 4, 5, including his famous words, "Woe to them that . . . trust in the mountain of Samaria," 6:1); and Hosea.

Isaiah of Judah pronounced an oracle against Samaria when he wrote on a large tablet the name of his second son, Maher-shalal-hash-baz" ("spoil speeds, prey hastens"), suggesting that before the boy could talk Samaria would be plundered by Assyria (Isa. 8:1–4). Micah of Judah uttered judgments against Samaria (1:1–4, 6–9). History tells that the city of Samaria was not actually razed but that more than 20,000 of its inhabitants were deported.

In Jesus' time Samaria was north of Judaea, in one of the political divisions of Palestine, which the will of Herod the Great had partitioned. Samaria, along with Judaea and N. Idumaea, went, on Herod's death, to his son Archelaus. Augustus then made Archelaus ethnarch of Palestine until he should become worthy of the royal title; then, critical of the unrest, he deposed him in A.D. 6 and gave Samaria into the custody of a Roman procurator.

Jesus often avoided Samaria because of its Hellenistic culture, its worldly materialism, and its lack of concern for spiritual progress. He sometimes used the N.-S. footpaths along the Jordan to go from Galilee to Judaea. He experienced the extreme inhospitality of Samaritans on the occasion described by Luke (9:51–56). Yet it is recorded (Luke 17:11–19) that in a Samaritan village he cleansed 10 lepers, one of whom came back to thank him. When Jesus was in Samaria, at the Sychar* well of Jacob, he cut the Gordian knot of dispute between Jews and Samaritans concerning the place where they should worship, by declaring to a woman of Samaria that it was actually unimportant whether people worshipped God in Jerusalem or at Samaria (John 4:21–24), because God is a spirit and they that worship Him must worship Him in spirit and in truth.

In the early Apostolic age persecuted Christians of Jerusalem fled to Samaria and other regions. Philip came to Samaria and there preached Christ (Acts 8:1, 5), winning many converts, including Simon Magus (vv. 9–13), healing many, and bringing great joy to that city (vv. 7 f.).

Samaritan Pentateuch, the. See SAMARITANS.

Samaritans, in the O.T. inhabitants of the city or district of Samaria (II Kings 17:29). After the deportation of "27,290" Israelites by the Assyrian Sargon II (722/1 B.C.), colonies of non-Jews from Babylonia, Syria, Elam, and elsewhere, were settled in Samaria (II Kings 17:24). The record of II Kings 17:24 tallies with Sargon's own annals preserved at Khorsabad near Nineveh, but historical perspective has reduced the total number of people removed from Israel. Though thousands of the ruling class and the craftsmen were carried off, thousands more of the peasant class were left behind. The bringing in of foreigners resulted in a racially mixed population (Ezra 4:2, cf. vv. 9 f.) without the Hebrew standards of racial and religious purity; the situation was ripe for a schism between those who lived in Samaria and the orthodox Jews whose capital was Jerusalem. Matters worsened when Sanballat*, a man of Cutha who had been set up by the Persians as governor of Samaria, and others proffered help in the rebuilding of the Jerusalem Temple* and were rebuffed (Neh. 6); this rebuff may be reflected in Isa. 63:16 f. Within a century and a half of this incident Samaritans had erected a temple of their own on Mt. Gerizim* and organized themselves into a schismatic sect, in the later Nablus and the vicinity of Shechem. This apparently took place in the 4th century B.C., when Alexander the Great of Macedon carried his brilliant campaign through Palestine and possibly gave permission for the new temple. Some authorities date it earlier by a century and a half.

The Samaritans' own version of their origin is different from that of the Jews. They claim the derivation of their name from *shomerim* ("observant"), and their descent from those Israelites who remained loyal to Yahweh at the time when Eli "seduced" their brethren into constructing the apostate shrine at Shiloh*, instead of at God's chosen holy mountain, Gerizim (I Sam. 1:3, etc.).

The Jews, after the 4th century schism and the establishment of the religious state of Ezra and Nehemiah, forbade the Samaritans to present votive or freewill offerings at Jerusalem; to buy large cattle or unmovable property; to marry a Jew; or to circumcise a Jew. In brief, there were no dealings between Samaritans and Jews, even in Jesus' day (John 4:9). (See SAMARIA, DISTRICT OF.)

Dark hours in the history of Samaria included the sacking of Shechem by Alexander the Great, followed by an invasion by Demetrius (Poliorcetes) I (296–295 B.C.); deportation of Samaritans to Egypt under Ptolemy I; persecutions under Antiochus Epiphanes IV; invasion (c. 128 B.C.) by the Maccabean John Hyrcanus; destruction of the Samaritan temple on Mt. Gerizim (never rebuilt); and the razing of the capital 20 years later by sons of Hyrcanus (cf. Mic. 1:6). Samaria came under Roman rule (63 B.C.–A.D. 6), and Herod*, King of the Jews, received it from Octavian. Eleven thousand Samaritans were slaughtered by the Roman general Vespasian during an attempted revolt against Rome in the 7th decade of the 1st century, and 20,000 by the Byzantine Emperor Justinian (A.D. 527–65). Cruelties were rife under Moslem invaders, with the exception of the clement Fatimids. During the Crusades Samaritans were part of the small Christian kingdom of Godfrey de Bouillon, but were subdued by Saracens in 1184 and retaken by Christians in 1242, to be controlled by Mongols in 1259. Matters became worse under Turkish administration. The persecuted people continued to dwindle. Groups of Samaritans were living in 1616 in Cairo, Gaza, and Damascus, as well as at Nablus; today a considerable number may survive in the tiny community on the edge of Nablus.

The *religious beliefs* of the Samaritans had much in common with those of the Jews, e.g., the Sabbath* and sacred feasts*, circumcision*, and the conviction that a Messiah* or "Restorer" will come (but to convert

358. A Samaritan high priest and kinsfolk at Nablus.

all nations to Samaritanism). Samaritans, however, based their religion on the Pentateuch alone, and rejected the rest of the O.T. They had faith in (1) God (Who is unique and "without associate"); (2) Moses; (3) the Torah; (4) the sanctity of Mt. Gerizim; and (5) future reward and punishment. They believed that the whole Pentateuch was written by God. Their veneration of Mt. Gerizim as sacrosanct, and the true abode of God on earth, was the crux of their debate with the Jews, who venerated the mount at the Jebusite city which became Jerusalem. To Gerizim Samaritans assigned many O.T. events attributed by the Jewish O.T. to Moriah*. They declared that it was the home of Abraham (Gen. 22); the place where he was about to sacrifice Isaac; the place of Jacob's vision (cf. Gen. 31:13); Joseph's burial place (Josh. 24:32); the Bethel where Jacob "went up" to pray; and the "Mount of Blessing" (Deut. 11:29). (Jacob, son of Aaron, a Samaritan high priest of the present century [all Samaritan priests have claimed direct descent from Aaron], asserts that the Shekinah* was established during the lifetime of Aaron on Mt. Gerizim, which has been a sanctuary since the time of Moses; that it is the sanctuary indicated in Deut. 12:26.) To Gerizim Samaritans applied "twice seven" names: "the Ancient Mountain," "Bethel," "the House of Angels," "the Gate of Heaven," "Luzah" ("To God is This Place"), "Sanctuary," "Mt. Gerizim," "Beth-yhwh—the very name of the Highest," "the Beautiful Mountain," "the Chosen place," "the Highest in the World," "the First of Mountains," "God is Seen," and "the Mountain of the Inheritance of the Shekinah."

On Gerizim the small remnant of Samaritans still sacrifice; sanctify themselves in obedience to Deut. 33:18 f.; celebrate the Passover with an ancient ritual; and wait for the appearance of the prophet-leader of the world, who will bring again upon Gerizim the Shekinah in the second kingdom, when God will look with favor on His people and forgive them.

Samaritans have always been devoted to their sacred literature, consisting of the Pentateuch, liturgies, commentaries on the Pentateuch, homilies, treatises on ritual, etc. They used a form of western Aramaic, and after the Moslem conquest also Arabic, into which they translated their Targum. They claim that the Samaritan Pentateuch is as old as the sect itself. Scholars recognize it as a special recension of the Hebrew Pentateuch. Since it is actually not a translation of the Hebrew original it is therefore not properly a version. It is a Hebrew text, written in a modified old Phoenician alphabet which the Jews had discarded soon after 200 B.C., in script similar to the old Hebrew characters (Phoenician), and maintained independently of the Jewish tradition since the 4th century B.C. (see TEXT). The Samaritan Targum is an important paraphrase of the Pentateuch, the final form of which dates from about the 4th century A.D.

samech, the 15th letter of the Heb. alphabet.

Samgarnebo (săm′gär-nē′bō), a high officer of Nebuchadnezzar, who sat with other Babylonian princes, e.g., Sarsechim, at the middle gate of besieged Jerusalem (Jer. 39:3).

Samos (sā′mŏs), a mountainous Mediterranean island separated from the mainland of E. Asia Minor by a mile-wide strait. It lies athwart the trade routes from Asia Minor to the W. and from the Pontus and Aegean regions to Egypt. As early as the 7th century B.C. Samos was an important Greek commercial center. It carried on its silver coins a head of its famous philosopher son, Pythagoras. Paul, returning from his Second Missionary Journey, sailed S. from Mitylene on the island of Lesbos to Samian Trogyllium, where he tarried a day before proceeding S. to the city of Miletus in SW. Asia Minor (Acts 20:15).

Samothrace (săm′ō-thrās), a small island between Troas in Asia Minor and Neapolis in European Macedonia, touched by Paul on his Second Missionary Journey as he proceeded by boat to Philippi (Acts 16:11). The famous Greek statue, the Winged Victory (c. 200 B.C., Louvre, Paris), was found in Samothrace.

Samson, a hero of the Tribe of Dan, whose home near Beth-shemesh ("house of the sun") may account for the error by which his name has sometimes been based on *shemesh* ("sun") —Heb. *shimshon.* The brilliant author of the J source drew on popular oral folk tales for his story of Samson's life (Judg. 13–16). Robert H. Pfeiffer (*Introduction to the Old Testament*, pp. 319 f.) has suggested that these colorful folk tales—almost "unique in early literature as examples of rustic fiction"

—were told by traveling story-tellers who went from village to village, presenting their tales of the strong man who was too weak to resist feminine wiles, and who in the end heroically caused his own death. Although Samson's feats have a fabulous quality, like those of Hercules in Greek mythology, Melkarth in the Tyrian epics, and Peer Gynt in Norwegian literature, the story-tellers believed him to have been a real man. The words, "he judged Israel twenty years" (Judg. 16:31b) are significantly not part of J's document.

Additions made by J to old folk tales show this famous Danite, the last "judge" of Israel, as living in a specific era, between 1150 and 1050 B.C. (Pfeiffer), near Zorah*, and buried in the plot of his father, Manoah, between Zorah and Eshtaol (16:31). Samson appeared at a time when the great judges of Israel had done noble service, rallying Israel to meet outside foes, and welding them into a fairly united group, in a sort of league with the once dreaded Canaanites*. The Philistines* were then occupying the coastal plain from Gaza almost to Mt. Carmel, keeping strong garrison posts, and by their monopoly of iron preventing the Israelites from making weapons (I Sam. 13:19 ff.). The Philistines did not tax them heavily, but wore down their spirits and their faith in Yahweh. Into this situation Samson came.

Samson's life story, presented in Judg. 13–16, runs as follows. He was born to the barren wife of Manoah, who at the suggestion of an angel of the Lord adopted the Nazirite (see NAZIRITES) vow before his birth (13:2–24); and Samson was encouraged to live by the austere Nazirite ideals (cf. Judg. 16:17). His almost supernatural strength resulted in amazing feats: rending a lion with his hands (14:5 f.); slaying single-handed 30 men of Ashkelon to pay the promised reward to the Philistines of Timnah for guessing his riddle of the honey in the lion's carcass (14:12–19); killing 1,000 Philistines with the jawbone of an ass (15:14–17); carrying off the gates of Gaza to a hill in the direction of Hebron (16:3); pushing down the pillars of the temple of Dagon with his bare hands (16:30). His cunning resourcefulness showed up in his device for wreaking vengeance on his father-in-law's people by setting fire to their grainfields and orchards with firebrands tied between the tails of pairs of foxes (? jackals) (15:4 f.). The weakness of Samson's moral fibre appeared in his relations with women: the woman of Timnah (15:1 ff.); a Gaza harlot (16:1 ff.); and Delilah of Sorek (16:4–20), a tool of Philistine lords, who used her to precipitate his downfall by getting the secret of his strength (chap. 16). Samson was clearly of different caliber from the other judges of Israel, who were real leaders of their people in time of crisis. He had little of their mystical fellowship with God. Perhaps his own lack of deep moral conviction accounted for his failure to arouse it in Israel. He never himself claimed to be a judge. Samson did not deliver Israel from the Philistines, but performed melodramatic feats.

One of the great values of the Samson cycle is the light it sheds on social customs of the period just before the Hebrew Monarchy: marriage rites, with feasts lasting through days of eating and drinking and telling riddles (14:9 ff.); the role of the parents in securing a son's wife (14:2–4); the giving of an unpopular wife to someone else (15:2); the effective wiles of a woman used as a tool by Philistine war lords (16:5 ff.); the social side of Philistine sacrifices to the god Dagon* (16:23).

The great contribution of J was, in Pfeiffer's opinion, to infuse the "crude rustic tales" with the elements of patriotic fervor, and to show God's calling of Samson without spoiling the freshness of the oral originals. A spiritual highlight in the narrative is the reverence shown for the appearances of the angel of the Lord to Manoah and his wife (Judg. 13:3, 9, 13–21).

The consummate skill with which the J writer narrated Samson's life inspired the use of part of his material by the artists Rembrandt and Rubens; the poet Milton, in his *Samson Agonistes;* Saint-Saens in his opera, *Samson et Delilah;* and Handel in an oratorio.

Samuel ("name of God"), the last of the judges (I Sam. 7:15; Acts 13:20), and the first of the prophets after Moses (II Chron. 35:18; Jer. 15:1), a seer (I Sam. 9:9; I Chron. 26:28), and an 11th century B.C. priest (I Sam. 2:18, 27, 35, 7:9 f.). His story is set forth in the first book which bears his name (I Sam. 1–25). The complex origin of I Samuel* and the variety of its sources account for the conflicts in the story; though these can be somewhat harmonized.

Samuel was the child of Elkanah, an Ephraimite (I Sam. 1:1) and his wife Hannah* (1:2). Only after prayer (1:26), annual pilgrimages to Shiloh* (1:7) and a vow by Hannah to consecrate her first-born to Yahweh (1:11), was Samuel born. At Shiloh he was trained by Eli* the priest (2:11, 18–21, 3:1–10). Samuel voiced the condemnation of Yahweh against the shrine at Shiloh and the house of Eli (3:11–18) because of the pagan fertility cult practiced there with its drunkenness (1:13); sexual immoralities (2:22); and sacrilegious feastings (2:12–17). Later, in fulfillment of Samuel's ethical prognostications, Eli's irresponsible sons were slain (4:11), the Ark of God was captured by the Philistines (4:17), and Eli died from a broken neck (4:18). Samuel's position as a prophet in Israel became well established (3:20). Ramah* was his headquarters, but he traveled every year to Bethel, Gilgal, and Mizpah (7:16 f.).

The prophet was greatly concerned over the threat to Israel's national independence (7:3), and as a judge summoned the people to assemble at Mizpah to consider the encroachments of the Philistines*. The latter, using this occasion to attack the Israelites, were thrown into panic by a providential thunderstorm and defeated by the pursuing Israelites, whose morale had been strengthened by the words and deeds of Samuel, serving as priest to the nation (7:5–11). When the prophet's sons demonstrated their unfitness to succeed him as leaders in Israel's fight against the Philistines (8:1–3), the people demanded a king. Samuel was commanded by God to anoint Saul of Benjamin king (9:15, 10:1). The people ratified this choice.

The break between King Saul and Samuel came when the king assumed some of Samuel's priestly prerogatives (13:8–14), and refused to obey his warnings concerning the Amalekites* (15:1–23). The open repudiation of Saul by Samuel led to the king's repentance and a temporary reconciliation of both to Yahweh (15:24–31); but the earlier close association between the two was never resumed. Samuel anointed David—secretly, for reasons of personal security (16:2)—as the king to succeed Saul (vv. 3–13). Later, seeking to escape the madness of Saul, David found asylum at the home of Samuel at Ramah (19:18–23). At his death Samuel was buried there (25:1, 28:3). When Saul sought the services of the necromancer of Endor, the spirit of Samuel rebuked the king and told him of his approaching doom (28:8–19).

Samuel's foresightedness, spiritual insight, and ability to inspire others at a most critical period in Israel's development made him one of the great leaders of Israel. The fact that the books of I and II Samuel are named for him, though they include events that happened long after his death, reveals the high regard in which he was held. Rabbinical literature loves to dwell on his life and deeds, and mistakenly associates him with the authorship of Judges and Ruth. Nebī* Samwîl, 5 m. NE. of Jerusalem, one of the highest points in Palestine (2,935 ft. above sea level) has unsubstantiated traditions concerning the prophet, including a mosque containing his supposed tomb; and his name attached to this noteworthy elevation further reflects the high regard in which Samuel has always been held by Jew, Moslem, and Christian.

Samuel, I and II, in the original Hebrew canon formed one book, called "Samuel." In the LXX it was divided into two books for convenience, as was also done with the single book of Kings: for in Gk.—in which the vowels are written, in contrast with ancient Heb.—two scrolls of papyrus were required. Thus in the Greek version Samuel and Kings are four books. They are entitled "Kingdoms I–IV."

I and II Samuel deal with the beginnings of the Hebrew Monarchy in the times of Samuel, Saul, and David. They may be briefly summarized thus:

I Sam. 1:1–7:2—The birth, childhood, training, and early experiences of Samuel; the Ark* and the priests of Shiloh.

I Sam. 7:3–15:35—Samuel and Saul.

I Sam. 16:19–II Sam. 1—Saul and David.

II Sam. 2–24—David as king: (1) of Judah (II Sam. 2–4); (2) of United Israel (II Sam. 5–24).

I and II Samuel are compilations of various historical materials. Early and late sources* have been incorporated—often side by side or interwoven, in spite of their differing and often conflicting details and points of view. Glosses and insertions are added by later readers and editors to harmonize discrepancies or to equate ancient times with post-Exilic Judaism. This composite authorship leads to confusion and debate unless the sources are separated and used with discrimination. Thus in the early source will be found the most accurate and brilliant historical writing in the O.T.; and this dependable history should be kept distinct from later reactions to and interpretations of the events recorded.

Evidences of the use of several sources are especially conspicuous in I Samuel. Some incidents are recorded twice, with considerable difference in details. Saul is anointed king privately by Samuel (I Sam. 9:26–10:1); and twice in public (10:17–24, 11:15). Likewise Saul is twice deposed from the throne (13:14, 15:26–29), but continues to rule until the day of his death. David is introduced twice to Saul (16:14–23, 17:55–58); twice is offered a daughter of Saul in marriage (18:17–19, 22–29); twice escapes Saul's court, the second time forever (19:12, 20:42); and three times makes a covenant with Jonathan (18:3, 20:16, 42, 23:18). Goliath is slain by David (17; 21:9), but also by Elhanan, one of David's henchmen (II Sam. 21:19). The Chronicler endeavored to solve this contradiction by saying that Elhanan slew "Lahmi, the brother of Goliath" (I Chron. 20:5). Evidently Hebrew writers had a praiseworthy desire to preserve all information concerning the nation's highly revered early personalities, and thus legends multiplied and became more popular than the actual facts reported in the oldest records.

The composite character of the book is also seen in the different viewpoints incorporated in I Samuel concerning the Monarchy. Yahweh, in order to deliver the Israelites from the Philistines, ordered Samuel to anoint Saul king (I Kings 9:1–10:16, 10:27–11:11). Elsewhere, however, the Monarchy is considered a calamity, a concession to the pagan customs of the times (I Sam. 10:25–27, 11:12 f., 12). In the former view Samuel is portrayed as a village seer; in the latter, as a mighty prophet and ruler in Israel. Such differences disclose the contrast between the idealization of the Monarchy at its enthusiastic inception, and the disillusionment which followed its actual operation. The foundations of modern democracy, involving the right to criticize and disagree, are projected into this story of the Monarchy, in which the people, the prophets, and the will of God all find expression.

I Samuel begins with material derived in the main from N. Israel or Ephraimitic sources (I Sam. 1–7:2). Samuel dominates this record. The beautiful story of the idealized childhood of Samuel is legendary and late, for such details would be recorded only after the hero had attained high popular regard. The unknown writer or writers from N. Israel who patriotically penned this record may be recognized by: (1) the condemnation of the Monarchy (I Sam. 8; cf. Hos. 8:4, 13:11); (2) a fondness for northern centers, e.g., Shiloh* (I Sam. 1:3, 2:14, 3:21, 4:4), Gilgal* (7:16, 10:8, 11:14 f., 15:33; II Sam. 19:15); and Ramah* (I Sam. 1:19, 2:11, 7:17, 8:4, 15:34, 16:13, 19:18–23). In his *Introduction to the Old Testament*, p. 362

(Harper & Brothers), Robert H. Pfeiffer says, "We may date I Sam. 1 with some assurance c. 750 B.C., . . . and tentatively I Sam. 17 and 20 in their original form, somewhere in the following century. The rest [of the northern sources] seems to belong to the century 650–550 B.C."

The Judaean sources incorporated in I and II Samuel are older than the above-mentioned Ephraimitic ones, and reflect a contemporary view of Saul (chaps. 8–14), and especially of David (I Sam. 15–II Sam. 20). Freed from later additions, such as the late source and contributions made by the Deuteronomic editor, this earlier source stands out as a vivid record of actual history, from the first battle between Israelites and Philistines to the accession of Solomon (c. 1050–961 B.C.). The author made such good use of his available sources of information and his personal observations that he can be called the "father of history" in a much truer sense than Herodotus, half a millennium later. This recital of events is dominated by a great idea—love of country and of God—and centers in the personality of David. The Chronicler guessed that David's biography was written by Samuel, Nathan, and Gad (I Chron. 29:29). Some modern scholars have nominated as candidates for this authorship two priests of David's era, Abiathar* (II Sam. 15:27–29), or Ahimaaz* (17:17–21, 18:19–32), because the vividness of the narrative indicates a contemporary author who witnessed the events he described, and the highly intelligent character of the history indicates an educated man who, in those days, would have been a priest. Whoever the author was, he wrote without any previous model as a guide a "masterpiece unsurpassed in historicity, psychological insight, literary style, and dramatic power." Before this time poetry had been the vehicle used to preserve historic happenings; but Hebrew prose now emerged in its first and best form as a record of history.

The account of Jonathan's attack on the Philistine garrison (I Sam. 14:1–23, 13:5) was recorded with such accuracy and detail that Field Marshal Edmund Allenby, Viscount of Megiddo, while conducting his Palestine campaign of January-March 1918, was able as a result of his Bible study to identify the crag "on the north in front of Michmash, and the other on the south in front of Geba" (A.S.V. I Sam. 14:5). The Viscount stopped his pursuit of the Turks long enough to give a talk to his staff on Jonathan's strategy and the terrain so accurately recorded in this passage (*Allenby, a Study in Greatness*, Archibald Wavell, p. 236).

The O.T. writer's graphic attention to details extended also to a penetrating treatment of persons. Though the kings of Babylonia, Assyria, and Egypt in this period are known to us only from formal records inscribed on monuments, temples, rocks, and tablets, Saul and David are depicted by this historian as human beings, capable of generosity and faithfulness, but also subject to moods of malice and selfishness. David, in his exalted position, was not exempt from the sorrows of mourning (II Sam. 18:33) and of remorse (II Sam. 12:1–7, 13). Kings are not regarded as gods, as in Egypt and elsewhere; individuals, whatever their station, are not exempted from God's ethical demands (I Sam. 15:24–28; II Sam. 12:7). The democracy that assures individual freedom is manifest in the moral standards and religious revelations in these historical narratives, which pave the way for later prophetic thought.

Sanballat (săn-băl′ăt), a Horite leader, possibly a resident at Beth-horon in Samaria. He repeatedly tried to halt Nehemiah's efforts to rebuild the Jerusalem walls. It "grieved" him to think that someone had arrived "to seek the welfare of the children of Israel" (Neh. 2:10). He and Tobiah suggested that Nehemiah was planning revolt against the Babylonian king (2:19). Next Sanballat (v. 20) and his henchmen used derision, suggesting that even a fox could break down the repaired walls (Neh. 4:1, 7). Foiled in his plot to lure Nehemiah to Ono for physical hurt, Sanballat received the brave retort, "I am doing a great work, so that I cannot come down" (6:2 f.; cf. the further threats of vv. 10–13). Sanballat and his friends "were cast down in their own eyes" when the repairs were completed within 52 days (v. 15). The Horite's daughter married the son of a high priest, Joiada (Neh. 13:28). Apocryphal legend credits Sanballat with establishing the colony of Samaritans*.

sanctification, like holiness, has the root idea of "separateness" or "apartness." In the N.T. the idea is carried to its completeness. The "sanctity" or "holiness" made possible to men through Jesus Christ goes beyond anything described in the O.T., because faith in Christ releases energies of the Holy Spirit not otherwise experienced, and it is through the Holy Spirit that sanctification comes to pass (II Thess. 2:13 f.; I Pet. 1:2; cf. Rom. 8:1–17, 26 f.). The terms "sanctify," "holy," and their derivatives are much more common in the O.T. than in the N.T., but that is because in the O.T. the terms are used ritualistically and are applied to things and places, whereas in the N.T. the use is limited chiefly to persons. The N.T. describes a Saviour whose own sanctification—that is, his separateness from all sin and his consecration to God—was so complete that it could avail to bring about a like sanctification for sinful men. The O.T. exhortation, "sanctify yourselves therefore, and be ye holy, for I am holy" (Lev. 11:44), is repeated in the N.T. (I Peter 1:15), but in circumstances which give a depth of meaning to the N.T. usage far exceeding that in the O.T. It is the difference between the formal and the vital. The sanctification of the Christian is not anything formal: it is increased "participation" in Christ; it is the growing realization of that which was symbolized in baptism and "imputed" in justification. The justified person, whom God "reckons" to be righteous (Rom. 4:5), is but as "a babe in Christ" (I Cor. 3:1), and it belongs to him to undergo "perfecting," to come "unto a fullgrown man, unto the measure of Christ," and the power by which this "increase" takes place is "love" (Eph. 4:12–16). This "increase" is increase in sanctification, which is why the degree of Christian sanctity is in the degree of Christian love. Perfect love is perfect holiness, or "entire sanctification" (I John 3:6, 9, 4:7–13, 16–19). See HOLINESS; JUSTIFICATION; REGENERATION. E. L.

sanctuary, a sacred place believed to offer personal security, like the six cities* of refuge provided by Hebrew law for unintentional killers. Very early sanctuaries were set up in places where some natural grandeur moved people to worship or where they had theophanies, like Jacob at Bethel*. (Cf. Peter's desire to erect three "tabernacles" at Caesarea Philippi, Mark 9:5.) After the time of Solomon (c. 961–922 B.C.) Hebrews regarded their Temple* as the one great sanctuary where they could always be sure of the ear of a listening God.

Sanctuaries were not peculiar to Israel. Long before the Patriarchal Age primitive tribes at Athens built their first sanctuaries on the sacred hill later known as the Acropolis*. Beneath the rocky summit of that elevation was a sanctuary of the Furies (Eumenides), which later Christians converted into a church in honor of Dionysius, Paul's convert (Acts 17:34). Beneath the Acropolis wall at Eleusis, Greek mystery cult center known to Paul, there had been built in very early times a sanctuary sacred to Pluto, god of the underworld.

sand, the small, loose debris from disintegrating rocks, conspicuous in the shifting dunes along the Mediterranean shores of S. Palestine and Egypt, as well as in desert wilderness areas. Its innumerable particles were used frequently in Scripture to symbolize a great quantity, or a numerical multitude, e.g., the descendants promised to Abraham (Gen. 22:17) and to Jacob (Gen. 32:12); or the corn stored by Joseph against famine (Gen. 41:49); or the number of Midianite camels (Judg. 7:12); or the Philistine fighters (I Sam. 13:5); or the length of Job's years (29:18); or the quails sent by Yahweh (Ps. 78:27); or the thoughts of the righteous toward God (Ps. 139:18). Sand, especially in the form of shifting dunes, was recognized as providing a good hiding place for men or treasures (Ex. 2:12; Deut. 33:19). It was heavy (Job 6:3; Prov. 27:3). It disintegrated when it became wet, like the foundation of the foolish man's house (Matt. 7:26).

Sandahanna, Tell. See MARESHAH (Gk. Marisa).

sandal, a kind of shoe (see SHOES).

Sanhedrin (săn'hē̍-drĭn) (from Gk. *synedrion*, Aramaicized to Sanhedrin), the chief judicial council* or supreme court of the Jews. Successor to the Great Synagogue*, it met from some time in the 3d century B.C., or possibly earlier; after the fall of Jerusalem to the Romans (A.D. 70) it lost its authority.

According to the Chronicler (c. 250 B.C.) the Sanhedrin was organized by King Jehoshaphat* of Judah (c. 873–849 B.C.). Some scholars see in II Chron. 19:5–11 the first reference to what became the Sanhedrin: a group of Levites, priests, and chief fathers of Israel (v. 8) under the executive leadership of a high priest were to sit in Jerusalem, hearing cases of disagreements which had come up in provincial courts. The Chronicler warns them to make scrupulous decisions. Amariah, the chief priest, was to be supreme in matters of God, and Zebadiah, son of Ishmael, ruler of the house of Judah, was to be in control of all the king's matters. The officers of this council were to be Levites (v. 11). There seems almost a suggestion here of two sanhedrins, one for religious, one for civil affairs. But the later Sanhedrin had governing as well as judicial functions, whereas the old council was merely judicial. Cf. the number of members in the Sanhedrin (70 plus one or two) with the "seventy men of the elders of Israel," and Moses (Num. 11:16). The first mention of the Sanhedrin is attributed to the Jewish historian Josephus, who wrote of the division of Palestine into five *synedria* (57 B.C.). (See SEPPHORIS.)

The functions and the personnel of the Sanhedrin varied in different periods. In pre-Maccabean times it was aristocratic, ecclesiastical, and imperialistic. Its members were priests, Levites, and the heads of the leading families of Israel—Sadducees (Ezra 10:15; II Chron. 19:8). But—as I. G. Matthews points out (*The Religious Pilgrimage of Israel*, p. 250, Harper & Brothers)—by the opening of the Roman age in Palestine (c. 63 B.C.) the Sanhedrin was taking on the tone of a "layman's movement," for the unsympathetic, pro-Hellenistic priesthood had lost touch with the people and the Sanhedrin was drawn in large measure from the middle class, devoted to the Law, but interpreting it by intelligence. Under Herod many Pharisees became members of the Sanhedrin. Over the Great Sanhedrin pairs of leaders (teachers, or scribes) presided who held rival points of view, as do the conservative and liberal leaders of a parliament. The leaders of the ultralegalistic party in the 1st century A.D. were called "Beth Shammai," and of the more liberal opposition "Beth Hillel." Far more questions were brought for solution than were ever decided, but discussion clarified many legal points.

The Sanhedrin met in impressive chambers of hewn stone in the colonnade of the Jerusalem Temple Area, and was accessible to all Jews who sought enlightenment on the complicated details of the Jewish Law as it had developed through the centuries. In the Roman era, though it could not hold sessions in the absence of the Roman procurator, the area in which its decisions were valid was very wide. The learned council sat in a semicircle with the accused in front of them; attended by court clerks; and observed by three rows of disciples who might be candidates for the body. The prisoner was appareled in mourning garments.

The Sanhedrin could pronounce even capital punishment in cases of the violation of major Jewish Law, but might not execute the sentence without the sanction of the Roman procurator. In the time of Jesus the Sanhedrin had authority only in Judaea; therefore it could not lay hands on Jesus while he was working in Galilee and the

Peraea. Its charge of blasphemy against him was typical of its arraignments, for it was the court of highest appeal in matters based on the Mosaic Law. But it was able, working hand-in-glove with the Roman procurator, to bring about the Crucifixion of Jesus. Not the Jewish people as a whole, nor the Roman Empire alone, but a group of bigoted Jewish religious leaders and an unscrupulous foreign administrator seeking favor with the population, bear the responsibility for history's greatest tragedy. The Sanhedrin ("council") appears in the following Gospel narratives dealing with the Trial of Jesus: Matt. 26:59; Mark 14:55, 15:1; Luke 22:66; John 11:47. It must be noted that the Sanhedrin of Jesus' day included men like the sincere Pharisee Nicodemus*, who not only sought out Jesus to inquire about his Kingdom (John 3:1–21), but pleaded with the Sanhedrin for greater fairness in its treatment of Jesus (John 7:50–52). Nicodemus carried 100 pounds of myrrh and aloes to prepare the body of the crucified Jesus for burial (John 19:39). Joseph* of Arimathaea, also a well-to-do member of the Sanhedrin and a secret disciple of Jesus, went personally to Pontius Pilate to ask permission to place Jesus' body in his new tomb near Golgotha (John 19:38).

After the death of Jesus the Sanhedrin continued its policy of persecuting those of the Way. Peter, John, and other apostles were questioned by the Sanhedrin, commanded not to preach in the name of Jesus, threatened, and beaten (Acts 4:5–21, 5:17–41). Stephen was haled before the Sanhedrin (Acts 6:12), as was Paul later (22:30, 23:15, 24:20).

The Sanhedrin ceased to function as such when Jerusalem fell to the Romans.

Sansannah (săn-săn′*ȧ*) ("palms") (Khirbet esh-Shamsanīyât), a town N. of Beer-sheba, in the extreme S. of Judaea; part of the inheritance of the Tribe of Judah* (Josh. 15:31).

Saph (săf) (Sippai), one of four gigantic Philistines slain by David's henchmen (II Sam. 21:18; I Chron. 20:4).

Sapphira (să-fī′rȧ) (Aram., "beautiful"), the wife of Ananias* (Acts 5:1 ff.).

sapphire (possibly intended for lapis lazuli). See JEWELRY; also BREASTPLATE.

Sarah (a later form of Sarai, perhaps "princess"). (1) The wife and half-sister of Abraham* the Patriarch (Gen. 11:29, 20:12, 16:1). Sarah shared with her husband and his relatives the epochal journey from Ur* of the Chaldees into Haran and ultimately to Canaan, some time in the 20th or 19th century B.C. (Gen. 11:31).

Sarah's great beauty (Gen. 12:14) was the cause for Abraham's twice palming her off as his sister: (a) during the short descent into Egypt, when Sarah was taken into Pharaoh's house (Gen. 12:15) and Abraham was well treated for her sake by the Egyptian (v. 16), but Pharaoh and his household were punished with "great plagues" (v. 17); and (b) when Abraham, on a later journey south to Gerar, deceived King Abimelech by representing the fair Sarah as his sister, thus bringing down punishment on Abimelech's household. These two narratives may be variant records of the same incident.

Sarah's part in the Patriarchal customs of hospitality is seen in her personal attention to the baking of fresh bread for guests, even though the household had servants (Gen. 18:6, 9). When God promised Abraham, after the circumcision covenant, that he should have a son named Isaac*, who should be the heir of the covenant and the father of a great nation, Sarai's name was changed to Sarah (Gen. 17:15). Sarah, already "old" (Gen. 18:13), laughed to scorn the announcement that she would become a mother—and then, in fear, denied that she had derided the Lord's announcement (vv. 12, 15). She bore Isaac (Gen. 21:2 f.; cf. 24:36; Isa. 51:2; Rom. 4:19, 9:9) and became the first of the four Hebrew matriarchs. Sarah cruelly sent her Egyptian handmaid, Hagar*, and her young son, Ishmael, into the desert when irked by Hagar's mockery during Isaac's weaning feast. Sarah had given Hagar to Abraham as secondary wife (Gen. 16), an act allowable by the custom of the day.

Sarah must have rejoiced in the blessing pronounced by the angel when her son Isaac was spared from sacrifice, "I will multiply thy seed as the stars of the heaven, and as the sand which is upon the sea shore" (Gen. 22:17). During Sarah's lifetime, as Gen. 25:1 suggests, she was the principal wife of the Patriarch, who after her death married Keturah. She alone is mentioned as resting beside the Patriarch in the Machpelah tomb (Gen. 49:31). These narratives suggest at least a tendency toward monogamy, except where the wife was childless (see MARRIAGE).

Sarah, after sharing her husband's life near Beer-sheba, died at a ripe old age ("an hundred and seven and twenty years") at Hebron* (Kirjath-arba) and was mourned by Abraham. He bought for her burial place the Cave of Machpelah*, from Ephron the Hittite, in a field near Mamre (Gen. 23). Isaac's devotion to Sarah's memory is indicated by his bringing his bride Rebekah to his mother's own tent (Gen. 24:67).

Sarah's name is mentioned in Jewish homes today in the parental blessing of girls on Sabbaths and holidays. Her story is amplified in the Talmud and Islamic writings.

(2) Asher's daughter, Sarah (Serah) (Gen. 46:17; Num. 26:46; I Chron. 7:30).

sarcophagus. See BURIAL.

Sardis (sär′dĭs), a highland city of W. Asia Minor, located about 60 m. E. of Smyrna, one of the seven cities to whom messages are addressed in the Book of Revelation (1:11, 3:1, 4). It was founded probably as early as 1200 B.C. Situated at the trade crossroads running E. and W. through the powerful Kingdom of Lydia* of which it was the capital, Sardis was enriched by commerce, productive plains of Hermus and Pactolus Rivers, and by extensive manufacture of textiles and gold jewelry. It is credited with minting the first coins, under the fabulously rich Croesus. From Sardis the Greeks probably learned the art of coinage. In spite of its almost impregnable acropolis, Sardis was overcome by Cyrus* the Great (546 B.C.) and by Antiochus the Great (218 B.C.). Sardis was within the Roman Province of Asia, organized in 129 B.C. Its rich citizens were patrons of the mystery* cults, including that of Cybele, which claimed power to restore life to the dead. Hence the point of Rev. 3:4, praising the "few" who, even in Sardis, "have not defiled their garments," but were worthy of walking in white with Christ. The Christian colony degenerated until the majority had reverted to paganism.

359. Sardis.

Portions of the temple of Artemis, excavated for Princeton 1910–14, Howard C. Butler, survive. He excavated the early church adjacent to temple. Temple of Zeus, supposedly adjacent to temple, has not yet been found. T. L. Shear excavated for Princeton, 1920–22.

The Chester Beatty Papyri dating from the 2d to the 4th century A.D., and found in Egypt in 1931, include a sermon or religious discourse by Melito of Sardis.

sardius (sär′dĭ-ŭs), a precious stone, possibly a ruby (see A.S.V. Ezek. 28:13), in the breastplate* of the Jewish high priest (see also JEWELRY). Symbolically the sardius was used by the prophet Ezekiel in describing the beauty of Tyre (Ezek. 28:13); and by the author of Revelation to convey the glory of the foundation walls of the holy city, Jerusalem (21:20).

Sarepta (să-rĕp′tă) ("smelting place") (the modern Sarafand), the Gk. N.T. form in the A.V. of Zarephath* (A.S.V., R.S.V. Luke 4:26), the Phoenician city where Elijah lodged with a widow during a famine and restored her son (I Kings 17:8–24). It was situated between Sidon and Tyre.

Sargon (sär′gŏn) **I** (*Shargani-shar-ali*), of Agade (Accad*), "the first great Semitic leader in history" (J. H. Breasted). He lived **c.** 2360 B.C. His origin is uncertain. Legend says that as an infant he was set adrift on open water (like Moses), was found by a gardener, and became cupbearer to a king of Mesopotamian Kish. He established a great new empire, which included both Sumer* and Accad, and reached from Elam to the Mediterranean and up the Tigris and Euphrates toward Armenia. Sargon I and his son Naram-sin received homage from the ancient cities of Nippur*, Kish*, Babylon*, and Erech*. Some of the innovations in Sargon's reign were: a change from living in tents to living in huts of sun-dried brick; the first efforts at writing a Semitic language—an art adapted from the Sumerians; the making of metal helmets for war; the tradition of dedicating a royal princess to the service of the great gods, like En-khe-du-an-na, daughter of Sargon. An alabaster disk depicting this daughter of Sargon has been excavated at Ur and is in the University Museum at Philadelphia. This priestess and wife of the moon god Nannar learned the god's secrets after a night with him in the empty shrine at the top of the *ziggurat** (stage tower). Sargon's subjects and their successors developed marvelous skill in carving seals; they were especially adept in depicting animals.

Sargon II, the "king of Assyria" mentioned by name in Isa. 20:1; he lived 772–705 B.C. He was successor of Shalmaneser V and father of Sennacherib, who succeeded him in 705 B.C. Sargon II completed (722–1 B.C.) Shalmaneser's three-year siege of Samaria* (II Kings 17:5); the final surrender was made c. "the ninth year of King Hoshea" (reigned c. 732–724 B.C.). Sargon's records claim that he deported 27,290 chief citizens. According to II Kings 17:6 he settled them in "Halah and in Habor by the river of Gozan, and in the cities of the Medes." The downfall of the Kingdom of Israel at his hands was attributed to the people's sins, including apostasy (v. 7). He settled immigrants from Babylonia, Elam, and Syria (v. 24) in the homes of the deported Israelites; and in 715 B.C. brought in more colonists from Arab communities. He also conquered the Hittite capital, Carchemish* (717), warred bitterly against Armenia, levied taxes on Egypt, and received tribute from King Hezekiah of Judah (c. 715–687 B.C.).

The leading kings of the dynasty of Sargon II were:

Sargon II	722–705 B.C.
Sennacherib	705–681 B.C.
Esar-haddon	681–669 B.C.
Ashurbanipal (Gk. Sardanapalus)	669–633 B.C.

Sargon II used several cities for his successive capitals: Assur*, his first residence; the Biblical Calah* (Nimrûd), his second; Nineveh*, his third; and Dur-Sharrukin ("Sargonsburg"), which he founded, 10 m. N. of Nineveh. Excavation of Dur-Sharrukin (Khorsabad, as the ruined Iraqi city is called) has brought to light immense quantities of sculpture and inscribed records in the royal archives.

Sargon's capital at Dur-Sharrukin exceeded anything built by Babylon in its proudest epoch. Its ruins have been excavated by the French government and the University of Chicago. Sargon's palace stood partly within and partly without the city walls, on a vast, two-acre platform. Sargon's chariot entered the royal precinct via a ramp inside the walls. His palace rooms were grouped around open courts. His thousands of subjects lived below the palace but inside the city walls. Colossal human-headed, winged bulls in pairs guarded the palace entrance; one is in the Museum of the O.I., Chicago. It is skillfully wrought out of calcareous stone, similar to alabaster, 16 ft. high, and weighs 30 tons. The pair of which it was one flanked the portal leading from the courtyard to the throne room. The side walls of the doorway were formed by two larger human-headed winged bulls which faced the court. Wall reliefs found in Sargon's palace both inside and out show events in his campaigns; processions of captives bearing tribute; and the building of Sargonburg.

Sargon II began the great collection of thousands of clay tablets continued by his great-grandson, Ashurbanipal, found in the famous library of the latter at Nineveh. Clay tablets from Sargon to his son Sennacherib have been recovered.

360. From the palace of Sargon II, a relief depicts captives leading horses.

Sarid (sā'rĭd), possibly Tell Shadud, SW. of Nazareth, and just N. of the Plain of Esdraelon. It was a border village of the territory of Zebulun (Josh. 19:10, 12).

Sarsechim (sär'sē-kĭm), an unidentified official of Nebuchadnezzar who entered Jerusalem (Jer. 39:3).

Satan, the name given in the Scriptures to the evil power that stands in opposition to God, but which in the end is always subject to His will. Other names are "the evil one" (N.E.B. Matt. 6:13, 13:19; Eph. 6:16; I John 2:13, 5:18, 19); "the devil" (Matt. 4:1, 13:39, 25:41; John 8:44; Eph. 4:27); "the old serpent" (Rev. 12:9).

In the intertestamental literature there is a marked development of the idea; due, it is usually believed, to Persian influences. The Persians had an elaborate angelology and demonology, and much of this seems to have passed over into later Jewish thought. The O.T. is singularly free from it, though it does present us with the conception of a heavenly "adversary" (Heb. *satan*). That conception is present in the first two chapters of the Book of Job, where Satan is described as "one of the sons of God" (divine agents) who has the special function, assigned him by God, of bringing calamities on good men to test their integrity. God sets a limit, however, to the amount of evil Satan may inflict (1:12). In the Book of Job Satan really means "the adversary," and should be named "the *satan*." The term "adversary" or "adversaries" is frequent in earlier O.T. books, but is used in the general sense of "enemy" (Ex. 23:22). In the Balaam story, where the angel is called "an adversary," the Heb. word here being "a satan," the meaning is not the same as in Job (see Num. 22:22). In I Kings the word "adversary" occurs four times (5:4, 11:14, 11:23, 11:25), and each time the Heb. says "a satan," but in each case the reference is to a human enemy. In Zech. 3:1 f., "the adversary" (N.E.B.) plays the same role as in Job; he is the one who acts as prosecuting attorney and brings an accusation against the high priest Joshua. But in I Chron. 21:1 the role is a different one, that of tempting men to sin; the Chronicler has introduced him in order to avoid making Yahweh responsible for David's wrongdoing (cf. II Sam. 24:1). Here the Hebrew omits the article "the" so one must either translate the expression "*an* adversary" or, with greater likelihood, as a proper name "Satan." It is only in this place, in one of the latest books of the O.T., that the word is used with this particular nuance. From this time on, Satan and other demonic figures begins to appear in Jewish thought; Satan now becomes God's "adversary," not merely men's, and is held responsible for sin and evil.

It is this personalizing of the conception that is so conspicuous in the Apocalyptic writings. The Book of Enoch supposes "the demons" to be the offspring of angels and women (cf. Gen. 6:1:4). There are frequent references in these writings to Asmodeus and Satan and Sammael, as the "ruler" of the demons—perhaps to be identified with the Apollyon of Rev. 9:11 and "the old serpent" of Rev. 12:9. To these writings we owe the tradition, so dramatically employed by Milton in *Paradise Lost*, that Satan was once an angel in heaven who led a revolt against God, and was banished with his followers for the offense (cf. Isa. 14:12–15 A.V.), the archangel Michael being his chief foe (see Jude 9; Rev. 12:7).

The N.T. reflects the widespread influence of the Satan idea. He is definitely "personal," as in the account of the temptation of Jesus, where he is also called "the devil" (the Gk. is "the *diabolos*") and "the tempter" as well as "satan" (Matt. 4:1–11). Whether the "evil [one]" of the Lord's Prayer (Matt. 6:13) refers to Satan is not certain (cf. R.S.V., N.E.B.); but Beelzebub, meaning perhaps "lord of flies," undoubtedly means Satan (Matt. 12:24). Jesus himself very evidently believed in a kingdom of evil spirits under its own powerful ruler, and he said that this is what he had come to destroy (Mark 3:22–27; cf. John 16:11; I John 3:8 f.). He even seems to have recognized "demon-possession" (Matt. 12:43–45, 17:14–18; Mark 5:1–20); and he gave his disciples "authority over unclean spirits" (Matt. 10:1). The disciples' power over demons he described as proof of "Satan falling as lightning from heaven" (Luke 10:17–20).

Paul recognizes Satan and his function to lead men astray (I Cor. 7:5; cf. II Cor. 11:14). He speaks of "the fiery darts of the evil one" (Eph. 6:16). He calls Satan "the serpent" (II Cor. 11:3). He makes use of the promise in Gen. 3:15 that Satan shall be "bruised" (Rom. 16:20). Paul's phrase, "the sons of disobedience" may reflect the belief in "fallen angels" (cf. Eph. 6:11–13). As we should expect, Revelation uses all these various names, such as "the devil" (2:10); "Satan" (2:9, 13, 24); perhaps also the rider "Death, followed by Hades" (6:8; cf. 20:14); Apollyon and Abaddon (9:11); "a great red dragon" (12:3); "a beast" (13:1, 14:9, 16:13; cf. this chapter with Dan. 7). In 20:2 the four names are given as synonyms: "the dragon, the old serpent, the Devil, and Satan." The final fate of the devil and all his agents was to be "cast into the lake of fire and brimstone" (20:10–15), in contrast to the triumph of "the Lamb"—meaning Christ—by whom "the beast" is at last overcome.

The Bible teaching as a whole therefore seems to mean that there is a malign power of evil at work in the world, attempting to pervert the purposes of God, especially His purposes for mankind; but there is a limit to this evil power. Against it God employs all His resources; and His chief resource is Jesus Christ, who was "manifested that he might destroy the works of the devil" (I John 3:8). See APOCALYPTIC; BAALZEBUB; LUCIFER; DEVIL. E. L./R. C. D.

satrap (sā′trăp), the governor of a province in the ancient Persian Empire (R.S.V. Esther 3:12; A.V. "lieutenants"). This title was also given to high officials in the Babylonian Empire and in the realm of Darius the Mede (R.S.V. Dan. 3:2, 6:1; A.V. "princes").

satyr (săt′ẽr), a riotous, lascivious deity in Mediterranean mythology, represented as half man and half goat. This word is used in Isa. 13:21 in a prophetic picture of the impending desolation of Babylon.

Saul. (1) The son of the Benjamite Kish, and the 1st king of Israel (c. 1020–1000 B.C.). His life story is recorded in I Sam. 9–31 in sometimes contradictory narratives which come from three sources*: (a) The older, more vivid, and perhaps more reliable source, consisting mainly of chaps. 9–14. (b) Narratives written from the viewpoint of later political and religious interpreters are scattered through I Sam. 10–15:3. (c) Information concerning Saul is included in the popular David stories (17:12–31:13).

Saul's prestige was derived from his family's wealth (A.S.V. margin I Sam. 9:1, 3:5); his imposing presence (9:2); and his deeply religious nature (I Sam. 9:6, 14:37, 28:3–25). He worked on his father's farm (11:5) and cared for the stock (9:3). The Philistines* were pressing hard on the Israelites when Samuel*, the leading seer of the time, seeking for a leader to revive the spirit of the harassed people, was impressed by the qualifications of Saul (I Sam. 9:17). He secretly anointed him for the task (10:1), and admitted him into his prophetic school (10:11–13). When Jabesh-gilead was besieged by the Ammonites*, the city asked Saul for help (11:1–7); and he raised an army and relieved it (11:11). This exploit led a large part of the people to acclaim him king (11:15). He established his capital at Gibeah*, where his excavated citadel on the summit of Tell el-Fûl, 3 m. N. of Jerusalem, is the oldest datable Israelite fortification. He defeated the Philistines at Geba (13:3, 5), and with the aid of his son Jonathan at Michmash* (13:16, 14:1–16). But no decisive victory over the Philistines was possible, because the latter possessed a monopoly of iron* manufacture (13:19–22). Meanwhile Saul extended his sway over the Israelites by warring against all their other enemies (14:47 f.).

Saul's reign would have been more extensive and successful but for his temperament. He alternated between bursts of energy (14:36, 15:7 f.) and fits of depression (16:14, 23); and his moody, suspicious temperament led him to quarrel with others. The rift between Samuel and Saul, of which the Bible gives several versions, was a clash of authority between prophet and king (13:13 f., 15:17–23, 35). David, who came to Saul's court as a skilled musician, married the king's daughter, and developed into a renowned chieftain in border warfare; Saul suspected him of treason (I Sam. 18:6–8); attempted to kill him; and drove him out of his kingdom (23:19–26). Not even his own beloved son Jonathan (II Sam. 1:23) escaped Saul's jealousy (I Sam. 14:44 f., 20:30–33). The innocent priests of Nob were slaughtered by Saul's order for unwittingly aiding his son-in-law (22:11–21). Saul was reputed to be a foe of necromancy (28:3), but himself succumbed to its appeal (vv. 8–25) (see MAGIC).

The Philistines, taking advantage of the instability of Saul and his kingdom, attacked Israel through the Valley of Jezreel and encountered Saul at Mt. Gilboa. In this battle the army of Israel was defeated, the sons of the king were killed, and Saul fell by his own hand (31:1–6). The Amalekite who testified to David that he had killed Saul (II Sam. 1:1–16) lied, in the hope of receiving a reward. The Philistines circulated Saul's head among their villages, put his armor in the temple of the Ashtaroth, and fastened his body to the walls of Beth-shan*, from where, under cover of night, the grateful men of Jabesh-gilead rescued it, together with the bodies of his three sons, and buried their bones under an oak (I Sam. 31:8–13).

The reign of Saul awoke Israel to a conscious need for leadership, brought closer union among the Tribes, and prepared the way for his abler successor, David. The personality, achievements, and failures of Saul have called forth various rabbinical and theological treatments; some in praise, others in condemnation. The emotional depths and heights of Saul's nature inspired Rembrandt's portrait, Handel's oratorio, and Browning's poem. The modern psychiatrist finds in Saul's complex character much material for study.

(2) Saul of Tarsus. See PAUL.

Saviour, the term applied to Jesus Christ to express his central significance for mankind. In the O.T. it is used occasionally of God Himself, to refer to His activity as the deliverer of His people in time of need (Ps. 106:21; Isa. 43:1–13, 63:7–9). It is also used there occasionally of national heroes (II Kings 13:5; Neh. 9:27; Isa. 19:20; Obad. 21). The root meaning of the word in the O.T. is "helper" or "preserver," and this meaning is carried over into the Gospel story in the name given to Jesus. The proper name "Jesus" is the Greek form of the Hebrew word that means "to help," "to preserve," "to save." Jesus therefore bore a name that described his office.

Jesus was to be the Saviour, however, in a very special sense. Although the Christian salvation is intended to embrace the whole of life (cf. the metaphor of leaven, Matt. 13:33), its fundamental form is salvation from sin. Jesus Christ is Saviour primarily because he brings God and man together in a fellowship of love. This experience, properly understood, affects life in all its aspects; it has had an incalculable influence on civilization. The saving work of Christ has brought a new conception of personality and of its rich possibilities (cf. Luke 12:7, 13:10–17, 14:12–14, 18:9–14, 21:1–4). It has created in the world a new social sense. Great numbers of men who appear to be entirely indifferent to Jesus Christ owe him more than they can ever know; in countless ways he has been their "saviour." These, however, are derivative aspects of Christ's saving work, not its fundamental aspect. A person may, because of

361. The Saviour: Byzantine mosaic in dome of Daphni Church, on the road between Athens and Corinth.

the influence on the world of Jesus Christ, have found freedom from many of the evils of life, and still not have found what Paul calls "freedom from the yoke of bondage" (Gal. 5:1; cf. 4:1–7).

In the first Christian sermon he preached, Peter defined the saving work of Christ in terms of "remission of sins" (Acts 2:38 f.; cf. 3:13–26), a work that roots in the eternal purpose of God (Eph. 1:7–14). In the divine purpose to create is the divine purpose to complete creation by salvation (Rom. 8:28–30). It is what John means when he says that the throne of God is shared by a slain Lamb (Rev. 5:6, 7:17). The theme of the Epistle to the Hebrews is that all the O.T. sacrifices for sin were but imperfect foreshadowings of the final and perfect sacrifice offered in Christ (9:11–14; 10:1–14, 20). The salvation that men have sought in other religions finds its completion only in him (Acts 17:22–31). Hence he is not properly called simply "*a* saviour," for there are many saviours in the secondary sense; he is properly to be called "*the* Saviour," since "in none other is there salvation" (Acts 4:12, 10:36–43). He came into the world expressly to save it; he could save it because he was the Son of God in the flesh; and the root and center of the salvation is a "personal experience" which in its turn is the promise of both that perfect conformity to the will of God which is the purpose of man's existence, and of that relation to other men which is essential to the realized family of God. See JESUS CHRIST; MESSIAH; REDEMPTION; WORSHIP. E. L.

savour. (1) The "sweet savour" of freshly roasted meats or newly baked loaves, offered to Yahweh on altars, is frequently mentioned in the O.T.: Ex. 29:18, 25, 41; Lev.

1:9, 3:5, 4:31, 8:21. The fragrance of offerings burned by fire, and acceptable to God, included also the sacred incense*. Ezekiel referred to the sweet savour of offerings made to idols by apostate Israel (6:13; cf. 16:19). Christ was sacrificed "to God for a sweet-smelling savour" (Eph. 5:2).

(2) In the N.T. "savour" means to enjoy with relish, as a Christian enjoys the things of God (Matt. 16:23). "Savour" as used in II Cor. 2:14–16 suggests the sweet fragrance of incense rising from a triumphal procession, as God's messengers bring before Him the sweet odor of Christ—which, however, is a fatal odor to the unheeding, whose portion is death. (3) The savour lost when salt deteriorated gave Christ an effective metaphor for the Christian who is so weak and ineffective that, like insipid salt, he is not fit for anything but to be cast out (Luke 14:34 f.).

savoury, the adjective applied to the aged Isaac's favorite meat dish, served with bread (Gen. 27:4, 7), usually prepared for him by his son Esau. The scheming Rebekah made a substitute dish of the tender meat of kids (vv. 9, 14, 17) for her favorite son, Jacob, to present to his father.

scall, a skin disease; "ringworm" (A.V. Lev. 13:30 and *passim*).

scapegoat. See ATONEMENT, DAY OF; AZAZEL.

scarlet, a favorite color in Bible lands, whose soil is often drab, stony, and treeless. Secured from the cochineal insect, scarlet for dyeing was a luxury ware of merchants (Rev. 18:12, 16). Textiles mentioned as used in Israel's Tabernacle were of scarlet, purple, and blue (Ex. 25:4). Scarlet, along with hyssop, cedar wood, and slain birds, was used in cleansing lepers' houses (Lev. 14:49–52). A scarlet thread hung at the window identified Rahab's house at Jericho to Israel's spies (Josh. 2:18, 21; cf. Song of Sol. 4:3). Scarlet was used for fine textiles (Prov. 31:21) for family apparel; people of importance were spoken of as being clothed in scarlet, like Saul (II Sam. 1:24); and Daniel (5:7, 16, 29). Matthew describes the robe placed on Jesus by mocking Roman soldiers as of scarlet (27:28). For the woman in scarlet and purple of the Apocalypse, see Rev. 17:4.

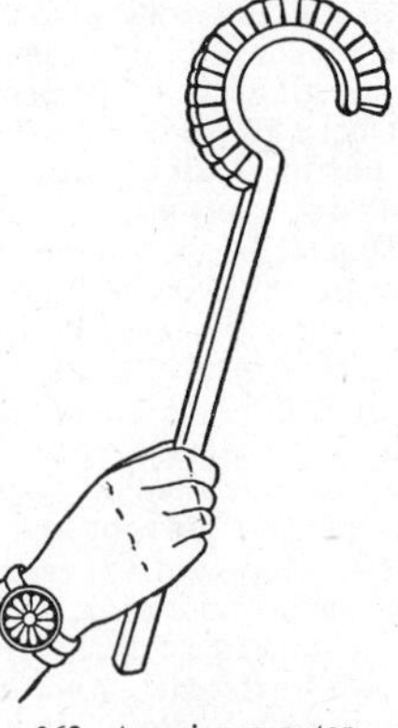

362. Assyrian scepter, 850 B.C.

scepter, a staff borne by a ruler to indicate his authority; it is depicted on many bas-reliefs of Assyrian and Persian kings of the Biblical period. Scepters were sometimes long, topped by symbolic insignia, and sometimes short, like a mace. No member of the Persian king's entourage could approach his inner court unless the ruler extended his golden scepter in invitation (Esther 4:11, 5:2, 8:4). To "hold the scepter" meant to possess sovereignty, e.g., "the scepter of Judah" (Gen. 49:10) or of Ashkelon (Amos 1:8). The word "scepter" was used of the promised Messiah (Num. 24:17), and of God (Ps. 45:6). A mock scepter of reed was given to Jesus by Roman soldiers (Matt. 27:29).

Sceva (sē′vȧ), a Jew belonging to a high-priestly family, whose seven sons (Acts 19:14 ff.)—or two (v. 16 A.S.V.)—were itinerant exorcists working near Ephesus. Adjuring evil spirits to depart in the name of Jesus, they built up prestige among both Greeks and Jews (v. 17). The author of Acts emphasizes this story as part of the triumph of Christianity over magic (vv. 18 ff.). The narrative indicates the belief in demonic possession prevalent in the Apostolic Age.

schism (sĭz'm), a formal division inside a religious group; or a sect* formed by such a division. The word occurs only in I Cor. 12:25. Both Judaism and early Christianity were rife with schisms. See HERESY.

school (Gk. *scholē*, "leisure," and therefore use of leisure for study), an institution for teaching. Schools in the sense of buildings were not characteristic of life in Palestine until the synagogue* developed, after Israel's return from Exile and the work of Ezra* was established (5th century B.C.). Schools are not mentioned in the Bible, except in A.V., A.S.V. Acts 19:9, where "the school of Tyrannus" (R.S.V. hall) is named as the place where Paul continued his daily teaching at Ephesus. The Palestinian "schools of the prophets" ("sons of the prophets," I Sam. 10:11–13; II Kings 4:1, 6:1) were not schools, but guilds of itinerant religious teachers, e.g., Samuel. The allusion to teachers and schools in II Chron. may be a thrusting back into the time of Jehoshaphat (c. 873–849 B.C.) of a later custom.

In the Patriarchal age fathers gave their sons and daughters practical schooling in farming, animal husbandry, handicrafts (Gen. 4:22), trades—e.g., masonry, carpentry, building; and the elements of ceramics and textile making. Life itself taught Hebrew boys and girls such elementary things as how to keep wolves from the flock, how to find food under emergencies, and how to get along with people. In early O.T. times mothers and fathers were the children's first teachers, as indicated by the fact that the precepts of Proverbs were addressed largely to them (Prov. 1:8, 4:1, 7:1, 13:1, 15:5, 19:20, 23:12). God Himself was thought of as the great Teacher (Isa. 28:26; cf. I Cor. 2:16); children were taught that fear of Him was the beginning of wisdom, and that "knowledge of the holy is understanding" (Prov. 9:10). (See EDUCATION.)

In Babylonia during the Exile the Hebrews developed a form of adult education in the *Kallah* assembly, where they could hear discussions by religious authorities. Egypt had educational centers, where even outsiders like Moses the Hebrew might become versed in "the wisdom of the Egyptians" (Acts 7:22). The latter may have included not only religious concepts, principles of government, social laws, cultural studies in writing, etc., but "world" events, and science—such as astronomy and mathematics—as well as magic*, divination, etc.

After the return of the Exiles to their homes in Palestine every synagogue had a place where adults and youth were instructed in the Law. After the adoption of the Law in Ezra's time, priests and Levites were teachers, and education was largely a matter of religious education; but elements of reading, writing, and music were also included in the curriculum. Elementary schools are said to have been introduced into Judaea by the Hasmonean queen Alexandra* (c. 75 B.C.), under the inspiration of her brother, the teacher Ben-shetah. School attendance was compulsory for boys between 6 and 16 but optional for girls. The Sanhedrin played a large role in the schooling of the people on matters of the Law.

Schools gave oral instruction; passersby could hear the pupils droning out their memorized lessons. Teachers sat on benches, pupils on the floor, near low stands holding copies of the Scriptures. In Palestine, as in Greece during the teaching years of the peripatetic philosophers—e.g., Plato in his Athenian open-air academy near the Dipylon Gate—schooling was teacher-centered. The teacher (usually unpaid) was always honored in his community. Teaching priests and prophets made bold to instruct even kings, as Nathan taught David (II Sam. 12:1–7); Jehoiada, Jehoash (II Kings 12:2); and Shemaiah, Rehoboam (II Chron. 12:5).

Judaism maintained in Talmudic times schools for advanced study, which functioned in every world capital where Jews were allowed to live, e.g. Alexandria and Rome, and in such other centers as Nisibis, Jamnia, and Tiberias on the Sea of Galilee. At Jerusalem, between c. 150 B.C. and A.D. 70, two schools centered in two great teachers of the 2d half of the 1st century B.C.—Shammai, who interpreted the Law in an extremely legalistic manner, and Hillel, who allowed consideration of human interests in specific situations. It was at the feet of Gamaliel, grandson of the great Hillel (c. 70 B.C.–A.D. 10) that Saul of Tarsus studied when he was a student in Jerusalem. Gamaliel is said to have been the first man to whom the title *Rabban* ("master," "teacher") was given (see RABBI). (For his intervention in the Sanhedrin on behalf of the Disciples of Jesus see Acts 5:34 ff.) The Talmudic schools attracted thousands of Gentiles; and such pupils bore tribute to the value of the teacher, as compared to the priest. I. G. Matthews (*The Religious Pilgrimage of Israel*, p. 268, Harper & Brothers) says: "The teachers (rabbis) in the schools and their disciples in a thousand synagogues in every center throughout the [Roman] Empire, were the instructors in the Torah. They had long guided the Dispersion in the rules for personal and social conduct, and in an understanding of the world order. They had taught them to sing the songs of Zion in strange tongues and in strange lands, and had led them to worship, in spirit and in truth, the God who tabernacled in the hearts of good men everywhere. They had been the bearers of light to the Gentiles. Their lofty ethical ideals, their appealing philosophy, and their missionary zeal had been rewarded by many proselytes, who forsook paganism for the better way. Thus Judaism, the religion of the book, and of a people scattered to the four corners of the earth but united in allegiance to the one God, was well equipped to succeed in the struggle of existence."

A boy like Jesus of Nazareth would have had his schooling in the synagogue classroom; in private study if his parents had resources to afford that opportunity; and at the feet of wise and pious men in his community. He might have had access to a few privately owned scrolls or parchments. Such a boy would have longed to sit in the midst of the learned doctors in Jerusalem (Luke 2:46 f.); this was his "Father's business" to which Jesus referred (v. 49).

It was as teacher (*Rabban*, "master") that Jesus was perhaps best known by his contemporaries (Luke 3:12); and it was concerning what Jesus began to teach, as well as to do, that Luke wrote his Gospel (Acts 1:1). Jesus taught out-of-doors (Matt. 5:1 ff.), and also "in the synagogue" (John 6:59). The record of Mark 6:2 states what was customary for the teacher: "And when the sabbath day was come, he began to teach in the synagogue." The Pharisee Nicodemus*, himself a teacher of Israel, brought a profound query to him one night, and went away from the interview declaring, "Rabbi, we know that thou art a teacher come from God" (John 3:2). This learned Pharisee, recognizing that Jesus possessed more wisdom than he had learned in any school, acknowledged that this power must come from God.

Paul's schooling began in the synagogue school of Tarsus. He may also have studied in Gentile schools, where he learned the Gk. language (used in all his Epistles), heard about Hellenistic mystery cults of the Resurrection, and studied the principles of Stoic (see STOICS) philosophy. Possibly in his Hebrew home he learned Aramaic. At Jerusalem he studied to become a scribe, and he was proud to sit at the feet of Gamaliel (Acts 22:3). Saul's preparation as a teacher of the Jewish religion was turned to good use when he became a missionary of Christ and a formulator of Christian belief.

In Jesus' day—in fact ever since the return of the Jews from Exile—there was a scarcity of schools and teachers in Palestine; this scarcity continued into the Apostolic Age [see PHILIP (6), Acts 8:26–39, and his teaching ministry].

Christian catechetical schools for the training of youth were maintained by the early Church Fathers, like Clement of Alexandria (born c. A.D. 150); and Origen (c. 185–254), who conducted a school first at Alexandria, then, when ousted from that city, at Caesarea. Ever since, Christian education of youth has been a primary concern of all the Christian churches.

science, used twice in the A.V. for "knowledge" (Dan. 1:4; I Tim. 6:20).

scorpion, any one of numerous arachnids (spiderlike creatures) of the order *Scorpiones*, with a venomous sting at the end of its long, narrow tail. They are especially numerous in the hot wilderness of Judaea (Deut. 8:15). The scorpion referred to by King Rehoboam (I Kings 12:11; II Chron. 10:14) was probably a whip or scourge tipped with spikes.

scourge. (1) A whip of cords or thongs, used as an instrument of punishment in O.T. times (Josh. 23:13; Heb. 11:36), and by irate Jews in their synagogues (Matt. 10:17, 23:34). Its use is specially associated with the Roman period in Palestine. It was usual to scourge a condemned prisoner before crucifying him, as Pilate did with Jesus (Matt. 20:19, 27:26; Mark 15:15; John 19:1). Roman law allowed an ordinary prisoner to be scourged during trial, to force confession, as the chief captain at Jerusalem commanded to be done with Paul (Acts 22:24). But it was not lawful to scourge an uncondemned Roman citizen (v. 25). The scourge itself was sometimes a whip of small cords such as Jesus used to drive from the Temple the illicit money-changers and sellers of animals (John 2:15). Romans made it by attaching leather thongs to a handle. The thongs were sometimes tipped with metal, or knotted.

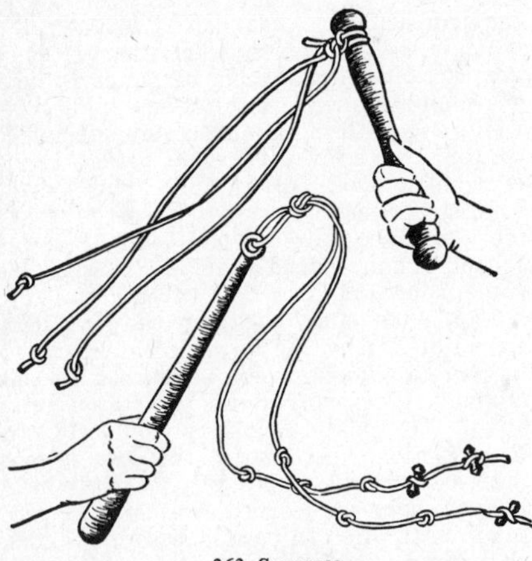

363. Scourges.

(2) "Scourge" is also used in Scripture in the figurative sense of calamity sent for punishment: a plague of disease, an invasion (Josh. 23:13), or any other form of disaster popularly viewed as a God-sent catastrophe (Job 9:23; Isa. 10:26, 28:15, 18). (For scourge in the sense of a tongue lashing, see Job 5:21.)

scribes. (1) In the primary sense, penmen or copyists, like the sidewalk letter-writers still seen on streets in the Near East. Scribes were important in Babylonian life, where they not only cared for the temple archives of sacred literature, but served as royal secretaries, recording (on clay* tablets) land boundaries and business transactions. Sometimes governors of districts were royal Mesopotamian scribes. Similarly in Egypt scribes kept account of the contents of royal granaries, recorded the Nile flood times, and wrote ancient religious texts on papyri, like the Book of the Dead and the venerable Wisdom writings. The equipment of Egyptian scribes is shown in wall reliefs from Saqqârah near Memphis (c. 2750–2625 B.C.). It included a

364. Slate palette; water jug; pen or brush case. Fifth Egyptian Dynasty.

palette with a groove for reed brushes, and two depressions for red and black ink. (See WRITING). In O.T. Palestine scribes served as secretaries, recorders, and clerks to kings, governments, and the Temple organization (II Kings 12:10, 19:2; Ezra 4:8; II Chron. 34:8, 13; Jer. 36:18).

(2) The role of scribe was at its height just after the Return of the Jews from Exile. The prophetic age had closed. The Pentateuch, which was adopted as the basic Law of Judaism, needed interpreters to bring its meaning to the people (Neh. 8:8), who were busy re-establishing their homes. The priestly *soferim*, or scholars, formed a link in the chain of Hebrew tradition between Moses (cf. Matt. 23:2, "in Moses' seat") and the sages and prophets, and Jesus, who reminded his hearers that many scribes had been scourged in synagogues, and persecuted from city to city and crucified and killed (Matt. 23:34).

Before Ezra's time and the canonization of the Pentateuch, the professional teachers had been called "sages," "wise men" (*hakāmîm*)—a word which recurred in the 2d century A.D. to designate "learned men," but was eventually succeeded by "rabbi."

As R. H. Pfeiffer points out (*Introduction to the Old Testament*, and *History of New Testament Times*, Harper & Brothers), Israel's scribes were men who made acceptable copies of the Scriptures, and also interpreted and taught them. The Chronicler, himself a Biblical scholar (c. 300 B.C.), viewed Ezra the priest as the first scribe (Neh. 8:1 ff., 12:26, 36; Ezra 7:6, 11) and Zadok as the second (Neh. 13:13); and made Ezra the founder of the guild of scribes at Jerusalem—a guild formed only after the canonization of the Pentateuch (c. 400 B.C.). In the dramatic scene in Neh. 7:73b–8:18 Ezra, standing on a wooden pulpit, read the Law to the attentive people and saw it ratified in "the street that was before the water gate" at Jerusalem.

Joshua, son of Eleazar, son of Sira (Gk. Sirach), author of the Apocryphal Book of Ecclesiasticus (written in an early decade of the 2d century B.C.), has been called an ideal scholar and scribe of his time. Scribes not only investigated and mastered every portion of the Scriptures, but possessed general wisdom; shared human problems and activities; traveled; lectured in synagogues; were accepted in the best society; were often themselves writers; and, if not of independent means (scribes were unpaid), were diligent enough to pursue a trade as well as perform their scribal duties.

In the 2d century B.C. the Pharisees began to dispute the prestige of the priestly scribes. Lay *soferim*, or scholars, taught the Law without direct reference to the Scriptures. By at least the middle of the 1st century A.D. the *soferim* were replaced by "sages" and "rabbis," who taught the Bible in primary schools. The phrase "scribes of the Pharisees" suggests that the Sadducees as well as the Pharisees had scribes.

In the N.T. scribes were laymen, not priests, but they worked with the hereditary priesthood. They had seats in the Sanhedrin (Matt. 16:21, 26:3; Luke 22:66; Acts 4:5). The scribes, like the Pharisees with whom their name is often linked in the N.T., were opposed to Jesus (Matt. 7:29), because he sometimes cut across their ancient traditions and exposed their unwarranted claims to prestige. Scribes played a conspicuous role in bringing about his Crucifixion (Mark 14:43, 15:1; Luke 23:10), though a few of them believed in his teaching (Matt. 8:19). Some of the scribes of the Pharisees sided with Paul in the uproar in the Sanhedrin concerning the Resurrection (Acts 23:9); but many allied themselves with the rulers and elders to persecute Peter and John (Acts 4:5), and Stephen (6:12).

scrip (skrĭp), the small wallet or bag of leather or homespun in which shepherds carried bread and other food, and stones to attract the attention of wandering sheep (I Sam. 17:40). In A.V. Matt. 10:10 and Luke 9:3, 10:4, 22:35 f., "scrip" is used in the sense of a wallet used to carry money or bread.

scripts. See WRITING.

Scripture (Lat. *scriptura*, "writing"), used by Hebrews to indicate their sacred writings ("Holy Scriptures") or the O.T., and by Christians to indicate both the O.T. and the N.T. In the N.T. "Scripture" or "Scriptures" refers to the O.T. (cf. II Pet. 3:15 f.). When the singular word is used, evidently the group of sacred writings is thought of as a whole, e.g. in John 2:22, 19:24; Acts 8:32; Gal. 4:30; Jas. 2:23; I Pet. 2:6. When "Scriptures" is used the composite authorship of the O.T. may be in the writer's mind (Matt. 21:42; Rom. 1:2). See BIBLE; CANON; NEW TESTAMENT; OLD TESTAMENT; REVELATION.

scroll, the roll of an ancient book*, written on skin, papyrus, or parchment. Much of the O.T. and the N.T. was written on rolls, as were many other religious, scientific, and literary documents of the ancient Near East. The rolls were made of sheets usually from 9 to 11 in. high and 5 or 6 in. wide, sewed together to make a long strip, which was rolled around a stick. The reader held the roll in his right hand, and with his left hand wound it around another stick (cf. Isa. 34:4; Rev. 6:14). Two parallel rolls of paper toweling would give an idea of what an ancient scroll looked like. Some papyrus rolls were as much as 144 ft. long. The Edwin Smith Surgical Papyrus, Library of N. Y. Academy of Medicine, copied in the 17th century B.C. from an original made between c. 3000 and 2500 B.C., is 15 ft. 3½ in. long and has 21 columns of hieratic Egyptian 15 in. high. The Dead Sea Scroll of Isaiah (see SCROLLS, THE DEAD SEA) is 23.75 ft. long and 10.25 in. high. Documents were usually stored together in a jar or chest. Sometimes the last column was damaged, as seems to have happened with the Gospel of Mark, which from early times ended abruptly at 16:8. Titles were sometimes attached to the top edge of the roll. Scrolls were marked with lines to guide the pen of the writers (Isa. 8:1); such lines are clearly visible on the Dead Sea Scroll of Isaiah. Scrolls were copied by professional scribes, and sometimes by slaves. They were costly in labor, time, and often in money.

The most famous O.T. narrative concerning the writing of a scroll is Jer. 36.

For Ezekiel's symbolic eating of a roll of lamentations, see Ezek. 3:1 ff.

The winged "flying roll" of Zech. 5:1 ff. signified the spread of a curse over the face of the earth. A royal pottery jar handle excavated at Lachish*, and stamped with a two-winged scroll (rather than the four-winged Egyptian scarab) may reflect Josiah's reforms (c. 640–609 B.C.), when he stamped out foreign cults and stressed the Law (II Kings 22:8; II Chron. 34:14–33).

Scroll of the Law, a term used by Jews for the Torah* (Pentateuch).

Scrolls, the Dead Sea (also called the Qumran manuscripts), the fragmentary remains of what was once a large library that belonged to a Jewish sect, evidently the Essenes*. One group of the sect lived in caves around the Wâdī Qumrân at the northwestern corner of the Dead Sea, where the Scrolls were found. Other manuscript fragments of the Byzantine Age have been found farther south around the next main valley, the Wâdī en-Nar. Still others, chiefly from the period of the second Jewish Revolt (A.D. 132–135), including correspondence of the Revolt's leader, Simeon ben Kosbah (Bar Kochba), have appeared in caves still farther south in the Wâdī Murabba'at. Generally, however, the term refers to the remains of the Essene library noted above.

1. *The Discovery.* The Scrolls from Qumran are now believed to be the greatest find ever made in the field of biblical archaeology, and one of the greatest in any field. The first cave was accidentally discovered in the spring of 1947 by a member of the Bedouin tribe of the area. While looking for a lost sheep or goat, he threw a stone at a venture and shattered a jar in a cave. It proved to be a vessel that had once contained manuscripts; other vessels and actual manuscripts were found. The latter eventually got into the hands of scholars at the American School of Oriental Research and at the Hebrew University in Jerusalem for study. These included two manuscripts of the Book of Isaiah, one of them almost perfectly preserved (1QIs[a]; 1Q means Cave 1 at Qumran; Is[a] means the first scroll of Isaiah found in that cave.) There were also commentaries on Genesis (a paraphrase) and Habakkuk, the book of rules or discipline of the sect, a scroll containing Thanksgiving Psalms, and a document which describes the final eschatological war between "the children of light and the children of darkness." Since 1949 the search for more manuscripts has been carried on in the area; hundreds of caves have been searched by archaeologists and Bedouin, the latter working when the former had quit the field, and having by far the greater success in the search.

Of most importance was the discovery by Bedouin of Cave 4 (4Q) in 1952, from which the largest group of fragments has come. In the same year archaeologists of the American School found two tightly rolled copper scrolls in Cave 3 which together once formed a single plaque over 8 ft. long. Some ten different manuscript-bearing caves have been discovered (by the end of 1955) in the Qumran area.

The Palestine Archaeological Museum, on the Jordan side of Jerusalem, is now the center of Scroll study. There the fragments are studied by an international team of scholars under the supervision of Mr. Lankester Harding, Director of the Jordan Department of Antiquities, and Father R. de Vaux of the Dominican Biblical School in Jerusalem.

The scope of the total find is quite large—thousands of fragments of varying sizes, the equivalent of several baskets full. To be sure, most of the pieces are very small and complete documents are few in number. That is because the library was repeatedly robbed in antiquity. Yet when all have been fitted together, read and interpreted, their significance for biblical studies will be tremendous and in many ways revolutionary. Most of the fragments are from a large number of non-biblical works which are otherwise unknown. Biblical manuscripts are readily identified by the fine quality and color of the leather used and by the careful book-hand in which they are written. The leather sheets were sewn together to make a roll, the columns for the text measured off, the lines for each column ruled and the letters written hanging from the line. The great Isaiah scroll (1QIs[a]) was made of 17 pieces of leather sewn together to make a roll some 24½ ft. long, averaging 10 5/16 in. in width, with 54 columns of text, each having between 28 and 32 lines.

365. Five Dead Sea Scrolls. At left, Dr. John C. Trever, holding Isaiah Scroll as Archbishop Athanasius Yeshue Samuel looks on. At far right, The Sectarian Manual of Discipline; in right foreground, ms. first identified as "Lamech Apocalypse," with Habakkuk Commentary above it.

Portions of over 100 scrolls of O.T. books have appeared; Cave 4 had fragments of every book except Esther, which thus far has not come to light. The most popular books were, of course, Deuteronomy, Isaiah and Psalms, a dozen or more scrolls of each having been found. The linen in which the rolls of Cave 1 were wrapped has been dated by its radioactive carbon to A.D. 33, with a possible error either way of 200 years. Scholars studying the documents in the light of the evolution of ancient writing have dated the earliest fragments to about 200 B.C. (4QSam[b] and 4QJer[a]). The main Isaiah scroll is dated about 100 B.C. whereas many other scrolls were copied in the 1st century A.D. At least three different scrolls of Daniel existed; the earliest dates from the early 1st century B.C.; that is, within a century of when the book was written!

Khirbet Qumran, the sect's living, study and worship center, has been excavated. In one room a large clay table, with bench, two inkpots and a washbasin were recovered; this was undoubtedly where the scrolls were copied. More than 400 coins were found on the site, dating from John Hyrcanus (135–104 B.C.) to Agrippa II (c. A.D. 86). The place was abandoned after a great earthquake in 31 B.C., rebuilt some years later, but destroyed by the 10th Roman legion in A.D. 68. After that a fort was erected and used for a time as an outpost. The neighboring cemetery of the settlement has been investigated; it contains over 1000 graves. Apparently the community was a large one, with many of its members living in caves in the surrounding cliffs. The central buildings were used for worship, study, meals, etc.

2. *Significance of the Discovery.* The importance of the find is to be assessed in two directions: (a) One is the new knowledge concerning the text of the O.T. that is made available; (b) the other is with regard to the people of the scrolls and their influence on the Early Christian Movement.

(a) Before the Qumran discovery, the oldest fairly complete manuscripts of the Hebrew O.T. were mediaeval; that is, from c. the 10th century A.D. The Qumran discoveries provide biblical texts in Hebrew a thousand years older than anything previously known, except for one small fragment. Furthermore, the present Hebrew text was edited and standardized in earlier times so that it preserves only one text tradition with a few variants. The new finds show that this standardization occurred in the latter part of the 1st century or the beginning of the 2d century A.D. While most of the Qumran manuscripts reflect the same tradition as that of the received text, certain scrolls show a great many differences; that is, they represent a real variant textual tradition which is very close to that of the Septuagint or Gk. translation in certain books (particularly I & II Sam. in 4QSam[a]). Indeed, the indications are that the textual tradition these fragments represent may antedate both that of the Septuagint and that of the standardized Hebrew Bibles. That the people of Qumran were acquainted with the Septuagint is suggested by the fact that one piece of this translation in leather and several in papyrus have been found. The real meaning of these remarks is that the Qumran manuscript discovery enables the scholar to penetrate far behind the present Hebrew text into a period before variant textual traditions died out. This already is causing the demise of some older views, and the introduction of new ones.

(b) Of far more dramatic interest are the people of the Scrolls themselves. They were the Essenes*, the only sect of Judaism which did not receive condemnation in the N.T. The sect spoke of their founder as "the teacher of righteousness." Under his leadership the group withdrew to the wilderness to prepare the way of the Lord (Isa. 40:3). They were organized like a "salvation army," accepting a rigorous discipline, studying the law continually, while awaiting the coming of the priestly and Davidic Anointed Ones (Messiahs). A large number of features of the community are so close to characteristics of the Early Christian group in Jerusalem that a relationship of influence is almost certain. All property was held in common, and holy poverty was idealized; both had sacramental meals, followed "The Way" (e.g., Acts 9:2), and occasionally used as a name for themselves "The Many" (Acts 4:32); both criticized the Sadducees and Pharisees, considered themselves members of "The New Covenant." Further, the Essenes and Stephen's followers among the Christians refused sacrificial worship at the Temple; both studied the Scriptures with an attitude of expectancy, had lists of messianic proof-texts, and looked to their times for fulfillment of prophecy.

The Qumran Essenes believed that the present life is the battleground between two opposing realms, those of good and evil, light and darkness, truth and error. The terminology in which the conflict is described is very close to that found especially in the Johannine literature of the N.T. (e.g., John 8:12, 12:36; I John 4:6). These and many other resemblances lead one to conclude that the early Christians in Jerusalem and the Johannine wing of Christian teaching were especially influenced in some direct or indirect way (whether through Jesus himself, or John the Baptist, or the Jewish "Hellenists" is uncertain) by the Essenes.

Yet in spite of the influence the Christians were still radically different: the Gospel of God's love is very different from the Qumran new righteousness in the New Covenant. Christ was no "teacher of righteousness" in this sense; his saving work was for the outcast and sinners, not for the elect few; and he suffered and died but did not reign in earthly splendor. In fact, the Gospel of John is now interpreted by some as a Christian answer to the Essene question, though whether this is too narrow a view of the Gospel must await further study. (See also ESSENES.)

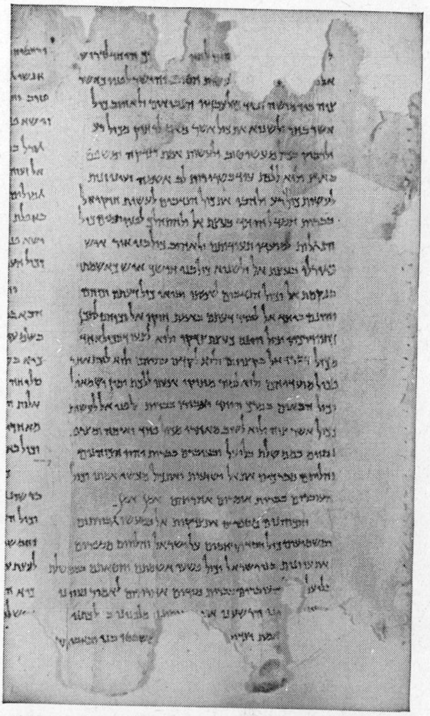

366. Portion of The Sectarian Manual of Discipline, one of the Dead Sea Scrolls. It begins with initiation ceremony for those who "enter into the Covenant," ends with punishments (mainly temporary rejection from the community) for infringement of rules.

See: Millar Burrows, *The Dead Sea Scrolls*, 1955; A. Dupont-Sommer, *The Jewish Sect of Qumran and the Essenes*, 1954; and various issues of the *BA* and *BASOR*; especially Frank M. Cross, Jr., "The Manuscripts of the Dead Sea Caves," *BA* XVII, 1 (Feb. 1954), pp. 2–21.

G. E. W.

sculpture, the art of carving or modeling representations of objects and people, in relief or in the round. This skill did not develop among Hebrews, who obeyed the Second Commandment: "Thou shalt not make unto thee any graven image, or any likeness of anything that is in heaven above, or that is in the earth beneath, or that is in the water under the earth" (Ex. 20:4). Where sculpture was used it was imported from outside sources—Phoenician, Syrian, Egyptian, Mesopotamian, Greek, or Roman. Sumerians (see SUMER) were the first to develop statues carved in the round. Assyrians were never excelled in their massive winged statues, as at Khorsabad (see SARGON II), and Persians in their large-scale reliefs depicting historic events and personages, as at Persepolis*. See SEAL; SYMBOL; TEMPLE.

Scythians, a people who lived in ancient times N. and E. of the Black Sea. Hordes of Scythians, leaving desolation in their wake as they pushed S. on their drive toward Egypt, threatened Judah c. 626 B.C. Both Jeremiah and Zephaniah were appalled at this menace. Jeremiah prophesied that his country would be laid desolate (4:5–31, 5:15–17, 6:1–8, 22–26). Zephaniah saw in the coming of these northern barbarians the imminent approach of the Day of the Lord (1:7, 8, 14–18). But the Scythians used the coastal route, were bribed by Pharaoh Psamtich I, and returned N. by the same route without touching Judah. They are also referred to in Col. 3:11.

Scythopolis. See BETH-SHAN.

sea, a large body of deep water. When no qualifying name is used, "the sea" means the Mediterranean (II Chron. 20:2).

Few Hebrews ventured to sea until the era of commercial expansion under Solomon. But see Judg. 5:17: "why did Dan remain in ships? Asher continued on the sea shore, and abode in his breaches" (A.S.V. "creeks"). Do these words indicate that some Hebrews caught the sea fever of their maritime neighbors, the Phoenicians? Fear of the ancient Semitic (? Sumerian) sea monster Tiâmat may be reflected in such utterances as Ps. 46:2, 89:9; Isa. 17:12; Jer. 49:23, etc. Out of the great sea came the four beasts of Daniel's vision (7:2 ff.), and the blasphemous beast of Revelation (13:1).

See DEAD SEA; GALILEE, SEA OF; MEDITERRANEAN; RED SEA (also EXODUS, for "Sea of Reeds"); ARABAH. For "brasen" or "molten" sea, see TEMPLE.

sea monster (Heb. *tannīn*), any great fish or prodigious creature of the deep (Lam. 4:3 A.V., A.S.V. "jackals"). The "great whales" of Gen. 1:21 is rendered "sea monsters" by A.S.V.; similarly with the symbolic "whale" of Job 7:12.

seah, (1) unit of dry volume measure, about ⅕ U.S. bushel, ⅓ the standard unit *ephah;* the "measure" of Matt. 13:33; Lk. 13:21; (2) the area which would normally be sown with a *seah* of barley seed, about ⅕ acre.

seal (Lat. *sigillum*). (1) An implement for imprinting an impression on clay or wax; (2) the impression made by the seal. Thousands of tiny seals have been excavated in the Near East, 10,000 in Mesopotamia alone. It is hard to overestimate the importance of seals in the ancient Near East. The collection of cylinder seals in the Pierpont Morgan Library, New York, is the largest in the United States and one of the greatest in the world. It has enabled scholars to observe the evolution of designs from the Uruk and Jedmet Nasr periods (c. 3200–2800 B.C.) on to the closing scenes of seal history in Persian Palestine (c. 538–333 B.C.). Mesopotamian seals look like small spools—often only 4/5 in. long and 2/5 in. in diameter, or less; engraved with religious symbols and scenes, social customs, trades, apparel, and characteristic animals.

367. Seals: Top, Impression from hematite cylinder seal, 18 mm. high and 8 mm. in diameter, from end of First Babylonian Dynasty, probable era of Hammurabi. In center, god with mace, facing unidentified deity; nude female figure at right and left of impression; at her left, a mongoose (?) above bow-legged dwarf; at her right, star above small scimitar. Property of Madeleine S. and J. Lane Miller. Center, Silver seal of Tarqumuwa, King of Mera, 12th century B.C., showing two writing systems used by Hittites: cuneiform adopted from Mesopotamians (around edge) and a complex picture-writing of their own (center). Bottom, Early Christian and Roman seals, such as were mounted in rings: at left, symbolic ship with cross in mast; at right, popular symbol of Christ, the Good Shepherd.

There are three types: (1) the primitive *button stamp seal* from which developed the later Egyptian scarabs and Palestinian Graeco-Roman flat seals or signets; (2) the *cylinder seal,* typical of Mesopotamian cultures from the 4th millennium B.C. to the Hellenistic period; and (3) the *Persian stamp seal,* conical at the top for easy handling. Seal engravers, whose skill produced what is called the glyptic art, were spared in battle whenever possible. They developed their art from mere brocade patterns to vivid scenes from epic myths.

The Uses of Seals.—(1) Seals were used to affix the ancient equivalent of written signatures to documents, as when numerous princes, priests, and Levites of Jerusalem sealed the written covenant of Nehemiah (Neh. 9:38–10:27). Seals had an advantage over signatures, in that they could be passed around among deputies. In ancient Mesopotamia and Palestine, when cuneiform statements had been imprinted with a stylus (a pointed writing instrument) on wet clay tablets, witnesses were called by the scribe, and the negotiator's personal cylinder seal was rolled over the document to legalize it. (Cf. Jeremiah's use of a stamp seal for the deed for his Anathoth field, 32:10, 14.) Cuneiform tablets with cylinder seal impressions of the writer or sender are specially revealing. As early as the Patriarchal period in Palestine, men like Judah had their personal seals—clearly of the Mesopotamian type, worn on a cord around the neck (or affixed to the wrists), as in the narrative of A.S.V. Gen. 38:18, where Tamar asks of Judah a pledge in the form of his signet and his cord; this is the first O.T. reference to a seal. The ring of Pharaoh which was entrusted to Joseph the Hebrew prime minister was his scarab seal (Gen. 41:42).

Near Eastern seal engraving appears in the 12 stones set on the shoulders of the priest's ephod* of "onyx stones, inclosed in settings of gold, graven with the engravings of a signet, according to the names of the children of Israel" (A.S.V. Ex. 39:6). Israel's seals, whether used as ornaments, personal signatures, or protective devices for safeguarding bales, jars, or tombs (Matt. 27:66), had no symbols which might be considered images.

368. Cylinder seal.

The "signets" of the O.T. were seal stamps, not cylinders. (See Hag. 2:20–23, where the Lord tells Zerubbabel, governor of Judah, that on the coming great Day of the Lord He will make him as a signet on His hand, deputized with His purposes and authority; cf. Jer. 22:24.) In 9th-century Israel "Jezebel wrote letters in Ahab's name, and sealed them with his seal" (I Kings 21:8). At the Persian court of Esther's day King Ahasuerus signed his documents with "the king's ring," so that no man might revoke their contents (Esther 3:12, 8:8, 10). This ring would probably have been a Persian signet seal, such as was also used in Daniel's time (Dan. 6:9, 17). Seals of rulers were familiar. That of Darius shows the king in his chariot, between two date palms, with bow and arrow aimed at a lion—one already lying under his chariot. At the top center is the winged disk, with letters denoting the god, "Ahura-Mazda"; at the left is a trilingual inscription, "I am Darius the great king."

The Parable of the Prodigal Son may refer to the ancient system of signing by sealing with a signet ring; when the father placed a ring on his son's finger (Luke 15:22) he put him in a position to transact business as an accepted member of the community. The ownership implied in sealing appears symbolically in the Bible, where God seals His own (John 6:27; Rom. 15:28; II Cor. 1:22; Eph. 4:30). The redeemed are described in the Apocalypse as having seals stamped "in their foreheads" (Rev. 7:3 ff.). The "book of the Lamb" was sealed with seven seals, which no man was found worthy to break open until the Lamb himself opened them (6:1, 3 etc., through 8:1).

(2) Seals were also widely used whenever security from molestation was important. To protect wine, olive oil, and other commodities for shipment, a stopper was placed in the mouth of the jar, tied in place with cord or linen bands, then covered with a lump of clay, over which an inspector's cylinder seal was rolled or a stamp seal pressed down; finally the jar top was capped with plaster, stamped with the royal seal. Sealing was so important that unions or guilds of sealers were maintained. More than 2,000 handles from Rhodian wine jars were found at luxury-loving Samaria. Bales of goods were similarly sealed. A sealed bag was mentioned by Job (14:17), who also spoke symbolically of the natural world, turned to God "as clay to the seal" (38:14).

A remarkable jar-handle seal found in Babylonia is preserved in the Museum of the Oriental Institute, Chicago. It carries one of the oldest known quotations of a Hebrew Biblical text: "Moab hath been at ease from his youth, and he hath settled on his lees, and hath not been emptied from vessel to vessel, neither hath he gone into captivity; therefore his taste remained in him, and his scent is not changed" (Jer. 48:11). An impression from the royal jasper seal found at Megiddo carries a well-executed lion and the words in Hebrew, "Belonging to Shema, servant of Jeroboam" (Jeroboam II, c. 775 B.C.). The famous Seal of Gedaliah*, from the Lachish mound, still bears traces of the papyrus "weave" of the document to which the seal was affixed in the 6th century B.C. (Jer. 40:5, 8). A jar handle stamped, "Belonging to Eliakim, boy [steward] of Jokin" (Jehoiachin*), carried to Babylon (597 B.C.) was found at Tell Beit Mirsim, and an identical one at 'Ain Shems. This Eliakim may have been the official left in charge of the young king's property during the reign of his uncle Zedekiah. Nelson Glueck found at Ezion-geber a seal stamped on pottery, "Qosanal, servant of the king," possibly the royal customs officer (? Edomite) of this important industrial port of Solomon.

W. F. Albright (*The Archaeology of Palestine*, p. 143, Penguin Books) tells of jars of the Persian and early Hellenistic periods in Palestine stamped with "Yehed" or "Yerushalem." A winged-scroll design and the name "Hebron" have been found at Tell ed-Duweir (Lachish) on a jar handle attributed to the era of David. (See illus. 54, *An Encyclopedia of Bible Life*, Madeleine S. and J. Lane Miller, Harper & Brothers; also *BASOR* 53, p. 21.)

The Making of Seals.—The seal-cutters used crude "graving tools" (cf. Ex. 32:4) made of copper, until the introduction of iron into the Near East c. 1000 B.C. Dr. Henri Frankfort describes a kit of Accadian tools discovered in a pot: a copper chisel, a whetstone, and two sharply pointed implements. Bow-drills for boring holes through the length of the seals, and powder ground in for finishing were also used. Cylinder seals were carved in reverse, like mirror writing.

Various materials were used for seals. Primitive Egyptian seals may have been made of wood; baked clay; or relatively soft material like marble and serpentine (hydrous magnesium silicate). Most of the recovered seals—from the end of the 4th millennium B.C. to the era when they were supplanted by the stamp type of seal (c. 700 B.C. in Mesopotamia, though stamp seals had always been preferred among some peoples, like the Hittites and Palestinians)—were engraved in hard, semiprecious stones believed to possess magical properties: siliceous hematite, limonite, magnetite, steatite, jasper, carnelian, chalcedony, copper covered with silver, crystal, ivory faïence (glazed clay), and in later eras gold and silver.

When Edith Porada, an authority in this field, was asked about the way seals were rolled over the damp clay, she replied, "A rolling with the palm of the hand would be most likely . . . only if the seal were rubbed with a drop of oil could the clay be prevented from sticking to the stone." Occasionally Assyrian or Egyptian cylinders had a small wire swivel through their center perforation for a handle, as with modern lawn rollers. Miss Porada believes that the "ancients cared little about the way in which they rolled the seal, provided that—in case of an inscribed seal—the inscription had been clearly impressed, or, in other cases, the characteristic, recognizable part of the design had left its mark on the tablet."

Excellent publications concerning seals of the ancient Near East are available. To the standard work by Henri Frankfort of the Oriental Institute (*Cylinder Seals*, The Macmillan Company, London) and the volumes of Léon Legrain of the University of Pennsylvania, there have been added as Volume I of a five-volume work, *Corpus of Ancient Near Eastern Seals in North American Collections* (in two volumes, one of text, one of plates) entitled *The Collection of the Pierpont Morgan Library* (The Bollingen Series XIV), catalogued and edited by Edith Porada, in collaboration with Briggs Buchanan, and with a preface by Albrecht Goetze of the Yale Babylonian Collection; and a brief but authoritative brochure, *Mesopotamian Cylinder Seals*, by Edith Porada. Maurice Dunand published in Lebanon *Byblia Grammata*, reproducing with analysis all the known Chalcolithic seal impressions, some of which carry impressions in a formerly unknown pictographic script from the late 4th millennium B.C.

Seal of Solomon, the, a Jewish symbol used as a decorative motif on early Palestinian synagogues, as at Tell Hûm (Capernaum). It is a five-pointed star whose every point touches a circle (see SYMBOL, illus. 405). It is also called "Seal of Jacob," and is to be distinguished from the six-pointed "Star of David," a modern Jewish symbol. (See also HEBREWS, illus. 177.)

season. (1) As a division of the year when a particular type of weather prevails, there are only two seasons in Palestine—the dry (April-September, in most sections); and the rainy (October-March). Though the Bible mentions seedtime, harvest (Gen. 8:22), "earing time" (Ex. 34:21), etc., these are actually only parts of the two seasons. The Song of Solomon (2:8–17) pictures early spring. (See PALESTINE, *climate.*) Dr. James H. Breasted called attention to the fact that the first three seasons ever recognized in the Nile country were the Egyptian four-month periods known as "the inundation," "the coming forth," and "the harvest."

(2) "Season" is also used in the sense of "time," e.g., "in due season" (Ps. 104:27; Matt. 24:45 f.); "for a season" (Acts 13:11); "a little season" (Rev. 20:3); "the Lord in his appointed season" (Num. 9:2, 7, 13).

(3) Seasoning food with salt*, condiments, etc., has always been important to Near Easterners (Mark 9:50). For the use of seasoning in meat oblations see Lev. 2:13.

Seba, a dialectal variation of Sheba. See SABA.

Sebat (sē′băt) (Shebat), the 11th month of the Hebrew year (Zech. 1:7), corresponding approximately to January-February.

Secacah (sē-kā′kȧ) ("thicket"), a wilderness town in Judah (Josh. 15:61).

Second Coming of Christ, the. See ESCHATOLOGY; MILLENNIUM; PAROUSIA.

sect, a group of persons having a set of doctrines differing from those of an established organization. Sects were sometimes formed by schisms (see SCHISM) within a religious body. (See HERESY.) The N.T. refers to "the sect of the Sadducees" (Acts 5:17); "the sect of the Pharisees" (15:5); "the sect of the Nazarenes" (24:5). Prominent Jews in Rome called Christianity "this sect" (Acts 28:22).

Secundus (sē̆-kŭn′dŭs), a man from Greece who accompanied Paul to Jerusalem with offerings for the poor (Acts 20:4; cf. II Cor. 8:23). He, like Aristarchus, may have represented the church at Thessalonica; the name of one Secundus has been found inscribed in that city.

security. (1) Freedom from war, such as the ease-loving Sidonians (see SIDON) and the people of Laish enjoyed (Judg. 18:7, 10, 27; cf. Mic. 2:8). (2) The sense of inner confidence characteristic of the man who trusts in God (Job 11:18), and yearns for hiding under the shadow of His wings (Ps. 17:8). Not national defense (Ps. 20:7, 44:6); nor political alliances (Ps. 146:3; Isa. 36:6); nor wealth (I Tim. 6:17) could produce this inner security. (3) Surety or bail, which the officials of Thessalonica took of Jason before allowing Paul and Silas to leave the city (Acts 17:9).

seed. (1) A plant's unit of reproduction (Gen. 1:11 f., 47:19, 23 f.; Jer. 35:7; Hag. 2:19).

(2) Human progeny (Gen. 3:15, 13:15 f.). Abraham's "seed" was in Isaac (Gen. 21:12, 28:14). The seed of God's people Israel was

to be established forever (Ps. 89:4). Christ was the seed of David (II Tim. 2:8).

(3) Christ used stories about seeds in the parables: the Seeds and the Sower (Matt. 13:3–23; Luke 8:5–15); the Seed and the Tares (Matt. 13:24–39); the Mustard Seed (Matt. 17:20 f.); the Mystery of Growth (Mark 4:26–29). Paul taught of the Resurrection in terms of grain which is sown, dies, and lives again in fruition (I Cor. 15:20–23, 35–58).

seer, a clairvoyant or diviner of Israel's early history. A prophet was at first called a seer (I Sam. 9:11), but later a distinction was made between them (I Sam. 9:9); the seer was known for his ecstatic visions, but the prophet as the spokesman of God. Amaziah called Amos a seer in a disparaging sense (Amos 7:12). See PROPHET.

Segub (sē′gŭb). (1) The youngest son of Hiel the Bethelite. He died (perhaps as a human sacrifice) when his father rebuilt the Jericho gates (I Kings 16:34), as Joshua had prophesied (Josh. 6:26). (2) The son of Hezron by a daughter of Machir (I Chron. 2:21, 22).

Seir (sē′ĭr) ("hairy"). (1) The large mountain mass of Edom (especially Mt. Seir), S. of the Dead Sea and running down the E. side of the Arabah* depression almost to the head of the Gulf of Aqabah. The route of the Exodus passed through Seir (Deut. 2:1). The Lord rose up from Mt. Seir and revealed Himself to Israel (the Blessing of Moses, Deut. 33:2). Seir was regarded as the home of Esau*, rival of the Jacob tribes—"Esau dwelt in mount Seir; Esau is Edom" (Gen. 36:8). In Joshua's farewell address he spoke of God's giving Mt. Seir to Esau (Josh. 24:4); yet chieftains of the Horites* were called "the children of Seir in the land of Edom" (Gen. 36:21, 30, cf. Ezek. 35:2 ff.). The people called in the O.T. "Horites in their mount Seir" (Gen. 14:6) were Hurrians, non-Semites who between 1750 and 1600 B.C. invaded N. Mesopotamia from the eastern highlands, and in the 15th and 14th centuries spread over Palestine and Syria. Esau is represented as dispossessing the Horites of Mt. Seir (Gen. 32:3, 36:20 f.; Deut. 2:1–29; Josh. 24:4). Simeonites pushed out the Amalekites* who had hidden in Seir (I Chron. 4:42 f.).

The majesty of God was associated with the awesome grandeur of Mt. Seir (Deut. 33:2; Judg. 5:4).

The Chronicler tells how King Amaziah of Judah (c. 800–783 B.C.) went to the Valley of Salt and slew 10,000 men of Seir but paid homage to their gods (II Chron. 25:11–24). Isaiah's words, "Watchman, what of the night?" came from Seir (21:11).

(2) A mountain elevation, possibly Saris, SW. of Kirjath-jearim on the N. border of Judah NW. of Jerusalem (Josh. 15:10).

Seirath (sē̇-ī′răth) (Seirah) (sē̇-ī′rȧ), a town of unknown site, possibly in the highlands of Ephraim, to which Ehud escaped after murdering Eglon, King of Moab (Judg. 3:26).

Sela (sē′lȧ) (Selah) (II Kings 14:7) (A.S.V. marg. "rock"), the rock-cut Edomite city called by the Greeks Petra. See NABATAEA.

selah (Heb. *sālal,* "to lift up"), a word used 71 times in the Heb. Psalter, once in connection with *Higgāyōn* (Ps. 9:16); and in Hab. 3:3, 9, 13. Its significance is uncertain, but, like "amen" and "hallelujah" (Ps. 46:3) it may have been a cry of worshippers at the close of the liturgy of worship, or at a specified point in it (Ps. 3:2, 4, etc.). It may have been used as a signal for the singers to "lift up" their voices, or for the orchestra to "lift up, loud," with their music, after they had been playing softly to accompany the singers' voices. The "selah" may have come into use in the Persian period, when liturgical forms were highly developed, to indicate the points at which priests were to utter benedictions.

Seleucia (sē̇-lū′shĭ-ȧ) (Selûqiyeh). (1) The port of Syrian Antioch*, established by Seleucus I (Nicator) (see SELEUCIDS). Seleucia was built on level ground at the foot of Mt. Pieria, 5 m. N. of the mouth of the Orontes River, and 16 m. W. of Antioch. It was one of the most important commercial harbors of the eastern Mediterranean in N.T. times. Paul and Barnabas embarked there for Cyprus on the First Missionary Journey (Acts 13:4). It was heavily fortified, especially in the Roman period, when it became a "free city." The harbor silted up in mediaeval times.

(2) A town in the Bashan highlands, NE. of the Sea of Galilee.

(3) A town (Silifke) in SE. Asia Minor, on the coast of Cappadocia.

(4) A city opposite Ctesiphon, winter capital of the Sassanian kings, on the Tigris River, 20 m. N. of modern Baghdad; founded by Seleucus I. It became the chief city of the Seleucid Kingdom, more impressive even than Babylon. It was destroyed by Rome (A.D. 162).

Seleucids (sē̇-lū′sĭds), **the**, a dynasty (312–64 B.C.) which ruled over Bactria, Persia, Babylonia, Syria, and part of Asia Minor.

Seleucus I, Nicator, son of Antiochus, was a cavalry officer of Philip of Macedon (359–336 B.C.), a brilliant military leader, who as a young man accompanied Alexander the Great (336–323 B.C.) in his Asiatic and India campaigns. In the breakup of Alexander's empire Seleucus acquired the greater part, from Thrace to the border of India (but exclusive of Macedonia, Egypt, and the Greek Aegean), and Bithynia, the Pontus, and Galatia in Asia Minor. The empire which Seleucus established was known as the Seleucid Empire (312–64 B.C.). Its tyrannical, turbulent rulers claimed to be veritable gods in the flesh and played dark roles in the unhappy Middle East. Their capital was Syrian Antioch*, founded by Seleucus I, and named, like the numerous other Antiochs, for his father, Antiochus.

The Seleucids ruled in the Hellenistic Age, when the late and often pseudocultural influences of the classic Greek culture prevailed, except in conservative Jewish circles and rural districts. Palestine came under Seleucid rule in 198 B.C., when Antiochus III the Great was victorious over Egypt in a battle near the Jordan headwaters. From the time of Antiochus Epiphanes (175–163 B.C.)

to the coming of the Roman conquerors (63 B.C.) the fate of Palestine was closely linked with that of Syria. (See MACCABEES.)

Emperors of the Seleucid Dynasty

Seleucus I	312–280 B.C.
Antiochus I	280–262/1
Antiochus II	261–246
Seleucus II	246–226
Seleucus III Soter	226–223
Antiochus III "the Great"	223–187
Seleucus IV Philopater	187–175
Antiochus IV Epiphanes	175–163
Antiochus V	163–162
Demetrius I	162–150
Alexander Balas	150–145
Demetrius II	145–139/8
Antiochus VI	145–142/1
Antiochus VII	139/8–129

The dynasty ended with Pompey's reduction of Syria to a Roman province (64 B.C.).

The Seleucid emperor most closely connected with the history of Biblical Palestine is Antiochus IV Epiphanes, grandson of Antiochus III "the Great." Events which made his reign hateful to the Jews included the appointing of high priests not of high-priestly lineage (e.g., Jason and Menelaus); forcing Hellenistic cults and culture on them (I Macc. 1:44–53); plundering Jerusalem, even to the stripping of treasures from the Temple; forcing Jews to violate the Mosaic Law (II Macc. 4:15–26); murdering orthodox Jews in the sacred area; annulling feasts; and belittling Judaism (I Macc. 1:14–40). He erroneously believed that he could exact political loyalty by dominating religious views. Seleucus I was expected to be worshipped as "Zeus victorious"; Antiochus I was Soter ("saviour"); Antiochus IV was Epiphanes ("god manifest"), and was portrayed on his coins as Olympian Zeus. The policy of Antiochus Epiphanes precipitated the patriotic-religious revolt of the Jews led by the Maccabean family (the Hasmoneans) (I Macc. 1:54–64, cf. II Macc. 6). He tried a similar procedure against the Samaritans* in their sacred stronghold of faith, Mt. Gerizim (II Macc. 6:2). The brief period of freedom won by the Jews under the leadership of the Maccabees (I Macc. 5:1–9:22) was one of the very few periods in history when the Jews as a nation have enjoyed political independence. Even this was embittered by strife between the rival groups of Pharisees* and Sadducees. The Seleucids are referred to in the Book of Daniel; the two-horned ram (8:20) is the Medo-Persian Empire, and the great horn of this ram is Alexander (v. 21). The great horn broke up into four (vv. 8, 22), representing the four kingdoms of Alexander's successors; the "little horn" (v. 9) which branched out from one of the four was the devastating Antiochus Epiphanes. His doom was foreshadowed in v. 25: "he shall be broken without hand."

Hellenistic culture in the Middle East centered in the great cities the Seleucids established, e.g., in Syria, Antioch; in Mesopotamia, Seleucia, greatest city of its era, surpassing even Babylon; also Edessa, Dura-Europos; and still others in Lydia, Caria, Phrygia, Media, and Iran. The rural sections of Palestine, however, scarcely felt the Hellenistic trends and tastes, and Hellenism in Palestine was eradicated by the victory of Judas Maccabaeus.

self-control. See TEMPERANCE.

Semites, a term (first used by A. L. Schlözer in 1781) derived from Gen. 10:22, where the sons of Shem are named as Elam, Asshur, Arphaxad (i. e., Hebrews and Arabs), Lud (i.e., Lydia), and Aram. The Semites are a group of nations who lived in Western Asia S. of the Taurus and Armenia, and W. of Iran. They constitute a linguistic unit (like the Indo-Europeans) but by no means a racial unit. The Semitic languages are classified as follows: (1) East Semitic (Akkadian, Babylonian, Assyrian). (2) North Semitic: (a) Aramaic group (Eastern), Syriac, Mandaean, the language of the Babylonian Talmud; (Western) Aramaic inscriptions, Biblical Aramaic, Palestinian Jewish and Christian Aramaic, Palmyrene, Nabataean; (b) Canaanitic or Amoritic group, Phoenician, Ugaritic, Hebrew, Moabitic; also Punic (Carthage). (3) South Semitic: (a) Arabic (Northern), inscriptions, classical Arabic, modern dialects; (Southern), Minaean and Sabaean inscriptions; also Ethiopic.

It is generally thought that the Arabian peninsula was the original homeland of the Semites, though Babylonia, North Africa, and Amurru (in the Lebanon region) have also been suggested. It is widely held that the Semites poured out of Arabia in great waves about 3000 B.C. (Amorites), 2500 (Akkadians), 2000 (Canaanite-Phoenicians), 1500 (Arameans and Hebrews), 500 (Nabataeans)—as the Arabian Moslems set forth after the death of Mohammed in A.D. 632. Even if such was the case, with the exception of the Bedouin Arabs, none of the Semitic nations (Babylonians, Assyrians, Syrians, Phoenicians, Canaanites, Israelites, Moabites, Ammonites, Edomites, etc.,) in historic times exhibits the anthropological characteristics of a supposed Semitic racial group; only their languages are closely related. The religions of these nations, like their cultures, vary profoundly and should be studied individually. Since the three great monotheistic religions of salvation (Judaism, Christianity, and Islam) arose on Semitic soil out of the religion of the primitive Semites (directly out of the prophetic reformation of the religion of Israel), it may be said, as E. Renan did, "the tent of the Semitic patriarch was the starting point of mankind's religious progress."

It has been said that the earliest Semitic religion was monotheism (E. Renan, M. J. Lagrange), totemism (W. Robertson Smith), ancestor worship (Herbert Spencer), or polydaemonism (J. Wellhausen); the original significance of animal sacrifice would correspond to any one of these theories. Though traces of all these notions may be detected in the polytheistic systems of Semitic nations in historic times, polydaemonism seems to have prevailed among the early Semites. They regarded stones, trees, springs, mountains, and other natural objects as the domiciles of spirits (*numina loci*), each of which was generically called an *il* (Arab. *ilah*, Heb. *el*) and resembled the jinn of later Arabs. A few among them, like the el of a spring who saved Hagar and Ishmael from death in the desert (Gen. 16:13–14) and the el of a stone who made Jacob rich (Gen. 31:13, 35:7, 15), through such outstanding acts acquired a personality and a history, were given a personal name (El Roi and El Bethel ["the el of the domicile of the el"], respectively), and received regular worship: thus they emerged from the anonymous class of the els and bebecame gods. Some of the gods remained attached to their domicile, which became the goal of pilgrimages (Arabic *khaj*, Hebrew khag [festival]), and were worshipped by passing tribes; others were adopted by certain tribes as their gods, and thus moved about with their tribe. Eventually El (or Ilah) was used as a proper name for a particular god, so among the Phoenicians (in the Ras Shamrah poems El, "the father of years," is the supreme god; Philo of Byblos identifies him with Kronos), among the Arameans (Panammu's inscription on a statue of Hadad, found at Zenjirli), among the Arabs (Allah [i.e., al-Ilah, the God] was becoming the supreme god even before Mohammed), and in the Book of Job (El is the one true God). The strong sense of tribal solidarity among the nomadic Semites (manifested in blood revenge, circumcision [an ancient initiation rite], and particularly in war) was based, at least in principle, on ties of blood. Accordingly the tribal god was regarded as the father (or some other relative) of the tribe. Just as blood sealed the covenant between two parties in Arabia (Herodotus III:8), so Yahweh became the god of Abraham by walking between the two bleeding halves of sacrificial victims (Gen. 15:9–12, 17 f.). The earliest sanctuaries were natural objects (springs, trees, mountains, stones) inhabited by a god. The rites of worship (purifications in approaching a sacred spot, sacrifices, offerings, prayers), the pilgrimages, and the celebration of the festivals (with dancing and feasting), did not at first require a regular priesthood; the earliest Semitic priests were probably diviners. The integrity of the clan was secured by the iron rule of ancestral customs, in which no distinction was made between social, legal, ethical, and religious obligations or tabus. Out of such crude beginnings arose the polytheism of the civilized Semitic kingdoms, and later the great monotheistic religions.

(*Reprinted from "An Encyclopedia of Religion,"* Robert H. Pfeiffer, *by permission of the author, the Philosophical Library, and Vergilius Ferm, editor.*)

Senaah (sḗ-nā'*ȧ*), an unidentified town site to which the Exiles returned after their Captivity in Babylon (Ezra 2:35; Neh. 7:38). It may have been adjacent to Jericho. Some people of this colony (Hassenaah, Neh. 3:3) repaired the Fish Gate in the Jerusalem wall.

Senate of the Children of Israel, a term used only in Acts 5:21 for the Sanhedrin*.

Seneh (sē'nĕ), a well-known crag in the Michmash* pass (I Sam. 14:4).

Senir (sē'nĭr) (Shenir), the Amorite name of Mt. Hermon in A.V. Deut. 3:9 (Sidonian "Sirion"). In other O.T. passages, like Song of Sol. 4:8, "Senir" probably refers to the whole Anti-Lebanon range. In I Chron. 5:23 it is a boundary of Manasseh, E. of the Jordan. Fir trees from Senir were used for the famous boats of Tyre (Ezek. 27:5).

Sennacherib (sĕ-năk'ẽr-ĭb) ("Sin [moon god] has increased the brothers"), a son of Sargon II, who ascended the Assyrian throne on the 12th of Ab, 705 B.C., and reigned until he was assassinated in 681 B.C. by two of his sons, jealous of their brother Esar-haddon* (II Kings 19:37; II Chron. 32:21). He was the grandfather of Ashurbanipal. Sennacherib was "one of the great statesmen of the early Orient" (J. H. Breasted). Secular histories record his conquests, and his levy of vast tribute from people as far W. as the Ionian Greek isles and as far N. as Tarsus, which he plundered soon after 700 B.C. Records are confused concerning the sequence of his conquests. After dominating Babylon (703/702) he faced W., where his subject provinces had rebelled and made alliances with Egypt. These restless subjects included Hezekiah*, King of Judah (contemporary of Isaiah), and lords of the Philistine cities. Moving to the Mediterranean coasts c. 701 B.C., he isolated Tyre and reduced Phoenician cities—Ashkelon, Timnath, and Ekron. Moving into Judaea, he captured (if we accept his own records) 46 walled cities and 200,150 prisoners. The record of II Kings 18 tells of his approach toward Jerusalem, incident to which he besieged the frontier fortress of Lachish*, now excavated. There (according to II Kings 18:14–16) he received emissaries from King Hezekiah, "in the fourteenth year" of his reign (v. 13), i.e., 701 B.C. The Jewish monarch offered to pay heavy tribute in gold and silver (v. 14), which he later sent—even gold from the Temple pillars and doors (v. 16). Pfeiffer sees in II Kings 18:13, 17–19:8, 36 f., a story unequaled in interest among extant remains of Judah's royal history. But he points out that two other stories have been combined with the above narrative: one (18:14–16) tells of Hezekiah's submission to Sennacherib, and tallies rather well with Assyrian records; the other (19:9b–35; Isa. 37:9b–36) contains what may be a lengendary story of how 185,000 Assyrian soldiers were slain by a sudden epidemic (? bubonic plague). The threatened advance of Sennacherib on Jerusalem and the danger of a siege occasioned the construction of the Siloam* Tunnel.

One section of Sennacherib's annals inscribed in cuneiform on a clay prism records his eight campaigns, and gives his version of his expedition against King Hezekiah in the summer of 701 B.C. A copy of this prism may be seen in the Museum of the Oriental Institute of the University of Chicago. The account, written in 689 B.C., reads in part: "As for Hezekiah the Jew, who did not submit to my yoke, forty-six of his strong, walled cities, as well as the small cities in their neighborhood, which were without number—by constructing a rampart out of trampled earth and by bringing up battering-rams, by the attack of infantry, by tunnels, breaches, and [the use of] axes, I besieged and took [those cities]. Two hundred thousand one hundred and fifty people, great and small,

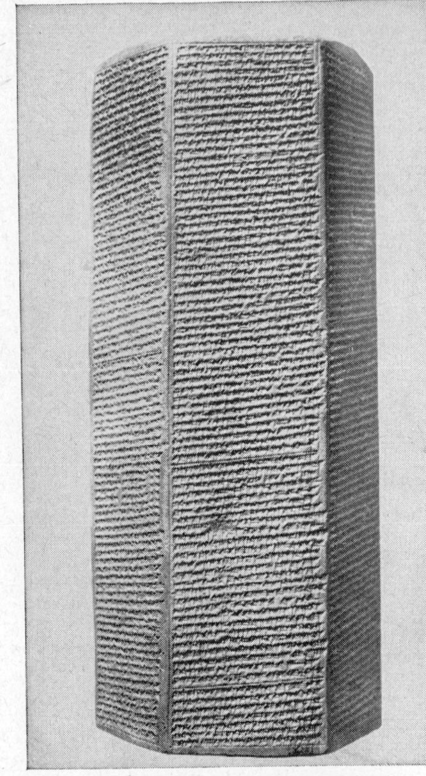

369. Column 3 of Sennacherib's Prism.

male and female, horses, mules, asses, camels, cattle, and sheep without number, I brought away from them and counted as spoil. Himself like a caged bird I shut in Jerusalem his royal city. Earthworks I threw up against him; the one coming out of the city gate I turned back to his misery." This inscription corroborates the Biblical account of II Kings 18–19 and Isaiah 36–37.

Sennacherib improved his people's water supply and irrigation. He introduced the *shadûf* or well-sweep from Egypt, and built the Aqueduct of Jerwan which made Nineveh a garden city (see WATER, illus. 476). (For details see *Sennacherib's Aqueduct of Jerwan* by Jacobson and Lloyd, University of Chicago Press.) It was the first Mesopotamian aqueduct known, and brought water 30 m. by a 1,000 ft. causeway over the Gomer River. The arches of this aqueduct are considered the world's oldest bridge. Its fabric may have required two million blocks of stone, some of which bear historic inscriptions. Sennacherib gave his subjects other gardens and canals, and offered similar boons to Jerusalem. He built Nineveh's wall and Kouyunjik palace.

Sephar (sē′fär), a border of Joktan's territory (Gen. 10:30), probably in S. Arabia, though some identify it as in the region of the Syrian Desert associated with "Children of the east."

Sepharad (sē̆-fā′răd), a place to which Jerusalem captives were deported (Obad. 20). It may be (1) Sardis* in W. Asia Minor, NE. of Smyrna, or (2) a section of Media, SW. of the Caspian.

Sepharvaim (sĕf′är-vā′ĭm), a place near Riblah*, site unknown, from which the Assyrians transported Sepharvites to replace captives taken from Samaria (II Kings 17:24, 31). It may be the same place referred to in 18:34, 19:13.

Sepphoris (the modern Saffûriyeh), an agricultural village in Galilee 4 m. N. of Nazareth, not mentioned by any known name in Scripture, but certainly familiar to Jesus and his family. Herod Antipas, early in his rule (4 B.C.–A.D. 39) as tetrarch of Galilee and Peraea, used the beautified city of Sepphoris as his capital until he moved to Tiberias on the Sea of Galilee. When Sepphoris revolted against Rome in A.D. 6 it was razed by Varus. It was soon rebuilt, and gave employment to carpenters and masons from Nazareth. Jesus avoided the Hellenistic Sepphoris, as well as Tiberias. Sepphoris was a rabbinic center. Gabinius, Roman proconsul in Syria, established there in 55 B.C. one of the Sanhedrins he organized in each of the five districts (Jerusalem, Gazara, Amathus, Jericho, and Sepphoris) of Palestine.

A Roman theater, an underground reservoir, and evidences of occupation of the town from soon after 200 B.C. have been found here.

Septuagint (sĕp′tū-*ȧ*-jĭnt), the Gk. version of the O.T., prepared by a group of scholars at Alexandria in the 3d century B.C. H. S. Gehman of Princeton Theological Seminary made a study of the vocabulary, idioms, and syntax used in the Septuagint, which led him to believe that the work is in "translation Greek," a type understood only by Jews, who had probably heard extemporaneous oral renderings from the Heb. O.T. in their synagogues. Thus, believes Dr. Gehman, the religious vernacular of Greek Jews absorbed Hebraic idioms. "The Septuagint was the Bible of the Greek-speaking world in the times of Christ and the apostles," as Ira M. Price stated. When N.T. writers wished to quote from the O.T., they usually employed the Septuagint as their source. This text was the one used by the early Church in the Mediterranean lands. It serves today as a suitable check against the *Textus Receptus* ("received text") of the Gk. New Testament published in seven editions between 1624 and 1678 (Elzevir). (See TEXT.)

Sepulcher, Church of the Holy, one of the most historic shrines in Christendom, a tottering structure composed of many buildings in the NW. section of the walled Arab city of Jerusalem. It was begun c. A.D. 326 by Queen Helena, mother of Constantine the Great, over what she believed to be the true Calvary*, adjacent to the Garden of Joseph of Arimathaea in whose "new tomb" Jesus was laid (John 19:38–42). Substantial scholarship favors this site as authentic, although it is inside the present city walls, rather than "without the gate" (Heb. 13:12) where crucifixions took place; it may well have been outside the walls of Jesus' time. The only rival site is "Gordon's Calvary" and the adjacent "Garden Tomb," selected in the nineteenth century by General "Chinese" Gordon, who thought they looked exactly as "the place of the skull" and an adjacent garden tomb would look. "Gordon's Calvary" is outside Herod's Gate, not far from the site of the American Schools of Oriental Research. (See also TOMB OF JESUS.)

The twenty-two chapels of the Church of the Holy Sepulcher are shared by several eastern churches, each of which has its allotment of space. It is hoped that room will eventually be provided for Protestants. The heart of the structure is the marble Chapel of the Holy Sepulcher, perpetually lighted by forty-three lamps provided by various religious groups. The Sacristy contains priceless relics of the Crusades, which poured out of Europe during the Middle Ages to free this church from the Moslems. The treasures include the sword and spurs of Godfrey de Bouillon (1099), who preferred to be known as "Guardian of the Sepulcher of Christ," rather than as "King of Jerusalem."

Serabit el-Khadem, a lonely, mountainous desert region on the Sinai Peninsula, 2,000 ft. above sea level, c. 50 m. from the traditional Mt. Sinai, important for its ancient turquoise mines and its "proto-Sinaitic" inscriptions.

NW. Semitic slaves or captives between c. 1500 B.C. and 1200 B.C. came from Merkhah, the Egyptian Red Sea port, to the almost inaccessible mines at Serabit el-Khadem. They extracted lumps of turquoise, imbedded in the matrix of not too hard rock, not far from the famous Temple of the Egyptian goddess Hathor, high above the Wâdī Serabit. As early as the Third Egyptian Dynasty (the reign of Snefru), again during the Twelfth Dynasty, and particularly during the brilliant Eighteenth Dynasty (c. 1570–1310 B.C.) and the Nineteenth, the Serabit mines yielded turquoise for jewelry, amulets, and ornamented palace furnishings. Merchants came from afar to the well-defended, Egyptian-controlled mines.

A group of c. 25 inscriptions were discovered at Serabit el-Khadem by Sir Flinders Petrie in 1904–5, in the course of clearing the Serabit Temple of Hathor. They were found on well-worn sandstone slabs from the burial cairns of the miners, who had literally worked themselves to death. One large, important inscription is inside Mine L. Petrie dated the inscriptions c. 1500 B.C., but was unable to derive any meaning from the marks made in a "previously unknown alphabetic script, but one which had strong affinities to the Egyptian hieroglyphic." The British Egyptologist Alan Gardiner detected the acrophonic nature of several of the markings, and made out "[belonging] to Ba'lat"—chief Canaanite goddess of Byblos—the Hathor of the Egyptians. W. F. Albright suggested that Hebrew letters had developed from pictures of objects with initial consonants that give the phonetic value of the picture (as primary school children today know the "c" in "cat" and the "d" in "dog"). Dr. Albright in 1947 deciphered the proto-Sinaitic inscriptions, and showed that a Canaanite Semitic alphabetic script had been used by the NW. Semites held as slaves or as captive laborers by Thutmose III and Queen Hatshepsut at Serabit el-Khadem. It is possible, if not likely, that Moses could have written in a Semitic script (Ex. 34:28). The slaves, possibly levied from Canaan and collected near the Egyptian Delta city of Tanis (now identified as Raamses*, a Hyksos center of c. 1720–c. 1550 B.C.) may have been subjected to the same sort of bondage as that endured by the Israelites in Egypt before their Exodus early in the 13th century B.C. The cairn burials of the Serabit miners seem to have continued up to c. 1200 B.C.

370. Serabit el-Khadem.

The inscriptions from Serabit el-Khadem are the oldest known documents written in the alphabet from which the Eng. alphabet was finally derived, via the Lat., Gk., Phoen., and Heb. The thoughts expressed on the slabs include wistful appeals to deities, including possibly the serpent lady, and to the mine foremen to befriend the buried miners, lest in the life to come they be compelled to endure hardships comparable to their wretched lot in this world. (See *Bulletin* No. 110, April 1948, ASOR, article by W. F. Albright, pp. 6 ff.)

The proto-Sinaitic inscriptions are not to be confused with the Sinaitic inscriptions, which include numerous Nabataean ones from the 1st centuries of the Christian era.

See chart showing evolution of the alphabet, under WRITING.

Serah (sē'rȧ), a "daughter" or clan of the tribe of Asher (Gen. 46:17; Num. 26:46, A.V. Sarah*).

Seraiah (sē-rā′yȧ) ("Jehovah persists"). (1) One of David's scribes or recorders, perhaps called "Sheva," "Shisha," and "Shavsha"* (II Sam. 8:17; I Kings 4:3; I Chron. 18:16). (2) A son of Kenaz, of the house of Judah (I Chron. 4:13 f.). (3) A son of Asiel, of the Tribe of Simeon (I Chron. 4:35). (4) A chief priest at Jerusalem in Zedekiah's time (598–587 B.C.), carried to Riblah by Nebuchadnezzar, who slew him there (II Kings 25:18; Jer. 52:24; I Chron. 6:14). He may have been Ezra's ancestor (7:1). (5) A son of Tanhumeth, and captain of a band not taken by Nebuchadnezzar (Jer. 40:8); he clung to Gedaliah in Judah (II Kings 25:23). (6) A son of Azriel, one of the Jerusalem group sent to arrest Baruch the scribe and Jeremiah the prophet (Jer. 36:26). (7) A "quiet prince" (A.V. Jer. 51:59, or better, in the A.S.V., "chief chamberlain"), son of Neriah. He accompanied King Zedekiah of Judah to Babylon (vv. 59, 61), and carried to that city the prophecy of Jeremiah (v. 64). (8) A priest who came back from Exile to Jerusalem with Zerubbabel (Ezra 2:2; Neh. 12:1, 12). (9) A priest who sealed the covenant in Nehemiah's time (Neh. 10:2). (10) A son of Hilkiah, who was "ruler of the house of God" (Neh. 11:11).

371. Six-winged seraph from Tell Halaf, late Hurrian (Provincial Assyrian), c. 1000 B.C.

seraphim (sĕr′ȧ-fĭm) (plural noun; A.V., incorrectly, "seraphims"), celestial beings, an order of angels who, along with cherubim and ophanim, were thought of as guarding the throne of God. In Isaiah's early vision (chap. 6) six-winged seraphim stood above the throne. Seraphim had voices, for the seraph which carried a coal from the Temple altar to cleanse Isaiah's lips spoke of the purification as accomplished. The exact origin and symbolic meaning of seraphim is uncertain; possibly they were derived from the serpent-like creatures of Assyrian mythology, symbolic of lightning, or from the Egyptian "guardian griffins." For Isaiah, certainly, they were moral beings, not personifications of nature, performing an atoning ministry, and by their cries disclosing the attribute of holiness* in God. They praised the holiness and the glory of the Lord of hosts in accents so vigorous that the thresholds trembled and the holy place was filled with smoke (vv. 3 f.). There is no other information about them in Scripture.

Serapis (sē-rā′pĭs), a male deity of Egypt. His cult, blending features of Eleusinian and Osirian mysteries, was influential in the Hellenistic world. He was associated with Aesculapius and was consulted in times of illness, at his sanctuary (Serapion), of which there were many in the eastern Mediterranean world. One is now in ruins between Puteoli, where Paul landed in Italy (Acts 28:13), and Naples. R. H. Pfeiffer compares the Serapion with Lourdes or St. Anne de Beaupré.

372. Serapis Temple, near Naples.

sergeants, petty Roman officers (lictors; R.S.V. "police") sent by the Jerusalem magistrates to release Paul from jail (Acts 16:35, 38).

Sergius Paulus (sûr′jĭ-ŭs pô′lŭs). See PAULUS, SERGIUS.

Sermon on the Mount, The, the teachings of Jesus concerning the character and conduct of the true disciple. It is found in Matt. 5:3–7:27, and is the first of five long discourses which are a feature of this Gospel (see chaps. 10, 13, 18, 24–25). Some scholars regard the Sermon as a compilation of separate, scattered sayings of Jesus grouped around a main theme; others, as a digest of a discourse actually given by Jesus. It probably belongs in the first half of Jesus' Galilean ministry. It is addressed to those who are already disciples, yet it is delivered in the hearing of "the multitudes." Luke (6:12–20) indicates that it followed the appointment of the twelve Disciples. As the scene of this teaching (? Hattîn) is a mountain (Matt. 5:1), it suggests Mt. Sinai and the giving of the old Law to Moses. A shorter form of the so-called Sermon on the Mount is found in Luke 6:20–49, where the setting is a plain

SERPENT

(6:17). Both accounts of this body of teaching may be derived from Q*.

The Beatitudes, the "Golden Rule," and the Lord's Prayer are well-known parts of the Sermon. Both Matthew and Luke open with the Beatitudes, of which Matthew gives eight, while Luke gives four, with four woes, not found in Matthew. The "Golden Rule," in Matt. 7:12 and Luke 6:31, summarizes the teaching of the Law and the prophets concerning human relationships. The Lord's Prayer, in Matt. 6:9–13, is not included in Luke's Sermon on the Plain, but is in Luke 11:2–4.

The Sermon on the Mount presents the ideal life of the real disciple, and is concerned with true righteousness, and with the New Law of the Kingdom of Heaven. Basically the New Law is the law of love. Jesus did not present this New Law as a new set of specific commandments similar to the old Law of Moses which was being replaced. Instead, he pronounced upon the true disciple a series of blessings which carried the idea of love rather than of exaction.

He explained the difference between the old righteousness and the new: "It was said by them of old time,"—"but I say unto you." He taught that the final test of a man is not what he has done or omitted to do, but what his character is and his deepest aspirations are. The higher righteousness is not attained by a larger total of good deeds, but it is the fruit of a life transformed by the grace of God.

The Sermon on the Mount may be outlined as follows:

(1) The true disciple Matt. 5:3–16
- (a) His portrait in the Beatitudes
- (b) His task: to be "salt" and "light"

(2) How the higher righteousness of the New Law fulfills the old Law in respect to: 5:17–48
- (a) Murder
- (b) Adultery
- (c) Divorce
- (d) Truthfulness
- (e) Revenge
- (f) Love of neighbor

(3) How the new righteousness affects acts of piety 6:1–18
- (a) Almsgiving
- (b) Prayer
- (c) Fasting

(4) Trust in God and devotion to the Kingdom 6:19–34

(5) The right attitude toward others 7:1–12

(6) The test of true righteousness: doing God's will 7:13–27
- (a) Two ways
- (b) Two kinds of teachers
- (c) Two kinds of disciples
- (d) Two kinds of houses

serpent, a snake, of which there are 30 or more species in Palestine and the desert areas S. of this region. In the Bible serpents are called by almost a dozen names in addition to the generic *nāchāsh*. The serpent of the Garden of Eden narrative (Gen. 3:1 f., 4, 13 f.) is a symbol of evil (see SATAN). John the Baptist mentioned the viper in his condemnation of the Pharisees and scribes (Matt. 3:7). Jesus contrasted the serpent to the wholesome fish (Matt. 7:10). Many snakes of the Near East are harmless; others have a "fiery" bite (Isa. 14:29, cf. Prov. 23:32). All of them, lurking in damp places near homes, were feared. In primitive times they were often supplied with milk to appease them, as in the kitchen prayer-niches of 1st-century Pompeians.

373. Cultic painting of serpent, Pompeii, in Naples Museum.

Desert nomads were fearful of serpents. It is easy to see why Moses might have fashioned a metal serpent intended to appease the creature they feared, and to remind his company that the Lord was able to heal and to protect (Num. 21:9). The veneration of the metal serpent continued among Hebrews, and they burned incense to this idol-symbol until the reforms of Hezekiah abolished it (II Kings 18:4). (See Christ's allusion to the serpent lifted up in the Wilderness, John 3:14.)

Serpent cults were popular among all Semites. The primitive story of Moses' rod turning into a serpent in Egypt is typical of primitive religion tinged with magic (Ex. 4:2–4).

In Hebrew symbolism the serpent denoted Dan (Gen. 49:17); and Assyria and Babylonia, hostile to God's plans (Isa. 27:1).

Because serpents or snakes lurk in damp places, their names were given to springs, e.g., the Dragon's Spring (or well) near Jerusalem (Neh. 2:13). The "serpent's stone" (Zoheleth) was near the En-rogel spring adjacent to Jerusalem (R.S.V. I Kings 1:9).

The cunning of the serpent was hinted by Jesus (Matt. 10:16). In Greek mythology it had long been associated with Aesculapius, deity of healing, and is today a symbol* of the medical profession.

The serpent was a symbol in Near Eastern fertility cults. A six-inch bronze serpent has been dug from Gezer*, and cult stands decorated with snakes and the mother goddess from Beth-shan* of the 13th century B.C. Megiddo also has yielded a cult stand decorated with serpent and goddess, both of which together symbolized the Earth mother. In the Egyptian pantheon of many gods the uraeus-serpent was so venerated that it decorated the pharaoh's thrones, as seen in ancient reliefs. The cobra was especially honored.

servant, one who serves under command. In the sense of one who labors for another, the servant is represented in the Bible by several words, commonest of which is *'ebhedh* ("worker"). This term, as well as *'āmāh* (for a female servant) and *shiphhāh* ("handmaid"), imply bondage. The *na'ar* was "a young person" who toiled. A *sākhār* was one who worked for wages. (Cf. the hired servants of the Prodigal's father, Luke 15:17). The Hebrew Patriarchs had servants who had been captured or bought as slaves. Sometimes Israelites became slave servants, e.g., the maid of the Syrian Naaman's wife

374. Wooden model of servants, Eleventh Egyptian Dynasty.

(II Kings 5:2). The Patriarchal society depicted in the O.T. shows servants moving freely in the family tent colony, as if they were displaced persons sheltered by the charitable family. The record of Abraham entertaining angelic visitors implies that his servants brought water for their feet (Gen. 18:4). Abraham dispatched trusted servants led by the eldest, or a steward, to Mesopotamia to seek a wife for his son (Gen. 24). Sarah had as one of her servants an Egyptian handmaid, Hagar*, whom she gave to Abraham as secondary wife, to bear him offspring (Gen. 16). Laban gave to his daughter Leah the handmaid Zilpah, and Bilhah to his younger daughter Rachel. Both servants bore to Jacob sons who became heads of tribes (Gen. 30). Jacob the Patriarch bade his servants come and go (Gen. 32:16). Boaz, the rich farmer of Bethlehem, had servants who worked as harvesters (Ruth 2:5 f.). Saul, as a young landsman hunting his father's lost asses, was accompanied by a servant carrying money in his girdle when Saul carried none (I Sam. 9:5, 8). Elisha's Gehazi shows that even prophets had servants, who sometimes overstepped their stations (II Kings 5:20–27).

Servants were included in the kindly provisions of the O.T. Law; for example, they were mentioned among those exempted from labor on the Sabbath (Ex. 20:10). The freeing of slave servants at the Jubile* was written into legislation, if not always carried out (Lev. 25:55) (see FREEMAN). Servants sometimes received inheritances from the family (Gen. 15:2 f.); and were given as husbands to daughters of the household (I Chron. 2:35).

In the Roman world of Jesus' day slaves and servants formed a sizable part of the population of the average city. They included many intellectuals who had suffered adversity. Jesus was familiar with servants of Roman households, and did not hesitate to help them, as when he cured the centurion's servant (Matt. 8:6 ff.). There were probably servants in the Capernaum household which was often his headquarters. Zebedee, fisherman-father of James and John, had hired servants (Mark 1:20). Though none are mentioned in the Nazareth home of Joseph the carpenter, possibly the Cana household had servants (see Mary's role at the wedding, John 2:5). Mary, the mother of John Mark, had in her Jerusalem home, where early Christian gatherings were held, at least one servant—Rhoda (Acts 12:13–15). High priests had trusted servants—e.g. Malchus, whose ear was cut off in Gethsemane (John 18:10), and others with whom Peter sat in the palace, warming himself (Mark 14:66; John 18:16–18). Jesus often mentioned servants in his parabolic teaching (Luke 14:17, 20:9–18; Matt. 10:24, 18:23–35, 24:45–51, 25:14–46, Mark 13:34–37). Jesus himself became a living parable of the servant in the towel-girding incident at the Last Supper, and spoke of himself as the "servant of all."

The concept of the "Suffering Servant" first appears in the O.T. (see ISAIAH). Israel was viewed as a servant of Yahweh, Who had brought His people out of Egypt (Lev. 25:55; Isa. 42:1). After the fall of their nation and the experience of Exile, Israel continued to serve through suffering (Isa. 48:20). The Synoptists saw in Jesus the fulfillment of the "Suffering Servant" prophecy and ideal (cf. Matt. 12:18 with Isa. 42:1 ff.; and Luke 22:37 with Isa. 53:12). The early Church saw in Jesus the "approved Servant" (see GUILT; KINGDOM OF GOD; MESSIAH; SON OF MAN).

The word "servant" is also used in Scripture to indicate one who is an adherent or a chosen agent of Deity or of a ruler. Abraham was God's servant (Ps. 105:42); so, too were Moses (Ex. 4:10; Num. 12:7; Josh. 8:31), Solomon (I Kings 1:26), Paul (Titus 1:1), James (1:1), and Jude (1).

All slaves were servants, but not all servants were slaves in the sense of being the property of or wholly subject to another.

service, a term, conspicuous in the vocabulary of modern Christians, which stems from two Biblical concepts: (1) a ritual or liturgy for the worship of God, administered by men who served as staff at Tabernacle* and Temple*, e.g., the Kohathites (see KOHATH) (Num. 4:4), and the aged prophetess Anna, at the Temple of Christ's time (Luke 2:37 A.V.); (2) "spiritual service" (A.S.V. Rom. 12:1) or "spiritual worship" (R.S.V.), which may include the dedication of oneself to Christ's kingdom. The life of Jesus, from his first recorded miracle at Cana to his final act of world redemption on Calvary, was one of service—"I am among you as he that serveth" (Luke 22:27); whosoever "would be great among you must be your servant" (R.S.V. Matt. 20:26; see SERVANT). "Ye cannot serve God and Mammon" (Matt. 6:24).

Seth, the third son of Adam, born after the death of Abel (Gen. 4:25 f. J source; 5:2–8 P source). He became father of Enos, and is in the genealogical table of I Chron. 1. Luke's table makes him an ancestor of Christ (3:38). Nothing is told of Seth except that he was parent of many children.

seven, seventy. See NUMBERS.

seven words from the Cross, the seven sentences spoken by Jesus on the Cross. The 1st, addressed to God, concerned Christ's enemies: "Father, forgive them; for they know not what they do" (Luke 23:34). The next two were spoken to people: (1) to the penitent thief: "Verily, I say unto thee, To-day shalt thou be with me in Paradise" (Luke 23:43); (2) to the mother of Christ and to John: "Woman, behold thy son . . . Behold thy mother" (John 19:26 f.). The 4th was a cry to God in the words of Ps. 22:1: "Eli [Eloi] Eli [Eloi], lama sabachthani? . . . My God, my God, why hast thou forsaken me?" (Matt. 27:46; Mark 15:34) (see ELI, ELI). The 5th was a simple statement of physical need: "I thirst" (John 19:28). The 6th also was a statement: "It is finished" (John 19:30). The 7th, like the 1st, was addressed to God in words echoing Ps. 31:5: "Father, into thy hands I commend my spirit" (only in Luke 23:46).

Seveneh (sĕ-vē′nĕ). See SYENE.

Shaalbim (shȧ-ăl′bĭm) (Shaalabin) (shā′ȧ-lăb′ĭn), the modern Selbit, a town of central Palestine, between Jerusalem and Lydda, won from the Amorites by the Hebrews (Judg. 1:35). Several centuries later it became headquarters for one of Solomon's commissary officers (I Kings 4:9). It may be Shaalbon, the home of one of David's heroes, "the Shaalbonite" (II Sam. 23:32).

Shaaraim (shā′ȧ-rā′ĭm) ("the two gates"). (1) A town in the Shephelah near Azekah, at the border of Judah and Dan, mentioned in the annals of warfare between the Israelites and the Philistines (I Sam. 17:52). (2) A town of Simeon (I Chron. 4:31) (see SHILHIM).

Shaashgaz (shā-ăsh′găz), the chamberlain in charge of the harem of Ahasuerus at Shushan in Esther's day (Esther 2:14).

Shabbethai (shăb′ĕ-thī), a Levite who did not agree with Ezra's proposals for marriage reforms (Ezra 10:15).

Shaddai (shăd′ī). See EL SHADDAI; GOD.

Shadrach (shā′drăk), the name given the Hebrew Hananiah by the prince of eunuchs at Babylon (Dan. 1:7). He was honored with official responsibilities (2:49), but, along with Abednego and Meshach, was thrown into a fiery furnace when he refused to bow down before the golden image set up by Nebuchadnezzar (3:1–30).

Shaharaim (shā′hȧ-rā′ĭm), a man of Benjamin's tribe (I Chron. 8:8).

Shalem (shā′lĕm) (Heb., "peace"). A town near Shechem* (Gen. 33:18) to which Jacob came. The R.S.V. omits, reading, "And Jacob came safely to the city of Shechem."

Shalim (shā′lĭm) (A.V. I Sam. 9:4; A.S.V. Shaalim), a region probably not far from the N. boundary of Benjamin's territory, where young Saul hunted his father's lost asses.

Shalisha (shȧ-lī′shȧ) (A.S.V. Shalishah), the region N. or NW. of Mt. Ephraim* through which Saul hunted his father's asses (I Sam. 9:4).

Shallum (shăl′ŭm) ("recompense"). (1) The eponymous head of a group of Simeonites (I Chron. 4:25); of a clan of Naphtali (I Chron. 7:13); and of a Jerahmeelite family (I Chron. 2:40 f.). (2) A gatekeeper or family of porters at the Jerusalem Temple (I Chron. 9:17 ff.). (3) A son of Jabesh and the murderer of King Zechariah* of Israel (c. 746–745 B.C.), whom he succeeded, but for only one month before he was himself assassinated by Menahem, his successor (II Kings 15:8–15). (4) Father of Jehizkiah (II Chron. 28:12). (5) An ancestor of Ezra, called Meshullam* (I Chron. 9:11). (6) A son of Tikvath and husband of the prophetess Huldah, and keeper of the priests' or possibly the royal robes in the time of King Josiah of Judah (c. 640–609 B.C.) (II Kings 22:14; II Chron. 34:22). (6) Jeremiah's uncle, and father of Hanameel (Jer. 32:7 f.). (7) The alternate name of Jehoahaz II, son of King Josiah of Judah (II Kings 23:30; cf. Jer. 22:11); he reigned three months (609 B.C.). (8) A temple porter who put away his foreign wife during Ezra's reforms (Ezra 10:24, 42). (9) An official in charge of half of Jerusalem. With his daughters, he helped repair the city wall (Neh. 3:12).

Shalmai (shăl′mī), the founder of a Nethinim* family (Ezra 2:46; Neh. 7:48); R.S.V. reads "Shamlai" at Ezra 2:46.

Shalman (shăl′măn), possibly a contraction of the name of Shalmaneser* of Assyria, who despoiled Beth-arbel (Hos. 10:14), or of the Moabite monarch Salamanu, named in an inscription of Tiglath-pileser III and alive in Hosea's time.

Shalmaneser (shăl′măn-ē′zẽr) (Assyr., "the god Shulman is chief"), the name of five Assyrian kings, two of whom appear in O.T. narratives.

(1) Shalmaneser III (859–824 B.C.), son of Ashurnasirpal; considered the great Assyrian emperor of his century, he crossed the Euphrates with territorial ambitions early in his reign, wasting Hittite cities as far as the Mediterranean. A few years later he was confronted at Karkar (853) in Syria by a coalition, headed by Ben-hadad* (Hadadezer), King of Damascus, which included contingents from Hamath, the coastal city-states, and Israel. Ahab* of Israel (c. 869–850 B.C.) is said to have supplied 10,000 troops and 2,000 chariots. Though Shalmaneser did not follow up the advantage he claimed then to have won over the coalition, he returned periodically, without lasting successes. Finally the Syrian league was weakened by confusion inside Damascus, and especially within Israel following the reforms advocated by Elijah and Elisha. Ahab and Ben-hadad were both swept from their thrones (II Kings 8:7–15, 9, 10). Ben-hadad's successor, Hazael, was routed at Mt. Hermon in 841. Shalmaneser's black obelisk, on the 2d of its five rows of relief, shows either King Jehu of Israel (c. 842–815 B.C.) or one of his emissaries kissing the ground at the feet of Shalmaneser and offering him as tribute bars and vessels of

gold, silver, and lead. The kings of Tyre and Sidon hastened to add their tokens of submission. The obelisk, found in 1845 at Nimrûd (the Biblical Calah* on the Tigris) in the palace of the king, is now in the British Museum; a cast is in the Museum of the Oriental Institute in Chicago. (See JEHU, illus. 206.)

375. Replica of obelisk of Shalmaneser III (original in British Museum), describing expeditions and conquests of his 35-year reign.

(2) Shalmaneser V, successor of Tiglath-pileser III (II Kings 17:3, 18:9), warred against Phoenicia, capturing Sidon, Acre, and the mainland portions of Tyre. He received tribute from Hoshea*, last ruler of the Northern Kingdom (Israel) (c. 732–724 B.C.), as had his predecessor. When Hoshea made an about-face and allied himself with So of Egypt and refused to continue payment to Shalmaneser, the latter seized and imprisoned the king and besieged Israel's capital, Samaria*, for three years but died before it fell to his successor, Sargon* II, in 722/1 B.C.

Shama (shā′mȧ), one of David's heroic comrades (I Chron. 11:44).

shame is rendered by many Heb. and Gk. words in the O.T. and the N.T. The sense of shame felt by an individual arises from a consciousness of guilt or impropriety or of having injured one's reputation; e.g., from nakedness (Ex. 32:25; Rev. 3:18); or from adversities heaped upon him by others (Ps. 69:19). Prophets longed for the wicked to be brought to a sense of shame (Ezek. 16:52). In various ages and communities ideas of what constitute shame have changed. Crucifixion was regarded in Roman times as an ignominious, shameful method of death (Heb. 12:2). Women praying with uncovered heads or speaking in public worship were considered shameful by 1st-century Christians (I Cor. 11:6).

Shamed (shā′mĕd) (A.S.V. Shemed), a Benjamite who, with the help of Eber and Misham, helped rebuild Ono and Lod (I Chron. 8:12).

Shamgar (shăm′gär) (possibly a Hittite or Phoenician name), a son of Anath. He was a "deliverer" or minor judge of Israel, who by his prowess with an ox goad cleared dangerous roads of marauding neighbors and encouraged the resumption of normal travel in the days shortly before Deborah (Judg. 3:31, 5:6).

Shamir (shā′mẽr). (1) A town in the highlands of Judah (Josh. 15:48). (2) The home and burial place of the Israelite judge Tola, possibly the same as Samaria (Judg. 10:1 f.). (3) A man of the Kohathite division (I Chron. 24:24).

Shamma (shăm′ȧ), a man of the tribe of Asher (I Chron. 7:37).

Shammah (shăm′ȧ). (1) A son of Reuel and grandson of Esau and Bashemath (Gen. 36:13, 17). He became a tribal leader in Edom. (2) The third son of Jesse (I Sam. 16:9). With his two older brothers Shammah fought with Saul against the Philistines (17:13). This man is the Shimeah who was father of Jonadab (II Sam. 13:3); and Shimma, mentioned in A.V. I Chron. 2:13, identical with Shimei (A.S.V.), father of the Jonathan who killed a giant of Gath (II Sam. 21:21). (3) A son of Agee the Hararite, who held out single-handed against the Philistines (II Sam. 23:11 f.) and was rewarded by David with a position of leadership (v. 33). (4) Probably the same as (3). A Harodite, one of David's mighty men, probably the Shammoth of I Chron. 11:27 and the Shamhuth of I Chron. 27:8.

Shammai (shăm′ȧ-ī) (Shemaiah). (1) A male descendant of Jerahmeel (I Chron. 2:28, 32). (2) A son of Rekem (I Chron. 2:44 f.). (3) A man of the Tribe of Judah (I Chron. 4:17).

Shaphan (shā′făn). (1) A son of Azaliah, of King Josiah's time (c. 640–609 B.C.), who served as scribal secretary of state and was responsible for turning over to Hilkiah the priest the moneys paid by the people for repairing the Temple (II Kings 22:3–7). Shaphan received from Hilkiah the lost book of the Law (our Deuteronomy* substantially), accidentally found during the reconstruction at the Temple (vv. 8 f.). After reading it to the king Shaphan was dispatched by Josiah* to inquire of the prophetess Huldah what was God's will concerning the book (vv. 9–14). Shaphan probably was prominent in the ensuing reforms. (2) The father of Ahikam (Jer. 26:24, 39:14), possibly the same as (1). (3) The father of Jaazaniah (Ezek. 8:11), perhaps the same as (1).

Shaphat (shā′făt) ("he has judged"). (1) A Simeonite sent by Joshua to survey the land of Canaan (Num. 13:5). (2) A member of Gad's Tribe (I Chron. 5:12). (3) A valley herdsman for David (I Chron. 27:29). (4) The father of Elisha, from Abel-meholah (I Kings 19:16, 19). (5) A descendant of David (I Chron. 3:22).

Sharai (shȧ-rā′ī), a son of Bani rebuked by Ezra (10:40) for taking a foreign wife.

Sharezer (shȧ-rē′zẽr). (1) A son of the Assyrian King Sennacherib*, who with his brother Adrammelech slew the famous monarch while he was at worship "in the house of Nisroch his god," according to the record of II Kings 19:36 f. (cf. Isa. 37:38). Records of Babylonian origin agree with this account. (2) A man (A.V. Sherezer) sent from Bethel to Jerusalem in Zechariah's time to inquire of the Lord whether the Jews should continue fasting on the anniversary of the fall of Jerusalem (Zech. 7:2).

Sharon, the Plain of (possibly from a word meaning "level country"), the most fertile part of the coastal plain of Palestine. It extended c. 50 m. N. (from near the present

376. Plain of Sharon.

Joppa) to the headland of Mt. Carmel* just S. of Haifa. Its width varies from c. 6 to 12 m. It extends east to the edge of the Samaria highlands. The Plain of Sharon lay within the Kingdom of Israel after the division of Solomon's United Monarchy. Its fertility was proverbial in Bible times. Its roses (see ROSE), possibly the narcissus (*Narcissus tazetta*), or the autumn crocus (*Colchicum autumnale*), are mentioned in the Song of Solomon (2:1). Its "excellency" was used to describe the Messianic hope (Isa. 35:2). In O.T. times oak forests grew in its N. portions, but successive wars reduced the area to treeless prairie. Broad valleys gave access to Sharon from the interior. Water was plentiful; in fact, in ancient times marshes dotted the Plain. Flocks grazed in Sharon after the grain was cut. In David's state, Shitrai the Sharonite was in charge of the royal flocks that fed there (I Chron. 27:29). In spring a profusion of gay flowers carpeted the Plain of Sharon and made it a garden. In the Plain today there are extensive citrus groves and farm lands among the numerous Jewish settlements.

Among the Biblical cities in the Plain of Sharon were Joppa, Lydda, Dor, Caesarea, Antipatris, and Rakkon. Up and down its coastal road and over miles of its sandy beach moved caravans to and from Egypt, Arabia, Babylonia, Assyria, and all parts of the Middle East. Through Sharon successive currents of religious and cultural influences flowed into other parts of Palestine.

The Plain of Sharon was one of the most ancient homes of man in Palestine (see MUGHÂRAH, WÂDĪ EL-). E. L. Sukenik, of the Hebrew University in Jerusalem, discovered in 1934 near Khudheirah a cave burial place ascribed by W. F. Albright to the Ghassulian Age, i.e., the 1st half of the 4th millennium B.C. The cave contained ossuaries* shaped like little houses standing on piles (as if in marshland) with ridged roofs and doors.

Sharuhen (shȧ-rōō′hĕn), a strongly fortified town on the main N.–S. route between Palestine and Egypt. Amosis (c. 1570–1546 B.C.) besieged the city for three years when he drove the Hyksos out of Egypt (*ANET*³, p. 233). The Hyksos garrison is alluded to by Tuthmosis III (1504–1450 B.C.) in the introduction to his first military campaign into western Asia (*ANET*³, p. 235), suggesting that the site lay unoccupied after Amosis' victory. At the time of the Hebrew conquest, it was assigned to the tribe of Simeon (Josh. 19:6). In parallel lists it occurs as Shilhim (Josh. 15:32) and Shaaraim (I Chron. 4:31).

Sharuhen has been identified by W. F. Albright with Tell el-Far'ah (S) ("S" for South, to distinquish it from the other Tell el-Far 'ah (N), Biblical Tirzah, near Nablus), a mound 15 m. S. of Gaza on the Wâdī Ghazzeh (*BASOR* 33, 1929, p. 7). It was excavated by W. M. F. Petrie from 1928–30 as Beth-pelet (*Beth-pelet*, I, 1930; E. Macdonald, *et al.*, *Beth-pelet*, II, 1932). Petrie exposed a massive earthen rampart, an 80-ft.-wide ditch, and a three-buttress gateway of the late "Hyksos" period (17th cen. B.C.). An Egyptian "residency" (c. 1150 B.C.) and tombs with Philistine pottery and anthropoid clay coffins were also found. Persian, Hellenistic, and Roman remains covered the summit of the mound. W. P. A.

Shaul (shā′ŭl) ("asked for"). (1) An ancestor of a Simeonite clan, the Shaulites (Num. 26:13), who married a Canaanitess (Gen. 46:10; Ex. 6:15). (2) A king of Edom*, possibly an Aramaean, "from Rehoboth by the river" (I Chron. 1:48 f.). (3) A descendant of Levi (I Chron. 6:24, the "Joel" of v. 36).

Shaveh (shā′vĕ), **Valley of,** a broad, defenseless valley (King's Valley) where King of Sodom* met Abram as he returned from rescuing his nephew Lot (Gen. 14:17). It may be same King's Valley as one near Jerusalem where Absalom reared a memorial to himself (II Sam. 18:18).

Shaveh-kiriathaim (shā′vĕ-kĭr′yȧ-thā′ĭm), the scene of Chedorlaomer's rout of the Emim (Gen. 14:5).

shaving, cutting the hair close to the skin. Hebrew men wore beards*, which in nomadic periods were of necessity long and untrimmed. When village and town life developed, hair was trimmed (Ezek. 44:20) and beards carefully groomed. Shaving the body was part of the ceremony for cleansing an Israelite about to become a Levite* (Num. 8:7). Shaving was prescribed in the ritual for cleansing those afflicted with the plague (Lev. 13:33), or with leprosy (Lev. 14:8 f.). Nazirites*, who vowed to leave their hair uncut until their vow had been fulfilled (Num. 6:18; Acts 21:24), were expected to shave their heads in case they suddenly came into contact with the dead (Num. 6:9). When a female slave was about to be married she shaved her head to designate the termination of stigma (Deut. 21:12). Mourners shaved their heads and part of their beards (Deut. 14:1; Jer. 41:5), unless they were priests (Lev. 21:5; Ezek. 44:20).

Assyrians wore beards. Upper-class Egyptians cut their hair short, shaved their faces, and in public wore ceremonial wigs and sometimes artificial beards. Greeks and Romans were clean-shaven, and preferred to have even their slaves shaved.

See RAZOR.

Shavsha (shăv′shȧ), a scribe in David's organization (I Chron. 18:16) entrusted with state records; possibly the Seraiah of II Sam. 8:17 and the Shisha of I Kings 4:3. His Aram. name suggests that David employed linguists on his secretarial staff.

Sheal (shē′ăl), one of the priestly group of Ezra's time who offered to put away their foreign wives and make a trespass offering (Ezra 10:29).

Shealtiel (shė-ăl′tĭ-ĕl) ("I have asked of God"), a son of King Jeconiah (Jehoiachin*) and father of Zerubbabel, according to Ezra 3:2, 8, 5:2; Neh. 12:1; Hag. 1:1, 12, 14, 2:2, 23. I Chron. 3:19, however, makes Pedaiah, brother of Salathiel (R.S.V. Shealtiel) the father of Zerubbabel. In either case, he is the link in the chain of royal succession between Jeconiah and Zerubbabel. The A.V. of Matt. 1:12 and Luke 3:27 also lists this name as Salathiel.

Sheariah (shē′ȧ-rī′ȧ), a son of Azel, descendant of Jonathan, the son of Saul (I Chron. 8:38).

Shear-jashub (shē′är-jä′shŭb) ("a remnant shall return"), the symbolic name given by Isaiah to his elder son (Isa. 7:3, cf. 10:21 f.), to express the prophet's confidence in the ultimate return of at least a remnant of the Jews to Palestine from their Babylonian Exile.

Sheba (shē′bȧ). (1) A town named in A.V. Josh. 19:2 as included in Simeon's inheritance, along with Beer-sheba and Moladah. The A.S.V. suggests that Sheba was Beer-sheba (see SHIBAH). (2) A man of Belial, son of Bichri of the Tribe of Benjamin. He led a revolt against David after the quelling of Absalom's rebellion. He had hoped to seize N. Israel, but was pursued by Joab and his henchmen and was decapitated by a "wise woman" of the town of Abel-beth-maacah (II Sam. 20). (3) A man of the Tribe of Gad (I Chron. 5:13).

Sheba, the Queen of. See SABA.

Shebah. See SHIBAH.

Shebaniah (shĕb′ȧ-nī′ȧ) (possibly "Jehovah has brought me back"). (1) A Temple trumpeter (I Chron. 15:24). (2) A Jerusalem Levite who in Ezra's time joined in exclamations exalting God (Neh. 9:4). (3) A priest who sealed the covenant between Israel and God at Jerusalem after the Exile (Neh. 10:4, 12:14; the Shecaniah of 12:3). (4) Another Levite, possibly Shechaniah (Neh. 10:10).

Shebat. See SEBAT.

Shebna (shĕb′nȧ) (Shebnah), a scribe or secretary at the court of King Hezekiah of Judah (c. 715–687 B.C.) (II Kings 18:18, 26, 37, 19:2). Isaiah refers to him as treasurer "over the house," rebukes him, and foretells his captivity (Isa. 22:15–17).

Shebuel (shė-bū′ĕl), the founder of a family of Gershonite Levites (I Chron. 23:16, 26:24; Shubael, 24:20, 25:20). In I Chron. 26:24–27 Shebuel is in charge of treasures in the "house of the Lord" (the Tabernacle). (2) One of the fourteen sons of the musical family of Heman, in David's organization of worship (I Chron. 25:4).

Shecaniah (shĕk′ȧ-nī′ȧ) ("Jehovah hath taken up His abode"). (1) A man descended from David (I Chron. 3:21; cf. Ezra 8:3). His descendants returned from Exile with Ezra (Ezra 8:5). (2) The chief of the 10th course of priests in the Davidic religious organization of Israel (I Chron. 24:11). (3) A priest in Hezekiah's time (II Chron. 31:15). (4) A Hebrew who, during Ezra's abolition of marriage* with foreigners, confessed his sin (Ezra 10:2). (5) A keeper of the Jerusalem East Gate, who helped repair the wall under Nehemiah* (Neh. 3:29); he may be the same as (1). (6) A son of Arah and the father-in-law of Tobiah the Ammonite (Neh. 6:18). (7) The eponymous head of a family of priests or Levites who returned to Palestine from Babylon with Zerubbabel (Neh. 12:3).

Shechem (shē′kĕm). (1) "The son of Hamor the Hivite" from whose Canaanite clan Jacob bought a parcel of land (Gen. 33:18 f.; cf. Acts 7:16) and with whom he entered into alliance (Gen. 34). In the latter story the Hebrews in the patriarchal period and the people of Shechem are symbolized by individuals. At Shechem the Hebrews first came into contact with the Canaanites and entered into amicable relations with the ruling Hivites (Horites?), closely related to the Hurrians. Later Abimelech made an alliance with "the men of Hamor" at Shechem (Judg. 9). (2) The traditional ancestor of Manassites in an old tribal list (Num. 26:31; cf. Josh. 17:2), showing that "Shechemites" were eventually incorporated into the territory of Manasseh. (3) Shemidah's son (I Chron. 7:19).

(4) A city in the hill country of Ephraim near the S. border of Manasseh. Its ruins still stand beside the modern village of Balâṭah 41 m. N. of Jerusalem, at the E. end of the pass between Mts. Ebal* and Gerizim.* Strategically situated at the junction of the main commercial highways, it overlooked "the plain of Shechem" which extends a considerable distance to the N., S. and E. It was near Jacob's well at Sychar*, which is called "Shechem" in the old Syriac Gospels.

During most of the 2d millennium B.C., Shechem was one of the chief cities of Canaan, for Mt. Gerizim, overlooking it, was called "the navel of the land" (Judg. 9:37, ASV marg.). Egyptian texts from the 19th cent. B.C. suggest that the city had great influence in the area and may have been the center of opposition to Egyptian control. During the Amarna period (c. first half of the 14th century) it was ruled by Lab'ayu and his sons, who controlled the whole area from Megiddo on the north to Bethel and Gezer on the south.

Shechem was the first place visited by Abraham (Gen. 12:6), although it was associated primarily with the northern tribal heroes, Jacob and Joseph (Gen. 33:18–20, 35:1–4, 37:12–14, 48:22; Josh. 24:32). At this place, where the Hebrews first came into contact with Canaanite culture (see above on Gen. 34), Joshua united the tribes in the Israelite Covenant Confederacy (Josh. 24), an organization which persisted until the foundation of the monarchy in Samuel's time. The fact that there is no known account of Israel's seizure of Shechem at the Conquest has led many scholars to believe that the city was already under the control of people friendly to the Israelites, perhaps since the Amarna period. Shechem was the scene of Abimelech's abortive attempt to found a kingdom, modeled on Canaanite standards which violated the ideals of the Covenant Confederacy (Judg. 9). Here Rehoboam came to be crowned by the northern tribes (I Kings 12), only to stir up the revolutionary feelings of tribes who longed for the days of freedom under the Confederacy. Jeroboam I established his first royal residence at Shechem, and it remained under Israel's control until the fall of the northern kingdom to Assyria (722–21 B.C.). Although Deuteronomic literature contains echoes of the religious importance of Shechem (Deut. 11:26–32, 27:1–26; Josh. 8:30–37), the city fell into obscurity after the time of Jeroboam I. In the post-exilic period it regained much of its ancient prestige when, in the middle of the 4th cent. B.C., the Samaritans built their Temple on Gerizim.

Excavations were first made at the site by Germans, including Ernst Sellin, between 1913 and 1934, and lately have been resumed by the Drew-McCormick Expedition under the direction of G. Ernest Wright. The significance of the earlier excavation was largely eclipsed by failure to establish accurate chronology on the basis of pottery analysis and stratigraphy. Sellin unearthed the NW. city gate, which had three entryways and was bonded into a cyclopean wall, so called because of its huge stones. This massive fortification was erected c. 1650 B.C. and was one of the strongest defense systems of the period. Also a fortress-temple, probably the one referred to in Judg. 9:4 and similar in structure to a contemporary building at Megiddo, was erected about the same time. C. 68 ft. long, 84 wide, and with walls 17 ft. thick, it is the largest temple known in Palestine from the pre-Roman period. On each side of the door and by the altar in the court were installations for sacred standing stones (*massebot.*)

The East Gate, partially explored by the Germans, was investigated during the first two Drew-McCormick campaigns (1956–57). Four pairs of huge basalt blocks (7x5x5½) form its two entryways. Adjacent to the gate, in an untouched area, the remains of one of the southern towers were uncovered. Pottery and other evidence indicated that the East Gate and towers, with accompanying city wall, were erected c. 1600 B.C. to double the strength of the earlier wall, during an age when foreigners in Egypt—aided by the new military weapon of the horse-drawn chariot—made Shechem one of their major cities, encircling it with a great earthen mound covered over with plaster (*terre pisée*). Excavation further suggested that the tower, later destroyed, had been rebuilt probably by Jeroboam I (I Kings 12:25). Another layer of charcoal-filled earth indicated another destruction by the Assyrians c. 724–23 B.C. Pottery and coins nearer the surface indicated that the gate was in use during the Hellenistic period, at which time the city was the Samaritan capital and rival of Jerusalem, until John Hyrcanus destroyed it, probably in his conquest of Samaria in 107 B.C. From that day to this the site has been unoccupied except by a small village around the copious spring. (For excavation reports see *BA*, vols. XX, XXIII; *BASOR*, nos. 144, 148, 161.) B.W.A.

Shedeur (shĕd′ē-ẽr) ("Shaddai is light"), a Reubenite chief (Num. 1:5, 2:10, 7:30, 10:18), commander of the tribal army.

sheep in earliest Biblical times were important members of the quartette of domestic animals: the *Bovidae* (including both sheep and goats [see GOAT]); the ass-donkey group; the cattle (also of the *Bovidae*); and the camel (see CAMELS). The sheep was domesticated much earlier than the camel. An Asiatic *moufflon* is seen on a Sumerian vase of c. 3000

377. Sheep and shepherd.

B.C. Poor indeed was the Palestine family which did not own at least one lamb or sheep (see II Sam. 12); and "very rich" in sheep were Patriarchs like Abraham (Gen. 13:2).

Three *types of sheep* found in Palestine are: (1) the short-tailed, horned (both rams and ewes), and short-wool sheep. (2) The curling-horned, broad-tailed sheep whose tail (cf. Ex. 29:32) valued for food fats, often weighs as much as 15 lbs. Its deep wool is usually cream or white, sometimes parti-colored black and white (see Gen. 30:33, 35). The broad-tailed sheep may have come into Palestine from Kurdistan, at the head of the Tigris-Euphrates Valley. (3) The Egyptian-bred, long-legged, short-fleeced sheep of Asia.

Ownership of sheep was by the head of the family or clan, who often numbered his animals in tremendous figures. After the settlement in Palestine, it was customary to buy two lambs at each Passover season, one being killed and eaten at the celebration of the Exodus* anniversary and the other kept for later uses. The pet lamb slept with the children or father, and ate tender grasses from their hands and from their cups (II Sam. 12:4). Sometimes community shepherds were hired to care for the animals of several families, grazing them by day and letting them run home at night.

In O.T. times sheep which wandered into a neighbor's land might be legally claimed if they remained there over a period of time specified in the Law Code (Deut. 22:1). Bedouin raiders still prey on sheep, as Midianites and Amalekites did on ancient Israel's flocks.

The *traits of sheep*, as depicted in the Bible, are affection for the shepherd, whose voice they know (John 10:2–5)—a characteristic lacking in camels; meekness, submission (Isa. 53:7); helplessness (Jer. 11:19; Mic. 5:8) in the presence of enemies, e.g., lions, (Mic. 5:8), wolves (Matt. 10:16; John 10:12), snakes, jackals, and bears. They are apt to fall into pits (Matt. 12:11); and to suffer under faithless or careless shepherds (Ezek. 34:5–8; Matt. 9:36; Mark 6:34), and unscrupulous hirelings (John 10:13).

Terrain especially favorable for sheep raising were the Judaean highlands and the S. country (Negeb); Moab; the region near Haran; Anatolia; the hills of Syria; Midian; Trans-Jordan; and inland Arabia.

Uses of the sheep are manifold: (1) for food—its meat, its milk and the great amount of fat in its tail; (2) for clothing, both in the whole skin, worn as a cloak by shepherds and wanderers (Heb. 11:37), and in cut wool, which after being cleaned and spun on hand spindles, was woven (see WEAVING) into garments for the entire family (Prov. 31:13, 19, 21; Ezek. 34:3); (3) for oil and unguent flasks made from horns (I Sam. 16:1), and for the sacred shophar* or horn used to call Israel to worship (Josh. 6:4); (4) for tent covering (Ex. 26:14); (5) for offerings sacrificed to God (Ex. 12:3–10; Mic. 6:6–8) (see WORSHIP).

Sheepshearing (Gen. 38:12, 31:19; I Sam. 25:2; II Sam. 13:24 f.) was done in shearing-houses (II Kings 10:12, 14) after the spring lambing season (Isa. 53:7; Acts 8:32). The firstlings of flocks were sacred to God and were not to be sheared (Deut. 15:19). Sheep-shearing time was a festive occasion, when friends were invited to engage in the offering of new wool (Deut. 18:4) and to share a communal meal. Part of the joy was due to the revenue which came at shearing time to the owners of the flocks. There may be a connection between the spring Passover* Feast and the ancient lambing festivals.

Valuable flocks were often protected by good-hearted freebooters, like David's men at Carmel, when Nabal's sheep were being sheared (I Sam. 25:2 ff.). There was profit for such volunteers.

See ROD, SHEPHERD.

Sheep Gate, the, was situated in the N. course of the Jerusalem city walls near the tower of Hammeah (Neh. 12:39). Through it animals were driven to the Temple area for sacrifice. It was near the now excavated Pool of Bethesda, formerly used to bathe the sheep, and in Jesus' day an arcaded place of healing to which invalids were carried to wait for the intermittent "troubling of the waters" (John 5:2–4).

Shehariah (shē′hȧ-rī′ȧ), a Benjamite (I Chron. 8:26).

shekel (shĕk′ĕl), originally an ancient Babylonian unit of weight equal to c. ½ ounce or 1/50 or 1/60 of a mina; later a coin of this weight, the chief Hebrew silver coin. See MONEY; WEIGHTS AND MEASURES.

Shekinah (shė-kī′nȧ) (from Heb. root *shkn*) ("to dwell," whence "that which abides"), a word not found in the Bible, but one employed in late Jewish times to denote God's dwelling among His people, like the thick cloud enclosing a devouring flame on Mt. Sinai (Ex. 24:16–18). The Shekinah was thought of as a cloud which rested above the Tabernacle* by day, and the fire which supplanted that cloud by night (Ex. 40:34 f.). When the cloud went up from over the Tabernacle it was a sign that Israel should go onward in their Wilderness wanderings (vv. 36 f.). Behind the Shekinah was the idea of the divine transcendence; God was too holy to be within human touch. Philo, the Jewish philosopher (c. 20 B.C.–A.D. 50), emphasized the eternal, abstract, unchangeable nature of God which was at the basis of the Shekinah concept. Though the word is not in the N.T., "glory"* conveys a similar thought (Rom. 6:4; Heb. 1:3, 9:5; Jas. 2:1; I Pet. 4:14; see especially II Cor. 4:6, "the light of the knowledge of the glory of God in the face of Jesus Christ").

Shelah (shē′lȧ). (1) The youngest son of Judah, by Shuah* (Gen. 38:5, 14, 26; I Chron. 2:3, 4:21). The family of Shelanites (Num. 26:20), possibly the same as "Shiloni" (Neh. 11:5), were descendants of Shelah. (2) A son of Arphaxad (I Chron. 1:18, 24; A.S.V. Gen. 10:24; Luke 3:35). (3) The name given in A.S.V. Neh. 3:15 to the pool by the king's garden (A.V. Siloah).

Shelemiah (shĕl′ē-mī′ȧ). (1) One drawn by lot to be a Tabernacle doorkeeper (I Chron. 26:14); possibly the same as Meshelemiah, eponymous ancestor of a family of Korahite doorkeepers (I Chron. 9:21, 26:1). (2) and (3) Sons of Bani who had taken foreign wives in Ezra's time (Ezra 10:39, 41). (4) The father of Hananiah who repaired part of the Jerusalem wall (Neh. 3:30). (5) A priest who was appointed treasurer by Nehemiah (Neh. 13:13). (6) The father of Netheniah (Jer. 36:14). (7) A son of Abdeel, ordered by Jehoiakim to take Jeremiah and his secretary Baruch into custody (Jer. 36:26). (8) The father of Jehucal, sent by King Hezekiah to ask Jeremiah to pray to the Lord on behalf of Judah (Jer. 37:3). (9) The father of Irijah (Jer. 37:13).

Sheleph (shē′lĕf), a descendant of Joktan, and therefore a member of an unidentified S. Arabian tribe (Gen. 10:26; I Chron. 1:20).

Shelesh (shē′lĕsh), a member of Asher's tribe (I Chron. 7:35).

Shelomi (shē-lō′mī), the father of an Asherite chieftain (Num. 34:27).

Shelomith (shē-lō′mĭth) ("peacefulness"). (1) The Danite mother of a blasphemous Israelite (Lev. 24:11). (2) A Levite, son of Shimei (I Chron. 23:9). (3) A Gershonite Levite (I Chron. 23:18), Shelomoth (24:22). (4) A descendant of Eliezer, son of Moses, placed in custody of the dedicated treasures in David's bureaucracy (I Chron. 26:25). (5) A son of King Rehoboam* of Judah (c. 922–915 B.C.), by his favorite, Maachah (II Chron. 11:20). (6) An ancestor of a family who returned from Exile (Ezra 8:10). (7) A daughter of Zerubbabel, a leader of Jews who returned to Jerusalem after the Exile (I Chron. 3:19), and sister of Meshullam and Hananiah.

Shelumiel (shē-lū′mĭ-ĕl) ("God is counselor"), a son of Zurishaddai; a chieftain of the Tribe of Simeon (Num. 1:6, 2:12).

Shem (shĕm) ("renown"), the eldest son of Noah, brother of Ham and Japheth (Gen. 5:32, 10:1). His loyalty to his father in the latter's sin after the Flood* (Gen. 9:21–27) was rewarded by the promise that the worship of the true God would continue among his descendants: "God shall . . . dwell in the tents of Shem" (Gen. 9:27). Shem is called the "ancestor" of the Hebrews, Aramaeans, and Arabs; "Semites" ("Shemites") has been applied since the middle of the 18th century to peoples who speak the Semitic languages, and "Semitic" has also been used in a racial as well as in a philological sense. (See SEMITES.) Sometimes, however, the inclusion of people as descendants of Shem (like the Elamites) was on a geographical or political rather than a linguistic or racial basis.

Shema (shē mȧ) ("hearing, report"). (1) A town in the Negeb, site unknown; possibly the same as "son" of Hebron (I Chron. 2:43). (2) A man of the Tribe of Reuben (I Chron. 5:8). (3) A man who helped rout the people of Gath* (I Chron. 8:13). (4) One of the colleagues of Ezra (Neh. 8:4). (5) A town of Judah (Josh. 15:26).

Shema (shĕ-mä′) ("Hear thou!"), the watchword of Jewish monotheism, a confession of faith based on three O.T. passages, introduced by Deut. 6:4 ("Hear, O Israel, the Lord our God is one Lord"). The three sections are: Deut. 6:4–9, 11:13–21; Num. 15:37–41 (cf. Matt. 19:16 ff.). It is an ancient Jewish custom that the Shema is recited by the dying or by those gathered at their side. Jewish liturgy prescribes the reading of the Shema twice daily, at the morning prayer (*Shaharith*) and at the evening prayer (*'Arbith*). The Shema opens with the *barechu* ("Praise ye"), an ancient invitation to worship. The essential sections of the Jewish liturgy are the Shema and the Amidah Prayer (see PEACE, 5).

Shemaah (shē-mā′ȧ), a man of Gibeah, father of two of David's chief bowmen, Ahiezer and Joash (I Chron. 12:3).

Shemaiah (shē-mā′yȧ) ("Jehovah has heard"). (1) The father of Hattush (I Chron. 3:22). (2) The head of a Reubenite family (I Chron. 5:4). (3) A Levite in David's regime (I Chron. 24:6). (4) A Levite (I Chron. 9:14). (5) A Levite (I Chron. 9:16). (6) A Kohathite chief in David's day (I Chron. 15:8, 11). (7) A son of Nethaneel, who recorded the assignment of priests (I Chron. 24:6). (8) The eldest son of Obededom (I Chron. 26:4, 6, f.). (9) A prophet who advised Rehoboam not to fight Israel (I Kings 12:22, II Chron. 11:2), and led the people to repent when Shishak* of Egypt invaded Judah (II Chron. 12:5–7). (10) A Levite in Jehoshaphat's time (c. 873–849 B.C.) (II Chron. 17:8). (11) A son of Jeduthun who helped in the Temple cleansing under Hezekiah (c. 715–687 B.C.). (12) The father of the prophet Urijah (Jer. 26:20). (13) A false prophet (Jer. 29:24–32). (14) The father of Delaiah, a man of Jerusalem in the time of Baruch and Jeremiah (Jer. 36:12). (15), (16) Levites (II Chron. 31:15, 35:9). (17), (18), (19). Men of Ezra's day (Ezra 8:13, 16, 10:31). (20) A priest who had married a foreign wife (Ezra 10:21). (21)–(26) Men who played various roles in Nehemiah's rebuilding and dedication of the Jerusalem wall (Neh. 3:29, 6:10 ff., 10:8, 12:6, 18, 34, 35, 36, 42).

Shemariah (shĕm′ȧ-rī′ȧ) ("Jehovah has kept") Shamariah, II Chron. 11:19. (1) A Benjamite bowman who joined David at Ziklag (I Chron. 12:5). (2) A son of Rehoboam, son of Solomon (II Chron. 11:19). (3), (4) Two Jews who were persuaded by Ezra to put away foreign wives (Ezra 10:32, 41).

Shemeber (shĕm-ē′bẽr), King of Zeboiim, who with the confederated kings of the cities of the Dead Sea Plain was defeated by Chedorlaomer (Gen. 14:2, 8–10).

Shemer (shē′mẽr) (Shamer in Chronicles) ("watcher"). (1) The founder of a clan in the tribe of Asher (I Chron. 7:34, Shomer 7:32). (2) The owner of the hill purchased by King Omri of Israel (c. 876–869 B.C.) for his capital, Samaria* (I Kings 16:24).

Shemida (shē-mī′dȧ) (Shemidah I Chron. 7:19), a Gileadite, founder of the family of Shemidaites (Num. 26:32; Josh. 17:2).

Sheminith (shĕm′ĭ-nĭth), a musical term, used in connection with harps in I Chron. 15:21, and referring perhaps to eight strings, rather than octaves or eighths—as some have believed. The word also occurs in the titles of Ps. 6 and 12.

Shemiramoth (shĕ-mĭr′ȧ-mŏth). (1) A Levite musician in David's organization (I Chron. 15:18, 20, 16:5). (2) A Levite teacher in the time of King Jehoshaphat of Judah (c. 873–849 B.C.) (II Chron. 17:8).

Shemuel (shē-mū′ĕl) ("name of God"). (1) A Simeonite chieftain, son of Ammihud, who received an inheritance in Canaan (Num. 34:20). (2) The traditional founder of a clan of Issachar's Tribe (I Chron. 7:2). (3) An ancestor of a singer in David's organization, probably Samuel* (I Chron. 6:33).

Shen (shĕn), an unidentified site adjacent to the place where Samuel erected the stone "Ebenezer"* (I Sam. 7:12).

Shenazar (shĕ-năz′är), a descendant of Jeconiah (Jehoiachin), King of Judah for three months in 598 B.C. (I Chron. 3:18).

Sheol (shē′ōl), the Hebrew counterpart of the Greek and Roman gloomy underworld of departed spirits, Hades*, Tartarus. See HELL; GEHENNA.

Shepham (shē′făm), an unidentified site on the border of Canaan (Num. 34:10 f.).

Shephatiah (shĕf′*ȧ*-tī′*ȧ*). (1) The 5th son of David, by Abital, at Hebron (II Sam. 3:4; I Chron. 3:3). (2) A Haruhite who came to the ranks of David at Ziklag when he was at odds with Saul (I Chron. 12:5). (3) A son of Maachah who became ruler over Simeon's Tribe in David's reign (I Chron. 27:16). (4) One of the sons of King Jehoshaphat of Judah (c. 873–849 B.C.). He received treasures of gold and silver and fenced towns, but the crown went to his eldest brother, Jehoram* (II Chron. 21:2 f.). (5) The father of Meshullam, a Benjamite of Jerusalem (I Chron. 9:8). (6) One of the group at Jerusalem who urged the king to kill Jeremiah the prophet, because his pronouncement of impending doom at the hands of the Babylonian army was damaging the morale of defenders of the city (Jer. 38:1). (7) A man of the family of Perez living in Judah, apparently before the Exile (Neh. 11:4). (8) The founder of a large family group which returned from Babylonian exile with Zerubbabel (Ezra 2:4; Neh. 7:9). (9) A man whose descendants returned from Babylon with Zerubbabel (Ezra 2:57; Neh. 7:59).

Shephelah (shĕ-fē′l*ȧ*), **the** ("lowland"), the low hills E. of the Maritime or Coastal Plain of Palestine*, separated from the highlands of Judaea and Ephraim by the Valleys of Ajalon, Sorek, Eleh, Zephathath, and, farther S., the valleys guarded by Gath, Lachish, Eglon, and Debir. Shephelah valleys produced grain, and olives and grapes grew on the higher reaches. The Shephelah contained the strategic defense towns of Lachish*, Debir*, Libnah, and Beth-shemesh*, which controlled the approach to Judaea. The word "Shephelah" appears in I Macc. 12:38 and 10 times in the R.S.V., but is not mentioned by name in the A.V.

Shepher (shē′fẽr), a camp site of Israel en route to Canaan (Num. 33:23 f.).

shepherd, the, preceded the farmer and sooner or later came into conflict with him, for grazing and crop raising cannot go on side by side. The first murder recorded in Scripture (Gen. 4:1–8) was provoked by rivalry between Abel, who brought the firstlings of the flock to the Lord, and Cain, his brother, who brought of the fruit of the ground. Comity was often worked out by letting sheep graze after the crops were cut, as below Bethlehem in the Shepherds' Field today, or near Madeba and 'Ammân in the Kingdom of Jordan.

Ps. 23 reveals shepherd ways. "The Lord is my shepherd; I shall not want" expresses man's gratitude for God's mercies. The Psalmist, whatever his identity, certainly knew "the green pastures," such as exist below the terraced farms of Bethlehem. He knew how to walk at the head of the flock, leading them—not following them, as Western shepherds do. He knew the "still waters" of wells, pools, quiet rivulets, or sheltered sand

378. Shepherd, wearing heavy, hand-woven cloak (*abayeh*), veil, and side locks; he carries rod and water bottle.

bars, such as are still used by shepherds where the Dog River enters the Mediterranean.

The "paths of righteousness" were age-old sheep-walks. "The valley of the shadow," which called for extra shepherding, was the deep rock-cleft wâdī where serpents lurked. The sheep* felt the touch of the shepherd's hooked staff, lifting them over perilous stones. The familiar stout, short rod "rodded" them into the stone-walled fold at nightfall. The shepherd was able to "prepare tables" in safe grassy spots, in the presence of the sheep's hereditary enemies—venomous snakes, which bit the faces of unsuspecting ones. Hence the necessity of having their injured heads "anointed with oil" or butter.

An example of the "cup" which ran over is the Well of the Star (illus. 487) on the N. outskirts of Bethlehem. It is a stone trough—a round section of Pilate's stone conduit, in this instance—placed beside the well from which the shepherd dipped water to fill the "cup." The "dwelling in the house of the Lord" reflects the return to the village after the summer grazing period, when families prepare to go up to the House of God, in mended garments and new-made shoes, to thank Him for His "goodness and loving kindness" and to entreat Him to let these blessings follow the family forever.

Shepherds of Bible times were of two *types:* (1) nomads (from Gk. word meaning "to graze"), who, after exhausting pasturage in one area, or finding insufficient water, led their flocks to better ground, and (2) shepherds who lived in villages, like the well-known shepherds' village Beit Sahur, below Bethlehem (Luke 2:8–20). In the highlands of the Kingdom of Jordan today are walled hilltop villages, where owners of herds and flocks live in winter, while their underlings lead the animals to warmer grazing grounds on lower terrain. The Hebrew Patriarchs were nomads who, with many helpers, led flocks and families on journeys as far as from Ur around the Fertile* Crescent into Canaan, or down to Egypt and back to Palestine. The people could advance only as fast as their flocks could walk.

Shepherds' apparel in earliest times was a roughly tanned whole skin with the wool left on (cf. Matt. 7:15). Later shepherds wore an under tunic and an outer mantle or cloak, often seamless, measuring about 4x4 ft. This garment, called an *abayeh* or *aba*, shielded them from sun, rain, and snow, or, pulled over the head tent-wise, made a night shelter. It was usually woven with broad gray and black stripes by the shepherd's wife or daughters, and might serve a lifetime. The shepherd wore a fabric girdle in whose folds was a pocket in which he carried money, and pebbles tossed to attract the sheep's attention. His veil or *kheffiyeh* was a yard-square piece of material folded into a triangle and kept in place by a black *agal* or ring of twisted goat's hair. Shepherds wore beards and long hair, as a matter of convenience. The shepherd carried a bag, or scrip, with food for several days—cheese, olives, dried raisins, and bread. His rod* was a stout club c. 3 ft. long, sometimes studded with metal to beat off enemies of his sheep. Under his rod he caused his sheep to pass one by one, for counting. His staff was a longer stick, used for guiding. His dog rounded up stragglers, for the shepherd himself walked ahead of the sheep, leading them (John 10:27). While resting, he fashioned or played reed pipes, which—with the ram's horn—were Israel's earliest musical instruments. The unkempt shepherd brothers of Joseph were looked down on by the clean Egyptians at Pharaoh's court (Gen. 43:32). When they and their flocks multiplied they became "an abomination" (Gen. 46:34) in the Delta, whose farmers knew that grazing and agriculture were incompatible. Yet Pharaoh had not excluded them, because he sensed that some of these Hebrews might be "men of activity" (Gen. 47:6), who could be useful in managing his cattle. See SHEEP, illus. 377.

Shepherds' shelter was in caves; as below Bethlehem, or at 'Ain Fashka, where the Dead Sea Scrolls* were found, or the Cave of Pan at Banias (Caesarea Philippi); or in light, portable tents (Song of Sol. 1:8; Isa. 38:12); or in huts ("cottages," Zeph. 2:6, which possibly should read "caves"). Sometimes the shepherd slept in the open field, placing his own body across the door of the stone-enclosed sheepfold; in a group of shepherds each took his turn at the watch. Shepherd groups consisted of wise old sheikhs, mature men, and young boys like David. In Patriarchal times shepherdesses sometimes looked after their father's flocks near home, as Rachel did (Gen. 29:9).

Characteristics of the good shepherd included faithfulness, even to a willingness to lay down his life for the sheep (John 10:11); tenderness, which prompted him to carry the lambs in his arms and to lead gently those that were with young (Isa. 40:11); binding up the broken, strengthening the sick (Ezek. 34:16); diligence, which sought out, in dark and cloudy weather, sheep grazing on too high places, and brought them to folds and good watering-places (Ezek. 34:11–16); and wisdom which made people turn to him for advice (Ezek. 34:17). The integrity of the shepherd is reflected in Ps. 78:70–72.

References to shepherds abound in sacred writings. Truths Moses learned as a shepherd in Midian can be found in much that he taught Israel (Ex. 22:1, 30; Num. 27:15–17; Deut. 7:13, 15:19, 28:4, 18, 31, 51, etc.). The Psalms use shepherd customs to reveal spiritual truths, as in Ps. 23. Prophets reminded kings that they were shepherds (pastors) of their subjects (Jer. 23:4 f., 25:34 ff.; Ezek. 34:2, 5, 8 ff.; Zech. 10:2 f., 11:3, 5, 8, 15 f.). Jesus not only used familiar details of shepherd life to impart his eternal truths in parables but spoke of himself as "the good shepherd" (Matt. 25:32 f.; Luke 15:4; John 10:2 ff.). He was the Lamb of God (John 1:29; Rev. 13:8), and to his early Disciples a "shepherd" (Heb. 13:20; I Pet. 2:25, 5:4).

Outstanding Pastoral Passages in Scripture

The Shepherd Psalm	Ps. 23
Shepherd of Israel	Ps. 80:1–5
"He shall feed his flock"	Isa. 40:11
"as a lamb to the slaughter"	Isa. 53:7; cf. Acts 8:32; Rom. 8:36; Rev. 13:8
God's care of His flock Israel	Ezek. 34:7–31
"one shepherd"	Ezek. 37:24
The Shepherds' Christmas	Luke 2:8–20
Christ's Parables:	
The Good Shepherd	John 10:2–18, 25-29
The Lost Sheep	Matt. 18:11–14; Luke 15:4–7
The Sheep and the Goats	Matt. 25:31–46
Jesus, the "great shepherd"	Heb. 13:20; I Pet. 2:25, 5:4
Jesus, "Lamb of God"	John 1:29, 36; Rev. 7:17

Christian ministers are called "pastors" because they look after the "sheep" of their flocks (I Pet. 2:25).

For sheep and shepherds in Christian iconography, see SYMBOL.

Shephi (shē'fī) (Shepho Gen. 36:23), a man or tribe of Shobal*, descended from a Horite of Seir (I Chron. 1:40).

Sherah (shē'rȧ) (A.V.; R.S.V. Sheerah [shē'ē-rȧ]), an Ephraimitic group, credited with establishing the Beth-horons and the unidentified Uzzen-sheereh (I Chron. 7:24).

Sherebiah (shĕr'ē-bī'ȧ), a Levite prominent in Ezra's time (Ezra 8:18, 24; Neh. 8:7, 9:4 f., 10:12, 12:8, 24).

Sheshach (shē'shăk), a cryptic name for Babylon* (Jer. 25:26, 51:41).

Sheshai (shē'shī), a son or family of Anak, driven from Hebron by Caleb (Josh. 15:14).

Sheshan (shē'shăn), a man of the Tribe of Judah, who gave his daughter in marriage to his Egyptian servant (I Chron. 2:31, 34 f.).

Sheshbazzar (shĕsh-băz'ēr), possibly a cryptogram for Zerubbabel. To this prince of Judah Cyrus entrusted the sacred vessels of the Jerusalem Temple which Nebuchadnezzar had carried to Babylon. After bringing the treasures back, Sheshbazzar was made governor and began rebuilding the Temple (Ezra 1:8, 11, 5:14, 16).

Sheth (shĕth) ("sons of tumult"), an epithet applied to the warlike Moabites (Num. (24:17). Also a form of Seth*, third son of Adam (I Chron. 1:1).

Sheva (shē'vȧ). (1) A man or a clan descended from Caleb*, living at Machbenah and Gibea (I Chron. 2:49). (2) A scribe in David's organization (II Sam. 20:25).

shewbread, the term used in the A.V. for the 12 loaves of consecrated unleavened bread placed on a table in the Holy Place of the Tabernacle* and Temple* (Ex. 25:30; Lev. 24:5–9). See WORSHIP.

Shibah (shī'bȧ) (A.V. Sheban, "seven," "an oath"), the well dug by Isaac's servants, so named because of the oath he had made with Abimelech (Gen. 26:26–33). The name of Beer-sheba* came from this well.

shibboleth (shĭb'bŏ-lĕth) ("stream in flood"), the word used by Jephthah* to test whether fugitives were Ephraimites or his own Gileadites (Judg. 12:4–6). Ephraimites could not pronounce "sh," and said "s" instead. In modern usage "shibboleth" means the test or catchword of a party, sect, or class.

shield. See SPEAR.

Shiggaion (shĭ-gā'yŏn) (pl. Shigionoth, Hab. 3:1), an obscure word used in the title of Ps. 7, whose meaning is not definitely known.

Shihor (shī'hôr), a branch of the Nile, possibly the Pelusiac, near the E. border of Egypt; or the Wâdī el-Arish, called "the Brook [or River] of Egypt," the boundary between Palestine and Egypt (I Chron. 13:5).

Shihor-libnath (shī'hôr-lĭb'năth), a boundary of Asher, location unknown, but apparently near Mt. Carmel*. It may have been a stream, the Zerqa ("Crocodile River"), 6 m. S. of Dor, and just N. of Caesarea (Josh. 19:26).

Shiloah (shī-lō'ȧ). See SILOAM.

Shiloh (shī'lō) (possibly "tranquillity"), an important sanctuary town established by Israel in the hill country of Ephraim between Bethel and Lebonah, E. of the main road from Shechem to Jerusalem (Judg. 21:19). It has been identified with Khirbet Seilun, 9 m. N. of Bethel. To this place Joshua brought the Tribes of Israel at the close of the main phase of their Conquest. At the entrance to the tent of meeting, in the presence of Yahweh, he cast lots for the "assignment" of territory to the Tribes of Israel (Josh. 18:1 ff.). The new town flourished throughout the period of the Judges, and became Israel's headquarters (Josh. 21:2, 22:9, 12). At a vintage festival in Shiloh remnants of the Benjamites hid in the vineyards and captured for marriage Shiloh girls who were dancing among the vines (Judg. 21:15–24). Shiloh's Tabernacle became the resting place of the Ark*, and was administered by resident priests, like Eli and his sons, Hophni and Phinehas (I Sam. 2:12–17). Here Samuel was established as a prophet (I Sam. 3:20).

During the Philistine war Israel took the Ark from Shiloh to their camp at Ebenezer. The Philistines captured the Ark (c. 1050 B.C.) and killed Eli's two sons who were guarding it (I Sam. 4). Their priestly descendants evidently moved to Nob (I Sam. 14:3, 22:11). When the Philistines returned the Ark to Israel it was not placed again in Shiloh (I Sam. 6:21–7:2).

379. Shiloh, looking south.

Excavations of Khirbet Seilun by H. Kjaer in 1926, 1929, and 1932 indicated that following a limited settlement in Middle Bronze II (18th–17th cen. B.C.), the site was next occupied toward the beginning of Iron I (late 13th–early 12th cen. B.C.). No trace of Late Bronze Age settlement was reported, and following the destruction of the Iron I town in the 11th century B.C., no trace of further occupation was identified until Roman times (see H. Kjaer, *PEFQS*, 1927, pp. 202–213; *JPOS* 10, 1930, pp. 87–174; *PEFQS*, 1931, pp. 71–88). Combining the archaeological and Biblical evidence, Albright and others concluded: (1) that Seilun/Shiloh was settled by the Israelites at the time of the Conquest (13th cen. B.C.); (2) that there was no longer any doubt that "Shiloh was destroyed by the Philistines about 1050 B.C. . . ." (*BASOR* 35, 1929, p. 4); and (3) that the absence of Iron II forms confirmed that the site was not rebuilt for centuries (cf. Jer. 7:12, 14, 26:6, 9; Ps. 78:60). Albright then asserted that Samuel was the founder of the prophetic movement in Israel, replacing the central sanctuary at Shiloh with "places" at Bethel, Gilgal, and Mizpah (most recently, *Yahweh and the Gods of Canaan*, 1968, pp. 209 ff.).

This interpretation, however, fails to consider the fact that other Biblical references indicate that Shiloh was occupied—and may even have had a shrine (at least a prophetic clan)—during the time of Jeroboam I (c. 922–901 B.C.) (I Kings 11:29, 12:15, 14:2 ff.). It also appears to have been inhabited as late as the time of Jeremiah (Jer. 41:5).

The Danish excavations have recently been restudied, along with the results of a new campaign in 1963 (M-L. Buhl and S. Holm-Neilsen, *Shiloh: The Danish Excavations at Tall Sailūn, Palestine*, 1969). The authors have reached entirely new conclusions (see esp. chaps. VI–VII): (1) extensive MB II occupation; (2) minor occupation during LB II; (3) little or no Iron I; (4) but "richly represented" Iron II (9th–6th cen. B.C.) remains (i.e., they redated the previous Iron I material to Iron II). They have thus discounted Albright's thesis. It should be noted, however, that some of the parallels drawn in the final publication are questionable, such that the conclusions reached must be accepted with caution (cf. *JNES* 31, 1972, pp. 384–385). Coupled with the realization that the stratigraphy of the site is anything but clear, it is evident that neither Albright's thesis, nor the latest excavations, provide a solution to the problem. W. P. A.

Shilshah (shĭl′shȧ), a man descended from Asher (I Chron. 7:37).

Shimea (shĭm′ē-ȧ). (1) A son of a Merarite Levite, Shimei (I Chron. 6:30). (2) A brother of David (I Chron. 20:7). (3) A son of David and Bath-sheba, the Shammuah of II Sam. 5:14; I Chron. 3:5.

Shimeath (shĭm′ē-ăth), the Ammonite mother of Jozachar (II Kings 12:21) (Zabad, II Chron. 24:26), one of the murderers of King Joash* of Judah.

Shimeathites (shĭm′ē-ăth-īts), a family of scribes descended from Kenites through Hammath (I Chron. 2:55).

Shimei (shĭm′ē-ī), the name of at least 18 men in the O.T., including: (1) a Gershonite (Num. 3:18) after whom a minor group, Shimeites (Zech. 12:13) or Shimites (A.V. Num. 3:21) was named; (2) a son of Gera, of the house of Saul, who threatened David with curses, stones, and dust, met with non-resistance by the king (II Sam. 16:5–13), and apologized later at the Jordan ferry crossing (II Sam. 19:16–23); (3) a son of Ela, faithful to David during the revolt of Adonijah (I Kings 1:8), and later a commissary officer of Solomon (I Kings 4:18); (4) a son of Pedaiah (I Chron. 3:19); (5) a Simeonite, the father of sixteen sons and six daughters (I Chron. 4:26 f.); (6) the head of an important group of Merarite Levites (I Chron. 6:29); (7) a Benjamite chieftain (Shimhi, A.V. I Chron. 8:21); (8) the assistant treasurer of tithes and offerings under King Hezekiah of Judah (II Chron. 31:12); (9) a Levite who married a foreign wife in Ezra's time (Ezra 10:23); (10) a Benjamite ancestor of Mordecai (Esther 2:5).

Shimeon (shĭm′ē-ŭn), a son of Harim, who had married a foreign wife in the time of Ezra (Ezra 10:31).

Shimon (shī′mŏn), the eponymous founder of a family of Judah (I Chron. 4:20); father of Amnon, Rinnah, Ben-hanan, and Tilon.

Shimrath (shĭm′răth), a descendant of Benjamin (I Chron. 8:21).

Shimri (shĭm′rī) (Simri, A.V. I Chron. 26:10). (1) The father of Jediael, and one of David's "valiant men of the armies" (I Chron. 11:26, 45). (2) The "chief" (though not the first-born) son of Hosah (I Chron. 26:10), the eponymous founder of a family of porters. (3) A Levite contemporary of King Hezekiah of Judah (c. 715–687 B.C.) (II Chron. 29:13).

Shimrith (shĭm′rĭth), a woman of Moab (II Chron. 24:26), whose son was one of the assassins of King Joash (Jehoash) of Judah (c. 837–800 B.C.). She may be identical with Shomer* (II Kings 12:21).

Shimron (shĭm′rŏn). (1) The 4th son of Issachar, and founder of the Shimronites (Gen. 46:13; Num. 26:24). (2) An unidentified town in Zebulun. One of its kings was summoned by Jabin*, King of Hazor, to halt the conquests of Joshua in S. Palestine (Josh. 11:1). Possibly the same as Shimron-meron, a Canaanite town W. of the Jordan, whose king was defeated by Joshua (Josh. 12:20).

Shimshai (shĭm′shī), a Persian official—secretary or "scribe"—stationed in Syria, who with others voiced a protest to Artaxerxes I against the rebuilding of the Jerusalem walls by Exiles returned from Babylon about the middle of the 5th century B.C. (Ezra 4:8 f., 17, 23). As a result of the protest the work ceased "until the second year of Darius, king of Persia" (Ezra 4:24).

shin (sin), the 21st letter of the Heb. alphabet. It is ordinarily pronounced *sh*. A special form of the letter, called *sin*, is pronounced *s*. See WRITING.

Shinab (shī′năb), a king of Admah, a city near the Dead Sea (Gen. 14:2).

Shinar, Plain of, an alluvial lowland surrounding Babylon (Gen. 11:2, 14:1, 9). Sumerian peoples entered this region c. 4000 B.C. and developed a high civilization, based on wonderfully fertile soil. Later "Shinar" became virtually synonymous with Babylonia (the modern Iraq), whose great cities—Babel, Erech, Accad, and Calneh—are attributed by the Genesis narrative to Nimrod,

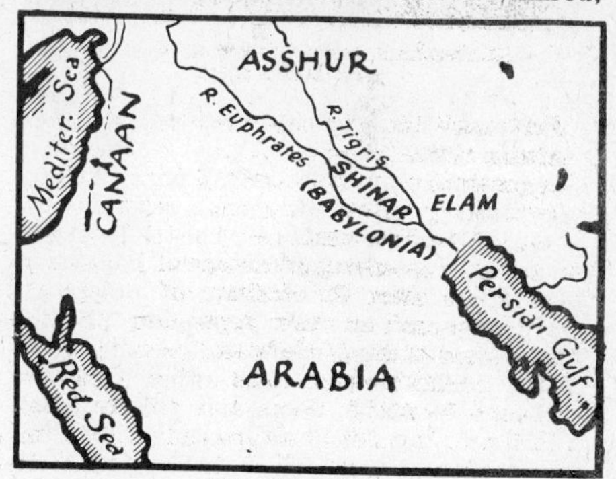

380. Plain of Shinar.

son of Cush (Gen. 10:8–10). Sumer*—the country from which Terah and his son Abraham are said to have migrated (Gen. 11:31)—was in the S. part of the plain of Shinar. Assyrian followers of the god Asshur* departed from the Plain of Shinar to found Nineveh*, Rehoboth, and Calah (10:11). The recording of the settlement in the Plain of Shinar of the first generations after Noah (11:2) indicates that the Genesis writers desired to stress the early origin of cities that became famous. Amraphel, King of Shinar in Abraham's time, is no longer identified with the great Hammurabi*. Isaiah prophesied that Jews exiled to Shinar would be saved as part of a righteous remnant (11:11; Zech. 5:11). Nebuchadnezzar transported Temple treasures stripped from Jerusalem to the Shinar area (Dan. 1:2). In the Talmud Shinar designates Babel and Baghdad, as it still does to Oriental Jews.

Shion (shī'ŏn), a town of Issachar (Josh. 19:19).

Shiphi (shī'fī), a Simeonite prince (I Chron. 4:37).

Shiphrah (shĭf'rȧ) ("splendor"), a Hebrew midwife in Egypt who refused to kill the sojourners' male infants (Ex. 1:15).

Shiphtan (shĭf'tăn), the father of Kemuel, a leader in Ephraim (Num. 34:24).

ships. See BOATS.

Shishak (shī'shăk), a pharaoh of Egypt, whose Egyptian name was Sheshonk (Sheshonq) I, founder of the Twenty-second Dynasty (Libyan). Sheshonk ruled 935–914 B.C., according to the most recent chronology (accepted by the Metropolitan Museum of Art). Other excellent authorities (see Steindorff and Seele, in *When Egypt Ruled the*

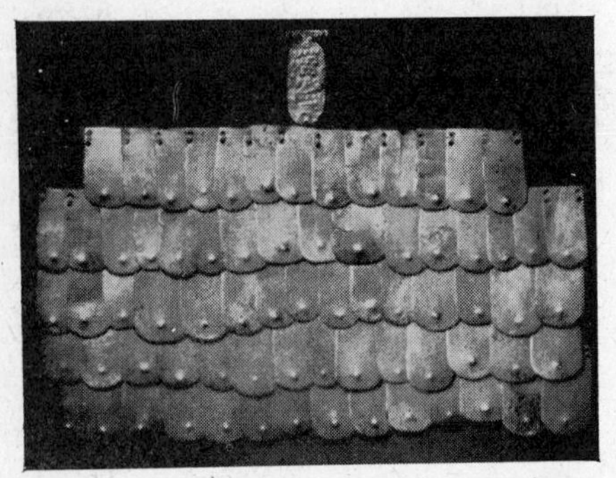

381. Iron scale armor of Shishak I, carrying his cartouche.

East) make his accession year 945 B.C. and others c. 924. A contemporary of Solomon, he gave refuge to Jeroboam* (I Kings 11:40), apparently without disrupting relations between the two countries. The O.T. represents him as taking advantage of Palestine's weakness after the division of Solomon's kingdom and invading Jerusalem "in the fifth year of king Rehoboam," seizing Solomon's golden shields and other treasures (I Kings 14:25 f.). Some date this invasion c. 926 B.C.; but this date presents difficulties for those accepting W. F. Albright's well-established dates for Rehoboam (c. 922–915 B.C.). The gold-masked body of Shishak was found A.D. 1938–39 in his intact burial chamber at Tanis (see RAAMSES). One of his carved reliefs at Karnak shows captives taken in his Palestinian campaign (see *Les Temples de Karnak*, by Léon Legrain, Fig. 44).

Shitrai (shĭt'rī), a man of Sharon who had charge of David's flocks (I Chron. 27:29).

shittah (shĭt'ȧ) (sing.), the tree with hard, orange-toned branches which yielded the shittim (pl.) wood used for the Ark (Ex. 37:1) and the fittings of the Tabernacle (Ex. 25, 26, 27:1). It has been identified with the desert acacia (*seyal*), which even in waste places grows 20 ft. high and produces feathery flowers. It may have been the "burning bush" of Moses. The Heb. word for acacia, *seneh*, is said to have given the name to Sinai* (Sinah, Seneh). Shittim wood was insect-resisting, and was used for clamps for mummy cases, for tanning leather, and for fuel. The *Acacia senegal* of Africa provided gum Arabic.

Shittim (shĭt'ĭm) (Tell el-Hammâm), a camp site of Israel in the high plains of Moab E. of the NE. end of the Dead Sea, opposite Jericho, occupied after the conquest of Sihon and Og, and before the Jordan crossing (Num. 25:1, 33:49; Josh. 2:1, 3:1; Mic. 6:5). From this place, N. of Mt. Nebo* and NW. of Heshbon, Joshua dispatched spies to survey the Promised Land. The evil conduct of the Israelites during their stay at Shittim, and their punishment, are narrated in Num. 25:1–16. Other events of the sojourn there are narrated in Num. 24–36. [See ABEL (2).]

Joel's "valley of Shittim" (3:18) should be rendered "valley of acacias" (shittah* trees), i.e., an unfruitful valley where only the shittah tree will grow. When the Day of the Lord comes, the nations shall be made desolate, while Judah shall flourish and her dry places be rich with waters and new growth. It is doubtful whether Joel referred to a specific valley.

Shiza (shī'zȧ), the father of a leader of a Reubenite group (I Chron. 11:42).

Shoa (shō'ä), a people mentioned in association with Babylonians, Chaldaeans, and Assyrians (Ezek. 23:23). They may be the Sutu of the Amarna* Letters, Syrian nomads who were pushed E. of the Tigris and, allied with Aramaean groups, were never subdued by the Assyrians.

Shobab (shō'băb). (1) A son born to David in Jerusalem (II Sam. 5:14; I Chron. 3:5, 14:4). (2) A son (or clan) of Caleb, begotten of his wife Azubah (I Chron. 2:18).

Shobach (shō'băk), the commander of the army of King Hadarezer of Zobah. When this Aramaean group supported the Ammonites against David, the latter killed or put to flight large numbers of Shobach's men, even though they were equipped with chariots. Shobach was killed in battle at Helam, E. of the Jordan (II Sam. 10:16–18; cf. I Chron. 19:16, 18, Shophach).

Shobai (shō'bī), the founder of a group of sanctuary doorkeepers who returned from Exile in Babylon (Ezra 2:42; Neh. 7:45).

Shobal (shō'băl). (1) The eponymous ancestor of a clan of Horites* (Gen. 36:20–29; I Chron. 1:38–40); a descendant of "Seir in the land of Edom." (2) A family of Calebites in Judah (I Chron. 4:1 f.; cf. 2:50).

Shobek (shō'bĕk), a man who sealed the covenant after the return of deported Jews (Neh. 10:24) from Exile.

Shobi (shō'bī), a man who lived E. of the Jordan, a son of Nahash, an Ammonite king of Rabbah. Shobi brought supplies to David when David was a fugitive from his home in Judaea during his son Absalom's revolt (II Sam. 17:27 f.). Possibly David had placed Shobi in charge of food at Rabbah (Rabbath-ammon), which the Hebrew king had occupied (II Sam. 12:29 f.).

shoes in Bible times were usually very crude. Those worn by Moses and the Patriarchs were probably like the footgear of Bedouins today—simply pieces of hide drawn together with thongs or cord, with no "right" or "left." In the Roman period sandals were worn by soldiers and the upper classes. The simplest form of sandal was a leather (sometimes wooden) sole fastened to the foot by a thong or shoe latchet (Gen. 14:23; Mark 1:7, etc.). Women wore leather footgear in Ezekiel's time (16:10). Royal Egyptian sandals from the Eighteenth Dynasty (c. 1570–1310 B.C.) are extant. Assyrians preferred

382. Shoes: 1. Egyptian, 1200 B.C.; 2. Egyptian; 3. Babylonian; 4. Assyrian, 900 B.C.; 5. Greek *krepis;* 6. Greek *pediba;* 7. Roman *calceus;* 8. Roman *crepeda.*

sandals with heel caps, as seen in their obelisk reliefs; their warriors wore laced boots (A.S.V. margin Isa. 9:5).

Shoes were removed in the house and in places of worship (Ex. 3:5; cf. Acts 7:33; Josh. 5:15), and during mourning (II Sam. 15:30). Moslems today remove shoes at their mosque doors, or place slippers over their street shoes before stepping onto prayer rugs.

When a Hebrew bought property he removed his shoe and handed it to the seller, to express symbolically the act of transference (Ruth 4:7). The shoe also played a part in the ceremony of levirate marriage*, whereby a brother agreed to rear children by the widow (Deut. 25:5–10; cf. Ps. 60:8 and 108:9—the figure of taking over Edom). Terra cotta shoes were excavated from the Athenian agora (1948); placed in a grave of c. 900 B.C., they probably were worn in that period; they resemble modern snow boots. Two eyelets at each side of the front opening were provided for laces. The soles were thick and stout, as if intended for walking.

Shoham (shō′hăm), a descendant of Merari (I Chron. 24:27).

Shomer (shō′mẽr) ("keeper"). (1) A descendant of Heber, and the eponymous head of a group in the tribe of Asher (I Chron. 7:32). (2) The mother of Jehozabad, one of the murderers of King Joash of Judah (c. 837–800 B.C.) (II Kings 12:21). In II Chron. 24:26 she is called "Shimrith* a Moabitess." Her origin is mentioned in order to show the dire consequences of marrying a foreign wife.

shophar (Heb."horn"), the ram's horn trumpet which was probably the oldest musical instrument (see MUSIC) of Israel. The horn was flattened with heat, and turned up at the end. In early times it was used to sound alarms, to signal attacks (Josh. 6:5), to dismiss the army, and to authorize a return of warriors to their homes. It proclaimed the accession of a king (II Sam. 15:10; I Kings 1:34; II Kings 9:13). Throughout Hebrew history it summoned the congregation to worship in the Tabernacle (I Chron. 25:5) and at the Jerusalem Temple (Ps. 98:6; 150:3). Its chief use was at Rosh Hashanah, the New* Year Festival, to which it called people on the 1st day of Tishri (Lev. 23:24; Num. 29:1), at the beginning of the Ten Days of Penitence which end on the Day of Atonement* (Yom Kippur). The shophar was associated with God's revelation of His will and Law at Sinai (Ex. 19:16), and with the proclamation of His judgment of the world. Some communities, in an effort to prepare themselves for the period of repentance culminating in the Day of Atonement, blow the ram's horn a month before the New Year Festival and also at the end of the solemn service of Yom Kippur. Shophars usually produce three sequences of notes. Some Reform temples use a cornet or an organ in place of a shophar. In 1940 a mouthpiece to facilitate the blowing of notes was officially allowed by the Union of American Hebrew congregations.

In ancient synagogue mosaics and frescoes the shophar often appears along with Menorah and lulab symbols.

Shoshannim (shō-shăn′ĭm) ("lilies"), Shoshannim Eduth ("lilies, a testimony"), words which appear in the titles of Ps. 45, 69, 80. The A.V. translation "upon Shoshannim" suggests an accompaniment on a lily-shaped instrument. But the A.S.V. translation, "set to Shoshannim," is probably correct, referring to well-known tunes known as "Lilies" and "Lilies, a Testimony." (Cf. the heading of Ps. 60, *Shushan-eduth,* "the Lily of Testimony".) See LILY.

shovel. (1) A utensil in the Tabernacle* equipment, possibly of copper or bronze, used to remove ashes from the altar (Ex. 27:3, 38:3; Num. 4:14). Hiram made shovels for Solomon's Temple (I Kings 7:40); they were among the booty carried off to Babylon when Jerusalem was destroyed (II Kings 25:14). (2) Broad, wooden forks (scoop-shaped in Egypt) with which farmers tossed threshed grain into the wind to separate the kernels from the chaff. (See FAN, illus. 141.)

showbread. See SHEWBREAD.

shrines, sacred places or altars. An early shrine is pictured on the cylinder seals from Sumerian Ur in the British Museum, showing a reed altar or offering table, with a bull rampant occupying a position similar to the famous "rams caught in a thicket" (cf. Gen. 22:13) excavated from the royal cemetery of Ur (c. 2900 or 2500 B.C.).

All Mediterranean peoples invoked the favor of their deities by the erection of open-air or enclosed shrines on impressive elevations, as at the Italian Cumae and the Greek

Delphi, or at the sources of springs. Market places like the Roman forums and the agora of every Greek city were sometimes littered with shrines, some of which became architectural wonders. (See TEMPLES.)

The "shrines" of Diana of Ephesus* (Acts 19:24) were images of the goddess encased in small silver, marble, or terra cotta reproductions of her temple.

See SYNCRETISM.

Shuah (shōō'ȧ) (Shua) ("depression"). (1) A descendant of Abraham by Keturah (Gen. 25:2), i.e., a member of an Arabian tribe (Shuhites) wandering near the land of Uz, or possibly S. of Carchemish, on the right bank of the Euphrates. (2) The father of a Canaanite whom Judah took as wife or concubine and who bore the Hebrew three sons—Er, Onan, and Shelah (Gen. 38:2–5; but cf. I Chron. 2:3). (3) An Asherite, daughter of Heber (I Chron. 7:32). (4) Job's friend Bildad was a Shuhite (Job 2:11).

Shual (shōō'ăl). (1) A man of Asher's tribe (I Chron. 7:36). (2) A region, "the land of Shual," N. of Michmash*, to which a foraging party of Philistines advanced (I Sam. 13:17).

Shuham (shōō'hăm), a son of Dan; founder of the Shuhamites (Num. 26:42 f.; I Chron. 2:53).

Shulamite. See SHUNEM; SHUNAMMITE.

Shunammite (shōō'năm-īt), one who resided in the town of Shunem. (1) Abishag, the "fair damsel" who was companion-nurse to David in his old age (I Kings 1:3 f.). She is, perhaps, alluded to as the Shulamite in the Song of Solomon (6:13); Shulem is perhaps a poetic name for Shunem, whose women were "Shunammites." However, E. J. Goodspeed and H. H. Rowley interpret "the Shulamite" as the feminine of Solomon ("Solomoness"). (2) The wealthy woman of Shunem* whose guest room was available to the tired prophet Elisha (II Kings 4).

Shunem (shōō'nĕm) (the modern Sûlem), a town on the SW. slope of Jebel Dahî (Little Hermon, 1,843 ft.) just E. of the main N.-S. road from Nazareth across the Plain of Esdraelon to Jenîn and Jerusalem. Shunem was on the border of Issachar (Josh. 19:18), c. 5 m. S. of Mt. Tabor and 3 m. N. of Jezreel. The Philistines encamped there before their battle against Saul and Israel at Mt. Gilboa* (I Sam. 28:4). It was the home of the "great woman" and her husband whose well-equipped guest room (II Kings 4:10) was at the disposal of the prophet Elisha. The narratives concerning the Shunammite (II Kings 4:8–37, 8:1–6) shed light on the customs of Elisha's day.

Abishag (I Kings 1:3 f.) was a native of Shunem. See SHUNAMMITE.

Shuni (shōō'nī), the eponymous ancestor of the Shunites (Num. 26:15), a clan of Gad's Tribe (Gen. 46:16).

Shupham (shōō'făm) (Shephuphan, I Chron. 8:5, Muppim, Gen. 46:21), the founder of a Benjamite clan, the Shuphamites (Num. 26:39).

Shur (shōōr) ("wall"), **Wilderness of,** a region near the NE. border of Egypt, at the NW. tip of the Sinai* Peninsula. Beside one of its springs (Gen. 16:7) the angel of the Lord found Hagar*. Between Shur and Kadesh Abraham tented on his way to Gerar (Gen. 20:1). Adjacent to the Wilderness of Shur was the Ishmaelite land (Gen. 25:18) which Israel crossed after passing over the Sea of Reeds (Ex. 15:22). Saul and David both smote the Amalekites, ancient inhabitants of the borderlands of "Shur, that is over against Egypt" (I Sam. 15:7, 27:8).

Shushan (shōō'shăn) (Gk. Susa), a city on the Karkheh River, c. 150 m. N. of the head of the Persian Gulf, one of the three capitals of the Persian Empire maintained by Darius*

383. Excavations showing Old Testament Susa.

the Great. This city—the royal winter residence, as Ecbatana was the summer one—was the scene of Biblical events in the time of Nehemiah (Neh. 1:1), and of Esther, consort of King Ahasuerus (Xerxes) (Esther 1:2, 2:3, 5, 8, 3:15, 4:8, 16, 8:14 f., 9:6–18). Shushan was also the scene of Daniel's imprisonment and vision (Dan. 8:2) under Belshazzar. Colonists from Shushan (Susanchites) were planted in Samaria by Ashurbanipal (A.V. Asnapper, R.S.V. Osnapper, Ezra 4:9b–10a). Shushan was in existence in the 23d century B.C., and was at one time the capital of Elam*. Natives call it today "Shush" (perhaps its ancient name).

Excavation at Shushan shows bricks and pavements from the palace begun by Darius I and enlarged by his successors. The palace had three courts surrounded by many rooms which were decorated with panels of glazed bricks, showing spearmen and symbolic winged bulls and griffins. In the excavated area a copy of the Code of Hammurabi* was found in 1901 by de Morgan.

Shushan Eduth (shōō' shăn ē'dŭth). See SHOSHANNIM.

Shuthelah (shōō-thē'lȧ). (1) The eponymous ancestor of an Ephraimitic clan, the Shuthalites (A.V.; A.S.V. Shulethites), numbered at the time of Israel's inheritance in Canaan (Num. 26:35 f.). (2) Another descendant of Ephraim (I Chron. 7:20 f.).

shuttle. See WEAVING.

Sia (sī'ȧ) (Siaha, Ezra 2:44, A.S.V. margin Sia), the eponymous founder of a company of Nethinim who returned from the Captivity in Babylon (Neh. 7:47).

Sibbecai (sĭb'ĕ-kī) the Hushathite, one of

David's mighty men (I Chron. 11:29; Mebunnai, II Sam. 23:27), who slew the powerfully built Philistine Saph (II Sam. 21:18; I Chron. 20:4).

Sibmah (sĭb′mȧ), (Sebam R.S.V. Num. 32:3; Shebam, Shibmah A.V.), a town assigned to Reuben (Num. 32:38; Josh. 13:19); famous for grapes (Isa. 16:8–9; Jer. 48:32).

sickle, a short-handled reaping implement, of flint in very ancient times (3000–2000 B.C.), later of metal. Men and women reapers harvested small tufts of grain by grasping them with their left hands and cutting them with sickles held in their right (Deut. 16:9; Joel 3:13; Mark 4:29). The cut grain was then bound into bundles or sheaves (tied with tufts of its own straw), ready to be carted to the nearest community threshing* floor. Sometimes grain was pulled up by the roots instead of being cut.

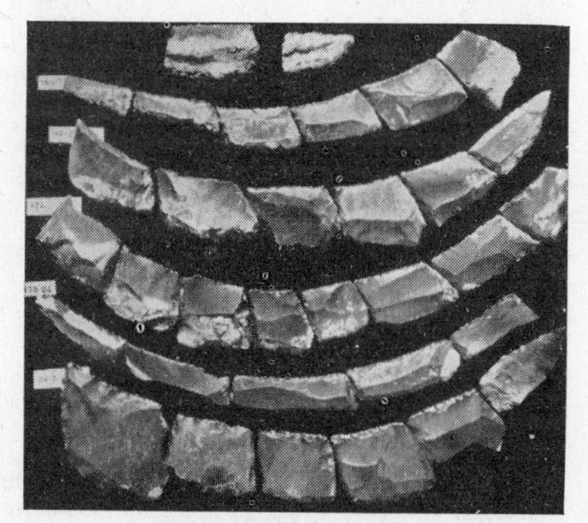

384. Flint sickles from Gerar.

Siddim, Vale of, the region S. of the peninsula "the Tongue," which projects into the Dead Sea from its E. shore. It was flooded in the time of Abraham, when its cities (Sodom, Gomorrah, Admah, Zeboiim, and Zoar) became submerged. It is mentioned in Genesis as the battleground of the "four kings versus five kings" (14:3, 8, 10).

side locks (Heb. *pe'ŏth*, "corners"), hairs left uncut over a man's temples and ears (Lev. 19:27) to indicate that he is a Jew.

Sidon (sī′dŏn) (Zidon sometimes in the A.V.), an ancient Phoenician city (the modern Saida in the Republic of Lebanon), on a small headland which extends into the Mediterranean, c. 24 m. S. of Beirut. It had an excellent harbor to the N., with an outer and inner port, and another, less well protected one, to the S. (A. Poidebard and J. Lauffray, *Sidon: Aménagements Antiques du Port de Saida*, 1951). According to Biblical tradition, Sidon is the oldest of the Phoenician cities (Gen. 10:15, 19; I Chron. 1:13). Its character was determined by the commerce of the sea and, along with Tyre, it was an active sea power by the latter half of the 2d millennium B.C. From an Amarna Letter (EA 85), it is known that at least one Egyptian pharaoh, either Tuthmosis IV or Amenophis III, visited Sidon in the late 15th or early 14th century B.C. Other letters shed light on the political intrigue at this time between Zimrida, King of Sidon (c. 1370–1355 B.C.), and the kings of Byblos and Tyre (see Jidejian, *Sidon*, pp. 18–23). The shrine of Elath of Sidon is referred to along with that of Asherah of Tyre in the Ugaritic Legend of King Keret (*ANET*³, p. 145). Sidon is also mentioned in the late 13th century Papyrus Anastasi I (*ANET*³, p. 477), in Hittite incantations (*ANET*³, p. 352), and in the Tale of Wen-Amon (c. 1100 B.C.) (*ANET*³, p. 27).

385. Sidon waterfront and promontory. Crusader castle at left.

References to Sidon in the Bible, as in Homer (Jidejian, *Sidon*, pp. 28, 30), rarely refer to the city itself, but more often to Phoenicia ("Sidonians") as a whole (e.g., Judg. 10:12, 18:7; I Kings 5:6, 11:1, 5) or to the N. border of Israel ("Sidon," or "Great Sidon"; e.g., at the time of the Conquest in Josh. 11:8, 13:6; for the boundary of Asher, Josh. 19:28; Judg. 1:31; or in the Davidic census, II Sam. 24:6–7).

Historical references to Sidon during the 1st millennium B.C. come mainly from the annals of the Assyrian and Babylonian kings. Tiglath-pileser I (c. 1114–1076 B.C.) was the first to receive tribute from Sidon (*si-du-nu; ANET*³, p. 276), and invited its delegates to the inauguration of his palace at Calah (Nimrud; *ANET*³, p. 560). Shalmaneser III (858–824 B.C.) exacted tribute from Sidon, Tyre, and Jehu of Israel in his 18th year (c. 841 B.C.) and from Sidon and Byblos in his 21st year (c. 838 B.C.) (*ANET*³, pp. 280 f.). Adad-Nirari III (c. 810–783) conquered Sidon (*ANET*³, p. 281), as did Sennacherib (c. 704–681), who in 701 B.C. on his way to lay siege to Jerusalem forced Luli, the King of Sidon (c. 715–701 B.C.) to flee to Cyprus (*ANET*³, pp. 287 f.), and installed Ethba 'al (Taba 'lu) as his successor. Esar-haddon (c. 680–669 B.C.) captured the city in his 4th year (677 B.C.), beheaded Abdimilkutte, its king, completely destroyed the city, deported its people, and built a new city in its place, Kar-Esarhaddon (*ANET*³, pp. 290 ff., 302 f.). Both Jeremiah (25:22, 27:3) and Ezekiel (27:8, 28:21 ff.) forecast the destruction of Sidon by Nebuchadnezzar II (c. 605–562 B.C.). The King of Sidon is listed as one of Nebuchadnezzar's court "officials" (*ANET*³, p. 308), probably some time after 587 B.C. Under Persian rule, Sidon became the center of the Fifth Satrapy, and supplied the Persian army with ships. Inscriptions of several Sidonian kings are known, including those of Tabnit (late 6th or early 5th cen. B.C.), and his son, Eshmun'azar II (5th cen. B.C.)

(*ANET*3, p. 662). The latter is the longest Phoenician inscription known, inscribed on the black basalt sarcophagus of this king (*ANEP*2, No. 283) found by M. Peretié in 1855 (see Jidejian, *Sidon*, pp. 1 f. and plates 4–9). Late in the Persian period, a revolt headed by Tennes, King of Sidon (c. 362–351 B.C.), led to the destruction of Sidon by Artaxerxes III (see Jidejian, *Sidon*, pp. 50 ff.). Sidon experienced prosperity during the Hellenistic (c. 330–64 B.C.) and Roman periods (64 B.C.–A.D. 300). While few architectural elements are preserved, several inscriptions, steles, and sarcophagi illustrate the wealth and artistry of the age (see Jidejian, *Sidon*, chaps. 6–7). Under Roman rule, Sidon was a free city, and was famed for her bronze and glass industries, as well as for her sculpture.

According to the N.T., Christ visited the region of Tyre and Sidon on his northernmost journey (Mark 7:24, 31), and referred indirectly to their wickedness (Matt. 11:21 f.). On his way to Rome as a prisoner Paul was allowed to visit his friends there (Acts 27:3). Early excavations (see Table of Excavated Sites in Bible Lands, p. 40; also Jidejian, *Sidon*, chap. 1) uncovered inscriptions, works of art, and a rich collection of anthropoid sarcophagi (see Jidejian, *Sidon*, chap. 9 and plates 6–168), but little architecture. Excavations since 1963, however, have provided the following: (1) the remains of several apsidal houses of the Chalcolithic Age (4th millennium B.C.) recently unearthed along the shore of the S. harbor (Jidejian, *Sidon*, plates 171–174); (2) the monumental Temple of Eshmun, built by Eshmun'azar III (5th cen. B.C.) and restored as late as the Roman period (see Jidejian, *Sidon*, pp. 59–62 and plates 175–191). See various studies and excavation reports in *Berytus*, *Syria*, *BMB* and elsewhere; for general survey, see N. Jidejian, *Sidon Through the Ages*, Beirut, 1971. W. P. A.

siege. See DEFENSE; WAR; also examples of Biblical sites under siege, e.g., Samaria*, Lachish*, Jerusalem*.

sieve, a sifting device used in grain harvesting. When metals came into general use grain was separated from chaff with sieves, c. 20 in. wide, which consisted of meshed material held in wooden rims. Primitive sieves had been made of woven horsehair or other coarse materials. (For "sifting" the hearts of men, see Isa. 30:28; Amos 9:9; Luke 22:31.) See also FAN; FARMING, illus. 142; WINNOWING.

sign, a supernatural or unusual event interpreted as having profound significance, like the rainbow after the Flood, regarded as a token of the covenant between God and His people (Gen. 9:12); and the rite of circumcision*, viewed as a pledge between the men of Israel and their Maker (17:11). Men of early Israel sought signs or tokens (Rom. 4:11) by which they might learn the will of God in specific situations, like Gideon (Judg. 6:17–24); and Saul (I Sam. 10:7). God also initiated signs to communicate His will, as to Aaron (Ex. 4:6–9). The birth of Jesus as a swaddled child lying in a manger was announced to the shepherds as "a sign" of the Saviour (Luke 2:12; cf. SIMEON). Many hearers of Jesus saw in his miracles "signs and wonders" which confirmed his power as Son* of God (John 3:2, 4:54). Jesus rebuked sensation-loving scribes and Pharisees who looked for spectacular confirmation of his mission (Matt. 12:38, 16:1; John 4:48). When he said, "An evil and adulterous generation seeketh after a sign; and there shall no sign be given to it, but the sign of the prophet Jonas," he probably referred to Jonah's preaching of repentance to Gentiles (Matt. 12:39, 41). Early Christians looked for spectacular signs and wonders to herald the Second Coming of Christ and the "End" (Rev. 12:1, 13:13, etc.).

The Spirit of God manifested Himself in the Apostolic Age through wonders, signs, mighty works, miracles, and amazing deeds wrought by the witnessing leaders (Acts 2:19, 22, 43, 4:30, 5:12, 7:36, 8:13; Rom. 15:19; II Cor. 12:12; Heb. 2:4).

See SYMBOL.

signet. See SEAL.

Sihon (sī'hŏn), a king of the Amorites, with headquarters at Heshbon, near Madeba, E. of the Jordan, not far from Mt. Nebo. This redoubtable ruler refused to give Israel permission to pass through his territory en route to the Jordan Valley (Num. 21:21 ff.); thereupon the Israelites and Amorites clashed at Jahaz (v. 23). The narrative declares that Sihon's territory, between the Arnon and Jabbok rivers, fell to the new arrivals, and the king and his sons and many of his subjects were slain (Deut. 1:4). This victory became proverbial in Israel (Num. 21:26–31; Deut. 2:24, 26, 30–32). As late as Solomon's day (961–922 B.C.) Gilead, the rich food-producing district placed under the supervision of Geber, is said to be "in the country of Sihon" (I Kings 4:19; see also Ps. 135:11, 136:19). Even after the return from Exile the Jews were still talking about the winning of Sihon's land (Neh. 9:22). The region came under the pronouncement by Jeremiah (48:45) of the woe in store for Moab.

Israel's victory over Sihon provided a pattern for Israel's subsequent hopes (Deut. 3:2, 6, 4:46, 29:7, 31:4; Josh. 2:10). It is associated in their annals with their other outstanding victory over Og*, king of Bashan (Josh. 9:10). The "assignment" of Sihon's and Og's lands to tribal heads of Israel is mentioned in Deut. 29:8; Josh. 12:6, 13:15 ff.: "we . . . gave it for an inheritance unto the Reubenites, and to the Gadites, and to the half-tribe of Manasseh." This territory included the plain of Medeba (Josh. 13:16), which in early Christian centuries became an important seat of the new faith.

Silas, the original Semitic (? Aram.) name of a man whose activities are narrated in Acts, but who in the N.T. Epistles is Silvanus (probably an adopted Roman form). Silas was a prominent member of the 1st group of Christian leaders at Jerusalem, a "prophet," who preached and exhorted (Acts 15:32). He was sent with Paul and Barnabas to Antioch with the decision of the Jerusalem

Council concerning entrance requirements for members of the Church (Acts 15:1–35). After the disagreement between Paul and Barnabas, Paul chose Silas to accompany him on the Second Missionary Journey (the account of which begins with Acts 15:40 and merges into the Third at 18:23). Silas may have been a Roman citizen (Acts 16:37). He sang (v. 25) and was eloquent (v. 31 f.). He traveled with Paul through S. Galatia. At Philippi he was jailed with Paul (Acts 16:16–40), and helped convert the jailer and his family. He moved on with Paul to Thessalonica and Berea (17:1–14). For some reason Silas and Timothy were left behind when Paul went on alone to Athens (v. 15). Silas was with him in Corinth (II Cor. 1:19). As indicated by Paul's letters to the Thessalonians, Silas seems to have had some part in sending the messages (I Thess. 1:1; II Thess. 1:1). Some authorities believe Silas was the bearer of the First Epistle of Peter (I Pet. 5:12). The last three verses of this document indicate that Silas was the amanuensis, and possibly the author of I Peter; Silas may have ministered to Peter after Paul's death. See PETER, FIRST EPISTLE OF.

Siloam (sĭ-lō′ăm) (Shiloah, Isa. 8:6; Siloah, A.S.V. Shelah Neh. 3:15 are all Heb. and Gk. equivalents of the modern Arab. Silwan). (1) A village, Silwan, clinging to a hillside above the juncture of the Kidron* and Hinnom Valleys of Jerusalem. It overlooks the ancient En-rogel* Spring. It is inhabited now only by Arabs, some in ancient houses, others still living in caves once used as tombs in the Kidron Valley. Silwan is not the Biblical Siloam (Shiloah), which was perhaps a district of Jerusalem proper. See also KING'S GARDEN, illus. 229.

(2) The Siloam Tunnel was constructed in the 8th century B.C. by King Hezekiah's

386. Siloam Tunnel and Pool of Siloam.

(c. 715–687 B.C.) engineers when the Jerusalem water supply was threatened by the approach of Sennacherib's* army (701 B.C.). Until that time the intermittently flowing Virgin's Fount (the Spring Gihon*), in the exposed Kidron Valley, had been the main water supply of the inhabitants, who went down 33 rock-cut steps to fill their water jars from a basin 11½ ft. by 11 ft. As early as the Jebusite occupation of the hill on which Jerusalem was later built, or under David or Solomon, a surface canal (found by Shick in 1891) conveyed water from the Virgin's Fount to the Old Pool of Siloam, situated just inside the SE. corner of the old city.

SILOAM

This Old Pool of Siloam is the oldest open reservoir in Jerusalem. The phrase "the waters of Shiloah that go softly" (Isa. 8:6) may mean the flowing current of the channeled brook that ran from the Spring Gihon by a serpentine course to the Pool, in contrast to the turbulent Euphrates (v. 7).

Canaanites dug a tunnel from near the top of the elevation where Jerusalem was built, down to the Spring Gihon, to protect people filling their water jars. It is possible that this is the watercourse through which David's men made their entrance into the city when they seized it (II Sam. 5:8). Later a surface aqueduct* ("brook," II Chron. 32:4) was constructed (cf. Isa. 7:3) from Gihon to the lower or Old Pool.

When Hezekiah* realized the imminent threat of Sennacherib he built the Siloam Tunnel or conduit to convey water from Gihon to the new upper pool or Pool of Siloam on "the west side of the City of David" (II Chron. 32:30), and probably enclosed the new pool with a new section of wall at the exposed SE. to defend it in case of siege (II Chron. 32:4–8, 30; Isa. 22:9 f.; II Kings 20:20). The achievement of Hezekiah's engineers resulted in one of the most amazing devices for water supply in the Biblical period, comparable to the tunnels at Megiddo* and Gezer*. The two groups of workmen who started from opposite ends used hand picks, and worked in a zig-zag. They excavated 583 yds. to go only 366, perhaps trying to avoid some site, possibly the supposed Tombs of the Kings; or perhaps they followed the natural fissure, where the water trickled through. They finally met, as told in a remarkable contemporary inscription, carved in the rock c. 19 ft. from the Siloam end of the aqueduct. The six lines, beautifully cut in classical Heb. (c. 701 B.C.)—one of the oldest Heb. inscriptions known—are preserved in the Turkish Archaeological Museum at Istanbul. The inscription was accidentally discovered in 1880 by two boys wading in the pool:

"The boring through is completed. Now this is the story of the boring through. While the workmen were still lifting pick to pick, each toward his neighbor, and while three cubits remained to be cut through, each heard the voice of the other who called his neighbor, since there was a crevice in the

387. Siloam inscription.

rock on the right side. And on the day of the boring through the stonecutters struck, each to meet his fellow, pick to pick; and there flowed the waters to the pool for a thousand and two hundred cubits, and a hundred cubits was the height of the rock above the heads of the stone-cutters."

Archaeologists and engineers, including Col. C. R. Conder, M. Clermont-Ganneau, and Sir Charles Warren, studied and cleared the Tunnel. Père L. Hughes Vincent photographed it (see his *Jerusalem Underground*, 1911). The 1,777-ft. long tunnel is at places barely more than 20 in. wide; its average height is 6 ft.

Hezekiah's defense measure against Sennacherib proved unnecessary, for by payment of heavy tribute Jerusalem escaped siege. Moreover, by another account, a strange calamity sent the King of Assyria home (II Chron. 32:21).

(3) The Pool of Siloam, to which the Tunnel leads from the Virgin's Fount, is an open-air basin c. 30x20 ft. Steps lead down to it. Broken columns remain from a Byzantine church erected by Empress Eudoxia. A 5th century basilica has been found N. of the pool, and probably a Herodian bath. In the time of Jesus sick persons were brought to bathe in the Pool of Siloam (John 9:7–11). The tower, which fell on 18 people and killed them—an incident evidently well-known in the time of Jesus and used by him as an illustration (Luke 13:4)—was probably on the Ophel ridge, near the pool; ruins of a round stone structure are sometimes pointed out as this tower.

The upper pool of Siloam, inside the fortification of Hezekiah's day, is sometimes called "the King's Pool," because the king had a garden in a fertile tract at the mouth of the Tyropoeon watershed, which was watered by the overflow of the Pool of Siloam. It is still carefully cultivated with vines and vegetables (II Kings 18:17; Isa. 36:2; see Neh. 2:14, 3:15).

Silvanus. See SILAS.

silver (Heb. *keseph*), a ductile, white, precious metal known to people of Bible lands from ancient times. Sumerians made silver lyres, pipes, statuettes, and filigree jewelry in the 3d millennium B.C., as seen in treasures excavated at Ur and now in the University Museum, Philadelphia. Silver ornaments of the 4th millennium B.C. have been excavated in Chaldaea.

The heavy silver deposits of W. Asia Minor were worked c. 2500 B.C.; Aegean island veins were among the earliest known sources. Greeks discovered silver deposits at Laurion near Athens as early as 1000 B.C.—an explanation of their ability to excel later in minted coins (see LYDIA; MONEY). Egypt had silver in her early dynasties, but Eighteenth Dynasty merchants imported it, as evidenced by the quantities of silver objects and jewelry in the world's great Egyptian collections, e.g., the Egyptian National Museum, Cairo; the Metropolitan Museum of Art, New York; and the British Museum, London. Joseph the Hebrew, during his premiership at Pharaoh's court, had a silver cup (for drinking and divining) which he ordered hid in his brother's sack (Gen. 44:2, 5, 12, 16). He also gave Benjamin "three hundred pieces [shekels] of silver" (45:22). At the Exodus the departing Israelites carried from Egypt silver jewelry acquired from their neighbors (Ex. 3:22, 11:2, 12:35). They were often tempted to copy the silver gods and amulets of their neighbors (Ex. 20:23). The metal was plentiful in the Babylonian centers where Hebrews acquired their first minted money. Phoenicians and Romans used the Spanish silver mines.

The first mention of silver in Scripture is in Gen. 13:2: "Abram was very rich . . . . in silver" (see also 20:16). Abraham paid 400 shekels of weighed silver money to Ephron for the Cave of Machpelah (Gen. 23:16). The Book of Joshua tells of wedges (bars or "tongues") of silver sinfully appropriated by Achan* from war booty (7:21). Midianite merchants bought Joseph from his brothers for "twenty pieces of silver" (Gen. 37:28; cf. Judas' price in silver for Jesus, Matt. 26:15). Two talents' weight of silver were offered to Gehazi, servant of Elisha, by the cured Syrian, Naaman (II Kings 5:23).

The uses of silver mentioned in the Bible include its conversion into bars or coins of money; sacred musical instruments (Num. 10:2); images (Ex. 20:23; Judg. 17:1–5; Acts 19:24 ff.); and portable ornaments in buildings. Silver went into the sockets, pillar trim, fillets, and hooks of the Tabernacle (Ex. 26:19, 21, 32, 27:10, 11, 17), and into the vessels used in the Tabernacle and the Temple (Num. 7:13; II Sam. 8:11). The Chronicler tells how David turned over to his son Solomon a great abundance of silver (I Chron. 22:14–16) for the candlesticks and tables (I Chron. 28:14–16, 29:2). The valuable metal he accumulated for the craftsmen was probably acquired as booty (II Sam. 8). Solomon, by his far-flung commerce, acquired so much silver that in Jerusalem this shining metal was "as plenteous as stones" (II Chron. 1:15). The Temple silver tempted invaders or was offered by frightened kings to aggressors to buy them off, e.g., King Asa of Judah to Ben-hadad (I Kings 15:18); Ahaz to the Assyrian Tiglath-pileser (II Kings 16:7 f.); King Hezekiah to Sennacherib (II Kings 18:14); Jehoiachin and Zedekiah to Nebuchadnezzar (II Kings 25:15; Jer. 52:19) and King Hoshea to So of Egypt (II Kings 17:4). Silver and vessels were easily transferred to Babylon under Nebuchadnezzar and back to Jerusalem under Cyrus (Ezra 1:6, 9). The cash booty looted by invaders was generally the offerings paid by the people to the Temple. The shekel* was long the medium of payment of sacred taxes (cf. Matt. 17:24). Sometimes the money was used for repairing the Temple (II Kings 12:4–16, 22:3–7); again, part of it went to priests, or was handed down from royal fathers to their heirs, as in Jehoshaphat's case (II Chron. 21:3).

Foundation deposits of silver plates, inscribed in cuneiform with events of the reigns of Near Eastern kings, were found by the Oriental Institute under the NE. and SE. corners of the vast audience hall of Darius the Great at Persepolis*. The plates are of solid silver, over 13 in. square, and are duplicated in plates of gold (cf. I Cor. 3:12).

Glimpses of the processes of refining silver are given in the O.T.—frequently with symbolic connotation: "fining" (see FINING-POT) (Prov. 17:3, 27:21; Isa. 48:10; Mal. 3:3; Zech. 13:9); taking away the dross (Prov.

25:4); the righteous sold for silver (Amos 2:6, 8:6); the futility of silver to buy God's favor (Zeph. 1:18).

N.T. teaching belittled silver and the money made of it. It was "corruptible" (I Pet. 1:18); and "cankered" (James 5:2, 3). In revolt against the materialism of the prosperous Roman Age, Jesus taught his Disciples not to carry money in their bags when they traveled (Matt. 10:9). Yet he revealed people's concern for their coins in his Parable of the Lost Coin (Luke 15:8); and provided money for his own Roman taxes (Matt. 17:24–27). Peter told a lame man whom he healed at the Gate Beautiful of the Temple, "silver and gold have I none" (Acts 3:6).

One of the most valuable pieces of silver art work discovered by archaeologists is the elegant Persian bowl in the Metropolitan Museum of Art carrying around its rim a cuneiform inscription, saying that it was made for Artaxerxes I, the Achaemenian (465–424 B.C.). See also ANTIOCH, THE CHALICE OF, illus. 19, and BOWL, illus. 66.

Simeon (perhaps "hearing"). (1) A Hebrew Patriarch, the 2d son of Jacob and his wife Leah* (Gen. 29:33). The tribal group named after him were Simeonites. He was not one of the major figures in Israel's history, and his destiny is linked with that of his brother Judah, with whose territory and interests those of Simeon seemed to blend. Along with his full brothers Reuben, Levi, and Judah, Simeon was a leader in avenging the rape of their sister Dinah by Shechem* (Gen. 34). Simeon was retained as hostage by Joseph in Egypt, when he sent the others back for young Benjamin. Simeon had six sons, each of whom (except Ohad) headed a tribal group (Gen. 46:10; Num. 26:12–14; I Chron. 4:24).

The Tribe of Simeon was probably absorbed by Judah. It is not mentioned in the Song of Deborah (Judg. 5), but it is listed as one of the group pronouncing blessings at Mt. Gerizim* (Deut. 27:12). The sons of Leah (Reuben, Simeon, Levi, and Judah) fare poorly at the hands of the writers of the early sources* on which the whole Jacob-Joseph cycle (as we have it in our Bible) is based. As the 12 sons of Jacob in this literature are at least as much personifications of the 12 tribes as they are individual persons (except Joseph), one is led (with R. H. Pfeiffer) to assume an origin for such slanderous tales as found in Gen. 34, 35:21 f., 38 among peoples who had little use for the four tribes involved. Nevertheless these tales made their way into the common oral tradition of Judah and were allowed to stand by the compiler of the J document (c. 850 B.C.), repulsive as their import must have been to him.

(2) An ancestor of Jesus in Luke's genealogical list (3:30, A.S.V. Symeon).

(3) A name of Simon Peter (A.V. Acts 15:14, A.S.V. and II Pet. 1:1 Symeon).

(4) The aged and pious man, "just and devout," who recognized the infant Jesus, presented at the temple by his parents, as the long-expected Messiah (Luke 2:22–34). His recognition of the "child . . . set for the fall and rising again of many in Israel" (v. 34) was the "sign"* which made him feel ready to depart from this world "in peace" (v. 29). Simeon's words, echoing Isa. 49:6, are the *Nunc Dimittis* of Christian liturgy.

(5) "Simeon that was called Niger," a Christian of Antioch listed next after Barnabas as a prophet and teacher (Acts 13:1).

Simon, the name of several men in the Bible. (1) Simon Peter (see PETER). (2) One of the Twelve, Simon the Canaanite (Matt. 10:4; Mark 3:18), or "the Zealot"* (Luke 6:15; Acts 1:13), i.e., a member of a Jewish nationalistic party. (3) A brother of Jesus (Matt. 13:55; Mark 6:3). (4) A leper cured by Jesus, who entertained Jesus in his home at Bethany (Mark 14:3–9). The anointing by "a woman having an alabaster box of ointment" took place in Simon's house. (5) The man from Cyrene in N. Africa who was compelled to carry the cross of Jesus (Mark 15:21 and parallels). He was father of Alexander and Rufus, who probably became prominent Christians. (6) A Pharisee who was entertaining Jesus in his home when an unnamed woman anointed the guest (Luke 7:36 ff.); undoubtedly a Lukan variation on (4). (7) Simon Iscariot, father of Judas the betrayer of Jesus (John 6:71, 13:26). (8) A tanner of Joppa, at whose seaside house Peter lodged (Acts 9:43, etc.). (9) A Samaritan sorcerer, Simon Magus (see separate article).

Simon Maccabaeus, a Hasmonaean ruler in Palestine (142–134 B.C.) (see HASMONAEANS).

Simon Magus, described in Acts 8:9–24 as a Samaritan magician (hence "magus") partly converted to Christianity who wanted to buy the power of imparting the Holy Spirit; rebuked by the apostle Peter, Simon was at least momentarily penitent. At an earlier time the Samaritans called Simon "that power of God which is called the Great." Such a notion seems to have led to the later belief that Simon, the unknown Father, had generated a female creative principle which was imprisoned by the powers she had produced for making the world, and had been incarnate in such women as Helen of Troy. To rescue her, Simon had descended—in Judaea as Son, in Samaria as Father, elsewhere as Holy Spirit. He freed her and his disciples, who live by grace, not by works (cf. Eph. 2:8–9) and therefore disregard the Jewish Law. The Simonian system seems to be a mixture of distorted Christianity and earlier Samaritan religion. The author of Acts either disregarded Simonianism or wrote before it developed. Later legends describe Simon's encounters with various apostles and their victories over him.

R.M.G.

simple, the translation of Heb. *pethī*, "naïve," or easily led into wrong-doing, often used in Proverbs; of *tōm*, "integrity," "freedom from evil intent," as in II Sam. 15:11; of a Gk. word meaning "innocent" (Rom. 16:18); and of a Gk. word meaning "sincerity of purpose" (A.V. Rom. 12:8: II Cor. 1:12, 11:3).

Sin, a fortress in Egypt (Ezek. 30:15 f.), probably Pelusium in the Nile Delta. This strategic stronghold had to be taken by any army seeking to penetrate Egypt. Herodotus recorded being told by Egyptian priests that Sennacherib's attack upon it, during the reign of Hezekiah in Judah, had to be left off because a plague of field mice ate up his archers' bowstrings. Esar-haddon captured it c. 671 B.C., and then overran Egypt. Assyrian annals list the Assyrian military personnel to whom the fortress was entrusted during the reigns of Esar-haddon and Ashurbanipal.

sin is essentially a religious idea; it always presupposes God and His law; this is why the conception of God determines what is regarded as sinful. Always in the Bible teaching sin has a God-reference. Men are sinners because they have gone contrary to the will of God, or to what they took His will to be, or to what they might have known His will to be. This rebelliousness is charged to all: "There is none righteous, no not one" (Rom. 3:10). Sin, however, goes deeper than the will: it is primarily a matter of the heart. The sinful deed expresses a still deeper sinfulness, and the problem lies with that deeper sinfulness, that is, with "the natural disposition." This accounts for the Biblical stress on "the clean heart" (Ps. 51:6–10; Acts 15:8 f.; cf. Prov. 4:23, 20:9). The account of the Fall of Adam and Eve may be regarded as typical (Gen. 3:1–8). There was a divine command to begin with, and there was a knowledge of that command; later the command was disobeyed. But the sin was not simply in the taking and eating of the forbidden fruit—it was in the prior dallying with the thought of it, in the willingness to entertain the temptation. Adam and Eve had "fallen" before they ate; the sin was *in them* before it was done *by them*—the outward act sprang from the inward "desire"—as it always does. The Bible is clear in teaching that the fundamental problem of sin is with human nature itself. Jesus made this perfectly plain when he contrasted the Mosaic "Thou shalt not *do*" with his own "Thou shall not *intend*" (Matt. 5:21 ff.).

There is in the Bible, however, the recognition not only of individual sin but of corporate or general sin as well. Corporate sin presupposes such an intimate relationship among the members of a group that the sin of one becomes the sin of all. Adam's sin becomes the sin of all his posterity (Rom. 5:12); the sin of Achan made all his family guilty (Josh. 7; see especially v. 11, "Israel [the nation] hath sinned," though actually it was only one man). Note, however, the significant act of Moses in identifying himself with the sin of his people (Ex. 32:30–35); the corporate principle works in both directions—which is its ultimate justification. If, says Paul, one man can make many sinful, one man can also make many righteous (Rom. 5:15–21). Repeatedly in the O.T. what is rebuked is the sin of the nation, and punishment for sin is threatened on the nation, even though the nation included persons who protested against the sin, and persons—like little children—who were in fact innocent of it. But in the same way blessings come to the nation as a reward for righteousness, though many in the nation had done little enough to deserve it.

The social consequences of sin are especially emphasized in the prophets—as a part of their vivid realization of God's ethical character. In the period when the Hebrew nation was being formed there were all kinds of excesses, as may be seen from the Books of the Kings, excesses due chiefly to the failure of the people to distinguish clearly between the character of their God, Yahweh, and that of the numerous gods of their neighbors. It sufficed if Yahweh was worshipped at the shrines; and even that worship was often attended with gross immoralities (II Kings 21:1–18). The so-called nonwriting prophets —Samuel, Micaiah, Elijah, and Elisha— stood against these perversions, but they were often like voices in the wilderness. With Amos—the first of the writing prophets—the character of Yahweh Himself was immensely exalted, and with that came a corresponding ethical demand on the people. To ignore that demand was to come inevitably under the law of retribution, and that law no man could bribe.

This ethical insistence of the prophets, however, was all too often undermined by the priestly insistence that what was all-important was the strict observance of the religious ceremonies. For the priest "sin" was likely to mean some ritualistic failure. The contrast between the priestly ritualistic and the prophetic ethical is nowhere more forcibly set forth than in Mic. 6:6–8. It is true that in a man like Ezekiel we have a combination of both the priest and the prophet, an equal stress on the moral law and the ceremonial (chaps. 13, 14; cf. 40, 45, 46), but the ultimate influence of Ezekiel was the deepening of the cult practices, and the creating of that meticulous formalism to which Jesus was to oppose himself so resolutely.

The Biblical teaching on sin, however, is never isolated from the question of forgiveness. The God of the O.T., for all the stress on His righteousness, is still "a God merciful and gracious, slow to anger, and abundant in lovingkindness and truth" (Ex. 34:6); and the God of the N.T. is "the God and Father of our Lord Jesus Christ" (II Cor. 11:31). Repentance, confession, regeneration, propitiation, reconciliation, transformation, empowerment, sanctification—all these are involved in the question of the relation of the sinful man to God and His will.

Jesus was chiefly occupied with sin as something at once unfilial and unfraternal. For him God was the Father of all men, even though they might ignore Him; and if all were sons, then all were also brothers— fatherhood, sonship, brotherhood, were for Jesus inseparable truths. Hence such parables as the Prodigal Son and the Good Samaritan (Luke 15:11–32, 10:25–37). The dreadful denunciations of Matt. 23 are directed against those who do not properly see God as their Father, and consequently are without the spirit of sonship and so of brotherhood. The priestly-prophetic opposition of the O.T.

is here made sharper yet, though Matt. 23:23 indicates that the opposition is not absolute (but cf. Matt. 5:20). Jesus finds the roots of sin in the human heart; his metaphor of "the good tree" and "the corrupt tree" in Matt. 7:16–20 means this—figs are not produced by thistles, nor good deeds by an evil heart. Jesus' answer to the deep-seated human moral weakness is love; in love to God and love to men is the secret of a redeemed world (Matt. 22:34–40). But such love does not come of itself. Jesus himself perfectly expressed it, which authenticates his claim that he came into the world to create love in others. He would create it by his own complete self-giving, a self-giving which stopped short of nothing (Matt. 20:25–28, 26:42; cf. Phil. 2:5–8). "Love is the fulfillment of the law" (Rom. 13:10; cf. John 13:34; Jas. 2:8–10).

The apostolic teaching in the N.T. is concerned to show that the destruction of sin is the work of God's love. Christ died for sinners because he loved them, and because he would deliver them from the dominion of sin by bringing them under the constraint of love (Rom. 5:8, 6:14, 22, 8:35–39; II Cor. 5:14 f.; I John 3:4–24, 4:7–21). Love is born of love, and where love is in command the pride and self-centeredness and disobedience which are the essence of sin can no longer continue. The Bible sets the reign of love over against the reign of sin, and sees Jesus Christ as God's supreme means for creating love.

See GRACE; GUILT; HOLINESS; JUSTIFICATION; REGENERATION. E. L.

sin offering. See WORSHIP.

Sin, Wilderness of, a desert plain at the foot of the Sinai plateau, possibly Debbet er-Ramleh, inland from the Red Sea, in the W. central area of the Sinai* Peninsula. Through this rugged region Israel passed, journeying between Elim and Mt. Sinai (Ex. 16:1; cf. 17:1; Num. 33:11 f.). An area on the coastal desert plain, el-Markhah, has also been suggested; which would be a more plausible setting for the quails sent by God in answer to the Hebrews' hunger-mutiny in the Wilderness (Ex. 16:2 ff.). If the Israelites came through the Wilderness of Sin (not to be confused with the Wilderness of Zin*) they would naturally have passed inland at Wâdī Feiran. See EXODUS.

Sinai (sī'nī) (etymology uncertain—possibly from *seneh*, "thorn bush," or from the ancient male moon god Sin).

(1) The Sinai Peninsula is a 260-m.-long triangle at whose southern apex the Gulf of Aqabah joins the Gulf of Suez at the head of the Red Sea. Its inverted base extends 150 m. along the Mediterranean, forming the border between Palestine and Egypt. The Sinai Peninsula is characterized by extraordinary beauty of line and color, with granite peaks rising 8,000 ft. above sea level. Its terrain is rugged. Across the middle of the peninsula ran the old caravan route between Memphis on the Nile and Ezion-geber* at the head of the Gulf of Aqabah, from which the King's Highway ran north into Edom, Moab, Ammon, and the other countries E. of Jordan. From a point about halfway up the W. side of the peninsula, at the head of the Gulf of Suez, there ran SE. the main route used by miners of the famous Sinai copper and turquoise (malachite) veins at Serabit* el-Khadem and by the Egyptian soldiers who guarded the mines and also the sources of pearls, peridot, and other semi-precious stones. (Modern engineers are extracting oil, manganese, etc. from Sinai.)

Sinai has three types of terrain: (a) a 15-m.-wide band of sandy dunes reaching S. from the Mediterranean; (b) a high plateau of limestone and gravel intersected by dry streambeds (wâdīs) and running 150 m. S. of the sand belt; (c) a granite mountainous mass reaching 8,000 ft. above sea level at the apex of the triangular peninsula. Sandy loam E. of el-'Arîsh supplies soil suitable for crops, and—in the view of those who accept Gebel Hellal (Arab. "lawful") as the Mount of the Law—could have yielded corn for Israel, and a date crop after the quail and manna ceased, and adjacent grazing ground for flocks.

Four wilderness areas are notable inside the Sinai Peninsula: (a) in the N., directly E. of the Land of Goshen*, and lying directly W. of the small stream at the border of Palestine known in the A.V. as "The River of Egypt," lay the Wilderness of Shur; (b) the Wilderness of Sin lay about two-thirds down the W. side of the Peninsula; (c) the Wilderness of Paran was in the E. portion of Sinai, reaching E. toward the Arabah*; (d) the Wilderness of Zin was at the NE. tip, where Sinai joins S. Palestine, NE. of the traditional Kadesh-barnea.

The population of Sinai, very sparse in early times, increased after the domestication of the camel, late in the 2d millennium B.C., because there was plenty of plant food suitable for vast herds of camels there.

El-'Arîsh, the capital of Sinai (part of Egypt), is near the Mediterranean entrance of the Biblical "Valley of Egypt" (A.V. "River of Egypt"), and is a thriving town of some 10,000 people who cultivate date-palm groves on one of the world's oldest highways, "the Way of the Land of the Philistines"—used by pharaohs and by modern conquerors. El-'Arîsh was the Roman Rhinocolura, and an early Christian see. Its low mound survives.

(For proto-Sinaitic script, see SERABIT EL-KHADEM. See also *Bulletin* 109, ASOR, Feb. 1948, "Exploring in Sinai with the University of California African Expedition," W. F. Albright.)

(2) Mt. Sinai is the name used by the J and P sources* for the sacred mountain named by E and D "Horeb" (Ex. 3:1, 17:6; Deut. 1:6, 4:10). Mt. Sinai is repeatedly referred to in the O.T. as the awesome elevation (possibly volcanic, cf. Ex. 19:16) where Moses received the revelation of the Ten Commandments (v. 20, 34:4; see also Ex. 16:1, 24:16; Lev. 25:1).

Several elevations have been suggested for Mt. Sinai. (a) Critics who say that Israel's leaders would not have escorted the unwieldy company to the traditional southern Sinai (Mt. Moses) near the Serabit copper and turquoise mines, because of the presence of Egyptian soldiers there, favor a northern route into Palestine, and therefore suggest Jebel Hellal, 30 m. S. of el-'Arîsh, rising abruptly 2,000 ft. from its alluvial plain, and looking impressive enough to fit Ex. 19:16 as Sinai. (b) Jewish scholars incline to identify Mt. Sinai with volcanic Mt. Seir, S. of Palestine, in Edomite country probably not far from Kadesh* (cf. Deut. 33:2; Judg. 5:4 f.). This region is near enough to Midian for Moses to have led his flocks there (Ex. 3:1) and distant from Canaan by only three covenient treks for flocks (Num. 10:33). (c) The oldest Christian tradition, based on Eusebius, identifies Mt. Sinai with Jebel Serbal, an inaccessible 6,750-ft. peak having on its N. a small, well-watered oasis, the Wâdī Feiran—possibly too small, however, to accommodate as large a company as is suggested by the Exodus narratives. (d) Preponderant tradition points to Jebel Mûsā, "the Mountain of Moses," part of a granite range beginning with the rugged mass of Râs es-Safsâf, as Sinai. The tradition favoring this range dates from at least the time of Emperor Justinian (A.D. 527–564). The desert (or "wilderness that is before Sinai") mentioned in Ex. 19:2 and Num. 33:16, may be the small, arid plain extending from the base of Râs es-Safsâf. Overlooking a valley on the E. side of the range, at the foot of Jebel Mûsā in the Wâdī ed-Deir 5,000 ft. above sea level, is the famous Monastery of St. Catherine (portions of which may date from A.D. 330 or 335), where Count Tischendorf in 1844 and 1859 found the famous Codex Sinaiticus (see TEXT). In 1950, scholars from the Expedition of the American Foundation for the Study of Man (including Wendell Phillips, Wallace Wade, K. W. Clark, and Aziz Atiya) microfilmed for the Library of Congress c. 500,000 pages of MSS. in Gk., Lat., Arab., Syr., etc. This enterprise was part of the International Project to Establish a New Critical Apparatus for N.T. Gk. Manuscripts ("The International N.T. MSS. Project").

388. Mt. Sinai and Monastery of St. Catherine, occupied for the past 1500 years.

sinew, a tendon, e.g., the sciatic muscle, in contrast to bone structure (Job. 10:11, 30:17; Ezek. 37:6, 8), "the sinew which shrank, which is upon the hollow of the thigh" (Gen. 32:32). This portion of meat was forbidden food to Israelites, in line with the taboo mentioned in connection with Jacob's limping after wrestling with an angel at Peniel (Gen. 32:24 ff.). But the law codes of the Pentateuch make no such restriction. The sinew or tendon of the neck is mentioned in Isa. 48:4.

Sinim (sī'nĭm), a remote, unknown area from which Jewish Exiles would return (Isa. 49:12).

Sinites, a Canaanite people (Gen. 10:17; I Chron. 1:15), listed between the people of Arka and those of Arvad. Their home may have been Sinna (Siannis), named in an Assyrian inscription—a fortress at the foot of the Lebanons; or a site c. 80 m. N. of Sidon.

Sion, a name of Mt. Hermon in the Anti-

Lebanons, or of a portion of that elevation (Deut. 4:48) (cf. SENIR; SIRION). To be distinguished from Zion*, one of the hills on which Jerusalem was built, though spelled "Sion" in Maccabees and the A.V. of the N.T. (e.g., Matt. 21:5; John 12:15; Rom. 9:33, 11:26; Heb. 12:22; I Pet. 2:6; Rev. 14:1).

Sirach, Son of (Wisdom of). See APOCRYPHA, "ECCLESIASTICUS."

Sirah (sī′rȧ), **the Well of,** a cistern near Siret el-Bella', N. of Hebron, from which Abner was summoned by Joab (II Sam. 3:26).

Sirion (sĭr′ĭ-ŏn), the name given to Mt. Hermon* by Sidonians (Deut. 3:9; Ps. 29:6). (Cf. Senir [Shenir], the Amorite name for Hermon.)

Siron. See SENIR; SION.

Sisamai (sĭs′ȧ-mī) (A.S.V. Sismai), a son of Eleash, a Jerahmeelite (I Chron. 2:40).

Sisera (sĭs′ẽr-ȧ), a Canaanite chieftain of the 12th century B.C., who became a general of Jabin's hosts (Judg. 4:7) in the war against the Israelites, and whose defeat by the armies of Deborah* and Barak at the Kishon ended Canaanite domination in the N. (Judg. 5:31). A prose account (Judg. 4) and an earlier poetic one (Judg. 5) describe this decisive battle. Sisera, with the latest war equipment, consisting of "nine hundred chariots of iron," massed on the Plain of Esdraelon*, faced the united hosts of Israel, who had no chariots. Torrential rains turned the Esdraelon Plain into a quagmire and made the heavy chariots useless. Infantry and possibly some horsemen of Deborah and Barak, with drawn swords, spread confusion and death among the Canaanites, many of whom perished in the flood waters of the Kishon as they tried to escape. Sisera fled on foot to the tent of Jael, wife of Heber the Kenite, an ally of the Canaanitish cause (Judg. 4:11 f.). After offering Sisera the customary hospitality (Judg. 4:18 f., 5:25), Jael murdered him in her tent. The poetic narrative closes with a moving account of Sisera's mother, looking in vain through the lattice of her harem for the return of her warrior son, while her maidens-in-waiting tried to allay her fears with their chatter about the spoils of battle.

sisters play a minor role in the Bible. Among those who emerge with an individuality of their own are: Rebekah, the sister of Laban (Gen. 24:29, 25:20); Rachel, and her elder sister, Leah (Gen. 29:16 ff.); Miriam, the sister of Moses (Ex. 2:4, 7, 15:20 f., etc.); Zeruiah and Abigail, sisters of David (I Chron. 2:16); the sisters of Lazarus (John 11:3). For "sisters of Jesus" see Matt. 13:56; Mark 6:3; Paul's sister, Acts 23:16.

sit. See GESTURE.

Sitnah (sĭt′nȧ) ("hostility"), a well dug by Isaac between Gerar and Rehoboth SW. of Beer-sheba, contended for by herdsmen of Gerar (Gen. 26:21).

Sivan (sē-vän′), the 3d month (May-June) of the Babylonian and Hebrew year. The name is Accadian in origin and appears in Scripture only in Esther 8:9.

six, an unimportant number (see NUMBERS) in Scripture. Sixty is used to indicate an indefinite number (Song of Sol. 3:7, 6:8). Food considered ritually unclean (unfit for consumption) was, by traditional procedure, pure if mixed with clean food 60 times its quantity. The cryptic number of the "beast," 666 (Rev. 13:18), was intended to convey the name of a specific person who would be recognized by contemporary readers from the context of the Apocalypse.

skirt, used in I Sam. 24:4 f. for the corner of Saul's robe, cut off by David.

skull, place of the. See CALVARY.

slavery, a state of involuntary servitude. The Holiness Code, embodied in Leviticus, provided that Israelites who had been sold into slavery for debt were to be released or redeemed in the Year of Jubilee (Ex. 21:2; Deut. 15:12); redemption was through the negotiation of kinsmen or by the simple act of the owner's freeing the enslaved. Non-Israelite slaves, however, were to remain indefinitely in the status of bondsmen. The Covenant Code deals with the sale of daughters into slavery (Ex. 21:7–11). (For laws on the bondwoman, see Deut. 15:12, 17b; and for the death penalty for persons who had stolen human beings for sale, see Deut. 24:7.) A provision of the Deuteronomic Law concerning shelter given to a runaway slave is given in Deut. 23:15 f. See FREEMAN.

sled (or sledge), a term sometimes applied to the threshing* board.

slime used for mortar for the Mesopotamian Tower of Babel (Gen. 11:3) may have been bitumen*. Slime was commonly used in that region for setting bricks together or for holding the mosaic tesserae of limestone, like the mosaic frieze of a milking scene from a Sumerian First Dynasty temple at al-'Ubaid, 4 m. W. of Ur (c. 1900 B.C.), now in the University Museum at Philadelphia. The "slime" with which Moses' mother calked his little ark of bulrushes at the Nile may have been bitumen (as A.S.V. margin of Ex. 2:3). "Pitch" in the Bible means bitumen (Gen. 6:14; Isa. 34:9). For "slime pits" (bitumen pits) near the Dead Sea, see SIDDIM, VALE OF.

sling, a leather thong or a band woven of rushes, animal sinews, or hair, wider at the center and hollowed to receive the smooth round slingstone from brook or valley. It had a string attached to each end, for twirling. When one string was let go, the stone flew to its mark, as when David's brook stone struck Goliath's forehead (I Sam. 17:40, 48–50). Small boys and shepherds were the first slingers, and developed amazing accuracy. Shepherds carried their slings attached to their staffs, and slingstones in garment folds or scrip (bag) (I Sam. 17:40). Sometimes the sling thong was worn around the forehead or the waist when not in use. Benjamin's left-handed slingers were famous (Judg. 20:16). Israel's kings, who did not have heavily armed infantry or chariots,

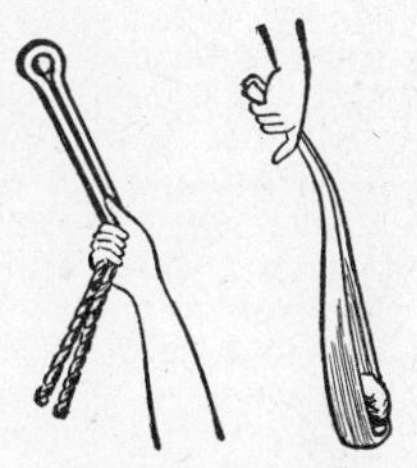

389. Slings: At left, Assyrian (900 B.C.); right, Roman (100 B.C.).

maintained bands of accurate slingers (II Kings 3:25; II Chron. 26:14); and bands of trained slingers were used by many early Mediterranean peoples in warfare—Egyptians, Syrians, Assyrians, Persians, Sicilians, and Roman mercenaries. (For the figurative

390. Sling-stone from Megiddo.

use of slings in the Bible, see Job 41:28; Jer. 10:18; Zech. 9:15.) Flint slingstones, often carefully worked, have been excavated from Tell Beit Mirsim, Megiddo and other Palestine sites. They usually measure c. 10 centimeters and weigh c. 1 kilogram.

smith, a craftsman, an artificer in metals. Smiths did not appear early in Israel, for in their mainly pastoral period the Hebrews did not need metal products (but see CAIN; TUBAL-CAIN; and KENITES, for traveling tinkers in the "Valley of the Smiths," the Arabah); smiths developed their crafts when metals became available. Copper*, one of the first metals they used, had been introduced into the Middle East in the Chalcolithic Age (c. 4000–3300 B.C.); bronze appeared in the first historical period (c. 3300–2000 B.C.); iron came into general use among Israelites after the 11th century B.C. Many allusions in the A.V. to "brass" and "brazen" objects should probably be translated "copper" or "bronze," e.g., in descriptions of the Jerusalem Temple* equipment (I Kings 7:14–16, 27, 30, 38).

The Hebrews found their Canaanite foes using iron-rimmed chariots (Judg. 4:13). Later, in the period of the Judges, their farmers were compelled to visit Philistine blacksmiths to have their plowshares sharpened (I Sam. 13:19 ff.). After David's victories over the Philistines (c. 1000 B.C.), iron became available to the Hebrews. Solomon's trade alliance with Hiram of Tyre gave him access to the Jordan Valley copper and iron mines. (See EZION-GEBER; ARABAH.)

The first Hebrew smiths leaned over their charcoal furnaces holding bits of metal with tongs, encouraging the flame with hand bellows. They beat the hot metal on an anvil with a hammer to fashion teraphim, idols, or simple household hardware (Isa. 44:12). They knew how to solder (Isa. 41:7); to cast for images (II Chron. 34:3 f.; Nahum 1:14) and to draw out gold to thread-fineness for weaving into textiles and for embroidery (Ex. 28:6, 39:3). They were skillful in beating, overlaying, and plating with gold (I Kings 6:20 ff.). By the 6th century B.C. smiths had become so adept that they were desirable captives for Babylonian builders to deport from Palestine (Jer. 24:1). (See MINES; GOLD.)

W. F. Albright (in *Archaeology and the Religion of Israel*, pp. 207 ff., Penguin Books) states that traveling smiths, such as appear in the tableau of Beni-hasan (1892 B.C.), show us how Biblical nomadic metalworkers traveled. They took along asses, bellows, and tools, living by their craftsmanship and the income from music and their women's fortunetelling. He believes that the early Hebrews were in part, at least, related to such groups, traveling with their weapons, bellows, and musical instruments. Even in Greece traveling smiths were familiar figures; Homer gives them a place in his epics of the Mediterranean world. Wayfaring prospectors, dealers, and craftsmen traveled all over the Middle East, starting trends which in time assumed local characteristics in developing the metals.

Smyrna (the modern Izmir, an important Aegean port of W. Anatolian Turkey), the seat of one of the "seven churches that are in Asia" to whom the Book of Revelation was addressed (1:11). Words directed to Chris-

391. Smyrna: Roman statue of Poseidon and Demeter.

tians in Smyrna (Rev. 2:8–10) suggest their material poverty and their tribulations, due to their refusal to worship the Roman emperor. Their spiritual riches are mentioned in 2:9. Smyrna, founded in the 12th century B.C. by Aeolic Greeks, had grown rich on trade between Asia and the W. Alexander the Great designed its rebuilding. Its public buildings rivaled those of Ephesus and Pergamum. It minted its own coins, from Augustus to Gallienus. Its first Christians were converts of Jewish proselytes (cf. Rev. 2:9). Although some Jews of 1st-century Smyrna are called members of the "synagogue of Satan" (2:9), Christians of the city are praised almost more than those of the other "seven cities." Suffering had kept them noble; and they would attain "a crown of life" (2:10). Polycarp, Bishop of Smyrna in the 1st half of the 2d century, suffered martydom there c. A.D. 155. Smyrna was the last city in Asia Minor to yield to the Moslem conquest. Greek and Armenian Christians continued to be numerous.

snail, one of the unclean animals (not fit for food) in Israel's Levitical Code, listed with other creeping things—chameleon, lizard, mole (Lev. 11:30). In the A.S.V. of this passage the animal is "sand lizard" (*hōmet*). The evanescence of life is compared in Ps. 58:8 to a snail which "melts" (Heb. *shabbelūl*).

snare, a noose-cord trap for catching small game and birds by their feet (Prov. 7:23); one of four types of trap listed by Job (18:8–10). Snares are often mentioned in Scripture, usually in a figurative sense, e.g., wicked people lay snares to entrap others (Josh. 23:13; Ps. 119:110); the devil also (cf. I Tim. 3:7). Death snares the living according to Wisdom* writers (Ps. 18:5; Eccles. 9:12). A hated prophet is called "a snare of a fowler" (Hos. 9:8). Ps. 11 warned that God would "rain snares" upon the wicked (v. 6); the man who trusts in Yahweh will be delivered "from the snare of the fowler" (91:3). Jesus warned worldly Jerusalemites that the judgments of God would come as suddenly as snares closing about birds (Luke 21:35).

snow is seen even in summer on Mt. Hermon, from points as far S. as the Sea of Galilee; and falls in elevated areas of Palestine in January and February (cf. Prov. 26:1). It seldom lies deeper than a few inches, though a blanket 15 in. deep covered the N. shores of the Dead Sea in February 1950. The hot sun soon melts Palestine snow. In ancient times—and also in the Middle Ages—snow was in some way conveyed from the Lebanons to the plains to refresh people. In Scripture snow is a symbol of purity and whiteness (Ps. 51:7; Isa. 1:18). The garments of the transfigured Jesus were said to be "white as snow" (Matt. 28:3; cf. Rev. 1:14). Ice and snow over brooks are mentioned by Job (6:16). The model O.T. housewife prepared warm scarlet clothing for her family and was therefore "not afraid of the snow" (Prov. 31:21).

snuffers. See TEMPLE.

So, the "king of Egypt" (II Kings 17:4) to whom King Hoshea* of Israel sent emissaries and thus gave a pretext to Israel's overlord, Shalmaneser of Assyria, to besiege Samaria* (v. 5). Since "So" has not been identified with any Egyptian pharaoh known to history, the epithet may be an error; possibly a high official or petty prince was meant. He may be the same as Sib'i, ally of the rebel Hanum of Gaza in 720 B.C. He is not to be identified with the Ethiopian Egyptian King Shabaka.

soap, the substance mentioned in Jer. 2:22 and Mal. 3:2 was not the fat-potash-soda sort which is made in Palestine today (notably olive oil soap at Neapolis*). It was evidently a cleansing material compounded by fullers from vegetable alkali (see FULLER).

sobriety. See DRUNKENNESS; VINE.

Socho (Socoh). (1) A son of Heber (I Chron. 4:18). (2) A town (Khirbet 'Abbâd) in Judah (Josh. 15:35) NW. of Adullam. (3) A mountain town (Khirbet Shuweikeh) of S. Judah, SE. of Kiriath-sepher and c. 10 m. SW. of Hebron (Josh. 15:48).

sod (sŏd), (p. tense and p. part. of *seethe*), boiled slowly, simmered (Gen. 25:29; II Chron. 35:13).

Sodom (Sodoma, Rom. 9:29), the twin city of infamy with Gomorrah, which, with Admah, Zeboiim, and Zoar (Gen. 14:2; Deut. 29:23) constituted the "cities of the plain" (Gen. 13:12) in the "vale of Siddim"* (14:3). These five cities were located on what is now the S. portion of the Dead Sea, below the tongue of land protruding from the E. shore. Once this was all above water. An earthquake along the Jordan-Dead Sea fault caused the catastrophe which destroyed the cities (presumably c. 1900 B.C.). Archaeologists favor this location for the destroyed cities because (1) only here do fresh-water streams flow from the mountains of Moab into the Dead Sea with sufficient force to maintain five cities without intercity friction; (2) such fresh water for irrigation was necessary to support vegetation as lush as that which Lot beheld (Gen. 13:10); (3) Zoar, on the SE. end of the Dead Sea, with no evidence of pre-Christian occupation, evidently moved to higher ground to escape the waters of the Dead Sea which inundated the Vale of Siddim and continued to rise through the centuries. The author of Genesis plainly records that the "vale of Siddim" was the "salt sea" (Gen. 14:3).

Lot's testimony to the productivity and fertility of this lower Jordan Valley (in the Middle Bronze Age, c. 2000–1500 B.C.) has been substantiated by archaeologists. Four Mesopotamian kings under Chedorlaomer considered it worth while to make war on the five cities of the plain, sacked Sodom and Gomorrah, and captured Lot (Gen. 14:1–12). Abraham pursued the conquerors to Damascus, recovered his brother's son, the captured loot, and the townsfolk, and on his return was given a great welcome by the King of Sodom (Gen. 14:13–24). "Slime pits" (Gen. 14:10), "brimstone and fire" (Gen. 19:24), and "the smoke of a furnace" (19:28)—all mentioned by the Genesis writer—in conjunction with the petroleum and gases now known to have been in this general region, could have furnished all the necessary devastating accompaniments to the geological activity which settled the floor of the Vale at this point. The wickedness of the Sodomites was so debasing as to become proverbial (Gen. 13:13; Isa. 3:9; Lam. 4:6); sometimes this condemnation was shared with the residents of Gomorrah (Gen. 18:20; II Peter 2:6; Jude 7).

The fate of Sodom and Gomorrah is referred to by Jesus as a warning to those who are inhospitable to the Gospel (Matt. 10:15). Sodom is a symbol for dead bodies lying in the street of a city (Rev. 11:8).

sodomy, unnatural carnal copulation. Sodom was so closely associated with sex perversion that its name became permanently identified with perverts and their sin. This vice, popularized in Sodom (Gen. 19:5; II Pet. 2:6–8), fastened itself on Israel (I Kings 14:24) and the ancient world (Rom. 1:26 f.) in violation of Deut. 23:17; debased religion (II Kings 23:7); and was the object of reforms (I Kings 15:12, 22:46) and the purifying powers of the Holy Spirit (I Thess. 4:4–8).

Sojourn, the, the period of temporary residence of the Jacob tribes in Egypt, from the time of the descent narrated in Gen. 47:4 and Deut. 26:5 (cf. Isa. 52:4) to the Exodus* under Moses (cf. Ex. 12:40). Other periods of sojourn in Egypt are mentioned in Gen. 12:10; cf. Jer. 42:15, 43:2, 44:12, 14.

sojourner. See FOREIGNER; GENTILES; STRANGER.

soldier, a person engaged in military service. Successive armies of aggression and occupation contended for millennia to hold the strategic bridgehead of an economically unimportant Palestine. Pharaoh's soldiers pursued Israel as this people made its Exodus from the Delta. Bands of soldiers "fit to go out for war and battle" are mentioned by the Chronicler (I Chron. 7:4, 11). The exiled Jews felt the famous armed power of Babylonia. Ezra knew that the Persian king would send a protective band of soldiers with the returning Exiles, but he hesitated to request the escort, lest it discount his faith in God's power (Ezra 8:22). The First Isaiah was familiar with the armed soldiers of Moab (15:4).

In N.T. times the soldiers of Rome were familiar to all the inhabitants of Palestine and Syria. Every Palestinian peasant knew that a soldier could compel him to carry his pack for one mile; hence the virtue of volunteering to go a second mile (Matt. 5:41). Some Roman soldiers were kindly, noble, even devout and God-fearing (see CENTURION); others were ruthless, e.g., the Roman soldiers who arrested Jesus (John 18:12), conducted him to the praetorium (Mark 15:16), mocked and scourged him (John 19:2 f.), nailed him to his cross, and gambled for his garments (Mark 15:24).

In the early Apostolic age Herod set four quaternions (see QUATERNION) of Jerusalem soldiers to guard the Apostle Peter (Acts 12:4, 6–18). Again, Roman soldiers restored order and exerted protective custody when mob violence broke out against Paul (Acts 21:32, 35, 23:10), and gave him safe conduct between Jerusalem and Caesarea (vv. 23, 31). Credit must be given to the centurion and the soldiers on board the Alexandrian grain ship carrying Paul to Rome for their efforts to save passengers and cargo (Acts 27:31 f.), though later they advised killing the prisoners lest they escape (v. 42).

In the Roman military organization a centurion was the commander of a century or group of 100 soldiers. A legion numbered 3,000 to 6,000 men, usually combined with 300 to 700 cavalrymen.

Ancient art depicts soldiers fully armed, or engaged in attack—as on the Medinet Habu relief of the Egyptian siege on a Canaanite city (Tunip) in Syria, or bringing in captives and compelling them to bow the neck in homage—as on the obelisk of Shalmaneser* III.

See ARMS; DEFENSE; DRESS; WAR.

solemn assembly, a term at first applied to any religious gathering of the Congregation Israel, as in Amos 5:21; R.S.V. Isa. 1:13; II Kings 10:20; but later used to indicate only the 7th day of the Feast of Unleavened Bread (Deut. 16:8) and the 8th day of the Feast of Booths (Lev. 23:36; Num. 29:35). No servile work was done on days of solemn assembly; but meat and drink offerings were offered to the Lord and vows made. See FESTIVALS.

Solomon ("peaceable"), the 3d king of Israel (c. 961–922 B.C.), son of David and Bath-sheba; called "Jedidiah" ("beloved of Jehovah") by Nathan the prophet (II Sam. 12:24 f.). His peaceful reign made "Solomon" his more popular name.

The chief sources for Solomon are the above-cited passage and I Kings 1–11; the account given in I Chron. 22–II Chron. 9 is a pious 3d century B.C. revision of the 600 B.C. edition of the account in I Kings. The latter rests on earlier works, e.g., "the Acts of Solomon" (I Kings 11:41), material from "chronicles of the kings of Judah" (I Kings 14:29), and early Temple records in I Kings 7:13–8:66. The story of his famous judgment concerning two mothers and a disputed child is narrated in I Kings 3:16–28. Solomon was a glamorous personality with power and pomp seen through the mist of awe and legend.

David preferred Solomon as his successor rather than his older son Adonijah* (I Kings 1:15–31). Forthwith Solomon, with appropriate ecclesiastical pomp, was anointed king at Gihon Spring in the Valley of the Kidron (1:38–40). A palace revolt instigated by the disappointed Adonijah was suppressed, but led to a demonstration of clemency by Solomon toward the usurper (1:52 f.) and his fellow conspirator, the priest Abiathar (2:26 f.). Joab, the military leader of the unsuccessful coup, did not fare so well at the hands of the young king (2:28–34). Later, when Adonijah—with Bath-sheba as his intermediary—asked to be given Abishag* as his wife, Solomon grew suspicious—interpreting the request as a political threat to his own position—and had him executed (2:19–25).

The story of Solomon's pilgrimage to Gibeon* and the oracle he received from Yahweh at this high place reveal his early attitude toward God and life (3:4–15). His desire for an understanding heart, in order to discern between good and evil and to judge his people rightly, was approved by God and became the basis of one of his claims to fame (vv. 16–28). Solomon specialized in the literary proverb; and he was assisted by a court group of wise men (4:30 f.). Three thousand pithy observations about life have been accredited to him. The number of songs he is said to have composed also reached fantastic proportions (4:32). Because Solomon was considered to be an "authority" on trees, beasts, birds, fish, etc., his court was visited by the intellectually alert from neighboring nations (4:33, 10:24). The Queen of Sheba (see SABA) was as amazed by his wisdom as by his opulence (10:1, 3 f., 7 f.). Solomon was the father of what was later called Hebrew Wisdom Literature, even as David was considered the father of the Psalter. The Book of Proverbs* has traditionally been attributed to this kingly philosopher.

392. Solomon, in stained-glass window, Hanson Place Central Methodist Church, Brooklyn, N. Y.

The tradition of Solomonic splendor and grandeur current in Christ's time (Matt. 6:29) rests on historic, economic, and social facts which have been verified. Solomon inherited from David a kingdom extending from Homs in the N. to the Gulf of Aqabah in the S. Never before or after was the territory of Israel so extensive. Peace characterized this vast domain, mainly because Israel's powerful neighbors, especially Assyria and Egypt, were at this period in a weakened or quiescent condition. Solomon took advantage of this situation and embarked on profitable ventures on land and sea.

The commercial aspects of sea transportation were developed by Israel in Solomon's day. By a trade alliance with Hiram* I of Tyre, who controlled Mediterranean commerce, Solomon developed Ezion-geber* on the Gulf of Aqabah to such a degree as to make this the front door of Israel for trade with Arabia and Africa (I Kings 9:26–28).

Revolutionary changes in land transportation also brought wealth to Solomon. The domestication of the camel (see CAMELS) (c. 12th century B.C.) made increased caravan travel possible through deserts where adequate water supplies were days' journeys apart. Solomon's control of the frontier districts of Zobah, Damascus, Hauran, Ammon, Moab, and Edom meant that he controlled the entire caravan trade between Arabia and the N. (4:21). Horses from the Hittite Cilicia (a better translation of 10:28 f.) and chariots from Egypt were handled at a fixed price by Solomon's merchants, who controlled the land and sea routes. When Solomon built a chain of chariot cities* for national defense (I Kings 9:19, 10:26), he required both chariots and cavalry, items in the national budget with costly price-tags (I Kings 10:28–29; II Chron. 1:16–17, 9:28). See GEZER, MEGIDDO.

Copper mining and refining in the Arabah*, at and around Ezion-geber, and from Succoth to Zarthan in the Jordan Valley (I Kings 7:46), carried on under the skilled co-operation of Phoenician workmen, made Solomon one of the early copper kings. To the wealth which all this industry and commerce brought Israel must be added the regular tribute paid yearly by subject states (4:21–28).

Solomon conscripted labor from the population for his building projects (5:13–17, 9:19–21). Israel's products of wheat and oil, never in surplus supply, he exported to Phoenicia* in exchange for skilled labor, timber, and gold (5:7–11, 9:14). Finally he was compelled to make up a deficit in his trade balance with Hiram by ceding him 20 towns in Galilee (9:10–13). When Solomon died, after a 38-year reign (11:43), the international situation had changed (11:14–25), and many of the sources of national income failed while defense and government expenses remained high.

Solomon, through his international business and political policies, fostered a *cosmopolitanism* which profoundly affected Israel. Early in his reign he had married the daughter of an Egyptian pharaoh (3:1). As her dowry he obtained the stronghold of Gezer, which the pharaoh had taken from the Canaanites (9:16 f.). This Egyptian princess remained his favorite queen; he built her house close to his own (9:24). Solomon made numerous other alliances with neighboring states through marriage (11:1–3) with women of prominence in their homelands, who contributed to the atmosphere of cosmopolitanism in the court and country. Tradition outside Biblical literature transformed the visit of the Queen of Sheba into a romance. Though polygamy (see MARRIAGE) was the matrimonial standard of the time among those who could afford it, rabbis later interpreted the fact that Solomon had only one son —Rehoboam*—as a judgment sent by God for his violation of monogamy. Solomon's wives and consorts had their own private chapels. Ashtoreth (see ASHERAH) of the Sidonians, Molech* of the Ammonites, and Chemosh* of the Moabites (11:5–7), were among the foreign gods who had their shrines, priests, and court patrons at Jerusalem. Such feminine influence—with perhaps even open proselyting in the court—had its effect on the purity of Solomon's religion (vv. 9 f.). The breakup of the United Monarchy was attributed not to economic collapse, but to Solomon's disobedience to God and his interest in foreign deities (vv. 9–11).

At the outset of Solomon's reign the old tribal system had given way to one of centralized control (4:7–19). The elders "that stood before Solomon" petitioned Solomon's successor, Rehoboam, to ease the tax burden imposed by his father. His refusal led to the dividing of the Monarchy (12:1–19); thus economic forces which made the Solomonic splendor also broke it.

Solomon's *building program* became his outstanding attainment. Though he failed to increase the agricultural productivity of the land or raise the standard of living, Solomon, through his vast wealth and his control of the country's economy, brought it distinction by inaugurating a vast building program. For the protection of trade and national defense, he constructed store- and chariot cities. His public works in Jerusalem included repairing the breaches in the city walls which David had made when he captured the city from the Jebusites (see JEBUS) (3:1); and the building of Millo*, a fortress tower in the N. section of the old "City of David" (9:15, 24). On the site of the present Haram esh-Sherif (the Temple Area in Jerusalem) he erected, beginning in the S., and running northward in the following order, the House of the Forest of Lebanon, characterized by cedar-wood construction (7:2–5); Solomon's Porch of Pillars (v. 6), which continued as an architectural feature of the Temple Area in the time of Christ (John 10:23) and the Apostles (Acts 3:11, 5:12); the throne room and hall of judgment (I Kings 7:7); Solomon's own palace (3:1, 7:1, 8); the palace of his Egyptian queen (7:8); and the Temple. For these buildings on Jerusalem's acropolis which brought Solomon such enduring fame he employed foreign architects and builders (5:18, 7:13), and demonstrated his openmindedness to new ideas (5:2–10). See also RESERVOIR, illus. 344.

In the ceremonies in connection with the transfer of the Ark* of the Covenant from the lower City of David up the Temple hill, past the buildings under construction, to the inner sanctuary of the Temple, and in the subsequent dedication of the Temple itself, Solomon testified to and demonstrated his faith in God. This ceremony was evidently the high point of his religious career. Though much of the language of the prayer and the addresses is in the style of the Deuteronomist, Solomon's enthusiasm and devotion is apparent (8:22–66). To perform the function of priest to his people was in keeping with his religious nature and early training. Three times each year thereafter he offered sacrifices in the Temple which he had built (9:25).

This Temple in time eclipsed all other shrines in the land; and its site has probably been used continually for worship over a longer period of time than any other. The God Whom neither heaven nor the heaven of heavens nor any Jerusalem temple could contain (8:27) was honored in this house which Solomon built for the worship of Yahweh.

Solomon, the Song of, whose full title is "The Song of Songs which is Solomon's" (1:1), is the last of five O.T. poetic books in the English Bible. It stands between Job and Ruth in the Writings (Hagiographa), as the 1st of the "Five Scrolls" in the Hebrew Scriptures. "Canticles," another title for this book, is a translation of the Vulgate title, *Canticum Canticorum* (1:1). The book is a poem or collection of poems characterized by enchanting imagery, appreciation of nature, great literary skill, and a keen understanding of romantic and nuptial love. In some modern editions of the Bible the arrangement of Canticles in poetic form, with breaks between the paragraphs and the various episodes, aids in the understanding of its form and structure.

The book may be outlined thus:

Songs of the bride—1:2–8.
Dialogue between the groom and the bride—1:9–2:7.
Reminiscences of the bride—2:8–3:5.
The procession of the bridegroom—3:6–11.
Songs of the lover—4:1–5:1.
The lost bridegroom—5:2–6:3.
The beauty of the bride—6:4–7:9.
Songs of the bride—7:10–8:4.
Miscellaneous love lyrics—8:5–14.

The tradition that Solomon was the author is due to the use of his name in the book (1:5, 3:9, 11), and to his fame as a song writer (I Kings 4:32). Solomon's brunette Egyptian wife may be indicated in 1:5, 9–11, and a Shunammite* (Shulamite) maiden renowned for her beauty is mentioned in 6:13–7:9 (cf. I Kings 3:1, 1:3 f.). But it is more likely that these ancient characters furnished only idealized personalities for the lyrics. The bridegroom depicted as a king, and the bride as the most beautiful of women, reflect typical Middle Eastern wedding customs, and express typical feelings at peasant wedding feasts.

The variety of subjects and situations portrayed, the repetitions and parallels (3:1–5, 5:2–8), and the lack of logical order indicate that the book is a collection of love and marriage lyrics. Sometimes the background is Judaean (1:14, 2:7, 3:11), again N. Israelite (2:1, 6:4, 7:5), again Trans-Jordanic (4:1, 6:5, 7:4). Some of the poems dramatize special occasions, e.g., the coming of the bridegroom (3:6–11, cf. Matt. 25:6); the dance of the bride (6:13–7:5); the lost bridegroom (5:2–6:3). The influence of Egyptian love poetry is seen in the addressing the bride as "my sister" (4:9 f., 12, 5:1 f.); and in the rapturous admiration of flowers, trees, doves, gazelles, and gardens.

The name of God does not appear in the book except perhaps as a symbol of power (8:6). If the practices depicted belonged originally to earlier fertility cults taken over by the Hebrews from the agricultural Canaanites (Judg. 21:19–23), as some scholars maintain, their original pagan cultic terms and sensual indecencies have been eliminated by a purifying Hebrew monotheism*. Such an origin for parts of this book would antedate Solomon (c. 961–922 B.C.). On the other hand, Aram. and Gk. expressions indicate the Greek period. Although very ancient customs are referred to, and Solomon and his love for a country lass may be depicted, some unknown author or authors wove together this anthology of erotic poems c. 250 B.C. against the background of springtime and the charming Palestinian countryside. The notion that the book is a drama is obsolete.

Many poetic lines and phrases in the book have become familiar in Eng., e.g., 1:15, 2:1, 4:6. This book is one of the first to label and diagnose "love sickness" (2:5, 5:8). A famous description of springtime is found in 2:11–13.

Allegorical interpretation, by discovering a deeper meaning beneath the love poetry, and thereby imparting some religious value to the Song of Solomon, made possible the canonization of the book (see CANON). Since Hosea's time married love was a symbol in the O.T. of the relations between Yahweh and His people (Hos. 1–2; Jer. 2:2, 3:1–13; Isa. 50:1; Ezek. 16, 23). In the Talmud (A.D. 500) the bridegroom of Canticles is taken to be God, and the bride the congregation Israel. Most early Christian interpreters—among them Origen (d. A.D. 254), Jerome (d. 420), and Augustine (d. 430)—perpetuated this allegorical interpretation but changed the figure to the love of Christ for his Church.

The scope of interpretations about this little book surpasses by far that of any other book in the Bible. For a detailed exposition of all interpretations, see R. H. Pfeiffer, *Introduction to the Old Testament*, Harper.

"Solomon's Pools," three pools (constructed probably not later than the 2d century B.C.), near the junction of the Jerusalem-Hebron road with the road to Bethlehem. From these reservoirs, one of which measures 582x207x50 ft., two aqueducts carried water 7 m. to Jerusalem. In Roman times Pontius Pilate repaired them, and repairs in modern times have kept this system working as part of Jerusalem's water supply. See RESERVOIR, illus. 344.

Solomon's Porch, a magnificent colonnade running along the E. side of the Temple* Area on a platform built up from Kidron Valley materials. The one seen in N.T. times was so called because people believed it to be on the site of a similar arched passage erected by Solomon. In that porch Jesus walked in winter, which is cold in highland Jerusalem (John 10:23). In it assembled "all the people" to see the cripple whom Peter and John had healed (Acts 3:11). Acts 5:12 suggests that Solomon's Porch was the scene of Apostolic "signs and wonders" after the Resurrection of Jesus.

Solomon's Seal. See SEAL OF SOLOMON, THE.

Solomon's servants, foreign slaves used by Solomon in his Temple Area for menial tasks (Ezra 2:55, 58; Neh. 7:57, 60, 11:3). They were similar to the Nethinim* (Ezra 8:20) who helped the Levites after the Exile.

Solomon's Temple. See TEMPLE, THE.

son, male offspring. The hundreds of allusions to sons in the O.T. and the N.T. reveal their importance in Hebrew society. On the son rested the perpetuation of clan, tribe, and nation, and the guarantee of the land on which they lived (see INHERITANCE; OWNERSHIP). To be without a son was reproach and tragedy; to give birth to a son was cause for rejoicing, as with Sarah*, Hannah*, Elisabeth*, and Mary* of Nazareth (see FAMILY; GENEALOGY).

"Son" is used in many figurative senses: (1) of remoter relatives, e.g., grandsons and descendants; (2) of members of musical guilds, like "sons of Korah" (heading Ps. 47, 48, 49, etc.); "sons" of apothecaries; "sons" of the prophets (II Kings 2:3, 5; cf. Amos 7:14); (3) of followers of certain deities, e.g., "sons of Chemosh" (Num. 21:29); and of dwellers in specific places, e.g., "sons of Javan" (Gen. 10:4).

Loyalty and respect for parents were early inculcated in Hebrew children (Ex. 20:12); Wisdom literature is especially rich in precepts encouraging filial relationships. The Book of Proverbs uses the phrase "my son" to introduce its exhortations (2:1, 3:1, 5:1, 6:1, 7:1); and the theme of wise sonship resounds through its collection of ancient maxims: "A wise son heareth his father's instruction" (13:1). Its closing chapter describes the deference paid by a son to his worthy mother (31:1 f.). Cf. the devotion of Jesus to his mother Mary (John 19:26 f.).

Sonship in the O.T. appears in the profoundly moving love revealed by Joseph, prime minister at the court of Pharaoh, for his shepherd father, Jacob (Gen. 45:13–15, 46:29–34, 47:12); contrast with this Absalom's* disloyal sonship. The great N.T. revelation of a filial relationship broken and then restored is seen in Christ's Parable of the Prodigal Son (Luke 15:11–32).

Son of God, the, is a term used in the Scriptures in a variety of senses. It is applied to superhuman beings (Gen. 6:2, 4; Job 1:6, 2:1, 38:7; Dan. 3:25); to faithful Israelites (Hos. 1:10, cf. Isa. 63:16, 64:8); to the Israelite king and then later, by extension, to the future Messianic king (II Sam. 7:14; Ps. 2:7, 89:26 f.); and to Christian believers (Rom. 8:14; Gal. 3:26, cf. John 1:12; I John 3:2).

But in a special and unique sense the term is applied to Jesus Christ. He is not Son of God as any Christian might be, since it is through him that the Christian comes to the relation of sonship. It is the difference between a sonship that is natural (John 16:28) and a sonship that is acquired (17:22; Gal. 4:5, "the adoption of sons"). When Paul calls Jesus Christ "the firstborn among many brethren" (Rom. 8:29), he does not mean that he was just the first of a succession of like persons, but that he was "the One Son" (John 1:18) who made all the others possible. Such a Son had rights and prerogatives which were his alone; they could never be taken from him or shared; they rooted in his fundamental nature as uncreated and eternal; he could, however, in pursuance of the will of the Father, temporarily lay them aside. This is the doctrine of the "self-emptying of the Son" (Phil. 2:5–11), and is similar to John's teaching about the Logos. Paul further elaborates and sharpens it in Col. 1:13–17, and the conception is in substance repeated in Heb. 1:1–4. The teaching involves what is known as the preexistence of Christ with the Father, and is a presupposition of the story of his Virgin Birth (Luke 1:26–35), of his Resurrection from the dead, of his final departure without dying (24:44–52; cf. Acts 1:1–11), and of his promise to return as a Presence and to remain in the world as a redeeming power.

The full development of the doctrine that Jesus, as son, is the second person of the Trinity is a product of the later Church, but the N.T. itself contains the seed from which it grew. From the beginning Jesus was conscious of a unique filial relationship with God which was perhaps undefined at first even in his own mind. The simple directness with which he spoke of God as "Father" or "my Father" is unprecedented in Jewish piety (Matt. 7:21, 26:42; Luke 2:49, 10:21 f., 23:34, 46, 24:49). Even more striking is his use of the informal, affectionate Aramaic word "Abba" to address God (Mark 14:36), a use he then bequeathed to his disciples (Rom. 8:15 ff.; Gal. 4:6). The Gospels relate that he heard God addressing him as "Son" both at the Baptism (Mark 1:11) and Transfiguration (Mark 9:7). The evidence that he felt himself to be in a unique Father-Son relationship to God from the beginning of his career is too widespread to be explained away, but the full implications of this feeling may well have been subject to considerable change and growth in his own mind, as they certainly were in the minds of the N.T. writers and those of the post-Apostolic Church.

It is not impossible that Jesus himself first interpreted his sense of special sonship in terms of a Messianic vocation, since, as we have noted, the Israelite king was called God's son in the O.T. and, after the end of the Monarchy, the same appellation was naturally given to the expected Messiah of David's line. The words of the "Messianic" second Psalm (v. 7) "You are my son . . ." are evidently echoed in the formula of Jesus' Baptism, "Thou art my beloved son . . ." (Mark 1:11). The story of the Temptation, in its Matthaean form (4:1–11), can be interpreted as reflecting a struggle within the soul of Jesus as he endeavored to understand the nature of his "sonship" or "Messiahship." Whatever Jesus himself may have thought on this subject, there can be no doubt that the later Church understood that as God's "Son" his Messiahship was purely spiritual, not political; it was to be interpreted in terms of the Suffering Servant of Isa. 42:1–4, 49:1–6, 50:4–9, 52:13–53:12 (a figure who, in O.T. thought, was not the Messiah at all). The second part of the baptismal address "with thee I am well pleased" (Mark 1:11) is an obvious reference to Isa. 42:1. So there developed, in the mind of the N.T. Church at least, the thought that Jesus as "Son of God" was Messiah, but a *suffering* Messiah, an idea for which there was no precedent in Judaism. The last stage in the attempt of the N.T. writers to understand him was to conceive of his "sonship" in terms of an eternal metaphysical relationship to the Father. This is perhaps implied in Jesus' own consciousness of being God's son in a special sense and is set forth clearly in a number of passages in the Gospels and the rest of the N.T. (Luke 10:22; John 1:14, 18, 3:16 ff.; Rom. 8:3, 32; Heb. 1:1–4).

The Resurrection appearances began in the minds of the disciples a process which was to evolve into the conviction that the Master with whom they had been privileged to live for a while was much more than the "Son of God" of Messianic tradition —a mere national deliverer: he was instead the eternal Son of the eternal Father, who had come into the world to share the human lot in order to accomplish a salvation from sin in which all men everywhere could share. The N.T. reflects the emergence of this conviction and of the associated faith. The first impact on the mind of the disciples was made by the human Jesus, the historical Jesus, the "man of sorrows," whose final act of self-giving—over their protest—was the Cross. Actually the impact left them confused. The crucifixion saw them disillusioned and discouraged (see Luke 24:18–21). It was the Resurrection that began the work of clarification, inspiration, and transformation; when they began, in the light of this new experience, to look at the Jesus they had known and lost, everything took on a different meaning: the crucified Jesus became for them the Lord of Glory. His death appeared to them as a sacrifice for sin. The kingdom they had hoped he would establish, which vanished with his death, they now saw to be a kingdom "not of this world" (John 18:36). The salvation he had accomplished far transcended the political and economic one they had once hoped for: they now saw it as a salvation from all the evil forces of existence; as a new relationship of man to God and of man to man; and therefore as a promise of "a new humanity" (Eph. 2:13–22).

It is only from the standpoint of this conviction of the universal redeeming significance of Jesus Christ that the declaration that he is the eternal son of the eternal Father—"the Word made flesh"—becomes intelligible. This is not mere philosophy—it is a doctrine of faith, a truth required by faith, and a truth which only the faith that creates it can authenticate.

The Gospel of John, where this is set forth, is to be read accordingly. This Gospel was written within the circle of faith itself, and is not to be understood otherwise. Similarly with great passages like Rom. 8:29–39; I Cor. 15:12–28; II Cor. 4:7–18; Gal. 4:1–7; Eph. 1:15–23, 2:4–10; Phil. 2:5–11; Col. 1:12–20; Heb. 1:1–4, 9:11–15; I Pet. 1:13-25; Rev. 1:9–18. These passages assign him a position for just one reason: faith finds in him the promise and power of both individual and universal redemption. He is the living center around which swings God's eternal purpose respecting mankind. The N.T. declaration, which is continued in the testimony of the Church itself, attests the need of faith to protect its own validity.

See JESUS CHRIST; MEDIATOR; MESSIAH; SAVIOR; SON OF MAN; TRINITY.

E. L./R. C. D.

son of man, a phrase used frequently in the O.T. to indicate a human being pure and simple—just "a man" (Ps. 8:4, 80:17, 144:3, 146:3; Isa. 56:2; Jer. 51:43; in the plural, see Ps. 31:19, 33:13; Prov. 8:4; Eccl. 3:18 f., 8:11, 9:12). The term occurs with great frequency in Ezekiel—almost a hundred times—to indicate the prophet himself as addressed or commissioned by God: "Son of man, stand upon thy feet, and I will speak with thee" (2:1).

The term occurs once, however, in the O.T. in what may be a special sense. It is in Dan. 7:13, 14: "One like the Son of man came with the clouds of heaven.... And there was given him dominion, . . . an everlasting dominion." Earlier in Daniel the symbols of various world-empires were beasts (see 7:1–8). This figure "like the Son of man" is a symbol of a new kind of empire, that of the Israel of God brought to fulfillment. The term in Daniel may therefore be said to have a Messianic significance. In other Jewish Apocalyptic writings not included in the O.T. a figure appears, especially in what is known as the Similitudes of the Book of Enoch, who is called variously "the Elect One," "the Anointed One," and "the Son of Man." He will serve as God's agent in that Day of the Lord with which will come final victory. In some of these writings this is also described as "the manifestation of the Son of Man."

We meet the title many times in the Gospels, but only on the lips of Jesus and as applied to himself (Matt. 8:20, 9:6, 11:19, 12:8, etc.). In the references just made he uses it in connection with his earthly mission; but he also uses it of himself frequently when he is describing his ultimate triumph as Redeemer and Judge (Matt. 16:27 f., 19:28, 24:30, 25:31; cf. Luke 12:8–10, 18:8). Its use in the latter sense is generally taken to mean that Jesus borrowed the term from the apocalypses; but if it was borrowed, it was given a new connotation, because the Gospels represent Jesus as associating it with his death and, therefore, with the concept of the "Suffering Servant" of Isa. 53 (Mark 10:45).

Outside the Gospels the term occurs only once, on the lips of Stephen (Acts 7:56). This curious silence about a concept which the Gospels connect so closely with Jesus' own self-understanding is probably due to the fact that it was not intelligible to people who did not speak one of the Semitic languages. Paul's use of the term "man" for Jesus may be an attempt to translate the Semitic idiom into its Greek equivalent (I Cor. 15:21, 45, 47). On the whole Gentiles preferred to express their faith in Christ by means of the Greek term "the Lord." The modern use of "Son of Man" to express the idea of Jesus' human, as opposed to his divine, nature is without warrant in Scripture.

See JESUS CHRIST; JUDGMENT, DAY OF; MESSIAH; PAROUSIA; SON OF GOD.

E. L./R. C. D.

Song of degress, A (A.S.V., R.S.V. "A Song of Ascents," Moff. "A pilgrim song"), any one of Psalms 120 through 134, sung by the males of Judah on their pilgrimages to the Jerusalem Temple for the Festival of Booths, the Passover, and the Festival of Weeks.

Song of Songs, the. See SOLOMON, THE SONG OF.

songs. See MUSIC; PSALMS; PRIESTS; also SCROLLS, THE DEAD SEA, for the previously unknown collection of Thanksgiving Psalms ("DST") found in 1947 in a cave near 'Ain Fashka above the Dead Sea.

sons of God, children of God, phrases whose implication is divine Fatherhood. The Bible does not teach, however, that men are "naturally" the sons of God; they must be creatures of God's power before they can become consciously sons of His love. Nothing can ever destroy the relation of Creator and creature; that remains in spite of indifference to God or of rebellion against His commands, because the relation is independent of man's will.

The father-son relation, however, is different: different because it calls for the attitude of faith, obedience, and love on the man's part. It also calls for a certain attitude on God's part. This is apparent even in the O.T., where the few references to God as Father denote His special relation to the people of Israel. In Ps. 68:5 God is called "a father of the fatherless," but the meaning is really that of Ps. 10:14, "the helper of the fatherless" (cf. Ps. 103:13). The "Everlasting Father" of Isa. 9:6 is a reference to the expected Messiah. The meaning of "Father" in Isa. 63:16 f. is explained by "servants" and by "holy people." The metaphor of "clay and potter" in Isa. 64:8 indicates that "Father" here means little more than "Sovereign." The relation suggested by Jer. 3:4 and 31:9 is perhaps more intimate, but it is still "natural," as implied by "firstborn."

It is with the coming of Christ that the Fatherhood of God takes on its true meaning. About his own Sonship to God he had no least doubt (Luke 23:34, 46). His usual way of referring to God was as "my Father," "your Father," "our Father" (Matt. 7:21, 6:32, 6:9), but he always used the word as expressing a special relation. He believed it was God's purpose to bring men to a conscious sonship with Him as their Father, and consequently to brotherhood with each other (see John 17). Both the sonship and the brotherhood were relations to be acquired, not relations that came "by nature." Hence, "Ye must be born again" (John 3:7). He believed he had come into the world to make these relations possible. The case is exactly stated in John 1:12 f., where "the children of God" are those who have "received" Christ as "the true light."

This teaching pervades the N.T. There is "one Lord, one faith, one baptism, one God and Father of all" (Eph. 4:5–7), but the "all" means those who know this "faith" of which the object is Christ, who is "the Head of the Church" (Col. 1:18). This Church is a "household" or family (Gal. 6:10; cf. II Thess. 3:13–15), a "brotherhood" (I Pet. 2:17) or "fellowship" (Acts 2:42–47) centered in Christ, who makes believers "children of God" and his own "joint-heirs" (Rom. 8:16 f., 19–21).

Paul sometimes used the word "adoption" to illustrate Christian sonship. He finds the analogy in current Roman procedure: an outsider could, by a prescribed ceremony, be taken into a Roman family as a son, and given the family name and all the rights and privileges of sonship (cf. Rev. 14:1); even a slave might be thus adopted—and this seems to be the allusion in the word "redeem" in Gal. 4:4–7. Thus Christian sonship is a status "conferred" on men through Christ.

See REGENERATION; SACRAMENTS; SALVATION. E. L.

sons of the prophets. See PROPHET.

soothsayer, a foreteller of events. See MAGIC AND DIVINATION. For contrast, see PROPHET.

sop, a piece of thin bread, often bent to make a spoon, and dipped into a juicy meat stew or other liquid. Two or more friends honored one another by dipping from the same earthen sop dish. Judas attempted to conceal his disloyalty to Jesus by dipping his hand in the same dish with him (Matt. 26:23). In the Johannine account Jesus dips the bread—or possibly a piece of meat—into the dish and hands it to Judas (John 13:26–30). See MEALS.

Sopater (sō′pȧ-tẽr). See SOSIPATER.

Sophereth (sǒ-fē′rĕth), a family descended from "Solomon's servants" or staff (Ezra 2:55; Neh. 7:57), Nethinim* who returned from their Babylonian Exile.

sorcery. See MAGIC AND DIVINATION.

Sorek (sō′rĕk), Valley of, one of the transverse brook valleys (wâdīs) which cut through the Shephelah* foothills between the Philistine Plain and the highlands of Judaea. This Wâdī es-Sarâr lay S. of the Valley of Ajalon and N. of the Valley of Elah. The Valley of Sorek was protected by Ekron and Gezer in the Plain. One of its chief cities was Beth-shemesh*. Samson's home was at the Danite Zorah (Josh. 19:41) in this valley; that of his first wife at Timnath (Judg. 14); and Delilah's also in the Valley of Sorek (Judg. 16:4). In this valley Samson performed some of his famous exploits, like the fox brands feat (Judg. 15:4–8). Its defiles were scenes of battles between Israel and the Philistines (I Sam. 4–7). Through this valley came the Ark of Israel when it was being returned from the Philistines (I Sam. 6:15). The Valley of Sorek, the most natural approach to Jerusalem from the coastal Joppa, supplied in modern times the railway roadbed.

Sosipater (sǒ-sĭp′ȧ-tẽr), a man named in the postcript of Romans (16:21) as a "kinsman"—fellow countryman—of the author. He encloses greetings to "God's beloved in Rome" (R.S.V. 1:7) to whom the message is addressed. He may be the Sopater of Berea who was Paul's companion on his last visit to Jerusalem (Acts 20:4).

Sosthenes (sǒs′thĕ-nēz), the president of a synagogue at Corinth* during Paul's residence there. He was probably the successor of Crispus after Crispus's conversion (Acts 18:8). When Gallio refused to pursue the case of irate Jews against Paul, whose Christian preaching they resented (vv. 12–17) the angered mob seized Sosthenes and beat him before the judgment seat. This Sosthenes may be the same one mentioned in I Cor. 1:1 as sending greetings to "the Church of God which is at Corinth"; if so, he had become a Christian some time after the violent scene before Gallio. He may have been one of the Seventy.

soul, generally the translation of the Heb. *nephesh* ("breath") and the Gk. *psyche.* "Soul" is used in so many senses in Scripture that it should be rendered by even more Eng. words than are used in the various translations. Sometimes *nephesh* is used in connection with animals, e.g., Gen. 2:19. Both *nephesh* and *psyche* are used also in the sense of persons, or men (Gen. 2:7; I Chron. 5:21; Acts 2:41). It is apparent that N.T. concern for the saving of "souls" (often "life" in the R.S.V., e.g., Matt. 16:26) is something different from what many O.T. passages suggest by "soul." Yet even in many O.T. passages the word translated "soul" usually means something living, something which could be "cut off" from the Congregation Israel (Num. 15:30)—something which seeks God with all its might (Deut. 10:12); which is humbled by fasting (Ps. 35:13); and which is healed of sin (41:4) or cast down in despair (42:5). The soul was recognized as having a faculty for friendship (I Sam. 18:1).

The Jews after their return from Exile definitely believed that the soul was man's immortal part. Jesus taught that human forces are unable to kill the soul (Matt. 10:28), and that it is wiser to retain the soul's integrity than to gain the whole material world (Matt. 16:26). Mark quotes Jesus' words in Gethsemane: "My soul is exceeding sorrowful, even unto death" (A.S.V. 14:34). The work of the early Apostles included "confirming the souls of the disciples" (Acts 14:22) at Antioch, etc.

See FLESH AND SPIRIT; HADES; HEAVEN; HELL; IMMORTALITY; MAN; PUNISHMENT; RESURRECTION.

sources, the documents from which the O.T. editors made up their narratives. The backbone of the O.T. is a great historical and legal work originally in nine volumes, relating the vicissitudes of early mankind and of the Children of Israel from the Creation (Gen. 1) to the destruction of Jerusalem in 587 B.C. (587, Albright) and the deliverance of Jehoiachin in 561 B.C. (II Kings 25). These nine volumes were Genesis, Exodus, Leviticus, Numbers, Deuteronomy, Joshua, Judges, Samuel, and Kings. Samuel and Kings were originally (in Heb.) two volumes, but in the Gk. translation were divided into four books because the Heb. text written without vowels could be contained in two scrolls of papyrus, whereas the Gk., in which the vowels are written, required four scrolls. About 400 B.C. the first five books, called the Pentateuch ("five scrolls"), were separated from the rest and canonized as the Law of Moses, after being edited substantially as we now have them. The other four books (Joshua to Kings) were repeatedly copied and edited until their final publication and canonization about 200 B.C. under the title of "The Former Prophets"; "The Latter Prophets" are the books of Isaiah, Jeremiah, Ezekiel, and "the Twelve [Minor Prophets]." They were likewise canonized c. 200 B.C.; that is why Jesus called the Bible of his time "The Law and the Prophets" (Matt. 22:40; Luke 16:16; etc.).

Modern scholars speak of a "Hexateuch" ("six scrolls") because they are convinced that the same sources continue through the Pentateuch into Joshua; but the Jews never had such a volume—only Genesis to Kings before 400 B.C. and Genesis to Deuteronomy and Joshua to Kings after that time. Since the five books of the Pentateuch are extant in their edition of c. 400 B.C. and the four historical books Joshua to Kings in their edition of c. 200 B.C., we may expect to find material from 1250 to 400 B.C. in the Pentateuch and material from 1200 to 200 B.C. in the historical books. Every book was—at least in part—compiled out of previously existing written sources; but when the Greek practice of citing one's sources was unknown none of the authors mentioned his sources. The author of Kings, however, does refer to "the book of the acts of Solomon" (I Kings 11:41), to "the book of the chronicles of the kings of Judah" (14:29, and 14 other times), and to "the book of the chronicles of the kings of Israel" (14:19, and 15 other times) for additional information; and two ancient anthologies from which poems are quoted are mentioned, "the book of Jasher" or "the Upright" (Josh. 10:13; II Sam. 1:18; in the Gk. text following I Kings 8:53 it is called—probably correctly—"the book of song," reading *sh-y-r* instead of *y-sh-r*), and "the book of the wars of the Lord" (Num. 21:14). The only actual citation of a source is in II Kings 14:6 (quoting Deut. 24:16), though some writings of Moses are mentioned in the Pentateuch (Ex. 17:14, 24:4; Num. 33:2; Deut. 31:9–13, 24–26). But modern research has rejected the traditional authorship of the nine volumes with which we are here concerned (as given in the Talmud, *Baba Bathra* 14b): that Moses wrote the Pentateuch (except for Deut. 34:5–12, ascribed to the pen of Joshua); Joshua wrote his own book; Samuel wrote Judges and Samuel; and Jeremiah wrote Kings.

(1) *The Sources of the Pentateuch.* Jean Astruc (d. 1766), regius professor of medicine at Paris, seems to have been the first to have discovered that earlier sources were utilized in the writing of the Pentateuch; in 1753 he published anonymously in Brussels a French book entitled, *Conjectures on the original memoirs which Moses seems to have used in composing the Book of Genesis.* Since then the two chief sources he identified in Genesis by their use of *Yahweh* (Jehovah) and *Elohim* (deity) for the God of Israel have been determined more accurately, and are still called J (Jehovistic or Yahwistic) and E (Elohistic, from which the Priestly Code or P was eventually separated) in accordance with the divine name prevalently used in them; though we should perhaps more correctly regard J as the abbreviation of Judaic and E as the abbreviation of Ephraimitic, from their place of origin.

(a) *The J Document.* The author of the J Document was a Judaean who lived in Jerusalem c. 950–850 B.C., when Judah was enjoying great power and prosperity, and the outlook for the future was most promising. With the assurance that Yahweh would continue to guide and protect Israel as He had in the past, the J author wrote a superb epic, which magnificently expressed the national pride of Israel, and thus kept it alive to the present day. At the very beginning, in the three promises of Yahweh to Abraham, the author presented the contents and plan of his work (Gen. 12:1–4a, 7): "I will make of thee a great nation, . . . and in thee shall all the families of the earth be blessed. . . . Unto thy seed will I give this land." In Gen. 12–33 J shows how from Abraham the Twelve Tribes of Israel were descended; in Gen. 37–50 how through Joseph all nations were blessed by being saved from starvation; and in Ex. 1–Judg. 1 how Jehovah gave to the seed of Abraham the land of Canaan. The J author drew his material from traditions (mostly N. Israelitic) which were circulating orally. The genuine traditions of the Tribes of Israel did not reach back beyond the deliverance from Egyptian bondage (Moses is the first genuinely historical character mentioned by J). In Genesis J utilized ancient Canaanitic traditions about Abraham, Isaac, and Jacob—the founders of the ancient sanctuaries at Hebron, Beer-sheba, and Bethel, respectively—and composed the brilliant novel about Joseph, to explain how the Children of Israel happened to be oppressed in Egypt until Yahweh sent Moses to deliver them. This epic, showing how Israel overcame all obstacles under the guidance of its God, was penned by the J author in a brilliant but unobtrusive style, combining his own nobility and sophistication with the simplicity of his naïve sources. His fascinating story is built around the heroic figures of Abraham, Jacob, Joseph, and Moses—to mention but the main characters (the story of the conquest of Canaan at the end has been for the most part suppressed and lost). Heirs of divine promises, the characters of J are men of destiny, triumphant through Yahweh's invincible help.

(b) *The S Document.* The stories about the creation of Adam, the Garden of Eden, Cain and his descendants, the birth of the giants, Noah and his sons, and the Tower of Babel (in Gen. 2–11, omitting P) are usually assigned to the J document, though their pessimism and sense of divine indifference—if not hostility—toward human beings are notably different from the enthusiasm of J. These stories, as well as some others in Genesis which disclose indifference and hostility to Israel, and cannot be fitted into J or E (Gen. 14, 19, 34, 35:21–22a, 36, 38, for the most part), seem to be part of a distinct document, possibly composed in Edom, called S (from

South or Seir). Judging from the historical list of the kings of Edom (Gen. 36:31–39) who ruled before Saul or David, we may date the S document in the 1st half of the 10th century B.C.

(c) *The E Document.* This is the epic composed in N. Israel, presumably by a priest at Bethel, about 750 B.C., not long before the end of the kingdom in 722 B.C. when Sargon of Assyria took Samaria. Though similar to J in contents (from Abraham to Joshua), E is subtly different in its ardent nationalism and in the classic beauty of its style. The style no longer combines nobility and simplicity; it is more refined, more sentimental, more reflective, more prolix; compare Gen. 31:3 (J) with 31:11, 13 (E). God no longer appears visibly to men (except to Moses), but reveals Himself in dreams or through an angel; the Patriarchs no longer (as in J) have recourse to lies, tricks, and questionable actions, but achieve their safety and success through divine blessing; miracles, lacking in J, are frequently performed by Moses. The cult, disregarded by J, is stressed by E, whose masterpiece is the story of the sacrifice of Isaac (Gen. 22:1–13, 19) ignored by J.

(d) *The D Document.* In 622 B.C. Hilkiah the high priest found the book of the Law of Moses in the collection box at the entrance of the Temple in Jerusalem; King Josiah read the book before the Judaeans, and they made a covenant to observe Yahweh's commandments written in it (II Kings 22–23). That book was the Deuteronomic Code (D), found in Deut. 4:44–8:20, 10:12–11:25, 12–26, 28:1–24, 43–46, 29:1. Written by a priest in Jerusalem shortly before it was found, D is really a sermon of Moses—one which did not exist before—a redaction of what the author felt had been the final prophetic oracle of Moses in the plains of Moab. The Ten Commandments (Deut. 5:6–21; in a later edition in Ex. 20:2–17) and the special laws (Deut. 12–26) are not set down in the juristic style of a code but in the hortatory style of a preacher. D has the standard sermonic divisions: introduction (Deut. 5–11), exposition (Deut. 12–26), peroration (Deut. 28). To the noble nationalism of J and the priestly interests of E, D adds the stern reproof and inspired prophetic exhortation of Amos, Hosea, Micah, and Isaiah, whose books were known to the author.

(e) *The P Document.* The Priestly Code (P) is a concise, dogmatic history of God's organization of His holy congregation through Moses, and its establishment in Canaan through Joshua, written by a priest in Jerusalem c. 450 B.C. Except in reporting the four revelations of God (to Adam, Noah, Abraham, and Moses) and His two covenants (with Noah and with Abraham), and Joshua's distribution of the territory to the Twelve Tribes, almost no details are given. Ritual legislation is the essential part of P, and it carried out the author's main purpose—to keep the Jews, without a state and country of their own, separate from the Gentiles as the Lord's own people.

(f) *Codes of Law.* In addition to D, the Ten Commandments, and P, the following codes are included, at least in part of the Pentateuch. The Covenant Code (Ex. 20:22–23:33) contains those parts of an ancient code of civil laws (1200–1100 B.C.) which had not been utilized in D, an equally ancient ritual decalogue (given also, in a revised edition dating from about 550 B.C., in Ex. 34), and other early codes. The anathemas in Deut. 27:15–26 (omitting 27:15 and 26) probably date from the 9th or 8th century. The Holiness Code (Lev. 17–26) dates from about 550, but utilized a sanctuary code, known also to Ezekiel, earlier than D.

(2) *The Sources of the Historical Books.*

(a) *Joshua.* A few isolated verses may be ascribed to J; Josh. 1–12 and 24 is mostly based on E, thoroughly rewritten by the Deuteronomistic redactor about 550 B.C. (he wrote chap. 23); most of Josh. 13–20 is P, and chaps. 21–22 belong for the most part to the 3d century.

(b) *Judges.* In Judg. 1:1–2:5 we have a late and corrupt summary of J's account of the conquest of Canaan, which was suppressed in favor of E's more attractive report of an immediate conquest under the command of Joshua (Josh. 1–12). The Deuteronomistic redactor of Judg. 2:6–15:20 (550 B.C.) utilized a book in which an early source (similar to J) and a later source (similar to E) were combined. The early stories in chaps. 9, 16, 17–21 (950–850 B.C.), the Song of Deborah (chap. 5, about 1125 B.C.), and 1:1–2:5 were added after 400 B.C.

(c) *Samuel.* The early source of Samuel, which is essentially a biography of King David presumably written by his contemporary Ahimaaz, son of Zadok, about 950 B.C., is the unsurpassed, as well as the earliest, masterpiece of historical writing; it is found in the following passages (slightly rearranged): I Sam. 4:1–7:1, 9:1–10:16, 10:27b–11:11, 15, 13:2–7a, 15b–18, 23, 14:1–46, 16:14–23, 18:6–9, 20, 22–29a, 19:11–17, 21:1–9, 22:6–23, 23:1, 5–14a, 25:2–44, 26–27, 29, 30, 28, 31; II Sam. 1–5, 21:15–22, 23:8–39, 6, 24, 21:1–14, 9–20; I Kings 1, 2:13–46a. The rest of Samuel consists of poems dated between 1000 and 300 B.C., and miscellaneous stories or summaries written between 750 and 250 B.C.

(d) *Kings.* The book was written about 600 B.C. and supplemented, with earlier and later material, from then to 250 B.C. The original author utilized the following sources: A biography of Solomon, a history of the kings of Judah (based on the official annals of the kings of Judah), a history of the kings of Israel (likewise based on the annals of the kings of Israel), and a chronicle of the Temple in Jerusalem written by its priests. Later editors added the biographies of Elijah (I Kings 17–19; chap. 21 had been in the original book) and Elisha (II Kings 2–8, 13:14–21 for the most part), dating from about 800 B.C. and 750, respectively.

(3) *The Sources of the Hexateuch* (Chapter and verse references are to the Eng. Bible; secondary material is in parenthesis.)

(a) *The J Document.* Gen. 12:1–4a, 6–20, 13:1–2, 4–5, 7a, 8–10a (11a, 13–18), 16:1–2,

4–6, 7a (7b), 8, 11–14, 18:1–33, 19:27–28, 21:1a, 2a, 7, 33, 24:1–67, 25:21–26a, 27–34, (26–27, JE), 28:10, 13–16, 19a, 29:2–14, 26, 31–35, (30–32, JE), 33:1–17; 37 (JE), 39:1–23; 41–42 (JE), 43:1–13, 15–34; 44, 45 (JE), 46:1a, 28–34, 47:1–4, 5a, 6b, (12–27a), 29–31, 48:2b, 10, 13–14, 17–19, 50:(1–11), 14.

Ex. 1:6, 8–10, 2:11–23a, 3:2–4a, 5, 7, 8a, (18?), 4:19–20a, 24–26, 5:1–2, 5–23, 7:14, 15a, 16 (17a), 18, 21a, 8:1–4, 8–15a, 20–24, 28–32, 9:1–7, 13, 17–18, 23b, 24b, 25b–29a, 33–34, 10:1a, (3–10), 13aB, 14aB, 15a, 16–19, 11:4–8, 12:29–33, 38, 13:21–22, 14:(5–6), 10abA, 11–12, 13–14, 19b, (20), 21a, 24, 25b, 27aBb, 28b, 30, 15:22–25a, 27; 16–18 (JEP) (19:2b, 18, 20a, 21, 34:1a, 2, 4, 28).

Num. 10:29–32, 11:4–34 (JE), 13:17b, 19, 22a, 28, 30–31 (14:1b, 3–4, 31–32, 40–45), 20:1–13 (JEP) (21:1–14; 32).

Deut. 34:4 (?).

Josh. (5:13–14, 9:6–7, 10:12–13a), 13:13, 15:13–19, 63, 16:10, 17:11–18, 19:47.

Judg. 1:1–3, 5–7, 10b–17, 19–21 (22), 23–35.

(b) *The S Document.* Gen. 2:5–9 (10–14), 15–25, 3:1–24 (4:1–16), 4:17–24 (4:25–26) (5:29, 6:5–8, 7:1–5, 7–10, 12, 16b, 17b, 22–23, 8:2b–3a, 6–12, 13b, 20–22), 6:1–4, 9:20–27 (10:1b, 8–19, 21, 24–30), 11:1–9 (11:28–30), 14:1–17 (18–20), 21–24, 19:1–26, 30–38, (25:1–4), 34:1–31, 35:5, 35:21–22a, 36:(9–19), 20–39, 38:1–30.

(c) *The E Document.* Gen. 15:1–3, 5–6, 11, 12a, 13–14, 16 (the rest of the chapter is secondary), 20:1–17, 21:6a (6b), 8–21 (25–32a, 34), 22:1–13, 19; (26–27, JE), 28: 11–12, 17–18, 20–22, 29:1, 15–18 (19–23, 25, 27, 28a, 30), 30:1–3, 4b–8, 17–20a, 21, 22b–23, 26, 28 (31–35, 38–40 JE), 31:2, 4–11, 13–17, 19, 24, 25a, 26, 28–31a, 32–35, 36b–37, 41–43, 32:13b–21, 23a, 24a, 25a, 26b, 27–28, 31–32, 33:5, 11a, 18aAb, 19–20 (35:1–4, 6b–7), 35:14, 16–20, 37:5a, 6–11 (12–18, JE), 19–20, 22, 24, 28aAb–30, 32–34a, 35b, 36, 40:2–3a, 4, 5a, 6–15a, 16–23; 41 (traces of J, 41:46a P), 42:1, 3, 4a, 8–26, 29–37 (traces of J), 43:12a, 13–14, 15aBb, 23b, 45:1b, 3, 5aBb, 7a, 8, 9a, 13, 15–18, 20 (21), 24b, 25–27, 46:1b, 2–5a, 47:7, 48:1, 2a, 8–9, 11–12, 15–16, 20–22, 50:15–26.

Ex. 1:11–12, 15–22, 2:(1), 2–10, 3:1, 4b, 6 (9–22), 4:1–17, 18, 20b (21–23), 27–31, 5:3–4 (traces in 5:6–19), 7:15aBb, 17b, 20b, 8:25–27, 9:22–23a, 25a (35), 10:8–9, 11 (12–15), 20–27, 11:1–3, 12:35–36, 13:17–19, 14:(5–7), 15–16, 19a, 20a, 21a, 22a, (23), 25a, 31, 15:20–21; 16–18 (JEP), 24:12–13, 18b, 31:18, 32:5b, 6, 15–19a, 25–29 (the rest of 32 is secondary) (33).

Num. 10:33, 35–38 (11:1–3, 25–30; 12), 13–14 (JEP), 16:1b, 2aA, 12–15, 25–26, 27b–34 (JE), 20:1b, 14–21 (20:19–20 J?), 21:4b–9, 11b–15, 21–25 (33–35), 22:2–21, 35b–41, 23:1–30, 24:25, 25:1–5 (JE), 32:(1–5), 16–17, 20–27, 34–41.

Deut. 31:14–15, 23, 34:3, 5–6, 10 (in part).

Josh. 2–11, 14:6–14, 19:49–50, 24 (all edited by the JE and Deuteronomistic editors).

(d) *The Priestly Code (P).* Gen. 1:1–2:4, 5:1–28, 30–32, 6:9–22, 7:6, 11, 13–16a, 17a, 18–21, 24, 8:1–2a, 3b–5, 13a, 14–19, 9:1–17, 28–29, 10:1a, 2–5, 6–7, 20, 22–23, 31–32, 11:10–26, 27, 31–32, 12:4b–5, 13:6, 11b–12, 16:3, 15–16, 17, 19:29, 21:1b, 2b–5, 23, 25:7–11a, 12–17, 19–20, 26b, 26:34–35, 27:46–28:9, 29:24, 28b–29, 30:4a, 9b, 22a, 31:18aBb, 33:18aB, 35:6a, 9, 13, 15, 22b–29, 36:1–8, 40–43, 37:1–2, 41:46a, 46:6–7 (8–27), 47:5b (LXX), 6a, 8–11, 27b–28, 48:3–6 (7), 49:1a, 28b–33aAb, 50:12–13.

Ex. 1:1–5, 7, 13–14aA, 2:23b–25, 6:2–12 (13–30), 7:1–13, 19–20aA, 21b–22, 8:5–7, 16–19, 9:8–12 (11:9–10), 12:(1–28), 40–51, 13:1–2, 20, 14:1–2, 4, 8–9, 10bB (in part: 14:15–18, 21–23, 26–29); 16 (with traces of JE), 17:1abA, 19:1–2a, 24:15b–18a, 25:1–31:17 (34:29–35) (35–40).

Lev. 1–27, including earlier codes like the Holiness Code (H) in 17–26.

Num. (1:1–10:10), 10:11–12 (13–28), 13:1–17a, 21, 25–26a, 32abA, 14:1a, 2, 5–7, 10, most of 14:26–38, 15, 16:1a, 2aBb, 3–11, 16–24, 27a, 35–50, 17:1–13, 18:1–32 (19:1–22), 20:1aA, 2, 3b–4, 6–8a, 10, 11bB, 12–13, 22–29, 21:4a, 10–11a, 22:1 (25:6–18) (26) (27:1–23) (28:1–30:16) (31) (32:1a, 2b, 4a, 6–15, 18–19, 28–33) (33:1–36:13).

Deut. 32:48–52, 34:1–4 (in part), 34:7–9.

Josh. 4:10, 16, 19, 5:10–12, 9:15b, 17–21, 27a, 12:1–24, 13:15–33, 14:1–2 (3–5), 15:1–12, 20–62, 16:4–8, 17:1–6, 18:1–21:42 (22:9–34).

(e) *Codes of Law:* Covenant Code (Ex. 20:22–23:19); Ritual Decalogue (34:10–26, 22:29b–30a, 23:12, 15–19); Twelve Curses (Deut. 27:14–26); Ten Commandments (5:6–21; Ex. 20:1–17); the Deuteronomic Code (Deut. 12–26 for the most part); the Holiness Code (Lev. 17–26); the Priestly Code (Exodus, Leviticus, Numbers; see above).

(f) *Original Poems.* (*a*) About 1250–1050 B.C.—Gen. 4:23–24, 9:25–27; Ex. 15:21, 17:14, 16; Num. 10:35–36, 21:14–15, 17–18, 27–30.

(*b*) About 1050–950 B.C.—Gen. 49:2–27; Num. 24:3–9, 15–19 (20–24).

(*c*) About 950–722 B.C.—Num. 23:7–10, 18–24; Deut. 33:6–25.

(*d*) About 650–400 B.C.—Ex. 15:1–18; Num. 6:24–26, 12:6–8; Deut. 32:1–43, 33:2–5, 26–29.

(g) *Redactors.* (*a*) The JE redactor.—Gen. 12:9, 13:1, 3–4, 14–17, 16:9–10, 22:14, 26:1, 2b, 15, 18, 28:14, 21b, 32:9–12, 32, 39:1, 20aG, 40:3b, 15bB, 45:19–20 (21), 46:1, 3b. Ex. 3:20, 4:14aB–16, 21–23, 7:17a, 8:10b, 9:14b–16, 19–21, 29b, 10:1b, 19:22–24, 32:19b, 34:1, 4; Num. 23:13b, 23.

(*b*) The Deuteronomistic redactor.—Gen. 15:18–21, 26:5; Ex. 3:8, 17, 12:24–27a, 13:3–16, 15:26, 19:3b–8 (in part), 23:23. 28, 32:7–14, 33:1b–3a, 34:6–17, 24; Num. 14:11–44, 32:33a, 40.

(*c*) The Priestly redactor.—Slight retouches in: Gen. 15:7 (Ur of the Chaldees), 24:67 ("his father" changed to "his mother"), 27:46; Ex. 6:6–9 (recast), 9:35b, 11:9–10, "the tables of testimony" in 31:18, 32:15, 34:29; Num. 10:34.

(*d*) The S redactor.—Gen. 3:20, 4:25–26,

5:29, 6:4, 9:18–19, 10:9, 14, 16–18a, 24, 11:9, 28–30, 14:12, 18:17–19, 22b, 25:6.
R. H. P.

South, the, (the Southland), the Negeb*.

sowing, the scattering or planting of seeds. The winter seeds of Palestine are wheat and barley, planted in late January and February; the summer seeds include sesame, millet, melons, and various vegetables. Mixed and ceremonially unclean seeds were forbidden to Hebrews (Lev. 11:37 f., 19:19; Deut. 22:9), but landsmen might plant several sorts of seed on one field. Sowing was done by the sower with his right hand, from a bag suspended over his left hip. In order to protect precious seed from ants, the sower often followed behind the plowman and laid his seed in furrows, which were then plowed in or harrowed by the driving of flocks over them to press the seed into the soil; this was a popular method in Egypt. See Christ's Parable of the Sower (Mark 4:26–29).

Spain, mentioned twice in Paul's Letter to the Romans (15:24, 28) as a region he hoped to visit, evidently with the co-operation of Roman Christians. Whether the Apostle ever reached Spain is not definitely known. He may have been martyred at Rome before the journey was undertaken.

Spain in Paul's day was the most thoroughly Romanized province in the Empire. Paul was evidently more eager to go there than to Gaul or Africa.

span. See WEIGHTS AND MEASURES.

sparrow, a word used in the Bible for any small, twittering bird. The Psalmist honored the home-building sparrow, nesting near the Temple altar (Ps. 84:3). In N.T. times, as now, sparrows are so plentiful as to be sold "two for a farthing" (Matt. 10:29; "five for two farthings," Luke 12:6 f.). Jesus used God's care for these humble birds to make men understand His greater solicitude for them.

spear, a sharp-headed weapon on a long wooden pole, first used by primitive hunters. Joshua's spear may have been made entirely of wood (Josh. 8:18–26), or it may have had a flint* head. Egyptians using spears and two-edged swords (see SWORD) drove back the threatening Indo-European peoples (c. 1200 B.C.). From the beginning of the Iron Age (c. 1200 B.C.), Greeks used spears and round shields as characteristic weapons, rather than the bow and arrows used by Mesopotamians. The Hebrews used metal-tipped spears after David's victories over the Philistines made metal available (cf. Judg. 5:8). David's own spears and shields were hung "in the temple of the Lord" (II Kings 11:10; II Chron. 23:9). Rehoboam, son of Solomon, strengthened his defense of Jerusalem by arming the men of the towns in Judah with "shields and spears" (II Chron. 11:12). King Asa of Judah (c. 913–873 B.C.) is said to have had an enormous army equipped with "targets and spears" (II Chron. 14:8). King Amaziah (c. 800–783 B.C.), successor of Jehoash, gave spears and shields to all the men able to go to war (II Chron. 25:5).

A Roman soldier pierced the side of the crucified Jesus with a spear (John 19:34). The Roman occupation force of Palestine included companies of spearmen, or javelin-throwers, such as the 200 who escorted the prisoner Paul to Antipatris (Acts 23:22).

In a figurative sense spears are mentioned in Ps. 35:3, 46:9. Isaiah and Micah refer to pruning hooks made of spears (cf. Joel 3:10).

Shields were usually carried on the left arm of the spearmen; "spear and shield" is an O.T. term (I Sam. 17:45; II Chron. 25:5; Job 39:23). Sometimes they were carried in front of important leaders to protect them in battle. Primitive shields were of wood, or of leather tightened on wooden frames; later they were made of metal, e.g., bronze, copper (I Kings 14:27) or gold combined with base metal (I Kings 10:17; II Chron. 9:16). Shields were round, oval, or oblong. Figurative allusions to shields appear in Ps. 3:3, 28:7; Prov. 30:5—where God is the shield of those who put their trust in Him.

spelt, a kind of wheat, named in A.S.V. Ex. 9:32; Isa. 28:25 for "rie" of the A.V. Rye does not normally grow in Palestine.

sphinx, the Gk. name for a composite creature with the body of a lion and a human head (usually). The Hebrews during their Sojourn in Egypt saw sphinxes—usually recumbent, on guard at temple entrances in pairs, or lining the avenue of approach, as at Memphis* in the Delta. The most famous Egyptian sphinx is at Gizeh, adjacent to the

393. Alabaster sphinx at Memphis.

Great Pyramids. Carved from desert rock, it stretches 189 ft. along the sand, from which it has frequently to be dug. Its head, 66 ft. high, may be that of Khafre, builder of the Second Pyramid. Between its paws it guards a temple, where articles were stored for the ruler's use in the after-world. The temple has been excavated in recent times, and the whole surrounding area has been studied by Dr. George Reisner and others.

Assyrian sphinxes were winged, with either bearded male heads or female features, as seen in the palace of Esar-haddon. Greek sphinxes had wings and female breasts. Phoenicia and the E. Mediterranean islands had sphinxes in sculpture or carved on gems.

spices, aromatic vegetable substances so highly valued by the people of Bible lands that extensive trade in them developed. The caravan routes by which they were conveyed from one country to another became highways for the spread of ideas and culture (see TRADE). Spices were used (1) for seasoning food, like various Arabian spices, including myrrh and cinnamon, black cummin, or dill, and mint; (2) for making cosmetics* and unguents, like aloes, precious spikenard (Mark 14:3 f.; John 12:3), saffron (Song of Sol. 4:14), cassia (Ps. 45:8); (3) for sacred incense*, like frankincense, stacte, galbanum, onycha, calamus, and sweet cane; (4) for the preparation of bodies for burial, like the "mixture of myrrh and aloes" which Nicodemus brought for Jesus' burial (John 19:39 f.), and the "spices and ointments" which the women brought to the sepulcher of Jesus (Luke 23:55–24:1).

spies, secret scouts, e.g., the 12 men dispatched into Canaan by Moses from Kadesh, as narrated in the composite account of Num. 13; Deut. 1:22 f.; the two sent by Joshua to test the strength of Jericho (Josh. 2:1 ff.); and the spies stationed by Absalom throughout the Tribes of Israel to spread the news, at the trumpet blast, that he was made king in Hebron (II Sam. 15:10). Gideon was sent to eavesdrop at the Midianites' camp (Judg. 7:9 ff.).

spikenard, an aromatic plant, growing in spiky heads and yielding a fragrant, essential oil used in expensive perfumes* and unguents, such as Mary used to anoint the feet of Jesus (John 12:3). See COSMETICS; OINTMENTS.

spinning. See WEAVING.

spirit. See FLESH AND SPIRIT; HOLY SPIRIT; SOUL.

spitting. See GESTURE.

sponge, the absorbent skeleton of certain aquatic animals that are plentiful along the Palestinian coast. A sponge dipped in vinegar and attached to a reed was offered as an anodyne to Jesus on the Cross (Matt. 27:48; Mark 15:36; John 19:29).

springs. See WATER; also CAESAREA PHILIPPI; EN-GANNIM; EN-GÊDI; EN-ROGEL; GIHON; JERICHO; PEIRENE; SILOAM.

394. Stables of King Ahab.

stable, a building for housing and feeding beasts. Pillared buildings at Megiddo, once thought to be "Solomon's stables" (Figs. 394, 395) can no longer be identified as such (see MEGIDDO). The stable at Bethlehem where Jesus was born was quite likely a rock-hewn cave stable on the hillside of Bethlehem overlooking the Field of the Shepherds. Bethlehem caves are still used for stables, whose

395. Reconstruction model of King Ahab's Stables, by Olaf Lind.

mangers (Luke 2:7) are hollowed-out rocks, placed on the ground where animals can eat from them comfortably; or niches hewn out of the cave wall itself.

Stachys (stā′kĭs), one of Paul's Christian friends in Rome (Rom. 16:9).

stacte (stăk′tē) (Heb. *nāṭāph*), a solid resin having a vanillalike fragrance, exuded in drops from a plentiful desert bush. It may be the storax (*opobalsamum*), which was an ingredient of the holy incense placed "before the testimony in the tabernacle of the congregation" (Ex. 30:34–36).

staff. See ROD.

stairs, flights of stone steps which led from the typical one-story Palestinian house to its

396. Stairs from street to house, Bethlehem.

flat roof. They were constructed on the outside of the dwelling, and rose either from the street or the house court. Some stairs had a landing, from which the mezzanine or family level was reached, while the animal quarters were entered from the ground. Some houses had two flights of stairs—one leading from the inner court to the roof, one from the street to an upper story. The top steps of Jehu's house were a vantage place for the conspirators against Joram (II Kings 9:13).

The "stairs of the city of David, at the going up of the wall, above the house of David, even unto the water gate eastward" (Neh. 12:37) have been identified to the satisfaction of many at the S. end of the E. ridge on which Jerusalem stands. The remarkable stone steps of Gezer*, leading down the stone shaft to the water supply, were so worn in antiquity that hand grips were cut inside the tunnel. The famous steps leading down to the Megiddo water supply were prepared between c. 1250 and 1050 B.C. to protect water carriers.

Flights of steep steps gave impressiveness to temple entrances, as can be seen today at Jerash (Gerasa*) and at the Acropolis* at Athens, and to civic centers, as at the agora of Corinth. The wide platform, enlarged by artificial masonry for the Temple Area at Jerusalem, is still featured by flights of steps as in O.T. times (cf. Ezek. 43:17).

A flight of six steps led to the dais of Solomon's throne; two lions stood on each step, right and left (I Kings 10:19 f.; II Chron. 9:18 f.).

The characteristic triclinia or cultic banquet couches seen at Nabataean high places were rock-cut steps.

stall, a compartment in a stable for one animal, or a shed for several horses, cattle, or "all manner of beasts" (II Chron. 32:28). When the Palestinian farmer's stalls were full of calves, the times were prosperous (Amos 6:4). Prov. 15:17 favored "a dinner of herbs where love is" over "a stalled (fatted) ox and hatred therewith." The common man kept his animals in the yard, or in a cave-stable nearby, or in the lower portion of his house. Solomon is said to have had 40,000 stalls of horses for his chariots (I Kings 4:26), probably an exaggeration; II Chron. 9:25 gives the number as 4000 stalls for horses and chariots. See STABLE.

stars, celestial bodies which impressed the Hebrew people with their intense beauty and apparent nearness. Wisdom writers mentioned them: Job heard God speak of the morning stars singing together (38:7); the Psalmist considered the stars as fashioned by the "fingers" of God (Ps. 8:3; cf. Gen. 1:16), Who counted and named them (Ps. 147:4); the author of Ecclesiastes glorified the brilliance of the stars (12:2). "As many as the stars" was an expression frequently used to indicate vast multitudes (Gen. 22:17, 26:4; I Chron. 27:23; Neh. 3:16; Heb. 11:12). Many peoples of the East believed that the destinies of human beings were in some way determined by "their" stars; adherents of astrology believed in star-guided events. Mesopotamian gods, e.g., Moloch and Chiun —the latter being possibly Saturn—had their stars (Amos 5:26; Acts 7:43). Jesus was called "the bright and morning star" (Rev. 22:16).

There are many beautiful allusions to stars in Scripture—e.g., Neh. 4:21. Stars are used symbolically, e.g., the daystar rising in men's hearts (II Pet. 1:19; see also Rev. 2:28, 8:10, 12:1). Several constellations are mentioned in the Bible. Arcturus (A.V.), or the Great Bear; Orion, and the Pleiades in Job (9:9; cf. 38:31 f.); Orion and "the seven stars" in Amos 5:8 are Orion and the Pleiades.

Astrology, the art of interpreting the influence of heavenly bodies on human events, interested all Near Eastern peoples. Though the Hebrews classed "astrologers, the stargazers, and the monthly prognosticators" with magicians and diviners (see MAGIC) (Isa. 47:13), they often adopted the cult of "the queen of heaven" (Jer. 7:18)—probably Venus or Ishtar. "The host of heaven" was popular in N. Israel (II Kings 17:16); the sun* and Sin, the moon god, had been worshipped, especially in Israel's nomadic days.

Egyptians observed stars for purposes of worshipping the brilliant heavenly bodies (astrolatry). Babylonian interest in stars began on the magical and the astrological level, but developed scientific precision; they observed planets, predicted eclipses, and achieved the division of time into years and months. It is natural that out of a Babylonian setting should come such words as in Dan. 12:3: "they that turn many to righteousness [shall shine] as the stars forever and ever."

Some people regard the "star in the east" which led the Wise Men to the manger-cradle of Christ (Matt. 2:2, 7, 9 f.) as a beautiful symbol*; others view it as a miracle. Scientists, who are able nowadays to describe the appearance of the heavens at specific times in past centuries, are thwarted in this instance because the year of Christ's birth is not definitely known (many accept 7 B.C. or 6 B.C.). The Hayden Planetarium, New York, has issued a pamphlet, "The Christmas Star," by Catherine E. Barry, Asst. Curator, Dept. of Astronomy, which suggests several possibilities. The Star of the Wise Men may have been (1) a bright meteor—yet meteors are too transient to have lighted so long a journey as these travelers (from Persia or Arabia) seem to have taken; (2) a comet—Halley's appeared in 11 B.C., and another such heavenly spectacle appeared in 4 B.C., but these years do not fit the chronology of Christ's life—and besides, comets viewed by the naked eye are not seen for more than a few months at the most; (3) a nova—not a new star, but perhaps an old one which suddenly burst into exceptional brilliance; or (4) an unusual conjunction or assembling of planets—Saturn, which was especially meaningful to Hebrews, and Jupiter, joined later by a third. "After the sun had passed the configuration of Mars, Jupiter, and Saturn in late February, 6 B.C., Mars moved away from the others but Venus came into the picture. Considering its brilliance and its relation to these planets in the 'house of the Hebrews,' the brightest of the planets might well have been taken as the sign of the Nativity" (quoted by permission).

stater (Gk. *statēr*), an ancient Greek coin having various values. Sometimes, in gold, it was worth 20 drachmas. The "piece of money" of Matt. 17:27 reads "stater" in the A.S.V.

margin (half an ounce of silver, in value 2s. 6d.) See MONEY.

stealing. See ROBBERY.

stele (stē′lē) (Gk., "standing block"), a thin, upright slab or small stone column, with an inscription or incised design, set up to commemorate an event, or mark a grave, or carry

397. Stele of warrior, and modern Greek soldier, near the Mound of Marathon.

the votive likeness of a deity. No Israelite stelae have as yet come to light, though a fragment of one with a single well-carved Heb. word has been found at Samaria. Egyptian stelae have been found in various levels at Beth-shan*. A Hyksos limestone stele was found in a house at Tell Beit Mirsim, with a relief portrait of a serpent goddess—the first found in Palestine. The stele of Mesha*, King of Moab (c. 835 B.C.), discovered in 1868 at Beth-shan by Clermont-Ganneau, was inscribed with a record of his triumph over Israel after the downfall of the Omri Dynasty.

Stephen (Gk., "crown"), probably a Hellenistic Jew of Jerusalem. His zeal ("faith and power," Acts 6:5) led to his becoming the first Christian martyr. He was one of "the seven," usually regarded as the first deacons, appointed to distribute food and other necessities to the poor of the growing Christian community in Jerusalem, in order to give the Apostles more time for the spiritual activities of their ministry. But "the seven" were apparently expected not only to "serve tables" but to teach and preach, as Stephen did in the synagogues. Members of the Hellenistic group within the synagogue of the Libertines, and others who were jealous of Stephen's wisdom and consecrated spirit, trumped up a charge that he was speaking blasphemously against Moses (Acts 6:9 ff.), stirred up the Jewish elders, and had him haled before the Sanhedrin*. There false witnesses accused him of saying that Jesus would destroy the holy place of Jerusalem "and change the customs which Moses . . . delivered." Stephen's opponents expressed exactly what the new Christian era was already bringing to pass. He made no apology for his faith, but based his defense on an interpretation of Scripture (7:2–53). He made four points: (1) God had made His greatest revelation of truth not in the Jerusalem Temple, but actually outside Palestine. (2) Israel had always rebelled against God and rejected His ministers. (3) It was in keeping with this that the "Just One," the prophet whose coming Moses predicted, had been betrayed and killed. (4) The Law was holy, but they had not kept it. At least part of his famous statement to the Sanhedrin is preserved in Acts 7:2–53. His rebuke to his opponents cut them to the heart (v. 54); gnashing their teeth at him, they stopped their ears while he spoke of his vision of Jesus standing at the side of God. To them this was blasphemy, and according to the Law punishable by death. Though it was unlawful for them to execute a man without permission from the Romans, the mob seized

398. St. Stephen's Gate, Jerusalem.

Stephen and stoned him to death at a place adjacent to the city wall which may be near the present Stephen's Gate, in the E. wall. Praying for forgiveness for his murderers, Stephen died, and was buried with "great lamentation" by devout men. The garments of the men who stoned Stephen were laid at the feet of a young Jew named Saul of Tarsus, who by his presence "was consenting unto his death" (7:58–8:2).

Stephen's teaching showed clearly the difference between Judaism and Christianity. This led to the end of the early phase of Christianity, in which it appeared to be merely a Jewish sect, and to the emergence of a distinctive Christian Church. Stephen's martyrdom touched off a persecution which scattered Christians to Samaria (8:1) and probably as far as Damascus (9:1, 2), thus laying the foundations for the extension of Christianity to the Gentile world. Paul, the Apostle chiefly responsible for the mission to the Gentiles, experienced a Christian conversion that is closely linked with Stephen's martyrdom.

Stephanas (stĕf′ȧ-năs), the first man who, with his family, was baptized by Paul in

Achaia (Greece) (I Cor. 1:16, 16:15, 17). This household seems to have devoted itself to the Christian message. Together with Achaicus and Fortunatus, Stephanas made a personal visit to Paul at Ephesus, and may have carried a letter from the Corinthians to whom the Apostle addressed the reply preserved in I Corinthians. Stephanas and his two colleagues may also have carried this Letter to Corinth. See the subscription in the A.V. I Corinthians—not in the A.S.V. or the R.S.V.

steward, the overseer of a large household, as Eleazar of Damascus was for Abraham (Gen. 15:2) and Joseph for Potiphar (39:4). O.T. narratives mention stewards of Joseph's Egyptian household (Gen. 43:19 ff., 44:1, 4). The office is illustrated in the N.T. by Chuza, Herod's steward (Luke 8:3). Jesus' parable of the unjust steward (Luke 16:1–8) reveals customs of household administration of rich men of Jerusalem. In the pastoral Epistles bishops were stewards of God (Tit. 1:7). Christian leaders were "stewards of the mysteries of God" (I Cor. 4:1 f.). Every man might be a steward of "the grace of God" (I Pet. 4:10).

The Christian principle of the stewardship of possessions, time, and personality is the outgrowth of the fundamental teachings of Jesus concerning a man's obligation to make any needful sacrifice for the progress of God's kingdom*; see his advice to a wealthy man to sell all his goods and give them to the poor (Mark 10:17–22 and parallels); his commendation of Zacchaeus for giving half his means to the needy, and for returning fourfold what he had illegally exacted from taxpayers (Luke 19:8 f.); his parables of the Good Samaritan (Luke 10:30–37) and of the faithful and unfaithful servants (or of the talents) (Matt. 25:14–30, cf. Luke 19:11–28).

stoa, a portico or covered walk where Greeks and Romans promenaded and talked politics, philosophy, religion, and business. Stoae usually faced the agora* or market place, and contained small shops behind the promenading area. Often they possessed great architectural beauty, made possible by gifts of wealthy citizens, e.g., the stoa of Attalos in Athens, presented to the city by King Attalos II of Pergamum (159–138 B.C.) in the 2d century

399. Restoration drawing of the Stoa of Attalos II, by G. P. Stevens.

B.C., and prepared for reconstruction after World War II to house the Museum of 50,000 antiquities excavated by the American School of Classical Studies in their 20 years of investigation. Paul knew and used the stoae of Athens and of Corinth for his peripatetic teaching of Christianity. The largest stoa of Greece was the South Stoa at Corinth*, which in Hellenistic and Roman times had space for 33 shops and was more than 500 ft. long. This Stoa was decorated with a colonnade of 71 Doric columns and an inner row of 34. Each shop had a storeroom and a well.

See AGORA; AREOPAGUS; STOICS; TEMPLE.

400. Stoa at Corinth, with Temple of Apollo at upper left.

Stoics, Greek philosophers who, with Epicureans, disputed with Paul at Athens, ridiculing him as a "babbler" and a promoter of "strange gods," because he preached Jesus and the Resurrection (Acts 17:18 ff.). Stoics were very influential in the Roman Empire during the N.T. period. Seneca, Epictetus, and Marcus Aurelius were Stoics. This school of philosophy, founded by Zeno of Citium in the 4th century B.C., took its name from the stoa* at Athens—the painted colonnade or porch which ran along the market place (agora*)—where Zeno taught.

The aim of the Stoics was to shape men's characters to meet the difficulties of the world, and their doctrines were designed to this end. Their system of philosophy comprised three branches: logic, physics, and ethics. Logic included a theory of knowledge and expression. In physics, or the study of nature, they taught that everything is material, even God and the human soul. God is the soul of the world and the motive power of the universe. He watches over the world, hence everything in nature is rational and good. The ethics of Stoicism taught that man's soul is part of the divine soul and that a life of virtue is conformity to nature. This leads to the central idea of Stoicism that the supreme goal of human life is virtue, and that men can attain virtue only by bringing their wills into conformity with the laws of nature. This "life in harmony with nature" demanded that passion, unjust thoughts, and indulgence be put aside, and that duty be performed with the proper disposition; it required an unending battle with the self. Stoicism, as taught by Epictetus, grew to a belief in God as the all-pervasive Force in the universe. For this worship no altars, temples, images, or prayers were necessary, only purity in life and thought. The Stoics objected to anthropomorphic and superstitious elements in the popular religion of their day. Stoicism made the individual self-sufficient, independent of externals, and master of himself. Its four cardinal virtues were wisdom, courage, self-restraint, and justice.

Many of the teachings of Stoicism were

parallel to those of Christianity, e.g., that the best worship of God is that which takes place in a man's own heart (cf. John 4:23); the vanity of life (cf. Jas. 1:10); heroic resignation to the will of God (cf. John 5:30); the brotherhood of all men (cf. I Pet. 2:17); the rule of divine Providence. Seneca's (4 B.C.–A.D. 65) letters and essays were widely read within the Christian Church.

stone, abundant in Palestine, Lebanon, Syria, Jordan, and Assyria, was put to manifold uses mentioned in the Bible. Stonecutters and masons* of the Near East became able craftsmen, e.g., those of Byblos (see GEBAL) (Gebalites) (Ezek. 27:9) and those of Solomon and Hiram (I Kings 5:15–18). Some of the stones cut for the Temple* were 8 to 10 cubits (14 to 18 ft.) long (I Kings 7:9–12). Nearly every hill village of Palestine engaged in quarrying and making lime. The mountains of Assyria were quarries for palaces, temples, and reliefs, as were the rock cliffs of Egypt. Stone was used for emergency pillows (Gen. 28:18); well curbs (Gen. 29:2); knives—especially flinty stone (Ex. 4:25); storage vessels for wine or grain (Ex. 7:19; cf. John 2:6); houses (Lev. 14:42); walls and parapets (Neh. 4:3; Hab. 2:11); plummets (A. S. V. Isa. 34:11); millstones (Deut. 24:6); city wall foundations and cornerstones (Ps. 118:22; Mark 12:10); pavements and roads (II Kings 16:17; cf. GABBATHA); boundary stones and topographical landmarks* (Deut. 19:14; Josh. 15:6; I Sam. 7:12); milestones; weights (Deut. 25:14); missiles, e.g., slingstones (I Sam. 17:49; II Sam. 16:6, 13; I Chron. 12:2); siege "engines" (II Chron. 26:15; I Macc. 6:51); idols (Lev. 26:1; Deut. 29:17; II Kings 19:18; Isa. 57:6); altars (I Sam. 6:16 f.; Ex. 20:25; Deut. 27:5 f.); pillars (Gen. 13:18); and material on which letters were carved (Ex. 24:12; Deut. 27:2 f.; Josh. 8:30 ff.). Stones were also used in burial rites, e.g., for tomb doors (Matt. 27:60, 28:2; John 11:38 f.), or to heap over bodies (Josh. 7:26, 8:29), and as "witnesses" of important events (Gen. 28:22, 31:46; Josh. 4:19–22, 24:26 f.).

Still other uses, known from excavations but not mentioned in the Bible, were for sheepfolds and mangers; measuring units; and harbors, moles, and quays, as now apparent at Corinth, Rome, Ephesus, Ostia, Jerusalem, Jerash, Megiddo, etc.

Stones worked into masonry supply archaeologists with clues of dates and builders; even casual observers can detect the differences in the Ahab, Omri, and Roman construction at Samaria*. The Hebrew walls of Lachish are inferior to its Persian masonry, and Hyksos construction is still different. The walls of Jerusalem reveal work done by Jebusites and David and Solomon—all inferior to the great Herodian courses. The mediaeval courses of Suleiman near the top are equally distinctive. Solomonic masonry at Megiddo* has recognizable sequences of long, narrow blocks of stone placed alternately in groups of two or three headers and stretchers; and it is characterized by the use of quoins, i.e., larger corner blocks, and of supporting piers. The excavation of Shechem has revealed a casemated or chambered wall which may date from the 11th century B.C., in the time of Abimelech, whose crowning at Shechem is narrated in Judg. 9. Masonry excavated at N.T. Jericho* in 1950 shows the smooth edges and rough centers of stones used by 1st century Herodian builders.

"Stone" is used symbolically in Scripture for the weight that sinks (Ex. 15:5, cf. Neh. 9:11; Jer. 51:63); fear that petrifies (Ex. 15:16; I Sam. 25:37); firmness and strength (Job 6:12, 41:24); dumbness (Hab. 2:19, cf. Luke 19:40); hardness of heart (Ezek. 11:19, 36:26); hindrance to farming (Matt. 13:5; Mark 4:15 f.); rocklike personalities (John 1:42); and the "living stone" of God's spiritual house (I Pet. 2:4–8).

See BREASTPLATE; JEWELRY; ROCK.

stoning, the form of capital punishment prescribed by the Law (Lev. 20:2). Blasphemy (Lev. 24:16); idolatry (Deut. 13:10, 17:5–7), and adultery (Deut. 22:22; John 8:5) were punishable by stoning. Israel tolerated the stoning to death of a man who, like Achan*, had stolen spoil, "the accursed thing" (Josh. 7). In King Rehoboam's time (c. 922–915 B.C.) Israel openly stoned to death Adoram, who was "over the tribute" at the time of Israel's secession from the United Monarchy (I Kings 12:18). Zechariah, son of Jehoiada the priest, was stoned "in the court of the house of the Lord" (II Chron. 24:21). Jews picked up stones to hurl at Jesus for what they considered his blasphemous statement (John 8:58 f.). Stephen, the first Christian martyr, died by stoning (Acts 7:58). Paul was stoned at Lystra (Acts 14:19).

storage. (1) There is ample evidence in the Bible and at excavated sites of surpluses built up in times of prosperity to cover periods of scarcity (for the typical store-cities of Egypt, "treasure cities," Ex. 1:11, see CITIES; PITHOM; RAAMSES). David constructed storage centers for tribute and taxes in kind (oil, grain, wine, etc.) (I Chron. 27:25, 31). Solomon built store-cities on a larger scale, like Tadmor*, the Beth-horons, Baalat, etc. (I Kings 9:19, 10:26; II Chron. 8:4, 9:26). Jehoshaphat, who ruled Judah c. 50 years after Solomon, stored his "exceedingly" rich wares in places of safety (II Chron. 17:12). Temple staffs at Jerusalem had storage space for surplus offerings brought to "the house of the Lord" (II Chron. 31:10). Hundreds of jar handles, stamped to indicate capacity or place of origin, have been found in Palestine, with 325 specimens dug from Lachish* alone. These are believed to come from the time of Hezekiah, Manasseh, Josiah, and his successors (from the early 8th century B.C., for at least another hundred years), and indicate the extent of the storage of commodities.

(2) Traders and farmers erected warehouses or storehouses (Gen. 41:56), sometimes at the caravanserais, where goods were accumulated for safekeeping and distribution (cf. Mal. 3:10). Paul must have known about the tremendous storehouses (*horrea*) of rich Ostia*, pantry and harbor of Rome.

(3) Individual capitalists of Christ's day built larger and larger barns to hold their ever-increasing crops (see the Parable of the

True Treasure, Luke 12:16–21, cf. v. 24).

(4) Repositories for storing clay tablets inscribed with business accounts of temples and rulers have been found at Gezer, Tell el-Hesi (near the Egyptian border), Samaria, etc. Ancient libraries like the temple school at Ras Shamrah* (Ugarit), Ashurbanipal's library at Nineveh*, and the great library of papyri at Alexandria, were storehouses of contemporary learning.

stork, a bird listed in O.T. Law as unclean, i.e., unfit for food (Lev. 11:19; Deut. 14:18) —possibly because it feeds on reptiles and offal. It nested in fir trees (Ps. 104:17), and flew fearlessly over houses, shrines, and cemeteries in the Mediterranean lands, as it does today. Storks, usually white, heronlike birds 3 to 4 ft. high, are gentle with their young. They mate for life. Male and female repair their nests. Since early Bible times storks have been migrating from inner Africa across the Red Sea, tarrying in Palestine to feed on small water animals along the Jordan before flying on to Europe. Jeremiah referred to the stork in the heavens knowing "her appointed times" (8:7).

stove, a device for heating and cooking. Household stoves were often made of clay. They had a lower section where sticks of wood or bits of charcoal were burned, and a rimmed lid where the clay or metal cooking pots rested. A small hole provided necessary draft. Stoves were easily portable, and were sometimes carried on women's heads—as is still done in rural villages. They were used in courtyards, on roofs, or inside the one-roomed house. Houses of the well-to-do had metal stoves or braziers, as in the Jerusalem winter palace of Jehoiakim (Jer. 36:22 f.) and in the court of the Jerusalem high priest where Peter warmed himself during the Trial of Jesus (Mark 14:54). See BAKER; OVEN.

strakes (A.S.V. "streaks"; Moffatt "patches") were believed to appear on plague-ridden house walls (Lev. 14:37). This archaic form also appears in A.V. Gen. 30:37.

stranger (usually sojourner A.S.V. in O.T. passages), one not a Hebrew, but living among them on friendly terms and with certain rights and duties. The stranger was to be distinguished from foreigners living only temporarily in a Hebrew community (see FOREIGNER). Kindness to strangers (Num. 15:11–16) may have been due to the remembrance of the years when Israel itself lived on foreign soil (Ex. 20:10, 22:21, 23:9, 12 etc.). Sojourners might enter the Court of the Gentiles at the Temple*. At the time when the D document was written, sojourners were allowed to attend the three great feasts (Deut. 16:11 ff.), but might not marry Hebrews. The P document placed the sojourner almost on a footing with Hebrews, expecting him to observe the Sabbath; attend the Day of Atonement rites, as well as the three great feasts; but not allowing him to be part of the actual Congregation of Israel unless he submitted to circumcision. (Cf. the regulations concerning the second Temple, Ezek. 43:7–9 vs. I Kings 6:1–10, 7:7–13). The post-Exilic exclusiveness and the reforms of Ezra and Nehemiah caused the sojourner to become the proselyte of the N.T. The ultimate winning of all foreigners into Israel was the hope of the Hebrew people.

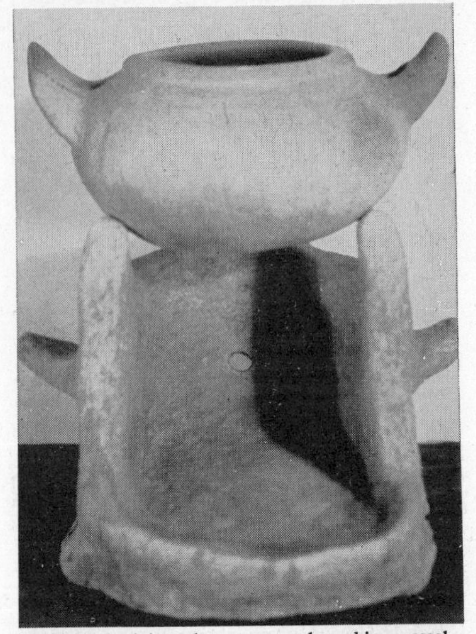

401. Palestinian clay stove and cooking vessel.

402. Pompeian brazier (Naples Museum).

In the N.T. a stranger is either an alien or one who is merely unknown (John 10:5; Luke 17:16, 18; Acts 2:10; Eph. 2:19). In A.V. I Pet. 1:1 the word is used for an Israelite of the Dispersion.

strangled animals were forbidden as food—in a pastoral letter from the Jerusalem Council to Gentile Christians (Acts 15:20,

29, 21:25). This was a strong Jewish food taboo, which in modern times is observed by the orthodox in the use of kosher meat.

straw, the stalks of grains, used for the bedding and provender of animals. It was supplied to the flocks of a guest by the host in the Patriarchal period (Gen. 24:25, 32) and later (Judg. 19:19). Solomon's commissary officers provided straw and provender for his "forty thousand stalls of horses" (I Kings 4:26, 28). Cf. Isa. 11:7, 65:25. Straw was also used as a binder in the making of mud bricks in Palestine and Egypt. Pharaoh's taskmasters required the Israelites to gather the straw they needed for brickmaking (Ex. 5:7, 10 f.).

stripes, wounds inflicted by rods or scourges for punishment (Ex. 21:25). Deuteronomic Law allowed a judge to beat the condemned man not more than 40 stripes (Deut. 25:3). Jews frequently punished by lashing with a triple-headed whip (Luke 12:47 f.; II Cor. 11:23 f.). Pilate inflicted stripes on Jesus with flagellation thongs (Matt. 27:26; Mark 15:15; John 19:1). Cf. Isa. 53:5 and I Pet. 2:24 ("with his stripes we are healed").

stumbling blocks, obstructions that might cause falls, were forbidden by Levitical Law to be put in the way of the blind (Lev. 19:14). The merciful removed stumbling blocks (Isa. 57:14). O.T. writers used "stumbling blocks" in a figurative sense—iniquity in the way of the righteous (Ezek. 3:20, 7:19, 14:3 f.; Rev. 2:14). Paul realized that the idea of a crucified Christ was a stumbling block to Jews (I Cor. 1:23). He also taught strong-willed Christians to refrain from things which, though not wrong in themselves, might become stumbling blocks to weaker men (I Cor. 8:9).

suburbs (Heb. *mighrāsh*) of towns in the O.T. were pastures and farmlands radiating out from settled sites, "for their cattle, and for their goods, and for all their beasts" (Num. 35:2–5). Importance was attached to these "suburbs," as shown by the lists of allotted lands, e.g., Josh. 21:13 ff.; I Chron. 6:55 ff.

Succoth (sŭk′ŏth) ("booths"). (1) A town E. of the Jordan in the territory of Gad (Josh. 13:27). The origin of its name is explained in terms of the booths erected by Jacob on his return from Padan-aram (Gen. 33:17). It lay near a ford over which Gideon pursued the Midianites (Judg. 8:4 f.), and when Succoth refused to provide food for his army, Gideon retaliated against them (Judg. 8:5 ff., 13 ff.). From these verses, it is clear that Succoth lay near the Jordan and along the road which led into the Trans-Jordanian highlands along the River Jabbok (see Y. Aharoni, *The Land of the Bible*, 1967, pp. 53, 57). At the time of Solomon, it marked the S. boundary, "in the plain of the Jordan . . . between Succoth and Zarethan," where the bronze vessels for the Jerusalem Temple were cast (I Kings 7:46; II Chron. 4:17). The Vale of Succoth is twice referred to in the Psalms (Ps. 60:6, 108:7).

Succoth is generally identified with Tell Deir 'allā, an impressive mound on the E. side of the Jordan, c. 2 m. N. of the Wâdī Zerqa (Bib. Jabbok), dominating the rich valley between the Wâdī Zerqa and the Wâdī Rajeb (see N. Glueck, *AASOR* 25/28, 1951, pp. 308–310, 347–350). It was excavated on a limited but intensive scale by H. J. Franken from 1960–64. Evidence indicates that the site was first occupied early in the Late Bronze Age (16th cen. B.C.), when an artificial platform for a sanctuary was constructed. This sanctuary remained in use until the beginning of the 12th century B.C., when it was completely destroyed by an earthquake and fire. A faience vase in the debris bore the cartouche of the Egyptian Queen Tewosret (c. 1209–? 1200 B.C.). According to Franken, a new culture of itinerant metalworkers then occupied the site, the only structures of the period limited to courtyards and furnaces used for the smelting and casting of copper/bronze (Franken's "1st Iron Age period," c. 12th cen. B.C.). While this indicates that metal vessels were produced in the area, the evidence is some two centuries earlier than the time of Solomon (cf. I Kings 7:46). These seminomads were replaced by a group who built a small, walled town and whose ceramic repertoire points to a homeland further East (Franken's "2d Iron Age period," c. 11th–10th cen. B.C.). The site was then abandoned for an unknown length of time, after which a fully developed ceramic repertoire of 7th century B.C. Palestine appeared. A sanctuary was again constructed on the mound, and occupation continued well into the Persian period (c. 4th cen. B.C.). The tell was then unoccupied until the Middle Ages.

Because of inconsistencies between the archaeological and literary evidence, Franken doubts that Tell Deir 'allā is Succoth, and instead inclines toward the possibility of identifying the tell with ancient Gilgal (*Excavations at Tell Deir 'Allā*, I, 1969, pp. 4–8). An alternative for the site of Succoth is neighboring Tell Ekhsâs ("Mound of the Booths"), 1 m. away, which preserves the ancient name (cf. Abel, *RB*, 1910, pp. 555 f.). As with Zaphon, Zarethan, and other sites in the Jordan Valley, the identification of Succoth must await further developments. Perhaps the site of Tell es-Sa 'īdīyeh should be given serious consideration (M. Ottosson, *Gilead*, p. 224, n. 60; see ZARETHAN). See H. J. Franken, *Excavations at Tell Deir 'Allā, I. The Early Iron Age Pottery*, 1969, esp. pp. 2 ff., 19 ff.; also *VT* 10, 1960, pp. 386–393; 11, 1961, pp. 361–372; 12, 1962, pp. 378–382; 14, 1964, pp. 417–422; *CAH*³, Vol. II, chap. XXVIb.

(2) A site in Egypt on the E. edge of the Nile Delta given as the first station on the route of the Hebrew Exodus (Ex. 12:37, 13:20; Num. 33:5–6). It has long been equated with Egyptian Tjeku, an important border fortress near the E. end of the Wâdī Tumilat (see *ANET*³, p. 259), and identified with the site of Tell el-Maskhûtah (Gardiner, *JEA* 6, 1920, p. 109). The latter was excavated by E. Naville in 1883 and produced 19th Dynasty, and later, remains. While the identification is acceptable, it has yet to be

verified, so that the location of Succoth must remain uncertain. W. P. A.

Succoth-benoth (sŭk′ŏth-bē′nŏth), a processional image or idol brought into Samaria by Babylonians (II Kings 17:30; cf. Amos 5:26). It may have been a depiction of the Chaldaean goddess Zirbanit, wife of Merodach*.

Sukkoth ("booths"), the Feast of Tabernacles, celebrated beginning with the 15th of Tishri (or Ethanim—September to October; see TIME). At first it lasted seven days; later an 8th day (of solemn assembly) was added. Stemming from a harvest celebration, the "feast of ingathering" (Ex. 34:22), it became a high peak in the year's joyous occasions; sometimes it was called simply "the festival." On the Sukkoth festival a pilgrimage was made to Jerusalem, to offer first fruits and tithes, and to enjoy festival meals and happy dances. The exact date of the celebration at first may have varied in various parts of Palestine, according to the climate and local harvest times, but was later standardized on the 15th of the month. Remembering Israel's tent life during their wanderings, the people erected booths or huts on roofs or roads and lived in them during Sukkoth. Processions waving lulabs (palm branches) and ethrog (citron) and singing happy songs marked the celebrations. See FEASTS.

Sumer (sū′mẽr), the land at the head of the Persian Gulf which became the seat of the oldest civilization in the Fertile Crescent. It occupied the southern part of the rich alluvial plain between the Tigris and the Euphrates, while Accad* occupied the northern area of the region. These two countries comprised the later Babylonia. Sumer and its people are important to students of the Bible because their pictographic and semipictographic inscriptions and their Accadian cuneiform documents describe life in the city of Ur* in the time of Abraham the Hebrew Patriarch, who was probably born there (Gen. 11:31). Abraham lived between the era of the kings of Isin and Larsa (city-states) and the First Dynasty of Babylon.

403. Sumerian head of warrior, probably from Kish.

Sumerian cities include the Biblical Ur and Erech* (Uruk, Warka), 50 m. NW. of Ur (Gen. 10:10, 11:10–27 f., 15:7) and Calah* (Nimrûd) "in the land of Shinar" (10:11 f.); also Lagash* (Tello)—50 m. N. of Ur—Eridu, Tell al 'Ubaid, etc.

Sumerians were of mixed blood, but are believed by most authorities to have been non-Semites, whereas Accadians were Semites. They may have come to the river plain before 4000 B.C. from the highlands between India and the Plain of Shinar; or, as others believe, from the region between the Caspian and Black seas. Their own claim to fabulous antiquity gives no clue to an earlier home elsewhere. Their love of their native mountains is reflected in their erection of artificial hillocks (*ziggurats*) in low Babylonia to serve as staged platforms for temples. The fertility of their flooded land in S. Babylonia and their boat trade in the Persian Gulf produced the wealth on which their extremely early culture was based—a culture inherited by several peoples of W. Asia, e.g., Cassites, Hittites, Mittani, Horites (Hurrians), Syro-Hittites, Persians, etc. This culture expressed itself in writing, language, law, religion, architecture, art, science (including mathematics and astronomy); engineering (for flood control and irrigation canals); military and civil administration. Sumerian culture dates from at least the middle of the 4th millennium B.C. Its centers were independent city-states, protected by local gods and ruled by *patesis*, or high priest-princes.

One of the greatest contributions of the Sumerians was their language and literature, stumbled upon about the middle of the 19th century by Henry Rawlinson and others who were trying to find the significance of the clay tablets in Ashurbanipal's library at Nineveh. Information about Sumerian literature began to be published by Samuel Noah Kramer of the Babylonian Department of the University of Pennsylvania in 1938. Kramer edited and reconstructed the great Sumerian epics of the 3d millennium B.C.—the world's oldest literary narratives—like the Gilgamesh and creation epics, which greatly influenced the language and later sacred literature of such Semites as the Accadians, the Aramaic peoples, and the Hebrews, whose Bible contains many words of Sumerian origin. Even after the Accadians had conquered the Sumerians the Sumerian tongue continued to be used as the learned and sacred language of Mesopotamia until shortly before the Christian era, when cuneiform records were no longer used. Down to the Greek period Babylonian scribal schools persisted in their study and teaching of Sumerian.

Sumerian literature on clay preserves memories of three lower Mesopotamian floods. One of these (at Kish or at Shuruppak, home of the Sumerian Noah) is briefly reflected in the famous Sumerian king list, which names the eight sovereigns who reigned (for fabulously long terms) before the Deluge. Their Flood legend, preserved in a fragment from Nippur, was later incorporated in the Gilgamesh epic, and survived—stripped of baser elements—in the Hebrew Flood story of Gen. 6:5–9:17. The Sumerian king list ascribes 24,510 years to the 23 kings of the First Dynasty of Kish, but it becomes more historical as it progresses to the later kings.

The Sumerians and all others in Babylonia were subdued by the Semitic Sargon* I in "the old Accadian period" (c. 2360–2180 B.C.). Under his grandson Naram-Sin art developed, as illustrated by his victory stele in the Louvre. Naram-Sin's empire was soon overrun by the Gutians, a Caucasus people from eastern hill tribes. At about the same time a remarkable Sumerian, Gudea of Lagash, a governor both kindly and able, had initiated a renaissance of Sumerian splendor (c. 2100 B.C.). This flowered in the famous Third Dynasty of Ur, which built c. 2000 B.C. under King Ur-Nammu, "King of Sumer and Accad," the great *ziggurat** of Ur, still surviving as the best example of the terraced artificial hill or platform crowned by a temple, forerunner of the Tower of Babel at Babylon. It must have been a conspicuous feature of Ur in the time of Abraham, who lived probably several centuries after its initial construction.

Disaster befell the Sumerians when the Elamites swept down on Ur and destroyed it. During feuds between several rival city-states an Amorite founded the first Dynasty of Babylon. Hammurabi* belonged to this Dynasty, and during his reign Rim-Sin of Sumer was defeated and the S. portion of the River plain fell to Hammurabi's empire (c. 1728–1686 B.C.).

Treasures recovered from Sumer are displayed in the University Museum at Philadelphia (which shared some of its material with Ankara, Turkey); in the British Museum, jointly with the University of Pennsylvania—fruits of Sir Leonard Woolley's finds; in the Museum of the Oriental Institute of the University of Chicago; and in the Chicago Natural History Museum. The Louvre holds evidences of Sumerian culture excavated at Tello. In 1947 the Iraq Department of Antiquities found at the site of the Sumerian Eridu a series of temples dating from the earliest cultural levels of S. Iraq—the protohistorical 'Ubaid period—which had been overlaid by the *ziggurat* of the Third Dynasty of Ur. The 7th level revealed a temple whose central room had an altar and a bench, evidently for offerings.

sun, the heavenly body around which the earth travels and from which it receives light and heat, was recognized by early Semites as part of the handiwork of God (Gen. 1:16). People were aware of its rising (Gen. 19:23) and setting (Gen. 15:12), its ability to foster agriculture (Deut. 33:14), its convenience for telling time on sun dials (Isa. 38:8), and its noonday heat (Ps. 121:6; cf. II Kings 4:18 f.). Its radiance was a figure used to describe deity (Ps. 84:11). "The righteous" shone as the sun (Matt. 13:43). The sun was as a strong man running a race, having a circuit to the ends of the earth, whose remotest portions it heated (Ps. 19:5 f.). Realizing the essential qualities of the sun, the Hebrews, like other Semites, at times worshipped sun images (Lev. 26:30; Isa. 17:8). Shamash was a great sun god of the ancient Middle East. Sun worship is indicated in specific place names, like Beth-shemesh* ("house of the sun"). Phoenicia adored a sun Baal, Baal-hammon. In the Nile Valley worship of the sun was especially popular and influential. (See AKHENATON; AMARNA; EGYPT; ON; RE.)

One of the most beautiful descriptions of the Messiah longed for by the Hebrews appears in the last chapter of the O.T., Mal. 4:2 ("the sun of righteousness . . . with healing in its wings").

Supper, the Lord's. See LORD'S SUPPER, THE; SACRAMENTS.

surety, one who made himself responsible, not always wisely, for the debts or obligations of another (Prov. 6:1, 11:15, 17:18, 20:16, 22:26, 27). A surety might be offered for a service to be rendered (Gen. 44:32).

Susa. See SHUSHAN.

Susanna. (1) A woman who gave of her means to Jesus and the Twelve, to aid in their ministry (Luke 8:3). (2) See APOCRYPHA, The Story of Susanna.

swaddling, the practice in which a newborn Hebrew child, like the infant Jesus (Luke 2:7, 12), was washed and rubbed with salt, and laid on a square of cloth, his head in one corner and his feet in the corner diagonally opposite; the cloth was folded over his sides and up over his feet, and the swaddling bands were then tied round the bundle. His hands were fastened to his sides. During the day the cloth was occasionally loosened and the child rubbed with olive oil and dusted with powdered myrtle leaves. Swaddling was continued until the baby was several months old. The little Palestinian "papoose" was thus conveniently carried by his swaddling bands to field work, or strapped to his mother's back. At night he slept in a home-made cradle of wool swung from two forked sticks. For figurative uses of "swaddling" see Ezek. 16:4; also Job 38:9.

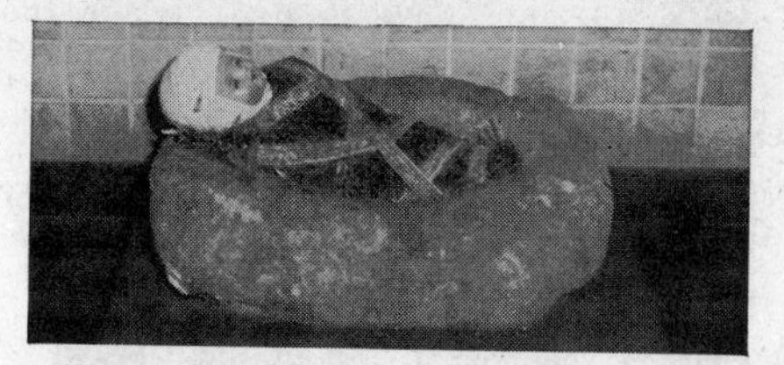

404. Swaddling clothes, shown here in ancient stone manger from Bethlehem, now in Children's Chapel, the Hanson Place Central Methodist Church, Brooklyn, N. Y.

swallow, a generic term used to translate the names of several domestic Palestinian birds. (1) In Ps. 84:3 and Prov. 26:2 it is the *deror*, which likes to nest in or near dwellings or houses of prayer, as now in the old Temple Area of Jerusalem. (2) In Isa. 38:14 the swallow is the cheerful *agur*, mentioned with the chattering crane. (3) In Jer. 8:7 the swallow is the *sus, sis* ("crane" A.V.). The writers of these passages used the common swallow to express the unerring ability of certain birds to return every spring to their nests at predictable times. Swallows rear two broods each summer.

swan, a bird listed in O.T. Law as unclean, i.e., unfit for food (Lev. 11:18; Deut. 14:16; R.S.V. "water hen").

swearing. See OATH.

swine (Heb. *chazir*). These omnivorous mammals were forbidden to be used as food by Israel (Lev. 11:7, etc.), probably because they were sacred to neighboring peoples from whose sacrifices and gods the Hebrews wished to keep their people separate. Swine were used for food and offerings by Canaanites and Syrians, and were sacrificed at Gezer*, as known from many bones excavated there. Phoenicians, Egyptians, and Ethiopians, however, also deemed them unclean. In Roman times they were favorite sacrificial animals, as indicated by depictions of them on an altar in the Forum at Rome. Classifications of swine as "unclean" (inedible) may also have been partly due to their filthy habits, which led them to eat offal and carrion, and to live even in tombs. Experience may have taught the Hebrews that the eating of swine's flesh was related to certain diseases, esp. of the skin. References to swine in Scripture (Prov. 11:22; II Peter 2:22, etc.) always reflect the Jew's aversion to this animal, as in the story of the Prodigal Son, who could sink no lower than to care for swine and to crave the food they ate (Luke 15:15 f.). (See the Gergesene or Gadarene demoniac's story, Matt. 8:28–34; Luke 8:26–39, where the devils went out of the afflicted man and rushed into swine.)

sword, a handled weapon with a metal blade (iron, bronze, copper, or steel)—long or short, single- or double-edged. Specimens of many types have been excavated in Bible lands. The first mention of a sword in Scripture is the symbolic "flaming sword" which guarded the tree of life in the Garden of Eden (Gen. 3:24). O.T. narratives of the Conquest of Canaan refer to the sword of Joshua, by which he smote enemies all the way from Kadesh-barnea to Gaza, "all the country of Goshen, even unto Gibeon." Such a leader might have acquired an Egyptian sword by booty or purchase, yet it is anachronistic to state that groups of the Children of Israel, in eras before the Monarchy, took cities by the use of swords (Judg. 1:8, 25; 4:15 f.); for not until David's victories over the Philistines—who held a monopoly over iron and its manufacture—did iron become plentiful enough to equip Israel's fighters with swords (I Sam. 13:19). Saul had probably seized the sword on which he fell (I Sam. 31:4) from a beaten enemy, as David won his from Goliath (I Sam. 17:51). A Philistine sword factory, with its smeltery and furnace, was excavated by the Flinders Petries at Gerar*.

Cretan Philistines and Sardinians, who had access to metals, were threatening Egypt with battle swords as early as 1200 B.C.

The prophet Ezekiel was familiar with Mesopotamian swords (Ezek. 25:13). The "sword of the king of Babylon" was to him more than a figure of speech (32:11). Roman swords were short and usually two-edged—legions stationed in Palestine were equipped with these in the time of Jesus, and such a one was seized by a companion of Jesus (Matt. 26:51) to cut off the ear of a servant of the high priest in Gethsemane. Jesus rebuked his impetuousness: "Put up again thy sword into his place; for all they that take the sword shall perish with the sword" (v. 52). A few moments later, Jesus challenged a mob of Jews and others crossing the Kidron Brook to arrest him, "Have you come out as against a robber, with swords and clubs to capture me?" (R.S.V. Matt. 26:55). Luke's narrative says that Jesus had previously advised his disciples, in view of the approaching "end," to sell their garments and buy swords (22:36–38).

Symbolic mention of the sword is made in Ps. 55:21; Isa. 1:20; Joel 3:10; Mic. 4:3. In Christian symbolism the sword—e.g., in the statue of Paul in the courtyard of the Basilica of St. Paul-without-the-Walls in Rome—denotes spiritual warfare against the forces of evil (Matt. 10:34; Rev. 1:16, 19:21). In Eph. 6:17 "the sword of the Spirit" is "the word of God."

sycamine the tree mentioned by Jesus to the Disciples (Luke 17:6); a mulberry.

Sychar (sī′kär), a village of Samaria "near to the parcel of ground that Jacob gave to his son Joseph," adjacent to Jacob's well (John 4:5 f.). Jacob's well is on the S. edge of modern Balata, a village that owns and lies on the edge of the tell that was once the city of Shechem*. Hence when it is said that Jesus came to Jacob's well, the location of which is given by a village name, one would expect the latter to be Sychem (Shechem), a reading actually preserved in the Old Syriac and defended in early times. In any case, the modern identification of Sychar with the village of 'Askar, on the slope of Mt. Ebal some distance away across the plain of Shechem, has little to commend it either topographically or linguistically.
G.E.W.

Sychem. See SHECHEM.

sycomore (*Ficus sycomorus*), a Near Eastern tree related to the common or wild fig. It produces scarcely edible fruit, but gives welcome shade, for its strong trunk grows as high as 40 ft. Such a tree Zacchaeus climbed (Luke 19:4). Amos of Tekoa was a dresser or ripener (by incision) of sycomore figs (Amos 7:14). Sycomores grew abundantly in stony patches near Jerusalem (I Kings 10:27) and in "low plains" (I Chron. 27:28). They were blighted by frost (Ps. 78:47), and were not as highly valued as cedars (Isa. 9:10), though their timber was useful. The sycomore is to be distinguished from the American sycamore—a species of plane—and from the English sycamore or maple.

Syene (sī-ē′nē) (A.S.V. Seveneh), an Egyptian town, Swn (the modern Aswān), situated on the border of Egypt and Ethiopia, on the Ethiopian side of the First Cataract. This fortress, opposite the island of Elephantine (capital of the first nome—province—of Upper Egypt) is mentioned in Ezekiel's pronouncement of the doom threatening Egypt: "from Migdol to Syene" (A.S.V. 29:10, 30:6). As now known from the Elephantine Aramaic papyri (found in 1903), Jews maintained at Elephantine their own temple to Yahweh in the Persian period (c. 538–333 B.C.), and were given permission by Achaemenid rulers to celebrate the Passover as enjoined by Ex. 12:1–20.

symbol (Gk. *symbolon*, a "mark," "token," "ticket"), a visible material representation of an immaterial object, idea, or personality suggested by a sign* or mark. Symbolism is the practice of expressing ideas by symbols; iconography (Gk. *eikōn*, "image") is the expression in art or other visible form of an idea, a person, or an event. Peoples of Bible lands and times were prone to express their religious beliefs by symbols. Countless symbols made over a period of 4,000 years or more have been found on cylinder seals (see SEAL), clay tablets, jar handles, plaques, reliefs, statuettes, figurines* and amulets (see AMULET), mosaics (see MOSAIC), glazed bricks, jewelry, and weapons. Among emblems of great cities and personalities which became familiar throughout the Near East were: the fish inside a city wall, which meant Nineveh on the Tigris; a roaring lion, accompanied by certain marks, the emblem of an officer of King Jeroboam II of Judah; winged lions and griffins, which represented the aggressive power of Babylonia.

405. Solomon's Seal, from stone synagogue, Capernaum.

The Canaanites made a myriad of gods in the form of men, like the storm god Baal or Hadad; Dagon, the grain god; El, king of the gods; and his wife Asherah, primarily a sea goddess, but associated also with sex and war, often depicted—as on a clay cult-stand excavated from Megiddo—in the form of a nude, lewd woman, with a dove and a serpent. This widely popular Canaanite goddess was often shown holding a lily (purity) in one hand and a serpent (fertility) in the other. Material excavated at Ras Shamrah has revealed many Canaanite symbols.

In spite of the Second Commandment and the efforts of the prophets to wean Israel away from the symbols of the polytheistic pantheons, the people showed a penchant for the serpent, symbolic of the earth in which it seems to live, and the bull, typifying the powers of generation and productivity (see I Kings 11:1–6, 12:32). Though the bull belongs to the agricultural phase of Israel's life, the snake cult may be a survival of the fear of snakes lurking on their nomad paths, and calling for propitiation and worship (cf. the fiery serpent staff, bronze or copper, used by the nomad Moses) (Num. 21:8 f.; II Kings 18:4, "Nehushtan," cf. Gen. 3:1–24). In Egypt, the serpent (sometimes the cobra) was an emblem of kingship.

By about the 3d century A.D. the Jews who built the synagogue at Dura-Europos on the Euphrates in Syria (now in the Damascus Museum) interpreted the Second Commandment liberally. They executed wall paintings which constitute the oldest known pictorial depictions of Biblical scenes. The Dura synagogue frescoes manifest "the growing freedom of expression in the whole Jewish world" (*The Messianic Theme in the Paintings of the Dura Synagogue*, Rachel Wischnitzer, Univ. Chicago Press).

Hebrew Symbolism.—Hebrew symbols of greatest importance were the Sabbath* (Ex. 31:16 f.); and circumcision* (Gen. 17:10), both expressive of God's covenants with Israel.

(1) Hebrews developed objective symbols in *amulets* which were worn to give magical protection from evil forces. There were many kinds of amulets. The *sahărôn*, in the form of the crescent moon, was worn by Midianite kings and camels (Judg. 8:21, 26) and by women of Jerusalem (Isa. 3:18) to protect them from the strength of the waxing moon. The earrings and "strange gods" ordered abandoned by Jacob (Gen. 35:2–4) were related to the *teraphim** (II Kings 23:24) and the *lehashîm* (Isa. 3:20 f.) (objects associated with whispered incantations). Tinkling *bells*, worn on the skirts of high priests (Ex. 28:33 f.), were relied on to drive away lurking evil spirits (cf. those worn by the mincing daughters of Zion, Isa. 3:16). Mesopotamian and Egyptian *gods* were secretly worn, and Judas Maccabaeus attributed the Jews' military defeat to them (II Macc. 12:39 f.). *Tôtâphôth* or phylacteries were possibly at first stones worn on the forehead to drive away evil (Ex. 13:9, 16), but were considered by the Samaritans as only symbolical, and not to be actually worn (Deut. 6:8). The *mezuzah* was a parchment containing Deut. 6:4–9, 11:13–21, rolled up in a case and attached to the door frame. The *zizith*, a tassel or lock of hair or fringe (Num. 15:38; Deut. 22:12) of prehistoric origin, symbolized submission to the Lord or deliverance from Egyptian bondage, or a reminder of the Law as a warning against idolatry. Samaritans wore fringes only when the sacred scroll was exhibited.

(2) The *Temple* and its furnishings employed symbols later used in synagogue

decoration. The two *cherubim* hovering over the Ark (the only "images") symbolized the presence of God, Whose glory they guarded. The *bronze sea* (I Kings 7:23 f.) had what W. F. Albright called "a cosmic significance" —from the sea came all life and all fertility. The 12 *bulls* (oxen) on which the sea stood (v. 25) were decorative symbols of fecundity, arranged in four groups to represent the seasons. The portable copper *laver* or platform on which Solomon stood to pray may be associated with an early idea of the foundation of the earth. The two enigmatic *pillars* Jachin and Boaz at the entrance to the Temple symbolized "the permanence of

406. Italian wayside cross showing symbols identified with the Crucifixion: cup, cock, city gate, crown of thorns, ladder, hand, spear, sponge on reed, etc.

the Davidic dynasty" (Albright, *Archaeology and the Religion of Israel*, p. 155). Archaeology has thus far not produced any objects clarifying "altars for all the host of heaven" in the Temple courts (II Kings 21:5), or the horses and chariots of the sun (II Kings 23:11). The *showbread table* symbolized dependence on God for sustenance, wherefore all creatures were to praise Him. The *candlestick* stood not for the seven planets, as some suggest, but for the congregation of the people of God, or for the creation of the world by God in six days and His rest on the 7th, or Sabbath. The *altar of incense* denoted prayer. The four-horned *altar of sacrifice* stood for the place where God was revealed; His protection might be gained by grasping one of its horns (I Kings 1:50, 2:28). The *sacrifices* were symbols: the burnt offering (Lev. 14:20), perfection; the thank offering (II Chron. 29:31) (and the meal and wave offerings), fellowship between God and Israel; the sin offering (Lev. 4:14), atonement; the guilt offering, an awakened sense of wrong-doing. The *cedar* and *hyssop* used in the ritual for cleansing lepers expressed the dependence of high and low on God.

(3) The eight *garments* of the priests were symbolic of sanctity; the one-piece coat was joy, in contrast to the rent garments of mourning; the girdle was a sign of the servant of the Lord; the bared feet, the sanctity of the Temple; etc.

(4) *Numbers** were used symbolically.

(5) *Gestures* were also symbolic (see GESTURE).

(6) *Metals* symbolized: gold (Heb. 9:4), divine or celestial light; silver, spiritual innocence (Isa. 1:22; Jer. 6:30); "brass" or copper, firmness, hardness, strength (Lev. 26:19; Job 40:18; Jer. 15:12).

(7) Among *colors*, green symbolized God's indwelling; purple, power, dignity, royal glory, or purification from sin; crimson or scarlet stood for blood and life, joy and happiness, but also for sin (Gen. 38:28; Josh. 2:18); white represented complete intellectual and physical purity (Song of Sol. 5:10; Dan. 7:9; Zech. 6:3, 6).

(8) Prophetic and Apocalyptic books are full of symbolic *words*, as are the Proverbs and the Psalms. The O.T. tells of numerous symbolic acts, e.g., Isaiah's going barefoot and half clad, posing as a captive to dramatize the uselessness of relying on Egypt and Ethiopia for help against Sargon (20:1–6); Jeremiah's wearing a wooden yoke to symbolize Jerusalem's unending calamity (28:12); and buying a field at Anathoth even while he was in prison, to symbolize the coming of a freer day for Israel (32:6–15; see also Jer. 51:63 f., the sinking of Jeremiah's prophecy in the Euphrates). In his allegories he talked of Tyre as a great ship; kings as eagles or tops of trees; cities as harlots; he gave symbolic meaning to a seething kettle and a blossoming almond tree (1:11–16). Daniel at Babylon explained the symbolism of Nebuchadnezzar's dream (4:4–18, 19–27), and read the symbolic writing on the walls at Belshazzar's banquet (chap. 5). Kings were "horns" (7:7, 20, 24); but his symbolic language to describe historic events is often confusing (2:7, 8). In the eschatological language of Zechariah's oracles the prophet became a shepherd of the flock (the people) about to be slaughtered (11:4–6).

(9) Devout Hebrews saw in their Feasts* symbols of their national religious experiences.

(10) The *coins* struck by the Jews in their brief period of independence have Jewish symbols. Shekels and quarter, third, and half shekels and tetradrachmas date from c. 139 B.C. to A.D. 135, in the Maccabean period and the time of the first and second revolts, and express the longings and beliefs of the people

SYMBOL

at the time—eloquent insights into their psychology. Some Jewish symbols were retained on Herodian coins. Among the symbols used were:

Design	*Meaning*
Lulab	Palm rising from center of bundle of plants carried in Sukkoth* festivals
Palm	Dignity, royal honor, rejoicing
Basket of fruits (*bikkurim*)	First fruits, brought by pilgrims to the Temple
Cornucopia	Plenty; same as fruit baskets
Omer (cup)	The cup of manna; or cup of sacrificial blood; or measuring cup for Passover barley
Wreath of olive	Worn to Passover Feast by pilgrims
Lily, rose	Temple decoration denoting righteousness, purity
Pomegranate (single or three buds on stem)	On Temple priests' robe, rain and fertility; piety
Four vertical lines and a horizontal line	The Temple Area (Ex. 26:33) entrance, the Ark inside; or the Gate Beautiful
Menorah (7-branched candlestick)	The company of Israel; or the 6 days of God's creation and the 7th (Sabbath) of rest
Clay oil lamps	The light of the Lord
Hydra (water jar)	Water libations—tinged with magical efforts to induce rain at autumn festival
Vine leaf	First fruits, vintage
Temple and Ark	Propaganda for rebuilding the Temple
Grapes	Israel, husbandry; symbol of blessing spoken over wine, in later Jewish symbolism
Trumpets (unique in numismatics)	Reminder of Temple worship
Lyre (3 or 6 strings, "*chelys*") (3 strings, *cithara*)	Reminder of praise and priests, Levites
Star (8-pointed or 8-rayed)	Sun rays or morning star on coins Alexander Jannaeus or Bar Kochba's, possible allusions to "the star," Messiah
Almond	Blossoming hope

(*Jewish Symbols on Ancient Jewish Coins*, Paul Romanoff, Dropsie College, Phila., 1944.)

Symbolism developed in rich detail in the countries forming the periphery of Palestine. Egypt was especially rich in its iconography, expressed in amulets worn on the person from birth to death, and then tossed into the grave; in reliefs, paintings, manuscripts, and architectural monuments. Canaanite Syria, Asia Minor, and the Mesopotamian Valley were almost equally prolific in symbols.

A study of symbols found in excavated synagogues in Galilee, as at Tell Hûm (Capernaum), where eagles, lions, griffins, cherubim, menorahs, a temple shrine on wheels (possibly the Ark), and other emblems appear, demonstrates the gradual lessening of inhibitions against graphic art. In the first three or four centuries before the invasions of the iconoclastic Moslems, the Jews distinguished between depicting live creatures for worship and using them for mere decoration or symbolic purposes.

Jewish symbols are used extensively in all synagogues. Typical is the Temple of the Congregation Emanu-El of New York City. The Ark of the Testimony is at the rear center of the altar. Suspended in front of the Ark is the *Ner Tamid* (perpetual light), symbolic of the eternal application of the truths of the Torah. The Ten Commandments are in the grille of the Ark, on each side of which is the menorah (7-branched candlestick). Other symbols in windows and elsewhere are the 6-pointed Star of David, the lion of Judah, the royal crown, fruit and flowers. Symbols of the Twelve Tribes on the bronze doors are: gate in tower, Simeon; unicorn, Ephraim; bull, Manasseh; wolf, Benjamin; ship, Zebulun; ass, Issachar; olive tree, Asher; snake, Dan; breastplate, Levi; mandrake, Reuben; lion, Judah; deer, Naphtali.

407. Silver ichthus on fish-scale chain.

Christian symbolism.—

(1) The *Cross** is the principal symbol of Christianity among the nations. This, however, was not the earliest emblem of the new faith, except as the *sign* of the cross was made by believers, or a pectoral cross was secretly worn.

(2) The oldest Christian symbols are probably found in excavated early churches in Syria; in 1st–century Pompeii; in the catacombs along Rome's Appian and Ostian Ways; and in the recently discovered Chris-

tian mausolea beneath Vatican crypts in Rome. (See *BA*, Vol. XII, No. 1, Feb. 1949, "Recent Excavations underneath the Vatican Crypts," Roger T. O'Callaghan, S. J.) Catacomb frescoes depict, for example, the *orans* or praying figure (male or female) standing, full face, with arms extended, symbolizing adoration, soul in Paradise; or the Church itself. The *ichthus* (Gk. "fish") was very early used (possibly introduced from Alexandria); an acrostic, the five Gk. letters of which stand for the initials of the words meaning, "Jesus Christ, Son of God, Saviour." The *dolphin*, friend of man and of shipwrecked sailors, was early a Christian emblem; sometimes carved on gems, with a shepherd's crook on its left, and a *palm branch* (symbol of victory), on its right. The *good shepherd*, showing Jesus carrying a lamb over his shoulder, is derived from Hellenistic art. The *ship* in which souls of the faithful are carried safely over life's sea to bliss symbolizes the Church, also missionary expansion; the masts form a cross. The *anchor*, symbol of hope, is sometimes shown resting on a fish—Christian hope based on Jesus Christ. Various forms of the sacred monogram were placed on the *labarum* or standard of Constantine. A Gk. X (chi) was superimposed on P (rho)—the first two letters in the Gk. word χριστος ("Christ").

The Byzantine *mosaics* used symbols, as at S. Sophia, Constantinople; in the churches of Ravenna—S. Vitale, S. Apollinare in Classe, S. Apollinare Nuovo, and the charming little baptistry of Empress Galla Placidia —and at Medeba in Jordan. Early Christian *sarcophagi* are carved with palms of victory,

408. Symbols: 1. "Jesus Christ." First two letters are first and last letters of Greek word for "Jesus," second two are first and last letters of Greek word for "Christ." 2. A figure combining the Greek word *ichthus* and its related symbol, a fish, used by ancient peoples of the sea as a symbol of a familiar deity. Read as an acrostic, *ichthus* spells out "Jesus Christ, Son of God, Saviour." 3. The sacred monogram "Chi Rho" resting on an anchor, the symbol of hope. 4. The initial letters of the Latin *Iesus Hominorum Salvator* (Jesus, Saviour of men.) 5. Symbol of the Latin superscription above the head of the crucified Jesus: *Iesus Nazarenus, Rex Iudaeorum* ("Jesus of Nazareth, King of the Jews").

the peacock of immortality, the sheep of Christ's flock, and the Alpha and Omega emblem—"Christ, the beginning and the end" (Rev. 1:8, 11, 21:6, 22:13).

Symbols of the Twelve Apostles

Keys	Peter
X-shaped cross	Andrew
Cross with two loaves of bread; or cross and carpenter's square	Philip
Flaying knife on Bible	Bartholomew
Saw	James the Less
Spear and square	Thomas
Fish	Simon
Chalice with serpent	John
Book and axe	Matthias
Three money bags	Matthew
Pilgrim's hat and staff	James the Major
Carpenter's square and boathook; ship	Jude

Symbols of the Four Evangelists

Winged man	Matthew
Winged lion	Mark
Winged ox	Luke
Eagle	John

Symbolic Colors

White	Creator, perfection, peace
Blue	Heavenly truth, sanctification
Red	Divine zeal, creative fire, love of God
Purple	Dignity, mourning
Purple-red	Severity
Purple-blue	Tranquillity
Green	Eternal youth, hope
Gold	Worth, virtue, glory of God
Bright yellow	Truthfulness, beneficence
Dull yellow	Deceitfulness (Judas—dung color)
Black	Penitence
Violet	Humility, suffering, sympathy

The Hand in Early Christian and Modern Art Forms

In clouds	First Person of the Trinity
Holding bolts and rays	First Person of the Trinity
With first two fingers and thumb extended	The Trinity
Reaching down	Offer of help

Other Christian Symbols

The nimbus (Lat. for "cloud")	A halo used for Christ or for saints; or for Deity when the upper three bars of a Greek cross (square) are within the circle
Star: 5-pointed	Nativity, sign of Christ
6-pointed	The Creator (cf. Star of David)
Water: Jordan	Baptism
Rushing from rock	Moses
Circle	Eternity
Shell	Pilgrimage (Crusades)
All-seeing eye	God
Dove	Holy Spirit
Tongues of fire	Pentecost
Pomegranates	Fruits of the Spirit; also the Early Church (as full of vitality as this fruit is of seeds)
Skull and crossbones, beneath cross	Death overcome by immortality

Phoenix	Immortality
Pelican	Sacrificial Christ
Tablet	Ten Commandments
Sword	Spiritual warfare
Trees: oak	Place of angelic visions; strength
cedar	Incorruptibility
palm	Victory over flesh
fig	Fruitfulness, good works
willow	Desperation, grief
apple	First sin; in hand of infant Jesus, redemption
acacia	Friendship
aspen	Judas; fear

Since Christian symbolism has become too detailed to be discussed fully here, reference books should be consulted. See especially *The Cross in Tradition and History*, William Wood Seymour; *The Voices of the Cathedral*, Sartell Prentice; *A Treasury of the Cross*, by Madeleine S. Miller. Princeton University is also making a study of Christian iconography.

Symeon. See SIMEON.

synagogue (Gk. *proseuchē*, Acts 16:13, "place of prayer," "sanctuary"; Hellenistic Gk. *synagōgē*, "a gathering of people," "a congregation"), a Jewish religious community, or sanctuary.

(1) The *origin* of the synagogue is unknown. Jews exiled to Babylonia in the 6th century B.C. were separated from their Temple, where alone sacrifices might be offered. It is believed that they met in local groups to study and discuss the Pentateuch, in an effort to fulfill the ancient Law*. Such may have been the origin of the synagogue as a place, not of sacrifice, but for instruction and prayer. R. H. Pfeiffer and others believe that the synagogue may have been "derived from the addresses of Ezekiel to the Babylonian exiles" (*History of New Testament Times*, Harper & Brothers, p. 50). Gatherings in the prophet's house (Ezek. 8:1, 20:1–3) may be the prototype of later meetings in the synagogue (cf. Jer. 39:8, "houses of the people"). These early "house synagogues" are comparable to the "house churches" of early Apostolic times (as in Acts 2:1 f.; Col. 4:15).

Synagogues are not mentioned in the O.T. except in a doubtful allusion in the A.V. of the Maccabean Psalm 74:8: "they have burned up all the synagogues of God" (A.S.V. margin, "places of assembly"; cf. Enoch 39:6). "It is possible that the Chronicler's description of Ezra's reading from the Law of Moses (Neh. 8) was inspired by the synagogue practice of his day; if so, this is our earliest source (c. 250 B.C.) on the subject" (R. H. Pfeiffer, *Introduction to the Old Testament*, p. 81).

There are more than 50 references in the N.T. to the synagogue in the sense of (a) a community of persons organized for a religious purpose, e.g., the synagogue of the Freedmen at Jerusalem (Acts 6:9), and the numerous ones at Damascus and other chief cities of W. Asia and the eastern Mediterranean in the time of Paul (Acts 9:2); (b) a building in which gatherings for such purposes were held (Matt. 4:23). (For such structures see ARCHITECTURE.)

(2) The *rapid growth* of synagogues in Palestine and elsewhere after the Return from Exile was due to the fact that the synagogue was the place where the Pentateuch was read and studied. It was Israel's conviction that her hopes would not be realized until people lived in accordance with God's Law as revealed in the Scriptures; hence it became necessary to teach the divine revelation to all Jews. By A.D. 70 Jerusalem had scores of synagogues; and they were functioning in rural towns like Nazareth (Luke 4:16–30). Damascus had many (Acts 9:2). It is estimated that from four to seven million Jews of the Diaspora had more than 1,000 synagogues by A.D. 70. Egypt had many synagogues by c. 250 B.C.; one is known (from a Greek manuscript) to have been dedicated to Ptolemy III (246–221 B.C.) and Bernice at Shedia. Inscriptional evidence has revealed at least 11 in ancient Rome.

The oldest extant trace of a Palestinian synagogue is an inscription dating probably from before 70 A.D. It was found in 1914 by Raymond Weill at Jerusalem. It tells of the erection of a synagogue by "Theodotus, son of Vettenus." This may have been the synagogue of the Freedmen (Acts 6:9), a group so orthodox that it gave support to the persecutors of Stephen. The inscription, whose text and translation were published by Pfeiffer in 1921, commemorates the opening of this synagogue and its housing accommodations for Jews from abroad; it was a hostel synagogue.

In Palestine no "house synagogue" remains have been found, though they existed, as shown by N.T. evidence. The ruins excavated usually conform to the basilica type, whose main portion contains a nave and two aisles, separated by two rows of columns.

(3) The *functions* of the synagogue were several: (a) It was "a little sanctuary" (Ezek. 11:16) where people living nearby gathered for worship and instruction. (b) It was a place where both adults and children learned the Law, and received instruction concerning God's will for their daily lives (see SCHOOL). (c) It was a social center, where community problems were discussed and solved, where legal transactions of interest to the congregation were posted, where funerals were held, and alms received. It has been called "the spiritual home of the Jew." (d) It was a place of trial and punishment (Matt. 10:17). In times of political unrest synagogues were also opinion-making centers.

(4) The *organization* of the synagogue: Minimum quorum for public prayer was 10 adult males. Men in the same neighborhood or occupation might join to organize a synagogue. A private home was usually used for worship until funds were raised for erection of a separate building. The head of the synagogue was its *rosh hakeneseth* or ruler (Acts 18:8; Mark 5:22), some of whose duties are described in Luke 13:14. The ruler was in charge of worship services, and selected the men who in turn led prayers, read from the Torah, and preached (Luke 4:16 ff.; Matt. 4:23; Acts 13:15). Sometimes the office was hereditary. It exacted so much time that in the Roman

period the synagogue ruler was exempted from his usual public obligations. In later times the ruler was done away with and his functions administered by several officers. A sexton or *shammash* carried out orders of the ruler or the officers, such as caring for the sacred scrolls (Luke 4:20). A quorum (*minyan*)–10 adult males–of the congregation (*tzibbur*) was essential.

(5) The synagogue *services of worship* were held principally on Sabbath mornings; attendance at the evening service, after the family meal, was at first optional. The ritual used at morning worship in most synagogues at the beginning of the Christian era began with psalms and benedictions; the *Shema** *Yisrael* (the Jewish creed) was recited; then the Amidah Prayer ("18 Benedictions") was recited; and on certain days prescribed portions of the Law and of the Prophets were read. These were often followed by a sermon or interpretation by any member of the synagogue or by a guest (Luke 4:16 ff.). Next the head or ruler of the synagogue pronounced a blessing, the congregation engaged in praise, and the service closed with the Aaronic blessing (Num. 6:24–26). The atmosphere was joyous and reminiscent, as the assembly faced in the direction of the Jerusalem Temple—E., for most of the Diaspora.

The portions of the Pentateuch appointed to be read were at first so divided in most synagogues as to enable it to be completed in about three years; later the Babylonian cycle of lessons, which enabled the reading to be finished in one year, was adopted. The passage was first read in Heb. and then translated into Aram., one verse at a time.

The synagogue fostered development of the Psalter, which, as Pfeiffer says (*Introduction to the Old Testament*, p. 620, Harper & Brothers), was a "religious anthology for the reverent Jew, prepared for the purpose of stimulating that personal piety which became characteristic of the Pharisees." It reflected the religious atmosphere of the synagogue, rather than of the Temple, expressed " the religious emotions of the laity rather than the rituals performed in the sanctuary by the clergy. Even the doxologies, liturgies, and hymns sung in the Temple service, which are included in the Psalter, were selected because they were suitable for private devotion."

409. Mosaic floor of ancient synagogue at Tiberias. In foreground, signs of the Zodiac; in background, Herod's Temple and two seven-branched candlesticks.

(6) The synagogue is closely *related to the church*. Jesus both learned and taught in his local synagogue at Nazareth (yet see his prophecy in John 16:2). His first followers continued to worship in the Jerusalem Temple for a time (Acts 3:1), but they used the synagogues as teaching places and centers for gathering new recruits; as Paul did at Corinth (Acts 18:4), Cyprus (13:5), Antioch (13:14), and in practically every city he entered (see 13:14–52 for details of a synagogue service in Paul's time). The Apostles recruited from synagogues Gentile adherents or "fearers of God" (10:2, 13:16), who had accepted the moral teachings of Judaism but had not become full adherents through circumcision. From the synagogue the Church took over its Scripture reading, prayer, and preaching; the synagogue gave the Church more than did any other Jewish institution. (See article in *BA* Vol. VII, No. 4, Dec. 1944, pp. 77–87, by Floyd V. Filson.)

(7) In most towns the synagogues were the most important structures, as seen in excavations at Capernaum (Tell Hûm), where the elegant white limestone synagogue from c. A.D. 200 or later—possibly the suc-

cessor of the one where Jesus taught—has been reconstructed from ruins found on the site. This beautiful structure faced the Sea of Galilee, a short distance away, and was oriented toward Jerusalem. Its decorative motifs show greater freedom than many others—palms, vines, eagles, lions, stars, and boys carrying garlands. Evidently by this time Jewish antipathy was only against making animals for *worship;* for ornamentation they were permissible.

Other synagogues in Palestine have been found in Galilee, at Beth Alpha in the Jezreel Valley; at Chorazin, 2 m. upland from Capernaum; and at Bethsaida Julias, just E. of the entrance of the Jordan into the sea, 2½ m. across the lake from Capernaum. Another has been discovered at Meirôn; and one of "the most perfect remains" at Kefr Bir'im. There are literary allusions to synagogues at Lydda, Beth-shan, Caesarea, and Kefar Tiberias. Early data on the Samaritans has been yielded by a Samaritan synagogue of the 4th and 5th centuries A.D., excavated in 1949, by Prof. E. L. Sukenik, the outstanding authority on synagogues in Palestine. This synagogue, 18 m. NW. of Jerusalem, between Latrun and Ramleh, 45 ft. long, had a courtyard, an outer hall, and a prayer hall. Its elegant mosaic flooring, ornamented with symbolic reference to Mt. Gerizim, flanked by two candelabra, was removed to the Hebrew University, where the inscriptional material, including a verse of the Song of Moses (Ex. 15:18) in the Samaritan version, was studied.

The Corinthian synagogue where Paul preached (Acts 18:4) is thought by many to have stood on the excavated Lechaeum Road, opposite the shops which line the W. side of this famous street, close to the elevation where the Temple of Apollo still stands. A heavy stone has been found, inscribed crudely, "Synagogue of the Jews." This may have fallen from its place in the now lost structure, which stood "hard by" the house of Titus Justus in this residential district near the agora and judgment seat of Gallio.

syncretism, the reconciliation or union of different principles, practices, or beliefs; the mingling of religious faiths. Sometimes it is the deliberate weaving of varied strands of faith and practice to form a new religion; often it is an unconscious process of change which occurs when faiths come into contact with one another. The role syncretism played in the Jewish-Christian religion has been carefully studied.

The conquest of Canaan by nomadic Israelites led to the absorption by the latter of Canaanite practices. The desire for success and recreation partly motivated this syncretism. The Israelites, anxious to succeed as farmers, took over the agricultural techniques and also the agricultural cults of the Canaanites. The Hebrews enjoyed the festival moods of the older settlers (Judg. 9:27), and the dances which were originally part of the fertility cults but later gained respectability and sanction (Judg. 11:34, 21:19–23; II Sam. 6:14). Sacred places, the centers of fertility cults, became the sites for altars (Judg. 6:19–24, 13:19; I Sam. 6:13–15). Shrines, erected where local priests presided, became the property of Israel and centers of Yahweh worship (I Sam. 1:1–3:21; Judg. 17:5, 18:30). Gideon personified the transformation of the nomad to the farmer; when, in addition to a kid from his flocks, he offered the unleavened cakes of the farmer, both of which were accepted by God, he had a syncretistic experience that contributed to Israel's religious progress (Judg. 6:19–24). Ritualism in early Israel received new content from such syncretism.

The many figurines* representing the Canaanite mother-fertility goddess found in Israelitish sites give evidence of popular syncretism among the common people. Yet these gods did not displace Yahweh as Israel's national and all-controlling God. In the tons of debris removed from Israelitish occupation levels, statuettes of male deities—found in abundance in Canaanite levels—have been significantly absent. The antiquity of the Second Commandment, and Israel's obedience to it, thus receive strong support, in spite of apparent ritualistic syncretism.

Solomon, by his political policies and international marriages, furthered a syncretism in Israel which took many years to eradicate (I Kings 11:7 f., 18:19). Jeroboam, jealous of the popular appeal of the Temple at Jerusalem, built competing shrines at Bethel and Dan, reviving earlier, discredited Israelitish practices (I Kings 12:28). King Ahaz sacrificed his own son to Molech*, like the people of E. Syria (II Kings 16:3, 17:31). The recognition of a conqueror's gods by a conquered king was syncretism under pressure. Two stories in I Kings 13, 14 illustrate the budding prophetic movement that opposed syncretism. Under Josiah (640–609 B.C.) the Baal cultic vessels were removed which Solomon's tolerance had brought into the Temple (II Kings 22:4–20). Ezek. 8 is an exposure of (1) an Egyptian cult practiced by highly respectable Jerusalem citizens in fantastic surroundings (vv. 7–12); (2) a Sumerian-Accadian fertility religion which made its appeal to childless women (vv. 13 f.); and (3) an Eastern sun-worship cultic group which met regularly in the portico of the Temple.

The syncretism of the Persian period in Palestine and Syria is extremely complex. (See *The Haverford Symposium of Archaeology and the Bible,* ASOR, p. 33.) Apostolic Christianity is a syncretism of the religion of Israel and the revelation of God in Jesus Christ. Three elements in Gnosticism* were considered deviations from Apostolic Christianity: Jewish speculations, Oriental theosophy, and Greek religious philosophy. A dangerous syncretism prevailed in Asia Minor when Colossians was written (Col. 2), and later when the Pastoral Epistles took form (II Tim. 1:8–18; Titus 3:8–11). At these times certain people lost sight of the Christian fundamental of a right relationship to God through Christ, and preached a theory or belief which was revealed only to a select group of the "understanding." The Book of Revelation has a syncretistic background, especially in its mythological ideas, not all of which have been traced to their sources or even fully recognized. Because of the inability of readers to analyze the syncretistic thought of the writer, much of the book is mystifying, misinterpreted, and misunderstood.

synoptic problem, the, refers to a consideration of the sources from which the first three Gospels were derived, and the relationship of the material common to the three. See GOSPEL, illus. 171; NEW TESTAMENT; MATTHEW, GOSPEL OF; Q.

Syntyche (sĭn′tĭ-chē), a Greek Christian of Philippi whose difficult disposition led Paul to send an exhortation to her (Phil. 4:2). See EUODIAS.

Syracuse, the chief Greek city of Sicily, where Paul spent three days (Acts 28:12) en route from Malta to Rhegium on his journey to Rome. Syracuse, founded by Corinth, possibly as early as the 8th century B.C., is at the SE. corner of the Mediterranean's largest island. Paul may have seen the Temple of Athena (5th century B.C.) and the rock-cut, semicircular theater begun before 420 B.C., and built with geometric precision. A new amphitheater had been erected in the Augustan period.

410. A silver *dekadrachma* (405–345 B.C.) struck to commemorate the victory of Syracuse over the Athenian fleet, and given as a prize to contenders in the Asinarion games. Rev., flying Nike (Victory) and armor booty; obv., Arethusa, surrounded by four dolphins emblematic of the city's insularity and sea power.

Syria (diminutive of "Assyria," or the Bab. Suri), the region S. of the Taurus Mountains and N. of Bashan, centering in Damascus*: "the head of Syria is Damascus" (Isa. 7:8)—still the capital of the modern Republic of Syria. Syria is not mentioned under this name in the Heb. Bible, but is given a name translated "Aram,"* in such passages as Deut. 26:5; II Kings 18:26, etc. (However, "Aram" and "Syria" cannot be regarded as synonyms.) The Greeks called the Syrians *Syrioi*, i.e., tribes ruled by Assyrians. The area of Syria varied at different times, but usually included territory at the arch of the Fertile* Crescent, bounded on the W. by the Mediterranean; on the S. by what became Galilee and Bashan; and on the E. by the Arabian Desert. Syria has always been richer, much larger, and more powerful than Palestine. Its abundant fruit orchards and terraced farms of grain, vines, and olives are watered by the Orontes, the Pharpar and Abana, the upper Euphrates, and many small streams springing from the twin ranges of the Lebanons, enclosing the high plain of the Beka'a or Coele Syria. Its grazing land supports large flocks of sheep and goats. Its wool, silk fabrics, and metal wares have always been famous. Its cities included, in addition to Damascus, Antioch, Hama on the Orontes, Homs, Byblos, and at times Tyre and Sidon; Aleppo (ancient Berea); Palmyra and Carchemish.

It is hard to overestimate the religious, cultural, and business influence of Syria on Palestine. Syria, herself overrun by many conquerors, developed a cosmopolitanism of thought and outlook that reached S. into Palestine. The gods of the Syrian pantheon—Baal-hadad, the fertility goddesses and the rest—came into conflict with the Yahweh of Israel and Judah.

In the 3d millennium B.C. the Amorites were powerful in Syria. In the 2d millennium Aryan Hittites* and Mitanni* occupied NE. Syria. The Hyksos* dominated Syria c. 1720 B.C., and were followed by Egyptian masters—beginning with Amenhotep I and Thutmose I. These allowed the Syrian princes and petty rulers who did not rebel to remain. An Aramaean invasion out of Arabia came in the period of the Judges of Israel (c. 1200–1020 B.C.). In the 12th century B.C. "sea peoples" held Syria. The relationship between Syria and Palestine was usually antagonistic, but at times co-operative. David took Aramaean towns from Hadadezer of Zobah (II Sam. 8:3 ff.), and conquered and garrisoned Damascus. Solomon, however, could not hold his father's gains. Israel, which lay nearer Syria than the Kingdom of Judah, had closer political relations with Syria. King Asa* of Judah (c. 913–873 B.C.) bought the help of Ben-hadad* of Syria against Baasha, King of Israel. King Ahab of Israel (c. 869–850 B.C.) put Ben-hadad of Syria to flight (I Kings 20:20; cf. vv. 26–29), and made a covenant for bazaar streets in the merchant city of Damascus (v. 34, cf. Ezek. 27:16). In a later war, when Ahab allied himself with King Jehoshaphat against Syria, he was killed at Ramoth-gilead (I Kings 22). Again, a king of Israel, Jehoram (c. 849–842 B.C.), allied himself with Ahaziah of Judah, warred against a Syrian king, Hazael; and was wounded (II Chron. 22:5). During the reign of Ahaz (Jehoahaz I), of Judah (c. 735 B.C.), the Syrian Rezin* allied himself with King Pekah of Israel against Judah "but could not overcome him" (II Kings 16:5; see Isa. 7:1).

But in this era the Syrians gained the strategic port of Elath on the Gulf of Aqabah (v. 6; see EZION-GEBER). In the 1st half of the 8th century B.C. Tiglath-pileser* III conquered the Kingdom of Damascus; and in 720 Sargon* II took the region around Hamath. Then ensued a struggle between Babylonia and Egypt for the riches of Syria, after which it came under Persian rule. The Macedonian Alexander the Great became master of Syria when he defeated the Persians at the battle of Issus (333 B.C.). In c. 300 B.C. the Seleucids* made Antioch a royal city, and from 280 B.C. controlled most of Syria; however the region S. of the Lebanons including Palestine was governed by the Egyptian Ptolemies. The Roman Empire established the three-pronged Province of Syria (64 B.C.): Syria, Syria-Phoenice, and Syria-Palestina. It reached from the Taurus Mountains to Egypt, and from the Euphrates to the Mediterranean. Rome found Syria disturbed enough to require the presence of four legions—19,200 men, together with their auxiliary forces.

Jesus never visited Syria, except the region of Tyre and Sidon. He referred to the healing of a leprous Syrian captain, Naaman, by Elisha (Luke 4:27, cf. II Kings 5). The conversion of Paul took place in Syria, on the edge of Damascus (Acts 9). Through numerous Syrian towns he and Christians journeyed, preaching and winning converts to Christ. The new faith spread rapidly through Syria in the 2d century.

The religious and cultural influences of Syria on Palestine are revealed by the famous clay tablets inscribed with the "lost Canaanite literature," found at Ras Shamrah* (Ugarit) in N. Syria and by information discovered at Byblos, Antioch, Tell Halâf, Baalbek, Dura-Euphrates, Palmyra, and Carchemish. Scholars find traces of what may be Syrian influences in the architecture of the Jerusalem Temple (see *BA*, Vol. IV, No. 2, May 1941).

Syriac versions. See TEXT.

Syro-Phoenician, a, a name applied in the A.V. to a Gentile woman living near the old Phoenician cities of Tyre and Sidon who urged Jesus, when he was in that "foreign" neighborhood, to cure her daughter (Mark 7:26, cf. Matt. 15:22). In the R.S.V. she is called "a Greek, a Syrophenician by birth" in the Mark passage; in the Matthew account, "a Canaanite woman from that region." The general location of the scene is on the picturesque Phoenician coast (now Lebanon), at various times under full or partial control of Syria.

Syrtis (sûr'tĭs), banks of quicksands off the African coast, dreaded by Mediterranean sailors (Acts 27:17). The Greater Syrtis (Gulf of Sidra) stretches c. 234 m. along the eastern part of the great depression in the N. African shore opposite Sicily. The Lesser Syrtis (Gulf of Cabes) extends c. 69 m. between two islands. Winds and tides make navigation perilous; ships were often sucked into the quicksands.

T

Taanach (tā'ȧ-năk), a Canaanite and later Israelite town on the S. edge of the Esdraelon Plain, modern Tell Ta 'annak, 5 m. SE. of Megiddo. It guarded the westernmost of three main passes over the Carmel ridge between the Plain of Sharon and the Plain of Esdraelon (Yadin, *The Land of the Bible*, 1967, pp. 47, 53). Tuthmosis III rejected this route when he attacked Megiddo c. 1482 B.C., preferring instead the shorter but more dangerous 'Aruna pass (*ANET*³, p. 235; see MEGIDDO). The King of Taanach is listed among those defeated by Joshua (12:21) at the time of the Hebrew Conquest, though Manasseh—to whom it was allocated (Josh. 7:11; cf. I Chron. 7:29)—was unable to occupy it (Judg. 1:27). It was also designated a Levitical city (Josh. 21:25).

Tell Ta'annak was first excavated for the Kaiserlichen Akademie der Wissenschaften, Vienna, by E. Sellin in 1902–04 (for bibliography, see *BASOR* 173, 1964, p. 5, n. 4). More recent excavations were carried out in 1963, 1966, and 1968 by a joint Concordia Seminary-ASOR expedition under the direction of P. W. Lapp. The site was first occupied in Early Bronze Age II (c. 2700 B.C.), and was an active fortified town for two centuries before being abandoned in EB III (c. 2500 B.C.). The EB Age defenses were substantial, and underwent several phases of repairs. Taanach was not extensively occupied again until the latter part of the 17th century B.C., when a second period of prosperity was experienced during MB IIC (c. 1650–1550 B.C.). The fortifications constructed at this time consisted of a packed earthen embankment sealed by plaster, typical of the period, surmounted by a wall. The latter, which continued in use through two phases into LB I, is the earliest known example in Palestine of a casemate wall, and to Lapp indicates the arrival of new people (*BASOR* 195, 1969, pp. 17–22). Also dated to this period is the substantial two-story building on the W. side of the mound excavated by Sellin and considered to be the house of the local ruler. At the end of the Middle Bronze Age (c. 1550 B.C.), several areas of the town were destroyed, while others, best represented by a large building complex and adjacent street S. of the west building, continued without apparent break into the early phases of the LB Age. The entire town was destroyed early in the 15th century, probably when Tuthmosis III attacked Megiddo (c. 1482; *ANET*³, p. 235). The next half-century was represented by less pretentious occupation. This period is perhaps reflected in the topographical lists of Tuthmosis III (*ANET*³, p. 243) as well as in the allocation of beer and corn to foreign envoys from Taanach and other towns of Syria-Palestine recorded in an Egyptian papyrus of about the same date (*JEA* 49, 1963, p. 50). The 7 tablets and 5 fragments written in Accadian cuneiform and discovered by Sellin in 1903–04 are to be assigned to this period (Albright, *BASOR* 94, 1944, pp. 12–27), on the basis of an additional tablet discovered by Lapp in 1968 (*BASOR* 204, 1971, pp. 17–30). This material is of extreme importance for understanding the political, economic, and social framework of the LB Age in Palestine, as well as in interpreting the later 14th century B.C. Amarna Letters.

Evidence indicates that Taanach was unoccupied from the late 15th to the late 14th century B.C., which, if correct, makes the supposed reference to the town in Amarna Letter EA 248 unlikely. Several substantial buildings of the 12th century B.C. were excavated, though large areas of the mound do not appear to have been occupied. A courtyard area with a drainage system and a possible grain-storage area belong to this phase. From the latter came a small baked tablet bearing an invoice/receipt for grain inscribed in alphabetic cuneiform (Hillers, *BASOR* 173, 1964, pp. 45–50; cf. Lapp, *ibid.*, p. 23; 185, 1967, pp. 19 f.; also F. M. Cross, Jr., *BASOR* 190, 1968, pp. 41–46). This 12th century B.C. phase ended with a vast destruction, considered by Lapp to be reflected in the Hebrew victory celebrated in the Song of Deborah (Judg. 5), which records a battle "at Taanach, by the waters of Megiddo" (v. 19). Following a period of abandonment, several important structures dated to the 10th century B.C. were constructed. At this time Taanach was included within the fifth administrative district of Solomon (I Kings 4:12). An enigmatic cultic installation (*BASOR* 173, 1964, pp. 26–32, 35 ff.; 185, 1967, pp. 27–30) and two incense altars—one discovered by Sellin in 1902, the other by Lapp in 1968 (*BASOR* 195, 1969, pp. 42–44) —are assigned to this phase. It was violently destroyed, perhaps at the hands of Pharaoh Sheshonk I (Shishak) c. 918 B.C.(see *ANET*³, p. 243). Only scattered remains of Iron II (c. 900–587 B.C.) are represented. Part of a substantial building and a number of stone-lined pits date to the Persian period, which ends the occupation of the site except for an impressive Arabic fortress of the 11th–12th centuries A.D. See P. W. Lapp, *BASOR* 173, 1964, pp. 4–44 (1963 season); 185, 1967, pp. 2–39 (1966 season); 195, 1969, pp. 2–49 (1968 season); also *BA* 30, 1967, pp. 2–27.

W. P. A.

Tabeal (Aram. "God is good"). The father of the man whom Rezin of Damascus and Pekah of Judah attempted to place on the throne of Ahaz of Judah (c. 735–715 B.C.) (Isa. 7:6 A.V., R.S.V. Tabeel).

Tabeel (tā'bē-ĕl), an official at the court of Persia (Ezra 4:7; cf. R.S.V. Isa. 7:6).

Tabernacle (Lat. *taberna*, "hut"), the portable sanctuary that served as a place of worship for the Israelites during their Wilderness wanderings, variously called in Ex. 33:7 "the tabernacle of the congregation" (A.V.), the "tent of meeting" (A.S.V.), and the "Trysting tent" (Moffatt). Other names for it are in Ex. 23:19, 26:9, 39:32; I Chron. 6:48, 9:23, 17:5; II Chron. 24:6.

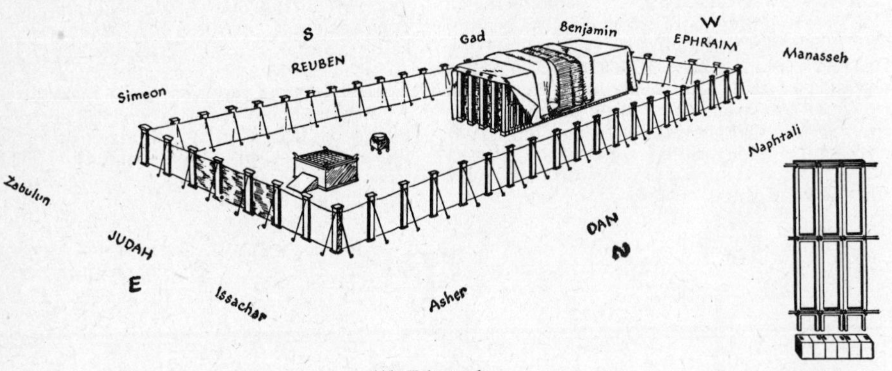

411. Tabernacle.

The description and specifications of the Tabernacle are in Ex. 26, 27, 35–38. Ten strips of linen (Ex. 26:1–6) covered with goat's-hair cloth (vv. 7–13), topped with a canopy of animals' skins (v. 14), were to be supported by a construction of "boards" (vv. 15–30). A veil was to hang between the "holy" place and the "most holy" place (vv. 31–35). Specifications were given for the court of the Tabernacle (27:9–21). The entrance faced E. Immediately within stood the altar of burnt offering (27:1–8). Beyond was a "brazen" laver containing water for priestly ablutions (30:17–21). The curtained enclosure at the W. end of the Tabernacle was the Holy of Holies or Most Holy Place. The table of the shewbread (25:23–30), the seven-branched candlestick* (Menorah) (25:31–39), and the altar of incense (30:1–10) were E. of the veil or curtain (26:31). The Holy of Holies beyond the veil contained only the Ark* of the Covenant (25:10–22).

Moses received at Sinai divine revelations about constructing and furnishing the Tabernacle (25:40). Bezaleel, Aholiab, and a number of divinely enlightened associates (31:2–6) did the work. When it was completed "a cloud covered the tent" (40:34–48; Num. 9:17 f.). The Tabernacle is seldom mentioned in Jewish historical records after the Wilderness wanderings (Josh. 18:1, 19:51; I Sam.

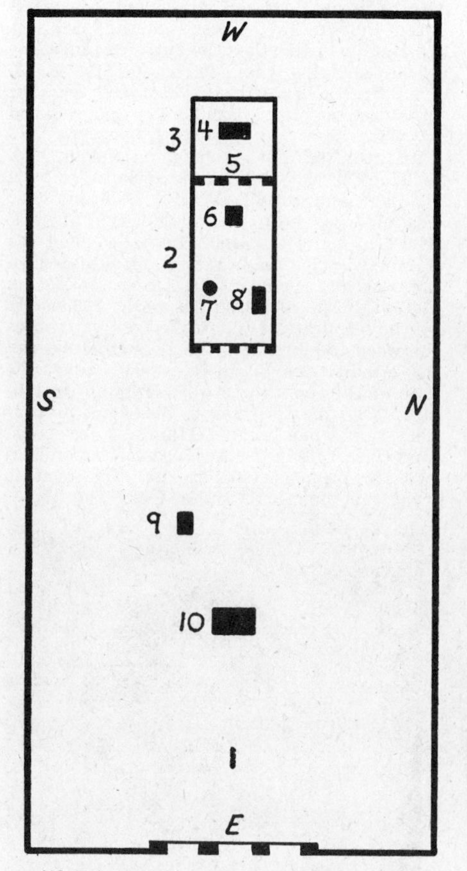

412. Tabernacle: 1. Court; 2. Holy Place; 3. Holy of Holies; 4. Ark of the Covenant; 5. Veil; 6. Altar of Incense; 7. Candelabrum; 8. Table of Shewbread; 9. Laver; 10. Altar of Burnt Offering.

3:3), though the Ark appears frequently. Those who view all this above as a historical record believe that the first Tabernacle was destroyed when the Philistines defeated Israel and captured the Ark at Shiloh (I Sam. 4:10 f.; I Chron. 17:5).

The disappearance of the Tabernacle from the historical sections of the Bible—except the P strand and the sources* associated with it—casts doubt on the historicity of the Tabernacle as described in the Hexateuch. The description of the simple Tent "without the camp," where Moses and those who "sought the Lord" could retire for meditation (Ex. 33:7–10), is from the E or early Ephraimite source, and is consistent with nomadic life. But the details of elaborate construction, trappings, and trimmings, all requiring highly skilled workers, expensive materials, and engineering precision (chaps. 26, 27, 35, 38) do not fit into the life of migrants; and the elaborate system of priests* and Levites, presumably inaugurated with the Tabernacle in the Wilderness (Num. 2 and 3) disappears when the wanderers arrive in Canaan. These considerations lead to a search for the real motive for this account.

During the Babylonian Exile and the years immediately afterward an effort was made to centralize and re-establish the Jewish faith. Ideas of local sanctuaries and priesthood of an earlier Israel were gone (Judg. 6:24, 11:11, 21:2–4; I Sam. 9:12–14, 11:15, 16:5, 21:1; II Sam. 15:7–9, 30–32; I Kings 3:4). The doctrine of a single sanctuary and a nationwide priestly caste became the rallying point for national restoration and unity. The P writers attempted to gain support for this new doctrine by appealing to the past. They enlarged the earliest tradition of worship (Ex. 33:7–11), transferred to the period of the Wilderness all the new institutions considered necessary for national rehabilitation, and used the popular figure of Moses as their authority. The priest here gained ascendancy over the prophet. Some scholars believe that the P writers in their Tabernacle narrative also tried to justify the leadership assumed by Judah after Ephraim, the Northern Kingdom, fell 722/1 B.C. In the earliest Israelitish history Ephraim had played the major role, and Joshua the Ephraimite was custodian of the first "tent of meeting" (Ex. 33:11). The P writers, in describing the allocation of positions "about the Tabernacle," showed Judah in the place of honor adjacent to its eastern entrance (Num. 2:3). Leah's sons, officiating in the Aaronic priesthood and as Levites acting as Tabernacle guards, had similar assignments of honor (Num. 3:38 f.). Thus the patriotic religious writers endeavored to prepare public opinion for Judah's important role. Ezekiel (48:1–7, 23–27), in his vision of the restored Temple (written c. 573 B.C.), locates the tribes in exactly the same position in relation to the Temple as P does with relation to the Tabernacle.

The religious significance of the Tabernacle, whether viewed as history or as symbol, influenced Jewish as well as Christian thinking in N.T. times (John 1:14; Heb. 9:2–12; Rev. 22:3, and elsewhere).

Tabernacles, Feast of (Sukkoth). See FEASTS, BOOTHS, SUKKOTH.

Tabitha (tăb′ĭ-thȧ), a woman disciple at Joppa. See DORCAS.

tables of the Law (also called tablets of the Law) (Heb. *luhoth haberith* and *luhoth ha-eduth*), the large slabs of stone on which the Biblical narratives of Ex. 24:12, 32:15 f., etc., state that the Ten* Commandments given by the Lord to Moses and Israel at Mt. Sinai were written. (See p. 724, illus. 413.)

Tabor (tā′bẽr). (1) A limestone mountain (Arab. Jebel et-Tûr) in Galilee, c. 5 m. E. of Nazareth and 12 m. W. of the S. end of the Sea of Galilee, at the juncture of the territory of Issachar (Josh. 19:22), Zebulun, and Naphtali. Its isolated situation makes its rounded summit a conspicuous landmark (Jer. 46:18), though its altitude is only 1,843 ft. above sea level. A strategic valley (the scene of Gideon's defeat of Midianite camel raiders) leads E. between Tabor and the Hill of Moreh to the Jordan. From Tabor's summit one looks down on the Plain of Esdraelon*, W. to Mt. Carmel, and N. toward snowy Hermon. From the region of Tabor Barak* and Deborah recruited their forces to advance against Sisera, captain of the army of Jabin the Canaanite (Judg. 4:6, 5:15).

413. Moses showing (or destroying) the Tablets of the Law (Ten Commandments), *by Rembrandt Van Rijn.*

The attack advanced down its slopes, carrying the battle to the swollen river Kishon (5:21) in the Plain of Esdraelon. Today the ascent of Mt. Tabor zigzags perilously for motorists, but leads to a roomy summit where an elegant, modern Franciscan Church (with the ground plan of a Crusader cross) and its hospitable hostel testify to the belief held by many since the 3d century A.D. that this mountain top (and not Mt. Hermon) was the scene of Christ's Transfiguration. This event is portrayed in exquisite mosaics over a cave-like holy place inside the church. Deut. 33:19 suggests that Mt. Tabor was the site of an early sanctuary; and its commanding and remote summit makes such use probable. Antiochus the Great, Josephus, the Romans, and Saladin fortified Mt. Tabor; but the Crusaders met defeat in their attempt to gain it. Olive, fig, oak, and terebinth trees grow on Mt. Tabor, but they are not as abundant as the beautiful forest which in the Biblical period characterized the elevation, strong and high as God's right hand (Ps. 89:12 f.). A village of cubical stone houses on the slope of Tabor carries in its name, Deborîyeh, the memory of the woman judge who guided the affairs of young Israel from beneath her palm tree (Judg. 4:4 ff.).

(2) The plain of Tabor (I Sam. 10:3, A.S.V. "oak of Tabor") was where Saul was instructed by Samuel to look for three men going up to Bethel. (3) A village in Zebulun given to Merarite Levites (I Chron. 6:77).

tabret, a musical instrument similar to a tambourine (Gen. 31:27; I Sam. 10:5; Job 17:6; Isa. 5:12, 24:8, 30:32; Jer. 31:4; Ezek. 28:13).

tache, an archaic noun, equivalent to "clasp," used in the A.V. in the plural. "Golden taches" held together the two sets of Tabernacle curtains (Ex. 26:6, 35:11, 36:13, 39:33); "taches of brass" fastened together its outer covering (Ex. 26:11) and the veil (v. 33).

Tadmor (tăd′môr), a city mentioned in A.V. I Kings 9:18, where it was confused with Tamar*, and in A.V., R.S.V. II Chron. 8:4). Tadmor has been identified with Palmyra, the Gk. name by which Romans called the fabulously rich trade metropolis situated on an oasis at the edge of the Arabian steppe, c. 140 m. NNE. of Damascus and c. 120 m. W. of the Euphrates. It controlled caravan routes between the Red Sea, the Persian Gulf, and the Mediterranean. In Patriarchal times the site was on the trail between Haran in Padan-aram, Damascus, Hazor, Shechem, Jerusalem, and what became Mamre, Beer-sheba, and Gerar. Its importance led the Chronicler, with his propensity for exaggeration, to state that Solomon had founded it. The Kings

414. The Transfiguration, depicted in the Franciscan Church on Mt. Tabor.

narrative states that Solomon fortified "Tamar," which may have been a position S. of the Dead Sea strengthened to protect Jerusalem (see Ezek. 47:19, 48:28). The greatest era of Palmyra-Tadmor began with the downfall of the Nabataean Petra (A.D. 105), and reached its peak under Odenatus and his famous widow, Zenobia. Its influence as an independent kingdom was felt from Armenia to Egypt (last half of the 3d century A.D.). Its spectacular wealth from trade and heavy taxes tempted Roman emperors. In the contest between Parthians and Romans Palmyra leaned to the Romans, who naturally honored her citizens with grants of Roman prestige. Palmyra was finally destroyed, however, by a Roman army led by Aurelian (A.D. 273). A mile of its magnificent ruins includes remnants of its famous Temple of the Sun (Shamash), its colonnade of rose-white lime-

415. Tadmor (Palmyra): colonnaded street.

stone Corinthian columns, an aqueduct, and walls erected by Justinian. Some of its characteristic tomb-chambers carved with heads of the deceased are in the Damascus Museum.

A living town, Tudmur, thrives ½ m. from the ruins of Palmyra, an important station on the Iraq-Tripoli oil pipe line.

Tahpanhes (tä′păn-hēz) (Tahapanes) (A.V. Jer. 2:16), Tehaphnehes (Ezek. 30:18), the modern Tell Defenneh, an Egyptian frontier town fortified in the Delta at the most easterly mouth of the Nile. Herodotus states that Psammeticus I (Psamtik I) (663–609 B.C.) settled some Greek mercenaries there. Jeremiah, his secretary Baruch, and a group of Jewish refugees from Jerusalem fled there after the murder of the puppet governor of Jerusalem, Gedaliah (Jer. 40–41:3), whom Nebuchadnezzar had appointed after the fall of Jerusalem (587 B.C.). Jews continued to live in this protected fertile corner of NE. Egypt (Jer. 43:9). Sir Flinders Petrie excavated Tahpanhes and verified the site.

Tahpenes (tä′pē-nēz), the queen of a pharaoh contemporary with Solomon; her husband gave her sister in marriage to Hadad the Edomite, adversary of Solomon (I Kings 11:14, 19 f.).

Tahtim-hodshi (tä′tĭm-hŏd′shī), a place E. of Jordan in the land of the Hittites; the vicinity of the Kadesh (Tell Nebi Mend) visited by David's staff of census takers (II Sam. 24:6).

tale, an archaic word used in the A.V. for "number," or "total," as "the tale of the bricks" (Ex. 5). See also Ex. 5:18; I Sam. 18:27; I Chron. 9:28.

talebearing, a gossipy form of slander prevalent in the Near East. This was legislated against in the code of Lev. 19:16, and condemned in Prov. 11:13, 18:8, 20:19, 26:20, 22. Men as well as women were talebearers (Ezek. 22:9). The reports of the Resurrection of Jesus brought by the women were at first discredited as "idle tales" (Luke 24:11).

talent. See MONEY; WEIGHTS AND MEASURES; also PARABLE.

talitha cumi (tăl′ĭ-thȧ kōō′mē) (*taleitha coum*), an Aram. phrase ("damsel, arise") in the text of Mark 5:41. The author of the Second Gospel tended to use Aram. phrases (cf. 7:11, 14:36, 15:22).

Talmai (tăl′mī). (1) A clan, descended from Anak, which lived near Hebron and was driven from home by the Israelites at the Conquest (Num. 13:22; Josh. 15:14; Judg. 1:10). (2) Son of Ammihud and King of Geshur*, whose daughter Maacah married David and bore him Absalom (II Sam. 3:3, 13:37; I Chron. 3:2). Absalom fled to Talmai after having his brother Amnon put to death because of Amnon's rape of Tamar, Absalom's sister.

Talmud (from Heb. word meaning "learning"), a compilation of Jewish tradition. It is made up of two parts: the *Mishnah**, published in Palestine by Judah ha-Nasi (who died c. A.D. 220) and his disciples, and consisting of 63 tractates dealing with prayer, marriage, festivals, agriculture, etc.; and the *Gemara*, a commentary on the *Mishnah*. The so-called Palestinian Talmud was finished c. A.D. 450, the Babylonian Talmud, which is nearly four times as large, c. A.D. 500; both Talmuds are made up of *Mishnah* and *Gemara*. See also LAW; TIBERIAS.

Tamar (tā′mẽr) ("date palm"). (1) The wife of Er, son of Judah (Gen. 38:6). After her husband's death she was given to his younger brother, Onan. When Onan died she remained a neglected widow until her father-in-law, Judah*, saw her veiled in an open place, mistook her for a harlot, and became by her the father of twins, Pharez and Zerah (Gen. 38:29 f.; I Chron. 2:4). The story of Tamar as told in Gen. 38 illustrates marriage* customs in early Israel: the father selecting his son's wife (v. 6); the giving of a widow to a brother of her deceased husband (v. 8); pledges given to a woman, like a signet, bracelets, a staff (v. 18); and the harlotry of veiled women, by the wayside, in sheep-shearing time (v. 14). It may have been maliciously circulated by a tribe unfriendly to the tribe of Judah. Tamar and her son Pharez are cited (without any imputation of shame) in Ruth 4:12. (2) Absalom's sister (II Sam. 13:1–32; I Chron. 3:9), who was raped by her half-brother, Amnon—later Amnon was put to death by Absalom (II Sam. 13:29). To escape David's anger Absalom fled to the home of his grandfather, Talmai. (3) The daughter of Absalom, "of a fair countenance," possibly named for his sister (II Sam. 14:27).

(4) An unidentified borderland site, mentioned in Ezekiel's narrative of the restored Israel (Ezek. 47:19, 48:28). See TADMOR.

tamarisk (*Tamarix*, esp. *gallica*), a bush or tree having ornamental, feathery branches and small pink and white flowers in spring. Some 20 species occur in Palestine. The tamarisk is also plentiful (in the neighborhood of water) in Sinai and Trans-Jordan. Though not mentioned in the A.V., it is found in the A.S.V. as the name of the tree planted by Abraham at Beer-sheba* (Gen. 21:33); and in connection with the Ramah residence of Saul (I Sam. 22:6) and the burial place of Saul and Jonathan in Jabesh-gilead E. of the Jordan (I Sam. 31:13). Some authorities see in the exudations of tamarisks a source of manna*. The tamarisk had sacred associations in O.T. times, as it does today among Arabs, who like to sit under it and hear it say in the breeze "Allah, Allah."

Tammuz (tăm′ŭz) (Thammuz), an ancient Accadian (see ACCAD) god whose worship spread through Babylonia, Assyria, Palestine, and Phoenicia. Tammuz became a powerful member of various Semitic pantheons. Women wailing for the dead god Tammuz at the Jerusalem N. Temple Gate are named in Ezekiel's vision of "abominations" (8:14). Tammuz was the Sumerian Dumuzi, god of pasture and flocks, of the subterranean ocean, and of vegetation. He was husband and brother of Ishtar* (Asherah*), goddess of fertility. Babylonian epics preserve the saga of the annual dying of Tammuz in the autumn when vegetation withered; his departure to the underworld; his recovery by the mourning Ishtar; and his springtime return to the fertilized upper world. Tammuz gave his name to the 4th Babylonian month, Tammuz (July), a word applied in post-Biblical times by Jews to their 4th month (June-July; cf. Zech. 8:19, "fast of the fourth month" and the "cheerful feasts"). Tammuz was similar to the Greek god Adonis (from Canaanite *Adon*), and the Egyptian Osiris* (cf. the Pluto-Persephone-Ceres cult of the Eleusinian Mysteries). There may be allusions to the mourning rites associated with Tammuz cults in Jer. 22:18; Amos 8:10; Zech.12:11.

The symbolic rites of the Tammuz-Ishtar, Dumuzi-Inaana cult included, in Babylonia, the divine marriage of the king each year to the fertility goddess in the person of a priestess, a union from which came the "life of all lands," and even the continuity of time and the moon's renewals. Byblos (the Phoenician city from which the word "Bible" is derived) was for centuries a center of Adonis worship similar to that of Tammuz. The annual feast (Adonia) mourned his death and rejoiced at his resurrection. The cult worked its way into the folkways of Christian peasants, who wept over the lost Adonis and participated in lewd festivities.

Tanis. See RAAMSES.

tanning, the process of converting the hides of animals (goat, sheep, pig, camel, calf, etc.) into leather for containers (see BAGS) for water (Gen. 21:14), milk (Judg. 4:19), wine (Matt. 9:17 ff.), oil, and other liquids. Tanned leather was also prepared for footwear, shields, helmets, girdles, etc. The parchments used for documents were skins, prepared by men who considered their task a noble one. Artisan tanners, however, had an odorous and loathsome task (especially when they were tanning hides of animals tabooed by their religion as "unclean"). They were compelled to find quarters outside of towns, preferably near water, like Simon* the tanner, who lived on the shore at Joppa (Acts 10:6); or the many tanners of Galilee, adjacent to the lake. The fact that Simon Peter lodged with Simon (Acts 9:43, 10:9 ff.) proved how far the Apostle had overcome his intolerance against the ceremonially unclean. A similar attitude marked the "devout soldier" (v. 7) who was willing to lodge overnight at the tanner's in order to escort Peter to his centurion master's at Caesarea (22 ff.).

Glimpses of the ancient process of tanning appear in Egyptian literature. For three days the skins were treated with salt and flour to free them from foreign matter. Hair was removed by soaking the skin in a mixture of water and lime, or in the acrid juice of a desert plant, *Periploca secamine;* sometimes oak bark was used in the bath. After drying for a few days, the skin was treated with a solution of pods of *Acacia nilotica* or of common desert barks and leaves, like sumac.

Taphath (tā′făth), a daughter of Solomon who married a son of Abinadad, one of her father's commissary officers stationed in the productive district of Dor (I Kings 4:11) on the Plain of Sharon.

Tappuah (tăp-pū′*a*) ("apple tree"). (1) A town in the Shephelah whose king was beaten by Joshua (Josh. 12:17; cf. I Chron. 2:43, "son" of Hebron, suggesting that the place had been established by kinsmen of the Calebites of Hebron). (2) A Canaanite town which later stood on the border of Manasseh and Ephraim (Josh. 16:8, 17:7 f., En-Tappuah).

tares, any variety of vetch, but in the N.T. probably bearded darnel, a pestiferous weed which spreads of itself, yet is capable of having its seeds sowed by an "enemy" of the farmer (Matt. 13:25–52). Not until the seed of the tares ripens and grows yellow can this weed be distinguished from the wheat among which it grows; hence the practical advice of the householder in the parable to allow both to grow together until the harvest. Farmers

416. Tares.

assign to their wives and children the tedious task of pulling out the tare kernels one by one from the good grain after the harvesting. If tares are ground into meal they spoil the flour, and often cause dizziness and nausea when eaten. The bundled tares are burned (v. 40) or fed to chickens.

target, a small shield (A.V. I Kings 10:16) or buckler (A.S.V.).

Targums. See TEXT.

Tarshish (tär'shĭsh) (in A.V. 4 times Tharshish) (Phoen. for "mine," "smeltery"; from Bab. word for "smelting plant" or "refinery"). (1) "Tarshish" is used several times in the O.T. in association with ships and ports. Solomon and his Phoenician trade ally, Hiram* I of Tyre, maintained at Ezion-geber* (Tell Kheleifeh) at the head of the Gulf of Aqabah a refinery (smeltery) and shipbuilding center for Tarshish ships (I Kings 9:26–28, 10:22). There were apparently other Tarshish stations maintained for such ships by Phoenicians in Sardinia, SW. Spain (Tartessus), and possibly in the Near East, where cargoes (II Chron. 9:21) from India could be transshipped. The fact that in a Genesis genealogical list (10:4; cf. I Chron. 1:7) Tarshish is a son of Javan (? Greece), suggests that the large Tarshish ships sailed among the Greek isles. Tarshish trade was also attempted (unsuccessfully) by Jehoshaphat (c. 873–849 B.C.) (I Kings 22:49 f.; II Chron. 20:36 f.). Ships of Tarshish were symbols of Mediterranean trade* and traders (Isa. 2:16; Ezek. 38:13; Ps. 48:7, 72:10). They carried silver (Jer. 10:9), iron, tin, and lead to trade at such ports as Tyre* (Ezek. 27:12, 25). They were among the best-known vessels of the Mediterranean and Red Sea in the Biblical period.

A slab bearing a Phoenician inscription (9th century B.C.) was found (1773) at ancient Nora in Sardinia. It mentions a Tarshish or "smelting plant" in this island. Smeltery fleets or Tarshish ships sailed to this as they did in the 10th and 9th centuries B.C. to Ezion-geber on the Gulf of Aqabah.

It is possible that Tarshish was originally a city which developed a sea-going trade in minerals. If so, this city may be Tartessus near Gibraltar in Spain, for Phoenicians developed it because of its mineral wealth. However, the evidence for this is very weak, especially as most of the A.V. renderings indicating that Tarshish is a destination (e.g., II Chron. 9:21, 20:36) are paraphrases for passages (e.g. I Kings 10:22, 22:48) in which Tarshish is not the name of a place but the term used to describe the ships.

(2) A man (A.V. "Tharshish"), a son of Bilhan of Benjamin (I Chron. 7:10).

(3) A high-ranking Persian prince at Susa (Shushan) (Esther 1:14).

Tarsus, the capital of Cilicia* and the birthplace of Paul (Acts 9:11, 21:39, 22:3). The city was built on the banks of the swift Cydnus River, 10 m. from the Mediterranean and 30 m. S. of the Taurus ("silver") Mountains, which were veined with lead and silver. Cold waters from melting snows of these Asia Minor ranges cascaded to the plain where Tarsus sprawled 70 ft. above sea level, and, below the city, formed a harbor lake, accessible and safe for Mediterranean shipping. This unique waterway gave inland Tarsus a thriving maritime trade. In 41 B.C. on this inland lake Cleopatra met and captivated Mark Antony, as described by Petrarch in *Antony* and by Shakespeare in *Antony and Cleopatra* (Act II, Scene 2).

The ancient trade route from the Euphrates joined the highway from Antioch and the E. Mediterranean 50 miles E. of Tarsus, passed through the Cilician capital, and turned N. through the Taurus Mountains to the Asia Minor uplands. The Tarsians and their neighbors accomplished c. 1000 B.C. the great engineering feat of cutting through rock wall to broaden a narrow, natural pass to these uplands—the "Cilician Gates" (a series of defiles), one of the most famous mountain passes of the ancient world. Highways by land and sea made Tarsus one of the most important meeting places of E. and W.

417. Roman road from Tarsus to Cilician Gates.

The foundations of Tarsus are legendary. The Assyrians entered Cilicia c. 850 B.C. Tarsus is mentioned on the Black Obelisk as having been captured by Shalmaneser. Under the Persian Empire Tarsus was ruled by satraps or subject kings. Xenophon (c. 430–355 B.C.) called Tarsus "a great and prosperous city." The coming of Alexander the Great to Tarsus in 334 B.C. fostered the Greek elements which had always been there. Antiochus Epiphanes IV visited Cilicia (c. 171 B.C.) to put down an insurrection. In order to encourage Greek rather than oriental influences, he made Tarsus an autonomous Greek city. Following the custom of these Seleucids in the early days of their reign, he planted in Tarsus a colony of Jews to encourage industry and commerce, and gave them equal rights with Greeks. When Pompey reconstituted the Province of Cilicia in 64 B.C., Tarsus became the headquarters of a Roman government. Antony bestowed full Roman citizenship on all its inhabitants, exempted them from taxation, and gave them self-government; and Augustus confirmed these privileges. Coins minted at Tarsus and neighboring Cilician cities verify the mixture and struggle of E. and W. in this section.

Tarsus had a university which was, as elsewhere in Graeco-Roman cities, supported by the state. Strabo (b. c. 63 B.C.) wrote that the Tarsians had an enthusiasm for education and philosophy which surpassed that of the Athenians and the Alexandrians, and that moreover the Cilician students were natives and did not come from other lands, as was the case in these other two cities. Under the leadership of the political-minded Stoic philosopher Athenodorus (c. 74 B.C.-A.D. 7), a native of Cilicia, a counselor and teacher of Caesar Augustus, Tarsus exemplified the Platonic ideal of a state. When Athenodorus in 15 B.C., with the prestige of his long relationship with the emperor, retired to Tarsus, the task of restoring some of the democratic processes in the city fell to this able philosophical leader. As a result Tarsus developed a high degree of civic consciousness which many of its citizens treasured (Acts 21:39). John Chrysostom, however, writing about Tarsus a century later, deplored the non-Hellenistic character of the town, and commented on the oriental custom of the veiling of women when walking in its streets.

Paul* was born and grew up in Tarsus, and after his conversion spent perhaps 10 years there (Acts 9:30; Gal. 1:21). During this later period he must have had opportunities to observe what aspects of the Gospel were acceptable to Jews and to Greeks. This experience would have made him useful to Barnabas at Antioch (Gal. 1:22 f.; Acts 11:25), and later would have helped him on his Greek missions. At Tarsus Paul learned his trade of Cilician cloth-making that furnished him support during his evangelistic labors (Acts 18:3, 20:34; I Thess. 2:9; II Thess. 3:8). Paul's quotations of O.T. Scripture come from the Septuagint, and demonstrate the Greek affiliation of his Judaism. His readiness of speech in Aramaic was due to the fact that he knew the vernacular of the E. (Acts 20:40). The multiple culture of Tarsus left its mark on Paul. While the strictness of his Pharisaical upbringing prohibited his participation in the university life of Tarsus, yet it furnished the youthful Paul with the pattern for his education (Acts 22:3). Greek philosophy was not alien to him (Acts 17:18, 28). His ideas about women (see WOMAN) reflect the Oriental attitude of Tarsus toward them (I Cor. 11:3–6). Paul considered the veil as the protection and honor which society accorded them (v. 10). He shared the free-born Roman citizenship which came to his family no doubt from the edict of Antony; and the announcement of his status altered the attitude of Roman authorities toward him (Acts 22:28 f.).

418. Taurus Mountains.

Today Tarsus is the Anatolian Turkish Tersoos, a city of c. 20,000 inhabitants. The Cydnus River no longer flows through the town; the ancient river bed has silted up, and Rhegma, the harbor lake, is now a vast marsh 30 m. wide. Remains of the ancient city lie 15–20 ft. below the surface of the modern town. Miles away, in the open country, bits of the old city wall stand in fields of cotton and thick vegetation. A street of weavers in Tersoos is a living link with Paul. Many ancient loom weights (to keep fabric uniform), spindle whorls, lamps, coins, and figurines have been unearthed recently at Tarsus. Goat's-hair still comes from the herds in the Taurus Mountains, and the Cilician haircloth woven from it has always been famous for its strength and durability. Beneath the American-sponsored Tarsus College there are enormous vaults which may have belonged to the Hippodrome of Roman times. At the SE. edge of the town is the large mound of *Gözlü Kule* excavated by Hetty Goldman (see volumes,

Tarsus, Hetty Goldman, Princeton University Press, especially "Excavations at Gözlü Kule, Tarsus," Vol. 1, "The Hellenistic and Roman periods").

Tartan, one of Sennacherib's emissaries (see RABSARIS).

Taurus Mountains. See TARSUS.

Taverns, the Three, a landmark on the old Appian Way, 30 m. from Rome, where Paul, on his 130-m. journey from the harbor of Puteoli* to the capital, was greeted by a group of Christians. The Three Taverns was 10 m. nearer Rome than the market of Appius* (*Appii Forum*) (Acts 28:15).

tax. See MONEY; PUBLICANS; TRIBUTE; TREASURES; WORSHIP.

teaching, the process of instruction. The N.T. presents Jesus as the "teacher come from God" (John 3:2), the one who taught rightly "the way of God" (Matt. 22:16; Mark 12:14; Luke 20:21). According to the Fourth Gospel Jesus taught his Disciples that he was their Lord and Teacher: "You call me Teacher and Lord; and you are right, for so I am" (R.S.V. John 13:13).

In the Apostolic Church the teacher was one of the Christian orders: "apostles, prophets, evangelists, pastors, teachers" (R.S.V. Eph. 4:11; cf. I Cor. 12:28 f.). Older women were encouraged to be "teachers of good things" (Tit. 2:3). Teachers in N.T. times were rebuked for failure to measure up to the highest standards of their Christian calling (Heb. 5:12; I Tim. 1:7; II Pet. 2:1). Paul was criticized by Jews for teaching—they said—against the Mosaic Law and the Temple (Acts 21:28). The Apostle's statement concerning the keystone of his teaching—"nothing . . . except Jesus Christ and him crucified" —and the source of true wisdom in "the depths of God," taught to men not by means of "human wisdom but taught by the Spirit" —is found in I Cor. 2 (see R.S.V.).

See EDUCATION; FAMILY; RABBI; SANHEDRIN; SCHOOL; SYNAGOGUE.

teeth, hard, bony appendages in the jaws of mammals. (1) The teeth of carnivorous animals, like lions, are mentioned in the O.T. (Deut. 32:24; Job 4:10; Joel 1:6; Rev. 9:8). (2) The teeth of human beings were valued because the general population had little knowledge of oral care or access to dental medicine; to lose a tooth was a misfortune, and none were extracted without dread. Hence, when one man destroyed another's tooth it was lawful for him to retaliate in like manner—"a tooth for a tooth" (Ex. 21:24, 27; Lev. 24:20; Deut. 19:21; and cf. Christ's transformation of this vengeful attitude, Matt. 5:38–41). To ask God to break the teeth of the wicked (Ps. 58:6) was an imprecation, literal and symbolic (cf. Lam. 3:16). (3) The gnashing of teeth in anger was proverbial (Ps. 35:16, 27:12, 112:10; Matt. 8:12, 13:42, 22:13, 25:30; Mark 9:18). So, too, were "escaped with the skin of my teeth" (Job 19:20) and "the children's teeth are set on edge" (Jer. 31:29, cf. 31:30). A metaphor of famine was "cleanness of teeth" (Amos 4:6). People who had no compassion for the needy were said to have teeth like knives, "to devour the poor" (Prov. 30:14).

(4) Dental art was practiced in Egypt very early. Excavated papyri speak of physicians who evidently were also dentists, like "Chief Treater of the Toothers of the Royal Palace" (c. 2500 B.C.). From a Gizeh tomb (c. 2500 B.C.) a jawbone was excavated (now in the Peabody Museum, Cambridge, Mass.) showing the first known "dental operation," the draining of an abscessed molar. Phoenician dentists pioneered in devising dental prostheses, of which two specimens have been excavated near Sidon—crude replacement of lost teeth, and the tightening of loose ones. Hebrews also used bridgework and crowns, fashioned by artisans. The Talmud gives formulae for oral hygiene and suggestions for combating tooth decay. In the days of the prophets these holy men were the sole consultants of many suffering from toothache. Their practical prescription for treating abscesses (oral or otherwise) is hinted at in Isa. 38:21. Hebrews in Babylon during the Exile undoubtedly learned the medical (including dental) technique of Babylonia. Babylonian prescriptions for cleaning the teeth have been discovered.

Tekoa (tē-kō′*ȧ*) (Tekoah), a wilderness desert SE. of Bethlehem, and the town in its midst, the birthplace of the herdsman-prophet Amos (1:1), c. 6 m. S. of Bethlehem. This austere, stony region, sparsely dotted with olives and a poor quality of sycomore figs, and traversed today only by sure-footed donkeys and pedestrians, was fortified by Rehoboam to protect Jerusalem (II Chron. 11:6). Its elevation led to its use as a station for trumpet-blown signals (Jer. 6:1). Tekoites included the "wise woman" used by Joab to persuade David to allow his estranged son Absalom to return home (II Sam. 14); and Ira, son of Ikkesh (II Sam. 23:26; I Chron. 27:9). Tekoites went 10 m. to help rebuild the Jerusalem walls under Nehemiah (Neh. 3:5, 27). There is nothing interesting about the ruins of Tekoa except a polygonal baptismal font in the stony desert, which indicates that there were early Christians there. The donkey-back journey from Bethlehem leads past Frank's Mountain (site of Herod's pleasure palace). From Tekoa one can see Nebī Samwil N. of Jerusalem, and Mt. Nebo E. beyond the Dead Sea dunes. Tekoa desert land is, in certain areas, tilled by tent colonies of Bedouins who raise dhourah (durra), a coarse millet, harvested in July.

tell (Arab.), a flat-topped, artificial mound made by the successive tumbling down of the houses and walls of a town and the rebuilding on the same site. A *tell* thus contains layers of evidence of occupation by successive groups of human beings across centuries or millenniums. This evidence is in the form of broken pottery*, various artifacts, masonry of houses and temples, ostraca*, coins, idols and figurines, fragments of decorative ivory, jewelry, etc. A *tell* is distinguishable from a natural hillock in that its top is a flat, relatively level surface instead of conical; the solid material in the upper layer of a *tell* prevents it from becoming eroded. The oldest level of occupation is at the bottom of the *tell*. Some excavated mounds (see ARCHAEOLOGY) have revealed as many as 18 layers of successive occupation over a period of 4000 years, like Beth-shan*, whose glowering Tell el-Husn guards the approach to the Jordan. Universities, museums, and learned societies of various countries have excavated many *tells* in Palestine and Jordan, such as Tell el-'Ajjûl (Beth-eglaim), Tell ed-Duweir (Lachish), Tell el-Fûl (Gibeah), Tell el-Hesī (Eglon), Tell Hûm (Capernaum), Tell Jemmeh (Gerar), Tell Jezer (Gezer); Tell Beit Mirsim (Debir); Tell en-Nasbeh (?Mizpah); Tell Sandahannah (Marisa); Tell es-Sultân (O.T. Jericho), Tell Tulûl Abū el-'Alâyiq (N.T. Jericho), Tell el-Qedah (Hazor), etc. (See separate articles under Biblical place names.) For many *tells* identified and studied by Nelson Glueck, especially Tell el-Kheleifeh (Ezion-geber), see his *The River Jordan* (Westminster Press). *Tells* are also numerous in Egypt, like Tell el-Amarna*; and in Mesopotamia, like Tepe Gawra and many others.

419. Tell el-Judeideh in Syria, showing typical "step-trench" excavated up the slope of artificial "mound of many cities," the accumulation of thousands of years of occupation, opened by the Syrian Expedition of the Oriental Institute of the University of Chicago. Arrows indicate objects found at the various levels. Near the base of the trench, beneath the walls of a building that collapsed before 3200 B.C., 6 copper statuettes (3 male, 3 female) were found, along with traces of the fabric in which they had been bundled together. These figures, the oldest known representation in metal of human figures, symbolize fertility.

Tell Beit Mirsim (Kiriath-sepher). See DEBIR.

temperance, the translation in the A.V. of various N.T. words, like the Gk. *enkrateia*, more accurately rendered "self-control," as in R.S.V. Acts 24:25; Gal. 5:23, where it is one of the fruits of the Spirit; and II Pet. 1:6 ("knowledge with self-control, and self-control with steadfastness"). Self-control is mastery of self, abstinence from excess, in the realms of drinking and brawling, speech, conceit, acquisitiveness, etc. (I Tim. 3:3–8); see I Cor. 9:25, "self-control in all things." In the N.T. the Christian is not known by what he eats or drinks primarily. Jesus was not an ascetic, as were the Essenes; he said that John the Baptist was thought to have a devil because he did not eat or drink; but that he, Jesus, who accepted hospitality, was called by his enemies a "glutton and a drunkard" (R.S.V. Matt. 11:19). But Jesus embodied that temperance (Gk. *nēphalios*) which the early Disciples taught as desirable (I Tim. 3:2; Tit. 2:2). Sobriety and self-control became deeply ingrained in those who, walking in the Spirit, could not fulfill fleshly lusts (R.S.V. I Pet. 2:11 "passions of the flesh"). (See FLESH AND SPIRIT.) There are numerous protests against drunkenness in the O.T. Nazirites* and Rechabites (see RECHAB) in protest against the pagan excesses of Canaanite civilization, advocated abstinence from wine (see DRUNKENNESS; VINE).

Temple, the, the Jerusalem Temple, mentioned in 23 of the O.T. and 11 of the N.T. books, which became the religious center of world Jewry. Most O.T. "temple" references allude to this Temple (but cf. I Sam. 1:9,

3:3; II Sam. 22:7). Shiloh, Nob, Bethel, Shechem, and possibly Gibeon probably had more "permanent" structures than many other sites sacred to early Israel; yet these shrines were insignificant compared to what developed at Jerusalem, in a structure distinguished from other Near Eastern temples in that it contained no idol, but had for its holy treasure a boxlike Ark* containing two stone tablets symbolizing the Law and the presence of Yahweh (I Kings 6:19). One Jewish tradition claims that the Ark of the Tabernacle also contained a pot of manna, Aaron's rod (Ex. 25:16; Deut. 10:5; Heb. 9:4) and a Torah* scroll.

Information concerning the Jerusalem Temple in the era of the Hebrew United Monarchy is confused in the accounts of I Kings and II Chronicles and the scanty outside sources available. But recent archaeological finds have somewhat enriched our information (see *BA* Vol. IV, No. 2, May 1951, article by G. Ernest Wright). In *BA* Vol. XIV, No. 1, 1951, in a significant article, "Reconstructing Solomon's Temple," Paul L. Garber, of Agnes Scott College, gives the author's answer to Dr. Wright's question, "What did Solomon's Temple look like?" Professor Garber's study summarizes several years' study of the O.T. text and material gleaned from archaeological findings. His work resulted in the construction of an accurate scale model (⅜ in. to the cubit) by E. G. Howland, and in the preparation of a 35 mm. film-strip of the model (South-eastern Films, Atlanta 3, Ga.).

There were two Temples: the first one built by Solomon, 960–950 B.C. and destroyed by the Babylonians under Nebuchadnezzar c. 587 B.C.; the second built by Zerubbabel in 516 B.C., rebuilt by Herod, and destroyed by the Romans under Titus in A.D. 70. (See also the ideal temple of Ezek. 40 ff.) It is hard to overestimate the importance attached to the Temple by Jews for 1,000 years. "Beautiful in elevation" (A.S.V. Ps. 48:2), it was "the joy of the whole earth." Situated on Temple Hill (the eastern hill, 2,470 ft. above sea level), it looked E. to the point where the sun rose over the Mount of Olives (200 ft. higher than the eastern hill). Little wonder that a disciple of Jesus exclaimed as they beheld the Temple Area together, "Look, Teacher, what wonderful stones and what wonderful buildings!" (R.S.V. Mark 13:1). The inspiring site, the stepped plateau-platform on which the Temple stood, is reflected in the Hymns of Pilgrimage (Ps. 84, 122) and of Zion (48, 87, 46, 76). The supreme Temple Psalm (84) contains these lines (A. S. V.):

> "How lovely are thy tabernacles,
> O Jehovah of hosts!
> My soul longeth, yea, even fainteth
> for the courts of Jehovah. . . .
> For a day in thy courts is better
> than a thousand.
> I had rather be a doorkeeper in the
> house of my God,
> Than to dwell in the tents of wickedness."

The experiences of worshippers at the Temple were sometimes recorded in other Psalms used in liturgy at the "house of pilgrimage," e.g., 23:6, 27:4, 42:4, 66:13, 119:54, 122:1. The musical service that developed in Solomon's Temple ultimately enriched the liturgy of the Christian Church.

From boyhood Jesus visited the Temple (Luke 2:41–51). During his ministry there were seasons when he walked daily in the Temple Area, available to all inquirers (Matt. 26:55; Mark 14:49; Luke 22:53), even in winter, when Solomon's eastern porch or stoa was thronged with strollers enjoying the sun (John 10:23). In the Temple Area he taught and uttered rebukes (Mark 12:35; Luke 19:45; John 7:28–36, etc.), and healed (Matt. 21:14). Apostles taught and healed in Solomon's Porch (Acts 5:12–16, 25), and were arrested there (Acts 4, 5). Paul was falsely accused of bringing Gentiles into the Temple and a riot ensued there (Acts 21). The sanctity of the Temple was unique in that only there could sacrifices be offered in obedience to the Law (see WORSHIP).

420. The Dome of the Rock. The interior, 150 ft. in diameter, of the 7th century structure is arranged in three concentric circles, richly adorned with mosaics by Byzantine artists of 10th-11th centuries, and with 36 stained-glass windows (16th century) of brilliant beauty. Moslems believe that at the judgment God's throne will be located on this Rock.

No tangible vestiges of either of the Jerusalem Temples survive, except the 52-yard stretch of massive limestone blocks from the outer wall of Herod's Temple Area, known today as the Western or Wailing Wall. The location of the Temple is definitely known, however, because the sacred Rock Moriah, where, according to many scholars, the sacrificed animals were burned on the altar of burnt offering, exists today under the Moslem Dome of the Rock (recently restored). This natural scarp (c. 58x51 ft.) was a focal point just E. of the Temple building; Solomon's and Herod's Temples were both oriented with relation to it. Traditions locate this venerable Rock Moriah (II Chron. 3:1) as adjacent to the Jebusite threshing floor bought by David from Ornan (Araunah*) for "six hundred shekels of gold by weight," for the rearing of an altar to mark the end of the plague that followed his census of Israel (II Chron. 21:14–20; cf. II Sam. 24:18–25). Legendary claims make it also the scene of Melchizedek's sacrifice (Gen. 14:18); and of Abraham's offering of Isaac (Gen. 22:2-14). Beneath the Rock and approached by 11 steps is a cavity which might have been used to drain off blood and refuse from the altar of burnt offerings into the Kidron Valley below. Some scholars who reject Moriah as the site of the great altar locate the Holy of Holies around this rock. (Dr. W. F. Albright believes that the sacred Rock under the Dome of the Rock was the Holy of Holies.)

(1) *Solomon's Temple*, described in the narratives of I Kings 5:1–9:25, II Chronicles 2:1–7:22, and Ezek. 40–46, is surrounded with unsolved problems. The Chronicler narrates how David brought the Ark to Jerusalem, Israel's future capital, and placed it in a tent (I Chron. 16:4 f.), and how he developed an elaborate organization of priests, Levites, singers, and orchestra to minister before it (I Chron. 16:4 f., 25:1–7). But when he told

421. Solomon's Temple, as reconstructed in Howland-Garber scale model, ⅜" to cubit. Front elevation and interior as seen from court. Pillars Jachin and Boaz flank the Porch entrance. Treasures were stored in side chambers. At left, model of Molten Sea (see illus. 273); at right, Altar of Burnt Offering (see illus. 423).

Nathan, the court prophet, that he desired to build a house for the Ark, as he had already built a palace for himself, Nathan, instructed by the Lord in a vision, advised against the project; God preferred to have David's son Solomon build His house (I Chron. 17:1–12). David, however, provided enormous amounts of weighed money and material of various sorts, acquired by "gifts" and tribute from vassals dwelling between the Nile and the Euphrates (18:5–13, 22:6–17). With this capital, and his own vast resources acquired by commercial and industrial expansion in co-operation with his ally, King Hiram* of Tyre, Solomon began to build the Temple (I Kings 5). He had already erected the royal structures S. of the Temple site on his acropolis on the eastern hill N. of Ophel and David's City. Between the 4th and 11th years of his reign (c. 961–922 B.C.) Solomon completed the small but elegant Temple, which at first may have served as his own royal chapel. It was beautiful and costly, but smaller than Herod's Temple, erected some nine centuries later on the same site, and the Greek Parthenon and Temple of Jupiter at Baalbek. It was not designed to admit worshippers, who went "unto" the house of the Lord (A.S.V. Ps. 122:1) rather than *into* it. The high priests are known to have entered its holiest chambers only on Atonement Day, Priestly activities in other portions of the House were usually in connection with replenishing supplies of oil, incense, and bread. Yet it must be remembered that to the pious Jew the whole Temple Area was "the house of the Lord" (Ps. 66:13). Solomon's Temple stood less than 400 years; in 587 B.C. it was burned by Nebuchadnezzar's general Nebuzaradan, 11 years after he had carried captive to Babylon Judah's young King Jehoiachin, the flower of the capital's citizens, and the Temple treasures (II Kings 24:10–16) (for the furnishings plundered from the Temple, see II Kings 25:13–17). It had impressed even the affluent Queen of Sheba (I Kings 10:4 f.).

Solomon's Temple was built by Phoenician craftsmen from the model of a Phoenician-Canaanite (or Syro-Palestinian) chapel, possibly like the one excavated at Tell Tainat (the ancient Hattina), though Egyptian and other Near Eastern influences also left impacts on its design. This chapel, used by 8th century kings who were contemporaries of the kings of Israel, gives a better idea of Solomon's Temple than any ruin found in Palestine of the era between 1000 and 600 B.C.

Solomon's Temple was long and narrow. The entrance was at one end, the Holy of Holies at the other. It was probably c. 100 ft. long and 30 ft. wide. It stood on a 9-ft.-high platform possibly 7½ ft. wider than the Temple. It was constructed of elegant white limestone finished at the quarries (I Kings 5:6, 18, 6:7) by thousands of conscripted Hebrew and Phoenician laborers; some of the limestone may have come from Jerusalem quarries. The interior was lined or wainscoted with choice, durable cedar from Lebanon's mountain forests. Carpenters, possibly from Gebal (Byblos), contributed their expert craftsmanship (I Kings 6:5–36; cf. 5:6).

Ten broad steps led up to the entrance. Two landings in the flight provided dramatic space for ceremonial processions of singers. To right and left of the steps were the famous enigmatic, symbolic pillars Jachin* and Boaz, standing free of the walls. To enter the Temple proper, the priest passed through tall, narrow doors perhaps 33x15 ft. The cypress doors were carved with symbolic cherubim, palm trees, and open flowers inlaid with gold (I Kings 6:18, 32, 35). There were doorkeepers (Ps. 84:10). The Temple layout comprised three elements: (a) The *Ulam*, or vestibule porch from which the priest walked into (b) the main chamber, called the *Hekal*, or Holy Place, into which light filtered from high clerestory ("Tyrian") windows, slatted, broad within and narrow without (I Kings 6:4). The Holy Place was about 45 ft. high, 30 ft. wide, and 60 ft. long. It was floored with cypress and panelled throughout with cedar, which was decorated with carvings of cherubim, palms, and garlands of flowers. Lavish use of gold leaf, inlaid, highlighted the solemn interior (I Kings 6:21 ff.). The flat roof was of planks and beams of cedar (I Kings 6:9) and may have been covered with a layer of beaten earth. It also may have been surrounded with a crenelated parapet or battlement, a practice common in ancient Israel (Deut. 22:8). (c) A small cedar altar stood in front of steps leading to a windowless, cubical, cavelike room c. 30 ft. square, the *Debir*, Holy of Holies, or Oracle, the special abode of the Lord (II Chron. 3:8–13); it had a raised floor. Inside the Holy of Holies were two 15-ft.-high guardian cherubim, made of olivewood and adorned with gold. On the floor beneath them stood the Ark of the Covenant. In the Holy of Holies dwelt the invisible presence of the Lord. While later interpreters described the cherubim as winged children, they probably were winged human-headed lions or bulls such as those described by Ezekiel (1:22–25) and often found in Mesopotamian architecture. See CHERUB.

Small doors led from the Temple by interior or exterior stairways to the upper stories of lateral buildings which may have surrounded the Temple on all sides except the front, and provided storage chambers (cf. *Denkmäler Palästinas*, Carl Watzinger, Leipzig, J. C. Heinrichsche).

The *equipment of Solomon's Temple*, much of which is attributed to Hiram of Tyre (the architect-craftsman whose mother was of the tribe of Naphtali), included the great altar of burnt offering in the open courtyard E. of the Temple. This altar, which stood either on the rock of Ornan or right beside it, is mentioned in I Kings 8:64 and 9:25 and is described in detail in II Chron. 4:1. It was made of bronze and was about 34 feet square and 17 feet high. shaped somewhat like a small *ziggurate**. Ezekiel (43:14) speaks of a horn at each of its four corners, such as excavated Canaanite altars are known to have had (see illus. 193). South of the altar of sacrifice stood the huge molten sea of cast copper alloy ("brass," A.S.V. II Chron. 4:1), 3½ in. thick, c. 15 ft. in diameter and perhaps 7½ ft. high. Its brim curved gracefully as a lily (I Kings 7:26). It stood on the backs of 12 metal bulls or calves (A.S.V., A.V. "oxen"), three facing in each of the four directions, and suggesting the sequence of seasons. The 12 bulls were not only decorative, but symbolic of fecundity and associated with Hadad (Baal), the rain-sender throughout the Middle East. Similar animal supports for thrones and sacred objects were common in the Iron Age. The molten* sea may not have been intended primarily for ceremonial washings by priests at the sacrifices, but to express symbolically that water or the sea is the source of life. Its capacity is estimated at c. 10,000 gal. and its weight may have been 25 to 30 tons. This unique Sea was fashioned in the Jordan Valley near Adamah, "between Succoth and Zarthan" (I Kings 7:46), where the clay was suitable for molding the metals found in the valley. W. F. Albright suggested that the portable, chariot-wheeled platform on which the molten sea and its supporting animals stood may have had amplifying effects useful to Solomon in his public addresses. (For further material on the molten sea see *BA*, Vol. XII, No. 4, Dec. 1949, pp. 86–90.) Ultimately the sea was carried off by captors and diverted to other uses (II Kings 16:17). Near the sea there stood on wheel stands ten lavers, probably similar in shape but smaller, and used by the priests for washing utensils of the burnt offerings.

The smaller furnishings of Solomon's Temple included fleshhooks, snuffers, shovels, firepans, and tongs—types of which have been excavated on other sites. There were articles inside the sanctuary which remained

422. Solomon's Temple, as reconstructed in Howland-Garber scale model, ⅜" to cubit. Roof tips back to reveal the Porch (*Ulam*), the Holy Place (*Hekal*), and Holy of Holies (*Debir*). Side chambers do not show in this view. The Holy Place, with its latticed windows and tall pilasters crowned by volute or "Proto-Ionic" capitals, contains ten 7-branched lampstands. Steps lead to the Holy of Holies, where the Ark is guarded by huge cherubim.

in position. (a) Ten golden candlesticks (I Kings 7:49; II Chron. 4:7), ancestors of the seven-branched candlestick (menorah) of the later priestly regulations (Lev. 24:1–4; Num. 8:1–4; Ex. 25:31–40). These candlesticks might better be called "lamp holders" (see LAMP, illus. 236, which shows the tripod base, slender shaft, and seven-spouted lamps, like those found at Megiddo). The Tabernacle had only one candlestick (Ex. 37:17). The Second Temple had only one candelabrum, which was stolen by Antiochus Epiphanes, replaced by the Maccabeans, and finally carried off to Rome in A.D. 70, where its likeness may be seen today, carved on the Arch of Titus in the Forum. (b) A golden table for the twelve loaves of shewbread* ("bread of the Presence" in R.S.V. Ex. 25:30). This is called in I Kings 6:20 the "altar of cedar-wood," which was plated with gold. (Fresh loaves were brought every Sabbath, and the old loaves were eaten by the priests.) (c) The portable incense altar (carried by staves) was adorned with gold. It was probably "horned."

Courts and gates characterized the sacred area. More is known of these, since they also existed in Herod's Temple (see below).

Solomon's Temple was dedicated (I Kings 8:12 ff.; II Chron. 6) during a Feast of the Tabernacles. The king's prayer on that occasion, was, according to R. H. Pfeiffer, a four-line poem preserved in "the Book of Song." But the expanded form in which Solomon's dedication now appears (the work of a post-Exilic editor of c. 550 B.C., see reference to the Exile in I Kings 8:44–56) is an eloquent, devout utterance worthy of the occasion.

The furnishings of Solomon's Temple were doubtless pilfered and replaced from time to time, e.g., after Shishak had raided it in Rehoboam's reign (c. 922–915 B.C.) (I Kings 14:25 f.). Evil Queen Athaliah (c. 842–837 B.C.) is credited with having introduced Baal worship and its trappings into the precincts of the Temple. The reforming King Ahaz (c. 735–715 B.C.) remodeled the interior, ordering an altar patterned after one in Damascus, and making other alterations (II Kings 16:10–18). Hezekiah (c. 715–687 B.C.) discarded the metal serpent of Moses (Nehushtan) (II Kings 18:4). Manasseh (c. 687–642 B.C.) introduced pagan innovations (largely Assyrian) (II Kings 21:4 f.), which were abolished during the reforms of Josiah (c. 640–609 B.C.) (Jer. 7:30), after the finding of the lost Book of the Law (essentially Deuteronomy) in the building. Josiah, going beyond Solomon's centralization policy, ruled out local shrines, and gave their staffs duties to perform at Jerusalem (cf. Deut. 12:2–28).

(2) *The Second or Zerubbabel's Temple* was completed c. 515 B.C., at the insistence of the prophets Haggai and Zechariah, while Jeshua was high priest and Zerubbabel, grandson of the exiled King Jehoiachin, governor of Judaea. The latter served under Persian authorities who had permitted displaced persons living in Babylon to return home if they so desired. Families, busy rebuilding their own dwellings, delayed for several years before restoring the Temple (Ezra 1–6). The structure they erected was poor in comparison

423. Altar of Burnt Offering, as reconstructed in Howland-Garber scale model, ⅜" to cubit. For detailed description of model, see article by Paul L. Garber in *The Biblical Archaeologist*, Vol. XIV, No. 1, Feb. 1951.

to Solomon's. Aged people who recalled the First disparaged the Second, and called it "as nothing" (Hag. 2:3). But Haggai encouraged the builders, and looked on Zerubbabel as a possible Messiah. The Second Temple had no Ark, which had evidently been destroyed in 587 B.C. The Holy of Holies was empty of all save the presence of the invisible God. It had one candlestick or lampstand, instead of ten. The vessels stolen by Nebuchadnezzar were returned (Ezra 1:5–11). Outside the Temple the altar of sacrifice was repaired. The desecration of this structure by Antiochus Epiphanes precipitated the Jewish Revolt. Maccabean enthusiasts repaired it, and it stood until replaced by Herod's magnificent structure.

(3) *Herod's Temple* replaced the shabby structure which had survived the plundering of Pompey and Crassus. Deeming such an edifice unworthy of the splendor of his rebuilt Jerusalem, Herod the Great completed within 18 months (20–19 B.C.) the sanctuary proper; but his enlargement of the sacred area to four *stadia* by means of artificial supports, so that it approximated something less than its present size (35 acres), and his construction of buildings auxiliary to the Temple, required more than half a century (cf. John 2:20). Specially trained priests built it; and it was not entirely finished when it was destroyed by Titus. Herod's was the Temple Jesus knew.

Moslem conservatism prevents scientific examination of the impressive substructures beneath the Dome of the Rock area (the old Temple Area) which would give modern Biblical scholarship material on which to base an imaginative reconstruction of Herod's Temple. The Bible itself supplies even less descriptive matter than the data for Solomon's Temple found in I Kings and II Chronicles. If, however, archaeology could produce evidence to lay alongside the literary material found in *The Jewish Antiquities* by Flavius Josephus, born less than a century after the Temple was completed, truth might be served. Albright says, "I see no escape from the arguments of Galling and others who identify the sacred rock under the Dome of the Rock as the Holy of Holies." He adds that the other possibility is that the top of the hill was cut down more than supposed.

A walk around the present Haram esh-Sherîf, whose wall measures 1,601 ft. on the W., 1,530 on the E., 1,024 on the N., and 922 on the S., gives one a sense of Herod's spacious enclosure. The line of the E. wall, facing the Mount of Olives, cannot have varied much down the centuries, because the scarp drops down to the Kidron Valley. Along this edge of the plateau Herod built walls so broad that they held the elegant double halls (stoae) which housed a synagogue, shops, booths for sacrificial animals, and money-changers' tables. People liked to walk and talk in such a sheltered arcade, typical of a Greek city. The area also contained the meeting-place of the Great Sanhedrin*. When Jesus walked into Herod's Temple Area, he might have entered by the spacious Court of the Gentiles, just inside the wall. Beyond this point Gentiles might not go; notices to that effect were posted (see illus. 181)—two of these inscribed signs have been found. Jesus proceeded to the inner courts, which rose in terraces, until he came to a small terrace leading to the main forecourt, which had no fewer than eight gates, one of which was known as the "Beautiful Gate" (Acts 3:2, 10). A wall separated the forecourt into an eastern section, the Court of the Women, and a western Court of the Israelites, i.e., of men. The men's court was reached by perhaps 15 semicircular steps suggesting a threshing floor. On these the Levites stood to sing all of Ps. 120–134, the *Shir Hamaaloth*. Still nearer the sanctuary proper was the Court of Priests, where stood the laver and the huge altar of burnt offering. At this altar, in Jesus' day, lambs for the Passover were slain (cf. Luke 22:7–13). Twelve more steps led to the Temple, a structure considerably larger than its predecessors, but having, like them, a portico, a Holy, and a Most Holy Place, the former containing the candelabrum, the table of shewbread, and the altar of incense. The Holy of Holies was empty and dark; separated from the Holy Place by a veil (double curtains), which was "rent" at the Crucifixion of Jesus (Mark 15:38). The exterior material of Herod's Temple has been described as "slabs of white, or variegated, marble." Much gold went into its ornamentation, which gleamed with dazzling effect when touched by rays from the rising sun over the Mount of Olives.

The tractate Middoth includes detailed descriptions from the Jewish viewpoint of the elevation on which Herod's Temple stood, omitting discussion of the porticoes and the fortress Antonia. It tells of the Temple guard and the locations in which the nine sections of guards were stationed; describes the various courts, platforms, buildings, and their chambers, including the treasuries, gatehouses, positions of the 21 Levites stationed at outside gates, corners of the outermost court, platform gates, and other strategic posts. The structures associated especially with Herod's improvements to the ancient worship center are seen in the SW. corner of the area, even as those of Solomon were more toward the SE. The impressive E. wall and Solomon's porches were features shared by the Temples of Solomon and Herod.

The limited observations modern scholars have been permitted to make in the substructures of the Temple Area indicate that Herod's Temple, like Solomon's, used an amazing system of fountains and underground cisterns for storing water used in religious ceremonials and for flushing away debris from the sacrifices.

Herod's Temple was destroyed by burning in A.D. 70, by the armies of Titus*, which could not spare it because the Jews were fighting furiously in the area. Its sacred treasures were carried to Rome, where depictions of them are seen on the Arch of Titus today in the Forum (see illus. 444). Its destruction brought an end to Jerusalem as the religious capital of world Jewry, to the function and revenue of the priesthood, and to Sadducean prestige.

Herod's Temple appears on the silver shekel of the Second Revolt—a tetradrachma. Four pillars on the coin represent the inner portion of the structure described by Josephus. The dotted design between the columns suggests the place where the Ark had stood behind the veil. The two circles in the Ark designate the staves by which it was carried. Oval lines above the Ark symbolize the covering, or the cherubim. A star over the Temple suggests divine glory. The three rooms of the Temple are indicated by three squares.

(4) *Ezekiel's Temple* did not have objective reality, but was seen by him in a vision, when he was carried in the spirit from Babylon to Jerusalem, on New Year's Day (October 573 B.C.), and was shown the ideal temple of the future (Ezek. 40:1 ff.). The details of the Temple, its decoration and furnishings as recorded in Ezek. 40–46, provide probably one of the best descriptions of Solomon's Temple. The prophet may have gained his information by walking around the ruins of the Temple, rather than from a documentary source. His *ziggurat*-like altar of burnt offerings (43:13–17) had three square stages, each with a side two cubits shorter than the stage below it (proportions which tally with the Chronicler's account). Biblical archaeologists, studying the text of Ezek. 40:5–16 (the prophet's description of the East Gate of the Temple), found striking similarities between the structure there described and a gate actually found in Solomon's Megiddo*, level IV B, with its two vestibules and over-all measurements similar to those recorded by Ezekiel. Iron Age gates found at Carchemish and at the early Monarchy level of Lachish, as well as the 10th-century gate excavated by Nelson Glueck at Ezion-geber, suggest that the type of gate described in Ezekiel's vision of the Jerusalem Temple is of the type constructed during and just after Solomon's reign. These data point to the "traditional date for the prophet Ezekiel, viz., the first half of the 6th century B.C.," for he must have lived at least part of his life prior to the destruction of the Solomonic East Gate, destroyed during the siege of Jerusalem (587 B.C.) (C. G. Howie, in *BASOR* No. 117, Feb. 1950, pp. 13 ff.).

The temple erected on Mt. Gerizim in Samaria developed under uncertain circumstances and at a debatable date. When, in 722 B.C., Samaria became a military colony peopled by the remnant of Jews who had not been deported by Sargon II and of colonists brought in from Babylonia and N. Syria, the question of a worship center became acute. The offer of certain Samaritans to help rebuild the Jerusalem Temple under Zerubbabel's leadership sanctioned by Cyrus (c. 538 B.C.) was rejected (Ezra 4:1–6). The rift widened in the 5th century when Nehemiah expelled a member of the high priestly family for marrying a Samaritan girl (Neh. 13:28 f.). Apparently about one century after the incident recorded in this passage, the Samaritans erected their own temple on a traditionally favored site on the summit of Mt. Gerizim, where God's chosen people had received the blessing (Deut. 11:29). Samaritans tried to bring prestige to their temple by assigning its foundation, or its sanctioning, to Alexander the Great (2d half of the 4th century B.C.). The Jewish historian Josephus emphasized this claim. During political disorders in the time of the Maccabean, John Hyrcanus (c. 134–104 B.C.), the temple was destroyed, but Samaritans continued to worship on the old favorite site down to the time of Christ (John 4:1–42, especially "neither in this mountain, nor yet at Jerusalem"). Today a vanishing colony of Samaritans maintains a small synagogue in Nablus.

Before the Exile, temples had been established by the Jewish Diaspora. At the Egyptian Elephantine a temple erected before c. 525 B.C. was destroyed in 411 B.C. and rebuilt after 408. Here the Biblical system of sacrifices was maintained without realization that the Deuteronomic Law forbidding sacrifices outside Jerusalem was being violated. A Jewish temple built at the Egyptian Leontopolis, excavated by Sir Flinders Petrie, may have duplicated the dimensions of the Jerusalem Temple.

424. The Parthenon, from Temple of Zeus.

Hebrew prophets warned against putting too much trust in the Temple and its sacrifices (Isa. 66:1–4; Jer. 7:1–15). Their teaching is carried further in Hebrews 10, where Christ is presented as the all-effective sacrifice.

See LEVITES; MUSIC; PRIESTS; STOA.

temples (in the O.T. from Heb. *hekal* and *bayith*, meaning, approximately, "house" or "palace"; and in the N.T. from Gk. *hieron*, *naos*, connoting "sacred enclosure," "sanctuary") were erected to house gods in ancient times from the Mesopotamian Valley to the Mediterranean and its islands, from Asia to Egypt. The first shrines were very crude—of reeds in the southern Tigris-Euphrates basin, and of mud in pre-dynastic Egypt. Primitive temples were small, for they were not intended to accommodate assemblies of worshippers, but only to contain the likeness of the honored deity and to provide room for priests to perform their offices, while gift-bringing worshippers stood outside, glimpsing the rites and sometimes the cultic figure within. As time went on larger temples were built, some of large proportions, like the Great Hall at Karnak, the Temple of Diana at Ephesus (Acts 19:27, 34 f.) that of Artemis at Gerasa (Jerash), and the temple of Olympian Zeus at Athens. These "temples made with hands" (Acts 17:24) were characterized by architectural perfection, as seen in the Parthenon ruins. Usually temples were the best edifices of the community, except the palaces in Persia, where the worship of the fire god Ahura-Mazda required only simple altars on which the sacred fires burned. Whether crude or elaborate, temples were places where a man tried to enter into communion with the deity in whom he believed, and whose favor, protection, and guidance he sought to win with offerings from his flock or farm, or with gifts of metal.

Most pagan temples of the Near East contained a statue or other graphic depiction of the god there honored. Most worshippers did not believe that the image incarnated the deity, but that he lived in it.

(1) *Recent archaeological exploration* has revealed the ground plans, and a little of the superstructures, equipment, and cultic paraphernalia of many temples of the ancient Near East. Reliefs, seals, and paintings show some of these. Clay and papyrus documents recovered from temple archives indicate the ritual and contain some of the sacred epics. The oldest extant brick structures were places dedicated to gods millenniums ago. The Second Dynasty Egyptian temple found at the Phoenician Byblos (in the present

Republic of Lebanon) is believed to be the oldest stone structure, antedating even the Saqqârah and Gizeh pyramids. From the mound of Beth-shan* have been excavated temples erected during 4,000 years of history, beginning with c. 4000 or 3500 B.C., and including "the most complete series of Canaanite temples yet discovered, from five different levels and periods," with at least six sanctuaries on one section of the mound. These temples, remarks C. C. McCown, "throw a flood of light upon the religion of the Canaanites whom the Israelites supplanted and absorbed, for they were built during a period when Egypt was strongly under Syrian influence, and though erected by Egyptian officials, they exhibit Canaanite worship under a thin veneer." Bible students are especially interested in temples of Stratum V of Beth-shan, which were standing when King Saul's headless body was affixed to the Beth-shan city wall. The temple of 'Anat may be the one where Saul's armor was presented as an offering by his Philistine enemies (I Sam. 31:10). Similarly at Megiddo the various excavated layers have yielded numerous Canaanite and other Temples from c. 3500 to c. 450 B.C. or a little later. In Lachish were found a series of three small Egyptian (or later) temples built in the Hyksos fosse, in the Late Bronze period (15th–13th centuries B.C.). Their ground plans have been traced, and some of the apparatus of their ritual found. The 3d fosse temple, destroyed by fire, may have been ruined by invading Israelites (Josh. 10:32). The Persian period temple at Lachish was small and simple. Excavation of Roman Samaria makes clear the Severan reconstruction of the huge Augusteum, or Temple of Zeus Olympius, erected by Herod the Great in honor of his patron, the Roman emperor, Caesar Augustus. The jumbled mass of temple ruins at

425. Temple ruins at Baalbek, showing approach to Temple of Zeus.

Syrian Baalbek (in Coele Syria) shows this center to be one of the longest used syncretistic worship sites in the Near East, where temples were erected to Baal, the Greek *Helios* (sun), the Roman Jupiter, Mercury, Venus, Bacchus, etc. At ancient Damascus a temple of Rimmon (II Kings 5:18) became a Christian church and then a mosque.

Around the square or rectangular temple were built accessory structures, housing priests, musicians, administrators, keepers of the archives of sacred literature and of business transactions, moneys, and official mints.

In vicinities where many gods were worshipped a large number of shrines existed. Peasants confined their worship to simple rustic altars, sacred trees, springs, rocks, or mountains. Vast power was exerted by Near Eastern temple complexes, and they controlled economic life.

(2) Excellent brief treatments of *basic temple types* of the ancient Near East appear in *BA* (ASOR) for Sept. and Dec. 1944.

(a) *The Mesopotamian temple* developed from reed huts built in the marshes of S. Mesopotamia about the end of the 4th millennium B.C. Their early altars were of reed.

426. Thirty-foot pillars from Moon Temple at Mareb, visited by Americans for the first time in 1951.

The use of sun-dried bricks and of bitumen-laid mosaics gave dignity and beauty to some of these temples. On new earthen mounds, suggestive of a mountain rising above the watery wastes, builders erected three-naved temples, their doors opening in three directions to enable people to view the statue of the god. The usual Mesopotamian temple consisted of a zoned temple tower or *ziggurat** (see BABEL; SUMER; UR), where the deity alighted; and a building on the ground level, patterned after a S. Babylonian private dwelling, where the god lived while on earth. Although several *ziggurats* have survived, like Etemenanki at Babylon, begun in the 3d millennium B.C., none of the upper structures remain. Many believe that the top room was the marriage chamber of the "god" and a priestess. The lower or "living room," containing the image of the god in gorgeous apparel, could be seen by worshipping crowds through impressive portals. Where one temple was shared by several gods, the chief deity had the main room, and the lesser ones had smaller shrines. In both Babylonia and Assyria the temples and royal palaces were similar in design. In both the chief figure was seen across an impressive vista of court and doors.

(b) *Egyptian temples* at Memphis*, Saqqârah, (center of apis bull worship), Heliopolis, and Gizeh may have been seen by Hebrews on their sojourn in the Delta. Hebrew laborers may have helped to build

427. Palm-leaf column, 19th Egyptian Dynasty, Ramesses II, from Ahnaŝ el-Medîneh.

some Egyptian temples. In Palestine there were many Egyptian temples. Throughout Egypt temples were built to house the statues of powerful deities like Osiris, Isis, Horus, Hathor, Amun (Re), Ptah, and many lesser deities. Each statue was housed in its own *naos* or shrine, from which on feast days it was conveyed on the shoulders of a priest or floated on the Nile in a sacred boat. Even deities which in early times had been given animal forms were later given human bodies with heads of the sacred crocodile, falcon, lioness, etc. Many Egyptian temples were parts of elaborate mortuary structures, like Queen Hatshepsut's at Deir el-Bahri. On many sites they were reared primarily for elaborate rituals exalting specific deities, as at sumptuous "hundred-gated" Thebes (the Biblical No or No-amon, Jer. 46:25; Ezek. 30:14; Nah. 3:8). The Temple of Amun, erected by Amenhotep III at Luxor (the S. quarter of E. Thebes), with its colossal hypostyle hall erected by Seti I and Ramesses II, had pillars, open courts, chapels, ambulatories, and chambers of the god's house. This temple was connected by a mile-long avenue, lined with ram-headed sphinxes with the imperial Temple of Amun at Karnak. Two towers, called "pylons," flanked the entrance to many temples. These pylons, erected on rectangular bases and sloping inward, had the appearance of truncated pyramids. The actual entrance portal between the towers gave access, by inner stairways, to small rooms inside the pylons and to the roof. Since almost every pharaoh from Amenhotep I on had a part in building the Temple of Amun at Karnak, it represents what George Steindorff and Keith C. Seele (*When Egypt Ruled the East*, University of Chicago Press) aptly termed a gigantic chronicle in stone of Egypt's Golden Age. Obelisks and gigantic statues, like the talking colossus of Memnon at W. Thebes, were also typical of Egyptian temples, as were sacred lakes, botanical gardens, and impressive ramps.

Egyptian temples, with their lotus and papyrus capitals, were houses of the gods, yet a deity like Amun of Karnak also lived in many other temples, inside and outside of Egypt, wherever the pharaoh ruled. Similarly, the sun god Re*, whose special dwelling was at Heliopolis, had many local temples, for gods were not confined in either shrines or images. Services of worship were not for the people, but for and by the pharaoh, from whom the god-given blessings of health, prosperity, power, victory, and longevity flowed out to his subjects. The common man saw the god-images on feast days, addressed petitions to the king of the gods, and paid back-breaking tribute for the erection and maintenance of temples.

(c) *Canaanite temples* were often of the "broad house" type, with a door in the long side. Such temples have been excavated at Megiddo, Jericho, and Ai (c. 3000–1900 B.C.). By 1500 B.C. they were square, with an entrance portico and a special room at the rear reached by steps. This was the housing place of deity (represented by a statue) and a forerunner of the "Holy of Holies" in Solomon's Temple. The main sanctuary room, as seen at Lachish, had benches where offerings were laid; an incense altar; libation stands;

TEMPTATION

and lamps. Phoenician-Canaanite temples influenced Solomon's Temple at Jerusalem.

(d) *Graeco-Roman* temples at Antioch*, Ephesus*, throughout Asia Minor, in Thrace, and in Achaia were seen by Paul and his Apostolic companions. Beholding the perfection of the Parthenon at Athens and its

428. Poseidon's Temple, Cape Sunium, Greece.

companion temples on the Acropolis, as well as in the lower city, Paul exclaimed, "God that made the world and all things therein . . . dwelleth not in temples made with hands, neither is he served by men's hands, as though he needed anything, seeing he himself giveth to all life" (A.S.V. Acts 17:24, 25).

Roman temples were usually erected in a forum. They stood some 25 ft. above the surrounding area, and were approached by impressive steps at the foot of which an altar stood. The temple had a single *cella* or room containing—if it were dedicated to the Capitoline triad (Jupiter, Juno, Minerva)—three spaces at the rear for statues of these deities. In front of these was a narrow platform for offerings of cultic objects. The threshold was often of marble; the floor, of marble or mosaic. The interior was frequently decorated with pilasters. Around the *cella* ran a portico of fluted columns. Under the platform on which the temple stood were rooms entered from the rear and lighted by loopholes. An example of this type of Roman temple is seen today in Ostia, port of ancient Rome.

429. Doric columns of the Temple of Apollo at Corinth, which was standing in Paul's day.

Paul used the figure of a temple, familiar to his converts at Corinth in the archaic Temple of Apollo, to convey his teaching about man's relation to God: "what agreement hath a temple of God with idols? for we are a temple of the living God; even as God said, I will dwell in them, and walk in them; and I will be their God, and they shall be my people" (A.S.V. II Cor. 6:16; cf. Eph. 2:20–22—believers built together—Christ the chief cornerstone, "into a holy temple in the Lord . . for a habitation of God in the Spirit").

temptation, used in the English Bible to convey the idea of (1) testing, or making trial of (from root *nissāh*, "to prove," or "to test out"), as in Gen. 22:1, where God is said to tempt Abraham to offer his son as a sacrifice; in Ex. 17:2, 7, where Israel in the Wilderness is said to tempt God, to see whether He acts in accord with His character and His purpose; and in Isa. 7:12, where Ahaz refused to tempt (test) God; (2) enticing to sin* (from Gk. verb used in the N.T., *peiradzo*, which means to test, or to lure toward sin), as in Matt. 4:1, in connection with the Temptation of Jesus; and in Rev. 2:10, where Satan tries the faithful.

The Temptation of Jesus (Matt. 4:1–11; Mark 1:12 f.; Luke 4:1–13) is an example of the effort of Satan* to mar the personality of Jesus at the opening of his ministry. The nature of Jesus being unique, he could not be tempted after the manner of ordinary men. His wilderness temptation was an assault on his role as Son of God and Saviour of men. (1) The suggestion that he command a desert stone to be made bread (Luke 4:3) (and there is an external resemblance between the two)—was an effort to induce him to deny the spiritual nature of the Kingdom of God, and to win men in an easy way, i.e., by catering to their physical needs. This type of temptation recurred (John 6:1–15). (2) The temptation to cast himself down from the SE. tower of the Temple Area (a leap of some 100 ft. to the colonnades, and more than that to the Kidron Valley) was an effort to have him use spectacular methods to establish the Kingdom of God (Luke 4:9 f.). A recurrence of this temptation is seen in Matt. 16:1; John 6:30. (3) The proffered bribe, of "all the kingdoms of the world, and the glory of them" if he would fall down and worship Satan (Matt. 4:8 f.), brought from Jesus a stinging rebuke of the evil one and his declaration of his own reliance on God. The temptations of Jesus did not cease after the first victorious encounter even though angels came to his aid (v. 11), for Satan departed only "for a season" (Luke 4:13).

Jesus was likewise tempted by man, especially in the form of questions which might elicit answers harmful to him. Hypocrites tempted or tried him (Matt. 22:18). Scribes and Pharisees tested him with captious questions, trying to ensnare him in his own words (Matt. 22:15–46; Luke 21:7 ff.). Jesus must have been tempted frequently to fear lest his Disciples fail him (see his Gethsemane warning, Mark 14:37 f.). At the Last Supper Jesus declared to his Disciples, "Ye are they which have continued with me in my temptations" (Luke 22:28). His outcry from the cross, "My God, my God, why hast thou forsaken me?" (Mark 15:34) may express a temporary testing of his supreme faith in the fellowship of the Father with him. His teaching the Twelve to pray "Lead us not into temptation" is not a statement of his belief that God places men on the brink of pitfalls; the clause may be interpreted, "Help us not to succumb to temptation when it inevitably comes." When Jesus told Peter that he had prayed for him when Satan was trying to win him, he supplied a pattern whereby Christians everywhere can fortify their brothers (Luke 22:31 f.).

The Epistles of the N.T. tell how to overcome temptations which come to all men, but which need not lead to sin. Most important is probably I Cor. 10:13: "There hath no temptation taken you but such as is common to man: but God is faithful, who will not suffer you to be tempted above that ye are able; but will with the temptation also make a way to escape, that ye may be able to bear it." (See also Jas. 1:12; I Thess. 3:5; II Pet. 2:9; Rev. 3:10, 12, 21.)

ten. See NUMBERS.

Ten Commandments, the (sometimes called the Decalogue, Gk. *deka logos* "the ten words," but to be distinguished from the ritual Decalogue of Ex. 34:1–26 and Ex. 22:29b–30, 23:12, 15–19; see COVENANT; LAW), a body of social and spiritual wisdom which was long considered to be distinctive of Israel (Deut. 4:6, 8; Ezra 7:25). It contains clues to the good life, and summarizes much O.T. teaching. The Exodus Decalogue as we now have it is in two forms: a Deuteronomistic statement (Deut. 5:6–21) (c. 621 B.C.) and a priestly reworking (Ex. 20:2–17) (c. 451 B.C.); the earlier statement is the more humane. Both may be revisions of a briefer and older original set of laws (cf. Lev. 19:2–4, 11–13). The offenses condemned in commandments five to nine are also found in other ancient law codes. The two versions of the commandments differ in the basis assigned for observance of the Sabbath: Deut. 5:14 f. bases its command to grant rest to laborers and animals on gratitude for deliverance from Egyptian bondage; Ex. 20:11 bases it on the sanctification of God's day of rest after His creation of the world in six days. All the commandments except two (observing the Sabbath and honoring parents) are in negative form. The only one with a promise attached is the fifth.

The Priestly Code transferred all covenants and legislation to a setting on Sinai, and disregarded the covenant of Moses in the plains of Moab (R. H. Pfeiffer, *Introduction to the Old Testament*, p. 183, Harper & Brothers).

The Ten Commandments inscribed on the Tables of the Law, according to Biblical record, were first pronounced by God orally to Moses, and then committed to writing (Ex. 31:18–32:16, E source) on two stone tablets when Moses had ascended Mt. Sinai. The writing was on both sides of the tablets. But when Moses, after 40 days of communion with God on the Mount, returned to the camp, he found his people worshipping a golden calf; this so angered him that he shattered the tablets. After the congregation had been purged of apostasy, Moses, at God's command, went again into the Mount, carrying two new tablets, on which the leader wrote again the commandments of the Lord (Ex. 34). These he read to the people, with a veil over his face. The second set of tablets was deposited in the Ark* of the Covenant. (See TABLES OF THE LAW, illus. 413.)

According to the E account (c. 750 B.C.) of Ex. 31:18, God prepared two tablets of testimony and also wrote upon them with His "finger"; but in the P account of Ex. 34:27 f. Moses prepared the tablets and God wrote on them. The D (c. 622 B.C.) account of Deut. 10:1–5 repeated this material; but in Ex. 34:27 f. Moses not only prepared the tablets but wrote on them, as God's amanuensis. Now that the early use of writing among people in and near Sinai (see SERABIT) has been proved (see WRITING), it is clear that Moses could have inscribed the tablets.

The Mosaic authorship of the Ten Commandments has been assailed by critics, who have based their attacks in part on the inclusion of the 2d commandment, when Moses himself used a bronze serpent, Nehushtan* (Num. 21:4–9); on his emphasis on the Sabbath*, originally a Canaanite farm institution rather than one practical for nomads; and on other points. The offenses condemned in commandments five to nine are also condemned in many other ancient law codes; yet some critics find less reason to doubt the Mosaic origin of the 6th, 7th, and 8th commandments or "words." Interesting as is the effort to assign a date to the written form of the Ten Commandments, this concern is less vital than the early origin of the ethical Decalogue, for, as I. G. Matthews pointed out (*The Religious Pilgrimage of Israel*, p. 128, note, Harper & Brothers), "the essential features of this code were a part of the social inheritance of each tribe of the federation long before the time of Moses." And regardless of one's ideas concerning Mosaic "authorship," many scholars are in accord with W. F. Albright, who feels that there is no ground for denying that Moses was the individual who founded the commonwealth of Israel and framed its religious system (*From the Stone Age to Christianity*, W. F. Albright, p. 196, The Johns Hopkins Press).

As pointed out in *The Jews, Their History, Culture, and Religion* (ed. by Louis Finkelstein, vol. 1, article by Robert Gordis, pp. 466 f., Harper & Brothers), even if there had been no tradition of a legislator like Moses it would have been necessary to invent one. The leading of a mass of captives from a country like Egypt, the transforming of a crowd of cowed helots into a mighty people, the unifying of clans united in worship of the same God, presuppose a liberator who was also a lawgiver. Moreover, the people could be convinced of the type of life they were to live only by receiving the exalted principles of the Decalogue and the mundane details of ritual, civil, and criminal law.

The present arrangement of the Ten Commandments is that of the early Jewish and the early Christian Church. However, the Western Church from the era of Augustine to the Reformation, and also the Roman and the Lutheran churches today, follow the arrangement of the Massoretic Hebrew text in making the 1st and 2d commandments one and the 10th two.

The N.T. reveals Jesus as honoring and quoting the Ten Commandments (Matt. 5:21 f., 27 f.; Mark 7:10, 10:19; John 7:19) and even making them more stringent. Yet for his liberal interpretation of the Sabbath he came into violent conflict with the Pharisees, who had an excessive regard for the Mosaic Law (John 9:28; cf. Matt. 23:2).

tent of meeting. See TABERNACLE.

tents, "houses of hair," as desert families call tents today, were the homes of Israel after their settlement in Patriarchal groups in Palestine. Their worship center was a sacred tent of meeting (see TABERNACLE). The tents still used by Bedouins are probably similar to those of early Hebrews in Palestine.

The *material* used in tents was—and is—hand-woven goat's-hair material which shrinks taut with rain. Goat's-hair and woven reed cloth were the first fabrics used by Hebrews, sheep's-wool having been used ultimately for garments. Weaving* usually follows sheep- and goat-shearing time; old tents are then patched, and if the family has grown, or if new sets of relatives have joined the encampment, new tents are set up—forerunners of the "bridal canopy" used today for Jewish marriages (see Ps. 19:5; Joel 2:16; cf. II Sam. 16:22). The cloth is dark brown or black; hence the saying "black as the tents of Kedar" (Song of Sol. 1:5). The addition of fresh material gives a striped effect when the sun has baked the original to a golden brown. In Bible times women and men wove tent cloth in narrow strips on homemade looms. Stone spinning whorls and loom weights of stone and clay have frequently been found in excavated deposits from the Early Bronze Age (c. 3300–2000 B.C.).

430. Bedouin tent at coffee time.

The Apostle Paul is the most famous maker of tent cloth in the Bible. His native town, Tarsus in Cilicia, was noted for its *cilicium*, or goat's-hair cloth. As a boy Paul learned to weave it, and as a man he used this trade to support him and others while he devoted his leisure to preaching the Gospel of Christ. As Saul, he, like every obedient Jew, purified himself after the ceremonial pollution of handling goat's-hair: "as to every garment, and all that is made of skin, and all work of goats' hair . . . ye shall purify yourselves" (A. S. V. Num. 31:20).

The *pitching* of tents is in the same manner used by campers everywhere. The top is spread smoothly on the ground, ropes are straightened out, and pegs are driven with a hammer into ground firm enough to give support; then the workers get underneath the cloth and lift it up onto poles. To the women falls the task of pitching, as well as the making, the patching, and the loading of nomads' tents. Isaiah's exhortation to the Hebrews to "lengthen . . . cords" and "strengthen stakes" and "enlarge the place of the tent" and stretch forth the curtains takes on vivid meaning when barefooted Bedouin women are seen today pitching tents near the Jordan.

Poles are usually nine in number, arranged in three rows. The middle row may be 7 ft. high, while the other two rows are only 6 ft.; thus the roof of the tent slopes from the center ridge of the cloth toward the back and the front. Wooden rings sewed inside the top of the tent are fastened to the ropes which run to the tent pins. In early O.T. times the tent pins and hammer were of wood. (See the story of Jael, Heber's wife, who with tent pins killed Sisera, captain of the Canaanite king who oppressed Israel in the time of Deborah, Judg. 4.)

Mesopotamian sculpture shows a conical type of soldiers' tent used by royal warriors. It had a center pole with two arms; and the king's rectangular pavilion (cf. I Kings 20:12, 16) had walls (probably of linen) and elegant tasselled tops of embroidery or richly woven fabrics.

Inside the tent home there is little privacy. Most activities go on near or just outside the tent door. Bedouin tents in daytime are generally left open to the breeze, with cloth flaps rolled up. Sometimes they have "walls," or screens, of woven reed or wattle, about 4 ft. high. The floor is the earth itself, or handwoven matting, or (in the quarters of rich sheikhs) hand-woven carpets. The "rooms" are two: one for the men, used also as a reception room for guests; and an inner room for women. The latter apartment, to which only the male head of the family has access, is also a storage place for the cooking pots and simple utensils of nomads. The door, or opening, faces the direction from which strangers might be expected to approach. Young goats and calves enter at one end of the tent, and the family at the other. Old cows in the night sit by the smoldering embers of campfires. For protection tents are usually pitched in groups. Only affluent wives have a separate tent. It was from the seclusion of her own tent at Mamre or the compartment of Abraham's which was her kitchen that Sarah eavesdropped on the conversation of the angelic visitors, and laughed when they told her husband that she, "stricken in age," would bear a son (Gen. 18:10). In the betrothal story of Isaac and Rebekah, when the young damsel arrived by camel from Mesopotamia, Isaac brought her into the tent of his deceased mother (Gen. 24:67). Gen. 31:33 tells of separate tents for maidservants.

Equipment of tent homes is extremely simple. Stoves for baking daily bread are a sheet of metal, or a few stones set up at the tent door, or holes in the ground, heated with charcoal until hot enough to bake the thin, flat loaves placed there. Changes of garments are few; hence clothes chests are not necessary. A few earthen pots and bowls; a stone grain mill*, or mortar and pestle; water jars (now often replaced by tin oil cans); a lamp of pleated cloth treated with paraffin and fastened to a brass lid and bottom; bed mats, which are piled in a corner of the tent by day and unrolled on the ground at night—these are the essentials. A woolen cradle may swing from two of the inner tent poles. Chickens, dogs, and children wander in and out among the women sitting on the floor at their tasks. Grandfathers, unable to work, dandle infants on their shoulders. Hideous scavenger dogs ward off approaching strangers.

Tents are expensive. Only the rich among Sinai Bedouins can afford them. Israel during the Exodus may have had very few.

Tents in Scripture. The finest picture of tent life in Patriarchal times is found in Gen. 18. Abraham had been born in a city of comfortable, well-built, two-storied houses—Ur of the Chaldees, on the Euphrates. Abraham voluntarily became a wanderer for God, a sojourner by faith "in the land of promise, as in a land not his own, dwelling in tents . . . for he looked for the city which hath the foundations, whose builder and maker is God" (A.S.V. Heb. 11:9). Abraham pitched his tents and built his altars to Yahweh time and again as he became a very rich herdsman of sheep and cattle. He usually looked for a clump of oaks for his site, as at Mamre* near Hebron in S. Palestine. The details of tent life depicted in Gen. 18 include the favorite seat of the father at the tent door, his hospitality to strangers, and the tasks of the women.

These oak-shaded sites are sought after today. Often they conceal vestiges of ancient cities and of former nomads. If in addition to trees wells* were near, the privilege of pitching camp was often contested; the "herdsmen of Gerar strove with Isaac's herdsmen, saying 'The water is ours'" (A. S.V. Gen. 26:20). A good camping ground was far different from wilderness wastes. Isaiah, wishing to picture the desolation to which Babylon would be reduced, declared that not even the Arabian would pitch tent there: "neither shall shepherds make their flocks to lie down there" (A.S.V. Isa. 13:20).

After the Hebrews had ceased to be roving herders, and had begun to live in villages, they returned to their well-loved tents during summer harvest seasons; or they built tent booths on their roof tops for comfort (see FEASTS). Many Arab farm families of Jordan today leave their winter towns on walled hilltops and take to their tents on the edge of their vast acres of ripe grain.

Terah (tē′rȧ). (1) A son of Nahor, and father of Abraham, another Nahor, and Haran (Gen. 11:26; I Chron. 1:26 f.). The Terachites lived at first in the vicinity of the early Babylonian (Sumerian) city of Ur*. In the 3d quarter of the 20th or the 19th century B.C. they migrated NW. to Haran (Harran), a town at the heart of the area called by later Israel Padan-aram ("field of Aram," Aram-naharaim, or Aram of the Two Rivers, of Gen. 24:10 A.S.V. margin). Haran was at the arch of the Fertile* Crescent. It is known from cuneiform records to have been flourishing in the 19th century B.C. Terah died there at an advanced age (Gen. 11:32 f.). The statement of Josh. 24:2 that the Terah family had worshipped "other gods" at Ur (? the moon god Sin and entourage) may have been written to high-light, by contrast, the piety of young Abraham. A town near Haran was given the name of Terah.

(2) An unidentified camp site of Israel (Tarah A.V. Num. 33:27 f.), between Tahath and Mithkah.

teraphim (literally, "vile things," W. F. Albright), figurines, not necessarily cultic or obscene, as were many lewd depictions of Astarte, used as good-luck charms for expectant mothers, or as family gods (comparable to the penates of the Romans, which stood on the family god shelf). These images in human form may be a survival of ancestor worship, as may be the small teraphim ("images," Gen. 31:19, "teraphim," margin; "gods" v. 30), stolen by Rachel* and hidden under her saddle when she left her father Laban's home in Padan-aram (Haran) for Canaan with her husband, Jacob (vv. 31–35). Her possession of them does not seem to have conflicted with the family's worship of Yahweh, but her removing them from Laban's home was not condoned. Teraphim evidently had sacred traditions in families, and were believed to be endued with certain rights. The fact that the Danites stole Micah's priest and teraphim when moving to a new home in the N. suggests that such figurines had a tribal value. The teraphim of Micah* of Ephraim (Judg. 17:5) may have been images of gods in human form, used for oracular purposes, as was the ephod (v. 5). Teraphim continued to be used through the time of Samuel (I Sam. 15:23, A.S.V.) and long after. Hosea apparently did not see in them any rival to Yahweh (3:4); but Zechariah denounced the superstitious use of teraphim to secure rain (10:2). Babylonian kings used teraphim (Ezek. 21:21). Josiah's reforms (c. 640–609 B.C.) officially outlawed teraphim (II Kings 23:24 A.S.V.), but the images remained popular until after the Exile. (See also IDOLS.)

431. Teraphim.

terebinth (*Pistacia terebinthus*), a large shade tree not mentioned in the A.V., but appearing in A.S.V. Isa. 6:13 (some versions have "teil" tree); Hos. 4:13 (elsewhere sometimes "elm"); and in Ecclus. 24:16 (for "turpentine"). Elim (Ex. 15:27) means "terebinth." Some versions translate "terebinth" as "oak." The oaklike terebinth yields resinous sap. Its shade made it popular for cultic rites. It was a "sacred tree" (A.S.V. Gen. 12:6; Deut. 11:30). Under a terebinth or oak at Shechem Jacob hid the strange gods of his idolatrous household. Under a terebinth (A.S.V. margin Judg. 9:6) Abimelech was made "prince over Israel" for a three-year reign in the period of the Judges. A terebinth gave its name to the valley of Elah ("terebinth" A.S.V. margin I Sam. 17:2), where David took up the challenge of Goliath.

Tertius (tûr′shĭ-ŭs), Paul's secretary who penned the Epistle to the Romans and inserted in it a personal greeting (16:22).

Tertullus (tẽr-tŭl′*us*), the prosecuting attorney (probably Roman) who, at the behest of Jews, made the charge against Paul before Felix*, the governor resident at Caesarea. His speech (Acts 24:2–8) is true to Roman form, and may have been delivered in Latin, though Greek was permitted in the law courts. After flowery phrases of compliment to Felix—who was actually under constant criticism by the Jews—he castigated the prisoner as "a pestilent fellow" who provoked sedition among Jews throughout the world, was ringleader of "the sect of the Nazarenes," and had attempted to profane the Temple (vv. 5 f.). Tertullus, after making his charge, dropped out of sight in the subsequent stages of the trial.

testament (Gk. *diathēkē*), "a will," as in Heb. 9:16 f.; "a covenant," as in Heb. 8:6–10, 13, 9:1, 4. See COVENANT; NEW TESTAMENT; OLD TESTAMENT.

Testaments of the Twelve Patriarchs, a composite work of the Pseudepigrapha (see APOCRYPHA). This work of one (or two) Pharisaic Jews was composed between c. 200 B.C. and A.D. 100, or between c. 130 B.C. and A.D. 10. It contains high ethical teaching, uttered as if proceeding from the mouths of the 12 sons of Jacob. It is believed by many that Jesus knew this work and its encouragement to love of God and man, its emphasis on social obligations and the rewards of righteousness. There are close parallels between Matt. 22:37–39 and statements in these Testaments.

testimony, the rendering in the O.T. of three Heb. words derived from the root *'ūdh*, "to bear witness," "to testify." (See ARK; TABLES. See also Ruth 4:7, where "testimony" is used of a piece of property offered as evidence in a business transaction—cf. Matt. 8:4 and Isa. 8:16, 20, prophetic utterance as witness to God's truth.) In the N.T. three Gk. words used for "testimony" are clear in their context, as in I Cor. 1:6, testimony of Christ; II Tim. 1:8, testimony of the Lord; Heb. 11:5, of Enoch.

teth (tāth), the 9th letter of the Heb. alphabet, early written as a cross in a circle. The Greek *theta* was derived from this letter. Teth stands at the beginning of the 9th part of Ps. 119, and begins each verse (in the Heb.) of this 9th part. See WRITING.

tetrarch, etymologically, the governor of the 4th part of a Greek and later of a Roman province (a tetrarchy), but also used loosely in the sense of a petty prince, ruler of a small district. Herod* Antipas, son of Herod the Great, was tetrarch of Galilee and Peraea (Matt. 14:1; Luke 3:1, 19, 9:7; Acts 13:1) Herod Philip, brother of Antipas, was tetrarch of Ituraea and Trachonitis (Luke 3:1). Lysanias was tetrarch of Abilene (3:1). After the death of Herod Palestine was divided among three rulers, two of whom (Antipas and Philip) were called "tetrarchs"; the third, Archelaus, who was assigned Judaea, Samaria, and Idumaea, was given a superior title, "ethnarch," and the hope (never attained) of achieving the title "king," held by his father. Instances of a tetrarch being given the courtesy title of "king" appear in Matt. 14:1, cf. v. 9; Mark 6:14.

text, versions, manuscripts, editions. (See also CODEX; ENGLISH BIBLE.) The *text* of the Bible comprises the original words of its authors. Although many early manuscripts of the O.T. and N.T. survive, no autograph of any portion of the Bible has ever been found, hence the original text cannot be determined with complete accuracy. During centuries of copying it was subject to changes arising from scribal errors, editorial revisions, and additions. It has been found, however, that no essential N.T. teaching is seriously affected by any of these variants. Nevertheless the textual critic tries to restore or reconstruct a text as close as possible to the original. For this purpose ancient *manuscripts* of the text and of its early versions are sought, studied, and compared. Any translation of the Heb. text of the O.T. or of the Gk. text of the N.T. is known as a *version.*

The Old Testament

(1) *The Hebrew Text.* This was the work of many authors from about the 13th to the 1st century B.C. (See articles on the individual books.) The writing of one portion of it is described in Jer. 36. Writing was done with ink and a reed pen on papyrus or leather scrolls. Early books were written in the old Heb. alphabet, which contained only consonants and was somewhat cursive like that of the ostraca* of Samaria and Lachish. In the 1st century B.C. the Pentateuch was copied in the "squared" letters similar to Aram. characters. This must have been the alphabet used in Jesus' time, for his reference to "jot" as the smallest of letters (Matt. 5:18) is correct for the "square" but not for the old Heb. alphabet. The Nash Papyrus of the late Maccabean period and part of the Dead Sea Scrolls of the 2d and 1st centuries B.C are written in "square" Heb.-Aram.

The Samaritan Pentateuch is a Heb. text, not a translation. Because it was transmitted by the Samaritan community in independence of Jewish tradition since the Samaritan schism of the 4th century B.C., it is a check on errors that had crept into the Heb. text. The final canonization of the Pentateuch must have taken place before the schism, for these writings were sacred Scripture to both Jews and Samaritans. The expulsion of Manasseh from Jerusalem (Neh. 13:23–30) and the building of a rival temple on Mt. Gerizim marked a lasting separation in which "the Jews have no dealings with the Samaritans" (John 4:9). The last few survivors of the Samaritan community now live in Neapolis*.

Of the 6,000 differences between the Samar. and Heb. texts only 1,000 are important. Some are alterations made by the Samaritans for doctrinal purposes, such as the substitution of the name of their sacred mountain, "Gerizim," for "Ebal" (Deut. 27:4). The importance and value of the Samaritan variations have long been debated by scholars.

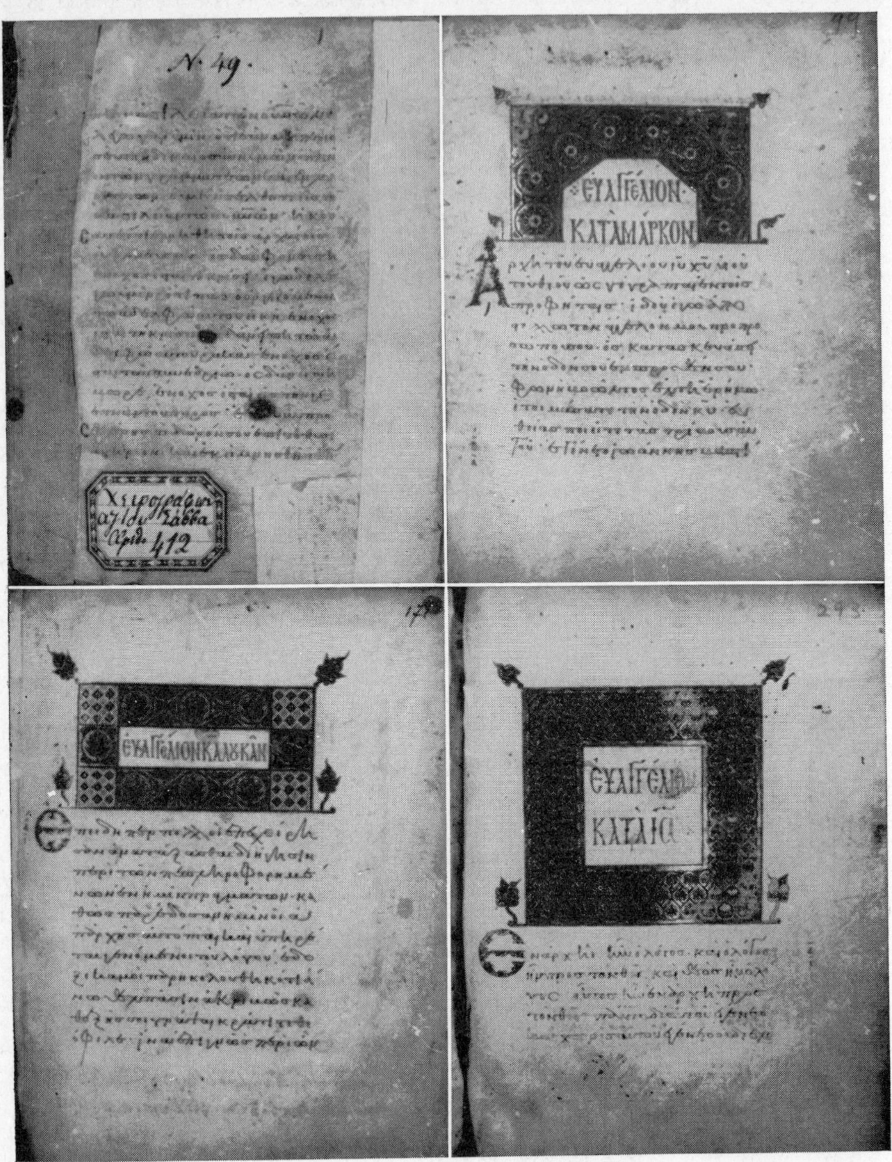

432. Jerusalem Greek Orthodox Patriarchate, Saba MS. Gr. 412. (Pages are 6½ x 5¼", bound between wooden boards covered with black leather, tied with a pair of leather thongs.) Recto of first extant leaf, 49: text of "Sermon on the Mount" (Matt. 5:19-23) in the original Greek. An 11th-century scribe made this copy, in a parchment book containing all four Gospels. The first chapters of Matthew have been lost. Recto of folio 99: the beginning of the Gospel of Mark (1:1-4a). A copy written 900 years ago, containing all four Gospels. Ornament and initial were illuminated in bright colors. An ancient chapter division (*B* or *2*) was written in gold ink opposite the bottom line. Recto of folio 171: the beginning of the Gospel of Luke (1:1-4a). The 11th-century artist painted in bright colors the frame for the title, and the initial *E*. An ancient chapter arrangement is indicated by the small gold *a* in the left margin. Recto of folio 293: the beginning of the Gospel of John (1:1-3). Title frame and initial *E* brightly illuminated by 10th-century artist. Small gold *a* in right margin indicates ancient chapter arrangement.

TEXT, VERSIONS

The variants may all be corruptions or deliberate changes made by the Samaritans for doctrinal and other purposes. Some variants, however, especially those that agree with the Septuagint or other versions, may represent original readings from which the Hebrew text diverged.

Manuscripts of the Samaritan Pentateuch

date from the 13th century A.D., although a few are earlier. The synagogue at Nablus ascribes its manuscript to the 1st century A.D., but scholars give it a more conservative date; as it was "rediscovered" in the 14th century, its origin was evidently several centuries earlier. The first specimen of the Samaritan Pentateuch was brought to Europe in 1616 by Pietro della Valle. Later he succeeded in purchasing two copies from the Samaritans in Damascus. One was placed in the library of the Oratory of Paris and its text was published in the Paris Polyglot in 1632. In 1914–18 von Gall published a text for which he collated 80 manuscripts and fragments from the 14th and 15th centuries.

The *transmission* of the Heb. text before the middle of the 3d century B.C. was subject to many changes and errors. When copyists realized the importance of guarding the text they adopted elaborate measures to insure the accuracy of each copy; by that time early corruptions made it impossible to recapture the original wording, but further changes were halted. Three stages in this concern about the text can be distinguished: (a) Canonization of the books saved them from deliberate alterations (see CANON). (b) An authoritative text, close to the present one, seems to have been finally determined by the Jewish text critics at the beginning of the 2d century A.D. (c) The preservation of the authoritative text was the responsibility of the Massoretes, the famous school of textual scholars. They accumulated a vast body of notes on the occurrence of words, features of writing, directions for pronunciation; and they created a system of vowel sounds, for written Heb. had theretofore included only consonants. They also devised accentual marks to serve as punctuation. The Massoretes were active in Babylonia and in Tiberias of Palestine. Their work was brought to a conclusion at the beginning of the 10th century by Moses ben Asher and his son Aaron.

Manuscripts embodying the completed work of the Massoretes survive, on which the study of the later history of the Heb. text of the O.T. is based. Paul Kahle has shown that four of the most important surviving old manuscripts are the work of the ben Ashers. The Codex of the Former and Latter Prophets, belonging to the Karaite synagogue in Cairo, was written in Tiberias in A.D. 895 by Moses ben Asher. His son Aaron early in the 10th century wrote some 131 of the 186 folios of the British Museum Codex of the Pentateuch, numbered Or. 4445. A manuscript of the entire O.T. numbered 19a in the Public Library in Leningrad, though copied in Cairo in A.D. 1008 or 1009 by Samuel ben Jacob, is, as he has stated, "from the corrected clear books prepared by the master Aaron ben Mosheh ben Asher." The codex of the synagogue of the Sephardim in Aleppo is also believed to be Aaron ben Asher's work.

Until 1947 few Heb. manuscripts more ancient than these were known to survive, owing to the Jewish custom of destroying worn-out scrolls to save them from impious hands. The oldest known were fragments: (a) The Nash Papyrus, containing the Ten Commandments and the Shema (Deut. 6:4), was found in Egypt and is now in Cambridge, England. It is dated by some in the late Maccabean period. (b) Fragments of Biblical manuscripts from the 6th and following centuries A.D. were found in the Old Cairo Genizah. All these reproduce a text older than that of the Massoretes.

A discovery of major importance to textual criticism was made in 1947 when about a dozen leather scrolls* and hundreds of manuscript fragments were found in a high cave at 'Ain Fashka on the E. slope of the Judaean plateau just W. of the Dead Sea, a few miles from the modern resort of Kallia, by Bedouins of the Ta'amira tribe. The Dead Sea Scrolls, as these documents came to be called, date from the two centuries before the disaster of A.D. 70. They include: The Sectarian Manual of Discipline, the Habakkuk Commentary, the St. Mark's Isaiah manuscript, the Hebrew University Isaiah manuscript (last third), a "midrash of Genesis," the Thanksgiving Psalms, and the War of the Sons of Light with the Sons of Darkness. Some of the fragments, including a few on papyrus, which have survived the wrecks of time, have been identified as coming from Genesis, Leviticus, Deuteronomy, and Judges. Some scholars believe the Leviticus fragments are the oldest specimen of Bible text, having been written in Palaeo-Hebrew about the 2d half of the 5th century B.C., which would make them older than any known Targum and older than the LXX by almost two centuries. Others believe the fragments to be Samaritan, from the 1st half of the 1st century B.C. or c. 100 B.C. (see *BASOR* No. 118, April 1950, pp. 20–30). Many of the fragments are from unknown documents. This discovery gives us, for parts of the O.T., a text a thousand years or so nearer the original Heb. text than the Massoretic text of the ben Ashers. (See SCROLLS, DEAD SEA.)

Printed Heb. Bibles depend largely on the system of ben Asher. The entire O.T. with vowel points and accents was first published at Soncino in 1488. The standard edition of the Massoretic text was edited by Jacob ben Chayim and printed by Daniel Bomberg at Venice in 1524–25. Rudolph Kittel's 3d edition of the *Biblia Hebraica* issued in 1937 abandoned the ben Chayim tradition and printed the text of the Leningrad manuscript 19a; this has become the text used by students of the Heb. O.T.

(2) *The Ancient Versions of the O.T.* These are of importance because many were translated from texts older than those used by the Massoretes, and also because the surviving manuscripts of these ancient versions are, with a few exceptions, much older than those of the Heb. Bible. The principal versions used by textual scholars are: the Gk. Septuagint and other Gk. translations, the "Old Latin" and the Vulgate, the Syr. Peshitta, the Aram. Targums, and a group of other Eastern versions.

a. *Greek Versions*

The *Septuagint** is by far the oldest and most important. Septuagint means "of the seventy," and is commonly designated LXX, but the origin of the name is unknown. A legendary explanation in the *Letter of Aristeas*, c. 100 B.C., states that the translation was made about 250 B.C. for the great library at Alexandria by 72 scholars sent from Jerusalem at the request of Ptolemy Philadelphus. It is more probable that the translation was made, not for the monarch, but for the large Greek-speaking Jewish community in Alexandria. The translation of the Pentateuch was followed by that of the rest of the O.T. over a period of about 150 years. This unique achievement outgrew its original purpose of providing a Bible for the Jews of Alexandria, and was used by Jews throughout the eastern Mediterranean. It was the Bible of Paul, the Apostles, and the early Church. The LXX was quoted in the N.T. and used in the arguments of the Church fathers, and for this reason it ceased from about A.D. 100 to be an authority to the Jews. From its text other important translations were made. It has been the Bible of the Greek Church to the present day.

Aquila, *Theodotion*, and *Symmachus* made three Gk. translations in the 2d century A.D. Aquila, a proselyte to Judaism, made an exceedingly literal translation which became the official Gk. version for the Jews. Theodotion, a Christian of Pontus, made a translation between A.D. 180 and 192 which follows parts of the LXX so closely that it may be a revision rather than a new translation. Theodotion's was a free rendering in idiomatic Gk., and became popular in the Christian Church. His version of Daniel was often substituted for that of the LXX in ancient manuscripts. About A.D. 200 Symmachus, an Ebionite, made a third Gk. translation of which only a few fragments survive. His work, expressed in elegant Gk., is faithful to the original Heb. Jerome says of the three Gk. versions: "Aquila translates word for word, Symmachus follows the sense, and Theodotion differs slightly from the Septuagint."

The *Hexapla* (six-fold), an arrangement in six parallel columns of the Gk. and Heb. texts, current about A.D. 240, was made in Caesarea by Origen, the greatest Biblical scholar of the early Church. Having observed that every manuscript contained a different text from every other, Origen decided to compare the versions and produce from them the best one possible. In the 1st column Origen copied the Heb. text of his day—which is practically the same as the Massoretic text of today—and in the 2d column he wrote this Heb. text in Gk. letters. The 3d, 4th, and 6th columns were the translations of Aquila, Symmachus, and Theodotion. The 5th column was Origen's own revision of the Septuagint. For some churches this became the authoritative Gk. O.T. It was studied in Caesarea by Jerome c. A.D. 400 and by other copyists.

Greek manuscripts of the O.T. survive which are six to eight centuries older than our earliest complete Heb. Bible. Hence the Septuagint supplies important evidence for the early Heb. text. The earliest Gk. manuscripts are written on papyrus*. From the 4th century A.D. vellum began to be used. Gk. vellum manuscripts are divided into two classes according to their script: the "uncials," written in separate capital letters, and dating in general from the 3d to the 10th century A.D.; and the "cursives" or "miniscules," written in a small, running hand, mainly from the 9th to the 16th century A.D.

The oldest known fragments of the Septuagint are from a papyrus roll of Deuteronomy which was torn up to provide scraps for a mummy cartonnage. These fragments, assigned to c. 150 B.C., are now in the John Rylands Library, Manchester, England.

The Chester Beatty Biblical Papyri, in addition to 126 leaves of N.T. books, contain parts of eight O.T. books, written with one exception in cursive script and dated from the 2d to the 4th century A.D. They were purchased in Egypt and brought to England in 1931 by A. Chester Beatty. As some of these papyri were written before Origen revised the Septuagint, they are a valuable indication of its original text.

A papyrus manuscript of the minor prophets, dated between the middle and end of the 3d century A.D., found in Egypt, is now in the Freer collection, Washington, D.C. It is written in a sloping uncial.

Uncial manuscripts are generally designated by capital letters. Of the 30 or so known uncials, none is complete. The principal uncials are:

B, Codex Vaticanus, written about the middle of the 4th century A.D., possibly at Alexandria. It contains the O.T. and N.T., and is more nearly complete than any other known manuscript. It lacks Gen. 1–46; Ps. 106–138; Heb. 9–13; the Pastoral Epistles; and Revelation. Its early history is unknown. Old catalogues show that it was in the Vatican Library as early as the 15th century.

S (or Aleph), Codex Sinaiticus, ranks in age with B, but the fragmentary character of its O.T. reduces its value for O.T. textual study. It was discovered by Tischendorf in 1844 in the Monastery of St. Catherine at Mt. Sinai and placed in the royal library at St. Petersburg (Leningrad). It was purchased from the Soviet Government in 1933 and placed in the British Museum.

A, Codex Alexandrinus, a 5th-century manuscript, given to James I in 1624, but not brought to England until 1628 in the reign of Charles I, is now in the British Museum. This was the first uncial used by modern Biblical scholars.

C, Codex Ephraemi, is a palimpsest or twice-used parchment, the underneath writing of which is a 5th-century Gk. Bible. Only 64 of its O.T. leaves survive. It is now in the Bibliothèque Nationale in Paris.

The cursive or miniscule manuscripts date mainly from the 9th to the 16th century A.D., and are designated by Arabic numerals. There are more than 1,500 cursives, but only those copied from early uncials, now lost, are of importance to the textual critic.

The first printed edition of the Septuagint was the Complutensian Polyglot, completed 1514–17 under the supervision of Cardinal Ximenes and published in 1522. Next came the Sixtine edition of 1587, prepared for Pope Sixtus V and depending on Codex Vaticanus. The most common edition of the Septuagint today is that published (1887–1894) by Henry Barclay Swete at Cambridge, England, in three volumes. It generally employs the text of the Vaticanus, but notes the variants of three or four other manuscripts. The *Larger Cambridge Septuagint* edited by A. E. Brooke and N. McLean was begun in 1906 and is nearing completion. It employs Swete's text but gives a full critical apparatus. Alfred Rahlfs of Göttingen published in 1935 a preliminary edition of the Septuagint. The text is based on a collation of A, B, and S.

The purpose of scholars as they work on the Gk. translation of the O.T. is (a) to determine, by a study of all the manuscripts and other evidence, the text of the LXX as it was originally translated from the Heb.; (b) to discover, by this means, the text of the Heb. O.T. from which the LXX was made; and (c) to learn so far as possible, by a comparison of this with the Massoretic text, the original words of the O.T. books. The LXX is thus a tool for the recovery of the original text of the Heb. Bible.

b. *Latin Versions*

The "Old Latin" version probably originated among Latin-speaking Jews of Carthage in North Africa, and was adopted by Christians. A Lat. translation of the entire Bible circulated in Carthage by A.D. 250. The writings of the Church fathers and various manuscripts give evidence of a variety of Lat. versions current before Jerome's day. Three types of Old Lat. text are identified: the African, the European, and the Italian—which is probably a revision of the European. These Old Lat. versions are valuable because they are translations of the Septuagint before Origen revised its text.

The Vulgate was produced by Jerome, an accomplished Biblical scholar from Dalmatia, and is still the current Lat. Bible. In A.D. 382 Pope Damasus commissioned Jerome to make an official revision of the Old Lat. Bible. Jerome corrected the Lat. text of the Gospels and probably the rest of the N.T. by comparing it with the original Gk. With the O.T. the case was different. He made two revisions of the Old Lat. Psalms by comparing them with the LXX. The 1st was the "Roman Psalter," still the official Psalter in St. Peter's in Rome and in Milan. The 2d, known as the "Gallican Psalter" because it was first adopted in Gaul, is now in the Vulgate. For the "Gallican Psalter" Jerome used the LXX and Origen's Hexapla. In Bethlehem, in a cave adjacent to what he believed to be the Grotto of the Nativity, Jerome made a Lat. version of the O.T. directly from the Heb., but with reference to the Gk. versions. Jerome's version became the Bible of Western Christendom, and was called the Vulgate or "common edition." It was virtually without a rival for a thousand years. Jerome's translation did not generally equate word for word, but usually gave the thought of the original in idiomatic, graceful Lat. This freedom of translation, together with the fact that the Heb. text Jerome used was approximately the form we know today, diminishes the value of the Vulgate to the O.T. textual critic.

About 8,000 *manuscripts* of the various Latin versions survive. None of the Old Lat. Bibles is complete. The Vulgate manuscripts, many of them Gospels, are largely 13th- and 14th-century documents of little critical value.

The first *printed edition* of the Vulgate was the Gutenberg Bible, also known as the "Bible of 42 Lines" or "Mazarin Bible." It was published before August 1456, and believed to be the first book of importance ever printed. Significant though this achievement was, the text was full of errors. Scholars labored for years to produce an authoritative text of the Vulgate. A critical edition of the Vulgate is being prepared by the Benedictine Order, and the O.T. books from Genesis to Psalms have already been published by the Vatican press.

The standard edition of the Old Lat. remains that of Pierre Sabatier, *Bibliorum Sacrorum latinae versiones antiquae seu vetus italica*, issued 1743–49.

c. *Syriac Versions*

The O.T. of the Syriac Bible, called the *Peshitta*, was in use by Syriac Christians by the 3d century A.D. The work of translation was probably done either in the city of Edessa, in northern Mesopotamia, or in Adiabene, the region E. of the Tigris River. Some scholars believe that parts of the O.T. are of Jewish origin, though the translation as a whole was made for Christians. The Peshitta was edited in the light of the Septuagint, but its O.T. is basically an independent translation from the Hebrew, and consequently of considerable value to text critics. Many manuscripts of the Peshitta survive, notably the 6th- or 7th-century codex in the Ambrosian Library, Milan. This is considered to be the most valuable Syriac authority for the entire O.T. text. In the British Museum there is a Syriac manuscript of Genesis, Exodus, Numbers, and Deuteronomy which bears a date corresponding to A.D. 464. This is the earliest date on any known manuscript of the Bible. This manuscript was obtained in 1842 from the monastery of St. Mary Deipara in Egypt. Most printed texts are uncritical.

The *Syro-Hexaplar* version is Gk. in origin, being a Syriac translation by Bishop Paul of Tella in A.D. 616–617 of the 5th column of Origen's Hexapla. A number of manuscripts of different parts of the O.T. survive. As this is a very literal rendering, it is our chief authority for reconstructing the Hexapla.

d. *The Targums*

The Targums were originally oral interpretations or translations in Aram. (sometimes improperly called "Chaldee") accompanying the reading of the Heb. Scriptures. They became necessary when Heb. ceased to be the spoken language of the Jews and Aram. took its place in the period preceding the Christian era. In time these extemporary translations or paraphrases were written down and became important evidence of the O.T. text read in the early synagogues. Besides translation, the Targums contain explanations and religious instructions. The great Targums on the Pentateuch and the Prophets attained their final form in Babylonia about the 5th century A.D. and were accepted in Palestine in the 9th century. But it is probable that the Targums as we know them are related to pre-Christian written translations, themselves the crystallization of a long oral tradition. The three Pentateuchal Targums are: the Targum of Onkelos (or Babylonian Targum); the Jerusalem (pseudo-Jonathan) Targum; and the Fragmentary Targum, which is a remnant of the old Palestinian Targum. The Targum on the Prophets, though attributed to Jonathan ben Uzziel, a pupil of Hillel of the 1st century A.D., is actually a continuation of the Targum of Onkelos.

e. *Other Eastern Versions*

The oldest of the many eastern versions were made for Christians, and are an evidence of the spread of Christianity.

The *Coptic* versions were made for the Christians of Egypt. The earliest Coptic version was in the Sahidic dialect of Upper Egypt. Scholars date this about the middle of the 3d century, though some assign it to the 2d century. The later Bohairic version was used in the Delta. Both translations were made from a LXX text. Early manuscripts of both versions survive, the earliest of the Sahidic manuscripts dating from the 4th century.

The *Ethiopic* version was made from a Gk. text in the 4th or 5th century, when Christianity became the state religion. Due to upheavals in Abyssinia resulting from the spread of Islam, the great number of manuscripts of the Ethiopic Bible which survive are no older than the 13th century. They are revisions of the original Ethiopic text, and as they were made with the help of the Peshitta, the Arabic translation, and the Massoretic text, they are of little use to the textual scholar.

The *Gothic* version, prepared by Ulfilas from a Gk. text c. A.D. 350, is the first written literature of the Goths. Only fragments of its O.T. survive among a dozen or so known manuscripts.

The *Armenian* version, made for the Christian communities of eastern Asia Minor c. A.D. 400, was translated from the LXX but later revised with the help of the Heb. and Syr. This version is said to be exceptionally beautiful and accurate. It is believed to have been made by Mesrop, the inventor of the Armenian alphabet.

The *Georgian* version of the 5th or 6th century is doubtless made from the Gk. with some influences from the Syr. The Georgian church separated from the Armenian at the end of the 6th century, and the Georgian Bible has been called the "twin sister of the Armenian." Legend credits Mesrop with making the Georgian version. A manuscript of the whole Bible is preserved in two volumes in the Iberian monastery on Mt. Athos.

The *Slavonic* version, attributed to two Greek brothers, Cyril and Methodius, is not older than the 9th century. Though 10th- or 11th-century manuscripts survive, the oldest manuscript of the whole Bible, the Codex Gennadius, now in Moscow, is dated 1499.

The *Arabic* version, made necessary by the great Arabic conquests of the 7th and 8th centuries, was begun in the 10th century by Saadya. He was born in Upper Egypt A.D. 892, but became head of the great Jewish school in Babylonia. His translation of the Pentateuch was from the Heb., but the rest of the Arab. O.T. was from the Peshitta and the LXX.

The New Testament

(1) *The original text* of the N.T.* was written by Paul, Luke, Mark, John, and other Christians in the 1st century and possibly the early years of the 2d century A.D. (See articles on the individual books.) The language of Jesus was Aramaic, and his sayings must have been transmitted at first in this language. Aramaic words and expressions occur in the Gospels; but the theory that the N.T. books were originally written in Aramaic is considered doubtful by most scholars. As Christianity spread to the Graeco-Roman world, Greek became the language of the early Church, and it is in Greek that the Epistles and Gospels have come down to us.

The century and a half between the original writing of the N.T. and the copying of our earliest manuscripts, though a much shorter interval than is the case with the O.T., is the period which produced the greatest variations. Scribes were untrained, and the documents had not yet become sacred Scripture. It was not considered wrong to interpolate, expand, contract, or omit. When the N.T. canon* was defined there were efforts to standardize the text. Five general types of text have been identified in the early manuscripts: Alexandrian, Western, Caesarean, Eastern, and Byzantine. The first four were current in the 2d to the 4th centuries; the Byzantine is a "standardized" edition used from the 5th century on. There is much mixture of so-called types even in a single manuscript. The basic text of all these types is about 90% the same; of a total of about 150,000 known variants only 400 affect the sense and only 50 are of real significance. No essential N.T. teaching is greatly affected by any of these variants.

(a) *Greek manuscripts* of the N.T. survive in such great numbers that the N.T. is by far the best preserved ancient document in the world. There survive about 175 papyri from the 2d to the 4th centuries; over 200 uncial documents, including all fragments, from the 2d to the 9th century; and about 2,500 cursive manuscripts from the 9th century to the invention of printing in the 15th. Though few of these contain the entire text, and a number, especially some of the papyrus documents and early uncials, are fragmentary, it remains true that no other Gk. or Lat. book is supported by as many early manuscripts as those which undergird the text of the N.T.

TEXT, VERSIONS

The papyri are the oldest Gk. manuscripts of the N.T. Most of these are in the codex or book form adopted by Christians in the 2d century in place of the scroll. The oldest surviving fragment is believed to be part of a single papyrus leaf assigned to a date before A.D. 150 and containing only John 18:31–33, 37 f., now in the John Rylands Library in Manchester, England. The Chester Beatty Papyri, in addition to the O.T. described above, contain three codices with portions of 15 N.T. books in uncials ascribed to the 3d century. This is the oldest extensive text in existence. The codex of the Gospels and Acts (P 45) contains 30 of an original 220 leaves, dating from the early 3d century. The text varies, being Caesarean, Alexandrian, and Western. The codex of the Pauline letter (P 46) contains 86 of an original 104 leaves, dating A.D. 200. The text is more Alexandrian than Western. The leaves of this codex are divided between the British Museum and the University of Michigan. The codex of Revelation (P 47) has 10 of an original 32 leaves, from the end of the 3d century. Its text is generally Alexandrian.

The oldest uncial vellum codices are complete Bibles which have been described above. Their N.T. characteristics are:

B, Codex Vaticanus, the best representative of the Alexandrian type of text, contains the N.T. to Hebrews 9:14. It dates from the 1st half of the 4th century A.D.

S (or *Aleph*), Codex Sinaiticus (4th century A.D.), one of our two complete uncial N.Ts., contains also the Epistle of Barnabas and the Shepherd of Hermas. Its text resembles that of B.

A, Codex Alexandrinus (5th century A.D.), contains an almost complete N.T. and also I and II Clement. The text is Alexandrian in Paul, but Byzantine in the Gospels.

C, Codex Ephraemi Rescriptus (4th century A.D.), contains 145 of an original 238 N.T. leaves. Its text is generally Alexandrian with a mixture of later readings.

D, Codex Bezae, written in the 5th or 6th century, is a Gk.-Lat. manuscript of the Gospels and Acts. Its text is the most important representative of the Western type. Theodore Beza secured it in 1562 at Lyons and gave it to the University of Cambridge, where it is today. Two other Gk.-Lat. uncials, textually similar to D, are: Codex Claromontanus (D_2), a 6th-century copy of the Pauline Epistles, now in the Bibliothèque Nationale, Paris; and Codex Laudianus (E_2), a 6th- or 7th-century manuscript of Acts, now in the Bodleian Library, Oxford, England.

W, Washington Codex, a 4th- or 5th-century copy of the Gospels, was obtained in Egypt in 1906 by C. L. Freer and is now in the Freer Gallery, Washington, D.C. The text is a mixture of Byzantine, Alexandrian, Western, and Caesarean types.

I, The Washington Manuscript of Pauline Epistles in the Freer Gallery is a vellum codex of 84 fragmentary leaves written in the 5th or 6th century. It contains an Alexandrian text of the Pauline letters except Romans.

Θ, Codex Koridethi, is a 9th-century vellum codex of the four Gospels now in the Library of Tiflis. It is an important witness to the Caesarean text and helped to identify this textual family.

The cursive manuscripts, being later than the uncials and generally reflecting a Byzantine text, are of less value to the textual critic. They are consulted when weightier authorities disagree. Some are of significance for their illustrations and illuminations. Cursives which agree closely with each other in unusual readings are thought to be copies of a lost uncial and are grouped in "families." Family 1 (including the cursives 1, 22, 118, 131, 209, 1582, 2193) forms a group whose relationship was first shown by Kirsopp Lake. This family takes its name from Codex 1, a Basle manuscript of the 10th to 12th century, used slightly by Erasmus for his 1516 Greek N.T. Family 13 (including 13, 69, 124, 346) is known as the Ferrar group—for W. H. Ferrar, who first discovered the common ancestry of these cursives. Eight more MSS. have been added to this family. These two families are Caesarean.

Codex 33, called by Eichhorn the "Queen of the Cursives," is a 9th- or 10th-century Paris manuscript of the N.T. with fragments of the prophets. It has an Alexandrian text.

Lectionaries and *patristic writings* are two other sources of information for the N.T. Gk. text. The uncial and cursive lectionaries were books containing a selection of Scripture to be read in church services. They sometimes use a very early text. The patristic writings or works of the early Church fathers contain quotations often not written from memory but copied from very ancient manuscripts.

(b) *Printed editions of the Gk. text* appeared before many of the oldest and best documents described above had been discovered and before the real work of textual criticism had begun. Consequently they reproduced a late medieval text. The earliest printed Gk. N.T. was that incorporated in the Complutensian Polyglot, printed in 1514–17, but not issued until 1522, in six large and expensive volumes. Erasmus, the Dutch scholar, edited the first published Gk. text in 1516. His text, based on two late and inferior documents, was corrected in four later editions, and widely used by early leaders of the Reformation. Robert Stephanus (Estienne) of Paris, published several editions beginning in 1546, basing his text on Erasmus, the Complutensian Polyglot, and 15 manuscripts in the Paris Library. The third edition (1550) of Stephanus, known as the "*editio regina*," became the standard text of Britain. Next Theodore Beza produced 10 editions with a text almost identical with Stephanus's. Two Dutch printers, the Elzevir brothers, between 1624 and 1678 published seven editions based on Stephanus and Beza; their form of text became the standard one on the Continent. The preface to their 2d edition claimed that their text was "accepted [*receptum*] by everyone." From this claim came the name "Textus Receptus" or "received text." This text differed from the Stephanus 1550 edition used in Britain by only an estimated 287 instances. Based as it was on a few fairly late manuscripts, it was not likely to be an exact reproduction of original N.T. documents. This became apparent when older manuscripts were discovered and their evidence of an earlier text was printed in the editions of K. Lachmann, C. Tischendorf, and others. In 1881–2 two British scholars, Dr. F. J. A. Hort and Bishop B. F. Westcott, published a Gk. text which supplanted the Textus Receptus.

Since the appearance of the Westcott-Hort text, important manuscripts have been found, textual theory has advanced, and new editions by Hermann von Soden, Scrivener, Eberhard Nestle, and others have been published. As long as it appears possible to detect and remove ancient scribal errors and editorial changes and to recover a text more closely approaching the original writings than the text we now possess, the extremely complicated work of textual criticism will go on.

(2) *Versions of the N.T.* began to appear in the middle of the 2d century as Christianity spread into the Latin-speaking areas of North Africa and the Syriac-speaking kingdom of Edessa beyond the Euphrates where the two oldest versions originated. The Latin and Syriac N.T. give important indirect evidence of the 2d-century Gk. text from which they were made, a text 200 years older than the Codex Vaticanus.

(a) *Latin Versions*

The *Old Latin* is believed to have been made at Carthage between A.D. 160 and 200. From the nearly 40 manuscripts and fragments of this version which survive and from quotations of it in the Church fathers it can be almost entirely recovered. It is one of the chief witnesses to the Western type of text.

The *Vulgate* was made by Jerome at the behest of Pope Damasus to correct the wide variations which had appeared in the Old Lat. text. Jerome's revised Gospels appeared in 383 or 384, followed by the rest of the N.T. There is some difficulty in ascribing the entire N.T. to Jerome. The Vulgate and Old Lat. versions circulated together for several centuries and consequently became somewhat intermixed.

Of the thousands of Vulgate manuscripts now extant one of the best for the entire Bible is the Codex Amiatinus, copied at Wearmouth or Jarrow, England, in the 8th century, and taken to Rome as a gift to the Pope. It is now in Florence.

The 1st printed edition of the Vulgate, the Gutenberg Bible of about 1456, was made from inferior manuscripts. Subsequent editions showed an effort to restore the text of Jerome with the help of early manuscripts. After the Council of Trent in 1546 decreed the Vulgate to be the official Bible text and called for an amended edition of it, Pope Sixtus V published a three-volume edition in 1590. In 1592 Pope Clement VIII withdrew the Sixtine edition and reissued it in a slightly revised form. The Clementine Vulgate of 1592 became the authoritative Bible of the Roman Catholic Church.

The Vulgate was the basis for many of the early vernacular versions, among them the 1st English Bible* of Wyclif.

(b) *Syriac Versions*

The *Diatessaron*, a harmony of the four Gospels, produced about A.D. 170 by Tatian, was so vigorously replaced by the "separated" Gospels in the 5th century that there are now only Arab. and Arm. translations of it. A 3d-century vellum fragment of the Diatessaron in Gk. was found at Dura-Europos on the Euphrates.

The *Old Syr. Gospels*, originating in the late 2d or early 3d century, are a significant witness to the primitive Gk. text. Two manuscripts of the Old Syr. version survive. One is the 4th-century "Sinaitic Syriac" palimpsest discovered at the Monastery of St. Catherine at Mt. Sinai by Mrs. A. S. Lewis and Mrs. A.D. Gibson. The "Curetonian Syriac" manuscript of the middle of the 5th century was discovered by Dr. W. Cureton at the Convent of St. Mary Deipara W. of Cairo. It is now in the British Museum.

The *Peshitta* was a revision of divergent manuscripts of the Old Syr. in accord with Gk. manuscripts, and has been in continuous use in the Syrian Church from the 5th century. Fifteen of its surviving 250 manuscripts are from the 5th and 6th centuries.

(c) *Other ancient eastern versions* of importance to the textual study of the N.T. are the Coptic, Ethiopic, Gothic, Armenian, and Georgian.

Based on *The Ancestry of Our English Bible*, Ira Maurice Price, third revised edition, William A. Irwin and Allen P. Wikgren, Harper & Brothers, 1956.

The entire Bible or portions of it have been translated into more than 1,118 ancient and modern languages and dialects.

(See ENGLISH BIBLE.)

In 1949–50, in connection with the preparation of a new apparatus of variant readings for the Gk. N.T., an elaborate international organization of scholars microfilmed (1) c. 150 MSS. in the Jerusalem Library of the Greek Orthodox Patriarchate, one of the oldest libraries in the world; (2) some 3,000 MSS. in the monastery of St. Catherine at Mt. Sinai. The latter task was considered the largest microfilming project of its kind ever attempted. About 2,000 miniatures illustrating the MSS. were also photographed at Mt. Sinai. Prof. Kenneth Clark of Duke University, Annual Professor of the ASOR in Jerusalem, was in charge of work on the manuscripts from the Jerusalem Library, and the photographic work was done by Wallace Wade of the Library of Congress. The second project was sponsored by the Library of Congress and the American Foundation for the Study of Man (Wendell Phillips, Director).

Thaddaeus, a little-known disciple of Jesus. He is listed among the Twelve* in Matt. 10:3 and Mark 3:18, but not in Luke 6:16 or Acts 1:13. In the last two passages—later listings—the name "Judas, son of James" occurs instead of Thaddaeus. Lebbaeus is used as his main name in A.V. Matt. 10:3, but is dropped in the A.S.V. and R.S.V. in favor of Thaddaeus only. This variety of names in the listing of the Twelve has led to various theories. (1) Scribal errors in early transmission have led to irreconcilable confusion. (2) He had 3 names: Thaddaeus, Lebbaeus, and Judas the son of James. (3) The last listing of the Disciples (Acts 1:13) reflects a change in personnel among the Twelve. The fact that Thaddaeus is not mentioned elsewhere suggests that he was succeeded by Judas, son of James (John 14:22).

Apocalyptic literature concerning Thaddaeus supplies traditions which circulate in the Eastern Church. He was a Hebrew, born in Edessa, who came to Jerusalem in the days of John the Baptist, and was baptized by him. He was a companion of Jesus until just before the Crucifixion, when he returned to Edessa to evangelize the Syrians and the Armenians. He is said to be buried in Beirut.

thank offering. See WORSHIP.

Tharshish. See TARSHISH.

theater (from Lat. *theatrum*, Gk. *theatron*, "place for seeing"), a place for dramatic performances. In the Hellenistic cities of the Near East theaters were often the largest structures of the community. They were not only "places for seeing" Greek dramas and Roman satirical comedies, but places of civic assembly and public controversy, as Paul learned at Ephesus* (Acts 19:29). The scene of the events narrated in Acts 12:20–23 was, if Josephus be correct, the theater at Caesarea. Wherever Romans traveled, they wanted their theater, where in late afternoon and early evening the businessmen of the Empire could be diverted by a play and inspired by a natural setting of mountain and sea—often more impressive than the play. The unroofed theater was usually dug into a hillside overlooking a level place, which might have been an old threshing floor or meadow near an altar. The famous Theater of Dionysus (5th century B.C.), on the lower SE. reaches of the Acropolis hill at Athens, is the prototype of the outdoor theater. In that place the drama developed from a spring feast in honor of the wine god Dionysus. Rows of seats, at first of wood, then of stone and marble (for officials) ranged around the hard-surfaced circle (later a semicircle), from which developed the orchestra circle of modern theaters. On the orchestra area the chorus danced and sang. A small stage developed behind the orchestra, from a booth or tent (Gk. *skene*, "scene"), where actors dressed or retired. The stage cut off a portion of the curving orchestra opposite the audience. To the stage was gradually added a platform and a portico. In Greek theaters the space for the chorus was usually circular, as at Epidaurus, the largest extant Greek theater, with seats for 25,000 (4th century B.C.). In Roman theaters the orchestra was semicircular, as now in the Odeum of Herodes Atticus at Athens, probably connected by a portico or stoa with the Dionysiac theater. The narrative was developed by the chorus, alternating with dialogue by actors (usually men. wearing grotesque masks, as can be seen at excavated Ostia*).

433. Theater of Dionysus, Athens.

Theaters which functioned in the Biblical period can be seen at Corinth, Athens, Antioch, Jerash, Amman, Italian Ostia, and Pompeii. At Rome there are vestiges of a theater begun by Pompey (55 B.C.), and the imposing theater of Marcellus, completed by Augustus. The theater of Ephesus where Paul was mobbed is more impressive since the excavation of the straight road *Arkadiane*, leading from the theater to the harbor.

Amphitheaters were as popular as theaters.

Events in these places for gladiatorial combats and athletic contests are reflected in Paul's notes on personal experiences, as in I Cor. 9:24–27; II Tim. 4:7 f.

434. Pergamum Theater.

The now obliterated public works of Herod the Great at Jerusalem must have included a theater and a stadium, for which there was hillside space overlooking the valleys of the Hinnom and Kidron. Early in the excavation of N.T. Jericho (Tulûl Abū el-'Alâyiq, a mile W. of modern Jericho, at the mouth of the Wâdī Qelt), Dr. James L. Kelso, director of the 1950 campaign, reported the finding in this winter capital of Herod Archelaus (4 B.C.–A.D. 6) and his father, Herod the Great, a civic center having a grand façade at whose center "was a large exedra which looks like an outdoor theater with tiers of very low terrace walls or benches running up the slope."

435. Marble masks at Ostia Theater.

The exedra was apparently used also as an outdoor garden, for flower pots were found on the seats (*Bul.* ASOR No. 120, p. 17, Dec. 1950).

Thebes. See NO.

Thebez (thē'bĕz) (the modern Tūbâs), a town c. 10 m. N. of Nablus and NE. of Tirzah and Shechem on the road to Beth-shan. In the period of the Judges it was in Manasseh's holdings. Just after Abimelech* had seized Thebez he was killed by a piece of millstone which was hurled down on him by a woman who, with her townsfolk, had taken refuge in a strong tower (Judg. 9:50–56; II Sam. 11:21).

theft. See ROBBERY.

Theodotus (thē-ŏd'ō-tŭs.) See SYNAGOGUE.

theophany, a manifestation of God to an individual. as to Moses out of a burning bush (Ex. 3:2), and on Sinai* when the Law was given (Ex. 19:20). Sometimes the communication was by means of angelic visitors, as to Abraham (Gen. 18:2–22); or by direct conversation of the Lord with an individual, as with Abraham (Gen. 18:23–33), and Jacob (35:1). A dream theophany came to Solomon (I Kings 3:5–14, cf. 9:2–9). Elijah heard God speak in "a still small voice" on stormy Mt. Horeb (I Kings 19:9–18). Ezekiel heard the word of the Lord "in the land of the Chaldaeans by the river Chebar" (Ezek. 1:3).

Theophanies experienced by individuals of the O.T. were temporary. But the manifestation of the Lord in the pillar of cloud and the pillar of fire lasted through the Wilderness experience of Israel, and perpetuated itself in the Tabernacle and in the Temple of Solomon, in whose Holy of Holies God was thought of as manifesting His presence between the cherubim which hovered over the Ark*.

God spoke directly to Jesus at his Baptism (Mark 1:11); but the constant manifestations of the Father to him throughout his life are not to be regarded as theophanies such as other men experienced—they grew out of his unique nature in relation to God (see INCARNATION). The voice which spoke at the Transfiguration was addressed to his Disciples, Peter, James, and John (Mark 9:7; cf. II Pet. 1:17 f.).

Theophanies came to spiritual people, as to Paul on the Damascus road (Acts 9:4–6). Any evaluation of them is determined by our knowledge of the previous life, personality, and social background of the individual receiving it. The writers of the early books of the O.T. told of theophanies in which God appeared to be anthropomorphic, talking with human beings as man to man, and walking away again after the communication. Again, God spoke through angelic messengers, as He continued to do in N.T. times—as to Mary (Luke 1:26–38), and Joseph (Matt. 2:13, 19); or through the media of dreams and visions. Some of the instances of God's speaking may refer to His coming into the mind of a prophet, with the conviction that he ought to do thus and so. Post-Biblical Judaism taught that theophanies in general had ceased.

Theophilus (thē-ŏf'ĭ-lŭs) ("friend of God"). (1) The man to whom the Third Gospel and the Book of Acts are addressed. The use of "most excellent" in Luke 1:3 may be the equivalent of "Right Honorable" in English usage. Theophilus may have been a Gentile (Roman) official, sympathetic to Christianity, for Christians did not use such terms in addressing one another. The fact that "most excellent" does not appear in Acts 1:1 ("O Theophilus") leads many to believe that the official had become a Christian some time between the writing of the two books. Theophilus is the Christian, not the Roman, name of the individual.

(2) The Patriarch of Alexandria in A.D. 391, who, by destroying the statue of Serapis* and the Serapeum, outlawed this influential cult in Alexandria and helped pave the way for the spread of Christianity in Hellenistic centers.

Thessalonians, First Epistle of Paul to the, the 13th book in the N.T. and the Apostle's 1st letter; the earliest of all N.T. writings to reach us in its original form. It was written from Corinth about A.D. 50 during Paul's Second Missionary Journey.

Occasion. The founding of the church in Thessalonica* by Paul is recorded in Acts 17:1–10. A riot provoked by the Jews there forced Paul and his helpers, Timothy and Silvanus (Silas), to withdraw hastily. Paul's itinerary after Thessalonica included Berea, Athens, and Corinth. Concerned over the unfinished work among the Thessalonians, but unable to return there himself (I Thess. 2:17, 18), Paul sent Timothy back to Thessalonica from Athens (3:1–5). Both Timothy and Silas rejoined Paul at Corinth (Acts 18:5). Timothy brought an encouraging report of the Thessalonian church (3:6–10) and thereupon Paul wrote them this Letter. He associated Timothy and Silvanus with him in the salutation and throughout the Epistle (I Thess. 1:1, 2, 2:4, 18; etc.).

Paul's chief *purpose* in writing was to express his thankfulness for the loyalty and spiritual progress of the Thessalonians in the face of heavy odds (1:2, 3, 6–8, 3:6–9). Timothy had evidently reported several problems that had arisen, and Paul took this opportunity to deal with them. The Jews in Thessalonica were undermining the loyalty of the Christians to Paul by attacking his character. Paul answered their insinuations by defending his motives and acts (2:1–16). There was danger of sexual laxity in a young church whose members had so recently been pagans and who continued to live in a pagan environment; Paul instructed them in Christian morals (4:1–12). There were difficulties resulting from their belief that the second coming of Christ was near. The early death of some members of the Church had led others to worry lest the departed should miss some of the blessings of the new age. Paul assured them that the dead in Christ would share the eternal companionship of their Master (4:13–18). There was a tendency for some to quit work and idly await the Parousia*; this placed a burden on industrious Christians and caused outsiders to ridicule them. Paul met this problem with advice about work (4:11, 12).

An *outline* of I Thessalonians follows:

(1) Salutation—1:1.
(2) Thanksgiving for their spiritual progress —1:2–10.
(3) Defense of his message and mission against Jewish insinuations—2:11–16.
(4) Narrative of events—2:17–3:10:
 (a) Paul's absence from them—2:17–20;
 (b) Timothy's mission—3:1–5;
 (c) Timothy's report—3:6–10.
(5) Paul's prayer for them—3:11–13.
(6) Concerning problems of the Thessalonians—4:1–5:22:
 (a) moral injunctions—4:1–12;
 (b) the Second Coming—4:13–5:11;
 (c) church life and conduct—5:12–22.
(7) Final prayer and conclusion—5:23–28.

The outstanding *features* of Paul's two Letters to the Thessalonians are similar and may be considered together. Both are intensely personal letters. They do not deal with points of doctrine, but provide insights into Paul's own thoughts and character. They show him as a man possessed by Christ (I Thess. 5:10), and eager to bring others into relationship with his Lord. In these letters Paul reveals his great joy in his converts and his affection for them. He is proud of them and yet aware that they are not yet perfect (3:10). He is as eager to praise (1:7), encourage (4:1), and comfort (4:13) as to exhort (4:3), admonish (II Thess. 2:2), or rebuke (3:14).

These letters reflect more clearly than any other N.T. book except Acts the missionary preaching of the early Church. They lack the developed doctrine of Romans, Galatians, and Corinthians, but they contain the Gospel Paul preached. This agrees with the sermon summaries of Acts. The Gospel told of the fatherhood of God (I Thess. 1:3; II Thess. 1:2), and of His Son Jesus (I Thess. 1:10); who died for all (5:10) and rose from the dead (4:14) to bring salvation to those who accept him as Lord (5:9). Salvation, beginning in the purpose of God (II Thess. 2:13), is mediated by the preaching of the Gospel (2:14). It begins on earth as life with Christ (I Thess. 5:10), and ends in perfect fellowship with Christ in glory (4:17; II Thess. 2:14). History approaches an impending crisis (I Thess. 1:10), in which Christ will return to banish the wicked (II Thess. 1:8, 2:12), and to gather his own people (I Thess. 4:16). For those who deny him it will be a day of terror (2:16; II Thess. 1:9), but for those who acknowledge him the fulfillment of all hope (I Thess. 5:9; II Thess. 1:10). Those who would be Christ's in the New Age must live worthy of him (I Thess. 4:1) in faith, love, and hope (1:3), and in self-discipline (4:3); doing honest work (II Thess. 3:12), and remaining in peace with one another (I Thess. 5:13), in accordance with the precepts of the Apostles (II Thess. 3:6).

The prominence of *eschatological teaching* in these Letters indicates that it was an important feature of early Christian belief; confidence in the return of Christ is constantly expressed (I Thess. 1:10, 2:19, 3:13, 4:16, 5:23; II Thess. 1:7, 2:1, 3:5). Paul attempted not to formulate a system of belief concerning the last things, but to answer particular questions of his converts who had already received teaching on this subject (I Thess. 5:1; II Thess. 2:5). In I Thess. 4:13–5:10 Paul answered the question, What share will those who have already died in the Lord have in the Parousia? They will rise first, and with those who are still alive be united with Christ forever. Though this picture of the Parousia is colored by the imagery of Jewish apocalyptic literature, it is permeated with the conviction that Christ's Resurrection is the guarantee of the resurrection of Christians (4:14). In the so-called "Pauline Apocalypse" (II Thess. 2:1–12) Paul answered the question: what will be the signs of the end? There will be a "falling away" or apostasy; and the "man of sin," incarnating evil, will sit in the Temple and claim to be God. This "mystery of iniquity," already at work (2:7), was checked by a restraining force (2:6). Restraint will cease, but in the end the Lord will destroy the lawless one "with the brightness of his coming" (2:8).

Thessalonians, Second Epistle of Paul to the is a 2d message addressed by Paul to this Macedonian church, sent from Corinth c. A.D. 50.

Authorship. The similarity of this Letter to I Thessalonians, especially in salutation, chief topic, prayer, and conclusion, is accepted by most scholars as evidence of Paul's authorship. There are, however, aspects of II Thessalonians which cast doubt on its authenticity. This Letter lacks the affectionate tone of the 1st. It employs O.T. phraseology not found in the 1st. Its "little apocalypse" (2:1–12) tells of the events which will precede the Second Coming, while I Thess. 5:2 indicates that the end will come unannounced, "as a thief in the night." Finally, it contains fantastic apocalyptic ideas which are difficult to assign to Paul. Among the various theories which have been advanced to account for these differences are the following: (1) that the second Epistle antedates the first; (2) that it is a forgery; (3) that it was written by Timothy or Silvanus; (4) that it was sent to a Jewish group in the Thessalonican church. With all these theories there are difficulties. The solution with the fewest difficulties is that Paul wrote this Epistle soon after I Thessalonians and addressed it to the same readers. It is possible that he had received reports from Thessalonica that his exhortation in the 1st Epistle (5:1 ff.), to be ready for the imminent return of Christ, had produced excitement, anxiety, and increased idleness, and that Paul wrote the 2d Letter to deal with this situation.

For the outstanding *features* and eschatological *teaching* of this Epistle see THESSALONIANS, FIRST EPISTLE.

The *contents* of II Thessalonians may be outlined as follows:

(1) Salutation—1:1, 2.
(2) Thanksgiving for their progress—1:3–10.
(3) Prayer for them—1:11, 12.
(4) Instruction as to the Second Coming—2:1–12:
  (a) not immediate—2:1–4;
  (b) the preceding events—2:5–12.
(5) The eternal purpose of God—2:13–17.
(6) Various counsels—3:1–15:
  (a) request for prayer—3:1, 2;
  (b) a word of encouragement—3:3–5;
  (c) the injunction to work—3:6–15.
(7) Closing prayer, signature, and benediction—3:16–18.

Thessalonica (thĕs′ȧ-lō-nī′kȧ), now Salonika, was a chief city of Macedonia* on the site of ancient Therma ("hot springs"), whose name was preserved in the Thermaic Gulf, now the Gulf of Salonika. As viewed from the Gulf of Salonika, Thessalonica rises from the water's edge and sprawls like an amphitheater. The ancient Egnatian Way, passing through it, linked it with Macedonian cities and markets. Land and sea connections made it a commercial and strategic center, and it has remained so to this day.

Refounded by Cassander c. 315 B.C., it was named after his wife Thessalonica, sister of Alexander the Great. Under the Romans it became the leading city of Macedonia. It was a strong naval base, and during the first civil war the headquarters of Pompey and the Senate. It was made a free city because of its allegiance to Octavius and Antony in their victorious struggle with Brutus and Cassius. The wisdom of Paul's policy of establishing Christianity in the governing and commer-

436. Thessalonica.

cial centers of the Empire was demonstrated and successfully realized in Thessalonica (I Thess. 1:8). As a free city Thessalonica enjoyed autonomy in internal affairs. Luke's accuracy in designating the "rulers of the city" "politarchs"—an unusual appellation in the Graeco-Roman world (Acts 17:6, 8)—has been corroborated by an inscription on the fine triple carved Arch of Galerius (early 4th century A.D.) which spans the Egnatian Way.

During the Second Missionary Journey Paul arrived at Thessalonica via the Egnatian Way and founded its Christian church. Jews in large numbers had been attracted to this city because of its commercial opportunities. Their prominence, wealth, and influence can be gauged (1) by their synagogue (Acts 17:1, cf. 16:13); (2) by the number of Greeks who had accepted the Jewish faith, or attended the synagogue as God-seekers; (3) and by the ease with which they influenced the city crowd (Acts 17:4 f.). Three weeks of instruction in the synagogue (17:2) and much personal work (I Thess. 2:11) brought "some" results among the Jews, "a great multitude" of adherents among "the devout Greeks," and of the "chief women not a few" (Acts 17:4). Political expediency used against Paul by the politarchs under pressure from the Jews resulted in the Apostle's quitting the city. Later this action was characterized by Paul in I Thess. 2:18.

Paul revisited Thessalonica (I Cor. 16:5). Its church suffered persecution (I Thess. 2:14). Its members known by name are: Jason, Gaius (Acts 19:29), Secundus (Acts 20:4), Aristarchus, and perhaps Demas. In the post-Apostolic period the city became one of the strongholds of eastern Christendom, and was called "the orthodox city."

Because of its strategic position in the Balkan Peninsula it played an important role in World Wars I and II. Today it has a population of more than 200,000. A large part of its Jewish section today is Sephardic (Spanish-Portuguese) Jews who speak a vernacular dialect of Spanish called "Ladino." They came to Thessalonica when expelled from Spain in the latter part of the 15th century. The main thoroughfare of the city now coincides with a stretch of the Via Egnatia; and a street and a chapel are named for St. Paul. The fame of the city rests on the Epistles of Paul which bear its ancient name.

Theudas (thū′d*ǎ*s), a man referred to by the learned Pharisee Gamaliel* in addressing the Sanhedrin* during the arrest of the Apostles (Acts 5:36). Reminding his audience that the boaster Theudas, who had attached 400 to himself, came to naught, Gamaliel went on to mention one "Judas of Galilee," who in the time of the taxing drew many adherents, and "he also perished" (v. 37). The historian Josephus also mentions a Theudas with a similar career, and thought by some to be the same man; unless there is an error in one of the accounts, however, the two seem to have lived at different times.

thigh (Heb. *yārēk*, Gk. *mēros*), the part of the leg between knee and trunk. This member is given special significance in the O.T. Because Jacob after wrestling with an angel at the Jabbok limped on a strained thigh, traditional Jews, following the Mishna (the precepts on which the Talmud is based), do not eat "the sinew of the hip" (Gen. 32:25–32). The hand was placed under the thigh when oaths were taken (Gen. 24:2, 9, 47:29), because special veneration was given the organs of generation (Judg. 8:30 LXX). People in sorrow or fear beat on their thighs (Jer. 31:19).

thistle. See THORNS.

Thomas, one of the Twelve Disciples of Jesus. He is named only "Thomas" in Matt. 10:3; Mark 3:18; Luke 6:15; Acts 1:13; but in John 11:16, 20:24, 21:2 he is further identified as Didymus ("twin"). No incident is recorded about him in the Synoptics or in Acts, but in the Fourth Gospel he becomes prominent in the closing scenes. Thomas displayed courage and loyalty when Jesus proposed to return to Judaea in spite of Jewish hostility (John 11:8, 16). In the conversation with Jesus after the Last Supper, Thomas revealed his spiritual limitation (John 14:5). Both of these attitudes came to their logical conclusion and conflict, when Thomas, on the evening of the Resurrection day, was unable to accept the testimony of the other Disciples concerning the risen Lord (John 20:24 f.). A week later, when Jesus again appeared, Thomas made the most forthright and all-inclusive confession of faith to be found in the Gospels (John 20:26–29). Thomas is mentioned in John 21:2 ("There were together Simon Peter, and Thomas....") as one of the group to whom Jesus appeared in Galilee. Tradition declares that he was a missionary to Parthia or to India.

Thomas was evidently the quiet, reflective type, inclined to think that bad situations were worse than they really were, yet possessed of a loyalty that made him steadfast in spite of danger. His pessimism had this as a redeeming virtue, that even in the darkest days he did not separate himself from Jesus or the Apostolic company. He refused, however, to accept the testimony of his friends, and insisted on finding the truth for himself. The willingness of Christ to have his nail prints investigated banished the incredulity of Thomas, and supplied him with the assurance that eliminated all doubt. The record does not specifically say that Thomas actually placed his hand in the Master's side (John 20:27 f.). See THOMAS, GOSPEL OF, pp. 234 f.

thorns (sometimes associated in Scripture with thistles) exist in many more varieties in Palestine than in most lands (Jer. 4:3); George E. Post believed that not less than 200 species and 50 genera of plants of Palestine and Syria have thorns, spikes, or stinging hairs.

Gen. 3:18 mentions them as the most undesirable yield of the soil—part of Adam's curse (see also Job 5:5). Camels and goats eat thorns and thistles. Thistles bear giant lavender blooms in the fertile Plain of Esdraelon and elsewhere. Thorns were used in O.T. times by nomads, as by Bedouins now, for quick-burning fuel. They are carried in bundles on the heads of desert walkers, or on the backs of animals, to fire ovens or limekilns (Ex. 22:6; Ps. 58:9, 118:12; Eccles. 7:6; Isa. 9:18, 10:17, 27:4, 33:12). Thorns were symbols of vexation ("thorns in your sides," Num. 33:55, or "in your eyes," Josh. 23:13), or of things which could not be grasped with hands (II Sam. 23:6). Thorns were evidence of misfortune (Ezek. 2:6); and of God's judgment on evil people (Nah. 1:10). Arranged as prickly hedges they were effective barriers (Prov. 15:19, 22:5; Hos. 2:6). If allowed to spread in fields or vineyards (Prov. 24:31; Isa. 5:6, 7:19–25, 32:13, 34:13; Jer. 12:13) they became pestiferous. In the N.T. thorns continued to express the idea of a fruitless nuisance, a curse ("grapes of thorns, or figs of thistles," Matt. 7:16). They choked good seed (13:22 and parallels).

The crown of thorns placed on the head of the condemned Jesus by mocking Roman soldiers (Matt. 27:29) may have been platted of *Calycotome villosa*, grown near Jerusalem, or of *Rhamnus punctata*. Crusaders identified it with *spina-christi* or Paliurus, a shrub plentiful in Judaea.

thousand, a symbolic number used scores of times in the O.T., as in Ps. 84:10, 90:4; Ezek. 45:1, 3, 5 f., 47:3–5; Dan. 7:10; and in mystical passages of the N.T., as in Jude 14 and Rev. 5:11, where Satan is to be cast into an abyss to remain a thousand years, until the Second Coming of Christ. In Apocryphal literature of the 1st century B.C. days made up of 1,000 years are divisions of world history. In the O.T. "thousand" is used as a round number meaning "many" in passages which otherwise would appear as exaggerations (I Sam. 21:11; II Chron. 15:11; Eccles. 6:6). In the society of Israel "thousand" and "family" are often synonymous (Judg. 6:15, A.S.V. margin; Num-

10:4); the "thousand" was a subdivision of a tribe. It was also a military unit (I Sam. 8:12; I Chron. 13:1).

Thrace, a kingdom and later a Roman province in SE. Europe, between the Danube and the Strymon rivers, and between the Black Sea and Macedonia. It is mentioned in II Macc. 12:35.

three. See NUMBERS; TRINITY.

Three Holy Children, The Song of the. See APOCRYPHA.

threshing. (1) Threshing was done by beating ripe grain spread on the ground or on a stone wine-press floor (Judg. 6:11) with a staff or rod (Isa. 28:28). A flail (still used by backward farmers) is a hand-threshing instrument consisting of a wooden staff from which swings a short, thick stick.

(2) Threshing was used figuratively in the sense of bruising, pounding, or running over enemies, like Babylon (Jer. 51:33); many enemies of Zion (Mic. 4:13); and "the heathen" (Hab. 3:12). The chaff of the summer threshing floor (Hos. 13:3), which the afternoon breeze blows away and separates from the ripe kernels of grain, is referred to in Daniel's interpretation of Nebuchadnezzar's dream (Dan. 2:35).

See FARMING. For references to individual threshing floors see Judg. 6:11 (Gideon); I Chron. 21:15–30 (Araunah*, and David).

threshold, the plank or stone at the entrance of a building; the doorsill. This was viewed with superstitious or religious awe in the Biblical period, as now, among primitive peoples, who carry brides over the thresholds of new homes. Superstitious people leaped over their temple or domestic thresholds rather than step on them (I Sam. 5:1–5; Zeph. 1:9). Foes were thought of as being outside; inside was security and peace, safeguarded by gods. To placate the evil forces outside, an offering—sometimes even the life of a child—was made when the construction of a house was begun (cf. Josh. 6:26; I Kings 16:34). The temples of Assyria, Babylonia, and Egypt had their entrances flanked by gigantic carved bulls, eagles, lions, dragons, or sphinxes to make the ingress safe for worshippers. The Jerusalem Temple entrance was protected by outer courts, officials, and safeguarding rites. Royal palaces had guards at their entrances, as in the story of Joash (II Kings 11:4–11). The Temple Area had priestly guards, keepers of the watch, at the thresholds to protect the sacred treasures (II Kings 12:9, cf. 22:4, 23:4, "keepers of the door").

throne. (1) The chair of a reigning monarch, like Pharaoh's (Ex. 11:5, 12:29); Solomon's (I Kings 1:46, 10:18–20); or that of Ahasuerus (Esther 1:2; see also Jer. 1:15). The throne chair of Eighteenth Dynasty Tutankh-amun is preserved in the Egyptian Museum at Cairo. The most elegant throne described in Scripture is Solomon's, ivory trimmed and overlaid with gold, and approached by six steps, each flanked by two lions. Many extant reliefs and paintings portray thrones of Assyria, Babylonia, Persia, and Egypt. (2) Sometimes the "throne" denotes royal power, rather than a place of administration; as the throne of David (II Sam. 3:10; Ps. 122:5), especially in Messianic passages referring to Jesus (Luke 1:32). Jesus promised his Twelve that they should have thrones beside his in the Kingdom of God, judging the Twelve Tribes of Israel (Matt. 19:28; Luke 22:30). God's holy, eternal throne is figuratively mentioned in Ps. 47:8, 89:4; Isa. 6:1–4. Jeremiah termed Jerusalem "the throne of the Lord" (3:17; cf. Rev. 4:2–4, God's throne in heaven, as in Isa. 66:1).

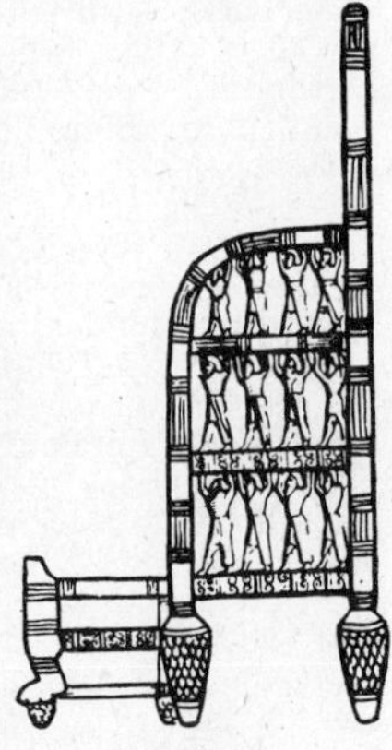

437. Throne.

thumb, the first digit of the hand. The thumb of the right hand was valued as essential to man's work. As part of the consecration rite, the right thumbs of Aaron and his sons were sprinkled with the blood of a ram (Ex. 29:20; Lev. 8:23). The ceremonial for cleansing lepers included the application of the blood of a lamb from the trespass offering, and also oil, to their right thumbs (Lev. 14:14, 17, 25, 28). Both the thumbs and great toes of Adoni-bezek were removed by men of Judah, even as he himself had cut off the thumbs and toes of 70 kings who had gathered their food under his table (Judg. 1:6 f.).

thummim. See URIM AND THUMMIM; BREASTPLATE.

thunder was associated by early Hebrews with manifestations of the power of God. He not only caused thunder (Ex. 9:23, 28), but He Himself "thundered" (I Sam. 7:10; Ps. 77:18; Isa. 29:6). Winter thunder among the crags of Near Eastern desert mountains and deep river valleys boomed with terrifying reverberation. Writers attempting to depict theophanies included thunder among their supernatural accompaniments, as at Sinai (Ex. 19:16, 20:18). Prophetic pronouncements concerning the Day of the Lord were sometimes couched in terms of thunder, tempest, and devouring flames (Isa. 29:6); cf. the Apocalypse (Rev. 4:5, 6:1, 8:5, 14:2, 19:6).

thunder, sons of, an epithet applied to James and John (Boanerges) (Mark 3:17), whose fiery disposition led them to ask Jesus if he wished them to "command fire to come down from heaven, and consume" the inhospitable Samaritans of a certain village (Luke 9:52–56).

Thutmose (Thothmes), the name of four pharaohs of the brilliant Eighteenth Dynasty of Egypt*, centering at Thebes*. Under their rule Egypt attained her greatest power. The dates assigned them by excellent authorities vary. Those of the great Thutmose III are: Borchardt-Edgerton, c. 1490–1436 B.C.

The two whose activities were linked with the destiny of Palestine and Syria were (1)

Thutmose I, 2d ruler of the Dynasty, whose Syrian campaign determined Egyptian foreign policy for centuries to come. In his plan for bringing SW. Asia under his control, Thutmose I crossed Syria without opposition, and near the upper reaches of the Euphrates won a victory that netted him tremendous booty and many captives. In commemoration of this triumph he erected on the river bank a boastful inscription. He had royal burial places prepared in the isolated Libyan Valley of the Tombs of the Kings. (2) Thutmose III, 5th of the Eighteenth Dynasty, ruled for some 18 years after having ruled jointly with the powerful Queen Hatshepsut, half-sister and wife of Thutmose II and stepmother and mother-in-law of Thutmose III. Innovations of his age included the introduction of horses and chariots*, marriage with Asiatic wives, adoption of Asiatic gods, and cultivation of close political relations with W. Asia. In the 22d year of his reign he led his army across the Egyptian border at the fortress Tjaru, on a pretext of crushing rebels threatening the borders of his kingdom, but his real foe was a confederacy of 330 princes of central and northern Palestine, led by the king of Kadesh. Crossing at the present Qantara on the Suez Canal, Thutmose swept up the ancient road along the Mediterranean, marched through Gaza, Ashkelon, Ashdod, and Jamnia, and followed an old caravan road to the foot of Mt. Carmel. Having selected strategic Megiddo*, overlooking the Plain of Esdraelon, as his objective in battle, Thutmose decided to use the most dangerous of the three approaches. His spectacular triumph over the king of Kadesh and his confederates, and his unbelievable booty in animals, treasure, and prisoners, are recorded in inscriptions in the great temple at Karnak. Joppa fell after long resistance, and the Egyptians pressed on into Syria, the land of the Mitanni*, and the Euphrates country, which after a total of 17 campaigns Thutmose established as the northern boundary of Egypt. Although he conquered Palestine (through his victory at Megiddo), Phoenicia, and Syria to the 36th parallel, and marched as far as Carchemish*, this city as well as Aleppo remained in the hands of the Mitanni. (For the monuments he erected in Egypt to mark these victories, see OBELISK.) Thutmose III is the pharaoh who above all others seemed worthy of being called "the great." (For an account of his era, see *When Egypt Ruled the East*, Steindorff and Seele, University of Chicago, chaps. V–VII.)

Thyatira (thī′*ȧ*-tī′r*ȧ*) (possibly "town of Thya"), the modern Akhisar, a city of ancient Lydia in W. Asia Minor (now Anatolian Turkey). Thyatira was situated on an elevation in the Lycus River valley SE. of Pergamum*, with which it was closely linked, and NW. of Sardis. It was on a key highway of commerce. Established evidently in the 3d century B.C. by Seleucus I, who brought in a colony of Macedonians, the town gained prestige from its guilds of weavers and dyers of wool and linen textiles for clothing, and for its leather-workers and metal craftsmen (Rev. 2:18). Lydia, Paul's first convert in Europe, was a cloth merchant from Thyatira, who did business in Macedonian Philippi (Acts 16:14). She probably belonged to one of the city's guilds, and to a synagogue. From the large Jewish colony in Thyatira a cell of devout Christians was formed. Thyatira, one of the seven churches of Asia to whom the Apocalypse was addressed (Rev. 2:18–29), was praised for its good works, charity, faith, and patience, but chastised because some of its members, following the advice of "the prophetess Jezebel," had practiced fornication, and had eaten things sacrificed to idols (2:20 ff.; cf. Acts 15:20).

thyine, a prized ornamental "sweet" wood, derived from *Callitris quadrivalvis*, mentioned among other luxury products of symbolic Babylon (Rev. 18:12; cf. R.S.V.).

Tiâmat, a Babylonian chaos monster, or dragon, who is overcome by Marduk in the Babylonian creation epic. (Cf. Gen. 1:6, the separation of waters from the firmament, with Marduk's formation of heaven and earth from the cleft body of Tiâmat; also cf. Job 26:12). The word "deep" (Heb. *tehom*) in Gen. 1:2, 7:11, 8:2 may be connected with the name Tiâmat. (Cf. Isa. 27:1, "leviathan," 51:9 f.)

Tiberias (Heb., Teveriah), a city established by Herod Antipas, who made it his capital (after using Sepphoris). He named it in honor of Emperor Tiberius* (1st quarter of the 1st century A.D.). It lies on the W. shore of the Sea of Galilee, c. 12 m. S. of the entrance of the Jordan into that body, and 6 m. N. of the river's exit from the sea; along the shore, 681 ft. below sea level, on a low shelf at the foot of hills rising in the direction of Cana and Nazareth, with the Horns of Hattîn (the traditional Mount of Beatitudes) visible behind the town. Its exposed position has been fortified by conquerors, e.g., Herod, Josephus, Omar al-Daher, and Crusaders. Because it was on the edge of an ancient walled town, Rakkath (Josh. 19:35) or Hammath, whose cemetery lies under it, Tiberias was in Jesus' time shunned by pious Jews. There is no

438. Tiberias: ancient city walls along the shore of the Sea of Galilee.

record of his having visited it, though much of his ministry was spent in nearby towns. He avoided the lax, Hellenistic atmosphere of this famous hot-water bath resort, as he usually did that of pagan Gentile cities. After the fall of Jerusalem in A.D. 70 Tiberias became a Jewish metropolis and center of rabbinic learning; by the 2d century A.D. it was recognized, with Jerusalem, Hebron, and Sepphoris, as one of four sacred cities of the Jews, the seat of the great Sanhedrin, the school of the Talmud, and the court of the Hebrew Patriarch of the W. In Tiberias, at the opening of the 3d century, was published the Mishnah (collection of ancient Hebrew traditional Law), made by Judah ha-Nasi (c. A.D. 135–220), which, with the Gemara (commentary on the Mishnah), also compiled at Tiberias, constitutes the Jerusalem Talmud*. Important developments in the Massoretic text of the O.T., including the preservation of pronunciation by means of vowel points, took place at Tiberias. Crusaders in the 12th century made it the capital of Galilee. Its fall to the Moslem Saladin in 1187 precipitated the Battle of Hattîn, disastrous to the Christians. The famous Jewish philosopher and physician Maimonides (d. A.D. 1204), forerunner of scientific medicine, and a man whose obedience to Biblical precepts of faith and love was notable, is buried at Tiberias. The hot baths of Tiberias which attracted people in N.T. times have been modernized and are still popular.

The vicinity of Tiberias is rich in archaeological possibilities. In addition to portions of the ancient town wall (partly Herodian) and an ancient synagogue, masonry of various dates remains between the modern town and the famous hot springs of Tiberias. Just S. of here Prof. E. L. Sukenik of the Hebrew University found a round structure, possibly of Hadrian's time, which may have stood at the crossing of an ancient city. Archaeological sites in the southern environs of Tiberias are Hammâm Tabarîyeh (the Hammath in Naphtali, Josh. 19:35, and the Ammathus of N.T. times); and Khirbet Kerak, a huge site (Beth-yerah*), where strata of occupation from the 4th and the 3d millenniums B.C. have been unearthed by the Israel Exploration Society.

Tiberias, Sea of, an alternate name of the Sea of Galilee (John 6:1, 21:1).

Tiberius (Tiberius Claudius Nero), the 2d Roman emperor (A.D. 14–37), and the one referred to as "Caesar" in the Gospels except in Luke 2:1; he is mentioned by name only in Luke 3:1 (see Matt. 22:17; Mark 12:14; Luke 20:22; John 19:12). He was a son of an officer of Julius Caesar and of Livia, of the Claudian family. He became consul at 29, but he subsequently spent most of his time in the army, where he became "the first soldier of the Empire." He campaigned for Rome along the Danube and the Rhine, went into retirement for study in Rhodes, then emerged for further marches into Germany, and established the imperial organization in Europe. He was appointed military governor of the Roman provinces in A.D. 12 by Caesar Augustus*, whose stepson, adopted son, son-in-law (he married Julia), and heir he became. He was made *Imperator* A.D. 14, at the age of 56, and ruled until A.D. 37, when he died after years of what Tacitus depicts as debauchery at Capri. He was succeeded by Caligula. He was noted for his strict punishment of officers who tolerated the unprovoked oppression of their subjects, for leniency in taxation, and for rigid economy of administration. He fostered trade and communication. Tiberius was emperor during the procuratorship of Pontius Pilate (A.D. 26–36), and at the time therefore of the Crucifixion of Jesus. See TIBERIAS.

439. Emperior Tiberius.

Tidal (tī′dăl), a king of Goiim (A.V. "the nations"), allied with Chedorlaomer in the Dead Sea encounter described in Gen. 14. He may have been a Hittite.

Tiglath-pileser III (tĭg′lăth-pĭ-lē′zẽr), king of Assyria (745–727 B.C.), and founder of a new dynasty. He is erroneously named Tilgath-pilneser in Chronicles. He is identified, with the aid of Babylonian records, as "Pul" of II Kings 15:19, who received tribute from King Menahem of Israel (c. 745–738 B.C.); perhaps this was his original name. King Ahaz* of Judah, when the anti-Assyrian alliance of Pekah* and Rezin of Damascus turned against him for not joining them, appealed to Tiglath-pileser for assistance, contrary to the advice of Isaiah*, who urged dependence on the God of Israel. In 733 Tiglath-pileser, apparently delighted at the opportunity and the excuse, captured many of the northern cities of Israel, carrying off captives to Assyria, and punished the Philistine city-states, which had attacked Judan cities while Ahaz was in the midst of his difficulties. In 732 he captured Damascus*, killed Rezin and transported the inhabitants of the Syrian capital wholesale to Assyria as a part of his policy of breaking down national feeling in neighboring states. Ahaz's gifts (II Chron. 28:20) perhaps saved Jerusalem from a similar fate. Some time after Damascus' fall the pro-Assyrian party in Israel murdered Pekah, and Hoshea took the throne. All the petty kingdoms of Palestine and Syria were now vassal states. Ahaz went to Damascus and paid homage (II Kings 16:8), offering tribute of silver and gold from the Temple. Tiglath-pileser had brought Assyria to glorious heights of power. He died in 727, and was succeeded by Shalmaneser V.

Tigris River (or Idiglat), the Hiddekel (Heb.) of Gen. 2:14. It was described by the author of this passage as the 3d of the four heads of the river which watered the garden of Eden ("that is it which goeth toward the east of Assyria"); and is mentioned in Dan. 10:4 ("the great river, which is Hiddekel"). The 1,146–m. Tigris is one of two rivers which frame the region known as Mesopotamia ("the land between the rivers"), comprising Assyria in the N. and Babylonia (the ancient Accad and Sumer) in the S.; the other stream is the Euphrates*. In O.T. times the Tigris and Euphrates flowed so close together that irrigation canals were built linking the two; at Baghdad the distance between the streams is only 35 m. They once had two mouths, but now they meet at Kurnah and flow 100 m. as one stream to the Persian Gulf. The streams which feed the Tigris rise on the S. slopes of the Taurus Mountains, whence the river crosses Armenia and flows SE. through the heart of what was the Assyrian Empire. It was the barrier between Babylonia and Susiana. On its banks, frequently lined with palms, pomegranates, and jungles of reed, stood the ancient city of Nineveh*, almost opposite the modern Mosul; Asshur*; Calah* (Gen. 10:11); Samarra; Baghdad; Ctesiphon; and Seleucia, capital of the Seleucids' kingdom. Source also has two headstreams, the most distant one the Turkish Dicle rising in a mountain lake about 15 miles SE. of Elâzig. There it is just a few miles from the channel of the Euphrates, which makes a wide sweep from W. to E. Although shorter than the Euphrates, it is much swifter and of greater volume, with many rapids. It is far less navigable, only by small boats and rafts and has never been so important as the Euphrates as a line of traffic. The Tigris was an important factor in the economy that shaped the cultural, religious, and military history of a large section of the Near East. Iraq is the modern country through whose heart the Tigris flows.

440. Tigris River at Baghdad.

Tilgath-pilneser. See TIGLATH-PILESER.

Timaeus (tī-mē′ĕs), the father of the blind beggar Bartimaeus, cured by Jesus on the highway near Jericho (Mark 10:46).

timbrel, a tambourinelike musical instrument, usually played by women and girls: Miriam and her companions (Ex. 15:20); Jephthah's daughter (Judg. 11:34); David's musicians (II Sam. 6:5; I Chron. 13:8; "damsels," Ps. 68:25). (See MUSIC.)

time was marked in the early Biblical period, as among Bedouins today, by sunrise and sunset, phases of the moon, and location of a few constellations; but there was no accurate knowledge of years, nor names for months and days. The first Biblical allusion to time is the Genesis account of God's separation of light from darkness (1:5), and His creation of "the greater light" (the sun) to rule the day, and the "lesser light" (the moon) to rule the night, with "the stars also" (vv. 14–16). These luminaries were "for signs, and for seasons, and for days, and years," as these demarcations later developed. Men became aware of seasons when they began to farm. "While the earth remaineth, seedtime and harvest, and cold and heat, and summer and winter, and day and night shall not cease" (Gen. 8:22). The recurring seasons are indicated in the Gezer* Calendar, late 10th century B.C., a piece of soft limestone on which a boy had evidently scratched a ditty about the farmer's almanac as he knew it from watching farm activities. For the mention of seasons see Gen. 8:22; Ex. 34:21 ("earing time" and "harvest"); Lev. 26:5 ("vintage" and "sowing time"); Ps. 74:17, and cf. Zech. 14:8 ("summer" and "winter"); Ruth 1:22 and II Sam. 21:9 ("barley harvest").

Eras were measured by the Jews in terms of epochal events in their history, like the Exodus, the Sojourn in Egypt (Ex. 12:40); the Babylonian Exile (Ezek. 33:21; 40:1), sometimes called "the seventy years"; the Temple building time (I Kings 6:1); the period between the two Temples; and by sudden events, like an "earthquake in the

TIME

days of Uzziah, king of Judah" (Amos 1:1; cf. Zech. 14:5). The years of the reigns of the kings of Israel and of Judah were numbered with reference to each other (II Kings 3:1, 13:1, 10, etc.) (see CHRONOLOGY).

Modern Jews date religious documents with reference to the Creation, as did ancient Jews. The year A.D. 1960 corresponds generally to 5720 *Anno Mundi*. In modern secular writings Jews omit "B.C." and "A.D." and use instead "B.C.E." ("Before the Christian Era") and "C.E." ("Common Era" or "Christian Era").

The year among early Hebrews was lunar, the first day of each month being set at the new moon. The early Canaanites and Israelites gave the months names, four of which survive in the Bible: Abib, Ziv, Ethanim, and Bul

441. "Tower of the Winds," Athens, erected before Paul's day at east end of Roman Agora. This horologion was topped by a weathercock in the form of Triton; the frieze represented the winds; it contained a water clock to tell time in cloudy weather, while sundials faced the sun.

(see chart). Later, probably during the Exile, they used numbers. Babylonian names of months (Nisan, etc.) came after the Exile. Later the Hebrews used a solar year, based on revolutions of the sun; but the old lunar month of 29½ days was retained for their religious calendar. In order to reconcile the lunar and the solar years they adopted the Metonic cycle of 19 years, whereby an extra (intercalary) month ("Second Adar") was added to the 3d, 6th, 8th, 11th, 14th, 17th, and 19th years. Babylonians used the "intercalated" month, and surrounding nations borrowed it from them. Greeks and Romans also used the extra month, until the calendar reform of Julius Caesar. The recurrent February 29 in our calendar is a vestige of the Babylonian solution of the lunar month problem.

Before the Exile the Hebrew year began in the autumn, with the ingathering of crops. In post-Exilic times a secular calendar began with the vernal equinox (see NEW YEAR FESTIVAL). Both the ecclesiastical and civil calendars were used.

Sacred Year	*Civil Year*	*Jewish Calendar*	*Farm Seasons*
mo.	mo.		
1	7	Abib or Nisan (March-April) (Neh. 2:1; Esther 3:7). 1st—New Moon; beginning of the SACRED YEAR. 14th—preparation for PASSOVER—paschal lamb eaten in the evening. 15th—Sabbath and Holy Convocation; Week of Unleavened Bread begins. 16th—the offering of OMER or FIRST SHEAF (Lev. 23:10–12). 21st—Holy Convocation.	Latter or spring rains (Deut. 11:14). Barley harvest begins in some localities (Ruth 1:23).
2	8	Iyyar or Ziv (April-May) (I Kings 6:1). 1st—New Moon. 14th—SECOND or LITTLE PASSOVER. 18th—33rd day of the Omer*, a minor holiday.	Barley harvest (Ruth 1:23).
3	9	Sivan (May-June) (Esther 8:9). 1st—New Moon. 6th and 7th—PENTECOST or FEAST OF WEEKS, marking the close of harvest.	Wheat harvest.
4	10	Tammuz (June-July) (Ezek. 8:14). 1st—New Moon. 17th—FAST to commemorate breach in Jerus. wall (Jer. 52:5).	
5	11	Ab (July-August). 1st—New Moon. 9th—FAST for the destructions of Temple by Babylon, Rome.	Grapes, figs, olives ripen.
6	12	Elul (August-September) (Neh. 6:15; I Macc. 14:27). 1st—New Moon.	Vintage begins. Maize harvest. Pomegranates ripen.
7	1	Tishri or Ethanim (September-October) (I Kings 8:2). 1st—New Moon. NEW YEAR'S DAY. Beginning of the CIVIL YEAR. FEAST OF TRUMPETS. 10th—YOM HA—KIPPURIM or DAY OF ATONEMENT. 15th–22d—FEAST OF TABERNACLES or BOOTHS. 21st—FEAST OF BRANCHES OR PALMS.	Former or early rains. (Joel 2:23). Plowing and sowing begin.
8	2	Marchesvan or Bul (October-November) (I Kings 6:38). 1st—New Moon.	Sowing of wheat and barley.
9	3	Chislev (November-December) (Neh. 1:1; Zech. 7:1; I Macc. 1:54). 1st—New Moon. 25th—HANUKKAH (II Macc. 1:9). FEAST OF DEDICATION.	
10	4	Tebeth (December-January) (Esther 2: 16). 1st—New Moon. 10th—FAST commemorating the beginning of Nebuchadnezzar's siege of Jerusalem (II Kings 25:1).	

Sacred Year	Civil Year	Jewish Calendar	Farm Seasons
mo.	mo.		
11	5	Sebat (January-February) (Zech. 1:7; I Macc. 16:14). 1st—New Moon. 15th—Jewish Arbor Day.	Blossoming of trees.
12	6	Adar (February-March) (Ezra 6:15; Esther 3:7). 1st—New Moon. 13th—FAST OF ESTHER. 14th–15th—FEAST OF PURIM.	Blossoming of almonds.
13		Veadar or Second Adar (intercalary month).	

The week of the Jews consisted of seven days, ending with the Sabbath* on which God had rested from His creative work (Ex. 20:11), and which memorialized liberation from Egyptian bondage. (Deut. 5:14 f.). Israel does not assign names to days of the week, but uses ordinal numbers. In dating letters, Jews often identify day and week by the selection from the Torah designated to be read on the following Sabbath.

The day, divided into 24 hours of 60 minutes of 60 seconds, was the gift of the sexagesimal system (later combined with a decimal system) of the ancient Sumerians.

442. Fourth-century A.D. mosaic in Beth Alpha Synagogue, Palestine. Helios in sun chariot, surrounded by signs of the Zodiac. Winged figures at corners represent the four seasons.

Chaldaeans named the days for the sun, moon, and other celestial bodies. Their day of the planet Saturn became what is now known as our Saturday. A Chaldaean astronomer, Nabu-rimannu, using files kept by Chaldaean astronomers for a long period, made tables of the motions of the sun and moon from which he dated eclipses and estimated a year's length of 365 days, 6 hrs., 15 min., 41 sec.—only 26 min. 55 sec. too long. In the Biblical period most Near Easterners began their day with sunrise and ended it with sunset, to which night hours were added incidentally—divided into three or four watches (see Judg. 7:19, "middle watch"; Ex. 14:24, "the morning watch," cf. I Sam. 11:11; Luke 12:38, "second," "third" watch). The Romans had four military night watches: evening, midnight, cockcrowing (between midnight and 3 A.M.), and morning (from 3 A.M. to dawn; see Mark 13:35; Matt. 14:25). The 12-hour day of N.T. times appears in John 11:9. The sixth hour (Matt. 27:45 and parallels) was noon.

Jews based their sacrifice times on daybreak (cf. Lev. 7:15). In laws involving a period of time, such as mourning, a part of the day is counted as a whole. Holy days and the Sabbath begin and end at twilight.

Clocks or *timekeepers* of various types were used by Jews in the Biblical period. They had several sorts of sundials (II Kings 20:11; Isa. 38:8), like the shadow clock, an Egyptian specimen of which, c. 3,400 years

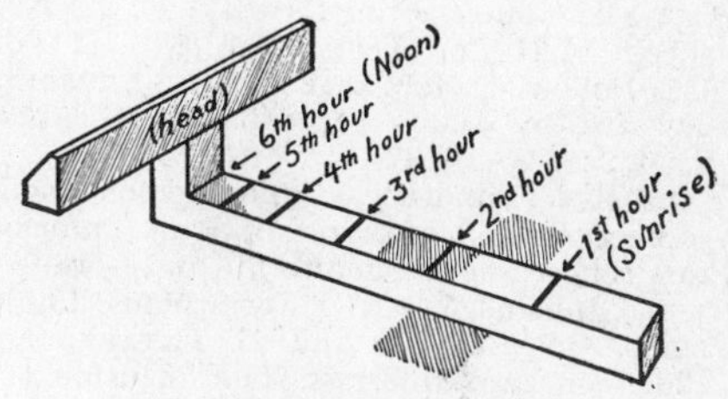

443. Egyptian shadow clock.

old, is in the Berlin Museum. It consists of a short piece of wood turned toward the E. in the morning, so that its shadow falls on a long arm fastened to it at right angles, and carrying a scale by which time (from the 1st hour until noon) over a period of six hours could be read by means of the shadow of the shorter bar on the longer piece. At noon the head (the shorter bar) was turned to the W., and the lengthening afternoon shadows measured on the long bar. From such shadow clocks the 12-hour clock was worked out in Europe. The Greeks often used the water clock (*clepsydra*), also invented by the Egyptians; this worked on the hour-glass principle. One of these hydraulic clocks was kept as a public timepiece in the (still extant) 1st century tower of the winds (*hōrologion*) in Athens, where the water flowing into a cistern of standard size in a specific period gave the time.

Timna (twice in the A.V. Timnah). (1) An eponymous concubine of Esau's 2d son, Eliphaz, and ancestress of Amalek (Gen. 36:12, 22; I Chron. 1:36); a tribal mother who was daughter of Seir and sister of Lotan (I Chron. 1:39). (2) A chieftain (A.V. "duke") of Edom* (Gen. 36:40; I Chron. 1:51).

Timnah (Timnath eight times in the A.V., once Thimnathah). (1) A region in the hill country of Judah where Judah pastured sheep (Gen. 38:12–14), perhaps Tibnah, 12 m. SW. of Jerusalem; possibly the town mentioned in Josh. 15:57, although the context of the latter would place it S. of Hebron. (2) A town of the N. border of Judah (Josh. 15:10), part of the inheritance of Dan (Josh. 19:43). The Philistines dominated it in Samson's day (Judg. 14:2), and captured it in the reign of King Ahaz of Judah (c. 735–715 B.C.) (II Chron. 28:18). Samson's wife was from Timnah (Judg. 14:1 f., 15:6). Sennacherib captured it on his march to Jerusalem in 701 B.C. (*ANET*³, p. 288). It has been identified with Tell el-Batashi, c. 4 m. NW. of Beth-shemesh. (3) See TIMNATH-SERAH.

Timnath-serah (tim'nath-se'rȧ), part of Joshua's inheritance in the hill country of Ephraim (Josh. 19:50); and his burial place (24:30) (Timnath-heres in Judg. 2:9). Most authorities identify it with Khirbet Tibnah, 12 m. NE of Lydda, where Late Bronze and Iron I pottery has been found. It is probably the Timnath fortified by Bacchides (I Macc. 9:50).

Timon, one of "the Seven" selected by the Apostles to assist in "the daily ministration" of relief to needy Christians (Acts 6:1–5).

Timotheus (tĭ-mō'thē-ŭs). (1) The Greek name of Timothy*, in the A.V. of the N.T. except in II Cor. 1:1; I Tim. 1:2; II Tim. 1:2; Philem. 1; Heb. 13:23. (2) An Ammonite defeated by Judas Maccabaeus (II Macc. 8:30, 9:3, 10:24–37).

Timothy (Timotheus) ("honorer of God"), companion and assistant of Paul. Information concerning this man's life and work is in Acts, Romans, I and II Corinthians, Philippians, Colossians, I and II Thessalonians, Philemon, and Hebrews. The inclusion of I and II Timothy* and Titus* as historical sources about him depends on the view held of these Pastoral Epistles.

Timothy was Paul's "beloved son" (I Cor. 4:17; I Tim. 1:2–18; II Tim. 1:2) and "fellowlabourer in the gospel" (I Thess. 3:2). He was the son of a Greek father and a devoted Jewish mother (Acts 16:1, Eunice, II Tim. 1:5). He lived in either Lystra* or Derbe*, where, during Paul's First Missionary Journey, he was converted (c. A.D. 48). In the Second Missionary Journey Paul desired this young man to be his secretary and helper (Acts 16:1–4). He was duly ordained (II Tim. 1:6). To make Timothy more acceptable to the Jews, Paul circumcised him (Acts 16:3). Paul's affection for and confidence in Timothy soon became known to all (I Cor. 4:17; II Tim. 3:10 f.). When Paul fled from Berea Timothy and Silas remained there (Acts 17:14). Summoned by Paul to join him at Athens (Acts 17:15), they overtook the Apostle at Corinth (Acts 18:1, 5), where the Church learned to know Timothy (II Cor. 1:19). After another sojourn at Ephesus Paul sent Timothy into Macedonia (I Thess. 3:6), with Corinth as his destination, to deal with the disorders of the church there (Acts 19:22; I Cor. 4:17, 16:11). But the situation was too difficult for Timothy, and he was replaced by Titus (II Cor. 7:6, 13 f., 8:6, 16, 23, 12:18). Yet even in the letter which records Titus as replacing Timothy, Paul mentions Timothy in his greetings and the body of the letter (II Cor. 1:1), as he had previously done in I Thess. 1:1 and II Thess. 1:1. Timothy helped to organize the offering for the church at Jerusalem, and accompanied Paul as far as Troas (Acts 20:4–6); it is not clear whether he went with Paul to Jerusalem. There is no reference to Timothy during Paul's imprisonment at Rome, to which the closing chapters of Acts lead. Timothy is present with the Apostle and shares in the writing of Philippians, Colossians, and Philemon. For lack of data this period and Timothy's later life must remain confused, and be subjected to theories which, however plausible, do not answer all questions.

The references to Timothy in the books which bear his name present confusing information. Timothy is addressed as a young man still in his formative years with much to learn, yet in charge of churches in the neighborhood of Ephesus (I Tim. 1:3). The Apostle is in prison and writes for Timothy to come to him (II Tim. 4:11, 13). In view of the fact that Timothy was with Paul when he wrote three of his prison Epistles, as referred to above, a release from prison and a 2d imprisonment climaxed by the Apostle's martyrdom would be necessary to account for these details. Perhaps before this 2d imprisonment Paul visited Crete (Titus 1:5), Macedonia (I Tim. 1:3), Greece, Asia, and Troas, where he had left his cloak, of which he felt the need in Rome (II Tim. 4:13). Though it overcomes one difficulty, this theory fails to reconcile the Timothy of the historical record of Luke and the Letters of Paul with the Timothy of the Pastoral Epistles. The latter was languid in performing his duties (I Tim. 4:14–16, 6:13–16), yielded to love of money (6:6–11), was a fanatical ascetic (5:23), was timid (II Tim. 1:17), and shrank from hardship (2:3). The gulf between the "beloved Timothy" of Paul and the Timothy of these Letters is very great; some scholars indeed, think these two Timothys irreconcilable. The last glimpse of Timothy is in Hebrews 13:23, where it is announced that he has been set free from prison, into which he may have been thrown as he shared the last, triumphant days of the doomed Paul.

Tradition declares that Timothy was the 1st bishop of Ephesus.

Timothy, I and II Epistles to, and **Titus, Epistle to,** three N.T. books attributed to Paul, and grouped together as "the Pastoral Epistles" since the 18th century. Their theme is the "care of the church" (I Tim. 3:5). In them all the Apostle gives his assistants directions for their missionary work. The Pastoral Epistles all deal with the same problems, exhibit the same peculiarities of language, and agree in religious and ethical teaching. The same man evidently wrote the three Pastorals during the same period, against the same background, and for closely related purposes. II Timothy appears to be the earliest of the three letters, because (1) it has the greatest freshness and power; (2) it contains more of the genuine Pauline passages; and (3) its expression of certain ideas which reappear in I Timothy and Titus is more original than in those Epistles. II Timothy deals with Christian life and character; I Timothy, with Church administration; and Titus, with the need for right doctrine.

Paul's *authorship* of these three Epistles is seriously questioned on historical, theological, ecclesiastical, and literary grounds; historical arguments are the most important. The general historical situation in the Pastorals cannot be fitted into the record of Paul's life as it is recorded in Acts and the other

Epistles. I Timothy purports to be written from Macedonia to Timothy, whom the Apostle had left behind in Ephesus (I Tim. 1:3). But we know of only one journey Paul made from Ephesus to Macedonia (Acts 20:1; II Cor. 2:13), and on that occasion Timothy had preceded Paul into Macedonia (II Cor. 1:1). The Epistle to Titus presupposes that Paul was in Crete long enough to found churches in many cities (Titus 1:5). Acts, however, is silent about a Pauline mission in Crete, and mentions only the brief visit Paul made to the island when the ship on which he travelled as a prisoner to Rome waited at Fair Havens for a change of wind (Acts 27:7, 8). II Timothy appears to have been written while Paul was a prisoner in Rome (II Tim. 1:17) awaiting imminent death (II Tim. 4:6–8). Yet immediately after his solemn farewell Paul apparently forgets he may die at any time and asks Timothy to come to him before winter and bring Mark (II Tim. 4:9, 11, 21). Paul also mentions events of five or six years before: his cloak left at Troas; Erastus remaining at Corinth; and Trophimus falling sick at Miletus (II Tim. 4:13, 20).

Those who uphold the traditional Pauline authorship meet these difficulties by assigning the Pastorals to a period outside the record in Acts. In the 4th century there was a belief—probably derived from the Pastorals themselves—that Paul's trial in Rome resulted in acquittal, after which he resumed his missionary work; then was arrested and brought to Rome a second time and put to death. As this period between the two trials is hypothetical, it can be filled in with an itinerary which explains all the historical difficulties in the Pastorals. The three chief objections to this theory of an extra unrecorded period in Paul's life are: (1) There is no record of Paul's acquittal in Rome, which would surely have left a deep impression on the Church. (2) Paul intended to proceed from Rome to Spain (Rom. 15:24), yet the Pastorals show him continuing work in the E. (3) The author of Acts definitely states that at Paul's leavetaking the elders of Ephesus were sorrowful "that they should see his face no more" (Acts 20:25, 38).

The *character* of the Pastoral Epistles, as well as their historical setting, casts doubt on the Pauline authorship. The theological outlook is not that of Paul. The author does not understand what Paul meant by the Law (I Tim. 1:8–10); puts loyalty to Church tradition in the supreme place Paul put faith; disregards the conflict between flesh and spirit; forgets the value Paul attached to the Cross; and lacks Paul's mysticism. Paul uses "spirit" more than 85 times, while the author of the Pastorals uses it but 3 times (R.S.V. I Tim. 4:1; II Tim. 1:14; Tit. 3:5). The ecclesiastical organization in the background of these Epistles is more formal and elaborate than in Paul's time. The author mentions "bishops" (I Tim. 3:1–7), or "elders" (cf. Tit. 1:5–7); "deacons" (I Tim. 3:8–13), and an official staff of "widows" (I Tim. 5:9–13). The language of the Pastorals is unlike Paul's in grammar and vocabulary. Even Pauline ideas are expressed in a manner foreign to Paul in his other Epistles.

There are, however, passages in these Epistles that appear to be the genuine work of Paul, like I Tim. 1:1, 2; II Tim. 1:1–11, 15–18, 2:1–13, 4:9–21; Tit. 3:1–7, 12 f. They conform in literary style to Paul's other Epistles; they contain names and allusions which sound authentic; and they do not fit into their context, especially II Tim. 4:9, 11, 21; cf. II Tim. 4:6–8. These may be fragments of personal notes written by Paul and used by a later writer as the nucleus of the Pastoral Epistles which he issued in Paul's name c. A.D. 100.

The *purpose* of the Pastoral Epistles is suggested by their attribution to Paul. The unknown author was evidently an ardent admirer of Paul, who, he believed, taught and practiced true Christianity. At a time when the Church was building up its organization, combating the moral standards of its pagan converts, and encountering heretical speculations, this writer attempted to preserve pure Christianity by applying Paul's doctrines and practical teachings to the conditions of the time. In this he largely succeeded. Like Paul he insisted that true faith shows itself in Christian living. He took Paul's fundamental ideas and made a place for them in the creed of the Church.

Teachings. The author has much to say about church officials, but he is chiefly concerned with their personal character and with the conscientious performance of their duties. He does not attempt to issue a code of ecclesiastical law. Regarding right belief as the foundation of Christian living, he gives summaries of "sound doctrine" as preached by Paul (I Tim. 3:16; II Tim. 1:8–10, 2:11–14; Tit. 2:11–14, 3:5–7). Along with right belief he also insists on ethical behavior, on courage, loyalty, uprightness, seemly action, honorable discharge of duties. Paul declared that action must arise directly from the impulse of the Spirit (Rom. 14:23), but this author thinks of morality as something by itself. He does not rely, like Paul, simply on the direction of the Spirit, but thinks out rules for Christian living. According to E. F. Scott in *The Moffatt New Testament Commentary* (Harper & Brothers), in the Pastoral Epistles "the precepts of the Gospels, the aspirations of Paul and John, are transposed into a lower key. But it may truly be said of this writer that while he compromises he does not abandon anything that is essential. He insists on the great Christian beliefs; he allows no debasing of the moral standards; he seeks to adapt the Church to existing conditions. . . . Because he has thus made Christianity a working religion for ordinary men, the author of the Pastorals may justly be ranked among the great Christian teachers."

Tiphsah (tĭf′sȧ) ("ford"). (1) Probably Thapsacus, an important crossing of the middle Euphrates, on the W. bank of the river, situated on a great E.-W. trade route. It was at the NE. edge of Solomon's territory (I Kings 4:24). (2) An unidentified town attacked by Menahem, King of Israel (c. 745–738 B.C.) (II Kings 15:16).

Tiras (tī′răs), people said to have descended

from Japheth, 3d son of Noah (Gen. 10:2; I Chron. 1:5). The group and their place of habitation have sometimes been associated with the Aegean islands and coast land, and with Thrace, Tarsus, and Tarshish.

Tirhakah (Taharka in Egyptian king lists), an Ethiopian prince mentioned in II Kings 19:9 (he was not yet "king") and Isa. 37:9, as advancing against Sennacherib* while the Assyrian was threatening the existence of Judah, following his conquest of Philistia (688 B.C.). Tirhakah was defeated at Eltekeh, but became (c. 685 B.C.) the 3d king in the Twenty-fifth Egyptian Dynasty, the Ethiopian period (715–663 B.C.). Against Sennacherib's son, the invading Esar-haddon*, he was at first successful, but three years later (671) he was routed, driven from Memphis*, and never returned. He maintained himself in Upper Egypt until his death in 664, when the Twenty-sixth Dynasty came to power with Psamtik I. Tirhakah appeared in Biblical history at the tense moment in 701 B.C. when Isaiah was battling to maintain faith in God among the people of Jerusalem, hard pressed as they were between the jaws of a nut-cracker—Assyria and Egypt.

Tirzah (tûr′zȧ) (*tirtsāh*, "pleasure"). (1) A daughter of Zelophehad, a man whose five girls inherited territory in Canaan (Num. 26:33, 27:1, 36:1–13)—an unusual instance of women gaining property rights in the O.T. period. (2) A royal Canaanite city on Mt. Ephraim, taken by Joshua (12:24). It was the home of King Jeroboam (I Kings 14:17) after his residence at Shechem (I Kings 12:25), and was made into the capital city of the Northern Kingdom (Israel) by successive rulers including Baasha (c. 900–877 B.C.), Elah (c. 877–876 B.C.), Zimri (seven days in c. 876 B.C.), and Omri (c. 876–869 B.C.)—who took it by siege (I Kings 16:17) and reigned there until he removed to Samaria. King Menahem of Israel (c. 745–738 B.C.) used Tirzah as a base of attack on Shallum (ruler for one month c. 745 B.C.) (II Kings 15:14, 16). In the Song of Solomon the beauty of Tirzah is compared with that of Jerusalem (6:4).

Tirzah was tentatively identified in 1931 by W. F. Albright with Tell el-Far 'ah (N), a large mound 7 m. NE. of Nablus at the head of the Wâdī Fâr 'ah (*JPOS* 11, 1931, pp. 241–251). It controlled the important route through the Wâdī Fâr 'ah from the Jordan Valley to the hill country of Ephraim, where other roads led N. to Beth-shan and S. to Shechem (Y. Aharoni, *The Land of the Bible*, 1967, pp. 31, 53, 56). Excavation of the mound for the École Biblique in Jerusalem by R. de Vaux from 1946–60 has tended to confirm this identification (de Vaux, *AOTS*, 1967, pp. 379–382). The site was first occupied in the Neolithic and Chacolithic periods, but took on an urban character at the beginning of the Early Bronze Age when it developed into a well-planned, fortified town (EB I–II, c. 3100–2600 B.C.). Houses of rectangular plan and straight streets equipped with drains were enclosed by a substantial wall and fortified gateway. A pottery kiln of this period is the oldest yet discovered in Palestine (see *ANEP*², No. 786). The site was abandoned at the end of EB II (c. 2600 B.C.), and remained unoccupied until Middle Bronze IIA (19th cen. B.C.). Toward the end of the 18th century B.C. (MB II), a defensive wall was again erected, enclosing only the W. half of the mound. Other than a gateway with a right-angle approach and the wall—protected on the N. by a stone glacis and on the W. by a packed-earth rampart—little was preserved. The Late Bronze Age was also poorly represented.

More substantial evidence for the initial Iron Age occupation of the tell (Stratum III, 10th cen. B.C.) was provided by well-designed houses erected in orderly fashion along well-defined streets. The houses were of similar plan, with a courtyard—entered from the street—on each side of which were arranged one or more rooms. These houses were violently destroyed, after which new structures appeared in some areas. One large building was begun but never completed, and the site was abandoned for a short time. It has been suggested by de Vaux (see *AOTS*, pp. 380–381) that Omri was responsible for the destruction of Stratum III, at which time the usurper Zimri died in the flames of his palace (c. 885 B.C.; I Kings 16:17 f.); and that the following, intermediate phase represents a reconstruction by Omri, which was left incomplete when he transferred his capital to Samaria (I Kings 16:23 f.).

After a period of abandonment, the mound was again intensively occupied (Stratum II), possibly beginning with the reigns of Joash and Jeroboam II (8th cen.), as de Vaux suggests. A large building was erected near the city gate, possibly a residency or administrative structure. A group of attractive dwellings followed the pattern of the 10th-century examples, but were of much better construction. This quarter was separated by a wall from an area of smaller, less substantial structures. This phase was destroyed by the Assyrians when they besieged Samaria in 732 B.C. (cf. II Kings 17:5). The walls and other structures of Stratum II were demolished and burned. A brief unfortified settlement (Stratum I) followed which was characterized by a ceramic repertoire of Assyrian origin. The site was abandoned c. 600 B.C. and never reoccupied. See preliminary reports in *RB* 54, 1947, pp. 394 ff., 573 ff.; 55, 1948, pp. 544 ff.; 56, 1949, pp. 102 ff.; 58, 1951, pp. 393 ff., 566 ff.; 59, 1952, pp. 551 ff.; 62, 1955, pp. 541 ff.; 64, 1957, pp. 552 ff.; 68, 1961, pp. 393 ff.; 69, 1962, pp. 212 ff.; see also de Vaux, *PEQ*, 1956, pp. 125–140 and *AOTS*, 1967, pp. 371–383.

M. S. M./W. P. A.

Tishbite, a term applied repeatedly in the O.T. to Elijah* (I Kings 17:1, 21:17; II Kings 1:3, 8, 9:36). Nelson Glueck, explorer of lands E. of the Jordan, gives as his reading of I Kings 17:1, "Elijah the Jabeshite, from Jabesh-gilead." The latter town was a few miles W. of Abel-meholah. Glueck's view suggests that the Brook Cherith*, by which Elijah sojourned, may be a small branch of the Jabesh which flows into the Jordan.

Tishri, a month in the Hebrew calendar. See TIME.

tithe, the tenth part of one's income set aside for a specific use. From the earliest times tithes of the year's yields from fields, fruits, and flocks were offered for various objectives, by peoples in lands from Babylonia to Rome. Among the Hebrews during the early Monarchy it was the fixed tax paid by the people to the government (I Sam. 8:15–17). When a conqueror subjected a people he levied as tribute* the tithe of their possessions. But usually the tithe in the Bible implies a religious objective. The submission of Jacob to God was expressed by a tithe (Gen. 28:22). Abraham, in offering one-tenth of his spoils of war to Melchizedek, King of Salem (Gen. 14:20), gave the tithe both a political and a religious significance; and implications of the latter extended into N.T. times (Heb. 7:2, 4–6).

The lack of uniformity in the Bible concerning the tithe law is due to the fact that the general principle of giving was practiced in different ways in different eras, and was subject to regulations which changed under ecclesiastical and political pressures. Even the Genesis passages, though referring to very ancient historical incidents, may give specific details of a later period, when these incidents were cast in their present literary form. Throughout Hebrew history, however, the obligation persists to give not the last and the least, but the first and the best. In the Covenant Code, parts of which date from before 1200 B.C. (edited c. 650 B.C.), offerings are authorized, but tithing is not specified (Ex. 23:16, 19). The Deuteronomic Code (c. 622 B.C.) authorized tithe offerings of the first fruits of the earth (Deut. 26:2–4, 10, 12). The paying of the tithe took on a social aspect. Servants, orphans, widows, propertyless Levites, casual strangers, were invited to the tithing banquet and festival (Deut. 12:17–19, 14:22–29). In the Jerusalem Temple the tithe was designated for the benefit of the priests (Lev. 27:32 f.; Neh. 10:36); the high priest (Num. 18:26–28); and the Levites (Deut. 26:12 f.; Neh. 10:37 f.). In hard times and periods of religious depression, tithing as a financial method of supporting organized religion was difficult (Mal. 3:8, 10).

The Talmudic rabbis solved contradictions in the O.T. concerning the tithe by supposing two separate tithes to be presented every year. The first was to be given to the Levites; the second was to be expended in feasts at Jerusalem, except in the 3d and 6th years of the Sabbatical cycle of seven (Amos 4:4), when it was designated for the poor. According to this rabbinical interpretation the heavy burden caused by the double tithe or one-fifth (Gen. 47:24, 26) of income caused the situation referred to in Mal. 3:8, 10.

In a period of religious revival King Hezekiah (c. 715–687 B.C.) by royal command ordered payment of the tithes, and had chambers built in the Temple precincts to store the offerings (II Chron. 31:4–12). The underground chambers in the present Jerusalem Temple Area known as "Solomon's Stables" suggest how similar cellars may have stored perishable food tithes. The early English law (A.D. 786) authorizing the tithe tax for the Church led to the erection of tithe barns.

In N.T. times tithing was the orthodox procedure among the Pharisees (Luke 18:12). Jesus chided them for their minute exactness in regard to the lesser details of the tithing law, in contrast to their disregard for the inner and more important virtues of justice, mercy, and faith (Matt. 23:23). But he also taught that the tithe, as well as other O.T. institutions of divine origin, was binding on the Jews of his day (Luke 11:42). The doom pronounced on the foolish rich man (Luke 12:13–21) was in part due to his lack of giving (v. 18) as an acknowledgment of God's ownership and man's stewardship. Percentage deductions allowable to the individual in the U.S. tax law for gifts to religious, charitable, educational, scientific organizations, etc., are a modern recognition and acceptance of this ancient practice of proportional giving.

title. See SUPERSCRIPTION.

tittle (a variant spelling of "title"), a dot or other small stroke or mark used in writing or printing, e.g., as a diacritical mark. In Gk. such marks denote accents. In Heb. they were a means of distinguishing one letter from another. Some rabbis (teachers) stressed such marks excessively. "Tittle," along with "jot,"* was used by Jesus to express a very small measure or amount (Matt. 5:18).

Titus, a Greek convert to Christianity and one of Paul's chief associates (II Cor. 8:23). He is not mentioned in Acts; facts about him are found in Galatians and II Corinthians. Whether the Epistles of II Timothy and Titus contain other than general historical statements concerning his character depends on the view held concerning these Pastoral Epistles. (See TIMOTHY, I AND II EPISTLES TO, AND TITUS, EPISTLE TO.)

Titus, whose home was probably in Antioch* or its neighborhood, was born of Gentile parents (Gal. 2:3) and was a convert of Paul (Tit. 1:4). As a delegate from Antioch he accompanied the Apostle to Jerusalem at the time of the council (Acts 15:6) at which Paul argued so effectively against the necessity of circumcision (Gal. 2:3–5). The case of Titus seems to have been a *cause célèbre;* the Judaistic party within the Church wished to have Titus circumcised, but the Apostle and "certain other of them" (Acts 15:2) resisted, and the decision of the Church was in their favor (Acts 15:23–29). Titus is referred to in the Epistle to the Galatians, because he was well-known among these churches as Paul's traveling companion (Gal. 2:1, 3). When trouble broke out in the church at Corinth, Paul replaced Timothy (I Cor. 4:17, 16:10) with Titus, whose labors for peace were effective (II Cor. 7:5 f.). As a result of his services, there sprang up between Titus and the Corinthian church a deep affection (II Cor. 8:16). This relationship Paul utilized when he again sent Titus to finish taking the collection for the saints at Jerusalem (v. 6), and gave him that portion of II Corinthians which is an appeal for Christian giving (chaps. 8, 9).

On the basis of statements in the Epistle of Titus, it would appear that Paul assigned the difficult field of Crete* to his trusted "partner and fellow helper." No reason for Titus' recall from Crete is given, other than Paul's desire to see "mine own son after a common faith" (1:4). Later tradition calls Titus the bishop of Crete, and claims that he also carried on a mission in Dalmatia (in the present Yugoslavia) (II Tim. 4:10).

Titus, Epistle to. See TIMOTHY, I AND II EPISTLES TO, AND TITUS, EPISTLE TO.

Titus, Flavius Sabinius Vespasianus, the son of Vespasian, b. A.D. 40 or 41. He became one of the three Flavian emperors. He grew to be an able soldier, and commanded a legion under his father in the Jewish War which was precipitated by the revolt of A.D. 66–70. Titus directed the siege of Jerusalem which resulted in the fall of the city (Sept. 8, A.D. 70) and the destruction of the Temple—never rebuilt. Titus carried the Temple treasures to Rome; some of these are

444. Arch of Titus, Roman Forum.

pictured in carvings on the Arch of Titus in the *Forum Romanum,* erected after the triumphal festivities accorded Titus and his father. Titus became emperor in A.D. 79. His reign, which lasted until 81, was in the main peaceful. Titus was lenient to the Dalmatians and generous to the Pompeians, to whose ruined city he personally brought relief after the destruction of A.D. 79. Titus had the Colosseum completed in A.D. 80, later the scene of the persecution of many Christians.

Titus Justus. See JUSTUS.

Tob (tŏb), a small, unidentified region occupied by Aramaeans, possibly in the Hauran E. of the Jordan, to which Jephthah* fled and where he lived as an outlaw (Judg. 11:3, 5). Tob sent men to help the Ammonites fight David (II Sam. 10:6 ff.).

Tobiah ("Jehovah is good"), a partly Jewish Ammonite governor who allied himself with Sanballat* the Samaritan in opposing Nehemiah's* work of rebuilding the Jerusalem walls (Neh. 2:10, 4:3, 7, 6:1–19). When Nehemiah found that during his own absence in Babylon (13:6) Tobiah had been given by a priestly relative a room in the Temple area formerly used to store offerings, he tossed out Tobiah's "household stuff," evicted him, cleansed the room, and placed in it vessels, meat offerings, and frankincense (Neh. 13:6–9).

The Tobiads were a family which returned from exile in Babylonia (Ezra 2:60, cf. Neh. 7:62). Dr. W. F. Albright states (*The Archaeology of Palestine,* Penguin Books) that the most revealing monument of the Seleucid period is the family mausoleum of the Tobiads found at 'Araq el-Emir in central Jordan. It carries in deep-cut Aram. characters of the 3d century B.C. the name of a "Tobiah"—evidently a descendant of Nehemiah's enemy, and a man who like his ancestor two centuries earlier was governor of Ammon. Near this tomb is a structure whose details suggest that it belongs to the era when Hyrcanus, the last of the Tobiads, was active on the eve of the Maccabean period. The Tobiads are thought to have been tax collectors. The family lost its prestige after Syria seized Palestine and Antiochus Epiphanes plundered the land.

Tobijah. (1) A Levite dispatched by the pious and prosperous King Jehoshaphat (c. 873–849 B.C.) to teach the people of Judah from the "book of the law of the Lord" (II Chron. 17:8 f.). (2) One of the men who brought back gifts of gold and silver from Babylon to Jerusalem (Zech. 6:10) and was memorialized (v. 14).

Tobit, the Book of. See APOCRYPHA.

Togarmah (tō̆-gär′mȧ), a group said to have descended from Japheth*, son of Noah, through Gomer (Gen. 10:3; I Chron. 1:6). They lived "in the uttermost parts of the north" (A.S.V. Ezek. 38:6)—possibly SW. Armenia, S. of the Black Sea. They traded war horses and mules for luxury wares of Tyre (Ezek. 27:14).

Tola (tō′lȧ) (from a word meaning "worm," the type yielding crimson dye). (1) A descendant of Issachar and founder of the tribal family of Tolaites (Gen. 46:13; Num. 26:23; I Chron. 7:1 f.), related to the clan Puah. (2) A hero in the era of the Judges, the 1st of five unimportant judges, son of Puah of Issachar (Judg. 10:1 f.; cf. Tola, "brother" of Puah, Gen. 46:13).

Tomb of Jesus, the, the burial place of Jesus in the tomb of Joseph* of Arimathaea (John 19:38–42), of which two sites have been pointed out. (1) The site known as "the Garden Tomb," adjacent to "Gordon's Calvary," has no archaeological or historical evidence to support it. When General "Chinese" Gordon, living in Jerusalem in the 19th century, identified what he believed to be

Calvary*—a knoll near Jeremiah's Grotto—the "Garden Tomb" was thought to be the place of Christ's burial, a rock-hewn garden tomb (John 19:41 f.). (2) The other site is beneath the rotunda of the ancient Church of the Holy Sepulcher* inside the present old walled city, reached from the Jaffa Gate by means of stepped David Street and Christian Street. This most historic church of Christendom was begun by Constantine the Great after the Palestinian pilgrimage of his mother Helena in the early 4th century. Confirmation of the Church of the Holy Sepulcher as the location of Christ's Tomb awaits proof that

445. Tower of Crusaders' Church, traditional site of the tomb of Jesus.

this site was *outside* the N. wall of Jerusalem at the time of the Crucifixion. The rock-cut tomb where Christ's body was placed is believed by many to be under the rotunda of the Church. The hillock Calvary is also thought by many to be adjacent to the sepulcher—its site within the same church. The freeing of this most historic church of Christendom from Moslems was one of the purposes of the Crusades. The Chapel of the Holy Sepulcher, 26 ft. long and 17½ ft. wide, is at the center of the 65-ft.-wide rotunda. It is entered by a low doorway from an E. vestibule leading to the Angels' Chapel. The so-called Tomb of Jesus, which covers a rock-cut sepulcher, has been for centuries encased in marble. The eminent Dominican archaeologist Père Vincent claims that a genuine tomb of some unknown person is under the 5-ft. marble "Tomb of Christ." In the Angels' Chapel five Orthodox, five Latin, and four Armenian lamps burn constantly. The ceremony of the Lighting of the Holy Fire each Easter season is celebrated with holy excitement—and with danger. The tottering structure of the Church of the Holy Sepulcher is actually a group of buildings facing a spacious court, long used for processions and worship services. It is overtopped by the minaret of the true Mosque of Omar (A.D. 1216) (not to be confused with the Dome of the Rock). With a fair degree of comity, encouraged by an old Moslem family of key-keepers at the main portal, the altars and 22 chapels in the Church of the Holy Sepulcher are maintained by Latins, Greek Orthodox, Copts, Jacobites, Armenians, and Abyssinians (whose chapel is on the roof of the structure). A plan launched by Franciscans in 1949 called for extensive redesigning of the complex structure, whereby in addition to the religious groups already having altars there opportunity would be given for Lutherans, Anglicans, and others to have a worship space within the Church of the Holy Sepulcher.

For detailed studies of the Church of the Holy Sepulcher see the works of Père Hughes

446. The Entombment, *by Fra Angelico.*

Vincent, archaeologist of the Dominican Biblical School of Jerusalem.

See JERUSALEM ("WALLS").

tombs. See ARCHITECTURE; BURIAL; MARESHAH; NABATAEA; OSSUARIES; SIDON; TADMOR; THUTMOSE; TOMB OF JESUS.

tongue. (1) Mentioned in Scripture in the sense of spoken language (Gen. 10:5, 11:1, 9; Deut. 28:49; Acts 2:8; Rev. 7:9, 10:11, 17:15) or of a specific language, e.g., the Syrian (Ezra 4:7); the Hebrew (Acts 21:40, 22:2, 26:14). (See LANGUAGES; WRITING.) (2) Used also with reference to the act or manner of speaking, as "none moved his tongue against him" (Josh. 10:21). Mention is made of the rash and stammering tongue (Isa. 32:4, 33:19); the dumb tongue (Isa. 35:6; Mark 7:35; Luke 1:64); the tongue of the crafty (Job 15:5); the deceitful tongue (27:4); the backbiting tongue (Ps. 15:3); the tongue of the kindly (Prov. 31:26). People sin with their tongue (Ps. 39:1), or speak praise with it (35:28), or use it in singing (126:2). The N.T. warned specifically against the evil of an uncontrolled and uncharitable tongue (Jas. 1:26, 3:5–18). (3) Animals' tongues enabled them to lap food (Judg. 7:5). The bite of the viper's tongue was fatal (Job 20:16). (4) A wedge-shaped lump of precious metal used for money by Mesopotamians. (5) A conspicuous peninsula, at the E. shore of the Dead Sea, which the Israelites called the vale of Siddim (Gen. 14:3). See TONGUES OF FIRE; TONGUES, SPEAKING WITH.

tongues of fire, a phrase symbolically used in descriptions of Pentecost, when "cloven tongues like as of fire" sat upon believers and "they were all filled with the Holy Ghost, and began to speak with other tongues, as the Spirit gave them utterance" (Acts 2:3 f., 6–18, 10:46). Peter interpreted the phenomenon as the fulfillment of Joel's prophecy (Joel 2:28; Acts 2:16 f.). Speaking with tongues (see next entry) was part of the mystical, ecstatic, and often unintelligible jargon of mystery cults of the Hellenistic world.

tongues, speaking with, inarticulate and unintelligible speech, meaningless sounds, jargon, uttered in times of extreme emotional excitement or religious frenzy, apparently in consequence of the belief that the speaker is literally possessed by a spirit not his own, as the spirit of God; otherwise styled *glossolalia*, "gift of tongues." This well-known phenomenon is conspicuous as a characteristic of early Christianity. A clear and revealing picture of it is found in I Cor. 12–14. Though Paul does not question the reality of the phenomenon (he himself confesses to having the gift in a marked degree) he warns his readers of the danger of immoderate employment of it. Primarily of value to the man himself and to be exercised in private, if it is to be tolerated at all in church services, it must be under the strictest supervision and discipline. Under no circumstance may more than three Christians practice the gift during any one church service, and not at all unless one competent to interpret it be present (I Cor. 14:27 f.). Unbridled use of this gift may well lead to a most unfortunate misunderstanding of the Gospel (R.S.V. v. 23): "If, therefore, the whole church assembles and all speak in tongues, and outsiders or unbelievers enter, will they not say that you are mad?" It is far preferable to speak five intelligible words than 10,000 words in this ecstatic and meaningless babble (v. 19). Though he does not question the belief that this phenomenon is directly connected with the spirit of God—in fact, he regularly styles it one of the "gifts of the spirit"—he clearly regards it as subordinate to the "fruits of the spirit," that is, those qualities of life (virtues) which will be of aid and value to others.

In the account of the reception of the spirit by the early Christians at Pentecost the same phenomenon is to be seen, although our account has been drastically rewritten. That underlying the present account is the picture of a period of emotional excitement characterized by frenzy and uncontrolled speech in the form of unintelligible gibberish is clear from the gibe of some of the spectators: "These men are full of new wine" (Acts 2:13), a remark quite unexplainable on the basis of the present form of the story but perfectly clear in the light of Paul's description of the phenomenon.

In the story of Pentecost as it now stands in Acts 2 the author interprets "speaking with tongues" as a linguistic miracle, in which folk, each using a different language, hear Peter speaking in their native speech. Opinions differ as to the cause of this transformation of the earlier narrative. To some it is an evidence that the author of Acts was unfamiliar with the ecstatic phenomenon and consequently misunderstood his source. By others it is regarded as a deliberate rewriting of an older narrative to provide a foretaste of the coming success of the Gentile mission and the future triumph when once again all men will speak the same language, as was the case before sin led to the creation of different—that is, foreign—languages ("confusion of speech") at Babel. In support of this view it is customary to cite "And ye shall be for a people of the Lord *and one tongue*, and there shall not be a spirit of deceit of Belial" (*Testaments of the XII Patriarchs, Judah* 25:3). In addition it is to be observed that in Jewish thinking Pentecost was regarded as the anniversary of the giving of the law on Sinai to all peoples. "Although the ten commandments were promulgated with a single sound, it says 'All people heard the *voices*'; it follows then that when the voice went forth it was divided into seven voices and then went into seventy tongues, and every people received the law in their own language" (*Midrash Tanḥuma* 26c).

Other references to the occurrence of *glossolalia* are found in Acts 10:46, 19:6, and probably in the late ending of Mark (Mark 16:17). That this phenomenon is by no means restricted to early Christianity is universally recognized. It was common in the Christian movement as late as Tertullian and Irenaeus. By the time of Chrysostom it had apparently died out; at least the good bishop found difficulty in understanding what it really was. This, however, was but temporary. In later years it appeared again, and has been the seemingly inevitable consequence of all extended seasons of "revival." Conspicuous examples of it are to be seen among the Jansenists, the Camisards of the Cévennes, the Irvingites, and during early American revivals of the frontier days. It may still be seen at meetings of the Pentecostals, Holy Rollers, and other highly emotional groups.

tools used in O.T. Palestine were the same as those used by most peoples in their early phases of settled farm and village life (see specific trades and crafts). Numerous specimens of prehistoric and later tools have been found in the Middle East. (1) Sharp, flaked flints (see FLINT) were valuable for knives; disc-shaped scrapers; sharp-edged, narrow hoes; and the semicircular "reaping hooks" with serrated flint teeth set in plaster, excavated at Gerar*. Flints were also mounted for use as small saws. Tiny flints known as "microliths" or miniature blades, whose use is still a mystery, were left by the first occupants of Jericho millenniums ago. The Iraq Department of Antiquities has excavated at Hassuna, N. of Ur, a perfectly preserved flint sickle used c. 8,000 years ago, at the dawn of farming activities in the Middle East; its edge of matched pieces of flint

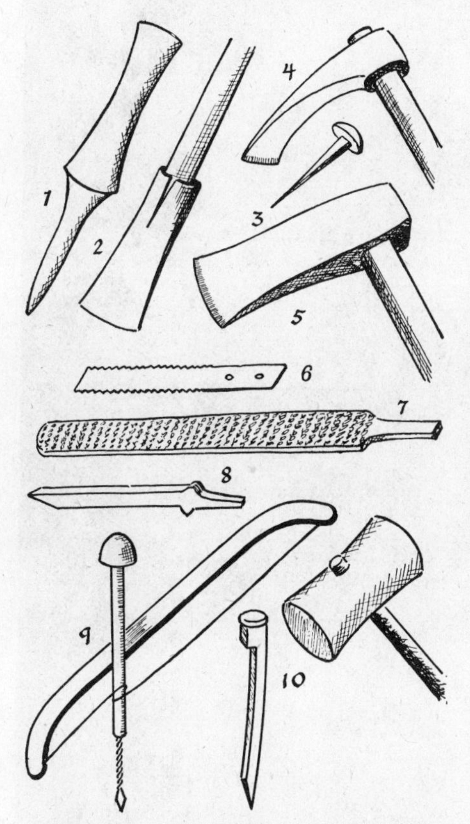

447. Tools: Palestinian, 1. Awl; 2. Chisel; 3. Nail; 4, 5. Iron adze and bronze ax blades from Gezer (800–100 B.C.); Assyrian iron tools: 6. Double-edged saw; 7. Rasp; 8. Small chisel; 9. Ancient Egyptian drill; 10. Tent-nail and mallet.

glued together with bitumen (pitch) could still cut corn easily. Flint continued to be used for sickles and strike-a-lights in Palestine even after metal became plentiful (after c. 1000 B.C.). (2) Bronze tools known from excavated specimens to have been used in early Palestine were axes, knives, chisels, and saws. (3) Iron tools, like knives, chisels, pruning-hooks, and saws, and combinations of ax and adze with a hole in the middle for the handle, are known to have been used by Israel's workmen. (4) Stone was used for hammers (metal ones being rare until the Monarchy); for cone-shaped pestles and their bowl-shaped stones used in grinding meal, prior to and concurrent with millstones of the saddle-shaped quern type; and for rotary millstones.

(For types of presses, see OLIVE and VINE.)

Nelson Glueck, exploring the Jordan Valley, found evidence of the use of heavy stone hammers and wooden wedges for quarrying great limestone slabs, some as much as 7 ft. long, 5 ft. wide, and 2 ft. thick, erected for dolmens (tombs) like those still standing near the Biblical Adamah (see ADAM).

Topheth (tō′fĕth), a high place in the Valley of Hinnom* at Jerusalem, where in the lifetime of Isaiah and Jeremiah people sacrificed their children by burning them in idolatrous rites sacred to Molech* (Jer. 7:31 f.; II Kings 23:10). This primitive custom was given royal support by King Manasseh* (c. 687–642 B.C.). The pyre of wood and brimstone (Isa. 30:33) was built up from a large hole in the ground. The reformer-king Josiah (c. 640–609 B.C.) abolished this heathen rite but it was revived later. Jeremiah predicted that the Hinnom Valley would be known as the Valley of Slaughter (Jer. 7:31 f., 19:6, 11–15).

Torah (from Heb. root *yarah*, "to cast," as a lot for oracular guidance), "instruction," "law," applied to (1) the five "Books of Moses," (see HEXATEUCH); (2) the entire O.T.; (3) the whole body of religious literature of Judaism, derived through priests, prophets, and sages. The written Torah, regarded by the Sadducees as a completed book, was supplemented, in the view of Pharisees and rabbinic Judaism, by oral matter; these groups believed in a dual Torah, one written and one oral. The latter contained guidance in the specific application of the general principles of the written Torah. The Torah is regarded by devout Jews as fundamental in the life of Israel. (See LAW.)

The reading of the Torah (i.e., the Pentateuch) according to a cycle, arranged so that its contents can be covered within a year, is one of the characteristics of Jewish worship, in Orthodox and Conservative and in some Reformed congregations (see SYNAGOGUE). Christianity and Islam both followed the Jewish practice of reading sacred literature in the regular worship services.

Velvet mantles, often brocaded and ornamented, are thrown over the scrolls before they are placed in the ark of the synagogue. (Among Oriental Jews Torah scrolls are usually protected by a metal case, *tik*, often carved or jeweled.) Apertures are left in the top of the mantle through which the rollers of the Torah scrolls are inserted, though the Dead Sea Scrolls* had no rollers when found in the 'Ain Fashka cave in **1947**.

See illus. 448, p. 770.

Tou (tō′o͞o), a king of Hamath on the Syrian river Orontes, who by sending his son Hadoram with congratulatory messages and gifts to David after David's victory over Hadadezer (Hadarezer) (I Chron. 18:9 f.; cf. II Sam. 8:9 ff.), brought himself under the authority of the Hebrew.

tow (tō), the short fibers of flax or hemp (Judg. 16:9; Isa. 1:31).

towers. (1) Elevated structures of mud, brick, or stone erected to provide places where watchmen could distinguish between approaching enemies and friends (II Chron. 14:7; Isa. 21:12); and where populations could take refuge from invaders, as the people of Thebez* did in Abimelech's time (Judg. 9:51 f.). Towers were integral parts of the walled city (II Kings 17:9; II Chron. 14:7, 26:9); they were also remote outposts to protect the approach (II Kings 17:9; II Chron. 20:24). (See Saul's stronghold tower at Gibeah, built before c. 1000 B.C. at Gaza, II Kings 18:8. For "David's Tower" see JERUSALEM.) Canaanite fortresses had massive fort towers, vestiges of which have been excavated from the c. 1300 B.C. level at Beth-shan*. Similar towers existed also at Lachish and Megiddo. (For the towers of Jerusalem's historic walls, see JERUSALEM.) Numerous towers, whose sites have not yet been found, are mentioned in the Bible: the tower of Jezreel (II Kings 9:17); and the towers of Tyre and Syene (Ezek. 26:4, 29:10). David and his sentry watched from a high place for news of the end of Absalom's revolt (II Sam. 18:24–33). (For the story of the fall of the Tower of Siloam, Luke 13:4, see SILOAM.)

448. Torah (Scroll of the Law), showing Lev. 10:17-13:7.

A tremendous Hellenistic tower occupied most of the mound of N.T. Jericho* (Tulûl Abu el-'Alâyiq) when it was opened in 1950. This oldest building on the site where the Wâdī Qelt enters the Jericho Plain was unique, in that it was square, with a circular interior; the tower was c. 20 meters square, with an interior c. 15 meters in diameter. The wall measured c. 2.20 meters at its thinnest point. Nowhere else in Palestine has such military construction been excavated. The circular interior of the tower had nine rooms. The masonry showed large, crudely cut stones alternating with courses of wâdī boulders. In the age of Herod the Great this tower had been leveled off to form a substructure for the elaborate hillside civic center of Herod the Great and his son Archelaus. (See *BASOR* No. 120, Dec. 1950, pp. 11 ff.) In the Mesopotamian Tepe Gawra, in one of the oldest groups of social structures yet excavated, a unique tower refuge has been found standing to a considerable height, built as a place of safety probably between 4000 and 3000 B.C.

(2) Towers in the form of zoned, stepped platforms were characteristic of Babylonian temples (see BABEL, TOWER OF; ZIGGURAT). Egyptian pylons were often towers near the approach to temples.

(3) Farmers built leafy watchtowers from which they could guard vines and crops. Jesus referred to this in his parable of the husbandman who prepared a winepress and guarded it with a tower (Matt. 21:33). Such watchtowers are still seen in S. Palestine and the highlands of old Samaria, especially during harvest season.

town clerk (Gk. *grammateus*), a responsible official in Graeco-Roman cities of the 1st century, as at Ephesus (Acts 19:35). His many duties included responsibility for law and order. Popular demonstrations or illegal assemblies which might tend toward disorder were feared by the town clerk. Several inscriptions mention the *grammateus*.

towns were distinguished from cities in that they were usually without walls, moats, or ramparts. Their area was very limited. Cities which figure prominently in Scripture, like Jericho, Megiddo (12 or 13 acres), Beth-shan, Lachish (15 acres), and Samaria, were small in area compared to modern cities; Khirbet Kerak in Galilee, with its 60 acres, was exceptional. Jerusalem within its strong walls was "compactly builded together" for easier defense, in an area about the size of New York's Central Park. Canaanite towns captured by Israel were repaired and reoccupied, but on a smaller scale. The large, two-story court type of house once used by a single family became multiple dwellings of several Hebrew agricultural families living under a somewhat patriarchal head—as in some Arab towns of Palestine today. Outlying town sections became grazing lands and grain storage areas. After the Conquest new Israelite towns used the newly adopted water-supply system of cisterns, which made towns independent of outside wells and springs.

Towns—though sometimes walled (I Sam. 23:7)—were usually farm or market centers, often near large threshing floors, like the towns of Galilee—Cana, Nain, etc. (see Mark 6:6, 56; Acts 8:25). Even the busy lake port of Capernaum was less of a city than a commercial town. Typical highland towns of Judaea were Bethany, "the town of Mary and her sister Martha" (John 11:1), and Bethphage (Luke 19:29 f.). Persia, too, had her unwalled towns and villages (Esther 9:19). Towns beyond the cities supplied them with food and merchandise, as towns and villages near the old walled city of Jerusalem in modern times furnish vegetables and commodities to the bazaars. We read of "Beth-shan and her towns" (Josh. 17:11); "Shechem and her towns" (I Chron. 7:28); "Gaza and her towns" (I Chron. 7:28); "Gath and her towns" (18:1). The first two kings of Judah, Saul and David, both came from towns, not cities. John the Baptist came from a hilltop town of Judaea.

Villages were even smaller and weaker than towns—often mere groups of crude houses or huts clustering together for protection. Shepherds lived in villages, as now in Beit Sahûr below Bethlehem.

Trachonitis (trăk′ō-nī′tĭs) an area of c. 370 sq. m. between the Anti-Lebanons and the highlands of Batanaea. It consists of lava deposits from prehistoric volcanic action; S. of Damascus, N. of Hauran, E. of Bashan, and N. of Galilee. It was governed by the tetrarch Herod* Philip (Luke 3:1) and later by his nephew Herod Agrippa I, who was crowned king by the Roman emperor Caligula. The region included Bethsaida Julias and Caesarea Philippi.

trade and transportation developed together. Nomadic Hebrews had little to trade except surplus animals and their products; grazing routes and migration trails were their primary communications need. Even now nomads visit markets only when seeking essential commodities. Then they go to their nearest center of small *sûks*, such as Bethlehem, Gaza, Amman, or Homs. As agricultural and village communities developed, and stocks of simple pottery, tools, textiles, dyes, metal or leather articles, grains, wines, oil, etc., accumulated to be sold and bought, markets sprang up. To reach these markets, roads broadened out from the time-worn footpaths and sheep walks.

(1) *Markets* and *merchants* developed as roads and wares increased. Commercial stands grew up near shrines, where gifts for deity and articles for family consumption were available. Worship centers like Jerusalem (Neh. 13:20), Damascus, Samaria, and Jerash were also trading centers. Early Israel was not a merchant people, as the Phoenicians, Aramaeans, and Canaanites were (A.S.V. margin Prov. 31:24). Yet during the reign of Solomon* in the 10th century B.C., the Hebrews enriched themselves by transshipping merchandise—chariots and horses e.g.—between Egypt and Asia Minor, and acting as middlemen. A trade agreement between Solomon and Hiram of Tyre gave the latter rights in Israel's port of Ezion-geber* in return for sailors, ships, and luxury wares (I Kings 9, 10).

Markets were lively, noisy places (Matt. 11:16 f.), where news circulated, constituencies were built up (Mark 12:38), laborers hired (Matt. 20:3 ff.), and disorders quelled (Acts 16:19 ff.) (see AGORA; STOA). Peddlers, hawkers, and merchants became familiar figures in Near Eastern life (Gen. 37:28; Prov. 31:24; Neh. 3:32, 13:20; Matt. 13:45). They accumulated and distributed money (Gen. 23:16). Cities like Tyre* (Ezek. 27:1–36) and Damascus (27:18) were centers for large-scale merchants whose emporiums were scattered throughout the Mediterranean world. After the Exile in Babylonia the Jews engaged in trade and finance, for they had learned the secrets of Babylonian trade and banking. By N.T. times influential guilds had developed, such as the cloth guild of Thyatira*, to which Lydia may have belonged (cf. I Chron. 4:21; Neh. 3:8).

(2) *Methods of Conveyance.* (a) Before the 4th millennium B.C. wheeled vehicles arrived at the Mediterranean coast from the Indus region. At Tepe Gawra, level VIII, a model of a four-wheeled covered wagon came to light which may mark the first appearance of a wheeled conveyance. Excavations at Ur have revealed the four-wheeled carts used by Queen Shubad's court several centuries before Abraham. In Gen. 45 there are references to wagons which Pharaoh instructed Joseph to send N. for his father Jacob and his family. (b) In rugged mountain terrain, as in Crete, the palanquin became the favorite vehicle of the Minoan sea kings when visiting their ports. In Egypt also palanquins were popular for royalty—used by Queen Hetep-heres, mother of Khufu, builder of the Great Pyramid (30th century B.C.). The gold casing of her disintegrated wooden carrying-chair was found by George Reisner's Harvard-Boston University Expedition near the pyramid, and is now restored in the Egyptian Museum; a replica is in the Boston Museum of Fine Arts. (c) Peasants in Egypt carried burdens on heads or in hands. The backs of porters were a common conveyance for unbelievably heavy burdens; hamals even now bend almost double under loads of fresh summer grapes shipped from Hebron to the Jerusalem markets. Christ knew this type of burdenbearer (Matt. 11:28). (d) Horses were introduced into Egypt by the Hyksos, and by the Eighteenth Dynasty were common. Among the Hebrews of Palestine they became popular in the reign of Solomon, horse fancier and trader. The "new cart" mentioned in II Sam. 6:3 as transporting the Ark was probably drawn by asses. The horses of Persian warriors came from the rough, cold mountains south of the Caucasus and the horse-breeding "land of the Mitanni." For their prisoners and war material the Assyrians used baggage wagons. Camel transport did not develop until possibly 1100 or 722 B.C.

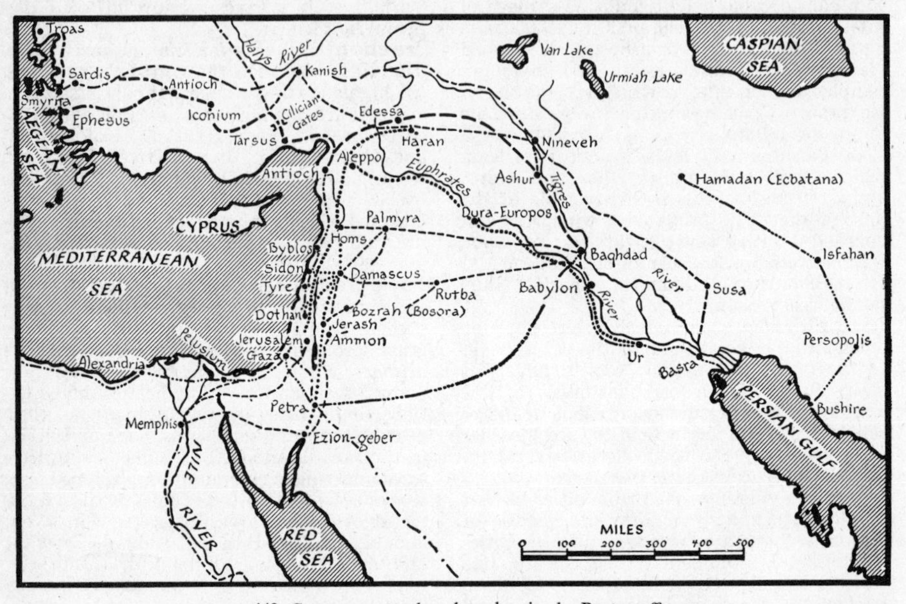

449. Caravan routes, based on drawing by Rostovzeff.

450. Camel caravan crossing plain below the Horns of Hattîn.

(3) *Roads.* Much of the Bible was written by, about, and for road-minded people. These were "in journeyings often" (II Cor. 11:26), like Abraham trekking from Ur to Haran and Canaan; Joseph carried to Egypt by Midianite camel traders; Israel making the Exodus from Egypt; the Apostles, risking perils of land and sea to promote the Gospel. The O.T. and the N.T. contain hundreds of allusions to roads and ways. Prophets gave practical hints for road improvement (Isa. 40:3 f.; cf. John 1:23). Malachi, familiar with messengers sent out ahead of their lords to clear roads of highway thugs, furnished the author of Matt. 11:10 with terms to express the relation of John the Baptist to Jesus (cf. Heb. 6:20). The road robbers of Luke 10:30 and those implied in Judg. 5:6 are types which still persist. Jesus called himself the "way, the truth, and the life" (John 14:6). His followers were known as people of "the Way" (cf. Acts 19:23).

Because Palestine has no navigable rivers, and because during most of her history her people have not been sea-minded, traders took to land routes for business. Roads lead-

TRADE AND TRANSPORTATION

ing to many countries crossed Palestinian plains, like Esdraelon, Sharon, Gennesaret. These roads were controlled by her mountain-walled passes, as at Megiddo. Numerous Biblical narratives mention the great caravan trails of the Middle East, which still exist. (a) When Abraham and his clans moved north from Ur in lower Babylonia to Canaan, they probably grazed NW. along the Euphrates—river valleys made easier going for their animals—to Haran, at the arch of the Fertile Crescent. They grazed ultimately to Syrian Hamath, south to Shechem, Bethel, and finally to their nomadic headquarters at Hebron S. of Bethlehem. Some of the Abraham tribes ranged near Damascus and E. of the Jordan. (b) Often in Old Testament narratives we read such sentences as: "And there was a famine in the land: and Abram went down into Egypt to sojourn there; for the famine was sore" (A.S.V. Gen. 12:10) Again, "all countries came into Egypt to Joseph to buy grain, because the famine was sore in all the earth" (Gen. 41:57). And Jacob said unto his sons, "I have heard that there is grain in Egypt: get you down thither, and buy for us" (Gen. 42:1 f.). The route from Palestine lay along the coast to the Egyptian frontier. (For the return route of Israel and their allies, see EXODUS.) (c) The deportation route to Babylon was perhaps via the E.-W. caravan routes across the Syrian "saddle," or by way of the Fertile Crescent. One course runs E. from Homs to Palmyra; SE. to the present Baghdad; then S. to Babylon. Another caravan route, now a motor bus run around the Syrian desert saddle, goes S. of the above trail, from Damascus to Rutba, joining the Homs route at the Euphrates. A third route ran—and still runs—SE. from Aleppo along the Euphrates. Still other roads near Jerash and Amman in Trans-Jordan join trails at Rutba for Baghdad. Over these same desert stretches—from India, Persia, Palestine, Syria, Egypt, Greece, and the W.—there are now many airline routes. Exiles must have gone afoot. Nehemiah represents the craftsmen, servants, singers, and businessmen on their return from the Exile as bringing 736 horses, 245 mules, 435 camels, and 6,720 asses (Neh. 7:66–69).

The *Great West Road* or *Way of the Sea* (or *Way to the Sea*) had various branches. One fork came down from Damascus, along Mount Hermon, crossed the Jordan between Merom and Galilee near the present Bridge of the Daughters of Jacob, and went on to Dothan. One branch turned W. to Safed, went down the valley between upper and lower Galilee, and on to Accho (the present Acre, just N. of Haifa). Another branch went S. to Capernaum and the Plain of Gennesaret, joining the W. branch at Ramah. Still another left Capernaum for Arbela (? Irbid), wound between Mt. Tabor and the hills of Nazareth to the Plain of Esdraelon; crossed to Megiddo, then followed the Mediterranean down the Plain of Sharon, into the Philistine Plain, and so to Egypt. A 5th branch of the Way of the Sea ran from Capernaum to Tiberias on Galilee, thence to Beth-shan and the Plain of Esdraelon.

A *N.-S. trade route* ran N. from Mt. Carmel up the coast to Antioch. This way, used by Paul and his companions, is now a motor highway running from Palestine to Lebanon, and into Asiatic Turkey. The "Face of God" promontory is one of the conspicuous features of its narrow roadbed, near Byblos (see GEBAL). Caravans used brooks and soft plains along rivers like the Nile, the Orontes, and some courses of the Jordan; they avoided regions known to be robber-infested.

The N.-S. caravan routes linked Asia Minor, Syria, Palestine, and Egypt with the spice routes from Arabia. (1) Gen. 37:25 is explicit about the itinerary of the Ishmaelites who bought Joseph: "a company of Ishmaelites came from Gilead with their camels bearing spicery [gum tragacanth] and balm [mastic] and myrrh [laudanum], going to carry it down to Egypt." (2) The road over which the Queen of Sheba travelled from her realm in SW. Arabia tallies with what W. F. Albright calls the Sabaean continuation of Arabian camel trade, which in Solomon's time competed with the former Red Sea commerce. Her presents of gold, spices, and

451. Fork of Roman roads to Samaria and Caesarea, c. 4 m. N. of Jerusalem.

precious stones (I Kings 10:10) were products of her rich caravan kingdom; hers was "a very great train" that tinkled into Solomon's magnificent new capital, Jerusalem. Jars like those which contained her spice gifts have been excavated in E. Palestine by Nelson Glueck; they carry S. Arabian inscriptions. (3) The Wise Men from the East, mentioned by Matthew (2:1–12) as seeking the newborn Christ, may have come from star-worshipping Chaldaea, to which their gifts had been brought from India, or Arabia. Possibly they were wealthy Arabian frankincense traders. At any rate, they were familiar with more than one road, for, warned not to return home by way of Jerusalem because of Herod, they "departed into their own country another way" (Matt. 2:12). Caravans of spice and of myrrh in O.T. times went from the Persian Gulf across Arabia to Nabataean Petra, thence to Gaza, and up the Mediterranean or along the east shore of the Dead Sea and the Jordan to Damascus. In addition to the N.-S. trade route across the Jordan, one used in the Early Bronze Age turned W. at Feinan, for Sinai. Even central Africa sent out rich wares by caravan to Egypt and Syria.

TRADE AND TRANSPORTATION

In Trans-Jordan Roman roads survive that are parts of the ancient N.-S. route from the border of Syria to the Gulf of Aqabah; Trajan rebuilt highways for his prosperous Nabataean subjects in the 2d century A.D. that are strategic today in the Hashemite Kingdom of Jordan. Engineers often turn up Roman milestones in this area. Some Jordan roads were perhaps used by the messengers of Moses to the king of the Amorites, to beg that the wandering Israelite nomads be allowed to use peaceably the essential links in the royal highroads (Num. 27:21–23).

The growth of caravan trade after the 11th century B.C. led to the building of fabulously rich, architecturally embellished *caravan cities*. Palmyra, one of the younger cities (II Chron. 8:4 Tadmor* "in the wilderness"), was enlarged for Solomon's trade in Cilician horses and other items gathered at the hump of the Syrian saddle. Through it the wealth of the Tigris-Euphrates valley flowed into

452. Roman road at Ostia.

Syria and Palestine. In centuries when its rival, Petra, was weak, Palmyra was the one link between Yemen, central Arabia, SW. Palestine, and Syria. Several major caravan routes intersected at Palmyra, one coming from Aleppo diagonally across to the Euphrates. (Palmyra has yielded no excavated material thus far which can be dated earlier than the 9th century B.C.) Far older than Palmyra was Petra, most wonderful of the caravan cities. It was situated off the actual caravan routes, but sat snugly at the end of its narrow gorge (see NABATAEA). Jerash (see GERASA), one of the Greek cities which spread out fanlike from Beth-shan, was not built as a caravan city, but was nevertheless one of the most prosperous trade centers in the centuries just before Christ and during the early Christian period. In its columned oval forum, parts of which survive, caravan wealth was distributed. Other caravan cities included Damascus, whose caravanserais are today still picturesque, if odorous; Amman in Trans-Jordan; Tyre and Sidon on the Phoenician coast; Baghdad; and Dura-Europos. The busy trading street in the Syrian Homs (Emessa) gives the atmosphere of this ancient caravan center, whose road leading to Hamath and Aleppo is one of the oldest in the world.

The Tell-el-Amarna Letters, written c. 1400 B.C. by petty Egyptian vassals, are replete with accounts of caravans and lists of articles sent by kings of Egypt to rulers of Babylon. O.T. writers were aware of the habits of caravans. Isaiah referred to troops of camels and asses (21:7); and to caravans of Dedanites from NW. Arabia, lodging in forests (21:13). Job—who may have been a man of Edom, land of pack trains—spoke of the waylaying of caravans passing through hostile country; he suggests that "companies of Sheba," in Arabia, "waited for them" (6:19). I Kings 10:28 refers to Solomon's imports of horses and chariots from Egypt for export through traders to other kings.

Military roads were built by early Near Eastern strategists, like the Great West Road constructed by Hittites* (c. the 14th century B.C.). This way followed an early trade route, with an exit probably at Smyrna, a branch to Ephesus on the Aegean, and the main arm running down the Meander valley, as indicated by Hittite monuments along the way. A natural terminus of the Hittite military road was Miletus, overlooking the Aegean islands. Paul, with his preference for low roads, may have used some of the Hittite routes along the rivers of Pisidia flowing toward the Mediterranean. Caravans from Babylonia and Assyria brought cultural influences to the barbarian Hittites, who by the 12th century B.C. had become one of the great powers of W. Asia. The Turks—who claim descent from the Hittites—are doing much to improve roads all over the archaeologically rich "hunting ground" once controlled by these ancient people; they have made passable Alexander the Great's route through the Cilician Gates over the Taurus Mountains.

Another example of military highways is the Highway of the Conquerors at Dog River, Syria, known as the Nahr el-Kelb; the road runs through a steep gorge. This timeless road carried the armies of Phoenicia, Egypt, Persia, Babylonia, Greece, Rome, and nations of modern Europe, who have left, cut in the rock, records of their triumphs.

(4) *Sacred ways* led to the famous worship centers of the Middle East. In Egypt they usually led to great temples. Alabaster sphinxes lined the approach to the Temple of Ptah at Memphis. A mile-long causeway connected the great temple at Luxor with the vast Temple of Amun at Karnak. A ram-flanked road led from the Temple of the goddess Mut to the gate of the mighty Temple of Amun. A famous sacred street led from the complex of shrines at Karnak to a quay on the Nile. In Akhenaton's new City of the Horizon of Aton (Akhetaton), at Amarna, a sacred way connected the palace of the king with residences of courtiers and with the Temple of Aton. At Heliopolis there was a sumptuous approach and obelisk-trimmed court.

Babylon, too, had its sacred way, where Hebrew captives saw celebrants bearing images of Marduk—as Greeks carried a likeness of Athena to their Parthenon. This holy thoroughfare, called Procession Street, passed temples, palaces, and hanging gardens on its way out through the Ishtar Gate.

 TRADE AND TRANSPORTATION

The sacred road to Eleusis ran 12 m. W. from Athens. When the season came for the celebration of the Greek mysteries at Eleusis the procession went out through the Dipylon Gate of the capital, along the way lined with tombs of famous citizens, and topped the pass over Mount Aegaleos. The celebrants halted at a temple of Apollo (succeeded in Byzantine times by the monastery Church of Daphni, with its story-telling Biblical mosaics). After resting at the salt springs the procession came into the squalid village of Eleusis, birthplace of the great Greek dramatist Aeschylus. When it reached the hall of the mysteries, or telesterion, the participants joined in rites honoring Persephone, daughter of Zeus and Demeter, who had been carried off to the underworld by Pluto. Paul—if he walked to Corinth from Athens instead of taking a boat across the Saronic Gulf—must have passed through Eleusis (cf. I Cor. 15).

453. The Bazaar in the Old City of Jerusalem.

In Athens, the sacred route of pan-Athenaic processions terminated at the Acropolis. The famous Dromos, or "broad way," leading to this high place of temples, was discovered in the region of the *kerameikós* by the American School of Classical Studies. This stretch, paved with large blocks in the Roman period, extended from the Dipylon Gate past the Altar of the Twelve Gods in the agora, which

TRADE AND TRANSPORTATION

served as a milestone for measuring distances from this heart of the Hellenic world. Near the Dromos excavators found a boundary stone indicating the sacred way to the Temple of Apollo at Delphi, used by processions from the 4th century B.C.

Rome had her Via Sacra running through the Forum Romanum from the Arch of Titus through the maze of temples to Castor and Pollux, Vesta Faustina, and Julius Caesar, on past the great rostrum, past the Basilica Julia and the Temple of Saturn, then up to the Capitoline Hill, passing on its way the circular construction known as the *Umbilicus Urbis Romae*, center of the capital. The Apostle Paul was familiar with the Roman Via Sacra; it was only a few feet from the Mamertine prison, traditionally associated with Paul.

454. "Street which is called Straight," Damascus.

Cumae had its sacred way to an acropolis above the Tyrrhenian Sea 12 miles W. of Naples. This portion of the Domitian Way still shows its polygonal stone paving, and makes a picturesque approach to the tunnel of the Cumaean sibyl, the Temple of Apollo, vestiges of early Christian churches, and their baptistries. When Paul was at Puteoli, where he landed for Rome, he was just below the sacred way of Cumae, the town which was given credit for founding Puteoli.

The holiest sacred way in Bible lands to Christians is Jerusalem's Via* Dolorosa, whose 1st-century level is now buried under 30 ft. of debris. It went from Pilate's judgment hall or praetorium up to Calvary, which many believe to be under the present Church of the Holy Sepulcher. Each Friday afternoon a procession of scholars, clergy, soldiers, and civilians retraces the "stations of the cross" (see TRIAL OF JESUS).

"Streets of sepulchers" were built just outside the gates of Roman cities in Paul's time. Paul must have seen the one in Athens, near the Dipylon Gate in the Potters' Section, with its gems of Greek funerary art (many still extant). He must have noticed on the last stretches of the Appian* Way as he came into Rome the varied mausolea and tombs of eminent Romans. In Ostia, port of Rome, which had been improved just before Paul came to Italy, a *Via dei Sepolcri* ran parallel to the Ostia Road from Rome. Amedeo Maiuri reported of the noted Street of the Sepulchers in 1st-century *Pompeii*, near the Street of Consolation, "400 metres of the road have been laid bare, flanked by villas and monumental tombs for private and public use." Located just outside the Herculaneum Gate, this street shows mausolea surrounded by statues, exedra with stone seats, plain niches, garden tombs, and almost every variety of sepulcher known in that century. In Jerusalem, outside the Golden Gate and Stephen's Gate, along both walls of the Kidron Valley through which runs the Jericho road, there are myriads of graves—Jewish ones on the E. and Moslem ones on the W. of this valley of sepulchers.

(5) *Traits of 1st-Century Roman Roads.* Both Jesus and Paul enjoyed the convenience of the best highways civilians and traders had ever known. Built primarily to maintain the *Pax Romana* and to guarantee prompt delivery of Roman post dispatches, these thoroughfares were worth while to taxpayers. Roman roads almost always took the straight-

TRADE AND TRANSPORTATION

est line between two important objectives. One of the finest examples of the engineering directness of a Roman street to be seen today is the *Decumanus Maximus* at Ostia. Another example of the straight Roman "Main Street" such as Paul used is the *Strada di Nola* of Pompeii, running directly across the center of the town, which was flourishing in the Apostle's time. In Graeco-Roman Jerash the long *Decumanus Maximus* intersects the Cardo, or Street of a Thousand Columns. In the Asiatic Greek cities the old streets still twisted then as they had in early centuries.

Roman highways were well drained and were curbed, often with travertine. They had wells at convenient intervals. They were kept in good repair, under the supervision of reliable "curators of roads," who were willing to spend the equivalent of $4,500 per Roman mile—430 ft. shorter than our mile—for durable construction. On a rubble foundation flat stones were laid in lime, and covered with a layer of rubble; the top paving was of polygonal blocks of silex or basaltic lava neatly fitted into concrete, intersticed with basaltic stone. In some instances roads were paved with blocks of stone instead of polygonal units. Roman streets were made comfortable for pedestrians by narrow, elevated footpaths, which, together with stepping-stones at street corners, kept people's feet out of the water that collected in chariot ruts. Mileage from Rome was indicated on milestones. The milestone from which roads running out from the Empire's capital were measured was called the "Golden Milestone," or *Miliarium Aureum*, in the Forum Romanum. An example of a Palestinian Roman milestone is at the entrance of the monastery at Abū Ghôsh (one of the Emmaus sites, Luke 24:13); two others stand on Rome's Capitoline Hill.

First-century roads were used by Jesus. He seems to have avoided Roman highways whenever possible, even as he sometimes avoided Samaria, and used the heavily shaded walk down along the Jordan to Jerusalem. He doubtless enjoyed the informal ancient foot trails through grainfields gay with spring flowers. During his youth at Nazareth he lived at the crossroads of caravan routes and Roman military ways.

One road came into Nazareth from the Mediterranean N. of the present Haifa, skirted the N. edge of the great Plain of Esdraelon, passed through Harosheth of the Gentiles and Sepphoris, and came S. from Japhia into Nazareth. Another ran along the S. part of Esdraelon, below Megiddo, converging with the road from Jerusalem across the plain, and entered Nazareth by a steep N. climb past the traditional Hill of Precipitation.

Leaving Nazareth in a NE. direction, a road dropped down to the Sea of Galilee, by way of Cana, where Jesus had many friends. This is a sacred little highway because it passes the Horns of Hattîn, a saddle-shaped hillock where Jesus may often have taught his Disciples (Matt. 5, 6, 7), which now runs between well-tended gardens, from which opens one of the most impressive vistas to the lake. Once he had reached the blue-green misty sea, Jesus took winding, tree-shaded footpaths as he walked from one seaside village to the next—Magdala, Tabgha (Bethsaida), Capernaum, etc. Boats, sailed or rowed across the lake, put him in touch with the roads of eastern Palestine. From Sepphoris, NW. of Nazareth, he could get the road to the Phoenician coast towns near Tyre, Sidon, and Zarephath—which, however, he seldom visited. We can picture him turning more frequently E. along the Valley of Jezreel below Beth-shan to cross the Jordan for the Decapolis cities. Leaving that region, he could have come down the impressive Wâdī Nimrin to the vicinity of Jericho, taking the weird, difficult climb up through the Wâdī Qelt, whose barren wastes resemble photographs of the moon more than portions of the earth. The road from Jericho enters Jerusalem through the lower Garden of Gethsemane, and winds into the city at the NE. corner of the wall, where it passes the Palestine Archaeological Museum.

During his ministry near Jerusalem Jesus was again at the intersection of roads that brought loaded caravans from distant cities. Merchants from such trains may even have been among the throngs of worshippers "from every nation under heaven" (Acts 2:5) who came not only at Pentecost but long before that for religious festivals. They followed trade routes from Mesopotamia, Cappadocia, Phrygia, Egypt, Libya, and upper Galilee.

Paul used Roman roads on his four famous land journeys. Though he was sometimes "treated" to an ass or a horse or a "two-horsed carriage"—as suggested by one translation of Acts 21:15—most of the Apostle's land travel was on foot. The stretch of road he used most often was between the two Antiochs—Pisidian and Syrian—passing through his birthplace at Tarsus, and through Lystra, Derbe, and Iconium. On his western travels he used the famous Egnatian Road, running from Dyrrachium on the Adriatic, opposite the heel of Italy, across Illyrium (in the present Yugoslavia), Macedonia, and Thrace, into Thessalonica, Berea, Apollonia, Amphipolis, Neapolis, and Philippi at the head of the Aegean. His route time and again among the cities of Asia Minor was a few miles off the great E.-W. Persian Imperial Highway, which in most ancient times led from Ephesus on the Aegean to cities on the Euphrates. He has left no record of ever going to Colossae. The old Appian Way from Rome to Brindisi, by which Paul entered Rome, can be travelled today. See APPIAN WAY, illus. 23, and TARSUS, illus. 417.

Some famous 1st-century streets still survive, like The Street Called Straight in Damascus. It is a straightaway artery of trade E. and W. across the once-walled capital, south of the Omaiyid Mosque and N. of St. Paul's Chapel, roughly paralleling the Barada River; it is known to Arabs as Derb el-Mustakim. It begins at the Eastern Gate (whose narrow portal is one of three formerly used), and is used by heavily laden camels and jostling pedestrians. Motor cars halt at the square tower near the silk-weaving studios. Another interesting street in Damascus is the road winding along the SE. city wall, on which is built a house similar to the one from which Paul "was let down in a basket" (Acts 9:25). Paul is also remembered in the Greek Boulevard of St. Paul at Athens. On the narrow streets in the *kerameikós* section—where potters made their famous Greek vases and oil jars—Paul is sure to have walked as he arrived from the harbor of the city. He must have walked on the Lechaeum Road in Corinth, a city where he lived as long as 18 months at a time. This broad, impressive road, paved with large blocks of the original stones, is wider than the usual 1st-century streets, but one would expect this in the twin-harbored commercial center of Corinth. The Lechaeum Road, now shaded by eucalyptus trees, was in Paul's day lined with little shops, a Jewish synagogue, and the offices of wholesalers. It leads by impressive steps to the agora and to the various springs, temples, altars, and vast colonnaded shops, or stoae, and it joins Corinth with its W. harbor town. The most splendid street of Ephesus (the *Arkadiane*) led from the great theater to the sea.

Other Near Eastern Roads. (a) Persian. One of the oldest highways in the world runs from the interior of Persia (the present Iran), to link Ecabatana (Hamadan), Isfahan, Persepolis, and Shiraz with Bushires on the Persian Gulf; thence to Basra, Ur, and Babylon. Long before written records began, pack trains carried woven goods, foods, and mountain wares from this remote land below the Caspian Sea. Darius constructed a royal road 1,500 m. from Susa to Sardis, extending from N. of Basra to the vicinity of Smyrna. Paul used part of this route on journeys through Asia Minor. (b) Egyptian. Since the Nile provided 4,000 miles of safe and cheap transportation, Egypt spent little on road construction. Her roads consisted mainly of much-used, time-hardened footpaths along the Nile, and vital canals winding through rich grain fields. The Delta was a network of tracks. (c) Greek. Except for roads built while Rome dominated Greece, the highways of the rugged Greek peninsula never amounted to much; it was no wonder that her thriving commerce turned early to sea paths. The unique trade asset of Greece was Corinth, on an isthmus commanding the W. from her harbor of Lechaeum on the Gulf of Corinth, and the E. from Cenchreae on the Saronic Gulf. Some overland trade routes ran from Athens NW. into Macedonia and Thrace. The Euxine or Black Sea region supplied slaves, hides, bronze, and certain foods, including fish. From the Crimea Greece sent agents overland for Baltic amber. Greek coins have been found in Prussia. Yet Greeks were loath to exchange their handsome silver money for barbarian goods if they could barter. Greek caravans met their ships, and continued in use until the time of Alexander the Great in the 4th century B.C. Many Greek sea lanes had as their objectives Tyre and Sidon, from which old roads radiated.

For sea lanes and river routes, see BOATS.

For additional material pertaining to trade centers and transportation see ANTIOCH; AQABAH; CORINTH; DAMASCUS; EPHESUS; EZION-GEBER; GEBAL; GERASA; JOPPA. Also see BUSINESS; CUNEIFORM; MONEY; OWNERSHIP; SABA; SEAL; WEIGHTS AND MEASURES.

trades. See individual entries.

Trajan (Marcus Ulpius Nerva Trajanus), b. A.D. 53? in Spain, rose to the position of the ablest soldier of the Roman Empire, and became emperor A.D. 98, an office which he held until his death (A.D. 117). Trajan—successor of Nerva, who followed Domitian—brought the Roman Empire to its maximum extent. He added the provinces of Dacia (whose conquest is depicted in reliefs on Trajan's Column in his great Roman Forum); Armenia, Mesopotamia, Assyria, and Arabia (following the restlessness of the Nabataean tribes in Arabia Petraea). Practically all of Asia Minor, Syria, and Palestine were under the direct or indirect control of Rome. During his reign Ignatius, Bishop of Antioch, wrote his *Letters*. Trajan decreed that Christians should not be hunted out for persecution, but that if legally prosecuted and convicted they must be executed. This policy probably did not originate with Trajan, but with Vespasian (A.D. 69–79) or some other Flavian emperor, who had ruled that Christian worship was a crime against the Empire. During the reign of Trajan Christianity expanded and its literature developed.

455. Emperor Trajan.

Transfiguration, the, a supernatural experience of Jesus (Matt. 17:1–13; Mark 9:2–13; Luke 9:28–36). Six or eight days after he first told his Disciples of his imminent sacrifice (Mark 8:27–38), Jesus went with Peter, James, and John up into a high mountain, identified by many as snow-crowned Mt. Hermon*, not far from Caesarea Philippi. (Mt. Tabor* in Galilee has also been suggested, and has for centuries been accepted by many; but this elevation presents geographical difficulties with reference to preceding incidents; the Mount of Olives, suggested by some, is not at all likely.) But the locale is less important than the revelation which came to the three Disciples. The Transfiguration of Jesus was not merely an experience of the Master, but a marvel observed by all three of his companions. It increased their confidence in him to hear God address him, "This is my beloved Son . . . hear ye him" (Matt. 17:5); and it established him in his Disciples' sight as one who was in the line of Elijah and Moses. The Transfiguration is viewed as one of the manifestations by which God sought to reveal Jesus as His Son, even as He had done at his birth, and at his Baptism, and as He would do at his Resurrection. The details of the Transfiguration as narrated by Luke are: The going of the four to the mountain top to pray (9:28); the change which came over the face of Jesus, and the glistening of his garments (v. 29); the talking of Moses and Elijah with Jesus (v. 30); the drowsiness of the three Disciples (v. 32, cf. the Gethsemane narrative, Mark 14:37); their awakening to see the two prophets standing by Jesus; the suggestion of Peter that they build three tabernacles—as if to prolong the glory of the experience (v. 33); the coming of a shadowing cloud over the four, as a voice spoke from it, saying, "This is my beloved Son: hear him"

456. The Transfiguration, *by Titian*, in church of S. Salvatore, Venice.

(v. 35). The sequel to this mystical experience was the case of the epileptic or otherwise "tormented" boy, brought to Jesus the next day in the valley below, and cured by him (v. 42).

The Transfiguration is referred to in II Peter 1:16-18, which is a reflection of Peter's experience—regardless of the authorship of this Epistle.

transgression. See FLESH AND SPIRIT; MAN; PARDON; PUNISHMENT; REPENTANCE; SALVATION; SIN.

Trans-Jordan, the large plateau E. of the Jordan, sometimes called Eastern Palestine, comprised in the modern Hashemite Kingdom of Jordan, successor to the Trans-Jordan of the British Mandate, and first ruled by King Abdullah ibn Hussein (b. 1882), 2d son of the late King Hussein of the Hejaz. In N.T. times it was usually thought of as the Peraea and the Decapolis. The area lies S. of Damascus and the River Abana, N. of the River Zered, and is bounded on the E. by Iraq and Saudi Arabia, on the S. by the border of Egypt and Saudi Arabia. It reaches down to the head of the Gulf of Aqabah, whose ancient port, Ezion-geber, was used by several kings of Judah. In the Biblical period this extensive highland contained Moab*, Ammon (see AMMONITES), Gilead*, and Bashan*.

The *topography* of Jordan is rugged terrain which reaches an elevation of 2,644 ft. at Mt. Nebo*—itself 3,800 ft. above the surface of the Dead Sea. The plateau of Trans-Jordan, forming the E. wall of the river gorge, is cut into five sections by four streams: the Yarmuk, the Zerka (the Biblical Jabbok), the Môjib (the Biblical Arnon), and the Hesā (the Biblical Zered). Many small streams flow down toward the Jordan valley, and make the highland, especially in Gilead, suitable for large-scale grain production, even without the irrigation formerly used there. S. Trans-Jordan is suited for the grazing of sheep, goats, and camels (II Kings 3:4). The highlands N. of the Jabbok were formerly wooded. Eastern Palestine has always been more productive than the land occupied by Israel W. of the Jordan.

This lofty, relatively remote section is associated with the O.T. personalities who moved across it from Egypt and Sinai en route to Canaan, and who, during the era of the Judges and the Hebrew Monarchy, had profound spiritual experiences. (See JORDAN for a chart of the Biblical events which took place in Eastern Palestine.) In Trans-Jordan was the strategic plateau through which Moses was leading Israel and their confederates and flocks and herds when he requested permission from the king of Edom to allow the group to pass peacefully along the "Highway of the King" (later Trajan's Roman road from Syria to the Red Sea, and today a paved thoroughfare)—a request which was refused (Num. 20:14–21). Two and one-half Tribes of Israel received allotted territory within Trans-Jordan. Reuben and Gad settled for a time in land formerly held by King Sihon, E. of the N. end of the Dead Sea and the S. end of the Jordan. Half of the tribe of Manasseh located N. of Gad, in what had been the kingdom of Og (Josh. 13), but they never drove out the previous owners, for they found the country already controlled by other Semites. Even when David had made extensive conquests E. of the river he and his son Solomon had trouble holding them, for the approaches from Judah to the eastern areas were much more difficult than those from the Northern Kingdom, Israel, via the pass at Beth-shan, for example. Kings of Israel were able to hold and to drain the resources of Eastern Palestine for centuries.

Some time after their liberation by Pompey (c. 63 B.C.), nine Hellenistic cities banded together into a trade league east of Jordan which, with one city W. of the River (Beth-shan), comprised the Decapolis, designed to protect the plateau from desert tribes. There was always antagonism between this league of Hellenistic cities and the Nabataeans, and between them and the Jews; who after their return from Exile had gained political strength under the Hasmonaeans (the Maccabees), (166–63 B.C.), who seized Gadara and Jerash (Gerasa), controlled almost all of Trans-Jordan, and built up the mighty fortress Machaerus against the Nabataeans. The Romans checked Nabataean power when its dynasty ended with Malchus III in A.D. 106 and Nabataean territory became part of the Roman Province of Arabia. Nelson Glueck examined some 70 ancient sites E. of the Jordan, many of which are connected with events in the Israelitish period (the 13th century B.C.). Rich deposits of ore containing both iron and copper explain the economic strength of Eastern Palestine and the Arabah in O.T. times. Many old mines and their camps for slave labor have been excavated.

For more detailed information concerning eastern Palestine see Nelson Glueck, *The*

Other Side of the Jordan (ASOR) and *The River Jordan* (Westminster Press).

translation. See TEXT; ENGLISH BIBLE.

transportation. See TRADE AND TRANSPORTATION.

travail (trăv'āl), the pain and labor of childbirth, referred to in Gen. 35:16, 38:27 f.; Ps. 48:6; Jer. 4:31; Mic. 4:9, etc. From its primary meaning travail took on a symbolic meaning, as in "Zion travailed" (Isa. 66:8); "The wicked man travaileth" (Job 15:20); Paul labored and travailed, preaching the Gospel (I Thess. 2:9), and spoke of "the whole creation" groaning and travailing in the process of redemption* (Rom. 8:22).

travel. See TRADE AND TRANSPORTATION.

treasures in the Bible included (1) valuable *secular* objects ("treasure in your sacks," Gen. 43:23); "precious things" (Jer. 20:5); Solomon's royal treasures of golden shields, etc. (I Kings 14:26); treasures of the Persian kings (Ezra 5:17, 7:20, etc.); the treasures of Tyre (Ezek. 28:4); commodities transported by camel (Isa. 30:6, 39:4); treasures presented by the Wise Men to Jesus—gold, frankincense, and myrrh (Matt. 2:11); the choice treasures of Egypt (Heb. 11:26); and (2) *sacred* "treasures of the house of the Lord," offered as oblations by the faithful of Israel, but plundered time and again by conquerors, like Shishak of Egypt (I Kings 14:25); Ben-hadad of Syria (I Kings 15:18); Sennacherib (II Kings 18:13-16); and Nebuchadnezzar (II Kings 24:11–13). Temple treasures at Jerusalem included the gold trim of portals; articles fashioned of choice metals; vessels; and money (II Chron. 36:18; Neh. 12:44). Other countries also had collections of sacred treasures, as Babylonia (Dan. 1:2).

Treasuries (used in some passages of the A.V. where the more accurate word would be "treasures") belonged (1) to kings, like Solomon, whose store of luxury articles amazed even the Queen of Sheba (I Kings 10); and Hezekiah, who showed his spying Babylonian guests all his palace treasure—silver, gold, spices, ointments, jewels, and armor (Isa. 39:2); (2) to the house of the Lord, like the portable equipment of the Tabernacle and the Temple—always a temptation to invaders—and the contributions of tithed oil, grain, wine, and other offerings in kind, as well as gold, silver, golden dishes, garments, and various types of "oblations" dedicated to the maintenance and repair of the house of God (Neh. 7:70 f.). In some A.V. passages "treasuries" meant also the *structures* where the choice wares were housed. The treasury at the Jerusalem Temple was an edifice in the court of the sacred Area, probably in or near the Court of the Women. To this section of the enclosure both men and women were admitted. Into its trumpet-shaped receptacles the poor (Mark 12:41, 43) and the rich (Luke 21:1) cast their offerings of money. Jesus spoke in the Temple treasury (John 8:20). The treasuries of the Persian court in the time of Esther were places where currency (weighed silver talents and coins) were stored (Esther 3:9, 4:7). Cyrus and Darius at Babylon also had treasure-houses (archives), where their official documents were safeguarded (Ezra 5:17). Treasuries were in the broadest sense warehouses of precious commodities, even as "*treasure cities*" (A.V. Ex. 1:11) were storecities (A.S.V.). (See PITHOM and RAAMSES, constructed to house valuable goods.)

Treasurers were officers in charge of the royal and religious stocks of precious articles and moneys, like Azmaveth in David's day (I Chron. 27:25), Abijah the Levite, who guarded the Lord's treasures; and Mithredath of the Persian regime of Cyrus, who was ordered to deliver thousands of treasured articles to the exiles returning to Jerusalem (Ezra 1:8, cf. 7:21). An Ethiopian eunuch was treasurer for Queen Candace (Acts 8:27); and Erastus was city chamberlain or treasurer at Corinth (Rom. 16:23).

Symbolically "treasure" was spoken of as Israel is "his peculiar treasure" (Ps. 135:4; see also Prov. 15:6, 16, 21:20; Job 38:22, "treasures of the snow"; Isa. 45:3; Jer. 10:13; Rom. 2:5). Jesus said of a man's relation to his material treasures, "Where your treasure is, there will your heart be also" (Matt. 6:21; see also Matt. 12:35, 13:44, 52, 19:21; Luke 12:21). He made a clear-cut distinction between the man who lays up treasure "for himself" and the one who is "rich toward God" (Luke 12:21).

tree of life, a symbolic plant whose fruit was supposed to confer immortality on persons eating it. (1) It grew in the Garden of Eden (Gen. 2:9, 3:22, 24), but Adam and Eve partook only of the fruit of the Tree of Knowledge and thus failed to become immortal. The tree of life is a figure of success and happiness in Prov. 3:18, 11:30, 13:12, 15:4. (2) In apocalyptic visions, the tree of life is reserved for the righteous after the Last Judgment (Enoch 24:4, 25:4–6; Apocalypse of Moses [Life of Adam and Eve] 19:2, 22:3, 28:2, 4; Testaments of the Twelve Patriarchs, Levi 18:11). "For you is paradise opened, the tree of life is planted; the time to come is prepared, plenteousness is made ready; a city is builded, a rest is allowed . . ." (II Esdras 8:52). "To him that overcometh will I give to eat of the tree of life, which is in the midst of the paradise of God" (Rev. 2:7; see also 22:2, 14). (3) All ancient civilized nations wondered why man should be mortal and explained how man lost his chance of achieving immortality. The food of the gods, insuring their immortality, was *soma* in India, *haoma* in Iran, and *ambrosia* in Greece. In the Babylonian epic of Gilgamesh, Gilgamesh, after obtaining the plant of immortality, lost it when it was stolen by a snake; likewise the myth of Adapa (similar to Adam's failure to attain immortality) is a story of such a failure. (4) The tree of life or the sacred tree is a well-known motif in ancient art. It appears often on Assyrian bas-reliefs and much earlier it occurs in Near-Eastern and Cretan art as a tree surrounded by two goats eating from its branches. Persian artists represent it as a holy symbol. For the early Church Fathers it is the Cross, whose fruit is Christ, the source of immortality. Armenian Christians have frequently used the tree of life in their manuscripts (since the 9th century) and in their glazed tiles.

457. The Tree of Life, depicted in glazed tiles by an Armenian Christian, Jerusalem.

trees. (1) In Palestine, much of which was desert, and in Babylonia, with its watery lowlands unfavorable to them, trees were considered sacred. The totemism of Semitic Arabs put spirits in trees; trees in oases were dwelling places of Deity. Veneration of specific trees in Patriarchal times is suggested in A.S.V. Gen. 12:6 f., 13:18, 21:33, 23:17, 35:4, 8. (See also Ex. 3:2; Deut. 12:2; Judg. 4:5, Deborah's palm; II Kings 16:4; Jer. 2:20.) For generations the religious leaders of Israel protested against the groves on Canaanite hills which concealed cultic rites. The *asherah* was supposed to have been a tree or a post, associated with the fertility goddess. Isaiah vigorously decried the worship of trees and gardens, popular among Canaanites, and continued in some forms in Christian times in Syria (Isa. 1:29–31). Trees were so reverently regarded by Hebrews as gifts of God that their first fruits were offered to Him (Ex. 22:29). Levitical Law forbade the fruit of new trees to be eaten for the first four years (Lev. 19:23–25). Enemies cut down fruit orchards. (2) Trees were used in O.T. and N.T. parables: Jotham's fable (Judg. 9:7–15); the fable of Jehoash (II Kings 14:9); Christ's parables of the unproductive tree (Matt. 3:10, 7:17–20, 12:33). There are many other symbolic allusions to trees, e.g., in Isa. 65:22; Ezek. 17:22–24, 20:47; Job 19:10; Jude 12. The olive was especially revered, because before the old tree is dead it sends up new shoots to continue its life (cf. Job 14:7–9). (For Nebuchadnezzar's dream concerning a tree, and Daniel's interpretation, see Dan. 4:10–27.) (3) The tree is used five times in the N.T. to mean the Cross on which Jesus died (Acts 5:30, 10:39, 13:29; Gal. 3:13; I Pet. 2:24). Trees were not used as gallows for hanging criminals, but after the condemned man's death his body was hung on a tree to show that punishment had been meted out, and to warn others against similar offenses.

See ALMOND; APPLE; CEDARS; CYPRESS; FIG TREE; FIR TREE; MULBERRY; OAK; OLIVE; PALM; PINE; PLANE; POMEGRANATE; SYCOMORE; TAMARISK; TEREBINTH; WILLOW; etc.

trespass offering. See WORSHIP.

trespasses. See PUNISHMENT; SIN; TRANSGRESSION.

trial. See TEMPTATION.

Trial of Jesus, the, precipitated by (1) the growing restlessness of the Jews gathered at Jerusalem for the Passover festival over his failure to proclaim himself the earthly king (Messiah*) for whom they had long been looking; (2) the antagonism of Jewish religious leaders, including the Pharisees, Sadducees, elders of the people, and lawyers, who joined forces with the Herodians in their irritation over the mounting popularity of Jesus, especially after his Palm Sunday acclaim by the people (Mark 11:1–10); (3) the Roman hearings on charges not initiated by Roman officials, but credited by them (Luke 23:1–3) lest they be blamed for tumult in Jerusalem (Matt. 27:24); and (4) the betrayal of Jesus by one of his intimate disciples, Judas*, motivated (a) by his disappointment over his friend's failure to proclaim himself Messiah; and (b) by his resentment at Christ's rebuke after Judas's criticism of the extravagance of the anointing of Jesus (John 12:4–8).

Point (2) above merits fuller consideration. The Gospel narratives of the last days of Jesus clearly show the mounting antagonism of Jewish religious leaders because of his popularity (Mark 11:1–11 and parallels) and his authoritativeness, e.g., in cleansing the Temple (Matt. 21:12–16), and by his rebuttal of their challenge of his authoritativeness (vv. 23–27). They were also offended by his pointed parables, uttered in part in condemnation of priests and scribes (Luke 20:19)—the Parable of the Vineyard (vv. 9–16); of the Two Sons (Matt. 21:28–32); and of the Slighted Wedding Invitation (Matt. 22:1–14). Opposition to Jesus was increased by the temporary amalgamation of often noncooperative groups, like the Pharisees and the Herodians (Matt. 22:15 f.), who nevertheless found themselves amazed at the replies of Jesus (Luke 20:26); by the efforts of the Sadducees to ensnare him in talk concerning resurrection (Matt. 22:23–33); and by a Pharisee lawyer (Mark 12:28–34). After the answer of Jesus to his combined critics "no one was able to answer him a word, neither durst any man from that day forth ask him any more questions" (Matt. 22:46).

Steps in the Arrest, Trial, and Crucifixion of Jesus
(all within 10 hours)

(1) His *arrest* in the Garden of Gethsemane by Roman soldiers escorted by Judas, who had previously conspired with Jewish religious rulers to betray Jesus for 30 pieces of silver (Matt. 26:14–16).

(2) His *Trial*—before Jewish religious authorities—

(a) In the residence of Annas, former high

priest, and father-in-law of the current high priest Caiaphas (John 18:13): a brief examination.

(b) In the house of Caiaphas (which possibly adjoined that of Annas in the Temple Area, and shared the same small court in which the denial of Peter took place at cock-crowing time, Matt. 26:69–75 and parallels). Here, in an illegal predawn session of a partial roster of Sanhedrin* members presided over by Caiaphas, Jesus was questioned, spat upon, buffeted (Mark 14:65), and mocked (Luke 22:54–64).

(c) At daybreak (Luke 22:66) Jesus was led away to the council or Sanhedrin, composed of elders of the people, chief priests, and scribes (Luke 22:66), where their gibes drew from him the admission that he was the Son* of God (v. 70). This brought about his condemnation by the Jewish religious leaders, who, however, had no authority to execute their sentence of death, this being a Roman prerogative. Therefore he was taken to the Roman procurator (governor), Pontius Pilate*.

(3) His *Trial*—before Roman authorities—

(a) At the praetorium (a part of the castle fortress at the NW. corner of the Temple Area not far from the residences of Annas, Caiaphas, and the Sanhedrin council chamber) Pilate sat in his judgment seat on the stone pavement of the military courtyard (see GABBATHA), and weighed the evidence of the leaders accusing Jesus of perverting the people; of opposing payment of tribute to Caesar; and of setting himself forth as King of the Jews (Luke 23:1 f.)—which latter charge Jesus admitted (v. 3).

(b) His Trial before Herod* Antipas, tetrarch of Galilee and Peraea, under whose jurisdiction Jesus came because he was a Galilean, and Galilee had been a center of his activity (Luke 23:6). This phase of the Trial was the result of an impulse of Pilate's when he heard Jesus' name linked with Galilee; Pilate wished to dodge responsibility for this dangerous case. Herod had come to Jerusalem for the Passover, and now was eager to see Jesus personally—and perhaps even to see him perform a miracle (Luke 23:8). The previously unfriendly rulers, Pilate and Herod, became friends during the Trial of Jesus (v. 12). Herod, some of whose massive masonry survives today near Jaffa Gate, at "The Tower of David," remained silent at the vehement Jewish accusations against the prisoner (Luke 23:10). Soldiers arrayed Jesus in gorgeous garments of mock royalty (v. 11); but Herod, having found no fault in him (cf. Luke 23:15), sent him back to Pilate at the Roman praetorium, situated in the Fortress Antonia, north of the Temple Area.

(c) Back again before Pilate's judgment seat, Jesus heard this ruler tell the chief priests and rulers of the people that he found no guilt in him in the matters charged against him (Luke 23:14), and suggest that he have the prisoner chastised and released (v. 16). But the accusers demanded the release, instead, of Barabbas*, an imprisoned insurrectionist, a murderer (vv. 18 f.), and a robber (John 18:40). The infuriated crowd, impatient with Pilate's repeated offer of clemency (Mark 15:9), shouted for his crucifixion (Matt. 27:22 f.)—the Roman method of execution. A third effort was made by Pilate to spare Jesus (Mark 15:12), for he had been warned by his wife's dream to have nothing to do with "that righteous man" (R.S.V., A.S.V. Matt. 27:19). But, at last outvoiced, he symbolically washed his hands in the praetorium court, where the mob could see his efforts to impress them with his own neutrality, as he declared, "I am innocent of the blood of this just person: see ye to it" (Matt. 27:24).

(d) Pilate delivered Jesus to the soldiers to be scourged and crucified (Mark 15:15).

(e) His trial before Pilate ended when soldiers led Jesus into the hall called the praetorium and engaged in cruel mockery and abuse (Mark 15:16–20).

(f) His *Crucifixion* took place at once on what became "Good Friday," on a low mound outside the N. wall of Jerusalem, called Golgotha (see Calvary) (Matt. 27:32–56).

(g) His *burial* was made on Friday afternoon, as soon as death had overtaken Jesus. He was laid in the new rock-cut garden tomb adjacent to Golgotha belonging to a rich Jew, Joseph* of Arimathaea, who had begged his body from Pilate. Nicodemus*, a member of the Sanhedrin who had once come to Jesus by night, brought 100 lb. of myrrh and aloes for the preparation of his body for burial (John 19:39). The speed with which the body was placed in the stone-sealed and guarded sepulcher (Matt. 27:63–66) was due to Jewish deference for the oncoming Sabbath, which began Friday evening (Luke 23:54–56). Preparation of the body for entombment was deferred until the day after the Sabbath.

(h) The *Resurrection* of Jesus Christ was discovered by ministering women disciples on "the first day of the week, very early in the morning"—on the world's first Easter (Luke 23:55–24:12 and parallels).

Tribes, the, were definite social units among Semitic peoples. In the development of Israel they played both a historical and a psychological role.

The tribe was a corporate personality, consisting of clans, which in turn were made up of families, held together by kinship or blood-brotherhood. All the members of these groups—whether by birth, adoption, association with a group, or prolonged residence as a stranger—acknowledged the sheikh as father. The Patriarch* held his leadership by virtue of blood and birth; though guided at times by the counsel of elders, his will was absolute. The tribe was also communal. Customs concerning marriage*, flocks, wells, strangers, murder, theft, etc., became fixed and authoritative. Religion found expression in terms of this tribal environment. Times, places, and rare experiences became associated with the occult. Taboos, magic and divination, miracles, ceremonials, and intercessions found expression in tribal religious life. The deity of the tribe was at times believed to repose in its physical ancestor

(Num. 21:29). The tribal religion of Israel was influenced by Abraham's superior understanding of the divine (Gen. 12:1, 15:1, 17:1–10, 21:33). The Genesis narratives of the journey of Abraham from Ur to Haran, to Shechem, and on to Egypt record the migrations of nomadic and seminomadic peoples according to the tribal pattern. Tribal laws are readily discernible—e.g., the peaceful division of a tribe and a clan for economic purposes (Gen. 13:1–12); tribal revenge (Gen. 14:13–16); peaceful penetration of another's land (Gen. 20:14 f., 21:22–34); etc.

The tribe of Israel descended into Egypt as one tribe, Jacob-Israel, with Jacob as Patriarch, perhaps better described as a tribe of 12 households. At the Exodus* not only had the tribal divisions been preserved but out of them a distinct people, Israel, had been created through multiplication of offspring and a combination of factors of environment and of the unique nature of Jacob-Israel. Historically the process started with the appearance of the Hyksos* (Semites and shepherds) on the Egyptian scene, c. 1720 B.C. In time they gained control of Egypt, reigning for two centuries. For one of the Hyksos pharaohs Joseph*, after a series of desperate adventures and happy outcomes, became prime minister. Jacob and his sons, driven out of Palestine by famine, were reunited with Joseph, and given land in Goshen, a borderland between the Arabian Desert and the Nile Valley. There they multiplied under favorable conditions, acquired servants (Gen. 30:43, 32:5, 45:10), who after circumcision (Gen. 17:12 f.) were taken into the tribe and (later) entitled to share in the Passover (Ex. 12:44), and with whom marriage was acceptable (Num. 12:1; cf. Gen. 16:1, 30:4). Then a new king arose, "who knew not Joseph," signifying the end of the friendly Hyksos' dynasty. The new rulers transformed the Hebrews from herdsmen into a subject people; forced labor was exacted from them (Ex. 1:11, 14, 5:6–8). Out of oppression arose a leader, Moses; the lines are drawn sharply between Egyptian and Hebrew; tribal organization (probably abetted by enforced service by tribes under Egyptian *gauleiters*) emerged in a sharply developed form; Israel was ready to be led, not as a shapeless mob, but as the hosts or armies of the Lord.

While this history was developing, Joseph begot two sons—Ephraim* and Manasseh*, who were partly Egyptian (Gen. 41:45, 50 f.); these were assimilated into Jacob's family. These sons became heads of tribes in lieu of their father; the increase of an extra tribe thereby is later compensated by the denial to the sons of Levi* of any territory within the Promised Land because the Levites were chosen (Ex. 28:41; Num. 3:6 ff.) for service in the elaborate labors requiring many hands in the Tabernacle* and in the Temple*. Solomon divided his kingdom (exclusive of royal Judah) into 12 districts, each supporting the court for a month. Ephraim and Manasseh may have been counted as one (Joseph).

The family tree of the Twelve Tribes can be charted thus:

TRIBES, THE

Leah

Reuben Simeon Levi Judah Issachar Zebulun

Rachel — Joseph Benjamin

Zilpah — Gad Asher

Bilhah — Dan Naphtali

Joseph — Ephraim Manasseh

Leah and Rachel were the full wives of Jacob; Zilpah and Bilhah his concubines.

The Exodus from Egypt was a tribal revolt led by Moses (Ex. 3:11; cf. Gen. 47:11). The sons of Jacob were joined in their revolt and Wilderness trek by a "mixed multitude" (Ex. 12:38), a historic addition which made the event something more than a Jacob-Israel family affair (see ISRAEL). Just as the early days of any nation are remembered, honored, and idealized, so the tribal units and the men who gave them their names have been perpetuated in Hebrew history.

The variations in the accounts of the Tribes, their number, their location, composition, etc., are due to the mixture of fact and fancy, and differences in the date of composition and in the degree of literary craftsmanship. The Song of Deborah (Judg. 5), the most reliable contemporary survey of the Palestine of its period (the 12th century B.C.), lists ten Tribes, only five of which (vv. 14 f.) fought Sisera. Judah is not mentioned. The similarities and variations between Judg. 1 and Josh. 15–17:13, both of which give accounts of the location of the Tribes in Canaan, can best be explained by postulating a common source used by the authors, who, however, added supplementary data and their editorial viewpoint at the time. The blessing of Moses (Deut. 33) names 11 Tribes, omitting Simeon; the blessing of Jacob (Gen. 49) names 12. Some scholars have suggested that the stereotyped expression the "Twelve Tribes" sprang from the division of the nation by Solomon into 12 administrative districts (I Kings 4:7–19). This historical fact inspired the later writers of early Hebrew history (in this view) to associate the number of tribes with this feature of the United Kingdom's most glamorous days. In a similar human way, this theory argues, the destruction of Ephraim by Assyria and the deportation of the people of the Northern Kingdom, contrasted with the independent survival of Judah for more than another 100 years, its weathering of Captivity and leadership in the Return of the Jews to Israel, led the historians to stress in pride the importance of Judah in the nation's earlier history. This tendency is evidenced in the "blessings" (Gen. 49:2–27; Deut. 33:6–25), both of which in their present expanded form, it is commonly agreed, were late literary productions and not contemporary with their settings in history.

Though the tribal boundaries disappeared during the Monarchy, the tribal concept of pioneer days persisted. Ezekiel, in his idealistic state, apportioned the land among the Twelve Tribes (Ezek. 48). The N.T. perpetuated the tribal appeal. The promise to the Twelve Apostles as to how they should judge the Twelve Tribes of Israel (Matt. 19:28; Luke 22:30) indicates how Jesus employed current apocalyptic tribal notions. The mention of the tribal pedigree of persons indicates a religious aristocracy of blood (Luke 2:36; Acts 13:21). The Messianic claims of Jesus were strengthened by the citation of his descent from the Tribe of Judah and its royal family (Matt. 2:6; Heb. 7:14; Rev. 5:5). The reference in the Epistle of James (1:1) to the "twelve tribes" evidences the early Christian habit of referring to themselves as the spiritual Israel, the true descendants of Abraham.

For accounts of the separate tribes, see individual entries.

tribute, tax, and **toll,** enforced contributions to individuals, governments, or institutions—like the Temple.

Tribute took the form of (1) *human labor,* conscripted for such public works as the erection of Egyptian store-cities by Hebrew *corvée* (Ex. 5), or the mining of turquoise at Serabit* for the pharaohs who exploited Sinai; or for such menial tasks as were imposed on Canaanites subdued by Israel (Josh. 16:10, 17:13; Judg. 1:28); or the

458. Wooden model from El Bersheh of tribute bearers, Twelfth Egyptian Dynasty.

work of "strangers" in David's and Solomon's kingdom, impressed to work in the Lebanons preparing material for the Temple construction, etc. (I Chron. 22:2; II Chron. 2); or the toil of remnants of conquered peoples living in Israel's domain—Hittites, Amorites, Perizzites, Hivites, Jebusites, etc. (II Chron. 8:7 f.); (2) *enforced contributions* of precious metals, works of art, commodities, or slaves, exacted of Israel by invaders, like Syrians (I Kings 20:1–7), Assyrians (II Kings 17:1–6), and Chaldaeans for "the king's tribute" (Neh. 5:4). Jews frequently had to mortgage their homes or farms in order to pay tribute and taxes. The powerful King Ahasuerus of Persia, following the example of his predecessors, "laid a tribute upon the land, and upon the isles of the sea" (Esther 10:1). Ancient art offers many examples of long lines of vanquished peoples (including Hebrews), waiting their turn to present offerings to their captors, as shown on the Shalmaneser obelisk, and on Egyptian reliefs and paintings, showing Nubians and Syrians, for example, paying homage gifts to Tut-ankh-amun (depicted in the Tomb of Huy at Thebes), or the offering bearers in the Twelfth Dynasty wooden models recovered from El Bersheh.

Taxes for secular ends were exacted by Egyptian pharaohs, who actually owned the state, from peasants who paid in kind from their produce of field, flock, and crafts. Egypt collected taxes for every animal owned, every palm tree, every vineyard. Such great quantities of taxes in kind were brought to the overseers like Joseph the Hebrew (Gen. 41:25–57) that viziers had to erect larger granaries and store-cities. In the early Hebrew Monarchy taxation may have been the real reason for David's disastrous census taking (II Sam. 24). His son Solomon was the first actually to introduce taxes. These were gathered by heads of the well-organized bureaucracy of chariot cities, and by men in charge of the royal trading stations and metal-producing areas (I Kings 4; II Chron. 9:13–28). Israel's burden of taxes became so heavy that when Rehoboam succeeded his father (c. 922 B.C.) the people hoped for a lighter yoke (I Kings 12:1 ff.); however, they were taxed even more heavily (v. 14). Little wonder that Adoram, "who was over all the tribute," was stoned to death (v. 18), and the N. portion of Solomon's kingdom withdrew permanently from the "house of David unto this day" (v. 19). King Jehoshaphat became exceedingly rich because of the Philistine "presents" or tribute in silver, and the Arabian flocks of rams and goats, the profits from which he used to build additional store-cities and fortified strongholds in Judah (II Chron. 17:11 f.).

In the N T. there are many evidences of *Roman taxes.* A census for the purpose of estimating levies occasioned the journey of Joseph and Mary to Bethlehem on the eve of Christ's birth (Luke 2:1–3; cf. Acts 5:37). In Palestine at Christ's time there were taxes on water, meat, salt, land, etc. In addition there was a road tax, and often a town tax. The customary poll tax may be referred to in Christ's advice about payment to Caesar (Luke 20:25).

Tolls or customs duties were collected at border towns on exported goods. Matthew* was a customs officer (Matt. 9:9) who became a disciple. Jesus dined with many tax collectors because he felt their need of him (Matt. 9:10–13). Publicans* who farmed the tolls for Rome are said to have collected c. $720,000 a year from Judaea, Peraea, and Idumaea.

Sanctuary taxes. Rome expected Jews to pay for their own Temple* maintenance. A *didrachma* or half-shekel was exacted of every Hebrew male, as his share annually for the expenses of Temple administration (Matt. 17:24–27). The faithful of Israel had been disciplined to generosity by exactions made in the past, during major repairs to the Temple fabric, as in Josiah's reforms of the 7th century B.C., and in the time of Nehemiah some two centuries later. "Atonement money" had been specified in Israel's Law codes (Ex. 30:11–16), reckoned in terms of a weighed shekel* as ransom for each man's soul and as his contribution to the maintenance of sanctuary services. It corresponded in a way to the later Temple tax collected by Rome. After the fall of the Jerusalem Temple the old tax continued to be imposed, and was directed to the upkeep of the Temple of Jupiter Capitolinus in Rome.

See TITHE; and WORSHIP.

Trinity, the, the union of three divine Persons in the Godhead. The term means that the divine life is characterized by interior personal relationships, whose sources are described as Father, Son, and Holy Spirit.

The common supposition that this amounts to the assertion of three gods, or tritheism, and therefore involves the surrender of monotheism, is based on a complete misunderstanding. Tritheism would mean three gods each of whom had some independence of the others. In the Trinity as properly understood no such independence is possible; all three Persons must exist in order for any one of the Persons to exist; because God's existence as a Trinity is as necessary as His mere existence. God does not choose to exist, and He could not choose not to exist. He does not choose the manner of His existence, nor could He change the manner. He *must* be *what* He is and *how* He is. None of the three Persons can exist or act save in relation to the other two. The manner of God's existence as triune is not the result of mutual agreement, and it could not be changed by agreement. The Father *must be* the Father; the Son *must be* the Son; the Holy Spirit *must be* the Holy Spirit; and God *must be* such a threefold Being as this involves.

It is true that Christianity speaks of the Father as the First Person, and of the Son as the Second Person, and of the Holy Spirit as the Third Person; but "first," "second," and "third" here do not represent a time order—rather the order of necessary relationships. It is of the nature of the Son to depend on the Father, and it is the nature of the Holy Spirit to depend on the Father and Son. A certain order is therefore implied, and "first," "second," and "third" represent that order; but the dependence and the order are alike necessary: nothing could change either. This, in fact, is the fundamental divine unchangeability; any other sense in which God is unchangeable rests on this.

The conception is admittedly a difficult one; but what is chiefly important about it is that it makes God a perfect Personal Fellowship; He is social rather than solitary. The conception enables us to see how His essential nature can be love. Love means not only someone who loves, but also someone who is loved; and then—because love unshared is never perfect since it tends to selfishness—a third is required to complete the circle of love in perfection. The life of the Trinity is therefore the basis of the perfected social life of men. The community of love which is the Kingdom of God brought to fulfillment is at the same time the most complete expression of the inner nature of God, eternally Father, Son, and Holy Spirit, and therefore eternally the one God of perfect love.

The term Trinity does not occur in the Scriptures, and it is often objected to on that ground. But though the term is not Scriptural the Scriptures do contain the rich truths which the term was devised to protect and harmonize. We are confronted with a great body of historical and experiential fact which is indispensable to the Christian faith, and which is recorded chiefly in the Scriptures; and from early times the Church felt that the idea of the Trinity as explained above was the comprehensive truth to which it all pointed. Devout men, committed to the faith that the personal activity of God in Christ was a revelation through the Holy Spirit, sought to weave together what is said in the O.T. about the one God Who chose Israel, and Who through Israel sought a final universal kingdom, with all that is said in the N.T. about the will of the Father, and the loving obedience of the Son "even unto death" (Phil. 2:8), and the selfless ministry of the Holy Spirit (John 16:13); and to see all of these as the activities of one and the same God. When it is remembered that to all this was added the testimony of their own deep experience in Christ, the reasons for their arrival at the idea of the Trinity become clear. Indeed even before the idea was fully thought through and made an article of Christian faith, the Apostolic benediction, "The grace of the Lord Jesus Christ, and the love of God, and the communion of the Holy Spirit, be with you all" (II Cor. 13:14; cf. Gal. 1:1–5), and baptism "in the name of the Father, and of the Son, and of the Holy Spirit," were in general use throughout the Church. See HOLY SPIRIT; MONOTHEISM; SON OF GOD. E. L.

triumphal arch, a stone structure characteristic of cities of the Graeco-Roman world. A great triple arch, erected in honor of Hadrian, c. A.D. 120, has been found and studied at Jerash (Gerasa*). It incorporated fragments from an earlier Jewish building apparently destroyed c. A.D. 68. This arch,

459. Triumphal Arch of Constantine, erected in Rome A.D. 312 after his victory over Maxentius. Colosseum in background.

when approached from the S., gave a magnificent vista along the stadium wall to a triple-arched gate through which the temple of Artemis was seen crowning the highest hill. The Arch of Titus* in Rome is only one of several in the forums of the capital, all of which were designed to accent vistas. The arch with curved sides had been known in cities of the Tigris-Euphrates valley by 4000 B.C., and was used by the Assyrians for monumental gateways; but the Romans developed the form of triumphal arch which spread across the centuries into the modern world.

Troas, Alexandria, a chief city and port of the Roman Province of Asia, on the Aegean coast on the Troas promontory of NW. Asia Minor, c. 2 m. S. of the Dardanelles; its modern name is Eskistanbul. Alexandria Troas lies SW. of the ancient Ilium or Troy of Homer's *Iliad,* excavated by Heinrich Schliemann and others. Paul first sailed to Europe from Alexandria Troas, where he had seen a man beckoning him to come over into Macedonia (Acts 16:8–11). Some believe that Luke may have been associated in some way with the man of Paul's dream, and Paul presumably met Luke at Troas. During the Apostle's return trip from his Third Missionary Journey he spent a week at Troas preaching and teaching (Acts 20:6–12), and the incident of the young man Eutychus* occurred during that sojourn. Structures excavated at Alexandria Troas are typical of the Roman period—theater, temple, baths, and aqueduct.

troglodytes, cave men or cave dwellers who lived in natural caverns in the 100,000 or more years of the Stone Ages. Examples of caves so used (which have yielded skeletal and other evidences of occupation) are the three at the mouth of the Wâdī el-Mughârah on the W. face of Mt. Carmel* 18 m. S. of Haifa, where studies of the "Carmel man" have proved these caves to be one of the most important prehistoric sites yet examined; the Mughâret ez-Zuttieh ("Cave of the Gipsy Woman") near the N. side of the Plain of Gennesaret, where pieces of the skull of the "Galilee man" were found; others at Umm el-Qatafah, SE. of Bethlehem, near Jebel Fureidis (Frank Mountain), on the left side of the Wâdī Khareitûn, where five geological levels came to light. At the traditional Mount of Precipitation, 1½ m. SE. of Nazareth, deposits left perhaps 100,000 years ago were found (the same age as the "Carmel man").

Trogyllium (trŏ-jĭl′ĭ-ŭm), a promontory extending into the Aegean Sea S. of Ephesus, almost opposite the island of Samos. The A.V. (Acts 20:15) mentions it as a place where Paul's coastal ship put in for a brief time en route S. to Miletus, Cos, Rhodes, and ultimately to Tyre (Third Missionary Journey).

Trophimus (trŏf′ĭ-mŭs), a Gentile Christian of Ephesus, who accompanied Paul on missionary work in Asia (Acts 20:4) and to Jerusalem, bringing gifts to the church. Jews who saw Trophimus in the city with the Apostle thought that he had also been brought into the inner court of the Temple, past the barrier with its sign forbidding Gentiles to proceed farther; and the uproar of accusation against Paul precipitated his arrest (Acts 21:30 ff.). Trophimus several years later was left ill at Miletus (II Tim. 4:20).

trumpet. See MUSIC; SHOPHAR.

Trumpets, Feast of, celebrated at the 1st new moon* of Tishri, the 1st civil month and the 7th or Sabbatical month in the religious year. It was attributed to Moses (Lev. 23:24 f., P), and reckoned the holiest of the various new moon festivals. People were summoned to the holy convocation by trumpets—possibly of a different sort from those used for ordinary signals (see SHOPHAR). Offerings in addition to the usual daily and monthly gifts were presented; no servile work was done (Num. 29:1–7).

trust. See FAITH.

truth, according to the Gk. philosophical conception, the sum total of the reality of the universe of God, and the correspondence of the known facts of existence with that reality. In the O.T. truth is *ĕmeth, emūnāh,* i.e., "stability," "reliability," in contrast to "capriciousness." According to the Hebrew view, "truth" is that which can be depended upon, and the word is not used in the O.T. in any other sense. The "God of truth" (Isa. 65:16) is the God whose very name is "Fidelity" (cf. Ps. 31:5 A.V., R.S.V.). In most places where the word "truth" occurs, some such word as "faithfulness" would give a better sense (cf. A.V., R.S.V. on Ps. 25:10, 33:4). The O.T. concept of truth is, therefore, not so much an intellectual as a moral one.

At the core of Judaism is the conviction that whatever is true is also good and beautiful; even as in Hellenistic thought whatever was beautiful was also true and good. Judaism, with a pragmatic emphasis, insisted that the moral tenets of its teaching were valid because they benefited human society. Truth-telling was emphasized, for example, in Wisdom* Literature (Prov. 12:19, 17:20, etc.). Truth to one's neighbor and truthful justice toward fellow men were the conditions of true community (Zech. 8:16). By such insights Judaism advanced beyond a mere utilitarian basis for its ethics ("be good and truthful because it pays"), declaring that truth was the command of God.

Both the O.T. and the N.T. praise truthfulness and condemn all forms of falsifying: Ex. 20:16; Prov. 6:17, 8:7, 12:17, 19, 22, 19:5, 9, 30:8; I Cor. 5:8; Eph. 4:15, 25; Phil. 4:8; Col. 3:9; I Tim. 4:2; Jas. 3:14; I John 2:21; Rev. 22:15.

In the N.T. truth (Gk. *alētheia*) is represented, especially in the Fourth Gospel, in the life and personality of Jesus, who, in spite of his silence in the face of Pilate's question, "What is truth?" (John 18:38a), was the incarnation of truth. He was not only "full of grace and truth," but he *was* "the way, the truth, and the life." Although the word in John's Gospel is Greek, it has overtones of the Hebrew concept also. The phrase "grace and truth" echoes a common O.T. expression found, for example, in Ps. 25:10 (see above). Jesus was at one and the same time the goal of man's perfection ("the life"), the path by which it was attained ("the way"), and the dependable reality ("the truth") which nourished that life (John 14:6). To communicate truth to his followers was his purpose; they were to know the truth, and truth would make them free (8:32). Jesus revealed that the ideal atmosphere of the worship of God, the Spirit, was to be "in spirit and truth" (John 4:24). Lying and the devil were one (John 8:44). The "Spirit of truth" (John 14:17, 15:26) was the Comforter, whom Jesus promised to send to his Disciples after his death. But the world would not receive the Spirit of truth, because the world neither saw nor knew him, as Christ had taught his followers to know him. Christ called himself the "true vine," and his faithful the "branches" of that true vine (John 15:1, 5). When the Spirit of truth came he would lead the faithful into the totality of truth: "he will show you things to come" (John 16:13).

Tryphena (trī-fē′nȧ), a woman greeted along with Tryphosa in Paul's Letter to the Romans (16:12). The two may have been sisters, diligent about the Lord's work. Both names have been found in a Roman cemetery where servants of the imperial family were interred; Tryphena and Tryphosa may have been among the "saints in Caesar's household" (Phil. 4:22).

Tryphosa. See TRYPHENA.

Tubal-cain, a son of Lamech and Zillah (Gen. 4:22). The narrative of Gen. 4:19–26 (the J source) suggests that the ancient craft of traveling metal smiths was established by Tubal-cain. He may have been a Kenite (see KENITES)—a people whose name has the same root as "Cain," and who were related to the Amalekites and Midianites. They apparently lived SE. of the Dead Sea and knew the rich copper and iron mines of the Arabah*. They probably gave Israel their first lessons in metallurgy (Gen. 4:22). Traveling tinkers persist in the Near East today—the Sulaib. These despised wayfaring people wear on their foreheads a T-shaped cross—an ancient Accadian cuneiform symbol for "god" and "iron." These tinkering gypsies, states W. F. Albright, show us how the Biblical Kenites traveled, carrying bellows and tools on their asses, and increasing their livelihood by music and fortunetelling. Nelson Glueck believes that Kenites lived in "the Valley of the Smiths"—the Wâdī Arabah—which is full of recently discovered ruins of copper- and iron-smelting sites.

tunic, a straight, shirt-like garment worn by men and women of the Biblical period under other apparel. See DRESS.

turban, a man's brimless headdress formed by draping a scarf of wool, cotton, or other fabric around the head or around a tight-fitting cap. The turban is typical of Near Easterners, from Persia to Palestine; and is popular among conservative Moslem sheikhs in modern times. See DRESS.

turquoise, a blue or green-blue mineral containing copper and iron, highly prized for jewelry in the Biblical period. Famous Egyptian turquoise mines, worked at Serabit* in the Sinai Peninsula, have recently yielded valuable information concerning the evolution of writing.

turtle. See TURTLEDOVE.

turtledove (*Turtur communis*), a herald of spring, arriving about April (A.V. turtle, Jer. 8:7; Song of Sol. 2:12). A palm turtledove (*Turtur senegalensis*) is found in Jerusalem. Hebrews often used this bird for offerings to the Lord (Gen. 15:9; Lev. 1:14, 5:7, 11, 12:6, 14:22, 30; Luke 2:24). The

460. Turtledoves male and female.

"turtle" specified in the A.V. for purification of women after childbirth (Lev. 12:8, 15:29) and men whose Nazirite vow had been broken (Num. 6:10), is probably also the turtledove cf. A.S.V., R.S.V.).

Twelve, the. See APOSTLE, and the accompanying chart; also individual entries. For one account of Christ's selection of the Twelve, see Luke 6:12 ff.

Twin Brothers, the (Gk. *Dioskouroi*), the ensign of the Alexandrian grain ship which carried Paul from Malta to Puteoli, port of Rome (A.S.V. Acts 28:11). Mediterranean ships had "signs" (A.S.V. v. 11, R.S.V. "figure-heads") even before writing developed. In Roman mythology the Twin Brothers (*Gemini*) were Castor and Pollux (A.V. Acts 28:11), sons of Zeus and Leda. They were guardians of sailors, to whom they appeared in a constellation.. Likenesses of Castor and Pollux can still be seen in statues on the Capitoline Hill in Rome.

two. See NUMBERS.

Tychicus (tĭk′ĭ-kŭs), a man of Roman Asia who, along with Trophimus*, accompanied Paul on a missionary journey through his home province (Acts 20:4) after the Apostle's three months in Greece (v. 3), subsequent to the Ephesus riot. Eph. 6:21 makes Tychicus the bearer of the Epistle to the Ephesians. The similar role he played in the safe delivery of Colossians is evidence of his relationship to Paul as a "beloved brother, and a faithful minister and loved fellowservant in the Lord," sent by Paul to inquire for the Christians at Colossae and bring them spiritual comfort (Col. 4:7 f.). He may have been scheduled to assist Titus in Crete (Tit. 3:12), but he was appointed to Ephesus (II Tim. 4:12).

Tyrannus (tī-răn′ŭs) (Lat., from Gk. *tyrannos*, "tyrant"), the name of a Greek teacher or lecturer in Ephesus*, in whose room (or in a well-known building named for him) Paul preached every day to Jews and proselytes after being expelled from the synagogue where he had preached for three months (Acts 19:8 f.). If Tyrannus was still living in Paul's time he probably conducted popular discussion groups in the cool morning hours, as Eastern teachers were wont to do. In this case Paul could have hired his hall for Christian gatherings in the hotter part of the day, or the evening. Paul continued to teach at Ephesus for two years, so that "all they that dwelt in Asia heard the word of the Lord Jesus, both Jews and Greeks" (Acts 19:10).

Tyre (Tyrus, A.V. Ezek. 26–28; Heb. *Tzôr*; mod. Arab. *Sûr*, "rock"), an ancient and important seaport of Phoenicia, situated in antiquity on an offshore island, c. 25 m. S. of Sidon. Like other Phoenician cities, it had legendary founding (Jidejian, *Tyre*, p. 94); according to Herodotus (5th cen. B.C.), the city was founded c. 2750 B.C. The O.T. appears to indicate that it was settled by Sidon (Isa. 23:12). The first clear historical reference to Tyre occurs in the 14th century B.C. Amarna Letters, in which Tyre's king. Abi-Milki (c. 1365–1358 B.C.) pleads for assistance against Zimrida of Sidon (*ANET*³, EA 147, p. 484; see Jidejian, *Tyre*, pp. 17–20). "The shrine of Asherah of Tyre" is mentioned in the Legend of King Keret from Ugarit (*ANET*³, p. 145). The name of Tyre also appears in the Tale of Wen-Amon (c. 1100 B.C.) (*ANET*³, p. 56), an Egyptian record from the time of Merenptah (*ANET*³, p. 258), topographical lists of Sethos I and Ramesses II of Egypt (*ANET*³, p. 243), a Hittite incantation (*ANET*³, p. 352), and in the late 13th century B.C. Papyrus Anastasi I (*ANET*³, p. 477).

461. Tyre.

two harbors, a natural one to the N. improved by the addition of a seawall, and a second, artificial harbor to the S. (A. Poidebard, *Un grand port disparu: Tyr*, 1939). There was also a settlement on the mainland, called Ushu in Assyrian annals. For most of the 1st millennium B.C., Tyre was the chief city of the Phoenician homeland, a cosmopolitan port and a center of Mediterranean trade. It took the lead in founding colonies and opening up commercial contacts in the E. Mediterranean world. Carthage, the most important of these, was founded, according to tradition, in 814 B.C. Tyre's most famous product was Tyrian purple, a dye extracted from the murex, a marine snail (see Jidejian, *Tyre*, chap. 9). It also traded in timber, oil, wine, metals, slaves, horses, and other commodities. In his oracle against Tyre, Isaiah alludes to the city's greatness (Isa. 23). It was an "exultant city whose origin is from days of old, whose feet carried her to settle afar . . . whose merchants were princes, whose traders were the honored of the earth . . . " (R.S.V. Isa. 23:7 f.). Ezekiel pictured Tyre as a ship of treasures soon to be wrecked by storms (Ezek. 26–28). It was a "city renowned, that was mighty on the sea," (R.S.V. 26:17); she was "the signet of perfection, full of wisdom and perfect in beauty" (28:12). Indeed, as the apex of cultural achievement, she seems to have drawn the full wrath of the Hebrew prophets (e.g., Ezek. 27:25 ff., 28:6 ff.; Amos 1:9 f.; Zech. 9:3 f.).

In later times, Tyre was accorded a

Tyre is first referred to in the O.T. as a "fortified city" on the border of Asher (Josh. 19:29). It was the home of Hiram, King of Tyre (c. 970–936 B.C.), the ally of David and Solomon (I Kings 5:1), who supplied Solomon with cedar and gold for the Temple (I Kings 9:11 ff.; II Chron. 2:3 ff.); and of Hiram, the worker in bronze (I Kings 7:13; II Chron. 4:11). Ahab of Israel (c. 869–850 B.C.) married Jezebel, the daughter of Ithobaal of Tyre (c. 888–856 B.C.) (Bib. Ethbaal, "king of the Sidonians"; (I Kings 16:31).

The history of Tyre in the 1st millennium B.C. is known primarily from the records of Assyrian and Babylonian kings: Ashurnasirpal II (c. 883–859 B.C.) exacted tribute from Tyre (*ANET*³, p. 276) and invited its representatives to the dedication of his palace at Calah (*ANET*³, p. 560); Shalmaneser III (c. 858–824 B.C.) received tribute from Tyre (*ANET*³, p. 280), an event depicted on the bronze gate of Balawat (*ANEP*², No. 356); Tiglath-pileser III (c. 744–727 B.C.) exacted tribute from Metenna of Tyre (*ANET*³, p. 282) and from Hiram II (p. 283); Sennacherib (c. 704–681 B.C.) took the mainland settlement of Ushu (*ANET*³, p. 287); Esar-haddon (c. 680–669 B.C.) besieged Tyre in his 10th year (*ANET*³, pp. 290 f.) and signed a treaty with its king, Ba'lu (*ANET*³, pp. 533 f.); Ashurbanipal

(c. 668–633 B.C.) conquered Ushu and besieged Tyre in his 3d year (*ANET*³, pp. 295, 300); and Nebuchadnezzar (c. 605–562 B.C.) held Tyrian captives at Babylon and included Tyrians within his official court (*ANET*³, p. 308). Perhaps Tyre's most famous siege was that by Alexander the Great in 332 B.C. Alexander solved the military problem by building a mole or causeway, nearly ¼ mile long, from mainland to island. This mole stands today, though it has been widened by the accumulation of drifting sands. Tyre never again was free from the empires that succeeded Alexander's; it nevertheless enjoyed a portion of its earlier prosperity for some centuries (see Jidejian, *Tyre*, chaps. 6–8).

Jesus visited the region about Tyre (Mark 7:24–31) and was well-received (cf. Luke 3:8). Paul once landed at Tyre and remained there seven days; when he was about to sail away, his disciples escorted him to his ship and knelt on the shore in prayer (Acts 21:3–7).

Excavation of Tyre has produced few remains earlier than the Graeco-Roman period. Massive destructions, extensive Roman and Byzantine alterations, and recent wall-robbing have all but obliterated the Phoenician city. Earlier exploration in the area unearthed sarcophagi, tombs (including the "Kabr-Hiram," the traditional "Tomb of Hiram," probably of Persian date), inscriptions, and other finds. Since 1947, however, excavations directed by Emir Maurice Chehab, Director General of Antiquities of Lebanon, have brought to light a large part of Roman and Byzantine Tyre, including: (1) an extensive Roman-Byzantine necropolis; (2) a section of the Roman city, including streets, colonnades, a bath, gymnasium, etc.; (3) a monumental archway; (4) a Crusader Church; and (5) most recently a vast hippodrome, or racecourse. See W. Fleming, *The History of Tyre*, 1915; M. Chehab, prelim. reports in *BMB* and *Sarcophagus à Relief de Tyr*, 1969; N. Jidejian, *Tyre Through the Ages*, 1969 (with further bibliography). W. P. A.

Tyropoeon Valley. See JERUSALEM, illus. 213.

Tyrus. The Latin name of Tyre* (Jer. 25:22).

tzade, the 18th letter of the Heb. alphabet.

U

Ucal (ū′kăl), a son or pupil of Agur (Prov. 30:1).

Uel (ū′ĕl), a son of Bani; he put away his foreign wife (Ezra 10:34).

Ugarit. See RAS SHAMRAH.

Ulai (ū′lī), a river beside which Daniel saw himself in a vision (Dan. 8:2). Of the three streams near Susa (Shushan) the Eulaeus is undoubtedly the one referred to; it passed close by Susa before joining the Choaspes R.

uncle, the brother of one's father or mother. In Hebrew society an uncle could redeem a nephew who had sold himself, because of poverty, to a stranger or a sojourner (Lev. 25:49). Uncles mentioned in Scripture include: (1) Laban, brother of Rebekah and uncle of Jacob and Esau (Gen. 24:29 ff., 29:22 ff., 30:25 ff.); (2) Uzziel, uncle of Aaron (Lev. 10:4); (3) Abner, uncle of Saul (I Sam. 10:14–16, 14:50); (4) Jonathan, a scribe, wise man, and counsellor, uncle of David (I Chron. 27:32); (5) Abihail, father of Esther and uncle of Mordecai (Esther 2:15); (6) Shallum, uncle of Jeremiah (Jer. 32:7 ff.); (7) Abraham, according to P (Gen. 11:27, 31, 12:5) uncle of Lot, son of Haran. Sometimes in the O.T. a kinsman other than an uncle was called by this term to show respect.

unclean. See ANIMALS; PURITY.

unction, anointing as a religious rite (see ANOINT).

unicorn (Lat. *unicornus*, "having one horn"), a fabulous animal whose name is used in the A.V. of the O.T. to mean a horned (Deut. 33:17), very strong (Num. 23:22, 24:8), wild animal, difficult to catch and to domesticate (Job 39:9 f.). The animal intended may be the wild ox (*urus*) that roamed Mediterranean lands in Assyrian times but is now extinct (see also Ps. 29:6, 92:10). The A.S.V. translates "unicorn" "wild ox" in Num. 24:8; Deut. 33:17; Job 39:9; in Num. 23:22 (margin) it reads "ox antelope."

unknown God, an (A.V. "the unknown God"), the inscription on an altar at Athens referred to by Paul (Acts 17:23) in his message about the true God. The Greek custom of dedicating some altars to anonymous deities is recorded in a 3d century biography of the philosopher Apollonius (born near the beginning of the Christian era), who praised the wisdom of the Athenians in speaking well of all the gods.

unleavened, a word applied to bread made without yeast. See LEAVEN; PASSOVER.

Unleavened Bread, the Feast of, originally a solar agricultural festival, later combined with the Passover. See FEASTS; PASSOVER.

Unni (ŭn′ī). (1) One of the musicians "of the second degree" appointed by David to the group of psaltery players who accompanied the Ark to Jerusalem (I Chron. 15:18, 20). (2) A Levite watchman who went up to Jerusalem with Zerubbabel (Neh. 12:9 A.V., A.S.V. Unno).

unpardonable sin, the, a term which does not appear in Scripture but which is often applied to the sin of blasphemy against the Holy* Spirit. This sin was condemned by Jesus after the Pharisees had accused him of casting out demons by the power of Beelzebub instead of by the power of God (Matt. 12:24–32); the "unpardonable sin" consisted in ascribing to the forces of evil what was really done by the Spirit of God. The roots of the concept of an unpardonable sin lie in the O.T., as in Num. 15:30 f., where the man who willfully violates the known laws of God is doomed to separation from the mercies of Yahweh (cf. Ps. 19:13).

upharsin. See MENE.

Uphaz (ū′făz), a place where gold was obtained (Jer. 10:9; Dan. 10:5), possibly confused with Ophir. Most modern translations render "Ophir."

Upper Room, the, the large, furnished upper room designated by Jesus as the place where he would eat his last Passover (Luke 22:12), was either the guest room on the second floor of a spacious Jerusalem house, or a chamber erected on the wall or on the roof, penthouse fashion. Most Palestinian houses were one-storied, except in crowded cities which were built in small, walled areas. There houses were two or more stories high, as in walled Jerusalem today and in Bethlehem, or in ancient Jericho (see II Kings 4:10; cf. I Kings 17:19). Christian tradition and the testimony of such travelers as the Bordeaux Pilgrim located the Upper Room, *Coenaculum*, on the hill Zion, S. of the present Zion Gate and the Armenian quarter, and adjacent to the "Palace of Caiaphas"* (a modern structure containing tombs of Armenian patriarchs). This site, occupied today by the Mosque En-Neby Dâûd (adapted from a 14th-century Gothic church), claimed by some Moslems as "the Tomb of David," may

462. Entrance to a typical upper room in old Jerusalem.

well have been that of the house where the Last Supper was held (Mark 14:14 f.) and the place to which Christian believers returned after the Ascension of Jesus (Acts 1:12–14). Many believe that this first gathering place of Christians was the home of John Mark's mother (Acts 12:12). See LORD'S SUPPER, THE.

Ur (Accad. Uri), one of the oldest cities of ancient Sumer, and generally recognized as the ancestral home of Abraham (Gen. 11:28, 31, 15:7; Neh. 9:7), although a northern location for the latter is upheld by some (cf. C. H. Gordon, *JNES* 17, 1958, pp. 28 ff. with the reply by H. W. F. Saggs, *Iraq* 22, 1960, pp. 200 ff.). The ruins of this once revered city are marked by the mound of Tell el-Muqaiyar ("mound of pitch"), whose main feature is the well-preserved remains of a ziggurat begun by Ur-Nammu (c. 2113–2096 B.C.). Situated in southern Iraq about 10 m. W. of the present course of the Euphrates and 100 m. NW. of Bosra, the mound occupies an oval space about 1300 yds. long and 740 yds. wide. Archaeological examination of the site was begun by J. E. Taylor in 1853–54. Additional soundings were made by R. C. Thomson (1918), and H. R. Hall (1919). From 1922–34, Ur was systematically excavated by the British Museum and the Museum of the University of Pennsylvania under the direction of C. L. Woolley (see his summary of the work, *Excavations at Ur*, 1954). In the course of this work, the *ziggurat* and *temenos* area were thoroughly explored, numerous structures were uncovered and identified, the city plan in its major stages was defined, and thousands of cuneiform

463. *Ziggurat* at Ur, the best-preserved in Mesopotamia. Solid brick mass 200 ft. x 150 ft. x c. 70 ft. high. Begun by Ur-Nammu (c. 2000 B.C.), completed by Nabonidus.

tablets were discovered. Soundings indicate that the earliest settlement dates from the 'Ubaid period (c. 4300–3500 B.C.), represented by a number of terra cotta female figurines with human bodies and reptilian heads (see *ANEP*², No. 510). Above this were found deposits of "clean water-laid sand," thought by Woolley to be evidence of the great Flood of Babylonian tradition. Although these and similar deposits at other sites have raised questions concerning their significance, the Ur deposits (c. 3500 B.C.) appear to be too early to accord with the literary and inscriptional evidence. The latter would place the origin of the Flood tradition c. 2900 B.C., at the end of Early Dynastic I (see *CAH*³, Vol. I, 1970, p. 354 and Part II, 1971, pp. 243 f.; also *Iraq* 26, 1964, pp. 62 ff.).

According to the Sumerian King List, Ur was the seat of the Third Sumerian Dynasty after the Flood (*ANET*³, p. 266; see *CAH*³, Vol. I, Part I, 1970, pp. 200 f., 222 ff., 236). The first recorded ruler of this First Dynasty of Ur is Mesannipada, known from his own inscriptions to date c. the middle of the Early Dynastic III period (c. 2550 B.C.). The most sensational discovery at Ur, the "Royal Cemetery," is to be dated earlier than, and perhaps in part contemporary with, the reign of Mesannipada (*CAH*³, Vol. I, Part I, 1970, pp. 351 ff.; Part II, 1971, pp. 244 f., 282 ff.). The graves of the "Royal Cemetery" produced art treasures of exquisite beauty and expert craftsmanship, such as: the "Royal Standard of Ur," decorated in shell and lapis lazuli with scenes of peace and war (*ANEP*², Nos. 303–304); the electrum helmet of Meskalamdug (*ANEP*², No. 160); and a lyre decorated with a golden bull's head (*ANEP*², Nos. 192–193). The most famous grave is that of Queen "Shub-ad" (Pu-abi), who was buried with her royal attendants and carriage as well as an extraordinary treasure of gold and silver vessels and jewelry (see C. L. Woolley, *The Royal Cemetery*, 1934).

Ur achieved its greatest political power at the time of the Third Dynasty, founded by Ur-Nammu. Cuneiform texts indicate that its control extended as far as Susa in SW. Iran and Byblos along the Mediterranean coast. The city of this period was extensive, surrounded by a sloping mud brick rampart crowned by a burnt-brick wall. It had two harbors, one to the N. along an arm of the Euphrates, and the other to the W., along a navigable canal. Within the walls were sections of densely packed and irregularly planned residential quarters. The average house was a one-story mud-brick building with several rooms around an open courtyard, though there were others which were more elaborate, with two stories and plastered walls (see Fig. 464).

The heart of the city was at all times the sacred *temenos* area to the NW., dominated by its lofty *ziggurat*. A rectangular three-stage tower, it was constructed of a solid mass of brickwork faced with an outer layer of burnt brick set in bitumen. Its orientation was to the NE., where was located the main gate and the temple of the moon god, Nanna, with its spacious outer court surrounded by numerous small chambers. S. of this was located the E-nummah, dedicated to both Nanna and Ningal, and further S. the temple of Ningal. Between the temple buildings and the S. wall of the *temenos* stood the palace of Ur-Nammu. The sacred area underwent many phases of reconstruction, the last major changes at the time of Nebuchadnezzar II (c. 605–561 B.C.) and Nabonidus (c. 555–539 B.C.). Under Cyrus the Great, Ur received its final alterations before the changed course of the Euphrates led to its ruin.

464. Model of Ur street scene (c. 2000 B.C.) with *ziggurat* in distance.

See C. L. Woolley, *Ur Excavations*, II. *The Royal Cemeteries*, 1934; IV. *The Early Periods*, 1955; V. *The Ziggurat and Its Surroundings*, 1939; VIII. *The Kassite Period, etc.*, 1965; M. E. L. Mallowan, IX. *The Neo-Babylonian and Persian Periods*, 1962; B. W. Buchanan, *JAOS* 74, 1954, pp. 147 ff.; M. E. L. Mallowan and D. J. Wiseman (eds.), "Ur in Retrospect," *Iraq* 22, 1960; ref. to Ur in *CAH*[3]. W. P. A.

Uri (ū′rī). An abbreviation of Uriah*. Bearers of this shortened name are mentioned in Ex. 31:2; I Kings 4:19; Ezra 10:24.

Uriah (ū-rī′*ȧ*) (Urijah) ("Jehovah is light"). (1) A man of Hittite ancestry, like many others prominent in Jerusalem (cf. Ezek. 16:3), but a worshipper of Israel's God, as suggested by his name. Uriah (Urias A.V. Matt. 1:6) as one of David's warriors participated in his victories over Ammon and Syria. David treated Uriah shamefully, taking his wife Bath-sheba*, and ordering him to such an exposed position during the siege of Rabbath-ammon (the present 'Ammân, capital of Jordan) that his death was inevitable (II Sam. 11, 12). (2) A high priest (Urijah) in the reign of Ahaz (Jehoahaz I) of Judah (c. 735–715 B.C.). He carried out innovations for his king, like the installation of an altar similar to one seen by Ahaz in Damascus (II Kings 16:10–16). (3) A son of Shemaiah, a prophet of Kiriath-jearim. His rebuke of King Jehoiakim (c. 609–598 B.C.) and his prediction of the destruction of Jerusalem necessitated his flight to Egypt, whence he was brought back, slain, and buried in a common grave (Jer. 26:20–23). Professor Harry Torczyner of the Hebrew University, Jerusalem, considered this Uriah (Urijah) to be "the prophet" of the Lachish* Letters, concern for whose fate runs through the famous correspondence on potsherds. Lachish Letter IV seems to have been addressed to him, but never received, because the crisis of 598 B.C. prevented its being forwarded by Ya'ush. Uriah may already have been apprehended in Egypt by officers of the King of Judah. (4) A priest, father of Meremoth, contemporary of Nehemiah (Ezra 8:33; Neh. 3:4). (5) A priest who stood beside Ezra in Jerusalem when he read the Law to the returned Exiles (Neh. 8:4).

Uriel (ū′rĭ-ĕl) ("my light is El"). (1) A prominent Kohathite Levite who helped bring the Ark from the home of Obed-edom to Jerusalem (I Chron. 6:24, 15:5, 11). (2) A man of Gibeah whose daughter was the mother of King Abijah of Judah (II Chron. 13:2). (3) An angel in II Esdras (4:1–11).

urim and thummim ("oracle and truth") various unidentified objects—possibly small carved, or otherwise marked stones worn in a pouch over the high priest's heart under the frame of his breastplate*. They were used as sacred lots, consulted when the priest wished an oracle of God's will under specific circumstances (I Sam. 14:41 f.; see also Ex. 28:29 f.; Deut. 33:8; Lev. 8:7 f.; Num. 27:21; I Sam. 28:6). There may have been two oracular objects (one for negative, one for positive counsel), or three (one for a neutral position). They were used in pre-Exilic times (but see Ezra 2:63; Neh. 7:65), but were later abandoned in favor of advice given by the prophets of Israel. Some authorities believe that urim and thummim were Hebrew adaptations of the Babylonian tablets of destiny, known as *Urtu* and *Tamitu*. See EPHOD.

Uruk. See ERECH.

usury, lending at interest; later, at an exorbitant rate. The laws of Israel forbade lending to a needy Hebrew, with expectation that principal plus interest would be returned, in the form of "money, food, or anything else" (Moffatt Deut. 23:19). Many poor Hebrew farmers would have been in a desperate plight had they not received generous loans in commodities or in weighed money* (later coins) (Deut. 23:19; see also Ex. 22:25; Lev 25:36 f.; Ps. 15:5; Ezek. 18:8, 13, 17). There was no compunction about lending at interest to foreigners or strangers, for such transactions involved risk (Deut. 23:20). Nehemiah was grieved when the well-to-do of his day took advantage of poor Jews returned from Exile, who had mortgaged their farms and vineyards to pay Persian taxes. He constrained the prosperous to desist from usury, and to return vineyards, orchards, and houses, together with the hundredth part of the "money, and the grain, the new wine, and the oil" exacted. This shows that interest was paid in commodities as well as in money as late as the 5th century B.C. Coinage of money fostered usury. Small coins which enabled farmers to secure some of the commodities that had not been available when they had had only agricultural products to offer in payment, made it now possible to borrow and to become involved in debt*.

Babylonian bankers were not only skilled financiers, but often exorbitant usurers, charging as much as 20% per annum in money or in grain. Hammurabi's letters include instructions for the suppression of extortion. At Athens in the 5th century B.C. people paid from 12 to 20%. In Rome, early in the Christian era, capital was plentiful and rates lower; but in the Roman provinces interest was high. In Egypt 30% was often paid. The Fourteenth Egyptian Dynasty pharaoh Harmhab ordered those who made illegal exactions from the poor to have their noses cut off and to be exiled.

Jesus in his Parable of the Talents did not condemn putting money out to legitimate interest at the banker's (Matt. 25:27; Luke 19:23). When the agricultural society of O.T. times was succeeded by a commercial society engaged in extensive business transactions, the borrowing and lending of money became necessary and legitimate.

Uthai (ū'thī). (1) Son of Ammihud (I Chron. 9:4). (2) A member of the family of Bigvai who accompanied Ezra from Babylon (Ezra 8:14).

Uz, the unidentified homeland of Job*, hero of the O.T. book that bears his name. Some scholars consider NW. Arabia as a possible location of the Land of Uz (Job 1:1); some, weighing Jer. 25:20, place it somewhere between Egypt and Philistia. Others, considering the suggested environments of Job's friends (Eliphaz of Teman, 2:11), Bildad the Shuhite (cf. Gen. 25:2), and Elihu the Buzite (Gen. 22:21), believe that Uz was either Edom* or a portion of the Hauran, the fertile highland E. of the Sea of Galilee and the Upper Jordan. Lam. 4:21 speaks of the "daughter of Edom, that dwellest in the land of Uz."

Clues to the origin of Uz as a place name may possibly be found in the book of Genesis: according to 10:23, Uz is a tribe descended from Aram; an individual named Uz (A.V. Huz, 22:21) was the eldest son of Milcah and Nahor, Abraham's brother; in 36:28 Uz is a man or tribe descended from Dishan, a "duke" of Edom.

Uzal (ū'zăl), an Arabian tribe descended from Joktan in the genealogical list of Gen. 10:27. San'â, ancient capital of the kingdom of Yemen in SW. Arabia, was once called Azal (a kindred name, according to Arabian tradition).

Uzza (ŭz'ȧ), the name of the original owner of a garden in which Manasseh and Amon, kings of Judah, were buried (II Kings 21:18, 26). See UZZAH.

Uzzah, (1) A son of Abinadab, who was suddenly killed in punishment for touching the Ark* to steady it when the oxen carrying it stumbled on Nachon's threshing floor (II Sam. 6:6 f.; I Chron. 13:11). David, angered at the incident, named the place Perez-uzzah ("the breach of Uzzah") (v. 11). (2) A son of Merari (I Chron. 6:29).

Uzzen-sherah (ŭz'ĕn-shē'rȧ), an unidentified place said to have been built by Beriah's daughter, Sherah, to whom the building of the upper and lower cities named Beth-horon are attributed by the Chronicler (I Chron. 7:24).

Uzzi (ŭz'ī) (abbreviated from Uzziah), the name of several honorable family heads of Issachar and Benjamin, and of priests and Levites (I Chron. 6:5 f., 51, 7:2 f., 9:8; Neh. 11:22, 12:19, 42).

Uzziah (ŭ-zī'ȧ) (Azariah), a king of Judah. Uzziah ("Jehovah is my strength") is used in II Kings 15:32–34; Isa. 7:1; Hos. 1:1; Amos 1:1; Zech. 14:50. The alternative Heb. name Azariah ("Jehovah hath helped"), is found in II Kings 14:21, 15:1, 6–8, 17, 23–27; I Chron. 3:12. Many believe that this king had only one name, Uzziah, but that an early mistake in copying corrupted the text and perpetuated the error.

Uzziah, son of King Amaziah (c. 800–783 B.C.), became king at the age of six (II Kings 15:2). His rule over Judah (c. 783–742 B.C.) was contemporaneous with the reign of Jeroboam II of Israel (c. 786–746 B.C.) (II Kings 15:1). The Deuteronomic redactor writes favorably of Uzziah's reign in spite of the king's syncretism* (v. 4). His brief record of this half-century reign (14:22, 15:5–7) has specific details supplied by the Chronicler (II Chron. 26:1–23): (1) Uzziah developed Judah's agricultural resources (II Chron. 26:10); (2) he raised a large, well-equpped army for the nation's protection (vv. 11–14); (3) he strengthened the walls of Jerusalem (v. 9), and supplied the city with military defenses (v. 15); (4) he carried on successful military campaigns against the Philistines and their cities in the W. (vv. 6 f.); (5) he recovered Elath (see EZION-GEBER, II Kings

14:22), which his father had once conquered, and led a successful campaign against the Arabians in the S. (II Chron. 26:7); and (6) he received tribute from the Ammonites in the E. (v. 8). His reign covered a period of great material prosperity (II Chron. 26:22, cf. Isa. 2, 3). A severe earthquake during his reign was remembered as an outstanding event (Amos 1:1; Zech. 14:5).

The historical account from the annals of Judah recorded by the Deuteronomist attributes Uzziah's death to leprosy (II Kings 15:5). The Chronicler believed the illness was retribution for Uzziah's interference as head of the state with the functions within the province of religious authorities (II Chron. 26:16–20); violations of the Priestly Code* were as liable to punishment as those of the moral. The narrative is a record of ancient leprosy*—its first symptoms, the quarantine it imposed on its victim, and the limitation it exacted on the burial even of a king (vv. 20–23). The death from leprosy of this king was an event so charged with emotion that it contributed to the prophet's call described in Isa. 6:1, 5–8.

Uzziel (ŭ-zī′ĕl) ("God is strong"). (1) The traditional founder of the important group of Kohathite Levites, the Uzzielites (Ex. 6:18, 22; Lev. 10:4; Num. 3:19, 30; I Chron. 6:2, 18, 23:12, 20, 24:24). A group of Uzzielites organized by David assisted in bringing the Ark to Jerusalem (I Chron. 15:10). (2) A man of the tribe of Simeon (I Chron. 4:42). (3) One who founded a Benjamite family (I Chron. 7:7). (4) An instrumentalist, of the sons of Heman, in David's musical organization (I Chron. 25:4; Azareel in v. 18). (5) A Levite of the Jeduthun group (II Chron. 29:14). (6) A goldsmith, son of Harhaiah, who helped to rebuild the Jerusalem wall (Neh. 3:8).

V

vagabond (Lat. *vagari*, "to wander"), the term used in A.V. and A.S.V. Ps. 109:10 in a plea for vengeance on the slanderous enemies of David; and in A.V. Gen. 4:12, 14 for the fugitive murderer Cain (A.S.V. "wanderer"). The "vagabond Jews" of A.V. Acts 19:13 reads "strolling Jews" in the A.S.V.

vail. See VEIL.

vale, valley, the translation of more than a half-dozen Heb. and Gk. words used in the Bible to convey the idea of low-lying ground —a plain*, a gorge, a ravine, a wâdī. The most conspicuous and extensive valleys of Palestine are the Shephelah, the Jordan, and the Valley of Jezreel. See JERUSALEM; PALESTINE; WÂDĪ; and many individual valleys like EUPHRATES; HINNOM; JEHOSHAPHAT, VALLEY OF; KIDRON; MUGHÂRAH; NILE; ORONTES; REPHAIM, VALLEY OF; SIDDIM; TIGRIS; ZEDEK; ZERED. For the valley between the Lebanons and the Anti-Lebanons see COELE SYRIA.

vanity, the translation of several Heb. and Gk. words in Scripture. Its root idea is suggested by the Lat. *vanus* ("emptiness"). In O.T. Wisdom Literature the Heb. *hebhel* ("vapor," "breath") is translated "vanity" to convey the notion of the transitory nature of man (Ps. 144:4, 8, 11), or of futility (Eccles. 1:2, 12:8). The Heb. word translated in the A.V. "vanity" in Job 15:35; Ps. 10:7 is translated "iniquity" in the A.S.V. (R.S.V. Job 15:35 reads "evil"). The emptiness of lies is indicated by the Heb. word *shav'* in A.V. Ps. 41:6 (A.S.V. "falsehood"). *Riq*, which in the Heb. indicates a sense of empty failure, is in Ps. 4:2 and Hab. 2:13. The Heb. *tōhū* conveys the idea of wasteful confusion such as characterizes the makers of idols (Isa. 40:17, 23, 44:9). In the N.T. "vain" and "vanity" are translations of three Gk. words, *kenos* ("empty"), as in I Cor. 15:10, *mataios* ("worthless"), as in Acts 14:15, and the noun *mataiotes* (Rom. 8:20; Eph. 4:17; II Pet. 2:18).

Vashni (vâsh′nī). According to A.V. I Chron. 6:28, Vashni was the eldest son of Samuel*. Cf. v. 33, and I Sam. 8:2, where Joel is named as Samuel's first born. Apparently in transmission "Joel" dropped out of the text of I Chron. 6:28 and a Heb. word meaning "and the second" was transformed into a proper name, Vashni.

Vashti, the queen of Ahasuerus (Xerxes I) in the Book of Esther* (1:9, etc.).

vau (vav, or waw), the 6th letter of the Heb. alphabet, pronounced in ancient Hebrew as a *w*, later as *v*; used as heading of the 6th part of Ps. 119. See WRITING.

Veadar (vē′*ā*-där), an intercalary (inserted) month, "the second Adar," introduced seven times in the cycle of each 19 years of the Jewish calendar, in order to make the average length of the year correct. It falls in late March or early April. See TIME.

veil, a fabric used for concealment. (1) An article of dress*, used by women to cover their head or person, as when Rebekah "took a veil and covered herself" before meeting her future husband Isaac for the first time (Gen. 24:65). This custom still prevails in conservative sections (Moslem areas) of the Near East. Veils were also used by shepherds, travelers, and farmers to protect the back of the head and the neck from excessive heat. This is illustrated by Ruth's veil, which was large enough to hold "six measures of barley" (Ruth 3:15).

Many Christian wives of Bethlehem today wear long white veils or mantles, flowing down from the high red tarboosh (a fez-like cap), almost to the hem of their blue garments. Veils are also worn by Bedouins and cameleers, who wrap head and face with folded square *kufiyehs* to protect themselves from dust and glare. Moses veiled his face while speaking at Sinai, but removed the veil when he went before the Lord (Ex. 34:30–35; cf. II Cor. 3:13).

Paul taught that women praying or prophesying in public ought to be veiled, even as men (made in the image of God) ought not to be veiled when so engaged (I Cor. 11:4–16). Woman, he said, should have "a sign of authority on her head because of the angels" (A.S.V. I Cor. 11:10). This difficult passage may mean: (1) that the veil would protect women from the evil angels of late Jewish speculation; or (2) that the veil, as an aid to seemliness, would be well-pleasing to the angels who are invisible helpers and witnesses (cf. Heb. 1:13 f., 12:1). The veil may even have been Paul's common-sense recommendation to prevent the distraction of men worshippers by the beauty of women's uncovered hair. (Cf. I Cor. 11:15, "if a woman have long hair, it is a glory to her: for her hair is given her for a covering.")

(2) In both Tabernacle* and Temple* a beautiful, hand-woven veil separated "the holy place" from "the most holy" (Ex. 26:31–37). The veil described in Ex. 26:31–35 was of "blue, and purple, and scarlet, and fine twined linen of cunning work: with cherubims." Hung from pillars of shittim wood overlaid with gold, by golden hooks on sockets of silver (v. 32), at a point 20 cubits from the E. end, it was so arranged that the Ark* could be carried inside it (Ex. 30:6, 40:3). The table and the candlestick were outside the veil; and the functions of the priests took place outside the veil (Ex. 27:21; Lev. 4:6, 24:3). Successive Temples, including Herod's, had the double veil of parallel curtains, three cubits apart. The one nearest the Holy Place was open at its N. end, allowing the high priest to enter the Holy of Holies (the Most Holy Place) on Atonement Day without letting the Most Holy Place be seen. This custom is referred to in Heb. 9, 10, where Jesus is spoken of as high priest and Saviour; he consecrated a new and living way by which men could with boldness enter "the holiest" through the "veil" of "his flesh," and thus he did away with the old custom.

During the Crucifixion of Jesus "the veil of the temple was rent in twain from the top to the bottom" (Matt. 27:51 and parallels).

For symbolic allusion "within the veil," see Heb. 6:19.

vengeance, revenge or punishment inflicted on one who has caused suffering or injury. An example of this is the O.T. practice of blood revenge, whereby an individual or a tribe wreaks vengeance on a murderer. Time and again Judah or Israel as a nation was thought to be chastised for wrongs committed by their rulers. Usually vengeance was viewed as the prerogative of the Lord: "vengeance is mine, saith the Lord" (Deut. 32:41, 43; Judg. 11:36; I Sam. 25:32–39; Isa. 34:8); a divine vengeance which was looked on as justifiable (II Sam. 3:39). In some O.T. and inter-Testamental writings (Prov. 25:21 f.) a new ideal appeared of returning good for evil, practicing forbearance and kindly self-control, and heaping "coals of fire." In the N.T. this became a high point in Christ's ideal, expressed in the Sermon on the Mount and elsewhere (Matt. 5:38–41, 6:14 f., 18:15–17, 21–35; Rom. 12:14, 17–21; I Cor. 13:4–7; I Thess. 5:15; Eph. 4:2, 32; Col. 3:13; I Pet. 3:9).

See also BLOOD; MURDER; PARDON; PUNISHMENT; RECONCILIATION.

venison, the meat of deer and other animals, a favorite food of Isaac, served to him by his hunter son Esau* (Gen. 25:28, 27:3–31).

vermilion, a brilliant red color associated in Scripture with luxurious settings, like the painted ceiling of the house described in Jer. 22:14; and the dyed apparel of Chaldaeans (Ezek. 23:14). The pigment was obtained by pulverizing the mineral cinnabar, or less effectively from a mixture of red clay and oxide of iron.

versions. See TEXT.

vessel, container for food, like the earthen cooking vessels and dishes used for a family's daily food—oil (Matt. 25:4), wine, grain, fish (Matt. 13:48), etc.; or for sacred materials used in the ritual of Tabernacle* and Temple, or (in archaic A.V. use) object (Acts 10:11) or wife (I Thess. 4:4). Vessels were made of wood or stone (Ex. 7:19; brass, A.V. 27:3, 39:39—more accurately copper or bronze); iron (Josh. 6:19, 24); silver and gold (I Kings 7:51; I Chron. 18:10); and ivory (Rev. 18:12). "Pleasant vessels" (Hos. 13:15), Temple furnishings of precious metals and the tablewares of the king (II Chron. 36:18) were often taken away as treasure by invaders.

Precious vessels from the Biblical period include a silver bowl* (Metropolitan Museum of Art) carrying a cuneiform inscription, telling that it was made for Artaxerxes I, the Achaemenian (465–424 B.C.); and Queen Shubad's fluted gold tumbler and spouted gold libation cup, excavated from the royal cemetery of Ur from the early dynastic period of Sumerian culture (University Museum, Philadelphia). (See CUP, illus. 104.)

vesture, an archaic word for garments, like the fine vestures given to Joseph the Hebrew by Pharaoh (Gen. 41:42). (See Deut. 22:12, "fringes . . . of thy vesture," Ps. 22:18 and Matt. 27:35, where mention is made of lots cast upon vesture.) Metaphorical allusions to vestures occur in Ps. 102:26; Heb. 1:12; Rev. 19:13, 16.

Via Dolorosa ("the Way of Sorrow"), the traditional route taken by Christ from Pilate's judgment hall to Calvary*. In Christ's time a business street, it is today a steep, narrow, Jerusalem street, used since the 14th century by pilgrims to dramatize the events of Christ's passion. The authenticity of the street as the Via Dolorosa is doubtful because of (1) its late recognition as a sacred way; (2) the fact that the 1st-century street actually traversed by Jesus is buried at least 30 ft. below the present street level; (3) the question as to the definite location of Pilate's praetorium (see ARCHITECTURE). Nevertheless every Friday pilgrims from all over the world, from every church and creed—scholars, clergy, soldiers, travelers, and peasants—join in the sacred procession through the narrow, picturesque street, and pause for devotions at the stations of the Cross clearly marked on the side of ancient buildings and in various portions of the Church of the Holy Sepulcher. Of the 14 stations of the Cross, four are borrowed from tradition (4, 6, 7, and 9); the

465. Via Dolorosa.

others come from Scripture freely interpreted, as noted below:

1. The condemnation by Pilate—Mark 15:16, 20; John 19:13–16.
2. Christ bears his Cross—John 19:17.
3. Christ falls under his Cross—Luke 23:26.
4. Christ meets Mary.
5. Simon shares the Cross—Luke 23:26.
6. Veronica, wiping the sweat from Christ's brow, finds the imprint of Christ's face on her handkerchief.
7. Christ's second fall.
8. The women of Jerusalem are exhorted—Luke 23:28.
9. The third fall of Christ.
10. The division of Christ's garments—Mark 15:24; John 19:23 f.
11. Christ is nailed to the Cross—Matt. 27:35.
12. The death of Christ—Matt. 27:33–54; Mark 15:22–39; Luke 23:33–47; John 19:18–30.
13. The descent from the Cross—John 19:38.
14. The burial of Christ—Matt. 27:59.

The Roman Catholic Church in its edifices, or sometimes in the open air, by a series of pictures or images representing the closing scenes in the passion of Christ encourages the dramatization of devotion by the use of these 14 stations of the Cross. This usage originated with the Franciscans, who were the custodians of many of Jerusalem's sacred places. (See also TRADE AND TRANSPORTATION.)

vial, a small flask or vessel for anointing oil. It was sometimes the horn of an animal, such as a shepherd might use, or a rustic prophet like Samuel (I Sam. 10:1) or Elisha (II Kings 9:1). (See Ps. 23:5.) Sometimes vials were of alabaster*, clay, or precious metal. (Cf. Rev. 15:7, 16:1 ff., 17:1, 21:9, vials filled with "the wrath of God.")

villages. See TOWNS.

vine, a slender-stemmed plant that trails or climbs by means of tendrils clasping a support. In the O.T. several kinds of vine are mentioned: melons (Num. 11:5), gourds (Jonah 4:6 ff.; II Kings 4:39), and cucumbers (Isa. 1:8). The Biblical vine par excellence is the grape, *Vitis vinifera,* the common European species of woody stems bearing clusters of grapes. The large-clustered red and the white varieties are preferred. The tiny black grapes that flourish at Corinth have long been exported as "currants" (Fr. "*raisins de Corinthe*"). At Smyrna seedless raisins have for centuries been cultivated. The neighborhood of Scutari, opposite Istanbul, boasts the finest grapes of the Middle East. Armenia and the Lebanons are also

466. Palestinian husbandman pruning vine.

centers of viticulture (Hos. 14:7). Egyptian viticulture was always intensive. Ancient Judah was famous for its enormous clusters of grapes, found in the Valley of Eshcol* ("grapes") by spies dispatched by Moses (Num. 13:23 f.); in this valley bunches weighing several pounds each are still plentiful. Early Israel had encountered grapes before crossing the Jordan, for their messengers agreed not to molest the vineyards of Sihon, King of the Amorites, if he would allow the company to pass through his land (Num. 21:22); and the Canaanites were probably raising grapes in abundance before Israel entered (cf. Gen. 14:18). The Rechabites' protest against strong drink may have risen from the excesses they had seen among the Canaanites.

The soil of Palestine has always been favorable to viticulture. Vines flourished on high, stone-walled terraces, as at Samaria (Jer. 31:5), and also on low land, like the plains of Jericho and Esdraelon (still so cultivated). Early Israelites, coming in from deserts, saw the vine-shaded homes of Canaanites and yearned for a time when they, too, would sit under their own "vine and fig tree"—a dream which for centuries was a reality (I Kings 4:25; II Kings 18:31; Isa. 36:16).

Cultivation of the vine (some details of which are described in Isa. 5:1–7 and in several parables of Jesus) begins with digging a ditch 3–4 ft. wide around the proposed vineyard. In this trench stout posts are set, to which are attached the intertwined branches that will start a hedge or fence (Mark 12:1). Sometimes the fence is reinforced with uncemented stone, or sun-dried brick, or mounds of earth; sometimes on boundary fences thorny shrubs or small trees are planted. Next the soil of the enclosure is dug up with a triangular-bladed, long-handled spade—the chief expense of the new vineyard (see Christ's Parable of the Laborers in the Vineyard, hired at the "eleventh hour"—one hour before sunset—Matt. 20:1–15). Young vines are soaked in water for several days before being planted. Then they are set in rows about 8 ft. apart; are pruned with pruning hooks (Joel 3:10) every spring (Lev. 25:3; John 15:2) and kept low, with the main stem trailing along the ground, and the fruit-bearing branches supported slightly above the earth (Ezek. 17:6). As soon as the vines are under cultivation, jackal scares of small, piled, whitewashed stones are put in place; also fox traps. No other plants are cultivated in the vineyard (Deut. 22:9). The 7th and 50th years' resting of the vines (Sabbatical* and Jubilee Years), is based on scientific as well as religious motives. Some Palestinian vineyards have been cultivated for centuries, with periodic renewal of some of the vines. Not until a vineyard has proved utterly unproductive is it given over to wild animals or marauders (cf. Isa. 16:8); even then the dry old vines make excellent fuel and charcoal (Ezek. 15:2 ff.; John 15:6).

The *watchtower* or leaf-covered wooden booth built on a high spot overlooking the vineyard (Mark 12:1) is occupied by members of the family all through the vintage season (Job 27:18), and sometimes by a watchman during the winter. Often a cottage is erected in the vineyard which the family lives in during the summer but abandons in the winter (Isa. 1:8). See BOOTH, illus. 63.

The first buds appear on the vine in March; blossoms come in April; grapes mature from July until late November, depending on the type and location of the vineyard. Carts and baskets (Jer. 6:9) carried by women, men, and children, conveyed the grapes in Bible times to the wine presses (Hos. 9:2).

Wine presses were square or oblong, sometimes cut in solid limestone, and lined with mortar or small stones. The tank had a hole near the bottom of one side, through which juice flowed to a smaller basin below. Rock-cut wine presses have been found at Beit Jibrîn in S. Palestine and elsewhere. Juice was extracted by several vintage helpers at a time stamping on the grapes with their bare feet (Amos 9:13); they held onto ropes suspended over their heads as they tramped, shouted in unison, and sang (Isa. 16:10; Jer. 25:30, 48:33). Egyptian wall paintings and reliefs show clearly the operation of wine presses in the large vine-producing areas of the Delta. In Palestine wine was stored in clay jars or in skin bottles*—principally goatskin bags* (made by drawing the body of the killed animal out from its skin after air had been blown between skin and flesh, and by tying the neck and feet). Fermenting wine was safest when stored in strong new skins (see Jesus' allusion to new wine bursting old skins, Matt. 9:17). Hundreds of pottery or skin containers of wine were stored in the cellars of the prosperous. Grapes were also used to produce certain types of vinegar* which result when acetous fermentation is not controlled by the use of lime or other fixative.

467. Wall painting of vintage, in Tomb of Apuy, sculptor, Nineteenth Egyptian Dynasty. At left, treading grapes; storage jars in center; grape pickers at right.

Vintage time (Sept.-Dec.) was, like sheep-shearing, a joyous season (Jer. 25:30, 48:33). People sang vintage songs—a portion of one possibly appears in Isa. 65:8; they danced; they courted; they became drunk and engaged in excesses (Judg. 9:27). Vine festivals were incorporated into Israel's Feast of Tabernacles (see FEASTS) in the month Tishri (Sept.-Oct.), when families lived in booths on roofs or on roadways to remind themselves of Israel's early tent life.

Tax collectors were alert at grape harvesting to claim their share of the yield (I Sam. 8:14), for debts were sometimes paid in terms of Palestinian wine, as Solomon did to Hiram (II Chron. 2:10). Men engaged in the vintage were exempt from military duty.

The *uses of the grape* are various. (1) White grapes are eaten in the hand. When they first come into the markets of Bethlehem and Hebron, for example, people cannot get enough of them. Clusters weigh several pounds each. (2) Grapes are dried for future eating in the form of masses of raisins or raisin cakes (A.V. I Sam. 25:18, 30:12; A.S.V. I Chron. 16:3), sometimes associated with Canaanite cults (cf. A.S.V. Hos. 3:1). (3) Grapes are also made into thin, honeylike jelly, *dibs*, by boiling down the juice. (4) But most of the crop is pressed into juice for wine—the light, sweet wines (cf. Matt. 26:29) (including unfermented "must") which with bread was staple food; and the heavier, fermented wines, excessive use of which is frequently inveighed against in the O.T. and the N.T. Wine was regarded as a gift from the Lord (Ps. 80:8). Kings delighted in their own royal vineyards—David (I Chron. 27:27);

Ahab (I Kings 21); Uzziah (II Chron. 26:10). Palestine also imported wines from Mediterranean islands—as recently attested, for example, by the many Rhodian jar handles bearing the name of the current magistrate and the date of bottling. Sacramental wines were made in both O.T. and N.T. times. In Zikron Ya'aqov region today carts loaded with grapes pull up to unload at this famous center for the manufacture of Jewish sacramental wine, destined for various countries.

Hebrew laws specified that the tenth of every man's vines belonged to the Lord (Deut. 12:17, 14:23; see also Num. 15:10). Drink offerings of wine were specified for every Sabbath (Num. 28:14). The fallen fruit was not gleaned, but was left for the poor and the sojourner (Lev. 19:10). The D Code provided that a man might eat grapes from his neighbor's vineyard, but not carry any home in a vessel (Deut. 23:24). Wine was not allowed to priests ministering at the sanctuary (Lev. 10:9), or to magistrates on duty. By teaching and by legislation, warnings were issued against excessive drinking of wine (Gen. 9:21 ff.; II Sam. 13:28; Prov. 20:1, 21:17, 23:20, 30; Isa. 5:11–17, 28:1; I Cor. 5:11, 6:10; Gal. 5:21; I Pet. 4:3). At banquets the strength of wine was one of the matters regulated by the "governor of the feast" (John 2:9 f.). Water was mixed with wine when Greek customs were followed (John 2:7–10; cf. Isa. 1:22). (For Rechabites* and wine see Jer. 35:5 ff.)

When Jesus engaged in normal sociability in an effort to win publicans and sinners, he was criticized as "a winebibber" (Matt. 11:19; cf. Prov. 23:20). The ascetic John the Baptist had been accused of having "a devil" because he followed an unsocial policy (Matt. 11:18).

Jesus in his parables used figures drawn from the vineyard: the Parable of the Vineyard rented by a cultivator (Mark 12:1–11); the Parable of the Fig in the Vineyard (Luke 13:6–9); of New Wine in Old Bottles (Matt. 9:17); of Laborers in the Vineyard (Matt. 20:1–16); of the Two Sons (Matt. 21:28–32); of the Wicked Husbandmen (vine cultivators) (Matt. 21:33; Mark 12:1–11). Jesus couched numerous other teachings in terms of viticulture: men do not "of a bramble bush gather . . . grapes" (Luke 6:44). His Parable of the Vine was spoken in the Upper Room a few hours before his arrest: "I am the true vine, and my Father is the husbandman. Every branch in me that beareth not fruit he taketh away," etc. (John 15:1–8). Following this utterance, Jesus honored the vine by taking the cup filled with its juice, as generations of Jews had done at the Passover*, and passed it to his Disciples, saying, "Drink ye all of it; for this is my blood of the new testament [covenant], which is shed for many for the remission of sins. But I say unto you, I will not drink henceforth of this fruit of the vine, until that day when I drink it new with you in my Father's kingdom" (Matt. 26:27 ff.). The Passover wine became the sacramental new wine of the Christian Communion.

Vines as symbols spelled prosperity among ancient Hebrews. Their prophets, like Habakkuk, foretold times of invasion in terms of vines not fruiting. Coins of the Maccabees, in the brief period of Jewish independence from Rome in the 2d century B.C., carry vines symbolic of restored Hebrew political power. Flavius Josephus in *The Jewish Antiquities* described Herod's decorative use of a golden vine, whose branches hung down from a great height at the Jerusalem Temple doors, under the crown-work of the "interwoven pillars of the doors," adorned with embroidered veils. Synagogues were sometimes adorned with carved vines. Rabbis used the vine symbol to represent the Torah, the Messiah, and spiritual leaders. Christian art used the popular motif of grape-bearing vines to suggest the union of Christ with his Disciples, and also the Christian Eucharist.

Vine of Sodom, the vines of the wicked in the Song of Moses; "Their grapes are grapes of gall, their clusters are bitter" (Deut. 32:32). If the phrase is not wholly figurative, a plant with luscious-looking fruit but powdery insides or a bitter flavor is probably meant.

vinegar, sour liquid obtained by acetous fermentation from wine, cider, beer, etc., used in condiments or as a preservative. "Vinegar of wine, and vinegar of strong drink" were forbidden to the Nazirites (Num. 6:3). Acetic acid in vinegar made it a beverage administered as a punishment (Ps. 69:21). Diluted wine was used by farm families of Palestine as a relish into which parched corn was dipped (Ruth 2:14); it was considered injurious to the teeth (Prov. 10:26). Vinegar —probably acetum, the sour wine of soldiers' rations—was offered Jesus on his cross, as an anodyne to pain (Mark 15:36; John 19:29 f.); this was different from the "wine mixed with myrrh" that he had refused earlier in his agony (Mark 15:23; cf. A.V. Matt. 27:34, "vinegar . . . mingled with gall").

viol. See MUSIC.

viper (Heb. *'eph'eh*), any poisonous snake of the genus *Vipera*. Isaiah used the viper as a symbol of evil (30:6, 59:5), as did Job (20:16). John the Baptist called "the multitudes which came forth to be baptized of him" a "generation of vipers" (Matt. 3:7)—R.S.V. "brood of vipers." Matthew records that Jesus castigated the Pharisees (12:34) and the scribes and Pharisees (23:33) as a "generation of vipers," as does Luke 3:7. The viper which "came . . . out of the heat, and fastened on his (Paul's) hand" at Malta (Acts 28:3) may have been an asp, or the common viper of Mediterranean shores. The people watching thought at first that this was a sign of vengeance against Paul and that he must therefore be a murderer, but they decided, when he showed no ill effects, that he must be a god.

virgin (Heb. *bethūlāh*, "separated"), a young and unmarried woman, like Rebekah (Gen. 24:16; Ex. 22:16 f.), Tamar (II Sam. 13:2); or (Heb. *'almāh* "mature") one of marriageable age (Gen. 24:43; Song of Sol. 1:3, 6:8; Isa. 7:14). (See IMMANUEL.)

The marriage* customs of early Israel provided that a bride who was bought by payment of 50 shekels to the father must be a virgin. If such proved not to be the case she might be stoned (Deut. 22:13–20). If a husband wrongly accused his wife of being "not a maid" (v. 14) he was chastised and fined for having besmirched the reputation of Israel (v. 19; cf. Ex. 22:16 f.). In the N.T. "virgin" is used to mean unmarried woman (cf. R.S.V. I Cor. 7:25, 28, 34, 36 f.).

In a symbolic sense "virgin daughter" is used of the city of Tyre (founded by Sidon) in Isa. 23:12; of Jerusalem (Jer. 14:17); and of "the virgin daughter of Babylon" (Isa. 47:1). The early Church was to Paul like "a chaste virgin" whom he presented to Christ (II Cor. 11:2). See MARY, THE VIRGIN.

virtue (Lat. *virtus*), a word used in Scripture in its usual sense of righteousness, conformity to known good, chastity. In Ruth 3:11 it connotes one who is capable and admirable. The "virtuous woman" described in Prov. 31 has many commendable qualities in addition to chastity: integrity and helpfulness (vv. 11 f.); industry (vv. 13–16, 19–22, 24, 27); business ability (vv. 14, 24); and talent for home-making (v. 27). "Virtue" in Mark 5:30 and Luke 6:19, 8:46 is more adequately translated "power" (*dynamis*) in the A.S.V. and R.S.V. "Virtue" A.V. Phil. 4:8 ("if there be any virtue, and if there be any praise, think on these things"), is "excellence" in the R.S.V.; and "virtue" in A.S.V. II Pet. 1:3 is "excellence" in the R.S.V.; but in v. 5 "virtue" is kept in the R.S.V. and the A.S.V.

Seven cardinal virtues were listed by early Christian writers, who added to the four virtues of Plato and the Stoics (prudence, temperance, fortitude, and justice), three "theological virtues" (faith, hope, and love).

vision, a sight presented to the mind through dream, trance, or some other nonobjective stimulus. There are scores of visions recorded in Scripture, most of them conveying revelations from God (theophanies—see THEOPHANY). Prophets especially were in communion with Deity, and their visions conveyed God's will in pictorial form. The visions of Ezekiel and of Daniel were in scenic form to clarify their God-sent revelations to their hearers or readers. The vision method of conveying truth is especially characteristic of Apocalyptic* literature.

(1) Visions in the O.T. include those of Amos: the vision of locusts (7:1–3) and fire or drought (7:4–6); the plumb line (7:7 f.); and the basket of summer fruit (8:1 f.)—the last of uncertain authenticity. For Hosea's vision of Israel's coming glory, see 2:14–23. Visions of the First Isaiah appear in 6:1–11. For the visions of Jeremiah see 1:11–16. Ezekiel's visions recorded in chaps. 1–3 are dated by some July 597 B.C., and those in chaps. 8–11 Sept. 592. His vision of the valley of dry bones appears in 37:1–10; and those concerning the Temple are in 40:1–44:3. Joel's "apocalyptic dreams" (R. H. Pfeiffer) are mentioned in 2:28–3:21. Zechariah's eight visions are contained in chaps. 2–7. Daniel's four, concerning the collapse of pagan empires and the coming Kingdom of God, in chaps. 7–12.

Other types of O.T. visions were that of the sleeping Abraham, promised an endless line of descendants (Gen. 15:1–3, 5 f., 11, 12a, 13 f., 16); of Balaam (Num. 22–24); of Samuel (I Sam. 3:3 f.); of Solomon (I Kings 3:5, 9:2–9, 11:9); and of Job (4:12–20).

Elisha's experience recorded in II Kings 3:11–20 has been called a "trance-vision," induced by the playing of a minstrel.

(2) The N.T. mentions several types of vision by which people of mystical temperament felt that they were being guided by the Lord. Sometimes the visions were marked by the appearance of angelic messengers, like the one which spoke to Zacharias in the Temple before the birth of John the Baptist (Luke 1:8–23); and those who announced the nativity of Jesus to the Bethlehem shepherds (2:8–14). Matthew referred to the Transfiguration as a "vision" (17:9). The Roman centurion Cornelius had a vision at Caesarea, prior to Peter's on the Joppa roof top (Acts 10:3, 10:10–19, cf. 11:5, 12:9). Paul's "heavenly vision" along the Damascus way was of a different sort (Acts 9:3–9, reflected in 26:19; cf. Gal. 1:11–17; I Cor. 9:1, 15:8). For other visions of Paul see Acts 16:9, 18:9; II Cor. 12:1. The Book of Revelation (see especially 9:17) is an Apocalyptic vision of the Lord and His approaching Kingdom.

vow (expressed by the Heb. *neder*, in connection with something dedicated to the Lord, and *'issar*, to indicate voluntary abstinence in honor of God), a solemn promise, especially to God. Vows were common very early among all Near Eastern peoples. (1) They were voluntarily entered into (Deut. 23:22) as a sort of bargain, whereby the individual promised to do thus and so, in return for a favor granted by Deity; as when Jacob vowed at Bethel that if the Lord would guarantee his peaceful entry to the land of his fathers he would own Him as his God and would give Him "the tenth." This vow, the oldest recorded in the O.T., was witnessed by Jacob's erection of a stone pillar (Gen. 28:16–22). Similar vows were Hannah's (I Sam. 1:11), when she promised that if God would grant her a son she would "give him unto the Lord all the days of his life," and there would no razor come upon his head (see NAZIRITES); and Absalom's, who vowed at Geshur that if God would bring him to Jerusalem he would serve Him (II Sam. 15:8); and the vow of Israel, led by Saul on the eve of the battle of Michmash, not to eat until evening (I Sam. 14:24 f., 36 f.), a forswearing which threatened grave consequences (vv. 32–35a). Breaking such a voluntary vow involved the death penalty (I Sam. 14:44; cf. Num. 30:2; Deut. 23:21–23). Rash vows, like that of Jephthah, were frowned upon (Judg. 11:30 ff.). The making of vows was often accompanied by gifts (like Jacob's pillar), or freewill offerings (Deut. 12:6, 23:23). But nothing was valid as a bond for a vow unless it truly belonged to the individual offering it (Lev. 27:26–30), or was of good quality (Mal. 1:14). It was a sin for an individual to appropriate "the devoted things." For restrictions on vows made by women, see Num. 30:2 ff. Persons might terminate vows by paying the redemption price (Lev. 27:26–30), or by repeating a certain formula.

(2) Vows of "devoted" material, turned over from battle spoils, for example, for the use of Yahweh (the support of priests, etc.), were not to be seized by individuals. The dire effects of Achan's stealing a Babylonish mantle, etc., are narrated in Josh. 7. (3) Nazirites vowed abstinence.

By N.T. times vow-making had become so corrupt that hypocrites used as an excuse for not supporting their aged parents (Ex. 20:12; I Tim. 5:8) the fact that they had vowed such and such possessions to the Lord, i.e., had made them "corban"*; this practice was exposed by Jesus (Matt. 15:3–5; Mark 7:6–13).

Vulgate, the Lat. version of the Bible, prepared by Jerome late in the 4th century. See TEXT.

vulture, the name given several kinds of large birds of prey, often bare-necked, and usually feeding on carrion. The vulture listed among "unclean" animals in A.V. Lev. 11:14 is a "kite" in the A.S.V. (see also Deut. 14:13, A.V.; Isa. 34:15). The far-visioned

468. Vultures.

eye of the vulture is mentioned by Job (28:7 A.V.—A.S.V. "falcon").

W

wâdī, an Arabic word used in Palestine, Syria, Jordan, N. Africa, etc., for (1) the channel of a watercourse, usually stony and dry, and sun-baked except during

469. Wâdī Nimrim leading to Jordan.

and immediately after the rainy season; (2) the river or stream itself. Many wâdīs are rimmed with wild white or pink oleander bushes which signal their presence to travelers miles away. Examples of wâdīs are the Arabah*, Wâdī Jabbok*, Wâdī Qelt, etc.

wafers, thin cakes of flour; sometimes made with honey (Ex. 16:31), as a sweet. Unleavened wafers rubbed with oil were part of Israel's meal oblations used in various offerings (Ex. 16:31, 29:2; Lev. 2:4, 7:12, 8:26; Num. 6:15, 19). Wafers are used in the Eucharist by Roman Catholics and others.

wages, regular payment for work or service rendered, was unknown in the nomadic and early Patriarchal period of Israel; the "wages" arranged between Laban and Jacob in Padanaram were unusual (Gen. 29:15, 30:28, 32 f.). Egyptian wages were paid to the mother of Moses by Pharaoh's daughter (Ex. 2:9). The usual wages paid in O.T. times in Palestine consisted of food and clothing distributed by the family head to servants, as well as to children and wives; cf. the "bread enough and to spare" of the "hired servants" in the Parable of the Prodigal Son (Luke 15:17).

Hebrew law codes provide for the payment of fair compensation for the day's work at the end of the day (Lev. 19:13; Deut. 24:14 f.). (For the wages of poor Hebrews toiling for rich sojourners or foreigners see Lev. 25:47–53.) Neighbors who helped build new barns or harvest crops expected to receive wages (cf. Jer. 22:13). O.T. prophets spoke of wages in times of inflation as being put "into a bag with holes" (Hag. 1:6).

It is to be assumed that wages in some form were customarily paid to Israelite hired laborers: Ammon hired many Syrian soldiers (II Sam. 10:6); masons and carpenters were hired to repair the Temple (II Chron. 24:12); counsellors were hired in Ezra's time (4:5). The O.T. refers to "the hire of a harlot" (Mic. 1:7). Zebedee of Galilee hired fishermen (Mark 1:20). Jesus referred to hirelings for flocks (John 10:12 f.).

Free labor co-existed alongside slave labor in the construction of Mesopotamian palaces and business places. Privately owned slaves were often apprenticed to Mesopotamian masters for as much as five or six years, so that they might become skilled in weaving, dyeing, working leather, fulling, or cutting gems. During this period the owner clothed and fed the pupil-slave. Yet Babylonians could employ free craftsmen almost as cheaply as they could maintain slaves (I. Mendelsohn, in *BASOR*, No. 89). A recovered clay tablet reveals a strike of Neo-Babylonian free gem-cutters, caused by their dissatisfaction over the wages paid by their king. The Code of Hammurabi is specific about wages to be paid farm laborers, brickmakers, herdsmen, etc.

In N.T. times wages were agreed on between servants and masters. According to Tobit 5:14, the drachm, about 20 cents in silver, was the usual daily wage. A working day was from sunrise to sunset. John the Baptist declared that soldiers should be content with their wages (Luke 3:14). Employers of laborers for vineyards went out into the market place and engaged day workers, sometimes as late as "the eleventh hour." In the latter portion of the Parable of the Workers in the Vineyard (Matt. 20:1–16), Jesus portrays an enlightened employer who keeps in mind the need of the late-coming laborers: if they return home with only an hour's wage, their families will go hungry. Perhaps not every employer can do this, but God can and does in His rewards. Earthly criteria of merit are arbitrary and often issue in the lovelessness of the full-day workers; God (and the employer of the parable) has other criteria, expressive of divine love for the late recruit. Not only fair wages, but just relationships between employers and employed (servants and masters) were advocated by leaders in N.T. times (Matt. 10:24 f.; Luke 17:7–9; John 13:16, 15:20; Eph. 6:5–9; Col. 3:22–25; I Tim. 6:1 f.; Tit. 2:9 f.; I Pet. 2:18 ff.).

wagon. See CART.

wallet, a bag used by shepherds and travelers to carry food, sandals, extra coat, etc. (A.S.V. and R.S.V. I Sam. 17:40; A.S.V. Matt. 10:10 and parallels; Luke 10:4, 22:35 f.; R.S.V. "bag," A.V. "scrip"). Money was carried in a purse of soft leather or fabric tucked into the girdle.

walls are often mentioned in Scripture. (1) *Vineyards and farms* had walls (Gen. 49:22; Num. 22:24 f.) made of stones set in mud or mortar, or made of thorny branches or mud (see VINES).

(2) *House walls* in Palestine were of mud, crude or baked brick, or stone. In early

470. Wall of O.T. Jericho.

Babylonia they were of reeds or wattles. Many houses in Bethlehem today have been standing for centuries, apparently impervious to the vicissitudes of time and weather, and look good for centuries more. Houses were required by Hebrew law to have a parapet or low battlement* to safeguard people on the roof top, and to protect passersby from objects that might fall into the street (Deut. 22:8) (see ROOFS). Sanitary and religious laws provided for the cleansing of the walls of houses where lepers had lived (Lev. 14:37).

(3) The *walls of "fenced" towns and fortified cities* were a chief means of defense in the Biblical period. They were usually of stone;

471. Hollow wall at Samaria, with transverse wall; Hellenistic wall in background.

sometimes of brick, as at Lachish*. Before crossing the Jordan into Canaan Israel encountered in Bashan King Og's "cities fenced with high walls, gates, and bars" (Deut. 1:28, 3:5). Israel's first building of walled cities was in Trans-Jordan (Num. 32:17). Walled cities existed at Philistine Gaza in the time of Samson. Spies sent into W. Palestine reported apparently impregnable Canaanite cities, whose great walls seemed to reach to heaven (Deut. 1:28). Canaanite construction excavated from such strategic sites as Beth-shan*, Lachish, and Tell el-Fâr'ah verify the reports of Israel's spies.

Hyksos walls were also formidable for young Israel. At Tell el-Fâr'ah, a frontier town 18 m. S. of Gaza on the important highway between Palestine and Egypt, the 150-ft. elevation was ringed with a trench 80 ft. wide. It had also a steeply sloping outer earthwork, as well as an inner sloping glacis, such as is seen today protecting the Crusader castle at the Syrian Krak des Chevaliers. The Hyksos had built a wall inside the earthwork, and Ramesses II constructed inside of it yet another wall of brick—a superb example of Eighteenth Dynasty Egyptian defense construction work in Palestine. A later Pharaoh, Shishak*, threw up a wall for this stronghold 22 ft. thick. Inside of it stood structures nearly 80 ft. long. When the

Romans came they raised a strong stone fort as a top layer, and built a stout revetment below. (Flinders Petrie believed that Tell el-Fâr'ah was Beth-pelet, but W. F. Albright favored Sharuhen*.) The rubble found here makes it understandable that O.T. writers like Isaiah should have mentioned reducing city walls to "heaps" (Isa. 24:12, 25:2, 12, 26:5).

The walls of cities are mentioned frequently in O.T. narratives. O.T. Jericho's* brick walls, which were wide enough to have houses built on them (Josh. 2:15), or to have their two rings of brick "tied together" by dwellings, fell "flat" (or "under it" or "in its place"—A.S.V.) at the historic invasion by Joshua's Israelites (6:5, 20; Heb. 11:30). Excavations at O.T. Jericho have demonstrated that this commanding city on the Jordan plain—one of the first sites inhabited in Palestine—was ringed by a double wall, like those at Lachish and other sites. The space between the walls was used for patrols, conferences of councilors, activities of merchants, and as a refuge for terrified citizens. Such walls were strong-gated and towered. From wall towers bowmen shot their arrows (II Sam. 11:20, 24), and heavy material like millstones was thrown down on attacking enemies (II Sam. 11:21). The walls of Beth-shan—many courses of which have been excavated by the University of Pennsylvania—were used by the enemies of Saul and Jonathan to display the slain bodies of this royal pair (I Sam. 31:10, 12). Some O.T. cities whose walls are specifically mentioned in Scripture are: Jezreel (I Kings 21:23); Gath; Ashdod (II Chron. 26:6); Rabbah (the present 'Ammân, capital of the Kingdom of Jordan) (Amos 1:14); Damascus (Jer. 49:27; Acts 9:25; II Cor. 11:33); Babylon (Jer. 51:44, 58); and Tyre (Ezek. 26:4).

472. Wall over Damascus Gate, Jerusalem.

Jerusalem's historic walls, with their ancient rubble and present 2½ m. circuit of masonry, 34 towers, 8 gates, and variegated construction, reveal much of the city's 30 centuries of history. The walls still convey to the observer the atmosphere of the typical walled city of the Near East, even though most of what is now standing is of 16th century construction (Suleiman the Magnificent). The S. and SE. stretches retain massive layers which no doubt Jesus saw, including the famous cornerstone*. (See II Sam. 5:6–9 for David's early wall at the Jebusite stronghold; and Solomon's wall construction, I Kings 3:1, 9:15). Jehoash, King of Israel (c. 801–786 B.C.), battered the wall (II Kings 14:13). The Chronicler tells of Jerusalem's walls being defended in the time of King Hezekiah (c. 715–687 B.C.) when Sennacherib made his threatening advance (II Chron. 32:18). King Manasseh repaired them before the close of his reign c. 642 B.C. (II Chron. 33:14). Chaldaeans pounded them (II Chron. 36:17–19), and precipitated by their fall the end of the Kingdom of Judah. The most famous Jerusalem "wall" chapters concern the night ride of inspection made by Nehemiah after Artaxerxes had allowed him to return to Jerusalem, and the subsequent repairs he and his adherents made within 52 days, in spite of taunts and obstructions (Neh. 1:3, 2:8, 2:12–20, 3, 4, 6:15). Titus (A.D. 70) defeated the Jews by destroying these long-cherished Jerusalem* walls.

The Apocalypse describes the walls of the heavenly Jerusalem, high and twelve-gated (Rev. 21:12 ff.).

Not mentioned in the Bible, but excavated

at Gibeah* (Tell el-Fûl), King Saul's rustic stronghold, was an outer citadel whose walls were 8 to 10 ft. thick, with distinctive casemated walls and tower construction. The walls of Gezer were 14 ft. thick.

One of the most dreadful pronouncements a prophet could hurl against Jerusalem or any other fenced city was that it would become as a "town without walls" (Zech. 2:4). One of the most effective enemy measures for accomplishing this disaster was to ring the walls with burning trees. This is known to have been the technique used in destroying Lachish in S. Judaea, for fragments of burned ripe olivewood have been excavated—revealing the season of year when the disaster took place (v. 5).

Outside of Palestine many cities were famous for their walls—not mentioned in the Bible, but familiar to Biblical persons. Paul saw the walls of Athens, long famous for

473. Damascus city wall (Acts 9:25).

protecting the path to the harbors of Piraeus and Phaleron. He saw also the ancient Corinthian walls built on the lofty Acrocorinthus above the merchant city. These powerful, gated defenses were effective in early times, and down the centuries to the Roman period of Paul; even through Byzantine and Turkish days they continued effective—with successive additions. A few vestiges of these early Greek walls can still be seen. Down in the commercial city, beautifully revealed by American archaeologists, are traces of the city wall, including the Isthmian Gate and part of the long, double wall joining Corinth with its harbor at Lechaeum.

The Greek colonial city of Syracuse, founded by Corinth on the island of Sicily, had mighty fortifications in the Biblical period, built by Dionysius the Elder (402–397 B.C.). This "Castle of Euryelos," constructed about a half-century after Nehemiah's restoration of the walls of Jerusalem, held at bay for 38 years the armed semi-barbarians of Carthage and thus protected Hellenic culture in the mid-Mediterranean.

war, as depicted in Scripture, was waged for the same purposes that have motivated wars ever since O.T. times—desire to enlarge territory (II Sam. 8; II Kings 17:5, etc.), increase material resources, liquidate enemies, and establish political and religious ideologies. The settlement of Canaan by the Hebrews was marked by barbaric struggles with previous settlers (Josh. 11:3; Judg. 3:3; II Sam. 24:7, etc.), many of whom continued to live in their old homes alongside Israel. Their presence tested the faithfulness of Israel to God (Judg. 2:22). The God of the Conquest was depicted by O.T. writers as the protagonist of a violently espoused cause. Ruthlessness was characteristic of many of Israel's war leaders—Joshua, Deborah and Barak, Gideon, Jephthah, Samson, Saul, even David.

Not only did these warriors endeavor to determine the will of God before going into

474. War captives, shown in glazed tiles from palace of Ramesses III. Left to right: Syrian, Philistine, Syrian, Negro, Hittite, in native apparel.

battle by oracles, (Judg. 1:1, 20:23, 27 f.; I Sam. 23:2; I Kings 22:6) the "wise" (II Sam. 14), the lot (I Sam. 14:41 f.), the urim and thummim, or by sacrifice (I Sam. 7:8 f., 13:12) and fasting (II Chron. 20:3–13), but they sometimes even carried the Ark* of the Lord into battle (I Sam. 4:1–3). Priests and warriors thanked God, in festivals and ritual, for victory. "Singers unto the Lord" preceded armies (II Chron. 20:21). It was not considered inconsistent to display war trophies in sacred places (II Sam. 8:11). Specific portions of booty were dedicated to the Lord and His priests (Num. 31:37–41; cf. Josh. 6:19, 7). Captives—even kings—were cruelly killed or obliged to bend the knee and bow the neck to their captors. Successful warriors were honored by their king, as David honored his general Joab, victor in many engagements (II Sam. 20:22 f.). The extermination of whole town populations was believed necessary to the establishment of the true concepts of God and to the building of a nation dedicated to His purposes (Judg. 6:1; II Chron. 14:9–15, 21:16, etc.). If war brought out the worst in the tribes (II Sam. 20:10; I Chron. 20:3), it also—according to O.T. writers—served to develop strong leaders, to amalgamate loosely knit Hebrew groups (I Sam. 14:47 f.), and to foster stamina and morale in a pioneering people. Yet the price paid was very high, as in David's case (I Chron. 22:8 f.).

The O.T. is outspoken in its denunciation of killing (Ex. 20:13; Lev. 24:17, 19 f., etc.) and in extolling the blessings of peace* (Lev. 26:6; I Kings 2:31–33; II Chron. 14:1 f.; Jer. 29:7). Throughout the Bible facts are recorded which demonstrate that "all who take the sword will perish by the sword" (R.S.V. Matt. 26:52). Scores of passages show war as a weapon used by the Lord to punish wayward Israel for apostasies and disobedience (Judg. 6:1; II Kings 15:37; II

Chron. 21:4–10). The builders and restorers of the Temple and its worship, like Solomon (II Chron. 3–6), Joash (II Chron. 24), and Josiah (II Chron. 34, 35), were not primarily warriors.

Aggressive warfare, which has chronically devastated Palestine (despite the enthusiasm of Deut. 8:7–9) was due to its location at the crossroads of ancient highways. This is illustrated graphically by carvings visible today in the rock wall of Dog River Pass (Nahr el-Kelb) in Lebanon between Tripoli and Beirut. It was taken for granted that when spring set in kings would go forth to battle (II Sam. 11:1). Weather determined the outcome of chariot warfare (Judg. 4:15, 5:21), and terrain decided whether horsemen or footmen would be used. (For the chief aggressors who moved across Palestine on their way to some richer prize, or to rob whatever was in the coffers of this poor country, see BEN-HADAD; NEBUCHADNEZZAR; SELEUCIDS; SENNACHERIB; SHALMANESER; THUTMOSE; TIGLATH-PILESER; TITUS, etc.)

Israel's defenses. Under the Hebrew kings, large standing armies composed of "hundreds" and "thousands" (I Chron. 12:14) led by captains were maintained by draft and fed by systematic chains of food depots, especially under Solomon (I Kings 4). This king became famous for his horses and war chariots stationed in chariot cities (I Kings 9:19, 10:26) like the now excavated Megiddo* overlooking the great battle plain, Esdraelon. Faulty translation or enthusiastic exaggeration account for the enormous numbers attributed to the forces of certain Hebrew kings, like Abijah, Jeroboam (II Chron. 13:3), and Asa (II Chron. 14:8). Techniques employed in O.T. warfare included the use of strategy, like Gideon's terrifying attack by night (Judg. 7:15–22); spies; the use of signal towers placed so that messages could be flashed from height to height (as revealed in the Lachish Letters excavated at the S. frontier of Judah); battle cries and terrifying war trumpets; and the protection of water supplies from invaders (see SILOAM). Defense* measures included throwing up extra mounds in front of towns, adding extra rings of wall (as demonstrated today by excavated masonry), maintaining battering-rams* and scaling ladders, and stock-piling weapons*. Not until the opening of the Iron Age in Palestine under the early Monarchy, and the availability of raw materials for metal weapons following the exploits of David, could Israel compete with her armed neighbors. (See *An Encyclopedia of Bible Life*, Madeleine S. and J. Lane Miller, Harper & Brothers, Section 8.)

War songs in the O.T. are enumerated by R. H. Pfeiffer (*An Introduction to the Old Testament*, Harper & Brothers, p. 274): the Song of Lamech (Gen. 4:23 f.); Samson's war song (Judg. 15:16); the Song of Miriam (Ex. 15:21); an insertion from The Book of the Wars of the Lord (Num. 21:14 f.); a eulogy of Moab's devastation (Num. 21:27–30); an oracle against the Amalekites (Ex. 17:14); and a liturgy for bringing the Ark into battle (Num. 10:35 f.). Hymns of peace are found in numerous Psalms (30, 122, 125, 133, etc.).

Wars of the Lord, Book of the, a lost work from which quotation is made in Num. 21:14 f., and possibly in vv. 17 f. ("The Song of the Well") and vv. 27–30. It is scarcely to be considered identical with the Book of Jashar, as some have suggested.

wash (Luke 7:38, 44; R.S.V., A.S.V. wet), a reference to the Palestinian custom of providing water for the bathing of guests' road-dusty feet. The woman who was a sinner did with tears what Jesus' host had failed to do with water. See also BATHING; WATER.

watch. See TIME.

watchman. See WATCHTOWERS. For figurative use of "watchman" see Isa. 21:11 f., 52:8, 56:10; Ezek. 3:17; Mic. 7:4.

watchtowers were built at crossroads and on the outskirts of cities like Jerusalem to conceal or shelter sentries, like those of King Jehoshaphat (II Chron. 20:24). Sometimes the king's watchtower was "on the roof over the gate unto the wall," like David's at Jerusalem (II Sam. 18:24). (For watchtowers in vineyards, see VINE.) The prophet Habakkuk spoke figuratively of having a watchtower where he was alert for signs of God's revelation (2:1). See TOWERS.

water was even more valued by people in Palestine than in most other parts of the ancient world—because scarcer. (1) Adequate *sources of water* determined the sites of early settlement in the Near East. Palestine, in spite of its description in Deuteronomy as "a good land, a land of brooks of water, of fountains and depths that spring out of valleys and hills" (8:7), has always been hampered by

475. Gigantic water-wheel for irrigation at Hama (biblical Hamath).

scant rainfall, frequent droughts, and inadequate water supply. Miles of parched desert have caused many mass migrations to the well-watered Nile* Valley and to the regions of the children of "the east" (Gen. 29:1). Trans-Jordan (now the Kingdom of Jordan) has many more useful rivers than Palestine despite the latter's seasonal brooks (see WÂDĪ). The highlands of Trans-Jordan lent themselves to irrigation (see Nelson Glueck, *The Other Side of the Jordan*, ASOR, and *The River Jordan*, Westminster Press). The Romans found terrain in Eastern Palestine where their expert engineers could work out water supply techniques; land along the

Jordan in W. Palestine was too low to lend itself to irrigation; not until modern times has large-scale irrigation been projected or effected in Israel.

Archaeology has revealed that water determined settlement on such strategic sites as Gezer, Jericho, Jerusalem (see EN-ROGEL; GIHON; SILOAM), and Megiddo (Judg. 5:19). Rabbah (the present 'Ammân) was known as "the city of waters" (II Sam. 12:27). Amazing underground water conduits and foot tunnels leading to protected springs have been excavated at Gezer, Jerusalem, and Megiddo. (See *An Encyclopedia of Bible Life*, Madeleine S. and J. Lane Miller, Harper & Brothers, Section 21, "Water Supply.")

(Gen. 21:14, 19, the story of Hagar; Ex. 17:1, 6, cf. "no water for the people," Num. 20:2; Judg. 4:19, Sisera); of flocks (Gen. 29:2, 7); and of plant life (Job 8:11). (See also Elijah, in time of drought, I Kings 17:10; David, in battle near Bethlehem, I Chron. 11:17; Jeremiah, in a Jerusalem dungeon, 38:6; Jesus, thirsting on his Cross, John 19:28.) Water was even bought by migrant peoples, as Moses vainly attempted to do from Sihon, King of Heshbon (Deut. 2:28), and as is still done in Palestine during drought. God was the One Who watered the hills (Ps. 104:13); hence water was sacred. It was very early an element in *ritual and worship*. Hebrew laws found in the O.T.

476. Reconstruction drawing by Seton Lloyd of aqueduct built c. 700 B.C. by Sennacherib. Enormous masonry construction (c. 1000 ft. long x 80 ft. wide) allowed water to flow in broad channel, and formed part of a canal 45 m. long. From *Sennacherib's Aqueduct at Jerwan*, by Jacobson and Lloyd, University of Chicago Press.

The economic greatness of Corinth in N.T. times and for centuries earlier is explained not only by the twin harbors of her isthmus, facing E. and W., but by the rushing waters of her fountains—the Peirene, the Triglyph, and others. The wealth of S. Babylonia was due to fertile flood deposits in its marshes; and the irrigating canals of Babylonia contributed to its wealth. Rulers from Hammurabi on prided themselves on adding conduits and reservoirs for drinking water and irrigation. Sennacherib's Aqueduct of Jerwan was one of the earliest in history (excavated by the Oriental Institute); it made possible the beauty of the garden capital, Nineveh*. There were times when the Tigris was joined to the Euphrates by irrigating canals.

Jerusalem's modern water supply is pumped 30 m. through pipes attached to copious springs at Râs el-'Ain—the ancient Antipatris, briefly visited by Paul (Acts 23:31).

Certain O.T. streams had marked characteristics: "the waters of Megiddo" (Judg. 5:19), near the battlegrounds of Taanach and other sites on the Plain of Esdraelon, were linked with political destinies wrought out in battles; these waters both slaked the thirst of warriors and bogged their chariots down in Kishon mud. Isaiah mentioned the "waters of Shiloah [Siloam] that go softly" (8:6). Jeremiah knew the rapid waters of the lively Wâdī Nimrim* (48:34).

(See also TADMOR; TARSUS—for their water supplies; WELLS; CISTERNS; FOUNTAIN.)

(2) Water is mentioned more frequently in Scripture than any other natural resource. It was recognized by writers of the early O.T. books as essential to the life of man

codes were common-sense provisions for sanitation, as well as for religious rites: the ceremony for cleansing lepers (Lev. 14:8; cf. the story of Naaman); for ridding people of the taboo of uncleanness due to illness (15:5–8, 10–13), or to eating unclean animals* (17:15 f.). Holy water, made according to a Levitical formula, was used to test marital fidelity (Num. 5:17 ff.). (See WATER OF BITTERNESS; WATER OF SEPARATION.)

(3) Water was a favorite symbol*. The tremendous copper sea in Solomon's Temple Area was symbolic of God's creative "heavenly acts" (cf. Gen. 1:2), and of water as the source of all life. It thus had a "cosmic significance" rather than a ritualistic function of cleansing, such as the portable laver had. W. F. Albright associated the copper sea with the Mesopotamian *apsu*, the fresh-water body from which all living creatures were derived. Shrines always tended to be established near springs or other sources of water.

In the O.T. water was also a symbol of instability (Gen. 49:4), and of the fleeting quality of life (Job 11:16; Ps. 58:7). It typified Assyria's overflowing of Judah (Isa. 8:7 f.).

In N.T. times, water was essential for baptism*, which denoted the washing away of sin (Matt. 3:6, 11, 13 ff.). The divine sonship of Jesus was manifested at his Baptism at the Jordan (Matt. 3:16). John baptized at Aenon because there was "much water" there (cf. "Bethany beyond the Jordan," "Betharabah," A.S.V. John 1:28 and margin). A small wayside spring was similarly used by Philip in baptizing the Ethiopian eunuch (Acts 8:36). In N.T. iconography water was a symbol of baptism.

Jesus used water metaphorically when he said to Nicodemus that "Except one is born of water [baptism] and the Spirit, he cannot enter the kingdom of God" (R.S.V. John 3:5); and to a woman at the Sychar well he mentioned "living water" as a symbol of the

477. Flocks at ancient Roman reservoir.

eternal life which springs up within the redeemed (John 4; cf. Matt. 5:6).

The "cup of water" given in Christ's name describes Christian charity (Mark 9:41; cf. Matt. 25:35) (and see Pilate's ceremonial use of water at the Trial of Jesus, Matt. 27:24). Paul spoke of watering the planted seed of the Church (I Cor. 3:6—"I planted, Apollos watered") (see also Tit. 3:5). The "great voice" of one "like unto the Son of man" (Rev. 1:11–15) was "as the sound of many waters" (see also 7:14). At its climax the Apocalypse describes the "river of the water of life" (Rev. 22:1 f., 17).

(4) Water was used to show hospitality (Gen. 18:4, 24:32; II Sam. 11:8; Luke 7:38, 44; John 13:6, 8, 10, 14) (see WASH).

watercourse. (1) A natural channel through which water flows, like the "upper watercourse of Gihon" (II Chron. 32:30) (see WÂDĪ). (2) An artificial conduit or canal made for conveying water, like the Siloam* Tunnel; the conduit which carried a supply from Solomon's pools near Bethlehem to Jerusalem; the Gezer tunnel; the Megiddo water system; the aqueduct of Sennacherib at Jerwan.

water of bitterness, a drink consisting of "holy water" and dust from the Tabernacle floor, administered in a "jealousy ordeal" to test a wife suspected of unfaithfulness (Num. 5:11–31).

water of separation, liquid used in the ancient ritual of cleansing from the deflement which the Hebrews believed was incurred by touching a dead body. The water-of-separation rite was incorporated into the P Code* (Num. 19). It used living or running water, mixed with the ashes of an unblemished, reddish-brown heifer which had never felt the yoke, and which had been burned under specific regulations by a man appointed by the high priest. The water of separation was sprinkled on the contaminated person with a sprig of ceremonial hyssop* on the 3d and 7th days after the deflement had taken place. Then, after the individual had washed his body and his garments, he returned as an acceptable member of the community.

waterpot, a clay vessel, sometimes two-handled, sometimes pitcherlike, used for transporting water to the house from wells, cisterns, springs, or streams (John 2:6 f., 4:28); or for pouring water into troughs for animals (Gen. 24:45 f., cf. 29:6–10). Waterpots, usually carried by women (John 4:7) and girls (but cf. Luke 22:10), were securely and gracefully poised on the shoulder or the head. Their capacity was several gallons. The type of waterpot used for storing and purifying water, as at the Cana wedding, was often of stone and held "two or three firkins" (A.V. John 2:6 f.; cf. R.S.V.); a firkin in the Graeco-Roman world was c. 10.3 U.S. gallons. See POTTERY, illus. 328.

wave offering. See WORSHIP.

waw. See VAU.

way, a word used to translate various Heb. and Gk. words in Scripture: (1) for a path, a road (Gen. 18:16), or a route (Ex. 13:17, "way of the land of the Philistines"; I Sam. 6:9, 12; II Kings 3:20; Jer. 2:18; Matt. 2:12); (2) for a human life ("my way" Gen. 24:56), or a manner of living (II Chron. 20:32; Prov. 2:8); (3) as a figure of speech, for "the way everlasting" to reach God (I Kings 2:4; Job 17:9); "the way of the Lord" (Isa. 40:3) in contrast to "the evil way" (Jonah 3:8; Ps. 139:24); His plan for a righteous universe (Gen. 18:19; John 1:23) frequently expressed in the O.T. and the N.T. (Acts 18:25 f.). (See KINGDOM OF GOD; KINGDOM OF HEAVEN.)

In the N.T. Jesus spoke of himself as being not only "the way" but the goal to which that way led: "I am the way, the truth, and the life" (John 14:4–6). Hence his followers were known as "people of the way" (cf. Acts 19:23). The Greek world knew various philosophical ways of life—Stoic, Cynic, Orphic, etc., but it was still waiting for something better than a new way of conduct; it looked expectantly for "the way of salvation" (Acts 16:17), "a new and living way" (Heb. 10:20), of which Isaiah's highway of holiness (35:8) had given a foreglimpse.

wayfaring man, a traveler (Judg. 19:17; II Sam. 12:4; Isa. 33:8, 35:8). Wayfaring men included merchants, metal smiths, musicians, idlers, and sojourners (Jer. 9:2, 14:8). They disappeared in times of unsettled political conditions (Judg. 5:6).

"we" source. (See ACTS.)

wealth in the nomadic phase of Hebrew history consisted of great flocks, such as Abraham, Lot, Isaac, Jacob, and Laban possessed (Gen. 13:2, 5 ff., 26:11–14, 29:3 ff., 32:5). As Israel became a settled agricultural people fenced land was an evidence of riches. Those who had farms and orchards often desired more, as King Ahab* did when he coveted his neighbor Naboth's vineyard. In post-Exilic times land was eagerly reclaimed (Neh. 5:3). Large families, and companies of servants, slaves, and secondary wives were income-producing resources. Metals, in the form of rings and wedges or "tongues" of gold used as uncoined money*;

vessels of valuable metal; weapons; garments; well-stocked markets; armed retainers—were all part of the rich man's wealth. Solomon is the only O.T. example of a wealthy Israelite merchant. Egypt grew wealthy through trade (see TRADE AND TRANSPORTATION).

Palestine as a land was never as rich as the enthusiastic words of Deut. 8:7–9 indicate; only parts of the country, and at specific times, "flowed with milk and honey." The hills containing metals were E. of the Jordan, rather than in Palestine.

Biblical teaching concerning wealth varied. Riches were regarded as coming from the Lord (I Sam. 2:7). Wealth given by God was not to be avoided, nor was it to dominate a man's interests. The wisdom of Prov. 30:8 exalted "neither poverty nor riches." The Essenes and other ascetic groups avoided material wealth.

The noblest Hebrews have always viewed wealth as a responsibility and something to be shared with the poor and the community; the revised Union Prayer Book of modern Jews enjoins the stewardship before God of all that a man possesses.

Jesus did not condemn wealth per se, though he condemned the man whose chief concern was in building larger barns (Luke 12:16–21); and he stressed the handicap of wealth to one entering the Kingdom of God (Matt. 19:24, Luke 16:19–31); he did not wish it to be an all-absorbing interest. He therefore taught "where your treasure is, there will your heart be also" (R.S.V. Matt. 6:21); and "seek first his kingdom, and his righteousness; and all these things shall be yours as well" (R.S.V. Matt. 6:33; cf. Luke 12:22–34). He did not decline to dine with men of wealth. One rich Jew, Joseph of Arimathaea (Mark 15:43), honored him at the last. Yet Christ's compassion for the poor was one of his most characteristic traits. "The poor ye have always with you" was a truth well-known to him. He praised the poor widow who gave her all to the Temple treasury (Mark 12:41–44). He fed hungry multitudes (Mark 8:1–9). Though Jesus owned no property (Luke 9:58; John 7:53, 8:1), the Twelve carried a common purse (except on unusual occasions, as in Matt. 10:10), replenished by his followers (Luke 8:3). The Apostolic Church did not condemn wealth, for it collected funds to minister to its poor and to stranded foreigners seeking the Way (Acts 6:1 f.); yet such utterances as the Epistle of James are bitter against the adulation paid to ring-wearing, extravagantly attired worshippers, and against accumulated riches (2:1–8, 5:1–5). The author of I Timothy, who was in contact with the rich cities of the Graeco-Roman world, warned against the pitfalls of wealth (6:9 f., 17–19; see also Rev. 3:17).

weaning, accustoming a child to food other than its mother's milk. Hannah said of her young son Samuel, "I will not go up until the child be weaned, and then will I bring him, that he may appear before the Lord, and there abide forever" (I Sam. 1:22). Hebrews often weaned their children at the age of two or three. Weaning festivals were popular (Gen. 21:8). Late weaning continues in primitive sections of the Near East.

weapons, instruments of combat, were of various kinds. *Stones* (I Sam. 17:49) were the earliest and commonest of weapons; they are still used on the slightest pretext in certain regions of Palestine, Syria, and more remote areas. *Slingballs* of stone and of flint were also used. Many of these have been excavated. The stone *hand axes* or *coups-de-poing* used in very early Palestine have not been found in *tells*, whose rubble was built up at later dates.

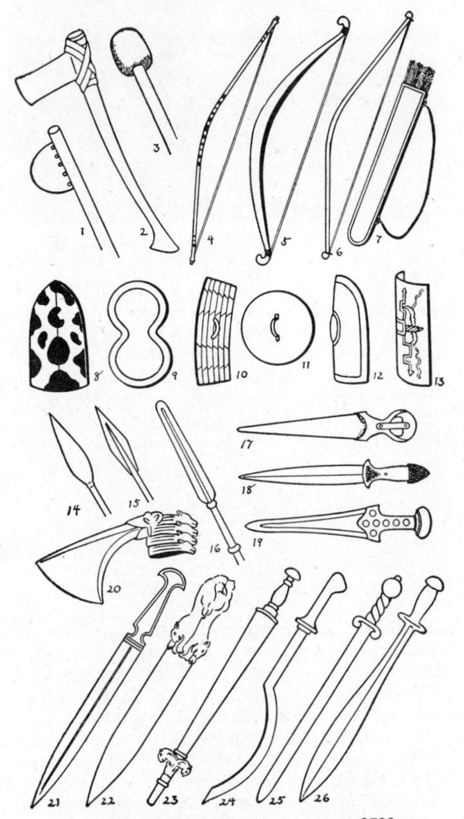

478. Weapons: 1. Egyptian poleax, c. 2700 B.C.; 2. Egyptian ax, 1580 B.C.; 3. Type of ancient stone mace; 4. Type of Egyptian bow, 1430 B.C.; 5. Assyrian bow, 1200 B.C.; 6, 7. Assyrian bow and quiver with arrows, 850 B.C.; Ancient shields, 1/30 to 1/40 size: 8. Egyptian, 2000 B.C.; 9. Late Minoan, 1580-1100 B.C.; 10. Assyrian, 700 B.C.; 11. Assyrian, 650 B.C.; 12. Roman, 100 B.C.; 13. Roman, 300 B.C.; 14. Assyrian spear; 15. Syrian spear; 16. Egyptian spear, 1600 B.C.; 17. Egyptian dagger, 2000 B.C.; 18. Sumerian dagger; 19. Late Minoan dagger, 1600-1100 B.C.; 20. Type of sword with curved blade coming from mouth of animal forming hilt, c. 3000 B.C.; 21. Sword of Marduk-shapik-zeri, 1250 B.C.; 22. Sword with straight blade, two lions forming hilt, c. 3000 B.C.; 23. Assyrian sword, 900 B.C.; 24. Ancient Palestinian scimitar; 25. Type of ancient Roman sword; 26. Type of ancient Greek sword.

Flint *knives* and slingballs were used in a late period, as well as in very early O.T. times. *Daggers*, double-edged knives, were common in the period of the Judges (Judg. 3:16–22); and became plentiful as soon as the Iron Age in Palestine made metal available. Philistines at the time of David's conquests (10th century B.C.) were using daggers, whose handles were inlaid with ivory; their sheaths were attached to the warrior's arm. Daggers were favorite weapons of the Hittites. Some of these weapons were excavated in the debris of the level of Thutmose III at Beth-shan*. Daggers from Crete and Cyprus were treasured Hyksos weapons. *Spears* with tips of barbed bronze or iron became common in Palestine, as in central Mediterranean lands. (For Saul's use of a spear, see I Sam. 26:7.) In Iron Age Palestine bronze arrowheads were made and used. *Javelins* (possibly of wood) were used by Joshua and his men at the siege of Bethel-Ai. (See Saul's use of a javelin, I Sam. 20:33; cf. "dart," II Sam. 18:14; Eph. 6:16). *Swords** are often mentioned as having been used by Joshua, to "smite" his enemies; these references may be anachronistic. *Bows and arrows* were commonly employed in Israel's warfare (I Sam. 20:20 ff.). They had been in wide use among the Sumerians more than 1,000 years before Joshua, as seen in many bas-reliefs of archers in chariots. The battle bow continued to be a favorite weapon of Babylonians and Persians down to the Battle of Marathon, where Persian bows were matched against Greek spears; spears won out in that memorable contest of 490 B.C. Extant bas-reliefs show archers in the armies of a Shalmaneser, for example, laying siege to a Syrian city; or in the ranks of Sennacherib attacking Lachish, or an Egyptian stronghold in the 7th century B.C. Job, apparently a dweller in Edom, felt as if encompassed with archers (16:13). Zechariah, envisioning a Messianic era of peace, hoped for the disappearance of weapons—battle bow, chariot, arrow, and slingstones (9:10; cf. Isa. 2:4).

Jonathan presented to his friend David his royal sword, bow, and girdle—standard equipment for at least the king's household (I Sam. 18:4). We know that some also possessed helmet and cuirass, for Saul offered to lend David his armor for the contest with the Philistine giant Goliath, who was fully armed with metal from the crown of his head to his knees, and probably wore leather shin guards. An enormous round *shield* was bound to his forearm by two bands of metal or leather. I Samuel 17:5–7 relates that "he had an helmet of brass upon his head, and he was armed with a coat of mail; and the weight of the coat was five thousand shekels of brass [copper or bronze]. And he had greaves of brass upon his legs, and a target of brass [bronze] between his shoulders. And the staff of his spear was like a weaver's beam . . . and one bearing a shield went before him." The armor of Saul, which David declined in favor of his slingstones, was also of bronze or possibly copper. In earlier times armor of leather or quilted fabric had been used. Sumerians sometimes made helmets (Isa. 59:17) of gold, as known from that of King Meskalam-dug (c. 2500 B.C.) excavated at Ur. Their use of copper gave them—as it did the Egyptians—superior weapons at an early date.

A cache of typical weapons unearthed from a *tell* or a tomb of the Hebrew Monarchy period would include a broad-bladed dagger, a curved scimitar of Babylonian type, sling-balls, a stone-headed mace (common in Egypt), darts, and leaf-shaped bronze arrow tips. Clubs, sometimes metal-studded, were used in strife, as well as by shepherds protecting their flocks. Iron arrowheads were not common until almost the Roman era. Halberds (axlike spears), hatchets, and boomerangs (popular in Egypt) were not typically Palestinian. (For weapons in a symbolic sense, see Eph. 6:11–17.)

The Flinders Petries excavated at Gerar, where there was a sword-blade factory, several spearheads, arrowheads, and daggers (dating c. 1300–800 B.C.).

See ARMS; BATTERING-RAM; CHARIOTS; DEFENSE; SLING.

weasel, a small, carnivorous quadruped, allied to the ferret, listed with the mouse and lizard among unclean animals* (Lev. 11:29).

weather, the meteorological phenomena of the atmosphere. Many Bible passages show an awareness of weather conditions natural to people who spent a large part of their time in the open. The keen observer, Job, remarked, "Fair weather cometh out of the north" (37:22; see also his comments about clouds, v. 16, and garments that feel too warm in the S. wind, v. 17). Cold winter weather is mentioned in an allusion to garments (Prov. 25:20). Jesus said to Sadducees and Pharisees seeking "a sign from heaven" concerning current situations, "When it is evening, ye say, It will be fair weather: for the sky is red. And in the morning, It will be foul weather today, for the sky is red and lowring" (Matt. 16:2 f.).

The great topographical diversity of Palestine gives it a variety of weather on any given date. Even the hottest summer day is tempered by refreshing breezes from the Mediterranean, blowing far inland, beginning in midmorning; this breeze is priceless to farmers winnowing in the wind. The warm sunshine and invigorating air of summer are preferable to the long, depressing, wet weather of the winter months, except in such regions as lower Jericho, the Dead Sea, and the Jordan plains, which are intolerable in summer. Jerusalem summers are pleasant because of the elevation of the city; and the long noon siestas make Palestine summers tolerable for all types of work. Viscount Allenby referred to "the burning heat of summer on the plains." Evenings under the Palestinian stars are memorable.

In the Wilderness of Judaea, and on the slopes and plains of Galilee, myriads of short-lived summer wild flowers follow on the heels of late winter—often soon after the snow. The flowers are followed by burned-up layers of brown vegetation in desert areas, and by grain in fertile zones.

(See FARMING; SEASON; SNOW; WINDS.)

Weather determined the outcome of the chariot battles in O.T. Palestine (Judg. 5:19–21).

weaving and spinning, two ancient processes that are basic in the preparation of cloth for garments, textiles for tents, cur-

WEAVING AND SPINNING

tains for shrines, etc. Even before early Biblical times until now, weaving has been done by both men and women; materials for the Tabernacle were woven by men and women (Ex. 26:1–13, 35:35); and Aquila, Paul, and Prisca at Corinth did weaving (Acts 18:2). Well-organized guilds of weavers developed in large commercial and market centers from which retail cloth merchants, like Lydia* of Thyatira, secured stocks. Evidences of extensive weaving industry have been excavated from Byblos, Tell Beit Mirsim, and Lachish, where loom weights have been found near dyeing vats, and spinning whorls have been dug up. These centers were small in comparison with Egyptian and Babylonian ones, where the Hebrews became proficient during the Sojourn and the Exile. Egypt very early developed large-scale weaving centers for linen, and heavier cloths for palace and temple hangings and awnings.

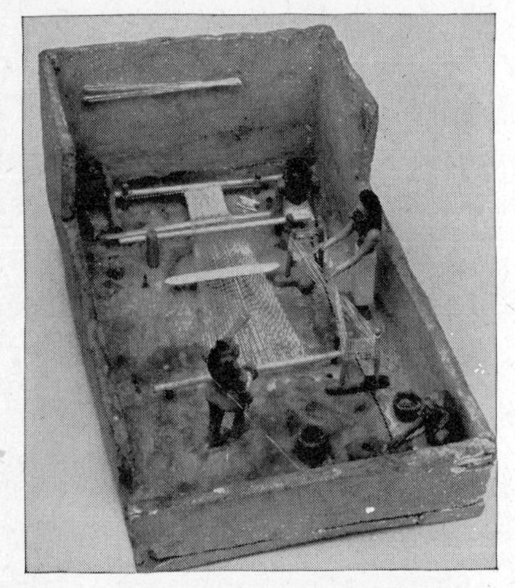

479. Egyptian horizontal loom.

Herodotus tells of one Egyptian type of linen so fine that each thread contained 360 fibers. At least one Babylonian who ruled as early as c. 2320 B.C. is known from clay records to have had his own "factory" for weaving textiles. Babylonian mantles were coveted and stolen by poor Palestinians who saw them in battle (Josh. 7:20 ff.). Mesopotamian weaving was done by women —often slaves. The Hebrews learned from the Canaanites, who knew how to weave and dye well; and from the color-loving Amorites.

Materials cultivated for weaving include sheep's wool, goats' hair, camels' hair, flax, hemp, and ramie—but, according to many authorities, not cotton until at least the era of Alexander the Great.

Sheep's wool was the chief material woven into family garments. Camels' hair made light, warm cloaks (*abayehs*). Goats'-hair cloth made durable tents and rugged mantles for shepherds. Sackcloth was woven from coarse flax, hemp, or dark goats' hair. The exceptionally strong goats'-hair *cilicium* cloth was made in the Taurus Mountains, where Paul the Cilician learned weaving.

Spinning was preliminary to weaving. Once the fibers of wool, flax, or hair had been washed and combed with a comb such as wool carders still use in Mediterranean lands, a mass of them was hooked onto a distaff (Prov. 31:19), a small wooden rod, and held under the spinner's left arm. From the distaff wisps of the material were drawn out until there was sufficient to attach in the form of thread to the spindle. This was a rounded wooden rod 9–15 in. long, tapering at both ends, with its upper portion hooked to catch hold of the yarn during the twisting. Part way down the spindle was a whorl or disc of stone, bone, clay, wood, or broken pottery heavy enough to help keep the spindle rotating steadily. The spinner, having attached a few fibers to the spindle, then set it in motion by rolling it against the thigh or by twirling it between his right thumb and finger. It continued to twirl as the yarn fibers were drawn out from the mass held under the left arm and were twisted into thread by both hands. The twisted material was wound into fairly uniform thread until the spindle was full. Spinners of Bible lands became so adept that they

480. Distaff.

481. Woman spinning, Corinth.

could spin while they walked or rode on donkeys. They attained amazing dexterity in producing smooth yarns for the looms.

The loom was the apparatus on which the spun yarn was woven into fabric, by intersecting threads of flexible material (the warp, or "that which is thrown across") and the weft (also called "the woof," i.e., "that which is woven"; see Lev. 13:48–59). The setting up of the family loom outdoors under trees, on the roof, or inside the house was always an event. Upright looms were made by pegging out on the ground two heavy beams (see Samson's spear "like a weaver's beam," I Sam. 17:7) fastened at the top by a cross-

482. Syrian at his loom.

beam; the threads of the warp were suspended from the top beam, and kept tight by small loom weights of stone or clay fastened to their lower ends. Numerous loom weights have been excavated from Kiriath-sepher. The usual upright loom of N.T. Palestine had a 3d crossbeam near the bottom, onto which woven cloth was wound; thus a longer, heavier piece could be woven than if all hung from the top beam. A horizontal loom used in ancient Egypt is still a favorite type in the Near East.

When the threads were fastened to the beam of the loom the weaver was ready to run the shuttle through, very quickly (Job 7:6). The shuttle was a boat-shaped wooden object containing the bobbin of weft thread, which was deftly passed through the "shed" made by keeping the warp threads separate in two series, by means of a heddle or heald. After each new thread had been pulled through by the shuttle, the weaver pushed it firmly against the growing fabric by a reed bar, a batten—supplanted in later times by a heavy comblike device. Patterns were made with various colors of yarn or thread. Sometimes gold and silver "wire" threads were woven in (Ex. 39:3). In Palestine usually just sufficient length was woven to make the traditional "seamless cloak" or coat (John 19:23). The fastened threads at the end of the piece were cut by the weaver (A.S.V. Isa. 38:12: "I have rolled up, like a weaver, my life; he will cut me off from the loom.")

The woven cloth, if fine enough, next went to the fuller* and then to the dyer (see DYEING).

Wide use of woven textiles is indicated in Scripture: for the Tabernacle (Ex. 26:1, 7, 27:16); for priests' apparel (Ex. 28:31 f., 39:3–5, 27; Lev. 19:19); for pagan shrines (II Kings 23:7); for Christ's seamless robe (John 19:23); and for Paul's warm winter cloak (II Tim. 4:13).

wedding, the ceremony of marriage*, and the celebration which often accompanies it. The securing of a wife for the son of a Hebrew Patriarch was important enough for the sending of a personal representative into the distant homeland among "the children of the east" (see the narratives concerning bride-quests for both Isaac and Jacob, Gen. 24, 29). We know nothing of the wedding ceremony at this early time, other than the bringing of the veiled, jewel-bedecked bride (Gen. 24:22, 65) into the groom's tent, which was sometimes that of a deceased mother (Gen. 24:67). The tent ceremony has been perpetuated in modified form down to the present time among Jews who are married under the traditional wedding canopy (*huppah*, cf. Joel 2:16). Weddings in Israel were often joyous occasions, long planned for. They were community festivals, marked by singing. The Song of Solomon may be "a collection of folk songs sung at rural weddings" (R. H. Pfeiffer).

Traditional Jews still prefer an outdoor ceremony. Where the four poles of the *huppah* are not fixed, they are usually held by four unmarried young men. The bride is customarily conducted under it by the two mothers, the groom by the two fathers.

Weddings were also celebrated with dancing, asking of riddles—as at Samson's wedding feast (Judg. 14:10 ff.)—eating large quantities of food, consuming so much wine that the "governor of the feast" (John 2:9) was often faced with problems of an exhausted supply, and intoxicated guests. As shown in Christ's Parable of the King's Wedding Feast (Matt. 22:1–13), invitations were sent to guests by personal messengers. Acceptance was expected, and excuses were considered insults. Festive apparel was demanded of wedding guests; for a man to come in his work clothes was cause for his ejection (v. 13). If he owned nothing but the one customary garment, he might easily borrow, for borrowing was prevalent in the old East (cf. Ex. 11:2, the borrowing of jewels). The suggestion has been made that grooms sometimes distributed to prospective guests textiles from which they were expected to fashion guest wedding garments; and if a man arrived wearing some other material, not recognized by the groom, he was cast out as an uninvited person. The wedding garment in the Parable of the Wedding Feast teaches that at the coming of the Messianic King some men will be fit for sharing in his Kingdom and others not.

The bride, after receiving ceremonial washings by her maidens, was beautified with cosmetics* (Ruth 3:3; Ezek. 23:40; Eph. 5:26 f.), dressed in often elaborately embroidered wedding garments, including the traditional girdle (Isa. 3:24, 49:18; Jer. 2:32), put on, probably, with the old traditional wish (Ruth 4:11). Jewels were donned (Isa. 61:10). Sometimes the bride was veiled (Gen. 24:65). When "all things [were] now ready" (Luke 14:17), the groom—who had dressed in his finest (or borrowed) robes at his own home (Ps. 19:5; Isa. 61:10)—engaged in preliminary celebrations with men friends (? "the bachelor's dinner"); proceeded joyfully from his own quarters (Joel 2:16; cf. Jer. 7:34, 16:9, 25:10, 33:11); and came to the place of the wedding feast, in the home of a friend or of his father. Often he wore a garland Isa. 61:10). He was escorted by companions carrying torches, like those still used to light wedding parties in valleys near Jerusalem. He distributed free sweetmeats as he proceeded. The weary attendants of the bride, some grown sleepy with waiting, went forth to meet the bridegroom when they heard he was coming. As told in Christ's Parable of the Ten Virgins, the wise ones provided themselves with tiny clay hand lamps and small containers for extra oil (swung from their fingers by a cord). These girls continued on to the wedding; the foolish, improvident ones were shut out in the dark (Matt. 25:10–12). (See LAMP.)

No religious ceremony is indicated in the O.T., but there were often witnesses (Ruth 4:11); and after the Exile sometimes written contracts. Festivities for the couple and their friends continued for seven days after the wedding night, or longer (cf. Gen. 29:27; Judg. 14:12). The setting up of a new Hebrew family* was always important. New matches were begun at weddings. Such occasions were bright spots in the drab lives of agricultural villagers, as shown in the narrative of the wedding at Cana of Galilee (John 2:1–11).

For the apocalyptic "marriage supper of the Lamb," see Rev. 19:7–9.

wedge (of metal). See TONGUE; also MONEY.

week. See TIME.

Weeks, Feast of, See FEASTS.

Weights and Measures. The metrological terms and standards named in the Bible do not belong to a single unified system. The meaning of the terms, their values, and the ratios which related them varied during the approximately twelve centuries while the Bible was taking literary form. Allowance must be made for local usage, for differences between customary, commercial, and official values, for depreciation and revaluation, and for the influence through commerce and conquest of the systems of neighboring peoples. To begin with, some of the terms like *cubit* (forearm), *homer* (heap, donkey-load) and *hin* (jar, Egyptian) originated as imprecise "natural" measures, and were later defined and integrated into official systems to meet the needs of taxation, architecture, international trade, and tribute to foreign powers. The pre-Exilic kings and post-Exilic temple authorities established their own standards (II Sam. 14:26; Num. 3:47; I Chron. 23:29). The coordination of formerly independent units would modify them to bring them into a simple mathematical relation, as the English mile of 5000 ft. was changed to 5280 ft. in Tudor times to make it eight times the rood. Moreover, the same term might be differently defined for different purposes, like the ounce troy and the ounce advp., as in Ezek. 40:5. Old systems which had been replaced might be restored (II Chron. 3:3).

Biblical metrology is thus beset by many uncertainties and pitfalls of which the Bible student should be aware. Tables of values and ratios derived indiscriminately from widely different periods and sources of unequal value are highly misleading. Nevertheless careful comparative study of the Biblical data and its

483. Babylonian duck weight, second millennium B.C.

correlation with literary evidence from extra-Biblical ancient authors and with the constantly augmented archaeological evidence makes it possible to understand broadly (and sometimes with precision) the values and relations of the weights and measures referred to. For obvious reasons the Old Testament evidence must be examined before that of the New Testament.

Old Testament

(1) *Weights.* It is important to observe that weights were primarily for the measurement of metals and metallic objects rather than of other commodities, which were measured usually by size or quantity. Silver by weight was the common standard of value and medium of exchange (Jer. 32:9) until the introduction of coinage (originally an officially certified weight of silver) in the fifth century B.C. Many of the stone weights against which silver was measured on the balances have come to light in Palestinian excavations. The word translated "money" in the English versions is "silver," and "thirty pieces of silver" meant silver thirty shekels in weight. Some confusion results from the fact that the principal unit of weight, the shekel, gave its name to a coin later derived from it which represented not a weight but a *value* in a bimetallic monetary system (about 3/40 of a gold shekel). It is possible, also, that there was a "heavy" shekel which was double the weight of the "light" shekel, as in Babylonia; the commercial, royal, and sanctuary shekels

WEIGHTS AND MEASURES

would be different definitions of the "light" shekel.

The units of weight mentioned in the Old Testament are the *shekel*; its fractions the *pim* (⅔, I Sam. 13:21), the *beka* (½, Exod. 38:26) and the *gerah* (1/20 according to Ezek. 45:12); and its multiples the *mina* (50 or 60, Neh. 7:70–71) and the *talent* (II Kings 15:19, 2500 or 3000, though possibly one-tenth this size originally). The shekel and the gerah were Babylonian units, though differing there in value; the pim is of unknown and probably local origin, the beka is possibly Egyptian, the mina is Sumero-Babylonian, and the talent of Sumerian origin though this name was given it by the Greeks. It has generally been assumed that the Hebrew system was adapted from an original Sumerian system based on a sexagesimal arithmetic (i.e., a reckoning by sixties) : 1 gun (talent) = 60 ma-na (minas) = 3600 gin (shekels). From Exod. 38:25–26 it can be calculated that the talent was assumed by the writers of the Priestly document to contain 3000 shekels, and in Exod. 30:13 these are defined as "sanctuary shekels" of 20 gerahs. The same definition appears in Ezek. 45:10, where it is linked with what appears to be a redefinition of the mina as sixty shekels of twenty gerahs in place of fifty shekels of twenty-four gerahs. This "sanctuary shekel" was thus ⅚ the shekel in common use, but the mina was unchanged. The talent of Exod. 30:13 must then have contained 50 minas of 60 sanctuary shekels, replacing one of 50 minas of 50 common shekels. There is evidence from Ugarit for a mina of fifty shekels.

The mina, in fact, is mentioned only by Ezekiel and later writers. It will be observed that large weights are reckoned in tens, fifties, hundreds, and thousands of shekels, and the largest also in talents. The Heb. word translated "talent" is, however, ambiguous; *kikkar* means "circle, disc, ring," and is used in other senses than as a weight or monetary unit (e.g., Gen. 13:10; Zech. 5:7). When referring to the payment of foreign tribute (e.g., II Kings 18:14) it must mean the "light" or the "heavy" talent of Babylonia (about 66 lbs. or 132 lbs. avdp. respectively). But it is improbable that David wore a golden crown of even the lesser of these weights (II Sam. 12:30). One of the el Amarna tablets (Knudtzon's no. 41) suggests that an earlier *kikkar* might represent five minas rather than fifty, which may solve the problem of David's crown.

The sexagesimal system of weights—1 talent = 60 minas = 3600 shekels—was established by the Sumerians in the third millenium B.C. and persisted with modifications down to the Graeco-Roman period. Nebuchadnezzar II (605–562 B.C.) certified that his "heavy" mina was of the standard established by Shulgi, king of Ur (c. 2000 B.C.); it weighs 978 gm. or 2 lbs., 2¼ oz. avdp., and yields a corresponding "heavy" talent of 58.68 kgm. or 129 lbs. avdp. An Assyrian weight yields a "heavy" talent of 131½ lbs. Weights representing the "light" talent average 66 lbs. Whereas the Babylonian shekel was 1/3600 of the talent, archaeological evidence from Syria and Palestine indicates that prior to Ezekiel and Judah's subjugation by the Babylonians the shekel there was 1/2500 the Sumero-Babylonian talent. A bronze weight in the shape of a bull from Ugarit, inscribed "twenty," yields a unit which is 1/2500 of a "heavy" talent of 128.8 lbs. avdp. (see Fig. 485).

484. Hebrew measures. Dry measures: 1. 1⅓ omer; 2. 1⅔ hin; Liquid measures: 3. 1⅓ omer; 4. ½ hin; 5. 1 bath; 6. 1 kab.

The pre-Exilic Hebrew shekel appears to have been related to the Babylonian "light" talent in the same 1/2500 ratio. Its actual weight can be determined with fair accuracy from inscribed stone weights found in Palestine, allowance being made for the variable factors mentioned above. We know from Exod. 38:26 that the *beka* was counted a half-shekel. Six weights inscribed "beka" average 5.94 gm., indicating a shekel of 11.88 gm., slightly over ⅖ oz. avdp. This enables us to identify as shekels or multiples of a shekel seventeen weights in the (unit) range 11.3—12.25 gm. which bear a symbol resembling a "figure 8" with the upper loop open. The symbol may represent the tied bag or purse (Prov. 7:20) in which silver or small weights were carried, or it may be the Egyptian hieroglyphic sign for *SS*. The average weight of the stones with the shekel sign is 11.42 gm., a figure confirmed by a large stone weight found at Tell Beit Mirsim weighing 4565 gm., or 400 shekels at 11.41 gm., almost exactly ⅖ oz. avdp. This average weight of the pre-Exilic Israelite shekel probably had depreciated from about 12 gm. (.42 oz.), which is 1/2500 the Babylonian "light" talent. The smaller shekel of Ezekiel 45:12 and Exod. 38:25–26 was 1/3000 talent; it is represented by a series of weights marked "n-c-p" (a word not found in the Bible), averaging 9.86 gm. or about ⅛ oz. A few weights of nearly 13 gm. may be shekels reckoned as 1/7 of the Egyptian unit the *deben*, which weighed 91 gm.

The establishment of the monarchy, the development of international trade, and especially the imposition of tribute in the Assyrian period made necessary an adjustment of the Hebrew shekel to bring it into relation with the weight-monetary systems of the great powers. As with the deben in Egypt, the shekel was the primary unit, and large weights were calculated originally in hundreds and thousands of shekels. (Judg. 8:26; II Kings 5:5; Isa. 7:23). The word *kikkar*, later used for the standard Babylonian talent, was at this time used for a ring or disc of precious metal of undetermined weight, as well as for other circular objects. The adjustment of the shekel to a value of 11.4–11.9 gm. enabled it to be related to both systems and reckoned at 8 to the Egyptian *deben* and 2500 to the Babylonian "light" talent.

(2) *Linear Measures*. Approximate distances as distinguished from measured lengths were indicated by expressions drawn from common experience, such as "a bowshot" (Gen. 21:16), "a furrow's length" (I Sam. 14:14), "a day's journey" (Num. 11:31) "A three days' journey" (Exod. 5:3) meant a considerable distance but within the normal range of travel, whereas Elijah's journey of "forty days and forty nights" (I Kings 19:8) suggests a destination extremely remote.

The most important linear measure was the *'ammāh*, which we know from its Latin name as the *cubit*. As a readily available "natural" measure, the length of a man's arm from the bent elbow to the finger tips, this was called "a man's cubit" (Deut. 3:11) and sufficed to indicate the height of a man (I Sam. 17:4), the depth of water (Gen. 7:20) or the approximate size of an object (Est. 7:19). Larger but still inexact lengths were sometimes expressed in hundreds or thousands of cubits (II Kings 14:13; Neh. 3:13). A specific unit of measurement was required by architects and craftsmen, and by far the greater number of references to the cubit occur in passages prescribing measurements of the Tabernacle and

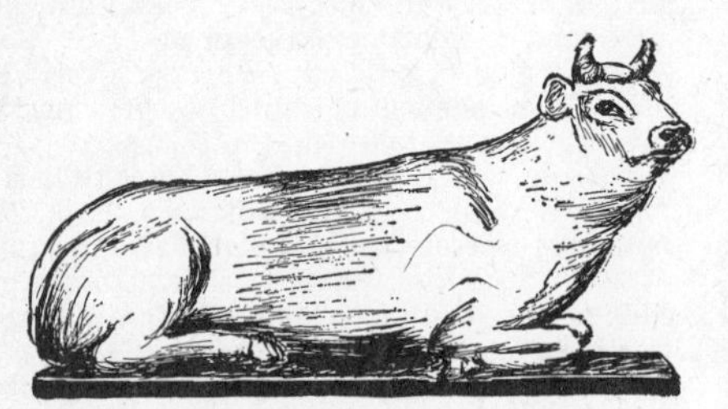

485. Ugaritic bull weight (one mina).

the Temple and their furnishings (Exod. 25–27; I Kings 6–7; II Chron. 3–4; Ezek. 40–43). Just as in Egypt and Babylonia there was a "royal" cubit longer than the common cubit, so—in the post-Exilic period—there was a sanctuary cubit of seven handbreadths instead of six. (Ezek. 40:5). Apparently this is meant by "the old standard" mentioned in II Chron. 3:3, which may have been derived from Egypt in the time of Solomon and later fell out of use. The Great Pyramid is laid out in cubits of 20.65 in., whereas the rise and fall of the Nile was measured in cubits of 17.7 in. Herodotus (Hist. i:178) tells of a Babylonian "royal" cubit which was three finger-breadths longer than the common cubit.

Fortunately, archaeological evidence from Palestine enables us to fix the size of the Israelite common cubit—and hence of its related units—fairly accurately. The Siloam inscription discovered in 1880 in Hezekiah's surviving water tunnel (II Kings 20:20) states that the tunnel is 1200 cubits in length. The most careful modern measurement arrived at a figure of 533.1 meters or 1749 ft., and hence at a cubit of 444 mm. or 17.47 in. This figure when applied to the excavated remains of large public buildings or land enclosures of the Israelite period not infrequently yields significant measurements: a Megiddo palace was 50 cubits square and a courtyard 123 cubits (20½ reeds of six cubits) square; and at Lachish the citadel platform was 12 reeds or 72 cubits square. Omri's enclosure wall on the summit of the hill of Samaria measures about 178 x 89 meters, which would be 400 x 200 cubits of 445 mm., 17.51 in. From this standard, about 17.5 in., of the common cubit under the monarchies, Ezekiel's long cubit would be 518 mm. = 20.4 in. Both cubits are very slightly shorter than their Egyptian counterparts.

The remaining linear units were the *reed* of six cubits (Ezek. 40:5); the *span* (I Sam. 17:4), roughly one-half the common cubit; the *handbreadth* or palm of four *fingers* (Jer. 52:21), there being six palms in the shorter and seven in the longer (like the Egyptian units which were defined as of 24 and of 28 fingers respectively). In summary, based on a common cubit of 17.5 in.,

4 fingers = 1 handbreadth = 2.9 in.
6 handbreadths = 1 short or common cubit = 17.5 in.
7 handbreadths = 1 long or sanctuary cubit = 20.4 in.
6 short cubits = 1 short reed = 8 ft. 9 in.
6 long cubits = 1 long reed = 10 ft. 2½ in.

In Judg. 3:16 a unique word *gōmedh* is translated "cubit," but the meaning of the term is unknown. It cannot have been more than ½ or ⅔ the common cubit, since the context makes clear that a dagger rather than a sword is in question.

(3) *Measures of Area*. The "acre" of I Sam. 14:14 and Isa. 5:10 is literally "a yoke," i.e., the area which a yoke of oxen could plow in one day. In Mesopotamia a corresponding term was later defined as an area equivalent to about ⅖ an English acre, and in Roman times as ⅝ acre. A second method of area measurement was by the quantity of barley needed to seed a field of that size (Lev. 27:16; I Kings 18:32; Isa. 5:10). A *seah* would be about ⅕ acre, a *homer* about 6 acres. The only exactly defined area is the planned pasture lands of the Levitical cities (Num. 35:4–5). The passage is rather obscure but seems to mean that there were to be blocks of land 1000 cubits deep on four frontages of 2000 cubits each.

(4) *Measures of Capacity.* In addition to informal measures such as "a bowlful" (Judg. 6:38) and "a handful" (I Kings 20:10), most of the specific units of capacity were derived from items in common use. The *homer* was a heap or donkey-load, the *hin* a jar or pot, and the *ephah* a basket. These and other units were later given specific values and brought into an arithmetical relation to each other.

(i) *Liquid Measures.* The standard unit was the *bath,* and it alone is mentioned in pre-Exilic writings. Of the smaller units, the *hin,* traditionally ⅙ bath, is mentioned first by Ezekiel; the *log,* traditionally 1/12 hin or 1/72 bath, is mentioned in the Bible only in Lev. 14. The ratios of these units to the bath is derived from post-Biblical information which may not be accurate for the Biblical period but can be adopted provisionally. The size of the bath has been calculated from Josephus' equation of the log with the Graeco-Roman *xestēs—sextarius* as 10.3 U.S. gallons (8.6 imper. gals.). However, at this point Palestinian archaeology has something to say if we could be sure what it is. From fragments of large jars found at Lachish and Tell Beit Mirsim and inscribed "royal" or "royal bath", Inge has calculated that the bath = about 12 U.S. gallons (10 imper. gals.). Albright holds that this is about twice the correct figure of 5.8 U.S. gallons. Albright's figure gains some support from the figures given in I Kings 7:23–26 for the dimensions and capacity of the "molten sea." If it is correct, the *hin* would hold 7¾ U.S. liquid pints, and the *log* about ⅔ pint; if the *bath* should prove to have been larger these figures would be correspondingly increased.

(ii) *Dry Measures.* In Ezekiel's attempt to standardize the Hebrew units after the catastrophe of the Babylonian Exile, a "true ephah" (dry measure) and a "true bath" (liquid measure) are equated in capacity and rated as 1/10 *homer.* Though the homer was not a liquid measure, this equation gives the best available evidence of the sizes of the several dry measures. The *cor* is of the same capacity as the homer, (Ezek. 45:14) but is used only as a unit of account for large quantities (I Kings 5:11) whereas the homer is used for amounts which could be visualized. The *seah* or "third" (Gen. 18:6; Isa. 40:12) was ⅓ ephah, the *omer* or "sheaf" was 1/10 ephah (Exod. 16:36). The *kab,* mentioned only in II Kings 6:25, is traditionally 1/18 ephah. The *lethech* is translated "half-cor" in the Vulgate; we have no other means of determining its size.

In summary, the measures of capacity and their modern equivalents based on the hypothetical identification of the bath as 5.8 U.S. gals. are:

Liquid measures	(liters)
	220
	110
bath 5.8 U.S. gals.	22
	7.3
hin 3.86 U.S. qts.	3.66
	2.2
	1.2
log ⅔ U.S. liquid pint	.3

Dry measures		
homer—cor	6¼	U.S. bushels
lethech	3⅛	" "
ephah	⅗	" "
seah—"third"	⅕	" "
omer	4	U.S. dry pints
kab	2²⁄₉	" " "

New Testament

New Testament weights and measures are considered separately because the New Testament comes from a later time, when Graeco-Roman units have been introduced alongside the old but altered Hebrew units which themselves are in Greek dress.

(1) *Weights.* The only specific weight mentioned (John 12:3; 19:39) is the Roman pound (Greek *litra,* Latin *libra*), which weighed slightly less than 11½ oz. avdp. The reference in Rev. 16:21 to hailstones heavy as a talent weight (R.S.V. "hundredweight") is, of course, figurative; the Roman talent was 90 lbs. avdp. In the Parable of the Talents (Matt. 25:14–30) and its parallel the Parable of the Minas (R.S.V. "pounds", Luke

486. "Good measure" (Luke 6:38).

19:12–27) sums of money rather than weights are meant; so with "the half-shekel tax" (Matt. 17:24). The thirty pieces of silver," which in Zech. 11:13 meant silver 30 shekels in weight, is interpreted in Matt. 27:9 30 coined shekels or tetradrachmae.

(2) *Linear Measures.* The *cubit* is named only three times—in Matt. 6:27 (with its parallel Luke 12:25) where its use is figurative, John 21:8, and in Rev. 21:17 in the apocalyptic vision of the heavenly city. In any case the Roman cubit coincided with the Jewish common cubit of 17.5 in. The remaining metrical units mentioned are Graeco-Roman: the *fathom* or "arm-stretch" of four cubits or 70 in. (Acts 27:28); the *stade* of 600 Greek ft. or 202½ modern yards (Luke 24:13, etc.); there were eight stades in the Roman *mile* (Matt. 5:41) of 1620 yds. The distance of "a Sabbath day's journey" (Acts

1:12) was 2000 long cubits or about ⅔ the modern mile.

(3) *Measures of Capacity.* Three Old Testament terms reappear in Greek form, and probably with somewhat altered values—the *bath* as *batos* (Luke 16:6), the *cor* as *koros* (Luke 16:7), and the *seah* as *saton* (Matt. 13:33; Luke 13:21). The English translation "measures" obscures the facts that the first was a liquid measure and the others dry measures, and that the koros was thirty times the size of the saton. Four Graeco-Roman measures also are named—the *modius* (Matt. 5:15), a grain measure equal to about a peck or ¼ bushel; the *xestēs* (Mark 7:4, a pint or, as here, a pint-sized jug); the *choinix* (Rev. 6:6), roughly a dry quart; and the *metrētēs* (A. V. "firkin", John 2:6), slightly more than 10 U.S. gallons. R.B.Y.S.

See MONEY; SABBATH DAY'S JOURNEY.

"Well of the Star," a name sometimes given to the old stone-curbed drinking place on the N. outskirts of Bethlehem, on the ancient five-mile road from Jerusalem. It is today a busy halting place for shepherds and cameleers, for it has beside it a low stone basin or "cup" into which they pour water

487. Well of the Star.

for their thirsty animals. Ancient legend says that the Wise Men, en route to Bethlehem, lost their guiding star, but found it again when they saw its reflection in this unfailing well. It is also sometimes called "Mary's Well," though the best-known one bearing the Virgin's name is at Nazareth.

wells, man-curbed, natural springs; or water supplies secured by digging holes in the earth (see FOUNTAIN). The digging of new wells was occasion for rejoicing and singing in early Biblical times; "The Song of the Well" (Num. 21:17) is one of the famous lyrics of the O.T. Wells, however, were also causes of strife, as were the still functioning Beersheba* wells, between Abraham and Abimelech's servants, and between Isaac and the herdsmen of Gerar (Gen. 26:15 ff.). These famous wells, at whose digging Abraham had sacrificed seven ewe lambs (Gen. 21:29 f.), and which the Philistines had clogged up (Gen. 26:18), had been reopened by Isaac, who also dug new wells (vv. 19, 21 f.).

Wells made excellent hiding places, as in the strategy of Jonathan and Ahimaaz (II Sam. 17:18–21).

For wells famous in Biblical narratives, see those which figure in the courtship of Isaac and Rebekah (Gen. 24:11 ff.) and of

488. Hundred-foot well on edge of Lachish mound, besieged by Sennacherib and Nebuchadnezzar.

Rachel (29:2 ff.); and the Bethlehem well known to David (I Chron. 11:17).

See EN-ROGEL; GIHON; JERUSALEM; LACHISH; PEIRENE; NAZARETH (for Mary's Well); SYCHAR (for Jacob's Well); WELL OF THE STAR; WATER.

whale, the word used in Job 7:12; Ezek. 32:2; Matt. 12:40 for a great fish; cf. Jonah 1:17. The A.S.V. of Job 7:12 and A.S.V. margin of Matt. 12:40 read "sea monster," while the A.S.V. text, R.S.V. and Moffatt use "whale" at Matt. 12:40. The A.S.V. of Ezek 32:2 reads "monster in the seas." "Great whales" of A.V. Gen. 1:21 is "great sea-monsters" in the A.S.V. and Moffatt.

wheat of several species was grown in ancient Palestine. This grain is first mentioned in Scripture in Gen. 30:14, in the story of Reuben and his mandrakes plucked for his mother Leah. It was cultivated in Egypt of Moses' day (Ex. 9:32). The finest of the new wheat crop was dedicated to Yahweh (Num. 18:12; see Ezra 6:9, rededication of the Temple). Moses' characterization of the Promised Land as one capable of producing wheat and many other desired products (Deut. 8:8) was found true when Israel entered Canaan. Instances of men working on their wheat-threshing floors in the pre-Monarchy era include Gideon (Judg. 6:11); Ornan, Araunah* (I Chron. 21:20). Ruth gleaned wheat (2:23; see also I Sam. 6:13, 12:17). By the time of the Monarchy wheat was being raised on such a large scale that Solomon included in his payments to his trade-ally, Hiram of Tyre, "twenty thousand measures of beaten wheat" (II Chron. 2:10, 15). Jotham levied tribute on Ammon in terms of wheat, grown in territory which today is still a great wheat-producing territory E. of the Jordan (II Chron. 27:5). Artaxerxes commanded wheat to be sent to the men rebuilding the Temple (Ezra 7:22).

Christ in his Parable of the Tares depicted a curse of wheat cultivation (Matt. 13:25, 29 f.; see also Luke 3:17). To Greeks he said a short while before his death, "unless a grain of wheat falls into the earth and dies, it remains alone; but if it dies, it bears much fruit" (R.S.V. John 12:24).

wheels. (1) Chariot* wheels, like the primitive Sumerian ones (c. 2900 B.C.) were wooden disks made of two semicircular pieces clapped around a central core with copper; Sumerian chariots had either two wheels or four. Light Egyptian chariots (Ex. 14:25) had six-spoked wheels which were larger than the eight-spoked wheels of Etruscan chariots. Canaanite chariot wheels were listened for in vain by the waiting mother of Sisera (Judg. 5:28). The metal lavers in Solomon's Temple had spoked wheels similar to chariot wheels (I Kings 7:30–33). Isaiah's poem (5:28) stresses the whirlwind speed of wheels. Jeremiah mentioned the wheels of the famous Philistine chariots (47:3). (For the wheels of Ezekiel's Apocalyptic vision of cherubim see 10:9 ff.; Dan. 7:9, wheels of the throne of "the Ancient of days," and Nah. 3:2, the rattling of Nineveh's chariot wheels.) (2) Potters' (see POTTERY) wheels were their most important tools (Jer. 18:3, etc.). (3) Ropes drawn over well and cistern wheels facilitated the movement of water buckets (Eccles. 12:6).

whirlwinds (Ezek. 1:4; Hos. 8:7), were any violent winds, as in Jas. 3:4 (A.V. "fierce winds," A.S.V. "rough winds," R.S.V. "strong winds"). These seem to be characteristic of the land—not of the sea gales that hindered travel, as Paul learned when he encountered "contrary winds" (Acts 27:4). The Sea of Galilee has always been known for its sudden, perilous squalls, such as Jesus and his Disciples experienced (Luke 8:25).

whore, a prostitute or harlot* (Gen. 38:15; Lev. 19:29; Deut. 23:18; Isa. 57:3; Hos. 2:2, 4, 4:11). Paul in his Ephesian Letter classed whoremongers and idolaters together among those who would have no inheritance in the Kingdom* of God (5:5).

Time and again in Scripture Israel's apostasies are described as "going whoring" after strange gods, devils, idols, and the sundry paraphernalia of pagan cults (Ex. 34:15 f.; Lev. 17:7, 20:5 f.; Deut. 31:16; Judg. 2:17, 8:27, 33; I Chron. 5:25; II Chron. 21:13; Ps. 73:27; Hos. 1:2). Ezekiel is especially vehement in symbolizing Israel's pursuit of heathen cults in terms of "going whoring," as, for example, in his lurid allegory of Aholah and Aholibah (Ezek. 23), and the judgment of the Lord upon them. (See also Ezek. 6:9 ff., 23:30, condemning Israel's pollution through idols.) "Whoring after other gods" took place in varying degrees throughout Israel's religious progress toward ethical monotheism from the era of Moses to N.T. times.

wickedness. See REDEMPTION; REGENERATION; RESTITUTION; SIN; etc.

widows from earliest Bible times were looked upon with sincere pity. They were protected by special legislation, along with "the fatherless" and "the stranger" (Deut. 16:11, 26:12, 27:19; cf. Ps. 146:9; Zech. 7:10; Matt. 23:14). They were permitted to glean in fields and orchards (Deut. 24:19 f.), and to participate in community sacrifices and feasts (14:29). The tithe of the "third year" was divided with them. A childless widow was required to engage in levirate marriage*, in order to raise up seed to her childless husband's line by his brother. They wore recognized widows' weeds (Gen. 38:14, 19), whose confiscation was as illegal (Deut. 24:17) as the appropriating of their ox (Job 24:3). Jesus praised the generosity of the widow who gave her whole income to the Temple (Luke 21:2–4). In the Apostolic Church widows were not only recipients of systematic charity when they were aged, or had no relatives to support them (Acts 6:1; I Tim. 5:3–16), but many belonged to a religious order ministering to women (see Acts 9:39, widows weeping over Dorcas).

Some widows mentioned in Scripture were Tamar, Abigail, Naomi, Ruth, Orpah and Anna; the "widow woman" of Zarephath, near Sidon, whose son was raised by Elijah (I Kings 17:9–24; Luke 4:26); the widowed Naphtalite mother of the famous craftsman, Hiram of Tyre (I Kings 7:14); the widow of a son of the prophets, blessed by Elisha (II Kings 4:1–7); Mary of Nazareth (cf. John 2:1); and the widow of Nain, whose son was restored to life by Jesus (Luke 7:11–17).

wife. See FAMILY; MARRIAGE; WOMAN; and individual entries by name.

wilderness in the Near East of the Biblical period meant a wild, almost treeless area of scant vegetation except at certain seasons when rain had provided temporary pasturage (cf. margin A.S.V. Ps. 106:9, "pasture-land") for nomads' flocks. Cultivation on a large scale was impossible. Wildernesses were thinly peopled, except by wandering groups. In them many caravans perished (Job 6:18). The wildernesses of Sinai and Palestine, unlike the densely wooded wildernesses of early America, were treeless except for palms in the oases (Ex. 15:27, Elim), and bushes like acacia, and inferior trees like tamarisks, etc.

489. Wilderness of Judaea, near Inn of the Good Samaritan.

The wilderness par excellence of the Biblical narratives is the Wilderness of the Wandering of the congregation (people) Israel and the "mixed multitude" associated with them under the leadership of Moses and Aaron. Other wildernesses named in the O.T. are Beer-sheba* (Gen. 21:14); Beth-aven (Josh. 18:12); Damascus (I Kings 19:15); Judah (Judaea) or Jeshimon—a natural desert bar-

WILLOW

rier guarding the approach to Jerusalem from the S., a hideout for fugitives (Judg. 1:16 etc.); Maon (I Sam. 23:24 f.); Moab (Num. 21:11; Deut. 2:8); Tadmor (I Kings 9:18; II Chron. 8:4); and Tekoa, on the western edge of the Wilderness of Judaea. (See individual entries; also ARABAH; NEGEB; and allegorical allusions to wilderness conditions brought about by calamities to once-flourishing cities, Isa. 64:10, etc.)

The Wilderness of the Wandering includes the deserts of Sinai* Peninsula and some wilderness regions E. and N. of this. The Sinai Peninsula itself contains four wildernesses: the Wilderness of Shur*; of Sin* (possibly a plain, Debbet er-Ramleh, at the edge of the Sinai plateau); the Wilderness of Paran*; and the Wilderness of Zin*. These all figure in the O.T. narratives of the years during which Israel and its associates were making their way toward the Promised Land. The itinerary of their grazing pilgrimage is not accurately known. Many of the places listed in Num. 33, as touched between Raamses and the plains by the Jordan near Jericho, are unidentified. The list of halting places in the following chart is contingent on the route chosen for the Exodus; two routes are suggested in the article EXODUS.

A Tentative Itinerary for the Exodus of the Children of Israel from Egypt to Canaan—based on the narratives of Genesis, Exodus, Num. 33, and Deuteronomy

Halting Places	*Possible Identification*	*References*
1. Raamses	Tanis	Gen. 47:11; Ex. 1:11 f.; Num. 33:3, 5
2. Succoth	Tell el-Maskhûtah	Ex. 12:37–13:20; Num. 33:5 f.
3. Etham	in Wâdī Tumeilat	Ex. 13:20; Num. 33:6 f.
4. Pi-hahiroth		Ex. 14:2–9; Num. 33:7 f.
5. Marah	probably 'Ain Hawarah or Wâdī Amarah	Ex. 15:23; Num. 33:8 f.
6. Elim	Wâdī Gharandel	Ex. 15:27–16:1; Num. 33:9 f.
7. By the Sea of Reeds (*Yam Suph*)	near Succoth and Lake Timsah	Num. 33:10
8. In the Wilderness of Sin	El Markha	Ex. 16:1–17:1; Num. 33:11 f.
9. Dophkah	? Serabit el-Khadem	Num. 33:12 f.
10. Alush	? Serabit el-Khadem	Num. 33:13 f.
11. Rephidim	Wâdī Refâyid	Ex. 17:1, 8, 19:2; Num. 33:14 f.
12. Mt. Sinai	Sufsafeh Mts., perhaps Jebel Musa ("Mt. Moses")	Ex. 16:1, 19:1 f., 11, 18, 20, 23, 24:16, 31:18, 34:2, 4, 29, 32; Lev. 7:38, 25:1, 26:46, 27:34; Num. 1:1, 19, 3:1, 4, 14, 9:1, 5, 10:12, 26:64, 28:6, 33:15 f, Deut. 33:2; Judg. 5:5; Neh. 9:13; Ps. 68:8, 17; Acts 7:30, 38; Gal. 4:24 f.;
13. Taberah	Site unknown	Num. 11:3; Deut. 9:22
14. Kibroth-Hattaavah	Site unknown	Num. 11:34 f.; 33:16 f.; Deut. 9:22
15. Hazeroth	? 'Ain Khadrā	Num. 11:35, 12:16, 33:17 f., Deut. 1:1
16. Wilderness of Paran	NW. of the head of the Aqabah	Gen. 21:21; Num. 10:12, 12:16, 13:3, 26; Deut. 1:1, 33:2; I Sam. 25:1; I Kings 11:18; Hab. 3:3
17. Kadesh-barnea	? 'Ain Qedeis in Wilderness of Zin	Num. 13:26, 20:1, 14, 22, 27:14, 32:8, 33:36, 37, 34:4; Deut. 1:2, 19, 46, 2:14, 9:23, 32:51; Josh. 10:41, 14:6, 7, 15:3; Judg. 11:16 f.; Ps. 29:8; Ezek. 47:19, 48:28
18. Rimmon-parez	?	Num. 33:19
19. Libnah	?	20
20. Rissah	?	21
21. Kehelathah	?	22
22. Mt. Shapher	?	23
23. Haradah	?	24
24. Makheloth	?	25
25. Tahath	?	26
26. Tarah	?	27
27. Mithcah	?	28
28. Hashmonah	?	29
29. Moseroth	?	30
30. Bene-Jaakan	?	31
31. Hor-hagid-gad	?	32
32. Jotbathah	?	Num. 33:33 f.; Deut. 10:7
33. Ebronah	?	Num. 33:34
34. Ezion-geber	head of the Gulf of Aqabah	Num. 33:35 f.; Deut. 2:8; I Kings 9:26, 22:48; II Chron. 8:17, 20:36
35. Kadesh-barnea	'Ain Qedeis	Num. 33:36
36. Mt. Hor	uncertain	Num. 20:22, 23, 25, 27, 21:4, 33:37–41; Deut. 32:50
37. Zalmonah	probably Alem Maan	Num. 33:41
38. Punon	Feinân, E. of Central Arabah	Num. 33:42
39. Oboth	S. of the entrance of Brook Zered to the Dead Sea	Num. 21:10 f., 33:43 f.
40. Ije-abarim	in the desert E. of Moab	Num. 21:11, 33:44 f.
41. Dibon or Dibon-gad	Dhībân, N. of the Arnon	Num. 21:30, 32:3, 34, 33:45 f.; Josh. 13:9, 17; Isa. 15:2; Jer. 48:18, 22
42. Almon-dib-lathain	?	Num. 33:46; Ezek. 6:14
43. Nebo	near Pisgah and the mountains of Moab	Num. 32:3, 38, 33:47; Deut. 32:49, 34:1; I Chron. 5:8; Ezra 2:29, 10:43; Neh. 7:33; Isa. 15:2; Jer. 48:1, 22
44. In the Plains of Moab, near the Jordan	part of El-ghor, or the Valley of the Jordan	Num. 22:1, 33:48

The N.T. refers to a desert region in the Jordan Valley not far N. of the Dead Sea. This was the scene of the preaching and some of the baptisms of John the Baptist (Matt. 3:1; Mark 1:3 f.), who was identified by the author of the Gospel of Matthew as the one mentioned by the prophet Isaiah: the voice of one crying "in the wilderness" (40:3). The Wilderness of Judaea was the scene of the Temptation of Jesus (Matt. 4 and parallels). This region, arid except in the brief springtime when it is carpeted by frail but brilliant flowers, looks as if it had once been part of a dessicated, dead planet. It is generally waterless, in spite of steep wâdīs running down to the Dead Sea; the Wâdī Qelt* is an exception. Wild animals infest the Wilderness of Judaea. No natural food is available. The "wilderness" above the Sea of Galilee where Jesus fed the multitudes (A.V. Matt. 15:33) is "desert" in the R.S.V.

willow, a word used in the O.T. to indicate a type of tree growing along a brook or near water (Lev. 23:40; Job 40:22; Ezek. 17:5, where it translates a generic term, *tsaphtsāphāh*). Ps. 137:2 tells of captive Israelites hanging their harps on willows which grew along the river or canals of Babylon.

Willows, Brook of the, a portion of the willow-shaded Wâdī el-Hesa, a Trans-Jordan brook, the Zered* that formed the boundary between Edom and Moab.

winds made Palestinians so wind-conscious that when Jerusalem Christians at Pentecost felt supernatural manifestations they described them as being like the "rush of a mighty wind" (R.S.V. Acts 2:2; cf. John 3:8). From the southern deserts scorching winds blew across Palestine. These were recognized by Jesus as bringers of heat: "When ye see a south wind blowing, ye say, There will be a scorching heat" ("hot wind" A.S.V. margin Luke 12:55). South winds were "terrible" (Isa. 21:1). The noted sirocco is a desert wind, of which one type makes the sky ominous with blinding sand clouds and violent blowing; the other tortures by quiet, intense burning (see Hos. 13:15, as evidence of a hot SE. wind, evidently "from the wilderness"). The powerful E. wind had a role in the pushing back of the Sea of Reeds at the crossing of Israel during the Exodus* (Ex. 14:21); and in the breaking up of Tarshish ships (Ps. 48:7). The E. and SE. winds (the *hamsin* of the Arabs) blast crops (Gen. 41:6). N. winds bring cool, merciful breezes; their whirlwind (Ezek. 1:4), rain-bringing character was noted by the author of Prov. 25:23. N. winds blowing across Palestine from the Mediterranean not only help threshers to winnow grain comfortably in late afternoon hours, but also bring moisture, welcome to everyone in summer. The blowing of winds from the Mediterranean to the mountains and back again to the sea makes possible the dews which save vegetation.

Symbolically wind expresses the disorganizing effects of war (Jer. 18:17); and conveys the transiency of life (Job 7:7; Ps. 78:39) and of the wicked (Prov. 10:25). Apocalyptic passages use the four winds to denote the scattering of peoples (Jer. 49:36; Dan. 7:2; Matt. 24:31); or the gathering of the elect from the four winds of the earth (Rev. 7:1).

Mediterranean peoples have been wind-conscious since very early times. The Greeks built at Athens, near the Agora, a Tower of the Winds, which served as a sort of meteorological station (see TIME, illus. 441). Roman artists paid homage to the enriching trade winds of Sicily by depicting the three-legged wind messenger of the triangular island in floor mosaics at the chamber of commerce in Ostia, one of the ports of ancient Rome.

wine. See VINE; for wine offerings see WORSHIP, "Sacrifice and Offerings."

winebibbers, tipplers, those who make merry with excessive consumption of wine, such as those denounced in Prov. 23:20. See VINE, concerning Matt. 11:19.

wine press. See VINE.

wineskin. See VINE; also BAGS; BOTTLES.

winnowing, a favorite Palestinian method (still used) to separate the kernels of threshed grain from the chaff. By means of a wooden fork the farmer throws bunches of wheat, barley (Ruth 3:2), etc., into the breeze-stirred air of his threshing floor in late afternoon. The grain falls to the ground, to be heaped together by means of wooden threshing shovels (Isa. 30:24), for garnering into barns (Ps. 1:4, 35:5; Dan. 2:35; Hos. 13:3). The chaff is blown away to be gathered later into a heap for burning or for fodder. Winnowing is one of the most picturesque aspects of old Palestinian farm ways surviving today (see FARMING).

wisdom (Heb. *hokmâh*) is used in Scripture in the sense of knowledge of the principles of right living gained through observation, experience, and reflection. The wisdom of a human being reached its peak, in the estimate of the author of I Kings, in Solomon. His wisdom enabled him to make profitable trade alliances, as with King Hiram of Tyre; to develop a rich, well-governed, materially splendid kingdom which was the envy of contemporary rulers (I Kings 10); to offer brilliant solutions for problems that distressed his subjects (I Kings 3:16–28); and to evaluate "an understanding heart" as the greatest boon he could ask of God (I Kings 3:9, 11). He possessed a substantial deposit of the wisdom lore of his people: "he was wiser than all men . . . he spake three thousand proverbs; and his songs were a thousand and five." He knew elements of botany and zoölogy; he spoke of "trees, from the cedar tree that is in Lebanon even unto the hyssop that springeth out of the wall: he spake also of beasts, and of fowl, and of creeping things, and of fishes" (I Kings 4:31–34). Cf. the remarkable natural science observations of another impressive Wisdom figure, Job (chaps. 38–41).

Wisdom in early Hebrew thought was characterized by such "mundane" virtues as industry, honesty, sobriety, chastity, and concern for good reputation. (See the Book of Ruth; and Prov. 31.) It was gradually perceived in Hebrew society that to be "wise" was to act nobly. The foolish deliberately chose to do evil (Prov. 1:7). The Hebrews reached their highest conception of wisdom in Ps. 111:10 (cf. Job 28:28), "The fear of the Lord is the beginning of wisdom."

The chief allusions to "wisdom" in the Bible are as an attribute of God and in connection with man's striving for the good life. Wisdom, along with power (Job 26:12), was one of the two main characteristics ascribed to the Creator: "the Lord by wisdom hath founded the earth" (Prov. 3:19; cf. Ps. 104:24, 136:5). He is the source of "wisdom, and knowledge, and joy" (cf. Eccles. 2:26). God gives wisdom to His sons: Solomon (I Kings 4:29–34); Ezra (7:25); and others (Prov. 2:6) who strive to "get wisdom . . . for wisdom is the principal thing" (4:5, 7). Wisdom was thought of as belonging to sages and wise men of many peoples (Eccles. 1:9 f.; cf. Ps. 105:22). It was the antithesis of vanity* and "vexation of the spirit" (Eccles. 2:26). Wisdom rose to such heights of veneration that certain writers personified it (Prov. 4:8 f., 8:11–31; cf. Matt. 11:19, where Jesus remarks that "wisdom is justified of her children"). To an even greater degree wisdom was exalted by the author of the Apocryphal book The Wisdom of Solomon. The Apocryphal Ecclesiasticus identifies wisdom with the Law of Moses. The Logos of John 1:1–18 has kinship with the wisdom of Prov. 8:22–31. In portions of The Wisdom of Solomon wisdom and the Logos are related.

Wisdom may be communicated, provided the learner has the capacity to receive it (Job 28:28; Ps. 111:10; Prov. 1:7, 15:33).

The literature which grew out of the intellectual curiosity about nature, man, and God is called Wisdom Literature. It is one of five types of writing distinguishable in the O.T., the other four being historical, legal, devotional, and prophetic. Separate books exemplifying the type are Proverbs, Job, Ecclesiastes and the Apocryphal Ecclesiasticus, and Wisdom of Solomon. Two aspects of wisdom are found in the Wisdom Literature that is preserved in Scriptures—the *practical* and the *theoretical.* Practical wisdom consists of sound advice applicable to every individual in handling the problems of daily life. Though perhaps based on legislation or custom, it is suggestive rather than mandatory, and occasionally metaphorical rather than literal. As with much of the O.T. Scriptures, practical wisdom developed orally, in the form of folk wisdom, before it was adopted by literary men. The popular proverb was the standard form of folk wisdom. Ahab taunted Benhadad with the folk epigram best translated (with Pfeiffer): "Let not the one putting on his armour boast like the one taking it off" (I Kings 20:11). Other fine examples of folk wisdom are quoted in I Sam. 10:12, 24:13; Jer. 23:28, 31:29 f.; Ezek. 16:44. The riddle (Samson, Judg. 14:18), the fable (Jotham, Judg. 9:7–21; Jehoash, II Kings 14:9), and the parable (Nathan, II Sam. 12:1–4; Isaiah's vineyard, Isa. 5:1–6) are employed as framework for folk wisdom. Eventually Hebrew sages began to compile collections of maxims and reflections following Egyptian and Babylonian models, especially *The Instruction of Ptahhotep*, the oldest collection of Egyptian maxims, dating from the Old Kingdom, and consisting of advice given to a worldly young man eager for success. There is a strong trace of the more spiritual *Wisdom of Amenemope* in Prov. 22:17–23:22. In their first phases both Egyptian and Hebrew wisdom were purely utilitarian: "success" in life is the end, and the means are correct manners, tact, respect for superiors, fidelity in matters of trust, etc. Work and wealth, relaxation and amusements, marriage and family life, and friendship are the main themes of the Book of Proverbs. In its later stages the wisdom of Israel became more ethical and pious: examples of a real identification of morality with religion are numerous in Proverbs; the utilitarian note, however, is never entirely missing. This *practical* strain in the Wisdom Literature eventually became a part of the orthodox piety of normative Judaism. (See APOCRYPHA, Ecclesiasticus.)

The *theoretical* aspect of wisdom dealt with questions universal in scope, at first through myths (e.g. Gen. 2–11) and then through speculative literature. It also concerned itself with questions pertaining to the origins of specific Hebrew customs and institutions; from this curiosity and literary instinct came the numerous sagas and legends of early racial events strewn throughout the books of Genesis and Exodus. Much of the great philosophical literature (esp. Gen. 2–11 and Job) apparently came from Edomitic sages; before 587 B.C., at least, there is no evidence of any interest on the part of Israelites and Judaeans in questions of extra-national scope. The Deuteronomic Code of 622 B.C. did not speculate about the ultimate origins of the world and man; it was not until c. 450 B.C. that the tenets of theoretical wisdom on such matters were finally incorporated in the work of the Priestly Code*. Edom, in the meanwhile, was viewed as a land in which wisdom flourished (Obad. 8; Jer. 49:7). Job* then, as an Edomitic book of Wisdom, is not typically Hebraic, however high it may be rated. His "wisdom" is basically pessimistic in tone and argument, and his God is almost too transcendent to be comprehended. Ecclesiastes*, the wisdom writing of an unorthodox Jewish philosopher, carried Job's doubts to a point of complete skepticism. Job, however, contains the conviction that God is creator and upholder of all that exists, and it is possible that this book had an important influence on the Second Isaiah, who first gave this doctrine in fully developed terms to the Jews. Otherwise the *theoretical* strain died out with the abject defeatism of Ecclesiastes.

Wisdom Literature in the N.T. appears in the sayings of Jesus, who had inherited a rich deposit of the Wisdom of his people's sages, undoubtedly fostered by parental teachings, but through whom God imparted new and tremendous truths, concealed from the learned and those wise in their own conceits. Jesus burst the bonds of ultilitarianism and piety in which wisdom had become encased with a Gospel of the Kingdom of Heaven which gave men an entirely new light in which to examine the realities of life and death, yet he did not discard the valid insights of the Jewish tradition and of Wisdom, but rather built on them and the teaching method with which the people were familiar. There are identifiable 16 "Wisdom Parables"* of Jesus, which he taught informally in the open, or in the home of a learner (Mark 2:15–22), or at the tables of Pharisees (Luke 11:37–54; see Luke 10:30–36, the Good Samaritan, and 18:10–25, the Pharisee and the Publican). Time and again the ancient proverbial wisdom of his people appeared in his practical teaching: "A city that is set on a hill cannot be hid" (Matt. 5:14); "Take no thought for the morrow" (Matt. 6:34); "Those who are well have no need of a physician" (R.S.V. Matt. 9:12).

Jesus the sage was exalted by Paul to the point of being considered wisdom personified; he was "the wisdom of God," "our wisdom" (I Cor. 1:24, 30); in him were hidden "the treasures of wisdom and knowledge" (Col. 2:3). The author of the Gospel of John equates Jesus with the Logos*, a Greek concept of "the Word" not entirely unrelated to the personified Jewish Wisdom. The Epistle of James also embodies Wisdom concepts, and has been interpreted as a "body of Wisdom teachings" dictated and sent as a General Epistle (T. Y. Mullins, *JBL* Dec. 1949, p. 338).

Paul, in touch with keen-minded Greek contemporaries, was able to meet them at Athens on their own level (Acts 17). He was overwhelmed, soon after, with a remorseful sense that true wisdom consisted not in "excellency of speech," or in "wisdom of men," but in "demonstration of the Spirit and of power" (I Cor. 2:1, 4 f.). His failure to secure many converts in Athens or to establish an early church there led him to the conviction that his function was to "be ignorant of everything except Jesus Christ, and Jesus Christ the crucified"; for what he said "did not rest on any plausible arguments of 'wisdom' but on the proof supplied by the Spirit and its power." The wisdom that he will discuss is "the mysterious Wisdom of God, that hidden wisdom which God decreed from all eternity for our glory" (Moffatt), which none of the intellectual leaders of Judaism knew, or they would not have crucified Jesus. To Paul wisdom was one of the "gifts of the Spirit." His goal was to establish hearers with faith resting in "the power of God, rather than in the 'wisdom' of men" (v. 5).

See WISE MEN.

Wisdom of Jesus, the Son of Sirach (Ecclesiasticus). See APOCRYPHA.

Wisdom of Solomon, the. See APOCRYPHA.

wise men were sages who received and imparted abiding spiritual truths which had practical value. Wise men are listed in Jer. 18:18, along with priests and prophets, as expert in giving counsel. They knew the Torah, but were not so much interested in the ritual of Temple rites as in teaching. Just as priests fostered legal literature now embodied

490. Wise Men, in mosaic frieze, Church of Sant' Apollinare Nuovo, Ravenna, begun as the Arian Cathedral by Theodoric the Goth, A.D. 500.

in the O.T., and prophets participated in bringing about the prophetic books, so wise men gave posterity the "Wisdom Literature." Wise men were not limited to Palestine. The author of I Kings 4:31, speaking of Solomon's advance over men previously rated very wise, lists four whose fame "was in all nations round about." Wise women also are spoken of (II Sam. 14:2 ff., 20:16 ff.). Some so-called wise men proved to be charlatans, like Simon Magus (Acts 8:9 ff.). (See MAGIC AND DIVINATION.)

Sometimes wise men's ideals were tinged with materialism. Sometimes they were pessimistic, as reflected in Ecclesiastes and large portions of Job. The wise man of Edom declared that the Lord uttered "things too wonderful" for him to comprehend, so that he abhorred himself and repented in dust and ashes (Job 42:1–6), overwhelmed by the wisdom of God (36:5). He climaxed his enthusiasm for divine wisdom thus: "Behold, the fear of the Lord, that is wisdom; and to depart from evil is understanding" (28:28).

The "wise men from the east" (Magi, from *magikos*, magician, magic) mentioned in the Gospel of Matthew (2:1 ff.) as journeying to Bethlehem at the time of Christ's birth, were (if not entirely legendary) part of a stream of wisdom-seekers in the ancient Near East. Following the best light they knew—the light of a star—they sought a prophesied world-deliverer, whose destiny would transform the existing world order. They were stargazers, possibly from a priestly caste of Media, who worshipped fire and were versed in astrology and magic, and believed that the appearance of new stars heralded the coming of great world leaders, like Alexander. They were familiar with the main caravan roads, and may have been enriched by trade along the Arabian frankincense routes. They showed their practical wisdom by returning to their own country "another way," in spite of Herod's request to report to him concerning the child they expected to find (Matt. 2:8). The names of the three Wise Men assigned by legend—Gaspar ("white"), Melchior ("light"), and Balthasar ("the lord of the treasury") —are as unhistorical as the report that their skulls were discovered by Queen Helena, mother of Constantine the Great, taken to Constantinople, and thence to Cologne, whose cathedral has for centuries claimed them to be deposited in its Chapel of the Three Wise Men.

(For the "Wise Men's Well" on the edge of Bethlehem, see WELL OF THE STAR.)

witch, one (usually a woman) who practices the black art of witchcraft. A witch's power was thought to be obtained by compact with an evil spirit. Witchcraft, like all forms of magic*, was an abomination to the Lord (Deut. 18:10) and was forbidden to Israel on pain of death (Ex. 22:18). Saul, in spite of his people's sacred law, consulted a witch at Endor (I Sam. 28:7 ff.). Jezebel, wife of King Ahab of Israel (c. 869–850 B.C.), fostered witchcraft (II Kings 9:22); Manasseh of Judah, some two centuries later, resorted to similar forms of sorcery, which was commonly practiced in Egypt, Assyria (Nahum 3:4), and Babylonia (Isa. 47:9; Dan. 2:2). Simon Magus (=Magician) and Bar-Jesus were sorcerers in apostolic times (Acts 8:9–24, 13:6–12).

withe (wĭth), a flexible twig or branch; a willow or osier twig; a band consisting of a twisted twig or twigs (Judg. 16:7–9).

withered hand, a hand wasted away for lack of nourishment, caused by some form of atrophy; cured by Jesus (Mark 3:1–6).

witness (Heb. *'ēd;* Gk. *martys*). (1) One who beholds a transaction or testifies to a truth. Bearing false witness against one's neighbor in any capacity was forbidden by the Ninth Commandment (Ex. 20:16). Mosaic Law demanded at least two witnesses in all civil and criminal cases. (See Num. 35:30; Deut. 17:6; Heb. 10:28; cf. Matt. 26:60). In the drawing of contracts, or the writing of letters by professional scribes, it was a sensible precaution to have one or more witnesses.

People who declared their faith in Christian truth were said to "witness" to it (Heb. 10–12:1). The risen Christ told his Disciples that they had been witnesses of his ministry and his purposes (Luke 24:48), and that they should witness concerning him—after they had received the Holy Spirit—"in Jerusalem, and in all Judaea, and in Samaria, and unto the uttermost part of the earth" (Acts 1:8, 2:32, 3:15).

491. Bethlehem's Church of the Nativity, first built by Constantine c. 330 A.D. 330 and rebuilt by Justinian about 230 years later. The traditional site of the manger is in a cave beneath the choir.

The "cloud of witnesses" mentioned in Heb. 12:1 suggests massed observers at athletic contests in Graeco-Roman stadia. "Martyr," in the sense of one who dies for his faith in the life and Resurrection of Jesus, is derived from the Gk. word for "witness" (see Acts 22:20).

God is sometimes called on to be a witness (Rom. 1:9; A.S.V. II Cor. 1:23). The O.T. prophet Malachi refers to God as a wedding witness (2:14).

(2) A material marker, such as a heap or cairn or altar of stones, erected to acknowledge and remind people of an important spiritual experience (Gen. 31:46–49; Josh. 22:26–34, 24:26 f.).

witness of the Spirit, the Christian's awareness of God's leading and revelation; a sense of infallible divine communication, which also accords with one's own best judgment. The witness of the Spirit comes directly to the individual—not through any other person or any institution; no one but the person affected can affirm the validity of the experience (see Rom. 8:16; I John 5:6–10; cf. "the Comforter," John 14:26; "the Spirit of truth," John 15:26, 16:13 f.).

wizard, a magician or a sorcerer, male or female (Lev. 19:31, 20:6, 27; I Sam. 28:3, 9; II Kings 21:6, 23:24; II Chron. 33:6; Isa. 8:19, 19:3). See MAGIC AND DIVINATION.

woes, the seven Messianic, the seven condemnations of the religious leaders of Judaism, spoken by Jesus (Matt. 23:13–32) to the "multitude, and to his disciples." Oracles beginning "Woe unto . . . " were frequently used by Hebrew prophets (Isa. 5:8, 11, 18 f., 20, 21, 22, 23 [cf. 10:1]—also seven in number; Amos 5:18). In oracular usage, "Woe unto . . . !" is a form of curse, an anathema. The point of the seven woes of Jesus may be summarized thus: (1) The Kingdom* of God was near at hand; the scribes by their teaching and living were hindering men from getting ready to enter it (Matt. 23:13). (2) The scribes and Pharisees were leaving no stone unturned to make new proselytes, narrower than even they themselves (v. 15). (3) They were "blind guides," quibbling over inconsequential matters (v. 16). (4) They strove for worthless virtues, and omitted such vital matters as mercy and faith (v. 23). (5) External decencies mattered nothing if inner spiritual integrity was lacking (the clean outside of the cup) (v. 25). (6) Outward proprieties ("whited sepulchres") cannot conceal heart evils (v. 27). (7) Like their ancestors who built fine tombs for prophets who had been killed by their forebears, so the Jewish nation would cry "Crucify!" when Jesus came to trial (vv. 29, 34).

wolf, a variety of *Canis lupus*, an enemy of flocks in the Biblical period and a symbol of the judgments which prophets announced as coming to punish Jewry and Jerusalem for their sin. Jer. 5:6 and Zeph. 3:3 both associate wolves' prowlings with evening. The wolf is no longer seen in modern Palestine.

woman, as presented in the Bible, runs the gamut from the great matriarchs Sarah, Rebekah, and Rachel in the Patriarchal narratives, to the infamous Jezebel, Athaliah, and Herodias in the Monarchy and N.T. periods.

(1) In the transition from barbarism in the Near East to the Neolithic Age woman played a creative role. V. Gordon Childe, in *What Happened in History,* gives her credit for working out many steps in taming the land, devising agricultural tools, working out ways to store crops, and making grains into foods. Ethnographic evidence points to her large part in making the family's first pots, working out "the physics of spinning," inventing the loom, and learning the value of flax. In very early Mesopotamia women were priestesses at prominent temples, tending the flocks of goddesses, and engaging in crafts for deities. Throughout history the shoulders and heads of women have provided a mode of transportation for burdens. In the Porch of the Maidens on the Athenian Acropolis, figures of draped maidens (Caryatids) support the entablature instead of the usual columns.

(2) In the O.T. period there were times, as during the political crisis of Israel in the era of the Judges, when women rose to a position of leadership. Deborah counseled her people under a palm tree, and personally inspired the charge down Mt. Tabor against the Canaanites. In the arts the women of O.T. times sometimes excelled, like Miriam with her music and dance at the Sea of Reeds. Women created fine clothing and choice textiles (Prov. 31:13, 19–22). In business they were often efficient (Prov. 31:24; Acts 16:12–15). They had generous concern for the needy (Prov. 31:20). Their marital devotion was normally above reproach, yet they also sank to degrading jealousy, as in Sarah's cruel treatment of Hagar (Gen. 21).

Women in O.T. times were tireless drudges whose lot was little better than that of cattle or slaves. Yet their primary function was that of wife and mother; childlessness was reproach and woe. In tent life woman played the role of homemaker, from weaving the fabric of the "house of hair" to clothing its occupants, preparing their food, imparting to their children such religious fundamentals and tried maxims as they had inherited. The average O.T. woman of the villages participated in the folk festivals and religious feasts and pilgrimages of her people, and enjoyed the rustic dances and seasons of rejoicing at weddings, weanings, and the arrival of guests from far-off places. The lot of Hebrew women of any age was usually better than that of their contemporaries in Mesopotamia, Arabia, or Egypt, unless the latter were of royal rank. Even in Athens of the 5th century B.C. the wives of prominent citizens lived in virtual retirement.

Hebrew legislation protected women, even servants and slaves, as shown in the Ten Commandments (5th and 10th). The Deuteronomic Code included provisions for improving the lot of women, as well as that of men (Deut. 15:12–18, 23:17 f., 24:17). The safeguarding of women's chastity was a matter of concern to those who formulated the laws in Deut. 22:13–21, 24:1–5; violation of a woman's chastity was punishable by death. Girls taken prisoners in war were protected by what was considered a decent standard for such an age (20:14, 21:10–14). Prostitution and all forms of sexual vice were banned (22:22–30). The laws of levirate marriage* (Deut. 25:5–10) provided somewhat for the future of widows*.

(3) In the N.T. women moved on a plane more equal with men. The home of John Mark's mother may have been the meeting place of the first Christians (Acts 1:13 f., 12:12). Christian groups which became the Church felt that in Christ there was neither male nor female (Gal. 3:28). Jesus had honored woman by his courteous understanding and sympathetic ministry. Paul used marriage as a symbol of Christ's relationship to the Church (Eph. 5:22–33; cf. I Tim. 2:9–15). Women in the early Church served as prophetesses, deaconesses, teachers, fellow workers with the Apostles, helpful wives (I Cor. 9:5), and consecrated business women. The Graeco-Roman world in which they moved was accustomed to women who used their intellectual and spiritual gifts.

(See FAMILY; HARLOT. Also individual women under their proper names.) Other women of the Bible, whose names are unknown, include Jephthah's daughter (Judg. 11:30–40); the witch of Endor (I Sam. 28:1–25); the wise woman of Tekoa (II Sam. 14:2–9); the deliverer of Abel-beth-maachah (II Sam. 20:16 ff.); the Hebrew maid of the Syrian Naaman's wife (II Kings 5:2 ff.); the mother of Zebedee's sons (Matt. 4:21); Peter's wife and her mother (Matt. 8:14); the Syro-Phoenician woman blessed by Jesus (Mark 7:26–30); Jairus' daughter (Mark 5:22 ff.); the woman of Samaria Jesus met at the well of Sychar (John 4:1–42); the adulteress forgiven by him (John 8:3–11); the sinful woman who anointed him (Luke 7:36–50); Pilate's wife, who counseled caution at his Trial (Matt. 27:19); and Paul's sister (Acts 23:16). See also Pharaoh's daughter, the wife of Solomon (I Kings 3:1; cf. "The Marriage Psalm," 45); the Shulamite sweetheart in the Song of Solomon; the Shunammite hostess of Elisha (II Kings 4:8 ff., 8:1 ff.); the strange woman "whose house is the way to Sheol" (A.S.V. Prov. 7:5–27); and the ideal wife and mother (Prov. 31). See also *All of the Women of the Bible*, by Edith Deen (Harper & Brothers).

wonders. See SIGNS.

woods were cherished in Biblical Palestine and Jordan. The woods of various trees were used for boats* (cf. Gen. 6:14) on the Nile and the Tigris-Euphrates, as well as for very early coastal ships plying between Byblos and Egypt, and between Ezion-geber and Red Sea ports. Wood was also vital to burnt offerings (Gen. 22:3, 6 f., 9; Lev. 1:7; see also the use of cedar wood in the ritual of Lev. 14:51). The incense altar of the Tabernacle was made of shittim wood (Ex. 37:25); cedar adorned palaces and Solomon's Temple. Wood went into food vessels (Lev. 11:32); yokes for draught animals (cf. Jer. 28:13) and carts (I Sam. 6:14), as well as idols (Deut. 29:17; II Kings 19:18; Isa. 45:20), furniture, farm implements, and musical instruments. It was wantonly consumed for fuel (Prov. 26:20 f.; Isa. 37:19; Jer. 7:18 f.). So much timber was destroyed in Palestine wars that the hills were denuded. Large-scale reforestation was inaugurated in the 20th century.

In marshy Babylonia wood was precious and scarce, but it was abundant in the Assyrian highlands. Early Sumerian temples and houses used columns of reeds bundled together for wooden supports. Lashed reeds were also used for early Babylonian boats.

See individual woods: CEDARS; CYPRESS; OAK; OLIVE; PINE; SHITTAH; THYINE; etc.

wool, the fleece or soft hair of sheep* (and a few other animals), used in Bible times for textiles and many other purposes. Wool was often a medium for the payment of debts and of tribute, as with Mesha, the sheep-master King of Moab, and King Jehoram of Israel (c. 849–842 B.C.) (II Kings 3:4). (See WEAVING.) Fine wool was bought in large markets, as at Tyre (Ezek. 27:18) or Tarsus.

word. (1) See LOGOS. (2) The Word of God, the Scriptures, the Bible. (3) "The word of the Lord" is a phrase which recurs throughout Scripture. It usually means the will or purpose or plan of God, revealed to individuals, as to Abraham in a vision (Gen. 15:1); to Moses in a desert theophany* (Num. 3:14–16); to Saul (I Sam. 15:23, 26) through the voice of Samuel; to Zechariah the prophet during the Temple rebuilding (Zech. 7:8). The "word of God" was expressed through oracles, revealed laws, visions, spoken and written prophecies and teachings, and events in history. The Bible discloses how the "word of God" operated during more than a thousand years of Israel's history.

world, the, is a term used in several senses in the English Bible, and translates various Heb. and Gk. words: "the earth, the present age or time, the inhabited earth" in Heb.; and "the present and future ages, the earth, the cosmos, the inhabited earth" in Gk.

(1) Two accounts of the origin of the world, or cosmogonies, occur in Genesis: 1:1–2:5 (the beginning of the P source*) and 2:5–25 (variously assigned to the J, or J1 or L and J, or S sources). According to P, God created the four parts of the world (light, firmament, seas, and land) and their respective inhabitants (heavenly bodies, birds, fishes, and animals as well as human beings) in six days and rested on the seventh. The order in the creation of living beings (plants, fishes, birds, cattle, man) is more in harmony with modern science than the sequence in chap. 2 (man, vegetation, animals, and woman). Unless the second account is incomplete, it confines itself to the origins of mankind, taking the world (which in the Bible, as before in Sumerian literature, is called "heaven and earth") for granted. In the first account God creates by fiat, in the second by fashioning living beings out of existing materials. In view of the reference to chaos in Gen. 1:2, it is not known with certainty whether God created the world out of nothing or out of chaos. The following references to God's work of creation are earlier than Gen. 1: Isa. 45:7, 18, 44:24; likewise, presumably, the considerably different cosmologies in Job 38–39 and Ps. 104. The parallels of Gen. 1 with the Babylonian creation myth are vague and doubtful, but the fight of Marduk with Tiâmat before the

creation of the world has left some echoes in Job, Ps. 104, Isaiah, Ezekiel, etc.

In the Book of Job, God created the world by imposing upon the turbulent elements of chaos the rational norms of Wisdom. He founded the earth by means of pillars over the waters of the abyss, and stretched over it the tent-like expanse of the firmament*. The waters of the ocean, which threatened to cover the earth, were confined around the circular rim of the flat surface of the earth, below which God formed the springs and recesses of the sea; and deeper still He placed the Underworld with its gates and gatekeepers. Over the heavenly dome God built the chambers containing snow, hail, rain, and, lower, winds. Sun and moon move under the firmament, to which the stars are attached. The first man was "made before the hills" (Job 15:7). Needless to say, the Biblical cosmology, though magnificent in its poetry and profound in its faith, reflects a science which has long been obsolete.

The chief difference between the two Testaments with regard to the cosmogony or creation of the world is that in the N.T., aside from numerous allusions to the O.T. teaching (Mark 13:19; Acts 7:50, 17:24; Heb. 3:4; Rev. 4:11, 10:6, etc.), the world was created by God's word (II Pet. 3:5–7), the *Logos* (Word, Reason) which in John 1:1–14 is identified with Christ; Christ is said to have been the creator of the world in: I Cor. 8:6; Col. 1:16; cf. Eph. 3:9.

(2) In English the term "world" may mean "mankind," and it occurs in this sense in the Bible, particularly in the phrase, "God will judge the world," or the like (Ps. 9:8, 96:13, 98:9; Acts 17:31; Rom. 3:6; cf. John 12:47; I Cor. 6:2), and in other contexts (Matt. 5:14; John 1:29, 8:12, 9:5; Acts 17:6).

(3) Beginning with Daniel (chap. 7), in apocalyptic writings the history of mankind was divided into two periods: the present age and the future age, which in the A.V. and A.S.V. of the N.T. are called "this world" and "the world to come."

This world is subject to the devil, "the god of this world" (II Cor. 4:4) or "the prince of this world" (John 12:31, 14:30, 16:11), and his evil spirits (I Cor. 2:6, 8). It is consequently filled with sin and suffering (Matt. 13:22; Mark 4:19; Luke 16:8, 20:34; Rom. 12:2; I Cor. 1:20, 3:18–19, 5:10, 7:31; Gal. 1:4; Eph. 2:2; I Tim. 6:17; II Tim. 4:10; Tit. 2:12; cf. Rom. 8:18).

The world to come will begin after "the end of this world" (Matt. 13:39–40, 49, 24:3, 28:20; I Cor. 10:11). This Messianic age will bring salvation and bliss to the redeemed (Matt. 12:32; Mark 10:30; Luke 18:30, 20:35; Eph. 1:21, 2:7; Heb. 6:5).

(4) Thus "the world" (meaning the present age) becomes synonymous with what is temporal, carnal, wicked—the antithesis of the Kingdom of God. This sense of the term is found especially in the writings of Paul (Rom. 11:12; I Cor. 1:27 f., 2:12, 5:10, 7:31–34; II Cor. 7:10; Gal. 6:14; Eph. 2:2) and of John (John 7:7, 8:23, 14:17, 15:18 f., 17:14; I John 2:15–17, 5:4; see also James 4:4; II Pet. 2:20).

(5) The world of the O.T. reached Spain (Tarshish) in the W., Elam and Persia in the E., Greece in the N., and Ethiopia (Cush) in the S. The nations of the 7th c. B.C. are classified by P as the sons of Noah's three sons, Shem, Ham, and Japheth (Gen. 10:1–7, 20, 22 f., 31). The sons of Shem ("Semites") are: the Elamites (non-Semitic), the Assyrians, the Hebrews (Arphaxad), the Lydians (non-Semitic), the Aramaeans, and, among the descendants of Arphaxad, some of the Arabs. The sons of Ham ("Hamites") are: the Ethiopians, the Egyptians, Put (the inhabitants of Punt, on the west coast of the Red Sea?), the Canaanites (Semitic), and, among the sons of Cush, the South Arabians. The sons of Japheth (Indo-Europeans) are: the Cimmerians, Magog (unknown), the Medes, the Greeks, the Tibarenes, the Moschians (both on the southern shores of the Black Sea), and the Tyrrhenians or Etruscans; the Scythians (Ashkenaz) are sons of Gomer (the Cimmerians); the Cypriotes (Elishah and Kittim), the Tartessians in southern Spain (Tarshish), and the Rhodians (Dodanim, an error for Rodanim) are the sons of Javan (the Greeks, i.e., Ionians). Nations which had ceased to exist before 700 B.C. (like the Philistines) and those that became prominent later (like the Persians) are not included.

The world of the N.T. is slightly more extensive, including the southern portions of the Roman Empire (Italy is unknown in the O.T.). Aside from Paul's journeys (confined to lands where the olive grows), we may gain an idea from the list of Jewish pilgrims from the Diaspora in Acts 2:9–11: Parthians, Medes, Elamites, Mesopotamians, Cappadocians, Pontians, Anatolians, Phrygians, Pamphilians, Egyptians, Lybians, Cyrenians, Romans, Cretans, and Arabians.

Our world has expanded immensely since Biblical times, but the final instructions of Jesus to his disciples have lost none of their challenging urgency: "Go ye therefore, and teach all nations, baptizing them in the name of the Father, and of the Son, and of the Holy Ghost: teaching them to observe all things whatsoever I have commanded you" (Matt. 28:19 f.). R. H. P.

worms. (1) Larvae of insects which eat organic matter, like bread (Ex. 16:24) or wool (Isa. 51:8); vegetable matter (Jonah 4:7); or the human body (Job 19:26, 21:26). (2) Possibly maggots such as proved fatal to Herod Agrippa I (Acts 12:23). (3) Symbolically, expressive of man's insignificance—"less than a worm" (Job 25:6; cf. Ps. 22:6; Isa. 41:14).

wormwood, the wastelands plant *Artemisia* (Heb. *la'anah*, Lat. *Artemisia absinthium*), characterized by a bitter taste (Deut. 29:18; Prov. 5:4; Lam. 3:15). It is mentioned in association with water of gall (? hemlock) as a beverage of affliction (Jer. 9:15, 23:15; Lam. 3:19; cf. Jer. 8:14). Wormwood is symbolic of bitter experience (Prov. 5:4).

worship in the A.V. means honor paid to man (Luke 14:10) or to God. This term translates Hebrew words meaning, "to make images (Jer. 44:19), to serve, to bow down, to prostrate oneself," and Greek words meaning, "to revere, to serve, to wait on, to do obeisance, to venerate."

In antiquity the basic notion of worship is service: we still speak of "religious services" long after the notion of worship has been radically changed; in antiquity the words for "worship" in Hebrew, Greek, and other languages all mean originally "service." The Hebrew Prophets, Jesus, and Paul substituted right living, love, and faith for ritual acts; prayer eventually took the place of sacrifice as the center of worship.

(1) *Before Amos* (750 B.C.). Among the ancient Israelites, as among all contemporary ancient nations, worship meant domestic service for the gods, providing them with what they needed, notably food, shelter, and whatever makes life pleasant. The Hittite *Instructions for Temple Officials*, written long before Moses, explain this notion of religion clearly. "Is the disposition of men and gods at all different? No. . . . When a slave stands before his master, he is washed and wears clean clothes; and he gives him something to eat or something to drink. And his master eats and drinks something, and he is refreshed in spirit and gracious toward him. If, however, the servant is neglectful and not observant, his disposition toward him is different. If the slave annoys his master, they either kill him, or injure his nose, his eyes, his ears. . . ."

As this text lucidly explains, the correct worship involved in antiquity two requirements: the slave is "washed and wears clean clothes" and "he gives his master something to eat or something to drink." The ancient religion of Israel, like the others, had a negative and a positive phase: avoidance of what annoys the deity, such as any kind of dirt and impurity; performance of what pleases the deity, such as provision of food and drink. The negative phase consists of purifications, the positive of sacrifices and oblations.

Purifications. The deity was holy and was surrounded by a zone of holiness: impertinent intrusion of the holy domain or intolerable pollution could result in instant death. So Uzzah was killed for touching the Ark (II Sam. 6:7) and seventy men of Beth-shemesh were killed for looking into it (I Sam. 6:19). The mere sight of God may kill (Ex. 33:20; Judg. 13:22; Isa. 6:5). This is why in ancient Israel and even later religion was called "the fear of God" (Neh. 5:9, 15; Job 6:14; Ps. 5:7, 34:11; Prov. 1:29, 8:13; Isa. 11:2, 3, 29:13, etc.). The most obvious defense against the danger of holy places was distance from them (Ex. 19:21, 20:18, 21). But in the immediate vicinity of the deity a person covered his face (Ex. 3:6; I Kings 19:13); in an orthodox synagogue men still keep their hats on, and women must keep their heads covered in Roman Catholic churches (cf. I Cor. 11:10). In regular worship, as in the case of the servant in the Hittite text, one must be clean and wear clean garments, lest dirt offend the deity. This cleansing in the O.T. is referred to by the expression "to sanctify oneself" (Ex. 28:41, 30:29; Josh. 7:13; Job 1:5, etc.). Some types of impurity were removed with a bath (Lev. 14:9, 15:11, 17:15 f.; II Sam. 11:2, 12:20); in several of these instances, washing the garments was also required; special garments could be worn. In an attenuated form these purifications survive in baptism (a symbolical cleansing) and in "Sunday clothes." Sandals were removed on holy ground (Ex. 3:5; Josh. 5:15), as still in Mohammedan mosques. To remove any remaining impurity after these purifications, special sacrifices could be offered (Lev. 12:6 f., 15:13–15; Deut. 21:1–9). The national rite of purification took place on the Day of Atonement, when a goat loaded with the sins of Israel was sent into the wilderness to Azazel (Lev. 16).

Sacrifices and offerings. As God's servant man should not only be clean in His presence, but supply what He desires. In a literal and primitive sense this occurred when God placed Adam in the garden of Eden "to dress it and keep it" (Gen. 2:15) and when the Lord "smelled the sweet savour" of Noah's sacrifice (Gen. 8:21), having been deprived of the nourishment of sacrifice during the Flood. Moreover, in ancient Israel the shewbread was provided for the Lord's table (I Sam. 21:6), a rite likewise known in Babylonia; it survived after the Exile (Ex. 25:30, 35:13; II Chron. 4:19, etc.). Sacrifices and offerings were supposed to provide God with His necessary food, until they became purely symbolical ceremonies. In its original meaning sacrifice was a sacred meal eaten either by the deity alone or by both deity and worshipper together. The most common and probably most primitive sacrifice was the "peace offering" (*shelem*) in which the blood of the victim was poured on the altar or on the ground, the fat and other parts were burned on the altar likewise for the deity, and the meat (often boiled; I Sam. 2:15–16; I Kings 19:21) provided a feast for the lay sacrificer, his family, and his friends. In the burnt offering (*'olah*, *kalil*) the whole animal was burned on the altar unto Yahweh, who enjoyed its sweet savor. The general term *minchah* (incorrectly rendered "meat offering" 131 times in the A.V.) is almost always used for a cereal offering (oblation). It could be offered in conjunction with animal sacrifices; if it was a separate offering, it often was presented as a propitiation to placate an angry deity.

In ancient times (probably until the destruction of Jerusalem and the Exile in 587 B.C.) the head of the family offered sacrifice; priests participated only in claiming part of the animal and its hide as their compensation when the sacrifice was offered at a temple (I Sam. 1:4, 2:13–16).

Human sacrifice was exceptional among the ancient Hebrews, although we still read, "The firstborn of thy sons shalt thou give unto me" (Ex. 22:29b, cf. 13:2). The Israelites very early substituted, like Abraham (Gen. 22:13), an animal sacrifice to "redeem" the first-born (Ex. 13:13–15, 34:20; Num. 18:15). Nevertheless, in a desperate crisis, the first-born was sacrificed as the supreme gift to the deity, as Mesha king of

Moab did (II Kings 3:27). The immolation of Jephthah's daughter (Judg. 11:30–40), which has been compared to Agamemnon's proposed sacrifice of his daughter Iphigenia (saved by Artemis), is the result of a vow made to the deity to obtain victory. Prisoners of war were occasionally sacrificed either for blood revenge (Judg. 8:18–21) or as part of the ban (I Sam. 15:33). Both these barbaric ancient rites were regarded as sacrifices to the deity: the first is an expiation (II Sam. 21:1–9), the second is a wholesale sacrifice of the persons and property of the enemy vowed to the deity before the battle (Num. 21:2), as a reward for victory. Human sacrifice, although extremely rare among the ancient Semites, except among the Carthaginians, was revived in the "Molech" worship in the time of Ahaz and Manasseh (II Kings 16:3, 21:6), provoking the protest of the prophets (Mic. 6:7).

Hymns and prayers in ancient times were not an essential part of the worship, like sacrifice. The Pentateuch knows nothing of vocal and orchestral music in the worship aside from the blowing of trumpets (Num. 10:1–10); except for the denunciation of temple music in Amos 5:23, there is no allusion to it before the Exile. Prayers were offered outside of the regular worship as occasion demanded (Gen. 24:12–15). The earliest prayers were personal petitions unto God, offered either in a sanctuary (I Sam. 1:10) or elsewhere (II Sam. 15:31), for help in difficulties, for the welfare of another (II Sam. 12:16), or for success in an undertaking (Gen. 24:12–14). Prayers for the nation were equally ancient (cf. Amos 7:2, 5), but confessions of sin and prayers of thanksgiving apparently came later. The only known pre-Exilic prayer offered as part of the worship is that of Solomon (I Kings 8:25–39); likewise the only hymn sung in the Jerusalem Temple before the Exile was apparently Ps. 24:7–10, probably sung when the Ark was brought into the Holy of Holies of Solomon's temple.

Places of worship. In the desert, during the nomadic period, the ancient Hebrews before Moses worshipped local deities dwelling in stones (Gen. 28:10–12, 16–22), mountains (Sinai-Horeb, "the mountain of God," Ex. 3:1), springs (Gen. 16:9–14), and other natural objects. In Canaan the Israelites adopted the sanctuaries in which the Canaanites worshipped the Baals. Some of them, particularly in the largest cities, were temples (as at Shiloh, Nob, Bethel, Shechem, etc.); but most of them were "high places," or open-air enclosures in which stood an altar, a stone pillar, and a wooden post or a tree. This worship was regarded as legitimate not only before Solomon built the Temple (I Kings 3:2), but actually until 622 B.C., when Josiah (in obedience to the newly found Book of the Law; see Deut. 12:2–7) destroyed all sanctuaries of the Lord except one and centralized the worship in the Jerusalem Temple (II Kings 23:8). Henceforth sacrifices and offerings could be presented to the Lord only there, in "the place which the Lord your God shall choose out of all your tribes to put his name there" (Deut. 12:5, and often).

Times of worship. During the nomadic period the Hebrews were shepherds, and their principal festivals occurred on the two occasions in which shepherds were rewarded for their labors: the birth of the lambs in the spring, celebrated on the Passover; and sheepshearing. Both were family festivals, observed in the home, and not in a sanctuary. In Canaan the nomadic festival of the Passover was combined with the agricultural festival of Unleavened Bread (Deut. 16:1–8; Ezek. 45:21; for the later observance see Ex. 12); although Deut. 16:5–6 ordered that the Passover be celebrated only in the Jerusalem Temple, after the Exile (Ex. 12) it was again celebrated in the family, and could thus continue to be observed as a family meal after the destruction of the Temple in A.D. 70. Such rites as the following, explained through the Exodus from Egypt, are extremely ancient: nothing should be left over till morning; the blood of the lamb should be smeared on the door-posts. Its original purpose seems to have been to ward off by means of blood the plague from people and flocks. The feast of sheepshearing (Gen. 31:19, 38:12 f.; I Sam. 25:4–12, 36; II Sam. 13:23 f.) lacked the mystical characteristics of the Passover, connected with the mysteries of birth and disease, and with the supposed power of blood to avert evil; therefore it ceased to be observed after the Exile.

In Canaan the Israelites adopted the three annual festivals of the farmers (Unleavened Bread, Harvest, and Ingathering; Ex. 23:15–17) and named them: Passover, Weeks or Pentecost, and Booths or Tabernacles (Deut. 16). The feast of the New Moon was observed from the earliest times (I Sam. 20:5 f.; II Kings 4:23; Isa. 1:14; Hos. 2:11; Amos 8:5). Conversely the Sabbath, which was originally a day of rest from farm labors (Ex. 23:12), began to be observed after the settlement in Canaan (cf. Hos. 2:11–13) and developed eventually from a day of rest to a holy day (Ex. 20:8–11; Deut. 5:12–15; Isa. 58:13 f.; Ezek. 20:20), consecrated to the Lord and His worship.

In ancient times the celebration of religious festivals was neither solemn nor lugubrious, as after Ezekiel stressed repentance and atonement on sacred days. The feasts were occasions for eating and drinking (Judg. 9:27; I Sam. 1:3, 9, 13, 25:36), as also dancing by the maidens (Judg. 21:19–21).

(2) *The teaching of the prophets about worship.* Amos (750 B.C.) was the first and greatest of those reforming prophets who denounced the current religious tenets and practices of Israel and advocated a worship "in spirit and in truth." From time immemorial religion had consisted in providing the gods with what they needed and what pleased them. In the time of Amos the Israelites regarded the ritual of worship, notably sacrifice, as the effective means for preserving or restoring the favor of Yahweh. Morality before Amos had never been regarded as an essential element in religion, with the single exception of the following words of an Egyptian sage, Meri-ka-Re (about 2100 B.C.), "More acceptable (to God)

is the character of one upright of heart than the (sacrificial) ox of the evildoer." This expresses the new teaching of Amos, which is later echoed succinctly as follows, "Does Jehovah delight in burnt-offerings and sacrifices, as in listening to the voice of Jehovah? Behold, obedience is better than sacrifice, and hearkening than the fat of rams" (I Sam. 15:22). The time of Amos was prosperous, following the successful wars of Jeroboam II against the Aramaeans of Damascus, and the rich lived luxuriously (Amos 3:12, 15, 4:1, 6:4–6); callously indifferent to the suffering of the needy (5:11; 6:6), they enjoyed offering lavish sacrifices in the sanctuaries of Yahweh (4:4 f.). Incidentally, whereas Amos complained about the abundance of sacrifices in a time of prosperity, Malachi (about 460 B.C.) lamented that in a time of acute depression the people were remiss in bringing tithes and sacrifices to the temple. Post-Exilic prophets like Haggai and Malachi assured the people that the best way to appease the Lord in times of distress was to build His Temple and bring to it the regular offerings, promising that by so doing they would be rewarded by Yahweh with unbelievable prosperity. Thus the old-fashioned religion continued in spite of Amos and the other great prophets; it has not disappeared in Judaism and Christianity even in our time. In this religion the worship of God consisted essentially in sacrifices and offerings, or other ritual acts. Sacred rites, as they had been learned from the fathers, were thought to have been ordained by God Himself, Who allegedly rewarded through the generations those who faithfully performed them. Sincere and earnest pious men placed their confidence in the effectiveness of sacrifices and other rites, but wicked men likewise believed that through ritual ceremonies they could induce God to overlook their iniquities, just as a king's anger might be placated by a gift or a judge may be corrupted by a bribe. Such notions of religion degraded God to the level of a "shyster" lawyer devoid of integrity, blind to the elementary principles of justice.

The reforming prophets from Amos to Jeremiah (750–600 B.C.) not only denounced corruption and wickedness connected with the worship at the various sanctuaries, but even questioned the efficacy of sacrificial rites in gaining God's favor. With righteous indignation they inveighed against sacred prostitution (Amos 2:7; Hos. 4:13 f.; cf. I Kings 14:24, 15:12, 22:46; Deut. 23:17 f.); against using in the worship what had been taken from the needy (Amos 2:8); against the worship of the Canaanite Baals, the lovers after whom Israel went awhoring, forsaking Yahweh, her true husband (Hos. 2:2–13; Jer. 3:1); against the wickedness of priests (Hos. 4:4–10) and their intemperance (Isa. 28:7 f.); against the sacrifice of children to Molech in Tophet (Jer. 7:31, 32:35; Ezek. 16:20 f.; cf. Deut. 18:10; Lev. 18:21). But aside from such abominable practices, the great prophets questioned the religious value of sacrifice, the central rite of the worship. The people enjoyed the festivals at the sanctuaries, when they offered especially abundant sacrifices and banqueted merrily (Amos 4:4 f.; Hos. 4:13; Isa. 22:13), but Yahweh was revolted by their revelry and refused to accept their sacrifices (Amos 5:21–24; Hos. 5:6, 8:11–13; Isa. 1:11–15; Jer. 6:20). For Yahweh preferred loyalty to sacrifice and knowledge of God to burnt offerings (Hos. 6:6), and when He delivered Israel from Egyptian bondage He demanded of them obedience and not sacrifices (Jer. 7:21–23). He does not require numerous sacrifices, but "to do justly, and to love mercy, and to walk humbly with thy God" (Mic. 6:6–8). "For thou desirest not sacrifice, . . . ; thou delightest not in burnt offering. The sacrifices of God are a broken spirit; a broken and contrite heart, O God, thou wilt not despise" (Ps. 51:16 f.).

Many Biblical scholars have concluded from these statements that the prophets intended to abolish sacrifice, festivals, and all ritual worship completely, substituting morality for religious ceremonies. But if they had intended to establish a purely spiritual worship, a religion without public cult, it is difficult to understand the central position that sacrifice retained in the Second Temple at Jerusalem, from its inauguration in 515 B.C. to its destruction by Titus in A.D. 70. It is true that they shifted the center of gravity in religion from external correctness to inner uprightness, and that for them righteousness, God's primary requirement, did not consist in prescribed acts but in an attitude of mind, in the inner motives of one's actions. They obviously did not equate peace offerings and burnt offerings to intrinsically abominable deeds such as sacred prostitution and infant sacrifice. But they were convinced that the whole religious ritual was offensive to Yahweh if it was not accompanied by honesty and mercy for the needy, if it was performed with the expectation of inducing God to overlook one's iniquities by payment of what amounted to a bribe. The prophets are opposed to the misuse of sacrificial worship, not to the institution as such; and that is why they did not substitute a different order of service, such as the synagogue service which after the destruction of the Temple remained the sole worship in Judaism and influenced deeply the Christian worship. The book found in the Temple in 622 B.C., which was profoundly influenced by the prophetic teaching, retained sacrifice as all-important in the worship; but far from being a gift or tribute presented to Yahweh, it was merely the expression of gratitude for God's blessings and rejoicing in His presence (Deut. 12:11 f., 16:1–17, 26:10 f.). In conclusion the pre-Exilic prophets did not wish to abolish sacrifices and other rites because they were performed in the wrong spirit, any more than Jesus wished to abolish prayer because of the perverse prayer of a Pharisee (Luke 18:11 f.). Like the prayer of the publican (Luke 18:13), the acts of worship—worse than useless as empty forms—were significant for the prophets only in so far as they were an expression of an upright life, of true repentance, of a desire to do God's will, and of full trust in God.

(3) *Worship in the Second Temple* (516 B.C.–A.D. 70). The noble teaching of the prophets was not forgotten in the post-Exilic period: God does not require sacrifice but obedience to His will and repentance (Ps. 40:6–11, 51:16 f.; Prov. 21:3; cf. Prov. 15:8, 21:27), for God owns every beast of the forest and is not hungry for the meat of bulls (Ps. 50:8–13); "Offer unto God thanksgiving" (v. 14). Moreover the worship was spiritualized in some of the Psalms (26:6 f., 27:6, 66:13–20, 107:22).

Ritual worship, however, retained its central importance not only for the people in general, but even for such prophets as Ezekiel, Haggai, Zechariah; see in particular, Mal. 1:7–14, 3:3 f., 8–10; Joel 1:9, 13. Except for minor changes in later times (such as sacred vocal and instrumental music in the Temple, which is very important in Chronicles but is unknown in the Pentateuch; and some new festivals, like Dedication [165 B.C.] and Purim [about 125 B.C.]), the ritual of the Temple worship was fixed in the Priestly Code (about 450 B.C.), which embodied earlier codes and some very early rituals (like the "scapegoat" rite on the Day of Atonement, Lev. 16) and some later supplements. It is both a concise history of God's kingdom on earth, from the creation of the world (Gen. 1) to the settlement of Israel in Canaan (Josh. 13–22), and the definitive codification of Israel's ritual laws. Living under the liberal rule of the Persian empire, the authors did not dream of a future independent Messianic kingdom of the Jews, but willingly accepting foreign rule, they did not interfere with the civil administration, and created for the Jews a spiritual commonwealth to which the Persian authorities did not object in the least. They showed how the only God in existence, Who created heaven and earth, became the sovereign of the Jewish community by separating Israel from the Gentiles through the covenant with Abraham (Gen. 17), by revealing His Law to Moses, and by giving to Israel the land of Canaan. As the charter of the holy commonwealth of Israel under the rule of God, the Priestly Code, reversing the teaching of the prophets, shifted again the emphasis from morality to the ritual worship, and regarded religion as the recognition that God owns the property, the time, the land, and the very persons of the Israelites, who must consequently obey blindly the enactments of their divine sovereign, whether they seem sensible or incomprehensible, under penalty of exile (excommunication) or death. Thus the Priestly Code created a holy state within the empire, the first organized church in history, chiefly by fixing exactly the ritual of public and private devotions.

The whole ritual system is based on two immemorial notions: physical holiness, based on God's ownership of everything; and arbitrary divine enactment, inflexible though unintelligible, which allowed men to use what they needed for living without robbing God of His property. Thus God said, "The land is mine" (Lev. 25:23), but allowed Israel to use most of it provided they paid to God the firstlings, the first fruits, the tithes, etc., as a sort of rent. The festivals and the sabbaths were a tax paid to God for the use of time. All Israelites were slaves of God, since He redeemed them from Egyptian bondage: they could be virtually free, however, by devoting to God the Tribe of Levi, redeeming the firstborn at the price of five shekels (Num. 18:16), and paying a yearly tax of half a shekel to the sanctuary, beginning with the age of twenty (Ex. 30:11–16). For the use of their property the Israelites paid the following taxes to God, for the benefit of the priests and Levites. To the priests belonged: heave offerings, meal offerings, sin offerings, trespass offerings, wave offerings, the first fruits and the choice produce of the fields, the first-born of man and beast (redeeming the first-born of men and unclean beasts, Num. 18:8–15, 17 f.). The Levites received the tithes of the Israelites (Num. 18:21, 24a), but had to pay the best tenth of them to the high priest (Num. 18:25–32).

Thus the whole sacrificial system, except for some personal optional offerings, was a list of taxes and fines, national or private. The taxes paid by the Israelites for the support of the Temple, listed above, were not sacramental in character, but such were the national taxes, of which the most important was the *tamid* (perpetual), the daily burnt offering of a yearling lamb, a cereal oblation, and a libation of wine, presented morning and evening in the Temple (Ex. 29:38–42; Num. 28:1–8).

Besides taxes, every government exacts fines. The other public and private sacrifices prescribed in the Priestly Code are to be classed as fines. For Israel an annual expiation for all sins is prescribed on the Day of Atonement (Lev. 23:26–32; Num. 29:7–11; Lev. 16); and also a sin offering of a he-goat on new moons and festivals (Num. 28:15, 22, 29:15–38); and the sin offering of a bullock at the consecration of priests (Ex. 29:14, 36) followed by a burnt offering of a ram (Ex. 29:18, 25), and of another ram as a heave offering (Ex. 29:19–28); and a sin offering and a burnt offering of bullocks for the Levites (Num. 8:8–12); and sin offerings for the high priest (Lev. 4:1–35; Num. 15:22–31).

The following sacrifices were fines for individual transgressions: the *sin offering* (*hattath*) for violation of taboos or involuntary sins (Lev. 4:27–5:6; Num. 15:22–29), and for certain purifications (Lev. 12:6, 14:10–20, 15:14 f., 29 f.), etc. The *trespass* or *guilt offering* (*asham*) atoning for theft of human or divine property (Lev. 5:14–16, 6:1–7), after restitution, plus one-fifth, had been made. Other private sacrifices were more or less optional: the *burnt offering* (Lev. 1:1–17), the *peace offering* (Lev. 3, 7:11–34, 22:21–25), the *meal offering* consisting of flour and oil kneaded together or variously cooked (Lev. 2), and *oblations* as substitutes for burnt offerings (Lev. 5:11–13), or as vows and freewill offerings (Lev. 2, 7:9 f.; Num. 7). In conclusion, the sacrificial worship in the Priestly Code was conceived in part as payment of what was due to God and in part as expiation of sin. Since God had made Israel a holy nation (Ex. 19:6), it was imperative for it to observe the ritual enactments punctiliously, even when incomprehensible, lest God in His holy anger destroy His people. The "legalism" of the Priestly Code preserved the Jews as a separate nation without state and country through the centuries.

(4) *The synagogue worship.* The synagogue originated in the 4th cen. B.C., unless its roots reached back to Ezekiel's meetings in Babylonia (Ezek. 8:1, 18, 33 f.; cf. especially 33:30–33). Except for Ps. 74:8 (possibly referring to destruction of synagogues by Antiochus IV Epiphanes in 168–165), synagogues are not mentioned before the Christian era except in Greek inscriptions from Egypt dated about 230 B.C. and later. A Gk. inscription probably dating from before A.D. 70 found in Jerusalem in 1920, records the founding of a synagogue, probably the "Synagogue of the Libertines" (Acts 6:9), by Theodotus of the family of Vettenus: he "built the synagogue for the reading of the law [i.e., the Pentateuch] and for the teaching of the commandments." Such was indeed the chief and original purpose of the synagogue. It became the seat of a rational worship without sacrifices and offerings: its central feature was instruction in religion, and eventually it became the model of Christian and Moslem public worship. The synagogue service included the reading of a portion of the Pentateuch, its translation into the vernacular (Aramaic in Palestine, Greek in Egypt), a homily (expository or edifying), and eventually a reading from the Prophets (Luke 4:16–22; Jesus read at Nazareth Isa. 61:1 f. and preached on it), prayer ("the Eighteen [Benedictions]," *Shemoneh 'Esreh*), and the priestly benediction.

(5) *Christian worship in the New Testament.* At first Jesus and the Apostles worshipped in the Jewish Temple and synagogues (Luke 4:16–22; Matt. 26:55; Mark 11:11, 15; Luke 21:37 f., 24:53; Acts 2:46, 3:1, 20:16, 21:26, etc.). Eventually St. Paul established among his Gentile converts a Christian worship. The New Testament does not give us a full description of it, but we may glean from Paul's epistles the following elements in the service: occasional glossolalia (speaking with tongues), to which Paul greatly preferred prophecy or an understandable message (I Cor. 14) of teaching or of exhortation (Rom. 12:7 f.); singing of psalms (I Cor. 14:26), or psalms, hymns, and spiritual songs (Eph. 5:19; Col. 3:16); and the celebration of the Lord's Supper or Eucharist (I Cor. 11:23–34; Mark 14:22–25; Matt. 26:26–29; Luke 22:15–20). The two sacraments mentioned in the New Testament (both modifications of Jewish rites) are baptism and the Lord's Supper. The earliest description of Christian worship is in Justin Martyr's *First Apology,* 65–67 (about A.D. 150): On Sunday all the believers meet together; the memoirs of the Apostles (the Gospels) and the writings of the prophets (the O.T.) are read; a sermon follows; the congregation prays audibly; the Eucharist is celebrated, including the prayer of consecration of the elements, and ending with the "Amen" of the congregation.

See entries on GOD; JESUS CHRIST; POLYTHEISM; PROPITIATION; SACRAMENTS. For the pantheons of various countries see BABYLON; CANAAN; EGYPT; ROMAN EMPIRE; SUMER, etc.

R. H. P.

wrath, the rendering of several Heb. and Gk. words used in Scripture to express anger: (1) the wrath of men, like that of Jacob against Rachel (Gen. 30:2); of Balaam against his ass (Num. 22:27); of Eliab* against David (I Sam. 17:28); of Saul against Jonathan (I Sam. 20:30, 33); of Jonathan against his father (I Sam. 20:34); and (2) the anger of Yahweh, as an ethical and justifiable reaction of a wholly righteous God against His sinful people and against evil in all forms. This anger was consistent with the early, anthropomorphic conceptions of the Lord. It manifested itself against Moses (Ex. 4:14); against Aaron and Miriam (Num. 12:9); against the wicked cities of the Dead Sea rim (Deut. 29:23); against Israel at Ai (Josh. 7:1); against Uzzah, for touching the sacred Ark (II Sam. 6:7); and against Israel on countless other occasions. The wrath of Yahweh was tempered by mercy, understanding love, and kindly yearning for man's repentance. The anger of God as described in certain Psalms was "slow" to display itself, because of His "great kindness" (Ps. 103:8; cf. Joel 2:13). The prophets often linked God's anger with His more merciful aspects, as in Nah. 1:3. This teaching was a step toward the N.T. revelation of a God Whose main quality was love, embodied in and revealed through His Son, Jesus Christ. To Jesus anger was so sinful that it was only one step removed from killing (Matt. 5:21); though he recognized justifiable anger (v. 22), and he himself expressed it against illicit practices in the Temple (John 2:15). See LOVINGKINDNESS; PARDON.

wrestle, to contend by grappling, like Jacob and the angel at the Jabbok (Gen. 32). Wrestling matches were popular in Mediterranean lands of the 1st century A.D. Paul may have seen them at Corinth and Puteoli. He used their imagery in presenting the Christian way of life (Eph. 6:12). See GAMES.

writing, invented in Mesopotamia, probably by Sumerians (non-Semites who arrived there possibly 6,000 years ago), is a major milestone in civilization. The oldest known "ABC" (14th century B.C.) was found at the Syrian Ras Shamrah by C.F.A. Schaeffer in a three-line cuneiform inscription. As early as c. 2500 B.C. Sumerians had a form of primitive linear writing (nonalphabetic); from their pictographic messages cuneiform* developed. Countless examples of very early cuneiform have been dug from Warka (Erech, Gen. 10:10). Pricked on wet clay with a wedge-shaped stylus, cuneiform messages were used in everyday business transactions by many peoples of the Near East (including Palestine) for centuries. The thousands of cuneiform tablets excavated at Nippur by the University of Pennsylvania represent the oldest written literature recovered in any significant quantity. They supply unique information about spiritual and business conditions in Babylonia in the 2d millennium B.C.

WRITING

In Egypt, a cradle of near-alphabetic writing, hieroglyphs (conventionalized pictures) were in use long before the Israelites descended to the Delta to escape famine. And long after these hieroglyphs were current, cursive hieratic and demotic writing developed in Egypt. (See ROSETTA STONE.)

Thousands of years of experimenting with writing by Near Eastern peoples lay behind men's ability to reduce to writing the material now embodied in Scripture. Efforts to write resulted in nonalphabetic systems of pictographs (pictures of objects); ideographs (symbols denoting ideas by conventionalized pictures, as in Egyptian hieroglyphs); phonograms (symbols representing speech sounds); and also in alphabetic scripts. Over the years people of different countries assimilated and modified the forms of writing employed by their neighbors.

SINAITIC SCRIPT	DESCRIPTION OF SIGN	CANAANITE SCRIPT OF 13th CENT. B.C.	CANAANITE SCRIPT OF c. 1000 B.C.	SOUTH ARAB SCRIPT OF IRON AGE	MODERN HEBREW SCRIPT	PHONETIC VALUE
	OX-HEAD				א	ʾ
	HOUSE				ב	b
?					ג	g
	FISH				ד	d
	MAN PRAYING				ה	h
?					ו	w
?					ז	z
	?				ד	ḏ
	FENCE?				ח	ḥ
	DOUBLE LOOP				ח	ḫ
?					ט	ṭ
?					י	y
	PALM OF HAND				כ	k
	"OX-GOAD"				ל	l
	WATER				מ	m
	SERPENT				נ	n
?					ס	s
	EYE				ע	ʿ
?					ע	ǵ
	THROW STICK				פ	p
?					צ	ṣ
	BLOSSOM				צ	ḍẓ
	?				ק	q
	HUMAN HEAD				ר	r
	BOW				ש	ṯ ś
	?				ש	š
	MARK OF CROSS				ת	t

HEBREW NAME	PHOENICIAN SCRIPT OF 8th CENT. B.C. BAAL LEBANON KARATEPE		OLD GREEK SCRIPT OF 8th CEN. B.C.	HEBREW CURSIVE OF c. 600 B.C.	GREEK NAME	MODERN GREEK SCRIPT	MODERN ROMAN SCRIPT
ALEPH					ALPHA	A	A
BETH					BETA	B	B
GIMEL					GAMMA	Γ	G
DALETH					DELTA	Δ	D
HE					EPSILON	E	E
WAW							V
ZAYIN					ZETA	Z	Z
HETH					ETA	H	H
TETH					THETA	Θ	
YODH					IOTA	I	I
KAPH					KAPPA	K	K
LAMEDH					LAMDA	Λ	L
MEM					MU	M	M
NUN					NU	N	N
SAMEKH					XI	Ξ	
AYIN					OMICRON	O	O
PE					PI	Π	P
SADE							
QOPH							Q
RESH					RHO	P	R
SHIN					SIGMA	Σ	S
TAW					TAU	T	T

492. Writing Chart, drawn by Frank M. Cross, Jr., for *The Archaeology of Palestine*, by William F. Albright, Penguin Books.

The Development of the Alphabet

The word "alphabet" is derived from the Gk. words *alpha* from the Phoenician *aleph* ("ox"), and *beta*, from *beth* ("house").

New materials bearing on the evolution of alphabetic writing have been made accessible by the patient and brilliant research of Biblical archaeologists and their colleagues, including gifted native helpers. Prior to 1914 the alphabet could not be traced in Palestine farther back than c. 835 B.C. (the Moabite* Stone) or c. 950–910 B.C. (the Gezer* Calendar). But now a wealth of new material bearing on the development of alphabetic writing is coming to light, from the 1949 expedition of the University of California to Serabit el-Khadem; the related studies of W. F. Albright; and the microfilming by the ASOR, the American Foundation for the Study of Man, and the Library of Congress, of almost forgotten MSS. in Gk., Arm., Georg., Syr., and Arab. (mostly N.T. text) in patriarchal archives in Jerusalem; and of thousands of MSS. in the Monastery of St. Catherine at Sinai.

The alphabet is known to possess a far greater antiquity than was for centuries believed, since several Sinai research expeditions followed up the discovery by Sir Flinders Petrie (1904) of 25 pieces of fragmentary writing left c. 1500 B.C. by possibly the foreman of a lonely band of oppressed miners of turquoise at Serabit el-Khadem. These miners, who had evidently been in touch with Egyptian hieroglyphic writing in the 2d millennium B.C., worked out or stumbled on—by the acrophonic principle—the prototype of an alphabet from which Heb. and many other languages, including Eng., ultimately developed. This proto-Sinaitic writing is in the earliest known alphabet. It is now evident that the words, scratched in Canaanite dialect on desert sandstone some 3,500 years ago, were a major factor in the evolution of the alphabet.

Wendell Phillips calls the Serabit finds "the oldest known groups of documents in the alphabet from which our own is descended." (For an exhaustive and scholarly study of the development of systems of writing see *The Alphabet*, David Diringer, Philosophical Library, New York.) For a succinct and authoritative consideration of writing as it evolved in the lands where the Bible was first set down, see *The Archaeology of Palestine*, Chap. VIII, pp. 185–196, W. F. Albright, Penguin Books. On this material the next section of this article is based. See the chart on p. 829, showing the developments from the Sinaitic script through to the Canaanite scripts of the 13th century B.C. and c. 1000 B.C.; the script of the South Arabians of the Iron Age (from c. 1200 B.C.); the Heb. cursive (600 B.C.); Phoenician (8th century B.C.); Old Gk. (8th century B.C.); and modern Heb., Gk., Roman, and European scripts.

Development of Writing in Palestine

As pointed out by W. F. Albright in *The Archaeology of Palestine*, pp.185–196 (Penguin Books), Palestine experimented with a variety of scripts: (1) pictograms near the end of the 4th millennium B.C., as illustrated by the seal impressions discovered by Maurice Dunand at Byblos on jar handles excavated from a cemetery; (2) "pseudo-hieroglyphic" syllabic scripts seen on recovered bits of stone stelae, tablets, and bronze objects ranging apparently from the 18th century B.C. to the 15th, and showing a relationship to Egyptian hieroglyphs; (3) cuneiform script used by Mesopotamians. This script appears also on the Balu'ah stele found in Moab in 1930. Other scripts known to have developed in Palestine and Syria include: (1) the Ugaritic (Ras Shamrah) cuneiform; and (2) the linear alphabet used by Phoenicians and transmitted by them to Western peoples. Examples of the former script have been excavated not only from Ugarit, but from the Palestinian Beth-shemesh (on a narrow tablet of clay), and from near Mt. Tabor (on a copper knife). Of the 2d script that developed in Palestine (used on the Mesha stone c. 835 B.C.) and the Ahiram sarcophagus (c. 1000 B.C.), the ancestry seems to go back to the lonely turquoise mines of Serabit el-Khadem. Megiddo and Lachish have also supplied links in the evolution of the alphabets used in Palestine and Syria.

Versatile Canaanites living in Palestine in the Late Bronze Age (c. 1550–1200 B.C.) were using four or five sorts of writing to convey their messages: (1) Mesopotamian (Accadian cuneiform); (2) hieroglyphs of Egypt; (3) a linear alphabetic writing, ancestor of our own; (4) the Ugaritic alphabetic cuneiform system; (5) the Byblos syllabic script. Messages were usually written on small, practically imperishable clay* tablets, such as have been excavated at Gezer, Shechem, Taanach, Tell-el-Hesī, Jericho, and elsewhere.

Chester C. McCown points out in *The Ladder of Progress in Palestine*, p. 117 (Harper & Brothers), that Hebrews living during the Monarchy (c. 1020–587 B.C.) used one type of handwriting at Samaria and another at Jerusalem. At about the time of the Second Temple, erected after the Exile, the sacred books were written in the "square" characters of current Aram. (Syr. *'ashurith*), which were ultimately "frozen" by the Massoretes in the form of the Heb. alphabet used today. The Aram. script came to be regarded as "holy" in the copying of O.T. books; the old Heb. letters were "profane." The old Heb. was based on the Phoen. alphabet (c. 1500 B.C. or earlier) and was borrowed by Israelites from the Canaanites (Phoenicians). Cuneiform writing had been discontinued for daily business several centuries before Christ; merchants preferred the easier Aram. An Aram. inscription, giving the "autograph" of Jesus as he would have signed it, has been found on a Jerusalem ossuary (bone box). All the Dead Sea Scrolls found within the past few years date nearer the time of Jesus than any now-known Aram. documents. The "square" characters, more conveniently read, were used in manuscripts and in the printed forms which ultimately developed. Heb. is always written from right to left. A cursive form of Heb. is used for secular correspondence. (See JESUS, illus. 217.)

The chart on p. 829, showing the Heb. alphabet and the probable meaning of its letters, contains clues about the life of the people in whose society it originated. *Aleph* (A) is based on an ox-head; *beth* (B), a house; *gimel* (C), a camel; *mem* (M) water; *ayin* (a sound having no equivalent in Western alphabets) appears to be an eye or a well; *nun* (N) a fish; *taw* (Y) a cross, etc.

The ancient Heb. alphabet consisted of 21 consonants and the silent *aleph* (') used at the beginning of certain words to suggest that it started with a vowel sound. The 22 letters originally represented about 27 sounds. Until about the 6th century B.C. only consonants were used; subsequently there developed under Jewish scholars (Massoretes) a system of seven vowel points, employed singly or in combination with one another and with a *vau* or a *yodh*. This establishing of the vowel-point system was completed A.D. 700. The 12th century saw its adoption into general use.

Hebrew writers used letters of the alphabet to designate numerals in a decimal system: 1 is *aleph*, 2 is *beth*, and so on, to 10, which is *yod*. Greeks also used their alphabet for numerals. Maccabean coins illustrate this early use of letters as numerals.

Biblical Allusions to Writing

One of the earliest is: "And the Lord said unto Moses, Write this for a memorial in a book" (Ex. 17:14; cf. 24:4, "And Moses wrote all the words of the Lord"). Num. 33:2 mentions Moses' writing a record of the Wilderness journeys of Israel. A written Book of the Law on tables (small stone stelae coated with limestone composition) is mentioned as having been given by Moses to Levites to be placed in the Ark of the Covenant (Deut. 31:24–26; cf. Josh. 8:31). His writing of a song (which he taught the children of Israel before his death) is mentioned in Deut. 31:22. The evidence found at Serabit* indicates that writing was done by non-literary persons at the time of the Exodus. The Book of Joshua tells of this leader's writing on altar stones a copy of the law of Moses (Josh. 8:32). (For glyptic writing on gems, see SEAL; BREASTPLATE.) Metal plates (like the gold and silver plates built into foundation deposits of the palace of Darius the Great at Persepolis) were engraved. (For evidence of writing attributed to the period of the Judges, see allusion to the young man of Succoth, Judg. 8:14 and A.S.V. margin.) The "Song of Deborah" (12th century B.C.) speaks of those who "handle the pen of the writer" as coming out of Zebulun (Judg. 5:14).

The existence of the O.T. prophetic books is evidence that the Hebrew literary or "writing" prophets and their scribes were able to write (see Acts 7:42; and the "ready writer," Ps. 45:1). Jeremiah referred to a "diamond" pointed, metal pen (17:1); to ink (36:18); and to a knife (36:23) used for erasures. Mention is made of sealing written witnessed books of purchase and storing them in earthen vessels (32:12–14). Ezekiel mentioned a man's inkhorn, worn on the thigh (9:2) (see also 24:2, 37:16, 43:11).

(For allusions to writing in the Persian period see Ezra 1:1 ff.; also the letter written "in the Syrian tongue" to Artaxerxes by men opposing repairs to the Jerusalem Temple, Ezra 4:7–10, cf. 4:6; and the written decrees of the Persian Ahasuerus, Esther 3:9–14, 8:8 ff. For state correspondence of the era of Darius see Ezra 5:6, 6:1; Dan. 5:7 ff.—the Belshazzar incident; 6:8–10.)

Writing Materials

In the Biblical period these included tables of stone; tablets of wood covered with wax (Luke 1:63); skins of animals, parchment; vellum; bricks; clay tablets; bits of broken pottery (shards, ostraca); papyrus; gems; and metal plates. (See SCROLL. For writers and their activities, see SCRIBES.) Before such clearly written Biblical documents as the pre-Massoretic Nash Papyrus (possibly 2d half of 2d century B.C.) and the Dead Sea Scrolls* could have been produced there must have been a long process of development of Hebrew writing and writing materials.

The Apostolic Letters were written in Gk., probably on papyrus* with ink* (II Cor. 3:3; II John 5, 12, etc.; see also Luke 1:3; I Cor. 4:14, 14:37; II Cor. 1:13, 3:2; I John 2:14; Gal. 1:20; Rev. 1:11, 2:1 f., 3:12. The Romans used parchment for ordinary correspondence, II Tim. 4:13 A.V., A.S.V. R.S.V.).

In reply to the query, "Did Jesus write?" cf. John 7:14 f., "How knoweth this man letters, having never learned?"; also John 8:6, "with his finger wrote on the ground."

(See BIBLE; GEBAL; RAS SHAMRAH; SUPERSCRIPTION, John 19:19 f.)

WRITINGS, THE

Some Epigraphic Date Pegs for Script

Material	*Date*
Byblos pseudo-hieroglyphic script (80 or more syllabic characters)	Probable, 23d–22d cen. B.C.
Byblos copper script (Early Canaanite-Phoenician)	Probable, c. 22d–21st cen. B.C.
Byblos Ahiram Sarcophagus	Before 975 B.C.
Proto-Sinaitic alphabet, Serabit, ("earliest known attempt at purely alphabetic writing," Semitic origin—forebear of Phoenician, Hebrew, Greek, Latin, English. Similar to Gezer jar-handle script and Beth-shemesh fragment.)	c. 1500 B.C.
Ras Shamrah alphabet, N. Syria (Ugarit), (less than 30 alphabetic cuneiform letters)	c. 15th cen. B.C.
Ras Shamrah tablets (indicating parallels with O.T. vocabulary and style)	c. 15th–14th cen. B.C.
Tell ed-Duweir (Lachish, S. Palestine) ewer and bowl inscriptions. Letters (18) in ink on clay potsherds, in non-literary Hebrew, Jeremiah era, ancient Phoenician script	14th–13th cen. B.C. 588 B.C.
Megiddo material	c. 1150 B.C.
Gezer Calendar	Late 10th cen. B.C.
Moabite Stone, recording in alphabet resembling Biblical Hebrew wars between Israel and neighbors; events in reign of Mesha, King of Moab, subsequent to death of Ahab, King of Israel. Writing called "Israelite alphabet," in distinction to later "Hebrew alphabet."	c. 835 B.C.
Samaria ostraca, Jeroboam II and Amos era	c. 786–746 B.C.
Siloam Tunnel inscription (Jerusalem) indicates alphabet used by some Hebrew prophets. Same as sacred script of Samaritan worshippers at Nablus.	701 B.C.
Note: inscriptions on jar handle seals and stamps have yielded hundreds of personal names from the Biblical period.	

Writings, the. See HAGIOGRAPHA.

X

Xerxes (zûrk'sēz) (Gk. form of the Pers. *Khshayarsha* and Heb. *Ahasuerus**, Esther 1:1 f.; Ezra 4:6), the name of two Persian kings of the Achaemenid Dynasty, the 1st of whom is generally considered to be the Ahasuerus referred to above.

493. Xerxes, standing behind his father, Darius, as he gives audience to a Median petitioner. From a monumental relief found in a courtyard in Persepolis, Iran.

Y

Yahweh (yä'wĕ). See GOD.

Yam Suph, the term used in the Heb. Bible, Ex. 13:18, and translated (probably incorrectly) in most English versions, "Red Sea." Yam Suph means literally "Reed Sea" or "Marsh Sea." See EXODUS.

Yarmuk, Wâdī el- (Sherî'at el-Menâdireh), one of the four somewhat parallel streams cutting Trans-Jordan into five highland regions: Bashan, Gilead, Ammon, Moab, and Edom. The Yarmuk, though not mentioned in Scripture, is a conspicuous feature of the landscape, entering the Jordan a short distance S. of the Sea of Galilee. Its deep gorge contains masses of limestone over which volcanic lava is deposited. At certain seasons a torrential river flows through the Wâdī el-Yarmuk in gorgeous cascades.

A unique Pottery Neolithic culture was discovered by M. Stekelis at Sha'ar ha-Golan, N. of the Yarmuk near its outlet into the Jordan. Called "Yarmukian," it dates c. 4500 B.C. and is characterized by its art, which consists of engraved and incised pebbles and small stone and clay figurines. Many of the latter are schematic portrayals of human figures, particularly of women. Existence was based on hunting, fishing, and farming. The pottery was coarse, heavy, and decorated, if at all, only by incision—especially bands filled with a herringbone design. See M. Stekelis, *IEJ* 1, 1960, pp. 1 ff.; E. Anati, *Palestine Before the Hebrews*, 1963, pp. 263 ff.; R. de Vaux, *CAH*³, Vol. I, Part I, 1970, pp. 513 ff.

year. See TIME.

yodh (yōd) ("hand"), the 10th letter of the Heb. alphabet. Like *y* in the Latin alphabet, it could serve as either a consonant (pronounced as in "yes") or a vowel (as in "rhythm"). It is the smallest character in the "square" Heb. script (see WRITING). See also JOT.

yoke (Heb. *ol*). (1) A wooden frame for joining two oxen or other draft animals, consisting of a crosspiece and two bows which fit around the necks of the animals (Num. 19:2; Deut. 21:3). A "yoke" of oxen is a pair (I Sam. 14:14; Luke 14:19).

(2) A symbol of subjection of one individual to another, as Esau to Jacob (Gen. 27:40). A yoke was placed literally on the neck of one reduced to submission (Jer. 28:10); cf. the yoke placed on Israel by Solomon and Rehoboam (I Kings 12:9 f.). The humiliation of one nation by another was tantamount to bringing them "under the yoke," like the Jews to the yoke of the King of Babylon (Jer. 27:8, 11 f., 28:4). Jesus, who may have worked with his father making yokes at Nazareth, offered the heavy-laden of his day peace of soul in terms of an "easy" yoke and a "light" burden (Matt. 11:29 f.); in contrast, see the yoke of sin suggested in Lam. 1:14. The N.T., referring to the relationship of a servant to his master, spoke of his being under a yoke of authority (I Tim. 6:1).

496. Yoke.

In rabbinic literature, "taking the yoke of the kingdom of heaven," or yielding to the complete sovereignty of God's will, is used, and also "taking the yoke of the commandments," i.e., doing right for the sake of righteousness.

yokefellow (Gk. *synzugŏs*), a proper name, or the characterization applied by the writer of Phil. 4:3 to the bearer of the Epistle to the Philippians. This man had been a partner with Paul in Christian work in the city and was urged to assist the women, Euodia and Syntyche, and the rest of Paul's fellow workers. The "yokefellow" may have been Luke—but not Epaphroditus, Barnabas, or Silas, since these were apparently elsewhere at the time.

Yom Kippur. See ATONEMENT, DAY OF.

Y-R-S-L-M, letters used on a pentagram seal to indicate the captured Jerusalem.

Z

Zaanannim (zā′ȧ-năn′ĭm) (Zaanaim, Judg. 4:11), a frontier town of Naphtali (Josh. 19:33), probably located N. or NE. of Mt. Tabor.

Zabad (zā′băd) ("He has given"), the name of several O.T. minor characters. (1) A son of Nathan, son of Attai, of the Tribe of Judah (I Chron. 2:36 f.), and possibly one of David's heroes (I Chron. 11:41). (2) A man of the Shuthelah group of Ephraimites (I Chron. 7:21). (3) A son of an Ammonitess (Shimeath); a conspirator against King Joash of Judah (837–800 B.C.) in the plot to avenge the death of Zechariah, son of the priest Jehoiada (II Chron. 24:26); the same as Jozachar (II Kings 12:21). (4) The name of three men, all of whom were compelled by the reforms of Ezra to separate from foreign wives (Ezra 10:27, 33, 43).

Zabbai (zăb′ā-ī), one who renounced his foreign wife under the marriage reforms inaugurated by Ezra (Ezra 10:28). His son or kinsman Baruch repaired the portion of the Jerusalem wall which was near the house of the high priest Eliashib (Neh. 3:20).

Zabdi (zăb′dī). (1) A progenitor of Achan of Judah, whose sin in appropriating spoils highlights the narrative of Josh. 7. (2) A man of the line of Benjamin (I Chron. 8:19). (3) A manager of David's vineyards (I Chron. 27:27). (4) A member of a musical family in post-Exilic Jerusalem (Neh. 11:17).

Zabdiel (zăb′dĭ-ĕl) (1) Father of Jashobeam (I Chron. 27:2). (2) Son of Haggedolim (Neh. 11:14). (3) Murderer of the usurper, Alexander Balas, king of the Seleucid empire (I Macc. 11:17).

Zacchaeus (ză-kē′ŭs) ("pure"), a citizen of Jericho who became a disciple of Jesus, known only in Luke 19:1–10. As head tax collector at the important road center of Jericho, Zacchaeus had amassed a fortune by methods which his conscience did not unreservedly approve (vv. 2, 8). When Jesus came to Jericho, Zacchaeus, being "little of stature," "climbed up into a sycomore tree" in order to see, over the heads of the crowd, the Master as he passed by (vv. 3 f.). Jesus, observing his eagerness, brushed aside local prejudices and invited himself to be the house guest of the unpopular publican (vv. 5–7), and his friendliness led to Zacchaeus' conversion (vv. 9 f.).

Zachariah. See ZECHARIAH.

Zacharias. (1) The father of John the Baptist (Luke 1:5–25, 57–80, 3:2). He belonged to the priestly course of Abia (Luke 1:5, Abijah I Chron. 24:10), the 8th of the 24-family divisions listed by the Chronicler and assigned after the return from Babylon to officiate at stated times in the Jerusalem Temple. His marriage to Elisabeth, a daughter of the Aaronic line, evidenced his deep regard for the marriage law of priests (Lev. 21:7–14). They lived in an unnamed town in the hill country of Judah (Luke 1:23, 39 f.)—possibly Ain* Karem.

While keeping his scheduled appointment in the Temple, and burning incense in the Holy Place, the aged Zacharias had a vision (vv. 11–17) in which the birth of a son to the childless (v. 7) pair was promised. His emotional reactions to this unbelievable announcement produced temporary paralysis (v 21). When he emerged from the sacred place and stood before the people, he could gesticulate a blessing, but remained speechless (v. 22). A few months later, however, after his return to the quiet of his hilltop home, Zacharias recovered his speech when the new-born child was named (v. 64).

The wonder of the people, when the 8-day-old boy was circumcised, was in part due to the recovery of Zacharias and also because he declined to name his belated offspring after himself, preferring "John" ("the grace of Jehovah"). In a song of praise and thanksgiving, "The Benedictus" (vv. 68–79), Zacharias prophesied the fulfillment of Israel's Messianic expectations.

(2) A Jewish martyr mentioned by Jesus (Matt. 23:35; Luke 11:51). The reference is to the death of Zechariah, son of Jehoiada (II Chron. 24:20–24). Inasmuch as Chronicles is the last book of the Jewish Canon, as in Jesus' day, his use of the phrase "from Abel to Zechariah" was equivalent to our all-inclusive expression "from A to Z," or "from Genesis to Revelation." In II Chron. 24:20 Zechariah is "the son of Jehoiada"; in Matt. 23:35 Zacharias is "the son of Barachias," who is, according to Zechariah 1:1, the father of the prophet. Luke in 11:51 omits giving the ancestry of the martyred priest. This confusion is due either to the faulty oral tradition of the age, to an error by the evangelist, or to a mistake of the scribe in copying.

Zadok (zā′dŏk). (1) The father of Ahimaaz (II Sam. 18:19–23) and Jerushah (II Kings 15:23 f.); a priest in the time of David and Solomon, and at first of equal rank with Abiathar* (II Sam. 15:24–29, 35, 17:15, 19:11, 20:25). During the rebellion of Absalom, both priests guarded the Ark at Jerusalem (II Sam. 15:24–29, 35) and were jointly ordered by David to spread propaganda favorable to him (II Sam. 19:11). In the struggle for the throne which followed Absalom's death Abiathar joined with Adonijah (I Kings 1:7), but Zadok supported Solomon (I Kings 1:8). For his loyal services in anointing Solomon (I Kings 1:32–39, 45) Zadok was made chief priest (I Kings 2:35).

The Chronicler's account, based on the historic record in Kings but biased in favor of the priests of Jerusalem, portrays Zadok as a colorful war veteran (I Chron. 12:28).

Zadok's genealogy, traced from Eleazar (I Chron. 6:4–15, 50–52), aimed to show that the descendants of Zadok belonged to the elder branch of Aaron's descendants. The figures in connection with the priesthood, as elsewhere throughout this book, are fantastic. The record, however, shows that after the return from Exile the "sons" of Zadok were not only more numerous, but had the best assignments in the Temple (I Chron. 24:2 f., 27:17, 29:22). Ezekiel considered the sons of Zadok the only legitimate priests (Ezek. 40:46, 43:19, 44:15, 48:11). I Sam. 2:27–36 is considered by some as a spurious prophecy inserted by a late editor to refute all priestly claims made for Eli and his house, and to support the exclusive monopoly attained by the sons of Zadok in the Temple at Jerusalem.

(2) A son of Baana, a helper of Nehemiah (Neh. 3:4). (3) A son of Immer, who built a wall before his house near the Horse Gate (Neh. 3:28 f.). (4) A scribe appointed treasurer by Nehemiah (Neh. 13:13). (5) A chief who sealed the Covenant (Neh. 10:21). (6) A high priest (Neh. 11:11; Ezra 7:2–5).

Zair (zā′ĭr), a place in, or in the direction of, Edom where Joram of Judah encamped before attacking the Edomites (II Kings 8:21); perhaps Sa'īr, 5 m. NE. of Hebron.

Zalmon. (1) An elevation, possibly a peak of Mt. Gerizim* (Judg. 9:48). (2) One of David's heroes (II Sam. 23:28).

Zalmonah (zăl-mō′nȧ), an unidentified camp site of Israel en route to Canaan from Egypt, somewhere in the Arabah near Punon, whose location is also unidentified (Num. 33:41 f.).

Zalmunna (zăl-mŭn′ȧ), a Midianite king slain by Gideon* (Judg. 8:4–28; Ps. 83:11).

Zamzummims ("noise makers"), giants "of old time" (see REPHAIM) who lived in a region later claimed by the Ammonites (Deut. 2:20).

Zanoah (zȧ-nō′ȧ). (1) A town in the lowland of Judah (Josh. 15:34; Neh. 11:30). (2) A town in the highlands of Judah (Josh. 15:56; I Chron. 4:18).

Zaphnath-paaneah (zăf′năth-pā-ȧ-nē′ȧ) (Tsaphenath-pa'nekh), the Egyptian name assigned to Joseph the Hebrew, according to the narrative of Gen. 41:45. Egyptologists believe that the term represents the Egyptian name which could be rendered *Djed-pa-Neter-ef-'onekh*, which would mean, "Says the God: he will live"—"he" being the new-born bearer of the name. This sort of name was common in late-dynastic Egypt (c. 1000–500 B.C., Metropolitan Museum of Art chronology), when the O.T. was being put into written form. Such a name, however, was not used in the time of Joseph (perhaps c. 1600 B.C.), and must have been a later addition or alteration of the saga. According to the Midrash*, the name means "revealer of secrets." Some translate it as "Minister of Agriculture."

Zaphon (zā′fŏn), a town of Gad (Josh. 13:27) on the E. side of the Jordan Valley N. of Succoth, formerly in the kingdom of Sihon, King of Heshbon (cf. Num. 25:15—"Zephon" and Gen. 46:16—"Ziphion," a son of Gad). Jephthah was at Zaphon when a quarrel with Ephraim broke out (Judg. 12:1), and according to the LXX version of Judg. 12:7, was buried there. It appears as Ṣapuna, city of the "Mistress of the Lion," in a 14th century B.C. Amarna Letter (No. 274; Albright, *BASOR* 89, 1943, pp. 15–17). It also appears in the list of Canaanite towns conquered by Shishak (Aharoni, *The Land of the Bible*, 1967, pp. 284–287). The name is probably to be connected with Ba 'al-safôn, a Canaanite deity (Albright, *AASOR* 6, 1926, pp. 45–46).

Identification is uncertain. N. Glueck equated it with Tell el-Qôs, a large mound overlooking the Wâdī Râjeb c. 3 m. N. of Tell Deir 'allā (*BASOR* 90, 1943, pp. 19–23; *AASOR* 25/28, 1951, pp. 299–301, 350–355). W. F. Albright, however has long identified Zaphon with Tell es-Sa'īdîyeh (*AASOR* 6, 1926, p. 46; *BASOR* 89, 1943, pp. 15–17). Y. Aharoni accepts this latter suggestion (*The Land of the Bible*, 1967, p. 115). W. P. A.

Zarah, see Zerah.

Zared (zā′rĕd) (Num. 21:12). See Zered.

Zarephath (zăr′ė-făth) (? "smelting place") (Accad. *Sariptu*, from *ṣarāpu*, "to refine [metals]," "to fire [bricks]") (Gk. *Sarepta*), a Phoenician city belonging to Sidon, named in I Kings 17:8 ff. as the place where Elijah lodged with a widow during a famine, and restored her son. The incident is referred to in Luke (4:25 f.). Obadiah (v. 20) considers Zarephath the N. boundary of the restored Israel. Its name appears in Ugaritic texts of the 14th century B.C., and along with other Phoenician cities in the late 13th century B.C. Papyrus Anastasi I (*ANET*³, p. 477). It was one of the Phoenician cities captured by Sennacherib in 701 B.C. (Zarebtu, *ANET*³, p. 287), and again by Esar-haddon (c. 680–669 B.C.), who gave it to Ba' li, King of Tyre. Classical and medieval sources note its fame as a source of purple dye, its wine, and its "holy god" (see J. B. Pritchard, "Sarepta in History and Tradition," in J. Reumann, ed., *Understanding the Sacred Text*, 1971, pp. 101–114).

The site of ancient Zarephath/Sarepta is situated on the Lebanese coast, c. 8 m. S. of Sidon (modern Saida), on a promontory with two harbors—a Phoenician trademark—directly below the modern village of Sarafand, which preserves the ancient name. A seal inscribed with the name of the city in Phoenician script (SRPT), discovered in 1971, confirms the identification.

Excavation of the site was begun in 1969 for the Museum of the University of Pennsylvania by J. B. Pritchard. Four seasons of excavation have revealed a history of occupation extending back to the close of the Middle Bronze Age. A series of Iron Age levels were discovered which are of great importance in understanding Phoenician economy and culture, and for establishing ties between Phoenicia on the one hand and Syria-Palestine and the W. Mediterranean on the other. Similarities in pottery, architecture, art, and religious symbolism serve to provide archaeological links between the Phoenician homeland and its W. Mediterranean colonies and ports of trade (see

Pritchard, *Expedition* 14–1, Fall, 1971, pp. 14–23). Numerous kilns, potters' workshops, and dumps attest to a large pottery manufacturing area, perhaps reflected in the name of the site. Evidence for metallurgy and the purple-dye industry is also present. A small shrine with numerous votive objects and the "Sign of Tanit" stamped on a piece of glass provide evidence for Phoenician religious symbolism and practice.

The remains of a Hellenistic city (3d–2d cen. B.C.) overlie the Phoenician city. A port used in Late Roman and Byzantine times was located 540 yds. to the W. of the Iron Age city. See also *AJA* 74, 1970, p. 202; 76, 1972, p. 216; *Archaeology* 24, 1971, pp. 61–63.
W. P. A.

495. Excavated covered stairway at Zarethan.

Zarethan (zăr'ē-thăn) (R.S.V.; A.V. Zaretan, Josh. 3:16; Zartanah, Zarthan, I Kings 4:12, 7:46), a city in the middle Jordan Valley associated with the miraculous crossing of the Jordan by the Israelites (Josh. 3:16). The Midianites fled in this direction when chased by Gideon (Judg. 7:22, R.S.V. Zererah, A.V. Zererath). Later, it formed a part of Solomon's fifth administrative district (I Kings 4:12). It also marks the N. boundary of the region "in the plain of the Jordan . . . between Succoth and Zarethan" —where the bronze vessels for Solomon's Temple at Jerusalem were cast (I Kings 7:46; II Chron. 4:17, R.S.V. Zeredah, A.V. Zeredathah).

Various identifications have been proposed (see Glueck, *AASOR* 25/28, 1951, pp. 339 ff.). A location on the E. bank of the Jordan and N. of Succoth appears best to fit the evidence, though this cannot be taken as certain. Indeed, J. Simons (*Geographical and Topographical Texts of the O.T.*, 1959, pp. 292 f.) and others have proposed the site of Qarn Sartabeh, approximately opposite Tell ed-Dâmīyeh (Adam/Adamah), or some other site on the W. bank. These, however, have generally been rejected. Albright tentatively identified Zarethan with "the fine mound of Sleihat," N. of the Wâdī Kufrinjeh (*AASOR* 6, 1926, p. 47), and Aharoni has suggested Tell Umm Ḥamad (*The Land of the Bible*, 1967, pp. 31, 115, 241).

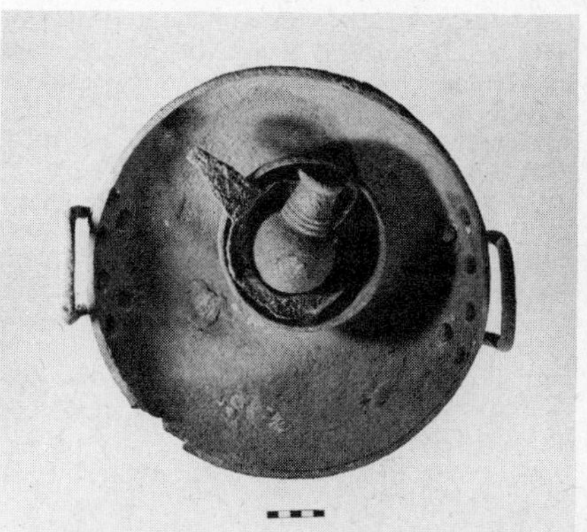

496. Bronze laver, drinking bowl, strainer, and jug, probably used as a wine service, found at Zarethan in 1964.

Since the identification proposed by N. Glueck, most authorities have located the Biblical Zarethan at Tell es-Sa 'īdîyeh (but see Zaphon), c. 1 m. E. of the Jordan midway between the Dead Sea and the Lake of Tiberias and overlooking the Wâdī Kufrinjeh to the N. (*BASOR* 90, 1943, pp. 5–14; *AASOR* 25/28, 1951, pp. 339–347; most recently in *AOTS*, 1967, p. 431, where the identification is believed "confirmed").

Excavations were carried out on this large 138-ft.-high double mound (for description, see Glueck, *AASOR* 25/28, 1951, pp. 290–295) by J. B. Pritchard for the Museum of the University of Pennsylvania between 1964 and 1967. Work on the upper mound disclosed an entire block of row-houses, identical in size and plan, of the 8th century B.C. (see *BA* 28, 1965, pp. 11–12; *Expedition*, 7–4, 1965, pp. 30–33). Numerous objects were recovered from the floors of these buildings. The 8th-century phase was violently destroyed by fire and never extensively rebuilt. The area subsequently served as a threshing floor during the 7th century B.C. An impressive Persian citadel (c. 5th cen. B.C.) was later erected on the acropolis (see *Expedition* 11–1, 1968, pp. 20–22). A well-built stairway was found on the N. slope, constructed to provide access from inside the city to a spring a short distance from the base of the mound. Cut into the side of the tell and lined with stones, it had a mud-brick wall in the center to support a roof and divide the stairway for descending and ascending traffic (see *BA* 28, 1965, pp. 12–14; *Expedition* 6–4, 1964, pp. 3–5).

A cemetery on the N. edge of the lower mound, transitional from Late Bronze to

Iron I (c. 1200 B.C.), produced remains indicative of a rich cosmopolitan culture—Mycenaean imports, Egyptian pottery forms, and above all, numerous metal objects (see *BA* 28, 1965, pp. 14–17; *Expedition* 7–4, 1965, pp. 26–33). The most impressive tomb was that of a wealthy young woman, containing grave goods of ivory, pottery, gold, carnelian, and seven examples of bronze work (see Pritchard, in W. A. Ward, ed., *The Role of the Phoenicians*, 1968, pp. 99–112). The large number of bronzes recovered from these tombs suggests the availability, and perhaps the manufacture, of bronze in the area. The preliminary results of the excavations in the light of the tradition preserved in I Kings 7:45–46 appears to strengthen Glueck's identification of Zarethan with Tell es-Sa ʻIdîyeh. Despite this added support, however, the identification must remain uncertain until more data are available (cf. M. Ottosson, *Gilead*, 1969, pp. 216 f.). The lack of clarity in the Biblical statements and the presence of numerous unexplored mounds in the N. Jordan Valley make any present identification precarious. W. P. A.

Zattu (zăt′ū), founder of a family of some importance in the time of Ezra (2:8, 10:27; Neh. 7:13, 10:14).

Zayin (zä′yĭn) (A.V. zain), 7th letter of the Heb. alphabet, pronounced like *z*. The original meaning of the word may have been "weapon," or it may have been a form of *zayit*, "olive". See WRITING.

Zealot, an epithet applied to the Simon of Luke 6:15 and Acts 1:13 A.S.V. and R.S.V. (Zelotes A.V. is from Gk. *zēlōtes*). The same Disciple is called "the Cananaean" (cf. Aram. *qan'an*, "zealot") in Matt. 10:4 and Mark 3:18 A.S.V. and R.S.V. Either epithet was primarily a means of distinguishing him from Simon Peter. A Zealot was a member of one of the parties or sects that loosely formed what Josephus called "the fourth philosophy," i.e., the fourth group in Judaism, thus distinguishing them from the Pharisees, Sadducees, and Essenes. "The fourth philosophy" was simply a movement, largely unorganized, of Jewish patriots irked by outside political control. Josephus' first explicit use of the term "Zealot" is of one group of these anti-Roman patriots who started a reign of terror in A.D. 66 under John of Gischala. Some hold that the Zealot party was formed at the time of the revolt of Judas of Galilee against the enrollment of citizens under Quirinius*, but there is little to support this view. It seems clear that Palestine had its home-rule fanatics from the first days of Roman domination; and complete identification of the Zealots with these irreconcilable patriots, either at a particular time or throughout the history of the abortive struggles against Rome, is not possible.

Zebadiah ("Jehovah has given"), the name of several minor O.T. characters. Three Benjamites are mentioned (I Chron. 8:15, 17, 12:7). One Zebadiah was a Temple doorkeeper (I Chron. 26:2). Another was an officer of David (I Chron. 27:7). Two more Zebadiahs appear in narratives of Jehoshaphat's reign (c. 873–849 B.C.) (II Chron. 17:8, 19:11); two others are named as Ezra's contemporaries (Ezra 8:8, 10:20).

Zebah (zē′bȧ), a Midianite king who, along with King Zalmunna of Midian, was pursued and slain by Gideon* and his son in a vigorous campaign E. of the Jordan.

Zebedee (zĕb′ĕ-dē) ("Jehovah has given"), the husband of Salome* (Matt. 27:56; Mark 15:40), and the father of two Apostles, James* and John* (Mark 3:17, 14:33). Zebedee appears to have been a fisherman of some substance (Mark 1:19 f.). When Jesus called the brothers they left Zebedee, and nothing more is heard of him.

Zeboim (zė-bō′ĭm) (? "hyaena") (1) A city now submerged somewhere under the Dead Sea, exact site unknown. Its king allied himself with the kings of Sodom*, Gomorrah, Admah, and Zoar (Gen. 14) against four confederate kings (Amraphel, Arioch, Chedorlaomer, and Tidal) in the time of Abraham. This was the struggle in the Vale of Siddim, in which Lot was captured and later rescued by Abraham, who pursued as far N. as Hobah, near Damascus. It was destroyed by fire from heaven. (See Gen. 10:19; Deut. 29:23; Hos. 11:8.) (2) A village near Hadid in Judaea, where the Jews lived after their return from Exile (Neh. 11:34).

Zeboim (zė-bō′ĭm), **Valley of.** The Wâdī Abū Dab'a, near Debir, or possibly a tributary of the Valley of Achor (I Sam. 13:18). Out of it the Philistines came into the Wilderness of Judah to threaten Saul and Jonathan. It is also known as "the Valley of Serpents."

Zebul (zē′bŭl), governor of Shechem, faithful to Abimelech at the time of Gaal's conspiracy (Judg. 9:28 ff.).

Zebulun (N.T. Zabulun) ("dwelling"). (1) The 6th son of Leah and Jacob, and the 10th of Jacob (Gen. 30:20); full brother of Reuben, Simeon, Levi, Judah, and Issachar (35:23). His sons were Sered, Elon, and Jahleel (46:14), through whom Zebulun was represented in the group that descended to Egypt in the migration of the Jacob tribes.

(2) The Tribe of Zebulun held territory described in "Jacob's blessing" (date uncertain), as being "at the haven of the sea" (Gen. 49:13), with easy access to harbors. Though actually cut off from the Mediterranean by Asher, and from the Sea of Galilee by Naphtali and Issachar, Zebulunites were in convenient reach of rich markets like Sidon. Their territory, though not large, was fertile, including a small portion of the Plain of Esdraelon*, and such rich farm land as the present region of Nazareth. Zebulun's holdings were traversed by the age-old international highway "The Way of the Sea." Unlike Judah and Simeon, Zebulun failed to dispossess the native Canaanites ("Kitron" and "Nahalol," Judg. 1:27–30). This Tribe aided Barak and Deborah against Sisera (Judg. 4:10–16, 5:18), and rushed aid to Gideon against the Midianites; otherwise their history was undistinguished. Many Zebulunites were carried into captivity by the Assyrian Tiglath-pileser. A Jerusalem gate in Ezekiel's vision, near the gates of Simeon and Issachar, (Ezek. 48:33), was named for them.

Zechariah ("Jehovah hath remembered"), the name of 29 persons in the Bible; 4 times (in A.V.) spelled Zachariah. Those more than merely identified are (1) The son of Jehoiada the priest, who after his father's death reproved the people for their idolatry and was stoned to death by command of King Joash of Judah (c. 837–800 B.C.) (II Chron. 24:20, 22). (2) A son of King Jeroboam II of Israel (c. 786–746 B.C.) (II Kings 14:29, 15:8–12). His six months' reign (c. 746–745 B.C.) was preceded by confusion and followed by complete anarchy, precipitated when he was assassinated by a claimant to the throne, ending the dynasty of Jehu (II Kings 10:30).

(3) The son of Berechiah and grandson of Iddo, who was head of a priestly family which returned from Exile (Zech. 1:1, 7; Neh. 12:4); see ZECHARIAH, BOOK OF.

Zechariah, the Book of, the 11th among the books of the Minor Prophets. Zechariah was a contemporary of Haggai*. The book bearing his name supplies the background and the nature of his life work in chaps. 1–8. Haggai (2:6–9) and Zechariah (2:6 ff.) reveal the unsettled condition of the empire in the early years of the reign of Darius the Persian. In Jerusalem the work on the Temple restoration undertaken by earlier returned Jews had halted (6:15, 8:9). Haggai began his utterances in behalf of Temple rebuilding in 520 B.C. (Hag. 1:1), and Zechariah, his "twin" prophet, perhaps inspired by this 10th minor prophet, carried on over a two-year period (Zech. 1:1, 7:1) the same urgent appeal to rebuild. He also called on the people to repent (1:2 ff.). The influence of the prophet of the Exile, Ezekiel*, is strong in Zechariah. The superhuman mediators (Ezek. 40 ff.) for the first time become angels (Zech. 1:9, 12, 19, 2:3, 3:1, 4:1, 5, 5:5, 6:4) who control the destiny of men and nations. The historic desire of the Jews for a descendant of David (Isa. 7:14–16, 9:7, 11:1; Jer. 23:5, 33:15; Zech. 3:8) to become God's regent on earth caused political agitation in Zechariah's day. Haggai had nominated Zerubbabel* (Hag. 2:23). Zech. 6:9–15—a passage censored or corrupted in transmission—records how Zechariah supported the coronation of Governor Zerubbabel as the Messiah. But the plot was thwarted by the Persian secret police, Zerubbabel disappeared, and Bethel-sar-eser, a Babylonian, was appointed civil administrator of Judaea. Thus the Jews' sixth-century dream of a sovereign, independent state was thwarted, though the reconstruction of the Temple, which the Persian authorities permitted, was completed in 515 B.C. While the rebuilding of the Temple (Zech. 8:9) and the revival of the ritual (8:18–20) were Zechariah's major aims, the prophet showed deep social sympathies (7:9–12).

But underneath such aspirations for material things were enduring spiritual principles (4:8, 8:22). Haggai spoke as an old man, whereas Zechariah's Apocalyptic visions were those of a younger, more visionary personality. The first part of the book (chaps. 1–8) may be outlined as follows:

497. Zacharias (Zechariah), by *Michelangelo*, Sistine Chapel, Rome.

Introduction—1:1–7—Repentance urged.
Eight visions—
- 1:7–17—the horseman;
- 1:18–21—four horns and four smiths;
- 2:1–5—the measuring line;
- 3:1–10—the High Priest in filthy garments;
- 4:1–3—the candlestick and olive trees;
- 5:1–4—the flying scroll;
- 5:5–11—the woman inside a bushel;
- 6:1–8—the four chariots.

Historical statement—
- 6:9–15—the coronation of Zerubbabel (or of Joshua).

Prophetic messages for the coming restoration—7:1–8–8:23.

The Second Zechariah (chaps. 9–14) marks a complete change in background from that of the 1st half of the book. It represents the Greek (not the Persian) period (9:13), following the conquests of Alexander the Great (336–323 B.C.) (10:10 f.). In that period the Jews of the Diaspora went when possible on annual pilgrimages to Jerusalem (14:16). Other indications point to the 3d century B.C.: the scarcity of true prophets (13:2–6); strict ritual observances (9:7, 14:19); and the Apocalyptic* style, typical of this period. The editors of the Minor Prophets apparently collected some anonymous utterances and grouped them under three divisions, each called a "burden" or oracle (9:1, 12:1; Mal. 1:1). Two of these constitute Second Zechariah, which can be briefly outlined as follows:

Chap. 9—the coming of the Greeks.
10—restoration of scattered Israel.
11—the parable of the shepherds.
12, 13, 14—visions of Israel's future.

Moslem ideas of final judgment (see ESCHATOLOGY) are similar to Zech. 14:4. Second Zechariah contains sayings precious to Christians (13:1, 9, 14:7), especially prophecies later judged to pertain to the Christ who came 200 years later:

His triumphant entry into Jerusalem (9:9; Matt. 21:5; John 12:15).
His betrayal for 30 pieces of silver (11:12; Matt. 27:9, 10—where it is incorrectly ascribed to Jeremiah).
His pierced hands (12:10, 13:6; John 19:37).
The smitten shepherd (13:7; Matt. 26:31; Mark 14:27).
His universal reign (9:10).

Zedek Valley, the name suggested for a small but topographically important, artificial valley discovered c. 1923, cut into the W. side of the eastern hill of Jerusalem c. 325 yds. S. of the present city wall. This valley had evidently been cut through the crest of the hill to protect that portion of the city later known as "the City of David" at Millo. The city was well safeguarded from every direction but the N., and this small valley was necessary to complete its defense. It may have served its purpose between c. 2000 and 1600 B.C., when it became filled up with potsherds and other debris and the city moved northward, on up the eastern hill. R. A. S. Macalister explained the derivation of the name for the little artificial valley, "Zedek Valley," from the old city deity whose name appears in Melchizedek* and Adonizedek.

Zedekiah ("righteousness of Jehovah"). (1) A son of Chenaanah, one of Ahab's 400 court prophets (I Kings 22:11, 24; II Chron. 18:10–23 f.). (2) A prophet, son of Maaseiah, deported to Babylon with Ahab, son of Koliah. Both men were burned to death because of their immoralities and political agitations (II Kings 24:12–16; Jer. 29:21–23). (3) A son of Hananiah, a prince in the reign of King Jehoiakim of Judah (c. 609–598 B.C.) (Jer. 36:12).

(4) The last king of Judah (c. 597–587 B.C.). The account of his 11-year reign is found in II Kings 24:17–25:7; Jer. 39:4–13, 52:1–27; II Chron. 36:10–21. In addition to these historical passages there are incidents, details, and observations concerning Zedekiah in the contemporary writings of Jeremiah* and Ezekiel*.

Zedekiah, the son of King Josiah (c. 640–609 B.C.), succeeded his much older brothers Jehoahaz II (c. 609 B.C.) and Jehoiakim, and his nephew, Jehoiachin, on the throne of Judah (II Kings 23:31, 24:18; II Chron. 36:10; "brother" in II Chron. 36:9 f. should be read "kinsman"). When Nebuchadnezzar* subdued Judaea and captured Jerusalem (597 B.C.), he deported Jehoiachin and many of his important subjects to Babylon (II Kings 25:27; Jer. 27:20, 52:31; Ezek. 1:2), and made Zedekiah regent at Jerusalem, changing his name from Mattaniah to Zedekiah (Jer. 37:1). An oath of allegiance to the King of Babylon was exacted from Zedekiah, which—according to Ezekiel—he repeatedly violated (II Chron. 36:13; Ezek. 17:15–18). Zedekiah, weak by nature (Ezek. 19:14), was under the constant pressure of his subjects, who had recently come into a new sense of their own importance when their real leaders were carried to Babylon (Jer. 24). They urged Zedekiah to seek the aid of Egypt against Judah's Chaldaean master (Jer. 27:12–22). The king consulted Jeremiah (Jer. 21:1–7), who opposed the Egyptian party and an alliance with Pharaoh (Jer. 37:6–10, 38:14–28). Zedekiah showed some strength of character and purpose in his personal attitude toward Jeremiah (Jer. 37:16–21, 38:7–13).

Zedekiah sent an embassy to Nebuchadnezzar to assure him of his fidelity (Jer. 29:3–7). In the 4th year of his reign the king was summoned to Babylon to report in person upon conditions (Jer. 51:59). Finally, because of Judah's rebellion, the Chaldaean armies besieged Jerusalem in the 8th year of Zedekiah's regime (II Kings 25:1; Jer. 32:24, 52:4; Ezek. 4:2). Pestilence, famine, even cannibalism characterized the siege (Jer. 19:9, 21:6–9, 32:36, 34:17, 52:6; Ezek. 5:10–17). The siege was interrupted for a time by the advance of the Egyptian army (Jer. 37:5), but in the 10th year of Zedekiah's reign the city capitulated to the Chaldaeans (II Kings 25:2–4; Jer. 52:4–6). In the confusion that followed Zedekiah tried to escape (II Kings 25:4), but was captured by the Chaldaeans at Jericho and brought to trial before the King of Babylon at Riblah in N. Palestine (Jer. 39:1–5). Zedekiah saw his sons murdered; then his own eyes were put out. He was fettered and carried to Babylon (II Kings 24:17–20, 25:1–7; II Chron. 36:11-21; Jer. 39:6–14), and imprisoned until his death (Jer. 52:11). The year 587 B.C. marked the end not only of a dynasty but of an age.

Zeeb (zē′ĕb), a Midianite prince, captured and slain by Gideon (Judg. 7:25). See OREB.

Zelophehad (zĕ-lō′fĕ-hăd), a man of Manasseh, whose only heirs were daughters. The inheritance by these girls may represent the origin of legislation allowing this procedure (Num. 26:33, 27:1–11, 36; Josh. 17:3; I Chron. 7:15). Female heirs were expected to marry within the tribe to safeguard the group inheritance* (Num. 36:3).

Zelzah (zĕl′zȧ), an unidentified place near Rachel's Tomb at the border of Benjamin and Ephraim, where Saul received a sign of his royalty from the Lord after his anointing by Samuel the prophet (I Sam. 10:2).

Zenas, a Jewish lawyer or a Roman advocate journeying with Apollos in Crete. Paul enjoined Titus to assist them (Tit. 3:13). Zenas and Apollos may have been the bearers of the Epistle to Titus*.

Zephaniah ("Jehovah has hidden" or "protected"). (1) A 7th-century prophet (see ZEPHANIAH, BOOK OF). (2) A son of Tahath, a Kohathite (I Chron. 6:36). (3) A son of Maaseiah and second priest under King Zedekiah (II Kings 25:18; Jer. 52:24). Though he belonged to the court party, which was opposed to making terms with

Babylon, and therefore was in opposition to Jeremiah's policies, at the king's request he carried on important conferences with Jeremiah (Jer. 21:1, 29:25, 29, 37:3). After the fall of Jerusalem he was taken with others to Riblah*, where he was put to death by Nebuchadnezzar (Jer. 52:24–27). (4) A contemporary of Zerubbabel*, and the father of Josiah, whose house in Jerusalem was a rendezvous of Jews returning from Babylon (Zech. 6:10, 14).

Zephaniah, the Book of, the 9th among the books of the Minor Prophets. The only biographical material concerning the prophet whose name the book bears, is Zeph. 1:1, and what can be deduced from the book's more revealing passages. Zephaniah, the son of Cushi, was a direct descendant in the 4th generation of King Hezekiah (c. 715–687 B.C.). His detailed knowledge of the localities and customs of Jerusalem argues for his residence there (1:4 f., 10). The close-up view of life in the homes of the well-to-do indicates his aristocratic background (1:8 f., 13). The severe judgment, characteristic of those portions of the book that are recognized as his utterances (1:2–18), reflect the moral earnestness of a youth as yet untempered by the tolerance of middle life or old age. Under King Josiah (c. 640–609 B.C.) a sweeping reform (622 B.C.) corrected many of the customs that Zephaniah condemned. Therefore it has been assumed that before this reform Zephaniah, a youthful prophet of princely blood, had boldly denounced the social clique with which he was identified, and the prevailing perverted religious life of his time. He was a contemporary of Jeremiah.

The book may be outlined as follows:

Chap. 1:1—Title of the book.

1:2 f.—The world judgment.

1:4–2:3—Judgment on Judah and Jerusalem:
- for religious syncretism (1:4–6);
- for social and moral corruption (vv. 7–9);
- the sorry plight of the population (vv. 10–13);
- the imminence of the Day of Wrath (vv. 14–18);
- last call to repentance (2:1–3).

2:4–15—Judgment on the nations:
- Philistia (vv. 4–7);
- Moab and Ammon (vv. 8–11);
- Ethiopia (i.e., Egypt) (v. 12);
- Assyria (vv. 13–15).

3:1–7—Judgment on Jerusalem:
- the city's apostasy (vv. 1–4);
- Jehovah's rejected overtures (vv. 5–7).

3:8–14—The effects of judgment:
- nations will be transformed (vv. 8–10);
- Judah will have a righteous remnant (vv. 11–13).

3:14–20—A psalm of praise to Yahweh
- for the defeat of His enemies
- and for Israel's redemption.

The international background revealed in Zephaniah reflects the period prior to 621 B.C. The Scythians, bands of wild horsemen from the Black Sea regions, which Zephaniah, like Jeremiah, does not specifically name (Jer. 4:6, 13, 29) overran western Asia and brought terror to its peoples (c. 630–624 B.C.). The speed of their blows and the cruelty and destructiveness of their onslaughts preyed on the imagination of those not yet attacked; this is the terror reflected in Zephaniah. Having devastated the Philistine cities (2:4–7), the Scythians threatened Egypt (2:12) (called "Ethiopians" because the Twenty-fifth Dynasty of Egypt, c. 712–633 B.C., had been Ethiopian). According to Herodotus the Egyptians stopped these invaders at the border by paying them a heavy indemnity. Assyria (2:13–15) and Moab and Ammon (vv. 8–11) are considered by some as included in Zephaniah's original oracle; others consider the 1st passage an accurate description of Nineveh and its environs after its destruction, and the 2d passage a later reflection of the traditional unfriendliness of Moab and Ammon toward Judah. A third group of scholars would harmonize these two by considering the record a blend of prophetic forecast and historic realities.

Zephaniah's sensitive moral and religious spirit was overwhelmed by the impending doom that awaited the disobedient; in such a spiritual atmosphere disaster was sure. The Day of Wrath (1:14–18)—borrowed from Amos (5:18–20) and Isaiah—here for the first time became prophecy plus apocalypse, a new note in the literature of Judaism. The Day of the Lord became not only the Day of Wrath, but the Last Day. The shallow optimism and indifference of people to all the moral issues of life (1:12) here gave way to stark pessimism; doom was inevitable. The prophet's words inspired "Dies Irae—Dies Illa," the mediaeval hymn written by Thomas of Celano and formerly sung throughout the Christian world. Zephaniah envisaged an attitude of life in which there remains nothing but the judgment of an outraged God.

The few hope-filled passages in the book are considered by many to be later additions (2:3, 3:5, 12 f., 14–20). They reveal the hope of the righteous remnant* (3:13) which shines eternally in men of faith.

Zerah (zē'rȧ) (A.V. Zarah). (1) An Edomitic descendant of Esau (Gen. 36:13, 17; I Chron. 1:37). (2) The father of a king of Edom (Gen. 36:33; I Chron. 1:44), associated with Bozrah*. (3) A twin son of Tamar* and Judah, founder of the Zeraphites or Zarhites (Gen. 38:30; Num. 26:20; Josh. 7:1; cf. Neh. 11:24). (4) The founder of a Simeonite clan, Zarhites (Num. 26:13; I Chron. 4:24). (5) The name of two Levites (I Chron. 6:21, 41). (6) An Ethiopian or Cushite who led a large chariot-riding force against King Asa of Judah (c. 913–873 B.C.) but was defeated at Mareshah (II Chron. 14:8–15). Some Egyptian scholars identify this Zerah with one of the Osorkons of the Twenty-second Dynasty.

Zered (zē'rĕd), **the Brook** (Wâdī el-Hesā), (Zared, Num. 21:12) a river which enters the Dead Sea at its SE. corner, and formed the boundary between Edom* and Moab*; one of the last obstacles overcome by Israel en route to Canaan from Egypt (Deut. 2:13 f.). See WILLOWS, BROOK OF THE.

Zeresh (zē′rĕsh), Haman's wife (Esther 5: 10, 14, 6:13).

Zerqa, the modern name for Biblical Jabbok* River. The iron mines on its N. bank have been worked from O.T. to modern times.

Zeruah (zĕ-rōō′*à*), mother of Jeroboam I (I Kings 11:26).

Zerubbabel (N.T. Zorobabel) ("begotten in Babylon," or "offspring of Babylon"), son of Shealtiel or Salathiel (Ezra 3:2, 8; Hag. 1:1; Matt. 1:12), or of Pedaiah (I Chron. 3:19), grandson of Jehoiachin, captive king of Judah (I Chron. 3:17). Zerubbabel returned to Jerusalem with the first band of Exiles, and with Joshua the High Priest set up an altar for burnt offerings; kept the Feast of Tabernacles; and took steps to rebuild the Temple (Ezra 3). After "the adversaries of Judah and Benjamin"—perhaps the Samaritans or those Jews who had not been taken into Exile and were now unfriendly—had been rebuffed in their proffer to co-operate in the enterprise (Ezra 4:1–5), 17 years of inactivity in Temple rebuilding followed, until work was resumed in 520 B.C. under the stimulus supplied by Haggai* and Zechariah* (Ezra 5:1 f.). According to Hag. 1:1, 14 Zerubbabel was governor of Judaea when this rebuilding began; but when the Temple was dedicated in 515 B.C. his name was not mentioned (Ezra 6:15 ff.). Zech. 6:9–15 describes an event taking place (between 520 and 515 B.C.), in which the High Priest is to be given the pre-eminence which Haggai felt should have been Zerubbabel's. However, the text of Zech. 6:11 almost certainly once read "Zerubbabel, the son of Shealtiel," for Zerubbabel, not Joshua, was the Messianic branch (v. 12) or scion of the royal house (Hag. 2:20, 23). Probably a change was made later in v. 11 when it was known that Zerubbabel did not attain the throne, and when Joshua was pre-eminent as the religious authority. Secular control remained in Persian hands. Whatever caused Zerubbabel's disappearance, his influence was so great in bringing the Second Temple into being that historians refer to it as "Zerubbabel's Temple." At times Zerubbabel has been identified as "the suffering servant" (Isa. 53). He was in the direct line of the ancestry of Jesus (Luke 3:27).

Zeruiah (zĕr′ōō-ī′*à*) (Zeruia), the mother of Joab, Abishai, and Asahel (I Sam. 26:6; II Sam. 2:13, 18; I Kings 1:7; I Chron. 2:16). She was either a woman of outstanding qualities, or else the mention of her, rather than of the father of these sons, is due to an old custom of tracing ancestry through the maternal line. She is said (II Sam. 17:25) to have been the daughter of Nahash (or read, possibly, "of Jesse"; or perhaps Zeruiah was a daughter of David's mother by a marriage with Nahash before her marriage to Jesse).

Zeus (zūs), the chief deity of the ancient Greeks, corresponding to the Roman Jupiter. People of Lystra, where there was a temple of this god, likened Barnabas to Jupiter (Zeus R.S.V. and A.S.V. margin, Acts 14:12 f.) after a miraculous healing by Paul. Jupiter was regarded as ruler of the heavens, whence the Ephesians believed their statue of Diana had fallen (Acts 19:35).

498. Plaster scale model (Agora Museum, Athens) of Stoa of Zeus, late 5th century B.C., a landmark in Paul's time. "If this building was also known as the Royal Stoa (a view for which there is much to be said), it was occasionally used for meetings of the Council of the Areopagus." Homer A. Thompson.

Paul and his Apostolic colleagues were familiar with many temples and statues of Zeus in the Hellenistic cities where they preached; famous shrines to this god were at Baalbek, Gerasa, Athens, Rome, Sebaste, etc. Ras Shamrah excavations show that in that city Zeus was called Zabul*. Attributes of the thunderbolt-bearing Zeus were accredited to Syrian and other Near Eastern deities, like the Nabataean Zeus-hadad, consort of Atargatis. Likenesses of this deity excavated at Khirbet et-Tannûr by Nelson Glueck show Hellenistic-Parthian influences in the eclectic culture of this trade center on the River Zered in Jordan, E. of the SE. end of the Dead Sea.

The erection by Antiochus Epiphanes IV in 168 B.C. of an altar to Zeus on the altar of

499. Bronze statuette of Zeus, Roman period.

burnt offering in the Jerusalem Temple Area touched off the revolt led by the victorious Maccabees.

Ziba (zī'bȧ), one of Saul's household staff who was turned over by David, along with all the servants under him, to Saul's lame son, Mephibosheth* (II Sam. 9:2–12). During David's flight from Jerusalem incident to Absalom's revolt, Ziba professed loyalty to David and was rewarded by the king with Mephibosheth's estates. Ziba had craftily told David that Mephibosheth was disloyal and was about to seize the throne of Judah in the king's absence (II Sam. 16:1–4). David, after his return from Trans-Jordan, received expressions of loyalty from Mephibosheth, whereupon the king suggested a new and equal disposition of the property at issue (II Sam. 19:17–29).

Zichri (zĭk'rī), name of 11 O.T. men, 2 of whom are worthy of note: (1) Father of Amasiah, one of Jehoshaphat's captains (II Chron. 17:16), and of Elishaphat who aided Jehoida in turning out Athaliah (II Chron. 23:1). (2) One of Pekah's warriors, who killed a royal prince and 2 officials of Judah in a battle against King Ahaz (II Chron. 28:7). For others named Zichri, see Ex. 6:21; I Chron. 8:19, 23, 27; 9:15 (who may also be "Zaccur" in I Chron. 25:2, 10; Neh. 12:35, and "Zabdi" in Neh. 11:17, through careless textual copying); I Chron. 26:25, 27:16; Neh. 11:9, 12:17.

Zidon. See SIDON.

zif, ziv, 2d month of the Hebrew sacred year, later called *iyar*. See TIME.

ziggurat (zĭg'ōō-răt) (from Assyr.-Bab., "pinnacle"), a feature of very early Sumerian temples* which became the chief characteristic of Mesopotamian temples. It was an artificial brick platform (suggesting a small hillock in the flatlands) constructed in several receding stages or terraces to give the effect of a truncated, stepped pyramid. The *ziggurat* or tower was topped by the small temple, or heavenly house of the god, reached by impressive outer staircases (sometimes of 100 steps, as at Ur*) on various faces of the platform. In early Sumero-Babylonian *ziggurats* the terraces had sloping walls; in Assyrian and Neo-Babylonian ones the walls were vertical. The *ziggurat* was surrounded by a strong-gated outer wall; there was space between the wall and the tower for shrines to minor deities. On the various terraces there were also shrines. One of the oldest of the score or so of known *ziggurats* is at Uruk (Warka, the Biblical Erech*, Gen. 10:10), the 2d royal city after the Flood, ruled by Gilgamesh, hero of the Sumerian epic; it stands more than 36 meters high. It was constructed by King Ur-Nammu of the Third Dynasty of Ur (2060–1950 B.C.). One of the most significant *ziggurats* known today is at Ur, early home of Abraham (Gen. 11:31), built by Ur-Nammu before 2000 B.C. and repaired by Nabonidus of Babylon (556–539 B.C.). An amazing contemporary record of the erection of the Ur *ziggurat* has been found—a stele which also preserves the oldest known depiction of an angel.

The *ziggurat* of Babylon was the Biblical Tower of Babel* (Gen. 11:3 ff.).

See NIPPUR.

Ziklag (zĭk'lăg) (Ziglag), a town probably in S. Judah, site unknown, but possibly Tell el-Khuweilfeh SE. of Gaza, between Beer-sheba and Debir. At the time of Israel's entrance into the Promised Land it seems to have been assigned to the Tribe of Simeon (Josh. 19:5; I Chron. 4:30) but either was never taken or was later lost. A Philistine ruler, Achish, gave this once Philistine city to David at the time of his banishment by Saul (I Sam. 27:6). There David performed the heroic exploits told in I Sam. 30, and there the fugitive lived until Saul's death (II Sam. 1:1, 4:10). Ziklag was occupied by Jews returned from Exile in Babylonia (Neh. 11:28).

Zillah (zĭl'ȧ), a wife of Lamech* and mother of Tubal-cain* (Gen. 4:19–23).

Zilpah, a handmaid whom Laban gave to his daughter Leah (Gen. 29:24), who gave her to Jacob as a concubine (Gen. 30:9). While in Padan-aram (Haran*), Zilpah bore two sons, Gad and Asher (30:10–13, 35:26, 37:2).

Zilthai (zĭl'thī) (A.S.V. Zillethai). (1) A direct descendant of Benjamin (I Chron. 8:20). (2) A military leader from the Tribe of Manasseh who joined David at Ziklag (I Chron. 12:20).

Zimran (zĭm'răn), a son of Abraham and Keturah (Gen. 25:2; I Chron. 1:32).

Zimri (zĭm'rī). (1) An Israelite, son of Salu. This Simeonite leader was slain by Phinehas, grandson of Aaron, for bringing a pagan Midianite woman named Cozbi within sight of the congregation of the children of Israel, near the Tabernacle (Num. 25:6–8, 14 f.). (2) A son of Zerah of Judah and forebear of Achan (I Chron. 2:6), the Zabdi of Josh. 7:1, 17 f. (3) A descendant of King Saul (I Chron. 8:36, 9:42). (4) A kingdom or region whose ruler was destined to feel the divine fury (Jer. 25:25).

(5) The most important Zimri was the seven-day King of Israel (c. 876 B.C.), a chariot captain who came to the throne after his palace conspiracy against and murder of King Elah*, son of King Baasha (I Kings 16:8–20). He justified his act by stressing the sins of Baasha and Elah, and carried on a campaign of atrocity (v. 11). Attacked by Omri, captain of the host, who had been absent on a campaign against the Philistines, Zimri set fire to the palace at Tirzah* and died in the wreckage (v. 18). He was succeeded by Omri (c. 876–869 B.C.).

Zin, Wilderness of, one of the four wildernesses of the Sinai Peninsula (not to be confused with the Wilderness of Sin). This region was situated SW. of the Dead Sea, across the Arabah from Edom (Josh. 15:1; Num. 34:3). Kadesh-barnea* was situated on its edge (Num. 27:14, 33:36). Spies sent to Canaan by Moses operated in this area (Num. 13:21). Israel murmured against the Lord in the Wilderness of Zin (Num. 27:14).

Zion (probably "fortress" or "citadel") (see also SION) was originally the scarp of rock on the S. tip of the ridge between the Kidron and the Tyropoeon valleys of Jerusalem*; but in time the name was applied to the entire E. ridge up which early Jerusalem spread. Later Zion was still farther expanded to include the whole city of Jerusalem (Ps. 126:1; Isa. 1:26 f., 10:24; see map, JERUSALEM). In the N.T. it became a symbolic word with Apocalyptic* implications (Heb. 12:22; I Pet. 2:6; Rev. 14:1). After the 4th century A.D. Zion was erroneously associated with the S. portion of the W. ridge of Jerusalem, between the Tyropoeon and Hinnom valleys.

The rocky scarp at the point of the E. ridge between the Kidron and the Tyropoeon valleys was a formidable natural Jebusite stronghold (Judg. 19:11 f.). The proximity of the Spring Gihon (now called 'Ain Sittī Maryam or the Fountain of the Virgin), and En-rogel (now Bir Ayyûb or Job's Well), supplied the water necessary for the existence of any town site. When David laid siege to this Jebusite acropolis he was defied with taunts and jeers (II Sam. 5:6, 8; I Chron. 11:5). "Nevertheless David took the stronghold of Zion: the same is the city of David" (II Sam. 5:7; I Chron. 11:5–8). Excavations in this section have revealed the part that underground water conduits played in the early days of Zion's defense, as they did at Gezer and Megiddo. Despite a badly corrupted and enigmatic text at this point (II Sam. 5:8), it is clear that the underground "gutter" (A.V.) or "watercourse" (A.S.V.) was used by David's men to gain entrance by stealth into the fortification. Scriptural evidence, buttressed by archaeological findings, locates the original Zion on the spur of the E. ridge, rather than on the W. hill—as championed by traditions of the early Christian centuries.

In Zion David built his palace (II Sam. 5:11; Neh. 12:37); erected a tent for the Ark (II Sam. 6:12, 17; I Kings 8:1); and when he died, was buried there (I Kings 2:10). In the development of Zion David acquired, farther up on the ridge, the elevated, rocky threshing floor of Araunah* (Ornan) the Jebusite, on which he erected the altar of sacrifice (II Sam. 24:18, 24 f.), and where later Solomon built the Temple. The evolution of Zion from a fortress-stronghold to a holy site is traceable in both Scripture and archaeology.

Though Zion is sometimes referred to as a definite section of Jerusalem (Ps. 51:18; Isa. 30:19, 64:10; Amos 1:2; Mic. 3:12), there are Scripture passages which do not have meaning if Zion and the Temple area were not one. Zion is "the holy hill" (Ps. 2:6), the "habitation of the Lord" (Ps. 9:11, 76:2, 132, 137; Isa. 8:18, 60:14), where He must be worshipped (Ps. 65:1; Jer. 31:6). The Babylonians requested their Hebrew captives to "sing . . . one of the songs of Zion" (Ps. 137:3). Though this passage could refer to any Hebrew song, it probably referred to one of the melodies that expressed the captives' nostalgic devotion to the Temple environs. Ps. 48 is the diary of a pilgrim's thoughts and emotions as, traveling from the E., he views Mt. Zion from the Mount of Olives.

500. Zion Gate, southernmost entrance to present-day walled Jerusalem.

In spite of the Diaspora the "fountains" of faith of the scattered people were in Zion (Ps. 87).

Growing Jerusalem later took in the W. ridge (II Chron. 33:14). Christian tradition located the house of John Mark's mother in this section of the city. As early as the 4th century A.D. this meeting place of the infant Church was called "the Church of the Apostles," or "the Church of Zion." The Syrian and Armenian churches especially cherish this SW. corner of Jerusalem as Zion.

Zionism, the modern movement to resettle Jews in their earlier homeland and to make the State of Israel an influential member in the family of nations. The Scriptural motivation for Zionism is found mainly in the later Psalms and prophetic writings (Ps. 69:35, 126:1, 132:13; Isa. 24:23, 30:19, 52:8; Jer. 3:14, 31:1–14, 50:4–6; Joel 2:32). To some Bible students such passages are only historical records expressing the hopeful yearnings for the return of Jews to Jerusalem after their Babylonian Exile, from where God would rule the nations and restore Israel to its rightful position. Many Christian interpreters think that these aspirations were spiritually fulfilled in Christ and the Messianic Kingdom he established among believers. Religious Zionists have always seen in their sacred Scriptures a heretofore unfulfilled promise for their nation concerning Palestine. Premillennarian Christians also consider the return of the Jews to Palestine as preliminary to Christ's second coming (see PAROUSIA). Jewish literature throughout the centuries has abetted the Zionistic urge. Judah Halevi, b. c. 1080 in Spain, the greatest Hebrew poet of the Middle Ages, voiced in his *Zionides* the religious aspirations of the Jews for their motherland. Modern Zionism, fed by many streams of influence and emphasis, economic, social, and political, as well as religious, dates from Theodor Herzl (1860–1904), a Viennese. The Balfour Declaration, promulgated in the midst of World War I (Nov. 2, 1917), put Great Britain on record as in favor of "the establishment in Palestine of a national home for the Jewish people." The General Assembly of the United Nations on Nov. 29, 1947, recommended the partition of Palestine into two separate states, Arab and Jewish. In conformity with this action, the Jewish National Council proclaimed on May 14, 1948, a Jewish state in Palestine to be called Israel.

Ziph. (1) A town identified as ez-Zeifeh in the Idumaean wilderness W. of the Dead Sea and near the "Ascent of Akkrabim" which leads to the Wilderness of Zin; part of the inheritance of the Tribe of Judah (Josh. 15:24, 55). (2) A plains town (Tell Zif) SE. of Hebron, near which David hid when he was pursued by Saul (Josh. 15:55; I Sam. 23:14 ff., 26:2). This town was fortified by King Rehoboam (c. 922–915 B.C.) to guard the approach to Jerusalem from the S. (II Chron. 11:8). Its citizens were Ziphites. (3) A son of Jehaleleel, of the Tribe of Judah (I Chron. 4:16).

Zipporah (zĭ-pō′rȧ), one of the seven shepherdess daughters of Jethro, a Midianite priest. According to the J source, Zipporah became the wife of Moses while he was a fugitive in Midian after slaying an Egyptian taskmaster (Ex. 2:11 ff.). She bore him a son, Gershom (Ex. 2:22). According to the E source (Ex. 18:3 f.), she also bore him Eliezer. By circumcising her son with a flint knife she appeased Yahweh, who was believed to be angered against Moses (Ex. 4:18–26). Sources are confused concerning the story of Zipporah, with some authorities attempting to identify her with the Cushite (Ethiopian) wife of Moses (Num. 12:1).

Zoan (zō′ ăn) (Egypt. *Dja'ne;* Gk. *Tanis*), the capital of Egypt's 21st Dynasty, and an important commercial center down to the time of Alexander the Great, located near the NE. frontier of Egypt on the E. side of the Tanaitic branch of the Nile, c. 73 m. NE. of Cairo. The region of Tanis, "the fields of Zoan," was central to the Exodus tradition (Ps. 78:12, 43). Tanis appears as early as the 11th century B.C. in the Tale of Wen-Amon (*ANET*[3], p. 26). It was a center of Egyptian government at the time of Isaiah (c. 740–687 B.C.; Isa. 19:11, 13, 30:4), and important as late as the time of Ezekiel (30:14) (cf. *ANET*[3], pp. 294 f.).

The ruins of ancient Tanis, San el-Hagar, were explored by W. M. F. Petrie in 1884 and more extensively by P. Montet between 1929 and 1933. Settled as early as the 6th Dynasty, it was rebuilt and enlarged during the 12th Dynasty (c. 1991–1786 B.C.). Numerous remains, all in fragmentary condition, were found dating to the time of Ramesses II (c. 1304-1237 B.C.). A great temple, and the tomb of Psusennes I and Amenemope, attest to its importance under the 21st Dynasty (c. 1085-945 B.C.).

Based on archaeological and literary evidence such as the "Stela of the Year 400" (*ANET*[3], pp. 252 f.), many scholars identify Tanis with both Avaris*, the Hyksos capital of Egypt (see *ANET*[3], pp. 230 ff.), and Pi-Ramesses (Biblical Raamses*), taking Avaris —Raamses—Tanis as successive names of the same site (P. Montet, *RB* 39, 1930, pp. 5–28; *Syria* 17, 1936, pp. 200–202, and *Le drame d'Avaris*, 1940; A. H. Gardiner, *JEA* 19, 1933, pp. 122–128). This is far from certain, however, and a number of objections have been raised (see R. Weill, *JEA* 21, 1935, pp. 10–25; J. Van Seters, *The Hyksos*, 1966, pp. 132 ff.). As far as Raamses is concerned, identification with Qantir, S. of Tanis, has much to commend it (see RAAMSES). W. P. A.

Zoar (zō′ẽr), one of the 5 cities of the Plain on the E. side of the Dead Sea. In early Biblical times it was ruled by a king whom Chedorlaomer* defeated (Gen. 13:10, 14:2, 8). For Lot and his relations with Zoar, see Gen. 19:20–23. Zoar still existed in Moab in the era of the great prophets (Isa. 15:5; Jer. 48:34). By N.T. times the site of Zoar had moved to the S. end of the Dead Sea; perhaps the Genesis site now lies beneath the Dead Sea waters.

Zobah, an important Aramaean state N. of Damascus sometimes called Aram-zobah, whose frontiers (II Sam. 8:3) extended to the Euphrates c. 1000 B.C., when it was threatening Assyrian territory. Saul fought the people of Zobah, and David subdued them and their king Hadadezer, son of Rehob, even though a large contingent of Syrians came to their aid (II Sam. 8:5; I Chron. 18:3, 5, 7, 9). The diversion of Zobah's pressure from Assyria strengthened that power, so that ultimately it conquered the whole Fertile Crescent. Zobah lay in the metal-rich Anti-Lebanons (see II Sam. 8:8, an allusion to David's capturing much copper—A.V. "brass"). The principality of Zobah was rich in silver. Its army used horses and chariots in warfare (I Chron. 19:6). It was subjugated by Assyria (c. 733/2 B.C.), but its Aramaean traders remained influential figures in Western Asia.

Zoheleth (zō′hĕ-lĕth) a stone by En-rogel* (I Kings 1:9). R.S.V. reads "Serpent's Stone."

Zorah (Zoreah A.V. Josh. 15:33, Zareah A.V. Neh. 11:29), a town and its valley, Wâdī es-Sar'ah. The valley provided easy approach from the Mediterranean to Jerusalem, and has been used in modern times as a railroad bed from Jaffa (Joppa*) to the capital, 18 m. E. of Zorah. Zorah (within the holdings of Dan before the Tribe moved north), was the home of Samson's father, Manoah (Judg. 13:2, 25); and Samson's family buried him between Zorah and Eshtaol (Judg. 16:31). A group of Jews who returned from the Babylonian Exile resettled at Zorah (Neh. 11:29). The Chronicler mentions Rehoboam's strengthening Zorah's defenses for the protection of Judah (II Chron. 11:10).

Zuar (zū′ẽr), father of Nethaneel, a prince of the Tribe of Issachar (Num. 1:8, 2:5, 7:18, 23, 10:15).

Zur (zûr), a prince of Midian; ally of Sihon; father of the Cozbi who was taken by Zimri of Israel to wife at Baal-peor* with dire results (Num. 25:1–15).

A LIST OF ILLUSTRATIONS

WITH ACKNOWLEDGEMENTS

LIST OF ILLUSTRATIONS

LIST OF ILLUSTRATIONS

LIST OF ILLUSTRATIONS

LIST OF ILLUSTRATIONS

MAP INDEX

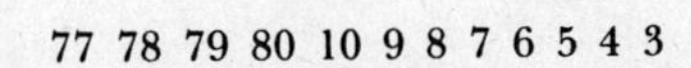
77 78 79 80 10 9 8 7 6 5 4 3

Map 1

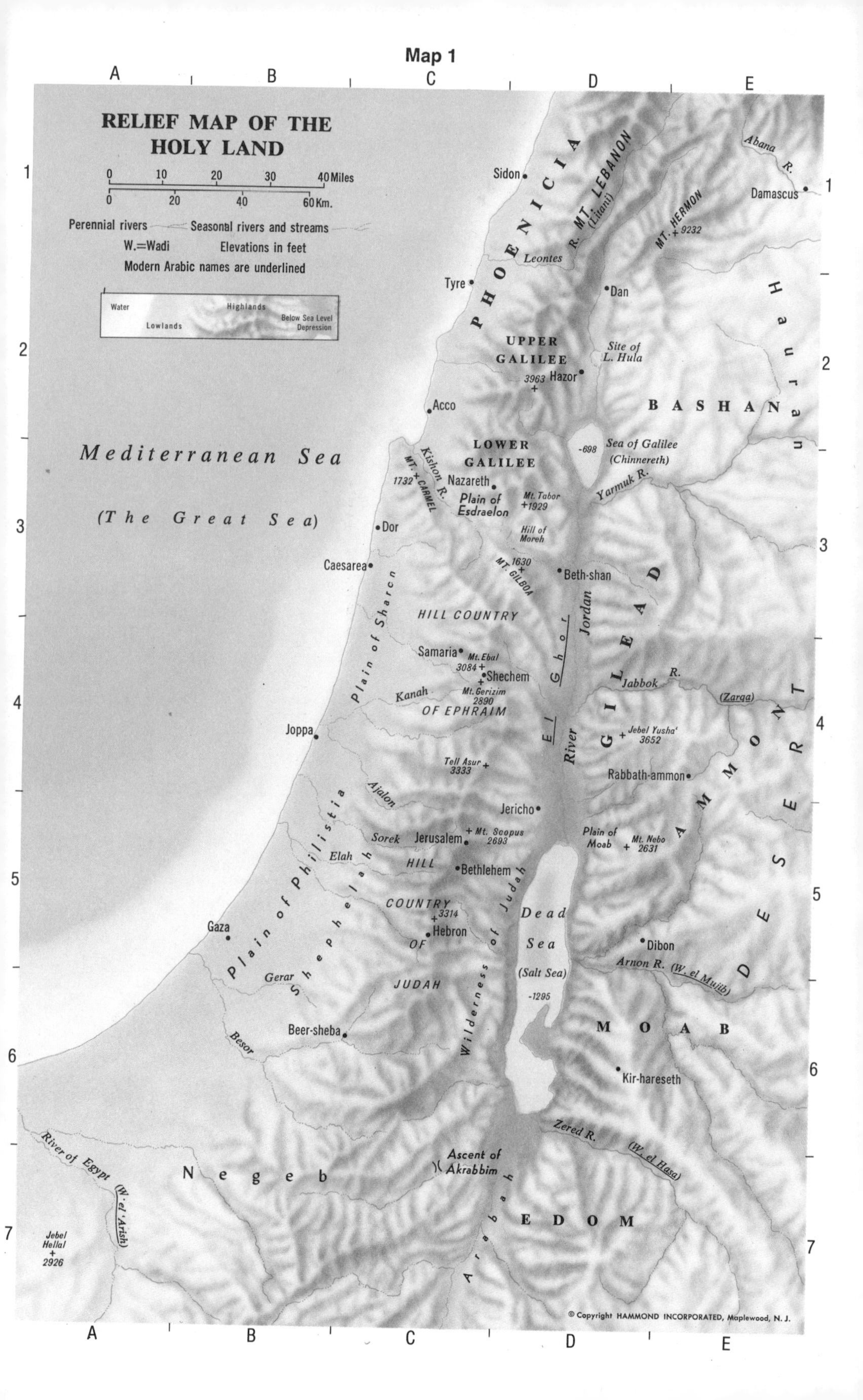
RELIEF MAP OF THE HOLY LAND
0 10 20 30 40 Miles
0 20 40 60 Km.
Perennial rivers
Seasonal rivers and streams
W.=Wadi
Elevations in feet
Modern Arabic names are underlined
Water
Highlands
Lowlands
Below Sea Level Depression
Mediterranean Sea
(The Great Sea)
PHOENICIA
MT. LEBANON
R. (Litani)
Leontes
Sidon
Tyre
Dan
Abana R.
Damascus
MT. HERMON 9232
Hauran
UPPER GALILEE
Site of L. Hula
3963
Hazor
Acco
BASHAN
LOWER GALILEE
-698
Sea of Galilee (Chinnereth)
Kishon R.
MT. CARMEL 1732
Nazareth
Plain of Esdraelon
Mt. Tabor 1929
Yarmuk R.
Dor
Hill of Moreh
Caesarea
1630 MT. GILBOA
Beth-shan
Plain of Sharon
HILL COUNTRY
El Ghor
Jordan River
GILEAD
Samaria
Mt. Ebal 3084
Shechem
Mt. Gerizim 2890
Kanah
OF EPHRAIM
Jabbok R.
(Zarqa)
Joppa
Jebel Yusha' 3652
Tell Asur 3333
Rabbath-ammon
AMMON
Ajalon
Jericho
Sorek
Jerusalem
Mt. Scopus 2693
Plain of Moab
Mt. Nebo 2631
Elah
HILL
Bethlehem
Plain of Philistia
COUNTRY
3314
Hebron
OF
JUDAH
Shephelah
Wilderness of Judah
Dead Sea (Salt Sea)
-1295
DESERT
Gaza
Gerar
Dibon
Arnon R. (W. el Mujib)
Beer-sheba
Besor
MOAB
Kir-hareseth
Zered R. (W. el Hasa)
River of Egypt (W. el 'Arish)
Negeb
Ascent of Akrabbim
Arabah
EDOM
Jebel Hellal 2926
A B C D E
1 2 3 4 5 6 7

Map 2

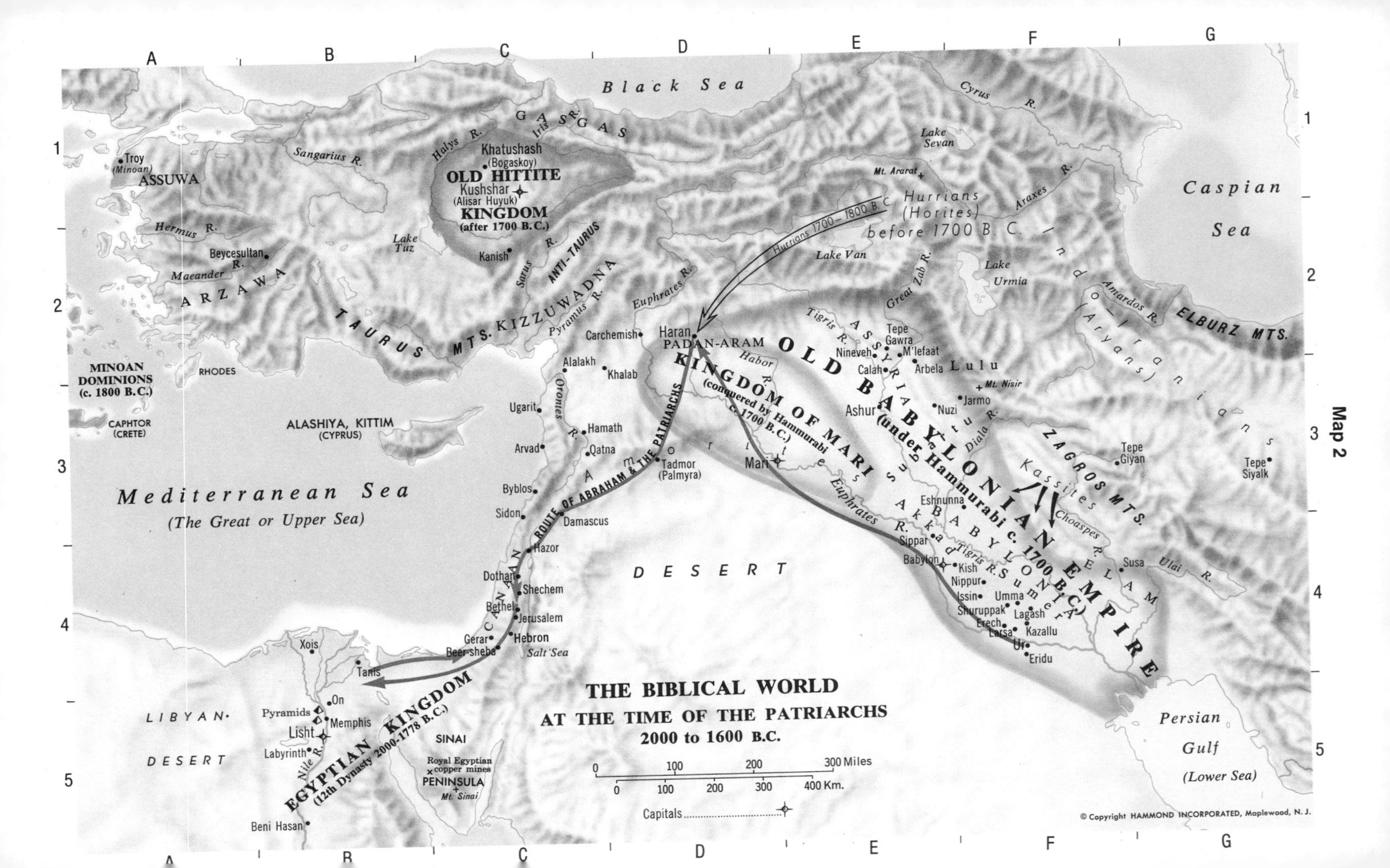
THE BIBLICAL WORLD
AT THE TIME OF THE PATRIARCHS
2000 to 1600 B.C.
0 100 200 300 Miles
0 100 200 300 400 Km.
Capitals
Black Sea
Caspian Sea
Mediterranean Sea
(The Great or Upper Sea)
Persian Gulf
(Lower Sea)
OLD HITTITE KINGDOM
(after 1700 B.C.)
Khatushash
(Bogaskoy)
Kushshar
(Alisar Huyuk)
Kanish
GASGAS
Halys R.
Iris R.
Sangarius R.
Troy
(Minoan)
ASSUWA
Hermus R.
Beycesultan
Maeander R.
ARZAWA
Lake Tuz
TAURUS MTS.
KIZZUWADNA
ANTI-TAURUS
Sarus R.
Pyramus R.
Euphrates R.
MINOAN DOMINIONS
(c. 1800 B.C.)
RHODES
CAPHTOR
(CRETE)
ALASHIYA, KITTIM
(CYPRUS)
Carchemish
Haran
PADAN-ARAM
Habor R.
KINGDOM OF MARI
(conquered by Hammurabi c. 1700 B.C.)
Mari
Alalakh
Khalab
Ugarit
Orontes R.
Hamath
Arvad
Qatna
Tadmor
(Palmyra)
Amorites
ROUTE OF ABRAHAM & THE PATRIARCHS
Byblos
Sidon
Damascus
Hazor
CANAAN
Dothan
Shechem
Bethel
Jerusalem
Hebron
Salt Sea
Gerar
Beer-sheba
DESERT
Xois
Tanis
On
Pyramids
Memphis
Lisht
Labyrinth
Nile R.
Beni Hasan
LIBYAN DESERT
EGYPTIAN KINGDOM
(12th Dynasty 2000-1778 B.C.)
SINAI
Royal Egyptian copper mines
PENINSULA
Mt. Sinai
Lake Sevan
Cyrus R.
Mt. Ararat
Araxes R.
Hurrians
(Horites)
before 1700 B.C.
Hurrians 1700-1800 B.C.
Lake Van
Lake Urmia
Great Zab R.
Indo-Iranians
(Aryans)
Amardos R.
ELBURZ MTS.
Tigris R.
ASSYRIA
Tepe Gawra
Nineveh
M'lefaat
Calah
Arbela
Lulu
Mt. Nisir
Jarmo
Ashur
Nuzi
Diala R.
OLD BABYLONIAN EMPIRE
(under Hammurabi c. 1700 B.C.)
Euphrates R.
Sippar
Eshnunna
Akkad
BABYLONIA
Babylon
Kish
Tigris R.
Sumer
Nippur
Issin
Umma
Shuruppak
Lagash
Erech
Larsa
Kazallu
Ur
Eridu
ZAGROS MTS.
Kassites
Choaspes R.
ELAM
Susa
Ulai R.
Tepe Giyan
Tepe Siyalk

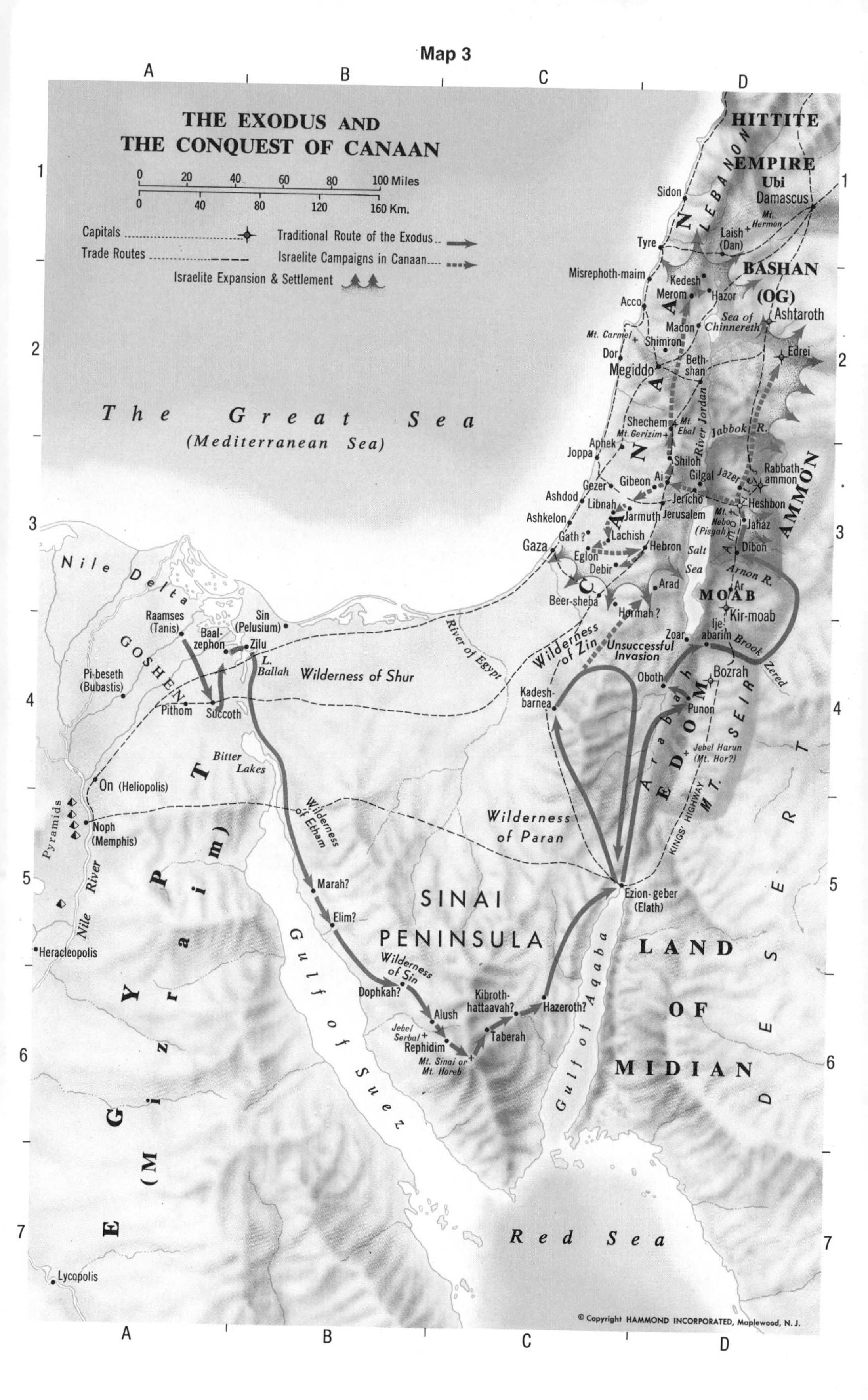
THE EXODUS AND
THE CONQUEST OF CANAAN
0 20 40 60 80 100 Miles
0 40 80 120 160 Km.
Capitals
Trade Routes
Traditional Route of the Exodus
Israelite Campaigns in Canaan
Israelite Expansion & Settlement
The Great Sea
(Mediterranean Sea)
HITTITE EMPIRE
Ubi
Damascus
Mt. Hermon
Sidon
LEBANON
Tyre
Laish (Dan)
BASHAN (OG)
Misrephoth-maim
Kedesh
Merom
Hazor
Acco
Sea of Chinnereth
Ashtaroth
Madon
Mt. Carmel
Shimron
Edrei
Dor
Megiddo
Beth-shan
Shechem
Mt. Ebal
Mt. Gerizim
River Jordan
Jabbok R.
Aphek
Joppa
Shiloh
Rabbath-ammon
AMMON
Gezer
Gibeon
Ai
Gilgal
Jazer
Ashdod
Libnah
Jericho
Heshbon
Jarmuth
Jerusalem
Ashkelon
Mt. Nebo (Pisgah)
Jahaz
Gath?
Lachish
Gaza
Eglon
Hebron
Salt Sea
Dibon
Debir
Arnon R.
Arad
Ar
MOAB
Beer-sheba
Hormah?
Kir-moab
CANAAN
Nile Delta
Raamses (Tanis)
Sin (Pelusium)
Baal-zephon
Zilu
L. Ballah
River of Egypt
Wilderness of Zin
Unsuccessful Invasion
Zoar
Ije-abarim
Brook Zered
GOSHEN
Wilderness of Shur
Pi-beseth (Bubastis)
Kadesh-barnea
Oboth
Bozrah
Pithom
Succoth
Punon
EDOM
MT. SEIR
Arabah
Bitter Lakes
Jebel Harun (Mt. Hor?)
On (Heliopolis)
Wilderness of Etham
Pyramids
Noph (Memphis)
Wilderness of Paran
KINGS' HIGHWAY
Nile River
Marah?
Ezion-geber (Elath)
SINAI PENINSULA
Elim?
EGYPT (Mizraim)
Heracleopolis
Wilderness of Sin
Dophkah?
Gulf of Suez
Gulf of Aqaba
LAND OF MIDIAN
Kibroth-hattaavah?
Hazeroth?
Alush
Jebel Serbal
Rephidim
Taberah
Mt. Sinai or Mt. Horeb
DESERT
Red Sea
Lycopolis
A B C D
1 2 3 4 5 6 7

Map 4
A
B
C
D
E
THE TWELVE TRIBES
IN CANAAN
0 10 20 30 40 Miles
0 20 40 60 Km.
1
2
3
4
5
6
7
Sidon
Phoenicians
MOUNT LEBANON
Leontes R.
Zarephath
MT. HERMON
Damascus
Abana R.
Tyre
Abel-beth-maachah
DAN
Laish or Leshem (Dan)
Kanah
Bashan
Hammon
En-hazor
Kedesh
Misrephoth-maim
Iron
Achzib
Abdon
Hazor
Beth-emek
Ramah
ASHER
NAPHTALI
Acco
Karnaim
Argob
Achshaph
Cabul
Hukkok
Chinnereth
Ashtaroth
Aphek
Rimmon
Madon
Sea of Chinnereth
Geshur
Aphek
Golan?
Kishon
MT. CARMEL
Hannathon
ZEBULUN
Gath-hepher
Hammath
Shimron
Harosheth
Sarid
Mt. Tabor
Jabneel
Yarmuk R.
Jokneam
Chesulloth
En-dor
Edrei
Dor
Plain of Jezreel
Shunem
Havoth-jair
MANASSEH
ISSACHAR
Camon
Megiddo
Jezreel
Harod (spring)
Ramoth-gilead
Shihor-libnath
Taanach
Mt. Gilboa
Beth-shan
Pella
Ibleam
Jordan
Gilead
Plain of Sharon
Dothan
Jabesh-gilead
Bezek
The Great Sea
MANASSEH
Abel-meholah
Tirzah?
Thebez
Zaphon
Mt. Ebal
Shechem
Succoth
Mahanaim
AMMON
Mt. Gerizim
Jabbok R.
Pirathon
Taanath-shiloh
River
Penuel
Kanah
Tappuah
Janohah
Mizpeh
Gath-rimmon?
Aphek
Lebonah
Shiloh
Adam
Joppa (Japho)
Bene-berak
EPHRAIM
Ataroth
GAD
Jogbehah
Ono
Timnath-serah
Betonim
Ajalon
Ophrah
Naarath
Jazer
Rabbath-ammon
DAN
Lod
Lower Beth-horon
Bethel
Ai
Mizpah?
Gilgal
Beth-nimrah
Jabneel
Ekron
Gezer
Ramah
Gibeon
Geba
Jericho
Abel-shittim
Elealeh
Sorek
Gibbethon
Kirjath-jearim
BENJAMIN
Gibeah
Heshbon
Eltekeh
Zorah
Beth-jeshimoth
Ashdod
Timnah
Beth-shemesh
Jebus (Jerusalem)
Mt. Nebo
Makkedah
Jarmuth
Bethlehem
Medeba
Philistines
Libnah
Azekah
Etam
Baal-meon
Jahaz
Ashkelon
Tekoa
Gath?
Mareshah
Keilah
Beth-zur
REUBEN
JUDAH
Ataroth
Eglon
Lachish
Hebron
Kiriathaim
Salt Sea
Gaza
Dibon
Debir
Caleb
Ziph
En-gedi
Arnon R.
Aroer
Juttah
Carmel
Gerar
Ziklag
Anab
Eshtemoh
Madmannah
Jattir
Raphia
Sharuhen
Arad
Ar?
Cherethites
Beer-sheba
Moladah
Kenites
MOAB
Hormah
Beth-palet?
Kir-hareseth
Aroer
SIMEON
Rehoboth
Brook Zered
Ascent of Akrabbim
EDOM
© Copyright HAMMOND INCORPORATED, Maplewood, N. J.

Map 5

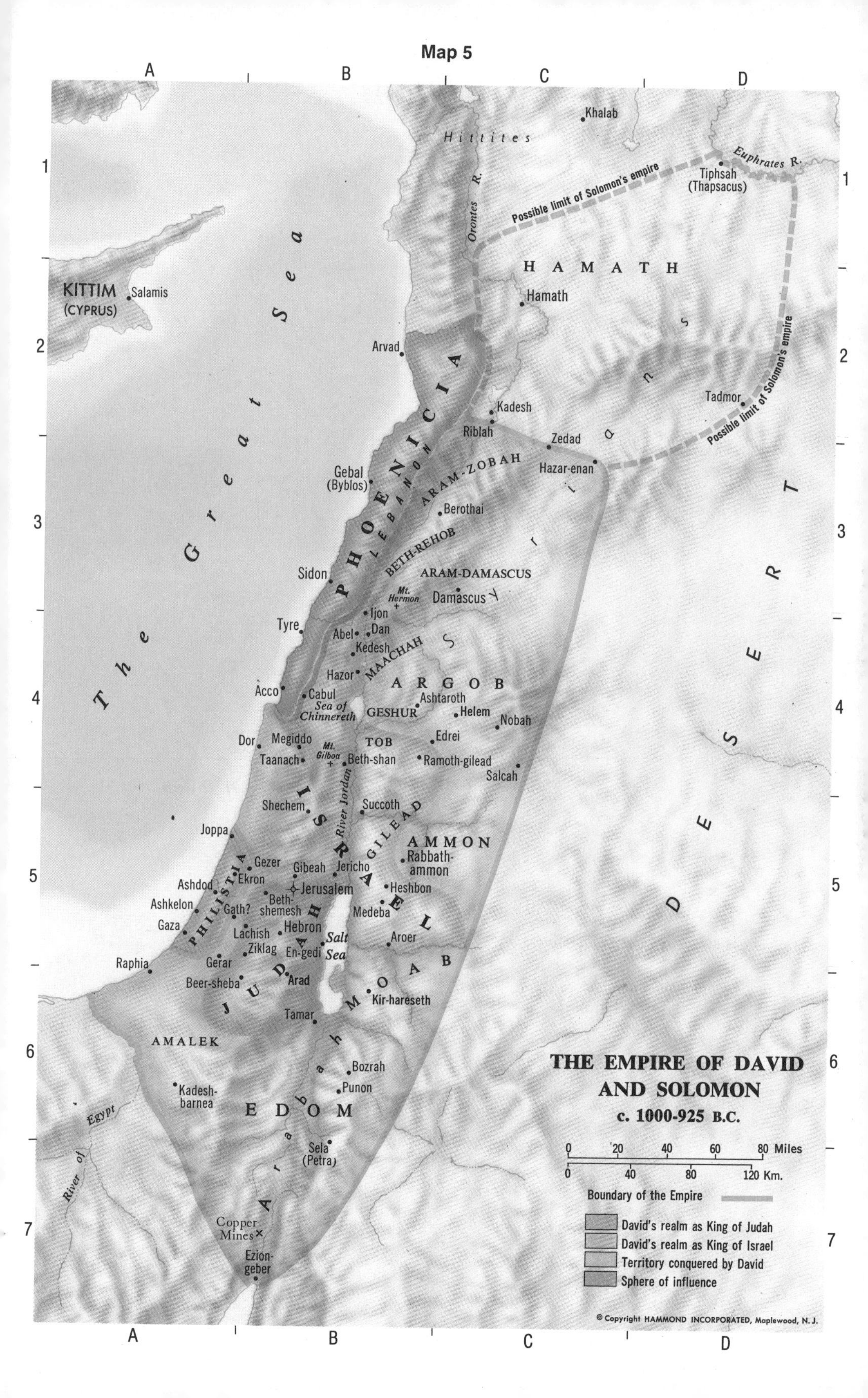

THE EMPIRE OF DAVID AND SOLOMON
c. 1000-925 B.C.
0 20 40 60 80 Miles
0 40 80 120 Km.
Boundary of the Empire
David's realm as King of Judah
David's realm as King of Israel
Territory conquered by David
Sphere of influence
The Great Sea
KITTIM (CYPRUS)
Salamis
Hittites
Khalab
Orontes R.
Euphrates R.
Tiphsah (Thapsacus)
Possible limit of Solomon's empire
HAMATH
Hamath
Arvad
PHOENICIA
Kadesh
Riblah
Tadmor
Zedad
Hazar-enan
Gebal (Byblos)
LEBANON
ARAM-ZOBAH
Berothai
BETH-REHOB
ARAM-DAMASCUS
Damascus
Sidon
Mt. Hermon
Syrians
Tyre
Ijon
Dan
Abel
Kedesh
MAACHAH
Hazor
ARGOB
Acco
Cabul
Sea of Chinnereth
GESHUR
Ashtaroth
Helem
Nobah
Dor
Megiddo
TOB
Edrei
Taanach
Mt. Gilboa
Beth-shan
Ramoth-gilead
Salcah
Shechem
Succoth
River Jordan
GILEAD
Joppa
ISRAEL
AMMON
Gezer
Gibeah
Jericho
Rabbath-ammon
Ashdod
Ekron
Jerusalem
Heshbon
Ashkelon
Gath?
Beth-shemesh
Medeba
Gaza
PHILISTIA
Lachish
Hebron
Salt Sea
Aroer
Ziklag
En-gedi
Raphia
Gerar
MOAB
Beer-sheba
Arad
JUDAH
Kir-hareseth
Tamar
AMALEK
Bozrah
Punon
Kadesh-barnea
EDOM
Arabah
River of Egypt
Sela (Petra)
Copper Mines
Ezion-geber
DESERT
A B C D
1 2 3 4 5 6 7

Map 6

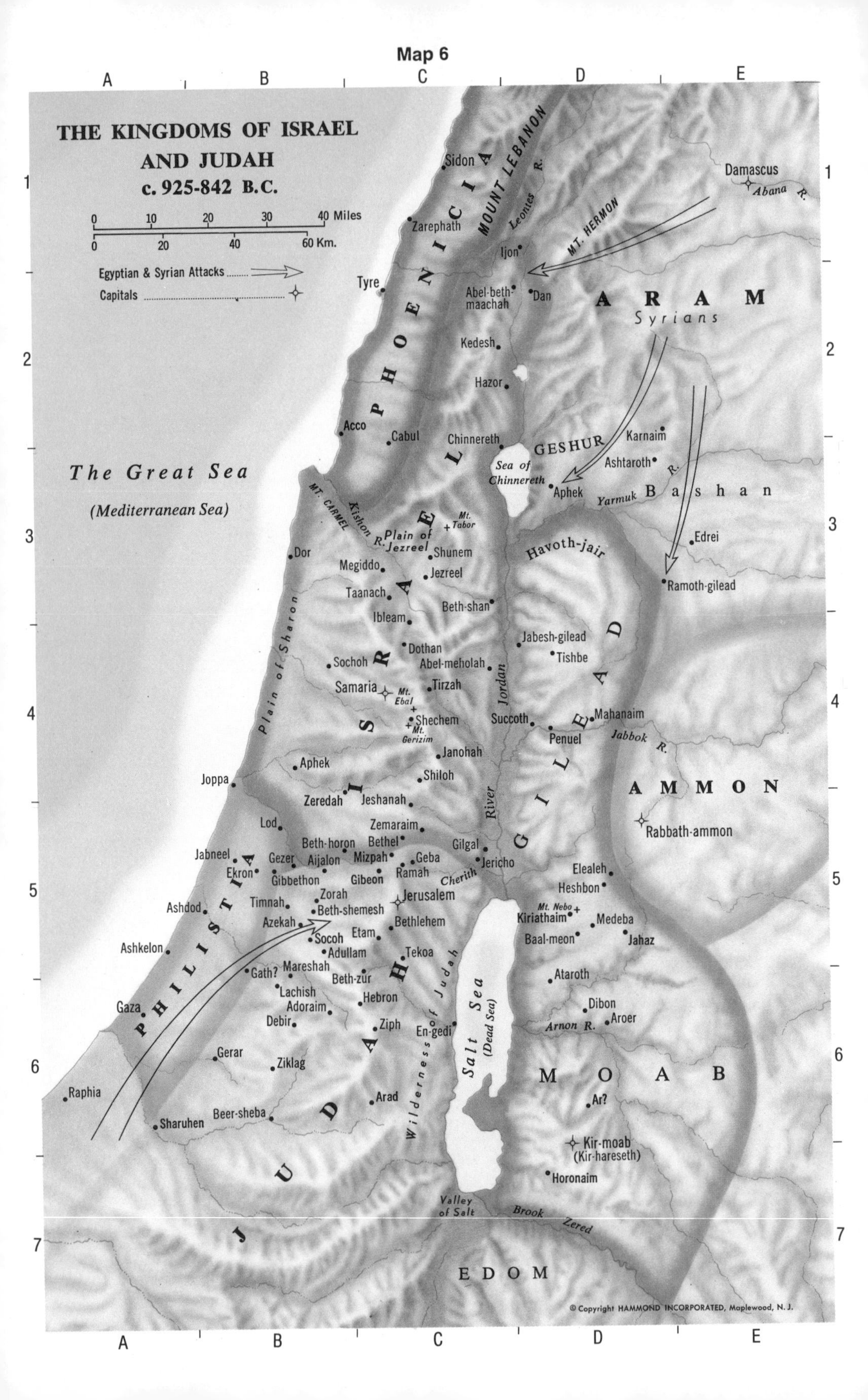
THE KINGDOMS OF ISRAEL AND JUDAH
c. 925-842 B.C.
0 10 20 30 40 Miles
0 20 40 60 Km.
Egyptian & Syrian Attacks
Capitals
The Great Sea
(Mediterranean Sea)
PHOENICIA
MOUNT LEBANON
Leontes R.
MT. HERMON
Sidon
Zarephath
Tyre
Ijon
Abel-beth-maachah
Dan
Damascus
Abana R.
ARAM
Syrians
Kedesh
Hazor
Acco
Cabul
Chinnereth
GESHUR
Karnaim
Ashtaroth
Sea of Chinnereth
Aphek
Yarmuk R.
Bashan
MT. CARMEL
Kishon R.
Plain of Jezreel
Mt. Tabor
Edrei
Havoth-jair
Dor
Shunem
Megiddo
Jezreel
Ramoth-gilead
Taanach
Beth-shan
Ibleam
ISRAEL
Plain of Sharon
Dothan
Jabesh-gilead
Tishbe
Sochoh
Abel-meholah
GILEAD
Samaria
Mt. Ebal
Tirzah
Jordan River
Shechem
Mt. Gerizim
Succoth
Mahanaim
Penuel
Jabbok R.
Janohah
Aphek
Shiloh
Joppa
AMMON
Zeredah
Jeshanah
Rabbath-ammon
Lod
Zemaraim
Beth-horon
Bethel
Gilgal
Jabneel
Gezer
Aijalon
Mizpah
Geba
Jericho
Ekron
Gibbethon
Gibeon
Ramah
Cherith
Elealeh
Heshbon
Zorah
Jerusalem
Ashdod
Timnah
Beth-shemesh
Mt. Nebo
Kiriathaim
Medeba
Azekah
Bethlehem
Etam
Socoh
Baal-meon
Jahaz
Ashkelon
Adullam
Tekoa
PHILISTIA
Gath?
Mareshah
Beth-zur
Ataroth
Lachish
Hebron
Salt Sea (Dead Sea)
Gaza
Adoraim
Dibon
Debir
Ziph
Wilderness of Judah
Arnon R.
Aroer
En-gedi
Gerar
Ziklag
MOAB
Raphia
Arad
Ar?
JUDAH
Sharuhen
Beer-sheba
Kir-moab (Kir-hareseth)
Horonaim
Valley of Salt
Brook Zered
EDOM
A B C D E
1 2 3 4 5 6 7

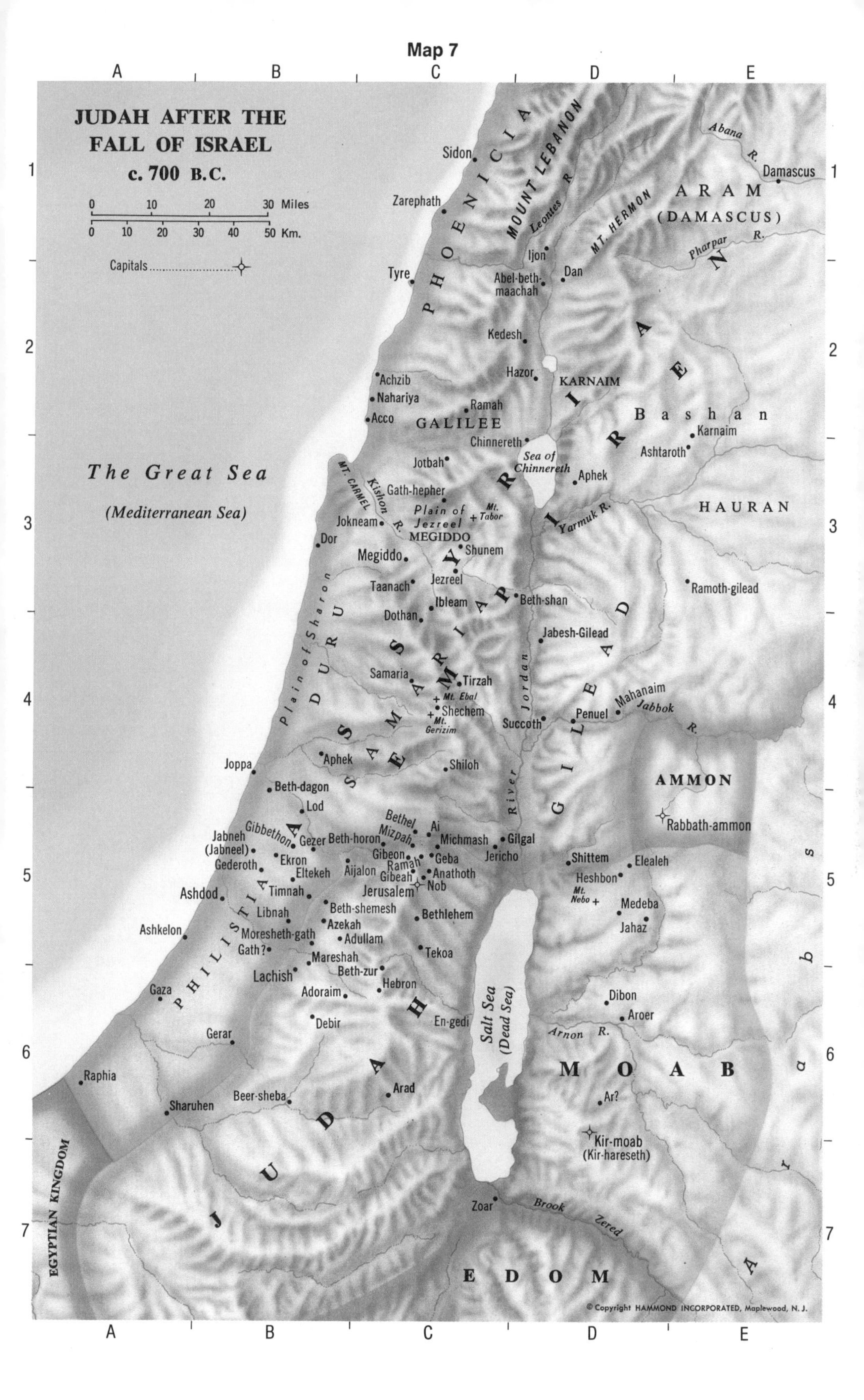
JUDAH AFTER THE FALL OF ISRAEL
c. 700 B.C.
0 10 20 30 Miles
0 10 20 30 40 50 Km.
Capitals
The Great Sea
(Mediterranean Sea)
PHOENICIA
MOUNT LEBANON
Leontes R.
MT. HERMON
ARAM
(DAMASCUS)
Abana R.
Pharpar R.
Damascus
Sidon
Zarephath
Tyre
Ijon
Dan
Abel-beth-maachah
Kedesh
Hazor
KARNAIM
Achzib
Nahariya
Acco
Ramah
GALILEE
Chinnereth
Sea of Chinnereth
Bashan
Karnaim
Ashtaroth
Jotbah
Aphek
MT. CARMEL
Kishon R.
Gath-hepher
Plain of Jezreel
Mt. Tabor
HAURAN
Jokneam
MEGIDDO
Yarmuk R.
Dor
Megiddo
Shunem
Jezreel
Taanach
Ramoth-gilead
Ibleam
Beth-shan
Dothan
Jabesh-Gilead
Plain of Sharon
DURU
SAMARIA
GILEAD
Samaria
Tirzah
Mt. Ebal
Shechem
Mt. Gerizim
Jordan River
Mahanaim
Penuel
Jabbok R.
Succoth
Aphek
Shiloh
Joppa
AMMON
Beth-dagon
Lod
Rabbath-ammon
Bethel
Ai
Gibbethon
Mizpah
Jabneh (Jabneel)
Gezer
Beth-horon
Michmash
Gilgal
Jericho
Ekron
Gibeon
Geba
Ramah
Shittem
Elealeh
Gederoth
Eltekeh
Aijalon
Gibeah
Anathoth
Heshbon
Timnah
Jerusalem
Nob
Mt. Nebo
Ashdod
Beth-shemesh
Medeba
Libnah
Bethlehem
Jahaz
Azekah
Ashkelon
Moresheth-gath
Adullam
Gath?
Tekoa
Mareshah
Beth-zur
Lachish
Hebron
PHILISTIA
Gaza
Adoraim
Salt Sea (Dead Sea)
Dibon
Debir
En-gedi
Aroer
Arnon R.
Gerar
MOAB
Raphia
Arad
Beer-sheba
Ar?
Sharuhen
Kir-moab (Kir-hareseth)
JUDAH
EGYPTIAN KINGDOM
Zoar
Brook Zered
EDOM
ARABS
ARAMAEANS
© Copyright HAMMOND INCORPORATED, Maplewood, N. J.

Map 7

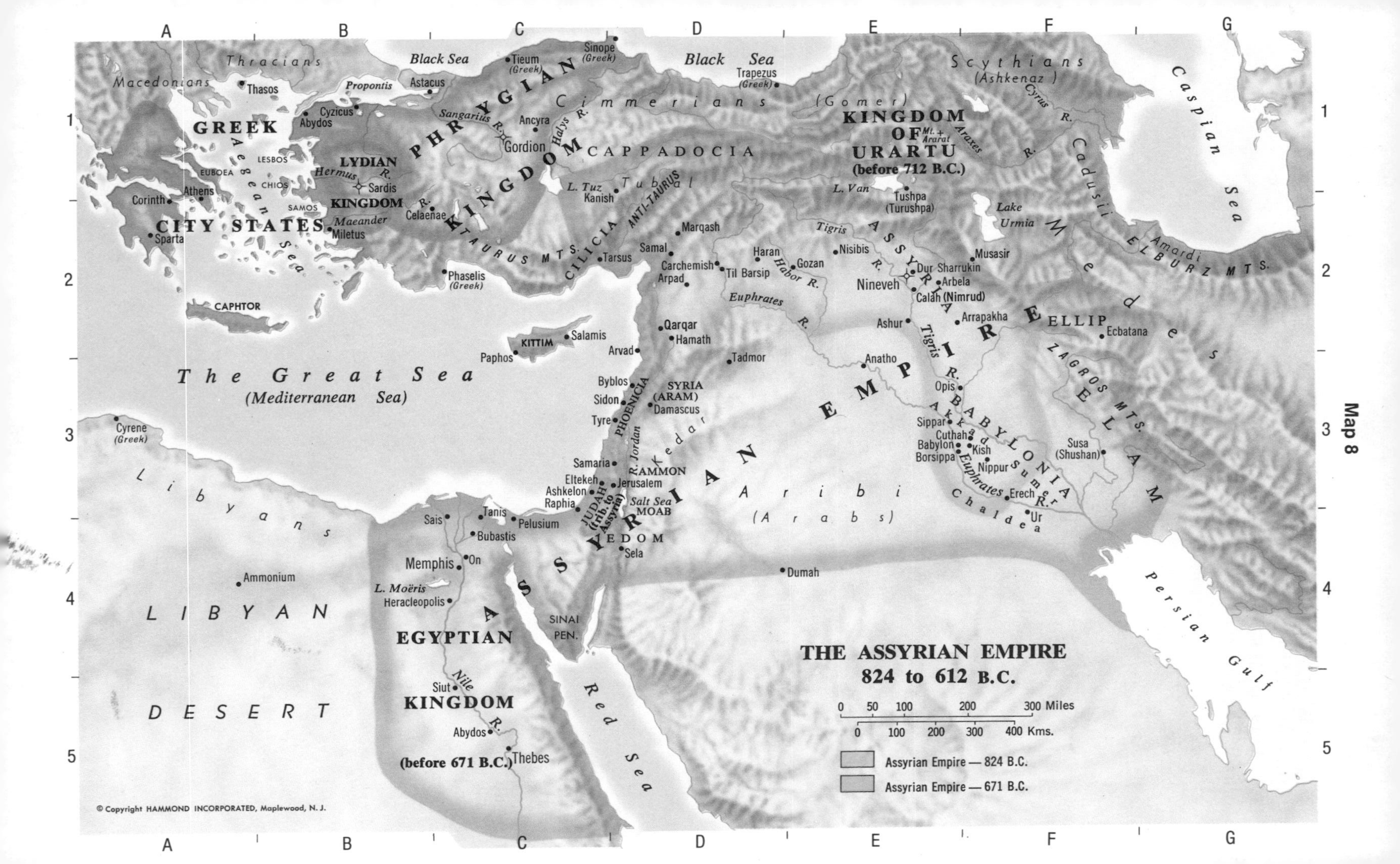
THE ASSYRIAN EMPIRE
824 to 612 B.C.
0 50 100 200 300 Miles
0 100 200 300 400 Kms.
Assyrian Empire — 824 B.C.
Assyrian Empire — 671 B.C.
ASSYRIAN EMPIRE
GREEK CITY STATES
LYDIAN KINGDOM
PHRYGIAN KINGDOM
KINGDOM OF URARTU
(before 712 B.C.)
EGYPTIAN KINGDOM
(before 671 B.C.)
CAPPADOCIA
CILICIA
PHOENICIA
SYRIA (ARAM)
BABYLONIA
ELAM
ELLIP
AMMON
MOAB
EDOM
JUDAH (trib. to Assyria)
Akkad
Sumer
Chaldea
Medes
Cimmerians
(Gomer)
Scythians
(Ashkenaz)
Thracians
Macedonians
Cadusii
Amardi
Tubal
Kedar
Aribi
(Arabs)
Libyans
LIBYAN DESERT
Black Sea
Caspian Sea
Persian Gulf
Red Sea
The Great Sea
(Mediterranean Sea)
Aegean Sea
Proportis
Lake Urmia
L. Van
L. Tuz
L. Moëris
Salt Sea
ELBURZ MTS.
ZAGROS MTS.
TAURUS MTS.
ANTI-TAURUS
Mt. Ararat
SINAI PEN.
CAPTHOR
KITTIM
LESBOS
CHIOS
SAMOS
EUBOEA
Tigris R.
Euphrates R.
Habor R.
Nile R.
Jordan R.
Halys R.
Sangarius R.
Hermus R.
Maeander R.
Araxes R.
Cyrus R.
Thasos
Cyzicus
Abydos
Athens
Corinth
Sparta
Miletus
Sardis
Celaenae
Astacus
Tieum (Greek)
Sinope (Greek)
Trapezus (Greek)
Ancyra
Gordion
Kanish
Phaselis (Greek)
Tarsus
Samal
Marqash
Carchemish
Til Barsip
Arpad
Haran
Gozan
Nisibis
Nineveh
Dur Sharrukin
Arbela
Calah (Nimrud)
Musasir
Tushpa (Turushpa)
Ashur
Arrapakha
Ecbatana
Anatho
Opis
Sippar
Cuthah
Babylon
Kish
Borsippa
Nippur
Erech
Ur
Susa (Shushan)
Qarqar
Hamath
Tadmor
Arvad
Byblos
Sidon
Tyre
Damascus
Samaria
Elteke
Jerusalem
Ashkelon
Raphia
Sela
Dumah
Salamis
Paphos
Cyrene (Greek)
Sais
Tanis
Pelusium
Bubastis
On
Memphis
Heracleopolis
Ammonium
Siut
Abydos
Thebes
A B C D E F G
1 2 3 4 5

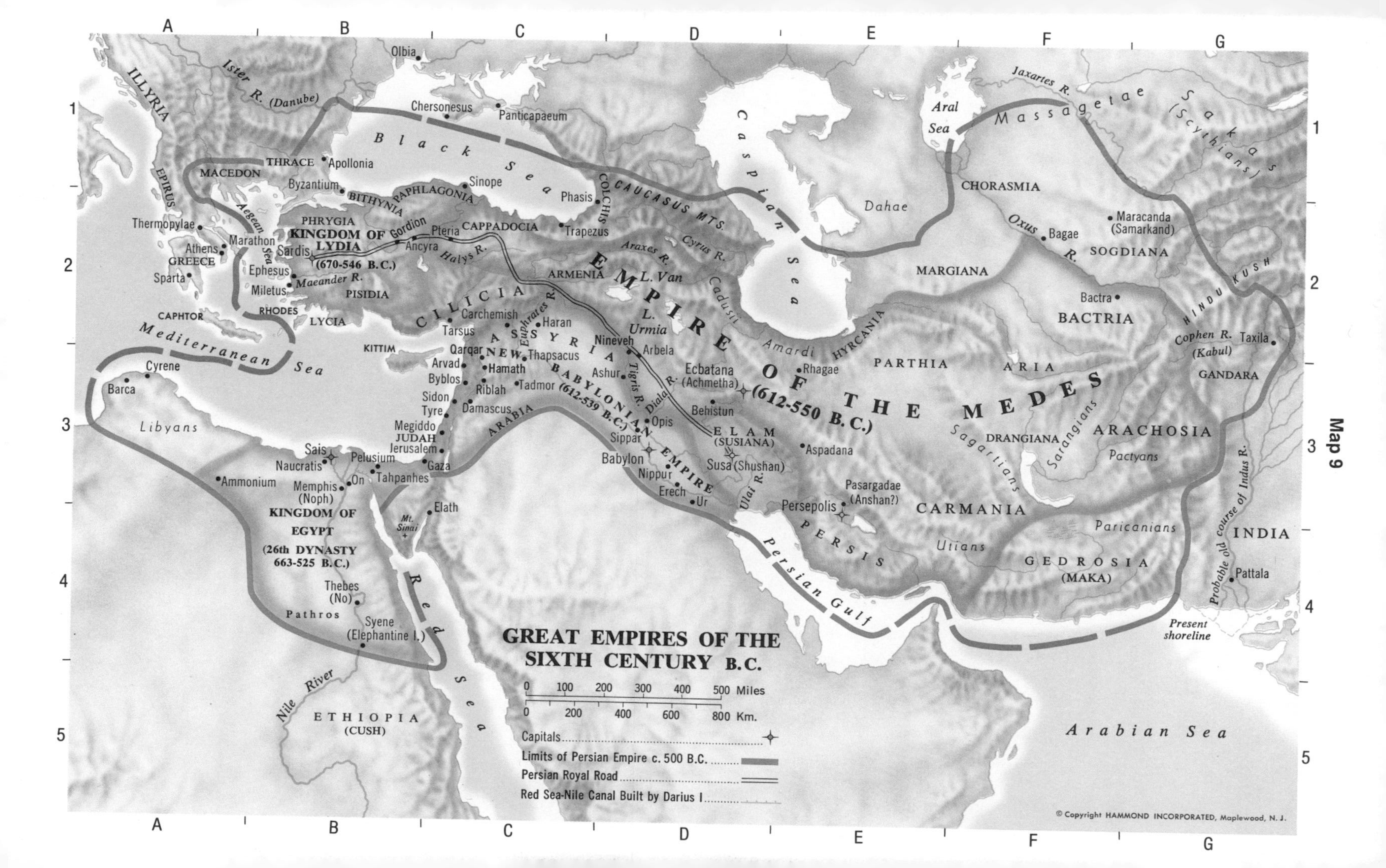
GREAT EMPIRES OF THE SIXTH CENTURY B.C.
0 100 200 300 400 500 Miles
0 200 400 600 800 Km.
Capitals
Limits of Persian Empire c. 500 B.C.
Persian Royal Road
Red Sea-Nile Canal Built by Darius I
EMPIRE OF THE MEDES (612-550 B.C.)
NEW BABYLONIAN EMPIRE (612-539 B.C.)
KINGDOM OF LYDIA (670-546 B.C.)
KINGDOM OF EGYPT (26th DYNASTY 663-525 B.C.)
ILLYRIA
Ister R. (Danube)
Olbia
Chersonesus
Panticapaeum
Black Sea
Caspian Sea
Aral Sea
Jaxartes R.
Massagetae
Sakas (Scythians)
EPIRUS
MACEDON
THRACE
Apollonia
Byzantium
Sinope
Phasis
COLCHIS
CAUCASUS MTS.
Dahae
CHORASMIA
Oxus R.
Bagae
Maracanda (Samarkand)
SOGDIANA
Thermopylae
Athens
Marathon
Aegean Sea
GREECE
Sparta
PHRYGIA
BITHYNIA
PAPHLAGONIA
Gordion
Pteria
CAPPADOCIA
Trapezus
Sardis
Ancyra
Halys R.
Ephesus
Maeander R.
Miletus
PISIDIA
RHODES
LYCIA
CAPTOR
Mediterranean Sea
KITTIM
CILICIA
Carchemish
Tarsus
Haran
Euphrates R.
ARMENIA
Araxes R.
Cyrus R.
L. Van
L. Urmia
Cadusii
MARGIANA
Bactra
BACTRIA
HINDU KUSH
Cophen R. (Kabul)
Taxila
GANDARA
ASSYRIA
Nineveh
Arbela
Qarqar
Hamath
Thapsacus
Arvad
Byblos
Riblah
Tadmor
Ashur
Tigris R.
Diala R.
Amardi
HYRCANIA
Rhagae
Ecbatana (Achmetha)
Behistun
PARTHIA
ARIA
Cyrene
Barca
Libyans
Sidon
Tyre
Damascus
Megiddo
JUDAH
Jerusalem
Gaza
ARABIA
Opis
Sippar
Babylon
Nippur
Erech
Ur
ELAM (SUSIANA)
Susa (Shushan)
Ulai R.
Aspadana
Sagartians
DRANGIANA
Sarangians
ARACHOSIA
Pactyans
Sais
Naucratis
Pelusium
Tahpanhes
On
Ammonium
Memphis (Noph)
Elath
Mt. Sinai
Pasargadae (Anshan?)
Persepolis
PERSIS
CARMANIA
Utians
Paricanians
GEDROSIA (MAKA)
INDIA
Probable old course of Indus R.
Pattala
Persian Gulf
Present shoreline
Thebes (No)
Pathros
Syene (Elephantine I.)
Red Sea
Nile River
ETHIOPIA (CUSH)
Arabian Sea
A B C D E F G
1 2 3 4 5

Map 10

A
B
C
D
E
1
2
3
4
5
6
7
THE RESTORATION OF JUDAH
c. 445 B.C.
0 10 20 30 40 Miles
0 20 40 60 Km.
Route of the Returning Exiles
Sidon
SIDON
MOUNT LEBANON
Phoenicians
Damascus
Arameans
MT. HERMON
From Babylonia
Leontes R.
Tyre
Kedesh
Achzib
Hazor
Bashan
KARNAIM
Karnaim
Acco
GALILEE
Lake
Gennesaret
Kishon R.
MT. CARMEL
Yarmuk R.
Beth-yerah
Megiddo
Mt. Tabor
Edrei
Dor
The Great Sea
(Mediterranean Sea)
Ramoth-gilead
Plain of Sharon
DOR
Beth-shan
Pella
GILEAD
SAMARIA
River Jordan
Samaria
Mt. Ebal
Shechem
Jabbok R.
Mt. Gerizim
Joppa
Ono
Neballat
Rabbath-ammon
Lod
Hadid
Gath ?
Mizpah
Gibeon
Bethel
Ai
Gilgal
Araq el-Amir
Gezer
Beth-horon
Michmash
Jericho
AMMON
Ekron
Emmaus
Chephirah
Geba
Azmaveth
Ramah
Kirjath-jearim
Anathoth
Heshbon
Ashdod
Beth-haccherem
Jerusalem
Zanoah
JUDAH
Medeba
Jarmuth
Bethlehem
Ashkelon
Azekah
Adullam
Keilah
Tekoa
ASHDOD
Mareshah
Nebo
Beth-zur
Lachish
Hebron
Dibon
Gaza
Philistines
En-gedi
Salt Sea
(Dead Sea)
Arnon R.
Gerar
Ziklag
En-rimmon
MOAB
Raphia
Jeshua
Moladah
Beer-sheba
Edomites
Beth-phelet?
Kir-moab
(Kir-hareseth)
Arabs
Brook Zered
ARABS

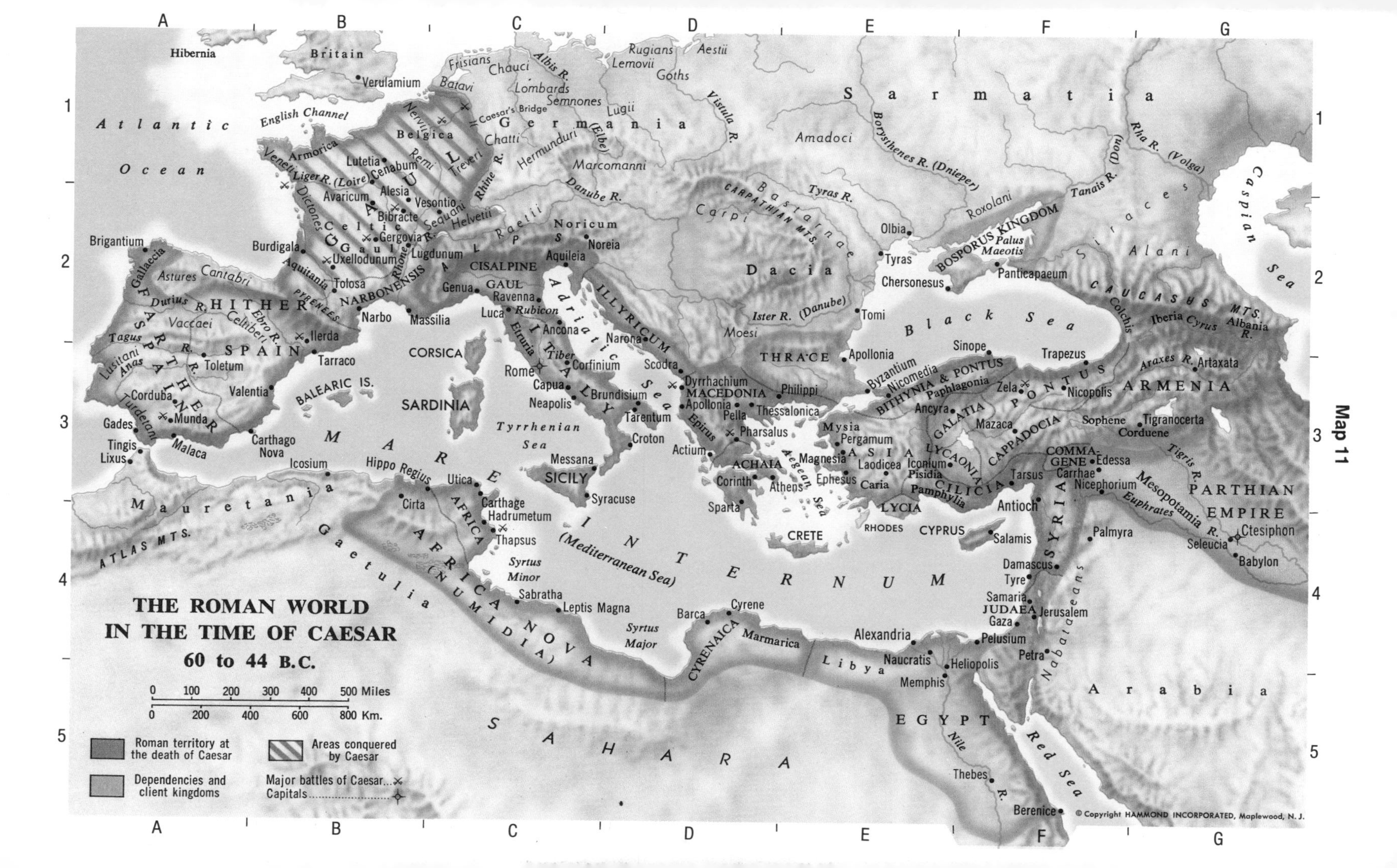
THE ROMAN WORLD
IN THE TIME OF CAESAR
60 to 44 B.C.
0 100 200 300 400 500 Miles
0 200 400 600 800 Km.
Roman territory at the death of Caesar
Dependencies and client kingdoms
Areas conquered by Caesar
Major battles of Caesar
Capitals
Atlantic Ocean
Hibernia
Britain
Verulamium
English Channel
Sarmatia
Germania
Gaul
Belgica
Celtic Gaul
Aquitania
NARBONENSIS
HITHER SPAIN
FARTHER SPAIN
CISALPINE GAUL
ITALY
ILLYRICUM
Noricum
Dacia
THRACE
MACEDONIA
ACHAIA
Black Sea
Caspian Sea
BOSPORUS KINGDOM
ARMENIA
PARTHIAN EMPIRE
PONTUS
BITHYNIA & PONTUS
GALATIA
CAPPADOCIA
ASIA
CILICIA
SYRIA
JUDAEA
Arabia
EGYPT
Libya
CYRENAICA
AFRICA
AFRICA NOVA (NUMIDIA)
Mauretania
Gaetulia
SAHARA
MARE INTERNUM (Mediterranean Sea)
Adriatic Sea
Tyrrhenian Sea
Aegean Sea
Red Sea
CORSICA
SARDINIA
SICILY
BALEARIC IS.
CRETE
CYPRUS
RHODES
Rome
Carthage
Alexandria
Athens
Jerusalem
Antioch
© Copyright HAMMOND INCORPORATED, Maplewood, N. J.

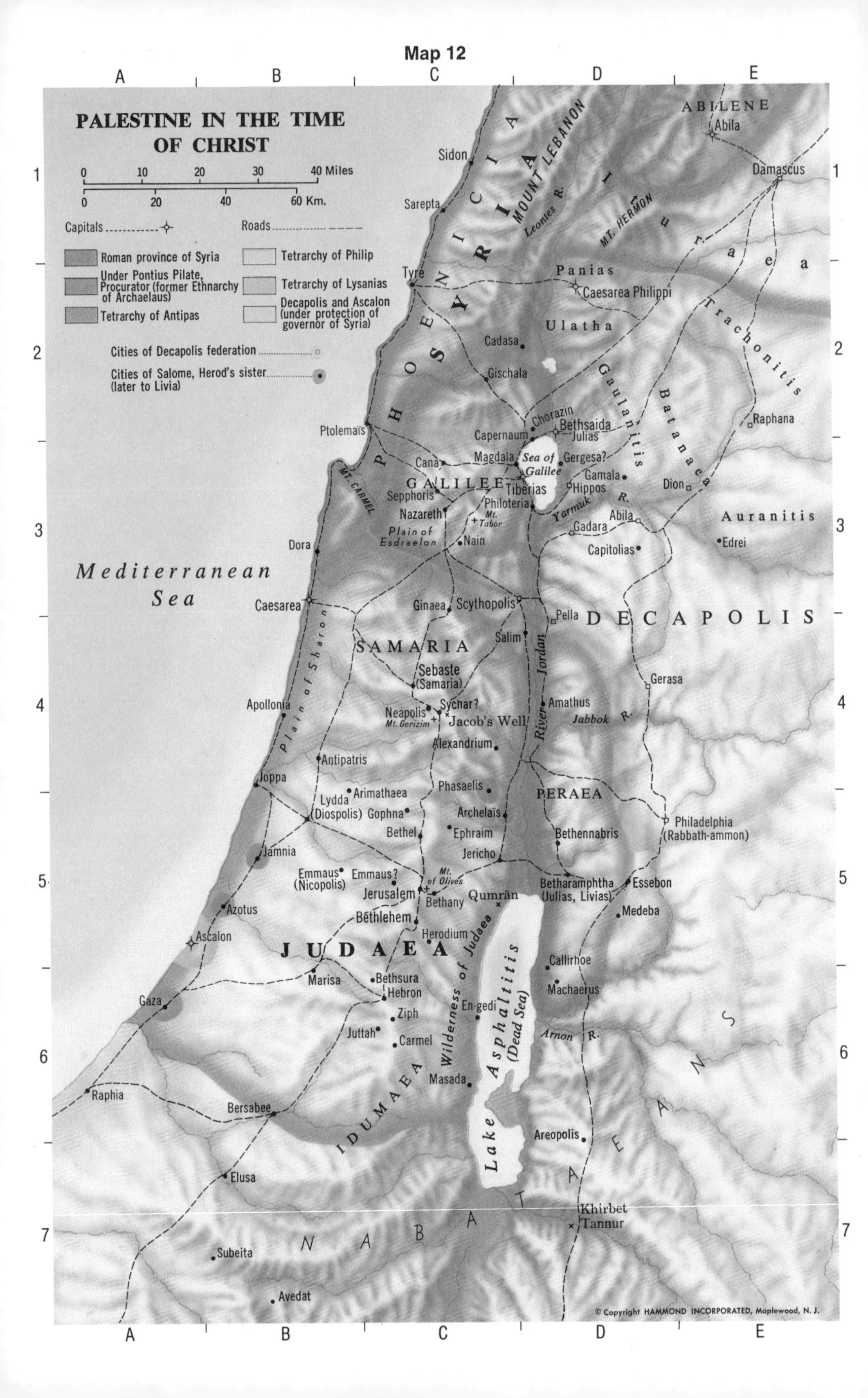
PALESTINE IN THE TIME OF CHRIST
0 10 20 30 40 Miles
0 20 40 60 Km.
Capitals
Roads
Roman province of Syria
Under Pontius Pilate, Procurator (former Ethnarchy of Archaelaus)
Tetrarchy of Antipas
Tetrarchy of Philip
Tetrarchy of Lysanias
Decapolis and Ascalon (under protection of governor of Syria)
Cities of Decapolis federation
Cities of Salome, Herod's sister (later to Livia)
Mediterranean Sea
PHOENICIA
SYRIA
MOUNT LEBANON
Leontes R.
MT. HERMON
Ituraea
ABILENE
Abila
Damascus
Sidon
Sarepta
Tyre
Panias
Caesarea Philippi
Ulatha
Cadasa
Gischala
Trachonitis
Gaulanitis
Batanaea
Raphana
Ptolemaïs
MT. CARMEL
Chorazin
Capernaum
Bethsaida Julias
Magdala
Sea of Galilee
Gergesa?
Cana
GALILEE
Tiberias
Gamala
Hippos
Dion
Sepphoris
Philoteria
Yarmuk R.
Nazareth
Mt. Tabor
Plain of Esdraelon
Nain
Abila
Gadara
Capitolias
Auranitis
Edrei
Dora
Caesarea
Ginaea
Scythopolis
Pella
DECAPOLIS
Salim
SAMARIA
Plain of Sharon
Sebaste (Samaria)
Gerasa
Apollonia
Neapolis
Mt. Gerizim
Sychar?
Jacob's Well
Amathus
River Jordan
Jabbok R.
Alexandrium
Antipatris
Joppa
Phasaelis
Lydda (Diospolis)
Arimathaea
Gophna
PERAEA
Archelaïs
Bethel
Ephraim
Philadelphia (Rabbath-ammon)
Bethennabris
Jamnia
Jericho
Emmaus (Nicopolis)
Emmaus?
Mt. of Olives
Jerusalem
Bethany
Qumrân
Betharamphtha (Julias, Livias)
Essebon
Azotus
Bethlehem
Medeba
Herodium
Ascalon
JUDAEA
Wilderness of Judaea
Lake Asphaltitis (Dead Sea)
Callirhoe
Marisa
Bethsura
Hebron
Machaerus
Gaza
Ziph
En-gedi
Juttah
Carmel
Arnon R.
IDUMAEA
Masada
Raphia
Bersabee
Areopolis
NABATAEANS
Elusa
Khirbet Tannur
Subeita
Avedat

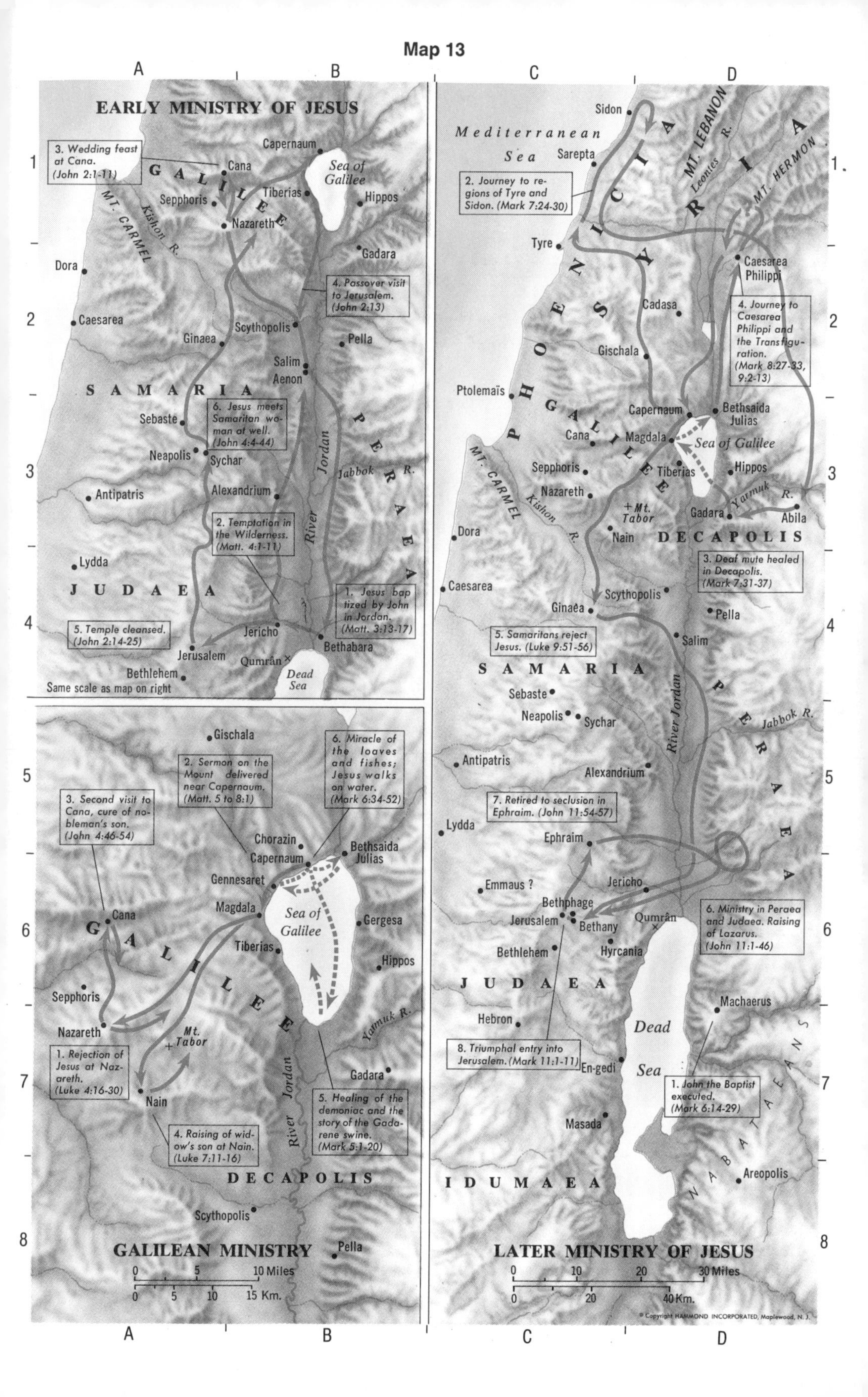

Map 13
EARLY MINISTRY OF JESUS
3. Wedding feast at Cana. (John 2:1-11)
Capernaum
Cana
GALILEE
Sea of Galilee
Tiberias
Hippos
Sepphoris
Nazareth
MT. CARMEL
Kishon R.
Gadara
Dora
4. Passover visit to Jerusalem. (John 2:13)
Caesarea
Scythopolis
Ginaea
Pella
Salim
Aenon
SAMARIA
6. Jesus meets Samaritan woman at well. (John 4:4-44)
Sebaste
PERAEA
Neapolis
Sychar
River Jordan
Jabbok R.
Antipatris
Alexandrium
2. Temptation in the Wilderness. (Matt. 4:1-11)
Lydda
JUDAEA
1. Jesus baptized by John in Jordan. (Matt. 3:13-17)
5. Temple cleansed. (John 2:14-25)
Jericho
Bethabara
Jerusalem
Qumrân
Dead Sea
Bethlehem
Same scale as map on right
Gischala
2. Sermon on the Mount delivered near Capernaum. (Matt. 5 to 8:1)
6. Miracle of the loaves and fishes; Jesus walks on water. (Mark 6:34-52)
3. Second visit to Cana, cure of nobleman's son. (John 4:46-54)
Chorazin
Capernaum
Bethsaida Julias
Gennesaret
Magdala
Cana
Sea of Galilee
Gergesa
GALILEE
Tiberias
Hippos
Sepphoris
Yarmuk R.
Nazareth
Mt. Tabor
1. Rejection of Jesus at Nazareth. (Luke 4:16-30)
Gadara
Nain
River Jordan
5. Healing of the demoniac and the story of the Gadarene swine. (Mark 5:1-20)
4. Raising of widow's son at Nain. (Luke 7:11-16)
DECAPOLIS
Scythopolis
GALILEAN MINISTRY
Pella
0 5 10 Miles
0 5 10 15 Km.
Sidon
Mediterranean Sea
Sarepta
PHOENICIA
SYRIA
MT. LEBANON
Leontes R.
MT. HERMON
2. Journey to regions of Tyre and Sidon. (Mark 7:24-30)
Tyre
Caesarea Philippi
Cadasa
4. Journey to Caesarea Philippi and the Transfiguration. (Mark 8:27-33, 9:2-13)
Gischala
Ptolemaïs
GALILEE
Capernaum
Bethsaida Julias
Cana
Magdala
Sea of Galilee
MT. CARMEL
Sepphoris
Tiberias
Hippos
Nazareth
Kishon R.
Mt. Tabor
Yarmuk R.
Gadara
Abila
Dora
Nain
DECAPOLIS
3. Deaf mute healed in Decapolis. (Mark 7:31-37)
Caesarea
Scythopolis
Ginaea
Pella
5. Samaritans reject Jesus. (Luke 9:51-56)
Salim
SAMARIA
PERAEA
Sebaste
Neapolis
Sychar
River Jordan
Jabbok R.
Antipatris
Alexandrium
7. Retired to seclusion in Ephraim. (John 11:54-57)
Lydda
Ephraim
Emmaus ?
Jericho
Bethphage
Jerusalem
Bethany
Qumrân
6. Ministry in Peraea and Judaea. Raising of Lazarus. (John 11:1-46)
Bethlehem
Hyrcania
JUDAEA
Machaerus
Hebron
Dead Sea
8. Triumphal entry into Jerusalem. (Mark 11:1-11)
En-gedi
1. John the Baptist executed. (Mark 6:14-29)
Masada
NABATAEANS
IDUMAEA
Areopolis
LATER MINISTRY OF JESUS
0 10 20 30 Miles
0 20 40 Km.
© Copyright HAMMOND INCORPORATED, Maplewood, N. J.

Map 14

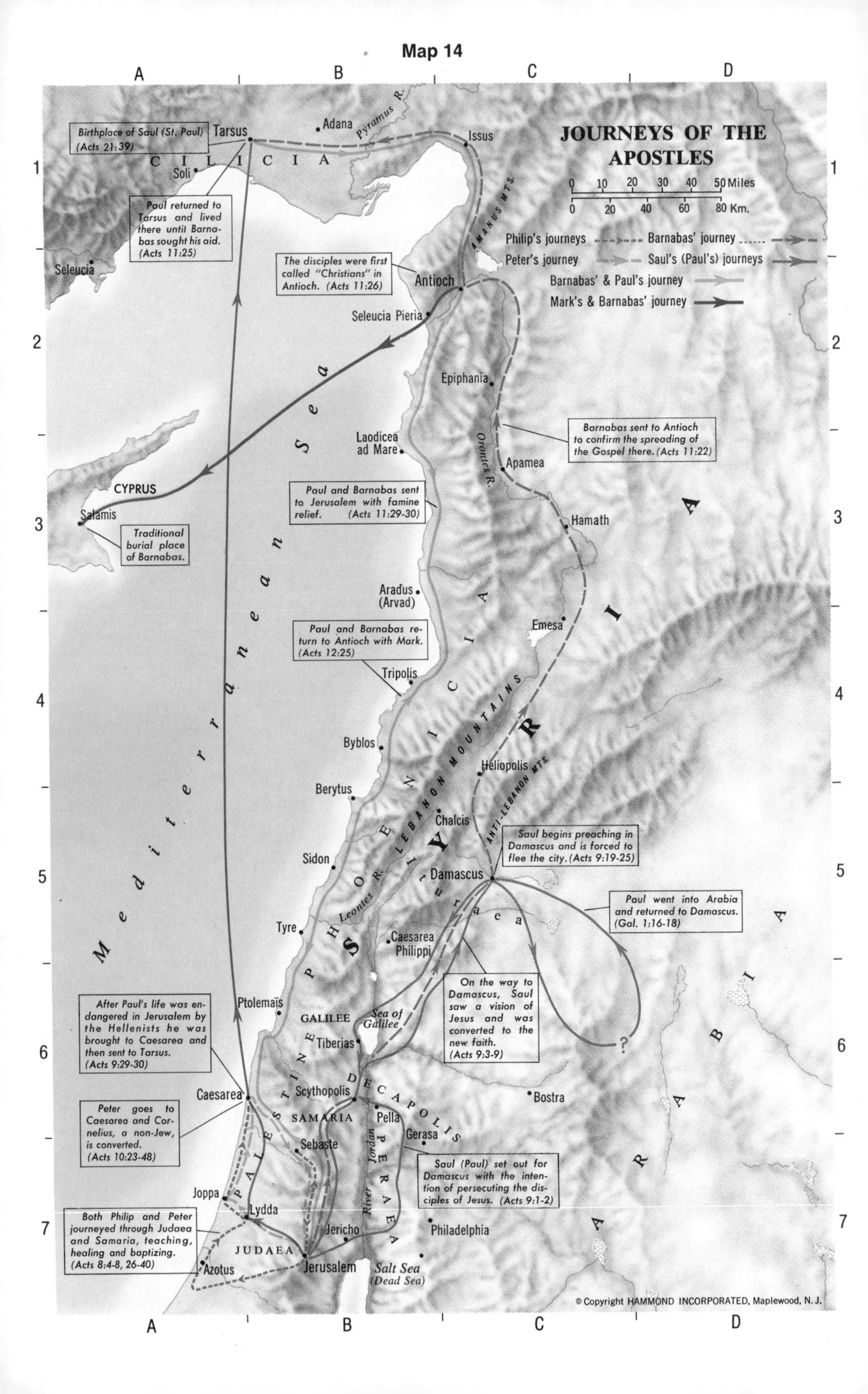

JOURNEYS OF THE APOSTLES
0 10 20 30 40 50 Miles
0 20 40 60 80 Km.
Philip's journeys
Barnabas' journey
Peter's journey
Saul's (Paul's) journeys
Barnabas' & Paul's journey
Mark's & Barnabas' journey
Birthplace of Saul (St. Paul) (Acts 21:39)
Paul returned to Tarsus and lived there until Barnabas sought his aid. (Acts 11:25)
The disciples were first called "Christians" in Antioch. (Acts 11:26)
Barnabas sent to Antioch to confirm the spreading of the Gospel there. (Acts 11:22)
Paul and Barnabas sent to Jerusalem with famine relief. (Acts 11:29-30)
Traditional burial place of Barnabas.
Paul and Barnabas return to Antioch with Mark. (Acts 12:25)
Saul begins preaching in Damascus and is forced to flee the city. (Acts 9:19-25)
Paul went into Arabia and returned to Damascus. (Gal. 1:16-18)
On the way to Damascus, Saul saw a vision of Jesus and was converted to the new faith. (Acts 9:3-9)
After Paul's life was endangered in Jerusalem by the Hellenists he was brought to Caesarea and then sent to Tarsus. (Acts 9:29-30)
Peter goes to Caesarea and Cornelius, a non-Jew, is converted. (Acts 10:23-48)
Saul (Paul) set out for Damascus with the intention of persecuting the disciples of Jesus. (Acts 9:1-2)
Both Philip and Peter journeyed through Judaea and Samaria, teaching, healing and baptizing. (Acts 8:4-8, 26-40)
Tarsus
Adana
Pyramus R.
Issus
CILICIA
Soli
AMANUS MTS.
Seleucia
Antioch
Seleucia Pieria
Mediterranean Sea
Epiphania
Laodicea ad Mare
Orontes R.
Apamea
CYPRUS
Salamis
Hamath
Aradus (Arvad)
Emesa
Tripolis
Byblos
Berytus
Heliopolis
LEBANON MOUNTAINS
ANTI-LEBANON MTS.
Chalcis
PHOENICIA
SYRIA
ARABIA
Sidon
Damascus
Leontes R.
Ituraea
Tyre
Caesarea Philippi
Ptolemaïs
GALILEE
Sea of Galilee
Tiberias
Scythopolis
DECAPOLIS
Bostra
Caesarea
SAMARIA
Pella
Gerasa
Sebaste
PALESTINE
River Jordan
PERAEA
Joppa
Lydda
Jericho
Philadelphia
JUDAEA
Jerusalem
Azotus
Salt Sea (Dead Sea)

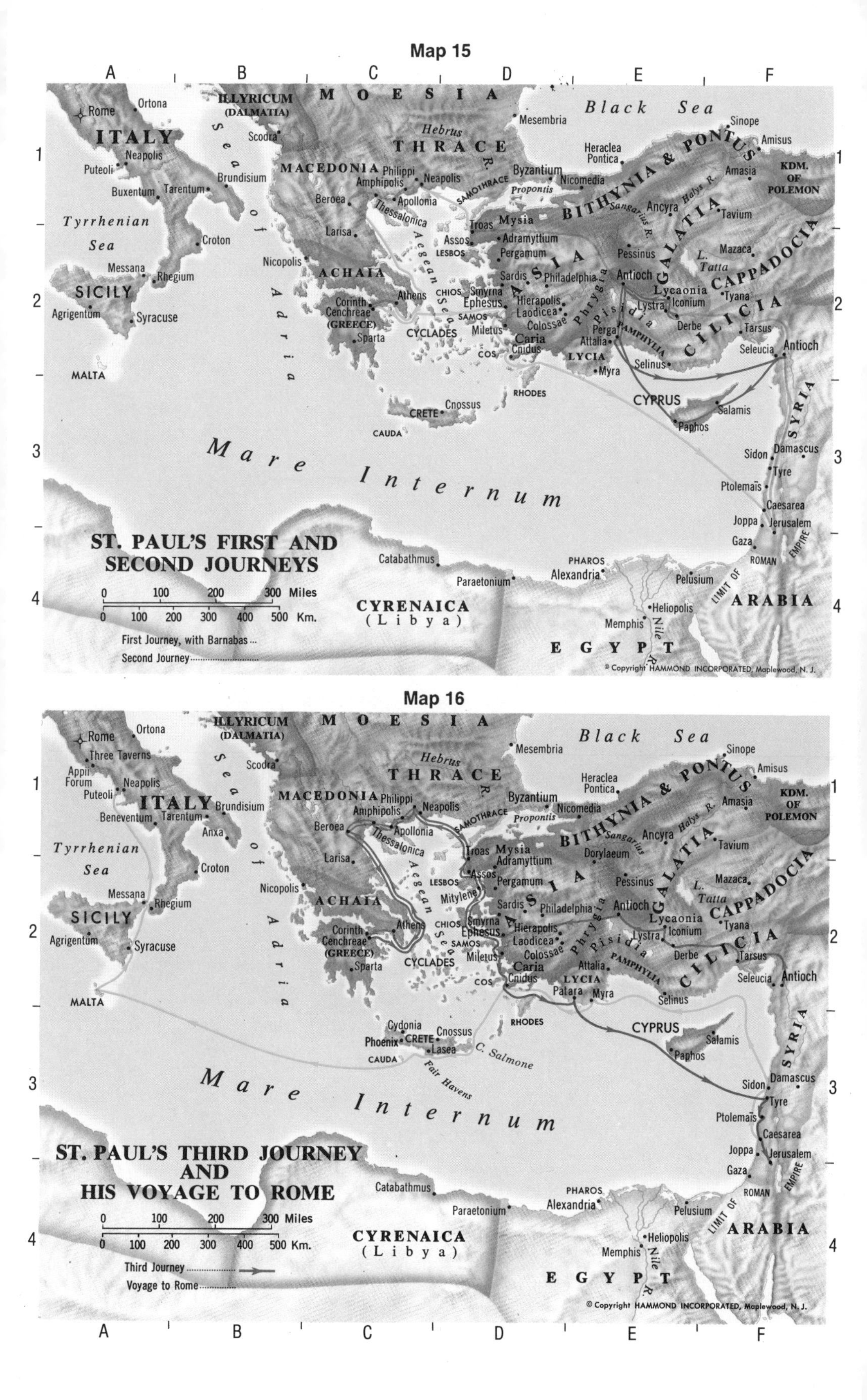

Map 15
ST. PAUL'S FIRST AND SECOND JOURNEYS
First Journey, with Barnabas
Second Journey
0 100 200 300 Miles
0 100 200 300 400 500 Km.
ITALY
Rome
Ortona
Neapolis
Puteoli
Buxentum
Tarentum
Brundisium
Croton
Messana
Rhegium
SICILY
Agrigentum
Syracuse
MALTA
Tyrrhenian Sea
ILLYRICUM (DALMATIA)
Scodra
Sea of Adria
MOESIA
THRACE
Hebrus R.
MACEDONIA
Philippi
Amphipolis
Neapolis
Beroea
Apollonia
Thessalonica
Larisa
Nicopolis
ACHAIA
Corinth
Cenchreae
(GREECE)
Athens
Sparta
CYCLADES
Aegean Sea
SAMOTHRACE
Mesembria
Black Sea
Byzantium
Propontis
Nicomedia
Heraclea Pontica
Sinope
Amisus
Amasia
KDM. OF POLEMON
BITHYNIA & PONTUS
Sangarius R.
Halys R.
Ancyra
Tavium
GALATIA
Troas
Mysia
Assos
Adramyttium
LESBOS
Pergamum
ASIA
CHIOS
Smyrna
Ephesus
Sardis
Philadelphia
Hierapolis
Laodicea
Colossae
SAMOS
Miletus
Caria
Cnidus
COS
RHODES
Phrygia
Pisidia
Antioch
Pessinus
Mazaca
L. Tatta
CAPPADOCIA
Lycaonia
Iconium
Lystra
Derbe
Tyana
Perga
Attalia
PAMPHYLIA
LYCIA
Myra
CILICIA
Tarsus
Selinus
Seleucia
Antioch
CYPRUS
Salamis
Paphos
SYRIA
Sidon
Damascus
Tyre
Ptolemaïs
Caesarea
Joppa
Jerusalem
Gaza
LIMIT OF ROMAN EMPIRE
CRETE
Cnossus
CAUDA
Mare Internum
Catabathmus
Paraetonium
PHAROS
Alexandria
Pelusium
Heliopolis
Memphis
Nile R.
CYRENAICA (Libya)
EGYPT
ARABIA
© Copyright HAMMOND INCORPORATED, Maplewood, N. J.
Map 16
ST. PAUL'S THIRD JOURNEY AND HIS VOYAGE TO ROME
Third Journey
Voyage to Rome
0 100 200 300 Miles
0 100 200 300 400 500 Km.
Rome
Ortona
Three Taverns
Appii Forum
Neapolis
Puteoli
ITALY
Beneventum
Tarentum
Brundisium
Anxa
Croton
Messana
Rhegium
SICILY
Agrigentum
Syracuse
MALTA
Tyrrhenian Sea
Dorylaeum
Mitylene
Patara
Cydonia
Phoenix
CRETE
Cnossus
Lasea
CAUDA
C. Salmone
Fair Havens
Mare Internum
CYPRUS
Salamis
Paphos
Sidon
Damascus
Tyre
Ptolemaïs
Caesarea
Joppa
Jerusalem
Gaza
CYRENAICA (Libya)
EGYPT
ARABIA
© Copyright HAMMOND INCORPORATED, Maplewood, N. J.

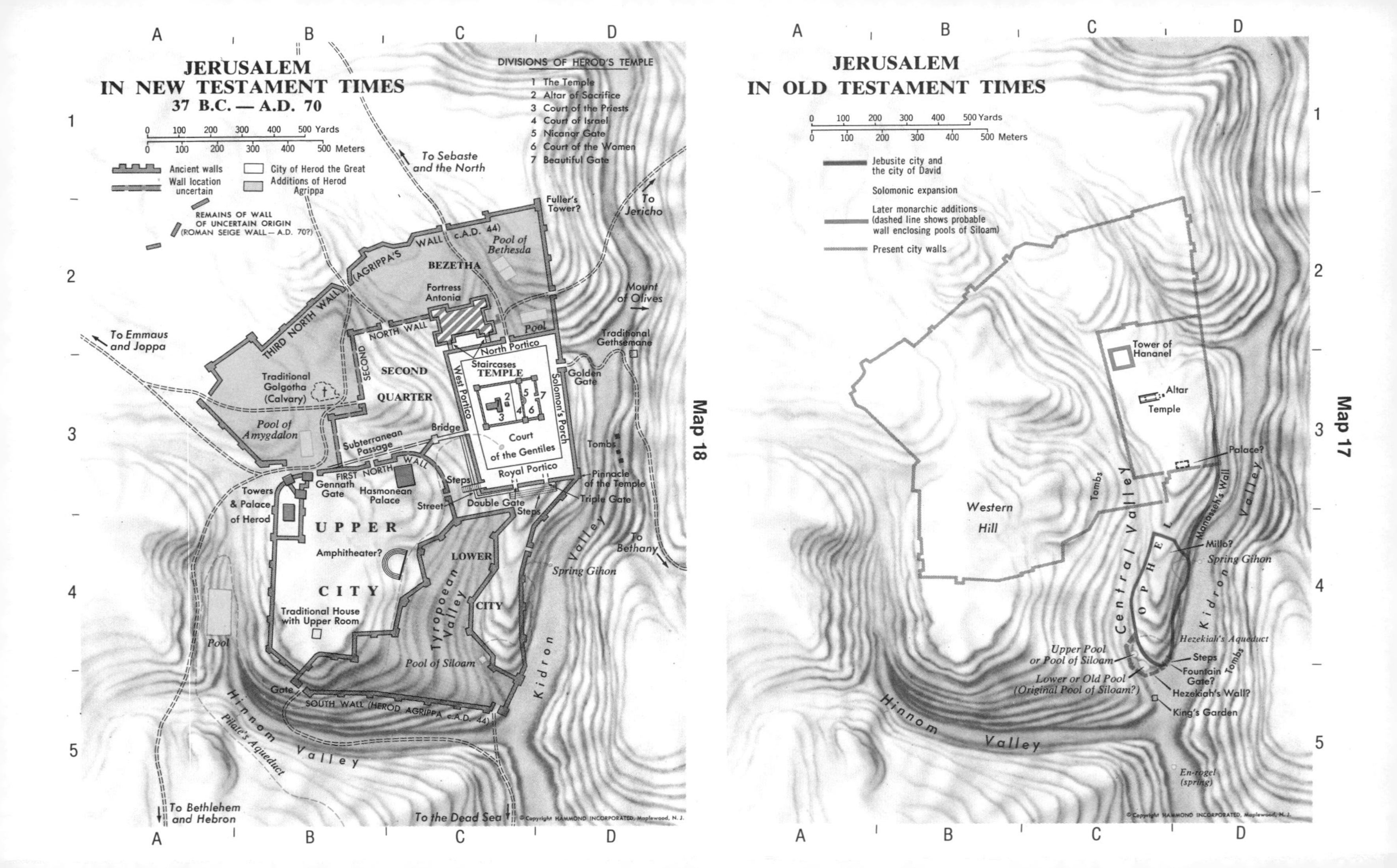
Map 18
JERUSALEM
IN NEW TESTAMENT TIMES
37 B.C. — A.D. 70
0 100 200 300 400 500 Yards
0 100 200 300 400 500 Meters
Ancient walls
Wall location uncertain
City of Herod the Great
Additions of Herod Agrippa
REMAINS OF WALL OF UNCERTAIN ORIGIN (ROMAN SEIGE WALL — A.D. 70?)
DIVISIONS OF HEROD'S TEMPLE
1 The Temple
2 Altar of Sacrifice
3 Court of the Priests
4 Court of Israel
5 Nicanor Gate
6 Court of the Women
7 Beautiful Gate
To Sebaste and the North
To Emmaus and Joppa
To Jericho
Mount of Olives
Traditional Gethsemane
Fuller's Tower?
AGRIPPA'S WALL c.A.D. 44
Pool of Bethesda
BEZETHA
Fortress Antonia
Pool
THIRD NORTH WALL
NORTH WALL
SECOND
SECOND QUARTER
Traditional Golgotha (Calvary)
Pool of Amygdalon
North Portico
Staircases
TEMPLE
West Portico
Solomon's Porch
Golden Gate
Court of the Gentiles
Royal Portico
Bridge
Subterranean Passage
FIRST NORTH WALL
Steps
Tombs
Pinnacle of the Temple
Triple Gate
Double Gate
Gennath Gate
Hasmonean Palace
Towers & Palace of Herod
Street
UPPER CITY
Amphitheater?
LOWER CITY
Tyropoean Valley
Kidron Valley
To Bethany
Spring Gihon
Traditional House with Upper Room
Pool
Pool of Siloam
Gate
SOUTH WALL (HEROD AGRIPPA c.A.D. 44)
Hinnom Valley
Pilate's Aqueduct
To Bethlehem and Hebron
To the Dead Sea
©Copyright HAMMOND INCORPORATED, Maplewood, N. J.
Map 17
JERUSALEM
IN OLD TESTAMENT TIMES
0 100 200 300 400 500 Yards
0 100 200 300 400 500 Meters
Jebusite city and the city of David
Solomonic expansion
Later monarchic additions (dashed line shows probable wall enclosing pools of Siloam)
Present city walls
Tower of Hananel
Altar
Temple
Palace?
Western Hill
Tombs
Central Valley
Manasseh's Wall
Kidron Valley
Millo?
Spring Gihon
OPHEL
Hezekiah's Aqueduct
Upper Pool or Pool of Siloam
Lower or Old Pool (Original Pool of Siloam?)
Steps
Fountain Gate?
Tombs
Hezekiah's Wall?
King's Garden
Hinnom Valley
En-rogel (spring)
©Copyright HAMMOND INCORPORATED, Maplewood, N. J.